Street by Street

LONDON

C000049209

3rd edition July 2003
© Automobile Association Developments Limited 2004

Original edition printed May 2001

Ordnance Survey® This product includes map data licensed from Ordnance Survey ® with the permission of the Controller of Her Majesty's Stationery Office. © Crown copyright 2004. All rights reserved. Licence number 399221.

Published by AA Publishing (a trading name of Automobile Association Developments Limited, whose registered office is Millstream, Maidenhead Road, Windsor, Berkshire, SL4 5GD. Registered number 1878835).

Mapping produced by the Cartography Department of The Automobile Association. (A02257)

A CIP Catalogue record for this book is available from the British Library.

Printed by GRAFIASA S.A., Porto, Portugal

The contents of this atlas are believed to be correct at the time of the latest revision. However, the publishers cannot be held responsible for loss occasioned to any person acting or refraining from action as a result of any material in this atlas, nor for any errors, omissions or changes in such material. This does not affect your statutory rights. The publishers would welcome information to correct any errors or omissions and to keep this atlas up to date. Please write to Publishing, The Automobile Association, Fanum House (FH17), Basing View, Basingstoke, Hampshire, RG21 4EA.

ML038y

Key to map pages	ii–iii
Key to map symbols	iv–1
Enlarged map pages	2-19
Main map pages	20-217
Index – towns & villages	218-219
Index – streets	219-297
Index – featured places	297-316
Acknowledgements	316

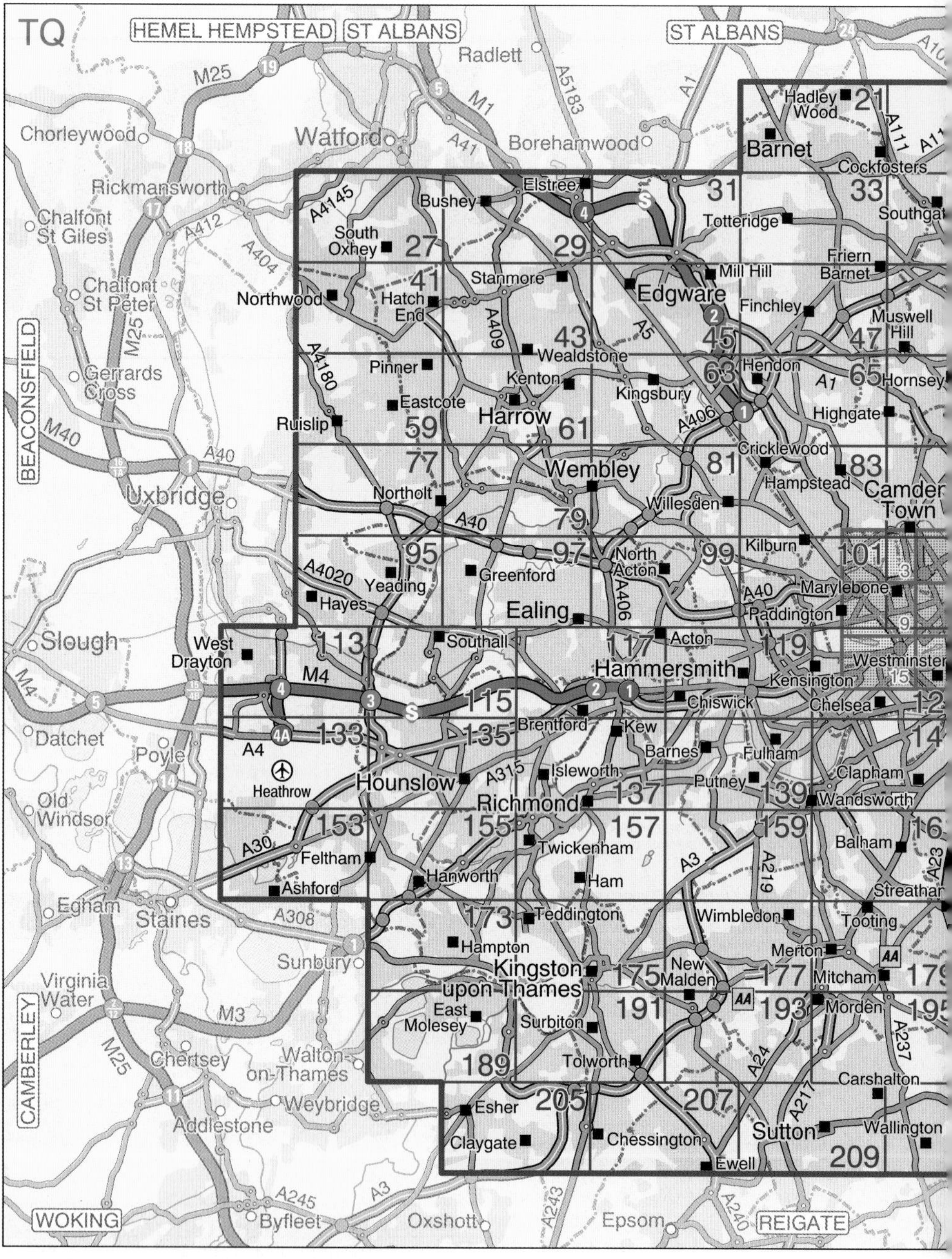

Scale of enlarged map pages 1:10,000 6.3 inches to 1 mile

0 1/4 miles 1/2

0 1/4 1/2 kilometres 3/4 1

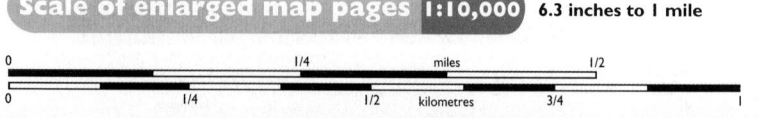

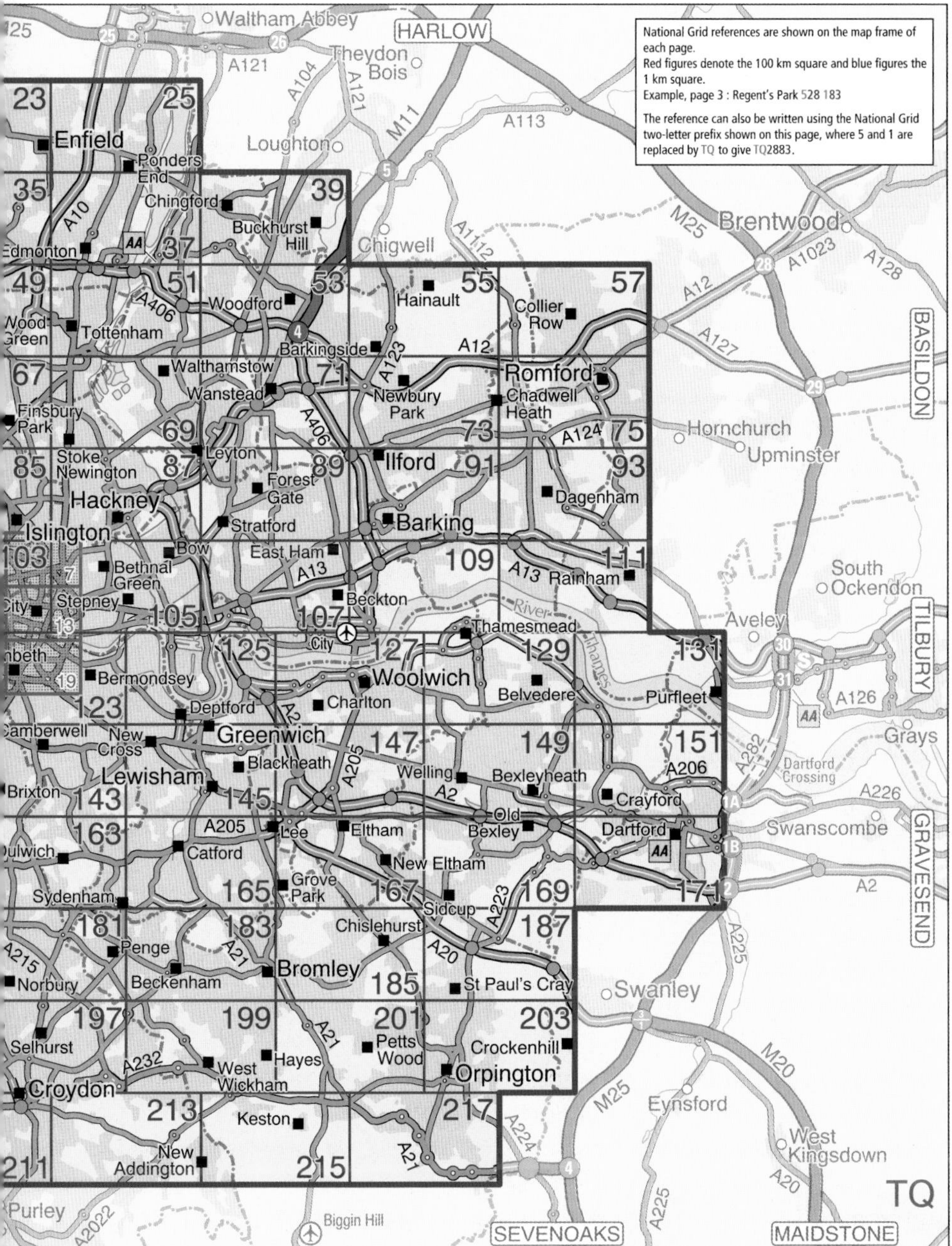

3.6 inches to 1 mile

Scale of main map pages 1:17,500

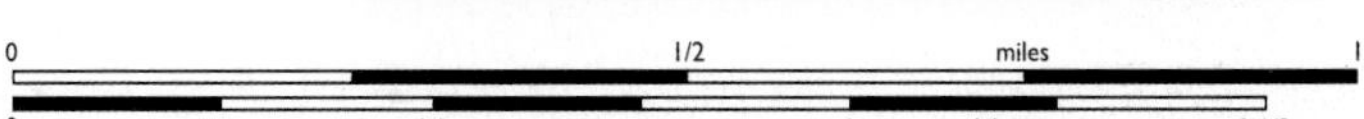

Junction 9	Motorway & junction
Services	Motorway service area
	Primary road single/dual carriageway
Services	Primary road service area
	A road single/dual carriageway
	B road single/dual carriageway
	Other road single/dual carriageway
	Minor/private road, access may be restricted
	One-way street
	Pedestrian area
	Track or footpath
	Road under construction
	Road tunnel
AA	AA Service Centre
P	Parking
P+	Park & Ride
	Bus/coach station
	Railway & main railway station
	Railway & minor railway station

	Underground station
	Light railway & station
	Preserved private railway
LC	Level crossing
	Tramway
	Ferry route
	Airport runway
	County, administrative boundary
	Congestion Charging Zone *
	Mounds
93	Page continuation 1:17,500
7	Page continuation to enlarged scale 1:10,000
	River/canal, lake, pier
	Aqueduct, lock, weir
465 Winter Hill	Peak (with height in metres)
	Beach
	Woodland
	Park
	Cemetery

* The AA central London Congestion Charging map is also available

Built-up area

Featured building

City wall

A&E — Hospital with 24-hour A&E department

PO — Post Office

Public library

Tourist Information Centre

Petrol station, 24 hour
Major suppliers only

Church/chapel

Public toilets

Toilet with disabled facilities

PH — Public house
AA recommended

Restaurant
AA inspected

Theatre or performing arts centre

Cinema

Golf course

Camping
AA inspected

Caravan site
AA inspected

Camping & caravan site
AA inspected

Theme park

Abbey, cathedral or priory

Castle

Historic house or building

Wakehurst Place NT — National Trust property

Museum or art gallery

Roman antiquity

Ancient site, battlefield or monument

Industrial interest

Garden

Arboretum

Farm or animal centre

Zoological or wildlife collection

Bird collection

Nature reserve

Aquarium

Visitor or heritage centre

Country park

Cave

Windmill

Distillery, brewery or vineyard

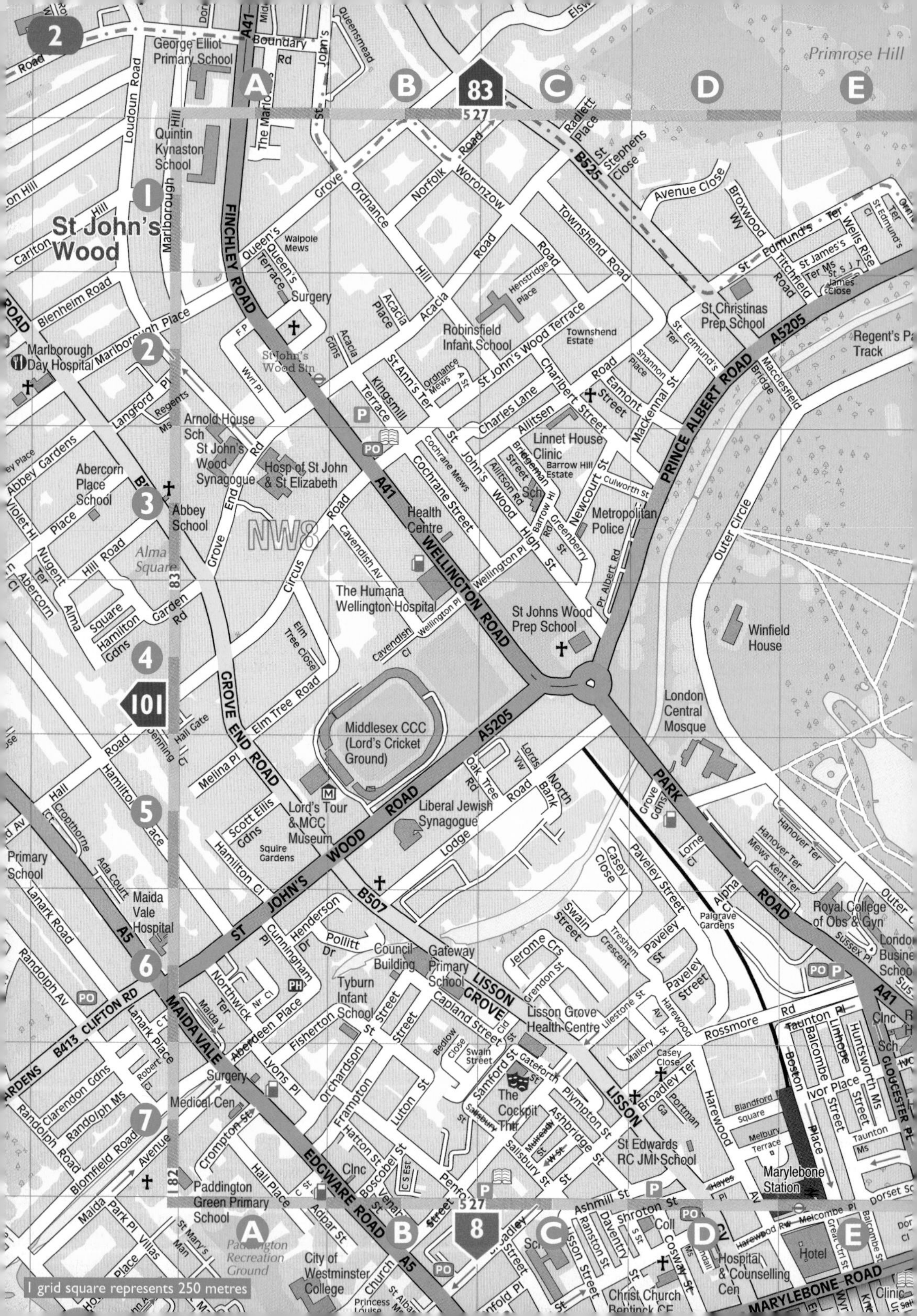

2
83
527
8
101
A
B
C
D
E
1
2
3
4
5
6
7
82
83
Primrose Hill
St John's Wood
NW8
George Elliot Primary School
Quintin Kynaston School
Boundary Rd
Queensmead
St John's
The Marlborough
Marlborough Hill
Loudoun Road
Carlton Hill
Blenheim Road
Marlborough Place
Marlborough Day Hospital
FINCHLEY ROAD
A41
Queen's Grove
Queen's Terrace
Walpole Mews
Surgery
Ordnance Hill
Norfolk Road
Woronzow Road
Radlett Place
St Stephens Close
B525
Avenue Close
Broxwood Wy
St Edmund's Ter
Wells Rise
St James's Ter Ms
St James Close
Titchfield Road
St Christinas Prep School
Regent's Park Track
Townshend Road
Townshend Estate
Henstridge Place
Acacia Road
Acacia Place
Acacia Gdns
Robinsfield Infant School
St John's Wood Terrace
St John's Wood Stn
Wyrl Pl
FP
Kingsmill Terrace
St Ann's Ter
Ordnance Mews
Charles Lane
Charlbert Street
Allitsen Road
Eamont Street
Shannon Place
Mackennal St
St Edmund's Ter
PRINCE ALBERT ROAD
A5205
Macclesfield Bridge
Langford Pl
Regents Ms
Arnold House Sch
St John's Wood Synagogue
Hosp of St John & St Elizabeth
PO
Cochrane Mews
Cochrane Street
St John's Wood High St
Linnet House Clinic
Barrow Hill Estate
Bridgeman Street
Allitson Rd
Barrow Hl Rd
Sch
Newcourt St
Culworth St
Greenberry St
Metropolitan Police
Pr Albert Rd
Outer Circle
Abbey Gardens
Abercorn Place School
Abbey School
Abercorn Place
Violet Hl
Nugent Ter
Abercorn Cl
Hill Road
Alma Square
Grove End Rd
Circus Road
Cavendish Av
Health Centre
WELLINGTON ROAD
Wellington Pl
The Humana Wellington Hospital
St Johns Wood Prep School
Winfield House
Hamilton Gdns
Garden Rd
Elm Tree Close
Cavendish Cl
Elm Tree Road
GROVE END ROAD
Middlesex CCC (Lord's Cricket Ground)
London Central Mosque
Hall Gate
Denning Cl
Hall Road
Hamilton Terrace
Melina Pl
Lord's Tour & MCC Museum
Oak Tree Rd
Lords Vw
North Bank
ST JOHN'S WOOD ROAD
Liberal Jewish Synagogue
Lodge Road
PARK ROAD
Grove Gdns
Scott Ellis Gdns
Squire Gardens
Hamilton Cl
Casey Close
Paveley Street
Lorne Cl
Hanover Ter
Hanover Ter Mews
Kent Ter
Cropthorne Ct
Ada Court
Primary School
Maida Vale Hospital
Lanark Road
A5
B507
Henderson Dr
Pollitt Dr
Cunningham Pl
Council Building
Gateway Primary School
Swain Street
Tresham Crescent
Jerome Crs
Paveley St
Alpha Cl
Palgrave Gardens
Royal College of Obs & Gyn
Sussex Pl
London Business School
Randolph Av
PO
B413 CLIFTON RD
MAIDA VALE
Maida V
Northwick Ter
Nr Cl
PH
Tyburn Infant School
Aberdeen Place
Fisherton Street
Capland Street
LISSON GROVE
Grendon St
Lisson Grove Health Centre
Lilestone St
Harewood Av
Rossmore Rd
Taunton Pl
Balcombe St
Linhope Street
Huntsworth Ms
GLOUCESTER PL
Clnc
Sch
Lanark Place
Robert Cl
Clarendon Gdns
Randolph Ms
Randolph Road
Blomfield Road
Surgery
Lyons Pl
Orchardson St
Frampton Street
Luton St
Bedlow Close
Swain Street
Samford St
Gateforth St
Plympton St
Mallory St
Casey Close
Broadley Ter
Portman Ga
Harewood Av
Ivor Place
Boston Place
Blandford Square
Melbury Terrace
Taunton Ms
Medical Cen
Crompton St
Hatton St
Boscobel St
Clnc
Salisbury St
The Cockpit Thtr
Ashbridge St
Mulready St
W St
St Edwards RC JMI School
Marylebone Station
Dorset Sq
Avenue
Paddington Green Primary School
Hall Place
Adpar St
C St
EDGWARE ROAD
Venables St
C S Est
Penfold Street
Ashmill St
Shroton St
Coll
Hayes Pl
Melcombe Pl
Harewood Rw
Great Ctrl St
Balcombe St
Maida Av
Park Pl Villas
St Mary's Mans
Paddington Recreation Ground
City of Westminster College
Church St
St Albans
Princess Louise
Broadley Street
Sch
Lisson Street
Ranston St
Daventry St
S St
Cosway St
Ms
Hospital & Counselling Cen
Hotel
MARYLEBONE ROAD
Clinic
Christ Church Bentinck CE
Penfold Pl
1 grid square represents 250 metres

Primrose Hill
84
28
29
F
G
H
J
K
Princess Rd
Primrose Hill School
Cecil Sharpe House
Gloucester Crs
Inverness St
Odeon
The Cavendish School
PKWY
Mornington Sports & Fitness Cen
London Capital
BAYHAM ST
A400
St Martin's Cl
Kingstown St
Kingstown Street
Auden Place
Calvert St
Manley St
Park Road
Albert Terrace
Albert Ter
St Mark's Sq
Friends of the Hebrew University
The Jewish Museum
Arlington Road
Underhill St
PRATT ST
Pratt
Bayham
Plender Street
Surgery
PRINCE ALBERT A5205 ROAD
Regal Lane
DELANCEY ST A503
Delancey Passage
Mary Ter
CAMDEN HIGH ST
King's Ter
Grand Union Canal
Outer Circle
North Bridge House Senior School
Mornington Terrace
Albert Street
Arlington
Miller St
Carlow St
Camden T
Park Village East
Mornington St
Nelsons Yard
Mornington Crs
Mornington Crescent Stn
EVERSHOLT ST
London Zoo
City of Westminster
Camden
Gloucester Gate
Gloucester Ga
Gloucester Ga Ms
Pk Village W
Regent's Park Barracks
NW1
Mornington Place
Clarkson Row
Harrington Sq
Ampthill Medical
Ampthill Estate
Regent's Park
Cumberland Terrace
Cm T Ms
Outer Circle
A4201
ALBANY STREET
Christ Church School
Redhill Street
Augustus Street
Granby Ter
Harrington St
Silverdale
HAMPSTEAD ROAD
A400
Cumberland Gate
Chester Pl
Redhill St
Stanhope Parade
Mackworth St
Harrington Street
Regent's College
Chester Terrace
Chester Cl North
Nash St
Cumberland Medical Cen
Varndell St
Market
Robert St
Everton Buildings
Open Air Theatre
Inner Circle
Chester Road
Chester Cl South
Compton Close
Clarence Gdns
Netley St
Prince Regent Mews
School
The Holme
Queen Mary's Garden
Chester Ga
Cambridge Ter
William Road
Police Station
Cambridge Ga Ms
Cambridge Ga
Colosseum Terrace
Munster Sq
Coll
Camden Peoples Thtr
Drummond
University of Westminster
Royal College of Physicians
Albany St
Longford St
Hotel
Euston Centre
Euston Tower
St Andrew's Pl
Park Sq East
Peto Pl
Osnaburgh St
Diana Place
Works
EUSTON
A501
Clarence Gate
Regent's College
York Bridge
Steiner
Outer Circle
Park Square
Warren Street Stn
Royal Academy of Music
International Community School
Sherlock Holmes Mus
Cornwall Terrace
Cornwall Ter Ms
Allsop Pl
York Ter East
York Ter West
Nottingham Terrace
Brunswick Place
Clinic
P S Ms
Park Sq West
Ulster Pl
Upr Harley St
Regent's Park Stn
Regent's Clnc
PK CR
Great Portland Street Stn
Warren St
Hosp
Grafton Ms
LT Lost Property Office
Madame Tussaud's Planetarium
College
Emb of Latvia
MARYLEBONE ROAD
A501
Hlth Cen
The London Clnc
Surg
Central London Co Court
PORTLAND PL
Royal National Orthopaedic Hosp
Park Crs Ms E
Bolsover St
Emb of Croatia
Emb of Mozambique
Medical Cen
London Foot Hosp
W1
BAKER ST
Baker Street Stn
Melcombe St
Mry Rd
Siddons Lane
Glentworth St
A501
28
Hosp
Consulate of Chile
Devonshire Place
Devonshire St
Clipstone Ms
Clipstone St
Cleveland St
British Telecom Twr
Lisson Grove
Chiltern St
Univ of Westmi
High Comm of The Maldives
Oldbury Pl
Marylebone High St
Devonshire Hospital
9
Clnc
Emb of China
RIBA
Hotel
Hanson St
University of Westminster
High Comm of Seychelles
Screen on Baker St
Surgery
Nottingham St
Emb of Poland
College
University
Clipstone St
Cen Synagogue
Sch
Luxborough St
Bingham Pl
Nottingham Pl
Devonshire Ms
Upr Wimpole St
Devonshire Ms S
Bridford Ms
Great Titchfield St
Fitzroy St
Maple St
Cleveland Ms
Whitfield Pl
Grafton Way
Grafton Ms
Warren St
Fitzroy St
A41
B524
King Edward VII

4
84
A
B
C
D
E
30
PKWY
Carol St
St Michael's CE Prim Sch
Works
Primary School
Pratt St
College Place
Mandela Street
COLLEGE STREET
ST PANCRAS WAY
Camley Street
London Capital College
Mornington Sports & Fitness Cen
The Cavendish School
Friends of the Hebrew University
The Jewish Museum
Arlington Road
Underhill
BAYHAM
A400
PRATT ST
Pratt Ms
Bayham
Royal Veterinary College
Granary Street
St Pancras Hospital
Depot
Central School Speech & Drama
DELANCEY ST
Delancey Passage
Mary Ter
CAMDEN HIGH ST
King's Ter
Plender Street
Bayham Pl
Surgery St
Richard Cobden Primary School
Albert Street
Mornington Terrace
Miller St
Carlow St
College
Camden Thtr
CROWNDALE ROAD
Blakeney Close
Goldington Crs
A5202
PANCRAS
Camley Street
Goods Way
Park Village East
Mornington
Nelsons Yard
Mornington Crs
Mornington Crescent Stn
EVERSHOLT ST
Oakley Sq
OAKLEY SQ
Crowndale Hlth Cen
Chalton St
Unity Ms
Charrington St
Medburn St
Penryn St
Goldington St
Platt St
Purchese St
Chenies Pl
Clyde Court
Community School
Regent's Park Barracks
NW1
Mornington Place
Clarkson Row
Mornington Crs
Harrington Sq
Surgery
A400
Ampthill Square Medical Centre
Cranleigh St
Bridgeway St
Werrington St
Somers Town
Hampden Close
Coopers Lane
Battle Br Rd
Stanley Passage
Cheney Rd
ROAD
Community Sports Cen
Edith Neville Primary School
Regent's Park
A4201
ALBANY
Christ Church School
HAMPSTEAD ROAD
Granby Ter
Ampthill Estate
Ampthill Square
EVERSHOLT
Aldenham St
School
Polygon Rd
St Mary & St Pancras CE Primary School
Ossulston Street
Brill Place
Midland Rd
Weller's Ct
Barnby Street
Silverdale
Harrington Sq
Augustus Street
Redhill Street
Chester Pl
Phoenix Rd
Maria Fidelis Convent Upper School
St Aloysius RC Infant School
St Pancras Station
British Library
Stanhope Parade
Mackworth St
Harrington Street
Stanhope
Drummond Crs
Chalton St
Churchway
EUSTON ROAD
Chester Terrace
Outer Circle
Chester Cl North
Redhill St
Varndell St
STREET
Doric Way
St Pancras International Youth Hostel
Camden Town Hall & St Pancras Library
Nash St
Robert St
National Temperance Hospital
Lower School
Cardington Street
Euston Station
Lancing St
A4200
Grafton Place
Elizabeth Garrett Anderson Hosp
Bidborough Street
Hastings Street
B504
Compton Close
Everton Buildings
Hotel
Chester Cl South
Netley Primary School
Netley St
Prince Regent Mews
Starcross St
Cobourg St
Melton Street
Fire Station
Duke's Road
Flaxman Ter
University
Uni Coll Sch of Fine Art
Cartwright Gdns
Sandwich St
Thanet St
Chester Ga
William Road
A501
UPR WOBURN PL
Woburn Walk
Police Station
Cambridge Ga Ms
Cambridge Ga
Munster Sq
Camden Peoples Thtr
George Ms
N Gower St
Euston Street
Euston Sq
Friends House
Endsleigh Gdns
University College
Ends St
WC1H
Burton Pl
Burton St
Leigh St
Colosseum Terrace
Albany St
Coll
Drummond St
University of Westminster
Tolmer's Sq
Foundry Ms
Stephenson Wy
College
Wellcome Institute
Tavistock Sq
British Medical Association
Woolf Mews
Marchmont Street
Kenton St
St Andrew's Pl
Hotel
Triton Sq
Euston Centre
Euston Tower
ROAD
Gower Pl
Gordon St
Taviton Street
Tavistock Sq
Tavistock
Herbrand Street
Park Sq East
Euston Centre
Euston Square Station
Bloomsbury Theatre
Birkbeck Coll
End Pl
Gordon Sq
A4200 WOBURN PLACE
TAVISTOCK SQ
Diana Place
Works
EUSTON
Beaumont Pl
A&E
Percival David Fndtn
University of London
Marchmont Street
Peto Pl
A501
Warren Street Stn
GRAFTON WY
GOWER ST
University College London
Dep of Clinical Haematology
Uni Church
Coram Street
Hotel
Fitzroy St
Street
Whitfield Pl
Htl
University Coll Hosp
Mus
Gordon Sq
Woburn Sq
College
Russell Square Station
Regent's Pk Stn
Great Portland Street Stn
Hosp
Warren St
Grafton Ms
Grafton Wy
Coll
Obstetrics Hosp
Byng Pl
Bedford Wy
PK CR
Cleveland St
Emb of Croatia
Emb of Mozambique
Medical Cen
Grafton Wy
London Foot Hosp
UCL Hospitals
Huntley St
Chenies Ms
College
Malet Pl
Torrington Pl
Birkbeck Coll
Thornhaugh St
Hotel
Royal National Orthopaedic Hosp
Park Crs Ms W
Htl
Bolsover
Union of Liberal & Prog Synagogues
Queen's Yd
WC1E
TOTTENHAM
Vanbrugh Thtr
RADA
School
RUSSELL SQ
A4200
PORTLAND PL
Clipstone
Coll
Torrington Sq
Malet St
Bloomsbury
Bridford Ms
Hallam
Maple
Cleveland Ms
Howland St
Fitzroy St
Howland Ms
10
A400
Ridgmount Gdns
British Telecom Twr
RIBA
Hotel
Emb of Chile
University Westminster
Med Sch
UCL
Astor Coll
Charlotte St
Chitty St
Pollock's Toy Mus
Alfred Mews
North Crs
CHENIES ST
Drill
Coll
Ridgmount St
Eckerd Coll
London Sch of Hygiene & Tropical Medicine
Uni of London
Keppel St
MONTAGUE PLACE
RUSSELL SQ
E
Royal Coll of Anaes
Cen Synagogue
1 grid square represents 250 metres

85
11
F
G
H
J
K
31
Pentonville
FINSBURY
St Pancras
Clerkenwell
YORK WAY
A5200
COPENHAGEN ST B514
WHARFDALE ROAD
PENTONVILLE ROAD
A501
PENTON RISE
KING'S CROSS RD
GRAY'S INN RD
SWINTON STREET
ACTON STREET
GRAY'S INN ROAD
THEOBALD'S ROAD
GUILFORD STREET
CALTHORPE STREET
FARRINGDON ROAD
ROSEBERY AVENUE
CLERKENWELL ROAD
A5201
B521
SKINNER ST
B502
PERCIVAL ST
ST JOHN ST
A401
UPPER STREET
A1
CITY ROAD
WAKLEY STREET
ISLINGTON GREEN
B515 LIVERPOOL ROAD
Richmond Avenue
Barnsbury Rd
Caledonian Road
Carnegie Street
Wynford Road
Copenhagen St
Tolpuddle St
White Lion St
Donegal Street
Chapel Market
Amwell St
Myddelton Square
Lloyd Baker St
Great Percy Street
Margery Street
Exmouth Market
Northampton Rd
Mount Pleasant (Postal Sorting Office)
King's Cross Thameslink Stn
Angel Station
Farringdon Station
Royal National Throat Nose & Ear Hosp
Eastman Dental Hosp
The Foundling Museum
Coram's Fields Playground
The Charles Dickens Mus
National Hosp for Sick Children (Great Ormond St)
Royal London Homeopathic Hosp
The London Canal Museum
Sadler's Wells Theatre
Lillian Baylis Thtr
City Uni
The City University
Crafts Council
The Business Design Centre
N1 Shopping Centre
Screen on the Green Cinema
Pop Up Theatre
Kingsway College
Magistrates Court
Police Stn
Family Records Centre
Town Hall
Finsbury Health Cen
Records Office
House of Detention
Central School of Ballet
London Weather Centre
WC1X
WC1N
WC1R
EC1R
EC1M

N1
Kings Head Theatre
Moon St
Theberton Street
LIVERPOOL ROAD
B515
Gibson Sq
Milner Place
Stonefield Street
Samuel Rhodes School
Cloudesley Sq
Doves Yd
Cloudesley Street
Cloudesley Pl
Batchelor St
Sch
Ritchie St
Barnsbury
Bromfield Street
Parkfield St
N1 Shopping Centre
White Conduit St
Chapel Pl
Chapel Market
Bradley's Close
Consulate of Eritrea
Angel Station
Crafts Council
BARON ST
ROAD
A501
UPPER STREET
A1
Water Tower Pl
Providence Place
Coll
Screen on the Green Cinema
St Alban's Place
Islington Gn
ISLINGTON GREEN
Islington Green Medical Cen
Anderson Square
Gaskin St
Horse Yd
St Mary's Pth
Draper Place
Dagmar Ter
Dagmar Passage
Business Design Centre
Berners Rd
Charlton Pl
Pierrepoint Row
School
Camden Walk
Clerkenwell Co Court
Duncan St
Duncan Ter
Colebrooke Rw
Gerrard Road
Noel Road
Vincent Terrace
Bridel Mews
Torrens St
Elia Street
Elia Mews
Quick St
Sudeley St
Rocliffe St
City Gdn Rw
Graham Street
Boreas Walk
Theseus Walk
Nelson Pl
Nelson Ter
Remington St
Coombs St
Haverstock St
Falcon Court
City Gdn Rw
City University
Pickering
Dibden St
Popham
Rosemary Primary School
Bishop St
Basire St
Holland Passage
Ridgewell
Steeple Walk
Rawreth Walk
NEW NORTH ROAD
Surgery
Primary School
Shepperton Road
Canonbury Business Centre
Islington Business Centre
Coleman Flds
Rydon St
St Philip's Way
Wilton Sq
Wilton Vls
Baring St
Rees St
Packington St
Queen's Head St
Elliott's Pl
Raleigh Mews
Colebrooke Place
Cruden St
Raleigh Street
Chantry Street
Lambs Mews
Surgery
Colebrooke Works
Primary School
St Peter's St
Devonia Road
Grantbridge Street
Danbury St
Islington Green School
Rheidol Ter
Rheidol Ms
St Paul St
Packington Square
Prebend St
Rector St
Canon St
Union Sq
Paul St
Mary St
Linton St
Arlington Square
Arlington Av
Clock Tower Mews
Bevan Street
Museum of London (Archaeological Research Centre)
Frome St
Dame St
Burgh St
Baldwin Ter
Hanover Primary School
Wharf Road
Faircharm Trading Estate
Shepherdess Wk
Wenlock Road
Brewery Industrial Estate
Sturt St
Taplow St
SHEPHERDESS WALK
B144
EAGLE WHF ROAD
Parr St
Bracklyn St
Niagara Cl
Bletsoe Walk
Forston St
Godwin Close
Napier Grove
Primary School
Wimbourne St
Cropley St
Shaftesbury St
Cavendish Street
Wenlock Street
Bletchley St
Evelyn Walk
Grove
Murray Walk
Britannia Walk
Provost St
Fairbank
Provost Estate
Crusoe House Sch
Underwood St
Unwd Row
Micawber St
Thoresby St
Windsor Terrace
Wellesley Ter
Nile Street
Police Station
Westland Pl
Eb St
Britannia Walk
VESTRY
CITY ROAD
A501
Wakley Street
Sidney Gv
City Uni
London Open College
Pop Up Theatre
Claremont Cl
Myddelton Square
Amwell St
Chadwell St
River St
Myddelton Passage
Lillian Baylis Thr
Sadler's Wells Theatre
Owen's Rw
Friend St
Paget St
Hermit St
Rawstorne St
City Uni
ST JOHN ST
A1
B83
GOSWELL ROAD
Hall St
New Charles Street
Pickard St
Moreland Street
Gard St
Central Street
Macclesfield Road
Earlstoke Estate
Mason's Pl
Moreland Primary School
King Sq
Wynyatt St
Lloyd's Row
Spencer Street
The City University
Ashby St
Goswell Place
City University
Sebastian St
Northampton Sq
Wyclif St
Berry Pl
Tompion Street
B502
City Business Coll
City Central Estate
Dingley Rd
Dingley Pl
Mora Street
EC1V
LEVER STREET
City & Islington College
Moorfields Eye Hospital
Cayton St
BATH STREET
Galway Street
Peerless St
Baldwin St
St Luke's Estate
Old St Station
Ironmonger Row
Ironmonger Row Baths
Norman St
Radnor Street
Lizard St
Primary School
Finsbury Leisure Centre
Bartholomew Square
St Luke's Cl
Europa Pl
H St
FINSBURY
Primary School
Hardwick Primary School
Family Records Centre
Gloucester Way
Garnault Pl
Town Hall
ROSEBERY AVENUE
ROSOMAN ST
SKINNER ST
Joseph Trotter Close
Finsbury Estate
Whiskin St
Meredith St
Skinner St
JOHN STREET
B502
PERCIVAL ST
Agdon St
Malta St
Cyrus St
Mt Mills
Seward Street
Masons Yard
Central St
Mitchell St
Helmet Rw
St Luke's
A5201
OLD STREET
Mallow St
Martha's Bldgs
Surgery
Featherstone St
Moorfields Primary Sch
Wesley's Chapel House & Museum
Exmouth Market
Rosoman Place
Finsbury Health Cen
Northampton Rd
Record Office
EC1R
Rosemary Secondary Sch
Kingsway Place
Kingsway Coll
House of Detention
Sans Wk
Sekforde St
Woodbridge St
Compton Street
Compton Passage
Enclave Court
School
Primary Sch
Brewhouse Yard
Dallington St
Dallington Square
Northburgh St
Berry St
Peartree Street
City Uni
Bastwick St
Gee St
Garrett St
Baird St
Roscoe Street
Whitecross Street
Banner St
Chequer Street
Chequer St
BUNHILL ROW
University
Dufferin St
Errol Street
Honourable Artillery Company
Clerkenwell
Bowling Gn La
Pear Tree Ct
Clerkenwell Cl
Newcastle Row
St James Wk
Aylesbury St
Works
Jerusalem Passage
Crawford Pas
CLERKENWELL ROAD
Farringdon La
Ray St
Herbal Hl
Back Hl
Central Sch of Ballet
St John's Sq
Gt Sutton St
St John's Path
Clerkenwell Heritage Cen
Hat & Mitre Court
Mus of the Order of St John
St Bartholomews Medical Sch
Charterhouse Buildings
Glasshouse Yd
Golden Lane Estate
Golden Lane
EC1Y
Baltic St E
Baltic St W
Memel St
Crescent Rw
Fortune Street
Prior Western Primary School
Cherry Tree Walk
Lamb's Pas
Guildhall School of Music & Drama
College
Fann St
Brackley St
Viscount St
Exhibition Halls
Broad Yard
Britton St
Dickens Mews
Briset St
Albion Pl
Eagle Ct
Benjamin St
Charterhouse Sq
Arnot Abbey
Barbican Station
Faculty of Medicine
White Lyon Court
BEECH ST
City University Business Sch
Barbican Theatre
Barbican Cinema
Silk St
Milton St
Milton Court
Ropemaker St
B100
CHISWELL ST
Finsbury
HATTON GARDEN
Hatton Pl
Hatton Wall
Saffron Hill
Leather La
Cross St
Farringdon Station
Cowcross St
EC1M
B521
Turnmill St
A1 ALDERSGATE
A B C D E
85
532
12
1 grid square represents 250 metres

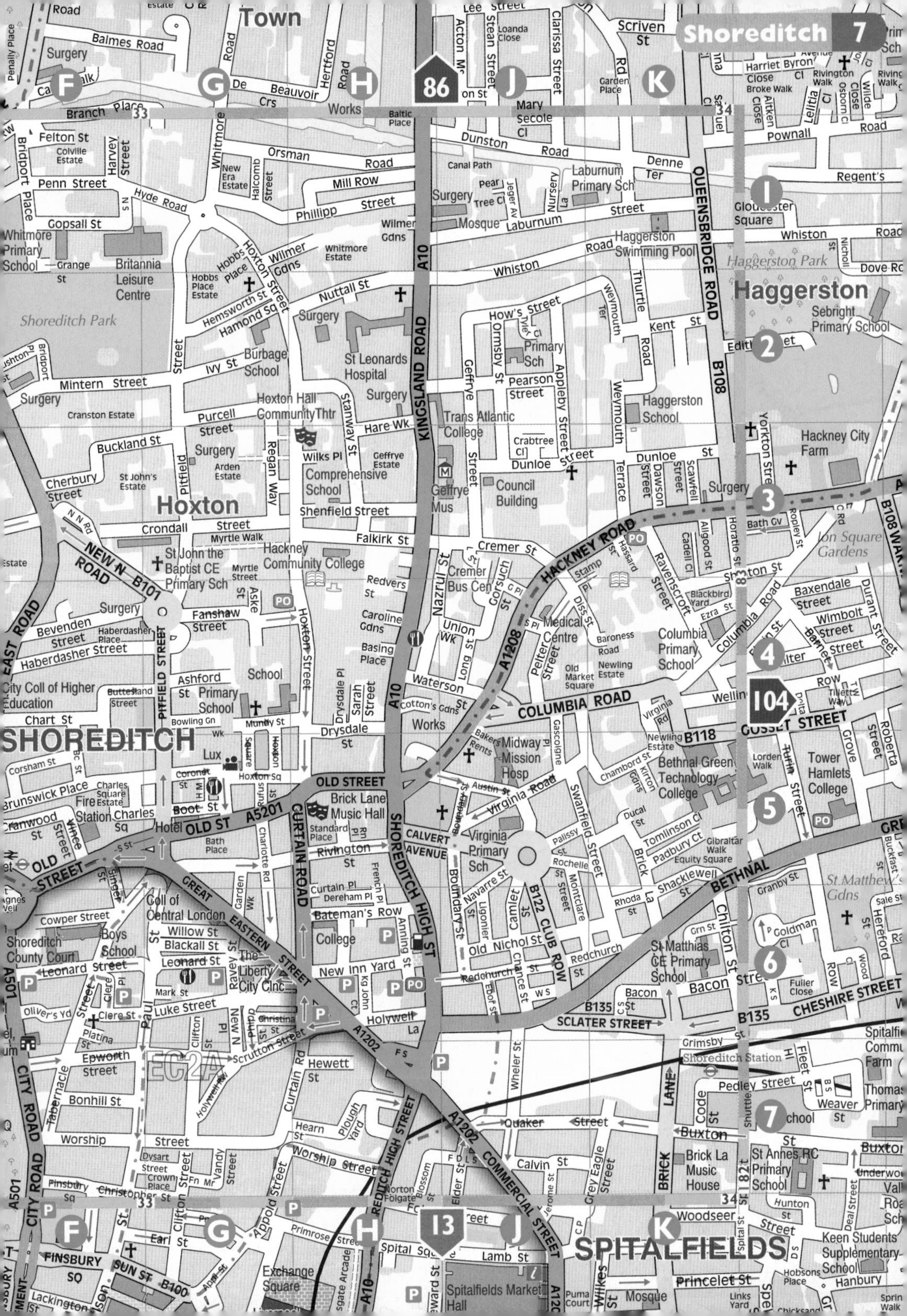
Town
Balmes Road
Surgery
De Beauvoir Crs
Hertford Road
Branch Place
Works
Baltic Place
86
Acton Mews
Stean Street
Loanda Close
Clarissa Street
Scriven St
Garden Place
Mary Secole Cl
Dunston Road
Felton St
Colville Estate
Harvey Street
Bridport Place
Penn Street
Hyde Road
Orsman Road
New Era Estate
Halcomb Street
Whitmore Road
Mill Row
Phillipp Street
Canal Path
Pear Tree Cl
Jeger Av
Nursery La
Laburnum Primary Sch
Denne Ter
Regent's
Gopsall St
Whitmore Primary School
Grange St
Britannia Leisure Centre
Hobbs Place Estate
Hoxton Street
Wilmer Gdns
Whitmore Estate
Mosque
Laburnum Street
Gloucester Square
Whiston Road
Haggerston Swimming Pool
Haggerston Park
Haggerston
Shoreditch Park
Hemsworth St
Hamond Sq
Nuttall St
Surgery
St Leonards Hospital
KINGSLAND ROAD
A10
How's Street
Tyler Cl
Ormsby St
Primary Sch
Weymouth Ter
Thurtle Road
Kent St
QUEENSBRIDGE ROAD
B108
Sebright Primary School
Edith Street
Burbage School
Ivy St
Mintern Street
Surgery
Cranston Estate
Purcell Street
Hoxton Hall Community Thtr
Stanway St
Hare Wk
Geffrye Street
Pearson Street
Appleby Street
Haggerston School
Trans Atlantic College
Yorkton Street
Hackney City Farm
Buckland St
Surgery
Arden Estate
Regan Way
Wilks Pl
Geffrye Estate
Comprehensive School
Crabtree Cl
Dunloe Street
Dunloe St
Dawson Street
Scawfell Street
Surgery
Cherbury Street
St John's Estate
Pitfield Street
Geffrye Mus
Council Building
Hoxton
Shenfield Street
Crondall Street
Myrtle Walk
Falkirk St
HACKNEY ROAD
Bath Gv
Ropley St
Ion Square Gardens
B108 WARNER
NEW N ROAD B101
St John the Baptist CE Primary Sch
Hackney Community College
Redvers St
Cremer St
Cremer Bus Cen
Nazrul St
Gorsuch St
Ravenscroft Street
Allgood St
Cadell Cl
Horatio St
Shipton St
Baxendale Street
Durant Street
Surgery
Bevenden Street
Haberdasher Place
Haberdasher Street
Fanshaw Street
Aske St
Caroline Gdns
Union Wk
Long St
A1208
Diss St
Medical Centre
Pelter Street
Baroness Road
Newling Estate
Columbia Primary School
Blackbird Yard
Ezra St
Columbia Road
Wimbolt Street
Barnet Street
EAST ROAD
PITFIELD STREET
City Coll of Higher Education
Buttesland Street
Ashford St
Primary School
School
Basing Place
Drysdale Pl
Sarah Street
Waterson St
Old Market Square
COLUMBIA ROAD
Virginia Rd
Wellington Row
104
Tillett Way
Chart St
Bowling Gn Wk
Mundy St
Hoxton St
Drysdale St
Cotton's Gdns
Works
SHOREDITCH
Corsham St
Lux
Coronet St
Hoxton Sq
OLD STREET
Bakers Rents
Midway Mission Hosp
Gascoigne Pl
Newling Estate
Chambord St
Kirton Gdns
B118
Bethnal Green Technology College
GOSSET STREET
Lorden Walk
Turin Street
Tower Hamlets College
Grove
Roberta Street
Brunswick Place
Charles Square Estate
Fire Station
Charles Sq
Boot St
Rufus St
Brick Lane Music Hall
Austin St
Virginia Road
Swanfield Street
Ducal St
Tomlinson Cl
Hotel
OLD ST A5201
Bath Place
Charlotte Rd
CURTAIN ROAD
Standard Place
Rivington St
SHOREDITCH HIGH ST
CALVERT AVENUE
Boundary St
Virginia Primary Sch
Palissy St
Rochelle St
Padbury Ct
Gibraltar Walk
Equity Square
Cranwood St
Vince Street
OLD STREET
Singer St
GREAT EASTERN STREET
French Pl
Curtain Pl
Dereham Pl
Navarre St
Ligonier St
Camlet St
Montclare St
Brick Lane
Shacklewell St
BETHNAL GREEN
Granby St
St Matthew's Gdns
Buckfast St
Coll of Central London
Cowper Street
Willow St
Blackall St
Leonard St
Garden Wk
Bateman's Row
College
Anning St
Old Nichol St
B122 CLUB ROW
Rhoda St
Grn St
St Matthias CE Primary School
Chilton St
Goldman Cl
Hereford St
Shoreditch County Court
Boys School
Leonard Street
The Liberty City Clnc
New Inn Yard
Redchurch St
Bacon St
Bacon Street
Fuller Close
CHESHIRE STREET
A501
Mark St
Luke Street
Ravey St
Holywell La
Chance St
B135
SCLATER STREET
Oliver's Yd
Clere St
Platina St
Christina St
Scrutton Street
A1202
Grimsby St
Shoreditch Station
Fleet St
Spitalfields Community Farm
Epworth Street
Clifton St
EC2A
Hewett St
Pedley Street
Weaver St
Thomas Primary
Bonhill St
Holywell Row
Curtain Rd
Wheler St
Code St
Tabernacle Street
Hearn St
Plough Yard
Quaker Street
Buxton St
School
Worship Street
Worship Street
A1202 COMMERCIAL STREET
Calvin St
Grey Eagle Street
Brick La Music House
St Annes RC Primary School
Dysart Street
Crown Place
Vandy Street
Norton Folgate
Blossom St
Elder St
Jerome St
BRICK LANE
Underwood Valance Road
Finsbury Sq
Christopher St
Appold Street
Hunton St
Deal Street
CITY ROAD
Earl St
Primrose St
13
Lamb St
Woodseer St
Spital Street
Keen Students Supplementary School
FINSBURY SQ
SUN ST B100
Exchange Square
Spital Square
Spitalfields Market Hall
Puma Court
Wilkes St
SPITALFIELDS
Princelet St
Mosque
Links Yard
Hobsons Place
Hanbury St
Lackington St
A10
33
34

1 grid square represents 250 metres

MARYLEBONE
Mayfair
Lisson Grove
MARYLEBONE ROAD
A501
PORTLAND PL
PK CR
Regent's Park Stn
Great Portland Street
Madame Tussaud's
Planetarium
LT Lost Property Office
Baker Street Stn
Univ of Westminster
High Comm of The Maldives
High Comm of Seychelles
Emb of Honduras
Emb of Latvia
Central London Co Court
Consulate of Chile
Medical Express Clnc
Devonshire Hospital
King Edward VII Hosp for Officers
Emb of Poland
High Comm of Kenya
Emb of China
RIBA
Cen Synagogue
University of Westminster
British Telecom Twr
Emb of Croatia
Emb of Mozambique
London Foot Hosp
Coll Nurses Home
PADDINGTON ST
B524
W1G
W1U
W1W
W1H
W1C
W1S
W1K
W1J
GLOUCESTER PLACE
BAKER STREET
MARYLEBONE HIGH ST
THAYER ST
WELBECK ST
GT PORTLAND STREET
REGENT ST
MORTIMER ST
CAVENDISH PL
The Heart Hosp
Eye Clnc
High Comm of Namibia
British Dental Ass
Queens Coll
Lister Ho Clinic
Wallace Collection
High Comm of Antigua & Barbuda
Wigmore Hall
Emb of Slovenia
High Comm of Belize
Emb of Bosnia
Consulate of Colombia
London Fo Temple
High Comm of Sierra Leone
RIBA Library Drawings & Manuscript Collection
PORTMAN SQUARE
Royal Society of Medicine
WIGMORE STREET
A5204
OXFORD ST
Oxford Circus Station
Bond Street Stn
Marble Arch Station
High Comm of Botswana
(0700-1900 Mon-Sat Buses and taxis only)
Palladium Thtr
High Comm of Cyprus
PORTMAN ST
ORCHARD ST
NEW BOND STREET
The Ford College
Handel's House
Emb of Brazil
Emb of Argentina
Emb of Italy
High Comm of Malawi
High Comm of Angola
Roosevelt Memorial
Grosvenor Square
Emb of USA
Emb of Indonesia
Emb of Angola
Consulate of Guinea
Speakers Corner
MARBLE ARCH
CUMBERLAND GATE
PARK LA
City of Westminster Vehicle Pound
Brook Gate
Grosvenor Gate
PARK LANE
A4202
Royal Institution Faraday Museum
Royal Academy of Arts
Royal Arcade
Burlington Arcade
PICCADILLY
A4
Emb of Myanmar
Emb of Saudi Arabia
Emb of Qatar
High Comm of Bahamas
Crewe Ho
Emb of Egypt
Emb of Mexico
Consulate of Panama
Emb of Japan
Green Park Station
Spencer House
St Curzon
Berkeley Sq
Primary School
Hotel

10
4
9
16
A
B
C
D
E
529
30
Bloomsbury
Mayfair
Soho
St Giles
China Town
St James
W1T
WC1E
W1G
W1W
WC1B
W1S
W1F
W1D
WC2H
WC2E
W1J
SW1Y
PORTLAND PL
GT PORTLAND STREET
REGENT STREET
REGENT ST
OXFORD STREET (restricted)
A40
NEW OXFORD ST
MORTIMER ST
A5204
GOODGE ST
TOTTENHAM COURT RD
A400
CHARING CROSS RD
SHAFTESBURY AV
PICCADILLY
PICCADILLY CIRCUS
PALL MALL
HAYMARKET
NEW BOND STREET
CONDUIT ST
RUSSELL SQ
MONTAGUE PLACE
Montague Street
BEDFORD SQ
GOWER ST
ST GILES HIGH ST
LONG ACRE
ST JAMES'S ST
A4
A4201
A3212
B506
Russell Square Station
Goodge St Station
Tottenham Court Road Stn
Oxford Circus Station
Leicester Square Stn
Piccadilly Circus Stn
Green Park Station
Covent Gdn Station
British Museum
University of London
UCL Hospital
Pollock's Toy Mus
British Telecom Twr
University of Westminster
Middlesex Hosp
Royal National Orthopaedic Hosp
London Sch of Hygiene & Tropical Medicine
RADA
Vanbrugh Thtr
Centre Point
Dominion Thtr
Palladium Thtr
Marshall Clnc
Prince Edward Thtr
Phoenix Thtr
Queens
Gielgud
Apollo
Lyric
Piccadilly
Criterion
Her Majesty's
Trocadero Cen
London Pav
Eros
Royal Academy of Arts
Faraday Museum
National Gallery
National Portrait Gal
Trafalgar Square
Nelson's Column
Coliseum
Garrick
Donmar Wa
Whitehall Thtr
Admiralty Arch
Old Admiralty
ICA
Mall Galleries
Duke of York Column
Carlton House
Schomberg House
Waterloo Place
Horse Guards Parade
Old War Office
Government Offices
Privy Council
Canada House
High Com of Uganda
High Comm of South Africa
High Comm of New Zealand
High Comm of Papua New Guinea
High Comm of Singapore
High Comm of Malta
High Comm of Sierra Leone
High Comm of Belize
High Comm of Namibia
High Comm of Barbados
Emb of Bosnia
Emb of Turkmenistan
Consulate of Colombia
Emb of Mozambique
Emb of Croatia
Emb of China
Emb of Egypt
1 grid square represents 250 metres

Soho 11
F
G
H
5
J
K
National Hosp for Sick Children (Great Ormond St)
Royal London Homeopathic Hosp
SOUTHAMPTON ROW
THEOBALD'S ROAD
ROSEBERY AV
CLERKENWELL ROAD
Central School of Ballet
London Weather Centre
HATTON GARDEN
EC1M
WC1R
Gray's Inn
Farringdon Station
Cowcross St
Kensington School of Business
Inns of Court School of Law
EC1N
Chancery Lane Stn
Holborn
HIGH HOLBORN
HOLBORN CIRCUS
CHARTERHOUSE
Central London Mkts
2
WC1V
Holborn Station
Holborn Town Hall
Staple Inn Bldgs
Gresham Coll
Daily Mirror Office
City Temple
Coll of Organists
A40 HOLBORN VIAD
Cock Police Station
Sir John Soane's Mus
Lincoln's Inn
WC2A
KINGSWAY
CHANCERY LA
EC4A
FARRINGDON STREET
3
Fleet Place
Central Criminal Court
Royal College of Surgeons
Old Curiosity Shop
Public Record Office
Gough Square
Dr Johnson's House
City Thameslink Station
New London Thtr
Kings Coll
New Connaught Rooms
The Peacock Thtr
WC2B
Royal Courts of Justice
London School of Economics
FLEET ST
Fleet Street
High Comm of Nigeria
4
12
Ludgate
Royal Ballet School
Fortune Thtr
Royal Opera House
Thtr Royal
Aldwych
Bush Ho (BBC)
Australia House
STRAND
Inns of Court and Chancery
Temple
Middle Temple Hall
Inner Temple
Sion Coll
Tudor St
NEW BRIDGE STREET
Covent Garden Piazza
LT Mus
The Mkt
Jubilee Mkt
St Peter's Hosp
Strand
Duchess
Lyceum
ALDWYCH
Courtauld Institute
Kings College London
WC2R
Somerset House
Gilbert Collection
Roman Bath
Temple Place
Temple Stn
EC4Y
VICTORIA EMB
5
Blackfriars Station
Blackfriars Stn
HMS President
Blackfriars Millennium Pier
City of London
Southwark
HQS Wellington (Master Mariners)
EMBANKMENT
LANCASTER PL
STRAND A4
Savoy Thtr
Royal Society of Arts
VICTORIA
Thames Police Station
Entrance to Strand Underpass (northbound only)
WATERLOO BRIDGE
Savoy Pier
Victoria Embankment Gardens
Cleopatra's Needle
York Water Gate
Embankment Pier
Charing Cross Stn
Embankment Station
The Playhouse
Waterloo Bridge
6
A201
Oxo Tower Wharf
Thames Path
The London Television Centre (LWT)
Royal National Theatre
National Film Theatre
Festival Pier
Queen Elizabeth Hall
Hungerford Bridge
Hispaniola
Royal Festival Hall
Hayward
BFI London IMAX Cinema
17
London City College
Schiller International School
STAMFORD ST
London Nautical School
7
Christchurch Industrial Centre
BLACKFRIARS
Paris Gdn
Rennie Street
Upper Ground
WC2N
Concert Hall Ap
Whittlesey Street
Roupell
Isabella
Southwark

12
6
532
A
B
C
D
E
EC1Y
EC1M
EC1N
EC1A
EC2Y
EC2V
EC2R
EC4A
EC4M
EC4N
EC4Y
EC4V
1
2
3
4
5
6
7
11
Central School of Ballet
Clerkenwell Heritage Cen
Mus of the Order of St John
St Bartholomews Medical
Charterhouse Buildings
Golden Lane Estate
Fortune Street
Errol Street
Cherry Tree Walk
Prior Weston Primary School
Guildhall School of Music & Drama
College
Honourable Artillery Company
CLERKENWELL ROAD
A5201
B521
HATTON GARDEN
Hatton Wall
Hatton Pl
Saffron Hill
Kirby St
Cross St
Leather Lane
Broad Yard
Dickens Mews
Turnmill St
Britton St
Briset St
Benjamin St
Albion Pl
Eagle Ct
Charterhouse
Sch of Medicine
Arnot Abbey
Fann St
Brackley St
Viscount St
Exhibition Halls
B100
CHISWELL
White Lyon Court
BEECH ST (BELOW)
City University Business Sch
Barbican Theatre
Silk St
Milton St
Milton Court
Ropemaker
Farringdon Station
Kensington School of Business
Cowcross St
Charterhouse St
Surgery
Long La
Hayne St
Lindsey St
Barbican Station
Middle St
Newbury St
A1 ALDERSGATE ST
Barbican Cinema
The Barbican
Barbican
City of London School for Girls
Guildhall School
Moor La
New Union St
Moorgate Stn
Moorfields Highwalk
Greville St
Ely Place
Central London Mkts
Cloth Court
Cloth Fair
Hall
St Bartholomew's the Great
Barber Surgeons' Hall
Surgery
Salters' Hall
Fore St
Wood St
Alphage Gdn
Alphage Highwalk
A201
FARRINGDON RD
CHARTERHOUSE ST
HOLBORN
HOLBORN CIRCUS
W Smithfield
Smithfield St
Hosier La
Snow Hl
Giltspur St
Lti Britain
A Wy
Mus of London
Ironmongers Hall
Sch of Music & Drama
MNTO ST
LONDON WALL
A1211
Roman Wall Remains
Brewers' Hall
Girdlers' Hall
Armourers Braziers'
Gresham Coll
Daily Mirror Office
Dyer's Buildings
Norwich St
Fetter Lane
NEW FETTER LA
ST ANDREW ST
City Temple
Plumtree Court
Shoe La
A40 HOLBORN VIAD
Cock La
Police Station
St Bartholomews Hospital
Little Britain
Postman's Park
Pewterers' Hall
Oat La
Clock Museum
Basinghall Avenue
Coleman St
Moorgate
Coll of Organists
Pigh Pl
N Cl
A4208
STONECUTTER ST
Fleet Place
A40 NEWGATE ST
KING EDWARD ST
Angel St
BT Centre
ST M LE GRAND
ALDERSGATE
Gresham St
Noble St
Haberdashers' Hall
Guildhall
Art Gal
Guildhall Yard
Guildhall Buildings
Mason's Avenue
Goldsmiths' Hall
Carey La
Waxchandlers' Hall
Rolls Buildings
SHOE LANE
FARRINGDON STREET
ST BRIDE ST
A4208
Old Fleet La
B Ct
Central Criminal Court
Cutlers' Hall
Warwick La
Foster La
G St
Mumford Ct
Gough Square
Red Lion Court
Crane Court
Dr Johnson's House
FETTER LA
A4
Lm La
Old Bailey
Am C
Stationers' Hall
St Paul's Station
Paternoster Rw
St Paul's Cathedral School
Saddlers Hall
Trump St
King St
Ironmonger La
Grocers' Hall
Prince's Street
Lothbury
Poppins Ct
City Thameslink Station
Ludgate Hill
St Paul's Cathedral
Cheapside
Bank of England Ext
Mercers' Hall
Fleet Street
High Comm of Nigeria
Bride La
NEW BRIDGE STREET
Yth Hostel
Bread St
Watling Street
Groveland Court
Well Court
Queen St
Poultry
Magistrates Court
Mansion Ho
Bouverie St
Temple Lane
Dorset Ri
The Bridewell Thtr
Black Friars La
Hall
Playhouse Yd
Carter Lane
Faraday Building
Addle Hl
Knightrider St
Cannon St
College of Arms
Bow Lane
Mansion House Station
Qu Victoria St
Temple of Mithras
Inner Temple
Sion Coll
Tudor St
Temple Av
John Carpenter St
Hotel
Kingscote St
QU VICTORIA ST
Queen Victoria St
Distaff La
Friday St
Budge Row
Navigation Coll
Oxford Ct
St Swithin's La
Tallis St
Blackfriars Station
PUDDLE DOCK
Mermaid
Castle
Baynard
Booth Lane
Salvation Army Heritage Centre
Huggin Hl
Lti Trinity La
Garlick Hl
Apostle
Med Cen
Sports Club
Halls
Cannon Street Stn
Bush La
Suffolk La
VICTORIA EMB
School
Peter's Hill
UPPER THAMES ST
Trig La
Skinners La
Med Cen
Innholders Hall
Dowgate Hl
Vinters' Hall
Games Path
HMS President
Blackfriars Millennium Pier
Blackfriars Stn
Blackfriars Pier
Blackfriars UP
White Lion Hill
CITY OF LONDON
Stew La
Gardners La
Queenhithe
Kennett Whf La
QUEEN ST PLACE
Bell Wharf Lane
Cousin La
Allhill La
City of London
Southwark
River Thames
Queenhithe Stairs
Southwark Bridge Stairs
Millennium Bridge
Southwark Bridge
Steelyard Passage
London Bridge Sports Centre
Fish Hal
A201
Blackfriars Bridge
Thames Path
South Bank
Marigold Alley
Panorama Pier
Bankside Jetty
Swan Pier
Oxo Tower Wharf
Bargehouse St
Upper Gnd
Milroy Walk
Rennie Street
Bankside Gallery
Hopton St
Shakespeare's Globe Theatre
Bankside
Golden Hinde Educational Museum
Glaziers Scientific Instrument Makers
Gabriel's Wharf
Broadwall
Ducky St
Invicta Plaza
Purdy Hicks Gallery
Holland Street
Tate Modern
Park St
New Globe Wk
Bear Gdns
Rose Aly
Financial Times
Hotel
Bank End
Clink Exhib
Clink St
SOUTHWARK BRIDGE ROAD
Coin St
A3200
STAMFORD ST
Duchy St
Hatfields
Christchurch Industrial Centre
Paris Gdn
Kings College London
Emerson St
Rose Thr Exhibition
Sumner St
Porter St
Vinopolis, City of Wine
Mus Montag Cl
Winchester Wk
Southwark Cath
Coin Street
Aquinas St
London Nautical School
Colombo St
Burrell St
Chancel St
Bear La
School
Zoar St
Falcon Cl
Industrial Cen
St Christopher House
Perkins Sq
Gatehouse Square
Borough Market
Miller Walk
Surgery
Surgery
Price's St
SOUTHWARK
STREET
Kings Coll London
Bramah's Tea & Coffee Mus
Hotel
Operating Theatre Museum
Theed St
Whittlesey St
Meymott St
BLACKFRIARS
Nicholson Street
Brinton Walk
Gambia St
Great Suffolk St
Farnham Pl
Loving
Works
Ewer St
Hotel
Guildford St
Thrale St
Maiden La
A3200
White Hart Yard
1 grid square represents 250 metres
Roupell St
Scoresby St
Grande Vitesse Industrial Cen
Wardens Grove
Isabella St
Southwark
Maidstone Buildings
Talbot
Southwark

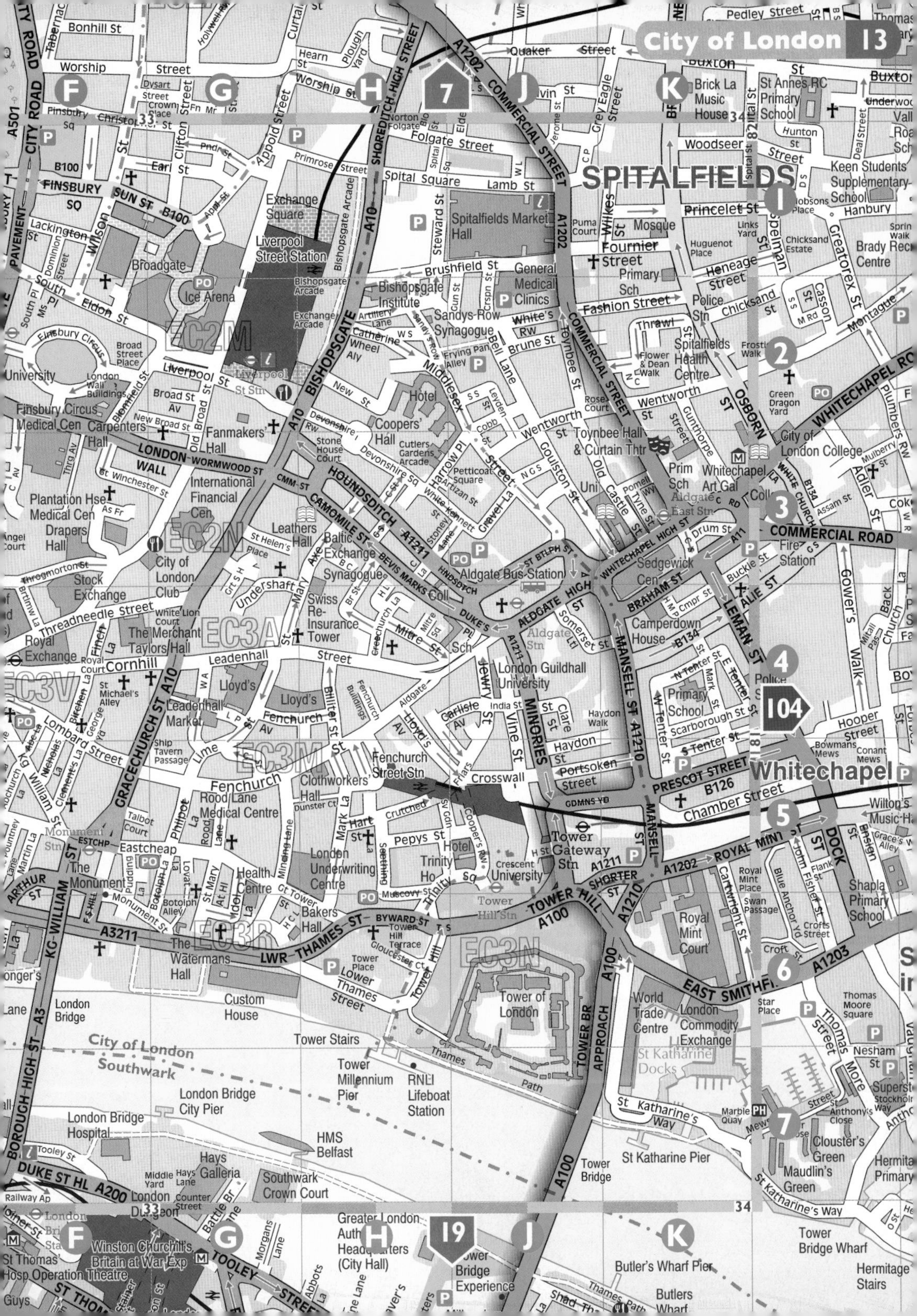
SPITALFIELDS
Whitechapel
City of London
Southwark
Bonhill St
Worship Street
City Road
Finsbury Sq
Finsbury Sq
Sun St
Appold Street
Shoreditch High Street
Commercial Street
Quaker Street
Pedley Street
Buxton St
Brick La Music House
St Annes RC Primary School
Folgate Street
Primrose Street
Spital Square
Lamb St
Exchange Square
Liverpool Street Station
Broadgate
Ice Arena
Spitalfields Market Hall
Princelet St
Mosque
Fournier Street
Hanbury
Brady Recreation Centre
Brushfield St
General Medical Clinics
Bishopsgate Institute
Sandys Row Synagogue
Fashion Street
Heneage Street
Chicksand St
Spitalfields Health Centre
Finsbury Circus
Liverpool St
Bishopsgate
Middlesex Street
Wentworth St
Toynbee Hall & Curtain Thtr
Osborn St
Whitechapel Art Gal
City of London College
Whitechapel Rd
Finsbury Circus Medical Cen
London Wall
Fanmakers' Hall
Coopers' Hall
Houndsditch
International Financial Cen
Plantation Hse Medical Cen
Drapers Hall
Leathers Hall
Baltic Exchange
Bevis Marks
Aldgate Bus Station
Aldgate High St
Whitechapel High St
Commercial Road
Fire Station
Sedgewick Cen
Braham St
Leman St
Alie St
Gower's Walk
Stock Exchange
City of London Club
Threadneedle Street
The Merchant Taylors Hall
Royal Exchange
Cornhill
Leadenhall Street
Swiss Re-Insurance Tower
Mitre St
Aldgate Stn
Camperdown House
Mansell St
London Guildhall University
Lloyd's
Leadenhall Market
Lombard Street
Gracechurch St
Fenchurch St
Fenchurch Street Stn
Minories
Haydon St
Portsoken Street
Prescot Street
Chamber Street
Hooper Street
Wilton's Music Hall
Clothworkers' Hall
Crosswall
Rood Lane Medical Centre
Monument Stn
Eastcheap
The Monument
London Underwriting Centre
Trinity Ho
Crescent University
Tower Gateway Stn
Tower Hill Stn
Royal Mint St
Cartwright St
Shapla Primary School
Health Centre
Byward St
Lwr Thames St
Tower Hill
Royal Mint Court
East Smithfield
The Watermans Hall
Custom House
Tower of London
Lower Thames Street
London Bridge
Tower Bridge Approach
World Trade Centre
London Commodity Exchange
St Katharine Docks
Thomas More Street
Tower Stairs
Tower Millennium Pier
RNLI Lifeboat Station
London Bridge City Pier
London Bridge Hospital
HMS Belfast
Hays Galleria
St Katharine's Way
St Katharine Pier
Tower Bridge
Southwark Crown Court
Duke St Hl
London Dungeon
Winston Churchill's Britain at War Exp
Tooley Street
Greater London Auth Headquarters (City Hall)
Tower Bridge Experience
Butler's Wharf Pier
Butlers Wharf
Tower Bridge Wharf
Hermitage Stairs
St Thomas' Hosp Operation Theatre
Borough High St
KG William St
EC2M
EC2N
EC3A
EC3V
EC3M
EC3R
EC3N
F
G
H
J
K
1
2
3
4
5
6
7
19
104
33
34

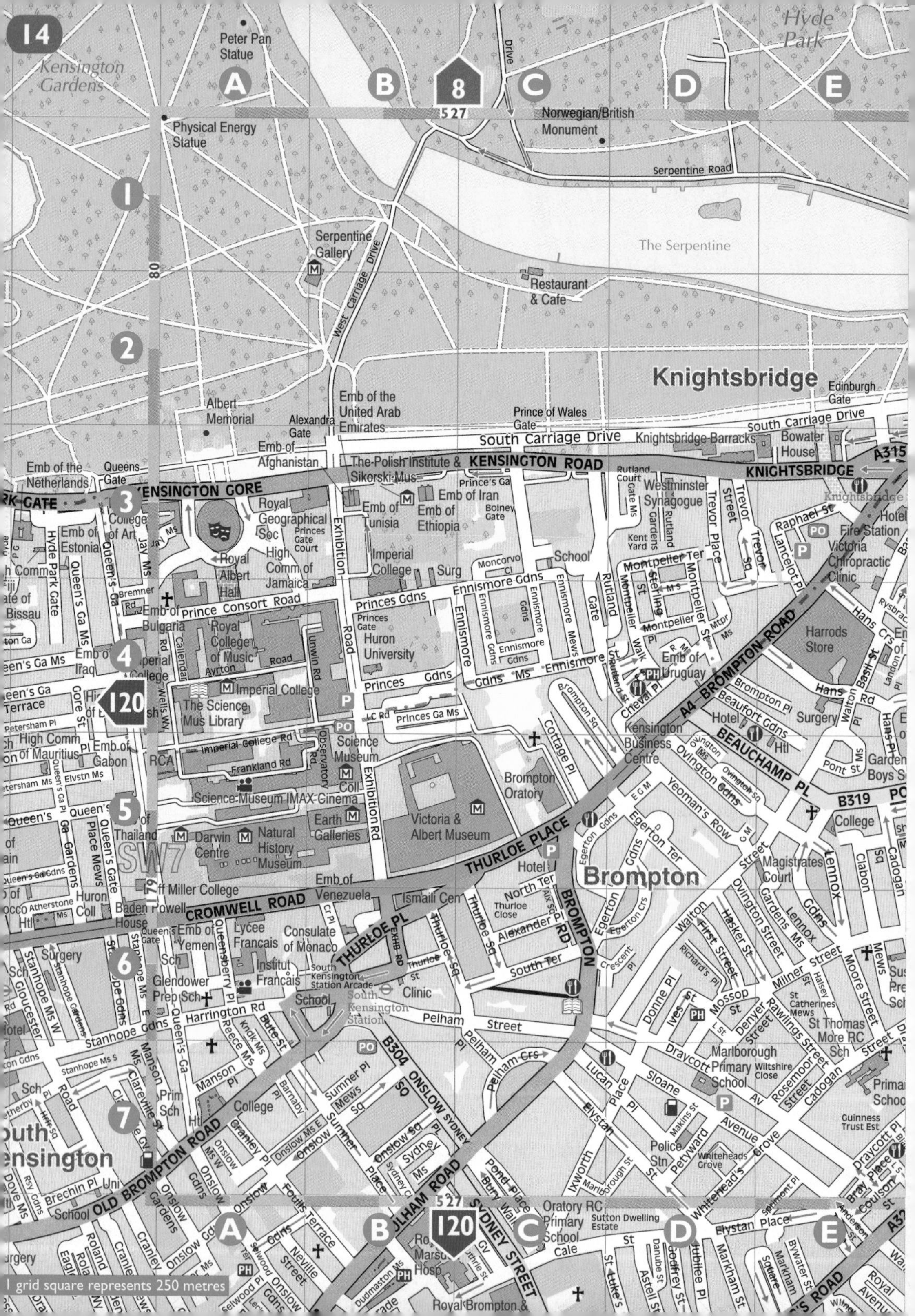
Kensington Gardens
Hyde Park
Peter Pan Statue
Physical Energy Statue
Norwegian/British Monument
Serpentine Road
The Serpentine
Serpentine Gallery
West Carriage Drive
Restaurant & Cafe
Knightsbridge
Edinburgh Gate
Albert Memorial
Alexandra Gate
Emb of the United Arab Emirates
Prince of Wales Gate
South Carriage Drive
Knightsbridge Barracks
Bowater House
Emb of Afghanistan
Emb of the Netherlands
Queens Gate
The Polish Institute & Sikorski Mus
KENSINGTON ROAD
KNIGHTSBRIDGE
KENSINGTON GORE
Rutland Court
Westminster Synagogue
Royal Geographical Soc
Princes Gate Court
Emb of Tunisia
Emb of Iran
Emb of Ethiopia
Boiney Gate
College of Art
Emb of Estonia
Hyde Park Gate
Royal Albert Hall
High Comm of Jamaica
Imperial College
Surg
Exhibition Road
School
Montpelier Ter
Trevor Place
Trevor Sq
Raphael St
Fire Station
Victoria Chiropractic Clinic
Emb of Bulgaria
Prince Consort Road
Royal College of Music
Princes Gdns
Huron University
Ennismore Gdns
Ennismore Mews
Montpelier Walk
Emb of Uruguay
Harrods Store
A4 BROMPTON ROAD
Imperial College
The Science Mus Library
Unwin Rd
Princes Ga Ms
Brompton Sq
Kensington Business Centre
Beaufort Gdns
BEAUCHAMP PL
Surgery
High Comm of Mauritius
Emb of Gabon
RCA
Imperial College Rd
Frankland Rd
Science Museum
Science Museum IMAX Cinema
Victoria & Albert Museum
Brompton Oratory
Cottage Pl
Ovington Gdns
Yeoman's Row
Pont St
Garden Boys Sch
B319
College
Queen's Gate
SW7
Darwin Centre
Natural History Museum
Earth Galleries
Exhibition Rd
THURLOE PLACE
Hotel
Brompton
Egerton Ter
Magistrates Court
Lennox Gdns
Clabon Ms
Cadogan Sq
Emb of Thailand
Emb of Venezuela
Ismaili Cen
CROMWELL ROAD
Baden Powell House
Huron Coll
Emb of Yemen
Lycee Francais
Consulate of Monaco
Institut Francais
THURLOE PL
Thurloe Close
Alexander Pl
North Ter
South Ter
BROMPTON RD
Egerton Crescent
Walton Street
First Street
Hasker St
Ovington Street
Milner Street
Moore Street
St Catherines Mews
St Thomas More RC Sch
Glendower Prep Sch
South Kensington Station Arcade
South Kensington Station
Clinic
Pelham Street
Harrington Rd
Stanhope Gdns
Gloucester Rd
Manson Pl
Prim Sch
College
B304 ONSLOW SQ
Sumner Pl
Pelham Crs
Lucan Place
Sloane Av
Draycott Av
Marlborough Primary School
Wiltshire Close
Rawlings Street
Rosemoor Street
Cadogan Street
Primary School
Guinness Trust Est
Police Stn
Whiteheads Grove
Elystan Pl
Ixworth Pl
Makins St
South Kensington
OLD BROMPTON ROAD
FULHAM ROAD
SYDNEY STREET
Onslow Gardens
Onslow Sq
Foulis Terrace
Neville Street
Brechin Pl
School
Oratory RC Primary School
Sutton Dwelling Estate
Elystan Place
Markham St
Bywater St
Royal Marsden Hosp
Royal Brompton &
Dudmaston Ms
Astell St
Jubilee Pl
1 grid square represents 250 metres

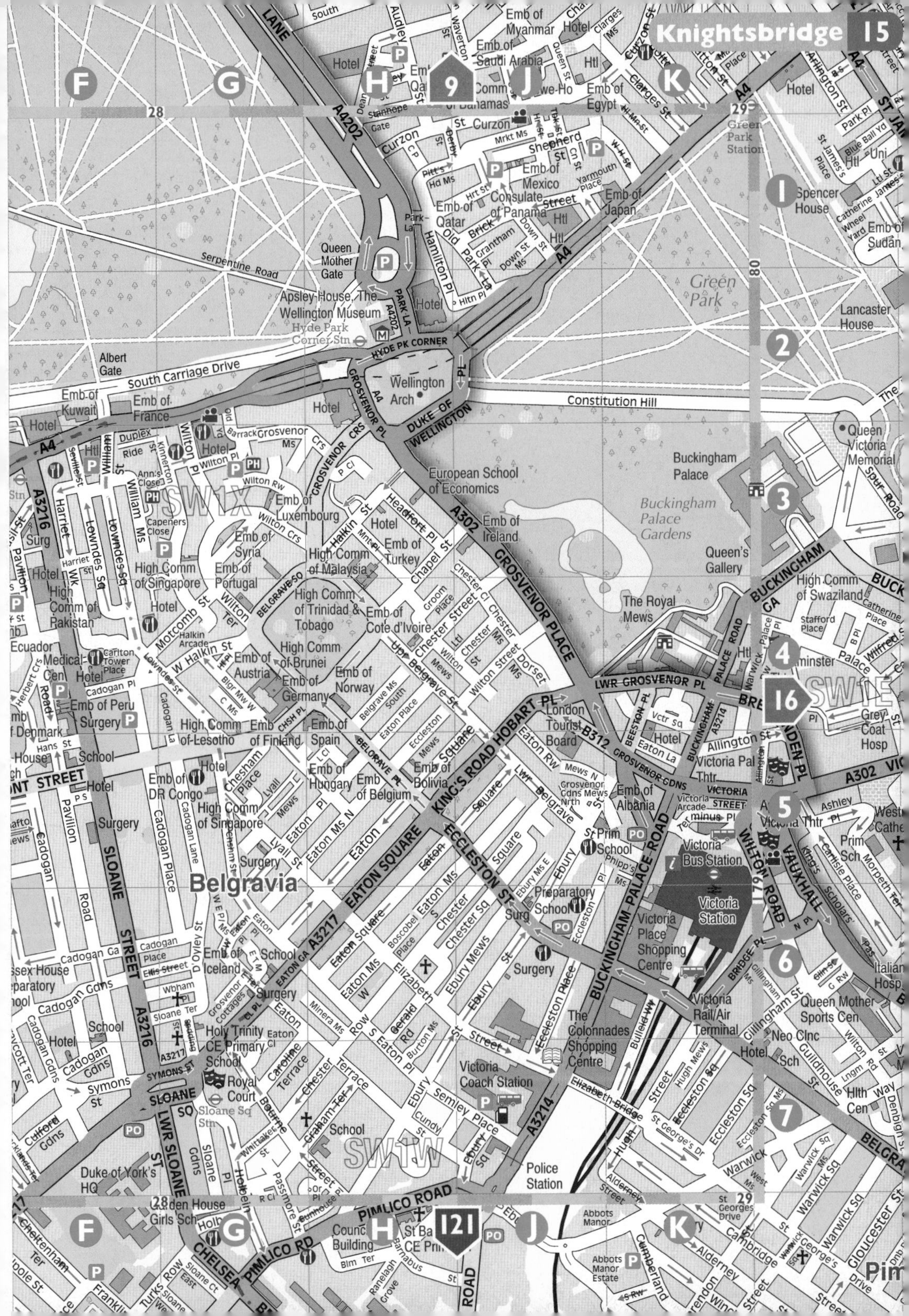

F
G
H
J
K
I
2
3
4
5
6
7
9
16
121
28
29
80
Hyde Park
Serpentine Road
Queen Mother Gate
Apsley House, The Wellington Museum
Hyde Park Corner Stn
HYDE PK CORNER
Albert Gate
South Carriage Drive
Wellington Arch
Constitution Hill
Green Park
Green Park Station
Spencer House
Lancaster House
Queen Victoria Memorial
Buckingham Palace
Buckingham Palace Gardens
Queen's Gallery
The Royal Mews
European School of Economics
Emb of Ireland
PARK LA
A4202
A4
DUKE OF WELLINGTON
GROSVENOR PL
GROSVENOR CRS
A302
GROSVENOR PLACE
LWR GROSVENOR PL
HOBART PL
B312
GROSVENOR GDNS
BUCKINGHAM PALACE ROAD
VICTORIA STREET
WILTON ROAD
VAUXHALL
BRESSENDEN PL
BUCKINGHAM GATE
Victoria Bus Station
Victoria Station
Victoria Place Shopping Centre
Victoria Rail/Air Terminal
Victoria Coach Station
The Colonnades Shopping Centre
Victoria Pal Thtr
Victoria Thtr
London Tourist Board
Emb of Albania
Police Station
Queen Mother Sports Cen
Neo Clnc
Grey Coat Hosp
High Comm of Swaziland
SW1X
SW1E
SW1W
Belgravia
Emb of Kuwait
Emb of France
Emb of Luxembourg
Emb of Syria
Emb of Portugal
High Comm of Singapore
High Comm of Pakistan
Emb of Ecuador
Emb of Turkey
High Comm of Malaysia
High Comm of Trinidad & Tobago
Emb of Cote d'Ivoire
High Comm of Brunei
Emb of Austria
Emb of Germany
Emb of Norway
Emb of Spain
Emb of Finland
High Comm of Lesotho
Emb of Peru
Emb of Denmark
Emb of DR Congo
Emb of Hungary
Emb of Belgium
Emb of Bolivia
Emb of Iceland
Emb of Myanmar
Emb of Saudi Arabia
Emb of Egypt
Emb of Mexico
Consulate of Panama
Emb of Qatar
Emb of Japan
Emb of Sudan
Carlton Tower Hotel
Halkin Arcade
BELGRAVE SQ
BELGRAVE PL
KING'S ROAD
EATON SQUARE
A3217
ECCLESTON ST
SLOANE STREET
A3216
SLOANE SQ
Sloane Sq Stn
Royal Court
Holy Trinity CE Primary School
LWR SLOANE ST
PIMLICO ROAD
PIMLICO RD
CHELSEA BRIDGE RD
Duke of York's HQ
Cadogan Gdns
Cadogan Place
Cadogan Lane
Chesham Place
Lowndes Sq
Lowndes St
Wilton Crs
Wilton Pl
Motcomb St
Halkin St
Chapel St
Chester Square
Elizabeth St
Ebury St
Ebury Bridge
Eccleston Place
Eccleston Sq
Warwick Sq
St George's Dr
Cambridge St
Alderney St
Abbots Manor Estate
Curzon St
Clarges St
Shepherd St
Hamilton Pl
Old Park La
Stanhope Gate
Dean St
Audley St
Arlington St
St James's Place
Pavilion Road
Hans St
Harriet Wk
William St
Pimlico

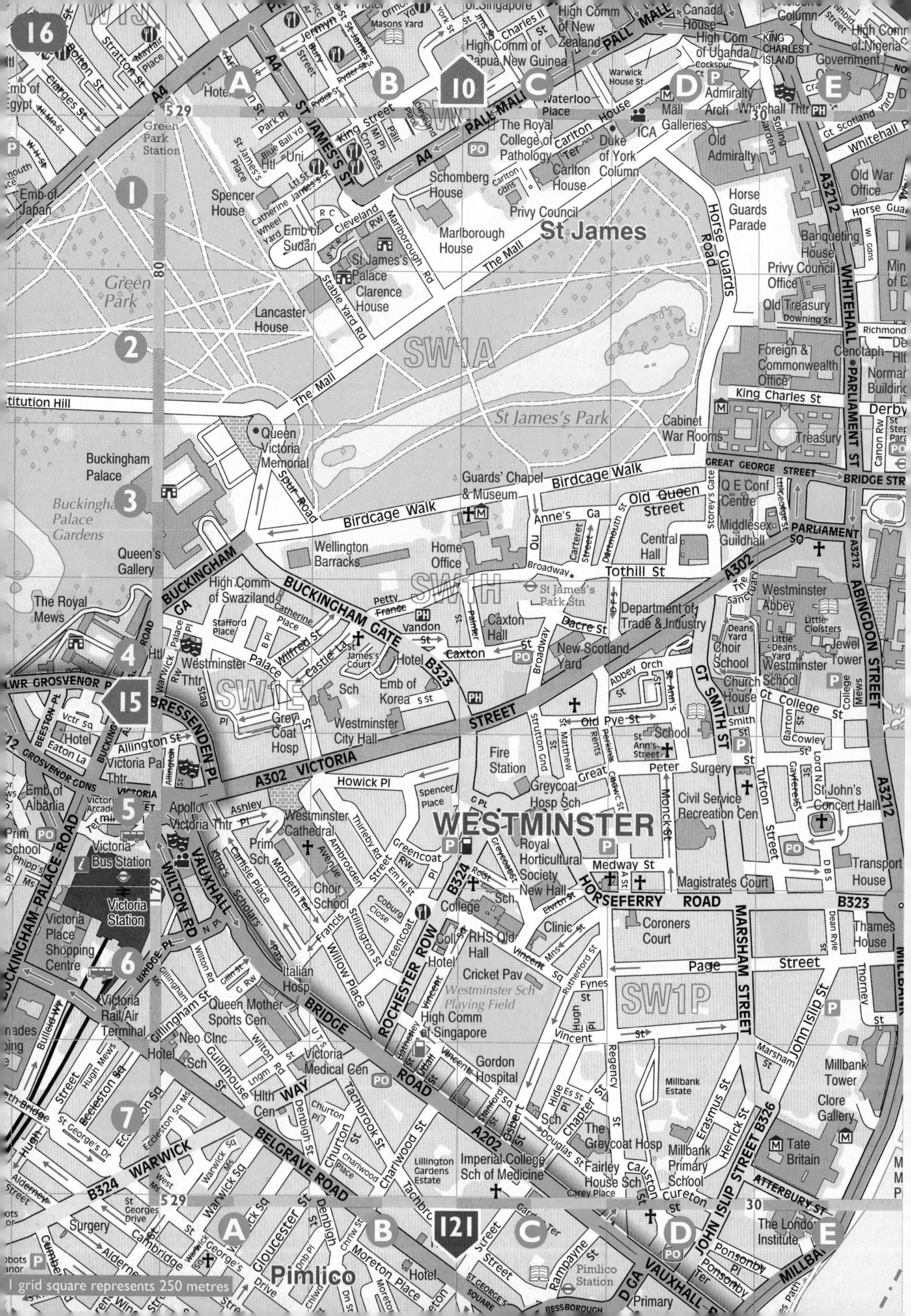

1 grid square represents 250 metres

Charing Cross Stn
Embankment Pier
Embankment Station
Festival Pier
Royal National Theatre
Television Centre (LWT)
National Film
Playhouse
Queen Elizabeth Hall
Hungerford Bridge
Hayward Gallery
Royal Festival Hall
Hispaniola
WC2N
BFI London IMAX Cinema
Concert Hall Ap
Schiller International School
London City College
Stamford St
Coin Street
Aquinas St
Miller Walk
London Nautical School
Industrial Centre
Paris Gdn
Burrell St
Colombo St
Chancel St
Blackfriars
Nicholson Street
Brinton Walk
Scoresby St
Meymott St
Surgery
Cornwall
School
Theed St
Whittlesey Street
Roupell St
Brad St
Exton St
Secker St
Isabella St
Joan Street
Southwark Station
Works
Jubilee Gardens
Shell Centre
Belvedere Road
Mepham St
Alaska St
Sandell St
Waterloo East Stn
Wootton Street
Greet St
Southwark Coll
Burrows Ms
The Cut
Young Vic Theatre
Nelson Sq
British Airways London Eye
Chicheley Street
Hotel
International Rail Terminal
Waterloo Station
York Road
A3200
Waterloo Rd
Surrey
Pocock
Friars Prim Foundation School
Valentine Place
Works
Dali Universal Exhibition
County Hall
Saatchi Gallery
London Aquarium
Forum Magnum Square
Leake Street
Holmes Ter
Pear Pl
Spur Road
Mitre Rd
Ufford
Chaplin Close
Gray St
Webber Street
Old Vic Theatre
B300
Westminster Pier
Portcullis House
Westminster Station
A302
A23
Westminster Bridge Road
The Nightingale School
Marsh
Lower Marsh
Coral St
A301
Baron's Place
Webber Row
Big Ben
Westminster Bridge
Florence Nightingale Museum
Grindal St
Launcelot St
Johanna Primary School
Waterloo Health Centre
Murphy Street
Baylis Road
Frazier St
Cooper Close
Morley St
South Bank University
St George's Circus
Houses of Parliament
A&E
Upper Marsh
Creeham Cl
Pearman Street
Gerridge St
Dodson St
Emery St
Cottesloe Mews
Lambeth North Station
Royal Street
Newnham Terrace
Westminster Br Rd
A3202
St George's Cathedral RC Primary School
St Thomas's Hospital
Metropolitan Hospital
United Medical & Dental Schools
Victoria Tower Gardens
City of Westminster
Lambeth
Thames Path
Lambeth Palace Road
Carlisle Lane
Centaur St
Virgil St
Hercules Rd
LAMBETH
Police Stn
Mead Row
Oakey Lane
Kg Edward Wk
Churchill Clinic
St George's Cathedral
18
Gladstone St
Sch
Collinson St
Garden Row
A3036
Archbishop's Park
Cosser Street
McAuley Cl
Morton Place
Hotel
Road
Council Building
Imperial War Museum
Geraldine Mary Harmsworth Park
A302
Sidford Place
Lambeth
Surgery
Newington
West Sq
Lambeth Palace
A3203
Museum of Garden History
Pratt Walk
Sall Street
Walk
Kennington
Harmsworth Mews
IWM Annexe
Brook Drive
Southwark
Lambeth
Austral St
Orient St
Hayles Street
Hedger St
Lamlash St
A3203
Lambeth Bridge
Hotel
Norfolk Row
Juxon St
Hornbeam Cl
Walnut Tree Walk
Walcot Sq
Old Paradise St
Ingram Cl
Saperton Walk
Fitzalan
Walnut Tree Walk Primary School
Bishop's Ter
St Mary's Wk
St Mary's Gdns
Sullivan Rd
Polperro Ms
Brook Dr
Castlebrook Close
Fire Brigade HQ
Lambeth High Street
Whitgift Street
Newport Street
Ravent Road
Lambeth Walk
Lollard Street
Saunders St
Street
Oakden St
Monkton St
Nightingale Ms
Gilbert Rd
Heralds Place
Renfrew Road
Wincott St
The Michael Tippett School
Works
Salamanca Place
Black Prince
Gibson Road
Distin St
Archbishop Sumners CE Primary School
Knights
London College of Further Edu
Salamanca Street
Lillian Baylis School
Ethelred Estate
Lollard St
Reedworth Street
K Rd
Cotton Garden Estate
A3204
Lilliac Pl
Beaufoy Walk
Marylee Way
SE11
Hinley Clinic
Opal St
Millbank Millennium Pier
Randall Road
Randall Rw
School
Road
Hotspur Street
A23
Chester Way
Embankment
St Thomas Childrens Day Ho
Denny St
Denny Crs
Kennington Lane
Cottington St
Othello Cl
Kennington Park Rd
Citadel Place
Surgery
Nathan Street
Sancroft Street
A3036 Albert
Tinworth Street
Graphite Square
Vauxhall
Worgan St
Tyers
Wickham St
Orsett St
Seaton Close
Tavy Close
White Hart Street
Works
Thames Path
Glasshouse
Lambeth County
Kennington
F
G
H
J
K
I
2
3
4
5
6
7
11
31
122

A3200
STAMFORD ST
Christchurch Industrial Centre
Kings College London
School
Zoar St
Industrial Cen
Financial Times
Hotel
Rose Thtr Exhibition
Sumner St
Vinopolis, City of Wine
Mus
Montague Cl
Southwark Cath
Borough Market
12
532
SOUTHWARK STREET
St Christopher House
Price's St
Farnham Pl
Lavington St
Hotel
Works
Kings Coll London
Bramah's Tea & Coffee Mus
Thrale St
Old Operating Theatre Museum
Hatfields
London Nautical School
Coin St
Aquinas St
Duchy St
Colombo St
BLACKFRIARS ROAD
Burrell St
Chancel St
Bear La
Surgery
Meymott St
Nicholson Street
Brinton Walk
Scoresby St
Gambia St
Grande Vitesse Industrial Cen
Theed St
Whittlesey Street
Roupell St
Brad St
Waterloo East Stn
Wootton Street
Isabella St
Joan Street
Southwark Station
Works
B300
UNION STREET
Wardens Grove
Guildford St
Ewer St
Southwark Bridge Bus Cen
Maidstone Buildings Mews
White Hart Yard
Talbot Yard
York Clinic
Young Vic Theatre
THE CUT
Southwark Coll
Burrows Ms
Nelson Sq
Works
Copperfield St
Loman Street
Pepper St
Fire Brigade Mus
Crown Court at the Borough
Fire Stn
Ayres Street
Redcross Wy
School
Davies's College
Newcomen St
Mermaid Ct
Chapel Court
Old Vic Theatre
Mitre Rd
Ufford St
Surrey Row
Pocock St
Chaplin Close
Valentine Place
Works
Friars Primary Foundation School
Rushworth St
King's Bench St
Glasshill Street
Great Suffolk Street
Sawyer St
Sturge St
BRIDGE
Quilp St
Mint St
Weller St
Lant St
MARSHALSEA RD
Disney St
Primary School
Southwark Coroners Court
HIGH ST A3
Tabard Garden Estate
Borough Stn
Webber Street
Coral St
B300
A301
Baron's Place
Webber Row
Silex St
Boyfield Street
Lancaster Street
Kg James St
Sudrey St
Toulmin St
School
Pickwick Street
Great Suffolk St
Collinson Street
Collinson Walk
The Borough
Sterry St
Pilgrimage Street
Cooper Close
Morley St
Dodson St
WATERLOO ROAD
Gerridge St
Emery St
Pearman Street
Cottesloe Mews
South Bank University
ST GEORGE'S CIRCUS
Davidge St
Milcote St
Mathieson Court
Scovell Rd
McCoid Way
Borough Square
Police Stn
Surgery
BOROUGH
Hulme Place
Surg
Swan St
Trinity St
Cole St
Globe St
Becket St
WESTMINSTER BR RD A3202
BOROUGH ROAD
South Bank University
SOUTHWARK
A3
NEWINGTON CSWY
SE1
Trinity Church Sq
Merrick Sq
GREAT DOVER ST
Metropolitan Hospital
St George's Cathedral RC Primary School
A201
Rotary St
Kell St
Thomas Doyle St
Keyworth St
Gaunt St
Inner London Sessions Ho (Crown Court)
Newington Gardens
Brockham St
HARPER RD
Alderney Mews
Spurgeon St
Chettle Close
Oakey Lane
Churchill Clinic
17
Girls School
Gladstone St
Sch
Kg Edward Wk
ROAD
Council Building
Geraldine Mary Harmsworth
LONDON RD
Eden College
Ontario St
GARDEN RW
A302
Tiverton St
Bath Terrace
Tarn St
Falmouth Rd
B240
Geoffrey Chaucer School
Burbage Close
Deverell St
Imperial War Museum
Newington
A302
ST GEORGE'S RD
West Sq
Sch
Gaywood St
Princess St
Elephant and Castle Stn
Newington Court Business Cen
Arch Street
Rockingham St
South Bank University
Joseph Lancaster School
Theobald St
Harmsworth Mews
IWM Annexe
Brook Drive
Southwark
Lambeth
A201
Austral St
Orient St
Hayles Street
London Coll of Printing
Elliott's Rw
Oswin St
Elephant & Castle Shopping Centre
Elephant and Castle Stn
County Street
NEW KENT ROAD
Walcot Sq
Metropolitan Tabernacle
Castle Industrial Est
Heygate Estate
Rodney Pl
Balfour St
Munton Road
Victory Primary School
John Maurice Cl
Henshaw Street
Walcot Sq
Bishop's Ter
St Mary's Gdns
Oakden St
Hedger St
Lamlash St
Brook Drive
Castlebrook Close
Elephant & Castle Leisure Cen
Churchyard Rw
Elephant Rd
Deacon Way
Victory Place
Chatham St
Salisbury Cl
Wincott St
Monkton St
Nightingale Ms
Gilbert Rd
Heralds Place
Renfrew Road
Dante Rd
Holyoak Rd
NEWINGTON BUTTS
Draper Estate
Wollaston Close
Howell Wk
Hampton St
Heygate Street
Brandon St
Rodney Road
The Michael Tippett School
Archbishop Sumners CE Primary School
Knights Walk
Cotton Gardens Estate
London College of Further Education
A3204
Marlborough Close
WALWORTH
Walworth Town Hall
Wansey St
Larcom St
Content St
Wadding St
Stead St
English Martyrs Primary School
Reedworth Street
Chester Way
Hinley Clinic
KENNINGTON PARK ROAD
Newington Industrial Est
Canterbury Place
Peacock St
Surg
The Cuming Mus
Sch
John Smith House
Charleston St
Cotham St
Morecambe Street
Nursery Row
Orb St
Denny St
Opal St
Penton St
Wesley Close
Crampton Primary Sch
532
122
Crampton St
Police Station
Browning Street
King And Queen St
Tw St
KENNINGTON LANE
Cottington St
Othello Cl
Tavy Close
Seaton Close
Alberta Street
Iliffe St
Place
Alberta Estate
Thrush St
Manor Place
Occupation Road
Surgery
Robert Browning Primary Sch
Pilton Place
Blackwood St
Surgery
Lambeth County
Kennington
1 grid square represents 250 metres

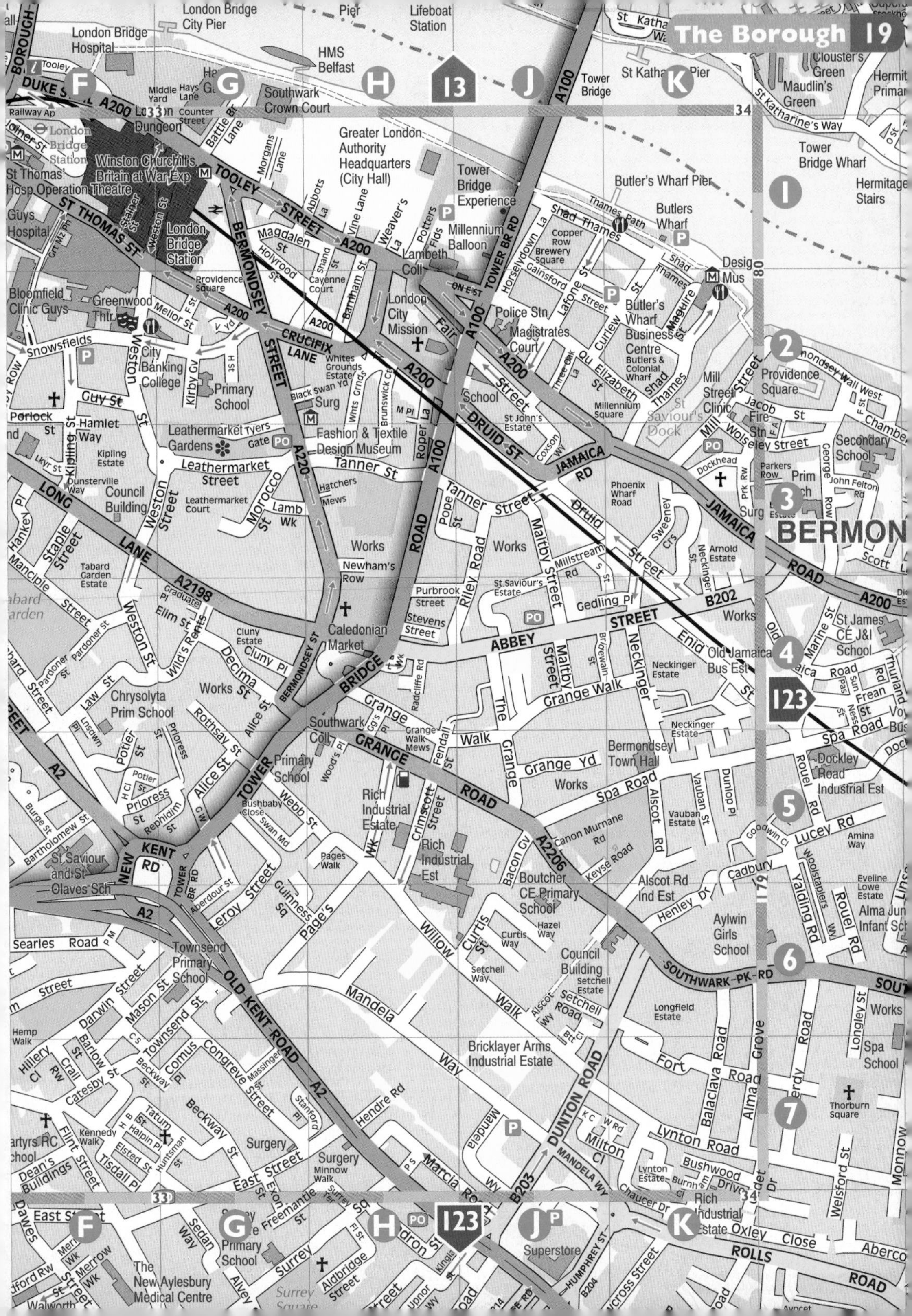
London Bridge City Pier
Pier
Lifeboat Station
London Bridge Hospital
HMS Belfast
13
Tower Bridge
St Katharine Pier
Clouster's Green
Maudlin's Green
Hermitage Primary
St Katharine's Way
Tooley St
DUKE ST HILL
A200
Middle Yard
Hays Lane
Counter Street
Southwark Crown Court
F
G
H
J
K
I
Railway Ap
33
34
London Dungeon
Joiner St
London Bridge Station
Battle Br Lane
Winston Churchill's Britain at War Exp
Greater London Authority Headquarters (City Hall)
Tower Bridge Experience
Tower Bridge Wharf
Hermitage Stairs
St Thomas' Hosp Operation Theatre
TOOLEY STREET
Morgans Lane
Abbots La
Vine Lane
Weaver's La
Potters Fids
Butler's Wharf Pier
Guys Hospital
ST THOMAS ST
Stainer St
Weston St
London Bridge Station
BERMONDSEY STREET
Magdalen St
Holyrood St
Shand St
Barnham St
Lambeth Coll
Millennium Balloon
TOWER BR RD
Horselydown La
Thames Path
Shad Thames
Copper Row
Brewery Square
Gainsford St
Butlers Wharf
Design Mus
Providence Square
Cayenne Court
ON E ST
Lafone St
Curlew St
Maguire St
Butler's Wharf Business Centre
Butlers & Colonial Wharf
80
Bloomfield Clinic Guys
Greenwood Thtr
Mellor St
F St
V Yd
London City Mission
Fair St
A100
Police Stn
Magistrates Court
Three Oak La
Qu Elizabeth St
Shad Thames
Mill Street
Mill Street Clinic
St Saviour's Dock
2
Bermondsey Wall West
Providence Square
Snowsfields
Weston St
City Banking College
Kirby Gv
H St
CRUCIFIX LANE
Whites Grounds Estate
Whts Grnds
Brunswick Ct
A200
School
St John's Estate
Millennium Square
Jacob St
Fire Stn
Wolseley Street
Chambers
Guy St
Porlock St
Hamlet Way
Primary School
Black Swan Yd
Surg
M Pl
Roper La
DRUID ST
Coxson Wy
JAMAICA RD
Secondary School
Kipling St
Kipling Estate
Leathermarket Gardens
Tyers Gate
Fashion & Textile Design Museum
Dockhead
George Row
Parkers Row
Prim Sch
John Felton Rd
Lkyr St
Dunsterville Way
Leathermarket Street
Leathermarket Court
Morocco St
Lamb Wk
A220
Tanner St
Hatchers Mews
Phoenix Wharf Road
Prk Rw
Surg
3
BERMON
Council Building
Weston Street
Tanner Street
Pope St
Maltby Street
Druid Street
Sweeney Crs
JAMAICA ROAD
LONG LANE
Hankey Pl
Staple Street
Tabard Garden Estate
Works
Newham's Row
ROAD
Riley Road
Works
Millstream Rd
S St
Neckinger St
Arnold Estate
Scott
A2198
Mancipie Street
Tabard Garden
Graduate Pl
Elim St
Weston St
Purbrook Street
Stevens Street
St Saviour's Estate
Gedling Pl
B202
A200
Caledonian Market
Cluny Estate
Cluny Pl
Wild's Rents
Pardoner St
BERMONDSEY ST
ABBEY STREET
Bridgewain St
Maltby Street
Neckinger
Works
Enid St
Old Jamaica Bus Est
Marine St
St James CE J&I School
Old Jamaica Road
4
Tabard Street
Law St
Decima St
Works
Chrysolyta Prim School
BRIDGE
L Wk
Radcliffe Rd
Neckinger Estate
Grange Walk
The Grange
Pas
Sun
Thurland Rd
Frean St
Nesss St
123
Spa Road
Potier St
Prioress St
Rothsay St
Alice St
Southwark Coll
Grange Walk Mews
Gg's Pl
Fendall St
Walk
Neckinger Estate
Bermondsey Town Hall
Dockley Road Industrial Est
Rouel Rd
A2
Lansdown Pl
Potier St
H Cl
Prioress St
Rephidim St
Alice St
TOWER
Primary School
Wood's Pl
GRANGE ROAD
Rich Industrial Estate
Crimscott Street
Grange Yd
Works
Spa Road
Alscot Rd
Vaubar St
Dunlop Pl
Vauban Estate
5
Lucey Rd
Goodwin Cl
Amina Way
Burge St
Bartholomew St
KENT RD
NEW
TOWER BR RD
Bushbaby Close
Swan Md
Webb St
Pages Walk
Wk
Rich Industrial Est
A2206
Canon Murnane Rd
Keyse Road
Bacon Gv
Alscot Rd Ind Est
Cadbury
Woolstaplers Wy
Yalding Rd
Rouel Rd
Eveline Lowe Estate
St Saviour and St Olaves Sch
Aberdour St
Leroy Street
Guinness Sq
Page's
Boutcher CE Primary School
Henley Dr
Aylwin Girls School
Alma Jun Infant Sch
A2
Searles Road
Townsend Primary School
Willow
Curtis St
Curtis Way
Hazel Way
Council Building
172
6
SOUTHWARK PK RD
SOUT
Setchell Way
Setchell Estate
Street
Darwin Street
Mason St
OLD KENT ROAD
Mandela
Walk
Alscot Wy
Setchell Road
Longfield Estate
Longley St
Works
Hemp Walk
Hillery Cl
Barlow St
Crail Rw
Townsend St
Comus Pl
Congreve Street
Massinger St
Way
Bricklayer Arms Industrial Estate
Fort Road
Balaclava Road
Grove
Alma
Road
Spa School
Catesby St
Beckway St
Tatum St
Halpin Pl
Beckway St
Stanford Pl
Hendre Rd
Mandela
DUNTON ROAD
K C
W Rd
7
Thorburn Square
Kennedy Walk
Flint Street
Elsted St
Huntsman St
Surgery
Milton Cl
Lynton Road
Welsford St
Monnow
Martyrs RC School
Dean's Buildings
Tisdall Pl
Surgery
Minnow Walk
East Street
Exon St
Marcia Road
B203
MANDELA WY
Lynton Estate
Burnham Cl
Bushwood Drive
Cadet Dr
East Street
Freemantle St
Surrey Ter
Chaucer Dr
Rich Industrial Estate
Oxley Close
Abercorn
Dawes
Merrow Wk
Sedan Way
Primary School
Aldbridge Street
Surrey Sq
Surrey Square
Kinglake
Superstore
HUMPHREY ST
B204
ROLLS ROAD
The New Aylesbury Medical Centre
Merrow Wk
Walworth
Upnor
Street
Street
Avocet

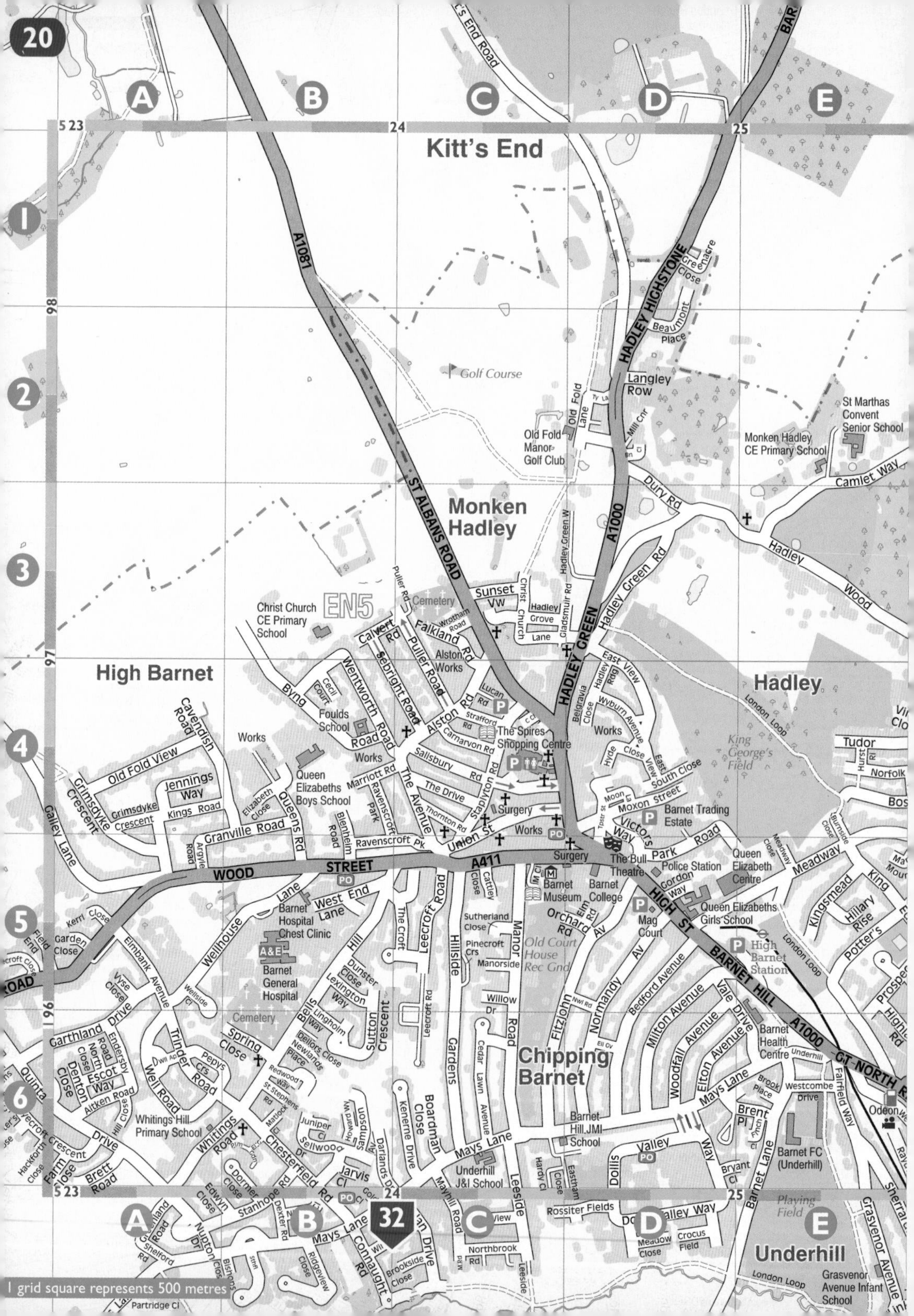

1 grid square represents 500 metres

Wood
Wagon Road
F
G
H
J
K
26
27
28
Claremont Road
Helena Close
Hadley Wood Primary School
Courtleigh Avenue
Duchy Road
Kingwell Road
Hotel
Hadley Wood
Hadley Wood Station
Lancaster Avenue
Bartrams Lane
PO
Crescent West
Crescent East
St Ronans Close
Parklands Close
Beech Hill
Ferny Hill
A111
COCKFOSTERS ROAD
Corbar Close
Walmar Close
Hadley Wood Golf Club
Camlet Way
Beech Hill Avenue
Wd Ride
Musgrave Cl
Newman's Way
Greenbrook Av
Covert Way
Golf Course
Pagitts Grove
Broadgates Avenue
Parkgate Crs
Parkgate Av
EN4
Greenoak Pl
Monken Hadley Common
Enfield
Barnet
Coombehurst Close
Bakers Hill
Hadley Common
Road
The Crs
Latimer Rd
Clifford Road
Hadley Road
Woodville Road
Julian Cl
Bournwell Close
Fairgreen
Somercoates Cl
East Barnet School
Livingstone Primary School
Hertford Close
Hertford Road
Westbrook Crescent
Westbrook Close
Armstrong Crescent
Castlewood Road
Arundel Rd
Northfield Rd
Linthorpe Road
Grove Road
Games Road
Baring Road
Lawton Road
Galdana Av
Boleyn Way
Lichfield Close
Verwood Drive
Catcombe Way
Cockfosters Sports Ground
St Mark's Cl
Potter's Road
Cromer Road JMI School
Cromer Rd
Artesian Grove
St James Road
Fordham Road
Appletree Gardens
Kenley Close
Edgeworth Road
Southgate Compton Cricket
Langford Road
Wilton Road
Chalk Lane
Park Road
Pendall Cl
Bevan Road
Langford Crescent
Belmont Close
Hexham Road
Lytton Road
Albert Rd
Glyn Avenue
Pymms Brook Drive
Hamilton Close
Hamilton Road
Mount Pleasant
Trent CE Primary School
Bulwer Road
Plantagenet Road
Works
Victoria Road
Alexander Close
Crescent Road
Silvercliffe Gardens
Herons Rise
Carson Road
Norrys Road
Evelyn Road
Calvay Close
Duncan Close
Mulberry Cl
Margaret Road
Ibsley Way
Eccleston Cl
Leicester Road
Warwick Road
Abbotts Road
A110
EAST BARNET ROAD
STATION ROAD
County Court
Station Ap
Lancaster Road
Margaret Rd
Red Rose Trading Estate
Edward Road
Victoria Cl
Mount Rd
Rolfe Close
High Trees
Avenue Road
Hddn Rd
Heddon Court Avenue
Mowbray Rd
Somerset Road
New Barnet Stn
Warwick Cl
St Wilfrid's Rd
Pymmes Brook Trail
Park Road
Pilgrim's Rise
Keely Close
Cockfosters
Ashurst Road
Freston Gardens
New Barnet
Richmond Road
Lyonsdown School
York Road
Henry Road
Ind Est
East Barnet Health Cen
Caddington Close
Brookhill Close
Belmont Avenue
96
98
Greenhill
Gloucester Road
Hill Side
Denewood
Kingston Rd
Berkeley Crs
Crsc Rl
CAT HILL
Museum of Domestic Design & Architecture
Dinsdale Gdns
Park Road
Barnet Synagogue
East Barnet Road
Crescent Road
Doggetts Ct
Chestnut Grove
Lyonsdown Road
Eversleigh Road
Pank Av
PRICKLERS HILL
GREAT
Haslemere Gdns
The Fairway
B19
LONGMORE AVENUE
33
Primary School
East Barnet School
Works
Dale Close
Hillier Close
Cherry Hill
LYONSDOWN RD
The Drive
Lyonsdown Avenue
Monks Avenue
Calton Road
Dalmeny Rd
Netheriand
Sycamore
Smf Gv
Welbeck
Middle Rd
BARNET
Jackson Rd
Churchmead
St.Marys CE Primary School
Eton Avenue
Bohun Grove
Windsor Drive
Ridgeway Avenue
Littlegrove
Oakland CP School
Daneland
Mansfield Av
Lakeside Crs
Willenhall Avenue
Shurland Avenue
Cranbrook
The Way
22

London Loop
A1005
THE R
A
B
C
D
E
528
29
30
1
2
3
4
5
6
98
96
Hadley Road
Hill
Hadley R
London Loop
University of Middlesex
Trent Country Park
21
Snakes Lane
Golf Course
ENFIELD ROAD
ENFIELD RD
COCKFOSTERS ROAD
Cockfosters Sports Ground
Trent Park Cemetery
Southgate Compton Cricket Club
Chalk
Lane
Cockfosters Station
Belmont Close
A111
Norfolk Close
West Close
East Close
Trent Park Golf Club
A110
South Lodge Crs
Lakeside
Greystoke Gdns
Lowther Drive
Culgaith Gardens
Merryhills Drive
Lonsdale
South Lodge Drive
Brayton Gdns
Curthwaite Gdns
Drive
North
Galva Close
Mount Close
Cockfosters Road
Surgery
Road
Gloucester Gardens
Kent Drive
Westpole Avenue
Way
Southgate School
Sussex
Oakwood Medical Cen
Oakwood Station
Belgrave Gdns
Grosvenor Gdns
Prince
Carlton Av
Brantwood Gardens
Clifton Gardens
Lonsdale Drive
Bayliss Cl
Freston Gardens
Leys Gdns
Avenue
BRAMLEY ROAD
Harper Cl
Chase
Gerrards Cl
George
Sheringham Av
South Lodge Drive
South Ldg Dr
Overton Road
Penning
HILL
Museum of Domestic Design & Architecture
Chicken Shed Theatre
Bramley Close
Priory Close
Peace Cl
Homestead Paddock
Stafford Cl
Tregenna Close
Reservoir
Road
Wolverton Wy
Lakenheath
Close
Chestnut
Ashmead
The Vineries
Merrivale
Chase
A111
CHASE SIDE
Mansfield Av
Vernon Crs
Lakeside Crs
Middlesex University
34
De-Bohun
Green
The Fairway
Masefield Crs
Cowper Gardens
Linden Close
Highfield Court
Wayside Cl
Saxon Wy
Oakwood
Sheringham Avenue
Oakwood
Hood
Trent
De Bohun
Ave
Dalry
1 grid square represents 500 metres

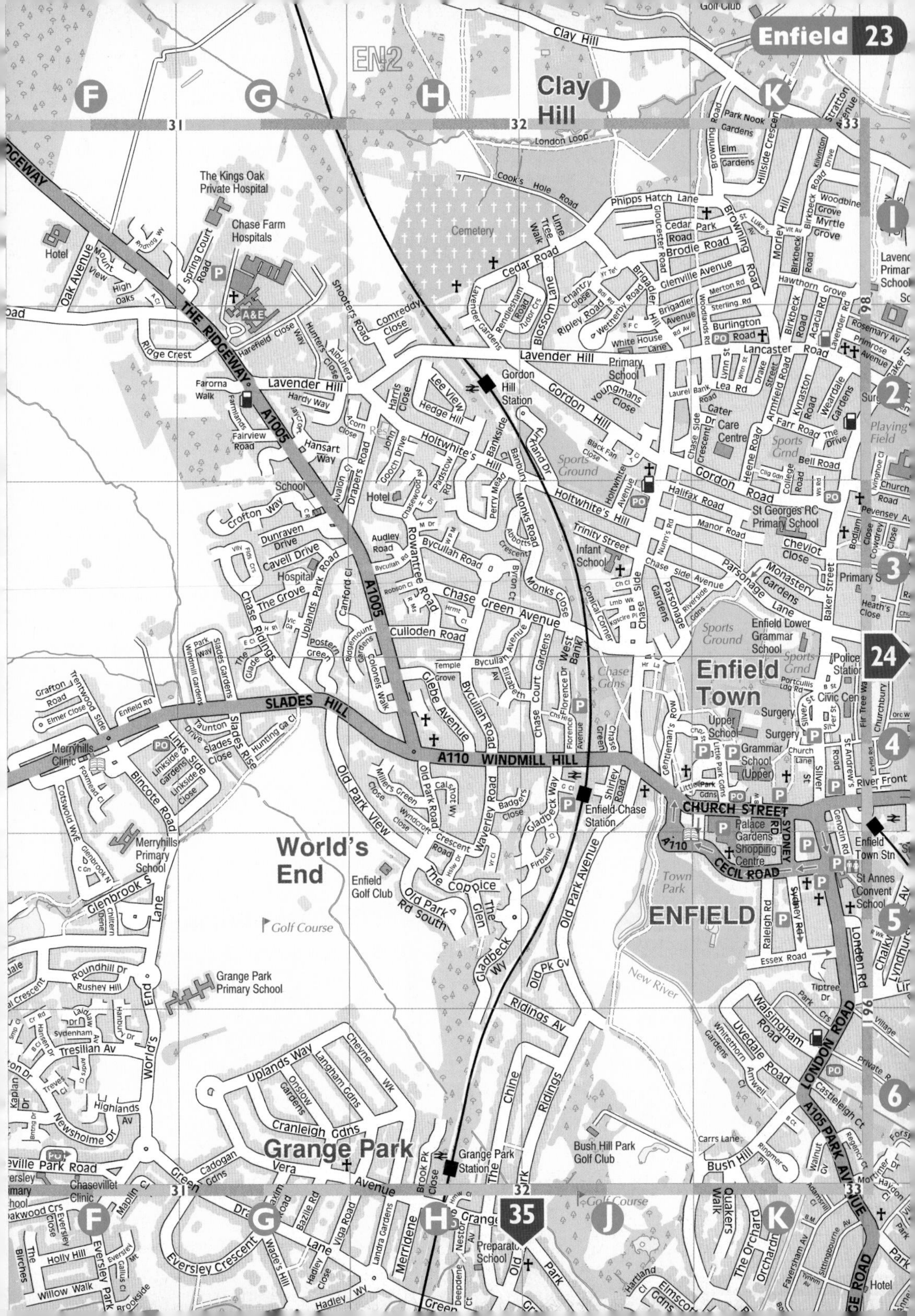
Clay Hill
EN2
F
G
H
J
K
31
32
33
The Kings Oak Private Hospital
Chase Farm Hospitals
A&E
Hotel
Oak Avenue
Mount View
High Oaks
Spring Court Road
THE RIDGEWAY
A1005
Ridge Crest
Harefield Close
Farorna Walk
Farmlands
Fairview Road
Lavender Hill
Hardy Way
Hansart Way
London Loop
Cook's Hole Road
Cemetery
Lime Tree Walk
Cedar Road
Phipps Hatch Lane
Cedar Park Road
Brodie Road
Glenville Avenue
Gloucester Road
Browning Road
Park Nook Gardens
Elm Gardens
Hillside Crescent
Stratton Avenue
Morley Hill
Birkbeck Road
Woodbine Grove
Myrtle Grove
Hawthorn Grove
Acacia Rd
Lavender Rd
Rosemary Av
Primrose Avenue
Burlington Road
Lancaster Road
Comreddy Close
Shooters Road
Albuhera Close
Hunter's Close Way
Lavender Gardens
Rendlesham Road
Tudor Crs
Blossom Lane
Chantry Close
Ripley Road
Wetherby Road
Brigadier Hill
Brigadier Avenue
White House Lane
Primary School
Gordon Hill Station
Gordon Hill
Youngmans Close
Lee View
Hedge Hill
Harris Close
Holtwhite's Hill
Bankside
Padstow Rd
Gooch Drive
Hotel
Chaseville
School
Crofton Way
Dunraven Drive
Cavell Drive
Hospital
The Grove
Uplands Park Road
Chase Ridings
Audley Road
Byculla Road
Rowantree Road
Drapers Road
Avalon Cl
Acorn Close
Kirkland Dr
Banbury
Perry Mead
Monks Road
Abbotts Crescent
Byron Ct
Monks Close
Sports Ground
Lea Rd
Laurel Bank Road
Gater Dr
Care Centre
Chase Side Crescent
Armfield Road
Kynaston Road
Weardale Gardens
Farr Road
The Drive
Heene Road
Sports Grnd
College Road
Bell Road
Playing Field
Gordon Road
Halifax Road
Holtwhite Avenue
Holtwhite's Hill
Manor Road
St Georges RC Primary School
Trinity Street
Infant School
Parsonage Lane
Monastery Gardens
Cheviot Close
Baker Street
Chase Side Avenue
Chase Side
Chase Green Avenue
Culloden Road
Canford Cl
Postern Green
Ridgemount Gardens
Colonels Walk
Conical Corner
Parsonage Gardens
Riverside Gdns
Sports Ground
Enfield Lower Grammar School
Police Station
Enfield Town
Upper School
Surgery
Grammar School (Upper)
Civic Cen
Little Park Gdns
Church Lane
Silver St
Gentleman's Row
Chase Gdns
Chase Green
Chase Court Gardens
Florence Avenue
West Bank
Bycullah Avenue
Bycullah Road
Elizabeth Av
Glebe Avenue
Temple Grove
24
Grafton Road
Trentwood Side
Elmer Close
Enfield Rd
SLADES HILL
Slades Gardens
Windmill Gardens
Park Way
Taunton Drive
Slades Close
Slades Rise
Hunting Ga Cl
Links Side
Linkside Gardens
Linkside Close
Merryhills Clinic
Bincote Road
Cotswold Wy
Foxmead Cl
A110 WINDMILL HILL
Old Park View
Millers Green Close
Old Park Road
Calshot Wy
Wyndcroft Close
Crescent Road
Waverley Road
Badgers Close
Gladbeck Way
Firbank Cl
Enfield Chase Station
Shirley Road
CHURCH STREET
Palace Gardens Shopping Centre
A110
CECIL ROAD
SYDNEY RD
Genotin Rd
Enfield Town Stn
St Annes Convent School
Town Park
ENFIELD
Raleigh Rd
Sydney Rd
Essex Road
London Rd
Merryhills Primary School
Glenbrook N
Glenbrook S
Chiltern Dene
World's End Lane
World's End
Enfield Golf Club
Golf Course
The Coppice
Old Park Rd South
The Glen
Gladbeck Wy
Old Park Avenue
Old Pk Gv
New River
Tiptree Dr
Walsingham Road
Uvedale Road
Whitethorn Gardens
Amwell
LONDON ROAD
Castleleigh Ct
A105 PARK AVENUE
Roundhill Dr
Rushey Hill
Grange Park Primary School
Tresilian Av
Sydenham Av
Highlands Av
Newsholme Dr
Kaplan Dr
Ridings Av
Uplands Way
Cheyne Wk
Langham Gdns
Onslow Gardens
Cranleigh Gdns
Chine
Ridings
Grange Park
Grange Park Station
Brook Pk Close
Vera Avenue
Cadogan Gdns
Green
Chaseville Park Road
Chasevillet Clinic
Oakwood Crs
Eversley Close
Maplin Cl
Holly Hill
Eversley Park
Willow Walk
Brookside
The Birches
Eversley Crescent
Wade's Hill
Hadley Close
Bazile Rd
Viga Road
Landra Gardens
Merridene
Nestor Av
Deepdene Ct
Preparatory School
Old Park
Bush Hill Park Golf Club
Carrs Lane
Bush Hill
Quakers Walk
The Orchard
Ringmer Pl
Walnut Gv
Faversham Av
Sittingbourne Av
Regency Ct
Private Rd
Village
Hotel
35
Golf Course
Hartland Cl
Elmscott Gdns
Lyndhurst
Chalkwell
Church Road
Pevensey Av
Bodiam Close
Cowdrey Close
Primary School
Heath's Close
Churchbury
Fir Tree Wk
River Front
St Andrew's Road
Lavender Primary School
Surgery
Golf Club
Clay Hill

24
23
36
Forty Hill
Enfield
Ponders End
Bush Hill Park
EN1
Enfield Playing Fields
Bush Hill Park
Recreation Ground
Forty Hill CE Primary School
Enfield Crematorium
Worcesters Primary School
Lavender Primary School
Chace Community School
Adath Yisroel Cemetery
Queen Elizabeth Stadium
Sports Centre & Swimming Pool
Russet House School
Carterhatch Primary School
Durants School
Bishop Stopford School
Suffolks Primary School
Enfield College
Enfield Business Centre
Northgate Business Centre
George Spicer Primary School
Kingsmead School
UGC
Superstore
Works
Haslemere Business Centre
Martinbridge Industrial Estate
Great Cambridge Industrial Est
Southbury Station
Enfield Town Stn
St Annes Convent School
Enfield Cricket Club
Martindale Ind Estate
Bush Hill Park Primary School
Infant School
Waverley School
Asquith Sch
Queensway Business Cen
University
Cemetery
Playing Field
Civic Cen
Surgery
GREAT CAMBRIDGE ROAD
A10
SOUTHBURY ROAD
A110
HERTFORD ROAD
A1010
HERTFORD ROAD HIGH ST
NAGS HEAD
LONDON ROAD
A105 PARK AVENUE
Carterhatch Lane
Hoe Lane
Lincoln Road
Goat Lane
Baker Street
Willow Road
Tenniswood Road
Donkey Lane
Brick Lane
Crown Road
Baird Road
Southbury Av
Main Av
Northfield Road
Southfield Road
Elmcroft Avenue
Oaklands Av
Queensway
Chalkwell Pk Av
Wellington Road
A
B
C
D
E
1
2
3
4
5
6
533
34
35
1 grid square represents 500 metres

Lock
Ordnance Road
Surgery
Enfield Lock Stn
LC
Rotherfield Road
Fairoaks Grove
Uckfield Road
Titchfield Road
Catisfield Road
Chesterfield Road
Bradley Road
Newbury Avenue
Soham Road
Prince of Wales Primary School
Salisbury Road
Medcalf Road
Warwick Road
A1010
Kettering Road
St Stephens Road
Beaconsfield Road
Standard Road
Preston Gdns
Albany Road
London Loop
Connop Road
Enfield Wash
Albany School
Albany Pool
Lytton Avenue
Marrilyne Avenue
Bideford Road
Eastfield Road
Eastfield Primary School
Bell Lane
Elmore Rd
Leda Avenue
Grove Gardens
Meadow Close
Redlands Road
Castle Road
Brimsdown Avenue
Bilton Way
Works
A1055
Park Avenue
The Sunny Road
The Brightside
Nursery Close
Road
Shaw Road
Nursery Gardens
Greenwood Avenue
Meads Road
Croft Road
Brancroft Way
Lansbury Road
The Hatch
Fouracres
Wheatfields
Lockfield Avenue
Enterprise Works
Highway
Westmoor Gardens
Westmoor Road
Swan Way
Leyland Avenue
Sharon Road
Carterhatch Road
Walcot Road
Watermill Business Cen
Edison Road
Bowood Road
PO
EN3
Millmarsh Lane
MOLLISON AVENUE
Vis Av
Mayfield Road
Brimsdown
Leaside Business Centre
Osborne Road
Goldsdown Road
Brimsdown Station
Stonycroft
Street
Ponders End Industrial Estate
Goldsdown Close
Jute Lane
Plaza Business Centre
Green Street
Works
Stockingswater Lane
Sovereign Business Centre
Hunts Mead
Ambleside Crescent
Brimsdown Primary School
Celadon Close
Enstone Road
Braithwaite Road
Dundee Way
Westfield Close
Avondale Crescent
Alma Road
Works
King George's Reservoir
Lea Valley Walk
Exeter Road
Ride
Durants Pk Av
Arbour Road
Brookfields
Alexandra Road
Alexandra Business Centre
Works
Mill River Trading Estate
Suez Road
Jeffreys Road
Ponders End Industrial Estate
Bursland Rd
Charcroft Gdns
Holmbridge Gdns
Trafalgar Trading Est
Centenary Rd
Durants
St Marys RC Primary School
Road
Kg Edward's Rd
Aden Rd
Duck Lees La
Alpha Rd
A110
Scotland Gn Rd N
Duck Lees Lane
Gilda Av
Clydesdale
Redcote Road
Scotland Gn Rd
Curzon Av
Freemantle Av
Surg
Alma Primary School
Works
Keats Close
Percy Gdns
Tennyson Cl
Scotland Rd
Napier Road
South
Ponders End Station
Works
Street
Woodall Road
Falcon
Wharf Rd
Sutherland Road
Nelson Road
Riverside Industrial Est
Redburn Industrial Est
Woodall Rd
Works
LEA VALLEY
Ordnance Rd
Barrass Cl
Martini Dr
Smtn Rd
Baddeley Cl
Sten Cl
Thorneycroft Dr
Pritchett Cl
Manton Rd
Fogerty Cl
Aldridge Avenue
Eden Cl
Lee Sq
Harston Drive
Metford Crescent
Hide Cl
Cnge Cl
Bd Gv
Swan and Pike Road
Heron Md
Waterways Business Centre
Joslyn Close
Lloyd Ms
Ostell Crs
Brunswick Rd
Crompton Pl
London Loop
Lee Valley Campsite
Mill Lane
A112
SEWARDSTONE ROAD
Enfield
Essex County
River Lea or Lee
Sewardstone Road
Gilwell Cl
Boardman Av
Antlers Hill
Deerleap Gv
Yardley La
Yardley Primary School
Hawkwood Crescent
Avenue
Hawkdene
Epping Way
A112
F G H J K
36 37 38
98 97 96
1 2 3 4 5 6
37

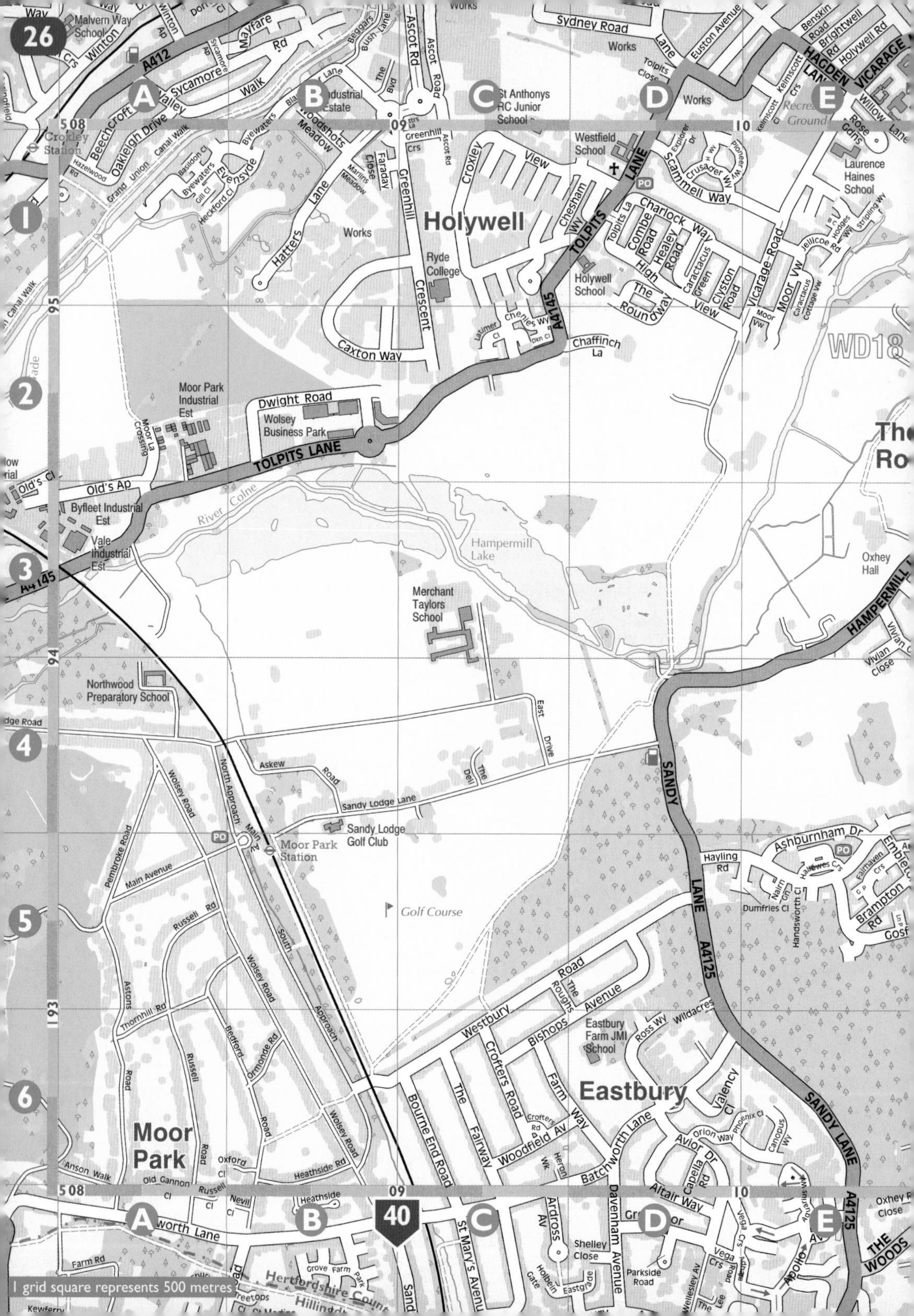
26
40
A
B
C
D
E
1
2
3
4
5
6
508
09
10
95
94
93
Holywell
Moor Park
Eastbury
WD18
Croxley Station
Moor Park Station
Malvern Way School
St Anthonys RC Junior School
Westfield School
Laurence Haines School
Ryde College
Holywell School
Moor Park Industrial Est
Wolsey Business Park
Byfleet Industrial Est
Vale Industrial Est
Merchant Taylors School
Northwood Preparatory School
Sandy Lodge Golf Club
Golf Course
Eastbury Farm JMI School
Hampermill Lake
River Colne
Oxhey Hall
Works
Industrial Estate
Recreation Ground
A412
A4145
A4125
TOLPITS LANE
SANDY LANE
HAMPERMILL LANE
HAGDEN LANE
VICARAGE
THE WOODS
Sydney Road
Euston Avenue
Benskin Road
Brightwell Rd
Holywell Rd
Kelmscott Crs
Willow Lane
Rose Gdns
Winton Ap
Mayfare
Sycamore Ap
Sycamore Rd
Valley Walk
Beechcroft
Oakleigh Drive
Byewaters
Evensyde
Basildon Cl
Gill Cl
Heckford Cl
Grand Union Canal Walk
Hazelwood Rd
Woodshots Meadow
Hatters Lane
Marlins Meadow
Faraday Close
Greenhill Crescent
Greenhill Crs
Ascot Rd
Ascot Road
The Bvd
Bush Lane
Beggars
Croxley View
Chesham Wy
Tolpits Close
Scammell Way
Crusader Wy
Pioneer Wy
Explorer Dr
Charlock Way
Combe Road
Healey Road
High View
Caractacus Green
Clyston Road
Vicarage Road
Moor Vw
Jellicoe Rd
Hodges Wy
Stripling Wy
Caractacus Cottage Vw
The Roundway
Tolpits La
Caxton Way
Latimer Cl
Chenies Wy
Dkn Cl
Chaffinch La
Dwight Road
Moor La Crossing
Old's Ap
Old's Cl
Vivian Close
East Drive
The Dell
Askew Road
Sandy Lodge Lane
North Approach
Main Av
South Approach
Wolsey Road
Pembroke Road
Main Avenue
Russell Rd
Astons Road
Thornhill Rd
Bedford Road
Ormonde Rd
Oxford Cl
Heathside Rd
Heathside
Anson Walk
Old Gannon Cl
Nevil Cl
Ashburnham Dr
Hayling Rd
Hallowes Crs
Nairn Gn
Handsworth Cl
Dumfries Cl
Fairhaven Crs
Brampton Rd
Westbury Road
The Roughs
Bishops Avenue
Crofters Road
Crofters Rd
Farm Way
Woodfield Av
Heron Wk
Ross Wy
Wildacres
Valency Cl
Batchworth Lane
Bourne End Road
The Fairway
Phoenix Cl
Orion Way
Canopus Wy
Avior Dr
Capella Rd
Altair Way
Vega Crs
Vega Road
Apollo Av
Oxhey Close
St Mary's Avenue
Ardross Av
Davenham Avenue
Shelley Close
Holbein Gate
Eastgrade
Parkside Road
Wellesley Av
The Lee
Grove Farm Park
Farm Rd
Treetops Cl
Kewferry
1 grid square represents 500 metres

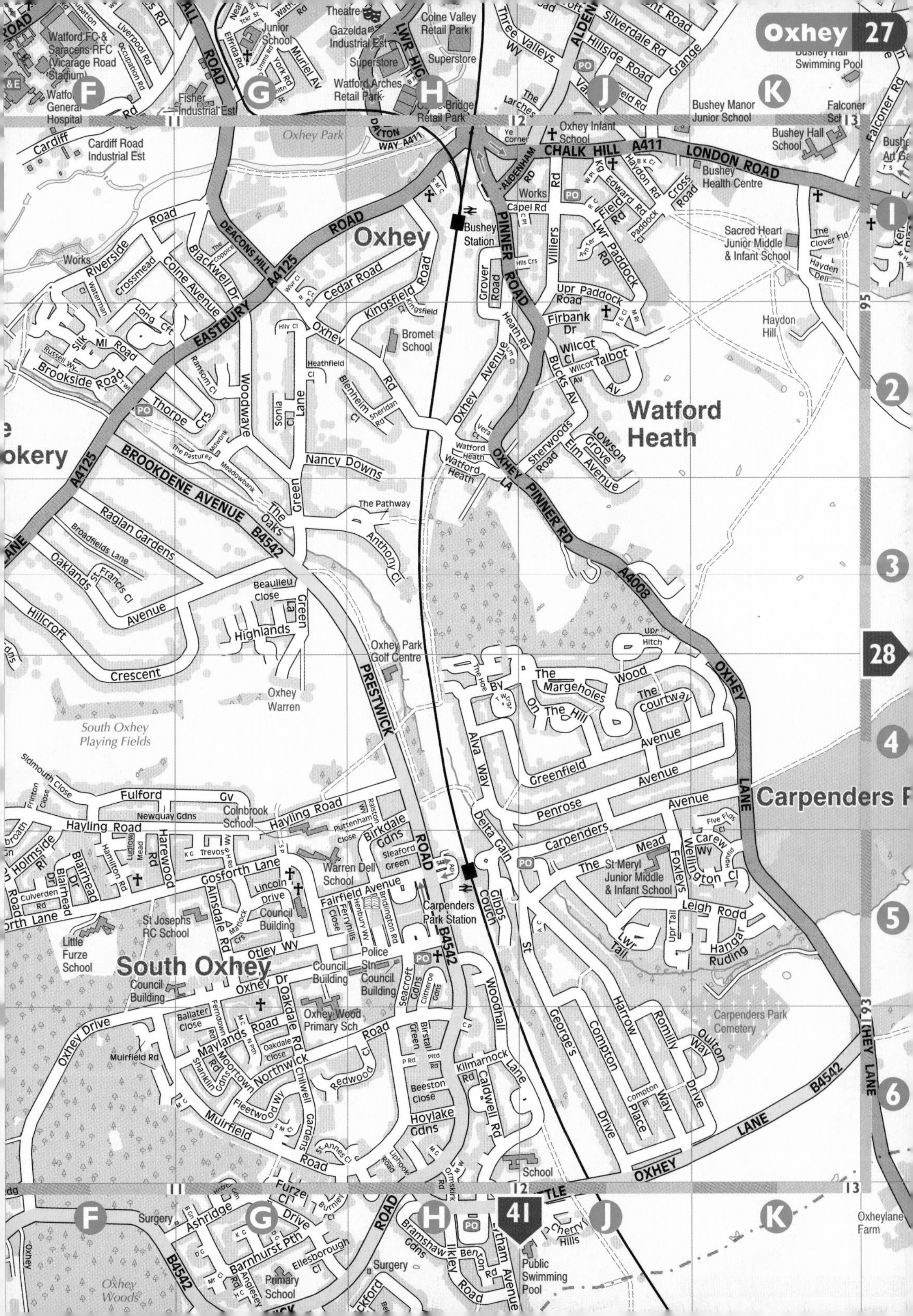

Watford FC & Saracens RFC (Vicarage Road Stadium)
Watford General Hospital
Liverpool Rd
Occupation Rd
Junior School
Elfrida Rd
York Rd
Muriel Av
Fisher Industrial Est
Theatre
Gazelda Industrial Est
Colne Valley Retail Park
Superstore
Watford Arches Retail Park
Colne Bridge Retail Park
LWR HIGH
Three Valleys Wy
Silverdale Rd
Hillside Road
Grange
The Larches
Bushey Hall Swimming Pool
Bushey Manor Junior School
Falconer Rd
Bushey Hall School
Cardiff Road Industrial Est
Cardiff
Oxhey Park
DALTON WAY A411
Ye Corner
Oxhey Infant School
ALDENHAM RD
CHALK HILL A411
LONDON ROAD
Haydon Rd
Edward Rd
Cross Road
Bushey Health Centre
Capel Rd
Works
Villiers Rd
Lwr Paddock Rd
Paddock Cl
Sacred Heart Junior Middle & Infant School
The Clover Fld
Hayden Dell
Riverside Road
Works
DEACONS HILL
ROAD
Oxhey
Bushey Station
PINNER ROAD
Crossmead
Colne Avenue
Blackwell Dr
EASTBURY
A4125
Cedar Road
Kingsfield Road
Kingsfield Ct
Grover Road
Hls Crs
Upr Paddock Road
Firbank Dr
Haydon Hill
Waterman Cl
Long Cft
Silk Mill Road
Russell Wy
Brookside Road
Ransom Cl
Woodwaye
Oxhey Rd
Heathfield Cl
Bromet School
Heath Rd
Oxhey Avenue
Wilcot Cl
Wilcot Av
Talbot Av
Bucks Av
Thorpe Crs
Sonia Cl
Lane
Blenheim Cl
Sheridan Rd
Watford Heath
Sherwoods Road
Lowson Grove
Elm Avenue
The Pastures
Meadowbank
Nancy Downs
Green
okery
A4125
BROOKDENE AVENUE
B4542
The Oaks
The Pathway
Anthony Cl
OXHEY LA
PINNER RD
A4008
Raglan Gardens
Broadfields Lane
Oaklands
St Francis Cl
Hillcroft
Avenue
Crescent
Beaulieu Close
Green La
Highlands
Oxhey Park Golf Centre
PRESTWICK
Oxhey Warren
South Oxhey Playing Fields
Upr Hitch
The Hoe
By Wy
The Margeholes
Wood
The Courtway
On The Hill
Alva Way
Greenfield Avenue
OXHEY LANE
Carpenders P
Sidmouth Close
Frinton Close
Fulford Gv
Newquay Gdns
Colnbrook School
Hayling Road
Raliston Wy
Puttenham Close
Birkdale Gdns
Delta Gain
Penrose Avenue
Five Flds Cl
Carpenders
Holmside Ri
Blairhead Dr
Hamilton Rd
Ludlow Mead
Harewood Rd
Trevos
Sleaford Green
ROAD
Gosforth Lane
Warren Dell School
Carpenders Park Station
The Mead
St Meryl Junior Middle & Infant School
Foxleys
Carew Wy
Wellington Cl
Culverden Rd
Blairhead Dr
Lincoln Drive
Fairfield Avenue
Ferryhills Close
Henbury Wy
Bridlington Rd
Gibbs Couch
Leigh Rodd
Council Building
Ainsdale Rd
Matlock Crs
St Josephs RC School
Little Furze School
B4542
Lwr Tail
Upr Tail
Hangar Ruding
South Oxhey
Otley Wy
Police Stn
Council Building
St
Council Building
Seacroft Gdns
Clitheroe Gdns
Woodhall
Oxhey Dr
Oakdale Rd
Ballater Close
Ferndown
Maylands Road
Oxhey Wood Primary Sch
Road
Birstal Green
Harrow
Compton
Romilly
Oulton Way
Carpenders Park Cemetery
Oxhey Drive
Oakdale Close
Moortown Rd
Northwick
Chilwell
Redwood Cl
Pitd Rd
Kilmarnock Rd
Lane
George's
Muirfield Rd
Shanklin Gdns
Fleetwood Wy
Gardens
Beeston Close
Caldwell Rd
Compton Pl
Way
Drive
B4542
Muirfield
Hoylake Gdns
Drive
Place
LANE
OXHEY
Road
St Annes Cl
Liphook Road
School
Ormskirk Rd
Furze Cl
Burnley Cl
Ashridge
Surgery
Drive
Barnhurst Pth
Ellesborough Cl
B4542
Anglesey
Primary School
Surgery
Bramshaw Gdns
Ilkley Road
Benton Rd
Lytham Avenue
Cherry Hills
Public Swimming Pool
Oxhey Woods
Oxheylane Farm
F
G
H
J
K
I
2
3
4
5
6
11
12
13
95
93
28
41

BUSHEY
Bushey Heath
Merry Hill
WD23
Bushey Golf & Country Club
Golf Course
Hartsbourne Golf & Country Club
Hertfordshire County
Harrow
Harrow Weald Common
The Kiln
Grims Dyke Golf Club
Oxheylane Farm
Hotel
Bournehall Junior & Infant School
Meadow Wood School
Meads School
Falconer School
Little Redding Primary School
Bushey Mus & Art Gallery
St Hildas School
Ashfield Junior School
Police Station
St Margarets School
Council Building
Bushey & District Synagogue
Primary School
Immanuel College
Rosary Priory School
Westwood School
Hartsbourne JMI School
Peterborough & St Margarets High School
Works
HIGH STREET
A411
SPARROWS HERNE
ELSTREE RD
HIGH ROAD
A4140
COMMON ROAD
A409
MAGPIE HALL RD
OXHEY LANE
A41
M1
Old Redding
Ass House La
Merry Hill Road
Chestnut Ri
Steeplands
Ashfield
Kg George Av
Coldharbour
Cotswold Avenue
Chiltern Avenue
Oundle Avenue
Pentland Rd
Little Bushey Lane
Rossway Dr
Finch Lane
Falconer Rd
Herkomer Road
Melbourne Road
Bournehall Av
Bourne Rd
Clapgate Rd
Herne Road
Cooks Md
Herne Rd
Kemp Place
Rudolph Road
Park Road
Castle Cl
Milner Ct
Perry Md
Highland Dr
Catsey Lane
Catsey Wd
Somers Way
Brooke Cl
Richfield Road
Clarks Md
Coombe Rd
Garratts Rd
Wayside Av
Albany Cl
Woodfield Rise
Potters
Caldecote Gdns
Rosary Gdns
Tate Gdns
Otway Gdns
Hollygrove
Titian Av
Windmill Street
Windmill Lane
Rutherford Way
The Rutts
Belle Vue
California Lane
Florida Close
Giant Tree Hl
Downalong
Warren Road
Comyns
Rose Lawn
Beamish Drive
Robinson Crs
Allard Crs
Finucane Rise
Gleed Av
Prowse Avenue
Hartsbourne Av
Hartsbourne Road
Hive Rd
Broadfield Ct
Elder Ct
Lime Tree Walk
Alpine Wk
Tanglewood Cl
Clamp Hill
Brookshill
Brookshill Av
Brook Drive
Victoria Rd
Rosebery Rd
School Lane
Swallow Cl
Ash Hl Close
Merry Hill Road
Wren Crs
Woodpecker Close
Goldcrest Wy
Vega Rd
Pasture Close
Claybury
Fair Cl
Risingholme Cl
Springfield
Howton Pl
Nicholson Dr
Treacy Close
Lake Dr
Laurino Pl
Greenacres
The Squirrels
Rockingham Ga
Dunsmore Wy
Cheviot Close
Mendip Rd
Woburn Close
Chiltern Close
Aston Cl
Bridgewater Wy
Greensward
Wendover Way
The Birches
Goodison Cl
Edridge Cl
Redding Av
Moatfield Rd
Meadow Road
Little Martins
Nightingale Rd
Bournehall La
Frobisher Cl
Palmer Av
Lake
Coles Green
Larken Dr
The Lake
Nimmo Dr
Langmead Dr
Pickets Cl
Everett Cl
The Pantiles
St Peter's Cl
Priory Vw
Howard Cl
Warwick Cl
Clay Ln
Montrose Rd
Hayden Dell
The Clover Fld
Heathbourne
42
27
1 grid square represents 500 metres

F
G
H
J
K
16
17
18
(TYLERS WAY)
Dagger Lane
Aldenham Reservoir
Elst
Surgery
The Bartons
St Nicholas Cl
School
Lands' End
Hertsmere Progressive Synagogue
WATFORD ROAD
HIGH ST
ELSTREE HILL SOUTH
A5183
Schubert Rd
Britten Cl
Rodgers Cl
Delius Cl
Beethoven Rd
Elgar Close
Sullivan Way
Coates Rd
Summer Gv
May Gdns
Fortune La
West View Gardens
M1
ELSTREE ROAD
A411
Lismarrine Industrial Park
A411 ELSTREE ROAD
N WESTERN AV (WATFORD BY-PASS) A41
Centennial Avenue
Caldecote Lane
Caldecote Hill
A409
Paynesfield Rd
HEATHBOURNE ROAD
ELSTREE HL S
Brockley Hill Farm
Junction 4
Royal National Orthopaedic Hospital
Stanmore Common
Works
A5 BROCKLEY HILL
Barnet
Harrow
Nutt Gv
A41
EDGWARE
30
Wood Lane
Warren Lane
THE COMMON
Priory Drive
Priory Cl
Harrow RFC
Bentley Priory
Springfield Close
Park La
Hilltop Wy
Fallowfield
A4140
Aylmer Cl
Aylwards Rise
Heriots Cl
Pine Cl
Hall Farm Cl
Dennis Lane
Spring Lake
Old Forge Cl
Adelaide Cl
St Johns CE Middle School
First School
STANMORE HILL
Hill Close
Eaton Close
Surgery
Stangate Gdns
Rec Gnd
Embry Close
Embry Way
Green Lane
Halsbury Cl
Knights Road
Valencia Road
Arran Dr
Kerry Av
Glanleam Road
Stanmore Synagogue
London Rd
LONDON ROAD
A410
Snaresbrook Dr
Stanmore Station
Tintagel Drive
Berry Hill
Rees Dr
Newlands Close
Grantham Close
1
2
3
4
5
6
95
93
Bentley Wood Girls School
Flecker Close
Bridges Rd
Oldfield Close
Winscombe Wy
Ben Hale Cl
Woodside Cl
Holland Wk
Old Ldg Way
Deanne Close
Bowls Close
Tennis Club
43
Dennis Gdns
THE BROADWAY
CHURCH ROAD
Ray Gdns
Hall
Glebe Rd
Tel Ex
London Rd
Copley Rd
Merrion Av
Dene Gdns
Marsh Rd
Craigwell Dr
Sandymount Av
Beech Tree Close
Pangbourne Dr
Dovercourt Gardens
Aylward First & Middle Schools
STANMORE
PO
P

30
29
44
A
B
C
D
E
1
2
3
4
5
6
518
19
20
95
193
Elstree
Deacons Hill
Edgware
Cemetery
St Nicholas School
Hertsmere Progressive Synagogue
The Rise
Nicholas Road
Wentworth
Shiremeade
Sheraton Cl
Alwyn Close
Clare Cl
Hadley Cl
Summer Hl
Hartfield Cl
Ascot Cl
Berkeley Cl
Byron Av
Vale Av
Masefield Av
Carrington Av
Furzehill
Linster Gv
Burghley Avenue
BARNET LANE
A411
Deacons Hts
Fortune La
May Gdns
Summer Gv
London Loop
Hotel
Edgwarebury Lane
M1
Hertfordshire County
Barnet
London Gateway (Scratch
Bury Farm
Edgwarebury Cemetery
Broadfields Junior School
Broadfields Infant School
Bushfield Crescent
Meadfield
Bushfield Close
Springwood Crs
Burrell Close
Warrens Shawe La
Luther Close
Hartland Drive
Hartland Close
Hamonde Cl
Pentland Av
Tayside Dr
Rosh Pinah School
Aldridge Avenue
Kenilworth Road
Morley Crescent
Bellamy Close
Franklyn Gardens
Harrowes Meade
Bullescroft Road
Parsons Cres
Parsons Cv
Glengall Rd
Edgwarebury Park
Marlborough Av
Warwick Av
Harcourt Avenue
Fairmead Crescent
Wolmer Gdns
Broadfields Avenue
Beulah Close
Cranmer Rd
Rosens Wk
Wyre Grove
Crossgate
Windsor Av
Lynford Gardens
Blackwell Gdns
Parkside Dr
Parnell Cl
EDGWARE WAY (WATFORD BY-PASS)
A41
Grantham Close
Newlands Close
Hamlyn Close
Pipers Gn Lane
Brockley Avenue
HILL
Berry Hill
Rees Dr
SPUR ROAD A410
The Edgware School
Edgware Way
Sterling Avenue
Hillside Gardens
Glendale Avenue
Ranelagh Cl
Ashcombe Gdns
Shelley Cl
Mowbray Rd
Holland House School
Surgery
Broadhurst Av
Edgware United Synagogue
Highview Avenue
Highview Gardens
Riverdene
Hazel Gdns
Hillcrest Avenue
The Grove
Priory Field Drive
Fairview Wy
Edgwarebury Lane
London Rd
LONDON ROAD
Lacey Dr
Stone Grove
The Spinney
Snaresbrook Dr
Court Dr
Brockley Cl
Tintagel Dr
Pangbourne Dr
Edgware Reform Synagogue
Green Lane
Kings Drive
Upcroft Av
Stoneyfields Lane
Ash Close
Gibbs
Pangbourne Dr
Dovercourt Gardens
Heronslea Dr
Stonegrove Gdns
STONE GROVE
Orchard Dr
Park Grove
Purcells Av
Savoy Cl
Princes Cl
The Drive
The Rise
HA8
Penshurst Gardens
St Margarets Road
A5100
HALE LANE
Farm Road
Alders Cl
Cloister Gdns
Orchard Crs
Grange Hill
Stone Grove Park
Queen's Cl
Heronsgate
1 grid square represents 500 metres

Barnet Gate
Arkley
Highwood Hill
Mill Hill
NW7
F
G
H
J
K
1
2
3
4
5
6
21
22
23
95
93
32
45
Rowley Green Road
Meadowbanks
Meadowlands
Glebe Lane
Ripon Way
Dacre Gdns
Drive
Hackney Cl
Clydesdale Cl
Halter Close
Stirling Industrial Cen
Farriers
Works
Shetland Close
Percheron Rd
Retail Park
Stirling Way
BARNET LANE
BARNET WAY
Sports Ground
Windmill La
Dingle Close
Wylo Dr
Rockways
Brickfield Lane
A411 BARNET ROAD
Winifred Cl
Barnet Gate Lane
Chantry Close
B552
Mays Lane
Althorp Cl
HENDON WOOD LANE
London Loop
A1
Hyver Hill
BARNET WAY (BARNET BY-PASS)
Service Area
Golf Course
Tot Gre
Nan Clark's Lane
Crown Close
TOTTERIDGE COMMON
A5109
HIGHWOOD HILL
Mill Hill County High School
Mill Hill Golf Club
Courtland JMI Sch
Fairway Primary School
Fairway JMI School
Ramillies Road
Bedford Road
Hankins Lane
Worcester Crs
Norbury Road
Norbury Gv
Glenwood Road
Courtland Avenue
Robin Close
The Fairway
Laleham Avenue
North Dene
Westmere Drive
Stockton Gardens
Ellesmere Avenue
Fernside Avenue
Middle Dene
South Dene
Laurel Gdns
Westfield Rd
Croft Cl
MARSH LANE
The Lincolns
Abbey View
Hinton Cl
Marsh Close
Lawrence Gdns
The Reddings
Reddings Cl
Lawrence Street
St Marys Abbey
Belmont (Mill Hill Junior School)
Millers Close
Austell Gdns
Tretawn Gardens
Tretawn Park
Sunnyfield
Lawrence Av
Uphill Grove
Uphill Road
Green Av
Pike Rd
A41
St Pauls CE JMI School
Works
HAMMERS LANE
St Joseph's RC College
Shakespeare Road
Mill Hill School
THE RIDGEWAY
St Vincent RC Prima School
WATFORD WAY (BARNET BY-PASS)
Foxwood Cl
Glendor Gdns
Northolm
Oakmead Gdns
SELVAGE LANE
A5109
Sunbury Av
Sunbury Gardens
Maxwelton Cl
Maxwelton Av
Highwood Gv
Manor Drive
Hale Grove Gdns
HALE LANE
Matilda Marks School
Russell Grove
Mill
Newcombe Pk
St Martins School
Goodwyn Av
Victoria Road
Milton Rd
The Homoeopathic Health Cen
Byron Rd
Marion Road
DAWS LANE B1461
Wills Grove
Hollies End
Vineries Bank
Mount School
High St
Hartley Av
Surg
THE BROADWAY

Barnet
BARNET
Underhill
Ducks Island
Totteridge Green
Totteridge
Woodside Park
N20
Whitings Hill Primary School
Barnet Hill JMI School
Underhill J&I School
Ravenscroft School
Grasvenor Avenue Infant School
St Andrews CE JMI School
Woodridge Primary School
St Vincents RC Primary School
Rhodes Farm Clinic
Mount School
The Mill Hill Cricket Club
Totteridge Cricket Club
South Herts Golf Club
Woodside Park Golf Club
Golf Course
Playing Field
London Loop
TOTTERIDGE COMMON
A5109
TOTTERIDGE VILLAGE
A5109 TOTTERIDGE
RIDGEWAY
B552
Mays Lane
Barnet Lane
Dollis Valley Way
Rossiter Fields
Oaklands Road
Priory Close
White Orchards
The Pastures
Badgers Croft
Lime Gv
Wykeham Rise
Grange Avenue
Horseshoe Lane
Chestnut Lane
Northcliffe Dr
Pine Grove
Harmsworth Way
The Close
Willow End
Greenway Close
Coppice Walk
Laurel
Southover
Chiddingfold
Arlington
Framfield Cl
Shortgate
Michleham Down
Pycombe Corner
Chanctonbury
Burtonhole Lane
Burtonhole Cl
Hillview Road
Eleanor Crescent
Lullington
Rodmell Slope
Offham Slope
Garth
Cissbury Ring North
Wolstonbury
Ring South
Saddlescombe Wy
Argyle
Partingdale Lane
Reading Way
Approach La
Chesterfield Rd
Connaught Rd
Alan Drive
Brookside Close
Windsor Rd
Ridgeview Close
Bishops Close
Nupton Dr
Greenland Road
Shelford Rd
Partridge Cl
Edwyn Close
Dormer Close
Stanhope Rd
Dexter Rd
Niton Cl
Jarvis Cl
Juniper Cl
Sampson
Boardman Close
Mayhill Road
Valley View
Northbrook Rd
Leeside
Eastham Close
Hardy Cl
Dollis
Meadow Close
Crocus Field
Brent Pl
Bryant
Westcombe Drive
Fairfield Way
Grasvenor Avenue
Brett Road
Farm Close
Hackforth Close
Vecroft Crescent
Aitken Road
Escot Way
Denton Close
Well Road
Whitings Road
1 grid square represents 500 metres

20
31
46

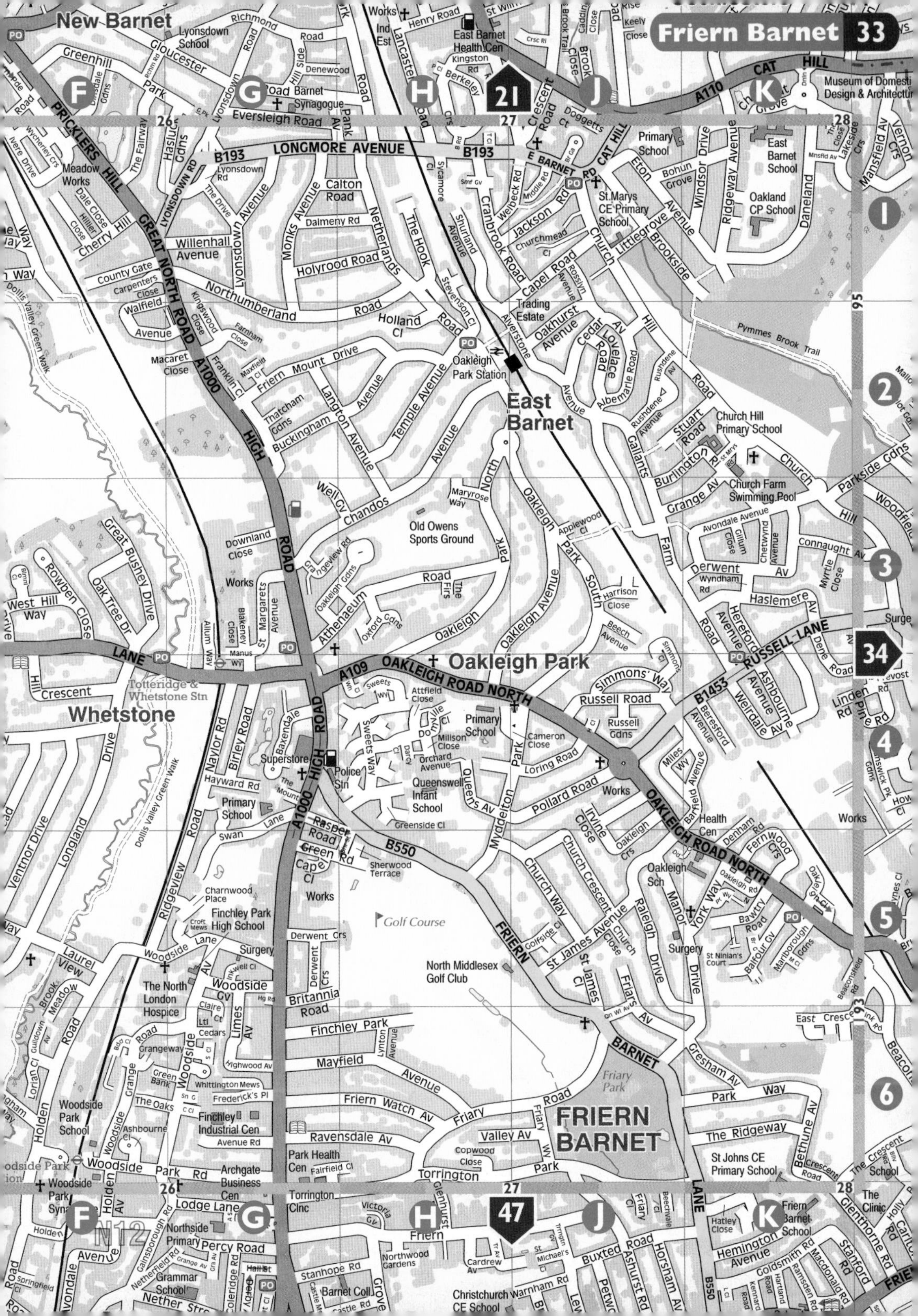
New Barnet
East Barnet
Oakleigh Park
Whetstone
FRIERN BARNET
21
34
47
F
G
H
J
K
1
2
3
4
5
6
26
27
28
95
93
GREAT NORTH ROAD
A1000
HIGH ROAD
A1000 HIGH ROAD
LONGMORE AVENUE
B193
CAT HILL
A110
E BARNET RD
OAKLEIGH ROAD NORTH
A109
RUSSELL LANE
B1453
B550
FRIERN BARNET LANE
PRICKLERS HILL
LYONSDOWN RD
Oakleigh Park Station
Totteridge & Whetstone Stn
Woodside Park Stn
Museum of Domestic Design & Architecture
East Barnet Health Cen
East Barnet School
Oakland CP School
St.Marys CE Primary School
Church Hill Primary School
Church Farm Swimming Pool
Old Owens Sports Ground
Queenswell Infant School
Finchley Park High School
The North London Hospice
Woodside Park School
North Middlesex Golf Club
Golf Course
Friary Park
St Johns CE Primary School
Friern Barnet School
Christchurch CE School
Barnet Coll
Northside Primary School
Grammar School
Archgate Business Cen
Finchley Industrial Cen
Park Health Cen
Torrington Clnc
Lyonsdown School
Road Barnet Synagogue
Meadow Works
Trading Estate
Pymmes Brook Trail
Dollis Valley Green Walk
Superstore
Police Stn
Health Cen
Oakleigh Sch
Surgery
Works
The Clinic
N12

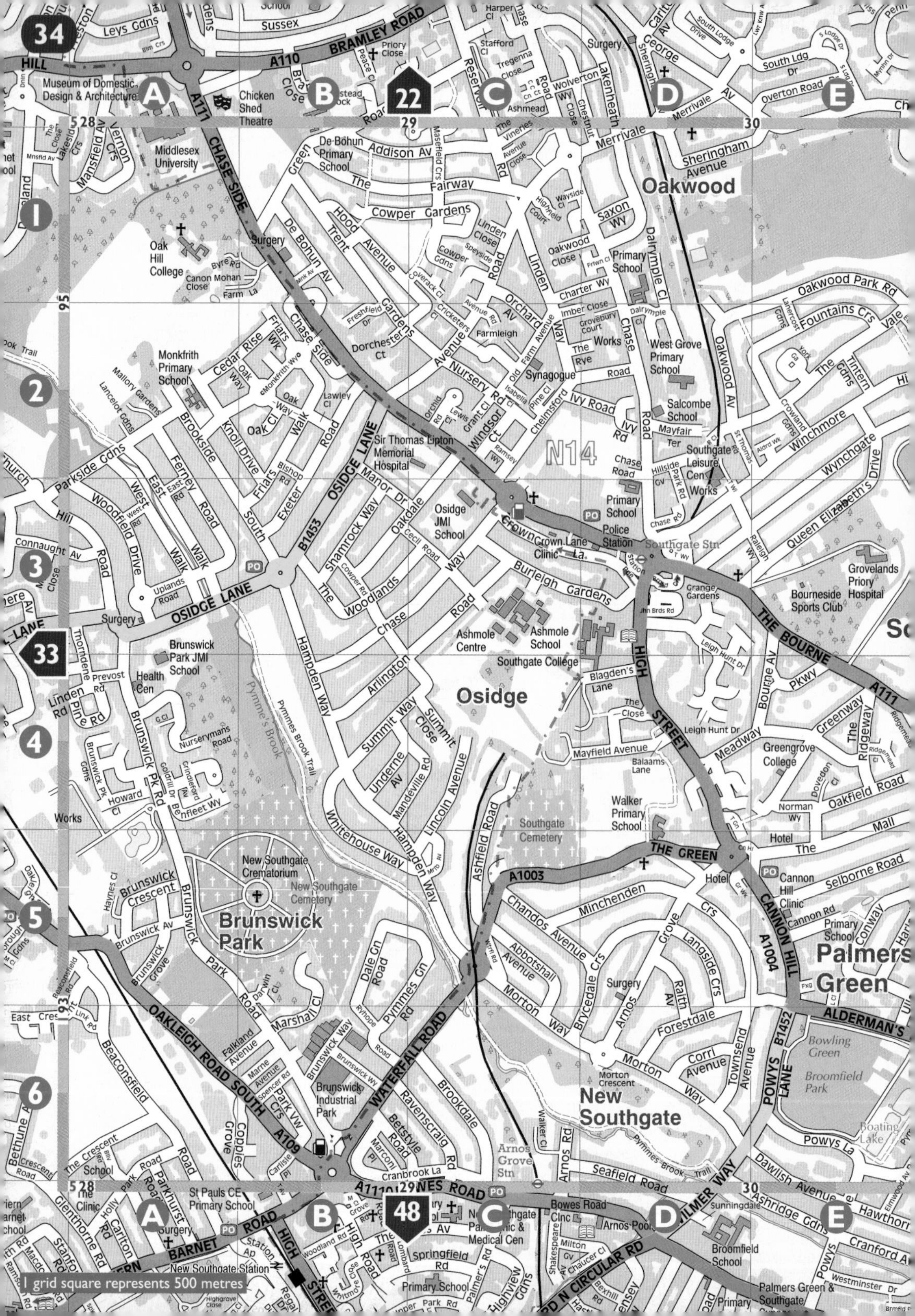
34
22
33
48
A
B
C
D
E
1
2
3
4
5
6
28
29
30
95
93
Oakwood
N14
Osidge
Palmers Green
New Southgate
Brunswick Park
HILL
A110 BRAMLEY ROAD
A111 CHASE SIDE
B1453 OSIDGE LANE
OSIDGE LANE
HIGH STREET
THE BOURNE
A111
THE GREEN
A1003
CANNON HILL
A1004
ALDERMAN'S
POWYS LANE
B1452
OAKLEIGH ROAD SOUTH
A109
WATERFALL ROAD
A1110 BOWES ROAD
BARNET ROAD
HIGH STREET
N CIRCULAR RD
WILMER WAY
LANE
Museum of Domestic Design & Architecture
Chicken Shed Theatre
Middlesex University
Oak Hill College
De Bohun Primary School
Monkfrith Primary School
Sir Thomas Lipton Memorial Hospital
Osidge JMI School
Brunswick Park JMI School
Health Cen
Primary School
West Grove Primary School
Salcombe School
Southgate Leisure Cen
Police Station
Southgate Stn
Crown Lane Clinic
Ashmole Centre
Ashmole School
Southgate College
Grovelands Priory Hospital
Bourneside Sports Club
Greengrove College
Walker Primary School
Southgate Cemetery
New Southgate Crematorium
New Southgate Cemetery
Brunswick Industrial Park
Arnos Grove Stn
Cannon Hill Clinic
Hotel
Bowling Green
Broomfield Park
Boating Lake
Broomfield School
Bowes Road Clinc
Arnos Pool
New Southgate Polyclinic & Medical Cen
St Pauls CE Primary School
New Southgate Station
The Crescent School
The Clinic
Primary School
Palmers Green & Southgate
Synagogue
Surgery
Works
Leys Gdns
Sussex
Priory Close
Stafford Cl
Tregenna Close
Wolverton Wy
Lakenheath
Reservoir Rd
George
Merrivale
Sheringham Av
South Lodge Drive
South Ldg Dr
Overton Road
Addison Av
The Fairway
Cowper Gardens
Hood Avenue
Trent Gardens
De Bohun Av
Linden Close
Linden Way
Oakwood Close
Saxon Wy
Charter Wy
Dalrymple Cl
Chase Road
Orchard Av
Avenue Rd
Farmleigh
Nursery Rd
Windsor Ct
Chelmsford
Ivy Road
Ivy Rd
Mayfair Ter
Oakwood Park Rd
Fountains Crs
Oakwood Av
Lancelot Gdns
Tintern
Winchmore
Wynchgate
Queen Elizabeth's Drive
Cedar Rise
Friars Wk
Oak Way
Oak Cl
Lawley Cl
Chase Side
Dorchester Ct
Mallory Gardens
Lancelot Gdns
Parkside Gdns
Brookside
Ferney Road
Knoll Drive
Friars Walk
East Walk
West Walk
Woodfield Drive
Hill Road
Connaught Av
Uplands Road
South Exeter
Bishop Rd
Manor Dr
Shamrock Way
Oakdale
Cecil Road
The Woodlands
Chase Road
Chase Way
Burleigh Gardens
Crown La
Grange Gardens
Leigh Hunt Dr
Bourne Av
Pkwy
Greenway
The Ridgeway
Blagden's Lane
The Close
Mayfield Avenue
Balaams Lane
Meadway
Oakfield Road
Norman Wy
The Mall
Selborne Road
Cannon Rd
Conway
Thorndene
Prevost Rd
Linden Rd
Pine Rd
Brunswick Pk Rd
Nurserymans Road
Brunswick Pk Gdns
Howard Cl
Benfleet Wy
Hampden Way
Arlington
Summit Way
Summit Close
Underne Av
Mandeville Rd
Lincoln Avenue
Whitehouse Way
Ashfield Road
Pymmes Brook Trail
Pymme's Brook
Minchenden Crs
Chandos Avenue
Abbotshall Avenue
Brycedale Crs
Grove
Langside Crs
Raith Av
Morton Way
Forestdale
Arnos
Corri Avenue
Townsend Avenue
Morton Crescent
Brunswick Crescent
Brunswick Av
Brunswick Grove
Brunswick Park Road
Darwin Cl
Marshall Cl
Dale Gn Road
Pymmes Gn Rd
Rynope Road
Brunswick Way
Falkland Avenue
Marne Avenue
Spencer Rd
Park Vw Crs
Coppies Grove
Brookdale
Ravenscraig Rd
Betstyle Road
Marconi Pl
Cranbrook La
Beaconsfield Road
Beaconsfield
East Cres
Link Rd
Bethune Av
Crescent Rd
Park Road
Parkhurst Road
Glenthorne Rd
Holly Pk
Carlton Rd
Stanford
Walker Cl
Arnos Rd
Seafield Road
Powys La
Dawlish Avenue
Ashridge Gdns
Hawthorn
Cranford Av
Westminster Dr
Sunningdale
Shakespeare Av
Milton Gv
Chaucer Cl
Bexhill
Springfield Rd
Palmer's Rd
Highview Gdns
Lombard
Woodland Rd
Station Ap
1 grid square represents 500 metres

Grange Park
Winchmore Hill
N21
N13
23
36
49
Grange Park Station
Winchmore Hill Station
Palmers Green Station
Bush Hill Park Golf
Golf Course
Edmonton Cemetery
Winchmore School
Winchmore Hill Cricket Club
Highfield Primary School
Moor Primary School
Preparatory School
Palmers Green High School
Firs Farm Primary School
Aylward School
St Annes Catholic High School
Hazelwood Junior School
Hazelwood Infant School
Sports Ground
Great Cambridge Junction
Millfield Thtr
Chasevillet Clinic
Gainsborough Clinic
Ridge Ho Clinic
Winchmore Hill Clnc
Bus Garage
Works
Green Lane
Ridge Avenue
Park Avenue
Village Road
Church Street
Great Cambridge Road
Bourne Hill
Hedge Lane
North Circular
Sterling Way
A105
A111
A406
A10
A1004
B154
Houndsden Road
Church Hill
Dragon Lane
Grange Park Avenue
Bush Hill
Firs Lane
Compton Rd
Broad Walk
Fox Lane
Eversley Crescent
Old Park Ridings
Vicar's Moor Lane
Sherbrook Gardens
Highfield Rd
Farm Road
Hyde Park Avenue
Firs Park Avenue
Barrowell Green
Fernleigh Road
Woodberry Av
Caversham Avenue
Derwent Road
Lakeside Road
Grovelands Road
Westerham Ave
Huxley
Henley
Silver
Sterling
F
G
H
J
K
I
2
3
4
5
6
31
32
33

1 grid square represents 500 metres

F
G
H
J
K
25
36
37
38
I
2
3
4
5
6
38
51
Keats Close
Percy Gdns
Tennyson Cl
Scotland Gn
Napier Road
Alma Primary School
Ponders End Station
South Street
Woodall Road
Wharf Rd
Riverside Industrial Est
Redburn Industrial Est
Woodall Rd
Sutherland Road
Nelson Road
Gardiner Cl
Falcon Crs
Morson Rd
Works
Riverside Industrial Estate
Mottingham Rd
Road
Avenue
Chelsfield Av
PO
Hall La
Coran Cl
Winton Cl
Grove
Road
Cambourne
Warren Cl
Penfold Road
Chariton
MERIDIAN WAY
A1055
UCI
Lee Valley Leisure Golf Club
Lee Valley Leisure Centre Camping & Caravan
Golf Course
Lea Valley Walk
William Girling Reservoir
LEA VALLEY ROAD
A110
Dunnock Cl
Horizon Business Cen
Dominion Business Pk
Lock La
Pickett's Lock La
Pymmes Brook Trail
Lea Valley Wk
Ardra Rd
Works
River Lea
River Lea or Lee
Lea Va Wk
Yardley La
Yardley Primary School
Hawkwood Crescent
Epping Way
Mark Av
Amsbry Dr
Drysdale Avenue
Margaret Av
Dells Cl
South Av
Markfield Gdns
Harford Rd
Holly Drive
Merryhill Cl
Maida Wy
Maida Avenue
KINGS HEAD HILL
Hawksmouth
Blandford Crs
A112
Low Hall Cl
College Gardens
Sunset Av
Seymour Rd
Mount Echo Drive
Mount Echo Av
Chingford School
Nevin Drive
Chingford RFC
A1037
WALTHAM WAY
Valley side
MANSFIELD HILL
Surgery
Silverthorn Gardens
Lawrence Hl
B169
Eatons Md
Lambourne Gdns
Lansdowne Rd
Denner Road
Mulberry Cl
Peel Cl
ROAD
Heriot Av
St Catherines Road
Walmer Cl
Leadale Avenue
Wellington Avenue
Chingford Avenue
OLD CHURCH
Brindwood Road
Priory Close
Mayhew Close
Rectory Close
Moreland Wy
Heathcote Gv
Cemetery
Priory Avenue
Cherrydown Close
Cherrydown Avenue
Middleton Close
Middleton Avenue
Hurst Av
Hurst Cl
Churchill Terrace
Alpha Road
Salisbury Rd
Morris Court
Flaxen Road
Harold Rd
Mount Av
Templeton Avenue
Chivers Rd
St John's Rd
Suffield Rd
Grove
Marmion Cl
Medical Centre
Windsor Rd
Brook Crs
Primary School
Brook Crs
Brook Gdns
Marmion Avenue
Russell Road
NEW ROAD
A1009
HALL LANE
Drive
Hall Gdns
Chingford Health Centre
Works
Normanshire
Waverley Av
Chase Lane Primary School
Albert Av
Chase Gdns
Orchard Cl
Tufton Road
Larkswood Road
Ainslie Wood Gdns
Bourne Gdns
Larkswood Playing Fields
Frankland Road
Surgery
Chingford Industrial Cen
Lee Park Way
Advent Way
Lwr
Norbury Rd
Kingsley Gdns
Genever Cl
Palace Vw Rd
Underwood Road
A406
AA
Service Centre
Burnham Road
Warwick Rd
Finch Gdns
COOKS FERRY ROUNDABOUT
Ainslie Wood Road
PO

1 grid square represents 500 metres

The Warren
F
G
H
J
K
Hill Reform Synagogue
Albion Hill
Albion Park
Pollards Close
High View Close
Surgery
Oaklands School
Forest Medical Centre
Roding Valley High School
Meadow Road
Lower Park Road
Algers Rd
Algers Mead
Algers Close
Crescent Vw
Loughton Station
Roding Road
Stonards Hill
Barncroft
Algiers Road
Oakwood
River
South Vw Road
Three Forests
41
42
43
Spring Grove
Newnham Close
The Crescent
The Avenue
Road
Summerfield Road
Hillcrest Road
Lancaster Dr
Roding Gardens
Boleyn
Valley Close
Valley Hill
Malvern Gardens
Kenilworth Gardens
Highland Ave
Southern Drive
Avondale Drive
Broomfield
Witham Cl
Cheltenham Gardens
Dunmow Close
Danbury Road
Nevill Wy
Drayton Ave
Elmhurst Way
Avondale Close
White Bridge Primary School
Felstead Rd
Greensted Rd
Valley Hill
Sutton Close
Roydon Close
Greensted Road
Thaxted Rd
Blackmore Rd
Pentlow Way
Bradwell Road
Rous Rd
Boxted Close
Tennis Centre
Guru Gobind Singh Khalsa College
New Barns Farm
HIGH ROAD
A121
EPPING NEW ROAD
A104
Manor Road
North Farm
Swan Lane
Treetops Vw
Kings Pl
Harvest Lane
Fallow Flds
The Chase
Woodcote Mews
Regents Place
The Drive
North End
Hotel
Powell Rd
Roebuck Lane
Little Plucketts Way
Stradbroke Grove
Roding View
Way
River Road
Rous Road
Dene Rd
Surgery
Hurst Road
Buckhurst Hill FC
RODING LANE
Ardmore Lane
Braeside Senior School
Braeside Junior School
Luctons Avenue
Greenhill
Forest Side
Ormonde Rise
Fernside
Epping New Rd
St Johns CE Primary School
Works
Fernbank
Church Rd
Gladstone Road
St John's Court
High Rd
Amberley Road
The Meadway
Russell Road
Scotland Road
Palace Gardens
Loughton Way
Trent Rd
Osborne Rd
Hill's Road
Chequers
Loyola Preparatory Sch
Westbury Rd
Daiglen Sch
Fairfield Clinic
PALMERSTON RD
B170
Surgery
Surg
Devon Close
Westbury Lane
Buckhurst Hill Station
Langfords
Victoria Rd
Stag Lane
Queen's Road
Surgery
Andrews Cl
Works
IG9
Princes Road
Albert Road
Alfred Road
The Windsors
Buckhurst Hill Primary School
Lower Queen's Road
Chandos Cl
Beech Av
Holly House Private Hospital
Wimborne Cl
Woodside
Princes Way
Monarch Place
Briar Close
Mountbatten Court
Elgar Cl
Cedar Cl
Cascade Rd
Knighton Lane
Elm Cl
Lime Cl
Buckhurst Hill
Lord's Bushes
Woodland Cl
Maple Close
Oak Rise
Birch Close
Council Building
Willow Close
Holly Close
Buckhurst Way
Chestnut Ave
Hornbeam Road
Edge
Forest
Woodland Way
Dell Close
The Dell
The Glade
Woodford Wells
Field Close
Broadfield Way
Farm Close
Farm Way
Walnut Way
Station Way
Works
Roding Valley Station
Forest Way
Denehurst Gardens
Gardens
Dale
Knighton Close
Monkham's Lane
Orchard Lane
Beresford Drive
Cherry Tree Rise
Bush Road
Old Bancroftians FC
Luxborough Lane
M11
Princes Avenue
Worcester Crescent
Malvern Drive
Avenue
Hawthorn Road
Ridge Way
Heath Way
95
94
93
I
2
3
4
5
6
53
Park Ave
Tudor Close
Monkham's
Worcester Crescent
Queen's Ave
Broad Oak
King's
Fairway
Glebeway
Seaforth Gdns
Durham Ave
Oxford Road
Essex County
Redbridge
West Hatch High School
St Marys Way

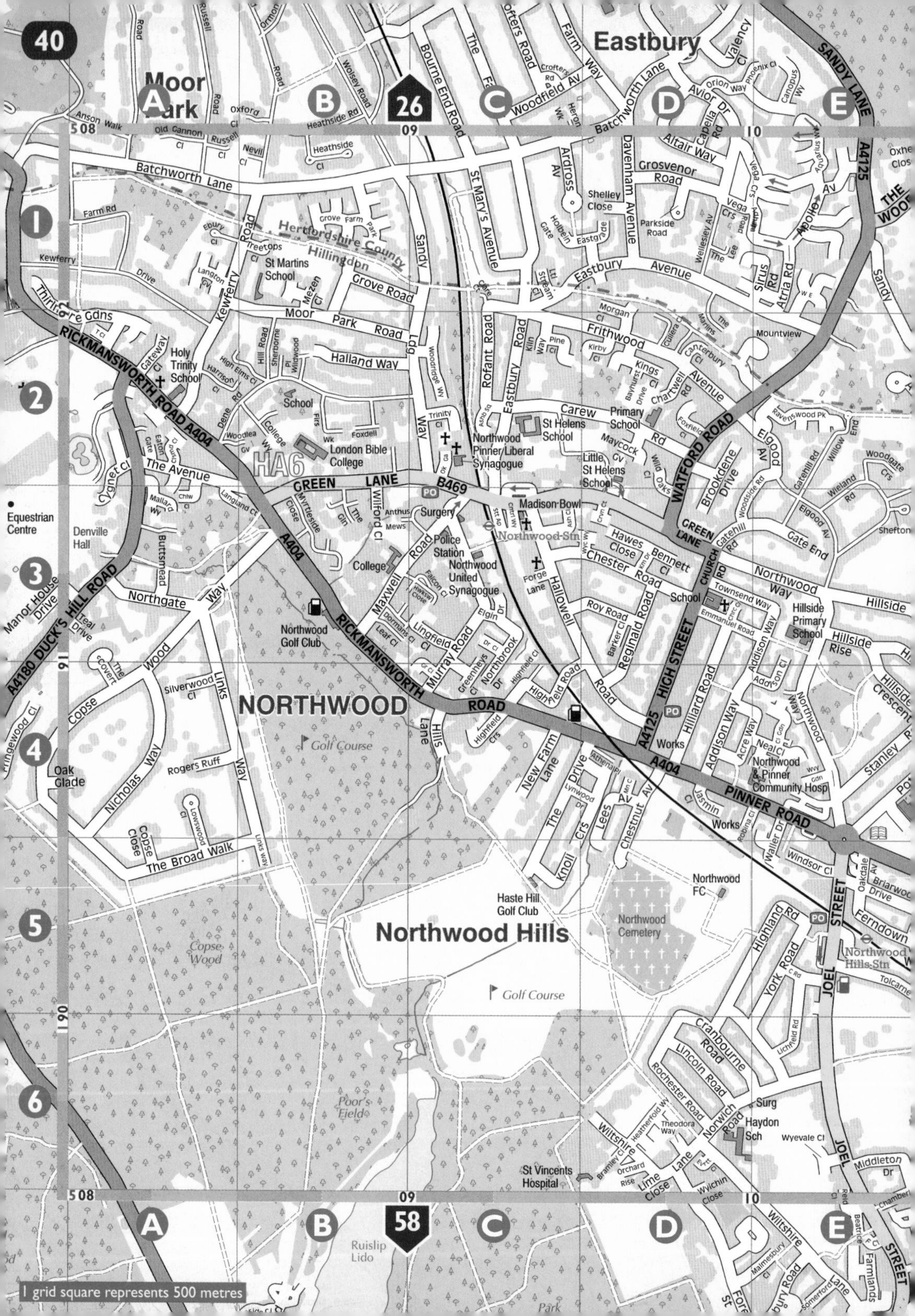
40
Moor Park
Eastbury
26
58
A
B
C
D
E
1
2
3
4
5
6
508
09
10
91
190
Batchworth Lane
Hertfordshire County
Hillingdon
Kewferry Road
Kewferry Drive
Farm Rd
St Martins School
Grove Farm Park
Grove Road
Moor Park Road
Halland Way
Sandy Lodge Way
St Mary's Avenue
Bourne End Road
Woodfield Av
Batchworth Lane
Ardross Av
Shelley Close
Davenham Avenue
Grosvenor Road
Eastbury Avenue
Altair Way
Avior Dr
Capella Rd
Parkside Road
Wellesley Av
Sirus Rd
Atria Rd
Apollo Av
SANDY LANE
A4125
THE WOOD
Thirlmere Gdns
RICKMANSWORTH ROAD A404
Holy Trinity School
Gateway Cl
Dene Rd
College Wy
School
Foxdell
London Bible College
HA6
GREEN LANE
B469
PO
Surgery
Police Station
Northwood United Synagogue
Northwood Pinner Liberal Synagogue
St Helens School
Little St Helens School
Madison Bowl
Northwood Stn
Primary School
Carew Rd
Rofant Road
Eastbury Road
Frithwood Avenue
Chartwell Rd
Maycock Gv
WATFORD ROAD
Brookdene Drive
Elgood Av
Ravenswood Pk
Woodgate Crs
Wieland Rd
Gatehill Rd
Gate End
Mountview
Equestrian Centre
Denville Hall
The Avenue
Cygnet Cl
Buttsmead
Northgate Way
Manor House Drive
A4180 DUCK'S HILL ROAD
Teal Drive
College
Maxwell Road
Lingfield Cl
Murray Road
Northbrook Dr
Elgin Dr
Hallowell Road
Forge Lane
Chester Road
Hawes Close
Bennett Cl
Roy Road
Reginald Road
School
CHURCH RD
HIGH STREET
A4125
Northwood Way
Hillside Primary School
Hillside Rise
Hillside Crescent
Townsend Way
Emmanuel Road
Addison Way
Hilliard Road
Northwood Golf Club
RICKMANSWORTH ROAD
NORTHWOOD
Golf Course
Copse Wood Way
Links Way
Silverwood Cl
Rogers Ruff
Nicholas Way
Oak Glade
Copse Close
The Broad Walk
Hills Lane
Highfield Road
Highfield Crs
New Farm Lane
The Drive
Lees Av
Chestnut Av
Knoll Crs
A404
PINNER ROAD
Works
Northwood & Pinner Community Hosp
Acre Way
Neal Cl
Stanley
Windsor Cl
Briarwood Drive
Ferndown
Oakdale Av
Northwood FC
Haste Hill Golf Club
Northwood Hills
Northwood Cemetery
Northwood Hills Stn
JOEL STREET
Highland Rd
York Road
Tolcarne
Golf Course
Copse Wood
Poor's Field
Cranbourne Road
Lincoln Road
Rochester Road
Norwich Road
Haydon Sch
Surg
Wyevale Cl
Middleton Dr
Wiltshire Lane
St Vincents Hospital
Lime Grove
Orchard Close
Theodora Way
Ruislip Lido
Malmesbury Rd
Somerford Cl
Farmlands
Beatrice
1 grid square represents 500 metres

Muirfield Rd
Northwick
Moortown
Chilwell
Redwood
Beeston Close
Kilmarnock
Caldwell Rd
Lane
Fleetwood Wy
Muirfield
Hoylake Gdns
Gardens
St Annes Cl
Road
Liphook
Compton Place
Way
Drive
LANE
OXHEY
LITTLE
F
G
H
J
K
27
12
13
11
Oxheylane Farm
I
Furze Cl
Drive
Burnley Cl
Ashridge
Surgery
Hindhead
Barnhurst Pth
Ellesborough Cl
ROAD
Bramshaw Gdns
Ilkley
Benton Rd
Lytham Avenue
Cherry Hills
Public Swimming Pool
B4542
Oxhey
Oxhey Woods
Primary School
Anglesey
Surgery
Blackford Rd
Belfairs
Foxgrove Pth
Road
PRESTWICK
Heysham Dr
Bowring Green
Bramley Gdns
Hertfordshire County
Harrow
Pinnerwood House
92
Royston
Royston
Oakleigh Road
Witney Close
Kennedy
The Avenue
Newland Cl
Sylvia Avenue
Derwent Av
Lyndon Av
Grimsdyke First & Middle School
Colburn Avenue
Colburn Av
Hillview Road
Hillview Close
Walpole Cl
Hatch End Station
2
South
View
Potter Street
Pinner Hill Golf Club
St Johns School
Park View Road
Harrow
Hillingdon
Road
Pinner Hill
Hatch End
Westfield Park
Drive
Meredith Cl
Staplefield Cl
Grimsdyke
Road
Ferndown Cl
Wessex Drive
A410
3
Golf Course
Pinnerwood Park
Albury
Scot Gv
Langland Dr
Hallam Gdns
Woodridings Cl
THE BROADWAY
Dove Pk
Potters Hts Close
Woodhall
Drive
Felden Close
Cornwall Rd
Anselm Road
Hillside Road
Evelyn
Avenue
Lytton Road
Altham Rd
The Broadway
Road
Towers Rd
Devonshire Rd
42
Gardens
Street
Lyndhurst Gardens
Southacre Way
Albury Drive
Marsworth
Linkway
Gate
Tooke Cl
Woodhall Drive
UXBRIDGE RD (HATCH END)
Wellington Road
Park
Woodridings Avenue
Surg
Seymour Close
Athol Cl
Pinner
Buckland Ri
Blythwood Road
Murray Crs
Old S Cl
A404
Nugent's Park
Nugent's Park
4
Northwood School
Dale Cl
Alandale Drive
Athol Gardens
Albury Drive
Latimer Gdns
Latimer Cl
Norman Crescent
Murray Crs
Limedene
Old Hall Dr
ST THOMAS' DRIVE
River Pinn
Northwood Sports Centre
Lyndhurst Avenue
Pinner Wood Primary School
Hill
Poplar Cl
UXBRIDGE ROAD (PINNER)
Woodhall Av
Old Hall Cl
Holly Gv
Pinner Park
Greenway
Jubilee
Cherry Ct
Bryants Cl
Valley Close
Crossway
Jubilee Cl
Pinner Green
Willow Dene
Lawn Vale
Barrow Point
Paine's
Moss Ltl Moss Lane
Pinner Park Farm
A404
GEORGE V AVENUE
Deacons Cl
RICKMANSWORTH ROAD
Road
Willows Cl
Olwen Ms
Waxwell
The Dell
Barrow Point
Oakhill Av
Hazelwood Dr
Oakwood
Ashley Cl
Rd
Maycroft
Mill Farm Close
Antoneys Cl
Oakhill Avenue
Lane
Moss Close
5
Woodford Crs
Wynlie Gdns
Tanworth Gdns
Audley Ct
Tudor Rd
PINNER GREEN
Elm Pk
Haywood Cl
Lane
Avenue
Surgery
90
Abbey Cl
Ash Hl Dr
Bell Cl
Millman Cl
HA5
East End Way
Cemetery
Harlyn
Harlyn School
Hazeldene Drive
West
Elm Park Road
Waxwell Lane
Love La
School
Avenue Rd
Leighton Av
Burlington Pl
Nursery Rd
Nursery Rd
Granville Pl
Mayfield Sch
Paines Cl
Moss
Terrilands
6
Lawson Gdns
Clovelly Cl
CUCKOO HILL
Starling Cl
Cuckoo Hill
Drive
End
Bridge St
M S Business Centre
Estgl
Anglesmede Wy
Drive
Henley Gdns
Chamberlain Way
Raisins Hl
Sweetmans Av
Westbury Ldg
High Street
Church
Bch
Ingle Close
Amberley Cl
Wakehams Hill
The Squirrels
Linslade
Selway Close
Catlin's
Raisins Hl
Ashdene
View
Lane
Chapel Lane
Station Ap
Surg
Lane
Sh Cl
Lane
High
North Way
West Wy
13
Cemetery
Pinner Station
School
Pinner
59
Pinner & District Synagogue
F
G
H
J
K
Arden Mnr
Daymer Gdns
Birchmead Avenue
Northfield Av
Gilbert Rd
West Lodge School
Dickson Fold
Grange Gdns
The Cha
Capel Gdns
Copperfield Wy
Lane
High Rd Eastcote
Larkswood
Pushmoor
Crest Vw
Hillcrest Av
West End
End Av
Ashridge Gdns
Holwell Pl
Wentworth
Pinn Medical
Cecil Park Clinic
Cecil Park
Marsh Rd
Reddiford School
Pinner

42
28
41
60
Golf Course
Grims Dyke Golf Club
Oxheylane Farm
Old Redding
Ass House La
Kiln
Hotel
Clamp Hill
Brookshill Drive
Brookshill Av
A409
OXHEY LANE
A4008
Saddlers Close
Park Road
Royston Park
Royston Grove
Oakleigh Road
Thornton Grove
Clonard Way
Rowlands
Hazelcroft
Oakmeade Drive
Ashcroft
Highbanks Rd
Sequoia Pk
Pinewood Av
Oxhey La
Avenue
Walpole Cl
Cedar Drive
Furham Field
Sherington Av
Milne Fld
Hatch End Station
Surgery
The Lawns
UXBRIDGE RD (HATCH END)
A410
UXBRIDGE ROAD (HARROW WEALD)
UXBRIDGE RD (HARROW
Superstore
Hatch End Swimming Pool
Harrow Arts Centre
Winston Ct
Boniface Wk
Boniface Gdns
Ufford Rd
Courtenay Av
Tillotson Road
Hatch End High School
Shaftesbury School
School
Roger Bannister Sports Ground
Bannister Stadium
Birch Pk
Ross Close
Hutton Wk
Mepham Crs
Chicheley Road
Langton Rd
Whittlesea School
Cedars First School
Cedars Middle School
Whittlesea Road
Stafford Rd
Boxtree Rd
Hutton Lane
Belsize Road
Bellfield Av
West Drive
West Dr Gdns
Lakeland Cl
Timbers Clinic
Harrow Weald Pk
Weald College
BROOKSHILL
Park Dr
Harrow Weald Cemetery
All Saints Ms
Clamp Hill
Fontwell Cl
Kelvin Crs
Monro Gdns
Boxtree Road
Kynaston Close
High Road
Silver Cl
Lane
Colmer Place
Blackwell Cl
Elm Ter
Marlcas Av
Hitherwell Drive
Creer Rd
Weighton Road
A409 HIGH ROAD
Superstore
Harrow Weald
College Rd
College Avenue
Park Crescent
The Meadow Wy
Elms Rd
College Hill Road
Long Elmes
Stanhope Av
Stox Md
Derby Av
Mead Cl
Clewer Crs
Windsor Road
Hampden Road
Carmelite Road
Sefton Av
Weald Lane
Medical Centre
Enderley Rd
Headstone Lane Station
Augustine Road
Headstone Lane
Chantry Rd
Chantry Pl
Mullion Cl
Fernleigh Ct
Randon Close
Broadfields
Barmor Cl
Surgery
Parkfield Avenue
Verwood Rd
Fullbeck Wy
Parkfield Crs
Almond Wy
Pinner Pk Av
Pinner Pk Gdns
Bancroft Rd
Avenue
Brinsley Road
Bengarth Dr
Toorack Road
Nicola Cl
Whitefriars Dr
Tudor Rd
Leighton Rd
Athelstone Rd
Risingholme Rd
Salvatorian College
Spencer Road
School
Claremont Road
Bruce Road
Ladysmith Road
HIGH ST
Whitefriars Trading Est
Whitefriars Trading Est
Sch
Barrett Way Industrial Est
Barrett Wy
Graham Rd
Wellington Rd
Havelock Road
Wolseley Rd
Gordon Road
Police Stn
Old Millhillians Sports Ground
River
Pinner Park
Pinner Park Farm
Pinner Park Primary School
Melbourne Av
Holmwood Close
Greystoke Av
Manor Pk Dr
Birkdale Av
Greenfield Way
Holmdene Av
Parkfield Gdns
Harrow Heritage Museum
Downing Cl
Waverley Industrial Est
Hailsham Dr
Cecil Rd
George V Av
GEORGE V AVENUE
Anglesmede Crs
Elmcroft Crescent
Surgery
Headstone Manor Recreation Ground
Victor Road
Albert Rd
Edward Road
Sidney Rd
Atherton Pl
Harrow View
Harrow Crown Courts
Headstone Drive
Ellen Webb Dr
Princes Dr
Harrow & Wealdstone Station
Hillview Gdns
Cemetery
A404
Headstone
Headstone Gdns
Pinner View
Priory Way
Manor Way
Brook Drive
Moat Drive
Harley Road
Harley Crs
Walton Road
Walton Cl
Queens Walk
Dukes Avenue
Earls Crs
Kings Way
Sandridge Cl
Marlborough
Civic Centre
Pinner Court
Hazelwood
1 grid square represents 500 metres

STANMORE
Belmont
Wealdstone
HA7
HA3
St Johns CE Middle School
First School
Surgery
Spring Lake
Stanmore Hill
Embry Way
Eaton Close
Knights Road
London Road
Kerry Av
Valencia Road
Snaresbrook Dr
Stanmore Station
Westbere Dr
Morecambe Gdns
Pangbourne Dr
Tintagel Drive
Aylward First & Middle Schools
North London Collegiate School
Dalkeith
Bentley Wood Girls School
Masefield Avenue
Flecker Close
Bridges Rd
Sitwell Gv
Binyon Crs
Brockhurst Cl
Chenduit Way
Algar Cl
White Orchards
Bentley Way
Oldfield Close
Winscombe Wy
Holland Wk
Ben Hale Cl
Woodside Cl
Green Lane
Tennis Club
Pynnacles Cl
Rav Gdns
Church Road
The Broadway
Dennis Gdns
Hall
Tel Ex
A410
A4140
Marsh Lane
Marsh Road
London Rd
Dene Gdns
Merrion Avenue
Craigwell Cl
Sandymount Avenue
Charlbury Av
Beech Tree Close
Elizabeth Gdns
Malcolm Ct
Haig Rd
Elm Park
Nelson Road
Du Cros Drive
Peters Cl
Howberry Rd
Cheyneys Avenue
Wychwood Avenue
Wychwood Close
Wychwood Av
Howberry Cl
Cloyster Wd
Longcrofte Road
Cornbury Road
Howberry Road
Surgery
Stanmore Marsh
Watersfield Wy
B461
Uxbridge Road (Stanmore)
Douglas Cl
Elliott Rd
Boyle Av
Lady Aylesford Avenue
Rectory Lane
Rectory Cl
Tudor Well Close
Old Church La
Cherry Tree Wy
Stanmore College
Beatty Road
Bernays Cl
Silverston Way
Silverston Wy
The Ridgeway
Lansdowne Road
Barn Crs
Gas Works
Jellicoe Gdns
Conway Close
Dowding Pl
Embry Drive
Robb Rd
Trenchard Cl
Temple Md Close
Capuchin Cl
Leavesden Rd
Ashdale Gv
Kenneth Gardens
The Chase
Cairn Wy
Chartley Avenue
Holme Wy
Heather Wy
Woodlands Dr
Winston Cl
Gordon Av
Georgian Close
Maytree La
Woodward Gdns
Weymouth Wk
Links Vw Cl
Sunningdale Cl
Greenacres Drive
Gordon
Gleneagles Cl
Rosedale Cl
Water Gdns
September Wy
Wolverton Rd
Stanmore Golf Club
Golf Course
Old Church Lane
Courtenay
Cranmer Cl
Gn Verges
Golf Cl
Abercorn Road
Sports Ground
Acorn Close
Belmont Lane
Stanburn Middle Sch
Wemborough Road
Bromefield
Brick La
My Cl
Bush Gv
Honeypot Lane
Honeypot Lane Centre
Kenton Lane
Richmond Gdns
Dromey Gdns
Drummond
Daventer Dr
Alton Av
The Hwy
The Drive
Woodcroft Av
Weald First & Middle School
Robin Hood Drive
Laurel Wk
Kingshill
Weald Rise
Woodpecker Cl
Chestnut Dr
The Avenue
Three Mdw Ms
Mountside
Vernon Drive
St Edmunds Drive
Hermitage Way
Honister Gdns
Honister Close
Honister Pl
Floriston Close
Floriston Gdns
Coledale Drive
Braithwaite Gdns
St Andrews Dr
Gyles Park
Bromefield
Lyon Meade
Bush Grove
Pickett Cft
Parr Rd
Carlisle Road
Wigton Gdns
College Hill Rd
Adderley Rd
Connaught Rd
Dryden Rd
Kenton Road
Beverley Gardens
Curzon Av
Felbridge Av
Bellamy Dr
Weston Drive
Ventnor Av
York Avenue
Wetheral Drive
Kynance Gdns
Crowshott Av
Lamorna Grove
Ladycroft Walk
Anmersh Grove
Pearswood Gardens
Thistlecroft Gdns
Burnell Gardens
Church Lane
Bishop Ken Road
Fisher Road
Hibbert Road
Lime Close
Dobbin Cl
Belmont First & Middle School
School
Clifton Av
Kingshill Drive
Tenby Avenue
Elgin Avenue
Grange Avenue
Derwent Crs
Culver Grove
High School
Carisbrooke Close
Portland Crescent
Broadcroft Avenue
Langland Crescent
Fairways
Byron Road
Warham Road
Lorne Rd
Locket Road
Sancroft Road
Radcliffe Road
Borrowdale Av
Grasmere Gardens
Cross Rd
Rocklands Dr
Jersey Avenue
Ivanhoe Drive
Hillary Gdns
Talbot Road
Charmian Av
Morley Crs East
Morley Crs West
Clydesdale Av
Streatfield Rd
Portland Crs
Medical Centre
Priestmead First & Middle Schools
Queens Avenue
Ennerdale Av
Uppingham Av
Formby Avenue
Dudley Avenue
Stirling Rd
Aberdeen Rd
Grant Road
Archery Cl
Avondale Road
Belmont Road
Ronart St
Works
Canning Road
Peel Road
Stuart Rd
Pembroke Av
Irvine Av
Hartford Avenue
Radstock Av
Alveston Av
Oakfield Av
Larkfield Av
Streatfield Road
Moorhouse Road
Wagborn Road
Cody Cl
Kenmore Park School
Warneford Road
Court Cl
Liddell
Kenmore Avenue
Hinkler Road
Brancker Road
Rowland Avenue
Hamel Cl
Cemetery
Palmerston Road
Oxford Rd
Driving School & Road Safety Centre
Beaufort Avenue
Kenmore Avenue
The Bridge
Railway App
Masons Av
Herga Road
Christchurch Av
Forward Dr
The Hollies
Coxe Pl
Burnham Cl
Christchurch Avenue
Wykeham
Bradenham Rd
Boxmoor Rd
Brampton Grove
Cullington Close
Paulhan Rd
Hunters Grove
Kenton Pk Crs
Kenton Cricket Club
Westfield Gdns
Charlton Road
D'Arcy Gardens
Glebe First & Middle School
Glebe Lane
Mag Cts
F
G
H
J
K
I
2
3
4
5
6
16
17
18
29
44
61

44
30
43
62
A
B
C
D
E
1
2
3
4
5
6
Edgware
HA8
Canons Park
Little Stanmore
QUEENSBURY
STONE GROVE
A5
EDGWARE RD
HIGH ST
BURNT OAK BROADWAY
STATION ROAD
A5100
HALE LANE
A5109 DEANSBROOK RD
DEAN'S LANE
WHITCHURCH LANE
B461
HONEYPOT LANE
A4140
LONDON ROAD
Stone Grove Park
The Lake
The Basin
Chandos Recreation Ground
William Ellis Sports Ground
North London Collegiate School
Edgware Reform Synagogue
Masorti Synagogue
Yeshurun Synagogue
Edgware Station
Bus Station & Depot
Belle Vue Cinema
Broadwalk Shopping Cen
Edgware Clnc
Telephone Exchange
Junior School
Infant School
Police Stn
Boys' Club
The Forum
War Meml
Sharp Sports Cen
Edgware FC & Wealdstone FC
Blood Transfusion Centre
TA Centre
Edgware Community Hospital
Oak Lodge Medical Centre
Broadway Clnc
Burnt Oak Station
Watling Medical Centre
Barnfield Primary School
The Menorah Foundation School
Deansbrook Primary School
Canons Park Station
Honeypot Business Cen
Little Stanmore First & Middle School
Canons High School
Tenby Rd Clinic
Honeypot Medical Centre
Medical Centre
Kenmore Park School
Queensbury Station
Superstore
Bowman Trading Est
Capitol Ind Park
Colindale Business Park
Capitol Industrial Park
Stag Lane Medical Cen
Kingsbury Hospital
Kingsbury High School
Roe Green J&I School
Hay Lane School
Glebe First & Middle School
St Bernadettes RC First & Middle School
Works
Surgery
1 grid square represents 500 metres

Mill Hill
Burnt Oak
Colindale
A41
WATFORD WAY
BARNET BY-PASS
A1
A5109 SELVAGE LANE
HALE LANE
A5100
THE BROADWAY
DAWS LANE B1461
RIDGEWAY
St Joseph's RC College
Mill Hill School
St Vincent RC Primary School
Goodwyn School
The Homoeopathic Health Cen
St Martins School
Matilda Marks School
Paradise Swimming Pools
Mill Hill Broadway Station
Mill Hill Synagogue
The Annunciation RC Junior School
Langley Park
Granard Business Cen
Mill Hill Industrial Estate
Parkmead Gardens
Mill Hill Park
Pentavia Retail Park
Copthall School
Woodcroft Primary School
Watling Clinic
Goldbeaters Primary School
Hendon College
Barnet Copthall Pool & Stadium
Hasmonean High School
Junction 2
FIVE WAYS JUNCTION
GREAT NORTH WAY (BARNET BY-PASS)
Grahame Park Junior & Infant School
Grahame Park Health Cen
Hurricane Trading Centre
Police Station
Primary School
Royal Air Force Museum
Birch Court Colindale Hosp
Willow Court Colindale Hosp
Silk Stream
Bus Cen
Colindale Hospital
Colindale Station
British Library Newspaper Library
Rankin Close
Metropolitan Police Track (Hendon)
Metropolitan Police Training School, Hendon
Air Call Business Centre
Beis Yaakov Primary School
Superstore
THE HYDE
EDGEWARE ROAD
A5
COLINDEEP LANE
A5150
Sunny Hill Park
St Georges Medical Cen
Church Farm House Museum
High School
Surgery
Works
Grove Park Industrial Estate
Colindale Primary School
Central Hendon Clinic
CHURCH ROAD
M1
31
46
63
F
G
H
J
K
1
2
3
4
5
6
21
22
23

Golf Course
Park
Michleham Down
Twineham Green
Woodside Park Golf Club
Southover
St Vincents RC Primary School
Rhodes Farm Clinic
A
B
C
D
E
32
Burtonhole Lane
Hillview Rd
Eleanor Crescent
Pycombe Cnr
Chanctonbury Way
523
24
25
RIDGEWAY
Rodmell Slope
Cissbury Ring North
Garth
Offham Slope
Wolstonbury
Cissbury Ring South
Lullington
Approach La
Mount School
B552
Partingdale Lane
Reading Way
Reading Wy
Argyle
Saddlescombe Wy
Poynings Wy
Steynings Wy
Folkington Corner
Cissbury
Walmington Fold
Singleton Scarp
Mill Hill Cemetery
Woodcote Avenue
Bittacy Park Av
Sevright Drive
Charles
Henry Darlot Dr
Holmes Av
Ross Av
Roberts Road
Lidbury Rd
Price Kenny Cl
Warren Way
Rushden Gdns
Bittacy Cl
Curry Rise
Kelly Rd
Drew Av
Twinn Rd
Westlinton Close
Golf Course
Linkside
Chesterfield Road
Westbury
Nethercourt Av
Milespit Hill
Salcombe Gdns
Engel Park
Bittacy Rise
BITTACY HILL B552
Road
Brav Wy
Walden
Frith Lane
Fursby Avenue
Brookfield Av
Moreton Close
Brookfield Ct
Road
Surgery
Sanders Rd
Bittacy
Bittacy Business Centre
Mill Hill East Station
Finchley Golf Club
Brent Way
West Avenue
Hamilton Wy
Penstemon Cl
Finchley Wy
The Dr
Surgery
Dollis Infant School
Dollis Junior School
Sanders Lane
Grants Cl
Oakdene Pk
Lansdowne Road
Nether Street
Howcroft Crescent
Hendon Golf Club
Ashley Lane
Osborn Gdns
Devonshire Crs
Devonshire Road
New Road
Lee Rd
Vineyard Avenue
Abercorn Road
Gordon Road
Grosvenor Rd
Eversleigh Road
Elm Park Road
Nether Cl
Sellers Hall Close
Links Vw
Cornwall Av
Golf Course
Aberdare Gardens
Oakhampton Rd
Mallow Md
Frith Court
B1462 DOLLIS RD
B1462
Surgery
Falkland Av
The Grove
45
Barnet Copthall Stadium
The Metro Golf Centre
Hendon Crematorium
Hendon Cemetery
Golf Course
Thornfield Av
Christ's College Playing Fields
St Marys CE Primary School
Dollis Av
Crescent Rd
NETHER ST
Popes Dr
Shopping Precinct
Telephone Exchange
Finchley Central Synagogue
Finchley Central Stn
Dorset
Redbourne
Claremont Pk
Lyndhurst Gardens
Grass Park
Tennis & Squash Club
Dollis Park
Church Crs
Clifton Av
Victoria Hall
Victoria Av
County Court
Works
Station
Lichfield
N3
FIN
Holders Hill
HILL ROAD
Hwth Ms
Hendon Avenue
Grenville Close
Rectory Close
Ratngar Close
Arcadia Avenue
Surgery
Glenhill Cl
Church
BARNET-BY-PASS
Ashley Close
Woodtree Close
Linksway
Village Rd
Cyprus Gardens
Freston Pk
Works
St Mary's Av
HENDON LANE
GRAVEL HL
REGENT'S PK ROAD
School
Spencer Cl
Playing Fields
5
B552 HOLDERS
Holders Hl Gdns
Holders Hl Dr
Dollis Valley Gn Wk
Cyprus Av
Bibsworth Rd
A504 EAST END ROAD
Sunningfields Crs
Sunny Gardens Road
Meadow Dr
A1
Ashley La
Manor Av Hall
Manor Hall Dr
Garrick Pk
Hasmonean High School
Windsor Road
Kensit Memorial Coll
Wickliffe Av
Cyprus Road
North Crs
Salisbury Av
A598
Stanhope Avenue
Cavendish Av
Templars Crs
Holmwood Gdns
Avenue
Rowsley Avenue
Downage
Sherwood Rd
Garrick Dr
Ashley Lane
Holders Hl Crs
Holders Hl Av
Broughton Av
Rawlins Cl
Arden Road
Mountfield Rd
Surg
Sunningfield Road
Surg
Sherwood Road
Surgery
PARSON STREET B552
Westchester Dr
GREAT NORTH WAY (BARNET
Waverley Gv
A504
Fitzalan Road
Regents Pk Rd
Holly Park Gdns
Cavendish Av
Orchard Avenue
Windermere
Amberden Avenue
Nursery Wk
Gardens
St Marys CE High School
Cedars Close
Tenterden Drive
Dollis Brook
HENDON LANE
Allandale Avenue
REGENT'S PARK ROAD
Holly Park
Kingsgate Avenue
Clandon Gdns
6
Church Ter
High School
Road
Mulberry Cl
Hanbury Close
Preparatory School
Tenterden Gardens
Crooked Usage
Highview Gdns
Drive
Parklands
Chalgrove Gdns
Chalgrove Primary School
Chessington Av
Fairholme Gdns
Haslemere Gardens
Kinloss Gardens
Finchley Synagogue
CHARTER WY
Tillingbourne Gdns
Beechwood Avenue
Edge Hill
NORTH CIRCULAR
Church End
Florence St
Tenterden Gv
Garrick Way
Linfield Cl
24
64
25
CHURCH ROAD
FINCHLEY
Alexandra
Second Av
First
Babington Rd
Ravenshurst Av
BRENT
Hillcrest Gardens
Fairholme Close
A1
A406
NORTH CIRCULAR
Beaufort Drive
Connaught Drive
Gloucester Drive
Brookland Ri
Jews College London
Greenbank Cl
Dollis Valley Green Walk
Southbourne Crs
Kings Cl
Bell Lane JMI School
Boyne Av
Albert
Road
Surgery
Addison
Monkville Avenue
Theatre
1 grid square represents 500 metres

FRIERN BARNET
Friary Park
North Finchley
Colney Hatch
East Finchley
Fortis Green
N12
N2
33
48
65
F
G
H
J
K
1
2
3
4
5
6
26
27
28
92
90
Mayfield Avenue
Friern Watch Av
Friary Road
Ravensdale Av
Torrington Park
The Ridgeway
Woodside Park School
Woodside Park Synagogue
Woodside Grange
Holden Road
Holden Av
Lodge Lane
Archgate Business Cen
Finchley Industrial Cen
Whittington Mews
Frederick's Pl
Green Bank
The Oaks
Ashbourne Cl
Park Health Cen
Torrington Clnc
Copwood Close
St Johns CE Primary School
Bethune Av
The Crescent
Friern Barnet School
The Clinic
Hatley Close
Hemington Avenue
Goldsmith Rd
Stanford Rd
Glenthorne Rd
Friern Park
Buxted Road
Ashurst Rd
Horsham Avenue
Petworth Road
Lewes Road
Bramber Road
Hilton Avenue
Fenstanton Av
Grove Road
Northwood Gardens
Cardrew Av
Christchurch CE School
Warnham Rd
Woodhouse Sixth Form College
Barnet Coll
Stanhope Rd
Castle Rd
Northside Primary
Percy Road
Grammar School
Nether Street
Finchley Progressive Synagogue
Dale Gv
Hutton Gv
Alexandra Grove
Hillcourt Av
Moss Hall Grove
Primary School
West Finchley Stn
Woodhouse Road
A1003
Colney Hatch Lane
B550
Lane
Queens Pde
Hillside Av
Asher Loftus Way
Lyndhurst Av
Ferncroft Av
Thurlestone Av
Hollickwood Av
Ribblesdale Av
Firs Av
Poplar
Churchfield Av
Superstore
High Road
A1000
Christchurch Avenue
Woodberry Grove
Woodberry Way
Sandringham Gdns
Woodgrange Avenue
Addington Drive
Kenver Av
Fallow Ct Av
Eton Av
Ingleway
Crossway
Summerside JMI School
Crescent Way
The Compton School
Sports Centre
Summers Lane
Sunny Wy
Legion Way
Coppetts Close
Sports Club
Wingate & Finchley FC
Ballards Lane
Finchley Reform Synagogue
Granville Road
Seymour Road
Police Stn
Surg
Chislehurst Avenue
Etchingham Park Road
Holdenhurst Avenue
Victoria Park
Finchley Memorial Hospital
Leisure Wy
Swimming Pool
A406
Our Lady of Lourdes RC Primary School
Warner Village
TA Centre
Surgery
Old Farm Rd
Nursery Rd
St Pancras and Islington Cemetery
Islington Crematorium
Greenfields Special School
Coppetts Wood Primary School
Coppetts Wood Hospital
Coppetts Rd
Osier Crs
Marriot Road
Barrenger Road
Steeds Road
Hill Road
Everington Rd
Coldfall Wood
Coldfall Avenue
Nelson Mandela
Park Crs
Woodlands Avenue
Queen's Av
Clifton Road
Bow Lane
The Ridgeway
St Paul's Way
Willow Way
Parkside
Long Lane
Millers Yd
Dukes Av
Vines Av
Oakfield Rd
Park Vw Rd
Park Av
Manorside Primary School
Dickens Av
Glebe Rd
Tudor Primary School
North Circular Road
Queen's Road
Squires Lane
Vineyard
Strathmore Gdns
Montpelier Road
Cromwell Road
Abingdon Road
Nursery Avenue
Long Lane
Strawberry Vale
Lankaster Gdns
Lewis Gdns
Exit Rd
North Road
East Road
Joint Road
Wesley Rd
Raleigh Road
Chapel Hill
Centre Avenue
Church Circle
Church Rd South
West Road
Viaduct
Sylvester Rd
Fallows Cl
Tarling Road
Oak Lane
Central Av
Chandos Road
Martin Infant School
Creighton Avenue
Fortismere School
Eastwood Road
Burlington Road
Secondary School
Church Vale
Beech Drive
Ringwood Av
Twyford Avenue
Ante Natal Cli
Police Station
FINCHLEY
Church End
Manor View
Rosemary Av
Finchley Cricket Club
Tangle Tree Cl
Brighton Rd
Brendon Gv
Taunton Dr
New Oak Rd
New Trinity Rd
Challoner Cl
William Cl
Bishop Douglas RC School
St Mary's Green
Clare Cl
Helen Cl
Christs College School
Hamilton Road
Brackenbury Road
Sedgemere Av
Manor Pk Road
Church Lane
Trinity Rd
Leopold Road
Leslie Road
Park Gate
Creigton Avenue
School
Hertford Road
Bedford Road
Huntingdon Road
Leicester Rd
Lincoln Road
Durham Road
Great North Road
Finchley Youth Theatre
Kitchener Rd
Market Pl
Primary School
East End Road
St Marylebone Crematorium
Denison Close
Christs College
East Finchley Cemetery
Moat Crescent
Brookland Primary School
Holyoake Walk
Neale Close
Oak Lodge School
Ossulton Way
Heath View
Pulham Av
Deaney Close
A504
Fortis Green
Med Cen
Phoenix
Baronsmere Road
Ingram Road
Summerlee Avenue
Springcroft Avenue
Western Road
Eastern Road
Lynmouth Rd
Lauradale Road
Midhurst Av
Collingwood Av
Southern Road
Summerlee Gardens
Cherry Tree Road
Shakespeare
Greenfield Dr
Brompton Gr
East Finchley Station
Cedar Drive
Abbots Gdns
Howard Walk
Brim Hill
Heath View
The Leys
Ludlow Way
Brookland Rise
Hill Top

1 grid square represents 500 metres

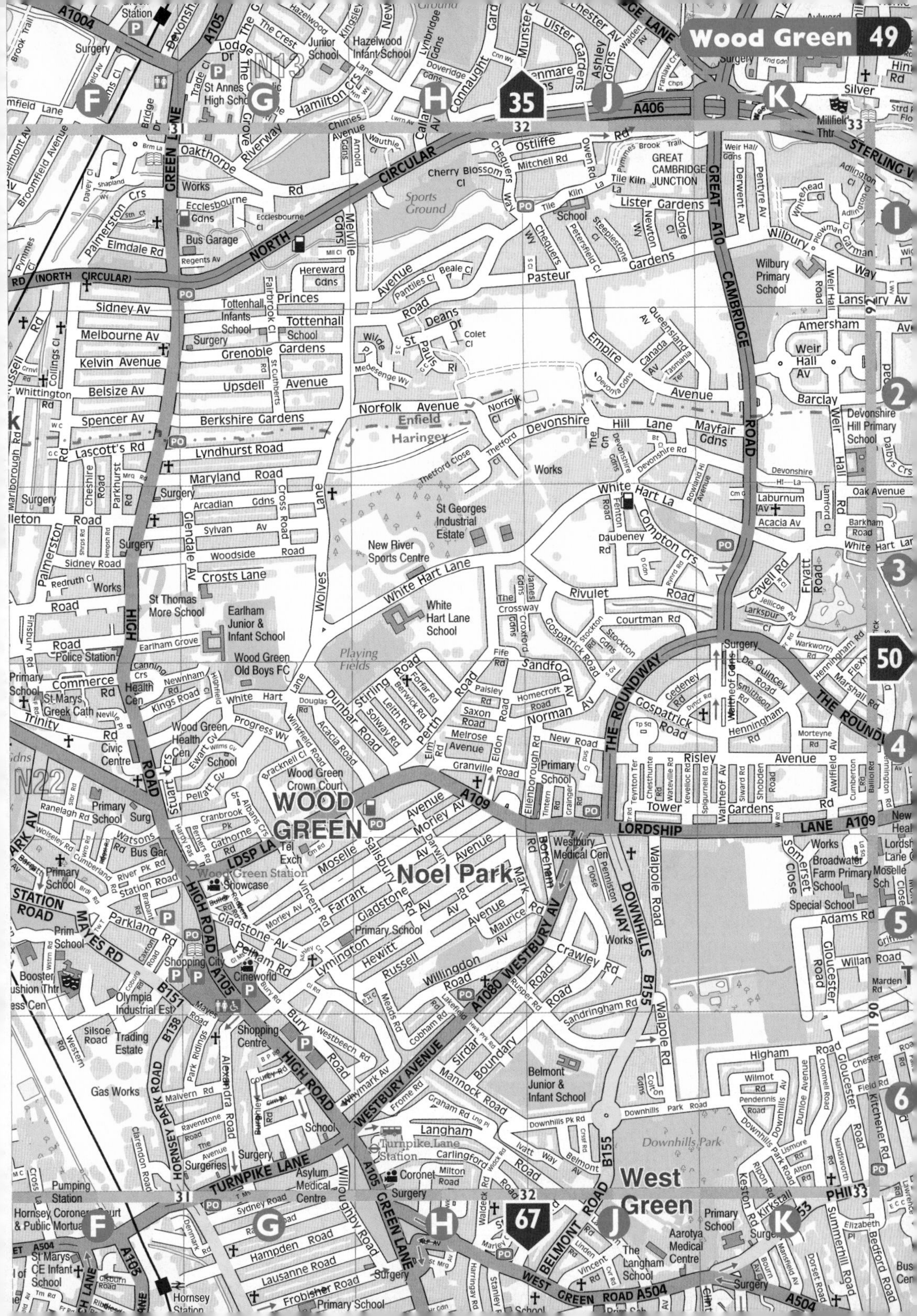

A1004
Station
Devonshire
A105
Lodge Dr
The Crest
Hazelwood
Junior School
Hazelwood Infant School
Kingsley
Lynbridge Gdns
Doveridge Gdns
Connaught
Munster
Ulster Gardens
Ashley Gdns
Walden Av
Surgery
N13
Trade Cl
St Annes Catholic High School
The Grove
Hamilton Crs
Chimes Avenue
Arnold Gdns
Callard Av
Wauthier Cl
35
32
A406
Ostliffe Rd
Owen Rd
Pymmes Brook Trail
GREAT CAMBRIDGE JUNCTION
Millfield Thtr
33
STERLING WAY
Silver
F
G
H
J
K
Brook Trail
Lane
Bridge Dr
GREEN LANE
31
Oakthorpe Rd
Riverway
NORTH CIRCULAR
Broomfield Avenue
Davey Cl
Shapland Wy
Palmerston Crs
Works
Ecclesbourne Gdns
Ecclesbourne Cl
Bus Garage
Regents Av
Elmdale Rd
Pymmes Cl
RD (NORTH CIRCULAR)
Melville Gdns
Mill Cl
Sports Ground
Cherry Blossom Cl
Chequers Way
Mitchell Rd
Tile Kiln La
Lister Gardens
School
Petersfield Cl
Steeplestone Cl
Newton Wy
Lodge Cl
GREAT CAMBRIDGE ROAD A10
Weir Hall Gdns
Derwent Av
Pentyre Av
Whitehead Cl
Adlington Cl
Plowman Cl
Garman
Wilbury Way
Wilbury Primary School
Hereward Gdns
Avenue
Beale Cl
Pantiles Cl
Pasteur Gardens
Chequers Wy
Sidney Av
Tottenhall Infants School
Fairbrook Cl
Princes
Tottenhall School
Melbourne Av
Collings Cl
Kelvin Avenue
Surgery
Grenoble Gardens
Upsdell Avenue
St Cuthberts Rd
Belsize Av
Whittington Rd
Wilde Pl
St Pauls Pl
Deans Dr
Colet Cl
Medesenge Wy
Empire Avenue
Queensland Av
Canada Av
Tasmania Ter
Devonia Gdns
Amersham Av
Weir Hall Av
Barclay
Lansbury Av
Spencer Av
Berkshire Gardens
Norfolk Avenue
Norfolk Cl
Enfield
Haringey
Devonshire Hill Lane
Mayfair Gdns
Devonshire Hill Primary School
Dalbys Crs
Lascott's Rd
Lyndhurst Road
Thetford Cl
Thetford Close
The Gn
Devonshire Gdns
Devonshire Rd
Marlborough Rd
Cheshire Road
Parkhurst Rd
Maryland Road
Works
Devonshire Hl La
Weir Hall Rd
Surgery
Cross Road
Lane
White Hart La
Fenton Rd
Rowland Hl Avenue
Laburnum Av
Lamford Cl
Oak Avenue
Palmerston Road
Arcadian Gdns
Sylvan Av
St Georges Industrial Estate
Compton Crs
Acacia Av
Barkham Road
Glendale Av
Woodside Road
New River Sports Centre
Daubeney Rd
White Hart Lane
Sidney Road
Redruth Cl
Works
Crosts Lane
White Hart Lane
Wolves Lane
Rivulet Road
Cavell Rd
Fryatt Road
Jellicoe Rd
Larkspur Cl
St Thomas More School
Earlham Junior & Infant School
White Hart Lane School
James Gdns
The Crossway
Croxford Gdns
Courtman Rd
Finsbury Road
Road
Police Station
Earlham Grove
Wood Green Old Boys FC
Playing Fields
Gospatrick Road
Stockton Gdns
Stockton Rd
Surgery
Warkworth Rd
Henningham Rd
50
Primary School
Commerce Rd
Canning Crs
Health Cen
Newnham Rd
Kings Road
Highfield Rd
White Hart Lane
Douglas Rd
Dunbar Road
Stirling Road
Forfar Rd
Berwick Rd
Leith Rd
Solway Rd
Perth Road
Fife Rd
Sandford Av
Paisley Rd
Homecroft Road
Saxon Road
Norman Av
THE ROUNDWAY
Gedeney Rd
De Quincey Road
Smithson Rd
Waltheof Gdns
Dyncr Rd
Gospatrick Road
Henningham Road
Marshall Rd
St Marys Greek Cath
Trinity Rd
Nevill Pl
Civic Centre
Wood Green Health Cen
Progress Wy
Ewart Gv
Wilms Gv
School
Winkfield Road
Acacia Road
Elm Rd
Melrose Avenue
Eldon Road
Ellenborough Rd
New Road
Primary School
Tp Sq
Risley Avenue
Morteyne Rd
Awlfield Av
N22
Stuart Crs
Bracknell Cl
Wood Green Crown Court
Granville Road
Teynton Ter
Chesthunte Rd
Watevile Rd
Keveloc Rd
Spigurnell Rd
Waltheof Av
Siward Rd
Shobden Rd
Cumberton Rd
Ranelagh Rd
Primary School
Surgery
Pellatt Gv
St Albans Crs
WOOD GREEN
Avenue
Morley Av
A109
Tintern Rd
Grainger Rd
Tower Gardens Rd
Park Av
Watsons Rd
Cranbrook Pk
Gathorne Rd
Hardy Pas
Berners Rd
LORDSHIP LANE A109
Works
Broadwater Farm Primary School
Lordship Lane
Moselle Sch
Cumberland Rd
Bus Garage
River Pk Rd
LDSP LA
Tel Exch
Moselle Av
Salisbury Av
Darwin Rd
Avenue
Noel Park
Mark Rd
Boreham Rd
Westbury Medical Cen
Penniston Close
Walpole Road
Somerset Close
Special School
Primary School
Station Road
Wood Green Station
Showcase
Vincent Rd
Farrant Av
Gladstone Av
Av
Avenue
Maurice Rd
DOWNHILLS WAY
Adams Rd
Gloucester Road
Primary Sch
STATION ROAD
MAYES RD
Parkland Rd
Brabant Rd
Caxton Rd
Morley Av
Gladstone Av
Primary School
Lymington
Hewitt Av
Russell Av
Willingdon Road
A1080 WESTBURY AV
Crawley Rd
Works
Willan Road
Marden Rd
Booster Cushion Thtr
Shopping City
Pelham Rd
Ashley Crs
Cineworld
Olympia Industrial Est
B151
Bury Rd
Rusper Rd
Road
Road
B155
Walpole Rd
Sandringham Rd
Silsoe Road
Trading Estate
B138
Park Ridings
Alexandra Road
Shopping Centre
Bury Road
Westbeech Rd
Meads Rd
Cobham Rd
Lakefield Rd
Sirdar Rd
Boundary Road
Belmont Junior & Infant School
Colton Gdns
Higham Road
Chester Rd
Field Rd
Wilmot Rd
Pendennis Road
Gas Works
HORNSEY PARK ROAD
Malvern Rd
HIGH ROAD
WESTBURY AVENUE
Whymark Av
Frome Rd
Graham Rd
Mannock Road
Downhills Park Road
Downhills Pk Rd
Downhills Avenue
Dunloe Avenue
Clonmell Road
Kitchener Road
Ravenstone Road
Clarendon Road
The Avenue
Surgeries
Surgery
School
Langham Pl
Turnpike Lane Station
Carlingford Road
Ivatt Way
Belmont Av
Downhills Park
Lismore Rd
Alton Rd
Handsworth Road
Cross
Pumping Station
TURNPIKE LANE
Asylum Medical Centre
Coronet
Milton Road
Wolsey Rd
Wroxham Rd
West Green
Ripon Rd
Keston Rd
Kirkstall
PHII33
Hornsey Coroners Court & Public Mortuary
Sydney Road
G
Willoughby Road
A105
GREEN LANE
Surgery
H
67
Waldeck Rd
BELMONT ROAD
J
Primary School
Surgery
K
Summerhill Road
Elizabeth Pl
Bedford Road
F
A504
St Marys CE Infant School
A103
Hampden Road
Lausanne Road
Frobisher Road
Surgery
Primary School
Haringey Rd
Stanley Rd
Marlow Rd
The Langham School
Aarotya Medical Centre
Vincent Rd
Linden Rd
Mansfield Av
Dorset Road
WEST GREEN ROAD A504
Surgery
Hornsey Station
Oxford Rd
1
2
3
4
5
6

A
B
C
D
E
1
2
3
4
5
6
36
49
68
N18
N17
Upper Edmonton
TOTTENHAM
Tottenham Hale
STERLING WAY (NORTH CIRCULAR)
A406
ANGEL RD
(NORTH CIRCULAR)
CONDUIT LANE
MERIDIAN WAY
WATERMEAD WAY
FORE STREET
HIGH ROAD
A1010
HIGH RD
A10
LORDSHIP LANE
A109
BRUCE GROVE
THE ROUNDWAY
MONUMENT WAY
HALE ROAD
THE HALE
BROAD LANE
FERRY LANE
FOREST ROAD
A503
A1055
B137
Silver Street Station
White Hart Lane Station
Angel Road Station
Northumberland Park Station
Bruce Grove Stn
Tottenham Hale Station
North Middlesex Hospital
Medical Centre
County Court
Playing Field
Gas Works
Superstore
Glover Drive
Lea Valley Trading Est
Crispin Industrial Cen
Triumph Trading Est
Lake Business Cen
The Royal London Est
Hotspur Industrial Est
Northumberland Park Industrial Est
Leeside Trading Est
Leeside Works
Mowlem Trading Est
Unicorn Works
Wingate Trading Est
Tottenham Hotspur FC (White Hart Lane)
Peacock Industrial Est
Gibson Business Centre
The Gibson Business Cen
Langhedge Lane Industrial Est
Frontier Works
Devonshire Hill Primary School
Cemetery
Bruce Castle Park
Bruce Castle Museum
Magistrates Court
Lordship Lane Clinic
Health Centre
Down Lane Recreation Ground
Lockwood Reservoir
Lockwood Ind Park
Milmead Industrial Cen
Tottenham Hale Retail Park
Fountayne Business Centre
Haringey Hlth Care
College of North East London
Tottenham Gn Leisure Cen
Town Hall
Police Station
Bus Garage
Retail Park
Lea Valley Walk
Waltham Forest
Haringey
Ferry Lane Industrial
White Hart Lane
Creighton Road
Park Lane
Church Rd
Bridport Road
Shaftesbury Road
Brantwood Road
Leeside Road
Stockton Road
Leyburn Road
Poynton Road
Rosebery Av
Lansdowne Road
Hampden Road
Holcombe Road
Scales Road
Sperling Rd
St Loy's Rd
Willan Road
Philip Lane

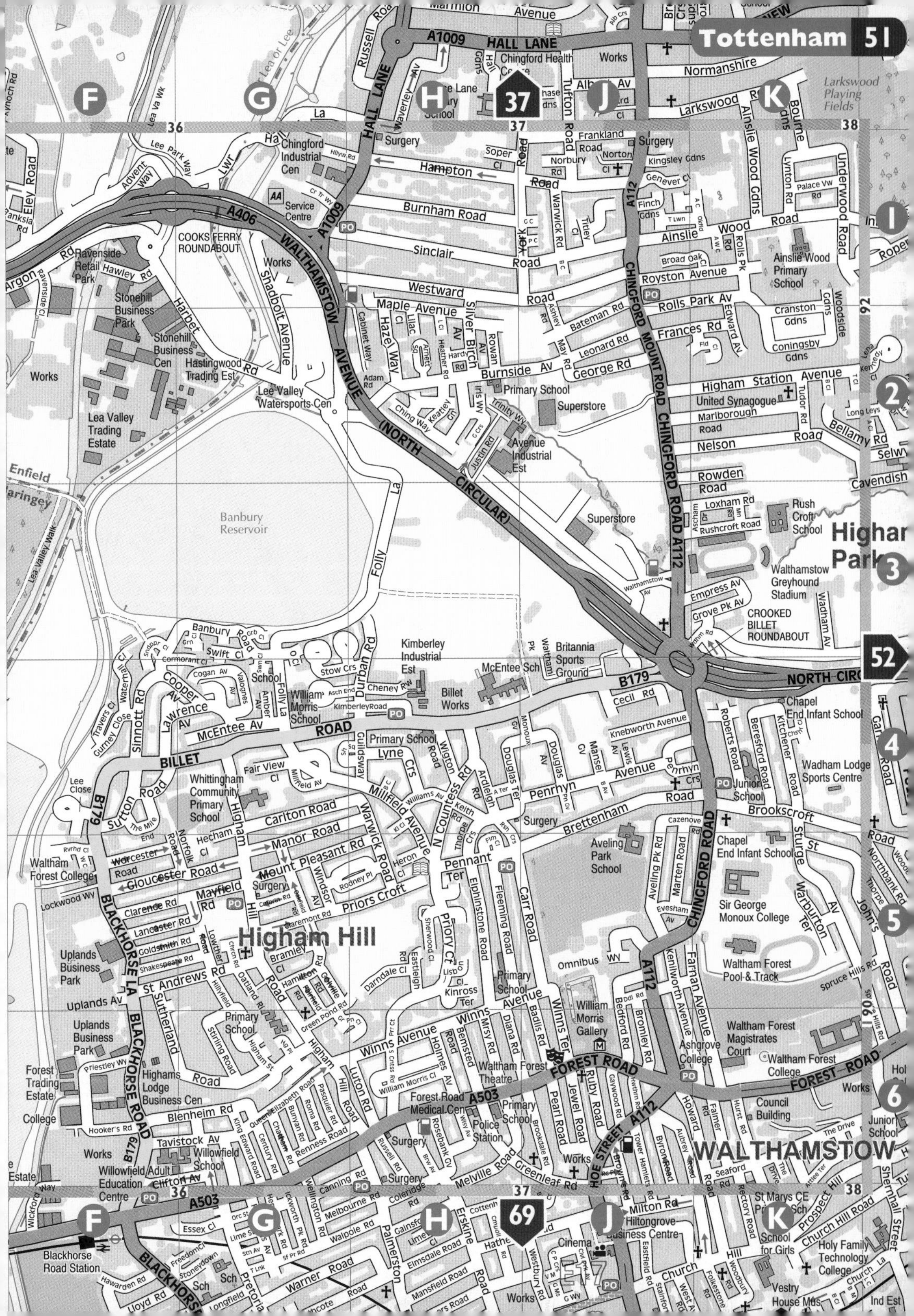
F
G
H
J
K
36
37
38
37
52
69
92
90
2
3
4
5
6
HALL LANE
A1009
Chingford Health Centre
Works
Normanshire
Larkswood Playing Fields
Larkswood
Lea or Lee
Lea Va Wk
Chingford Industrial Cen
Surgery
Hampton
Soper Cl
Frankland Road
Norbury Rd
Kingsley Gdns
Lee Park Way
Advent Way
Eley Road
Service Centre
Burnham Road
A406
WALTHAMSTOW AVENUE
COOKS FERRY ROUNDABOUT
Ravenside Retail Park
Argon Rd
Hawley Rd
Sinclair Road
Westward Road
Warwick Rd
Titley
York Road
Ainslie Wood Road
Ainslie Wood Gdns
Lynton Rd
Underwood Road
Palace Vw Rd
Ainslie Wood Primary School
Broad Oak Cl
Royston Avenue
Rolls Park Av
Bateman Rd
Frances Rd
Leonard Rd
George Rd
Cranston Gdns
Coningsby Gdns
Woodside Gdns
Stonehill Business Park
Stonehill Business Cen
Harbet Rd
Shadbolt Avenue
Hastingwood Trading Est
Maple Avenue
Hazel Way
Lilac
Silver Birch Av
Rowan
Burnside Av
Primary School
Works
Lea Valley Trading Estate
Lee Valley Watersports Cen
Ching Way
Keatley Gn
Justin Rd
Trinity Wy
Avenue Industrial Est
Superstore
Higham Station Avenue
United Synagogue
Tudor Rd
Marlborough Road
Nelson Road
Bellamy Rd
Rowden Road
Cavendish
Loxham Rd
Rushcroft Road
Rush Croft School
Higham Park
CHINGFORD MOUNT ROAD
CHINGFORD ROAD A112
(NORTH CIRCULAR)
Enfield
Haringey
Lea Valley Walk
Banbury Reservoir
Folly La
Superstore
Walthamstow Greyhound Stadium
Empress Av
Grove Pk Av
Wadham Av
CROOKED BILLET ROUNDABOUT
Banbury Road
Swift Cl
Cogan Av
Cooper Av
Valognes Av
Lawrence Av
McEntee Av
BILLET ROAD
B179
Kimberley Industrial Est
Stow Crs
Durban Rd
Cheney Rw
William Morris School
Kimberley Road
Britannia Sports Ground
McEntee Sch
Billet Works
Cecil Rd
NORTH CIRC
Chapel End Infant School
Knebworth Avenue
Roberts Road
Beresford Road
Kitchener Road
Primary School
Lyne Crs
Wigton Road
Guildsway
Douglas Av
Penrhyn Avenue
Mansel Gv
Lewis Av
Wadham Lodge Sports Centre
Junior School
Whittingham Community Primary School
Fair View Cl
Millfield Avenue
Sutton Road
Lee Close
Higham Hill
Carlton Road
Warwick Road
N Countess Rd
Ardleigh Rd
Penrhyn Road
Brettenham Road
Surgery
Brookscroft
Sturge
St
Worcester Road
Norfolk Road
Hecham Cl
Manor Road
Mount Pleasant Rd
Waltham Forest College
Gloucester Road
Mayfield Rd
Surgery
Windsor Av
Priors Croft
Pennant Ter
Aveling Park School
Aveling Pk Rd
Marten Road
Chapel End Infant School
Lockwood Wy
Clarence Rd
Lancaster Rd
Goldsmith Rd
Shakespeare Rd
Higham Hill
Elphinstone Road
Fleeming Road
Carr Road
Evesham Av
Sir George Monoux College
Warburton Ter
John's Road
BLACKHORSE LA
Uplands Business Park
St Andrews Rd
Bramley Cl
Priory Ct
Darndale Cl
Eastleigh Rd
Omnibus Wy
Kenilworth Avenue
Farnan Avenue
Waltham Forest Pool & Track
Spruce Hills Rd
Uplands Av
Sutherland Road
Hamilton Rd
Kinross Ter
Primary School
Winns Avenue
William Morris Gallery
Bedford Rd
Bromley Rd
Ashgrove College
Waltham Forest Magistrates Court
Waltham Forest College
Uplands Business Park
Primary School
Stirling Road
Higham St
Bemsted Rd
Diana Rd
Badlis Rd
Winns Ter
FOREST ROAD
Forest Trading Estate
Highams Lodge Business Cen
Road
Waltham Forest Theatre
Ruby Road
Jewel Road
Pearl Road
Works
College
Blenheim Rd
Queen Elizabeth Road
Hill Road
Lutton Rd
Forest Road Medical Cen
A503
Primary School
Council Building
Junior School
Hooker's Rd
BLACKHORSE ROAD
Tavistock Av
Willowfield School
Renness Road
Rosebank Gv
Police Station
HOE STREET A112
Howard Road
Falmer Rd
Hurst Rd
Works
Willowfield Adult Education Centre
Clifton Av
Surgery
Melville Road
Greenleaf Rd
Works
WALTHAMSTOW
Estate
Wickford Way
Canning Rd
Coleridge Rd
Seaford Rd
The Drive
Prospect Hill
Shernhall Street
A503
Essex Cl
Melbourne Rd
Walpole Rd
Erskine Road
Milton Rd
Hiltongrove Business Centre
St Marys CE Prim Sch
Church Hill Road
Blackhorse Road Station
Palmerston Road
Elmsdale Road
Cinema
School for Girls
Holy Family Technology College
Warner Road
Mansfield Road
Westbury Rd
Church Hill
Eastfield Rd
Woodbury Rd
Hawarden Rd
Lloyd Rd
Pretoria
Works
Vestry House Mus
Ind Est

Chingford Hatch
38
Larkswood Playing Fields
A
B
C
D
E
538
39
40
Jubilee Sports Ground
LARKSHALL ROAD
B160
CHINGFORD LANE A1009
Woodford Golf Club
Woodford Green Primary School
Mornington Road
High School
Primary School
Trinity Catholic Lower High School
HIGH RD WOODFORD
Avon House School
1
2
3
4
5
6
92
Inks Green
Ropers Avenue
Underwood Road
Coolgardie Avenue
Richmond Avenue
Castle Avenue
Falmouth Av
Handsworth Avenue
Nightingale Av
Forest Glade
Montalt Road
Wood Lane
Henry's Avenue
Beechwood Drive
Charter Road
Hickman Av
Works
Handsworth Hlth Clinic
Highams Park School
Highams Park Station
Primary School
Hale End
Woodford County High School
Woodford Green Prep School
A1009 BROADMEAD ROAD
Snakes Lane
Selwyn Avenue
Selwyn Primary School
Cavendish Rd
Haldan Road
Hale End Road
Special School
Primary School
Hollywood Way
Oak Hill
Armstrong Av
Highams Park
WINCHESTER ROAD
Hotel
WOODFORD NEW ROAD
St Aubyns School
Woodford
Forest Drive
Empress Av
Fuller's Road
Derby Road
Chelmsford Road
51
NORTH CIRCULAR
SOUTHEND ROAD (NORTH CIRCULAR)
FULBOURNE ROAD
Garner Road
Primary School
Whitefield School & Leisure Centre
A104
Peel Road
Walpole Road
Carnarvon Road
Stanley
Malmesbury Road
Buckingham Road
A11 HIGH RD WOODFORD GN
South Woodford Health Centre
Churchfields J&I School
College
A406
Grove Road
Superstore
Odeon
South Woodford
GEORGE LANE
Walthamstow Business Cen
Surgery
A503
FOREST ROAD
Hyland House School
NEW ROAD
High View Rd
Byron Avenue
Raymond Avenue
Wordsworth Avenue
Greenheys Drive
E18
Snaresbrook Coll
Woodford Progressive Synagogue
Junior School
Medical Centre
Holy Family College
Broadwalk
Cheyne Avenue
WOODFORD ROAD
Tavistock Road
Wood Street Station
70
Upper Walthamstow
Holy Family Technology College
Primary School
1 grid square represents 500 metres

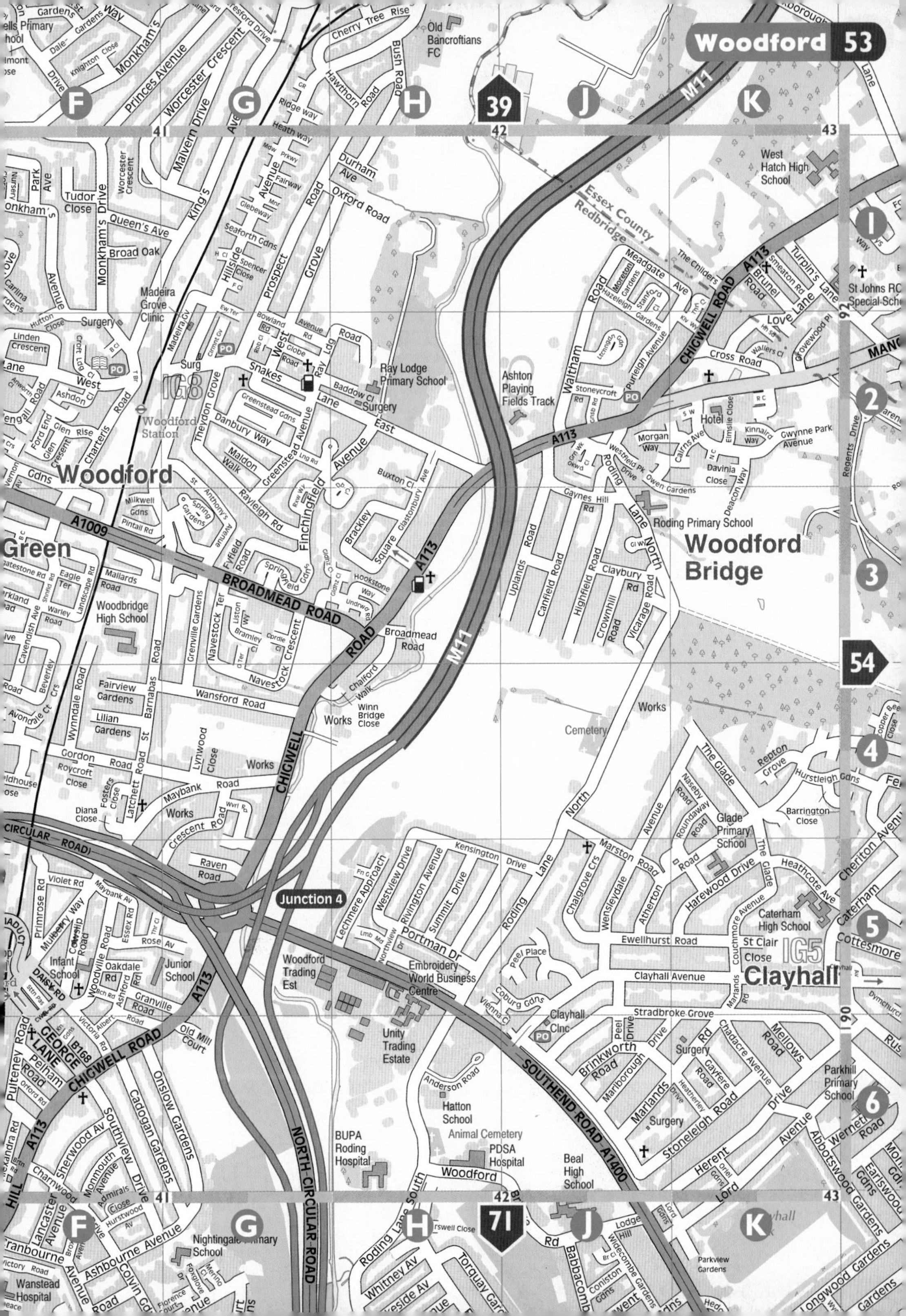

F
G
H
J
K
39
41
42
43
54
71
1
2
3
4
5
6
Woodford
Green
Woodford Bridge
Clayhall
IG8
IG5
M11
A113
A1009
A1400
B168
Junction 4
Old Bancroftians FC
West Hatch High School
St Johns RC Special School
Essex County
Redbridge
Madeira Grove Clinic
Woodford Station
Ray Lodge Primary School
Surgery
Ashton Playing Fields Track
Hotel
Roding Primary School
Woodbridge High School
Works
Winn Bridge Close
Cemetery
Glade Primary School
Caterham High School
Parkhill Primary School
Infant School
Junior School
Woodford Trading Est
Embroidery World Business Centre
Unity Trading Estate
Hatton School
Animal Cemetery
PDSA Hospital
BUPA Roding Hospital
Beal High School
Clayhall Clnc
Nightingale Primary School
Wanstead Hospital
Parkview Gardens
Cherry Tree Rise
Bush Road
Hawthorn Road
Ridge Way
Heath Way
Durham Ave
Oxford Road
Prospect Road
Grove
Princes Avenue
Worcester Crescent
Monkham's Avenue
Malvern Drive
King's Avenue
Tudor Close
Queen's Ave
Broad Oak
Monkham's Drive
Hillside
Spencer Close
Seaforth Gdns
Glebeway
Fairway
Snakes Lane East
West Grove
Ray Lodge Road
Baddow Cl
Greenstead Gdns
Greenstead Avenue
Danbury Way
Maldon Walk
Theydon Grove
Finchingfield Avenue
Buxton Cl
Glastonbury Ave
Brackley Square
Hookstone Way
Broadmead Road
Rayleigh Rd
St Anthony's Avenue
Spring Gardens
Springfield Gdns
Fyfield Road
Milkwell Gdns
Pintail Rd
Mallards Road
Eagle Ter
Landscape Rd
Warley Road
Cavendish Ave
Beverley Crs
Avondale Ct
Wynndale Road
Fairview Gardens
Lilian Gardens
St Barnabas Road
Grenville Gardens
Navestock Ter
Navestock Crescent
Liston Wy
Bramley Cl
Wansford Road
Lynwood Close
Chalford Walk
Gordon Road
Roycroft Close
Fosters Close
Latchett Road
Diana Close
Maybank Road
Crescent Road
Raven Road
Chigwell Road
North Circular Road
Circular Road
Violet Rd
Primrose Rd
Mulberry Way
Cowslip Road
Maybank Av
Essex Rd
Woodville Road
Oakdale Rd
Rose Av
Ashford Rd
Granville Road
Victoria Rd
Albert Road
Old Mill Court
George Lane
Pelham Road
Pulteney Road
Daisy Rd
Onslow Gardens
Cadogan Gardens
Southview Drive
Sherwood Av
Monmouth Avenue
Charnwood
Lancaster Avenue
Admirals Close
Hurstwood Av
Ashbourne Avenue
Colvin Gdns
Cranbourne
Victory Road
Hutton Close
Linden Crescent
West Cl
Ashdon Cl
Charteris Road
Glen Rise
Glen Crescent
Ford End
Vernon Gdns
Waltham Road
Meadgate Ave
Moreton Gardens
Hazeleigh Gardens
Stanford Cl
Purleigh Avenue
Stoneycroft Rd
The Childers
Brunel Road
Smeaton Rd
Turpin's Lane
Love Lane
Cross Road
Wallers Cl
Grovewood Pl
Morgan Way
Cairns Ave
Elmslie Close
Kinnaird Way
Gwynne Park Avenue
Westfield Pk Drive
Roding Lane North
Owen Gardens
Davinia Close
Deacon Way
Regents Drive
Gaynes Hill Rd
Uplands Road
Canfield Road
Highfield Road
Claybury Rd
Crownhill Road
Vicarage Road
The Glade
Repton Grove
Hurstleigh Gdns
Barrington Close
Naseby Road
Roundaway Road
Marston Road
Avenue
Heathcote Ave
Harewood Drive
Cheriton Avenue
Caterham Ave
Cottesmore
Chalgrove Crs
Wensleydale
Atherton
Couchmore Avenue
Ewellhurst Road
St Clair Close
Clayhall Avenue
Stradbroke Grove
Marlands Rd
Peel Place
Peel Drive
Coburg Gdns
Vienna Cl
Kensington Drive
Westview Drive
Rivington Avenue
Summit Drive
Lechmere Approach
Portman Dr
Northview Dr
Roding Lane
Brinkworth Road
Marlborough Drive
Gayfere Road
Chadacre Avenue
Mellows Road
Heatherley Drive
Marlands Road
Stoneleigh Road
Herent Drive
Lord Avenue
Abbotswood Gardens
Wernet Road
Earlswood Gdns
Longwood Gardens
Anderson Road
Woodford Bridge Rd
Roding Lane South
Whitney Av
Torquay Gardens
Babbacombe
Widecombe Gardens
Coniston Gdns
Lodge Hill
Orlel Gdns
Manor Road

A
B
C
D
E
1
2
3
4
5
6
543
44
45
Golf Course
HAINAULT ROAD
HIGH ROAD
A113
Tudor Cl
Lechmere Avenue
Hycliffe Gardens
Hainault Grove
Dacre Gdns
Fontayne Avenue
Great Oaks
Mount Pleasant Road
Grange Hill Station
Friars Close
Fairview Road
Fairview Dr
Long Green
Chigwell Golf Club
A123
Lechmere Avenue
Manor Road
Linkside
B173
MANOR ROAD
Grange Crescent
Oak Lodge Avenue
Millwell Crs
Northdene
Forest Ave
Emmaus Way
St Marys Way
Forest Lane
St Winifred's Close
View Close
High Meadows
Manford Way
Raven Way
Brocket Way
Stanway Close
Oakmoor Way
Karina Close
Hazelwood Park Close
Woodman Path
Ely Place
St Johns RC Special School
Turpin's Lane
Grovewood Pl
The Shrubberies
Limes Av
Chigwell & Hainault Synagogue
Council Building
Trotwood
Clayside
Limes Ave
Shrublands Close
Orange Grove
Keats Close
Limes Farm Primary School
Copperfield
Robinia Close
Chestnut Grove
Beech Grove
MANOR ROAD
New Forest Lane
Stradbroke
Drive
Bracken Drive
Glenside
Murtwell Drive
FENCEPIECE ROAD
Grange Hill
Tomswood Road
Audleigh Place
Clarence Gate
Regents Drive
Wynne Park Avenue
Tudor Crescent
Tower Close
Nonsuch Cl
Culpepper Close
Stradbroke Park
Shakespeare Sq
Knights Way
Yeomen Way
Anne Way
Westmede
The Holt
Vincent Close
Fencepiece Rd
Laurel Close
Bernards Close
Copperfield
Franklyn Gardens
Thurlow Gardens
Ascot Close
Clinton Crescent
Kirby Close
New North Road
Inverness Drive
Kelsie Way
Rosebury Sq
The Bvd
Richmond Dr
Hampstead Av
Copthorne Avenue
Wolsey Gardens
Boleyn Way
Montfort Gardens
Works
Laing Close
Hainault Station
Aragon Drive
Merlin Grove
Wannock Gardens
Tomswood Hill
Katherine Gdns
Marlon Cl
Maypole Crs
New North Road
Trehearn Road
Hazelbrouck Gardens
Walden Way
Davids Way
Brunswick Gardens
Hanover Gardens
Colvin Gardens
Cleves Walk
Surgery
Saltash Road
Trelawney Road
Fairlop Gdns
Greenwood Gdns
Benrek Close
Surgery
Forest Ind Park
Stalham Wy
Hoveton Way
Tomswood Hill
Fairlop Primary School
Kingsley Road
Fairlop
Ravensbourne Gardens
Copper Beech Close
Caernarvon Drive
Calne Ave
Ludham Cl
Martham Cl
Carrick Drive
Meriden Close
Neville Road
Addison Road
Forest Road
Redbridge Sports Centre
Fairlop Station
Fullwell Avenue
Surgery
Bysouth Close
Exmoor Cl
Oakhurst Cl
Marlowe Close
A123
Fullwell Cross
IG6
Hurstleigh Gdns
Felstead Av
Barrington Close
Basildon Avenue
Clifford Av
Gilbert Colvin Primary School
Kelston Rd
Lane
Fullwell Avenue
Greystone Gdns
Fullwell Cross Health Cen
King Solomon High School
Heathcote Ave
Cheriton Avenue
Dovedale Avenue
Ryecroft Avenue
Lamerton Road
Mossford
School
Fair Oak Pl
Pintree Crs
Caterham
Strafford Avenue
Dacre Av
Jerningham Av
Emsworth Road
Waterloo Rd
Road
Craven Gdns
Starch House Lane
Kirkland
Sheldon Ave
Belvedere Avenue
Ashley Avenue
Ilford County High School
Pool & Rec Cen
School
Cottesmore Av
Berkeley Close
Purley Close
Dunspring Lane
Hobart Rd
Sydney Rd
IG5
Clayhall Av
Fairlop
Mossford Green Primary School
Westminster Gardens
Clayhall Avenue
Fremantle Rd
Dymchurch Cl
Tiptree Crs
Wincanton Gdns
Hatfield Cl
Looe Gdns
HIGH STREET
Waverley Gdns
Tiverton Av
Beaminster Gardens
Trinity Rd
Horace Rd
Baron Gdns
Heybridge Drive
Rushden
Tiptree Crescent
Mossford Green
Sandringham Gdns
Tollesbury Gdns
Craven Gardens
Parkhill Primary School
Barkingside Cemetery
Cranbourne Gdns
Barkingside
Ilford Jewish Primary School
Werneth Hall Road
Wray Av Gardens
Longwood Gardens
Greenleafe Drive
Oakleafe Gdns
Mapleleafe Gardens
Tanners Lane
Court Wy
Evesham Wy
Dellwood Gdns
Monkswood Gdns
Abbotswood
Surgery
Woodville Gdns
Carlton Drive
Rachel Cl
Station Rd
Superstore
Earlswood Gardens
Beattyville Gdns
Glenthorne Gdns
Brandville Gdns
CRANBROOK ROAD
Barkingside FC
Barkingside Station
Aldborough Hatch
Rosedene
Queenborough Gardens
Thorpdale Gdns
Sunnymede
Georgeville Gdns
Gearies
Haigville Gdns
Civic Way
Barnardo Drive
Walnut
Crown Road
Princes Rd
Hatley Aven
Surgery
Mulberry Way
Coronation
School
1 grid square represents 500 metres

53

72

Park School
School Lane
Brocket Way
Brocket Cl
Bearing Way
Bearing Cl
Verderers Rd
Baywood Square
Lakeland Close
Yellowpine Way
Manford Way
Coppice Path
Tercel Path
ROMFORD ROAD
A1112
F
G
H
J
K
46
47
48
Fox
Fox Burrow Rd
Road
Holt Way
Holt Close
Crossbow Rd
The Burrow
Lowe Cl
North
Agister Road
Coppice Primary School
Manford
Regarder Rd
New North Road
Harbourer Rd
Branch Road
Falconer Road
Marlyon Road
Hainault Industrial Estate
Beaver Road
Fowler Road
Works
Parkes Rd
Arrowsmith Road
Fawn Road
Robert Close
Burrow Road
Fletcher
Pollard Cl
Lowe
Manford Cross
Hainault Forest High School
Surgery
Huntsman Road
Peregrine
Tufter Road
Hind Cl
Hart Crescent
Fallow Cl
Hursley Road
Manford Way
PO
Frmrk Cl
Manford Wayn Health Cen
Kielder Close
Stoke Avenue
New North Road
Tunstall Avenue
Burslem Avenue
Burnside Industrial Estate
Hog Hill
Hainault Forest Golf Club
Lime Grove
Covert Road
Kesteven Cl
Inglewood Cl
Wickets Way
Dryden Close
Newcastle Avenue
Roebuck Road
Roebuck Road Trading Estate
Elmbridge Road
Forest Road
Trentbridge Close
Grace Close
John Bramston Primary School
Penrith Road
Rover Ave
Hainault
Kennylands Road
Forest Road
Bracken Industrial Est
L P R Sports Club
Hainault Road
Hainault Works
Fairlop Waters
Hainault Farm
Seven Kings Water
Redbridge
Barking and Dagenham
Painters Road
Hainault Road
Red House Farm
Billet Road
Rowan Way
Coral Close
Uplands Road
Danbury Close
Newhouse Av
Bardfield Av
Rosehatch Av
Tantony Grove
Arneways Av
Longhayes Av
Kingston Cl
Hazel Gv
I
2
3
56
4
5
6
92
90
rough
73
Little Heath School
Little Heath
Hope Cl
Nash Rd
Gregory Rd
Cavalier Cl
Surgery
Crabtree Avenue
Roles Grove
Sheepcotes Road
Woodrush Way
Lake Rd
Applegarth Drive
Peters Close
A12
EASTERN AVENUE

Golf Course
Havering
Redbridge
River Rom
Carter Drive
Thistledene Av
Pinewood Primary School
Lulworth Drive
Craven Gdns
Lodge Lane
Morant Gardens
Patmore Way
Ray Road
Cornell Way
Firbank Road
St Johns Road
Warden Av
Wensley Cl
Oates Road
Ravenswood Close
Boxmoor Road
Clitheroe Road
Prestwood Dr
Trescoe Gdns
Portmore Gdns
Bamford Way
Fox Close
Hunter's Grove
Silvermere Ave
Avenue
Fry Close
Navarre Gdns
Charlotte Gardens
Victoria Avenue
Kingshill
Braddock Close
Hillrise
Abridge Gardens
Stapleford Gardens
Larchwood Avenue
Larchwood Close
Harlow Gdns
Hendon Gdns
Dominion Drive
Highfield Close
Highfield
Lynwood Cl
Udall Gardens
Defoe Wy
RM5
Judith Avenue
Clockhouse Primary School
Clockhouse Lane
Burland Road
Ascension Road
Bacon Link
Lynwood Drive
Turpin Avenue
Felstead Rd
Gabriel Cl
Carter Close
Carter Drive
Sheila Road
Surgery
Frinton Road
Lodge Lane
Taylor Cl
Penn Gardens
Downham Close
Riversdale Road
Sunny Ms
CHASE
Hamlet Road
Hamlet Close
Ramsden Dr
Gelsthorpe Rd
Irons Way
Berkeley Avenue
Eaton Drive
Burchwall Cl
Fullers Cl
Brockley Crs
Virginia Close
Lawns
HOG HILL ROAD
ROMFORD ROAD B174
COLLIER ROW ROAD
Hazell Crs
Mill Rd
Birds Fm Av
Ash Cl
Erith Crs
Selsdon Cl
Collier Row
Lowshoe Lane
Collier Row Clinic
B174
Playfield Av
Surgery
Hulse Avenue
Cook's Cl
Horndon Green
Goring Cl
Hillfoot Avenue
School
Hood Walk
Elizabeth Close
Clovelly Gardens
Lynton Avenue
COLLIER ROW LANE
Hillfoot Road
Horndon Road
Works
Collier Row FC
Collier Row Road
Providence Place
White Hart Lane
Rodney Way
Nelson Cl
Argus Close
Elm Close
Ashdown Walk
Mowbrays Close
Mowbrays Road
Orchard Rd
Victory Way
Peartree Gardens
C Wk
Norman Cl
Kenway
Elm Road
Marks Gate
Northgate Ind Park
Crownfield Primary School
Anson Close
Mawney Rd
Maidstone Av
Hayden Way
Ferndale Road
Redriff Road
Prspct Pl
Wainfleet Av
Surgery
Oak
F F C
Billet Road
Vanguard Close
Barham Close
Walmer Close
Dunster Cl
Dover Cl
B174
Beansland Gv
Kingston Hill Avenue
Mawney Close
Percy Rd
Linley Crs
Rosedale
Hazel Cl
Kingston Cl
Abbotts Cl
Mawney Road
Gibbfield Close
Kings Oak
Birch Road
Birch Close
Barking and Dagenham
Havering
Marks Gate Junior School
Cemetery
Hlth Service Clinic
Forest Road
Cross Road
Hubbinet Ind Est
King George Cl
Tantony Grove
Longhayes Av
Silver Way
Epping Close
Susan Cl
Lawn Farm Gv
Essex Road
Beaufort Cl
EASTERN AVENUE
Bagleys Spring
Roles Grove
Rams Gv
Pitcairn Close
Surgery
Blenheim Cl
Amberley Way
Edinburgh's Dr
Rose Lane
Sheepcotes Road
Marlborough Road
Blandford Close
Poplar Street
Willow
Winston Close
Warren Farm
A12
RM6
1 grid square represents 500 metres
WHALEBONE LANE NORTH A1112
A1112
ROMFORD ROAD
Five Oaks Lane
Hainault Forest Golf Club
Marks Gate
5 48
49
50
92
90
A
B
C
D
E
1
2
3
4
5
6
55
74
PO

Country Park
Bower House
F
G
H
J
K
51
52
53
ORANGE TREE HILL
Kiln Wood Lane
B175 HAVERING ROAD
Noak Hill Road
Appleby
Stanwyck Gardens
Straight Road
Bedfords Park
Lower Bedfords Road
St Ursulas RC Junior School
RC Infant School
Ashvale Gdns
Merlin Road
Merlin Gdns
Avelon Road
Mount Pleasant Rd
Immanuel School
Merlin Close
Gobions JMI School
Bower Park School
Chase Cross
B1459
CROSS ROAD
Chelmsford Avenue
Broomfield Close
Gobions Avenue
Campbell Close
Glenton Way
Glenton Cl
Greenock Way
Helmsdale Rd
Nevis Close
Seaforth Close
Helmsdale Close
Risebridge Chase
Grange Road
Hale End
Archway
Hilldene Primary School
Meynell Rd
Morris Rd
Cowley Rd
Sheridan Cl
Chaucer Road
Heaton Avenue
Haydon Cl
Coleridge Road
Tennyson Road
Heaton Cl
Dyers Way
Keats
Ruskin Gdns
Elliott Gdns
Harrow Crescent
Bell Avenue
Robin Close
Bower Close
Faircross Avenue
Carry Way
Tweed Wy
Esk Way
Moray Cl
Spey Way
Moray Way
Garry Close
Cree Way
Risebridge Golf Club
Golf Course
Bartlow Gardens
HAVERING
Ayr Way
Ayr Gn
Clyde Way
Rise Park Primary School
Annan Way
Deveron Way
Dee Way
Rise Park
Tay Way
Mashiters Hill
Pettits Lane
Heather Cl
Clyde Way
Beauly Way
Rise Park Boulevard
AVENUE EAST
A12
Ramsay Gdns
Masefield Cl
North
Heather Way
Heather Gardens
Pettits Bvd
EASTERN
Millbrook Gardens
Park Bvd
Brook Cl
Brook Road
Heaton Gra
Risebridge Road
Heath Drive
Gidea Park Sports G
Takeley Close
Heather Drive
Linton
Rise Pk Pde
Roslyn Gdns
Netherpark Drive
Reed Pond Wk
Parkway
Golf Course
Heather Avenue
Portnoi Close
Heather Glen
The Elkins
Meadway
Mead Cl
Priests Av
Pettits Cl
Fairoak Gdns
Marshalls Park School
Gidea Park
Hockley Dr
Links Avenue
Surgery
Ashmour Gardens
Hamilton Avenue
Parkside Avenue
Fontayne Avenue
Parkland Avenue
Raphael Avenue
Broadway
A118
MAIN ROAD
RM1
Marshalls Drive
HAVERING RD B174
EASTERN AV EAST
Primary School
Hill Grove
McIntosh Road
Cedric Av
Wayside Close
Sorrel Walk
Lake Rise
Rosemary Av
Woodlands Road
Elm Wk
Gidea Cl
Gidea Avenue
Heath Close
Romford Golf Club
Severn Av
Castellan Avenue
Pemberton Av
RM2
Hall Road
Seymer Road
Dorset Av
The Chase
Drive
Mashiters Walk
College
Tudor Avenue
Balgores Crs
Crossways
Wallenger Av
St Marys Hare Park School
St Peters Catholic Primary School
Havering
Oaklands Avenue
St Ivians Dr
Repton Gdn
Repton Avenue
Squirrel's Heath Av
Compton Avenue
WEST
A125
NORTH STREET
St Edwards CE Primary School
75
Gidea Park School
Stanley Cl
Tudor Gdns
Balgores
Brook Dr
Chesham Cl
Park Drive
Romford County
The Ridgeway
Avenue
Gidea Park Station
Works
The Av
North Havering College of Adult Education
Brunel Cl
Woodfield Drive
Station Road
Diane Matthews Clinic
Medora Road
Brooklands
Dunton Rd
Havering Magistrates Court
Park End Road
Romford Clinic
Gilbert Road
Erroll Road
The Dolphin Leisure Centre
Lane
Chalforde Gdns
Church
I
2
3
4
5
6
92
91
90

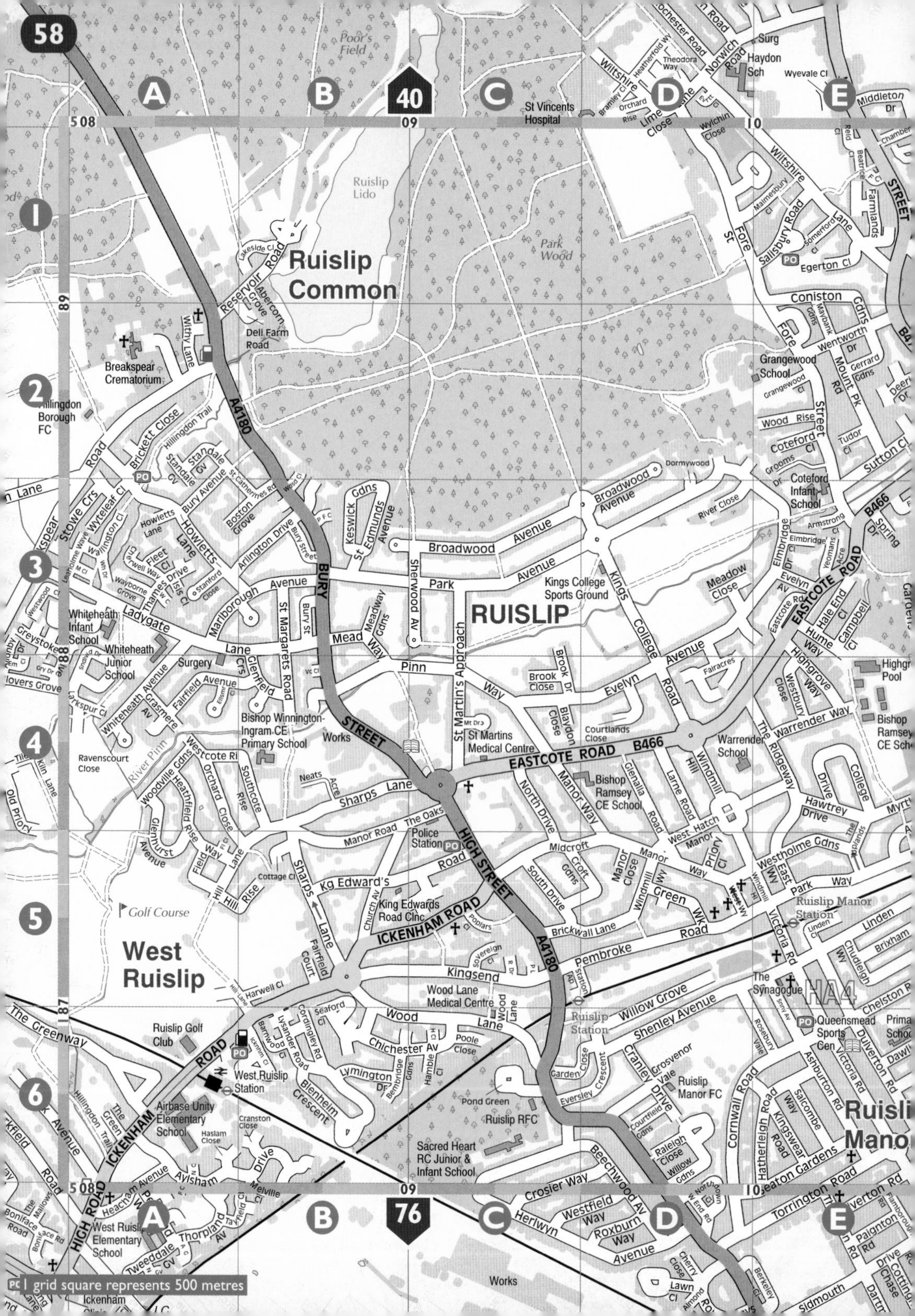

1 grid square represents 500 metres

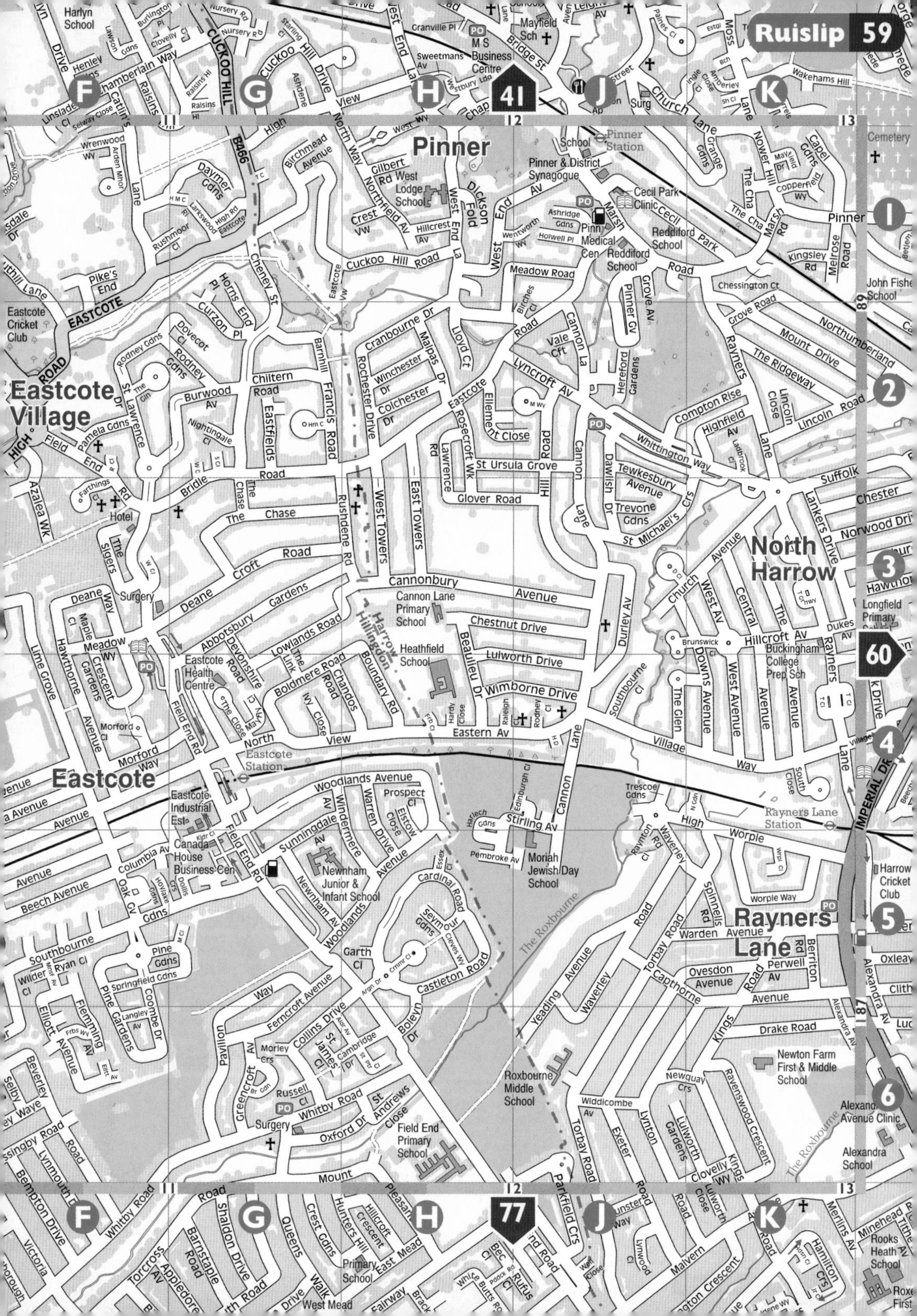
Pinner
Eastcote Village
Eastcote
North Harrow
Rayners Lane
Pinner Station
Eastcote Station
Rayners Lane Station
Cemetery
Harlyn School
M S Business Centre
Mayfield Sch
West Lodge School
Pinner & District Synagogue
Cecil Park Clinic
Pinner Medical Cen
Reddiford School
John Fisher School
Eastcote Cricket Club
Hotel
Surgery
Cannon Lane Primary School
Heathfield School
Eastcote Health Centre
Longfield Primary
Buckingham College Prep Sch
Eastcote Industrial Est
Canada House Business Cen
Newnham Junior & Infant School
Moriah Jewish Day School
Harrow Cricket Club
Newton Farm First & Middle School
Roxbourne Middle School
Field End Primary School
Alexandra Avenue Clinic
Alexandra School
Primary School
Rooks Heath School
The Roxbourne
Harrow
Hillingdon
41
60
77
12
11
13
68
87
F
G
H
J
K
I
2
3
4
5
6
EASTCOTE ROAD
HIGH ROAD
CUCKOO HILL
B466
IMPERIAL DR
Cuckoo Hill Road
Cuckoo Hill Drive
High View
West End Lane
Bridge St
Church Lane
Marsh Road
Cecil Park
Whittington Way
Cannon Lane
Village Way
Cannonbury Avenue
Field End Rd
Rushdene Rd
West Towers
East Towers
Deane Croft Road
The Chase
Bridle Road
Chiltern Road
Francis Road
Rochester Drive
Lincoln Road
Northumberland
Mount Drive
The Ridgeway
Yeading Avenue
Torbay Road
Capthorne Avenue
Drake Road
Alexandra Av
Kings Road
Ravenswood Crescent
Lulworth Gardens
Parkfield Crs
Whitby Road
Woodlands Avenue
Beech Avenue
Southbourne
Lime Grove
Hawthorne Avenue
Castleton Road
Cardinal Road
Newnham Av
Boundary Rd
Beaulieu Dr
Chestnut Drive
Lulworth Drive
Wimborne Drive
Eastern Av
North View
Durley Av
Hillcroft Av
West Avenue
Central Avenue
Downs Avenue
Worple Way
Warden Avenue
Ovesdon Avenue
Exeter Road
Lynton Road
Widdicombe Av
Newquay Crs
Mount Road
Pleasant Way
Queens Walk
Crest Gdns
Hunters Hill
Hillcroft Crescent
East Mead
West Mead
Shaldon Drive
Barnstaple Road
Torcross Av
Bempton Drive
Victoria Road
Merlins Av
Minehead Road
Hamilton Crs
Rufus Cl
Malvern Av
Lynwood Cl
Munster Way

42
59
78
A
B
C
D
E
1
2
3
4
5
6
513
14
15
88
87
Headstone
HARROW
West Harrow
Roxeth
South Harrow
HA2
Harrow Heritage Museum
Waverley Industrial Est
Harrow Crown Courts
Headstone Recreation Ground
Cemetery
Nower Hill High School
John Fisher School
Harrow Superbowl
School
North Harrow Station
Old Lyonian Sports Ground
Pinner View Medical Centre
Caryl Thomas Clnc
Harrow & Wealdstone Station
Marlborough School
Civic Centre
Civic Medical Cen
Alpha Prep School
Buckingham College School
Norbury First & Middle School
St Georges Shopping Centre & Cinema
Hotel
Warner Village
St Ann's Shopping Cen
Harrow-on-the-Hill Station
Middlesex New Synagogue
Bus Vlg
Longfield Primary School
Vaughan First & Middle School
West Harrow Station
The Harold Macmillan Medical Cen
West Harrow Recreation Ground
Medical Cen
St Anselms School
Harrow School
Grove Fields
Whitmore High School
Harrow Town Cricket Club
Grange First & Middle School
John Lyon School
Shaftesbury Medical Centre
Middle School
First & Middle School
Police Stn
Council Building
Archdale Business Cen
Works
Bowden House Clinic
College
Alexandra Avenue Clinic
Alexandra School
Roxbourne Medical Centre
Rooks Heath School
Eastcote Lane Cem
South Harrow Station
The Purcell School
Orley Farm School
Surgery
A404
A4090
A4005
A312
B458
PINNER ROAD
COLLEGE ROAD
LOWER ROAD
ROXETH HILL
LONDON ROAD
HIGH STREET
BESSBOROUGH ROAD
LOWLANDS ROAD
IMPERIAL DRIVE
ALEXANDRA
GEORGE V AV
Headstone Drive
Headstone Gdns
Pinner View
Kingsfield Avenue
Cambridge Road
Northumberland Road
Whitmore Road
Rayners Lane
Shaftesbury Avenue
Ridgeway
Eastcote Av
Roxborough Park
Hindes Road
Harrow View
Cunningham Park
1 grid square represents 500 metres

Wealdstone
Greenhill
Kenton
North Wembley
Preston
HA1
Cemetery
Driving School & Road Safety Centre
Elmgrove First & Middle School
Kenton Recreation Ground
Kenton Cricket Club
Glebe First & Middle School
Cody Park School
Surgery
Mag Cts
Harrow Central Mosque
Phoenix Industrial Est
Safari Cinema & Bingo
TA Centre
Troy Ind Est
Hotel
Greenhill Coll
Magistrates Court
Hall
College
Harrow High School
Medical Centre
Superstore
Kenton Station
Asquith Court School
St Gregorys High School
Kenton Synagogue
Uxendon M School
Mount Stewart Primary School
Northwick Park Station
University of Westminster (Harrow Campus)
Northwick Park
Northwick Park Hospital & Clinical Research Centre
A&E
Golf Course
Playing Fields
Rifle Range
Football La
Brent
Harrow
South Kenton Station
Byron Court Primary School
Preston Park Primary Sch
East Lane Business Park
Littleton Crescent
Clementine Churchill Hospital
St Georges RC First & Middle School
Wembley High School
Council Building
Community North
43
62
79
16
17
18
F
G
H
J
K
1
2
3
4
5
6
THE BRIDGE
RAILWAY APP
STATION ROAD
SHEEPCOTE ROAD
A409
KENTON ROAD
A4006
A404
WATFORD ROAD
SUDBURY COURT DRIVE A4127
A4088
EAST LANE
Belmont
Canning Road
Peel Road
Palmerston Rd
Oxford Rd
Masons Av
Herga Road
Christchurch Av
Forward Dr
The Hollies
Cullington Close
Christchurch Gdns
Christchurch Avenue
Wykeham Road
Boxmoor Rd
Brampton Grove
Prestwood Av
Beaufort Avenue
Kenmore Avenue
Irvine Av
Hartford Avenue
Radstock Av
Kingshill Avenue
Alveston Av
Oakfield Av
Larkfield
Kenton Lane
Formby Av
Dudley Avenue
Streatfield Road
Rowland Avenue
Shooters Avenue
Hunters Grove
Paulhan Road
Brancker Road
Hinkler Road
Hamel Cl
Kenton Pk Crs
Westfield Lane
Westfield Gdns
Westfield Dr
Charlton Road
D'Arcy Gardens
D'Arcy Dr
Lodge
Alicia Gardens
Alicia Avenue
Elmsleigh Avenue
Prestwood Close
Penn Cl
Kenton Pk Rd
Kenton Pk Av
Kenton Pk Cl
Hughenden Av
Addiscombe Close
Kenton Gdns
St Leonards Av
St Marys Vw
Woodgrange Av
Retreat Cl
Brookside Cl
Gooseacre La
Liddling Rd
Brookfield Crs
Hillview
Becmead Avenue
Hillbury Avenue
Willowcourt Av
Mayfield Av
Carlton Avenue
Elmwood Avenue
Totternhoe Cl
Sedgecombe Av
Briar Road
Norcombe Gdns
Winchfield Cl
Woodcock Hill
Illmington Rd
Donnington Road
Upton Gdns
Northwick Cir
Dovedale Avenue
Draycott Close
Wellacre Road
Nash Wy
Greystone Gdns
Lapstone Gdns
Mentmore Close
Ashridge Close
Ebrington Road
Woodhill Crs
Shaftesbury
Sheridan Gdns
Bouverie Gdns
Carlisle Gdns
The Ridgeway
Draycott Avenue
Aston Av
Stewart Avenue
Mount Stewart
Bulmer Gdns
Abercorn Gdns
Caverley Gdns
Manning Gdns
Trevelyan Crs
Woodcock Dell Avenue
Woodcock Hill Ct
Silverholme Cl
Lulworth Av
Conway Gdns
Derwent Gdns
Coniston Gdns
Rydal Gdns
Grasmere Avenue
Ambleside Gdns
Arnside Gdns
Windermere Avenue
Thirlmere Gardens
Montpelier Rise
College Road
Ennerdale Gdns
Glendale Gdns
The Link
Hawthorn Centre
Crystal Wy
Woodlands Rd
Elmgrove Crs
Glenwood
Moelyn Ms
Francis Road
Catherine Pl
Duffield Cl
Richards Cl
Hill Crs
Hill Rd
Courtfield Crs
Grange Rd
Crofts Road
Bonnersfield Lane
Manor Road
Bonnersfield La
Woodway Crs
Gerard Road
Hawthorne Av
Flambard Road
Rufford Cl
Rushout Av
Churchill Avenue
Northwick Pk Rd
Gayton Road
St John's Road
Lyon Rd
Ashburnham Av
Northwick Avenue
Kenton Av
Ntgale Av
Norval Road
Audrey Gdns
Spencer Road
Nathans Road
Abbotts Drive
Fairway Avenue
Carlton Avenue West
Langham Gardens
Oldborough Road
The Crs
Paxford Road
The Road
Blockley Road
Pasture Road
Shelley Gdns
Strathcona Road
Eskdale Close
Carlton Avenue
Third Av
Second Av
First Av
Warren
Logan R
Edison Dr
Pebworth Road
Mulgrave Road
Amery Road
The Green
Littleton Road
Heritage View
Bengeworth Road
Sudbury Court
St Georges Cl
Stapenhill Rd
Pasture Close
Byron Road
Peel Road
Hutchinson
Sudbury Hill

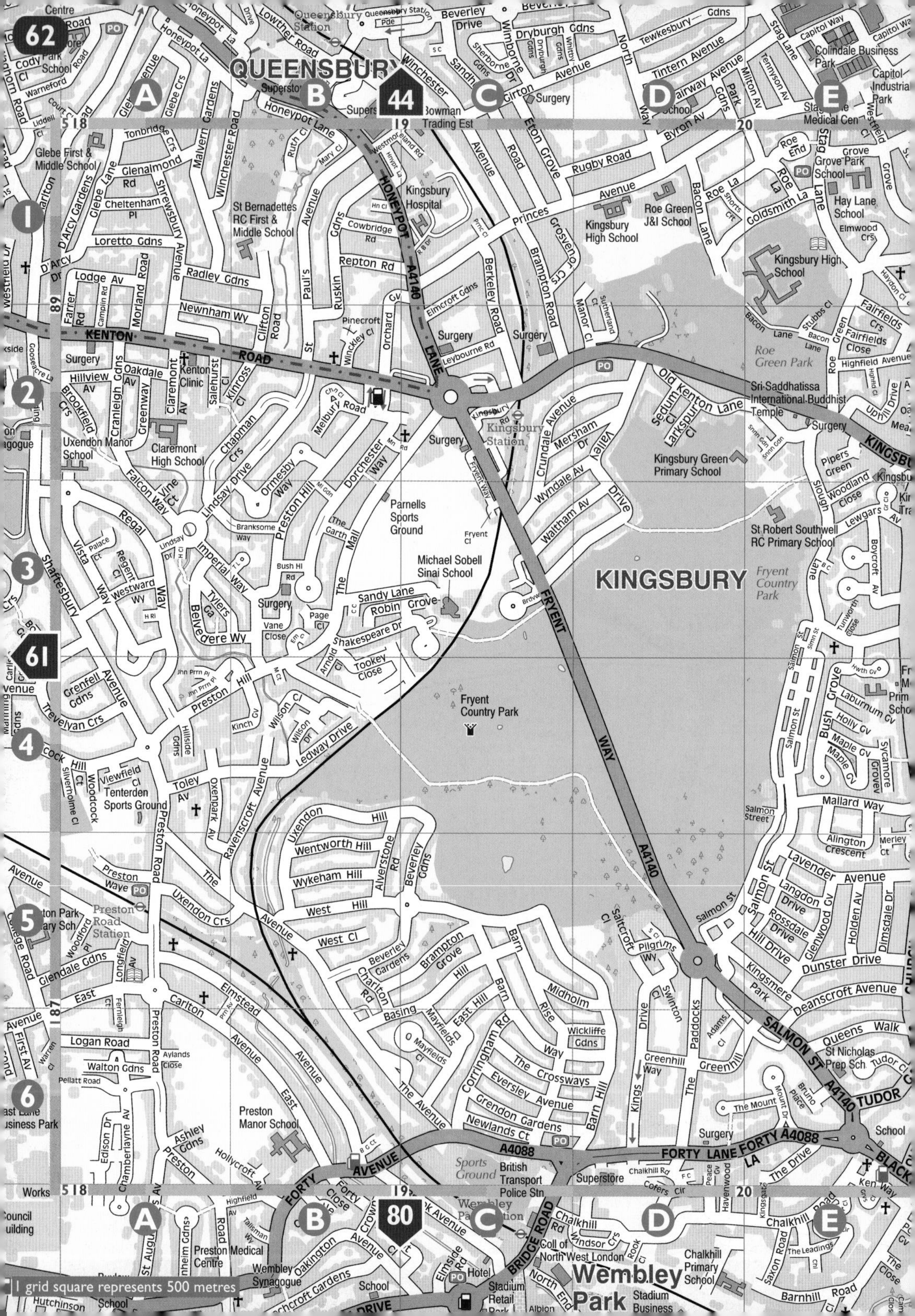

1 grid square represents 500 metres

44
61
80

Colindale
The Hyde
HENDON
West Hendon
Welsh Harp
Dollis Hill
NW9
West Hendon Playing Fields
Brent Reservoir
Silk Stream
Malcolm Park
Barnet Brent
Junction 1
45
64
81
F
G
H
J
K
21
22
23
1
2
3
4
5
6
British Library Newspaper Library
Metropolitan Police Track (Hendon)
Metropolitan Police Training School, Hendon
Rankin Close
Aerodrome Road
Denmark Hill Dr
Rowan Drive
Surgery
Hendale Avenue
Greyhound Hill
Church Farm House Museum
Medical Cen
Church Ter
High School
Church End
Primary School
Fuller St
Superstore
Annesley Av
Works
Colindale Av
Cecil Rd
Ajax Av
Chequers
Air Call Business Centre
Beis Yaakov Primary School
Capitol
Edgware Road
Colindeep Lane
Surgery
Beaulieu Close
Manor Way
Colin Park Road
Court Way
Sheaveshill Avenue
The Loning
Clovelly Avenue
Colindale Primary School
Lynton Avenue
Poolsford Rd
Rushgrove Avenue
A5150
M1
Selborne Gdns
Watford Way
A41
Sherrock Gardens
University
Church Road
The Burroughs
Central Hendon Clinic
Babington Rd
St Josephs Grove
Egerton Gdns
Little Theatre
Primary School
Brampton Grove
Evelyn Avenue
Rose Glen
Superstore
Grove Park Industrial Estate
Crescent
Hay Lane
Hayland Cl
Pear Cl
Ridge Cl
Larkway
Summit Cl
The Ridgeway
Edgware Rd The Hyde
Colin Close
New Way Rd
Woodfield Avenue
Hillfield Avenue
Crossway
Gardens
Crescent
Endersleigh Gdns
Barton Close
Colindeep Gdns
Richmond Gdns
Grosvenor Hospitals
Prothero Gdns
Hendon United Synagogue
Wykeham Rd
Hillside
Lane
Mount View
Wakemans
Summit Av
Hill View
Road
The Grove
Buck Lane
Gdns
Hill Avenue
Stancroft
Forest Gate
Highcroft
Springfield Mount
Lodore Gardens
Ennerdale Drive
Crummock Gardens
Rydal Gdns
The Hyde
Silkfield Road
Scottwell Drive
Colin Drive
Connaught Business Centre
Rookery Way
Works
The Hyde Industrial Estate
Edgeworth Avenue
Vaughan Avenue
Faber Gardens
Woodward Av
Talbot Crescent
Station Road
A504
Neeld Crescent
Rundell Crescent
Alderton Crs
Hendon Secretarial College
Infant School
Hendon Central Station
Queen's
Tree Dell
Coniston Gardens
Oliver Goldsmith Primary School
Springfield Gdns
Mardale Dr
St Johns CE School
Garrick Industrial Centre
The Hyde School
Hyde Est Road
Wilberforce Rd
Malcolm Crs
Alderton Wy
Vivian Avenue
Sevington
Foscote
Crespigny
Allington
The Albany College
Synagogue
Bowater Cl
Road
A4006
Derwent Ri
Goldsmith
Hyde Crs
Reets Farm Cl
Avenue
Fryent Flds
Superstore
Hendon Station
Audley
Hillview Cl
Pain Relief Clnc
Cheyne
North London Tutorial Co
Barningham Way
Burgess Avenue
Northgate Clinic
Snowden Drive
Puthin Cl
Fryent Crs
Fryent Grove
Gadsbury Close
Superstore
A5
The Broadway
Garrick Rd
Russell Rd
Surgery
Montagu Road
Graham Rd
Algernon Rd
Bertram Road
Dartmouth Rd
Surgery
Elthorne Wy
Marsh Drive
West Hendon Clinic
Marriotts Close
Herbert Rd
Perryfield Wy
Vicarage Road
Elliot Road
Fairfield Av
London Gender Clinic
Elthorne Road
Sunnymead Road
Meadowbank Rd
Tyrrel Way
Warner Cl
Rosemead
Brent View Road
Brent Park
Mount Road
Park Place
Daniel Place
Avenue
Parkfield JMI School
Sturgess Avenue
Sturgess Park
Brent Cross Shopping
Surgery
Reeves Av
Queensbury Road
Kingsmead Av
Wood Close
Townsend Lane
Kinloch Drive
Perth Av
Rannock Av
Winston Av
Blair Av
Hillway
Cool Oak Bridge
Cool Oak Lane
Dehar Crs
Esmar Crs
Seelig Av
Stuart Av
Woolmead Av
Dallas Road
Riverside
Layfield Crs
Layfield Road
Layfield Close
Park Road
Tempel
Wood Lane
B454
Church Dr
Dors Cl
Doreen Avenue
Parkfields Av
Glenwood Av
Woodfield School
Police Station
Priestley Wy
JVC Business Park
Aquarius Business Park
North Circular
Tilling Rd
Leith Cl
St Andrews Rd
Wells Drive
London Group Business Park
Staples Corner Business Park
UCG Cinemas
Superstore
Works
Harp Business Centre
Waterloo Road
Streakes Field Road
Coles Green Road
Kelceda Close
Eyhurst Cl
Atlas Business Centre
Oxgate Lane
Edge Business Centre
Geron Way
Old Church La
Church Walk
Birchen Grove
R Clr
Apsley Way
Shepherds Walk
Horseshoe Cl
Humber Trading Estate
Humber Rd
A406
Review Road
Heather Road
Dawpool Road
Warren Road
Ballards Road
Tadworth Road
Brook Road
Selsdon Road
Alder Gv
Road
Tankridge Rd
Chipstead Gardens
Oxgate Gardens
Conway
Church Lane
Harp Island Close
Braemar Av
Links Rd
North Circular Road
Crest Road
Paddock Road
Comber Close
Byron Rd
Walton Close
Bird Hill
Coombe Rd
Lyndhurst Close
Kelly Cl
Press Rd
Janson Close
Abovne Road
Attewood Av
Avondale Av
Randall Avenue
Braincroft Primary School
John Kelly Boys & Technol College
Nurfield
Rylandes Road
Forbes Close
Ainsworth Close
Newfield Ri
Applewood Close
Worcester Cl
Dollis Hill Lane
Mount
Neasden Lane
Primary School
Ardley Cl
The Cir
Kenwyn Drive
Cairnfield Avenue
Vincent Gdns
Pippin Close
Junior School
The Crs
Hill Avenue
Park Gardens
Oxleys Road
Wykeham Primary School
Annesley Cl
Jackman Ms
Eastleigh Close
Ashcombe
Flowers Cl
Hawarden
A409

1 grid square represents 500 metres

East Finchley
Hampstead Garden Suburb
Fortis Green
North End
Sandy Heath
West Heath
Vale of Health
Hampstead Heath
Kenwood House
St Marylebone Crematorium
Christs College School
Christs College
Brookland Primary School
Oak Lodge School
Abbots Gdns
East Finchley Station
Edmunds Walk
Works
Kerem House School
The Kerem School
Hampstead Garden Suburb Synagogue
Henrietta Barnett School
Golders Hill Health Centre
Annemount School
Golf Course
Highgate Golf Club
Highgate Private Hospital
Highgate Pre-Preparatory School
Highgate School
Highgate Junior School
Athlone House Hospital
Hampstead Golf Club
Golders Green Health Centre
King Alfred School
Manor House Hospital
Middlesex University
Golders Hill Park
Spaniards Inn
Highgate Ponds
Whitestone Pond
Police Station
Med Cen
Phoenix
Surgery
Primary School
EAST END ROAD
GREAT NORTH ROAD
FORTIS GREEN
A504
LYTTELTON ROAD
A1
AYLMER ROAD
CHERRY TREE HILL
ARCHWAY ROAD
HAMPSTEAD LANE
SPANIARDS ROAD
B519
NORTH END WAY
A502
NORTH END ROAD
HEATH STREET
Winnington Road
Bishops Avenue
Kingsley Way
Wildwood Road
Hampstead Way
Ingram Avenue
Sheldon Avenue
Stormont Road
Denewood Road
Broadlands Road
Bishopswood Road
Courtenay Avenue
Compton Avenue
Camden
Haringey
Barnet
N6
F
G
H
J
K
26
27
28
47
66
83
2
3
4
5
6
68
87

1 grid square represents 500 metres

Gas Works
Pumping Station
Hornsey Coroners Court & Public Mortuary
St Marys CE Infant School
Hornsey Station
College of North East London
Police Stn
School for Girls
Hornsey Vale
Weston Park Primary School
Harringay
Harringay Station
Stroud Green
St Aidans Primary School
Crouch Hill Station
Finsbury Park
Finsbury Park Station
Finsbury Park Track
N4
Poole's Park Primary School
RSPCA Animal Hospital
Police Station
Andover Medical Cen
City & Islington College
Germal College
Harringay Green Lanes Stn
Arena Estate
Crusader Industrial Estate
St Ann's General Hospital
Police Station
St Mary's RC Primary School
Woodlands Park Primary School
West Green
Downhills Park
The Langham School
Aarotya Medical Centre
Belmont Junior & Infant School
Turnpike Lane Station
Coronet
Asylum Medical Centre
Euro Way School London
Woodbury Down Primary School
Manor House Station
John Scott Health Centre
Finsbury Park District Synagogue
Watersports Centre
Parkwood Primary School
Yeshivo Horomo Talmudical College
Sir Thomas Abney Primary School
Avigdor Primary School
Clissold Park
Lordship Terrace
Barton House Hlth Cen
Bnois Jerusalem School
Mednurs Clinic
Synagogue
Hornsey County School
Junior School
Arsenal
TURNPIKE LANE
GREEN LANES
WEST GREEN ROAD A504
ST ANN'S ROAD B152
SEVEN SISTERS ROAD
STROUD GREEN ROAD A1201
BLACKSTOCK ROAD
BROWNSWOOD ROAD
LORDSHIP PARK
WIGHTMAN ROAD B138
TOTTENHAM LANE
CHURCH LANE
ENDYMION ROAD B150
49
68
85
F
G
H
J
K
I
2
3
4
5
6

Tottenham Hale
50
South Tottenham
N15
Stamford Hill
Upper Clapton
STOKE NEWINGTON
N16
E5
67
86
A B C D E
1 2 3 4 5 6
34 35
HIGH ROAD
WEST GREEN ROAD
BROAD LANE
A503 FOUNTAYNE RD
A503 FERRY LANE
FOREST ROAD
SEVEN SISTERS ROAD
ST ANN'S ROAD
B152
AMHURST PARK
A107
CLAPTON COMMON
STAMFORD HILL
A10
MANOR ROAD
B105
NORTHWOLD ROAD
B111
UPPER CLAPTON ROAD
RECTORY ROAD
STOKE NEWINGTON HIGH ST
STOKE NEWINGTON CH ST
Seven Sisters Station
South Tottenham Stn
Stamford Hill Stn
Stoke Newington Station
Rectory Road Station
Clapton Stn
Tottenham Hale Station
Lockwood Ind Park
Tottenham Hale Retail Park
Tottenham Gn Leisure Cen
Town Hall
College of North East London
Haringey Hlth Care
Fountayne Business Centre
High Cross Centre
Ferry Lane Primary School
South Tottenham District Synagogue
Gladesmore Community School
Warwick Reservoir
Copper Mills Works
Coppermill Lane
Nature Reserve
Springfield Park
Lea Valley Walk
Abney Park Cemetery
Sir Thomas Abney Primary School
Beth Hamedrash Skver Synagogue
Holmleigh Primary School
St Thomas CE Primary School
Oldhill Medical Centre
Jubilee JMI School
Yetev Lev Day School for Boys
Fountayne Road Health Cen
Healy Medical Cen
Knightland Road Synagogue
Council Building
Ickburgh School
Community College
Clapton Synagogue
West Hackney Synagogue
Grazebrook Primary School
Fire Station
Barton House Hlth Cen
George Downing Estate
Satmer Trust Sch
Jewish School
Beis Rochel D'satmar Girls School
Bnois Jerusalem School
United Synagogue
Boys School
FOB School
Ziam Trading Estate
Lea Bridge
Waltham Forest
Hackney
Walthamstow Marsh
Superstore
Warwick Grove
Mount Pleasant Hill
Southwold Road
Gunton Road
Cleveleys Road
Casimir Road
Kenninghall Road
Evering Road
Brooke Road
Narford Road
Reighton Road
Lynmouth Road
Dunsmure Road
Northfield Road
Linthorpe Road
Olinda Road
Ravensdale Road
Craven Park Road
Clifton Gdns
Lealand Road
Ferndale Road
Crowland Road
Gladesmore Road
Wargrave Av
Norfolk Av
Fairview Rd
Elm Park Av
Castlewood Road
Moundfield Road
Leadale Road
Lingwood Road
Ashtead Road
Spring Hill
Springfield
Jessam Avenue
Moresby Road
Forburg Road
Filey Avenue
Chardmore Road
Fountayne Road
Osbaldeston Road
Cazenove Road
Alkham Road
Darenth Road
Kyverdale Road
Heathland Rd
Cranwich Road
Durley Road
West Bank
Bethune Road
Lordship Road
Yoakley Rd
Bouverie Road
Grayling Rd
Dumont Rd
Kynaston Rd
Lavers Rd
Oldfield Rd
Leswin Rd
Daleview Road
Vartry Road
Eastbourne Rd
Richmond Rd
Franklin St
St John's Rd
Culvert Road
Southey Road
Greenfield Rd
Beaconsfield Road
Lawrence Rd
Bedford Road
Summerhill Road
Seaford Road
Roslyn Road
Elmar Rd
Antill Road
Talbot Road
Rangemoor Rd
Wakefield Rd
Markfield Road
Stamford Rd
Ashby Rd
Newton Rd
Colless Rd
Armadale Cl
Yarmouth Crs
Jarrow Road
Reedham Cl
Bream Cl
Mount Pleasant Lane
Theydon Road
Riverside Close
Leaside Road
Grosvenor Way
Spring Lane
Monument Way
Chesnut Rd
Scales Road
Police Station
Bus Garage
Clinic
1 grid square represents 500 metres

Walthamstow 69
51
70
87
WALTHAMSTOW
Lea Bridge
Hackney
F
G
H
J
K
2
3
4
5
6
36
37
38
E17
E10
FOREST ROAD
A503
BLACKHORSE ROAD
A1006
HOE STREET
A112
MARKHOUSE ROAD
LEA BRIDGE ROAD
A104
CHURCH ROAD
HIGH ROAD
HIGH ROAD LEYTON
Blackhorse Road Station
Walthamstow Central Station
Walthamstow Queens Road Stn
St James St Stn
Waltham Forest Theatre
Forest Road Medical Cen
Police Station
Willowfield School
Willowfield Adult Education Centre
Highams Lodge Business Cen
Forest Trading Estate
The Hiltongrove Business Centre
Cinema
St Marys CE Primary Sch
School for Girls
Holy Family Technology College
Vestry House Mus
Coppermill Primary School
Alpha Business Cen
St James's Health Cen
Cemetery
Coroners Court
Kelmscott Leisure Centre
Kelmscott School
Low Hall Sports Ground
Barn Croft Primary School
Forest Business Park
Leyton Industrial Village
Roxwell Trading Park
Cromwell Industrial Estate
Burwell Industrial Est
Dorma Tdg Park
Fairways Business Park
Lea Park Trading Est
Leyton FC
St Saviours CE Primary School
Church Mead Junior School
St Josephs Catholic Infant School
Leyton Business Cen
Orient Ind Park
George Mitchell School
Leyton Youth Sports Ground
Leyton Leisure Centre
Leyton Orient FC (Matchroom Stadium)
River Lea or Lee
Orient Way
Marsh Lane
Ive Farm Lane
Coppermill Lane
Markhouse Av
Markmanor Avenue
Argall Av
Lammas Rd
Mandeville St
Caldecott Way

70
52
69
88
A
B
C
D
E
1
2
3
4
5
6
538
39
40
Upper Walthamstow
Leytonstone
LEYTON
E11
Holy Family College
Medical Centre
Woodlands Road
Waverley Rd
Wyatt's Lane
Junior School
Havant Road
Turner Rd
B160
WOOD STREET
Wood Street Station
Fyfield Road
Avon Road
Bistern Avenue
Upper Walthamstow Road
Broadwalk
Cheyne Avenue
Bushey Avenue
Clarenndon Road
Lansdowne
Cleveland
Tavistock Road
Beechwood Park
WOODFORD NEW ROAD
WOODFORD ROAD
The
Prospect Hill
Church Hill Road
Shernhall Street
Works
Marlowe Rd
Vallentin Road
Greenway Avenue
Forest Rise
Saint Peters Path
Oakhurst Gardens
College Place
Forest School
The Forest
Forest Ct
Centenary Walk
Bradwell Cl
Rivenhall Gardens
Hermitage Cl
Hermitage Wk
Laurel Way
Meadow Walk
Primary School
Falcon Way
Avon Way
Holy Family Technology College
Church La
Ind Est
Brookfield Av
Barrett Road
Grevile Rd
Brooke Rd
School for Boys
Works
The Risings
Morgan Av
Salters Road
Foresters Drive
Lucern Cl
Woodside Pk Av
Buxton Dr
Snaresbrook Road
Snaresbrook Rd
Eagle Lane
Trafalgar Place
Malcolm Way
Sylvan Road
HERMON
A11
HOLLYBUSH HILL
A113
Summit Rd
Surgery
Ferndale Av
Oliver Rd
Junior School
Infant School
Addison Rd
Wilson St
Brunswick St
Beulah Road
Maynard Road
Raglan Rd
A104
LEA BRIDGE ROAD
Barclay Road
Cromwell Rd
Salisbury
Shernhall Street
Western Rd
Eastern Rd
Elm Rd
W End Av
Halford Road
Eatington Road
Fulready Rd
Forest Glade
Snaresbrook Crown Court
The Rise
Hollybush Close
Forest Close
Snaresbrook Station
Station App
Wanstead CE Primary School
Ellesmere Cl
Selworthy Cl
Church Path
Surgery
NEW WANSTEAD
Wanstead Place
Police Station
Spratt Hall Road
Wellesley
Wellington
Surgery
Fraser Rd
Copeland Rd
Merton Rd
College Road
Carnarvon Rd
Liverpool Rd
Peterborough Road
A114
WHIPPS CROSS ROAD
A&E
Whipps Cross Hospital
Greg Cl
Matlock
Nottingham Road
Essex Road
Leyton VI Form College
Barclay Junior & Infant School
James Lane
Leytonstone School
Forest Glade
Fladgate Road
Maple Road
Dyson Road
Preston Road
Poppleton Road
Colworth Road
Chadwick Road
Teesdale
Surgery
Voluntary Pl
Chaucer Rd
Addison Road
Dangan Road
Gordon Road
Chestnut Dr
Highstone Avenue
Convent School
Primary School
Cambridge Park Road
Cambridge Road
Lonsdale Rd
A12
Knotts Green Rd
Belmont Park School
Belmont Park Road
LEYTON GREEN ROAD
Epsom Road
Griggs Road
Chesterfield Road
Canterbury Road
Sandringham Road
Forest Drive East
James Lane
Hainault Rd
Wadley Rd
Lytton Road
Esther Road
Ashbridge Road
Corbicum
HIGH ROAD
Leyton Leisure Centre
Cheltenham Road
Ely Road
Colchester
Cromer Road
Essex Road S
Gwyn Jones Primary School
Woodriffe Road
Percy Road
Kingswood Rd
Selsdon Road
Woodcote Road
Felstead
Surgery
Abbotts Park Road
Lyndhurst Dr
Leigh Road
James Lane
Forest Drive West
Forest Road
Fairlop Road
Wallwood Road
Allum Medical Centre
King's Road
Queen's Road
Superstore
BUSH RD
A114
BUSH ROAD A114
SMA Medical Cen
Works
A112
Fletcher Lane
Wesley Rd
Goodman Rd
Midland Road
Serbin Close
Hainault Road
Hawbridge Road
Clarendon Road
A106
GAINSBOROUGH RD
Bus Cen
Kirkdale Rd
Leytonstone Stn
Browning Road
Beacontree Road
Bushwood
Skelton's La
Tilbury Rd
Cooper's La
School
Leyton Midland Road Station
Leyton Youth Sports Ground
The Sidings
Cavendish Road
Bulwer Rd
Chelmsford Road
Southwest Road
The Synagogue
Church Lane
College
Superstore
Aylmer
Leytonstone Mosque
Hartley Rd
Woodville Rd
Harvey Rd
Surg
Leyspring Rd
BLAKE HALL ROAD
Police Cadet School
Brewster Road
Belgrave Rd
Grosvenor Rd
Norlington Road
Norlington Sch
Scarborough Rd
Drayton Rd
Fillebrook Rd
GROVE GN RD
Primary School
Barclay Rd
Stanmore Road
Mornington Rd
Leybourne Rd
Bushwood
LEYTON
Kings Edward Rd
Lawton Road
Scott's Road
Morley Road
Claude Road
Pretoria Road
Connaught Rd
Girls School
Harold Rd
Vernon Rd
Michael Road
Lister Road
Bushwood
Belgrave Road
Surgery
Jesse Rd
Police Station
Albert Road
Jersey Rd
Twickenham Rd
Kimberley Rd
Rhodesia Road
Madeira Rd
Leytonstone High Road Stn
Brockway Cl
LEYTONSTONE ROAD
Davies Lane
Works
Davies Lane Infant School
Centenary Walk
Windsor Road
Tennyson
HIGH ROAD
Primary School
B161
Dawlish Road
Surgery
Newport Rd
Newport J&I School
St Anne's Rd
Richmond Road
Thornton Rd
Trinity Cl
Health Cen
Ferndale Road
Malvern Road
Richmond Way
Road
GRANGE PK RD
Buckland Rd
Sedgwick Road
Murchison Road
FRANCIS ROAD
Oakdale Road
Pearcroft Road
Ashville Rd
Central Av
A106 GROVE GREEN ROAD
Norman Road
Woodlands Rd
Granleigh Road
Park Gv Road
Melford Rd
Lancaster Rd
Cookes Close
Montague Road
House
Tyndall Road
Huxley Road
Surgery
Sadbury Rd
Leyton Park Road
Elm Road
Mayville Rd
Southwell Gv Rd
Police Station
Lansdowne Rd
Brisbane Road
Balmoral
Sidmouth Road
St Mary's Road
B161
Marchant Rd
Lincoln St
Junior School
Lynn Ms
ROAD
Cecil Road
Acacia Road
Briscoe Cl
Cobden Road
Centenary Walk
Lake
Osborne
Buckingham Road
Lyttelton Rd
Oliver Road
St George's Rd
A106 WARREN ROAD
GROVE GREEN RD
Colville Rd
A12
Cemetery
Hollydown Way
Infant School
CATHALL RD
Beachcroft
Acacia Business Cen
Surgery
B161
BARROW ROAD
Terling Cl
School
Cobbold Rd
Neville Cl
Primary School
Pear Gv
Apple Rd
Melon Rd
HIGH RD
Chichester
Matcham Rd
Woodhouse Rd
1 grid square represents 500 metres

F
G
H
J
K
41
42
43
53
72
89
1
2
3
4
5
6
Redbridge
WANSTEAD
Aldersbrook
Gants Hill
NORTH CIRCULAR ROAD
A406
SOUTHEND ROAD A1400
A1400 WOODFORD AVENUE
EASTERN AVENUE A12
ALDERSBROOK ROAD
BEEHIVE LANE
B192
CHIGWELL
HIGH ST
A113
Hatton School
Anderson Road
Animal Cemetery
BUPA Roding Hospital
Woodford Bridge Road
High School
Carswell Close
Roding Lane South
Clayhall Park
Parkview Gardens
Nightingale Primary School
Wanstead Hospital
Victory Road
Cranbourne Avenue
Lancaster Avenue
Monmouth Avenue
Southview Drive
Onslow Gardens
Cadogan Gardens
Ashbourne Avenue
Colvin Gdns
Rodney Road
Elmcroft
Rutland Rd
Warwick Rd
Leicester Road
Hereford Road
Gloucester Road
Buckingham Rd
Lorne Gdns
Deynecourt Gardens
Eaton Rise
Nutter Lane
Eaton Manor RFC
Preston Drive
Reydon Av
Grove Park
The Avenue
Nightingale Lane
Cowley Rd
Grosvenor Rd
Eastway
Gardner Cl
Wanstead Station
Mansfield Road
Chester Rd
Oak Hall Rd
Redbridge Lane West
Wigram Road
Drummond Rd
Corbett Rd
River Close
Wanstead Leisure Centre
Wanstead High School
St Mary's Av
Draycot Road
Langley Drive
Langley Crs
Warren Road
Colebrooke Drive
Overton Drive
Wanstead Golf Club
Wanstead Cricket Club
The Warren Dr
Raynes Avenue
Golf Course
Whitney Av
Lakeside Av
Leigh Avenue
Merrivale Avenue
Peaketon Avenue
Mighell Avenue
Fowey Avenue
Tryfan Close
Falmouth Gardens
Torquay Gardens
Braintree Avenue
Bergholt Av
Works
Cobbetts Av
Vista Drive
Rosemary Drive
Fernhall Drive
Fairmead Gdns
Edwina Gdns
Redbridge Lane East
Margaret Way
Redbridge Station
Hotel
Studley Drive
Royston Gdns
Evanston Gardens
Surgery
Castle Drive
Castle View Gardens
Preston Gdns
Hill Vw Crs
Devonport
The Drive
Wanstead Lane
Carlisle Gdns
Stonehall Avenue
Wakefield Gdns
Ripon Gdns
Worcester Gdns
Hereford Gdns
Canterbury Avenue
Gloucester Gardens
Lincoln Gardens
Chelmsford Gdns
Chichester Gdns
Rochester Gdns
Exeter Gdns
Truro Gdns
Wells Gdns
Lincoln Island
Wanstead Park
Babbacombe Gdns
Coniston Gdns
Derwent Gdns
Widecombe Gardens
Keswick Gdns
Primary School
Ambleside Gdns
Brantwood Gardens
Grasmere Gardens
College Gdns
Grangeway Gardens
Ridgeway Gardens
Highcliffe Gardens
Windermere Gardens
Ellesmere Gdns
Danehurst Gdns
Inglehurst Gardens
Somersby Gdns
Gosford Primary School
Beehive Preparatory School
Hedgeley
Lodge Hill
Lord Gdns
Herent Drive
Stoneleigh Avenue
Marlands
Abbotswood Gardens
Longwood Gardens
Highwood Gardens
Beechwood Gardens
Collinwood Gardens
Wycombe Road
Avery Gdns
Ethelbert Gdns
Radnor Crs
Sussex Cl
Clarence Avenue
St Helen's Road
Cranbrook Rise
St Edmund's Road
Ilford Synagogue
St George's Road
St Andrew's Road
Wilson Rd
Vaughan Gardens
Cowley Road
Clarendon Gardens
Arlington Gardens
Ranelagh
Redcliffe Gardens
Infant Sch
Highlands Gardens
Prim Sch
Stanhope Gardens
Sackville Gdns
Seymour Gdns
Seymour Gardens
Medical Centre
Kensington Gardens
Endsleigh Gdns
Belgrave Road
De Vere Gardens
Courtland Avenue
Mayfair Avenue
Empress Avenue
Wanstead Pk Road
Westbury Rd
York
Ilford Golf Club
Woodlands Avenue
Queenswood Gdns
St Gabriel's Cl
Brading Crs
Burden Way
Alders Cl
Park Road
Primary Sch
Northumberland Av
Secondary Sch
Ingatestone Rd
Albury Mews
Harpenden Road
Margaretting Road
Dover Road
Herongate Road
Wanstead Park Avenue
Clavering Road
Arran Drive
Westmorland Close
Sunderland Way
St Margaret's Road
Empress Avenue
Merlin Road
Heatherwood Close
City of London Cemetery
City of London Crematorium
Wanstead Flats
PO
IG4

72
54
71
90
Barkingside
Barkingside Cemetery
Ilford Jewish Primary School
Tanners Lane
Superstore
Station Rd
Barkingside FC
Barkingside Station
Aldborough Hatch
Fullwood Primary School
Cranbrook Road
A123
Gants Hill
Gants Hill Station
Gants Hill Medical Cen
Woodford Avenue
A12
Eastern Avenue
Newbury Park
Newbury Park Station
Newbury Park Health Centre
Newbury Park Primary School
South-West Essex Reform Synagogue
Geuries Junior School
Infant School
Lower School
Odeon Cinema
Valentine High School
Ilford Synagogue
Valentines Park
Cranbrook
Seven Kings High School
St Aidans RC Primary School
Kings Gardens
Downshall Primary School
Canon Palmer RC High School
Seven Kings Health Cen
Christchurch Primary Sch
Cranbrook College
College High School
New Rush Hall School
Ilford County Court
Ilford Swimming Pool
Buckingham Road Cemetery
Cricklefield Stadium
South Park Bus Cen
Ilford Retail Park
The Business Centre
The Exchange
High Road
Green Lane
A1083
A118
Ilford Station
Kenneth More Theatre
Winston Way
Ilford Medical Cen
Gordon Infant School
Maytime School
South Circular Road
South Park
IG1
IG2
A
B
C
D
E
1
2
3
4
5
6
1 grid square represents 500 metres

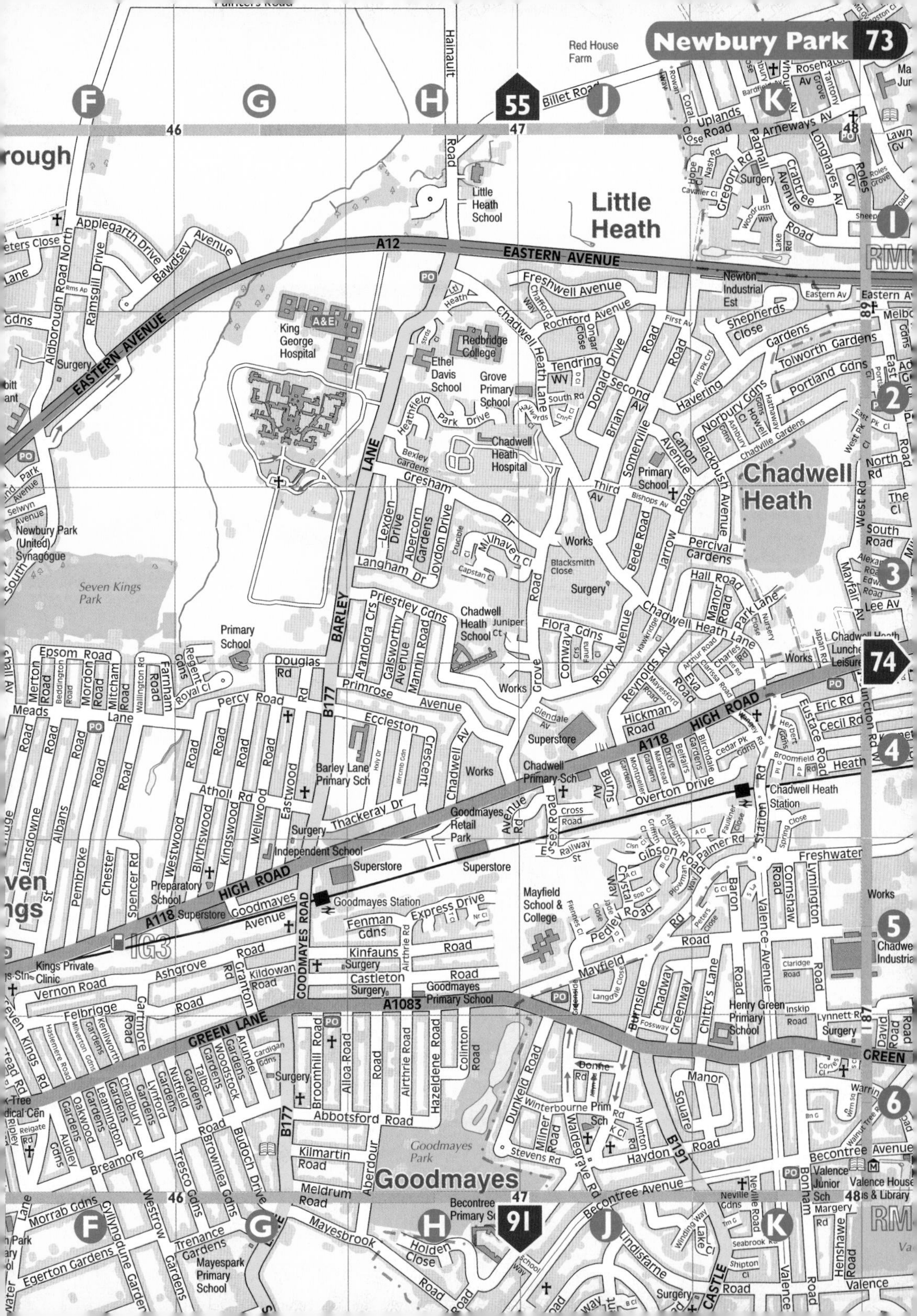
Red House Farm
Hainault Road
Billet Road
55
F
G
H
J
K
46
47
48
Little Heath School
Little Heath
Applegarth Drive
Bawdsey Avenue
Aldborough Road North
Ramsgill Drive
A12
EASTERN AVENUE
Newton Industrial Est
Shepherds Close
Uplands Road
Arneways Av
Padnall Road
Gregory Rd
Surgery
Crabtree Avenue
Longhayes Av
Roles Gv
Lake Rd
Freshwell Avenue
Rochford Avenue
Ongar Close
Chafford Way
Chadwell Heath Lane
Donald Drive
Second Av
First Av
Havering Gardens
Tolworth Gardens
Portland Gdns
Norbury Gdns
Chadville Gardens
Hathaway
King George Hospital
A&E
Redbridge College
Ethel Davis School
Grove Primary School
Tendring Wy
South Rd
Heathfield Park Drive
Chadwell Heath Hospital
Bexley Gardens
Gresham Dr
Lexden Drive
Abercorn Gardens
Joydon Drive
Millhaven Cl
Capstan Cl
Langham Dr
Brian Av
Somerville Avenue
Canon Avenue
Blackbush Avenue
Primary School
Third Av
Bishops Av
Chadwell Heath
Works
Blacksmith Close
Bede Road
Jarrow Road
Percival Gardens
Hall Road
Manor Road
Park Lane
Surgery
Seven Kings Park
Newbury Park (United) Synagogue
Primary School
BARLEY LANE
Priestley Gdns
Arandora Crs
Galsworthy Avenue
Mannin Road
Chadwell Heath School
Juniper Ct
Flora Gdns
Conway
Roxy Avenue
Grove Road
Reynolds Av
Chadwell Heath Lane
Epsom Road
Merton Road
Mordon Road
Mitcham Road
Farnham Road
Royal Cl
Douglas Rd
Percy Road
Primrose Avenue
Eccleston Crescent
Chadwell Av
Works
Glendale Av
Superstore
Hickman Road
Eva Road
Mayesford Road
Eric Rd
Cecil Rd
Eustace Road
Heath
74
Meads Lane
A118 HIGH ROAD
Barley Lane Primary Sch
Chadwell Primary Sch
Burns Av
Overton Drive
Chadwell Heath Station
Lansdowne Road
Albans Road
Pembroke Road
Chester Road
Spencer Rd
Westwood Road
Blythswood Road
Kingswood Road
Wellwood Road
Eastwood Rd
Atholl Rd
Thackeray Dr
Goodmayes Retail Park
Cross Road
Railway St
Gibson Road
Palmer Rd
Station Rd
Freshwater
Independent School
Superstore
Superstore
Preparatory School
Seven Kings
Goodmayes Avenue
Goodmayes Station
Express Drive
Fenman Gdns
Mayfield School & College
Crystal Way
Pedley Road
Baron Rd
Valence Avenue
Cornshaw Road
Lymington Road
Works
IG3
Kings Private Clinic
Ashgrove Road
Granton Rd
Kildowan Road
GOODMAYES ROAD
Kinfauns Road
Castleton Road
Surgery
Goodmayes Primary School
Mayfield
Burnside
Chadway
Greenway
Chitty's Lane
Claridge Road
Vernon Road
Felbrigge Road
Gartmore Road
A1083
GREEN LANE
Henry Green Primary School
Inskip Road
Lynnett Rd
Surgery
Arundel Gardens
Woodstock Gardens
Talbot Gardens
Nutfield Gardens
Lynford Gardens
Charlbury Gardens
Leamington Gardens
Oakwood Gardens
Audley Gdns
Broomhill Road
Alloa Road
Airthrie Road
Hazeldene Road
Colinton Road
Dunkeld Road
Donne Rd
Winterbourne Prim Sch
Manor Square
Abbotsford Road
Kilmartin Road
Aberdour Road
Goodmayes Park
Goodmayes
Milner Road
Waldegrave Rd
Stevens Rd
Haydon Road
B191
B177
Becontree Avenue
Valence Junior Sch
Valence House & Library
Breamore Road
Tresco Gdns
Brownlea Gdns
Budoch Drive
Meldrum Road
Becontree Primary Sch
91
Neville Gdns
Neville Road
Bonham Road
Margery Rd
Morrab Gdns
Westrow Gardens
Trenance Gardens
Mayespark Primary School
Mayesbrook Road
Holden Close
Lindisfarne
Egerton Gardens
Gylingdune Gardens
Surgery
CASTLE
Henshawe Road
Valence
1
2
3
4
5
6

74
56
73
92
A
B
C
D
E
1
2
3
4
5
6
48
49
50
89
87
RM6
RM7
RM8
Barking and Dagenham
Havering
Kingston Cl
Gibbfield Close
Marks Gate Junior School
Hlth Serv Clinic
Cemetery
Tantony Grove
Longhayes Av
Lawn Farm Gv
Roles Gv
Roles Grove
Thatches Grove
Bagleys Spring
Rams Gv
Sheepcotes Road
Rose Lane
Padnall Rd
Hatch Grove
WHALEBONE LANE NORTH
Warren Farm
Birch Road
Birch Close
Forest Road
Kings Oak
Cross Road
Silver Way
Epping Close
Essex Road
Works
Essex Close
Pitcairn Close
Marlborough Road
Amberley Way
Blandford Close
Winston Close
Hubbinet Ind Est
George Cl
Susan Cl
Beaufort Cl
Surgery
Blenheim Cl
EASTERN AVENUE
Edinburgh's Dr
Poplar Street
Willow
Cedar
Maple St
Beech St
Vine St
Lime Cl
Pretoria Rd
Oak St
Mildmay Rd
Palm Road
Barkwood Close
EASTERN AVENUE WEST A12
Eastern Av
Eastern Avenue West
Melbourne Gdns
Henley Gdns
Cedar Av
Yew Tree Gdns
North Gardens
Portland Gdns
East Rd
Adelaide Gdns
Geneva Gardens
Pemberton Gdns
Warren Comprehensive School
Warren Sports Centre
Warren Junior School
East Pk Cl
West Pk Cl
North Rd
Lansbury Avenue
Morley Road
Kelly Way
Cvndsh Gdn
Beresford Gdns
Surg
A1112
The Cl
South Road
West Rd
Hainault Gore
Millbrook Gdns
Whalebone Avenue
Whalebone Gv
Gordon Road
Albany Road
Hainault Road
Sylvan Av
Kings Avenue
Mill Lane
Willow Road
Ashton Gardens
Alexandra Road
Edward Road
Mayfair Av
Eagle Close
Cromer Road
Tenby Road
Lee Av
Forsters Cl
Furze Infant School
HIGH ROAD
A118 LONDON ROAD
Salcombe Drive
Coombewood Drive
Saville Road
Grantham Gdns
Chadwell Heath Leisure Cen
Back La
Tenby Close
Woodlands Av
Farrance Road
Bennett Rd
Wadeville Av
St Chad's Gdns
Morden Road
Merten Road
Burlington Gdns
Eric Rd
Cecil Rd
Junction Rd W
Kenneth Road
Heath Road
Mirravale Trading Estate
Coppen Road
Selinas Lane
Works
Superstore
Eldenwall Industrial Estate
Freshwater Road
Lymington Road
Chadwell Heath Industrial Park
Jubilee Avenue
Jubilee Close
Marks
Recreation Av
Lowland Gdns
Marina Gdns
Spring Gdns
Richards Avenue
Primary School
Southern Way
Fernden Way
Stanford Close
Bear Cl
Weald Way
Jutsums Lane
Crowlands Avenue
Burlington Avenue
Aston Av
Lonsdale Av
Derby Av
Lessington Av
Cromer Rd
Norfolk Road
Kensington Rd
Kimberley Av
Sheringham
St Edwards CE Comprehensive School
Bracken Ms
Eddy Close
Jutsums Av
Ainsley Av
Bridport Av
Viking Business Centre
Danes Road
Bernard Rd
Maldon Rd
Beechfield Gardens
Braithwaite Av
Vignoles Rd
Crow Lane
Romford Cemetery
Limbourne Avenue
Warley Avenue
Rosslyn Av
Laneside Avenue
Alan Gdns
Goldsmith Avenue
Seabrook Gardens
Stanley Avenue
Torrington Road
Mount Road
Gray Av
Grosvenor Road
Whalebone La S
Temple Avenue
Pembridge Rd
WHALEBONE LANE SOUTH
Purland Cl
Rosemary Gdns
Brendon Road
Albert Rd
James Av
Emerald Gdns
Meadow Road
Bell House Road
Rush Gn
Clv Rd
RUSH
Wood Lane Sports Centre
All Saints Catholic School
A124
Barton Av
Legon Av
Lamberhurst Rd
Winifred Road
Gerald Rd
Ross Avenue
Tenterden Road
Robert Clack School
Turnage Road
Lynnett
Surgery
David Road
Joan Road
Joan Gdns
Grafton Gdns
Fordyke Rd
Gosfield Road
Terling Road
Wisdons Cl
WOOD LANE
Dagenham Civic Centre
GREEN LANE A1083
Stockdale Rd
Green La
Laburnum Health Centre
Althorne Way
Bradwell Av
Stour Rd
Central Park
Warrington Road
Walnut Tree Rd
Hitherfield Road
Bentry Road
Bentry Cl
Surgery
Morris Road
Dagenham Swimming Pool
Trefgarne Road
Calverley Crs
William Bellamy Junior & Infant School
RAINHAM ROAD NORTH A1112
Becontree Avenue
Becontree Day Hospital
Grafton Primary School
Homestead Road
Valence Junior Sch
Valence House Museum Library
Boulton Rd
Blomville Rd
Stanhope Road
Nicholas Road
Rowlands Rd
Stone Cl
Danette
Stansgate Road
Listowel Road
Bull Lane
Margery Rd
Henshawe Road
Valence Park
Grafton Road
Brittain Road
Coote Rd
Surgery
Five Elms Primary School
Marston Avenue
Uvedale Road
Kershaw Road
Listowel Road
Lawrence Crescent
Hamden Crescent
Rusholme Avenue
Fels Cl
Woodshire Rd
Highland Av
Wheel Farm Dr
Park Drive
Ely Gdns
Birch Gdns
Bell Farm Avenue
Wood Lane
Weylond Road
Dunbar
Woodshire
1 grid square represents 500 metres

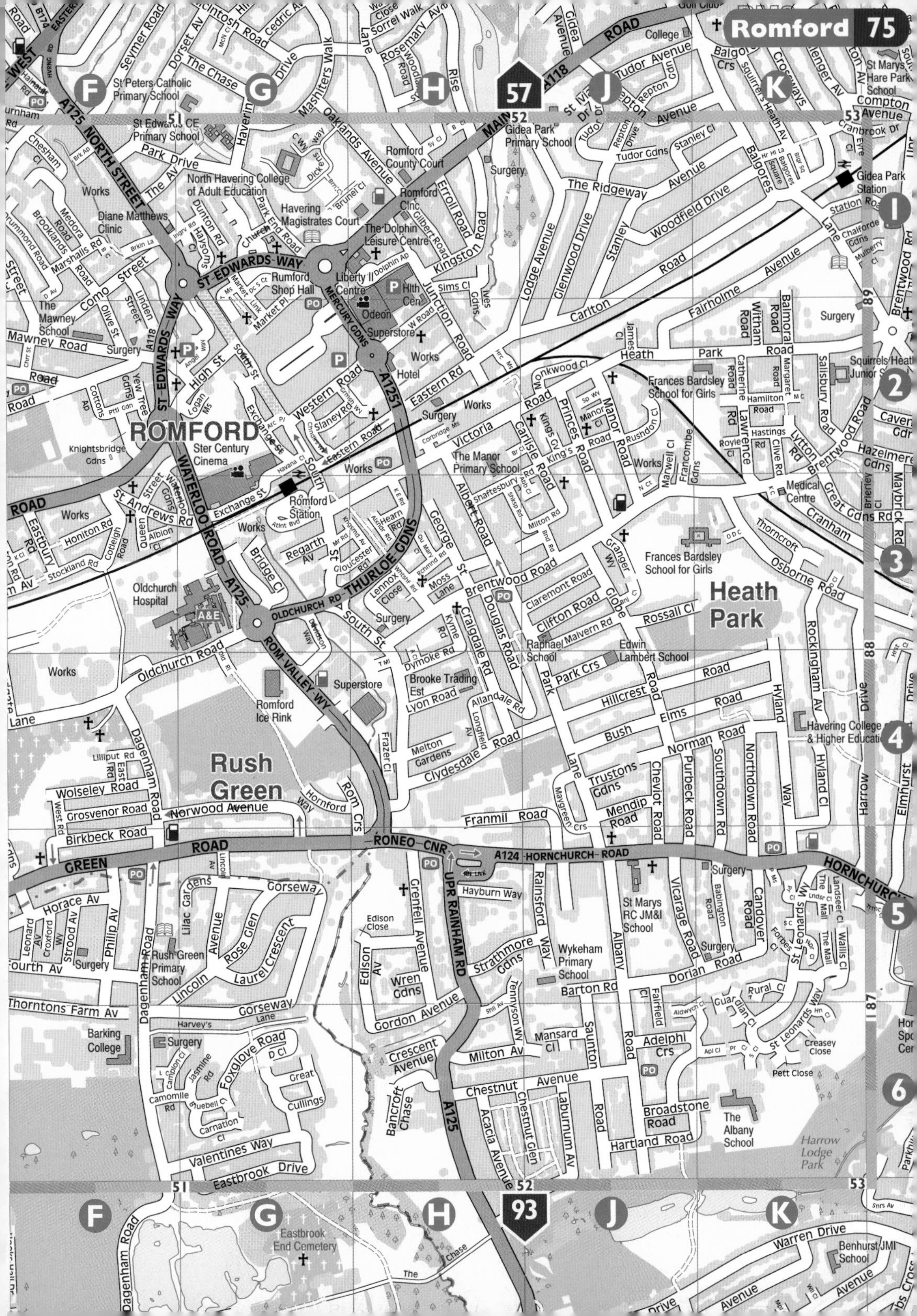
57
93
F
G
H
J
K
I
2
3
4
5
6
51
52
53
89
88
87
ROMFORD
Heath Park
Rush Green
North Havering College of Adult Education
St Peters Catholic Primary School
St Edwards CE Primary School
Gidea Park Primary School
Romford County Court
Havering Magistrates Court
The Dolphin Leisure Centre
Romford Clinic
Liberty Centre
Romford Shop Hall
Odeon
Superstore
Hotel
Works
Surgery
Diane Matthews Clinic
The Mawney School
Knightsbridge Gdns
Ster Century Cinema
Romford Station
Gidea Park Station
Oldchurch Hospital
A&E
Romford Ice Rink
Brooke Trading Est
The Manor Primary School
Frances Bardsley School for Girls
Raphael School
Edwin Lambert School
Squirrels Heath Junior School
St Marys Hare Park School
College
Medical Centre
Havering College of Further & Higher Education
St Marys RC JM&I School
Wykeham Primary School
Rush Green Primary School
Barking College
The Albany School
Harrow Lodge Park
Eastbrook End Cemetery
Benhurst JMI School
A125
A118
A1251
A124
A12
NORTH STREET
ST EDWARDS WAY
WATERLOO ROAD
MAIN ROAD
MERCURY GDNS
THURLOE GDNS
OLDCHURCH RD
ROM VALLEY WY
RONEO CNR
HORNCHURCH ROAD
UPR RAINHAM RD
GREEN ROAD
Eastern Rd
Victoria Road
South St
Western Road
Exchange St
High St
Market Pl
Como Street
Mawney Road
Cottons Ap
Park Drive
The Avenue
Havering Drive
The Chase
Mashiters Walk
Oaklands Avenue
Erroll Road
Kingston Road
Junction Road
Sims Cl
Lodge Avenue
Glenwood Drive
Stanley Avenue
Woodfield Drive
The Ridgeway
Carlton Road
Fairholme Avenue
Heath Park Road
Balgores Lane
Brentwood Road
Cranham Road
Osborne Road
Rockingham Av
Hyland Way
Harrow Drive
Manor Road
Princes Road
Carlisle Road
Albert Road
George St
Douglas Road
Craigdale Rd
Clydesdale Road
Brentwood Road
Claremont Road
Clifton Road
Malvern Rd
Rossall Cl
Park Lane
Park Crs
Hillcrest Road
Elms Road
Bush Elms Road
Norman Road
Cheviot Road
Purbeck Road
Southdown Rd
Northdown Road
Mendip Road
Franmil Road
Oldchurch Road
Dagenham Road
Wolseley Road
Grosvenor Road
Norwood Avenue
Birkbeck Road
Hornford Way
Rom Crs
Gorseway
Lilac Gardens
Rose Glen
Laurel Crescent
Lincoln Avenue
Horace Av
Fourth Av
Philip Av
Strood Av
Thorntons Farm Av
Foxglove Road
Valentines Way
Eastbrook Drive
Grenfell Avenue
Hayburn Way
Edison Av
Wren Gdns
Gordon Avenue
Crescent Avenue
Bancroft Chase
Milton Av
Chestnut Avenue
Acacia Avenue
Laburnum Av
Strathmore Gdns
Rainsford Way
Albany Road
Saunton Road
Broadstone Road
Hartland Road
Vicarage Road
Candover Road
Dorian Road
Barton Rd
Adelphi Crs
St Leonards Way
Warren Drive

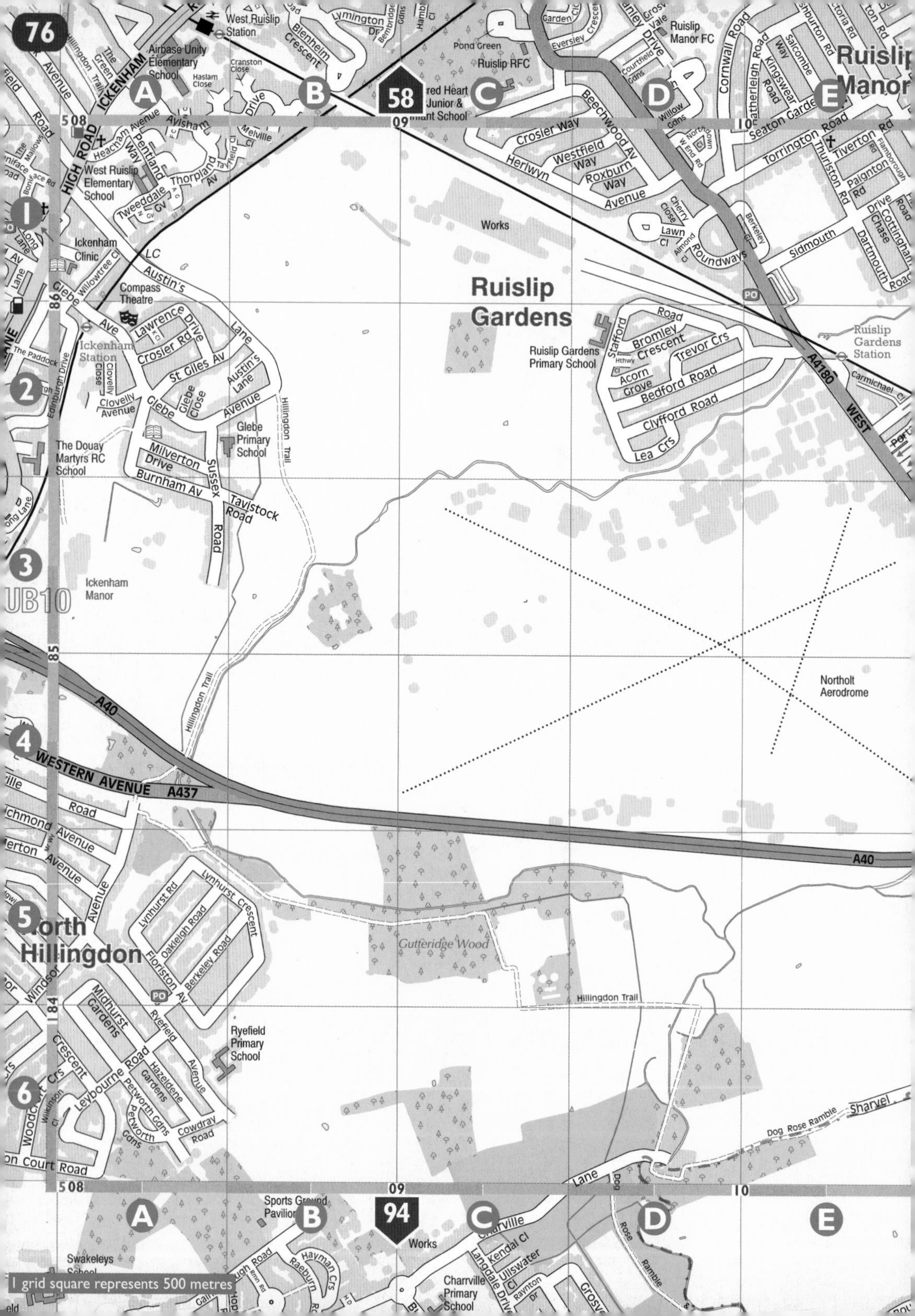
West Ruislip Station
Airbase Unity Elementary School
ICKENHAM
HIGH ROAD
Blenheim Crescent
Lymington Dr
Pond Green
Ruislip RFC
Sacred Heart Junior & Infant School
58
Ruislip Manor FC
Ruislip Manor
Cornwall Road
Kingsweal Road
Salcombe Way
Seaton Gardens
Torrington Road
Tiverton Rd
Thurlston Rd
Paignton Rd
Aylsham
Heacham Avenue
Pentland Way
West Ruislip Elementary School
Tweeddale Gv
Thorpland Av
Crosier Way
Beechwood Av
Westfield Way
Roxburn Way
Herlwyn Avenue
Cherry Close
Lawn Cl
Almond Cl
Roundways
Berkeley Cl
Sidmouth
Dartmouth Road
Cottingham Chase
Works
Ickenham Clinic
Willowtree Cl
LC
Austin's Lane
Glebe Ave
Compass Theatre
Lawrence Drive
Crosier Rd
St Giles Av
Ickenham Station
Clovelly Close
Clovelly Avenue
Glebe Close
Glebe Avenue
Glebe Primary School
Hillingdon Trail
Ruislip Gardens
Stafford Road
Bromley Crescent
Trevor Crs
Acorn Grove
Bedford Road
Clyfford Road
Lea Crs
Ruislip Gardens Primary School
Ruislip Gardens Station
Carmichael Cl
A4180
WEST
The Paddock
Edinburgh Drive
The Douay Martyrs RC School
Milverton Drive
Burnham Av
Sussex Road
Tavistock Road
UB10
Ickenham Manor
Northolt Aerodrome
A40
WESTERN AVENUE
A437
Richmond Avenue
Road
Avenue
North Hillingdon
Windsor
Lynhurst Rd
Lynhurst Crescent
Oakleigh Road
Berkeley Road
Floriston Av
PO
Ryefield Avenue
Ryefield Primary School
Midhurst Gardens
Leybourne Road
Hazeldene Gardens
Petworth Gdns
Cowdray Road
Crescent
Woodcroft Crs
Court Road
Gutteridge Wood
Hillingdon Trail
Dog Rose Ramble
Sharvel
Lane
508
09
10
A
B
C
D
E
1
2
3
4
5
6
86
85
84
Sports Ground Pavilion
94
Works
Charville Lane
Kendal Cl
Ullswater Cl
Langdale Drive
Charville Primary School
Hayman Crs
Raeburn
Swakeleys School
Rose Ramble
1 grid square represents 500 metres

Roxbourne Middle School
59
Field End Primary School
Surgery
Whitby Road
Oxford Dr
St Andrews Close
Mount
Parkfield Crs
Torbay Road
Exeter Road
Lynton
Lulworth Gardens
Clovelly Wy
Kings Road
Alexandra School
Avenue Clinic
Bempton Drive
Lynmouth Drive
Victoria
Whitby Road
Shaldon Drive
Barnstaple Road
Queens Walk
Crest Gdns
Hunters Hill
Hillcroft Crescent
Pleasant
East Mead
Primary School
Field End Road
Dunster Way
Lynwood Cl
Malvern
Avenue
Leamington Crescent
Hamilton Crs
Merlins Av
Minehead Rd
Rooks Heath
Torcross Av
Appledore
Exmouth Road
Bideford Road
Hartland Drive
Melthorne Drive
West Mead Clinc
Med Cen
Fairway
Abbot Close
Brackenbridge Drive
White Butts Road
Rufus Cl
Bec Cl
Thistledene Av
Stuart Avenue
Veldene Wy
Stiven Crs
Primrose Close
Mirren Cl
Bodmin Close
Eastcote
Medical Cen
Lane
Tregenna
Bridgwater Road
Manningtree Rd
Braintree Road
Tiptree Rd
West Mead
The Croft
Crossway
The Vale
Down Barns Road
Long Drive
Royal Crescent
Palace Rd
Rosebery Av
Brookside
Kenilworth Avenue
Ivy Close
Walton Avenue
Ludlow Close
Carlyon
Corfe Av
South Ruislip
Braintree Road Industrial Estate
Angus Drive
Rydal Wy
Jubilee Drive
Princes Way
Diamond Rd
The Ct
Holyrood Avenue
Warwick Avenue
Earlsmead
Harrow Borough FC
Earlsmead First & Middle School
Works
Long Drive
Deanesfield Primary School
Queensmead School
Road
Superstore
Arundel
South Ruislip Station
Victoria
Queensmead Sports Centre
Victoria Road
Crown Rd
Stonefield Cl
Stonefield Way
Walton Av
Somervell
Trenchard Av
Odyssey Business Park
The Runway
Superstore
Civic Way
Crown Rd
Victoria Retail Park
Bradfield Road
Field End Rd
END ROAD
Cavendish Av
Canfield Dr
Dudley Dr
Bourne Court
Station Approach
Primrose Gdns
Manor Gardens
Great Central Avenue
Greenacre Cl
Martin Drive
Mallet Dr
Gaylor Road
Silverdale Cl
Hornbeam
Hill
Lane
Hardy Avenue
Mahlon Avenue
Northolt Avenue
Deane Avenue
Bourne Avenue
Edwards Avenue
Priors Gardens
Cedar Av
Bourne CP School
Rabournmead Drive
Wilsmere Dr
Sandown Way
Medical Cen
Doncaster Drive
Hurst Cl
78
Wingfield Way
Frazer Av
Nairn Rd
South Pk Way
Fld End
Newbury Way
Northolt High School
Newbury Close
Dabbs
Walnut Way
Masson Avenue
Mandeville Special School
Haydock Av
Weldon Cl
Warsaw Cl
Glebe Avenue
Hillingdon
Ealing
Willow Tree Primary School
Arnold Fld
Stroud
Attewood Rd
Abbott Close
Millway Gdns
Mandeville Special School
Eastcote Lane
Priors Farm
Laymead Close
New Park Close
Fortunes Mead
Cowings Mead
Road
Eastcote
Moat Farm Road
The Farmlands
WESTERN AVENUE
Gauntlet Close
Yeoman Rd
Manor
UB5
Lane
C & L Leisure Centre
Islip Manor
Islip Gdns
Dog Rose Ramble
Golf Course
C & L Golf & Country Club
Harvey Road
A40
Dukes Av
Manor Av
Alderney Gardens
Lytton Cl
Kng Dr
MANDEVILLE ROAD
WEST END ROAD
Northolt Primary School
John Chilton School
Harewood Av
A312
CHURCH ROAD
Church Rd
Ealing
Golf Course
Kingston Close
Vicarage Cl
Dog Rose Ramble
Compton Crs
Compton Leisure Centre
Walford Secondary School
Bishops Drive
Eskdale Avenue
Rectory Gdns
Lane
Downe Barns Farm
Lime Trees Park Golf Club
Irving Av
Bengarth Road
Godfrey Av
Garden Close
Gulliver Close
Henson Place
Maurier Close
Laing Dean
Perry Garth
Laughton Road
Hindhead Gdns
Hawthorn Farm Av
Canford Av
Lilliput Av
A4180
RUISLIP ROAD
Bancroft Court
Thorndike Avenue
Kentford Way
ROAD
Clifford
Makepeace Rd
Huxley Close
Road
Vanbrough Crs
Rubens Road
Lynne Wy
CHURCH
95
Parkfield Road
Parkfield Close
Hazelmere Wk
Dolphin Rd
Hazelmere Rd
Hazelmere Close
Hazelmere Drive
Barn Close
Grange Ct
Edward
Watery Lane
Newdene Av
Church
Academy Gdns
Parkfield Drive
Gifford Primary School
Kensington
St Raphaels School
Greenhill Gdns

78
Roxeth
South Harrow
Northolt
60
77
96
A
B
C
D
E
1
2
3
4
5
6
513
14
15
184
Alexandra Avenue Clinic
Alexandra School
Newton Close
Learner Drive
Roxbourne Medical Centre
Eastleigh Avenue
Coles Crescent
Swift Cl
Franklins Ms
Works
Archdale Business Cen
Brember Rd
Stanley
Sherwood Road
Police Stn
Council Building
Roxeth Hill
Harrow School
Bowden House Clinic
Park
Georgian Way
Mount Pk Avenue
College
Cowen Avenue
Jullan Hill
Sandringham Crs
Alexandra Avenue
Merlins Av
Minehead Road
Tithe Farm Close
Tithe Farm Av
Rooks Heath School
Roxeth Manor First School
Eastcote Lane
Eastcote Lane Cem
Cross Rd
Rowe Wk
Windsor Close
Windsor Crs
Medical Centre
Tregenna Avenue
Carlyon
Corfe Av
Balmoral
Earlsmead
Harrow Borough FC
Earlsmead First Middle School
Arundel
Somervell Road
The Heights
Lane
Park Lane
Park Mead
Torrington Drive
Brendon Gdns
Paddocks Close
Beechwood Av
Northolt Road Clinic
Middle School
Northolt Road
A312
Roxeth Gv
Wood End Av
Westwood Av
Cadogan Cl
Stroud Ga
Northolt Rd
Whitby Road
Eastcote Road
Scarsdale Rd
Kingsley Road
Wargrave Rd
Parkfield Road
South Harrow Station
Brooke Av
South Hl Av
Sackville Cl
Arden Cl
Ashneal Gdns
Ingleby Dr
The Purcell School
Orley Farm School
South Hill Avenue
Wendela Ct
Gooden Court
Fircroft Gdns
A4005
Harrow Field Gardens
South Hill Av
Runnelfield
Orley Farm Road
Harrow Cricket Club
South Vale
Tyrell Cl
Hartington Cl
Cavendish Avenue
Wood End
Harrow
Ealing
East
Northolt Park Station
Acock Grove
Hollydale Cl
Halsbury Rd W.
Halsbury Road
Dorchester Rd
Clauson Avenue
Russell Road
Killowen Avenue
Gdns
Bannister Close
Ealing Northern Sports Centre
Sudbury Hill Station
Greenford Road
A4090
Pett's Hill
Surgery
Dane mead Gv
Reading Road
Whitton Av West
Wood End Gdns
Wood End Way
Mary Peters Dr
Bedser Drive
Lilian Board Wy
Primary School
Wood End J&I Schools
Merton Av
Keble Cl
Dimmock Drive
Vernon Rise
Greenford Green Clinic
Gainsborough Gdns
Wincanton Crs
Newmarket Avenue
Bangor Cl
Infant School
Mildred Av
Wood End Lane
Ascot Close
Plumpton Close
Kempton Avenue
Ripon Cl
Redcar Close
Wetherby Cl
Haydock Av
Southwell Close
Thirsk Close
Cheltenham
Sussex Crescent
Lewes Close
Tenby Gdns
Eastcote Lane Nth
Mandeville Special School
Northolt Swimarama
Mandeville Road
Surgery
Briar Crs
Ribblesdale Av
Castle
Blenheim Road
Lancaster Road
Newnham Cl
Newnham Gdns
Barnabas Medical Cen
Girton Road
Gorville Crs
Oriel Way
Girton Close
Clamis Way
The Fairway
Carr Road
Currey Road
Wadham Gardens
Worcester Gdns
Rothesay Av
Clare Road
Hadden Way
Malden Avenue
Rugby Av
Oldfield Lane North
Berkeley Avenue
Ennismore Avenue
Sherwood
Burwell Av
Horsenden Primary School
Berkeley Av
The Farmlands
Moat Farm Road
Northolt Station
Carr Road
Road
Auriol Drive
Grand Union Canal
Belvue Cl
Belvue Road
Belvue Business Cen
Cherry Gdns
Sandringham Rd
Summit Rd
Court Farm Rd
Ealing Road
Church Rd
Vicarage
Fort Rd
Dog Rose Ramble
Rowdell Road
Rectory Gdns
Fairway Dr
Station Approach
Allington Close
Taunton Road
Derby Road
Greenford Industrial Estate
Halifax Road
Hill
Drive
Birkbeck Avenue
Stanley Avenue
Lincoln Close
Rise
Belle Vue
Birkbeck Way
Hillbeck Wy
Greenford Station
Rockware Business Cen
Works
Uneeda Drive
Rockware
Bennetts Avenue
Lyon Way
Bridport Road
Bristol Road
Norwich Road
Field Way
Kelvin Ind Est
Superstore
Long Drive
Chartwell Cl
Olympic Wy
Jeymer Drive
Oldfield La North
Ingram Way
Oldfield Farm Gdns
Community Rd
Courthope Rd
Downing Drive
Greenford Road Medical Centre
Belvue School
Ealing Rd
A40
Western Avenue
Dolphin Rd
Hazelmere Rd
Hotspur Rd
Farrier Road
Meadow Close
Union Road
Evesham Close
Chesterton Close
Melrose Av
Melrose Cl
Chinnor Crs
Bledlow Rise
Gdns
Oldfield Primary School
Middleton Avenue
Hotel
Darlington Drive
Runnymede
Conway
Cayton Rd
1 grid square represents 500 metres

Sudbury
WEMBLEY
HA0
Perivale
East Lane Business Park
Clementine Churchill Hospital
St Georges RC First & Middle School
Surgery
Thomas a'Beckett Close
Sudbury Hill (Harrow Station)
SUDBURY HILL
SUDBURY COURT DRIVE A4127
WATFORD ROAD
A404
HARROW ROAD
A4005
A4088
EAST LANE
Wembley High School
Playing Fields
Sudbury Court Sports Club
Community Centre
North Wembley Station
Council Building
Works
Vale Farm Sports Centre
Wembley FC
Perrin Road Clnc
Sudbury Primary School
Sudbury & Harrow Road Station
Barham Park
Health Centre
Lancelot Medical Cen
Police Station
Fire Station
Wembley Hospital
Ambulance Station
Barham Primary School
Sudbury Town Station
A4090
WHITTON AVENUE EAST
BRIDGEWATER ROAD
Horsenden Hill Golf Club
Sudbury Golf Club
Golf Course
Alperton Cem
Alperton High School
Abercorn Trading Estate
Alperton Station
Grand Union Canal
Phoenix Trading Est
Superstore
Capital Business Centre
Athlon Industrial Estate
Perivale Industrial Park
Perivale Ind Park
Perivale Station
Selborne School
Fleetway Business Park
Sheraton Business Cen
Silicon Business Cen
Primary School
Horsenden Lane North
Horsenden Lane South
Rosebank Avenue
Fernbank Av
Maybank Avenue
Greenbank Av
Eastcote Avenue
District Road
Central Road
Saunderton Road
Roundtree Road
Harrow Road
Chaplin Road
Farm Avenue
Eagle Road
Bowrons Ave
Braemar Av
Jordan Road
Bilton Road
Jubilee Road
George V Way
Walmgate Road
Fraser Rd
Federal Rd
Wadsworth Road
Tavistock Av
Colwyn Av
Woodhouse Av
Buckingham Av
Sunley Gdns
Ashness Gdns
Orchard Gate
Woodland Rise
Robin Hood Way
Drew Gdns
Bourne View
Cambridge Av
Elton Avenue
Northwood Gdns
Priory Gdns
Priory Crs
Homefield Road
Medway Gdns
Eton Avenue
Rugby Avenue
Beaumont Avenue
Charterhouse Avenue
Sylvester Road
Pettsgrove Av
Crawford Avenue
Copland Av
Talbot Road
Napier Road
Ranelagh Road
Swinderby Road
Norton Road
Scarle Road
Thurlby Road
Bassingham Road
Holland Road
Danethorpe Rd
Lincoln Rd
Lancelot Road
Llanover Road
Harrowdene Road
Sudbury Avenue
Peel Road
Byron Road
Oldborough Road
Holt Road
Blockley Road
Paxford Road
Carlton Avenue
Pasture Road
Bengeworth Road
Elms Lane
Mulgrave Road
Pebworth Road
Stilecroft Gardens
Woodfield Avenue
West Avenue
Langham Gardens
Shelley Gdns
Hutchinson Ter
Clarendon Gdns
Meadow Way
Keswick Gdns
Milford Gdns
Lantern Road
Market
Mosque
Cem
F G H J K
1 2 3 4 5 6
16 17 18
61
80
97
EALING ROAD
A4089

1 grid square represents 500 metres

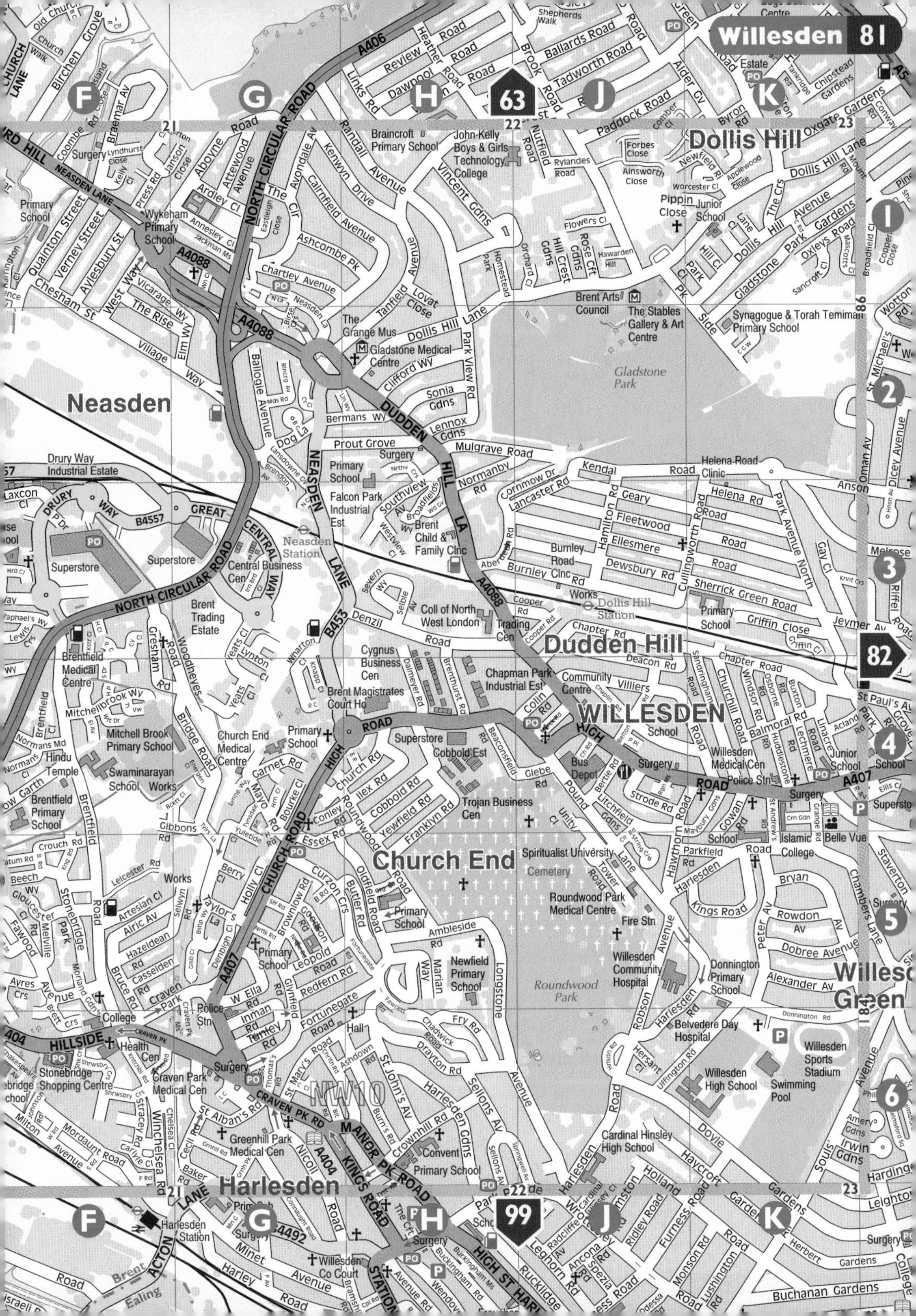
Dollis Hill
Neasden
Dudden Hill
WILLESDEN
Church End
Harlesden
Willesden Green
Gladstone Park
Roundwood Park
NW10
63
82
99
North Circular Road
A406
A4088
A407
A404
B453
B4557
B4492
Neasden Lane
Dudden Hill La
High Road
Church Road
Craven Pk Rd
Manor Pk Road
Kings Road
Harlesden Road
Dollis Hill Lane
Dollis Hill Avenue
Gladstone Park Gardens
Park View Rd
Mulgrave Road
Kendal Road
Denzil Road
Chapter Road
Sherrick Green Road
Neasden Station
Dollis Hill Station
Harlesden Station
Brent Arts Council
The Stables Gallery & Art Centre
The Grange Mus
Gladstone Medical Centre
Coll of North West London
Brent Magistrates Court Ho
Brent Trading Estate
Drury Way Industrial Estate
Cygnus Business Cen
Chapman Park Industrial Est
Trojan Business Cen
Spiritualist University
Cemetery
Roundwood Park Medical Centre
Willesden Community Hospital
Willesden Sports Stadium
Swimming Pool
Willesden High School
Cardinal Hinsley High School
Stonebridge Shopping Centre
Hindu Temple
Swaminarayan School
Islamic College
Belle Vue
Willesden Medical Cen
Bus Depot
Fire Stn
Superstore
Braincroft Primary School
John Kelly Boys & Girls Technology College
Wykeham Primary School
Mitchell Brook Primary School
Brentfield Primary School
Newfield Primary School
Donnington Primary School
Synagogue & Torah Temimah Primary School
Convent Primary School
Belvedere Day Hospital
Greenhill Park Medical Cen
Craven Park Medical Cen
Willesden Co Court
Brent
Ealing
F
G
H
J
K
1
2
3
4
5
6
21
22
23

82
81
64
100
86
A
B
C
D
E
1
2
3
4
5
6
NW2
NW6
Cricklewood
Brondesbury
Brondesbury Park
Willesden Green
Kilburn
Kensal Rise
Queens Park
EDGWARE ROAD CRICKLEWOOD BROADWAY
CRICKLEWOOD BROADWAY
CRICKLEWOOD LANE
HENDON WAY
FINCHLEY ROAD
WALM LANE
CHICHELE ROAD
SHOOT-UP HILL
WILLESDEN LANE
KILBURN HIGH ROAD
BRONDESBURY ROAD
IVERSON ROAD
FORTUNE GN RD
QUEX RD
A5
A41
A407
A4003
B150
B451
B520
Barnet
Camden
Brent
Clitterhouse Primary School
Cricklewood Station
Cricklewood Trading Estate
Broadway Retail Park
Britannia Business Centre
The Mosque & Islamic Centre of Brent
Childs Hill Primary School
All Saints CE Primary School
Greenfield Medical Centre
Welbeck Clinic
Hampstead School
Cemetery
Anson Primary School
Cricklewood Synagogue
Walm Lane Clinic
Willesden Green Station
Mulberry House Sch
Kilburn Station
Brondesbury Station
West Hampstead Station
Mill Lane Medical Cen
Solent Road Health Cen
Shomrei Hadath Synagogue
Police Stn
Tricycle Cinema
Kingsgate Primary School
North West London Jewish J&I School
Council Building
London Welsh School
Emb of Senegal
Cricket Ground
South Hampstead Cricket Club
Avenue Primary School
Brondesbury College for Boys
Malorees Junior & Infant School
Queens Park Community School GM
Brondesbury Park Station
Islamia Girls School
Bus Park
Coll of North West London
Charteris Road Sports Centre
Kilburn Square
St Marys RC Primary School
Kilburn Park Stn
Queens Park Station
Park House Medical Centre
Kensal Rise
Willesden Sports Stadium
Belle Vue
Superstore
Synagogue
Surgery
Works
1 grid square represents 500 metres

West Heath
Vale of Health
HAMPSTEAD
Hampstead Pond
Whitestone Pond
Parliament Hill
Parliament Hill Fields Athletics Track
Hampstead Hill School
Hampstead Heath Stn
Keats House Museum
Royal Free Hospital
Belsize Park Stn
Maitland Park
The Village School
West Hampstead
Finchley Road & Frognal Station
Hampstead Cricket Club
Finchley Road Station
West Hampstead Station
South Hampstead
Swiss Cottage Stn
South Hampstead Station
Kilburn High Road Station
Primrose Hill
St John's Wood
Hampstead Theatre
Freud Mus
The Portman Clinic
Tavistock Clinic
Belsize Square Synagogue
South Hampstead Synagogue
Chalk Farm Station
Heath Street
Rosslyn Hill
Haverstock Hill
Finchley Road
Fitzjohn's Avenue
Belsize Road
Adelaide Road
Avenue Road
Prince Albert Road
Abbey Road
Hilgrove Road
Fleet Rd
Agincourt Rd
Mansfield Road
Malden Road
Constantine Rd
Pond St
Willow Road
Christchurch Hill
Frognal Lane
Arkwright Road
Lyndhurst Road
Wedderburn Rd
Belsize Av
Belsize Pk Gardens
Lambolle Rd
Eton Av
Fellows Road
Aberdare Gardens
Goldhurst Ter
Springfield Road
Boundary Road
Greville
Regent's Park Track
Grand Union Canal
Outer Circle
65
84
101
26
27
28

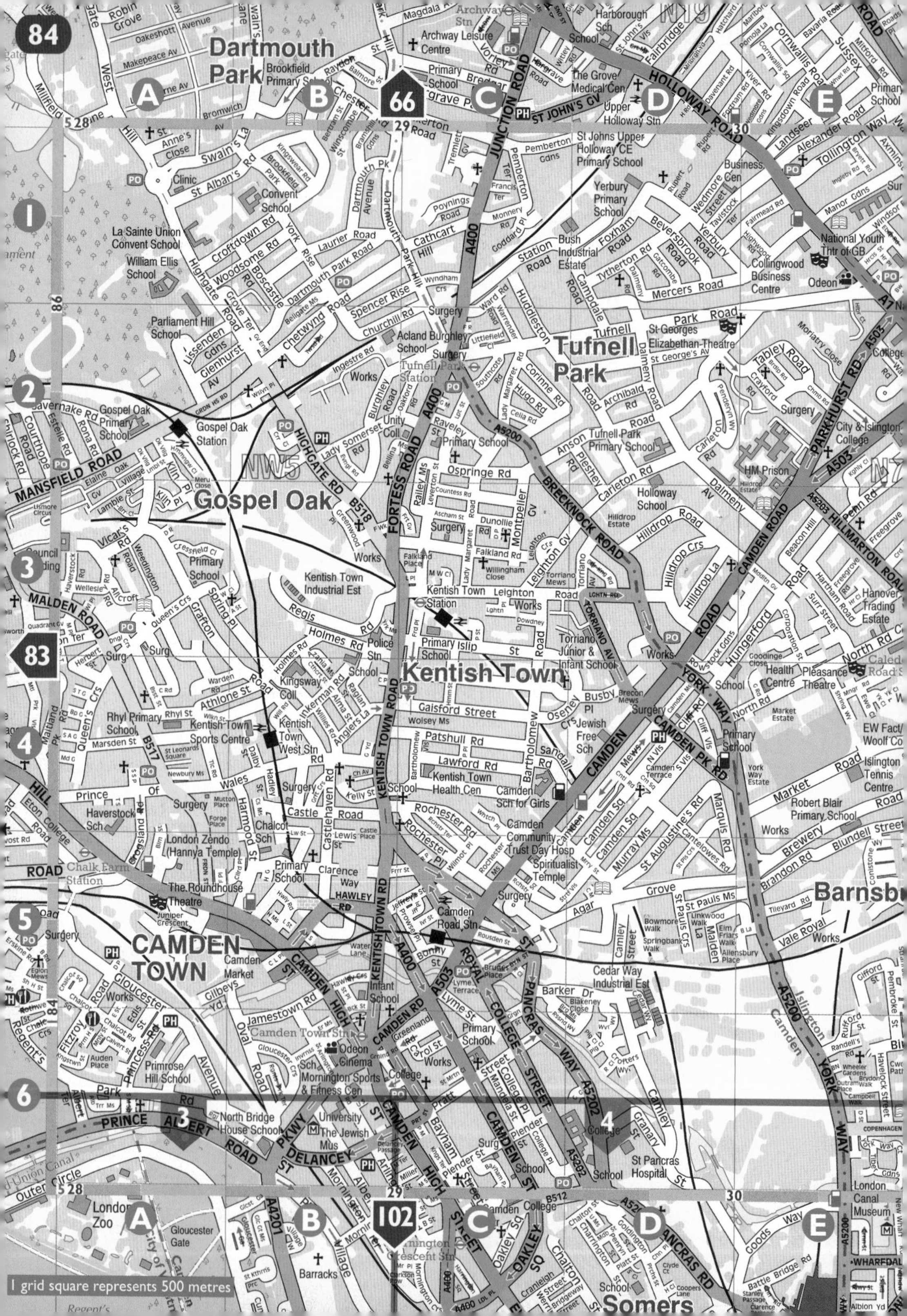

1 grid square represents 500 metres

Lower Holloway
Highbury
Canonbury
ISLINGTON
Hoxton
N5
N1
67
86
103
Park Station
Finsbury Park
Blackstock Road
Seven Sisters Road
Isledon Rd
Hornsey Road
Holloway Road
Tollington Road
Caledonian Road
Liverpool Road
Upper Street
Essex Road
Canonbury Road
Highbury Grove
Highbury Park
St Paul's Rd
Balls Pond Road
New North Road
Southgate Road
Albion Road
Newington Grn Rd
Mildmay Grove North
Northchurch Road
Baring Street
Eagle Whf Road
Clissold Park
Clissold Leisure Cen
Arsenal Station
Arsenal FC (Highbury)
Drayton Park Station
Highbury Fields
Highbury Pool
Highbury & Islington Stn
Highbury Corner
Canonbury Stn
Caledonian Road & Barnsbury Stn
Essex Road Station
Holloway Road Stn
Islington Town Hall
Almeida Thtr
Kings Head Thtr
Little Angel Thtr
Tower Theatre
Theatre De Complicite
HM Prison
Magistrates Court
Council Building
The Business Design Cen
Islington Bus Cen
Canonbury Bus Cen
N1 Shopping Centre
The Anna Scher Thtr
Crafts Council
Britannia Leisure Centre
Ecclesbourne Primary School
Highbury Grove School
Highbury Fields School
St Andrews Primary School
Sobell Leisure Centre
Aksaray Sports Club
Trabzon Spor FC
Clissold Crs
Carysfort Road
Grosvenor Av
Compton Rd
Alwyne Road
Barnsbury Park
Barnsbury Sq
Thornhill Road
Richmond Av
Cloudesley Rd
Chapel Market
White Lion St
Noel Road
Danbury St
Packington St
Arlington Av
Downham Rd
Englefield Road
Ockendon Road
Mitchison Rd
Petherton Road
Poet's Rd
Ferntower Rd
Pyrland Rd
Beresford Road
Aberdeen Park
Highbury New Park
Riversdale Road
Gillespie Road
Elwood St
Aubert Park
Drayton Park
Benwell Road
Hornsey Rd
Roman Way
Mackenzie Road
Sheringham Rd
Huntingdon Street
Bridgeman Road
Hemingford Road
Carnegie St
Muriel St
Rodney Street
Killick St
Collier St
Maygood St
Tolpuddle St
Duncan St
Vincent Terrace
Mintern St
Buckland St
Poole St
Bridport Place
Penn St
Wilton Sq
Shepperton Rd
Elmore St
Oakley Road
Ufton Rd
Lawford Rd

86
STOKE NEWINGTON
68
85
104
7
A
B
C
D
E
1
2
3
4
5
6
34
35
533
Shacklewell
Hackney Downs
Kingsland
Dalston
De Beauvoir Town
HACKNEY
South Hackney
London Fields
E5
E8
NORTHWOLD ROAD
UPPER CLAPTON ROAD
LOWER CLAPTON ROAD
STOKE NEWINGTON HIGH ST
STOKE NEWINGTON ROAD
KINGSLAND HIGH ST
KINGSLAND ROAD
RECTORY ROAD
ALBION ROAD
BALLS POND ROAD
DALSTON LANE
A1207 GRAHAM ROAD
AMHURST RD
PEMBURY RD A104
CRICKETFIELD RD
MARE STREET
MORNING LANE
WELL ST
VICTORIA PARK ROAD
URSWICK RD
QUEENSBRIDGE ROAD
SOUTHGATE ROAD
Queensbridge Road
Downs Park Road
Sandringham Road
Shacklewell La
Evering Road
Brooke Road
Southwold Road
Cleveleys Road
Amhurst Rd
Foulden Rd
Sydner Rd
Barbauld Road
Howard Road
Matthias Rd
Mildmay Road
Ridley Road
Richmond Road
Lansdowne Drive
Forest Rd
Middleton Road
Albion Drive
Haggerston Road
Regent's Row
Whiston Road
Andrews Road
Kingsland Shopping Cen
Hackney Downs Stn
Hackney Ctrl Stn
London Fields Stn
Dalston Kingsland Stn
Rectory Road Station
Hackney Empire Variety Thtr
Town Hall
Sutton House
Haggerston Swimming Pool
Homerton House School
Lower Clapton Health Centre
1 grid square represents 500 metres

Lea Bridge
Clapton
Clapton Park
Hackney Marsh
Temple Mills
Hackney Wick
Homerton
Old Ford
Victoria Park
Stratford Marsh
BOW
Orient Ind Park
Leyton Orient FC (Matchroom Stadium)
New Spitalfields Market
Hackney Sports Centre
Homerton Hospital
Hackney Hospital
Homerton Stn
Hackney Wick Station
Pudding Mill Lane Station
Carpenters Business Park
Bow Industrial Park
Marshgate Trading Estate
Victoria Park Industrial Cen
Crown Close Business Cen
Axis Business Centre
Sorsby Health Cen
Mandeville Primary School
Cardinal Pole RC School
Cardinal Pole RC Secondary Lower School
St Dominics RC J&I School
Gainsborough Primary School
Lauriston Primary School
Mother Baby Clnc
Council Building
Victory Works
Leisure Cen
Roman Indoor Mkt
A104 LEA BRIDGE
A102 HOMERTON HIGH STREET
HOMERTON ROAD B112
MARSH HILL
A106 EASTWAY
EASTWAY
RUCKHOLT ROAD
CHAPMAN ROAD
WICK ROAD
KENWORTHY ROAD
CASSLAND ROAD
VICTORIA PARK ROAD
EAST CROSS ROUTE
WHITE POST LANE A115
CARPENTERS
OLD FORD ROAD B118
GROVE ROAD A1205
PARNELL ROAD
TREDEGAR RD
FAIRFIELD ROAD
A12
Orient Way
Temple Mills Lane
Quartermile Lane
Waterden Road
Lee Conservancy Road
River Lea or Lee
Lee Navigation
Thames Path
Hackney
Newham
Tower Hamlets
St Marks Gate
Marshgate Lane
Wansbeck Rd
Wick Lane
Cadogan Terrace
Osborne Rd
Trowbridge Rd
Felstead St
Eastway
Oriel Road
Hassett Road
Ballance Road
Redwald Road
Overbury Street
Glyn Road
Mandeville St
Oswald St
Elderfield Road
Lockhurst Street
Brooksby's Walk
Coopersale Road
Mabley St
Kingsmead Wy
Buckingham Road
Oliver Road
Dunedin Road
Lyttelton Rd
Windsor Rd
Clays Lane
F
G
H
J
K
36
37
38
69
88
105
2
3
4
5
6

88
70
87
106
A
B
C
D
E
1
2
3
4
5
6
538
39
40
86
84
LEYTON
Forest Gate
Stratford New Town
STRATFORD
Stratford Marsh
HIGH ROAD LEYTON
A112
LEYTON ROAD
ANGEL LANE
LEYTONSTONE RD
HIGH ROAD
A11
THE GROVE
WATER LANE
ROMFORD ROAD
A118
CHOBHAM ROAD
MAJOR RD
EASTERN ROAD
BROADWAY
HIGH ST
VICARAGE LA
WEST HAM LANE
NEW PLAISTOW RD
PLAISTOW ROAD
PORTWAY
B165
STOPFORD ROAD
A114
MANOR ROAD
GROVE GREEN RD
A106 WARREN ROAD
RUCKHOLT RD
HARROW ROAD
B161
DAMES ROAD
A12
B164
Cemetery
Superstore
Langthorne Hospital
Drapers Sports Ground
Stratford Station
Stratford Shopping Cen
Maryland Stn
Forest Gate Station
Plaistow Station
West Ham Park
Atherton Leisure Centre
Ramgarhia Sikh Gurdwara Temple
Axis Business Centre
Vanguard Trading Est
Marsh Gate Business Centre
Channelsea Business
1 grid square represents 500 metres

F
G
H
J
K
71
41
42
43
90
107
1
2
3
4
5
6
City of London Cemetery
City of London Crematorium
Wanstead Flats
Centenary Walk
ALDERSBROOK ROAD
FOREST DRIVE
A117
A116
E12
E7
NORTH CIRCULAR ROAD
Heronga
St Margaret's Road
Surgery
Park Avenue
Empress
Merlin Road
Avenue
Heatherwood Close
Aldersbrook Lane
Daines Close
A118
Capel Road
Tylney Road
Cranmer Road
Latimer Road
Lorne Road
Ridley Road
Chestnut Avenue
Forest Side
Barwick
Godwin Road
Godwin Junior Sch
Wanstead Park Stn
Kubrick Business Estate
Sebert Road
Woodgrange Infant School
Works
Balmoral Road
Manor Park Crematorium
Manor Park Cemetery
Manor Park Station
The Chase
Whitta Road
Gladding Road
Forest View Road
Rabbits Rd
Washington Av
Romford Rd
Carlyle Road
Ravandos Sikh Temple
Mosque
Manor Park
Station Rd
Durham Road
Albany Road
Carlton Road
Manor Pk
Clarence Road
Avenue Primary School
High St North
Snowshill Road
Nine Acres Close
Church Rd
First Avenue
Second Avenue
Third Avenue
Fourth Avenue
Fifth Avenue
Sixth Avenue
Seventh Avenue
Eighth Avenue
Harcourt Avenue
Sheringham Avenue
Dersingham Avenue
LTL Ilford Lane
B165
Junior School
Wolferton Rd
Trevelyan Av
Dersingham Infant School
Primary School
London Sri Murugan Temple
Morris Av
Little Ilford School
Rectory Road
Church
Hampton Road
Osborne Road
Claremont Road
Windsor Road
Richmond Road
Claremont Clinic
Romford Road
Woodgrange Park Stn
Salisbury Road
Bluebell Avenue
Woodgrange Park Cemetery
Queensberry Pl
Tenbury Cl
Quakers Pl
Police Station
Post Office
Green Street
Sandringham Road
Primary School
Henderson Rd
Katherine Road Medical Centre
Health Cen
Rosedale Road
Birchdale Road
Nigel Road
Monega Primary School
Sherrard Road
Halley Road
Monega Road
Strone Road
Shrewsbury Road
Plashet Jewish Cemetery
Warwick Road
Berkeley Road
Stanley Road
Coleridge Avenue
Ruskin Avenue
Goldsmith Avenue
Rosebery Avenue
Sheridan Road
Browning Road
Dashmesh Darbar Sikh Temple
Shakespeare Crescent
Kensington Avenue
Upton La
Palmerston Rd
Westbury Road
Vale Road
Glenparke Road
Whyteville Road
Medical Centre
Studley Road
Kitchener Road
Grosvenor Road
RC Sch
6th Form Centre
St George's Road
Sherrard
Halley
Monega
Strone
South Esk Road
B167
Green Street
Colston Rd
Clifton Rd
Bath Rd
Prim School
Bristol Road
Stafford Road
Woodhouse Grove
Plashet
Shelley Avenue
Byron Avenue
Kensington Avenue
Gladstone Avenue
East Avenue
Wordsworth Avenue
Tennyson Avenue
Shrewsbury Road Health Centre
Plashet Park
Marlborough Road
Rothsay Road
Lansdown Road
Woodstock Road
Derby Road
Rutland Road
Chester Road
Prestbury Road
Cromwell Road
Shaftesbury Road
Surgery
Primary School
B109
Elmhurst Road
Elmhurst Primary School
Upton Park Road
Upton
Independent School
East Ham Memorial Hospl
Plashet School
Plashet Grove
Sibley Grove
East Ham Stn
Keppel Road
Bridge Road
Shoebury Road
Springfield Road
Northfield Road
Ashford Road
Leigh Road
Wall End
Stukeley Road
Plashet Road Medical Centre
St Stephens Road
Wortley Road
School
Milton Avenue
Heigham Road
Colvin Rd
Bendish Road
Lathom Road
Lathom Junior School
Clements Road
Caulfield Road
Altmore Avenue
Altmore Infant School
Caledon Road
Skeffington Road
Holla
Plashet Road
B165
Lucas Avenue
Thorngrove Road
Pengo Road
Katherine Road
Elizabeth Road
Victoria Avenue
Lawrence Road
Outram Road
Malvern Road
Stamford Road
Oakfield Road
Ron Leighton Way
High Street North
Kempton Road
Latimer Avenue
Streatfeild Avenue
Norfolk Road
Bedford Road
Calverton Road
Gwendoline Avenue
Claude Road
Dacre Road
Harold Road
Upton Cross Primary School
Upton Park Station
Park Road
King's Rd
Redclyffe Road
William Morley Close
Primary School
Grangewood Street
Eversleigh Road
Spencer Road
Works
The Shop Hall
Wakefield Street
Campbell Road
Hartley Avenue
Aintree Avenue
Winter Av
Primary School
Queens Road West
Queen's Ter
Rochester Av
Waghorn Road
Tudor Road
Priory Rd
Surgery
Arragon Road
Abbots
St Bernard's Road
Friar's
Barking Road
A124
East Ham Leisure Cen
Wellington
Didsbury
Napier Road
Ranelagh Road
Lister Community
Southern Rd Primary School
Southern Road
Plaistow Hosp
Credon Road
Selsdon Road
Bushey Road
Upton Park
West Ham United FC (Upton Park)
Newham Medical Centre
Castle St
Cinema
Boleyn Rd
Rochford
Dickens Rd
Thackeray Road
Macaulay Road
Kimberley Avenue
Gillett Avenue
Ernald Avenue
Nelson St
College
Henry Road
Market Street
St Michaels RC Primary School
Tilbury Road
East
Central Park Road
Central
Eastern Road
Edinburgh Road
Glasgow Road
Tweedmouth Road
Stirling Road
St Mary's Road
Nightingale Clinic
Surgery

90
72
89
108
ILFORD
Little Ilford
Loxford
BARKING
Wallend
NORTH CIRCULAR ROAD
A406
HIGHBRIDGE ROAD
ILFORD LANE
A123
FANSHAWE AVENUE
NORTHERN RELIEF ROAD
LONGBRIDGE ROAD
A124
A118
WINSTON WAY
ILFORD HL
CHAPEL RD
HIGH ROAD
GREEN LANE
A1083
ALFRED'S WAY
ABBEY RD
ST PAULS RD
LONDON ROAD
Ilford Station
Barking Station
The Exchange
Ilford Retail Park
Kenneth More Theatre
Ilford Medical Cen
Cricklefield Stadium
South Park
Barking Park
Barking Abbey Comprehensive School
Eastbury Comprehensive School
Loxford School of Science and Technology
Woodlands Infant & Junior School
Hyleford School
South Park Clinic
Jamia Mosque
Singh Sabha Temple
The Vicarage Field Shopping Cen
Magistrates Court
Abbey Sports Centre
Barking Abbey Industrial Est
Fresh Wharf Est
NTGB Sports Ground
New England Industrial Est
Lyon Business Pk
Buckingham Road Cemetery
St Peter & Pauls RC Primary School
Gordon Infant School
Dersingham Infant School
Uphall Primary School
Northbury Primary School
St Margarets Primary School
St Josephs RC Primary School
Ripple Junior & Infant School
Altmore Infant School
Maytime School
Infant College
The Orchard Health Cen
Health Clinic
Medical Cen
Primary School
Langdon School
Works
Surgery
Superstore
Hotel
1 grid square represents 500 metres

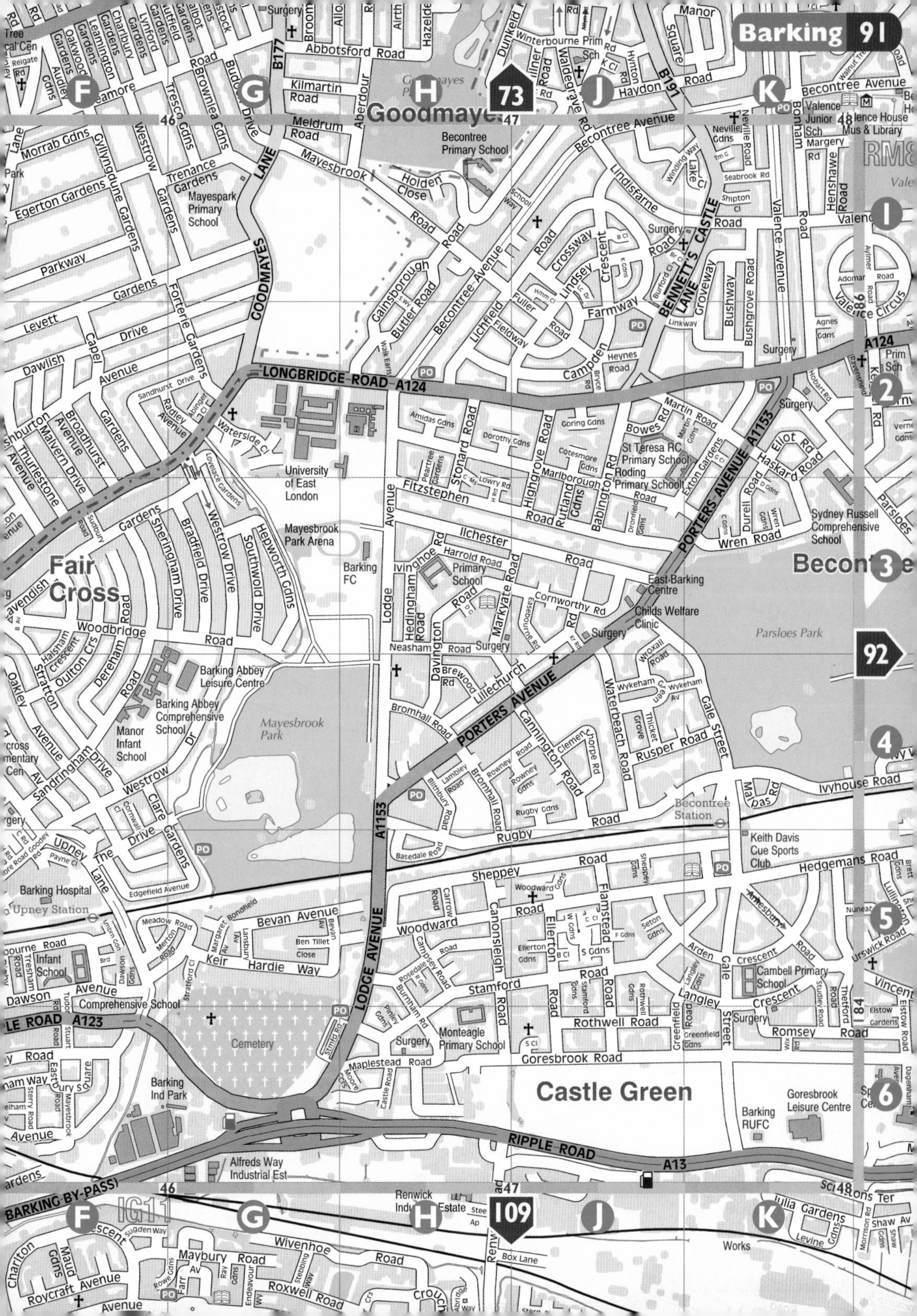
Goodmayes
Fair Cross
Castle Green
Becontree
73
109
92
46
47
48
F
G
H
J
K
1
2
3
4
5
6
IG11
RM8
Abbotsford Road
Kilmartin Road
Meldrum Road
Mayesbrook Road
Becontree Primary School
Holden Close
Mayespark Primary School
Morrab Gdns
Egerton Gardens
Trenance Gardens
Westrow Gardens
Parkway
Levett Gardens
Capel Drive
Dawlish Avenue
Forterie Gardens
Goodmayes Lane
B177
Longbridge Road A124
University of East London
Mayesbrook Park Arena
Barking FC
Waterside Cl
Radley Avenue
Broadhurst Gardens
Malvern Drive
Thurlestone Avenue
Sheringham Drive
Bradfield Drive
Westrow Drive
Southwold Drive
Hepworth Gdns
Woodbridge Road
Oulton Crs
Dereham Road
Stratton
Barking Abbey Leisure Centre
Barking Abbey Comprehensive School
Manor Infant School
Mayesbrook Park
Sandringham Drive
Westrow Drive
Clare Gardens
Upney Lane
Barking Hospital
Upney Station
Edgefield Avenue
Bevan Avenue
Keir Hardie Way
Ben Tillet Close
Dawson Avenue
Comprehensive School
A123
Cemetery
Barking Ind Park
Alfreds Way Industrial Est
Barking-By-Pass
Ripple Road
A13
Renwick Industrial Estate
Box Lane
Wivenhoe Road
Maybury Road
Roxwell Road
Roycraft Avenue
Lodge Avenue
A1153
Porters Avenue
Becontree Avenue
Gainsborough Road
Butler Road
Lichfield
Fieldway
Crossway
Farmway
Lindsey
Crescent
Campden
Heynes Road
Bennett's Castle Lane
Groveway
Bushway
Bushgrove Road
Valence Avenue
Valence Circus
Valence Junior Sch
Valence House Mus & Library
Haydon Road
Winterbourne Prim Sch
Waldegrave Rd
B191
Lindisfarne Road
Surgery
Amidas Gdns
Stonard Road
Dorothy Gdns
Highgrove Road
Goring Gdns
Cotesmore Gdns
Martin Road
Bowes Rd
St Teresa RC Primary School
Roding Primary School
Marlborough Road
Fitzstephen Road
Rutland Gdns
Babington Rd
Ilchester Road
Harrold Road Primary School
Ivinghoe Rd
Hedingham Road
Davington Road
Markyate Road
Cornworthy Rd
East Barking Centre
Childs Welfare Clinic
Neasham Road
Brewood Rd
Lillechurch
Bromhall Road
Cannington Road
Waterbeach Road
Wykeham Green
Rusper Road
Gale Street
Parsloes Park
Haskard Road
Eliot Rd
Sydney Russell Comprehensive School
Wren Road
Ivyhouse Road
Becontree Station
Rugby Road
Keith Davis Cue Sports Club
Hedgemans Road
Sheppey Road
Woodward Road
Canonsleigh Road
Ellerton Road
Flamstead Road
Stamford Road
Rothwell Road
Arden Crescent
Langley Crescent
Cambell Primary School
Romsey Road
Goresbrook Road
Monteagle Primary School
Maplestead Road
Goresbrook Leisure Centre
Barking RUFC
Works
Julia Gardens
Vincent Road
Urswick Road
Parsloes Avenue

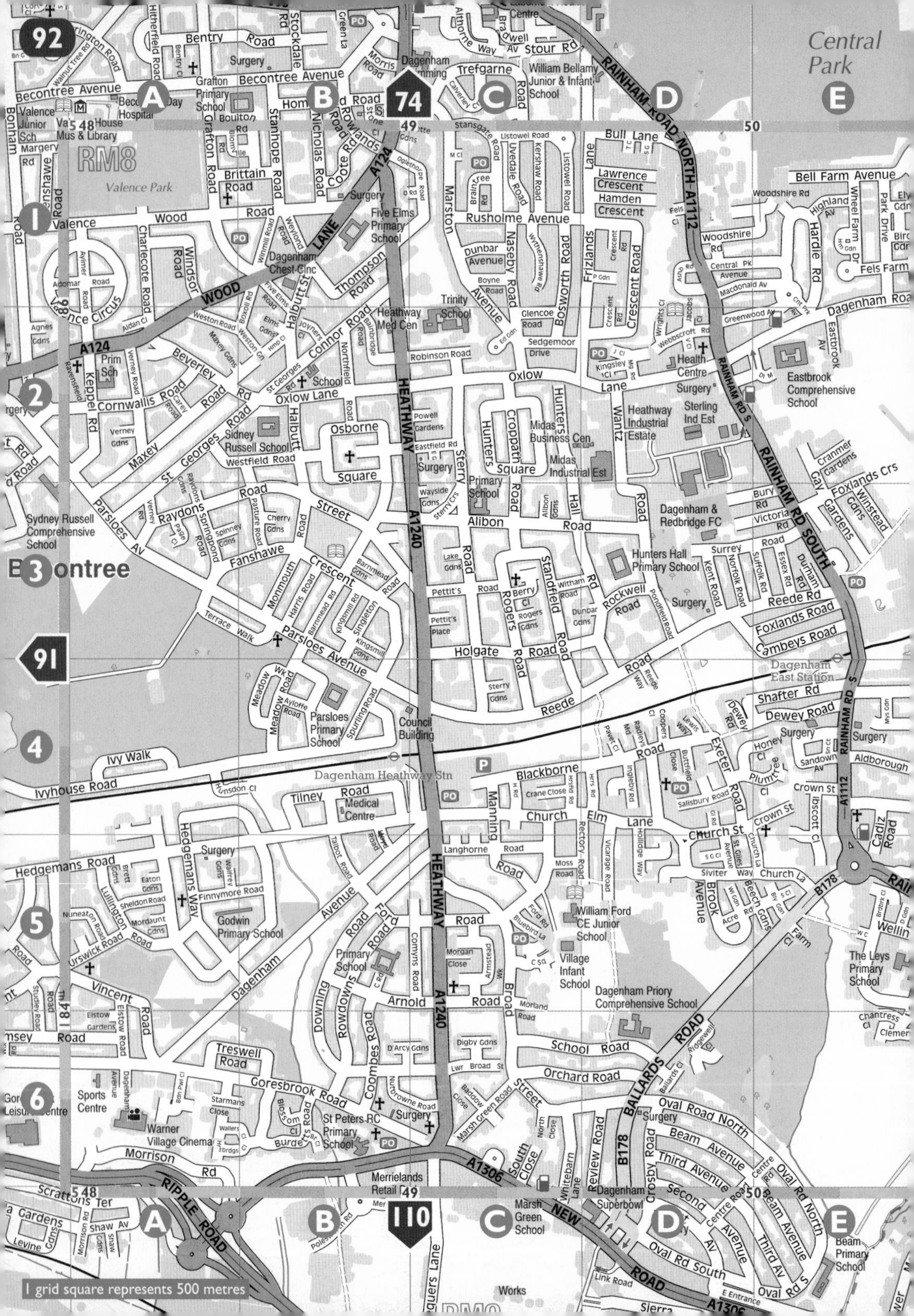
92
74
91
110
Central Park
A
B
C
D
E
1
2
3
4
5
6
48
49
50
RM8
Valence Park
Bentry Road
Stockdale Rd
Green La
Althorne Way
Bradwell Av
Stour Rd
Centre
Hitherfield Road
Walnut Tree Rd
Surgery
Becontree Avenue
Morris Road
Dagenham Swimming
Trefgarne Road
William Bellamy Junior & Infant School
RAINHAM ROAD NORTH A1112
Grafton Primary School
Becontree Day Hospital
Valence Junior Sch
Valence House Mus & Library
Bonham Road
Margery Rd
Home Road
Nicholas Road
Rowlands Road
Coote Rd
Boulton Rd
Grafton Road
Stanhope Road
Brittain Road
Calverley Cl
Stansgate Road
Listowel Road
Bull Lane
Lawrence Crescent
Hamden Crescent
Bell Farm Avenue
Woodshire Rd
Highland Av
Wheel Farm Dr
Park Drive
Uvedale Road
Kershaw Road
Braintree Rd
Marston
Oglethorpe Road
Five Elms Primary School
Valence Wood Road
Windsor Road
Charlecote Road
Weylond Road
Winmill Road
Dagenham Chest Clnc
WOOD LANE
A124
Thompson Road
Rusholme Avenue
Dunbar Avenue
Boyne Road
Naseby Road
Wythenshawe Rd
Bosworth Road
Frizlands Lane
Crescent Road
Fels Cl
Woodshire Rd
Central Pk Avenue
Macdonald Av
Hardie Rd
Fels Farm
Valence Circus
Adomar Road
Aylmer Road
Agnes Gdns
Aldan Cl
Weston Road
Maxey Gdns
Boxoll Rd
Five Elms Rd
Elms Gdns
Halbutt St
Joyners Cl
Connor Road
Heathway Med Cen
Bainbridge Rd
Trinity School
Avenue
Glencoe Road
Sedgemoor Drive
Crescent Rd
Wrights Cl
Webbscroft Rd
Greenwood Av
Dagenham Road
Eastbrook Av
Ravensfield
Keppel Rd
Prim Sch
Verney Road
Beverley Road
St Georges Rd
School
Northfield Road
Robinson Road
Kingsley Cl
Health Centre
Surgery
Eastbrook Comprehensive School
Cornwallis Road
Carey Road
Oxlow Lane
Oxlow Lane
HEATHWAY
Powell Gardens
Hunters Square
Cropath Road
Hunters Hall Road
Wantz Road
Heathway Industrial Estate
Sterling Ind Est
RAINHAM RD S
Verney Gdns
Maxey Road
St Georges Road
Sidney Russell School
Halbutt Street
Osborne Square
Eastfield Rd
Surgery
Sterry Road
Midas Business Cen
Midas Industrial Est
Cranmer Gardens
Foxlands Crs
Westfield Road
Parsloes Av
Raydons Gdns
Raydons Road
Pasture Road
Springpond Road
Spinney Gdns
Cherry Gdns
Street
Wayside Gdns
Sterry Crs
Primary School
Alibon Road
Alibon Gdns
Bury Rd
Victoria Rd
Gay Gardens
Winstead Gdns
Dagenham & Redbridge FC
Sydney Russell Comprehensive School
Becontree
Fanshawe Crescent
Monmouth Road
Barnmead Gdns
A1240
Lake Gdns
Berry Cl
Standfield Road
Witham Road
Rockwell Road
Hunters Hall Primary School
Surrey Road
Kent Road
Norfolk Road
Suffolk Rd
Essex Rd
Durham Av
Reede Rd
Harris Road
Barnmead Rd
Kingsmill Rd
Singleton Road
Pettit's Road
Rogers Road
Rogers Gdns
Dunbar Gdns
Pondfield Road
Surgery
Foxlands Road
Cambeys Road
Terrace Walk
Parsloes Avenue
Kingsmill Gdns
Pettit's Place
Holgate Road
Reede Way
Dagenham East Station
Meadow Wk
Meadow Road
Ayloffe Road
Parsloes Primary School
Spurling Road
Sterry Gdns
Council Building
Reede Road
Shafter Rd
Dewey Rd
Dewey Road
Mvs Gdn
Coopers Road
Lewis Way
Radleys Md
Pavet Cl
Exeter Road
Honey Cl
Surgery
Surgery
Sandown Av
Aldborough
Ivy Walk
Ivyhouse Road
Hunsdon Cl
Dagenham Heathway Stn
Tilney Road
Medical Centre
Blackborne Road
Crane Close
Manning Road
Inglby Rd
Buttsbury Rd
Close
Salisbury Road
Plumtree Cl
Crown St
A1112
Ibscott Cl
Cadiz Road
Hedgemans Way
Surgery
Walfrey Gdns
Church Elm Lane
Rectory Road
Vicarage Road
Hollidge Way
Church St
St Giles Av
Church La
Crown St
Hedgemans Road
Brett Gdns
Eaton Gdns
Langhorne Road
Talbot Road
Moss Road
Siviter Way
Church La
B178
Lullington Road
Sheldon Road
Finnymore Road
Mordaunt Gdns
Godwin Primary School
Avenue
Ford Road
Bluebird La
Ford Rd
William Ford CE Junior School
Brook Avenue
Acre Rd
Beech Gdns
Farm Cl
Welling
Nuneaton Road
Urswick Road
Dagenham Road
Primary School
Comyns Road
Morgan Close
Armstead Road
Broad Road
Village Infant School
Dagenham Priory Comprehensive School
The Leys Primary School
Vincent Road
Elstow Gardens
Elstow Road
Studley Road
Downing Road
Rowdowns Road
Arnold Road
Morland Road
Chantress Cl
Clements
Ramsey Road
Coombes Road
D'Arcy Gdns
Digby Gdns
School Road
Ridgewell Cl
Treswell Road
Lwr Broad St
BALLARDS ROAD
Orchard Road
Sports Centre
Dagenham Avenue
Goresbrook Road
Nutbrowne Road
Baddow Close
Marsh Green Road
Street
Ballards Cl
Oval Road North
Gorseb Leisure Centre
Starmans Close
Surgery
Surgery
Beam Avenue
Warner Village Cinema
Blossom Cl
St Peters RC Primary School
North Close
Crosby Road
Third Avenue
Centre Rd
Oval Rd North
Morrison Rd
Burdetts Road
South Close
Whitebarn Lane
Review Road
B178
Second Avenue
Centre Road
Beam Avenue
Merrielands Retail Pk
A1306
Dagenham Superbowl
Scrattons Ter
RIPPLE ROAD
Marsh Green School
NEW ROAD
Avenue
Third Av
Beam Primary School
Gardens
Morrison Rd
Shaw Av
Shaw Av
Levine Gdns
Polesworth Rd
Oval Rd South
Link Road
Oval Rd S
Works
E Entrance
Sierra
A1306
1 grid square represents 500 metres

Great Cullings
Camomile Rd
Jasmine Rd
Foxglove
Bluebell Cl
Carnation Cl
Valentines
Eastbrook Drive
Bancroft Chase
Chestnut Avenue
Acacia Avenue
Laburnum Av
Broadstone Road
Portland Road
The Albany School
Harrow Lodge Park
F
G
H
J
K
75
51
52
53
Dagenham Road
Eastbrook End Cemetery
The Chase
Eastbrookend Country Park
Works
RM10
Barking & Dagenham
Havering
UPPER RAINHAM ROAD
A125
Warren Drive
Benhurst JMI School
Avenue
Eyhurst
St Nicholas Av
Benhurst
Woodcote Avenue
Northwood Avenue
Elm Park Avenue
Brian Close
Diban
Cowdray Way
Carfax Rd
Yale Wy
Petworth Wy
Kings Estate
Elm Park Station
The Broadway
Woburn Av
Ayloff Primary School
Spring Gdns
Maylands Av
Farm Way
Andrews Avenue
Windermere Avenue
Carnforth Gardens
Dunningford Primary School
Coniston Wy
Ullswater Way
School
Langdale Gdns
Rosewood Av
Ambleside Av
Coronation Dr
Arbour Way
Calbourne Av
South End Road
Lancaster
Laburnum
Elm Park
Kendal Cft
Ennerdale Avenue
Furness Wy
Surgery
Easedale Dr
Silverdale Dr
Rosewood Medical Centre
Maybank
Wood Lane
Penrith Crs
Kilmartin Way
Morecambe Cl
West Malling Way
Northolt
R J Mitchell Primary School
Gray Gdns
Lovell Walk
Stephen Av
Boulter Gdns
Finucane Gdns
Malan Sq
Astra Cl
Park Lane
Cavendish Av
Tangmere Crs
Wells Gdns
Sowrey Av
Ryder Gdns
Mungo Park Road
Deere Avenue
Gillam Wy
Bader Way
Cavendish Crs
Tuck Rd
Deere Av
Eagle Cl
Bretons
ROAD
Simpson Road
Hugo Gdns
Stapleton Crs
Fulmar Rd
Flight Av
Heron Flight Av
Airfield Way
Coltishall Rd
John Perry Primary School
Auriel Av
Western Avenue
Norton Rd
Charles Rd
Goring Road
Surgery
Road
Dagenham
Beamway
Kingaby Gdns
Elm Cl
Elmer Gardens
Sunningdale Rd
Jersey Rd
Princes Park
South End Rd
Mermagen Dr
Hayes Dr
Dowding Close
School
RAINHAM
Brittons School
Willoughby Dr
Fontayne Av
Castle Av
A1112
DAGENHAM RD
Newtons Cl
Ford Lane
Ford Cl
Trinidad Gdns
Canberra Crs
Canberra
Beam River
South Hornchurch
Thorogood Way
Ongar Wy
Fyfield Road
Dunmow Drive
Danbury Rd
Harlow Road
Oliver Rd
Whybridge Junior School
Whybridge Infant School
Grove Park Road
Gainsborough Road
Avelon Road
Albyns Farm
Canfield Rd
Surgery
Blacksmith's Lane
South End Road
Guysfield Drive
Health & Welfare Clinic
Stanley Road
Whybridge Close
Blake Cl
Alexandra Road
Hood Rd
North
Trafalgar Rd
Nelson Road
Lane
111
Lowen Road
Frederick Road
Newtons Primary School
Maytree Cl
Victory Rd
Stanhope Rd
I
2
3
4
5
6
86
85
84

76
113
A
B
C
D
E
1
2
3
4
5
6
508
09
10
83
82
81
Sharvel
Dog Rose Ramble
Dog Rose Ramble & Hillingdon Trail
Yeading Brook
Leybourne Road
Hazeldene Gardens
Petworth Road
Petworth Gdns
Cowdray Road
Avenue
Sports Ground Pavilion
Works
Swakeleys School
Highfield School
Gainsborough Road
Hayman Crs
Raeburn Rd
Rmn Rd
Hoppner Road
Lawrence Rd
Charville Lane
Charville Lane
Hill Road
Harrow View
Charville Lane
Kendal Cl
Langdale Drive
Ullswater Cl
Charville Primary School
Bury Avenue
Raynton Dr
Grosvenor Avenue
Coshawk Gardens
Hedgewood School
Weymouth Road
Dorset Avenue
Lansbury Drive
Exmouth Rd
Weald Way
Portland Road
Bradenham Rd
Adelphi Crs
Kenmore Crs
Brook House FC
Percy Gdns
Kingshill Avenue
Raynton Dr
Byron Way
Dale Dr
Fairholme Crs
Frogmore Avenue
Mansfield Dr
Raynton Drive
Hayes Park Junior & Infant School
Leamington Place
Fairholme Crs
Warwick Crs
Fredora Av
Surgery
Grange Park Primary School
Grange Park Clinic
Park Lane
Frogmore Gardens
Balmoral Dr
Derwent Drive
Wrays Way
Hurstfield Crs
Woodrow Avenue
Haven Cl
Westacott
Cavendish Close
Park Road
Woodstock Gdns
Lansbury Drive
Whittington Avenue
Gledwood Dr
Burns Close
Melrose Cl
Shelley Close
Marvell Av
Balmoral Road
Keats Close
Johnson Drive
Gledwood Av
Chaucer Av
Gledwood Gdns
Spencer Av
Marshall Dr
Kenilworth Gdns
Uxbridge Co Court
Grange Rd
Grange Cl
Mellow Lane East
Mellow Lane School
Hewens Road
Blacklands Drive
Meadow View Road
Hayes End
Hayes End Dr
Hayes End Rd
Mead House Lane
Wilmar Close
Newport Road
Nelson Rd
Marlborough Rd
Pole Hill
Star Road
Heath Rd
Uxbridge Road
Butler St
Westbourne Road
Charles Street
Neilgrove Rd
New Road
Fountain Cl
Hillingdon Heath
Sibley Ct
Haig Road
West Drayton Rd
Green Lane
WEST DRAYTON ROAD
HAYES
Morgan's La
Angel La
Mellina Cl
Church Cl
Middleton Rd
Pronto Trading Estate
Wood End Green
Kingsway
Surgery
Saxony Pde
Hanover Circle
Tudor Square
Waylands
North Rd
Wood End Green Road
Stuart Crs
Normandy Drive
Tudor Road
Victoria Road
Cranmer Road
Cromwell Road
Commonwealth Av
York Avenue
Bishop's Road
Albion Road
Queens Road
The Beck Theatre
Wood End
Hayes Cricket Club
The Hayes Manor School
Hayes Stadium Sports Centre
Leven Way
Botwell Crs
Botwell Lane
Church Walk
Wood End
Swift Cl
Acacia Avenue
Church Road
Dr Tripletts School
Addison Road
Rectory Road
Manor Road
Hesa Avenue
Harrow View
Hesa Road
Wesley
Uxbridge College
College Way
Orchard Road
Craven Close
The Warren
UXBRIDGE ROAD
Warley Avenue
Belmore Av
Coleridge Way
Uxbridge Road
Avenue
Cherry Grove
White Heart Av
B465 WEST
Lonsdale Cl
Cromer Cl
Dawley Av
Harlington Road
HARLINGTON ROAD
Lansdowne Rd
Titmus Cl
Corwell Lane
Corwell Gdns
St Jerome's Gv
Gould's Gn
A437
Judge Heath Lane
Junior Sch
Mcmillan Clinic
Princes Park Avenue
Princes Pk Cl
Princes Pk Pde
Princes Pk Cir
Princes Pk La
Ash Gv
Beechwood Av
Juniper Way
Lime Grove
Burbage Cl
Ulac Gdns
Freemans Lane
Sycamore Avenue
Hall Road
Almond Close
Chestnut Close
Manton Close
Willenhall Dr
Botwell Common Road
Hemmen Lane
Lych Gate Walk
Kerstin Cl
St Mary's Rd
St Mary's Crs
North Av
Central Avenue
Longmead Road
Hayes FC
Hayes Social and Sports Club
West Avenue
Compton Road
Townfield Sq
Ninth Av
Lane
Golf Course
Stockley Park Golf Club
DAWLEY ROAD
UB11
Forris Avenue
Moray Avenue
Lannock Road
Church Road
First Av
Sixth Av
Second Av
Third Av
Seventh Av
Eighth Av
East Wy
Silverdale Industrial Estate
Birchway
Rostrever Gardens
Hayes
Business Centre
Bolingbroke Way
1 grid square represents 500 metres

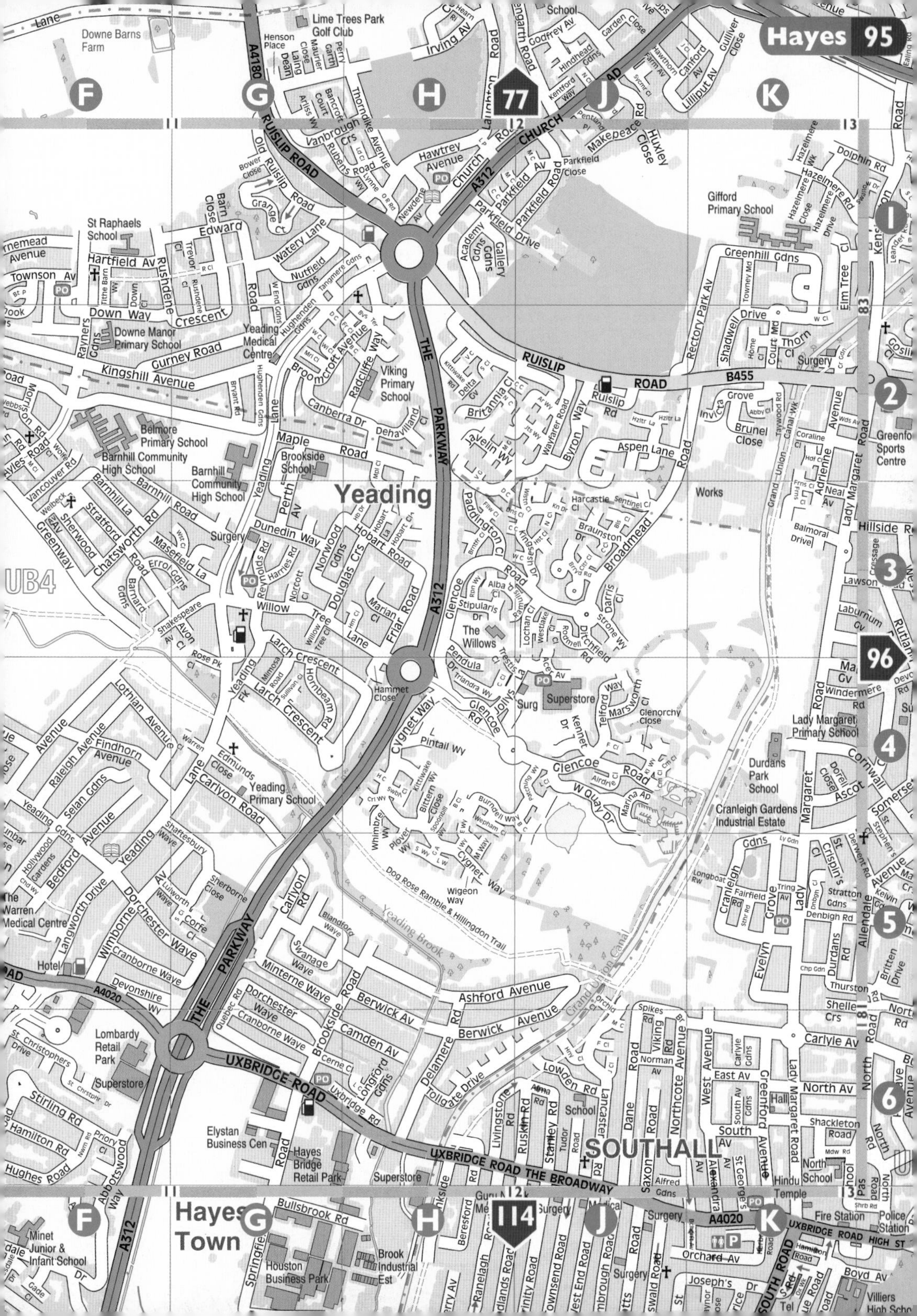
Downe Barns Farm
Lime Trees Park Golf Club
Henson Place
A4180
RUISLIP ROAD
CHURCH ROAD
A312
77
F
G
H
J
K
Irving Av
Godfrey Av
Garden Close
Hindhead Gdns
Canford Av
Gulliver Close
Lilliput Av
Makepeace Rd
Huxley Close
Vanbrough Crs
Thorndike Avenue
Rubens Road
Hawtrey Avenue
Old Ruislip Road
Grange Ct
Watery Lane
Parkfield Av
Parkfield Road
Parkfield Close
Parkfield Drive
Academy Gdns
Gallery Gdns
Gifford Primary School
Hazelmere Rd
Dolphin Rd
Greenhill Gdns
Elm Tree Cl
Rectory Park Av
Shadwell Drive
Court Md
Thorn
Surgery
St Raphaels School
Edward
Hartfield Av
Townson Av
Rushdene Crescent
Down Way
Nutfield Gdns
Downe Manor Primary School
Gurney Road
Yeading Medical Centre
Kingshill Avenue
THE PARKWAY
Broomcroft Avenue
Radcliffe Way
Viking Primary School
Canberra Dr
Dehavilland Cl
RUISLIP ROAD B455
Britannia Cl
Delta Gv
Javelin Wy
Wayfarer Road
Byron Way
Ruislip Rd
Aspen Lane
Brunel Close
Grove
Invicta
Coraline
Adrienne Av
Lady Margaret Road
Greenford Sports Centre
Belmore Primary School
Barnhill Community High School
Maple Road
Brookside School
Yeading
Perth Av
Works
Grand Union Canal Wk
Neal Av
Balmoral Drive
Hillside Rd
Vancouver Rd
Barnhill Road
Stratford Rd
Chatsworth Rd
Sherwood Av
Greenway
Dunedin Way
Hobart Road
Norwood Gdns
Douglas Crs
Harcastle Cl
Braunston Dr
Broadmead
UB4
Masefield La
Errol Gdns
Barnard Gdns
Reynolds Rd
Harries Rd
Norcott Cl
Marian Cl
Friar Road
Glencoe Road
Alba Cl
Stipularis Dr
The Willows
Lochan Cl
Darris Cl
Strone Wy
Ditchfield Rd
Lawson
Laburnum Gv
Rutland
Shakespeare Av
Avon Cl
Willow Tree Lane
Larch Crescent
Rose Pk Cl
Yeading Fk
Mimosa Road
Hornbeam Rd
Hammet Close
Pendula Dr
Triandra Wy
Trestis Cl
Jollys La
Acer Av
Superstore
Surg
Telford Way
Marsworth Cl
Kennet Dr
Glenorchy Close
96
Windermere Rd
Lady Margaret Primary School
Lothian Avenue
Raleigh Avenue
Findhorn Avenue
Warren
Edmunds Close
Lane
Caryon Road
Yeading Primary School
Cygnet Way
Pintail Wy
Kittiwake
Bittern Close
Burnell Way
Glencoe Road
W Quay Dr
Marina Ap
Durdans Park School
Cranleigh Gardens Industrial Estate
Margaret Dorell Close
Ascot
Cornwall
Somerset
Yeading Gdns
Selan Gdns
Bedford Avenue
Hollywood Gardens
Shaftesbury Wayne
Sherborne Close
The Warren Medical Centre
Langworth Drive
Wimborne Av
Dorchester Waye
Lulworth Waye
Corfe Cl
Wigeon Way
Dog Rose Ramble & Hillingdon Trail
Yeading Brook
Carlyon Rd
Blandford Waye
Swanage Waye
Plover Wy
Whimbrel Wy
Longboat Rw
Cranleigh Gdns
Fairfield Av
Tring Av
Grove
Lady Cl
St Crispin's
Stratton Gdns
Kelvin
Allendale Avenue
Denbigh Rd
Durdans Rd
Evelyn
Britten Drive
Thurston
Hotel
Cranborne Waye
Devonshire Wy
A4020
Minterne Waye
Brookside Road
Ashford Avenue
Berwick Av
Berwick Avenue
Delamere Rd
Camden Av
Lombardy Retail Park
Superstore
St Christophers Drive
Dorchester Waye
Cranborne Waye
Quebec Rd
Cerne Cl
Longford Gdns
Tollgate Drive
Grand Union Canal
Spikes Bridge Rd
Viking Rd
Norman Av
Northcote Avenue
West Avenue
East Av
Carlyle Gdns
Carlyle Av
South Av
Greenford Avenue
Shelley Crs
North Road
North Av
Hall
Shackleton Road
UXBRIDGE ROAD
Uxbridge Rd
Stirling Rd
Hamilton Rd
Hughes Road
Priory Cl
Abbotswood Way
Elystan Business Cen
Hayes Bridge Retail Park
Superstore
Lowden Rd
Livingstone Rd
Ruskin Rd
Stanley Rd
Tudor Rd
School
Lancaster Rd
Dane Road
Saxon Road
South Av
Alexandra Av
St George's
SOUTHALL
North School
Hindu Temple
UXBRIDGE ROAD THE BROADWAY
Alfred Gdns
Hayes Town
A312
Minet Junior & Infant School
Gade Cl
Bullsbrook Rd
Houston Business Park
Brook Industrial Est
Springfield
Beresford Rd
Ranelagh Rd
Guru Nanak Rd
114
Surgery
Medical
Townsend Road
West End Road
Orchard Av
Joseph's
Fire Station
Police Station
UXBRIDGE ROAD HIGH ST
SOUTH ROAD
Hamilton Road
Boyd Av
Villiers High School

96
78
95
115
A
B
C
D
E
1
2
3
4
5
6
513
14
15
83
81
WESTERN AVENUE
Belvue School
Greenford Industrial Estate
Kelvin Ind Est
Bridport Road
Halifax Road
Bristol Road
Field Way
Chartwell Cl
Stanley Avenue
Lincoln Close
Jeymer Drive
Uneeda Drive
Oldfield La North
Rockware
Bennetts Avenue
Lyon Way
Works
Station
Downing Drive
Courthope Rd
Greenford Road Medical Centre
Oldfields Primary School
Middleton Avenue
Hotel
Daryngton Drive
Runnymede Gdns
Cayton Rd
Conway
Dolphin Rd
Hazelmere Rd
Kensington Road
Farrier Road
Union Road
Hotspur Rd
Horse Shoe Crs
Meadow Close
Paddock Close
Old Br Close
Pump Close
Grand Union Canal
Evesham Close
Chesterton Close
Melrose Av
Melrose Cl
Chinnor Crs
Bledlow Rise
Ferrymead Avenue
Ferrymead Gdns
Goring Way
Ormsby Gdns
Girls School
South Lane
Wordsworth
Wessex La
Cowgate
Leaver Gardens
Anthony Rd
Hicks Avenue
David Av
South Greenford Station
Perivale Park Athletics Track
Perivale Park Golf Club
Golf Course
UB6
Elm Tree Cl
Surgery
Gosling Cl
Rosedene Avenue
Crossmead Avenue
Primary School
Greenway Gardens
Beechwood Avenue
Eastmead Avenue
Marnham Crs
Millet Road
Penn Cl
Barnham Road
Farndale Crs
E Betham CE Primary School
Costons La
Costons Av
Shelley Av
Kelvin Ind Est
Greenford Gardens
Ravenor Park Road
Greenford Synagogue
Croyde Av
Oldfield Lane
Greenford Sports Centre
Greenford High School
RUISLIP ROAD
Allenby Rd
Stickleton Cl
Pembroke Rd
Surgery
Oakfield Gdns
Costons Lane
Wedmore Road
Betham Road
Locarno Rd
Clifton Rd
A4127
GREENFORD
Lady Margaret Road
Neal Av
Adrienne Avenue
Hillside Road
Enmore Rd
Towers Rd
Verulam Rd
Ruislip Close
B455
Cressage Close
Lawson Road
Westbury Avenue
Selby Gdns
Rosecroft Rd
Rose Gdns
Braund Avenue
Avon Road
Upper Town Rd
Mornington Road
Garrick Road
Lyric Dr
Warren Dr
School
RUISLIP ROAD
Brentside High School
Riverside
Laburnum Gv
Rutland Road
Bycroft Road
Portland House Medical Centre
Ellesmere Rd
Otter Rd
GREENFORD ROAD
Our Lady of the Visitation RC Combined Primary School
Brentside Primary School
Brants Wk
Cuckoo
Devonshire Avenue
Windermere Rd
Sunnycroft Road
Cedar Gv
Ash Gv
Allenby Road
Fermoy Rd
Purcell Rd
Mansell Rd
Portland Crs
Stanhope Road
Bingley Rd
The Cardinal Wiseman ARC School Technology and Art College
Brookbank Av
Elmbank Way
Cuckoo Dene
Gifford Gardens
Beechmount Av
Beresford Av
Kennedy Road
Elfwine Rd
Laurie Rd
Hillyard Road
Greenford Avenue
Lady Margaret Primary School
Hart Gv
Surgery
Cornwall Gdns
Somerset Road
Windmill Lane
River Brent
Brent River Pk Wk
Bridge Avenue
Greenford Park Cemetery
Canterbury Close
Dale Road
Keats Way
Hurley Road
Barbican Rd
Ascot Cl
Dorrell Close
St Peter's Road
Jubilee Gdns
Greenford Avenue Medical Centre
Mayfield Gardens
Hanway Rd
Highland Av
High Lane
Mayfield Primary School
St Stephen's Avenue
St Ursula Rd
Bassett Wy
Queen's Av
The Gv
King's Avenue
Hobbayne Rd
Studland Road
Westview
Grove Avenue
Greenford Avenue
Allenby Infant School
Manaton Crs
Kelvin Gdns
Stratton Gdns
Waxlow Crs
Dormer's Av
Allendale Avenue
Dormers Wells School
Dormers Wells Leisure Centre
Lovell Rd
Whittle Cl
Swan Rd
Wallis Road
Darwin Dr
Edison Dr
Howard Rd
Osborne Rd
Kings Avenue Medical Cen
Fleming Road
Marconi Way
Telford Rd
Longridge Lane
Dormers Ri
Whitecote Rd
Redcroft Rd
Durdans Rd
Britten Drive
Mount Av
Thurston Rd
Medical Centre
Dormer's Wells La
Faraday Rd
Panhard Place
Haldane Rd
Baird Avenue
Elmwood Gardens
Brent Valley Golf Club
Surgery
Cuckoo Lane
North Road
Masefield Av
Carlyle Av
Burns Avenue
Farm Cl
Brindley Way
Dormer's Wells
KS Medical Centre
Church Road
Oakley Close
Manor Ct Road
Golden Manor
Manor House
Palgrave Avenue
Kingsley Avenue
Oakwood Av
Kenton Av
Milford Road
Longford Avenue
Atherton Pl
Dormers Wells Primary School
West Middlesex Golf Club
Shackleton Road
North School
UB1
Dormer's Wells Lane
Golf Course
Alwyne Rd
Campbell Rd
Hanwell Stn
Hanwell
York Av
Fire Station
Police Station
Park View
Uxbridge Rd
UXBRIDGE ROAD
Brentvale Av
Blackmore Av
Works
A4020
Conolly Rd
Lawn Gdns
Myrtle Gdns
Laurel Gdns
Half Acre Rd
Southall
Boyd Av
Knowsley Avenue
Morland Gdns
Argyll Av
Green Dr
Windmill Lane
Hamilton Road
1 grid square represents 500 metres

Perivale
79
98
116
EALING
W5
W13
W7
West Ealing
F
G
H
J
K
1
2
3
4
5
6
16
17
18
A40
B456
B455
B452
A4020
ARGYLE ROAD
EAST
SCOTCH COMMON
KENT GARDENS
CASTLEBAR HILL
CASTLEBAR ROAD
HAVEN GN
THE BROADWAY
NEW BROADWAY
UXBRIDGE ROAD
BROADWAY
ALPERTON LANE
DRAYTON GREEN ROAD
HIGH STREET
BOND ST
MADELEY ROAD
EALING GREEN
Bilton Road
Horsenden Lane South
Buckingham Av
Perivale Industrial Park
Works
Perivale Station
Sunley Gdns
Selborne Gdns
Woodhouse Cl
Woodhouse Av
Selborne School
Thames Avenue
Medway Drive
Hodder Drive
Barmouth Avenue
Rhyl Rd
Scorton Av
Colwyn Av
Ealing Central Sports Ground
Welland Gdns
Tavistock Av
Dawlish Avenue
Bideford Av
Superstore
Perivale Ind Park
Wadsworth Road
Fleetway Business Park
Sheraton Business Cen
Silicon Business Cen
Primary School
Wadsworth Business Cen
Perivale New Business Cen
Sarsfield Road
Aintree Road
Perimeade Road
Federal Rd
Fairfield Dr
Brooklands Dr
Manor Farm Rd
Athlon Rd
Athlon Industrial Estate
Alperton Sports Ground
Phoenix Trading Est
Grand Union
Glacier Way
Capital Business Centre
Eden Close
Pleasant Way
Primrose Way
Lily Gdns
May Gardens
W Links
Nagi Business Centre
Marsh Road
Crescent
Rydal
Coniston Avenue
Thirlmere Av
St John Fisher School
Stockdove Way
Haymill Close
Perivale Lane
Wicket Road
Hotel
Ealing Golf Club
Golf Course
River Brent
Brent River Pk Wk
Gurnell Leisure Centre
Gurnell Gv
Brentside Close
Argyle Close
Avalon Road
Crossway
Downside Crescent
Royle Crs
Avalon Cl
Vallis Way
Hathaway Primary School
Castlebar Special School
Castle Bar Park Station
Fosse Way
Bruton Way
Hathaway Gdns
Claremont Road
Cleveland Road
Harp Road
Greatdown Road
Copley Close
Templeman Road
Alcott Close
Cavendish Avenue
Cavendish Special School
Kingsley Av
Lynton Av
Highview Road
Springhallow School
Rosemount Rd
Rosebery Gdns
Courtfield Gdns
Homefarm Road
Framfield Road
Dryden Av
Browning Av
Drayton Br Road
Drayton Green Station
Drayton Manor High School
Middle School
Cowper Road
Shakespeare Road
Milton Road
Allingham Cl
Tennyson Road
Works
Ealing Liberal Synagogue
Berners Dr
Sutherland Rd
Drayton Gdns
Drayton Green
Manor Road
West Ealing Station
West Ealing Business Centre
Felix Road
St Johns Primary School
Alexandria Road
Bedford Road
Kirchen Rd
Cemetery
Church Rd
Holly Pk
Mag Ct
Witham Rd
Meadvale Road
Perivale Gdns
Bellevue Rd
Brentcot Cl
Woodbury Pk Rd
Curzon Road
Harrow Vw
Selby Road
Barnfield Road
Lindfield Rd
Holyoake Walk
Denison Rd
Ludlow Road
Neville Rd
Brunswick Road
Mulgrave Rd
Kingsfield Rd
Fowler's Walk
Brentham Way
Lynwood Road
Clarendon Rd
Ainsdale Rd
Pitshanger Lane
Primary School
Glencairn Dr
Albert Rd
Castlebar Mews
Queen's Gdns
Queen's Walk
Princes Gdns
Mount Pleasant Rd
Woodfield Rd
Woodfield Crs
St Gregorys RC Primary School
Buckingham Cl
Lanark Close
Helena Road
Mount Avenue
Montpelier Primary School
Montpelier Road
Eaton Rise
Montpelier Av
St Benedicts School
The Firs
Kent Avenue
The Md
The Dene
Templewood
Castlebar Rd
Victoria Rd
Park
Edgehill Rd
High School
The Knoll
Ealing Abbey Scriptorium
Ealing Abbey
St Stephen's Rd
Stephen's Av
Hollingbourne Gdns
North Avenue
Sherborne Gdns
Wimborne Gdns
Egerton Gardens
Bradley Gdns
Avenue House School
Waldeck Rd
Ealing College Upper School
Arlington Road
Albany Road
The Avenue
Montague Road
Mortimer Road
Amherst Avenue
Amherst Rd
White Ledges
Sports Ground
Denbigh Road
Saint Leonard's Road
Carlton Road
Carlton Gdns
Longfield Rd
Harvington School
Blakesley Av
Charlbury Gv
Marchwood Crs
Eaton Rise
Elmcroft Close
Mount Pk Road
Durston House School
Kings Av
Kings Road
Park Hill
Queen's Rd
Aston House School
Haven Green
Haven Green Clnc
Mountfield Rd
Ealing Broadway Stn
Sports Cen
Hillcroft Crs
Croft
West Rd
Gordon Road
Langham Gardens
Arcadia Shopping Centre
Spring Br Rd
Town Hall
Middle School
Ealing Civic Centre
Craven Avenue
Craven Road
Bowling Club
Police Station
College
UGC
Clifton Lodge Sch
The Questors Theatre
Hastings Road
Hartington Rd
Broughton Road
Denmark Rd
Arden Rd
Fire Station
St Leonard's Rd
Ealing Broadway Centre
Oxford Rd
Windsor Road
Harriers Rd
Surg
Pitshanger Manor Mus
Tertiary College
Telephone Exchange
University
Ealing Film Studios
Walpole Park
Ealing & Acton Synagogue
Grange
Webster Gdns
Park Pl
Balmain Close
Gordon House Hlth Cen
Snooker Club
St Johns Ambulance Station
Culmington
Churchfield
Somerset Rd
Leeland Terrace
Shirley Gdns
Nightingale Road
Azalea
Michael Gaynor Cl
Grosvenor
Surg
Hlth Cen
Uxbridge Road
B452

98
80
97
117
A
B
C
D
E
1
2
3
4
5
6
518
19
20
Alperton
Park Royal
Lower Place
West Acton
NORTH CIRCULAR ROAD
HANGER LANE
WESTERN AVENUE
A40
A406
EALING ROAD
CORONATION ROAD
PARK ROYAL ROAD
ACTON LANE
HORN LANE
UXBRIDGE RD
UXBRIDGE ROAD
THE BROADWAY
THE MALL
GUNNERSBURY AVENUE
Hanger Lane Station
Park Royal Stn
North Ealing Station
West Acton Station
Acton Station
Ealing Broadway Stn
Ealing Common Stn
Central Middlesex Hospital
Abbey Industrial Est
Northfields Industrial Est
Grand Union Industrial Estate
Grand Union Ind Estate
Mill Trading Estate
Townsend Industrial Estate
Lower Place Business Centre
Cumberland Business Park
AMC Business Cen
Western Trading Est
Western Avenue Business Park
Heron Trading Est
Concord Business Cen
Westpoint Trading Est
Warner Village
Acton Superbowl
West Twyford Primary School
St Augustines Priory School
Pavilion Barclays Sports Ground
Ealing Cricket Club
Ellen Wilkinson School for Girls
West Acton Primary School
The Japanese School
The Shamrock Sports Club
Acton Central Industrial Est
Twyford CE High School
Twyford Sports Cen
Ealing Common
Ealing Broadway Centre
Grand Union Canal Walk
River Brent
1 grid square represents 500 metres

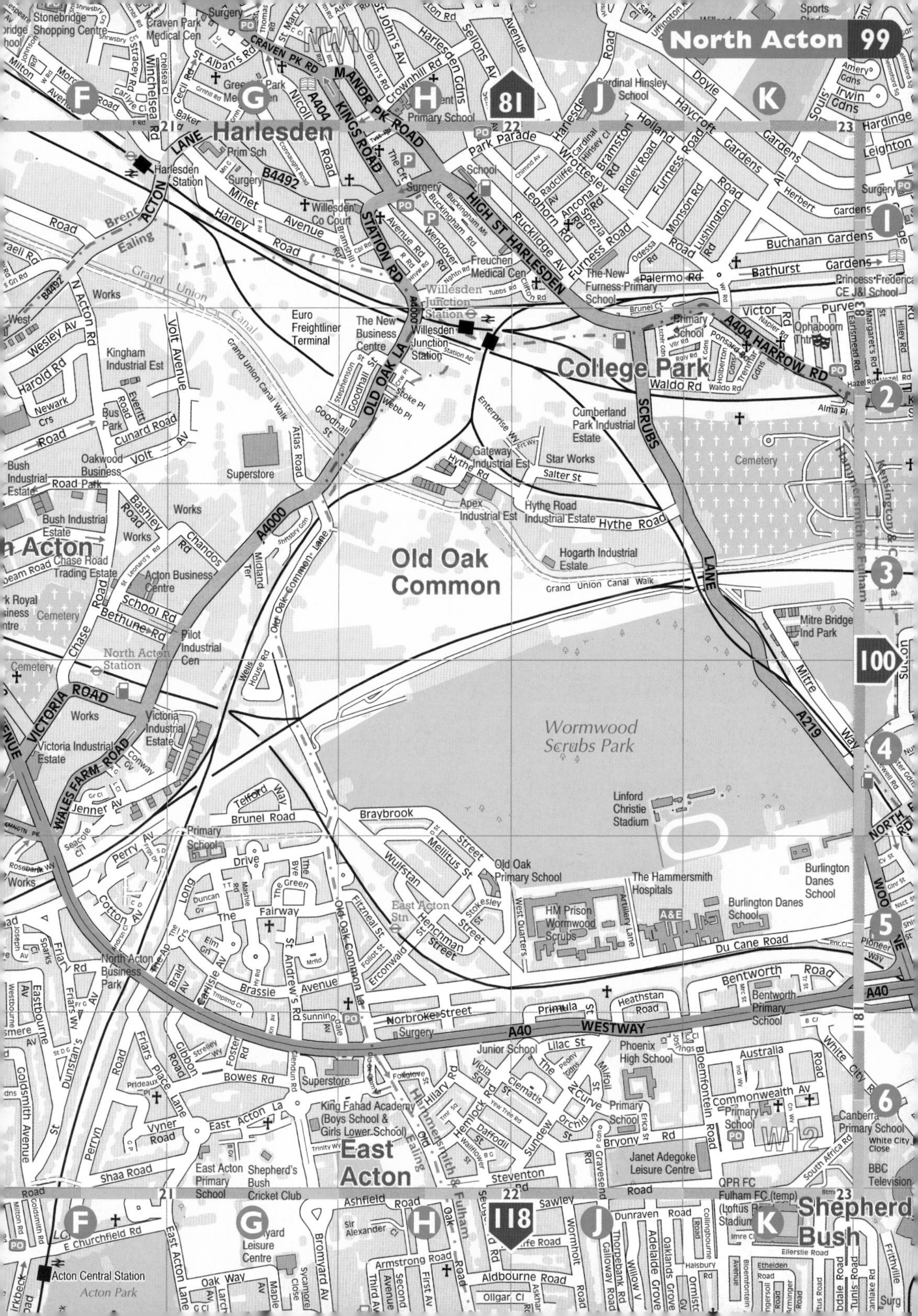

Harlesden
NW10
College Park
Old Oak Common
Wormwood Scrubs Park
North Acton
East Acton
Shepherd's Bush
W12
81
100
118
F
G
H
J
K
21
22
23
1
2
3
4
5
6
Stonebridge Shopping Centre
Craven Park Medical Cen
Craven Pk Rd
Manor Pk Road
Kings Road
Station Rd
High St Harlesden
Acton Lane
Harlesden Station
Willesden Junction Station
Willesden Co Court
Freuchen Medical Cen
Cardinal Hinsley School
Euro Freightliner Terminal
The New Business Centre
Grand Union Canal
Grand Union Canal Walk
Old Oak La
A4000
A404
A404 Harrow Rd
B4492
Scrubs Lane
Kingham Industrial Est
Superstore
Oakwood Business Park
Bush Industrial Estate
Chase Road Trading Estate
Acton Business Centre
Pilot Industrial Cen
North Acton Station
Victoria Road
Victoria Industrial Estate
Wales Farm Road
Cemetery
Cumberland Park Industrial Estate
Gateway Industrial Est
Star Works
Apex Industrial Est
Hythe Road Industrial Estate
Hogarth Industrial Estate
Mitre Bridge Ind Park
Mitre Way
A219
Linford Christie Stadium
Braybrook Street
Old Oak Primary School
The Hammersmith Hospitals
HM Prison Wormwood Scrubs
Burlington Danes School
Du Cane Road
A40 Westway
East Acton Stn
Primula St
Bentworth Primary School
Phoenix High School
Commonwealth Av
White City Road
Canberra Primary School
BBC Television
Janet Adegoke Leisure Centre
QPR FC Fulham FC (temp) (Loftus Rd Stadium)
King Fahad Academy (Boys School & Girls Lower School)
East Acton Primary School
Shepherd's Bush Cricket Club
Acton Central Station
Acton Park
E Churchfield Rd
East Acton La
Hammersmith & Ealing
Hammersmith & Fulham
Wood Lane
North Pole Rd
Kensington & Chelsea
Ealing
Brent

100
82
99
119
A
B
C
D
E
1
2
3
4
5
6
523
24
25
Brondesbury Park
Kilburn
Queens Park
Kensal Rise
Kensal Green
West Kilburn
Westbourne Green
Kensal Town
North Kensington
Notting Hill
Shepherd's Bush
W10
W11
HARVIST ROAD
KILBURN LANE
BRONDESBURY ROAD
CARLTON VALE
HARROW ROAD
A404
B451
B413
B412
B450
A40
WESTWAY
MORTIMER RD
LADBROKE GROVE
ST QUINTIN AVENUE
NORTH POLE RD
WOOD LANE
WEST CROSS ROUTE A3220
WESTBOURNE PK RD
GT WESTERN RD
CHEPSTOW ROAD
PEMBRIDGE VILLAS
KENSINGTON PK RD
HOLLAND PK AVENUE
Grand Union Canal Walk
Kensal Rise Station
Kensal Green Station
Queens Park Station
Kilburn Park Stn
Westbourne Park Station
Ladbroke Grove Stn
Latimer Road Station
White City Station
Notting Hill Gate Stn
Holland Park Stn
St Charles Hospital
BBC Television Centre
Portobello Market
Golborne Med Cen
City of Westminster College
1 grid square represents 500 metres

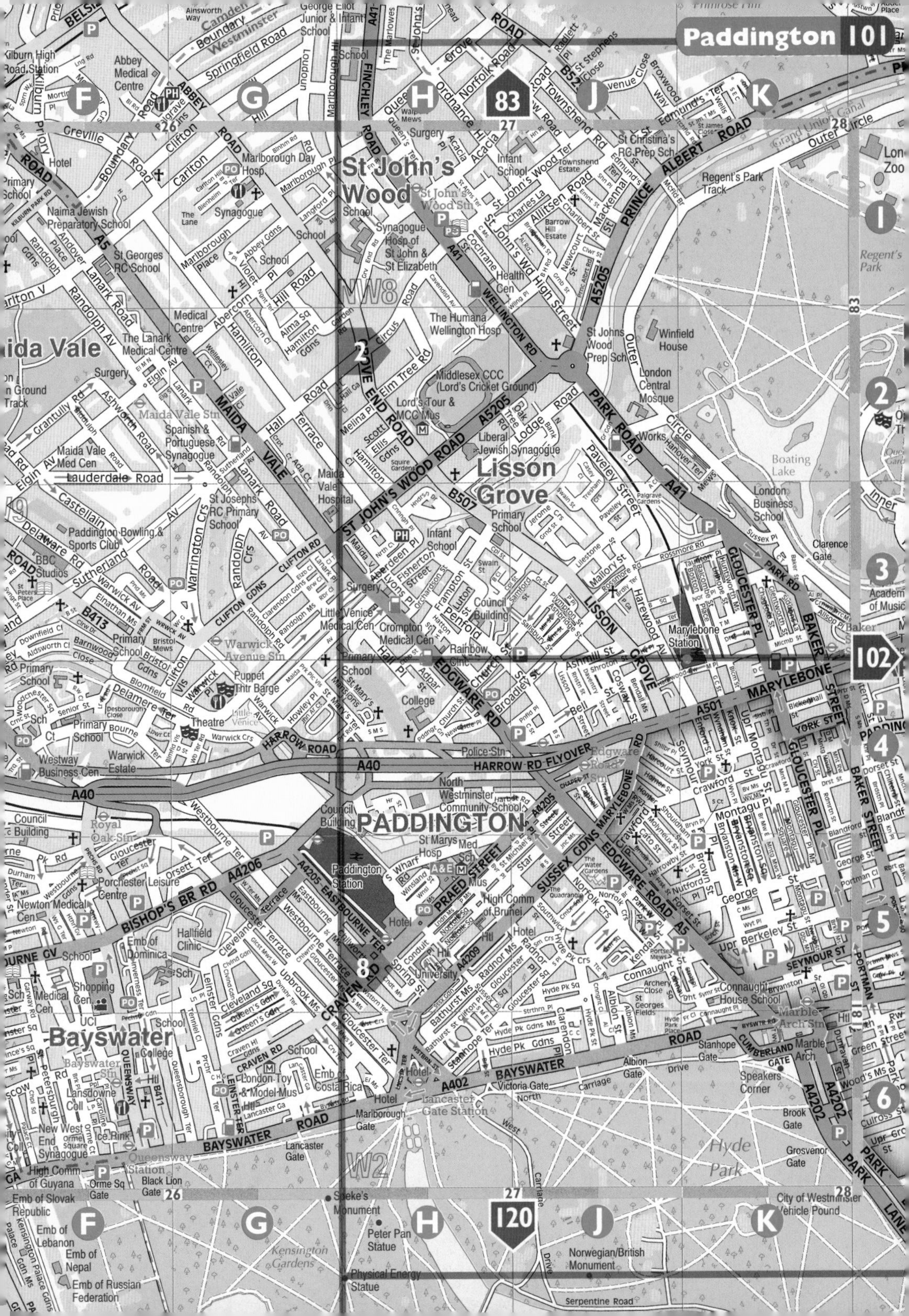

St John's Wood
NW8
Maida Vale
Lisson Grove
PADDINGTON
Bayswater
W2
Regent's Park
Hyde Park
Kensington Gardens
London Zoo
Grand Union Canal
Outer Circle
Middlesex CCC (Lord's Cricket Ground)
Lord's Tour & MCC Mus
London Central Mosque
Winfield House
Boating Lake
London Business School
Marylebone Station
Paddington Station
Edgware Road Stn
Marble Arch Stn
Lancaster Gate Station
Queensway Station
Bayswater Stn
Royal Oak Stn
Warwick Avenue Stn
Maida Vale Stn
St John's Wood Stn
Little Venice
Puppet Thtr Barge
BBC Studios
Paddington Bowling & Sports Club
Spanish & Portuguese Synagogue
The Humana Wellington Hosp
Hosp of St John & St Elizabeth
Liberal Jewish Synagogue
St Marys Hosp
London Toy & Model Mus
Speakers Corner
Speke's Monument
Peter Pan Statue
Physical Energy Statue
Norwegian/British Monument
City of Westminster Vehicle Pound
Emb of Slovak Republic
Emb of Lebanon
Emb of Nepal
Emb of Russian Federation
High Comm of Guyana
High Comm of Brunei
Emb of Costa Rica
Emb of Dominica
Victoria Gate
Albion Gate
Stanhope Gate
Brook Gate
Grosvenor Gate
Clarence Gate
Marlborough Gate
Lancaster Gate
Black Lion Gate
Orme Sq Gate
Marble Arch
MAIDA VALE
EDGWARE RD
ST JOHN'S WOOD ROAD
PRINCE ALBERT ROAD
PARK ROAD
BAKER STREET
GLOUCESTER PL
MARYLEBONE RD
HARROW RD FLYOVER
HARROW ROAD
BAYSWATER ROAD
BISHOP'S BR RD
PRAED STREET
SUSSEX GDNS
EASTBOURNE TER
CRAVEN RD
QUEENSWAY
PARK LANE
FINCHLEY ROAD
GROVE END ROAD
WELLINGTON RD
CLIFTON GDNS
A40
A5
A41
A501
A402
A4202
A4205
A4206
A5205
B507
83
102
120
F G H J K
26 27 28
1 2 3 4 5 6

102

1 grid square represents 500 metres

84
101
121

85
104
122
Hoxton
Pentonville
FINSBURY
Clerkenwell
St Luke's
Holborn
CITY
Barbican
PENTONVILLE ROAD
CITY ROAD
GOSWELL ROAD
OLD STREET
CLERKENWELL ROAD
FARRINGDON ROAD
GRAY'S INN ROAD
KING'S CROSS ROAD
ROSEBERY AVENUE
HOLBORN
HOLBORN VIADUCT
NEWGATE
LONDON WALL
CHEAPSIDE
CANNON ST
FLEET ST
ALDWYCH
KINGSWAY
CHANCERY LANE
VICTORIA EMBANKMENT
UPPER THAMES STREET
SOUTHWARK STREET
STAMFORD STREET
BLACKFRIARS ROAD
SOUTHWARK BRIDGE ROAD
KG WILLIAM ST
FINSBURY PAVEMENT
MOORGATE
BUNHILL ROW
CHISWELL ST
SHEPHERDESS WALK
NEW NORTH ROAD
EAST ROAD
VESTRY STREET
Angel Stn
Old Street Station
Farringdon Stn
Barbican Stn
Moorgate Stn
St Paul's Station
Mansion House Stn
Cannon Street Station
Bank Stn
Monument Stn
Blackfriars Station
City Thameslink Stn
Chancery Lane Stn
Holborn Stn
Temple Station
London Bridge
Southwark Bridge
Millennium Bridge
Blackfriars Bridge
Waterloo Bridge
St Paul's Cathedral
Bank of England (& Mus)
The Monument
City Road Basin
PO Sorting Office
London Weather Centre
Gray's Inn
Lincolns Inn
Somerset House
Courtauld Institute
Kings College London
HQS Wellington (Master Mariners)
HMS President
Oxo Tower Wharf
Bankside Gallery
Shakespeare's Globe Theatre
Vinopolis City of Wine
Golden Hinde Educational Museum
Royal National Theatre
National Film Theatre
Royal Festival Hall
Queen Elizabeth Hall
Hayward Gallery
The London Television Centre (LWT)
Cleopatra's Needle
London Dungeon
Hays Galleria
Mus of Tea & Coffee
Entrance to Strand Underpass (northbound only)
F G H J K
1 2 3 4 5 6
31 32 33

104
86
103
123
13
7
A
B
C
D
E
1
2
3
4
5
6
533
34
35
Haggerston
SHOREDITCH
BETHNAL GREEN
SPITALFIELDS
St George in the East
Shadwell
Wapping
South Hackney
E2
E1
E1W
KINGSLAND ROAD
A10
SHOREDITCH HIGH ST
HACKNEY ROAD
A1208
COLUMBIA ROAD
B118 GOSSET STREET
BETHNAL GREEN ROAD
A1209
OLD STREET
GT EASTERN STREET
A1202
COMMERCIAL STREET
BRICK LANE
B135
CHESHIRE STREET
DUNBRIDGE ST
SCLATER STREET
WHITECHAPEL ROAD
A11 MILE END
COMMERCIAL ROAD
A13
CABLE STREET
THE HIGHWAY
A1203
EAST SMITHFIELD
ROYAL MINT ST
LEMAN ST
MANSELL STREET
MINORIES
BISHOPSGATE
A10 BISHOPSGATE
HOUNDSDITCH
LEADENHALL ST
FENCHURCH ST
THAMES ST
CAMBRIDGE HEATH ROAD
A107
MARE ST
VICTORIA PARK
OLD FORD ROAD
Liverpool Street Station
Shoreditch Station
Aldgate East Stn
Aldgate Stn
Tower Gateway Stn
Tower Hill Stn
Fenchurch St Stn
Whitechapel Stn
Bethnal Green Stn
Cambridge Heath Stn
Shadwell Stn
Monument Stn
Old Spitalfields Market Hall
The Royal London Hospital
Tower of London
Tower Bridge
London Bridge
World Trade Centre
News International
Tobacco Dock
River Thames
Thames Path
1 grid square represents 500 metres

Ford
Old Ford Road
B118
87
Bow
Globe Town
Grove Road
A1205
Roman Road
B119
Bow Road
A11
A12
Bromley
Mile End
Mile End Hospital
Queen Mary & Westfield College
Half Moon Theatre
Stepney Green Station
St Clements Hospital
Cemetery
Bow Common
Burdett Road
St Paul's Way
Ben Jonson Road
Stepney
Mile End Stadium
Limehouse
Commercial Road
A13
East India Dock Road
Limehouse Link
Ratcliff
Poplar
West India Dock Rd
Westferry Rd
Narrow Street
Free Trade Wharf
Chimnocks Wharf
Victoria Wharf
Dunbar Wharf
Tower Hamlets
Southwark
Limehouse Town Hall
Poplar Station
A1261
E14
E3
West India Quay Station
Museum in Docklands
Canada Square
Canary Wharf
Billingsgate Fish Market
Rotherhithe Street
Salter Road
Nelson Dock Museum
Devons Rd Stn
St Andrews Hospital
106
124
Heron Industrial Estate
Blackwall Tunnel
F
G
H
J
K
2
3
4
5
6
36
37
38

106
88
105
125
A
B
C
D
E
1
2
3
4
5
6
538
39
40
Mill Meads
Plaistow
South Bromley
Blackwall
Axis Business Centre
Vanguard Trading Est
Marsh Gate Business Centre
Hedges & Butler Estate
Invicta Industrial Estate
Three Mill Lane
Three Mills Heritage Centre
Superstore
Channelsea Business Centre
Gas Works
Works
Bromley by Bow Station
Ian Mikardo High School
St Andrews Hospital
Barratt Industrial Park
Datapoint Business Cen
Pylon Trading Estate
Industrial Estate
Business Centre
Blackwall Trading Estate
River Lea or Lee
Culloden Primary School
Financial Times
Poplar Business Park
Blackwall Station
East India Station
Canning Town Station
West Ham Station
Plaistow Station
Royal Victoria Station
Mace Gateway
Royal Victoria Docks Watersports Centre
East London Crematorium
East London Cemetery
Memorial Recreation Ground
East London RUFC
Ranelagh Primary School
Portway Primary School
Grange Infant School
St Helens RC Primary School
Community School
Community College
Comprehensive School
Primary School
St Luke's Health Cen
Mint Business Park
Balaam Leisure Centre
Health Cen
Surgery
Abbey Rd Health Cen
Secondary School
Health Centre
Mosque
Billingsgate Fish Market
HIGH STREET
A118
BLACKWALL TUNNEL NORTHERN APPROACH
A102
MANOR ROAD
A1011
STEPHENSON STREET
NEW PLAISTOW RD
PLAISTOW ROAD
A112
HIGH ST
STOPFORD ROAD
BARKING ROAD
A124
NEWHAM WAY
A13
EAST INDIA DOCK ROAD
ABBOTT ROAD
B125
LEAMOUTH RD
A1020
LOWER LEA CROSSING
SILVERTOWN WAY
ASPEN WAY
COTTON STREET
PRESTON'S ROAD
Dock Road
Crows Road
Abbey Lane
Twelvetrees Crescent
Cody Road
North Crescent
South Crescent
Oban Street
Grange Road
Howard's Road
Stratford Road
Corporation Street
Jack Clow Road
Holland Rd
Memorial Av
Gainsborough Rd
Kimberley Rd
Bethell Avenue
Chargeable Lane
Star Lane
Malmesbury Rd
Fife Road
Fords Park Road
Radland Rd
Boreham Av
Victoria Dock Rd
Tower Hamlets
Greenwich
Newham
River Thames
1 grid square represents 500 metres

Upton Park
EAST HAM
Beckton
Custom House
E13
E6
E16
Upton Park Station
Upton Cross Primary School
West Ham United FC (Upton Park)
Newham Medical Centre
Cinema
Nightingale Clinic
Plaistow Hosp
Lister Community School
Southern Rd Primary School
University of East London
Greengate Medical Cen
Police Station
Newham Sixth Form College
Newham General Hospital
A&E
Kingford Community School
Brampton Manor School
Tollgate Primary School
Terence McMillan Stadium
Newham Leisure Centre
East Ham Industrial Est
Roman Road Primary School
Brampton Primary School
East Ham Jewish Cemetery
Synagogue
Central Park
East Ham Leisure Cen
College
Canning Town Recreation Ground
Rosetta Primary School
Scott Wilkie Primary School
West Becton Health Cen
King George V Park
Beckton Special School
Beckton Globe
Beckton District Park
East Beckton District Centre
Superstore
Health Centre
East London RFC
Beckton Station
Beckton Ski Centre
New Beckton Park
Winsor Primary School
Custom House for ExCeL Station
Prince Regent Station
Royal Albert Station
Beckton Park Station
ExCeL Exhibition Centre
Royal Victoria Dock
Royal Albert Dock
London City Airport
Drew Primary School
St Marks Industrial Estate
BARKING ROAD
A124
CENTRAL PK ROAD
B167
RANCLIFFE RD B167
HIGH STREET SOUTH A117
GREENGATE ST
PRINCE REGENT LANE
A112
NEWHAM WAY A13
VICTORIA DOCK RD
ROYAL ALBERT WAY A1020
CONNAUGHT BR
CONNAUGHT RD
Lonsdale Avenue
Stokes Road
Roman Road
Humberstone Road
Tunmarsh Lane
Strait Road
Dock Road
89
108
126
F G H J K
41 42 43
1 2 3 4 5 6

108
90
107
127
A124
A406
A13
A1020
A117
NORTH CIRCULAR ROAD
ROYAL DOCKS ROAD
NEWHAM WAY
ALFRED'S WAY
EAST HAM AND BARKING BY-PASS
WOOLWICH MNR WAY
WOOLWICH MNR
WOOLWICH MANOR WAY
ROYAL ALBERT WAY
ROYAL ALBERT RD
ST PAULS RD
Wallend
E6
Creekmouth
St Josephs RC Primary School
Abbey Sports Centre
Surgery
Medical Cen
Primary School
Morley Road
King Edward Road
Jackson Road
Greatfields Road
Movers Lane
Perth Road
Keith Road
Wheelers Cross
Devon Rd
Wedderburn Road
Gordon Road
Sutton Rd
Alfred's
Sussex Road
Langdon School
Langdon Crs
Primary Sch
Works
St Michaels RC Primary School
Abbey Park Industrial Est
The Shaftesburys
The Orchard Health Cen
Boundary Road
Gascoigne Road
St Ann's
New England Industrial Est
Jenkins Lane
Spur Road
Showcase Newham Cinema
Abbey Wharf Industrial Estate
Ind Est
River Road Business Park
Westminster Gdns
Waverley Gdns
River Road
Lyon Business Park
Katella Trading Est
Cromwell Business Cen
Barking Creek
Vicarage Lane
Gooseley Lane
Folkestone Road
Brighton Road
Eastbourne Rd
St Alban's Avenue
Mountfield Road
Charlemont Rd
Norman Road
Hameway
South
Beckton Triangle Retail Park
Eric Clarke Lane
Claps Gate Lane
Superstore
East Ham Nature Reserve
Beckton Ski Centre
Gateway Retail Park
Eastbury Road
Alpine Bus Cen
GX Superbowl
Alpine Way
The London Ind Estate
Aaron Hill Road
Roding Road
London Ind Park
County Rd
Henry Addlington Cl
Winsor Terrace
Stonewall
Beckton Station
Cygnet Clinic
Beckton
Gallions Primary School
Knok
Newark
Bradymead
Downings
Covelees Wall
Oxleas
Horse Leaze
Warwall
Health Centre
Beckton District Centre
Frobisher Road
Savage Gardens
Winsor Primary School
New Beckton Park
Pennyroyal Avenue
Royal Docks Medical Cen
Renfrew Cl
Strait Road
Cyprus Place
Cyprus Station
University of East London Campus
University Way
Gallions Reach Station
Armada Way
Gallions Road
Royal Albert Dock
King George V Dock
Margaret or Tripcock Ness
Newham
Greenwich
1 grid square represents 500 metres
Brixham St
Storey

Castle Green
Goresbrook Road
Maplestead Road
Barking Ind Park
Alfreds Way Industrial Est
A13
Barking RUFC
Renwick Industrial Estate
Renwick Road
Box Lane
Scrattons Ter
Julia Gardens
Levine Gdns
Works
Crescent
Maybury Road
Wivenhoe Road
Roxwell Road
Roycraft Avenue
Bastable Avenue
Thames View Clinic
Thames View Junior & Infant School
Stanley Avenue
Curzon Crs
Alderman Av
Stern Close
Keel Close
Choats Road
Blessing Way
Wanderer Drive
Sovereign Road
Gt Galley Close
Skillion Business Park
Riverside Industrial Est
Estuary Cl
Thames Road
River Road Business Park
Radford Way
Crossness Road
Callions Cl
Bankside Park Industrial Est
Marine Dr
Galleons Drive
Mallards Rd
Marine Drive
Atlantis Cl
Buzzard Creek Industrial Est
Creek Road
Creekmouth Industrial Park
Long Reach Road
River Road
Works
Trafalgar Business Centre
Anglian Industrial Estate
Balmoral Trading Estate
Buzzard Creek Industrial Estate
Atcost Road
Creekmouth
River Thames
Barking and Dagenham
Newham
Bexley
Barking Reach
Greenwich
Cross Ness
St Andrews Cl
Fairway Drive
Voyagers Cl
Thamesbank Place
Copperfield Rd
Watersmeet Way
Castilion Primary School
Crossway
Manordene Road
Summerton Way
Cherbury Close
Greenhaven Drive
Thamesmead Leisure Centre
Superstore
Primary School
Thamesmere Dr
Thamesmead Shopping Centre
Central Way
Bishop John Robinson CE Primary
Goldcrest Close
Kingfisher Close
Walsham Cl
Crossway
Haldane Road
Titmuss Avenue
Police Station
Carlyle Road
Crowden Way
Glendale Way
Jubilee Primary School
Hawksmoor Primary School
Waldstock Rd
Hutchins Road
A2041
Thamesmead
Newmarsh Rd
Woolwich Polytechnic School
SE28
Bentham Road
Austen Close
Byron Cl
Belvedere Road
Green Chain Walk
IG11
91
110
128
F G H J K
1 2 3 4 5 6
46 47 48
83 81

110
Sports Centre
Warner
Goresbrook Road
Starmans Close
St Peters RC Primary School
Surgery
92
Orchard Road
Lwr Broad St
BALLARDS
Oval Road North
Beam Avenue
Surgery
A
B
C
D
E
548
49
50
Merrielands Retail Park
Merrielands Crs
Polesworth Rd
Scrattons Ter
Gardens
Morrison Rd
Shaw Av
Levine Gdns
RIPPLE ROAD
A1306
NEW ROAD
Marsh Green Road
Street
South Close
North Close
Whitebarn Lane
Review Road
B178
Crosby Road
Dagenham Superbowl
Marsh Green School
Second Avenue
First Avenue
Centre Road
Beam Avenue
Third Av
Oval Rd North
Oval Rd South
Oval Rd S
Surgery
Beam Primary School
Link Road
E Entrance
Sierra Drive
Works
RM9
Dagenham Dock Station
LC
Chequers Lane
Kent Avenue
A13
Ford Industrial Park
Thames Avenue
Breach Lane
Power Station
Choats Road
Hindmans Way
Lake Road
Works
Fiesta Drive
Courier
Hindmans
Industrial Estate
Thunderer Road
Thames Av
Hornchurch Marshes
109
Works
River Thames
Halfway Reach
St Andrews Cl
Lytham Cl
Riverside Golf Club
Cherbury Close
Longworth Cl
Golf Course
Courtland
Fleming Way
Works
1
2
3
4
5
6
83
81
129
Road
A2016
Capital Industrial
1 grid square represents 500 metres

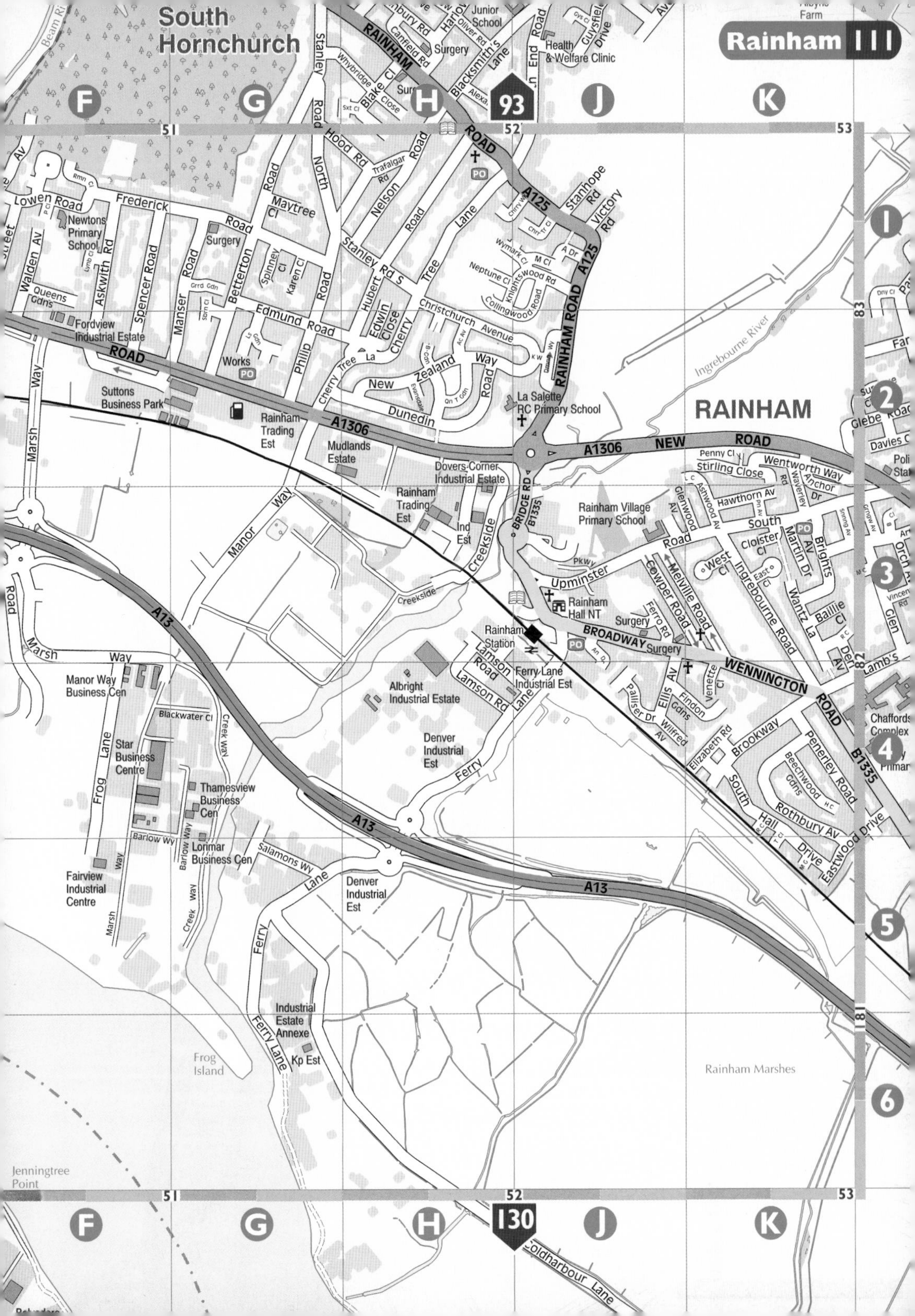
South Hornchurch
Junior School
Surgery
Health & Welfare Clinic
Rainham Road
Blacksmith's Lane
Whybridge Close
Blake Cl
Canfield Rd
Oliver Rd
Stanley Road
Guysfield Drive
93
F
G
H
J
K
51
52
53
Hood Rd
North Road
Trafalgar Rd
Nelson Road
PO
A125
Stanhope
Victory Rd
Rmn Cl
Lowen Road
Frederick Road
Newtons Primary School
Maytree Cl
Tree Lane
Stanley Rd S
Surgery
Walden Av
Askwith Rd
Spencer Road
Manser Road
Betterton Road
Spinney Cl
Karen Cl
Road
Hubert Rd
Cherry
Wymark Cl
M Cl
A Dr
Neptune Cl
Knights Wood Rd
Collingwood Road
Rainham Road
Queens Gdns
Edmund Road
Philip Road
Edwin Close
Christchurch Avenue
Fordview Industrial Estate
Road
Works
PO
Cherry Tree La
New Zealand Way
Road
Dunedin
Suttons Business Park
Rainham Trading Est
A1306
La Salette RC Primary School
Ingrebourne River
RAINHAM
A1306 New Road
Penny Cl
Stirling Close
Wentworth Way
Anchor Dr
Waverley
Mudlands Estate
Dovers Corner Industrial Estate
Rainham Trading Est
Ind Est
Creekside
Bridge Rd
B1335
Rainham Village Primary School
Glenwood Av
Ashwood Av
Hawthorn Av
South
Road
Cloister Cl
West Cl
East Cl
Martin Dr
Av
Brights
Ingrebourne Road
Wantz La
Baillie Cl
Upminster
Pkwy
Melville Road
Cowper Road
Ferro Rd
Manor Way
Marsh Way
Road
A13
Marsh Way
Creekside
Rainham Hall NT
Surgery
Rainham Station
Broadway
Surgery
PO
Wennington Road
Lamson Road
Lamson Rd
Ferry Lane Industrial Est
Albright Industrial Estate
Lane
Ellis Av
Findon Gdns
Venette Cl
Palliser Dr
Wilfred Av
Elizabeth Rd
Brookway
Penerley Road
B1335
Manor Way Business Cen
Blackwater Cl
Creek Way
Star Business Centre
Frog Lane
Thamesview Business Cen
Denver Industrial Est
Ferry
Beechwood Gdns
South Hall Drive
Rothbury Av
Eastwood Drive
A13
Barlow Wy
Barlow Way
Lorimar Business Cen
Salamons Wy
Lane
Fairview Industrial Centre
Way
Marsh
Creek Way
Denver Industrial Est
A13
Ferry
Industrial Estate Annexe
Kp Est
Ferry Lane
Frog Island
Rainham Marshes
Jenningtree Point
1
2
3
4
5
6
83
82
81
Glebe Road
Davies Cl
Lamb's
Chaffords Complex
Orchard
Glen
130
Coldharbour Lane

112
Yiewsley
Tapling Trading Estate
Rainbow Industrial Estate
Chantry Close
Surgery
Otterfield
Yew
Castle Av
Poplar Av
Whitethorn
Acacia Avenue
Laburnum
Willow
Elm Grove
Lime Av
Uxbridge FC
Goulds
Trout
Lane
Works
Tavistock
Padcroft Rd
Wimpole Rd
Winnock Road
Bentinck Rd
St Stephen's Rd
Primary School
High St
Fairfield Rd
Albert Rd
Colham Avenue
Edgar Rd
Maple Avenue
School
Providence Road
Aspen Close
Whitehorn Place
Stone Close
Horton Road
Crown Way
Crown Business Cen
Yiewsley Health Centre
Horton Rd
Knowles Cl
Roberts Cl
Independent Industrial Est
Horton Br Rd
Horton Ind Park
Horton Close
Iron Bridge Road North
Longwalk Road
Station Ap
West Drayton Station
Fairway Avenue
Sunray Av
Colne Av
Lawn Avenue
Colnham Ml
Weirside Gdns
Warwick Rd
Cherry Orch
Lantern Wy
Furzeham Road
Ruffle Cl
Holly Gdns
Iron Br Road S
Grand Union Canal W
Frays Avenue
Ferrers Avenue
Swan Road
Osprey Cl
Bellclose Road
Station Road
Newcourt Dr
Primary School
Kingston Lane
Boxwood Cl
Hawthorne Crs
Rutters Close
Berrite Works
Emden Cl
Mulberry Crs
Briar Way
Jasmine Ter
Lavender Rise
Stockley Rd
Stockley Cl
A408
Old Farm Rd
Wren Dr
Drayton Gdns
Bagley Close
Kings Rd
Queens Road
London Area Terminal Control Centre
St Catherines RC Primary School
Medical Centre
Church Road
Porters Way
Mulberry Pde
Works
Money La
Brooklyn Wy
The Green
Copse Close
Church Close
West Drayton Park Avenue
Police Station
Hanson Cl
Percy Rd
Brickfields Wy
Starveall Close
South Cl
Almond Av
Oak Av
Hazel Av
Golf Course
Stockley Farm Rd
Frays Cl
Mill Cl
Pippins Cl
Avenue Close
The Closes Recreation Ground
Thornton Av
Napier Cl
West Road
South Road
Thornton Close
Walnut Av
Smaldon Cl
STOCKLEY ROAD
St Martin's Cl
Mill Road
West Drayton
Elnuge
Wiltheys Place
Stainby Cl
Sipson Road
Chapman Cl
Bell Av
Fir Tree Av
Heathpark Golf Club
Longmead Primary School
Cemetery
Dell Road
Myrtle Cl
Thornton Avenue
Beech Cl
Blackthorn Av
Cricketfield Road
West Drayton Cricket Club
Primrose Dr
Tulip Wy
Lily Dr
Wise Lane
Treeside Close
Laurel Lane
Maxwell Road
East Road
Hotel
Rosesary Close
Berberis Walk
Benty
The Glebe
UB7
Cherry Lane
Cherry Lane Primary School
Blossom Way
Hotel
Byron Wy
Scott Close
Coleridge Way
Keats Way
Harmondsworth Road
Magnolia Street
Wise La
Rowan Road
Great Brambles
The
Milton Wy
Wordsworth Way
Vine Close
HOLLOWAY LANE
Shepiston
M4
Lupin Cl
Little Benty
Junction 4
Hotel
HOLLOWAY LANE
SIPSON ROAD
Holloway Close
Sipson
Russell Gdns
Harmondsworth
Heathrow Primary School
Vineries Cl
Sipson Lane
Meadowlea Cl
Acacia Mews
Priory Wy
A3044
Harmondsworth Lane
Blondell Cl
High St
Cambridge Cl
Hollycroft Close
A408
Vincent Cl
Hollycroft Gardens
Chambers Business Park
M4
Lane
School Rd
Summerhouse La
Moorland Road
Sipson Cl
Candover Close
Cumberlands River
LANE
SIPSON
132
Bomer Close
Ashby Way
HATCH
Airport Gate Business Centre
ROAD
Hotel
1 grid square represents 500 metres
A B C D E
1 2 3 4 5 6
506 07 80 79 78

Golf Course
Stockley Park Golf Club
UB11
Stockley Park Business Centre
Furzeground Way
The Square
Roundwood Av
Bolingbroke Way
DAWLEY ROAD
A437
Botwell Common Road
Princes Pk Pde
Princes Pk Cir
Beechwood
Juniper Way
Lime Grove
Barra Hall Road
Sycamore Avenue
Chestnut Close
Egan Wy
Walnut Close
Almond Close
Orwell
Badgers Cl
Manton Close
Willenhall Dr
Botwell Lane
94
Hayes FC
Hayes Social and Sports
Longmead Road
Churchfield Cl
Drenon Sq
Chard Road
Hitherbroom Road
Hamilton
Hughes R
Uxbridge
Townfield Sq
Centre Avenue
Ninth Av
Sixth Av
Eighth Av
Seventh Av
First Av
Second Av
Third Av
Fourth Av
Church Road
Moray Avenue
Forris Avenue
Lannock Road
Central Avenue
East Avenue
Coldharbour Lane
Minet Clinic
Minet Junior
Avondale
Birchway
Silverdale Industrial Estate
Hermon Gv
Halsway
Minet Drive
West Wk
Hunters Grove
East Walk
Fairdale Gdns
Mount Rd
Silverdale
Pump Lane
Pump L Industr
Trading
Provident Ind Est
Regent Business C
Rostrever Gardens
Golden Crs
Hayes Pool
Rec Gnd
Sikh Temple
Botwell La
Primary School
St Anselms Road
Nield Road
Crown Close
Austin Road
Little Rd
Superstore
Chailey Industrial Est
Silverdale Industrial Est
Silverdale Rd
Peter James Business Cen
Halls Business Cen
Johnsons Industrial Estate
Trinity Trading Est
Grand Union Canal Wk
Swallowfield Wy
Rigby Lane
Works
Speedway Industrial Est
Aberglen Industrial Est
Betam Rd
Kestrel Way
Adler Ind Est
Warnford Industrial Est
Caxton Trading Est
Crown Trading Cen
Printinghouse Lane
Clayton Road
Fairview Industrial Est
Blyth Rd
Frogmore Industrial Est
Station Rd
Cranford Park Primary School
Hayes & Harlington Station
UB3
Denbigh Dr
Stormount Dr
Snowdon Crs
Conway Drive
Clevedon Gdns
Burnham Gdns
Marlow Gdns
Windsor Gdns
Guinness Cl
Bourne Avenue
Glamis Crs
Waltham Avenue
Colbrook Av
Colbrook Cl
Skipton Drive
Carnarvon Drive
Seaton Road
Wentworth Crs
Mildred Avenue
Elers Road
Elers Clinic
Ross Cl
Dawley Road
Woodhouse Cl
N HYDE RD
Keith Road
Millington Rd
Millington Road
Albert Rd
Station Road
Old Station Rd
Squirrels Trading Est
Viveash Cl
Nestle's Avenue
North Hyde Gardens
Bull's Bridge
114
Northfield Pk
Fairey Av
Hyde Way
Dallas Ter
Harold Av
Gordon Crs
A312 NORTH HYDE RD
Pinkwell Lane
Pinkwell Avenue
Pinkwell Primary School
Harlington Community School
Redmead Rd
Copthorne Ms
Bushey Rd
STATION ROAD
Monmouth Road
Crowland Avenue
Crane Gdns
Granville Road
Blair Cl
Wyre Gv
Laburnum Rd
Coronation Rd
Cranford Drive
Waterspash Lane
A312
Oakington Avenue
Repton Avenue
Clement Gdns
Bedwell Gdns
Woolacombe Wy
Lundy Dr
Croyde Avenue
Cleave Avenue
Phelps Way
Cranford Park Junior School
Carfax Rd
Hillborne Cl
Hillborne Road
Roseville
St Dunstans Cl
Fuller Wy
Moston Cl
Wilkins Close
Hillingdon Trail
Savoy Av
Carlton Av
Hotel
Bedwell Gardens
Lane
M4
Juncti 5
St Pauls Cl
St Peters Wy
Heathrow Medical Centre
HARLINGTON
STREET
HIGH
Gravel Works
Bletchmore Cl
Victoria Lane
Brickfield La
Imperial College Athletic Ground
William Byrd School
Hudson Road
Richards Cl
Sipson Lane
Hillingdon
Hounslow
Cranford Park
Cranford Lane
Shortlands
Manse Close
Harlington
High St
Manor La
THE
08
09
10
78
80
F
G
H
J
K
1
2
3
4
5
6
133
Cranford
Field
End
The Crescent
Gilpin
Lane
Raywood Close
Croft Cl
Pennine Way
Browngraves Road
New
Little Elms
Works
Acorn Gv
Saunton Av
Pendell Av
Langley Crs
The Cedars Primary School
Brunel Cl
Cranford

114
113
95
134
Uxbridge College
Superstore
Stirling Rd
Hamilton Rd
Priory Cl
Hughes Road
Hitherbroom Road
Prec Rd
Abbotsford Way
Abbey Cl
A312
UXBRIDGE ROAD
Uxbridge Rd
Elystan Business
Hayes Bridge Retail Park
Superstore
Longford Gdns
Delamere
Tollgate Drive
Lowden Rd
Alma Rd
Livingstone Rd
Ruskin Rd
Stanley Rd
Tudor Rd
School
Lancaster Rd
Dane Rd
Norman Av
Northcote Av
West Av
East Av
South Av
Greenford Road
Lady Margaret Road
North Av
Hall
Shackleton Road
SOUTHALL
UXBRIDGE ROAD THE BROADWAY
Saxon Rd
Alfred Gdns
Alexandra Av
St George's
Hindu Temple
North School
Mdw Rd
A4020
UXBRIDGE ROAD
Fire Stat
Hayes Town
Minet Clinic
Minet Junior & Infant School
Avondale Dr
Bourton
Clivesdale Dr
Gade Cl
Hermon Gv
Halsway
Cherry Gv
East Walk
Showers Way
Bullsbrook Rd
Springfield Road
Houston Business Park
Brook Industrial Est
Beaconsfield Road
Beaconsfield Primary School
Yeading FC
Bankside
Beresford
Ranelagh Road
Woodlands Road
Trinity Road
Townsend Road
West End Road
Hambrough Road
Abbotts Road
Oswald Road
Guru Nanak Medical Cen
Surgery
Medical Centre
Cherry Av
Blaire Peach School
Beaconsfield Road
Orchard Av
Joseph's Dr
Raynor Close
Beatrice Rd
SOUTH ROAD
A3005
Hambrough Primary Sch
Tel Ex
Avenue Road
Villiers Road
Hamilton Road
Herbert Road
Park Av
Milan Rd
Works
Grange Rd
Lewis Rd
Hanson Gdns
Surgery
Middle School
The Crs
Southall Stn
Arches Business Cen
Pump Lane Industrial Est
Trading Est
Pasadena Cl
Bilton Wy
Regent Business Cen
Peter James Business Cen
Halls Business Cen
Trinity Trading Est
Hillingdon
Ealing
Grand Union Canal
White St
The Straight
Southbridge Wy
Hortus Road
Kingston Rd
Bridge
Hortus Cen
Dairy Meadow Prim School
Featherstone Industrial Est
Dilloway Industrial Est
The Green
Queen's Rd
Dokal Industrial Est
Spencer St
Clarence St
Dudley Rd
Balfour Rd
Balfour Business Cen
Johnson Street
Works
Brent Park Industrial Estate
Brent Road
Featherstone Road Hlth Clinic
Hakim Qureshi Clnc
School
Church Av
Cem
Marlow Rd
Havelock Primary School
Trident Wy
Rubastic Rd
Scotts Rd
Caxton Rd
Lonsdale Rd
Marlborough Road
International Trading Est
Sussex Rd
Primary School
Waltham Rd
King St
Havelock Road
Surgery
Emerald Sq
Western Rd
Belmont Av
Dagmar Rd
Hammond Road
Victoria Road
Rectory Rd
MERRICK ROAD
A3005
UB2
Bull's Bridge
Boeing Way
Trident Way
Derley Road
Greenland Crs
Albert Rd
Florence Rd
The Mosque
Norwood Road
Superstore
Bulls Bridge Road
Bullsbridge Industrial Estate
Bullsbridge Industrial Est
Tilney Road
Three Bridges Primary School
Leonard Rd
Tachbrook Rd
Featherstone School
Montague Road
Road
Adelaide Rd
Clifton Rd
Endsleigh Rd
School
Ellison Gdns
Witley Gdns
Grand Union Canal
Talbot Rd
HYDE RD
Christopher Rd
Market Trading Est
Hayes Rd
Western Road
Manor Wy
Leamington Rd
Recreation Rd
Stratford Rd
George St
Endsleigh Industrial Est
Witley Industrial Est
Wolf Fields Primary School
A312
The Common
Wentworth Road
Regina Rd
Lea Road
Gordon Rd
Williams Rd
Grand Union Canal Walk
Burket Cl
Barnes Av
Kingsbridge Road
North Hyde
Southall Lane
Airlinks Golf Club
Convent Way
Surgery
Raleigh Road
Penbury Road
Ditton Rd
Norwood Green Infant School
Norwood Green Junior School
Thorncliffe
Craneswater Pk
The Gln
Junction 3
Spitfire Way
International Av
Victory Way
Shannon Cl
Holly Farm Road
N Hyde Lane
Ringway
Kings Arbour
Rost Gdns
Ringway
Dade Wy
Hadley Gardens
Crosslands Av
Clunbury Avenue
Brandon
Lane
Fern
Watersplash Lane
Church Road
Golf Course
Air Links Industrial Estate
North Hyde La
Grange Cl
The Alders
Durham Av
The Hartlands
Heston Services
M4
Cranford Community College
Crane Lodge Road
Parkway Trading Estate
North Road
TW5
Heston Gra La
West Pk Cl
Heston Park Cricket Club
Rosary RC Primary Sch
Heston Pool
Harlech Gdns
Phoenix Way
Berkeley Primary School
The Vale
Berkeley Waye
Somerset Waye
Blossom Waye
Heston Av
The Cft
Worthing Rd
Memorial Cl
Heston Rd
Parkway Trading Estate
High Street
Quinton Close
Cranford
Bleriot Rd
Cobham Road
Wright Rd
Fairmead
Cranford Lane
Scott Gdn
Beechcroft Cl
Whytecroft
Speart La
Orch Av
Oak Av
New Heston Rd
Heston
The Andrew Ewing Primary School
Westbrook Road
Heston Ind Mall
Devon Wave
Warren
The Cedars Primary School
Brunel Cl
THE PARKWAY
Johnson
Sopwith Rd
Whittle Rd
Alcock
Norman Crs
1 grid square represents 500 metres

Dormer's Wells
Burns Avenue
Palgrave Avenue
Kingsley Avenue
Oakwood Av
Milford Road
Kenton Av
Longford Avenue
Atherton Pl
Dormer's Lane
K S Medical Centre
Dormers Wells Primary School
Greenford Road
West Middlesex Golf Club
Golf Course
96
F
G
H
J
K
Manor Ct
Manor House School
Tennyson Road
Hanwell Stn
Hanwell
Primary School
York Av
Balfour Av
Church Rd
Alwyne Rd
Conolly Rd
Lawn Gdns
Myrtle Gdns
Laurel Gdns
Station Rd
Half Acre Rd
Broadway
Uxbridge Road
Police Station
High St
Park View Rd
Melrose Dr
Uxbridge Rd
Southall Park
Villiers High School
Barrett Ind Park
Green Drive
Argyll Av
Knowsley Avenue
Park Avenue
Morland Gdns
Uxbridge Road
A4020
Brentvale Av
Blackmore Av
Works
Windmill Business Centre
Windmill Lane
Iron Br Cl
Ellis Road
Alderson Place
Alexander Cl
West Park Road
A&E
Ealing Hospital
Chaucer Clinic
Chevy Rd
Navigator Drive
PO
A3002
Boston Rd
Factory
Westminster Rd
Jessamine Road
Walker Cl
St Marks Primary School
Great Western Industrial Park
Dean Way
Armstrong Way
Three Bridges Business Centre
A4127
Green Lane
Bishop's Rd
St Mark's Road
St Dunstan's Road
Rosebank Road
Osterley Park Rd
Studley Grange Rd
Humes Avenue
St Margaret's Road
Billetts Hart
Belvedere Rd
Trumpers
Middlesex Business Cen
The Bridge Business Cen
Glade
Grand Union Canal Walk
Cookham Cl
Baxter Cl
Post Lane
McNair Rd
Works
Quaker La
Hunt Rd
Hillary Rd
Wylie Rd
Gregory Rd
Sybil Elgar School
Havelock Road
Trubshaw Rd
Poplar Av
Wolsey Cl
Osterley RFC
Tentelow Lane
The Waterside Trading Cen
Grand Union Canal Wk
Boston Business Park
River Brent Business Park
116
Windmill Lane
The Aviary
Three Bridges Primary School
Melbury Avenue
Shaftesbury Avenue
Stour Av
Minterne Av
Dorset Av
Sherborne Av
Blandford
Ealing
Hounslow
Norwood Green
Wimborne Av
Manston Av
Cranborne Avenue
St Marys Av
Norwood Road
Norwood Gn Rd
St Marys Av
Osterley Lane
Osterley Lane
The Lawn
Boundary Cl
Green Wk
Windmill Lane
B454
Osterley Lane
Osterley Park House
Osterley Park
Ferraro Cl
Biscoe Cl
Wheatlands
Old Cote Drive
Heston Junior School
Heston Community Sports Hall
Heston Infant School
Heston Community School
Jersey Road
Ashley Dr
Lingwood Gardens
Wood Lane
Grasshoppers RFC
Crown Close
Osterley
135
Jersey Road
Bassett Gdns
Thistleworth Cl
Thornbury
St Mary's Crs
Osterley Av
Great West Road
Great W Rd
Brunel University (Osterley Campus)
Church Road
Eldon Av
Hogarth Gdns
13
14
15
1
2
3
4
5
6

116
115
97
136
W13
W7
TW8
EALING
West Ealing
Brentford End
BRENTFORD
A B C D E
1 2 3 4 5 6
516
17
Shakespeare Road
Milton Road
Allingham Cl
Tennyson Road
Manor House School
Drayton Gdns
Drayton Av
Manor Road
West Ealing Station
West Ealing Business Centre
Works
St Johns Primary Sch
Drayton Green Road
Cemetery
Ecclestone Road
Felix Rd
Endsleigh Rd
Tewkesbury Rd
Mag Ct
Witham Rd
Green Man La
Kirchen Rd
Bedford Rd
Harrington Rd
Hastings Road
Broughton Road
Denmark Rd
Arden Rd
Dane Rd
Fire Station
Craven Avenue
Craven Road
Bowling Club
Police Station
College
UGC
Clifton Lodge Sch
The Questors Theatre
Ealing Civic Centre
Town Hall
Middle School
New Broadway
The Broadway
Bond St
High Street
Ealing Broadway Centre
Oxford Rd
Western Rd
Grove Rd
Uxbridge Road
Broadway A4020
Singapore Road
Church Rd
Holly Pk Rd
Netheravon Road
Shirley Gdns
Nightingale Road
Azalea
Balfour Av
York Av
Primary School
Hlth Cen
Michael Gaynor Cl
Barchester Cl
Boston Road
B455
Mattock Lane
Pitshanger Manor Mus
Ealing Tertiary College
Telephone Exchange
University
Ealing Film Studios
Walpole Park
Gosai
Snooker Club
Dean Gdns
Leeland Terrace
Gordon House Hlth Cen
St Johns Ambulance Station
Culmington Road
Churchfield Rd
Somerset Rd
Lavington Rd
Loveday Rd
Rathgar Av
Waldemar Av
Ealing Green
University
Balmain Close
Ealing & Grange
Acton Synagogue
Park Pl
The Park
Disraeli Road
Sunnyside Road
Cairn Av
Lammas Pk Gdns
Thames Valley University
St Mary's Rd
Beaconsfield Rd
Ranelagh Rd
Church Place
Grange Primary School
Church Gdns
Liverpool Rd
St James Av
Regina Road
Sydney Rd
Westfield Road
Seaford Rd
Sherwood Close
Surg
Grosvenor Road
Jessamine Road
Montague Av
Montague Road
St George's Road
Dean's Rd
City of Westminster Cemetery
Works
Oaklands Primary School
Oaklands Road
Croft Gdns
Seward Road
Coldershaw Rd
St Kilda Road
Adelaide Rd
Westfield
Leighton Road
Hessel Road
Northfield Rd
Balfour Road
Salisbury Road
Mayfield Avenue
Graham Av
Northcroft Rd
Bernard Av
Glenfield Rd
Dudley Gardens
Kingsdown Av
Camborne Av
Leyborne Av
Carew Rd
Walpole Cl
Lyncroft Gdns
Northfield Avenue B452
St Aidan's Rd
Elers Rd
Clovelly Rd
Gloucester Rd
Coningsby Rd
Lothair Rd
South Ealing Rd
B452
Cumberland Rd
Manton Avenue
Elthorne Avenue
Elthorne Pk Rd
Surgery
Whitehall Rd
Balmoral Gdns
Walmer Gdns
Midhurst Rd
Erlesmere Gdns
Claygate Rd
Wyndham Rd
Altenburg Avenue
Green Av
Fielding Primary School
Cranmer Av
Belsize Av
Ridley Av
Fulmer Wy
Woodstock Av
Mervyn Rd
Raymond Rd
Haslemere Av
Clitherow Av
Chepstow Rd
Cantley Rd
Christopher Gdns
Cardiff Rd
Windermere Road
Weymouth Avenue
Trent Av
Devonshire Rd
Overdale Rd
Dorset Rd
South Ealing Stn
Works
Surgery
Airedale Rd
Netherbury Rd
Creighton Rd
Northfields Station
Bramley Rd
York Rd
Hereford Rd
Primary School
Wellington Rd
Julien Rd
Temple Rd
Durham Rd
Pope's
Maple Gv
Lilac Gdns
Olive Road
Rose Gdns
Chestnut Gv
Hawthorn Rd
Studley Grange Rd
Osterley Vw Rd
Rosebank Road
Humes Avenue
Belvedere Rd
Trumpers Way
Townholm Crescent
Elthorne Park High School
Elthorne Sports Centre
Grand Union Canal
Boston Business Park
Wyke Gdns
Southdown Avenue
A3002
Chalfont Wy
Burnham Way
Cawdor Crs
Blondin Avenue
Niagara Av
Laurel Clinic
B4491 Little Ealing Lane
Chandos Avenue
North Rd
South Road
Ealing Park Health Cen
Radbourne Av
Lawrence Rd
Junction Rd
King Fahad Academy (Girls Upper School)
Occupation La
River Brent
Wellmeadow Rd
Boston Manor Station
Boston Gardens
Boston Manor Road
Swyncombe Av
Windmill Road
Gumleigh Rd
Convent Gdns
Ealing Park Gdns
Murray Road
Carlyle Road
Darwin Road
Whitestile Road
Enfield Road
Ealing Road
Claypond Gdns
Chestnut Av
The Ride
Clitherow Rd
Gunnersbury Catholic School
Reynard Mills Trading Estate
Burden Close
Our Lady of St Johns
Grove Rd
Eastbourne Rd
Challis Rd
Golf Course
M4
Transport Avenue
York Rd
Brook La N
Layton Rd
Brook Lane Bus Cen
Brentford Stn
Glenhurst Rd
Orchard Rd
Hamilton Rd
Clifden Rd
Brentford FC London Rd (Griffin Pk)
Riverbank Wy
Church St
Health Cen
Robin Gv
Willow Cl
Somerset Rd
The Butts
Brentford School for Girls
Lateward Rd
Half Acre
St Paul's CE Primary School
Wyke Green Golf Club
Centaurs RFC
Centaurs Business Cen
Syon Lane B454
Oaklands Avenue
Grasshoppers RFC
Crowntree Close
Wyke Cl
Superstore
Macfarlane Lane
Grant Wy
Shield Drive
Amalgamated Dr
West Cross Way
Harlequin Avenue
Superstore
Great West Trading Estate
Rock Works
Commerce Road
Grand Union Canal Walk
Wood Lane
Braybourne Dr
Syon Pk Gdns
Hotel
Great W Rd
A4
Syon La B454
Syon Lane
Works
Superstore
Warkworth Gdns
Cherry Crs
Almond Av
Rowan Rd
Hornbeam
Beech Av
Brentford Business Cen
A315
Brentford Medical Cen
Catherine Wheel Rd
Brentford County Court
Pump Alley
The Ham
Augustus
Justin
1 grid square represents 500 metres
(Osterley Campus)

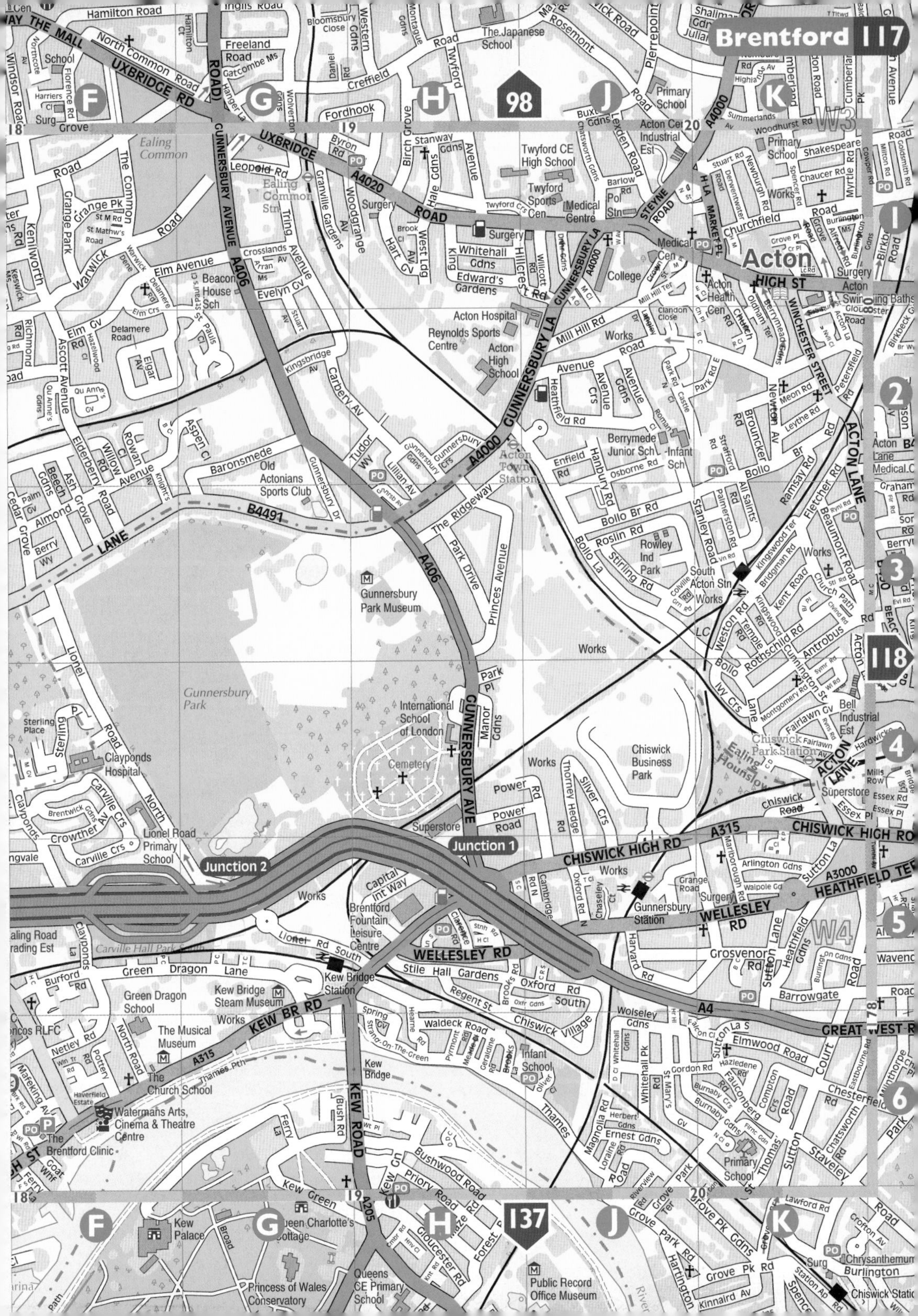

Brentford 117
98
118
137
F
G
H
J
K
1
2
3
4
5
6
18
19
20
W3
W4
Acton
HIGH ST
Hamilton Road
North Common Road
UXBRIDGE RD
THE MALL
Freeland Road
Gatcombe Ms
Creffield
Twyford
The Japanese School
Rosemont
Primary School
Ealing Common
Leopold Rd
Ealing Common Stn
UXBRIDGE
A4020
ROAD
GUNNERSBURY AVENUE
A406
Twyford CE High School
Twyford Sports Cen
Medical Centre
Acton Central Industrial Est
A4000
STEYNE ROAD
Churchfield
Shakespeare
Chaucer Rd
Woodhurst Rd
Summerlands
Surgery
Whitehall Gdns
Edward's Gardens
College
Medical Cen
Acton Health Cen
Acton Swimming Baths
WINCHESTER STREET
GUNNERSBURY LA
Acton Hospital
Reynolds Sports Centre
Acton High School
Mill Hill Rd
Heathfield Rd
Berrymede Junior Sch
Infant Sch
Bollo Br Rd
Rowley Ind Park
South Acton Stn
Works
Acton Town Station
ACTON LANE
Elm Avenue
Beacon House Sch
Warwick Road
Kenilworth Rd
Grange Park
The Common
Delamere Road
Elm Gv
Ascott Avenue
Elderberry Road
Baronsmede
Old Actonians Sports Club
B4491
LANE
Carbery Av
Kingsbridge Av
Gunnersbury Park Museum
Gunnersbury Park
The Ridgeway
Park Drive
Princes Avenue
GUNNERSBURY AVE
International School of London
Cemetery
Manor Gdns
Park Pl
Chiswick Business Park
Chiswick Park Station
Power Rd
Power Road
Thorney Hedge Rd
Silver Crs
Claypond Hospital
Sterling Place
Lionel Road Primary School
Junction 1
Junction 2
Superstore
CHISWICK HIGH RD
A315
Gunnersbury Station
WELLESLEY RD
Heathfield Gdns
Sutton Lane
Grosvenor Rd
Barrowgate
A3000
HEATHFIELD TER
Capital Int Way
Brentford Fountain Leisure Centre
Lionel Rd South
Kew Bridge Station
Green Dragon Lane
Green Dragon School
Kew Bridge Steam Museum
The Musical Museum
KEW BR RD
Stile Hall Gardens
Oxford Rd South
Chiswick Village
A4
GREAT WEST R
Elmwood Road
Court
Chesterfield Rd
Waldeck Road
Strand-On-The-Green
Kew Bridge
KEW ROAD
Infant School
Thames
The Church School
Waterman's Arts, Cinema & Theatre Centre
The Brentford Clinic
Thames Pth
Ferry La
Bush Rd
Bushwood Road
Priory Road
Kew Green
Kew Palace
Queen Charlotte's Cottage
Princess of Wales Conservatory
Queens CE Primary School
Gloucester Rd
Forest Rd
Public Record Office Museum
Grove Park Rd
Grove Park Gdns
Hartington Rd
Kinnaird Av
Primary School
Chiswick Station
Burlington
Chrysanthemum
Staveley Rd
Sutton Court
St Thomas' Rd
Magnolia Rd
Ernest Gdns
Whitehall Pk
Bell Industrial Est
Essex Pl
Mills Row

118
99
117
138
A
B
C
D
E
1
2
3
4
5
6
W3
W12
W6
SW13
521
22
East Acton
Shepherd's Bush
Bedford Park
Acton Green
CHISWICK
Acton Central Station
Acton Park
King Fahad Academy (Boys School & Girls Lower School)
East Acton Primary School
Shepherd's Bush Cricket Club
Bromyard Leisure Centre
Janet Adegoke Leisure Centre
QPR FC Fulham FC (temp) (Loftus Road Stadium)
Acton Park Industrial Est
Vale Park Industrial
Acton Park Industrial Est
Southfield First & Middle Sch
Cobbold Primary School
Gayford Road Primary School
Acton Lane Medical Cen
Southfield Medical Centre
Orchard House School
Queen Charlottes & Chelsea Hosp
John Betts Primary School
Ravenscourt Square
Brackenbury Health Cen
Stamford Clinic
Flora Gardens Primary School
The Craven Clinic
Turnham Green Stn
Stamford Brook Stn
Ravenscourt Park Stn
Airedale Physiotherapy Clnc
UGC Cinema
Town Hall
Hogarth's House
Hogarth Business Park
Chiswick House
St Pauls Preparatory School
Swedish School
Lowther Prim Sch
Harrodian School
Chiswick Community School
Cavendish Primary School
Chrysanthemum Clnc
Hammersmith Bridge
Hounslow
Richmond upon Thames
Hammersmith & Fulham
Thames Path
UXBRIDGE ROAD A4020
THE VALE A4020
B491 SOUTHFIELD ROAD
B491 THE AVENUE
B409 BATH ROAD
B409 SOUTH PDE
ACTON LANE
GOLDHAWK RD A402
STAMFORD BROOK RD
PADDENSWICK RD
DALLING RD
GLENTHORNE
KING STREET
A315 CHISWICK HIGH ROAD
A3000 HEATHFIELD TER
GREAT W ROAD
GREAT WEST ROAD CHISWICK A4
GREAT WEST RD ELLESMERE RD GT W RD HOGARTH LA
A316 CHISWICK LANE
TURNHAM GN TER
BURLINGTON LANE
A316
ASKEW ROAD B408
B350
CASTELNAU
LONSDALE
1 grid square represents 500 metres

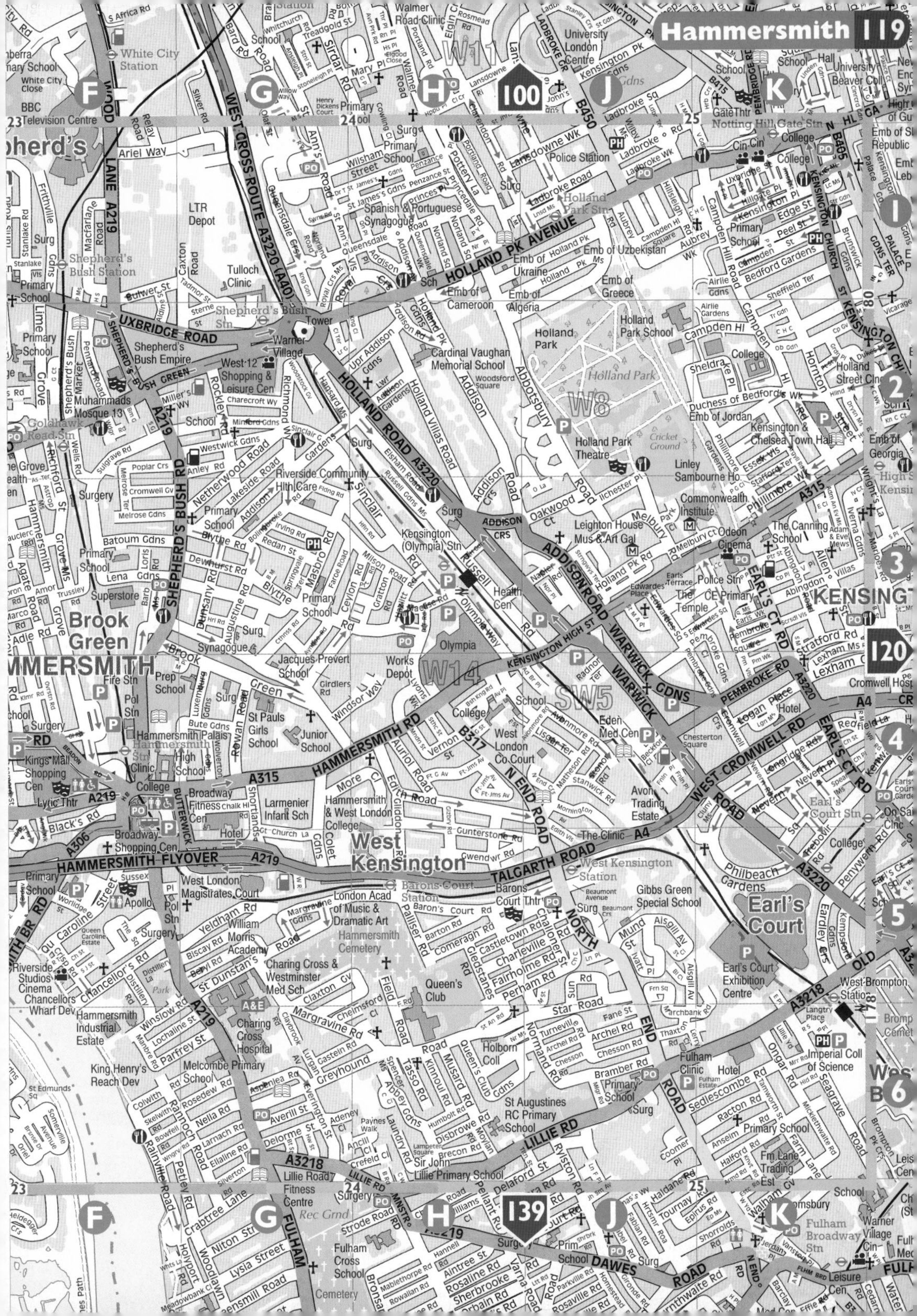
100
120
139
W11
W8
W14
SW5
White City Station
BBC Television Centre
Shepherd's Bush
Shepherd's Bush Station
Uxbridge Road
Shepherd's Bush Empire
West Cross Route A3220 (A40)
Holland Pk Avenue
Holland Park
Holland Park School
Holland Road A3220
Kensington (Olympia) Stn
Olympia
Kensington High St
Addison Road
Notting Hill Gate Stn
Ladbroke Road
Holland Park Stn
Commonwealth Institute
Leighton House Mus & Art Gal
Kensington & Chelsea Town Hall
Brook Green
Hammersmith
Hammersmith Rd
Hammersmith Flyover
Talgarth Road
West Kensington
West Kensington Station
Barons Court Station
Queen's Club
Charing Cross Hospital
Fulham Palace Road
Lillie Rd
West Cromwell Rd
Warwick Road
Earl's Court
Earl's Court Exhibition Centre
Earl's Court Stn
West Brompton Station
North End Road
Fulham Broadway Stn
Dawes Road
Kensington

120
101
119
140
A
B
C
D
E
1
2
3
4
5
6
Kensington Gardens
Hyde Park
Round Pond
The Serpentine
Serpentine Road
Knightsbridge
KENSINGTON
Brompton
South Kensington
West Brompton
SW7
SW10
BAYSWATER ROAD
KENSINGTON RD
KENSINGTON CHURCH ST
HYDE PK GA
KENSINGTON GORE
KNIGHTSBRIDGE
GLOUCESTER RD
PALACE GA
EXHIBITION ROAD
CROMWELL ROAD
CROMWELL RD
BROMPTON ROAD
BROMPTON RD
THURLOE PL
SLOANE STREET
PONT ST
FULHAM ROAD
KING'S RD
REDCLIFFE GDNS
FINBOROUGH RD
OLD BROMPTON
EDITH GV
BEAUFORT ST
OAKLEY ST
SYDNEY ST
ROYAL HOSPITAL ROAD
CHELSEA
Kensington Palace
Albert Memorial
Royal Albert Hall
Royal Geographical Society
Imperial Coll
Science Mus
Natural History Mus
Victoria & Albert Mus
Brompton Oratory
Serpentine Gallery
Speke's Monument
Peter Pan Statue
Physical Energy Statue
Norwegian/British Monument
Speakers Corner
High Street Kensington Stn
Gloucester Road Stn
South Kensington Stn
Knightsbridge Stn
Queensway Station
Lancaster Gate Station
Earl's Court Stn
West Brompton Station
Brompton Cemetery
Royal Marsden Hosp
Royal Brompton & National Heart Hospitals
Chelsea Physic Garden
Chelsea Old Town Hall
Carlyle's Ho. (NT)
Duke of York's HQ
National Museum
Albert Bridge
Battersea Bridge
Kensington & Chelsea
Wandsworth
Thames Path
Chelsea Reach
Peace Pagoda
Chelsea FC (Stamford Bridge)
1 grid square represents 500 metres

Mayfair
St James
WESTMINSTER
Belgravia
Pimlico
CHELSEA
Vauxhall
SW1W
102
141
122
9
15
10
16
11
17
F
G
H
J
K
28
29
30
1
2
3
4
5
6
PICCADILLY
PICCADILLY CIRCUS
HAYMARKET
STRAND
EMBANKMENT
National Gallery
Nelson's Column
Trafalgar Sq
Charing Cross Stn
Embankment Station
Cleopatra's Needle
Hungerford Bridge
NORTHUMBERLAND AV
COCKSPUR ST
WATERLOO PL
PALL MALL
Admiralty Arch
The Mall
Horse Guards Parade
WHITEHALL
Ministry of Defence
Downing St
British Airways London Eye
Saatchi Gallery
London Aquarium
Cabinet War Rooms
Treasury
Westminster Stn
BRIDGE ST
WESTMINSTER BR
Big Ben
Westminster Bridge
Westminster Hall
St Thomas' Hospital
PARLIAMENT SQ
Westminster Abbey
Westminster School
Houses of Parliament
Victoria Tower Gardens
City of Westminster
Lambeth
Museum of Garden History
Lambeth Bridge
MILLBANK
Tate Britain
Millbank Millennium Pier
River Thames
Vauxhall Bridge
Vauxhall Station
St George Wharf
PARRY ST
Covent Garden Flower Mkt
New Covent Garden Market
WANDSWORTH RD
NINE ELMS LANE
FENTIMAN RD
Green Park
Green Park Station
St James's Palace
Clarence House
Constitution Hill
Queen Victoria Memorial
Buckingham Palace
Buckingham Palace Gardens
Queen's Gallery
The Royal Mews
Birdcage Walk
St James's Park
St James's Park Stn
BUCKINGHAM GA
VICTORIA ST
Victoria Station
Victoria Coach Station
Cath
Playing Field
VAUXHALL BRIDGE ROAD
HORSEFERRY RD
Apsley House, The Wellington Museum
Hyde Park Corner Stn
HYDE PARK CORNER
Wellington Arch
Queen Mother Gate
GROSVENOR PLACE
BELGRAVE SQ
EATON SQ
ECCLESTON ST
BUCKINGHAM PALACE ROAD
Sloane Square Stn
PIMLICO RD
CHELSEA BR ROAD
EBURY BR RD
Chelsea Barracks
Museum
Ranelagh Gardens (site of Chelsea Flower Show)
The Lister Hospital
GROSVENOR ROAD
Pimlico Station
BELGRAVE ROAD
Chelsea Bridge
Grosvenor Bridge
QUEENSTOWN ROAD
Battersea Power Station (disused)
Battersea Dogs' Home
Battersea Park
Millennium Arena
Chelsea Bridge Gate
Tideway Industrial Est
South Bank Business Cen
Thames Path
City of Westminster Wandsworth
Nine Elms

122
103
121
142
A
B
C
D
E
1
2
3
4
5
6
VICTORIA EMBANKMENT
A3211
HQS Wellington (Master Mariners)
HMS President
Blackfriars Bridge
Millennium Bridge
Shakespeare's Globe Theatre
Cannon Street Station
The Monument
Southwark Bridge
London Bridge
Panorama Pier
Temple Station
Gilbert Collection
Entrance to Strand Underpass (northbound only)
Waterloo Bridge
Cleopatra's Needle
Embankment Station
The London Television Centre (LWT)
National Film Theatre
Royal National Theatre
Queen Elizabeth Hall
Royal Festival Hall
Hayward Gal
Hungerford Bridge
Tate Modern
Golden Hinde Educational Museum
Vinopolis City of Wine
Mus of Tea & Coffee
STAMFORD STREET
SOUTHWARK STREET
A3200
UPPER GROUND
Waterloo East Stn
Southwark Stn
UNION STREET
B300
Shell Centre
British Airways London Eye
County Hall
Saatchi Gallery
London Aquarium
Waterloo Station
International Rail Terminal
THE CUT
WATERLOO ROAD
BLACKFRIARS ROAD
A201
YORK RD
Guys Hospital
Borough Stn
The Borough
BOROUGH HIGH ST
MARSHALSEA RD
A2198 LONG LANE
GREAT DOVER STREET
WESTMINSTER BR RD
A302
Westminster Bridge
Florence Nightingale Museum
St Thomas' Hospital
A&E
United Medical & Dental Schools
LAMBETH PALACE RD
A3036
BAYLIS RD
A3202
BOROUGH RD
ST GEORGES CIRCUS
LAMBETH
LAMBETH ROAD
Imperial War Museum
Newington
ST GEORGE'S RD
LONDON RD
Elephant and Castle Stn
Elephant & Castle Station
Elephant & Castle Shopping Cen
NEW KENT ROAD
Archbishop's Park
Lambeth Palace
Museum of Garden History
A3203
Lambeth Bridge
NEWINGTON BUTTS
KENNINGTON LA
KENNINGTON ROAD
A23
WALWORTH RD
Newington Industrial Est
SE11
SE17
Kennington Stn
Vauxhall
London Balloon
Vauxhall Station
ALBERT EMB A3036
HARLEYFORD ROAD
Kennington
KENNINGTON OV
Surrey CCC (The Oval)
Oval Stn
A3 KENNINGTON PARK ROAD
Walworth
ALBANY ROAD
CAMBERWELL ROAD A215
FENTIMAN ROAD
Young England RFC
Royal National Thtr
CAMBERWELL
1 grid square represents 500 metres

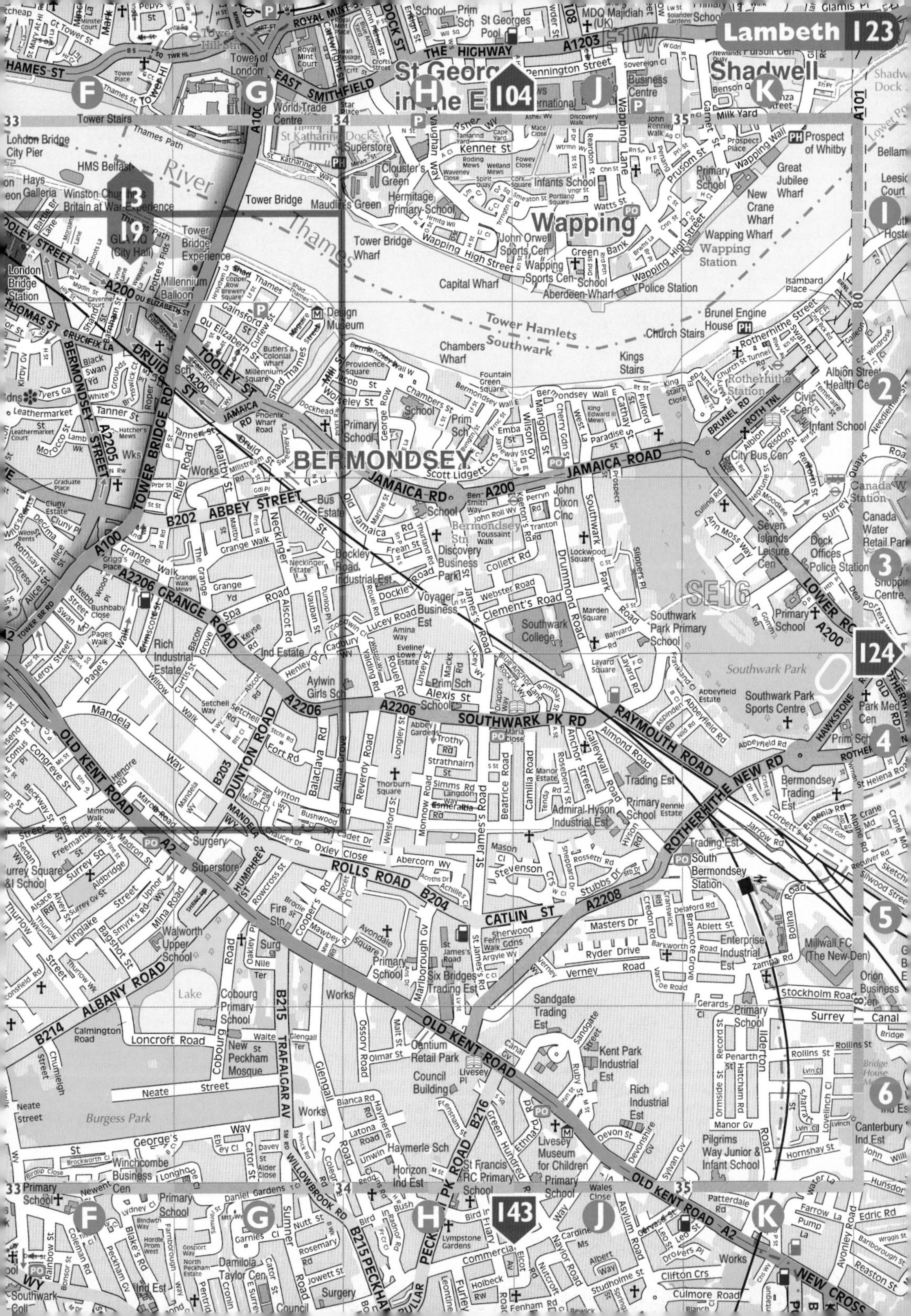

Shadwell
St George in the East
Wapping
BERMONDSEY
River Thames
Tower of London
Tower Bridge
HMS Belfast
Hays Galleria
London Bridge Station
London Bridge City Pier
Design Museum
Tower Hamlets
Southwark
SE16
Southwark Park
Burgess Park
THE HIGHWAY
EAST SMITHFIELD
Wapping High Street
Wapping Lane
TOOLEY STREET
TOWER BRIDGE RD
JAMAICA ROAD
ABBEY STREET
GRANGE ROAD
SOUTHWARK PK RD
RAYMOUTH ROAD
ROTHERHITHE NEW RD
LOWER ROAD
OLD KENT ROAD
ALBANY ROAD
ROLLS ROAD
CATLIN ST
DUNTON ROAD
BERMONDSEY STREET
Drummond Road
St James's Road
Verney Road
Ilderton Road
Rotherhithe Station
Bermondsey Stn
South Bermondsey Station
Wapping Station
Canada Water Station
Southwark Park Sports Centre
Millwall FC (The New Den)
Livesey Museum for Children
Surrey Canal
104
124
143
13
19
F
G
H
J
K
I
2
3
4
5
6
33
34
35

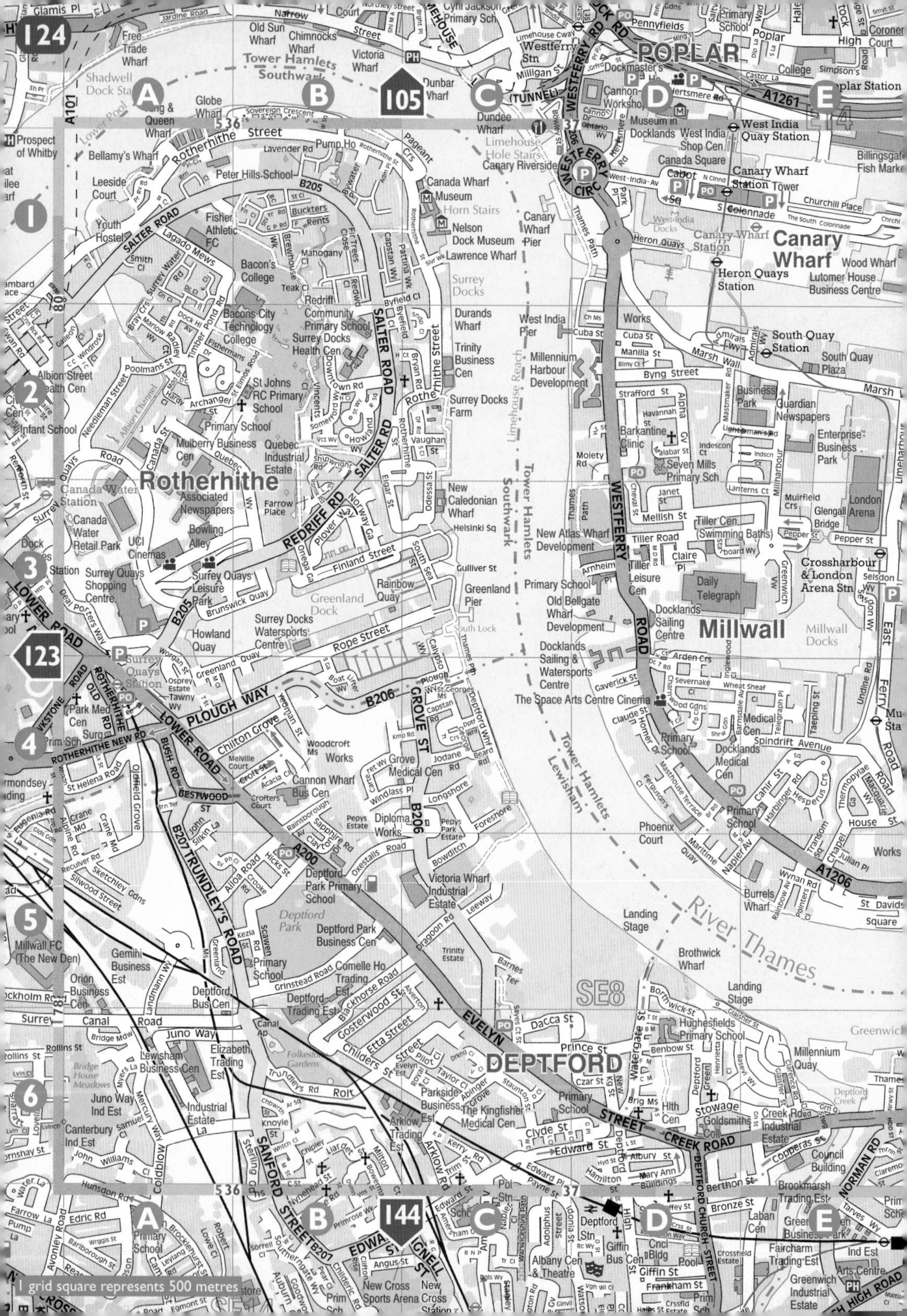

124
105
123
144
A
B
C
D
E
1
2
3
4
5
6
536
37
Shadwell Dock Stair
Lower Pool
Tower Hamlets
Southwark
King & Queen Wharf
Globe Wharf
Free Trade Wharf
Old Sun Wharf
Chimnocks Wharf
Victoria Wharf
Dunbar Wharf
Dundee Wharf
Narrow Street
Glamis Pl
Jardine Road
Prospect of Whitby
Bellamy's Wharf
Rotherhithe Street
Pump Ho
Lavender Rd
Pageant Crs
Peter Hills School
Leeside Court
Youth Hostel
SALTER ROAD
Lagado Mews
Fisher Athletic FC
Bacon's College
Bacons City Technology College
Canada Wharf Museum
Horn Stairs
Nelson Dock Museum
Lawrence Wharf
Surrey Docks
Durands Wharf
Trinity Business Cen
Surrey Docks Farm
Limehouse Hole Stairs
Canary Riverside
Canary Wharf Pier
Thames Path
Redriff Community Primary School
Surrey Docks Health Cen
St Johns RC Primary School
Primary School
Mulberry Business Cen
Quebec Industrial Estate
Rotherhithe
Canada Water Station
Canada Water Retail Park
Associated Newspapers
Bowling Alley
UCI Cinemas
Surrey Quays Shopping Centre
Surrey Quays Leisure Park
Surrey Quays Station
REDRIFF RD
Finland Street
Greenland Dock
Rainbow Quay
Greenland Pier
New Caledonian Wharf
Helsinki Sq
Surrey Docks Watersports Centre
Howland Quay
Rope Street
South Lock
PLOUGH WAY
B206
GROVE ST
LOWER ROAD
ROTHERHITHE NEW RD
Chilton Grove
Woodcroft Ms
Works
Grove Medical Cen
Cannon Wharf Bus Cen
Pepys Estate
Diploma Works
Victoria Wharf Industrial Estate
Deptford Park
Deptford Park Primary School
Deptford Park Business Cen
Trinity Estate
Comelle Ho Trading Est
Deptford Trading Est
Primary School
Grinstead Road
A200
EVELYN
DEPTFORD
SE8
Millwall FC (The New Den)
Gemini Business Est
Orion Business Cen
Deptford Bus Cen
Juno Way
Canal Road
Lewisham Business Cen
Elizabeth Trading Est
Juno Way Ind Est
Industrial Estate
Canterbury Ind Est
Bridge House Meadows
Folkestone Gardens
TRUNDLEY'S ROAD
SANFORD STREET
Arklow Trading Est
Parkside Business Est
The Kingfisher Medical Cen
Primary School
Hlth Cen
Goldsmiths Coll
Creek Rd Industrial Estate
CREEK ROAD
DEPTFORD CHURCH STREET
Council Building
Brookmarsh Trading Est
NORMAN RD
Deptford Stn
Giffin Bus Cen
Albany Cen & Theatre
Laban Cen
Green Business Park
Faircharm Trading Est
Arts Centre
Greenwich Industrial Estate
New Cross Sports Arena
Primary School
Hughesfields Primary School
Millennium Quay
Deptford Creek
Landing Stage
Brothwick Wharf
River Thames
Tower Hamlets
Lewisham
Limehouse Reach
Burrels Wharf
Phoenix Court
Primary School
Docklands Medical Cen
Medical Cen
The Space Arts Centre Cinema
Docklands Sailing & Watersports Centre
Old Bellgate Wharf Development
Docklands Sailing Centre
Millwall
Millwall Docks
Daily Telegraph
Tiller Leisure Cen
Tiller Cen (Swimming Baths)
Crossharbour & London Arena Stn
Glengall Bridge
London Arena
Enterprise Business Park
Guardian Newspapers
Business Park
New Atlas Wharf Development
Primary School
WESTFERRY ROAD
Seven Mills Primary Sch
Barkantine Clinic
Millennium Harbour Development
West India Pier
Works
South Quay Station
South Quay Plaza
Marsh Wall
Heron Quays Station
Canary Wharf Station
Canary Wharf
Lutomer House Business Centre
Wood Wharf
West India Docks
Canary Wharf Station Tower
Churchill Place
Cabot Sq
West India Quay Station
West India Shop Cen
Canada Square
Museum in Docklands
Cannon Workshops
Dockmaster's Ho
POPLAR
Westferry Stn
Pennyfields
Primary School
Poplar Station
A1261
A1206
Billingsgate Fish Market
WESTFERRY CIRC
(TUNNEL)
Cyril Jackson Primary Sch
St Davids Square
Works
1 grid square represents 500 metres

India Station
Newport Av
Jamestown Way
Naval Rw
Health Centre
Blackwall Station
ASPEN
Poplar Business Park
Blackwall Wy
Paul Julius Close
F
G
H
J
K
106
Blackwall
39
40
River Thames
Tower Hamlets
Greenwich
Newham
Greenwich
SILVERTOWN WAY
Dock Road
Royal Victoria Docks Watersports Centre
Gateway
Trafalgar Way
Boardwalk Pl
Poplar Dock
PRESTON'S ROAD
A102
Blackwall Reach
Landons Cl
Blackwall Basin
Lovegrove Wk
Lancaster Dr
A1206
Coldharbour
Horatio Pl
Sai Medical Cen
Wood Wharf Business Park
S W India Dock Entrance
Dome
Delta Wharf
Tunnel Avenue Trading Est
North Greenwich Station
Hanover Av
Wesley Avenue
Evelyn
Dock Road
Bell Lane
Works
Fisons Road
Minerva Works
Greenshields Industrial Est
Greenshields Industrial Estate
Knights Rd
Bradfield Road
Works
Bugsby's Reach
1
2
3
4
5
6
Pumping Station
Folly Wall
Capstan Square
River Barge Close
Stewart Street
Island Clinic
Ferry Road
Plevna St
Chipka St
New Union Cl
Tunnel Avenue
Ordnance Crs
Edmund Halley
West
East
Millennium Way
Parkside
Annandale Primary School
River Wy
John Harrison Wy
Thames Path
Gas Works
Dreadnought St
Boord St
A102
Marshfield St
Adult Education Cen
Amsterdam Rd
Rotterdam Dr
Cubitt Town Primary School
Friars Md
Rembrandt Cl
Millennium Dr
Schooner Cl
Millennium Wharf Development
Pier
Superstore
Cubitt Town
Mudchute City Farm
Millwall Park
Pier St
Sextant Av
Plymouth Whf
Storers Quay
Primary School
Caledonian Wharf Road
Empire Whf Rd
Seyssel St
Kingfield St
Billson St
Parsonage St
Glengarnock Av
ROAD
ISLE OF DOGS
Community Centre (Island History Trust)
Island Gardens Station
Stebondale Street
Saunders Ness Rd
Grosvenor Whf Rd
Newcastle Drawdock
MANCHESTER
Manchester Grove
George Green Mixed School
Ferry St
Morden Whf Road
Tunnel Avenue
Peterboat Cl
Lawrence Trading Est
Maritime Mus
A2203
Tunnel Av
BUGSBY'S WAY
W Parkside
Peartree Wy
Horn Link Wy
UCI Filmworks Cinema
Brocklebank Industrial Estate
Willoughby Way
BUGSBY'S WAY
A102
Horn Lane
Angerstein Business Park
Superstore
Peninsular Pk Rd
Feltram Way
Ind Est
126
Mauritius Road
Azof Street
BLACKWALL LANE
Armitage Rd
Lenthorp Rd
Glenforth St
Fingal St
Chilver St
Glenister Rd
East Greenwich Christ Church CE Prim Sch
Cadet Pl
Derwent St
Bellot St
Flavell Ms
Lovell's Wharf
Banning St
Pelton Road
Commerell St
Prim School
Enderby St
Hadrian St
Christchurch Wy
Whitworth St
Caradoc St
Lassell St
Hoskins St
Trinity Hospital
GREENWICH
Fearon St
Dandridge Cl
Tunnel Av
A206
WOOLWICH ROAD
Combedale Rd
Kemsing Rd
Halstow Rd
Chevening Rd
Annandale Road
Calvert Rd
Greenwich Hospital
A&E
Vanbrugh Hill
TRAFALGAR ROAD
Tyler St
Colomb St
Redmore St
Primary School
Police Stn
Fairthorn Rd
Gurdon Road
Westcombe Park Station
Station Crs
Ormiston Rd
Primary School
Humber Road
Greenwich Foot Tunnel
Greenwich Pier
Cutty Sark Clipper Ship
Thames Path
University
Old Royal Naval College
Trinity College of Music
Park Row
Meridian Prim Sch
Surg
Tuskar St
Woodlands Pk Rd
Earlswood St
Annandale Rd
Dinsdale Rd
Arches Leisure Cen
School
Maze Hill Station
Restell Close
Park Vista
Maze Hill
Cutty Sark Station
Gypsy Moth
Thames St
Library
ROMNEY ROAD
CREEK ROAD
Bardsley Lane
The Queens House
National Maritime Museum
Royal Observatory Greenwich
SE10
Greenwich Park
Council Building
Roan St
A206
Hotel
Greenwich Theatre & Art Gallery
Fan Mus
Welfare Clinic
Police Stn
Flamsteed House Museum
145
Ulundi Rd
Foyle Road
Webb Rd
Coleraine Road
Hardy Rd
Beaconsfield Road
Mycenae Road
Ruthin Road
Glenluge Rd
Westcombe Hill
Kirkside
John Roan Lower School
Invicta Primary School
Invicta Rd
Sandtoft
Eversley
Eastcombe Av
Westcombe Park Rd
Blackheath High Senior School
Highmore Rd
Vanbrugh Pk Rd W
Wycherley Cl
Vanbrugh Park
VANBRUGH PK B210
Mary Lawrencson
Heathway
CHARLTON RD
B210
B211
OLD DOVER
Dornberg Cl
St John's Park
ROYAL HILL
Circus St
Conduit House
Croom's Hill
King George St
Great Cross Av
Blackheath Av
Old Royal Observatory
St Ursulas
Greenwich Natural
School
Burney St
Nevada St
Randall

126
107
125
146
A
B
C
D
E
1
2
3
4
5
6
541
42
E16
SE7
ExCeL Exhibition Centre
Royal Albert Station
Beckton Park Station
Western Gateway
Dockside Road
Royal Victoria Dock
CONNAUGHT BR
A112
London City Airport
Hartmann Road
Drew Primary School
Camel Road
Drew Rd
Parker St
CONNAUGHT RD
ALBERT RD
Newland Street
Wesley Avenue
Evelyn Road
Primary School
Boxley St
Fort St
Mill Road
NORTH WOOLWICH ROAD
A1020
N Woolwich Rd
St Marks Industrial Estate
Thames Road
Factory Rd
Thameside Ind Est
Silvertown & City Airport Stn
Standard Industrial Estate
Thameside Industrial Estate
Factory Road
Greenshields Industrial Est
Bradfield Road
Works
Silvertown
Thames Barrier
River Thames
North Woolwich
Newham
Greenwich
Woolwich Reach
Thames Barrier Visitor Centre
Thames Path
Harrington Wy
Unity Way
Westminster Ind Est
Bowater Rd
Warspite Road
Harlinger Street
Anchorage Point Industrial Estate
Herringham Road
Riverside
Ruston Rd
Dockyard Industrial Est
WOOLWICH CHURCH STREET
Fire Station
Lord Warwick St
Westfield St
Mellish Ind Est
Faraday Wy
Eastmoor Pl
Lombard Wall
Anchor and Hope Lane
Derrick Gdns
VIP Trading Estate
Ashleigh Commercial Estate
Lombard Trading Estate
Brocklebank Industrial Estate
Willoughby Way
Meridian Trading Estate
A2052
ANCHOR & HOPE LANE
Ropery Business Park
Stone Lake Retail Park
New Charlton
A206
Woolwich Coll
Pett Street
Marshalls Gv
Woolwich Dockyard Stn
Cardwell Primary School
Maryon Rd
Prospect V
Woodhill Primary School
Samuel St
Frances Street
Ogilby St
Maritime Industrial Estate
Superstore
Gallions Rd
Greenwich Industrial Estate
WOOLWICH ROAD
Hickin Cl
Barney Close
Troughton Road
Charlton Stn
Mosque
Harvey Gardens
The Former Health Centre
Health & Fitness Cen
Charlton Athletic FC (The Valley)
Floyd Rd
Valley Gv
Pound Pk Rd
Green Chain Walk
Woodland Ter
Heathwood Gardens
Kinveachy Gardens
HILLREACH B210
Green Hill
Thorntree Primary School
Maryon Wilson Park
Charlton
LITTLE HEATH B210
Flamsteed Rd
McCall Crs
Gurdon Road
Victoria Way
Rathmore Rd
Delafield Rd
Sundorne Rd
Swallowfield Road
Inverine Rd
Priolo Road
Wellington Gardens
Charlton Church Lane
Lansdowne Mews
Wolfe Crs
Westcombe Park Station
Eastcombe Avenue
Primary School
The Birches
Tallis Gv
Nadine St
Collogly Terrace
Ellscombe Road
The Heights
Lansdowne La
Grove
Meridian Locality Mental Health Centre
St Alfege Rd
Beacham Close
Park Dr
Cemetery Lane
Repository Rd
Sandtoft Road
Eversley Road
Bramshot Avenue
Highcombe
Bramhope Lane
Wyndcliff Rd
Primary School
Copse Close
Mascalls Rd
Fletching Rd
THE VILLAGE
B210 CHARLTON PK RD
Fairfield
Charlton House
Charlton Park
Charlton School
Cemetery
Ha-Ha
Springfield Gv
Sherington Primary School
CHARLTON ROAD B210
Canberra Road
Charlton Park Lane
Queen Elizabeth Hospital
A&E
Invicta Primary School
The Rectory Field
Fairlawn
Montcalm Rd
Meridian Sports Club
Stadium Road
Shrapnel Cl
Woolwich Common
Blackheath Bluecoat CE School
Rectory Field Crescent
The Glade
Sutlej Road
Nigeria Rd
Charlton Park Lane
Greenbay Rd
Prince Henry Road
Charlton Dene
Cherry Orchard Primary School
Russell Cl
St John's Park
Hornfair Park
Mansergh Close
Green Chain Walk
1 grid square represents 500 metres

Cyprus Station
University of East London Campus
University Way
Gallions Road
F
G
H
108
J
K
Newham
Greenwich
43
44
45
King George V Dock
Thames
WOOLWICH MANOR WAY
Storey Primary School
Rymill St
Woodman St
ALBERT ROAD
Dockland St
ALBERT RD
A112
A117
North Woolwich Station
Old Station Museum
PIER ROAD
Barge House Rd
Woolwich Manorway
Grimsby Gv
Fisherguard Wy
Gallions Reach
WOOLWICH FERRY
Warepoint Dr
Ridge Close
Martin St
Delisle Rd
Battery Rd
New Acres Rd
Kentlea Rd
WESTERN WAY
Nuthatch Gardens
Harrier Mews
Avocet Ms
Magistrates Court
Woolwich Crown Court
HM Prison Belmarsh
Camelot Cl
Pier Way
Temple Cl
Whinchat Road
Goldfinch Road
WESTERN WAY A2016
Heronsgate Primary School
Boughton Road
Hadden Road
Works
Nathan Way
Waterfront Leisure Centre
Bell Water Gate
NEW FERRY AP
A2204
A206
WOOLWICH HIGH ST
Bingo
County Court
Powis Street
Marlborough Road
Cadogan Rd
Cornwallis Rd
Royal Arsenal Rd
Firepower (Museum of Artillery)
Wellington Av
Tom Cribb Road
BERESFORD STREET
Primary School
Mag Ct
Outdoor Market
Indoor Market
Essex St
Seymour St
A206 PLUMSTEAD ROAD
Woolwich College
Polthorne Gv
Plumstead Station
PETTMAN CRESCENT
WESTERN WAY
North Road
128
JOHN WILSON ST
Rectory Place
University
Town Hall
WELLINGTON ST
WOOLWICH NEW ROAD
Spray St
Community College
Burrage Gv
Walker Cl
Walmer Terrace
Theatre
Woolwich Arsenal Station
Arthur Gv
Invermore Place
London Lei Zang Si Temple
St Patricks RC Primary School
Conway Primary School
PLUMSTEAD HIGH STREET
White Hart Road
Primary School
Police Stn
ARTILLERY PL
School
Cncl Bldg
GRAND DEPOT RD
A205
S E H A Hindu Temple
Dawson Close
Glyndon Rd
Conway Road
Conway Medical Cen
Military Barracks
Crescent Road
Conduit Rd
St Peters RC Primary School
Foxfield Prim Sch
Sandbach Place
Surgery
Nineacres Sch Prim School
Raglan Road
Brewery Road
Frederick Place
Burrage Place
Works
Plumstead
Waverley Rd
Durham Ri
Majendie Rd
Ancona Rd
Philimore Close
GRAND DEPOT ROAD
Gunner La
Brookhill Rd
Elmdene Rd
Ed Cen
Med Cen
Primary School
Shree KS Swaminarayan Temple
Plumstead Manor School
Heavitree Rd
Chestnut Rise
Community College
Nightingale Pl
Plumstead Common Rd
St Margarets CE Prim Sch
Green Chain Walk
St John's Ter
Mill Rd
Negus 6th Form Centre
Winn Common Road
WOOLWICH COMMON
Primary School
Plumstead Common Road
Wernbrook St
Common
Greenslade Primary School
King's
WOOLWICH
Surgery
Kempt St
Ritter St
Eglinton
Ripon Road
Genesta Road
Wrottesley Road
Vernham Rd
Isla Rd
Plumcroft Primary School
Macoma Road
Tuam Road
Chelsworth Drive
Erindale
The Slade
Kirkham St
Surgery
Melling Street
Timbercroft
Junior School
Infant School
Nithdale Road
Rowton Rd
147
Alabama Street
Timbercroft Primary School
Rockcliffe Manor Primary School
Camdale
Irwin Avenue
Thornhill Av
Eastview Av
Dallin Road
Cantwell Road
Brent Rd
Whitworth Road
Plum
Brinklow Crs
Ashridge Crs
Clothworkers Rd
Garland
Raymere Gardens
Landstead Road
Warland
Ancaster St
Duncroft
Matchless
SE18
I
2
3
4
5
6

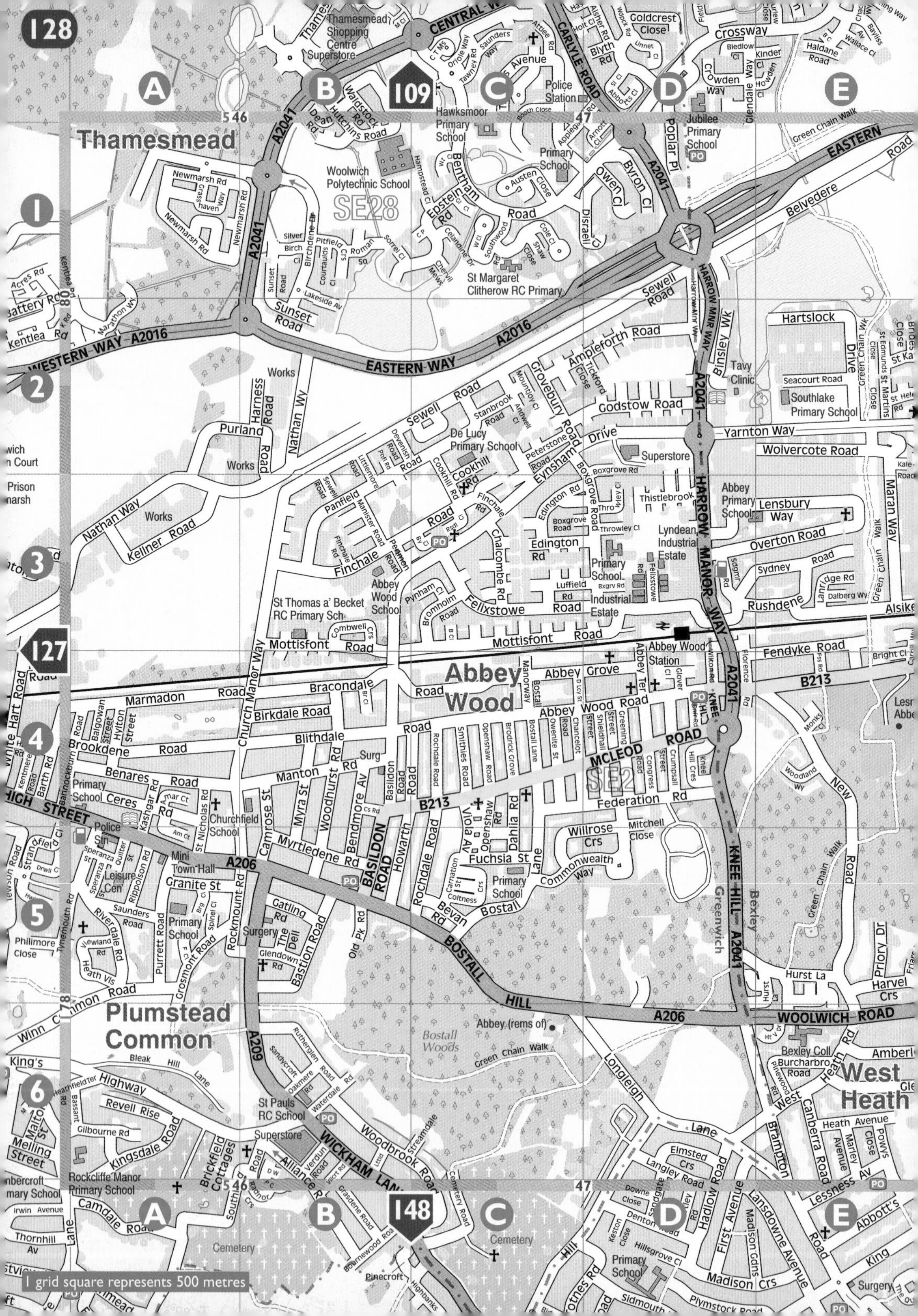
109
A
B
C
D
E
1
2
3
4
5
6
546
47
Thamesmead
Thamesmead Shopping Centre
Superstore
CENTRAL WAY
Goldcrest Close
Crossway
Haldane Road
Police Station
CARLYLE ROAD
Hawksmoor Primary School
Jubilee Primary School
Poplar Pl
Green Chain Walk
EASTERN WAY
Belvedere Road
Woolwich Polytechnic School
SE28
Newmarsh Rd
Grasshaven Way
Bentham Road
Austen Close
Owen Cl
Byron Cl
Disraeli Cl
Primary School
Epstein Rd
Southwood Rd
St Margaret Clitherow RC Primary
A2041
A2016
WESTERN WAY
Sunset Road
Kentlea Rd
Battery Rd
Acres Rd
Marathon Wy
Sewell Road
Ampleforth Road
HARROW MNR WAY
Binsley Wk
Hartslock Drive
Seacourt Road
Southlake Primary School
Tavy Clinic
Works
Harness Road
Nathan Way
Purland Road
Grovebury Road
Godstow Road
Yarnton Way
Wolvercote Road
De Lucy Primary School
Eynsham Drive
Superstore
Kellner Road
Nathan Way
Cookhill Rd
Finchale Road
Thistlebrook
Abbey Primary School
Lensbury Way
Maran Way
Edington Rd
Boxgrove Road
Lyndean Industrial Estate
HARROW MANOR WAY
Overton Road
Sydney Road
Abbey Wood School
Felixstowe Road
Industrial Estate
Rushdene
St Thomas a' Becket RC Primary Sch
Mottisfont Road
Abbey Wood Station
Fendyke Road
127
B213
Abbey Wood
Abbey Grove
Abbey Wood Road
Bracondale Road
Marmadon Road
Church Manor Way
Birkdale Road
Blithdale Road
Brookdene Road
MCLEOD ROAD
SE2
KNEE HILL
Federation Rd
Benares Road
Manton Rd
Primary School
Ceres Rd
HIGH STREET
Police Stn
Churchfield School
Camrose St
Myrtledene Rd
BASILDON ROAD
Howarth
Rochdale Road
Willrose Crs
Mitchell Close
Commonwealth Way
Fuchsia St
Primary School
Mini Town Hall
Leisure Cen
Granite St
A206
Primary School
Gatling Rd
The Dell
Bastion Road
BOSTALL HILL
Bostall Lane
Greenwich
Bexley
Green Chain Walk
New Road
Priory Dr
Hurst La
WOOLWICH ROAD
Philimore Close
Riverdale Rd
Grosmont Road
Rockmount Rd
Plumstead Common
Winn Common Road
A209
Abbey (rems of)
Bostall Woods
Green Chain Walk
Longleigh Lane
Bexley Coll
Burcharbro Road
West Heath
King's Highway
Bleak Hill Lane
Revell Rise
Kingsdale Road
St Pauls RC School
Superstore
WICKHAM LANE
Woodbrook Road
Melling Street
Rockcliffe Manor Primary School
Camdale Road
Cemetery
Elmsted Crs
Langley Road
Heath Avenue
Canberra Road
Lessness Av
148
Abbott's Road
First Avenue
Lansdowne Avenue
Madison Crs
Primary School
Thornhill Av
Irwin Avenue
1 grid square represents 500 metres

F
G
H
110
J
K
48
49
50
Jennington Point
Works
WAY
A2016
Erith Marshes
Thamesmead Community College
DA18
East Thamesmead Business Park
Waldrist Way
Yarnton Way
St John Fisher RC Primary School
Northwood Pl
Pkwy
Glimpsing Green
Leatherbottle Gn
Aspen Green
Northwood Primary School
Parkway Primary School
Centurian Way
Works
EASTERN WAY
A2016
Hailey Rd
Hailey Road Business Park
Hailey Road
Waterfield Close
Sutherland Road
Maida Rd
Dylan Rd
Station Rd
Belvedere Station
Norman Road
Norman Rd
PICARDY MANORWAY
North Road
Caldy Road
B253
Superstore
Capital Industrial Est
Crabtree Manorway North
Fisher's Way
Belvedere Industrial Estate
Anderson Way
St Thomas Rd
Crabtree Manorway South
Jenningtree Way
Mulberry Way
Works
BRONZE AGE WAY
Elbourne Trading Estate
Keats Rd
Cables Cl
Belvedere Link Business Park
Viking Way
Sikh Temple
Mitchell Cl
LOWER ROAD B213
130
Halifield Dr
Holcote Close
Beckett Cl
Tunstock Wy
Shortlands
Laymarsh Close
St Augustines Primary School
GILBERT ROAD B213
PICARDY ST
Paroma Road
Monarch Rd
Ambrook Rd
Coleman Rd
Ripley Rd
Edwards Rd
Sheridan Rd
Gertrude Rd
Lyndon Rd
B250
Lower Pk Rd
ROAD
Elstree Gardens
Kingswood Av
Hadley Road
St Augustine's Rd
Upper Abbey Road
Belvedere Primary School
Woodside Sch
Methuen Rd
Poplar Mt
Beltwood Rd
Bullbanks Rd
Mayfield Road
Ashburnham Road
Gordon Rd
Stanmore Road
Glendale Rd
Parkside Road
Halt Robin Road
Halt Robin Rd
Brigstock Rd
Green Chain Walk
Regent Sq
Capital Industrial Estate
Heathdene Drive
Elmbourne Drive
Fox House Rd
Trinity Sch Belvedere
Tower Rd
Valley Rd
Bramble Croft
Bexley College
Pembroke Road
Sandcliff Rd
Lesnes Abbey Woods
DA17
Hattersfield Cl
Heron Hill
Draper Cl
Clive Rd
Ruskin Road
Abbey Crs
Cowper Rd
Milton Rd
Orchard Rd
Kentish Road
PICARDY ROAD
Bunker's Hill
Fremantle Rd
Mossdown Close
Calvert Close
Upper Pk Rd
Belvedere
A206
Upr Holly Hl Rd
Holmhurst Rd
Raglan Rd
Wellington Rd
Napier Rd
Lessness Pk
Berkhampstead Rd
Smarden Cl
Essenden Rd
Eardley Road
ERITH ROAD
Surgery
Rutland Gate
Holly Hill Road
Church Rd
Crusoe Rd
Alford Rd
Athol Rd
FRASER ROAD
Hawthorn Pl
Nelson Rd
Walden Cl
Abbey Mt
Court Av
The View
Treetops Cl
Croft Cl
Tyeshurst Cl
WOOLWICH ROAD
Harold Avenue
Victoria St
Albert Rd
Alfred Rd
Med Cen
The Abbey Clinic
Surgery
Bedwell Rd
Hoddesdon Rd
Cheshunt Rd
Standard Rd
Stapley Rd
Roberts Rd
Salmon Road
Lessness Heath Primary School
Chapman Road
Brook St
Riverdale Road
Lumley Cl
Wadeville Cl
Milford Cl
Westergate Road
Osborne Road
Fairmont Cl
Albany Rd
Barnfield Rd
Nuxley Rd
Grosvenor Road
Lessness Heath
Cemetery
Silver Spring Cl
Kempton Cl
Thwaite Cl
Vicarage Close
Upper Gv
Grove Rd
Orchard Av
Orchard Avenue
Dryhill Rd
Stream Way
Walsingham Walk
Bedonwell Clinic
Bedonwell Road
Elmhurst
Leckwith Av
Clovelly Road
Bedonwell Primary School
Walk
Way
Road
Edwin Cl
Iris Crs
Redleaf Cl
Matfield Rd
Trosley Road
Cray Road
Swaylands Road
Bellring Close
Parsonage Manorway
Carlton Rd
Lochmere Cl
Collindale Av
Thorne Close
Cavendish Av
Oakdene Av
Carlton Road
Primary School
BEXLEY ROAD
Park Crs
Surgery
Ling Rd
Randall Cl
Erith Hosp
Northumberland Heath Medical
Pembury Road
Lenham Road
Stapleton Road
Brabourne Cres
Cemetery
Brantwood Av
Penda Road
Hengist Rd
Horsa Rd
Emes Rd
Buxton Rd
Hind Crs
Avenue Road
Harolds
Barry Av
Ashbourne Av
Chessington Avenue
Knowle Av
Whitfield Road
Chiddingstone Av
Cumberland
Hythe
The Pantiles
Hurlingham Rd
Shinglewell Rd
Lullingstone Road
Eastry Road
Plaxtol Road
149
Ightham Road
Nurstead Road
The Grove
Brook Street
Sussex Rd
Lawrence Road
Cookson Gv
Dickens
Primary School
Northumberland Park
Erith School
Erith School
Lwd
80
78
1
2
3
4
5
6
PO

Island
Rainham Marshes
A
B
111
C
D
E
Jenningtree Point
551
52
Coldharbour Lane
1
Fisher's Way
Belvedere Industrial Estate
80
Works
Way
2
Works
Erith Reach
Belvedere Link Business Park
Viking Way
Church Manorway
3
129
Works
Lower Rd
Corinthian Manorway
Galleon Close
4
Battle Rd
Valley Rd
Stanmore
Bramble Croft
Pembroke Road
Sandcliff Road
Jessett Cl
West Street
St Fidelis' Rd
Chandlers Dr
Bexley College
A2016
St. John's Rd
Vickers Rd
Church Rd
Crusoe Rd
Friday Rd
Alford Rd
Mildred Rd
Maxim Rd
Winifred Road
Maximfeldt Rd
Chichester Whf
PO
FRASER ROAD
5
Hawthorn Pl
Europa Trading Estate
Hamlet International Industrial Estate
Ind Park
Riverside Swimming Centre
Erith
Coldharbour
Erith Rands
Havering
Bexley
Cricketers Cl
Walnut Tree Rd
Erith High St
Library & Mus
Saltford Cl
Erith Theatre Guild
Erith Station
A206
178
Ron Gn Ct
A220
B252
Pier Road
Colebrk St
Business Centre
Superstore
James Watt Way
Wheatley Ter Road
Christ Church Av
Victoria Road
Arran Close
Debrabant Close
Park Crescent
Lesney
Meyer Rd
6
Glebe Way
QUEENS ROAD
Elrick Cl
Health Centre
ERITH HIGH ST
Crescent Road
Appold St
Works
Manor Road
Lesney Park Primary School
Lesney Park Road
Randall Cl
Ward Cl
Park Crs
ROAD
Surgery
Erith & District Hosp
Mortimer Road
Park
Grovebury Close
Clydon Close
Avenue Road
Erith Stadium
A206
Compton Pl
Britannia Cl
Alexandra Rd
Springhead Road
Lydia Rd
Aperfield Road
Cornwallis Close
Frobisher Rd
Turpin Lane
Manford Industrial Estate
Works
Ray Lamb Way
Ling Rd
Northumberland Heath Medical Cen
Erith Sports Centre
150
SOUTH ROAD
Reddy Road
Raleigh Close
Bilton Road
Emes Rd
Hind Crs
Buxton Road
Elm Cl
Avenue Road
Broadoak Road
Beechfield Rd
Coniston Close
Frinsted Road
Larner Rd
Badlow Cl
Waterhead Close
Festival Close
Ind Est
Boundary St
Arthur St
Canada Road
Snipe Cl
Jenningtree Rd
Sandpiper Dr
Longreach Rd
Beacon Rd
Widgeon Rd
Slade Green Primary School
Church Trading
Erith School
Valence
Mantle
Twigg Cl
BEXLEY
1 grid square represents 500 metres

Wennington
A13
SANDY LANE
Sandy Lane Farm
F
G
H
J
K
3
54
55
A13
A1306
Wennington Marshes
Purfleet Ind Park
Juliette Wy
LONDON RD
A1306
Havering
Thurrock
Kerry Avenue
Juliette Way
Purfleet Ind Park
LONDON ROAD
80
Aveley Marshes
A1306
Fanns Farm
LC
Milehams Industrial Estate
LONDON ROAD
79
ROAD
TANK HILL
Water
Surgery
Lane
Marlow Av
Fanns Rise
Quarry Ms
Long Ct
Thamley
Erith Ct
Halfway Court
Council Building
Marine Court
Crusader Close
Way
Centurion
Rapier Cl
Saladin
Chieftan Drive
PO
Comet Cl
Mulberry Drive
Tank Lane
Purfleet Primary School
A1090
The Limes
Church Lane
Hotel
Works
Harrisons Wharf
Purfleet Station
A1090
LC
78
River
Thames
Crayford Ness
Landau Way
Darent Industrial Park
Dayton Drive
Maypole Crescent
Road
Burnett
Ness Road
Works
Purfleet
Wallhouse Road
151
Dartford Marshes
I
2
3
4
5
6

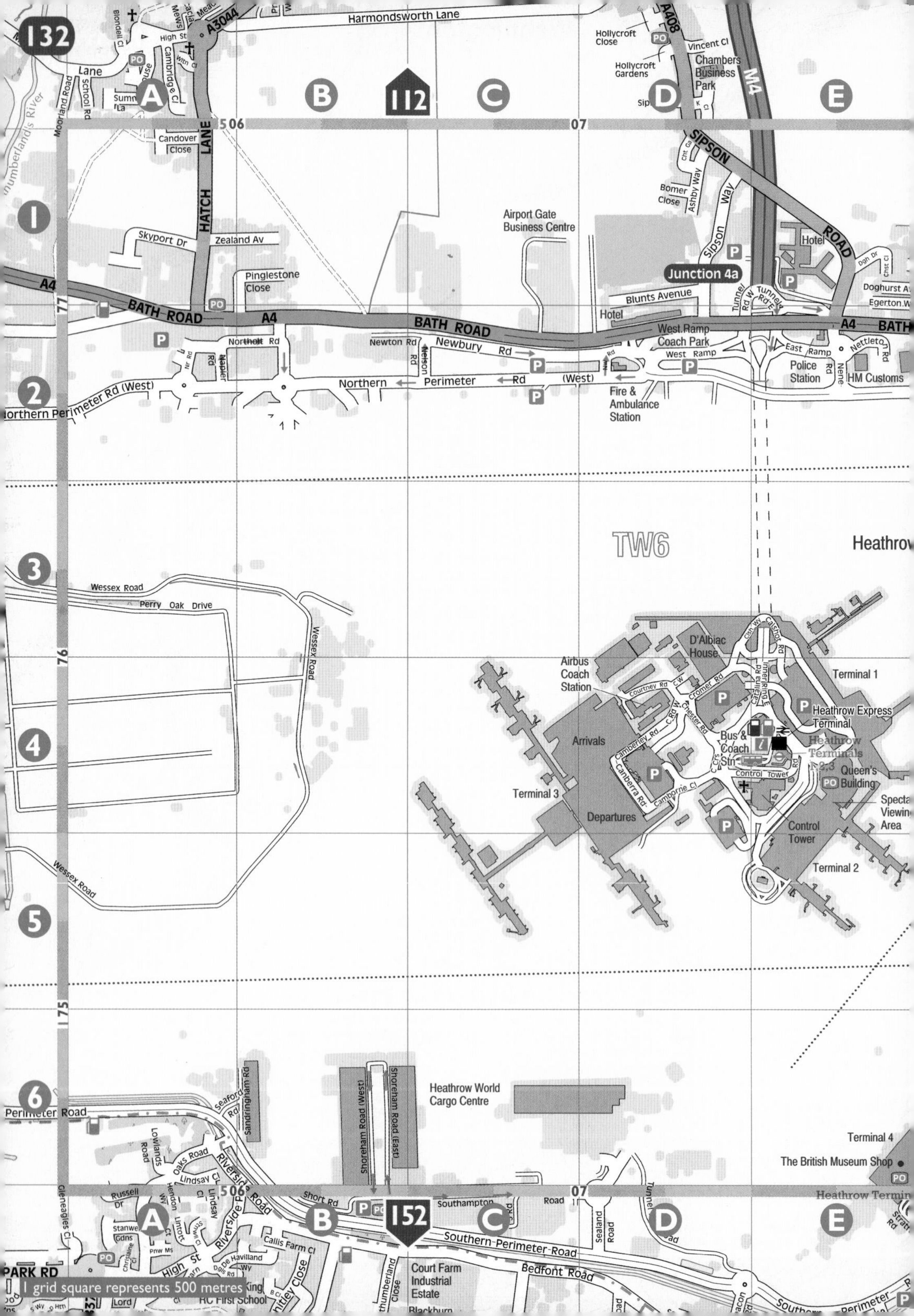

1 grid square represents 500 metres

Harlington
Cranford
Hatton
Airport
Sipson Lane
Richards Cl
Cranford Lane
Sportlands
Manse Close
Field Cl
West End Lane
The Crescent
Gilpin Way
Tasker Cl
Croft Cl
Raywood Close
Browngraves Road
Pennine Way
Pennine Wy
Cheviot
Hall La
High St
HIGH ST HARLINGTON
Little Elms
Marlborough Rd
Works
New Road
Brendon Cl
Heath Close
Hotel
Mondial Way
Triumph Cl
David Cl
Caroline Pl
Nobel Dr
Acorn Gv
Saunton Av
Pendell Av
Langley Crs
Eton Road
Winchester Road
Oxford Av
Malvern Road
Windsor Park Rd
Craneswater
The Cedars Primary School
Sheepcote Cl
Park Lane
Cole Gdns
The Avenue
Avenue Cl
Firs Dr
BATH ROAD
A4
ROAD
Norwood Crs
World Business Cen-Heathrow
Newall Road
Hatton Rd North
Northrop Road
Northern Perimeter Rd
Northern Perimeter Road
AA Heathrow Visitor Centre
Cranford Lane
Dudset Lane
Waye Av
Sandown Cl
Surgery
Berkeley Avenue
Waye Avenue
Meadowbank Gdns
Clevedon Gardens
Byron Ave
Eastern Perimeter Rd
Enfield Rd
E Crs
Esher Crs
Eastern Business Park
Eastchurch Rd
Cranford Infant School
Exeter Wy
Vanguard Wy
Exeter Road
Eastchurch Road
River Crane
Eastern Perimeter Road
Electra Av
Eagle Rd
Elmdon Rd
Cranford La
Girling Way
Sun Life Trading Estate
Eastern Perimeter Road
GREAT SOUTH-WEST RD
Viscount Way
Hatton Rd
GT SOUTH-WEST RD
Lithgow's Rd
Hatton Cross Stn
Turpin Wy
Dick
Dockwell Close
Faggs Rd
Green Man Lane
St Theresa's Road
St Anthony's Wy
Faggs Road
Hatton Gn
Heron Wy
CAUSEWAY
A312
A30
GREAT SOUTH-WEST ROAD
Hatton Road
Myrtle Av
Haslemere Industrial Estate
Armadale Rd
Space Wave
Space Waye
Chalmers Wy
Central
Works
Wellington Rd
Cain's Lane
Orchard Av
Unwin Av
Iverna Gdns
Edward Rd
The Marjory Kinnon School
Perimeter Road
Southern Perimeter Rd
Swindon Rd
Cem
FAGG'S ROAD
A312
Bowdon Road West
Sheffield
Swansea Road
Shrewsbury Road
Shrewsbury Rd
Scarborough Rd
Surgery
Hazelmere Cl
Bedfont J&I School
Marriott
Hillingdon
Hounslow
Peninsular Cl
Kingston Av
Elmcroft Cl
Engleheart Dr
Pentelow Gdns
Minimax Close
Avenue
F
G
H
J
K
113
134
153
08
09
10
1
2
3
4
5
6

1 grid square represents 500 metres

Osterley Park
115
Osterley
Spring Grove
Lampton
HOUNSLOW
Woodlands
TW3
136
155
Heston Junior School
Heston Community Sports Hall
Heston Infant School
Heston Community School
HESTON RD
CHURCH ROAD
Jersey Road
GREAT WEST ROAD
Osterley Station
Brunel University (Osterley Campus) Track
Brunel University
Isleworth & Syon School for Boys
Campion House College
Ashton House Sch
More House School
West Thames College
Metro Industrial Centre
SPRING GROVE ROAD B363
LONDON ROAD
A315
LAMPTON ROAD
A3005
Lampton School
Lampton Park
Civic Centre
Alexandra Junior School
Hounslow East Stn
Bus Depot
Hounslow Central Station
Hounslow Manor School
Sports Hall
Youth Centre
HIGH STREET
HANWORTH ROAD
GROVE ROAD
Police Station
The Treaty Centre
The Pountney Clnc
Primary School
Oaklands Sch
Inwood Park
Sikh Temple
Hounslow Business Park
Heath Business Cen
Inwood Business Cen
Hounslow Station
Maswell Park Health Centre
Chatsworth Junior & Infant School
Worton Hall Industrial Est
Wainwright Grove
The Orchard Junior School
B361 WHITTON RD
SOUTH A3063
A314
B358
KNELLER
Kneller Hall
Chase Bridge Primary School
Twickenham Stadium
Museum of Rugby & Twickenham Stadium Tours
Superstore
Harlequin Close
Whitton Dene
Grasshoppers RFC
Crowntree Close

136
116
135
156
BRENTFORD
Brentford End
ISLEWORTH
St Margarets
TW7
Syon Park
Syon House
River Thames
Hounslow
Richmond upon Thames
Thames Path
Old Deer Park
Golf Course
Royal Mid-Surrey Golf Club
Richmond Green
Richmond Theatre
Richmond Bridge
Twickenham Bridge
Isleworth Station
Syon Lane Station
St Margarets
Brunel University (Osterley Campus) Track
Brunel University
Middlesex University Hospital
Isleworth Recreation Centre
Victory Business Cen
Ivybridge Retail Park
Brentford Business Cen
Brentwaters Business Park
Great West Trading Estate
Centaurs Business Centre
Grasshoppers RFC
Centaurs RFC
Butterfly House
Syon Park School
The Green School for Girls
Marlborough Primary School
Smallberry Green Primary School
Isleworth Town Primary School
Brewery Mews Bus Centre
Convent School
Waterside Business Cen
University
Pools in the Park
Community College
Richmond Magistrates Court
Brentford School for Girls
St Paul's CE Primary School
Brentford County Court
Police Station
Brentford Medical Cen
Twickenham Park Health Cen
Film House
Museum
Odeon
SYON LANE
SPUR ROAD
LONDON ROAD
TWICKENHAM ROAD
TWICKENHAM RD
RICHMOND ROAD
ST MARGARET'S RD
ST JOHN'S ROAD
SOUTH STREET
THE AVENUE
A4
A310
A315
A316
A3004
B454
B363
1 grid square represents 500 metres

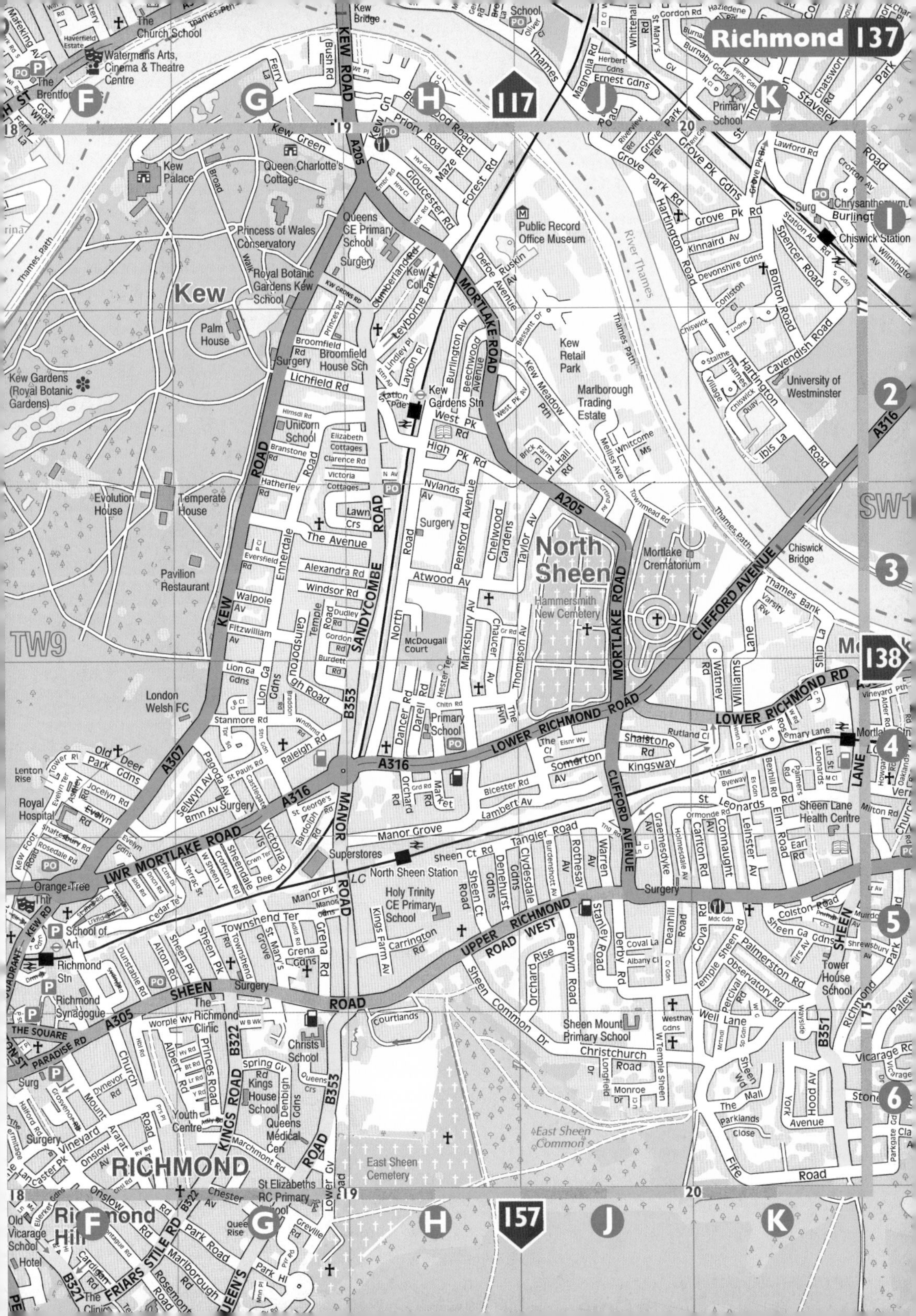

117
138
157
F
G
H
J
K
I
2
3
4
5
6
18
19
20
Kew Bridge
The Church School
Watermans Arts, Cinema & Theatre Centre
The Brentford
Kew
Kew Palace
Queen Charlotte's Cottage
Princess of Wales Conservatory
Royal Botanic Gardens Kew School
Palm House
Kew Gardens (Royal Botanic Gardens)
Evolution House
Temperate House
Pavilion Restaurant
TW9
London Welsh FC
Kew Green
KEW ROAD
A205
A307
Queens CE Primary School
Surgery
Kew Coll
Broomfield House Sch
Lichfield Rd
Unicorn School
Kew Gardens Stn
West Pk Rd
High Pk Rd
MORTLAKE ROAD
SANDYCOMBE ROAD
B353
North Road
The Avenue
Alexandra Rd
Windsor Rd
Walpole Av
Fitzwilliam Av
Gainsborough Road
Raleigh Rd
Stanmore Rd
A316
McDougall Court
Primary School
Atwood Av
Pensford Avenue
Chelwood Gardens
Taylor Av
North Sheen
Hammersmith New Cemetery
Mortlake Crematorium
Public Record Office Museum
Kew Retail Park
Marlborough Trading Estate
River Thames
Thames Path
Chiswick Bridge
CLIFFORD AVENUE
LOWER RICHMOND ROAD
LOWER RICHMOND RD
Chiswick Station
University of Westminster
Grove Park Rd
Hartington Road
Spencer Road
Bolton Road
Cavendish Road
Ibis La
A316
SW14
Mortlake
Thames Bank
Williams Lane
Sheen Lane Health Centre
SHEEN LANE
Royal Hospital
LWR MORTLAKE ROAD
Manor Grove
Superstores
North Sheen Station
MANOR ROAD
Holy Trinity CE Primary School
UPPER RICHMOND ROAD WEST
Orange Tree Thtr
School of Art
Richmond Stn
Richmond Synagogue
SHEEN ROAD
A305
THE SQUARE
PARADISE RD
The Richmond Clinic
B322
KINGS ROAD
Christs School
Kings House School
Queens Medical Cen
Youth Centre
RICHMOND
Courtlands
East Sheen Cemetery
East Sheen Common
Sheen Common Dr
Christchurch Road
Sheen Mount Primary School
Tower House School
Palmerston Rd
Observatory Rd
Well Lane
The Mall
Parklands Close
York Avenue
Hood Av
Fife Road
B351
St Elizabeths RC Primary School
Richmond Hill
Old Vicarage School
Hotel
FRIARS STILE RD
B321
Park Road
Rosemont Road
Marlborough Road

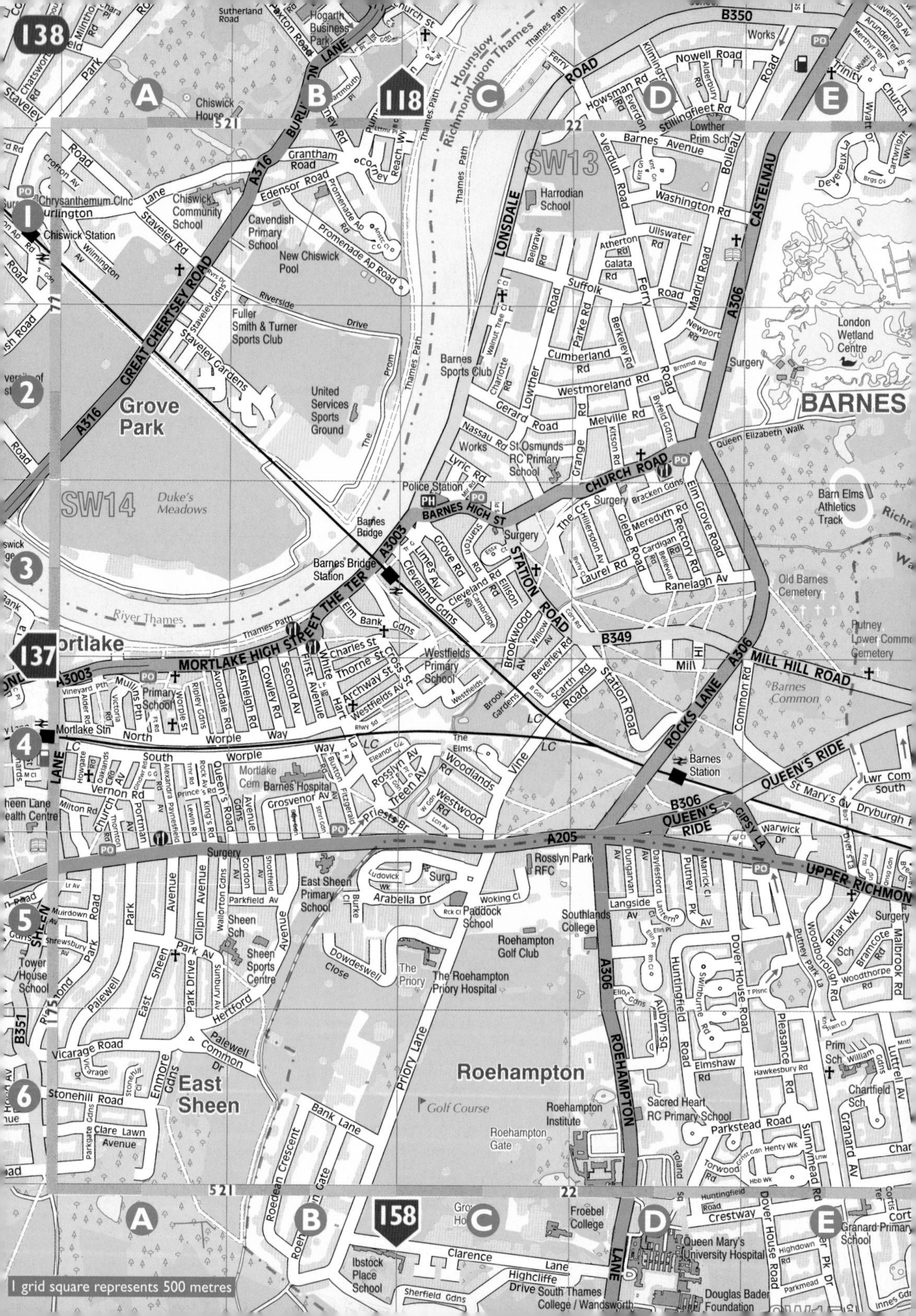
138
118
137
158
A
B
C
D
E
1
2
3
4
5
6
521
22
SW13
SW14
Grove Park
Duke's Meadows
BARNES
Roehampton
East Sheen
Mortlake
River Thames
Hounslow
Richmond upon Thames
Thames Path
Chiswick House
Chiswick Station
Chiswick Community School
Cavendish Primary School
New Chiswick Pool
Fuller Smith & Turner Sports Club
United Services Sports Ground
Hogarth Business Park
Sutherland Road
Burlington Lane
Great Chertsey Road
A316
Grantham Road
Edensor Road
Promenade Ap Road
Staveley Rd
Staveley Gardens
Riverside Drive
Chrysanthemum Clnc
Harrodian School
Lonsdale Road
Barnes Avenue
Washington Rd
Castelnau
A306
Boileau Rd
Lowther Prim Sch
Stillingfleet Rd
Nowell Road
Howsman Rd
B350
Works
Trinity Church
London Wetland Centre
Barnes Sports Club
Suffolk Road
Ferry Road
Madrid Road
Cumberland Rd
Westmoreland Rd
Gerard Road
Melville Rd
St Osmunds RC Primary School
Police Station
Barnes High St
Church Road
Queen Elizabeth Walk
Barn Elms Athletics Track
Barnes Bridge
Barnes Bridge Station
A3003
The Terrace
Mortlake High Street
Station Road
Laurel Rd
Ranelagh Av
Elm Grove Road
Old Barnes Cemetery
Putney Lower Common Cemetery
B349
Mill Hill Road
Rocks Lane
Barnes Common
Westfields Primary School
Mortlake Stn
North Worple Way
South Worple Way
Mortlake Cem
Barnes Hospital
Barnes Station
Queen's Ride
B306
Gipsy La
Upper Richmond Road
A205
Sheen Lane
Sheen Lane Health Centre
Rosslyn Park RFC
East Sheen Primary School
Paddock School
Southlands College
Roehampton Golf Club
The Priory
The Roehampton Priory Hospital
Sheen Sch
Sheen Sports Centre
Tower House School
Palewell Common Dr
Vicarage Road
Stonehill Road
Priory Lane
Bank Lane
Golf Course
Roehampton Institute
Roehampton Gate
Roehampton Lane
Sacred Heart RC Primary School
Parkstead Road
Dover House Road
Huntingfield Road
Froebel College
Queen Mary's University Hospital
Douglas Bader Foundation
Ibstock Place School
Clarence Lane
Highcliffe Drive
South Thames College / Wandsworth
Granard Primary School
Chartfield Sch
B351
1 grid square represents 500 metres

FULHAM
Walham Green
Parsons Green
PUTNEY
WANDSWO
SW6
River Thames
Thames Path
Hammersmith & Fulham
Richmond upon Thames
Wandsworth
FULHAM PALACE ROAD
FULHAM ROAD
DAWES ROAD
NEW KING'S ROAD
LWR RICHMOND ROAD
UPPER RICHMOND RD
PUTNEY BRIDGE ROAD
PUTNEY HIGH ST
PUTNEY HILL
WEST HILL A3
ARMOURY WY
BUCKHOLD RD
HARWOOD RD
FULHAM HIGH ST
FELSHAM RD
A3218
A3219
A304
A308
A219
A205
A218
B306
B318
Fulham FC (Craven Cottage)
Barn Elms Water Sports Centre
Putney Hospital
Bowls Club
Imperial College
Fulham Palace
Bishops Park
Museum of Fulham Palace
All Saints CE Primary School
Putney Bridge Station
Hurlingham House
Hurlingham Private School
Hurlingham Business Park
Hurlingham & Chelsea School
Wandsworth Park
Wandsworth County Court
East Putney Station
Putney Station
Parsons Green Stn
Fulham Broadway Stn
Lillie Primary School
Lillie Road Fitness Centre
Fulham Cross School
Henry Compton School
Putney Leisure Centre
Putneymead Medical Centre
Lion House School
Arts Theatre
South Thames College
Merlin School
Putney High School
Elliott Foundation School
ADT Technology College
The Roche School
St Josephs Primary School
Northfields Prospect Business Cen
Peterborough Primary School
Sulivan Primary School
Lady Margaret School
ABC Cinema
Fulham Clinic
Police Station
St Augustines RC Primary
F
G
H
J
K
1
2
3
4
5
6
23
24
25
119
140
159

140
West Brompton
SW10
139
120
160
A
B
C
D
E
1
2
3
4
5
6
526
27
175
Chelsea FC (Stamford Bridge)
Fulham Broadway Stn
Walham Green
FULHAM ROAD
KING'S RD
NEW KING'S ROAD
WANDSWORTH BR ROAD
CHEYNE WK
CHELSEA
Kensington & Chelsea
Wandsworth
Chelsea Physic Garden
Albert Bridge
Battersea Bridge
Chelsea Reach
Ransomes Dock
Albert Bridge Gate
BATTERS
ALBERT BRIDGE ROAD
BATTERSEA BR RD
VICARAGE CRS
WESTBRIDGE RD
Chelsea Harbour Dr
Harbour Avenue
Imperial Road
Gas Works
Chelsea College of Art & Design
Sands End
Battersea Reach
Kensington Wharf
Chelsea Wharf
YORK ROAD
LOMBARD RD
FALCON RD
LATCHMERE ROAD
SW11
Westland Heliport
Atlas Transport Est
Trading Estate
Townmead Business Cen
Consulate of Burkina Faso
Wandsworth Bridge
Carnwath Road Industrial Est
Clapham Junction Station
ST JOHN'S HL
SWANDON WY
Wandsworth Town Stn
Ferrier Industrial Est
Ram Brewery & Visitor Centre
WANDSWORTH HIGH ST
ARMOURY WY
FAIRFIELD ST
HUGUENOT PL
N SIDE WANDSWORTH COMMON
BATTERSEA RISE
EAST HL
WOODWELL ST
TRINITY RD
MILL RD SPENCER PARK
NORTHCOTE RD
St Mary's Cemetery
Emanuel School
Bolingbroke Hosp
The Wandsworth Arndale Centre
Arndale Health Centre
Lombard Business Park
Spencer Park
BROOMWOOD RD
ELSPETH RD
CLAPHAM COMM
LAVENDER
Police Station & Magistrates Court
1 grid square represents 500 metres

River Thames
Chelsea Bridge
Grosvenor Bridge
Battersea Power Station (disused)
Battersea Park
Boating Lake
Millennium Arena
Nine Elms
New Covent Garden Market
SW8
CLAPHAM
Battersea Park Stn
Queenstown Road Battersea Station
Wandsworth Road Station
Clapham High Street Stn
Clapham North Stn
Clapham Common Stn
Clapham South Station
Stockwell
Stockwell Stn
South Lambeth
SW4
Clapham Common
Clapham Park
NINE ELMS LANE A3205
BATTERSEA PK ROAD
BATTERSEA PARK ROAD
QUEENSTOWN ROAD A3216
WANDSWORTH ROAD A3036
SILVERTHORNE RD B224
CLAPHAM HIGH STREET
CLAPHAM COMMON NORTH SIDE A3 LONG ROAD
CLAPHAM COMMON SOUTH SIDE A24
CLAPHAM PK RD
THE AVENUE A205
CAVENDISH ROAD
SOUTH LAMBETH RD A203
CLAPHAM RD A3
BEDFORD ROAD B221
KINGS AV B221
CEDARS ROAD A3216
OLD TOWN
NORTH ST
Lambeth
Wandsworth
121
142
161
28
29
30
F
G
H
J
K
1
2
3
4
5
6

142
Kennington
Surrey CCC (The Oval)
Ken Barrington Cen
Kennington Ov
Young England RFC
Fentiman Road
Archbishop Tenison's School
Theatre
Oval Stn
A3 Kennington
122
Meadow Road
Royal Road
Cook's Rd
Lorrimore Road
John Ruskin Primary School
Camberwell Road A215
Albany Road
Westmoreland Rd
Keesey Street
A
B
C
D
E
531
32
Hillingdon St
Grosvenor Terrace
Grosvenor Pk
John Ruskin St
Bethwin Rd
Southampton Way
Bowyer New Church Rd
Burgess Ind Pk
Rita Road
Heyford Av
Dorset Rd
Meadow Pl
Usborne Mews
B301
Handforth Rd
Crewdson Rd
Royal National Thtr
Foxley Road
Cranmer Rd
Chryssell Rd
Kendal Close
Primary School
Camberwell New Road
Wyndham Road
College
Surgery
Primary Sch
Calvary Temple
Works
Blucher Rd
Crown St
Primary School
Camberwell Business Cen
Elmington Road
South Lambeth
Reay Primary School
Island Pl
Mowll St
Caldwell St
Vassall Road
Myatts Field Clnc
Frederick Crs
Salisbury Place
Langton Rd
Medlar St
Cambridge Rd
Camberwell Gn
Leisure Centre
Vicarage Gv
Lambeth Rd A203
South Lambeth Rd
Portland Gv
Hampson Way
Durand Prim Sch
Stockwell Park Road
The Type Museum
Isabel St
Hackford Road
Cranworth Gdns
Southey Rd
Liberty St
Morat St
Hillyard St
Brixton Road A23
Gosling Way
Cowley Road
Primary School
Eythorne Road
Fountain Pl
Cromwell Rd
Lothian Rd
Upper School
Akerman Rd
Cormont Road
Calais St
Halsmere Rd
Baldwin Crs
Sacred Heart RC Sch
A202
Surg
Camberwell Church St
Denmark Hl
Knatchbull Rd
Camberwell Station Rd
Valmar Trading Est
Wren Rd
Grove Lane
Stockwell Park School
Groveway
Normandy Rd
Mostyn Road
Lower School
Brief St
Upstall St
Inglis St
Camberwell Trading Est
Warner Road
Valmar Primary School
Temple of Bacchus
Kerfield Crs
Love Walk
Camberwell
Stockwell Stn
Clapham Rd
Rose McAndrew Clnc
Stockwell Gdns
Stockwell Pk Crs
Lorn Road
Ingleton St
Evesham Wk
Akerman Road
Burton Rd
Claribel Rd
Penford St
Templar St
Flaxman Sports Cen
Lowth Road
Crawford Rd
SE5
De Crespigny Pk
Primary School
College
Stockwell Road
Robsart St
Thornton St
Sidney Road
Aytoun Pl
Aytoun Road
Stockwell Pk Rd
Wynne Rd
Loughborough Road
Lilford Road
Fiveways Rd
Crownhurst
SW9
Prim Sch
Minet Rd
Elam St
Flaxman Rd
Industrial Est
Coldharbour Ind Est
Bessemer Rd
The Maudsley Hosp
A&E
School of Medicine
King's College Hospital
Champion Pk
A2216
Denmark Hill Stn
141
Primary School
Works
Surgery
Lansdowne Sch
Overton Rd
Primary School
Peckford Pl
Villa Rd
Angell Rd
Angell Pk Gdns
Barrington Road
Styles Gdns
Rupert Gdns
Gordon Gv
Loughborough Junction Stn
Eastlake Rd
A2217
Southwell Rd
Surgery
Higgs Industrial Est
Northway Rd
Kemerton Rd
Champion Hl
Jewish Community Theatre
Welfare Clnc
Psychiatric Home
Stansfield Rd
Chantrey Rd
A203
Stockwell Pk Wk
Brixton Mosque
St Helens RC Prim Sch
St John's Crs
IQRA Ind Sch
Wiltshire Rd
St James's Crs
Gresham Road
Western Rd
Millbrook Rd
Ridgway Rd
Lane
Hinton Rd
Shakespeare Business Centre
Wanless Rd
Herne Hill Rd
Primary School
Finsen Road
Acland Crs
Deepdene Rd
Brixton Academy
Police Stn
Canterbury Crs
Brixton Rec Cen
Fire Stn
Brixton Station Rd
Mahatma Gandhi Industrial Est
Pulross Rd
CPFC Soccer & Sports Cen
Almshouses
Nursery Rd
Brixton Stn
Atlantic Road
Coldharbour Lane
Moorland Road
Hillmead Primary School
Works
Electric Av
Ritzy
Rushcroft Rd
Saltoun Road
Brixton
Brighton Terrace
Acre Lane
War Mem
Effra Rd
Kellett Rd
Mervan Rd
Eurolink Business Cen
Effra Road Retail Park
B223
Railton Road
Industrial Estate
Railton Road Clnc
Bessemer Park Industrial Estate
Infant School
Jessop Primary School
Milkwood Road
Lowden Road
Fawnbrake Avenue
Brantwood Road
Dorchester Dr
Ruskin House School
Casino Avenue
Danecroft Road
Frankfurt Road
Herne Hill
Denmark Hill
A215
Sunray Avenue
Willowfield Sch
Heron Rd
Poplar Rd
Ferndene
Sunset Rd
Primary School
Sudbourne Road
Hayter Road
College
Horsford Rd
Trent Road
Hastings Clnc
Brixton Water Lane
St Matthew's Road
Crownstone Rd
Effra Parade
Chaucer Road
Spenser Road
Shakespeare Road
Milton Road
Trelawn Rd
Morval Road
Brixton Water La
Dulwich Road
Surgery
Kestrel Av
Rollscourt Av
Surgery
Hollingbourne Rd
Holmdene Av
Elfindale Road
Beckwith Road
The Charter School
James Allen's Prep Girls Sch
North Dulwich Station
Herne Hill Station
School
Ruskin Wk
Hill
Lambert Rd
Glanville Rd
Josephine Av
Arodene Road
Helix Rd
Appach Road
Brixton Primary School
Windmill
Blenheim Gardens
162
Regent Rd
St Jude's CE
Brockwell
Rymer St
Carver Rd
Half Moon Lane
Herne Hill
Surgery
Winterbrook Rd
Stradella
Kings College Sch of Medicine & Dentistry
Herne Hill Stadium
Dulwich Ha
Moon
Pond
SE24
Bath
A204
John Ashby Cl
Waterworks Rd
Prison
1
2
3
4
5
6
1 grid square represents 500 metres

CAMBERWELL
Peckham
SE15
East Dulwich
Nunhead
Burgess Park
Peckham Rye Park
Cemetery
Golf Course
123
144
163
F
G
H
J
K
2
3
4
5
6
33
34
35
PECKHAM ROAD
PECKHAM HIGH ST
A202
QUEEN'S ROAD
OLD KENT ROAD A2
NEW CROSS RD
RYE LANE A2215
B215 PECKHAM HILL STREET
PECKHAM PK ROAD B216
EAST DULWICH RD
A2214
NUNHEAD LANE
EVELINA ROAD
DOG KENNEL HILL
A2216
GROVE LANE
LORDSHIP LANE
PECKHAM RYE B238
FOREST HILL ROAD
LAUSANNE ROAD
POMEROY STREET
KENDER ST
B2227
Peckham Rye Stn
Queen's Road Peckham Stn
Nunhead Stn
East Dulwich Stn
Camberwell College of Arts
South London Gallery
Livesey Museum for Children
Dulwich Hamlet FC
Dulwich Hospital
Dulwich Leisure Centre
Goose Green Trading Est
Waverley Lower Secondary School
Waverley School
Premier Cinema
Aylesham Centre
Bellenden Rd Retail Park
Peckham Mosque

144
124
143
164
DEPTFORD
New Cross Gate
New Cross
St Johns
Ladywell
Brockley
Nunhead
Honor Oak
Honor Oak Park
SE14
SE4
NEW CROSS RD
A2
NEW CROSS
DEPTFORD BROADWAY
BLACKHEATH RD A2
LEWISHAM WAY
LOAMPIT HILL
THURSTON RD
BROCKMILL RD
DEPTFORD CHURCH STREET
CREEK ROAD
B2142 DRAKEFELL ROAD
BROCKLEY ROAD
B218
MALPAS ROAD
ADELAIDE AV
B236
LADYWELL ROAD
LEWISHAM HIGH ST
A21
SANFORD STREET
EDWARD ST
PAGNELL ST
AMERSHAM RD
FLORENCE ROAD
BESSON STREET
KENDER ST
LAUSANNE ROAD
GELLATLY RD
New Cross Gate Stn
New Cross Station
Deptford Stn
Deptford Bridge Station
St Johns Stn
Brockley Stn
Crofton Park Station
Ladywell Stn
Goldsmiths College
University of London
Lewisham College
Haberdashers Askes Hatcham College
Telegraph Hill School
Prendergast School
Ladywell Cemetery
Honor Oak Crematorium
Hilly Fields Crs
University Hospital
A&E
Crofton Leisure Centre
Ladywell Arena
Aquarius Golf Club
536
37
A
B
C
D
E
1
2
3
4
5
6
1 grid square represents 500 metres

125
146
165
SE10
SE3
SE13
Greenwich Park
Blackheath
Blackheath Park
LEWISHAM
Hither Green
Lee
CREEK ROAD
ROMNEY ROAD
The Queens House
National Maritime Museum
Royal Observatory Greenwich
Greenwich Theatre & Art Gallery
Fan Mus
Welfare Clinic
Police Stn
Greenwich Cinema
Greenwich Coll
Greenwich Station
Cutty Sark Station
Maze Hill Station
Park Vista
Flamsteed House Museum
Old Royal Observatory Greenwich
Conduit House
St Ursulas Convent School
Greenwich Natural Health Cen
Rangers House (The Wernher Collection)
John Roan School
John Roan Lower School
Blackheath High Senior School
Invicta Primary School
Westcombe Park Rd
Vanbrugh Park
VANBRUGH PK B210
CHARLTON RD
St John's Park
Langton Way
STRATHEDEN ROAD
HYDE VALE
ROYAL HL
CHARLTON WAY
SHOOTERS HILL RD A2
SHOOTERS HILL ROAD A2
BLACKHEATH HILL A2
Christs College
Long Pond Road
Blackheath Business Est
Hare And Billet Road
Mounts Pond Road
All Saints CE Primary Sch
Kidbrooke Gardens
Morden College Homes
Blackheath High School GDST
Wemyss Rd Prep School
Camden Ho Clinic
Primary School
Blackheath Stn
Blackheath Park
Brooklands Primary School
Wingfield Primary School
LEWISHAM RD A2211
Superstore
Lewisham Centre
Clock Tower
Our Lady of Lourdes RC Primary School
St Josephs Academy RC School
Christ the King 6th Form College
LEE TERRACE
BELMONT HILL B220
Blackheath Hosp
Surgery
LEE ROAD B212
Huntsman Sports Club
The Blackheath Clinic
Sports Ground
MOLESWORTH ST A21
HIGH ROAD
LEE
Goldsmiths Coll
Northbrook CE School
Riverston School
ELTHAM ROAD A20
Lyme Farm Road
Old Colfeian Sports Club
Ladywell Leisure Centre
Ennersdale Primary School
St Winifreds RC Infant School
BURNT ASH ROAD A2212
Hither Green Stn
Lee Manor Primary School
Chiltonian Industrial Est
Lee Station
Colfes Prep School

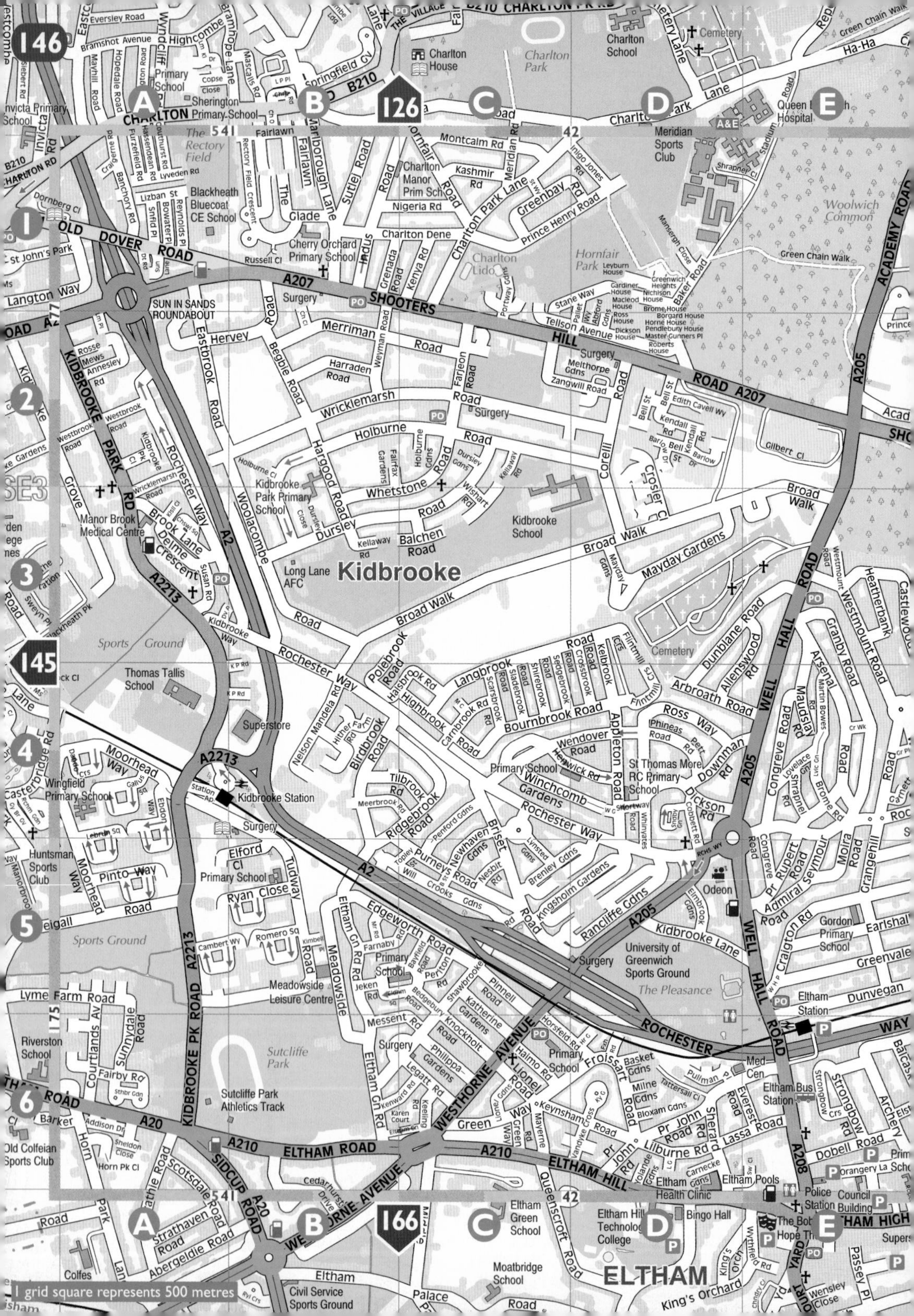
146
126
145
166
A
B
C
D
E
1
2
3
4
5
6
Kidbrooke
ELTHAM
SE3
Charlton House
Charlton Park
Charlton School
Cemetery
Queen Elizabeth Hospital
Meridian Sports Club
Woolwich Common
Green Chain Walk
Charlton Manor Prim Sch
Blackheath Bluecoat CE School
Cherry Orchard Primary School
Sherington Primary School
Wyndcliff Primary School
The Rectory Field
Charlton Lido
Hornfair Park
SUN IN SANDS ROUNDABOUT
OLD DOVER ROAD
SHOOTERS HILL ROAD A207
ACADEMY ROAD
A205
WELL HALL ROAD
KIDBROOKE PARK RD
Rochester Way
A2
A2213
Kidbrooke School
Long Lane AFC
Broad Walk
Mayday Gardens
Kidbrooke Park Primary School
Manor Brook Medical Centre
Thomas Tallis School
Superstore
Kidbrooke Station
Wingfield Primary School
Huntsman Sports Club
Elford Cl Primary School
Sports Ground
Meadowside Leisure Centre
Sutcliffe Park
Sutcliffe Park Athletics Track
Riverston School
Old Colfeian Sports Club
KIDBROOKE PK ROAD
ELTHAM ROAD
A20
A210
SIDCUP ROAD
WESTHORNE AVENUE
ELTHAM HILL
University of Greenwich Sports Ground
The Pleasance
Kidbrooke Lane
Odeon
Eltham Station
Eltham Bus Station
Rochester Way
Gordon Primary School
St Thomas More RC Primary School
Primary School
Eltham Green School
Eltham Hill Technology College
Bingo Hall
Eltham Health Clinic
Eltham Pools
Police Station
Council Building
Moatbridge School
Civil Service Sports Ground
Colfes
King's Orchard
Court Yard
A208
Eltham Palace Road
Queenscroft Road
Strathaven Road
Abergeldie Road
Scotsdale Road
Lyme Farm Road
Courtlands Av
Sunnydale Road
Moorhead Way
Pinto Way
Ryan Close
Tudway
Weigall Road
Edgeworth Road
Rancliffe Gdns
Kingsholm Gardens
Brenley Gdns
Winchcomb Gardens
Appleton Road
Ross Way
Bournbrook Road
Langbrook Road
Arbroath Road
Dunblane Road
Westmount Road
Granby Road
Congreve Road
Admiral Seymour Road
Craigton Rd
Dunvegan
Greenvale
Wricklemarsh Road
Holburne Road
Whetstone Road
Dursley Road
Balchen Road
Merriman Road
Harraden Road
Eastbrook Road
Begbie Road
Corelli Road
Woolacombe Road
Prince Henry Road
Charlton Park Lane
Marlborough Lane
Sutlej Road
Charlton Dene
Nigeria Rd
Kashmir Rd
Montcalm Rd
Springfield Gv
B210
Langton Way
Invicta Primary School
Westbrook Road
Rochester Way
Brook Lane
Delme Crescent
Nelson Mandela Rd
Birdbrook Road
Ridgebrook Road
Tilbrook Rd
Westhorne Avenue
Briset Road
Purneys Road
Knockholt Road
Phillippa Gardens
Legatt Rd
Keynsham Road
Sherard Road
Lilburne Rd
Lassa Road
Dobell Road
Archery
Strongbow
1 grid square represents 500 metres

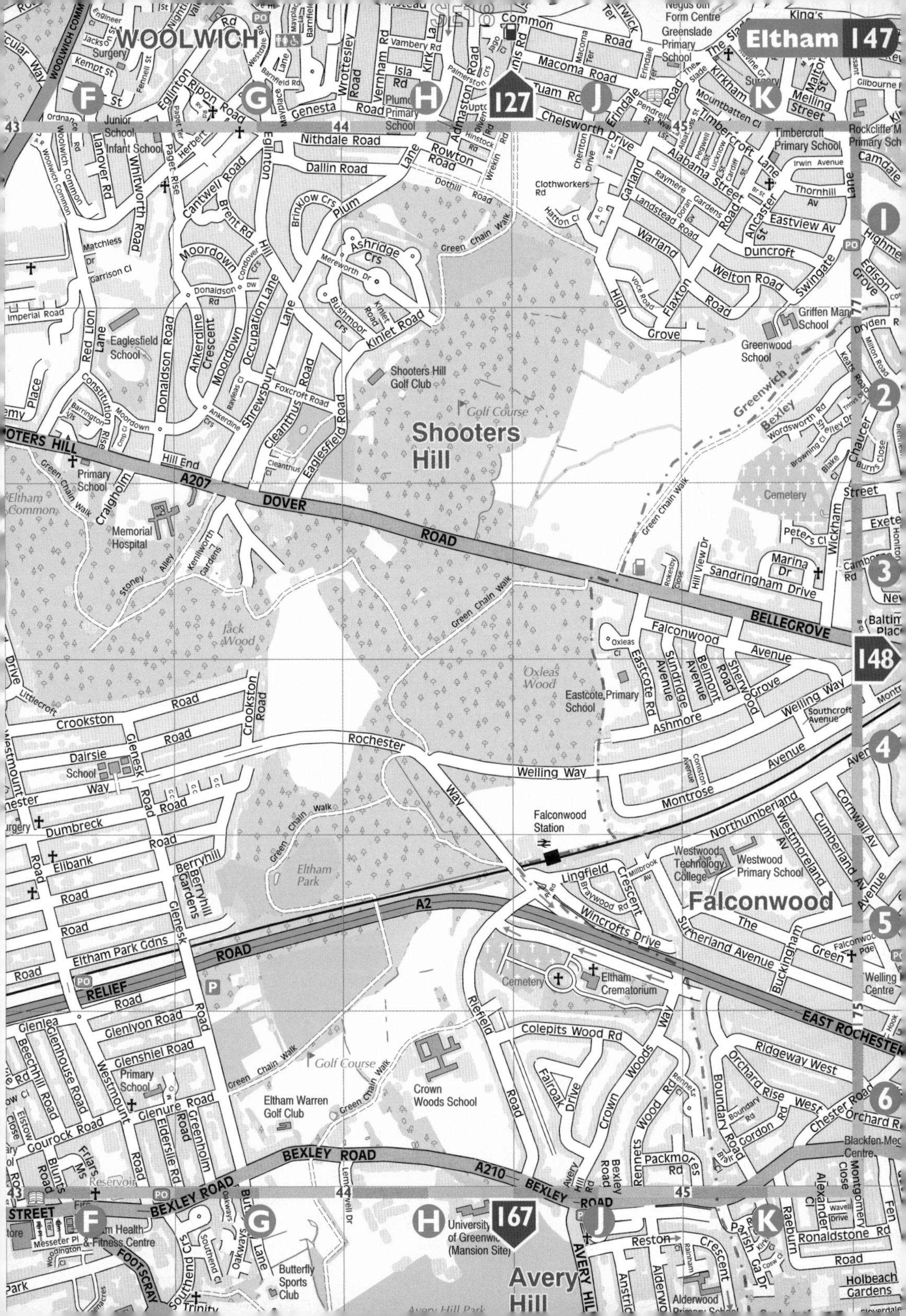
WOOLWICH
SE18
Shooters Hill
Falconwood
Avery Hill
Shooters Hill Golf Club
Golf Course
Jack Wood
Oxleas Wood
Eltham Common
Eltham Park
Memorial Hospital
Eltham Warren Golf Club
Crown Woods School
Eltham Crematorium
Cemetery
Falconwood Station
Eastcote Primary School
Westwood Technology College
Westwood Primary School
Eaglesfield School
Dairsie School
Primary School
Junior School
Infant School
Timbercroft Primary School
Greenwood School
Griffen Manor School
Greenslade Primary School
Plumcroft Primary School
University of Greenwich (Mansion Site)
Butterfly Sports Club
Reservoir
Blackfen Medical Centre
Welling Centre
A207 DOVER ROAD
BELLEGROVE ROAD
ROCHESTER WAY RELIEF ROAD
A2
EAST ROCHESTER WAY
A210 BEXLEY ROAD
BEXLEY ROAD
Welling Way
Rochester Way
Green Chain Walk
Greenwich
Bexley
F
G
H
J
K
I
2
3
4
5
6
43
44
45
127
148
167

148
128
147
168
A
B
C
D
E
1
2
3
4
5
6
546
47
East Wickham
Welling
BEXLEY
DA16
West Heath
Bleak Hill Lane
Highway
Revell Rise
Gilbourne Rd
Kingswood
Rockcliffe Manor Primary School
Brickfield Cottages
Southland Road
Superstore
St Pauls RC School
Alliance Road
Vicarage Road
Waterdale Rd
Oakmere Rd
Wickham Lane
Grasdene Road
Bournewood Road
Cemetery Road
Cemetery
Camdale Road
Highmead
Edison Grove
Combside
Pinecroft
Highbanks Cl
Patricia Court
Green Chain Walk
Dryden Road
Milton Road
Keats Road
Edison Road
Glenmore Road
Chaucer Road
Wycliffe Close
Blenheim Drive
Peregrine Court
Rosemary Road
East Wickham Primary School
Rippersley Road
Wickham Street
Beal Cl
Darenth Road
Ridley Rd
Anthony Road
Linton Cl
Lovel Avenue
Doverdale Close
Victoria Business Centre
Queen's Road
Church Rd
East Rd
Leigh Pl
Graves Yard Industrial Estate
Health & Welfare Clinic
Olyffe Av
Burnell Av
Norfolk Place
Bennett Cl
Exeter Road
Monkton Road
Awliscombe Road
Central Avenue
Tidford Road
Camborne Rd
Newlyn Rd
Lulworth Road
Cleveland Rd
Vaughan Road
Baltimore Place
Welling Stn
Station Approach
Station Ap
Surgery
Ruskin Av
Primary School
Deepdene Road
Edmund Rd
The Welling Clinic
Coton Road
New Road
Springfield Rd
Orchard Rd
Carlton Rd
Bull Aly
Welling High Street
Police Stn
Montrose Cl
Southcroft Avenue
Faraday Road
Kelvin Rd
Hook Lane Primary School
Churchfield Road
Leonards Cl
Danson Road
St John's Rd
Darwin Road
Tyndall Road
Cavendish Avenue
Marne Av
Newton Road
Maxwell Road
Huxley Road
Hook Lane
Merlin Road N
Monmouth Close
Portnkerry Av
Lancelot Road
Surgery
Danson Crescent
Selwyn Crs
Park Ap
Penpool Lane
Roseacre Road
Welling United FC
Danson Mead
Park View Road
Clinton Av
Dansington Road
Lakeview Rd
Little Danson Welfare Clinic
Danson Primary School
Bradenham Av
Fairwater Av
Birch Grove
Wendover Way
Merlin Rd
Cowper Close
Bexley Grammar School
Danson Park
Cumberland Av
Cambridge Av
Dorset Av
Hook Lane
Yorkland Av
Westwood Lane
Gloucester Av
Somerset Av
Kent Av
Falconwood Pde
Welling Medical Centre
Sutherland Avenue
East Rochester Way
A2
Ingleton Avenue
Radnor Avenue
Groombridge Cl
Tyrrell Avenue
Wellan Close
Ridgeway East
Chester Road
Orchard Rise E
Leechcroft Avenue
Lyndon Avenue
Blackfen Medical Centre
Blackfen Road
Superstore
Park Mead
Lakeside Close
Danson Up
Overcourt Cl
Westerham Drive
A210
A221
Works
Blackfen Rd
Blendon Rd
Blackfen School for Girls
Sherwood Park Primary School
Alexander Cl
Montgomery Close
Ronaldstone Rd
Queenswood Road
Hawthorn Terrace
Sycamore Av
Days Lane
Maple Crs
Wellington Ave
Penshurst
Burns Av
Ramillies
Blackfen
Woodside
Lane
Blendon Road
Margaret Rd
Brook Lane
Cedar Grove
Longleigh Lane
Langley Road
Hartley Rd
Downe Close
Sandgate Road
Denton Road
Keston Close
Hillsgrove Cl
Hadlow Road
First Avenue
Madison Gdns
Madison Crs
Lansdowne Avenue
Primary School
Plymstock Road
Sidmouth Road
Seaton Road
Totnes Rd
Bideford Road
Lodge Hill
Exmouth Road
Budleigh Crescent
Okehampton Crescent
Axminster Crescent
Lyme Road
Charmouth Road
Tavistock Road
Saltash Road
St Michaels CE Primary School
Selsey Crescent
Colyton Close
Tenby Road
Bognor Rd
Brixham Road
Gipsy Road
Preston Drive
Berkeley Avenue
Mayfair Avenue
Teviot Cl
Stuart Rd
Douglas Road
Bruce Close
Kay Street
Berwick Road
Wrotham Road
Welling School
Swanley Road
Teignmouth Rd
Normanhurst Avenue
Farnham Road
Elsa Road
Fosters Primary School
Balliol Road
Somerhill Road
Kenmere Road
Hazeldene Road
Ivedon Road
Avondale Road
Sutcliffe Road
Holmesdale Road
Stevedale Rd
Fairlawn Avenue
Lynmere Rd
Northdown Road
Barrington Road
Barrington Primary School
Winchester Road
Alexander Rd
Brampton Primary School
Upper Wickham Lane
A209
A207
A221
Clifton Rd
Westbrooke Crs
Westbrooke Road
Foster's Primary School
Fox Hollow Dr
Marlborough Road
Palmeira Road
Warwick Road
Stuart Evans Cl
Lewis Rd
Granville Rd
Bethel Road
S Gipsy Road
Westbrooke School
Crook Log Sports Centre
Brampton Road
Park View Road
Crook Log
Splashworld Swimming Centre
Crook Log Primary School
Dallin Road
North Close
South Close
The Gv
Sydney
Askern Cl
Bean Road
Danson Road
Danson Watersports Centre
Iverhurst Cl
Green Vale
Brasted Close
Sandhurst Rd
Wellington Rd
Lodge La
Pengarth Rd
Heath Avenue
Canberra Road
Powys Close
Lessness Av
Abbott's
King
Surgery
The Quad
Brampton Road
West Heath
Burcharbro Road
1 grid square represents 500 metres

129
150
169
F
G
H
J
K
48
49
50
1
2
3
4
5
6
Bexleyheath
DA6
DA7
Northumberland Heath
Bedonwell Clinic
Bedonwell Primary School
Belmont Primary School
Erith School
Erith School Community Sports Centre
Bursted Wood Primary School
Bursted Wood
Barnehurst Station
Bexleyheath Station
St Thomas More RC Primary School
Pickford Lane Medical Centre
Upland Primary School
Bexleyheath School
Playing Field
Cemetery
Russell Park
Pelham Primary School
London Transport Bus Depot
Fire Stn
Amb Stn
The Medical Centre
Police Station
Shopping Centre
Clock Tower
Broadway Sh Ctr
Superstore
Super Bowl
Bexleyheath Centre
Upton Day Hospital
Civic Offices
Cineworld
Gravel Hill Primary School
St Catherines RC Girls School
St Columbas RC Boys School
Bexleyheath Golf Club
Golf Course
Upton Road School
Upton Primary School
Townley Grammar School for Girls
Bexley Erith Technical High School
Recn Gnd
Hall Place
A220
A207
A221
A2
BROADWAY
ALBION ROAD
WATLING STREET
GRAVEL HILL
ERITH ROAD
BEXLEY ROAD
MAYPLACE RD W
EAST ROCHESTER WAY
BOURNE ROAD
ARNSBERG WAY
Long Lane
Little Heath Road
Pembury Road
Lenham Road
Bedonwell Road
Belmont Road
Brook Street
Rydal Drive
Long Lane
Woolwich Road
Belvedere Road
Mayplace Road East
Barnehurst Road
Merewood Road
Northall Road
Halcot Avenue
Upton Road
Hansol Road
Pickford Lane
Church Road
Lion Road
Oaklands Road
Townley Road
Horsham Rd
Midhurst Hill
Broomfield Road
Latham Road
Station Road
Woodlands Road
Sheldon Road
Dunwich Road
Hurlingham Rd
Ightham Road
Nurstead Road
Swanton Road
Silecroft Road
Swanbridge Rd
Lavernock Rd
Haslemere Road
Garden Avenue
Nursery Avenue
Bowness Rd
Silverdale Road
Brantwood Road
Lyndhurst Road
Martens Avenue
Leysdown Avenue
Stephen Road
Mayplace Road
Hillingdon Road
Eastleigh Rd
Westfield Road
Beverley Road
Coniston Rd
Grasmere Road
Windermere Rd
Heath Way
Colyers La
Hengist Rd
Horsa Rd
Sussex Rd
Carlton Road
Manorway
Arcadian Av
Basing Drive
Iris Av

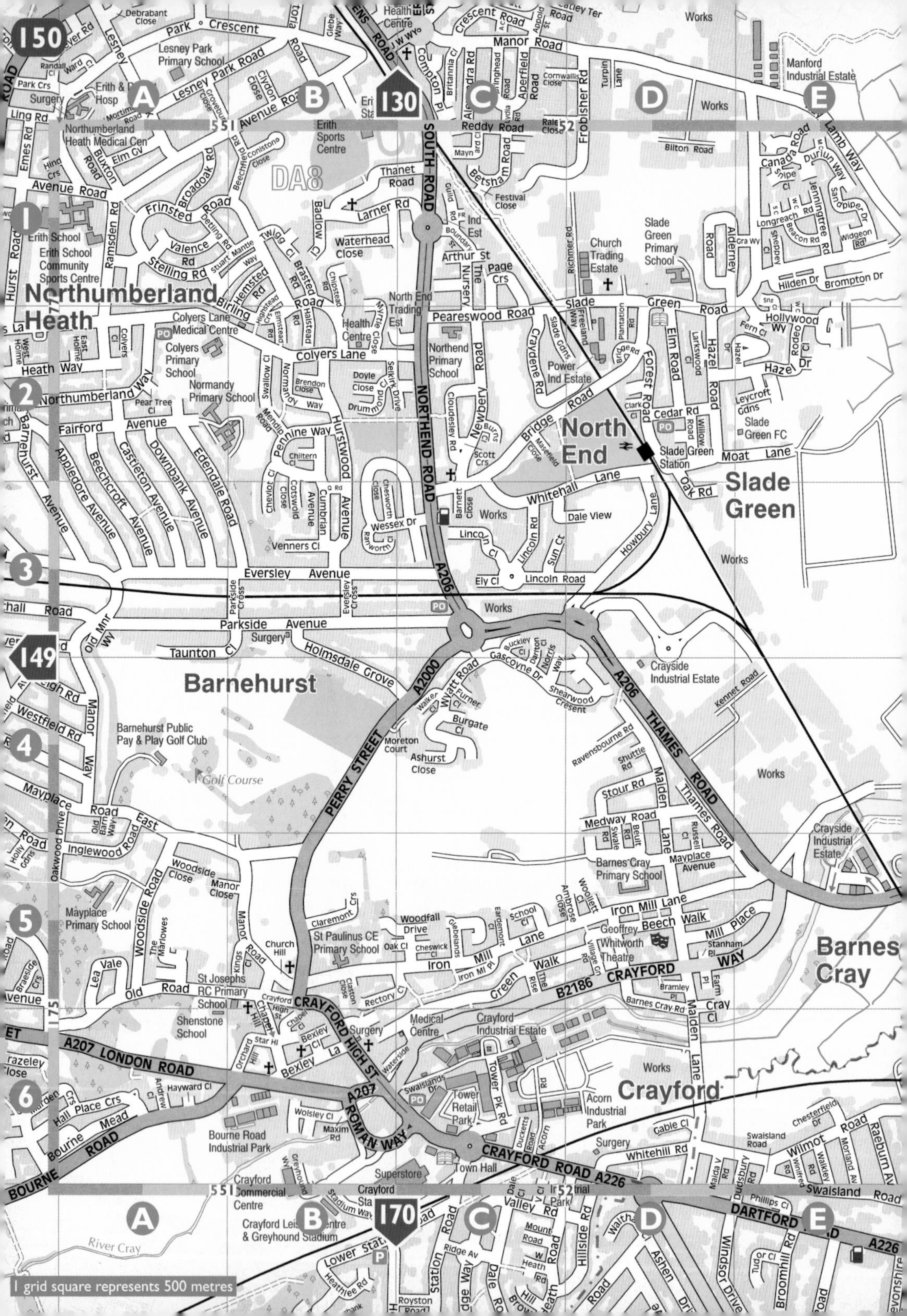
150
130
149
170
A
B
C
D
E
1
2
3
4
5
6
551
552
175
DA8
Northumberland Heath
North End
Slade Green
Barnehurst
Barnes Cray
Crayford
Erith School
Erith School Community Sports Centre
Erith Sports Centre
Lesney Park Primary School
Northumberland Heath Medical Cen
Colyers Lane Medical Centre
Colyers Primary School
Normandy Primary School
Northend Primary School
North End Trading Est
Health Centre
Church Trading Estate
Slade Green Primary School
Power Ind Estate
Slade Green FC
Slade Green Station
Manford Industrial Estate
Works
Crayside Industrial Estate
Barnehurst Public Pay & Play Golf Club
Golf Course
Mayplace Primary School
Barnes Cray Primary School
St Paulinus CE Primary School
St Josephs RC Primary School
Shenstone School
Geoffrey Whitworth Theatre
Crayford Industrial Estate
Bourne Road Industrial Park
Tower Retail Park
Acorn Industrial Park
Town Hall
Superstore
Crayford Commercial Centre
Crayford Leisure Centre & Greyhound Stadium
River Cray
Park Crescent
Lesney Park Road
Avenue Road
Manor Road
Crescent Road
Reddy Road
Bilton Road
Frobisher Rd
South Road
Northend Road
A206
Thames Road
A2000
Perry Street
Crayford High St
A207 London Road
Roman Way
Crayford Road A226
B2186 Crayford Way
Dartford Rd
A226
Bourne Road
Mayplace Road East
Eversley Avenue
Parkside Avenue
Holmsdale Grove
Colyers Lane
Peareswood Road
Slade Green Road
Bridge Road
Whitehall Lane
Moat Lane
Lincoln Road
Iron Mill Lane
Maiden Lane
Old Road
Swaisland Road
Crayford Sta
1 grid square represents 500 metres

F
G
H
131
J
K
53
54
55
Burnett
Ness Road
Works
Wallhouse Road
Dartford Marshes
Darent Valley Path
Joyce Green Lane
Crayford Marshes
Kent County
Bexley
Marsh Street
A206 UNIVERSITY WAY
A206
UNIVERSIT
McCudden Rd
Salmon Rd
Grovehurst Rd
Atlas Rd
Cornwall Rd
Cemetery
Joyce Green Lane
Strickland Av
Sharp Wy
Barnwell Rd
M Rd
Marsh St
Chaucer Wy
Wodehouse Road
Hardy Gv
Wordsworth Way
Henderson Drive
Hall Road
Green Lane
Wellcome Av
Spielman Road
Bronte Gv
Browning Road
Osterberg Rd
Joyce
Trevelyan Cl
Blake Gdns
Keyes Road
Sheridan Ct
Trevithick Drive
Perry Gv
Farnol Rd
Dunkin Rd
Dickens Av
Cavell Cres
Coleridge Rd
Shakespeare Rd
Shaftesbury La
Edmunds Rd
St
Thames Gate
Primary School
Pilgrims Ct
F Rd
Littlebrook Manor Way
Tennyson Rd
Masefield Rd
Eliot Rd
Hilltop Gdns
Primary School
Surgery
PO
P
Temple Hl Sq
Temple Hill
Mallard Cl
Falcon Cl
Lansbury Crs
Morris Gdns
Kingsley Av
Attlee Drive
Ruskin Gv
A282
Industrial Estate
Works
Central Road
Bus Garage
Works
Dartford Station
Knights Manor Way
Norfolk Cl
Sandpit Road
Swan Business Park
Millside Industrial Estate
Burnham Trading Estate
DA1
A206
Temple Hill
Riverside Industrial Estate
Riverside Way
Darent Valley Path
Shirley Cl
Burnham Crs
Alan Cl
Eton Way
Arundel Rd
Lagonda Wy
Chatsworth Rd
Chtsw Rd
Lawson Rd
Lawson Gdns
Priory Road
Cairns Cl
Invicta Sports Club
Kenwyn Rd
Avonmouth Rd
Humber Rd
Victoria Industrial Park
Business Centre
Hythe St
Holmleigh Av
Mayfair Rd
Savoy Road
A2026 BURNHAM ROAD
Holy Trinity CE Primary School
Francis Rd
Grsvnr Crs
VICTORIA ROAD
Stanham Road
Gainsborough Avenue
Turner Ct
Marcet Rd
Lawford Gdns
Rayford Cl
Priory Cl
Avenue
Priory Gdns
Anne of Cleves Rd
Firmin Road
Hallford Way
Kingswood Close
Kingsridge Gdns
Kg Edward Avenue
West Hill Primary School
Hill Dr
The Homestead
Lodge Av
Primary School
Sanctuary Cl
Priory Pl
Prospect Pl
Superstore
A2026
Civic Centre
Station Ap
Superstore
A226
Mill Pond
171
Fulwich Road
New Town
Bow Lane
Vincents
Gladstone Rd
Lavinia Rd
St Martin's Road
Queen St
Carrington Road
Bayly Road
Syndridge Cl
Osbourne Rd
Carlisle Road
Angel Centre
Kent Rd
Westgate Rd
Twisleton
WEST HILL
Cross Rd
Nelson Rd
Wellington Road
County Court
Orchard
Overy
PO
1
2
3
4
5
6
74
75
76
77

132
Perimeter Road
Heathrow World Cargo Centre
Terminal 4
The British Museum Shop
Heathrow Terminal
Shoreham Road (West)
Shoreham Road
Sandringham Rd
Seaford Rd
A
B
C
D
E
506
07
Oaks Road
Lindsay Cl
Riverside Road
Short Rd
Southampton Road
Sealand Road
Tunnel Link Road
Southern Perimeter Road
Bedfont Road
Russell Dr
Stanwell Gdns
Hendon Wy
Lintott Ct
Lindsay Rd
Riverside Pl
Callis Farm Cl
Northumberland Close
Court Farm Industrial Estate
Gleneagles Cl
High St
De Havilland Wy
Dutch Barn Cl
Christ the King RC First School
Whitley Close
Blackburn Trading Estate
St Marys CE Junior School
Lord Knyvett Cl
Falcon Dr
Clare Road
Crane Road
Sanctuary Rd
Beacon Rd
Southern Perimeter Road
Scylla Rd
Longford River
Heath Cl
Trinity Close
Hadfield Road
Everest Road
TOWN LA B378
St Mary's Crs
Comet Rd
Corsair Rd
St Annes Primary School
West Bedfont
Long Lane
Brook Cl
Hillingdon
Surrey County
Stanwell
St Davids Health Centre
Hadrian Way
Britannia Way
Hannibal Road
Frobisher Crs
Cordelia Rd
Cordelia Gdns
Jubilee Cl
Beech Cl
Town Farm Primary School
Cambria Gdns
Cambria Gdns
Cemetery
Vibia Close
Elizabethan Wy
Argosy La
Canopus Way
East Bedfont
Jordans Close
St Anne's Av
Diamedes Avenue
Viscount Road
Hadrian Wy
Cranford Av
Caledonia Rd
Hillingdon Av
Osborne Av
Short Lane
Clare Road
Ensign Cl
Explorer Av
Ravensbourne Av
Masefield Way
Elm Cl
Clyde Road
Longford Way
Genesis Cl
Mulberry Avenue
Holywell Way
LANE
TOWN
Kingsway
Holywell Cl
Long Lane
A30
Clockhouse Industrial Estate
Scots Cl
Viola Avenue
Viola Avenue
Ashford Sports Club
Harrow Road
Ascot Road
Works
B378
Ashdale Cl
Willowbrook Rd
Cemetery
LONDON ROAD
B3003
Albain Crs
Superstore
London Rd
Edward Way
Orchard Way
Desford Way
LANE
Ellies Ms
Ashford Hospital
A&E
PO
Lodge Way
A30
Works
Seaton Dr
Gordon Road
Road
London Rd
Kenilworth
Cumberland Road
STANWELL ROAD
Ashford High School
CLOCKHOUSE
Hounslow
Surrey County
Rennie Cl
Hengrove Crs
Avondale Road
Dorset Road
Portland Road
Ashford Crescent
Salcombe Rd
Thetford Rd
Ashford Clinic
St Davids School
Anglesey Cl
Anglesey Cl
Clarendon Primary School
Ashford Station
Station Crescent
Stanwell Road
Village Way
Glen Av
Parkland Rd
Reedsfield Road
Grays Lane
Chattern Hill
Ashford Park Primary School
Windsor Dr
Sandringham Dr
Tudor Close
Queens Walk
CHURCH
Station Rd
TW15
Meadway
Grove
Clifford Gv
Clockhouse La
Rosary Gdns
Works
West Cl
Coleridge Road
Clarendon Rd
Spelthorne Sixth Form College
Studholme Medical Cen
Ashford Sports Club
Woodthorpe Rd
The Wickets
Chaucer Road
Ford Rd
ROAD
Brownrigg Rd
Parkland
Exeforde Av
Echelforde Dr
Rosa Av
Chestnut Cl
Surgery
Chestnut Rd
Wolsey Road
Muncaster Cl
FELTHAM
Ruggles-Brise Road
Chesterfield Road
Dudley Rd
Fordbridge Medical Cen
CHURCH
FELTHAM RD
Oakfield Rd
Margarets Av
Chalmers Rd
Woodthorpe Road
Adelaide Road
Marlborough Road
Townsend Road
Warwick Road
Stanley Road
Stanley Rd
Princes Road
B377
Percy Av
TOWN TREE RD
CONVENT RD
Tennyson Rd
Springfield Rd
Arlington Rd
ASHFORD
St Michaels RC School
Muncaster Road
Echelford Primary School
BY-PASS
Nelson Road
Gables Av
Fontmell Park
Fontmell Cl
Metcalf Road
1 grid square represents 500 metres
Fernside Road
Talbot Rd
Hilda's Av
Fairholme Rd
The Crs
ROAD
Manor
Feltham Hl Rd
St Michaels Rd
Elm Tree Cl
Dingle Rd
B378
1
2
3
4
5
6
74
73
72

133
154
F
G
H
J
K
08
09
10
2
3
4
5
6
Hillingdon
Hounslow
Lower Feltham
TW14
GREAT SOUTH-WEST ROAD
A30
A315
STAINES ROAD
BEDFONT LANE
B3377
BEDFONT LA
NEW RO
A312
A244
HIGH STREET
ASHFORD HIGH ST
ASHFORD RD
ASHFORD ROAD
CHERTSEY ROAD
Chertsey Road
Southern Perimeter Rd
Swindon Rd
Scarborough Rd
Snowdon Road West
Sheffield Rd
Swansea Road
Shrewsbury Rd
Shrewsbury Road
Cain's Lane
Orchard Av
Unwin Av
Iverna Gdns
Edward Rd
Wellington
The Marjory Kinnon School
Surgery
Bedfont J&I School
Hazelmere Cl
The Gardens
Marriott Cl
Cem
Engineheart Dr
Clive Road
Minimax Close
Pentelow Gdns
Central
Work
Peninsular Cl
Northumberland Crs
Target Cl
Kingston Av
Richmond Av
Longford Avenue
Elmcroft Cl
White Br
Burns Avenue
Shaftesbury Avenue
Rosslyn Av
Buckingham Av
Gladstone Av
Bedfont Cl
Montrose Rd
Horsham Rd
North Rd
North Cl
New Road
Page Road
East Road
West Road
Hatton Road
Benedict Dr
Dorchester Dr
Bethany Wave
Staines Rd
Ruskin Av
Cassiobury Avenue
Shakespeare Avenue
Feltham & Hounslow Boro FC
Longford Community School
Letchworth Av
Tachbrook Rd
Link Rd
Fruen Road
Feltham Athletics Arena
Road
Stanwell Rd
Spinney Drive
West View
Longleat Wy
Pates Mnr Dr
Staines Road
Burlington Cl
Gould Rd
Warfield Rd
Imperial Road
Colonial Rd
Bedfont Health Clinic
Fairholme
Grovestile Wave
St Mary's Drive
Natalie Cl
Elm Road
Sherborne Rd
Cedar Rd
Kilross Rd
Padbury Cl
Lox Wood Cl
Bowden Close
Elsworth Close
Beech Road
Monarch Cl
Southville Road
Southville Close
Southville Crs
Sandy Dr
Ash Gv
Oak Way
Watermead
Walker Cl
Westmacott Dr
Stone Crs
Chandlers Close
Beattie Cl
Southville Junior School
Shore Cl
Hawkes Rd
Gibbins Rd
Locomotive Dr
Station Est Rd
Pacific Cl
Westminster Cl
Ashmead Rd
Southern Av
Proctors Cl
Sandycombe Rd
Jubilee Wy
Eldridge Cl
Trevithick Cl
Grsmr Cl
Derwent Cl
Westmacott Drive
Waterloo Cl
Padstow Walk
Grove Village Medical Cen
Hatchett Rd
Fawns Manor Rd
Peacock Avenue
Dudley Road
Bedfont Green Close
Fairholme J&I School
Cemetery
Bedfont Road
Industrial Estate
Bedfont Lakes Country Park
Edward Pauling School
Railway Terrace
Cardinal Rd Infant School
Highfield Road
Plum Cl
Hanover Av
Guildford Av
Southcote Av
Cravan Av
Granville Av
Rochester Av
Superstore
Manor La
Rose Gdns
Redford Close
Raleigh Road
Lancing Rd
Vernon Road
Percival Road
Princes Road
Westbourne Rd
Maple Industrial Est
Ordn Cl
Vineyard Rd
Francis Av
Poplar Wy
Maple Wy
Tawny Cl
Parkfield Road
Parkfield Crs
Challenge Road
HM Young Offender Institution
Feltham Hill Infant School
Feltham Hill Junior School
St Dunstan's Rd
Av Rd
Hayling Av
Craigwell Avenue
April Close
Harvest Road
Brookside Cl
Badger Cl
Sycamore Cl
Deerhurst Close
Bedfont Industrial Park
Portland Crs
Field Vw
Ashford Industrial Estate
Shield Road
The Clumps
Spring Rd
Cemetery
Sunbury Road
Shelson Av
Walton Gdns
Ryland Close
Ludlow Rd
Shelson Avenue
Ellington Road
Denison Road
Cranleigh Road
Hamilton Road
Highland Pk
Felthamhill
Staines RFC
Hamilton Close
Chattern Road
Fernhurst Road
Duke's Cl
Anderson Dr
ROAD
Vinegrove Av
Sandell's Av
Wren's Av
Neil Cl
Coolgardie Rd
New Pk Rd
Poplar Road
Ashgrove Road
Newhaven Crs
Priory Gdns
Beech Cl
Kinross Dr
Kinross Cl
Groveley Rd
Oakhall Dr
Hounslow
Surrey County

154
134
153
172
A
B
C
D
E
1
2
3
4
5
6
12
TW13
North Feltham
FELTHAM
Hanworth
Hounslow Heath
Hanworth Park
Golf Course
Golf Club
Industrial Est
Superstore
Works
Central Way
Mill Way
River Gardens
Roman Cl
Staines Road
Harlington Road West
Harlington Road East
Hounslow Road
A312
A244
A314
A316
B3377
Minimax Close
Lansbury Av
Field Road
Becketts Cl
Baber Dr
Beeston Way
Bywrd Av
The Vale
Viola Av
Carlton Avenue
Denham Rd
Sparrow Farm Dr
Sparrow Farm Drive
Sparrow Farm Infant School
Sparrow Farm Junior School
Fareham Rd
Cygnet Av
Cygnet Avenue
Finch Dr
Durham Rd
Rosslyn Av
Buckingham Av
Gladstone Av
Shaftesbury Avenue
Helen Avenue
The Dell
Walsham Rd
Clymping Dene
Brainton Av
Feltham & Hounslow Boro FC
Feltham Athletics Arena
Nursery Close
Fern Grove
Park Wy
Works
Station Est Rd
Locomotive Dr
Manor Pl
New Road
Feltham Station
Surgery
Queen's Rd
Cromwell Rd
Kings Rd
Hanworth Road
Cardinal Road Infant School
Cardinal Rd
Florence Rd
Ashfield Av
Danesbury Road
Camden Av
Alfred Rd
Gloucester Rd
Norfolk Rd
Hereford Road
Boundaries Road
Salisbury Rd
De Broome Rd
Slattery Rd
Wyatt Cl
Elthorne Court
Junior School
Victoria Rd
School
The Gn
Cineworld Cinema
St Lawrence Business Cen
Feltham Superbowl
Browell's Lane
Feltham Community College
Uxbridge Road
Forest Road
Works
Maple Industrial Est
Elmwood Av
Sandalwood Rd
Pinewood Rd
Felthambrook Industrial Estate
Felthambrook Wy
Rookeries Cl
Plane Tree Crs
Poplar Wy
Maple Wy
Aspen Wy
Five Ways Business Cen
Sycamore Cl
Badger Cl
Foxwood Cl
Roebuck Cl
Beagle
Deerhurst Close
Brookside
Felthambrook Way
Fernside Av
Clifton
Camrose Av
Castle Way
Seymour Gdns
Elizabeth Way
Moat Side
Queens Wy
Queens Av
Shakespeare Wy
Felthamhill Road
Staines RFC
Raleigh Wy
Sunbury Wy
Country Way
Nailhead Road
Dickenson Rd
Godfrey Way
Hounslow Cem
Mill Farm Business Park
Curtis Rd
Millfield Rd
Farm Road
Grafton Cl
Mill Farm Crs
South West Middlesex Crematorium
Wigley Road
Westbury Rd
Pevensey Rd
Amesbury Road
Marlborough Rd
Eastbourne Rd
Bexhill Cl
Meadow Rd
Little Pk Dr
Woodlawn Dr
Oaks Av
Surgery
Mount Medical Cen
Feltham Airparcs Leisure Centre
Hampton Road West
Sunningdale Av
Canterbury Rd
Saxon Av
Norman Av
Braid Cl
Towfield Rd
Crane Junior School
Crane Infant School
Barnlea Cl
Hampton Fm Industrial Est
Bel La
Mt Rd
Hanworth Trading Est
Winslow Way
Oriel Primary School
Cottington Rd
Cresswell Rd
Devonshire Rd
Swift Rd
Popham Cl
Apex Retail Park
Little Eden & Eden High School
Park Rd
Hounslow College Independent School
Twickenham Road
Crispen Rd
Cross Rd
Riverdale Rd
Millbourne Road
Hampton La
St John's Road
Shepherd Cl
Swan Cl
The Alders
St George's Rd
Grove Crs
Oxford Wy
Bear Road
Conway Rd
Malthouse Dr
Lebanon Av
Osborne Cl
Green Lane
New Rd
New Cl
Holly Cl
Forge La
Armstrong Rd
Fir Rd
Birch Rd
Surgery
Robin Cl
Street
Wraysbury Close
Dorney Wy
Raglan Cl
Beaulieu Cl
Garrison Cl
Sheridan Court
Beresford Gardens
Yew Tree Wk
Avondale Gardens
Heathland School
Simpson Rd
Edgar Rd
Hanworth Road
Heathside
Lea Cl
Pembridge Av
Chester Avenue
Glasbrook Av
Albemarle Av
Villiers Av
Cheyne Av
Ellerman Av
Waverley
Saxon Av
Nene Gdns
Fountains Cl
Winchester Road
Bideford Cl
Lincoln Rd
York Wy
Exeter Rd
Stourton Av
Fairlawn Cl
Superstore
Wordsworth Rd
Browning Cl
Byron Cl
Rectory Rd
Buckingham Rd
Richmond House
1 grid square represents 500 metres

Whitton
TWICKENHAM
TW2
Strawberry Hill
Hampton Hill
135
156
173
F
G
H
J
K
1
2
3
4
5
6
13
14
15
74
72
Twickenham Stadium
Museum of Rugby & Twickenham Stadium Tours
Chase Bridge Primary School
Kneller Hall
Richmond upon Thames College
NEC Harlequins RFC (The Stoop Memorial Ground)
Whitton Station
Twickenham Cemetery
Bishop Perrin CE Prim Sch
Heathfield Primary School
Nelson Primary School
Primary School
Whitton Health Cen
Whitton Health Clinic
Whitton School
Whitton Sports & Fitness Centre
Richmond upon Thames
Hounslow
River Crane
Cemetery
Jack & Jill School
Trafalgar Primary School
Waldegrave Girls School
The Mall School
St James RC Primary School
Strawberry Hill Station
Strawberry Hill Golf Club
Golf Course
Fulwell Golf Club
Fulwell Station
Superstore
Stanley Junior School
Stanley Infant School
Teddington Cemetery
Twickenham Golf Club
Medical Centre
Hampton Community
Hampton School
The Lady Eleanor Holles School
Surgery
Works
Health Centre
KNELLER RD
B361 WHITTON RD
CHERTSEY ROAD A316
HOSPITAL BR ROAD
B358
NELSON RD
WHITTON RD
HOUNSLOW RD
STAINES ROAD A305
SIXTH CROSS ROAD
HAMPTON ROAD A311
WELLINGTON ROAD A311
FULWELL ROAD B360
SOUTH ROAD
UXBRIDGE ROAD A312
PARK ROAD A313
CHURCH ROAD B360
THE GREEN
TWICKENHAM ROAD A305
SOUTH RD A3063
A314
A309
Warren Road
Constance Rd
Montrose Avenue
Bridge Way
Crane Way
Nelson Road
Percy Road
Ross Road
Selkirk Road
Lincoln Avenue
Staines
Burton's Road
Pigeon Lane
Queen's Rd
Victor Road
York Road
Shacklegate La
Grove Rd
Wellesley Rd
Tower Rd
Twining Avenue
Fortescue Avenue
Fielding Avenue
River Meads Avenue
Beech Way
Glebe Wy
Butts Crs
Mill Road
Lisbon Av
Fulwell Park Av

St Margarets
Cole Park
Ham
Twickenham Stn
St Margaret's Stn
Strawberry Hill Station
River Thames
Eel Pie Island
Marble Hill Park
Marble Hill House
Orleans Park School
Orleans House Gallery
Ham House (NT)
Deutsche Schule
The Russell School
Strathmore School
Grey Court School
St Richards with St Andrews CE Primary School
Meadlands Prim Sch
Teddington Lock
St Marys University College
Newland House School
The Waldegrave Clinic
Teddington Pool & Fitness Centre
The Cassel Hospital
Ham & Petersham Cricket Club
Dysart School
St Georges Industrial Est
Twickenham Trading Est
Ivybridge Retail Park
Superstore
Richmond Adult & Community College
St Margarets Business Centre
Mary Wallace Theatre
Civic Centre
Council Building
Oak Lane Medical Cen
Cambridge Park Bowling & Sports Club
Twickenham Park Health Cen
Ham Health Clinic
St Catherines School
Heatham Park
Moormead Recn Ground
Junior School
Primary School
TW1
CHERTSEY RD A316
THE AVENUE A316
LONDON ROAD A310
ST MARGARET'S RD
CROWN RD A3004
RICHMOND ROAD A305
HEATH ROAD A305
YORK ST
KING ST
CROSS DEEP A310
WALDEGRAVE ROAD A309
STRAWBERRY V
TWICKENHAM RD A310
UPR HAM ROAD A307
B360 CHURCH ROAD
SHACKLEGATE LA
HIGH STREET
FERRY RD
Ham Street
Ham Common
Riverside Drive
Sandy Lane
Dukes Avenue
Thames Path
Richmond Bridge
136
155
174
A B C D E
1 2 3 4 5 6
1 grid square represents 500 metres

RICHMOND
Richmond Hill
Petersham
TW10
Richmond Park
East Sheen Cemetery
East Sheen Common
St Elizabeths RC Primary School
Kings House School
Queens Medical Centre
Youth Centre
Surgery
Old Vicarage School
Hotel
The Clinic
The Vineyard Primary School
Richmond College
Htl
Hotel
Star & Garter Home
Nightingale La
Hobart Place
Bog Lodge
Sawyer's Hill
Queen's Road
Pen Ponds
Pembroke Lodge
Golf Course
The Richmond Golf Club
Sudbrook Gardens
Isabella Plantation
Ham Common
Ham Gate Av
Parkgate House
HAM GATE AVENUE
B352
Church Road
PETERSHAM ROAD
A307
STAR AND GARTER HILL
RICHMOND HILL
FRIARS STILE RD
QUEEN'S ROAD
KINGS ROAD
B353
B321
B322
Park Road
Marlborough Rd
Rosemont Road
Cambrian Rd
Chisholm Rd
Kingsmead
Kg George Sq
Stafford Pl
Queen's Rise
Chester Av
Onslow Rd
Greville Rd
Park Hl
Lower Gro Rd
Vineyard
Mount Ararat Rd
Dynevor Rd
Grosvenor Rd
Halford Rd
Sudbrook Lane
Dickens Cl
Bute Av
Ashfield Cl
Cedar Hts
Meadow Cl
Beechrow
The Shires
Tudor Drive
Aragon Rd
Anne Boleyn's Wk
Bainbridge Cl
Latchmere Cl
Garthside
Sopwith Cl
Hatch Pl
Cowper Rd
Parklands Close
Avenue
Fife Road
Parkgate Gdns
KINGSTON HILL
A308
Kingston Hl Pl
Cedar Cl
Coombe Pk
Richmond upon Thames
Kingston upon Thames
137
158
175
F
G
H
J
K
18
19
20
1
2
3
4
5
6
74
72

158
East Sheen
Roehampton
Golf Course
Roehampton Institute
Sacred Heart RC Primary School
Parkstead Road
Chartfield Sch
Bank Lane
138
Roehampton Gate
Roedean Crescent
Grove House
Froebel College
Queen Mary's University Hospital
Granard Primary School
Crestway
Dover House Road
Clarence Lane
Ibstock Place School
Highcliffe Drive
South Thames College / Wandsworth Adult College
Douglas Bader Foundation
SW15
Westmead
Sherfield Gdns
Tunworth Crs
Surgery
Tangley Gv
Minstead Gdns
School
Danebury
Richmond Park Golf Club
Harbridge Av
Police Stn
Avenue
Laverstoke Gdns
Roehampton High St
Medfield St
A306
Roehampton Church School
Roehampton Recreation Centre
Westmoor Community Clnc
Royal Hospital & Home
Fontley Way
Ibsley Gdns
Alton Rd
Bessborough Rd
Dilton Gdns
Primary School
Arnewood Cl
Wandsworth
Richmond upon Thames
Richmond Park
The Royal Ballet School
Beverley Brook
Golf Course
157
ROEHAMPTON LANE
KINGSTON
Norstead Pl
Putney Vale Crematorium
Putney Vale Cemetery
Superstore
A3
ROEHAMPTON VALE
Friars Av
Stag Lane
Stroud Crescent
Putney Vale
Hall School Wimbledon
London Scottish Golf Club
Wandsworth
Merton
Golf Course
Wimbledon Common
KINGSTON VALE
Robinwood Place
Robin Hood Lane
Robin Hood Way
Derwent Avenue
Grasmere Avenue
Ullswater Crs
Vale Crs
A308
ROBIN HOOD
Robin Hood Road
Golf Course
HILL
521
22
176
Robin Hood Rd
Sunset Road
Wimbledon Common Golf Club
Windermere Rd
Bowness Crescent
Keswick Avenue
Coombe
1 grid square represents 500 metres

Cambalt Road
South Thames College
Castello Av
Genoa Av
Simon's Av
Cherrywood Dr
Westleigh Avenue
Elliott Foundation School
Tildesley Rd
Hayward Gdns
Surgery
Putney Heath
Heath
Putney Heath
Wildcroft
Road
Putney Hill
Putney High School
Carlton
Merlin School
Tintern Cl
Mercier Road
Rayner's Rd
Redgate
Surgery
Holmbush Rd
Grove
Dromore
Kersfield Road
Rusholme Road
Putney Heath La
Prospect House Sch
Ronald Rose Primary Sch
Royal Orch Cl
Linstead Wy
Arnal Crs
Bell Dr
Beaumont
Castlecombe Dr
Mere Cl
West Hill
A3
Tibbet's Ride
A219
Heathview Gdns
Portsmouth Road
Road
Works
East Putney Station
Keswick Road
Buttermere
Penrith Close
Askill
139
A205
Technology College
West Hill
A3
Station
Fire Station
Amb Stn
PO
Schubert Rd
Galveston Rd
Merton Rd
A218
Buckhold Rd
Wandsworth
Hardwick's Wy
Works
Prim Sch
Lebanon Gdns
Ringford Road
Haldon Rd
Ameriand Rd
Valonia Gdns
Sispara Gdns
Hill
The Southfields Clnc
Southfields Rd
Arndale Health Centre
The Way Arndale
Mapleton
Wandle Recreation Centre
Tennis Courts
Longstaff Crs
Brathway Rd
Wandsworth Trading Estate
SW18
Roehampton Institute
Whitefield Cl
Royal Hospital for Neuro-Disability
Strathan Cl
Cromer Vls Rd
Melrose
Viewfield Road
Seymour Rd
Primary School
Wimbledon Pk Road
Limes Gdns
Morris Gdns
Surgery
West Hill
Granville Road
Granville Rd
Camborne Rd
Wincanton Rd
Hambledon Rd
Gatwick Rd
Pulborough Rd
Wimbledon Park Road
Sutherland Grove
Girdwood Rd
Skeena Hill
Keevil Dr
Princes Way
John Paul II RC School
Primary School
Tudor Lodge Health Cen
Victoria Dr
Beaufort Cl
Portsmouth Rd
A3
Road
Balvernie Gv
Smeaton Rd
The Baulk
Longfield St
Grammar School
Kimber
Merton Road Industrial Estate
Standen Road
Sheringdale Primary School
Bowman Ms
School
Riverside Business Centre
Burr Rd
Community School
Southfields
Pirbright Rd
Replingham Road
Surgery
Southfields Station
Combemartin Road
Whitlock Drive
Stapleford Cl
Windlesham Grove
Southmead Primary School
Southmead Rd
Augustus Road
Manningtree
Linden Lodge School
Theatre of the Dispossessed
Fulwood Wk
Inner Park Road
Tilford Gdns
Limpsfield Av
Selhurst Cl
Surg
Albemarle Primary School
Albert Dr
Peterstow Cl
Southdean Gardens
Gartmoor Gdns
Kingscliffe Gdns
Surgery
Eisenham Street
Clonmore Street
Engadine Street
Elborough Street
Trentham Street
Astonville Street
Brookwood Rd
Heythorp Street
Lavenham Road
Surgery
Hanford Cl
Arragon Rd
Bodmin
Strathville Rd
160
Merton Road
Durnsford Road
Surgery
Revelstoke Road
Woodspring Rd
Wimbledon Park
Wimbledon Park Athletics Track
Kingsmere Rd
Albyn Rd
Sawkins Cl
Murfett Cl
Thursley Gdns
Blincoe Cl
Inner Pk Rd
Glen
Synagogue
Queensmere Road
Penner Cl
Campen Cl
Frimley
Wimbledon
Braemar Av
Normanton Av
Alverstone Av
Wolseley Av
Ashen Grove
Stuart Road
Stroud Road
Avenue
Ryfold Rd
Mount Rd
Lucien Rd
Havana Rd
Wellington
Wimbledon Primary Sch
Gresham Way
Gresham Way Industrial Est
A218
Castle Cl
Castle Md
Haven Cl
Beltane Dr
Seymour Road
Windmill Road
Clockhouse Cl
Alfreton Cl
Apostolic Nuncio
Parkside Hospital
Lincoln Av
Bathgate Road
Oakfield Rd
The All England Lawn Tennis & Croquet Club
Church Road
Boating Lake
Wimbledon Park Golf Club
Crescent Gdns
The Crs
Wimbledon Park Station
Durnsford Rd
Somerset Rd
Cedar Ct
Newstead Wy
Somerset Road
Greenoak Way
Coach House La
Burghley
Calonne Road
Atherton Dr
Parkside Gardens
Parkside
A219
Golf Course
Home Park Road
Arthur Road
Surgery
Squires Ct
Arthur Rd
Lambourne Av
Camelot Cl
Vineyard Hill Road
Kenilworth Avenue
Strathearn Road
Buddhapadipa Temple
Deepdale
Road
Road
SW19
Burghley Road
Marryat Pl
Welford Pl
Rectory Orch
Steeple
Arthur Road
Currie Hl Cl
Parkhouse Middle School
Leopold Road
Dora Road
177
WIMBLEDON
High School
Landgrove
Primary School
Leopold Rd
Gap Road
Margin Drive
Marryat
Lancaster Gdns
Lancaster Rd
Belvedere Avenue
Alan Rd
Highbury Rd
St Mary's
Church Hl
St Aubyn's
Lake Rd
Ricards Rd
Bernard Gardens
Leopold Rd
Road
Preparatory School
B281
West Pl
The Causeway
Camp Road
Haydon Pk Rd
Avondale Rd
Cromwell
Woodside
Haydons Rd
Albany
F
G
H
J
K
I
2
3
4
5
6
23
24
25

160
140
159
178
A
B
C
D
E
1
2
3
4
5
6
27
26
Wandsworth High St
Ram Brewery & Visitor Centre
Town Hall
Huguenot Pl
N Side Wandsworth
Spencer Park
Windmill Rd
Trinity Road
Emanuel School
Bolingbroke Grove
Bellevue Rd
Buckhold Rd
The Wandsworth Arndale Centre
Arndale Health Centre
Wandle Recreation Centre
Sergeant Industrial Est
SW18
Wandsworth Trading Estate
King George's Park
Garratt Lane
Earlsfield Road
Magdalen Road
HM Prison
Heathfield Square
Wandsworth Common
Northcote Lodge School
Highfield School
Wandsworth Common Station
Wandsworth Cemetery
Earlsfield
Beatrix Potter Primary School
Southfields
Riverside Business Centre
Community School
Earlsfield Station
Earlsfield Primary School
Haslemere Industrial Est
Burntwood Lane
Central London Golf Club
Burntwood School
Summerstown
Golf Course
Nightingale School
St Walter & St John Sports Ground
Upper Tooting Independent High School
Finton House Sch
Springfield Hospital
Ernest Bevin School
Upper Tooting
Upper Tooting Road
Balham Preparatory School
Rufus Business Centre
Wimbledon Park Primary School
River Wandle
Gresham Way Industrial Est
Wimbledon Stadium Business Cen
Wimbledon Stadium
Streatham Cemetery
SW17
Lambeth Crematorium
Superstore
Durnsford Road
Wimbledon (Gap Road) Cemetery
Plough Lane
Smallwood Primary School
Broadwater Primary School
Tooting Leisure Centre
Tooting Broadway Stn
St Georges Hospital
A&E
Gap Road
South Wimbledon
Lambeth Cemetery
Tooting Graveney
Haydons Road Station
Secondary School
1 grid square represents 500 metres

141
162
179
F
G
H
J
K
28
29
30
2
3
4
5
6
Clapham Park
Streatham Hill
Streatham Park
Furzedown
STREATHAM
SW12
THE AVENUE
CLAPHAM COMMON SOUTH SIDE
Clapham Common W Side
Windmill Drive
Council Building
NIGHTINGALE LANE
Nightingale Wk
Clapham South Station
College
CAVENDISH ROAD
A24 BALHAM HILL
BALHAM HIGH RD
A205 POYNDERS ROAD
ATKINS RD
STREATHAM PL
B221 KINGS AV
KINGS AVENUE
THORNTON AV
STREATHAM HILL
A23
BRIXTON
Balham Station
Balham Station Rd
Fernlea Road
Emmanuel
BEDFORD HILL
B242
Tooting Bec Common
Lido
GARRAD'S ROAD
TOOTING BEC ROAD
A214
CHURCH LANE
Tooting Bec Athletics Track
Dr Johnson Avenue
STREATHAM HIGH RD
TOOTING BEC GDNS
AMBLESIDE AV
MITCHAM LANE
Streatham Station
Streatham Swimming Pool
Streatham Hill Station
STERNHOLD AV
Megabowl
Telford Avenue
Wandsworth Lambeth
Waldorf School of S W London
Streatham & Clapham High School
South London Liberal Synagogue
Girls School
Zennor Road Industrial Est
Primary School
Glenbrook Primary School
Rowan High School
HM Prison
Aspen House Secondary & Primary Sch
Balham Leisure Centre
Balham Health Cen
Battersea Tutorial College
Hornsby House School
Trinity St Marys Primary School
Telferscot Primary School
St Bedes RC Infant Sch
Woodentops School
Mortimer School
Beechwood School
St Leonards CE Primary School
Police Stn
Odeon
ABC
Bowls Club
Balham Mosque
Radha Krishna Temple
Bethel Temple
Natural Therapy Clnc
Tooting Bec Stn

162
142
161
180

1 grid square represents 500 metres

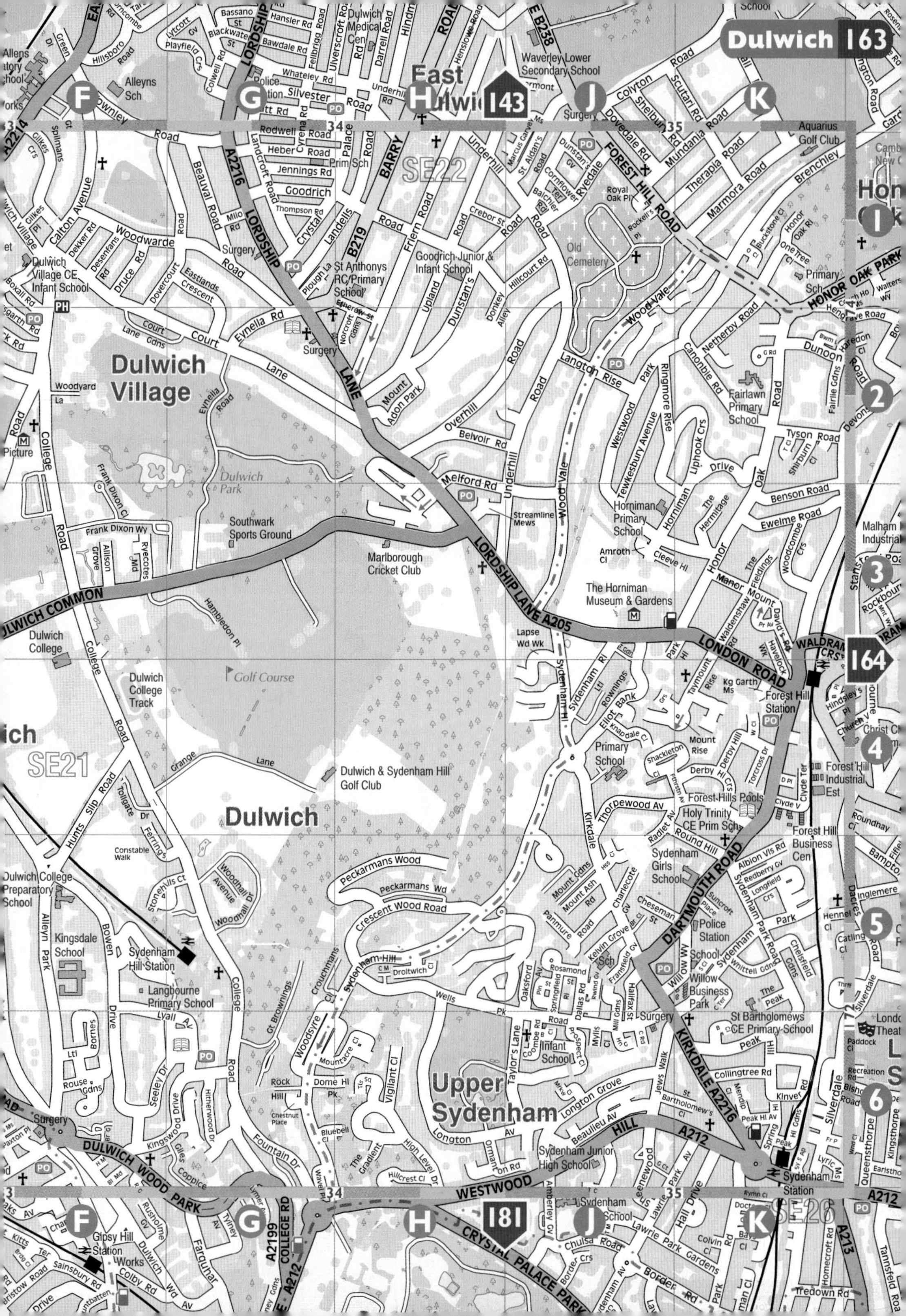

East Dulwich
143
SE22
Dulwich Village
Dulwich Park
Southwark Sports Ground
Marlborough Cricket Club
Golf Course
Dulwich College
Dulwich College Track
Dulwich & Sydenham Hill Golf Club
Dulwich
SE21
Upper Sydenham
Sydenham Hill Station
Sydenham Station
Forest Hill Station
The Horniman Museum & Gardens
Horniman Primary School
Fairlawn Primary School
Old Cemetery
Goodrich Junior & Infant School
St Anthonys RC Primary School
Dulwich Village CE Infant School
Alleyns Sch
Waverley Lower Secondary School
Aquarius Golf Club
Kingsdale School
Langbourne Primary School
Dulwich College Preparatory School
Sydenham Girls School
Holy Trinity CE Prim Sch
Forest Hills Pools
Sydenham Junior High School
St Bartholomews CE Primary School
Willow Business Park
Forest Hill Business Cen
Forest Hill Industrial Est
Malham Industrial
Police Station
LORDSHIP LANE A205
LONDON ROAD
DARTMOUTH ROAD
KIRKDALE A2216
FOREST HILL ROAD
HONOR OAK PARK
DULWICH COMMON
DULWICH WOOD PARK
WESTWOOD HILL A212
CRYSTAL PALACE PARK
COLLEGE RD A2199
College Road
Sydenham Hill
Crescent Wood Road
Peckarmans Wood
Lordship Lane
Court Lane
Eynella Rd
Underhill Road
Wood Vale
Honor Oak Road
Langton Rise
Westwood Park
Tewkesbury Avenue
Ringmore Rise
Kirkdale
Thorpewood Av
Longton Grove
Alleyn Park
Hunts Slip Road
Grange Lane
Calton Avenue
Woodwarde Road
Barry Road
Crystal Palace Road
SE26
F G H J K
1 2 3 4 5 6
34 35
164
181

164
144
163
182
Honor Oak
Honor Oak Park
Forest Hill
Lower Sydenham
Bell Green
Bellingham
SE23
Honor Oak Crematorium
Camberwell New Cemetery
Aquarius Golf Club
Honor Oak Park Station
Crofton Park Station
Catford Bridge Station
Catford Station
Bellingham Stn
Lower Sydenham
Sydenham Station
Stillness Primary School
Crofton Leisure Centre
Crofton School
St Dunstans College
Phoenix Leisure Centre
ABC Cinema
Rushey Green Prim Sch
Catford Cricket & Sports Club
Priory House School
Catford Trading Estate
Bromley Road Retail Park
Catford Cyphers Cricket Club
Athelney Primary School
Bellingham Trading Est
Council Building
Elfrida Primary School
Kilmorie Primary School
The Vale Medical Centre
Greenvale School
Brent Knoll School
Forest Hill School
London Living Theatre
Our Lady & St Philip Neri RC Primary School
Christ Church CE Primary School
Forest Hill Industrial Est
Forest Hill Business Cen
Malham Road Industrial Est
Jenner Health Cen
Rathfern Primary School
Holbeach Primary School
Ladywell Arena
Lambeth Southwark & Lewisham Health Authority
University Hospital A&E
Register Office
The Bridge Leisure Centre
Kangley Business Cen
Lower Sydenham Industrial Est
Broomsleigh Business Park
Cornhill Sports Club
London Ladies & Girls FC
Gardener Industrial Est
Superstore
HONOR OAK PARK
HONOR OAK PK
STONDON PK
BROCKLEY RI
BROCKLEY ROAD
B218
STANSTEAD ROAD
A205
CATFORD ROAD
A212 CATFORD HILL
PERRY HILL
A212
PERRY VALE
PERRY RISE
B227
BELL GN
SOUTHEND LA
STANTON WY
A2218
SOUTHEND LANE
BROMLEY ROAD A21
RUSHEY GN
PLASSY RD
LEWISHAM HIGH ST
A21
SYDENHAM
A213
WALDRAM PK RD
SUNDERLAND RD
536
37
Ravensbourne River
Pool River
A
B
C
D
E
1
2
3
4
5
6
1 grid square represents 500 metres

Hither Green
Lee
CATFORD
Southend
SE13
SE12
SE6
145
166
183
Hither Green Stn
Lee Station
Beckenham Hill Stn
Mountsfield Park
Hither Green Cemetery
Lewisham Crematorium
Cemetery
BROWNHILL ROAD A205
ST MILDREDS ROAD A205
WESTHORNE AVENUE
BURNT ASH ROAD
BURNT ASH HILL
BARING ROAD A2212
BROMLEY ROAD
A21
Whitefoot Lane
Green Chain Walk
Ennersdale Primary School
Northbrook CE School
Lee Manor Primary School
Complementary Health Cen
Chiltonian Industrial Est
St Winifreds Junior School
Baring Primary School
Sandhurst Primary School
Holy Cross RC Primary School
Torridon Primary School
Catford Girls School
Forster Park Primary School
New Woodlands School
St John the Baptist CE Primary School
Downderry Primary School
Bonus Pastor School
Downham Health Centre
Good Shepherd RC Primary School
Malory School
Launcelot Primary School
Rangefield Primary School
Police Station
South Lewisham Health Centre
Catford Wanderers Sports Club
Old Colfeian Sports Club
Baring Road Medical Centre
Business Centre
Grove Park Stn

166
146
165
184
A
B
C
D
E
1
2
3
4
5
6
Sutcliffe Park Athletics Track
Old Colfeian Sports Club
Colfes Prep School
Civil Service Sports Ground
Old Brockleians Sports Ground
Leathersellers Sports Ground
Horn Park Primary School
Eltham Green School
Eltham Hill Technology College
Moatbridge School
Bingo Hall
Eltham Health Clinic
Eltham Pools
Eltham Bus Station
Police Station
Council Building
The Bob Hope Theatre
ELTHAM
King's Orchard
Eltham Palace (remains)
Royal Blackheath Golf Club
Middle Park Primary School
Woodmere
Mottingham Station
Hadlow College
Surgery
Eltham College Junior School
Eltham College
Eric Liddell Sports Centre
Mottingham
London Guildhall University Sports Ground
City of London Polytechnic School Sports Ground
Central YMCA
Infant School
Grove Park
Grove Park Stn
Primary School
Mottingham Primary School
Mottingham Community Hlth Clinic
Cemetery
Castlecombe Primary School
Elmstead Woods
Greenwich
Bromley
Lewisham
A20
A210
A205
A208
A2212
B226
ELTHAM ROAD
ELTHAM HILL
ELTHAM HIGH
SIDCUP ROAD
WESTHORNE AVENUE
KIDBROOKE
COURT YARD
COURT ROAD
GROVE PARK ROAD
MOTTINGHAM ROAD
CHINBROOK ROAD
BURNT ASH LANE
Green Chain Walk
Mottingham Lane
Woodyates Rd
Burnt Ash Hill
Dunkery Road
Court Farm Road
Beaconsfield Road
Castlecombe Road
1 grid square represents 500 metres

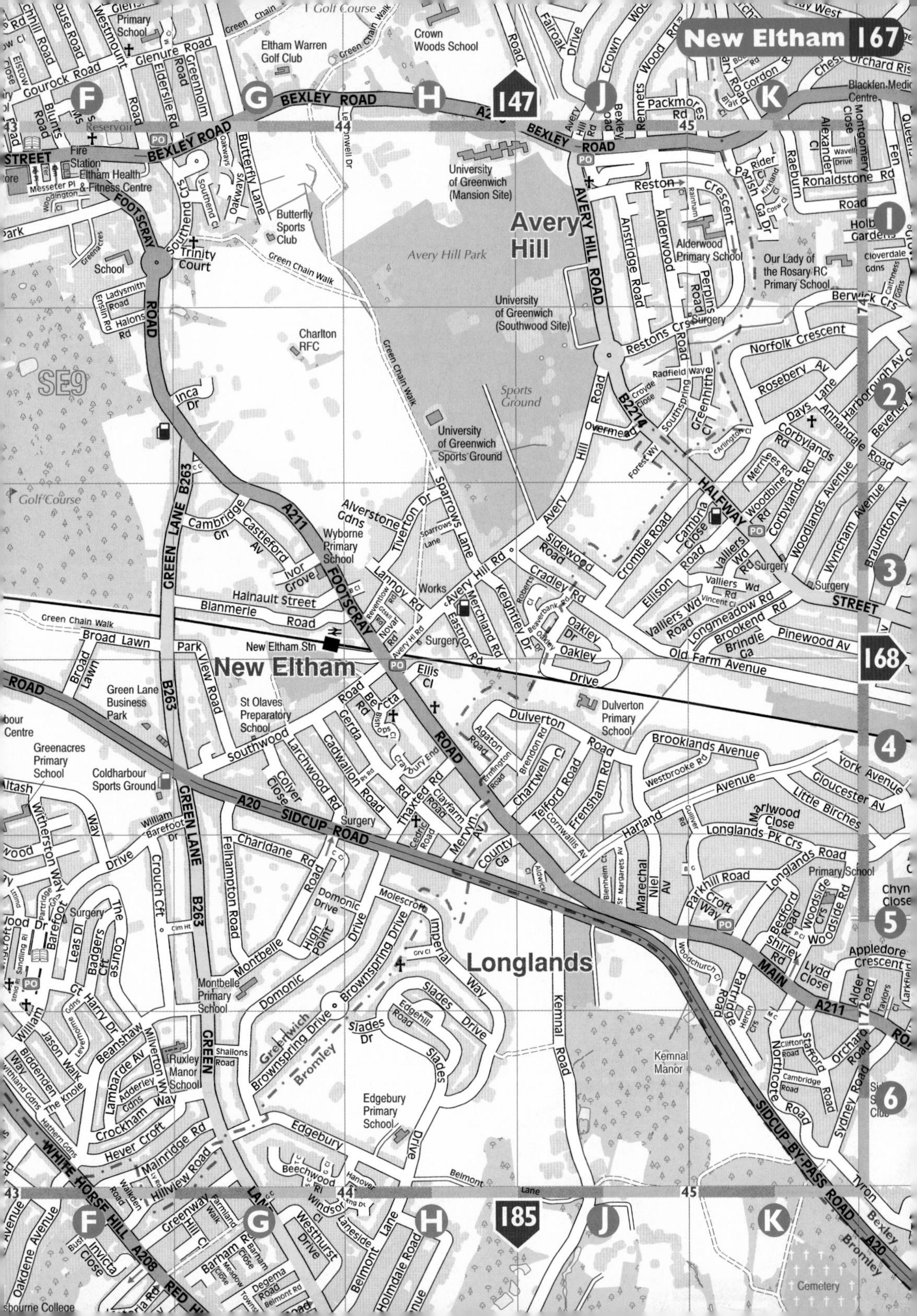
F
G
H
J
K
147
168
185
1
2
3
4
5
6
43
44
45
BEXLEY ROAD
A210
Golf Course
Eltham Warren Golf Club
Crown Woods School
Primary School
Westmount
Glenure Road
Eldersile Rd
Greenholm Road
Gourock Road
Blunts Road
Elstow Close
Reservoir
STREET
Fire Station
Eltham Health & Fitness Centre
Messeter Pl
Woodington Cl
FOOTSCRAY ROAD
Southend Crs
Southend Cl
Oakways
Butterfly Lane
Butterfly Sports Club
Trinity Court
Green Chain Walk
Greenacres
School
Ladysmith Road
Enslin Rd
Halons Rd
Charlton RFC
SE9
Inca Dr
Golf Course
GREEN LANE B263
Cambridge Gn
Castleford Av
Ivor Grove
A211
Wyborne Primary School
Alverstone Gdns
Tiverton Dr
Sparrows Lane
Lannoy Rd
Works
Avery Hill Rd
Merchland Rd
Eastnor Rd
Keightley Dr
Hainault Street
Blanmerle Road
Broad Lawn
Park View Road
New Eltham Stn
New Eltham
Surgery
Ellis Cl
Green Lane Business Park
St Olaves Preparatory School
Southwood Road
Bercta Rd
Gerda Road
Cadwallon Road
Larchwood Rd
Colyer Close
Craybury End
Thaxted Rd
Clayfarm Road
Cedric Road
Mervyn Av
Agaton Road
Emmington Road
Brendon Rd
Chartwell Cl
Telford Road
Frensham Rd
Dulverton Road
Dulverton Primary School
Brooklands Avenue
Westbrooke Rd
York Avenue
Gloucester Av
Little Birches
Harland Avenue
Marlwood Close
Longlands Pk Crs
Longlands Road
Parkhill Road
Croft Way
Primary School
Woodside Crs
Woodside Rd
Bedford Road
Shirley Rd
Lydd Close
Appledore Crescent
Alder Road
Taylors Cl
Larkfield
Chyn Close
MAIN ROAD A211
University of Greenwich (Mansion Site)
Avery Hill
Avery Hill Park
AVERY HILL ROAD
University of Greenwich (Southwood Site)
Sports Ground
University of Greenwich Sports Ground
Hill Road
Overmead
B2214
Reston Crescent
Anstridge Road
Alderwood Road
Rainham Cl
Alderwood Primary School
Perpins Road
Restons Crs
Surgery
Radfield Way
Croyde Close
Southspring
Greenhithe Cl
Forest Wy
Arlington Cl
HALFWAY STREET
Crombie Road
Cambria Close
Woodbine Rd
Corbylands Rd
Merrilees Rd
Ellison Road
Valliers Wd Rd
Vincent Cl
Longmeadow Rd
Brookend Rd
Brindle Ga
Pinewood Av
Old Farm Avenue
Oakley Dr
Oakley Drive
Cradley Rd
Roberts Cl
Beaverbank Rd
Sidewood Road
Woodlands Avenue
Wyncham Avenue
Braundton Av
Annandale Road
Days Lane
Rosebery Av
Harborough Av
Beverley
Norfolk Crescent
Berwick Crs
Our Lady of the Rosary RC Primary School
Cloverdale Gdns
Caithness Gdns
Holbe Gardens
Ronaldstone Rd
Raeburn Road
Alexander Cl
Montgomery Close
Wavell Drive
Rider Cl
Parish Ga Dr
Kirkland Cl
Blackfen Medical Centre
Gordon Rd
Packmores Rd
Rennets Wood Rd
Crown Woods
Falroak Drive
Orchard Rise
Bexley Road
Greenacres Primary School
Coldharbour Sports Ground
Witherston Way
A20 SIDCUP ROAD
William Barefoot Dr
Crouch Cft
Charldane Rd
Felhampton Road
Domonic Drive
High Point
Molescroft
Imperial Way
Brownspring Drive
Longlands
Kemnal Road
Marechal Niel Av
Blenheim Cl
St Margarets Av
Cornwallis Av
County Ga
Aldwick Cl
Woodchurch Cl
Partridge Road
Heron Crs
Montbelle Road
Montbelle Primary School
Surgery
Barefoot Dr
The Course
Badgers Cft
Leas Dl
Harry Dr
Jason Walk
Beanshaw
Milverton Way
Lambarde Av
Adderley Gdns
Ruxley Manor School
Crockham Way
Shallons Road
Greenwich
Bromley
Slades Drive
Edgehill Road
Slades Dr
Edgebury Primary School
Edgebury
Hever Croft
Mainridge Rd
Hillview Road
Beechwood Ri
Hanover
Windsor
Belmont Lane
Kemnal Manor
SIDCUP BY-PASS ROAD
A20
Northcote Road
Stafford Road
Clifton Road
Cambridge Road
Orchard Road
Sydney Road
Tyron
Bexley
Bromley
Cemetery
WHITE HORSE HILL
A208
The Knole
Biddenden Way
Hathern Gdns
Walkden Road
Greenway
Farmland Walk
Hill Cl
Barham Rd
Barham Close
Meadow Close
Westhurst Drive
Laneside
Belmont Lane
Holmdale Road
Degema Road
Belmont Rd
Invicta Close
Oakdene Avenue
RED HILL
Sandling Ri
Witherston Way
Altash
Edgebury
Avenue

168
148
167
186
A
B
C
D
E
1
2
3
4
5
6
A2
BLACKFEN ROAD
A210
EAST ROCHESTER WAY
A221
BLACKFEN RD
BLENDON RD
BLENDON ROAD
PENHILL ROAD
HURST ROAD
A222
STATION ROAD
B2214
STREET
A211
ROAD
HIGH STREET
ELM ROAD
THE GREEN
A2001
CHISLEHURST RD
SIDCUP HILL
BY-PASS ROAD
A20
Blackfen
SIDCUP
DA15
DA14
Ridgeway East
Orchard Rise E
Lyndon Avenue
Burleigh Av
Beechcroft
Curran Avenue
Blackfen Medical Centre
Montgomery Close
Alexander Cl
Wavell Drive
Queenswood Road
Hawthorn Terrace
Sycamore Av
Ronaldstone Rd
Holbeach Gardens
Fen Grove
Cloverdale Gdns
Caithness Gdns
Berwick Crs
Crescent
Harman Dr
Days Lane
Days Lane Primary School
Elmcroft Av
Burnt Oak Lane
Ashcroft Av
Ashcroft Crs
Willow Av
Maple Crs
Wellington Avenue
Superstore
Groombridge Cl
Ingleton Av
Tyrrell Avenue
Wells Close
Mead
Park
Overcourt Cl
Shorne Cl
Penshurst Av
Burns Av
Claywood Cl
Ramillies
Blackfen School for Girls
Sherwood Park Primary School
Westerham Drive
Lakeside Close
Danson Up
Works
Watersports Centre
Green Vale
Brasted Cl
Sandhurst Rd
Wellington Rd
Brook Lane
Margaret Rd
Lodge La
Woodside Lane
Cedar Grove
Beechway
The Sanctuary
Blendon Drive
The Crs
Drive
Sherwood Cl
Harcourt Avenue
Portland Av
Bowes Rd
Health & Welfare Clinic
Sherwood Park Avenue
Meadow View Road
Burnt Oak Lane
Cedar Av
Beech Av
The Oval
Rutland Av
Cavendish Av
Montrose Avenue
Somerhill Av
Hill Crest
Haddon Grove
Surgery
Oaklands Avenue
Harborough Av
Beverley Av
Annandale Road
Shuttle Cl
Avenue
Lacebark Cl
Acacia Wy
White Oak Gdns
Redwood Close
Cypress Tree Cl
Elder Cl
Willersley Close
Willersley Av
Braundton Av
Penhurst Avenue
Woodlands Avenue
Rowanwood Av
School
Chatsworth Avenue
Welbeck Avenue
Collindale Av
Marlborough Park Av
Chatsworth Infant School
Golf Course
Rose Bruford College of Speech & Drama
Lamorbey Park
Hurstmere School
Rowley Avenue
Dene Av
Oakley Park
Oakley Pk
The Rise
Viewfield Road
Bladindon Drive
Albany Cl
Albany Rd
Howard Avenue
Shirley Av
Crofton Avenue
Montpelier Av
Dorchester Avenue
Hurst Primary School
Murchison
Health & Welfare
Stansted Crs
Carisbrooke Avenue
Cottage Fld Cl
Foots Cray Lane
Eynsford Crs
Festival Close
Cemetery
Cotleigh Avenue
Albany Park Station
Chaucer Road
Blenheim Road
Abbeyhill Road
Canterbury Avenue
Maple Leaf Dr
Firside Gr
Baytree Cl
Larch Gv
Marrabon Cl
Primary School
Burnt Oak Junior School
Chislehurst & Sidcup Grammar School
Sidcup Golf Club
Lamorbey Swimming Centre
Hollies Av
Lamorbey Cl
Lingey Cl
Old Farm Rd West
Old Farm Rd East
Chestnut Cl
Old Farm Avenue
Bursdon Cl
York Avenue
Gloucester Av
Little Birches
Sidcup Station
Jubilee Way
Kingsmead Close
Longlands Road
Faraday Avenue
Hemmings Cl
Cleeve Park Gdns
Parkside
Melville Road
Longmead Drive
Cherrydown Road
Onslow Drive
Eaton Rd
Goodwin Drive
Kimberley Drive
Bexley Lane
Hatherley Crs
Alma Rd
Austral Close
Ham Shades Cl
Grange Cl
Manor Road
Birkbeck Primary School
Lewis Road
Luton Rd
Heatherside Road
Harefield Road
Royal Road
Drive
St Andrews Road
Chyngton Close
Priestlands Park Road
Crescent Road
Christchurch Road
Laurel Close
Langford Pl
Becks Rd
Gresswell Cl
Birkbeck Rd
Clarence Rd
Clarence Crs
Lansdown Rd
Damon Cl
Birchwood Av
The Chevenings
Walton Road
Camborne Road
Wren Road
Princes Cl
Maylands
Cleve Road
Ladbrooke Crs
Appledore Crescent
Lydd Close
Sandhurst Rd
West Lodge Preparatory School
Hatherley Road
Aston Cl
Stanley Rd
Tarling Close
Embassy Ct
Denberry Dr
Warren Road
Cleeve Park School
Alder Road
Taylors Cl
Larkfield Rd
Updale Road
Lyminge Close
Priestlands Pk Road
Victoria Road
Benedict Ho Prep Sch
Nevill Cl
Stanhope Rd
Hamilton Road
Shelbury Cl
Sidcup Health Centre
Ash Cl
St John's Rd
Highview Road
The Drive
Farwell Road
Stafford Road
Orchard Road
Albany Clinic
Granville Road
Granville Mews
Belton Road
Hadlow Road
Sydney Road
Sidcup Sports Club
The Crs
Sharman Court
Nelson Place
Back Rd
Carlton Road
Grassington Rd
Church Road
Craybrooke Rd
Medical Centre
Selborne Road
Charles Close
Rectory Cl
Rectory Lane
Rectory Business Centre
Old Forge Wy
Knoll Road
Merton Court Preparatory School
Church Rd
Tyron Way
Felton Lea
Upperton Rd
Langdon Shaw
St Mary and St Josephs
Sidcup Pl
Durham Road
Lincoln Rd
Sussex Rd
Warwick Rd
Oxford Road
Studley Court
Frimley Court
Caerleon Cl
St Peter Chanel RC
David Lloyd Tennis Centre
Bexley
Bromley
546
472
47
1 grid square represents 500 metres

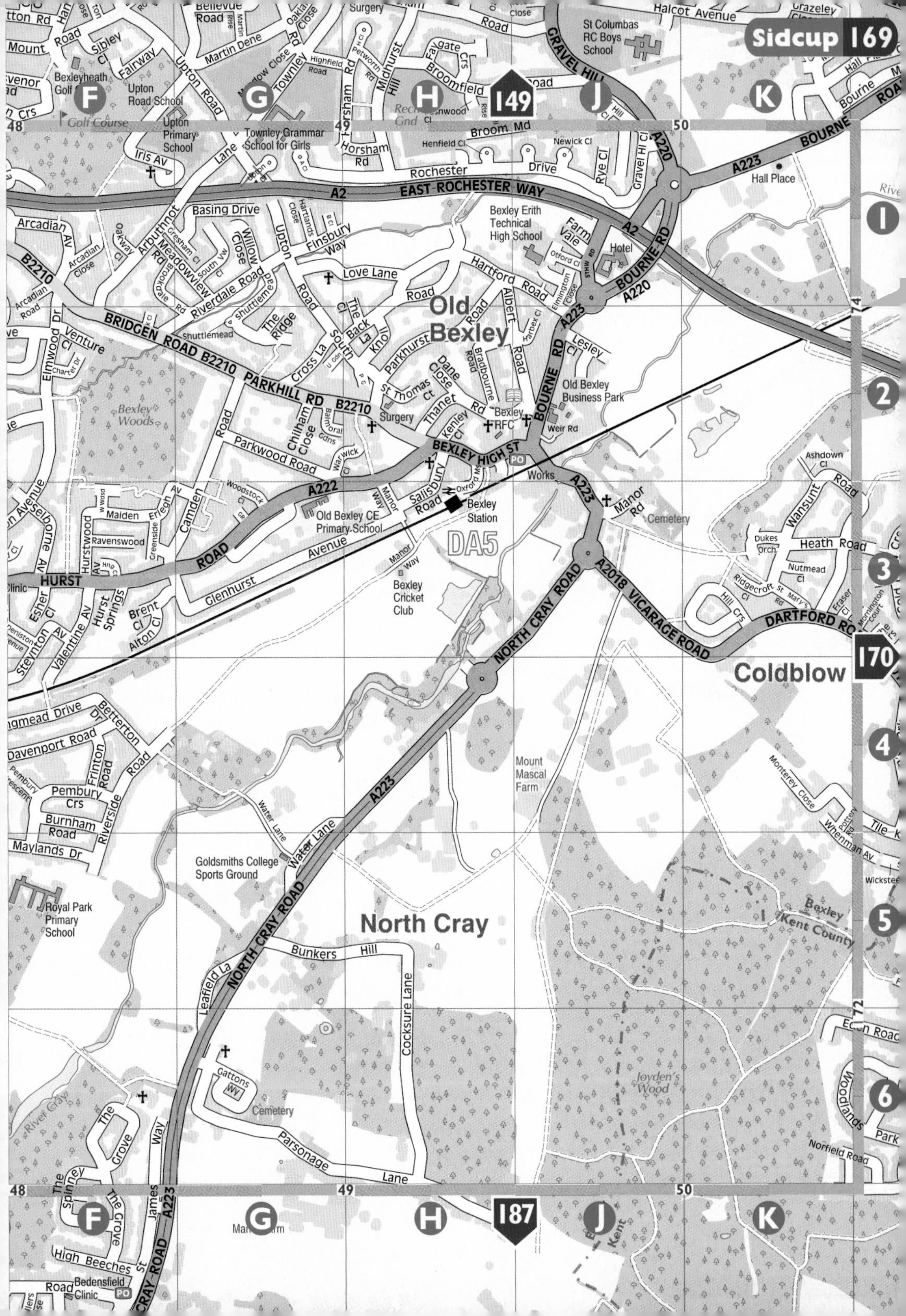
149
187
170
Old Bexley
North Cray
Coldblow
DA5
Bexley Woods
Joyden's Wood
Mount Mascal Farm
Goldsmiths College Sports Ground
Royal Park Primary School
Bexley Cricket Club
Bexley Station
Old Bexley CE Primary School
Old Bexley Business Park
Bexley RFC
Surgery
Cemetery
Works
Hall Place
Hotel
Bexley Erith Technical High School
St Columbas RC Boys School
Townley Grammar School for Girls
Upton Primary School
Upton Road School
Bexleyheath Golf Course
Bedensfield Clinic
A2 EAST ROCHESTER WAY
A223 BOURNE RD
A220
BRIDGEN ROAD B2210
PARKHILL RD B2210
BEXLEY HIGH ST
A222
HURST ROAD
NORTH CRAY ROAD
A2018 VICARAGE ROAD
DARTFORD ROAD
GRAVEL HILL
Bexley
Kent County
River Cray
Rochester Drive
Broom Md
Upton Road
Love Lane
Hartford Road
Albert Road
Glenhurst Avenue
Parkwood Road
Riverdale Road
Bunkers Hill
Cocksure Lane
Parsonage Lane
Water Lane
Leafield La
Gattons Wy
Riverside Road
Davenport Road
Burnham Road
Maylands Dr
Pembury Crs
Heath Road
Wansunt Road
Monterey Close
Whenman Av
Norfield Road
Woodlands Park
High Beeches
The Grove
The Spinney
James St
48
49
50
F
G
H
J
K
1
2
3
4
5
6

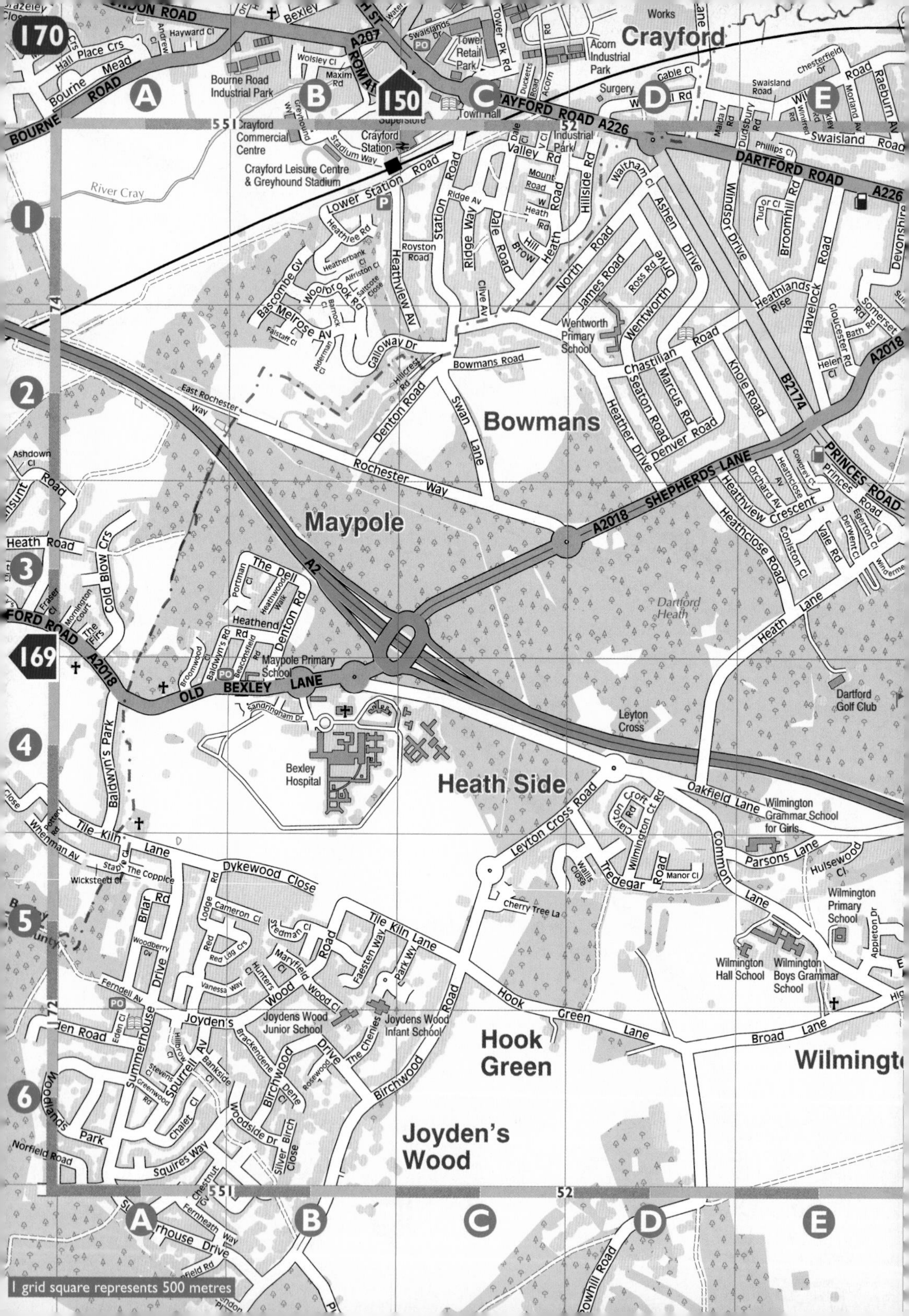

1 grid square represents 500 metres

151
F
G
H
J
K
53
54
55
I
2
3
4
5
6
73
74
172
DARTFORD
New Town
Hawley
DA2
Victoria Road
Dartford Station
West Hill
A226
Shepherds Lane
Spital St
High St
Instone Rd
Lowfield Street
Hawley Road
A225
A296
A2
B258
B260
A282
A226 Home Gdns
A296 Park Road
East Hill
Overy
Liberty
Church Hill B258
High Road B258
Highfield Rd
Heath Lane
Heath Street
Phoenix Pl
Powder Mill Lane
Darenth Road
Fawkes Avenue
Butterfly Av
Pearson Way
Wilks Av
Saunders Way
Applegarth Dr
Darent Valley Path
River Darent
Brooklands Lake
Central Park
Central Park Arena
Fairfield Pool & Leisure Centre
Cranford Road
Ingram Rd
Superstore
Works
Council Building
Orchard Theatre
Angel Centre
Civic Centre
Priory Shopping Cen
Dartford Mus & Lib
County Court
Natural Health Centre
Lowfield Medical Centre
Police Stn
Sikh Temple
Surgery
Magistrates Ct
Health Centre
School for Boys
Becket Sports Centre
Dartford Grammar School for Girls
Dartford West Technology College
NW Kent College of Technology
Westgate Primary School
West Hill Primary School
Primary School
Livingstone Hospital
Adult Ed Cen
York Road Junior School
Cemetery
Cem
Fulwich Road
Colney Road
Carrington Rd
St Martin's Road
Gladstone Rd
Lavinia Rd
Tufnall Rd
Little Queen St
Marriott Rd
Brandon Rd
Shenley Road
Howard Rd
Mildred Cl
Carlisle Road
Bayly Road
St Vincents Road
Bow Arrow Lane
Norfolk Cl
Knights Manor Way
Mill Pond Rd
Attlee Drive
Lansbury Crs
Brent Lane
Dene Road
Sussex Road
Cumberland Dr
Dorchester Cl
Berkeley Crs
Princes View
Brentlands Dr
Marina Dr
Rochester Rd
Bedford Rd
Carleton Rd
Downs Av
Pilgrims Way
Wayville Rd
Oakwood Rd
(West Campus)
(East Campus)
The Leigh City Technology College
University of Greenwich
University
Oakfield Primary School
Oakfield Park Road
Oakfield Place
The Spires
Monks Orchard
Golf Course
Rowhill School
Laburnum Av
Linden Av
Rowan Crs
Acacia Rd
Elm Road
Elm Cl
Cedar Road
Ash Rd
Mead Crs
Beech Rd
Hazel Rd
Hawthorn Rd
Maple Rd
Myrtle Road
Walnut Tree Av
Brooklands
Norman Road
Olive Road
Laurel Cl
Links View
Willow Road
Holly Rd
Sycamore Rd
Chestnut Rd
Larch Rd
Highfield Road South
Landale Gdns
Service Centre
Sackville Rd
Chave Road
Mitchell Cl
Warren Road
Gothic Cl
Church Fld
Curates Wk
Garden Place
Langworth Close
Orchard Way
South Vw Rd
Albert Rd
Hurlfield
The Close
Martin Rd
Martin Row
Taylor Row
Whitehead Cl
Rowlatt Cl
Gerdview Dr
Stock Lane
Brewers Field
Meadow Wk
Capel Pl
Burnt House Lane
Saxon Rd
Ethelbert Rd
Alfred Road
Harold Road
Ash Road
May Rd
Bott Rd
Cross Rd
Mill Road
Shirehall Road
Royal Road
Hallford Way
Firmin Road
Stanham Road
Marcet Rd
Rayford Cl
Priory Cl
Priory Hill
Priory Pl
Kg Edward Avenue
Kingsridge Gdns
Lodge Av
Lawrence Hill Rd
Miskin Road
Penney Close
Summerhill
Christchurch
Cross Rd
Blenheim Rd
Nelson Rd
Roseberry Gdns
Pencroft Dr
Rosedene Cl
Victoria Industrial Park
Business Centre
Bus Garage
Sports Club
Francis Rd
Anne of Cleves Rd
Prospect Pl
Vauxhall Place
Gordon St
Temple Hi Sq
Mallard Cl
Falcon Cl
Surgery
Estate
Mount Pleasant Rd
West View Rd
St Alban's Rd
Great Queen St
Waldeck Rd
York Rd
Chaucer Park

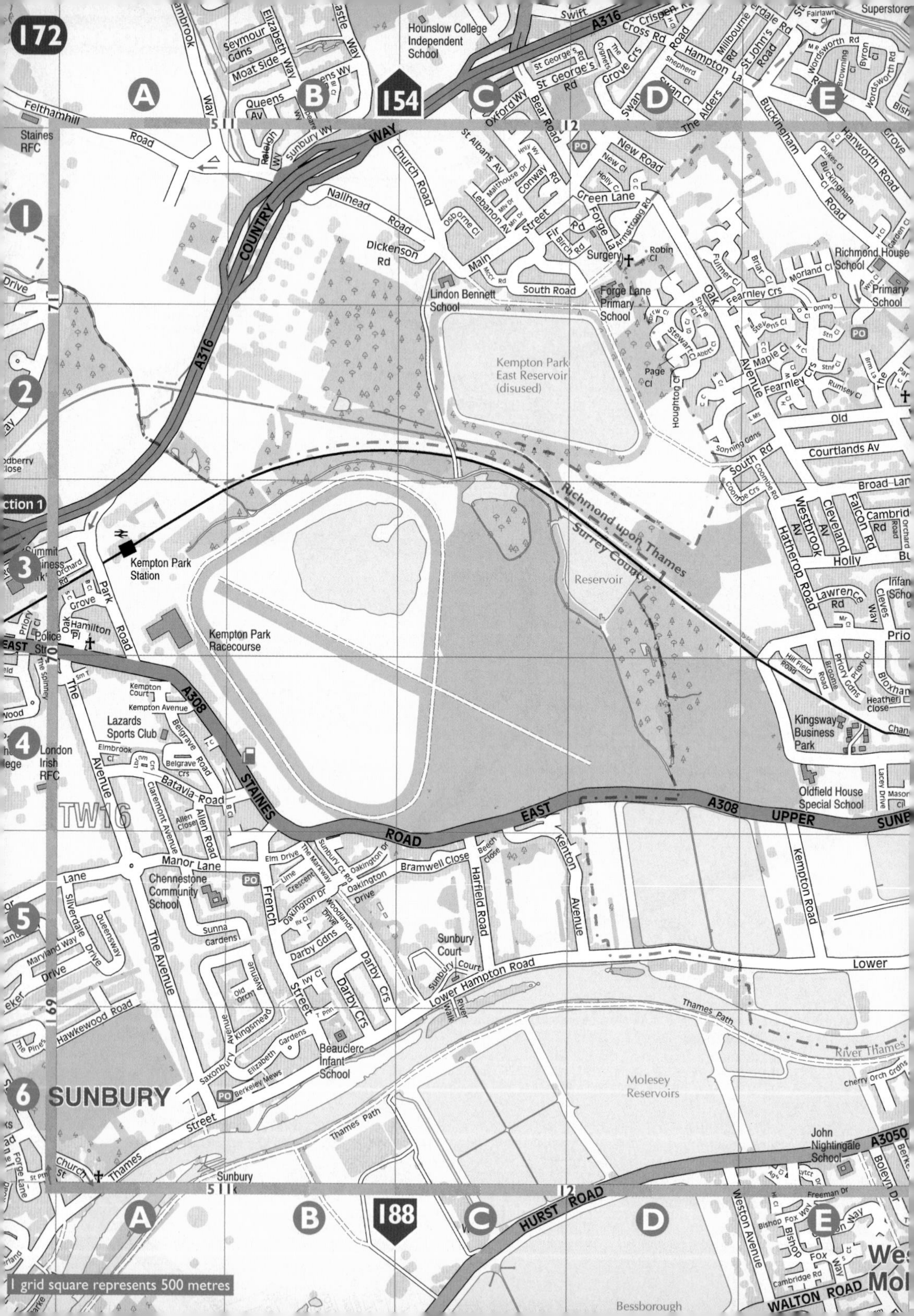
154
188
A
B
C
D
E
1
2
3
4
5
6
511
12
70
71
169
Hounslow College Independent School
Seymour Gdns
Elizabeth Way
Moat Side
Queens Av
Felthamhill Road
Staines RFC
Sunbury Wy
COUNTRY WAY
A316
Church Road
Nallhead Road
Dickenson Rd
Main Street
St Albans Av
Lebanon Av
Osborne Cl
Conway Rd
Bear Road
Oxford Wy
St George's Rd
Cross Rd
Crispen Rd
Grove Crs
Hampton La
Shepherd Cl
Swan Cl
Swan Rd
St John's Road
Millbourne Rd
The Alders
New Road
New Cl
Holly Cl
Green Lane
Forge La
Armstrong Rd
Fir Rd
Birch Rd
South Road
Surgery
Robin Cl
Lindon Bennett School
Forge Lane Primary School
Stewart Cl
Page Cl
Houghton Cl
Buckingham Road
Hanworth Road
Dukes Cl
Richmond House School
Primary School
Fulmer Cl
Briar Cl
Morland Cl
Fearnley Crs
Oak Avenue
Maple Cl
Rumsey Cl
Sonning Gdns
South Rd
Coombe Rd
Coombe Crs
Old
Courtlands Av
Broad Lane
Westbrook Av
Cleveland Av
Falcon Rd
Cambridge Rd
Hatherop Road
Holly
Lawrence Rd
Cleves Way
Hill Field Road
Broome Road
Priory Gdns
Heather Close
Bloxham
Kingsway Business Park
Oldfield House Special School
Lacey Drive
Kempton Park East Reservoir (disused)
Richmond upon Thames
Surrey County
Reservoir
Kempton Park Station
Kempton Park Racecourse
Park Road
Summit Business Park
Orchard
Grove
Hamilton Pl
Oak
Priory
Police Stn
The Spinney
The
Kempton Court
Kempton Avenue
A308
STAINES ROAD EAST
A308 UPPER SUNBURY
Lazards Sports Club
Belgrave Road
Belgrave Crs
Elmbrook Cl
London Irish RFC
Batavia Road
Avenue
TW16
Claremont Avenue
Allen Close
Allen Road
Manor Lane
Chennestone Community School
Elm Drive
Lime Crescent
The Markway
Sunbury Ct Rd
Oakington Dr
Oakington Drive
Bramwell Close
Beech Close
Harfield Road
Kenton Avenue
Kempton Road
Lower
Woodlands Drive
Darby Gdns
Darby Crs
Ivy Cl
French Street
Sunna Gardens
Sunbury Court
Lower Hampton Road
River Walk
Thames Path
River Thames
Molesey Reservoirs
Cherry Orch Grdns
Silverdale Drive
Queensway
Maryland Way
Drive
Hawkewood Road
The Pines
The Avenue
Old Orch
Avenue
Kingsmead
Saxonbury Avenue
Elizabeth Gardens
Beauclerc Infant School
Berkeley Mews
SUNBURY
Thames Street
Church St
Forge Lane
Sunbury
HURST ROAD
Weston Avenue
John Nightingale School
A3050
Boleyn Dr
Freeman Dr
Bishop Fox Way
Cambridge Rd
WALTON ROAD
Bessborough
Superstore
Wordsworth Rd
Byron
Browning Cl
Section 1
1 grid square represents 500 metres

155
174
189
F
G
H
J
K
1
2
3
4
5
6
TEDDINGTON
Hampton
Hampton Hill
Hurst Park
Bushy Park
TW12
KT8
UXBRIDGE ROAD
A312
PARK ROAD
A313
HAMPTON ROAD
HIGH STREET
A311
CHURCH STREET
THAMES STREET
HAMPTON COURT ROAD
A308
HURST ROAD
A3050
WALTON ROAD
B369
FULWELL ROAD
B360
STANLEY ROAD
CHURCH ROAD
B358
RIVERBANK
Burton's Road
Queen's Road
Pigeon Lane
Hampton Community College
Hampton School
The Lady Eleanor Holles School
Hanworth Road
Acacia Road
Nightingale Road
Jack & Jill School
Clarendon School
Carlisle Infant School
Longford Industrial Estate
Broad Lane
Marlingdene Close
Templar Place
Hampton Cem
Percy Road
Ripley Road
Chestnut Avenue
Tudor Road
Wensleydale Road
Gloucester Road
Denmead School
The Hampton Medical Centre
Athelstan House Sch
Hampton Station
Oldfield Road
Hammond Close
Station Road
Ormond Avenue
Ormond Drive
Ormond Crescent
Manor Gardens
Cardinal's Wk
Warwick Close
Hampton Open Air Pool
Hampton FC
King's Paddock
Hogarth Way
Thames Cl
St Clare Business Park
Windmill Rd
Cross St
Connaught Road
Parkside
Works
Laurel Road
Blandford Road
National Physical Laboratory
Teddington Memorial Hospital
Teddington Clinic
New Kelvin Av
Rayleigh Av
Bartons Cottage
Cobbler's Walk
Golf Club
Wellington Rd
Clonmel Rd
Winchendon Rd
Wilcox Rd
Shacklegate La
Victor Road
Royal Road
Windsor Rd
Mays Rd
Oxford Rd
Anlaby Road
Kent Dr
Gloucester Rd
Surgery
Primary School
BROAD ST
Sunbury Road
Richmond upon Thames
Surrey County
Thames Path
Sadlers Ride
Buckingham Avenue
Buckingham Gdns
Beldham Gardens
Tufton Gdns
Rivermead
Tagg's Island
Ash Island
East Molesey Cricket Club
Graburn Way
Hurst Park School
Park Way
The Fairway
Dunstall Way
Kings Chase
Molesey Lock
Hotel
Balmoral Crescent
Mole Abbey Gdns
Dundas Gdns
Palace Road
St Lawrence Junior School
Vine Medical Centre
Cemetery
Rosemary Avenue
Cherry Orchard Road
Hurstfield Rd
Windsor Avenue
Wilton Gardens
Cannon Way
High Street
Third Close
Pemberton Road
Park Road
Kent Road
Manor Road
Arnison Road
Bridge Rd
Creek Rd
Hampton Court Station
River Thames
Feltham Road

174
156
172
190
A
B
C
D
E
1
2
3
4
5
6
Teddington Lock
Newland House School
Waldegrave Road
Waldegrave Park Road
Twickenham Rd
Manor Road
Ferry Rd
Dukes Avenue
Maguire Dr
Beaufort Rd
Lammas Rd
Burnell Av
Dysart Avenue
Dysart School
Ham & Petersham Cricket Club
Parkleys
Weald La
St Georges Industrial Estate
River Thames
Thames Path
Broom Road
The Hawker Centre
Richmond
Kingston upon Thames
Richmond upon Thames
Trowlock Island
Trowlock Av
Trowlock Wy
Teddington School
The Waldegrave Clinic
Works
Teddington Pool & Fitness Centre
Teddington Business Park
High Street
Broad St
Primary School
Teddington Station
Park Lane
Surgery
Park Road
Clarence Road
Queen's Road
Admiralty Rd
Park Road B358
Sandy Lane
TW11
Cromwell Road
Collis Primary School
Sacred Heart RC Primary School
Harrowdene Gardens
Fairfax Road
Kingston Road A310
St Winifred's Road
Atbara Road
King Edward's Grove
Munster Road
Holmesdale Road
Fairways
Hampton Wick Infant School
Normansfield Av
St John the Baptist CE Junior Sch
Cedars Rd
Vicarage Road
Upr Teddington Rd
Hampton Wick Stn
Hampton Wick
Bushy Park
Chestnut Avenue
Diana Fountain
Hampton Court Road A308
Hampton Court Palace
Hampton Court Station
Stud House
Horse Fair
Church Grove
Guildhall
Pol Stn
Kingston Hall Rd
High Street
Portsmouth Road
A307
TAVR Centre
Riverside Close
Anglesea Road
Queens Promenade
Hampton Court Park
1 grid square represents 500 metres

Ham Common
Church Road
Ham Gate Av
Queen's Rd
Parkgate House
F
G
H
J
K
157
19
20
Latchmere Cl
Beechrow
The Shires
Garthside
Barnfield Gdns
Tudor Drive
Aragon Rd
Anne Boleyn's Wk
Bainbridge Cl
Ham Ridings
Cowper Rd
Sopwith Cl
Hatch Pl
Wilmer Cl
Wilmer Crs
Beard Rd
Garth Rd
Garth Road
Lane
Parkfields Rd
Woodcote Cl
Park Gdns
Surgery
Cranmer Rd
Cardinal Avenue
Hollybush Road
Latchmere Cl
Queen's Road
Thatched House Lodge
Richmond upon Thames
Kingston upon Thames
Kingston Hill
A308
Coombe Pk
Coombe Wd Rd
Corscombe Cl
Coombe Ridings
Laddersstile Ride
Warboys Road
Canbury Sch
Wrby Ap
Fairlawn Cl
Cotswold Cl
Magnolia Cl
Astor Close
Haygreen Cl
Warren Road
Warren Pk
Tiffin Girls School
Wolsey Drive
Primary School
The Vine Clinic
Durlston Road
St Albans Rd
Latchmere J&I School
Aldersbrook Dr
Cranleigh Gdns
Wingfield Rd
Kelvedon Cl
Upper Park Rd
St Agatha's Drive
St Agathas RC Primary School
The Keep
Bockhampton Road
Dinton Rd
Bertram Road
Wyndham Rd
Park Rd
Liverpool Road
Handle Cl
Winchester Road
Renfrew Rd
Kings Pk
A308
St Albans Rd
Surgery
Archer Cl
Park Farm Road
Burton Road
Chesfield Road
Staunton Road
King's Road
New Road
Queen's Road
Crescent
Deer Pk Close
Boyd Cl
Eaton Drive
George Road
Hotel
Coombe Wood Golf Club
Holy Cross Preparatory School
The Drive
Stoke Rd
Rokeby Road
Rokeby School
Catehouse Cl
Marymount Int Sch
Bank Lane
Berkeley
Woodside Rd
Chestnut Road
Osborne Road
Windsor Road
Thorpe Rd
Bearfield Road
King's Road
Acre Road Hlth Clinic
Cross Rd
Shortlands Road
Tudor Road
Alexandra Rd
Infant Sch
Jnr Sch
Park Hill School
Surgery
Berystede
Blenheim Gdns
KT2
Golf Course
176
Eastbury Road
Richmond Road Medical Centre
Richmond Park Road
Gibbon Road
Elm Rd
York Rd
St George's Rd
Florence Rd
Princes Rd
Art Rd
The Farthings
Lowther Road
Dagmar Rd
Park Cl
Borough Road
Glenville Road
Brunswick Road
Hosp
Willoughby Road
Clifton Road
Craven Rd
Beresford Rd
Canbury Avenue
Works
East Road
Acre Road
Primary School
Canbury Medical Cen
Kingsgate Business Centre
Canbury 2000 Bus Pk
Deacon Road
Elton Road
Surgery
Kingston Hill
Wolverton Avenue
A&E
Kingston Hospital
Galsworthy Road
Wolsey Close
Brook Gdns
Coombe Ridge
Orchard Rise
West Road
Southwood Avenue
Crown Road
Woodlands Av
Coombe Lane West
A238
Albion Road
High Drive
Richmond Road
Kingsgate Rd
Sopwith Way
Kingston Stn
Elm Gv
Sigrist Square
Business Cen
Canbury
Park Road
Gordon Road
Telephone Exchange
Medical Cen
Manorgate Road
Norbiton Station
Coombe Road
Old London Rd
Wood Street
Cromwell Rd
Odeon
Hardman Rd
ABC
Lovekyn Cl
Tiffin School
Birkenhead Avenue
Tithe Barn Cl
A238
Chatham Rd
Chesham Road
Cobham Road
Norbiton Av
Jemmett Cl
Revell Road
Beechcroft Avenue
Branksome Way
The Rotunda
Fife Rd
Clarence St
London Road
L Rd
Norbiton
Homersham Road
Neville Road
Norbiton Avenue
Arundel Rd
Kenley Road
Cardinal Crs
Arundel Road
Dickerage Road
Oliver Road
Overdale Avenue
Eden Walk Shopping Centre
Adams Walk
Fairfield North
Old London Rd
Church Road
Clevedon Road
Ayliffe Close
Cambridge Gardens
Grammar School
Fairfield E
Caversham Rd
Minerva Rd
Albert Road
Victoria Road
Cambridge Road
Gloucester Road
Porchester Road
Orme Road
Clarence Av
Myrtle Gv
The Cl
Laburnum Gv
5
Lady Booth Rd
Ashdown
Fairfield W
Fairfield Road
Sports Centre
St Josephs RC Primary School
Hawks Road
School Rd
Washington Rd
Portman Rd
Eureka Rd
Burritt Road
Ernest Rd
Douglas Road
Rosebery Road
Charter Road
Charter Sq
Wheatfield Way
Orch Rd
Fairfield South
KT1
Linden Crs
Somerset Road
Willingham Way
Cambridge Grove Road
Vincent Road
Waters Road
King Henry's Road
Fleetwood Road
Fleetwood Square
Muybridge Road
Middleton Road
Long Walk
Mount Rd
Pleasant Road
The Crescent
Dickerage Hill
A240
Palmer Crs
Grange Road
Knight's Park
Avenue Road
Mill Street
Mill Place
Livesey Cl
Winery Lane
Rowlis Road
Bonner Hill
Road
Gladstone Road
Hampden Road
Works
Boundary Close
A2043
Kingston Rd
Archdale Pl
Dickerage Lane
Stafford Rd
Superstore
Council Building
Primary School
University
Dawson Rd
Cemetery
Kingsmeadow Athletics Centre
Kingstonian FC
The Mount Infant School
Cheltenham Av
Northcote Road
6
Grove Crs
Denmark Road
Springfield Rd
Portland Road
Horace Rd
Herbert Rd
Villiers Road
Old Mill Road
Fairfield Industrial Estate
Kingston Crematorium
Hogsmill River
Superstore
Avenue Ter
St Johns Rd
Wellington Crs
Health Clinic
Penrhyn Road
Kingston University
Bloomfield Rd
Alfred Road
Works
Athelstan Road
Kingston upon Thames
Grove Lane
Beaufort Road
Geneva Rd
Grove Cl
Balmoral Road
Buckingham Road
191
Windrush
Willow Road
Georgia Road
Beresford Road
Dunbar Road
Roselands Clinic
Lingfield Avenue
Lower Marsh Lane
Surbiton Cemetery
Park Avenue
Potters Grove
A240
Works

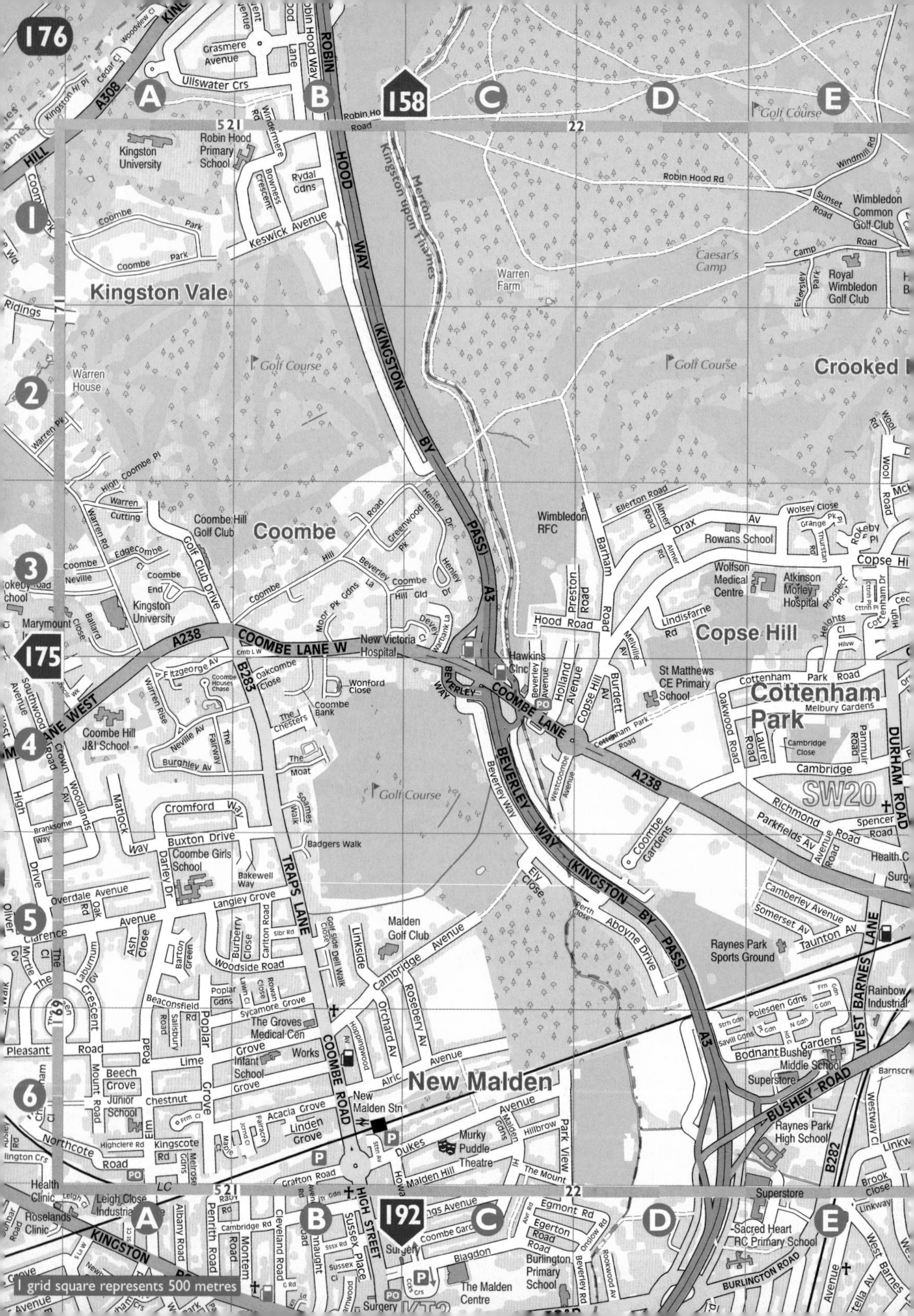
158
175
192
A
B
C
D
E
1
2
3
4
5
6
521
22
Kingston Vale
Coombe
Crooked
Copse Hill
Cottenham Park
New Malden
SW20
Kingston University
Robin Hood Primary School
Grasmere Avenue
Ullswater Crs
Robin Hood Way
Robin Hood Road
Windermere Rd
Bowness Crescent
Rydal Gdns
Keswick Avenue
Coombe Park
Kingston upon Thames
Merton
ROBIN HOOD WAY (KINGSTON BY PASS)
A3
A308
Cedar Cl
Woodview Cl
Kingston Hill Pl
Robin Hood Rd
Windmill Rd
Sunset Road
Wimbledon Common Golf Club
Camp Road
Caesar's Camp
Warren Farm
Royal Wimbledon Golf Club
Eversley Park
Golf Course
Ridings
Warren House
Warren Pk
High Coombe Pl
Warren Cutting
Warren Rd
Coombe Hill Golf Club
Golf Club Drive
Edgecombe Cl
Coombe Neville
Coombe End
Kingston University
Ballard Close
Marymount
Coombe Hill Road
Greenwood Pk
Henley Dr
Beverley La
Coombe Hill Gld
Moor Pk Gdns
Devey Cl
Warbank La
New Victoria Hospital
A238
COOMBE LANE W
COOMBE LANE WEST
Cmb L W
Fitzgeorge Av
Coombe Houses Chase
Warren Rise
Oakcombe Close
Wonford Close
Coombe Bank
The Chesters
The Moat
B283
Southwood Avenue
Coombe Hill J&I School
Neville Av
The Fairway
Burghley Av
Crown Road
Woodlands Av
Matlock Way
Cromford Way
Buxton Drive
Darley Dr
Coombe Girls School
Bakewell Way
TRAPS LANE
Soames Walk
Badgers Walk
Branksome Way
High Drive
Overdale Avenue
Oak Rd
Langley Grove
Avenue
Ash Close
Burberry Close
Carlton Road
Slbr Rd
Golf Side Close
Dell Walk
Linkside
Malden Golf Club
Cambridge Avenue
Barton Green
Woodside Road
Clarence
Myrtle Gv
The Crescent
Laburnum Gv
Poplar Gdns
Lawn Cl
Rowan Close
Sycamore Grove
Beaconsfield Road
Salisbury Road
Poplar Grove
The Groves Medical Cen
Hoppingwood Av
Orchard Av
Rosebery Av
COOMBE ROAD
Pleasant
Road
Mount Road
Beech Grove
Junior School
Lime
Grove Infant School
Works
Alric Avenue
Chestnut
Grove
Acacia Grove
Linden Grove
New Malden Stn
Northcote Road
Highclere Rd
Kingscote Rd
Melrose Gdns
Crafton Road
Dukes
Murky Puddle Theatre
Malden Hill
Malden Gdns
Avenue
Hillbrow
Park View
The Mount
Health Clinic
Leigh Close Industrial
Roselands Clinic
KINGSTON
Raby Rd
Penrith Road
Albany Road
Cambridge Rd
Montem Road
Cleveland Road
Sussex Rd
Sussex Place
Sussex Cl
HIGH STREET
Connaught Rd
Coombe Gardens
Egmont Rd
Egerton Road
Burlington Primary School
Blagdon Road
Beverley Rd
Onslow Rd
Rookwood Av
The Malden Centre
Surgery
Wimbledon RFC
Ellerton Road
Almer Road
Barham Road
Preston Road
Drax Av
Rowans School
Wolsey Close
Grange Pk Pl
Thurstan Rd
Rokeby Pl
Copse Hill
Wolfson Medical Centre
Atkinson Morley Hospital
Prospect Pl
Cottenham Dr
Hood Road
Lindisfarne Rd
Melville Av
Heights Cl
Hawkins Clnc
Beverley Avenue
Holland Avenue
Copse Hill Av
Burdett
St Matthews CE Primary School
Cottenham Park Road
Melbury Gardens
BEVERLEY WAY
COOMBE LANE
Cottenham Park Road
Oakwood Road
Laurel Road
Panmuir Road
Cambridge Close
Cambridge
DURHAM ROAD
Westcoombe Avenue
Beverley Way
BEVERLEY WAY (KINGSTON BY PASS)
Coombe Gardens
Richmond Road
Parkfields Av
Spencer Road
Avenue Road
Ely Close
Perth Close
Aboyne Drive
Camberley Avenue
Somerset Av
Taunton Av
Raynes Park Sports Ground
WEST BARNES LANE
Rainbow Industrial
Polesden Gdns
Savill Gdns
Bodnant Gardens
Bushey Middle School
Superstore
BUSHEY ROAD
Raynes Park High School
B282
Westway Cl
Linkway
Brook Close
Sacred Heart RC Primary School
BURLINGTON ROAD
West Barnes
1 grid square represents 500 metres

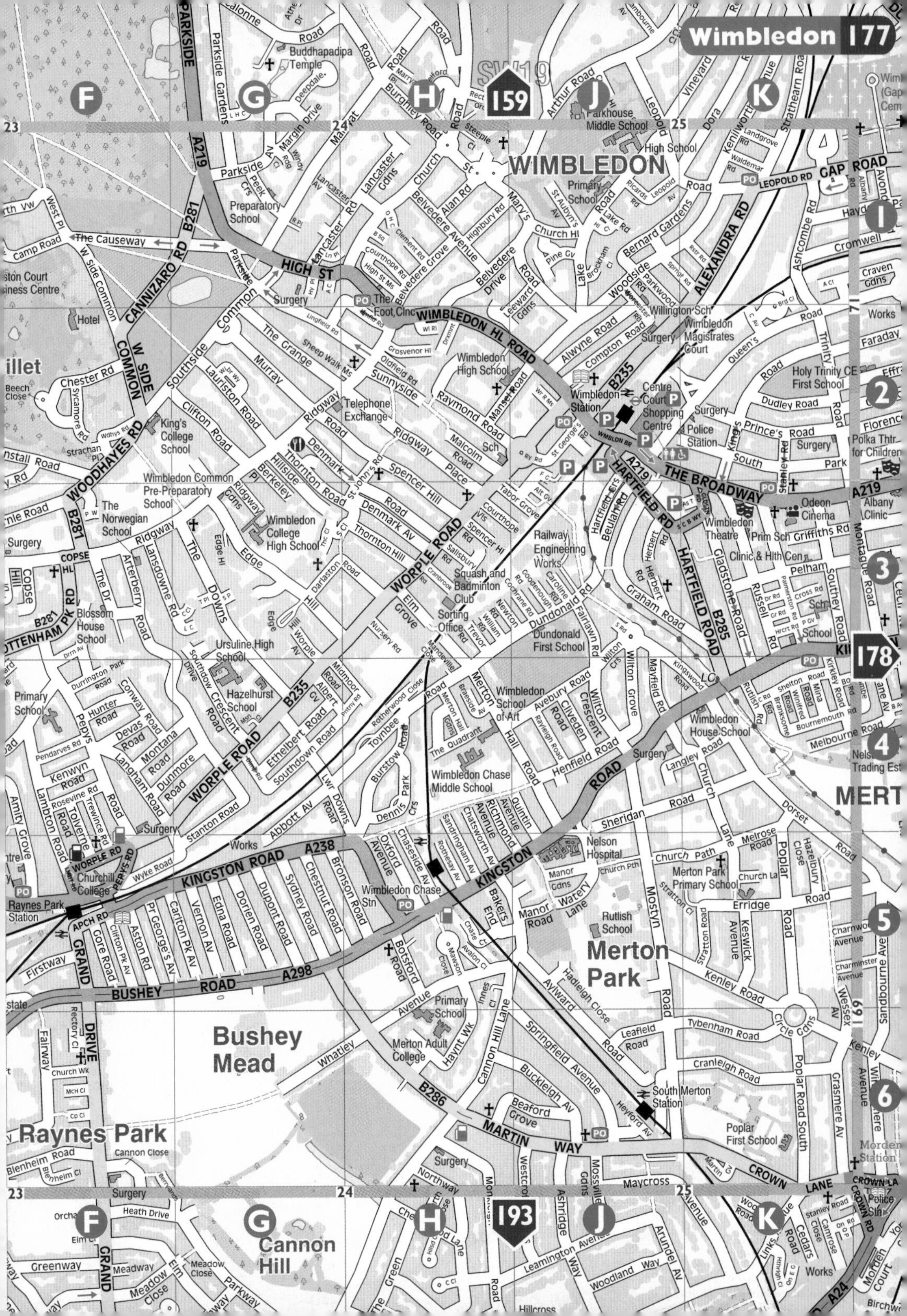
SW19
159
WIMBLEDON
Buddhapadipa Temple
Parkhouse Middle School
High School
Primary School
Peek Crs Preparatory School
HIGH ST
WIMBLEDON HL ROAD
The Causeway
Camp Road
CANNIZARO RD
W SIDE COMMON
WOODHAYES RD
PARKSIDE
A219
B281
Hotel
Wimbledon High School
Wimbledon Station
Centre Court Shopping Centre
Police Station
THE BROADWAY
Wimbledon Magistrates Court
Willington Sch
ALEXANDRA RD
LEOPOLD RD
GAP ROAD
Holy Trinity CE First School
Polka Thtr for Children
Odeon Cinema
Wimbledon Theatre
Albany Clinic
Clinic & Hlth Cen
HARTFIELD RD
HARTFIELD ROAD
B285
King's College School
Wimbledon Common Pre-Preparatory School
The Norwegian School
Wimbledon College High School
Telephone Exchange
WORPLE ROAD
B235
Squash and Badminton Club
Sorting Office
Railway Engineering Works
Dundonald First School
Ursuline High School
Hazelhurst School
Blossom House School
Primary School
Wimbledon School of Art
Wimbledon Chase Middle School
Wimbledon House School
178
MERT
Nelson Trading Est
Nelson Hospital
Merton Park Primary School
Rutlish School
Merton Park
KINGSTON ROAD
A238
KINGSTON
Wimbledon Chase Stn
Raynes Park Station
Churchill College
BUSHEY ROAD
A298
Bushey Mead
Merton Adult College
Primary School
South Merton Station
MARTIN WAY
B286
CROWN LANE
Poplar First School
Raynes Park
Cannon Hill
193
Morden Station
Police Stn
A24
Works
F
G
H
J
K
23
24
25
1
2
3
4
5
6

178
160
177
194
A
B
C
D
E
1
2
3
4
5
6
26
27
1 grid square represents 500 metres
South Wimbledon
Tooting Graveney
Collier's Wood
MERTON
TOOTIN
Wimbledon Stadium
Superstore
Wimbledon (Gap Road) Cemetery
Lambeth Crematorium
Lambeth Cemetery
Durnsford Road
Plough Lane
B235
A218
Gap Road
Haydon Park Road
Avondale Rd
Cromwell Road
Havelock Road
Kingsley Rd
Kohat Rd
Haydon's Rd
Haydons Road Station
Regent Pl
Caxton Rd
Priory CE Middle School
Queen's Road
Craven Gdns
Works
Faraday Road
Evelyn Rd
Birkbeck Rd
Cowdrey Rd
Tennyson Rd
Garfield Road
Garfield Primary School
Shree Ghanapathy Temple
Dryden Rd
Milton Rd
Cowper Rd
Edith Rd
York Rd
Effra Road
Ashley Rd
Clarence Road
Florence Road
Holy Trinity CE First School
Trinity Road
Surgery
Polka Thtr for Children
Wimbledon Recreation Centre
Wycliffe Rd
Cardigan Rd
Haccombe Rd
Latimer Rd
Ridley Rd
A219
Albany Clinic
Odeon Cinema
Griffiths Rd
Montague Road
Merton Road
Quicks Road
Trafalgar Rd
Hamilton Rd
Hardy Road
Nelson Road
Victory Road
Deburgh Rd
All Saints Rd
Hanover Rd
First School
Laburnum Rd
Grove Rd
Norman Rd
Hotham Rd
Gilbert Rd
Leyton Rd
Holmes Rd
Wandle Bank
East Road
Downside Cl
South Rd
Bewley St
North Rd
Mead Path
Autumn Cl
Halles Cl
Lecock Cl
Cecil Rd
Balfour Rd
Kingston Road
South Wimbledon Station
Merton High Street
A238
Abbey Rd
Croft Rd
Mill Rd
Meadow Rd
Dane Rd
Hilborough Rd
Nelson Grove Road
Station Rd
Milner Road
Haywards Cl
Brisbane Av
Mina Rd
Bournemouth Rd
High Path
Merantun Way
First School
Nelson Trading Estate
Lee Rd
Merton Ind Park
Jubilee Way
Lyon Road
Riverside Business Park
Abbey Mills
Watermill Wy
Runnymede
Liberty Avenue
Windsor Avenue
Saxon Business Centre
Brangwyn Cr
Primary School
Sheldrick Cl
Hogarth Crs
Lombard Road
Lombard Business Park
Deer Park
Willmore End
Nursery Road
Covey Cl
Hazelbury Close
Charnwood Avenue
Charminster Avenue
Sandbourne Avenue
Daybrook Road
A24
Morden Road
Morden Road Clinic
Morden Hall Medical Centre
Kenley Road
Windermere Avenue
Grasmere Av
Morden Station
Crown La
Crown Rd
Police Stn
Aberconway Road
Morden Hall Road
Morden Hall Park
Stanley Road
Camrose Close
York Close
Bardney Rd
Beeleigh Rd
Bayham Road
Central Medical Centre
A239
Morden Road
Rutter Gdns
Ravensbury Grove
Birchwood
Lambeth Crematorium
Smallwood Road
Foss Rd
Alston Road
Worslade Rd
Bertal Rd
Khartoum Road
Fairlight Road
Tooting Leisure Centre
Broadwater Primary School
Broadwater Rd
Khama Rd
Gatton Road
Selkirk Road
Graveney Rd
Gilbey Road
Garratt Ter
217
Coverton Road
Fountain Rd
Cranmer Ter
Blackshaw Road
Kiln Ms
St Georges Hospital
A&E
Tooting Broadway Stn
Superstore
Effort St
Hoyle Rd
Tooting Gv
Laurel Cl
Salvador
Nutwell St
Woodbury St
Bickley Street
Mellison Road
Brightwell Crs
Himley Rd
Sellincourt Rd
Sellincourt School
Tooting High St
College
Surgery
Moffat Rd
Blackenham Rd
Chasefield Road
Cowick Rd
Letchworth St
Totterdown Street
Longmead Rd
Ashvale Rd
School
Med Cen
Undine St
Valnay St
Secondary School
Dewey St
Vant Road
Mitcham Rd
Trident Business Cen
Maybury St
Aldis St
Carlwell St
Kenlor Road
Kimble Rd
Dinton Rd
Kipling Dr
Acre Rd
Waterfall Cottages
Briscoe Rd
Boundary Rd
Miller Rd
Boyd Rd
Carter Rd
Denison Rd
College Rd
University Rd
Walpole Rd
Bygrove Rd
High St Colliers Wood
Tooting High Street
A24
Robinson Road
Clive Road
Warren Rd
Marlborough Rd
Park Road
Norfolk Road
Harewood Rd
Wilton Rd
Birdhurst Rd
Longley Road
Charlmont Rd
Trevelyan Rd
Lyveden Rd
Bickersteth Rd
Byton Rd
Avarn Rd
Stella Rd
Loubet St
Glasford St
Renmuir Street
A217
Tooting Station
Finborough Rd
Arnold Rd
Swains Rd
Pitcairn Rd
Crusoe Rd
Singleton Cl
Devonshire Road
Cavendish Road
Collier's Wood Stn
Baltic Cl
Hotel
North Gdns
South Gdns
Valley Gdns
Singlegate First School
Colwood Gdns
Christchurch Rd
Priory Rd
Clarendon Rd
Myrna Cl
Fleming Mead
Courtney Rd
Alexandra Rd
Taylor Rd
Waldo Pl
Island Rd
Friday Rd
Road
Fortescue Road
Victoria Road
Cemetery
Priory Retail Park
Works
Tandem Centre
Wheatstone Cl
Brailsford Cl
Lister Cl
Fairfield Cl
Heathfield Dr
Wilson Avenue
Hawkes Road
Turner Av
Stuart Place
Border Gdns
Steers Mead
Dennis Reeve Close
Pr Georges Road
College Fields Business Cen
Chelsea Fields Industrial Est
Heathfield Drive
Wilkins Cl
Veals Mead
Biggin Avenue
Rose Av
Poplar Av
Silbury Av
Oakmead Pl
Lavender Park
Mortlake Drive
Reynolds Close
Farewell Pl
Western Road
Roan Industrial Estate
Lavender Grove
Lavender Avenue
Playing Fields
Mortimer Road
Plummer Lane
Eveline Road
Blenheim Business Centre
Sunshine Way
Bond Road School
Menin Works
Bond First School
Downe Road
Armfield Cres
London Road
Surgery
Heyford Rd
Laings Av
Dorset Rd
Liberty Middle School
Lowry Crs
Borough Road
Bond Road
Mount Rd
Church Road
Hawthorne Av
Ashtree Avenue
Oakwood Av
Dalton Avenue
Homefield Gdns
Haslemere Av
Thornville Gv
Phipp's Bridge Road
Roslyn Close
Primary School
Foxton Grove
Park Vw
Bourne Dr
Rock Cl
Lewis Road
Glebe Av
Abbeyfield Cl
Bank Av
Rodney Rd
Seaton Rd
Portland Road
Boundary Bus Park
Batsworth Road
Goodwin Cl
Collingwood Rd
Miles Road
Edmund Rd
Merlin Cl
Frimley Gdns
Belgrave Wk
Illingworth Cl
Oxted Close
Queen's Road
New Close
Sadler Cl
A236
Holborn Wy
Upper Gn W
Raleigh Gdns
St Marks Prim Sch
A217
Works
Elmwood Rd
Whitford Gdns
Albert Road
Langdale Avenue
Kingsleigh Place
Love Lane
Russell Rd
Harwood Av
Glebe Path
Church Rd
Love La
Surgery
Benedict Rd
Hallowfield Wy
Church Pth
Gunns Gdns
Vicarage Gdns
Melrose Special School
Nursery Rd
Fire Stn
Lower Gn W
Vestry Hall
Cricket Green
Birches Close
Chart Close
The Canons Leisure Centre
Cricket Green
Cranmer
Madeira
Mitcham Cricket Club
Pol Stn
Baron Gv
Linden Pl
Taplow Ct
White Br Av
Works

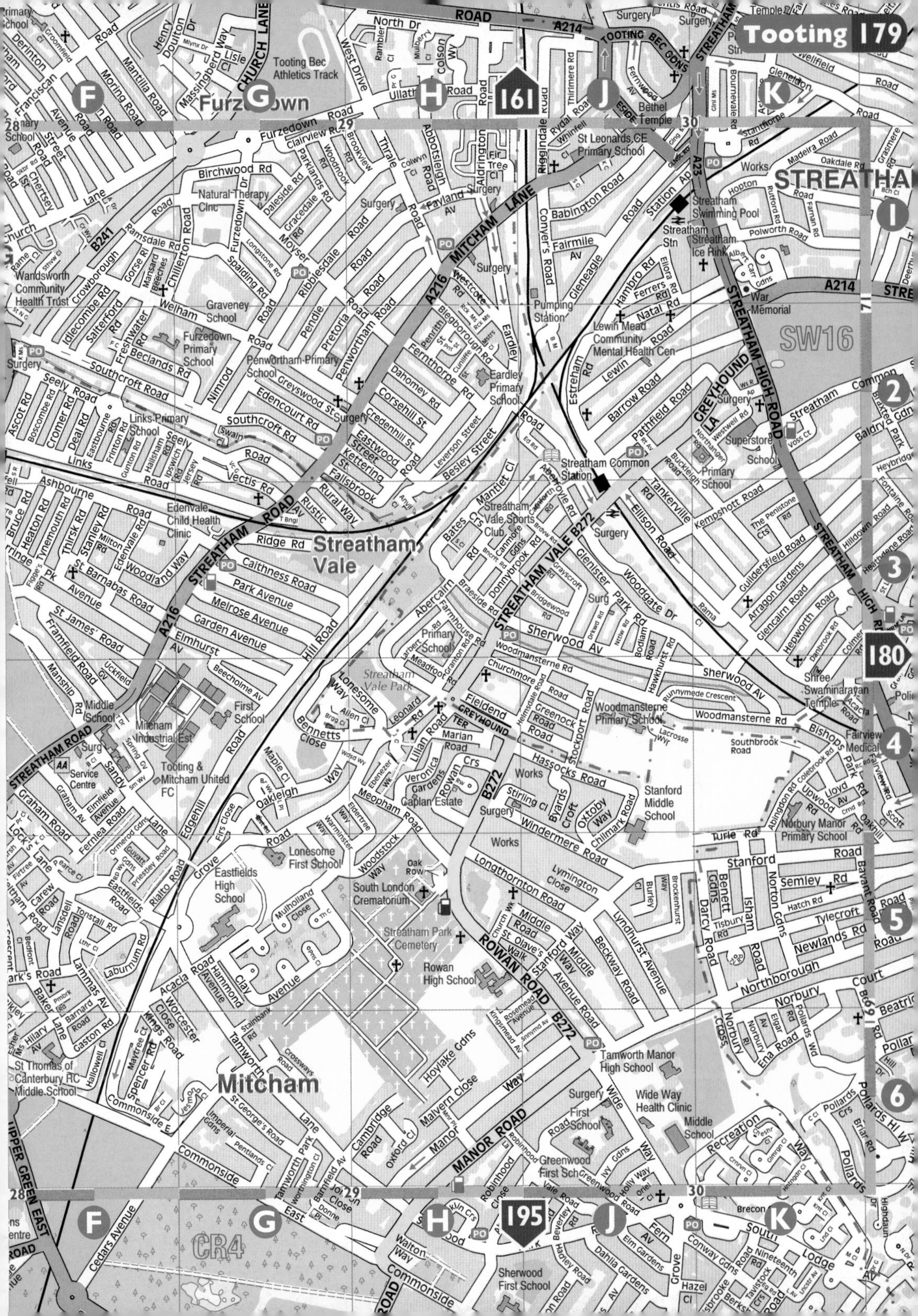
Furzedown
Tooting Bec Athletics Track
161
Tooting Bec Gdns
Bethel Temple
St Leonards CE Primary School
STREATHAM
Streatham Swimming Pool
Streatham Stn
Streatham Ice Rink
War Memorial
SW16
Streatham Common
Mitcham Lane
A216
A214
A23
Natural Therapy Clinc
Wandsworth Community Health Trust
Graveney School
Furzedown Primary School
Penwortham Primary School
Eardley Primary School
Pumping Station
Lewin Mead Community Mental Health Cen
Links Primary School
Streatham Common Station
Edenvale Child Health Clinic
Streatham Vale Sports Club
Streatham Vale
Superstore
Primary School
Streatham Vale Park
Middle School
First School
Mitcham Industrial Est
Tooting & Mitcham United FC
Service Centre
Woodmansterne Primary School
Stanford Middle School
Norbury Manor Primary School
Shree Swaminarayan Temple
Fairview Medical
Caplan Estate
Lonesome First School
Eastfields High School
South London Crematorium
Streatham Park Cemetery
Rowan High School
St Thomas of Canterbury RC Middle School
Mitcham
Tamworth Manor High School
Wide Way Health Clinic
Middle School
First School
Greenwood First Sch
Sherwood First School
CR4
180
195
Streatham Road
Streatham Vale B272
Rowan Road B272
Manor Road
Streatham High Road
Greyhound La
Upper Green East
Cedars Avenue
Commonside
F
G
H
J
K
I
2
3
4
5
6
28
29
30

180
162
179
196
A
B
C
D
E
1
2
3
4
5
6
531
32
West Norwood
STREATHAM
Norwood New Town
Upper Norwood
Norbury
SW16
CR7
A214 STREATHAM COMMON NORTH
CROWN LANE A214
A214 CROWN DALE
CENTRAL HILL
A215 KNIGHT'S HILL
NORWOOD HIGH ST
B232 ELDER ROAD
BEULAH HILL
A215
B273 GREEN LANE
B273 PARCHMORE ROAD
A23 LONDON ROAD
STREATHAM HIGH RD
GRANGE ROAD
A212
B266
HIGH ST
ROAD
Sunnyhill Primary School
Surgery
Julians Primary School
Bishop Thomas Grant School
Crown Lane Primary School
Norwood School
St Josephs RC Infant School
St Josephs RC Junior School
Virgo Fidelis Convent Sch
Rockmount School
St Josephs College
Downsview Primary School
Westwood High School for Girls
David Livingstone Primary School
Norbury Manor Secondary Girls School
Kensington Ave Primary School
Norbury Complementary Therapy Clinic
Fairview Medical Cen
Norbury Station
Police Stn
Shree Swaminarayan Temple
Norbury Trading Est
Norbury Health Centre
Sports Ground
St James The Great RC Primary School
Infant School
Parchmore Medical Centre
Thornton Heath Pools & Fitness Cen
Thornton Heath Health Centre
St Lukes School
Works
Primary School
Kingswood Primary School
College
Valleyfield Road
Belltrees Grove
Cheviot Rd
Roxburgh Road
Truslove Road
Lakeview Road
Dassett Road
Linton Grove
Eylewood Road
Norwood Park Rd
Copgate Path
Ryecroft Road
Gibson's Hill
Covington Way
Crescent Way
Strathbrook Road
Groveland Av
Hillcote Avenue
Christian Fields
Norbury Hill
Biggin Hill
Marston Way
Downsview Road
Waddington Way
Dale Park Rd
Beauchamp Road
Norbury Avenue
Kensington Avenue
Virginia Road
Florida Road
Maryland Road
Georgia Road
Carolina Road
Springfield Road
Ingram Road
Northwood Road
Highbury Avenue
Westminster Av
Craignish Av
Norbury Crescent
Beatrice Avenue
Pollards Hill North
Pollards Hill South
Melrose Av
Kilmartin Avenue
Strathyre Avenue
Warwick Road
Bridport Road
Melfort Road
Windsor Road
Bensham Grove
Heath Road
Woodville Road
Livingstone Road
Wharfedale Gdns
Richmond Rd
Brook Road
1 grid square represents 500 metres

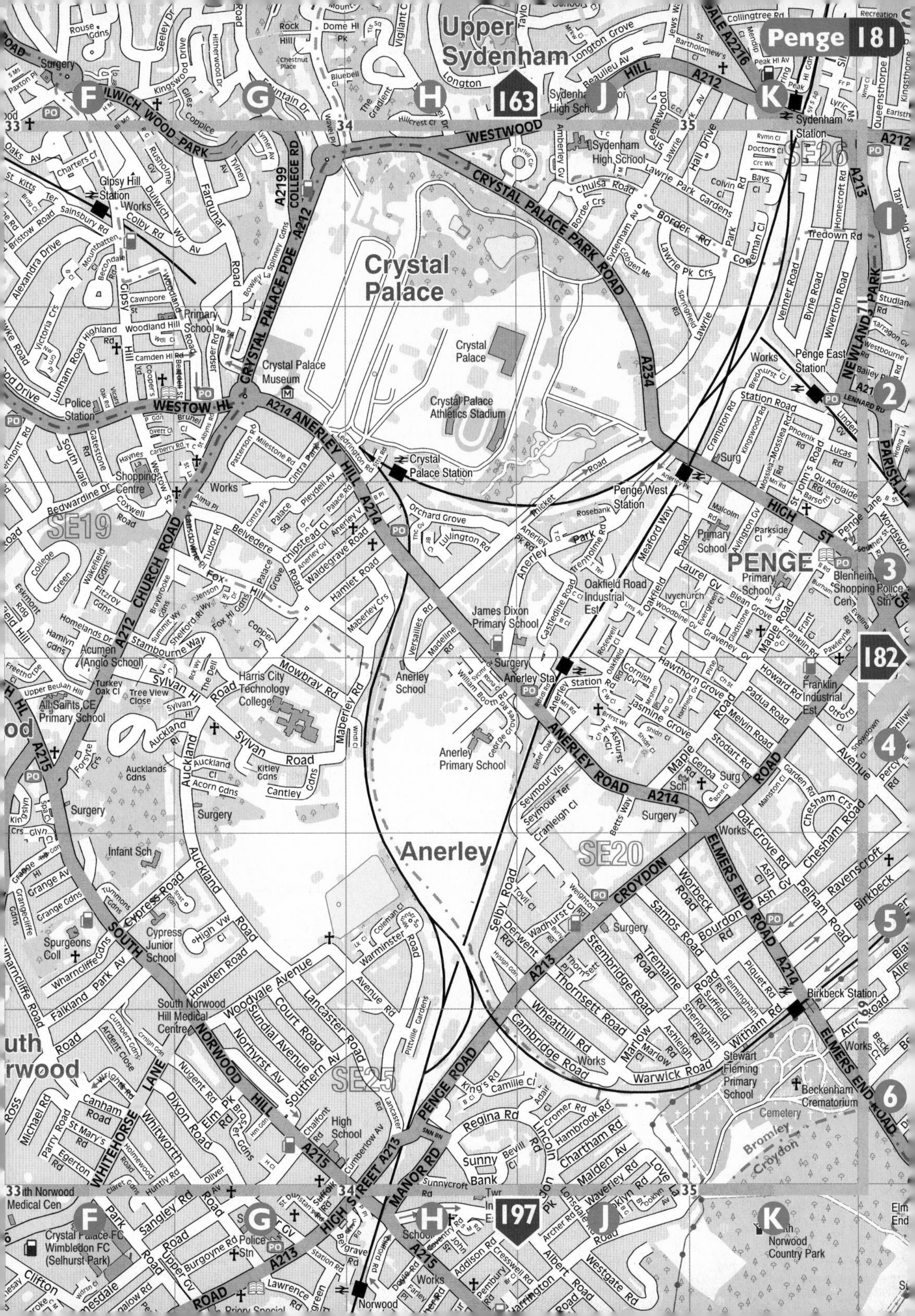

Penge 181
Upper Sydenham
163
182
197
F
G
H
J
K
33
34
35
I
2
3
4
5
6
Crystal Palace
Crystal Palace Museum
Crystal Palace Athletics Stadium
Crystal Palace Station
Penge West Station
Penge East Station
Sydenham Station
Gipsy Hill Station
Anerley Station
Birkbeck Station
Norwood
Anerley
PENGE
SE19
SE20
SE25
SE26
South Norwood
CRYSTAL PALACE PARK ROAD
CRYSTAL PALACE PDE A212
WESTWOOD
WESTOW HL
A214 ANERLEY HILL
ANERLEY ROAD A214
CHURCH ROAD A212
SOUTH NORWOOD HILL
NORWOOD HILL A215
CROYDON
A213
PENGE ROAD
HIGH STREET A213
MANOR RD
ELMERS END ROAD A214
HIGH ST
DULWICH WOOD PARK
NEWLANDS PARK
WHITEHORSE LANE
Sydenham High School
James Dixon Primary School
Anerley School
Anerley Primary School
Harris City Technology College
Acumen (Anglo School)
All Saints CE Primary School
Cypress Junior School
Spurgeons Coll
South Norwood Hill Medical Centre
Stewart Fleming Primary School
Beckenham Crematorium
Cemetery
Oakfield Road Industrial Est
Franklin Industrial Est
Blenheim Shopping Cen
Crystal Palace FC Wimbledon FC (Selhurst Park)
South Norwood Country Park
High School
Bromley
Croydon

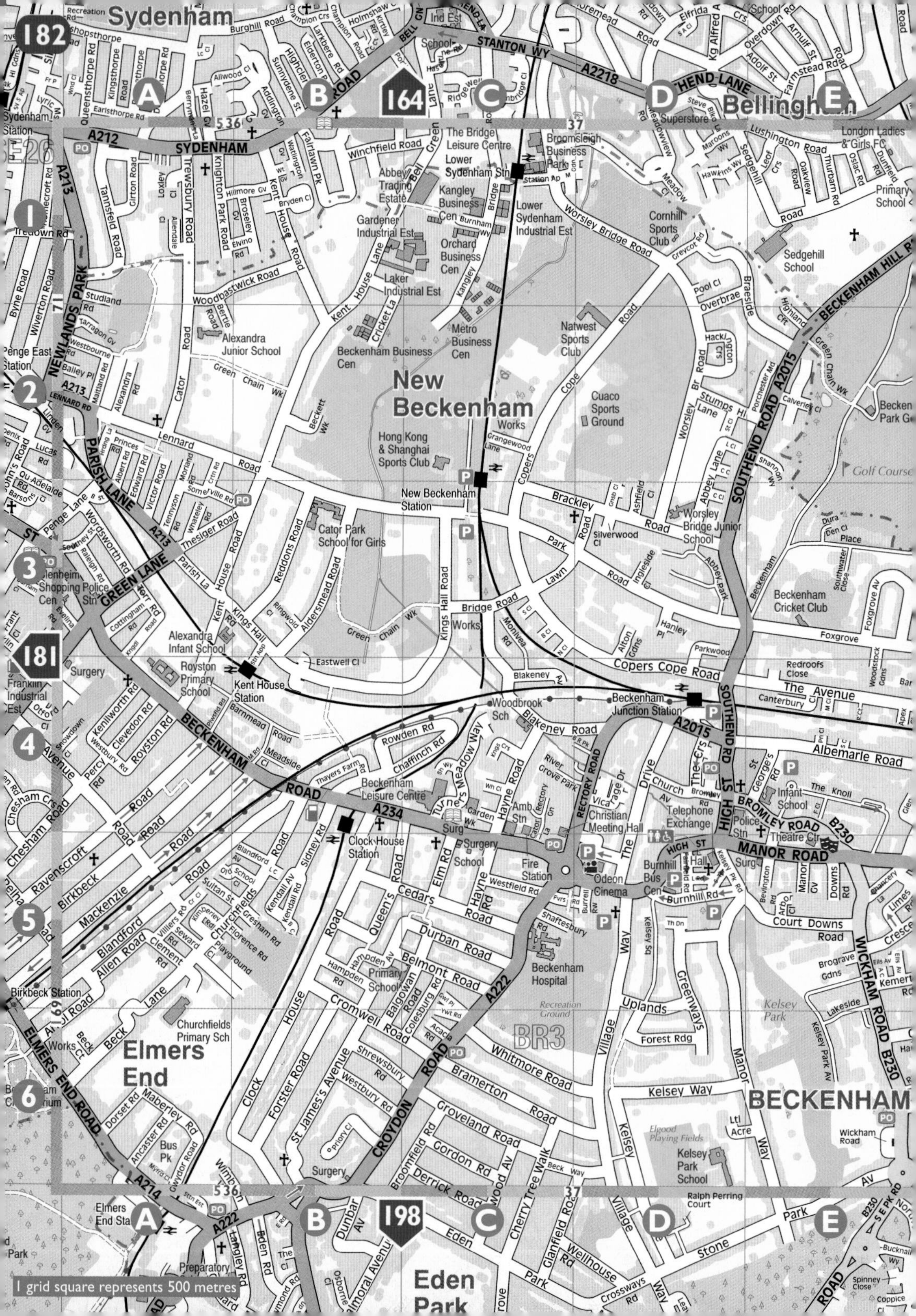

1 grid square represents 500 metres

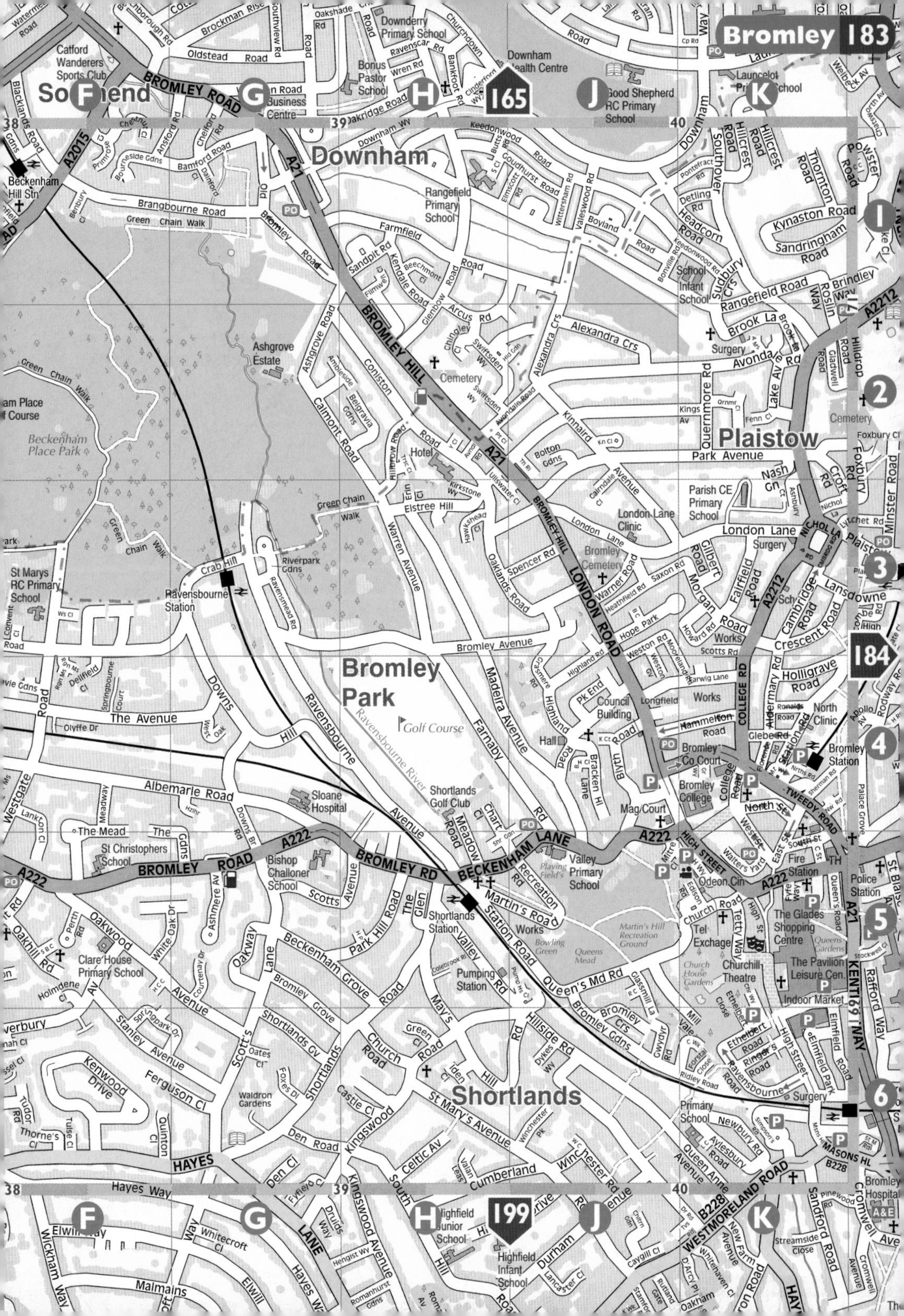
Downham
Bromley Park
Plaistow
Shortlands
Beckenham Place Park
Ashgrove Estate
Catford Wanderers Sports Club
Beckenham Hill Stn
Ravensbourne Station
Shortlands Station
Bromley Station
BROMLEY ROAD
BROMLEY HILL
LONDON ROAD
BROMLEY RD
BECKENHAM LANE
HIGH STREET
COLLEGE RD
TWEEDY ROAD
KENTISH WAY
WESTMORELAND ROAD
NICHOL LA
HAYES LANE
A21
A222
A2015
A2212
B228
Downderry Primary School
Bonus Pastor School
Downham Health Centre
Good Shepherd RC Primary School
Launcelot Primary School
Rangefield Primary School
Parish CE Primary School
London Lane Clinic
Bromley Cemetery
Cemetery
Hotel
St Marys RC Primary School
Golf Course
Ravensbourne River
Shortlands Golf Club
Sloane Hospital
St Christophers School
Bishop Challoner School
Clare House Primary School
Valley Primary School
Martin's Hill Recreation Ground
Queens Mead
Bowling Green
Pumping Station
Council Building
Bromley Co Court
Bromley College
Mag Court
Odeon Cin
Tel Exchange
Churchill Theatre
Church House Gardens
The Glades Shopping Centre
The Pavilion Leisure Cen.
Indoor Market
Fire Station
Police Station
North Clinic
Surgery
Works
Waldron Gardens
Highfield Junior School
Highfield Infant School
Primary School
Bromley Hospital
A&E
Green Chain Walk
Brangbourne Road
Oldstead Road
Brockman Rise
Oakridge Road
Keedonwood Road
Downham Wy
Farmfield Road
Ashgrove Road
Coniston Road
Calmont Road
Warren Avenue
Elstree Hill
Bromley Avenue
Madeira Avenue
Farnaby Rd
Ravensbourne Avenue
Downs Hill
The Avenue
Albemarle Road
Westgate Road
Oakwood Avenue
Stanley Avenue
Ferguson Cl
Kenwood Drive
Scott's Lane
Beckenham Grove
Park Hill Road
Church Road
Station Road
Martin's Road
Recreation Rd
Queen's Md Rd
Bromley Gdns
Hillside Rd
St Mary's Avenue
Cumberland Rd
Winchester Rd
Queen Anne Avenue
Aylesbury Rd
Newbury Rd
Ravensbourne Road
Ethelbert Road
Elmfield Road
Rafford Way
Sandford Road
Cromwell Avenue
Masons Hl
Kingswood Avenue
Hayes Way
Malmains Way
Wickham Way
Den Road
Durham Avenue
Rangefield Road
Sudbury Crs
Headcorn Road
Hillcrest Road
Thornton Road
Kynaston Road
Sandringham Road
Avondale Rd
Alexandra Crs
Kinnaird Avenue
Park Avenue
London Lane
Gilbert Road
Morgan Road
Fairfield Road
Cambridge Road
Crescent Road
Lansdowne
Holligrave Road
Aldermary Rd
Hammelton Road
Glebe Rd
North St
East St
West St
Highland Road
Blyth Road
Oaklands Road
Spencer Rd
Warner Road
Saxon Rd
Hope Park
Chart Cl
Meadow Road
Valley Rd
Tetty Way
Mill Vale
Ridley Road
Foxbury Rd
Minster Rd
Croft Rd
Quernmore Rd
Brook La
Avonda Rd
Hilldrop
165
184
199
F
G
H
J
K
I
2
3
4
5
6
38
39
40

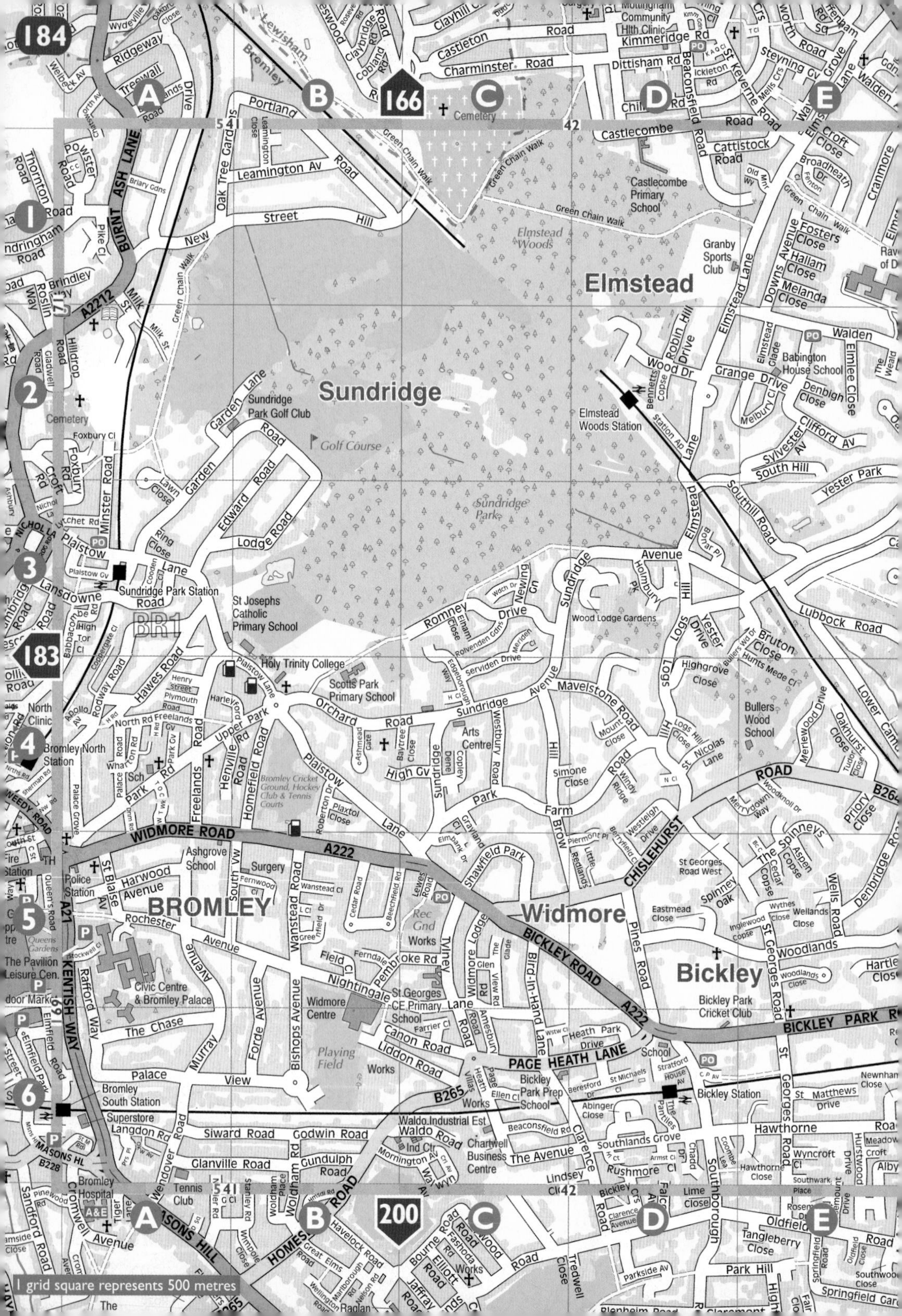

1 grid square represents 500 metres

167
186
201
Chislehurst West
Foxbury
CHISLEHURST
BR7
Chislehurst Common
Golf Course
Chislehurst Golf Club
Petts Wood
Hawkwood Farm
Tongs Farm
Jubilee Country Park
Cemetery
WHITE HORSE HILL
A208
RED HILL
CHISLEHURST HIGH ST
B263
PRINCE IMPERIAL RD
CENTRE COMMON ROAD
BROMLEY ROAD
A222
BROMLEY LANE
ROYAL PARADE
WATT'S LANE
MANOR PARK ROAD
OLD HILL
B264
BROMLEY RD
SUMMER HILL
ST PAUL'S CRAY ROAD
ORPINGTON ROAD
PERRY STREET
SIDCUP BY-PASS ROAD
A20
Edgebury Primary School
Mead Road Infant School
Chislehurst Natural Health Centre
The Willows Clinic
Junior School
Surgery
Old Elthamians Sports Club
St Barts Hospital Sports Ground
Beaverwood School for Girls
Farrington & Stratford House School
Coopers School
Chislehurst Caves
Chislehurst Station
Bromley High School
Middlesex Hospital Sports Gr
Hoblands End
Kemnal Road
Foxbury Av
Belmont Lane
Edgebury
Woodside Avenue
Holmdale Road
Westhurst Drive
Wilderness Road
Camden Close
School Road
Church Row
Bull Lane
Holbrook Lane
Cardinal Cl
Hawkwood Lane
Botany Bay Lane
Gosshill Road
Station Approach
Hazelmere Road
Birchwood Road
Thornet Wood Road
Golf Road
Otford Close
Beaverwood Rd
St Paul's Wood Hill
The Drive
Leesons Hill
Beddington Rd
Marlings Park Av
Kevington
F
G
H
J
K
1
2
3
4
5
6
44
45

186
185
168
169
202
Sidcup Sports Club
A211
HIGH STREET
ELM ROAD
Nelson Place
Selborne Road
Rectory Lane
Surgery
DA14
A
B
C
D
E
1
2
3
4
5
6
THE GREEN
A2001
Church Av
Old Forge Wy
Merton Court Preparatory School
David Lloyd Tennis Centre
Felton Lea
Upperton Rd
Langdon Shaw
St Mary and St Josephs GM School
CHISLEHURST RD
SIDCUP HILL
Durham Road
Lincoln Rd
Sussex Rd
Warwick Rd
Oxford Road
Knoll Road
Caerleon Cl
St Peter Chanel RC Primary School
Baugh Road
Rectory Lane
Harenc School
Middlesex Hospital Sports Ground
Frognal Corner
A222
Frognal Av
Queen Marys Hospital
A&E
Frognal Place
Sidcup Hill Primary School
Middleton Av
Wingate Rd
Amberley Ct
Waring Rd
Suffolk Road
Granton Rd
FOOTS CRAY HIGH ST
Evry Rd
MAIDSTONE ROAD
Beaverwood Rd
Leas Green
STREET
A20
SIDCUP BY-PASS ROAD
Frognal Avenue
Foots Cray
CRAY ROAD
A224
Works
Ruxley Corner Industrial Estate
Watery Lane
Haven Close
Superstore
Powerscroft Road
M Wy
A223 EDGINGTON WAY
Scadbury Park
Lullingstone Crescent
Wisley Road
Grovelands Road
Midfield Primary School
The Avenue
Kemnal Technology College
Cornwall Drive
Superstore
Sandy Lane
Bostall Road
Valley Road
The Drive
Midfield Way
Croxley Road
Grays Farm Road
Horsell Road
Ski Slope
St Paul's Wood Hill
Whitewebbs Way
Blythe Hill
Breakspears Drive
Spring Shaw Road
Athelstan Way
Croxley Green
Grays Farm Primary School
Golf Course
Crayfields Business Park
New Mill Road
Main Road
Ruxley Park Golf Centre
Beddington Road
Beddington Green
Brenchley Road
Thorndon Close
Leith Hill
Mickleham
Giggs Hill
Chipperfield Road
Cotmandene Crs
Shoreham Rd
Whippendell Way
Whippendell Close
Walsingham Road
Palewell Cl
Broom Avenue
Dawson Avenue
Tilbury Close
Scadbury Gardens
Chorleywood Crescent
St Pauls Cray Health Clinic
Broad Oak Close
Goose Green Close
Croxley Cl
Rectory Paddock School
Crayfield Industrial Park
Riverside Close
Gardiner Close
Broomwood Road
SEVENOAKS WAY
Chapman's
St Paul's Cray
Leesons Way
Petersham Drive
Rushet Road
Ravenscourt Road
Surgery
Longbury Drive
Wateringbury Cl
Saxville Road
Kelsey Road
Normanhurst Rd
Pleasance Road
Wynford Grove
Farrington Av
Vernon Close
Chalk Pit Avenue
Paulinus Close
Ethelbert Rd
Augustine Road
Martins Close
Edmunds Avenue
St Justin Cl
Barnfield Road
St Laurence Close
Bridgewater
The Drive
Highfield Road
Manorfields Close
Southfield Road
Harvel Close
Leesons Hill
Arbrook Close
Leesons Primary School
Ringshall Road
Silverdale Road
Swan Cl
Curtismill Way
Curtismill Close
Robin Way
Murray Business Centre
Murray Road
Sevenoaks Way Industrial Estate
The Landway
Springfield Way
Millwood Road
Francis Road
St Pauls Cray CE Primary School
Brantwood Way
Craylands
Springvale Retail Park
Wren Cl
Avenue
Park
Clarendon Way
Leesons Hill
Clarendon Green
Clarendon Path
Batchwood Green
Berens Way
Sayes Court
Hyde
Millfields Cl
Chipperfield Road
Hearns Rd
Veryan Cl
Teal Av
B258
Orpington Retail Park
MILL BROOK
Surgery
Star Lane
Marlings Park Av
Marlings Close
Kevington
Station Approach
Cray Station
Amherst Cl
Scotsdale
Drive
Works
Sandway
Wotton Gn
1 grid square represents 500 metres

169
203
F
G
H
J
K
48
49
50
1
2
3
4
5
6
70
71
Gattons Wy
Cemetery
Parsonage Lane
River Cray
The Grove
The Spinney
James St
Way
NORTH CRAY ROAD
A223
High Beeches
Bedensfield Clinic
PO
Bullers Close
Burdett Close
Road
Orvill Rd
Fowler Close
Thursland Road
Bedens Rd
Honeyden Road
Cornell Close
N Cray Rd
Barton Rd
North Cray Primary School
Ruxley
Whitney Walk
Manor Farm
Bexley
Kent
Norfield Road
Park
Golf Course
Stonehill Green
Chalk Wood
Birchwood Park Golf Club
Bexley
Bromley
MAIDSTONE ROAD
B2173
Old Maidstone Road
A20
A20(T)
Birchwood Rd
Works
Harfst Way
Selah Dr
Leyden
Conifer Way
Russett Way
Upper Hockenden
Cookham Road
Cray Valley Golf Club
Golf Course
MAIDSTONE ROAD
B2173
LONDON
Lawn Cl
Crescent Gdns
Woodview Rd
Heathwood Gdns
Cedar Close
Kent County
Bromley
Ash Cl
Way
Lane
Chapman's Lane
Hockenden Lane
Hockenden
The Croft
The Dale Road
Sermon Drive
Brook Road
Laburnum Av
Lavender
Bourne Way
Farm Avenue
Lynden
Cherry Ave
Star Lane
Sheepcote Lane

UNBURY
Molesey Reservoirs
172
Thames Path
Street
Church St
Forge Lane
Thames Street
Lock
HURST ROAD
A305
Works
Weston Avenue
John
Bishop Fox Way
Grafton Way
Freeman Dr
Cambridge Rd
WALTON ROAD
Bessborough Reservoir
Knight Reservoir
Upper Farm Road
Molesey Avenue
Armfield Close
Central Avenue
Eastco
Works
Sand & Gravel Works
Walton Casuals FC
River Thames
Waterside Drive
Elmbridge Leisure Centre
Parke Road
B369
WALTON ROAD
The Dene
Ivydene
Monks Avenue
Molesey Road
Pool Road
Fleetside
Sunnyside
Rivernook Close
A3050 TERRACE ROAD
Waterside Drive
Dunsmore Road
Franklyn Rd
River Walk
Franklyn Road
Grovelands School
Spicer Close
Cambridge Road
Sandy Lane
Vicarage Fields
First Avenue
Second Av
Carlton Rd
Works
Queen Elizabeth II Reservoir
Russell Road
TERRACE ROAD
Garden Road
Orchard Close
Carlton Road
Vanbrugh Drive
Telford Dr
Pankhurst Rd
Shaw Drive
Walton Business Centre
Terrace Road
Works
A3050
Lancaster Court
Grove Crs
Cottimore Lane
Willowhayne Drive
Florence Road
Fox Grove
Braycourt Avenue
Field Common
Mellor Close
Homefield Road
Hurtwood Road
Oakbank Avenue
Netley Dr
Fernbank Av
Westfield Road
Byron Close
Works
Fieldcommon Lane
Sand & Gravel Works
Fir Close
Montague Close
Egmont Road
Fairfax Close
Cottimore Crs
Cottimore Avenue
Monks Crescent
Cromwell Close
Hillary Crs
Sidney Road
Esher Av
Royston Close
WALTON-ON-THAMES
Misty's Fld
Regency Gdns
Stuart Av
Langport Ct
Swansmere School
Holly Avenue
Ambleside Avenue
Ambleside Junior School
Rydens Road
Screen Cinema
Walton Swimming Pool
Oakfields
Chestnuts
Preston Court
St Johns Dr
Cardinal Drive
Wolsey Drive
Tudor Dr
King George Avenue
Kings Road
Crutchfield Lane
Cromwell Road
Rodney Road
Worcester Ct
Branksome Close
Normanhurst Rd
North Weylands Industrial Est
Health Centre
Rydens Close
The Furrows
Meadowside
Devoke Way
Bowes Road
Rodney Rd
Rydens Park
Walton Pk La
York Gardens
Esher RFC
Maitland Cl
Walton & Hersham FC
The Grange
Midway
Walton Community Hospital
Newhall Gdns
Rydens Avenue
Brunswick Close
Rydens Road
Walton Park
Hurley Close
Danesfield Manor School
Rydens
Beecot Lane
Holwood Close
Severn Drive
Denton Gv
Elland Road
Hersham Trading Estate
Lyon Road
HERSHAM
Surgery
Crossway
Sidney Road
Council Building
Rydens
Home Farm Gdns
Lindley Road
Saxon Rd
Lindley Rd
Works
Ashley Park
Rydens Rd
St Martins Dr
Crofton Avenue
Winslow Way
Shaldon Way
Stoke Road
Kenilworth Dr
Milton Rd
Hersham Station
Adelaide Road
Betley Ct
Long Lodge Dr
Danesfield Cl
Stoke Rd
Broad Cl
Abbotts Tilt
Russet Cl
Assher Road
Arch Rd
Wynton
St Vincent Rd
1 grid square represents 500 metres
Works

East Molesey
KT8
Lower Green
West Green
173
190
204
F
G
H
J
K
2
3
4
5
6
13
14
15
HURST ROAD
A3050
WALTON ROAD
B369
HAMPTON COURT WAY
A309
ESHER ROAD
B3379
EMBER LANE
EMBER LANE STATION ROAD
B364
A307
PORTSMOUTH ROAD
KINGSTON
Island Barn Reservoir
River Ember
River Mole
Golf Course
Littleworth Common
Sandown Park Racecourse
Esher Station
Hampton Court Station
Thames Ditton Station
Molesey Hospital
Chandlers Field Primary School
Primary School
Glenlyn Medical Cen
The Teddington Theatre Club
The Orchard School
Grist Memorial Sports Club
Old Tiffinians Sports Ground
Imber Court Trading Estate
Metropolitan Police FC
St Pauls RC Primary School
Esher College
Ember Sports Club
Weston Green School
River Mole Business Park
Sandown Industrial Park
Vine Medical Centre
Lawrence Junior School
Council Building
Cemetery
Surgery
Works
Hotel
Beauchamp Road
Molesey Road
Grove Way
Imber Park Road
Douglas Road
Mill Road
Lower Green Road
Weston Green Road
Orchard Lane
Broadfields
Summer Road
Palace Road
Wolsey Road
Vine Road
Bridge Rd
Creek Rd
Riverbank
Cranbrook Drive
Cranleigh Road
The Woodlands
Parkwood Avenue
Oaklands Avenue
Orchard Gate
Alma Road
Chestnut Avenue
Lime Tree Av
Elm Tree Av
Ember Farm Way
Spencer Road
Seymour Road
Green Lane
Ray Road
Grange Road
Arnison Road
Matham Road
Bell Road
Manor Road
Kent Road
Park Road
Pemberton Road
Clinton Avenue
Langton Road
Faraday Road
High Street
Ennismore Gardens
Southfields
Couchmore Avenue
Montgomery Avenue
Westmont Rd
Hillmont Rd
Eastmont Road
Esher Gn Drive
Sandown Gate
Farm Road
Blair Avenue
Arran Way
Woodend

190
174
189
205
HAMPTON
Hampton Court Palace
Hotel
Hampton Court Station
HAMPTON COURT WAY
A309
River Thames
Thames Path
Hampton Court Park
Stud House
Golf Course
Home Park Golf Club
Thames Ditton Island
Works
Richmond upon Thames
Kingston upon Thames
Surrey County
PORTSMOUTH ROAD
A307
Seething Wells
Thames Ditton
Giggshill
Weston Green
Long Ditton
SURBITON
Hinchley Wood
KINGSTON BY-PASS
A309
HOOK UNDE
KT7
Summer Road
Speer Road
Aragon Avenue
Queen's Road
Alexandra Rd
River Bank
Riversdale Rd
Warwick Rd
Warwick Gdns
Leaf Close
Thistledene
Sterry
Elsworthy
Thames Ditton Infant School
Church Walk
St Nicholas Rd
Old School Sq
Ashley Rd
Harvest La
Council Building
High St
Boyle Farm Road
Fitzgerald
Burtenshaw Road
Queen's Drive
Kings Drive
Ferry Road
Cholmley Road
Ditton Reach
Ferry
STATION ROAD
Thames Ditton Station
Basingfield Rd
Basing Way
Basing Close
WATTS ROAD
Ditton Close
Portsmouth Avenue
River Avenue
St Leonard's Road
Mercer Close
Thames Ditton Junior School
GIGGS HILL RD
Giggs Hill Rd
Raphael Drive
Savile Cl
Hayward Rd
Surgery
Longmead Rd
Camm Gdns
Home Farm Close
Green Road
College Drive
Onslow
Newlands
Westville Rd
Southville Road
Rushett Rd
Rushett Close
Thorkhill Road
Thorkhill Gdns
Angel Road
Quinton Rd
Ditton Lawn
Orchard Street
Ewell Road
Kingston Liberal Synagogue
Effingham Road
Windmill Lane
Windmill Close
Houston Rd
Southbank
Vaughan Rd
Alston Cl
Prospect Rd
Simpson Way
Seething Wells Lane
Hastings Dr
Akerman Road
Balaclava Road
Chadwick Pl
Williams Dv
St James Sq
Savery Dr
Jennings Cl
Endsleigh Gdns
Victoria Avenue
Electric Parade
Surbiton Business Centre
BRIGHTON ROAD
A243
VICTORIA ROAD
UPPER
Lovelace Gardens
Lovelace Road
Lwr Sand Hills
Beechwood Cl
Woodlands Road
Sylvan Gdns
Lissant Cl
Copse Glade
Southborough Close
St Chads Cl
St Mary's Road
Saxonbury Gardens
Sharon Close
Pound Close
Fleece Road
King's Road
Infant School
Ditton Hill Rd
Highfield Cl
St Marys CE Junior School
Betts Way
Rectory Lane
Rectory Cl
St Scott Farm Close
St Andrews Cl
Sugden Road
Sugden Close
Mayfield Close
Orchard Avenue
Bankside Drive
Greenwood Cl
Greenwood Road
Dene Gardens
North Dene Gdns
Paget Pl
Brkin Rd
Lynwood Road
Woodfield Road
Macaulay Avenue
Bourne Cl
Wessex Cl
Lynwood
Eastmont Road
Claygate Lane
Hinchley Wood School
Cumberland Drive
Chesterfield Drive
Cotswold Close
Manor Road
Manor Drive
Severn Drive
Hill Rl
Cemetery
Church Road
Church Meadow
Woodstock Lane North
Ditton Hill
Ditton Grange Drive
Ditton Gra Cl
Oaks Way
Devonshire Drive
Saffron Way
Mandeville Drive
Summerfield Lane
Wentworth Close
Shrewsbury House School
Herne
Catherine Road
Grove Road
Cadogan Road
St Leonard's Rd
Cleaveland Road
Westfield Road
The Mall
St Andrew's Sq
St Andrew's Road
St Mary's Road
Cottage Gv
Maple Infant School
Synagogue
Uxbridge Road
Palace Road
Belgravia Mews
Anglesea Road
Riverside Close
TAVR Centre
SURBITON ROAD
B3365
Woodbines Av
Milner Road
South La
Queens Promenade
Hinchley Way
Southwood Gdns
Claygate La
Hillmont Rd
Station Ap
KINGSTON
PH
PO
1 grid square represents 500 metres

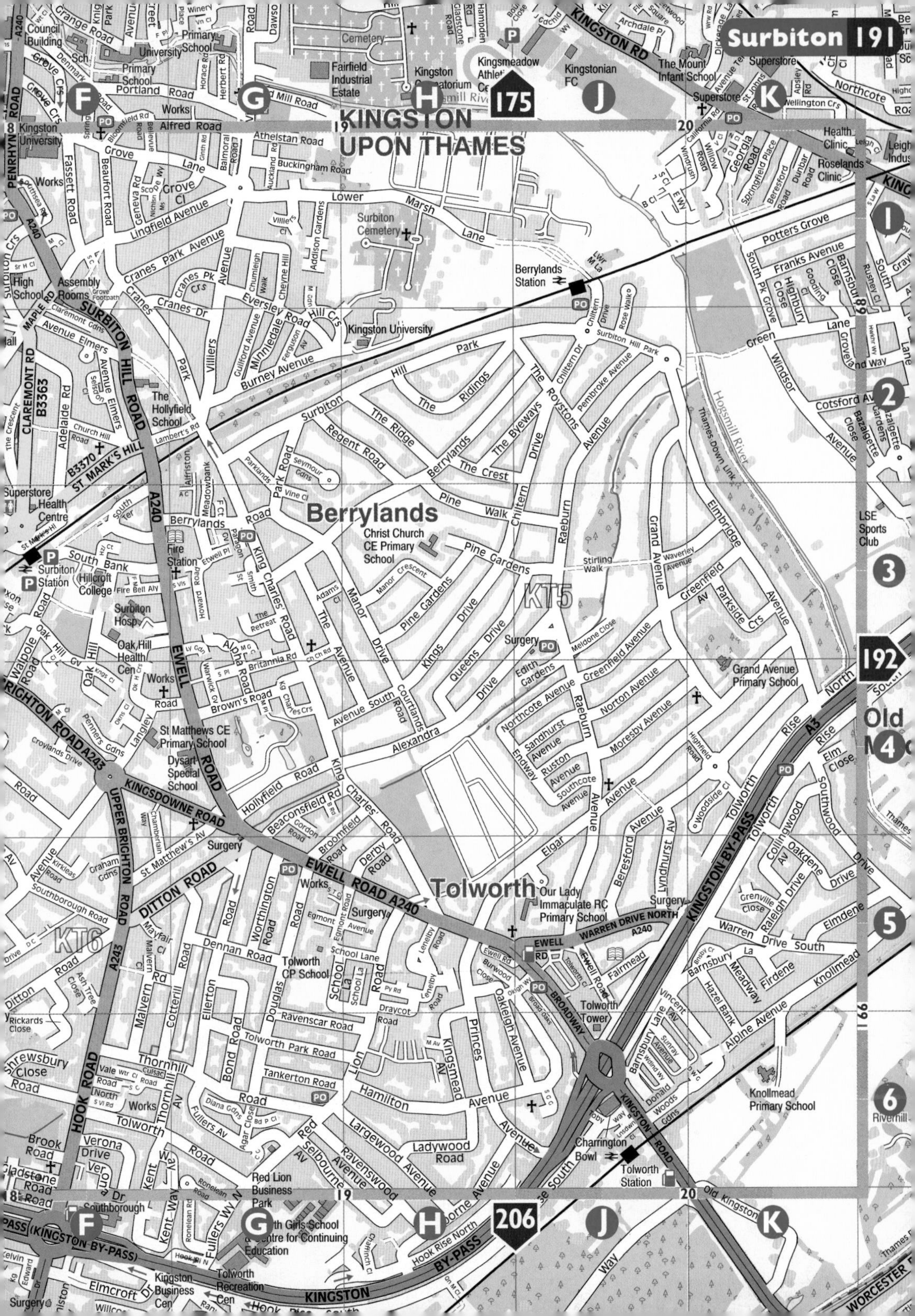
KINGSTON UPON THAMES
Berrylands
Tolworth
KT5
KT6
175
192
206
F
G
H
J
K
19
20
1
2
3
4
5
6
Surbiton Station
Berrylands Station
Tolworth Station
Kingston University
Surbiton Cemetery
Cemetery
Fairfield Industrial Estate
Kingston Crematorium
Kingstonian FC
The Mount Infant School
Superstore
Health Clinic
Roselands Clinic
LSE Sports Club
Hogsmill River
Thames Down Link
Christ Church CE Primary School
Grand Avenue Primary School
Our Lady Immaculate RC Primary School
St Matthews CE Primary School
Dysart Special School
The Hollyfield School
Hillcroft College
Surbiton Hosp
Oak Hill Health Cen
Fire Station
High School
Assembly Rooms
Council Building
Tolworth CP School
Tolworth Tower
Charrington Bowl
Knollmead Primary School
Red Lion Business Park
Tolworth Recreation Cen
Kingston Business Cen
Surgery
Works
KINGSTON RD
PENRHYN ROAD
SURBITON HILL ROAD
EWELL ROAD
EWELL ROAD A240
KINGSDOWNE ROAD
UPPER BRIGHTON ROAD
BRIGHTON ROAD A243
DITTON ROAD
HOOK ROAD
KINGSTON BY-PASS
WARREN DRIVE NORTH
BROADWAY
CLAREMONT RD B3363
ST MARK'S HILL
Alfred Road
Lower Marsh Lane
Cranes Park Avenue
Lingfield Avenue
Berrylands
King Charles' Road
Manor Drive
Pine Walk
Pine Gardens
Chiltern Drive
Raeburn Avenue
Grand Avenue
Elmbridge Avenue
Alexandra Drive
Hollyfield Road
Tolworth Rise
Hamilton Avenue
Ravenscar Road
Tolworth Park Road
Tankerton Road
Princes Avenue
Oakleigh Avenue
Largewood Avenue
Ladywood Road
Ravenswood Avenue
Alpine Avenue
Knollmead
Warren Drive South
Worthington Road
Douglas Road
Thornhill Road
Verona Drive
Southborough Road
Potters Grove
Franks Avenue
Windsor Avenue
Cotsford Av
Surbiton Hill Park
The Ridings
The Ridge
Regent Road
The Crest
The Byeways
The Roystons
Greenfield Avenue
Northcote Avenue
Norton Avenue
Moresby Avenue
Beresford Avenue
Lyndhurst Av
Elgar Avenue
Derby Road
Broomfield Road
Beaconsfield Rd
Dennan Road
Ellerton Road
Cotterill Road
Malvern Rd
Old Kingston Road
WORCESTER

192
176
191
207
New Malden
New Malden Stn
KINGSTON ROAD
HIGH STREET
BURLINGTON ROAD
BUSHEY ROAD
KINGSTON BY PASS
MALDEN WAY
A3
A2043
MALDEN ROAD
Motspur Park
Motspur Park Station
University of London Athletics Ground
Old Malden
Malden Manor Station
Malden Manor Junior School
CHURCH ROAD
CENTRAL ROAD
Worcester Park
Worcester Park Station
OLD MALDEN LANE
KT3
KT4
Raynes Park High School
Sacred Heart RC Primary School
Burlington Primary School
The Malden Centre
Holy Cross Convent School
The Study School
Beverley School
LSE Sports Club
Green Lane Primary School
Malden Parochial Primary School
Manor Drive Health Centre
Cuddington Cemetery
Cheam Common Infant School
Linden Bridge School
Riverhill
Merton
Sutton
A
B
C
D
E
1
2
3
4
5
6
521
22
1 grid square represents 500 metres

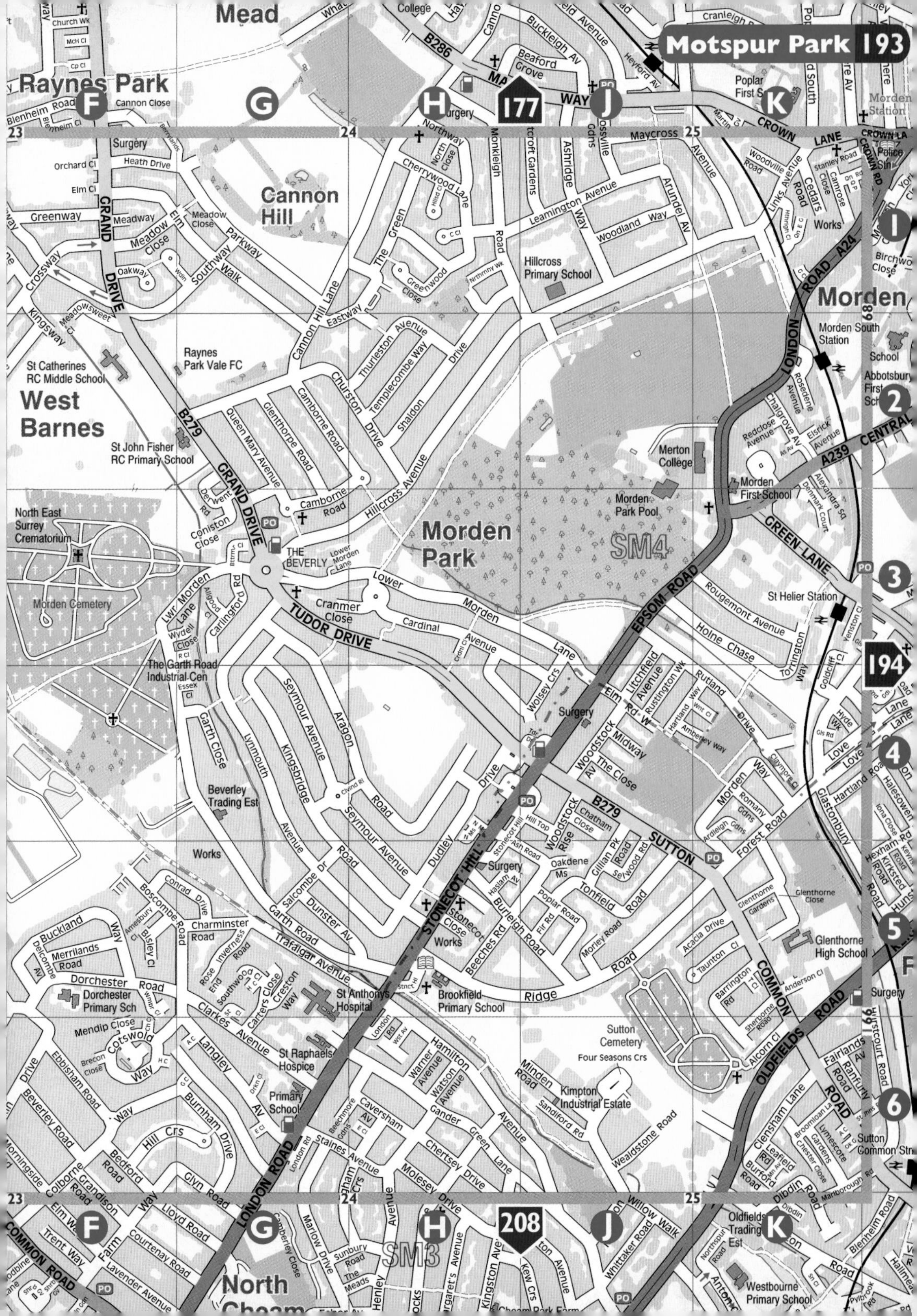

Motspur Park 193
177
194
208
Raynes Park
Mead
Cannon Hill
West Barnes
Morden
Morden Park
North Cheam
SM4
SM3
F
G
H
J
K
I
2
3
4
5
6
23
24
25
B286
B279
A24
A239
Blenheim Road
Cannon Close
Church Wk
Crossway
Kingsway
Meadowsweet Cl
Greenway
Meadway
Meadow Close
Elm Close
Oakway
Southway
Parkway
Walk
Grand Drive
Orchard Cl
Elm Cl
Heath Drive
Surgery
Raynes Park Vale FC
St Catherines RC Middle School
St John Fisher RC Primary School
Cannon Hill Lane
Eastway
Northway
North Close
Cherrywood Lane
The Green
Greenwood Close
Monkleigh Road
Leamington Avenue
Ashridge Way
Woodland Way
Arundel Av
Maycross Avenue
Crown Lane
Hillcross Primary School
Thurleston Avenue
Templecombe Way
Churston Drive
Shaldon
Camborne Road
Glenthorpe Road
Queen Mary Avenue
Hillcross Avenue
Drive
Derwent Rd
Coniston Close
North East Surrey Crematorium
Morden Cemetery
THE BEVERLY
Lower Morden Lane
Lwr Morden Lane
Carlingford Rd
Cranmer Close
Cardinal Avenue
Tudor Drive
Lower Morden Lane
Wydell Close
The Garth Road Industrial Cen
Essex Cl
Garth Close
Lynmouth Avenue
Kingsbridge
Seymour Avenue
Aragon Road
Beverley Trading Est
Works
Merton College
Morden Park Pool
Epsom Road
London Road
Morden South Station
Rosedene Avenue
Chalgrove Av
Redclose Avenue
Elsrick Avenue
Morden First School
Green Lane
Central
Alexandra Sq
Dennark Court
St Helier Station
Rougemont Avenue
Holne Chase
Tortington Way
Litchfield Avenue
Rustington Wk
Rutland Drive
Hartland Way
Amberley Way
Woodstock Av
Midway
The Close
Morden Way
Romany Gdns
Ardleigh Gdns
Forest Road
Glastonbury
Hartland Road
Love Lane
Halesowen
Hexham Rd
Kirksted Road
Wolsey Crs
Elm Rd W
Surgery
Stonecot Hill
Hill Top
Chatham Close
Woodstock Rise
Ash Road
Oakdene Ms
Gillian Pk Road
Selwood Rd
Tonfield Road
Poplar Road
Burleigh Road
Sutton
Common Road
Dudley Drive
Salcombe Dr
Dunster Av
Garth Road
Trafalgar Avenue
Stonecot Close
Beeches Rd
Morley Road
Acacia Drive
Taunton Cl
Barrington Rd
Sherborne Road
Anderson Cl
Glenthorne Gardens
Glenthorne Close
Glenthorne High School
Oldfields Road
Ridge Road
Brookfield Primary School
St Anthonys Hospital
St Raphaels Hospice
Sutton Cemetery
Four Seasons Crs
Kimpton Industrial Estate
Minden Road
Sandiford Rd
Weaidstone Road
Alcorn Cl
Conrad Drive
Boscombe Road
Buckland Way
Merrilands Road
Delcombe Av
Amesbury Cl
Bisley Cl
Charminster Road
Dorchester Road
Dorchester Primary Sch
Rose End
Inverness Road
Southwood
Carters Close
Creston Way
Clarkes Avenue
Mendip Close
Cotswold Way
Brecon Close
Langley Avenue
Ebbisham Road
Beverley Road
Burnham Drive
Hill Crs
Bedford Road
Glyn Road
Colborne Way
Grandison Road
Morningside Road
Lloyd Road
Courtenay Road
Lavender Avenue
Trent Way
Common Road
Farm Way
Primary School
Hamilton Avenue
Warner Avenue
Watson Avenue
Gander Green Lane
Caversham Av
Staines Avenue
Chertsey Drive
Molesey Drive
Marlow Drive
Sunbury Road
The Meads
Henley Avenue
Kingston Avenue
Kew Crs
Whittaker Road
Willow Walk
Clensham Lane
Leafield Road
Burford Road
Broomloan La
Lymescote Gardens
Chester Close
Dibdin Road
Marlborough Road
Hurstcourt Road
Fairlands Av
Ranfurly Road
Sutton Common Stn
Oldfields Trading Est
Westbourne Primary School
Northspur Road
Blenheim Road
Poplar First S
Heyford Av
Beaford Grove
Buckleigh Av
Woodville Road
Links Avenue
Cedars Road
Camrose Close
Stanley Road
Police Stn
Crown Rd
Works
Birchwood Close
School
Abbotsbury First School
Surgery
Goldcliff Cl
Hyde Wk
Yenston Cl

194
178
193
209
196
A
B
C
D
E
1
2
3
4
5
6
526
27
Morden
Morden Station
Morden Hall Medical Centre
Morden Hall Road
Aberconway Road
Crown La
Crown Rd
Police Stn
Morden Road
A239
Central Road
A24
Central Medical Centre
Morden South Station
Abbotsbury First School
School
Surgery
Phoenix College
Bishopsford Road
St Helier Avenue
A217
Reigate Avenue
Green Lane
Middleton Road
Malmesbury Middle School
Primary School
Garth Primary School
Watermeads High School
London Road
Mitcham Cricket Club
Cricket Green
Lower Gn W
Vestry Hall
Fire Stn
Melrose Special School
Primary Sch
Cranmer School
Cranmer
Madeira
Capital Business Cen
Connaught Business Centre
Abbey Industrial Est
The Willow Centre
Grace Business
Eagle Trading Estate
Wandle Trading Est
Mill Green Business
River Wandle
Wandle Way
Riverside Drive
Brookfields Av
Tramway Path
Mitcham Park
Works
Green Wrythe Primary School
Green Wrythe Lane
Tweeddale Junior School
Infant School
Sutton Arena
St Helier
St Helier Hospital
A&E
Rosehill
Rosehill Avenue
B2230
B278
Rose Hill
Wrythe Lane
Carshalton High School for Boys
Greenshaw High School
Muschamp Primary School
The Wrythe
Carshalton High School
Sutton Common Stn
Angel Hill
Benhilton
Nightingale
Arlington Drive
Buckhurst Avenue
Culvers Way
Connaught Road
Pr of Wales' Road
Westminster Road
Winchcombe Road
Middleton Road
Shaftesbury
Peterborough
Shrewsbury Road
Selby Green
Watermead La
Maynooth Gdns
Wates Way
Poulton Av
Gassiot Way
1 grid square represents 500 metres

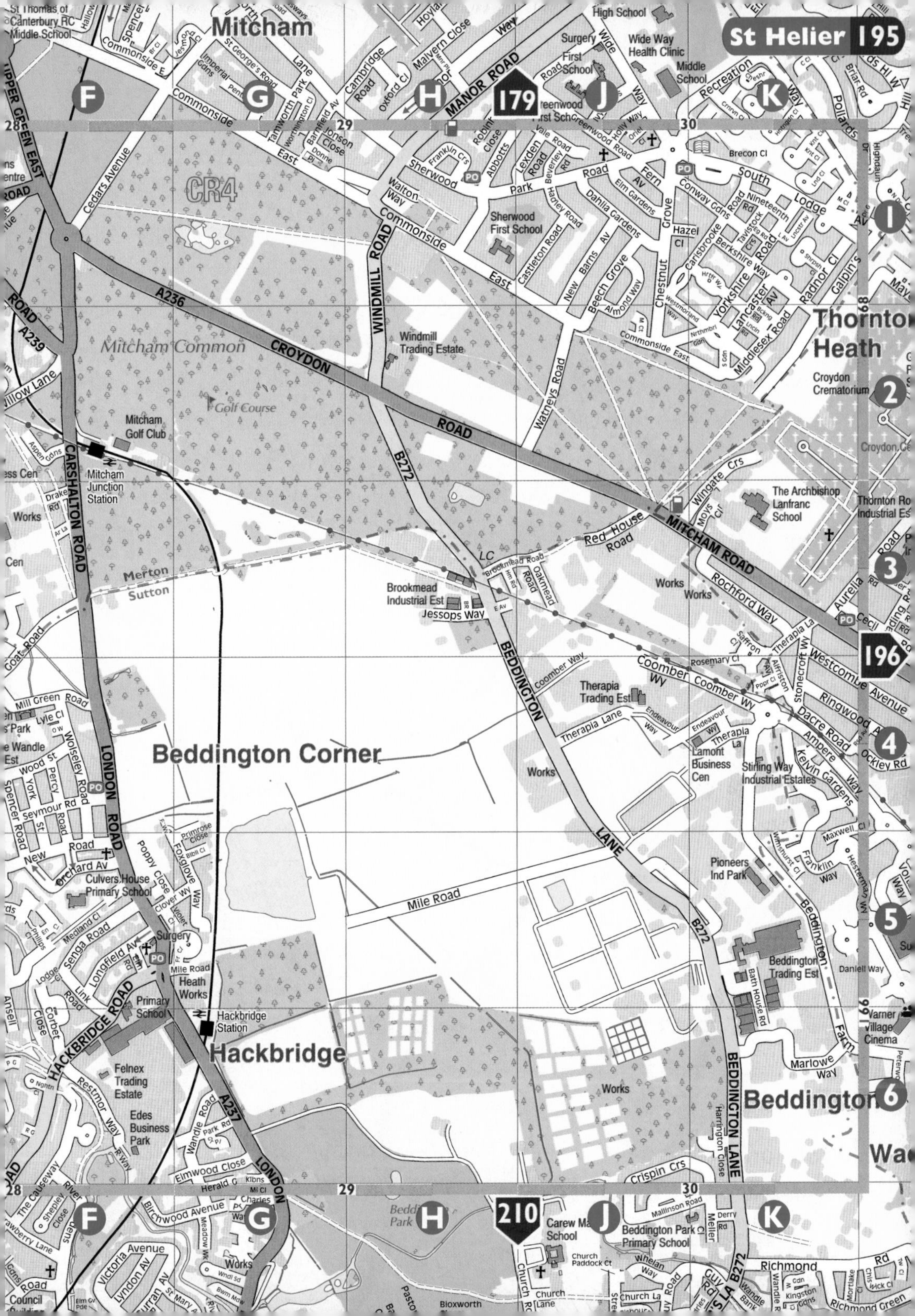
Mitcham
Beddington Corner
Hackbridge
Beddington
Thornton Heath
Mitcham Common
Golf Course
Mitcham Golf Club
Mitcham Junction Station
Hackbridge Station
CR4
A236
CROYDON ROAD
MITCHAM ROAD
WINDMILL ROAD
B272
BEDDINGTON LANE
LONDON ROAD
A237
CARSHALTON ROAD
HACKBRIDGE ROAD
A239
MANOR ROAD
Commonside East
Mile Road
Merton
Sutton
Windmill Trading Estate
Brookmead Industrial Est
Therapia Trading Est
Lamont Business Cen
Stirling Way Industrial Estates
Pioneers Ind Park
Beddington Trading Est
Felnex Trading Estate
Edes Business Park
Culvers House Primary School
Sherwood First School
The Archbishop Lanfranc School
Croydon Crematorium
Wide Way Health Clinic
Beddington Park Primary School
Carew Manor School
Varner Village Cinema
Thornton Road Industrial Est
Works
179
196
210
F
G
H
J
K
28
29
30
2
3
4
5
6

196
180
195
211
A
B
C
D
E
1
2
3
4
5
6
Thornton Heath
Selhurst
Broad Green
Wandle Park
Waddon
Thornton Heath Station
Thornton Heath Pools & Fitness Cen
Thornton Heath Health Centre
Parchmore Medical Centre
HIGH ST
B266
BRIGSTOCK ROAD
THORNTON ROAD
A23
A235
LONDON ROAD
A212
WHITEHORSE ROAD
NORTHCOTE ROAD
A222
WINDMILL ROAD
ST JAMES'S RD
WELLESLEY ROAD
PURLEY WAY
MITCHAM ROAD
A236
A213 SUMNER ROAD
ROMAN WAY
Croydon Cemetery
Queen's Rd Cemetery
Gonville Primary School
St Lukes School
Junior Girls School
Brigstock Medical Centre
Streatham & Croydon RFC
Ecclesbourne Primary School
Manor School
Croydon Mosque & Islamic Cen
Mayday University Hospital
North Croydon Medical Cen
London Road Medical Centre
Eversley Medical Cen
Thornton Road Industrial Est
Peall Road Industrial Est
West Thornton Primary School
Lombard Business Park
Council Building
Hampton Rd Ind Park
St James Medical Cen
St Marys High School
Croydon Hlth Authority
West Croydon Stn
Whitgift Shopping Centre
Whitgift Almshouses
Drummond Shopping Centre
St Marys RC Junior School
St Marys RC Infant School
East Croydon Station
Warehouse Thtr
Croydon Coll
Fairfield Halls
The Law Courts
Police Stn
Clocktower
Katharine St
Taberner House
Town Hall
Old Palace School
Mill Lane Trading Est
Superstore
Warner Village Cinema
Progress Business Park
Pilton Estate
Primary School
Works
Mosque
Safari
The BRIT School
CROY
1 grid square represents 500 metres

SE25
181
198
212
CR0
Woodside
Addiscombe
Shirley
Monks Orchard
South Norwood Country Park
South Norwood Medical Cen
Crystal Palace FC Wimbledon FC (Selhurst Park)
Priory Special School
Norwood Junction Stn
South Norwood Primary School
Heavers Farm Primary School
St Chads RC Primary School
Selhurst Station
Follys End Christian High School
Pools & Fitness Centre
Health Cen Portland Medical Cen
Ryelands Primary School
Croydon Sports Arena
Croydon FC
Croydon Road Industrial Est
Tollgate Primary School
Ashburton Primary School
Ashburton High School
Council Building
Davidson J&I School
Junior School
Shirley Park Golf Club
Trinity School
Shirley Clinic
Peabody Close
Addiscombe Cricket Club
Golf Course
High School
Bank Twr Industrial Est
SELHURST ROAD
WHITEHORSE LANE
HIGH STREET A213
PORTLAND ROAD
WOODSIDE GREEN
SPRING LANE
LONG LANE
SHIRLEY ROAD
LOWER ADDISCOMBE ROAD
MORLAND ROAD
ADDISCOMBE ROAD
CHEPSTOW ROAD
WICKHAM
A215
A213
A222
A232
B243
F
G
H
J
K
33
34
35
1
2
3
4
5
6

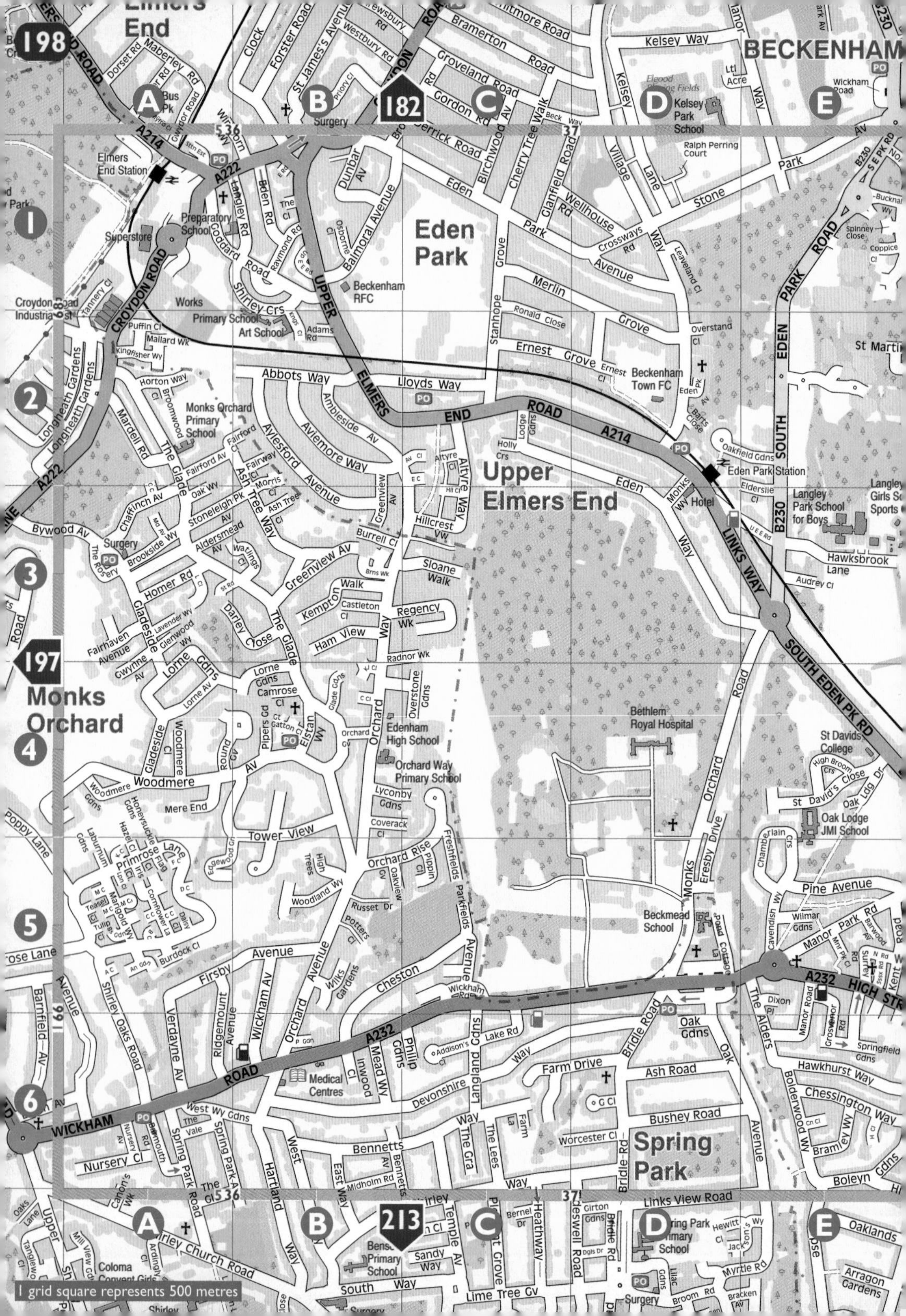

1 grid square represents 500 metres

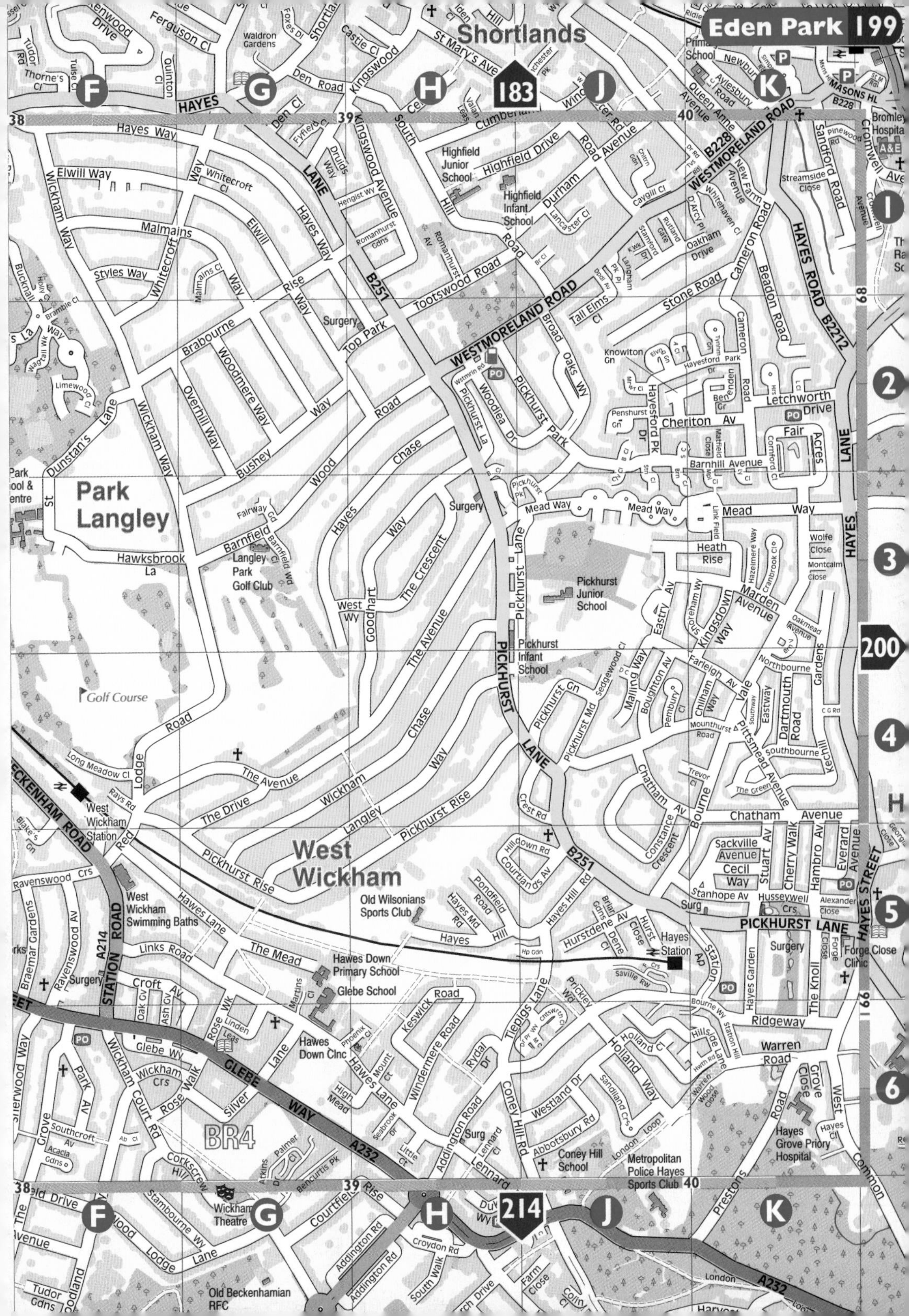

Shortlands
183
Park Langley
West Wickham
BR4
200
214
F
G
H
J
K
38
39
40
66
68
1
2
3
4
5
6
Hayes Way
Elwill Way
Wickham Way
Malmains Way
Styles Way
Whitecroft Way
Brabourne Rise
Woodmere Way
Overhill Way
Bushey Way
Hayes Lane
Kingswood Avenue
Den Road
Den Cl
Ferguson Cl
Quinton Cl
Tulse Cl
Thorne's Cl
Tudor Rd
Waldron Gardens
Foxes Dl
Shortlands
Castle Cl
St Mary's Ave
Cumberland Road
Winchester Rd
Highfield Drive
Highfield Junior School
Highfield Infant School
Durham Road
Lancaster Cl
Tootswood Road
Westmoreland Road
Romanhurst Av
Romanhurst Gdns
Hengist Wy
Druids Way
Fyfield Cl
Queen Anne Avenue
Aylesbury Road
Newbury Rd
Primary School
Masons Hl
Bromley Hospital
A&E
Cromwell Ave
Sandford Road
Streamside Close
Pinewood Rd
Hayes Road B2212
New Farm Avenue
Whitehaven Cl
D'Arcy Pl
Oakham Drive
Cameron Road
Beadon Road
Stone Road
Tall Elms Cl
Rutland Gate
Stamford Dr
Langham
Caygill Cl
Broad Oaks Wy
Knowlton Gn
Hayesford Park Dr
Penshurst Gn
Cheriton Av
Letchworth Drive
Fair Acres
Cornford Cl
Matfield Close
Barnhill Avenue
Mead Way
Link Field
Heath Rise
Wolfe Close
Montcalm Close
Hazelmere Way
Cranbrook Cl
Marden Avenue
Oakmead Avenue
Northbourne
Gardens
Hayes Lane
Kingsdown Way
Eastry Av
Pickhurst Junior School
Pickhurst Infant School
Pickhurst Lane
Pickhurst Park
Pickhurst Pk
Pickhurst La
Woodlea Dr
Wstmrln Rd
PO
Surgery
Top Park
Wood Road
Hayes Chase
Hayes Way
The Crescent
West Wy
Goodhart Way
The Avenue
Fairway
Barnfield
Barnfield Wd
Langley Park Golf Club
Hawksbrook La
Dunstan's Lane
Golf Course
Lodge Road
Long Meadow Cl
Rays Rd
West Wickham Station
Beckenham Road
Blake's Gn
The Drive
Wickham Chase
Langley Way
Pickhurst Rise
Pickhurst Gn
Pickhurst Mead
Sedgewood Cl
Malling Way
Boughton Av
Pembury Cl
Chilham Way
Farleigh Av
Vale
Eastway
Dartmouth Road
Mounthurst Road
Pittsmead Avenue
Southbourne
Kechill
The Green
Trevor Cl
Chatham Av
Chatham Avenue
Bourne
Constance Crescent
Crest Rd
Hilldown Rd
Courtlands Av
B251
Hayes Hill Rd
Sackville Avenue
Stuart Av
Cherry Walk
Hambro Av
Everard Avenue
Cecil Way
Stanhope Av
Husseywell Crs
Alexander Close
Hayes Street
Pickhurst Lane
Forge Close
Forge Clinic
Hurst Close
Hurstdene Av
Dene Close
Briar Gdns
Hayes Station
Station Ap
Saville Rw
Hayes Garden
The Knoll
Ridgeway
Warren Road
Grove Close
West Common
Hayes Cl
Hayes Grove Priory Hospital
Prestons Road
Warren Wood Close
Hillside Lane
Station Hill
Bourne Wy
Old Wilsonians Sports Club
Pondfield Road
Hayes Md Rd
Hayes Hill
Hayes Lane
The Mead
Links Road
Hawes Down Primary School
Glebe School
Martins Cl
Hawes Down Clnc
Hawes Lane
Keswick Road
Windermere Road
Rydal Dr
Tiepigs Lane
Prickley Wd
Holland Cl
Holland Way
Sandiland Crs
Westland Dr
Abbotsbury Rd
Coney Hill Rd
Coney Hill School
London Loop
Metropolitan Police Hayes Sports Club
Lennard Rd
Addington Road
Surg
High Mead
Seabrook Dr
Little Ct
Phoenix Cl
Mount Ct
West Wickham Swimming Baths
Station Road A214
Ravenswood Crs
Ravenswood Av
Braemar Gardens
Croft Av
Oak Gv
Ash Gv
Glebe Wy
Glebe Way A232
Rose Wk
Rose Walk
Linden Leas
Silver Lane
Wickham Crs
Wickham Court Rd
Sherwood Way
Park Av
Grove
Southcroft Av
Acacia Gdns
Corkscrew Hill
Atkins Dr
Palmer Cl
Bencurtis Pk
Courtfield Rise
Stambourne Wy
Wickham Theatre
Lodge Lane
Addington Rd
Croydon Rd
South Walk
Farm Close
Old Beckenhamian RFC
Tudor Gdns
A232
London

200
184
199
215
Bromley South Station
Superstore
Palace View
Works
Bickley Park Prep School
Bickley Station
Waldo Industrial Est
Siward Road
Godwin Road
Langdon Rd
Glanville Road
MASONS HL
B228
B265
Bromley Hospital
A&E
Tennis Club
MASONS HILL
HOMESDALE ROAD
Cromwell Avenue
Sandford Road
Wendover Road
Woldham Road
Havelock Road
Great Elms Road
Jaffray Road
Raglan Primary School
Southlands Road
Cowper Road
Bourne Road
Haywood Road
Elliott Road
Fashoda Rd
Vincent Close
Fletchers Close
The Ravensbourne School
HAYES LANE
A21
The Avenue
Rushmore Cl
Clarence Road
Southborough Road
Hawthorne Road
Hawthorne Close
Oldfield Road
Tangleberry Close
Park Hill
Parkside Av
Tredwell Close
Blenheim Road
Claremont Road
Burford Road
Waldegrave Road
Mayfield Road
Woodside Road
Sunningdale Rd
Highfield Road
Springfield Gardens
Southwood Close
Fairmead
Homemead
Brookmead
Cloisters Avenue
Ringmer Way
Birdham Close
Cowper Close
Whitehall Road
Brooklyn Road
Union Road
Herbert Road
Balfour Road
Albert Road
Victoria Road
Salisbury Road
Mosslea Road
Chatterton Rd
Addison Road
Bloomfield Road
Chantry Lane
Walpole Rd
Pope Road
Johnson Rd
Waverley Close
Crown Lane
Crown Lane Spur
Newton Terrace
Surgery
PO
BROMLEY COMMON
Hook Farm Road
Old Bromlians Cricket Club
Bromley FC
Norman Park
Norman Park Athletics Track
Rookery Lane
Bromley College of Further & Higher Education
Bromley Common
Lavender Close
Turpington Lane
Green Way
Sunray Avenue
Mons Wy
Manor Way
Narrow Way
Mosul Way
Rayfield Close
Turpington Close
Link Way
Magpie Hall Lane
Cemetery
Golf Course
Bromley Golf Club
Austin Av
Southborough Lane
Holmcroft Way
Holbrook Way
Parkfield Way
Willow Close
Stiles Cl
South
Oakley House
HAYES LANE
HAYES ROAD B2212
Hayes
George Lane
Georgian Close
Hayes Wood Avenue
Glebe House Drive
Hayes Primary School
HAYES STREET
Forge Close
Clinic
Everard Avenue
Hambro Av
Burwood Avenue
Hayes School
Baston School
Redgate Drive
Park House RFC
Barnet Wood Road
BR2
Church Lane
Prince's Plain
Brewery Road
Cottage Av
Lower Gravel Road
Trinity Close
Jackson Road
Daerwood Cl
Lennard Road
Randolph Road
Bradford Close
Copthorne Avenue
Weald Close
Cherry Orchard Road
Knowle Road
Barnet Drive
Cross Road
Doves Cl
Beverley Road
Gravel Road
OAKLEY ROAD
HASTINGS ROAD
Keston Mark
Ravens Wood School
Oakley Drive
Cedar Close
Cedar Crescent
Lakeside Drive
Rowan Walk
Hollydale Drive
The Drift
Five Elms Road
BASTON ROAD
Common
A233
541
42
68
66
A
B
C
D
E
1
2
3
4
5
6
1 grid square represents 500 metres

185
202
216
A208
A232
Petts Wood
Crofton
Locksbottom
Jubilee Country Park
Bromley High School
St James RC Primary School
Southborough Primary School
Petts Wood Station
Orpington Station
Newstead Wood School for Girls
Darrick Wood Swimming Pool
London Loop
Southborough Lane
Franks Wood Avenue
Lakeswood Road
Woodhurst Av
Nightingale Rd
Queensway
Chesham Avenue
Oxhawth Crescent
Faringdon Av
Prescott Avenue
Rolleston Avenue
Hollingworth Road
Laburnum Way
Larch Way
Almond Way
Whitebeam Avenue
Ash Row
Birch Row
Hazel Walk
Lovelace Avenue
Thorn Cl
Felton Close
Diameter Rd
Crescent Drive
Shepperton Road
Transmere Road
Kenilworth Road
Rycroft Rd
Jersey Dr
Towncourt Lane
Kydbrook Cl
Eynsford Cl
Rolleston Close
Fairoak Close
Ember Close
Woodland Way
Great Thrift
Little Thrift
Silverdale Road
Manor Way
Hazelmere Road
Towncourt Crescent
Crossway
Birchwood Road
Wood Ride
Kingsway
Petts Wood Road
Greencourt Road
Princes Avenue
Willett Way
Ladywood Avenue
The Chenies
Grosvenor Road
Sutherland Close
West Way
Maple Close
Acacia Close
Hawthorn Close
Ash Cl
Fairway
Tudor Way
Priory Avenue
St Georges Rd
St John's Road
Beaumont Road
Eastbury Road
Fieldway
Fairfield Road
Homesdale Road
Buckingham Close
The Covert
Crofton Lane
Lynwood Grove
Dale Wood Road
Derwent Drive
Greenfield Gardens
Broadcroft Road
Heath Side
Branston Crs
Kennedy Close
Honeybourne Way
Sparrow Drive
Beckford Drive
Place Farm Av
Tandridge Drive
Allington Road
Andover Road
Cathcart Drive
Oregon Square
Yeovil Close
York Rise
Kelvin Parade
Abbots Close
Monks Way
St Thomas' Drive
Romany Rise
Gumping Road
Clareville Road
Lansdowne Avenue
Drayton Av
Rose Dale
Lime Grove
Wistaria Close
Poplar Avenue
Fairbank Av
Jasmine Close
St Anthony's Court
Bramley Close
Wyndham Close
Ormond Av
Morley Cl
Birch Mead
Wood Way
Hazel Grove
Sunnydale
Larch Dene
Mere Cl
Munnery Way
Burlington Close
Mereside
Nuthfield Way
Crofton Road A232
Glen
Meadow Way
Grasmere Gardens
Starts Close
Red Oak Close
Mada Road
Percival Road
Pondfield Road
Lovibonds
Highwood Dr
Highwood Cl
Oakwood Road
Oakwood Gardens
Crofton Avenue
Grange Road
Foxfield Road
Broughton Road
Torver Way
Darrick Wood Road
Pound Court Drive
The Ridge
Hilltop Gardens
Newstead Avenue
Willersley Avenue
Ruskin Drive
Reed Avenue
Tile Farm Road
Tubbenden Lane
Woodhead Drive
Sherlies Av
Thorpe Close
Telscombe Close
Orchard Green
Hillview Crescent
Surgery
Hall
Chislehurst Road
Blackbrook Lane
Northumberland Gardens
Thornwood Road
Golf Road
Otford Close
Barfield
Marlings Park Av
Marlings Close
Scotsdale Close
Sefton Close
Sefton Road
Melbourne Close
Westholme
Mayfield
Bancroft Gardens
Bicknor Road
Denver Cl
Stables End
Masefield View
Partridge Drive
Normar Close
F G H J K
1 2 3 4 5 6
43 44 45

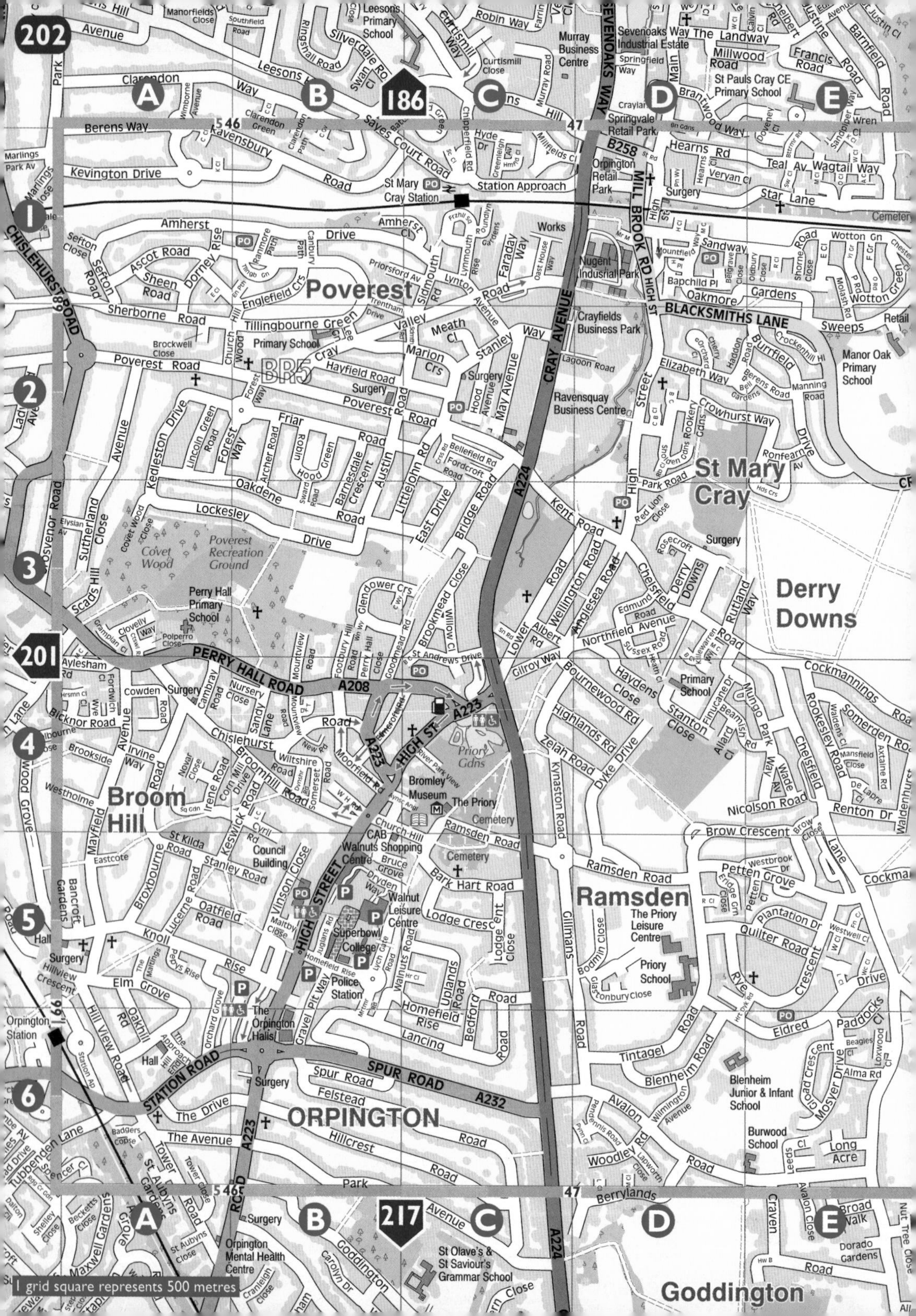
202
186
201
217
A
B
C
D
E
1
2
3
4
5
6
546
47
1 grid square represents 500 metres
Poverest
BR5
St Mary Cray
Derry Downs
Broom Hill
Ramsden
ORPINGTON
Goddington
Leesons Primary School
Manorfields Close
Southfield Road
Avenue
Park
Clarendon Way
Leesons Hill
Ringshall Road
Silverdale Rd
Swan Rd
Curtismill Way
Curtismill Close
Robin Way
Murray Business Centre
Murray Road
SEVENOAKS WAY
Sevenoaks Way Industrial Estate
The Landway
Springfield Way
Main Rd
Millwood Road
Francis Road
Barnfield Road
St Pauls Cray CE Primary School
Brantwood Way
Berens Way
Ravensbury Road
Clarendon Green
Clarendon Path
Sayes Court Road
Chipperfield Rd
Hyde Dr
Millfields Cl
Springvale Retail Park
B258
Hearns Rd
Wren Cl
Teal Av
Wagtail Way
Marlings Park Av
Marlings Close
Kevington Drive
St Mary Cray Station
Station Approach
Orpington Retail Park
MILL BROOK RD
Surgery
Veryan Cl
Star Lane
Cemetery
CHISLEHURST ROAD
A208
Amherst Drive
Amherst Cl
Sefton Close
Sefton Road
Ascot Road
Sheen Road
Dorney Rise
Ranmore Path
Canbury Path
Lynmouth Rise
Sidmouth Rd
Faraday Way
Works
Oast House Way
Nugent Indusrial Park
HIGH ST
Sandway
Mountfield Way
Bapchild Pl
Oakmore Gardens
Wotton Gn
Wotton Green
Shorne Close
Priorsford Av
Lynton Avenue
Englefield Crs
Sherborne Road
Tillingbourne Green
Trentham Drive
Valley Road
Meath Cl
Stanley Way
CRAY AVENUE
Crayfields Business Park
BLACKSMITHS LANE
Sweeps
Retail
Brockwell Close
Primary School
Church Hill
Wood Way
Cray
Marion Crs
Lagoon Road
Elizabeth Way
Orchard Gro
Burrfield
Crockenhill
Manor Oak Primary School
Poverest Road
Hayfield Road
Hood Avenue
May Avenue
Ravensquay Business Centre
Berens Road
Manning Road
Kedleston Drive
Lincoln Green Road
Forest Way
Friar Road
Robin Hood Green
Archer Road
Littlejohn Rd
Bellefield Rd
Fordcroft Road
Crowhurst Way
Rookery Gdns
Ronfearn Av
Drive
Barnesdale Crescent
Austin Road
East Drive
Bridge Road
A224
Park Road
High Street
Oakdene Road
Lockesley Drive
Grosvenor Road
Sutherland Close
Elysian Av
Covet Wood Close
Covet Wood
Poverest Recreation Ground
Kent Road
Red Lion Close
Rosecroft Cl
Derry Downs
Chelsfield Road
Rutland Way
Scads Hill
Perry Hall Primary School
Glendower Crs
Brookmead Close
Willow Cl
Wellington Road
Anglesea Road
Edmund Road
Northfield Avenue
Clovelly Way
Grampian Cl
Polperro Close
PERRY HALL ROAD
Mountview Road
Footbury Hill Road
Perry Hall Close
Goodmead Rd
St Andrews Drive
Lower Rd
Albert Rd
Gilroy Way
Sussex Road
Heath Cl
Primary School
Cockmannings Road
Aylesham
Fordwich Cl
Wye Cl
Cowden Road
Cambray Road
Nursery Close
Sandy Lane
Bournewood Rd
Haydens Close
Finucane Dr
Mungo Park Way
Rookesley Road
Somerden Road
Bicknor Road
Chislehurst Road
Elmcroft Rd
A223
HIGH ST
Highlands Rd
Stanton Close
Beamish Rd
Allard Cl
Mansfield Close
Axtaine Rd
Brookside
Irvine Way
Novar Close
Irene Road
Corn Mill Drive
Broomhill Road
Wiltshire Road
New Rd
Moorfield Rd
River Park View
Priory Gdns
Zelah Road
Dyke Drive
Wade Av
Chelsfield Lane
De Lapre Cl
Westholme
Keswick Road
Somerset Road
Bromley Museum
The Priory
Cemetery
Kynaston Road
Nicolson Road
Renton Dr
Waldenhurst
Mayfield
Cyril Rd
Church Hill
Ramsden Road
Brow Crescent
Brow Close
Wood Grove
St Kilda Road
Stanley Road
Council Building
CAB
Walnuts Shopping Centre
Bruce Grove
Dryden Way
Cockmannings
Westbrook Dr
Petten Grove
Petten Cl
Broxbourne Road
Eastcote
Bancroft Gardens
Lucerne Road
Oatfield Road
Vinson Close
Bark Hart Road
Walnut Leisure Centre
Lodge Crescent
Lodge Close
Gillmans Road
The Priory Leisure Centre
Plantation Dr
Quilter Road
Westwell Cl
Hall
Surgery
Knoll Rise
Maltby Close
HIGH STREET
Superbowl
College
Bodmin Close
Priory School
Crescent
Hillview Crescent
Pepys Rise
The Maltings
Homefield Rise
Lych Gate Road
Walnuts Road
Elm Grove
Oakhill Rd
Police Station
Uplands Road
Bedford Road
Glastonbury Close
Rye
Drive
Orpington Station
Hill View Road
Orchard Grove
The Orpington Halls
Gravel Pit Way
Homefield Rise
Eldred
Paddocks Cl
Beagles Cl
Lancing Road
Tintagel Road
Blenheim Road
Blenheim Junior & Infant School
Alma Rd
Mosyer Drive
Gladwood Crescent
Station Ap
The Approach
STATION ROAD
SPUR ROAD
Spur Road
A232
Felstead Road
Avalon Road
Wilmington Avenue
Pendennis Road
Burwood School
Long Acre
Leeds Cl
Woodley Rd
Lapworth Close
The Drive
The Avenue
Badgers Copse
Tubbenden Lane
Spencer Cl
Tower Road
Tower Close
Hillcrest Road
Park Avenue
Berrylands
Broad Walk
Craven Road
Avalon Close
Nut Tree Close
St Aubyns Gardens
ROAD
Surgery
Orpington Mental Health Centre
Goddington Lane
Carolyn Dr
St Olave's & St Saviour's Grammar School
Dorado Gardens
Road
Maxwell Gardens
Beckets Close
Shelley Close
Dalton Cl
St Aubyns Close
Cranleigh Close
Close

187
F
G
H
J
K
48
49
50
Star Lane
Sheepcote Lane
Bourne Wood
Sheepcote Farm
Shawcroft School
Kevingtown
CROCKENHILL ROAD
B258
Waldens Road
Crouch Farm
Bromley
Kent
CRAY ROAD B258
MAIN RD
Bransell Close
Crockenhill Primary School
GREEN COURT
Stones Cross
Tylers Green Road
Darns Hill
Old Chapel Road
Tudor Court
Church Road
Harvest Way
Woodmount
East Hall Road
Lane
Lone Barn
Gorse Road
Daltons Road
Crown Wood
Skeet Hill Lane
Kibbs Lane
Lynden
Laburnum
Avenue
Cherry Ave
Furness
Swanley
1
2
3
4
5
6
66
67
68
PO

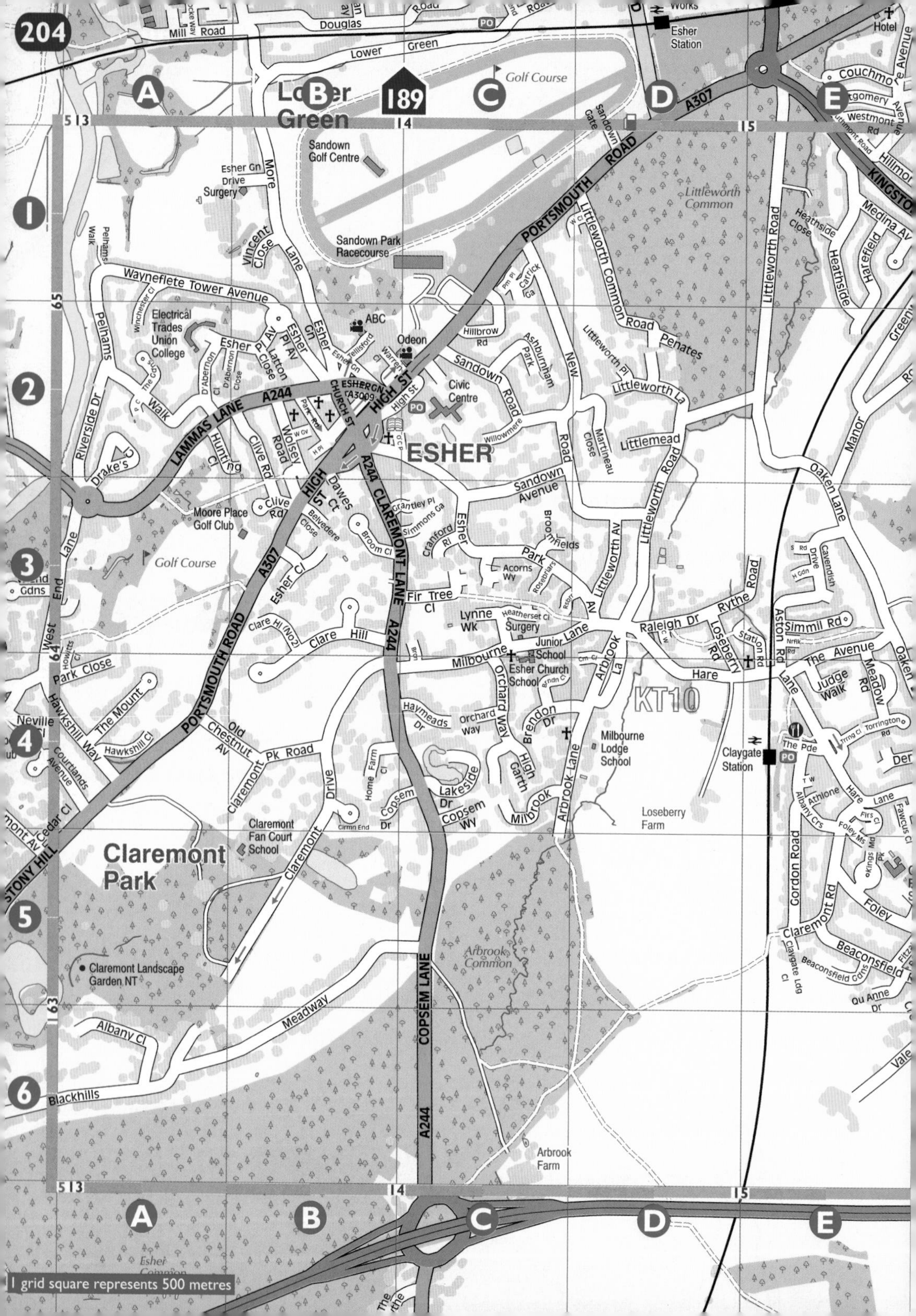
189
A
B
C
D
E
1
2
3
4
5
6
513
14
15
65
64
63
Lower Green
Esher Station
Golf Course
Sandown Golf Centre
Sandown Park Racecourse
Littleworth Common
ESHER
Civic Centre
Odeon
ABC
Electrical Trades Union College
Moore Place Golf Club
Golf Course
Esher Church School
Junior School
Surgery
Milbourne Lodge School
KT10
Claygate Station
Loseberry Farm
Claremont Fan Court School
Claremont Park
Claremont Landscape Garden NT
Arbrook Common
Arbrook Farm
Esher Common
PORTSMOUTH ROAD
A307
A244
HIGH ST
LAMMAS LANE
CLAREMONT LANE
COPSEM LANE
STONY HILL
Wayneflete Tower Avenue
Littleworth Common Road
Littleworth Road
Littleworth Av
Sandown Avenue
Sandown Road
Esher Park Av
Milbourne Lane
Hare Lane
Raleigh Dr
Rythe Road
Loseberry Rd
Station Rd
Aston Rd
Oaken Lane
The Avenue
Claremont Drive
Claremont Pk Road
Meadway
Blackhills
Albany Cl
Arbrook Lane
West End Lane
Pelhams Walk
Riverside Dr
More Lane
Clare Hill
Fir Tree Cl
Orchard Way
Brendon Dr
Lakeside Dr
Copsem Wy
Gordon Road
Claremont Rd
Beaconsfield Rd
Hare Lane
Park Close
Hawkshill Way
The Mount
Old Chestnut Av
1 grid square represents 500 metres

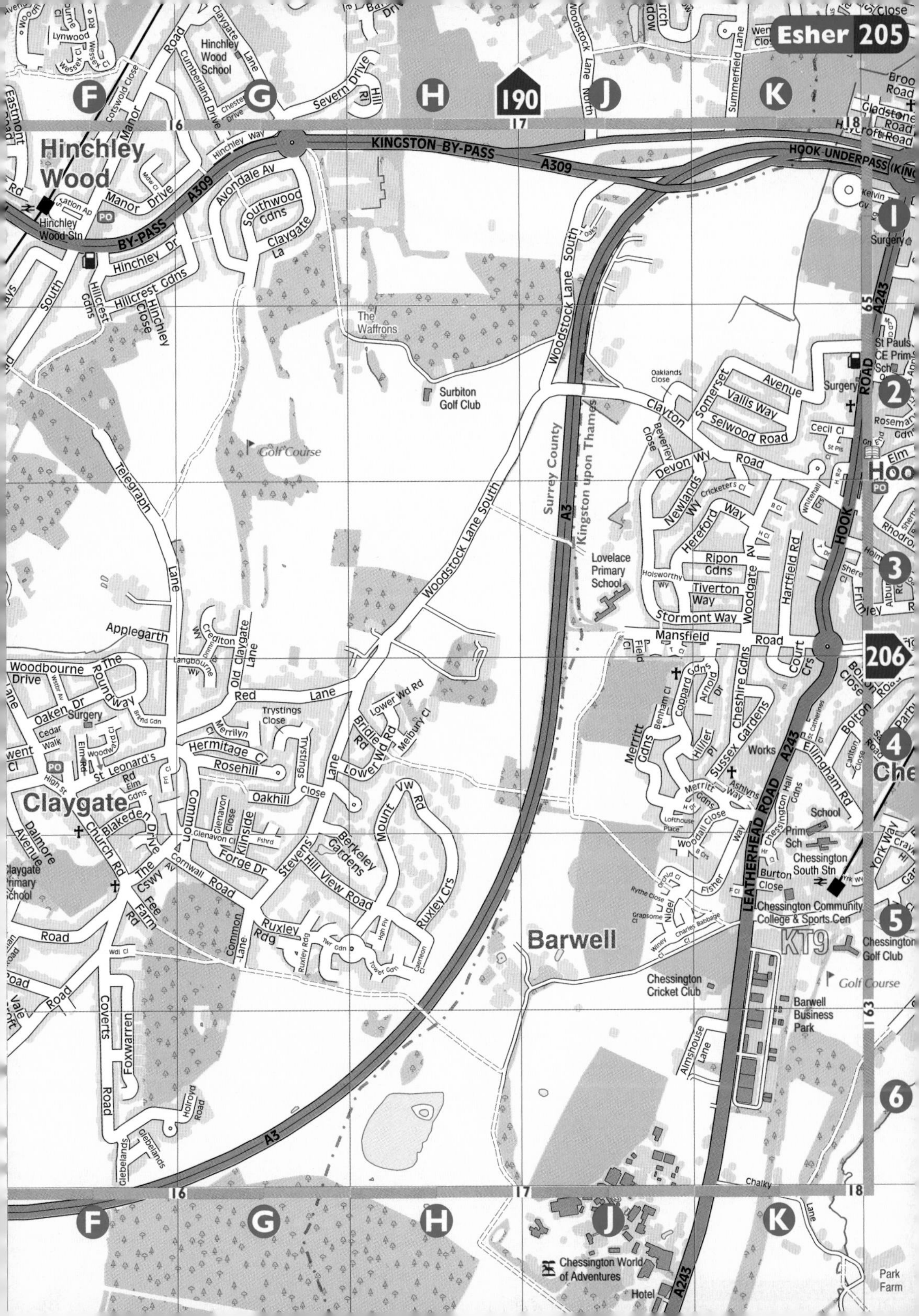

Hinchley Wood
Hinchley Wood Stn
Hinchley Wood School
Lynwood
Wessex Cl
Eastmont Road
Cotswold Close
Manor Road
Cumberland Drive
Chester Drive
Claygate Lane
Severn Drive
Hill Rd
Woodstock Lane North
Summerfield Lane
190
F
G
H
J
K
16
17
18
KINGSTON BY-PASS
A309
HOOK UNDERPASS
Brook Road
Gladstone Road
Haycroft Road
Hinchley Way
Station Ap
PO
Manor Drive
Avondale Av
Southwood Gdns
Claygate La
BY-PASS
Hinchley Dr
Hillcrest Gdns
Hinchley Close
Hillcrest Gdns
South
Kelvin Gv
Surgery
A243
The Waffrons
Woodstock Lane South
Surbiton Golf Club
Golf Course
Telegraph Lane
Oaklands Close
Somerset Avenue
Vallis Way
Selwood Road
Clayton Road
Beverley Close
Devon Wy
Cecil Cl
St Pauls CE Prim Sch
Surgery
ROAD
HOOK
Hoo
Surrey County
Kingston upon Thames
A3
Newlands Wy
Cricketers Cl
Hereford Way
Hartfield Rd
Lovelace Primary School
Ripon Gdns
Tiverton Way
Holsworthy Wy
Woodgate Av
Stormont Way
Mansfield Road
Court Crs
206
Applegarth
Crediton Wy
Old Claygate Lane
Langbourne Wy
Woodbourne Drive
The Roundway
Oaken Dr
Surgery
Cedar Walk
Red Lane
Trystings Close
Lower Wd Rd
Bridle Rd
Melbury Cl
Merrilyn Cl
Hermitage Cl
Rosehill
St Leonard's Rd
Elm Rd
Woodward Cl
High St
Claygate
Blakeden Drive
Common Lane
Trystings Close
Oakhill
Glenavon Close
Kinlside
Forge Dr
Stevens Lane
Berkeley Gardens
Mount Vw Rd
Hill View Road
Ruxley Crs
Cornwall Road
Church Rd
The Cswy
Fee Farm Rd
Dalmore Avenue
Claygate Primary School
Ruxley Rdg
Common Lane
Road
Wdl Cl
Coverts Road
Foxwarren
Holroyd Road
Glebelands
Merritt Gdns
Benham Cl
Coppard Gdns
Arnold Dr
Cheshire Gdns
Cheshire Gardens
Hillier Pl
Sussex Gardens
Works
Ashlyns Way
Lofthouse Place
Woodall Close
Fisher Way
LEATHERHEAD ROAD
Chessington Hall Gdns
Bolton Close
Bolton Road
Ellingham Rd
Carlton Close
4
Che
School
Prim Sch
Chessington South Stn
York Way
Burton Close
Chessington Community College & Sports Cen
Rythe Close
Grapsome Cl
Nigel
Charles Babbage
Barwell
KT9
Chessington Golf Club
Golf Course
Chessington Cricket Club
Barwell Business Park
Almshouse Lane
63
65
1
2
3
5
6
Chalky Lane
Chessington World of Adventures
Hotel
Park Farm

Hook
Chessington
191
205
KT19
Tolworth Station
Chessington North Stn
Chessington South Stn
Kingston By-Pass
Hook Underpass (Kingston By-Pass)
Hook Road
A243
Hook Rise South
Hook Rise North
Old Kingston Road
Kingston Road
Jubilee Way
Cox Lane
Moor Lane
Bridge Road
Chessington Road
B284 Ruxley Lane
B284
Green Lane
Horton Lane
Long Grove
Thames Down Link
Red Lion Business Park
Tolworth Girls School & Centre for Continuing Education
Tolworth Recreation Cen
Kingston Business Cen
Hook Rise South Industrial Park
Corinthian Casuals FC
Knollmead Primary School
St Pauls CE Prim Sch
Gosbury Hill Health Cen
Buckland Infant School
Moor Lane Junior School
St Marys CE Primary School
Epsom & Ewell High School
Danetree School
Horton Park Golf & Country Club
Horton Country Park
Horton Park Farm
Chessington Golf Club
Golf Course
Cemetery
St Ebba's Hospital
Kingston upon Thames
Surrey County
Southborough Sch
Surgery
Works
Poplar Farm Close
Gainsborough Road
1 grid square represents 500 metres

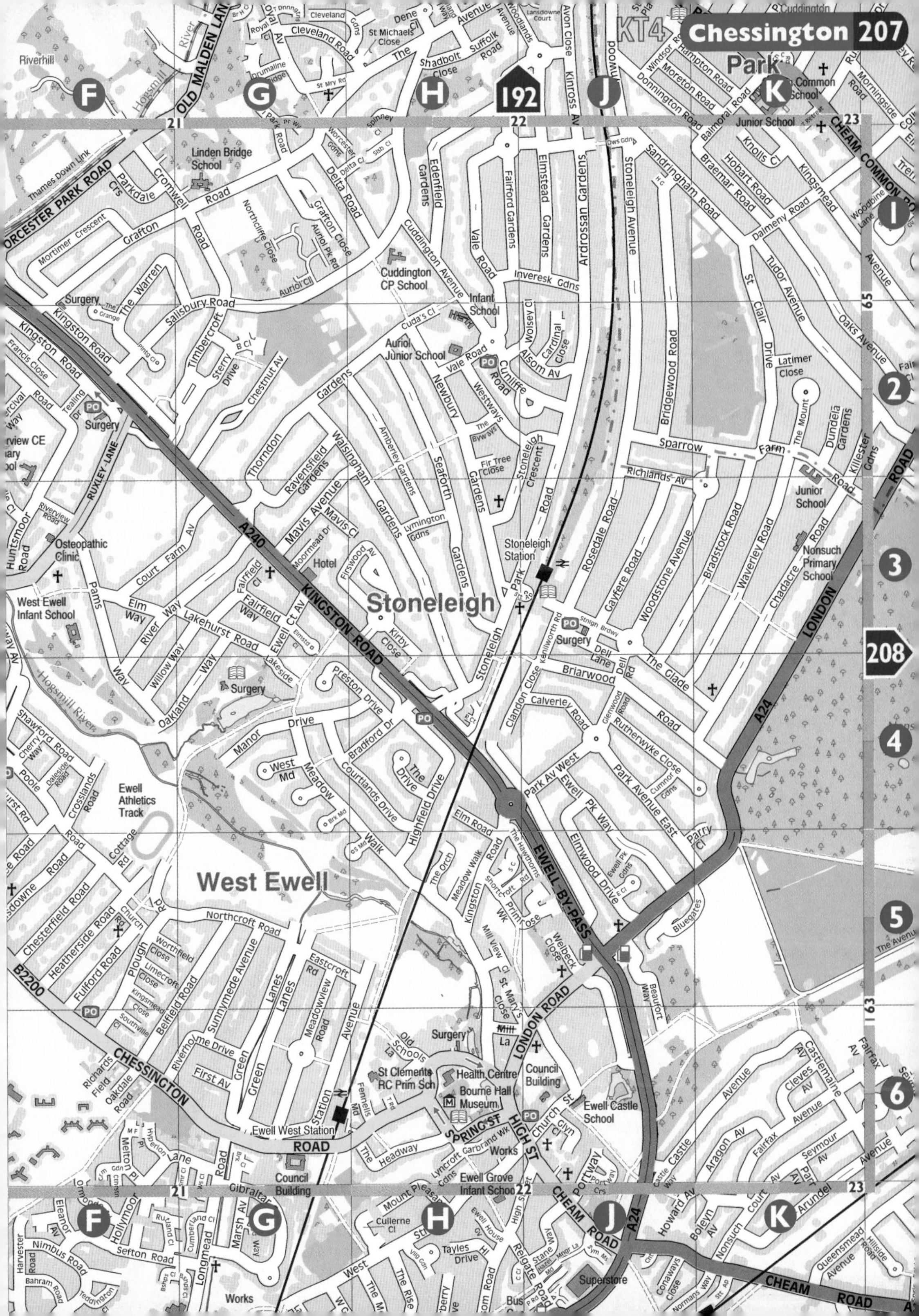
KT4
Park
192
208
F
G
H
J
K
I
2
3
4
5
6
21
22
23
65
63
Riverhill
Hogsmill River
OLD MALDEN LANE
Cleveland Road
St Michaels Close
Dene Cl
The Avenue
Shadbolt Close
Suffolk Road
Avon Close
Kinross Av
Lansdowne Court
Woodlands Avenue
Lynwood
Cuddington
Hampton Road
Moreton Road
Donnington Road
Windsor Rd
Balmoral Road
Cuddington Common
Junior School
CHEAM COMMON ROAD
Knolls Cl
Hobart Road
Braemar Road
Kingsmead
Morningside Road
Dalmeny Road
Tudor Avenue
Woodbine Lane
Oaks Avenue
Thames Down Link
WORCESTER PARK ROAD
Linden Bridge School
Cromwell Road
Parkdale Crs
Mortimer Crescent
Grafton Road
Northcliffe Close
Auriol Pk Rd
Auriol Cl
Grafton Close
Delta Road
Delta Cl
Worcester Gdns
Edenfield Gardens
Cuddington Avenue
Fairford Gardens
Elmstead Gardens
Ardrossan Gardens
Stoneleigh Avenue
Sandringham Road
Vale Road
Inveresk Gdns
Cuddington CP School
Infant School
Bridgewood Road
St Clair Drive
Surgery
The Grange
The Warren
Salisbury Road
Kingston Road
Francis Close
Timbercroft
Sterry Drive
Chestnut Av
Cuda's Cl
Auriol Junior School
Wolsey Cl
Cardinal Close
Alsom Av
Cunliffe Road
Westways
Newbury Gardens
Latimer Close
The Mount
Dundela Gardens
Killester Gdns
Sparrow Farm Road
Richlands Av
Perceival Road
Tealing Dr
PO
Ruxley Lane
Riverview Road
Huntsmoor Road
Osteopathic Clinic
Thorndon Gardens
Ravensfield Gardens
Walsingham Gardens
Amberley Gardens
Seaforth Gardens
The Byways
Fir Tree Close
Stoneleigh Crescent
Junior School
A240
Mavis Avenue
Mavis Cl
Lymington Gdns
Moormead Dr
Hotel
Firswood Av
Stoneleigh Station
Stoneleigh Park Road
Rosedale Road
Gayfere Road
Woodstone Avenue
Bradstock Road
Waverley Road
Chadacre Road
Nonsuch Primary School
LONDON ROAD
A24
West Ewell Infant School
Pams Way
Court Farm Av
Elm Way
River Way
Fairfield Cl
Fairfield Way
Lakehurst Road
Ewell Ct Av
Elmstd Cl
KINGSTON ROAD
Stoneleigh
Kirby Close
Kenilworth Rd
Stnigh Brdwy
Dell Lane
Dell Rd
The Glade
Briarwood Road
Willow Way
Oakland Way
Lakeside
Surgery
Preston Drive
Clandon Close
Calverley Road
Glenwood Road
Rutherwyke Close
Shawford Road
Cherry Way
Dalestde Road
Poole Road
Crosslands Road
Manor Drive
West Md
Meadow Walk
Bradford Dr
Courtlands Drive
The Drive
Highfield Drive
Park Av West
Ewell Pk Way
Park Avenue East
Cumnor Gdns
Parry Cl
Ewell Athletics Track
Cottage Rd
Elm Road
The Hawthorns
EWELL-BY-PASS
Elmwood Drive
Ewell Pk Gdns
West Ewell
The Orch
Meadow Walk
Kingston Road
Shortcroft Rd
Primrose Wk
Chesterfield Road
Heatherside Road
Church Rd
Northcroft Road
Worthfield Close
Limecroft Close
Plough
Fulford Road
Belfield Road
Sunnymede Avenue
Green Lanes
Eastcroft Rd
Meadowview Road
Avenue
Mill View Cl
St Mary's Close
Welbeck Close
Beaufort Way
Bluegates
The Avenue
B2200
Kingsmead Close
Southville Cl
Riverholme Drive
First Av
Old Schools La
Surgery
Mill La
LONDON ROAD
Council Building
Castlemaine Av
Fairfax Av
Cleves Av
CHESSINGTON
Richards Field
Oakdale Road
St Clements RC Prim Sch
Health Centre
Bourne Hall Museum
Ewell West Station
Fennells Md
SPRING ST
HIGH ST
Church St
Glyn Cl
Ewell Castle School
Castle Avenue
Aragon Av
Fairfax Avenue
Seymour Av
Parr Av
Avenue
Hyperion
Melton Pl
Lane
Road
ROAD
The Headway
Garbrand Wk
Works
Portway
Lyncroft Gdns
Ewell Grove Infant School
Council Building
Gibraltar
Mount Pleasant
High St
CHEAM ROAD
Howard Av
Boleyn Av
Nonsuch Court Av
Arundel
Ormond
Eleanor Av
Hollymoor
Cumberland Cl
Marsh Av
Longmead
Cullerne Cl
Ewell House Gv
Tayles Hl
Drive
Reigate Road
Stane Way
Conaways Close
Normans Way
Queensmead Avenue
Hillside
Harvester Road
Nimbus Road
Sefton Road
Bahram Road
Teddington
Works
West
The Rise
Superstore
Bus
CHEAM ROAD

208
193
207
A
B
C
D
E
1
2
3
4
5
6
523
24
25
65
163
North Cheam
Cheam
SUTTON
SM3
SM2
East
CHEAM COMMON ROAD
LONDON ROAD
MALDEN ROAD
A2043
ST DUNSTAN'S HILL
A217
CHEAM ROAD
HIGH STREET
EWELL ROAD
THE BROADWAY
STATION WAY
SANDY LANE
B283
BELMONT RISE
BURDON LANE
A232
Beverley Road
Morningside Road
Colborne Way
Grandison Road
Bedford Road
Burnham Drive
Hill Crs
Glyn Road
Lloyd Road
Elm Way
Trent Way
Farm Way
Courtenay Road
Lavender Avenue
Woodbine Lane
Oaks Avenue
Wellington Avenue
Leicester Close
Lingfield Avenue
Senhouse Road
Camberley Close
Marlow Drive
Sunbury Road
The Meads
Henley Avenue
Brocks Drive
St Margaret's Avenue
Kingston Avenue
Kew Crs
Walton Avenue
Kimpton Road
Whittaker Road
Willow Walk
Watson Avenue
Cander Green Lane
Caversham Av
Molesey Drive
Sandiford Rd
Kimpton Industrial Estate
Baldstone Road
Primary School
Superstore
Esher Av
Hilbert Road
Wrayfield Road
Frogmore Close
Windsor Avenue
Cheam Park Farm Junior School
Works
Hayes Crs
Church Hill Road
Buxton Crescent
Carlton Crescent
Abbots Road
Chartwell Place
Chelsea Gdns
Hanover Cl
Matlock Crescent
Matlock Gdns
Alberta Av
Alma Crescent
Surgery
D'Arcy Rd
Malden Road Baths
Cheam Leisure Cen
Priory Crs
Priory Av
Priory Road
Fairlight Close
Hemingford Rd
The Spinney
Wordsworth Drive
Kenley Walk
Chatsworth Road
Cheam High Sch
Cheam Fields Prim Sch
Dundela Gardens
Killester Gdns
Palmer Avenue
Wickham Avenue
Newbolt Avenue
Stoughton Av
Netley Close
Tilehurst Road
Kingsdown Road
Fromondes Road
Lumley Road
Tudor Close
Ashmere Close
Nonsuch Park
Surrey County
Sutton
Cookes Lane
Mickleham Gdns
Cheam Pk Way
Park Lane
Parkside
Surg
Park Road
Love Lane
Stafford Close
Sunningdale Road
Gander Green Lane
Westfield Road
Silverdale Cl
Elmbrook Rd
St Albans Road
Jeffs Road
Hilldale Road
Frederick Road
Denbigh Close
Shearwater Rd
Cheam Works
Grebe Ct
Park Rd
Antrobus Close
Carlisle Road
Fairholme Road
Revell Road
Quarry Road
Quarry Rise
Cecil Road
Rosebery Road
Derby Road
Hotel
Summerville Gdns
Bridgefield Road
Landseer Road
Beggar's Roost Lane
Grove Road
Grove Av
Tormead Close
St James' Rd
Salisbury Avenue
Recreation Ground
Sutton United FC
West Sutton Station
Sydney Road
Beulah Rd
Beauchamp Road
Orchard Road
Wings Cl
Collingwood Road
Chaucer Gdns
Milton Road
Alexandra Av
Westbourne Primary School
Anton Crs
Northspur Road
Oldfields Trading Est
Stayton Road
Dibdin Road
Clensham Lane
Burford Road
Broomloan La
Lymescote Gardens
Bus Depot
Bushey Road
St James Av
St James Road
Norman Road
Sutton West Centre
Robin Hood
School
Sherwood Park Road
Western Road
Tate Road
Cricket Ground
Gander Gn Lane
Petersham
Surgery
Heather Gdns
York Road
Village Rw
Overton Road
Worcester Road
Frampton Cl
Chalcot Cl
Grange Road
Wyndham Cl
Sackville Rd
Holland Avenue
Cornwall Road
Beresford Road
Mulgrave Road
Hillside Rd
Arundel Road
Manor Road
Burdon Pk
Cheam Station
Upr Mulgrave Rd
Tabor Gdns
Scotsdale Cl
St Dunstans CE Primary School
Kings Rd
Forge La
Jubilee Rd
Queens Acre
Anne Boleyn's Walk
Fir Walk
Nonsuch High School for Girls
The Avenue
Old Barn Close
Peaches Close
Cheam Sports Club
Holmwood Close
Villiers Gv
Glebe Road
Wonersh Wy
Merrow Road
Bramley Road
Ranmore Road
Walk
West Drive
The Glade
Sandy Lane
The Wray Rd
Devon Road
Meadowside Road
Harefield Avenue
Rugby Lane
Fairfax Av
Seymour Av
Holmwood Road
Abinger Avenue
Ewhurst Close
Buckland Road
Albury Avenue
Nonsuch
Hays Walk
South Drive
Cheam Close
Northey Avenue
Shirley Av
Cheyham Gardens
Shere Av
Gomshall Rd
Hillside Road
Queensmead Avenue
Dorset Road
Courtenay Av
Henderson Hosp
Moore Way
Sutton Bowling Club
Balmoral Way
The Avenue Primary School
Cross Rd
PO
1 grid square represents 500 metres

194
210
SM1
SM5
Benhilton
The Wrythe
Carshalton
Carshalton Beeches
Belmont
Greenshaw High School
Muschamp Primary School
Carshalton College of FE
Council Building
Carshalton High School for Girls
Carshalton AFC
War Mem Sports Ground
Junior Sch
Carshalton Station
St Marys Infant School
St Marys RC Infant School
St Philomenas RC High School
Benhill Recreation Ground
Palmerston Business Cen
Grammar School
Prim Sch
Times Square Shopping Centre
St Nicholas Centre
Sports Club
Superbowl
Health Cen
Manor Park
Gas Works
Police Stn
Sutton Station
Hotel
Cemetery
Carshalton War Memorial Hospital
Carshalton Beeches Station
Stanley Park Primary School
Devonshire Primary School
Stowford College
Overton Grange School
Barrow Hedges Primary School
Queen Marys Hospital for Children
Sutton General Hospital
Royal Marsden Hospital
Belmont Station
The Warren
Carshalton Park
Stanley Park
CARSHALTON ROAD
HIGH STREET
ANGEL HILL
ROSE HILL
ST NICHOLAS WAY
THROWLEY WAY
BRIGHTON ROAD
HIGH ST
PARK HILL
THE BEECHES AV
WOODMANSTERNE
WEST STREET
NORTH STREET
POUND ST
NIGHTINGALE ROAD
COTSWOLD ROAD
A232
B2230
B278
B277
26
27
28
F
G
H
J
K
I
2
3
4
5
6

210
195
209
Felnex Trading Estate
Edes Business Park
Restmor Way
Works
Bedding
BEDDINGTON LANE
Harrington Close
Crispin Crs
Beddington Park
Elmwood Close
Birchwood Avenue
Wandle Road
Carew Manor School
Beddington Park Primary School
Mallinson Road
Church Paddock Ct
Whelan Way
Richmond
Church Road
Church Lane
Streeters La
Church La
Guy Road
HILLIER'S LA B272
Wandle Rd
Kingston Gdns
Bridle Pth
Sherwood Park School
NIGHTINGALE ROAD
Strawberry Lane
The Causeway
River Gardens
Shepley Close
Victoria Avenue
Lyndon Av
Curran Av
Burleigh Av
St Mary Av
Leechcroft Rd
Butter Hill
Riverside
Lake Gdns
Paston Close
Bampfylde Close
Bloxworth Close
Wallington Grammar School
Council Building
Denmark Rd
Dover Gdns
School
Mill Lane
Papermill Cl
Clinic
Station Rd
Westcroft Leisure Centre
The Grove
Westcroft Road
Scawen Close
Council Building
Lewis Clinic
HIGH STREET
A232
ACRE LANE
CROYDON ROAD
A237
MANOR ROAD
Quinton Close
Derek Av
Chestnut Mnr
Harcourt Fld
Harcourt Road
The Mnr Way
Beddington Infants School
Dell Close
Evelyn Way
Lytton Gdns
Rookwood Av
Raleigh Av
Ferrers Av
Sandhills
Royston Av
Iberian Av
Qu Elizabeth's Wk
Beddington Medical Cen
Hallowell Av
Bridges Lane
Tritton Av
The Link Day Prim School
Garratt Cl
The Holt Junior School
Infant School
Bond Gardens
Rectory Lane
Demesne Road
Bute Road
Northway
Southway
Darcy Av
Arran Close
Montagu Gardens
Queenswood Avenue
Collyer Av
Oakley Av
Bristow Road
Claydon Dr
B272
Bandon Hill Cemetery
Crichton Avenue
Hotel
Lavender Road
Bernard Rd
Mint Rd
Lodge Rd
Alcester Road
Maldon Road
Morton Gardens
The Bridle Way
Parkgate Road
Queen's Rd
Surgery
Park Road
Osmond Gdns
Bute Gdns
Bandonhill
PLOUGH LANE
Gomshall Av
Reigate Av
Central Av
Primary School
Works
Upper Road
Sandy La N
Beddington Gv
Tharp Road
RUSKIN ROAD B271
Talbot Road
Rotherfield Road
Brookside
Park Lane
Taylor Road
St George's Road
Clifton Road
Belmont Road
Bute Gdns W
Springfield Rd
Collingwood Prep Sch
Clarence Rd
Melbourne Road
Carshalton Park
Woodstock Road
PARK LANE B271
Wallington
Mellows Road
SM6
Bandon Ri
Surgery
Garden Cl
Ashcombe Road
Grosvenor Road
Ross Road
Clarendon Road
Clyde Road
Carew Road
Police Station
STAFFORD ROAD
Bandon Hill Prim Sch
South Beddington
Wilson
Mollison Drive
Park Av
Grosvenor Avenue
Wallington Station
Beddington Gdns
Magistrates Court
Shotfield
Superstore
Chandos Bus Cen
Elgin Rd
Works
Link Lane
The Mead
Lavender Vale
Chalice Cl
Milton Road
Hinton Road
Francis Road
Charlotte Road
SANDY LANE S
Beddington Gdns
Northwood Rd
Woodfield Av
Anglesey Gdns
Anglesey Ct Road
BOUNDARY ROAD
Stanley Park High School
Holmwood Gardens
Shotfield Health Clinic
B271
Blenheim Gardens
Cowper Gdns
Wordsworth Road
Waterer Rise
Redford Av
Cobham Cl
Mcintosh Cl
Douglas Cl
Olley Cl
Stanley Park
Stanley Park Primary School
STANLEY PARK RD B271
Stanley Gdns
Cranley Gdns
Cosdach Av
Foresters Primary School
Barlow Cl
Hermes Way
Carter Cl
Shaw Way
Avenue
Defiant Wy
Avro Wy
De Havilland Rd
Hawthorn Road
Park Road
Turpin Way
Willow Rd
WOODCOTE ROAD
Grosvenor Gardens
Onslow Gardens
B272
FORESTERS DRIVE
Foresters Close
Brown Close
Surg
Mollison Drive Health Cen
Mollison Drive
Kingsford Av
Stanley Rd
The Av
Hawthorne Av
Dalmeny Road
Windborough Road
Heathdene Road
Hillside Gdns
South Lane
Oaklands Way
Tudor Cl
Fir Tree Gro
Stanhope Rd
Road Hill
The Newlands
Lindbergh Rd
Brabazon Av
Gull Cl
Amy Johnson Primary Sc
Oaks Way
Brambledown
A237
Carshalton on the Hill
Woodcote Avenue
Avenue Rd
Marchmont Road
Elystan Cl
Ingleby Way
Carleton Avenue
Moore Cl
Bristol Cl
Lawford Cl
Mariette Wy
Pine Ridge
Mount Park
Boundary Road
Hall Road
Glen Rd
Dower Av
Shirley Rd
Sandy Lane
Mallard Way
Alington Grove
Sunkist Wy
Apeldoorn Drive
Clarice Wy
Stanley Square
Cranfield Rd East
St Rd
Mount Close
Mount Way
High School
Oakwood
Woodcote Gn
Buckingham Way
Hamilton Way
Stratton Avenue
Ambrey Way
Sprucedale Gdns
Kenny Dr
Briar Lane
Bramble Banks
Briar Bank
Lawson Wk
Tillis La
Woodcote Park
The Drive
Great Woodcote Park
Woodcote Green
Ridge Park
Goldcrest Way
John Fisher Sch
Church Road
Lordsbury Field
Farm Cl
Linden Way
Purley Sports Club
The Ridge
Peaks
Track
A237 WOODCOTE
Grassmere
1 grid square represents 500 metres
A
B
C
D
E
1
2
3
4
5
6
28
29
30
63
64
65

Wandle Park
Waddon
CROYDON
South Croydon
Roundshaw
Russell
196
212
F
G
H
J
K
I
2
3
4
5
6
31
32
33
ROMAN WAY
PARK LA
ADDISCOMBE
FAIRFIELD RD
BARCLAY RD
A236 OLD TOWN
THE CROYDON FLYOVER A232
DUPPAS HILL ROAD A232
COOMBE ROAD
LWR COOMBE ST
SOUTHBRIDGE ROAD
ST PETER'S ROAD
SOUTH PARK HILL ROAD
DENNING AVENUE B275
WARHAM ROAD B275
PURLEY WAY A23
PURLEY WAY
EPSOM RD
STAFFORD RD
SELSDON ROAD
SOUTH END
CROHAM RD
BRIGHTON ROAD
SANDERSTEAD ROAD
A235
A212
A232
B243
B272
Commerce Way
Progress Business Park
Mill Lane Trading Est
Superstore
Waddon Station
The Link Secondary School
Sayer Clinic
Whitgift Almshouses
Drummond Shopping Centre
Croydon Coll
Fairfield Halls
Clocktower
Old Palace School
Parish Church CE Prim Sch
Fire Station
Police Stn
Occupational Health Centre
Howard Primary School
Croydon Indoor Bowling Club
Whitgift School
Duppas Junior School
Waddon Clinic
Waddon Infant School
Stafford Cross Business Park
Silver Wing Industrial Estate
Connaught Business Cen
Croydon Airport Industrial Estate
St Giles School
Regina Coeli RC Primary School
Haling Manor High School
South Croydon Medical Cen
Purley Oaks Primary School
Selsdon Rd Ind Estate
Two Bridges Business Park
South Croydon Station
Elmhurst School
Cumnor House Sch
Sanderstead Station
Purley Oaks Stn
Junior School
Margaret Roper RC Primary School
Christ Church
Croydon
Sutton
Waddon Way
Coldharbour Rd
Layton Crs
Cooper Road
Park Road
Pampisford Road
Kingsdown Av
Mount Park Avenue
Blenheim Park Road
Churchill Road
Highfield Road
Edgehill
Imperial Way
Lysander Rd
Foss Av
Whitgift Av
Haling Park
St Augustine's Avenue
Avondale Rd
Chatsworth Rd
Heathhurst Road
Carlton Rd
Sussex Road
Mayfield Road
Brantwood Rd
Grange Road
Norman Avenue
Kendall Avenue South
Montpelier Road

212
197
211
A
B
C
D
E
1
2
3
4
5
6
34
35
533
65
63
CROYDON
Shirley
Upper Shirley
Addiscombe Road
ADDISCOMBE ROAD
A232
FAIRFIELD RD
CHEPSTOW ROAD
Fitzjames Avenue
Upfield
Harland Av
Sandilands
Grimwade Avenue
Mapledale Avenue
Shirley Park Golf Club
Trinity School
SHIRLEY ROAD
Golf Course
The Law Courts
Park Hill Junior Sch
Chichester Rd
Selborne Road
Addiscombe Cricket Club
Archbishop Tenisons CE School
Ranmore Av
Deepdene Av
Occupational Health Centre
PARK HILL ROAD
A2039
Brownlow Road
Steep Hill
Water Tower Hill
A212
COOMBE ROAD
SOUTH PARK HILL ROAD
B243
Birdhurst Road
Birdhurst Rise
Hotel
Elmhurst School
South Croydon Station
South Croydon Sports Club
Campden Road
Spencer Road
Croham Park Avenue
Castlemaine Avenue
Ballater Road
Melville Avenue
Binfield Rd
Blossom
Vanguard Way
Oaks Road
Conduit Lane
COOMBE LANE
Sunken Rd
London Loop
Croham Road
Hollycroft
Croham Hurst School
Pilgrim's Way
Bench Fld
Manor Way
Ballards Way
Royal Russell School
Ballards Farm Road
Hollingsworth Road
Croham Valley Road
Croham Hurst Golf Club
Winchelsey Ri
Manor Gdns
Bankside
Harewood Road
Rayleigh Ri
Normanton Road
St Peters Primary School
Surgery
Hurst Wy
Croham Manor Road
Hurst Vw Rd
B275
Carlton Av
Carlton Rd
High Beech
Lytchgate Cl
Croham Hurst
Ruffetts Close
Crest Rd
The Ruffetts
Chapel Vw
Chestnut Gv
The Gallop
Croham Va Rd
Heathfield
Essenden Road
Sandhurst Way
UPPER SELSDON ROAD
Brambledown Rd
Heathhurst Road
Farley Road
Littleheath
Brent Rd
Sanderstead Station
Beechwood
West Hill
Barnfield Road
Elmfield Way
Ellenbridge Way
Ewhurst Avenue
Wisborough Rd
Arkwright Road
Moir Cl
Ridgeway Primary School
Selsdon Primary School
Foxearth
Queenhill Rd
Rylandes Rd
Surgery
Southcote Road
Day's Acre
Morley Road
The Ridge
East Hill
Courtlands
Langley Oaks Av
Arundel Avenue
Byron Road
Dulverton Road
Sundale
Elmpark Gdns
Montana
A2022
1 grid square represents 500 metres

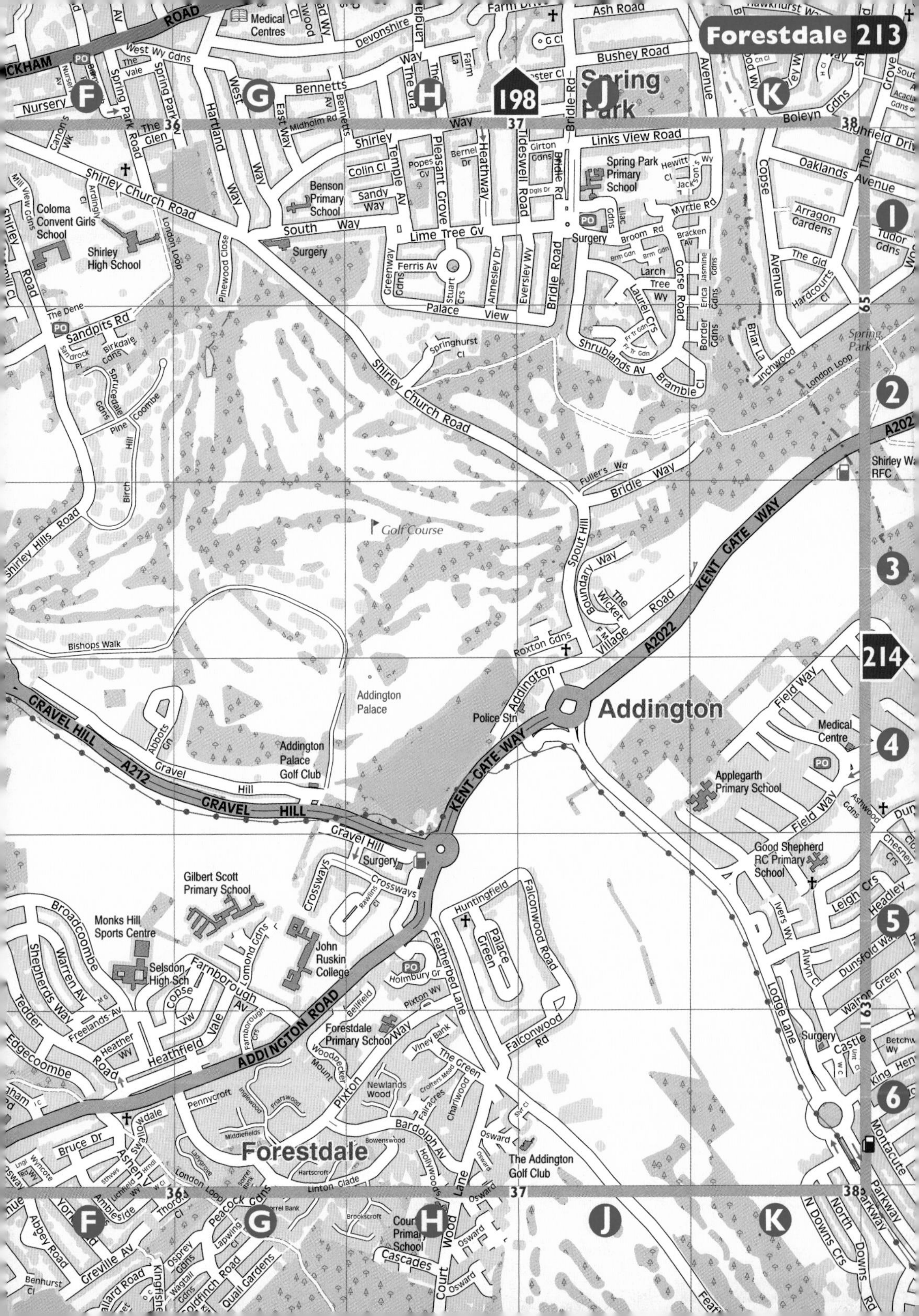

Medical Centres
Devonshire
Ash Road
Bushey Road
Spring Park
198
West Wy Gdns
The Vale
Spring Park Road
Nursery
Bennetts Av
Bennetts Way
East Way
Midholm Rd
West Way
Hartland Way
The Glen
Canon's Wk
Shirley Way
Shirley Church Road
Coloma Convent Girls School
Shirley High School
London Loop
Pinewood Close
Benson Primary School
Colin Cl
Temple Av
Sandy Way
Popes Gv
Pleasant Grove
Bernel Dr
Heathway
Tideswell Road
Girton Gdns
Bridle Rd
Links View Road
Spring Park Primary School
Hewitt Cl
Jackson's Wy
Myrtle Rd
Lilac Gdns
Broom Rd
Bracken Av
Surgery
South Way
Lime Tree Gv
Ferris Av
Greenway Gdns
Stuart Crs
Annesley Dr
Eversley Wy
Bridle Road
Palace View
Larch Tree Wy
Laurel Crs
Gorse Road
Jasmine Gdns
Erica Gdns
Border Gdns
Shrublands Av
Bramble Cl
Briar La
Inchwood
London Loop
Spring Park
Copse Avenue
Oaklands Avenue
Arragon Gardens
The Glade
Hardcourts Cl
Tudor Gdns
Boleyn Gdns
Highfield Drive
The Dene
Sandpits Rd
Sandrock Pl
Birkdale Gdns
Sprucedale Gdns
Pine Coombe
Birch Hill
Shirley Hills Road
Springhurst Cl
Shirley Church Road
Fuller's Wa
Bridle Way
Spout Hill
Golf Course
Boundary Way
The Wicket
Village Road
Kent Gate Way
A2022
Shirley Way RFC
Bishops Walk
Roxton Gdns
Addington Palace
Addington Palace Golf Club
Abbots Gn
Gravel Hill
A212
Police Stn
Addington
Field Way
Medical Centre
Applegarth Primary School
Ashwood Gdns
214
Gravel Hill
Surgery
Crossways
Rawlins Cl
Gilbert Scott Primary School
Monks Hill Sports Centre
Broadcoombe
Shepherds Way
Warren Av
Selsdon High Sch
Farnborough Av
Lomond Gdns
John Ruskin College
Copse Vw
Freelands Av
Heather Wy
Heathfield Vale
Edgecoombe
Tedder Road
Addington Road
Holmbury Gr
Bellfield
Pixton Wy
Forestdale Primary School
Woodpecker Mount
Pixton Way
Featherbed Lane
Huntingfield
Palace Green
Falconwood Road
Falconwood Rd
Viney Bank
The Green
Newlands Wood
Fairacres
Chariwood
Bardolph Av
Hollywoods
Good Shepherd RC Primary School
Chesney Crs
Leigh Crs
Headley
Ivers Wy
Alwyn Cl
Dunsfold Way
Walton Green
Lodge Lane
Surgery
Castle
Betchworth Wy
King Henry's
Montacute
Pennycroft
Inglewood
Friarswood
Middlefields
Bowenswood
Forestdale
Hartscroft
Oswald
The Addington Golf Club
Bruce Dr
Ashen Vale
Swallowdale
Wyncote
Ambleside
London Loop
Linton Glade
Peacock Gdns
Sorrel Bank
Brookscroft
Court Primary School
Court Wood Lane
Cascades
York Road
Abbey Road
Greville Av
Benhurst Cl
Osprey Gdns
Lapwing Cl
Goldfinch Road
Quail Gardens
Kingfisher
North Downs Crs
North Downs Road
Parkway
36
37
38
65
63
F
G
H
J
K
1
2
3
4
5
6

214
199
213
A
B
C
D
E
1
2
3
4
5
6
538
39
40
65
63
BR4
GLEBE WAY
Wickham Crs
Rose Walk
Silver
Park Av
Grove
Southcroft Av
Acacia Gdns
Court Rd
Corkscrew Hill
Wickham Theatre
Stambourne Wy
Highfield Drive
Oaklands Avenue
The Way
Wood Lodge Lane
Woodland Way
Tudor Gdns
Old Beckenhamian RFC
Courtfield Rise
Addington Rd
Bencurtis
Hawes Lane
High Mead
Seabrook Dr
Little Ct
Windermere
Addington Road
Surg
Lennard Cl
Lennard Av
Dukes Av
Coney Hill Rd
Westland Dr
Abbotsbury Rd
Sandiland Crs
Coney Hill School
Metropolitan Police Hayes Sports Club
London Loop
Prestons Road
Grove Close
West
Hayes Cl
Hayes Grove Priory Hospital
Warren Wood Close
Croydon Rd
South Walk
Farm Close
Colin Cl
Church Drive
Kingsway
Princes Way
A232
Harvest Bank Road
Robins Grove
Hartfield Crescent
Hartfield Rd
Lawrence Road
Gates
Spring Park
ADDINGTON ROAD
A2022
Shirley Wanderers RFC
London Loop
St John Rigby Catholic College
Coney Hall
Layhams Road
Sylvan Way
Hawthorn Dr
Chestnut Avenue
Birch Tree Avenue
Lime Tree Walk
Cherry Tree Wk
Monarch Cl
Queensway
Rouse Farm
Bromley
Croydon
North Pole Lane
Nash Lane
Medical Centre
Ashwood Gdns
Dunley Drive
Ripley Close
Witley Crs
Burford Wy
Merrow Wy
Pirbright Crs
Claygate Crs
Alford Gn
Surgery
Chesney Crs
Headley Drive
Netley Close
Frimley Close
Brockham Crs
Mickleham Wy
Thursley Crs
Frensham Drive
Dunsfold Way
Horsley Dr
Frimley Crs
Avenue
New Addington
Goldcrest Wy
Hill
Tilford Av
Castle
Betchworth Wy
King Henry's Drive
Wolsey Crescent
Aldrich Crescent
Shaxton Crescent
Grenville Road
Montacute
Queen Elizabeth's Drive
Kestrel Way
Rowdown Crs
Vulcan Business Cen
Godric Crs
Stowell Av
Rothwell Road
Gascoigne Road
Parkway
North Downs Crs
Walsingham Rd
Salcot Crs
Vulcan Way
Addington Business Centre
Layhams Farm
Works
1 grid square represents 500 metres

Keston Mark
Keston
Nash
Hayes School
Baston School
Park House RFC
Ravens Wood School
Keston CE Primary School
Heathfield College
Hayes Common
Baston Manor
Keston Court
Holwood
Holwood Farm
Lower Hook Farm
CROYDON ROAD
BASTON ROAD
HEATHFIELD ROAD
WESTERHAM ROAD
A233
A232
A21
B265
Barnet Wood
Five Elms Road
Commonside
Lakes Road
Fishponds Road
Church Road
Downe Road
New Road Hill
Farthing Street
Shire Lane
Jackass Lane
Blackness Lane
Rectory Road
Fox Hill
Heritage
Leafy Grove
Fox Lane
Keston Av
Greys Park Cl
Regents Drive
Oakfield Lane
Stour Cl
Windmill Drive
Keston Gdns
Hassock Wood
Swires Shaw
Rolinsden Way
Poulters Wood
Beechwood Drive
Brockdene Dr
The Dale
Rushley Close
Mark Close
Longdon Wood
Forest Drive
Forest Ridge
Keston Park Close
Ebury Close
Pine Glade
Beech Dell
Holwood Park Av
Lakeside Drive
Rowan Walk
Kemble Drive
Hollydale Drive
Cedar Crescent
Oakley Drive
Cedar Close
Cheyne Cl
Gravel Road
Cross Road
Doves Cl
Barnet Dr
Quiet Nook
Phoenix Dr
The Drift
Redgate
West Common Road
Baston Manor Road
Rookery
Redgate
200
216
BR2
F
G
H
J
K
1
2
3
4
5
6
41
42
43
63
65

216
201
215
A232
Allington Road
Orchard Green
Fairbank Av
Hazel Grove
Wood Way
Sunnydale
Larch Dene
Mere Cl
Oakwood Road
Crofton Avenue
Grange Road
Foxfield Road
Broughton Road
Darrick Wood Road
The Ridge
Hilltop Gardens
Telscombe Av
Sherlies Avenue
Tubbenden Cl
Woodhead Drive
Red Oak Close
Mada Road
Pondfield Road
Lovibonds Avenue
Avonstowe Close
Partridge Drive
Masefield View
Norman Close
Torver Way
Rusland Avenue
Newstead Wood School for Girls
Newstead
Willersley Avenue
Ruskin Drive
Southcroft Rd
Surgery
Tile Farm Road
Avebury Rd
Winterborne Avenue
Reed Avenue
Sandy Bury
Roseberry Gdns
Ridgeway
CROFTON ROAD A232 CROFTON ROAD
Windermere Rd
Grasmere Gardens
Meadow Way
Starts Close
Willow Walk
Locksbottom
Darrick Wood Swimming Pool
Darrick Wood School
Darrick Wood Sports Centre
Darrick Wood
Darrick Wood Primary School
Stables End
Pallant Way
Bromley Hospitals
Crofton Rd
Dene
Wellbrook Road
Hilda Vale Road
Starts Hill
Bassetts Way
Broadwater Gardens
Bridle Way
Isabella Drive
Attlington Close
Hale Close
Cherrycot Rise
Tubbenden Lane
Ashbourne Rise
Curzon Close
Leamington Av
Tunstall Close
Borkwood Way
Northlands Avenue
North D
St Leonards Rise
Southlands Avenue
Pinewood Drive
South Drive
Oakleigh
Haywood Rise
Ashley Gardens
Ninhams Wood
Holwood Park Av
Wolds Drive
The Birches
Vale Cl
Winton Road
FARNBOROUGH COMMON A21
FARNBOROUGH WAY A21
Pinecrest Gardens
Acorn Way
Arden Gv
Starts Hill Av
Orchard Rd
Elgal Cl
Limes Row
Clifton
Ladycroft Way
Green Gdns
Hartington Cl
Peel Road
Gladstone Rd
Palmerston Road
Cobden Rd
Pitt Rd
Tubbenden Lane South
Chartwell Dr
Dane Cl
Hilborough Way
Darwin Cl
Ferndale Way
Oleander Cl
Durrant Way
Beechcroft Road
Conifer Cl
Fairview Drive
Melrose Crs
HIGH STREET
FARNBOROUGH HILL
B2158
Contessa
Farnborough
Pleasant View
Tye Lane
Farnborough Primary School
Church Road
Ramus Wd Av
Cocksett Av
Cleave Av
Kent Close
Beechwood Av
Beechwood Avenue
Old Hill
A21
The Larches
Shire Lane
Lower Hook Farm
North End Farm
High Elms Country Park
High Elms Golf Club
Green Street Green
Cudham Lane North
Street
Orange Court Lane
North End Lane
High Elms Road
Golf Course
Rookery
Gorringes
Cuckoo Wood
543
44
45
163
165
A
B
C
D
E
1
2
3
4
5
6
1 grid square represents 500 metres

ORPINGTON
Goddington
Pratt's Bottom
BR6
202
SPUR ROAD
A232
Spur Road
Felstead
STATION ROAD
Surgery
The Drive
The Avenue
Hillcrest
Road
A223
A224
Park Avenue
Blenheim Rd
Avalon
Pendennis Road
Wilmington Avenue
Woodley Rd
Lodworth Close
Burwood School
Leeds Cl
Berrylands
Craven
Avalon Close
Broad Walk
Nut Tree Close
Dorado Gardens
Road
Allandale Place
Badgers Copse
Tower Close
Aubyns Gardens
Road
Becketts Close
Arne Grove
Maxwell Gardens
St Aubyns Close
Orpington Mental Health Centre
Cranleigh Close
Carolyn Dr
Goddington
St Olave's & St Saviour's Grammar School
Warwick Cl
Wyvern Close
Dene Drive
COURT ROAD
(ORPINGTON BY-PASS)
Stapleton
Wayne Cl
Primary School
Cheltenham Rd
Sandhurst Road
Charterhouse
Lane
Durley Gdns
Goddington Chase
Goddington Lane
SEVENOAKS ROAD
Mitchell Road
Taylor Cl
Kings Road
Tregony Road
Padstow
Newlyn Cl
Trenear Cl
Repton Road
Haileybury Road
Abingdon Way
Roedean Close
Magdelan Grove
Harrow Gdns
Malvern Road
Stowe Road
Winchester Road
Saltwood Cl
PO
Amp Cl
Chelsfield Lane
Bromley Hospitals
Vancouver Cl
Holywell Cl
Penhale Cl
Crown Close
Eton Road
Gleeson Drive
Warren Road Primary School
Cloonmore Avenue
Arundel Drive
The Highway
The Highway Primary School
Warren Road
Edith Rd
Crown Rd
Albert Road
Warren Dr
Stirling Drive
Osgood Gdns
Wolsey Mews
Warren Gardens
The Brackens
Amberley Close
Rawlings Cl
Warnford Rd
Osgood Avenue
Linden Close
Aspen Close
Russett Cl
Kng Rdg
Warren Road
Briarswood Way
Henry Mews
Beblets Close
Martindale Avenue
Chestnut Close
Fox Cl
Goldfinch Close
Woodside
Green Farm Close
Fuller Cl
Edgewood Drive
Highfield Av
Glentrammon Close
Daleside
Station Approach
The Meadway
Chelsfield Station
HIGH STREET
Surgery
Glentrammon Gardens
Glentrammon Avenue
Steep Close
Foxbury Drive
Daleside Cl
Drive
Spring Gdns
The Woodlands
Court Lodge
Laxey Rd
Baker Mews
Pinchbeck
Waring Cl
Waring Drive
Windsor
High Beeches
The Retreat
Homestead Road
Oxenden Wood Road
Church Road
Lezayre Rd
Winnipeg Drive
Green St Green Prim School
Vine Road
Road
Linslade Road
Woodlands Road
Julian Rd
The Meadows
Kingsley Road
Moat Close
Dowlerville Road
Worlds End Lane
Ash Road
Elm Road
Oak Road
Beech Road
Holly Road
Brimstone Cl
Julian's Brimstone
Chelsfield Golf Cent
Rosenheath Close
Chelsfield Hill
The Hillside
SEVENOAKS ROAD
Broke Farm Drive
St Benjamins Drive
Grange Drive
Turnpike Drive
Stonehouse Lane
Stonehouse Road
Charmwood Farm
Orchard Road
Runciman Cl
Ringwood Av
Downs View Close
Stonehouse Farm
Rushmore
F
G
H
J
K
46
47
48
1
2
3
4
5
6
63
64
65

Abbey Wood 128 C4
Acton 117 K1
Acton Green 118 A4
Addington 213 J4
Addiscombe 197 G5
Aldborough Hatch 72 E1
Aldersbrook 71 G5
Alperton 80 A6
Anerley 181 H5
Avery Hill 167 H1
Balham 160 E2
Bandonhill 210 D3
Barking 90 D5
Barkingside 54 B6
Barnehurst 150 A4
Barnes 138 E2
Barnes Cray 150 E5
Barnet 32 D1
Barnet Gate 31 G1
Barnsbury 84 E5
Barwell 205 J5
Battersea 140 E1
Bayswater 101 F6
Beckenham 182 E6
Beckton 107 K5
Becontree 91 K3
Beddington 195 K6
Beddington Corner 195 F4
Bedford Park 118 C3
Belgravia 15 G6
Bell Green 164 C5
Bellingham 164 D6
Belmont 43 G5
Belmont 208 E6
Belvedere 129 J5
Benhilton 209 F1
Berrylands 191 G3
Bethnal Green 104 D2
Bexley 148 D5
Bexleyheath 149 G5
Bickley 184 D5
Blackfen 168 A1
Blackheath 145 J3
Blackheath Park 145 K5
Blackwall 106 B6
Bloomsbury 10 D1
The Borough 18 D3
Bow 105 J1
Bow Common 105 J4
Bowes Park 48 E2
Bowmans 170 C2
Brentford 116 E6
Brentford End 116 C6
Brimsdown 25 G3
Brixton 142 B5
Broad Green 196 C4
Brockley 144 C6
Bromley 105 K2
Bromley 184 A5
Bromley Common 200 C3
Bromley Park 183 H4
Brompton 14 C5
Brondesbury 82 C4
Brondesbury Park 82 B6
Brook Green 119 F3
Broom Hill 202 A4
Brunswick Park 34 A5
Buckhurst Hill 39 G5
Burnt Oak 45 F3
Bushey 28 C2
Bushey Heath 28 E2
Bushey Mead 177 G6
Bush Hill Park 36 A1
Caldecote Hill 29 F2
Camberwell 143 G2
Camden Town 84 A5
Canary Wharf 124 E1
Cannon Hill 193 G1
Canonbury 85 J4
Canons Park 44 A3
Carpenders Park 27 K4
Carshalton 209 J2
Carshalton Beeches 209 J6
Carshalton on the Hill 209 K5
Castle Green 91 J6
Catford 165 F3
Chadwell Heath 73 K2
Charlton 126 C5
Chase Cross 57 G2
Chattern Hill 152 E6
Cheam 208 D3
Chelsea 121 F5
Chessington 206 A4
Child's Hill 64 C6
China Town 10 C5
Chingford 38 A4
Chingford Green 38 A3
Chingford Hatch 38 C6
Chipping Barnet 20 C6
Chislehurst 185 H3
Chislehurst West 185 F2
Chiswick 118 C4
Church End 46 E5
Church End 81 H5
City of London 12 B5
Clapham 141 G3
Clapham Park 161 J1
Clapton Park 87 H2
Claremont Park 204 A5
Claygate 205 F4
Clayhall 53 K5
Clerkenwell 5 J6
Cockfosters 21 J6
Coldblow 169 K4
Coldharbour 130 D4
Cole Park 156 B1
Colindale 45 G6
College Park 99 J2
Collier Row 56 E4
Collier's Wood 178 C3
Colney Hatch 47 K2
Coney Hall 214 C2
Coombe 176 B3
Copse Hill 176 D3
Cottenham Park 176 E4
Cranbrook 72 A4
Cranford 133 K1
Cranley Gardens 66 A1
Crayford 150 D6
Creekmouth 108 E4
Cricklewood 82 B2
Crofton 201 J6
Crooked Billet 176 E2
Crouch End 66 C3
Croydon 211 K1
Crystal Palace 181 H1
Cubitt Town 125 F4
Custom House 107 J6
Dagenham 93 F5
Dalston 86 B5
Dartford 171 F2
Dartmouth Park 66 A6
Deacons Hill 30 C1
De Beauvoir Town 86 A6
Deptford 124 C6
Derry Downs 202 E3
Dollis Hill 81 K1
Dormer's Wells 96 B6
Downham 183 G1
Ducks Island 32 B2
Dudden Hill 81 J3
Dulwich 163 G4
Dulwich Village 163 F2
Ealing 97 J6
Earl's Court 119 K5
Earlsfield 160 B3
East Acton 99 H6
East Barnet 33 H2
East Bedfont 152 E2
Eastbury 26 D6
Eastcote 59 F4
Eastcote Village 59 F2
East Dulwich 143 H6
East Finchley 47 H6
East Ham 107 J1
East Molesey 189 H2
East Sheen 138 A6
East Wickham 148 B2
Eden Park 198 C1
Edgware 30 D6
Edmonton 36 A6
Elmers End 182 A6
Elm Park 93 K3
Elmstead 184 D1
Elstree 30 A1
Eltham 166 D1
Enfield 23 J5
Enfield Highway 24 E3
Enfield Town 23 K4
Enfield Wash 25 G1
Erith 130 C5
Esher 204 C2
Fair Cross 91 F3
Fairlop 54 E4
Falconwood 147 K5
Farnborough 216 B3
Feltham 154 A4
Field Common 188 E4
Finchley 46 E4
Finsbury 5 J4
Finsbury Park 67 F6
Foots Cray 186 C2
Forestdale 213 G6
Forest Gate 88 E3
Forest Hill 164 A3
Fortis Green 65 K1
Forty Hill 24 B2
Foxbury 185 J1
Friday Hill 38 B5
Friern Barnet 33 J6
Fulham 139 G1
Fullwell Cross 54 D4
Furzedown 161 G6
Gants Hill 71 K3
Gidea Park 57 H5
Giggshill 190 B4
Globe Town 105 F2
Goddington 217 J1
Golders Green 64 C3
Goodmayes 73 H6
Gospel Oak 84 A3
Grange Hill 54 D2
Grange Park 23 G6
Greenford 96 D3
Greenhill 61 F2
Green Street Green 216 E5
Greenwich 125 G5
Grove Park 138 A2
Grove Park 166 B5
Hackbridge 195 G6
Hackney 86 E4
Hackney Wick 87 J4
Hadley 20 E4
Hadley Wood 21 H1
Haggerston 7 K2
Hainault 55 F3
Hale End 52 B2
Ham 156 E5
Hammersmith 118 E4
Hampstead 83 H2
Hampstead Garden Suburb 65 F2
Hampton 173 G4
Hampton Hill 155 H6
Hampton Wick 174 C4
Hanwell 115 K1
Hanworth 154 C5
Harlesden 99 G1
Harlington 113 F6
Harringay 67 G2
Harrow 60 D3
Harrow on the Hill 60 E5
Harrow Weald 42 E3
Hatch End 41 J3
Hatton 133 H5
Hayes 94 A4
Hayes 200 A4
Hayes End 94 B3
Hayes Town 114 B1
Headstone 60 B1
Heath Park 75 K3
Heath Side 170 C4
Hendon 63 K2
Herne Hill 162 D1
Heston 134 E1
Higham Hill 51 G5
Highams Park 51 K3
High Barnet 20 A4
Highbury 85 H2
Highgate 65 K4
Highwood Hill 31 H4
Hinchley Wood 205 F1
Hither Green 165 H1
Hockenden 187 J6
Holborn 11 G2
Holders Hill 46 B4
Holywell 26 C1
Homerton 87 F4
Honor Oak 164 A1
Honor Oak Park 164 B1
Hook 206 A3
Hook Green 170 C6
Hornsey 66 E1
Hornsey Vale 67 F2
Hounslow 135 F3
Hounslow West 134 C4
Hoxton 7 G3
Hurst Park 173 H5
The Hyde 63 H2
Ilford 90 B1
Isle of Dogs 125 F4
Isleworth 136 C4
Islington 85 G6
Joyden's Wood 170 C6
Kennington 121 K6
Kensal Green 100 A1
Kensal Rise 100 B1
Kensal Town 100 C3
Kensington 119 K3
Kentish Town 84 C4
Kenton 61 J2
Keston 215 H2
Keston Mark 215 H1
Kevingtown 203 G3
Kew 137 G1
Kidbrooke 146 B3
Kilburn 82 C6
Kingsbury 62 D3
Kingsland 86 A5
Kingston upon Thames 175 G6
Kingston Vale 176 A1
Kitt's End 20 C1
Knightsbridge 14 D2
Knight's Hill 162 D3
Ladywell 144 D5
Lambeth 17 J4
Lampton 135 G2
Lea Bridge 87 F1
Lee 165 J1
Lessness Heath 129 J6
Lewisham 145 F5
Leyton 88 B1
Leytonstone 70 D5
Limehouse 105 H5
Lisson Grove 9 F1
Little Heath 73 J1
Little Ilford 90 A3
Little Stanmore 44 B4
Locksbottom 216 B1
Long Ditton 190 C5
Longlands 167 H5
Lower Clapton 86 E2
Lower Edmonton 36 A4
Lower Feltham 153 H5
Lower Green 189 G6
Lower Holloway 85 F3
Lower Place 98 E1
Lower Sydenham 164 A6
Loxford 90 C3
Maida Vale 100 E2
Maitland Park 83 K4
Manor Park 89 J2
Marks Gate 56 A5
Marylebone 9 G2
Mayfair 9 J6
Maypole 170 B3
Merry Hill 28 B3
Merton 177 K4
Merton Park 177 J5
Mile End 105 G3
Mill Hill 45 J1
Mill Meads 106 B1
Millwall 124 D3
Mitcham 179 G6
Monken Hadley 20 C3
Monks Orchard 197 K4
Moor Park 26 A6
Morden 193 K1
Morden Park 193 H3
Mortlake 137 K3
Motspur Park 192 D3
Mottingham 166 B4
Muswell Hill 48 A5
Nash 215 F4
Neasden 81 F2
New Addington 214 B5
New Barnet 21 F6
New Beckenham 182 B2
Newbury Park 72 D3
New Charlton 126 C4
New Cross 144 B3
New Cross Gate 144 B2
New Eltham 167 G4
Newington 17 K5
New Malden 176 C6
New Southgate 34 C6
New Town 171 J1
Nine Elms 141 J1
Noel Park 49 H5
Norbiton 175 G5
Norbury 180 C5
North Acton 98 E3
North Cheam 208 B1
North Cray 169 H5
North End 65 G5
North End 150 C2
North Feltham 134 A6
North Finchley 47 G2
North Harrow 59 K3
North Hyde 114 D4
North Kensington 100 B4
Northolt 78 A5
North Sheen 137 J3
Northumberland Heath 149 K1
North Wembley 61 H5
Northwood 40 A4
Northwood Hills 40 B5
North Woolwich 126 D2
Norwood Green 115 F4
Norwood New Town 180 E2
Notting Hill 100 C6
Nunhead 143 K5
Oakleigh Park 33 H4
Oakwood 34 D1
Old Bexley 169 H2
Old Ford 87 G6
Old Malden 192 A4
Old Oak Common 99 H3
Orpington 202 B6
Osidge 34 C4
Osterley 135 H1
Oxhey 27 H1
Paddington 8 A2
Palmers Green 34 E5
Park Langley 199 F3
Park Royal 98 C2
Parsons Green 139 K3
Peckham 143 J3
Penge 181 K3
Pentonville 5 H2
Perivale 79 J6
Petersham 157 F3
Petts Wood 201 J1
Pimlico 121 H5
Pinner 59 H1
Pinner Green 41 G5
Pinnerwood Park 41 G3
Plaistow 106 D2
Plaistow 183 K2
Plashet 89 H4
Plumstead 127 H5
Plumstead Common 128 A6
Ponders End 24 E6
Poplar 105 J6
Poverest 202 B1
Preston 61 K5
Primrose Hill 3 H1
Purfleet 131 K6
Putney 139 G6
Putney Heath 159 F2
Putney Vale 158 D5
Queensbury 44 A6
Queens Park 100 C1
Rainham 111 K2
Ramsden 202 D5
Ratcliff 105 G6
Rayners Lane 59 K5
Raynes Park 177 F6
Redbridge 71 G2
Regent's Park 3 K3
Richmond 137 F6
Richmond Hill 157 F1
Rise Park 57 G4
Roehampton 138 C6
Romford 75 F2
The Rookery 26 E2
Rosehill 194 A5
Rotherhithe 124 A3
Roundshaw 211 F4
Roxeth 60 C6
Ruislip 58 C3
Ruislip Common 58 B1
Ruislip Gardens 76 C1
Ruislip Manor 58 E6
Rush Green 75 G4
Ruxley 187 F2
Rydens 188 B6
St George in the East 104 C6
St Giles 10 D3
St Helier 194 B5
St James 16 C1
St Johns 144 D3
St Luke's 6 D6
St Margarets 156 D1
St Mary Cray 202 D2
St Pancras 5 F5
St Paul's Cray 186 B5
Sands End 140 B3
Sandy Heath 65 G6
Seething Wells 190 C3
Selhurst 196 E2
Seven Kings 72 E5
Shacklewell 86 C2
Shadwell 104 E6
Shepherd's Bush 118 E1
Shirley 197 K6
Shooters Hill 147 H2
Shoreditch 7 F5
Shortlands 183 H6
Sidcup 168 C6
Silvertown 126 B2
Sipson 112 C5
Slade Green 150 D3
Soho 10 C4
Somers Town 4 C3
Southall 95 J6
South Beddington 210 D4
Southborough 200 E3

South Bromley 106 B5
South Croydon 211 J4
Southend 165 F6
Southfields 159 K3
Southgate 34 E3
South Hackney 86 E6
South Hampstead 83 G5
South Harrow 78 B1
South Hornchurch 93 F6
South Kensington 120 B5
South Lambeth 141 K1
South Norwood 180 E6
South Oxhey 27 F5
South Ruislip 77 H2
South Tottenham 68 A2
South Wimbledon 178 B1
South Woodford 52 E5
Spitalfields 13 J1
Spring Grove 135 J2
Spring Park 198 D6
Stamford Hill 68 B4
Stanmore 43 H1
Stepney 104 E4
Stockwell 141 K4
Stoke Newington 68 B6
Stonehill Green 187 K2
Stoneleigh 207 H3
Strand 11 F5
Stratford 88 A5
Stratford Marsh 87 K6
Stratford New Town 88 A4
Strawberry Hill 155 J5
Streatham 179 K1
Streatham Hill 161 K3
Streatham Park 161 G6
Streatham Vale 179 G3
Stroud Green 67 G3
Sudbury 79 F3
Summerstown 160 C4
Sundridge 184 B2
Surbiton 190 E5
Sutton 208 E3
Teddington 173 J2
Temple Hill 151 G5
Temple Mills 87 K3
Thames Ditton 190 B4
Thamesmead 128 A1
Thornton Heath 195 K2
Tokyngton 80 D4
Tolworth 191 H5
Tooting 178 E1
Tooting Graveney 178 C1
Tottenham 50 A5
Tottenham Hale 50 B6
Totteridge 32 E3
Totteridge Green 32 A3
Tufnell Park 84 C2
Tulse Hill 162 C3
Twickenham 155 K3
Underhill 32 E1
Upper Clapton 68 C5
Upper Edmonton 36 C6
Upper Elmers End 198 C2
Upper Holloway 66 C6
Upper Norwood 180 E4
Upper Shirley 212 E2
Upper Sydenham 163 H6
Upper Tooting 160 D5
Upper Walthamstow 70 A1
Upton 89 F5
Upton Park 89 G6
Vale of Health 83 H1
Vauxhall 121 K5
Waddon 196 A6
Walham Green 139 K2
Wallend 90 A6
Wallington 210 B3
Walthamstow 51 J6
Walworth 122 D5
Wandle Park 196 B6
Wandsworth 139 K5
Wanstead 71 F4
Wapping 123 J1
Watford Heath 27 J2
Wealdstone 43 G6
Welling 148 C4
Welsh Harp 63 F5
Wembley 79 J3
Wembley Park 80 C1
West Acton 98 C5
West Barnes 193 F2
West Bedfont 152 C2
Westbourne Green 100 E3
West Brompton 120 A6
West Drayton 112 A3
West Dulwich 162 E4
West Ealing 116 B1
West Ewell 207 G5
West Green 49 J6
West Hampstead 82 E3
West Harrow 60 C4
West Heath 65 F6
West Heath 128 E6
West Hendon 63 J4
West Hill 159 H2
West Kensington 119 G5
West Kilburn 100 C2
Westminster 16 B5
West Molesey 188 E1
West Norwood 162 D6
Weston Green 189 K5
West Ruislip 58 A5
West Wickham 199 G5
Whetstone 33 F4
Whitechapel 13 K5
Whitton 155 H1
Widmore 184 C5
Willesden 81 J4
Willesden Green 81 K5
Wilmington 170 E6
Wimbledon 177 H1
Winchmore Hill 35 H3
Wood End 94 C5
Wood End Green 94 C4
Woodford 53 F2
Woodford Bridge 53 K3
Woodford Green 52 E3
Woodford Wells 39 F5
Wood Green 49 G4
Woodlands 135 J4
Woodside 197 H3
Woodside Park 32 E6
Woolwich 127 F6
Worcester Park 192 E6
World's End 23 G5
The Wrythe 194 D6
Yeading 95 G3

USING THE STREET INDEX

Street names are listed alphabetically. Each street name is followed by its postal town or area locality, the Postcode District, the page number, and the reference to the square in which the name is found.

Standard index entries are shown as follows:

Aaron Hill Rd *EHAM* E6 ....**108** A4

Street names and selected addresses not shown on the map due to scale restrictions are shown in the index with an asterisk:

Abbeville Ms *CLAP* * SW4 ......**141** J6

GENERAL ABBREVIATIONS

ACC ACCESS
ALY ALLEY
AP APPROACH
AR ARCADE
ASS ASSOCIATION
AV AVENUE
BCH BEACH
BLDS BUILDINGS
BND BEND
BNK BANK
BR BRIDGE
BRK BROOK
BTM BOTTOM
BUS BUSINESS
BVD BOULEVARD
BY BYPASS
CATH CATHEDRAL
CEM CEMETERY
CEN CENTRE
CFT CROFT
CH CHURCH
CHA CHASE
CHYD CHURCHYARD
CIR CIRCLE
CIRC CIRCUS
CL CLOSE
CLFS CLIFFS
CMP CAMP
CNR CORNER
CO COUNTY
COLL COLLEGE
COM COMMON
COMM COMMISSION
CON CONVENT
COT COTTAGE
COTS COTTAGES
CP CAPE
CPS COPSE
CR CREEK
CREM CREMATORIUM
CRS CRESCENT
CSWY CAUSEWAY
CT COURT
CTRL CENTRAL
CTS COURTS
CTYD COURTYARD
CUTT CUTTINGS
CV COVE
CYN CANYON
DEPT DEPARTMENT
DL DALE
DM DAM
DR DRIVE
DRO DROVE
DRY DRIVEWAY
DWGS DWELLINGS
E EAST
EMB EMBANKMENT
EMBY EMBASSY
ESP ESPLANADE
EST ESTATE
EX EXCHANGE
EXPY EXPRESSWAY
EXT EXTENSION
F/O FLYOVER
FC FOOTBALL CLUB
FK FORK
FLD FIELD
FLDS FIELDS
FLS FALLS
FLS FLATS
FM FARM
FT FORT
FWY FREEWAY
FY FERRY
GA GATE
GAL GALLERY
GDN GARDEN
GDNS GARDENS
GLD GLADE
GLN GLEN
GN GREEN
GND GROUND
GRA GRANGE
GRG GARAGE
GT GREAT
GTWY GATEWAY
GV GROVE
HGR HIGHER
HL HILL
HLS HILLS
HO HOUSE
HOL HOLLOW
HOSP HOSPITAL
HRB HARBOUR
HTH HEATH
HTS HEIGHTS
HVN HAVEN
HWY HIGHWAY
IMP IMPERIAL
IN INLET
IND EST INDUSTRIAL ESTATE
INF INFIRMARY
INFO INFORMATION
INT INTERCHANGE
IS ISLAND
JCT JUNCTION
JTY JETTY
KG KING
KNL KNOLL
L LAKE
LA LANE
LDG LODGE
LGT LIGHT
LK LOCK
LKS LAKES
LNDG LANDING
LTL LITTLE
LWR LOWER
MAG MAGISTRATE
MAN MANSIONS
MD MEAD
MDW MEADOWS
MEM MEMORIAL
MKT MARKET
MKTS MARKETS
ML MALL
ML MILL
MNR MANOR
MS MEWS
MSN MISSION
MT MOUNT
MTN MOUNTAIN
MTS MOUNTAINS
MUS MUSEUM
MWY MOTORWAY
N NORTH
NE NORTH EAST
NW NORTH WEST
O/P OVERPASS
OFF OFFICE
ORCH ORCHARD
OV OVAL
PAL PALACE
PAS PASSAGE
PAV PAVILION
PDE PARADE
PH PUBLIC HOUSE
PK PARK
PKWY PARKWAY
PL PLACE
PLN PLAIN
PLNS PLAINS
PLZ PLAZA
POL POLICE STATION
PR PRINCE
PREC PRECINCT
PREP PREPARATORY
PRIM PRIMARY
PROM PROMENADE
PRS PRINCESS
PRT PORT
PT POINT
PTH PATH
PZ PIAZZA
QD QUADRANT
QU QUEEN
QY QUAY
R RIVER
RBT ROUNDABOUT
RD ROAD
RDG RIDGE
REP REPUBLIC
RES RESERVOIR
RFC RUGBY FOOTBALL CLUB
RI RISE
RP RAMP
RW ROW
S SOUTH
SCH SCHOOL
SE SOUTH EAST
SER SERVICE AREA
SH SHORE
SHOP SHOPPING
SKWY SKYWAY
SMT SUMMIT
SOC SOCIETY
SP SPUR
SPR SPRING
SQ SQUARE
ST STREET
STN STATION
STR STREAM
STRD STRAND
SW SOUTH WEST
TDG TRADING
TER TERRACE
THWY THROUGHWAY
TNL TUNNEL
TOLL TOLLWAY
TPK TURNPIKE
TR TRACK
TRL TRAIL
TWR TOWER
U/P UNDERPASS
UNI UNIVERSITY
UPR UPPER
V VALE
VA VALLEY
VIAD VIADUCT
VIL VILLA
VIS VISTA
VLG VILLAGE
VLS VILLAS
VW VIEW
W WEST
WD WOOD
WHF WHARF
WK WALK
WKS WALKS
WLS WELLS
WY WAY
YD YARD
YHA YOUTH HOSTEL

POSTCODE TOWNS AND AREA ABBREVIATIONS

ABR/ST Abridge/Stapleford Abbotts
ABYW Abbey Wood
ACT Acton
ALP/SUD Alperton/Sudbury
ARCH Archway
ASHF Ashford (Surrey)
BAL Balham
BANK Bank
BAR Barnet
BARB Barbican
BARK Barking
BARK/HLT Barkingside/Hainault
BARN Barnes
BAY/PAD Bayswater/Paddington
BCTR Becontree
BECK Beckenham
BELMT Belmont
BELV Belvedere
BERM/RHTH Bermondsey/Rotherhithe
BETH Bethnal Green
BFN/LL Blackfen/Longlands
BGVA Belgravia
BKHH Buckhurst Hill
BKHTH/KID Blackheath/Kidbrooke
BLKFR Blackfriars
BMLY Bromley
BMSBY Bloomsbury
BORE Borehamwood
BOW Bow
BROCKY Brockley
BRXN/ST Brixton north/Stockwell
BRXS/STRHM Brixton south/Streatham Hill
BRYLDS Berrylands
BTFD Brentford
BTSEA Battersea
BUSH Bushey
BXLY Bexley
BXLYHN Bexleyheath north
BXLYHS Bexleyheath south
CAMTN Camden Town
CAN/RD Canning Town/Royal Docks
CANST Cannon Street station
CAR Carshalton
CAT Catford
CAVSQ/HST Cavendish Square/Harley Street
CDALE/KGS Colindale/Kingsbury
CEND/HSY/T Crouch End/Hornsey/Turnpike Lane
CHARL Charlton
CHCR Charing Cross
CHDH Chadwell Heath
CHEAM Cheam
CHEL Chelsea
CHIG Chigwell
CHING Chingford
CHSGTN Chessington
CHST Chislehurst
CHSWK Chiswick
CITYW City of London west
CLAP Clapham
CLAY Clayhall
CLKNW Clerkenwell
CLPT Clapton
CMBW Camberwell
CONDST Conduit Street
COVGDN Covent Garden
CRICK Cricklewood
CROY/NA Croydon/New Addington
CRW Collier Row
DAGE Dagenham east
DAGW Dagenham west
DART Dartford
DEN/HRF Denham/Harefield
DEPT Deptford
DUL Dulwich
E/WMO/HCT East & West Molesey/Hampton Court
EA Ealing
EBAR East Barnet
EBED/NFELT East Bedfont/North Feltham
ECT Earl's Court
ED Edmonton
EDGW Edgware
EDUL East Dulwich
EFNCH East Finchley
EHAM East Ham
ELTH/MOT Eltham/Mottingham
EMB Embankment
EMPK Emerson Park
EN Enfield
ENC/FH Enfield Chase/Forty Hill
ERITH Erith
ERITHM Erith Marshes
ESH/CLAY Esher/Claygate
EW Ewell
FARR Farringdon
FBAR/BDGN Friern Barnet/Bounds Green
FELT Feltham
FENCHST Fenchurch Street
FITZ Fitzrovia
FLST/FETLN Fleet Street/Fetter Lane
FNCH Finchley
FSBYE Finsbury east
FSBYPK Finsbury Park
FSBYW Finsbury west
FSTGT Forest Gate
FSTH Forest Hill
FUL/PGN Fulham/Parsons Green
GDMY/SEVK Goodmayes/Seven Kings
GFD/PVL Greenford/Perivale
GINN Gray's Inn
GLDGN Golders Green
GNTH/NBYPK Gants Hill/Newbury Park
GNWCH Greenwich
GPK Gidea Park
GSTN Garston
GTPST Great Portland Street
GWRST Gower Street
HACK Hackney
HAMP Hampstead
HARH Harold Hill
HAYES Hayes
HBRY Highbury
HCH Hornchurch
HCIRC Holborn Circus
HDN Hendon
HDTCH Houndsditch
HEST Heston
HGDN/ICK Hillingdon/Ickenham
HGT Highgate
HHOL High Holborn
HMSMTH Hammersmith
HNHL Herne Hill
HNWL Hanwell
HOL/ALD Holborn/Aldwych
HOLWY Holloway
HOM Homerton
HOR/WEW Horton/West Ewell
HPTN Hampton
HRW Harrow
HSLW Hounslow
HSLWW Hounslow west
HTHAIR Heathrow Airport
HYS/HAR Hayes/Harlington
IL Ilford
IS Islington
ISLW Isleworth
KENS Kensington
KIL/WHAMP Kilburn/West Hampstead
KTBR Knightsbridge
KTN/HRWW/WS Kenton/Harrow Weald/Wealdstone
KTTN Kentish Town
KUT Kingston upon Thames
KUTN/CMB Kingston upon Thames north/Coombe
LBTH Lambeth
LEE/GVPK Lee/Grove Park
LEW Lewisham
LEY Leyton
LINN Lincoln's Inn
LOTH Lothbury
LOU Loughton
LSQ/SEVD Leicester Square/Seven Dials
LVPST Liverpool Street
MANHO Mansion House
MBLAR Marble Arch
MHST Marylebone High Street
MLHL Mill Hill
MNPK Manor Park
MON Monument
MORT/ESHN Mortlake/East Sheen
MRDN Morden
MTCM Mitcham
MUSWH Muswell Hill
MV/WKIL Maida Vale/West Kilburn
MYFR/PICC Mayfair/Piccadilly
MYFR/PKLN Mayfair/Park Lane
NFNCH/WDSPK North Finchley/Woodside Park
NKENS North Kensington
NOXST/BSQ New Oxford Street/Bloomsbury Square
NRWD Norwood
NTGHL Notting Hill
NTHLT Northolt
NTHWD Northwood
NWCR New Cross
NWDGN Norwood Green
NWMAL New Malden
OBST Old Broad Street
ORP Orpington
OXHEY Oxhey
OXSTW Oxford Street west
PECK Peckham
PEND Ponders End
PGE/AN Penge/Anerley
PIM Pimlico
PIN Pinner
PLMGR Palmers Green
PLSTW Plaistow
POP/IOD Poplar/Isle of Dogs
PUR Purfleet
PUR/KEN Purley/Kenley
PUT/ROE Putney/Roehampton
RAIN Rainham (Gt Lon)
RCH/KEW Richmond/Kew
RCHPK/HAM Richmond Park/Ham
RDART Rural Dartford
REDBR Redbridge
REGST Regent Street
RKW/CH/CXG Rickmansworth/Chorleywood/Croxley Green
ROM Romford
ROMW/RG Romford west/Rush Green
RSLP Ruislip
RSQ Russell Square
RYLN/HDSTN Rayners Lane/Headstone
RYNPK Raynes Park
SAND/SEL Sanderstead/Selsdon
SCUP Sidcup
SDTCH Shoreditch
SEVS/STOTM Seven Sisters/South Tottenham
SHB Shepherd's Bush
SKENS South Kensington
SNWD South Norwood
SOCK/AV South Ockendon/Aveley
SOHO/CST Soho/Carnaby Street
SOHO/SHAV Soho/Shaftesbury Avenue
SRTFD Stratford
STAN Stanmore
STBT St Bart's
STHGT/OAK Southgate/Oakwood
STHL Southall
STHWK Southwark
STJS St James's
STJSPK St James's Park
STJWD St John's Wood
STKPK Stockley Park
STLK St Luke's
STMC/STPC St Mary Cray/St Paul's Cray
STNW/STAM Stoke Newington/Stamford Hill
STP St Paul's
STPAN St Pancras
STRHM/NOR Streatham/Norbury
STWL/WRAY Stanwell/Wraysbury
SUN Sunbury
SURB Surbiton
SUT Sutton
SWFD South Woodford
SWLY Swanley
SYD Sydenham
TEDD Teddington
THDIT Thames Ditton
THHTH Thornton Heath
THMD Thamesmead
TOOT Tooting
TOTM Tottenham
TPL/STR Temple/Strand
TRDG/WHET Totteridge/Whetstone
TWK Twickenham
TWRH Tower Hill
UED Upper Edmonton
UX/CGN Uxbridge/Colham Green
VX/NE Vauxhall/Nine Elms
WAB Waltham Abbey
WALTH Walthamstow
WALW Walworth
WAN Wanstead
WAND/EARL Wandsworth/Earlsfield
WAP Wapping
WAT Watford
WATW Watford west
WBLY Wembley
WBPTN West Brompton
WCHMH Winchmore Hill
WCHPL Whitechapel
WDGN Wood Green
WDR/YW West Drayton/Yiewsley
WEA West Ealing
WELL Welling
WEST Westminster
WESTW Westminster west
WFD Woodford
WHALL Whitehall
WHTN Whitton
WIM/MER Wimbledon/Merton
WKENS West Kensington
WLGTN Wallington
WLSDN Willesden
WNWD West Norwood
WOOL/PLUM Woolwich/Plumstead
WOT/HER Walton-on-Thames/Hersham
WPK Worcester Park
WWKM West Wickham
YEAD Yeading

1 - Aca

Index - streets

I

1 Av *WOOL/PLUM* SE18 127 G3

A

Aaron Hill Rd *EHAM* E6 108 A4
Abbess Cl *BRXS/STRHM* SW2 162 C3
Abbeville Ms *CLAP* * SW4 141 J6
Abbeville Rd *CEND/HSY/T* N8 66 D1
CLAP SW4 161 H1
Abbey Av *ALP/SUD* HA0 98 A1
Abbey Cl *HYS/HAR* UB3 114 A1
NTHLT UB5 95 K2
PIN HA5 41 F6
ROM RM1 75 H3
Abbey Crs *BELV* DA17 129 H4
Abbeydale Rd *ALP/SUD* HA0 80 B6
Abbey Dr *TOOT* SW17 179 F1
Abbeyfield Cl *MTCM* CR4 178 D5
Abbeyfield Est
BERM/RHTH SE16 123 K4
Abbeyfield Rd
BERM/RHTH SE16 123 K4
Abbeyfields Cl *WLSDN* NW10 98 C2
Abbey Gdns *BERM/RHTH* SE16 123 H4
HMSMTH W6 119 H6
STJWD NW8 101 G1
Abbey Gv *ABYW* SE2 128 C4
Abbeyhill Rd *BFN/LL* DA15 168 D3
Abbey La *BECK* BR3 182 D3
SRTFD E15 106 B1
Abbey Ms *WALTH* E17 69 J2
Abbey Mt *BELV* DA17 129 G5
Abbey Orchard St *WEST* SW1P 16 D4
Abbey Pk *BECK* BR3 182 D3
Abbey Pl *DART* * DA1 151 G6
Abbey Rd *BARK* IG11 90 B5
BELV DA17 128 E4
BXLYHS DA6 149 F5
CROY/NA CR0 211 H1
EN EN1 24 A6
GNTH/NBYPK IG2 72 D2
KIL/WHAMP NW6 83 F6
SRTFD E15 106 B1
WIM/MER SW19 178 B3
WLSDN NW10 80 D6
Abbey St *PLSTW* E13 106 E3
STHWK SE1 19 J4
Abbey Ter *ABYW* SE2 128 D3
Abbey Vw *MLHL* NW7 31 H5
Abbey Wk *E/WMO/HCT* KT8 173 G6
Abbey Wood Rd *ABYW* SE2 128 C4
Abbot Cl *RSLP* HA4 77 H1
Abbotsbury Cl *SRTFD* E15 106 A1
WKENS * W14 119 J2
Abbotsbury Gdns *PIN* HA5 59 G3
Abbotsbury Ms *PECK* SE15 143 K4
Abbotsbury Rd *MRDN* SM4 194 A1
WKENS W14 119 H2
WWKM BR4 199 J6
Abbots Cl *STMC/STPC* BR5 201 H5
Abbots Dr *RYLN/HDSTN* HA2 60 A6
Abbotsford Av *SEVS/STOTM* N15 67 J1
Abbotsford Gdns *WFD* IG8 52 E3
Abbotsford Rd *GDMY/SEVK* IG3 73 G6
Abbots Gdns *EFNCH* N2 65 H1
Abbots Gn *CROY/NA* CR0 213 F4
Abbotshade Rd
BERM/RHTH * SE16 124 A1
Abbotshall Av *STHGT/OAK* N14 34 C5
Abbotshall Rd *CAT* SE6 165 G3
Abbots La *STHWK* SE1 19 H1
Abbotsleigh Cl *BELMT* SM2 209 F5
Abbotsleigh Rd
STRHM/NOR SW16 161 H6
Abbots Mnr *PIM* * SW1V 121 G5
Abbotsmede Cl *TWK* TW1 156 A4
Abbots Pk *BRXS/STRHM* SW2 162 B3
Abbot's Pl *KIL/WHAMP* NW6 83 F6
Abbots Rd *CHEAM* SM3 208 C2
EDGE HA8 45 F3
EHAM E6 89 H6
Abbots Ter *CEND/HSY/T* N8 66 E3
Abbotstone Rd *PUT/ROE* SW15 139 F4
Abbot St *HACK* E8 86 B4
Abbots Wk *KENS* * W8 120 A3
Abbots Wy *BECK* BR3 198 B2
Abbotswell Rd *BROCKY* SE4 144 C6
Abbotswood Cl *BELV* DA17 129 F3
Abbotswood Gdns *CLAY* IG5 53 K6
Abbotswood Rd *EDUL* SE22 143 F5
STRHM/NOR SW16 161 J5
Abbotswood Wy *HYS/HAR* UB3 114 A1
Abbott Av *RYNPK* SW20 177 G5
Abbott Cl *HPTN* TW12 172 D2
NTHLT UB5 77 K4
Abbott Rd *POP/IOD* E14 106 A4
Abbotts Cl *IS* * N1 85 J5
ROMW/RG RM7 56 D6
THMD SE28 109 J6
Abbotts Crs *CHING* E4 38 B6
ENC/FH EN2 23 H3
Abbotts Dr *ALP/SUD* HA0 61 H6
Abbotts Md
RCHPK/HAM * TW10 156 D6
Abbotts Park Rd *LEY* E10 70 A4
Abbotts Rd *BAR* EN5 21 F5
MTCM CR4 195 H1
STHL UB1 114 D1
Abbott's Wk *BXLYHN* DA7 148 E1
Abchurch La *MANHO* EC4N 13 F5
Abdale Rd *SHB* W12 118 E1
Aberavon Rd *BOW* E3 105 G2
Abercairn Rd
STRHM/NOR SW16 179 H3
Aberconway Rd *MRDN* SM4 178 A6
Abercorn Cl *MLHL* NW7 46 C3
STJWD NW8 101 G2
Abercorn Crs *RYLN/HDSTN* HA2 60 B5
Abercorn Gdns *CHDH* RM6 73 H3
KTN/HRWW/W HA3 61 K4
Abercorn Gv *RSLP* HA4 58 B1
Abercorn Pl *STJWD* NW8 101 G2
Abercorn Rd *MLHL* NW7 46 C3
STAN HA7 43 J3
Abercorn Wy *STHWK* SE1 123 H5
Abercrombie Dr *EN* EN1 24 C2
Abercrombie St *BTSEA* SW11 140 D3
Aberdare Cl *WWKM* BR4 199 F6
Aberdare Gdns
KIL/WHAMP NW6 83 F5
MLHL NW7 46 B3
Aberdare Rd *PEND* EN3 24 E5
Aberdeen Cottages *STAN* * HA7 43 J3
Aberdeen La *HBRY* N5 85 H3
Aberdeen Pde *UED* * N18 50 D1
Aberdeen Pk *HBRY* N5 85 H3
Aberdeen Pl *STJWD* NW8 2 A7
Aberdeen Rd *CROY/NA* CR0 211 J2
HBRY N5 85 J2
KTN/HRWW/W HA3 43 F6
UED N18 50 D1
WLSDN NW10 81 H3
Aberdeen Ter *BKHTH/KID* SE3 145 G3
Aberdour Rd *BCTR* RM8 91 H1
Aberdour St *STHWK* SE1 19 G6
Aberfeldy St *POP/IOD* E14 106 A5
Aberford Gdns
WOOL/PLUM SE18 146 D2
Aberfoyle Rd
STRHM/NOR SW16 179 J2
Abergeldie Rd *LEE/GVPK* SE12 166 A1
Abernethy Rd *LEW* SE13 145 H5
Abersham Rd *HACK* E8 86 B3
Abery St *WOOL/PLUM* SE18 127 K4
Abingdon Cl *STHWK* * SE1 19 K7
WIM/MER SW19 178 B2
Abingdon Rd *FNCH* N3 47 G5
KENS W8 119 K3
STRHM/NOR SW16 179 K4
Abingdon St *WEST* SW1P 16 E3
Abingdon Vls *KENS* W8 119 K3
Abingdon Wy *ORP* BR6 217 H2
Abinger Av *BELMT* SM2 208 A6
Abinger Cl *BMLY* BR1 184 D6
CROY/NA CR0 214 A4
GDMY/SEVK IG3 91 G2
WLGTN SM6 210 E3
Abinger Gdns *ISLW* TW7 135 K4
Abinger Gv *DEPT* SE8 124 C6
Abinger Ms *MV/WKIL* W9 100 E3
Abinger Rd *CHSWK* W4 118 C3
Ablett St *BERM/RHTH* SE16 123 K5
Abney Park Ter
STNW/STAM * N16 68 B6
Aboyne Dr *RYNPK* SW20 176 D5
Aboyne Rd *TOOT* SW17 160 C5
WLSDN NW10 81 G1
Abridge Gdns *CRW* RM5 56 C2
Abridge Wy *BARK* IG11 109 H1
Abyssinia Cl *BTSEA* SW11 140 D5
Abyssinia Rd *BTSEA* * SW11 140 D5
Acacia Av *BTFD* TW8 136 C1
HCH RM12 75 H6
RSLP HA4 58 E5
TOTM N17 49 K3
WBLY HA9 80 A3
YEAD UB4 94 D5

Acacia Cl DEPT SE8 124 B4
KTN/HRWW/W HA3 42 E2
STMC/STPC BR5 201 J2
Acacia Dr CHEAM SM3 193 J5
Acacia Gdns STJWD NW8 2 B2
WWKM BR4 199 F6
Acacia Gv DUL SE21 162 E4
NWMAL KT3 176 B6
Acacia Ms WDR/YW UB7 112 A6
Acacia Pl STJWD NW8 2 B2
Acacia Rd ACT W3 98 E6
BECK BR3 182 C6
DART DA1 171 F3
ENC/FH EN2 23 K2
HPTN TW12 173 F2
MTCM CR4 179 F5
STJWD NW8 2 B2
STRHM/NOR SW16 179 K4
WALTH E17 69 G3
WAN E11 70 C6
WDGN N22 49 G4
The Acacias EBAR * EN4 21 H6
Acacia Wy BFN/LL DA15 168 A3
Academy Gdns CROY/NA CR0 197 G5
NTHLT UB5 95 H1
Academy Pl WOOL/PLUM SE18 146 E2
Academy Rd WOOL/PLUM SE18 146 E1
Acanthus Dr STHWK SE1 123 H5
Acanthus Rd BTSEA SW11 141 F4
Accommodation Rd
GLDGN NW11 64 D4
Ace Pde CHSGTN * KT9 206 A1
Acer Av YEAD UB4 95 J3
Acfold Rd FUL/PGN SW6 140 A2
Achilles Cl STHWK SE1 123 H5
Achilles Rd KIL/WHAMP NW6 82 E3
Achilles St NWCR SE14 144 B1
Acklam Rd NKENS W10 100 D4
Acklington Dr CDALE/KGS NW9 45 G4
Ackmar Rd FUL/PGN SW6 139 K2
Ackroyd Dr BOW E3 105 H4
Ackroyd Rd FSTH SE23 164 A2
Acland Cl WOOL/PLUM SE18 147 J1
Acland Crs CMBW SE5 142 E5
Acland Rd CRICK NW2 81 K4
Acock Gv NTHLT UB5 78 B2
Acol Crs RSLP HA4 77 F3
Acol Rd KIL/WHAMP NW6 82 E5
Acorn Cl CHING E4 51 K1
CHST BR7 185 H1
ENC/FH EN2 23 G2
HPTN TW12 173 G2
STAN HA7 43 H3
Acorn Gdns ACT W3 99 F4
NRWD SE19 181 G4
Acorn Gv HYS/HAR UB3 133 J1
RSLP HA4 76 D2
Acorn Pde PECK * SE15 143 J1
Acorn Rd DART DA1 150 C6
Acorns Wy ESH/CLAY KT10 204 C3
Acorn Wy FSTH SE23 164 A5
ORP BR6 216 B2
Acre Dr EDUL SE22 143 H5
Acre La BRXS/STRHM SW2 142 A5
CAR SM5 210 A2
Acre Rd DAGE RM10 92 D5
KUTN/CMB KT2 175 F4
WIM/MER SW19 178 C2
Acre Wy NTHWD HA6 40 D4
Acris St WAND/EARL SW18 140 B6
Acton Cl ED N9 36 C4
Acton Hill Ms ACT * W3 117 J1
Acton La CHSWK W4 117 K4
WLSDN NW10 98 E2
Acton Ms HACK E8 86 B6
Acton St FSBYW WC1X 5 G5
Acuba Rd WAND/EARL SW18 160 A4
Acworth Pl DART * DA1 171 F1
Ada Ct STJWD NW8 101 G2
Ada Gdns POP/IOD E14 106 B5
SRTFD E15 88 D6
Adair Cl SNWD SE25 181 J6
Adair Rd NKENS W10 100 C3
Adam & Eve Ms KENS W8 119 K3
Adam Rd CHING E4 51 H2
Adams Cl BRYLDS KT5 191 G3
CDALE/KGS NW9 62 D6
FNCH N3 46 E3
Adams Ms WDGN * N22 49 F3
Adamson Rd CAN/RD E16 106 E5
HAMP NW3 83 H5
Adams Pl HOLWY N7 85 F3
Adamsrill Rd SYD SE26 164 A6
Adams Rd BECK BR3 198 B2
TOTM N17 49 K5
Adam's Rw MYFR/PKLN W1K 9 H6
Adams Sq BXLYHS DA6 149 F4
Adam St TPL/STR WC2R 11 F6
Adams Wk KUT KT1 175 F5
Adams Wy SNWD SE25 197 G3
Adam Wk FUL/PGN * SW6 139 F1
Ada Pl BETH E2 86 C6
Adare Wk STRHM/NOR SW16 161 K4
Ada Rd ALP/SUD * HA0 79 J1
CMBW SE5 143 F1
Ada St HACK E8 86 D6
Adderley Gdns ELTH/MOT SE9 167 F6
Adderley Gv BTSEA SW11 141 F6
Adderley Rd KTN/HRWW/W HA3 43 F4
Adderley St POP/IOD E14 106 A5
Addington Dr NFNCH/WDSP N12 47 H2
Addington Gv SYD SE26 164 B6
Addington Rd BOW E3 105 J2
CAN/RD E16 106 C3
CROY/NA CR0 196 B5
FSBYPK N4 67 G4
WWKM BR4 214 A2
Addington Sq CMBW SE5 142 D1
Addington Village Rd
CROY/NA CR0 213 H4
Addis Cl PEND EN3 25 F2
Addiscombe Av
CROY/NA CR0 197 H4
Addiscombe Cl
KTN/HRWW/W HA3 61 J2
Addiscombe Court Rd
CROY/NA CR0 197 F5
Addiscombe Gv CROY/NA CR0 196 E6
Addiscombe Rd CROY/NA CR0 197 F6
Addison Av HSLW TW3 135 H2
NTGHL W11 119 H1
STHGT/OAK N14 34 B1
Addison Bridge Pl WKENS W14 119 H4
Addison Cl NTHWD HA6 40 E4
STMC/STPC BR5 201 H3
Addison Crs WKENS W14 119 H3
Addison Dr LEE/GVPK SE12 146 A6
Addison Gdns BRYLDS KT5 191 G1
WKENS W14 119 G3
Addison Gv CHSWK W4 118 B3
Addison Pl NTGHL W11 119 H1
Addison Rd BARK/HLT IG6 54 C4
HAYES BR2 200 C2
NTGHL W11 119 H2
PEND EN3 24 E2
SNWD SE25 197 H1
TEDD TW11 174 C2
WALTH E17 69 K2
WAN E11 70 E3
Addison's Cl CROY/NA CR0 198 C6
Addison Ter CHSWK * W4 117 K4
Addison Wy GLDGN NW11 64 D1
NTHWD HA6 40 E4
YEAD UB4 94 E5
Addle Hl BLKFR EC4V 12 B5
Addle St CITYW * EC2V 12 D3
Adecroft Wy E/WMO/HCT KT8 173 H6
Adela Av NWMAL KT3 192 E2
Adelaide Av BROCKY SE4 144 D5
Adelaide Cl EN EN1 24 A1
STAN HA7 29 G6
Adelaide Ct HNWL W7 116 A2
Adelaide Gdns CHDH RM6 74 A2
Adelaide Gv SHB W12 118 D1
Adelaide Rd CHST BR7 185 G1
HAMP NW3 83 K5
HEST TW5 134 D2
IL IG1 72 B6
LEY E10 88 A1
NWDGN UB2 114 D4
RCH/KEW TW9 137 G5
SURB KT6 191 F2
TEDD TW11 174 A2
WAND/EARL SW18 139 K6
WEA W13 116 B2
Adelaide St CHCR * WC2N 10 E6
Adelaide Ter BTFD * TW8 116 E5
Adela St NKENS W10 100 C3
Adelina Gv WCHPL E1 104 E4
Adelina Ms BAL SW12 161 J3
Adeline Pl RSQ WC1B 10 D2
Adeliza Cl BARK IG11 90 C5
Adelphi Crs HCH RM12 75 J6
YEAD UB4 94 C2
Adelphi Ter CHCR WC2N 11 F6
Adelphi Wy YEAD UB4 94 D2
Adeney Cl HMSMTH W6 119 G6
Aden Gv STNW/STAM N16 85 K2
Adenmore Rd CAT SE6 164 D2
Aden Rd IL IG1 72 B4
PEND EN3 25 G5
Adhara Rd NTHWD HA6 40 D1
Adie Rd HMSMTH W6 119 F3
Adine Rd PLSTW E13 106 E3
Adler St WCHPL E1 104 C4
Adley St HOM E9 87 G3
Adlington Cl UED N18 49 K1
Admaston Rd
WOOL/PLUM SE18 147 H1
Admiral Cl STMC/STPC BR5 202 E1
Admiral Ms NKENS W10 100 B3
Admiral Pl BERM/RHTH SE16 124 B1
Admirals Cl SWFD E18 71 F1
Admiral Seymour Rd
ELTH/MOT SE9 146 E5
Admiral's Ga GNWCH SE10 144 E2
Admiral Sq WBPTN * SW10 140 B2
Admiral St DEPT SE8 144 D2
Admiral's Wk HAMP NW3 83 G1
Admirals Wy POP/IOD E14 124 E2
Admiralty Rd TEDD TW11 174 A3
Admiral Wk MV/WKIL W9 100 E4
Adnams Wk RAIN RM13 93 J3
Adolf St CAT SE6 164 D6
Adolphus Rd FSBYPK N4 67 H6
Adolphus St DEPT SE8 144 C1
Adomar Rd BCTR RM8 91 K1
Adpar St BAY/PAD W2 8 A1
Adrian Ms WBPTN SW10 120 A6
Adrienne Av STHL UB1 95 K3
Advance Rd WNWD SE27 162 D6
Advent Wy UED N18 51 F1
Adys Lawn CRICK * NW2 81 K4
Adys Rd PECK SE15 143 G4
Aerodrome Rd CDALE/KGS NW9 45 H6
Aerodrome Wy HEST TW5 114 B6
Affleck St IS * N1 5 H3
Afghan Rd BTSEA SW11 140 D3
Aftab Ter WCHPL * E1 104 D3
Agamemnon Rd
KIL/WHAMP NW6 82 D3
Agar Cl SURB KT6 191 G6
Agar Gv CAMTN NW1 84 D5
Agar St CHCR WC2N 10 E6
Agate Cl CAN/RD E16 107 H5
Agate Rd HMSMTH W6 119 F3
Agatha Cl WAP E1W 123 J1
Agaton Rd ELTH/MOT SE9 167 H4
Agave Rd CRICK NW2 82 A2
Agdon St FSBYE EC1V 6 A6
Agincourt Rd HAMP NW3 83 K2
Agister Rd CHIG IG7 55 G1
Agnes Av IL IG1 90 A2
Agnes Cl EHAM E6 108 A6
Agnesfield Cl NFNCH/WDSP N12 47 J2
Agnes Gdns BCTR RM8 91 K2
Agnes Riley Gdns CLAP * SW4 161 H2
Agnes Rd ACT W3 118 C2
Agnes St POP/IOD E14 105 H5
Agnew Rd FSTH SE23 164 B2
Agricola Pl EN EN1 24 B6
Aidan Cl DAGW RM9 92 A2
Ailsa Av TWK TW1 136 B6
Ailsa Rd TWK TW1 136 C6
Ailsa St POP/IOD E14 106 A4
Ainger Rd HAMP NW3 83 K5
Ainsdale Cl ORP BR6 201 J5
Ainsdale Crs PIN HA5 42 A6
Ainsdale Dr STHWK SE1 123 H5
Ainsdale Rd EA W5 97 K3
OXHEY WD19 27 G5
Ainsley Av ROMW/RG RM7 74 E3
Ainsley Cl ED N9 36 A3
Ainsley St BETH E2 104 D2
Ainslie Wood Crs CHING E4 51 K1
Ainslie Wood Gdns CHING E4 37 K6
Ainslie Wood Rd CHING E4 51 J1
Ainsty St BERM/RHTH * SE16 123 K2
Ainsworth Cl CMBW * SE5 143 F3
CRICK NW2 81 J1
Ainsworth Rd CROY/NA CR0 196 C5
HOM E9 86 E5
Ainsworth Wy STJWD NW8 83 G6
Aintree Av EHAM E6 89 J6
Aintree Crs BARK/HLT IG6 54 C5
Aintree Rd GFD/PVL UB6 97 H1
Aintree St FUL/PGN SW6 139 H1
Airdrie Cl IS * N1 85 F5
YEAD UB4 95 J4
Airedale Av CHSWK W4 118 C5
Airedale Av South CHSWK * W4 118 C5
Airedale Rd BAL SW12 160 E2
EA W5 116 D3
Airfield Wy HCH RM12 93 K4
Airlie Gdns IL IG1 72 B5
KENS W8 119 K2
Air St REGST W1B 10 B6
Airthrie Rd GDMY/SEVK IG3 73 H5
Aisgill Av WKENS W14 119 J5
Aisher Rd THMD SE28 109 J6
Aislibie Rd LEW SE13 145 H5
Aiten Pl HMSMTH W6 118 D4
Aitken Cl HACK E8 86 C6
MTCM CR4 194 E4
Aitken Rd BAR EN5 20 A6
CAT SE6 164 E4
Aitman Dr CHSWK * W4 117 H5
Ajax Av CDALE/KGS NW9 45 G6
Ajax Rd KIL/WHAMP NW6 82 D2
Akabusi Cl SNWD SE25 197 H3
Akehurst St PUT/ROE SW15 158 D1
Akenside Rd HAMP NW3 83 H3
Akerman Rd CMBW SE5 142 C2
SURB KT6 190 D3
Alabama St WOOL/PLUM SE18 147 J1
Alacross Rd EA W5 116 D2
Alan Cl DART DA1 151 F5
Alandale Dr PIN HA5 41 F4
Alan Dr BAR EN5 32 C1
Alan Gdns ROMW/RG RM7 74 C4
Alan Hocken Wy SRTFD E15 106 C1
Alan Rd WIM/MER SW19 177 H1
Alanthus Cl LEE/GVPK SE12 165 J1
Alaska St STHWK SE1 17 J1
Alba Cl YEAD UB4 95 H3
Albacore Crs LEW SE13 164 E1
Alba Gdns GLDGN NW11 64 C3
Albain Crs ASHF TW15 152 B4
The Albany KUTN/CMB KT2 174 E2
Albany Cl BUSH WD23 28 D1
BXLY DA5 168 D2
ESH/CLAY KT10 204 A6
MORT/ESHN SW14 137 J5
SEVS/STOTM N15 67 H1
Albany Cottages HNWL * W7 115 K1
Albany Ctyd MYFR/PICC W1J 10 A6
Albany Crs EDGE HA8 44 C3
ESH/CLAY KT10 204 E4
Albany Ms BMLY BR1 183 K2
IS * N1 85 G5
KUTN/CMB * KT2 174 E2
SUT SM1 209 F3
WALW SE17 122 D6
Albany Pde BTFD * TW8 117 F6
Albany Pk PEND * EN3 25 F1
Albany Park Av PEND EN3 24 E2
Albany Park Rd KUTN/CMB KT2 174 E2
Albany Pl BTFD TW8 116 E6
HOLWY N7 85 G2
Albany Rd BELV DA17 129 G6
BTFD TW8 116 E6
BXLY DA5 168 D2
CHDH RM6 74 B3
CHST BR7 185 G1
CMBW SE5 122 E6
FSBYPK N4 67 F3
HCH RM12 75 J5
MNPK E12 89 H2
NWMAL KT3 192 A1
RCHPK/HAM * TW10 137 G6
UED N18 50 D1
WALTH E17 69 G3
WEA W13 97 H6
WIM/MER SW19 178 A1
Albany Rw EFNCH * N2 65 J1
Albany St CAMTN NW1 3 K4
Albany Ter RCHPK/HAM * TW10 137 G6
Albany Vw BKHH IG9 38 E3
Alba Pl NTGHL W11 100 D5
Albatross St WOOL/PLUM SE18 147 K1
Albemarle Ap GNTH/NBYPK IG2 72 B3
Albemarle Av WHTN TW2 154 E3
Albemarle Gdns
GNTH/NBYPK IG2 72 B3
NWMAL KT3 192 A1
Albemarle Pk BECK * BR3 182 E4
STAN * HA7 43 J1
Albemarle Rd BECK BR3 182 E4
EBAR EN4 33 J2
Albemarle St CONDST W1S 10 A6
Albemarle Wy FARR EC1M 6 A7
Alberon Gdns GLDGN NW11 64 D1
Alberta Av SUT SM1 208 C2
Alberta Est WALW SE17 122 C5
Alberta Rd BXLYHN DA7 149 K2
EN EN1 36 B1
Alberta St WALW SE17 122 C5
Albert Av CHING E4 37 J6
VX/NE SW8 142 A1
Albert Br BTSEA SW11 140 D1
Albert Bridge Ga BTSEA SW11 140 E1
Albert Bridge Rd BTSEA SW11 140 D1
CHEL SW3 120 D6
Albert Carr Gdns
STRHM/NOR SW16 179 K1
Albert Cl HOM E9 86 D6
WDGN N22 48 D4
Albert Cottages WCHPL * E1 104 C4
Albert Crs CHING E4 37 J6
Albert Dr WIM/MER SW19 159 H4
Albert Emb LBTH SE11 121 K5
Albert Gdns WCHPL E1 105 F5
Albert Ga KTBR SW1X 15 F2
Albert Gv WIM/MER SW19 177 G4
Albert Ms BROCKY * SE4 144 C5
FSBYPK * N4 67 F5
KENS W8 120 B3
POP/IOD * E14 105 G6
Albert Pl FNCH N3 46 E4
KENS W8 120 A2
Albert Rd BCTR RM8 74 B5
BELMT SM2 209 H3
BELV DA17 129 G5
BKHH IG9 39 H4
BXLY DA5 169 H1
CAN/RD E16 126 D1
EA W5 97 H3
EBAR EN4 21 G5
ELTH/MOT SE9 166 D5
FSBYPK N4 67 F5
HAYES BR2 200 C2
HDN NW4 64 B1
HPTN TW12 173 H1
HSLW TW3 135 F5
HYS/HAR UB3 113 H3
IL IG1 90 C1
KIL/WHAMP NW6 100 D1
KUT KT1 175 G5
LEY E10 70 A6
MLHL NW7 45 H1
MTCM CR4 178 E6
NWDGN UB2 114 C3
NWMAL KT3 192 C1
ORP BR6 217 G3
PGE/AN SE20 182 A3
RCHPK/HAM TW10 137 F6
RDART DA2 171 F5
ROM RM1 75 H3
RYLN/HDSTN HA2 42 C6
SEVS/STOTM N15 68 A3
SNWD SE25 197 J1
STMC/STPC BR5 202 C3
SWFD E18 53 F6
TEDD TW11 174 A2
TWK TW1 156 A3
WALTH E17 69 J2
WDGN N22 48 D4
WDR/YW UB7 112 B1
Albert Sq SRTFD E15 88 C3
VX/NE SW8 142 A1
Albert St CAMTN NW1 3 K1
NFNCH/WDSP N12 47 G1
Albert Ter CAMTN NW1 84 A6
EA * W5 97 H3
WLSDN * NW10 81 F6
Albert Wy PECK SE15 143 J1
Albion Av MUSWH N10 48 A4
VX/NE SW8 141 J3
Albion Cl BAY/PAD W2 8 D5
ROMW/RG RM7 75 F3
Albion Dr HACK E8 86 C5
Albion Est BERM/RHTH * SE16 123 K2
Albion Gdns HMSMTH W6 118 E4
Albion Ga BAY/PAD W2 8 D5
Albion Gv STNW/STAM N16 86 A2
Albion Ms BAY/PAD W2 8 D4
IS * N1 85 G5
Albion Pl FARR EC1M 12 A1
HMSMTH W6 118 E4
SNWD * SE25 181 H6
Albion Rd BELMT SM2 209 H4
BXLYHS DA6 149 G5
HSLW TW3 135 F5
HYS/HAR UB3 94 C5
KUTN/CMB KT2 175 K4
STNW/STAM N16 85 K3
TOTM N17 50 B5
WALTH E17 52 A6
WHTN TW2 155 K3
Albion Sq HACK E8 86 B5
Albion St BAY/PAD W2 8 D4
BERM/RHTH SE16 123 K2
CROY/NA CR0 196 C5
Albion Ter CHING * E4 25 K5
HACK E8 86 B5
Albion Villas Rd FSTH SE23 163 K5
Albion Wy LEW SE13 145 F5
STBT EC1A 12 C2
WBLY HA9 80 C1
Albion Yd IS N1 5 F3
Albrighton Rd EDUL SE22 143 F4
Albuhera Cl ENC/FH EN2 23 G2
Albury Av BELMT SM2 208 A6
BXLYHN DA7 149 F3
ISLW TW7 136 A1
Albury Cl HOR/WEW KT19 206 D6
HPTN TW12 173 F2
Albury Dr PIN HA5 41 G4
Albury Ms MNPK E12 71 G5
Albury Rd CHSGTN KT9 206 A3
Albury St DEPT SE8 124 D6
Albyfield BMLY BR1 184 E6
Albyn Rd DEPT SE8 144 D2
Alcester Crs CLPT E5 68 D6
Alcester Rd WLGTN SM6 210 B2
Alcock Cl WLGTN SM6 210 D5
Alcock Rd HEST TW5 134 C1
Alconbury Rd CLPT E5 68 C6
Alcorn Cl CHEAM SM3 193 K6
Alcott Cl HNWL W7 97 F4
Aldborough Rd DAGE RM10 92 E4
Aldborough Rd North
GNTH/NBYPK IG2 73 F2
Aldborough Rd South
GDMY/SEVK IG3 72 E5
Aldbourne Rd ACT W3 118 C1
Aldbridge St WALW SE17 123 F5
Aldburgh Ms MHST W1U 9 H3
Aldbury Av WBLY HA9 80 D5
Aldbury Ms ED N9 35 K2
Aldebert Ter VX/NE SW8 142 A1
Aldeburgh Pl WFD IG8 38 E6
Aldeburgh St GNWCH SE10 125 K5
Alden Av SRTFD E15 106 D2
Aldenham Rd OXHEY WD19 27 H1
Aldenham St CAMTN NW1 4 B3
Alden Md PIN * HA5 42 A3
Aldensley Rd HMSMTH W6 118 E3
Alderbrook Rd BAL SW12 161 G1
Alderbury Rd BARN SW13 118 D6
Alder Cl PECK SE15 123 G6
Alder Gv CRICK NW2 63 J6
Alderholt Wy PECK * SE15 143 F1
Alderman Av BARK IG11 109 G2
Aldermanbury CITYW * EC2V 12 D3
Aldermanbury Sq CITYW EC2V 12 D2
Alderman Cl DART DA1 170 B2
Alderman Judge Ml KUT * KT1 175 F5
Alderman's Hl PLMGR N13 34 E6
Aldermary Rd BMLY BR1 183 K4
Aldermoor Rd CAT SE6 164 C5
Alderney Av HEST TW5 135 G1
Alderney Gdns NTHLT UB5 77 K5
Alderney Ms STHWK SE1 18 E4
Alderney Rd ERITH DA8 150 D1
WCHPL E1 105 F3
Alderney St PIM SW1V 15 J7
Alder Rd MORT/ESHN SW14 138 A4
SCUP DA14 167 K5
The Alders FELT TW13 172 D1
NWDGN UB2 114 E6
STRHM/NOR * SW16 161 H6
WCHMH N21 35 G1
WWKM BR4 198 E5
Alders Av WFD IG8 52 C2
Aldersbrook Av EN EN1 24 A3
Aldersbrook Dr KUTN/CMB KT2 175 G2
Aldersbrook La MNPK E12 89 K1
Aldersbrook Rd MNPK E12 71 G6
Alders Cl EA W5 116 E3
EDGE HA8 44 E1
WAN E11 71 F6
Aldersey Gdns BARK IG11 90 D4
Aldersford Cl BROCKY SE4 144 A5
Aldersgate St STBT EC1A 12 C1
Aldersgrove E/WMO/HCT KT8 189 J2
Aldersgrove Av ELTH/MOT SE9 166 B5
Aldershot Rd KIL/WHAMP NW6 82 D6
Aldershot Ter
WOOL/PLUM * SE18 147 F1
Aldersmead Av CROY/NA CR0 198 A3
Aldersmead Rd BECK BR3 182 B3
Alderson Pl NWDGN UB2 115 H1
Alderson St NKENS W10 100 C3
Alders Rd EDGE HA8 44 E1
Alderton Cl WLSDN NW10 63 F6
Alderton Crs HDN NW4 63 K2
Alderton Rd CROY/NA CR0 197 G4
HNHL SE24 142 D4
Alderton Wy HDN NW4 63 K2
Alderville Rd FUL/PGN SW6 139 J3
Alderwick Dr HSLW TW3 135 J4
Alderwood Rd ELTH/MOT SE9 167 J1
Aldford St MYFR/PKLN W1K 9 G7
Aldgate FENCHST EC3M 13 H4
Aldgate Barrs WCHPL * E1 13 K3
Aldgate High St TWRH EC3N 13 J4
Aldine St SHB W12 119 F2
Aldingham Gdns HCH RM12 93 J3
Aldington Cl CHDH RM6 73 J4
Aldington Rd
WOOL/PLUM SE18 126 C3
Aldis Ms TOOT SW17 178 D1
Aldis St TOOT SW17 178 D1
Aldred Rd KIL/WHAMP NW6 82 E3
Aldren Rd TOOT SW17 160 B5
Aldrich Crs CROY/NA CR0 214 A6
Aldriche Wy CHING E4 52 A2
Aldrich Gdns CHEAM SM3 208 D1
Aldrich Ter WAND/EARL SW18 160 B4
Aldridge Av EDGE HA8 30 D5
PEND EN3 25 J1
RSLP HA4 59 G6
STAN HA7 44 A4
Aldridge Ri NWMAL KT3 192 B4
Aldridge Road Vls NTGHL W11 100 D4
Aldridge Wk STHGT/OAK N14 34 E2
Aldrington Rd
STRHM/NOR SW16 179 H1
Aldsworth Cl MV/WKIL W9 101 F3
Aldwick Cl CHST BR7 167 J5
Aldwick Rd CROY/NA CR0 211 F1
Aldworth Gv LEW SE13 165 F1
Aldworth Rd SRTFD E15 88 C5
Aldwych TPL/STR WC2R 11 G5
Aldwych Av BARK/HLT IG6 72 C1
Aldwych Cl HCH RM12 75 J6
Alers Rd BXLYHS DA6 148 E6
Alesia Cl WDGN N22 48 E3
Alestan Beck Rd CAN/RD E16 107 H5
Alexander Av WLSDN NW10 81 K5
Alexander Cl BFN/LL DA15 147 K6
EBAR EN4 21 H5
HAYES BR2 199 K5
NWDGN UB2 115 H1
WHTN TW2 155 K4
Alexander Evans Ms FSTH SE23 164 A4
Alexander Ms BAY/PAD W2 101 F5
Alexander Pl SKENS SW7 14 C6
Alexander Rd ARCH N19 84 E1
BXLYHN DA7 148 E3
CHST BR7 185 G2
Alexander Sq CHEL SW3 14 C6
Alexander St BAY/PAD W2 100 E5
Alexander Ter ABYW * SE2 128 C5
Alexandra Av BTSEA * SW11 141 F2
RYLN/HDSTN HA2 59 K5
STHL UB1 95 K6
SUT SM1 208 E1
WDGN N22 48 D4
Alexandra Cl RYLN/HDSTN HA2 78 A1
Alexandra Cottages
NWCR * SE14 144 C2
Alexandra Crs BMLY BR1 183 J2
Alexandra Dr BRYLDS KT5 191 H4
NRWD SE19 181 F1
Alexandra Gdns CAR SM5 210 A6
HSLW TW3 135 G3
MUSWH N10 66 B1
Alexandra Ga SKENS SW7 14 A2
Alexandra Gv FSBYPK N4 67 H5
NFNCH/WDSP N12 47 F1
Alexandra Ms EFNCH N2 47 K6
Alexandra Palace Wy
CEND/HSY/T N8 66 C1
Alexandra Pde
RYLN/HDSTN * HA2 78 B2
Alexandra Park Rd
MUSWH N10 48 B5
Alexandra Pl CROY/NA CR0 197 F5
SNWD SE25 196 E2
STJWD NW8 83 G6
Alexandra Rd BTFD * TW8 116 E6
CEND/HSY/T N8 49 G6
CHDH RM6 73 K3
CHSWK W4 118 A2
CROY/NA CR0 197 F5
ED * N9 36 D2
EHAM E6 108 A2
ERITH DA8 130 C6
HDN NW4 64 B1
HSLW TW3 135 G3
KUTN/CMB KT2 175 H3
LEY E10 88 A1
MORT/ESHN SW14 138 A4
MUSWH N10 48 B4
PEND EN3 25 F5
RAIN RM13 93 H6
RCH/KEW TW9 137 G3
ROM RM1 75 H3
SEVS/STOTM N15 67 K2
STJWD NW8 83 G5
SWFD E18 53 F6
SYD SE26 182 A2
THDIT KT7 190 A2
TWK TW1 156 D1
WALTH E17 69 H3
WIM/MER SW19 177 K1
WIM/MER SW19 178 D3
Alexandra Sq MRDN SM4 193 K2
Alexandra St CAN/RD E16 106 E4
NWCR SE14 144 B1
Alexandria Rd WEA W13 97 G6
Alexis St BERM/RHTH SE16 123 H4
Alfearn Rd CLPT E5 86 E2

Alford Gn CROY/NA CR0 214 B4
Alford Pl IS * N1 6 D3
Alford Rd ERITH DA8 129 K5
Alfoxton Av SEVS/STOTM N15 67 H1
Alfreda St BTSEA SW11 141 G2
Alfred Cl CHSWK W4 118 A4
Alfred Gdns STHL UB1 95 J6
Alfred Ms FITZ W1T 10 C1
Alfred Pl FITZ W1T 10 C1
Alfred Rd ACT W3 117 K1
BAY/PAD W2 100 E4
BELV DA17 129 G5
BKHH IG9 39 H4
FELT TW13 154 B4
KUT KT1 175 F6
RDART DA2 171 J6
SNWD SE25 197 H2
SRTFD E15 88 D3
SUT SM1 209 G3
Alfred's Gdns BARK IG11 108 E1
Alfred St BOW E3 105 H2
Alfred's Wy
(East Ham & Barking By-Pass)
BARK IG11 108 E1
Alfred Vls WALTH * E17 70 A1
Alfreton Cl WIM/MER SW19 159 G5
Alfriston BRYLDS KT5 191 G3
Alfriston Av CROY/NA CR0 195 K4
RYLN/HDSTN HA2 60 A3
Alfriston Cl BRYLDS KT5 191 G3
DART DA1 170 B1
Alfriston Rd CLAP SW4 140 E6
Algar Cl STAN HA7 43 F1
Algar Rd ISLW TW7 136 B4
Algarve Rd WAND/EARL SW18 160 A3
Algernon Rd HDN NW4 63 J3
KIL/WHAMP NW6 82 E6
LEW SE13 144 E5
Algiers Rd LEW SE13 144 D5
Alguin Ct STAN * HA7 43 J2
Alibon Gdns DAGE RM10 92 C3
Alibon Rd DAGE RM10 92 C3
Alice La BOW E3 87 H6
Alice Ms TEDD TW11 174 A1
Alice St STHWK SE1 19 G5
Alice Thompson Cl
LEE/GVPK SE12 166 B4
Alice Walker Cl HNHL * SE24 142 C5
Alice Wy HSLW TW3 135 G5
Alicia Av KTN/HRWW/W HA3 61 H1
Alicia Cl KTN/HRWW/W HA3 61 J1
Alicia Gdns KTN/HRWW/W HA3 61 H1
Alie St WCHPL E1 13 K4
Alington Crs CDALE/KGS NW9 62 E5
Alington Gv WLGTN SM6 210 D6
Alison Cl CROY/NA CR0 198 A5
EHAM E6 108 A5
Aliwal Ms BTSEA * SW11 140 D5
Aliwal Rd BTSEA SW11 140 D5
Alkerden Rd CHSWK W4 118 B5
Alkham Rd STNW/STAM N16 68 B6
Allan Barclay Cl
STNW/STAM N16 68 B3
Allan Cl NWMAL KT3 192 A2
Allandale Av FNCH N3 46 C6
Allandale Pl ORP BR6 217 K1
Allandale Rd EMPK RM11 75 H4
Allan Wy ACT W3 98 E4
Allard Cl STMC/STPC BR5 202 D4
Allard Crs BUSH WD23 28 C4
Allardyce St BRXN/ST SW9 142 A5
Allbrook Cl TEDD TW11 173 K1
Allcot Cl EBED/NFELT TW14 153 J3
Allcroft Rd KTTN NW5 84 A3
Allder Wy SAND/SEL CR2 211 H5
Allenby Av SAND/SEL CR2 211 J6
Allenby Cl GFD/PVL UB6 96 A2
Allenby Rd FSTH SE23 164 B5
STHL UB1 96 A5
Allen Cl MTCM CR4 179 G4
SUN TW16 172 A4
Allendale Av STHL UB1 96 A5
Allendale Cl CMBW SE5 142 E3
SYD SE26 182 A1
Allendale Rd GFD/PVL UB6 79 H4
Allen Edwards Dr VX/NE SW8 141 K2
Allen Rd BECK BR3 182 A5
BOW E3 105 H1
CROY/NA CR0 196 A4
STNW/STAM N16 86 A2
SUN TW16 172 A4
Allensbury Pl CAMTN NW1 84 D5
Allens Rd PEND EN3 24 E6
Allen St KENS W8 119 K3
Allenswood Rd ELTH/MOT SE9 146 D4
Allerford Rd CAT SE6 164 E6
Allerton Rd STNW/STAM N16 67 J6
Allestree Rd FUL/PGN SW6 139 H1
Alleyn Crs DUL SE21 162 E4
Alleyndale Rd BCTR RM8 73 J6
Alleyn Pk DUL SE21 162 E4
NWDGN UB2 114 E5
Alleyn Rd DUL SE21 162 E5
Allfarthing La
WAND/EARL SW18 160 B1
Allgood Cl MRDN SM4 193 G3
Allgood St BETH E2 7 K3
Allhallows La CANST EC4R 12 E6
Allhallows Rd EHAM E6 107 J5
All Hallows Rd TOTM N17 50 A4
Alliance Cl ALP/SUD HA0 79 K2
Alliance Rd ACT W3 98 D3
PLSTW E13 107 G3
WOOL/PLUM SE18 128 B6
Allied Wy ACT * W3 118 B2
Allingham Cl HNWL W7 97 F6
Allington Av TOTM N17 50 A2
Allington Cl GFD/PVL UB6 78 C5
WIM/MER SW19 177 G1
Allington Rd HDN NW4 63 K2
NKENS W10 100 C2
ORP BR6 201 K6
RYLN/HDSTN HA2 60 C2
Allington St WESTW SW1E 15 K5
Allison Cl GNWCH SE10 145 F2
Allison Gv DUL SE21 163 F3
Allison Rd ACT W3 98 E5
CEND/HSY/T N8 67 G2
Allitsen Rd STJWD NW8 2 C3
Allitson Rd STJWD NW8 2 C3
Allnutt Wy CLAP SW4 141 J6
Alloa Rd DEPT SE8 124 A5
GDMY/SEVK IG3 73 H6
Allonby Gdns WBLY HA9 61 J5
Alloway Rd BOW E3 105 G2
Allport Ms WCHPL * E1 104 E4
All Saints' Cl ED N9 36 B4
All Saints Dr BKHTH/KID SE3 145 J3
All Saints Ms KTN/HRWW/W HA3 42 E2
All Saints Pas
WAND/EARL * SW18 139 K6
All Saints' Rd ACT W3 117 K2
NTGHL W11 100 D4
SUT SM1 209 F1
WIM/MER SW19 178 B3
All Saints St IS N1 5 G2
Allsop Pl CAMTN NW1 3 F7
All Souls' Av WLSDN NW10 99 K1
All Souls' Pl REGST W1B 9 K2
Allum Wy TRDG/WHET N20 33 G3
Allwood Cl SYD SE26 164 A6
Alma Av CHING E4 52 A3
Almack Rd CLPT E5 86 E2
Alma Cl MUSWH * N10 48 B4
Alma Ct RYLN/HDSTN * HA2 60 D6
Alma Crs SUT SM1 208 C3
Alma Gv STHWK SE1 19 K7
Alma Pl NRWD SE19 181 G3
THHTH CR7 196 B2
WLSDN NW10 99 K2
Alma Rd CAR SM5 209 J3
ESH/CLAY KT10 189 K5
MUSWH N10 48 A3
PEND EN3 25 G6
SCUP DA14 168 B5
STHL UB1 95 J6
STMC/STPC BR5 202 E6
WAND/EARL SW18 140 B6
Alma Rw KTN/HRWW/W * HA3 42 D4
Alma Sq STJWD NW8 101 G2
Alma St KTTN NW5 84 B4
SRTFD E15 88 B4
Alma Ter BOW E3 87 H6
KENS * W8 119 K3
WAND/EARL SW18 160 C2
Almeida St IS N1 85 H6
Almeric Rd BTSEA SW11 140 E5
Almer Rd RYNPK SW20 176 D3
Almington St FSBYPK * N4 66 E5
Almond Av CAR SM5 194 E6
EA W5 117 F3
WDR/YW UB7 112 D3
Almond Cl HAYES BR2 201 F4
HYS/HAR UB3 94 C6
RSLP HA4 76 D1
Almond Gv BTFD TW8 136 C1
Almond Rd BERM/RHTH SE16 123 J4
TOTM N17 50 C3
Almonds Av BKHH IG9 38 E4
Almond Wy HAYES BR2 201 F4
MTCM CR4 195 J2
RYLN/HDSTN HA2 42 C5
Almorah Rd HEST TW5 134 C2
IS N1 85 K5
Almshouse La CHSGTN KT9 205 J6
Alnwick Gv MRDN SM4 194 A1
Alnwick Rd CAN/RD E16 107 G5
LEE/GVPK SE12 166 A2
Alperton La ALP/SUD HA0 97 K2
Alperton St NKENS W10 100 C3
Alphabet Gdns CAR SM5 194 C3
Alpha Cl CAMTN NW1 2 D6
Alpha Est HYS/HAR * UB3 113 H2
Alpha Gv POP/IOD E14 124 D2
Alpha Pl CHEL SW3 120 D6
KIL/WHAMP NW6 100 E1
MRDN * SM4 193 G4
Alpha Rd BRYLDS KT5 191 G3
CHING E4 37 J5
CROY/NA CR0 197 F5
HPTN TW12 173 J1
NWCR SE14 144 C2
PEND EN3 25 G5
UED N18 50 C2
Alpha St PECK SE15 143 H3
Alphea Cl WIM/MER SW19 178 D3
Alpine Av BRYLDS KT5 191 K6
Alpine Cl CROY/NA CR0 212 A1
Alpine Copse BMLY BR1 185 F5
Alpine Gv HOM * E9 86 E5
Alpine Rd BERM/RHTH SE16 123 K4
Alpine Vw SUT SM1 209 J3
Alpine Wk BUSH WD23 28 E4
Alpine Wy EHAM E6 108 A4
Alric Av NWMAL KT3 176 B6
WLSDN NW10 81 F5
Alroy Rd FSBYPK N4 67 G4
Alsace Rd WALW SE17 123 F5
Alscot Rd BERM/RHTH SE16 19 K5
Alscot Wy STHWK SE1 19 J6
Alsike Rd BELV DA17 128 E3
Alsom Av HOR/WEW KT19 207 H2
Alston Cl THDIT KT7 190 C4
Alston Rd BAR EN5 20 C4
TOOT SW17 160 C6
UED N18 50 D1
Altair Cl UED N18 50 B2
Altair Wy NTHWD HA6 40 D1
Altash Wy ELTH/MOT SE9 166 E4
Altenburg Av WEA W13 116 C3
Altenburg Gdns BTSEA SW11 140 E5
Alt Gv WIM/MER SW19 177 J3
Altham Ct RYLN/HDSTN * HA2 42 B4
Altham Rd PIN HA5 41 J3
Althea St FUL/PGN SW6 140 A3
Althorne Gdns SWFD E18 70 D1
Althorne Wy DAGE RM10 74 C6
Althorp Cl TRDG/WHET N20 31 J2
Althorpe Rd HRW * HA1 60 C2
Althorp Rd TOOT SW17 160 E3
Altmore Av EHAM E6 89 K5
Alton Av STAN HA7 43 F3
Alton Cl BXLY DA5 169 F3
ISLW TW7 136 A3
Alton Gdns BECK BR3 182 D3
WHTN TW2 155 J1
Alton Rd CROY/NA CR0 211 G2
PUT/ROE SW15 158 D3
RCH/KEW TW9 137 F5
TOTM N17 49 K6
Alton St POP/IOD E14 105 K4
Altyre Cl BECK BR3 198 C2
Altyre Rd CROY/NA CR0 196 E6
Altyre Wy BECK BR3 198 C2
Alvanley Gdns HAMP NW3 83 F3
Alva Wy OXHEY WD19 27 H4
Alverstone Av EBAR EN4 33 H2
WAND/EARL SW18 159 K4
Alverstone Gdns
ELTH/MOT SE9 167 G3
Alverstone Rd CRICK NW2 82 A5
MNPK E12 90 A2
NWMAL KT3 192 C1
WBLY HA9 62 B5
Alverston Gdns SNWD SE25 197 F2
Alverton St DEPT SE8 124 C5
Alveston Av KTN/HRWW/W HA3 43 H6
Alvey St WALW SE17 123 F5
Alvia Gdns SUT SM1 209 G2
Alvington Crs HACK E8 86 B3
Alway Av HOR/WEW KT19 206 E3
Alwold Crs LEE/GVPK SE12 166 B1
Alwyn Av CHSWK W4 118 A5
Alwyn Cl BORE WD6 30 B1
CROY/NA CR0 213 K5
Alwyne La IS * N1 85 H5
Alwyne Pl IS * N1 85 J4
Alwyne Rd HNWL W7 96 E6
IS N1 85 J5
WIM/MER SW19 177 J2
Alwyne Sq IS N1 85 J4
Alwyne Vls IS N1 85 H5
Alwyn Gdns ACT W3 98 D5
Alyn Bank CEND/HSY/T * N8 66 D3
Alyth Gdns GLDGN NW11 64 D3
Amalgamated Dr BTFD TW8 116 B6
Amanda Cl CHIG IG7 54 D2
Amanda Ms ROMW/RG RM7 74 E2
Amar Ct WOOL/PLUM SE18 128 A4
Amardeep Ct
WOOL/PLUM SE18 128 A5
Amazon St WCHPL E1 104 D5
Ambassador Cl HSLW TW3 134 D3
Ambassador Gdns EHAM E6 107 K4
Ambassador Sq POP/IOD E14 124 E4
Amber Av WALTH E17 51 G4
Amberden Av FNCH N3 46 E6
Ambergate St WALW SE17 122 C5
Amber Gv CRICK NW2 64 B5
Amberley Cl ORP BR6 217 F3
PIN HA5 41 K6
Amberley Ct SCUP DA14 186 D1
Amberley Gdns HOR/WEW KT19 207 H2
Amberley Gv CROY/NA CR0 197 G4
SYD SE26 163 J6
Amberley Rd ABYW SE2 128 E6
BKHH IG9 39 G3
EN EN1 36 B2
LEY E10 69 J4
MV/WKIL W9 100 E4
PLMGR N13 35 F4
Amberley Wy HSLWW TW4 134 B6
MRDN SM4 193 J4
ROMW/RG RM7 74 D1
Amberside Cl ISLW TW7 155 J1
Amber St SRTFD * E15 88 B4
Amberwood Cl WLGTN SM6 210 E3
Amberwood Ri NWMAL KT3 192 B3
Amblecote Cl LEE/GVPK SE12 166 A5
Amblecote Meadow
LEE/GVPK SE12 166 A5
Amblecote Rd LEE/GVPK SE12 166 A5
Ambler Rd FSBYPK N4 85 H1
Ambleside BMLY BR1 183 G2
Ambleside Av BECK BR3 198 B2
HCH RM12 93 K3
STRHM/NOR SW16 161 J6
WOT/HER KT12 188 B5
Ambleside Cl LEY E10 69 K4
Ambleside Crs PEND EN3 25 F4
Ambleside Dr EBED/NFELT
TW14 153 J3
Ambleside Gdns BELMT SM2 209 G4
REDBR IG4 71 J1
WBLY HA9 61 K5
Ambleside Rd BXLYHN DA7 149 H3
WLSDN NW10 81 H5
Ambrey Wy WLGTN SM6 210 D6
Ambrook Rd BELV DA17 129 H3
Ambrosden Av WEST SW1P 16 B5
Ambrose Av GLDGN NW11 64 D3
Ambrose Cl DART DA1 150 C5
ORP BR6 217 F1
Ambrose St BERM/RHTH SE16 123 J4
Amelia Cl ACT W3 117 J1
Amelia St WALW SE17 122 C5
Amen Cnr STP EC4M 12 B4
Amen Ct STP EC4M 12 B4
America Sq TWRH * EC3N 13 J5
America St STHWK SE1 18 C1
Amerland Rd WAND/EARL SW18 159 J1
Amersham Av UED N18 49 K2
Amersham Gv NWCR SE14 144 C1
Amersham Rd CROY/NA CR0 196 D3
NWCR SE14 144 C2
Amersham V NWCR SE14 144 C1
Amery Gdns WLSDN NW10 81 K6
Amery Rd HRW HA1 61 G6
Amesbury Av
BRXS/STRHM SW2 161 K4
Amesbury Cl WPK KT4 193 F5
Amesbury Dr CHING E4 37 K1
Amesbury Rd BMLY BR1 184 C6
DAGW RM9 91 K5
FELT TW13 154 C4
Ames Cottages POP/IOD * E14 105 G4
Amethyst Rd WAN E11 88 B2
Amherst Av WEA W13 97 J5
Amherst Cl STMC/STPC BR5 202 B1
Amherst Dr STMC/STPC BR5 202 A1
Amherst Gdns WEA * W13 97 J5
Amherst Rd WEA W13 97 J5
Amhurst Gdns ISLW TW7 136 A2
Amhurst Pde STNW/STAM * N16 68 B4
Amhurst Pk STNW/STAM N16 68 A4
Amhurst Rd STNW/STAM N16 86 B1
STNW/STAM N16 86 B2
Amhurst Ter HACK E8 86 C2
Amidas Gdns BCTR RM8 91 H2
Amiel St WCHPL E1 104 E3
Amies St BTSEA SW11 140 E4
Amina Wy BERM/RHTH SE16 123 H3
Amis Av HOR/WEW KT19 206 C4
Amity Gv RYNPK SW20 177 F4
Amity Rd SRTFD E15 88 D5
Ammanford Gn
CDALE/KGS * NW9 63 G3
Amner Rd BTSEA SW11 161 F1
Amor Rd HMSMTH W6 119 F3
Amott Rd PECK SE15 143 H4
Ampere Wy CROY/NA CR0 195 K4
Ampleforth Cl ORP BR6 217 J2
Ampleforth Rd ABYW SE2 128 C2
Ampthill Est CAMTN NW1 4 A3
Ampthill Sq CAMTN NW1 4 B3
Ampton St FSBYW WC1X 5 G5
Amroth Cl FSTH SE23 163 J3
Amroth Gn CDALE/KGS * NW9 63 G3
Amsterdam Rd POP/IOD E14 125 F3
Amwell Cl WCHMH N21 23 K6
Amwell St CLKNW EC1R 5 J4
Amyand Cottages TWK TW1 156 C1
Amyand Park Gdns TWK TW1 156 C2
Amyand Park Rd TWK TW1 156 B2
Amy Cl WLGTN SM6 210 E5
Amyruth Rd BROCKY SE4 144 D6
Amy Warne Cl EHAM E6 107 J4
Ancaster Crs NWMAL KT3 192 D3
Ancaster Rd BECK BR3 182 A6
Ancaster St WOOL/PLUM SE18 147 K1
Anchorage Cl WIM/MER SW19 177 K1
Anchor & Hope La CHARL SE7 126 A3
Anchor Cl BARK IG11 109 H2
Anchor Dr RAIN RM13 111 K2
Anchor St BERM/RHTH SE16 123 J4
Anchor Ter WCHPL * E1 104 E3
Anchor Yd FSBYE * EC1V 6 D6
Ancill Cl HMSMTH W6 119 G6
Ancona Rd WLSDN NW10 99 J1
WOOL/PLUM SE18 127 J5
Andace Park Gdns BMLY * BR1 184 B4
Andalus Rd BRXN/ST SW9 141 K4
Ander Cl ALP/SUD HA0 79 K2
Anderson Cl ACT W3 99 F5
CHEAM SM3 193 K5
WCHMH N21 23 F6
Anderson Dr ASHF TW15 153 F6
Anderson Rd HOM E9 87 F4
WFD IG8 53 H6
Anderson's Pl HSLW TW3 135 G5
Anderson Sq IS N1 6 A1
Anderson St CHEL SW3 120 E5
Anderson Wy BELV DA17 129 J2
Andover Av CAN/RD E16 107 H5
Andover Cl EBED/NFELT TW14 153 J3
GFD/PVL UB6 96 B3
Andover Pl KIL/WHAMP NW6 101 F1
Andover Rd HOLWY N7 67 F6
ORP BR6 201 K5
WHTN TW2 155 J3
Andover Ter HMSMTH * W6 118 E4
Andre St HACK E8 86 C3
Andrew Borde St
LSQ/SEVD * WC2H 10 D3
Andrew Cl BARK/HLT IG6 54 D3
DART DA1 150 A6
Andrewes Gdns EHAM E6 107 J5
Andrew Pl VX/NE SW8 141 J2
Andrews Cl BKHH IG9 39 G4
HRW HA1 60 D4
STMC/STPC BR5 186 E6
WPK KT4 193 G6
Andrews Rd HACK E8 86 D6
Andrew St POP/IOD E14 106 A5
Andrews Wk WALW SE17 122 C6
Andwell Cl ABYW SE2 128 C2
Anerley Gv NRWD SE19 181 G3
Anerley Hl NRWD SE19 181 G2
Anerley Pk PGE/AN SE20 181 J3
Anerley Park Rd PGE/AN SE20 181 J3
Anerley Rd NRWD SE19 181 H3
Anerley Station Rd
PGE/AN SE20 181 J4
Anerley V NRWD SE19 181 G3
Anfield Cl BAL SW12 161 H2
Angel Cl UED N18 50 B1
Angel Corner Pde UED * N18 50 C1
Angel Ct LOTH EC2R 13 F3
Angelfield HSLW TW3 135 G6
Angel Hl SUT SM1 209 F1
Angel Hill Dr SUT SM1 209 F1
Angelica Dr EHAM E6 108 A4
Angelica Gdns CROY/NA CR0 198 A5
Angel La HYS/HAR UB3 94 B4
SRTFD E15 88 B4
Angell Park Gdns BRXN/ST SW9 142 B4
Angell Rd BRXN/ST SW9 142 C4
Angell Town Est
BRXN/ST * SW9 142 B3
Angel Ms WCHPL E1 104 D6
Angel Pas CANST EC4R 12 E6
Angel Rd HRW HA1 60 E3
THDIT KT7 190 B5
Angel Rd (North Circular)
UED N18 50 C1
Angel Sq FSBYE * EC1V 6 A3
Angel St STBT EC1A 12 C3
Angel Wk HMSMTH W6 119 F4
Angel Wy ROM RM1 75 G2
Angerstein La BKHTH/KID SE3 145 J1
Anglers La KTTN NW5 84 B4
Anglers Reach SURB * KT6 190 E2
Anglesea Av WOOL/PLUM SE18 127 G4
Anglesea Rd KUT KT1 190 E1
STMC/STPC BR5 202 D3
WOOL/PLUM SE18 127 G4
Anglesey Cl ASHF TW15 152 D6
Anglesey Court Rd CAR SM5 210 A4
Anglesey Dr RAIN RM13 111 J3
Anglesey Gdns CAR SM5 210 A4
Anglesey Rd OXHEY WD19 41 G1
PEND EN3 24 D5
Anglesmede Crs PIN HA5 42 A6
Anglesmede Wy PIN HA5 41 K6
Angles Rd STRHM/NOR SW16 161 K6
Anglia Cl TOTM N17 50 D3
Anglian Rd WAN E11 88 B1
Anglo Rd BOW E3 105 H1
Angus Cl CHSGTN KT9 206 C3
Angus Dr RSLP HA4 77 G2
Angus Gdns CDALE/KGS NW9 45 F4
Angus Rd PLSTW E13 107 G2
Angus St NWCR SE14 144 B1
Anhalt Rd BTSEA SW11 140 D1
Ankerdine Crs
WOOL/PLUM SE18 147 G2
Anlaby Rd TEDD TW11 173 K1
Anley Rd HMSMTH W6 119 G2
Anmersh Gv STAN HA7 43 K4
Annabel Cl POP/IOD E14 105 K5
Anna Cl HACK E8 86 B6
Annandale Gv HGDN/ICK UB10 76 A1
Annandale Rd BFN/LL DA15 167 K2
CHSWK W4 118 B4
CROY/NA CR0 197 H6
GNWCH SE10 125 J6
Anna Neagle Cl FSTGT E7 88 E2
Annan Wy ROM RM1 57 F4
Anne Boleyn's Wk BELMT SM2 208 B5
KUTN/CMB KT2 175 F1
Anne Case Ms NWMAL * KT3 176 A6
Anne Compton Ms
LEE/GVPK SE12 165 J2
Anne of Cleves Rd DART DA1 151 G6
Annesley Av CDALE/KGS NW9 45 F6
Annesley Cl WLSDN NW10 81 G1
Annesley Dr CROY/NA CR0 213 H1
Annesley Rd BKHTH/KID SE3 146 A2
Anne St PLSTW E13 106 E3
Annette Cl KTN/HRWW/W HA3 42 E5
Annette Rd HOLWY N7 85 F2
Anne Wy BARK/HLT IG6 54 C2
Annexe Market WCHPL * E1 13 J1
Annie Besant Cl BOW * E3 87 H6
Anning St SDTCH EC2A 7 H6
Annington Rd EFNCH N2 47 K6
Annis Rd HOM E9 87 G4
Ann La WBPTN SW10 140 C1
Ann Moss Wy BERM/RHTH SE16 123 K3
Ann's Cl KTBR SW1X 15 F3
Ann St WOOL/PLUM SE18 127 J5
Annsworthy Av THHTH CR7 180 E6
Ansar Gdns WALTH E17 69 G2
Ansdell Rd PECK SE15 143 K3
Ansdell St KENS W8 120 A3
Ansdell Ter KENS W8 120 A3
Ansell Gv CAR SM5 194 E5
Ansell Rd TOOT SW17 160 D5
Anselm Cl CROY/NA CR0 212 B1
Anselm Rd FUL/PGN SW6 119 K6
PIN HA5 41 K3
Ansford Rd BMLY BR1 183 F1
Ansleigh Pl NTGHL W11 100 B6
Anson Cl ROMW/RG RM7 56 D5
Anson Rd CRICK NW2 81 K3
HOLWY N7 84 C2
Anson Wk NTHWD HA6 26 A6
Anstead Dr RAIN RM13 111 J1
Anstey Rd PECK SE15 143 H4
Anstice Cl CHSWK W4 138 B1
Anstridge Rd ELTH/MOT SE9 167 J1
Antelope Rd WOOL/PLUM SE18 126 E3
Anthony Cl OXHEY WD19 27 H3
Anthony Rd GFD/PVL UB6 96 E1
SNWD SE25 197 H3
WELL DA16 148 B2
Anthony's Cl WAP E1W 123 H1
Anthony St WCHPL E1 104 D5
Anthus Ms NTHWD HA6 40 B3
Antill Rd BOW E3 105 G2
SEVS/STOTM N15 68 C1
Antill Ter WCHPL E1 105 F5
Antlers Hl CHING E4 25 K6
Anton Crs SUT SM1 208 E1
Antoneys Cl PIN HA5 41 H5
Anton St HACK E8 86 C3
Antrim Rd HAMP NW3 83 K4
Antrobus Cl SUT SM1 208 D3
Antrobus Rd CHSWK W4 117 K4
Anvil Cl STRHM/NOR SW16 179 H3
Anworth Cl WFD IG8 53 F2
Apeldoorn Dr WLGTN SM6 210 E6
Aperfield Rd ERITH DA8 130 C6
Apex Cl BECK BR3 182 E4
Apex Pde MLHL * NW7 31 F6
Aplin Wy ISLW TW7 135 K2
Apollo Av BMLY BR1 184 A4
NTHWD HA6 40 E1
Apollo Cl EMPK RM11 75 K6
Apollo Pl WAN E11 88 C1
WBPTN * SW10 140 C1
Apollo Wy WOOL/PLUM SE18 127 J3
Apothecary St BLKFR * EC4V 12 A4
Appach Rd BRXS/STRHM SW2 142 B6
Apple Blossom Ct VX/NE * SW8 141 J1
Appleby Cl CHING E4 52 A2
SEVS/STOTM N15 67 K2
WHTN TW2 155 J4
Appleby Gdns
EBED/NFELT * TW14 153 J3
Appleby Rd CAN/RD E16 106 E5
HACK E8 86 C5
Appleby St BETH E2 7 J2
Appledore Av BXLYHN DA7 149 K2
RSLP HA4 77 F1
Appledore Cl EDGE HA8 44 C4
HAYES BR2 199 J2
TOOT SW17 160 E4
Appledore Crs BFN/LL DA15 167 K5
Appleford Rd NKENS W10 100 C3
Apple Garth BTFD TW8 116 E4
Applegarth ESH/CLAY KT10 205 F3
Applegarth Dr DART DA1 171 H4
GNTH/NBYPK IG2 73 F1
Applegarth Rd THMD SE28 128 C1
WKENS * W14 119 G3
Apple Gv CHSGTN KT9 206 A2
EN EN1 24 A4
Apple Ldg ALP/SUD * HA0 79 J1
Apple Market KUT KT1 174 E5
Apple Rd WAN E11 88 C1
Appleton Dr RDART DA2 170 E5
Appleton Gdns NWMAL KT3 192 D3
Appleton Rd ELTH/MOT SE9 146 D4
Appletree Cl PGE/AN SE20 181 J4
Appletree Gdns EBAR EN4 21 J5
Apple Tree Yd STJS SW1Y 10 B7
Applewood Cl CRICK NW2 81 K1
TRDG/WHET N20 33 J3
Appold St ERITH DA8 130 C6
SDTCH EC2A 13 G1
Apprentice Wy CLPT E5 86 D2
The Approach ACT W3 99 F5
EN EN1 24 D3
HDN NW4 64 B2
ORP BR6 202 A6
Approach La MLHL NW7 46 C1
Approach Rd BETH E2 104 E1
E/WMO/HCT KT8 189 F2
EBAR EN4 21 G5
RYNPK SW20 177 F5
Aprey Gdns HDN NW4 64 A1
April Cl FELT TW13 153 K5
HNWL W7 96 E6
ORP BR6 217 F3
April Gln FSTH SE23 164 A5
April St STNW/STAM N16 86 B2
Apsley Cl HRW HA1 60 C2
Apsley Rd NWMAL KT3 175 K6
SNWD SE25 197 J1
Apsley Wy CRICK NW2 63 J6
MYFR/PICC * W1J 15 J1
Aquarius TWK * TW1 156 C3
Aquarius Wy NTHWD HA6 40 E1
Aquila St STJWD NW8 2 B2
Aquinas St STHWK SE1 17 K1
Arabella Dr PUT/ROE SW15 138 B5
Arabia Cl CHING E4 38 A2
Arabin Rd BROCKY SE4 144 B5
Aragon Av EW KT17 207 K6
THDIT KT7 190 A2
Aragon Cl ENC/FH EN2 23 F1
HAYES BR2 200 E5
LOU IG10 39 J1
Aragon Dr BARK/HLT IG6 54 C3

RSLP HA4 59 H5
Aragon Rd KUTN/CMB KT2 175 F1
MRDN SM4 193 G4
Arandora Crs CHDH RM6 73 H4
Arbery Rd BOW E3 105 G2
Arbor Cl BECK BR3 182 E5
Arborfield Cl BRXS/STRHM SW2 162 A3
Arbor Rd CHING E4 38 B5
Arbour Rd PEND EN3 25 F5
Arbour Sq WCHPL E1 104 E5
Arbour Wy HCH RM12 93 K3
Arbroath Gn OXHEY WD19 26 E5
Arbroath Rd ELTH/MOT SE9 146 D4
Arbrook Cl STMC/STPC BR5 186 B6
Arbrook La ESH/CLAY KT10 204 D4
Arbuthnot La BXLY DA5 169 F1
Arbuthnot Rd NWCR SE14 144 A3
Arbutus St HACK E8 86 B6
The Arcade ELTH/MOT * SE9 167 F1
LVPST * EC2M 13 G2
WALTH * E17 69 J1
Arcade Chambers
ELTH/MOT * SE9 167 F1
Arcade Pde CHSGTN * KT9 206 A2
Arcade Pl ROM RM1 75 G2
Arcadia Av FNCH N3 46 E4
Arcadia Cl CAR SM5 210 A2
Arcadian Av BXLY DA5 169 F1
Arcadian Cl BXLY DA5 169 F1
Arcadian Gdns WDGN N22 49 G3
Arcadian Rd BXLY DA5 169 F2
Arcadia St POP/IOD E14 105 J5
Archangel St BERM/RHTH SE16 124 A2
Archbishop's Pl
BRXS/STRHM SW2 162 A1
Archdale Ct SHB W12 118 E1
Archdale Pl NWMAL KT3 175 J6
Archdale Rd EDUL SE22 143 G6
Archel Rd WKENS W14 119 J6
Archer Cl KUTN/CMB KT2 175 F3
Archer Rd SNWD SE25 197 J1
STMC/STPC BR5 202 B3
Archers Dr PEND EN3 24 E3
Archer Sq DEPT SE8 124 B6
Archer St SOHO/SHAV W1D 10 C5
Archery Cl BAY/PAD W2 8 D4
KTN/HRWW/W HA3 43 F6
Archery Rd ELTH/MOT SE9 146 E6
The Arches CHCR * WC2N 11 F7
RYLN/HDSTN HA2 60 B6
Archibald Ms MYFR/PICC W1J 9 H6
Archibald Rd HOLWY N7 84 D2
Arch St STHWK SE1 18 C5
Archway HARH RM3 57 K2
Archway Cl ARCH * N19 66 C6
CROY/NA * CR0 210 E1
NKENS W10 100 B4
WIM/MER SW19 160 A6
Archway Rd HGT N6 65 K2
Archway St BARN SW13 138 B4
Arcola St HACK E8 86 B3
Arctic St KTTN NW5 84 B3
Arcus Rd BMLY BR1 183 H2
Ardbeg Rd HNHL SE24 162 E1
Arden Cl BUSH WD23 29 F2
HRW HA1 78 D1
THMD SE28 109 K5
Arden Court Gdns EFNCH N2 65 H3
Arden Crs DAGW RM9 91 K5
POP/IOD E14 124 D4
Arden Est IS N1 7 G3
Arden Gv ORP BR6 216 B2
Arden Mhor PIN HA5 59 F1
Arden Rd FNCH N3 46 D6
WEA W13 97 J6
Ardent Cl SNWD SE25 181 F6
Ardfern Av STRHM/NOR SW16 180 B6
Ardfillan Rd CAT SE6 165 G3
Ardgowan Rd CAT SE6 165 H3
Ardilaun Rd HBRY N5 85 J2
Ardingly Cl CROY/NA CR0 213 F1
Ardleigh Gdns CHEAM SM3 193 K5
Ardleigh Rd IS N1 86 A4
WALTH E17 51 H4
Ardleigh Ter WALTH E17 51 H4
Ardley Cl FSTH SE23 164 B5
WLSDN NW10 81 G1
Ardlui Rd WNWD SE27 162 D4
Ardmay Gdns SURB * KT6 191 F2
Ardmere Rd LEW SE13 165 G1
Ardmore La BKHH IG9 39 F3
Ardmore Pl BKHH * IG9 39 F2
Ardoch Rd CAT SE6 165 G4
Ardra Rd ED N9 37 F5
Ardrossan Gdns WPK KT4 207 J1
Ardross Av NTHWD HA6 40 C1
Ardshiel Cl PUT/ROE SW15 139 G4
Ardwell Av BARK/HLT IG6 72 C2
Ardwell Rd BRXS/STRHM SW2 161 K4
Ardwick Rd CRICK NW2 82 E2
The Arena STKPK * UB11 113 F1
Arena Est FSBYPK * N4 67 H3
Argall Av LEY E10 69 G4
Argall Wy LEY E10 69 F5
Argenta Wy WLSDN NW10 80 D5
Argent Ct SURB * KT6 191 H6
Argon Ms FUL/PGN SW6 139 K1
Argon Rd UED N18 51 F1
Argosy La STWL/WRAY TW19 152 A2
Argus Cl ROMW/RG RM7 56 D4
Argus Wy NTHLT UB5 95 J2
Argyle Av HSLW TW3 155 F1
Argyle Cl WEA W13 97 F3
Argyle Cnr WEA * W13 97 H6
Argyle Pl HMSMTH W6 118 E4
Argyle Rd BAR EN5 20 A5
CAN/RD E16 107 F5
GFD/PVL UB6 97 F2
HSLW TW3 135 G6
IL IG1 72 A6
NFNCH/WDSP N12 46 E1
RYLN/HDSTN HA2 60 B3
SRTFD E15 88 C2
TOTM N17 50 C4
UED N18 36 C6
WCHPL E1 105 F3
Argyle Sq STPAN WC1H 5 F4
Argyle St CAMTN NW1 4 E4
Argyle Wk STPAN * WC1H 4 E5
Argyle Wy STHWK SE1 123 H5
Argyll Av STHL UB1 115 G1
Argyll Cl BRXN/ST SW9 142 A4
Argyll Gdns EDGE HA8 44 D5
Argyll Rd KENS W8 119 K2
WOOL/PLUM SE18 127 H3
Argyll St REGST W1B 10 A4
Arica Rd BROCKY SE4 144 B5
Ariel Rd KIL/WHAMP NW6 82 E4
Ariel Wy HSLWW TW4 134 A4
SHB W12 119 F1
Aristotle Rd CLAP SW4 141 J4
Arkell Gv NRWD SE19 180 C3
Arkindale Rd CAT SE6 165 F5
Arkley Crs WALTH * E17 69 H2
Arkley Rd WALTH E17 69 H2
Arklow Rd NWCR SE14 124 C6
Arkwright Rd HAMP NW3 83 G3
Arlesford Rd BRXN/ST SW9 141 K4
Arlingford Rd
BRXS/STRHM * SW2 142 B6
Arlington NFNCH/WDSP N12 32 E5
Arlington Av IS N1 6 D1
Arlington Cl BFN/LL DA15 167 K2
LEW * SE13 145 G6
SUT SM1 193 K6
TWK * TW1 156 D1
Arlington Ct HYS/HAR UB3 113 G5
Arlington Dr CAR SM5 194 E6
RSLP HA4 58 B3
Arlington Gdns CHSWK W4 117 K5
IL IG1 71 K4
Arlington Pde
BRXS/STRHM * SW2 142 A5
Arlington Rd CAMTN NW1 3 K1
RCHPK/HAM TW10 156 E4
STHGT/OAK N14 34 B4
SURB KT6 190 E3
TWK TW1 156 A6
TWK TW1 156 D1
WEA W13 97 H5
WFD IG8 52 E4
Arlington Sq IS N1 6 D1
Arlington St MYFR/PICC W1J 10 A7
Arlington Wy CLKNW EC1R 5 K4
Arliss Wy NTHLT UB5 77 G6
Arlow Rd WCHMH N21 35 G3
Armadale Cl TOTM N17 68 D1
Armadale Rd
EBED/NFELT TW14 133 K6
FUL/PGN SW6 139 K1
Armada St DEPT SE8 124 D6
Armada Wy EHAM E6 108 C5
Armagh Rd BOW E3 87 H6
Armfield Cl E/WMO/HCT KT8 188 E2
Armfield Crs MTCM CR4 178 E5
Armfield Rd ENC/FH EN2 23 K2
Arminger Rd SHB W12 118 E1
Armitage Rd GLDGN NW11 64 C5
GNWCH SE10 125 J5
Armour Cl HOLWY N7 85 F4
Armoury Rd DEPT SE8 144 E3
Armoury Wy WAND/EARL SW18 139 K6
Armstead Wk DAGE RM10 92 C5
Armstrong Av WFD IG8 52 C2
Armstrong Cl BCTR RM8 73 K4
BMLY BR1 184 D6
EHAM E6 107 K5
RSLP HA4 58 E3
Armstrong Crs EBAR EN4 21 H4
Armstrong Rd ACT W3 118 C1
FELT TW13 172 D1
Armstrong Wy NWDGN UB2 115 H2
Armytage Rd HEST TW5 134 C1
Arnal Crs WAND/EARL SW18 159 H2
Arncliffe Cl FBAR/BDGN N11 48 A2
Arne Gv ORP BR6 217 F1
Arne St LSQ/SEVD WC2H 11 F4
Arnett Sq CHING E4 51 H2
Arne Wk BKHTH/KID SE3 145 J5
Arneways Av CHDH RM6 73 K1
Arneway St WEST SW1P 16 D5
Arnewood Cl PUT/ROE SW15 158 D3
Arney's La MTCM CR4 195 F3
Arngask Rd CAT SE6 165 G2
Arnheim Pl POP/IOD E14 124 D3
Arnison Rd E/WMO/HCT KT8 189 J1
Arnold Av East PEND EN3 25 J1
Arnold Av West PEND EN3 25 H1
Arnold Cl KTN/HRWW/W HA3 62 B4
Arnold Crs ISLW TW7 135 J6
Arnold Dr CHSGTN KT9 205 K4
Arnold Est STHWK SE1 19 K3
Arnold Gdns PLMGR N13 49 H1
Arnold Rd BOW E3 105 J2
DAGW RM9 92 B5
NTHLT UB5 77 J4
TOOT SW17 178 E3
TOTM N17 50 B6
Arnold Ter STAN * HA7 43 F1
Arnos Gv STHGT/OAK N14 34 D6
Arnos Rd FBAR/BDGN N11 48 C1
Arnott Cl CHSWK W4 118 A4
THMD SE28 128 D1
Arnould Av CMBW SE5 142 E5
Arnsberg Wy BXLYHN DA7 149 H5
Arnside Gdns WBLY HA9 61 K5
Arnside Rd BXLYHN DA7 149 H2
Arnside St WALW SE17 122 D6
Arnulf St CAT SE6 164 E6
Arnull's Rd STRHM/NOR SW16 180 C2
Arodene Rd BRXS/STRHM SW2 162 A1
Arosa Rd TWK TW1 156 E1
Arragon Gdns
STRHM/NOR SW16 179 K3
WWKM BR4 213 K1
Arragon Rd EHAM E6 89 H6
TWK TW1 156 B2
WAND/EARL SW18 159 K3
Arran Cl ERITH DA8 130 A6
WLGTN SM6 210 C2
Arran Dr MNPK E12 71 H5
STAN HA7 29 J6
Arran Gn OXHEY * WD19 27 H6
Arran Ms EA W5 117 G1
Arran Rd CAT SE6 164 E4
Arran Wk IS N1 85 J5
Arran Wy ESH/CLAY KT10 189 G6
Arras Av MRDN SM4 194 B2
Arrol Rd BECK BR3 181 K6
Arrow Rd BOW E3 105 K2
Arrowsmith Rd CHIG IG7 55 F1
Arsenal Rd ELTH/MOT SE9 146 E3
Arterberry Rd RYNPK SW20 177 F3
Artesian Cl ROM RM1 75 H3
WLSDN NW10 81 F5
Artesian Gv BAR EN5 21 G5
Artesian Houses NTGHL * W11 100 E5
Artesian Rd BAY/PAD W2 100 E5
Arthingworth St SRTFD E15 88 D6
Arthurdon Rd LEW SE13 144 D6
Arthur Gv WOOL/PLUM SE18 127 H4
Arthur Rd CHDH RM6 73 J4
ED N9 36 B4
EHAM E6 107 K1
HOLWY N7 85 F2
KUTN/CMB KT2 175 H3
NWMAL KT3 193 F1
WIM/MER SW19 159 K6
Arthur St CANST EC4R 13 F6
ERITH DA8 150 C1
Artichoke Hl WAP E1W 104 D6
Artichoke Pl CMBW * SE5 142 E2
Artillery Cl GNTH/NBYPK IG2 72 C3
Artillery La LVPST EC2M 13 H2
SHB W12 99 J5
Artillery Pas WCHPL * E1 13 H2
Artillery Pl WOOL/PLUM SE18 126 E5
Artington Cl ORP BR6 216 C2
Artizan St WCHPL E1 13 H3
Arundel Av MRDN SM4 193 J1
Arundel Cl BTSEA SW11 140 D6
BXLY DA5 169 G1
CROY/NA * CR0 211 H1
HPTN TW12 173 G1
SRTFD E15 88 C2
Arundel Dr ORP BR6 217 H3
RYLN/HDSTN HA2 77 K2
WFD IG8 52 E3
Arundel Gdns EDGE HA8 45 F3
GDMY/SEVK IG3 73 G6
NTGHL W11 100 D6
WCHMH N21 35 G3
Arundel Gv STNW/STAM N16 86 A3
Arundel Pl IS N1 85 G4
Arundel Rd BELMT SM2 208 D5
CROY/NA CR0 196 E3
DART DA1 151 F5
EBAR EN4 21 J4
HSLWW TW4 134 B4
KUT KT1 175 K5
Arundel Sq HOLWY N7 85 G4
Arundel St TPL/STR WC2R 11 H5
Arundel Ter BARN SW13 118 E6
Arvon Rd HBRY N5 85 G3
Asbaston Ter IL IG1 90 C3
Ascalon St VX/NE SW8 141 H1
Ascension Rd CRW RM5 56 E2
Ascham Dr CHING E4 51 K3
Ascham End WALTH E17 51 G4
Ascham St KTTN NW5 84 C3
Aschurch Rd CROY/NA CR0 197 G4
Ascot Cl BARK/HLT IG6 54 E2
NTHLT UB5 78 A3
Ascot Gdns STHL UB1 95 K4
Ascot Ms WLGTN SM6 210 C6
Ascot Pde CLAP * SW4 141 K5
Ascot Rd ASHF TW15 152 D3
EHAM E6 107 K2
SEVS/STOTM N15 67 K2
STMC/STPC BR5 202 A1
TOOT SW17 179 F2
UED N18 36 C6
WATW WD18 26 C1
Ascott Av EA W5 117 F2
Ascott Ct PIN * HA5 58 E1
Ashanti Ms HACK * E8 86 D4
Ashborurne Sq NTHWD HA6 40 C2
Ashbourne Av BXLYHN DA7 149 F1
GLDGN NW11 64 D2
RYLN/HDSTN * HA2 60 D6
SWFD E18 71 F1
TRDG/WHET N20 33 K4
Ashbourne Cl EA W5 98 B4
NFNCH/WDSP N12 33 F6
Ashbourne Gv CHSWK W4 118 B5
EDUL SE22 143 G6
MLHL NW7 45 F1
Ashbourne Pde EA * W5 98 B3
GLDGN * NW11 64 D1
Ashbourne Ri ORP BR6 216 D2
Ashbourne Rd EA W5 98 B3
MTCM CR4 179 F2
Ashbourne Ter WIM/MER SW19 177 K3
Ashbourne Wy GLDGN NW11 64 D2
Ashbridge Rd WAN E11 70 C4
Ashbridge St STJWD NW8 2 C7
Ashbrook EDGE * HA8 44 B2
Ashbrook Rd ARCH N19 66 D5
DAGE RM10 92 D1
Ashburn Gdns SKENS SW7 120 B4
Ashburnham Av HRW HA1 61 F4
Ashburnham Cl EFNCH N2 47 H6
OXHEY * WD19 26 E5
Ashburnham Dr OXHEY WD19 26 E5
Ashburnham Gdns HRW HA1 61 F3
Ashburnham Gv GNWCH SE10 144 E1
Ashburnham Pk
ESH/CLAY KT10 204 C2
Ashburnham Pl GNWCH SE10 144 E1
Ashburnham Retreat
GNWCH SE10 144 E1
Ashburnham Rd BELV DA17 129 K4
RCHPK/HAM TW10 156 C5
WBPTN * SW10 140 B1
WLSDN NW10 100 A2
Ashburn Pl SKENS SW7 120 B4
Ashburton Av CROY/NA CR0 197 J5
GDMY/SEVK IG3 91 F2
Ashburton Cl CROY/NA CR0 197 H5
Ashburton Gdns CROY/NA CR0 197 H6
Ashburton Gv HOLWY N7 85 G2
Ashburton Rd CAN/RD E16 106 E5
CROY/NA CR0 197 H6
RSLP HA4 58 E6
Ashbury Ct BMLY BR1 183 K3
Ashbury Gdns CHDH RM6 73 K2
Ashbury Pl WIM/MER SW19 178 B2
Ashbury Rd BTSEA SW11 140 E4
Ashby Av CHSGTN KT9 206 C4
Ashby Gv IS N1 85 J5
Ashby Ms BROCKY SE4 144 C3
Ashby Rd BROCKY SE4 144 C3
SEVS/STOTM N15 68 C2
Ashby St FSBYE EC1V 6 B5
Ashby Wk CROY/NA CR0 196 D3
Ashby Wy WDR/YW UB7 132 D1
Ashchurch Gv SHB W12 118 D2
Ashchurch Park Vls SHB W12 118 D3
Ashchurch Ter SHB W12 118 C3
Ash Cl CAR SM5 194 E6
EDGE HA8 30 D6
NWMAL KT3 176 A5
PGE/AN SE20 181 K5
ROMW/RG RM7 56 D3
SCUP DA14 168 C5
STAN HA7 43 G2
STMC/STPC BR5 201 J2
SWLY BR8 187 K5
Ashcombe Av SURB KT6 190 E4
Ashcombe Gdns EDGE HA8 30 C6
Ashcombe Pk CRICK NW2 81 G1
Ashcombe Rd CAR SM5 210 A4
WIM/MER SW19 177 K1
Ashcombe Sq NWMAL KT3 175 K6
Ashcombe St FUL/PGN * SW6 140 A3
Ash Ct HOR/WEW KT19 206 E2
Ashcroft PIN HA5 42 A2
Ashcroft Av BFN/LL DA15 168 B1
Ashcroft Crs BFN/LL DA15 168 B1
Ashcroft Rd BOW E3 105 G2
CHSGTN KT9 206 B1
Ashdale Cl STWL/WRAY TW19 152 B4
WHTN TW2 155 G2
Ashdale Gv STAN HA7 43 F2
Ashdale Rd LEE/GVPK SE12 166 A3
Ashdene PIN HA5 41 G6
Ashdon Cl WFD IG8 53 F2
Ashdown WEA * W13 97 H4
Ashdown Cl BECK BR3 182 E5
BXLY DA5 169 K2
Ashdown Crs KTTN * NW5 84 A3
Ashdown Pl THDIT KT7 190 B3
Ashdown Rd KUT KT1 175 F5
PEND EN3 24 E4
WLSDN NW10 81 G6
Ashdown Wk ROMW/RG RM7 56 D4
Ashdown Wy TOOT SW17 161 F4
Ashenden Rd CLPT E5 87 G3
Ashen Dr DART DA1 170 D1
Ashen Gv WIM/MER SW19 159 K5
Ashen V SAND/SEL CR2 213 F6
Asher Loftus Wy
FBAR/BDGN N11 47 K2
Asher Wy WAP E1W 123 H1
Ashfield Av BUSH WD23 28 B1
FELT TW13 154 A3
Ashfield Cl BECK BR3 182 D3
RCHPK/HAM TW10 157 F3
Ashfield Ct EA * W5 98 A6
Ashfield La CHST BR7 185 H2
Ashfield Rd ACT W3 118 C1
FSBYPK N4 67 J3
STHGT/OAK N14 34 C5
Ashfield St WCHPL E1 104 E4
Ashfield Yd WCHPL * E1 104 E4
Ashford Av CEND/HSY/T N8 66 E1
YEAD UB4 95 H5
Ashford Cl ASHF TW15 152 B6
WALTH E17 69 H3
Ashford Crs ASHF TW15 152 B5
PEND EN3 24 E3
Ashford Gn OXHEY WD19 41 H1
Ashford Rd CRICK NW2 82 B2
EHAM E6 89 K4
FELT TW13 153 G6
SWFD E18 53 F5
Ashford St IS N1 7 G4
Ash Gv ALP/SUD HA0 79 G2
CRICK NW2 82 B2
EA W5 117 F2
EBED/NFELT TW14 153 H3
EN EN1 36 A2
HACK E8 86 D6
HEST TW5 134 C2
HYS/HAR UB3 94 B6
PGE/AN SE20 181 K5
PLMGR N13 35 J5
STHL UB1 96 A4
WWKM BR4 199 F6
Ashgrove Rd BMLY BR1 183 G2
GDMY/SEVK IG3 73 F5
Ash Hill Cl BUSH WD23 28 B3
Ash Hill Dr PIN HA5 41 G6
Ashingdon Cl CHING E4 38 A6
Ashington Rd FUL/PGN * SW6 139 J3
Ashlake Rd STRHM/NOR SW16 161 K6
Ashland Pl MHST W1U 9 G1
Ashlar Pl WOOL/PLUM SE18 127 G4
Ashleigh Gdns SUT SM1 194 A6
Ashleigh Rd MORT/ESHN SW14 138 B4
PGE/AN SE20 181 J6
Ashley Av BARK/HLT IG6 54 B5
MRDN SM4 193 K2
Ashley Cl HDN NW4 46 A5
PIN HA5 41 F5
Ashley Crs BTSEA SW11 141 F4
WDGN N22 49 G5
Ashley Dr ISLW TW7 115 K6
WHTN TW2 155 G3
Ashley Gdns ORP BR6 216 E3
PLMGR N13 35 J6
RCHPK/HAM TW10 156 E5
WBLY HA9 62 A6
Ashley La CROY/NA CR0 211 H2
MLHL NW7 46 A3
Ashley Pl WEST SW1P 16 A5
Ashley Rd ARCH N19 66 E5
CHING E4 51 J1
FSTGT E7 89 G5
HPTN TW12 173 F4
PEND EN3 24 E3
RCH/KEW TW9 137 F4
THDIT KT7 190 A3
THHTH CR7 196 A1
TOTM N17 50 C6
WIM/MER SW19 178 A2
Ashling Rd CROY/NA CR0 197 H5
Ashlin Rd SRTFD E15 88 B2
Ashlone Rd PUT/ROE SW15 139 F4
Ashlyns Wy CHSGTN KT9 205 K4
Ashmead STHGT/OAK N14 22 C6
Ashmead Ga BMLY BR1 184 B4
Ashmead Ms DEPT * SE8 144 D2
Ashmead Rd DEPT SE8 144 D3
EBED/NFELT TW14 153 K3
Ashmere Av BECK BR3 183 G5
Ashmere Cl CHEAM SM3 208 B3
Ashmere Gv CLAP SW4 141 K5
Ash Ms KTTN * NW5 84 C3
Ashmill St STJWD NW8 8 C1
Ashmole St VX/NE SW8 122 A6
Ashmore Cl PECK SE15 143 H1
Ashmore Gv WELL DA16 147 J4
Ashmore Rd MV/WKIL W9 100 D2
Ashmount Rd HGT N6 66 C4
SEVS/STOTM N15 68 B2
Ashmount Ter EA * W5 116 E4
Ashmour Gdns ROM RM1 57 F5
Ashneal Gdns HRW HA1 78 D1
Ashness Gdns GFD/PVL UB6 79 H4
Ashness Rd BTSEA SW11 140 E6
Ashridge Cl KTN/HRWW/W HA3 61 J3
Ashridge Crs WOOL/PLUM SE18 147 H1
Ashridge Dr OXHEY WD19 41 G1
Ashridge Gdns PIN HA5 59 J1
PLMGR N13 48 E1
Ashridge Wy MRDN SM4 193 J1
Ash Rd CROY/NA CR0 198 D6
DART DA1 171 G3
MRDN SM4 193 H5
ORP BR6 217 G5
RDART DA2 171 J6
SRTFD E15 88 C3
Ash Rw HAYES BR2 201 F3
Ashtead Rd CLPT E5 68 C4
Ashton Cl SUT SM1 208 E2
Ashton Gdns CHDH RM6 74 A3
HSLWW TW4 134 E5
Ashton Rd SRTFD E15 88 B3
Ashton St POP/IOD E14 106 A6
Ashtree Av MTCM CR4 178 C5
Ash Tree Cl CROY/NA CR0 198 B3
SURB KT6 191 F5
Ashtree Cl ORP BR6 216 B2
Ash Tree Dell CDALE/KGS NW9 62 E2
Ash Tree Wy CROY/NA CR0 198 B2
Ashurst Cl DART DA1 150 C4
NTHWD HA6 40 C3
PGE/AN SE20 181 J4
Ashurst Dr GNTH/NBYPK IG2 72 B3
Ashurst Gdns
BRXS/STRHM * SW2 162 B3
Ashurst Rd EBAR EN4 21 K6
NFNCH/WDSP N12 47 J1
Ashurst Wk CROY/NA CR0 197 J6
Ashvale Gdns CRW RM5 57 F1
Ashvale Rd TOOT SW17 178 E1
Ashville Rd WAN E11 70 B6
Ash Wk ALP/SUD HA0 79 J2
Ashwater Rd LEE/GVPK SE12 165 K3
Ashwin St HACK E8 86 B4
Ashwood Av RAIN RM13 111 K2
Ashwood Gdns CROY/NA CR0 213 K4
HYS/HAR UB3 113 J4
Ashwood Rd CHING E4 38 B5
Ashworth Cl CMBW SE5 142 E3
Ashworth Rd MV/WKIL W9 101 F2
Askern Cl BXLYHS DA6 148 E5
Aske St IS N1 7 G4
Askew Crs SHB W12 118 C2
Askew Rd NTHWD HA6 26 B4
SHB W12 118 C2
Askew Vls PLMGR * N13 35 H5
Askham Rd SHB W12 118 D1
Askill Dr PUT/ROE SW15 139 H6
Askwith Rd RAIN RM13 111 F1
Asland Rd SRTFD E15 88 B6
Aslett St WAND/EARL SW18 160 A2
Asmara Rd CRICK NW2 82 C3
Asmuns Hl GLDGN NW11 64 E2
Asmuns Pl GLDGN NW11 64 D2
Aspen Cl EA W5 117 G2
ORP BR6 217 G3
WDR/YW UB7 112 C1
Aspen Copse BMLY BR1 184 E5
Aspen Dr ALP/SUD HA0 79 G1
Aspen Gdns MTCM CR4 195 F2
Aspen Gn ERITHM DA18 129 G3
Aspen La NTHLT UB5 95 J2
Aspenlea Rd HMSMTH W6 119 G6
Aspen Wy FELT TW13 154 A5
POP/IOD E14 106 A6
Aspern Gv HAMP NW3 83 J3
Aspinall Rd BROCKY SE4 144 A4
Aspinden Rd BERM/RHTH SE16 123 J4
Aspley Rd WAND/EARL SW18 140 A6
Asplins Rd TOTM N17 50 C4
Asplins Vls TOTM * N17 50 C4
Asquith Cl BCTR RM8 73 J5
Assam St WCHPL E1 104 C5
Assata Ms IS N1 85 H4
Assembly Pas WCHPL E1 104 E4
Assembly Wk CAR SM5 194 D4
Ass House La KTN/HRWW/W HA3 28 B6
Astall Cl KTN/HRWW/W HA3 42 D4
Astbury Rd PECK SE15 143 K2
Astell St CHEL SW3 120 D5
Asteys Rw IS N1 85 H5
Astle St BTSEA SW11 141 F3
Astley Av CRICK NW2 82 A3
Aston Av KTN/HRWW/W HA3 61 J4
Aston Cl BUSH WD23 28 C1
SCUP DA14 168 B5
Aston Gn HEST TW5 134 B3
Aston Rd EA W5 97 K5
ESH/CLAY KT10 204 E3
RYNPK SW20 177 F5
Astons Rd NTHWD HA6 26 A5
Aston St WCHPL E1 105 G5
Aston Ter BAL * SW12 161 G1
Astonville St WAND/EARL SW18 159 K3
Astor Av ROMW/RG RM7 74 D3
Astor Cl KUTN/CMB KT2 175 J2
Astoria Pde ASHF * TW15 152 D6
STRHM/NOR * SW16 161 K5
Astoria Wk BRXN/ST SW9 142 B4
Astra Cl HCH RM12 93 K4
Astrop Ms HMSMTH W6 119 F3
Astrop Ter HMSMTH W6 119 F3
Astwood Ms SKENS SW7 120 A4
Asylum Rd PECK SE15 143 J1
Atalanta St FUL/PGN SW6 139 G2
Atbara Rd TEDD TW11 174 C2
Atcham Rd HSLW TW3 135 H5
Atcost Rd BARK IG11 109 G4
Atheldene Rd
WAND/EARL SW18 160 A3
Athelney St CAT SE6 164 D5
Athelstane Gv BOW E3 105 H1
Athelstane Ms FSBYPK N4 67 G5
Athelstan Gdns
KIL/WHAMP * NW6 82 C5
Athelstan Rd KUT KT1 191 G1
Athelstan Wy STMC/STPC BR5 186 B4
Athelstone Rd
KTN/HRWW/W HA3 42 D5
Athena Cl KUT KT1 175 G6
RYLN/HDSTN HA2 60 D6
Athenaeum Pl MUSWH N10 48 B6
Athenaeum Rd TRDG/WHET N20 33 G3
Athena Pl NTHWD HA6 40 D4
Athenlay Rd PECK SE15 144 A6
Athens Gdns MV/WKIL * W9 100 E3
Atherden Rd CLPT E5 86 E2
Atherfold Rd BRXN/ST SW9 141 K4
Atherley Wy HSLWW TW4 154 E2
Atherstone Ms SKENS * SW7 120 B4
Atherton Cl STWL/WRAY TW19 152 A1
Atherton Dr WIM/MER SW19 159 G6
Atherton Hts ALP/SUD HA0 79 J4
Atherton Ms FSTGT E7 88 E4
Atherton Pl RYLN/HDSTN HA2 42 C6
STHL UB1 96 A6
Atherton Rd BARN SW13 138 D1
CLAY IG5 53 J5

FSTGT E7 88 D3
Atherton St BTSEA SW11 140 D3
Athlone ESH/CLAY KT10 204 E4
Athlone Cl CLPT E5 86 D3
Athlone Ct WALTH E17 52 B6
Athlone Rd BRXS/STRHM SW2 162 A2
Athlone St KTTN NW5 84 A4
Athlon Rd ALP/SUD HA0 97 K1
Athol Cl PIN HA5 41 F4
Athole Gdns EN EN1 24 A6
Athol Gdns PIN HA5 41 F4
Atholl Rd GDMY/SEVK IG3 73 G4
Athol Rd ERITH DA8 129 K5
Athol Sq POP/IOD E14 106 A5
Atkins Dr WWKM BR4 214 B1
Atkinson Cl ORP BR6 217 G3
Atkinson Rd CAN/RD E16 107 G4
Atkins Rd BAL SW12 161 H2
LEY E10 69 K3
Atlanta Bvd ROM RM1 75 G3
Atlantic Rd BRXN/ST SW9 142 B5
Atlantis Cl BARK IG11 109 H2
Atlas Gdns CHARL SE7 126 B4
Atlas Ms HACK E8 86 B4
Atlas Rd DART DA1 151 J4
FBAR/BDGN N11 48 A2
PLSTW E13 106 E1
WBLY HA9 80 E2
WLSDN NW10 99 G2
Atley Rd BOW E3 87 J6
Atlip Rd ALP/SUD HA0 80 A6
Atney Rd PUT/ROE SW15 139 H5
Atria Rd NTHWD HA6 40 E1
Attenborough Cl OXHEY WD19 27 J5
Atterbury Rd FSBYPK N4 67 G3
Atterbury St WEST SW1P 16 D7
Attewood Av CRICK NW2 81 G1
Attewood Rd NTHLT UB5 77 J4
Attfield Cl TRDG/WHET N20 33 H4
Attlee Cl CROY/NA CR0 196 D3
NTHLT * UB5 95 F2
Attlee Dr DART DA1 151 K6
Attlee Rd THMD SE28 109 H6
YEAD UB4 94 E2
Attlee Ter WALTH E17 69 K1
Attneave St FSBYW WC1X 5 J6
Atwell Rd PECK * SE15 143 H3
Atwood Av RCH/KEW TW9 137 H3
Atwood Rd HMSMTH W6 118 E4
Aubert Pk HBRY N5 85 G2
Aubert Rd HBRY N5 85 H2
Aubrey Pl STJWD NW8 101 G1
Aubrey Rd CEND/HSY/T * N8 66 E2
KENS W8 119 J1
WALTH E17 51 J6
Aubrey Wk KENS W8 119 J1
Auburn Cl NWCR SE14 144 B1
Aubyn Hl WNWD SE27 162 D6
Aubyn Sq PUT/ROE SW15 138 D5
Auckland Av RAIN RM13 111 H2
Auckland Cl NRWD SE19 181 G4
Auckland Hl WNWD SE27 162 D6
Auckland Ri NRWD SE19 181 F4
Auckland Rd BTSEA SW11 140 D5
IL IG1 72 B5
KUT KT1 191 G1
LEY E10 87 K1
NRWD SE19 181 G4
Aucklands Gdns NRWD SE19 181 F4
Auckland St LBTH SE11 122 A5
Aucuba Vls WELL * DA16 148 C4
Audax CDALE/KGS * NW9 45 H5
Auden Pl CAMTN NW1 84 A6
CHEAM * SM3 208 A2
Audleigh Pl CHIG IG7 54 A2
Audley Cl MUSWH N10 48 B3
Audley Ct PIN HA5 41 G5
SWFD E18 70 D1
Audley Dr CAN/RD E16 126 A1
Audley Gdns GDMY/SEVK IG3 73 F6
Audley Pl BELMT SM2 209 F5
Audley Rd EA W5 98 B4
ENC/FH EN2 23 H3
HDN NW4 63 J3
RCHPK/HAM TW10 137 G6
Audley Sq MYFR/PKLN * W1K 9 H7
Audrey Cl BECK BR3 198 E3
Audrey Gdns ALP/SUD HA0 61 H6
Audrey Rd IL IG1 90 B1
Audrey St BETH E2 104 C1
Audric Cl KUTN/CMB KT2 175 H4
Augurs La PLSTW E13 107 F2
Augusta Cl E/WMO/HCT KT8 172 E6
Augusta Rd WHTN TW2 155 H4
Augustine Rd
KTN/HRWW/W HA3 42 B4
STMC/STPC BR5 186 E6
WKENS W14 119 G3
Augustus Cl BTFD TW8 136 E1
SHB W12 118 E2
Augustus Rd WIM/MER SW19 159 H3
Augustus St CAMTN NW1 3 K3
Aultone Wy CAR SM5 209 K1
SUT SM1 194 A6
Aulton Pl LBTH SE11 122 B5
Aurelia Gdns THHTH CR7 196 A2
Aurelia Rd CROY/NA CR0 195 K3
Auriel Av DAGE RM10 93 F4
Auriga Ms IS N1 85 K3
Auriol Cl HOR/WEW KT19 207 G1
Auriol Dr GFD/PVL UB6 78 D5
Auriol Park Rd WPK KT4 207 G1
Auriol Rd WKENS W14 119 H4
Austell Gdns MLHL NW7 31 G5
Austen Cl THMD SE28 128 C1
Austen Rd ERITH DA8 149 J1
RYLN/HDSTN HA2 60 B6
Austin Av HAYES BR2 200 D3
Austin Cl CAT SE6 164 B2
Austin Friars OBST EC2N 13 F3
Austin Friars Sq OBST * EC2N 13 F3
Austin Rd BTSEA SW11 141 F2
HYS/HAR UB3 113 J2
STMC/STPC BR5 202 B3
Austin's La HGDN/ICK UB10 76 A1
Austin St BETH E2 7 J5
Austral Cl BFN/LL DA15 168 A5
Australia Rd SHB W12 99 K6
Austral St LBTH SE11 18 A6
Austyn Gdns BRYLDS * KT5 191 J5
Autumn Cl EN EN1 24 D3
WIM/MER SW19 178 B2
Autumn Dr BELMT SM2 209 F6
Autumn St BOW E3 87 J6
Avalon Cl ENC/FH EN2 23 G3
ORP BR6 202 E6
RYNPK SW20 177 H5
WEA W13 97 G4
Avalon Rd FUL/PGN SW6 140 A2
ORP BR6 202 D6
WEA W13 97 G3
Avard Gdns ORP BR6 216 C2
Avarn Rd TOOT SW17 178 E2
Avebury Pk SURB * KT6 190 E3
Avebury Rd ORP BR6 216 D1
WAN E11 70 B5
WIM/MER SW19 177 J4
Avebury St IS N1 6 E1
Aveley Cl ERITH DA8 130 C6
Aveline St LBTH SE11 122 A5
Aveling Park Rd WALTH E17 51 J5
Avelon Rd CRW RM5 57 F2
RAIN RM13 93 J6
Avenell Rd HBRY N5 85 H1
Avening Rd WAND/EARL SW18 159 K2
Avening Ter WAND/EARL SW18 159 K1
Avenons Rd PLSTW E13 106 E4
The Avenue BAR EN5 20 C4
BECK BR3 182 E4
BELMT SM2 208 D6
BMLY BR1 184 C6
BRYLDS KT5 191 G3
BXLY DA5 168 E2
CAR SM5 210 A5
CEND/HSY/T N8 49 G6
CHING E4 52 B2
CHSWK W4 118 B3
CLAP SW4 141 F6
CROY/NA CR0 212 A1
ESH/CLAY KT10 204 E4
EW KT17 208 A5
FBAR/BDGN N11 48 B1
GNWCH SE10 145 G1
HEST TW5 133 K2
HPTN TW12 172 E2
HSLW TW3 135 G6
KIL/WHAMP NW6 82 B6
KTN/HRWW/W HA3 43 F4
LOU IG10 39 J1
MUSWH N10 48 C5
NTHWD HA6 40 A2
ORP BR6 202 A6
PIN HA5 41 K2
PIN HA5 59 K3
RCH/KEW TW9 137 G3
ROM RM1 75 F1
STMC/STPC BR5 186 C3
SUN TW16 172 A5
TOTM N17 50 A5
TWK TW1 156 C1
WAN E11 71 F3
WBLY HA9 62 A5
WEA W13 97 H6
WPK KT4 192 C6
WWKM BR4 199 G4
Avenue Cl HEST TW5 134 A2
STHGT/OAK N14 34 C1
STJWD NW8 2 D1
WDR/YW UB7 112 A3
Avenue Crs ACT W3 117 J2
HEST TW5 133 K2
Avenue Elmers SURB KT6 191 F2
Avenue Gdns ACT W3 117 J2
HEST * TW5 133 K1
MORT/ESHN SW14 138 B4
TEDD TW11 174 A3
Avenue Ga LOU IG10 39 G1
Avenue Ms MUSWH N10 48 B6
Avenue Pde SUN * TW16 172 A6
WCHMH * N21 35 K2
Avenue Park Rd WNWD SE27 162 C4
Avenue Rd ACT W3 117 J2
BTFD TW8 116 D5
BXLYHS DA6 149 F4
ERITH DA8 149 K1
FELT TW13 153 J5
FSTGT E7 89 F3
GDMY/SEVK IG3 73 H4
HGT N6 66 C4
HPTN TW12 173 G4
ISLW TW7 135 K2
KUT KT1 175 F6
NFNCH/WDSP N12 33 G6
NWMAL KT3 176 B6
PGE/AN SE20 181 K4
PIN HA5 41 J6
RYNPK SW20 176 E5
SEVS/STOTM N15 67 K2
SNWD SE25 181 H5
STHGT/OAK N14 34 C2
STHL UB1 114 E1
STJWD NW8 83 H6
STRHM/NOR SW16 179 J5
TEDD TW11 174 B3
WFD IG8 53 G2
WLGTN SM6 210 C5
WLSDN NW10 99 H1
Avenue South BRYLDS KT5 191 G4
Avenue Ter NWMAL KT3 175 K6
OXHEY WD19 27 J1
Averil Gv STRHM/NOR SW16 180 C2
Averill St HMSMTH W6 119 G6
Avern Gdns E/WMO/HCT KT8 189 G1
Avern Rd E/WMO/HCT KT8 189 G1
Avery Farm Rw BGVA * SW1W 15 J7
Avery Gdns GNTH/NBYPK IG2 71 K2
Avery Hill Rd ELTH/MOT SE9 167 H3
Avery Rw MYFR/PKLN W1K 9 J5
Aviary Cl CAN/RD E16 106 D4
Aviemore Cl BECK BR3 198 C2
Aviemore Wy BECK BR3 198 B2
Avignon Rd BROCKY SE4 144 A4
Avington Gv PGE/AN SE20 181 K3
Avington Wy PECK * SE15 143 G1
Avion Crs CDALE/KGS NW9 45 J5
Avior Dr NTHWD HA6 26 D6
Avis Sq WCHPL E1 105 F5
Avoca Rd TOOT SW17 161 F6
Avocet Cl STHWK SE1 123 G5
Avocet Ms THMD SE28 127 J3
Avon Cl SUT SM1 209 G2
WPK KT4 192 D6
YEAD UB4 95 G3
Avon Ct PIN * HA5 42 A3
Avondale Av CRICK NW2 81 G1
EBAR EN4 33 K3
ESH/CLAY KT10 205 G1
NFNCH/WDSP N12 47 F1
WPK KT4 192 C5
Avondale Cl LOU IG10 39 K2
Avondale Ct WFD IG8 53 F4
Avondale Crs PEND EN3 25 G4
REDBR IG4 71 H2
Avondale Dr HYS/HAR UB3 113 K1
LOU IG10 39 K1
Avondale Gdns HSLWW TW4 134 E6
Avondale Park Gdns
NTGHL * W11 100 C6
Avondale Park Rd NTGHL W11 100 C6
Avondale Pavement
STHWK * SE1 123 H5
Avondale Ri PECK SE15 143 G4
Avondale Rd ASHF TW15 152 A5
BMLY BR1 183 H2
CAN/RD E16 106 C4
ELTH/MOT SE9 166 D4
FNCH N3 47 G4
KTN/HRWW/W HA3 43 F6
MORT/ESHN SW14 138 A4
PLMGR N13 35 G4
SAND/SEL CR2 211 J4
SEVS/STOTM N15 67 H2
WALTH E17 69 J4
WELL DA16 148 D3
WIM/MER SW19 178 A1
Avondale Sq STHWK SE1 123 H5
Avonley Rd NWCR SE14 143 K1
Avonmore Gdns WKENS * W14 119 J4
Avonmore Pl WKENS W14 119 H4
Avonmore Rd WKENS W14 119 J4
Avonmouth Rd DART DA1 151 G6
Avonmouth St STHWK SE1 18 C4
Avon Rd BROCKY SE4 144 D4
GFD/PVL UB6 96 A3
WALTH E17 52 B6
Avonstowe Cl ORP BR6 216 C1
Avon Wy SWFD E18 52 E6
Avonwick Rd HSLW TW3 135 G3
Avril Wy CHING E4 52 A1
Avro Wy WLGTN SM6 210 E5
Awberry Ct WATW * WD18 26 B1
Awlfield Av TOTM N17 49 K4
Awliscombe Rd WELL DA16 148 A3
Axeholm Av EDGE HA8 44 D4
Axe St BARK IG11 90 C6
Axholme Av EDGE HA8 44 C4
Axminster Crs WELL DA16 148 D2
Axminster Rd HOLWY N7 84 E1
Axtaine Rd STMC/STPC BR5 202 E4
Aybrook St MHST W1U 9 G2
Aycliff Ct KUT * KT1 175 H5
Aycliffe Cl BMLY BR1 200 E1
Aycliffe Rd SHB W12 118 C1
Aylands Cl WBLY HA9 62 A6
Aylesbury Cl FSTGT E7 88 D4
Aylesbury Rd HAYES BR2 183 K6
WALW SE17 122 E5
Aylesbury St CLKNW EC1R 6 A7
WLSDN NW10 81 F1
Aylesford Av BECK BR3 198 B2
Aylesford St PIM SW1V 121 J5
Aylesham Cl MLHL NW7 45 J3
Aylesham Rd ORP BR6 201 K4
Ayles Rd YEAD UB4 95 F2
Aylestone Av KIL/WHAMP NW6 82 B5
Aylett Rd ISLW TW7 135 K3
SNWD SE25 197 J1
Ayley Cft EN EN1 24 C6
Ayliffe Cl KUT KT1 175 H5
Aylmer Cl STAN HA7 29 G6
Aylmer Dr STAN HA7 29 G6
Aylmer Pde EFNCH * N2 65 K2
Aylmer Rd BCTR RM8 92 A1
EFNCH N2 65 J2
SHB W12 118 B2
WAN E11 70 D4
Ayloffe Rd DAGW RM9 92 B4
Aylsham Dr HGDN/ICK UB10 58 A6
Aylton Est BERM/RHTH * SE16 123 K2
Aylward Rd FSTH SE23 164 A4
RYNPK SW20 177 J5
Aylwards Ri STAN HA7 29 G6
Aylward St WCHPL E1 105 F5
Aynhoe Rd WKENS W14 119 G4
Aynscombe Angle ORP BR6 202 B4
Ayres Cl PLSTW E13 106 E2
Ayres Crs WLSDN NW10 81 F5
Ayres St STHWK SE1 18 D2
Ayr Gn ROM RM1 57 G4
Ayrsome Rd STNW/STAM N16 86 A1
Ayrton Rd SKENS SW7 14 A4
Ayr Wy ROM RM1 57 G4
Aysgarth Rd DUL SE21 162 E1
Aytoun Pl BRXN/ST SW9 142 A3
Aytoun Rd BRXN/ST SW9 142 A3
Azalea Cl HNWL W7 116 A1
IL IG1 90 B3
Azalea Ct WFD * IG8 52 C3
Azalea Wk PIN HA5 59 F3
Azania Ms KTTN NW5 84 B3
Azenby Rd PECK SE15 143 G3
Azof St GNWCH SE10 125 H4

B

Baalbec Rd HBRY N5 85 H3
Babbacombe Cl CHSGTN KT9 205 K3
Babbacombe Gdns REDBR IG4 71 J1
Babbacombe Rd BMLY BR1 184 A4
Baber Bridge Pde
EBED/NFELT * TW14 154 B1
Baber Dr EBED/NFELT TW14 154 B1
Babington Ri WBLY HA9 80 C4
Babington Rd BCTR RM8 91 J3
HCH RM12 75 K5
HDN NW4 63 K1
STRHM/NOR SW16 179 J1
Babmaes St STJS SW1Y 10 C6
Bache's St IS N1 7 F5
Back Church La WCHPL E1 104 C5
Back Hl CLKNW EC1R 5 K7
Back La BTFD TW8 136 E1
BXLY DA5 169 H2
CEND/HSY/T N8 66 E2
CHDH RM6 74 A4
EDGE HA8 44 E4
HAMP NW3 83 G2
RCHPK/HAM TW10 156 D5
Backley Gdns SNWD SE25 197 H3
Back Rd SCUP DA14 168 B6
TEDD TW11 173 K3
Bacon Gv STHWK SE1 19 J6
Bacon La CDALE/KGS NW9 62 D1
EDGE HA8 44 C4
Bacon Link CRW RM5 56 D2
Bacon's La HGT N6 66 A5
Bacon St BETH E2 7 K6
BETH E2 104 C3
Bacton St BETH E2 104 E2
Baddow Cl DAGE RM10 92 C6
WFD IG8 53 H2
Baden Pl STHWK SE1 18 E2
Baden Powell Cl DAGW RM9 92 A6
SURB KT6 191 G6
Baden Rd CEND/HSY/T N8 66 D1
IL IG1 90 B3
Bader Wy HCH RM12 93 J4
Badger Cl FELT TW13 154 A5
HSLWW TW4 134 B4
Badgers Cl ENC/FH EN2 23 H4
HRW HA1 60 D3
HYS/HAR UB3 113 H1
Badgers Copse ORP BR6 202 A6
WPK KT4 192 C6
Badgers Ct WPK * KT4 192 C6
Badgers Cft ELTH/MOT SE9 167 F5
TRDG/WHET N20 32 C2
Badgers Wk NWMAL KT3 176 B5
Badlis Rd WALTH E17 51 J5
Badlow Cl ERITH DA8 150 B1
Badminton Cl HRW * HA1 60 E1
NTHLT UB5 78 A4
Badminton Ms CAN/RD E16 125 K1
Badminton Rd BAL SW12 161 F1
Badsworth Rd CMBW SE5 142 D1
Bagley Cl WDR/YW UB7 112 B2
Bagley's La FUL/PGN SW6 140 A2
Bagleys Spring CHDH RM6 74 A1
Bagshot Ct WOOL/PLUM * SE18 147 F2
Bagshot Rd EN EN1 36 B2
Bagshot St WALW SE17 123 F5
Baildon St DEPT SE8 144 C1
Bailey Cl WDGN N22 48 D4
Bailey Cottages POP/IOD * E14 105 G4
Bailey Crs CHSGTN KT9 205 K5
Bailey Pl SYD SE26 181 K2
Baillie Cl RAIN RM13 111 K3
Bainbridge Cl KUTN/CMB KT2 175 F1
Bainbridge Rd DAGW RM9 92 B2
Bainbridge St NOXST/BSQ WC1A 10 D3
Baines Cl SAND/SEL CR2 211 K3
Baird Av STHL UB1 96 B6
Baird Cl BUSH WD23 28 B1
CDALE/KGS NW9 62 E3
LEY E10 69 J5
Baird Gdns NRWD SE19 163 F6
Baird Memorial Cottages
STHGT/OAK * N14 34 D4
Baird Rd EN EN1 24 D4
Baird St STLK EC1Y 6 D6
Baizdon Rd BKHTH/KID SE3 145 H3
Baker La MTCM CR4 179 F5
Baker Ms ORP BR6 217 F4
Baker Rd WLSDN NW10 81 G6
WOOL/PLUM SE18 146 D1
Bakers Av WALTH E17 69 K3
Bakers End RYNPK SW20 177 H5
Bakers Gdns CAR SM5 194 D6
Bakers Hl BAR EN5 21 F3
CLPT E5 68 D5
Baker's Ms MHST W1U 9 G3
Bakers Rents BETH E2 7 J5
Baker's Rw CLKNW EC1R 5 J7
SRTFD E15 106 C1
Baker St CAMTN NW1 3 F7
EN EN1 23 K3
MHST W1U 9 G2
Baker's Yd CLKNW EC1R 5 J7
Bakery Cl BRXN/ST * SW9 142 A1
Bakewell Wy NWMAL KT3 176 B5
Balaams La STHGT/OAK N14 34 D4
Balaam St PLSTW E13 106 E2
Balaclava Rd STHWK SE1 19 K7
SURB KT6 190 D4
Bala Gn CDALE/KGS * NW9 63 G3
Balcaskie Rd ELTH/MOT SE9 146 E6
Balchen Rd BKHTH/KID SE3 146 C3
Balchier Rd EDUL SE22 163 J1
Balcombe Cl BXLYHS DA6 148 E5
Balcombe St CAMTN NW1 2 E6
Balcorne St HOM E9 86 E5
Balder Ri LEE/GVPK SE12 166 A4
Balderton St MYFR/PKLN W1K 9 H4
Baldock St BOW E3 105 K1
Baldry Gdns STRHM/NOR SW16 179 K2
Baldwin Crs CMBW SE5 142 D2
Baldwin Gdns HSLW TW3 135 H2
Baldwin's Gdns FSBYW WC1X 11 J1
Baldwin St FSBYE EC1V 6 E5
Baldwin Ter IS N1 6 C2
Baldwyn Gdns ACT W3 98 E6
Baldwyn's Pk BXLY DA5 170 A4
Baldwyn's Rd BXLY DA5 170 A4
Bale Rd WCHPL E1 105 G4
Bales Ter ED * N9 36 B5
Balfern Gv CHSWK W4 118 B5
Balfern St BTSEA SW11 140 D3
Balfe St IS N1 5 F3
Balfour Av HNWL W7 116 A1
Balfour Gv TRDG/WHET N20 33 K5
Balfour Ms ED N9 36 C5
MYFR/PKLN W1K 9 H7
Balfour Pl MYFR/PKLN W1K 9 H6
Balfour Rd ACT W3 98 E4
CAR SM5 209 K5
HAYES BR2 200 C2
HBRY N5 85 J2
HRW HA1 60 D2
HSLW TW3 135 G4
IL IG1 72 B6
NWDGN UB2 114 C3
SNWD SE25 197 H1
WEA W13 116 C2
WIM/MER SW19 178 A3
Balfour St STHWK SE1 18 E6
Balgonie Rd CHING E4 38 B3
Balgores Crs GPK RM2 57 K6
Balgores La GPK RM2 75 K1
Balgores Sq GPK RM2 75 K1
Balgowan Cl NWMAL KT3 192 B1
Balgowan Rd BECK BR3 182 B6
Balgowan St WOOL/PLUM SE18 128 A4
Balham Gv BAL SW12 161 F2
Balham High Rd BAL SW12 161 G3
Balham Hl BAL SW12 161 G2
Balham New Rd BAL SW12 161 G2
Balham Park Rd TOOT SW17 160 E3
Balham Rd ED N9 36 C4
Balham Station Rd BAL SW12 161 F3
Balkan Wk WAP * E1W 104 D6
Balladier Wk POP/IOD E14 105 K4
Ballamore Rd BMLY BR1 165 K5
Ballance Rd HOM E9 87 F4
Ballantine St WAND/EARL SW18 140 B5
Ballard Cl KUTN/CMB KT2 176 A3
Ballards Cl DAGE RM10 92 D6
Ballards Farm Rd
SAND/SEL CR2 212 C4
Ballards La FNCH N3 47 F3
Ballards Ri SAND/SEL CR2 212 C4
Ballards Rd CRICK NW2 63 J6
DAGE RM10 92 D6
Ballards Wy SAND/SEL CR2 212 C4
Ballast Quay GNWCH SE10 125 G5
Ballater Cl OXHEY WD19 27 G6
Ballater Rd CLAP SW4 141 K5
SAND/SEL CR2 212 B3
Ballina St FSTH SE23 164 A2
Ballingdon Rd BTSEA SW11 161 F1
Balliol Av CHING E4 38 B6
Balliol Rd NKENS W10 100 A5
TOTM N17 50 A4
WELL DA16 148 C3
Balloch Rd CAT SE6 165 G3
Ballogie Av WLSDN NW10 81 G2
Ballow Cl CMBW * SE5 142 E1
Ball's Pond Pl IS * N1 85 K4
Balls Pond Rd IS N1 85 K4
Balmain Cl EA W5 116 E1
Balmer Rd BOW E3 105 H1
Balmes Rd IS N1 85 K6
Balmoral Av BECK BR3 198 B1
FBAR/BDGN N11 48 A2
Balmoral Cl PUT/ROE * SW15 159 G1
Balmoral Crs E/WMO/HCT KT8 173 F6
Balmoral Dr STHL UB1 95 K3
YEAD UB4 94 C3
Balmoral Gdns BXLY DA5 169 G2
HNWL W7 116 B3
Balmoral Gv HOLWY N7 85 F4
Balmoral Ms SHB W12 118 C3
Balmoral Rd CRICK NW2 81 K4
FSTGT E7 89 G2
GPK RM2 75 K1
KUT KT1 191 G1
LEY E10 69 K6
RYLN/HDSTN HA2 78 A2
WPK KT4 207 K1
Balmore Crs EBAR EN4 22 A6
Balmore St ARCH N19 66 B6
Balmuir Gdns PUT/ROE SW15 139 F5
Balnacraig Av WLSDN NW10 81 G2
Balniel Ga PIM SW1V 121 J5
Baltic Cl WIM/MER SW19 178 C3
Baltic Pl IS N1 86 A6
Baltic St East STLK EC1Y 6 C7
Baltic St West FARR EC1M 6 C7
Baltimore Pl WELL DA16 148 A3
Balvaird Pl PIM SW1V 121 J5
Balvernie Gv WAND/EARL SW18 159 J2
Bamborough Gdns SHB W12 119 F2
Bamford Av ALP/SUD HA0 80 B6
Bamford Rd BMLY BR1 183 G1
Bamford Wy CRW RM5 56 D1
Bampfylde Cl WLGTN SM6 210 C1
Bampton Dr MLHL NW7 45 J3
Bampton Rd FSTH SE23 164 A5
Banavie Gdns BECK BR3 182 E4
Banbury Cl ENC/FH EN2 23 H2
Banbury Ct BELMT * SM2 208 E5
COVGDN * WC2E 10 E5
Banbury Rd HOM E9 87 F5
WALTH E17 51 G3
Banbury St BTSEA * SW11 140 D3
Banchory Rd BKHTH/KID SE3 146 A1
Bancroft Av EFNCH N2 65 J2
Bancroft Cha HCH RM12 75 H6
Bancroft Ct NTHLT UB5 77 G6
Bancroft Gdns
KTN/HRWW/W HA3 42 C4
ORP BR6 202 A5
Bancroft Rd
KTN/HRWW/W HA3 42 C5
WCHPL E1 104 E3
Bandon Ri WLGTN SM6 210 D4
Banfield Rd PECK SE15 143 J4
Bangalore St PUT/ROE SW15 139 F4
Bangor Cl NTHLT UB5 78 B3
Banim St HMSMTH W6 118 E3
Banister Rd NKENS W10 100 B2
The Bank HGT N6 66 B5
Bank Av MTCM CR4 178 C5
Bank Buildings CHING * E4 52 B2
Bank End STHWK SE1 12 D7
Bankfoot Rd BMLY BR1 165 H6
Bankhurst Rd CAT SE6 164 C2
Bank La KUTN/CMB KT2 175 F3
PUT/ROE SW15 138 B6
Banksia Rd UED N18 50 E1
Bankside ENC/FH EN2 23 H2
SAND/SEL CR2 212 B4
STHL UB1 114 C1
STHWK SE1 12 C6
Bankside Av NTHLT UB5 94 E1
Bankside Cl CAR SM5 209 J3
ISLW TW7 136 A5
RDART DA2 170 A6
Bankside Dr THDIT KT7 190 C6
Bankside Rd IL IG1 90 C3
Banks La BXLYHS DA6 149 G5
Bankton Rd BRXS/STRHM SW2 142 B5
Bankwell Rd LEW SE13 145 H5
Bank Willow RCHPK/HAM TW10 156 C5
Banner St STLK EC1Y 6 D7
Banning St GNWCH SE10 125 H5
Bannister Cl BRXS/STRHM SW2 162 B3
GFD/PVL UB6 78 D3
Bannister Gdns
STMC/STPC BR5 186 D6
Bannockburn Rd
WOOL/PLUM SE18 127 K4
Bannow Cl HOR/WEW KT19 207 G2
Banstead Gdns ED N9 35 K5
Banstead Rd BELMT SM2 209 H5
Banstead St PECK SE15 143 K4
Banstead Wy WLGTN SM6 210 E3
Banstock Rd EDGE HA8 44 E2
Banting Dr WCHMH N21 23 F6
Banton Cl EN EN1 24 D3
Bantry St CMBW SE5 142 E1
Banwell Rd BXLY DA5 168 E1
Banyard Rd BERM/RHTH SE16 123 J3
Baphchild Pl STMC/STPC BR5 202 D1
Baptist Gdns HAMP NW3 84 A4
Barandon Wk NTGHL * W11 100 B6
Barbara Hucklesbury Cl
WDGN N22 49 H5
Barbauld Rd STNW/STAM N16 86 A1
Barber Cl WCHMH N21 35 G2
Barbers Rd SRTFD E15 105 K1
Barbican BARB EC2Y 12 D1
Barbican Rd GFD/PVL UB6 96 B5

Barb Ms HMSMTH W6 119 F3
Barbon Cl BMSBY WC1N 11 F1
Barbot Cl ED N9 36 B5
Barchard St WAND/EARL SW18 140 A6
Barchester Cl HNWL W7 116 A1
Barchester Rd
KTN/HRWW/W HA3 42 D4
Barchester St POP/IOD E14 105 K4
Barclay Cl FUL/PGN * SW6 139 K1
WATW WD18 26 E1
Barclay Ov WFD IG8 38 E6
Barclay Rd CROY/NA CR0 211 K1
FUL/PGN SW6 139 K1
PLSTW E13 107 G3
UED N18 49 K2
WALTH E17 70 A2
WAN E11 70 D5
Barcombe Av
BRXS/STRHM SW2 161 K4
Barcombe Cl CHST BR7 186 B6
Barden St WOOL/PLUM SE18 147 K1
Bardfield Av CHDH RM6 55 K6
Bardney Rd MRDN SM4 194 A1
Bardolph Av CROY/NA CR0 213 H6
Bardolph Rd HOLWY N7 84 E2
RCH/KEW TW9 137 G5
Bard Rd NKENS W10 100 B6
Bardsey Pl WCHPL E1 104 E4
Bardsey Wk IS * N1 85 J4
Bardsley Cl CROY/NA CR0 212 B1
Bardsley La GNWCH SE10 125 F6
Barfett St NKENS W10 100 D3
Barfield Av TRDG/WHET N20 33 K4
Barfield Rd BMLY BR1 185 F6
WAN * E11 70 D5
Barford Cl HDN NW4 45 J5
Barford St IS N1 5 K1
Barforth Rd PECK SE15 143 J4
Barfreston Wy PGE/AN SE20 181 J4
Bargate Cl NWMAL KT3 192 D4
WOOL/PLUM SE18 128 A5
Barge House Rd CAN/RD E16 127 G2
Barge House St STHWK SE1 11 K7
Bargery Rd CAT SE6 164 E3
Barge Wk KUT KT1 174 E5
Bargrove Cl PGE/AN SE20 181 H3
Bargrove Crs CAT SE6 164 C4
Barham Cl ALP/SUD HA0 79 H4
CHST BR7 185 G1
HAYES BR2 200 D5
ROMW/RG RM7 56 D5
Barham Ct ALP/SUD HA0 79 J4
Barham Rd CHST BR7 185 G1
CROY/NA CR0 211 J2
DART DA1 171 K2
RYNPK SW20 176 D3
Baring Cl LEE/GVPK SE12 165 K4
Baring Rd BMLY BR1 166 A6
CROY/NA CR0 197 H5
EBAR EN4 21 H4
LEE/GVPK SE12 165 K3
LEE/GVPK SE12 166 A6
Baring St IS N1 6 E1
Barker Cl KUT KT1 191 J1
NTHWD HA6 40 D3
Barker Dr CAMTN NW1 84 C5
Barkham Rd TOTM N17 49 K3
Bark Hart Rd ORP BR6 202 C5
Barking Rd POP/IOD E14 106 C5
Bark Pl BAY/PAD W2 101 F6
Barkston Gdns ECT SW5 120 A5
Barkwood Cl ROMW/RG RM7 74 E2
Barkworth Rd
BERM/RHTH SE16 123 J5
Barlborough St NWCR SE14 144 A1
Barlby Gdns NKENS W10 100 B3
Barlby Rd NKENS W10 100 A4
Barley La GDMY/SEVK IG3 73 G3
Barley Mow Pas CHSWK W4 118 A5
Barlow Cl WLGTN SM6 210 E4
Barlow Dr WOOL/PLUM SE18 146 D2
Barlow Pl MYFR/PICC W1J 9 K6
Barlow Rd ACT W3 117 J1
CRICK NW2 82 D4
HPTN TW12 173 F3
Barlow St WALW SE17 19 F6
Barlow Wy DAGW RM9 111 F5
Barmeston Rd CAT SE6 164 E4
Barmor Cl RYLN/HDSTN HA2 42 B5
Barmouth Av GFD/PVL UB6 97 F1
Barmouth Rd CROY/NA CR0 198 A6
WAND/EARL SW18 160 B1
Barnabas Rd HOM E9 87 F4
Barnaby Cl RYLN/HDSTN HA2 60 C6
Barnaby Pl SKENS SW7 14 A7
Barnard Cl CHST BR7 185 J4
SUN TW16 172 A3
WLGTN SM6 210 D5
Barnard Gdns NWMAL KT3 192 D1
YEAD UB4 95 F3
Barnard Hl MUSWH N10 48 B5
Barnard Ms BTSEA SW11 140 D5
Barnardo Dr BARK/HLT IG6 72 C1
Barnardo Gdns WCHPL * E1 105 F5
Barnardo St WCHPL E1 105 F5
Barnard Rd BTSEA SW11 140 D5
EN EN1 24 D3
MTCM CR4 179 F6
Barnards Pl SAND/SEL CR2 211 H6
Barnby St CAMTN NW1 4 B3
SRTFD E15 88 C6
Barn Cl KTTN * NW5 84 D3
NTHLT UB5 95 G1
Barn Crs STAN HA7 43 J2
Barneby Cl WHTN TW2 155 K3
Barnehurst Av BXLYHN DA7 149 K2
Barnehurst Cl ERITH DA8 149 K2
Barnehurst Rd BXLYHN DA7 149 K3
Barn End Dr RDART DA2 171 F6
Barnes Av BARN SW13 138 D1
NWDGN UB2 114 E4
Barnes Br CHSWK W4 138 B3
Barnes Cl MNPK E12 89 H2
Barnes Cray Rd DART DA1 150 D5
Barnesdale Crs STMC/STPC BR5 202 B3
Barnes End NWMAL KT3 192 D2
Barnes High St BARN SW13 138 C3
Barnes Rd IL IG1 90 C3
UED N18 36 E6
Barnes St POP/IOD E14 105 G5
Barnes Ter DEPT SE8 124 C5
Barnet Dr HAYES BR2 200 D6
Barnet Gate La BAR EN5 31 H1
Barnet Gv BETH E2 104 C2
Barnet Hl BAR EN5 20 D5
Barnet La BORE WD6 30 B1
TRDG/WHET N20 32 D3
Barnet Rd MLHL NW7 31 G1
Barnett Cl ERITH DA8 150 C3
Barnetts Ct RYLN/HDSTN * HA2 78 B1
Barnett St WCHPL E1 104 D5
Barnet Wy (Barnet By-Pass)
MLHL NW7 31 F2
Barnet Wood Rd HAYES * BR2 215 F1
Barney Cl CHARL SE7 126 B5
Barn Fld HAMP * NW3 83 K3
Barnfield NWMAL KT3 192 B3
Barnfield Av CROY/NA CR0 197 K5
KUTN/CMB KT2 156 E6
MTCM CR4 195 G1
Barnfield Cl SWLY BR8 203 K4
Barnfield Gdns KUTN/CMB KT2 175 F1
WOOL/PLUM * SE18 127 G6
Barnfield Rd BELV DA17 129 G6
EA W5 97 J3
EDGE HA8 44 E4
SAND/SEL CR2 212 A6
STMC/STPC BR5 186 E6
WOOL/PLUM SE18 127 G6
Barnfield Wood Cl BECK BR3 199 G3
Barnfield Wood Rd BECK BR3 199 G3
Barnham Rd GFD/PVL UB6 96 C2
Barnham St STHWK SE1 19 H2
Barnhill PIN HA5 59 G2
Barn Hl WBLY HA9 62 D6
Barnhill Av HAYES BR2 199 K2
Barnhill La YEAD UB4 95 F2
Barnhill Rd WBLY HA9 80 E1
YEAD UB4 95 F3
Barnhurst Pth OXHEY WD19 41 G1
Barningham Wy
CDALE/KGS NW9 62 E3
Barnlea Cl FELT TW13 154 D4
Barnmead Gdns DAGW RM9 92 B3
Barnmead Rd BECK BR3 182 A4
DAGW RM9 92 B3
Barnock Cl DART DA1 170 B1
Barn Ri WBLY HA9 62 C5
Barnsbury Cl NWMAL KT3 191 K1
Barnsbury Crs BRYLDS KT5 191 K5
Barnsbury Est IS N1 5 H1
Barnsbury Gv HOLWY N7 85 F5
Barnsbury La BRYLDS KT5 191 J6
Barnsbury Pk IS N1 85 G5
Barnsbury Rd IS N1 5 J2
Barnsbury Sq IS N1 85 G5
Barnsbury St IS N1 85 G5
Barnsbury Ter IS N1 85 F5
Barnscroft RYNPK SW20 176 E6
Barnsdale Av POP/IOD E14 124 E4
Barnsdale Rd MV/WKIL W9 100 D3
Barnsley St WCHPL E1 104 D3
Barnstaple La LEW SE13 145 F5
Barnstaple Rd RSLP HA4 77 G1
Barnston Wk IS * N1 85 J6
Barn St STNW/STAM N16 68 A6
Barn Wy WBLY HA9 62 C5
Barnwell Rd DART DA1 151 J4
HNHL SE24 142 B6
Barnwood Cl MV/WKIL W9 101 F3
RSLP HA4 58 B6
Baron Cl FBAR/BDGN N11 48 A1
Baroness Rd BETH E2 7 K4
Baronet Gv TOTM N17 50 C4
Baronet Rd TOTM N17 50 C4
Baron Gdns BARK/HLT IG6 54 C6
Baron Gv MTCM CR4 194 D1
Baron Rd BCTR RM8 73 K5
The Barons TWK TW1 156 C1
Barons Cl IS * N1 5 J2
Baron's Court Rd WKENS W14 119 H5
Baronsfield Rd TWK * TW1 156 C1
Barons Ga EBAR EN4 33 J1
Barons Keep WKENS * W14 119 H5
Barons Md HRW HA1 60 E1
Baronsmead Rd BARN SW13 138 D2
Baronsmede EA W5 117 G2
Baronsmere Ct BAR * EN5 20 C5
Baronsmere Rd EFNCH N2 65 J1
Baron's Pl STHWK SE1 17 K3
Baron St IS N1 5 K3
Baron's Wk CROY/NA CR0 198 B3
Barque Ms DEPT SE8 124 D6
Barrack Rd HSLWW TW4 134 C5
Barra Hall Rd HYS/HAR UB3 94 C6
Barratt Av WDGN N22 49 F5
Barratt Wy KTN/HRWW/W HA3 42 D6
Barrenger Rd MUSWH N10 47 K4
Barrett Rd WALTH E17 70 A1
Barrett's Green Rd WLSDN NW10 98 E1
Barrett's Gv STNW/STAM N16 86 A3
Barrett St MBLAR W1H 9 H4
Barrhill Rd BRXS/STRHM SW2 161 K4
Barriedale NWCR SE14 144 B2
Barrier Point Rd CAN/RD E16 126 B1
Barringer Sq TOOT SW17 161 F6
Barrington Cl CLAY IG5 53 K4
KTTN NW5 84 A3
Barrington Rd BRXN/ST SW9 142 C4
BXLYHN DA7 148 E3
CEND/HSY/T N8 66 D2
CHEAM SM3 193 K5
MNPK E12 90 A4
Barrington Vls
WOOL/PLUM SE18 147 F2
Barrington Wk NRWD * SE19 181 F2
Barrow Av CAR SM5 209 K5
Barrow Cl WCHMH N21 35 H5
Barrowdene Cl PIN HA5 41 J5
Barrowell Gn WCHMH N21 35 H4
Barrowfield Cl ED N9 36 D5
Barrowgate Rd CHSWK W4 117 K5
Barrow Hedges Cl CAR SM5 209 J5
Barrow Hedges Wy CAR SM5 209 J5
Barrow Hl WPK KT4 192 B6
Barrow Hill Cl WPK KT4 192 B6
Barrow Hill Est STJWD NW8 2 C3
Barrow Hill Rd STJWD NW8 2 C3
Barrow Point Av PIN HA5 41 J5
Barrow Point La PIN HA5 41 J5
Barrow Rd CROY/NA CR0 211 G3
STRHM/NOR SW16 179 J2
Barrs Rd WLSDN NW10 81 F5
Barry Av BXLYHN DA7 149 F1
SEVS/STOTM N15 68 B3
Barry Cl ORP BR6 216 E1
Barry Pde EDUL * SE22 143 H5
Barry Rd EDUL SE22 163 H1
EHAM E6 107 J5
WLSDN NW10 80 E5
Barry Ter ASHF * TW15 152 C4
Barset Rd PECK SE15 143 K4
Barsons Cl PGE/AN SE20 181 K3
Barston Rd WNWD SE27 162 D4
Barstow Crs BRXS/STRHM SW2 162 A3
Barter St NOXST/BSQ WC1A 11 F2
Bartholomew Cl STBT EC1A 12 C2
WAND/EARL SW18 140 B5
Bartholomew La LOTH EC2R 13 F4
Bartholomew Rd KTTN NW5 84 C4
Bartholomew Sq FSBYE EC1V 6 D6
Bartholomew St STHWK SE1 19 F5
Bartholomew Vls KTTN NW5 84 C4
Barth Rd WOOL/PLUM SE18 127 K4
Bartle Av EHAM E6 107 J1
Bartle Rd NTGHL W11 100 B5
Bartlett Cl POP/IOD E14 105 J5
Bartlett Ct FLST/FETLN * EC4A 11 K3
Bartlett St SAND/SEL CR2 211 K3
Bartlow Gdns CRW RM5 57 F4
Barton Av DAGE RM10 74 E5
Barton Cl BXLYHS DA6 149 F6
HDN NW4 63 J2
PECK SE15 143 J4
Barton Gn NWMAL KT3 176 A5
Barton Mdw BARK/HLT IG6 72 B1
Barton Rd HCH RM12 75 J5
SCUP DA14 187 F2
WKENS W14 119 H5
The Bartons BORE WD6 29 K1
Barton St WEST SW1P 16 E5
Bartram Rd BROCKY SE4 144 B6
Bartrams La EBAR EN4 21 G1
Bartrip St HOM E9 87 G4
Barts Cl BECK BR3 198 D2
Barward Cl WOOL/PLUM SE18 127 F4
Barwell Ct CHSGTN * KT9 205 J5
Barwick Rd FSTGT E7 89 F2
Barwood Av WWKM BR4 198 E5
Bascombe Gv DART DA1 170 B2
Basden Gv FELT TW13 155 F4
Basedale Rd DAGW RM9 91 H5
Baseing Cl EHAM E6 108 A6
Basevi Wy DEPT SE8 124 D6
Bashley Rd WLSDN NW10 99 F3
Basil Av EHAM E6 107 J2
Basildene Rd HSLWW TW4 134 C4
Basildon Av CLAY IG5 54 A4
Basildon Cl BELMT SM2 209 F6
WATW WD18 26 A1
Basildon Rd ABYW SE2 128 B5
Basil Gdns CROY/NA CR0 198 A5
WNWD SE27 180 D1
Basilon Rd BXLYHN DA7 149 F3
Basil St CHEL SW3 14 E4
Basin Ap POP/IOD E14 105 G5
Basing Cl THDIT KT7 190 A4
Basingdon Wy CMBW SE5 142 E5
Basing Dr BXLY DA5 169 G1
Basingfield Rd THDIT KT7 190 A4
Basinghall Av CITYW EC2V 12 E3
Basinghall Gdns BELMT SM2 209 F6
Basinghall St CITYW EC2V 12 E3
Basing Hl GLDGN NW11 64 D5
WBLY HA9 62 B6
Basing Pl BETH E2 7 H4
Basing St NTGHL W11 100 D5
Basing Wy FNCH N3 46 E6
THDIT KT7 190 A4
Basire St IS N1 85 J6
Baskerville Gdns WLSDN NW10 81 G2
Baskerville Rd
WAND/EARL SW18 160 D2
Basket Gdns ELTH/MOT SE9 146 D6
Baslow Cl KTN/HRWW/W HA3 42 D4
Baslow Wk CLPT E5 87 F2
Basnett Rd BTSEA * SW11 141 F4
Bassano St EDUL SE22 143 G6
Bassant Rd WOOL/PLUM SE18 128 A6
Bassein Park Rd SHB W12 118 C2
Bassett Cl BELMT SM2 209 F6
Bassett Gdns ISLW TW7 135 H1
Bassett Rd NKENS W10 100 B5
Bassetts Cl ORP BR6 216 B2
Bassett St KTTN NW5 84 A4
Bassetts Wy ORP BR6 216 B2
Bassett Wy GFD/PVL UB6 96 B5
Bassingham Rd ALP/SUD HA0 79 K4
WAND/EARL SW18 160 B2
Basswood Cl PECK SE15 143 J4
Bastable Av BARK IG11 109 G1
Bastion Rd ABYW SE2 128 B5
Baston Manor Rd WWKM BR4 215 F1
Baston Rd HAYES BR2 200 A6
Bastwick St FSBYE EC1V 6 B6
Basuto Rd FUL/PGN SW6 139 K2
Batavia Cl SUN TW16 172 B4
Batavia Rd NWCR SE14 144 B1
SUN TW16 172 A4
Batchelor St IS N1 5 J2
Batchwood Gn STMC/STPC BR5 202 B1
Batchworth La NTHWD HA6 40 A1
Bateman Cl BARK IG11 90 C4
Bateman Rd CHING E4 51 J2
Batemans Cnr CHSWK * W4 118 A4
Bateman's Rw SDTCH EC2A 7 H6
Bateman St SOHO/SHAV W1D 10 C4
Bates Crs CROY/NA CR0 211 G4
STRHM/NOR SW16 179 H3
Bate St POP/IOD E14 105 H6
Bath Cl PECK SE15 143 J1
Bathgate Rd WIM/MER SW19 159 G5
Bath Gv BETH E2 104 C1
Bath House Rd CROY/NA CR0 195 K5
Bath Pas KUT KT1 174 E5
Bath Pl IS N1 7 G5
Bath Rd CHSWK W4 118 B4
DART DA1 170 E2
ED N9 36 D4
FSTGT E7 89 H4
HEST TW5 134 B2
WDR/YW UB7 132 A2
Baths Ap FUL/PGN * SW6 139 J1
Bath St FSBYE EC1V 6 D5
Bath Ter STHWK SE1 18 C5
Bathurst Av WIM/MER SW19 178 A4
Bathurst Gdns WLSDN NW10 99 K1
Bathurst Ms BAY/PAD W2 8 B5
Bathurst Rd IL IG1 72 B5
Bathurst St BAY/PAD W2 8 B5
Bathway WOOL/PLUM SE18 127 F4
Batley Cl MTCM CR4 194 E4
Batley Pl STNW/STAM N16 86 B1
Batley Rd STNW/STAM N16 86 B1
Batman Cl SHB W12 118 E1
Batoum Gdns HMSMTH W6 119 F3
Batson St SHB W12 118 D2
Batsworth Rd MTCM CR4 178 C6
Batten Cottages POP/IOD * E14 105 G4
Batten St BTSEA SW11 140 D4
Battersby Rd CAT SE6 165 G4
Battersea Br BTSEA SW11 140 C1
Battersea Bridge Rd
BTSEA SW11 140 D1
Battersea Church Rd
BTSEA SW11 140 C2
Battersea High St BTSEA SW11 140 C3
Battersea Park Rd BTSEA SW11 141 F2
Battersea Ri BTSEA SW11 140 D6
Battersea Sq BTSEA * SW11 140 D1
Battery Rd THMD SE28 127 K2
Battishill St IS N1 85 H5
Battle Bridge La STHWK SE1 19 G1
Battle Bridge Rd CAMTN NW1 4 E3
Battle Cl WIM/MER SW19 178 B2
Battledean Rd HBRY N5 85 H3
Battle Rd ERITH DA8 129 K4
Batty St WCHPL E1 104 C5
Baudwin Rd CAT SE6 165 H4
Baugh Rd SCUP DA14 186 D1
The Baulk WAND/EARL SW18 159 K2
Bavant Rd STRHM/NOR SW16 179 K5
Bavaria Rd ARCH N19 66 E6
Bavent Rd CMBW SE5 142 D3
Bawdale Rd EDUL SE22 143 G6
Bawdsey Av GNTH/NBYPK IG2 73 F1
Bawtree Rd NWCR SE14 144 B1
Bawtry Rd TRDG/WHET N20 33 K5
Baxendale TRDG/WHET N20 33 G4
Baxendale St BETH E2 104 C2
Baxter Cl NWDGN UB2 115 G3
Baxter Rd CAN/RD E16 107 G5
IL IG1 90 B3
IS N1 85 K4
UED N18 36 D6
Bay Ct EA * W5 117 F3
Baycroft Cl PIN * HA5 41 G6
Bayfield Rd ELTH/MOT SE9 146 C5
Bayford Ms HACK * E8 86 D5
Bayford Rd WLSDN NW10 100 B2
Bayford St HACK E8 86 D5
Bayham Pl CAMTN NW1 4 A1
Bayham Rd CHSWK W4 118 A3
MRDN SM4 194 A1
WEA W13 97 H6
Bayham St CAMTN NW1 4 A1
Bayhurst Dr NTHWD HA6 40 D2
Bayleaf Cl HPTN TW12 173 J1
Bayley St FITZ W1T 10 C2
Baylis Rd STHWK SE1 17 J4
Bayliss Av THMD SE28 109 K6
Bayliss Cl STHGT/OAK N14 22 E6
Bayly Rd DART DA1 171 K1
Bayne Cl EHAM E6 107 K5
Baynes Cl EN EN1 24 C2
Baynes Ms HAMP NW3 83 H4
Baynes St CAMTN NW1 84 C5
Baynham Cl BXLY DA5 169 G1
Bayonne Rd FUL/PGN SW6 119 H6
Bays Cl SYD SE26 181 K1
Bayston Rd STNW/STAM N16 86 B1
Bayswater Rd BAY/PAD W2 8 A6
Baythorne St BOW E3 105 H4
Baytree Cl BFN/LL DA15 168 A3
BMLY BR1 184 C4
Baytree Rd BRXS/STRHM SW2 142 A5
Bazalgette Cl NWMAL KT3 191 K2
Bazalgette Gdns NWMAL KT3 192 A2
Bazely St POP/IOD E14 106 A6
Bazile Rd WCHMH N21 35 G1
Beacham Cl CHARL SE7 126 C6
Beachborough Rd BMLY BR1 165 F6
Beachcroft Rd WAN E11 88 C1
Beach Gv FELT TW13 155 F5
Beachy Rd BOW E3 87 J5
Beacon Hl HOLWY N7 84 E3
Beacon Pl CROY/NA CR0 210 E1
Beacon Rd ERITH DA8 150 E1
HTHAIR TW6 152 D1
LEW SE13 165 G1
Beaconsfield Cl BKHTH/KID SE3 125 K6
CHSWK W4 117 K5
Beaconsfield Cottages
TRDG/WHET * N20 32 E5
Beaconsfield Gdns
ESH/CLAY KT10 204 E5
Beaconsfield Rd
BKHTH/KID SE3 125 K6
BMLY BR1 184 C6
BRYLDS KT5 191 G4
BXLY DA5 170 B4
CAN/RD E16 106 D3
CHSWK W4 118 A3
CROY/NA CR0 196 E3
EA W5 116 D2
ED N9 36 C5
ELTH/MOT SE9 166 D5
ESH/CLAY KT10 204 E5
HYS/HAR UB3 114 B1
LEY * E10 88 A1
NWMAL KT3 176 A5
SEVS/STOTM N15 68 A1
TRDG/WHET N20 33 K5
TWK TW1 156 C2
WALTH E17 69 H3
WALW SE17 122 E6
WLSDN NW10 81 H4
Beaconsfield Terrace Rd
WKENS W14 119 H3
Beaconsfield Wk FUL/PGN SW6 139 J2
Beacontree Av WALTH E17 52 B4
Beacontree Rd WAN E11 70 D4
Beadlow Cl MRDN SM4 194 C3
Beadman Pl WNWD * SE27 162 C6
Beadman St WNWD SE27 162 C6
Beadnell Rd FSTH SE23 164 A3
Beadon Rd HAYES BR2 199 K1
HMSMTH W6 119 F4
Beaford Gv RYNPK SW20 177 H6
Beagle Cl FELT TW13 154 A6
Beagles Cl STMC/STPC BR5 202 E6
Beak St REGST W1B 10 A5
Beal Cl WELL DA16 148 B2
Beale Cl PLMGR N13 49 H1
Beale Pl BOW E3 105 H1
Beale Rd BOW E3 87 H6
Beal Rd IL IG1 72 A6
Beam Av DAGE RM10 92 D6
DAGE RM10 110 E1
Beaminster Gdns BARK/HLT IG6 54 B6
Beamish Dr BUSH WD23 28 C3
Beamish Rd ED N9 36 C3
STMC/STPC BR5 202 D4
Beamway DAGE RM10 93 F5
Beanacre Cl HOM * E9 87 H4
Bean Rd BXLYHS DA6 148 E5
Beanshaw ELTH/MOT SE9 167 F6
Beansland Gv CHDH RM6 56 A5
Bear Cl ROMW/RG RM7 74 D3
Beardell St NRWD SE19 181 G2
Beardow Gv STHGT/OAK * N14 34 C1
Beard Rd RCHPK/HAM TW10 175 G1
Beardsfield PLSTW E13 88 E6
Beard's Hl HPTN TW12 173 F4
Beard's Hill Cl HPTN TW12 173 F4
Beardsley Wy ACT W3 118 A2
Bearfield Rd KUTN/CMB KT2 175 F3
Bear Gdns STHWK SE1 12 C7
Bear La STHWK SE1 12 B7
Bear Rd FELT TW13 154 C6
Bearstead Ri BROCKY SE4 144 C6
Bearstead Ter BECK * BR3 182 D4
Bear St LSQ/SEVD WC2H 10 D5
Beatrice Av STRHM/NOR SW16 180 A6
WBLY HA9 80 A3
Beatrice Cl PIN HA5 58 E1
PLSTW E13 106 E3
Beatrice Pl KENS W8 120 A3
Beatrice Rd ED N9 36 E2
FSBYPK N4 67 G4
RCHPK/HAM TW10 137 G6
STHL UB1 114 E1
STHWK SE1 123 H4
WALTH E17 69 J2
Beattie Cl EBED/NFELT TW14 153 J3
Beattock Ri MUSWH N10 66 B1
Beatty Rd STAN HA7 43 J2
STNW/STAM N16 86 A2
Beatty St CAMTN * NW1 4 A2
Beattyville Gdns CLAY IG5 54 A6
Beauchamp Pl CHEL SW3 14 D4
Beauchamp Rd BTSEA SW11 140 D5
E/WMO/HCT KT8 189 G2
FSTGT E7 89 F5
SUT SM1 208 E3
THHTH CR7 180 E4
TWK TW1 156 B2
Beauchamp St HCIRC EC1N 11 J2
Beauchamp Ter PUT/ROE SW15 138 E4
Beauclerc Rd HMSMTH W6 118 E3
Beauclerk Cl FELT TW13 154 A3
Beaufort EHAM E6 108 A4
Beaufort Av KTN/HRWW/W HA3 61 G1
Beaufort Cl CHING E4 51 K2
EA W5 98 B4
PUT/ROE SW15 159 F3
ROMW/RG RM7 74 E1
Beaufort Dr GLDGN NW11 64 E1
Beaufort Gdns CHEL SW3 14 D4
HDN NW4 64 A3
HEST TW5 134 D2
IL IG1 72 A5
STRHM/NOR SW16 180 A3
Beaufort Rd EA W5 98 B4
KUT KT1 191 F1
RCHPK/HAM TW10 156 D6
RSLP * HA4 58 B6
TWK TW1 156 D2
Beaufort St CHEL SW3 120 C6
Beaufort Wy EW KT17 207 J5
Beaufoy Rd TOTM N17 50 A3
Beaufoy Wk LBTH SE11 17 H7
Beaulieu Av CAN/RD E16 126 A1
SYD SE26 163 J6
Beaulieu Cl CDALE/KGS NW9 63 G1
CMBW SE5 142 E4
HSLWW TW4 134 E6
MTCM CR4 179 F4
OXHEY WD19 27 G3
TWK TW1 156 E1
Beaulieu Dr PIN HA5 59 H3
Beaulieu Gdns WCHMH N21 35 J2
Beaulieu Pl CHSWK W4 117 K3
Beauly Wy ROM RM1 57 G4
Beaumaris Gn CDALE/KGS * NW9 63 G3
Beaumont Av ALP/SUD HA0 79 J3
RCH/KEW TW9 137 G4
RYLN/HDSTN HA2 60 B3
WKENS W14 119 J5
Beaumont Cl KUTN/CMB * KT2 175 H3
Beaumont Ct ALP/SUD HA0 79 J3
Beaumont Crs RAIN RM13 93 J4
WKENS W14 119 J5
Beaumont Gdns HAMP NW3 82 E1
Beaumont Gv WCHPL E1 105 F3
Beaumont Ms MHST * W1U 9 H1
PIN * HA5 41 J6
Beaumont Pl BAR EN5 20 D2
FITZ W1T 4 B6
ISLW TW7 136 A6
Beaumont Ri ARCH N19 66 D5
Beaumont Rd CHSWK W4 117 K3
LEY E10 69 K4
NRWD SE19 180 D2
PLSTW E13 107 F2
STMC/STPC BR5 201 J3
WAND/EARL SW18 159 H2
Beaumont Sq WCHPL E1 105 F4
Beaumont St MHST W1U 9 H1
Beaumont Ter LEW * SE13 165 H2
Beaumont Wk HAMP NW3 83 K5
Beauvais Ter NTHLT UB5 95 H2
Beauval Rd EDUL SE22 163 G1
Beaverbank Rd ELTH/MOT SE9 167 J3
Beaver Cl HPTN TW12 173 G4
PGE/AN * SE20 181 H3
Beaver Rd BARK/HLT IG6 55 J1
Beavers Crs HSLWW TW4 134 C5
Beavers La HSLWW TW4 134 B4
Beaverwood Rd CHST BR7 185 K1
Beavor La HMSMTH W6 118 D4
Bebbington Rd
WOOL/PLUM * SE18 127 K4
Beblets Cl ORP BR6 217 F3
Beccles St POP/IOD E14 105 H5
Bec Cl RSLP HA4 77 H1
Beck Cl LEW SE13 144 E2
Beck Ct BECK BR3 182 A6
Beckenham Gdns ED N9 36 A5
Beckenham Gv HAYES BR2 183 G5
Beckenham Hill Rd BECK BR3 182 E2
Beckenham La HAYES BR2 183 H5
Beckenham Place Pk BECK BR3 182 E3
Beckenham Rd BECK BR3 182 A4
WWKM BR4 198 E4
Becket Av EHAM E6 108 A2
Becket Cl SNWD SE25 197 H3
WIM/MER * SW19 178 A4
Becket Fold HRW * HA1 61 F2
Becket Rd UED N18 36 E6
Becket St STHWK SE1 18 E4
Beckett Cl BELV DA17 129 F3
STRHM/NOR SW16 161 J4
WLSDN NW10 81 F4
Becketts Cl EBED/NFELT TW14 154 A1

ORP BR6 217 F1
Becketts Pl KUT KT1 174 E4
Beckett Wk BECK BR3 182 B2
Beckford Cl WKENS W14 119 J4
Beckford Dr STMC/STPC BR5 201 J4
Beckford Pl WALW * SE17 122 D5
Beckford Rd CROY/NA CR0 197 G3
Beck La BECK BR3 182 A6
Becklow Rd SHB W12 118 D2
Beck River Pk BECK BR3 182 C4
Beck Rd HACK E8 86 D6
Becks Rd SCUP DA14 168 B5
Beckton Rd CAN/RD E16 106 D4
Beck Wy BECK BR3 182 C6
Beckway Rd STRHM/NOR SW16 179 J5
Beckway St WALW SE17 19 G7
Beckwith Rd HNHL SE24 162 E1
Beclands Rd TOOT SW17 179 F2
Becmead Av KTN/HRWW/W HA3 61 H2
STRHM/NOR SW16 161 J6
Becondale Rd NRWD SE19 181 F1
Becontree Av BCTR RM8 91 H2
Bective Rd FSTGT E7 88 E2
PUT/ROE SW15 139 J5
Becton Pl ERITH DA8 149 J1
Bedale Rd ENC/FH EN2 23 J1
Bedale St STHWK * SE1 18 E1
Beddington Farm Rd
CROY/NA CR0 195 K5
Beddington Gdns CAR SM5 210 A4
Beddington Gn STMC/STPC BR5 186 A4
Beddington Gv WLGTN SM6 210 D3
Beddington La CROY/NA CR0 195 K6
MTCM CR4 195 H3
Beddington Rd GDMY/SEVK IG3 73 F4
STMC/STPC BR5 185 K4
Beddington Ter CROY/NA * CR0 196 A4
Bede Cl PIN HA5 41 H4
Bedens Rd SCUP DA14 187 F2
Bede Rd CHDH RM6 73 J3
Bedfont Cl EBED/NFELT TW14 153 F1
MTCM CR4 179 F5
Bedfont Green Cl
EBED/NFELT TW14 153 F3
Bedfont La EBED/NFELT TW14 153 H2
Bedfont Rd EBED/NFELT TW14 153 F3
STWL/WRAY TW19 152 C1
Bedford Av BAR EN5 20 D6
RSQ WC1B 10 D2
YEAD UB4 95 F5
Bedfordbury CHCR WC2N 10 E5
Bedford Cl CHSWK W4 118 B6
MUSWH N10 48 A3
Bedford Cnr CHSWK * W4 118 B4
Bedford Ct CHCR WC2N 10 E6
Bedford Gdns KENS W8 119 K1
Bedford Hl BAL SW12 161 G4
Bedford Pk CROY/NA CR0 196 D5
Bedford Pl CROY/NA CR0 196 E5
RSQ WC1B 10 E1
Bedford Rd BFN/LL DA15 167 K5
CEND/HSY/T N8 66 D3
CHSWK W4 118 A3
CLAP SW4 141 K5
DART DA1 171 K2
ED N9 36 D2
EFNCH N2 47 J6
EHAM E6 90 A6
HRW HA1 60 C3
IL IG1 90 B1
MLHL NW7 31 G4
NTHWD HA6 26 A6
ORP BR6 202 C6
RSLP HA4 76 D2
SEVS/STOTM N15 67 K1
SWFD E18 52 E5
WALTH E17 51 J5
WDGN N22 48 E4
WEA W13 97 H6
WHTN TW2 155 J5
WPK KT4 193 F6
Bedford Rw FSBYW WC1X 11 H1
Bedford Sq RSQ WC1B 10 D2
Bedford St COVGDN WC2E 10 E5
Bedford Vls KUT * KT1 175 G5
Bedford Wy STPAN WC1H 4 D7
Bedgebury Gdns
WIM/MER SW19 159 H4
Bedgebury Rd ELTH/MOT SE9 146 C5
Bedivere Rd BMLY BR1 165 K5
Bedlow Cl STJWD NW8 2 B7
Bedlow Wy CROY/NA CR0 211 F2
Bedonwell Rd BELV DA17 129 F6
Bedser Cl THHTH CR7 180 D6
VX/NE * SW8 122 A6
Bedser Dr GFD/PVL UB6 78 D3
Bedster Gdns E/WMO/HCT KT8 173 G5
Bedwardine Rd NRWD SE19 181 F3
Bedwell Gdns HYS/HAR UB3 113 H5
Bedwell Rd BELV DA17 129 H5
TOTM N17 50 A4
Beeby Rd CAN/RD E16 107 F4
Beech Av ACT W3 118 B1
BFN/LL DA15 168 B2
BKHH IG9 39 F4
BTFD TW8 136 C1
RSLP HA4 59 F5
TRDG/WHET N20 33 J3
Beech Cl CAR SM5 194 E6
DEPT SE8 124 C6
ED N9 36 C1
HCH RM12 93 K1
PUT/ROE SW15 158 D2
RYNPK SW20 177 F2
STWL/WRAY TW19 152 A2
SUN TW16 172 C5
WDR/YW UB7 112 D3
Beech Copse BMLY BR1 184 E5
SAND/SEL CR2 212 A3
Beech Ct ELTH/MOT * SE9 166 D1
Beechcroft CHST BR7 185 F3
Beechcroft Av BXLYHN DA7 150 A2
GLDGN NW11 64 D4
NWMAL KT3 175 K4
RKW/CH/CXG WD3 26 A1
RYLN/HDSTN HA2 60 A4
STHL UB1 114 E1
Beechcroft Cl HEST TW5 134 D1
ORP BR6 216 D2
STRHM/NOR SW16 180 A1
Beechcroft Gdns WBLY HA9 80 B1
Beechcroft Rd CHSGTN KT9 206 B2
MORT/ESHN * SW14 137 K4
ORP BR6 216 D2
SWFD E18 53 F5
TOOT SW17 160 E5
Beechdale WCHMH N21 35 F4
Beechdale Rd
BRXS/STRHM SW2 162 A1
Beech Dell HAYES BR2 215 K2
Beech Dr EFNCH N2 47 K6
Beechen Cliff Wy ISLW TW7 136 A3
Beechengrove PIN HA5 41 K6
Beechen Pl FSTH SE23 163 K4
The Beeches CHING * E4 38 B3
HNWL * W7 116 A2
The Beeches Av CAR SM5 209 J5
Beeches Cl PGE/AN SE20 181 K4
Beeches Rd CHEAM SM3 193 H5
TOOT SW17 160 D5
Beeches Wk CAR SM5 209 H6
Beechfield Gdns ROMW/RG RM7 74 E4
Beechfield Rd BMLY BR1 184 B5
CAT SE6 164 C3
ERITH DA8 150 B1
FSBYPK N4 67 J3
Beech Gdns DAGE RM10 92 D5
EA W5 117 F2
Beech Gv BARK/HLT IG6 54 E2
MTCM CR4 195 J2
NWMAL KT3 176 A6
Beech Hall Crs CHING E4 52 B3
Beech Hall Rd CHING E4 52 A3
Beech Hl EBAR EN4 21 H1
Beech Hill Av EBAR EN4 21 G2
Beechhill Rd ELTH/MOT SE9 147 F6
Beech House Rd CROY/NA CR0 211 K1
Beech Lawns
NFNCH/WDSP * N12 47 H1
Beechmont Cl BMLY BR1 183 H1
Beechmore Gdns CHEAM SM3 193 G6
Beechmore Rd BTSEA SW11 140 E2
Beechmount Av HNWL W7 96 D4
Beecholme Av MTCM CR4 179 G4
Beecholme Est CLPT * E5 86 E1
Beech Rd DART DA1 171 G3
EBED/NFELT TW14 153 H2
FBAR/BDGN N11 48 E2
ORP BR6 217 G5
STRHM/NOR SW16 179 K5
Beechrow KUTN/CMB KT2 157 F6
Beech St ROMW/RG RM7 74 E1
Beech St (Below) BARB EC2Y 12 C1
Beech Tree Cl IS N1 85 G5
STAN HA7 43 J1
Beech Tree Gld CHING E4 38 D3
Beech Tree Pl SUT SM1 209 F3
Beechvale Cl NFNCH/WDSP N12 47 J1
Beech Wk DART DA1 150 D5
MLHL NW7 45 F2
Beechway BXLY DA5 168 E1
Beech Wy FELT TW13 155 F5
WLSDN NW10 81 F5
Beechwood Av FNCH N3 46 D6
GFD/PVL UB6 96 B2
HYS/HAR UB3 94 B6
ORP BR6 216 E4
RCH/KEW TW9 137 H2
RSLP HA4 58 D6
RYLN/HDSTN HA2 78 B1
THHTH CR7 196 C1
Beechwood Cl EFNCH * N2 65 K1
MLHL NW7 45 G1
SURB KT6 190 D4
Beechwood Crs BXLYHN DA7 148 E4
Beechwood Dr HAYES BR2 215 H2
WFD IG8 52 D1
Beechwood Gdns CLAY IG5 71 K2
RAIN RM13 111 K4
RYLN/HDSTN HA2 78 B1
Beechwood Gv ACT W3 99 G6
Beechwood Ms ED N9 36 C4
Beechwood Pk SWFD E18 52 E6
Beechwood Ri CHST BR7 167 G6
Beechwood Rd CEND/HSY/T N8 66 D1
HACK E8 86 B4
SAND/SEL CR2 212 A6
Beechworth Cl HAMP NW3 65 F6
Beecot La WOT/HER KT12 188 B6
Beecroft La BROCKY SE4 144 B6
Beecroft Ms BROCKY SE4 144 B6
Beecroft Rd BROCKY SE4 144 B6
Beehive Cl BORE WD6 29 K1
HACK E8 86 B5
Beehive La REDBR IG4 71 K2
Beehive Pl BRXN/ST SW9 142 B4
Beeken Dene ORP BR6 216 C2
Beeleigh Rd MRDN SM4 194 A1
Beeston Cl HACK E8 86 C3
OXHEY WD19 27 H6
Beeston Pl BGVA SW1W 15 K5
Beeston Rd EBAR EN4 33 H1
Beeston Wy EBED/NFELT TW14 154 B1
Beethoven Rd BORE WD6 29 J2
Beethoven St NKENS W10 100 C2
Beeton Cl PIN HA5 42 A3
Begbie Rd BKHTH/KID SE3 146 B2
Beggar's Roost La SUT SM1 208 E4
Begonia Cl EHAM E6 107 J4
Begonia Pl HPTN TW12 173 F2
Beira St BAL SW12 161 G2
Bekesbourne St POP/IOD * E14 105 G5
Belcroft Cl BMLY BR1 183 J3
Beldham Gdns
E/WMO/HCT KT8 173 G6
Belfairs OXHEY WD19 41 H1
Belfairs Dr CHDH RM6 73 J4
Belfast Rd SNWD SE25 197 J1
STNW/STAM N16 68 B6
Belfield Rd HOR/WEW KT19 207 F6
Belford Gv WOOL/PLUM SE18 127 F4
Belfort Rd PECK SE15 143 K3
Belfry Cl BERM/RHTH * SE16 123 J5
Belgrade Rd HPTN TW12 173 G4
STNW/STAM N16 86 A2
Belgrave Cl ACT W3 117 K2
MLHL NW7 45 F1
STHGT/OAK N14 22 C6
STMC/STPC BR5 202 D1
Belgrave Crs SUN TW16 172 A4
Belgrave Gdns STHGT/OAK N14 22 D6
STJWD NW8 83 F6
Belgrave Ms South KTBR SW1X 15 H4
Belgrave Ms West KTBR SW1X 15 G4
Belgrave Pl KTBR SW1X 15 H5
Belgrave Rd BARN SW13 138 C1
HSLWW TW4 134 E4
IL IG1 72 A6
LEY E10 70 A5
MTCM CR4 178 C6
PIM SW1V 16 A7
PLSTW E13 107 G3
SNWD SE25 197 G1
SUN TW16 172 A4
WALTH E17 69 J3
WAN E11 70 E5
Belgrave Sq KTBR SW1X 15 G4
Belgrave St WCHPL E1 105 F5
Belgrave Wk MTCM CR4 178 C6
Belgravia Cl BAR EN5 20 D4
Belgravia Gdns BMLY BR1 183 H2
Belgravia Ms KUT KT1 190 E1
Belgrove St CAMTN NW1 4 E4
Belinda Rd BRXN/ST SW9 142 C4
Belitha Vls IS N1 85 G5
Bellamy Cl EDGE HA8 30 E5
POP/IOD E14 124 D2
WKENS W14 119 J5
Bellamy Dr STAN HA7 43 H4
Bellamy Rd CHING E4 51 K2
ENC/FH * EN2 23 K3
Bellamy St BAL SW12 161 G2
Bel La FELT TW13 154 D5
Bellasis Av BRXS/STRHM SW2 161 K3
Bell Av HARH RM3 57 K4
WDR/YW UB7 112 C3
Bell Cl PIN HA5 41 G6
Bellclose Rd WDR/YW UB7 112 B2
Bell Dr WAND/EARL SW18 159 H2
Bellefield Rd STMC/STPC BR5 202 C2
Bellefields Rd BRXN/ST SW9 142 A4
Bellegrove Cl WELL DA16 148 A3
Bellegrove Rd WELL DA16 147 K3
Bellenden Rd PECK SE15 143 G3
Belle Staines Pleasaunce
CHING E4 37 J4
Belleville Rd BTSEA SW11 140 E6
Belle Vue GFD/PVL UB6 78 D6
Belle Vue La BUSH WD23 28 D3
Bellevue Pk THHTH CR7 180 D6
Bellevue Pl WCHPL * E1 104 E3
Bellevue Rd BARN SW13 138 D3
BXLYHS DA6 149 G6
Belle Vue Rd CRW RM5 56 E2
Bellevue Rd FBAR/BDGN N11 34 A6
KUT KT1 175 F6
TOOT SW17 160 E2
Belle Vue Rd WALTH E17 52 B5
Bellevue Rd WEA W13 97 H3
Bellew St TOOT SW17 160 B5
Bell Farm Av DAGE RM10 92 E1
Bellfield CROY/NA CR0 213 H6
Bellfield Av KTN/HRWW/W HA3 42 D2
Bell Gdns LEY * E10 69 J5
STMC/STPC BR5 202 D2
Bellgate Ms KTTN NW5 84 B2
Bell Gn CAT SE6 164 B6
Bell Green La SYD SE26 182 C1
Bell House Rd ROMW/RG RM7 74 E5
Bellina Ms KTTN NW5 84 B2
Bellingham Gn CAT SE6 164 D5
Bellingham Rd CAT SE6 165 F5
Bell La CAN/RD E16 125 K1
HDN NW4 64 B1
PEND EN3 25 F1
TWK TW1 156 B3
WBLY * HA9 61 K6
WCHPL E1 13 J2
Bell Meadow NRWD SE19 163 F6
Bello Cl BRXS/STRHM SW2 162 C3
Bellot St GNWCH SE10 125 H5
Bell Pde HSLW * TW3 135 G5
WWKM * BR4 199 F6
Bellring Cl BELV DA17 129 H6
Bell Rd E/WMO/HCT KT8 189 J2
ENC/FH EN2 23 K2
HSLW TW3 135 G5
Bells Hl BAR EN5 20 B6
Bell St BAY/PAD W2 8 C1
WOOL/PLUM SE18 146 D2
Belltrees Gv STRHM/NOR SW16 180 A1
Bell Water Ga
WOOL/PLUM SE18 127 F3
Bell Wharf La CANST EC4R 12 D6
Bellwood Rd PECK SE15 144 A5
Bell Yd LINN WC2A 11 J4
Belmont Av ALP/SUD HA0 80 B6
EBAR EN4 21 K6
ED N9 36 C3
NWDGN UB2 114 D3
NWMAL KT3 192 D2
PLMGR N13 48 E1
TOTM N17 49 J6
WELL DA16 147 K3
Belmont Cir
KTN/HRWW/W * HA3 43 H4
Belmont Cl CHING E4 52 B1
CLAP SW4 141 H4
EBAR EN4 21 K5
TRDG/WHET N20 33 F3
WFD IG8 39 F6
Belmont Gv CHSWK W4 118 A4
LEW SE13 145 G4
Belmont Hl LEW SE13 145 G4
Belmont La CHST BR7 167 H6
STAN HA7 43 J3
Belmont Pde CHST * BR7 185 G1
GLDGN * NW11 64 D2
Belmont Pk LEW SE13 145 G5
Belmont Park Cl LEW SE13 145 H5
Belmont Park Rd LEY E10 69 K3
Belmont Ri BELMT SM2 208 D5
Belmont Rd BECK BR3 182 B5
CHST BR7 185 G1
CLAP SW4 141 H4
ERITH DA8 149 H1
IL IG1 90 C1
KTN/HRWW/W HA3 43 F6
SEVS/STOTM N15 67 J1
SNWD SE25 197 J2
WHTN TW2 155 J4
WLGTN SM6 210 C3
Belmont St CAMTN NW1 84 A5
Belmont Ter CHSWK W4 118 A4
Belmore Av YEAD UB4 94 E5
Belmore La HOLWY * N7 84 D3
Belmore St VX/NE SW8 141 J2
Beloe Cl BARN SW13 138 D5
Belsham St HOM E9 86 E4
Belsize Av HAMP NW3 83 J3
PLMGR N13 49 F2
WEA W13 116 C3
Belsize Ct Garages HAMP NW3 83 H3
Belsize Crs HAMP NW3 83 H3
Belsize Gdns SUT SM1 209 F2
Belsize Gv HAMP NW3 83 J4
Belsize La HAMP NW3 83 H4
Belsize Ms HAMP * NW3 83 H4
Belsize Pk HAMP NW3 83 H4
Belsize Park Gdns HAMP NW3 83 H4
Belsize Park Ms HAMP NW3 83 H4
Belsize Pl HAMP NW3 83 H3
Belsize Rd KIL/WHAMP NW6 83 G6
KTN/HRWW/W HA3 42 D3
Belsize Sq HAMP NW3 83 H4
Belsize Ter HAMP NW3 83 H4
Belson Rd WOOL/PLUM SE18 126 E4
Beltane Dr WIM/MER SW19 159 G5
Belthorn Crs BAL SW12 161 H2
Belton Rd FSTGT E7 89 F5
SCUP DA14 168 B6
TOTM N17 50 A6
WAN E11 88 C2
WLSDN NW10 81 J4
Belton Wy BOW E3 105 J4
Beltran Rd FUL/PGN SW6 140 A3
Beltwood Rd BELV DA17 129 K4
The Belvedere WBPTN * SW10 140 B2
Belvedere Av CLAY IG5 54 B5
WIM/MER SW19 177 H1
Belvedere Buildings STHWK SE1 18 B3
Belvedere Cl ESH/CLAY KT10 204 B3
TEDD TW11 173 K1
Belvedere Ct BELV DA17 129 G3
Belvedere Dr WIM/MER SW19 177 H1
Belvedere Gdns
E/WMO/HCT KT8 188 E2
Belvedere Gv WIM/MER SW19 177 H1
Belvedere Ms PECK SE15 143 K4
Belvedere Rd BXLYHN DA7 149 G4
HNWL W7 115 K3
LEY E10 69 G5
NRWD SE19 181 G3
STHWK SE1 17 G2
THMD SE28 128 E1
Belvedere Sq WIM/MER SW19 177 H1
Belvedere Strd CDALE/KGS NW9 45 H5
Belvedere Wy
KTN/HRWW/W HA3 62 A3
Belvoir Rd EDUL SE22 163 H2
Belvue Cl NTHLT UB5 78 A5
Belvue Rd NTHLT UB5 78 A5
Bembridge Cl KIL/WHAMP NW6 82 C5
Bembridge Gdns RSLP HA4 58 B6
Bemerton Est IS N1 85 F5
Bemerton St IS N1 85 F6
Bemish Rd PUT/ROE SW15 139 G4
Bempton Dr RSLP HA4 59 F6
Bemsted Rd WALTH E17 51 H6
Benares Rd WOOL/PLUM SE18 128 A4
Benbow Rd HMSMTH W6 118 E3
Benbow St DEPT SE8 124 D6
Benbury Cl BMLY BR1 183 F1
The Bench RCHPK/HAM * TW10 156 D5
Bench Fld SAND/SEL CR2 212 B4
Bencroft Rd STRHM/NOR SW16 179 H3
Bencurtis Pk WWKM BR4 214 B1
Bendall Ms CAMTN NW1 8 D1
Bendemeer Rd PUT/ROE SW15 139 G4
Bendish Rd EHAM E6 89 J5
Bendmore Av ABYW SE2 128 B5
Bendon Va WAND/EARL SW18 160 A2
Benedict Cl ORP BR6 216 E1
Benedict Dr EBED/NFELT TW14 153 G2
Benedict Rd BRXN/ST SW9 142 A4
MTCM CR4 178 C6
Benedict Wy EFNCH * N2 47 G6
Benedict Whf MTCM CR4 178 D6
Benenden Gn HAYES BR2 199 K2
Benett Gdns STRHM/NOR SW16 179 K5
Benfleet Cl SUT SM1 209 G1
Benfleet Wy FBAR/BDGN N11 34 A4
Bengal Rd IL IG1 90 B2
Bengarth Dr KTN/HRWW/W HA3 42 D5
Bengarth Rd NTHLT UB5 77 H6
Bengeworth Rd HRW HA1 61 G6
Ben Hale Cl STAN HA7 43 G1
Benham Cl BTSEA SW11 140 C4
CHSGTN KT9 205 J4
Benham Gdns HSLW TW3 134 E6
Benham Rd HNWL W7 96 E4
Benhill Av SUT SM1 209 G2
Benhill Rd CMBW SE5 142 E1
SUT SM1 209 H1
Benhill Wood Rd SUT SM1 209 G2
Benhilton Gdns SUT SM1 209 F1
Benhurst Av HCH RM12 93 K2
Benhurst La STRHM/NOR SW16 180 B1
Benin St LEW SE13 165 G2
Benjafield Cl UED N18 36 D6
Benjamin Cl EMPK RM11 75 J3
HACK E8 86 C6
Benjamin St FARR EC1M 12 A1
Ben Jonson Rd WCHPL E1 105 G4
Benledi St POP/IOD E14 106 B5
Bennelong Cl SHB W12 99 K6
Bennerley Rd BTSEA SW11 140 E6
Bennet Cl KUT KT1 174 D4
Bennetsfield Rd STKPK UB11 112 E1
Bennet's Hl BLKFR EC4V 12 B5
Bennett Cl NTHWD HA6 40 D3
WELL DA16 148 B3
Bennett Gv LEW SE13 144 E2
Bennett Pk BKHTH/KID SE3 145 J4
Bennett Rd CHDH RM6 74 A3
PLSTW E13 107 G3
Bennetts Av CROY/NA CR0 198 B6
GFD/PVL UB6 78 E6
Bennett's Castle La BCTR RM8 91 J2
Bennetts Cl MTCM CR4 179 G4
TOTM N17 50 B2
Bennetts Copse CHST BR7 184 D2
Bennett St CHSWK W4 118 B6
WHALL SW1A 10 A7
Bennetts Wy CROY/NA CR0 198 B6
Benningholme Rd EDGE HA8 45 F2
Bennington Rd TOTM N17 50 A4
WFD * IG8 52 C3
Benn St HOM E9 87 G4
Benrek Cl BARK/HLT IG6 54 C3
Bensbury Cl PUT/ROE SW15 158 E2
Bensham Cl THHTH CR7 196 D1
Bensham Gv THHTH CR7 180 D5
Bensham La THHTH CR7 196 C2
Bensham Manor Rd THHTH CR7 196 D1
Ben Smith Wy
BERM/RHTH SE16 123 H3
Benson Av PLSTW E13 107 G1
Benson Cl HSLW TW3 135 F5
Benson Quay WAP E1W 123 K6
Benson Rd CROY/NA CR0 211 G1
FSTH SE23 163 K3
Benthal Rd STNW/STAM N16 68 B6
Bentham Rd HOM E9 87 F4
THMD SE28 128 C1
Ben Tillet Cl BARK IG11 91 G5
CAN/RD * E16 126 E1
Bentinck Ms MHST W1U 9 H3
Bentinck Rd WDR/YW UB7 112 A1
Bentinck St MHST W1U 9 H3
Bentley Dr GNTH/NBYPK IG2 72 C3
Bentley Ms EN EN1 35 K1
Bentley Rd IS N1 86 A4
Bentley Wy STAN HA7 43 G1
WFD IG8 38 E5
Benton Rd IL IG1 72 D5
OXHEY WD19 41 H1
Benton's La WNWD SE27 162 D6
Benton's Ri WNWD SE27 180 E1
Bentry Cl BCTR RM8 74 A6
Bentry Rd BCTR RM8 74 A6
Bentworth Rd SHB W12 99 K5
Benwell Rd HOLWY N7 85 G2
Benwick Cl BERM/RHTH SE16 123 J4
Benworth St BOW E3 105 H2
Benyon Rd IS N1 85 K6
Berberis Wk WDR/YW UB7 112 B4
Berber Rd BTSEA * SW11 140 E6
Bercta Rd ELTH/MOT SE9 167 H4
Berenger Wk WBPTN * SW10 140 C1
Berens Rd STMC/STPC BR5 202 D2
WLSDN NW10 100 B2
Berens Wy CHST BR7 202 A1
Beresford Av ALP/SUD HA0 80 C6
BRYLDS KT5 191 J5
HNWL W7 96 D4
TRDG/WHET N20 33 K4
TWK TW1 156 D1
Beresford Dr BMLY BR1 184 C6
WFD IG8 39 G6
Beresford Gdns CHDH RM6 74 A2
EN EN1 24 A5
HSLWW TW4 134 E6
Beresford Rd BELMT SM2 208 D5
CEND/HSY/T N8 67 G2
CHING E4 38 C3
EFNCH N2 47 J6
HBRY N5 85 K3
HRW HA1 60 D2
KUTN/CMB KT2 175 G4
NWMAL KT3 191 K1
STHL UB1 114 C1
WALTH E17 51 K4
Beresford St WOOL/PLUM SE18 127 H3
Beresford Ter HBRY N5 85 J3
Berestede Rd HMSMTH W6 118 C5
Bere St WAP E1W 105 F6
Berger Cl STMC/STPC BR5 201 J3
Berger Rd HOM E9 87 F4
Berghem Ms WKENS W14 119 G3
Bergholt Av REDBR IG4 71 J2
Bergholt Crs STNW/STAM N16 68 A4
Bergholt Ms CAMTN NW1 84 C5
Bering Wk CAN/RD E16 107 H5
Berisford Ms WAND/EARL SW18 160 B1
Berkeley Av BXLYHN DA7 148 E2
CLAY IG5 54 A5
CRW RM5 56 E3
GFD/PVL UB6 78 E4
HEST TW5 133 K2
Berkeley Cl KUTN/CMB KT2 175 F3
ORP BR6 201 K4
RSLP HA4 76 E1
Berkeley Ct WLGTN SM6 210 C1
Berkeley Crs DART DA1 171 J3
EBAR EN4 21 H6
Berkeley Dr E/WMO/HCT KT8 172 E6
Berkeley Gdns ESH/CLAY KT10 205 G5
KENS * W8 119 K1
WCHMH N21 35 K2
Berkeley Ms MBLAR W1H 9 F3
SUN TW16 172 B6
Berkeley Pl WIM/MER SW19 177 G2
Berkeley Rd BARN SW13 138 D2
CDALE/KGS NW9 62 C1
CEND/HSY/T N8 66 D2
HGDN/ICK UB10 76 A5
MNPK E12 89 J3
SEVS/STOTM N15 67 K3
The Berkeleys SNWD * SE25 197 H1
Berkeley Sq MYFR/PICC W1J 9 K6
Berkeley St MYFR/PICC W1J 9 K6
Berkeley Waye HEST TW5 134 D1
Berkhampstead Rd BELV DA17 129 H5
Berkhamsted Av WBLY HA9 80 B4
Berkley Cl WHTN * TW2 155 K5
Berkley Rd CAMTN NW1 83 K5
Berkshire Gdns PLMGR N13 49 G2
UED N18 50 D1
Berkshire Rd HOM E9 87 H4
Berkshire Wy MTCM CR4 195 K1
Bermans Wy WLSDN NW10 81 G2
Bermondsey St STHWK SE1 19 G1
Bermondsey Wall East
STHWK SE1 123 H2
Bermondsey Wall West
STHWK SE1 123 H2
Bernal Cl THMD SE28 109 K6
Bernard Ashley Dr CHARL SE7 126 A5
Bernard Av WEA W13 116 C3
Bernard Cassidy St
CAN/RD * E16 106 D4
Bernard Gdns WIM/MER SW19 177 J1
Bernard Rd ROMW/RG RM7 74 E4
SEVS/STOTM N15 68 B2
WLGTN SM6 210 B3
Bernards Cl BARK/HLT IG6 54 C3
Bernard St BMSBY WC1N 4 E7
Bernays Cl STAN HA7 43 J2
Bernay's Gv BRXN/ST SW9 142 A5
Bernel Dr CROY/NA CR0 213 H1
Berne Rd THHTH CR7 196 C2
Berners Dr WEA W13 97 G6
Berners Ms FITZ W1T 10 B2
Berners Pl FITZ W1T 10 B3
Berners Rd IS N1 6 A1
WDGN N22 49 G4
Berners St FITZ W1T 10 B2
Berner Ter WCHPL * E1 104 C5
Berney Rd CROY/NA CR0 196 E4
Bernhart Cl EDGE HA8 44 E3
Bernwell Rd CHING E4 38 C5
Berridge Gn EDGE HA8 44 C3
Berridge Ms KIL/WHAMP NW6 82 E3
Berridge Rd NRWD SE19 180 E1
Berriman Rd HOLWY N7 85 F1
Berriton Rd RYLN/HDSTN HA2 59 K5
Berrybank Cl CHING E4 38 A4
Berry Cl DAGE RM10 92 C3
WCHMH N21 35 H3
WLSDN NW10 81 G5
Berry Cottages POP/IOD * E14 105 G5
Berrydale Rd YEAD UB4 95 J3
Berryfield Cl BMLY BR1 184 D4
Berry Field Cl WALTH E17 69 K1

Berryfield Rd WALW SE17 122 C5
Berryhill ELTH/MOT SE9 147 G5
Berry Hl STAN HA7 29 K6
Berryhill Gdns ELTH/MOT SE9 147 G5
Berrylands BRYLDS KT5 191 H2
ORP BR6 217 J1
RYNPK SW20 177 F6
Berrylands Rd BRYLDS KT5 191 G3
Berry La DUL SE21 162 E6
Berryman Cl BCTR RM8 91 J1
Berryman's La SYD SE26 164 A6
Berrymead Gdns ACT W3 117 K1
Berrymede Rd CHSWK W4 118 A3
Berry Pl FSBYE EC1V 6 B5
Berry St FSBYE EC1V 6 B7
Berry Wy EA W5 117 F3
Bertal Rd TOOT SW17 160 C6
Berthons Gdns WALTH * E17 70 B2
Berthon St DEPT SE8 144 D1
Bertie Rd SYD SE26 182 A2
WLSDN NW10 81 J4
Bertram Rd EN EN1 24 C5
HDN NW4 63 J3
KUTN/CMB KT2 175 H3
Bertram St KTTN NW5 84 B1
Bertrand St LEW SE13 144 E4
Bertrand Wy THMD SE28 109 H6
Bert Rd THHTH CR7 196 D2
Bert Wy EN EN1 24 B5
Berwick Av YEAD UB4 95 H6
Berwick Cl STAN HA7 43 F2
Berwick Crs BFN/LL DA15 167 K1
Berwick Rd CAN/RD E16 107 F5
WDGN N22 49 H4
WELL DA16 148 C2
Berwick St SOHO/CST W1F 10 B4
Berwyn Av HSLW TW3 135 G2
Berwyn Rd HNHL SE24 162 C3
RCHPK/HAM TW10 137 J5
Beryl Av EHAM E6 107 J4
Beryl Rd HMSMTH W6 119 G5
Berystede KUTN/CMB KT2 175 J3
Besant Cl CRICK * NW2 82 C1
Besant Rd CRICK NW2 82 C2
Besant Wy WLSDN NW10 80 E3
Besley St STRHM/NOR SW16 179 H2
Bessant Dr RCH/KEW TW9 137 J2
Bessborough Pl PIM SW1V 121 J5
Bessborough Rd HRW HA1 60 D5
PUT/ROE SW15 158 D3
Bessborough St PIM SW1V 121 J5
Bessemer Rd CMBW SE5 142 D3
Bessie Lansbury Cl EHAM E6 108 A5
Bessingby Rd RSLP HA4 58 E6
Besson St NWCR SE14 144 A2
Bessy St BETH * E2 104 E2
Best Ter SWLY * BR8 203 K2
Bestwood St DEPT SE8 124 A4
Beswick Ms KIL/WHAMP NW6 83 F3
Betam Rd HYS/HAR UB3 113 G2
Betchworth Cl SUT SM1 209 H3
Betchworth Rd GDMY/SEVK IG3 72 E6
Betchworth Wy CROY/NA CR0 214 A6
Betham Rd GFD/PVL UB6 96 D2
Bethany Waye
EBED/NFELT TW14 153 H2
Bethecar Rd HRW HA1 60 E2
Bethell Av CAN/RD E16 106 D3
IL IG1 72 A4
Bethel Rd WELL DA16 148 D4
Bethersden Cl BECK BR3 182 C3
Bethnal Green Rd BETH E2 7 K6
Bethune Av FBAR/BDGN N11 33 K6
Bethune Rd STNW/STAM N16 67 K4
WLSDN NW10 99 F3
Bethwin Rd CMBW SE5 142 C1
Betjeman Cl RYLN/HDSTN HA2 60 A1
Betjeman Ct WDR/YW * UB7 112 A1
Betony Cl CROY/NA CR0 198 A5
Betoyne Av CHING E4 38 C6
Betsham Rd ERITH DA8 150 C1
Betstyle Rd FBAR/BDGN N11 34 B6
Betterton Dr SCUP DA14 169 F4
Betterton Rd RAIN RM13 111 G1
Betterton St LSQ/SEVD WC2H 10 E4
Bettons Pk SRTFD E15 88 C6
Bettridge Rd FUL/PGN SW6 139 J3
Betts Cl BECK BR3 182 B5
Betts Rd CAN/RD E16 107 F5
Betts St WCHPL * E1 104 D6
Betts Wy PGE/AN SE20 181 J5
THDIT KT7 190 C5
Beulah Av THHTH * CR7 180 D5
Beulah Cl EDGE HA8 30 D5
Beulah Crs THHTH CR7 180 D5
Beulah Gv CROY/NA CR0 196 D3
Beulah Hl NRWD SE19 180 D2
Beulah Rd SUT SM1 208 E2
THHTH CR7 180 D6
WALTH E17 69 K2
WIM/MER SW19 177 J3
Beult Rd DART DA1 150 D4
Bevan Av BARK IG11 91 G5
Bevan Ct CROY/NA CR0 211 G3
Bevan Rd ABYW SE2 128 C5
EBAR EN4 21 K5
Bevan St IS N1 6 D1
Bev Callender Cl VX/NE SW8 141 G4
Bevenden St IS N1 7 F4
Beveridge Rd WLSDN NW10 81 G5
Beverley Av BFN/LL DA15 168 A2
HSLWW TW4 134 E5
RYNPK SW20 176 C4
Beverley Cl BARN SW13 138 D3
BTSEA SW11 140 C5
CHSGTN KT9 205 J2
WCHMH N21 35 J3
Beverley Ct BROCKY SE4 144 C4
Beverley Crs WFD IG8 53 F4
Beverley Dr EDGE HA8 44 D6
Beverley Gdns BARN SW13 138 C4
GLDGN NW11 64 C4
STAN HA7 43 G4
WBLY HA9 62 C5
WPK KT4 192 D5
Beverley La KUTN/CMB KT2 176 B3
Beverley Rd BARN SW13 138 C4
BXLYHN DA7 149 K3
CHING E4 52 B2
CHSWK W4 118 C5
DAGW RM9 92 A2
EHAM E6 107 H2
HAYES BR2 200 D6
KUT KT1 174 D4
MTCM CR4 195 J1
NWDGN UB2 114 D4
NWMAL KT3 192 D1
PGE/AN SE20 181 J5
RSLP HA4 59 F6
WPK KT4 193 F6
Beverley Wy NWMAL KT3 176 C4
Beverley Wy (Kingston By-Pass)
NWMAL KT3 176 C4
The Beverly MRDN SM4 193 G3
Beversbrook Rd ARCH N19 84 D1
Beverstone Rd
BRXS/STRHM SW2 142 A6
THHTH CR7 196 B1
Beverston Ms MBLAR W1H 8 E2
Bevill Cl SNWD SE25 181 H6
Bevin Cl BERM/RHTH SE16 124 B1
Bevington Rd BECK BR3 182 E5
NKENS * W10 100 C4
Bevington St BERM/RHTH SE16 123 H2
Bevin Rd YEAD UB4 94 E2
Bevin Sq TOOT SW17 160 E5
Bevin Wy IS N1 5 J3
Bevis Marks HDTCH EC3A 13 H3
Bewcastle Gdns ENC/FH EN2 22 E5
Bewdley St IS N1 85 G5
Bewick Ms PECK SE15 143 J1
Bewick St VX/NE SW8 141 G3
Bewley St WCHPL E1 104 D6
WIM/MER SW19 178 B2
Bewlys Rd WNWD SE27 180 C1
Bexhill Cl FELT TW13 154 D4
Bexhill Rd BROCKY SE4 164 C1
FBAR/BDGN N11 48 D1
MORT/ESHN SW14 137 K4
Bexley Cl DART DA1 150 B6
Bexley Gdns CHDH RM6 73 H2
ED N9 35 K5
Bexley High St BXLY DA5 169 H2
Bexley La DART DA1 150 B6
SCUP DA14 168 D4
Bexley Rd ELTH/MOT SE9 167 F1
ERITH DA8 149 K1
Beynon Rd CAR SM5 209 K3
Bianca Rd PECK SE15 123 G6
Bibsworth Rd FNCH N3 46 D5
Bibury Cl PECK SE15 123 F6
Bicester Rd RCH/KEW TW9 137 H4
Bickenhall St MHST W1U 9 F1
Bickersteth Rd TOOT SW17 178 E2
Bickerton Rd ARCH N19 66 B6
Bickley Crs BMLY BR1 200 D1
Bickley Park Rd BMLY BR1 184 E6
Bickley Rd BMLY BR1 184 C5
LEY E10 69 K4
Bickley St TOOT SW17 178 D1
Bicknell Rd CMBW SE5 142 D4
Bicknoller Rd EN EN1 24 B2
Bicknor Rd ORP BR6 201 K4
Bidborough Cl HAYES BR2 199 J2
Bidborough St STPAN WC1H 4 E5
Biddenden Wy ELTH/MOT SE9 167 F6
Bidder St CAN/RD E16 106 C4
Biddestone Rd HOLWY N7 85 F2
Biddulph Rd MV/WKIL W9 101 F2
SAND/SEL CR2 211 J6
Bideford Av GFD/PVL UB6 97 H2
Bideford Cl EDGE HA8 44 C4
FELT TW13 154 E5
Bideford Gdns EN EN1 36 A2
Bideford Rd BMLY BR1 165 J5
PEND EN3 25 H1
RSLP HA4 77 F1
WELL DA16 148 C1
Bidwell Gdns FBAR/BDGN N11 48 C4
Bidwell St PECK * SE15 143 J2
Biggerstaff Rd SRTFD E15 88 A6
Biggerstaff St FSBYPK N4 67 G6
Biggin Av MTCM CR4 178 E4
Biggin Hl NRWD SE19 180 C3
Biggin Wy NRWD SE19 180 C3
Bigginwood Rd
STRHM/NOR SW16 180 C3
Bigg's Rw PUT/ROE SW15 139 G4
Bigland St WCHPL E1 104 D5
Bignell Rd WOOL/PLUM SE18 127 G5
Bignold Rd FSTGT E7 88 E2
Bigwood Rd GLDGN NW11 65 F3
Billet Rd CHDH RM6 55 J6
WALTH E17 51 F4
Billetts Hart Cl HNWL W7 115 K2
Bill Hamling Cl ELTH/MOT SE9 166 E4
Billingford Cl BROCKY SE4 144 A5
Billing Pl WBPTN * SW10 140 A1
Billing Rd WBPTN SW10 140 A1
Billings Cl DAGW RM9 91 J5
Billing St WBPTN * SW10 140 A1
Billington Rd NWCR SE14 144 A1
Billiter Sq FENCHST * EC3M 13 H4
Billiter St FENCHST EC3M 13 H4
Billockby Cl CHSGTN KT9 206 B4
Billson St POP/IOD E14 125 F4
Bilton Rd ERITH DA8 150 D1
GFD/PVL UB6 79 H6
Bilton Wy HYS/HAR UB3 114 A2
PEND EN3 25 H2
Bina Gdns ECT SW5 120 B4
Bincote Rd ENC/FH EN2 23 F4
Binden Rd SHB W12 118 C3
Binfield Rd SAND/SEL CR2 212 B3
VX/NE SW8 141 K2
Bingfield IS N1 84 E6
Bingfield St IS N1 84 E6
Bingham Ct IS * N1 85 H5
Bingham Pl MHST W1U 3 G7
Bingham Rd CROY/NA CR0 197 H5
Bingham St IS N1 85 K4
Bingley Rd CAN/RD E16 107 G5
GFD/PVL UB6 96 C3
Binney St MYFR/PKLN W1K 9 H5
Binns Rd CHSWK W4 118 B5
Binsey Wk ABYW SE2 128 D2
Binstead Cl YEAD UB4 95 J4
Binyon Crs STAN HA7 43 F1
Birbetts Rd ELTH/MOT SE9 166 E4
Birchanger Rd SNWD SE25 197 H2
Birch Av PLMGR N13 35 J5
Birch Cl BKHH IG9 39 H5
BTFD TW8 136 C1
CAN/RD E16 106 C4
HSLW TW3 135 J4
ROMW/RG RM7 56 D6
TEDD TW11 174 B1
Birchdale Gdns CHDH RM6 73 K4
Birchdale Rd FSTGT E7 89 G3
Birchdene Dr THMD SE28 128 B1
Birchen Cl CDALE/KGS NW9 63 F6
Birchend Cl SAND/SEL CR2 211 K4
Birchen Gv CDALE/KGS NW9 63 F6
Birchen La BANK EC3V 13 F4
The Birches CHARL SE7 126 A6
CMBW * SE5 143 F4
HSLWW * TW4 154 E2
ORP BR6 216 A2
STHGT/OAK N14 35 F1
Birches Cl MTCM CR4 178 E6
PIN HA5 59 J2
Birchfield St POP/IOD E14 105 J6
Birch Gdns DAGE RM10 92 E1
Birch Gv ACT W3 117 H1
LEE/GVPK SE12 165 J2
WAN E11 88 C1
WELL DA16 148 B5
Birch Hl CROY/NA CR0 213 F3
Birchington Cl BXLYHN DA7 149 J2
Birchington Rd BRYLDS KT5 191 G4
CEND/HSY/T N8 66 D3
KIL/WHAMP NW6 82 E6
Birchlands Av BAL SW12 160 E2
Birch Md HAYES BR2 201 F6
Birchmead Av PIN HA5 59 G1
Birchmore Wk HBRY N5 85 J1
Birch Pk KTN/HRWW/W HA3 42 C3
Birch Rd FELT TW13 172 C1
ROMW/RG RM7 56 D6
Birch Rw HAYES BR2 201 F4
Birch Tree Av WWKM BR4 214 D3
Birch Tree Wy CROY/NA CR0 197 J6
Birch Wk MTCM CR4 179 G4
Birchway HYS/HAR UB3 113 K1
Birchwood Av BECK BR3 198 C1
MUSWH N10 48 A6
SCUP DA14 168 C5
WLGTN SM6 210 A1
Birchwood Cl MRDN SM4 194 A1
Birchwood Ct EDGE HA8 44 E5
Birchwood Dr HAMP NW3 83 F1
RDART DA2 170 B6
Birchwood Gv HPTN TW12 173 F2
Birchwood Rd RDART DA2 187 K3
STMC/STPC BR5 201 J1
TOOT SW17 179 G1
Birchwood Ter SWLY * BR8 187 K4
Birdbrook Cl DAGE RM10 92 E5
Birdbrook Rd BKHTH/KID SE3 146 B4
Birdcage Wk STJSPK SW1H 16 B3
Birdham Cl BMLY BR1 200 D2
Birdhurst Av SAND/SEL CR2 211 K2
Birdhurst Gdns SAND/SEL CR2 211 K2
Birdhurst Ri SAND/SEL CR2 212 A3
Birdhurst Rd SAND/SEL CR2 212 A3
WAND/EARL SW18 140 B5
WIM/MER SW19 178 D2
Bird In Bush Rd PECK SE15 143 H1
Bird-in-Hand La BMLY BR1 184 C5
Bird-in-Hand Pas FSTH * SE23 163 K4
Birdlip Cl PECK SE15 123 F6
Birds Farm Av ROMW/RG RM7 56 D4
Birdsfield La HOM E9 87 H6
Bird St MHST W1U 9 H4
Bird Wk WHTN TW2 154 E3
Birdwood Cl TEDD TW11 155 K6
Birkbeck Av ACT W3 98 E6
GFD/PVL UB6 78 C6
Birkbeck Gv ACT W3 118 A2
Birkbeck Hl DUL SE21 162 C4
Birkbeck Ms ACT * W3 99 F6
HACK E8 86 B3
Birkbeck Pl DUL SE21 162 C3
Birkbeck Rd ACT W3 118 A1
BECK BR3 182 A5
CEND/HSY/T N8 66 E1
EA W5 116 D4
ENC/FH EN2 23 K2
GNTH/NBYPK IG2 72 D2
HACK E8 86 B3
MLHL NW7 45 H1
NFNCH/WDSP N12 47 G1
ROMW/RG RM7 75 F5
SCUP DA14 168 B5
TOTM N17 50 B4
WIM/MER SW19 178 A1
Birkbeck St BETH E2 104 D2
Birkbeck Wy GFD/PVL UB6 78 D6
Birkdale Av PIN HA5 42 A6
Birkdale Cl BERM/RHTH * SE16 123 J5
ORP BR6 201 J4
Birkdale Gdns CROY/NA CR0 213 F2
OXHEY WD19 27 H5
Birkdale Rd ABYW SE2 128 B4
EA W5 98 A3
Birkenhead Av KUTN/CMB KT2 175 G5
Birkenhead St IS N1 5 F4
Birkhall Rd CAT SE6 165 G3
Birkwood Cl BAL SW12 161 J2
Birley Rd TRDG/WHET N20 33 G4
Birley St BTSEA SW11 141 F3
Birling Rd ERITH DA8 150 A1
Birnam Rd HOLWY N7 67 F6
Birse Crs WLSDN NW10 81 G2
Birstal Gn OXHEY WD19 27 H6
Birstall Rd SEVS/STOTM N15 68 A2
Biscay Rd HMSMTH W6 119 G5
Biscoe Cl HEST TW5 115 F6
Biscoe Wy LEW * SE13 145 G5
Bisenden Rd CROY/NA CR0 197 F6
Bisham Cl MTCM CR4 194 E4
Bisham Gdns HGT N6 66 A5
Bishop Butt Cl ORP BR6 217 F1
Bishop Cl RCHPK/HAM TW10 156 E5
Bishop Fox Wy
E/WMO/HCT KT8 188 E1
Bishop Ken Rd
KTN/HRWW/W HA3 43 F5
Bishop Kings Rd WKENS * W14 119 H4
WKENS W14 119 H4
Bishop Rd STHGT/OAK N14 34 B2
The Bishops Av EFNCH N2 65 H3
Bishops Av BMLY BR1 184 B6
CHDH RM6 73 J3
FUL/PGN SW6 139 G3
NTHWD HA6 26 C6
PLSTW E13 89 F6
Bishop's Bridge Rd
BAY/PAD W2 101 F5
Bishops Cl BAR EN5 32 B1
CHSWK W4 117 K5
ELTH/MOT SE9 167 H4
EN EN1 24 D3
SUT SM1 208 E1
WALTH E17 69 K1
Bishop's Ct STP EC4M 12 A3
Bishops Dr EBED/NFELT TW14 153 G1
NTHLT UB5 77 J6
Bishopsford Rd MRDN SM4 194 B4
Bishopsgate LVPST EC2M 13 H2
Bishopsgate Ar LVPST EC2M 13 G2
Bishops Gn BMLY * BR1 184 B4
Bishops Gv EFNCH N2 65 H3
HPTN TW12 154 E6
Bishop's Hall KUT KT1 174 E5
Bishops Md CMBW * SE5 142 D1
Bishop's Park Rd FUL/PGN SW6 139 G3
STRHM/NOR SW16 179 K4
Bishop's Pl SUT SM1 209 G3
Bishop's Rd CROY/NA CR0 196 C4
FUL/PGN SW6 139 J2
HGT N6 66 A3
HNWL W7 115 K2
HYS/HAR UB3 94 A5
Bishop's Ter LBTH SE11 17 K6
Bishopsthorpe Rd SYD SE26 163 K6
Bishops Wk CHST BR7 185 H4
CROY/NA CR0 213 F3
Bishop's Wy BETH E2 104 E1
Bishopswood Rd HGT N6 65 K4
Bishop Wy WLSDN NW10 81 G5
Bisley Cl WPK KT4 193 F5
Bispham Rd WLSDN NW10 98 B2
Bisson Rd SRTFD E15 106 A1
Bistern Av WALTH E17 52 B6
Bittacy Cl MLHL NW7 46 B2
Bittacy Hl MLHL NW7 46 B2
Bittacy Park Av MLHL NW7 46 B2
Bittacy Ri MLHL NW7 46 B2
Bittacy Rd MLHL NW7 46 B2
Bittern Cl YEAD UB4 95 H4
Bittern Pl WDGN * N22 49 F5
Bittern St STHWK SE1 18 C3
The Bittoms KUT KT1 174 E6
Bittoms Ct KUT * KT1 174 E6
Bixley Cl NWDGN UB2 114 E4
Blackall St SDTCH EC2A 7 G6
Blackberry Farm Cl HEST TW5 134 D1
Blackberry Fld STMC/STPC BR5 186 B4
Blackbird Hl CDALE/KGS NW9 62 E6
Blackbird Yd BETH E2 7 K4
Blackborne Rd DAGE RM10 92 C4
Black Boy La SEVS/STOTM N15 67 J2
Blackbrook La HAYES BR2 201 F2
Blackburne's Ms MYFR/PKLN W1K 9 G5
Blackburn Rd KIL/WHAMP NW6 83 F4
Blackbush Av CHDH RM6 73 K2
Blackbush Cl BELMT SM2 209 F5
Blackdown Cl EFNCH N2 47 G5
Blackdown Ter
WOOL/PLUM * SE18 146 E2
Blackenham Rd TOOT SW17 160 E6
Blackett St PUT/ROE SW15 139 G4
Black Fan Cl ENC/FH EN2 23 J2
Blackfen Pde BFN/LL * DA15 168 B1
Blackfen Rd BFN/LL DA15 148 A6
Blackford Cl SAND/SEL CR2 211 H6
Blackford Rd OXHEY WD19 41 H1
Blackfriars Br STHWK SE1 12 A6
Black Friars La BLKFR EC4V 12 A4
Blackfriars Pas BLKFR EC4V 12 A5
Blackfriars Rd STHWK SE1 12 A7
Blackfriars U/P BLKFR EC4V 12 B5
Blackheath Av GNWCH SE10 145 H1
Blackheath Gv BKHTH/KID SE3 145 J3
Blackheath Hl GNWCH SE10 145 F2
Blackheath Pk BKHTH/KID SE3 145 K4
Blackheath Ri LEW SE13 145 F3
Blackheath Rd GNWCH SE10 144 E2
Blackheath V BKHTH/KID SE3 145 H3
Black Horse Ct STHWK * SE1 19 F5
Blackhorse La CROY/NA CR0 197 H4
WALTH E17 51 F6
Black Horse Pde PIN * HA5 59 F2
Black Horse Rd SCUP DA14 168 B6
Blackhorse Rd DEPT SE8 124 B6
WALTH E17 51 F6
Blacklands Dr YEAD UB4 94 A3
Blacklands Rd CAT SE6 165 F6
Blacklands Ter CHEL SW3 14 E7
Black Lion Ga BAY/PAD W2 101 F6
Black Lion La HMSMTH W6 118 D4
Blackmans Cl DART DA1 171 F3
Blackmans Yd BETH * E2 7 K6
Blackmore Av STHL UB1 115 J1
Blackmore Rd BKHH IG9 39 J2
Blackmore's Gv TEDD TW11 174 B2
Blackness Cottages
HAYES * BR2 215 H6
Blackness La HAYES BR2 215 H6
Blackpool Gdns YEAD UB4 94 C3
Blackpool Rd PECK SE15 143 J3
Black Prince Rd LBTH SE11 17 G7
Black Rod Cl HYS/HAR UB3 113 J3
Blackshaw Rd TOOT SW17 178 C1
Blacksmith Cl CHDH RM6 73 J3
Blacksmith's La RAIN RM13 93 H6
STMC/STPC BR5 202 D2
Black's Rd HMSMTH W6 119 F5
Blackstock Rd FSBYPK N4 67 H6
Blackstone Est HACK E8 86 C5
Blackstone Rd CRICK NW2 82 A3
Black Swan Yd STHWK SE1 19 G2
Blackthorn Av WDR/YW UB7 112 D4
Blackthorn Ct HEST TW5 134 D1
Blackthorne Av CROY/NA CR0 197 K5
Blackthorne Dr CHING E4 38 B6
Blackthorn Gv BXLYHN DA7 149 F4
Blackthorn St BOW E3 105 J3
Blacktree Ms BRXN/ST * SW9 142 B4
Blackwall La GNWCH SE10 125 H5
Blackwall Tunnel Northern Ap
BOW E3 105 K2
Blackwall Wy POP/IOD E14 106 A6
Blackwater Cl RAIN RM13 111 F4
Blackwater St EDUL SE22 143 G6
Blackwell Cl CLPT E5 87 G2
KTN/HRWW/W HA3 42 D3
Blackwell Dr OXHEY WD19 27 G1
Blackwell Gdns EDGE HA8 30 C6
Blackwood St WALW SE17 122 E5
Bladindon Dr BXLY DA5 168 E2
Bladon Gdns RYLN/HDSTN HA2 60 B3
Blagden's La STHGT/OAK N14 34 D4
Blagdon Rd LEW SE13 164 E1
NWMAL KT3 192 C1
Blagdon Wk TEDD TW11 174 D2
Blagrove Rd NKENS W10 100 C4
Blair Av CDALE/KGS NW9 63 G4
ESH/CLAY KT10 189 H6
Blair Cl BFN/LL DA15 147 K6
HYS/HAR UB3 113 K4
IS N1 85 J4
Blairderry Rd
BRXS/STRHM SW2 161 K4
Blairhead Dr OXHEY WD19 27 F5
Blair St POP/IOD E14 106 A5
Blake Av BARK IG11 90 E6
Blake Cl CAR SM5 194 D5
NKENS W10 100 A4
RAIN RM13 93 H6
WELL DA16 147 K2
Blakeden Dr ESH/CLAY KT10 205 F5
Blake Gdns DART DA1 151 J5
FUL/PGN SW6 139 K2
Blakehall Rd CAR SM5 209 K4
Blake Hall Rd WAN E11 70 E5
Blakemore Rd STRHM/NOR SW16 161 K5
THHTH CR7 196 A2
Blakemore Wy BELV DA17 129 F3
Blakeney Av BECK BR3 182 C4
Blakeney Cl CAMTN NW1 4 C2
HACK E8 86 C3
TRDG/WHET N20 33 G3
Blakeney Rd BECK BR3 182 C4
Blaker Ct CHARL * SE7 146 B1
Blake Rd CAN/RD E16 106 D3
CROY/NA CR0 197 F6
FBAR/BDGN N11 48 C3
MTCM CR4 178 D6
Blaker Rd SRTFD E15 88 A6
Blakes Av NWMAL KT3 192 C2
Blake's Gn WWKM BR4 199 F4
Blakes La NWMAL KT3 192 C2
Blakesley Av EA W5 97 J5
Blakes Rd PECK * SE15 143 F1
PECK SE15 143 F1
Blakes Ter NWMAL KT3 192 D2
Blakesware Gdns ED N9 35 K2
Blakewood Cl FELT TW13 154 B6
Blanchard Cl ELTH/MOT SE9 166 D5
Blanchard Gv PEND EN3 25 J1
Blanchard Wy HACK * E8 86 C4
Blanch Cl PECK SE15 143 K1
Blanchedowne CMBW SE5 142 E5
Blanche St CAN/RD E16 106 D3
Blanchland Rd MRDN SM4 194 A2
Blandfield Rd BAL SW12 161 F1
Blandford Av BECK BR3 182 B5
WHTN TW2 155 G3
Blandford Cl CROY/NA CR0 210 E1
EFNCH N2 65 G2
ROMW/RG RM7 74 D1
Blandford Crs CHING E4 38 A2
Blandford Rd BECK BR3 182 A5
CHSWK W4 118 B3
EA W5 116 E2
NWDGN UB2 115 F4
TEDD TW11 173 J1
Blandford Sq CAMTN NW1 2 D7
Blandford St MHST W1U 9 F3
Blandford Waye YEAD UB4 95 G5
Bland St ELTH/MOT SE9 146 C5
Blaney Crs EHAM E6 108 B2
Blanmerle Rd ELTH/MOT SE9 167 G3
Blann Cl ELTH/MOT SE9 166 C1
Blantyre St WBPTN SW10 140 C1
Blantyre Wk WBPTN * SW10 140 C1
Blashford St LEW SE13 165 G2
Blawith Rd HRW HA1 60 E1
Blaydon Cl RSLP HA4 58 C4
TOTM * N17 50 D3
Blaydon Wk TOTM N17 50 D3
Bleak Hill La WOOL/PLUM SE18 128 A6
Blean Gv PGE/AN SE20 181 K3
Bleasdale Av GFD/PVL UB6 97 G1
Blechynden St NKENS * W10 100 B6
Bledlow Cl THMD SE28 109 J6
Bledlow Ri GFD/PVL UB6 96 C1
Bleeding Heart Yd HCIRC * EC1N 11 K2
Blegborough Rd
STRHM/NOR SW16 179 H2
Blendon Dr BXLY DA5 168 E1
Blendon Rd BXLY DA5 168 E1
Blendon Ter WOOL/PLUM SE18 127 H5
Blendworth Wy PECK SE15 143 F1
Blenheim CDALE/KGS * NW9 45 H5
Blenheim Av GNTH/NBYPK IG2 72 A3
Blenheim Cl DART DA1 171 F1
GFD/PVL * UB6 96 D1
OXHEY WD19 27 G2
ROMW/RG RM7 74 E1
RYNPK SW20 177 F6
WCHMH N21 35 J3
WLGTN SM6 210 C5
Blenheim Ct BFN/LL DA15 167 J5
WFD IG8 53 F3
Blenheim Crs NTGHL W11 100 C6
RSLP HA4 58 B6
SAND/SEL CR2 211 J5
Blenheim Dr WELL DA16 148 A2
Blenheim Gdns
BRXS/STRHM SW2 162 A1
CRICK NW2 82 A3
KUTN/CMB KT2 175 J3
WBLY HA9 80 A1
WLGTN SM6 210 C4
Blenheim Gv PECK SE15 143 G3
Blenheim Park Rd
SAND/SEL CR2 211 J6
Blenheim Pas STJWD NW8 101 G1
Blenheim Ri SEVS/STOTM * N15 68 B1
Blenheim Rd BAR EN5 20 B4
BFN/LL DA15 168 D3
CHSWK W4 118 B3
DART DA1 171 F1
EHAM E6 107 H2
HAYES BR2 200 D1
NTHLT UB5 78 B4
ORP BR6 202 D6
PGE/AN SE20 181 K3
RYLN/HDSTN HA2 60 B3
RYNPK SW20 177 F6
STJWD NW8 101 G1
SUT SM1 208 E1
WALTH E17 51 F6
WAN E11 88 C2
Blenheim St MYFR/PKLN W1K 9 J4
Blenheim Ter STJWD NW8 101 G1
Blenheim Wy ISLW TW7 136 B2
Blenkarne Rd BTSEA SW11 160 E1
Bleriot Rd HEST TW5 134 B1
Blessbury Rd EDGE HA8 44 E4
Blessington Rd LEW SE13 145 G5
Blessing Wy BARK IG11 109 J1
Bletchingly Cl THHTH CR7 196 C1
Bletchley St IS N1 6 D3
Bletchmore Cl HYS/HAR UB3 113 G5
Bletsoe Wk IS N1 6 D2
Blincoe Cl WIM/MER SW19 159 G4
Blissett St GNWCH SE10 145 F2
Bliss Ms NKENS W10 100 C2
Blisworth Cl YEAD UB4 95 J3
Blithbury Rd DAGW RM9 91 H4
Blithdale Rd ABYW SE2 128 B4

Blithfield St KENS W8 120 A3
Blockley Rd ALP/SUD HA0 61 H6
Bloemfontein Av SHB W12 118 E1
Bloemfontein Rd SHB W12 99 K6
Blomfield Rd MV/WKIL W9 101 F4
Blomfield St LVPST EC2M 13 F2
Blomfield Vls BAY/PAD W2 101 F4
Blomville Rd BCTR RM8 74 A6
Blondell Cl WDR/YW UB7 112 A6
Blondel St BTSEA SW11 141 F3
Blondin Av EA W5 116 D4
Blondin St BOW E3 105 J1
Bloomfield Crs GNTH/NBYPK IG2 72 B3
Bloomfield Pl MYFR/PKLN W1K 9 K5
Bloomfield Rd HAYES BR2 200 C2
HGT N6 66 A3
KUT KT1 191 F1
WOOL/PLUM SE18 127 G5
Bloomfield Ter BGVA SW1W 121 F5
Bloom Gv WNWD SE27 162 C5
Bloomhall Rd NRWD SE19 180 E1
Bloom Park Rd FUL/PGN SW6 139 J1
Bloomsbury Cl EA W5 98 B6
Bloomsbury Pl
NOXST/BSQ WC1A 11 F2
Bloomsbury Sq
NOXST/BSQ WC1A 11 F2
Bloomsbury St RSQ WC1B 10 D2
Bloomsbury Wy
NOXST/BSQ WC1A 10 E2
Blore Cl VX/NE SW8 141 J2
Blossom Cl DAGW RM9 92 B6
EA W5 117 F2
SAND/SEL CR2 212 B3
Blossom La ENC/FH EN2 23 J2
Blossom St WCHPL E1 13 H1
Blossom Wy WDR/YW UB7 112 D4
Blossom Waye HEST TW5 114 D6
Blount St POP/IOD E14 105 G5
Bloxam Gdns ELTH/MOT SE9 146 D6
Bloxhall Rd LEY E10 69 H5
Bloxham Crs HPTN TW12 172 E4
Bloxworth Cl WLGTN SM6 210 C1
Blucher Rd CMBW SE5 142 D1
Blue Anchor La
BERM/RHTH SE16 123 H4
Blue Anchor Yd WCHPL E1 104 C6
Blue Ball Yd WHALL SW1A 16 A1
Bluebell Av FSTGT E7 89 H3
Bluebell Cl HOM E9 86 E6
ORP BR6 201 H6
ROMW/RG RM7 75 G6
SYD SE26 163 G6
WLGTN SM6 195 G5
Bluebell Wy IL IG1 90 B4
Blueberry Cl WFD IG8 52 E2
Bluebird La DAGE RM10 92 C5
Bluebird Wy THMD SE28 127 J2
Bluefield Cl HPTN TW12 173 F1
Bluegates EW KT17 207 J5
Bluehouse Rd CHING E4 38 C5
Blue Riband Est CROY/NA * CR0 196 C6
Blundell Rd EDGE HA8 45 F4
Blundell St HOLWY N7 84 E5
Blunden Cl BCTR RM8 73 J5
Blunt Rd CROY/NA CR0 211 K3
Blunts Av WDR/YW UB7 132 D1
Blunts Rd ELTH/MOT SE9 147 F6
Blurton Rd CLPT E5 87 F2
Blyth Cl TWK TW1 156 A1
Blythe Cl CAT SE6 164 C2
Blythe Hl CAT SE6 164 C2
STMC/STPC BR5 186 A4
Blythe Hill La CAT SE6 164 C2
Blythe Hill Pl FSTH * SE23 164 B2
Blythe Ms WKENS * W14 119 G3
Blythe Rd WKENS W14 119 G3
Blythe V CAT SE6 164 C3
Blyth Rd BMLY BR1 183 J4
HYS/HAR UB3 113 H2
THMD SE28 109 J6
WALTH E17 69 H4
Blyth's Whf POP/IOD * E14 105 G6
Blythswood Rd GDMY/SEVK IG3 73 G5
Blythwood Rd FSBYPK N4 66 E4
PIN HA5 41 H4
Boadicea St IS N1 5 G1
Boardman Av CHING E4 25 K6
Boardman Cl BAR EN5 20 C6
Boardwalk Pl POP/IOD E14 125 F1
Boathouse Wk PECK SE15 143 G1
Boat Lifter Wy
BERM/RHTH SE16 124 B4
Bob Anker Cl PLSTW E13 106 E2
Bobbin Cl CLAP SW4 141 H4
Bob Marley Wy BRXN/ST SW9 142 B5
Bockhampton Rd
KUTN/CMB KT2 175 G3
Bocking St HACK E8 86 D6
Boddicott Cl WIM/MER SW19 159 H4
Bodiam Cl EN EN1 23 K3
Bodiam Rd STRHM/NOR SW16 179 J4
Bodley Cl NWMAL KT3 192 B2
Bodley Rd NWMAL KT3 192 B3
Bodmin Cl RYLN/HDSTN HA2 77 K1
STMC/STPC BR5 202 D5
Bodmin Gv MRDN SM4 194 A1
Bodmin St WAND/EARL SW18 159 K3
Bodnant Gdns RYNPK SW20 176 D6
Bodney Rd CLPT E5 86 D3
Boeing Wy NWDGN UB2 114 A3
Bognor Gdns OXHEY * WD19 41 G1
Bognor Rd WELL DA16 148 E2
Bohemia Pl HACK E8 86 E4
Bohn Rd WCHPL E1 105 G4
Bohun Gv EBAR EN4 33 J1
Boileau Rd BARN SW13 138 D1
EA W5 98 B5
Bolden St DEPT SE8 144 E3
Boldero Pl STJWD * NW8 2 C7
Bolderwood Wy WWKM BR4 198 E6
Boldmere Rd PIN HA5 59 G4
Boleyn Av EN EN1 24 D2
Boleyn Cl LOU IG10 39 J1
Boleyn Ct BKHH IG9 38 E3
WALTH E17 69 J1
Boleyn Dr E/WMO/HCT KT8 172 E6
RSLP HA4 59 H6
Boleyn Gdns DAGE RM10 92 E5
WWKM BR4 198 E6
Boleyn Rd EHAM E6 107 H1
FSTGT E7 88 E5
STNW/STAM N16 86 A3
Boleyn Wy BAR EN5 21 G4
BARK/HLT IG6 54 C2
Bolina Rd BERM/RHTH SE16 123 K5
Bolingbroke Gv BTSEA SW11 140 D6
Bolingbroke Rd WKENS W14 119 G3
Bolingbroke Wk BTSEA * SW11 140 C1
Bolingbroke Wy HYS/HAR UB3 113 G1
Bollo Bridge Rd ACT W3 117 J3
Bollo La ACT W3 117 J3
Bolney Ga SKENS SW7 14 C3
Bolney St VX/NE SW8 142 A1
Bolsover St GTPST W1W 3 K7
Bolstead Rd MTCM CR4 179 G4
Bolster Gv WDGN * N22 48 D4
Bolt Ct FLST/FETLN * EC4A 11 K4
Bolton Cl CHSGTN KT9 205 K4
Bolton Crs CMBW SE5 122 B6
Bolton Gdns BMLY BR1 183 J2
ECT SW5 120 A5
TEDD TW11 174 B2
WLSDN NW10 100 B1
Bolton Gardens Ms
WBPTN SW10 120 A5
Bolton Rd CHSGTN KT9 205 K4
CHSWK W4 137 K1
FSTGT E7 88 D4
HRW HA1 60 C1
KIL/WHAMP NW6 83 F6
UED N18 50 B1
WLSDN NW10 81 G6
The Boltons ALP/SUD HA0 79 F2
WBPTN * SW10 120 B5
WFD * IG8 38 E6
Bolton's La WDR/YW UB7 133 F1
Boltons Pl WBPTN SW10 120 B5
Bolton St MYFR/PICC W1J 9 K7
Bombay St BERM/RHTH SE16 123 J4
Bomer Cl WDR/YW UB7 132 D1
Bomore Rd NTGHL W11 100 B6
Bonar Pl CHST BR7 184 D3
Bonar Rd PECK SE15 143 H1
Bonchester Cl CHST BR7 185 F3
Bonchurch Cl BELMT SM2 209 F5
Bonchurch Rd NKENS W10 100 C4
WEA W13 116 C1
Bondfield Av YEAD UB4 94 E2
Bond Gdns WLGTN SM6 210 C2
Bond Rd MTCM CR4 178 E5
SURB KT6 191 G6
Bond St EA W5 97 K6
SRTFD E15 88 C3
Bondway VX/NE SW8 121 K6
Boneta Rd WOOL/PLUM SE18 126 E3
Bonfield Rd LEW SE13 145 F5
Bonham Gdns BCTR RM8 73 K6
Bonham Rd BCTR RM8 73 K6
BRXS/STRHM SW2 142 A6
Bonheur Rd CHSWK W4 118 A2
Bonhill St SDTCH EC2A 7 F7
Boniface Gdns
KTN/HRWW/W HA3 42 B3
Boniface Wk
KTN/HRWW/W HA3 42 B3
Bonita Ms BROCKY SE4 144 A4
Bonner Hill Rd KUT KT1 175 G6
Bonner Rd BETH E2 104 E1
Bonnersfield Cl HRW HA1 61 G3
Bonnersfield La HRW HA1 61 G3
Bonner St BETH * E2 104 E1
Bonneville Gdns CLAP SW4 161 H1
Bonnington Sq VX/NE SW8 122 A6
Bonny St CAMTN NW1 84 C5
Bonser Rd TWK TW1 156 A4
Bonsor St CMBW SE5 143 F1
Bonville Gdns HDN NW4 63 J1
Bonville Rd BMLY BR1 183 J1
Booker Rd UED N18 50 C1
Boones Rd LEW SE13 145 H5
Boone St LEW SE13 145 H5
Boord St GNWCH SE10 125 H3
Boothby Rd ARCH N19 66 D6
Booth Cl THMD SE28 109 H6
Booth La BLKFR EC4V 12 C5
Booth Rd CDALE/KGS NW9 45 F4
CROY/NA * CR0 196 C6
Boot Pde EDGE * HA8 44 C2
Boot St IS N1 7 G5
Bordars Rd HNWL W7 96 E4
Bordars Wk HNWL W7 96 E4
Borden Av WCHMH N21 35 K1
Border Crs SYD SE26 181 J1
Border Gdns CROY/NA CR0 213 K2
Border Ga MTCM CR4 178 D4
Border Rd SYD SE26 181 J1
Bordesley Rd MRDN SM4 194 A1
Bordon Wk PUT/ROE SW15 158 D2
Boreas Wk IS N1 6 B3
Boreham Av CAN/RD E16 106 E5
Boreham Rd WDGN N22 49 J4
Borgard House
WOOL/PLUM SE18 146 D2
Borgard Rd WOOL/PLUM SE18 126 E4
Borkwood Pk ORP BR6 217 F2
Borkwood Wy ORP BR6 216 E2
Borland Rd PECK SE15 143 K5
TEDD TW11 174 C2
Borneo St PUT/ROE SW15 139 F4
Borough High St STHWK SE1 18 D3
Borough Hl CROY/NA CR0 211 H1
Borough Rd ISLW TW7 135 K2
KUTN/CMB KT2 175 H4
MTCM CR4 178 D5
STHWK SE1 18 A4
Borough Sq STHWK SE1 18 C3
Borrett Cl WALW SE17 122 D5
Borrodaile Rd
WAND/EARL SW18 160 A1
Borrowdale Av
KTN/HRWW/W HA3 43 G5
Borrowdale Cl REDBR IG4 71 J1
Borthwick Ms WAN * E11 88 C2
Borthwick Rd CDALE/KGS NW9 63 H3
SRTFD E15 88 C2
Borthwick St DEPT SE8 124 D5
Borwick Av WALTH E17 51 H6
Bosbury Rd CAT SE6 165 F5
Boscastle Rd KTTN NW5 84 B1
Boscobel Pl BGVA SW1W 15 H6
Boscobel St BAY/PAD W2 8 B1
Boscombe Av LEY E10 70 B4
Boscombe Cl CLPT E5 87 G3
Boscombe Rd SHB W12 118 D2
TOOT SW17 179 F2
WIM/MER SW19 177 K4
WPK KT4 193 F5
Bosgrove CHING E4 38 A3
Boss St STHWK * SE1 19 J2
Bostall Heath ABYW * SE2 128 D5
Bostall Hl ABYW SE2 128 C5
Bostall La ABYW SE2 128 C5
Bostall Manorway ABYW SE2 128 C4
Bostall Park Av BXLYHN DA7 149 F1
Bostall Rd STMC/STPC BR5 186 C3
Boston Gdns BTFD TW8 116 B4
CHSWK W4 118 B6
Boston Gv RSLP HA4 58 A3
Boston Manor Rd BTFD TW8 116 B4
Boston Pde HNWL * W7 116 B4
Boston Park Rd BTFD TW8 116 D5
Boston Pl CAMTN NW1 2 E7
Boston Rd CROY/NA CR0 196 A3
EDGE HA8 44 E3
EHAM E6 107 J2
HNWL W7 115 K1
Bostonthorpe Rd HNWL * W7 115 K2
Boston V HNWL W7 116 B4
Boswell Cl STMC/STPC BR5 202 D3
Boswell Ct BMSBY WC1N 11 F1
Boswell Rd THHTH CR7 196 D1
Boswell St BMSBY WC1N 11 F1
Bosworth Cl WALTH E17 51 H4
Bosworth Rd BAR EN5 20 E4
DAGE RM10 92 C2
FBAR/BDGN N11 48 D2
NKENS W10 100 C3
Botany Bay La CHST BR7 185 H5
Botany Cl EBAR EN4 21 J5
Botany Ter PUR * RM19 131 K5
Boteley Cl CHING E4 38 B4
Botham Cl EDGE HA8 44 E3
Botha Rd PLSTW E13 107 F4
Bothwell Cl CAN/RD E16 106 E4
Bothwell St HMSMTH W6 119 G6
Botolph Aly MON EC3R 13 G6
Botolph La MON EC3R 13 G6
Botsford Rd RYNPK SW20 177 H5
Bott Rd RDART DA2 171 J6
Bott's Ms BAY/PAD W2 100 E5
Botwell Common Rd
HYS/HAR UB3 94 B6
Botwell Crs HYS/HAR UB3 94 C5
Botwell La HYS/HAR UB3 94 C6
Boucher Cl TEDD TW11 174 A1
Boughton Av HAYES BR2 199 J4
Boughton Rd THMD SE28 127 K3
Boulcott St WCHPL E1 105 F5
The Boulevard WFD IG8 54 A3
Boulogne Rd CROY/NA CR0 196 D3
Boulter Gdns RAIN RM13 93 J4
Boulton Rd BCTR RM8 74 A6
Boultwood Rd EHAM E6 107 K5
Bounces La ED N9 36 D4
Bounces Rd ED N9 36 D4
Boundaries Rd BAL SW12 160 E4
FELT TW13 154 B3
Boundary Av WALTH E17 69 H4
Boundary Cl BAR EN5 20 D2
GDMY/SEVK IG3 90 E2
KUT KT1 175 H6
NWDGN UB2 115 F5
Boundary La PLSTW E13 107 H3
WALW SE17 122 D6
Boundary Ms STJWD NW8 83 G6
Boundary Rd BARK IG11 90 D6
BARK IG11 108 C1
BFN/LL DA15 147 K6
ED N9 36 E1
PIN HA5 59 H3
PLSTW E13 107 G1
ROM RM1 75 J3
STJWD NW8 83 H6
WALTH E17 69 H4
WDGN N22 49 H6
WIM/MER SW19 178 C2
WLGTN SM6 210 A6
Boundary Rw STHWK SE1 18 A2
Boundary St BETH E2 7 J5
ERITH DA8 150 C1
Boundary Wy CROY/NA CR0 213 J3
Boundfield Rd CAT SE6 165 H5
Bounds Green Rd
FBAR/BDGN N11 48 D2
Bourchier St SOHO/CST W1F 10 C5
Bourdon Pl MYFR/PKLN W1K 9 K5
Bourdon Rd PGE/AN SE20 181 K5
Bourdon St MYFR/PKLN W1K 9 J6
Bourke Cl CLAP SW4 161 K1
WLSDN NW10 81 G4
Bourlet Cl FITZ W1T 10 A2
Bourn Av EBAR EN4 21 H6
SEVS/STOTM N15 67 K1
Bournbrook Rd BKHTH/KID SE3 146 C4
The Bourne STHGT/OAK N14 34 E3
Bourne Av HYS/HAR UB3 113 F3
RSLP HA4 77 G3
STHGT/OAK N14 34 E4
Bourne Cl ESH/CLAY KT10 190 A6
Bourne Ct RSLP HA4 77 F3
Bourne Dr MTCM CR4 178 C5
Bourne End Rd NTHWD HA6 26 C6
Bourne Est HCIRC * EC1N 11 J1
Bourne Gdns CHING E4 37 K6
Bournehall BUSH * WD23 28 A1
Bournehall La BUSH WD23 28 A1
Bournehall Rd BUSH WD23 28 A1
Bourne Hl PLMGR N13 35 F4
Bourne Hill Cl PLMGR * N13 35 F4
Bourne Md BXLY DA5 149 K6
Bournemead Av NTHLT UB5 94 E1
Bournemead Cl NTHLT UB5 94 E2
Bournemouth Cl PECK SE15 143 H3
Bournemouth Rd PECK SE15 143 H3
WIM/MER SW19 177 K4
Bourne Pde BXLY * DA5 169 J2
Bourne Rd BXLY DA5 169 J2
CEND/HSY/T N8 66 E3
FSTGT E7 88 D1
HAYES BR2 200 C1
Bourneside Crs STHGT/OAK N14 34 D3
Bourneside Gdns CAT SE6 183 F1
Bourne St BGVA SW1W 15 G7
CROY/NA CR0 196 C6
Bourne Ter BAY/PAD W2 101 F4
Bourne V HAYES BR2 199 K5
Bournevale Rd
STRHM/NOR SW16 161 K6
Bourne Vw GFD/PVL UB6 79 F4
Bourne Wy HAYES BR2 199 K6
HOR/WEW KT19 206 E2
SUT SM1 208 D3
SWLY BR8 187 K6
Bournewood Rd
STMC/STPC BR5 202 C4
WOOL/PLUM SE18 148 B1
Bournville Rd CAT SE6 164 D2
Bournwell Cl EBAR EN4 21 K4
Bourton Cl HYS/HAR UB3 113 K1
Bousfield Rd NWCR SE14 144 A3
Boutflower Rd BTSEA SW11 140 D5
Boutique Hall LEW * SE13 145 F5
Bouverie Gdns
KTN/HRWW/W HA3 61 K3
Bouverie Ms STNW/STAM N16 68 A6
Bouverie Pl BAY/PAD W2 8 B3
Bouverie Rd HRW HA1 60 C3
STNW/STAM N16 68 A6
Bouverie St EMB EC4Y 11 K4
Bouvier Rd PEND EN3 24 E1
Boveney Rd FSTH SE23 164 A2
Bovill Rd FSTH SE23 164 A2
Bovingdon Av WBLY HA9 80 C4
Bovingdon La CDALE/KGS NW9 45 G4
Bovingdon Rd FUL/PGN SW6 140 A2
Bow Arrow La DART DA1 171 K1
Bowater Cl BRXS/STRHM SW2 161 K1
CDALE/KGS NW9 63 F2
Bowater Pl BKHTH/KID SE3 146 A1
Bowater Rd WOOL/PLUM SE18 126 C3
Bow Bridge Est BOW E3 105 K2
Bow Churchyard STP * EC4M 12 D4
Bow Common La BOW E3 105 H3
Bowden Cl EBED/NFELT TW14 153 H3
Bowden St LBTH SE11 122 B5
Bowditch DEPT SE8 124 C5
Bowdon Rd LEY E10 69 J4
Bowen Dr DUL SE21 163 F5
Bowen Rd HRW HA1 60 C4
Bowen St POP/IOD E14 105 K5
Bowens Wd CROY/NA * CR0 213 H6
Bowenswood CROY/NA CR0 213 H6
Bower Av GNWCH SE10 145 H2
Bower Cl CRW RM5 57 F3
NTHLT UB5 95 G1
Bowerdean St FUL/PGN SW6 140 A2
Bowerman Av NWCR SE14 124 B6
Bower St WCHPL * E1 105 F5
Bowes Cl BFN/LL DA15 168 C1
Bowes Rd ACT W3 99 G6
BCTR RM8 91 J2
FBAR/BDGN N11 48 B1
WOT/HER KT12 188 A6
Bowes Rd (North Circular)
PLMGR N13 48 E1
Bowfell Rd HMSMTH W6 119 F6
Bowford Av BXLYHN DA7 149 F2
Bowhill Cl BRXN/ST SW9 142 B1
Bowie Cl CLAP SW4 161 J2
Bowland Rd CLAP SW4 141 J5
WFD IG8 53 G2
Bowland Yd KTBR * SW1X 15 F3
Bow La FNCH N3 47 G3
STP EC4M 12 D4
Bowley Cl NRWD * SE19 181 G2
Bowley La NRWD SE19 181 G1
Bowley St POP/IOD E14 105 H6
Bowling Green Cl PUT/ROE SW15 158 E2
Bowling Green Ct WBLY HA9 62 B6
Bowling Green La CLKNW EC1R 5 K7
Bowling Green Pl STHWK * SE1 18 E2
Bowling Green Rw
WOOL/PLUM * SE18 126 E4
Bowling Green St LBTH SE11 122 B6
Bowling Green Wk IS N1 7 G4
Bow Locks BOW * E3 106 A3
Bowls Cl STAN HA7 43 H1
Bowman Av CAN/RD E16 106 D5
Bowman Ms WAND/EARL SW18 159 J3
Bowmans Cl WEA W13 116 C1
Bowmans Lea FSTH SE23 163 K2
Bowman's Meadow
WLGTN SM6 210 B1
Bowman's Ms HOLWY N7 84 E1
WCHPL E1 104 C6
Bowman's Pl HOLWY N7 84 E1
Bowmans Rd DART DA1 170 C2
Bowmead ELTH/MOT SE9 166 E4
Bowmore Wk CAMTN NW1 84 D5
Bowness Cl HACK * E8 86 B4
Bowness Crs PUT/ROE SW15 176 B1
Bowness Dr HSLWW TW4 134 D5
Bowness Rd BXLYHN DA7 149 J3
CAT SE6 164 E2
Bowness Wy HCH RM12 93 J3
Bowood Rd CLAP SW4 141 F5
PEND EN3 25 F3
Bowring Gn OXHEY WD19 41 G1
Bow Rd BOW E3 105 J2
Bowrons Av ALP/SUD HA0 79 K5
Bowsley Ct FELT TW13 153 K4
Bow St COVGDN WC2E 11 F4
SRTFD E15 88 C3
Bowyer Cl EHAM E6 107 K4
Bowyer Pl CMBW SE5 142 D1
Bowyer St CMBW SE5 142 D1
Boxall Rd DUL SE21 163 F1
Boxelder Cl EDGE * HA8 44 E1
Boxgrove Rd ABYW SE2 128 C2
Box La BARK IG11 109 H1
Boxley Rd MRDN SM4 194 B1
Boxley St CAN/RD E16 126 A1
Boxmoor Rd CRW RM5 56 E1
KTN/HRWW/W HA3 61 H1
Boxoll Rd DAGW RM9 92 B2
Boxted Cl BKHH IG9 39 J3
Boxtree La KTN/HRWW/W HA3 42 C4
Boxtree Rd KTN/HRWW/W HA3 42 D3
Boxwood Cl WDR/YW UB7 112 C2
Boxworth Gv IS N1 85 F6
Boyard Rd WOOL/PLUM SE18 127 G5
Boyce Wy PLSTW E13 106 E3
Boycroft Av CDALE/KGS NW9 62 E3
Boyd Av STHL UB1 114 E1
Boyd Cl KUTN/CMB KT2 175 H3
Boydell Ct STJWD NW8 83 H5
Boyd Rd WIM/MER SW19 178 C2
Boyd St WCHPL E1 104 C5
Boyfield St STHWK SE1 18 B3
Boyland Rd BMLY BR1 183 J1
Boyle Av STAN HA7 43 G2
Boyle Farm Rd THDIT KT7 190 B3
Boyne Av HDN NW4 64 B1
Boyne Rd DAGE RM10 92 C1
LEW SE13 145 G4
Boyne Terrace Ms NTGHL * W11 119 J1
Boyson Rd WALW SE17 122 D6
Boyton Cl CEND/HSY/T N8 48 E6
WCHPL E1 105 F3
Boyton Rd CEND/HSY/T N8 48 E6
Brabant Rd WDGN N22 49 F5
Brabazon Av WLGTN SM6 210 E6
Brabazon Rd HEST TW5 134 B1
NTHLT UB5 96 A1
Brabazon St POP/IOD E14 105 K5
Brabourne Cl NRWD SE19 181 F1
Brabourne Crs BXLYHN DA7 129 G6
Brabourne Ri BECK BR3 199 G2
Brabourn Gv PECK SE15 143 K3
Bracewell Av GFD/PVL UB6 79 F3
Bracewell Rd NKENS W10 100 A4
Bracewood Gdns CROY/NA CR0 212 B1
Bracey St FSBYPK * N4 66 E6
The Bracken CHING E4 38 A4
Bracken Av BAL SW12 161 F1
CROY/NA CR0 213 J1
Brackenbridge Dr RSLP HA4 77 H1
Brackenbury Gdns
HMSMTH W6 118 E3
Brackenbury Rd EFNCH N2 47 G6
HMSMTH W6 118 E3
Bracken Cl EHAM E6 107 K4
WHTN TW2 155 F2
Brackendale WCHMH N21 35 F4
Brackendale Cl HEST TW5 135 G2
Brackendene BXLY DA5 170 B6
Bracken Dr CHIG IG7 54 B2
Bracken End ISLW TW7 135 J6
Bracken Gdns BARN SW13 138 D3
Brackenhill RSLP * HA4 77 J2
Bracken Hill Cl BMLY BR1 183 J4
Bracken Hill La BMLY BR1 183 J4
Bracken Ms ROMW/RG RM7 74 C3
The Brackens EN EN1 36 A2
ORP BR6 217 G3
Brackley Cl WLGTN SM6 210 E5
Brackley Rd BECK BR3 182 C3
CHSWK W4 118 B4
Brackley Sq WFD IG8 53 H3
Brackley St BARB EC2Y 12 D1
Brackley Ter CHSWK W4 118 B5
Bracklyn St IS N1 6 E2
Bracknell Cl WDGN N22 49 G4
Bracknell Gdns HAMP NW3 83 F3
Bracknell Wy HAMP NW3 83 F2
Bracondale ESH/CLAY KT10 204 C3
Bracondale Rd ABYW SE2 128 B4
Bradbourne Rd BXLY DA5 169 H2
Bradbourne St FUL/PGN SW6 139 K3
Bradbury Cl NWDGN UB2 114 E4
Bradbury St STNW/STAM N16 86 A3
Braddock Cl CRW RM5 56 E2
ISLW TW7 136 A4
Braddon Ct BAR * EN5 20 C4
Braddon Rd RCH/KEW TW9 137 G4
Braddyll St GNWCH SE10 125 H5
Bradenham Av WELL DA16 148 B5
Bradenham Cl WALW SE17 122 E6
Bradenham Rd
KTN/HRWW/W HA3 61 H1
YEAD UB4 94 C2
Braden St MV/WKIL W9 101 F3
Bradfield Dr BARK IG11 91 G3
Bradfield Rd CAN/RD E16 125 K2
RSLP HA4 77 J3
Bradford Cl HAYES BR2 200 E5
SYD SE26 163 J6
UED N18 50 B2
Bradford Dr HOR/WEW KT19 207 H4
Bradford Rd ACT W3 118 B2
IL IG1 72 D5
Bradgate Rd CAT SE6 164 E1
Brading Crs WAN E11 71 F6
Brading Rd BRXS/STRHM SW2 162 A2
CROY/NA CR0 196 A3
Brading Ter SHB W12 118 D3
Bradiston Rd MV/WKIL W9 100 D2
Bradley Cl HOLWY N7 84 E5
Bradley Gdns WEA W13 97 H5
Bradley Rd NRWD SE19 180 D2
PEND EN3 25 G1
WDGN N22 49 F5
Bradley's Cl IS N1 5 J2
Bradley Stone Rd EHAM E6 107 K5
Bradman Rw EDGE * HA8 44 E3
Bradmead VX/NE * SW8 141 G2
Bradmore Park Rd
HMSMTH W6 118 E3
Bradshaw Cl WIM/MER SW19 177 K2
Bradshaw Cottages
POP/IOD * E14 105 G5
Bradshaws Cl SNWD SE25 181 H6
Bradstock Rd EW KT17 207 K3
HOM E9 87 F4
Brad St STHWK SE1 17 K1
Bradwell Av DAGE RM10 74 C6
Bradwell Cl HCH RM12 93 K4
SWFD E18 70 D1
Bradwell Ms UED N18 36 C6
Bradwell Rd BKHH IG9 39 J3
Bradymead EHAM E6 108 A5
Brady St WCHPL E1 104 D3
Braemar Av ALP/SUD HA0 79 K5
BXLYHN DA7 149 K5
THHTH CR7 180 C6
WAND/EARL SW18 159 K4
WDGN N22 48 E4
WLSDN NW10 81 F1
Braemar Gdns BFN/LL DA15 167 J5
CDALE/KGS NW9 45 F4
WWKM BR4 199 F5
Braemar Rd BTFD TW8 116 E6
PLSTW E13 106 E3
SEVS/STOTM N15 68 A2
WPK KT4 207 K1
Braeside BECK BR3 182 D1
Braeside Av WIM/MER SW19 177 H4
Braeside Cl PIN HA5 42 A3
Braeside Crs BXLYHN DA7 149 K5
Braeside Rd STRHM/NOR SW16 179 H3
Braes St IS N1 85 H5
Braesyde Cl BELV DA17 129 G4
Brafferton Rd CROY/NA CR0 211 J2
Braganza St WALW SE17 122 C5
Bragg Rd TEDD TW11 173 K3
Braham St WCHPL E1 13 K4
Braid Av ACT W3 99 G5
Braid Cl FELT TW13 154 E4
Braidwood Rd CAT SE6 165 G3
Brailsford Cl WIM/MER SW19 178 D3
Brailsford Rd
BRXS/STRHM SW2 162 B1
Brainton Av EBED/NFELT TW14 154 A2
Braintree Av REDBR IG4 71 J2
Braintree Rd DAGE RM10 92 C1
RSLP HA4 77 F2
Braintree St BETH * E2 104 E2
Brair Bank CAR SM5 210 A6
Braithwaite Av ROMW/RG RM7 74 C4
Braithwaite Gdns STAN HA7 43 J4
Braithwaite Rd PEND EN3 25 H4
Bramall Cl SRTFD E15 88 D3
Bramber Rd NFNCH/WDSP N12 47 J1
WKENS W14 119 J6

Bramble Acres Cl BELMT SM2 208 E5
Bramble Banks CAR SM5 210 A6
Bramblebury Rd
WOOL/PLUM SE18 127 J5
Bramble Cl BECK BR3 199 F2
CROY/NA CR0 213 J2
SEVS/STOTM N15 68 C1
STAN HA7 43 K3
Bramble Cft ERITH DA8 129 K4
Brambledown Cl HAYES BR2 199 H3
Brambledown Rd CAR SM5 210 A5
SAND/SEL CR2 212 A5
Bramble Gdns SHB W12 99 H6
Bramble La HPTN TW12 172 E2
The Brambles CHIG IG7 54 C2
SUT * SM1 194 C6
WDR/YW UB7 112 A5
WIM/MER * SW19 177 J1
Brambles Cl BTFD TW8 136 C1
Bramblewood Cl CAR SM5 194 D5
The Bramblings CHING E4 38 B6
Bramcote Av MTCM CR4 194 E1
Bramcote Gv BERM/RHTH SE16 123 K5
Bramcote Rd PUT/ROE SW15 138 E5
Bramdean Crs LEE/GVPK SE12 165 K3
Bramdean Gdns
LEE/GVPK SE12 165 K3
Bramerton Rd BECK BR3 182 C6
Bramerton St CHEL SW3 120 D6
Bramfield Rd BTSEA SW11 160 D1
Bramford Rd WAND/EARL SW18 140 B5
Bramham Ct NTHWD * HA6 40 C1
Bramham Gdns CHSGTN * KT9 205 K3
ECT SW5 120 A5
Bramhope La CHARL SE7 126 A6
Bramlands Cl BTSEA SW11 140 D4
Bramley Cl HYS/HAR UB3 94 E6
ORP BR6 201 G5
RSLP HA4 40 D6
SAND/SEL CR2 211 H3
STHGT/OAK N14 22 B6
WALTH E17 51 G5
WFD IG8 53 G3
WHTN TW2 155 H1
Bramley Crs GNTH/NBYPK IG2 72 A3
VX/NE SW8 141 J1
Bramley Gdns OXHEY WD19 41 G2
Bramley Hl SAND/SEL CR2 211 J2
Bramley Hyrst SAND/SEL * CR2 211 J3
Bramley Ldg ALP/SUD HA0 79 K2
Bramley Pl DART DA1 150 D5
Bramley Rd BELMT SM2 208 B6
EA W5 116 D3
NTGHL W11 100 B6
STHGT/OAK N14 22 B6
SUT SM1 209 H3
Bramley Wy HSLWW TW4 134 E6
WWKM BR4 198 E6
Brampton Cl CLPT E5 68 D6
Brampton Gv HDN NW4 63 K1
KTN/HRWW/W HA3 61 G1
WBLY HA9 62 C5
Brampton La HDN NW4 64 A1
Brampton Park Rd WDGN N22 49 G6
Brampton Rd BXLYHN DA7 148 E4
CDALE/KGS NW9 62 C1
CROY/NA CR0 197 G4
EHAM E6 107 H3
FSBYPK N4 67 J2
OXHEY WD19 26 E5
Bramshaw Gdns OXHEY WD19 41 H1
Bramshaw Ri NWMAL KT3 192 B3
Bramshaw Rd HOM E9 87 F4
Bramshill Gdns ARCH N19 84 B1
Bramshill Rd WLSDN NW10 99 G1
Bramshot Av CHARL SE7 126 A6
Bramston Cl BARK/HLT IG6 55 F2
Bramston Rd WLSDN NW10 99 J1
Bramwell Cl SUN TW16 172 C5
Bramwell Ms IS N1 85 F6
Brancaster Dr MLHL NW7 45 J3
Brancaster Rd GNTH/NBYPK IG2 72 E3
STRHM/NOR SW16 161 K5
Brancepeth Gdns BKHH IG9 38 E4
Branch Hl HAMP NW3 83 G1
Branch Rd BARK/HLT IG6 55 H1
POP/IOD E14 105 G6
Branch St CMBW SE5 143 F1
Brancker Rd KTN/HRWW/W HA3 43 K6
Brancroft Wy PEND EN3 25 G2
Brand Cl FSBYPK N4 67 H5
Brandlehow Rd PUT/ROE SW15 139 J5
Brandon Est WALW SE17 122 C6
Brandon Ms BARB * EC2Y 12 E1
Brandon Rd DART DA1 171 K2
HOLWY N7 84 E5
NWDGN UB2 114 E5
SUT SM1 209 F2
WALTH * E17 70 A1
Brandon St WALW SE17 18 D7
Brandram Ms LEW * SE13 145 H5
Brandram Rd LEW SE13 145 H4
Brandreth Ct HRW * HA1 61 F3
Brandreth Rd EHAM E6 107 K5
TOOT SW17 161 G4
The Brandries WLGTN SM6 210 D1
Brand St GNWCH SE10 145 F1
Brandville Gdns BARK/HLT IG6 72 B1
Brandville Rd WDR/YW UB7 112 B2
Brandy Wy BELMT SM2 208 E5
Brangbourne Rd BMLY BR1 183 F1
Brangton Rd LBTH SE11 122 A5
Brangwyn Crs WIM/MER SW19 178 C5
Branksea St FUL/PGN SW6 139 H1
Branksome Av UED N18 50 B2
Branksome Cl WOT/HER KT12 188 C6
Branksome Rd
BRXS/STRHM SW2 141 K6
WIM/MER SW19 177 K4
Branksome Wy
KTN/HRWW/W HA3 62 B3
NWMAL KT3 175 K5
Bransby Rd CHSGTN KT9 206 A5
Branscombe Gdns WCHMH N21 35 G2
Branscombe St LEW SE13 144 E4
Bransdale Cl KIL/WHAMP NW6 82 E6
Bransell Cl SWLY BR8 203 K3
Bransgrove Rd EDGE HA8 44 B4
Branston Crs STMC/STPC BR5 201 J5
Branstone Rd RCH/KEW TW9 137 G2
Brants Wk HNWL W7 96 E3
Brantwood Av ERITH DA8 149 K1
ISLW TW7 136 B5
Brantwood Cl WALTH * E17 51 K6
Brantwood Gdns ENC/FH EN2 22 E5
REDBR IG4 71 J2
Brantwood Rd BXLYHN DA7 149 J3
HNHL SE24 142 D6
SAND/SEL CR2 211 J6
TOTM N17 50 C2
Brantwood Wy
STMC/STPC BR5 186 D6
Brasenose Dr BARN SW13 119 F6
Brasher Cl GFD/PVL UB6 78 D3
Brassey Cl EBED/NFELT * TW14 153 K3
Brassey Rd KIL/WHAMP NW6 82 D4
Brassey Sq BTSEA SW11 141 F4
Brassie Av ACT W3 99 G5
Brasted Cl BXLYHS DA6 148 E6
SYD SE26 163 K6
Brasted Rd ERITH DA8 150 B1
Brathway Rd
WAND/EARL SW18 159 K2
Bratley St WCHPL E1 104 C3
Braund Av GFD/PVL UB6 96 B3
Braundton Av BFN/LL DA15 168 A3
Braunston Dr YEAD UB4 95 J3
Bravington Pl MV/WKIL W9 100 D3
Bravington Rd MV/WKIL W9 100 D2
Braxfield Rd BROCKY SE4 144 B5
Braxted Pk STRHM/NOR SW16 180 A2
Brayard's Rd PECK SE15 143 J3
Braybourne Dr ISLW TW7 136 A1
Braybrooke Gdns NRWD SE19 181 F3
Braybrook St SHB W12 99 H4
Brayburne Av VX/NE SW8 141 H3
Braycourt Av WOT/HER KT12 188 B4
Bray Crs BERM/RHTH SE16 124 A2
Braydon Rd STNW/STAM N16 68 B5
Bray Dr CAN/RD E16 106 D6
Brayfield Ter IS N1 85 G5
Brayford Sq WCHPL * E1 104 E5
Bray Pl CHEL SW3 120 E5
Bray Rd MLHL NW7 46 B2
Brayton Gdns ENC/FH EN2 22 D5
Braywood Rd ELTH/MOT SE9 147 J5
Breach La DAGW RM9 110 C2
Bread St BLKFR EC4V 12 D5
Breakspears Dr
STMC/STPC BR5 186 B4
Breakspears Ms BROCKY SE4 144 D3
Breakspears Rd BROCKY SE4 144 C4
Bream Cl TOTM N17 68 D1
Bream Gdns EHAM E6 108 A2
Breamore Cl PUT/ROE SW15 158 D3
Breamore Rd GDMY/SEVK IG3 73 F6
Bream's Buildings LINN WC2A 11 J3
Bream St BOW E3 87 J5
Breamwater Gdns
RCHPK/HAM TW10 156 C5
Brearley Cl EDGE HA8 44 E3
Breasley Cl PUT/ROE SW15 138 E5
Breasy Pl HDN * NW4 63 K1
Brechin Pl SKENS SW7 120 B5
Brecknock Rd ARCH N19 84 C2
Brecknock Road Est ARCH * N19 84 D3
Brecon Cl MTCM CR4 195 K1
WPK KT4 193 F6
Brecon Gn CDALE/KGS * NW9 63 G3
Brecon Ms KTTN NW5 84 D4
Brecon Rd HMSMTH W6 119 H6
PEND EN3 24 E5
Brede Cl EHAM E6 108 A2
Bredgar Rd ARCH N19 66 C6
Bredhurst Cl PGE/AN SE20 181 K2
Bredon Rd CROY/NA CR0 197 G4
Breer St FUL/PGN SW6 140 A4
Breezer's Hl WAP * E1W 104 C6
Brember Rd RYLN/HDSTN HA2 60 C6
Bremer Ms WALTH E17 69 K1
Bremner Rd SKENS * SW7 120 B3
Brenchley Cl CHST BR7 185 F4
HAYES BR2 199 J2
Brenchley Gdns FSTH SE23 163 K1
Brenchley Rd STMC/STPC BR5 185 K4
Brenda Rd TOOT SW17 160 E4
Brende Gdns E/WMO/HCT KT8 189 G1
Brendon SCUP * DA14 168 B6
Brendon Av WLSDN NW10 81 G2
Brendon Cl ERITH DA8 150 B2
ESH/CLAY KT10 204 C4
HYS/HAR UB3 133 F1
Brendon Dr ESH/CLAY KT10 204 C4
Brendon Gdns RYLN/HDSTN HA2 78 B2
Brendon Gv EFNCH N2 47 G5
Brendon Rd BCTR RM8 74 B5
CHST BR7 167 J4
Brendon St MBLAR W1H 8 D3
Brendon Vls WCHMH * N21 35 J3
Brendon Wy EN EN1 36 A2
Brenley Cl MTCM CR4 179 F6
Brenley Gdns ELTH/MOT SE9 146 C5
Brent Cl BXLY DA5 169 F3
Brentcot Cl WEA W13 97 H3
Brent Crs WLSDN NW10 98 B1
Brent Cross F/O HDN NW4 64 A3
Brentfield WLSDN NW10 80 D5
Brentfield Cl WLSDN NW10 81 F4
Brentfield Gdns CRICK * NW2 64 B4
Brentfield Rd DART DA1 171 K1
WLSDN NW10 81 F4
Brentford Cl YEAD UB4 95 H3
Brent Gn HDN NW4 64 A2
Brentham Wy EA W5 97 K3
Brenthouse Rd HACK E8 86 D5
Brenthurst Rd WLSDN NW10 81 H4
Brentlands Dr DART DA1 171 K3
Brent La DART DA1 171 J2
Brent Lea BTFD TW8 136 D1
Brentmead Cl HNWL W7 96 E6
Brentmead Gdns WLSDN NW10 98 B1
Brenton St POP/IOD E14 105 G5
Brent Park Rd CDALE/KGS NW9 63 J5
Brent Pl BAR EN5 20 E6
Brent River Park Wk WEA W13 97 H2
Brent Rd BTFD TW8 116 D6
CAN/RD E16 106 E5
NWDGN UB2 114 B3
SAND/SEL CR2 212 D6
WOOL/PLUM SE18 147 G1
Brentside BTFD TW8 116 D6
Brentside Cl WEA W13 97 F3
Brent St HDN NW4 64 A1
Brent Ter CRICK NW2 64 A6
Brentvale Av ALP/SUD HA0 80 B6
STHL UB1 115 J1
Brent View Rd CDALE/KGS NW9 63 J3
Brent Wy BTFD TW8 136 E1
FNCH N3 46 E2
WBLY HA9 80 D4
Brentwick Gdns BTFD TW8 117 F4
Brentwood Cl ELTH/MOT SE9 167 H3
Brentwood Rd ROM RM1 75 H3
Brereton Rd TOTM N17 50 B3
Bressenden Pl WESTW SW1E 15 K4
Bressey Av EN EN1 24 C2
Bressey Gv SWFD E18 52 D5
Brett Cl NTHLT UB5 95 H2
STNW/STAM N16 68 A6
Brett Crs WLSDN NW10 81 F5
Brettell St WALW SE17 122 E5
Brettenham Av WALTH E17 51 J4
Brettenham Rd UED N18 36 C6
WALTH E17 51 J5
Brett Gdns DAGW RM9 92 A5
Brett Pas HACK E8 86 D3
Brett Rd BAR EN5 20 A6
HACK E8 86 D3
Brett Vls ACT * W3 99 F4
Brewers Fld RDART DA2 171 F6
Brewer St REGST W1B 10 B5
Brewery Cl ALP/SUD HA0 79 G3
Brewery Rd HAYES BR2 200 D5
HOLWY N7 84 E5
WOOL/PLUM SE18 127 J5
Brewery Sq STHWK SE1 19 J1
Brewhouse La WAP E1W 123 J1
Brewhouse Rd
WOOL/PLUM SE18 126 E4
Brewhouse St PUT/ROE SW15 139 H5
Brewhouse Wk
BERM/RHTH SE16 124 B1
Brewhouse Yd FSBYE EC1V 6 A6
Brewood Rd BCTR RM8 91 H4
Brewster Gdns NKENS W10 100 A4
Brewster Rd LEY E10 69 K5
Brian Cl HCH RM12 93 K2
Brian Rd CHDH RM6 73 J2
Briants Cl PIN HA5 41 J4
Briant St NWCR SE14 144 A2
Briar Av STRHM/NOR SW16 180 A3
Briarbank Rd WEA W13 97 G5
Briar Cl BKHH IG9 39 H4
EFNCH N2 47 G5
HPTN TW12 172 E1
ISLW TW7 136 A6
PLMGR N13 35 J5
Briar Crs NTHLT UB5 78 B4
Briardale Gdns CRICK NW2 82 E1
Briarfield Av EFNCH N2 47 F6
Briar Gdns HAYES BR2 199 J5
Briar La CAR SM5 210 A6
CROY/NA CR0 213 K2
Briar Rd BXLY DA5 170 A5
CRICK NW2 82 A2
KTN/HRWW/W HA3 61 J2
STRHM/NOR SW16 179 K6
WHTN TW2 155 K3
Briarswood Wy ORP BR6 217 F3
Briar Wk EDGE HA8 44 E3
NKENS * W10 100 C3
PUT/ROE SW15 138 E5
Briar Wy WDR/YW UB7 112 D2
Briarwood Cl CDALE/KGS * NW9 62 E3
FELT TW13 153 H5
Briarwood Ct WPK * KT4 192 D5
Briarwood Dr NTHWD HA6 40 E5
Briarwood Rd CLAP SW4 141 J6
EW KT17 207 J4
Briary Cl EDGE HA8 44 D5
HAMP * NW3 83 J5
Briary Ct SCUP DA14 186 C1
Briary Gdns BMLY BR1 184 A1
Briary La ED N9 36 A5
Brickbarn Cl WBPTN * SW10 140 B1
Brick Ct EMB * EC4Y 11 J4
Brickett Cl RSLP HA4 58 A2
Brick Farm Cl RCH/KEW TW9 137 J2
Brickfield Cl BTFD TW8 136 D1
Brickfield Cottages
WOOL/PLUM SE18 148 A1
Brickfield Farm Gdns ORP BR6 216 C2
Brickfield La BAR EN5 31 H1
HYS/HAR UB3 113 G6
Brickfield Rd BOW E3 105 K3
THHTH CR7 180 C4
WIM/MER SW19 160 A6
Brickfields RYLN/HDSTN HA2 60 D6
Brickfields Wy WDR/YW UB7 112 C3
Brickfield Vls SUT * SM1 209 J1
Brick Kiln Cl BUSH WD23 27 J1
Brick La EN EN1 24 D3
STAN HA7 43 K3
WCHPL E1 7 K7
Brick St MYFR/PICC W1J 15 J1
Brickwall La RSLP HA4 58 C5
Brickwood Cl SYD SE26 163 J5
Brickwood Rd CROY/NA CR0 197 F6
Brideale Cl PECK * SE15 123 G6
Bride Ct BLKFR * EC4V 12 A4
Bride La EMB EC4Y 12 A4
Bridel Ms FSBYE EC1V 6 A3
Bride St HOLWY N7 85 F4
Bridewain St STHWK SE1 19 J4
Bridewell Pl BLKFR EC4V 12 A4
WAP E1W 123 J1
Bridford Ms REGST W1B 9 K1
The Bridge EA * W5 117 G1
KTN/HRWW/W HA3 43 F6
Bridge Av HMSMTH W6 119 F5
HNWL W7 96 D4
Bridge Cl EN EN1 24 D3
NKENS W10 100 B5
ROM RM1 75 G3
Bridge Dr PLMGR N13 35 F6
Bridge End WALTH E17 52 A4
Bridgefield Rd SUT SM1 208 E4
Bridge Gdns E/WMO/HCT KT8 189 J1
Bridge Ga WCHMH N21 35 J2
Bridge House Quay
POP/IOD E14 125 F1
Bridgeland Rd CAN/RD E16 106 E6
Bridge La BTSEA SW11 140 D2
GLDGN NW11 64 C2
Bridgeman Rd IS N1 85 F5
TEDD TW11 174 B2
Bridgeman St STJWD NW8 2 C3
Bridge Mdw NWCR SE14 124 A6
Bridgenhall Rd EN EN1 24 B2
Bridgen Rd BXLY DA5 169 F2
Bridge Pde STRHM/NOR * SW16 179 K1
WCHMH * N21 35 J2
Bridge Pl CROY/NA CR0 196 E5
PIM SW1V 15 K6
Bridgeport Pl WAP * E1W 123 H1
Bridge Rd BECK BR3 182 C3
BXLYHN DA7 149 F4
CHSGTN KT9 206 A3
E/WMO/HCT KT8 189 K1
ED N9 36 C5
EHAM E6 89 K5
ERITH DA8 150 D2
HSLW TW3 135 J4
NWDGN UB2 114 E2
RAIN RM13 111 J3
SRTFD E15 88 B6
STMC/STPC BR5 202 C3
SUT SM1 209 F4
TWK TW1 156 C1
WALTH E17 69 H4
WBLY HA9 80 C1
WDGN N22 48 E4
WLGTN SM6 210 B3
WLSDN NW10 81 G4
Bridge Rw CROY/NA * CR0 196 E5
Bridges Ct BTSEA SW11 140 C4
Bridges La CROY/NA CR0 210 E2
Bridges Rd STAN HA7 43 F1
Bridge St CHSWK W4 118 A4
PIN HA5 41 H6
TWK TW1 156 E1
WEST SW1P 16 E3
Bridge Ter LEW * SE13 145 G5
SRTFD E15 88 B5
Bridgetown Cl NRWD SE19 181 F1
Bridgeview HMSMTH W6 119 F5
Bridge Vls WIM/MER * SW19 177 K1
Bridgewater Cl CHST BR7 185 K6
Bridgewater Gdns EDGE HA8 44 B5
Bridgewater Rd ALP/SUD HA0 79 H4
SRTFD E15 88 A6
Bridgewater Sq BARB * EC2Y 12 C1
Bridgewater St BARB EC2Y 12 C1
Bridgewater Wy BUSH WD23 28 B1
Bridgeway ALP/SUD HA0 80 A5
BARK IG11 91 F5
Bridge Wy GLDGN NW11 64 D2
WHTN TW2 155 H2
Bridgeway St CAMTN NW1 4 B3
Bridgewood Cl PGE/AN SE20 181 J3
Bridgewood Rd
STRHM/NOR SW16 179 J3
WPK KT4 207 J2
Bridgford St WAND/EARL SW18 160 B5
Bridgman Rd CHSWK W4 117 K3
Bridgwater Rd RSLP HA4 77 F2
Bridle Cl HOR/WEW KT19 206 E2
KUT KT1 190 E1
Bridle La SOHO/CST W1F 10 B5
TWK TW1 156 C1
The Bridle Pth WFD IG8 52 C3
Bridle Pth CROY/NA CR0 210 E1
Bridlepath Wy
EBED/NFELT TW14 153 H2
Bridle Rd CROY/NA CR0 213 J2
ESH/CLAY KT10 205 H4
PIN HA5 59 G3
The Bridle Wy WLGTN SM6 210 C2
Bridle Wy CROY/NA CR0 213 J3
ORP BR6 216 C2
Bridlington Rd ED N9 36 D2
OXHEY WD19 27 H5
Bridport Av ROMW/RG RM7 74 D3
Bridport Pl IS N1 7 F2
Bridport Rd NTHLT UB5 78 B6
THHTH CR7 180 B6
UED N18 50 A1
Bridstow Pl BAY/PAD W2 100 E5
Brief St CMBW SE5 142 C2
Brierley Av ED N9 36 E3
Brierley Cl SNWD SE25 197 H1
Brierley Rd BAL SW12 161 H4
WAN E11 88 B2
Brierly Gdns BETH * E2 104 E1
Brigade Cl RYLN/HDSTN HA2 60 D6
Brigade St BKHTH/KID * SE3 145 J3
Brigadier Av ENC/FH EN2 23 J2
Brigadier Hl ENC/FH EN2 23 J1
Briggeford Cl CLPT E5 68 C6
Briggs Cl MTCM CR4 179 G4
Bright Cl BELV DA17 128 E4
Brightfield Rd LEW SE13 145 H6
Brightling Rd BROCKY SE4 164 C1
Brightlingsea Pl POP/IOD E14 105 H6
Brightman Rd
WAND/EARL SW18 160 C3
Brighton Av WALTH E17 69 H2
Brighton Dr NTHLT * UB5 78 A4
Brighton Rd BELMT SM2 209 G5
EFNCH N2 47 G5
EHAM E6 108 A2
SAND/SEL CR2 211 J6
STNW/STAM N16 86 A2
SURB KT6 190 D3
Brighton Ter BRXN/ST SW9 142 A5
Brights Av RAIN RM13 111 K3
The Brightside PEND EN3 25 F2
Brightside Rd LEW SE13 165 G1
Bright St POP/IOD E14 105 K5
Brightwell Cl CROY/NA CR0 196 B5
Brightwell Crs TOOT SW17 178 E1
Brig Ms DEPT SE8 124 D6
Brigstock Rd BELV DA17 129 J4
THHTH CR7 196 C2
Brill Pl CAMTN NW1 4 D3
Brim Hl EFNCH N2 65 G1
Brimpsfield Cl ABYW SE2 128 C3
Brimsdown Av PEND EN3 25 G2
Brimstone Cl ORP BR6 217 J5
Brindle Ga BFN/LL DA15 167 K3
Brindley Cl BXLYHN DA7 149 H4
GFD/PVL UB6 79 J6
Brindley St NWCR SE14 144 C2
Brindley Wy BMLY BR1 183 K1
STHL UB1 96 B6
Brindwood Rd CHING E4 37 J5
Brinkburn Cl ABYW SE2 128 B4
EDGE HA8 44 D6
Brinkburn Gdns EDGE HA8 44 C6
Brinkley Rd WPK KT4 192 E6
Brinklow Crs WOOL/PLUM SE18 147 G1
Brinkworth Rd CLAY IG5 53 J6
Brinkworth Wy HOM * E9 87 H4
Brinsdale Rd HDN NW4 46 B6
Brinsley Rd KTN/HRWW/W HA3 42 D5
Brinsley St WCHPL * E1 104 D5
Brinsworth Cl WHTN TW2 155 J3
Brinton Wk STHWK SE1 18 A1
Brion Pl POP/IOD E14 106 A4
Brisbane Av WIM/MER SW19 178 A4
Brisbane Rd IL IG1 72 C4
LEY E10 69 K6
Brisbane St CMBW SE5 142 E1
Briscoe Cl WAN E11 70 D6
Briscoe Rd WIM/MER SW19 178 C2
Briset Rd ELTH/MOT SE9 146 C4
Briset St FARR EC1M 12 A1
Briset Wy HOLWY N7 67 F6
Bristol Cl STWL/WRAY TW19 152 B1
WLGTN SM6 210 E6
Bristol Gdns MV/WKIL W9 101 F3
Bristol Ms MV/WKIL W9 101 F3
Bristol Park Rd WALTH * E17 69 G1
Bristol Rd FSTGT E7 89 G4
GFD/PVL UB6 78 B6
MRDN SM4 194 B2
Briston Gv CEND/HSY/T N8 66 E3
Bristow Rd BXLYHN DA7 149 F2
CROY/NA CR0 210 E2
HSLW TW3 135 G4
NRWD SE19 181 F1
Britannia Cl CLAP SW4 141 J5
ERITH DA8 130 C6
NTHLT UB5 95 H2
Britannia Ga CAN/RD E16 125 K1
Britannia Rd BRYLDS KT5 191 G4
FUL/PGN SW6 140 A1
IL IG1 90 B1
NFNCH/WDSP N12 33 G5
POP/IOD E14 124 D4
Britannia Rw IS N1 85 H6
Britannia St FSBYW WC1X 5 G4
Britannia Wk IS N1 6 E4
Britannia Wy FUL/PGN SW6 140 A1
STWL/WRAY TW19 152 A2
WLSDN NW10 98 D3
British Est BOW E3 105 H2
British Gv CHSWK W4 118 C5
British Grove Pas CHSWK * W4 118 C5
British Legion Rd CHING E4 38 D4
British St BOW E3 105 H2
Brittain Rd BCTR RM8 92 A1
Britten Cl BORE WD6 29 K1
GLDGN NW11 65 F5
Brittenden Pde ORP * BR6 217 F4
Britten Dr STHL UB1 96 A5
Britten St CHEL SW3 120 D5
Britton Cl CAT SE6 165 G2
Britton St FARR EC1M 6 A7
Brixham Crs RSLP HA4 58 E5
Brixham Gdns GDMY/SEVK IG3 90 E3
Brixham Rd WELL DA16 148 E2
Brixham St CAN/RD E16 126 E1
Brixton Hl BRXS/STRHM SW2 162 A1
Brixton Hill Pl
BRXS/STRHM SW2 161 K2
Brixton Ov BRXN/ST SW9 142 B5
Brixton Rd BRXN/ST SW9 142 B3
LBTH SE11 122 B6
Brixton Station Rd
BRXN/ST SW9 142 B4
Brixton Water La
BRXS/STRHM SW2 142 B6
Broadbent St MYFR/PKLN * W1K 9 J5
Broad Bridge Cl
BKHTH/KID SE3 145 K1
Broad Common Est
STNW/STAM * N16 68 C5
Broadcoombe SAND/SEL CR2 213 F5
Broad Ct COVGDN * WC2E 11 F4
Broadcroft Av STAN HA7 43 K5
Broadcroft Rd STMC/STPC BR5 201 J4
Broadeaves Cl SAND/SEL CR2 212 A3
Broadfield Cl CRICK NW2 82 A1
ROM RM1 75 H2
Broadfield Ct BUSH WD23 28 E4
Broadfield La CAMTN NW1 84 E5
Broadfield Pde EDGE * HA8 30 D5
Broadfield Rd CAT SE6 165 H3
Broadfields E/WMO/HCT KT8 189 J3
PIN HA5 42 B5
Broadfields Av EDGE HA8 30 D6
WCHMH N21 35 G2
Broadfields Hts EDGE HA8 30 D6
Broadfields La OXHEY WD19 27 F3
Broadfield Sq EN EN1 24 D4
Broadfields Wy WLSDN NW10 81 H3
Broadfield Wy BKHH IG9 39 G5
Broadgates Av EBAR EN4 21 F2
Broadgates Rd
WAND/EARL SW18 160 C3
Broad Green Av CROY/NA CR0 196 C4
Broadhead Strd
CDALE/KGS NW9 45 H5
Broadheath Dr CHST BR7 184 E1
Broadhinton Rd CLAP SW4 141 G4
Broadhurst Av EDGE HA8 30 D6
GDMY/SEVK IG3 91 F2
Broadhurst Cl KIL/WHAMP NW6 83 G4
Broadhurst Gdns
KIL/WHAMP NW6 83 F4
RSLP HA4 59 G6
Broadlands FELT TW13 154 E5
Broadlands Av PEND EN3 24 D4
STRHM/NOR SW16 161 K4
Broadlands Cl HGT N6 66 A4
PEND EN3 24 D4
STRHM/NOR SW16 161 K4
Broadlands Rd BMLY BR1 166 A6
HGT N6 65 K4
Broadlands Wy NWMAL KT3 192 C3
Broad La HPTN TW12 172 E3
RDART DA2 170 E6
SEVS/STOTM N15 68 B2
Broad Lawn ELTH/MOT SE9 167 F4
Broadlawns Ct
KTN/HRWW/W HA3 43 F4
Broadley St STJWD NW8 8 C1
Broadley Ter STJWD NW8 2 D7
Broadmead CAT SE6 164 D5
Broadmead Av WPK KT4 192 D4
Broadmead Cl HPTN TW12 173 F2
PIN * HA5 41 J3
Broadmead Rd WFD IG8 52 E2
YEAD UB4 95 J3
Broad Oak WFD IG8 53 F1
Broad Oak Cl CHING E4 51 J1
STMC/STPC BR5 186 B5
Broadoak Rd ERITH DA8 150 A1
Broad Oaks SURB KT6 191 J5
Broad Oaks Wy HAYES BR2 199 J2
Broadstone Pl MHST W1U 9 G2
Broadstone Rd HCH RM12 75 J6
Broad St DAGE RM10 92 C5
TEDD TW11 174 A2
Broad Street Av LVPST EC2M 13 G2
Broad Street Pl LVPST EC2M 13 F2
Broadview CDALE/KGS NW9 62 C3
Broadview Rd
STRHM/NOR SW16 179 J3
Broad Wk BKHTH/KID SE3 146 B3
HEST TW5 134 C2
ORP BR6 217 K1
RCH/KEW TW9 137 G1
WCHMH N21 35 G3

Broadwalk RYLN/HDSTN * HA2 60 B2
SWFD E18 52 D6
Broadwalk La GLDGN NW11 64 D4
The Broad Wk KENS W8 120 B2
NTHWD HA6 40 A5
Broadwall STHWK SE1 11 K7
Broadwater Gdns ORP BR6 216 B2
Broadwater Rd TOOT SW17 160 D6
TOTM N17 50 A5
WOOL/PLUM SE18 127 J3
The Broadway ACT * W3 117 H2
BCTR RM8 74 B6
CDALE/KGS NW9 63 H3
CEND/HSY/T N8 66 E3
CHEAM SM3 208 C4
EA W5 97 K6
FBAR/BDGN * N11 47 K1
HCH RM12 93 K2
KTN/HRWW/W HA3 42 E5
MLHL NW7 45 G1
PIN HA5 41 K3
PLSTW E13 106 E1
RYLN/HDSTN * HA2 60 D6
STAN HA7 43 J1
THDIT KT7 189 K5
WFD IG8 53 F2
WIM/MER SW19 177 J2
Broadway BARK IG11 90 C6
BXLYHS DA6 149 F5
GPK RM2 57 J6
HNWL W7 115 K1
RAIN RM13 111 J3
SRTFD E15 88 B5
STJSPK SW1H 16 C4
SURB KT6 191 J5
SUT SM1 209 G2
Broadway Av CROY/NA CR0 196 E2
TWK TW1 156 C1
Broadway Cl WFD IG8 53 F2
Broadway Ct WIM/MER * SW19 177 K2
Broadway Gdns MTCM CR4 194 D1
Broadway Market HACK E8 86 D6
Broadway Market Ms HACK * E8 86 C6
Broadway Ms STNW/STAM N16 68 B4
Broadway Pde CHING * E4 52 A2
HYS/HAR * UB3 113 J2
RYLN/HDSTN * HA2 60 B2
WDR/YW * UB7 112 B2
Broadwell Pde
KIL/WHAMP * NW6 83 G4
Broadwick St SOHO/CST W1F 10 B4
Broadwood Av RSLP HA4 58 D3
Broadwood Ter WKENS * W14 119 J4
Broad Yd FARR EC1M 6 A7
Brocas Cl HAMP NW3 83 J5
Brockdene Dr HAYES BR2 215 H2
Brockdish Av BARK IG11 91 F3
Brockenhurst E/WMO/HCT KT8 188 E2
Brockenhurst Av WPK KT4 192 B5
Brockenhurst Gdns IL IG1 90 C3
MLHL NW7 45 G2
Brockenhurst Rd CROY/NA CR0 197 J4
Brockenhurst Wy
STRHM/NOR SW16 179 J5
Brocket Wy CHIG IG7 54 E1
Brockham Cl WIM/MER SW19 177 J1
Brockham Crs CROY/NA CR0 214 B5
Brockham Dr
BRXS/STRHM SW2 162 A2
GNTH/NBYPK IG2 72 C3
Brockham St STHWK SE1 18 D4
Brockhurst Cl STAN HA7 43 F2
Brockill Crs BROCKY SE4 144 B5
Brocklebank Rd CHARL SE7 126 A4
WAND/EARL SW18 160 B2
Brocklehurst St NWCR SE14 144 A1
Brocklesby Rd SNWD SE25 197 J1
Brockley Av EDGE HA8 30 A5
Brockley Cl STAN HA7 30 A6
Brockley Crs CRW RM5 56 E3
Brockley Cross BROCKY SE4 144 B4
Brockley Gv BROCKY SE4 144 C6
Brockley Hall Rd BROCKY SE4 164 B1
Brockley Hl STAN HA7 29 J4
Brockley Ms BROCKY SE4 144 B6
Brockley Pk FSTH SE23 164 B2
Brockley Ri FSTH SE23 164 B2
Brockley Rd BROCKY SE4 164 B1
Brockleyside STAN * HA7 30 A6
Brockley Vw FSTH SE23 164 B2
Brockley Wy FSTH SE23 144 A6
Brockman Ri BMLY BR1 165 G6
Brock Pl BOW E3 105 K3
Brock Rd PLSTW E13 107 F4
Brocks Dr CHEAM SM3 208 C1
Brockshot Cl BTFD TW8 116 E6
Brock St PECK * SE15 143 K4
Brockton Cl ROM RM1 75 H1
Brockway Cl WAN E11 70 C6
Brockwell Cl STMC/STPC BR5 202 A2
Brockwell Park Gdns
HNHL SE24 162 C2
Brockworth Cl PECK SE15 123 F6
Brodia Rd STNW/STAM N16 86 A1
Brodie Rd CHING E4 38 A3
ENC/FH EN2 23 J1
Brodie St STHWK SE1 123 G5
Brodlove La WAP E1W 105 F6
Brodrick Gv ABYW SE2 128 C4
Brodrick Rd TOOT SW17 160 D4
Brograve Gdns BECK BR3 182 E5
Broke Farm Dr ORP BR6 217 J6
Brokesley St BOW E3 105 H3
Broke Wk HACK * E8 86 C6
Bromar Rd CMBW SE5 143 F4
Bromborough Gn OXHEY WD19 41 G1
Bromefield STAN HA7 43 J4
Bromehead St WCHPL E1 104 E5
Brome House
WOOL/PLUM SE18 146 D1
Bromell's Rd CLAP SW4 141 H5
Brome Rd ELTH/MOT SE9 146 E4
Bromfelde Rd CLAP SW4 141 J4
Bromfield St IS N1 5 K2
Bromhall Rd DAGW RM9 91 H4
Bromhedge ELTH/MOT SE9 166 E5
Bromholm Rd ABYW SE2 128 C3
Bromley Av BMLY BR1 183 H3
Bromley Common HAYES BR2 200 D4
Bromley Crs HAYES BR2 183 J6
RSLP HA4 76 D2
Bromley Gdns HAYES BR2 183 J5
Bromley Gv HAYES BR2 183 G5
Bromley Hall Rd POP/IOD E14 106 A4
Bromley High St BOW E3 105 K2
Bromley Hl BMLY BR1 183 H2
Bromley La CHST BR7 185 H3
Bromley Rd BECK BR3 182 E4
CAT SE6 164 E5
CHST BR7 185 G4
HAYES BR2 183 H5
LEY E10 69 K3
TOTM N17 50 B4
UED N18 35 K6
WALTH E17 51 J6
Bromley St WCHPL E1 105 F4
Brompton Ar KTBR * SW1X 14 E3
Brompton Cl HSLWW TW4 134 E6
Brompton Cottages
WBPTN * SW10 120 B6
Brompton Dr ERITH DA8 150 E1
Brompton Gv EFNCH N2 65 J1
Brompton Park Crs
FUL/PGN SW6 120 A6
Brompton Pl CHEL SW3 14 D4
Brompton Rd CHEL SW3 14 C6
Brompton Sq CHEL SW3 14 C4
Brompton Ter
WOOL/PLUM * SE18 147 F2
Bromwich Av HGT N6 66 A6
Bromyard Av ACT W3 118 B1
Brondesbury Ms
KIL/WHAMP * NW6 82 E5
Brondesbury Pk CRICK NW2 82 A5
Brondesbury Rd
KIL/WHAMP NW6 100 D1
Brondesbury Vls
KIL/WHAMP NW6 100 D1
Bronhill Ter TOTM * N17 50 C4
Bronsart Rd FUL/PGN SW6 139 H1
Bronson Rd RYNPK SW20 177 G5
Bronte Cl ERITH DA8 149 J1
FSTGT * E7 88 E2
GNTH/NBYPK IG2 72 A2
Bronte Gv DART DA1 151 J5
Bronti Cl WALW SE17 122 D5
Bronze Age Wy BELV DA17 129 K3
Bronze St DEPT SE8 144 D1
Brook Av DAGE RM10 92 D5
EDGE HA8 44 D2
WBLY HA9 80 C1
Brookbank Av HNWL W7 96 D4
Brookbank Rd LEW SE13 144 E4
Brook Cl ACT W3 117 H1
GPK RM2 57 H4
HOR/WEW KT19 207 G6
RSLP HA4 58 C4
RYNPK SW20 176 E6
STWL/WRAY TW19 152 C2
TOOT SW17 161 F4
Brook Ct BECK * BR3 182 C4
Brook Crs CHING E4 37 J6
ED N9 36 D6
Brookdale FBAR/BDGN N11 34 C6
Brookdale Rd BXLY DA5 169 F1
CAT SE6 164 E2
WALTH E17 51 J6
Brookdene Av OXHEY WD19 27 F2
Brookdene Dr NTHWD HA6 40 D3
Brookdene Rd
WOOL/PLUM SE18 127 K4
Brook Dr RSLP HA4 58 C3
RYLN/HDSTN HA2 60 C1
STHWK SE1 17 K5
Brooke Av RYLN/HDSTN HA2 78 C1
Brooke Cl BUSH WD23 28 C2
Brookehowse Rd CAT SE6 164 E5
Brookend Rd BFN/LL DA15 167 K3
Brooke Rd CLPT E5 86 C1
WALTH E17 70 A1
Brooke's Market HCIRC * EC1N 11 J1
Brooke St HCIRC EC1N 11 J2
Brooke Wy BUSH WD23 28 C2
Brookfield Av EA W5 97 K3
MLHL NW7 45 K2
SUT SM1 209 J1
WALTH E17 70 A1
Brookfield Cl MLHL NW7 45 K2
Brookfield Crs
KTN/HRWW/W HA3 62 A2
MLHL NW7 45 K2
Brookfield Gdns
ESH/CLAY KT10 205 F4
Brookfield Pk KTTN NW5 84 B1
Brookfield Pth CHING E4 52 B2
Brookfield Rd CHSWK W4 118 A2
ED N9 36 C5
HOM E9 87 G4
Brookfields PEND EN3 25 F5
Brookfields Av MTCM CR4 194 D2
Brook Gdns BARN SW13 138 C4
CHING E4 37 K6
KUTN/CMB KT2 175 K4
Brook Ga BAY/PAD W2 9 F6
Brook Gn HMSMTH W6 119 F3
Brookhill Cl EBAR EN4 21 J6
Brook Hill Cl WOOL/PLUM SE18 127 G5
Brookhill Rd
WOOL/PLUM SE18 127 G5
Brookhouse Gdns CHING E4 38 C6
Brooking Cl BCTR RM8 91 J1
Brooking Rd FSTGT E7 88 E3
Brookland Cl GLDGN NW11 64 E1
Brookland Garth GLDGN NW11 64 E1
Brookland Hl GLDGN NW11 64 E1
Brookland Ri GLDGN NW11 64 E1
The Brooklands ISLW * TW7 135 J2
Brooklands DART DA1 171 H3
Brooklands Ap ROM RM1 75 F1
Brooklands Av BFN/LL DA15 167 J4
WAND/EARL SW18 160 A4
Brooklands Cl ROMW/RG RM7 75 F1
Brooklands Ct
KIL/WHAMP * NW6 82 D5
WCHMH N21 23 K6
Brooklands Dr GFD/PVL UB6 79 J6
Brooklands La ROMW/RG RM7 75 F1
Brooklands Pk BKHTH/KID SE3 145 K4
Brooklands Rd ROMW/RG RM7 75 F1
THDIT KT7 190 A5
Brook La BKHTH/KID SE3 146 A3
BMLY BR1 183 K2
BXLY DA5 168 E1
Brook La North BTFD TW8 116 E5
Brooklea Cl CDALE/KGS NW9 45 G4
Brooklyn Av SNWD SE25 197 J1
Brooklyn Cl CAR SM5 194 D6
Brooklyn Gv SNWD SE25 197 J1
Brooklyn Rd HAYES BR2 200 C2
SNWD SE25 197 J1
Brooklyn Wy WDR/YW UB7 112 A3
Brook Md HOR/WEW KT19 207 G4
Brookmead MTCM CR4 195 H3
Brookmead Av HAYES BR2 200 E2
Brookmead Cl ORP BR6 202 C4
Brook Meadow
NFNCH/WDSP N12 33 F6
Brook Meadow Cl WFD IG8 52 C2
Brookmead Rd CROY/NA CR0 195 H3
Brook Ms North BAY/PAD W2 101 G6
Brookmill Cl OXHEY * WD19 27 F2
Brookmill Rd DEPT SE8 144 D2
Brook Park Cl WCHMH N21 35 H1
Brook Pl BAR EN5 20 E6
Brook Rd BKHH IG9 38 E4
CEND/HSY/T N8 66 E1
CRICK NW2 63 J6
GNTH/NBYPK IG2 72 E3
GPK RM2 57 H5
SURB KT6 191 F6
THHTH CR7 196 D1
TWK TW1 156 B1
WDGN * N22 49 F5
Brook Rd South BTFD TW8 117 F6
Brooks Av EHAM E6 107 K3
Brooksbank St HOM * E9 87 F4
Brooksby Ms IS N1 85 G5
Brooksby St IS N1 85 G5
Brooksby's Wk HOM E9 87 F3
Brookscroft CROY/NA * CR0 213 H6
Brookscroft Rd WALTH E17 51 K4
Brookshill KTN/HRWW/W HA3 42 E2
Brookshill Av
KTN/HRWW/W HA3 42 D1
Brookshill Dr KTN/HRWW/W HA3 42 D1
Brookside BARK/HLT IG6 54 C2
CAR SM5 210 A3
EBAR EN4 33 J1
ORP BR6 202 A4
WCHMH N21 35 F1
Brookside Cl BAR EN5 32 B1
FELT TW13 153 K5
KTN/HRWW/W HA3 61 K2
RSLP HA4 77 J2
Brookside Crs WPK KT4 192 D5
Brookside Rd ED N9 36 D6
GLDGN NW11 64 C3
OXHEY WD19 27 F2
YEAD UB4 95 G6
Brookside South EBAR EN4 34 A2
Brookside Wy CROY/NA CR0 198 A3
Brooks La CHSWK W4 117 H6
Brook's Ms MYFR/PKLN W1K 9 J5
Brooks Rd CHSWK W4 117 H5
PLSTW E13 88 E6
Brook St BAY/PAD W2 8 B5
BELV DA17 129 J5
ERITH DA8 149 K1
KUT KT1 175 F5
MYFR/PKLN W1K 9 J5
Brooksville Av KIL/WHAMP NW6 82 C6
Brookview Rd
STRHM/NOR SW16 179 H1
Brookville Rd FUL/PGN SW6 139 J1
Brook Wk EDGE HA8 45 F2
EFNCH * N2 47 H4
Brook Water La HDN * NW4 64 B2
Brookway BKHTH/KID SE3 145 K4
RAIN RM13 111 K4
Brookwood Av BARN SW13 138 C4
Brookwood Cl HAYES BR2 199 J1
Brookwood Rd HSLW TW3 135 G3
WAND/EARL SW18 159 J3
Broom Av STMC/STPC BR5 186 C5
Broom Cl ESH/CLAY KT10 204 B3
HAYES BR2 200 D3
TEDD TW11 174 E3
Broomcroft Av NTHLT UB5 95 G2
Broome Rd HPTN TW12 172 E4
Broome Wy CMBW SE5 142 E1
Broomfield WALTH E17 69 H4
Broomfield Av LOU IG10 39 K1
PLMGR N13 35 F6
Broomfield Cl CRW RM5 57 F2
Broomfield Cottages
WEA * W13 116 C1
Broomfield La PLMGR N13 34 E6
Broomfield Pl WEA W13 116 C1
Broomfield Rd BECK BR3 198 B1
BRYLDS KT5 191 G5
BXLYHS DA6 149 H6
CHDH RM6 73 K4
PLMGR N13 48 E1
RCH/KEW TW9 137 G2
TEDD TW11 174 D2
WEA W13 116 C1
Broomfields ESH/CLAY KT10 204 C3
Broomfield St POP/IOD E14 105 J4
Broom Gdns CROY/NA CR0 213 J1
Broomgrove Gdns EDGE HA8 44 C4
Broomgrove Rd BRXN/ST SW9 142 A3
Broomhall Rd SAND/SEL CR2 211 K6
Broomhill Ri BXLYHS DA6 149 H6
Broomhill Rd DART DA1 170 E1
GDMY/SEVK IG3 73 G6
ORP BR6 202 B4
WAND/EARL SW18 139 K6
WFD IG8 52 E2
Broomhouse La FUL/PGN SW6 139 K3
Broomhouse Rd FUL/PGN SW6 139 K3
Broomloan La SUT SM1 193 K6
Broom Lock TEDD * TW11 174 D1
Broom Md BXLYHS DA6 169 H1
Broom Pk KUT KT1 174 E3
Broom Rd CROY/NA CR0 213 J1
TEDD TW11 174 C1
Broomsleigh St
KIL/WHAMP * NW6 82 E3
Broom Water TEDD TW11 174 D2
Broom Water West TEDD TW11 174 D1
Broomwood Cl BXLY DA5 170 A4
CROY/NA CR0 198 A2
Broomwood Rd BTSEA SW11 160 E1
STMC/STPC BR5 186 C5
Broseley Gv SYD SE26 182 B1
Broster Gdns SNWD SE25 181 G6
Brougham Rd ACT W3 98 E5
HACK E8 86 C6
Brougham St BTSEA SW11 140 E3
Brough Cl KUTN/CMB * KT2 174 E1
VX/NE SW8 141 K1
Broughton Av FNCH N3 46 C6
RCHPK/HAM TW10 156 D6
Broughton Dr BRXN/ST SW9 142 B5
Broughton Gdns HGT N6 66 C3
Broughton Rd FUL/PGN SW6 140 A3
ORP BR6 201 J6
THHTH CR7 196 B3
WEA W13 97 H6
Broughton Road Ap
FUL/PGN * SW6 140 A3
Broughton St VX/NE SW8 141 F3
Brouncker Rd ACT W3 117 K2
Brow Cl STMC/STPC BR5 202 E4
Brow Crs STMC/STPC BR5 202 D5
Browell's La FELT TW13 154 B4
Brown Cl WLGTN SM6 210 D5
Brownfield St POP/IOD E14 106 A5
Browngraves Rd WDR/YW UB7 133 F1
Brown Hart Gdns
MYFR/PKLN W1K 9 H5
Brownhill Rd CAT SE6 165 F2
Browning Av HNWL W7 97 F5
SUT SM1 209 J2
WPK KT4 192 E5
Browning Cl HPTN TW12 154 E6
MV/WKIL W9 101 G3
WALTH E17 70 A1
WELL DA16 147 K2
Browning Ms CAVSQ/HST * W1G 9 H2
Browning Rd DART DA1 151 J5
ENC/FH EN2 23 K1
MNPK E12 89 K4
WAN E11 70 D4
Browning St WALW SE17 122 D5
Browning Wy HEST TW5 134 C2
Brownlea Gdns GDMY/SEVK IG3 73 G6
Brownlow Ms FSBYW WC1X 5 H6
Brownlow Rd CROY/NA CR0 212 A2
FBAR/BDGN N11 48 E2
FNCH N3 47 F3
FSTGT E7 88 E2
HACK E8 86 B6
WEA * W13 116 B1
WLSDN NW10 81 G5
Brownlow St GINN WC1R 11 H2
Brownrigg Rd ASHF TW15 152 D6
Brownspring Dr ELTH/MOT SE9 167 G6
Brown's Rd BRYLDS KT5 191 G4
WALTH E17 51 J6
Brown St MBLAR W1H 8 E3
Brownswell Rd EFNCH N2 47 H5
Brownswood Rd FSBYPK N4 67 J6
Broxash Rd BTSEA SW11 161 F1
Broxbourne Av WAN E11 71 F1
Broxbourne House BOW E3 105 K3
Broxbourne Rd FSTGT E7 88 E1
ORP BR6 202 A5
Broxholm Rd WNWD SE27 162 B5
Broxted Rd CAT SE6 164 C4
Broxwood Wy STJWD NW8 2 D1
Bruce Castle Rd TOTM N17 50 B4
Bruce Cl NKENS W10 100 B4
WELL DA16 148 C2
Bruce Dr SAND/SEL CR2 213 F6
Bruce Gdns TRDG/WHET N20 33 K5
Bruce Gv ORP BR6 202 B5
TOTM N17 50 B5
Bruce Rd BAR * EN5 20 C4
BOW E3 105 K2
KTN/HRWW/W HA3 42 E5
MTCM CR4 179 F3
SNWD SE25 196 E1
WLSDN NW10 81 F5
Bruckner St NKENS W10 100 C2
Brudenell Rd TOOT SW17 160 E5
Bruffs Meadow NTHLT UB5 77 J4
Bruges Pl CAMTN NW1 84 C5
Brumfield Rd HOR/WEW KT19 206 E3
Brunel Cl HEST TW5 134 A1
NRWD SE19 181 G2
NTHLT UB5 95 K2
ROM RM1 75 G1
Brunel Ct WLSDN NW10 99 J2
Brunel Est BAY/PAD * W2 100 E4
Brunel Rd ACT W3 99 G4
WALTH E17 69 G3
WAP E1W 123 K1
WFD IG8 53 K1
Brunel St CAN/RD E16 106 D5
Brunel Wk WHTN TW2 155 F2
Brune St WCHPL E1 13 J2
Brunner Cl GLDGN NW11 65 F2
Brunner Rd EA W5 97 K3
WALTH E17 69 H2
Bruno Pl CDALE/KGS NW9 62 E6
Brunswick Av FBAR/BDGN N11 34 A5
Brunswick Cl BXLYHS DA6 148 E5
PIN HA5 59 J3
THDIT KT7 190 A5
WHTN TW2 155 J5
WOT/HER KT12 188 B6
Brunswick Ct STHWK SE1 19 H3
Brunswick Crs FBAR/BDGN N11 34 A5
Brunswick Gdns BARK/HLT IG6 54 C3
EA W5 98 A2
KENS W8 119 K1
Brunswick Gv FBAR/BDGN N11 34 A5
Brunswick Ms MBLAR W1H 9 F3
STRHM/NOR SW16 179 J2
Brunswick Pk CMBW SE5 142 E2
Brunswick Park Gdns
FBAR/BDGN N11 34 A4
Brunswick Park Rd
FBAR/BDGN N11 34 A4
Brunswick Pl CAMTN NW1 3 H7
IS N17 F5
NRWD SE19 181 H3
Brunswick Quay
BERM/RHTH SE16 124 A3
Brunswick Rd BXLYHS DA6 148 E5
EA W5 97 K3
KUTN/CMB KT2 175 H4
LEY E10 70 A5
PEND EN3 25 J1
SEVS/STOTM N15 68 A2
SUT SM1 209 F2
Brunswick Sq BMSBY WC1N 5 F6
Brunswick St WALTH E17 70 A2
Brunswick Vls CMBW SE5 143 F2
Brunswick Wy FBAR/BDGN N11 34 B6
Brunton Pl POP/IOD E14 105 G5
Brushfield St WCHPL E1 13 H1
Brussels Rd BTSEA SW11 140 C5
Bruton Cl CHST BR7 184 E3
Bruton La MYFR/PICC W1J 9 K6
Bruton Pl MYFR/PKLN W1K 9 K6
Bruton Rd MRDN SM4 194 B1
Bruton St MYFR/PICC W1J 9 K6
Bruton Wy WEA W13 97 G4
Bryan Av WLSDN NW10 81 K5
Bryan Rd BERM/RHTH SE16 124 C2
Bryanston Av WHTN TW2 155 G3
Bryanston Cl NWDGN UB2 114 E4
Bryanstone Rd CEND/HSY/T N8 66 D2
Bryanston Ms East MBLAR W1H 8 E2
Bryanston Ms West MBLAR W1H 8 E2
Bryanston Pl MBLAR W1H 8 E2
Bryanston Sq MBLAR W1H 8 E3
Bryanston St MBLAR W1H 8 E4
Bryant Cl BAR EN5 20 D6
Bryant Rd NTHLT UB5 95 G2
Bryant St SRTFD E15 88 B5
Bryantwood Rd HOLWY N7 85 G3
Brycedale Crs STHGT/OAK N14 34 D6
Bryce Rd BCTR RM8 91 J2
Bryden Cl SYD SE26 182 B1
Brydges Pl CHCR WC2N 10 E6
Brydges Rd SRTFD E15 88 B3
Brydon Wk IS N1 84 E6
Bryett Rd HOLWY N7 84 E1
Brymay Cl BOW E3 105 J1
Brynmaer Rd BTSEA SW11 140 E2
Bryn-y-Mawr Rd EN EN1 24 B5
Bryony Rd SHB W12 99 J6
Buchanan Cl WCHMH N21 23 F6
Buchanan Gdns WLSDN NW10 99 K1
Buchan Rd PECK SE15 143 K4
Bucharest Rd
WAND/EARL SW18 160 B2
Buckden Cl LEE/GVPK SE12 165 J1
Buckfast Rd MRDN SM4 194 A1
Buckfast St BETH E2 104 C2
Buckhold Rd WAND/EARL SW18 159 K1
Buckhurst Av CAR SM5 194 D5
Buckhurst St WCHPL E1 104 D3
Buckhurst Wy BKHH IG9 39 H5
Buckingham Av
E/WMO/HCT KT8 173 G5
EBED/NFELT TW14 154 A1
GFD/PVL UB6 79 G6
THHTH CR7 180 B4
TRDG/WHET N20 33 G2
WELL DA16 147 K5
Buckingham Cl EA W5 97 J4
EN EN1 24 A3
HPTN TW12 172 E1
STMC/STPC BR5 201 K4
Buckingham Ct BELMT * SM2 208 E6
Buckingham Dr CHST BR7 185 G1
Buckingham Gdns
E/WMO/HCT KT8 173 G5
STAN HA7 44 A3
THHTH CR7 180 B5
Buckingham Ga WESTW SW1E 16 A4
Buckingham La FSTH SE23 164 B2
Buckingham Ms WESTW * SW1E 16 A4
WLSDN NW10 99 H1
Buckingham Palace Rd
BGVA SW1W 15 J7
Buckingham Pde STAN * HA7 43 J1
Buckingham Pl WESTW SW1E 16 A4
Buckingham Rd EDGE HA8 44 B3
FELT TW13 154 E6
HRW HA1 60 D2
IL IG1 72 D6
IS N1 86 A4
KUT KT1 191 G1
LEY E10 87 K1
MTCM CR4 195 K2
RCHPK/HAM TW10 156 E4
SRTFD E15 88 D3
SWFD E18 52 D4
WAN E11 71 F1
WDGN N22 48 E4
WLSDN NW10 99 H1
Buckingham St CHCR WC2N 11 F6
Buckingham Wy WLGTN SM6 210 C6
Buckland Crs HAMP NW3 83 H5
Buckland Ri PIN HA5 41 G4
Buckland Rd CHSGTN KT9 206 B3
LEY E10 70 A6
ORP BR6 216 E2
Bucklands OXHEY * WD19 27 H5
Bucklands Rd TEDD TW11 174 D2
Buckland St IS N1 7 F3
Bucklands Whf KUT * KT1 174 E5
Buckland Wk MRDN SM4 194 B1
Buckland Wy WPK KT4 193 F5
Buck La CDALE/KGS NW9 63 F2
Buckleigh Av RYNPK SW20 177 J6
Buckleigh Rd
STRHM/NOR SW16 179 J2
Buckleigh Wy NRWD SE19 181 G4
Bucklersbury MANHO * EC4N 12 E4
Bucklers' Wy CAR SM5 209 K1
Buckle St WCHPL E1 13 K3
Buckley Cl DART DA1 150 C3
Buckley Rd KIL/WHAMP NW6 82 D5
Buckmaster Rd BTSEA SW11 140 D5
Bucknall St NOXST/BSQ WC1A 10 E3
Bucknall Wy BECK BR3 198 E1
Buckner Rd BRXS/STRHM SW2 142 A5
Buckrell Rd CHING E4 38 B4
Bucks Av OXHEY WD19 27 J2
Buckstone Cl FSTH SE23 163 K1
Buckstone Rd UED N18 50 C2
Buck St CAMTN NW1 84 B6
Buckters Rents
BERM/RHTH SE16 124 B1
Buckthorne Rd BROCKY SE4 164 B1
Budd Cl NFNCH/WDSP N12 33 F6
Buddings Cir WBLY HA9 80 E1
Bude Cl WALTH E17 69 H2
Budge La MTCM CR4 194 E4
Budge Rw MANHO EC4N 12 E5
Budleigh Crs WELL DA16 148 D2
Budoch Dr GDMY/SEVK IG3 73 G6
Buer Rd FUL/PGN SW6 139 H3
Bugsby's Wy GNWCH SE10 125 K4
Bulganak Rd THHTH CR7 196 D1
Bulinca St WEST * SW1P 16 E7
Bullace Rw CMBW SE5 142 E2
Bull Aly WELL DA16 148 C4
Bullar Cl PECK SE15 143 H1
Bullard Rd TEDD * TW11 174 A2
Bullards Pl BETH E2 105 F2
Bullbanks Rd BELV DA17 129 K4
Bulleid Wy PIM SW1V 15 K7
Bullen St BTSEA SW11 140 D3
Buller Rd BARK IG11 90 E5
THHTH CR7 180 E6
TOTM N17 50 C5
WDGN N22 49 G5
WLSDN NW10 100 B2
Bullers Cl SCUP DA14 187 F1
Bullers Wood Dr CHST BR7 184 D4
Bullescroft Rd EDGE HA8 30 C5
Bullivant St POP/IOD E14 106 A6
Bull La CHST BR7 185 J3
DAGE RM10 92 D1
UED N18 50 A1
Bull Rd SRTFD E15 106 D1
Bullrush Cl CROY/NA CR0 197 F3
Bulls Aly MORT/ESHN * SW14 138 A4

Bull's Br HYS/HAR UB3 113 K3
Bulls Bridge Rd NWDGN UB2 114 A3
Bullsbrook Rd HYS/HAR UB3 114 B1
Bull Yd PECK SE15 143 H2
Bulmer Gdns KTN/HRWW/W HA3 61 K4
Bulstrode Av HSLW TW3 134 E4
Bulstrode Gdns HSLW TW3 135 F4
Bulstrode Pl MHST W1U 9 H2
Bulstrode Rd HSLW TW3 135 F4
Bulstrode St MHST W1U 9 H3
Bulwer Court Rd WAN E11 70 B5
Bulwer Gdns BAR EN5 21 G5
Bulwer Rd BAR EN5 21 F5
UED N18 36 A6
WAN E11 70 B5
Bulwer St SHB W12 119 F1
Bunces La WFD IG8 52 D3
Bungalow Rd SNWD SE25 197 F1
The Bungalows
RYLN/HDSTN * HA2 77 K1
STRHM/NOR SW16 179 G3
Bunhill Rw STLK EC1Y 6 E6
Bunhouse Pl BGVA SW1W 121 F5
Bunkers Hl SCUP DA14 169 G5
Bunning Wy HOLWY * N7 84 E5
Bunn's La MLHL NW7 45 G2
Bunsen St BOW E3 105 G1
Bunting Cl ED N9 37 F3
MTCM CR4 194 E2
Bunton St WOOL/PLUM SE18 127 F3
Bunyan Rd WALTH E17 51 G6
Buonaparte Ms PIM SW1V 121 J5
Burbage Cl HYS/HAR UB3 94 B5
STHWK SE1 18 E5
Burbage Rd HNHL SE24 162 E1
Burberry Cl NWMAL KT3 176 B5
Burbridge Wy TOTM N17 50 C5
Burcham St POP/IOD E14 105 K5
Burcharbro Rd ABYW SE2 128 E6
Burchell Ct BUSH WD23 28 C2
Burchell Rd LEY E10 69 K5
PECK SE15 143 J2
Burchwall Cl CRW RM5 56 E3
Burcote Rd WAND/EARL SW18 160 C3
Burden Cl BTFD TW8 116 D5
Burdenshott Av
RCHPK/HAM TW10 137 J5
Burden Wy WAN E11 71 F6
Burder Cl IS N1 86 A4
Burder Rd IS N1 86 A4
Burdett Av RYNPK SW20 176 D4
Burdett Cl HNWL * W7 116 A1
SCUP DA14 187 F1
Burdett Rd BOW E3 105 H3
CROY/NA CR0 196 E3
RCH/KEW TW9 137 G3
Burdetts Rd DAGW RM9 92 B6
Burdock Cl CROY/NA CR0 198 A5
Burdock Rd TOTM N17 50 C6
Burdon La BELMT SM2 208 D6
Burdon Pk BELMT SM2 208 D6
Burfield Cl TOOT SW17 160 B6
Burford Cl BARK/HLT IG6 72 C1
BCTR RM8 91 J1
Burford Gdns PLMGR N13 35 F5
Burford Rd BMLY BR1 200 D1
BTFD TW8 117 F5
CAT SE6 164 C4
EHAM E6 107 J2
SRTFD E15 88 B5
SUT SM1 193 K6
WPK KT4 192 D4
Burford Wk FUL/PGN * SW6 140 A1
Burford Wy CROY/NA CR0 214 A5
Burgate Cl DART DA1 150 C4
Burges Gv BARN SW13 138 E1
Burges Rd EHAM E6 90 A5
Burgess Av CDALE/KGS NW9 63 F3
Burgess Cl FELT TW13 154 D6
Burgess Hl CRICK NW2 82 E2
Burgess Rd SRTFD E15 88 C2
SUT SM1 209 F2
Burgess St POP/IOD E14 105 J4
Burge St STHWK SE1 19 F5
Burghill Rd SYD SE26 164 A6
Burghley Av NWMAL KT3 176 A4
Burghley Hall Cl
WIM/MER * SW19 159 H3
Burghley Pl MTCM CR4 194 E1
Burghley Rd CEND/HSY/T N8 49 G6
KTTN NW5 84 B2
WAN * E11 70 C5
WIM/MER SW19 159 H6
Burgh St IS N1 6 B2
Burgon St BLKFR EC4V 12 B4
Burgon Street Hl BLKFR EC4V 12 B4
Burgos Cl CROY/NA CR0 211 G4
Burgos Gv GNWCH SE10 144 E2
Burgoyne Rd BRXN/ST SW9 142 A4
FSBYPK N4 67 H3
SNWD SE25 197 G1
Burham Cl PGE/AN SE20 181 K3
Burhill Gv PIN HA5 41 J5
Burke Cl PUT/ROE SW15 138 B5
Burke St CAN/RD E16 106 D5
Burket Cl NWDGN UB2 114 D4
Burland Rd BTSEA SW11 140 E6
CRW RM5 56 E2
Burleigh Av BFN/LL DA15 148 A6
WLGTN SM6 210 A1
Burleigh Gdns STHGT/OAK N14 34 C3
Burleigh Pde STHGT/OAK * N14 34 D3
Burleigh Pl PUT/ROE SW15 139 G6
Burleigh Rd CHEAM SM3 193 H5
EN EN1 24 A5
Burleigh St COVGDN WC2E 11 F5
Burleigh Wk CAT SE6 165 F3
Burleigh Wy ENC/FH EN2 23 K4
Burley Cl CHING E4 51 J1
STRHM/NOR SW16 179 J5
Burley Rd CAN/RD E16 107 G5
Burlington Ar CONDST W1S 10 A6
Burlington Av RCH/KEW TW9 137 H2
ROMW/RG RM7 74 D3
Burlington Cl
EBED/NFELT TW14 153 G2
EHAM E6 107 J5
MV/WKIL W9 100 E3
ORP BR6 201 G6
Burlington Gdns ACT W3 117 K1
CHDH RM6 74 A4
CHSWK W4 117 K5
CONDST W1S 10 A6
Burlington La CHSWK W4 137 K1
Burlington Ms ACT W3 117 K1
Burlington Pde CRICK * NW2 82 B2
Burlington Pl FUL/PGN SW6 139 H3
PIN HA5 41 F6
WFD IG8 38 E5
Burlington Ri EBAR EN4 33 J3
Burlington Rd CHSWK * W4 117 K5
ENC/FH EN2 23 K2
FUL/PGN SW6 139 H3
ISLW TW7 135 J2
MUSWH N10 48 A6
NWMAL KT3 192 C1
THHTH CR7 180 D5
TOTM N17 50 C4
Burma Rd STNW/STAM N16 85 K2
Burma Ter NRWD * SE19 181 F1
Burmester Rd TOOT SW17 160 B5
Burnaby Crs CHSWK W4 117 J6
Burnaby Gdns CHSWK W4 117 J6
Burnaby St WBPTN SW10 140 B1
Burnbrae Cl FNCH N3 47 F2
Burnbury Rd BAL SW12 161 H3
Burncroft Av PEND EN3 24 E4
Burndell Wy YEAD UB4 95 H4
Burnell Av RCHPK/HAM TW10 174 D1
WELL DA16 148 B3
Burnell Gdns STAN HA7 43 K5
Burnell Rd SUT SM1 209 F2
Burnell Wk STHWK * SE1 123 G5
Burnels Av EHAM E6 108 A2
Burness Cl HOLWY N7 85 F4
Burne St CAMTN NW1 8 C1
Burnett Rd ERITH DA8 131 G6
Burney Av BRYLDS KT5 191 G2
Burney St GNWCH SE10 145 F1
Burnfoot Av FUL/PGN SW6 139 H2
Burnham Av HGDN/ICK UB10 76 A2
Burnham Cl ENC/FH EN2 24 A1
KTN/HRWW/W HA3 61 G1
MLHL NW7 45 J3
STHWK SE1 19 K7
Burnham Crs DART DA1 151 F5
WAN E11 71 G1
Burnham Dr WPK KT4 193 G6
Burnham Gdns CROY/NA CR0 197 G4
HEST TW5 134 A2
HYS/HAR UB3 113 G3
Burnham Rd CHING E4 51 H1
DAGW RM9 91 H5
DART DA1 151 G6
MRDN SM4 194 A2
ROMW/RG RM7 56 E6
SCUP DA14 169 F4
Burnham St BETH E2 104 E2
KUTN/CMB KT2 175 H4
Burnham Ter DART * DA1 151 G6
Burnham Wy SYD SE26 182 C1
WEA W13 116 C4
Burnhill Rd BECK BR3 182 D5
Burnley Cl OXHEY WD19 41 G1
Burnley Rd BRXN/ST SW9 142 A3
WLSDN NW10 81 H3
Burnsall St CHEL SW3 120 D5
Burns Av BFN/LL DA15 168 C1
CHDH RM6 73 J4
EBED/NFELT TW14 153 K1
STHL UB1 96 A6
Burns Cl ERITH DA8 150 C2
WALTH E17 70 A1
WELL DA16 148 A2
WIM/MER SW19 178 C2
YEAD UB4 94 E4
Burnside Av CHING E4 51 H2
Burnside Cl BAR EN5 20 E4
BERM/RHTH SE16 124 A1
TWK TW1 156 B1
Burnside Crs ALP/SUD HA0 79 K6
Burnside Rd BCTR RM8 73 J6
Burns Rd ALP/SUD HA0 98 A1
BTSEA SW11 140 E3
WEA * W13 116 C2
WLSDN NW10 81 H6
Burns Wy HEST TW5 134 C2
Burnt Ash Hl LEE/GVPK SE12 165 J1
Burnt Ash La BMLY BR1 184 A1
Burnt Ash Rd LEE/GVPK SE12 145 J6
Burnt House La RDART DA2 171 H6
Burnthwaite Rd FUL/PGN SW6 139 J1
Burnt Oak Broadway EDGE HA8 44 D3
Burnt Oak Flds EDGE HA8 44 E4
Burnt Oak La BFN/LL DA15 168 B1
Burntwood Cl
WAND/EARL * SW18 160 C3
Burntwood Grange Rd
WAND/EARL SW18 160 C3
Burntwood La TOOT SW17 160 B5
Burntwood Vw NRWD * SE19 181 G1
Buross St WCHPL E1 104 D5
Burpham Cl YEAD UB4 95 H4
Burrage Gv WOOL/PLUM SE18 127 G4
Burrage Pl WOOL/PLUM SE18 127 G5
Burrage Rd WOOL/PLUM SE18 127 H4
Burrard Rd CAN/RD E16 106 E5
KIL/WHAMP NW6 82 E3
Burr Bank Ter RDART * DA2 171 F6
Burr Cl BXLYHN DA7 149 G4
WAP * E1W 123 H1
Burrell Cl CROY/NA CR0 198 B3
EDGE HA8 30 D4
Burrell Rw BECK BR3 182 D5
Burrell St STHWK SE1 12 A7
Burrfield Dr STMC/STPC BR5 202 E2
Burritt Rd KUT KT1 175 H5
The Burroughs HDN NW4 63 K1
Burroughs Cottages
POP/IOD * E14 105 G4
Burroughs Gdns HDN NW4 63 K1
Burrow Gn CHIG IG7 55 F1
Burrow Rd CHIG IG7 55 G1
EDUL SE22 143 F5
Burrows Ms STHWK SE1 18 A2
Burrows Rd WLSDN NW10 100 A2
Burr Rd WAND/EARL SW18 159 K3
Bursar St STHWK * SE1 19 G1
Bursdon Cl BFN/LL DA15 168 A4
Bursland Rd PEND EN3 25 F5
Burslem Av BARK/HLT IG6 55 G2
Burslem St WCHPL * E1 104 D5
Burstock Rd PUT/ROE SW15 139 H5
Burston Rd PUT/ROE SW15 139 G6
Burstow Rd RYNPK SW20 177 H4
Burtenshaw Rd THDIT KT7 190 B4
Burtley Cl FSBYPK N4 67 J5
Burton Bank IS * N1 85 K5
Burton Cl CHSGTN KT9 205 K5
THHTH CR7 180 E6
Burton Gdns HEST TW5 134 E2
Burton Gv WALW SE17 122 E5
Burtonhole Cl MLHL NW7 32 B6
Burtonhole La MLHL NW7 46 B1
NFNCH/WDSP N12 32 C6
Burton La BRXN/ST * SW9 142 B3
Burton Ms BGVA SW1W 15 H7
Burton Pl STPAN WC1H 4 D6
Burton Rd BRXN/ST SW9 142 C3
KIL/WHAMP NW6 82 D5
KUTN/CMB KT2 175 F3
SWFD E18 53 F6
Burtons Ct SRTFD E15 88 B5
Burton's Rd HPTN TW12 155 G6
Burton St STPAN WC1H 4 D6
Burt Rd CAN/RD E16 126 B1
Burtwell La WNWD SE27 162 E6
Burwash Cl STMC/STPC BR5 202 D2
Burwash Rd WOOL/PLUM SE18 127 J5
Burwell Av GFD/PVL UB6 78 E4
Burwell Cl WCHPL * E1 104 D5
Burwell Rd LEY E10 69 G5
Burwood Av HAYES BR2 200 A6
PIN HA5 59 G2
Burwood Cl SURB KT6 191 H5
Burwood Gdns RAIN RM13 111 H2
Burwood Pl BAY/PAD W2 8 D3
Bury Av RSLP HA4 58 A3
YEAD UB4 94 C1
Bury Cl BERM/RHTH SE16 124 A1
Bury Ct HDTCH EC3A 13 H3
Bury Gv MRDN SM4 194 A2
Bury Pl NOXST/BSQ WC1A 10 E2
Bury Rd DAGE RM10 92 E3
WDGN N22 49 G5
Bury St ED N9 36 B2
HDTCH EC3A 13 H4
RSLP HA4 58 B3
STJS SW1Y 10 A7
Bury St West ED N9 36 A2
Bury Wk CHEL SW3 14 C7
Busby Pl KTTN NW5 84 D4
Busch Cl ISLW TW7 136 C2
Bushbaby Cl STHWK SE1 19 G5
Bushberry Rd HOM E9 87 G4
Bush Cl GNTH/NBYPK IG2 72 D2
Bush Cottages
WAND/EARL SW18 139 K6
Bushell Cl BRXS/STRHM SW2 162 A4
Bushell Gn BUSH WD23 28 D4
Bushell Wy CHST BR7 185 F1
Bush Elms Rd EMPK RM11 75 J4
Bushey Av STMC/STPC BR5 201 J4
SWFD E18 52 D6
Bushey Cl CHING E4 38 A5
Bushey Hill Rd CMBW SE5 143 G2
Bushey La SUT SM1 208 E1
Bushey Lees BFN/LL * DA15 168 A1
Bushey Rd CROY/NA CR0 198 D6
HYS/HAR UB3 113 H4
PLSTW E13 107 G1
RYNPK SW20 177 F5
SEVS/STOTM N15 68 A3
SUT SM1 208 E2
Bushey Wy BECK BR3 199 G3
Bushfield Cl EDGE HA8 30 D4
Bushfield Crs EDGE HA8 30 D4
Bush Gv CDALE/KGS NW9 62 E4
STAN HA7 43 K4
Bushgrove Rd BCTR RM8 91 K2
Bush Hl WCHMH N21 35 J2
Bush Hill Pde EN * EN1 35 K2
Bush Hill Rd KTN/HRWW/W HA3 62 B3
WCHMH N21 35 K1
Bush La CANST EC4R 12 E5
Bushmead Cl SEVS/STOTM * N15 68 B1
Bushmoor Crs
WOOL/PLUM SE18 147 G1
Bushnell Rd TOOT SW17 161 G4
Bush Rd BERM/RHTH SE16 124 A4
BKHH IG9 39 H6
HACK E8 86 D6
RCH/KEW TW9 117 G6
WAN E11 70 D4
Bushway BCTR RM8 91 K2
Bushwood WAN E11 70 D4
Bushwood Dr STHWK SE1 19 K7
Bushwood Rd RCH/KEW TW9 117 H6
Bushy Park Gdns HPTN * TW12 173 J1
Bushy Park Rd TEDD TW11 174 C3
Bushy Rd TEDD TW11 173 K2
Butcher Rw POP/IOD E14 105 F6
Butchers Rd CAN/RD E16 106 E5
Bute Av RCHPK/HAM TW10 157 F4
Bute Gdns HMSMTH W6 119 G4
RCHPK/HAM * TW10 157 F3
WLGTN SM6 210 C3
Bute Gdns West WLGTN SM6 210 C3
Bute Rd BARK/HLT IG6 72 B2
CROY/NA CR0 196 B5
WLGTN SM6 210 C2
Bute St SKENS SW7 14 A6
Bute Wk IS * N1 85 K4
Butler Av HRW HA1 60 D4
Butler Rd BCTR RM8 91 H2
HRW HA1 60 C4
WLSDN NW10 81 H5
Butlers & Colonial Whf
STHWK SE1 19 K2
Butler St BETH * E2 104 E2
Buttercup Sq
STWL/WRAY * TW19 152 A3
Butterfield Cl
BERM/RHTH * SE16 123 H2
TOTM N17 49 J2
TWK TW1 156 A1
Butterfields WALTH E17 70 A2
Butterfield Sq EHAM E6 107 K5
Butterfly Av DART DA1 171 J4
Butterfly La ELTH/MOT SE9 167 G1
Butterfly Wk CMBW * SE5 142 E2
Butter Hl WLGTN SM6 210 A1
Butteridges Cl DAGW RM9 92 B6
Butterly Av DART * DA1 171 J4
Buttermere
Cl EBED/NFELT TW14 153 J3
MRDN SM4 193 G3
STHWK SE1 19 J6
WAN E11 88 B2
Buttermere Dr PUT/ROE SW15 139 H6
Buttermere Rd STMC/STPC BR5 202 E1
Buttermere Wk HACK * E8 86 B4
Butterwick HMSMTH W6 119 F4
Butterworth Gdns WFD IG8 52 E2
Butterworth Ter WALW * SE17 122 D5
Buttesland St IS N1 7 F4
Buttfield Cl DAGE RM10 92 D4
Buttmarsh Cl
WOOL/PLUM SE18 127 G5
Buttsbury Rd IL IG1 90 C3
Butts Crs FELT TW13 155 F5
Buttsmead NTHWD HA6 40 A3
Butts Piece NTHLT UB5 95 F1
Butts Rd BMLY BR1 183 H1
The Butts BTFD TW8 116 E6
Buxhall Crs HOM E9 87 H4
Buxted Rd EDUL SE22 143 F5
HACK E8 86 B5
NFNCH/WDSP N12 47 J1
Buxton Cl WFD IG8 53 H2
Buxton Crs CHEAM SM3 208 C2
Buxton Dr NWMAL KT3 176 A5
WAN E11 70 C1
Buxton Gdns ACT W3 98 D6
Buxton Pth OXHEY * WD19 27 G5
Buxton Rd ARCH N19 66 D5
CHING E4 38 B2
CRICK NW2 81 K4
EHAM E6 107 J2
ERITH DA8 150 A1
GNTH/NBYPK IG2 72 E3
MORT/ESHN SW14 138 B4
SRTFD E15 88 C3
THHTH CR7 196 C2
WALTH E17 69 G1
Buxton St WCHPL E1 7 K7
Byam St FUL/PGN SW6 140 B3
Byards Cft STRHM/NOR SW16 179 J4
Bychurch End TEDD * TW11 174 A1
Bycroft Rd STHL UB1 96 A4
Bycroft St PGE/AN SE20 182 A3
Bycullah Av ENC/FH EN2 23 H4
Bycullah Rd ENC/FH EN2 23 H4
The Bye ACT W3 99 G5
Byefield Cl BERM/RHTH SE16 124 B2
Byelands Cl BERM/RHTH SE16 124 A1
Byewaters WATW WD18 26 B1
The Byeway MORT/ESHN SW14 137 K4
The Bye Wy KTN/HRWW/W HA3 42 E4
The Byeways BRYLDS KT5 191 H2
Bye Ways WHTN TW2 155 G5
Byfeld Gdns BARN SW13 138 D2
Byfield Cl BERM/RHTH SE16 124 B2
Byfield Rd ISLW TW7 136 B4
Byford Cl SRTFD E15 88 C5
Bygrove Rd WIM/MER SW19 178 C2
Bygrove St POP/IOD E14 105 K5
Byland Cl ABYW SE2 128 C3
WCHMH N21 35 F2
Byne Rd CAR SM5 194 D6
SYD SE26 181 K2
Bynes Rd SAND/SEL CR2 211 K5
Byng Pl GWRST WC1E 4 D7
Byng Rd BAR EN5 20 B4
Byng St POP/IOD E14 124 D2
Bynon Av BXLYHN DA7 149 F4
Byre Rd STHGT/OAK N14 34 A1
Byrne Rd BAL SW12 161 G3
Byron Av CDALE/KGS NW9 62 D1
HSLWW TW4 134 A3
MNPK E12 89 J4
NWMAL KT3 192 D2
SUT SM1 209 H2
SWFD E18 52 D6
Byron Av East SUT SM1 209 H2
Byron Cl HACK E8 86 C6
HPTN TW12 154 E6
PGE/AN * SE20 181 J6
SYD * SE26 164 B6
THMD SE28 128 D1
WOT/HER KT12 188 D5
Byron Ct ENC/FH EN2 23 H3
Byron Dr EFNCH N2 65 H3
ERITH DA8 149 J1
Byron Gdns SUT SM1 209 H2
Byron Hill Rd RYLN/HDSTN HA2 60 D5
Byron Ms HAMP NW3 83 J3
Byron Rd ALP/SUD HA0 61 J6
CRICK NW2 63 K6
EA W5 117 G1
HRW HA1 60 E3
KTN/HRWW/W HA3 43 F6
LEY E10 69 K5
MLHL NW7 45 J1
WALTH E17 51 J6
Byron St POP/IOD E14 106 A5
Byron Ter ED * N9 36 E2
Byron Wy NTHLT UB5 95 J2
WDR/YW UB7 112 C4
YEAD UB4 94 C3
Bysouth Cl CLAY IG5 54 B4
By the Wd OXHEY WD19 27 H4
Bythorn St BRXN/ST SW9 142 A4
Byton Rd TOOT SW17 178 E2
Byward Av EBED/NFELT TW14 154 B1
Byward St MON EC3R 13 H6
Bywater Pl BERM/RHTH SE16 124 B1
Bywater St CHEL SW3 120 E5
The Byway BELMT SM2 209 H6
The Byways HOR/WEW KT19 207 H2
Bywell Pl GTPST * W1W 10 A2
Bywood Av CROY/NA CR0 197 K3

C

Cabbell St CAMTN NW1 8 C2
Cabinet Wy CHING E4 51 H2
Cable Pl GNWCH SE10 145 F2
Cables Cl BELV DA17 129 K3
Cable St TWRH EC3N 13 K5
WCHPL E1 104 D6
Cabot Sq POP/IOD E14 124 D1
Cabot Wy EHAM E6 89 H6
Cabul Rd BTSEA SW11 140 D3
Cactus Cl CMBW * SE5 143 F3
Cadbury Cl ISLW TW7 136 B2
Cadbury Wy BERM/RHTH SE16 19 K5
Caddington Cl EBAR EN4 21 J6
Caddington Rd CRICK NW2 82 C1
Caddis Cl STAN * HA7 43 F3
Cadell Cl BETH E2 7 K3
Cade Rd GNWCH SE10 145 G2
Cader Rd WAND/EARL SW18 160 B1
Cadet Dr STHWK SE1 123 G5
Cadet Pl GNWCH SE10 125 H5
Cadiz Rd DAGE RM10 92 E5
Cadiz St WALW SE17 122 D5
Cadman Cl BRXN/ST SW9 142 C1
Cadmer Cl NWMAL KT3 192 B1
Cadogan Cl HOM * E9 87 H5
RYLN/HDSTN HA2 78 B2
TEDD TW11 173 K1
Cadogan Ct BELMT SM2 209 F4
Cadogan Gdns CHEL SW3 15 F7
FNCH * N3 47 F4
SWFD E18 53 F6
WCHMH N21 23 G6
Cadogan Ga KTBR SW1X 15 F6
Cadogan La KTBR SW1X 15 G5
Cadogan Pl KTBR SW1X 15 F6
Cadogan Rd SURB KT6 190 E2
WOOL/PLUM SE18 127 H3
Cadogan Sq KTBR SW1X 14 E5
Cadogan St CHEL SW3 14 E7
Cadogan Ter HOM E9 87 H4
Cadoxton Av SEVS/STOTM N15 68 B3
Cadwallon Rd ELTH/MOT SE9 167 G4
Caedmon Rd HOLWY N7 85 F2
Caerleon Cl ESH/CLAY KT10 205 H5
SCUP DA14 186 D1
Caernarvon Cl MTCM CR4 179 K6
Caernarvon Dr CLAY IG5 54 A4
Caesars Wk MTCM CR4 194 E2
Cahill St STLK * EC1Y 6 D7
Cahir St POP/IOD E14 124 E4
Cain's La EBED/NFELT TW14 133 G6
Caird St NKENS W10 100 C2
Cairn Av EA W5 116 E1
Cairndale Cl BMLY BR1 183 J3
Cairnfield Av CRICK NW2 81 G1
Cairns Av WFD IG8 53 K2
Cairns Cl DART DA1 151 G6
Cairns Rd BTSEA SW11 140 D6
Cairn Wy STAN HA7 43 F2
Cairo New Rd CROY/NA CR0 196 C6
Cairo Rd WALTH * E17 69 J1
Caistor Park Rd SRTFD E15 88 D6
Caistor Rd BAL SW12 161 G2
Caithness Gdns BFN/LL DA15 168 A1
Caithness Rd MTCM CR4 179 G3
WKENS W14 119 G3
Calabria Rd HBRY N5 85 H4
Calais St CMBW SE5 142 C2
Calbourne Av HCH RM12 93 K3
Calbourne Rd BAL SW12 160 E2
Caldbeck Av WPK KT4 192 E6
Caldecote Gdns BUSH WD23 28 E1
Caldecote La BUSH WD23 29 F2
Caldecot Rd CMBW SE5 142 D3
Caldecott Wy CLPT E5 87 F1
Calder Av GFD/PVL UB6 97 F1
Calder Gdns EDGE HA8 44 C6
Calderon Rd WAN E11 88 A2
Calder Rd MRDN SM4 194 B2
Caldervale Rd CLAP SW4 141 J6
Calderwood St
WOOL/PLUM SE18 127 F4
Caldicote Gn CDALE/KGS * NW9 63 G3
Caldwell Rd OXHEY WD19 27 H6
Caldwell St BRXN/ST SW9 142 A1
Caldy Rd BELV DA17 129 J3
Caldy Wk IS * N1 85 J4
Caledonian Cl GDMY/SEVK * IG3 73 H5
Caledonian Rd HOLWY N7 85 F3
Caledonian Wharf Rd
POP/IOD E14 125 G4
Caledonia Rd
STWL/WRAY TW19 152 B3
Caledonia St IS N1 5 F3
Caledon Rd EHAM E6 89 K6
WLGTN SM6 210 A2
Cale St CHEL SW3 120 D5
Calidore Cl BRXS/STRHM * SW2 162 A1
California La BUSH WD23 28 D3
California Rd NWMAL KT3 191 K1
Callaby Ter IS * N1 85 K4
Callaghan Cottages
WCHPL * E1 104 E4
Callander Rd CAT SE6 164 E4
The Callanders BUSH * WD23 28 E3
Callard Av PLMGR N13 49 H1
Callcott Rd KIL/WHAMP NW6 82 D5
Callcott St KENS W8 119 K1
Callendar Rd SKENS SW7 14 A4
Callingham Cl POP/IOD E14 105 H4
Callis Farm Cl
STWL/WRAY TW19 152 B1
Callis Rd WALTH E17 69 H3
Callow St CHEL SW3 120 B6
Calmington Rd CMBW SE5 123 F6
Calmont Rd BMLY BR1 183 G2
Calne Av CLAY IG5 54 B4
Calonne Rd WIM/MER SW19 159 G6
Calshot Rd HTHAIR TW6 132 E3
Calshot St IS N1 5 G2
Calshot Wy ENC/FH EN2 23 H4
HTHAIR TW6 132 D3
Calthorpe Gdns EDGE HA8 44 B1
SUT SM1 209 G1
Calthorpe St FSBYW WC1X 5 H6
Calton Av DUL SE21 163 F1
Calton Rd BAR EN5 33 G1
Calverley Cl BECK BR3 182 E2
Calverley Crs DAGE RM10 74 C6
Calverley Gv ARCH N19 66 D5
Calverley Rd EW KT17 207 J4
Calvert Av BETH E2 7 H5
Calvert Cl BELV DA17 129 H4
SCUP DA14 187 F2
Calverton Rd EHAM E6 90 A6
Calvert Rd BAR EN5 20 B3
GNWCH SE10 125 J5
Calvert St CAMTN NW1 84 A6
Calvin Cl STMC/STPC BR5 186 E6
Calvin St WCHPL E1 7 J7
Calydon Rd CHARL SE7 126 A5
Calypso Wy BERM/RHTH SE16 124 C3
Camac Rd WHTN TW2 155 J3
Camarthen Gn
CDALE/KGS * NW9 63 G3
Cambalt Rd PUT/ROE SW15 139 G6
Camberley Av EN EN1 24 A5
RYNPK SW20 176 E5
Camberley Cl CHEAM SM3 208 B1
Camberley Rd HTHAIR TW6 132 D4
Cambert Wy BKHTH/KID SE3 146 A5
Camberwell Church St
CMBW SE5 142 E2
Camberwell Glebe CMBW SE5 142 E2
Camberwell Gn CMBW SE5 142 E2
Camberwell Gv CMBW SE5 142 E2
Camberwell New Rd
CMBW SE5 142 C1
Camberwell Rd CMBW SE5 122 D6
Camberwell Station Rd
CMBW SE5 142 D2
Cambeys Rd DAGE RM10 92 E3
Camborne Av WEA W13 116 C2
Camborne Cl HTHAIR TW6 132 D4
Camborne Crs HTHAIR TW6 132 D4
Camborne Rd BELMT SM2 208 E5
CROY/NA CR0 197 H4

MRDN SM4 193 G3
SCUP DA14 168 D5
WAND/EARL SW18 159 K2
WELL DA16 147 K3
Camborne Wy HEST TW5 135 F2
Cambourne Av ED N9 37 F2
Cambourne Ms NTGHL W11 100 C5
Cambray Rd BAL SW12 161 H3
ORP BR6 202 A4
Cambria Cl BFN/LL DA15 167 J3
HSLW TW3 135 F5
Cambria Ct EBED/NFELT TW14 154 A2
Cambria Gdns
STWL/WRAY TW19 152 B2
Cambrian Av GNTH/NBYPK IG2 72 E2
Cambrian Cl WNWD SE27 162 C5
Cambrian Gn CDALE/KGS * NW9 63 G2
Cambrian Rd LEY E10 69 J4
RCHPK/HAM TW10 157 G1
Cambria Rd CMBW SE5 142 D4
Cambria St FUL/PGN SW6 140 A1
Cambridge Av GFD/PVL UB6 79 F3
KIL/WHAMP NW6 100 E1
NWMAL KT3 176 C5
WELL DA16 148 A5
Cambridge Barracks Rd
WOOL/PLUM SE18 126 E4
Cambridge Cl HSLWW TW4 134 D5
RYNPK SW20 176 E4
WALTH E17 69 H3
WDGN * N22 49 G4
WDR/YW UB7 112 A6
WLSDN NW10 80 E1
Cambridge Crs BETH E2 104 D1
TEDD * TW11 174 B1
Cambridge Dr LEE/GVPK SE12 145 K6
RSLP HA4 59 G6
Cambridge Gdns EN EN1 24 C3
KIL/WHAMP NW6 100 E1
KUT KT1 175 H5
NKENS W10 100 B5
TOTM N17 49 K3
WCHMH N21 35 K2
Cambridge Ga CAMTN NW1 3 J5
Cambridge Gate Ms CAMTN NW1 3 K5
Cambridge Gn ELTH/MOT SE9 167 G3
Cambridge Gv HMSMTH W6 118 E4
PGE/AN * SE20 181 J4
Cambridge Grove Rd KUT KT1 175 H5
Cambridge Heath Rd BETH E2 104 D2
Cambridge Pde EN * EN1 24 C3
Cambridge Pk TWK TW1 156 E2
WAN E11 70 E3
Cambridge Park Rd WAN E11 70 E4
Cambridge Pas HOM E9 86 E5
Cambridge Pl KENS * W8 120 A2
Cambridge Rd BARK IG11 90 C5
BMLY BR1 183 K3
BTSEA SW11 140 E2
CAR SM5 209 J4
CHING E4 38 B3
E/WMO/HCT KT8 188 E1
GDMY/SEVK IG3 72 E5
HNWL W7 116 A2
HPTN TW12 172 E3
HSLWW TW4 134 D5
KIL/WHAMP NW6 100 E2
KUT KT1 175 H5
MTCM CR4 179 H6
NWMAL KT3 192 A1
PGE/AN SE20 181 H6
RCH/KEW TW9 137 H1
RYLN/HDSTN HA2 60 A2
RYNPK SW20 176 E4
SCUP DA14 167 K6
STHL * UB1 114 E1
TEDD TW11 156 B6
TWK TW1 156 E1
WAN E11 70 E3
WOT/HER KT12 188 A3
Cambridge Rd North
CHSWK W4 117 J5
Cambridge Rd South
CHSWK W4 117 J5
Cambridge Rw
WOOL/PLUM SE18 127 G5
Cambridge Sq BAY/PAD W2 8 C3
Cambridge St PIM SW1V 121 G5
Cambridge Ter CAMTN NW1 3 J5
ED * N9 36 B2
Cambridge Terrace Ms
CAMTN * NW1 3 K5
Cambridge Yd HNWL * W7 116 A2
Cambus Cl YEAD UB4 95 J4
Cambus Rd CAN/RD E16 106 E4
Camdale Rd WOOL/PLUM SE18 148 A1
Camden Av FELT TW13 154 B4
YEAD UB4 95 G6
Camden Cl CHST BR7 185 H4
Camden Gdns CAMTN * NW1 84 B5
SUT SM1 209 F3
THHTH CR7 180 C6
Camden Gv CHST BR7 185 G2
Camden High St CAMTN NW1 4 A1
Camden Hill Rd NRWD SE19 181 F2
Camdenhurst St POP/IOD E14 105 G5
Camden Lock Pl CAMTN NW1 84 B5
Camden Ms HOLWY N7 84 D4
Camden Park Rd CAMTN NW1 84 D4
CHST BR7 184 E3
Camden Pas IS N1 6 A2
Camden Rd BXLY DA5 169 G3
CAMTN NW1 84 B6
CAR SM5 209 K2
SUT SM1 209 F3
WALTH E17 69 H3
WAN E11 71 F3
Camden Rd Permanent Wy
CAMTN * NW1 4 C1
Camden Rw BKHTH/KID SE3 145 H3
PIN * HA5 41 G6
Camden Sq CAMTN NW1 84 D5
Camden St CAMTN NW1 84 B5
Camden Ter CAMTN NW1 84 D4
Camden Wk IS N1 6 A1
Camden Wy CHST BR7 184 E3
THHTH CR7 180 C6
Camelford Wk NTGHL * W11 100 C5
Camel Gv KUTN/CMB KT2 174 E1
Camellia Pl WHTN TW2 155 G2
Camellia St VX/NE SW8 141 K1
Camelot Cl WIM/MER SW19 159 J6
WOOL/PLUM SE18 127 J2
Camel Rd CAN/RD E16 126 D1
Camera Pl WBPTN SW10 120 C6
Cameron Cl BXLY DA5 170 A5
TRDG/WHET N20 33 J4
UED N18 36 D6
Cameron Rd CAT * SE6 164 C4
CROY/NA CR0 196 C3
GDMY/SEVK IG3 72 E5
HAYES BR2 199 K2
Cameron Ter LEE/GVPK * SE12 166 A5
Camerton Cl HACK E8 86 B4
Camilla Rd BERM/RHTH SE16 123 J4
Camille Cl SNWD SE25 181 H6
Camlan Rd BMLY BR1 165 J6
Camlet St BETH E2 7 J6
Camlet Wy EBAR EN4 20 E3
Camley St CAMTN NW1 4 D1
Camm Gdns KUT * KT1 175 G5
THDIT KT7 189 K4
Camomile Av MTCM CR4 178 E4
Camomile St HDTCH EC3A 13 H3
Camomile Rd ROMW/RG RM7 75 F6
Campana Rd FUL/PGN SW6 139 K2
Campbell Av BARK/HLT IG6 72 C1
Campbell Cl ROM RM1 57 G2
RSLP HA4 58 E3
STRHM/NOR * SW16 179 J1
WHTN TW2 155 J3
WOOL/PLUM SE18 147 F2
Campbell Cottages
MTCM * CR4 179 F5
Campbell Cft EDGE HA8 44 C1
Campbell Gordon Wy
CRICK NW2 81 K2
Campbell Rd BOW E3 105 J2
CROY/NA CR0 196 C4
EHAM E6 89 J6
HNWL W7 96 E6
SRTFD E15 88 C2
TOTM N17 50 B4
WALTH E17 69 H1
WHTN TW2 155 J4
Campbell Wk IS N1 84 E6
Campdale Rd ARCH N19 84 D1
Campden Crs ALP/SUD HA0 79 H1
BCTR RM8 91 J2
Campden Gv KENS W8 119 K2
Campden Hl KENS W8 119 J2
Campden Hill Gdns KENS W8 119 J1
Campden Hill Ga KENS * W8 119 K2
Campden Hill Pl KENS * W8 119 J1
Campden Hill Rd KENS W8 119 K2
Campden Hill Sq KENS W8 119 J1
Campden House Cl KENS W8 119 K2
Campden House Ter KENS * W8 119 K1
Campden Rd SAND/SEL CR2 212 A3
Campden St KENS W8 119 K1
Campden Ter CHSWK * W4 118 B5
Campen Cl WIM/MER SW19 159 H4
Camperdown St WCHPL E1 13 K4
Campfield Rd ELTH/MOT SE9 166 C2
Campion Cl EHAM E6 107 K6
KTN/HRWW/W HA3 62 B3
ROMW/RG RM7 75 F6
SAND/SEL CR2 212 A2
Campion Ct ALP/SUD * HA0 98 A1
Campion Gdns WFD IG8 52 E1
Campion Pl THMD SE28 128 C1
Campion Rd ISLW TW7 136 A2
PUT/ROE SW15 139 F5
Campion Wy EDGE HA8 30 E6
Camplin Rd KTN/HRWW/W HA3 62 A2
Camplin St NWCR SE14 144 A1
Camp Rd WIM/MER SW19 176 E1
The Campsbourne
CEND/HSY/T N8 66 E1
Campsbourne Pde
CEND/HSY/T * N8 66 E1
Campsbourne Rd
CEND/HSY/T N8 48 E6
Campsey Rd DAGW RM9 91 H5
Campshill Pl LEW SE13 145 F6
Campshill Rd LEW SE13 145 F6
Campus Rd WALTH E17 69 H3
Camp Vw WIM/MER SW19 176 E1
Cam Rd SRTFD E15 88 B6
Camrose Av ERITH DA8 129 J6
FELT TW13 154 A6
STAN HA7 44 A5
Camrose Cl CROY/NA CR0 198 B4
MRDN SM4 193 K1
Camrose St ABYW SE2 128 B5
Canada Av UED N18 49 J2
Canada Crs ACT W3 98 E4
Canada Park Pde EDGE * HA8 44 D4
Canada Rd ACT W3 98 E4
ERITH DA8 150 E1
Canada St BERM/RHTH SE16 124 A2
Canada Wy SHB W12 99 K6
Canadian Av CAT SE6 164 E3
Canal Ap DEPT SE8 124 B6
Canal Cl NKENS W10 100 B3
WCHPL E1 105 G3
Canal Gv PECK SE15 123 H6
Canal Pth HACK E8 7 J1
Canal Rd WCHPL E1 105 G3
Canal St CMBW SE5 122 E6
Canal Wk CROY/NA CR0 197 F3
IS N185 K6
WLSDN * NW10 80 E5
Canal Wy NKENS W10 100 B3
Canal Whf GFD/PVL * UB6 79 G6
Canal Yd NWDGN * UB2 114 A4
Canberra Cl DAGE RM10 93 F5
HDN NW4 45 J6
Canberra Crs DAGE RM10 93 F5
Canberra Dr NTHLT UB5 95 G2
Canberra Rd HTHAIR TW6 132 D4
ABYW SE2 128 E6
CHARL SE7 126 B6
EHAM E6 89 K6
Canbury Av KUTN/CMB KT2 175 G4
Canbury Ms SYD SE26 163 H5
Canbury Park Rd
KUTN/CMB KT2 175 F4
Canbury Pth STMC/STPC BR5 202 B1
Cancell Rd BRXN/ST SW9 142 B2
Candahar Rd BTSEA SW11 140 D3
Candler Ms TWK TW1 156 B2
Candler St SEVS/STOTM * N15 67 K3
Candover Cl WDR/YW UB7 132 A1
Candover Rd EMPK RM11 75 K5
Candover St GTPST * W1W 10 A2
Candy St BOW E3 87 H6
Caney Ms CRICK NW2 64 B6
Canfield Dr RSLP HA4 77 F3
Canfield Gdns KIL/WHAMP NW6 83 F5
Canfield Pl KIL/WHAMP NW6 83 G4
Canfield Rd RAIN RM13 93 H6
WFD IG8 53 J3
Canford Av NTHLT UB5 77 J6
Canford Cl ENC/FH EN2 23 G3
Canford Gdns NWMAL KT3 192 B3
Canford Pl TEDD TW11 174 D2
Canford Rd CLAP SW4 141 F5
Canham Rd CHSWK W4 118 B2
SNWD SE25 181 F6
Canmore Gdns
STRHM/NOR SW16 179 H3
Cann Hall Rd WAN E11 88 D2
Canning Crs WDGN N22 49 F4
Canning Cross CMBW SE5 143 F3
Canning Pl KENS W8 120 B3
Canning Place Ms KENS * W8 120 B3
Canning Rd CROY/NA CR0 197 G6
HBRY N5 85 H1
KTN/HRWW/W HA3 42 E6
SRTFD E15 106 C1
WALTH E17 69 G1
Cannington Rd DAGW RM9 91 J4
Cannizaro Rd WIM/MER SW19 177 F2
Cannonbury Av PIN HA5 59 H3
Cannon Cl HPTN TW12 173 G2
RYNPK SW20 177 F6
Cannon Dr POP/IOD E14 105 J6
Cannon Hl KIL/WHAMP NW6 83 F3
STHGT/OAK N14 34 E5
Cannon Hill La MRDN SM4 193 G2
Cannon La HAMP NW3 83 H1
PIN HA5 59 J2
Cannon Pl CHARL SE7 126 D5
HAMP NW3 83 G1
Cannon Rd BXLYHN DA7 149 F2
STHGT/OAK N14 34 E5
Cannon St STP EC4M 12 C4
Cannon Street Rd WCHPL E1 104 D5
Cannon Wy E/WMO/HCT KT8 189 F1
Canon Av CHDH RM6 73 J2
Canon Beck Rd
BERM/RHTH SE16 123 K2
Canonbie Rd FSTH SE23 163 K2
Canonbury Crs IS N1 85 J5
Canonbury Gv IS N1 85 J5
Canonbury La IS N1 85 H5
Canonbury Pk North IS N1 85 J4
Canonbury Pk South IS N1 85 J4
Canonbury Rd EN EN1 24 A2
IS N1 85 H5
Canonbury Sq IS N1 85 H5
Canonbury St IS N1 85 J5
Canonbury Vls IS N1 85 H5
Canon Mohan Cl EBAR EN4 34 A1
Canon Murnane Rd STHWK SE1 19 J5
Canon Rd BMLY BR1 184 B6
Canon Rw WHALL SW1A 16 E3
Canons Cl EDGE HA8 44 B2
EFNCH N2 65 H4
Canons Cottages EDGE * HA8 44 B2
Canons Ct EDGE * HA8 44 B2
Canons Dr EDGE HA8 44 B2
Canonsleigh Rd DAGW RM9 91 H5
Canon St IS N1 6 C1
Canon's Wk CROY/NA CR0 213 F1
Canopus Wy NTHWD HA6 26 E6
STWL/WRAY TW19 152 B2
Canrobert St BETH E2 104 D1
Cantelowes Rd CAMTN NW1 84 D4
Canterbury Av BFN/LL DA15 168 D4
IL IG1 71 J4
Canterbury Cl BECK BR3 182 E4
CMBW * SE5 142 D3
DART DA1 171 K2
EHAM E6 107 K5
GFD/PVL UB6 96 B4
NTHWD HA6 40 D2
Canterbury Crs BRXN/ST SW9 142 B4
Canterbury Gv WNWD SE27 162 C5
Canterbury Pl WALW SE17 18 B7
Canterbury Rd CROY/NA CR0 196 A4
FELT TW13 154 D4
HRW HA1 60 B2
KIL/WHAMP NW6 100 E1
LEY E10 70 A4
MRDN SM4 194 B3
Canterbury Ter
KIL/WHAMP NW6 100 E1
Cantley Gdns GNTH/NBYPK IG2 72 C3
NRWD SE19 181 G4
Cantley Rd HNWL W7 116 B3
Canton St POP/IOD E14 105 J5
Cantrell Rd BOW E3 105 J3
Cantwell Rd WOOL/PLUM SE18 147 G1
Canvey St STHWK SE1 12 C7
Cape Cl BARK IG11 90 B5
Capel Av WLGTN SM6 211 F3
Capel Cl HAYES BR2 200 D5
TRDG/WHET N20 33 G5
Capel Gdns GDMY/SEVK IG3 91 F2
PIN HA5 59 K1
Capella Rd NTHWD HA6 40 D1
Capel Pl RDART DA2 171 F6
Capel Rd EBAR EN4 33 J1
FSTGT E7 89 F2
OXHEY WD19 27 H1
Capeners Cl KTBR SW1X 15 F3
KTBR * SW1X 15 G3
Capern Rd WAND/EARL SW18 160 B3
Cape Rd TOTM N17 50 C6
Cape Yd WAP E1W 123 H1
Capital Interchange Wy
CHSWK W4 117 H5
Capitol Wy CDALE/KGS NW9 44 E6
Capland St STJWD NW8 2 C6
Caple Pde WLSDN * NW10 99 H1
Caple Rd WLSDN NW10 99 H1
Caprea Cl YEAD UB4 95 H4
Capri Rd CROY/NA CR0 197 G5
Capstan Cl CHDH RM6 73 H3
Capstan Ride ENC/FH EN2 23 G3
Capstan Rd DEPT SE8 124 C4
Capstan Sq POP/IOD E14 125 F2
Capstan Wy BERM/RHTH SE16 124 B1
Capstone Rd BMLY BR1 165 K6
Capthorne Av RYLN/HDSTN HA2 59 J5
Capuchin Cl STAN HA7 43 H2
Capulet Ms CAN/RD E16 125 K1
Capworth St LEY E10 69 J5
Caractacus Cottage Vw
WATW WD18 26 E2
Caractacus Gn WATW WD18 26 D1
Caradoc Evans Cl
FBAR/BDGN * N11 48 B1
Caradoc St GNWCH SE10 125 H5
Caradon Ct WAN * E11 70 C5
Caradon Wy SEVS/STOTM * N15 67 K1
Caravel Ms DEPT * SE8 124 D6
Caraway Cl PLSTW E13 107 F4
Caraway Pl WLGTN * SM6 210 B1
Carberry Rd NRWD SE19 181 F2
Carbery Av ACT W3 117 G2
Carbis Cl CHING E4 38 B3
Carbis Rd POP/IOD E14 105 H5
Carburton St GTPST W1W 9 K1
Cardale St POP/IOD E14 125 F3
Carden Rd PECK SE15 143 J4
Cardiff Rd HNWL W7 116 B3
PEND EN3 24 D5
WATW WD18 27 F1
Cardiff St WOOL/PLUM SE18 147 K1
Cardigan Gdns GDMY/SEVK IG3 73 G6
Cardigan Pl BKHTH/KID * SE3 145 G3
Cardigan Rd BARN SW13 138 D3
BOW E3 105 H1
RCHPK/HAM TW10 157 F1
WIM/MER SW19 178 B2
Cardigan St LBTH SE11 122 B5
Cardigan Wk IS * N1 85 J5
Cardinal Av KUTN/CMB KT2 175 F1
MRDN SM4 193 H3
Cardinal Bourne St STHWK * SE1 19 F5
Cardinal Cl CHST BR7 185 J4
EDGE HA8 45 F3
MRDN SM4 193 H3
WPK KT4 207 J2
Cardinal Crs NWMAL KT3 175 K5
Cardinal Dr BARK/HLT IG6 54 C2
WOT/HER KT12 188 C5
Cardinal Hinsey Cl WLSDN NW10 99 J1
Cardinal Pl PUT/ROE SW15 139 G5
Cardinal Rd FELT TW13 154 A3
RSLP HA4 59 H5
Cardinal's Wk HPTN TW12 173 H3
Cardinals Wy ARCH N19 66 D5
Cardinal Wy
KTN/HRWW/W * HA3 42 E6
Cardine Ms PECK SE15 143 J1
Cardington Sq HSLWW TW4 134 C5
Cardington St CAMTN NW1 4 B4
Cardozo Rd HOLWY N7 84 E3
Cardrew Av NFNCH/WDSP N12 47 H1
Cardross St HMSMTH W6 118 E3
Cardwell Rd HOLWY * N7 84 E2
Cardwell Ter HOLWY * N7 84 E2
Carew Cl HOLWY N7 67 F6
Carew Rd MTCM CR4 179 F5
NTHWD HA6 40 C2
THHTH CR7 180 C6
TOTM N17 50 C5
WEA W13 116 D2
WLGTN SM6 210 C4
Carew St CMBW SE5 142 D3
Carew Wy OXHEY WD19 27 K5
Carey Gdns VX/NE SW8 141 H2
Carey La CITYW EC2V 12 C3
Carey Pl WEST SW1P 16 C7
Carey Rd DAGW RM9 92 A2
Carey St LINN WC2A 11 H4
Carey Wy WBLY HA9 80 D2
The Carfax SYD * SE26 163 K5
Carfax Pl CLAP SW4 141 J5
Carfax Rd HCH RM12 93 H2
HYS/HAR UB3 113 K5
Carfree Cl IS N1 85 G5
Cargill Rd WAND/EARL SW18 160 B3
Cargreen Rd SNWD SE25 197 G1
Carholme Rd FSTH SE23 164 C3
Carisbrook Cl EN EN1 24 B2
Carisbrooke Av BXLY DA5 168 E3
Carisbrooke Cl STAN HA7 43 K5
Carisbrooke Ct NTHLT * UB5 77 K6
Carisbrooke Gdns PECK * SE15 143 G1
Carisbrooke Rd HAYES * BR2 200 B1
MTCM CR4 195 K1
WALTH * E17 69 G1
Carleton Av WLGTN SM6 210 D6
Carleton Cl ESH/CLAY KT10 189 J5
Carleton Gdns ARCH * N19 84 C3
Carleton Rd DART DA1 171 K2
HOLWY N7 84 D3
Carleton Vls KTTN * NW5 84 C3
Carlile Cl BOW E3 105 H1
Carlina Gdns WFD IG8 53 F1
Carlingford Rd HAMP NW3 83 H2
MRDN SM4 193 G3
SEVS/STOTM N15 49 H6
Carlisle Av ACT W3 99 G5
TWRH EC3N 13 H4
Carlisle Cl KUTN/CMB KT2 175 H4
Carlisle Gdns IL IG1 71 J3
KTN/HRWW/W HA3 61 K4
Carlisle La STHWK SE1 17 H4
Carlisle Pl FBAR/BDGN N11 34 B6
WEST SW1P 16 A5
Carlisle Rd CDALE/KGS NW9 44 E6
DART DA1 171 K1
FSBYPK N4 67 G5
HPTN TW12 173 G3
KIL/WHAMP NW6 82 C6
LEY E10 69 J5
ROM RM1 75 H2
SUT SM1 208 D4
Carlisle St SOHO/CST W1F 10 C4
Carlisle Wk HACK E8 86 B4
Carlisle Wy TOOT SW17 179 F1
Carlos Pl MYFR/PKLN W1K 9 H6
Carlow St CAMTN NW1 4 A2
Carlton Av EBED/NFELT TW14 154 B1
HYS/HAR UB3 113 H4
KTN/HRWW/W HA3 61 H2
SAND/SEL CR2 211 K5
STHGT/OAK N14 22 D6
Carlton Av East WBLY HA9 61 K6
Carlton Av West ALP/SUD HA0 61 H6
Carlton Cl CHSGTN KT9 205 K4
EDGE HA8 44 C1
HAMP NW3 64 E6
Carlton Crs CHEAM SM3 208 C2
Carlton Dene EW * KT17 207 K3
Carlton Dr BARK/HLT IG6 54 D6
PUT/ROE SW15 139 G6
Carlton Gdns EA W5 97 J5
STJS SW1Y 16 C1
Carlton Gn SCUP * DA14 168 A6
Carlton Gv PECK SE15 143 J2
Carlton Hl STJWD NW8 101 G1
Carlton House Ter STJS SW1Y 16 C1
Carlton Ms KIL/WHAMP * NW6 82 E3
Carlton Pde WBLY * HA9 62 A5
Carlton Park Av RYNPK SW20 177 F5
Carlton Rd CHSWK W4 118 A2
EA W5 97 J6
ERITH DA8 129 K6
FBAR/BDGN N11 48 A1
FSBYPK N4 67 G4
GPK RM2 75 J2
MNPK E12 89 H2
MORT/ESHN SW14 137 K4
NWMAL KT3 176 B5
SAND/SEL CR2 211 K5
SCUP DA14 186 A1
WALTH E17 51 G4
WAN E11 70 D5
WELL DA16 148 C4
WOT/HER KT12 188 A4
Carlton Sq WCHPL * E1 105 F3
Carlton St STJS SW1Y 10 C6
Carlton Ter SYD SE26 163 K5
UED * N18 35 K6
WAN * E11 71 F2
Carlton Tower Pl KTBR SW1X 15 F4
Carlton V KIL/WHAMP NW6 100 E2
Carlwell St TOOT SW17 178 D1
Carlyle Av BMLY BR1 184 C6
STHL UB1 95 K6
Carlyle Cl E/WMO/HCT KT8 173 G5
EFNCH N2 65 G3
WLSDN NW10 81 F6
Carlyle Ct WBPTN * SW10 140 B2
Carlyle Gdns STHL UB1 95 K6
Carlyle Rd CROY/NA CR0 197 H6
EA W5 116 D4
MNPK E12 89 J2
THMD SE28 109 H6
Carlyle Sq CHEL SW3 120 C5
Carlyon Av RYLN/HDSTN HA2 77 K2
Carlyon Cl ALP/SUD HA0 80 A6
Carlyon Rd ALP/SUD HA0 98 A1
YEAD UB4 95 G5
Carlys Cl BECK BR3 182 A5
Carmalt Gdns PUT/ROE SW15 139 F5
Carmel Ct KENS * W8 120 A2
Carmelite Rd KTN/HRWW/W HA3 42 C4
Carmelite St EMB EC4Y 11 K5
Carmen St POP/IOD E14 105 K5
Carmichael Cl BTSEA * SW11 140 C4
RSLP HA4 76 E2
Carmichael Rd SNWD SE25 197 H2
Carminia Rd BAL SW12 161 G4
Carnaby St REGST W1B 10 A5
Carnac St WNWD SE27 162 E6
Carnanton Rd WALTH E17 52 B4
Carnarvon Av EN EN1 24 B3
Carnarvon Dr HYS/HAR UB3 113 F3
Carnarvon Rd BAR EN5 20 C4
LEY E10 70 A3
SRTFD E15 88 D4
SWFD E18 52 D4
Carnation Cl ROMW/RG RM7 75 G6
Carnation St ABYW SE2 128 C5
Carnbrook Rd BKHTH/KID SE3 146 C4
Carnecke Gdns ELTH/MOT SE9 146 D6
Carnegie Cl PEND EN3 25 K1
SURB KT6 191 G6
Carnegie Pl WIM/MER SW19 159 G5
Carnegie St IS N1 5 G1
Carnforth Cl HOR/WEW KT19 206 D4
Carnforth Gdns HCH RM12 93 J3
Carnforth Rd
STRHM/NOR SW16 179 J3
Carnoustie Dr IS N1 85 F5
Carnoustie Cl THMD SE28 109 K5
Carnwath Rd FUL/PGN SW6 139 K4
Carolina Cl SRTFD E15 88 C3
Carolina Rd THHTH CR7 180 C5
Caroline Cl CROY/NA CR0 212 A2
STRHM/NOR SW16 162 A6
WDR/YW UB7 112 A2
Caroline Ct STAN * HA7 43 G2
Caroline Gdns BETH E2 7 H4
PECK * SE15 143 J1
Caroline Pl BAY/PAD W2 101 F6
HYS/HAR UB3 133 H1
OXHEY WD19 27 J1
VX/NE SW8 141 F3
Caroline Rd WIM/MER SW19 177 J3
Caroline St WCHPL E1 105 F5
Caroline Ter BGVA SW1W 15 G7
Caroline Wk HMSMTH W6 119 H6
Carol St CAMTN NW1 84 C6
Carolyn Dr ORP BR6 217 G1
Carpenders Av OXHEY WD19 27 J5
Carpenter Gdns WCHMH N21 35 H4
Carpenters Cl TRDG/WHET N20 33 F1
Carpenters Ms HOLWY * N7 84 E3
Carpenter's Pl CLAP SW4 141 J5
Carpenters Rd SRTFD E15 87 K5
Carpenter St MYFR/PKLN W1K 9 J6
Carrara Ms HACK E8 86 C3
Carr Gv WOOL/PLUM SE18 126 D4
Carriage Dr East BTSEA SW11 121 F6
Carriage Dr North BTSEA SW11 140 E1
Carriage Dr South BTSEA SW11 140 E2
Carriage Dr West BTSEA SW11 140 E1
Carriage Ms IL IG1 72 C6
Carrick Cl ISLW TW7 136 B4
Carrick Dr BARK/HLT IG6 54 C4
Carrick Gdns TOTM N17 50 A3
Carrick Ga ESH/CLAY KT10 204 C1
Carrick Ms DEPT SE8 124 D6
Carrill Wy BELV DA17 128 E4
Carrington Av HSLW TW3 135 G6
Carrington Cl CROY/NA CR0 198 B4
Carrington Gdns FSTGT E7 88 E2
Carrington Pl ESH/CLAY * KT10 204 B2
Carrington Rd DART DA1 171 J1
RCHPK/HAM TW10 137 H5
Carrington Sq
KTN/HRWW/W HA3 42 C3
Carrington St MYFR/PICC W1J 15 J1
Carrol Cl KTTN NW5 84 B2
Carroll Cl SRTFD E15 88 D3
Carronade Pl WOOL/PLUM SE18 127 H3
Carron Cl POP/IOD E14 105 K5
Carroun Rd VX/NE SW8 142 A1
Carroway La GFD/PVL UB6 96 D2
Carrow Rd DAGW RM9 91 H5
Carr Rd NTHLT UB5 78 B5
WALTH E17 51 H5
Carrs La WCHMH N21 23 K6
Carr St POP/IOD E14 105 G5
Carshalton Gv SUT SM1 209 H2
Carshalton Park Rd CAR SM5 209 K4
Carshalton Pl CAR SM5 210 A2
Carshalton Rd MTCM CR4 195 F2
SUT SM1 209 G3
Carsington Gdns DART DA1 171 G4
Carslake Rd PUT/ROE SW15 159 F1
Carson Rd CAN/RD E16 106 E4
DUL SE21 162 E4
EBAR EN4 21 K5
Carstairs Rd CAT SE6 165 F5
Carston Cl LEE/GVPK SE12 145 J6

Carswell Cl REDBR IG4 71 H1
Carswell Rd CAT SE6 165 F2
Carter Cl CRW RM5 56 D3
WLGTN SM6 210 D5
Carteret St STJSPK SW1H 16 C3
Carteret Wy DEPT SE8 124 B4
Carterhatch La EN EN1 24 B2
Carterhatch Rd PEND EN3 25 G3
Carter La BLKFR EC4V 12 B4
Carter Pl WALW SE17 122 D5
Carter Rd PLSTW E13 89 F6
WIM/MER SW19 178 C2
Carters Cl KTTN * NW5 84 D4
WPK KT4 193 G6
Carters Hill Cl ELTH/MOT SE9 166 B3
Carter St WALW SE17 122 D6
Carters Yd WAND/EARL * SW18 139 K6
Carthew Rd HMSMTH W6 118 E3
Carthew Vls HMSMTH W6 118 E3
Carthusian St FARR EC1M 12 C1
Carting La TPL/STR WC2R 11 F6
Cart La CHING E4 38 C3
Cartmel Cl TOTM N17 50 D3
Cartmel Ct NTHLT UB5 77 J4
Cartmel Gdns MRDN SM4 194 B2
Cartmel Rd BXLYHN DA7 149 H2
Cartwright Gdns STPAN WC1H 4 D5
Cartwright St TWRH EC3N 13 K5
Cartwright Wy BARN SW13 138 E1
Carver Rd HNHL SE24 162 D1
Carville Crs BTFD TW8 117 F5
Cary Rd WAN E11 88 C2
Carysfort Rd CEND/HSY/T N8 66 D2
STNW/STAM N16 85 K1
Cascade Av MUSWH N10 66 C1
Cascade Cl STMC/STPC BR5 186 D6
Cascade Rd BKHH IG9 39 H4
Casella Rd NWCR SE14 144 A1
Casewick Rd WNWD SE27 180 C1
Casey Cl STJWD NW8 2 D7
STJWD NW8 2 C5
Casimir Rd CLPT E5 86 D1
Casino Av HNHL SE24 142 D6
Caspian Street CMBW SE5 142 E1
Caspian Wk CAN/RD E16 107 H5
Cassandra Cl NTHLT UB5 78 D2
Casselden Rd WLSDN NW10 81 F5
Cassidy Rd FUL/PGN SW6 139 K1
Cassilda Rd ABYW SE2 128 B4
Cassilis Rd TWK TW1 156 C1
Cassiobury Av
EBED/NFELT TW14 153 J2
Cassiobury Rd WALTH E17 69 F2
Cassland Rd HOM E9 87 F5
THHTH CR7 196 E1
Casslee Rd CAT SE6 164 C2
Casson St WCHPL E1 104 C4
Castellain Rd MV/WKIL W9 101 F3
Castellan Av GPK RM2 57 K6
Castellane Cl STAN HA7 43 F3
Castello Av PUT/ROE SW15 139 F6
Castelnau BARN SW13 138 E1
Casterbridge Rd
BKHTH/KID SE3 145 K4
Casterton St HACK E8 86 D4
Castile Rd WOOL/PLUM SE18 127 F4
Castillon Rd CAT SE6 165 H4
Castlands Rd CAT SE6 164 C4
Castle Av CHING E4 52 B2
EW KT17 207 J6
RAIN RM13 93 G5
Castlebar Hl WEA W13 97 H4
Castlebar Ms EA W5 97 H4
Castlebar Pk EA W5 97 H4
Castlebar Rd WEA W13 97 J5
Castle Baynard St BLKFR EC4V 12 B5
Castlebrook Cl LBTH SE11 18 A6
Castle Cl ACT W3 117 J2
BUSH WD23 28 B1
HAYES BR2 183 G6
WIM/MER SW19 159 G5
Castlecombe Dr
WIM/MER SW19 159 G2
Castlecombe Rd ELTH/MOT SE9 184 D1
Castle Ct BANK * EC3V 13 F4
SYD SE26 164 B6
Castledine Rd PGE/AN SE20 181 J3
Castle Dr REDBR IG4 71 J3
Castleford Av ELTH/MOT SE9 167 G3
Castleford Cl UED N18 50 B2
Castlegate RCH/KEW TW9 137 G4
Castlehaven Rd CAMTN NW1 84 B5
Castle Hill Av CROY/NA CR0 213 K6
Castle Hill Pde WEA * W13 97 H6
Castle La WESTW SW1E 16 A4
Castleleigh Ct ENC/FH EN2 23 K6
Castlemaine Av EW KT17 207 K6
SAND/SEL CR2 212 B3
Castle Md CMBW * SE5 142 D1
Castle Ms CAMTN NW1 84 B4
NFNCH/WDSP N12 47 G1
Castle Pde EW * KT17 207 J5
Castle Pl CAMTN NW1 84 B4
Castlereagh St MBLAR W1H 8 E3
Castle Rd CAMTN NW1 84 B4
DAGW RM9 91 H6
ISLW TW7 136 A3
NFNCH/WDSP N12 47 G1
NTHLT UB5 78 B4
NWDGN * UB2 114 E3
PEND EN3 25 G2
Castle Rw CHSWK * W4 118 A5
Castle St EHAM E6 107 G1
KUT * KT1 175 F5
Castleton Av BXLYHN DA7 150 A2
WBLY HA9 80 A2
Castleton Cl CROY/NA CR0 198 B3
Castleton Gdns WBLY HA9 80 A1
Castleton Rd ELTH/MOT SE9 166 C6
GDMY/SEVK IG3 73 H5
MTCM CR4 195 J1
RSLP HA4 59 H5
WALTH E17 52 B5
Castletown Rd WKENS W14 119 H5
Castleview Cl FSBYPK N4 67 J5
Castle View Gdns IL IG1 71 J3
Castle Vls CRICK * NW2 81 J4
Castle Wk SUN * TW16 172 B6
Castle Wy FELT TW13 154 B6
WIM/MER SW19 159 G5
Castlewood Dr ELTH/MOT SE9 146 E3
Castlewood Rd EBAR EN4 21 H4
SEVS/STOTM N15 68 C3
Castle Yd HGT N6 66 A4
RCHPK/HAM TW10 136 E6
STHWK * SE1 12 B7
Castor La POP/IOD E14 105 K6
Catalina Rd HTHAIR TW6 132 E4
Caterham Av CLAY IG5 54 A5
Caterham Rd LEW SE13 145 F4
Catesby St WALW SE17 19 F7
Catford Broadway CAT SE6 164 E2
Catford Hl CAT SE6 164 C3
Catford Island CAT * SE6 164 E2
Catford Rd CAT SE6 164 D3
Cathall Rd WAN E11 70 B6
Cathay St BERM/RHTH SE16 123 J2
Cathcart Dr ORP BR6 201 K6
Cathcart Hl KTTN NW5 84 C1
Cathcart Rd WBPTN * SW10 120 A6
Cathcart St KTTN NW5 84 B4
Cathedral St STHWK SE1 12 E7
Catherall Rd HBRY N5 85 J1
Catherine Ct STHGT/OAK N14 22 C6
Catherine Dr RCH/KEW TW9 137 F5
Catherine Gdns HSLW TW3 135 J5
Catherine Griffiths Ct
CLKNW * EC1R 5 K6
Catherine Gv GNWCH SE10 144 E2
Catherine Pl HRW HA1 61 F2
WESTW SW1E 16 A4
WALTH E17 51 J4
Catherine Rd GPK RM2 75 K2
SURB KT6 190 E2
Catherines Cl WDR/YW * UB7 112 A2
Catherine St HOL/ALD * WC2B 11 G5
Catherine Vls RYNPK * SW20 176 E3
Catherine Wheel Aly
LVPST EC2M 13 H2
Catherine Wheel Rd BTFD TW8 136 E1
Catherine Wheel Yd
WHALL SW1A 16 A1
Cat Hl EBAR EN4 33 J1
Cathles Rd BAL SW12 161 G1
Cathnor Rd SHB W12 118 E2
Catling Cl FSTH SE23 163 K5
Catlin's La PIN HA5 41 F6
Catlin St BERM/RHTH SE16 123 H5
Cator La BECK BR3 182 C5
Cato Rd CLAP SW4 141 J4
Cator Rd CAR SM5 209 K3
SYD SE26 182 A2
Cator St PECK SE15 123 G6
Cato St MBLAR W1H 8 D2
Catsey La BUSH WD23 28 C2
Catsey Wd BUSH WD23 28 C2
Catterick Cl FBAR/BDGN N11 48 A2
Cattistock Rd ELTH/MOT SE9 184 D1
Cattley Cl BAR EN5 20 C5
Catton St RSQ WC1B 11 G2
Caudwell Ter
WAND/EARL * SW18 160 C1
Caulfield Rd EHAM E6 89 K5
PECK SE15 143 J3
The Causeway BELMT SM2 209 G6
CAR SM5 210 A1
CHSGTN KT9 206 A2
EFNCH N2 65 H1
ESH/CLAY KT10 205 F5
TEDD TW11 174 A2
WAND/EARL SW18 140 A6
WIM/MER SW19 177 F1
Causeway EBED/NFELT TW14 134 A5
Causeyware Rd ED N9 36 D2
Causton Cottages
POP/IOD * E14 105 G4
Causton Rd HGT * N6 66 B4
Causton Sq DAGE RM10 92 C5
Causton St WEST SW1P 16 D7
Cautley Av CLAP SW4 141 H6
Cavalier Cl CHDH RM6 73 J1
Cavalier Gdns HYS/HAR UB3 94 B5
Cavalry Crs HSLWW TW4 134 C5
Cavalry Gdns PUT/ROE SW15 139 H6
Cavan Pl PIN * HA5 41 K4
Cavaye Pl WBPTN SW10 120 B5
Cavell Crs DART DA1 151 K5
Cavell Dr ENC/FH EN2 23 G3
Cavell Rd TOTM N17 49 K3
Cavell St WCHPL E1 104 D4
Cavendish Av BFN/LL DA15 168 B2
ERITH DA8 129 K6
FNCH N3 46 E6
HCH RM12 93 K4
HRW HA1 78 D2
NWMAL KT3 192 E2
RSLP HA4 77 F3
STJWD NW8 2 B3
WEA W13 97 G4
WELL DA16 148 A4
WFD IG8 53 F3
Cavendish Cl KIL/WHAMP NW6 82 D4
STJWD NW8 2 B4
UED * N18 50 D1
YEAD UB4 94 C4
Cavendish Crs HCH RM12 93 K4
Cavendish Dr EDGE HA8 44 B2
ESH/CLAY KT10 204 E3
WAN E11 70 B5
Cavendish Gdns BARK IG11 91 F3
CHDH RM6 74 A2
CLAP * SW4 161 H1
IL IG1 72 A5
Cavendish Ms North REGST W1B 9 K1
Cavendish Ms South
GTPST * W1W 9 K2
Cavendish Pde CLAP * SW4 141 H5
HSLWW * TW4 134 D3
Cavendish Pl KIL/WHAMP NW6 82 B5
MHST W1U 9 J3
Cavendish Rd BAL SW12 161 G1
BAR EN5 20 A4
BELMT SM2 209 G5
CHING E4 51 K3
CHSWK W4 137 K2
CROY/NA CR0 196 C5
FSBYPK N4 67 H3
KIL/WHAMP NW6 82 C5
NWMAL KT3 192 C2
UED N18 50 D1
WIM/MER SW19 178 D3
Cavendish Sq CAVSQ/HST W1G 9 K3
Cavendish St IS N1 6 E3
Cavendish Ter BOW * E3 105 H2
FELT * TW13 153 K4
Cavendish Wy WWKM BR4 198 E5
Cavenham Gdns IL IG1 90 D1
Caverleigh Wy WPK KT4 192 D5
Caverley Gdns
KTN/HRWW/W HA3 61 K4
Cave Rd PLSTW E13 107 F1
RCHPK/HAM TW10 156 D6
Caversham Av CHEAM SM3 193 H6
PLMGR N13 35 G5
Caversham Rd KTTN * NW5 84 C4
KUT KT1 175 G5
SEVS/STOTM N15 67 J1
Caversham St CHEL SW3 120 E6
Caverswall St SHB W12 100 A5
Cawdor Crs HNWL W7 116 B4
Cawnpore St NRWD SE19 181 F1
Caxton Gv BOW E3 105 J2
Caxton Ms BTFD * TW8 136 E1
Caxton Rd NWDGN UB2 114 C3
SHB W12 119 G1
WDGN N22 49 F5
WIM/MER SW19 178 B1
The Caxtons CMBW * SE5 142 C1
Caxton St STJSPK SW1H 16 B4
Caxton St North CAN/RD E16 106 D5
Caxton Wy ROM RM1 75 G1
WATW WD18 26 B2
Cayenne Ct STHWK SE1 19 H2
Caygill Cl HAYES BR2 199 J1
Cayley Rd NWDGN UB2 115 G3
Cayton Rd GFD/PVL UB6 96 E1
Cayton St FSBYE EC1V 6 E5
Cazenove Rd STNW/STAM N16 68 B6
WALTH E17 51 J4
Cecil Av BARK IG11 90 D5
EN EN1 24 B5
WBLY HA9 80 B3
Cecil Cl CHSGTN KT9 205 K2
EA * W5 97 K4
Cecil Ct BAR EN5 20 B4
LSQ/SEVD WC2H 10 D6
Cecile Pk CEND/HSY/T N8 66 E3
Cecilia Cl EFNCH N2 47 G6
Cecilia Rd HACK E8 86 B3
Cecil Pk PIN HA5 59 J1
Cecil Pl MTCM CR4 194 E2
Cecil Rd ACT W3 98 E4
CDALE/KGS NW9 45 F6
CHDH RM6 73 K4
CROY/NA CR0 195 K3
ENC/FH EN2 23 K5
HSLW TW3 135 H4
IL IG1 90 B2
KTN/HRWW/W HA3 42 E6
MUSWH N10 48 B5
PLSTW E13 88 E6
STHGT/OAK N14 34 B3
SUT SM1 208 D4
WALTH E17 51 J4
WAN E11 70 C6
WIM/MER SW19 178 A3
WLSDN NW10 81 G6
Cecil Wy HAYES BR2 199 K5
Cedar Av BFN/LL DA15 168 B2
CHDH RM6 74 A2
EBAR EN4 33 J2
HYS/HAR UB3 94 E5
PEND EN3 24 E3
RSLP HA4 77 G3
WDR/YW * UB7 112 C1
WHTN TW2 155 G1
Cedar Cl BKHH IG9 39 H4
BOW E3 87 H6
CAR SM5 209 K4
DUL SE21 162 D3
HAYES BR2 215 J1
KUTN/CMB KT2 158 A6
ROMW/RG RM7 74 E1
SWLY BR8 187 K5
Cedar Copse BMLY BR1 184 E5
Cedar Ct CHARL * SE7 126 B6
ELTH/MOT * SE9 166 D1
WIM/MER SW19 159 G5
Cedar Crs HAYES BR2 215 J1
Cedarcroft Rd CHSGTN KT9 206 B2
Cedar Dr EFNCH N2 65 J1
PIN HA5 42 A2
Cedar Gdns BELMT SM2 209 G4
Cedar Gv BXLY DA5 168 E1
EA W5 116 E3
STHL UB1 96 A4
Cedar Hts RCHPK/HAM TW10 157 F3
Cedarhurst BMLY * BR1 183 H3
Cedarhurst Dr ELTH/MOT SE9 146 B6
Cedar Lawn Av BAR EN5 20 C6
Cedar Mt ELTH/MOT SE9 166 C3
Cedarne Rd FUL/PGN SW6 139 K1
Cedar Park Gdns CHDH RM6 73 K4
Cedar Park Rd ENC/FH EN2 23 J1
Cedar Pl CHARL SE7 126 B5
Cedar Ri STHGT/OAK N14 34 A2
Cedar Rd BELMT SM2 209 G4
BMLY BR1 184 B5
CRICK NW2 82 A2
CROY/NA CR0 197 F6
DART DA1 171 G3
E/WMO/HCT KT8 189 K1
EBED/NFELT TW14 153 G3
ENC/FH EN2 23 H1
ERITH DA8 150 D2
HEST TW5 134 B3
OXHEY WD19 27 G1
ROMW/RG RM7 74 E1
TEDD TW11 174 B1
TOTM N17 50 B4
The Cedars BKHH IG9 38 E3
HOM * E9 87 F5
SRTFD * E15 88 D6
TEDD TW11 174 A2
Cedars Av MTCM CR4 195 F1
WALTH E17 69 J2
Cedars Cl HDN NW4 46 B6
LEW SE13 145 G4
Cedars Cottages
PUT/ROE * SW15 158 D1
Cedars Ct ED N9 36 A4
Cedars Ms CLAP * SW4 141 G5
Cedars Rd BARN SW13 138 C3
BECK BR3 182 B5
CLAP SW4 141 G4
CROY/NA CR0 210 E1
E/WMO/HCT KT8 174 D4
ED N9 36 C4
MRDN SM4 193 K1
SRTFD E15 88 C4
WCHMH N21 35 H4
Cedar Ter RCH/KEW TW9 137 F5
Cedar Tree Gv WNWD SE27 180 C1
Cedarville Gdns
STRHM/NOR SW16 180 A2
Cedar Wk ESH/CLAY KT10 205 F4
Cedar Wy CAMTN NW1 84 D5
Cedric Av ROM RM1 57 G6
Cedric Rd ELTH/MOT SE9 167 H5
Celadon Cl PEND EN3 25 G4
Celandine Cl POP/IOD * E14 105 J4
Celandine Dr HACK E8 86 B5
THMD SE28 128 C1
Celandine Wy SRTFD E15 106 C2
Celbridge Ms BAY/PAD * W2 101 F5
Celestial Gdns LEW SE13 145 G5
Celia Rd ARCH N19 84 C2
Celtic Av HAYES BR2 183 H6
Celtic St POP/IOD E14 105 K4
Cemetery La CHARL SE7 126 D6
Cemetery Rd ABYW SE2 128 C6
FSTGT E7 88 D3
TOTM N17 50 A3
Cenacle Cl HAMP NW3 82 E1
Centaur Ct BTFD * TW8 117 F5
Centaur St STHWK SE1 17 H4
Centenary Rd PEND EN3 25 H5
Centenary Wk LOU IG10 39 F1
WAN E11 70 E6
WFD IG8 52 C2
Centennial Av BORE WD6 29 J2
Centennial Pk BORE * WD6 29 J2
Central Ar ASHF * TW15 152 C6
Central Av E/WMO/HCT KT8 188 E2
ED N9 36 A5
EFNCH N2 47 H5
EN EN1 24 D3
HSLW TW3 135 H5
HYS/HAR UB3 113 J2
PIN HA5 59 K3
WAN E11 70 B6
WELL DA16 148 B3
WLGTN SM6 210 E3
Central Buildings EA * W5 97 K6
Central Circ HDN NW4 63 K2
Central Hall Buildings
ARCH * N19 66 C6
Central Hl NRWD SE19 180 D1
Central Pde ACT * W3 117 H2
E/WMO/HCT * KT8 188 E1
GFD/PVL * UB6 97 G2
HRW HA1 61 F2
PEND * EN3 24 E3
PGE/AN * SE20 182 A3
SCUP * DA14 168 B5
STRHM/NOR * SW16 161 K6
SURB * KT6 191 F3
WALTH * E17 69 J1
Central Park Av DAGE RM10 92 E1
Central Park Est HSLWW * TW4 134 C5
Central Park Rd EHAM E6 107 H1
Central Pl SNWD * SE25 197 H1
Central Rd ALP/SUD HA0 79 H3
DART DA1 151 H6
MRDN SM4 193 K2
WPK KT4 192 D6
Central Sq E/WMO/HCT KT8 188 E1
GLDGN NW11 64 E3
Central St FSBYE EC1V 6 C5
Central Ter BECK * BR3 182 A6
Central Wy CAR SM5 209 J5
EBED/NFELT TW14 134 A6
NTHWD HA6 40 C3
THMD SE28 109 H6
WLSDN NW10 98 E2
The Centre FELT TW13 153 K4
Centre Av ACT W3 118 A1
EFNCH N2 47 J5
Centre Common Rd CHST BR7 185 H3
Centre Rd DAGE RM10 110 D1
WAN E11 70 E6
Centre St BETH E2 104 D1
Centre Wy ED N9 36 E4
Centric Cl CAMTN * NW1 84 B6
Centurian Wy ERITHM DA18 129 G3
Centurion Cl HOLWY N7 85 F5
Centurion Ct WLGTN * SM6 195 G6
Centurion La BOW E3 105 H1
Centurion Wy PUR RM19 131 J4
Century Cl HDN NW4 64 B2
Century Ct WATW * WD18 26 A2
Century Ms CLPT * E5 86 E2
Century Rd WALTH E17 51 G6
Cephas Av WCHPL E1 104 E3
Cephas St WCHPL E1 104 E3
Ceres Rd WOOL/PLUM SE18 128 A4
Cerise Rd PECK SE15 143 H2
Cerne Cl YEAD UB4 95 G6
Cerne Rd MRDN SM4 194 B3
Cervantes Ct BAY/PAD * W2 101 F5
NTHWD HA6 40 D3
Ceylon Rd WKENS W14 119 G3
Chadacre Av CLAY IG5 53 K6
Chadacre Rd EW KT17 207 K3
Chadbourn St POP/IOD E14 105 K4
Chadd Dr BMLY BR1 184 D6
Chadville Gdns CHDH RM6 73 K2
Chadway BCTR RM8 73 J6
Chadwell Av CHDH RM6 73 H4
Chadwell Heath La CHDH RM6 73 H1
Chadwell St CLKNW EC1R 5 K4
Chadwick Av CHING E4 38 B6
WCHMH * N21 23 F6
WIM/MER SW19 177 K2
Chadwick Cl TEDD TW11 174 B2
Chadwick Pl SURB KT6 190 D3
Chadwick Rd CMBW SE5 143 G3
IL IG1 90 B1
WAN E11 70 C4
WLSDN NW10 81 H6
Chadwick St WEST SW1P 16 C5
Chadwick Wy THMD SE28 109 K6
Chadwin Rd PLSTW E13 107 F4
Chadworth Wy ESH/CLAY KT10 204 D3
Chaffinch Av CROY/NA CR0 198 A3
Chaffinch Cl CROY/NA CR0 198 A2
ED N9 37 F3
SURB KT6 206 C1
Chaffinch La WATW WD18 26 D2
Chaffinch Rd BECK BR3 182 B4
Chafford Wy CHDH RM6 73 J1
Chagford St CAMTN NW1 2 E7
Chailey Av EN EN1 24 B3
Chailey Cl HEST TW5 134 C2
Chailey St CLPT E5 86 E1
Chalbury Wk IS N1 5 H2
Chalcombe Rd ABYW SE2 128 C3
Chalcot Cl BELMT SM2 208 E5
Chalcot Crs CAMTN NW1 83 K6
Chalcot Gdns HAMP NW3 83 K4
Chalcot Ms STRHM/NOR SW16 161 K5
Chalcot Rd CAMTN NW1 84 A6
Chalcot Sq CAMTN NW1 84 A5
Chalcott Gdns SURB * KT6 190 D5
Chalcroft Rd LEW SE13 145 H6
Chaldon Rd FUL/PGN SW6 139 H1
Chale Rd BRXS/STRHM SW2 161 K1
Chalet Cl RDART DA2 170 A6
Chalet Est MLHL * NW7 31 J6
Chalfont Av WBLY HA9 80 D4
Chalfont Gn ED N9 36 A5
Chalfont Rd ED N9 36 A5
HYS/HAR UB3 113 K2
SNWD SE25 181 G6
Chalfont Wk PIN * HA5 41 G5
Chalfont Wy WEA W13 116 C3
Chalford Cl E/WMO/HCT KT8 189 F1
Chalforde Gdns GPK RM2 75 K1
Chalford Rd DUL SE21 162 E6
Chalford Wk WFD IG8 53 H4
Chalgrove Av MRDN SM4 193 K2
Chalgrove Crs CLAY IG5 53 J5
Chalgrove Gdns FNCH N3 46 C6
Chalgrove Rd BELMT SM2 209 H5
HOM E9 86 E4
TOTM N17 50 D4
Chalice Cl WLGTN SM6 210 D4
Chalkenden Cl PGE/AN SE20 181 J3
Chalk Farm Pde HAMP * NW3 84 A5
Chalk Hl OXHEY WD19 27 J1
Chalk Hill Rd HMSMTH W6 119 G4
Chalkhill Rd WBLY HA9 62 D6
WBLY HA9 80 C1
Chalklands WBLY HA9 80 E1
Chalk La EBAR EN4 21 K4
Chalkley Cl MTCM CR4 178 E5
Chalk Pit Av STMC/STPC BR5 186 D6
Chalk Pit Rd SUT SM1 209 G3
Chalk Rd PLSTW E13 107 F4
Chalkstone Cl WELL DA16 148 B2
Chalkwell Park Av EN EN1 24 A5
Chalky La CHSGTN KT9 205 K6
Challenge Cl WLSDN NW10 81 G6
Challenge Rd FELT TW13 153 F5
Challice Wy BRXS/STRHM SW2 162 A3
Challin St PGE/AN SE20 181 K4
Challis Rd BTFD TW8 116 E5
Challoner Cl EFNCH N2 47 H5
Challoner Crs WKENS W14 119 J5
Challoners Cl E/WMO/HCT KT8 189 J1
Challoner St WKENS W14 119 J5
Chalmers Rd ASHF TW15 152 E6
Chalmers Rd East ASHF TW15 152 E6
Chalmers Wk WALW * SE17 122 C6
Chalmers Wy
EBED/NFELT TW14 134 A6
Chalsey Rd BROCKY SE4 144 C5
Chalton Dr EFNCH N2 65 G3
Chalton St CAMTN NW1 4 C2
Chamberlain Cl
WOOL/PLUM SE18 127 J3
Chamberlain Cottages
CMBW * SE5 142 E2
Chamberlain Crs WWKM BR4 198 E5
Chamberlain Gdns HSLW TW3 135 H2
Chamberlain La PIN HA5 58 E1
Chamberlain Pl WALTH * E17 51 G6
Chamberlain Rd ED N9 36 C5
EFNCH N2 47 G5
WEA W13 116 B2
Chamberlain St HAMP * NW3 83 K5
Chamberlain Wy PIN HA5 41 F6
SURB KT6 191 F4
Chamberlayne Av WBLY HA9 80 A1
Chamberlayne Rd WLSDN NW10 82 A6
Chamberlens Garages
HMSMTH * W6 118 E4
Chambers Gdns EFNCH N2 47 H4
Chambers La WLSDN NW10 81 K5
Chambers Rd HOLWY N7 84 E2
Chambers St BERM/RHTH SE16 123 H2
Chamber St WCHPL E1 13 K5
Chambon Pl HMSMTH W6 118 D4
Chambord St BETH E2 7 K5
Champion Crs SYD SE26 164 B6
Champion Gv CMBW SE5 142 E4
Champion Hl CMBW SE5 142 E5
Champion Pk CMBW SE5 142 E4
Champion Rd SYD SE26 164 B6
Champness Cl WNWD SE27 162 E6
Champness Rd BARK IG11 91 F5
Champneys OXHEY * WD19 27 J4
Champneys Cl BELMT SM2 208 D5
Chancellor Gdns SAND/SEL CR2 211 H6
Chancellor Gv DUL SE21 162 D4
Chancellor Pl CDALE/KGS NW9 45 H5
Chancellor's Rd HMSMTH W6 119 F5
Chancellors St HMSMTH W6 119 F5
Chancellors Whf HMSMTH * W6 119 F5
Chancelot Rd ABYW SE2 128 C4
Chancel St STHWK SE1 12 A7
Chancery La BECK BR3 182 E5
LINN WC2A 11 H2
Chance St BETH E2 7 J6
Chanctonbury Cl
ELTH/MOT SE9 167 G5
Chanctonbury Gdns
BELMT SM2 209 F5
Chanctonbury Wy
NFNCH/WDSP N12 32 E6
Chandler Av CAN/RD E16 106 E4
Chandler Cl HPTN TW12 172 E4
Chandlers Cl EBED/NFELT TW14 153 J2
Chandlers Ct LEE/GVPK * SE12 166 A4
Chandlers Dr ERITH DA8 130 A4
Chandlers Ms POP/IOD E14 124 D2
Chandler St WAP E1W 123 J1
Chandlers Wy ROM RM1 75 G2
Chandler Wy PECK SE15 143 G1
Chandos Av EA W5 116 D4
STHGT/OAK N14 34 C5
TRDG/WHET N20 33 H3
WALTH * E17 51 J5
Chandos Cl BKHH IG9 39 F4
Chandos Crs EDGE HA8 44 B3
Chandos Pl CHCR WC2N 10 E6
Chandos Rd CRICK NW2 82 A3
EFNCH N2 47 H5
HRW HA1 60 C2
PIN HA5 59 G4
SRTFD E15 88 B3
TOTM N17 50 A5
WLSDN NW10 99 G3
Chandos St CAVSQ/HST W1G 9 K2
Chandos Wy GLDGN NW11 65 F5
Channel Cl HEST TW5 135 F2
Channel Islands Est IS N1 85 J4
Channelsea Rd SRTFD E15 88 B6
Chantress Cl DAGE RM10 92 E6
Chantrey Cl SCUP DA14 187 F1
Chantrey Rd BRXN/ST SW9 142 A4
The Chantry CHING * E4 38 A3
Chantry Cl ENC/FH EN2 23 J1
KTN/HRWW/W HA3 62 B2
MLHL NW7 31 H2
MV/WKIL * W9 100 D3

Chantry La HAYES BR2 200 C2
Chantry Pl RYLN/HDSTN HA2 42 B4
Chantry Rd CHSGTN KT9 206 B3
KTN/HRWW/W HA3 42 B4
Chantry Sq KENS * W8 120 A3
Chantry St IS N1 6 B1
Chantry Wy MTCM CR4 178 C6
Chant Sq SRTFD * E15 88 B5
Chant St SRTFD E15 88 B5
Chapel Cl DART DA1 150 B6
Chapel Ct EFNCH N2 47 J6
STHWK SE1 18 E2
Chapel Farm Rd ELTH/MOT SE9 166 E5
Chapel Hl DART DA1 150 B5
EFNCH N2 47 J5
Chapel House St POP/IOD E14 124 E5
Chapel La PIN HA5 41 H6
Chapel Market IS N1 5 J2
Chapel Pl CAVSQ/HST W1G 9 J3
IS N1 5 K2
TOTM N17 50 B3
Chapel Rd BXLYHN DA7 149 H5
HSLW TW3 135 G4
IL IG1 90 A1
TWK TW1 156 C2
WEA W13 116 C1
WNWD SE27 162 C6
Chapel Side BAY/PAD W2 101 F6
Chapel St BAY/PAD W2 8 C2
ENC/FH EN2 23 J4
KTBR SW1X 15 H4
Chapel Vw SAND/SEL CR2 212 E5
Chaplemount Rd WFD * IG8 53 K2
Chaplin Cl ALP/SUD * HA0 79 K4
STHWK SE1 17 K2
Chaplin Rd ALP/SUD HA0 79 J4
CRICK NW2 81 J4
SRTFD E15 106 C1
TOTM * N17 50 B6
Chapman Cl WDR/YW UB7 112 C3
Chapman Crs
KTN/HRWW/W HA3 62 A2
Chapman Rd BELV DA17 129 H5
CROY/NA CR0 196 B5
HOM E9 87 H4
Chapmans Gn WDGN * N22 49 G4
Chapman's La STMC/STPC BR5 186 E5
SWLY BR8 187 H5
Chapman Sq WIM/MER SW19 159 G4
Chapman St WCHPL E1 104 D6
Chapman Ter WDGN * N22 49 H4
Chapter Rd CRICK NW2 81 J3
WALW SE17 122 C5
Chapter St WEST SW1P 16 C7
Chapter Wy HPTN TW12 155 F6
Chara Pl CHSWK W4 118 A6
Charcroft Gdns PEND EN3 25 F5
Chardin Rd CHSWK * W4 118 B4
Chardmore Rd STNW/STAM N16 68 C5
Chardwell Cl EHAM E6 107 J5
Charecroft Wy WKENS W14 119 G2
Charford Rd CAN/RD E16 106 E4
Chargeable La PLSTW E13 106 E3
Chargeable St CAN/RD E16 106 D3
Charing Cl ORP BR6 217 F2
Charing Cross CHCR * WC2N 10 E7
Charing Cross Rd
LSQ/SEVD WC2H 10 D5
Charlbert St STJWD NW8 2 C2
Charlbury Av STAN HA7 43 K1
Charlbury Gdns GDMY/SEVK IG3 73 F6
Charlbury Gv EA W5 97 J5
Charldane Rd ELTH/MOT SE9 167 G5
Charlecote Gv SYD SE26 163 J5
Charlecote Rd BCTR RM8 92 A1
Charlemont Rd EHAM E6 107 K2
Charles Babbage Cl
CHSGTN KT9 205 J5
Charles Barry Cl CLAP * SW4 141 H4
Charles Cl SCUP DA14 168 C6
Charles Cobb Gdns
CROY/NA CR0 211 G3
Charles Coveney Rd
PECK * SE15 143 G2
Charles Crs HRW HA1 60 D4
Charles Dickens Ter
PGE/AN * SE20 181 K3
Charlesfield ELTH/MOT SE9 166 B5
Charles Flemwell Ms
CAN/RD * E16 125 K1
Charles Grinling Wk
WOOL/PLUM SE18 127 F4
Charles Haller St
BRXS/STRHM SW2 162 B2
Charles II Pl CHEL * SW3 120 E5
Charles II St STJS SW1Y 10 C7
Charles La STJWD NW8 2 C3
Charles Pl CAMTN * NW1 4 B5
Charles Rd CHDH RM6 73 K4
DAGE RM10 93 F4
FSTGT E7 89 G5
WEA W13 97 G5
WIM/MER SW19 177 K4
Charles Sevright Dr MLHL NW7 46 B1
Charles Sq IS N1 7 F5
Charles Square Est IS N1 7 F5
Charles St BARN SW13 138 B4
CAN/RD E16 126 B1
CROY/NA CR0 211 J1
EN EN1 24 B6
HSLW TW3 134 E3
MYFR/PICC W1J 9 J7
Charleston Cl FELT TW13 153 K5
Charleston St WALW SE17 18 D7
Charleville Circ SYD SE26 181 H1
Charleville Rd WKENS W14 119 H5
Charlieville Rd ERITH DA8 149 K1
Charlmont Rd TOOT SW17 178 D2
Charlock Wy WATW WD18 26 D1
Charlotte Cl BXLYHS DA6 149 F6
Charlotte Despard Av
BTSEA SW11 141 G2
Charlotte Gdns CRW RM5 56 D2
Charlotte Ms ESH/CLAY * KT10 204 B2
FITZ W1T 10 B1
NKENS W10 100 B5
Charlotte Pde FSTH * SE23 164 B4
Charlotte Park Av BMLY BR1 184 D6
Charlotte Pl FITZ W1T 10 B2
Charlotte Rd BARN SW13 138 C2
IS N1 7 G5
WLGTN SM6 210 C4
Charlotte Rw CLAP SW4 141 H4
Charlotte St FITZ W1T 10 B1
Charlotte Ter IS N1 5 H1
Charlow Cl FUL/PGN SW6 140 B3
Charlton Church La CHARL SE7 126 B5
Charlton Crs BARK IG11 109 F1
Charlton Dene CHARL SE7 146 B1
Charlton King's Rd HOLWY N7 84 D3
Charlton La CHARL SE7 126 C5
Charlton Park La CHARL SE7 146 C1
Charlton Park Rd CHARL SE7 126 C6
Charlton Pl IS N1 6 A2
Charlton Rd BKHTH/KID SE3 126 A6
BKHTH/KID SE3 145 K1
ED N9 37 F3
KTN/HRWW/W HA3 61 K1
WBLY HA9 62 B5
WLSDN NW10 81 G6
Charlton Wy BKHTH/KID SE3 145 H2
Charlwood CROY/NA CR0 213 H6
Charlwood Cl
KTN/HRWW/W HA3 42 E2
Charlwood Pl PIM SW1V 16 B7
Charlwood Rd PUT/ROE SW15 139 G5
Charlwood St PIM SW1V 16 B7
Charlwood Ter PUT/ROE SW15 139 G5
Charmian Av STAN HA7 43 K6
Charminster Av
WIM/MER SW19 177 K5
Charminster Rd ELTH/MOT SE9 166 C6
WPK KT4 193 G5
Charmouth Rd WELL DA16 148 D2
Charnock Rd CLPT E5 86 D1
Charnwood Av WIM/MER SW19 177 K5
Charnwood Cl NWMAL KT3 192 B1
Charnwood Dr SWFD E18 53 F6
Charnwood Gdns POP/IOD E14 124 D4
Charnwood Pl TRDG/WHET N20 33 G5
Charnwood Rd SNWD SE25 196 E2
Charnwood St CLPT * E5 68 C6
Charrington Rd CROY/NA CR0 196 C6
Charrington St CAMTN NW1 4 C2
Charsley Rd CAT SE6 164 E4
Chart Cl CROY/NA CR0 197 K3
HAYES BR2 183 H4
MTCM CR4 194 E1
The Charter Rd WFD IG8 52 C2
Charter Av GNTH/NBYPK IG2 72 D5
Charter Crs HSLWW TW4 134 D5
Charter Dr BXLY DA5 169 F2
The Charterhouse FARR * EC1M 6 B7
Charterhouse Av ALP/SUD HA0 79 J3
Charterhouse Buildings
FARR EC1M 6 C7
Charterhouse Ms FARR EC1M 12 B1
Charterhouse Rd HACK E8 86 C3
ORP BR6 217 G1
Charterhouse St HCIRC EC1N 11 K2
Charteris Rd FSBYPK N4 67 F5
KIL/WHAMP NW6 82 D6
WFD IG8 53 F2
Charter Rd KUT KT1 175 J6
Charters Cl NRWD SE19 181 F1
Charter Sq KUT KT1 175 J5
Charter Wy GLDGN NW11 64 D1
STHGT/OAK N14 34 C1
Chartfield Av PUT/ROE SW15 138 E6
Chartfield Sq PUT/ROE * SW15 139 G6
Chartham Gv WNWD SE27 162 B5
Chartham Rd SNWD SE25 181 J6
Chart Hills Cl THMD SE28 110 A5
Chartley Av CRICK NW2 81 G1
STAN HA7 43 F2
Chartley Pde WLSDN * NW10 81 G1
Charton Cl BELV DA17 129 G6
Chartridge OXHEY * WD19 27 H4
Chartridge Cl BUSH WD23 28 C1
Chart St IS N1 7 F4
Chartwell Cl CHST BR7 167 J4
CROY/NA CR0 196 E5
GFD/PVL UB6 78 B6
Chartwell Dr ORP BR6 216 D3
Chartwell Pl CHEAM SM3 208 C2
RYLN/HDSTN HA2 60 D6
Chartwell Rd NTHWD HA6 40 D2
Chartwell Wy PGE/AN SE20 181 J4
Charville La HGDN/ICK UB10 94 A2
Charwood STRHM/NOR * SW16 162 B6
The Chase BMLY BR1 184 A6
BXLYHN DA7 149 J4
CLAP SW4 141 G4
DAGE RM10 93 F1
EDGE HA8 44 D4
LOU IG10 39 G2
MNPK E12 89 H2
PIN HA5 59 G3
PIN HA5 59 K1
ROM RM1 57 G6
STAN HA7 43 G2
STRHM/NOR SW16 180 A3
SUN TW16 172 A4
WLGTN SM6 210 E3
Chase Ct RYNPK SW20 177 H5
Chase Court Gdns ENC/FH EN2 23 J4
Chase Cross Rd CRW RM5 56 E3
Chasefield Rd TOOT SW17 160 E6
Chase Gdns CHING E4 37 J6
WHTN TW2 155 J1
Chase Gn ENC/FH EN2 23 J4
Chase Green Av ENC/FH EN2 23 H3
Chase Hl ENC/FH EN2 23 J4
Chase La BARK/HLT IG6 72 D2
Chaseley Ct CHSWK W4 117 J5
Chaseley St POP/IOD * E14 105 G5
Chasemore Cl MTCM CR4 194 E4
Chasemore Gdns CROY/NA CR0 211 G3
Chase Ridings ENC/FH EN2 23 G3
Chase Rd ACT W3 99 F3
STHGT/OAK N14 22 C6
Chase Side EBAR EN4 22 A6
ENC/FH EN2 23 J3
STHGT/OAK N14 34 A1
Chase Side Av ENC/FH EN2 23 J3
Chaseside Av RYNPK SW20 177 H4
Chaseside Cl ROM * RM1 57 G2
Chase Side Crs ENC/FH EN2 23 K2
Chaseville Pde WCHMH * N21 23 F6
Chaseville Park Rd WCHMH N21 22 E6
Chase Wy STHGT/OAK N14 34 B3
Chasewood Av ENC/FH EN2 23 H3
Chasewood Pk HRW * HA1 78 E1
Chastilian Rd DART DA1 170 D2
Chatfield Rd BTSEA SW11 140 B4
CROY/NA CR0 196 C5
Chatham Av HAYES BR2 199 K4
Chatham Cl CHEAM SM3 193 J4
GLDGN NW11 64 E2
Chatham Pl HOM E9 86 E4
Chatham Rd BTSEA SW11 160 E1
KUTN/CMB KT2 175 H5
SWFD E18 52 D5
WALTH E17 51 G6
Chatham St WALW SE17 18 E6
WOOL/PLUM SE18 127 G3
Chatsfield Pl EA W5 98 A5
Chatsworth Av BFN/LL DA15 168 B3
BMLY BR1 184 A1
HDN NW4 46 A5
RYNPK SW20 177 H4
WBLY HA9 80 B3
Chatsworth Cl CHSWK * W4 117 K6
HDN NW4 46 A5
WWKM BR4 199 J6
Chatsworth Crs HSLW TW3 135 J5
Chatsworth Dr EN EN1 36 C2
Chatsworth Est CLPT * E5 87 F2
Chatsworth Gdns ACT W3 98 D6
NWMAL * KT3 192 C2
RYLN/HDSTN HA2 60 B5
Chatsworth Pl MTCM CR4 178 E6
TWK TW1 156 B6
Chatsworth Ri EA W5 98 B3
Chatsworth Rd CHEAM SM3 208 B2
CHSWK W4 117 K6
CLPT E5 86 E1
CRICK NW2 82 B4
CROY/NA CR0 211 K2
DART DA1 151 F6
EA W5 98 B3
SRTFD E15 88 D3
YEAD UB4 95 F3
Chatsworth Wy WNWD SE27 162 C5
Chattern Hl ASHF TW15 153 F6
Chattern Rd ASHF TW15 153 F6
Chatterton Ms FSBYPK * N4 85 H1
Chatterton Rd FSBYPK N4 85 H1
HAYES BR2 200 C2
Chatto Rd BTSEA SW11 140 E6
Chaucer Av HSLWW TW4 134 A3
RCH/KEW TW9 137 H3
YEAD UB4 94 E4
Chaucer Cl FBAR/BDGN N11 48 C1
Chaucer Dr STHWK SE1 19 K7
Chaucer Gdns SUT SM1 208 E2
Chaucer Gn CROY/NA CR0 197 J4
Chaucer Pk DART DA1 171 J2
Chaucer Rd ACT W3 117 K1
ASHF TW15 152 B6
BFN/LL DA15 168 D3
FSTGT E7 88 E4
HARH RM3 57 K3
HNHL SE24 142 B6
SUT SM1 208 E2
WALTH E17 52 A4
WAN E11 70 E3
WELL DA16 148 A2
Chaucer Wy DART DA1 151 K5
Chauncey Cl ED N9 36 C5
Chaundrye Cl ELTH/MOT SE9 166 E1
Chauntler Rd CAN/RD E16 107 F5
Chave Rd DART DA1 171 H5
Cheam Common Rd WPK KT4 192 E6
Cheam Man CHEAM * SM3 208 C4
Cheam Park Wy CHEAM SM3 208 B4
Cheam Rd BELMT SM2 208 B6
Cheam St PECK * SE15 143 J4
Cheapside CITYW EC2V 12 D4
EFNCH * N2 47 K6
PLMGR N13 35 J6
WDGN * N22 49 G6
Cheddar Cl FBAR/BDGN N11 47 K2
Cheddar Waye YEAD UB4 95 F5
Cheddington Rd UED N18 36 A6
Cheeseman Cl HPTN TW12 172 D2
Cheesemans Ter WKENS * W14 119 J5
Chelford Rd BMLY BR1 183 G1
Chelmer Crs BARK IG11 109 H1
Chelmer Rd HOM E9 87 F3
Chelmsford Av CRW RM5 57 F3
Chelmsford Cl BELMT SM2 208 E6
EHAM E6 107 K5
HMSMTH W6 119 G6
Chelmsford Gdns IL IG1 71 J4
Chelmsford Rd STHGT/OAK N14 34 C2
SWFD E18 52 D4
WALTH E17 69 J3
WAN E11 70 B5
Chelmsford Sq WLSDN NW10 82 A6
Chelsea Br VX/NE SW8 121 G6
Chelsea Bridge Ga BTSEA SW11 121 F6
Chelsea Bridge Rd CHEL SW3 121 F5
Chelsea Cl HPTN TW12 173 H2
WLSDN NW10 81 F6
WPK KT4 192 D4
Chelsea Crs CRICK * NW2 82 D4
WBPTN * SW10 140 B2
Chelsea Emb CHEL SW3 120 E6
Chelsea Gdns BGVA * SW1W 121 F5
CHEAM SM3 208 C2
Chelsea Harbour Dr
WBPTN SW10 140 B2
Chelsea Manor Gdns
CHEL * SW3 120 D6
Chelsea Manor St CHEL SW3 120 D5
Chelsea Park Gdns
WBPTN SW10 120 C6
Chelsea Sq CHEL SW3 120 C5
Chelsea Towers CHEL * SW3 120 D6
Chelsea Village WBPTN * SW10 140 A1
Chelsfield Av ED N9 37 F2
Chelsfield Gdns SYD SE26 163 K5
Chelsfield Hl ORP BR6 217 J6
Chelsfield La ORP BR6 217 K2
STMC/STPC BR5 202 E4
Chelsfield Rd STMC/STPC BR5 202 D3
Chelsham Rd CLAP SW4 141 J4
SAND/SEL CR2 211 K5
Chelston Rd RSLP HA4 58 E6
Chelsworth Dr
WOOL/PLUM SE18 127 J6
Cheltenham Av TWK TW1 156 B2
Cheltenham Cl NTHLT UB5 78 B4
NWMAL KT3 175 K6
Cheltenham Gdns EHAM E6 107 J1
LOU IG10 39 J1
Cheltenham Pl ACT W3 117 K2
KTN/HRWW/W HA3 62 A1
Cheltenham Rd LEY E10 70 A3
ORP BR6 217 G1
PECK SE15 143 K5
Cheltenham Ter CHEL SW3 120 E5
Chelverton Rd PUT/ROE SW15 139 G5
Chelwood Cl CHING E4 37 K1
NTHWD HA6 40 A3
Chelwood Gdns RCH/KEW TW9 137 H3
Chenappa Cl PLSTW E13 106 E2
Chenduit Wy STAN HA7 43 F1
Cheney Rd CAMTN NW1 4 E3
Cheney Rw WALTH E17 51 H4
Cheneys Rd WAN E11 88 C1
Cheney St PIN HA5 59 G1
The Chenies ORP BR6 201 K3
RDART DA2 170 B6
Chenies Ms GWRST WC1E 4 C7
Chenies Pl CAMTN NW1 4 D2
Chenies St FITZ W1T 10 C1
Chenies Wy WATW WD18 26 C2
Cheniston Gdns KENS * W8 120 A3
Chepstow Cl PUT/ROE SW15 139 H6
Chepstow Cnr BAY/PAD * W2 100 E5
Chepstow Crs GDMY/SEVK IG3 72 E3
NTGHL W11 100 E6
Chepstow Gdns STHL UB1 95 K5
Chepstow Pl BAY/PAD W2 100 E6
Chepstow Ri CROY/NA CR0 212 A1
Chepstow Rd BAY/PAD W2 100 E5
CROY/NA CR0 212 A1
HNWL W7 116 B3
Chepstow Vls NTGHL W11 100 D6
Chepstow Wy PECK SE15 143 G2
The Chequers PIN * HA5 41 H6
Chequers BKHH IG9 39 F3
Chequers Cl CDALE/KGS NW9 45 G6
STMC/STPC BR5 202 A1
Chequers La DAGW RM9 110 B3
Chequers Pde PLMGR * N13 49 J1
Chequer St STLK EC1Y 6 E7
Chequers Wy PLMGR N13 49 H1
Cherbury Cl THMD SE28 109 K5
Cherbury St IS N1 7 F3
Cherimoya Gdns
E/WMO/HCT KT8 173 G6
Cherington Rd HNWL * W7 116 A1
Cheriton Av CLAY IG5 54 A5
HAYES BR2 199 J2
Cheriton Cl EA W5 97 J4
EBAR EN4 21 K4
Cheriton Ct WOT/HER KT12 188 B5
Cheriton Dr WOOL/PLUM SE18 147 J1
Cheriton Sq TOOT SW17 161 F4
Cherry Av STHL UB1 114 C1
Cherry Blossom Cl PLMGR N13 49 H1
Cherry Cl BRXS/STRHM * SW2 162 B2
CAR SM5 194 E6
EA W5 116 E3
MRDN SM4 193 H1
RSLP HA4 76 D1
Cherrycot Ri ORP BR6 216 C2
Cherry Ct PIN HA5 41 H5
Cherry Crs BTFD TW8 136 C1
Cherry Croft Gdns PIN * HA5 41 K3
Cherrydown Av CHING E4 37 H5
Cherrydown Cl CHING E4 37 H5
Cherrydown Rd SCUP DA14 168 E4
Cherrydown Wk ROMW/RG RM7 56 D5
Cherry Gdns DAGW RM9 92 B3
NTHLT UB5 78 B5
Cherry Garden St
BERM/RHTH SE16 123 J2
Cherry Garth BTFD TW8 116 E5
Cherry Gv HYS/HAR UB3 114 A1
UX/CGN UB8 94 A4
Cherry Hl BAR EN5 33 F1
KTN/HRWW/W HA3 42 E2
Cherry Hill Gdns CROY/NA CR0 211 F2
Cherry Hills OXHEY WD19 41 J1
Cherrylands Cl
CDALE/KGS * NW9 62 E6
Cherry La WDR/YW UB7 112 C4
Cherry Orch CHARL SE7 126 B6
WDR/YW UB7 112 B2
Cherry Orchard Cl
STMC/STPC BR5 202 D2
Cherry Orchard Gdns
CROY/NA CR0 196 E5
E/WMO/HCT KT8 172 E6
Cherry Orchard Rd
CROY/NA CR0 196 E6
E/WMO/HCT KT8 173 F6
HAYES BR2 200 D6
Cherry Rd PEND EN3 24 E1
Cherry St ROMW/RG RM7 75 F2
Cherry Tree Cl ALP/SUD HA0 79 G2
RAIN RM13 111 J1
Cherry Tree Ct CHARL * SE7 126 B6
Cherry Tree Dr
STRHM/NOR * SW16 161 K5
Cherry Tree Hl EFNCH N2 65 J2
Cherry Tree La RAIN RM13 111 H2
RDART DA2 170 C5
Cherry Tree Ri BKHH IG9 39 H6
Cherry Tree Rd EFNCH N2 65 K1
SRTFD E15 88 C3
Cherry Tree Wk BECK BR3 198 C1
STLK EC1Y 6 D7
WWKM BR4 214 D2
Cherry Tree Wy STAN HA7 43 H2
Cherry Wk HAYES BR2 199 K5
RAIN RM13 111 H1
Cherry Wy HOR/WEW KT19 207 F4
Cherrywood Cl BOW E3 105 G2
KUTN/CMB KT2 175 H3
Cherrywood Dr PUT/ROE SW15 139 G6
Cherrywood La MRDN SM4 193 H1
Chertsey Dr CHEAM SM3 193 H6
Chertsey Rd FELT TW13 153 H6
IL IG1 90 D2
TWK TW1 156 B1
WAN E11 70 B6
WHTN TW2 155 H3
Chertsey St TOOT SW17 179 F1
Chervil Cl FELT TW13 153 K5
Chervil Ms THMD SE28 128 C1
Cherwell Ct HOR/WEW KT19 206 E2
Cherwell Wy RSLP HA4 58 A3
Cheryls Cl FUL/PGN SW6 140 A2
Cheseman St SYD SE26 163 J5
Chesfield Rd KUTN/CMB KT2 175 F3
Chesham Av HAYES BR2 201 G3
Chesham Cl KTBR * SW1X 15 G5
ROMW/RG RM7 75 F1
Chesham Crs PGE/AN SE20 181 K4
Chesham Ms KTBR SW1X 15 G4
Chesham Pl KTBR SW1X 15 G5
Chesham Rd KUTN/CMB KT2 175 H4
PGE/AN SE20 181 K5
Chesham St KTBR SW1X 15 G5
WLSDN NW10 81 F1
Chesham Ter WEA W13 116 C2
Chesham Wy WATW WD18 26 C1
Cheshire Cl MTCM CR4 179 K6
WALTH E17 51 K4
Cheshire Gdns CHSGTN KT9 205 K4
Cheshire Rd WDGN N22 49 F3
Cheshire St BETH E2 104 C3
Chesholm Rd STNW/STAM N16 86 A1
Cheshunt Rd BELV DA17 129 H5
FSTGT E7 89 F4
Chesilton Rd FUL/PGN SW6 139 J2
Chesil Wy YEAD UB4 94 D2
Chesley Gdns EHAM E6 107 H1
Chesney Crs CROY/NA CR0 214 A5
Chesney St BTSEA SW11 141 F2
Chesnut Av North WALTH E17 70 B1
Chesnut Gv TOTM N17 50 C6
Chesnut Rd TOTM N17 50 C6
Chesnut Rw FNCH * N3 46 E3
Chessington Av BXLYHN DA7 149 F1
FNCH N3 46 C6
Chessington Cl HOR/WEW KT19 206 E4
Chessington Ct PIN HA5 59 K1
Chessington Hall Gdns
CHSGTN KT9 205 K5
Chessington Hill Pk
CHSGTN KT9 206 C4
Chessington Pde CHSGTN * KT9 205 K3
Chessington Rd CHSGTN KT9 206 C4
Chessington Wy WWKM BR4 198 E6
Chesson Rd WKENS W14 119 J6
Chesswood Wy PIN HA5 41 H5
Chester Av RCHPK/HAM TW10 157 G1
WHTN TW2 154 E3
Chester Cl BARN * SW13 138 E4
KTBR SW1X 15 H3
SUT SM1 193 K6
Chester Cl North CAMTN NW1 3 K4
Chester Cl South CAMTN NW1 3 K5
Chester Crs HACK E8 86 B3
Chester Dr RYLN/HDSTN HA2 60 A3
Chesterfield Cl STMC/STPC BR5 202 E1
Chesterfield Dr DART DA1 150 E6
ESH/CLAY KT10 190 B6
Chesterfield Gdns FSBYPK N4 67 H2
GNWCH * SE10 145 G1
MYFR/PICC * W1J 9 J7
Chesterfield Gv EDUL SE22 143 G6
Chesterfield Hl MYFR/PICC W1J 9 J6
Chesterfield Rd BAR EN5 20 B6
CHSWK W4 117 K6
FNCH N3 46 E2
HOR/WEW KT19 207 F5
LEY E10 70 A4
Chesterfield St MYFR/PICC W1J 9 J7
Chesterfield Wy
HYS/HAR * UB3 113 K2
PECK SE15 143 K1
Chesterford Gdns HAMP NW3 83 F2
Chesterford Rd MNPK E12 89 K3
Chester Gdns ED N9 36 D1
MRDN SM4 194 B2
WEA * W13 97 H5
Chester Ga CAMTN NW1 3 J5
Chester Ms KTBR SW1X 15 J4
Chester Pl CAMTN NW1 3 J4
NTHWD * HA6 40 C3
Chester Rd ARCH N19 66 B6
BFN/LL DA15 147 K6
CAMTN NW1 3 H5
CAN/RD E16 106 C3
ED N9 36 D3
FSTGT E7 89 H5
GDMY/SEVK IG3 73 F5
HSLWW TW4 134 A4
HTHAIR TW6 132 D4
NTHWD HA6 40 D3
TOTM N17 49 K6
WALTH E17 69 F2
WAN E11 71 F3
WIM/MER SW19 177 F2
Chester Rw BGVA SW1W 15 G7
Chester Sq BGVA SW1W 15 H6
Chester Square Ms
BGVA * SW1W 15 J5
The Chesters NWMAL KT3 176 B4
Chester St BETH * E2 86 C6
BETH E2 104 C3
KTBR SW1X 15 H4
Chester Ter CAMTN NW1 3 J4
Chesterton Cl GFD/PVL UB6 96 B1
WAND/EARL SW18 139 K6
Chesterton Ct EA * W5 97 K5
Chesterton Dr
STWL/WRAY TW19 152 C3
Chesterton Rd NKENS W10 100 B4
PLSTW E13 106 E2
Chesterton Sq WKENS W14 119 J4
Chesterton Ter KUT KT1 175 H5
PLSTW E13 106 E2
Chester Wy LBTH SE11 17 K7
Chesthunte Rd TOTM N17 49 J4
Chestnut Aly FUL/PGN * SW6 119 J6
Chestnut Av ALP/SUD HA0 79 H3
BKHH IG9 39 H5
BTFD TW8 116 E5
CEND/HSY/T N8 66 E2
E/WMO/HCT KT8 174 A6
EDGE HA8 44 A2
ESH/CLAY KT10 189 J4
FSTGT E7 89 F2
HCH RM12 75 H6
HOR/WEW KT19 207 G2
HPTN TW12 173 F3
MORT/ESHN * SW14 138 A4
NTHWD HA6 40 D5
TEDD TW11 174 A3
WWKM BR4 214 C3
Chestnut Av South WALTH E17 70 A1
Chestnut Cl ASHF TW15 152 E6
BFN/LL DA15 168 B4
BKHH IG9 39 H5
CAR SM5 194 E5
CAT SE6 165 F6
HYS/HAR UB3 94 C6
NWCR SE14 144 C2
ORP BR6 217 G3
STHGT/OAK N14 22 C6
STRHM/NOR SW16 162 B6
WDR/YW UB7 132 E1
Chestnut Cottages
TRDG/WHET * N20 32 C3
Chestnut Dr BXLYHN DA7 148 E4
KTN/HRWW/W HA3 43 F3
PIN HA5 59 H3
WAN E11 70 E3
Chestnut Gln HCH RM12 75 H6
Chestnut Gv ALP/SUD HA0 79 H3
BAL SW12 161 F2
BARK/HLT IG6 54 E2
EA W5 116 E3
EBAR EN4 21 K6
ISLW TW7 136 B5
MTCM CR4 195 J2
NWMAL KT3 176 A6

SAND/SEL CR2 212 D5
Chestnut La TRDG/WHET N20 32 C3
Chestnut Mnr WLGTN SM6 210 B2
Chestnut Pl SYD SE26 163 G6
Chestnut Ri BUSH WD23 28 B2
WOOL/PLUM SE18 127 K5
Chestnut Rd ASHF TW15 152 D6
DART DA1 171 G3
KUTN/CMB KT2 175 F3
RYNPK SW20 177 G5
WHTN TW2 155 K4
WNWD SE27 162 C5
The Chestnuts BECK * BR3 182 A6
PIN * HA5 41 K3
Chestnut Ter SUT * SM1 209 F2
Chestnut Wy FELT TW13 154 A5
Cheston Av CROY/NA CR0 198 B5
Cheswick Cl DART DA1 150 C5
Chesworth Cl ERITH DA8 150 B2
Chettle Cl STHWK SE1 18 E4
Chetwode Rd TOOT SW17 160 E5
Chetwynd Av EBAR EN4 33 K3
Chetwynd Rd KTTN NW5 84 B2
Chetwynd Vls KTTN * NW5 84 B2
Chevalier Cl STAN HA7 29 K5
Cheval Pl SKENS SW7 14 D4
Cheval St POP/IOD E14 124 D3
Cheveney Wk HAYES BR2 183 K6
Chevening Rd GNWCH SE10 125 J5
KIL/WHAMP NW6 100 B1
NRWD SE19 180 E3
The Chevenings SCUP DA14 168 C5
Cheverton Rd ARCH N19 66 D5
Chevet St HOM E9 87 G3
Chevington CRICK * NW2 82 D4
Cheviot Cl BELMT SM2 209 H6
BUSH WD23 28 C1
BXLYHN DA7 150 B3
ENC/FH EN2 23 K3
HYS/HAR UB3 133 G1
Cheviot Gdns GLDGN NW11 64 B6
Cheviot Ga EMPK RM11 75 J4
WNWD SE27 180 C1
Cheviot Wy GNTH/NBYPK IG2 72 E2
Chevron Cl CAN/RD E16 106 E5
Chevy Rd NWDGN UB2 115 H2
Chewton Rd WALTH E17 69 G1
Cheyne Av SWFD E18 52 D6
WHTN TW2 154 E3
Cheyne Cl HAYES BR2 215 J1
Cheyne Gdns CHEL SW3 120 D6
Cheyne Hl BRYLDS KT5 191 G1
Cheyne Ms CHEL SW3 120 D6
Cheyne Pth WEA W13 97 F4
Cheyne Pl CHEL * SW3 120 E6
Cheyne Rw CHEL SW3 120 D6
Cheyne Wk CHEL SW3 120 D6
CROY/NA CR0 197 H6
HDN NW4 64 A3
WBPTN SW10 140 C1
WCHMH N21 23 G6
Cheyneys Av EDGE HA8 43 K2
Chichele Gdns CROY/NA CR0 212 A2
Chichele Rd CRICK NW2 82 B3
Chicheley Rd KTN/HRWW/W HA3 42 C3
Chicheley St STHWK SE1 17 H2
Chichester Av RSLP HA4 58 B6
Chichester Cl BKHTH/KID SE3 146 B1
EHAM E6 107 J5
HPTN TW12 172 E2
Chichester Ct EW * KT17 207 H6
STAN HA7 44 A6
Chichester Gdns IL IG1 71 J4
Chichester Rd CROY/NA CR0 212 A1
ED N9 36 B3
KIL/WHAMP NW6 100 E1
WAN E11 88 C1
Chichester St PIM SW1V 121 H5
Chichester Wy
EBED/NFELT TW14 154 B2
POP/IOD E14 125 G4
Chichester Whf ERITH DA8 130 B5
Chicksand St WCHPL E1 13 K2
Chiddingfold NFNCH/WDSP N12 32 E5
Chiddingstone Av BXLYHN DA7 129 G6
Chiddingstone St FUL/PGN SW6 139 K3
Chieftan Dr PUR RM19 131 K4
Chieveley Pde BXLYHN * DA7 149 J4
Chieveley Rd BXLYHN DA7 149 J5
Chignell Pl WEA W13 116 B1
Chigwell Hl WAP E1W 104 D6
Chigwell Rd SWFD E18 53 F6
Chilcott Cl ALP/SUD HA0 79 J2
Childebert Rd TOOT SW17 161 G4
Childeric Rd NWCR SE14 144 B1
Childerley St FUL/PGN SW6 139 H2
The Childers WFD IG8 53 K1
Childers St DEPT SE8 124 B6
Childs Ct HYS/HAR UB3 94 E6
Childs La NRWD * SE19 181 F2
Child's Pl ECT SW5 119 K4
Child's St ECT SW5 119 K4
Child's Wk ECT * SW5 119 K4
Childs Wy GLDGN NW11 64 D2
Chilham Cl BXLY DA5 169 G2
GFD/PVL UB6 97 G1
Chilham Rd ELTH/MOT SE9 166 D6
Chilham Wy HAYES BR2 199 K4
Chillerton Rd TOOT SW17 179 F1
Chillingworth Gdns TWK * TW1 156 A4
Chillingworth Rd HOLWY N7 85 G3
Chilmark Gdns NWMAL KT3 192 C3
Chilmark Rd STRHM/NOR SW16 179 J5
Chiltern Av BUSH WD23 28 C1
WHTN TW2 155 F3
Chiltern Cl BUSH WD23 28 B1
BXLYHN DA7 150 B2
CROY/NA CR0 212 A1
WPK KT4 193 F6
Chiltern Dene ENC/FH EN2 23 F5
Chiltern Dr BRYLDS KT5 191 J3
Chiltern Gdns CRICK NW2 82 B1
HAYES BR2 199 J1
Chiltern Rd BOW E3 105 J3
GNTH/NBYPK IG2 72 E1
PIN HA5 59 G2
The Chilterns BELMT * SM2 209 F6
Chiltern St MHST W1U 9 G1
Chiltern Wy WFD IG8 38 E5
Chilthorne Cl CAT SE6 164 C2
Chilton Av EA W5 116 E4
Chilton Gv DEPT SE8 124 A4
Chilton Rd EDGE HA8 44 C2
RCH/KEW TW9 137 H4
Chilton St BETH E2 7 K6
Chilvers Cl WHTN TW2 155 K4
Chilver St GNWCH SE10 125 J5
Chilwell Gdns OXHEY WD19 27 G6
Chilworth Gdns SUT SM1 209 G1
Chilworth Ms BAY/PAD W2 101 G5
Chilworth St BAY/PAD W2 101 G5
Chimes Av PLMGR N13 35 G6
Chinbrook Crs LEE/GVPK SE12 166 A5
Chinbrook Rd ELTH/MOT SE9 166 B5
Chinchilla Dr HSLWW TW4 134 B3
The Chine ALP/SUD HA0 79 H3
MUSWH N10 66 C1
WCHMH N21 35 H1
Chingdale Rd CHING E4 38 C5
Chingford Av CHING E4 37 K5
Chingford La WFD IG8 38 C6
Chingford Mount Rd CHING E4 51 J1
Chingford Rd CHING E4 51 J3
WALTH E17 51 K5
Chingley Cl BMLY BR1 183 H2
Ching Wy CHING E4 51 H2
Chinnery Cl EN EN1 24 B1
Chinnor Crs GFD/PVL UB6 96 C1
Chipka St POP/IOD E14 125 F2
Chipley St NWCR SE14 124 B6
Chippendale St CLPT E5 87 F1
Chippenham Cl RSLP * HA4 58 D1
Chippenham Gdns
KIL/WHAMP NW6 100 E2
Chippenham Ms MV/WKIL * W9 100 E3
Chippenham Rd MV/WKIL W9 100 E3
Chipperfield Rd
STMC/STPC BR5 186 B5
Chipping Cl BAR EN5 20 C4
Chipstead Av THHTH CR7 196 C1
Chipstead Cl BELMT SM2 209 F6
NRWD SE19 181 G3
Chipstead Gdns CRICK NW2 63 K6
Chipstead Rd ERITH DA8 150 B1
Chipstead St FUL/PGN SW6 139 K2
Chirk Cl YEAD UB4 95 J3
Chisenhale Rd BOW E3 105 G1
Chisholm Rd CROY/NA CR0 197 F6
RCHPK/HAM TW10 157 G1
Chislehurst Av FNCH N3 47 G3
Chislehurst High St CHST BR7 185 G2
Chislehurst Rd BMLY BR1 184 D5
ORP BR6 202 B4
RCHPK/HAM TW10 157 F1
SCUP DA14 186 B1
STMC/STPC BR5 201 K1
Chislet Cl BECK BR3 182 D3
Chisley Rd SEVS/STOTM N15 68 A3
Chiswell Sq BKHTH/KID SE3 146 A3
Chiswell St STLK EC1Y 12 E1
Chiswick Br MORT/ESHN SW14 137 K3
Chiswick Cl CROY/NA CR0 211 F1
Chiswick Common Rd
CHSWK W4 118 A4
Chiswick High Rd CHSWK W4 117 J5
Chiswick House Grounds
CHSWK * W4 118 A6
Chiswick La CHSWK W4 118 B5
Chiswick La South CHSWK W4 118 C6
Chiswick Ml CHSWK W4 118 C6
Chiswick Pk CHSWK * W4 117 K3
Chiswick Pier CHSWK * W4 138 C1
Chiswick Quay CHSWK W4 137 K2
Chiswick Rd CHSWK W4 117 K4
ED N9 36 C4
Chiswick Sq CHSWK W4 118 B6
Chiswick Staithe CHSWK W4 137 J2
Chiswick Village CHSWK W4 117 H6
Chitterfield Ga WDR/YW UB7 132 D1
Chitty's La BCTR RM8 73 K6
Chitty St FITZ W1T 10 B1
Chivalry Rd BTSEA SW11 140 D6
Chivenor Gv KUTN/CMB KT2 174 E1
Chivers Rd CHING E4 37 K5
Choats Rd BARK IG11 109 J1
Chobham Gdns
WIM/MER SW19 159 G4
Chobham Rd SRTFD E15 88 C3
Cholmeley Cl HGT * N6 66 B4
Cholmeley Crs HGT N6 66 B4
Cholmeley Pk HGT N6 66 B5
Cholmley Gdns KIL/WHAMP NW6 82 E3
Cholmley Rd THDIT KT7 190 C3
Cholmley Ter THDIT * KT7 190 C4
Cholmley Vls THDIT * KT7 190 C4
Cholmondeley Av WLSDN NW10 99 J1
Chopwell Cl SRTFD * E15 88 B5
Chorleywood Crs
STMC/STPC BR5 186 A5
Choumert Gv PECK SE15 143 H3
Choumert Rd PECK SE15 143 G4
Chow Sq HACK * E8 86 B3
Chrislaine Cl STWL/WRAY TW19 152 A1
Chrisp St POP/IOD E14 105 K5
Christabel Cl ISLW TW7 135 K4
Christ Church Av ERITH DA8 130 A6
Christchurch Av ALP/SUD HA0 80 A4
KIL/WHAMP NW6 82 B6
KTN/HRWW/W HA3 61 G1
NFNCH/WDSP N12 47 G2
RAIN RM13 111 H1
TEDD TW11 174 B1
Christchurch Cl ENC/FH EN2 23 J3
NFNCH/WDSP * N12 47 H3
WIM/MER SW19 178 C3
Christchurch Gdns
KTN/HRWW/W HA3 61 G1
Christchurch Hl HAMP NW3 83 H1
Christ Church La BAR EN5 20 C3
Christchurch Ldg EBAR * EN4 21 K5
Christchurch Pk BELMT SM2 209 G5
Christchurch Pas HAMP NW3 83 H1
Christ Church Rd BECK * BR3 182 D5
BRYLDS KT5 191 G4
CEND/HSY/T N8 66 E3
Christchurch Rd BFN/LL DA15 168 A6
BRXS/STRHM SW2 162 A3
DART DA1 171 F2
IL IG1 72 B5
MORT/ESHN SW14 137 J6
WIM/MER SW19 178 C4
Christchurch Sq HOM E9 86 E6
Christchurch St CHEL SW3 120 E6
Christchurch Ter CHEL * SW3 120 E6
Christchurch Wy GNWCH SE10 125 H5
Christian Flds
STRHM/NOR SW16 180 B3
Christian St WCHPL E1 104 C5
Christie Dr SNWD SE25 197 H2
Christie Rd HOM E9 87 G4
Christina Sq FSBYPK N4 67 H5
Christina St SDTCH EC2A 7 G6
Christopher Av HNWL W7 116 B3
Christopher Cl BFN/LL DA15 148 A6
Christopher Gdns DAGW RM9 91 K3
Christopher Pl CAMTN * NW1 4 D4
Christopher Rd NWDGN UB2 114 A4
Christophers Ms NTGHL * W11 119 H1
Christopher St SDTCH EC2A 7 F7
Chryssell Rd BRXN/ST SW9 142 B1
Chubworthy St NWCR SE14 124 B6
Chudleigh Crs GDMY/SEVK IG3 90 E2
Chudleigh Gdns SUT SM1 209 G1
Chudleigh Rd BROCKY SE4 144 C6
KIL/WHAMP NW6 82 A5
WHTN TW2 155 K1
Chudleigh St WCHPL E1 105 F5
Chudleigh Wy RSLP HA4 58 E5
Chulsa Rd SYD SE26 181 J1
Chumleigh Gdns CMBW * SE5 123 F6
Chumleigh St CMBW SE5 123 F6
Chumleigh Wk BRYLDS KT5 191 G1
Church Ap DUL SE21 162 E5
Church Av BECK BR3 182 D4
CAMTN NW1 84 B4
CHING E4 52 B2
EFNCH N2 47 H5
MORT/ESHN SW14 138 A5
NTHLT UB5 77 K5
NWDGN UB2 114 D3
PIN HA5 59 J3
RSLP HA4 58 B5
SCUP DA14 186 B1
Churchbury Cl EN EN1 24 A3
Churchbury La EN EN1 24 A2
Churchbury Rd ELTH/MOT SE9 166 C2
EN EN1 24 A3
Church Cl EDGE HA8 44 E1
HSLW TW3 134 E3
KENS * W8 120 A2
NTHWD HA6 40 D3
TRDG/WHET N20 33 J5
WDR/YW UB7 112 B3
YEAD UB4 94 B4
Church Crs FNCH N3 46 D4
HOM E9 87 F5
MUSWH N10 66 B1
TRDG/WHET N20 33 J5
Churchcroft Cl BAL * SW12 161 F2
Churchdown BMLY BR1 165 H6
Church Dr CDALE/KGS NW9 63 F5
RYLN/HDSTN HA2 60 A3
WWKM BR4 214 C1
Church Elm La DAGE RM10 92 C4
Church End HDN NW4 45 K6
WALTH * E17 69 K1
Church Farm EBAR * EN4 33 K2
Church Farm La CHEAM SM3 208 C4
Church Fld DART DA1 171 G4
Churchfield Av
NFNCH/WDSP N12 47 G2
Churchfield Cl HYS/HAR UB3 94 D6
RYLN/HDSTN HA2 60 C1
Churchfield Rd ACT W3 117 K1
HNWL W7 115 K2
WEA W13 116 C1
WELL DA16 148 B4
Churchfields E/WMO/HCT KT8 173 F6
GNWCH SE10 125 F6
SWFD E18 52 E4
Churchfields Av FELT TW13 154 E5
Churchfields Rd BECK BR3 182 A5
Churchfield Wy
NFNCH/WDSP N12 47 G2
Church Gdns ALP/SUD HA0 79 G2
EA W5 116 E2
Church Garth ARCH * N19 66 D6
Church Ga FUL/PGN SW6 139 H4
Church Gn BRXN/ST * SW9 142 B3
HYS/HAR UB3 94 D5
Church Gv KUT KT1 174 D4
LEW SE13 144 E5
Church Hl CAR SM5 209 K3
DART DA1 150 B5
DART DA1 171 G5
HRW HA1 60 E5
ORP BR6 202 B4
WALTH E17 69 J1
WCHMH N21 35 F2
WIM/MER SW19 177 J1
WOOL/PLUM SE18 126 E3
Church Hill Rd CHEAM SM3 208 B2
EBAR EN4 33 J1
SURB KT6 191 F2
WALTH E17 69 K1
Church Hill Wd STMC/STPC BR5 202 A2
Church Hollow PUR RM19 131 K5
Church Hyde
WOOL/PLUM SE18 127 K6
Churchill Av KTN/HRWW/W HA3 61 H3
Churchill Cl EBED/NFELT TW14 153 J3
Churchill Gdns ACT W3 98 C5
Churchill Gardens Rd PIM SW1V 121 G5
Churchill Pl POP/IOD E14 124 E1
Churchill Rd CAN/RD E16 107 G5
CRICK NW2 81 K4
EDGE HA8 44 B2
KTTN NW5 84 B2
SAND/SEL CR2 211 J6
Churchill Ter CHING E4 37 J6
Churchill Wk HOM E9 86 E3
Churchill Wy BMLY BR1 183 K5
Church La CDALE/KGS NW9 62 E5
CEND/HSY/T N8 67 F1
CHSGTN KT9 206 B4
CHST BR7 185 H4
DAGE RM10 92 D4
ED * N9 36 C4
EFNCH N2 47 H6
ENC/FH EN2 23 K4
HAYES BR2 200 D5
KTN/HRWW/W HA3 43 F4
PIN HA5 41 J6
PUR RM19 131 K5
ROM RM1 75 G1
TEDD TW11 174 A1
THDIT KT7 190 A3
TOOT SW17 179 F1
TOTM N17 50 A4
TWK TW1 156 B3
WALTH E17 69 K1
WAN E11 70 C5
WEA W13 116 D2
WIM/MER SW19 177 K5
WLGTN SM6 210 D1
Churchley Rd SYD SE26 163 J6
Church Manor Wy ABYW SE2 128 B4
Church Manorway ERITH DA8 130 A3
Church Md CMBW * SE5 142 D1
Churchmead Cl EBAR EN4 33 J1
Church Meadow SURB KT6 190 D6
Churchmead Rd WLSDN NW10 81 J4
Churchmore Rd
STRHM/NOR SW16 179 H4
Church Mt EFNCH N2 65 H2
Church Paddock Ct WLGTN SM6 210 D1
Church Pde ASHF * TW15 152 C6
Church Pas BAR * EN5 20 D4
Church Pth CHSWK W4 117 K3
CROY/NA CR0 196 D6
MTCM CR4 178 D6
NFNCH/WDSP * N12 47 G1
RYNPK SW20 177 J5
WAN E11 70 E2
Church Pl EA W5 116 E2
MTCM CR4 178 D6
Church Ri CHSGTN KT9 206 B4
FSTH SE23 164 A3
Church Rd ACT W3 117 K2
ASHF TW15 152 C6
BARK IG11 90 C4
BARN SW13 138 D3
BKHH IG9 39 F3
BXLYHN DA7 149 G3
CHEAM SM3 208 C4
CROY/NA CR0 211 J1
E/WMO/HCT KT8 173 J6
EFNCH N2 47 H4
ERITH DA8 129 K5
ESH/CLAY KT10 205 F4
FELT TW13 172 B1
GNTH/NBYPK IG2 72 E3
HAYES BR2 183 H6
HAYES BR2 183 K5
HAYES BR2 215 H5
HDN NW4 63 K1
HEST TW5 114 A5
HEST TW5 135 F1
HNWL W7 96 E6
HOR/WEW KT19 207 F5
HYS/HAR UB3 113 J1
IS N1 85 J4
ISLW TW7 135 J2
KUT KT1 175 G5
LEY E10 69 J5
MNPK E12 89 K3
MTCM CR4 178 C5
NRWD SE19 181 F3
NTHLT UB5 95 H1
NTHWD HA6 40 D3
NWDGN UB2 114 E3
ORP BR6 216 C3
ORP BR6 217 K4
PEND EN3 36 E1
RCHPK/HAM TW10 137 F6
RCHPK/HAM TW10 157 F6
SCUP DA14 168 B6
STAN HA7 43 H1
SURB KT6 190 D5
TEDD TW11 155 K6
TOTM N17 50 A4
WALTH E17 51 F6
WDR/YW UB7 112 A2
WELL DA16 148 C3
WIM/MER SW19 159 H6
WLGTN SM6 210 C1
WLSDN NW10 81 G5
WPK KT4 192 B5
Church Rd South EFNCH N2 47 H5
Church Rw CHST BR7 185 H4
FUL/PGN * SW6 140 A1
HAMP NW3 83 G2
WAND/EARL * SW18 139 K6
Church Row Ms CHST BR7 185 H3
Church St BAY/PAD W2 8 B1
CHSWK W4 118 B6
CROY/NA CR0 211 H1
DAGE RM10 92 D5
ED N9 35 K3
ENC/FH EN2 23 J4
ESH/CLAY KT10 204 B2
EW KT17 207 J6
HPTN TW12 173 H4
HSLW TW3 135 H6
ISLW TW7 136 C4
KUT KT1 174 E5
SRTFD E15 88 C6
TWK TW1 156 B3
Church Street Est STJWD NW8 2 B7
Church St North SRTFD E15 88 C6
Church Ter FUL/PGN * SW6 140 A3
HDN NW4 45 K6
LEW SE13 145 H4
RCHPK/HAM TW10 136 E6
Church V EFNCH N2 47 K6
FSTH SE23 163 K4
Churchview Rd WHTN TW2 155 J3
Church Wk BTFD TW8 116 D6
BUSH WD23 28 A1
CDALE/KGS NW9 63 F6
CRICK NW2 82 D1
DART DA1 171 G5
HYS/HAR UB3 94 C5
RYNPK SW20 177 F6
STNW/STAM N16 85 K3
STNW/STAM N16 85 K1
STRHM/NOR SW16 179 H5
THDIT KT7 190 B3
Churchway CAMTN NW1 4 D5
Church Wy TRDG/WHET N20 33 J5
Churchyard Rw LBTH SE11 18 B6
Churston Av PLSTW E13 89 F6
Churston Cl BRXS/STRHM * SW2 162 C3
Churston Dr MRDN SM4 193 G2
Churston Gdns FBAR/BDGN N11 48 C2
Churton Pl CHSWK * W4 117 J6
PIM SW1V 16 B7
Churton St PIM SW1V 16 B7
Chyngton Cl BFN/LL DA15 168 A5
Cibber Rd FSTH SE23 164 A4
Cicada Rd WAND/EARL SW18 160 B1
Cicely Rd PECK SE15 143 H2
Cinderford Wy BMLY BR1 165 H6
Cinema Pde EDGE * HA8 44 C2
Cinnamon Cl CROY/NA * CR0 195 K4
Cinnamon St WAP E1W 123 J1
Cintra Pk NRWD SE19 181 G3
The Circle CRICK NW2 81 G1
MLHL NW7 45 F2
Circle Gdns WIM/MER SW19 177 K6
Circle Rd EFNCH N2 47 H5
The Circuits PIN HA5 59 G2
Circular Rd TOTM N17 50 B6
Circular Wy WOOL/PLUM SE18 126 E6
Circus Ms MBLAR * W1H 8 E1
Circus Pl LVPST * EC2M 13 F2
Circus Rd STJWD NW8 2 A4
Circus St GNWCH SE10 145 F1
Cirencester St BAY/PAD W2 101 F4
Cissbury Ring North
NFNCH/WDSP N12 46 D1
Cissbury Ring South
NFNCH/WDSP N12 46 D1
Cissbury Rd SEVS/STOTM N15 67 K2
Citadel Pl LBTH SE11 122 A5
Citizen Rd HOLWY N7 85 G1
Citron Ter PECK * SE15 143 J4
City Barracks SHB * W12 119 F1
City Gdn EDGE HA8 44 C2
City Garden Rw IS N1 6 B3
City Rd FSBYE EC1V 6 A3
SDTCH EC2A 13 F1
Civic Wy BARK/HLT IG6 72 C1
RSLP HA4 77 H3
Clabon Ms KTBR SW1X 14 E5
Clack St BERM/RHTH SE16 123 K2
Clacton Rd TOTM * N17 50 B5
WALTH E17 69 G3
Claire Ct NFNCH/WDSP N12 33 G5
Claire Gdns STAN HA7 43 J1
Claire Pl POP/IOD E14 124 D3
Clairvale Rd HEST TW5 134 C2
Clairview Rd TOOT SW17 179 G1
Clairville Gdns HNWL W7 115 K1
Clamp Hl KTN/HRWW/W HA3 28 D6
Clancarty Rd FUL/PGN SW6 139 K3
Clandon Cl ACT W3 117 J2
EW KT17 207 H4
Clandon Gdns FNCH N3 46 E6
Clandon Rd GDMY/SEVK IG3 72 E6
Clandon St DEPT SE8 144 D3
Clandon Ter RYNPK * SW20 177 G5
Clanricarde Gdns BAY/PAD W2 100 E6
Clapgate Rd BUSH WD23 28 B1
Clapham Common North Side
CLAP SW4 141 G5
Clapham Common South Side
CLAP SW4 161 G1
Clapham Common West Side
CLAP SW4 140 E5
Clapham Court Ter
BRXS/STRHM * SW2 141 K6
Clapham Crs CLAP SW4 141 J5
Clapham High St CLAP SW4 141 J5
Clapham Manor St CLAP SW4 141 H4
Clapham Park Est CLAP * SW4 161 J2
Clapham Park Rd CLAP SW4 141 H5
Clapham Park Ter
BRXS/STRHM * SW2 141 K6
Clapham Rd BRXN/ST SW9 141 K3
Clapham Rd South IS N1 85 K4
Claps Gate La EHAM E6 108 B3
Clapton Common
STNW/STAM N16 68 C4
Clapton Sq CLPT E5 86 E3
Clapton Ter STNW/STAM N16 68 C4
Clapton Wy CLPT E5 86 C2
Clara Pl WOOL/PLUM SE18 127 F4
Clare Cl BORE WD6 30 B1
EFNCH N2 47 G6
Clare Cnr ELTH/MOT SE9 167 G2
Clare Ct NTHWD HA6 40 C1
Claredale St BETH E2 104 C1
Clare Gdns BARK IG11 91 F4
FSTGT E7 88 E2
NTGHL * W11 100 C5
Clare Hl ESH/CLAY KT10 204 B3
Clare Hl (No 2) ESH/CLAY KT10 204 B3
Clare La IS N1 85 J5
Clare Lawn Av
MORT/ESHN SW14 138 A6
Clare Ms FUL/PGN SW6 140 A1
Claremont Av
KTN/HRWW/W HA3 62 A2
NWMAL KT3 192 E2
SUN TW16 172 A4
Claremont Cl BRXS/STRHM SW2 162 A3
CAN/RD E16 127 F1
IS N1 5 K3
ORP BR6 216 A2
Claremont Crs DART DA1 150 B5
Claremont Dr ESH/CLAY KT10 204 B5
Claremont End ESH/CLAY KT10 204 B4
Claremont Gdns GDMY/SEVK IG3 72 E6
SURB KT6 191 F1
Claremont Gv CHSWK W4 138 B1
WFD IG8 53 G2
Claremont House WATW * WD18 26 B1
Claremont La ESH/CLAY KT10 204 B3
Claremont Pk FNCH N3 46 C4
Claremont Park Rd
ESH/CLAY KT10 204 B4
Claremont Rd BMLY BR1 200 D1
CRICK NW2 64 A4
CROY/NA CR0 197 H5
EBAR EN4 21 G1
ESH/CLAY KT10 204 E5
FSTGT E7 89 F3
HGT N6 66 B4
KIL/WHAMP NW6 100 C1
KTN/HRWW/W HA3 42 E5
ROM RM1 75 J3
SURB KT6 191 F2
TEDD TW11 174 A1
TWK TW1 156 C2
WALTH E17 51 G5
WAN E11 88 B1
WEA W13 97 G4
Claremont Sq IS N1 5 J3
Claremont St GNWCH SE10 124 E6
UED N18 50 C2
Claremont Ter THDIT * KT7 190 C4
Claremont Vls CMBW * SE5 142 E1
KUT * KT1 175 G5
Claremont Wy CRICK NW2 64 A5
Clarence Av CLAP SW4 161 J2
HAYES BR2 200 D1
IL IG1 71 K3
NWMAL KT3 175 K5
Clarence Cl BUSH WD23 29 F2
EBAR EN4 21 H6
Clarence Ct MLHL * NW7 45 H1
Clarence Crs CLAP SW4 161 J1
SCUP DA14 168 C5
Clarence Gdns CAMTN NW1 3 K5
Clarence Ga CAMTN NW1 3 F6
WFD IG8 54 A2
Clarence La PUT/ROE SW15 158 C1
Clarence Ms CLPT E5 86 D3
Clarence Pas CAMTN * NW1 4 E3
Clarence Pl CLPT E5 86 D3
Clarence Rd BMLY BR1 184 D6
BXLYHS DA6 149 F5
CAN/RD E16 106 C3
CHSWK W4 117 H5

CLPT E5 86 D2
CROY/NA CR0 196 E4
DEPT SE8 124 E6
ELTH/MOT SE9 166 D4
FSTGT E7 89 G2
KIL/WHAMP NW6 82 D5
PEND EN3 24 E6
RCH/KEW TW9 137 G2
SCUP DA14 168 C5
SEVS/STOTM N15 67 J2
SUT SM1 209 F2
TEDD TW11 174 A2
WALTH E17 51 F5
WDGN N22 48 E3
WIM/MER SW19 178 A2
WLGTN SM6 210 B3
Clarence St KUT KT1 174 E5
NWDGN UB2 114 C3
RCH/KEW TW9 137 F5
Clarence Ter CAMTN NW1 3 F6
HSLW TW3 135 G5
Clarence Vls KUT * KT1 175 G5
Clarence Wk CLAP SW4 141 K3
Clarence Wy CAMTN NW1 84 B5
Clarendon Cl BAY/PAD * W2 8 C5
HOM E9 86 E5
STMC/STPC BR5 186 B6
Clarendon Crs WHTN TW2 155 J5
Clarendon Cross NTGHL W11 100 C6
Clarendon Dr PUT/ROE SW15 139 F5
Clarendon Gdns HDN NW4 45 J6
IL IG1 71 K5
MV/WKIL W9 101 G3
WBLY HA9 79 K1
Clarendon Ga BAY/PAD W2 8 C5
Clarendon Gn STMC/STPC BR5 186 B6
Clarendon Gv MTCM CR4 178 E6
STMC/STPC BR5 202 B1
Clarendon Ms BAY/PAD W2 8 C5
Clarendon Pth STMC/STPC BR5 202 B1
Clarendon Pl BAY/PAD W2 8 C5
Clarendon Ri LEW SE13 145 F4
Clarendon Rd ASHF TW15 152 C6
CEND/HSY/T N8 49 F6
CROY/NA CR0 196 C6
EA W5 98 A2
HRW HA1 60 E3
HYS/HAR UB3 113 J2
NTGHL W11 100 C6
SEVS/STOTM N15 67 H1
SWFD E18 52 E6
UED N18 50 C2
WALTH E17 69 K3
WAN E11 70 B5
WIM/MER SW19 178 D3
WLGTN SM6 210 C3
Clarendon St PIM SW1V 121 G5
Clarendon Ter MV/WKIL W9 101 G3
Clarendon Wy CHST BR7 186 A6
WCHMH N21 35 J2
Clarens St CAT SE6 164 C4
Clare Pde GFD/PVL * UB6 78 D4
Clare Rd GFD/PVL UB6 78 D4
HSLWW TW4 134 E4
NWCR SE14 144 C3
STWL/WRAY TW19 152 A3
WAN E11 70 B3
WLSDN NW10 81 J5
Clare St BETH E2 104 D1
Claret Gdns SNWD SE25 197 F1
Clareville Gv SKENS * SW7 120 B4
Clareville Grove Ms SKENS * SW7 120 B4
Clareville Rd STMC/STPC BR5 201 H6
Clareville St SKENS SW7 120 B4
Clare Wy BXLYHN DA7 149 F2
Clarges Ms MYFR/PICC W1J 9 J7
Clarges St MYFR/PICC W1J 9 K7
Claribel Rd BRXN/ST SW9 142 C3
Clarice Wy WLGTN SM6 210 E6
Claridge Rd BCTR RM8 73 K5
Clarissa Rd CHDH RM6 73 K3
Clarissa St HACK E8 86 B6
Clark Cl ERITH DA8 150 D2
Clarke Ms ED N9 36 D5
Clarkes Av WPK KT4 193 G5
Clarkes Ms CAVSQ/HST W1G 9 H1
Clarks Md BUSH WD23 28 C2
Clarkson Rd CAN/RD E16 106 D5
Clarkson Rw CAMTN NW1 3 K3
Clarkson St BETH * E2 104 D2
Clark's Rd IL IG1 72 D6
Clark St WCHPL E1 104 E5
Clark Wy HEST TW5 134 C1
Classon Cl WDR/YW UB7 112 B2
Claston Cl DART DA1 150 B5
Claude Rd LEY E10 70 A5
PECK SE15 143 J3
PLSTW E13 89 F6
Claude St POP/IOD E14 124 D4
Claudia Pl WIM/MER SW19 159 H3
Claughton Rd PLSTW E13 107 G1
Clauson Av NTHLT UB5 78 B3
Clavell St GNWCH SE10 125 F6
Claverdale Rd
BRXS/STRHM SW2 162 A2
Clavering Av BARN SW13 118 E6
Clavering Cl TWK TW1 156 B6
Clavering Rd MNPK E12 71 H5
Claverley Gv FNCH N3 46 E4
Claverley Vls FNCH N3 47 F3
Claverton St PIM SW1V 121 H5
Clave St WAP E1W 123 K1
Claxton Gv HMSMTH W6 119 G5
Clay Av MTCM CR4 179 G5
Claybank Gv LEW SE13 144 E4
Claybridge Rd LEE/GVPK SE12 166 B6
Claybrook Cl EFNCH N2 47 H6
Claybrook Rd HMSMTH W6 119 G6
Claybury BUSH WD23 28 B2
Claybury Rd WFD IG8 53 J3
Claydon Dr CROY/NA CR0 210 E2
Claydown Ms
WOOL/PLUM SE18 127 F5
Clayfarm Rd ELTH/MOT SE9 167 H4
Claygate Cl HCH RM12 93 J2
Claygate Crs CROY/NA CR0 214 A4
Claygate La ESH/CLAY KT10 190 B6
Claygate Lodge Cl
ESH/CLAY KT10 204 E5
Claygate Rd WEA W13 116 C3
Clayhall Av CLAY IG5 53 K5
Clayhill Crs ELTH/MOT SE9 166 C6
Claylands Pl BRXN/ST SW9 142 B1
Claylands Rd VX/NE SW8 122 A6
Clay La BUSH WD23 28 E2
Claymore Cl MRDN SM4 193 K4
Claypole Dr HEST TW5 134 D2
Claypole Rd SRTFD * E15 106 A1
Clayponds Av BTFD TW8 117 F4
Clayponds Gdns EA W5 116 E4
Clayponds La BTFD TW8 117 F5
Clayside CHIG IG7 54 D2
Clays La SRTFD E15 87 K3
Clays Lane Cl SRTFD E15 87 K3
Clay St MHST W1U 9 F2
Clayton Av ALP/SUD HA0 80 A5
Clayton Cl EHAM E6 107 K5
Clayton Crs BTFD TW8 116 E5
Clayton Croft Rd RDART DA2 170 D4
Clayton Dr DEPT SE8 124 B5
Clayton Fld CDALE/KGS NW9 45 G4
Clayton Ms GNWCH SE10 145 G2
Clayton Rd CHSGTN KT9 205 J2
HYS/HAR UB3 113 H2
ISLW TW7 135 K4
PECK SE15 143 H2
ROMW/RG RM7 74 E5
Clayton St LBTH SE11 122 B6
Clayton Ter YEAD * UB4 95 H4
Claytonville Ter BELV * DA17 129 K2
Clay Wood Cl ORP BR6 201 K4
Clayworth Cl BFN/LL DA15 168 C1
Cleanthus Cl WOOL/PLUM SE18 147 G2
Cleanthus Rd WOOL/PLUM SE18 147 G2
Clearbrook Wy WCHPL E1 104 E5
Clearwater Pl SURB KT6 190 D3
Clearwater Ter NTGHL W11 119 G2
Clearwell Dr MV/WKIL W9 101 F3
Cleave Av HYS/HAR UB3 113 H4
ORP BR6 216 E4
Cleaveland Rd SURB KT6 190 E2
Cleaverholme Cl SNWD SE25 197 J3
Cleaver Sq LBTH SE11 122 B5
Cleaver St LBTH SE11 122 B5
Cleeve Hl FSTH SE23 163 J3
Cleeve Park Gdns SCUP DA14 168 C4
Clegg St PLSTW E13 106 E1
WAP E1W 123 J1
Clematis Cottages SHB * W12 99 J6
Clematis Gdns WFD IG8 52 E1
Clematis St SHB W12 99 H6
Clem Attlee Ct FUL/PGN * SW6 119 J6
Clem Attlee Pde
FUL/PGN * SW6 119 J6
Clemence Rd DAGE RM10 92 E6
Clemence St POP/IOD E14 105 H4
Clement Av CLAP SW4 141 J5
Clement Cl CHSWK W4 118 A4
KIL/WHAMP NW6 82 A5
Clement Gdns HYS/HAR UB3 113 H4
Clementhorpe Rd DAGW RM9 91 J4
Clementina Rd LEY E10 69 H5
Clementine Cl WEA W13 116 C2
Clement Rd BECK BR3 182 A5
WIM/MER SW19 177 H1
Clements Av CAN/RD E16 106 E6
Clements Inn LINN WC2A 11 H4
Clements La IL IG1 90 B1
MANHO EC4N 13 F5
Clements Pl BTFD TW8 116 E5
Clements Rd
BERM/RHTH * SE16 123 H3
BERM/RHTH SE16 123 H3
EHAM E6 89 K5
IL IG1 90 B1
WOT/HER KT12 188 A6
Clendon Wy WOOL/PLUM SE18 127 J4
Clennam St STHWK * SE1 18 D2
Clensham La SUT SM1 193 K6
Clenston Ms MBLAR W1H 8 E3
Clephane Rd IS N1 85 J4
Clere Pl SDTCH EC2A 7 F6
Clere St SDTCH EC2A 7 F6
Clerkenwell Cl CLKNW EC1R 5 K7
Clerkenwell Gn CLKNW EC1R 6 A7
Clerkenwell Rd CLKNW EC1R 5 J7
Clermont Rd HOM E9 86 E6
Clevedon Gdns HEST TW5 134 A3
HYS/HAR UB3 113 G3
Clevedon Rd KUT KT1 175 H5
PGE/AN SE20 182 A4
TWK TW1 156 E1
Cleveland Av CHSWK W4 118 C4
HPTN TW12 172 E3
Cleveland Gdns BARN SW13 138 C3
BAY/PAD W2 101 G5
CRICK NW2 64 B6
FSBYPK N4 67 J2
WPK KT4 192 B6
Cleveland Gv WCHPL E1 104 E3
Cleveland Ms FITZ W1T 10 A1
Cleveland Park Av WALTH E17 69 J1
Cleveland Park Crs WALTH E17 69 J1
Cleveland Pl STJS SW1Y 10 B7
Cleveland Ri MRDN SM4 193 G4
Cleveland Rd BARN SW13 138 C3
CHSWK W4 117 K3
ED * N9 36 D2
IL IG1 90 B1
IS N1 85 K5
ISLW TW7 136 B5
NWMAL KT3 192 B1
SWFD E18 52 E6
WEA W13 97 G4
WELL DA16 148 A3
WPK KT4 192 B6
Cleveland Rw WHALL SW1A 16 B1
Cleveland Sq BAY/PAD W2 101 G6
Cleveland St CAMTN NW1 3 K7
Cleveland Ter BAY/PAD W2 101 G5
Cleveland Wy WCHPL E1 104 E3
Cleveley Crs EA W5 98 A1
Cleveleys Rd CLPT E5 86 D1
Clevely Cl CHARL SE7 126 C4
Cleverly Est SHB * W12 118 D1
Cleve Rd KIL/WHAMP NW6 82 E5
SCUP DA14 168 E5
Cleves Av EW KT17 207 K6
Cleves Cl LOU IG10 39 J1
Cleves Rd EHAM E6 89 H6
RCHPK/HAM TW10 156 D5
Cleves Wk BARK/HLT IG6 54 C3
Cleves Wy HPTN TW12 172 E3
RSLP HA4 59 H5
Clewer Crs KTN/HRWW/W HA3 42 D4
Clifden Rd BTFD TW8 116 E6
CLPT E5 86 E3
TWK TW1 156 A3
Cliffe Rd SAND/SEL CR2 211 K3
Clifford Av CHST BR7 184 E2
CLAY IG5 54 B4
RCH/KEW TW9 137 J4
WLGTN SM6 210 C2
Clifford Cl NTHLT UB5 77 J6
PLSTW * E13 107 F2
Clifford Dr BRXN/ST SW9 142 C5
Clifford Gdns HYS/HAR UB3 113 G4
WLSDN NW10 100 A1
Clifford Gv ASHF TW15 152 D6
Clifford Rd ALP/SUD HA0 79 K6
BAR EN5 21 F4
CAN/RD E16 106 D3
ED N9 36 E1
HSLWW TW4 134 C4
RCHPK/HAM TW10 156 E4
SNWD SE25 197 H1
WALTH E17 52 A5
Clifford St CONDST W1S 10 A6
Clifford Wy WLSDN NW10 81 H2
Cliff Rd HOLWY N7 84 D4
Cliff Ter DEPT SE8 144 D3
Cliffview Rd LEW SE13 144 D4
Cliff Vls HOLWY N7 84 D4
Cliff Wk CAN/RD E16 106 D4
Clifton Av FELT TW13 154 B5
FNCH N3 46 D4
KTN/HRWW/W HA3 43 H5
SHB W12 118 C2
WALTH E17 69 F1
WBLY HA9 80 B4
Clifton Cl ORP BR6 216 C3
Clifton Ct BECK * BR3 182 E4
Clifton Crs PECK SE15 143 J1
Clifton Gdns CHSWK W4 118 A4
ENC/FH EN2 22 E5
GLDGN NW11 64 D3
MV/WKIL W9 101 G3
SEVS/STOTM N15 68 B3
Clifton Ga WBPTN * SW10 120 B6
Clifton Gv HACK E8 86 C4
Clifton Hl STJWD NW8 101 G1
Clifton Ms SNWD SE25 197 F1
Clifton Pde FELT * TW13 154 B6
Clifton Park Av RYNPK SW20 177 F5
Clifton Pl BAY/PAD W2 8 B5
BERM/RHTH SE16 123 K2
KUTN/CMB * KT2 175 H4
WBPTN * SW10 120 B6
Clifton Ri NWCR SE14 144 B1
Clifton Rd CAN/RD E16 106 C4
CEND/HSY/T N8 66 D3
EMPK RM11 75 J3
FNCH N3 47 G4
FSTGT E7 89 H4
GFD/PVL UB6 96 C3
GNTH/NBYPK IG2 72 D3
HTHAIR * TW6 132 E5
ISLW TW7 135 K3
KTN/HRWW/W HA3 62 B2
KUTN/CMB KT2 175 H4
MV/WKIL W9 101 G3
NWDGN UB2 114 D4
SCUP DA14 167 K6
SNWD SE25 197 F1
TEDD TW11 155 K6
WDGN N22 48 C4
WELL DA16 148 D4
WIM/MER SW19 177 G2
WLGTN SM6 210 B3
WLSDN NW10 99 J1
Clifton St SDTCH EC2A 7 G7
Clifton Ter FSBYPK N4 67 G6
Clifton Vls MV/WKIL W9 101 F4
Clifton Wy ALP/SUD HA0 80 A6
PECK SE15 143 K1
Cline Rd FBAR/BDGN N11 48 C2
Clink St STHWK SE1 12 E7
Clinton Av E/WMO/HCT KT8 189 H1
WELL DA16 148 B5
Clinton Crs BARK/HLT IG6 54 E2
Clinton Rd BOW E3 105 G2
FSTGT E7 88 E2
SEVS/STOTM N15 67 K1
Clinton Ter DEPT * SE8 124 D6
SUT * SM1 209 G2
Clipper Cl BERM/RHTH SE16 124 A2
Clipper Wy LEW SE13 145 F5
Clippesby Cl CHSGTN * KT9 206 B4
Clipstone Ms GTPST W1W 4 A7
Clipstone Rd HSLW TW3 135 F4
Clipstone St GTPST W1W 9 K1
Clissold Crs STNW/STAM N16 85 K2
Clissold Rd STNW/STAM N16 85 K1
Clitheroe Av RYLN/HDSTN HA2 60 A5
Clitheroe Gdns OXHEY WD19 27 H5
Clitheroe Rd BRXN/ST SW9 141 K3
CRW RM5 56 E1
Clitherow Av HNWL W7 116 B3
Clitherow Rd BTFD TW8 116 C5
Clitterhouse Crs CRICK NW2 64 A5
Clitterhouse Rd CRICK NW2 64 A5
Clive Av DART DA1 170 C1
UED N18 50 C2
Clive Ct WLSDN * NW10 81 H5
Cliveden Cl NFNCH/WDSP N12 33 G6
Cliveden Pl BGVA SW1W 15 G6
Cliveden Rd WIM/MER SW19 177 J4
Clivedon Ct WEA W13 97 H4
Clivedon Rd CHING E4 52 C1
Clive Rd BELV DA17 129 H4
DUL SE21 162 E5
EBED/NFELT TW14 153 K1
EN EN1 24 C5
ESH/CLAY KT10 204 B2
GPK RM2 75 K2
TWK TW1 156 A6
WIM/MER SW19 178 D2
Clivesdale Dr HYS/HAR UB3 113 K1
Clive Wy EN EN1 24 C5
Cloak La BLKFR EC4V 12 D5
Clockhouse Av BARK IG11 90 C6
Clockhouse Cl WIM/MER SW19 159 F5
Clockhouse La ASHF TW15 152 D6
CRW RM5 56 E3
Clock House Pde PLMGR * N13 49 G1
Clockhouse Pl PUT/ROE SW15 139 H6
Clock House Rd BECK BR3 182 B6
Clock Pde EN * EN1 23 K6
Clock Tower Ms IS N1 6 D1
THMD SE28 109 H6
Clock Tower Pl HOLWY * N7 84 E4
Clock Tower Rd ISLW TW7 136 A4
Cloister Cl RAIN RM13 111 K3
TEDD TW11 174 C1
Cloister Gdns EDGE HA8 44 E1
SNWD SE25 197 J3
Cloister Rd ACT W3 98 E4
CRICK NW2 82 D1
Cloisters Av HAYES BR2 200 E2
Clonard Wy PIN HA5 42 A2
Clonbrock Rd STNW/STAM N16 86 A2
Cloncurry St FUL/PGN SW6 139 G3
Clonmel Cl RYLN/HDSTN HA2 60 D5
Clonmell Rd TOTM N17 49 K6
Clonmel Rd FUL/PGN SW6 139 J1
HPTN TW12 155 J6
Clonmore St WAND/EARL SW18 159 J3
Cloonmore Av ORP BR6 217 F3
Clorane Gdns HAMP NW3 82 E1
The Close ALP/SUD HA0 80 A4
BECK BR3 198 B1
BUSH * WD23 28 A1
BXLY DA5 169 H1
CAR SM5 209 J6
CHDH RM6 74 A3
CHEAM SM3 193 J4
CHING E4 52 A3
EBAR EN4 33 K1
GNTH/NBYPK IG2 72 E3
ISLW TW7 135 J3
MTCM CR4 194 E1
NWMAL KT3 175 K5
PIN HA5 59 G4
PIN HA5 59 K4
RCH/KEW TW9 137 J4
RDART DA2 171 F5
SCUP DA14 186 C1
SNWD * SE25 197 H3
STHGT/OAK N14 34 D4
STMC/STPC BR5 201 K3
SURB KT6 191 F4
TRDG/WHET N20 32 D4
WBLY HA9 80 E1
Closemead Cl NTHWD HA6 40 A2
Cloth Ct STBT EC1A 12 B2
Cloth Fair STBT EC1A 12 B2
Clothier St HDTCH * EC3A 13 H3
Cloth St STBT * EC1A 12 C1
Clothworkers Rd
WOOL/PLUM SE18 147 J1
Cloudesdale Rd TOOT SW17 161 G4
Cloudesley Pl IS N1 5 K1
Cloudesley Rd BXLYHN DA7 149 G2
ERITH DA8 150 C2
IS N1 5 J1
Cloudesley St IS N1 5 K1
Clouston Cl WLGTN SM6 210 E3
Clova Rd FSTGT E7 88 E4
Clove Crs POP/IOD E14 106 A6
Clovelly Av CDALE/KGS NW9 63 H1
HGDN/ICK UB10 76 A2
Clovelly Cl HGDN/ICK UB10 76 A2
PIN HA5 41 F6
Clovelly Gdns EN EN1 36 A2
ROMW/RG RM7 56 D4
Clovelly Rd BXLYHN DA7 129 F6
CEND/HSY/T N8 66 D1
CHSWK * W4 118 A2
HSLW TW3 135 F3
WEA W13 116 D2
Clovelly Wy ORP BR6 202 A3
RYLN/HDSTN HA2 77 K1
WCHPL E1 104 E5
Clover Cl WAN * E11 70 B6
Cloverdale Gdns BFN/LL DA15 168 A1
The Clover Fld BUSH WD23 27 K1
Clover Ms CHEL SW3 120 E6
Clover Wy WLGTN SM6 195 F5
Clove St PLSTW E13 106 E3
Clowders Rd CAT SE6 164 C5
Clowser Cl SUT SM1 209 G3
Cloysters Gn WAP * E1W 123 H1
Cloyster Wd EDGE HA8 43 K3
Club Gardens Rd HAYES BR2 199 K4
Club Rw BETH E2 7 J6
The Clumps FELT TW13 153 G6
Clunbury Av NWDGN UB2 114 E5
Cluny Est STHWK SE1 19 G4
Cluny Ms ECT SW5 119 K4
Cluny Pl STHWK SE1 19 G4
Clutton St POP/IOD E14 105 K4
Clydach Rd EN EN1 24 B5
Clyde Circ SEVS/STOTM N15 68 A1
Clyde Ct CAMTN NW1 4 D2
Clyde Flats FUL/PGN * SW6 139 J1
Clyde Pl LEY E10 69 K4
Clyde Rd CROY/NA CR0 197 G6
SEVS/STOTM N15 68 A1
STWL/WRAY TW19 152 A3
SUT SM1 208 E3
WDGN N22 48 D4
WLGTN SM6 210 C3
Clydesdale PEND EN3 25 F5
Clydesdale Av
KTN/HRWW/W HA3 43 K6
Clydesdale Cl ISLW TW7 136 A4
Clydesdale Gdns
RCHPK/HAM TW10 137 J5
Clydesdale Rd EMPK RM11 75 H4
NTGHL W11 100 D5
Clyde St DEPT SE8 124 C6
Clyde Ter FSTH SE23 163 K4
Clyde V FSTH SE23 163 K4
Clyde Wy ROM RM1 57 G4
Clydon Cl ERITH DA8 130 B6
Clyfford Rd RSLP HA4 76 D2
Clymping Dene
EBED/NFELT TW14 154 A2
Clyston Rd WATW WD18 26 D1
Clyston St VX/NE SW8 141 H3
Coach & Horses Yd CONDST W1S 9 K5
Coach House La HBRY * N5 85 H2
WIM/MER SW19 159 G6
Coach House Ms FSTH SE23 163 K1
NWCR * SE14 144 A2
Coach House Yd
WAND/EARL * SW18 140 A5
Coalecroft Rd PUT/ROE SW15 139 F5
Coates Av WAND/EARL SW18 160 D1
Coates Hill Rd BMLY BR1 185 F5
Coates Rd BORE WD6 29 K2
Coate St BETH E2 104 C1
Cobbett Rd ELTH/MOT SE9 146 D4
WHTN TW2 155 F3
Cobbetts Av REDBR IG4 71 H2
Cobbett St VX/NE SW8 142 A1
Cobble La IS N1 85 H5
Cobble Ms FSBYPK N4 85 J1
Cobbler's Wk TEDD TW11 173 K3
Cobblestone Pl CROY/NA CR0 196 D5
Cobbold Ms SHB * W12 118 C2
Cobbold Rd SHB W12 118 C2
WAN E11 88 D1
WLSDN NW10 81 H4
Cobb's Rd HSLWW TW4 134 E5
Cobb St WCHPL E1 13 J3
Cobden Ms SYD SE26 181 J1
Cobden Rd ORP BR6 216 D2
SNWD SE25 197 H2
WAN E11 88 C1
Cobham Av NWMAL KT3 192 D2
Cobham Cl BFN/LL DA15 168 C1
BTSEA * SW11 160 D1
EDGE HA8 44 D5
EN EN1 24 C4
HAYES BR2 200 D4
WLGTN SM6 210 E4
Cobham Ms CAMTN NW1 84 D5
Cobham Pl BXLYHS DA6 148 E6
Cobham Rd GDMY/SEVK IG3 72 E6
HEST TW5 134 B1
KUT KT1 175 H5
WALTH E17 52 A4
WDGN N22 49 H6
Cobland Rd LEE/GVPK SE12 166 B6
Coborn Rd BOW E3 105 H2
Coborn St BOW E3 105 H2
Cobourg Rd CMBW SE5 123 G6
Cobourg St CAMTN NW1 4 B5
Coburg Cl WEST SW1P 16 B6
Coburg Crs BRXS/STRHM SW2 162 A3
Coburg Dwellings WCHPL * E1 104 E6
Coburg Gdns CLAY IG5 53 H5
Coburg Rd WDGN N22 49 F5
Cochrane Ms STJWD NW8 2 B3
Cochrane Rd WIM/MER SW19 177 H3
Cochrane St STJWD NW8 2 B3
Cockcrow Hl SURB * KT6 190 E5
Cockerell Rd WALTH E17 69 G4
Cockfosters Pde EBAR * EN4 22 A5
Cockfosters Rd EBAR EN4 21 K1
Cock La STBT EC1A 12 A2
Cockmannings La
STMC/STPC BR5 202 E5
Cockmannings Rd
STMC/STPC BR5 202 E4
Cocks Crs NWMAL KT3 192 C1
Cocksett Av ORP BR6 216 E4
Cockspur Ct STJS SW1Y 10 D7
Cockspur St STJS * SW1Y 10 D7
Cocksure La SCUP DA14 169 H6
Code St WCHPL E1 7 K7
Codling Cl WAP E1W 123 H1
Codling Wy ALP/SUD HA0 79 K2
Codrington Hl FSTH SE23 164 B2
Codrington Ms NTGHL W11 100 C5
Cody Cl KTN/HRWW/W HA3 43 K6
WLGTN SM6 210 D5
Cody Rd CAN/RD E16 106 B3
Coe Av SNWD SE25 197 H3
Cofers Cir WBLY HA9 80 D1
Coffey St DEPT SE8 144 D1
Cogan Av WALTH E17 51 G4
Coin St STHWK SE1 11 J7
Coity Rd KTTN NW5 84 A4
Cokers La DUL SE21 162 D3
Coke St WCHPL E1 104 C5
Colbeck Ms SKENS SW7 120 A4
Colbeck Rd HRW HA1 60 C4
Colberg Pl STNW/STAM * N16 68 B4
Colborne Wy WPK KT4 208 A1
Colbrook Av HYS/HAR UB3 113 G3
Colbrook Cl HYS/HAR UB3 113 G3
Colburn Av PIN HA5 41 K2
Colburn Wy SUT SM1 209 H1
Colby Rd NRWD SE19 181 F1
Colchester Dr PIN HA5 59 H2
Colchester Rd EDGE HA8 44 E3
NTHWD HA6 40 E5
WALTH E17 69 J3
Colchester St WCHPL E1 13 K3
Coldbath Sq CLKNW EC1R 5 J7
Coldbath St LEW SE13 144 E3
Cold Blow Crs BXLY DA5 170 A3
Coldblow La NWCR SE14 144 A1
Coldershaw Rd HNWL W7 116 B2
Coldfall Av MUSWH N10 47 K5
Coldharbour POP/IOD E14 125 F1
Coldharbour Crest
ELTH/MOT * SE9 167 F5
Coldharbour La BRXN/ST SW9 142 B5
BUSH WD23 28 B1
HYS/HAR UB3 113 J2
RAIN RM13 130 D1
Coldharbour Pl CMBW SE5 142 D3
Coldharbour Rd CROY/NA CR0 211 G3
Coldharbour Wy CROY/NA CR0 211 G3
Coldstream Gdns
PUT/ROE SW15 159 J1
Colebeck Ms IS N1 85 H4
Colebert Av WCHPL E1 104 E3
Colebrooke Av WEA W13 97 H5
Colebrooke Dr WAN E11 71 F4
Colebrooke Pl IS N1 6 B1
Colebrooke Rw IS N1 6 A3
Colebrook Ri HAYES BR2 183 H5
Colebrook Rd
STRHM/NOR SW16 179 K4
Colebrook St ERITH DA8 130 C6
Colebrook Wy FBAR/BDGN N11 48 B1
Coleby Pth CMBW * SE5 142 E1
Cole Cl THMD SE28 128 C1
Coledale Dr STAN HA7 43 J4
Coleford Rd WAND/EARL SW18 140 B6
Cole Gdns HEST TW5 133 K1
Colegrave Rd SRTFD E15 88 B3
Colegrove Rd PECK SE15 123 G6
Coleherne Ms WBPTN SW10 120 A5
Coleherne Rd WBPTN SW10 120 A5
Colehill Gdns FUL/PGN * SW6 139 H2
Colehill La FUL/PGN SW6 139 H2
Coleman Cl SNWD SE25 181 H5
Coleman Flds IS N1 85 J6
Coleman Rd BELV DA17 129 H3
CMBW SE5 143 F1
Colemans Heath
ELTH/MOT SE9 167 F5
Coleman St LOTH EC2R 12 E3
Colenso Rd CLPT E5 86 E2
GNTH/NBYPK IG2 72 E5
Cole Park Gdns TWK TW1 156 B1
Cole Park Rd TWK TW1 156 B2
Colepits Wood Rd
ELTH/MOT SE9 147 J6
Coleraine Rd BKHTH/KID SE3 125 K6
CEND/HSY/T N8 49 G6
Coleridge Av MNPK E12 89 J4
SUT SM1 209 J2
Coleridge Cl VX/NE SW8 141 G3
Coleridge Gdns
KIL/WHAMP NW6 83 G5
Coleridge Rd ASHF TW15 152 B6
CEND/HSY/T N8 66 D3
CROY/NA CR0 197 K4
DART DA1 151 K5

FSBYPK N4 67 G6
HARH RM3 57 K3
NFNCH/WDSP N12 47 G1
WALTH E17 69 H1
Coleridge Sq WEA * W13 97 G5
Coleridge Wk GLDGN NW11 64 E1
Coleridge Wy ORP BR6 202 B3
WDR/YW UB7 112 C4
YEAD UB4 94 E5
Cole Rd TWK TW1 156 B1
Colesburg Rd BECK BR3 182 C6
Coles Crs RYLN/HDSTN HA2 60 B6
Coles Gn BUSH WD23 28 C3
Coles Green Rd CRICK NW2 63 J5
Coleshill Rd TEDD TW11 173 K2
Colestown St BTSEA SW11 140 D3
Cole St STHWK SE1 18 D3
Colet Cl PLMGR N13 49 H2
Colet Gdns WKENS W14 119 G5
Coley St FSBYW WC1X 5 H7
Colfe & Hatcliffe Glebe
LEW * SE13 144 E6
Colfe Rd FSTH SE23 164 B3
Colham Av WDR/YW UB7 112 B1
Colham Mill Rd WDR/YW UB7 112 A2
Colina Ms SEVS/STOTM N15 67 H1
Colina Rd CEND/HSY/T N8 67 H2
Colin Cl CDALE/KGS NW9 63 G1
CROY/NA CR0 213 H1
WWKM BR4 214 D1
Colin Crs CDALE/KGS NW9 63 H2
Colindale Av CDALE/KGS NW9 45 F6
Colindeep Gdns HDN NW4 63 J2
Colindeep La CDALE/KGS NW9 63 H1
Colin Dr CDALE/KGS NW9 63 H2
Colinette Rd PUT/ROE SW15 139 F5
Colin Gdns CDALE/KGS NW9 63 H2
Colin Park Rd CDALE/KGS NW9 45 G6
Colin Rd WLSDN NW10 81 J4
Colinton Rd BCTR RM8 73 H6
Coliston Rd WAND/EARL SW18 159 K2
Collamore Av
WAND/EARL SW18 160 D3
Collapit Cl RYLN/HDSTN HA2 60 B3
Collard Pl CAMTN NW1 84 B5
College Ap GNWCH SE10 125 F6
College Av KTN/HRWW/W HA3 42 E4
College Cl KTN/HRWW/W HA3 42 E4
UED N18 50 B1
WHTN TW2 155 J3
College Ct EA * W5 98 A6
College Crs KIL/WHAMP NW6 83 G4
College Cross IS N1 85 G5
College Dr RSLP HA4 58 E4
THDIT KT7 189 K4
College East WCHPL * E1 13 K2
College Gdns CHING E4 37 K2
ENC/FH EN2 23 K2
NWMAL KT3 192 C2
REDBR IG4 71 J2
TOOT SW17 160 D4
UED * N18 50 B1
College Gn NRWD SE19 181 F3
College Gv CAMTN NW1 4 C1
College Hl CANST * EC4R 12 D5
College Hill Rd
KTN/HRWW/W HA3 42 E3
College Ms IS N1 85 G5
WEST SW1P 16 E4
College Pde KIL/WHAMP * NW6 82 C6
College Park Cl LEW SE13 145 G5
College Pl CAMTN NW1 84 C6
WALTH E17 70 C1
WBPTN * SW10 140 B1
College Rd BMLY BR1 183 K4
CROY/NA CR0 196 E6
DUL SE21 163 F2
ENC/FH EN2 23 K3
HRW HA1 60 E3
ISLW TW7 136 A2
KTN/HRWW/W HA3 42 E4
NRWD SE19 181 G1
TOTM N17 50 B2
WALTH E17 70 A2
WBLY HA9 61 K5
WCHMH N21 35 G4
WEA W13 97 H5
WIM/MER SW19 178 C2
WLSDN NW10 100 A1
College St CANST * EC4R 12 D5
College Ter FNCH N3 46 D4
College Vw ELTH/MOT SE9 166 C3
College Wy ASHF TW15 152 C6
HYS/HAR UB3 94 E6
NTHWD HA6 40 B2
College Yd KIL/WHAMP * NW6 82 C6
KTTN * NW5 84 B3
Collent St HOM E9 86 E4
Colless Rd SEVS/STOTM N15 68 B2
Collett Rd BERM/RHTH SE16 123 H3
Collier Cl EHAM E6 108 B6
HOR/WEW KT19 206 C4
Collier Dr EDGE HA8 44 C5
Collier Row La CRW RM5 56 E4
Collier Row Rd CRW RM5 56 C4
Collier St IS N1 5 G3
Colliers Water La THHTH CR7 196 B2
Colliers Wd HAYES BR2 215 H3
Collindale Av BFN/LL DA15 168 B3
CDALE/KGS NW9 45 G6
ERITH DA8 129 J6
Collingbourne Rd SHB W12 118 E1
Collingham Gdns ECT SW5 120 A4
Collingham Pl ECT SW5 120 A4
Collingham Rd ECT SW5 120 A4
Collings Cl WDGN N22 49 F2
Collington St GNWCH * SE10 125 G5
Collingtree Rd SYD SE26 163 K6
Collingwood Av BRYLDS KT5 191 K5
MUSWH N10 48 A6
Collingwood Cl HSLW TW3 155 F2
Colling Wood Cl PGE/AN SE20 181 J4
Collingwood Rd MTCM CR4 178 D5
RAIN RM13 111 H1
SEVS/STOTM N15 68 A1
SUT SM1 208 E2
Collingwood St WCHPL E1 104 D3
Collins Av STAN HA7 44 A5
Collins Dr RSLP HA4 59 G6
Collinson St STHWK SE1 18 C3
Collinson Wk STHWK SE1 18 C3
Collins Rd HBRY N5 85 J2
Collins St BKHTH/KID SE3 145 H3
Collinwood Av PEND EN3 24 E4
Collinwood Gdns
GNTH/NBYPK IG2 71 K2
Coll's Rd PECK SE15 143 K2
Collyer Av CROY/NA CR0 210 E2
Collyer Pl PECK SE15 143 H2
Collyer Rd CROY/NA CR0 210 E2
Colman Pde EN * EN1 24 A4
Colman Rd CAN/RD E16 107 G4
Colmar Cl WCHPL E1 105 F3
Colmer Pl KTN/HRWW/W HA3 42 D3
Colmer Rd STRHM/NOR SW16 179 K3
Colmore Ms PECK SE15 143 J2
Colmore Rd PEND EN3 24 E5
Colnbrook St STHWK SE1 18 A5
Colne Av OXHEY WD19 27 F1
Colne Ct HOR/WEW KT19 206 E2
Colne Rd CLPT E5 87 F2
WCHMH N21 35 K2
WHTN TW2 155 K3
Colne St PLSTW E13 106 E2
Colney Hatch La
FBAR/BDGN N11 47 K2
Colney Rd DART DA1 171 J1
Cologne Rd BTSEA SW11 140 C5
Colombo Rd IL IG1 72 C5
Colombo St STHWK SE1 18 A1
Colomb St GNWCH SE10 125 H5
Colonels Wk ENC/FH EN2 23 H3
Colonial Av HSLW TW3 155 H1
Colonial Dr CHSWK W4 117 K4
Colonial Rd EBED/NFELT TW14 153 H2
The Colonnade DEPT * SE8 124 C4
Colonnade BMSBY WC1N 4 E7
Colosseum Ter CAMTN NW1 3 K6
Colson Rd CROY/NA CR0 196 E6
Colson Wy STRHM/NOR SW16 161 H6
Colsterworth Rd
SEVS/STOTM N15 68 B1
Colston Av CAR SM5 209 J2
Colston Rd FSTGT E7 89 H4
MORT/ESHN SW14 137 K5
Colthurst Crs FSBYPK N4 67 H6
Colthurst Dr ED N9 36 D5
Coltness Crs ABYW SE2 128 C5
Colton Gdns TOTM N17 49 J6
Colton Rd HRW HA1 60 E2
Columbas Dr HAMP * NW3 65 H5
Columbia Av EDGE HA8 44 D4
RSLP HA4 58 F6
WPK KT4 192 C4
Columbia Rd BETH E2 7 K4
PLSTW * E13 106 D3
Columbia Whf PEND * EN3 25 G6
Columbine Av EHAM E6 107 J4
SAND/SEL CR2 211 H5
Columbine Wy LEW * SE13 145 F3
Columbus Gdns NTHWD HA6 40 E4
Colvestone Crs HACK E8 86 B3
Colview Ct ELTH/MOT SE9 166 C3
Colville Est IS N1 7 F1
Colville Gdns NTGHL W11 100 D5
Colville Houses NTGHL * W11 100 D5
Colville Ms NTGHL W11 100 D5
Colville Pl FITZ W1T 10 B2
Colville Rd ACT W3 117 J3
ED N9 36 D3
NTGHL W11 100 D5
WALTH E17 51 G5
WAN E11 88 A1
Colville Sq NTGHL * W11 100 D5
Colville Square Ms
NTGHL * W11 100 D5
Colville Ter NTGHL W11 100 D5
Colvin Cl SYD SE26 181 K1
Colvin Gdns BARK/HLT IG6 54 C3
CHING E4 38 A5
SWFD E18 71 F1
Colvin Rd EHAM E6 89 J5
THHTH CR7 196 B2
Colwall Gdns WFD IG8 52 E1
Colwell Rd EDUL SE22 143 G6
Colwick Cl HGT N6 66 D4
Colwith Rd HMSMTH W6 119 F6
Colwood Gdns WIM/MER SW19 178 C3
Colworth Gv WALW SE17 18 D7
Colworth Rd CROY/NA CR0 197 H5
WAN E11 70 C3
Colwyn Av GFD/PVL UB6 97 F1
Colwyn Cl STRHM/NOR SW16 179 H1
Colwyn Crs HSLW TW3 135 H2
Colwyn Gn CDALE/KGS * NW9 63 G3
Colwyn Rd CRICK NW2 81 K1
Colyer Cl ELTH/MOT SE9 167 G4
Colyers Cl ERITH DA8 150 A2
Colyers La ERITH DA8 149 K2
Colyton Cl ALP/SUD HA0 79 J4
WELL DA16 148 E2
Colyton Rd EDUL SE22 143 J6
Colyton Wy UED N18 50 C1
Combe Av BKHTH/KID SE3 145 J1
Combedale Rd GNWCH SE10 125 K5
Combemartin Rd
WAND/EARL SW18 159 H2
Comber Cl CRICK NW2 81 J1
Comber Gv CMBW SE5 142 D1
Combermere Rd BRXN/ST SW9 142 A4
MRDN SM4 194 A3
Combe Rd WATW WD18 26 C2
Comberton Rd CLPT E5 68 D6
Combeside WOOL/PLUM SE18 148 A1
Combes Rd DAGW RM9 92 B5
Combwell Crs ABYW SE2 128 B3
Comely Bank Rd WALTH E17 70 A2
Comeragh Ms WKENS * W14 119 H5
Comeragh Rd WKENS W14 119 H5
Comerford Rd BROCKY SE4 144 B5
Comet Cl MNPK E12 89 H2
PUR RM19 131 K4
Comet Pl DEPT SE8 144 D1
Comet Rd STWL/WRAY TW19 152 A2
Comet St DEPT SE8 144 D1
Commerce Rd BTFD TW8 116 D6
WDGN N22 49 F4
Commerce Wy CROY/NA CR0 211 F1
Commercial Rd UED N18 50 A1
WCHPL E1 13 K3
Commercial St WCHPL E1 7 J7
Commercial Wy PECK SE15 143 G2
WLSDN NW10 98 D1
Commerell Pl GNWCH SE10 125 J5
Commerell St GNWCH SE10 125 H5
Commodore Pde
STRHM/NOR * SW16 180 A3
Commodore St WCHPL E1 105 F4
Commondale PUT/ROE SW15 139 F3
The Common EA W5 117 F1
NWDGN UB2 114 C4
STAN HA7 29 F4
Common La ESH/CLAY KT10 205 G5
RDART DA2 170 D4
Common Rd BARN SW13 138 D4
ESH/CLAY KT10 205 G4
STAN HA7 28 D5
Commonside HAYES BR2 215 G2
Commonside East MTCM CR4 179 F6
MTCM CR4 195 H1
Commonwealth Av
HYS/HAR UB3 94 B5
SHB W12 99 K6
Commonwealth Rd TOTM N17 50 C3
Commonwealth Wy ABYW SE2 128 C5
Community Cl HEST TW5 134 A2
Community Rd GFD/PVL UB6 78 C6
SRTFD E15 88 B3
Como Rd FSTH SE23 164 B4
Como St ROMW/RG RM7 75 F2
Compass Hl RCHPK/HAM TW10 156 E1
Compayne Gdns
KIL/WHAMP NW6 83 F5
Compton Av ALP/SUD HA0 79 H2
EHAM E6 107 H1
GPK RM2 57 K6
HGT N6 65 J4
IS N1 85 H4
Compton Cl CAMTN NW1 3 K5
CRICK NW2 82 B1
EDGE HA8 44 E3
ESH/CLAY KT10 204 D4
WEA W13 97 G5
Compton Crs CHSGTN KT9 206 A4
CHSWK W4 117 K6
NTHLT UB5 77 H6
TOTM N17 49 J3
Compton Pas FSBYE EC1V 6 B6
Compton Pl ERITH DA8 130 C6
OXHEY WD19 27 J6
STPAN WC1H 4 E6
Compton Ri PIN HA5 59 J2
Compton Rd CROY/NA CR0 197 J5
HYS/HAR UB3 94 C6
IS N1 85 H4
WCHMH N21 35 H3
WIM/MER SW19 177 J2
WLSDN NW10 100 B2
Compton St FSBYE EC1V 6 A6
Compton Ter IS N1 85 H4
WCHMH * N21 35 G3
Comreddy Cl ENC/FH EN2 23 H2
Comus Pl WALW SE17 19 G7
Comyn Rd BTSEA SW11 140 D5
Comyns Cl CAN/RD E16 106 D4
Comyns Rd DAGW RM9 92 C5
The Comyns BUSH WD23 28 C3
Conant Ms WCHPL E1 104 C6
Concanon Rd
BRXS/STRHM SW2 142 A5
Concert Hall Ap STHWK SE1 17 H1
Concord Cl NTHLT UB5 95 H2
Concorde Cl HSLW TW3 135 G3
Concorde Dr EHAM E6 107 K4
Concord Rd ACT W3 98 D3
PEND EN3 24 E6
Condell Rd VX/NE SW8 141 H2
Conder St POP/IOD E14 105 G5
Condover Crs
WOOL/PLUM SE18 147 G1
Condray Pl BTSEA SW11 140 D1
Conduit Ct COVGDN * WC2E 11 E6
Conduit La SAND/SEL CR2 212 C3
UED N18 50 E1
Conduit Ms BAY/PAD W2 8 A4
Conduit Pas BAY/PAD W2 8 A4
Conduit Pl BAY/PAD W2 8 A4
Conduit Rd WOOL/PLUM SE18 127 G5
Conduit St CONDST W1S 9 K5
Conduit Wy WLSDN NW10 80 E5
Conewood St HBRY N5 85 H1
Coney Acre DUL SE21 162 D3
Coney Burrows CHING E4 38 C4
Coney Hall Pde WWKM * BR4 214 C1
Coney Hill Rd WWKM BR4 199 H6
Coney Wy VX/NE SW8 122 A6
Conference Cl CHING E4 38 A4
Conference Rd ABYW SE2 128 D4
Congleton Gv
WOOL/PLUM SE18 127 H5
Congo Rd WOOL/PLUM SE18 127 J5
Congress Rd ABYW SE2 128 D4
Congreve Rd ELTH/MOT SE9 146 E4
Congreve St WALW SE17 19 G7
Conical Cnr ENC/FH EN2 23 J3
Conifer Av CRW RM5 56 D1
Conifer Cl ORP BR6 216 D2
Conifer Gdns EN EN1 35 K1
STRHM/NOR SW16 162 A5
SUT SM1 194 A6
Conifers Cl TEDD TW11 174 C3
Conifer Wy ALP/SUD HA0 79 J1
HYS/HAR UB3 94 E6
SWLY BR8 187 K4
Coniger Rd FUL/PGN SW6 139 K3
Coningham Ms SHB W12 118 D1
Coningham Rd SHB W12 118 E2
Coningsby Cottages EA W5 116 E2
Coningsby Gdns CHING E4 51 K2
Coningsby Rd EA W5 116 D2
FSBYPK N4 67 H4
SAND/SEL CR2 211 J6
Conington Rd LEW SE13 144 E3
Conisbee Ct STHGT/OAK N14 22 C6
Conisborough Crs CAT SE6 165 F5
Coniscliffe Cl CHST BR7 185 F4
Coniscliffe Rd PLMGR N13 35 J5
Coniston Av BARK IG11 90 E5
GFD/PVL UB6 97 H2
WELL DA16 147 K4
Coniston Cl BARN SW13 138 C1
BXLYHN DA7 149 K2
CHSWK W4 137 K2
DART DA1 170 E3
ERITH DA8 150 B1
MRDN SM4 193 G3
Coniston Ct BAY/PAD * W2 8 D4
Conistone Wy HOLWY N7 84 E5
Coniston Gdns BELMT * SM2 209 H4
CDALE/KGS NW9 63 F2
ED N9 36 E3
PIN HA5 58 E1
REDBR IG4 71 J1
WBLY HA9 61 J5
Coniston Rd BMLY BR1 183 H2
BXLYHN DA7 149 K2
CROY/NA CR0 197 H4
MUSWH N10 48 B5
TOTM N17 50 C2
WHTN TW2 155 G1
Coniston Wy CHSGTN KT9 206 A1
HCH RM12 93 J3
Conlan St NKENS W10 100 C3
Conley Rd WLSDN NW10 81 G4
Conley St GNWCH * SE10 125 H5
Connaught Av ASHF TW15 152 B6
CHING E4 38 B2
EBAR EN4 33 K3
EN EN1 24 A3
HSLWW TW4 134 D6
MORT/ESHN SW14 137 K4
Connaught Br CAN/RD E16 126 C1
Connaught Cl BAY/PAD W2 8 C4
EN EN1 24 A3
LEY * E10 69 G6
SUT SM1 194 C6
UX/CGN * UB8 94 A4
Connaught Dr GLDGN NW11 64 E1
Connaught Gdns MRDN SM4 194 B2
MUSWH N10 66 B2
PLMGR N13 35 H6
Connaught La IL IG1 72 C6
Connaught Ms FUL/PGN * SW6 139 H2
HAMP * NW3 83 J3
WOOL/PLUM SE18 127 F5
Connaught Pl BAY/PAD W2 8 E5
Connaught Rd BAR EN5 32 B1
CAN/RD E16 107 H6
CHING * E4 38 C2
FSBYPK N4 67 G4
HPTN TW12 173 J1
IL IG1 72 D6
KTN/HRWW/W HA3 43 F4
NWMAL KT3 192 B1
RCHPK/HAM * TW10 137 G6
SUT SM1 194 C6
WALTH * E17 69 J2
WAN E11 70 B5
WEA W13 97 H6
WLSDN * NW10 81 G6
WOOL/PLUM SE18 127 F5
Connaught Sq BAY/PAD W2 8 D4
Connaught St BAY/PAD W2 8 D4
Connaught Wy PLMGR N13 35 H6
Connell Crs EA W5 98 B3
Connemara Cl BORE * WD6 30 E1
Connington Crs CHING E4 38 B5
Connop Rd PEND EN3 25 F1
Connor Cl BARK/HLT IG6 54 C4
Connor Rd DAGW RM9 92 B2
Connor St HOM * E9 87 F6
Conolly Rd HNWL W7 115 K1
Conrad Dr WPK KT4 193 F5
Consfield Av NWMAL KT3 192 D1
Consort Cl FBAR/BDGN N11 47 K1
Consort Ms ISLW TW7 155 J1
Consort Rd PECK SE15 143 J3
Cons St STHWK * SE1 17 K2
Constable Av CAN/RD E16 126 A1
Constable Cl GLDGN NW11 65 F3
YEAD UB4 94 A1
Constable Crs SEVS/STOTM N15 68 C2
Constable Gdns EDGE HA8 44 C4
ISLW TW7 135 J6
Constable Ms BCTR RM8 91 H3
Constable Wk DUL SE21 163 F5
Constance Crs HAYES BR2 199 J5
Constance Rd CROY/NA CR0 196 C4
EN EN1 36 A1
SUT SM1 209 G2
WHTN TW2 155 G2
Constance St CAN/RD E16 126 D1
Constantine Rd HAMP NW3 83 J3
Constitution Hl WHALL SW1A 15 J2
Constitution Ri
WOOL/PLUM SE18 147 F2
Content St WALW SE17 18 D7
Contessa Cl ORP BR6 216 E3
Control Tower Rd HTHAIR TW6 132 D4
Convent Cl BECK BR3 183 F3
Convent Gdns EA W5 116 D4
NTGHL W11 100 D5
Convent Hl NRWD SE19 180 D2
Convent Wy NWDGN UB2 114 B4
Conway Cl RAIN RM13 93 J5
STAN HA7 43 G2
Conway Crs CHDH RM6 73 J4
GFD/PVL UB6 96 E1
Conway Dr BELMT SM2 209 F4
HYS/HAR UB3 113 F3
Conway Gdns ENC/FH EN2 24 A1
MTCM CR4 195 J1
WBLY HA9 61 J4
Conway Gv ACT W3 99 F4
Conway Ms FITZ W1T 10 A1
Conway Rd CRICK NW2 64 A6
FELT TW13 172 C1
HSLWW TW4 154 E2
RYNPK SW20 177 F4
SEVS/STOTM N15 67 J2
STHGT/OAK N14 34 E5
WOOL/PLUM SE18 127 J4
Conway St FITZ W1T 4 A7
Conybeare HAMP NW3 83 J5
Conyer's Rd STRHM/NOR SW16 179 J1
Conyer St BOW * E3 105 G1
Cooden Cl BMLY BR1 184 A3
Cookes Cl WAN E11 70 D6
Cookes La CHEAM SM3 208 C4
Cookham Cl NWDGN UB2 115 G3
Cookham Dene Cl CHST BR7 185 J4
Cookham Rd SWLY BR8 187 H4
Cookhill Rd ABYW SE2 128 C2
Cook's Cl CRW RM5 56 E4
Cooks Ferry Rbt UED N18 51 G1
Cook's Hole Rd ENC/FH EN2 23 H1
Cooks Md BUSH WD23 28 B1
Cookson Gv ERITH DA8 149 J1
Cook's Rd SRTFD E15 105 K1
WALW * SE17 122 C6
WALW SE17 122 C6
Coolfin Rd CAN/RD E16 106 E5
Coolgardie Av CHING E4 52 B1
Coolhurst Rd CEND/HSY/T N8 66 D3
Cool Oak Br CDALE/KGS NW9 63 H4
Cool Oak La CDALE/KGS NW9 63 H4
Coomassie Rd MV/WKIL W9 100 D3
Coombe Av CROY/NA CR0 212 A2
Coombe Bank NWMAL KT3 176 B4
Coombe Cl EDGE HA8 44 B5
HSLW TW3 135 F5
Coombe Cnr WCHMH N21 35 H3
Coombe Crs HPTN TW12 172 D3
Coombe Dr RSLP HA4 59 F5
Coombe End KUTN/CMB KT2 176 A3
Coombefield Cl NWMAL KT3 192 B2
Coombe Gdns NWMAL KT3 192 C1
RYNPK SW20 176 D5
Coombe Hill Gld KUTN/CMB KT2 176 B3
Coombe Hill Rd KUTN/CMB KT2 176 B3
Coombe House Cha
NWMAL KT3 176 A4
Coombehurst Cl EBAR EN4 21 K3
Coombe La CROY/NA CR0 212 D3
RYNPK SW20 176 D4
Coombe La West
KUTN/CMB KT2 175 K4
Coombe Lea BMLY BR1 184 D6
Coombe Ldg CHARL SE7 126 B6
Coombe Neville
KUTN/CMB KT2 175 K3
Coombe Pk KUTN/CMB KT2 175 K1
Coombe Ridings
KUTN/CMB KT2 175 K1
Coombe Ri KUTN/CMB KT2 175 K4
Coombe Rd BUSH WD23 28 C2
CHSWK W4 118 B5
HPTN TW12 172 E2
KUTN/CMB KT2 175 H5
NWMAL KT3 176 B6
SAND/SEL CR2 212 A2
SYD SE26 163 J6
WDGN N22 49 G5
WEA W13 116 C3
WLSDN NW10 81 F1
Coomber Wy CROY/NA CR0 195 K4
Coombes Rd DAGW RM9 92 B6
Coombe Vls
WAND/EARL * SW18 159 K2
Coombewood Dr CHDH RM6 74 B3
Coombe Wood Rd
KUTN/CMB KT2 175 K1
Coombs St IS N1 6 B3
Coomer Ms FUL/PGN * SW6 119 J6
Coomer Pl FUL/PGN SW6 119 J6
Cooperage Cl TOTM N17 50 B2
Cooper Av WALTH E17 51 F4
Cooper Cl STHWK SE1 17 K3
Cooper Crs CAR SM5 209 K1
Cooperdale Cl WFD IG8 53 G3
Cooper Rd CRICK NW2 81 J3
CROY/NA CR0 211 G3
HDN NW4 64 B3
Coopersale Rd HOM E9 87 F3
Coopers Cl DAGE RM10 92 D4
WCHPL E1 104 E3
Coopers La CAMTN NW1 4 D3
LEE/GVPK SE12 166 A4
LEY E10 69 K5
Cooper's Rd STHWK SE1 123 G5
Cooper's Rw TWRH EC3N 13 J5
Cooper St CAN/RD E16 106 D4
Cooper's Yd NRWD SE19 181 F2
Coote Rd BCTR RM8 92 B1
BXLYHN DA7 149 G2
Copeland Rd PECK SE15 143 H3
WALTH E17 69 K2
Copeman Cl SYD SE26 181 K1
Copenhagen Pl POP/IOD E14 105 H5
Copenhagen St IS N1 5 F1
Cope Pl KENS W8 119 K3
Copers Cope Rd BECK BR3 182 C3
Cope St BERM/RHTH SE16 124 A4
Copford Wk IS * N1 85 J6
Copgate Pth STRHM/NOR SW16 180 A2
Copland Av ALP/SUD HA0 79 K3
Copland Cl ALP/SUD HA0 79 J3
Copland Ms ALP/SUD HA0 80 A4
Copland Rd ALP/SUD HA0 80 A4
Copleston Rd PECK SE15 143 G4
Copley Cl HNWL W7 97 F4
WALW SE17 122 C6
Copley Dene BMLY BR1 184 C4
Copley Pk STRHM/NOR SW16 180 A2
Copley Rd STAN HA7 43 J1
Coppard Gdns CHSGTN KT9 205 J4
Coppelia Rd BKHTH/KID SE3 145 J5
Coppen Rd BCTR RM8 74 B4
Copperas St DEPT SE8 124 E6
Copper Beech Cl CLAY IG5 54 A4
STMC/STPC BR5 202 D2
Copper Cl NRWD SE19 181 G3
Copperdale Rd HYS/HAR UB3 113 K2
Copperfield CHIG IG7 54 D2
Copperfield Dr SEVS/STOTM N15 68 B1
Copperfield Rd BOW E3 105 G3
THMD SE28 109 J5
Copperfield St STHWK SE1 18 B2
Copperfield Wy CHST BR7 185 H2
PIN HA5 59 K1
Coppergate Cl BMLY BR1 184 A4
Coppermead Cl CRICK NW2 82 A1
Copper Mill Dr ISLW TW7 136 A3
Copper Mill La TOOT SW17 160 B6
Coppermill La WALTH E17 68 E3
Copper Rw STHWK SE1 19 J1
Coppetts Cl NFNCH/WDSP N12 47 K3
Coppetts Rd MUSWH N10 47 K4
The Coppice BAR * EN5 33 F1
BXLY DA5 170 A5
ENC/FH EN2 23 H5
OXHEY WD19 27 G1
Coppice Cl BECK BR3 198 E1
KTN/HRWW/W HA3 43 F2
RSLP * HA4 58 A3
RYNPK SW20 177 F6
Coppice Dr PUT/ROE SW15 158 D1
Coppice Wk TRDG/WHET N20 32 E5
Coppice Wy SWFD E18 70 D1
Coppies Gv FBAR/BDGN N11 34 B6
Copping Cl CROY/NA CR0 212 A2
The Coppins KTN/HRWW/W HA3 42 E2
Coppock Cl BTSEA SW11 140 D3
Coppsfield E/WMO/HCT KT8 173 F6
The Copse CHING E4 38 D3
EFNCH * N2 47 K6
Copse Av WWKM BR4 213 K1
Copse Cl CHARL SE7 126 A6
NTHWD HA6 40 A4
WDR/YW UB7 112 A3
Copse Gld SURB KT6 190 E5
Copse Hl BELMT SM2 209 F5
RYNPK SW20 176 D4
Copsem Dr ESH/CLAY KT10 204 B4
Copsem La ESH/CLAY KT10 204 C6
Copsem Wy ESH/CLAY KT10 204 C4
Copse Vw SAND/SEL CR2 213 F5
Copsewood Cl BFN/LL DA15 167 K1
Copse Wood Wy NTHWD HA6 40 A4
Coptefield Dr BELV DA17 128 E3
Copthall Av LOTH EC2R 13 F3
Copthall Dr MLHL NW7 45 J3
Copthall Gdns MLHL NW7 45 J3
TWK * TW1 156 B3
Copthorne Av BAL SW12 161 J2

BARK/HLT IG6 54 B2
HAYES BR2 200 E6
Copthorne Ms HYS/HAR UB3 113 H4
Coptic St NOXST/BSQ WC1A 10 E2
Copton Cl BOW E3 105 J4
Copwood Cl NFNCH/WDSP N12 33 H6
Coral Cl CHDH RM6 55 J6
Coraline Cl STHL UB1 95 K2
Coral St STHWK SE1 17 K3
Coram St STPAN WC1H 4 E7
Coran Cl ED N9 37 F2
Corban Rd HSLW TW3 135 F4
Corbar Cl EBAR EN4 21 H1
Corbet Cl WLGTN SM6 195 F5
Corbet Pl WCHPL E1 13 J1
Corbett Gv FBAR/BDGN N11 48 E3
Corbett Rd WALTH E17 52 B5
WAN E11 71 G3
Corbett's La BERM/RHTH SE16 123 K4
Corbicum WAN E11 70 C4
Corbin's La RYLN/HDSTN HA2 78 B1
Corbridge Crs BETH E2 104 D1
Corbridge Ms ROM RM1 75 H2
Corby Crs ENC/FH EN2 22 E5
Corbylands Rd BFN/LL DA15 167 K3
Corbyn St FSBYPK N4 66 E5
Corby Rd WLSDN NW10 98 E1
Cordelia Cl HNHL SE24 142 C5
Cordelia Gdns
STWL/WRAY TW19 152 B2
Cordelia Rd STWL/WRAY TW19 152 B2
Cordelia St POP/IOD E14 105 K5
Cordingley Rd RSLP HA4 58 B5
Cording St POP/IOD E14 105 K4
Cordova Rd BOW E3 105 G2
Cordwell Rd LEW SE13 145 G6
Corelli Rd BKHTH/KID SE3 146 D2
Corfe Av RYLN/HDSTN HA2 78 A2
Corfe Cl YEAD UB4 95 G5
Corfield Rd WCHMH N21 23 F6
Corfield St BETH E2 104 D3
Corfton Rd EA W5 98 A5
Coriander Av POP/IOD E14 106 B5
Cories Cl BCTR RM8 73 K6
Corinium Cl WBLY HA9 80 B2
Corinne Rd HOLWY N7 84 C2
Corinthian Manorway
ERITH DA8 130 A4
Corinthian Rd ERITH DA8 130 A4
Corkran Rd SURB KT6 190 E4
Cork St Ms CONDST W1S 10 A6
Corkscrew Hl WWKM BR4 199 F6
Cork Sq WAP E1W 123 H1
Cork St CONDST W1S 10 A6
Cork Tree Wy CHING E4 51 G1
Corlett St STJWD NW8 8 C1
Cormont Rd CMBW SE5 142 C2
Cormorant Cl WALTH E17 51 F4
Cormorant Rd FSTGT E7 88 D3
Cornbury Rd EDGE HA8 43 K3
Cornelia St HOLWY N7 85 F4
Cornell Cl SCUP DA14 187 F2
Cornell Wy CRW RM5 56 D1
The Corner EA * W5 117 F1
Corner Fielde
BRXS/STRHM * SW2 162 A3
Corner Gn BKHTH/KID SE3 145 K3
Corner Md CDALE/KGS NW9 45 H3
Corney Reach Wy CHSWK W4 138 B1
Corney Rd CHSWK W4 118 B6
Cornflower La CROY/NA CR0 198 A5
Cornflower Ter EDUL SE22 163 J1
Cornford Cl HAYES BR2 199 K2
Cornford Gv BAL SW12 161 G4
Cornhill BANK EC3V 13 F4
Cornish Gv PGE/AN SE20 181 J4
Corn Mill Dr ORP BR6 202 A4
Cornmill La LEW SE13 144 E4
Cornmow Dr WLSDN NW10 81 H3
Cornshaw Rd BCTR RM8 73 K5
Cornthwaite Rd CLPT E5 86 E1
Cornwall Av BETH E2 104 E2
ESH/CLAY KT10 205 F5
FNCH N3 46 E3
STHL UB1 95 K4
WDGN N22 48 E4
WELL DA16 147 K4
Cornwall Cl BARK IG11 91 F4
Cornwall Crs NTGHL W11 100 C6
Cornwall Dr STMC/STPC BR5 186 D3
Cornwall Gdns SKENS SW7 120 A3
SNWD * SE25 197 G1
WLSDN NW10 81 K4
Cornwall Gardens Wk
SKENS * SW7 120 A3
Cornwall Gv CHSWK W4 118 B5
Cornwallis Av BFN/LL DA15 167 J4
ED N9 36 D4
Cornwallis Cl ERITH DA8 130 C6
Cornwallis Gv ED N9 36 D4
Cornwallis Rd ARCH N19 66 E6
DAGW RM9 92 A2
ED N9 36 D4
WALTH E17 69 F1
WOOL/PLUM SE18 127 G3
Cornwallis Sq ARCH N19 66 E6
Cornwallis Wk ELTH/MOT SE9 146 E4
Cornwall Ms South SKENS SW7 120 B3
Cornwall Ms West SKENS * SW7 120 A3
Cornwall Rd BELMT SM2 208 D5
CROY/NA CR0 196 C6
DART DA1 151 J4
FSBYPK N4 67 G4
HRW HA1 60 C3
PIN HA5 41 K3
RSLP HA4 58 D6
SEVS/STOTM N15 67 K2
STHWK SE1 11 J7
TWK TW1 156 B2
UED N18 50 C1
Cornwall Sq LBTH * SE11 122 B5
Cornwall St WCHPL * E1 104 D6
Cornwall Ter CAMTN NW1 3 F7
Cornwall Terrace Ms
CAMTN NW1 3 F7
Corn Wy WAN E11 88 B1
Cornwood Cl EFNCH N2 65 H2
Cornwood Dr WCHPL E1 104 E5
Cornworthy Rd BCTR RM8 91 J3
Corona Rd LEE/GVPK SE12 165 K2
Coronation Cl BARK/HLT IG6 72 C1
BXLY DA5 168 E1
Coronation Dr HCH RM12 93 K3
Coronation Rd HYS/HAR UB3 113 J4
PLSTW E13 107 G2
WLSDN NW10 98 B2
Coronation Vls WLSDN * NW10 98 D3
Coronet Pde ALP/SUD * HA0 80 A4
Coronet St IS N1 7 G5
Corporation Av HSLWW TW4 134 D5
Corporation Rw CLKNW EC1R 5 K6
Corporation St HOLWY N7 84 E3
SRTFD E15 106 C1
Corrance Rd CLAP SW4 141 K5
Corri Av STHGT/OAK N14 34 D6
Corrib Dr SUT SM1 209 J3
Corrigan Cl HDN NW4 46 A6
Corringham Rd GLDGN NW11 64 E4
WBLY HA9 62 C6
Corringway EA W5 98 B4
GLDGN NW11 65 F4
Corris Gn CDALE/KGS * NW9 63 G3
Corsair Cl STWL/WRAY TW19 152 A2
Corsair Rd STWL/WRAY TW19 152 B2
Corscombe Cl KUTN/CMB KT2 175 K1
Corsehill St STRHM/NOR SW16 179 H2
Corsham St IS N1 7 F5
Corsica St HBRY N5 85 H4
Cortayne Rd FUL/PGN * SW6 139 J3
Cortina Dr DAGW RM9 110 E2
Cortis Rd PUT/ROE SW15 138 E6
Cortis Ter PUT/ROE SW15 138 E6
Corunna Rd VX/NE SW8 141 H2
Corunna Ter VX/NE SW8 141 H2
Corwell Gdns UX/CGN UB8 94 A5
Corwell La UX/CGN UB8 94 A5
Coryton Pth MV/WKIL W9 100 D3
Cosbycote Av HNHL SE24 142 D6
Cosdach Av WLGTN SM6 210 D5
Cosedge Crs CROY/NA CR0 211 G3
Cosgrove Cl WCHMH N21 35 H4
YEAD UB4 95 H3
Cosmo Pl RSQ WC1B 11 F1
Cosmur Cl SHB W12 118 C3
Cossall Wk PECK SE15 143 J2
Cosser St STHWK SE1 17 J4
Costa St PECK SE15 143 H3
Costons Av GFD/PVL UB6 96 D2
Costons La GFD/PVL UB6 96 D2
Cosway St CAMTN NW1 8 D1
Cotall St POP/IOD E14 105 J5
Coteford Cl PIN HA5 58 E2
Coteford St TOOT SW17 160 E6
Cotelands CROY/NA CR0 212 A1
Cotesbach Rd CLPT E5 86 E1
Cotesmore Gdns BCTR RM8 91 J2
Cotford Rd THHTH CR7 196 D1
Cotham St WALW SE17 18 D7
Cotherstone HOR/WEW KT19 207 F6
Cotherstone Rd
BRXS/STRHM SW2 162 A3
Cotleigh Av BXLY DA5 168 E4
Cotleigh Rd KIL/WHAMP NW6 82 E5
ROMW/RG RM7 75 F3
Cotman Cl EFNCH N2 65 G3
Cotmandene Crs
STMC/STPC BR5 186 C5
Cotman Gdns EDGE HA8 44 C5
Cotmans Cl HYS/HAR UB3 113 K1
Coton Rd WELL DA16 148 B4
Cotsford Av NWMAL KT3 191 K2
Cotswold Av BUSH WD23 28 C1
Cotswold Cl BXLYHN DA7 150 B2
ESH/CLAY KT10 190 A6
KUTN/CMB KT2 175 K2
Cotswold Gdns CRICK NW2 64 B6
EHAM E6 107 H2
GNTH/NBYPK IG2 72 D4
Cotswold Ga CRICK NW2 64 C5
Cotswold Gn ENC/FH EN2 23 F5
Cotswold Ri ORP BR6 202 A3
Cotswold Rd HPTN TW12 173 F2
Cotswold St WNWD SE27 162 C6
Cotswold Wy ENC/FH EN2 23 F4
WPK KT4 193 F6
Cottage Av HAYES BR2 200 D5
Cottage Cl RSLP HA4 58 B5
Cottage Field Cl SCUP DA14 168 D3
Cottage Gn CMBW SE5 142 E1
Cottage Gv BRXN/ST SW9 141 K4
SURB KT6 190 E3
Cottage Pl SKENS SW7 14 C4
Cottage Rd HOR/WEW KT19 207 F5
The Cottages EDGE * HA8 44 D3
Cottage St POP/IOD E14 105 K6
Cottenham Dr CDALE/KGS NW9 45 H6
RYNPK SW20 176 E3
Cottenham Park Rd
RYNPK SW20 176 D4
Cottenham Pl RYNPK SW20 176 E3
Cottenham Rd WALTH E17 69 H1
Cotterill Rd SURB KT6 191 G6
Cottesbrook St NWCR SE14 144 B1
Cottesloe Ms STHWK SE1 17 K4
Cottesmore Av CLAY IG5 53 K5
Cottesmore Gdns KENS W8 120 A3
Cottimore Av WOT/HER KT12 188 A5
Cottimore Crs WOT/HER KT12 188 A4
Cottimore La WOT/HER KT12 188 A4
Cottimore Ter WOT/HER KT12 188 A4
Cottingham Cha RSLP HA4 76 E1
Cottingham Rd PGE/AN SE20 182 A3
VX/NE SW8 142 A1
Cottington Rd FELT TW13 154 C6
Cottington St LBTH SE11 122 B5
Cotton Av ACT W3 99 F5
Cotton Cl DAGW RM9 91 J5
Cotton Gardens Est LBTH SE11 18 A7
Cottongrass Cl CROY/NA CR0 198 A5
Cotton Hl BMLY BR1 165 G6
Cotton Rw BTSEA SW11 140 B4
Cottons Ap ROMW/RG RM7 75 F2
Cotton's Gdns BETH E2 7 H4
Cotton St POP/IOD E14 106 A6
Couchmore Av CLAY IG5 53 K5
ESH/CLAY KT10 189 K6
Coulgate St BROCKY SE4 144 B4
Coulson Cl BCTR RM8 73 J5
Coulson St CHEL SW3 120 E5
Coulter Cl YEAD UB4 95 J3
Coulter Rd HMSMTH W6 118 E3
Councillor St CMBW SE5 142 D1
Counter St STHWK SE1 13 G7
Countess Rd KTTN NW5 84 C3
Countisbury Av EN EN1 36 B2
Country Wy FELT TW13 172 B1
County Ga CHST BR7 167 H5
TRDG/WHET N20 33 F1
County Gv CMBW SE5 142 D2
County Pde BTFD * TW8 136 E1
County Rd EHAM E6 108 B4
THHTH CR7 180 C5
County St STHWK SE1 18 D5
Coupland Pl WOOL/PLUM SE18 127 H5
Courcy Rd CEND/HSY/T N8 49 G6
Courier Rd DAGW RM9 110 E3
Courland Gv VX/NE SW8 141 J2
Courland St VX/NE SW8 141 J2
The Course ELTH/MOT SE9 167 F5
The Court MUSWH * N10 66 C1
RSLP HA4 77 J2
Courtauld Rd ARCH N19 66 D5
Courtaulds Cl THMD SE28 128 B1
Court Av BELV DA17 129 G5
Court Cl FELT TW13 155 G5
HAMP * NW3 83 H5
KTN/HRWW/W HA3 43 K6
Court Close Av FELT TW13 155 G5
Court Crs CHSGTN KT9 205 K4
Court Downs Rd BECK BR3 182 E5
Court Dr CROY/NA CR0 211 F2
STAN HA7 30 A6
SUT SM1 209 J2
Courtenay Av BELMT SM2 208 E6
HGT N6 65 J4
KTN/HRWW/W HA3 42 B3
Courtenay Dr BECK BR3 183 G5
Courtenay Ms WALTH E17 69 G2
Courtenay Rd PGE/AN SE20 182 A3
WALTH E17 69 F2
WAN * E11 88 D1
WBLY * HA9 79 K1
WPK KT4 208 A1
Courtenay Sq LBTH * SE11 122 B5
Courtenay St LBTH SE11 122 A5
Courten Ms STAN HA7 43 J3
Court Farm Av HOR/WEW KT19 207 F3
Court Farm Rd ELTH/MOT SE9 166 C4
NTHLT UB5 78 A5
Courtfield Av HRW * HA1 61 F2
Courtfield Crs HRW HA1 61 F2
Courtfield Gdns ECT SW5 120 A4
RSLP HA4 58 D6
WEA W13 97 G5
Courtfield Ms SKENS * SW7 120 B4
Courtfield Ri WWKM BR4 214 B1
Courtfield Rd SKENS SW7 120 B4
Court Gdns HOLWY N7 85 G4
Courthill Rd LEW SE13 145 F6
Courthope Rd GFD/PVL UB6 96 D1
HAMP NW3 83 K2
WIM/MER SW19 177 H1
Courthope Vls WIM/MER SW19 177 H3
Court House Rd FNCH N3 47 F2
Courtland Av CHING E4 38 D4
IL IG1 71 K6
MLHL NW7 31 F5
STRHM/NOR SW16 180 A3
Courtland Gv THMD SE28 109 K6
Courtland Rd EHAM E6 89 J6
Courtlands RCHPK/HAM TW10 137 H6
Courtlands Av HAYES BR2 199 H5
HPTN TW12 172 E2
LEE/GVPK SE12 146 A6
RCH/KEW TW9 137 J3
Courtlands Cl RSLP HA4 58 D4
Courtlands Dr HOR/WEW KT19 207 G4
Courtlands Rd BRYLDS KT5 191 H4
Court La DUL SE21 163 G2
Court Lane Gdns DUL SE21 163 F2
Courtleet Dr BXLYHN DA7 149 J2
Courtleigh Av EBAR EN4 21 H1
Courtleigh Gdns GLDGN NW11 64 C1
Courtman Rd TOTM N17 49 J3
Court Md NTHLT UB5 95 K2
Courtmead Cl HNHL SE24 162 D1
Courtnell St BAY/PAD W2 100 E5
Courtney Cl NRWD * SE19 181 F2
Courtney Crs CAR SM5 209 K5
Courtney Rd CROY/NA CR0 211 G1
HOLWY N7 85 G3
HTHAIR TW6 132 D4
WIM/MER SW19 178 D3
Courtney Wy HTHAIR TW6 132 D4
Courtrai Rd BROCKY SE4 164 B1
Court Rd ELTH/MOT SE9 166 E3
NWDGN UB2 114 E4
SNWD SE25 181 G5
Court Rd (Orpington By-Pass)
ORP BR6 217 H1
The Courts STRHM/NOR SW16 179 K3
Courtside CEND/HSY/T N8 66 D3
SYD * SE26 163 K5
Court St BMLY BR1 183 K5
WCHPL E1 104 D4
Court Vw HGT * N6 66 B6
The Courtway OXHEY WD19 27 J4
Court Wy ACT W3 98 E4
BARK/HLT IG6 54 C6
CDALE/KGS NW9 63 G1
WHTN TW2 156 A2
The Courtyard IS N1 85 F5
Court Yd ELTH/MOT SE9 166 E1
The Courtyards WATW * WD18 26 B2
Cousin La CANST EC4R 12 E6
Couthurst Rd BKHTH/KID SE3 126 A6
Coutts Av CHSGTN KT9 206 A3
Coutts Crs KTTN * NW5 84 A1
Coval Gdns MORT/ESHN SW14 137 J5
Coval La MORT/ESHN SW14 137 J5
Coval Rd MORT/ESHN SW14 137 K5
Covelees Wall EHAM E6 108 A5
Covent Gdn COVGDN WC2E 11 F5
Covent Garden Piazza
COVGDN WC2E 11 F5
Coventry Cl EHAM E6 107 K5
KIL/WHAMP NW6 100 E1
Coventry Cross Est BOW E3 106 A3
Coventry Rd IL IG1 72 B5
SNWD SE25 197 H1
WCHPL E1 104 D3
Coventry St MYFR/PICC W1J 10 C6
Coverack Cl CROY/NA CR0 198 B4
STHGT/OAK N14 34 C1
Coverdale Gdns CROY/NA CR0 212 B1
Coverdale Rd FBAR/BDGN N11 48 A2
KIL/WHAMP NW6 82 C5
SHB W12 118 E1
The Coverdales BARK IG11 108 D1
Coverley Cl WCHPL * E1 104 C4
Coverton Rd TOOT SW17 160 D6
The Covert NRWD * SE19 181 G3
NTHWD HA6 40 A4
ORP BR6 201 K3
Covert Rd BARK/HLT IG6 55 F2
Coverts Rd ESH/CLAY KT10 205 F5
Covert Wy EBAR EN4 21 G3
Covet Wood Cl
STMC/STPC BR5 202 A3
Covey Cl WIM/MER SW19 178 A5
Covington Gdns
STRHM/NOR SW16 180 C3
Covington Wy
STRHM/NOR SW16 180 B2
Cowbridge La BARK IG11 90 B5
Cowbridge Rd
KTN/HRWW/W HA3 62 B1
Cowcross St FARR EC1M 12 A1
Cowdenbeath Pth IS N1 84 E6
Cowden Rd ORP BR6 202 A4
Cowden St CAT SE6 164 D6
Cowdray Rd HGDN/ICK UB10 76 A6
Cowdray Wy HCH RM12 93 J2
Cowdrey Cl EN EN1 24 A3
Cowdrey Ct DART DA1 170 E2
Cowdrey Rd WIM/MER SW19 178 A2
Cowen Av RYLN/HDSTN HA2 60 D6
Cowgate Rd GFD/PVL UB6 96 D2
Cowick Rd TOOT SW17 160 E6
Cowings Md NTHLT UB5 77 J5
Cowland Av PEND EN3 24 E5
Cow La BUSH * WD23 28 A1
Cow Leaze EHAM E6 108 A5
Cowleaze Rd KUTN/CMB KT2 175 F4
Cowley Cl SAND/SEL CR2 212 E6
Cowley La WAN * E11 88 C1
Cowley Pl HDN NW4 64 A2
Cowley Rd ACT W3 118 C1
BRXN/ST SW9 142 B2
HARH RM3 57 K3
IL IG1 71 K4
MORT/ESHN SW14 138 B4
WAN E11 71 F2
Cowley St WEST SW1P 16 E5
Cowling Cl NTGHL W11 100 C6
Cowper Av EHAM E6 89 J5
SUT SM1 209 H2
Cowper Cl HAYES BR2 200 C1
WELL DA16 148 B6
Cowper Gdns STHGT/OAK N14 34 C1
WLGTN SM6 210 C4
Cowper Rd ACT W3 118 A1
BELV DA17 129 G4
HAYES BR2 200 C1
HNWL W7 97 F6
RAIN RM13 111 J3
RCHPK/HAM TW10 175 G1
STHGT/OAK N14 34 B3
STNW/STAM N16 86 A2
UED N18 50 C1
WIM/MER SW19 178 B2
Cowper St STLK EC1Y 7 F6
Cowper Ter NKENS * W10 100 B4
Cowslip Rd SWFD E18 53 F6
Cowthorpe Rd VX/NE SW8 141 J2
Coxe Pl KTN/HRWW/W HA3 61 G1
Cox La CHSGTN KT9 206 B2
HOR/WEW KT19 206 E3
Coxmount Rd CHARL SE7 126 C5
Coxson Wy STHWK SE1 19 J3
Coxwell Rd NRWD SE19 181 F3
WOOL/PLUM SE18 127 J5
Crabbs Croft Cl ORP * BR6 216 C3
Crab Hl BECK BR3 183 G3
Crabtree Av ALP/SUD HA0 98 A1
CHDH RM6 73 K1
Crabtree Cl BETH E2 7 J3
Crabtree La FUL/PGN SW6 139 G1
Crabtree Manorway North
BELV DA17 129 K2
Crabtree Manorway South
BELV DA17 129 K3
Craddock Rd EN EN1 24 B4
Craddock St CAMTN * NW1 84 A4
Cradley Rd ELTH/MOT SE9 167 J3
Cragie Lea MUSWH * N10 48 B5
Craigdale Rd ROM RM1 75 H3
Craigen Av CROY/NA CR0 197 J5
Craigerne Rd BKHTH/KID SE3 146 A1
Craig Gdns SWFD E18 52 D5
Craigholm WOOL/PLUM SE18 147 F3
Craigmuir Pk ALP/SUD HA0 80 B6
Craignair Rd BRXS/STRHM SW2 162 A2
Craignish Av STRHM/NOR SW16 180 A5
Craig Park Rd UED N18 36 D6
Craig Rd RCHPK/HAM TW10 156 D6
Craig's Ct WHALL SW1A 10 E7
Craigton Rd ELTH/MOT SE9 146 E5
Craigweil Cl STAN HA7 43 K1
Craigweil Dr STAN HA7 43 K1
Craigwell Av FELT TW13 153 K5
Crail Rw WALW SE17 19 F7
Cramer St MHST W1U 9 H2
Crammond Cl HMSMTH W6 119 H6
Crampton Rd PGE/AN SE20 181 K2
Cranberry Cl NTHLT UB5 95 H1
Cranberry La CAN/RD E16 106 C3
Cranborne Av NWDGN UB2 115 F4
SURB KT6 206 C1
Cranborne Rd BARK IG11 90 D6
Cranborne Waye YEAD UB4 95 F5
Cranbourne Av WAN E11 71 F1
Cranbourne Cl
STRHM/NOR SW16 179 K6
Cranbourne Dr PIN HA5 59 H2
Cranbourne Gdns BARK/HLT IG6 54 C6
GLDGN NW11 64 D2
Cranbourne Rd MNPK E12 89 J3
MUSWH N10 48 B5
NTHWD HA6 40 D6
SRTFD E15 88 A2
Cranbourn St LSQ/SEVD WC2H 10 D5
Cranbrook Cl HAYES BR2 199 K3
Cranbrook Dr ESH/CLAY KT10 189 H5
GPK RM2 75 K1
WHTN TW2 155 G3
Cranbrook La FBAR/BDGN N11 34 B6
Cranbrook Ms WALTH E17 69 H2
Cranbrook Pk WDGN N22 49 G4
Cranbrook Ri IL IG1 71 K3
Cranbrook Rd BXLYHN DA7 149 G2
CHSWK W4 118 B5
DEPT SE8 144 D2
EBAR EN4 33 H1
HSLWW TW4 134 E5
IL IG1 72 A4
THHTH CR7 180 D5
WIM/MER SW19 177 H3
Cranbrook St BETH E2 105 F1
Cranbury Rd FUL/PGN SW6 140 A3
Crane Av ACT W3 98 E6
ISLW TW7 136 B6
Cranebank Ms TWK * TW1 136 C6
Cranebrook WHTN TW2 155 H4
Crane Cl DAGE RM10 92 C4
Crane Ct FLST/FETLN EC4A 11 K4
MORT/ESHN * SW14 137 K5
Craneford Cl WHTN TW2 156 A2
Craneford Wy WHTN TW2 155 K2
Crane Gdns HYS/HAR UB3 113 J4
Crane Gv HOLWY N7 85 G4
Crane Lodge Rd HEST TW5 114 A6
Crane Md BERM/RHTH SE16 124 A4
Crane Park Rd WHTN TW2 155 G4
Crane Rd STWL/WRAY TW19 152 D1
WHTN TW2 155 K3
Cranesbill Cl CDALE/KGS NW9 45 F6
Cranes Dr BRYLDS KT5 191 F1
Cranes Pk SURB KT6 191 F1
Cranes Park Av SURB KT6 191 F1
Cranes Park Crs BRYLDS KT5 191 G1
Crane St PECK SE15 143 G2
Craneswater HYS/HAR UB3 133 J1
Craneswater Pk NWDGN UB2 114 E5
Crane Wy WHTN TW2 155 H2
Cranfield Dr CDALE/KGS NW9 45 G3
Cranfield Rd BROCKY SE4 144 C4
Cranfield Rd East CAR SM5 210 A6
Cranfield Rd West CAR * SM5 209 K6
Cranford Av PLMGR N13 48 E1
STWL/WRAY TW19 152 B2
Cranford Cl RYNPK * SW20 176 E4
STWL/WRAY TW19 152 B2
Cranford Cottages WAP * E1W 105 F6
Cranford Dr HYS/HAR UB3 113 J4
Cranford La HEST TW5 134 C1
HTHAIR TW6 133 J2
HYS/HAR UB3 113 G6
Cranford Park Rd
HYS/HAR UB3 113 J4
Cranford Ri ESH/CLAY KT10 204 C3
Cranford Rd DART DA1 171 H3
Cranford St WAP E1W 105 F6
Cranford Wy CEND/HSY/T N8 67 F2
Cranham Rd EMPK RM11 75 K3
Cranhurst Rd CRICK NW2 82 A3
Cranleigh Cl BXLY * DA5 169 J1
ORP BR6 217 G1
PGE/AN SE20 181 J5
Cranleigh Gdns BARK IG11 90 D5
KTN/HRWW/W HA3 62 A2
KUTN/CMB KT2 175 G2
LOU IG10 39 K1
SNWD SE25 181 F6
STHL UB1 95 K5
SUT SM1 194 A6
WCHMH N21 23 G6
Cranleigh Ms BTSEA SW11 140 D3
Cranleigh Rd ESH/CLAY KT10 189 H5
FELT TW13 153 J6
SEVS/STOTM N15 67 J2
WIM/MER SW19 177 K6
Cranleigh St CAMTN NW1 4 B3
Cranley Dr GNTH/NBYPK IG2 72 C4
RSLP HA4 58 D6
Cranley Gdns MUSWH N10 66 B1
PLMGR N13 35 F5
SKENS SW7 120 B5
WLGTN SM6 210 C5
Cranley Ms SKENS SW7 120 B5
Cranley Pl SKENS SW7 14 A7
Cranley Rd GNTH/NBYPK IG2 72 C3
PLSTW E13 107 F4
Cranley Ter HDN * NW4 46 B5
Cranmer Av WEA W13 116 C3
Cranmer Cl MRDN SM4 193 G3
RSLP HA4 59 H5
STAN HA7 43 J3
Cranmer Ct HPTN TW12 173 G1
Cranmer Farm Cl MTCM CR4 194 E1
Cranmer Gdns DAGE RM10 92 E2
Cranmer Rd BRXN/ST SW9 142 B1
CROY/NA CR0 211 H1
EDGE HA8 30 D5
FSTGT E7 89 F2
HPTN TW12 173 G1
HYS/HAR UB3 94 B5
KUTN/CMB KT2 175 F1
MTCM CR4 194 E1
Cranmer Ter TOOT SW17 178 C1
Cranmore Rd BMLY BR1 165 H5
CHST BR7 184 E1
Cranmore Wy MUSWH N10 66 C1
Cranston Cl HGDN/ICK UB10 58 B6
HSLW TW3 134 D3
Cranston Est IS N1 7 F2
Cranston Gdns CHING E4 51 K2
Cranston Rd FSTH SE23 164 B3
Cranswick Rd
BERM/RHTH SE16 123 J5
Crantock Rd CAT SE6 165 F4
Cranwell Cl BOW E3 105 K3
Cranwich Av WCHMH N21 35 K2
Cranwich Rd STNW/STAM N16 68 A4
Cranwood St FSBYE EC1V 7 F5
Cranworth Crs CHING E4 38 B3
Cranworth Gdns BRXN/ST SW9 142 B2
Craster Rd BRXS/STRHM SW2 162 A2
Crathie Rd LEE/GVPK SE12 166 A1
Cravan Av FELT TW13 153 K4
Craven Av WEA W13 97 J6
Craven Cl STNW/STAM * N16 68 C4
YEAD UB4 94 E5
Craven Gdns BARK IG11 108 E1
BARK/HLT IG6 54 D5
CRW RM5 56 C1
WIM/MER SW19 178 A1
Craven Hill Gdns BAY/PAD W2 101 G6
Craven Ms BTSEA SW11 141 F4
Craven Pk WLSDN NW10 81 F6
Craven Park Ms WLSDN NW10 81 G5
Craven Park Rd
STNW/STAM N16 68 B3
WLSDN NW10 81 G6
Craven Rd BAY/PAD W2 101 G6
CROY/NA CR0 197 J5
KUTN/CMB KT2 175 G4
ORP BR6 217 K1
WEA W13 97 J6
WLSDN NW10 81 F6
Craven St CHCR WC2N 10 E7
Craven Ter BAY/PAD W2 101 G6
Craven Wk STNW/STAM N16 68 C4
Crawford Av ALP/SUD HA0 79 K3
Crawford Cl ISLW TW7 135 K3
Crawford Gdns NTHLT UB5 95 K2
PLMGR N13 35 H5
Crawford Pas CLKNW EC1R 5 J7
Crawford Pl BAY/PAD W2 8 D3
Crawford Rd CMBW SE5 142 D3
Crawford St MBLAR W1H 8 E2
Crawley Rd ED N9 36 B2
LEY E10 69 K5
WDGN N22 49 J5

Crawthew Gv EDUL SE22 143 G5
Cray Av STMC/STPC BR5 202 C2
Craybrooke Rd SCUP DA14 168 C6
Craybury End ELTH/MOT SE9 167 H4
Cray Cl DART DA1 150 D6
Craydene Rd ERITH DA8 150 C2
Crayford High St DART DA1 150 B6
Crayford Rd DART DA1 150 C6
HOLWY N7 84 E2
Crayford Wy DART DA1 150 D5
Crayke Hl CHSGTN KT9 206 A5
Craylands STMC/STPC BR5 186 D6
Crayleigh Ter SCUP * DA14 186 D2
Cray Rd BELV DA17 129 H6
SCUP DA14 186 D2
SWLY BR8 203 K3
Crays Pde STMC/STPC * BR5 186 D5
Cray Valley Rd STMC/STPC BR5 202 B2
Crealock Gv WFD IG8 52 D1
Crealock St WAND/EARL SW18 160 A1
Creasey Cl EMPK RM11 75 K6
Crebor St EDUL SE22 163 H1
Credenhall Dr HAYES BR2 200 E5
Credenhill St STRHM/NOR SW16 179 H2
Crediton Hl KIL/WHAMP NW6 83 F3
Crediton Rd WLSDN NW10 82 B6
Crediton Wy ESH/CLAY KT10 205 G3
Credon Rd BERM/RHTH SE16 123 J5
PLSTW E13 107 G1
Creechurch La HDTCH EC3A 13 H4
Creechurch Pl HDTCH * EC3A 13 H4
Creed La BLKFR EC4V 12 B4
Creek Cottages
E/WMO/HCT * KT8 189 K1
Creek Rd BARK IG11 109 F2
DEPT SE8 124 D6
E/WMO/HCT KT8 189 K1
Creekside DEPT SE8 144 D1
RAIN RM13 111 H3
Creek Wy RAIN RM13 111 G4
Creeland Gv CAT SE6 164 C3
Cree Wy ROM RM1 57 G3
Crefeld Cl FUL/PGN SW6 119 G6
Creffield Rd EA W5 98 C6
Creighton Av EFNCH N2 47 K5
EHAM E6 107 H1
Creighton Cl SHB W12 99 K6
Creighton Rd EA W5 116 E3
KIL/WHAMP NW6 100 B1
TOTM N17 50 A3
Creigton Av EFNCH N2 47 J6
Cremer St BETH E2 7 J3
Cremorne Est WBPTN * SW10 120 C6
Cremorne Gdns HOR/WEW KT19 207 F6
Cremorne Rd WBPTN SW10 140 B1
The Crescent ACT W3 99 G5
ALP/SUD HA0 61 H6
BAR EN5 21 F4
BARN SW13 138 C3
BECK BR3 182 D4
BXLY DA5 168 D2
CRICK NW2 81 K1
E/WMO/HCT KT8 188 E1
FBAR/BDGN N11 33 K6
GNTH/NBYPK IG2 72 A3
HYS/HAR UB3 133 F1
LOU IG10 39 H1
NWDGN UB2 114 D2
NWMAL KT3 175 K5
RYLN/HDSTN HA2 60 C5
SCUP DA14 168 A6
SNWD SE25 196 E3
SURB KT6 191 F2
SUT SM1 209 H3
WALTH E17 69 G2
WIM/MER SW19 159 K5
WWKM BR4 199 H3
Crescent TWRH EC3N 13 J5
Crescent Ar GNWCH SE10 125 F6
Crescent Av HCH RM12 75 H6
Crescent Dr STMC/STPC BR5 201 H3
Crescent East EBAR EN4 21 G1
Crescent Gdns RSLP HA4 59 F4
SWLY BR8 187 K5
WIM/MER SW19 159 K5
Crescent Gv CLAP SW4 141 H5
MTCM CR4 194 D1
Crescent La CLAP SW4 141 J6
Crescent Pl CHEL SW3 14 C6
Crescent Ri EBAR EN4 21 J6
FNCH * N3 46 D4
WDGN N22 48 D4
Crescent Rd BECK BR3 182 E5
BFN/LL DA15 168 A5
BMLY BR1 183 K3
CEND/HSY/T N8 66 D3
CHING E4 38 C2
DAGE RM10 92 D2
EBAR EN4 21 H5
ED N9 36 C3
ENC/FH EN2 23 H5
ERITH DA8 130 C6
FBAR/BDGN N11 33 K6
FNCH N3 46 D4
KUTN/CMB KT2 175 H3
LEY E10 69 K6
PLSTW E13 88 E6
RYNPK SW20 177 G4
SEVS/STOTM * N15 49 H6
SWFD E18 53 G5
WDGN N22 48 D4
WOOL/PLUM SE18 127 G5
Crescent Rw STLK EC1Y 6 C7
Crescent St IS * N1 85 F5
Crescent Vw LOU IG10 39 H1
Crescent Wy BROCKY SE4 144 D4
ORP BR6 216 E3
STRHM/NOR SW16 180 A3
Crescentway NFNCH/WDSP N12 47 J2
Crescent West EBAR EN4 21 G1
Crescent Wood Rd SYD SE26 163 H5
Cresford Rd FUL/PGN SW6 140 A2
Crespigny Rd HDN NW4 63 K3
Cressage Cl STHL UB1 96 A3
Cresset Rd HOM E9 86 E4
Cresset St CLAP SW4 141 J4
Cressfield Cl KTTN NW5 84 A3
Cressida Rd ARCH N19 66 C5
Cressingham Gv SUT SM1 209 G2
Cressingham Rd EDGE HA8 45 F3
LEW SE13 145 F4
Cressington Cl STNW/STAM N16 86 A3
Cresswell Pk BKHTH/KID SE3 145 J4
Cresswell Pl WBPTN SW10 120 B5
Cresswell Rd FELT TW13 154 D5
SNWD SE25 197 H1
TWK TW1 156 E1
Cresswell Wy WCHMH N21 35 G2
Cressy Ct HMSMTH W6 118 E3
Cressy Houses WCHPL * E1 104 E4
Cressy Pl WCHPL E1 104 E4
Cressy Rd HAMP NW3 83 K2
Cressys Cnr HSLW * TW3 135 G4
The Crest BRYLDS KT5 191 H2
HDN NW4 64 A2
HOLWY * N7 84 D3
PLMGR N13 35 G6
Crestbrook Av PLMGR N13 35 H5
Crestbrook Pl PLMGR * N13 35 G5
Crest Dr PEND EN3 24 E1
Crestfield St CAMTN NW1 5 F4
Crest Gdns RSLP HA4 77 G1
Creston Wy WPK KT4 193 G5
Crest Rd CRICK NW2 63 J6
HAYES BR2 199 J4
SAND/SEL CR2 212 D5
Crest Vw PIN HA5 59 H1
Crest View Dr STMC/STPC BR5 201 G2
Crestway PUT/ROE SW15 158 D1
Crestwood Wy HSLWW TW4 134 E6
Creswick Rd ACT W3 98 D6
Creswick Wk GLDGN NW11 64 D1
Crewdson Rd BRXN/ST SW9 142 A1
Crewe Pl WLSDN NW10 99 H2
Crews St POP/IOD * E14 124 D4
Crewys Rd CRICK NW2 64 D6
PECK SE15 143 J3
Crichton Av WLGTN SM6 210 D3
Crichton Rd CAR SM5 209 K5
Crichton St VX/NE * SW8 141 H3
Cricketers Arms Rd
ENC/FH * EN2 23 J3
Cricketers Cl CHSGTN KT9 205 K3
ERITH DA8 130 B5
STHGT/OAK N14 34 C2
Cricketers Wk SYD SE26 181 K1
Cricketfield Rd CLPT E5 86 D2
Cricket Gn MTCM CR4 178 E6
Cricket Ground Rd CHST BR7 185 G4
Cricket La BECK BR3 182 B2
Cricket Rw EFNCH * N2 47 H6
Cricklade Av BRXS/STRHM SW2 161 K4
Cricklewood Broadway
CRICK NW2 82 A1
Cricklewood La CRICK NW2 82 C2
Cridland St SRTFD E15 88 D6
Crieff Rd WAND/EARL SW18 160 B1
Criffel Av BRXS/STRHM SW2 161 J4
Crimscott St STHWK SE1 19 H5
Crimsworth Rd VX/NE SW8 141 J2
Crinan St IS N1 5 F2
Cringle St VX/NE SW8 141 H1
Cripplegate St BARB * EC2Y 12 C1
Crispen Rd FELT TW13 154 D6
Crispian Cl WLSDN NW10 81 G2
Crispin Crs CROY/NA CR0 210 D1
Crispin Rd EDGE HA8 44 E2
Crispin St WCHPL E1 13 J2
Crisp Rd HMSMTH W6 119 F5
Cristowe Rd FUL/PGN * SW6 139 J3
Criterion Ms ARCH N19 66 D6
Cricketers Ms
WAND/EARL SW18 140 A6
Crockenhill Hl STMC/STPC BR5 202 E2
Crockenhill Rd STMC/STPC BR5 202 E3
Crockerton Rd TOOT SW17 160 E4
Crockham Wy ELTH/MOT SE9 167 F6
Crocus Cl CROY/NA CR0 198 A5
Crocus Fld BAR EN5 32 D1
The Croft ALP/SUD HA0 79 J3
BAR EN5 20 C5
CHING E4 38 C4
EA W5 98 A4
EDGE HA8 44 D4
HEST TW5 134 D1
RSLP HA4 77 G2
SWLY BR8 187 K6
WLSDN NW10 99 H1
Croft Av WWKM BR4 199 F5
Croft Cl BELV DA17 129 G5
CHST BR7 184 E1
HYS/HAR UB3 133 F1
MLHL NW7 31 G5
Croft Ct RSLP * HA4 58 D5
SUT * SM1 194 C6
Croftdown Rd KTTN NW5 84 A1
Crofters Cl ISLW TW7 135 J6
Crofters Ct DEPT SE8 124 B4
Crofters Md CROY/NA CR0 213 H6
Crofters Rd NTHWD HA6 26 C6
Crofters Wy CAMTN NW1 84 D6
Croft Gdns HNWL W7 116 B2
RSLP HA4 58 C5
Croft Lodge Cl WFD IG8 53 F2
Croft Ms NFNCH/WDSP N12 33 G5
Crofton Av BXLY DA5 168 E2
CHSWK W4 137 K1
ORP BR6 201 H6
Crofton Gate Wy BROCKY SE4 144 B6
Crofton Gv CHING E4 38 B6
Crofton La STMC/STPC BR5 201 J5
Crofton Park Rd BROCKY SE4 164 C1
Crofton Rd CMBW SE5 143 F2
ORP BR6 216 A2
PLSTW E13 107 F3
Crofton Ter RCH/KEW TW9 137 G5
Crofton Wy BAR * EN5 33 F1
ENC/FH EN2 23 G3
Croft Rd BMLY BR1 183 K2
PEND EN3 25 G2
STRHM/NOR SW16 180 B3
SUT SM1 209 H3
WIM/MER SW19 178 B3
Crofts Rd HRW HA1 61 G3
Crofts St WCHPL E1 104 C6
Croft St DEPT SE8 124 B4
WCHPL E1 104 C6
Croft Wy BFN/LL DA15 167 K5
RCHPK/HAM TW10 156 C5
Crogsland Rd CAMTN NW1 84 A5
Croham Cl SAND/SEL CR2 212 A4
Croham Manor Rd
SAND/SEL CR2 212 A5
Croham Mt SAND/SEL CR2 212 A5
Croham Park Av SAND/SEL CR2 212 B3
Croham Rd SAND/SEL CR2 211 K3
Croham Valley Rd
SAND/SEL CR2 212 C4
Croindene Rd
STRHM/NOR SW16 179 K4
Cromartie Rd ARCH N19 66 D4
Cromarty Rd EDGE * HA8 30 D4
Cromarty Vls BAY/PAD * W2 101 G6
Crombie Cl REDBR IG4 71 K2
Crombie Ms BTSEA * SW11 140 D3
Crombie Rd BFN/LL DA15 167 J3
Cromer Cl UX/CGN UB8 94 A5
Cromer Hyde MRDN * SM4 194 A2
Cromer Rd BAR EN5 21 G5
CHDH RM6 74 A3
HTHAIR TW6 132 D4
LEY E10 70 B4
ROMW/RG RM7 74 E3
SNWD SE25 181 J6
TOOT SW17 179 F2
TOTM N17 50 C5
Cromer Rd West HTHAIR TW6 132 D4
Cromer St STPAN WC1H 5 F5
Cromer Ter HACK E8 86 C3
Cromer Villas Rd
WAND/EARL SW18 159 J1
Cromford Cl ORP BR6 216 E1
Cromford Rd PUT/ROE SW15 139 J6
Cromford Wy NWMAL KT3 176 A4
Cromlix Cl CHST BR7 185 G5
Crompton Pl PEND EN3 25 J1
Crompton St BAY/PAD W2 2 A7
Cromwell Av HAYES BR2 184 A6
HGT N6 66 B5
HMSMTH W6 118 E5
NWMAL KT3 192 C2
Cromwell Cl CHSWK * W4 117 J5
EFNCH N2 65 H1
WOT/HER KT12 188 A5
Cromwell Ct ALP/SUD HA0 98 A1
Cromwell Crs ECT SW5 119 K4
Cromwell Gv HMSMTH W6 119 F3
Cromwell Ms SKENS * SW7 14 A6
Cromwell Pde ALP/SUD * HA0 98 A1
Cromwell Pl ACT W3 117 K1
HGT * N6 66 B5
MORT/ESHN SW14 137 K4
SKENS SW7 14 B6
Cromwell Rd ALP/SUD HA0 97 K1
BECK BR3 182 B5
BRXN/ST SW9 142 C2
CROY/NA CR0 196 E4
ECT SW5 120 A4
FELT TW13 154 A3
FNCH N3 47 G5
FSTGT E7 89 G5
HSLW TW3 135 F5
HYS/HAR UB3 94 B5
KUTN/CMB KT2 175 F4
MUSWH N10 48 A3
SKENS SW7 14 A6
TEDD TW11 174 B2
WALTH E17 70 A2
WIM/MER SW19 177 K1
WOT/HER KT12 188 A6
WPK KT4 207 F1
Cromwell St HSLW TW3 135 F5
Cromwell Ter HSLW * TW3 135 F5
Crondace Rd FUL/PGN SW6 139 K2
Crondall St IS N1 7 F3
Cronin St PECK SE15 143 G1
Crooked Billet Rbt CHING E4 51 K3
Crooked Usage FNCH N3 46 C6
Crooke Rd DEPT SE8 124 B5
Crookham Rd FUL/PGN SW6 139 J2
Crook Log BXLYHN DA7 148 E4
Crookston Rd ELTH/MOT SE9 147 G4
Croombs Rd CAN/RD E16 107 G4
Croom's Hl GNWCH SE10 145 G1
Croom's Hill Gv GNWCH SE10 145 F1
Cropley St IS N1 6 E2
Croppath Rd DAGE RM10 92 C2
Cropthorne Ct STJWD NW8 101 G2
Crosby Cl FELT TW13 154 D6
Crosby Rd DAGE RM10 110 D1
FSTGT E7 88 E4
Crosby Rw STHWK SE1 18 E3
Crosby Wk HACK E8 86 B4
Crosier Cl WOOL/PLUM SE18 146 D2
Crosier Rd HGDN/ICK UB10 76 A2
Crosier Wy RSLP HA4 76 C1
Crossbow Rd CHIG IG7 55 F1
Crossbrook Rd BKHTH/KID SE3 146 D3
Cross Deep TWK TW1 156 A5
Cross Deep Gdns TWK TW1 156 A4
Crossfield Est DEPT SE8 144 D1
Crossfield Rd HAMP NW3 83 H4
TOTM N17 49 J6
Crossfield St DEPT SE8 144 D1
Crossford St BRXN/ST SW9 142 A3
Crossgate EDGE HA8 30 C5
GFD/PVL UB6 79 H4
Cross Keys Cl MHST W1U 9 H2
Cross Lances Rd HSLW TW3 135 G5
Crossland Rd THHTH CR7 196 C3
Crosslands Av EA W5 117 G1
NWDGN UB2 114 E5
Crosslands Pde NWDGN * UB2 115 F5
Crosslands Rd HOR/WEW KT19 207 F4
Cross La BXLY DA5 169 G2
CEND/HSY/T N8 49 F6
Crosslet St WALW SE17 19 F6
Crosslet V GNWCH SE10 144 E2
Crossley St HOLWY N7 85 G4
Crossmead ELTH/MOT SE9 166 E3
OXHEY WD19 27 F1
Crossmead Av GFD/PVL UB6 96 A2
Crossness Rd BARK IG11 109 F2
Cross Rd BUSH WD23 27 J1
CHDH RM6 73 J4
CMBW SE5 143 F3
CROY/NA CR0 196 E5
DART DA1 171 F1
EN EN1 24 B5
FBAR/BDGN N11 48 B1
FELT TW13 154 D6
HAYES BR2 200 D6
HRW HA1 60 D1
KTN/HRWW/W HA3 43 G5
KUTN/CMB KT2 175 G3
RDART DA2 171 J6
ROMW/RG RM7 56 C6
RYLN/HDSTN HA2 78 A1
SCUP DA14 168 C6
STMC/STPC BR5 202 C2
SUT SM1 209 H3
WDGN N22 49 G2
WFD IG8 53 K2
WIM/MER SW19 177 K3
Cross St BARN SW13 138 B3
ERITH DA8 130 B6
HPTN TW12 173 H1
IS N1 85 H6
UED N18 50 C1
Crossthwaite Av HNHL SE24 142 E5
Crosswall TWRH EC3N 13 J5
The Cross Wy
KTN/HRWW/W HA3 42 E5
The Crossway ELTH/MOT SE9 166 C4
WDGN N22 49 H3
Cross Wy HYS/HAR UB3 113 K2
Crossway BCTR RM8 91 J1
CDALE/KGS NW9 63 H1
EN EN1 36 A2
NFNCH/WDSP N12 47 H2
NWMAL KT3 193 F1
PIN HA5 41 F5
RSLP HA4 77 G2
STMC/STPC BR5 201 J1
STNW/STAM N16 86 A3
THMD SE28 109 J6
WEA W13 97 F3
WOT/HER KT12 188 A6
Crossway Pde WDGN * N22 49 H3
The Crossways BRYLDS * KT5 191 J5
HEST TW5 134 E1
WBLY HA9 62 C6
Crossways BELMT SM2 209 H6
GPK RM2 57 K6
SAND/SEL CR2 213 H5
Crossways Rd BECK BR3 198 D1
MTCM CR4 179 G6
Crossways Ter CLPT * E5 86 E2
Croston St HACK E8 86 C6
Crosts La WDGN N22 49 G3
Crothall Cl PLMGR N13 35 F5
Crouch Av BARK IG11 109 H1
Crouch Cl BECK BR3 182 D2
Crouch Cft ELTH/MOT SE9 167 F5
Crouch End Hl ARCH N19 66 D4
Crouch Hall Rd CEND/HSY/T N8 66 D3
Crouch Hl ARCH N19 66 E4
Crouchmans Cl SYD SE26 163 G5
Crouch Rd WLSDN NW10 81 F5
Crowborough Pth OXHEY WD19 27 H6
Crowborough Rd TOOT SW17 179 F1
Crowden Wy THMD SE28 109 J6
Crowder St WCHPL E1 104 D6
Crowfoot Cl HOM E9 87 H3
Crowhurst Cl BRXN/ST SW9 142 B3
Crowhurst Wy STMC/STPC BR5 202 D2
Crowland Av HYS/HAR UB3 113 H4
Crowland Gdns STHGT/OAK N14 34 E2
Crowland Rd SEVS/STOTM N15 68 B2
THHTH * CR7 196 E1
Crowlands Av ROMW/RG RM7 74 D3
Crowland Ter IS N1 85 K5
Crowland Wk MRDN SM4 194 A3
Crow La ROMW/RG RM7 74 B4
Crowley Crs CROY/NA CR0 211 G3
Crowline Wk IS * N1 85 J4
Crown Ar KUT * KT1 174 E5
Crownbourne Ct SUT * SM1 209 F2
Crown Buildings CHING * E4 38 B3
Crown Cl BOW E3 87 J6
HYS/HAR UB3 113 J2
KIL/WHAMP NW6 83 F4
MLHL NW7 31 H4
ORP BR6 217 G2
WOT/HER KT12 188 B4
Crown Ct HOL/ALD WC2B 11 F4
Crown Dl NRWD SE19 180 D2
Crowndale Rd CAMTN NW1 4 B2
Crownfield Av GNTH/NBYPK IG2 72 E2
Crownfield Rd SRTFD E15 88 B3
Crown Hl CROY/NA * CR0 196 D6
Crownhill Rd WFD IG8 53 J3
WLSDN NW10 81 H6
Crown La CHST BR7 185 H4
HAYES BR2 200 C2
STHGT/OAK N14 34 C3
STRHM/NOR SW16 180 B1
WIM/MER SW19 177 K6
Crown Lane Gdns
WNWD * SE27 180 B1
Crown Lane Sp HAYES BR2 200 C3
Crown Office Rw EMB EC4Y 11 J5
Crown Pde MRDN * SM4 194 A1
STHGT/OAK * N14 34 C3
Crown Pas STJS SW1Y 16 B1
Crown Pl KTTN NW5 84 B4
SDTCH EC2A 7 G7
Crown Rd BARK/HLT IG6 72 D1
EN EN1 24 C4
MUSWH N10 48 A3
NWMAL KT3 175 K4
ORP BR6 217 G3
RSLP HA4 77 H3
SUT SM1 208 E2
TWK TW1 156 C1
WIM/MER SW19 193 K1
Crownstone Rd
BRXS/STRHM SW2 142 B6
Crown St ACT W3 117 J1
CMBW SE5 142 D1
DAGE RM10 92 E4
RYLN/HDSTN HA2 60 D5
Crown Ter CRICK * NW2 82 B2
RCH/KEW TW9 137 G5
STHGT/OAK * N14 34 D3
Crowntree Cl ISLW TW7 116 A6
Crown Vls ACT * W3 117 K2
Crown Wk WBLY HA9 80 B1
Crown Wy WDR/YW UB7 112 C1
Crown Woods Wy
ELTH/MOT SE9 147 J6
Crown Yd HSLW TW3 135 H4
Crowshott Av STAN HA7 43 J5
Crows Rd BARK IG11 90 B4
SRTFD E15 106 B2
Crowther Av BTFD TW8 117 F5
Crowther Rd SNWD SE25 197 H1
Crowthorne Cl
WAND/EARL SW18 159 J2
Crowthorne Rd NKENS W10 100 B5
Croxden Cl EDGE HA8 44 C6
Croxden Wk MRDN SM4 194 B3
Croxford Gdns WDGN N22 49 H3
Croxford Wy ROMW/RG RM7 75 F5
Croxley Cl STMC/STPC BR5 186 C5
Croxley Gn STMC/STPC BR5 186 C4
Croxley Rd MV/WKIL W9 100 D2
Croxley Vw WATW WD18 26 C1
Croxted Cl DUL SE21 162 D2
Croxted Rd DUL SE21 162 E4
Croyde Av GFD/PVL UB6 96 C2
HYS/HAR UB3 113 H4
Croyde Cl ELTH/MOT SE9 167 J2
The Croydon F/O CROY/NA CR0 211 H2
Croydon Gv CROY/NA CR0 196 C5
Croydon Rd BECK BR3 182 B6
CROY/NA CR0 198 A2
MTCM CR4 195 G2
PGE/AN SE20 181 J5
PLSTW E13 106 E3
WLGTN SM6 210 B2
WWKM BR4 214 C1
Croyland Rd ED N9 36 C3
Croylands Dr SURB KT6 191 F4
Crozier Ter HOM E9 87 F3
Crucible Cl CHDH RM6 73 H3
Crucifix La STHWK SE1 19 G2
Cruden St IS N1 6 B1
Cruickshank St FSBYW WC1X 5 J4
Cruikshank Rd SRTFD E15 88 C2
Crummock Gdns
CDALE/KGS NW9 63 G2
Crumpsall St ABYW SE2 128 D4
Crundale Av CDALE/KGS NW9 62 C2
Crunden Rd SAND/SEL CR2 211 K5
Crusader Cl PUR RM19 131 K4
Crusader Gdns CROY/NA CR0 212 A1
Crusader Wy WATW WD18 26 D1
Crusoe Ms STNW/STAM N16 67 K6
Crusoe Rd ERITH DA8 130 A5
MTCM CR4 178 E3
Crutched Friars TWRH EC3N 13 H5
Crutchfield La WOT/HER KT12 188 A6
Crutchley Rd CAT SE6 165 H4
Crystal Palace NRWD * SE19 181 H3
Crystal Palace Pde NRWD SE19 181 G2
Crystal Palace Park Rd
SYD SE26 181 H1
Crystal Palace Rd EDUL SE22 163 G1
Crystal Ter NRWD SE19 180 E2
Crystal Wy BCTR RM8 73 J5
HRW HA1 61 F2
Cuba Dr PEND EN3 24 E3
Cuba St POP/IOD E14 124 D2
Cubitt Sq NWDGN * UB2 115 H1
Cubitt St CROY/NA CR0 211 F3
FSBYW WC1X 5 H5
Cubitt Ter CLAP SW4 141 H4
Cuckoo Av HNWL W7 96 E3
Cuckoo Dene HNWL W7 96 D4
Cuckoo Hall La ED N9 36 E2
Cuckoo Hl PIN HA5 41 G6
Cuckoo Hill Dr PIN HA5 41 G6
Cuckoo Hill Rd PIN HA5 59 H1
Cuckoo La HNWL W7 96 E6
Cuda's Cl HOR/WEW KT19 207 H2
Cuddington Av WPK KT4 207 H1
Cudham St CAT SE6 164 E2
Cudworth St WCHPL E1 104 D3
Cuff Crs ELTH/MOT SE9 166 C2
Culford Gdns CHEL SW3 15 F7
Culford Gv IS N1 86 A4
Culford Ms IS N1 85 K4
Culford Rd IS N1 86 A6
Culgaith Gdns ENC/FH EN2 22 E5
Cullen Wy WLSDN NW10 98 E3
Cullera Cl NTHWD HA6 40 D2
Culling Rd BERM/RHTH SE16 123 K3
Cullington Cl KTN/HRWW/W HA3 61 G1
Cullingworth Rd WLSDN NW10 81 J3
Culloden Cl STHWK SE1 123 H5
Culloden Rd ENC/FH EN2 23 H3
Culloden St POP/IOD E14 106 A5
Cullum St FENCHST EC3M 13 G5
Culmington Pde WEA * W13 97 J6
Culmington Rd SAND/SEL CR2 211 J5
WEA W13 116 D1
Culmore Rd PECK SE15 143 J1
Culmstock Rd BTSEA SW11 141 F6
Culpepper Cl CHIG IG7 54 B2
Culross Cl SEVS/STOTM N15 67 J1
Culross St MYFR/PKLN W1K 9 G6
Culsac Rd SURB KT6 191 F6
Culverden Rd BAL SW12 161 H5
OXHEY WD19 27 F5
Culver Gv STAN HA7 43 J5
Culverhouse Gdns
STRHM/NOR SW16 162 A6
Culverlands Cl STAN HA7 29 H6
Culverley Rd CAT SE6 164 E3
Culvers Av CAR SM5 194 E6
Culvers Retreat CAR SM5 194 E5
Culverstone Cl HAYES BR2 199 J3
Culvers Wy CAR SM5 194 E6
Culvert Pl BTSEA SW11 141 F3
Culvert Rd BTSEA SW11 140 E3
SEVS/STOTM N15 68 A2
Culworth St STJWD NW8 2 C3
Cumberland Av WELL DA16 147 K4
WLSDN NW10 98 D2
Cumberland Cl BARK/HLT * IG6 54 C4
HACK E8 86 B4
RYNPK SW20 177 G3
TWK TW1 156 C1
Cumberland Dr BXLYHN DA7 149 F1
CHSGTN KT9 206 A1
DART DA1 171 J2
ESH/CLAY KT10 190 B6
Cumberland Gdns FSBYW WC1X 5 H4
HDN * NW4 46 B5
Cumberland Ga BAY/PAD W2 8 E5
CAMTN NW1 3 J4
Cumberland Market CAMTN NW1 3 K4
Cumberland Pk ACT W3 98 E6
Cumberland Pl CAMTN NW1 3 J4
CAT SE6 165 J3
Cumberland Rd ACT W3 98 E6
ASHF TW15 152 A5
BARN SW13 138 C2
ED N9 36 E3
HAYES BR2 199 H1
HNWL W7 116 A2
HRW HA1 60 B2
KTN/HRWW/W HA3 44 B6
MNPK E12 89 H2
PLSTW E13 107 F4
RCH/KEW TW9 137 H2
SNWD SE25 197 J3
WALTH E17 51 G5
WDGN N22 49 F5
Cumberland St PIM SW1V 121 G5
Cumberland Ter CAMTN NW1 3 J3
PGE/AN * SE20 181 J3
Cumberland Terrace Ms
CAMTN NW1 3 J3
Cumberlow Av SNWD SE25 181 H6
Cumberton Rd TOTM N17 49 K4
Cumbrae Gdns SURB KT6 190 E6
Cumbrian Av BXLYHN DA7 150 B3
Cumbrian Gdns CRICK NW2 64 B6
Cumming St IS N1 5 H3
Cumnor Cl BRXN/ST * SW9 142 A3
Cumnor Gdns EW KT17 207 J4
Cumnor Rd BELMT SM2 209 G4
Cunard Crs WCHMH N21 35 K1

Cunard Rd *WLSDN* NW10 **99** F2
Cundy Rd *CAN/RD* E16 **107** G5
Cundy St *BGVA* SW1W **15** H7
Cunliffe Rd *HOR/WEW* KT19 **207** H2
Cunliffe St *STRHM/NOR* SW16 **179** H2
Cunningham Cl *CHDH* RM6 **73** J2
WWKM BR4 **198** E6
Cunningham Pk *HRW* HA1 **60** D2
Cunningham Pl *STJWD* NW8 **2** A6
Cunningham Rd
SEVS/STOTM * N15 **68** C1
Cunnington St *CHSWK* W4 **117** K3
Cupar Rd *BTSEA* SW11 **141** F2
Cupola Cl *BMLY* BR1 **184** A1
Curates Wk *DART* DA1 **171** G5
Cureton St *WEST* * SW1P **121** J5
Curlew Cl *THMD* SE28 **109** K6
Curlew St *STHWK* SE1 **19** J2
Curlew Wy *YEAD* UB4 **95** H4
Curnick's La *WNWD* SE27 **162** D6
Curran Av *BFN/LL* DA15 **148** A6
WLGTN SM6 **210** A1
Currey Rd *GFD/PVL* UB6 **78** C4
Curricle St *ACT* W3 **118** B1
Currie Hill Cl *WIM/MER* SW19 **159** J6
Curry Ri *MLHL* NW7 **46** B2
Cursitor St *FLST/FETLN* EC4A **11** J3
Curtain Pl *SDTCH* EC2A **7** H6
Curtain Rd *SDTCH* EC2A **7** G7
Curthwaite Gdns *ENC/FH* EN2 **22** D5
Curtis Dr *ACT* W3 **99** F5
Curtis Field Rd
STRHM/NOR SW16 **162** A6
Curtis La *ALP/SUD* HA0 **80** A4
Curtismill Cl *STMC/STPC* BR5 **186** C6
Curtismill Wy *STMC/STPC* BR5 **186** C6
Curtis Rd *HOR/WEW* KT19 **206** E2
HSLWW TW4 **154** E2
Curtis St *STHWK* SE1 **19** J6
Curtis Wy *STHWK* SE1 **19** J6
The Curve *SHB* W12 **99** J6
Curwen Av *FSTGT* E7 **89** F2
Curwen Rd *SHB* W12 **118** D2
Curzon Av *PEND* EN3 **25** F6
STAN HA7 **43** G4
Curzon Cl *ORP* BR6 **216** D2
Curzon Crs *BARK* IG11 **109** F2
WLSDN NW10 **81** G5
Curzon Pl *MYFR/PKLN* W1K **15** H1
PIN HA5 **59** G2
Curzon Rd *EA* W5 **97** H3
MUSWH N10 **48** B5
THHTH CR7 **196** B3
Curzon St *MYFR/PICC* W1J **9** K7
MYFR/PKLN W1K **15** H1
Cusack Cl *TWK* * TW1 **156** A6
Custom House Reach
BERM/RHTH * SE16 **124** C3
The Cut *STHWK* SE1 **17** K2
Cutcombe Rd *CMBW* SE5 **142** D3
Cuthberga Cl *BARK* IG11 **90** C5
Cuthbert Gdns *SNWD* SE25 **181** F6
Cuthbert Rd *CROY/NA* CR0 **196** C6
UED N18 **50** C1
WALTH E17 **52** A6
Cuthbert St *BAY/PAD* W2 **2** A7
Cutlers Gardens Ar *LVPST* EC2M **13** H3
Cutler St *HDTCH* EC3A **13** H3
Cuxton Cl *BXLYHS* DA6 **149** F6
Cyclamen Cl *HPTN* TW12 **173** F2
Cyclamen Wy *HOR/WEW* KT19 **206** E3
Cygnet Av *EBED/NFELT* TW14 **154** C2
Cygnet Cl *NTHWD* HA6 **40** A3
WLSDN NW10 **81** F3
The Cygnets *FELT* TW13 **154** D6
Cygnet St *WCHPL* E1 **7** K6
Cygnet Wy *YEAD* UB4 **95** H5
Cymbeline Ct *HRW* * HA1 **61** F3
Cynthia St *IS* N1 **5** H3
Cypress Av *WHTN* TW2 **155** H2
Cypress Gdns *BROCKY* SE4 **144** B6
Cypress Gv *BARK/HLT* IG6 **54** E2
Cypress Rd *KTN/HRWW/W* HA3 **42** D5
SNWD SE25 **181** F5
Cypress Tree Cl *BFN/LL* DA15 **168** A3
Cyprus Av *FNCH* N3 **46** C5
Cyprus Cl *FSBYPK* N4 **67** G3
Cyprus Gdns *FNCH* N3 **46** C5
Cyprus Pl *BETH* E2 **104** E1
EHAM E6 **108** A6
Cyprus Rd *ED* N9 **36** B4
FNCH N3 **46** D5
Cyprus St *BETH* E2 **104** E1
Cyrena Rd *EDUL* SE22 **163** G1
Cyril Rd *BXLYHN* DA7 **149** F3
ORP BR6 **202** B4
Cyrus St *FSBYE* EC1V **6** B6
Czar St *DEPT* SE8 **124** D6

D

Dabbling Cl *ERITH* * DA8 **150** E1
Dabbs Hill La *NTHLT* UB5 **77** K4
D'abernon Cl *ESH/CLAY* KT10 **204** A2
Dabin Crs *GNWCH* SE10 **145** F2
Dacca St *DEPT* SE8 **124** C6
Dace Rd *BOW* E3 **87** J6
Dacre Av *CLAY* IG5 **54** A5
Dacre Cl *GFD/PVL* UB6 **96** B1
Dacre Gdns *LEW* * SE13 **145** H5
Dacre Pk *LEW* SE13 **145** H4
Dacre Pl *LEW* SE13 **145** H4
Dacre Rd *CROY/NA* CR0 **195** K4
PLSTW E13 **89** F6
WAN E11 **70** D5
Dacres Est *FSTH* * SE23 **164** A5
Dacres Rd *FSTH* SE23 **164** A5
Dacre St *STJSPK* SW1H **16** C4
Dade Wy *NWDGN* UB2 **114** E5
Daerwood Cl *HAYES* BR2 **200** E5
Daffodil Cl *CROY/NA* CR0 **198** A5
HPTN TW12 **173** F2
Daffodil Gdns *IL* IG1 **90** B3
Daffodil St *SHB* W12 **99** H6
Dafforne Rd *TOOT* SW17 **160** E5
Dagenham Av *DAGW* RM9 **92** A6
Dagenham Rd *DAGE* RM10 **92** E2
LEY E10 **69** H5
RAIN RM13 **93** F5
ROMW/RG RM7 **75** F4
Dagger La *BORE* WD6 **29** G1
Dagmar Av *WBLY* HA9 **80** B2
Dagmar Gdns *WLSDN* NW10 **100** B1
Dagmar Pas *IS* * N1 **85** H6
Dagmar Rd *CMBW* SE5 **143** F2
DAGE RM10 **92** E5
FSBYPK N4 **67** G4
KUTN/CMB KT2 **175** G4
NWDGN UB2 **114** D3
SEVS/STOTM N15 **67** K1
SNWD SE25 **197** F1
WDGN N22 **48** D4
Dagmar Ter *IS* * N1 **85** H6
Dagnall Pk *SNWD* SE25 **197** F2
Dagnall Rd *SNWD* SE25 **197** F2
Dagnall St *BTSEA* SW11 **140** E3
Dagnan Rd *BAL* SW12 **161** G2
Dagonet Rd *BMLY* BR1 **165** K5
Dahlia Gdns *IL* IG1 **90** B4
MTCM CR4 **195** J1
Dahlia Rd *ABYW* SE2 **128** C5
Dahomey Rd
STRHM/NOR SW16 **179** H2
Daimler Wy *WLGTN* SM6 **210** E5
Daines Cl *MNPK* E12 **89** K1
Dainford Cl *BMLY* BR1 **183** G1
Daintry Cl *KTN/HRWW/W* HA3 **61** G1
Dairsie Rd *ELTH/MOT* SE9 **147** F4
Dairy Cl *BMLY* * BR1 **184** A3
THHTH CR7 **180** D5
Dairy La *WOOL/PLUM* SE18 **126** E4
Dairyman Cl *CRICK* * NW2 **82** B2
Daisy Cl *CROY/NA* CR0 **198** A5
Daisy La *FUL/PGN* SW6 **139** K4
Daisy Rd *SWFD* E18 **53** F5
Dakota Cl *CROY/NA* CR0 **211** F5
Dakota Gdns *EHAM* E6 **107** J3
Dalberg Rd *BRXS/STRHM* SW2 **142** B6
Dalberg Wy *ABYW* SE2 **128** E3
Dalby Rd *WAND/EARL* SW18 **140** B5
Dalbys Crs *TOTM* N17 **50** A2
Dalby St *KTTN* NW5 **84** B4
Dalcross Rd *HEST* TW5 **134** D3
The Dale *HAYES* BR2 **215** H2
Dale Av *EDGE* HA8 **44** B4
HSLWW TW4 **134** D4
Dalebury Rd *TOOT* SW17 **160** E4
Dale Cl *BAR* EN5 **33** F1
BKHTH/KID SE3 **145** K4
DART DA1 **170** C1
PIN HA5 **41** F4
Dale Dr *YEAD* UB4 **94** D3
Dale Gdns *WFD* IG8 **39** F6
Dale Green Rd *FBAR/BDGN* N11 **34** B5
Dale Gv *NFNCH/WDSP* N12 **47** G1
Daleham Gdns *HAMP* NW3 **83** H3
Daleham Ms *HAMP* * NW3 **83** H4
Dale Park Av *CAR* SM5 **194** E6
Dale Park Rd *NRWD* SE19 **180** D4
Dale Rd *DART* DA1 **170** C1
GFD/PVL UB6 **96** B4
KTTN NW5 **84** A3
SUT SM1 **208** D2
SWLY BR8 **187** K6
WALW SE17 **122** C6
Dale Rw *NTGHL* W11 **100** C5
Daleside *ORP* BR6 **217** G3
Daleside Cl *ORP* BR6 **217** G4
Daleside Rd *HOR/WEW* KT19 **207** F4
STRHM/NOR SW16 **179** G1
Dale St *CHSWK* W4 **118** B5
Dale Vw *BAR* * EN5 **20** D4
ERITH DA8 **150** D3
Dale View Av *CHING* E4 **38** A4
Dale View Crs *CHING* E4 **38** A5
Dale View Gdns *CHING* E4 **38** B5
Daleview Rd *SEVS/STOTM* N15 **68** A3
Dalewood Gdns *WPK* KT4 **192** E6
Dale Wood Rd *ORP* BR6 **201** K4
Daley St *HOM* E9 **87** F4
Daley Thompson Wy
VX/NE SW8 **141** G3
Dalgarno Gdns *NKENS* W10 **100** A4
Dalgarno Wy *NKENS* W10 **100** A3
Dalkeith Gv *STAN* HA7 **43** K1
Dalkeith Rd *DUL* SE21 **162** D3
IL IG1 **90** C1
Dallas Rd *CHEAM* SM3 **208** C4
EA W5 **98** B4
HDN NW4 **63** J4
SYD SE26 **163** J6
Dallas Ter *HYS/HAR* UB3 **113** J3
Dallega Cl *HYS/HAR* UB3 **94** B6
Dallinger Rd *LEE/GVPK* SE12 **165** J1
Dalling Rd *HMSMTH* W6 **118** E4
Dallington Sq *FSBYE* EC1V **6** B6
Dallington St *FSBYE* EC1V **6** B6
Dallin Rd *BXLYHS* DA6 **148** E5
WOOL/PLUM SE18 **147** G1
Dalmain Rd *FSTH* SE23 **164** A3
Dalmally Rd *CROY/NA* CR0 **197** G4
Dalmeny Av *HOLWY* N7 **84** D2
STRHM/NOR SW16 **180** B5
Dalmeny Cl *ALP/SUD* HA0 **79** J4
Dalmeny Crs *HSLW* TW3 **135** J5
Dalmeny Rd *BAR* EN5 **33** G1
CAR SM5 **210** A5
ERITH DA8 **149** J2
HOLWY N7 **84** D2
WPK KT4 **207** K1
Dalmeyer Rd *WLSDN* NW10 **81** H4
Dalmore Av *ESH/CLAY* KT10 **205** F4
Dalmore Rd *DUL* SE21 **162** D4
Dalrymple Cl *STHGT/OAK* N14 **34** D2
Dalrymple Rd *BROCKY* SE4 **144** B5
Dalston Gdns *STAN* HA7 **44** A4
Dalston La *HACK* E8 **86** B4
Dalton Av *MTCM* CR4 **178** D5
Dalton Cl *ORP* BR6 **216** E1
YEAD UB4 **94** B3
Daltons Rd *SWLY* BR8 **203** K6
Dalton St *WNWD* SE27 **162** C4
Dalwood St *CMBW* SE5 **143** F2
Dalyell Rd *BRXN/ST* SW9 **142** A4
Damask Crs *CAN/RD* E16 **106** C3
Damer Ter *WBPTN* SW10 **140** B1
Dames Rd *FSTGT* E7 **88** E2
Dame St *IS* N1 **6** C2
Damien St *WCHPL* E1 **104** D4
Damon Cl *SCUP* DA14 **168** C5
Damsel Ct *BERM/RHTH* * SE16 **123** H2
Damson Dr *HYS/HAR* UB3 **94** E6
Damsonwood Rd *NWDGN* UB2 **115** F3
Danbrook Rd
STRHM/NOR SW16 **179** K4
Danbury Cl *CHDH* RM6 **55** K6
Danbury Ms *CAR* SM5 **210** B2
Danbury Rd *LOU* IG10 **39** J1
RAIN RM13 **93** H6
Danbury St *IS* N1 **6** B2
Danbury Wy *WFD* IG8 **53** G2
Danby St *PECK* SE15 **143** G4
Dancer Rd *FUL/PGN* SW6 **139** J2
RCH/KEW TW9 **137** H4
Dandelion Cl *ROMW/RG* RM7 **75** G6
Dando Crs *BKHTH/KID* SE3 **146** A4
Dandridge Cl *GNWCH* SE10 **125** J5
Danebury Av *PUT/ROE* SW15 **158** C2
Daneby Rd *CAT* SE6 **165** F5
Dane Cl *BXLY* DA5 **169** H2
ORP BR6 **216** D3
Danecourt Gdns *CROY/NA* CR0 **212** B1
Danecroft Rd *HNHL* SE24 **142** D6
Danehurst Gdns *REDBR* IG4 **71** J2
Danehurst St *FUL/PGN* SW6 **139** H2
Daneland *EBAR* EN4 **21** K6
Danemead Gv *NTHLT* UB5 **78** B3
Danemere St *PUT/ROE* SW15 **139** F4
Dane Pl *BOW* E3 **105** G1
Dane Rd *IL* IG1 **90** C3
STHL UB1 **95** J6
UED N18 **36** E6
WEA W13 **97** J6
WIM/MER SW19 **178** B4
Danesbury Rd *FELT* TW13 **154** A3
Danescombe *LEE/GVPK* SE12 **165** K3
Danescourt Crs *SUT* SM1 **194** B6
Danescroft Av *HDN* * NW4 **64** B2
Danescroft Gdns *GLDGN* NW11 **64** B2
Danesdale Rd *HOM* E9 **87** G4
Danes Ga *HRW* HA1 **42** E6
Danes Rd *ROMW/RG* RM7 **74** E4
Dane St *GINN* WC1R **11** G2
Daneswood Av *CAT* SE6 **165** F5
Danethorpe Rd *ALP/SUD* HA0 **79** K4
Danetree Cl *HOR/WEW* KT19 **206** E5
Danetree Rd *HOR/WEW* KT19 **206** E5
Danette Gdns *DAGE* RM10 **74** B6
Daneville Rd *CMBW* SE5 **142** E2
Dangan Rd *WAN* E11 **70** E3
Daniel Bolt Cl *POP/IOD* E14 **105** K4
Daniel Cl *HSLWW* TW4 **154** E2
UED N18 **36** E6
WIM/MER SW19 **178** D2
Daniel Gdns *PECK* SE15 **143** G1
Daniell Wy *CROY/NA* CR0 **195** K5
Daniel Pl *HDN* NW4 **63** K3
Daniel Rd *EA* W5 **98** B6
Daniel's Rd *PECK* SE15 **143** K4
Dan Leno Wk *FUL/PGN* * SW6 **140** A1
Dansey Pl *SOHO/SHAV* W1D **10** C5
Dansington Rd *WELL* DA16 **148** B5
Danson Crs *WELL* DA16 **148** C4
Danson La *WELL* DA16 **148** C5
Danson Md *WELL* DA16 **148** D4
Danson Rd *BXLYHS* DA6 **148** E6
Danson U/P *BFN/LL* DA15 **168** D1
Dante Rd *LBTH* SE11 **18** A6
Danube St *CHEL* SW3 **120** D5
Danvers Rd *CEND/HSY/T* N8 **66** D1
Danvers St *CHEL* SW3 **120** C6
Daphne Gdns *CHING* E4 **38** A5
Daphne St *WAND/EARL* SW18 **160** B1
Daplyn St *WCHPL* E1 **104** C4
D'arblay St *SOHO/CST* W1F **10** B4
Darby Crs *SUN* TW16 **172** B5
Darby Gdns *SUN* TW16 **172** B5
Darcy Av *WLGTN* SM6 **210** C2
Darcy Cl *TRDG/WHET* N20 **33** H4
D'arcy Dr *KTN/HRWW/W* HA3 **61** K1
D'arcy Gdns *DAGW* RM9 **92** B6
KTN/HRWW/W HA3 **62** A1
D'arcy Pl *HAYES* BR2 **199** K1
D'arcy Rd *CHEAM* SM3 **208** B2
ISLW TW7 **136** B2
STRHM/NOR SW16 **179** K5
Darell Rd *RCH/KEW* TW9 **137** H4
Darenth Rd *DART* DA1 **171** K4
STNW/STAM N16 **68** B4
WELL DA16 **148** B2
Darent Valley Pth *DART* DA1 **151** G2
Darfield Rd *BROCKY* SE4 **144** C6
Darfield Wy *NKENS* W10 **100** B6
Darfur St *PUT/ROE* SW15 **139** G4
Dargate Cl *NRWD* SE19 **181** G3
Darien Rd *BTSEA* SW11 **140** C4
Darlands Dr *BAR* EN5 **20** B6
Darlan Rd *FUL/PGN* SW6 **139** J1
Darlaston Rd *WIM/MER* SW19 **177** G3
Darley Cl *CROY/NA* CR0 **198** A3
Darley Dr *NWMAL* KT3 **176** A5
Darley Gdns *MRDN* SM4 **194** A3
Darley Rd *BTSEA* SW11 **160** E1
ED N9 **36** B3
Darling Rd *BROCKY* SE4 **144** D4
Darling Rw *WCHPL* E1 **104** D3
Darlington Rd *WNWD* SE27 **180** C1
Darlton Cl *DART* DA1 **150** C4
Darmaine Cl *SAND/SEL* CR2 **211** J5
Darndale Cl *WALTH* E17 **51** H5
Darnley Rd *HACK* E8 **86** D4
WFD IG8 **52** E4
Darnley Ter *NTGHL* W11 **119** G1
Darns Hl *SWLY* BR8 **203** K4
Darrell Rd *EDUL* SE22 **143** H6
Darren Cl *FSBYPK* N4 **67** F4
Darrick Wood Rd *ORP* BR6 **201** J6
Darris Cl *NTHLT* UB5 **95** J3
Darsley Dr *VX/NE* SW8 **141** J2
Dartford Av *ED* N9 **36** E1
Dartford Rd *BXLY* DA5 **169** K3
DART DA1 **170** D1
Dartford St *WALW* SE17 **122** D6
Dartmoor Wk *POP/IOD* * E14 **124** D4
Dartmouth Cl *NTGHL* W11 **100** D5
Dartmouth Gv *GNWCH* SE10 **145** F2
Dartmouth Hl *GNWCH* SE10 **145** F2
Dartmouth Park Av *KTTN* NW5 **84** B1
Dartmouth Park Hl *ARCH* N19 **66** B5
KTTN NW5 **84** B1
Dartmouth Park Rd *KTTN* NW5 **84** B1
Dartmouth Pl *CHSWK* W4 **118** B6
FSTH SE23 **163** K4
Dartmouth Rd *CRICK* NW2 **82** B4
HAYES BR2 **199** K4
HDN NW4 **63** J3
RSLP HA4 **76** E1
SYD SE26 **163** J5
Dartmouth Rw *GNWCH* SE10 **145** F3
Dartmouth St *STJSPK* SW1H **16** C3
Dartmouth Ter *GNWCH* SE10 **145** G2
Dartnell Rd *CROY/NA* CR0 **197** G4
Dartrey Wk *WBPTN* * SW10 **140** B1
Dart St *MV/WKIL* W9 **100** D2
Darville Rd *STNW/STAM* N16 **86** B1
Darwell Cl *EHAM* E6 **108** A1
Darwin Cl *FBAR/BDGN* N11 **34** B5
ORP BR6 **216** D3
Darwin Dr *STHL* UB1 **96** B5
Darwin Gdns *OXHEY* WD19 **41** G1
Darwin Rd *EA* W5 **116** D5
WDGN N22 **49** H4
WELL DA16 **148** A4
Darwin St *WALW* SE17 **19** F6
Darycngton Dr *GFD/PVL* UB6 **96** D1
Dashwood Cl *BXLYHS* DA6 **149** H6
Dashwood Rd *CEND/HSY/T* N8 **67** F3
Dassett Rd *WNWD* SE27 **180** C1
Datchelor Pl *CMBW* * SE5 **142** E2
Datchet Rd *CAT* SE6 **164** C5
Date St *WALW* SE17 **122** D5
Daubeney Gdns *TOTM* N17 **49** J3
Daubeney Rd *CLPT* E5 **87** G3
TOTM N17 **49** J3
Dault Rd *WAND/EARL* SW18 **160** B1
Davenant Rd *ARCH* N19 **66** D6
Davenant St *WCHPL* E1 **104** C4
Davenham Av *NTHWD* HA6 **26** D6
Davenport Cl *TEDD* * TW11 **174** B2
Davenport Rd *LEW* SE13 **164** E1
SCUP DA14 **168** E4
Daventer Dr *STAN* HA7 **43** F3
Daventry Av *WALTH* E17 **69** J3
Daventry St *CAMTN* NW1 **8** C1
Davern Cl *GNWCH* SE10 **125** J4
Davey Cl *HOLWY* N7 **85** F4
PLMGR N13 **49** F1
Davey Rd *HOM* E9 **87** J5
Davey St *PECK* SE15 **123** G6
David Av *GFD/PVL* UB6 **96** E2
David Cl *HYS/HAR* UB3 **133** G1
Davidge St *STHWK* SE1 **18** A3
David Ms *MHST* W1U **9** F1
David Rd *BCTR* RM8 **74** A6
Davidson Gdns *VX/NE* SW8 **141** K1
Davidson Rd *CROY/NA* CR0 **197** F5
Davidson Wy *ROMW/RG* RM7 **75** G3
David's Rd *FSTH* SE23 **163** K3
David St *SRTFD* E15 **88** B4
Davids Wy *BARK/HLT* IG6 **54** E3
David Twigg Cl *KUTN/CMB* KT2 **175** F4
Davies Cl *SNWD* SE25 **197** G3
Davies La *WAN* E11 **70** C6
Davies Ms *MYFR/PKLN* W1K **9** J5
Davies St *MYFR/PKLN* W1K **9** J5
Davies Wk *ISLW* TW7 **135** J2
Davington Gdns *BCTR* RM8 **91** H3
Davington Rd *BCTR* RM8 **91** H4
Davinia Cl *WFD* IG8 **53** K2
Davis Rd *ACT* W3 **118** C1
CHSGTN KT9 **206** C2
Davis St *PLSTW* E13 **107** F1
Davisville Rd *SHB* W12 **118** D2
Dawes Av *ISLW* TW7 **136** B6
Dawes Ct *ESH/CLAY* KT10 **204** B2
Dawes Rd *FUL/PGN* SW6 **139** J1
Dawes St *WALW* SE17 **122** E5
Dawley Pde *HYS/HAR* UB3 **94** A6
Dawley Rd *HYS/HAR* UB3 **94** B6
Dawlish Av *GFD/PVL* UB6 **97** G1
PLMGR N13 **34** E6
WAND/EARL SW18 **160** A4
Dawlish Dr *GDMY/SEVK* IG3 **91** F2
PIN HA5 **59** J2
RSLP HA4 **58** E6
Dawlish Rd *CRICK* NW2 **82** B4
LEY E10 **70** A6
TOTM N17 **50** C6
Dawnay Gdns
WAND/EARL SW18 **160** C4
Dawnay Rd *WAND/EARL* SW18 **160** B4
Dawn Cl *HSLWW* TW4 **134** D4
Dawn Crs *SRTFD* E15 **88** B6
Dawpool Rd *CRICK* NW2 **63** H6
Daws La *MLHL* NW7 **45** H1
Dawson Av *BARK* IG11 **91** F5
STMC/STPC BR5 **186** C5
Dawson Cl *HYS/HAR* UB3 **94** B4
WOOL/PLUM SE18 **127** H4
Dawson Dr *RAIN* RM13 **93** K5
Dawson Gdns *BARK* IG11 **91** F5
Dawson Pl *BAY/PAD* W2 **100** E6
Dawson Rd *CRICK* NW2 **82** A3
KUT KT1 **175** G6
Dawson St *BETH* E2 **7** K3
Dawson Ter *ED* * N9 **36** E2
Daybrook Rd *WIM/MER* SW19 **178** A5
Daylesford Av *PUT/ROE* SW15 **138** D5
Daymer Gdns *PIN* HA5 **59** G1
Daysbrook Rd
BRXS/STRHM SW2 **162** A3
Days La *BFN/LL* DA15 **167** K2
Dayton Dr *ERITH* DA8 **131** G6
Dayton Gv *PECK* SE15 **143** K2
Deacon Cl *PUR/KEN* CR8 **210** E6
The Deacon Est *CHING* * E4 **51** H2
Deacon Ms *IS* N1 **85** K5
Deacon Rd *CRICK* NW2 **81** J4
KUTN/CMB KT2 **175** G4
Deacons Cl *PIN* HA5 **41** F5
Deacons Hts *BORE* WD6 **30** C1
Deacons Hl *OXHEY* WD19 **27** G1
Deacons Leas *ORP* BR6 **216** D2
Deacons Ri *EFNCH* N2 **65** H2
Deacons Ter *IS* * N1 **85** J4
Deacons Wk *HPTN* TW12 **155** F6
Deacon Wy *WALW* SE17 **18** C6
WFD IG8 **53** K3
Deakin Cl *WATW* WD18 **26** C2
Deakins Ter *ORP* BR6 **202** B4
Deal Porters Wy
BERM/RHTH SE16 **123** K3
Deal Rd *TOOT* SW17 **179** F2
Deal St *WCHPL* E1 **104** C4
Dealtry Rd *PUT/ROE* SW15 **139** F5
Deal Wk *BRXN/ST* SW9 **142** B1
Dean Bradley St *WEST* SW1P **16** E5
Dean Ct *ALP/SUD* HA0 **79** H1
Deancross St *WCHPL* E1 **104** E5
Dean Dr *STAN* HA7 **44** A5
Deane Av *RSLP* HA4 **77** F3
Deane Ct *NTHWD* * HA6 **40** C4
Deane Croft Rd *PIN* HA5 **59** G3
Deanery Cl *EFNCH* N2 **65** J1
Deanery Ms *MYFR/PKLN* * W1K **9** H7
Deanery Rd *SRTFD* E15 **88** C4
Deanery St *MYFR/PKLN* W1K **9** H7
Deane Wy *RSLP* HA4 **59** F3
Dean Farrar St *STJSPK* SW1H **16** D4
Deanfield Gdns *CROY/NA* * CR0 **211** K2
Dean Gdns *WALTH* E17 **70** B1
Deanhill Ct *MORT/ESHN* * SW14 **137** J5
Deanhill Rd *MORT/ESHN* SW14 **137** J5
Dean Rd *CRICK* NW2 **82** A4
CROY/NA CR0 **211** K2
HPTN TW12 **173** F1
HSLW TW3 **135** G6
THMD SE28 **109** G6
Dean Ryle St *WEST* SW1P **16** E6
Deansbrook Cl *EDGE* HA8 **44** E3
Deansbrook Rd *EDGE* HA8 **44** E3
Dean's Buildings *WALW* SE17 **19** F7
Deans Cl *CHSWK* W4 **117** J6
CROY/NA CR0 **212** B1
EDGE HA8 **44** E2
Dean's Ct *BLKFR* EC4V **12** B4
Deanscroft Av *CDALE/KGS* NW9 **62** E6
Dean's Dr *MLHL* NW7 **45** F1
PLMGR N13 **49** H2
Deans Gate Cl *FSTH* SE23 **164** A5
Dean's La *EDGE* HA8 **44** E2
Dean's Ms *CAVSQ/HST* * W1G **9** K3
Dean's Rd *HNWL* W7 **116** A2
SUT SM1 **209** F1
Dean Stanley St *WEST* * SW1P **16** E5
Dean St *FSTGT* E7 **88** E3
SOHO/CST W1F **10** C3
Deansway *ED* N9 **36** A5
Deans Wy *EDGE* HA8 **44** E1
Deansway *EFNCH* N2 **65** H1
Deans Yd *WEST* SW1P **16** D4
Dean Trench St *WEST* * SW1P **16** E5
Dean Wy *NWDGN* UB2 **115** G2
Dearne Cl *STAN* HA7 **43** G1
De'arn Gdns *MTCM* CR4 **178** D6
Dearsley Rd *EN* EN1 **24** C4
Deason St *SRTFD* * E15 **88** A6
De Barowe Ms *HBRY* * N5 **85** H2
Debden Cl *KUTN/CMB* KT2 **174** E1
WFD IG8 **53** H3
De Beauvoir Crs *IS* N1 **86** A6
De Beauvoir Est *IS* * N1 **86** A6
De Beauvoir Rd *IS* N1 **86** A5
De Beauvoir Sq *IS* N1 **86** A5
Debnams Rd *BERM/RHTH* SE16 **123** K4
De Bohun Av *STHGT/OAK* N14 **34** B1
Deborah Cl *ISLW* TW7 **135** K2
Debrabant Cl *ERITH* DA8 **130** A6
De Broome Rd *FELT* TW13 **154** B3
Deburgh Rd *WIM/MER* SW19 **178** B3
Decima St *STHWK* SE1 **19** G4
Decimus Cl *SNWD* * SE25 **196** E1
Deck Cl *BERM/RHTH* SE16 **124** A1
Decoy Av *GLDGN* NW11 **64** C2
De Crespigny Pk *CMBW* SE5 **142** E3
Deeley Rd *VX/NE* SW8 **141** J2
Deena Cl *EA* W5 **98** B5
Deepdale *WIM/MER* SW19 **159** G6
Deepdale Av *HAYES* BR2 **199** J1
Deepdale Cl *FBAR/BDGN* N11 **48** A2
Deepdene Av *CROY/NA* CR0 **212** B1
Deepdene Cl *WAN* E11 **70** E1
Deepdene Ct *WCHMH* N21 **35** H1
Deepdene Gdns
BRXS/STRHM SW2 **162** A2
Deepdene Rd *HNHL* SE24 **142** D5
WELL DA16 **148** B4
Deepwell Cl *ISLW* TW7 **136** B2
Deepwood La *GFD/PVL* UB6 **96** D2
Deerbrook Rd
BRXS/STRHM SW2 **162** C3
Deerdale Rd *HNHL* SE24 **142** D5
Deere Av *RAIN* RM13 **93** J4
Deerhurst Cl *FELT* TW13 **153** K6
Deerhurst Crs *HPTN* TW12 **173** H1
Deerhurst Rd *KIL/WHAMP* NW6 **82** B5
STRHM/NOR SW16 **180** A1
Deerings Dr *PIN* HA5 **58** E2
Deerleap Gv *CHING* E4 **25** K6
Dee Rd *RCH/KEW* TW9 **137** G5
Deer Park Cl *KUTN/CMB* KT2 **175** J3
Deer Park Gdns *MTCM* * CR4 **194** C1
Deer Park Rd *WIM/MER* SW19 **178** A5
Deer Park Wy *WWKM* BR4 **199** J6
Deeside Rd *TOOT* SW17 **160** C5
Dee St *POP/IOD* E14 **106** A5
Dee Wy *ROM* RM1 **57** G4
Defiant Wy *WLGTN* SM6 **210** E5
Defoe Av *RCH/KEW* TW9 **137** H1
Defoe Cl *WIM/MER* SW19 **178** D2
Defoe Rd *BERM/RHTH* SE16 **124** C2
STNW/STAM N16 **68** A6
Defoe Wy *CRW* RM5 **56** C2
De Frene Rd *SYD* SE26 **164** A6
Degema Rd *CHST* BR7 **185** G1
Dehar Crs *CDALE/KGS* NW9 **63** H4
Dehavilland Cl *NTHLT* UB5 **95** H2
De Havilland Rd *EDGE* HA8 **44** D5
HEST TW5 **134** B1
WLGTN SM6 **210** E5
De Havilland Wy
STWL/WRAY TW19 **152** A1
Dekker Rd *DUL* SE21 **163** F1
Delacourt Rd *BKHTH/KID* SE3 **146** A1
Delafield Rd *CHARL* SE7 **126** A5
Delaford Rd *BERM/RHTH* SE16 **123** J5
Delaford St *FUL/PGN* SW6 **139** H1
Delamare Crs *CROY/NA* CR0 **197** K3
Delamere Gdns *MLHL* NW7 **45** F2
Delamere Rd *EA* W5 **117** F2
RYNPK SW20 **177** G4
YEAD UB4 **95** H6
Delamere St *BAY/PAD* W2 **101** G4
Delamere Ter *BAY/PAD* W2 **101** F4
Delancey Pas *CAMTN* NW1 **3** K1
Delancey St *CAMTN* NW1 **3** K1
De Lapre Cl *STMC/STPC* BR5 **202** E4
De Laune St *WALW* SE17 **122** C6
Delaware Rd *MV/WKIL* W9 **101** F3
Delawyk Crs *HNHL* SE24 **162** E1
Delcombe Av *WPK* KT4 **193** F5
Delhi Rd *EN* EN1 **36** B2
Delhi St *IS* N1 **5** F1
Delia St *WAND/EARL* SW18 **160** A2
Delisle Rd *THMD* SE28 **127** K2
Delius Cl *BORE* WD6 **29** J1
The Dell *ABYW* SE2 **128** B5
ALP/SUD HA0 **79** H3
BECK * BR3 **182** D3
BTFD TW8 **116** D6
BXLY DA5 **170** B3
EBED/NFELT TW14 **154** A2
NRWD SE19 **181** G4
NTHWD HA6 **26** C4
PIN HA5 **41** H5
WFD IG8 **39** F5
Dellbow Rd *EBED/NFELT* TW14 **134** A6
Dell Cl *SRTFD* E15 **88** B6
WFD IG8 **39** F5
WLGTN SM6 **210** C2
Dell Farm Rd *RSLP* HA4 **58** B2
Dellfield Cl *BECK* BR3 **183** F4

Dell La EW KT17 207 J3
Dellors Cl BAR EN5 20 B6
Dellow Cl GNTH/NBYPK IG2 72 D4
Dellow St WCHPL E1 104 D6
Dell Rd EW KT17 207 J4
PEND EN3 24 E1
WDR/YW UB7 112 C3
Dells Cl CHING E4 37 K2
Dell's Ms PIM * SW1V 16 B7
Dell Wk NWMAL KT3 176 B5
Dell Wy WEA W13 97 J5
Dellwood Gdns CLAY IG5 54 A6
Delme Crs BKHTH/KID SE3 146 A3
Delmey Cl CROY/NA CR0 212 B1
Deloraine St DEPT SE8 144 D2
Delorme St HMSMTH W6 119 G6
Delta Cl WPK KT4 207 G1
Delta Est BETH * E2 104 C2
Delta Gain OXHEY WD19 27 H4
Delta Gv NTHLT UB5 95 H2
Delta Rd WPK KT4 207 G1
Delta St BETH * E2 104 C2
De Luci Rd ERITH DA8 129 K5
De Lucy St ABYW SE2 128 C4
Delvers Md DAGE RM10 92 E2
Delverton Rd WALW SE17 122 C5
Delvino Rd FUL/PGN SW6 139 K2
De Mandeville Ga EN EN1 24 C5
Demesne Rd WLGTN SM6 210 D2
Demeta Cl WBLY HA9 80 E1
De Montfort Pde
STRHM/NOR * SW16 161 K5
De Montfort Rd
STRHM/NOR SW16 161 J4
De Morgan Rd FUL/PGN SW6 140 A4
Dempster Rd
WAND/EARL SW18 140 B6
Denberry Dr SCUP DA14 168 C5
Denbigh Cl CHST BR7 184 E2
NTGHL W11 100 D6
STHL UB1 95 K5
SUT SM1 208 D3
WLSDN NW10 81 G5
Denbigh Dr WDR/YW UB7 113 F2
Denbigh Gdns
RCHPK/HAM TW10 137 G6
Denbigh Pl PIM * SW1V 121 H5
Denbigh Rd EHAM E6 107 H2
HSLW TW3 135 G3
NTGHL W11 100 D6
STHL UB1 95 K5
WEA W13 97 H6
Denbigh St PIM SW1V 16 A7
Denbigh Ter NTGHL W11 100 D6
Denbridge Rd BMLY BR1 184 E5
Den Cl BECK BR3 199 G1
Dendy St BAL SW12 161 F3
The Dene CROY/NA CR0 213 F2
E/WMO/HCT KT8 188 E2
WBLY HA9 80 A2
WEA W13 97 H4
Dene Av BFN/LL DA15 168 C2
HSLW TW3 134 E4
Dene Cl BROCKY SE4 144 B4
HAYES BR2 199 J5
RDART DA2 170 B6
WPK KT4 192 C6
Dene Dr ORP BR6 217 H1
Dene Gdns STAN HA7 43 J1
THDIT KT7 190 B6
Denehurst Gdns ACT W3 117 J1
HDN NW4 64 A3
RCHPK/HAM TW10 137 H5
WFD IG8 39 F6
WHTN TW2 155 J2
Dene Rd BKHH IG9 39 J3
DART DA1 171 J2
NTHWD HA6 40 A2
TRDG/WHET N20 33 K3
Denewood BAR EN5 21 G6
Denewood Rd HGT N6 65 K3
Dengie Wk IS * N1 85 J6
Dengil Crs KTTN NW5 84 A3
Denham Crs MTCM CR4 194 E1
Denham Dr GNTH/NBYPK IG2 72 C3
Denham Rd EBED/NFELT TW14 154 B2
TRDG/WHET N20 33 K5
Denham Wy BARK IG11 90 E6
Denholme Rd MV/WKIL W9 100 D2
Denholme Wk RAIN RM13 93 H4
Denison Cl EFNCH N2 47 G6
Denison Rd EA W5 97 J3
FELT TW13 153 J6
WIM/MER SW19 178 C2
Deniston Av BXLY DA5 168 E3
Denleigh Gdns THDIT * KT7 189 K3
WCHMH N21 35 G2
Denman Dr ESH/CLAY KT10 205 G3
GLDGN NW11 64 E2
Denman Dr North GLDGN NW11 64 E2
Denman Dr South GLDGN NW11 64 E2
Denman Rd PECK SE15 143 G2
Denman St REGST W1B 10 B6
Denmark Av WIM/MER SW19 177 H3
Denmark Ct MRDN SM4 193 K2
Denmark Gdns CAR SM5 209 K1
Denmark Gv IS N1 5 J2
Denmark Hl CMBW SE5 142 E2
HNHL SE24 142 E5
Denmark Hill Dr CDALE/KGS NW9 45 J6
Denmark Rd BMLY BR1 184 A4
CAR SM5 209 K1
CEND/HSY/T N8 67 F1
CMBW SE5 142 D2
KIL/WHAMP NW6 100 D1
KUT KT1 175 F6
SNWD SE25 197 H2
WEA W13 97 H6
WHTN TW2 155 J5
WIM/MER SW19 177 G2
Denmark St LSQ/SEVD WC2H 10 D4
PLSTW E13 107 F4
TOTM N17 50 D4
WAN E11 88 C1
Denmark Ter EFNCH * N2 47 K6
Denmead Rd CROY/NA CR0 196 C5
Dennan Rd SURB KT6 191 G5
Denner Rd CHING E4 37 J4
Denne Ter HACK E8 7 K1
Dennett Rd CROY/NA CR0 196 B4
Dennett's Gv NWCR SE14 144 A3
Dennett's Rd NWCR SE14 143 K2
Denning Av CROY/NA CR0 211 G3
Denning Cl HPTN TW12 172 E2
STJWD NW8 101 G2
Denning Rd HAMP NW3 83 H2
Dennington Park Rd
KIL/WHAMP NW6 82 E4
The Denningtons WPK KT4 192 B6
Dennis Av WBLY HA9 80 B3
Dennis Gdns STAN HA7 43 J1
Dennis La STAN HA7 29 H6
Dennis Pde STHGT/OAK * N14 34 D3
Dennis Park Crs RYNPK SW20 177 H4
Dennis Reeve Cl MTCM CR4 178 E4
Dennis Rd E/WMO/HCT KT8 189 H1
Dennis Wy CLAP SW4 141 J4
Denny Crs LBTH SE11 122 B5
Denny Rd ED N9 36 D3
Denny St LBTH SE11 122 B5
Den Rd HAYES BR2 183 G6
Densham Rd SRTFD E15 88 C6
Densole Cl BECK * BR3 182 B4
Densworth Gv ED N9 36 E4
Denton Cl BAR EN5 20 A6
Denton Gv WOT/HER KT12 188 D6
Denton Rd CEND/HSY/T N8 67 F2
DART DA1 170 B2
TWK TW1 156 E1
UED N18 36 A6
WELL DA16 148 D1
Denton St WAND/EARL SW18 160 A1
Denton Ter BXLY * DA5 170 B4
Denton Wy CLPT E5 87 F1
Dents Rd BTSEA SW11 160 E1
Denver Cl ORP BR6 201 K3
Denver Rd DART DA1 170 D2
STNW/STAM N16 68 A4
Denyer St CHEL SW3 14 D6
Denzil Rd WLSDN NW10 81 H3
Deodar Rd PUT/ROE SW15 139 H5
Deodora Cl TRDG/WHET N20 33 J5
Depot Ap CRICK NW2 82 B2
Depot Rd HSLW TW3 135 J4
Depot St CMBW SE5 122 E6
Deptford Br GNWCH SE10 144 D2
Deptford Broadway DEPT SE8 144 D2
Deptford Church St DEPT SE8 124 D6
Deptford Gn DEPT SE8 124 D6
Deptford High St DEPT SE8 124 D6
Deptford Market DEPT * SE8 144 D1
Deptford Whf DEPT SE8 124 C4
De Quincey Rd TOTM N17 49 K4
Derby Av KTN/HRWW/W HA3 42 D4
NFNCH/WDSP N12 47 G1
ROMW/RG RM7 74 D3
Derby Ga WHALL SW1A 16 E2
Derby Hl FSTH SE23 163 K4
Derby Hill Crs FSTH SE23 163 K4
Derby Rd BRYLDS KT5 191 H5
CROY/NA CR0 196 C6
FSTGT E7 89 H5
GFD/PVL UB6 78 B6
HOM E9 87 F6
HSLW TW3 135 G5
MORT/ESHN SW14 137 J5
PEND EN3 24 D6
SUT SM1 208 D4
SWFD E18 52 D4
UED N18 50 E1
WIM/MER SW19 177 K3
Derbyshire St BETH E2 104 D2
Derby St MYFR/PICC W1J 15 H1
Dereham Pl CRW RM5 56 D2
SDTCH EC2A 7 H6
Dereham Rd BARK IG11 91 F4
Derek Av HOR/WEW KT19 206 C4
WBLY HA9 80 D5
WLGTN SM6 210 B1
Derek Cl HOR/WEW KT19 206 D3
Derek Walcott Cl HNHL * SE24 142 C6
Deri Av RAIN RM13 111 K3
Dericote St HACK E8 86 C6
Deri Dene Cl
STWL/WRAY * TW19 152 B1
Derifall Cl EHAM E6 107 K4
Dering Pl CROY/NA CR0 211 J2
Dering Rd CROY/NA CR0 211 J2
Dering St CONDST W1S 9 J4
Derinton Rd TOOT SW17 161 F6
Derley Rd NWDGN UB2 114 B3
Dermody Gdns LEW * SE13 145 G6
Dermody Rd LEW SE13 145 G6
Deronda Rd BRXS/STRHM SW2 162 C3
Deroy Cl CAR SM5 209 K4
Derrick Gdns CHARL SE7 126 B3
Derrick Rd BECK BR3 182 C6
Derry Downs STMC/STPC BR5 202 D3
Derry Rd CROY/NA CR0 210 E1
Derry St KENS W8 120 A2
Dersingham Av MNPK E12 89 K2
Dersingham Rd CRICK NW2 82 C1
Derwent Av CDALE/KGS NW9 63 G2
EBAR EN4 33 K3
MLHL NW7 45 F2
PIN HA5 41 J2
PUT/ROE SW15 158 B6
UED N18 49 K1
Derwent Cl DART DA1 170 E3
EBED/NFELT TW14 153 J3
ESH/CLAY KT10 204 E4
Derwent Crs BXLYHN DA7 149 H3
NFNCH/WDSP N12 33 G5
STAN HA7 43 J5
Derwent Dr STMC/STPC BR5 201 J4
YEAD UB4 94 C4
Derwent Gdns REDBR IG4 71 J1
WBLY HA9 61 J4
Derwent Gv EDUL SE22 143 G5
Derwent Ri CDALE/KGS NW9 63 G3
Derwent Rd EA W5 116 D3
MRDN SM4 193 G3
PGE/AN SE20 181 H5
PLMGR N13 35 F6
STHL UB1 95 K5
WHTN TW2 155 G1
Derwent St GNWCH SE10 125 H5
Derwentwater Rd ACT W3 117 K1
Derwent Wy HCH RM12 93 K3
Derwent Yd EA * W5 116 D3
De Salis Rd HGDN/ICK UB10 94 A3
Desborough Cl BAY/PAD W2 101 F4
Desenfans Rd DUL SE21 163 F1
Desford Rd CAN/RD E16 106 C3
Desford Wy ASHF TW15 152 C4
Desmond St NWCR SE14 124 B6
Despard Rd ARCH N19 66 C5
Detling Rd BMLY BR1 183 K1
ERITH DA8 150 A1
Detmold Rd CLPT E5 68 D6
Devalls Cl EHAM E6 108 A6
Devana End CAR SM5 209 K1
Devas Rd RYNPK SW20 177 F4
Devas St BOW E3 105 K3
Devema Cl CHST BR7 185 F4
Devenay Rd SRTFD E15 88 D5
Devenish Rd ABYW SE2 128 B2
De Vere Gdns IL IG1 71 K6
KENS W8 120 B2
Deverell St STHWK SE1 18 E5
De Vere Ms KENS * W8 120 B3
Devereux Ct TPL/STR WC2R 11 J4
Devereux La BARN SW13 138 E1
Devereux Rd BTSEA SW11 160 E1
Deveron Wy ROM RM1 57 G4
Devey Cl KUTN/CMB KT2 176 C3
Devizes St IS * N1 7 F1
Devoke Wy WOT/HER KT12 188 C6
Devon Av WHTN TW2 155 H3
Devon Cl BKHH IG9 39 F4
GFD/PVL UB6 79 J6
TOTM N17 50 B6
Devoncroft Gdns TWK TW1 156 B2
Devon Gdns FSBYPK N4 67 H3
Devonhurst Pl CHSWK * W4 118 A5
Devonia Gdns UED N18 49 J2
Devonia Rd IS N1 6 B2
Devon Man KTN/HRWW/W * HA3 61 J2
Devonport Gdns IL IG1 71 K3
Devonport Ms SHB * W12 118 E1
Devonport Rd SHB W12 118 E2
Devonport St WCHPL E1 104 E5
Devon Ri EFNCH N2 65 H1
Devon Rd BARK IG11 90 E6
BELMT SM2 208 C6
Devons Est BOW E3 105 K2
Devonshire Av BELMT SM2 209 G5
DART DA1 170 E1
Devonshire Cl CAVSQ/HST W1G 9 J1
SRTFD E15 88 C2
Devonshire Ct FELT * TW13 154 A4
Devonshire Crs MLHL NW7 46 B3
Devonshire Dr GNWCH SE10 144 E2
SURB KT6 190 E5
Devonshire Gdns CHSWK W4 137 K1
TOTM N17 49 J2
WCHMH N21 35 J2
Devonshire Gv PECK SE15 123 J6
Devonshire Hill La TOTM N17 49 K2
Devonshire Ms South
CAVSQ/HST W1G 9 J1
Devonshire Ms West
CAVSQ/HST W1G 3 H7
Devonshire Pl
CAVSQ/HST W1G 3 H7
CRICK NW2 82 E1
KENS W8 120 A3
Devonshire Place Ms MHST W1U 3 H7
Devonshire Rd BELMT SM2 209 G5
BXLYHS DA6 149 F5
CAN/RD E16 107 F5
CAR SM5 210 A2
CHSWK W4 118 B5
CROY/NA CR0 196 E4
EA W5 116 D3
ED N9 36 E3
ELTH/MOT SE9 166 D4
FELT TW13 154 D5
FSTH SE23 164 A2
GNTH/NBYPK IG2 72 D4
HRW HA1 60 D3
MLHL NW7 46 B3
ORP BR6 202 B4
PIN HA5 41 K4
PIN HA5 59 G3
PLMGR N13 35 F6
STHL UB1 96 A4
TOTM N17 49 J2
WALTH E17 69 J3
WIM/MER SW19 178 D3
Devonshire Rw LVPST EC2M 13 H2
Devonshire Sq HAYES BR2 200 A1
LVPST EC2M 13 H3
Devonshire St CAVSQ/HST W1G 9 H1
CHSWK W4 118 B5
Devonshire Ter BAY/PAD W2 101 G5
EDUL * SE22 143 H5
Devonshire Wy CROY/NA CR0 198 C6
YEAD UB4 95 F5
Devons Rd BOW E3 105 J4
Devon St PECK SE15 123 J6
Devon Wy CHSGTN KT9 205 J2
HOR/WEW KT19 206 D3
Devon Waye HEST TW5 134 E1
De Walden St CAVSQ/HST W1G 9 H2
Dewar St PECK SE15 143 H4
Dewberry Gdns EHAM E6 107 J4
Dewberry St POP/IOD E14 106 A5
Dewey Rd DAGE RM10 92 E4
IS N1 5 J2
Dewey St TOOT SW17 178 E1
Dewhurst Rd WKENS W14 119 G3
Dewsbury Cl PIN HA5 59 J3
Dewsbury Gdns WPK KT4 207 J1
Dewsbury Rd WLSDN NW10 81 J3
Dexter Rd BAR EN5 32 B1
Deyncourt Rd TOTM N17 49 J4
Deynecourt Gdns WAN E11 71 G1
D'eynsford Rd CMBW SE5 142 E2
Diadem Ct SOHO/SHAV * W1D 10 C3
Diamedes Av STWL/WRAY TW19 152 A2
Diameter Rd STMC/STPC BR5 201 G4
Diamond Cl BCTR RM8 73 J5
Diamond Rd RSLP HA4 77 H2
Diamond St PECK SE15 143 F1
WLSDN NW10 80 E5
Diana Cl DEPT SE8 124 C6
SWFD E18 53 F4
Diana Gdns SURB KT6 191 G6
Diana Pl CAMTN NW1 3 K6
Diana Rd WALTH E17 51 H6
Dianne Wy EBAR EN4 21 J5
Dianthus Cl ABYW * SE2 128 C5
Diban Av HCH RM12 93 K2
Dibden St IS N1 85 J6
Dibdin Cl SUT SM1 208 E1
Dibdin Rd SUT SM1 208 E1
Dicey Av CRICK NW2 82 A3
Dickens Av DART DA1 151 K5
FNCH N3 47 G4
Dickens Cl ERITH DA8 149 J1
HYS/HAR UB3 113 H4
RCHPK/HAM TW10 157 F4
Dickens Dr CHST BR7 185 H2
Dickens Est BERM/RHTH * SE16 123 H3
Dickens La UED N18 50 A1
Dickens Ms FARR EC1M 6 A7
Dickenson Cl ED N9 36 C3
Dickenson Rd CEND/HSY/T N8 66 E4
FELT TW13 172 B1
Dickenson's La SNWD SE25 197 H3
Dickenson's Pl SNWD SE25 197 H3
Dickens Rd EHAM E6 107 H1
Dickens Sq STHWK SE1 18 D4
Dickens St VX/NE SW8 141 G3
Dickens Wy ROM RM1 75 G1
Dickens Wood Cl NRWD SE19 180 C3
Dickerage Hl NWMAL KT3 175 K5
Dickerage La NWMAL KT3 175 K6
Dickerage Rd KUT KT1 175 K4
Dickson Fold PIN HA5 59 H1
Dickson House
WOOL/PLUM SE18 146 D2
Dickson Rd ELTH/MOT SE9 146 D4
Dick Turpin Wy
EBED/NFELT TW14 133 J5
Didsbury Cl EHAM E6 89 K6
Digby Crs FSBYPK N4 67 J6
Digby Gdns DAGE RM10 92 C6
Digby Pl CROY/NA CR0 212 B1
Digby Rd BARK IG11 91 F5
HOM E9 87 F4
Digby St BETH E2 104 E2
Diggon St WCHPL E1 105 F4
Dighton Rd WAND/EARL SW18 140 B6
Dignum St IS * N1 5 J2
Digswell St HOLWY * N7 85 G4
Dilhorne Cl LEE/GVPK SE12 166 A5
Dilke St CHEL SW3 120 E6
Dillwyn Cl SYD SE26 164 B6
Dilston Cl NTHLT UB5 95 C2
Dilton Gdns PUT/ROE SW15 158 D3
Dimes Pl HMSMTH W6 118 E4
Dimmock Dr GFD/PVL UB6 78 D3
Dimond Cl FSTGT E7 88 E2
Dimsdale Dr CDALE/KGS NW9 62 E5
EN EN1 36 C2
Dimson Crs BOW E3 105 J3
Dingle Cl BAR EN5 31 H1
Dingle Gdns POP/IOD * E14 105 J6
Dingley La STRHM/NOR SW16 161 J4
Dingley Pl FSBYE EC1V 6 D5
Dingley Rd FSBYE EC1V 6 C5
Dingwall Av CROY/NA CR0 196 D6
Dingwall Gdns GLDGN NW11 64 E3
Dingwall Rd CAR SM5 209 K6
CROY/NA CR0 196 E6
WAND/EARL SW18 160 B2
Dinmont St BETH E2 104 D1
Dinsdale Gdns BAR EN5 21 F6
SNWD SE25 197 F1
Dinsdale Rd BKHTH/KID SE3 125 J6
Dinsmore Rd BAL SW12 161 G2
Dinton Rd KUTN/CMB KT2 175 G3
WIM/MER SW19 178 C2
Diploma Av EFNCH N2 65 J1
Dirleton Rd SRTFD E15 88 D6
Disbrowe Rd HMSMTH W6 119 H6
Discovery Wk WAP E1W 104 D6
Dishforth La CDALE/KGS NW9 45 G4
Disney Pl STHWK SE1 18 D2
Disney St STHWK SE1 18 D2
Dison Cl PEND EN3 25 F2
Disraeli Cl THMD SE28 128 C1
Disraeli Rd EA W5 116 E1
FSTGT E7 88 E4
PUT/ROE SW15 139 H5
WLSDN NW10 98 E1
Diss St BETH E2 7 J4
Distaff La BLKFR EC4V 12 C5
Distillery La HMSMTH W6 119 F5
Distillery Rd HMSMTH W6 119 F5
Distin St LBTH SE11 17 J7
District Rd ALP/SUD HA0 79 H3
Ditchburn St POP/IOD E14 106 A6
Ditchfield Rd YEAD UB4 95 J3
Dittisham Rd ELTH/MOT SE9 166 D6
Ditton Cl THDIT KT7 190 B4
Dittoncroft Cl SAND/SEL CR2 212 A2
Ditton Grange Cl SURB KT6 190 E5
Ditton Grange Dr SURB KT6 190 E5
Ditton Hl SURB KT6 190 D5
Ditton Hill Rd SURB KT6 190 D5
Ditton Lawn THDIT KT7 190 B5
Ditton Pl PGE/AN * SE20 181 J4
Ditton Reach THDIT KT7 190 C3
Ditton Rd BXLYHS DA6 148 E6
NWDGN UB2 114 E5
SURB KT6 191 F5
Dixey Cottages EFNCH * N2 65 J2
Dixon Cl EHAM E6 107 K5
Dixon Pl WWKM BR4 198 E5
Dixon Rd NWCR SE14 144 B2
SNWD SE25 181 F6
Dobbin Cl KTN/HRWW/W HA3 43 G5
Dobell Rd ELTH/MOT SE9 146 E6
Dobree Av WLSDN NW10 81 K5
Dobson Cl KIL/WHAMP NW6 83 H5
Dockers Tanner Rd
POP/IOD E14 124 D4
Dockhead STHWK SE1 19 K3
Dock Hill Av BERM/RHTH SE16 124 A2
Dockland St CAN/RD E16 127 F2
Dockley Rd BERM/RHTH SE16 123 H3
Dock Rd BTFD * TW8 136 E1
CAN/RD E16 106 D6
Dockside Rd CAN/RD E16 107 H6
Dock St WCHPL E1 104 C6
Dockwell Cl EBED/NFELT TW14 133 K5
Doctors Cl SYD SE26 181 K1
Dodbrooke Rd WNWD SE27 162 B5
Doddington Gv WALW SE17 122 C6
Doddington Pl WALW SE17 122 C6
Dodsley Pl ED N9 36 E5
Dodson St STHWK SE1 17 K3
Dod St POP/IOD E14 105 H5
Doebury Wk WOOL/PLUM SE18 128 B6
Doel Cl WIM/MER SW19 178 B3
Doggett Rd CAT SE6 164 D2
Doggetts Ct EBAR EN4 21 J6
Doghurst Av WDR/YW UB7 132 E1
Doghurst Dr WDR/YW UB7 132 E1
Dog Kennel Hl EDUL SE22 143 F4
Dog La WLSDN NW10 81 G2
Dog Rose Ramble NTHLT UB5 76 E6
Dog Rose Ramble &
Hillingdon Trail
YEAD UB4 76 D6
Doherty Rd PLSTW E13 106 E3
Dolben Ct DEPT * SE8 124 C4
Dolben St STHWK * SE1 18 B1
Dolby Rd FUL/PGN SW6 139 J3
Dolland St LBTH SE11 122 A5
Dollary Pde KUT * KT1 175 J6
Dollis Av FNCH N3 46 D4
Dollis Crs RSLP HA4 59 G5
Dollis Hill Av CRICK NW2 81 K1
Dollis Hill Est CRICK * NW2 81 J1
Dollis Hill La CRICK NW2 81 H2
Dollis Pk FNCH N3 46 D4
Dollis Rd FNCH N3 46 C4
Dollis Valley Green Wk
GLDGN NW11 64 C1
TRDG/WHET N20 33 F1
Dollis Valley Wy BAR EN5 20 D6
Dolman Cl FNCH N3 47 G5
Dolman Rd CHSWK W4 118 A4
Dolman St BRXN/ST SW9 142 A5
Dolphin Ap ROM RM1 75 H1
Dolphin Cl SURB KT6 190 E3
THMD SE28 109 J5
Dolphin La POP/IOD E14 105 K6
Dolphin Rd NTHLT UB5 95 K1
Dolphin Sq CHSWK * W4 138 B1
PIM SW1V 121 H5
Dolphin St KUT KT1 175 F5
Dombey St BMSBY WC1N 11 G1
Dome Buildings
RCHPK/HAM * TW10 136 E6
Dome Hill Pk SYD SE26 163 G6
Domett Cl CMBW SE5 142 E5
Domingo St FSBYE EC1V 6 C6
Dominica Cl PLSTW E13 107 H2
Dominion Dr CRW RM5 56 D2
Dominion Pde HRW * HA1 61 F2
Dominion Rd CROY/NA CR0 197 G4
NWDGN UB2 114 D3
Dominion St LVPST EC2M 13 F1
Dominion Wy RAIN RM13 111 J2
Domonic Dr ELTH/MOT SE9 167 G5
Domville Cl TRDG/WHET N20 33 H4
Donald Dr CHDH RM6 73 J2
Donald Rd CROY/NA CR0 196 A3
PLSTW E13 89 F6
Donaldson Rd KIL/WHAMP NW6 82 D6
WOOL/PLUM SE18 147 F2
Donald Woods Gdns
BRYLDS KT5 191 J6
Doncaster Dr NTHLT UB5 77 K3
Doncaster Gdns FSBYPK * N4 67 J3
NTHLT UB5 77 K3
Doncaster Gn OXHEY WD19 41 G1
Doncaster Rd ED N9 36 D2
Donegal St IS N1 5 H3
Doneraile St FUL/PGN SW6 139 G3
Dongola Rd PLSTW E13 107 F2
TOTM N17 50 A6
WCHPL E1 105 G4
Dongola Rd West PLSTW E13 107 F2
Donington Av BARK/HLT IG6 72 C2
Donkey Aly EDUL SE22 163 H2
Donkey La EN EN1 24 C3
Donnefield Av EDGE HA8 44 A2
Donne Pl CHEL SW3 14 D6
MTCM CR4 195 G1
Donne Rd BCTR RM8 73 J6
Donnington Rd
KTN/HRWW/W HA3 61 K3
WLSDN NW10 81 K6
WPK KT4 192 D6
Donnybrook Rd
STRHM/NOR SW16 179 H3
Donoghue Cottages
POP/IOD * E14 105 G4
Donovan Av MUSWH N10 48 B5
Don Phelan Cl CMBW SE5 142 E2
Don Wy ROM RM1 57 G3
Doone Cl TEDD TW11 174 B2
Doon St STHWK SE1 17 J1
Dorado Gdns ORP BR6 217 K1
Doral Wy CAR SM5 209 K3
Dorando Cl SHB * W12 99 K6
Doran Gv WOOL/PLUM SE18 147 K1
Dora Rd WIM/MER SW19 177 K1
Dora St POP/IOD E14 105 H5
Dorchester Av BXLY DA5 168 E3
PLMGR N13 35 J6
RYLN/HDSTN HA2 60 C3
Dorchester Cl DART DA1 171 J2
NTHLT UB5 78 B3
STMC/STPC BR5 186 C3
Dorchester Ct CRICK NW2 82 B1
HNHL SE24 142 D6
STHGT/OAK N14 34 B2
Dorchester Dr
EBED/NFELT TW14 153 H1
HNHL SE24 142 D6
Dorchester Gdns CHING E4 37 J6
GLDGN * NW11 64 E1
Dorchester Gv CHSWK W4 118 B6
Dorchester Ms TWK TW1 156 D1
Dorchester Pde
STRHM/NOR * SW16 161 K4
Dorchester Rd MRDN SM4 194 A4
NTHLT UB5 78 B3
WPK KT4 193 F5
Dorchester Ter HDN * NW4 46 B5
Dorchester Wy
KTN/HRWW/W HA3 62 B3
Dorchester Waye YEAD UB4 95 G5
Dorcis Av BXLYHN DA7 149 F3
Dordrecht Rd ACT W3 118 B1
Dore Av MNPK E12 90 A3
Doreen Av CDALE/KGS NW9 63 F5
Dore Gdns MRDN SM4 194 A4
Dorell Cl STHL UB1 95 K4
Dorian Rd HCH RM12 75 J5
Doria Rd FUL/PGN SW6 139 J3
Doric Wy CAMTN NW1 4 C4
Dorien Rd RYNPK SW20 177 G5
Doris Av BXLYHN DA7 149 K2
Doris Rd FSTGT E7 88 E5
Dorking Cl DEPT SE8 124 C6
WPK KT4 193 G6
Dorlcote Rd WAND/EARL SW18 160 C2
Dorman Pl ED N9 36 C4
Dormans Cl NTHWD HA6 40 B3
Dorman Wy STJWD NW8 83 H6
Dormay St WAND/EARL SW18 140 A6
Dormer Cl BAR EN5 20 B6
SRTFD E15 88 D4
Dormer's Av STHL UB1 96 A5
Dormers Ri STHL UB1 96 B5
Dormer's Wells La STHL UB1 96 A5
Dormywood RSLP HA4 58 D2
Dornberg Cl BKHTH/KID SE3 145 K1
Dornberg Rd BKHTH/KID * SE3 146 A1
Dorncliffe Rd FUL/PGN SW6 139 H3
Dorney Ri STMC/STPC BR5 202 A1
Dorney Wy HSLWW TW4 134 D6
Dornfell St KIL/WHAMP NW6 82 D3
Dornton Rd BAL SW12 161 G4
SAND/SEL CR2 212 A3
Dorothy Av ALP/SUD HA0 80 A5

Dorothy Evans Cl BXLYHN DA7 149 J5
Dorothy Gdns BCTR RM8 91 H2
Dorothy Rd BTSEA SW11 140 E4
Dorrington St HCIRC EC1N 11 J1
Dorrit St STHWK * SE1 18 D2
Dorrit Wy CHST BR7 185 H2
Dors Cl CDALE/KGS NW9 63 F5
Dorset Av NWDGN UB2 115 F4
ROM RM1 57 F6
WELL DA16 148 A5
YEAD UB4 94 C2
Dorset Buildings EMB * EC4Y 12 A4
Dorset Cl CAMTN NW1 8 E1
YEAD * UB4 94 C2
Dorset Dr EDGE HA8 44 B2
Dorset Gdns STRHM/NOR SW16 196 A1
Dorset Ms FNCH N3 46 E4
KTBR SW1X 15 J4
Dorset Pl SRTFD E15 88 B4
Dorset Ri EMB EC4Y 12 A4
Dorset Rd ASHF TW15 152 A5
BECK BR3 182 A6
EA W5 116 D3
ELTH/MOT SE9 166 D4
HRW HA1 60 C3
MTCM CR4 178 D5
SEVS/STOTM N15 67 K1
VX/NE SW8 142 A1
WDGN N22 48 E4
WIM/MER SW19 177 K4
Dorset Sq CAMTN NW1 2 E7
Dorset St MHST W1U 9 G2
Dorset Wy WHTN TW2 155 H3
Dorset Waye HEST TW5 134 E1
Dorton Cl PECK * SE15 143 F1
Dorville Crs HMSMTH W6 118 E3
Dorville Rd LEE/GVPK SE12 145 K6
Dothill Rd WOOL/PLUM SE18 147 H1
Douai Gv HPTN TW12 173 H4
Doughty Ms BMSBY WC1N 5 G7
Doughty St BMSBY WC1N 5 G6
Douglas Av ALP/SUD HA0 80 A5
NWMAL KT3 192 E1
WALTH E17 51 J4
Douglas Cl STAN HA7 43 G1
WLGTN SM6 210 E4
Douglas Crs YEAD UB4 95 G3
Douglas Dr CROY/NA CR0 213 J1
Douglas Est IS * N1 85 J4
Douglas Ms CRICK NW2 82 C1
Douglas Pl POP/IOD * E14 125 F5
Douglas Rd CAN/RD E16 106 E4
CHING E4 38 C2
ESH/CLAY KT10 189 G6
GDMY/SEVK IG3 73 G4
HSLW TW3 135 G4
IS N1 85 J5
KIL/WHAMP NW6 82 D6
KUT KT1 175 J5
ROM RM1 75 H3
STWL/WRAY TW19 152 A1
SURB KT6 191 G6
WDGN N22 49 G4
WELL DA16 148 C2
Douglas Rd North IS N1 85 J4
Douglas Rd South IS * N1 85 J4
Douglas St WEST SW1P 16 C7
Douglas Ter WALTH E17 51 H4
Douglas Vis KUT * KT1 175 G5
Douglas Wy NWCR SE14 144 C1
Doulton Ms KIL/WHAMP NW6 83 F4
Dounesforth Gdns
WAND/EARL SW18 160 A3
Douro Pl KENS W8 120 A3
Douro St BOW E3 105 J1
Douthwaite Sq WAP E1W 123 H1
Dove Ap EHAM E6 107 J4
Dove Cl CROY/NA CR0 211 F5
MLHL NW7 45 J3
NTHLT UB5 95 H3
Dovecot Cl PIN HA5 59 G2
Dove Ct LOTH * EC2R 12 E4
Dovedale Av CLAY IG5 54 A5
KTN/HRWW/W HA3 61 J3
Dovedale Cl WELL DA16 148 B2
Dovedale Ri MTCM CR4 178 E3
Dovedale Rd EDUL SE22 143 J6
Dovedon Cl STHGT/OAK N14 34 E4
Dove House Gdns CHING E4 37 J4
Dovehouse Md BARK IG11 108 D1
Dovehouse St CHEL SW3 120 D5
Dove Ms ECT SW5 120 B4
Doveney Cl STMC/STPC BR5 202 E1
Dove Pk PIN HA5 41 K3
Dover Cl CRICK NW2 64 B6
ROMW/RG RM7 56 E5
Dovercourt Av THHTH CR7 196 B1
Dovercourt Est IS N1 85 K4
Dovercourt Gdns STAN HA7 44 A1
Dovercourt La SUT SM1 209 G1
Dovercourt Rd EDUL SE22 163 F1
Doverfield Rd
BRXS/STRHM SW2 161 K1
Dover Gdns CAR SM5 209 K1
Dover House Rd
PUT/ROE SW15 138 D5
Doveridge Gdns PLMGR N13 35 H6
Dove Rd IS N1 85 K4
Dove Rw BETH E2 104 C1
Dover Park Dr PUT/ROE SW15 158 E1
Dover Patrol BKHTH/KID SE3 146 A3
Dover Rd ED N9 36 E4
MNPK E12 71 G6
NRWD SE19 180 E2
WOOL/PLUM SE18 147 G3
Dover St MYFR/PICC W1J 9 K6
Dover Ter RCH/KEW * TW9 137 H3
Doves Cl HAYES BR2 200 D6
Doves Yd IS N1 5 J1
Doveton Rd SAND/SEL CR2 211 K3
Doveton St WCHPL E1 104 E3
Dowanhill Rd CAT SE6 165 G3
Dowdeswell Cl PUT/ROE SW15 138 B5
Dowding Cl HCH RM12 93 K5
Dowding Pl STAN HA7 43 G2
Dowdney Cl KTTN NW5 84 C3
Dower Av WLGTN SM6 210 B6
Dowgate Hl CANST EC4R 12 E5
Dowland St NKENS W10 100 C2
Dowlas St CMBW SE5 143 F1
Dowlerville Rd ORP BR6 217 F4
Dowman Cl WIM/MER SW19 178 A4
Downage HDN NW4 46 A6
Downalong BUSH WD23 28 D3
Downbank Av BXLYHN DA7 150 A2
Down Barns Rd RSLP HA4 77 H2
Down Cl NTHLT UB5 95 F2
Downderry Rd BMLY BR1 165 G5
Downe Cl WELL DA16 148 D1
Downend WOOL/PLUM SE18 147 G1
Downe Rd HAYES BR2 215 J6
MTCM CR4 178 E5
Downer's Cottages CLAP SW4 141 H5
Downes Cl TWK TW1 156 C1
Downes Ct WCHMH N21 35 G3
Downfield WPK KT4 192 C5
Downfield Cl MV/WKIL W9 101 F3
Down Hall Rd KUTN/CMB KT2 174 E4
Downham Cl CRW RM5 56 C3
Downham Rd IS N1 85 K5
Downham Wy BMLY BR1 183 H1
Downhills Av TOTM N17 49 K6
Downhills Park Rd TOTM N17 49 J6
Downhills Wy TOTM N17 49 J5
Downhurst Av MLHL NW7 45 F2
Downing Cl RYLN/HDSTN HA2 42 C6
Downing Dr GFD/PVL UB6 78 E6
Downing Rd DAGW RM9 92 B6
Downings EHAM E6 108 A5
Downing St WHALL SW1A 16 E2
Downland Cl TRDG/WHET N20 33 G3
Downleys Cl ELTH/MOT SE9 166 D4
Downman Rd ELTH/MOT SE9 146 D4
Down Pl HMSMTH W6 118 E4
Down Rd TEDD TW11 174 C2
The Downs RYNPK SW20 177 G3
Downs Av CHST BR7 184 E1
DART DA1 171 K2
PIN HA5 59 K3
Downs Bridge Rd BECK BR3 183 G4
Downs Court Pde CLPT * E5 86 D3
Downsell Rd WAN E11 88 B2
Downsfield Rd WALTH E17 69 G3
Downshall Av GDMY/SEVK IG3 72 E3
Downs Hl BECK BR3 183 G4
Downshire Hl HAMP NW3 83 H2
Downside BECK * BR3 182 D4
TWK TW1 156 A5
Downside Cl WIM/MER SW19 178 B2
Downside Crs HAMP NW3 83 J3
WEA W13 97 G3
Downside Rd BELMT SM2 209 H4
Downs La CLPT E5 86 D2
Downs Park Rd HACK E8 86 C3
Downs Rd BECK BR3 182 E5
CLPT E5 86 D2
EN EN1 24 A5
THHTH CR7 180 D4
Down St E/WMO/HCT KT8 189 F2
MYFR/PICC W1J 15 J1
Down Street Ms MYFR/PICC W1J 15 J2
Downs Vw ISLW TW7 136 A2
Downsview Gdns NRWD SE19 180 D3
Downsview Rd NRWD SE19 180 D3
The Downsway BELMT SM2 209 G6
Downsway ORP BR6 216 E3
Downton Av BRXS/STRHM SW2 162 A4
Downtown Rd
BERM/RHTH SE16 124 B2
Downway NFNCH/WDSP N12 47 J3
Down Wy NTHLT UB5 95 F2
Dowrey St IS N1 85 G6
Dowsett Rd TOTM N17 50 C5
Dowson Cl CMBW * SE5 142 E5
Doyce St STHWK * SE1 18 C2
Doyle Cl ERITH DA8 150 B2
Doyle Gdns WLSDN NW10 81 K6
Doyle Rd SNWD SE25 197 H1
D'oyley St KTBR SW1X 15 G6
Doynton St ARCH * N19 66 B6
Draco Ga PUT/ROE * SW15 139 F4
Draco St WALW SE17 122 D6
Dragonfly Cl PLSTW E13 107 F2
Dragon Rd PECK * SE15 123 F6
Dragoon Rd DEPT SE8 124 C5
Dragor Rd WLSDN NW10 98 E3
Drake Cl BERM/RHTH SE16 124 A2
Drake Crs THMD SE28 109 J5
Drakefell Rd NWCR SE14 144 A3
Drakefield Rd TOOT SW17 161 F5
Drake Ms HCH RM12 93 J5
Drake Rd BROCKY SE4 144 D4
CHSGTN KT9 206 C3
CROY/NA CR0 196 A4
MTCM CR4 195 F3
RYLN/HDSTN HA2 59 K6
Drake's Cl ESH/CLAY KT10 204 A3
Drakes Ctyd KIL/WHAMP NW6 82 D5
Drake St BMSBY WC1N 11 G2
ENC/FH EN2 23 K2
Drakewood Rd
STRHM/NOR SW16 179 J3
Draper Cl BELV DA17 129 G4
Draper Est WALW SE17 18 B6
Draper Pl IS N1 85 H6
Drapers Rd ENC/FH EN2 23 H3
SRTFD E15 88 A2
TOTM N17 50 B6
Drappers Wy BERM/RHTH SE16 123 H4
Draven Cl HAYES BR2 199 J4
Drawell Cl WOOL/PLUM SE18 127 K5
Drax Av RYNPK SW20 176 D3
Draxmont WIM/MER SW19 177 H2
Draycot Rd SURB KT6 191 H5
WAN E11 71 F3
Draycott Av CHEL SW3 14 D7
KTN/HRWW/W HA3 61 H3
Draycott Cl CRICK NW2 82 B1
KTN/HRWW/W HA3 61 H3
Draycott Pl CHEL SW3 14 E7
Draycott Ter CHEL SW3 14 E6
Dray Ct ALP/SUD * HA0 79 J4
Drayford Cl MV/WKIL * W9 100 D3
Draymans Wy ISLW TW7 136 A4
Drayson Ms KENS W8 119 K2
Drayton Av LOU IG10 39 K1
ORP BR6 201 G5
WEA W13 97 G6
Drayton Bridge Rd HNWL W7 97 F6
Drayton Cl HSLWW TW4 134 E6
IL IG1 72 D5
Drayton Ct WDR/YW * UB7 112 C4
Drayton Ct Chambers
WEA * W13 97 H6
Drayton Gdns WBPTN SW10 120 B5
WCHMH N21 35 H2
WDR/YW UB7 112 A2
WEA W13 97 G6
Drayton Gn WEA W13 97 G6
Drayton Green Rd WEA W13 97 H6
Drayton Gv WEA W13 97 G6
Drayton Pk HOLWY N7 85 G3
Drayton Park Ms HOLWY * N7 85 G3
Drayton Rd CROY/NA CR0 196 C6
TOTM N17 50 A5
WAN E11 70 B5
WEA W13 97 G5
WLSDN NW10 81 H6
Dreadnought St GNWCH SE10 125 H3
Drenon Sq HYS/HAR UB3 94 D6
Dresden Cl HAMP NW3 83 F4
Dresden Rd ARCH N19 66 C5
Dressington Av BROCKY SE4 164 D1
Drew Av MLHL NW7 46 C2
Drewery Ct BKHTH/KID * SE3 145 H4
Drew Gdns GFD/PVL UB6 79 F4
Drew Rd CAN/RD E16 126 D1
Drews Cottages BAL * SW12 161 J4
Drewstead Rd
STRHM/NOR SW16 161 J4
Driffield Rd BOW E3 105 G1
The Drift HAYES BR2 215 H1
The Driftway MTCM CR4 179 F4
Drinkwater Rd
RYLN/HDSTN HA2 60 B6
The Drive ACT W3 98 E5
BAR EN5 20 C4
BAR EN5 33 G1
BARK IG11 91 F5
BECK BR3 182 D5
BKHH IG9 39 G2
BXLY DA5 168 D1
CHING E4 38 B2
CHST BR7 186 A4
CHST BR7 186 A6
CRW RM5 57 F4
EBED/NFELT TW14 154 A2
EDGE HA8 44 C1
ENC/FH EN2 23 K2
ERITH DA8 149 J1
ESH/CLAY KT10 189 H5
FBAR/BDGN N11 48 C2
FNCH N3 46 E3
GLDGN NW11 64 C4
HGT N6 65 K2
HOLWY N7 85 F4
HOR/WEW KT19 207 H4
HSLW TW3 135 J3
IL IG1 71 J3
KUTN/CMB KT2 175 K3
MRDN SM4 194 B2
NTHWD HA6 40 C4
ORP BR6 202 A6
RYLN/HDSTN HA2 60 A4
RYNPK SW20 177 K2
SCUP DA14 168 C5
SURB * KT6 191 F4
SWFD E18 52 E6
THHTH CR7 196 E1
WALTH E17 51 K6
WBLY HA9 62 E6
WWKM BR4 199 G4
Drive Ct EDGE * HA8 44 C1
Dr Johnson Av TOOT SW17 161 G5
Droitwich Cl SYD SE26 163 H5
Dromey Gdns
KTN/HRWW/W HA3 43 F3
Dromore Rd PUT/ROE SW15 159 H1
Dronfield Gdns BCTR RM8 91 J3
Droop St NKENS W10 100 C3
Drovers Pl PECK SE15 143 J1
Drovers Rd SAND/SEL CR2 211 K3
Druce Rd DUL SE21 163 F1
Druid St STHWK SE1 19 J3
Druids Wy HAYES BR2 199 G1
Drumaline Rdg WPK KT4 192 B6
Drummond Av ROMW/RG RM7 75 F1
Drummond Cl ERITH DA8 150 B2
Drummond Crs CAMTN NW1 4 C4
Drummond Dr
KTN/HRWW/W HA3 43 F3
Drummond Ga PIM SW1V 121 J5
Drummond Rd
BERM/RHTH SE16 123 J3
CROY/NA CR0 196 D6
ROMW/RG RM7 74 E1
WAN E11 71 F3
Drummonds Pl RCH/KEW TW9 137 F5
Drummond St CAMTN NW1 4 A6
Drum St WCHPL E1 13 K3
Drury Crs CROY/NA CR0 196 B6
Drury La HOL/ALD WC2B 11 F4
Drury Rd HRW HA1 60 C4
Drury Wy WLSDN NW10 81 F3
Dryad St PUT/ROE SW15 139 G4
Dryburgh Gdns CDALE/KGS NW9 44 C6
Dryburgh Rd PUT/ROE SW15 138 E4
Dryden Av HNWL W7 97 F5
Dryden Cl BARK/HLT IG6 55 F2
Dryden Rd EN EN1 36 A1
KTN/HRWW/W HA3 43 F4
WIM/MER SW19 178 B2
WOOL/PLUM SE18 148 A2
Dryden St COVGDN WC2E 11 F4
Dryden Wy ORP BR6 202 B5
Dryfield Cl WLSDN NW10 80 E4
Dryfield Rd EDGE HA8 44 E2
Dryhill Rd BELV DA17 129 G6
Dryland Av ORP BR6 217 F2
Drylands Rd CEND/HSY/T N8 66 E3
Drysdale Av CHING E4 37 K1
Drysdale Cl NTHWD HA6 40 C3
Drysdale Dwellings HACK * E8 86 B3
Drysdale Pl BETH E2 7 H4
Drysdale St IS N1 7 H5
Dublin Av HACK E8 86 C6
Du Burstow Ter HNWL W7 115 K2
Ducal St BETH E2 7 K5
Du Cane Cl SHB * W12 100 A5
Du Cane Rd SHB W12 99 K5
Duchess Cl FBAR/BDGN N11 48 B1
SUT SM1 209 G2
Duchess Gv BKHH * IG9 39 F4
Duchess Ms CAVSQ/HST W1G 9 K2
Duchess of Bedford's Wk
KENS W8 119 J2
KENS * W8 119 K2
Duchess St REGST W1B 9 K2
Duchy Rd EBAR EN4 21 H1
Duchy St STHWK SE1 11 K7
Ducie St BRXN/ST SW9 141 K5
Duckett Rd FSBYPK N4 67 H3
Ducketts Rd DART DA1 150 C6
Duckett St WCHPL E1 105 F4
Ducking Stool Ct ROM RM1 75 G1
Duck La SOHO/CST W1F 10 C4
Duck Lees La PEND EN3 25 G5
Du Cros Dr STAN HA7 43 K2
Du Cros Rd ACT W3 118 B1
Dudden Hill La WLSDN NW10 81 H2
Dudden Hill Pde WLSDN * NW10 81 H2
Duddington Cl ELTH/MOT SE9 166 C6
Dudley Av KTN/HRWW/W HA3 43 J6
Dudley Dr MRDN SM4 193 H5
RSLP HA4 77 F3
Dudley Gdns RYLN/HDSTN HA2 60 D5
WEA W13 116 C2
Dudley Rd EBED/NFELT TW14 153 G3
FNCH N3 47 F5
IL IG1 90 B2
KIL/WHAMP NW6 100 C1
KUT KT1 175 G6
NWDGN UB2 114 C2
RCH/KEW TW9 137 G3
RYLN/HDSTN HA2 60 C6
WALTH E17 51 J5
WIM/MER SW19 177 K2
Dudley St BAY/PAD * W2 8 A2
Dudlington Rd CLPT E5 68 E6
Dudmaston Ms CHEL SW3 120 C5
Dudsbury Rd DART DA1 170 E1
Dudset La HEST TW5 133 K2
Dufferin Av STLK EC1Y 6 E7
Dufferin St STLK EC1Y 6 D7
Duffield Cl HRW HA1 61 F2
Duffield Dr SEVS/STOTM N15 68 B1
Duff St POP/IOD E14 105 K5
Dufour's Pl SOHO/CST W1F 10 B4
Duke Humphrey Rd
BKHTH/KID SE3 145 H2
Duke of Cambridge Cl
WHTN TW2 155 J1
Duke of Edinburgh Rd
SUT SM1 209 H1
Duke of Wellington Pl
WHALL SW1A 15 H3
Duke of York St STJS SW1Y 10 B7
Duke Rd BARK/HLT IG6 72 D1
CHSWK W4 118 A5
Duke's Av CHSWK W4 118 A5
EDGE HA8 44 B2
FNCH N3 47 F4
HRW HA1 60 E1
HSLWW TW4 134 D5
MUSWH N10 48 C6
NTHLT UB5 77 J5
NWMAL KT3 176 B6
PIN HA5 59 K3
RCHPK/HAM TW10 156 D6
Dukes Cl ASHF TW15 153 F6
HPTN TW12 172 E1
Dukes Ga CHSWK * W4 117 K4
Dukes La KENS W8 119 K2
Dukes La Chambers KENS * W8 120 A2
Dukes Lane Man KENS * W8 120 A2
Duke's Ms MHST W1U 9 H3
MUSWH N10 48 B6
Dukes Orch BXLY DA5 169 K3
Duke's Pl HDTCH EC3A 13 J4
Dukes Rd ACT W3 98 C3
CAMTN NW1 4 D5
EHAM E6 90 A6
Dukesthorpe Rd SYD SE26 164 A6
Duke St MBLAR W1H 9 H3
RCH/KEW TW9 136 E5
SUT SM1 209 H2
Duke Street Hl STHWK SE1 13 F7
Duke Street St James's
MYFR/PICC W1J 10 B7
Dukes Wy WWKM BR4 214 C1
Duke's Yd MYFR/PKLN W1K 9 H5
Dulas St FSBYPK N4 67 F5
Dulford St NTGHL W11 100 C6
Dulka Rd BTSEA SW11 140 E6
Dulverton Rd ELTH/MOT SE9 167 H4
RSLP HA4 58 E6
Dulwich Common DUL SE21 162 E3
The Dulwich Oaks DUL * SE21 163 G5
Dulwich Rd HNHL SE24 142 B6
Dulwich Village DUL SE21 162 E1
Dulwich Wood Av NRWD SE19 181 F1
Dulwich Wood Pk NRWD SE19 163 F6
Dumbarton Rd
BRXS/STRHM SW2 161 K1
Dumbleton Cl KUT KT1 175 J4
Dumbreck Rd ELTH/MOT SE9 147 F5
Dumfries Cl OXHEY WD19 26 E5
Dumont Rd STNW/STAM N16 86 A1
Dumpton Pl CAMTN NW1 84 A5
Dunbar Av BECK BR3 198 B1
DAGE RM10 92 C1
STRHM/NOR SW16 180 B5
Dunbar Cl YEAD UB4 94 E4
Dunbar Ct WOT/HER KT12 188 B6
Dunbar Gdns DAGE RM10 92 C3
Dunbar Rd FSTGT E7 88 E4
NWMAL KT3 191 K1
WDGN N22 49 G4
Dunbar St WNWD SE27 162 D5
Dunblane Rd ELTH/MOT SE9 146 D4
Dunboyne Rd HAMP NW3 83 K3
Dunbridge St BETH E2 104 C3
Duncan Cl BAR EN5 21 G5
Duncan Gv ACT W3 99 G5
Duncannon St CHCR WC2N 10 E6
Duncan Rd HACK E8 86 D6
RCH/KEW TW9 137 F5
Duncan St IS N1 6 A2
Duncan Ter IS N1 6 A3
Dunch St WCHPL * E1 104 D5
Duncombe Hl FSTH SE23 164 B2
Duncombe Rd ARCH N19 66 D5
Duncrievie Rd LEW SE13 165 G1
Duncroft WOOL/PLUM SE18 147 K1
Dundalk Rd BROCKY SE4 144 B4
Dundas Gdns E/WMO/HCT KT8 173 G6
Dundas Rd PECK SE15 143 K3
Dundee Rd PLSTW E13 107 F1
SNWD SE25 197 J2
Dundee St WAP E1W 123 J1
Dundee Wy PEND EN3 25 G4
Dundela Gdns WPK KT4 207 K2
Dundonald Cl EHAM E6 107 J5
Dundonald Rd WIM/MER SW19 177 J3
WLSDN NW10 82 B6
Dunedin Rd IL IG1 72 A4
LEY E10 87 K1
RAIN RM13 111 H2
Dunedin Wy YEAD UB4 95 G3
Dunelm Gv WNWD SE27 162 D6
Dunelm St WCHPL E1 105 F5
Dunfield Rd CAT SE6 182 E1
Dunford Rd HOLWY N7 85 F2
Dungarvan Av PUT/ROE SW15 138 D5
Dunheved Cl THHTH CR7 196 B3
Dunheved Rd North
THHTH CR7 196 B3
Dunheved Rd South
THHTH CR7 196 B3
Dunheved Rd West THHTH CR7 196 B3
Dunholme Gn ED N9 36 B5
Dunholme La ED N9 36 B5
Dunholme Rd ED N9 36 B5
Dunkeld Rd BCTR RM8 73 H6
SNWD SE25 196 E1
Dunkery Rd ELTH/MOT SE9 166 C6
Dunkin Rd DART DA1 151 K5
Dunkirk St WNWD * SE27 162 D6
Dunlace Rd CLPT E5 86 E3
Dunleary Cl HSLWW TW4 154 E2
Dunley Dr CROY/NA CR0 214 A4
Dunloe Av TOTM N17 49 K6
Dunloe St BETH E2 7 K3
Dunlop Pl BERM/RHTH SE16 19 K5
Dunmore Rd KIL/WHAMP NW6 82 C6
RYNPK SW20 177 F4
Dunmow Cl CHDH RM6 73 J2
FELT * TW13 154 D6
LOU IG10 39 J1
Dunmow Dr RAIN RM13 93 H6
Dunmow Rd SRTFD E15 88 B2
Dunmow Wk IS * N1 85 J6
Dunningford Cl HCH RM12 93 H3
Dunn Md CDALE/KGS NW9 45 H3
Dunnock Cl ED N9 37 F3
Dunnock Rd EHAM E6 107 J5
Dunn St HACK E8 86 B3
Dunollie Pl KTTN NW5 84 C3
Dunollie Rd KTTN NW5 84 C3
Dunoon Gdns FSTH * SE23 164 A2
Dunoon Rd FSTH SE23 163 K2
Dunraven Dr ENC/FH EN2 23 G3
Dunraven Rd SHB W12 118 D1
Dunraven St MYFR/PKLN W1K 9 F5
Dunsany Rd WKENS W14 119 G3
Dunsbury Cl BELMT SM2 209 F6
Dunsfold Wy CROY/NA CR0 213 K5
Dunsmore OXHEY * WD19 27 H4
Dunsmore Cl BUSH WD23 28 D1
YEAD UB4 95 H3
Dunsmore Rd WOT/HER KT12 188 A2
Dunsmore Wy BUSH WD23 28 C1
Dunsmure Rd STNW/STAM N16 68 A5
Dunspring La CLAY IG5 54 B5
Dunstable Ms CAVSQ/HST W1G 9 H1
Dunstable Rd E/WMO/HCT KT8 188 E1
RCH/KEW TW9 137 F5
Dunstall Rd RYNPK SW20 176 E2
Dunstall Wy E/WMO/HCT KT8 173 G6
Dunstall Welling Est
WELL * DA16 148 C3
Dunstan Cl EFNCH * N2 47 G6
Dunstan Gld STMC/STPC * BR5 201 J3
Dunstan Houses WCHPL * E1 104 E4
Dunstan Rd GLDGN NW11 64 D5
Dunstan's Gv EDUL SE22 163 J1
Dunstan's Rd EDUL SE22 163 H2
Dunster Av MRDN SM4 193 G5
Dunster Cl BAR EN5 20 B5
ROMW/RG RM7 56 E5
Dunster Ct FENCHST EC3M 13 G5
Dunster Dr CDALE/KGS NW9 62 E5
Dunster Gdns KIL/WHAMP NW6 82 D5
Dunsterville Wy STHWK SE1 19 F3
Dunster Wy RYLN/HDSTN HA2 77 J1
Dunston Rd BTSEA SW11 141 F4
HACK E8 7 J1
Dunston St HACK E8 86 B6
Dunton Cl SURB KT6 191 F5
Dunton Rd LEY E10 69 K4
ROM RM1 75 G1
STHWK SE1 19 J7
Duntshill Rd WAND/EARL SW18 160 A3
Dunvegan Cl E/WMO/HCT KT8 189 G1
Dunvegan Rd ELTH/MOT SE9 146 E5
Dunwich Rd BXLYHN DA7 149 G2
Dunworth Ms NTGHL * W11 100 D5
Duplex Ride KTBR SW1X 15 F3
Dupont Rd RYNPK SW20 177 G5
Dupont St POP/IOD E14 105 G5
Duppas Av CROY/NA CR0 211 H2
Duppas Hill Rd CROY/NA CR0 211 G2
Duppas Hill Ter CROY/NA CR0 211 H1
Duppas Rd CROY/NA CR0 211 G1
Dupree Rd CHARL SE7 126 A5
Dura Den Cl BECK BR3 182 E3
Durand Gdns BRXN/ST SW9 142 A2
Durand Wy WLSDN NW10 80 E5
Durants Park Av PEND EN3 25 F5
Durants Rd PEND EN3 24 E5
Durant St BETH E2 104 C1
Durban Gdns DAGE RM10 92 E5
Durban Rd BECK BR3 182 C5
GNTH/NBYPK IG2 72 E5
SRTFD E15 106 C2
TOTM N17 50 A2
WALTH E17 51 H4
WNWD SE27 162 D6
Durbin Rd CHSGTN KT9 206 A2
Durdans Rd STHL UB1 95 K5
Durell Gdns DAGW RM9 91 K3
Durell Rd DAGW RM9 91 K3
Durford Crs PUT/ROE SW15 158 D3
Durham Av HAYES BR2 199 J1
HEST TW5 114 E6
WFD IG8 53 H1
Durham Hl BMLY BR1 165 J6
Durham House St CHCR * WC2N 11 F6
Durham Pl CHEL * SW3 120 E5
Durham Ri WOOL/PLUM SE18 127 H5
Durham Rd CAN/RD E16 106 C3
DAGE RM10 92 E3
EA W5 116 E3
EBED/NFELT TW14 154 B2
ED N9 36 C4
EFNCH N2 47 J6
HAYES BR2 199 K1
HOLWY N7 67 F6
HRW HA1 60 B2
MNPK E12 89 H2
RYNPK SW20 176 E4
SCUP DA14 186 C1
Durham Rw WCHPL E1 105 F4
Durham St LBTH SE11 122 A5
Durham Ter BAY/PAD W2 101 F5
PGE/AN * SE20 181 J3
Durham Yd BETH * E2 104 D2
Durlun Wy ERITH DA8 150 E1
Durley Av PIN HA5 59 J3
Durley Gdns ORP BR6 217 H2
Durley Rd STNW/STAM N16 68 A4
Durlston Rd CLPT E5 68 C6
KUTN/CMB KT2 175 F2
Durnford St SEVS/STOTM N15 68 A2

Durning Rd NRWD SE19 180 E1
Durnsford Av
WAND/EARL SW18 159 K4
Durnsford Rd FBAR/BDGN N11 48 D3
WAND/EARL SW18 159 K4
Durrant Wy ORP BR6 216 D3
Durrell Rd FUL/PGN SW6 139 H2
Durrington Av RYNPK SW20 177 F3
Durrington Park Rd
RYNPK SW20 177 F4
Durrington Rd CLPT E5 87 G2
Dursley Cl BKHTH/KID SE3 146 B3
Dursley Gdns BKHTH/KID SE3 146 C2
Dursley Rd BKHTH/KID SE3 146 B3
Durward St WCHPL E1 104 D4
Durweston Ms MHST * W1U 9 F1
Dury Rd BAR EN5 20 D2
Dutch Barn Cl
STWL/WRAY TW19 152 A1
Dutch Gdns KUTN/CMB KT2 175 J2
Dutch Yd WAND/EARL SW18 139 K6
Duthie St POP/IOD E14 106 A6
Dutton St GNWCH SE10 145 F2
Duxford Cl HCH RM12 93 K4
Dwight Rd WATW WD18 26 B2
Dye House La BOW E3 87 J6
Dyer's Buildings
FLST/FETLN EC4A 11 J2
Dyers Hall Rd WAN E11 70 C5
Dyer's La PUT/ROE SW15 138 E4
Dyers Wy HARH RM3 57 J3
Dyke Dr STMC/STPC BR5 202 D4
Dykes Wy HAYES BR2 183 J6
Dykewood Cl BXLY DA5 170 A5
Dylan Cl BORE * WD6 29 K2
Dylan Rd BELV DA17 129 H3
Dylways CMBW SE5 142 E5
Dymchurch Cl CLAY IG5 54 A5
ORP BR6 216 E2
Dymock St FUL/PGN SW6 140 A4
Dymoke Rd ROM RM1 75 H4
Dyneley Rd LEE/GVPK SE12 166 B6
Dyne Rd KIL/WHAMP NW6 82 D5
Dynevor Rd RCHPK/HAM TW10 137 F6
STNW/STAM N16 86 A1
Dynham Rd KIL/WHAMP NW6 82 E5
Dyott St RSQ WC1B 10 D2
Dysart Av KUTN/CMB KT2 174 D1
Dysart St SDTCH EC2A 7 F7
Dyson Ct ALP/SUD HA0 79 G2
Dyson Rd FSTGT E7 88 D4
WAN E11 70 C3
Dyson's Rd UED N18 50 D1

E

Eade Rd FSBYPK N4 67 J4
Eagans Cl EFNCH * N2 47 H6
Eagle Av CHDH RM6 74 A3
Eagle Cl HCH RM12 93 K4
PEND EN3 24 E5
WLGTN SM6 210 E4
Eagle Ct FARR EC1M 12 A1
Eagle Dr CDALE/KGS NW9 45 G5
Eagle Hl NRWD SE19 180 E2
Eagle La WAN E11 70 E1
Eagle Ms IS N1 86 A4
Eagle Pl WBPTN SW10 120 B5
Eagle Rd ALP/SUD HA0 79 K5
HTHAIR TW6 133 J4
Eaglesfield Rd
WOOL/PLUM SE18 147 G2
Eagle St GINN WC1R 11 G2
Eagle Ter WFD IG8 53 F3
Eagle Wharf Rd IS N1 6 D2
Ealdham Sq ELTH/MOT SE9 146 B5
Ealing Gn EA W5 116 E1
Ealing Park Gdns EA W5 116 D4
Ealing Rd ALP/SUD HA0 98 A1
BOW E3 105 K2
EA W5 116 E4
NTHLT UB5 78 A6
Ealing Village EA W5 98 A5
Eamont St STJWD NW8 2 C2
Eardemont Cl DART DA1 150 C5
Eardley Crs ECT SW5 119 K5
Eardley Rd BELV DA17 129 H5
STRHM/NOR SW16 179 H2
Earl Cl FBAR/BDGN N11 48 B1
Earldom Rd PUT/ROE SW15 139 F5
Earle Gdns KUTN/CMB KT2 175 F3
Earlham Gv FSTGT E7 88 D3
WDGN N22 49 F3
Earlham St LSQ/SEVD WC2H 10 D4
Earl Ri WOOL/PLUM SE18 127 J5
Earl Rd MORT/ESHN SW14 137 K5
Earls Court Gdns ECT SW5 120 A4
Earl's Court Rd KENS W8 119 K3
Earl's Court Sq ECT SW5 120 A5
Earls Crs HRW HA1 60 E1
Earlsferry Wy IS N1 84 E5
Earlsfield Rd WAND/EARL SW18 160 B3
Earlshall Rd ELTH/MOT SE9 146 E5
Earlsmead RYLN/HDSTN HA2 77 K2
Earlsmead Rd SEVS/STOTM N15 68 B2
WLSDN NW10 99 K2
Earls Ter KENS W8 119 J3
Earlsthorpe Ms BAL SW12 161 F1
Earlsthorpe Rd SYD SE26 164 A6
Earlstoke Est FSBYE EC1V 6 A4
Earlstoke St FSBYE EC1V 6 A4
Earlston Gv HOM E9 86 D6
Earl St SDTCH EC2A 13 G1
Earls Wk BCTR RM8 91 H2
KENS W8 119 K3
Earlswood Av THHTH CR7 196 B2
Earlswood Gdns CLAY IG5 54 A6
Earlswood St GNWCH SE10 125 H5
Early Ms CAMTN NW1 84 B6
Earnshaw St NOXST/BSQ WC1A 10 D3
Earsby St WKENS W14 119 H4
Easby Crs MRDN SM4 194 A3
Easebourne Rd BCTR RM8 91 J3
Easedale Dr HCH RM12 93 K3
East Acton Ar ACT * W3 99 H5
East Acton La ACT W3 99 G6
East Arbour St WCHPL E1 105 F5
East Av CROY/NA CR0 211 F3
HYS/HAR UB3 113 J2
MNPK E12 89 J5
STHL UB1 95 K6
WALTH E17 69 K1
East Bank STNW/STAM N16 68 A4
Eastbank Rd HPTN TW12 173 H1
East Barnet Rd BAR EN5 21 G5
Eastbourne Av ACT W3 99 F5
Eastbourne Gdns
MORT/ESHN SW14 137 K4
Eastbourne Ms BAY/PAD W2 101 G5
Eastbourne Rd BTFD TW8 116 E5
CHSWK W4 117 K6
EHAM E6 108 A2
FELT TW13 154 C4
SEVS/STOTM N15 68 A3
SRTFD E15 88 C6
TOOT SW17 179 F2
Eastbourne Ter BAY/PAD W2 101 G5
Eastbournia Av ED N9 36 D5
Eastbrook Av DAGE RM10 92 E2
ED N9 36 E2
Eastbrook Dr DAGE RM10 93 G1
Eastbrook Rd BKHTH/KID SE3 146 A2
Eastbury Av BARK IG11 90 E6
EN EN1 24 A2
NTHWD HA6 40 C1
Eastbury Ct OXHEY * WD19 27 G2
Eastbury Gv CHSWK W4 118 B5
Eastbury Rd EHAM E6 108 A3
KUTN/CMB KT2 175 F3
NTHWD HA6 40 C2
OXHEY WD19 27 G2
ROMW/RG RM7 75 F3
STMC/STPC BR5 201 J3
Eastbury Sq BARK IG11 91 F6
Eastbury Ter WCHPL E1 105 F3
Eastcastle St GTPST W1W 10 A3
Eastcheap FENCHST EC3M 13 F5
East Churchfield Rd ACT W3 118 A1
Eastchurch Rd HTHAIR TW6 133 H4
East Cl EA W5 98 C3
EBAR EN4 22 A5
GFD/PVL UB6 96 C1
RAIN RM13 111 K3
Eastcombe Av CHARL SE7 126 A6
Eastcote ORP BR6 202 A5
Eastcote Av E/WMO/HCT KT8 188 E2
GFD/PVL UB6 79 G3
RYLN/HDSTN HA2 60 B6
Eastcote La NTHLT UB5 77 K4
RYLN/HDSTN HA2 77 K2
Eastcote La North NTHLT UB5 77 K4
Eastcote Rd PIN HA5 59 H2
RSLP HA4 58 C4
RYLN/HDSTN HA2 78 C1
WELL DA16 147 J3
Eastcote St BRXN/ST SW9 141 K3
Eastcote Vw PIN HA5 59 G1
East Ct ALP/SUD HA0 61 J6
East Crs EN EN1 24 A6
TRDG/WHET N20 33 K6
Eastcroft Rd HOR/WEW KT19 207 G5
East Cross Route HOM E9 87 H4
Eastdown Pk LEW SE13 145 G5
East Dr CAR SM5 209 J6
NTHWD HA6 26 C4
STMC/STPC BR5 202 C3
East Duck Lees La PEND EN3 25 G5
East Dulwich Gv EDUL SE22 143 F6
East Dulwich Rd EDUL SE22 143 H5
East End Rd FNCH N3 46 E5
East End Wy PIN HA5 41 J6
East Entrance DAGE RM10 110 D1
Eastern Av GNTH/NBYPK IG2 73 F2
PIN HA5 59 H4
REDBR IG4 71 H3
Eastern Av East ROM RM1 57 F6
Eastern Av West CHDH RM6 74 A1
ROMW/RG RM7 74 E1
Eastern Perimeter Rd
HTHAIR TW6 133 H3
Eastern Rd BROCKY SE4 144 D5
EFNCH N2 47 K6
PLSTW E13 107 F1
ROM RM1 75 H2
WALTH E17 70 A2
WDGN N22 48 E4
Easternville Gdns
GNTH/NBYPK IG2 72 C3
Eastern Wy THMD SE28 128 B2
East Ferry Rd POP/IOD E14 124 E4
Eastfield Gdns DAGE RM10 92 C2
Eastfield Rd CEND/HSY/T N8 48 E6
DAGE RM10 92 C2
PEND EN3 25 F1
WALTH E17 69 J1
Eastfields PIN HA5 59 G2
Eastfields Rd ACT W3 98 E4
MTCM CR4 179 F5
Eastfield St POP/IOD E14 105 G4
East Gdns WIM/MER SW19 178 D2
Eastgate Cl THMD SE28 109 K5
Eastglade NTHWD HA6 40 C1
PIN HA5 41 K6
East Hall Rd STMC/STPC BR5 203 F4
Eastham Cl BAR EN5 20 D6
East Ham Manor Wy EHAM E6 108 A5
East Harding St
FLST/FETLN EC4A 11 K3
East Heath Rd HAMP NW3 83 H1
East Hl DART DA1 171 J2
WAND/EARL SW18 140 B6
WBLY HA9 62 C6
East Hill Dr DART DA1 171 J2
Eastholm GLDGN NW11 65 F1
East Holme ERITH DA8 150 A2
Eastholme HYS/HAR UB3 113 K1
East India Dock Rd
POP/IOD E14 105 J5
Eastlake Rd CMBW SE5 142 C3
Eastlands Crs EDUL SE22 163 G1
East La ALP/SUD HA0 79 J1
BERM/RHTH SE16 123 H2
KUT KT1 174 E6
Eastlea Ms CAN/RD E16 106 C3
Eastleigh Av RYLN/HDSTN HA2 60 B6
Eastleigh Cl BELMT SM2 209 F5
CRICK NW2 81 G1
Eastleigh Rd BXLYHN DA7 149 K3
WALTH E17 51 H5
Eastleigh Wy
EBED/NFELT TW14 153 K3
Eastman Rd ACT W3 118 A2
East Md RSLP HA4 77 H1
Eastmead Av GFD/PVL UB6 96 B2
Eastmead Cl BMLY BR1 184 D5
Eastmearn Rd DUL SE21 162 D4
Eastmont Rd ESH/CLAY KT10 190 A6
Eastmoor Pl WOOL/PLUM SE18 126 C3
Eastmoor St CHARL SE7 126 C4
East Mount St WCHPL * E1 104 D4
Eastney Rd CROY/NA CR0 196 C5
Eastney St GNWCH SE10 125 G5
Eastnor Rd ELTH/MOT SE9 167 H3
Easton St FSBYW WC1X 5 J6
East Park Cl CHDH RM6 73 K2
East Parkside GNWCH SE10 125 H2
East Pl WNWD SE27 162 D6
East Pole Cottages EBAR * EN4 22 D5
East Poultry Av FARR EC1M 12 A2
East Rp HTHAIR TW6 132 E2
East Rd CHDH RM6 74 A2
EBAR EN4 34 A3
EBED/NFELT TW14 153 G2
EDGE HA8 44 E4
EFNCH N2 47 J4
IS N1 6 E5
KUTN/CMB KT2 175 F4
PEND EN3 24 E1
ROMW/RG RM7 75 F4
SRTFD E15 88 E6
WDR/YW UB7 112 C4
WELL DA16 148 C3
WIM/MER SW19 178 B2
East Rochester Wy
BFN/LL DA15 147 K6
DART DA1 170 A2
East Rw NKENS W10 100 C3
WAN E11 70 E3
Eastry Av HAYES BR2 199 J3
Eastry Rd ERITH DA8 149 H1
East Sheen Av
MORT/ESHN SW14 138 A6
East Side SHB * W12 119 F2
Eastside Rd GLDGN NW11 64 D1
East Smithfield WAP E1W 13 K6
East St BARK IG11 90 C5
BMLY BR1 183 K5
BTFD TW8 136 D1
BXLYHN DA7 149 H5
WALW SE17 122 D5
East Surrey Gv PECK SE15 143 G1
East Tenter St WCHPL E1 13 K4
East Ter BFN/LL * DA15 167 K3
East Towers PIN HA5 59 H3
East V ACT * W3 118 C1
East Vw BAR EN5 20 D4
CHING E4 52 A1
Eastview Av WOOL/PLUM SE18 147 K1
Eastville Av GLDGN NW11 64 D2
East Wk EBAR EN4 34 A3
HYS/HAR UB3 113 K2
East Wy CROY/NA CR0 198 B6
HYS/HAR UB3 113 K1
RSLP HA4 58 E5
Eastway HAYES BR2 199 K4
HOM E9 87 G6
HOM E9 87 H5
MRDN SM4 193 G2
WAN E11 71 F2
WLGTN SM6 210 B2
Eastwell Cl BECK BR3 182 B4
Eastwood Cl SWFD E18 52 E5
TOTM * N17 50 D3
Eastwood Dr RAIN RM13 111 K5
Eastwood Rd GDMY/SEVK IG3 73 G4
MUSWH N10 48 A5
SWFD E18 52 E5
Eastwood St STRHM/NOR SW16 179 H2
Eatington Rd LEY E10 70 B2
Eaton Cl BGVA SW1W 15 G6
STAN HA7 29 H6
Eaton Dr BRXN/ST SW9 142 C5
CRW RM5 56 D3
KUTN/CMB KT2 175 H3
Eaton Gdns DAGW RM9 92 A5
Eaton Ga BGVA SW1W 15 G5
NTHWD HA6 40 A2
Eaton La BGVA SW1W 15 K5
Eaton Ms North KTBR SW1X 15 H5
Eaton Ms South BGVA SW1W 15 H6
Eaton Ms West BGVA SW1W 15 H6
Eaton Park Rd PLMGR N13 35 G4
Eaton Pl KTBR SW1X 15 G6
Eaton Ri EA W5 97 J4
WAN E11 71 G2
Eaton Rd BELMT SM2 209 H4
EN EN1 24 A4
HDN NW4 64 A2
ISLW TW7 135 J5
SCUP DA14 168 E4
Eaton Rw BGVA SW1W 15 J4
Eatons Md CHING E4 37 J4
Eaton Sq BGVA SW1W 15 H6
Eaton Ter BGVA SW1W 15 G6
BOW * E3 105 G2
Eaton Terrace Ms KTBR SW1X 15 G6
Eatonville Rd TOOT SW17 160 E4
Eatonville Vls TOOT SW17 160 E4
Ebbisham Dr VX/NE SW8 122 A6
Ebbisham Rd WPK KT4 193 F6
Ebbsfleet Rd CRICK NW2 82 C3
Ebdon Wy BKHTH/KID SE3 146 A4
Ebenezer St IS N1 6 E4
Ebenezer Wk MTCM CR4 179 H4
Ebley Cl PECK SE15 123 G6
Ebner St WAND/EARL SW18 140 A6
Ebor St BETH E2 7 J6
Ebrington Rd
KTN/HRWW/W HA3 61 J3
Ebsworth St FSTH SE23 164 A2
Eburne Rd HOLWY N7 84 E1
Ebury Bridge Rd BGVA SW1W 121 F5
Ebury Cl HAYES BR2 215 J1
NTHWD HA6 40 A1
Ebury Ms BGVA SW1W 15 H6
Ebury Ms East BGVA SW1W 15 J6
Ebury Sq BGVA SW1W 15 J7
Ebury St BGVA SW1W 15 H7
Ecclesbourne Cl PLMGR N13 49 G1
Ecclesbourne Gdns PLMGR N13 49 G1
Ecclesbourne Rd IS N1 85 J5
THHTH CR7 196 D2
Eccles Rd BTSEA SW11 140 E5
Eccleston Cl EBAR EN4 21 J6
ORP * BR6 201 J5
Eccleston Crs CHDH RM6 73 H4
Eccleston Ct WBLY HA9 80 A3
Ecclestone Ms WBLY HA9 80 A3
Ecclestone Pl WBLY HA9 80 B3
Eccleston Ms KTBR SW1X 15 H5
Eccleston Pl BGVA SW1W 15 J7
Eccleston Rd HNWL W7 97 G6
Eccleston Sq PIM SW1V 15 K7
Eccleston Square Ms PIM SW1V 15 K7
Eccleston St BGVA SW1W 15 H5
Echelforde Dr ASHF TW15 152 D6
Echo Hts CHING * E4 37 K3
Eckford St IS N1 5 J2
Eckstein Rd BTSEA SW11 140 D5
Eclipse Rd PLSTW E13 107 F4
Ector Rd CAT SE6 165 H4
Edans Ct SHB W12 118 C2
Edbrooke Rd MV/WKIL W9 100 E3
Eddiscombe Rd FUL/PGN SW6 139 J3
Eddy Cl ROMW/RG RM7 74 D3
Eddystone Rd BROCKY SE4 144 B6
Ede Cl HSLW TW3 134 E4
Edenbridge Cl
BERM/RHTH * SE16 123 J5
STMC/STPC BR5 202 E1
Edenbridge Rd EN EN1 36 A1
HOM * E9 87 F5
Eden Cl ALP/SUD HA0 79 K6
BXLY DA5 170 A6
HAMP NW3 64 E6
KENS W8 119 K3
PEND EN3 25 J1
Edencourt Rd
STRHM/NOR SW16 179 G2
Edendale Rd BXLYHN DA7 150 A2
Edenfield Gdns WPK KT4 207 H1
Eden Gv HOLWY N7 85 F3
Edenham Wy MV/WKIL W9 100 D3
Edenhurst Av FUL/PGN SW6 139 J4
Eden Pde BECK * BR3 198 B1
Eden Park Av BECK BR3 198 C1
Eden Rd BECK BR3 198 B1
BXLY DA5 169 K6
CROY/NA CR0 211 K2
WALTH E17 69 K2
WNWD SE27 180 C1
Edensor Rd CHSWK W4 138 B1
Eden St KUT KT1 174 E5
Edenvale Rd MTCM CR4 179 F3
Edenvale St FUL/PGN SW6 140 B3
Eden Wk KUT * KT1 175 F5
Eden Wy BECK BR3 198 D2
Ederline Av STRHM/NOR SW16 180 A5
Edgar Kail Wy CMBW SE5 143 F4
Edgarley Ter FUL/PGN * SW6 139 H2
Edgar Rd BOW E3 105 K2
HSLWW TW4 154 E2
Edgeborough Wy BMLY BR1 184 C4
Edgebury CHST BR7 167 G6
Edgecombe Cl KUTN/CMB KT2 176 A3
Edgecoombe SAND/SEL CR2 213 F6
Edgecote Cl ACT W3 117 K1
Edgefield Av BARK IG11 91 F5
Edge Hl WIM/MER SW19 177 G3
WOOL/PLUM SE18 127 G6
Edge Hill Av GLDGN NW11 64 E1
Edgehill Ct WOT/HER * KT12 188 B5
Edgehill Gdns DAGE RM10 92 C2
Edgehill Rd CHST BR7 167 H5
MTCM CR4 179 G5
WEA W13 97 J5
Edgeley La CLAP SW4 141 J4
Edgeley Rd CLAP SW4 141 J4
Edgel St WAND/EARL SW18 140 A5
Edgepoint Cl WNWD * SE27 180 C1
Edge St KENS W8 119 K1
Edgewood Dr ORP BR6 217 F3
Edgewood Gn CROY/NA CR0 198 A5
Edgeworth Av HDN NW4 63 J2
Edgeworth Cl HDN NW4 63 J2
Edgeworth Rd EBAR EN4 21 J5
ELTH/MOT SE9 146 B5
Edgington Rd
STRHM/NOR SW16 179 J2
Edgington Wy SCUP DA14 186 D3
Edgwarebury Gdns EDGE HA8 44 C1
Edgwarebury La BORE WD6 30 B2
Edgware Rd BAY/PAD W2 2 A7
CDALE/KGS NW9 44 E6
CRICK NW2 82 A1
Edgware Rd Burnt Oak Broadway
EDGE HA8 44 D3
Edgware Rd High St EDGE HA8 44 C2
Edgware Rd The Hyde
CDALE/KGS NW9 63 G1
Edgware Wy (Watford By-Pass)
EDGE HA8 30 A4
Edinburgh Cl BETH E2 104 E1
PIN HA5 59 J4
Edinburgh Ct KUT * KT1 175 F6
Edinburgh Ga BAY/PAD W2 14 E1
Edinburgh Rd HNWL W7 116 A2
PLSTW E13 107 F1
SUT SM1 194 B6
UED * N18 50 C1
WALTH E17 69 J2
Edinburgh's Dr ROMW/RG RM7 74 E1
Edington Rd ABYW SE2 128 C3
PEND EN3 24 E3
Edison Av HCH RM12 75 H5
Edison Cl HCH RM12 75 H5
Edison Dr STHL UB1 96 B5
WBLY HA9 62 A6
Edison Gv WOOL/PLUM SE18 148 A1
Edison Rd CEND/HSY/T N8 66 D3
HAYES BR2 183 K5
PEND EN3 25 H3
WELL DA16 148 A2
Edis St CAMTN NW1 84 A6
Edith Cavell Wy
WOOL/PLUM SE18 146 D2
Edith Gdns BRYLDS KT5 191 J4
Edith Gv WBPTN SW10 120 B6
Edithna St BRXN/ST SW9 141 K4
Edith Rd CHDH RM6 73 K4
EHAM E6 89 H5
FBAR/BDGN N11 48 D3
ORP BR6 217 G3
SNWD SE25 196 E2
SRTFD E15 88 B3
WIM/MER SW19 178 A2
WKENS W14 119 H4
Edith Rw FUL/PGN SW6 140 A2
Edith St BETH E2 7 K2
Edith Ter WBPTN * SW10 140 B1
Edith Vls WKENS W14 119 J4
Edlson Cl WALTH E17 69 J2
Edmeston Cl HOM E9 87 G4
Edmund Gv FELT TW13 154 E4
Edmund Halley Wy
GNWCH SE10 125 H2
Edmund Hurst Dr EHAM E6 108 B4
Edmund Rd MTCM CR4 178 D6
RAIN RM13 111 G2
STMC/STPC BR5 202 D3
WELL DA16 148 B4
Edmunds Av STMC/STPC BR5 186 E6
Edmunds Cl YEAD UB4 95 G4
Edmund St CMBW SE5 142 E1
Edmunds Wk EFNCH N2 65 J1
Edna Rd RYNPK SW20 177 G5
Edna St BTSEA SW11 140 D2
Edrick Rd EDGE HA8 44 E2
Edrick Wk EDGE HA8 44 E2
Edric Rd NWCR SE14 144 A1
Edridge Rd CROY/NA CR0 211 J1
Edward Av CHING E4 51 K1
MRDN SM4 194 C2
Edward Cl ED N9 36 B2
HPTN TW12 173 H1
Edward Ct CAN/RD E16 106 E4
Edwardes Pl WKENS W14 119 J3
Edwardes Sq KENS W8 119 J3
Edward Gv EBAR EN4 21 H6
Edward Mann Cl East
WCHPL * E1 105 F5
Edward Mann Cl West
WCHPL * E1 105 F5
Edward Ms CAMTN * NW1 3 K4
Edward Pl DEPT SE8 124 C6
Edward Rd BMLY BR1 184 A3
CHDH RM6 74 A3
CHST BR7 185 G1
CROY/NA CR0 197 F4
EBAR EN4 21 H6
EBED/NFELT TW14 133 G6
HPTN TW12 173 H1
NTHLT UB5 95 G1
PGE/AN SE20 182 A3
RYLN/HDSTN HA2 42 C6
WALTH E17 69 F1
Edwards Av RSLP HA4 77 G3
Edwards Cl WPK KT4 193 G6
Edward's Cottages IS * N1 85 H5
Edward's La STNW/STAM N16 67 K6
Edwards Ms IS N1 85 H5
MBLAR W1H 9 G4
Edwards Pl FBAR/BDGN N11 48 D3
Edward Sq IS N1 5 G1
Edwards Rd BELV DA17 129 H4
Edward St CAN/RD E16 106 E3
DEPT SE8 124 C6
NWCR SE14 144 C1
Edward Temme Av SRTFD E15 88 D5
Edward Tyler Rd
LEE/GVPK SE12 166 A4
Edward Wy ASHF TW15 152 C4
Edwina Gdns REDBR IG4 71 J2
Edwin Av EHAM E6 108 A1
Edwin Cl BXLYHN DA7 129 G6
RAIN RM13 111 H2
Edwin Rd EDGE HA8 45 F2
RDART DA2 170 E5
WHTN TW2 155 K3
Edwin's Md HOM E9 87 G2
Edwin St CAN/RD E16 106 E4
WCHPL E1 104 E3
Edwin Ware Ct PIN * HA5 41 G5
Edwyn Cl BAR EN5 20 A6
Effie Pl FUL/PGN SW6 139 K1
Effie Rd FUL/PGN SW6 139 K1
Effingham Cl BELMT SM2 209 F5
Effingham Rd CEND/HSY/T N8 67 G2
CROY/NA CR0 196 A4
LEW SE13 145 H6
SURB KT6 190 C4
Effort St TOOT SW17 178 D1
Effra Pde BRXS/STRHM SW2 142 B6
Effra Rd BRXS/STRHM SW2 142 A5
WIM/MER SW19 178 A2
Egan Wy HYS/HAR UB3 94 C6
Egbert St CAMTN NW1 84 A6
Egerton Cl DART DA1 170 E3
PIN HA5 58 E1
Egerton Crs CHEL SW3 14 D6
Egerton Dr GNWCH SE10 144 E2
Egerton Gdns CHEL SW3 14 C6
GDMY/SEVK IG3 91 F1
HDN NW4 63 K1
WEA W13 97 H5
WLSDN * NW10 82 A6
Egerton Gardens Ms CHEL SW3 14 D5
Egerton Pl CHEL * SW3 14 D5
Egerton Rd ALP/SUD HA0 80 B5
NWMAL KT3 192 C1
SNWD SE25 181 F6
STNW/STAM * N16 68 B4
WHTN TW2 155 K2
Egerton Ter CHEL SW3 14 D5
Egerton Wy WDR/YW UB7 132 E1
Egham Cl CHEAM SM3 193 H6
Egham Crs CHEAM SM3 208 B1
Egham Rd PLSTW E13 107 F4
Eglantine Rd WAND/EARL SW18 140 B6
Egleston Rd MRDN SM4 194 A3
Eglington Rd CHING E4 38 B2
Eglinton Hl WOOL/PLUM SE18 127 G6
Eglinton Rd WOOL/PLUM SE18 127 F6
Egliston Ms PUT/ROE SW15 139 F4
Egliston Rd PUT/ROE SW15 139 F4
Eglon Ms CAMTN NW1 83 K5
Egmont Av SURB KT6 191 H5
Egmont Rd BELMT SM2 209 G5
NWMAL KT3 192 C1
SURB KT6 191 G5
WOT/HER KT12 188 A4
Egmont St NWCR SE14 144 A1
Egremont Rd WNWD SE27 162 B5
Egret Wy YEAD UB4 95 H5
Eider Cl FSTGT E7 88 D3
Eighteenth Rd MTCM CR4 195 K1
Eighth Av HYS/HAR UB3 113 K1
MNPK E12 89 K2
Eileen Rd SNWD SE25 196 E2
Eindhoven Cl MTCM CR4 195 F5
Eisenhower Dr EHAM E6 107 J4
Elaine Gv KTTN NW5 84 A3
Elam Cl CMBW SE5 142 C3
Elam St CMBW SE5 142 C3
Eland Rd BTSEA SW11 140 E4
CROY/NA CR0 211 H1
Elba Pl WALW * SE17 18 D6
Elberon Av CROY/NA CR0 195 H3
Elbe St FUL/PGN SW6 140 B3
Elborough Rd SNWD SE25 197 H2
Elborough St
WAND/EARL SW18 159 K3
Elbury Dr CAN/RD E16 106 E5
Elcho St BTSEA SW11 140 D1
Elcot Av PECK SE15 143 J1
Elder Av CEND/HSY/T N8 66 E2
Elderberry Rd EA W5 117 F2
Elder Cl BFN/LL DA15 168 A3
Elder Ct BUSH WD23 28 E4
Elderfield Rd CLPT E5 87 F2
Elderfield Wk WAN E11 71 F2
Elderflower Wy SRTFD E15 88 C5

Elder Oak Cl PGE/AN SE20 181 J4
Elder Rd WNWD SE27 180 D1
Elderslie Cl BECK BR3 198 D3
Elderslie Rd ELTH/MOT SE9 147 F6
Elder St WCHPL E1 13 J1
Elderton Rd SYD SE26 164 B6
Eldertree Wy MTCM CR4 179 G4
Elder Wk IS N1 85 H6
Eldon Av CROY/NA CR0 197 K6
HEST TW5 135 F1
Eldon Gv HAMP NW3 83 H3
Eldon Pde WDGN * N22 49 H4
Eldon Pk SNWD SE25 197 J1
Eldon Rd ED N9 36 E3
KENS W8 120 A3
WALTH E17 69 H1
WDGN N22 49 H4
Eldon St LVPST EC2M 13 F2
Eldon Wy WLSDN NW10 98 D1
Eldred Dr STMC/STPC BR5 202 E6
Eldridge Cl EBED/NFELT TW14 153 K3
Eleanora Ter SUT * SM1 209 G3
Eleanor Cl TOTM N17 50 B6
Eleanor Crs MLHL NW7 32 B6
Eleanor Gdns BAR EN5 20 B6
Eleanor Gv BARN SW13 138 B4
Eleanor Rd FBAR/BDGN N11 48 E2
HACK E8 86 D5
SRTFD E15 88 D4
Eleanor St BOW E3 105 J2
Electra Av HTHAIR TW6 133 J4
Electric Av BRXN/ST SW9 142 B5
Electric La BRXN/ST * SW9 142 B5
Electric Pde SURB KT6 190 E3
Elephant & Castle STHWK SE1 18 B6
Elephant La BERM/RHTH SE16 123 K2
Elephant Rd WALW SE17 18 C6
Elers Rd HYS/HAR UB3 113 F4
WEA W13 116 D2
Eley Rd UED N18 51 F1
Elfindale Rd HNHL SE24 142 D6
Elfin Gv TEDD TW11 174 A1
Elford Cl BKHTH/KID SE3 146 B5
Elfort Rd HBRY N5 85 G2
Elfrida Crs CAT SE6 164 D6
Elf Rw WAP E1W 104 E6
Elfwine Rd HNWL W7 96 E4
Elgal Cl ORP BR6 216 B3
Elgar Av BRYLDS KT5 191 J5
EA W5 117 F2
STRHM/NOR SW16 179 K6
WLSDN NW10 81 F4
Elgar Cl BKHH IG9 39 H4
BORE WD6 29 J2
DEPT SE8 144 D1
PLSTW E13 107 G1
Elgar St BERM/RHTH SE16 124 B2
Elgin Av KTN/HRWW/W HA3 43 H5
MV/WKIL W9 100 E3
SHB W12 118 D2
Elgin Crs HTHAIR TW6 133 H3
NTGHL W11 100 C6
Elgin Dr NTHWD HA6 40 C3
Elgin Ms NTGHL W11 100 C5
Elgin Ms North MV/WKIL W9 101 F2
Elgin Ms South MV/WKIL W9 101 F2
Elgin Rd CROY/NA CR0 197 G6
GDMY/SEVK IG3 72 E5
SUT SM1 209 G1
WDGN N22 48 C5
WLGTN SM6 210 C4
Elgood Av NTHWD HA6 40 E3
Elgood Cl NTGHL W11 100 C6
Elham Cl BMLY BR1 184 C3
Elia Ms IS N1 6 A3
Elias Pl LBTH SE11 122 B6
Elia St IS N1 6 A3
Elibank Rd ELTH/MOT SE9 147 F5
Elim St STHWK SE1 19 F4
Elim Wy PLSTW E13 106 D2
Eliot Bank FSTH SE23 163 J4
Eliot Dr RYLN/HDSTN HA2 60 B6
Eliot Gdns PUT/ROE SW15 138 D5
Eliot Hl LEW SE13 145 F3
Eliot Pk LEW SE13 145 F3
Eliot Pl BKHTH/KID SE3 145 H3
Eliot Rd DAGW RM9 91 K2
Eliot V BKHTH/KID SE3 145 G3
Elizabethan Wy
STWL/WRAY TW19 152 A2
Elizabeth Av ENC/FH EN2 23 H4
IL IG1 72 D6
IS N1 85 J5
Elizabeth Barnes Ct
FUL/PGN * SW6 140 A3
Elizabeth Br BGVA SW1W 15 J7
Elizabeth Cl BAR EN5 20 B4
MV/WKIL W9 101 G3
ROMW/RG RM7 56 D4
SUT SM1 208 D2
Elizabeth Clyde Cl
SEVS/STOTM N15 68 A1
Elizabeth Cottages
RCH/KEW TW9 137 G2
Elizabeth Gdns ACT W3 118 C1
STAN HA7 43 J2
SUN TW16 172 B6
Elizabeth Ms HAMP NW3 83 J4
Elizabeth Pl SEVS/STOTM N15 67 K1
Elizabeth Ride ED N9 36 D2
Elizabeth Rd EHAM E6 89 H6
RAIN RM13 111 K4
SEVS/STOTM N15 68 A2
Elizabeth Sq POP/IOD E14 105 G6
Elizabeth St BGVA SW1W 15 H6
Elizabeth Wy FELT TW13 154 B6
NRWD SE19 180 E3
STMC/STPC BR5 202 D2
Elkington Rd PLSTW E13 107 F3
The Elkins ROM RM1 57 G5
Elkstone Rd NKENS W10 100 D4
Ellaline Rd HMSMTH W6 119 G6
Ella Ms HAMP NW3 83 K2
Ellanby Crs UED N18 50 D1
Elland Rd PECK SE15 143 K5
WOT/HER KT12 188 C6
Ella Rd CEND/HSY/T N8 66 E4
Ellement Cl PIN HA5 59 H2
Ellenborough Pl
PUT/ROE SW15 138 D5
Ellenborough Rd SCUP DA14 186 E2
WDGN N22 49 J4
Ellenbridge Wy SAND/SEL CR2 212 A6
Ellen Cl BMLY BR1 184 C6
Ellen Ct ED N9 36 E4
Ellen St WCHPL E1 104 C5
Ellen Webb Dr
KTN/HRWW/W HA3 42 E6
Elleray Rd TEDD TW11 174 A2
Ellerby St FUL/PGN SW6 139 G2
Ellerdale Rd HAMP NW3 83 G3
Ellerdale St LEW SE13 144 E5
Ellerdine Rd HSLW TW3 135 H5
Ellerker Gdns
RCHPK/HAM TW10 157 F1
Ellerman Av WHTN TW2 154 E3
Ellerslie Rd SHB W12 118 E1
Ellerton Gdns DAGW RM9 91 J5
Ellerton Rd BARN * SW13 138 D2
DAGW RM9 91 J5
RYNPK SW20 176 D3
SURB KT6 191 G6
WAND/EARL SW18 160 C3
Ellery Rd NRWD SE19 180 E3
Ellery St PECK SE15 143 J3
Ellesborough Cl OXHEY WD19 41 G1
Ellesmere Av BECK BR3 182 E5
MLHL NW7 31 F5
Ellesmere Cl RSLP HA4 58 A4
WAN E11 70 D2
Ellesmere Gdns REDBR IG4 71 J2
Ellesmere Gv BAR EN5 20 D6
Ellesmere Rd BOW E3 105 G1
GFD/PVL UB6 96 C3
TWK TW1 156 D1
WLSDN NW10 81 J3
Ellesmere St POP/IOD E14 105 K5
Ellies Ms ASHF TW15 152 B4
Ellingfort Rd HACK E8 86 D5
Ellingham Rd CHSGTN KT9 205 K4
SHB W12 118 D2
WAN E11 88 B2
Ellington Rd FELT TW13 153 J6
HSLW TW3 135 G3
MUSWH N10 66 B1
Ellington St HOLWY N7 85 G4
Elliot Cl SRTFD E15 88 C5
WBLY HA9 80 B1
Elliot Rd HDN NW4 63 K3
Elliott Av RSLP HA4 59 F6
Elliott Gdns HARH RM3 57 K4
Elliott Rd BRXN/ST SW9 142 C1
CHSWK W4 118 B4
HAYES BR2 200 C1
STAN HA7 43 G2
THHTH CR7 196 C1
Elliott's Pl IS N1 6 B1
Elliott Sq HAMP NW3 83 J5
Elliott's Rw LBTH SE11 18 B6
Ellis Av RAIN RM13 111 J4
Ellis Cl CRICK NW2 82 A4
EDGE HA8 45 G2
ELTH/MOT SE9 167 H4
Elliscombe Mt CHARL * SE7 126 B6
Elliscombe Rd CHARL SE7 126 B5
Ellisfield Dr PUT/ROE SW15 158 C2
Ellison Gdns NWDGN UB2 114 E4
Ellison Rd BARN SW13 138 C3
BFN/LL DA15 167 J3
STRHM/NOR SW16 179 J3
Ellis Rd MTCM CR4 194 E3
NWDGN UB2 115 H1
Ellis St KTBR SW1X 15 F6
Ellis Wy DART * DA1 171 J4
Ellmore Cl HARH RM3 57 K4
Ellora Rd STRHM/NOR SW16 179 J1
Ellsworth St BETH * E2 104 D2
Elmar Rd SEVS/STOTM N15 67 K1
Elm Av EA W5 117 F1
OXHEY WD19 27 J2
RSLP HA4 58 E5
Elmbank WCHMH N21 34 E2
Elmbank Av BAR EN5 20 A5
Elmbank Dr BMLY BR1 184 C5
Elm Bank Gdns BARN SW13 138 B3
Elmbank Wy HNWL W7 96 D4
Elmbourne Dr BELV DA17 129 J4
Elmbourne Rd TOOT SW17 161 G5
Elmbridge Av BRYLDS KT5 191 K3
Elmbridge Cl RSLP HA4 58 E3
Elmbridge Dr RSLP HA4 58 E3
Elmbridge Rd BARK/HLT IG6 55 G2
Elmbridge Wk HACK * E8 86 C5
Elmbrook Cl SUN TW16 172 A4
Elmbrook Gdns ELTH/MOT SE9 146 D5
Elmbrook Rd SUT SM1 208 D2
Elm Cl BKHH IG9 39 H4
BRYLDS KT5 191 K4
CAR SM5 194 E5
DART DA1 171 F3
HDN NW4 64 B2
HYS/HAR UB3 94 E5
ROMW/RG RM7 56 D4
RYLN/HDSTN HA2 60 B3
RYNPK SW20 193 F1
SAND/SEL CR2 211 K4
STWL/WRAY TW19 152 A3
WAN E11 71 F3
WHTN TW2 155 G4
Elm Cottages MTCM * CR4 178 E5
Elmcourt Rd WNWD SE27 162 C4
Elm Crs EA W5 117 F2
KUTN/CMB KT2 175 F4
Elmcroft CEND/HSY/T N8 67 F2
Elmcroft Av BFN/LL DA15 168 A2
ED N9 36 D1
GLDGN NW11 64 D4
WAN E11 71 F2
Elmcroft Cl CHSGTN * KT9 206 A1
EA W5 97 K5
EBED/NFELT TW14 153 J1
Elmcroft Crs GLDGN NW11 64 B4
RYLN/HDSTN HA2 42 A6
Elmcroft Dr CHSGTN KT9 206 A1
Elmcroft Gdns CDALE/KGS NW9 62 C2
Elmcroft Rd ORP BR6 202 B4
Elmcroft St CLPT E5 86 E2
Elmdale Rd PLMGR N13 49 F1
Elmdene BRYLDS KT5 191 K5
Elmdene Cl BECK BR3 198 C2
Elmdene Rd WOOL/PLUM SE18 127 G5
Elmdon Rd HEST TW5 134 C3
HTHAIR TW6 133 J4
Elm Dr RYLN/HDSTN HA2 60 B3
SUN TW16 172 B5
Elmer Cl ENC/FH EN2 23 F4
RAIN RM13 93 J5
Elmer Gdns EDGE HA8 44 D3
ISLW TW7 135 J4
RAIN RM13 93 J5
Elmer Rd CAT SE6 165 F2
Elmer's Dr TEDD TW11 174 C2
Elmers End Rd BECK BR3 181 K6
Elmerside Rd BECK BR3 198 B1
Elmers Rd CROY/NA CR0 197 H4
Elmfield Av CEND/HSY/T N8 66 E2
MTCM CR4 179 F4
TEDD TW11 174 A1
Elmfield Cl HRW HA1 60 E6
Elmfield Pk BMLY BR1 183 K6
Elmfield Rd BAL SW12 161 G4
BMLY BR1 183 K6
CHING E4 38 A4
EFNCH N2 47 H6
NWDGN UB2 114 D3
WALTH E17 69 F3
Elmfield Wy MV/WKIL W9 100 D3
SAND/SEL CR2 212 B6
Elm Friars Wk CAMTN NW1 84 D5
Elm Gdns EFNCH N2 47 G6
ENC/FH EN2 23 K1
ESH/CLAY KT10 205 F4
MTCM CR4 195 J1
Elmgate Av FELT TW13 154 A5
Elmgate Gdns EDGE HA8 44 E1
Elm Gn ACT W3 99 G5
Elmgreen Cl SRTFD E15 88 C6
Elm Gv CEND/HSY/T N8 66 E3
CRICK NW2 82 B2
ERITH DA8 150 A1
KUTN/CMB KT2 175 F4
ORP BR6 202 A5
PECK SE15 143 H3
RYLN/HDSTN HA2 60 A4
SUT SM1 209 F2
WIM/MER SW19 177 H3
Elmgrove Crs HRW HA1 61 F2
Elmgrove Gdns HRW HA1 61 G2
Elm Grove Pde WLGTN SM6 210 A1
Elm Grove Rd BARN SW13 138 D2
EA W5 117 F2
Elmgrove Rd CROY/NA CR0 197 J4
HRW HA1 61 F2
Elm Hall Gdns WAN E11 71 F3
Elm Hatch PIN HA5 41 K3
Elmhurst BELV DA17 129 F6
Elmhurst Av EFNCH * N2 47 H6
MTCM CR4 179 F3
Elmhurst Crs EFNCH N2 47 H6
Elmhurst Dr SWFD E18 52 E5
Elmhurst Rd ELTH/MOT SE9 166 D4
FSTGT E7 89 F5
TOTM N17 50 A5
Elmhurst St CLAP SW4 141 J4
Elmhurst Wy LOU IG10 39 K2
Elmington Cl BXLY DA5 169 J2
Elmington Est CMBW SE5 142 D1
Elmington Rd CMBW SE5 142 E2
Elmira St LEW SE13 144 E4
Elm La CAT SE6 164 C4
Elmlee Cl CHST BR7 184 E2
Elmley St WOOL/PLUM SE18 127 J4
Elmore Cl ALP/SUD HA0 98 A1
Elmore Rd PEND EN3 25 F2
WAN E11 88 A1
Elmore St IS N1 85 K5
Elm Pde SCUP * DA14 168 B6
Elm Pk BRXS/STRHM SW2 162 A1
STAN HA7 43 H1
Elm Park Av HCH RM12 93 K2
SEVS/STOTM N15 68 B2
Elm Park Gdns HDN NW4 64 B2
WBPTN SW10 120 C5
Elm Park La CHEL SW3 120 C6
Elm Park Rd CHEL SW3 120 C6
FNCH N3 46 D3
LEY E10 69 G5
PIN HA5 41 G5
SNWD SE25 181 G6
WCHMH N21 35 J2
Elm Pl SKENS SW7 120 C5
Elm Rd BAR EN5 20 D5
BECK BR3 182 C5
CHSGTN KT9 206 A2
DART DA1 171 G3
EBED/NFELT TW14 153 G3
ERITH DA8 150 D2
ESH/CLAY KT10 205 F4
EW KT17 207 H4
FSTGT E7 88 D4
KUTN/CMB KT2 175 G4
MORT/ESHN SW14 137 K4
NWMAL KT3 176 A6
ORP BR6 217 G5
ROMW/RG RM7 56 D5
SCUP DA14 168 B6
THHTH CR7 196 D1
WALTH E17 70 A2
WAN E11 70 B6
WBLY HA9 80 A3
WDGN N22 49 H4
WLGTN SM6 195 F5
Elm Rd West MRDN SM4 193 J4
Elm Rw HAMP NW3 83 G1
The Elms BARN SW13 138 C4
ESH/CLAY * KT10 205 F5
NFNCH/WDSP * N12 47 J1
TOOT * SW17 161 F5
WLGTN * SM6 210 C2
Elms Av HDN NW4 64 A2
MUSWH N10 48 B6
Elmscott Gdns WCHMH N21 35 J1
Elmscott Rd BMLY BR1 183 H1
Elms Ct ALP/SUD HA0 79 F2
Elms Crs CLAP SW4 161 H1
Elmsdale Rd WALTH E17 69 H1
Elms Gdns ALP/SUD HA0 79 G2
DAGW RM9 92 B2
Elmshaw Rd PUT/ROE SW15 138 D6
Elmshurst Crs EFNCH N2 65 H1
Elmside Rd WBLY HA9 80 C1
Elms La ALP/SUD HA0 79 G2
Elmsleigh Av KTN/HRWW/W HA3 61 H1
Elmsleigh Rd WHTN TW2 155 J4
Elmslie Cl WFD IG8 53 K2
Elms Ms BAY/PAD W2 8 A5
Elms Park Av ALP/SUD HA0 79 G2
Elms Rd CLAP SW4 141 H6
KTN/HRWW/W HA3 42 E3
Elmstead Av CHST BR7 184 E1
WBLY HA9 62 A5
Elmstead Cl HOR/WEW KT19 207 G3
TRDG/WHET N20 32 E4
Elmstead Gdns WPK KT4 207 J1
Elmstead Gld CHST BR7 184 E2
Elmstead La CHST BR7 184 D3
Elmstead Rd ERITH DA8 150 B2
GDMY/SEVK IG3 72 E6
Elmsted Crs WELL DA16 128 D6
Elmstone Rd FUL/PGN SW6 139 K2
Elmstone Ter STMC/STPC * BR5 202 D1
Elm St FSBYW WC1X 5 H7
Elmsworth Av HSLW TW3 135 G3
Elm Ter CRICK NW2 82 E1
ELTH/MOT SE9 167 F1
KTN/HRWW/W HA3 42 D3
Elmton Wy STNW/STAM N16 86 C1
Elm Tree Av ESH/CLAY KT10 189 J4
Elm Tree Cl NTHLT UB5 95 K2
STJWD NW8 2 A4
Elm Tree Ct CHARL * SE7 126 B6
Elm Tree Rd STJWD NW8 2 A5
Elmtree Rd TEDD TW11 173 K1
Elm Vls HNWL * W7 96 E6
Elm Wk GPK RM2 57 J6
HAMP NW3 64 E6
ORP BR6 215 K1
RYNPK SW20 193 F1
Elm Wy FBAR/BDGN N11 48 A2
HOR/WEW KT19 207 F3
WLSDN NW10 81 G2
WPK KT4 208 A1
Elmwood Av FELT TW13 154 A5
KTN/HRWW/W HA3 61 G2
PLMGR N13 48 E1
Elmwood Cl EW KT17 207 J5
WLGTN SM6 195 G6
Elmwood Crs CDALE/KGS NW9 62 E1
Elmwood Dr BXLY DA5 169 F2
EW KT17 207 J5
Elmwood Gdns HNWL W7 96 E5
Elmwood Rd CHSWK W4 117 K6
CROY/NA CR0 196 C4
HNHL SE24 142 E6
MTCM CR4 178 E6
Elmworth Gv DUL SE21 162 E4
Elnathan Ms MV/WKIL W9 101 F3
Elphinstone Rd WALTH E17 51 H5
Elphinstone St HBRY N5 85 H2
Elrick Cl ERITH DA8 130 B6
Elrington Rd HACK E8 86 C4
WFD IG8 52 E1
Elruge Cl WDR/YW UB7 112 A3
Elsa Cottages POP/IOD * E14 105 G4
Elsa Rd WELL DA16 148 D3
Elsa St WCHPL * E1 105 G4
Elsdale St HOM E9 86 E4
Elsden Ms BETH * E2 104 E1
Elsden Rd TOTM N17 50 B4
Elsenham Rd MNPK E12 89 K3
Elsenham St WAND/EARL SW18 159 J3
Elsham Rd WAN E11 88 C1
WKENS W14 119 H2
Elsham Ter WKENS * W14 119 H2
Elsiedene Rd WCHMH N21 35 J2
Elsie Lane Ct BAY/PAD W2 100 E4
Elsiemaud Rd BROCKY SE4 144 C6
Elsie Rd EDUL SE22 143 G5
Elsinore Av STWL/WRAY * TW19 152 B2
Elsinore Gdns CRICK * NW2 82 C1
Elsinore Rd FSTH SE23 164 B3
Elsinore Wy RCH/KEW TW9 137 J4
Elsley Rd BTSEA SW11 140 E4
Elspeth Rd ALP/SUD HA0 80 A3
BTSEA SW11 140 E5
Elsrick Av MRDN SM4 193 K2
Elstan Wy CROY/NA CR0 198 B4
Elsted St WALW SE17 19 F7
Elstow Cl ELTH/MOT SE9 146 E6
RSLP HA4 59 H4
Elstow Gdns DAGW RM9 92 A6
Elstow Rd DAGW RM9 92 A5
Elstree Gdns BELV DA17 129 F4
ED N9 36 D3
IL IG1 90 C3
Elstree Hl BMLY BR1 183 H3
Elstree Hl South BORE WD6 29 K2
Elstree Pk MLHL * NW7 31 F1
Elstree Rd BUSH WD23 28 D3
Elswick Rd LEW SE13 144 E4
Elswick St FUL/PGN SW6 140 B3
Elsworth Cl EBED/NFELT TW14 153 H3
Elsworthy THDIT KT7 189 K3
Elsworthy Ri HAMP NW3 83 J5
Elsworthy Rd HAMP NW3 83 J6
Elsworthy Ter HAMP NW3 83 J5
Elsynge Rd WAND/EARL SW18 140 C6
Eltham Gn ELTH/MOT SE9 146 B6
Eltham Green Rd
ELTH/MOT SE9 146 B6
Eltham High St ELTH/MOT SE9 166 E1
Eltham Hl ELTH/MOT SE9 146 C6
Eltham Palace Rd
ELTH/MOT SE9 166 C1
Eltham Park Gdns
ELTH/MOT SE9 147 F5
Eltham Rd ELTH/MOT SE9 146 B6
Elthiron Rd FUL/PGN SW6 139 K2
Elthorne Av HNWL W7 116 A2
Elthorne Ct FELT TW13 154 B3
Elthorne Park Rd HNWL W7 116 A3
Elthorne Rd ARCH N19 66 D6
CDALE/KGS NW9 63 F4
Elthorne Wy CDALE/KGS NW9 63 F3
Elthruda Rd LEW SE13 165 G1
Eltisley Rd IL IG1 90 B2
Elton Av ALP/SUD HA0 79 H3
BAR EN5 20 D6
GFD/PVL UB6 79 F4
Elton Cl E/WMO/HCT KT8 174 D3
Elton Pl STNW/STAM N16 86 A3
Elton Rd KUTN/CMB KT2 175 G4
Eltringham St WAND/EARL SW18 140 B5
Elvaston Ms SKENS * SW7 120 B3
Elvaston Pl SKENS SW7 120 B3
Elveden Pl WLSDN NW10 98 C1
Elveden Rd WLSDN NW10 98 C1
Elvendon Rd FBAR/BDGN N11 48 E2
Elver Gdns BETH E2 104 C2
Elverson Ms DEPT * SE8 144 C1
Elverson Rd DEPT SE8 144 E3
Elverton St WEST SW1P 16 C6
Elvington Gn HAYES BR2 199 J2
Elvington La CDALE/KGS NW9 45 G4
Elvino Rd SYD SE26 182 A1
Elvis Rd CRICK NW2 82 A4
Elwill Wy BECK BR3 199 G1
Elwin St BETH E2 104 C2
Elwood St HBRY N5 85 H1
Elwyn Gdns LEE/GVPK SE12 165 K2
Ely Cl ERITH DA8 150 C3
NWMAL KT3 176 C5
Ely Cottages VX/NE * SW8 142 A1
Ely Gdns DAGE RM10 92 E1
Elyne Rd FSBYPK N4 67 G3
Ely Pl HCIRC EC1N 11 K2
WFD IG8 54 A1
Ely Rd CROY/NA CR0 196 E2
HSLWW TW4 134 B4
HTHAIR TW6 133 J3
LEY E10 70 A3
Elysian Av STMC/STPC BR5 201 K3
Elysium Pl FUL/PGN SW6 139 J3
Elysium St FUL/PGN SW6 139 J3
Elystan Cl WLGTN SM6 210 C6
Elystan Pl CHEL SW3 120 D5
Elystan St CHEL SW3 14 C7
Elystan Wk IS N1 5 J1
Emanuel Av ACT W3 98 E5
The Embankment TWK TW1 156 B3
Embankment PUT/ROE SW15 139 G4
Embankment Gdns CHEL SW3 120 E6
Embankment Pl CHCR WC2N 11 F7
Embassy Ct SCUP DA14 168 C5
WLGTN * SM6 210 B4
Emba St BERM/RHTH SE16 123 H2
Ember Cl STMC/STPC BR5 201 H4
Embercourt Rd THDIT KT7 189 K3
Ember Farm Av
E/WMO/HCT KT8 189 J3
Ember Farm Wy
E/WMO/HCT KT8 189 J2
Ember Gdns ESH/CLAY KT10 189 K4
Ember La ESH/CLAY KT10 189 J5
Embleton Rd LEW SE13 144 E5
OXHEY WD19 26 E5
Embry Cl STAN HA7 29 G6
Embry Dr STAN HA7 43 G2
Embry Wy STAN HA7 43 G1
Emden Cl WDR/YW UB7 112 D2
Emden St FUL/PGN SW6 140 A2
Emerald Cl CAN/RD E16 107 J5
Emerald Gdns BCTR RM8 74 C5
Emerald Sq NWDGN UB2 114 C3
Emerald St BMSBY WC1N 11 G1
Emerson Gdns
KTN/HRWW/W HA3 62 B3
Emerson St STHWK SE1 12 C7
Emerton Cl BXLYHS DA6 149 F5
Emery Hill St WEST SW1P 16 B5
Emery St STHWK SE1 17 K4
Emes Rd ERITH DA8 149 K1
Emilia Cl PEND EN3 24 D6
Emily Pl HOLWY N7 85 G2
Emily St CAN/RD E16 106 D5
Emlyn Rd SHB W12 118 B2
Emmanuel Rd BAL SW12 161 H3
NTHWD HA6 40 D3
Emma Rd PLSTW E13 106 D2
Emma St BETH E2 104 D1
Emma Ter RYNPK * SW20 177 F3
Emmaus Wy CHIG IG7 54 A1
Emmott Av BARK/HLT IG6 72 C2
Emmott Cl EFNCH N2 65 G3
WCHPL E1 105 G3
Emperor's Ga SKENS SW7 120 A3
Empire Av UED N18 49 J2
Empire Pde UED * N18 49 K2
WBLY * HA9 80 C1
Empire Rd GFD/PVL UB6 79 J6
Empire Wy WBLY HA9 80 B2
Empire Wharf Rd POP/IOD E14 125 G4
Empress Av CHING E4 51 K3
IL IG1 71 K6
MNPK E12 71 G6
WFD IG8 52 D3
Empress Dr CHST BR7 185 G2
Empress Pde CHING * E4 51 J3
Empress Pl ECT SW5 119 K5
Empress St WALW SE17 122 D6
Empson St BOW E3 105 K3
Emsworth Cl ED N9 36 E3
Emsworth Rd BARK/HLT IG6 54 B5
Emsworth St BRXS/STRHM SW2 162 A4
Emu Rd VX/NE SW8 141 G3
Ena Rd STRHM/NOR SW16 179 K6
Enbrook St NKENS W10 100 C2
Enclave Ct FSBYE EC1V 6 B6
Endale Cl CAR SM5 194 E6
Endeavour Wy BARK IG11 109 G1
CROY/NA CR0 195 K4
WIM/MER SW19 160 A6
Endell St LSQ/SEVD WC2H 10 E3
Enderby St GNWCH SE10 125 H5
Enderley Rd KTN/HRWW/W HA3 42 D4
Endersby Rd BAR EN5 20 A6
Endersleigh Gdns HDN NW4 63 J1
Endlebury Rd CHING E4 38 A4
Endlesham Rd BAL SW12 161 F2
Endsleigh Gdns IL IG1 71 K5
STPAN WC1H 4 C6
SURB KT6 190 D3
Endsleigh Pl STPAN WC1H 4 D6
Endsleigh Rd HNWL W7 116 B1
NWDGN UB2 114 D4
Endsleigh St STPAN WC1H 4 D6
Endway BRYLDS KT5 191 H4
Endwell Rd BROCKY SE4 144 B4
Endymion Rd
BRXS/STRHM SW2 162 A2
FSBYPK N4 67 H4
Energen Cl WLSDN NW10 81 G4
Enfield Rd ACT W3 117 J2
BTFD TW8 116 E5
EBAR EN4 22 D5
ENC/FH EN2 22 E4
HTHAIR TW6 133 H3
IS N1 86 A5
Enford St MBLAR W1H 8 E1
Engadine Cl CROY/NA CR0 212 B1
Engadine St WAND/EARL SW18 159 J3
Engate St LEW SE13 145 F5
Engel Pk MLHL NW7 46 A2
Engineer Cl WOOL/PLUM SE18 127 F6
Engineers Wy WBLY HA9 80 C2
England's La HAMP NW3 83 K4
England Wy NWMAL KT3 191 J1
Englefield Cl CROY/NA CR0 196 D3
ENC/FH EN2 23 G3
STMC/STPC BR5 202 A1
Englefield Crs STMC/STPC BR5 202 B2
Englefield Pth STMC/STPC BR5 202 B1
Englefield Rd IS N1 85 K5
Engleheart Dr
EBED/NFELT TW14 153 J1
Engleheart Rd CAT SE6 164 E2
Englewood Rd BAL SW12 161 G1
English St BOW E3 105 H3
Enid St STHWK SE1 19 K4
Enmore Av SNWD SE25 197 H2
Enmore Gdns
MORT/ESHN SW14 138 A6
Enmore Rd PUT/ROE SW15 139 F5
SNWD SE25 197 H2

STHL UB1 96 A3
Ennerdale Av HCH RM12 93 J3
STAN HA7 43 J6
Ennerdale Cl EBED/NFELT TW14 153 J3
SUT SM1 208 D2
Ennerdale Dr CDALE/KGS NW9 63 G2
Ennerdale Gdns WBLY HA9 61 J5
Ennerdale Rd BXLYHN DA7 149 H2
RCH/KEW TW9 137 G3
Ennersdale Rd LEW SE13 145 G6
Ennismore Av CHSWK W4 118 C4
GFD/PVL UB6 78 E4
Ennismore Gdns SKENS SW7 14 C4
THDIT KT7 189 K3
Ennismore Gardens Ms
SKENS SW7 14 B4
Ennismore Ms SKENS SW7 14 C3
Ennismore St SKENS SW7 14 C4
Ennis Rd FSBYPK N4 67 G5
WOOL/PLUM SE18 127 J6
Ensign Cl STWL/WRAY TW19 152 A3
Ensign Dr PLMGR N13 35 J5
Ensign St WCHPL E1 104 C6
Ensign Wy STWL/WRAY TW19 152 A3
Enslin Rd ELTH/MOT SE9 167 F1
Ensor Ms SKENS SW7 120 C5
Enstone Rd PEND EN3 25 G4
Enterprise Cl CROY/NA CR0 196 B5
Enterprise Rw SEVS/STOTM N15 68 B2
Enterprise Wy TEDD TW11 174 A1
WAND/EARL SW18 139 K5
WLSDN NW10 99 H2
Enterprize Wy DEPT * SE8 124 C4
Epcot Ms NKENS * W10 100 B2
Epirus Ms FUL/PGN SW6 139 K1
Epirus Rd FUL/PGN SW6 139 J1
Epping Cl POP/IOD E14 124 D4
ROMW/RG RM7 56 D6
Epping Gld CHING E4 38 A1
Epping New Rd BKHH IG9 39 F3
Epping Pl HOLWY N7 85 G4
Epping Wy CHING E4 37 K1
Epple Rd FUL/PGN SW6 139 J2
Epsom Cl BXLYHN DA7 149 J4
NTHLT UB5 77 K3
Epsom Rd CROY/NA CR0 211 G2
GDMY/SEVK IG3 73 F3
LEY E10 70 A3
MRDN SM4 193 J3
Epsom Sq HTHAIR * TW6 133 J3
Epstein Rd THMD SE28 128 C1
Epworth Rd ISLW TW7 136 C1
Epworth St SDTCH EC2A 7 F7
Equity Sq BETH E2 7 K5
Erasmus St WEST SW1P 16 D7
Erconwald St ACT W3 99 H5
Eresby Dr BECK BR3 198 D5
Eresby Pl KIL/WHAMP NW6 82 E5
Erica Gdns CROY/NA CR0 213 K2
Erica St SHB W12 99 J6
Eric Clarke La BARK IG11 108 B3
Ericcson Cl WAND/EARL SW18 139 K6
Eric Est BOW E3 105 H3
Eric Rd CHDH RM6 73 K4
FSTGT E7 88 E2
WLSDN NW10 81 H4
Eric St BOW E3 105 H3
Eridge Green Cl
STMC/STPC BR5 202 D5
Eridge Rd CHSWK W4 118 A3
Erin Cl BMLY BR1 183 H3
Erindale WOOL/PLUM SE18 127 J6
Erindale Ter WOOL/PLUM SE18 127 J6
Erin Ms WDGN * N22 49 H4
Erith Ct PUR RM19 131 K4
Erith Crs CRW RM5 56 E4
Erith High St ERITH DA8 130 B5
Erith Rd BELV DA17 129 J5
BXLYHN DA7 149 J4
Erlanger Rd NWCR SE14 144 A2
Erlesmere Gdns HNWL W7 116 B3
Erlich Cottages WCHPL * E1 104 E4
Ermine Cl HSLWW TW4 134 B3
Ermine Rd LEW SE13 144 E5
SEVS/STOTM N15 68 B3
Ermine Side EN EN1 24 C6
Ermington Rd ELTH/MOT SE9 167 H4
Ernald Av EHAM E6 107 J1
Erncroft Wy TWK TW1 156 A1
Ernest Av WNWD SE27 162 C6
Ernest Cl BECK BR3 198 D2
Ernest Gdns CHSWK W4 117 J6
Ernest Gv BECK BR3 198 C2
Ernest Rd KUT KT1 175 J5
Ernest St WCHPL E1 105 F3
Ernle Rd RYNPK SW20 176 E3
Ernshaw Pl PUT/ROE SW15 139 H6
Erpingham Rd PUT/ROE SW15 139 F4
Erridge Rd WIM/MER SW19 177 K5
Errington Rd MV/WKIL W9 100 D3
Errol Gdns NWMAL KT3 192 D1
YEAD UB4 95 F3
Erroll Rd ROM RM1 75 H1
Errol St STLK EC1Y 6 D7
Erskine Cl SUT SM1 209 J1
Erskine Crs TOTM N17 68 D1
Erskine Hl GLDGN NW11 64 E1
Erskine Ms HAMP * NW3 83 K5
Erskine Rd HAMP NW3 83 K5
SUT SM1 209 H2
WALTH E17 69 H1
Erwood Rd CHARL SE7 126 D5
Esam Wy STRHM/NOR SW16 180 B1
Escot Wy BAR EN5 20 A6
Escreet Gv WOOL/PLUM SE18 127 F4
Esher Av CHEAM SM3 208 B1
ROMW/RG RM7 74 E3
WOT/HER KT12 188 A5
Esher Cl BXLY DA5 169 F3
ESH/CLAY KT10 204 B3
Esher Crs HTHAIR TW6 133 J3
Esher Gn ESH/CLAY KT10 204 B2
Esher Green Dr ESH/CLAY KT10 204 A1
Esher Ms MTCM CR4 179 F6
Esher Park Av ESH/CLAY KT10 204 C3
Esher Place Av ESH/CLAY KT10 204 B2
Esher Rd E/WMO/HCT KT8 189 J3
GDMY/SEVK IG3 90 E1
Eskdale Av NTHLT UB5 77 K6
Eskdale Cl WBLY HA9 61 K6
Eskdale Rd BXLYHN DA7 149 H3
Eskmont Rdg NRWD SE19 181 F3
Esk Rd PLSTW E13 107 F3
Esk Wy ROM RM1 57 G3
Esmar Crs CDALE/KGS NW9 63 J4
Esmeralda Rd STHWK SE1 123 H4
Esmond Cl RAIN * RM13 93 K5
Esmond Gdns CHSWK * W4 118 A4
Esmond Rd CHSWK W4 118 A3
KIL/WHAMP NW6 82 D6
Esmond St PUT/ROE SW15 139 H5
Esparto St WAND/EARL SW18 160 A2
Essenden Rd BELV DA17 129 H5
SAND/SEL CR2 212 A5
Essendine Rd MV/WKIL W9 100 E2
Essex Av ISLW TW7 135 K4
Essex Cl MRDN SM4 193 G4
ROMW/RG RM7 74 D1
RSLP HA4 59 H5
WALTH E17 69 G1
Essex Ct BARN SW13 138 C3
TPL/STR * WC2R 11 J4
Essex Gdns FSBYPK N4 67 H3
Essex Gv NRWD SE19 180 E2
Essex Pk FNCH N3 47 F2
Essex Park Ms ACT W3 118 B1
Essex Pl CHSWK W4 117 K4
Essex Place Sq CHSWK * W4 118 A4
Essex Rd ACT W3 98 E6
BARK IG11 90 D5
CHDH RM6 73 J5
CHING E4 38 C3
CHSWK W4 118 A4
DAGE RM10 92 E3
DART * DA1 171 G1
ENC/FH EN2 23 K5
IS N1 85 H6
LEY E10 70 A3
ROMW/RG RM7 74 D1
SWFD E18 53 F5
WALTH E17 69 G3
WLSDN NW10 81 G5
Essex Rd South LEY E10 70 B4
Essex St FSTGT E7 88 E3
TPL/STR WC2R 11 J4
WOOL/PLUM SE18 127 H4
Essex Vls KENS W8 119 K2
Essex Whf CLPT * E5 69 F6
Essian St WCHPL E1 105 G4
Essoldo Wy EDGE HA8 44 B6
Estate Wy LEY E10 69 H5
Estcourt Rd FUL/PGN SW6 139 J1
SNWD SE25 197 J3
Estella Av NWMAL KT3 192 E1
Estelle Rd HAMP NW3 83 K2
Esterbrooke St WEST SW1P 16 C7
Este Rd BTSEA SW11 140 D4
Esther Cl WCHMH N21 35 G2
Esther Rd WAN E11 70 C4
Estoria Cl BRXS/STRHM SW2 162 B2
Estreham Rd
STRHM/NOR SW16 179 J2
Estridge Cl HSLW TW3 135 F5
Estuary Cl BARK IG11 109 H2
Eswyn Rd TOOT SW17 160 E6
Etchingham Park Rd FNCH N3 47 F3
Etchingham Rd SRTFD E15 88 A2
Etfield Gv SCUP DA14 186 C1
Ethelbert Cl HAYES BR2 183 K5
Ethelbert Gdns GNTH/NBYPK IG2 71 K2
Ethelbert Rd BMLY BR1 183 K6
ERITH DA8 149 K1
RDART DA2 171 H6
RYNPK SW20 177 G4
STMC/STPC BR5 186 E6
Ethelbert St BAL SW12 161 G3
Ethelburga St BTSEA * SW11 140 D2
Etheldene Av MUSWH N10 66 C1
Ethelden Rd SHB W12 118 E1
Ethelred Est LBTH SE11 17 J7
Ethel Rd CAN/RD E16 107 F6
Ethel St WALW * SE17 18 D7
Ethel Ter ORP * BR6 217 J6
Etheridge Rd CRICK NW2 64 A4
Etherley Rd SEVS/STOTM N15 67 J2
Etherow St EDUL SE22 163 H1
Etherstone Rd
STRHM/NOR SW16 162 A6
Ethnard Rd PECK SE15 123 J6
Ethronvi Rd BXLYHN DA7 149 F4
Etloe Rd LEY E10 69 J6
Eton Av ALP/SUD HA0 79 J2
EBAR EN4 33 J1
HAMP NW3 83 J5
HEST TW5 114 E6
NFNCH/WDSP N12 47 G3
NWMAL KT3 192 A2
Eton Cl WAND/EARL SW18 160 A2
Eton College Rd HAMP NW3 83 K4
Eton Garages HAMP NW3 83 J4
Eton Gv CDALE/KGS NW9 44 C6
LEW SE13 145 H4
Eton Pl HAMP * NW3 84 A5
Eton Ri HAMP * NW3 83 K4
Eton Rd HAMP NW3 83 K5
HYS/HAR UB3 133 J1
IL IG1 90 C2
ORP BR6 217 H2
Eton St RCHPK/HAM TW10 136 E6
Eton Vls HAMP NW3 83 K4
Eton Wy DART DA1 151 F5
Etta St DEPT SE8 124 B6
Etton Rd HSLW TW3 135 H6
Ettrick St POP/IOD E14 106 A5
Etwell Pl BRYLDS KT5 191 G3
Eugenia Rd BERM/RHTH SE16 123 K5
Eureka Rd KUT KT1 175 H5
Europa Pl FSBYE EC1V 6 C5
Europe Rd WOOL/PLUM SE18 126 E3
Eusdon Cl ED N9 36 D5
Eustace Pl WOOL/PLUM SE18 126 E4
Eustace Rd CHDH RM6 73 K4
EHAM E6 107 J2
FUL/PGN SW6 139 K1
Euston Rd CAMTN NW1 4 A6
CROY/NA CR0 196 B5
Euston Sq CAMTN NW1 4 C5
Euston St CAMTN NW1 4 B6
Evandale Rd BRXN/ST SW9 142 B3
Evangelist Rd KTTN NW5 84 B2
Evans Cl HACK E8 86 B4
Evansdale RAIN RM13 111 H2
Evans Gv FELT TW13 155 F4
Evans Rd CAT SE6 165 H4
Evanston Av CHING E4 52 A3
Evanston Gdns REDBR IG4 71 J3
Eva Rd CHDH RM6 73 J4
Evelina Rd PECK SE15 143 K4
PGE/AN SE20 181 K3
Eveline Lowe Est
BERM/RHTH SE16 123 H3
Eveline Rd MTCM CR4 178 E4
Evelyn Av CDALE/KGS NW9 63 F1
RSLP HA4 58 D4
Evelyn Cl WHTN TW2 155 G2
Evelyn Denington Rd EHAM E6 107 J3
Evelyn Dr PIN HA5 41 H3
Evelyn Est DEPT SE8 124 B6
Evelyn Gdns RCH/KEW TW9 137 F5
WBPTN SW10 120 B5
Evelyn Gv EA W5 117 G1
STHL UB1 95 K5
Evelyn Rd CAN/RD E16 125 K1
CHSWK W4 118 A3
EBAR EN4 21 K5
RCH/KEW TW9 137 F4
RCHPK/HAM TW10 156 D5
WALTH E17 70 A1
WIM/MER SW19 178 A1
Evelyn St DEPT SE8 124 C6
Evelyn Ter RCH/KEW TW9 137 F4
Evelyn Wk IS N1 6 E3
Evelyn Wy WLGTN SM6 210 D2
Evensyde WATW WD18 26 A1
Evenwood Cl PUT/ROE * SW15 139 H6
Everard Av HAYES BR2 199 K5
Everard Wy WBLY HA9 80 A1
Everatt Cl WAND/EARL * SW18 159 J1
Everdon Rd BARN SW13 118 D6
Everest Pl POP/IOD E14 106 A4
Everest Rd ELTH/MOT SE9 146 D6
STWL/WRAY TW19 152 A2
Everett Cl BUSH WD23 28 E3
PIN HA5 40 D6
The Everglades HSLW * TW3 135 H4
Everglade Strd CDALE/KGS NW9 45 H4
Evergreen Cl PGE/AN SE20 181 K3
Evergreen Ct
STWL/WRAY * TW19 152 A2
Evergreen Sq HACK E8 86 B5
Evergreen Wy HYS/HAR UB3 94 D6
STWL/WRAY TW19 152 A2
Everilda St IS N1 5 H1
Evering Rd CLPT E5 86 C1
Everington Rd MUSWH N10 47 K5
Everington St HMSMTH W6 119 G6
Everitt Rd WLSDN NW10 99 F2
Everleigh St FSBYPK N4 67 F5
Eve Rd ISLW TW7 136 B5
SRTFD E15 106 C1
TOTM N17 50 A6
WAN E11 88 C2
Eversfield Gdns EDGE HA8 45 G3
Eversfield Rd RCH/KEW TW9 137 G3
Eversholt St CAMTN NW1 4 A2
Evershot Rd FSBYPK N4 67 F5
Eversleigh Rd BAR EN5 21 G6
BTSEA SW11 140 E4
EHAM E6 89 H6
FNCH N3 46 D3
Eversley Av BXLYHN DA7 150 B3
WBLY HA9 62 C6
Eversley Cl WCHMH N21 35 F1
Eversley Crs ISLW TW7 135 J2
RSLP HA4 58 C6
WCHMH N21 35 F1
Eversley Cross BXLYHN DA7 150 B3
Eversley Mt WCHMH N21 35 F1
Eversley Pk WIM/MER SW19 176 E1
Eversley Park Rd WCHMH N21 35 F1
Eversley Rd BRYLDS KT5 191 G1
CHARL SE7 126 A6
NRWD SE19 180 E3
Eversley Wy CROY/NA CR0 213 J1
Everthorpe Rd PECK SE15 143 G4
Everton Buildings CAMTN NW1 4 A5
Everton Dr STAN HA7 44 B6
Everton Rd CROY/NA CR0 197 H5
Evesham Av WALTH E17 51 J5
Evesham Cl BELMT SM2 208 E5
GFD/PVL UB6 96 B1
Evesham Gn MRDN SM4 194 A3
Evesham Rd FBAR/BDGN N11 48 C1
MRDN SM4 194 A3
SRTFD E15 88 D5
Evesham St NTGHL W11 100 B6
Evesham Ter SURB * KT6 190 E3
Evesham Wk BRXN/ST SW9 142 B3
CMBW SE5 142 E3
Evesham Wy BTSEA SW11 141 F4
CLAY IG5 54 A6
Evry Rd SCUP DA14 186 D2
Ewald Rd FUL/PGN SW6 139 J3
Ewanrigg Ter WFD IG8 53 G1
Ewart Gv WDGN N22 49 G4
Ewart Pl BOW * E3 105 H1
Ewart Rd FSTH SE23 164 A2
Ewe Cl HOLWY N7 84 E4
Ewell By-Pass EW KT17 207 J5
Ewell Court Av HOR/WEW KT19 207 G3
Ewellhurst Rd CLAY IG5 53 J5
Ewell Park Gdns EW KT17 207 J5
Ewell Park Wy EW KT17 207 J4
Ewell Rd CHEAM SM3 208 B4
SURB KT6 191 G3
THDIT KT7 190 C4
Ewelme Rd FSTH SE23 163 K3
Ewen Crs BRXS/STRHM SW2 162 B2
Ewer St STHWK SE1 18 C1
Ewhurst Av SAND/SEL CR2 212 B6
Ewhurst Cl BELMT SM2 208 A6
WCHPL E1 104 E4
Ewhurst Rd BROCKY SE4 164 D1
Exbury Rd CAT SE6 164 D4
Excel Ct LSQ/SEVD WC2H 10 D6
Excelsior Cl KUT KT1 175 H5
Exchange Ar LVPST EC2M 13 G2
Exchange Ct COVGDN * WC2E 11 F6
Exchange Sq SDTCH * EC2A 13 H1
Exchange St ROM RM1 75 G3
Exeforde Av ASHF TW15 152 D6
Exeter Cl EHAM E6 107 K5
Exeter Gdns IL IG1 71 K5
Exeter Ms FUL/PGN * SW6 139 K1
Exeter Pde CRICK * NW2 82 C4
Exeter Rd CAN/RD E16 106 E4
CRICK NW2 82 C3
CROY/NA CR0 197 F4
DAGE RM10 92 D4
ED N9 36 E4
FELT TW13 154 E5
HTHAIR TW6 133 H4
PEND EN3 25 F4
RYLN/HDSTN HA2 59 J6
STHGT/OAK N14 34 B3
WALTH E17 69 J2
WELL DA16 148 A3
Exeter St COVGDN WC2E 11 F5
Exeter Wy HTHAIR TW6 133 H3
NWCR SE14 144 C1
Exford Gdns LEE/GVPK SE12 166 A3
Exford Rd LEE/GVPK SE12 166 A4
Exhibition Rd SKENS SW7 14 B3
Exit Rd EFNCH N2 47 H5
Exmoor Cl BARK/HLT IG6 54 C4
Exmoor St NKENS W10 100 B3
Exmouth Market CLKNW EC1R 5 J6
Exmouth Ms CAMTN * NW1 4 B5
Exmouth Pl HACK E8 86 D6
Exmouth Rd RSLP HA4 77 G1
WALTH E17 69 H2
WELL DA16 148 D2
YEAD UB4 94 C2
Exmouth St WCHPL E1 104 E5
Exning Rd CAN/RD E16 106 D3
Exon St WALW SE17 19 G7
Explorer Av STWL/WRAY TW19 152 B3
Explorer Dr WATW WD18 26 D1
Express Dr GDMY/SEVK IG3 73 H5
Exton Crs WLSDN NW10 80 E5
Exton Gdns BCTR RM8 91 K3
Exton St STHWK SE1 17 J1
Eyhurst Av HCH RM12 93 J1
Eyhurst Cl CRICK NW2 63 J6
Eylewood Rd WNWD SE27 180 D1
Eynella Rd DUL SE21 163 G2
Eynham Rd SHB W12 100 A5
Eynsford Cl STMC/STPC BR5 201 H4
Eynsford Crs SCUP DA14 168 D3
Eynsford Rd GDMY/SEVK IG3 72 E6
Eynsham Dr ABYW SE2 128 C3
Eynswood Dr SCUP DA14 186 C1
Eyot Gdns HMSMTH W6 118 C5
Eyre Cl GPK RM2 75 K1
Eyre Street Hl CLKNW EC1R 5 J7
Eythorne Rd BRXN/ST SW9 142 B2
Ezra St BETH E2 7 K4

F

Faber Gdns HDN NW4 63 J2
Fabian Rd FUL/PGN SW6 139 J1
Fabian St EHAM E6 107 K3
The Facade FSTH * SE23 163 K4
Factory La CROY/NA CR0 196 B6
TOTM N17 50 B5
Factory Pl POP/IOD E14 125 F5
Factory Rd CAN/RD E16 126 C1
Factory Yd HNWL W7 115 K1
Faesten Wy BXLY DA5 170 B5
Faggs Rd EBED/NFELT TW14 133 J5
EBED/NFELT TW14 133 K6
Fairacre ISLW * TW7 135 J2
NWMAL KT3 176 B6
Fair Acres HAYES BR2 199 K2
Fairacres CROY/NA CR0 213 H6
RSLP HA4 58 D4
Fairbank Av ORP BR6 201 G6
Fairbank Est IS N1 6 E3
Fairbanks Rd TOTM N17 50 C6
Fairbourne Rd TOTM N17 50 A6
Fairbridge Rd ARCH N19 66 D6
Fairbrook Cl PLMGR N13 49 G1
Fairby Rd LEE/GVPK SE12 146 A6
Fairchild Cl BTSEA SW11 140 C3
Fairchild Pl SDTCH * EC2A 7 H7
Fairchild St SDTCH EC2A 7 H7
Fair Cl BUSH WD23 28 B2
Fairclough St WCHPL E1 104 C5
Faircross Av BARK IG11 90 C4
CRW RM5 57 F3
Fairdale Gdns HYS/HAR UB3 113 K2
PUT/ROE SW15 138 E5
Fairey CDALE/KGS * NW9 45 H5
Fairey Av HYS/HAR UB3 113 J3
Fairfax Av EW KT17 207 K6
Fairfax Cl WOT/HER KT12 188 A5
Fairfax Gdns BKHTH/KID SE3 146 B2
Fairfax Ms CEND/HSY/T * N8 67 H1
PUT/ROE SW15 139 F5
Fairfax Pl KIL/WHAMP NW6 83 G5
Fairfax Rd CEND/HSY/T N8 67 G1
CHSWK W4 118 B3
KIL/WHAMP NW6 83 G5
TEDD TW11 174 B3
Fairfax Wy MUSWH * N10 48 A3
Fairfield Av EDGE HA8 44 D2
HDN NW4 63 K3
OXHEY WD19 27 G5
RSLP HA4 58 A4
WHTN TW2 155 G3
Fairfield Cl BFN/LL DA15 168 A1
HCH RM12 75 J5
HOR/WEW KT19 207 G3
NFNCH/WDSP N12 33 G6
PEND EN3 25 G5
WIM/MER SW19 178 D3
Fairfield Cnr KUT * KT1 175 G5
Fairfield Ct RSLP HA4 58 B5
Fairfield Crs EDGE HA8 44 D2
Fairfield Dr GFD/PVL UB6 79 J6
RYLN/HDSTN HA2 42 C6
WAND/EARL SW18 140 A6
Fairfield East KUT KT1 175 F5
Fairfield Gdns CEND/HSY/T N8 66 E2
Fairfield Gv CHARL SE7 126 C6
Fairfield North KUT KT1 175 F5
Fairfield Pth CROY/NA CR0 211 K1
Fairfield Pl KUT KT1 175 F6
Fairfield Rd BECK BR3 182 D5
BMLY BR1 183 K3
BOW E3 105 J1
BXLYHN DA7 149 G3
CEND/HSY/T N8 66 E2
CROY/NA CR0 211 K1
IL IG1 90 B4
KUT KT1 175 F5
STHL UB1 95 K5
STMC/STPC BR5 201 J4
UED N18 36 C6
WALTH E17 51 G5
WDR/YW UB7 112 B1
WFD IG8 52 E2
Fairfields CAT SE6 164 E2
Fairfields Cl CDALE/KGS NW9 62 E2
Fairfields Crs CDALE/KGS NW9 62 E1
Fairfield South KUT KT1 175 F6
Fairfield St WAND/EARL SW18 140 A6
Fairfield Wy BAR EN5 20 E6
HOR/WEW KT19 207 G3
Fairfield West KUT KT1 175 F5
Fairfoot Rd BOW * E3 105 J3
Fairford Av BXLYHN DA7 149 K2
CROY/NA CR0 198 A2
Fairford Cl CROY/NA CR0 198 A2
Fairford Ct BELMT * SM2 209 F5
Fairford Gdns WPK KT4 207 H1
Fairgreen EBAR EN4 21 K4
Fairgreen Ct EBAR * EN4 21 K4
Fairgreen Rd THHTH CR7 196 C2
Fairhaven Av CROY/NA CR0 198 A3
Fairhaven Crs OXHEY WD19 26 E5
Fairhazel Gdns KIL/WHAMP NW6 83 F4
Fairholme EBED/NFELT TW14 153 G2
Fairholme Av GPK RM2 75 J2
Fairholme Cl FNCH N3 64 C1
Fairholme Ct PIN * HA5 42 A2
Fairholme Crs YEAD UB4 94 D3
Fairholme Gdns FNCH N3 46 C6
Fairholme Rd CROY/NA CR0 196 B4
HRW HA1 60 E2
IL IG1 71 K4
SUT SM1 208 D4
WKENS W14 119 H5
Fairholt Rd STNW/STAM N16 67 K5
Fairholt St SKENS SW7 14 D4
Fairland Rd SRTFD E15 88 D4
Fairlands Av BKHH IG9 38 E4
SUT SM1 193 K6
THHTH CR7 196 A1
Fairlawn CHARL SE7 146 B1
Fairlawn Av BXLYHN DA7 148 E3
CHSWK W4 117 K4
EFNCH N2 65 J1
Fairlawn Cl ESH/CLAY KT10 205 F4
FELT TW13 154 E6
KUTN/CMB KT2 175 K2
STHGT/OAK N14 34 D1
Fairlawn Ct CHARL * SE7 146 B1
Fairlawn Dr WFD IG8 52 E3
Fairlawn Gdns STHL * UB1 95 K6
Fairlawn Gv CHSWK W4 117 K4
Fairlawn Pk SYD SE26 182 B1
Fairlawn Rd WIM/MER SW19 177 J3
Fairlawns TWK TW1 156 D1
Fairlea Pl EA W5 97 J4
Fairlie Gdns FSTH SE23 163 K2
Fairlight Av CHING E4 38 B4
WFD IG8 52 E2
WLSDN NW10 99 G1
Fairlight Cl CHING E4 38 B4
WPK KT4 208 A2
Fairlight Rd TOOT SW17 160 C6
Fairlop Cl HCH RM12 93 K4
Fairlop Gdns BARK/HLT IG6 54 C3
Fairlop Rd BARK/HLT IG6 54 C5
WAN E11 70 B4
Fairmead BMLY BR1 200 E1
SURB KT6 191 J5
Fairmead Cl BMLY BR1 200 E1
HEST TW5 134 C1
NWMAL KT3 176 A6
Fairmead Crs EDGE HA8 30 E6
Fairmead Gdns REDBR IG4 71 H2
Fairmead Rd CROY/NA CR0 196 B4
HOLWY N7 84 E1
Fairmile Av STRHM/NOR SW16 179 J1
Fairmont Cl BELV DA17 129 G5
Fairmount Rd
BRXS/STRHM SW2 162 A1
Fairoak Cl STMC/STPC BR5 201 G4
Fairoak Dr ELTH/MOT SE9 147 J6
Fairoak Gdns ROM RM1 57 G5
Fair Oak Pl BARK/HLT IG6 54 C5
Fairseat Cl BUSH WD23 28 E4
Fairstead Wk IS * N1 85 J6
Fair St HSLW TW3 135 H4
STHWK SE1 19 H2
Fairthorn Rd CHARL SE7 125 K5
Fairview ERITH DA8 150 C1
Fairview Av ALP/SUD HA0 79 K4
Fairview Cl SYD * SE26 164 B6
Fair View Cl WALTH E17 51 G4
Fairview Ct HDN * NW4 46 B5
Fairview Crs RYLN/HDSTN HA2 60 A5
Fairview Dr CHIG IG7 54 E1
ORP BR6 216 D2
Fairview Gdns WFD IG8 53 F4
Fairview Pl BRXS/STRHM SW2 162 A2
Fairview Rd ENC/FH EN2 23 G2
SEVS/STOTM N15 68 B3
STRHM/NOR SW16 180 A4
SUT SM1 209 H3
Fairview Vls CHING * E4 51 J3
Fairview Wy EDGE HA8 30 C6
Fairwater Av WELL DA16 148 B5
The Fairway ACT W3 99 G5
ALP/SUD HA0 61 H6
BAR EN5 33 F1
BMLY BR1 200 E2
E/WMO/HCT KT8 173 G6
HNWL * W7 96 E6
MLHL NW7 31 F5
NTHLT UB5 78 C4
NTHWD HA6 26 C6
NWMAL KT3 176 A4
PLMGR N13 35 J5
RSLP HA4 77 G2
STHGT/OAK N14 34 B1
Fairway BXLYHS DA6 149 F6
RYNPK SW20 177 F6
STMC/STPC BR5 201 J3
WFD IG8 53 G1
Fairway Av CDALE/KGS NW9 44 D6
Fairway Cl CROY/NA CR0 198 B2
GLDGN NW11 65 G4
HOR/WEW KT19 206 E2
Fairway Ct MLHL * NW7 31 F5
Fairway Dr GFD/PVL UB6 78 B5
THMD SE28 109 K5
Fairway Gdns BECK BR3 199 G3
IL IG1 90 C3
Fairways ISLW * TW7 135 K2
STAN HA7 44 A5
TEDD TW11 174 E3
WALTH * E17 70 A1
Fairweather Cl SEVS/STOTM N15 68 A1
Fairweather Rd
STNW/STAM N16 68 C3
Fairwyn Rd SYD SE26 164 B5
Faithfield BUSH * WD23 27 J1
Fakenham Cl MLHL NW7 45 J3
NTHLT UB5 78 A4
Fakruddin St WCHPL E1 104 C3
Falaize Av IL IG1 90 B2
Falcon Av BMLY BR1 184 D6
Falconberg Ct
SOHO/SHAV * W1D 10 C3
Falcon Cl CHSWK W4 117 J6
DART DA1 151 J6
NTHWD HA6 40 C3
STHWK SE1 12 B7

Falcon Ct IS N1 6 B3
Falcon Crs PEND EN3 25 F6
Falcon Dr STWL/WRAY TW19 152 A1
Falconer Rd BARK/HLT IG6 55 H1
BUSH WD23 28 A1
Falcon Gv BTSEA SW11 140 D4
Falcon La BTSEA SW11 140 D4
Falcon Rd BTSEA SW11 140 D4
HPTN TW12 172 E3
PEND EN3 25 F6
Falcon St PLSTW E13 106 E3
Falcon Ter BTSEA * SW11 140 D4
Falcon Wy CDALE/KGS NW9 45 G5
KTN/HRWW/W HA3 62 A2
WAN E11 70 E1
Falconwood Av WELL DA16 147 J3
Falconwood Pde WELL DA16 147 K5
Falconwood Rd CROY/NA CR0 213 H6
Falcourt Cl SUT SM1 209 F3
Falkirk Gdns OXHEY WD19 41 H1
Falkirk St IS N1 7 H3
Falkland Av FBAR/BDGN N11 34 A6
FNCH N3 46 E3
Falkland Park Av SNWD SE25 181 F6
Falkland Pl KTTN NW5 84 C3
Falkland Rd BAR EN5 20 C3
CEND/HSY/T N8 67 G1
KTTN NW5 84 C3
Falloden Wy GLDGN NW11 64 E1
Fallow Cl CHIG IG7 55 F1
Fallow Ct STHWK * SE1 123 H5
Fallow Court Av
NFNCH/WDSP N12 47 G3
Fallowfield STAN HA7 29 G5
Fallowfield Ct STAN HA7 29 G5
Fallow Flds LOU IG10 39 G2
Fallowfields Dr
NFNCH/WDSP N12 47 J2
Fallows Cl EFNCH N2 47 G5
Fallsbrook Rd
STRHM/NOR SW16 179 G2
Falman Cl ED N9 36 C3
Falmer Rd EN EN1 24 A5
SEVS/STOTM N15 67 J2
WALTH E17 51 K6
Falmouth Av CHING E4 52 B1
Falmouth Cl LEE/GVPK SE12 145 J6
Falmouth Gdns REDBR IG4 71 H1
Falmouth Rd STHWK SE1 18 D5
Falmouth St SRTFD E15 88 B3
Falstaff Cl DART DA1 170 B2
Fambridge Cl SYD SE26 164 C6
Fambridge Rd BCTR RM8 74 C5
Fane St WKENS W14 119 J6
Fanns Ri PUR RM19 131 K4
Fann St FARR EC1M 6 C7
Fanshawe Av BARK IG11 90 C4
Fanshawe Crs DAGW RM9 92 A3
Fanshawe Rd
RCHPK/HAM TW10 156 D6
Fanshaw St IS N1 7 G4
Fanthorpe St PUT/ROE SW15 139 F4
Faraday Av SCUP DA14 168 C4
Faraday Cl HOLWY N7 85 F4
WATW WD18 26 B1
Faraday Rd ACT W3 98 E6
E/WMO/HCT KT8 189 F1
NKENS W10 100 C4
SRTFD E15 88 D4
STHL UB1 96 B6
WELL DA16 148 B4
WIM/MER SW19 178 A2
Faraday Wy STMC/STPC BR5 202 C1
WOOL/PLUM SE18 126 C3
Fareham Rd EBED/NFELT TW14 154 B2
Fareham St SOHO/CST * W1F 10 C3
Farewell Pl MTCM CR4 178 C4
Faringdon Av HAYES BR2 201 F4
Faringford Rd SRTFD E15 88 C5
Farjeon Rd BKHTH/KID SE3 146 C2
Farleigh Av HAYES BR2 199 J4
Farleigh Pl STNW/STAM N16 86 B2
Farleigh Rd STNW/STAM N16 86 B2
Farley Dr GDMY/SEVK IG3 72 E5
Farley Pl SNWD SE25 197 H1
Farley Rd CAT SE6 165 F2
SAND/SEL CR2 212 D5
Farlington Pl PUT/ROE SW15 158 E2
Farlow Rd PUT/ROE SW15 139 G4
Farlton Rd WAND/EARL SW18 160 A2
The Farm WIM/MER * SW19 159 G2
Farman Ter KTN/HRWW/W * HA3 61 K1
Farm Av ALP/SUD HA0 79 J4
CRICK NW2 82 C1
RYLN/HDSTN HA2 60 A4
STRHM/NOR SW16 161 K6
SWLY BR8 187 K6
Farmborough Cl HRW HA1 60 D4
Farm Cl BELMT SM2 209 H5
BKHH IG9 39 G5
DAGE RM10 92 E5
FUL/PGN * SW6 139 K1
STHL UB1 96 B6
WWKM BR4 214 D1
Farmcote Rd LEE/GVPK SE12 165 K3
Farm Cottages
E/WMO/HCT * KT8 190 B1
Farmdale Rd CAR SM5 209 J5
GNWCH SE10 125 K5
Farm Dr CROY/NA CR0 198 C6
Farmer Rd LEY E10 69 K5
Farmers Rd CMBW SE5 142 C1
Farmer St KENS * W8 119 K1
Farmfield Rd BMLY BR1 183 H1
Farmhouse Rd
STRHM/NOR SW16 179 H3
Farmilo Rd WALTH E17 69 J4
Farmington Av SUT SM1 209 H1
The Farmlands NTHLT UB5 77 K4
Farmlands ENC/FH EN2 23 G2
PIN HA5 58 E1
Farmland Wk CHST BR7 185 G1
Farm La CROY/NA CR0 198 C6
FUL/PGN SW6 119 K6
STHGT/OAK N14 34 A1
Farmleigh STHGT/OAK N14 34 C2
Farm Pl DART DA1 150 D5
KENS W8 119 K1
Farm Rd BELMT SM2 209 H5
EDGE HA8 44 E1
ESH/CLAY KT10 189 F5
HSLWW TW4 154 D3
MRDN SM4 194 A2
NTHWD HA6 40 A1
WCHMH N21 35 J3
WLSDN NW10 81 F6
Farmstead Rd CAT SE6 164 E6
KTN/HRWW/W HA3 42 D4
Farm St MYFR/PICC W1J 9 J6
Farm V BXLY DA5 169 J1
Farmway BCTR RM8 91 J2
Farm Wy BKHH IG9 39 G6
HCH RM12 93 K2
NTHWD HA6 26 C6
WPK KT4 208 A1
Farnaby Rd BMLY BR1 183 H4
ELTH/MOT SE9 146 B5
Farnan Av WALTH E17 51 J5
Farnan Rd STRHM/NOR SW16 179 K1
Farnborough Av SAND/SEL CR2 213 G5
WALTH * E17 51 G6
Farnborough Cl WBLY HA9 62 D6
Farnborough Common
ORP BR6 215 K1
Farnborough Crs HAYES BR2 199 J5
SAND/SEL CR2 213 G6
Farnborough Hl ORP BR6 216 D3
Farnborough Wy ORP BR6 216 E4
PECK SE15 143 F1
Farncombe St
BERM/RHTH SE16 123 H2
Farndale Av PLMGR N13 35 H5
Farndale Crs GFD/PVL UB6 96 C2
Farnell Ms ECT SW5 120 A5
Farnell Rd ISLW TW7 135 J4
Farnham Cl TRDG/WHET N20 33 G2
Farnham Gdns RYNPK SW20 176 E5
Farnham Pl STHWK SE1 18 B1
Farnham Rd GDMY/SEVK IG3 73 F3
WELL DA16 148 D3
Farnham Royal LBTH SE11 122 A5
Farningham Rd TOTM N17 50 C3
Farnley Rd CHING E4 38 C2
THHTH CR7 196 E1
Farnol Rd DART DA1 151 K6
Faro Cl BMLY BR1 185 F5
Faroe Rd WKENS W14 119 G3
Farorna Wk ENC/FH EN2 23 G2
Farquhar Rd NRWD SE19 181 G1
WIM/MER SW19 159 K5
Farquharson Rd CROY/NA CR0 196 D4
Farrance Rd CHDH RM6 74 A3
Farrance St POP/IOD E14 105 J5
Farrant Av WDGN N22 49 G5
Farrant Cl ORP BR6 217 G5
Farr Av BARK IG11 109 G1
Farren Rd FSTH SE23 164 B4
Farrer Ms CEND/HSY/T N8 66 C1
Farrer Rd CEND/HSY/T N8 66 C1
KTN/HRWW/W HA3 62 A2
Farrier Cl BMLY BR1 184 C6
Farrier Rd NTHLT UB5 96 A1
Farrier St CAMTN NW1 84 B5
Farriers Wy BORE WD6 31 F1
Farrier Wk WBPTN * SW10 120 B6
Farringdon La CLKNW EC1R 5 K7
Farringdon Rd FARR EC1M 12 A2
FSBYW WC1X 5 J6
Farringdon St STBT EC1A 12 A3
Farrington Av STMC/STPC BR5 186 C6
Farrington Pl CHST BR7 185 J3
Farrins Rents BERM/RHTH SE16 124 B1
Farrow La NWCR SE14 143 K1
Farrow Pl BERM/RHTH SE16 124 B3
Farr Rd ENC/FH EN2 23 K2
Farthing Aly STHWK * SE1 123 H2
Farthing Flds WAP E1W 123 J1
The Farthings KUTN/CMB KT2 175 H4
Farthings Cl CHING E4 38 C5
PIN HA5 59 F3
Farthing St ORP BR6 215 K5
Farwell Rd SCUP DA14 168 C6
Farwig La BMLY BR1 183 K4
Fashion St WCHPL E1 13 J2
Fashoda Rd HAYES BR2 200 C1
Fassett Rd HACK E8 86 C4
KUT KT1 191 F1
Fassett Sq HACK E8 86 C4
Fauconberg Rd CHSWK W4 117 K6
Faulkner Cl BCTR RM8 73 K4
Faulkner St NWCR SE14 143 K2
Fauna Cl CHDH RM6 73 J3
Faunce St WALW SE17 122 C6
Favart Rd FUL/PGN SW6 139 K2
Faversham Av CHING E4 38 C3
EN EN1 35 K1
Faversham Rd BECK BR3 182 C5
CAT SE6 164 C2
MRDN SM4 194 A3
Fawcett Cl BTSEA SW11 140 C3
STRHM/NOR SW16 162 B6
Fawcett Est CLPT * E5 68 C5
Fawcett Rd CROY/NA CR0 211 H1
WLSDN NW10 81 H5
Fawcett St WBPTN SW10 120 B6
Fawcus Cl ESH/CLAY KT10 204 E4
Fawe Park Rd PUT/ROE SW15 139 J5
Fawe St POP/IOD E14 105 K4
Fawkes Av DART DA1 171 J4
Fawley Rd KIL/WHAMP NW6 83 F3
Fawnbrake Av HNHL SE24 142 C6
Fawn Rd CHIG IG7 55 F1
PLSTW E13 107 G1
Fawns Manor Rd
EBED/NFELT TW14 153 G3
Fawood Av WLSDN NW10 81 F5
Faygate Crs BXLYHS DA6 149 H6
Faygate Rd BRXS/STRHM SW2 162 A4
Fayland Av STRHM/NOR SW16 179 H1
Fearnley Crs HPTN TW12 172 D1
Fearon St GNWCH SE10 125 K5
Featherbed La CROY/NA CR0 213 H5
Feathers Pl GNWCH SE10 125 G6
Featherstone Av FSTH SE23 163 J4
Featherstone Rd MLHL NW7 45 K2
NWDGN UB2 114 D3
Featherstone St STLK EC1Y 6 E6
Featherstone Ter NWDGN UB2 114 D3
Featley Rd BRXN/ST SW9 142 C4
Federal Rd GFD/PVL UB6 97 J1
Federation Rd ABYW SE2 128 D4
Fee Farm Rd ESH/CLAY KT10 205 F5
Felbridge Av STAN HA7 43 G4
Felbridge Cl BELMT SM2 209 F6
STRHM/NOR SW16 162 B6
Felbrigge Rd GDMY/SEVK IG3 73 F6
Felday Rd LEW SE13 164 E1
Felden Cl PIN HA5 41 J3
Felden St FUL/PGN SW6 139 J2
Feldman Cl STNW/STAM N16 68 C5
Felgate Ms HMSMTH W6 118 E4
Felhampton Rd ELTH/MOT SE9 167 G5
Felix Av CEND/HSY/T N8 66 E3
Felix Rd HNWL W7 97 G6
Felixstowe Rd ABYW SE2 128 D3
ED N9 36 C6
TOTM N17 50 B6
WLSDN * NW10 99 K2
Felix St BETH * E2 104 D1
Fellbrigg Rd EDUL SE22 143 G6
Fellbrigg St WCHPL E1 104 D3
Fellbrook RCHPK/HAM TW10 156 C5
Fellmongers Yd CROY/NA CR0 211 J1
Fellowes Cl YEAD UB4 95 H3
Fellowes Rd CAR SM5 209 J1
Fellows Rd HAMP NW3 83 H5
Fell Rd CROY/NA CR0 211 J1
Felltram Wy CHARL SE7 125 K5
Felmersham Cl CLAP SW4 141 K5
Felmingham Rd PGE/AN SE20 181 K5
Felsberg Rd BRXS/STRHM SW2 161 K1
Fels Cl DAGE RM10 92 D1
Fels Farm Av DAGE RM10 92 E1
Felsham Rd PUT/ROE SW15 139 G4
Felspar Cl WOOL/PLUM SE18 128 A5
Felstead Av CLAY IG5 54 A4
Felstead Rd CRW RM5 56 E2
HOM E9 87 J4
LOU IG10 39 J2
ORP BR6 202 B6
WAN E11 70 E4
Felstead St HOM E9 87 H4
Felsted Rd CAN/RD E16 107 H5
Feltham Av E/WMO/HCT KT8 189 K1
Felthambrook Wy FELT TW13 154 A6
Felthamhill Rd FELT TW13 153 K6
Feltham Rd ASHF TW15 152 E6
MTCM CR4 178 E5
Felton Cl STMC/STPC BR5 201 G3
Felton Lea SCUP DA14 186 A1
Felton Rd BARK IG11 108 E1
WEA W13 116 D2
Felton St IS N1 7 F1
Fencepiece Rd BARK/HLT IG6 54 C2
Fenchurch Av FENCHST EC3M 13 G4
Fenchurch Buildings
FENCHST EC3M 13 H4
Fenchurch Pl FENCHST * EC3M 13 H5
Fenchurch St FENCHST EC3M 13 G5
Fendall Rd HOR/WEW KT19 206 E3
Fendall St STHWK SE1 19 H5
Fendt Cl CAN/RD E16 106 D5
Fendyke Rd ABYW SE2 128 E4
Fenelon Pl WKENS W14 119 J4
Fen Gv BFN/LL DA15 168 A1
Fenham Rd PECK SE15 143 H1
Fenman Ct TOTM N17 50 D4
Fenman Gdns GDMY/SEVK IG3 73 H5
Fenn Cl BMLY BR1 183 K2
Fennel Cl CAN/RD E16 106 C3
CROY/NA CR0 198 A5
Fennells Md HOR/WEW KT19 207 H6
Fennell St WOOL/PLUM SE18 127 F6
Fenner Cl BERM/RHTH SE16 123 J4
Fenner Sq BTSEA * SW11 140 C4
Fenning St STHWK SE1 19 G2
Fenn St HOM E9 87 F3
Fenstanton Av
NFNCH/WDSP N12 47 H1
Fen St CAN/RD E16 106 D6
Fentiman Rd VX/NE SW8 121 K6
Fenton Cl BRXN/ST * SW9 142 A3
CHST BR7 184 E1
HACK E8 86 B4
Fenton Rd TOTM N17 49 J3
Fenton's Av PLSTW E13 107 F2
Fenwick Gv PECK SE15 143 H4
Fenwick Pl BRXN/ST SW9 141 K4
SAND/SEL CR2 211 H5
Fenwick Rd PECK SE15 143 H4
Ferdinand Pl CAMTN NW1 84 A5
Ferdinand St CAMTN NW1 84 A5
Ferguson Av BRYLDS KT5 191 G2
Ferguson Cl BECK BR3 183 F6
Ferguson Dr ACT W3 99 F5
Ferguson's Cl POP/IOD E14 124 D4
Fergus Rd HBRY N5 85 H3
Ferme Park Rd CEND/HSY/T N8 66 E2
Fermor Rd FSTH SE23 164 B3
Fermoy Rd GFD/PVL UB6 96 B3
MV/WKIL W9 100 D3
Fern Av MTCM CR4 195 J1
Fernbank BKHH IG9 39 F3
Fernbank Av ALP/SUD HA0 79 F2
WOT/HER KT12 188 D4
Fernbank Ms CLAP SW4 161 G1
Fernbrook Dr RYLN/HDSTN HA2 60 B4
Fernbrook Rd LEW SE13 165 H1
Ferncliff Rd HACK E8 86 C3
Fern Cl ERITH DA8 150 E2
IS * N1 7 G2
Ferncroft Av HAMP NW3 82 E1
NFNCH/WDSP N12 47 J2
RSLP HA4 59 G6
Ferndale BMLY BR1 184 B5
Ferndale Av HSLWW TW4 134 D4
WALTH E17 70 B2
Ferndale Cl BXLYHN DA7 149 F2
Ferndale Rd CLAP SW4 141 K5
CRW RM5 56 E5
FSTGT E7 89 F5
SEVS/STOTM N15 68 B3
SNWD SE25 197 J2
WAN E11 70 D6
Ferndale St EHAM E6 108 B6
Ferndale Ter HRW HA1 61 F1
Ferndale Wy ORP BR6 216 D3
Ferndell Av BXLY DA5 170 A5
Ferndene Rd HNHL SE24 142 D5
Fernden Wy ROMW/RG RM7 74 D3
Ferndown NTHWD HA6 40 E5
Ferndown Av ORP BR6 201 J5
Ferndown Cl BELMT SM2 209 H4
PIN HA5 41 J3
Ferndown Rd ELTH/MOT SE9 166 C2
OXHEY WD19 27 G5
Ferney Meade Wy ISLW TW7 136 B3
Ferney Rd EBAR EN4 34 A2
Fern Gv EBED/NFELT TW14 154 A2
Fernhall Dr REDBR IG4 71 H2
Fernham Rd THHTH CR7 196 D1
Fernhead Rd MV/WKIL W9 100 D2
Fernhill Ct WALTH E17 52 B5
Fernhill Gdns KUTN/CMB KT2 174 E1
Fernhill St CAN/RD E16 126 E1
Fernholme Rd PECK SE15 144 A6
Fernhurst Gdns EDGE HA8 44 C2
Fernhurst Rd ASHF TW15 153 F6
CROY/NA CR0 197 H4
FUL/PGN SW6 139 H2
Fern La NWDGN UB2 114 E5
Fernlea Rd BAL SW12 161 G3
MTCM CR4 179 F5
Fernleigh Cl CROY/NA CR0 211 G2
MV/WKIL W9 100 D2
Fernleigh Ct RYLN/HDSTN HA2 42 B5
WBLY HA9 62 A5
Fernleigh Rd WCHMH N21 35 G4
Fernley Cl PIN HA5 58 E1
Fernsbury St FSBYW WC1X 5 J5
Fernshaw Cl WBPTN * SW10 120 B6
Fernshaw Rd WBPTN SW10 120 B6
Fernside BKHH IG9 39 F3
Fernside Av FELT TW13 154 A6
MLHL NW7 31 F5
Fernside Rd BAL SW12 160 E3
Ferns Rd SRTFD E15 88 C4
Fern St BOW E3 105 J3
Fernthorpe Rd
STRHM/NOR SW16 179 H2
Ferntower Rd HBRY N5 85 K3
Fern Wk STHWK SE1 123 H5
Fernways IL IG1 90 B1
Fernwood Av ALP/SUD HA0 79 J4
STRHM/NOR SW16 161 J6
Fernwood Cl BMLY BR1 184 B5
Fernwood Crs TRDG/WHET N20 33 K5
Ferny Hl EBAR EN4 21 K1
Ferranti Cl WOOL/PLUM SE18 126 C3
Ferraro Cl HEST TW5 115 F6
Ferrers Av WDR/YW UB7 112 A2
WLGTN SM6 210 D2
Ferrers Rd STRHM/NOR SW16 179 J1
Ferrestone Rd CEND/HSY/T N8 67 F1
Ferrey Ms BRXN/ST SW9 142 B3
Ferriby Cl IS N1 85 G5
Ferrier St WAND/EARL SW18 140 A5
Ferring Cl RYLN/HDSTN HA2 60 C5
Ferrings DUL SE21 163 F4
Ferris Av CROY/NA CR0 213 H1
Ferris Rd EDUL SE22 143 H5
Ferron Rd CLPT * E5 86 D1
Ferro Rd RAIN RM13 111 J3
Ferryhills Cl OXHEY WD19 27 G5
Ferry La BARN SW13 118 C6
BTFD TW8 117 F6
RAIN RM13 111 G5
TOTM N17 68 D1
Ferrymead Av GFD/PVL UB6 96 A1
Ferrymead Dr GFD/PVL UB6 96 A2
Ferrymead Gdns GFD/PVL UB6 96 C1
Ferrymoor RCHPK/HAM TW10 156 C5
Ferry Rd BARN SW13 138 D1
E/WMO/HCT KT8 173 F6
TEDD TW11 174 C1
THDIT KT7 190 C3
TWK TW1 156 C3
Ferry Sq BTFD TW8 117 F6
Ferry St POP/IOD E14 125 F5
Festing Rd PUT/ROE SW15 139 G4
Festival Cl BXLY DA5 168 E3
ERITH DA8 150 C1
Fetter La FLST/FETLN EC4A 11 K4
Ffinch St DEPT SE8 144 D1
Fidler Pl BUSH WD23 28 B1
Field Cl BKHH IG9 39 G5
BMLY BR1 184 B5
CHING E4 51 K2
CHSGTN KT9 205 J3
E/WMO/HCT KT8 189 G2
HSLWW TW4 134 A2
HYS/HAR UB3 133 F1
RSLP HA4 58 A5
Fieldcommon La
WOT/HER KT12 188 D5
Field Cottages EFNCH * N2 47 K6
FUL/PGN * SW6 139 J3
Field Ct GINN WC1R 11 H2
Field End RSLP HA4 77 G4
Fieldend TEDD TW11 156 A6
Field End Cl OXHEY WD19 27 J2
Field End Rd PIN HA5 59 F2
RSLP HA4 77 H1
Fieldend Rd STRHM/NOR SW16 179 H4
Fielders Cl EN EN1 24 A5
RYLN/HDSTN HA2 60 C5
Fieldfare Rd THMD SE28 109 J6
Fieldgate St WCHPL E1 104 C4
Fieldhouse Cl SWFD E18 53 F4
Fieldhouse Rd BAL SW12 161 H3
Fielding Av WHTN TW2 155 H5
Fielding Rd CHSWK W4 118 B3
WKENS W14 119 G3
The Fieldings FSTH SE23 163 K3
Fielding St WALW SE17 122 D6
Fielding Ter EA * W5 98 B6
Field La BTFD TW8 136 D1
TEDD TW11 174 B1
Field Md CDALE/KGS NW9 45 G3
Field Pl NWMAL KT3 192 C3
Field Rd EBED/NFELT TW14 154 A1
FSTGT E7 88 E2
HMSMTH W6 119 H6
OXHEY WD19 27 J1
TOTM N17 49 K6
Fieldsend Rd CHEAM SM3 208 C3
Fields Est HACK * E8 86 C5
Fieldside Cl ORP BR6 216 C2
Fieldside Cottages
TRDG/WHET * N20 32 D2
Fields Park Crs CHDH RM6 73 K2
Field St FSBYW WC1X 5 G4
Field Vw FELT TW13 153 G6
Fieldview WAND/EARL SW18 160 C3
Fieldview Cottages
STHGT/OAK * N14 34 D4
Fieldway BCTR RM8 91 H2
STMC/STPC BR5 201 J3
Field Wy CROY/NA CR0 213 K5
GFD/PVL UB6 78 B6
RSLP HA4 58 A5
WLSDN NW10 80 E5
Fieldway Crs HBRY N5 85 G3
Fiennes Cl BCTR RM8 73 J5
Fiesta Dr DAGW RM9 110 E3
Fife Rd CAN/RD E16 106 E4
KUT KT1 175 F5
MORT/ESHN SW14 137 K6
WDGN N22 49 H3
Fife Ter IS N1 5 H2
Fifield Pth FSTH SE23 164 A5
Fifth Av MNPK E12 89 K2
NKENS W10 100 C3
Fifth Cross Rd WHTN TW2 155 J4
Fifth Wy WBLY HA9 80 D2
Figge's Rd MTCM CR4 179 F3
Filby Rd CHSGTN KT9 206 B4
Filey Av STNW/STAM N16 68 C5
Filey Cl BELMT SM2 209 G5
Filey Waye RSLP HA4 58 E6
Fillebrook Av EN EN1 24 A3
Fillebrook Rd WAN E11 70 B5
Filmer Chambers
FUL/PGN * SW6 139 J2
Filmer Rd FUL/PGN SW6 139 J2
Finborough Rd TOOT SW17 178 E3
WBPTN SW10 120 A6
Finchale Rd ABYW SE2 128 C3
Fincham Cl HGDN/ICK UB10 76 A1
Finch Av WNWD SE27 162 E6
Finch Cl BAR EN5 20 E6
Finch Dr EBED/NFELT TW14 154 C2
Finch Gdns CHING E4 51 J1
Finchingfield Av WFD IG8 53 G3
Finch La BANK EC3V 13 F4
Finchley Cl DART DA1 171 K1
Finchley La HDN NW4 64 B1
Finchley Pk NFNCH/WDSP N12 33 G6
Finchley Pl STJWD NW8 2 A2
Finchley Rd GLDGN NW11 64 D2
HAMP NW3 82 E2
STJWD NW8 2 A1
Finchley Vls NFNCH/WDSP * N12 33 H6
Finchley Wy FNCH N3 46 E2
Finch Ms PECK * SE15 143 G2
Finden Rd FSTGT E7 89 F3
Findhorn Av YEAD UB4 95 F4
Findhorn St POP/IOD E14 106 A5
Findon Cl RYLN/HDSTN * HA2 78 B1
WAND/EARL SW18 159 K1
Findon Gdns RAIN RM13 111 J4
Findon Rd ED N9 36 D3
SHB W12 118 D2
Fingal St GNWCH SE10 125 J5
Finglesham Cl STMC/STPC BR5 202 E5
Finland Rd BROCKY SE4 144 B4
Finland St BERM/RHTH SE16 124 B3
Finlays Cl CHSGTN KT9 206 C3
Finlay St FUL/PGN SW6 139 G2
Finnis St BETH E2 104 D2
Finnymore Rd DAGW RM9 92 A5
Finsbury Av LVPST * EC2M 13 F2
Finsbury Circ LVPST EC2M 13 F2
Finsbury Cottages WDGN N22 48 E3
Finsbury Est CLKNW EC1R 5 K5
Finsbury Market SDTCH EC2A 7 G7
Finsbury Park Av FSBYPK N4 67 J3
Finsbury Park Rd FSBYPK N4 67 H6
Finsbury Pavement SDTCH EC2A 13 F1
Finsbury Rd WDGN N22 49 F4
Finsbury Sq SDTCH EC2A 7 F7
Finsbury St STLK EC1Y 12 E1
Finsbury Wy BXLY DA5 169 G1
Finsen Rd HNHL SE24 142 D5
Finstock Rd NKENS W10 100 B5
Finucane Dr STMC/STPC BR5 202 D4
Finucane Gdns RAIN RM13 93 J4
Finucane Ri BUSH WD23 28 C4
Fiona Ct ENC/FH * EN2 23 H4
Firbank Cl CAN/RD E16 107 H4
ENC/FH EN2 23 J5
Firbank Dr OXHEY WD19 27 J2
Firbank Rd CRW RM5 56 D1
PECK SE15 143 J3
Fircroft Gdns HRW HA1 78 E1
Fircroft Rd CHSGTN KT9 206 B2
TOOT SW17 160 E5
Firdene BRYLDS KT5 191 K5
Fir Dene ORP BR6 215 K1
Fire Bell Aly SURB KT6 191 F3
Firebell Ms SURB KT6 191 F3
Firecrest Dr HAMP NW3 83 F1
Firefly Gdns EHAM E6 107 J3
Fir Gv NWMAL KT3 192 C3
Firhill Rd CAT SE6 164 D5
Firmin Rd DART DA1 151 F6
Fir Rd CHEAM SM3 193 J5
FELT TW13 172 C1
The Firs BXLY DA5 170 A3
EA W5 97 K4
EBED/NFELT * TW14 153 H1
EDGE * HA8 31 F6
TRDG/WHET N20 33 H3
Firs Av FBAR/BDGN N11 48 A2
MORT/ESHN SW14 137 K5
MUSWH N10 48 A6
Firsby Av CROY/NA CR0 198 A5
Firsby Rd STNW/STAM N16 68 B5
Firs Cl ESH/CLAY KT10 204 E4
FSTH SE23 164 A2
MTCM CR4 179 G5
Firscroft PLMGR N13 35 J5
Firs Dr HEST TW5 134 A1
Firside Gv BFN/LL DA15 168 A3
Firs La PLMGR N13 35 J5
Firs Park Av WCHMH N21 35 K3
Firs Park Gdns WCHMH N21 35 K3
First Av ACT W3 118 C1
BXLYHN DA7 148 D1
CHDH RM6 73 J2
DAGE RM10 110 D1
E/WMO/HCT KT8 188 E1
EN EN1 24 B6
HDN NW4 64 A1
HOR/WEW KT19 207 G6
HYS/HAR UB3 113 J1
MNPK E12 89 J2
MORT/ESHN SW14 138 B3
MV/WKIL W9 100 D3
PLSTW E13 106 E2
UED N18 36 E6
WALTH E17 69 K2
WBLY HA9 61 K6
WOT/HER KT12 188 A3
First Cl E/WMO/HCT KT8 189 H1
First Cross Rd WHTN TW2 155 K4
First Dr WLSDN NW10 80 E5
First St CHEL SW3 14 D6
Firstway RYNPK SW20 177 F5
First Wy WBLY HA9 80 D2
Firs Wk NTHWD HA6 40 B2
WFD IG8 52 E1
Firswood Av HOR/WEW KT19 207 G3
Firth Gdns FUL/PGN SW6 139 H2
Firtree Av MTCM CR4 179 F5
Fir Tree Av WDR/YW UB7 112 D3
Fir Tree Cl EA W5 98 A5
ESH/CLAY KT10 204 C3
HOR/WEW KT19 207 H2
ORP BR6 217 F3
ROM RM1 57 F6
STRHM/NOR SW16 179 H1
Fir Tree Gdns CROY/NA CR0 213 J2
Fir Tree Gv CAR SM5 209 K5
Fir Tree Pl ASHF * TW15 152 D6

Fir Tree Rd *HSLWW* TW4 134 D5
Fir Trees Cl *BERM/RHTH* SE16 124 B1
Fir Tree Wk *EN* EN1 24 A4
Fir Wk *EW* KT17 208 B4
Fisher Cl *CROY/NA* CR0 197 G5
GFD/PVL UB6 96 A2
Fisherdene *ESH/CLAY* KT10 205 G5
Fisherman Cl
RCHPK/HAM TW10 156 D6
Fishermans Dr
BERM/RHTH SE16 124 A2
Fisher Rd *KTN/HRWW/W* HA3 43 F5
Fishers Ct *NWCR* SE14 144 A2
Fisher's La *CHSWK* W4 118 A4
Fisher St *CAN/RD* E16 106 E4
RSQ WC1B 11 G2
Fisher's Wy *BELV* DA17 129 K1
Fisherton St *STJWD* NW8 2 A7
Fishguard Wy *CAN/RD* E16 127 G1
Fishponds Rd *HAYES* BR2 215 H3
TOOT SW17 160 D6
Fish Street Hl *MON* EC3R 13 F6
Fisons Rd *CAN/RD* E16 125 K1
Fitzalan Rd *ESH/CLAY* KT10 204 E5
FNCH N3 46 C6
Fitzalan St *LBTH* SE11 17 H6
Fitzgeorge Av *NWMAL* KT3 176 A4
Fitz-george Av *WKENS* W14 119 H4
Fitzgerald Av
MORT/ESHN SW14 138 B4
Fitzgerald Rd
MORT/ESHN SW14 138 A4
THDIT KT7 190 B3
WAN E11 70 E2
Fitzhardinge St *MBLAR* W1H 9 G3
Fitzhugh Gv *WAND/EARL* SW18 160 C1
Fitzjames Av *CROY/NA* CR0 197 H6
Fitz-james Av *WKENS* W14 119 H4
Fitzjohn Av *BAR* EN5 20 C6
Fitzjohn's Av *HAMP* NW3 83 H3
Fitzmaurice Pl *MYFR/PICC* W1J 9 K7
Fitzneal St *ACT* W3 99 H5
Fitzroy Cl *HGT* N6 65 K5
Fitzroy Crs *CHSWK* * W4 138 A1
Fitzroy Gdns *NRWD* SE19 181 F3
Fitzroy Ms *GTPST* W1W 4 A7
Fitzroy Pk *HGT* N6 65 K5
Fitzroy Rd *CAMTN* NW1 84 A6
Fitzroy Sq *FITZ* W1T 4 A7
Fitzroy St *CAMTN* NW1 4 A7
FITZ W1T 10 A1
Fitzstephen Rd *BCTR* RM8 91 H3
Fitzwarren Gdns *ARCH* N19 66 C5
Fitzwilliam Av *RCH/KEW* TW9 137 G3
Fitzwilliam Ms *CAN/RD* E16 125 K1
Fitzwilliam Rd *CLAP* SW4 141 H4
Fitz Wygram Cl *HPTN* TW12 173 H1
Five Acre *CDALE/KGS* NW9 45 H5
Fiveacre Cl *THHTH* CR7 196 B3
Five Elms Rd *DAGW* RM9 92 B1
HAYES BR2 215 G1
Five Fields Cl *OXHEY* WD19 27 K4
Five Oaks La *CHIG* IG7 56 A2
Five Ways Jct *HDN* NW4 45 J4
Fiveways Rd *BRXN/ST* SW9 142 B3
Fladbury Rd *SEVS/STOTM* N15 67 K3
Fladgate Rd *WAN* E11 70 C3
Flag Cl *CROY/NA* CR0 198 A5
Flag Wk *PIN* HA5 58 E3
Flambard Rd *HRW* HA1 61 G3
Flamborough Rd *RSLP* HA4 76 E1
Flamborough St *POP/IOD* E14 105 G5
Flamingo Wk *HCH* RM12 93 J5
Flamstead Gdns *DAGW* RM9 91 J5
Flamstead Rd *DAGW* RM9 91 J5
Flamsted Av *WBLY* HA9 80 C4
Flamsteed Rd *CHARL* SE7 126 D5
Flanchford Rd *SHB* W12 118 C3
Flanders Crs *TOOT* SW17 178 E3
Flanders Rd *CHSWK* W4 118 B4
EHAM E6 107 K1
Flanders Wy *HOM* E9 87 F4
Flank St *WCHPL* E1 104 C6
Flask Wk *HAMP* NW3 83 G2
Flavell Ms *GNWCH* SE10 125 H5
Flaxen Cl *CHING* E4 37 K5
Flaxen Rd *CHING* E4 37 K5
Flaxley Rd *MRDN* SM4 194 A3
Flaxman Rd *CMBW* SE5 142 C3
Flaxman Ter *STPAN* WC1H 4 D5
Flaxton Rd *WOOL/PLUM* SE18 147 J2
Flecker Cl *STAN* HA7 43 F1
Fleece Dr *ED* N9 36 C6
Fleece Rd *SURB* KT6 190 D5
Fleece Wk *HOLWY* * N7 84 E4
Fleeming Cl *WALTH* E17 51 H5
Fleeming Rd *WALTH* E17 51 H5
Fleet Cl *E/WMO/HCT* KT8 188 E2
RSLP HA4 58 A3
Fleet Pl *STP* EC4M 12 A3
Fleet Rd *HAMP* NW3 83 J3
Fleetside *E/WMO/HCT* KT8 188 E3
Fleet Sq *FSBYW* WC1X 5 G5
Fleet St *EMB* EC4Y 11 K4
Fleet Street Hl *BETH* * E2 104 C3
Fleet Ter *CAT* * SE6 165 F2
Fleetwood Cl *CAN/RD* E16 107 H4
CHSGTN KT9 205 K5
CROY/NA CR0 212 B1
Fleetwood Rd *NWMAL* KT3 175 J6
WLSDN NW10 81 J3
Fleetwood Sq *NWMAL* KT3 175 J6
Fleetwood St *STNW/STAM* N16 68 A6
Fleetwood Wy *OXHEY* WD19 27 G6
Fleming Cl *MV/WKIL* W9 100 E3
WBPTN * SW10 120 B6
Fleming Ct *CROY/NA* CR0 211 G3
Fleming Md *WIM/MER* SW19 178 D3
Fleming Rd *STHL* UB1 96 B5
WALW SE17 122 C6
Fleming Wk *CDALE/KGS* * NW9 45 G5
Fleming Wy *ISLW* TW7 136 A4
THMD SE28 109 K6
Flemming Av *RSLP* HA4 59 F5
Flempton Rd *WALTH* E17 69 G5
Fletcher Cl *EHAM* E6 108 B6
Fletcher La *LEY* E10 70 A4
Fletcher Rd *CHIG* IG7 55 F1
CHSWK W4 117 K3
Fletchers Cl *HAYES* BR2 200 A1
Fletcher St *WCHPL* E1 104 C6
Fletching Rd *CHARL* SE7 126 C6
CLPT E5 86 E1
Fletton Rd *FBAR/BDGN* N11 48 E3
Fleur De Lis St *WCHPL* E1 7 J7
Flexmere Rd *TOTM* N17 49 K4
Flight Ap *CDALE/KGS* * NW9 45 H4
Flimwell Cl *BMLY* BR1 183 H1
Flint Cl *ORP* BR6 217 F4
Flint Down Cl *STMC/STPC* * BR5 186 B4
Flintmill Crs *BKHTH/KID* SE3 146 D3
Flinton St *WALW* SE17 123 F5
Flint St *WALW* SE17 19 F7
Flitcroft St *LSQ/SEVD* WC2H 10 D4
Flock Mill Pl *WAND/EARL* SW18 160 A3
Flockton St *BERM/RHTH* SE16 123 H2
Flodden Rd *CMBW* SE5 142 D2
Flood La *TWK* * TW1 156 B3
Flood St *CHEL* SW3 120 D5
Flood Wk *CHEL* SW3 120 D6
Flora Cl *POP/IOD* E14 105 K5
Flora Gdns *CHDH* RM6 73 J3
Floral Pl *IS* N1 85 K3
Floral St *COVGDN* WC2E 11 F5
Flora St *BELV* DA17 129 G5
Florence Av *ENC/FH* EN2 23 J4
MRDN SM4 194 B2
Florence Cl *WOT/HER* KT12 188 A4
Florence Ct *WAN* E11 71 F1
Florence Dr *ENC/FH* EN2 23 J4
Florence Gdns *CHSWK* W4 117 K6
Florence Rd *ABYW* SE2 128 D3
BECK BR3 182 A5
BMLY BR1 183 K4
CHSWK W4 118 A3
EA W5 98 A6
EHAM E6 89 G6
FELT TW13 154 A3
FSBYPK N4 67 F4
KUTN/CMB KT2 175 G3
NWCR SE14 144 C2
NWDGN UB2 114 C4
PLSTW E13 106 E1
SAND/SEL CR2 211 K6
WIM/MER SW19 178 A2
WOT/HER KT12 188 A4
Florence St *CAN/RD* E16 106 D3
HDN NW4 64 A1
IS N1 85 H5
Florence Ter *NWCR* SE14 144 C2
Florence Vls *HGT* * N6 66 B4
Florence Wy *BAL* SW12 160 E3
Florfield Rd *HACK* E8 86 D4
Florian Av *SUT* SM1 209 H2
Florian Rd *PUT/ROE* SW15 139 H5
Florida Cl *BUSH* WD23 28 D4
Florida Rd *THHTH* CR7 180 C4
Florida St *BETH* E2 104 C2
Florin Ct *UED* N18 36 A6
Floriston Av *HGDN/ICK* UB10 76 A5
Floriston Cl *STAN* HA7 43 H4
Floriston Gdns *STAN* HA7 43 H4
Floss St *PUT/ROE* SW15 139 F3
Flower & Dean Wk *WCHPL* E1 13 K2
Flower La *MLHL* NW7 45 H1
Flowers Cl *CRICK* NW2 81 J1
Flowers Ms *ARCH* N19 66 C6
Floyd Rd *CHARL* SE7 126 B5
Fludyer St *LEW* SE13 145 H5
Foley Ms *ESH/CLAY* KT10 204 E4
Foley Rd *ESH/CLAY* KT10 204 E5
Foley St *GTPST* W1W 10 A2
Folgate St *WCHPL* E1 13 H1
Foliot St *ACT* W3 99 H5
Folkestone Rd *EHAM* E6 108 A1
UED N18 36 C6
WALTH E17 69 K1
Folkingham La *CDALE/KGS* NW9 45 F4
Folkington Cnr
NFNCH/WDSP N12 46 D1
Follett St *POP/IOD* E14 106 A5
Folly La *WALTH* E17 51 G4
Folly Wall *POP/IOD* E14 125 F2
Fontaine Rd *STRHM/NOR* SW16 180 A2
Fontarabia Rd *BTSEA* SW11 141 F5
Fontayne Av *RAIN* RM13 93 G5
ROM RM1 57 G5
Fontenoy Rd *BAL* SW12 161 G4
Fonteyne Gdns *WFD* IG8 53 H5
Fonthill Ms *FSBYPK* N4 67 F6
Fonthill Rd *FSBYPK* N4 67 F6
Font Hills *EFNCH* N2 47 G5
Fontley Wy *PUT/ROE* SW15 158 D2
Fontwell Cl *KTN/HRWW/W* HA3 42 E3
NTHLT UB5 78 A4
Fontwell Dr *HAYES* BR2 201 F2
Football La *HRW* HA1 61 F5
Footbury Hill Rd *ORP* BR6 202 B4
The Footpath *PUT/ROE* * SW15 138 D6
Foots Cray High St *SCUP* DA14 186 D2
Foots Cray La *BXLY* DA5 168 D3
Footscray Rd *ELTH/MOT* SE9 167 F1
Forbes Cl *CRICK* NW2 81 J1
EMPK RM11 75 K5
Forbes St *WCHPL* E1 104 C5
Forbes Wy *RSLP* HA4 59 F6
Forburg Rd *STNW/STAM* N16 68 C5
Ford Cl *HRW* HA1 60 D4
RAIN RM13 93 H5
THHTH CR7 196 C3
Fordcroft Rd *STMC/STPC* BR5 202 C2
Forde Av *BMLY* BR1 184 B6
Fordel Rd *CAT* SE6 165 G3
Ford End *WFD* IG8 53 F2
Fordham Rd *EBAR* EN4 21 H4
Fordham St *WCHPL* E1 104 C5
Fordhook Av *EA* W5 98 B6
Fordingley Rd *MV/WKIL* W9 100 D2
Fordington Rd *HGT* N6 65 K1
Ford La *RAIN* RM13 93 H5
Fordmill Rd *CAT* SE6 164 D4
Ford Rd *ASHF* TW15 152 C6
BOW E3 105 G1
DAGE RM10 92 C5
Ford's Gv *WCHMH* N21 35 J3
Fords Park Rd *CAN/RD* E16 106 E5
Ford Sq *WCHPL* E1 104 D4
Ford St *BOW* E3 87 G6
CAN/RD E16 106 D5
Fordwich Cl *ORP* BR6 202 A4
Fordwych Rd *CRICK* NW2 82 C3
Fordyce Rd *LEW* SE13 165 F1
Fordyke Rd *BCTR* RM8 74 A6
Foreland Ct *HDN* NW4 46 C4
Foreland St *WOOL/PLUM* SE18 127 J4
Foremark Cl *BARK/HLT* IG6 55 F2
Foreshore *DEPT* SE8 124 C4
The Forest *WALTH* E17 70 C1
Forest Ap *CHING* E4 38 C2
WFD IG8 52 E3
Forest Av *CHIC* IG7 54 A1
CHING E4 38 C2
Forest Cl *CHST* BR7 185 F4
WAN E11 70 D2
WFD IG8 39 F6
Forest Ct *CHING* E4 38 D3
WAN E11 70 C1
Forestdale *STHGT/OAK* N14 34 D6
Forest Dr *HAYES* BR2 215 J2
MNPK E12 89 H1
WFD IG8 52 B3
Forest Dr East *WAN* E11 70 B4
Forest Dr West *WAN* E11 70 A4
Forest Edge *BKHH* IG9 39 G5
Forester Rd *PECK* SE15 143 J5
Foresters Cl *WLGTN* SM6 210 D5
Foresters Crs *BXLYHN* DA7 149 J5
Foresters Dr *WALTH* E17 70 B1
WLGTN SM6 210 D5
Forest Gdns *TOTM* N17 50 B5
Forest Ga *CDALE/KGS* NW9 63 G1
Forest Gld *CHING* E4 52 C1
WAN E11 70 C3
Forest Gv *HACK* E8 86 B5
Forest Hill Rd *EDUL* SE22 163 J1
Forestholme Cl *FSTH* * SE23 163 K4
Forest La *CHIG* IG7 54 A1
FSTGT E7 88 E3
Forest Mount Rd *WFD* IG8 52 B3
Fore St *BARB* EC2Y 12 E2
ED N9 36 C6
PIN HA5 58 D1
Forest Rdg *BECK* BR3 182 D6
HAYES BR2 215 J2
Forest Ri *WALTH* E17 52 B6
Forest Rd *BARK/HLT* IG6 54 E4
CHEAM SM3 193 K5
ED N9 36 D3
ERITH DA8 150 D2
FELT TW13 154 B5
FSTGT E7 88 E2
HACK E8 86 B4
RCH/KEW TW9 137 H1
ROMW/RG RM7 56 D6
WALTH E17 52 A6
WALTH E17 68 E1
WAN E11 70 B4
WFD IG8 38 E5
Forest Side *CHING* E4 38 D2
FSTGT E7 89 F2
WPK KT4 192 C5
Forest St *FSTGT* E7 88 E3
Forest Vw *CHING* E4 38 B2
WAN E11 70 D4
Forest View Av *WAN* E11 70 B2
Forest View Rd *MNPK* E12 89 J2
WALTH E17 52 A4
Forest Wy *BFN/LL* DA15 167 J2
STMC/STPC BR5 202 B2
WFD IG8 39 F6
Forfar Rd *BTSEA* SW11 141 F2
WDGN N22 49 H4
Forge Cl *HAYES* BR2 199 K5
Forge Cottages *EA* * W5 116 E1
Forge Dr *ESH/CLAY* KT10 205 G5
Forge La *BELMT* SM2 208 C5
FELT TW13 172 D1
NTHWD HA6 40 C3
Forge Ms *CROY/NA* CR0 213 J3
Forge Pl *CAMTN* NW1 84 A4
Forman Pl *STNW/STAM* N16 86 B2
Formby Av *KTN/HRWW/W* HA3 43 J6
Formosa St *MV/WKIL* W9 101 F3
Formunt Cl *CAN/RD* E16 106 D4
Forres Gdns *GLDGN* NW11 64 E3
Forrester Pth *SYD* SE26 163 K6
Forrest Gdns
STRHM/NOR SW16 180 A6
Forris Av *HYS/HAR* UB3 113 J1
Forset St *MBLAR* W1H 8 D3
Forstal Cl *HAYES* BR2 183 K6
Forster Cl *CHING* E4 52 B3
Forster Rd *BECK* BR3 182 B6
BRXS/STRHM SW2 161 K2
TOTM N17 50 B6
WALTH E17 69 G3
Forsters Cl *CHDH* RM6 74 B3
Forston St *IS* N1 6 D2
Forsyte Crs *NRWD* SE19 181 F4
Forsyth Gdns *WALW* SE17 122 C6
Forsythia Cl *IL* IG1 90 B3
Forsyth Pl *EN* EN1 24 A6
Forterie Gdns *GDMY/SEVK* IG3 91 G1
Fortescue Av *WHTN* TW2 155 H5
Fortescue Rd *EDGE* HA8 45 F4
WIM/MER SW19 178 C3
Fortess Gv *KTTN* NW5 84 C3
Fortess Rd *KTTN* NW5 84 B3
Fortess Wk *KTTN* NW5 84 B3
Forthbridge Rd *BTSEA* SW11 141 F5
Fortis Cl *CAN/RD* E16 107 G5
Fortis Gn *EFNCH* N2 47 K6
Fortis Green Av *EFNCH* N2 48 A6
Fortis Green Rd *MUSWH* N10 48 A6
Fortismere Av *MUSWH* N10 48 A6
Fortnam Rd *ARCH* N19 66 D6
Fortnums Acre *STAN* HA7 43 F2
Fort Rd *NTHLT* UB5 78 A5
STHWK SE1 19 K7
Fortrose Gdns
BRXS/STRHM SW2 161 K3
Fort St *CAN/RD* E16 126 A1
WCHPL * E1 13 H2
Fortuna Cl *HOLWY* * N7 85 F4
Fortunegate Rd *WLSDN* NW10 81 G6
Fortune Green Rd
KIL/WHAMP NW6 82 E3
Fortune La *BORE* WD6 29 K1
Fortunes Md *NTHLT* UB5 77 J4
Fortune St *STLK* EC1Y 6 D7
Fortune Wy *WLSDN* NW10 99 J2
Forty Acre La *CAN/RD* E16 106 E4
Forty Av *WBLY* HA9 80 B1
Forty Cl *WBLY* HA9 80 B1
Forty La *WBLY* HA9 62 E6
The Forum *E/WMO/HCT* KT8 189 G1
Forum Magnum Sq *STHWK* SE1 17 G2
Forumside *EDGE* HA8 44 C2
Forum Wy *EDGE* HA8 44 C2
Forval Cl *MTCM* CR4 194 E2
Forward Dr *KTN/HRWW/W* HA3 61 F1
Fosbury Ms *BAY/PAD* * W2 101 F6
Foscote Ms *MV/WKIL* W9 100 E3
Foscote Rd *HDN* NW4 63 K3
Foskett Rd *FUL/PGN* SW6 139 J3
Foss Av *CROY/NA* CR0 211 G3
Fossdene Rd *CHARL* SE7 126 A5
Fossdyke Cl *YEAD* UB4 95 J4
Fosse Wy *WEA* W13 97 G4
Fossil Rd *LEW* SE13 144 D4
Fossington Rd *BELV* DA17 128 E4
Foss Rd *TOOT* SW17 160 C6
Fossway *BCTR* RM8 73 J6
Foster La *CITYW* EC2V 12 C3
Foster Rd *ACT* W3 99 G6
CHSWK W4 118 A5
PLSTW E13 106 E3
Fosters Cl *CHST* BR7 184 E1
SWFD E18 53 F4
Foster St *HDN* NW4 64 A1
Foster Wk *HDN* NW4 64 A1
Fothergill Cl *PLSTW* E13 88 E6
Fothergill Dr *WCHMH* N21 22 E6
Fotheringham Rd *EN* EN1 24 B5
Foubert's Pl *SOHO/CST* W1F 10 A4
Foulden Rd *STNW/STAM* N16 86 B2
Foulden Ter *STNW/STAM* N16 86 B2
Foulis Ter *SKENS* SW7 14 A7
Foulser Rd *TOOT* SW17 160 E5
Foulsham Rd *THHTH* CR7 180 D6
Founders Gdns *NRWD* SE19 180 D3
Foundry Cl *BERM/RHTH* SE16 124 B1
Foundry Ms *CAMTN* NW1 4 B6
Foundry Pl *WAND/EARL* * SW18 160 A2
Fountain Cl *UX/CGN* UB8 94 A4
Fountain Dr *CAR* SM5 209 K6
NRWD SE19 163 G6
Fountain Green Sq *STHWK* SE4 123 H2
Fountain Ms *HAMP* * NW3 83 K4
Fountain Pl *BRXN/ST* SW9 142 B2
Fountain Rd *THHTH* CR7 180 D5
TOOT SW17 178 C1
Fountains Av *FELT* TW13 154 E5
Fountains Cl *FELT* TW13 154 E4
Fountains Crs *STHGT/OAK* N14 34 E2
Fountayne Rd *SEVS/STOTM* N15 68 C1
STNW/STAM N16 68 C6
Fount St *VX/NE* SW8 141 J1
Fouracres *PEND* EN3 25 G2
Fourland Wk *EDGE* HA8 44 E2
Fournier St *WCHPL* E1 13 K1
Four Seasons Cl *BOW* E3 105 J1
Four Seasons Crs *CHEAM* SM3 193 J6
Fourth Av *HYS/HAR* UB3 113 J1
MNPK E12 89 K2
NKENS W10 100 C3
ROMW/RG RM7 74 E5
Fourth Cross Rd *WHTN* TW2 155 J4
Fourth Wy *WBLY* HA9 80 E2
The Four Tubs *BUSH* WD23 28 D2
The Four Wents *CHING* E4 38 B4
Fowey Av *REDBR* IG4 71 H2
Fowey Cl *WAP* E1W 123 J1
Fowler Cl *BTSEA* SW11 140 C4
SCUP DA14 187 F1
Fowler Rd *BARK/HLT* IG6 55 J1
FSTGT E7 88 E2
IS N1 85 H6
Fowler's Wk *EA* W5 97 K3
Fownes St *BTSEA* SW11 140 D4
Fox And Knot St *FARR* * EC1M 12 B1
Foxberry Rd *BROCKY* SE4 144 B5
Foxborough Gdns *BROCKY* SE4 164 D1
Foxbourne Rd *TOOT* SW17 161 F4
Fox Burrow Rd *CHIG* IG7 55 J1
Foxbury Av *CHST* BR7 185 J2
Foxbury Cl *BMLY* BR1 184 A2
ORP BR6 217 G3
Foxbury Dr *ORP* BR6 217 G4
Foxbury Rd *BMLY* BR1 184 A2
Fox Cl *BORE* WD6 29 K1
CAN/RD E16 106 E4
CRW RM5 56 D1
ORP BR6 217 G3
WCHPL E1 104 E3
Foxcroft Rd *WOOL/PLUM* SE18 147 G2
Foxdell *NTHWD* HA6 40 B2
Foxearth Sp *SAND/SEL* CR2 212 E6
Foxes Dl *BKHTH/KID* SE3 145 K4
HAYES BR2 183 G6
Foxfield Cl *NTHWD* HA6 40 D2
Foxfield Rd *ORP* BR6 201 J6
Foxglove Cl *STHL* UB1 95 J6
STWL/WRAY TW19 152 A3
Foxglove Dr *WAN* E11 71 G1
Foxglove La *CHSGTN* KT9 206 C2
Foxglove Rd *ROMW/RG* RM7 75 G6
Foxglove St *ACT* W3 99 H6
Foxglove Wy *MTCM* CR4 195 F4
Foxgrove *STHGT/OAK* N14 34 E5
Fox Gv *WOT/HER* KT12 188 A4
Foxgrove Av *BECK* BR3 182 E3
Foxgrove Pth *OXHEY* WD19 41 H1
Foxgrove Rd *BECK* BR3 182 E3
Foxham Rd *ARCH* N19 84 D1
Fox Hl *NRWD* SE19 181 G3
Fox Hill Gdns *NRWD* SE19 181 G3
Foxhole Rd *ELTH/MOT* SE9 146 D6
Fox Hollow Cl
WOOL/PLUM SE18 127 K5
Fox Hollow Dr *BXLYHN* DA7 148 E4
Foxholt Gdns *WLSDN* NW10 80 E5
Foxhome Cl *CHST* BR7 185 F2
Fox House Rd *BELV* DA17 129 J4
Foxlands Crs *DAGE* RM10 92 E3
Foxlands Rd *DAGE* RM10 92 E3
Fox La *EA* W5 98 A4
HAYES BR2 215 F3
PLMGR N13 35 F4
Foxlees *ALP/SUD* HA0 79 G2
Foxley Cl *HACK* E8 86 C3
Foxley Rd *CMBW* SE5 142 B1
THHTH CR7 196 C1
Foxleys *OXHEY* WD19 27 J5
Foxley Sq *BRXN/ST* * SW9 142 C1
Foxmead Cl *ENC/FH* EN2 23 F4
Foxmore St *BTSEA* SW11 140 E2
Fox Rd *CAN/RD* E16 106 D4
Foxton Gv *MTCM* CR4 178 C5
Foxwarren *ESH/CLAY* KT10 205 F6
Foxwell St *BROCKY* SE4 144 B4
Foxwood Cl *FELT* TW13 154 A5
MLHL NW7 31 G6
Foxwood Green Cl *EN* EN1 36 A1
Foxwood Rd *BKHTH/KID* SE3 145 J5
Foyle Rd *BKHTH/KID* SE3 125 J6
TOTM N17 50 C4
Framfield Cl *NFNCH/WDSP* N12 32 E6
Framfield Rd *HBRY* N5 85 H3
HNWL W7 97 F5
MTCM CR4 179 F3
Framlingham Crs
ELTH/MOT SE9 166 D6
Frampton Cl *BELMT* SM2 208 E5
Frampton Park Rd *HOM* E9 86 E4
Frampton Rd *HSLWW* TW4 134 D6
Frampton St *STJWD* NW8 2 B7
Francemary Rd *LEW* SE13 144 D6
Frances Rd *CHING* E4 51 J2
Frances St *WOOL/PLUM* SE18 126 E4
Franche Court Rd *TOOT* SW17 160 B5
Francis Av *BXLYHN* DA7 149 H3
FELT TW13 153 K5
IL IG1 72 D6
Francis Barber Cl
STRHM/NOR * SW16 162 A6
Franciscan Rd *TOOT* SW17 161 F6
Francis Chichester Wy
BTSEA * SW11 141 F2
Francis Cl *HOR/WEW* KT19 207 F2
Francis Gv *WIM/MER* SW19 177 J2
Francis Ms *LEE/GVPK* * SE12 165 J1
Francis Rd *CROY/NA* CR0 196 C4
DART DA1 151 G6
EFNCH * N2 65 K1
GFD/PVL UB6 97 J1
HRW HA1 61 G2
HSLWW TW4 134 C3
LEY E10 70 A6
PIN HA5 59 G2
STMC/STPC BR5 186 E6
WLGTN SM6 210 C4
Francis St *SRTFD* E15 88 C3
WEST SW1P 16 B6
Francis Ter *ARCH* N19 84 C1
Francis Wk *IS* N1 85 F6
Francklyn Gdns *EDGE* HA8 30 C5
Francombe Gdns *ROM* RM1 75 J3
Franconia Rd *CLAP* SW4 141 H6
Frank Burton Cl *CHARL* SE7 126 A5
Frank Dixon Cl *DUL* SE21 163 F2
Frank Dixon Wy *DUL* SE21 163 F3
Frankfurt Rd *HNHL* SE24 142 D6
Frankham St *DEPT* SE8 144 D1
Frankland Cl *BERM/RHTH* SE16 123 J3
WFD IG8 53 G1
Frankland Rd *CHING* E4 51 J1
SKENS SW7 14 A5
Franklin Cl *KUT* KT1 175 H6
LEW SE13 144 E2
TRDG/WHET N20 33 G2
WNWD SE27 162 C5
Franklin Crs *MTCM* CR4 195 H1
Franklin Rd *BXLYHN* DA7 149 F2
PGE/AN SE20 181 K3
Franklins Ms *RYLN/HDSTN* HA2 60 C6
Franklin Sq *WKENS* W14 119 J5
Franklins Rw *CHEL* * SW3 120 E5
CHEL SW3 120 E5
Franklin St *BOW* E3 105 K2
SEVS/STOTM N15 68 A3
Franklin Wy *CROY/NA* CR0 195 K5
Franklyn Gdns *BARK/HLT* IG6 54 D2
Franklyn Rd *WLSDN* NW10 81 H5
WOT/HER KT12 188 A3
Franks Av *NWMAL* KT3 191 K1
Franks Wood Av
STMC/STPC BR5 201 G2
Franlaw Crs *PLMGR* N13 35 J6
Franmil Rd *EMPK* RM11 75 H4
Fransfield Gv *SYD* SE26 163 J5
Franshams *BUSH* * WD23 28 E4
Frant Cl *PGE/AN* SE20 181 K3
Franthorne Wy *CAT* SE6 164 E4
Frant Rd *THHTH* CR7 196 C2
Fraser Cl *BXLY* DA5 169 K3
Fraser Rd *ED* N9 36 D5
ERITH DA8 129 K5
GFD/PVL UB6 79 J6
WALTH E17 69 K2
Fraser St *CHSWK* W4 118 B5
Frating Crs *WFD* IG8 52 E2
Frays Av *WDR/YW* UB7 112 A2
Frays Cl *WDR/YW* UB7 112 A3
Frazer Av *RSLP* HA4 77 G3
Frazer Cl *ROMW/RG* RM7 75 H4
Frazier St *STHWK* SE1 17 J3
Frean St *BERM/RHTH* SE16 123 H3
Freda Corbett Cl *PECK* SE15 143 H1
Frederica Rd *CHING* E4 38 B2
Frederica St *HOLWY* N7 85 F5
Frederick Cl *BAY/PAD* W2 8 D5
SUT SM1 208 D2
Frederick Crs *BRXN/ST* SW9 142 C1
PEND EN3 24 E3
Frederick Gdns *CROY/NA* CR0 196 C3
SUT SM1 208 D3
Frederick Pl *WOOL/PLUM* SE18 127 G5
Frederick Rd *RAIN* RM13 111 F1
SUT SM1 208 D3
WALW SE17 122 C6
Frederick's Pl *LOTH* * EC2R 12 E4
NFNCH/WDSP N12 33 G6
Frederick Sq *POP/IOD* E14 105 G6
Frederick's Rw *FSBYE* EC1V 6 A4
Frederick St *FSBYW* WC1X 5 G5
Frederick Ter *HACK* * E8 86 B5
Frederic Ms *KTBR* * SW1X 15 G3
Frederic St *WALTH* E17 69 G2
Fredora Av *YEAD* UB4 94 D3
Freeborne Gdns *RAIN* RM13 93 J4
Freedom Cl *WALTH* E17 69 F1
Freedom St *BTSEA* SW11 140 E3
Freegrove Rd *HOLWY* N7 84 E3
Freeland Pk *HDN* NW4 46 C5
Freeland Rd *EA* W5 98 B6
Freelands Av *SAND/SEL* CR2 213 F6
Freelands Gv *BMLY* BR1 184 A4
Freelands Rd *BMLY* BR1 184 A4
Freeland Wy *ERITH* DA8 150 D2
Freeling St *IS* N1 85 F5
Freeman Cl *NTHLT* UB5 77 J5
Freeman Dr *E/WMO/HCT* KT8 188 E1
Freeman Rd *MRDN* SM4 194 C2
Freemans La *HYS/HAR* UB3 94 C6
Freemantle Av *PEND* EN3 25 F6
Freemantle St *WALW* SE17 123 F5
Freemasons Rd *CAN/RD* E16 107 F5
CROY/NA CR0 197 F5
Freesia Cl *ORP* BR6 217 F3
Freethorpe Cl *NRWD* SE19 181 F4
Freightmaster Est *RAIN* * RM13 130 D4
Freke Rd *BTSEA* SW11 141 F4
Fremantle Rd *BARK/HLT* IG6 54 B5
BELV DA17 129 H4
Fremont St *HOM* E9 86 E6
French Pl *SDTCH* EC2A 7 H5
French St *SUN* TW16 172 B5
Frendsbury Rd *BROCKY* SE4 144 B5
Frensham Cl *STHL* UB1 95 K3
Frensham Dr *CROY/NA* CR0 214 A5
PUT/ROE SW15 158 D5
Frensham Rd *BFN/LL* DA15 167 J4
Frensham St *PECK* SE15 123 H6
Frere St *BTSEA* SW11 140 D3

Freshfield Av HACK E8 86 B5
Freshfield Cl LEW SE13 145 G5
Freshfield Dr STHGT/OAK N14 34 B2
Freshfields CROY/NA CR0 198 C4
Freshford St TOOT SW17 160 B5
Freshwater Cl TOOT SW17 179 F2
Freshwater Rd BCTR RM8 73 K5
TOOT SW17 179 F2
Freshwell Av CHDH RM6 73 J1
Fresh Wharf Rd BARK IG11 90 B6
Freshwood Cl BECK BR3 182 E4
Freshwood Wy WLGTN SM6 210 C6
Freston Gdns EBAR EN4 22 A6
Freston Pk FNCH N3 46 D5
Freston Rd NKENS W10 100 B6
Freta Rd BXLYHS DA6 149 G6
Frewin Rd WAND/EARL SW18 160 C3
Friar Ms WNWD SE27 162 C5
Friar Rd STMC/STPC BR5 202 B2
YEAD UB4 95 H3
Friars Av PUT/ROE SW15 158 C5
TRDG/WHET N20 33 J5
Friars Cl CHING E4 38 A5
NTHLT UB5 95 G2
STHWK * SE1 12 B7
Friars Gdns ACT W3 99 F5
Friars Gate Cl WFD IG8 38 E6
Friars La RCH/KEW TW9 136 E6
Friars Md POP/IOD E14 125 F3
Friars Ms ELTH/MOT SE9 147 F6
Friars Place La ACT W3 99 F6
Friar's Rd EHAM E6 89 H6
Friars Stile Rd
RCHPK/HAM TW10 157 F1
Friars Wk ABYW SE2 128 E5
STHGT/OAK N14 34 B3
Friars Wy ACT W3 99 F5
Friars Wd CROY/NA * CR0 213 G6
Friarswood CROY/NA CR0 213 G6
Friary Cl NFNCH/WDSP N12 47 J1
Friary Est PECK * SE15 143 H1
Friary La WFD IG8 38 E6
Friary Pk TRDG/WHET * N20 33 J6
Friary Park Ct ACT * W3 98 E5
Friary Rd ACT W3 98 E5
NFNCH/WDSP N12 33 H6
PECK SE15 143 H1
Friary Wy NFNCH/WDSP N12 33 J6
Friday Hl CHING E4 38 C5
Friday Hl East CHING E4 38 C5
Friday Hl West CHING E4 38 C4
Friday Rd ERITH DA8 130 A5
MTCM CR4 178 E3
Friday St BLKFR EC4V 12 C5
Frideswide Pl KTTN NW5 84 C3
Friendly Pl GNWCH SE10 144 E2
Friendly St DEPT SE8 144 D2
Friendly Street Ms DEPT SE8 144 D3
Friends' Rd CROY/NA CR0 211 K1
Friend St FSBYE EC1V 6 A4
Friern Barnet La
FBAR/BDGN N11 47 K1
TRDG/WHET N20 33 H5
Friern Barnet Rd
FBAR/BDGN N11 48 A1
Friern Mount Dr
TRDG/WHET N20 33 G2
Friern Pk NFNCH/WDSP N12 47 H1
Friern Rd EDUL SE22 163 H1
Friern Watch Av
NFNCH/WDSP N12 33 H6
Frigate Ms DEPT SE8 124 D6
Frimley Av WLGTN SM6 210 E3
Frimley Cl CROY/NA CR0 214 A5
WIM/MER SW19 159 H4
Frimley Ct SCUP DA14 186 D1
Frimley Crs CROY/NA CR0 214 A5
Frimley Gdns MTCM CR4 178 D6
Frimley Rd CHSGTN KT9 205 K3
GDMY/SEVK IG3 90 E1
Frimley Wy WCHPL * E1 105 F3
Frinstead Gv STMC/STPC BR5 202 E1
Frinsted Rd ERITH DA8 150 A1
Frinton Cl OXHEY WD19 27 F4
Frinton Dr WFD IG8 52 B3
Frinton Ms IL IG1 72 A3
Frinton Rd CRW RM5 56 C3
EHAM E6 107 H2
SCUP DA14 169 F4
SEVS/STOTM N15 68 A3
TOOT SW17 179 F2
Friston St FUL/PGN SW6 140 A3
Friswell Pl BXLYHN DA7 149 H5
Fritham Cl NWMAL KT3 192 B3
Frith Ct MLHL NW7 46 C3
Frith La MLHL NW7 46 C2
Frith Manor Farm Cottages
NFNCH/WDSP * N12 46 C1
Frith Rd CROY/NA CR0 196 D6
WAN E11 88 A2
Frith St SOHO/SHAV W1D 10 C4
Frithville Gdns SHB W12 119 F1
Frithwood Av NTHWD HA6 40 D2
Frizlands La DAGE RM10 92 D1
Frobisher Cl BUSH WD23 28 A1
PIN HA5 59 H4
Frobisher Crs BARB * EC2Y 12 D1
STWL/WRAY TW19 152 B2
Frobisher Gdns LEY * E10 69 K3
Frobisher Rd CEND/HSY/T N8 67 G1
EHAM E6 107 K5
ERITH DA8 150 D1
Frog La DAGW RM9 111 F4
Frogley Rd EDUL SE22 143 G5
Frogmore WAND/EARL SW18 139 K6
Frogmore Av YEAD UB4 94 C3
Frogmore Cl CHEAM SM3 208 B1
Frogmore Est HBRY * N5 85 J2
Frogmore Gdns CHEAM SM3 208 C2
YEAD UB4 94 C3
Frognal HAMP NW3 83 G2
Frognal Av HRW HA1 61 F1
SCUP DA14 186 B2
Frognal Cl HAMP NW3 83 G3
Frognal Gdns HAMP NW3 83 G2
Frognal La HAMP NW3 83 F3
Frognal Man HAMP * NW3 83 G2
Frognal Pde HAMP NW3 83 G4
Frognal Pl SCUP DA14 186 B2
Frognal Ri HAMP NW3 83 G1
Frognal Wy HAMP NW3 83 G2
Froissart Rd ELTH/MOT SE9 146 D6
Frome Rd SEVS/STOTM N15 49 H6
Frome St IS N1 6 C2
Fromondes Rd CHEAM SM3 208 C3
Fromows Cnr CHSWK * W4 117 K5
Frostic Wk WCHPL E1 13 K2
Froude St VX/NE SW8 141 G3
Fruen Rd EBED/NFELT TW14 153 J2
Fryatt Rd TOTM N17 49 K3
Fry Cl CRW RM5 56 C1
Fryent Cl KTN/HRWW/W HA3 62 C3
Fryent Crs CDALE/KGS NW9 63 G3
Fryent Flds CDALE/KGS NW9 63 G3
Fryent Gv CDALE/KGS NW9 63 G3
Fryent Wy CDALE/KGS NW9 62 C3
Frying Pan Aly WCHPL E1 13 H2
Fry Rd EHAM E6 89 H5
WLSDN NW10 81 H6
Fryston Av CROY/NA CR0 197 H6
Fuchsia St ABYW SE2 128 C5
Fulbeck Dr CDALE/KGS NW9 45 G4
Fulbeck Wy RYLN/HDSTN HA2 42 C5
Fulbourne Rd WALTH E17 52 A5
Fulbourne St WCHPL E1 104 D4
Fulbrook Rd ARCH N19 84 C2
Fulford Gv OXHEY WD19 27 F4
Fulford Rd HOR/WEW KT19 207 F5
Fulford St BERM/RHTH SE16 123 J2
Fulham Broadway
FUL/PGN SW6 139 K1
Fulham Cl HGDN/ICK UB10 94 A3
Fulham Est FUL/PGN SW6 119 K6
Fulham High St FUL/PGN SW6 139 H4
Fulham Palace Rd
FUL/PGN SW6 139 G1
Fulham Park Gdns
FUL/PGN SW6 139 J3
Fulham Park Rd FUL/PGN SW6 139 J3
Fulham Rd FUL/PGN SW6 139 H3
WBPTN SW10 120 C5
Fullbrooks Av WPK KT4 192 C5
Fuller Cl BETH * E2 104 C3
ORP BR6 217 F3
Fuller Rd BCTR RM8 91 J1
Fullers Av SURB KT6 191 G6
WFD IG8 52 D3
Fullers Cl CRW RM5 56 E3
Fuller's Rd SWFD E18 52 D4
Fuller St HDN NW4 64 A1
Fullers Wy North SURB KT6 206 B1
Fullers Wy South CHSGTN KT9 206 A2
Fuller's Wd CROY/NA CR0 213 J3
Fullerton Rd CAR SM5 209 J6
CROY/NA CR0 197 G4
WAND/EARL SW18 140 B6
Fuller Wy HYS/HAR UB3 113 J5
Fullwell Av CLAY IG5 54 A4
Fullwood's Ms IS * N1 7 F4
Fulmar Ct BRYLDS KT5 191 G3
Fulmar Rd HCH RM12 93 J5
Fulmead St FUL/PGN SW6 140 A2
Fulmer Cl HPTN TW12 172 D1
Fulmer Rd CAN/RD E16 107 H4
Fulmer Wy WEA W13 116 C3
Fulready Rd LEY E10 70 B2
Fulstone Cl HSLWW TW4 134 E5
Fulthorp Rd BKHTH/KID SE3 145 K3
Fulton Ms BAY/PAD * W2 101 G6
Fulton Rd WBLY HA9 80 C1
Fulwell Park Av WHTN TW2 155 H4
Fulwell Rd HPTN TW12 155 J6
Fulwich Rd DART DA1 171 J1
Fulwood Av ALP/SUD HA0 98 B1
Fulwood Gdns TWK TW1 156 A1
Fulwood Pl GINN WC1R 11 H2
Fulwood Wk WIM/MER SW19 159 H3
Furber St HMSMTH W6 118 E3
Furham Fld PIN HA5 42 A3
Furley Rd PECK SE15 143 H1
Furlong Cl WLGTN SM6 195 G5
Furlong Rd HOLWY N7 85 G4
Furmage St WAND/EARL SW18 160 A2
Furneaux Av WNWD SE27 180 C1
Furner Cl DART DA1 150 C4
Furness Rd FUL/PGN SW6 140 A3
MRDN SM4 194 A3
RYLN/HDSTN HA2 60 B4
WLSDN NW10 99 J1
Furness Wy HCH RM12 93 J3
Furnival St FLST/FETLN EC4A 11 J3
Furrow La HOM E9 86 E3
The Furrows WOT/HER KT12 188 B6
Fursby Av FNCH N3 46 E2
Further Acre CDALE/KGS NW9 45 H5
Furtherfield Cl CROY/NA CR0 196 B3
Further Green Rd CAT SE6 165 H2
Furze Cl OXHEY WD19 41 G1
Furzedown Dr TOOT SW17 179 G1
Furzedown Rd TOOT SW17 179 G1
Furze Farm Cl CHDH RM6 56 A5
Furzefield Cl CHST BR7 185 G2
Furzefield Rd BKHTH/KID SE3 126 A6
Furzeground Wy STKPK UB11 113 F1
Furzeham Rd WDR/YW UB7 112 B2
Furzehill Sq STMC/STPC BR5 202 C1
Furze Rd THHTH CR7 180 D6
Furze St BOW * E3 105 J4
Fye Foot La BLKFR * EC4V 12 C5
Fyfe Wy BMLY BR1 183 K5
Fyfield Cl BECK BR3 199 G1
Fyfield Rd BRXN/ST SW9 142 B4
EN EN1 24 A4
RAIN RM13 93 H6
WALTH E17 52 B6
WFD IG8 53 G3
Fynes St WEST SW1P 16 C6

G

Gable Cl DART DA1 150 D6
PIN HA5 42 A3
Gable Ct SYD SE26 163 J6
The Gables NRWD * SE19 181 F4
WBLY HA9 80 B1
Gables Cl CMBW SE5 143 F2
LEE/GVPK SE12 165 K3
Gabriel Cl CRW RM5 56 E3
FELT TW13 154 D6
Gabrielle Cl WBLY HA9 80 B1
Gabriel St FSTH SE23 164 A2
Gabriel's Whf STHWK SE1 11 J7
Gad Cl PLSTW E13 107 F2
Gaddesden Av WBLY HA9 80 B4
Gade Cl HYS/HAR UB3 114 A1
Gadesden Rd HOR/WEW KT19 206 E4
Gadsbury Cl CDALE/KGS NW9 63 H3
Gadwall Cl CAN/RD E16 107 F5
Gage Rd CAN/RD E16 106 C4
Gainford St IS N1 85 G6
Gainsboro Gdns GFD/PVL UB6 78 E3
Gainsborough Av DART DA1 151 F6
MNPK E12 90 A3
Gainsborough Cl BECK BR3 182 D3
ESH/CLAY * KT10 189 J5
Gainsborough Ct SHB W12 119 F2
Gainsborough Gdns EDGE HA8 44 B5
GLDGN NW11 64 D4
HAMP NW3 83 H1
HSLW TW3 135 J6
Gainsborough Rd BCTR RM8 91 H2
CHSWK W4 118 C4
NFNCH/WDSP N12 47 F1
NWMAL KT3 192 A3
RAIN RM13 93 J6
RCH/KEW TW9 137 G3
SRTFD E15 106 C2
WAN E11 70 C4
WFD IG8 53 J2
YEAD UB4 94 A1
Gainsborough Sq BXLYHN DA7 148 E4
Gainsborough Ter
BELMT * SM2 208 D5
Gainsford Rd WALTH E17 69 H1
Gainsford St STHWK SE1 19 J1
Gairloch Rd CMBW SE5 143 F3
Gaisford St KTTN NW5 84 C4
Gaitskell Rd ELTH/MOT SE9 167 H3
Galahad Rd BMLY BR1 165 K5
Galata Rd BARN SW13 138 D1
Galatea Sq PECK SE15 143 J4
Galbraith St POP/IOD E14 125 F3
Galdana Av BAR EN5 21 G4
Galeborough Av WFD IG8 52 B3
Gale Cl HPTN TW12 172 D2
MTCM CR4 178 C6
Galena Rd HMSMTH W6 118 E4
Galen Pl NOXST/BSQ WC1A 10 E2
Galesbury Rd
WAND/EARL SW18 160 B1
Gales Gdns BETH E2 104 D2
Gale St BOW E3 105 J4
DAGW RM9 91 K4
Gales Wy WFD IG8 53 J3
Galgate Cl WIM/MER SW19 159 G3
Gallants Farm Rd EBAR EN4 33 J2
Galleon Cl BERM/RHTH SE16 123 K2
ERITH DA8 130 A4
Galleons Dr BARK IG11 109 G2
The Galleries IS * N1 6 A2
Gallery Gdns NTHLT UB5 95 H1
Gallery Rd DUL SE21 162 E3
Galleywall Rd
BERM/RHTH SE16 123 J4
Galleywood Crs CRW RM5 57 F2
Galliard Cl ED N9 36 C2
Galliard Rd ED N9 36 C2
Gallia Rd HBRY N5 85 H3
Gallions Cl BARK IG11 109 G2
Gallions Rd CAN/RD E16 108 B6
CHARL SE7 126 A4
Gallions View Rd THMD SE28 127 K2
Gallon Cl CHARL SE7 126 B4
The Gallop BELMT SM2 209 H6
SAND/SEL CR2 212 D5
Gallosson Rd WOOL/PLUM SE18 127 K4
Galloway Dr DART DA1 170 B2
Galloway Pth CROY/NA CR0 211 K2
Galloway Rd SHB W12 118 D1
Gallus Cl WCHMH N21 35 F1
Gallus Sq BKHTH/KID SE3 146 A4
Galpin's Rd THHTH CR7 195 K1
Galsworthy Av CHDH RM6 73 H4
Galsworthy Cl THMD SE28 128 C1
Galsworthy Crs
BKHTH/KID * SE3 146 B2
Galsworthy Rd CRICK NW2 82 C2
KUTN/CMB KT2 175 J4
Galton St NKENS W10 100 C3
Galva Cl EBAR EN4 22 A5
Galveston Rd PUT/ROE SW15 139 J6
Galway Cl BERM/RHTH * SE16 123 J5
Galway St FSBYE EC1V 6 D5
Gambetta St VX/NE SW8 141 G3
Gambia St STHWK SE1 18 B1
Gambole Rd TOOT SW17 160 D6
Games Rd EBAR EN4 21 J4
Gamlen Rd PUT/ROE SW15 139 G5
Gamuel Cl WALTH E17 69 J3
Gander Green Crs HPTN TW12 173 F4
Gander Green La CHEAM SM3 193 H6
SUT SM1 208 E4
Gandhi Cl WALTH E17 69 J3
Ganton St SOHO/CST * W1F 10 B4
Ganton Wk OXHEY * WD19 27 J6
Gantshill Crs GNTH/NBYPK IG2 72 A2
Gap Rd WIM/MER SW19 177 K1
Garage Rd ACT W3 98 C5
Garbrand Wk EW KT17 207 H6
Garbutt Pl MHST * W1U 9 H1
Garden Av BXLYHN DA7 149 G4
MTCM CR4 179 G3
Garden Cl BAR EN5 20 A5
CHING E4 51 J1
HPTN TW12 172 E1
LEE/GVPK SE12 166 A5
NTHLT UB5 77 J6
PUT/ROE SW15 158 E2
RSLP HA4 58 C6
WLGTN SM6 210 E3
Garden Ct TPL/STR * WC2R 11 J5
Gardeners Rd CROY/NA CR0 196 C5
Garden Flats HMSMTH * W6 119 G6
Gardenia Rd EN EN1 36 A1
Gardenia Wy WFD IG8 52 E2
Garden La BMLY BR1 184 A2
BRXS/STRHM SW2 162 A3
Garden Lodge Ct EFNCH * N2 47 H6
Garden Pl HACK E8 86 B6
RDART DA2 171 G5
Garden Rd BMLY BR1 184 A3
PGE/AN SE20 181 K4
RCH/KEW TW9 137 H4
STJWD NW8 101 G2
WOT/HER KT12 188 A3
Garden Rw STHWK SE1 18 A5
The Gardens BECK BR3 183 F5
CEND/HSY/T * N8 66 E1
EBED/NFELT TW14 153 G1
EDUL SE22 143 H5
ESH/CLAY KT10 204 A2
HRW HA1 60 C3
PIN * HA5 59 K3
STNW/STAM * N16 68 B4
Garden St WCHPL E1 105 F4
Garden Studios BAY/PAD * W2 101 G4
Garden Ter PIM * SW1V 121 J5
Garden Vls ESH/CLAY * KT10 205 F5
Garden Wk BECK BR3 182 C4
SDTCH EC2A 7 G6
Garden Wy WLSDN NW10 80 E4
Gardiner Av CRICK * NW2 82 A3
Gardiner Cl BCTR RM8 91 K2
PEND EN3 37 F1
STMC/STPC BR5 186 D5
Gardiner House
WOOL/PLUM SE18 146 D1
Gardner Cl WAN E11 71 F3
Gardner Pl EBED/NFELT TW14 154 A1
Gardner Rd PLSTW E13 107 F3
Gardners Cl FBAR/BDGN N11 34 A4
Gardners La BLKFR EC4V 12 C5
Gardnor Rd HAMP NW3 83 H2
Gard St FSBYE EC1V 6 B4
Garendon Gdns MRDN SM4 194 A4
Garendon Rd MRDN SM4 194 A4
Gareth Cl WPK KT4 193 G6
Gareth Gv BMLY BR1 165 K6
Garfield Rd BTSEA SW11 141 F4
CHING E4 38 B3
PEND EN3 24 E5
PLSTW E13 106 D3
TWK TW1 156 B3
WIM/MER SW19 178 B2
Garford St POP/IOD E14 105 J6
Garibaldi St WOOL/PLUM SE18 127 K4
Garland Rd STAN HA7 44 A2
WOOL/PLUM SE18 147 J1
Garlick Hl BLKFR EC4V 12 D5
Garlies Rd FSTH SE23 164 B5
Garlinge Rd CRICK NW2 82 D4
Garman Cl UED N18 49 K1
Garman Rd TOTM N17 50 E3
Garnault Ms CLKNW EC1R 5 K5
Garnault Pl CLKNW EC1R 5 K5
Garnault Rd EN EN1 24 B1
Garner Cl BCTR RM8 73 K5
Garner Rd WALTH E17 52 A4
Garner St BETH E2 104 C1
Garnet Rd THHTH CR7 196 D1
WLSDN NW10 81 G4
Garnet St WAP E1W 104 E6
Garnett Cl ELTH/MOT SE9 146 E4
Garnett Rd HAMP NW3 83 K3
Garnham St STNW/STAM N16 68 B6
Garnies Cl PECK SE15 143 G1
Garrad's Rd STRHM/NOR SW16 161 J5
Garrard Cl BXLYHN DA7 149 H4
CHST BR7 185 G1
Garrard Wk WLSDN * NW10 81 G4
Garratt Cl CROY/NA CR0 210 E2
Garratt La WAND/EARL SW18 160 A1
Garratt Rd EDGE HA8 44 C3
Garratts Rd BUSH WD23 28 C2
Garratt Ter TOOT SW17 160 D6
Garrett Cl ACT W3 99 F4
Garrett St STLK EC1Y 6 C7
Garrick Av GLDGN NW11 64 C3
Garrick Cl BTSEA SW11 140 B5
EA W5 98 A3
RCH/KEW TW9 136 D6
Garrick Crs CROY/NA CR0 197 F6
Garrick Dr HDN NW4 46 A5
WOOL/PLUM SE18 127 G3
Garrick Gdns E/WMO/HCT KT8 173 F6
Garrick Pk HDN NW4 46 B5
Garrick Rd CDALE/KGS NW9 63 H3
GFD/PVL UB6 96 B3
RCH/KEW TW9 137 H3
Garrick St COVGDN WC2E 10 E5
Garrick Wy HDN NW4 64 B1
Garrick Yd CHCR WC2N 10 E5
Garrison Cl HSLWW TW4 134 E6
WOOL/PLUM SE18 147 F1
Garrison La CHSGTN KT9 206 A5
Garry Cl ROM RM1 57 G3
Garry Wy ROM RM1 57 G3
Garsdale Cl FBAR/BDGN N11 48 A2
Garsdale Ter WKENS * W14 119 J5
Garside Cl HPTN TW12 173 G2
WOOL/PLUM SE18 127 J3
Garsington Ms BROCKY SE4 144 C4
The Garth HPTN TW12 173 G2
KTN/HRWW/W HA3 62 B3
NFNCH/WDSP * N12 47 F1
Garth Cl KUTN/CMB KT2 175 G1
MRDN SM4 193 G4
RSLP HA4 59 H5
Garth Ms EA * W5 98 A3
Garthorne Rd FSTH SE23 164 A2
Garth Rd CHSWK W4 118 A5
CRICK NW2 64 D6
KUTN/CMB KT2 175 G1
MRDN SM4 193 G5
Garthside KUTN/CMB KT2 175 F1
Garthway NFNCH/WDSP N12 47 J2
Gartmoor Gdns
WIM/MER SW19 159 J3
Gartmore Rd GDMY/SEVK IG3 73 F5
Garton Pl WAND/EARL SW18 160 B1
Gartons Cl PEND EN3 24 E6
Gartons Wy BTSEA SW11 140 B4
Garvary Rd CAN/RD E16 107 F5
Garway Rd BAY/PAD W2 101 F5
Gascoigne Gdns WFD IG8 52 C3
Gascoigne Pl BETH E2 7 J4
Gascoigne Rd BARK IG11 90 C6
Gascony Av KIL/WHAMP NW6 82 E5
Gascoyne Dr DART DA1 150 C4
Gascoyne Rd HOM E9 87 F5
Gaselee St POP/IOD E14 106 A6
Gasholder Pl LBTH SE11 122 A5
Gaskarth Rd BAL SW12 161 G1
EDGE HA8 44 E4
Gaskell Rd HGT N6 65 K3
Gaskell St CLAP SW4 141 K3
Gaskin St IS N1 85 H6
Gaspar Ms ECT SW5 120 A4
Gassiot Rd TOOT SW17 160 E6
Gassiot Wy SUT SM1 209 H1
Gastein Rd HMSMTH W6 119 G6
Gaston Bell Cl RCH/KEW TW9 137 G4
Gaston Rd MTCM CR4 179 F6
Gataker St BERM/RHTH SE16 123 J3
Gatcombe Ms EA W5 98 B6
Gatcombe Rd ARCH N19 84 D1
Gatcombe Wy EBAR EN4 21 K4
Gate Cottages EDGE * HA8 30 C4
Gate End NTHWD HA6 40 E3
Gateforth St STJWD NW8 2 C7
Gatehill Rd NTHWD HA6 40 E3
Gatehouse Cl KUTN/CMB KT2 175 K3
Gatehouse Sq STHWK SE1 12 D7
Gateley Rd BRXN/ST SW9 142 A4
Gate Ms SKENS SW7 14 D3
Gater Dr ENC/FH EN2 23 K2
Gates Ct WALW * SE17 122 D5
Gates Green Rd WWKM BR4 214 E2
Gateside Rd TOOT SW17 160 E5
Gatestone Rd NRWD SE19 181 F2
Gate St HHOL WC1V 11 G3
Gateway WALW SE17 122 D6
Gateway Ar IS * N1 6 A2
Gateway Cl NTHWD HA6 40 A2
Gateway Ms HACK * E8 86 B3
The Gateways RCH/KEW * TW9 136 E5
Gatfield Gv FELT TW13 155 F4
Gathorne Rd WDGN N22 49 G5
Gathorne St BETH E2 105 F1
Gatley Av HOR/WEW KT19 206 D3
Gatliff Cl BGVA * SW1W 121 F5
Gatliff Rd BGVA SW1W 121 G5
Gatling Rd ABYW SE2 128 B5
Gatonby St PECK SE15 143 G2
Gatton Cl BELMT * SM2 209 F6
Gatton Rd TOOT SW17 160 D6
Gattons Wy SCUP DA14 169 G6
Gatward Cl WCHMH N21 35 H1
Gatward Gn ED N9 36 A4
Gatwick Rd WAND/EARL SW18 159 J2
Gauden Cl CLAP SW4 141 J4
Gauden Rd CLAP SW4 141 J4
Gaumont Ter SHB * W12 119 F2
Gauntlet Cl NTHLT UB5 77 J5
Gauntlett Ct ALP/SUD HA0 79 G3
Gauntlett Rd SUT SM1 209 H3
Gaunt St STHWK SE1 18 B4
Gautrey Rd PECK SE15 143 K3
Gavel St WALW * SE17 19 F6
Gaverick St POP/IOD E14 124 D4
Gavestone Crs LEE/GVPK SE12 166 A3
Gavestone Rd LEE/GVPK SE12 166 A2
Gavina Cl MRDN SM4 194 D2
Gawber St BETH E2 104 E2
Gawsworth Cl SRTFD E15 88 D3
Gawthorne Av MLHL NW7 46 C1
Gay Cl CRICK NW2 81 K3
Gaydon La CDALE/KGS NW9 45 G4
Gayfere Rd CLAY IG5 53 K6
EW KT17 207 J3
Gayfere St WEST SW1P 16 E5
Gayford Rd SHB W12 118 C2
Gay Gdns DAGE RM10 92 E2
Gayhurst Rd HACK E8 86 C5
Gaylor Rd NTHLT UB5 77 K3
Gaynesford Rd CAR SM5 209 K5
FSTH SE23 164 A4
Gaynes Hill Rd WFD IG8 53 J3
Gay Rd SRTFD E15 106 B1
Gaysham Av GNTH/NBYPK IG2 72 A2
Gayton Crs HAMP NW3 83 H2
Gayton Rd HAMP NW3 83 H2
HRW HA1 61 G3
Gayville Rd BTSEA SW11 160 E1
Gaywood Cl BRXS/STRHM SW2 162 A3
Gaywood Rd WALTH E17 51 J6
Gaywood St STHWK SE1 18 B5
Gaza St WALW SE17 122 C5
Gearlesville Gdns BARK/HLT IG6 72 B1
Geary Rd WLSDN NW10 81 J3
Geary St HOLWY N7 85 F3
Geddes Pl BXLYHN DA7 149 H5
Gedeney Rd TOTM N17 49 J4
Gedling Pl STHWK SE1 19 J4
Geere Rd SRTFD E15 88 D6
Gees Ct MHST W1U 9 H4
Gee St FSBYE EC1V 6 C6
Geffrye Est IS N1 7 H3
Geffrye St BETH E2 7 J2
Geldart Rd PECK SE15 143 J1
Geldeston Rd CLPT E5 68 C6
Gellatly Rd PECK SE15 143 K3
Gelsthorpe Rd CRW RM5 56 D3
General Wolfe Rd GNWCH SE10 145 G2
Genesis Cl STWL/WRAY TW19 152 C3
Genesta Rd WOOL/PLUM SE18 127 G6
Geneva Dr BRXN/ST SW9 142 B5
Geneva Gdns CHDH RM6 74 A2
Geneva Rd KUT KT1 191 F1
THHTH CR7 196 D2
Genever Cl CHING E4 51 J1
Genista Rd UED N18 50 D1
Genoa Av PUT/ROE SW15 139 F6
Genoa Rd PGE/AN SE20 181 K4
Genotin Rd EN EN1 23 K4
Gentleman's Rw ENC/FH EN2 23 J4
Geoffrey Cl CMBW SE5 142 D3
Geoffrey Gdns EHAM E6 107 J1
Geoffrey Rd BROCKY SE4 144 C4
George Beard Rd DEPT SE8 124 C4
George Crs MUSWH N10 48 A3
George Downing Est
STNW/STAM N16 68 B6
George Gange Wy
KTN/HRWW/W HA3 42 E6
George Groves Rd
PGE/AN SE20 181 H4
George La HAYES BR2 200 A5
LEW SE13 165 F1
SWFD E18 52 E5
George Lowe Ct BAY/PAD * W2 101 F4
George Mathers Rd LBTH * SE11 18 A6
George Ms CAMTN NW1 4 A5
George Rd CHING E4 51 J2
KUTN/CMB KT2 175 K3
NWMAL KT3 192 C1
George Rw BERM/RHTH SE16 123 H2
Georges Md BORE WD6 30 A1
George's Rd HOLWY N7 85 F3
HOLWY N7 85 F4
George St BARK IG11 90 C5
CAN/RD E16 106 D5
CROY/NA CR0 196 E6
HNWL W7 115 K1
HSLW TW3 134 E3
MBLAR W1H 9 F3
NWDGN UB2 114 D4
RCHPK/HAM TW10 136 E6
ROM RM1 75 H3
Georgetown Cl NRWD SE19 180 E1
Georgette Pl GNWCH SE10 145 F1
George V Av PIN HA5 41 K5
Georgeville Gdns BARK/HLT IG6 72 B1
George V Wy GFD/PVL UB6 79 H5
George Wyver Cl
WAND/EARL SW18 159 H2
George Yd BANK EC3V 13 F4
MYFR/PKLN W1K 9 H5
Georgiana St CAMTN NW1 84 C6
Georgian Cl HAYES BR2 200 A5
STAN HA7 43 G3
Georgian Ct WBLY HA9 80 C4

Georgian Wy HRW HA1 60 D6
Georgia Rd NWMAL KT3 191 K1
THHTH CR7 180 C4
Georgina Gdns BETH * E2 7 K4
Geraint Rd BMLY BR1 165 K5
Geraldine Rd CHSWK W4 117 H6
WAND/EARL SW18 140 B6
Geraldine St LBTH SE11 18 A5
Gerald Rd BCTR RM8 74 B6
BGVA SW1W 15 H6
CAN/RD E16 106 D3
Gerard Av HSLWW TW4 155 F2
Gerard Gdns RAIN RM13 111 G1
Gerard Rd BARN SW13 138 C2
HRW HA1 61 G3
Gerards Cl BERM/RHTH SE16 123 K6
Gerda Rd ELTH/MOT SE9 167 G4
Gerdview Dr RDART DA2 171 F6
Germander Wy SRTFD E15 106 C2
Gernon Rd BOW E3 105 G1
Geron Wy CRICK NW2 64 A6
Gerrard Gdns PIN HA5 58 E2
Gerrard Pl SOHO/SHAV * W1D 10 D5
Gerrard Rd IS N1 6 A2
Gerrards Cl STHGT/OAK N14 22 C6
Gerrard St SOHO/SHAV W1D 10 C5
Gerridge St STHWK SE1 17 K3
Gertrude Rd BELV DA17 129 H4
Gertrude St WBPTN SW10 120 B6
Gervase Cl WBLY HA9 80 E1
Gervase Rd EDGE HA8 44 E4
Gervase St PECK SE15 143 J1
Ghent St CAT SE6 164 D4
Ghent Wy HACK E8 86 B4
Giant Arches Rd HNHL SE24 162 D2
Giant Tree Hl BUSH WD23 28 D4
Gibbfield Cl CHDH RM6 56 A6
Gibbins Rd SRTFD E15 88 A5
Gibbon Rd ACT W3 99 G6
KUTN/CMB KT2 175 F4
PECK SE15 143 K3
Gibbons Rd WLSDN NW10 81 F4
Gibbon Wk PUT/ROE * SW15 138 D5
Gibbs Av NRWD SE19 180 E2
Gibbs Cl NRWD * SE19 180 E1
Gibbs Couch OXHEY WD19 27 H5
Gibbs Gn EDGE HA8 30 E6
WKENS * W14 119 J5
Gibbs Rd UED N18 36 E6
Gibbs Sq NRWD * SE19 180 E1
Gibraltar Wk BETH E2 7 K5
Gibson Cl CHSGTN * KT9 205 J3
ISLW TW7 135 J4
WCHPL E1 104 E3
Gibson Gdns STNW/STAM * N16 68 B6
Gibson Rd BCTR RM8 73 J5
LBTH SE11 17 H7
SUT SM1 209 F3
Gibson's Hl STRHM/NOR SW16 180 B3
Gibson Sq IS N1 85 G6
Gibson St GNWCH SE10 125 H5
Gidea Av GPK RM2 57 J6
Gidea Cl GPK RM2 57 J6
Gideon Cl BELV DA17 129 J4
Gideon Ms EA * W5 116 E2
Gideon Rd BTSEA SW11 141 F4
Giesbach Rd ARCH N19 66 D6
Giffard Rd UED N18 50 A1
Giffin St DEPT SE8 144 D1
Gifford Gdns HNWL W7 96 D4
Gifford St IS N1 84 E5
Gift La SRTFD E15 88 C6
Giggs Hl STMC/STPC BR5 186 B5
Giggs Hill Gdns THDIT KT7 190 B5
Giggs Hill Rd THDIT KT7 190 B4
Gilbert Cl WIM/MER * SW19 178 A4
WOOL/PLUM SE18 146 E2
Gilbert Gv EDGE HA8 44 E4
Gilbert Pl NOXST/BSQ WC1A 10 E2
Gilbert Rd BELV DA17 129 H3
BMLY BR1 183 K3
LBTH SE11 17 K6
PIN HA5 59 H1
ROM RM1 75 H1
WIM/MER SW19 178 B3
Gilbert St HSLW TW3 135 H4
MYFR/PKLN W1K 9 H4
SRTFD E15 88 C2
Gilbey Rd TOOT SW17 160 D6
Gilbeys Yd CAMTN NW1 84 A5
Gilbourne Rd WOOL/PLUM SE18 128 A6
Gilda Av PEND EN3 25 G6
Gilda Crs STNW/STAM N16 68 C5
Gildea Cl PIN HA5 42 A3
Gildea St REGST W1B 9 K2
Gildersome St
WOOL/PLUM SE18 127 F6
Gilders Rd CHSGTN KT9 206 B5
Giles Coppice NRWD SE19 163 G6
Gilkes Crs DUL SE21 163 F1
Gilkes Pl DUL SE21 163 F1
Gillam Wy RAIN RM13 93 J4
Gillan Gn BUSH WD23 28 C4
Gillards Ms WALTH E17 69 J1
Gillards Wy WALTH E17 69 J1
Gill Av CAN/RD E16 106 E5
Gill Cl WATW WD18 26 A1
Gillender St BOW E3 106 A3
Gillespie Rd HBRY N5 85 G1
Gillett Av EHAM E6 107 J1
Gillett Pl HACK E8 86 B3
Gillett Rd THHTH CR7 196 E1
Gillett St STNW/STAM N16 86 A3
Gillham Ter TOTM N17 50 C2
Gillian Park Rd CHEAM SM3 193 J5
Gillian St LEW SE13 144 E6
Gillian Ter BRYLDS * KT5 191 G3
Gillingham Ms PIM SW1V 15 K6
Gillingham Rd CRICK NW2 82 C1
Gillingham Rw PIM SW1V 16 A6
Gillingham St PIM SW1V 15 K7
Gillison Wk BERM/RHTH * SE16 123 H3
Gillman Dr SRTFD E15 88 C6
Gillmans Rd STMC/STPC BR5 202 C5
Gill St POP/IOD E14 105 H5
Gillum Cl EBAR EN4 33 K3
Gilmore Rd LEW SE13 145 G5
Gilpin Av MORT/ESHN SW14 138 A5
Gilpin Cl MTCM CR4 178 D5
Gilpin Crs HSLW TW3 155 G2
UED N18 50 B1
Gilpin Rd CLPT E5 87 G2
Gilpin Wy HYS/HAR UB3 133 G1
Gilroy Cl RAIN RM13 93 H4
Gilroy Wy STMC/STPC BR5 202 C4
Gilsland Rd THHTH CR7 196 E1
Gilstead Rd FUL/PGN SW6 140 A3
Gilston Rd WBPTN SW10 120 B5
Gilton Rd CAT SE6 165 H5
Giltspur St STBT EC1A 12 B3
Gilwell Cl CHING E4 25 K5
Gippeswyck Cl PIN HA5 41 H4
Gipsy Hl NRWD SE19 181 F1
Gipsy La BARN SW13 138 D4
Gipsy Rd WELL DA16 148 E3
WNWD SE27 162 E6
Gipsy Road Gdns WNWD SE27 162 D6
Giralda Cl CAN/RD E16 107 H4
Giraud St POP/IOD E14 105 K5
Girdlers Rd WKENS W14 119 G4
Girdwood Rd
WAND/EARL SW18 159 H2
Girling Wy EBED/NFELT TW14 133 K4
Gironde Rd FUL/PGN SW6 139 J1
Girton Av CDALE/KGS NW9 44 C6
Girton Cl NTHLT UB5 78 C4
Girton Gdns CROY/NA CR0 213 J1
Girton Rd NTHLT UB5 78 C4
SYD SE26 182 A1
Gisbourne Cl WLGTN SM6 210 D1
Gisburn Rd CEND/HSY/T N8 67 F1
Gissing Wk IS * N1 85 G5
Gittens Cl BMLY BR1 165 J6
Glacier Wy ALP/SUD HA0 97 K1
Gladbeck Wy WCHMH N21 23 H5
Gladding Rd MNPK E12 89 H2
The Glade BELMT SM2 208 C6
BMLY BR1 184 C5
CHARL SE7 146 B1
CLAY IG5 53 K5
CROY/NA CR0 198 A2
ENC/FH EN2 23 G4
EW KT17 207 J4
HACK * E8 86 B4
NFNCH/WDSP * N12 33 H6
SHB * W12 118 E2
WCHMH N21 35 F1
WFD IG8 39 F5
WWKM BR4 213 K1
Glade Cl SURB * KT6 190 E6
Glade Gdns CROY/NA CR0 198 B4
Glade La NWDGN UB2 115 G2
Gladeside CROY/NA CR0 198 A4
WCHMH N21 35 F2
Gladesmore Rd
SEVS/STOTM N15 68 B3
Gladiator St FSTH SE23 164 B1
Glading Ter STNW/STAM N16 86 B1
Gladioli Cl HPTN TW12 173 F2
Gladsdale Dr PIN HA5 58 E1
Gladsmuir Cl WOT/HER KT12 188 B6
Gladsmuir Rd ARCH N19 66 C5
BAR EN5 20 C3
Gladstone Av
EBED/NFELT TW14 153 K1
MNPK E12 89 J5
WDGN N22 49 H5
WHTN TW2 155 J2
Gladstone Gdns HSLW TW3 135 H2
Gladstone Ms KIL/WHAMP NW6 82 D4
PGE/AN SE20 181 K3
WDGN N22 49 G5
Gladstone Pde CRICK * NW2 82 A1
Gladstone Park Gdns CRICK NW2 81 K1
Gladstone Pl BAR * EN5 20 B5
E/WMO/HCT * KT8 189 K2
Gladstone Rd BKHH IG9 39 G3
CHSWK * W4 118 A3
CROY/NA CR0 196 E4
DART DA1 171 J1
KUT KT1 175 H6
NWDGN UB2 114 D2
ORP BR6 216 C3
SURB KT6 190 E6
WIM/MER SW19 177 K3
Gladstone St STHWK SE1 18 A4
Gladstone Ter VX/NE * SW8 141 G2
WNWD * SE27 162 D6
Gladstone Wy
KTN/HRWW/W HA3 42 E6
Gladwell Rd BMLY BR1 183 K2
CEND/HSY/T N8 67 F3
Gladwyn Rd PUT/ROE SW15 139 G4
Gladys Rd KIL/WHAMP NW6 82 E5
Glaisher St DEPT SE8 124 E6
Glamis Crs HYS/HAR UB3 113 F3
Glamis Pl WAP E1W 104 E6
Glamis Rd WAP E1W 104 E6
Glamis Wy NTHLT UB5 78 C4
Glamorgan Cl MTCM CR4 179 K6
Glamorgan Rd KUT KT1 174 D3
Glanfield Rd BECK BR3 198 C1
Glanleam Rd STAN HA7 29 K6
Glanville Rd BRXS/STRHM SW2 141 K6
HAYES BR2 184 A6
Glasbrook Av WHTN TW2 154 E3
Glasbrook Rd ELTH/MOT SE9 166 C2
Glaserton Rd STNW/STAM N16 68 A4
Glasford St TOOT SW17 178 E2
Glasgow Rd PLSTW E13 107 F1
UED N18 50 D1
Glasgow Ter PIM SW1V 121 H5
Glasse Cl WEA W13 97 G6
Glasshill St STHWK SE1 18 B2
Glasshouse Flds WAP E1W 105 F6
Glasshouse St REGST W1B 10 B6
Glasshouse Wk LBTH SE11 121 K5
Glasshouse Yd STBT EC1A 6 C7
Glasslyn Rd CEND/HSY/T N8 66 D2
Glassmill La HAYES BR2 183 J5
Glass St BETH * E2 104 D3
Glass Yd WOOL/PLUM SE18 127 F3
Glastonbury Av WFD IG8 53 H3
Glastonbury Cl STMC/STPC BR5 202 D5
Glastonbury Pl WCHPL E1 104 E5
Glastonbury Rd ED N9 36 C3
MRDN SM4 193 K4
Glastonbury St KIL/WHAMP NW6 82 D3
Glaston Ct EA * W5 116 E1
Glaucus St BOW E3 105 K4
Glazbury Rd WKENS W14 119 H4
Glazebrook Cl DUL SE21 162 E4
Glazebrook Rd TEDD TW11 174 A3
The Glebe BKHTH/KID SE3 145 H4
CHST BR7 185 H4
STRHM/NOR * SW16 161 J6
WDR/YW UB7 112 B4
WPK KT4 192 C5
Glebe Av ENC/FH EN2 23 H4
HGDN/ICK UB10 76 A2
KTN/HRWW/W HA3 44 A6
MTCM CR4 178 D5
RSLP HA4 77 F4
WFD IG8 52 E2
Glebe Cl CHSWK * W4 118 B5
HGDN/ICK UB10 76 A2
Glebe Ct BKHTH/KID * SE3 145 H4
EA * W5 116 E1
STAN HA7 43 J1
Glebe Crs HDN NW4 64 A1
KTN/HRWW/W HA3 44 A6
Glebe Gdns NWMAL KT3 192 B4
Glebe House Dr HAYES BR2 200 A5
Glebelands DART DA1 150 C5
E/WMO/HCT KT8 189 G2
ESH/CLAY KT10 205 F6
Glebelands Av GNTH/NBYPK IG2 72 D4
SWFD E18 52 E5
Glebelands Cl CMBW * SE5 143 F4
Glebelands Rd
EBED/NFELT TW14 153 K2
Glebe La BAR EN5 31 J1
KTN/HRWW/W HA3 62 A1
Glebe Pth MTCM CR4 178 E6
Glebe Pl CHEL SW3 120 D6
Glebe Rd BARN SW13 138 D3
BELMT SM2 208 C6
BMLY BR1 183 K4
CAR SM5 209 K4
CEND/HSY/T N8 67 F1
DAGE RM10 92 D4
FNCH N3 47 G4
HACK * E8 86 B5
RAIN RM13 111 K2
STAN HA7 43 J1
WLSDN NW10 81 J4
Glebe Side TWK TW1 156 A1
Glebe Sq MTCM * CR4 178 E6
Glebe St CHSWK W4 118 A5
Glebe Ter BOW E3 105 K2
Glebe Wy ERITH DA8 130 B6
FELT TW13 155 F5
Glebeway WFD IG8 53 G1
Glebe Wy WWKM BR4 199 G6
Gledhow Gdns ECT SW5 120 B4
Gledstanes Rd WKENS W14 119 H5
Gledwood Av YEAD UB4 94 E4
Gledwood Crs YEAD UB4 94 D4
Gledwood Dr YEAD UB4 94 D4
Gledwood Gdns YEAD UB4 94 E4
Gleed Av BUSH WD23 28 D4
Gleeson Dr ORP BR6 217 F3
Glegg Pl PUT/ROE * SW15 139 G5
The Glen BELMT * SM2 209 G4
CROY/NA CR0 213 F1
ENC/FH EN2 23 H5
HAYES BR2 183 H5
NTHWD HA6 40 B3
NWDGN UB2 114 E5
ORP BR6 215 K1
PIN HA5 59 F2
PIN HA5 59 J4
WBLY HA9 79 K2
Glenaffric Av POP/IOD E14 125 F4
Glen Albyn Rd WIM/MER SW19 159 G4
Glenalla Rd RSLP HA4 58 D4
Glenalmond Rd
KTN/HRWW/W HA3 62 A1
Glenalvon Wy
WOOL/PLUM SE18 126 D4
Glena Mt SUT SM1 209 G2
Glenarm Rd CLPT E5 86 E2
Glen Av ASHF TW15 152 D6
Glenavon Cl ESH/CLAY KT10 205 G4
Glenavon Rd SRTFD E15 88 C5
Glenbarr Cl ELTH/MOT SE9 147 G4
Glenbow Rd BMLY BR1 183 H2
Glenbrook North ENC/FH EN2 23 F5
Glenbrook Rd KIL/WHAMP NW6 82 E3
Glenbrook South ENC/FH EN2 23 F5
Glenbuck Rd SURB KT6 190 E3
Glenburnie Rd TOOT SW17 160 E5
Glencairn Dr EA W5 97 H3
Glencairne Cl CAN/RD E16 107 H4
Glencairn Rd STRHM/NOR SW16 179 K3
Glencoe Av GNTH/NBYPK IG2 72 E4
Glencoe Rd BUSH WD23 28 A1
DAGE RM10 92 C2
YEAD UB4 95 H4
Glencorse Gn OXHEY * WD19 27 H6
Glen Crs WFD IG8 53 F2
Glendale Av CHDH RM6 73 J4
EDGE HA8 30 B6
WDGN N22 49 G3
Glendale Cl ELTH/MOT SE9 147 F4
Glendale Gdns WBLY HA9 61 K5
Glen Dale Ms BECK BR3 182 E4
Glendale Rd ERITH DA8 129 K4
Glendale Wy THMD SE28 128 D1
Glendall St BRXN/ST SW9 142 A4
Glendarvon St PUT/ROE SW15 139 G4
Glendevon Cl EDGE HA8 30 D5
Glendish Rd TOTM N17 50 C4
Glendor Gdns MLHL NW7 31 F6
Glendower Crs ORP BR6 202 B3
Glendower Gdns
MORT/ESHN SW14 138 A4
Glendower Rd CHING E4 38 B3
MORT/ESHN SW14 138 A4
Glendown Rd ABYW SE2 128 B5
Glendun Rd ACT W3 99 G6
Gleneagle Ms
STRHM/NOR SW16 179 J1
Gleneagle Rd
STRHM/NOR SW16 179 J1
Gleneagles STAN HA7 43 H2
Gleneagles Cl
BERM/RHTH * SE16 123 J5
ORP BR6 201 J5
OXHEY * WD19 41 H1
Gleneldon Ms
STRHM/NOR SW16 161 K6
Gleneldon Rd
STRHM/NOR SW16 161 K6
Glenelg Rd BRXS/STRHM SW2 141 K6
Glenesk Rd ELTH/MOT SE9 147 F5
Glenfarg Rd CAT SE6 165 G3
Glenfield Crs RSLP HA4 58 B4
Glenfield Rd BAL SW12 161 H3
WEA W13 116 C2
Glenfinlas Wy CMBW SE5 142 C1
Glenforth St GNWCH SE10 125 J4
Glengall Br POP/IOD E14 124 E3
Glengall Gv POP/IOD E14 124 E3
Glengall Rd BXLYHN DA7 149 F4
EDGE HA8 30 D5
KIL/WHAMP NW6 82 D6
PECK SE15 123 G6
WFD IG8 52 E2
Glengall Ter PECK SE15 123 G6
Glen Gdns CROY/NA CR0 211 G1
Glengarnock Av POP/IOD E14 125 F4
Glengarry Rd EDUL SE22 143 F5
Glenham Dr GNTH/NBYPK IG2 72 B2
Glenhead Cl ELTH/MOT SE9 147 G4
Glenhill Cl FNCH N3 46 E5
Glenhouse Rd ELTH/MOT SE9 147 F6
Glenhurst Av BXLY DA5 169 G3
KTTN NW5 84 A2
RSLP HA4 58 A4
Glenhurst Ri NRWD SE19 180 D3
Glenhurst Rd BTFD TW8 116 D6
NFNCH/WDSP N12 33 H6
Glenilla Rd HAMP NW3 83 J4
Glenister Park Rd
STRHM/NOR SW16 179 J3
Glenister Rd GNWCH SE10 125 J5
Glenlea Rd ELTH/MOT SE9 147 F6
Glenloch Rd HAMP NW3 83 J4
PEND EN3 24 E3
Glenluge Rd BKHTH/KID SE3 125 K6
Glenlyon Rd ELTH/MOT SE9 147 F6
Glenmere Av MLHL NW7 45 J3
Glenmore Lawns WEA * W13 97 G5
Glenmore Pde ALP/SUD * HA0 80 A6
Glenmore Rd HAMP NW3 83 J4
WELL DA16 148 A2
Glenmore Wy BARK IG11 109 G2
Glennie Rd WNWD SE27 162 B5
Glenny Rd BARK IG11 90 C4
Glenorchy Cl YEAD UB4 95 J4
Glenparke Rd FSTGT E7 89 F4
Glen Ri WFD IG8 53 F2
Glen Rd CHSGTN KT9 206 A1
PLSTW E13 107 G3
WALTH E17 69 H2
WLGTN SM6 210 B6
Glenrosa St FUL/PGN SW6 140 B3
Glenroy St SHB W12 100 A5
Glensdale Rd BROCKY SE4 144 C4
Glenshiel Rd ELTH/MOT SE9 147 F6
Glenside CHIG IG7 54 B2
Glentanner Wy TOOT SW17 160 C5
Glen Ter POP/IOD E14 125 F2
Glentham Cottages
BARN * SW13 118 D6
Glentham Gdns BARN SW13 118 E5
Glentham Rd BARN SW13 118 D6
Glenthorne Av CROY/NA CR0 197 K5
Glenthorne Cl CHEAM SM3 193 K5
Glenthorne Gdns BARK/HLT IG6 54 A6
CHEAM SM3 193 K5
Glenthorne Rd FBAR/BDGN N11 47 K1
HMSMTH W6 118 E4
KUT KT1 191 G1
WALTH E17 69 G2
Glenthorpe Rd MRDN SM4 193 G2
Glenton Cl ROM RM1 57 G3
Glenton Rd LEW SE13 145 H5
Glenton Wy ROM RM1 57 G3
Glentrammon Av ORP BR6 217 F4
Glentrammon Cl ORP BR6 217 F4
Glentrammon Gdns ORP BR6 217 F4
Glentrammon Rd ORP BR6 217 F4
Glentworth St CAMTN NW1 3 F7
Glenure Rd ELTH/MOT SE9 147 F6
Glenview ABYW SE2 128 E6
Glen View Rd BMLY BR1 184 C5
Glenville Av ENC/FH EN2 23 J1
Glenville Gv DEPT SE8 144 C1
Glenville Rd KUTN/CMB KT2 175 H4
Glenwood Av CDALE/KGS NW9 63 G5
RAIN RM13 111 J3
Glenwood Cl HRW HA1 61 F2
Glenwood Dr GPK RM2 75 J2
Glenwood Gdns
GNTH/NBYPK IG2 72 A2
Glenwood Gv CDALE/KGS NW9 62 E5
Glenwood Rd CAT SE6 164 C3
EW KT17 207 J4
HSLW TW3 135 J4
MLHL NW7 31 G5
SEVS/STOTM N15 67 H2
Glenwood Rw NRWD * SE19 181 G4
Glenwood Wy CROY/NA CR0 198 A3
Glenworth Av POP/IOD E14 125 G4
Gliddon Rd WKENS W14 119 H4
Glimpsing Gn ERITHM DA18 129 F3
Gload Crs STMC/STPC BR5 202 E6
Globe Pond Rd
BERM/RHTH SE16 124 B1
Globe Rd BETH E2 104 E2
EMPK RM11 75 J3
SRTFD E15 88 D3
WFD IG8 53 G2
Globe St STHWK SE1 18 E3
Globe Ter BETH E2 104 E2
Glossop Rd SAND/SEL CR2 211 K6
Gloster Rd NWMAL KT3 192 B1
Gloucester Av BFN/LL DA15 167 K4
CAMTN NW1 84 A5
WELL DA16 148 A6
Gloucester Circ GNWCH SE10 145 F1
Gloucester Cl THDIT * KT7 190 B5
WLSDN NW10 81 F5
Gloucester Ct MON EC3R 13 H6
MTCM * CR4 195 K2
RCH/KEW * TW9 137 H1
Gloucester Crs CAMTN NW1 84 B6
Gloucester Dr FSBYPK N4 67 H6
GLDGN NW11 64 E1
Gloucester Gdns BAY/PAD * W2 101 G5
EBAR EN4 22 A5
GLDGN NW11 64 D4
IL IG1 71 J4
SUT SM1 194 A6
Gloucester Ga CAMTN NW1 3 H2
Gloucester Gate Ms CAMTN NW1 3 J2
Gloucester Gv EDGE HA8 45 F4
Gloucester Ms BAY/PAD W2 101 G5
Gloucester Ms West
BAY/PAD W2 101 G5
Gloucester Pde BFN/LL * DA15 148 B6
HYS/HAR * UB3 113 F3
Gloucester Pl CAMTN NW1 2 E7
MHST W1U 9 F2
Gloucester Place Ms MBLAR W1H 9 F2
Gloucester Rd ACT W3 117 K2
BAR EN5 21 F6
BELV DA17 129 G5
CROY/NA CR0 196 E4
DART DA1 170 E1
EA W5 116 D2
ENC/FH EN2 23 J1
FELT TW13 154 B3
HPTN TW12 173 G3
HSLWW TW4 134 D5
KUT KT1 175 H5
LEY E10 69 J4
MNPK E12 89 K1
RCH/KEW TW9 137 H1
ROM RM1 75 G3
RYLN/HDSTN HA2 60 B2
SKENS SW7 120 B4
TEDD TW11 173 K1
TOTM N17 49 K6
UED N18 50 B1
WALTH E17 51 F5
WAN E11 71 F2
WHTN TW2 155 H3
Gloucester Sq BAY/PAD W2 8 B5
BETH E2 86 C6
Gloucester St PIM SW1V 121 H5
Gloucester Ter BAY/PAD W2 101 F5
STHGT/OAK * N14 34 D3
Gloucester Wk KENS * W8 119 K2
Gloucester Wy CLKNW EC1R 5 K5
Glover Cl ABYW SE2 128 D4
Glover Dr UED N18 50 E2
Glover Rd PIN HA5 59 H3
Glycena Rd BTSEA SW11 140 E4
Glyn Av EBAR EN4 21 H5
Glyn Cl EW KT17 207 J6
SNWD SE25 181 F5
Glyndebourne Pk ORP BR6 216 B1
Glynde Ms CHEL SW3 14 D5
Glynde Rd BXLYHN DA7 148 E4
Glynde St BROCKY SE4 164 C1
Glyndon Rd WOOL/PLUM SE18 127 H4
Glyn Dr SCUP DA14 168 C6
Glynfield Rd WLSDN NW10 81 G5
Glynne Rd WDGN N22 49 G5
Glyn Rd CLPT E5 87 F2
PEND EN3 24 E5
WPK KT4 193 G6
Glyn St LBTH SE11 122 A5
Goat La EN EN1 24 B1
Goat Rd MTCM CR4 195 F4
Goat Whf BTFD TW8 117 F6
Gobions Av CRW RM5 57 F3
Godalming Av WLGTN SM6 210 E3
Godalming Rd POP/IOD E14 105 K4
Godbold Rd SRTFD E15 106 C3
Goddard Pl ARCH N19 84 C1
Goddard Rd BECK BR3 198 A1
Goddards Wy IL IG1 72 D5
Goddington Cha ORP BR6 217 H2
Goddington La ORP BR6 217 G1
Godfrey Av NTHLT UB5 77 J6
WHTN TW2 155 J2
Godfrey Hl WOOL/PLUM SE18 126 D4
Godfrey Rd WOOL/PLUM SE18 126 E4
Godfrey St CHEL SW3 120 D5
SRTFD E15 106 A1
Godfrey Wy HSLWW TW4 154 D2
Goding St LBTH SE11 121 K5
Godley Rd WAND/EARL SW18 160 C3
Godliman St BLKFR * EC4V 12 B4
Godman Rd PECK * SE15 143 J3
Godolphin Cl PLMGR N13 49 H2
Godolphin Pl ACT W3 99 F6
Godolphin Rd SHB W12 118 E2
Godric Crs CROY/NA CR0 214 B6
Godson Rd CROY/NA CR0 211 G1
Godstone Rd SUT SM1 209 G2
TWK TW1 156 B1
Godstow Rd ABYW SE2 128 D2
Godwin Cl HOR/WEW KT19 206 E4
IS N1 6 D2
Godwin Rd FSTGT E7 89 F2
HAYES BR2 184 B6
Goffers Rd BKHTH/KID SE3 145 H3
Goidel Cl WLGTN SM6 210 D2
Golborne Gdns NKENS * W10 100 C3
Golborne Ms NKENS W10 100 C4
Golborne Rd NKENS W10 100 C4
Golda Cl BAR EN5 32 B1
Goldbeaters Gv EDGE HA8 45 G3
Goldcliff Cl MRDN SM4 193 K4
Goldcrest Cl CAN/RD E16 107 H4
THMD SE28 109 J6
Goldcrest Ms EA * W5 97 K4
Goldcrest Wy BUSH WD23 28 C3
CROY/NA CR0 214 B6
Golden Crs HYS/HAR UB3 113 H1
Golden Cross Ms NTGHL * W11 100 D5
Golden Hind Pl DEPT * SE8 124 C4
Golden La STLK EC1Y 6 C6
Golden Lane Est STLK EC1Y 6 C7
Golden Mnr HNWL W7 96 E6
Golden Pde WALTH * E17 52 A6
Golden Plover Cl CAN/RD E16 106 E5
Golden Sq SOHO/CST W1F 10 B5
Golden Yd HAMP * NW3 83 G2
Golders Cl EDGE HA8 44 D1
Golders Gdns GLDGN NW11 64 C4
Golders Green Crs GLDGN NW11 64 D4
Golders Green Rd GLDGN NW11 64 C3
Golders Hl HAMP * NW3 65 F6
Goldersiea GLDGN * NW11 64 E5
Golders Manor Dr GLDGN NW11 64 B3
Golders Park Cl GLDGN NW11 64 E5
Golders Ri HDN NW4 64 B2
Golders Wy GLDGN NW11 64 D4
Goldfinch Cl ORP BR6 217 G3
Goldfinch Rd THMD SE28 127 J3
Goldhawk Ms SHB W12 118 E2
Goldhawk Rd HMSMTH W6 118 C4
Goldhaze Cl WFD IG8 53 H3
Gold Hl EDGE HA8 45 F2
Goldhurst Ter KIL/WHAMP NW6 83 F5
Golding St WCHPL E1 104 C5
Goldington Crs CAMTN NW1 4 C2
Goldington St CAMTN NW1 4 C2
Gold La EDGE HA8 45 F2
Goldman Cl BETH E2 104 C3
Goldney Rd MV/WKIL W9 100 E3
Goldrill Dr FBAR/BDGN N11 34 A4
Goldsboro Rd VX/NE SW8 141 J2
Goldsborough Crs CHING E4 37 K4
Goldsdown Cl PEND EN3 25 G3
Goldsdown Rd PEND EN3 25 F3
Goldsmid St WOOL/PLUM SE18 127 K5
Goldsmith Av ACT W3 99 F6
CDALE/KGS NW9 63 G2
MNPK E12 89 J4
ROMW/RG RM7 74 C4
Goldsmith Cl RYLN/HDSTN HA2 60 A5
Goldsmith La CDALE/KGS NW9 62 E1
Goldsmith Pl KIL/WHAMP * NW6 83 F6
Goldsmith Rd ACT W3 118 A1
FBAR/BDGN N11 47 K1
LEY E10 69 K5
PECK SE15 143 H2
WALTH E17 51 F5

Goldsmiths Cl ACT * W3 118 A1
Goldsmith's Rw BETH E2 86 C6
Goldsmith St CITYW EC2V 12 D3
Goldsworthy Gdns
BERM/RHTH SE16 123 K4
Goldwell Rd THHTH CR7 196 A1
Goldwing Cl CAN/RD E16 106 E5
Golf Cl STAN HA7 43 J3
STRHM/NOR SW16 180 B4
Golf Club Dr KUTN/CMB KT2 176 A3
Golfe Rd IL IG1 90 D1
Golf Rd BMLY BR1 185 F6
EA * W5 98 B5
Golf Side WHTN TW2 155 J5
Golf Side Cl NWMAL KT3 176 B5
Golfside Cl TRDG/WHET N20 33 J5
Gollogly Ter CHARL SE7 126 B5
Gomer Gdns TEDD TW11 174 B2
Gomer Pl TEDD TW11 174 B2
Gomm Rd BERM/RHTH SE16 123 K3
Gomshall Av WLGTN SM6 210 E3
Gondar Gdns KIL/WHAMP NW6 82 D3
Gonson St DEPT SE8 124 E6
Gonston Cl WIM/MER SW19 159 H4
Gonville Crs NTHLT UB5 78 B4
Gonville Rd THHTH CR7 196 A2
Gonville St FUL/PGN SW6 139 H4
Goodall Rd WAN E11 88 A1
Gooden Ct HRW HA1 78 E1
Goodenough Rd
WIM/MER SW19 177 J3
Goodey Rd BARK IG11 91 F5
Goodge Pl FITZ W1T 10 B2
Goodge St FITZ W1T 10 B2
Goodhall St WLSDN NW10 81 H6
Goodhart Wy WWKM BR4 199 H3
Goodhew Rd SNWD SE25 197 H3
Gooding Cl NWMAL KT3 191 K1
Goodinge Cl HOLWY N7 84 E3
Goodinge Rd HOLWY N7 84 E4
Goodman Ct ALP/SUD * HA0 79 K2
Goodman Crs
BRXS/STRHM SW2 161 K4
Goodman Rd LEY E10 70 A4
Goodmans Ct ALP/SUD HA0 79 K2
Goodman's Stile WCHPL E1 104 C5
Goodman's Yd TWRH EC3N 13 J5
Goodmayes Av GDMY/SEVK IG3 73 G5
Goodmayes La GDMY/SEVK IG3 91 G2
Goodmayes Rd GDMY/SEVK IG3 73 G5
Goodmead Rd ORP BR6 202 B4
Goodrich Rd EDUL SE22 163 G1
Goodson Rd WLSDN NW10 81 G5
Goods Wy CAMTN NW1 4 E2
Goodway Gdns POP/IOD E14 106 B5
Goodwin Cl BERM/RHTH SE16 19 K5
MTCM CR4 178 C6
Goodwin Dr SCUP DA14 168 E4
Goodwin Gdns CROY/NA CR0 211 H4
Goodwin Rd CROY/NA CR0 211 H3
ED N9 36 E3
SHB W12 118 D2
Goodwins Ct CHCR WC2N 10 E5
Goodwin St FSBYPK N4 67 G6
Goodwood Cl MRDN SM4 193 K1
Goodwood Dr NTHLT UB5 78 A4
Goodwood Pde BECK * BR3 198 B1
Goodwood Rd NWCR SE14 144 B1
Goodwyn Av MLHL NW7 45 G1
Goodwyn's V MUSWH N10 48 A4
Goodyers Gdns HDN NW4 64 B2
Goosander Wy
WOOL/PLUM SE18 127 J3
Gooseacre La
KTN/HRWW/W HA3 61 K2
Goose Green Cl STMC/STPC BR5 186 B5
Gooseley La EHAM E6 108 A2
Goossens Cl SUT SM1 209 G3
Gophir La CANST * EC4R 12 E5
Gopsall St IS N1 7 F1
Gordon Av CHING E4 52 C2
HCH RM12 75 H6
MORT/ESHN SW14 138 B5
STAN HA7 43 F2
TWK TW1 136 B6
Gordonbrock Rd BROCKY SE4 144 D6
Gordon Cl WALTH E17 69 J3
Gordon Cottages KENS * W8 119 K2
Gordon Crs CROY/NA CR0 197 F5
HYS/HAR UB3 113 K4
Gordondale Rd WIM/MER SW19 159 K4
Gordon Gdns EDGE HA8 44 D5
Gordon Gv CMBW SE5 142 C3
Gordon Hl ENC/FH EN2 23 J2
Gordon House Rd KTTN NW5 84 A2
Gordon Pl KENS W8 119 K2
Gordon Rd ASHF TW15 152 B5
BARK IG11 90 E6
BECK BR3 182 C6
BELV DA17 129 K4
BFN/LL DA15 147 K6
BRYLDS KT5 191 G4
CAR SM5 209 K4
CHDH RM6 74 B3
CHING E4 38 C2
CHSWK W4 117 J6
DART DA1 171 G2
EA W5 97 J6
ED N9 36 D4
ENC/FH EN2 23 K2
ESH/CLAY KT10 204 E5
FBAR/BDGN N11 48 D3
FNCH N3 46 D3
HSLW TW3 135 H5
IL IG1 90 D1
KTN/HRWW/W HA3 42 E6
KUTN/CMB KT2 175 G4
NWDGN UB2 114 D4
PECK SE15 143 J3
RCH/KEW TW9 137 G3
SRTFD E15 88 A2
SWFD E18 53 F4
WAN E11 70 E3
Gordon Sq STPAN WC1H 4 D6
Gordon St PLSTW E13 106 E2
STPAN WC1H 4 C6
Gordon Wy BAR EN5 20 D5
BMLY BR1 183 K4
Gorefield Pl KIL/WHAMP NW6 100 E1
Gore Rd HOM E9 86 E6
RYNPK SW20 177 F5
Goresbrook Rd DAGW RM9 91 J6
Gore St SKENS SW7 120 B3
Gorham Pl NTGHL W11 100 C6
Goring Cl CRW RM5 56 E4
Goring Gdns BCTR RM8 91 J2
Goring Rd DAGE RM10 93 F4
FBAR/BDGN * N11 48 E2
Goring St HDTCH EC3A 13 H3
Goring Wy GFD/PVL UB6 96 C1
Gorleston Rd SEVS/STOTM N15 67 K2
Gorleston St WKENS W14 119 H4
Gorman Rd WOOL/PLUM SE18 126 E4
Gorringe Park Av MTCM CR4 178 E3
Gorse Ri TOOT SW17 179 F1
Gorse Rd CROY/NA CR0 213 J1
STMC/STPC BR5 203 H6
Gorseway ROMW/RG RM7 75 G6
Gorst Rd BTSEA SW11 160 E1
WLSDN NW10 98 E3
Gorsuch Pl BETH E2 7 J4
Gorsuch St BETH E2 7 J4
Gosberton Rd BAL SW12 160 E3
Gosbury Hl CHSGTN KT9 206 A2
Gosfield Rd BCTR RM8 74 C5
Gosfield St GTPST W1W 9 K1
Gosford Gdns REDBR IG4 71 K2
Gosforth La OXHEY WD19 26 E5
Gosforth Pth OXHEY WD19 26 E5
Goshawk Gdns YEAD UB4 94 C2
Goslett Yd SOHO/SHAV W1D 10 D3
Gosling Cl GFD/PVL UB6 96 A2
Gosling Wy BRXN/ST SW9 142 B2
Gospatrick Rd TOTM N17 49 J4
Gosport Rd WALTH E17 69 H2
Gosport Wy PECK SE15 143 G1
Gossage Rd WOOL/PLUM SE18 127 J5
Gosset St BETH E2 104 C2
Gosshill Rd CHST BR7 185 F5
Gossington Cl CHST BR7 167 G6
Gosterwood St DEPT SE8 124 B6
Gostling Rd WHTN TW2 155 F3
Goston Gdns THHTH CR7 180 B6
Goswell Pl FSBYE EC1V 6 B5
Goswell Rd FSBYE EC1V 6 B4
Gothic Cl DART DA1 171 G5
Gothic Ct HYS/HAR UB3 113 G6
Gothic Rd WHTN TW2 155 J4
Gottfried Ms KTTN NW5 84 C2
Goudhurst Rd BMLY BR1 183 H1
Gough Rd EN EN1 24 D3
FSTGT E7 88 D2
Gough Sq FLST/FETLN EC4A 11 K3
Gough St FSBYW WC1X 5 H6
Goulding Gdns THHTH CR7 180 D5
Gould Rd EBED/NFELT TW14 153 H2
WHTN TW2 155 K3
Gould Ter HACK E8 86 D3
Goulston St WCHPL E1 13 J3
Goulton Rd CLPT E5 86 D3
Gourley Pl SEVS/STOTM N15 68 A2
Gourley St SEVS/STOTM N15 68 A2
Gourock Rd ELTH/MOT SE9 147 F6
Govan St BETH E2 86 C6
Govier Cl SRTFD E15 88 C5
Gowan Av FUL/PGN SW6 139 H2
Gowan Rd WLSDN NW10 81 K5
Gower Cl CLAP SW4 161 H1
Gower Ms GWRST WC1E 10 D2
Gower Pl STPAN WC1H 4 B6
Gower Rd FSTGT E7 88 E4
ISLW TW7 116 A6
Gower St GWRST WC1E 4 B6
Gower's Wk WCHPL E1 104 C5
Gowland Pl BECK BR3 182 C5
Gowlett Rd PECK SE15 143 H4
Gowrie Rd BTSEA SW11 141 F4
Graburn Wy E/WMO/HCT KT8 173 J6
Grace Av BXLYHN DA7 149 G3
Gracechurch St BANK EC3V 13 F5
Grace Cl BARK/HLT IG6 55 F2
EDGE HA8 44 E3
ELTH/MOT SE9 166 C5
Gracedale Rd
STRHM/NOR SW16 179 G1
Gracefield Gdns
STRHM/NOR SW16 161 K5
Grace Jones Cl HACK * E8 86 B4
Grace Pl BOW E3 105 K2
Grace Rd CROY/NA CR0 196 D3
Grace's Ms CMBW SE5 142 E3
STJWD * NW8 101 G1
Grace's Rd CMBW SE5 143 F3
Grace St BOW E3 105 K2
The Gradient SYD SE26 163 H6
Graduate Pl STHWK SE1 19 G4
Graeme Rd EN EN1 24 A3
Graemesdyke Av
MORT/ESHN SW14 137 J4
Grafton Cl HSLWW TW4 154 D3
WEA W13 97 G5
WPK KT4 207 G1
Grafton Crs CAMTN NW1 84 B4
Grafton Gdns BCTR RM8 74 A6
FSBYPK N4 67 J3
Grafton Ms FITZ W1T 4 A7
Grafton Park Rd WPK KT4 192 B6
Grafton Pl CAMTN NW1 4 C5
Grafton Rd ACT W3 98 E6
BCTR RM8 74 A6
CROY/NA CR0 196 B5
ENC/FH EN2 23 F4
HRW HA1 60 C2
KTTN NW5 84 A3
NWMAL KT3 192 B1
WPK KT4 207 F1
Grafton Sq CLAP SW4 141 H5
Grafton St MYFR/PICC W1J 9 K6
Grafton Ter KTTN NW5 83 K3
Grafton Wy E/WMO/HCT KT8 188 E1
FITZ W1T 4 B7
GTPST W1W 10 A1
Grafton Yd KTTN NW5 84 B4
Graham Av MTCM CR4 179 F4
WEA W13 116 C2
Graham Cl CROY/NA CR0 198 D6
Grahame Park Wy MLHL NW7 45 H3
Graham Gdns SURB KT6 191 F5
Graham Rd BXLYHN DA7 149 G5
CHSWK W4 118 A3
HACK E8 86 C4
HDN NW4 63 K3
HPTN TW12 155 F6
KTN/HRWW/W HA3 42 E6
MTCM CR4 179 F4
PLSTW E13 106 E3
SEVS/STOTM N15 49 H6
WIM/MER SW19 177 J3
Graham St IS N1 6 B3
Graham Ter BFN/LL * DA15 168 C1
BGVA SW1W 15 H7
Grainger Cl NTHLT UB5 78 C3
Grainger Rd ISLW TW7 136 A3
WDGN N22 49 J4
Gramer Cl WAN E11 70 B6
Grampian Cl BELMT SM2 209 G5
HYS/HAR UB3 133 G1
ORP BR6 202 A3
Grampian Gdns CRICK NW2 64 C5
Granada St TOOT SW17 178 E1
Granard Av PUT/ROE SW15 138 E6
Granard Rd BAL SW12 160 E2
Granary Cl ED N9 36 E2
Granary Rd WCHPL E1 104 D3
Granary Sq IS * N1 85 G4
Granary St CAMTN NW1 4 C1
Granby Rd ELTH/MOT SE9 146 E3
WOOL/PLUM SE18 127 G3
Granby St BETH E2 7 K6
Granby Ter CAMTN NW1 4 A3
Grand Av BRYLDS KT5 191 J3
FARR EC1M 12 B1
MUSWH N10 66 A1
WBLY HA9 80 C3
Grand Av East WBLY HA9 80 D3
Grand Depot Rd
WOOL/PLUM SE18 127 F5
Grand Dr NWDGN UB2 115 H2
RYNPK SW20 177 F6
Granden Rd
STRHM/NOR * SW16 179 K5
Grandison Rd CLAP SW4 140 E6
WPK KT4 193 F6
Grand Junction Whf IS * N1 6 C3
Grand Pde FSBYPK * N4 67 H3
MORT/ESHN * SW14 137 K5
SURB * KT6 191 H5
WBLY * HA9 62 D6
Grand Union Canal Wk
HNWL W7 115 K3
MV/WKIL * W9 100 E4
NWDGN UB2 114 A3
STHL UB1 95 K3
STKPK UB11 112 E2
WLSDN NW10 98 D1
Grand Union Cl MV/WKIL W9 100 D4
Grand Union Crs HACK * E8 86 C6
Grand Union Wk CAMTN * NW1 84 B5
Grand Wk WCHPL * E1 105 G3
Granfield St BTSEA * SW11 140 C2
The Grange ALP/SUD HA0 80 C5
CROY/NA CR0 198 C6
HOR/WEW KT19 207 F2
NWMAL * KT3 192 D2
STHWK SE1 19 J4
WIM/MER SW19 177 G2
WKENS * W14 119 J4
WOT/HER KT12 188 A6
Grange Av EBAR EN4 33 J3
KTN/HRWW/W HA3 43 H5
NFNCH/WDSP N12 47 G1
SNWD SE25 181 F5
TRDG/WHET N20 32 C2
WFD IG8 52 E2
WHTN TW2 155 K4
Grangecliffe Gdns SNWD SE25 181 F5
Grange Cl BFN/LL DA15 168 B5
E/WMO/HCT KT8 189 G1
HYS/HAR UB3 94 C4
NWDGN UB2 114 E5
WFD IG8 52 E3
Grange Ct ALP/SUD * HA0 79 J3
BELMT * SM2 209 F5
HRW * HA1 79 F1
NTHLT UB5 95 G1
PIN * HA5 41 J6
WLGTN * SM6 210 B1
Grangecourt Rd
STNW/STAM N16 68 A5
Grange Crs CHIG IG7 54 D1
THMD SE28 109 J5
Grangedale Cl NTHWD HA6 40 C4
Grange Dr CHST BR7 184 D2
ORP BR6 217 J6
Grange Farm Cl
RYLN/HDSTN HA2 60 C6
Grange Gdns HAMP NW3 83 F1
PIN HA5 59 K1
SNWD SE25 181 F5
STHGT/OAK N14 34 D3
Grange Gv IS N1 85 J4
Grange Hl EDGE HA8 44 E1
SNWD SE25 181 F5
Grangehill Pl ELTH/MOT SE9 146 E4
Grangehill Rd ELTH/MOT SE9 146 E5
Grange Houses HBRY * N5 85 J2
Grange La DUL SE21 163 G4
Grange Ms FELT * TW13 153 G5
Grangemill Rd CAT SE6 164 D5
Grangemill Wy CAT SE6 164 D4
Grange Pk EA W5 117 F1
Grange Park Av WCHMH N21 35 H1
Grange Park Pl RYNPK SW20 176 E3
Grange Park Rd LEY E10 69 K6
THHTH CR7 180 E6
Grange Pl KIL/WHAMP NW6 82 E5
Grange Rd BARN SW13 138 D2
BELMT SM2 208 E5
CHSGTN KT9 206 A2
CHSWK W4 117 J5
E/WMO/HCT KT8 189 G1
EA W5 116 E1
EDGE HA8 45 F2
HARH RM3 57 K2
HGT N6 66 A3
HRW HA1 61 G3
HYS/HAR UB3 94 C5
IL IG1 90 C2
KUT KT1 175 F6
LEY E10 69 J5
ORP BR6 201 H6
PLSTW E13 106 E2
RYLN/HDSTN HA2 60 D6
SNWD SE25 180 E6
STHL UB1 114 D2
STHWK SE1 19 H5
TOTM N17 50 C2
WALTH E17 69 G2
WLSDN NW10 81 K4
Granger Wy ROM RM1 75 J3
Grange St IS N1 7 F1
Grange V BELMT SM2 209 F5
Grangeview Rd TRDG/WHET N20 33 G3
Grange Wk STHWK SE1 19 H4
Grange Walk Ms STHWK SE1 19 H5
The Grangeway WCHMH N21 35 H1
Grange Wy ERITH DA8 150 E1
Grangeway KIL/WHAMP NW6 82 E5
NFNCH/WDSP N12 33 G6
WFD IG8 39 G6
Grangeway Gdns REDBR IG4 71 J2
Grangewood BXLY DA5 169 G3
Grangewood Cl PIN HA5 58 E2
Grangewood La BECK BR3 182 C2
Grangewood St EHAM E6 89 H6
Grange Yd STHWK SE1 19 J5
Granham Gdns ED N9 36 B4
Granite St WOOL/PLUM SE18 128 A5
Granleigh Rd WAN E11 70 C6
Gransden Av HACK E8 86 D5
Gransden Rd SHB W12 118 C2
Grantbridge St IS N1 6 B2
Grantchester KUT * KT1 175 H5
Grantchester Cl HRW HA1 79 F1
Grant Cl STHGT/OAK N14 34 C2
Grantham Cl EDGE HA8 30 A5
Grantham Gdns CHDH RM6 74 B3
Grantham Pl MYFR/PICC W1J 15 J1
Grantham Rd BRXN/ST SW9 141 K4
CHSWK W4 138 B1
MNPK E12 90 A1
Grantley Pl ESH/CLAY KT10 204 B3
Grantley Rd HSLWW TW4 134 B3
Grantley St WCHPL E1 105 F2
Grantock Rd WALTH E17 52 B4
Granton Rd GDMY/SEVK IG3 73 G5
SCUP DA14 186 C2
STRHM/NOR SW16 179 H4
Grant Rd BTSEA SW11 140 D4
CROY/NA CR0 197 G5
KTN/HRWW/W HA3 42 E6
Grants Cl MLHL NW7 46 A3
Grant St IS N1 5 J2
PLSTW E13 106 E2
Grant Ter STNW/STAM * N16 68 C4
Grantully Rd MV/WKIL W9 101 F2
Grant Wy ISLW TW7 116 B6
Granville Ar BRXN/ST * SW9 142 B5
Granville Av ED N9 36 E5
FELT TW13 153 K4
HSLW TW3 135 F6
Granville Cl CROY/NA CR0 197 F6
Granville Gdns EA W5 117 G1
STRHM/NOR SW16 180 A4
Granville Gv LEW SE13 145 F4
Granville Ms SCUP DA14 168 B6
Granville Pk LEW SE13 145 F4
Granville Pl FUL/PGN * SW6 140 A1
MBLAR W1H 9 G4
NFNCH/WDSP * N12 47 G3
PIN HA5 41 H6
Granville Rd BAR EN5 20 A5
CRICK NW2 64 D6
FSBYPK N4 67 F3
HYS/HAR UB3 113 J4
IL IG1 72 B5
KIL/WHAMP NW6 100 E1
NFNCH/WDSP N12 47 G3
PLMGR N13 49 F2
SCUP DA14 168 B6
SWFD E18 53 F5
WALTH E17 69 K3
WAND/EARL SW18 159 K2
WDGN N22 49 H4
WELL DA16 148 D4
WIM/MER SW19 177 K3
Granville Sq PECK * SE15 143 F1
Granville St FSBYW WC1X 5 H5
Grape St LSQ/SEVD WC2H 10 E3
Graphite Sq LBTH * SE11 122 A5
Grapsome Cl CHSGTN KT9 205 J5
Grasdene Rd WOOL/PLUM SE18 148 B1
Grasmere Av ACT W3 98 E6
HSLW TW3 155 G1
ORP BR6 216 B1
PUT/ROE SW15 158 A6
RSLP HA4 58 A4
WBLY HA9 61 K4
WIM/MER SW19 177 K6
Grasmere Cl EBED/NFELT TW14 153 J3
Grasmere Ct WDGN N22 49 F2
Grasmere Gdns
KTN/HRWW/W HA3 43 G5
ORP BR6 216 B1
REDBR IG4 71 J2
Grasmere Rd BMLY BR1 183 J4
BXLYHN DA7 149 K2
MUSWH N10 48 B4
ORP BR6 216 B1
PLSTW E13 106 E1
SNWD SE25 197 J3
STRHM/NOR SW16 180 A1
TOTM N17 50 C2
Grasshaven Wy THMD SE28 128 A1
Grassington Cl FBAR/BDGN N11 48 A1
Grassington Rd SCUP DA14 168 B6
Grassmount FSTH SE23 163 J4
Grass Pk FNCH N3 46 D4
Grassway WLGTN SM6 210 C2
Grasvenor Av BAR EN5 32 E1
Grately Wy PECK * SE15 143 F1
Gratton Rd WKENS W14 119 H3
Gravel Hl BXLYHS DA6 149 J6
CROY/NA CR0 213 F4
FNCH N3 46 D5
Gravel Hill Cl BXLY DA5 169 J1
BXLYHS DA6 149 J6
Gravel La WCHPL E1 13 J3
Gravel Pit Wy ORP BR6 202 B6
Gravel Rd HAYES BR2 200 D6
WHTN TW2 155 K3
Gravelwood Cl CHST BR7 167 H5
Gravenel Gdns TOOT * SW17 178 D1
Graveney Gv PGE/AN SE20 181 K3
Graveney Rd TOOT SW17 160 D6
Gravesend Rd SHB W12 99 J6
Gray Av BCTR RM8 74 B5
Gray Gdns HCH RM12 93 J4
Grayham Crs NWMAL KT3 192 A1
Grayham Rd NWMAL KT3 192 A1
Grayland Cl BMLY BR1 184 C4
Grayling Cl CAN/RD E16 106 C3
Grayling Ct EA * W5 116 E1
Grayling Rd STNW/STAM N16 67 K6
Grayling Sq BETH * E2 104 C2
Grays Cottages
STMC/STPC * BR5 186 D4
Grayscroft Rd
STRHM/NOR SW16 179 J3
Grays Farm Rd STMC/STPC BR5 186 C4
Grayshott Rd BTSEA SW11 141 F4
Gray's Inn Rd FSBYW WC1X 5 F4
Gray's Inn Sq GINN WC1R 11 J1
Grays La ASHF TW15 152 E6
Gray St STHWK SE1 18 A2
Grayswood Gdns RYNPK SW20 176 E5
Gray's Yd MHST * W1U 9 H4
Graywood Ct NFNCH/WDSP N12 47 G3
Grazebrook Rd STNW/STAM N16 67 K6
Grazeley Cl BXLYHS DA6 149 K6
Great Benty WDR/YW UB7 112 B4
Great Brownings SYD SE26 163 G6
Great Bushey Dr
TRDG/WHET N20 33 F3
Great Cambridge Jct
PLMGR N13 49 J1
Great Cambridge Rd UED N18 49 K1
Great Castle St REGST W1B 10 A3
Great Central Av RSLP HA4 77 G3
Great Central St CAMTN NW1 8 E1
Great Central Wy WBLY HA9 80 E3
Great Chapel St SOHO/CST W1F 10 C3
Great Chertsey Rd CHSWK W4 138 A2
FELT TW13 154 E5
Great Church La HMSMTH W6 119 G5
Great College St WEST SW1P 16 E4
Great Cross Av GNWCH SE10 145 H1
Great Cullings ROMW/RG RM7 75 G6
Great Cumberland Ms
MBLAR W1H 8 E4
Great Cumberland Pl MBLAR W1H 8 E3
Great Dover St STHWK SE1 18 E4
Greatdown Rd HNWL W7 97 F4
Great Eastern Rd SRTFD E15 88 B5
Great Eastern St SDTCH EC2A 7 G5
Great Eastern Whf
BTSEA * SW11 140 D1
Great Elms Rd HAYES BR2 200 B1
Great Fld CDALE/KGS NW9 45 G4
Greatfield Av EHAM E6 107 K3
Greatfield Cl LEW SE13 144 D5
Greatfields Rd BARK IG11 90 D6
Great Galley Cl BARK IG11 109 H2
Great Gardens Rd EMPK RM11 75 K3
Great Gatton Cl CROY/NA CR0 198 B4
Great George St STJSPK SW1H 16 D3
Great Guildford St STHWK SE1 18 C1
Great Harry Dr ELTH/MOT SE9 167 F5
Great James St BMSBY WC1N 11 G1
Great Marlborough St
SOHO/CST W1F 10 A4
Great Maze Pond STHWK SE1 19 F1
Great New St FLST/FETLN * EC4A 11 K3
Great North Rd BAR EN5 33 F1
EFNCH N2 65 J1
Great North Wy (Barnet By-Pass)
HDN NW4 45 K4
Greatorex St WCHPL E1 104 C4
Great Ormond St BMSBY WC1N 11 F1
Great Percy St FSBYW WC1X 5 H4
Great Peter St WEST SW1P 16 C5
Great Portland St GTPST W1W 9 K1
Great Pulteney St
SOHO/CST W1F 10 B5
Great Queen St DART DA1 171 J1
HOL/ALD WC2B 11 G3
Great Russell St FITZ W1T 10 D3
Great St Helen's HDTCH EC3A 13 G4
Great St Thomas Apostle
BLKFR EC4V 12 D5
Great Scotland Yd WHALL SW1A 16 E1
Great Smith St WEST SW1P 16 D4
Great South-West Rd
EBED/NFELT TW14 153 F2
Great Spilmans EDUL SE22 143 F6
Great Strd CDALE/KGS NW9 45 H5
Great Suffolk St STHWK SE1 18 B2
Great Sutton St FSBYE EC1V 6 B7
Great Swan Aly LOTH EC2R 12 E3
Great Thrift STMC/STPC BR5 201 H1
Great Titchfield St GTPST W1W 3 K7
Great Tower St MON EC3R 13 G5
Great Trinity La BLKFR EC4V 12 D5
Great Turnstile HHOL * WC1V 11 H2
Great Western Rd BAY/PAD W2 100 D4
Great West Rd CHSWK W4 117 K6
HEST TW5 134 D3
HMSMTH W6 118 E5
Great West Rd Chiswick
CHSWK W4 118 C6
Great West Rd Ellesmere Rd
CHSWK W4 117 K6
Great West Rd Hogarth La
CHSWK W4 118 A6
Great Winchester St
OBST EC2N 13 F3
Great Windmill St
SOHO/SHAV W1D 10 C6
Greatwood CHST BR7 185 F3
Greaves Cl BARK IG11 90 D5
Greaves Cottages
POP/IOD * E14 105 G4
Greaves Pl TOOT SW17 160 D6
Grebe Av YEAD UB4 95 H5
Grebe Cl BARK IG11 109 G3
FSTGT E7 88 D3
WALTH E17 51 G3
Grebe Ct SUT SM1 208 D3
Grebe Ter KUT * KT1 175 F6
Grecian Crs NRWD SE19 180 C2
Greek St SOHO/SHAV W1D 10 D4
The Green ACT W3 99 G5
BKHH * IG9 39 F3
BXLYHN DA7 149 H2
CAR * SM5 210 A2
CROY/NA CR0 213 H6
ED N9 36 C4
FELT TW13 154 A4
HAYES BR2 199 K4
HEST TW5 115 F6
HGDN/ICK UB10 58 A6
HRW HA1 61 G6
MRDN SM4 193 H1
NWDGN UB2 114 E2
NWMAL KT3 175 K6
RCH/KEW TW9 136 E6
SCUP DA14 186 B1
SRTFD E15 88 D4
STHGT/OAK N14 34 D5
STMC/STPC BR5 186 C3
SUT SM1 209 F1
TOTM N17 49 J2
WAN E11 71 F3
WCHMH N21 35 G2
WDR/YW UB7 112 A3
WELL DA16 147 K5
WHTN TW2 155 K3
Greenacre Cl BAR EN5 20 D1
NTHLT UB5 77 K3
Greenacre Pl WLGTN SM6 195 G6
Greenacres BUSH WD23 28 D4
ELTH/MOT SE9 167 F1
Green Acres CROY/NA CR0 212 B1
SCUP * DA14 168 A6
Greenacres Cl ORP BR6 216 C2

Greenacres Dr STAN HA7 43 H3
Greenacre Sq
BERM/RHTH * SE16 124 A2
Greenacre Wk STHGT/OAK N14 34 D5
Green Arbour Ct STP * EC4M 12 A3
Green Av MLHL NW7 31 F6
WEA W13 116 C3
Greenaway Av UED * N18 51 F1
Greenaway Gdns HAMP NW3 83 F2
Green Bank NFNCH/WDSP N12 33 F6
WAP E1W 123 J1
Greenbank Av ALP/SUD HA0 79 G3
Greenbank Cl CHING E4 38 A4
Greenbank Crs FNCH N3 64 C1
Greenbanks DART DA1 171 H4
Greenbay Rd CHARL SE7 146 C1
Greenberry St STJWD NW8 2 C3
Greenbrook Av EBAR EN4 21 G2
Green Chain Wk BECK BR3 183 F3
CHARL SE7 126 C4
ELTH/MOT SE9 147 G6
SYD SE26 182 A2
THMD SE28 128 E1
Green Cl CAR SM5 194 E6
CDALE/KGS NW9 62 E3
EFNCH N2 65 G4
FELT TW13 172 D1
HAYES BR2 183 H6
Greencoat Pl WEST SW1P 16 B6
Greencoat Rw WEST SW1P 16 B5
Green Court Av CROY/NA CR0 197 J6
Greencourt Av EDGE HA8 44 C4
Green Court Gdns
CROY/NA CR0 197 J6
Greencourt Rd STMC/STPC BR5 201 K2
Greencroft EDGE HA8 44 E1
Greencroft Av RSLP HA4 59 G6
Greencroft Gdns EN EN1 24 A4
KIL/WHAMP NW6 83 F5
Greencroft Rd HEST TW5 134 E2
Green Dl EDUL SE22 143 F6
Green Dragon La BTFD TW8 117 F5
WCHMH N21 23 F6
Green Dragon Yd WCHPL E1 104 C4
Green Dr STHL UB1 115 F1
Green End CHSGTN KT9 205 K2
WCHMH N21 35 H4
Greenend Rd CHSWK W4 118 B2
Green Farm Cl ORP BR6 217 F3
Greenfell Man DEPT * SE8 124 C5
Greenfield Av BRYLDS KT5 191 J4
OXHEY WD19 27 J4
Greenfield Dr BMLY BR1 184 B5
EFNCH N2 65 K1
Greenfield Gdns CRICK NW2 64 C6
DAGW RM9 91 J6
STMC/STPC BR5 201 H4
Greenfield Rd DAGW RM9 91 J6
SEVS/STOTM N15 68 A2
WCHPL E1 104 C4
Greenfields STHL UB1 96 A6
Greenfield Wy RYLN/HDSTN HA2 42 B6
Greenford Av HNWL W7 96 E3
STHL UB1 95 K6
Greenford Gdns GFD/PVL UB6 96 B2
Greenford Rd GFD/PVL UB6 78 E3
STHL UB1 96 C6
SUT SM1 209 F2
Green Gdns ORP BR6 216 C3
Greengate GFD/PVL UB6 79 H4
Greengate St PLSTW E13 107 F1
Greenhalgh Wk EFNCH N2 65 G1
Greenham Cl STHWK SE1 17 J3
Greenham Crs CHING E4 51 H2
Greenham Rd MUSWH N10 48 A5
Greenhaven Dr THMD SE28 109 H5
Greenheys Cl NTHWD HA6 40 C4
Greenheys Dr SWFD E18 52 D6
Greenhill BKHH IG9 39 G3
HAMP NW3 83 H2
SUT SM1 194 B6
WBLY HA9 62 D6
Green Hl WOOL/PLUM SE18 126 E5
Greenhill Ct BAR * EN5 21 F6
Greenhill Crs WATW WD18 26 C1
Greenhill Gdns NTHLT UB5 95 K1
Greenhill Gv MNPK E12 89 J2
Greenhill Pde BAR * EN5 21 F6
Greenhill Pk BAR EN5 21 G6
WLSDN NW10 81 G6
Greenhill Rd HRW HA1 60 E3
WLSDN NW10 81 G6
Greenhill's Rents FARR * EC1M 12 A1
Greenhills Ter IS N1 85 K4
Greenhill Ter NTHLT * UB5 95 K1
Greenhill Wy HRW HA1 60 E3
WBLY HA9 62 D6
Greenhithe Cl ELTH/MOT SE9 167 K2
Greenholm Rd ELTH/MOT SE9 147 G6
Green Hundred Rd PECK SE15 123 H6
Greenhurst Rd WNWD SE27 180 B1
Greening St ABYW SE2 128 D4
Greenland Crs NWDGN UB2 114 B3
Greenland Ms DEPT SE8 124 A5
Greenland Pl CAMTN * NW1 84 B6
Greenland Quay
BERM/RHTH SE16 124 A4
Greenland Rd BAR EN5 32 A1
CAMTN NW1 84 C6
Greenlands HOR/WEW KT19 206 D3
Greenland St CAMTN * NW1 84 B6
Green La BCTR RM8 74 B6
CHSGTN KT9 206 A6
E/WMO/HCT KT8 189 G2
EDGE HA8 30 B6
ELTH/MOT SE9 167 F4
FELT TW13 172 D1
HDN NW4 64 B2
HNWL W7 115 K2
HSLWW TW4 134 B5
IL IG1 72 D6
MRDN SM4 194 A4
NTHWD HA6 40 B3
NWMAL KT3 191 K2
OXHEY WD19 27 G3
PGE/AN SE20 182 A3
STAN HA7 29 H6
THHTH CR7 180 C4
UX/CGN UB8 94 A4
WPK KT4 192 D5
Green La Cottages STAN * HA7 29 H6
Green La Gdns THHTH CR7 180 D5
Green Lanes CEND/HSY/T N8 49 H6
FSBYPK N4 67 H3
HOR/WEW KT19 207 G6
PLMGR N13 49 F1
WCHMH N21 35 H3
Greenlaw Ct EA * W5 97 K5
Greenlaw Gdns NWMAL KT3 192 C4
Green Lawns
NFNCH/WDSP * N12 47 F2
RSLP * HA4 59 G5
Greenlaw St WOOL/PLUM SE18 127 F3
Green Leaf Av WLGTN SM6 210 D2
Greenleaf Cl
BRXS/STRHM * SW2 162 B2
Greenleafe Dr BARK/HLT IG6 54 B6
Greenleaf Rd EHAM E6 89 G6
WALTH E17 51 H6
Greenlea Pk WIM/MER * SW19 178 D4
Greenleigh Av STMC/STPC BR5 202 C1
Green Man La
EBED/NFELT TW14 133 K5
WEA W13 97 G6
Greenman St IS N1 85 J5
Greenmead Cl SNWD SE25 197 H2
Green Moor Link WCHMH N21 35 H2
Greenmoor Rd PEND EN3 24 E3
Greenoak Pl EBAR EN4 21 K3
Green Oaks NWDGN * UB2 114 C4
Greenoak Wy WIM/MER SW19 159 G6
Greenock Rd ACT W3 117 J3
STRHM/NOR SW16 179 J4
Greenock Wy ROM RM1 57 G3
Green Pde HSLW * TW3 155 G1
Green Pond Cl WALTH E17 51 G6
Green Pond Rd WALTH E17 51 G6
Green Ride LOU IG10 38 E1
Green Rd STHGT/OAK N14 34 B1
TRDG/WHET N20 33 G5
Greens Ct NTGHL * W11 119 J1
SOHO/CST W1F 10 C5
Greens End WOOL/PLUM SE18 127 G4
Greenshank Cl WALTH E17 51 G3
Greenside BCTR RM8 73 J6
BXLY DA5 169 F3
Greenside Cl CAT SE6 165 G4
TRDG/WHET N20 33 H4
Greenside Rd CROY/NA CR0 196 B4
SHB W12 118 D3
Greenslade Rd BARK IG11 90 D5
Greenstead Av WFD IG8 53 G2
Greenstead Gdns
PUT/ROE SW15 138 D6
WFD IG8 53 G2
Greensted Rd LOU IG10 39 J2
Greenstone Ms WAN E11 70 E3
Green St FSTGT E7 89 F3
MYFR/PKLN W1K 9 F5
PEND EN3 25 F4
Green Street Green Rd
DART DA1 171 K3
Greenstreet Hl NWCR * SE14 144 A4
Greensward BUSH WD23 28 B1
Green Ter CLKNW EC1R 5 K5
Green V BXLYHS DA6 148 E6
EA W5 98 B5
Greenvale Rd ELTH/MOT SE9 146 E5
Green Verges STAN HA7 43 K3
Green Vw CHSGTN KT9 206 B5
Greenview Av BECK BR3 198 B3
Greenview Cl ACT W3 118 B1
The Green Wk CHING E4 38 A3
Green Wk DART DA1 150 C5
HDN NW4 64 B2
NWDGN UB2 115 F5
RSLP HA4 58 D5
STHWK SE1 19 G5
WFD IG8 53 J2
Green Wy ELTH/MOT SE9 146 C6
HAYES BR2 200 D3
Greenway BCTR RM8 73 J6
CHST BR7 185 F1
KTN/HRWW/W HA3 62 A2
PIN HA5 41 F5
RYNPK SW20 193 F1
STHGT/OAK N14 34 E4
TRDG/WHET N20 32 E4
WLGTN SM6 210 C2
YEAD UB4 95 F3
Greenway Av WALTH E17 70 B1
Greenway Cl CDALE/KGS NW9 45 F5
FBAR/BDGN N11 48 A2
FSBYPK N4 67 J6
TRDG/WHET N20 32 E4
Greenway Ct IL IG1 72 A5
Greenway Gdns CDALE/KGS NW9 44 E5
CROY/NA CR0 213 H1
GFD/PVL UB6 96 A2
Green Way Gdns
KTN/HRWW/W HA3 42 E5
The Greenways TWK * TW1 156 B1
Greenways BECK BR3 182 D5
ESH/CLAY KT10 204 E2
NFNCH/WDSP * N12 47 G2
The Green Wy
KTN/HRWW/W HA3 42 E4
The Greenway CDALE/KGS NW9 45 F5
HSLWW * TW4 134 E5
PIN HA5 59 K3
Greenwell St GTPST W1W 3 K7
Greenwich Church St
GNWCH * SE10 125 F6
Greenwich Crs EHAM E6 107 J4
Greenwich Foot Tnl
POP/IOD E14 125 F5
Greenwich Hts
WOOL/PLUM SE18 146 D1
Greenwich High Rd
GNWCH SE10 144 E1
Greenwich Park St
GNWCH * SE10 125 G6
Greenwich Quay DEPT SE8 124 E6
Greenwich South St
GNWCH SE10 144 E2
Greenwich Vw POP/IOD E14 124 E3
Greenwood Av DAGE RM10 92 D2
PEND EN3 25 G2
Greenwood Cl BFN/LL DA15 168 B4
MRDN SM4 193 H1
STMC/STPC BR5 201 K3
THDIT KT7 190 B5
Greenwood Dr CHING E4 52 A1
Greenwood Gdns BARK/HLT IG6 54 C3
PLMGR N13 35 H5
Greenwood La HPTN TW12 173 G1
Greenwood Pk KUTN/CMB KT2 176 B3
Greenwood Pl KTTN NW5 84 B3
Greenwood Rd BXLY DA5 170 A6
CROY/NA CR0 196 C4
HACK E8 86 C4
ISLW TW7 135 K4
MTCM CR4 179 J6
PLSTW E13 106 D1
THDIT KT7 190 B5
Greenwood Ter WLSDN * NW10 81 F6
Green Wrythe Crs CAR SM5 194 D5
Green Wrythe La MRDN SM4 194 C3
Green Yd FSBYW WC1X 5 H6
Greer Rd KTN/HRWW/W HA3 42 C4
Greet St STHWK SE1 17 K1
Greg Cl LEY E10 70 A3
Gregor Ms BKHTH/KID SE3 145 K1
Gregory Crs ELTH/MOT SE9 166 C2
Gregory Pl KENS W8 120 A2
Gregory Rd CHDH RM6 73 K1
NWDGN UB2 115 F3
Greig Cl CEND/HSY/T N8 66 E2
Greig Ter WALW SE17 122 C6
Grenaby Av CROY/NA CR0 196 E4
Grenaby Rd CROY/NA CR0 196 E4
Grenada Rd CHARL SE7 146 B1
Grenade St POP/IOD E14 105 H6
Grenadier St CAN/RD E16 127 F1
Grena Gdns RCH/KEW TW9 137 G5
Grenard Cl PECK * SE15 143 H1
Grena Rd RCH/KEW TW9 137 G5
Grendon Gdns WBLY HA9 62 C6
Grendon St STJWD NW8 2 C6
Grenfell Av HCH RM12 75 H5
Grenfell Ct MLHL * NW7 45 K2
Grenfell Gdns
KTN/HRWW/W HA3 62 A4
Grenfell Rd NTGHL W11 100 B6
TOOT SW17 178 E2
Grenfell Wk NTGHL W11 100 B6
Grennell Cl SUT SM1 194 C6
Grennell Rd SUT SM1 194 B6
Grenoble Gdns PLMGR N13 49 G2
Grenville Cl BRYLDS KT5 191 K5
FNCH N3 46 D4
Grenville Gdns WFD IG8 53 G3
Grenville Ms HPTN TW12 173 G1
Grenville Pl MLHL NW7 45 F1
SKENS * SW7 120 B3
Grenville Rd ARCH N19 66 E5
Grenville St BMSBY WC1N 5 F7
Gresham Av TRDG/WHET N20 33 K6
Gresham Cl BXLY DA5 169 F1
ENC/FH EN2 23 J4
Gresham Dr CHDH RM6 73 H2
Gresham Gdns CRICK NW2 64 C5
Gresham Rd BECK BR3 182 B5
BRXN/ST SW9 142 B4
CAN/RD E16 107 F5
EDGE HA8 44 B2
EHAM E6 107 K1
HEST TW5 135 H2
HPTN TW12 173 F2
SNWD * SE25 197 H1
WLSDN NW10 81 F3
Gresham St CITYW EC2V 12 C3
Gresham Wy WIM/MER SW19 159 K5
Gresley Cl SEVS/STOTM * N15 67 K1
WALTH E17 69 G3
Gresley Rd ARCH N19 66 C5
Gressenhall Rd
WAND/EARL SW18 159 J1
Gresse St FITZ W1T 10 C2
Gresswell Cl SCUP DA14 168 B5
Greswell St FUL/PGN SW6 139 G2
Gretton Rd TOTM N17 50 A3
Greville Cl TWK TW1 156 C2
Greville Ms KIL/WHAMP NW6 83 F6
Greville Rd KIL/WHAMP NW6 101 F1
RCHPK/HAM TW10 157 G1
WALTH E17 70 A1
Greville St HCIRC EC1N 11 K2
Grey Cl EFNCH N2 65 G3
Greycoat Pl WEST SW1P 16 C5
Greycoat St WEST SW1P 16 C5
Greycot Rd BECK BR3 182 D1
Grey Eagle St WCHPL E1 13 K1
Greyfell Cl STAN HA7 43 H1
Greyhound Hl HDN NW4 45 J6
Greyhound La
STRHM/NOR SW16 179 K2
Greyhound Rd HMSMTH W6 119 G6
SUT SM1 209 G3
TOTM N17 50 A6
WLSDN * NW10 99 K2
Greyhound Ter
STRHM/NOR SW16 179 H4
Greyhound Wy DART DA1 150 B6
Greyladies Gdns GNWCH * SE10 145 F3
Greys Park Cl HAYES BR2 215 G3
Greystead Rd FSTH SE23 163 K2
Greystoke Av PIN HA5 42 A6
Greystoke Cottages EA * W5 98 A3
Greystoke Gdns EA W5 98 A3
ENC/FH EN2 22 D5
Greystone Gdns BARK/HLT IG6 54 C5
KTN/HRWW/W HA3 61 J3
Greyswood Av UED * N18 51 F1
Greyswood St
STRHM/NOR SW16 179 G2
Grierson Rd FSTH SE23 164 B1
Griffin Centre
EBED/NFELT * TW14 154 A1
Griffin Cl WLSDN NW10 81 K3
Griffin Manor Wy THMD SE28 127 J3
Griffin Rd TOTM N17 50 A5
WOOL/PLUM SE18 127 J5
Griffith Cl CHDH RM6 73 J4
Griffiths Rd WIM/MER SW19 177 K3
Griggs Ap IL IG1 72 C6
Grigg's Pl STHWK SE1 19 H5
Griggs Rd LEY E10 70 A3
Grimsby Gv CAN/RD E16 127 G2
Grimsby St WCHPL E1 7 K7
Grimsdyke Crs BAR EN5 20 A4
Grimsdyke Rd PIN HA5 41 J3
Grimsel Pth CMBW SE5 142 C1
Grimshaw Cl HGT * N6 66 A4
Grimshaw Wy ROM RM1 75 G2
Grimston Rd FUL/PGN SW6 139 J3
Grimwade Av CROY/NA CR0 212 C1
Grimwood Rd TWK TW1 156 A2
Grindall Cl CROY/NA CR0 211 H2
Grindal St STHWK SE1 17 J3
Grindleford Av FBAR/BDGN N11 34 A4
Grindley Gdns CROY/NA * CR0 197 G3
Grinling Pl DEPT SE8 124 D6
Grinstead Rd DEPT SE8 124 B5
Grisle Cl ED N9 36 D6
Grittleton Av WBLY HA9 80 D4
Grittleton Rd MV/WKIL W9 100 E3
Grocers' Hall Ct LOTH * EC2R 12 E4
Groombridge Cl WELL DA16 148 B6
Groombridge Rd HOM E9 87 F5
Groom Cl HAYES BR2 200 A1
Groom Crs WAND/EARL SW18 160 C2
Groomfield Cl TOOT SW17 161 F6
Groom Pl KTBR SW1X 15 H4
Grooms Dr RSLP HA4 58 E2
Grosmont Rd
WOOL/PLUM SE18 128 A5
Grosse Wy PUT/ROE SW15 158 E1
The Grove BXLYHS DA6 148 E5
CDALE/KGS NW9 63 F2
CEND/HSY/T N8 66 D2
EA W5 116 E1
EDGE HA8 30 D6
ENC/FH EN2 23 G3
FNCH N3 46 E3
FSBYPK N4 67 F4
GFD/PVL UB6 96 C5
GLDGN NW11 64 C4
HGT N6 66 A5
ISLW TW7 135 K2
PLMGR N13 35 G6
SCUP DA14 169 F6
SCUP DA14 187 F1
SRTFD E15 88 C5
TEDD TW11 156 B6
WOT/HER KT12 188 A4
WWKM BR4 214 A1
Grosvenor Av CAR SM5 209 K4
HBRY N5 85 J3
MORT/ESHN SW14 138 B4
RYLN/HDSTN HA2 60 B4
YEAD UB4 94 D1
Grosvenor Br VX/NE SW8 121 G6
Grosvenor Cottages KTBR SW1X 15 G6
Grosvenor Crs CDALE/KGS NW9 62 C1
DART DA1 151 G6
KTBR SW1X 15 H3
Grosvenor Crescent Ms KTBR
SW1X 15 G3
Grosvenor Gdns BGVA SW1W 15 K5
CRICK NW2 82 A4
GLDGN NW11 64 D3
KUTN/CMB KT2 174 E2
MORT/ESHN SW14 138 B4
MUSWH N10 48 C6
STHGT/OAK N14 22 D6
WFD IG8 52 E2
WLGTN SM6 210 C5
Grosvenor Gardens Ms East
BGVA * SW1W 15 K4
Grosvenor Gardens Ms North
BGVA SW1W 15 J5
Grosvenor Ga BAY/PAD W2 9 F6
Grosvenor Hl MYFR/PKLN W1K 9 J5
WIM/MER SW19 177 H2
Grosvenor Pde EA * W5 117 H1
Grosvenor Pk CMBW SE5 142 D1
Grosvenor Park Rd WALTH E17 69 J2
Grosvenor Pl KTBR SW1X 15 H2
Grosvenor Ri East WALTH E17 69 K2
Grosvenor Rd BCTR RM8 74 B5
BELV DA17 129 G6
BTFD TW8 116 E6
BXLYHS DA6 148 E6
CHSWK W4 117 K5
ED N9 36 D3
FNCH N3 46 D3
FSTGT E7 89 F4
HNWL W7 116 B1
HSLW TW3 134 E4
IL IG1 90 C1
LEY E10 70 A5
MUSWH N10 48 B4
NTHWD HA6 40 D1
NWDGN UB2 114 E3
PIM SW1V 121 H6
RCHPK/HAM TW10 137 F6
ROMW/RG RM7 75 F4
SNWD SE25 197 H1
STMC/STPC BR5 201 K3
TWK TW1 156 B2
WAN E11 71 F2
WLGTN SM6 210 B4
WWKM BR4 198 E6
Grosvenor Sq MYFR/PKLN W1K 9 H5
Grosvenor St MYFR/PKLN W1K 9 H5
Grosvenor Ter CMBW SE5 142 D1
Grosvenor V RSLP HA4 58 D6
Grosvenor Wy CLPT E5 68 E6
Grosvernor Wharf Rd
POP/IOD E14 125 G4
Grote's Buildings
BKHTH/KID SE3 145 H3
Grote's Pl BKHTH/KID SE3 145 H3
Groton Rd WAND/EARL SW18 160 A4
Grotto Ct STHWK * SE1 18 C2
Grotto Pas MHST W1U 9 G1
Grotto Rd TWK TW1 156 A4
Grove Av HNWL W7 96 E5
MUSWH N10 48 C5
PIN HA5 59 J1
SUT SM1 208 E4
TWK TW1 156 A3
Grove Bank OXHEY * WD19 27 H3
Grovebury Cl ERITH DA8 130 A6
Grovebury Ct STHGT/OAK N14 34 C2
Grovebury Rd THMD SE28 128 C2
Grove Cl FSTH SE23 164 A3
HAYES BR2 199 K6
KUT KT1 191 F1
STHGT/OAK * N14 34 B2
Grove Cottages CHSWK * W4 118 B6
Grove Ct E/WMO/HCT KT8 189 J2
EA * W5 117 F1
Grove Crs CDALE/KGS NW9 62 E1
FELT TW13 154 D6
KUT KT1 175 F6
SWFD E18 52 D5
WOT/HER KT12 188 A4
Grove Crescent Rd SRTFD E15 88 B4
Grovedale Rd ARCH N19 66 D6
Grove Dwellings WCHPL * E1 104 E4
Grove End KTTN NW5 84 B2
SWFD E18 52 D5
Grove End La ESH/CLAY KT10 189 J5
Grove End Rd STJWD NW8 2 A4
Grove Farm Pk NTHWD HA6 40 B1
Grove Footpath SURB KT6 191 F1
Grove Gdns HDN * NW4 63 J2
PEND EN3 25 F2
STJWD NW8 2 D5
TEDD TW11 156 B6
Grove Green Rd LEY E10 88 A1
WAN E11 70 B6
Groveherst Rd DART DA1 151 J4
Grove Hl HRW HA1 60 E4
SWFD E18 52 D5
Grove Hill Rd CMBW SE5 143 F4
HRW HA1 61 F4
Grove House Rd CEND/HSY/T N8 66 E1
Groveland Av
STRHM/NOR SW16 180 A3
Groveland Ct STP EC4M 12 D4
Groveland Rd BECK BR3 182 C6
Grovelands E/WMO/HCT KT8 189 F1
Grovelands Cl CMBW SE5 143 F3
RYLN/HDSTN HA2 78 B1
Grovelands Rd PLMGR N13 35 F6
SEVS/STOTM N15 68 C3
STMC/STPC BR5 186 B3
Groveland Wy NWMAL KT3 191 K2
Grove La CMBW SE5 142 E2
KUT KT1 191 F1
Grove Market Pl
ELTH/MOT * SE9 166 E1
Grove Ms HMSMTH W6 119 F3
Grove Pk CDALE/KGS NW9 62 E1
CMBW SE5 143 F3
WAN E11 71 F2
Grove Park Av CHING E4 51 K3
Grove Park Br CHSWK W4 137 K1
Grove Park Gdns CHSWK W4 137 J1
Grove Park Rd CHSWK W4 137 K1
ELTH/MOT SE9 166 D4
RAIN RM13 93 J6
SEVS/STOTM N15 68 A1
Grove Park Ter CHSWK W4 137 J1
Grove Pl ACT W3 117 K1
BAL SW12 161 G1
HAMP NW3 83 H1
Grove Rd ACT W3 117 K1
BARN SW13 138 C3
BELV DA17 129 G6
BOW E3 105 G1
BTFD TW8 116 D5
BXLYHN DA7 149 K5
CHDH RM6 73 J4
CHING E4 38 A5
CRICK NW2 82 A4
E/WMO/HCT KT8 189 J1
EA W5 97 K6
EBAR EN4 21 J4
EDGE HA8 44 C2
FBAR/BDGN N11 48 B1
HOM E9 87 F6
HSLW TW3 135 G5
ISLW TW7 135 K2
MTCM CR4 179 G5
NFNCH/WDSP N12 47 H1
NTHWD HA6 40 B1
PIN HA5 59 K2
RCHPK/HAM TW10 157 G1
SEVS/STOTM N15 68 A2
SURB KT6 190 E2
SUT SM1 208 E4
SWFD E18 52 D5
THHTH CR7 196 B1
WALTH E17 69 K2
WAN E11 70 D4
WHTN TW2 155 J5
WIM/MER SW19 178 B3
Grover Rd OXHEY WD19 27 H1
Groveside Cl ACT W3 98 C5
CAR SM5 194 D6
Groveside Rd CHING E4 38 C5
Grovestile Waye
EBED/NFELT TW14 153 G2
Grove St BERM/RHTH SE16 124 C4
UED N18 50 B2
Grove Ter KTTN NW5 84 A1
STHL * UB1 96 A6
TEDD TW11 156 B6
Grove V CHST BR7 185 F2
EDUL SE22 143 F5
Groveway BCTR RM8 91 K2
BRXN/ST SW9 142 A2
Grove Wy ESH/CLAY KT10 189 H5
WBLY HA9 80 E3
Grovewood Pl WFD IG8 53 K2
Grummant Rd PECK SE15 143 G2
Grundy St POP/IOD E14 105 K5
Gruneisen Rd FNCH N3 47 F3
Guardian Cl EMPK RM11 75 K6
Gubyon Av HNHL SE24 142 D6
Guernsey Cl HEST TW5 135 F2
Guernsey Gv HNHL SE24 162 D2
Guernsey Rd IS N1 85 J4
LEY E10 70 B5
Guibal Rd LEE/GVPK SE12 166 A3
Guildersfield Rd
STRHM/NOR SW16 179 K3
Guildford Av FELT TW13 153 K4
Guildford Gv GNWCH SE10 144 E2
Guildford Rd CROY/NA CR0 196 E3
EHAM E6 107 J5
GDMY/SEVK IG3 72 E6
VX/NE SW8 141 K2
WALTH E17 52 A4
Guildford Wy WLGTN SM6 210 E3
Guildhall Buildings CITYW EC2V 12 D3
Guildhall Yd CITYW EC2V 12 D3
Guildhouse St PIM SW1V 16 A7
Guildown Av NFNCH/WDSP N12 33 F6
Guild Rd CHARL SE7 126 C5
ERITH DA8 150 C1
Guildsway WALTH E17 51 H4
Guilford Av BRYLDS KT5 191 G2
Guilford Pl BMSBY WC1N 5 G7
Guilford St BMSBY WC1N 5 G7
Guillemot Pl WDGN * N22 49 F5
Guilsborough Cl WLSDN NW10 81 G5
Guinness Cl HOM E9 87 G5
HYS/HAR UB3 113 G3
Guinness Ct CROY/NA * CR0 197 G6
Guinness Sq STHWK SE1 19 G5
Guinness Trust Est CHEL SW3 14 E7
SRTFD * E15 88 D6
STNW/STAM * N16 68 B5
Guion Rd FUL/PGN SW6 139 J3
Gulland Wk IS * N1 85 J4
Gull Cl WLGTN SM6 210 E5
Gulliver Cl NTHLT UB5 77 K6
Gulliver Rd BFN/LL DA15 167 J4
Gulliver St BERM/RHTH SE16 124 C3
Gumleigh Rd EA W5 116 D4
Gumley Gdns ISLW TW7 136 B4
Gumping Rd STMC/STPC BR5 201 H6
Gundulph Rd HAYES BR2 184 B6
Gunmakers La HOM E9 87 G6
Gunnell Cl SNWD SE25 197 G3
SYD * SE26 163 H6
Gunner La WOOL/PLUM SE18 127 F5
Gunnersbury Av ACT W3 117 H4
Gunnersbury Av
(North Circular Rd) EA W5 98 B6

Gunnersbury Cl *CHSWK* * W4 ....117 J5
Gunnersbury Crs *ACT* W3................117 H2
Gunnersbury Dr *EA* W5 ....117 G2
Gunnersbury Gdns *ACT* W3 ....117 H2
Gunnersbury La *ACT* W3 ....117 H2
Gunners Gv *CHING* E4......................38 A5
Gunners Rd *WAND/EARL* SW18 ....160 C4
Gunning St *WOOL/PLUM* SE18 ....127 K4
Gunstor Rd *STNW/STAM* * N16 ....86 A2
Gun St *WCHPL* E1............................13 J2
Gunter Gv *EDGE* HA8 ....45 F4
WBPTN SW10 ....120 B6
Gunterstone Rd *WKENS* W14 ....119 H5
Gunthorpe St *WCHPL* E1 ....13 K2
Gunton Rd *CLPT* E5 ....86 D1
TOOT SW17......................................179 F2
Gunwhale Cl *BERM/RHTH* SE16 ....124 A1
Gurdon Rd *CHARL* SE7 ....125 K5
Gurnell Gv *WEA* W13.........................97 F3
Gurney Cl *BARK* IG11 ....90 B4
SRTFD E15 ....88 C3
WALTH E17 ....51 F4
Gurney Crs *CROY/NA* CR0 ....196 A5
Gurney Dr *EFNCH* N2 ....65 G2
Gurney Rd *CAR* SM5 ....210 A2
FUL/PGN SW6....................................140 B4
NTHLT UB5 ....95 F2
SRTFD E15 ....88 C3
Guthrie St *CHEL* SW3......................120 D5
Gutter La *CITYW* EC2V......................12 C3
Guyatt Gdns *MTCM* CR4...................179 F5
Guy Barnett Gv *BKHTH/KID* SE3 ....145 K4
Guy Rd *CROY/NA* CR0 ....210 E1
Guyscliff Rd *LEW* SE13 ....145 F6
Guysfield Cl *RAIN* RM13 ....93 J6
Guysfield Dr *RAIN* RM13 ....93 J6
Guy St *STHWK* SE1 ....19 F2
Gwalior Rd *PUT/ROE* SW15 ....139 G5
Gwendolen Av *PUT/ROE* SW15 ....139 G6
Gwendoline Av *PLSTW* E13 ....89 F6
Gwendwr Rd *WKENS* W14 ....119 H5
Gweneth Cottages *EDGE* * HA8 ....44 C2
Gwillim Cl *BFN/LL* DA15 ....168 B1
Gwydor Rd *BECK* BR3 ....198 A1
Gwydyr Rd *HAYES* BR2 ....183 J6
Gwyn Cl *FUL/PGN* SW6 ....140 B1
Gwynne Av *CROY/NA* CR0 ....198 A4
Gwynne Park Av *WFD* IG8 ....53 K2
Gwynne Rd *BTSEA* SW11 ....140 C3
Gwynne Whf *CHSWK* W4 ....118 C6
Gylcote Cl *CMBW* SE5 ....142 E5
Gyles Pk *STAN* HA7 ....43 J4
Gyllyngdune Gdns
GDMY/SEVK IG3 ....91 F1

H

Haarlem Rd *WKENS* W14 ....119 G3
Haberdasher Pl *IS* N1.........................7 F4
Haberdasher St *IS* N1.........................7 F4
Haccombe Rd *WIM/MER* SW19.......178 B2
Hackbridge Park Gdns
CAR SM5 ....194 E6
Hackbridge Rd *CAR* SM5 ....195 F6
Hackford Rd *BRXN/ST* SW9 ....142 A2
Hackford Wk *BRXN/ST* SW9 ....142 A2
Hackington Crs *BECK* BR3 ....182 D2
Hackney Gv *HACK* E8 ....86 D4
Hackney Rd *BETH* E2 ....7 J4
Haddenham Ct *OXHEY* * WD19.........27 H5
Hadden Rd *THMD* SE28 ....127 K3
Hadden Wy *GFD/PVL* UB6 ....78 D4
Haddington Rd *BMLY* BR1...............165 G5
Haddon Cl *EN* EN1...........................36 C1
NWMAL KT3 ....192 C2
Haddon Gv *BFN/LL* DA15 ....168 B2
Haddon Rd *STMC/STPC* BR5 ....202 D2
SUT SM1 ....209 F2
Haddo St *GNWCH* SE10...................124 E6
Hadfield Cl *STHL* UB1 ....95 K2
Hadfield Rd *STWL/WRAY* TW19.......152 A1
Hadleigh Cl *RYNPK* SW20 ....177 J5
WCHPL E1 ....104 E3
Hadleigh Rd *BELMT* SM2..................208 E6
Hadleigh Rd *ED* N9 ....36 D2
Hadleigh St *BETH* E2.......................104 E3
Hadley Cl *WCHMH* N21.....................35 G1
Hadley Common *BAR* EN5................21 G3
Hadley Gdns *CHSWK* W4 ....118 A5
NWDGN UB2 ....114 E5
Hadley Gn *BAR* EN5...........................20 D4
Hadley Green Rd *BAR* EN5...............20 D3
Hadley Gn West *BAR* EN5 ....20 C3
Hadley Gv *BAR* EN5...........................20 C3
Hadley Highstone *BAR* EN5...............20 D2
Hadley Pde *BAR* * EN5 ....20 C4
Hadley Rdg *BAR* EN5 ....20 D4
Hadley Rd *BAR* EN5...........................21 F4
BELV DA17 ....129 G4
EBAR EN4 ....22 A1
ENC/FH EN2 ....22 E1
MTCM CR4 ....195 J1
Hadley St *KTTN* NW5........................84 B4
Hadley Wy *WCHMH* N21 ....35 G1
Hadley Wood Rd *BAR* EN5................20 E3
Hadlow Rd *SCUP* DA14...................168 B6
WELL DA16 ....148 D1
Hadrian Cl *STWL/WRAY* TW19 ....152 B2
Hadrian Est *BETH* * E2 ....104 C1
Hadrian's Ride *EN* EN1 ....24 B6
Hadrian St *GNWCH* SE10.................125 H5
Hadrian Wy *STWL/WRAY* TW19......152 B2
Hadyn Park Rd *SHB* W12 ....118 D2
Hafer Rd *BTSEA* SW11.....................140 E5
Hafton Rd *CAT* SE6 ....165 H3
Haggard Rd *TWK* TW1 ....156 C2
Hagger Ct *WALTH* * E17 ....52 B6
Haggerston Rd *HACK* E8 ....86 B5
Hague St *BETH* E2...........................104 C2
Ha-ha Rd *WOOL/PLUM* SE18 ....126 E6
Haig Rd *STAN* HA7 ....43 J1
Haig Rd East *PLSTW* E13 ....107 G2
Haig Rd West *PLSTW* E13...............107 G2
Haigville Gdns *BARK/HLT* IG6...........72 B1
Hailes Cl *WIM/MER* SW19...............178 B2
Haileybury Av *EN* EN1 ....36 B1
Haileybury Rd *ORP* BR6 ....217 G2
Hailey Rd *ERITHM* DA18 ....129 H2
Hailsham Av *BRXS/STRHM* SW2 ....162 A4
Hailsham Cl *SURB* KT6 ....190 E4
Hailsham Dr *HRW* HA1 ....42 D6
Hailsham Rd *TOOT* SW17 ....179 F2
Hailsham Ter *PLMGR* * N13..............49 K1
Haimo Rd *ELTH/MOT* SE9...............146 C6
Hainault Buildings *LEY* * E10............70 A5
Hainault Gore *CHDH* RM6 ....74 A2
Hainault Rd *CHDH* RM6 ....55 H3
CHDH RM6 ....74 B3
ROM RM1 ....57 F6
WAN E11 ....70 A5
Hainault St *ELTH/MOT* SE9 ....167 G3
IL IG1 ....72 B6
Haines Wk *MRDN* SM4 ....194 A4
Hainford Cl *BROCKY* SE4 ....144 A5
Haining Cl *CHSWK* W4....................117 H5
Hainthorpe Rd *WNWD* SE27 ....162 C5
Hainton Cl *WCHPL* E1 ....104 D5
Halbutt St *DAGW* RM9 ....92 B2
Halcomb St *IS* N1 ....7 G1
Halcot Av *BXLYHS* DA6 ....149 J6
Halcrow St *WCHPL* * E1 ....104 D4
Haldane Cl *MUSWH* N10...................48 B3
PEND EN3 ....25 K1
Haldane Pl *WAND/EARL* SW18.........160 A3
Haldane Rd *EHAM* E6 ....107 H2
FUL/PGN SW6..................................139 J1
STHL UB1 ....96 C6
THMD SE28.......................................109 K6
Haldan Rd *CHING* E4 ....52 A2
Haldon Rd *WAND/EARL* SW18 ....159 J1
The Hale *CHING* E4 ....52 B3
TOTM N17..50 C6
Hale Cl *CHING* E4 ....38 A5
EDGE HA8 ....44 E1
ORP BR6 ....216 C2
Hale Dr *EDGE* HA8 ....44 E2
Hale End *HARH* RM3 ....57 K2
Hale End Cl *RSLP* HA4.....................58 E3
Hale End Rd *WALTH* E17...................52 B4
Halefield Rd *TOTM* N17 ....50 C4
Hale Gdns *ACT* W3 ....117 H1
TOTM N17..50 C6
Hale Grove Gdns *MLHL* NW7 ....45 F1
Hale La *EDGE* HA8 ....44 E1
Hale Rd *EHAM* E6...........................107 J3
TOTM N17..50 C6
Halesowen Rd *MRDN* SM4...............194 A4
Hales St *DEPT* SE8 ....144 D1
Hale St *POP/IOD* E14 ....105 K6
Halesworth Rd *LEW* SE13 ....144 E4
Haley Rd *HDN* NW4 ....64 A3
Half Acre *BTFD* TW8 ....116 E6
Half Acre Ms *BTFD* TW8 ....136 E1
Half Acre Rd *HNWL* W7...................115 K1
Half Moon Crs *IS* N1 ....5 H2
Half Moon La *HNHL* SE24...............162 E1
Half Moon Pas *WCHPL* E1 ....13 K4
Half Moon St *MYFR/PICC* W1J...........9 K7
Halford Cl *EDGE* HA8........................44 D5
Halford Rd *FUL/PGN* SW6 ....119 K6
RCHPK/HAM TW10 ....137 F6
WALTH E17 ....70 B2
Halfway Ct *PUR* RM19 ....131 K4
Halfway St *BFN/LL* DA15 ....167 K3
Haliburton Rd *TWK* TW1.................136 B6
Haliday Wk *IS* N1 ....85 K4
Halifax Cl *TEDD* TW11 ....173 K2
Halifax Rd *ENC/FH* EN2 ....23 J3
GFD/PVL UB6 ....78 B6
Halifax St *SYD* SE26........................163 J5
Halifield Dr *BELV* DA17 ....129 F3
Haling Gv *SAND/SEL* CR2 ....211 J5
Haling Park Gdns
SAND/SEL CR2 ....211 H4
Haling Park Rd *SAND/SEL* CR2 ......211 H4
Haling Rd *SAND/SEL* CR2 ....211 K4
Halkin Ar *KTBR* SW1X........................15 G4
Halkin Ms *KTBR* * SW1X....................15 G4
Halkin Pl *KTBR* SW1X........................15 G4
Halkin St *KTBR* SW1X........................15 H3
The Hall *BKHTH/KID* SE3 ....145 K4
Hallam Cl *CHST* BR7 ....184 E1
Hallam Gdns *PIN* HA5 ....41 J3
Hallam Ms *REGST* W1B 9 K1
Hallam Rd *SEVS/STOTM* N15 ....67 H1
Hallam St *GTPST* W1W.......................9 K1
Halland Wy *NTHWD* HA6 ....40 B2
Hall Cl *EA* W5 ....98 A4
Hall Ct *TEDD* TW11..........................174 A1
Hall Dr *SYD* SE26 ....181 K1
Hall Rd *FSTGT* E7 ....89 G4
Halley St *POP/IOD* E14 ....105 G4
Hall Farm Cl *STAN* HA7 ....29 H6
Hall Farm Dr *WHTN* TW2 ....155 J2
Hallfield Est *BAY/PAD* * W2 ....101 G5
Hallford Wy *DART* DA1 ....171 F1
Hall Gdns *CHING* E4..........................37 H6
Halliday Sq *NWDGN* UB2 ....115 J1
Halliford St *IS* N1..............................85 J5
Halliwell Rd *BRXS/STRHM* SW2 ......162 A1
Halliwick Court Pde
FBAR/BDGN * N11 ....47 K1
Halliwick Rd *MUSWH* N10 ....48 A4
Hall La *CHING* E4 ....51 H1
HDN NW4 ....45 J5
HYS/HAR UB3...................................133 G1
Hallmead Rd *SUT* SM1 ....209 F1
Hall Oak Wk *KIL/WHAMP* NW6 ....82 D4
Hallowell Av *CROY/NA* CR0 ....210 E2
Hallowell Cl *MTCM* CR4 ....179 F6
Hallowell Rd *NTHWD* HA6 ....40 C3
Hallowes Crs *OXHEY* WD19 ....26 E5
Hallowfield Wy *MTCM* CR4 ....178 C6
Hall Pl *BAY/PAD* W2............................2 A7
Hall Place Crs *BXLY* DA5 ....149 K6
Hall Rd *CHDH* RM6 ....73 J3
DART DA1 ....151 J5
EHAM E6 ....89 K6
GPK RM2 ....57 K6
ISLW TW7 ....135 J6
STJWD NW8 ....101 G2
WAN E11 ....88 B2
WLGTN SM6 ....210 B6
Hallside Rd *EN* EN1 ....24 B1
Hall St *FSBYE* EC1V 6 B4
NFNCH/WDSP N12 ....47 G1
Hallsville Rd *CAN/RD* E16 ....106 D5
Hallswelle Pde *GLDGN* * NW11 ....64 D2
Hallswelle Rd *GLDGN* NW11.............64 D2
Hall Vw *ELTH/MOT* SE9...................166 C4
Hallywell Crs *EHAM* E6...................107 K4
Halons Rd *ELTH/MOT* SE9 ....167 F2
Halpin Pl *WALW* SE17 ....19 F7
Halsbrook Rd *BKHTH/KID* SE3........146 B4
Halsbury Cl *STAN* HA7 ....43 H1
Halsbury Rd *SHB* W12 ....118 E1
Halsbury Rd East *NTHLT* UB5 ....78 C2
Halsbury Rd West *NTHLT* UB5...........78 B3
Halsend *HYS/HAR* * UB3 ....114 A1
Halsey St *CHEL* SW3..........................14 E6
Halsham Crs *BARK* IG11 ....91 F4
Halsmere Rd *CMBW* SE5 ....142 C2
Halstead Cl *CROY/NA* CR0 ....211 J1
Halstead Gdns *WCHMH* N21 ....35 K3
Halstead Rd *EN* EN1 ....24 A5
ERITH DA8..150 B2
WAN E11 ....71 F2
WCHMH N21 ....35 K3
Halstow Rd *GNWCH* SE10...............125 K5
WLSDN NW10 ....100 B2
Halsway *HYS/HAR* UB3 ....113 K1
Halton Cl *FBAR/BDGN* N11 ....47 K2
Halton Cross St *IS* * N1.....................85 H6
Halton Rd *IS* N1 ....85 H5
Halt Pde *CDALE/KGS* * NW9 ....63 F1
Halt Robin Rd *BELV* DA17...............129 H4
The Ham *BTFD* TW8.........................136 D1
Hambalt Rd *CLAP* SW4 ....141 H6
Hamble Cl *RSLP* HA4 ....58 C6
Hambledon *WALW* * SE17 ....122 E6
Hambledon Ct *EA* * W5 ....98 A6
Hambledon Gdns *SNWD* SE25.........181 G6
Hambledon Pl *DUL* SE21 ....163 G3
Hambledon Rd
WAND/EARL SW18 ....159 J2
Hambledown Rd
ELTH/MOT * SE9 ....167 J2
Hamble St *FUL/PGN* SW6 ....140 A4
Hambleton Cl *WPK* KT4 ....193 F6
Hambro Av *HAYES* BR2...................199 K5
Hambrook Rd *SNWD* SE25...............181 J6
Hambro Rd *STRHM/NOR* SW16.......179 J2
Hambrough Rd *STHL* UB1 ....114 D1
Ham Common
RCHPK/HAM TW10 ....156 E5
Hamden Crs *DAGE* RM10 ....92 D1
Hamel Cl *KTN/HRWW/W* HA3...........61 K1
Hameway *EHAM* E6 ....108 A3
Ham Farm Rd
RCHPK/HAM TW10 ....156 E6
Hamfrith Rd *SRTFD* E15 ....88 D4
Ham Gate Av
RCHPK/HAM TW10 ....157 G6
Hamilton Av *BARK/HLT* IG6 ....72 B1
CHEAM SM3 ....193 H6
ED N9 ....36 C2
ROM RM1 ....57 F5
SURB KT6 ....191 H6
Hamilton Cl *BERM/RHTH* SE16 ....124 B2
EBAR EN4 ....21 J5
STJWD NW8 ....2 A5
TOTM N17..50 B6
Hamilton Ct *EA* W5 ....98 B6
Hamilton Crs *HSLW* TW3 ....135 G6
PLMGR N13 ....35 G6
RYLN/HDSTN HA2 ....77 K1
Hamilton Gdns *STJWD* NW8 ....101 G2
Hamilton Pde *FELT* * TW13 ....153 K6
Hamilton Pk *HBRY* N5 ....85 H2
Hamilton Pk West *HBRY* N5 ....85 H2
Hamilton Pl *MYFR/PKLN* W1K 15 H1
SUN TW16...172 A3
Hamilton Rd *BFN/LL* DA15..............168 B6
BTFD TW8 ....116 E6
BXLYHN DA7....................................149 F3
CHSWK W4 ....118 B3
EA W5 ....98 A6
EBAR EN4 ....21 J5
ED N9 ....36 C2
EFNCH N2 ....44 C6
GLDGN NW11 ....64 B4
GPK RM2..57 K4
HRW HA1 ....60 E2
HYS/HAR UB3....................................95 F6
IL IG1 ....90 B2
OXHEY WD19 ....27 F5
SRTFD E15 ....106 C2
STHL UB1 ....114 E1
THHTH CR7 ....180 E6
WALTH E17 ....51 G5
WHTN * TW2......................................155 K3
WIM/MER SW19...............................178 A3
WLSDN NW10.....................................81 J3
WNWD SE27 ....162 E6
Hamilton Road Ms
WIM/MER SW19................................178 A3
Hamilton Sq *NFNCH/WDSP* * N12.....47 G2
Hamilton St *DEPT* SE8 ....124 D6
Hamilton Ter *STJWD* NW8 ....101 G2
Hamilton Wy *FNCH* N3......................46 E2
PLMGR N13 ....35 H6
WLGTN SM6 ....210 D6
Hamlea Cl *BKHTH/KID* SE3 ....145 K6
The Hamlet *CMBW* SE5...................142 E4
Hamlet Cl *CRW* RM5 ....56 C3
LEW SE13 ....145 H5
Hamlet Gdns *HMSMTH* W6 ....118 D4
Hamlet Rd *CRW* RM5 ....56 C3
NRWD SE19 ....181 G3
Hamlet Sq *CRICK* NW2 ....82 C1
Hamlets Wy *BOW* E3 ....105 H3
Hamlet Wy *STHWK* SE1.....................19 F3
Hamlin Crs *PIN* HA5..........................59 G2
Hamlyn Cl *EDGE* HA8 ....30 A5
Hamlyn Gdns *NRWD* SE19 ....181 F3
Hammelton Rd *BMLY* BR1...............183 K4
Hammers La *MLHL* NW7....................31 J6
Hammersmith Br *HMSMTH* W6 ....118 E5
Hammersmith Bridge Rd
BARN SW13.......................................118 E6
Hammersmith Broadway
HMSMTH W6 ....119 F4
Hammersmith Emb
BARN * SW13 ....119 F5
Hammersmith F/O
HMSMTH W6 ....119 F5
Hammersmith Gv *HMSMTH* W6 ......119 F3
Hammersmith Rd *HMSMTH* W6 ......119 F4
Hammersmith Ter
HMSMTH * W6 ....118 D5
Hammet Cl *YEAD* UB4 ....95 H4
Hammett St *TWRH* EC3N 13 J5
Hammond Av *MTCM* CR4 ....179 G5
Hammond Cl *GFD/PVL* UB6 ....78 D3
HPTN TW12.......................................173 F4
Hammond Rd *EN* EN1 ....24 D4
NWDGN UB2 ....114 D3
Hammonds Cl *BCTR* RM8..................91 J1
Hammond St *KTTN* NW5 ....84 C4
Hamond Cl *SAND/SEL* CR2 ....211 H6
Hamonde Cl *EDGE* HA8.....................30 D4
Hamond Sq *IS* N1 ....7 G2
Ham Park Rd *FSTGT* E7 ....88 E5
Hampden Av *BECK* BR3 ....182 B5
Hampden Cl *CAMTN* NW1 ....4 D3
Hampden Gurney St *MBLAR* W1H 8 E4
Hampden La *TOTM* N17 ....50 B4
Hampden Rd *ARCH* N19 ....66 D6
BECK BR3 ....182 B5
CEND/HSY/T N8..................................67 G1
KTN/HRWW/W HA3............................42 C4
KUT KT1...175 H6
MUSWH N10.......................................48 A3
TOTM N17..50 C4
Hampden Wy *STHGT/OAK* N14 ....34 B3
Hampermill La *OXHEY* WD19 ....26 E3
Hampshire Cl *UED* N18.....................50 D1
Hampshire Hog La
HMSMTH * W6 ....118 E4
Hampshire Rd *WDGN* N22 ....49 F3
Hampshire St *KTTN* * NW5................84 D4
Hampson Wy *VX/NE* SW8 ....142 A2
Hampstead Av *WFD* IG8....................54 A3
Hampstead Cl *THMD* SE28..............128 C1
Hampstead Gdns *GLDGN* NW11 ....64 E3
Hampstead Ga *HAMP* NW3 ....83 G3
Hampstead Gn *HAMP* NW3 ....83 J3
Hampstead Gv *HAMP* NW3 ....83 G2
Hampstead Hill Gdns
HAMP NW3...83 J2
Hampstead La *HGT* N6......................65 K4
Hampstead Rd *CAMTN* NW1 ....4 A3
Hampstead Sq *HAMP* NW3 ....83 G1
Hampstead Wy *GLDGN* NW11 ....64 E2
Hampton Cl *FBAR/BDGN* N11 ....48 A1
KIL/WHAMP NW6..............................100 E2
RYNPK * SW20 ....177 F3
Hampton Ct *IS* N1 ....85 H4
Hampton Court Av
E/WMO/HCT KT8 ....189 J3
Hampton Court Crs
E/WMO/HCT * KT8...........................173 J6
Hampton Court Est *THDIT* * KT7.....189 K2
Hampton Court Rd *HPTN* TW12 ......173 J5
Hampton Court Wy
E/WMO/HCT KT8...............................189 K1
Hampton La *FELT* TW13 ....154 D6
Hampton Ri *KTN/HRWW/W* HA3.......62 A3
Hampton Rd *CHING* E4.....................51 H1
CROY/NA CR0...................................196 D3
FSTGT E7 ....89 F3
HPTN TW12......................................173 J1
IL IG1 ....90 C2
WAN E11 ....70 B5
WHTN TW2 ....155 J5
WPK KT4 ....192 D6
Hampton Rd East *FELT* TW13 ....154 E6
Hampton Rd West *FELT* TW13 ....154 D4
Hampton St *WALW* SE17 ....18 B7
Ham Ridings *RCHPK/HAM* TW10.....175 G1
Ham Shades Cl *BFN/LL* DA15..........168 A5
Ham St *RCHPK/HAM* TW10..............156 D4
Ham Vw *CROY/NA* CR0 ....198 B3
Ham Yd *SOHO/SHAV* * W1D 10 C5
Hanameel St *CAN/RD* E16 ....125 K1
Hanbury Cl *HDN* NW4 ....46 A6
Hanbury Ct *HRW* * HA1 ....61 F3
Hanbury Dr *WCHMH* N21 ....23 F5
Hanbury Rd *ACT* W3 ....117 J2
TOTM N17..50 D5
Hanbury St *WCHPL* E1 ....104 C4
Hancock Rd *BOW* E3 ....106 A2
NRWD SE19 ....180 E2
Handa Wk *IS* N1 ....85 J4
Hand Ct *HHOL* WC1V 11 H2
Handcroft Rd *CROY/NA* CR0 ....196 C5
Handel Cl *EDGE* HA8 ....44 B2
Handel Pde *EDGE* * HA8....................44 C2
Handel Pl *WLSDN* NW10...................81 F4
Handel St *BMSBY* WC1N......................4 E6
Handel Wy *EDGE* HA8.......................44 C3
Handen Rd *LEW* SE13 ....145 H6
Handforth Rd *BRXN/ST* SW9 ....142 B1
IL IG1 ....90 B1
Handley Gv *CRICK* NW2 ....82 B1
Handley Page Rd *WLGTN* SM6 ....211 F5
Handley Rd *HOM* E9 ....86 E5
Handowe Cl *HDN* NW4 ....63 J1
Handside Cl *WPK* KT4 ....193 G5
Handsworth Av *CHING* E4 ....52 B2
Handsworth Cl *OXHEY* WD19 ....26 E5
Handsworth Rd *TOTM* N17 ....49 K6
Handtrough Wy *BARK* IG11 ....108 B1
Hanford Cl *WAND/EARL* SW18.........159 K3
Hangar Ruding *OXHEY* WD19 ....27 K5
Hanger View Wy *ACT* W3..................98 C5
Hanger Gn *EA* W5 ....98 C3
Hanger La *EA* W5...............................98 A1
Hanger La (North Circular Rd)
EA W5 ....98 A2
Hanger Vale La *EA* W5 ....98 B5
Hankey Pl *STHWK* SE1 ....19 F3
Hankins La *MLHL* NW7 ....31 G4
Hanley Gdns *ARCH* N19 ....67 F5
Hanley Pl *BECK* BR3 ....182 D3
Hanley Rd *FSBYPK* N4 ....66 E5
Hannah Cl *BECK* BR3.......................182 E6
WLSDN * NW10 ....80 E2
Hannah Mary Wy *STHWK* * SE1 ....123 H4
Hannan Cl *WLSDN* NW10 ....80 E2
Hannards Wy *CHIG* IG7 ....55 H1
Hannay La *ARCH* N19 ....66 D4
Hannell Rd *FUL/PGN* SW6 ....139 H1
Hannen Rd *WNWD* * SE27 ....162 C5
Hannibal Rd *STWL/WRAY* TW19 .....152 B2
WCHPL E1 ....104 E4
Hannibal Wy *CROY/NA* CR0.............211 F3
Hannington Rd *CLAP* SW4 ....141 G4
Hanover Av *CAN/RD* E16 ....125 K1
FELT TW13 ....153 K3
Hanover Cir *HYS/HAR* UB3...............94 A5
Hanover Cl *CHEAM* SM3 ....208 C2
RCH/KEW TW9 ....137 H1
Hanover Dr *CHST* BR7....................167 H6
Hanover Gdns *BARK/HLT* IG6...........54 C3
LBTH SE11..122 B6
Hanover Pk *PECK* SE15 ....143 H2
Hanover Pl *COVGDN* WC2E...............11 F4
Hanover Rd *SEVS/STOTM* N15 ....68 B1
WIM/MER SW19................................178 B3
WLSDN NW10.....................................82 A5
Hanover Sq *CONDST* W1S 9 K4
Hanover Steps *BAY/PAD* * W2 ....8 D4
Hanover St *CONDST* W1S 9 K4
CROY/NA CR0...................................211 H1
Hanover Ter *CAMTN* NW1 ....2 D5
Hanover Terrace Ms *CAMTN* NW1.......2 D5
Hanover Wy *BXLYHN* DA7 ....148 E4
Hanover Yd *IS* * N1 ....6 B2
Hansard Ms *NTGHL* W11..................119 G2
Hansart Wy *ENC/FH* EN2 ....23 G2
Hans Crs *CHEL* SW3 ....14 E4
Hanselin Cl *STAN* HA7 ....43 F1
Hansen Dr *WCHMH* N21 ....23 F6
Hanshaw Dr *EDGE* HA8 ....45 F4
Hansler Gv *E/WMO/HCT* KT8 ....189 J2
Hansler Rd *EDUL* SE22 ....143 G6
Hansol Rd *BXLYHS* DA6...................149 F6
Hansom Ter *BMLY* * BR1 ....184 A4
Hanson Cl *BAL* SW12 ....161 G2
BECK * BR3 ....182 E2
MORT/ESHN SW14...........................137 K4
WDR/YW UB7 ....112 C3
Hanson Gdns *STHL* UB1 ....114 D2
Hanson St *GTPST* W1W......................10 A1
Hans Pl *KTBR* SW1X 14 E4
Hans Rd *CHEL* SW3 ....14 E4
Hans St *KTBR* SW1X..........................15 F5
Hanway Pl *FITZ* W1T 10 C3
Hanway Rd *HNWL* W7 ....96 D5
Hanway St *FITZ* W1T.........................10 C3
Hanworth Rd *FELT* TW13 ....154 A3
HPTN TW12.......................................154 E6
HSLW TW3 ....135 G5
HSLWW TW4.....................................154 E2
Hanworth Ter *HSLW* TW3 ....135 G5
Hapgood Cl *GFD/PVL* UB6 ....78 D3
Harben Pde *HAMP* * NW3 ....83 H5
Harben Rd *KIL/WHAMP* NW6............83 G5
Harberson Rd *BAL* SW12 ....161 G3
SRTFD E15 ....88 D6
Harberton Rd *ARCH* N19 ....66 C5
Harbet Rd *BAY/PAD* W2 ....8 B2
UED N18 ....51 F1
Harbex Cl *BXLY* DA5 ....169 J2
Harbinger Rd *POP/IOD* E14 ....124 E4
Harbledown Pl *STMC/STPC* BR5 ....202 D1
Harbledown Rd *FUL/PGN* SW6 ....139 K2
Harbord Cl *CMBW* SE5 ....142 E3
Harbord St *FUL/PGN* SW6 ....139 G2
Harborne Cl *OXHEY* WD19 ....41 G1
Harborough Av *BFN/LL* DA15 ....167 K2
Harborough Rd
STRHM/NOR SW16 ....162 A6
Harbour Av *WBPTN* SW10 ....140 B2
Harbourer Rd *BARK/HLT* IG6 ....55 H1
Harbour Rd *CMBW* SE5 ....142 D4
Harbour Yd *WBPTN* * SW10.............140 B2
Harbridge Av *PUT/ROE* SW15 ....158 C2
Harbury Rd *CAR* SM5 ....209 J6
Harbut Rd *BTSEA* SW11 ....140 C5
Harcastle Cl *NTHLT* UB5 ....95 J3
Harcombe Rd *STNW/STAM* N16 ....86 A1
Harcourt Av *BFN/LL* DA15 ....168 D1
EDGE HA8 ....30 E5
MNPK E12...89 K2
WLGTN SM6 ....210 B2
Harcourt Buildings *EMB* * EC4Y 11 J5
Harcourt Cl *ISLW* TW7 ....136 B4
Harcourt Fld *WLGTN* SM6...............210 B2
Harcourt Ms *ROM* RM1.....................75 H2
Harcourt Rd *BROCKY* SE4..............144 C5
BXLYHS DA6 ....149 F5
SRTFD E15 ....106 D1
THHTH CR7 ....196 A3
WDGN N22 ....48 D4
WIM/MER SW19................................177 K3
WLGTN SM6 ....210 B2
Harcourt St *CAMTN* NW1 ....8 D2
Harcourt Ter *WBPTN* SW10 ....120 A5
Hardcastle Cl *SNWD* SE25 ....197 H3
Hardcourts Cl *WWKM* BR4 ....213 K2
Hardel Wk *BRXS/STRHM* SW2 ....162 B2
Hardens Manorway
WOOL/PLUM SE18.............................126 C3
Harders Rd *PECK* SE15 ....143 J3
Hardess St *HNHL* SE24 ....142 D4
Hardie Cl *WLSDN* NW10 ....81 F3
Hardie Rd *DAGE* RM10 ....92 E1
Harding Cl *CROY/NA* CR0 ....212 B1
KUTN/CMB KT2 ....175 G4
WALW SE17......................................122 D6
Hardinge Rd *UED* N18 ....50 A1
WLSDN NW10.....................................82 A6
Hardinge St *WCHPL* E1 ....104 E5
WOOL/PLUM SE18.............................127 G3
Harding Rd *BXLYHN* DA7 ....149 G3
Hardings La *PGE/AN* SE20 ....182 A2
Hardman Rd *CHARL* SE7 ....126 A5
KUTN/CMB KT2 ....175 F5
Hardres Ter *STMC/STPC* * BR5 ....202 E6
Hardwick Cl *STAN* HA7 ....43 J1
Hardwicke Av *HEST* * TW5..............135 F2
Hardwicke Ms *FSBYW* * WC1X...........5 H5
Hardwicke Rd *CHSWK* W4 ....117 K4
PLMGR N13 ....48 E1
RCHPK/HAM TW10 ....156 D6
Hardwicke St *BARK* IG11 ....90 C6
Hardwick Gn *WEA* W13 ....97 H4
Hardwick St *CLKNW* EC1R 5 K5
Hardwick's Wy
WAND/EARL SW18.............................139 K6
Hardwidge St *STHWK* SE1 ....19 G2
Hardy Av *CAN/RD* E16 ....125 K1
RSLP HA4 ....77 F3
Hardy Cl *BAR* EN5 ....20 C6
BERM/RHTH SE16 ....124 A2
PIN HA5 ....59 H4
Hardy Cottages *GNWCH* * SE10 ......125 G6
Hardy Gv *DART* DA1 ....151 K5
Hardy Pas *WDGN* N22.......................49 F4
Hardy Rd *BKHTH/KID* SE3...............125 J6
CHING E4...51 H2
WIM/MER SW19................................178 A3
Hardy Wy *ENC/FH* EN2 ....23 G2
Hare & Billet Rd *BKHTH/KID* SE3 ....145 G2
Harebell Dr *EHAM* E6 ....108 A4
Hare Ct *EMB* * EC4Y 11 J4
Harecourt Rd *IS* N1...........................85 J4
Haredale Rd *HNHL* SE24................142 D5
Haredon Cl *FSTH* SE23 ....163 K2
Harefield *ESH/CLAY* KT10 ....204 E1
Harefield Av *BELMT* SM2 ....208 C6
Harefield Cl *ENC/FH* EN2 ....23 G2
Harefield Ms *BROCKY* SE4 ....144 C4
Harefield Rd *BROCKY* SE4 ....144 C4
CEND/HSY/T N8.................................66 D2
SCUP DA14 ....168 E4
STRHM/NOR SW16 ....180 A3
Hare Hall La *GPK* RM2......................75 K1
Hare La *ESH/CLAY* KT10 ....204 E4
Hare Marsh *BETH* E2.......................104 C3
Hare Rw *BETH* E2 ....104 D1
Haresfield Rd *DAGE* RM10 ....92 C4
Hare St *WOOL/PLUM* SE18 ....127 F3
Hare Wk *IS* N1 ....7 H3
Harewood Av *NTHLT* UB5 ....77 J5
STJWD NW8 ....2 D6
Harewood Cl *NTHLT* UB5 ....77 K5
Harewood Dr *CLAY* IG5 ....53 K5
Harewood Pl *CONDST* W1S 9 K4
Harewood Rd *ISLW* TW7 ....136 A1

OXHEY WD19 27 F4
SAND/SEL CR2 212 A4
WIM/MER SW19 178 D2
Harewood Rw CAMTN NW1 8 D1
Harewood Ter NWDGN UB2 114 E4
Harfield Gdns CMBW * SE5 143 F4
Harfield Rd SUN TW16 172 C5
Harford Cl CHING E4 37 K2
Harford Rd CHING E4 37 K2
Harford St WCHPL E1 105 G3
Harford Wk EFNCH N2 65 H1
Harfst Wy SWLY BR8 187 K4
Harglaze Ter CDALE/KGS * NW9 45 G6
Hargood Cl KTN/HRWW/W HA3 62 A3
Hargood Rd BKHTH/KID SE3 146 B2
Hargrave Pk ARCH N19 66 C6
Hargrave Rd ARCH N19 66 C6
Hargwyne St BRXN/ST SW9 142 A4
Haringey Pk CEND/HSY/T N8 66 E3
Haringey Rd CEND/HSY/T N8 66 E1
Harington Ter UED * N18 35 K6
Harkett Cl KTN/HRWW/W HA3 43 F5
Harland Av BFN/LL DA15 167 J5
CROY/NA CR0 212 B1
Harland Cl WIM/MER SW19 178 A6
Harland Rd LEE/GVPK SE12 165 K3
Harlands Gv ORP BR6 216 B2
Harlech Gdns HEST TW5 114 B6
RSLP HA4 59 H4
Harlech Rd STHGT/OAK N14 34 E5
Harlequin Av BTFD TW8 116 B6
Harlequin Cl ISLW TW7 135 K6
YEAD UB4 95 H4
Harlequin Ct WEA * W13 97 J6
Harlequin Rd TEDD * TW11 174 C3
Harlescott Rd PECK SE15 144 A5
Harlesden Gdns WLSDN NW10 81 H6
Harlesden Rd WLSDN NW10 81 J6
Harley Cl ALP/SUD * HA0 79 K4
Harley Crs HRW HA1 60 D1
Harleyford BMLY BR1 184 A4
Harleyford Rd LBTH SE11 122 A6
Harley Gdns ORP BR6 216 E2
WBPTN SW10 120 B5
Harley Gv BOW E3 105 H2
Harley Pl CAVSQ/HST W1G 9 J2
Harley Rd HAMP NW3 83 H5
HRW HA1 60 D1
WLSDN NW10 99 G1
Harley St CAVSQ/HST W1G 3 J7
Harley Vls WLSDN * NW10 99 G1
Harlinger St WOOL/PLUM SE18 126 D3
Harlington Cl HYS/HAR UB3 133 F1
Harlington Rd BXLYHN DA7 149 F4
Harlington Rd East
EBED/NFELT TW14 154 A2
Harlington Rd West
EBED/NFELT TW14 154 A1
Harlow Gdns CRW RM5 56 E2
Harlow Rd PLMGR N13 35 K5
RAIN RM13 93 H6
Harlyn Dr PIN HA5 41 F6
Harman Av WFD IG8 52 D3
Harman Cl CHING E4 38 B6
CRICK NW2 82 C1
STHWK * SE1 123 H5
Harman Dr BFN/LL DA15 168 A1
CRICK NW2 82 C1
Harman Rd EN EN1 24 B6
Harmondsworth La
WDR/YW UB7 112 B6
Harmondsworth Rd
WDR/YW UB7 112 B3
Harmony Cl GLDGN NW11 64 C2
WLGTN SM6 210 E6
Harmony Wy HAYES BR2 183 K5
HDN NW4 64 A1
Harmood Gv CAMTN NW1 84 B5
Harmood St CAMTN NW1 84 B4
Harmsworth Ms STHWK SE1 17 K5
Harmsworth St WALW SE17 122 C5
Harmsworth Wy
TRDG/WHET N20 32 D3
Harness Rd THMD SE28 128 B2
Harold Av BELV DA17 129 G5
HYS/HAR UB3 113 J3
Harold Rd CEND/HSY/T N8 67 F2
CHING E4 38 A5
NRWD SE19 180 E3
PLSTW E13 89 F6
RDART DA2 171 J6
SEVS/STOTM N15 68 B2
SUT SM1 209 H2
WAN E11 70 C5
WFD IG8 52 E4
WLSDN NW10 99 F2
Haroldstone Rd WALTH E17 69 F2
Harp Cross La MON EC3R 13 G6
Harpenden Rd MNPK E12 71 G6
WNWD SE27 162 C4
Harper Cl STHGT/OAK N14 22 C6
Harper Rd EHAM E6 107 K5
STHWK SE1 18 D4
Harpers Yd ISLW * TW7 136 A3
Harp Island Cl WLSDN NW10 63 F6
Harpley Sq WCHPL E1 104 E3
Harpour Rd BARK IG11 90 C4
Harp Rd HNWL W7 97 F3
Harpsden St BTSEA SW11 141 F2
Harpur St BMSBY WC1N 11 G1
Harraden Rd BKHTH/KID SE3 146 B2
Harrier Cl HCH RM12 93 K4
Harrier Ms THMD SE28 127 J2
Harriers Cl EA W5 98 A6
Harrier Wy EHAM E6 107 K4
Harries Rd YEAD UB4 95 G3
Harriet Cl BRXS/STRHM SW2 162 B2
HACK E8 86 C6
Harriet Gdns CROY/NA CR0 197 H6
Harriet St KTBR SW1X 15 F3
Harriet Wk KTBR SW1X 15 F3
Harriet Wy BUSH WD23 28 D2
Harringay Gdns CEND/HSY/T N8 67 H1
Harringay Rd CEND/HSY/T N8 67 H2
Harrington Cl CROY/NA CR0 195 K6
WLSDN NW10 81 F1
Harrington Ct MV/WKIL * W9 100 D2
Harrington Gdns ECT SW5 120 A4
Harrington Hl CLPT E5 68 D5
Harrington Rd SKENS SW7 14 A6
SNWD SE25 197 H1
WAN E11 70 C5
Harrington Sq CAMTN NW1 4 A2
Harrington St CAMTN NW1 4 A4
Harrington Wy
WOOL/PLUM SE18 126 C3
Harriott Cl GNWCH SE10 125 J4
Harris Cl ENC/FH EN2 23 H2
HEST TW5 135 F2
Harrison Cl NTHWD HA6 40 A2
TRDG/WHET N20 33 J3
Harrison Rd DAGE RM10 92 D4
Harrison's Ri CROY/NA CR0 211 H1
Harrison St STPAN WC1H 5 F5
Harrisons Whf PUR RM19 131 K5
Harris Rd BXLYHN DA7 149 F2
DAGW RM9 92 B3
Harris St CMBW SE5 142 E1
WALTH E17 69 H4
Harrods Gn EDGE * HA8 44 C1
Harrogate Rd OXHEY WD19 27 G5
Harrold Rd BCTR RM8 91 H3
Harrow Av EN EN1 36 B1
Harroway Rd BTSEA SW11 140 C3
Harrowby St MBLAR W1H 8 D3
Harrow Cl CHSGTN KT9 205 K5
Harrow Crs HARH RM3 57 K3
Harrowdene Cl ALP/SUD HA0 79 K2
Harrowdene Gdns TEDD TW11 174 B3
Harrowdene Rd ALP/SUD HA0 79 K2
Harrow Dr ED N9 36 B3
Harrowes Meade EDGE HA8 30 C5
Harrow Fields Gdns HRW HA1 78 E1
Harrow Gdns ORP BR6 217 H2
Harrowgate Rd HOM E9 87 G5
Harrow Gn WAN E11 88 C1
Harrow La POP/IOD E14 106 A6
Harrow Manor Wy THMD SE28 128 D1
Harrow Pk HRW HA1 60 E6
Harrow Pl WCHPL E1 13 H3
Harrow Rd ALP/SUD HA0 79 G2
ASHF TW15 152 D3
BARK IG11 90 E6
CAR SM5 209 J4
EHAM * E6 89 J6
IL IG1 90 C2
WAN E11 88 D1
WBLY HA9 80 B3
WLSDN NW10 99 K2
Harrow Road F/O BAY/PAD W2 8 B2
Harrow St CAMTN * NW1 8 D1
Harrow Vw HGDN/ICK UB10 94 A2
HYS/HAR UB3 94 E6
RYLN/HDSTN HA2 42 D6
Harrow View Rd EA W5 97 H3
Harrow Wy OXHEY WD19 27 J5
Harrow Weald Pk
KTN/HRWW/W HA3 42 D2
Harston Dr PEND EN3 25 J1
Hartcliff Ct HNWL * W7 116 A2
Hart Crs CHIG IG7 55 F1
Hart Dyke Rd STMC/STPC BR5 202 D6
Harte Rd HSLW TW3 134 E3
Hartfield Av NTHLT UB5 95 F1
Hartfield Crs WIM/MER SW19 177 J3
WWKM BR4 214 E1
Hartfield Gv PGE/AN SE20 181 J4
Hartfield Rd CHSGTN KT9 205 K3
WIM/MER SW19 177 J3
WWKM BR4 214 E2
Hartfield Ter BOW E3 105 J1
Hartford Av KTN/HRWW/W HA3 43 G6
Hartford Rd BXLY DA5 169 H1
HOR/WEW KT19 206 C4
Hart Gv ACT W3 117 H1
STHL UB1 96 A4
Hartham Cl HOLWY N7 84 E3
ISLW TW7 136 B2
Hartham Rd HOLWY N7 84 E3
ISLW TW7 136 A2
TOTM N17 50 B5
Harting Rd ELTH/MOT SE9 166 D6
Hartington Cl HRW HA1 78 E2
ORP BR6 216 C3
Hartington Rd CAN/RD E16 107 F5
CHSWK W4 137 J1
NWDGN * UB2 114 D3
TWK TW1 156 C2
VX/NE SW8 141 K2
WALTH E17 69 G3
WEA W13 97 H6
Hartismere Rd FUL/PGN SW6 139 J1
Hartlake Rd HOM E9 87 F4
Hartland Cl EDGE HA8 30 C4
WCHMH N21 35 J1
Hartland Dr EDGE HA8 30 C4
RSLP HA4 77 F1
Hartland Rd CAMTN * NW1 84 B5
FBAR/BDGN N11 47 K1
HCH RM12 75 J6
HPTN TW12 155 G6
ISLW TW7 136 B4
KIL/WHAMP NW6 100 D1
MRDN SM4 193 K4
SRTFD E15 88 D5
Hartland Rd Arches
CAMTN * NW1 84 A5
The Hartlands HEST TW5 114 A6
Hartlands Cl BXLY DA5 169 G1
Hartland Wy CROY/NA CR0 198 B6
MRDN SM4 193 J4
Hartley Av EHAM E6 89 J6
MLHL NW7 45 H1
Hartley Cl BMLY BR1 184 E5
MLHL NW7 45 H1
Hartley Rd CROY/NA CR0 196 D4
WAN E11 70 D5
WELL DA16 148 D1
Hartley St BETH E2 104 E2
Hartmann Rd CAN/RD E16 126 E1
Hartnoll St HOLWY N7 85 F3
Harton Cl BMLY BR1 184 C4
Harton Rd ED N9 36 D4
Harton St DEPT SE8 144 D2
Hartsbourne Av BUSH WD23 28 C4
Hartsbourne Cl BUSH WD23 28 D4
Hartsbourne Rd BUSH WD23 28 D4
Hartscroft CROY/NA CR0 213 G6
Harts Gv WFD IG8 52 E1
Hartshorn Gdns EHAM E6 108 A3
Harts La BARK IG11 90 B5
NWCR SE14 144 B1
Hartslock Dr ABYW SE2 128 E2
Hartsmead Rd ELTH/MOT SE9 166 E4
Hart Sq MRDN * SM4 194 A2
Hart St MON EC3R 13 H5
Hartsway PEND EN3 24 D5
Hartswood Gdns SHB * W12 118 A3
Hartswood Gn BUSH WD23 28 D4
Hartswood Rd SHB W12 118 C2
Hartsworth Cl PLSTW E13 106 D1
Hartville Rd WOOL/PLUM SE18 127 K4
Hartwell Dr CHING E4 52 A2
Hartwell St HACK E8 86 B4
Harvard Hl CHSWK W4 117 J5
Harvard Rd CHSWK W4 117 J5
ISLW TW7 135 K2
LEW SE13 145 F6
Harvel Cl CHST BR7 186 B6
Harvel Crs ABYW SE2 128 E5
Harvest Bank Rd WWKM BR4 214 E1
Harvesters Cl ISLW TW7 135 J6
Harvest La LOU IG10 39 H2
THDIT KT7 190 B3
Harvest Rd FELT TW13 153 K6
Harvest Wy SWLY BR8 203 K4
Harvey Dr HPTN TW12 173 G4
Harvey Gdns CHARL SE7 126 C5
Harvey Rd CEND/HSY/T N8 67 F2
CMBW SE5 142 E2
HSLWW TW4 154 E2
IL IG1 90 B3
NTHLT UB5 77 G5
WAN E11 70 C5
Harvey's La ROMW/RG RM7 75 F6
Harvey St IS N1 7 F1
Harvill Rd SCUP DA14 186 E1
Harvington Wk HACK * E8 86 C5
Harvist Rd KIL/WHAMP NW6 100 C1
Harwell Cl RSLP HA4 58 B5
Harwood Av BMLY BR1 184 A5
MTCM CR4 178 D6
Harwood Cl ALP/SUD HA0 79 K2
NFNCH/WDSP N12 47 J2
Harwood Ms FUL/PGN * SW6 140 A1
Harwood Rd FUL/PGN SW6 139 K1
Harwood Ter FUL/PGN SW6 140 A2
Hascombe Ter CMBW * SE5 142 E3
Haselbury Rd ED N9 36 A5
Haseley End FSTH * SE23 163 K2
Haselrigge Rd CLAP SW4 141 J5
Haseltine Rd SYD SE26 164 C6
Haselwood Dr ENC/FH EN2 23 H5
Haskard Rd DAGW RM9 91 K2
Hasker St CHEL SW3 14 D6
Haslam Av CHEAM SM3 193 H5
Haslam Cl HGDN/ICK UB10 58 A6
IS N1 85 G5
Haslam St PECK SE15 143 G2
Haslemere Av EBAR EN4 33 K3
HDN NW4 64 B3
HEST TW5 134 B3
HNWL W7 116 B3
MTCM CR4 178 C5
WAND/EARL SW18 160 A4
Haslemere Cl HPTN TW12 172 E1
WLGTN SM6 210 E3
Haslemere Gdns FNCH N3 46 D6
Haslemere Heathrow Est
HSLWW * TW4 134 A3
Haslemere Rd BXLYHN DA7 149 G3
CEND/HSY/T N8 66 E4
GDMY/SEVK IG3 73 F6
THHTH CR7 196 C2
WCHMH N21 35 H4
Hasler Cl THMD SE28 109 H6
Hasluck Gdns BAR EN5 33 G1
Hassard St BETH E2 7 K3
Hassendean Rd BKHTH/KID SE3 126 A6
Hassett Rd HOM E9 87 F4
Hassocks Cl SYD SE26 163 J5
Hassocks Rd STRHM/NOR SW16 179 J4
Hassock Wd HAYES BR2 215 H2
Hassop Rd CRICK NW2 82 B2
Hasted Rd CHARL SE7 126 C5
Hastings Av BARK/HLT IG6 72 C1
Hastings Cl ALP/SUD HA0 79 J2
BAR EN5 21 G5
PECK * SE15 143 H1
Hastings Dr SURB KT6 190 D3
Hastings Rd CROY/NA CR0 197 G5
FBAR/BDGN N11 48 C1
GPK RM2 75 K2
HAYES BR2 200 D5
TOTM * N17 49 K6
WEA W13 97 H6
Hastings St STPAN WC1H 4 E5
Hastings Ter SEVS/STOTM * N15 67 J2
Hastoe Cl YEAD UB4 95 J3
The Hatch PEND EN3 25 F2
Hatcham Park Ms NWCR SE14 144 A2
Hatcham Park Rd NWCR SE14 144 A2
Hatcham Rd PECK SE15 123 K6
Hatchard Rd ARCH N19 66 D6
Hatchcroft HDN NW4 45 K6
Hatchers Ms STHWK SE1 19 H3
Hatchett Rd EBED/NFELT TW14 153 F3
Hatch Gv CHDH RM6 74 A1
Hatch La CHING E4 38 B6
WDR/YW UB7 132 A1
Hatch Pl RCHPK/HAM TW10 175 G1
Hatch Rd STRHM/NOR SW16 179 K5
Hatch Side CHIG IG7 54 A1
Hatchwoods WFD IG8 38 D6
Hatcliffe Cl BKHTH/KID SE3 145 J4
Hatcliffe St GNWCH SE10 125 J5
Hatfield Cl BARK/HLT IG6 54 B6
BELMT SM2 208 E6
MTCM * CR4 194 C1
Hatfield Ct BKHTH/KID * SE3 145 K1
Hatfield Rd CHSWK W4 118 A2
HNWL W7 116 B1
SRTFD E15 88 C3
Hatfields STHWK SE1 11 K7
Hathaway Cl HAYES BR2 200 E5
RSLP HA4 76 D2
STAN HA7 43 G1
Hathaway Crs MNPK E12 89 K4
Hathaway Gdns CHDH RM6 73 K2
WEA W13 97 F4
Hathaway Rd CROY/NA CR0 196 C4
Hatherleigh Cl CHSGTN KT9 205 K3
MRDN SM4 193 K1
Hatherleigh Rd RSLP HA4 58 E6
Hatherley Crs SCUP DA14 168 B4
Hatherley Gdns CEND/HSY/T N8 66 E3
EHAM E6 107 H2
Hatherley Gv BAY/PAD W2 101 F5
Hatherley Rd RCH/KEW TW9 137 G2
SCUP DA14 168 B5
WALTH E17 69 H1
Hatherley St WEST SW1P 16 B7
Hathern Gdns ELTH/MOT SE9 167 F6
Hatherop Rd HPTN TW12 172 E3
Hathorne Cl PECK SE15 143 J3
Hathorne Ter ARCH * N19 66 D5
Hathway St PECK SE15 143 K3
Hatley Av BARK/HLT IG6 72 C1
Hatley Cl FBAR/BDGN N11 47 K1
Hatley Rd HOLWY N7 67 F6
Hat & Mitre Ct FARR EC1M 6 B7
Hatteraick St BERM/RHTH SE16 123 K2
Hattersfield Cl BELV DA17 129 G4
Hatters La WATW WD18 26 B1
Hatton Cl WOOL/PLUM SE18 147 J1
Hatton Cross Est HTHAIR * TW6 133 J5
Hatton Gdn CLKNW EC1R 5 K7
HCIRC EC1N 11 K1
Hatton Gdns MTCM CR4 194 E2
Hatton Gn EBED/NFELT TW14 133 K5
Hatton Gv WDR/YW * UB7 112 A2
Hatton Pl HCIRC EC1N 5 K7
Hatton Rd CROY/NA CR0 196 B5
EBED/NFELT TW14 153 F2
HTHAIR TW6 133 J5
Hatton Rd North HTHAIR TW6 133 G2
Hatton Rw STJWD * NW8 2 B7
Hatton St STJWD NW8 2 B7
Hatton Wall HCIRC EC1N 11 J1
Haunch of Venison Yd
MYFR/PKLN W1K 9 J4
Havana Cl ROM RM1 75 G2
Havana Rd WIM/MER SW19 159 K4
Havannah St POP/IOD E14 124 D2
Havant Rd WALTH E17 52 A6
Havelock Cl SHB * W12 99 K6
Havelock Pl HRW HA1 60 E3
Havelock Rd BELV * DA17 129 G4
CROY/NA CR0 197 G6
DART DA1 170 E2
HAYES BR2 200 B1
KTN/HRWW/W HA3 42 E6
NWDGN UB2 114 D3
TOTM N17 50 C5
WIM/MER SW19 178 B1
Havelock St IL IG1 72 B6
IS N1 84 E6
Havelock Ter VX/NE SW8 141 G1
Havelock Wk FSTH SE23 163 K3
The Haven RCH/KEW TW9 137 H4
Haven Cl ELTH/MOT SE9 166 E5
SCUP DA14 186 D2
WIM/MER SW19 159 G5
YEAD UB4 94 C4
Haven Ct BRYLDS * KT5 191 G3
Haven Gn EA W5 97 K6
Havenhurst Ri ENC/FH EN2 23 G3
Haven La EA W5 98 A5
Haven Rd ASHF TW15 152 E6
Haven St CAMTN NW1 84 B5
Havenwood WBLY HA9 80 D1
Haverfield Est BTFD TW8 117 F6
Haverfield Gdns RCH/KEW TW9 137 H1
Haverfield Rd BOW E3 105 F2
Haverford Wy EDGE HA8 44 B4
Havergal Vls CEND/HSY/T * N8 67 H1
Haverhill Rd BAL SW12 161 H3
CHING E4 38 A3
Havering Dr ROM RM1 75 G1
Havering Gdns CHDH RM6 73 J2
Havering Rd ROM RM1 57 F1
Havering St WCHPL E1 105 F5
Havering Wy BARK IG11 109 H2
Haversham Cl TWK TW1 156 E2
Haverstock Hl HAMP NW3 83 J4
Haverstock Pl IS N1 5 K3
Haverstock Rd KTTN NW5 84 A3
Haverstock St IS N1 6 B3
Haverthwaite Rd ORP BR6 216 D1
Havil St CMBW SE5 143 F2
Havisham Pl NRWD SE19 180 C2
Hawarden Gv HNHL SE24 162 D2
Hawarden Hl CRICK NW2 81 J1
Hawarden Rd WALTH E17 69 F1
Hawbridge Rd WAN E11 70 B5
Hawes Cl NTHWD HA6 40 D3
Hawes La WWKM BR4 199 F5
Hawes Rd BMLY BR1 184 A4
UED N18 50 D2
Hawes St IS N1 85 H5
Hawfield Bank ORP BR6 217 K1
Hawgood St BOW E3 105 J4
Hawkdene CHING E4 37 K1
Hawke Park Rd WDGN N22 49 H6
Hawke Pl BERM/RHTH * SE16 124 A2
Hawke Rd NRWD SE19 180 E2
Hawkesbury Rd PUT/ROE SW15 138 E6
Hawkesfield Rd FSTH SE23 164 B4
Hawkesley Cl TWK TW1 156 B6
Hawkes Rd EBED/NFELT TW14 153 K2
MTCM CR4 178 D4
Hawkesworth Cl NTHWD HA6 40 C3
Hawkewood Rd SUN TW16 172 A6
Hawkhurst Gdns CRW RM5 57 F2
Hawkhurst Rd
STRHM/NOR SW16 179 J4
Hawkhurst Wy NWMAL KT3 192 A2
WWKM BR4 198 E6
Hawkins Cl EDGE HA8 45 F1
HRW HA1 60 D4
Hawkins Rd TEDD TW11 174 C2
Hawkins Wy CAT SE6 182 D1
Hawkley Gdns WNWD SE27 162 C4
Hawkridge Cl CHDH RM6 73 J3
Hawksbrook La BECK BR3 198 E3
Hawkshead Cl BMLY BR1 183 H3
Hawkshead Rd CHSWK W4 118 B3
WLSDN * NW10 81 H5
Hawkshill Cl ESH/CLAY KT10 204 A4
Hawkshill Pl ESH/CLAY * KT10 204 A4
Hawkslade Rd PECK SE15 144 A6
Hawksley Rd STNW/STAM N16 85 K1
Hawks Ms GNWCH * SE10 145 F1
Hawksmoor Cl EHAM E6 107 J5
WOOL/PLUM SE18 127 K5
Hawksmoor Ms WCHPL E1 104 D6
Hawksmoor St HMSMTH W6 119 G6
Hawksmouth CHING E4 37 K2
Hawks Rd KUT KT1 175 G5
Hawkstone Rd
BERM/RHTH SE16 123 K4
Hawkwell Wk IS * N1 85 J6
Hawkwood Crs CHING E4 37 K1
Hawkwood La CHST BR7 185 H4
Hawkwood Mt CLPT E5 68 D5
Hawlands Dr PIN HA5 59 J4
Hawley Cl HPTN TW12 172 E2
Hawley Crs CAMTN NW1 84 B5
Hawley Ms CAMTN NW1 84 B5
Hawley Rd CAMTN NW1 84 B5
DART DA1 171 H4
UED N18 51 F1
Hawley Ter RDART * DA2 171 K6
Hawstead Rd LEW SE13 164 E1
Hawsted BKHH IG9 39 F2
Hawthorn Av PLMGR N13 48 E1
RAIN RM13 111 K3
THHTH CR7 180 C4
Hawthorn Cl HEST TW5 134 A1
HPTN TW12 173 F1
STMC/STPC BR5 201 J3
Hawthornden Cl
NFNCH/WDSP N12 47 J2
Hawthorndene Cl HAYES * BR2 199 J6
Hawthorndene Rd HAYES BR2 199 K6
Hawthorn Dr RYLN/HDSTN HA2 60 A3
WWKM BR4 214 C2
Hawthorne Av CAR SM5 210 A5
HOM E9 87 H6
HRW HA1 61 G3
MTCM CR4 178 C5
RSLP HA4 59 F3
Hawthorne Cl BMLY BR1 184 E6
IS N1 86 A4
Hawthorne Ct
STWL/WRAY * TW19 152 A2
Hawthorne Crs WDR/YW UB7 112 C2
Hawthorne Gv CDALE/KGS NW9 62 E4
Hawthorne Rd BMLY BR1 184 E6
UED N18 50 B2
WALTH E17 51 J6
Hawthorne Wy ED N9 36 B4
Hawthorn Farm Av NTHLT UB5 77 J6
Hawthorn Gdns EA W5 116 E3
Hawthorn Gv ENC/FH EN2 23 K1
PGE/AN SE20 181 J4
Hawthorn Hatch BTFD TW8 136 C1
Hawthorn Ms HDN NW4 46 C4
Hawthorn Pl ERITH DA8 129 K5
HYS/HAR * UB3 94 D6
Hawthorn Rd BKHH IG9 39 G6
BTFD TW8 136 C1
BXLYHS * DA6 149 G5
CEND/HSY/T N8 48 D6
DART DA1 171 G4
SUT SM1 209 H3
WLGTN SM6 210 B5
WLSDN NW10 81 J5
Hawthorns WFD IG8 38 E5
The Hawthorns EW KT17 207 H4
Hawthorn Ter BFN/LL DA15 168 A1
Hawthorn Wk NKENS W10 100 C3
Hawtrey Av NTHLT UB5 95 H1
Hawtrey Dr RSLP HA4 58 E4
Hawtrey Rd HAMP NW3 83 J5
Haxted Rd BMLY BR1 184 A4
Hayburn Wy HCH RM12 75 H5
Hay Cl SRTFD E15 88 C5
Haycroft Gdns WLSDN NW10 81 J6
Haycroft Rd BRXS/STRHM SW2 141 K6
SURB KT6 190 E6
Hay Currie St POP/IOD E14 105 K5
Hayday Rd CAN/RD E16 106 E4
Hayden Dell BUSH WD23 27 K1
Haydens Cl STMC/STPC BR5 202 D4
Hayden's Pl NTGHL W11 100 D5
Hayden Wy CRW RM5 56 E5
Haydock Av NTHLT UB5 78 A4
Haydock Gn NTHLT UB5 78 A4
Haydon Cl CDALE/KGS NW9 62 E1
EN EN1 36 A1
HARH RM3 57 K3
Haydon Dell Farm BUSH * WD23 27 K2
Haydon Dr PIN HA5 58 E1
Haydon Park Rd
WIM/MER SW19 177 K1
Haydon Rd BCTR RM8 73 J6
OXHEY WD19 27 J1
Haydon's Rd WIM/MER SW19 178 A1
Haydon St TWRH EC3N 13 J5
Haydon Wk WCHPL E1 13 J4
Haydon Wy BTSEA SW11 140 B5
Hayes Cha WWKM BR4 199 G3
Hayes Cl HAYES BR2 199 K6
Hayes Crs CHEAM SM3 208 B2
GLDGN NW11 64 D2
Hayes Dr RAIN RM13 93 K5
Hayes End Dr YEAD UB4 94 B4
Hayes End Rd YEAD UB4 94 B3
Hayesford Park Dr HAYES BR2 199 J2
Hayes Gdn HAYES BR2 199 K6
Hayes Hl HAYES BR2 199 H5
Hayes Hill Rd HAYES BR2 199 J5
Hayes La BECK BR3 183 G6
HAYES BR2 199 K3
Hayes Mead Rd HAYES BR2 199 H5
Hayes Pl CAMTN NW1 2 D7
Hayes Rd HAYES BR2 199 K1
NWDGN UB2 114 B4
Hayes St HAYES BR2 200 A5
Hayes Wy BECK BR3 199 F1
Hayes Wood Av HAYES BR2 200 A5
Hayfield Pas WCHPL E1 104 E3
Hayfield Rd STMC/STPC BR5 202 B2
Haygarth Pl WIM/MER SW19 177 G1
Haygreen Cl KUTN/CMB KT2 175 J2
Hay Hl MYFR/PICC W1J 9 K6
Hayland Cl CDALE/KGS NW9 63 F1
Hay La CDALE/KGS NW9 63 F1
Hayles St LBTH SE11 18 A6
Haylett Gdns KUT * KT1 190 E1
Hayling Av FELT TW13 153 K5
Hayling Cl STNW/STAM N16 86 A3
Hayling Rd OXHEY WD19 26 D5
Hayman Crs YEAD UB4 94 B1
Haymarket STJS SW1Y 10 C6
Haymeads Dr ESH/CLAY KT10 204 C4
Haymer Gdns WPK KT4 207 J1
Haymerle Rd STHWK SE1 123 H6
Haymill Cl GFD/PVL UB6 97 F2
Hayne Rd BECK BR3 182 C5
Haynes Cl BKHTH/KID SE3 145 H4
FBAR/BDGN N11 34 A5
TOTM N17 50 D3
Haynes Dr ED N9 36 D5
Haynes La NRWD SE19 181 F2
Haynes Rd ALP/SUD HA0 80 A5
Hayne St STBT EC1A 12 B1
Haynt Wk RYNPK SW20 177 H6
Hay Pl SWLY * BR8 203 K3
Hays La STHWK SE1 13 G7
Haysleigh Gdns PGE/AN SE20 181 H5
Hay's Ms MYFR/PICC W1J 9 J7
Haysoms Cl ROM RM1 75 G1
Haystall Cl YEAD UB4 94 C1
Hay St BETH E2 86 C6
Hayter Rd BRXS/STRHM SW2 141 K6
Hayton Cl HACK E8 86 B4
Hayward Cl DART DA1 150 A6
WIM/MER SW19 178 A3
Hayward Dr DART * DA1 171 J5
Hayward Gdns PUT/ROE SW15 159 F1
Hayward Rd THDIT KT7 190 A5
TRDG/WHET N20 33 G4
Haywards Cl CHDH RM6 73 J2

Hayward's Pl CLKNW * EC1R 6 A7
Haywood Cl PIN HA5 41 H5
Haywood Ri ORP BR6 216 E3
Haywood Rd HAYES BR2 200 C1
Hazel Av WDR/YW UB7 112 D3
Hazel Bank BRYLDS KT5 191 K5
Hazelbank Rd CAT SE6 165 G4
Hazelbourne Rd BAL SW12 161 G1
Hazelbrouck Gdns BARK/HLT IG6 54 D3
Hazelbury Cl WIM/MER SW19 177 K5
Hazelbury Gn ED N9 36 A5
Hazelbury La ED N9 36 A5
Hazel Cl BTFD * TW8 136 C1
CDALE/KGS NW9 45 H5
CROY/NA CR0 198 A4
HCH RM12 93 K1
MTCM CR4 195 J1
PLMGR N13 35 K5
WHTN TW2 155 H2
Hazelcroft PIN HA5 42 A2
Hazeldean Rd WLSDN NW10 81 F5
Hazeldene Dr PIN HA5 41 G6
Hazeldene Gdns HGDN/ICK UB10 76 A6
Hazeldene Rd BCTR RM8 73 H6
WELL DA16 148 D3
Hazeldon Rd BROCKY SE4 144 B6
Hazel Dr ERITH DA8 150 D2
Hazeleigh Gdns WFD IG8 53 J1
Hazel Gdns EDGE HA8 30 D6
Hazelgreen Cl WCHMH N21 35 H3
Hazel Gv ALP/SUD HA0 80 A6
CHDH RM6 56 A6
EN * EN1 36 C1
ORP BR6 201 G6
SYD SE26 164 A6
Hazelhurst BECK BR3 183 G4
Hazelhurst Rd TOOT SW17 160 B6
Hazell Crs ROMW/RG RM7 56 D4
Hazellville Rd ARCH N19 66 D4
Hazelmere Cl
EBED/NFELT TW14 153 G1
NTHLT UB5 95 K1
Hazelmere Dr NTHLT UB5 95 K1
Hazelmere Gdns EMPK RM11 75 K2
Hazelmere Rd KIL/WHAMP NW6 82 D6
NTHLT UB5 95 K1
STMC/STPC BR5 201 H1
Hazelmere Wk NTHLT UB5 95 K1
Hazelmere Wy HAYES BR2 199 K3
Hazel Rd DART DA1 171 G4
ERITH DA8 150 D2
SRTFD * E15 88 C3
WLSDN NW10 99 K2
Hazel Rw NFNCH/WDSP * N12 47 H1
Hazeltree La NTHLT UB5 95 J2
Hazel Wk HAYES BR2 201 F3
Hazel Wy CHING E4 51 H2
STHWK SE1 19 J6
Hazelwood Av MRDN SM4 194 A1
Hazelwood Cl CLPT E5 87 G1
EA W5 117 F2
RYLN/HDSTN HA2 60 B1
Hazelwood Ct SURB KT6 191 F3
Hazelwood Crs PLMGR N13 35 G6
Hazelwood Dr PIN HA5 41 F5
Hazelwood La PLMGR N13 35 G6
Hazelwood Park Cl
BARK/HLT IG6 54 E1
Hazelwood Rd EN EN1 36 B1
RKW/CH/CXG WD3 26 A1
WALTH E17 69 G2
Hazlebury Rd FUL/PGN SW6 140 A3
Hazledean Rd CROY/NA CR0 196 E6
Hazledene Rd CHSWK W4 117 K6
Hazlemere Gdns WPK KT4 192 D5
Hazlewell Rd PUT/ROE SW15 139 F6
Hazlewood Crs NKENS W10 100 C3
Hazlitt Cl FELT TW13 154 D6
Hazlitt Ms WKENS * W14 119 H3
Hazlitt Rd WKENS W14 119 H3
Heacham Av HGDN/ICK UB10 76 A1
Headcorn Rd BMLY BR1 183 J1
THHTH CR7 196 A1
TOTM N17 50 B3
Headfort Pl KTBR SW1X 15 H3
Headington Rd
WAND/EARL SW18 160 B3
Headlam Rd CLAP SW4 161 J2
Headlam St WCHPL E1 104 D3
Headley Ap IL IG1 72 A2
Headley Av WLGTN SM6 211 F3
Headley Cl CHSGTN KT9 206 C4
Headley Dr CROY/NA CR0 214 A5
GNTH/NBYPK IG2 72 B3
Headstone Dr HRW HA1 60 D1
Headstone Gdns
RYLN/HDSTN HA2 60 C1
Headstone La
KTN/HRWW/W HA3 42 B4
Headstone Pde HRW * HA1 60 D1
Headstone Rd HRW HA1 60 E3
Head St WCHPL E1 105 F5
The Headway EW KT17 207 H6
Headway Cl RCHPK/HAM TW10 156 D6
Heald St NWCR SE14 144 C2
Healey Rd WATW WD18 26 D1
Healey St CAMTN * NW1 84 B4
Healy Dr ORP BR6 217 F2
Hearne Rd CHSWK W4 117 H5
Hearn Ri NTHLT UB5 77 H6
Hearn Rd ROM RM1 75 H3
Hearn's Buildings WALW SE17 19 F7
Hearns Cl STMC/STPC BR5 202 D1
Hearns Rd STMC/STPC BR5 202 D1
Hearn St SDTCH EC2A 7 H7
Hearnville Rd BAL SW12 161 F3
The Heath HNWL * W7 115 K2
Heatham Pk WHTN TW2 156 A2
Heath Av BXLYHN DA7 128 E6
Heathbourne Rd STAN HA7 28 E4
Heath Brow HAMP NW3 83 G1
Heath Cl EA W5 98 B3
GLDGN NW11 65 F4
GPK RM2 57 J6
HYS/HAR UB3 133 G1
SAND/SEL CR2 211 H4
STMC/STPC BR5 202 D3
Heathclose Av DART DA1 170 E2
Heathclose Rd DART DA1 170 D3
Heathcote Av CLAY IG5 53 K5
Heathcote Gv CHING E4 38 A5
Heathcote Rd TWK TW1 156 C1
Heathcote St BMSBY WC1N 5 G6
Heathcote Wy WDR/YW UB7 112 A1
Heathcroft EA W5 98 B3
Heathcroft Gdns WALTH E17 52 B4
Heathdale Av HSLWW TW4 134 D4
Heathdene Dr BELV DA17 129 J4
Heathdene Rd
STRHM/NOR SW16 180 A3
WLGTN SM6 210 B5
Heath Dr BELMT SM2 209 G6
GPK RM2 57 J4
HAMP NW3 83 F2
RYNPK SW20 193 F1
Heathedge SYD * SE26 163 J4
Heathend Rd BXLY DA5 170 B3
Heather Av ROM RM1 57 F5
Heatherbank CHST BR7 185 F5
ELTH/MOT SE9 146 E3
Heatherbank Cl DART DA1 170 B1
Heather Cl EHAM E6 108 A5
HPTN TW12 172 E4
ISLW TW7 135 J6
LEW SE13 165 G2
ROM RM1 57 F4
VX/NE SW8 141 G4
Heatherdale Cl KUTN/CMB KT2 175 H2
Heatherdene Cl FNCH N3 47 G3
MTCM CR4 194 C1
Heather Dr DART DA1 170 D2
ENC/FH EN2 23 H3
ROM RM1 57 F5
Heatherfold Wy PIN HA5 40 D6
Heather Gdns BELMT SM2 208 E4
GLDGN NW11 64 C3
ROM RM1 57 F5
Heather Gln ROM RM1 57 F5
Heatherley Dr CLAY IG5 53 K6
Heather Park Dr ALP/SUD HA0 80 C5
Heather Park Pde
ALP/SUD * HA0 80 B5
Heather Pl ESH/CLAY KT10 204 B2
Heather Rd CHING E4 51 H2
CRICK NW2 63 H6
LEE/GVPK SE12 165 K4
The Heathers
STWL/WRAY TW19 152 C2
Heatherset Cl ESH/CLAY KT10 204 C3
Heatherset Gdns
STRHM/NOR SW16 180 A3
Heatherside Rd
HOR/WEW KT19 207 F5
SCUP DA14 168 D5
Heather Wk EDGE HA8 44 D1
NKENS W10 100 C3
Heather Wy ROM RM1 57 F4
SAND/SEL CR2 213 F6
STAN HA7 43 F2
Heatherwood Cl MNPK E12 71 F6
Heatherwood Dr YEAD UB4 94 B1
Heathfield CHING E4 38 A5
CHST BR7 185 H2
HRW * HA1 61 F4
Heathfield Av
WAND/EARL SW18 160 C2
Heathfield Cl CAN/RD E16 107 H4
HAYES BR2 215 G3
OXHEY WD19 27 G2
Heathfield Dr MTCM CR4 178 D4
Heathfield Gdns CHSWK W4 117 K5
CROY/NA * CR0 211 J2
GLDGN NW11 64 B3
WAND/EARL SW18 160 C1
Heathfield La CHST BR7 185 H2
Heathfield North WHTN TW2 155 K2
Heathfield Pk CRICK NW2 82 A4
Heathfield Park Dr CHDH RM6 73 H2
Heathfield Ri RSLP HA4 58 A4
Heathfield Rd ACT W3 117 J2
BMLY BR1 183 J3
BXLYHS DA6 149 G5
CROY/NA CR0 211 K3
HAYES BR2 215 G3
WAND/EARL SW18 160 B1
Heathfield South WHTN TW2 156 A2
Heathfield Sq
WAND/EARL SW18 160 C2
Heathfield Ter CHSWK W4 117 K5
WOOL/PLUM SE18 127 K6
Heathfield V SAND/SEL CR2 213 F6
Heath Gdns DART * DA1 171 F3
TWK TW1 156 A3
Heathgate GLDGN NW11 65 F3
Heathgate Pl HAMP NW3 83 K3
Heath Gv PGE/AN SE20 181 K3
Heathhurst Rd SAND/SEL CR2 212 A6
Heathland Rd STNW/STAM N16 68 A5
Heathlands Cl TWK TW1 156 A4
Heathlands Ct HSLWW TW4 134 D6
Heathlands Ri DART DA1 170 E2
Heathlands Wy HSLWW TW4 134 D6
Heath La BKHTH/KID SE3 145 G3
DART DA1 170 E3
Heathlee Rd BKHTH/KID SE3 145 J5
DART DA1 170 B1
Heathley End CHST BR7 185 H2
Heath Ldg BUSH * WD23 28 D3
Heathman's Rd FUL/PGN * SW6 139 J2
Heath Md WIM/MER SW19 159 G5
Heath Park Dr BMLY BR1 184 D6
Heath Park Rd GPK RM2 75 J2
Heath Ri HAYES BR2 199 K3
PUT/ROE SW15 159 G1
Heath Rd BXLY DA5 169 K3
CHDH RM6 73 K4
DART DA1 170 C1
HGDN/ICK UB10 94 A3
HRW HA1 60 C4
HSLW TW3 135 H5
OXHEY WD19 27 H2
THHTH CR7 180 D6
TWK TW1 156 A3
VX/NE SW8 141 G3
Heath's Cl EN EN1 23 K3
Heathside ESH/CLAY KT10 204 E1
HAMP NW3 83 H2
HSLWW TW4 154 E2
Heath Side STMC/STPC BR5 201 H5
Heathside Av BXLYHN DA7 149 F3
Heathside Cl ESH/CLAY KT10 204 E1
GNTH/NBYPK IG2 72 D2
NTHWD HA6 40 B1
Heathside Rd NTHWD HA6 26 B6
Heathstan Rd SHB W12 99 J5
Heath St DART DA1 171 G2
HAMP NW3 83 G2
Heath Vw EFNCH N2 65 G1
Heathview Av DART DA1 170 B1
Heath View Cl EFNCH N2 65 G1
Heathview Crs DART DA1 170 D2
Heath View Dr ABYW SE2 128 E6
Heathview Gdns
PUT/ROE SW15 159 F2
Heathview Rd THHTH CR7 196 B1
Heath Vls WAND/EARL * SW18 160 B3
WOOL/PLUM SE18 128 A5
Heathville Rd ARCH N19 66 E4
Heathwall St BTSEA SW11 140 E4
Heathway BKHTH/KID SE3 145 K1
CROY/NA CR0 213 H1
DAGW RM9 92 B2
Heath Wy ERITH DA8 149 K2
Heathway NWDGN * UB2 114 C4
WFD IG8 39 G6
Heathwood Gdns CHARL SE7 126 D4
SWLY BR8 187 K5
Heathwood Pde SWLY * BR8 187 K5
Heathwood Wk BXLY DA5 170 B3
Heaton Av HARH RM3 57 K3
Heaton Cl CHING E4 38 A5
Heaton Grange Rd GPK RM2 57 H4
Heaton Rd MTCM CR4 179 F3
PECK SE15 143 J4
Heaver Rd BTSEA * SW11 140 C4
Heavitree Cl WOOL/PLUM SE18 127 J5
Heavitree Rd WOOL/PLUM SE18 127 J5
Hebden Ter TOTM N17 50 A2
Hebdon Rd TOOT SW17 160 D5
Heber Rd CRICK NW2 82 B3
EDUL SE22 163 G1
Hebron Rd HMSMTH W6 118 E3
Hecham Cl WALTH E17 51 G5
Heckfield Pl FUL/PGN SW6 139 K1
Heckford Cl WATW WD18 26 A1
Heckford St WAP E1W 105 F6
Hector St WOOL/PLUM * SE18 127 K4
Heddington Gv HOLWY N7 85 F3
Heddon Cl ISLW TW7 136 B5
Heddon Court Av EBAR EN4 21 K6
Heddon Court Pde EBAR * EN4 22 A6
Heddon Rd EBAR EN4 21 K6
Heddon St CONDST W1S 10 A6
Hedge Hl ENC/FH EN2 23 H2
Hedge La PLMGR N13 35 H5
Hedgeley REDBR IG4 71 K1
Hedgemans Rd DAGW RM9 91 K5
Hedgemans Wy DAGW RM9 92 A4
Hedgerley Gdns GFD/PVL UB6 96 C1
Hedger's Gv HOM * E9 87 G4
Hedger St LBTH SE11 18 A6
Hedgewood Gdns CLAY IG5 72 A1
Hedgley St LEE/GVPK SE12 145 J6
Hedingham Cl IS N1 85 J5
Hedingham Rd BCTR RM8 91 H3
Hedley Rd WHTN TW2 155 F2
Hedley Rw HBRY N5 85 K3
Heenan Cl BARK IG11 90 C4
Heene Rd ENC/FH EN2 23 K3
Heidegger Crs BARN SW13 138 E1
Heigham Rd EHAM E6 89 H5
Heighton Gdns CROY/NA CR0 211 H3
The Heights BECK * BR3 183 F3
CHARL SE7 126 B5
NTHLT UB5 78 A3
Heights Cl RYNPK SW20 176 E3
Heiron St WALW SE17 122 C6
Helby Rd CLAP SW4 161 J1
Helder Gv LEE/GVPK SE12 165 J2
Helder St SAND/SEL CR2 211 K4
Heldmann Cl ISLW TW7 135 J5
Helena Pl HOM E9 86 D6
Helena Rd EA W5 97 K4
PLSTW E13 106 D1
WALTH E17 69 J2
WLSDN NW10 81 K3
Helena Sq POP/IOD E14 105 G6
Helen Av EBED/NFELT TW14 154 A2
Helen Cl DART DA1 170 E2
E/WMO/HCT KT8 189 G1
EFNCH N2 47 G6
Helenslea Av GLDGN NW11 64 E5
Helen's Pl BETH E2 104 E2
Helen St WOOL/PLUM * SE18 127 G4
Helford Cl RSLP HA4 58 C6
Heligan Cl ORP BR6 217 F2
Helix Gdns BRXS/STRHM SW2 162 A1
Helix Rd BRXS/STRHM SW2 162 A1
Hellings St WAP E1W 123 H1
Helme Cl WIM/MER SW19 177 J1
Helmet Rw FSBYE EC1V 6 D6
Helmore Rd BARK IG11 90 E5
Helmsdale Cl ROM RM1 57 G3
YEAD * UB4 95 J3
Helmsdale Rd ROM RM1 57 G3
STRHM/NOR SW16 179 H4
Helmsley Pl HACK E8 86 D5
Helmsley St HACK E8 86 D6
Helperby Rd WLSDN NW10 81 G5
Helsinki Sq BERM/RHTH SE16 124 C3
Helston Cl PIN HA5 41 K3
Helvetia St CAT SE6 164 C4
Hemans St VX/NE SW8 141 J1
Hemery Rd GFD/PVL UB6 78 D3
Hemingford Rd CHEAM SM3 208 A2
IS N1 85 F6
Heming Rd EDGE HA8 44 D2
Hemington Av FBAR/BDGN N11 47 K1
Hemlock Rd SHB W12 99 H6
Hemmen La HYS/HAR UB3 94 D6
Hemming Cl HPTN TW12 173 F4
Hemmings Cl SCUP DA14 168 C4
Hemming St WCHPL E1 104 C3
Hemmingway Cl KTTN NW5 84 A2
Hempstead Cl BKHH IG9 38 E4
Hempstead Rd WALTH E17 52 B6
Hemp Wk WALW SE17 19 F6
Hemsby Rd CHSGTN KT9 206 B4
Hemstal Rd KIL/WHAMP NW6 82 E5
Hemsted Rd ERITH DA8 150 B2
Hemswell Dr CDALE/KGS NW9 45 G4
Hemsworth St IS N1 7 G2
Henbury Wy OXHEY WD19 27 H5
Henchman St SHB W12 99 H5
Hendale Av HDN NW4 45 J6
Henderson Cl EMPK RM11 75 K6
WLSDN NW10 80 E4
Henderson Dr DART DA1 151 K5
STJWD NW8 2 A6
Henderson Rd CROY/NA CR0 196 E3
ED N9 36 D3
FSTGT E7 89 G4
WAND/EARL SW18 160 D2
YEAD UB4 94 E2
Hendham Rd TOOT SW17 160 D4
Hendon Av FNCH N3 46 C4
Hendon Gdns CRW RM5 56 E2
Hendon Gv HOR/WEW KT19 206 C6
Hendon Hall Ct HDN * NW4 46 B6
Hendon La FNCH N3 46 C6
Hendon Park Rw GLDGN * NW11 64 D3
Hendon Rd ED N9 36 C4
Hendon Wy CRICK NW2 64 C5
STWL/WRAY TW19 132 A6
Hendon Wood La MLHL NW7 31 J2
Hendren Cl GFD/PVL UB6 78 D3
Hendre Rd STHWK SE1 19 H7
Hendrick Av BAL SW12 160 E1
Heneage La HDTCH EC3A 13 H4
Heneage St WCHPL E1 13 K2
Henfield Cl ARCH N19 66 C5
BXLY DA5 169 H1
Henfield Rd WIM/MER SW19 177 J4
Hengelo Gdns MTCM CR4 194 C1
Hengist Rd ERITH DA8 149 K1
LEE/GVPK SE12 166 A2
Hengist Wy HAYES BR2 199 G1
Hengrave Rd FSTH SE23 163 K2
Hengrove Ct BXLY DA5 169 F3
Hengrove Crs ASHF TW15 152 A5
Henley Av CHEAM SM3 208 C1
Henley Cl BERM/RHTH * SE16 123 K2
GFD/PVL * UB6 96 C1
ISLW TW7 136 A2
Henley Dr BERM/RHTH SE16 19 K6
KUTN/CMB KT2 176 C3
Henley Gdns CHDH RM6 74 A2
PIN HA5 41 F6
Henley Rd CAN/RD E16 126 E2
IL IG1 90 C2
UED N18 36 A6
WLSDN NW10 82 A6
Henley St BTSEA SW11 141 F3
Henley Wy FELT TW13 172 C1
Hennel Cl FSTH SE23 163 K5
Hennessy Rd ED N9 36 E4
Henniker Gdns EHAM E6 107 H2
Henniker Ms CHEL SW3 120 C6
Henniker Rd SRTFD E15 88 B3
Henningham Rd TOTM N17 49 K4
Henning St BTSEA SW11 140 D2
Henrietta Cl DEPT SE8 124 D6
Henrietta Ms BMSBY WC1N 5 F6
Henrietta Pl CAVSQ/HST W1G 9 J3
Henrietta St COVGDN WC2E 11 F5
SRTFD E15 88 A3
Henriques St WCHPL E1 104 C5
Henry Addlington Cl EHAM E6 108 B4
Henry Cl ENC/FH EN2 24 A1
Henry Cooper Wy
ELTH/MOT SE9 166 C5
Henry Darlot Dr MLHL NW7 46 C1
Henry Dickens Ct NTGHL W11 100 B6
Henry Doulton Dr TOOT SW17 161 F6
Henry Jackson Rd
PUT/ROE SW15 139 G4
Henry Macaulay Av
KUTN/CMB KT2 174 E4
Henry Peters Dr TEDD TW11 173 K1
Henry Rd EBAR EN4 21 H6
EHAM E6 107 J1
FSBYPK N4 67 J5
Henry's Av WFD IG8 52 D1
Henryson Rd BROCKY SE4 144 D6
Henry St BMLY BR1 184 A4
Hensford Gdns SYD SE26 163 J6
Henshall St IS N1 85 K4
Henshawe Rd BCTR RM8 91 K1
Henshaw St WALW SE17 18 E6
Henslowe Rd EDUL SE22 143 H6
Henson Av CRICK NW2 82 A3
Henson Cl ORP BR6 201 G6
Henson Pl NTHLT UB5 77 G6
Henstridge Pl STJWD NW8 2 C2
Henty Cl BTSEA SW11 140 D1
Henty Wk PUT/ROE SW15 138 E6
Henville Rd BMLY BR1 184 A4
Henwick Rd ELTH/MOT SE9 146 C4
Henwood Side WFD IG8 53 K2
Hepburn Gdns HAYES BR2 199 J5
Hepple Cl ISLW TW7 136 C3
Hepscott Rd HOM E9 87 J4
Hepworth Gdns BARK IG11 91 G3
Hepworth Rd
STRHM/NOR SW16 179 K3
Herald Gdns WLGTN SM6 210 B1
Heralds Pl LBTH SE11 18 A6
Herald St BETH E2 104 D3
Herbal Hl CLKNW EC1R 5 K7
Herbert Crs KTBR SW1X 15 F4
Herbert Gdns CHDH RM6 73 K4
CHSWK W4 117 J6
WLSDN NW10 99 K1
Herbert Pl WOOL/PLUM SE18 127 G6
Herbert Rd BXLYHN DA7 149 F3
CDALE/KGS NW9 63 J3
FBAR/BDGN N11 48 E3
GDMY/SEVK IG3 72 E6
HAYES BR2 200 C2
KUT KT1 175 G6
MNPK E12 89 J2
SEVS/STOTM N15 68 B2
STHL UB1 114 E1
WALTH E17 69 H4
WIM/MER SW19 177 J3
WOOL/PLUM SE18 147 G1
Herbert St KTTN NW5 84 A4
PLSTW E13 106 E1
Herbrand St BMSBY WC1N 4 E7
Hercules Pl HOLWY N7 84 E1
Hercules Rd STHWK SE1 17 H5
Hercules St HOLWY N7 84 E1
Hereford Av EBAR EN4 33 K3
Hereford Gdns IL IG1 71 J4
PIN HA5 59 J2
WHTN * TW2 155 H3
Hereford Ms BAY/PAD * W2 100 E5
Hereford Pl NWCR * SE14 144 C1
Hereford Retreat PECK SE15 143 H1
Hereford Rd ACT W3 98 E6
BAY/PAD W2 100 E5
EA W5 116 D3
FELT TW13 154 B3
WAN E11 71 F2
Hereford Sq SKENS SW7 120 B4
Hereford St BETH E2 104 C3
Hereford Wy CHSGTN KT9 205 J3
Herent Dr CLAY IG5 53 K6
Hereward Gdns PLMGR N13 49 G1
Hereward Rd TOOT SW17 160 D6
Herga Rd KTN/HRWW/W HA3 61 F1
Heriot Av CHING E4 37 J4
Heriot Rd HDN NW4 64 A2
Heriots Cl STAN HA7 29 G6
Heritage Hl HAYES BR2 215 G3
Heritage Pl WAND/EARL * SW18 160 C1
Heritage Vw HRW HA1 79 F1
Herkomer Cl BUSH WD23 28 B1
Herlwyn Av RSLP HA4 76 C1
Herlwyn Gdns TOOT SW17 160 E6
Herm Cl ISLW TW7 135 H1
Hermes Cl MV/WKIL W9 100 E3
Hermes St IS N1 5 J3
Hermes Wy WLGTN SM6 210 D5
Hermiston Av CEND/HSY/T N8 66 E2
The Hermitage BARN * SW13 138 C2
FELT * TW13 153 J5
FSTH SE23 163 K3
KUT * KT1 190 E1
LEW * SE13 145 F3
RCHPK/HAM TW10 137 F6
Hermitage Cl ENC/FH EN2 23 H3
ESH/CLAY KT10 205 G4
RCHPK/HAM * TW10 136 E6
SWFD E18 70 D1
Hermitage Cottages STAN * HA7 42 E1
Hermitage Gdns HAMP NW3 82 E1
NRWD SE19 180 D3
Hermitage La CRICK NW2 82 E1
CROY/NA CR0 197 G4
STRHM/NOR SW16 180 A3
Hermitage Rd FSBYPK N4 67 J4
NRWD SE19 180 D3
Hermitage Rw HACK * E8 86 C3
Hermitage St BAY/PAD W2 8 A2
Hermitage Wk SWFD E18 70 D1
Hermitage Wall WAP E1W 123 H1
Hermitage Wy STAN HA7 43 G4
Hermit Rd CAN/RD E16 106 D4
Hermit St FSBYE EC1V 6 A4
Hermon Gv HYS/HAR UB3 113 K1
Hermon Hl WAN E11 70 E1
Herndon Rd WAND/EARL SW18 140 B6
Herne Cl WLSDN NW10 81 F3
Herne Ct BUSH * WD23 28 C3
Herne Hl HNHL SE24 142 D6
Herne Hill Rd HNHL SE24 142 D4
Herne Ms UED N18 36 C6
Herne Pl HNHL SE24 162 C1
Herne Rd BUSH WD23 28 B1
SURB KT6 190 E6
Heron Cl BKHH IG9 38 E3
WALTH E17 51 H5
WLSDN NW10 81 G4
Heron Ct HAYES BR2 200 B1
KUT * KT1 175 F6
Heron Crs SCUP DA14 167 K6
Herondale SAND/SEL CR2 213 F6
Herondale Av
WAND/EARL SW18 160 C3
Heron Dr FSBYPK N4 67 J6
Heron Flight Av HCH RM12 93 J5
Herongate Rd MNPK E12 71 G6
Heron Hl BELV DA17 129 G4
Heron Md PEND EN3 25 J1
Heron Ms IL IG1 72 B6
Heron Quays POP/IOD E14 124 D1
Heron Rd CROY/NA * CR0 197 F5
HNHL SE24 142 D5
TWK TW1 136 B5
Heronsforde WEA W13 97 J5
Heronsgate EDGE HA8 44 C1
Herons Lea HGT * N6 65 K3
Heronslea Dr STAN HA7 44 A1
Herons Pl ISLW TW7 136 C4
Herons Ri EBAR EN4 21 J5
Heron Wk NTHWD HA6 26 C6
Heron Wy EBED/NFELT TW14 133 K5
Herrick Rd HBRY N5 85 J1
Herrick St WEST SW1P 16 D7
Herries St NKENS W10 100 C1
Herringham Rd CHARL SE7 126 B3
Herrongate Cl EN EN1 24 A3
Hersant Cl WLSDN NW10 81 J6
Herschell Rd FSTH SE23 164 A2
Hersham Cl PUT/ROE SW15 158 D2
Hersham Rd WOT/HER KT12 188 A6
Hershell Ct MORT/ESHN * SW14 137 J5
Hertford Av MORT/ESHN SW14 138 A6
Hertford Cl EBAR EN4 21 H4
Hertford Ct STAN * HA7 43 K3
Hertford End Ct NTHWD * HA6 40 C1
Hertford Rd BARK IG11 90 B5
EBAR EN4 21 G4
ED N9 36 D3
EFNCH N2 47 J6
GNTH/NBYPK IG2 72 E3
IS N1 86 A6
PEND EN3 24 E2
Hertford Road High St
PEND * EN3 24 E5
Hertford St MYFR/PICC W1J 9 J7
MYFR/PKLN W1K 15 J1
Hertford Wy MTCM CR4 195 K1
Hertslet Rd HOLWY N7 85 F1
Hertsmere Rd POP/IOD E14 105 J6
Hertswood Ct BAR * EN5 20 C5
Hervey Cl FNCH N3 46 E4
Hervey Park Rd WALTH E17 69 G1
Hesa Rd HYS/HAR UB3 94 E5
Hesewall Cl VX/NE SW8 141 H3
Hesketh Pl NTGHL W11 100 C6
Hesketh Rd FSTGT E7 88 E1
Heslop Rd BAL SW12 160 E3
Hesper Ms ECT SW5 120 A5
Hesperus Crs POP/IOD E14 124 E4
Hessel Rd WEA W13 116 B2
Hessel St WCHPL E1 104 D5
Hesselyn Dr RAIN RM13 93 K5
Hestercombe Av FUL/PGN SW6 139 H3
Hesterman Wy CROY/NA CR0 195 K5
Hester Rd BTSEA SW11 140 D1
UED N18 50 C1
Hester Ter RCH/KEW TW9 137 H4
Heston Av HEST TW5 134 D1
Heston Grange La HEST TW5 114 E6
Heston Rd HEST TW5 135 F1
Heston St DEPT SE8 144 C2
Heswell Gn OXHEY * WD19 26 E5
Hetherington Rd CLAP SW4 141 K5
Hetley Rd SHB W12 118 E1
Heton Gdns HDN NW4 63 J1
Hevelius Cl GNWCH SE10 125 J5
Hever Cft ELTH/MOT SE9 167 F6
Hever Gdns BMLY BR1 185 F5
Heverham Rd
WOOL/PLUM SE18 127 K4
Heversham Rd BXLYHN DA7 149 H3
Hewens Rd HGDN/ICK UB10 94 A2
Hewer St NKENS W10 100 B4
Hewett Cl STAN HA7 29 H6
Hewett St SDTCH EC2A 7 H7
Hewish Rd UED N18 36 A6
Hewison St BOW E3 105 H1
Hewitt Av WDGN N22 49 H5

Hewitt Cl CROY/NA CR0 213 J1
Hewitt Rd CEND/HSY/T N8 67 G2
Hewlett Rd BOW E3 105 G1
The Hexagon HGT N6 65 K5
Hexal Rd CAT SE6 165 H5
Hexham Gdns ISLW TW7 136 B1
Hexham Rd BAR EN5 21 F5
MRDN SM4 194 A5
WNWD SE27 162 D4
Heybourne Rd TOTM N17 50 D3
Heybridge Av
STRHM/NOR SW16 180 A2
Heybridge Dr BARK/HLT IG6 54 D6
Heybridge Wy WALTH E17 69 G4
Heyford Av RYNPK SW20 177 J6
VX/NE SW8 141 K1
Heyford Rd MTCM CR4 178 D5
Heyford Ter VX/NE SW8 141 K1
Heygate Est WALW SE17 18 D6
Heygate St WALW SE17 18 C7
Heynes Rd BCTR RM8 91 J2
Heysham Dr OXHEY WD19 41 G1
Heysham La HAMP NW3 83 G1
Heysham Rd SEVS/STOTM N15 67 K3
Heythorp St WAND/EARL SW18 159 J3
Heywood Av CDALE/KGS NW9 45 G4
Heyworth Rd CLPT E5 86 D2
SRTFD E15 88 D3
Hibbert Rd KTN/HRWW/W HA3 43 F5
WALTH E17 69 H4
Hibbert St BTSEA SW11 140 B4
Hibernia Gdns HSLW TW3 135 F6
Hibernia Rd HSLW TW3 135 F5
Hichisson Rd PECK SE15 143 K6
Hickin Cl CHARL SE7 126 C4
Hickin St POP/IOD E14 125 F3
Hickling Rd IL IG1 90 B3
Hickman Av CHING E4 52 A2
Hickman Cl CAN/RD E16 107 H4
Hickman Rd CHDH RM6 73 J4
Hicks Av GFD/PVL UB6 96 D2
Hicks Cl BTSEA SW11 140 D4
Hicks St DEPT SE8 124 B5
Hidcote Gdns RYNPK SW20 176 E6
Hide Pl WEST SW1P 16 C7
Hide Rd HRW HA1 60 D1
Higham Hill Rd WALTH E17 51 G4
Higham Pl WALTH E17 51 G6
Higham Rd TOTM N17 49 K6
WFD IG8 52 E2
The Highams WALTH * E17 52 A4
Higham Station Av CHING E4 51 K2
Higham St WALTH E17 51 G6
Highbank Pl
WAND/EARL * SW18 160 A2
Highbanks Cl WELL DA16 148 B1
Highbanks Rd PIN HA5 42 B2
Highbank Wy CEND/HSY/T N8 67 G3
Highbarrow Rd CROY/NA CR0 197 G5
High Beech SAND/SEL CR2 212 A5
High Beeches ORP BR6 217 G4
SCUP DA14 187 F1
Highbridge Rd BARK IG11 90 A5
Highbrook Rd BKHTH/KID SE3 146 C4
High Broom Crs WWKM BR4 198 E4
Highbury Av THHTH CR7 180 B5
Highbury Cl NWMAL KT3 191 K1
WWKM BR4 198 E6
Highbury Cnr IS N1 85 H4
Highbury Crs HBRY N5 85 H3
Highbury Est HBRY N5 85 J3
Highbury Gdns GDMY/SEVK IG3 72 E6
Highbury Gra HBRY N5 85 H2
Highbury Gv HBRY N5 85 H3
Highbury Hl HBRY N5 85 H2
Highbury New Pk HBRY N5 85 H4
Highbury Pk HBRY N5 85 H2
Highbury Pl HBRY N5 85 H4
Highbury Qd HBRY N5 85 J1
Highbury Rd WIM/MER SW19 177 H1
Highbury Station Pde IS * N1 85 H4
Highbury Station Rd IS * N1 85 G4
Highbury Ter HBRY N5 85 H3
Highbury Terrace Ms HBRY N5 85 H3
High Cedar Dr RYNPK SW20 176 E3
Highclere Rd NWMAL KT3 176 A6
Highclere St SYD SE26 164 B6
Highcliffe Dr PUT/ROE SW15 158 C1
Highcliffe Gdns REDBR IG4 71 J2
Highcombe CHARL SE7 126 A6
Highcombe Cl ELTH/MOT SE9 166 C3
High Coombe Pl
KUTN/CMB KT2 176 A3
Highcroft CDALE/KGS NW9 63 G2
Highcroft Av ALP/SUD HA0 80 B5
Highcroft Gdns GLDGN NW11 64 D3
Highcroft Rd ARCH N19 66 E4
High Cross Rd TOTM N17 50 C6
Highdaun Dr STRHM/NOR SW16 196 A1
Highdown WPK KT4 192 B6
Highdown Rd PUT/ROE SW15 158 E1
High Dr NWMAL KT3 175 K4
High Elms WFD IG8 52 E1
High Elms Cl NTHWD HA6 40 A2
High Elms Rd ORP BR6 216 C6
Highfield OXHEY WD19 27 K5
Highfield Av CDALE/KGS NW9 62 E2
ERITH DA8 129 J6
GFD/PVL UB6 78 E3
GLDGN NW11 64 B4
ORP BR6 217 F4
PIN HA5 59 K2
WBLY HA9 80 A1
Highfield Cl CDALE/KGS NW9 62 E2
CRW RM5 56 E2
LEW SE13 165 G1
NTHWD HA6 40 C4
SURB KT6 190 D5
WDGN N22 49 G4
Highfield Ct STHGT/OAK N14 34 C1
Highfield Crs NTHWD HA6 40 C4
Highfield Dr HAYES BR2 199 H1
HOR/WEW KT19 207 H5
WWKM BR4 213 K1
Highfield Gdns GLDGN NW11 64 C3
Highfield Hl NRWD SE19 180 E3
Highfield Link CRW RM5 56 E2
Highfield Rd ACT W3 98 E4
BMLY BR1 200 E1
BRYLDS KT5 191 K4
BXLYHS DA6 149 G6
CRW RM5 56 E2
DART DA1 171 G2
FELT TW13 153 K3
GLDGN * NW11 64 C3
ISLW TW7 136 A2
NTHWD HA6 40 C4
STMC/STPC BR5 186 A6
SUT SM1 209 J3
WCHMH N21 35 H4
WFD IG8 53 J3
Highfield Rd South DART DA1 171 G2
Highfields Gv HGT N6 66 A5
High Foleys ESH/CLAY KT10 205 H5
High Garth ESH/CLAY KT10 204 C4
Highgate Av HGT N6 66 B4
Highgate Cl HGT N6 66 A4
Highgate Edge EFNCH * N2 65 J2
Highgate High St HGT N6 66 A5
Highgate Hl ARCH N19 66 B5
Highgate Rd KTTN NW5 84 A1
Highgate Spinney
CEND/HSY/T * N8 66 D3
Highgate West Hl HGT N6 66 A6
High Gv BMLY BR1 184 B4
WOOL/PLUM SE18 147 J1
Highgrove Cl CHST BR7 184 D4
FBAR/BDGN N11 48 A1
Highgrove Ms CAR SM5 209 J1
Highgrove Rd BCTR RM8 91 J3
Highgrove Wy RSLP HA4 58 E3
High Hill Ferry CLPT E5 68 D5
High Holborn HHOL WC1V 11 F3
Highland Av DAGE RM10 92 E1
HNWL W7 96 E5
LOU IG10 39 K1
Highland Cottages
WLGTN * SM6 210 B2
Highland Cft BECK BR3 182 E1
Highland Dr BUSH WD23 28 B2
Highland Pk FELT TW13 153 J6
Highland Rd BMLY BR1 183 J4
BXLYHS DA6 149 H6
NRWD SE19 181 F2
NTHWD HA6 40 E5
The Highlands BAR * EN5 21 F5
Highlands OXHEY WD19 27 G3
Highlands Av ACT W3 98 E6
WCHMH N21 23 F6
Highlands Cl HSLW TW3 135 G2
Highlands Gdns IL IG1 71 K5
Highlands Rd BAR EN5 20 E5
STMC/STPC BR5 202 C4
EDGE HA8 44 D5
Highland Ter LEW * SE13 144 E4
High La HNWL W7 96 D5
Highlea Cl CDALE/KGS NW9 45 G4
High Level Dr SYD SE26 163 H6
Highlever Rd NKENS W10 100 A4
High Limes NRWD * SE19 181 F2
High Md HRW HA1 60 E2
Highmead WOOL/PLUM SE18 148 A1
High Md WWKM BR4 199 G6
Highmead Crs ALP/SUD HA0 80 B5
High Meadow Cl PIN HA5 59 F1
High Meadow Crs
CDALE/KGS NW9 63 F2
High Mdw CHIG IG7 54 D1
High Meads Rd CAN/RD E16 107 H5
Highmore Rd BKHTH/KID SE3 145 H1
High Mt HDN * NW4 63 J3
High Oaks ENC/FH EN2 23 F1
The High Pde
STRHM/NOR * SW16 161 K5
High Park Rd RCH/KEW TW9 137 H2
High Pth WIM/MER SW19 178 A4
High Point ELTH/MOT SE9 167 G5
High Rdg MUSWH * N10 48 B4
Highridge Pl ENC/FH * EN2 23 F1
High Rd BKHH IG9 39 F4
BUSH WD23 28 D3
CHDH RM6 74 B3
FBAR/BDGN N11 48 B1
FNCH N3 47 G4
GDMY/SEVK IG3 73 G5
IL IG1 90 B1
KTN/HRWW/W HA3 42 E4
LEY E10 69 K3
NFNCH/WDSP N12 33 G5
RDART DA2 170 E5
SEVS/STOTM N15 68 B2
TRDG/WHET N20 33 G2
WBLY HA9 80 A3
WDGN N22 49 F3
WLSDN NW10 81 G4
High Rd Eastcote PIN HA5 59 F2
High Rd Great North Rd
EFNCH N2 47 H5
High Rd Ickenham
HGDN/ICK UB10 58 A6
High Rd Leyton LEY E10 69 K6
High Rd Leytonstone WAN E11 88 C1
High Rd Woodford Gn
SWFD E18 52 E4
WFD IG8 38 E6
Highshore Rd PECK SE15 143 H3
Highstead Crs ERITH DA8 150 B2
Highstone Av WAN E11 70 E3
High St ACT W3 117 K1
BAR EN5 20 D5
BARK/HLT IG6 54 C6
BECK BR3 182 D5
BELMT SM2 209 F4
BMLY BR1 183 K6
BORE WD6 29 K1
BTFD TW8 116 E6
BUSH WD23 28 A1
CAR SM5 209 K3
CEND/HSY/T N8 66 E1
CHEAM SM3 208 C4
CROY/NA CR0 211 J1
DART DA1 171 H1
E/WMO/HCT KT8 189 F1
EA W5 97 K6
ESH/CLAY KT10 204 B3
ESH/CLAY KT10 205 F4
EW KT17 207 H6
FBAR/BDGN N11 48 B1
FELT TW13 153 J5
HEST TW5 134 A1
HPTN TW12 173 G4
HRW HA1 60 E6
HSLW TW3 135 H4
HYS/HAR UB3 113 G6
KTN/HRWW/W HA3 42 E6
KUT KT1 174 D4
KUT KT1 174 E6
MLHL NW7 45 K1
NTHWD HA6 40 D4
NWMAL KT3 192 B1
ORP BR6 202 B5
ORP BR6 216 C3
PGE/AN SE20 181 K3
PIN HA5 41 J6
PLSTW E13 106 E1
ROM RM1 75 G2
RSLP HA4 58 C5
SCUP DA14 168 B6
SNWD SE25 197 G1
SRTFD E15 106 A1
STHGT/OAK N14 34 D3
STMC/STPC BR5 202 D1
STWL/WRAY TW19 152 A1
SUT SM1 209 F2
TEDD TW11 174 B1
THDIT KT7 190 B4
THHTH CR7 196 D1
WALTH E17 69 H1
WAN E11 71 F3
WBLY HA9 80 B2
WDR/YW UB7 112 A6
WDR/YW UB7 112 B1
WHTN TW2 155 H2
WIM/MER SW19 177 G1
WWKM BR4 198 E5
High St Collier's Wd
WIM/MER SW19 178 C3
High St Harlesden WLSDN NW10 99 H1
High St Harlington
HYS/HAR UB3 113 G6
High Street Ms WIM/MER SW19 177 H1
High St North MNPK E12 89 J4
High St South EHAM E6 107 K1
High Timber St BLKFR EC4V 12 C5
High Tor Cl BMLY BR1 184 A3
High Trees BRXS/STRHM SW2 162 B3
CROY/NA CR0 198 B5
EBAR EN4 21 J6
High Vw PIN HA5 59 G1
WATW WD18 26 D1
Highview Av EDGE HA8 30 E6
High View Av WLGTN SM6 211 F3
High View Cl NRWD SE19 181 G5
Highview Gdns EDGE HA8 44 E1
FBAR/BDGN N11 48 C1
FNCH N3 46 C6
High View Rd NRWD SE19 180 E2
SWFD E18 52 D5
Highview Rd SCUP DA14 168 C6
WEA W13 97 G5
Highview Ter DART * DA1 151 G6
The Highway BELMT SM2 209 G6
ORP BR6 217 H3
STAN HA7 43 F4
WAP E1W 104 C6
Highwood Av NFNCH/WDSP N12 33 G6
Highwood Cl ORP BR6 201 H6
Highwood Dr ORP BR6 201 H6
Highwood Gdns CLAY IG5 71 K2
Highwood Gv MLHL NW7 45 F1
Highwood Hl MLHL NW7 31 H5
Highwood Rd ARCH N19 84 E1
High Worple RYLN/HDSTN HA2 59 J4
Highworth Rd FBAR/BDGN N11 48 D2
Highworth St CAMTN * NW1 8 D1
Hilary Av MTCM CR4 179 F6
Hilary Cl BXLYHN DA7 149 J2
FUL/PGN * SW6 140 A1
Hilary Rd ACT W3 99 H6
Hilberry Ct BUSH * WD23 28 B2
Hilbert Rd CHEAM SM3 208 B2
Hilborough Cl WIM/MER SW19 178 B3
Hilborough Rd HACK E8 86 B5
Hilborough Wy ORP BR6 216 D3
Hilda Rd CAN/RD E16 106 C3
EHAM E6 89 H5
Hilda Ter BRXN/ST * SW9 142 B3
Hilda Vale Rd ORP BR6 216 A2
Hildenborough Gdns BMLY BR1 183 H2
Hilden Dr ERITH DA8 150 E1
Hildenlea Pl HAYES BR2 183 H5
Hildreth St BAL SW12 161 G3
Hildyard Rd FUL/PGN SW6 119 K6
Hiley Rd WLSDN NW10 100 A2
Hilgrove Rd KIL/WHAMP NW6 83 G5
Hiliary Gdns STAN HA7 43 J5
Hillary Crs WOT/HER KT12 188 B5
Hillary Dr ISLW TW7 136 A5
Hillary Ri BAR EN5 20 E5
Hillary Rd NWDGN UB2 115 F3
Hillbeck Cl PECK SE15 143 K1
Hillbeck Wy GFD/PVL UB6 78 D6
Hillborne Cl HYS/HAR UB3 113 K5
Hillborough Cl
WIM/MER * SW19 178 B3
Hillbrook Rd TOOT SW17 160 E5
Hill Brow BMLY BR1 184 C4
DART DA1 170 C1
Hillbrow NWMAL KT3 176 C6
Hillbrow Cl BXLY DA5 170 A6
Hillbrow Rd BMLY BR1 183 H3
ESH/CLAY KT10 204 C2
Hill Bunker's BELV DA17 129 H4
Hillbury Av KTN/HRWW/W HA3 61 H2
Hillbury Rd TOOT SW17 161 G5
Hill Cl BAR EN5 20 A6
CHST BR7 185 G1
CRICK NW2 81 K1
GLDGN NW11 64 E3
HRW HA1 78 E1
STAN HA7 29 H6
Hillcote Av STRHM/NOR SW16 180 B3
Hillcourt Av NFNCH/WDSP N12 47 F2
Hillcourt Rd EDUL SE22 163 J1
Hill Crs BRYLDS KT5 191 G2
BXLY DA5 169 K3
HRW HA1 61 G2
TRDG/WHET N20 33 F4
WPK KT4 193 F6
Hill Crest BFN/LL DA15 168 B2
SURB * KT6 191 F4
Hillcrest CMBW * SE5 142 E5
HGT N6 66 A4
WCHMH N21 35 H2
Hillcrest Av EDGE HA8 30 D6
GLDGN NW11 64 C2
PIN HA5 59 H1
Hillcrest Cl BECK BR3 198 C3
SYD SE26 163 H6
Hill Crest Gdns CRICK NW2 81 J1
Hillcrest Gdns ESH/CLAY KT10 205 F2
FNCH N3 64 C1
Hillcrest Rd ACT W3 117 H1
BMLY BR1 165 K6
DART DA1 170 B2
EA W5 98 A4
EMPK RM11 75 J4
LOU IG10 39 H1
ORP BR6 202 B6
WALTH E17 52 B5
Hillcrest Vw BECK BR3 198 C3
Hillcroft Av PIN HA5 59 K3
Hillcroft Crs EA W5 97 K5
OXHEY WD19 27 F3
RSLP HA4 77 H1
WBLY HA9 80 B2
Hillcroft Rd EHAM E6 108 B4
Hillcroome Rd BELMT SM2 209 H4
Hillcross Av MRDN SM4 193 H3
Hilldale Rd SUT SM1 208 D2
Hilldown Rd HAYES BR2 199 H5
STRHM/NOR SW16 179 K3
Hill Dr CDALE/KGS NW9 62 E5
STRHM/NOR SW16 180 A6
Hilldrop Crs HOLWY N7 84 D3
Hilldrop Est HOLWY N7 84 D3
Hilldrop La HOLWY N7 84 D3
Hilldrop Rd BMLY BR1 184 A2
HOLWY N7 84 D3
Hill End ORP BR6 202 A6
WOOL/PLUM SE18 147 F2
Hillersdon Av BARN SW13 138 D3
EDGE HA8 44 B1
Hillery Cl WALW SE17 19 F7
Hill Farm Rd NKENS W10 100 A4
Hillfield Av ALP/SUD HA0 80 A5
CDALE/KGS NW9 63 G2
CEND/HSY/T N8 67 F1
MRDN SM4 194 D3
Hillfield Cl RYLN/HDSTN HA2 60 C1
Hillfield La South BUSH WD23 28 E1
Hillfield Pde MRDN * SM4 194 C3
Hillfield Pk MUSWH N10 48 B6
WCHMH N21 35 G4
Hillfield Park Ms MUSWH N10 66 B1
Hill Field Rd HPTN TW12 172 E3
Hillfield Rd KIL/WHAMP NW6 82 D3
Hillfoot Av CRW RM5 56 E4
Hillfoot Rd CRW RM5 56 E4
Hillgate Pl BAL SW12 161 G1
KENS W8 119 K1
Hillgate St KENS * W8 119 K1
Hill Gv FELT TW13 154 E4
ROM RM1 57 G6
Hill House Av STAN HA7 43 F3
Hill House Cl WCHMH N21 35 G2
Hill House Dr HPTN TW12 173 F4
Hill House Rd
STRHM/NOR SW16 180 A1
Hilliard Rd NTHWD HA6 40 D4
Hilliard's Ct WAP E1W 123 K1
Hillier Cl BAR EN5 33 F1
Hillier Gdns CROY/NA CR0 211 G3
Hillier Pl CHSGTN KT9 205 K4
Hillier Rd BTSEA SW11 160 E1
Hillier's La CROY/NA CR0 210 E1
Hillingdon Av
STWL/WRAY TW19 152 B3
Hillingdon Rd BXLYHN DA7 149 K4
Hillingdon St WALW SE17 122 C6
Hillingdon Trail HYS/HAR UB3 113 K5
Hill La RSLP HA4 58 A5
Hillman St HACK E8 86 D4
Hillmarton Rd HOLWY N7 84 E3
Hillmarton Ter HOLWY * N7 84 E3
Hillmead Dr BRXN/ST SW9 142 C5
Hillmont Rd ESH/CLAY KT10 204 E1
Hillmore Gv SYD SE26 182 A1
Hillreach WOOL/PLUM SE18 126 E5
Hill Ri ED N9 36 D1
ESH/CLAY KT10 190 C6
GFD/PVL UB6 78 C6
GLDGN NW11 65 F1
RCHPK/HAM TW10 136 E6
RSLP HA4 58 A5
Hillrise Rd ARCH N19 66 E4
CRW RM5 56 E2
Hill Rd ALP/SUD HA0 79 H1
CAR SM5 209 J4
DART DA1 171 H4
HRW HA1 61 G2
MTCM CR4 179 G4
MUSWH N10 47 K4
NTHWD HA6 40 B2
PIN HA5 59 J3
STJWD NW8 101 G1
SUT SM1 209 F3
Hillsboro Rd EDUL SE22 143 F6
Hillsborough Gn OXHEY * WD19 26 E5
Hillsgrove Cl WELL DA16 148 D1
The Hillside ORP BR6 217 H6
Hill Side BAR EN5 21 G6
Hillside CDALE/KGS NW9 63 F1
ESH/CLAY * KT10 204 B3
WIM/MER SW19 177 G2
WLSDN NW10 81 F6
Hillside Av FBAR/BDGN N11 47 K2
WBLY HA9 80 B2
WFD IG8 53 G1
Hillside Cl KIL/WHAMP NW6 101 F1
MRDN SM4 193 H1
WFD IG8 53 G1
Hillside Crs ENC/FH EN2 23 K1
NTHWD HA6 40 E4
OXHEY WD19 27 H1
RYLN/HDSTN HA2 60 C6
Hillside Dr EDGE HA8 44 C2
Hillside Gdns BAR EN5 20 C5
BRXS/STRHM * SW2 162 B4
EDGE HA8 30 B6
FBAR/BDGN * N11 48 C2
HGT N6 66 A3
KTN/HRWW/W HA3 62 A4
NTHWD HA6 40 E3
WLGTN SM6 210 C5
Hillside Gv MLHL NW7 45 J3
STHGT/OAK N14 34 D2
Hillside La HAYES BR2 199 K6
Hillside Ri NTHWD HA6 40 E3
Hillside Rd BELMT SM2 208 D5
BRXS/STRHM SW2 162 A4
CROY/NA CR0 211 H3
DART DA1 170 D1
EA W5 98 A4
HAYES BR2 183 J6
NTHWD HA6 40 E3
STHL UB1 96 A3
STNW/STAM N16 68 A4
Hills La NTHWD HA6 40 C4
Hillsleigh Rd KENS W8 119 J1
Hills Ms EA * W5 98 A6
Hills Pl SOHO/CST W1F 10 A4
Hill's Rd BKHH IG9 39 F3
Hillstowe St CLPT E5 68 E6
Hill St MYFR/PICC W1J 9 J7
RCHPK/HAM TW10 136 E6
Hill Top GLDGN NW11 65 F1
MRDN SM4 193 J4
Hilltop WALTH * E17 51 K6
Hilltop Cottages SYD * SE26 163 J6
Hilltop Gdns DART DA1 151 J6
ORP BR6 201 K6
Hilltop Rd KIL/WHAMP NW6 82 E5
Hill Top Vw WFD * IG8 53 K2
Hilltop Wy STAN HA7 29 G5
Hillview RYNPK SW20 176 E3
Hillview Av KTN/HRWW/W HA3 62 A2
Hillview Cl PIN HA5 41 K2
Hill View Crs IL IG1 71 K3
Hillview Crs ORP BR6 201 K5
Hill View Dr WELL DA16 147 K3
Hill View Gdns CDALE/KGS NW9 63 F2
Hillview Gdns HDN NW4 64 B1
PIN HA5 42 A6
Hill View Rd ESH/CLAY KT10 205 G5
ORP BR6 202 A5
TWK TW1 156 B1
Hillview Rd CHST BR7 185 F1
MLHL NW7 32 B6
PIN HA5 41 K3
SUT SM1 209 G1
Hillway CDALE/KGS NW9 63 G5
HGT N6 66 A6
Hillworth BECK * BR3 182 E5
Hillworth Rd BRXS/STRHM SW2 162 B2
Hillyard Rd HNWL W7 96 E4
Hillyard St BRXN/ST SW9 142 B2
Hillyfield WALTH E17 51 G5
Hillyfield Cl HOM E9 87 G3
Hilly Flds BROCKY * SE4 144 D5
Hilly Fields Crs BROCKY SE4 144 D5
Hilsea St CLPT E5 86 E2
Hilton Av NFNCH/WDSP N12 47 H1
Himalayan Wy WATW WD18 26 D1
Himley Rd TOOT SW17 178 D1
Hinchley Cl ESH/CLAY KT10 205 F1
Hinchley Dr ESH/CLAY KT10 205 F1
Hinchley Wy ESH/CLAY KT10 205 G1
Hinckley Rd EDUL SE22 143 H5
Hind Cl CHIG IG7 55 F1
Hind Ct FLST/FETLN * EC4A 11 K4
Hind Crs ERITH DA8 149 K1
Hinde Ms MHST * W1U 9 H3
Hindes Rd HRW HA1 60 E2
Hinde St MHST W1U 9 H3
Hind Gv POP/IOD E14 105 J5
Hindhead Gdns NTHLT UB5 77 J6
Hindhead Gn OXHEY WD19 41 G1
Hindhead Wy WLGTN SM6 210 E3
Hindmans Rd EDUL SE22 143 H6
Hindmans Wy DAGW RM9 110 B3
Hindmarsh Cl WCHPL E1 104 C6
Hindrey Rd CLPT E5 86 D3
Hindsley's Pl FSTH SE23 163 K4
Hinkler Rd KTN/HRWW/W HA3 43 K6
Hinstock Rd WOOL/PLUM SE18 147 H1
Hinton Av HSLWW TW4 134 C5
Hinton Cl ELTH/MOT SE9 166 D3
Hinton Rd BRXN/ST SW9 142 C4
UED N18 36 A6
WLGTN SM6 210 C4
Hippodrome Pl NTGHL W11 100 C6
Hitcham Rd WALTH E17 69 H4
Hitherbroom Rd HYS/HAR UB3 113 K1
Hither Farm Rd BKHTH/KID SE3 146 B4
Hitherfield Rd BCTR RM8 74 A6
STRHM/NOR SW16 162 A4
Hither Green La LEW SE13 145 F6
Hitherwell Dr
KTN/HRWW/W HA3 42 D4
Hitherwood Dr DUL SE21 163 G6
Hive Rd BUSH WD23 28 D4
Hoadly Rd STRHM/NOR SW16 161 J5
Hobart Cl TRDG/WHET N20 33 J4
YEAD UB4 95 H3
Hobart Dr YEAD UB4 95 H3
Hobart Gdns THHTH CR7 180 E6
Hobart La YEAD UB4 95 H3
Hobart Pl BGVA SW1W 15 J5
RCHPK/HAM TW10 157 G2
Hobart Rd BARK/HLT IG6 54 C5
DAGW RM9 91 K2
WPK KT4 207 K1
YEAD UB4 95 H3
Hobbayne Rd HNWL W7 96 D5
Hobbes Wk PUT/ROE SW15 138 E6
Hobbs Gn EFNCH N2 47 G6
Hobbs Pl IS N1 7 G1
Hobbs Place Est IS N1 7 G2
Hobbs Rd WNWD SE27 162 D6
Hobday St POP/IOD E14 105 K5
Hoblands End CHST BR7 185 K2
Hobsons Pl WCHPL * E1 104 C4
Hobury St WBPTN SW10 120 B6
Hockenden La SWLY BR8 187 H6
Hocker St BETH * E2 7 J5
Hockley Av EHAM E6 107 J1
Hockley Dr GPK RM2 57 K5
Hockley Ms BARK IG11 108 E1
Hocroft Av CRICK NW2 82 D1
Hocroft Rd CRICK NW2 82 D2
Hocroft Wk CRICK NW2 82 D1
Hodder Dr GFD/PVL UB6 97 F1
Hoddesdon Rd BELV DA17 129 H5
Hodford Rd GLDGN NW11 64 D5
Hodges Wy WATW WD18 26 E1
Hodgkins Cl THMD SE28 109 K6
Hodister Cl CMBW SE5 142 D1
Hodson Cl RYLN/HDSTN HA2 77 K1
Hodson Crs STMC/STPC BR5 202 E3
Hodson Pl PEND * EN3 25 J1
Hoe La EN EN1 24 D1
The Hoe OXHEY WD19 27 H4
Hoe St WALTH E17 69 J2
Hoffman Sq IS * N1 7 F4
Hofland Rd WKENS W14 119 H3
Hogan Ms BAY/PAD W2 8 A1
Hogarth Cl CAN/RD E16 107 H4
EA W5 98 A4
Hogarth Crs CROY/NA CR0 196 D4
WIM/MER SW19 178 C4
Hogarth Gdns HEST TW5 135 F1
Hogarth Hl GLDGN NW11 64 D1
Hogarth Pl ECT * SW5 120 A4
Hogarth Rd BCTR RM8 91 H3
ECT SW5 120 A4
EDGE HA8 44 C5
Hogarth Ter CHSWK * W4 118 B6
Hogarth Wy HPTN TW12 173 H4
Hog Hill Rd CRW RM5 56 B3
Hogshead Pas WAP * E1W 104 D6
Hogsmill Wy HOR/WEW KT19 206 E3
Holbeach Gdns BFN/LL DA15 167 K1
Holbeach Rd CAT SE6 164 D2
Holbeck Rw PECK SE15 143 H1

Holbein Ga NTHWD HA6 40 C1
Holbein Ms BGVA SW1W 121 F5
Holbein Pl BGVA SW1W 15 G7
Holberton Gdns WLSDN NW10 99 K2
Holborn HCIRC EC1N 11 J2
Holborn Circ HCIRC EC1N 11 K2
Holborn Pl HHOL WC1V 11 G2
Holborn Rd PLSTW E13 107 F4
Holborn Viad STBT EC1A 12 A3
Holborn Wy MTCM CR4 178 E5
Holbrook Cl EN EN1 24 B2
Holbrooke Ct HOLWY N7 84 E1
Holbrook La CHST BR7 185 J3
Holbrook Rd SRTFD E15 106 D1
Holbrook Wy HAYES BR2 200 E3
Holburne Cl BKHTH/KID SE3 146 B2
Holburne Gdns BKHTH/KID SE3 146 C2
Holburne Rd BKHTH/KID SE3 146 B2
Holcombe Hl MLHL NW7 31 J5
Holcombe Rd TOTM N17 50 B6
Holcombe St HMSMTH W6 118 E5
Holcote Cl BELV DA17 129 F3
Holcroft Rd HOM E9 86 E5
Holden Av CDALE/KGS NW9 62 E5
NFNCH/WDSP N12 47 F1
Holdenby Rd BROCKY SE4 144 B6
Holden Cl BCTR RM8 91 H1
Holdenhurst Av FNCH N3 47 F3
Holden Rd NFNCH/WDSP N12 33 F6
Holden St BTSEA SW11 141 F3
Holdernesse Rd ISLW TW7 136 B2
TOOT SW17 160 E5
Holderness Wy WNWD SE27 180 C1
Holders Hill Av HDN NW4 46 B5
Holders Hill Crs HDN NW4 46 B6
Holders Hill Dr HDN NW4 46 B5
Holders Hill Gdns HDN NW4 46 B5
Holders Hill Pde HDN * NW4 46 C4
Holders Hill Rd HDN NW4 46 B5
Holford Ms FSBYW * WC1X 5 G4
Holford Rd HAMP NW3 83 G1
Holford St FSBYW WC1X 5 J4
Holford Yd IS * N1 5 J3
Holgate Av BTSEA SW11 140 C4
Holgate Rd DAGE RM10 92 C3
Holgate St CHARL SE7 126 C3
Holland Av BELMT SM2 208 E5
RYNPK SW20 176 C4
Holland Cl BAR EN5 33 H2
HAYES BR2 199 J6
ROMW/RG RM7 74 E2
STAN HA7 43 H1
Holland Dr FSTH SE23 164 B5
Holland Gdns WKENS W14 119 H3
Holland Gv BRXN/ST SW9 142 B1
Holland Pk KENS W8 119 J2
Holland Park Av GDMY/SEVK IG3 72 E3
NTGHL W11 119 H1
Holland Park Gdns NTGHL W11 119 H1
Holland Park Ms NTGHL W11 119 J1
Holland Park Rd WKENS W14 119 J3
Holland Park Ter NTGHL * W11 119 H1
Holland Pas IS N1 85 J6
Holland Pl KENS * W8 120 A2
Holland Pl Chambers
KENS * W8 120 A2
Holland Rd ALP/SUD HA0 79 K4
EHAM E6 89 K6
SNWD SE25 197 H2
SRTFD E15 106 C2
WKENS W14 119 G2
WLSDN NW10 81 J6
The Hollands WPK KT4 192 C5
Holland St KENS W8 119 K2
STHWK SE1 12 B7
Holland Villas Rd WKENS W14 119 H2
Holland Wk STAN HA7 43 G1
Holland Wy HAYES BR2 199 J6
Hollar Rd STNW/STAM N16 86 B1
Hollen St SOHO/CST W1F 10 B4
Holles Cl HPTN TW12 173 F2
Holles St CAVSQ/HST W1G 9 K3
Holley Rd ACT W3 118 B2
Hollickwood Av
NFNCH/WDSP N12 47 K2
Holliday Sq BTSEA SW11 140 C4
Hollidge Wy DAGE RM10 92 D5
The Hollies KTN/HRWW/W HA3 61 G1
Hollies Av BFN/LL DA15 168 A4
Hollies Cl STRHM/NOR SW16 180 B2
TWK TW1 156 A4
Hollies End MLHL NW7 45 K1
Hollies Rd EA W5 116 D4
Hollies Wy BAL * SW12 161 F2
Holligrave Rd BMLY BR1 183 K4
Hollingbourne Av BXLYHN DA7 149 G2
Hollingbourne Gdns WEA W13 97 H4
Hollingbourne Rd HNHL SE24 142 D6
Hollingsworth Rd
SAND/SEL CR2 212 D4
Hollington Crs NWMAL KT3 192 C3
Hollington Rd EHAM E6 107 K2
TOTM N17 50 C5
Hollingworth Cl
E/WMO/HCT KT8 188 E1
Hollingworth Rd
STMC/STPC BR5 201 G4
Hollman Gdns
STRHM/NOR SW16 180 C2
The Hollow WFD IG8 38 D6
Holloway Cl WDR/YW UB7 112 B5
Holloway La WDR/YW UB7 112 A6
Holloway Rd ARCH N19 66 D6
EHAM E6 107 K2
HOLWY N7 84 E1
WAN E11 88 B1
Holloway St HSLW TW3 135 G4
Holly Av STAN HA7 44 A5
WOT/HER KT12 188 C5
Holly Bank MUSWH * N10 66 C1
Hollybank Cl HPTN TW12 173 F1
Hollybrake Cl CHST BR7 185 J3
Hollybush Cl OXHEY WD19 27 G2
WAN E11 70 E2
Hollybush Gdns BETH E2 104 D2
Hollybush Hl WAN E11 70 D4
Holly Bush La HPTN TW12 172 E3
Hollybush Pl BETH E2 104 D2
Hollybush Rd KUTN/CMB KT2 175 F1
Hollybush St PLSTW E13 107 F2
Hollybush Ter NRWD * SE19 181 F2
Holly Bush V HAMP * NW3 83 G2
Holly Cl BECK BR3 199 F1
BKHH IG9 39 H5
FELT TW13 172 D1
WLSDN NW10 81 G5
Holly Crs BECK BR3 198 C2
WFD IG8 52 B3
Hollycroft Av HAMP NW3 82 E1
WBLY HA9 62 A6
Hollycroft Cl SAND/SEL CR2 212 A3
WDR/YW UB7 112 D6
Hollycroft Gdns WDR/YW UB7 112 D6
Hollydale Cl NTHLT UB5 78 B3
Hollydale Dr HAYES BR2 215 K1
Hollydale Rd PECK SE15 143 K3
Hollydown Wy WAN E11 88 B1
Holly Dr CHING E4 37 K2
Holly Farm Rd NWDGN UB2 114 D5
Hollyfield Av FBAR/BDGN N11 47 K1
Hollyfield Rd BRYLDS KT5 191 G4
Holly Gdns BXLYHN DA7 149 K5
WDR/YW UB7 112 C2
Hollygrove BUSH WD23 28 D2
Holly Gv CDALE/KGS NW9 62 E4
PECK SE15 143 G3
PIN HA5 41 J4
Hollygrove Cl HSLW TW3 134 E5
Holly Hedge Ter LEW SE13 145 F6
Holly Hl HAMP NW3 83 G2
WCHMH N21 35 F1
Holly Hill Rd BELV DA17 129 J5
Holly Lodge Gdns HGT N6 66 A6
Hollymead CAR SM5 209 K1
Holly Ms WBPTN SW10 120 B5
Holly Mt HAMP * NW3 83 G2
Hollymount Cl GNWCH SE10 145 F2
Holly Pk FNCH N3 46 D6
FSBYPK N4 66 E4
Holly Park Gdns FNCH N3 46 E6
Holly Park Rd FBAR/BDGN N11 48 A1
HNWL W7 116 A1
Holly Rd CHSWK * W4 118 A4
DART DA1 171 G3
HPTN TW12 173 H2
HSLW TW3 135 G5
ORP BR6 217 G5
TWK TW1 156 B3
Holly St HACK E8 86 B5
Hollytree Cl WIM/MER SW19 159 G3
Hollytree Pde SCUP * DA14 186 D1
Hollyview Cl HDN NW4 63 J3
Holly Vls HMSMTH * W6 118 E3
Holly Wk HAMP NW3 83 G2
Holly Wy MTCM CR4 195 J1
Hollywood Gdns YEAD UB4 95 F5
Hollywood Ms WBPTN * SW10 120 B6
Hollywood Rd CHING E4 51 G1
WBPTN SW10 120 B6
Hollywoods CROY/NA CR0 213 H6
Hollywood Wy ERITH DA8 150 E2
WFD IG8 52 B3
Holman Ct EW * KT17 207 J6
Holman Rd BTSEA SW11 140 C3
HOR/WEW KT19 206 E3
Holmbridge Gdns PEND EN3 25 F5
Holmbrook Dr HDN NW4 64 B2
Holmbury Cl BUSH WD23 28 E4
Holmbury Ct WIM/MER SW19 178 D3
Holmbury Gdns HYS/HAR UB3 113 J1
Holmbury Gv CROY/NA CR0 213 H5
Holmbury Mnr SCUP * DA14 168 B6
Holmbury Pk CHST BR7 184 D3
Holmbury Vw CLPT E5 68 D5
Holmbush Rd PUT/ROE SW15 159 H1
Holmcote Gdns HBRY N5 85 J3
Holmcroft Wy HAYES BR2 200 E2
Holmdale Gdns HDN NW4 64 B2
Holmdale Rd CHST BR7 185 H1
KIL/WHAMP NW6 82 E3
Holmdale Ter SEVS/STOTM N15 68 A3
Holmdene Av HNHL SE24 142 D6
MLHL NW7 45 J2
RYLN/HDSTN HA2 42 B6
Holmdene Cl BECK BR3 183 F5
Holmdene Ct BMLY BR1 184 D6
Holmead Rd FUL/PGN SW6 140 A1
Holmebury Cl BUSH * WD23 28 E4
Holme Lacey Rd
LEE/GVPK SE12 165 J1
Holme Rd EHAM E6 89 J6
Holmes Av MLHL NW7 46 C1
WALTH E17 51 H6
Holmesdale Av
MORT/ESHN SW14 137 J4
Holmesdale Cl SNWD SE25 181 G6
Holmesdale Rd BXLYHN DA7 148 E3
CROY/NA CR0 196 E2
HGT N6 66 B4
RCH/KEW TW9 137 G2
TEDD TW11 174 D3
Holmesley Rd BROCKY SE4 164 B1
Holmes Rd KTTN NW5 84 B4
TWK TW1 156 A4
WIM/MER SW19 178 B3
Holmes Ter STHWK SE1 17 J2
Holme Wy STAN HA7 43 F2
Holmewood Gdns
BRXS/STRHM SW2 162 A2
Holmewood Rd
BRXS/STRHM SW2 161 K2
SNWD SE25 181 F6
Holmfield Av HDN NW4 64 B2
Holmhurst Rd BELV DA17 129 J5
Holmleigh Av DART DA1 151 F5
Holmleigh Rd STNW/STAM N16 68 A5
Holm Oak Cl PUT/ROE SW15 159 J1
Holmsdale Gv BXLYHN DA7 150 B3
Holmshaw Cl SYD SE26 164 B6
Holmside Ri OXHEY WD19 27 F5
Holmside Rd BAL SW12 161 F1
Holmsley Cl NWMAL KT3 192 C3
Holmstall Av EDGE HA8 44 E5
Holmstall Pde EDGE * HA8 44 E5
Holmwood Cl BELMT SM2 208 B6
NTHLT UB5 78 B4
RYLN/HDSTN HA2 42 C6
Holmwood Gdns FNCH N3 46 E5
WLGTN SM6 210 B4
Holmwood Gv MLHL NW7 45 F1
Holmwood Rd BELMT SM2 208 A6
CHSGTN KT9 206 A3
GDMY/SEVK IG3 72 E6
Holne Cha EFNCH N2 65 G3
MRDN SM4 193 K3
Holness Rd SRTFD E15 88 D4
Holroyd Rd ESH/CLAY KT10 205 G6
PUT/ROE SW15 139 F5
Holstock Rd IL IG1 72 C6
Holsworth Cl RYLN/HDSTN HA2 60 C2
Holsworthy Sq FSBYW WC1X 5 H7
Holsworthy Wy CHSGTN KT9 205 J3
The Holt BARK/HLT IG6 54 C2
MRDN * SM4 193 K1
WLGTN SM6 210 C2
Holt Cl CHIG IG7 55 F1
MUSWH N10 66 A1
THMD SE28 109 H6
Holton St WCHPL E1 105 F3
Holt Rd ALP/SUD HA0 79 H1
CAN/RD E16 126 D1
Holt Wy CHIG IG7 55 F1
Holtwhite Av ENC/FH EN2 23 J3
Holtwhite's Hl ENC/FH EN2 23 H2
Holwell Pl PIN HA5 59 J1
Holwood Cl WOT/HER KT12 188 B6
Holwood Park Av ORP BR6 215 K2
Holwood Pl CLAP SW4 141 J5
Holybourne Av PUT/ROE SW15 158 D2
Holyhead Cl BOW E3 105 J2
Holyoake Ct BERM/RHTH SE16 124 B2
Holyoake Wk EA W5 97 J3
EFNCH N2 47 G6
Holyoak Rd LBTH SE11 18 A6
Holyport Rd FUL/PGN SW6 139 F1
Holyrood Av RYLN/HDSTN HA2 77 J2
Holyrood Gdns EDGE HA8 44 D5
Holyrood Rd BAR EN5 33 G1
Holyrood St STHWK SE1 19 G1
Holywell Cl BERM/RHTH * SE16 123 J5
BKHTH/KID SE3 125 K6
ORP BR6 217 G2
STWL/WRAY TW19 152 B3
Holywell La SDTCH EC2A 7 H6
Holywell Rw SDTCH EC2A 7 G7
Holywell Wy STWL/WRAY TW19 152 B3
Home Cl CAR SM5 194 E6
NTHLT UB5 95 K2
Home Ct FELT * TW13 153 K3
SURB * KT6 190 E2
Homecroft Rd SYD SE26 181 K1
WDGN N22 49 H4
Home Farm Cl ESH/CLAY KT10 204 B4
THDIT KT7 190 A4
Home Farm Gdns
WOT/HER KT12 188 B6
Homefarm Rd HNWL W7 96 E5
The Homefield MRDN * SM4 193 K1
Homefield Av GNTH/NBYPK IG2 72 E2
Homefield Cl STMC/STPC BR5 202 C1
WLSDN NW10 80 E4
YEAD UB4 95 H3
Homefield Gdns EFNCH N2 47 H6
WIM/MER SW19 178 B5
Homefield Ms BECK * BR3 182 D4
Homefield Pk SUT SM1 209 F4
Homefield Ri ORP BR6 202 B5
Homefield Rd ALP/SUD HA0 79 G2
BMLY BR1 184 B4
CHSWK W4 118 C4
EDGE HA8 45 F2
WIM/MER SW19 177 H2
WOT/HER KT12 188 E4
Homefield St IS * N1 7 G3
Home Gdns DAGE RM10 92 E1
DART DA1 171 H1
Homeland Dr BELMT SM2 209 F6
Homelands Dr NRWD SE19 181 F3
Home Lea ORP BR6 217 F3
Homeleigh Rd PECK SE15 144 A6
Home Md STAN HA7 43 J4
Homemead Rd CROY/NA CR0 195 H3
HAYES BR2 200 E2
Home Park Ct KUT * KT1 190 E1
Home Park Rd WIM/MER SW19 159 J6
Home Park Wk SURB KT6 190 E1
Homer Cl BXLYHN DA7 149 K2
Homer Dr POP/IOD E14 124 D4
Home Rd BTSEA SW11 140 D3
Homer Rd CROY/NA CR0 198 A3
HOM E9 87 G4
Homer Rw CAMTN NW1 8 D2
Homersham Rd KUT KT1 175 H5
Homer St CAMTN NW1 8 D2
Homerton Gv HOM E9 87 F3
Homerton High St HOM E9 87 F3
Homerton Rd HOM E9 87 H3
Homerton Rw HOM E9 86 E3
Homerton Ter HOM E9 86 E4
Homesdale Cl WAN E11 70 E2
Homesdale Rd HAYES BR2 200 B1
ORP BR6 201 K4
Homesfield GLDGN NW11 64 E2
Homestall Rd EDUL SE22 143 K6
The Homestead DART DA1 171 F1
Homestead Gdns
ESH/CLAY KT10 204 E3
Homestead Paddock
STHGT/OAK N14 22 B6
Homestead Pk CRICK NW2 81 H1
Homestead Rd BCTR RM8 74 B6
FUL/PGN SW6 139 J1
ORP BR6 217 H5
Homewillow Cl WCHMH N21 35 H1
Homewood Cl HPTN TW12 172 E2
Homewood Crs CHST BR7 185 K2
Homewood Gdns SNWD * SE25 197 F2
Honduras St FSBYE EC1V 6 C6
Honeybourne Rd
KIL/WHAMP NW6 83 F3
Honeybourne Wy
STMC/STPC BR5 201 H5
Honeybrook Rd BAL SW12 161 H2
Honey Cl DAGE RM10 92 E4
Honeyden Rd SCUP DA14 187 F2
Honeyman Cl CRICK NW2 82 B5
Honeypot Cl KTN/HRWW/W HA3 62 B1
Honeypot La CDALE/KGS NW9 62 B1
STAN HA7 43 K4
Honeysett Rd TOTM N17 50 B5
Honeysuckle Cl STHL UB1 95 J6
Honeysuckle Gdns
CROY/NA CR0 198 A4
Honeywell Rd BTSEA SW11 160 D1
Honeywood Rd ISLW * TW7 136 B5
WLSDN NW10 99 H1
Honeywood Wk CAR SM5 209 K2
Honister Cl STAN HA7 43 H4
Honister Gdns STAN HA7 43 H3
Honister Pl STAN HA7 43 H4
Honiton Gdns PECK * SE15 143 K3
Honiton Rd KIL/WHAMP NW6 100 D1
ROMW/RG RM7 75 F3
WELL DA16 148 A3
Honley Rd CAT SE6 164 E2
Honnor Gdns ISLW TW7 135 J3
Honor Oak Pk FSTH SE23 163 K2
Honor Oak Ri FSTH SE23 163 K1
Honor Oak Rd FSTH SE23 163 K3
Hood Av MORT/ESHN SW14 137 K6
STHGT/OAK N14 34 B1
STMC/STPC BR5 202 C2
Hood Cl CROY/NA CR0 196 C5
Hoodcote Gdns WCHMH N21 35 H2
Hood Rd RAIN RM13 93 G6
RYNPK SW20 176 C3
Hood Wk ROMW/RG RM7 56 D4
Hooker's Rd WALTH E17 51 F6
The Hook BAR EN5 33 H1
Hook Farm Rd HAYES BR2 200 C2
Hook Green La RDART DA2 170 C5
Hooking Gn RYLN/HDSTN HA2 60 B2
Hook La WELL DA16 148 A6
Hook Ri North SURB KT6 206 C1
Hook Ri South CHSGTN KT9 206 B1
Hook Rd CHSGTN KT9 205 K3
HOR/WEW KT19 206 E5
SURB KT6 191 F6
Hooks Hall Dr DAGE RM10 92 E1
Hookstone Wy WFD IG8 53 H3
Hook U/P (Kingston By-Pass)
SURB KT6 205 K1
Hook Wk EDGE HA8 44 E2
Hooper Rd CAN/RD E16 106 E5
Hooper's Ms ACT W3 117 K1
Hooper St WCHPL E1 104 C6
Hoop La GLDGN NW11 64 D4
Hop Ct ALP/SUD * HA0 79 J4
Hope Cl BTFD TW8 117 F5
CHDH RM6 73 K1
IS N1 85 J4
LEE/GVPK SE12 166 A5
SUT SM1 209 G3
Hopedale Rd CHARL SE7 126 A6
Hopefield Av KIL/WHAMP NW6 100 C1
Hope Pk BMLY BR1 183 J3
Hopes Cl HEST TW5 115 F6
Hope St BTSEA SW11 140 C4
Hopetown St WCHPL * E1 13 K2
Hopewell St CMBW SE5 142 E1
Hopewell Yd CMBW SE5 142 E1
Hop Gdns CHCR WC2N 10 E6
Hopgood St SHB W12 119 F1
Hopkins Cl MUSWH N10 48 A3
Hopkinsons Pl CAMTN * NW1 83 K6
Hopkins St SOHO/CST W1F 10 B4
Hoppers Rd WCHMH N21 35 G4
Hoppett Rd CHING E4 38 C5
Hopping La IS * N1 85 H4
Hoppingwood Av NWMAL KT3 176 B6
Hoppner Rd YEAD UB4 94 B1
Hopton Gdns NWMAL KT3 192 D3
Hopton Pde
STRHM/NOR * SW16 179 K1
Hopton Rd STRHM/NOR SW16 179 K1
WOOL/PLUM SE18 127 G3
Hoptons Gdns STHWK * SE1 12 B7
Hopton St STHWK SE1 12 B7
Hopwood Cl TOOT SW17 160 B5
Hopwood Rd WALW SE17 122 E6
Hopwood Wk HACK * E8 86 C5
Horace Av ROMW/RG RM7 75 F5
Horace Rd BARK/HLT IG6 54 C6
FSTGT E7 89 F2
KUT KT1 175 G6
Horatio Pl POP/IOD E14 125 F2
Horatio St BETH E2 7 K3
Horatius Wy CROY/NA CR0 211 F4
Horbury Crs NTGHL W11 100 E6
Horbury Ms NTGHL W11 100 D6
Horder Rd FUL/PGN SW6 139 H2
Hordle Prom East PECK SE15 143 G1
Hordle Prom North
PECK * SE15 143 G1
Hordle Prom West PECK SE15 143 F1
Horley Cl BXLYHS DA6 149 H6
Horley Rd ELTH/MOT SE9 166 D6
Hormead Rd MV/WKIL W9 100 D3
Hornbeam Cl IL IG1 90 D3
LBTH SE11 17 J6
MLHL NW7 31 H5
NTHLT UB5 77 K3
Hornbeam Crs BTFD TW8 136 C1
Hornbeam Gv CHING E4 38 C5
Hornbeam Rd BKHH IG9 39 H5
YEAD UB4 95 G4
Hornbeams Ri FBAR/BDGN N11 48 A2
Hornbeam Wy HAYES BR2 201 F3
Hornbuckle Cl RYLN/HDSTN HA2 60 D6
Hornby Cl HAMP NW3 83 H5
Horncastle Cl LEE/GVPK SE12 165 K2
Horncastle Rd LEE/GVPK SE12 165 K2
Hornchurch Cl KUTN/CMB KT2 174 E1
Hornchurch Rd EMPK RM11 75 K5
Horndean Cl PUT/ROE SW15 158 D3
Horndon Cl CRW RM5 56 E4
Horndon Gn CRW RM5 56 E4
Horndon Rd CRW RM5 56 E4
Horne House WOOL/PLUM SE18 146 D2
Horner La MTCM CR4 178 C5
Horne Wy PUT/ROE SW15 139 F3
Hornfair Rd CHARL SE7 126 C6
Hornford Wy ROMW/RG RM7 75 G4
Horniman Dr FSTH SE23 163 J3
Horniman Gdns FSTH * SE23 163 J3
Horning Cl ELTH/MOT SE9 166 D6
Horn La ACT W3 117 K1
GNWCH SE10 125 K4
WFD IG8 52 E2
Horn Link Wy GNWCH SE10 125 K4
Horn Park Cl LEE/GVPK SE12 146 A6
Horn Park La LEE/GVPK SE12 146 A6
Horns End Pl PIN HA5 59 G1
Hornsey Chambers CLPT * E5 68 D6
Hornsey La ARCH N19 66 C4
Hornsey Lane Est ARCH * N19 66 D4
Hornsey Lane Gdns HGT N6 66 C4
Hornsey Park Rd
CEND/HSY/T N8 49 F6
Hornsey Ri ARCH N19 66 D4
Hornsey Rise Gdns ARCH N19 66 D4
Hornsey Rd ARCH N19 66 E5
HOLWY N7 85 F1
Hornsey St HOLWY N7 85 F3
Hornshay St PECK SE15 123 K6
Horns Rd BARK/HLT IG6 72 C2
Hornton Pl KENS W8 119 K2
Hornton St KENS W8 119 K2
Horsa Rd ERITH DA8 149 K1
LEE/GVPK SE12 166 B2
Horsebridges Cl DAGW RM9 92 A6
Horsecroft Cl ORP BR6 202 C5
Horsecroft Rd EDGE HA8 45 F3
Horse Fair KUT KT1 174 E5
Horseferry Pl GNWCH SE10 125 F6
Horseferry Rd POP/IOD E14 105 G6
WEST SW1P 16 C5
Horse Guards Av WHALL SW1A 16 E1
Horse Guards Rd WHALL SW1A 16 D1
Horse Leaze EHAM E6 108 B5
Horsell Rd HBRY N5 85 G3
STMC/STPC BR5 186 B4
Horselydown La STHWK SE1 19 J2
Horsenden Av GFD/PVL UB6 78 E3
Horsenden Crs GFD/PVL UB6 79 F3
Horsenden La North
GFD/PVL UB6 78 E4
Horsenden La South
GFD/PVL UB6 79 G6
Horseshoe Cl CRICK NW2 63 K6
POP/IOD E14 125 F5
Horse Shoe Crs NTHLT UB5 96 A1
Horseshoe La ENC/FH EN2 23 J4
TRDG/WHET N20 32 B3
Horse Yd IS N1 85 H6
Horsfeld Gdns ELTH/MOT SE9 146 D6
Horsfeld Rd ELTH/MOT SE9 146 C6
Horsford Rd BRXS/STRHM SW2 142 A6
Horsham Av NFNCH/WDSP N12 47 J1
Horsham Rd BXLYHS DA6 169 G1
EBED/NFELT TW14 153 F1
Horsley Dr CROY/NA CR0 214 A5
KUTN/CMB KT2 174 E1
Horsley Rd BMLY BR1 184 A4
CHING E4 38 A4
Horsley St WALW SE17 122 E6
Horsmans Pl DART * DA1 171 H2
Horsman St CMBW SE5 122 D6
Horsmonden Cl ORP BR6 201 K4
Horsmonden Rd BROCKY SE4 144 C6
Hortensia Rd WBPTN SW10 120 B6
Horticultural Pl CHSWK W4 118 A5
Horton Av CRICK NW2 82 C2
Horton Bridge Rd
WDR/YW UB7 112 C1
Horton Cl WDR/YW UB7 112 C1
Horton Pde WDR/YW * UB7 112 B1
Horton Rd HACK E8 86 D4
WDR/YW UB7 112 B1
Horton St LEW SE13 144 E4
Horton Wy CROY/NA CR0 198 A2
Hortus Rd NWDGN UB2 114 E2
Hosack Rd BAL SW12 160 E4
Hoser Av LEE/GVPK SE12 165 K4
Hosier La STBT EC1A 12 A2
Hoskin's Cl CAN/RD E16 107 G5
HYS/HAR UB3 113 J5
Hoskins St GNWCH SE10 125 G5
Hospital Bridge Rd WHTN TW2 155 G4
Hospital Rd HSLW TW3 135 F4
Hospital Wy LEW SE13 165 G1
Hotham Cl E/WMO/HCT KT8 173 F6
Hotham Rd PUT/ROE SW15 139 F4
WIM/MER SW19 178 B3
Hotham St SRTFD E15 88 C6
Hothfield Pl BERM/RHTH SE16 123 K3
Hotspur Rd NTHLT UB5 96 A1
Houblon Rd RCHPK/HAM TW10 137 F6
Houghton Cl HACK * E8 86 B4
HPTN TW12 172 D2
Houghton Rd SEVS/STOTM N15 68 B1
Houghton St HOL/ALD * WC2B 11 H4
Houlder Crs CROY/NA CR0 211 H4
Houndsden Rd WCHMH N21 35 F1
Houndsditch HDTCH EC3A 13 H3
Houndsfield Rd ED N9 36 D2
Hounslow Av HSLW TW3 135 G6
Hounslow Gdns HSLW TW3 135 G6
Hounslow Rd
EBED/NFELT TW14 154 A2
FELT TW13 154 C5
HSLW TW3 155 G1
Houseman Wy CMBW SE5 142 E1
Houston Rd FSTH SE23 164 B4
SURB KT6 190 C3
Hove Av WALTH E17 69 H2
Hoveden Rd CRICK NW2 82 B3
Hove Gdns SUT SM1 194 A5
Hoveton Rd THMD SE28 109 J5
Hoveton Wy WFD IG8 54 B4
Howard Av BXLY DA5 168 D3
Howard Cl ACT W3 98 D5
BUSH WD23 28 E2
CRICK * NW2 82 C2
FBAR/BDGN N11 34 A4
HPTN TW12 173 H3
LOU IG10 39 J1
Howard Rd BARK IG11 90 D6
BMLY BR1 183 K3
BRYLDS KT5 191 G3
CRICK NW2 82 B2
DART DA1 171 K1
EHAM E6 107 K1
IL IG1 90 B2
ISLW TW7 136 A4
NWMAL KT3 176 B6
PGE/AN SE20 181 K4
SEVS/STOTM N15 68 A3
SNWD SE25 197 H2
STHL UB1 96 B5
STNW/STAM N16 85 K2
WALTH E17 51 J6
WAN E11 88 C1
Howards Cl PIN * HA5 41 F5
Howards Crest Cl BECK BR3 183 F5
Howard's La PUT/ROE SW15 139 F5
Howard's Rd PLSTW E13 106 E2
Howard St THDIT KT7 190 C4
Howard Wk EFNCH N2 65 G1
Howard Wy BAR EN5 20 B6
Howarth Rd ABYW SE2 128 B5
Howberry Cl EDGE HA8 43 K2
Howberry Rd EDGE HA8 43 K3
THHTH CR7 180 E4
Howbury La ERITH DA8 150 D3
Howbury Rd PECK SE15 143 K4
Howcroft Crs FNCH N3 46 E3
Howcroft La GFD/PVL UB6 96 D2
Howden Cl THMD SE28 109 J6
Howden Rd SNWD SE25 181 G5
Howden St PECK SE15 143 H4
Howe Cl ROMW/RG RM7 56 C4
Howell Cl CHDH RM6 73 K2
Howell Wk WALW SE17 18 B7
Howfield Pl TOTM * N17 50 B6
Howgate Rd MORT/ESHN SW14 138 A4
Howick Pl WEST SW1P 16 B5
Howie St BTSEA SW11 140 D1
Howitt Cl HAMP NW3 83 J4
Howitt Rd HAMP NW3 83 J4
Howitts Cl ESH/CLAY KT10 204 A4
Howland Ct PIN * HA5 42 A2
Howland Ms East FITZ W1T 10 B1
Howland St FITZ W1T 10 B1
Howland Wy BERM/RHTH SE16 124 B2

Howletts La *RSLP* HA4 58 A3
Howletts Rd *HNHL* SE24 162 D1
Howley Pl *BAY/PAD* W2 101 G4
Howley Rd *CROY/NA* CR0 211 H1
Howsman Rd *BARN* SW13 118 D6
Howson Rd *BROCKY* SE4 144 B5
Howson Ter
RCHPK/HAM * TW10 157 F1
How's St *BETH* E2 7 J2
Howton Pl *BUSH* WD23 28 D3
Hoxton Market *IS* N1 7 G5
Hoxton Sq *IS* N1 7 G5
Hoxton St *IS* N1 7 G1
Hoylake Gdns *MTCM* CR4 179 H6
OXHEY WD19 27 H6
RSLP HA4 59 F5
Hoylake Rd *ACT* W3 99 G5
Hoyland Cl *PECK* * SE15 143 J1
Hoyle Rd *TOOT* SW17 178 D1
Hoy St *CAN/RD* E16 106 D5
Hubbard Dr *CHSGTN* KT9 205 J4
Hubbard Rd *WNWD* SE27 162 D6
Hubbard St *SRTFD* E15 88 C6
Hubert Cl *WIM/MER* * SW19 178 B4
Hubert Gv *BRXN/ST* SW9 141 K4
Hubert Rd *EHAM* E6 107 H2
RAIN RM13 111 H2
Huddart St *BOW* E3 105 H4
Huddleston Cl *BETH* * E2 104 E1
Huddlestone Rd *CRICK* NW2 81 K4
FSTGT E7 88 D2
Huddleston Rd *ARCH* N19 84 C1
Hudson Cl *SHB* * W12 99 K6
Hudson Pl *WOOL/PLUM* SE18 127 H5
Hudson Rd *BXLYHN* DA7 149 G3
HYS/HAR UB3 113 G6
Huggin Hl *BLKFR* EC4V 12 D5
Huggins Pl *BRXS/STRHM* SW2 162 A3
Hughan Rd *SRTFD* E15 88 B3
Hugh Dalton Av
FUL/PGN * SW6 119 J6
Hughenden Av
KTN/HRWW/W HA3 61 H2
Hughenden Gdns *NTHLT* UB5 95 G2
Hughenden Rd *WPK* KT4 192 D4
Hughes Rd *HYS/HAR* UB3 95 F6
Hughes Ter *CAN/RD* * E16 106 D4
Hughes Wk *CROY/NA* CR0 196 D4
Hugh Gaitskell Cl
FUL/PGN * SW6 119 J6
Hugh Ms *PIM* SW1V 15 K7
Hugh Pl *WEST* SW1P 16 C6
Hugh St *PIM* SW1V 15 K7
Hugo Gdns *RAIN* RM13 93 H4
Hugon Rd *FUL/PGN* SW6 140 A4
Hugo Rd *ARCH* N19 84 C2
Huguenot Pl *WAND/EARL* SW18 140 B6
WCHPL E1 13 K1
Hullbridge Ms *IS* N1 85 K6
Hull Cl *BERM/RHTH* * SE16 124 A1
Hull St *FSBYE* EC1V 6 C5
Hulme Pl *STHWK* SE1 18 D3
Hulse Av *BARK* IG11 90 D4
ROMW/RG RM7 56 D4
Hulsewood Cl *RDART* DA2 170 E5
Humber Dr *NKENS* W10 100 B3
Humber Rd *BKHTH/KID* SE3 125 K6
CRICK NW2 63 K6
DART DA1 151 G6
Humberstone Rd *PLSTW* E13 107 G2
Humbolt Rd *HMSMTH* W6 119 H6
Humes Av *HNWL* W7 116 A3
Hume Wy *RSLP* HA4 58 E3
Humphrey Cl *CLAY* * IG5 53 K4
Humphrey St *STHWK* SE1 123 G5
Humphries Cl *DAGW* RM9 92 B2
Hundred Acre *CDALE/KGS* NW9 45 H5
Hungerdown *CHING* E4 38 A3
Hungerford Br *STHWK* SE1 11 G7
Hungerford Rd *HOLWY* N7 84 D4
Hungerford St *WCHPL* * E1 104 D5
Hunsdon Cl *DAGW* RM9 92 A4
Hunsdon Rd *NWCR* SE14 144 A1
Hunslett St *BETH* * E2 104 E1
Hunston Rd *MRDN* SM4 194 A5
Hunt Cl *BKHTH/KID* * SE3 145 K3
Hunter Cl *BAL* SW12 161 F3
STHWK SE1 19 F5
Hunter Ct *CMBW* * SE5 142 E5
Huntercrombe Gdns
OXHEY WD19 41 G1
Hunter Rd *RYNPK* SW20 177 F4
THHTH CR7 180 E6
Hunters Cl *BXLY* DA5 170 B5
Hunters Ct *RCH/KEW* TW9 136 E6
Hunter's Gv *CRW* RM5 56 D1
HYS/HAR UB3 113 K1
KTN/HRWW/W HA3 61 J1
ORP BR6 216 C2
Hunters Hall Rd *DAGE* RM10 92 C2
Hunters Hl *RSLP* HA4 77 G1
Hunters Meadow *NRWD* SE19 163 F6
Hunters Rd *CHSGTN* KT9 206 A1
IL IG1 90 B3
Hunters Sq *DAGE* RM10 92 C2
Hunter St *BMSBY* WC1N 5 F6
Hunters Wy *CROY/NA* CR0 212 A2
ENC/FH EN2 23 G2
Hunting Cl *ESH/CLAY* KT10 204 A2
Huntingdon Cl *MTCM* CR4 195 K1
Huntingdon Gdns *CHSWK* * W4 137 K1
WPK KT4 208 A1
Huntingdon Rd *ED* N9 36 E3
EFNCH N2 47 J6
Huntingdon St *CAN/RD* E16 106 D5
IS N1 85 F5
Huntingfield *CROY/NA* CR0 213 H5
Huntingfield Rd *PUT/ROE* SW15 138 D5
Hunting Gate Cl *ENC/FH* EN2 23 G4
Hunting Gate Dr *CHSGTN* KT9 206 A5
Hunting Gate Ms *WHTN* * TW2 155 K3
Huntings Rd *DAGE* RM10 92 C4
Huntland Cl *RAIN* RM13 111 K4
Huntley St *GWRST* WC1E 4 B7
Huntley Wy *RYNPK* * SW20 176 D5
Huntly Dr *FNCH* N3 46 E2
Huntly Rd *SNWD* SE25 197 F1
Hunton St *WCHPL* E1 104 C4
Hunt Rd *NWDGN* UB2 115 F3
Hunt's La *SRTFD* E15 106 A1
Huntsman Cl *FELT* TW13 154 A6
Huntsman Rd *BARK/HLT* IG6 55 H2
Huntsman St *WALW* SE17 19 G7
Hunts Md *PEND* EN3 25 F4
Hunts Mede Cl *CHST* BR7 184 E3
Huntsmoor Rd *HOR/WEW* KT19 207 F3
Huntspill St *TOOT* SW17 160 B5
Hunts Slip Rd *DUL* SE21 163 F5
Huntsworth Ms *CAMTN* NW1 2 E6
Hurdwick Pl *CAMTN* * NW1 4 A2
Hurley Cl *WOT/HER* KT12 188 A6
Hurley Rd *GFD/PVL* UB6 96 B4
Hurlfield *RDART* DA2 171 F5
Hurlingham Gdns
FUL/PGN SW6 139 J4
Hurlingham Pk *FUL/PGN* * SW6 139 J4
Hurlingham Rd *BXLYHN* DA7 149 G1
FUL/PGN SW6 139 J3
Hurlingham Sq *FUL/PGN* * SW6 139 K4
Hurlock St *HBRY* N5 85 H1
Hurlstone Rd *SNWD* SE25 196 E2
Hurn Court Rd *HEST* TW5 134 C3
Huron Cl *ORP* BR6 217 F4
Huron Rd *TOOT* SW17 161 F4
Hurren Cl *BKHTH/KID* SE3 145 H4
Hurricane Rd *WLGTN* SM6 211 F5
Hurry Cl *SRTFD* E15 88 C5
Hursley Rd *CHIG* IG7 55 F1
Hurst Av *CHING* E4 37 J5
HGT N6 66 C3
Hurstbourne Gdns *BARK* IG11 90 D4
Hurstbourne Rd *FSTH* SE23 164 B3
Hurst Cl *CHING* E4 37 J5
CHSGTN KT9 206 C3
GLDGN NW11 65 F3
HAYES BR2 199 J5
NTHLT UB5 77 K4
Hurstcourt Rd *SUT* SM1 194 A5
Hurstdene Av *HAYES* BR2 199 J5
Hurstdene Gdns
SEVS/STOTM N15 68 A4
Hurstfield *HAYES* BR2 199 K2
Hurstfield Crs *YEAD* UB4 94 C4
Hurstfield Rd *E/WMO/HCT* KT8 173 F6
Hurst La *ABYW* SE2 128 E5
E/WMO/HCT KT8 189 H1
Hurstleigh Gdns *CLAY* IG5 53 K4
Hurst Pl *DART* * DA1 171 F1
Hurst Ri *BAR* EN5 20 E4
Hurst Rd *BFN/LL* DA15 168 C4
BKHH IG9 39 H3
CROY/NA CR0 211 K3
E/WMO/HCT KT8 173 H6
ERITH DA8 149 K1
WALTH E17 51 K6
WCHMH N21 35 G3
WOT/HER KT12 188 C1
Hurst Springs *BXLY* DA5 169 F3
Hurst St *HNHL* SE24 162 C1
Hurst View Rd *SAND/SEL* CR2 212 A5
Hurst Wy *SAND/SEL* CR2 212 A4
Hurstway Wk *NKENS* * W10 100 B6
Hurstwood Av *BXLY* DA5 169 F3
ERITH DA8 150 B2
SWFD E18 71 F1
Hurstwood Dr *BMLY* BR1 184 E6
Hurstwood Rd *GLDGN* NW11 64 C1
Hurtwood Rd *WOT/HER* KT12 188 E4
Huson Cl *HAMP* * NW3 83 J5
Hussain Cl *HRW* HA1 79 F2
Hussars Cl *HSLWW* TW4 134 D4
Husseywell Crs *HAYES* BR2 199 K5
Hutching's St *POP/IOD* E14 124 D2
Hutchings Wk *GLDGN* NW11 65 F1
Hutchins Cl *SRTFD* E15 88 A5
Hutchinson Ter *WBLY* HA9 79 K1
Hutchins Rd *THMD* SE28 109 G6
Hutton Cl *GFD/PVL* UB6 78 D3
WFD IG8 53 F2
Hutton Gv *NFNCH/WDSP* N12 47 F1
Hutton La *KTN/HRWW/W* HA3 42 C3
Hutton Rw *EDGE* HA8 44 E3
Hutton St *EMB* EC4Y 11 K4
Hutton Wk *KTN/HRWW/W* HA3 42 C3
Huxbear St *BROCKY* SE4 144 C6
Huxley *UED* * N18 49 K1
Huxley Cl *NTHLT* UB5 95 J1
Huxley Dr *CHDH* RM6 73 H4
Huxley Gdns *WLSDN* NW10 98 B2
Huxley Pde *UED* * N18 49 K1
Huxley Pl *PLMGR* N13 35 H6
Huxley Rd *LEY* E10 70 A6
UED N18 35 K6
WELL DA16 148 A4
Huxley Sayze *UED* * N18 49 K1
Huxley St *NKENS* W10 100 C2
Hyacinth Cl *HPTN* TW12 173 F2
Hyacinth Rd *PUT/ROE* SW15 158 D3
The Hyde *CDALE/KGS* NW9 45 F6
Hyde Cl *BAR* EN5 20 D4
PLSTW E13 106 E1
Hyde Crs *CDALE/KGS* NW9 63 G2
Hyde Dr *STMC/STPC* BR5 202 C1
Hyde Estate Rd
CDALE/KGS NW9 63 H2
Hyde Farm Ms *BAL* SW12 161 J3
Hydefield Cl *ED* N9 35 K3
Hydefield Ct *ED* N9 36 A4
Hyde La *BTSEA* SW11 140 D2
Hyde Park Av *WCHMH* N21 35 J4
Hyde Park Cnr *MYFR/PICC* W1J 15 H2
Hyde Park Crs *BAY/PAD* W2 8 C4
Hyde Park Gdns *BAY/PAD* W2 8 B5
WCHMH N21 35 J3
Hyde Park Gardens
Ms *BAY/PAD* W2 8 B5
Hyde Park Ga *SKENS* SW7 120 B2
Hyde Park Gate Ms
SKENS * SW7 120 B2
Hyde Park Pl *BAY/PAD* W2 8 D5
Hyde Park Sq *BAY/PAD* W2 8 C4
Hyde Park St *BAY/PAD* W2 8 C5
Hyderabad Wy *SRTFD* E15 88 C5
Hyde Rd *BXLYHN* DA7 149 G3
IS N1 7 F1
RCHPK/HAM TW10 137 G6
Hydeside Gdns *ED* N9 36 B4
Hyde's Pl *IS* N1 85 H5
Hyde St *DEPT* SE8 124 D6
Hydethorpe Av *ED* N9 36 B4
Hydethorpe Rd *BAL* SW12 161 H3
Hyde V *GNWCH* SE10 145 F1
Hyde Wk *MRDN* SM4 193 K4
Hyde Wy *ED* N9 36 B4
HYS/HAR UB3 113 J4
Hyland Cl *EMPK* RM11 75 K4
Hylands Rd *WALTH* E17 52 B5
Hyland Wy *EMPK* RM11 75 K4
Hylton St *WOOL/PLUM* SE18 128 A4
Hyndewood *FSTH* * SE23 164 A5
Hyndman St *PECK* SE15 123 J6
Hynton Rd *BCTR* RM8 73 J6
Hyperion Pl *HOR/WEW* KT19 207 F6
Hyson Rd *BERM/RHTH* SE16 123 J5
Hythe Av *BXLYHN* DA7 149 G1
Hythe Cl *STMC/STPC* BR5 202 D1
UED N18 36 C6
Hythe Rd *THHTH* CR7 180 E5
WLSDN NW10 99 H2
Hythe St *DART* DA1 151 H6
Hyver Hl *MLHL* NW7 31 F1

I

Ibbotson Av *CAN/RD* E16 106 D5
Ibbott St *WCHPL* E1 104 E3
Iberian Av *WLGTN* SM6 210 D2
Ibis La *CHSWK* W4 137 K2
Ibis Wy *YEAD* UB4 95 H5
Ibscott Cl *DAGE* RM10 92 E4
Ibsley Gdns *PUT/ROE* SW15 158 D3
Ibsley Wy *EBAR* EN4 21 J6
Iceland Rd *BOW* E3 87 J6
Ickburgh Est *CLPT* * E5 68 D6
Ickburgh Rd *CLPT* E5 86 D1
Ickenham Cl *RSLP* HA4 58 B6
Ickenham Rd *RSLP* HA4 58 B5
Ickleton Rd *ELTH/MOT* SE9 166 D6
Icknield Dr *GNTH/NBYPK* IG2 72 B2
Ickworth Park Rd *WALTH* E17 69 G1
Ida Rd *SEVS/STOTM* N15 67 K2
Ida St *POP/IOD* E14 106 A5
Iden Cl *HAYES* BR2 183 H6
Idlecombe Rd *TOOT* SW17 179 F2
Idmiston Rd *SRTFD* E15 88 D3
WNWD SE27 162 D5
WPK KT4 192 C4
Idmiston Sq *WPK* KT4 192 C4
Idol La *MON* EC3R 13 G6
Idonia St *DEPT* SE8 144 C1
Iffley Rd *HMSMTH* W6 118 E3
Ifield Rd *WBPTN* SW10 120 A6
Ightham Rd *ERITH* DA8 149 H1
Ilbert St *NKENS* W10 100 C2
Ilchester Pl *WKENS* W14 119 J3
Ilchester Rd *BCTR* RM8 91 H3
Ildersly Gv *DUL* SE21 162 E4
Ilderton Rd *BERM/RHTH* SE16 123 K6
Ilex Cl *SUN* TW16 172 B5
Ilex Rd *WLSDN* NW10 81 H4
Ilex Wy *STRHM/NOR* SW16 180 B1
Ilford Hl *IL* IG1 90 A1
Ilford La *IL* IG1 90 B2
Ilfracombe Gdns *CHDH* RM6 73 H4
Ilfracombe Rd *BMLY* BR1 165 J5
Iliffe St *WALW* SE17 122 C5
Iliffe Yd *WALW* SE17 122 C5
Ilkley Cl *NRWD* * SE19 180 E2
Ilkley Rd *CAN/RD* E16 107 G4
OXHEY WD19 41 H1
Illingworth Cl *MTCM* CR4 178 C6
Illingworth Wy *EN* EN1 24 A6
Ilmington Rd *KTN/HRWW/W* HA3 61 K3
Ilminster Gdns *BTSEA* SW11 140 D5
Imber Cl *STHGT/OAK* N14 34 C2
Imber Cross *THDIT* * KT7 190 A4
Imber Gv *ESH/CLAY* KT10 189 J4
Imber Park Rd *ESH/CLAY* KT10 189 J5
Imber St *IS* N1 6 E1
Imperial Av *STNW/STAM* * N16 86 A2
Imperial Cl *RYLN/HDSTN* HA2 60 A3
Imperial College Rd *SKENS* SW7 14 A5
Imperial Dr *RYLN/HDSTN* HA2 60 A5
Imperial Gdns *MTCM* CR4 179 G6
Imperial Pl *CHST* BR7 185 F4
Imperial Rd *EBED/NFELT* TW14 153 H2
FUL/PGN SW6 140 A2
WDGN N22 48 E3
Imperial Sq *FUL/PGN* SW6 140 A2
Imperial St *BOW* E3 106 A2
Imperial Wy *CHST* BR7 167 H5
CROY/NA CR0 211 G4
KTN/HRWW/W HA3 62 A3
Imre Cl *SHB* W12 118 E1
Inca Dr *ELTH/MOT* SE9 167 G2
Inchmery Rd *CAT* SE6 164 E4
Inchwood *CROY/NA* CR0 213 K2
Independent Pl *HACK* E8 86 B3
Independents Rd
BKHTH/KID SE3 145 J4
Inderwick Rd *CEND/HSY/T* N8 67 F3
Indescon Ct *POP/IOD* E14 124 E2
India St *TWRH* EC3N 13 J4
India Wy *SHB* W12 99 K6
Indigo Ms *POP/IOD* * E14 106 A6
STNW/STAM N16 85 K1
Indus Rd *CHARL* SE7 146 B1
Ingal Rd *PLSTW* E13 106 E3
Ingate Pl *VX/NE* SW8 141 G2
Ingatestone Rd *MNPK* E12 71 G5
SNWD SE25 197 J2
WFD IG8 53 F3
Ingelow St *VX/NE* SW8 141 G3
Ingersoll Rd *PEND* EN3 24 E1
SHB W12 118 E1
Ingestre Pl *SOHO/CST* W1F 10 B4
Ingestre Rd *FSTGT* E7 88 E2
KTTN NW5 84 B2
Ingham Cl *SAND/SEL* CR2 213 F6
Ingham Rd *KIL/WHAMP* NW6 82 E2
SAND/SEL CR2 212 E6
Inglebert St *CLKNW* EC1R 5 J4
Ingleborough St *BRXN/ST* SW9 142 B3
Ingleby Dr *HRW* HA1 78 D1
Ingleby Rd *DAGE* RM10 92 D4
HOLWY N7 84 E1
IL IG1 72 B5
Ingleby Wy *CHST* BR7 185 F1
WLGTN SM6 210 D6
Ingle Cl *PIN* HA5 41 K6
Ingledew Rd *WOOL/PLUM* SE18 127 J5
Inglefield Sq *WAP* * E1W 123 J1
Inglehurst Gdns *REDBR* IG4 71 K2
Inglemere Rd *FSTH* SE23 164 A5
TOOT SW17 178 E3
Ingleside Cl *BECK* BR3 182 D3
Ingleside Gv *BKHTH/KID* SE3 125 J6
Inglethorpe St *FUL/PGN* SW6 139 G2
Ingleton Av *WELL* DA16 148 B6
Ingleton Rd *CAR* SM5 209 J6
UED N18 50 C2
Ingleton St *BRXN/ST* SW9 142 B3
Ingleway *NFNCH/WDSP* N12 47 H2
Inglewood *CROY/NA* CR0 213 G6
Inglewood Cl *BARK/HLT* IG6 55 F2
POP/IOD E14 124 D4
Inglewood Copse *BMLY* BR1 184 D5
Inglewood Rd *BXLYHN* DA7 150 A5
KIL/WHAMP NW6 82 E3
Inglis Rd *CROY/NA* CR0 197 G5
EA W5 98 B6
Inglis St *CMBW* SE5 142 C2
Ingram Av *EFNCH* N2 65 G4
Ingram Cl *LBTH* SE11 17 H6
STAN HA7 43 J1
Ingram Rd *DART* DA1 171 H3
EFNCH N2 65 J1
THHTH CR7 180 D4
Ingram Wy *GFD/PVL* UB6 78 D6
Ingrave Rd *ROM* RM1 75 F1
Ingrave St *BTSEA* SW11 140 C4
Ingrebourne Rd *RAIN* RM13 111 K3
Ingress St *CHSWK* W4 118 B5
Inigo Jones Rd *CHARL* SE7 146 C1
Inkerman Rd *KTTN* NW5 84 B4
Inks Gn *CHING* E4 52 A1
Inkwell Cl *NFNCH/WDSP* N12 33 G5
Inman Rd *WAND/EARL* SW18 160 B2
WLSDN NW10 81 G6
Inmans Rw *WFD* IG8 38 E6
Inner Cir *CAMTN* NW1 3 G5
Inner Park Rd *WIM/MER* SW19 159 G4
Inner Ring East *HTHAIR* TW6 132 E4
Innes Cl *RYNPK* SW20 177 H5
Innes Gdns *PUT/ROE* SW15 158 E1
Innes Yd *CROY/NA* CR0 211 J1
Inniskilling Rd *PLSTW* E13 107 G1
Innovation Cl *ALP/SUD* HA0 80 A6
Inskip Cl *LEY* E10 69 K6
Inskip Rd *BCTR* RM8 73 K5
Institute Pl *HACK* E8 86 D3
Instone Rd *DART* DA1 171 G2
Integer Gdns *WAN* * E11 70 B4
International Av *HEST* TW5 114 B5
Inver Ct *BAY/PAD* * W2 101 F5
Inveresk Gdns *WPK* KT4 207 H1
Inverforth Cl *HAMP* NW3 65 G6
Inverforth Rd *FBAR/BDGN* N11 48 B1
Inverine Rd *CHARL* SE7 126 A5
Invermore Pl *WOOL/PLUM* SE18 127 H4
Inverness Av *EN* EN1 24 A2
Inverness Dr *BARK/HLT* IG6 54 E2
Inverness Gdns *KENS* W8 120 A1
Inverness Pl *BAY/PAD* * W2 101 F6
Inverness Rd *HSLW* TW3 134 E5
NWDGN UB2 114 D4
UED N18 50 D1
WPK KT4 193 G5
Inverness St *CAMTN* NW1 84 B6
Inverness Ter *BAY/PAD* W2 101 F5
WDGN * N22 49 H4
Inverton Rd *PECK* SE15 144 A5
Invicta Cl *CHST* BR7 185 F1
EBED/NFELT TW14 153 J3
Invicta Gv *NTHLT* UB5 95 K2
Invicta Pde *SCUP* * DA14 168 C6
Invicta Plaza *STHWK* SE1 12 A7
Invicta Rd *BKHTH/KID* SE3 145 K1
Inville Rd *WALW* SE17 122 E5
Inwood Av *HSLW* TW3 135 H4
Inwood Cl *CROY/NA* CR0 198 B6
Inwood Rd *HSLW* TW3 135 H5
Inworth St *BTSEA* SW11 140 D3
Inworth Wk *IS* * N1 85 J6
Iona Cl *CAT* SE6 164 D2
MRDN SM4 194 A4
Ion Sq *BETH* * E2 104 C1
Ipswich Rd *TOOT* SW17 179 F2
Ireland Cl *EHAM* E6 107 K4
Ireland Pl *WDGN* N22 48 E3
Irene Ms *HNWL* * W7 116 A1
Irene Rd *FUL/PGN* SW6 139 K2
ORP BR6 202 A4
Ireton Cl *MUSWH* N10 48 A3
Ireton St *BOW* E3 105 J3
Iris Av *BXLY* DA5 169 F1
Iris Cl *CROY/NA* CR0 198 A5
EHAM E6 107 J4
SURB * KT6 191 G4
Iris Crs *BXLYHN* DA7 129 G6
Iris Rd *HOR/WEW* KT19 206 D3
Iris Wy *CHING* E4 51 H2
Irkdale Av *EN* EN1 24 B2
Iron Bridge Cl *NWDGN* UB2 115 H1
WLSDN NW10 81 G3
Ironbridge Rd *WDR/YW* * UB7 112 D1
Iron Bridge Rd *WDR/YW* * UB7 112 E1
Iron Bridge Rd North
WDR/YW UB7 112 D1
Iron Bridge Rd South
WDR/YW UB7 112 D2
Iron Mill La *DART* DA1 150 C5
Iron Mill Pl *DART* DA1 150 C5
WAND/EARL * SW18 160 A1
Iron Mill Rd *WAND/EARL* SW18 160 A1
Ironmonger La *CITYW* EC2V 12 E4
Ironmonger Rw *FSBYE* EC1V 6 D5
Ironside Cl *BERM/RHTH* SE16 124 A2
Irons Wy *CRW* RM5 56 E3
Irvine Av *KTN/HRWW/W* HA3 43 G6
Irvine Cl *TRDG/WHET* N20 33 J4
Irvine Wy *ORP* BR6 202 A4
Irving Av *NTHLT* UB5 77 H6
Irving Gv *BRXN/ST* SW9 142 A3
Irving Ms *IS* N1 85 J4
Irving Rd *WKENS* W14 119 G3
Irving St *LSQ/SEVD* WC2H 10 D6
Irwell Est *BERM/RHTH* * SE16 123 K2
Irwin Av *WOOL/PLUM* SE18 147 K1
Irwin Gdns *WLSDN* NW10 81 K6
Isabella Cl *STHGT/OAK* N14 34 C2
Isabella Ct *RCHPK/HAM* * TW10 157 G1
Isabella Dr *ORP* BR6 216 C2
Isabella Rd *HOM* * E9 86 E3
Isabella St *STHWK* SE1 18 A1
Isabel St *BRXN/ST* SW9 142 A2
Isambard Ms *POP/IOD* E14 125 F3
Isambard Pl *WAP* E1W 123 K1
Isham Rd *STRHM/NOR* SW16 179 K5
Isis Cl *RSLP* HA4 58 A3
Isis St *WAND/EARL* SW18 160 B4
Island Farm Av
E/WMO/HCT KT8 188 E2
Island Farm Rd *E/WMO/HCT* KT8 188 E2
Island Rd *MTCM* CR4 178 E3
Island Rw *POP/IOD* E14 105 H5
Isla Rd *WOOL/PLUM* SE18 127 H6
Islay Gdns *HSLWW* TW4 134 C6
Islay Wk *IS* * N1 85 J4
Islay Whf *POP/IOD* * E14 106 A4
Isledon Rd *HOLWY* N7 85 G1
Islehurst Cl *CHST* BR7 185 F4
Islington Gn *IS* N1 6 A1
Islington High St *IS* N1 6 A2
Islington Park Ms *IS* N1 85 H5
Islington Park St *IS* N1 85 G5
Islip Gdns *EDGE* HA8 45 F2
NTHLT UB5 77 J5
Islip Manor Rd *NTHLT* UB5 77 J5
Islip St *KTTN* NW5 84 C3
Ismailia Rd *FSTGT* E7 89 F5
Isom Cl *PLSTW* E13 107 F2
Ivanhoe Dr *KTN/HRWW/W* HA3 43 H5
Ivanhoe Rd *CMBW* SE5 143 G4
HSLWW TW4 134 C4
Ivatt Pl *WKENS* W14 119 J5
Ivatt Wy *SEVS/STOTM* N15 49 H6
Iveagh Av *WLSDN* NW10 98 C1
Iveagh Cl *HOM* E9 87 F6
WLSDN NW10 98 C1
Ivedon Rd *WELL* DA16 148 D3
Ive Farm Cl *LEY* E10 69 J6
Ive Farm La *LEY* E10 69 J6
Iveley Rd *CLAP* SW4 141 H3
Ivere Dr *BAR* EN5 33 F1
Iverhurst Cl *BXLYHS* DA6 148 E6
Iverna Ct *KENS* W8 119 K3
Iverna Gdns *EBED/NFELT* TW14 133 G6
KENS W8 119 K3
Iverson Rd *KIL/WHAMP* NW6 82 D4
Ivers Wy *CROY/NA* CR0 213 K5
Ives Gdns *ROM* RM1 75 H1
Ives Rd *CAN/RD* E16 106 C4
Ives St *CHEL* SW3 14 D6
Ivimey St *BETH* * E2 104 C2
Ivinghoe Cl *EN* EN1 24 A3
Ivinghoe Rd *BCTR* RM8 91 H3
BUSH WD23 28 D2
Ivor Gv *ELTH/MOT* SE9 167 G3
Ivor Pl *CAMTN* NW1 2 E7
Ivor St *CAMTN* NW1 84 C5
Ivory Ct *FELT* TW13 153 K4
Ivorydown *BMLY* BR1 165 K6
Ivybridge Cl *TWK* TW1 156 B1
Ivychurch Cl *PGE/AN* SE20 181 J3
Ivy Church La *STHWK* * SE1 123 G5
Ivy Cl *DART* DA1 171 K1
PIN HA5 59 G4
RYLN/HDSTN HA2 77 K2
SUN TW16 172 B5
Ivy Ct *STHWK* * SE1 123 H5
Ivy Crs *CHSWK* W4 117 K4
Ivydale Rd *BROCKY* SE4 144 A4
CAR SM5 194 E6
Ivyday Gv *STRHM/NOR* SW16 162 A5
Ivydene *E/WMO/HCT* KT8 188 E2
Ivydene Cl *SUT* SM1 209 G2
Ivy Gdns *CEND/HSY/T* N8 66 E3
MTCM CR4 179 J6
Ivyhouse Rd *DAGW* RM9 91 K4
Ivy La *HSLWW* TW4 134 E5
Ivymount Rd *WNWD* SE27 162 B5
Ivy Rd *BROCKY* SE4 144 C5
CAN/RD E16 106 E5
CRICK NW2 82 A2
HSLW TW3 135 G5
STHGT/OAK N14 34 D2
SURB * KT6 191 H6
TOOT SW17 178 D1
WALTH E17 69 J3
Ivy St *IS* N1 7 G2
Ivy Wk *DAGW* RM9 92 A4
NTHWD * HA6 40 C4
Ixworth Pl *CHEL* SW3 14 C7
Izane Rd *BXLYHS* DA6 149 G5

J

Jacaranda Cl *NWMAL* KT3 176 B6
Jacaranda Gv *HACK* E8 86 B5
Jackass La *HAYES* BR2 215 F4
Jack Clow Rd *SRTFD* E15 106 C1
Jack Cornwell St *MNPK* E12 90 A2
Jackman Ms *WLSDN* NW10 81 G1
Jackman St *HACK* E8 86 D6
Jackson Cl *HOM* E9 87 F5
Jackson Rd *BARK* IG11 90 D6
EBAR EN4 33 J1
HAYES BR2 200 D6
HOLWY N7 85 F2
Jackson's La *HGT* N6 66 A4
Jackson's Pl *CROY/NA* CR0 196 E5
Jackson St *WOOL/PLUM* SE18 127 F6
Jackson's Wy *CROY/NA* CR0 213 J1
Jack Walker Ct *HBRY* N5 85 H2
Jacobs Cl *DAGE* RM10 92 D2
Jacob St *STHWK* SE1 19 K2
Jacob's Well Ms *MHST* W1U 9 H3
Jacqueline Cl *NTHLT* UB5 77 J6
Jacqueline Creft Ter *HGT* * N6 66 A3
Jacqueline Vls *WALTH* * E17 70 A2
Jade Cl *BCTR* RM8 73 J5
CAN/RD E16 107 H5
CRICK NW2 64 B4
Jade Ter *KIL/WHAMP* * NW6 83 G5
Jaffe Rd *IL* IG1 72 C5
Jaffray Rd *HAYES* BR2 200 C1
Jaggard Wy *BAL* SW12 160 E2
Jago Cl *WOOL/PLUM* SE18 127 H6
Jago Wk *CMBW* SE5 142 E1
Jamaica Rd *BERM/RHTH* SE16 123 J3
STHWK SE1 19 J3
THHTH CR7 196 C3
Jamaica St *WCHPL* E1 104 E4
James Av *BCTR* RM8 74 B5
CRICK NW2 82 A3
James Cl *GLDGN* * NW11 64 C3
GPK RM2 75 J2
PLSTW E13 106 E1
James Collins Cl *MV/WKIL* W9 100 D3
James Gdns *WDGN* N22 49 J3
James Joyes Wk *HNHL* * SE24 142 C5
James La *LEY* E10 70 A4
James Lee Sq *PEND* EN3 25 J1
Jameson St *KENS* W8 119 K1
James Pl *TOTM* N17 50 B3
James Rd *DART* DA1 170 D2
James St *BARK* IG11 90 C5
COVGDN WC2E 11 F5
EN EN1 24 B6
HSLW TW3 135 J4
MHST W1U 9 H4
Jamestown Rd *CAMTN* NW1 84 B6
Jamestown Wy *POP/IOD* E14 106 B6
James Watt Wy *ERITH* DA8 130 C6
James Yd *CHING* * E4 52 B2
Jamuna Cl *POP/IOD* * E14 105 G4
Jane St *WCHPL* E1 104 D5
Janet St *POP/IOD* E14 124 D3

Janeway Pl BERM/RHTH SE16 ......123 J2
Janeway St BERM/RHTH SE16 ......123 H2
Janson Cl SRTFD E15......88 C3
WLSDN NW10......81 F1
Janson Rd SRTFD E15......88 C3
Jansons Rd SEVS/STOTM N15......50 A6
Japan Crs FSBYPK N4......67 F5
Japan Rd CHDH RM6......73 K3
Jardine Rd WAP E1W......105 F6
Jarrett Cl BRXS/STRHM SW2......162 C3
Jarrow Cl MRDN SM4......194 A2
Jarrow Rd BERM/RHTH SE16......123 K4
CHDH RM6......73 J3
TOTM N17......68 D1
Jarrow Wy HOM E9......87 G2
Jarvis Cl BAR EN5......20 B6
Jarvis Rd EDUL SE22......143 F5
SAND/SEL CR2......211 K4
Jasmin Cl NTHWD HA6......40 D4
Jasmine Cl HAYES BR2......201 G6
IL IG1......90 B3
STHL UB1......95 J6
Jasmine Ct LEE/GVPK SE12......165 K1
Jasmine Gdns CROY/NA CR0......213 K1
RYLN/HDSTN HA2......60 A6
Jasmine Gv PGE/AN SE20......181 J4
Jasmine Rd HOR/WEW KT19......206 D4
ROMW/RG RM7......75 G6
Jasmine Ter WDR/YW UB7......112 D2
Jasmin Rd HOR/WEW KT19......206 D4
Jason Wk ELTH/MOT SE9......167 F6
Jasper Cl PEND EN3......24 E1
Jasper Rd CAN/RD E16......107 H5
NRWD SE19......181 G2
Javelin Wy NTHLT UB5......95 H2
Jaycroft ENC/FH EN2......23 G2
Jay Gdns CHST BR7......166 E6
Jay Ms SKENS SW7......120 B2
Jean Batten Cl CROY/NA CR0......211 F5
Jebb Av BRXS/STRHM SW2......161 K1
Jebb St BOW E3......105 J1
Jedburgh Rd PLSTW E13......107 G2
Jedburgh St BTSEA SW11......141 F5
Jeddo Ms SHB * W12......118 C2
Jeddo Rd SHB W12......118 C2
Jefferson Cl GNTH/NBYPK IG2......72 B2
WEA W13......116 C3
Jeffrey's Pl CAMTN NW1......84 C5
Jeffrey's Rd CLAP SW4......141 K3
PEND EN3......25 H5
Jeffrey's St CAMTN NW1......84 B5
Jeffs Cl HPTN * TW12......173 G2
Jeffs Rd SUT SM1......208 D2
Jeger Av BETH E2......7 J1
Jeken Rd ELTH/MOT SE9......146 B5
Jelf Rd BRXS/STRHM SW2......142 B6
Jellicoe Gdns STAN HA7......43 G2
Jellicoe Rd TOTM N17......49 K3
WATW WD18......26 E1
Jemmett Cl KUTN/CMB KT2......175 J4
Jem Paterson Ct HRW * HA1......78 E2
Jengar Cl SUT SM1......209 F2
Jenkins La BARK IG11......108 B1
Jenkins Rd PLSTW E13......107 F3
Jenner Av ACT W3......99 F4
Jenner Rd STNW/STAM N16......68 B6
Jennett Rd CROY/NA CR0......211 G1
Jennifer Rd BMLY BR1......165 J5
Jennings Cl SURB KT6......190 D4
Jennings Rd EDUL SE22......163 G1
Jennings Wy BAR EN5......20 A4
Jenningtree Rd ERITH DA8......150 E1
Jenningtree Wy BELV DA17......129 K2
Jenny Hammond Cl WAN E11......88 D1
Jenson Wy NRWD SE19......181 G3
Jenton Av BXLYHN DA7......149 F2
Jephson Rd FSTGT E7......89 G5
Jephson St CMBW SE5......142 E2
Jephtha Rd WAND/EARL SW18......159 K1
Jeppo's La MTCM CR4......194 E1
Jerdan Pl FUL/PGN SW6......139 K1
Jeremiah St POP/IOD E14......105 K5
Jeremy's Gn UED N18......36 D6
Jermyn St STJS SW1Y......10 A7
Jerningham Av CLAY IG5......54 B5
Jerningham Rd NWCR SE14......144 B3
Jerome Crs STJWD NW8......2 C6
Jerome St WCHPL E1......13 J1
Jerrard St LEW SE13......144 E4
Jerrold St IS * N1......7 H3
Jersey Av KTN/HRWW/W HA3......43 H5
Jersey Dr STMC/STPC BR5......201 J3
Jersey Rd CAN/RD E16......107 G4
HEST TW5......135 G2
HNWL W7......116 B2
IL IG1......90 B2
IS N1......85 J4
LEY E10......70 B5
RAIN RM13......93 J5
TOOT SW17......179 G3
Jersey St BETH E2......104 D2
Jersey Vls HNWL * W7......115 K2
Jerusalem Pas CLKNW EC1R......6 A7
Jerviston Gdns
STRHM/NOR SW16......180 B2
Jesmond Av WBLY HA9......80 B4
Jesmond Cl MTCM CR4......179 G6
Jesmond Dene HAMP * NW3......83 G4
Jesmond Rd CROY/NA CR0......197 G4
Jesmond Wy STAN HA7......44 A1
Jessam Av CLPT E5......68 D5
Jessamine Rd HNWL W7......115 K1
Jessamine Ter SWLY * BR8......187 K4
Jesse Rd LEY E10......70 A5
Jessett Cl ERITH DA8......130 A4
Jessica Rd WAND/EARL SW18......160 B1
Jessop Av NWDGN UB2......114 E4
Jessops Wy MTCM CR4......195 H3
Jessup Cl WOOL/PLUM SE18......127 H4
Jetstar Wy NTHLT UB5......95 J2
Jevington Wy LEE/GVPK SE12......166 A3
Jewel Rd WALTH E17......51 J6
Jewry St TWRH EC3N......13 J4
Jews Rw WAND/EARL SW18......140 A5
Jews Wk SYD SE26......163 J6
Jeymer Av CRICK NW2......81 K3
Jeymer Dr GFD/PVL UB6......78 C6
Jeypore Rd WAND/EARL SW18......160 B2
Jillian Cl HPTN TW12......173 F3
Jim Bradley Cl
WOOL/PLUM SE18......127 F4
Joan Crs ELTH/MOT SE9......166 C2
Joan Gdns BCTR RM8......74 A6
Joan Rd BCTR RM8......74 A6
Joan St STHWK SE1......18 A1
Jocelyn Rd RCH/KEW TW9......137 F4
Jocelyn St PECK SE15......143 H2
Jockey's Flds FSBYW WC1X......11 H1
Jodane Rd DEPT SE8......124 C4
Jodrell Cl ISLW TW7......136 B2
Jodrell Rd HOM E9......87 H6
Joel St NTHWD HA6......40 E5
Johanna St STHWK * SE1......17 J3
John Adam St CHCR WC2N......11 F7
John Aird Ct BAY/PAD W2......101 G4
John Archer Wy
WAND/EARL SW18......160 C1
John Ashby Cl
BRXS/STRHM SW2......161 K1
John Austin Cl
KUTN/CMB KT2......175 G4
John Bradshaw Rd
STHGT/OAK N14......34 D3
John Burns Dr BARK IG11......90 E6
John Campbell Rd
STNW/STAM N16......86 A3
John Carpenter St EMB EC4Y......12 A5
John Felton Rd
BERM/RHTH * SE16......123 H2
John Fisher St WCHPL E1......104 C6
John Gooch Dr ENC/FH EN2......23 H2
John Goodchild Wy KUT KT1......175 J6
John Harrison Wy GNWCH SE10......125 J3
John Islip St WEST SW1P......16 E7
John Lamb Ct
KTN/HRWW/W HA3......42 E4
John Maurice Cl WALW SE17......18 E6
John McKenna Wk
BERM/RHTH * SE16......123 H3
John Parker Sq BTSEA * SW11......140 C4
John Penn St LEW SE13......144 E2
John Perrin Pl
KTN/HRWW/W HA3......62 A4
John Prince's St CAVSQ/HST W1G......9 K3
John Rennie Wk WAP E1W......104 D6
John Roll Wy BERM/RHTH SE16......123 H3
John Ruskin St CMBW SE5......142 C1
John's Av HDN NW4......64 A1
John's Cl ASHF TW15......153 F6
John Silkin La DEPT SE8......124 A5
Johns La MRDN SM4......194 B2
John's Ms BMSBY WC1N......5 H7
John Smith Av FUL/PGN SW6......139 J1
Johnson Cl HACK E8......86 C6
Johnson Rd CROY/NA CR0......196 E4
HAYES BR2......200 C2
HEST TW5......134 B1
WLSDN NW10......81 F6
Johnson's Cl CAR SM5......209 K1
Johnsons Dr HPTN TW12......173 H4
Johnson's Pl PIM SW1V......121 H5
Johnson St NWDGN UB2......114 B3
WCHPL E1......104 E5
Johnsons Wy WLSDN NW10......98 D3
John Spencer Sq IS * N1......85 H4
Johns Pl WCHPL E1......104 D5
John's Ter CROY/NA CR0......197 F5
Johnston Cl BRXN/ST SW9......142 A2
Johnstone Rd EHAM E6......107 K2
Johnston Rd WFD IG8......52 E1
John St BMSBY WC1N......5 H7
EN EN1......24 B6
HSLW TW3......134 D3
SNWD SE25......197 H1
SRTFD E15......88 D6
John Trundle Highwalk
BARB * EC2Y......12 C1
John Williams Cl NWCR SE14......124 A6
John Wilson St
WOOL/PLUM SE18......127 F4
John Wooley Cl LEW * SE13......145 H5
Joiners Arms Yd CMBW * SE5......142 E2
Joiner St STHWK SE1......18 E1
Joint Rd EFNCH N2......47 J4
Jollys La YEAD UB4......95 H4
Jonathan St LBTH SE11......122 A5
Jones Rd PLSTW E13......107 F3
Jonson Cl MTCM CR4......195 G1
YEAD UB4......94 E4
Jordan Cl RYLN/HDSTN HA2......77 K1
Jordan Rd GFD/PVL UB6......79 H6
Jordans Cl DAGE RM10......92 D2
Jordans Ms WHTN TW2......155 K4
Joseph Av ACT W3......99 F5
Josephine Av
BRXS/STRHM SW2......142 A6
Joseph Locke Wy
ESH/CLAY KT10......189 F6
Joseph Powell Cl BAL SW12......161 H1
Joseph Ray Rd WAN E11......70 C6
Joseph St BOW E3......105 H4
Joseph Trotter Cl CLKNW EC1R......5 K5
Joshua Cl MUSWH N10......48 B3
SAND/SEL CR2......211 H5
Joshua St POP/IOD E14......106 A5
Joslings Cl SHB W12......99 J6
Joslyn Cl PEND EN3......25 J1
Joubert St BTSEA SW11......140 E3
Jowett St PECK SE15......143 G1
Joyce Av UED N18......50 B1
Joyce Green La DART DA1......151 G2
Joyden's Wood Rd BXLY DA5......170 A6
Joydon Dr CHDH RM6......73 H3
Joyners Cl DAGW RM9......92 B2
The Jubilee GNWCH * SE10......144 E1
Jubilee Av CHING E4......52 A2
ROMW/RG RM7......74 E2
WHTN TW2......155 H3
Jubilee Cl CDALE/KGS NW9......63 F3
KUT KT1......174 D4
PIN HA5......41 G5
ROMW/RG RM7......74 D2
Jubilee Crs ED N9......36 C3
Jubilee Dr RSLP HA4......77 H2
Jubilee Gdns STHL UB1......96 A4
STHWK * SE1......17 H1
Jubilee Market COVGDN * WC2E......11 F5
Jubilee Pl CHEL SW3......120 D5
Jubilee Rd CHEAM SM3......208 B5
GFD/PVL UB6......79 H6
Jubilee St WCHPL E1......104 E5
Jubilee Ter FUL/PGN * SW6......139 H3
Jubilee Vls ESH/CLAY * KT10......189 K5
Jubilee Wy CHSGTN KT9......206 D1
EBED/NFELT TW14......153 K3
SCUP DA14......168 B4
WIM/MER SW19......178 A4
Judd St STPAN WC1H......4 E5
Jude St CAN/RD E16......106 D5
Judge Heath La HYS/HAR UB3......94 A5
Judges' Wk HAMP NW3......83 G1
Judge Wk ESH/CLAY KT10......204 E4
Judith Av CRW RM5......56 D2
Juer St BTSEA SW11......140 D1
Juglans Rd ORP BR6......202 B5
Jules Thorn Av EN EN1......24 C4
Julia Gdns BARK IG11......109 K1
Juliana Cl EFNCH N2......47 G6
Julian Av ACT W3......98 D6
Julian Cl BAR EN5......21 F4
Julian Hl HRW HA1......60 E6
Julian Pl POP/IOD E14......124 E5
Julian Rd ORP BR6......217 G4
Julian Tayler Pth FSTH * SE23......163 J4
Julien Rd EA W5......116 D3
Juliette Rd PLSTW E13......106 E1
Juliette Wy PUR RM19......131 J2
Julius Nyerere Cl IS N1......5 H1
Junction Ap BTSEA SW11......140 D4
LEW SE13......145 F4
Junction Ms BAY/PAD W2......8 C3
Junction Pl BAY/PAD * W2......8 B3
Junction Rd ARCH N19......84 C1
DART DA1......171 G1
EA W5......116 D4
ED N9......36 C3
HRW HA1......60 E3
PLSTW E13......89 F6
ROM RM1......75 H1
SAND/SEL CR2......211 K4
TOTM N17......50 C6
Junction Rd East CHDH RM6......74 A4
Junction Rd West CHDH RM6......73 K4
Juniper Cl BAR EN5......20 B6
CHSGTN KT9......206 B3
Juniper Ct CHDH RM6......73 H3
KTN/HRWW/W * HA3......43 F4
NTHWD * HA6......40 E4
Juniper Crs CAMTN NW1......84 A5
Juniper Gdns MTCM CR4......179 H4
Juniper La EHAM E6......107 J4
Juniper Rd IL IG1......90 A2
Juniper St WCHPL * E1......104 E6
Juniper Wy HYS/HAR UB3......94 B6
Juno Wy NWCR SE14......124 A6
Jupiter Wy HOLWY N7......85 F4
Jupp Rd SRTFD E15......88 B5
Jupp Rd West SRTFD E15......88 B6
Justice Wk CHEL SW3......120 D6
Justin Cl BTFD TW8......136 E1
Justin Rd CHING E4......51 H2
Jute La PEND EN3......25 G3
Jutland Rd CAT SE6......165 F2
PLSTW E13......106 E3
Jutsums Av ROMW/RG RM7......74 D3
Jutsums La ROMW/RG RM7......74 D3
Juxon Cl RYLN/HDSTN HA2......42 B4
Juxon St LBTH SE11......17 H6

K

Kaduna Cl PIN HA5......59 F2
Kale Rd ERITHM DA18......128 E2
Kambala Rd BTSEA SW11......140 C3
Kangley Bridge Rd SYD SE26......182 C1
Kaplan Dr WCHMH N21......23 F6
Kara Wy CRICK NW2......82 B2
Karen Cl RAIN RM13......111 G1
Karen Ct BMLY BR1......183 J4
ELTH/MOT SE9......146 B6
Karenza Ct WBLY * HA9......61 J4
Karina Cl CHIG IG7......54 E1
Kashgar Rd WOOL/PLUM SE18......128 A5
Kashmir Rd CHARL SE7......146 C1
Kassala Rd BTSEA SW11......140 E2
Katharine St CROY/NA CR0......211 J1
Katherine Cl BERM/RHTH SE16......124 A1
Katherine Gdns BARK/HLT IG6......54 C3
ELTH/MOT SE9......146 C5
Katherine Rd EHAM E6......89 H5
Katherine Sq NTGHL * W11......119 H1
Kathleen Av ACT W3......98 E4
ALP/SUD HA0......80 A5
Kathleen Rd BTSEA SW11......140 E4
Kayemoor Rd BELMT SM2......209 J5
Kay Rd BRXN/ST SW9......141 K3
Kays Ter SWFD * E18......52 D5
Kay St BETH E2......104 C1
SRTFD E15......88 B5
WELL DA16......148 C2
Kean St HOL/ALD WC2B......11 G4
Keatley Gn CHING E4......51 H2
Keats Av CAN/RD E16......126 A1
HARH RM3......57 K3
Keats Cl CHIG IG7......54 C2
PEND EN3......25 F6
STHWK SE1......19 J7
WAN E11......71 F2
WIM/MER SW19......178 C2
YEAD UB4......94 E4
Keats Est STNW/STAM * N16......68 B6
Keats Gv HAMP NW3......83 J2
Keats Pde ED * N9......36 C4
Keats Rd BELV DA17......129 K3
WELL DA16......147 K2
Keats Wy CROY/NA CR0......197 K3
GFD/PVL UB6......96 B4
WDR/YW UB7......112 C4
Keble Cl NTHLT UB5......78 C3
WPK KT4......192 C5
Keble Pl BARN SW13......118 E6
Keble St TOOT SW17......160 B6
Kechill Gdns HAYES BR2......199 K4
Kedleston Dr STMC/STPC BR5......202 A3
Kedleston Wk BETH E2......104 D2
Keeble Cl WOOL/PLUM * SE18......127 G6
Keedonwood Rd BMLY BR1......165 H6
Keel Cl BARK IG11......109 J1
BERM/RHTH SE16......124 A1
Keeley Rd CROY/NA CR0......196 D6
Keeley St HOL/ALD WC2B......11 G4
Keeling Rd ELTH/MOT SE9......146 C6
Keely Cl EBAR EN4......21 J6
Keemor Cl WOOL/PLUM * SE18......147 F1
Keens Cl STRHM/NOR SW16......179 J1
Keen's Rd CROY/NA CR0......211 J2
Keen's Yd IS N1......85 H4
The Keep BKHTH/KID SE3......145 K3
KUTN/CMB KT2......175 G2
Keepers Ms TEDD TW11......174 D2
Keesey St WALW SE17......122 E6
Keetons Rd BERM/RHTH * SE16......123 J3
BERM/RHTH SE16......123 J3
Keevil Dr WIM/MER SW19......159 G2
Keighley Cl HOLWY N7......84 E2
Keightley Dr ELTH/MOT SE9......167 H3
Keildon Rd BTSEA SW11......140 E5
Keir Hardie Est CLPT * E5......68 D5
Keir Hardie Wy BARK IG11......91 G5
YEAD * UB4......94 E2
Keith Connor Cl VX/NE SW8......141 G4
Keith Gv SHB W12......118 D2
Keith Rd BARK IG11......108 D1
HYS/HAR UB3......113 H3
WALTH E17......51 H4
Kelbrook Rd BKHTH/KID SE3......146 D3
Kelburn Wy RAIN RM13......111 J2
Kelceda Cl CRICK NW2......63 J6
Kelf Gv HYS/HAR UB3......94 D5
Kelfield Gdns NKENS W10......100 B5
Kelfield Ms NKENS W10......100 B4
Kelland Cl CEND/HSY/T * N8......66 D2
Kelland Rd PLSTW E13......106 E3
Kellaway Rd BKHTH/KID SE3......146 B3
Keller Cresent MNPK E12......89 H2
Kellerton Rd LEW SE13......145 H6
Kellett Rd BRXS/STRHM SW2......142 B5
Kelling Gdns CROY/NA CR0......196 C4
Kellino St TOOT SW17......160 E6
Kellner Rd THMD SE28......128 A3
Kell St STHWK SE1......18 B4
Kelly Av PECK SE15......143 G2
Kelly Cl WLSDN NW10......81 F1
Kelly Ms MV/WKIL * W9......100 D4
Kelly Rd MLHL NW7......46 C2
Kelly St CAMTN NW1......84 B4
Kelly Wy CHDH RM6......74 A2
Kelman Cl CLAP SW4......141 J3
Kelmore Gv EDUL SE22......143 H5
Kelmscott Cl WALTH E17......51 H4
WATW WD18......26 E1
Kelmscott Gdns SHB W12......118 D3
Kelmscott Rd BTSEA SW11......140 E6
Kelross Rd HBRY N5......85 H2
Kelsall Cl BKHTH/KID SE3......146 A3
Kelsey La BECK BR3......182 D6
Kelsey Park Av BECK BR3......182 E6
Kelsey Park Rd BECK BR3......182 D5
Kelsey Rd STMC/STPC BR5......186 C5
Kelsey Sq BECK BR3......182 D5
Kelsey St BETH E2......104 C3
Kelsey Wy BECK BR3......182 D6
Kelsie Wy BARK/HLT IG6......54 E2
Kelso Pl KENS W8......120 A3
Kelso Rd CAR SM5......194 B4
Kelston Rd BARK/HLT IG6......54 B5
Kelton Vls KUT * KT1......175 G5
Kelvedon Cl KUTN/CMB KT2......175 H2
Kelvedon Rd FUL/PGN SW6......139 J1
Kelvedon Wy WFD IG8......53 K2
Kelvin Av PLMGR N13......49 F2
Kelvinbrook E/WMO/HCT KT8......173 G6
Kelvin Cl HOR/WEW KT19......206 C4
Kelvin Crs KTN/HRWW/W HA3......42 E3
Kelvin Dr TWK TW1......156 C1
Kelvin Gdns CROY/NA CR0......195 K4
STHL UB1......96 A5
Kelvin Gv SURB KT6......205 K1
SYD SE26......163 J5
Kelvington Cl CROY/NA CR0......198 B4
Kelvington Rd PECK SE15......144 A6
Kelvin Pde ORP BR6......201 K5
Kelvin Rd HBRY N5......85 H2
WELL DA16......148 B4
Kember St IS N1......85 F5
Kemble Dr HAYES BR2......215 J1
Kemble Rd CROY/NA CR0......211 H1
FSTH SE23......164 A3
TOTM N17......50 C4
Kemble St HOL/ALD WC2B......11 G4
Kemerton Rd BECK BR3......182 E5
CMBW SE5......142 D4
CROY/NA CR0......197 G4
Kemey's St HOM E9......87 G3
Kemnal Rd CHST BR7......185 H2
Kempe Rd KIL/WHAMP NW6......100 B1
Kemp Gdns CROY/NA CR0......196 D3
Kemplay Rd HAMP NW3......83 H2
Kemp Pl BUSH WD23......28 A1
Kemps Dr NTHWD HA6......40 D3
POP/IOD E14......105 J6
Kempsford Gdns ECT SW5......119 K5
Kempsford Rd LBTH SE11......17 K7
Kempshott Rd
STRHM/NOR SW16......179 K3
Kempson Rd FUL/PGN SW6......139 K2
Kempthorne Rd DEPT SE8......124 B4
Kempton Av NTHLT UB5......78 A4
SUN TW16......172 A4
Kempton Cl ERITH DA8......129 K6
HGDN/ICK UB10......76 A2
Kempton Ct SUN TW16......172 A4
Kempton Pk SUN * TW16......172 B4
Kempton Rd EHAM E6......89 K6
HPTN TW12......172 E5
Kempton Wk CROY/NA CR0......198 B3
Kempt St WOOL/PLUM SE18......127 F6
Kemsing Cl BXLY DA5......169 F2
THHTH * CR7......196 D1
Kemsing Rd GNWCH SE10......125 K5
Kenbury St CMBW SE5......142 D3
Kenchester Cl VX/NE SW8......141 K1
Kendal Av ACT W3......98 C4
BARK IG11......90 E6
UED N18......35 K6
Kendal Cl CMBW SE5......142 C1
EBED/NFELT TW14......153 J3
WFD IG8......38 D4
YEAD UB4......94 C1
Kendal Ct ACT W3......98 C4
Kendal Cft HCH RM12......93 J3
Kendale Rd BMLY BR1......183 H1
Kendal Gdns SUT SM1......194 B6
UED N18......35 K6
Kendall Av BECK BR3......182 B5
SAND/SEL CR2......211 K6
Kendall Pl MHST W1U......9 G2
Kendall Rd BECK BR3......182 B5
ISLW TW7......136 B3
WOOL/PLUM SE18......146 D2
Kendalmere Cl MUSWH N10......48 B4
Kendal Pde UED * N18......35 K6
Kendal Pl PUT/ROE SW15......139 J6
Kendal Rd WLSDN NW10......81 J2
Kendal Steps BAY/PAD * W2......8 D4
Kendal St BAY/PAD W2......8 D4
Kender St NWCR SE14......143 K1
Kendoa Rd CLAP SW4......141 J5
Kendon Cl WAN E11......71 F2
Kendra Hall Rd SAND/SEL CR2......211 H5
Kendrey Gdns WHTN TW2......155 K1
Kendrick Ms SKENS SW7......14 A6
Kendrick Pl SKENS * SW7......14 A7
Kenelm Cl HRW HA1......79 G1
Kenerne Dr BAR EN5......20 C6
Kenilford Rd BAL SW12......161 G2
Kenilworth Av RYLN/HDSTN HA2......77 K2
WALTH E17......51 J5
WIM/MER SW19......177 K1
Kenilworth Crs EN EN1......24 A2
Kenilworth Gdns
GDMY/SEVK IG3......73 F6
LOU IG10......39 K1
OXHEY WD19......41 G1
STHL * UB1......95 K2
WOOL/PLUM SE18......147 G3
YEAD UB4......94 D4
Kenilworth Rd ASHF TW15......152 A5
BOW E3......105 G1
EA W5......117 F1
EDGE HA8......30 E4
EW KT17......207 J4
KIL/WHAMP NW6......82 D6
PGE/AN SE20......182 A4
STMC/STPC BR5......201 H3
Kenilworth Ter BELMT * SM2......208 E5
Kenley Av CDALE/KGS NW9......45 G4
Kenley Cl BXLY DA5......169 H2
CHST BR7......185 K6
EBAR EN4......21 J5
Kenley Gdns THHTH CR7......196 C1
Kenley Rd KUT KT1......175 J5
TWK TW1......156 B1
WIM/MER SW19......177 K6
Kenley Wk CHEAM SM3......208 B2
NTGHL * W11......119 H1
Kenlor Rd TOOT SW17......178 C1
Kenmare Dr MTCM CR4......178 E3
Kenmare Gdns PLMGR N13......35 J6
Kenmare Rd THHTH CR7......196 B3
Kenmere Gdns ALP/SUD HA0......80 C6
Kenmere Rd WELL DA16......148 D3
Kenmont Gdns WLSDN NW10......99 K2
Kenmore Av KTN/HRWW/W HA3......61 G2
Kenmore Crs YEAD UB4......94 D2
Kenmore Gdns EDGE HA8......44 D5
Kenmore Rd KTN/HRWW/W HA3......43 K6
Kenmure Rd HACK * E8......86 D3
Kenmure Yd HACK * E8......86 D3
Kennard Rd FBAR/BDGN N11......47 K1
SRTFD E15......88 B5
Kennard St BTSEA SW11......141 F2
CAN/RD E16......126 E1
Kennedy Av PEND EN3......36 E1
Kennedy Cl MTCM CR4......179 F5
PIN HA5......41 K2
PLSTW E13......106 E1
STMC/STPC BR5......201 J5
Kennedy Rd BARK IG11......90 E6
HNWL W7......96 E4
Kennedy Wk WALW SE17......19 F7
Kennet Cl BTSEA SW11......140 C5
Kennet Dr YEAD UB4......95 J4
Kenneth Av IL IG1......90 B2
Kenneth Crs CRICK NW2......81 K3
Kenneth Gdns STAN HA7......43 G2
Kenneth Moor Rd IL * IG1......90 B1
Kenneth Rd CHDH RM6......74 A4
Kennet Rd DART DA1......150 D4
ISLW TW7......136 A4
MV/WKIL W9......100 D3
Kennet St WAP E1W......123 H1
Kennet Wharf La BLKFR EC4V......12 D5
Kenninghall Rd CLPT E5......86 D1
UED N18......50 D1
Kenning St BERM/RHTH SE16......123 K2
Kennings Wy LBTH SE11......122 B5
Kennington Gdns KUT KT1......174 E6
Kennington Gv LBTH SE11......122 A6
Kennington La LBTH SE11......122 A5
Kennington Ov LBTH SE11......122 A6
Kennington Park Gdns
LBTH SE11......122 C6
Kennington Park Pl
WALW SE17......122 B6
Kennington Park Rd LBTH SE11......122 B6
Kennington Rd LBTH SE11......17 J5
Kenny Dr CAR SM5......210 A6
Kennylands Rd BARK/HLT IG6......55 G3
Kenny Rd MLHL NW7......46 C2
Kenrick Pl MHST W1U......9 G1
Kensal Rd NKENS W10......100 C3
Kensal Whf NKENS * W10......100 C3
Kensington Av MNPK E12......89 K4
THHTH CR7......180 B4
Kensington Church Ct
KENS W8......120 A2
Kensington Church St KENS W8......119 K2
Kensington Church Wk
KENS W8......120 A2
Kensington Cl FBAR/BDGN * N11......48 A1
Kensington Ct KENS W8......120 A2
Kensington Court Gdns
KENS * W8......120 A3
Kensington Court Ms
KENS * W8......120 A3
Kensington Court Pl KENS W8......120 A3
Kensington Dr WFD IG8......53 H5
Kensington Gdns IL IG1......71 K5
Kensington Gardens Sq
BAY/PAD * W2......101 F5
Kensington Ga KENS W8......120 B3
Kensington Gore SKENS SW7......120 B2
Kensington Hall Gdns
WKENS * W14......119 J5
Kensington High St
WKENS W14......119 H4
Kensington Ml KENS W8......119 K1
Kensington Palace KENS * W8......120 A1
Kensington Palace Gdns
KENS W8......120 A2
Kensington Park Gdns
NTGHL W11......100 D6
Kensington Park Ms
NTGHL W11......100 D5
Kensington Park Rd
NTGHL W11......100 D6
Kensington Pl KENS W8......119 K1
Kensington Rd KENS W8......120 A2
NTHLT UB5......96 A1
ROMW/RG RM7......74 E3
SKENS SW7......14 C3
Kensington Sq KENS * W8......120 A2
Kensington Ter SAND/SEL CR2......211 K5
Kent Av DAGW RM9......110 C3
WEA W13......97 H4
WELL DA16......148 A6
Kent Cl ORP BR6......216 E4
STRHM/NOR SW16......195 K1
Kent Ct CDALE/KGS * NW9......45 G5
Kent Dr EBAR EN4......22 A5
TEDD TW11......173 K1

Kentford Wy NTHLT UB5 ....77 J6
Kent Gdns RSLP HA4 ....58 E3
WEA W13 ....97 H4
Kent Gate Wy CROY/NA CR0 ....213 H4
Kent House La BECK BR3 ....182 B2
Kent House Rd BECK BR3 ....182 A3
Kentish Rd BELV DA17 ....129 H4
Kentish Town Rd CAMTN NW1 ....84 B5
Kentish Wy BMLY BR1 ....184 A5
Kentlea Rd THMD SE28 ....127 K2
Kentmere Rd
WOOL/PLUM SE18 ....127 K4
Kenton Av HRW HA1 ....61 F4
STHL UB1 ....96 A6
SUN TW16 ....172 C5
Kenton Gdns
KTN/HRWW/W HA3 ....61 J2
Kenton La
KTN/HRWW/W HA3 ....43 G4
Kenton Park Av
KTN/HRWW/W HA3 ....61 K1
Kenton Park Cl
KTN/HRWW/W HA3 ....61 J1
Kenton Park Crs
KTN/HRWW/W HA3 ....61 K1
Kenton Park Pde
KTN/HRWW/W * HA3 ....61 J2
Kenton Park Rd
KTN/HRWW/W HA3 ....61 J1
Kenton Rd HOM E9 ....87 F4
HRW HA1 ....61 F4
KTN/HRWW/W HA3 ....62 A2
Kenton St STPAN WC1H 4 E6
Kenton Wy YEAD UB4 ....94 C2
Kent Rd CHSWK W4 ....117 K3
DAGE RM10 ....92 D3
DART DA1 ....171 H1
E/WMO/HCT KT8 ....189 H1
KUT KT1 ....174 E6
RCH/KEW TW9 ....137 H1
STMC/STPC BR5 ....202 C3
WCHMH N21 ....35 K3
WWKM BR4 ....198 E5
Kent St BETH E2 ....7 K2
PLSTW E13 ....107 F2
Kent Ter CAMTN NW1 ....2 D5
Kent View Gdns GDMY/SEVK IG3 ....72 E6
Kent Wy SURB KT6 ....206 A1
Kentwell Cl BROCKY * SE4 ....144 B5
Kentwode Gn BARN SW13 ....138 D1
Kent Yd SKENS SW7 ....14 D3
Kenver Av NFNCH/WDSP N12 ....47 H2
Kenward Rd ELTH/MOT SE9 ....146 B6
Kenway ROMW/RG RM7 ....56 E5
Ken Wy WBLY HA9 ....62 E6
Kenway Rd ECT SW5 ....120 A4
Kenwood Cl GLDGN NW11 ....65 H5
WDR/YW UB7 ....112 D6
Kenwood Dr BECK BR3 ....183 F6
Kenwood Gdns CLAY IG5 ....72 A1
SWFD E18 ....53 F6
Kenwood Rd ED N9 ....36 C4
HGT N6 ....65 K3
Kenworthy Rd HOM E9 ....87 G3
Kenwyn Dr CRICK NW2 ....81 G1
Kenwyn Rd CLAP SW4 ....141 J5
DART DA1 ....151 G6
RYNPK SW20 ....177 F4
Kenya Rd CHARL SE7 ....146 C1
Kenyngton Pl
KTN/HRWW/W HA3 ....61 J2
Kenyon St FUL/PGN SW6 ....139 G2
Keogh Rd SRTFD E15 ....88 C4
Kepler Rd CLAP SW4 ....141 K5
Keppel Rd DAGW RM9 ....92 A2
EHAM E6 ....89 K5
Keppel St GWRST WC1E 10 D1
Kerbela St BETH E2 ....104 C3
Kerbey St POP/IOD E14 ....105 K5
Kerfield Crs CMBW SE5 ....142 E2
Kerfield Pl CMBW SE5 ....142 E2
Kerri Cl BAR EN5 ....20 A5
Kerrison Pl EA W5 ....116 E1
Kerrison Rd BTSEA SW11 ....140 D4
EA W5 ....116 E1
SRTFD E15 ....88 B6
Kerry Av PUR RM19 ....131 J2
STAN HA7 ....29 J6
Kerry Cl CAN/RD E16 ....107 F5
PLMGR N13 ....35 F4
Kerry Ct STAN HA7 ....29 K6
Kerry Pth NWCR SE14 ....124 C6
Kerry Rd NWCR SE14 ....124 C6
Kersfield Rd PUT/ROE SW15 ....159 G1
Kershaw Rd DAGE RM10 ....92 C1
Kersley Ms BTSEA SW11 ....140 E2
Kersley Rd STNW/STAM N16 ....86 A1
Kersley St BTSEA SW11 ....140 E3
Kerstin Cl HYS/HAR UB3 ....94 D6
Kerswell Cl SEVS/STOTM N15 ....68 A2
Kerwick Cl HOLWY N7 ....85 F5
Keslake Rd KIL/WHAMP NW6 ....100 B1
Kessock Cl TOTM N17 ....68 D2
Kesteven Cl BARK/HLT IG6 ....55 F2
Keston Av HAYES BR2 ....215 G3
Keston Cl UED N18 ....35 K5
WELL DA16 ....148 D1
Keston Gdns HAYES BR2 ....215 G2
Keston Park Cl HAYES BR2 ....215 K2
Keston Rd PECK SE15 ....143 H4
THHTH CR7 ....196 A3
TOTM N17 ....49 K6
Kestrel Av EHAM E6 ....107 J4
HNHL SE24 ....142 C6
Kestrel Cl CDALE/KGS NW9 ....45 G5
HCH RM12 ....93 K5
KUTN/CMB KT2 ....156 E6
WLSDN NW10 ....81 F3
Kestrel Pl NWCR * SE14 ....124 B6
Kestrel Wy CROY/NA CR0 ....214 B6
HYS/HAR UB3 ....113 G2
Keswick Av KUTN/CMB KT2 ....176 B1
WIM/MER SW19 ....177 K5
Keswick Cl SUT SM1 ....209 G2
Keswick Gdns REDBR IG4 ....71 J2
RSLP HA4 ....58 B3
WBLY HA9 ....80 A3
Keswick Ms EA W5 ....117 F1
Keswick Rd BXLYHN DA7 ....149 H3
ORP BR6 ....202 A5
PUT/ROE SW15 ....139 H6
WHTN TW2 ....155 H1
WWKM BR4 ....199 H6
Kettering St STRHM/NOR SW16 ....179 G2
Kettlebaston Rd LEY E10 ....69 H5
Kettlewell Cl FBAR/BDGN N11 ....48 A2
Kevelioc Rd TOTM N17 ....49 J4
Kevin Cl HSLWW TW4 ....134 C3
Kevington Cl STMC/STPC BR5 ....202 A1
Kevington Dr CHST BR7 ....202 A1
Kew Br RCH/KEW TW9 ....117 H6
Kew Bridge Arches
CHSWK * W4 ....117 H6
Kew Bridge Rd BTFD TW8 ....117 G6
Kew Crs CHEAM SM3 ....208 D1
Kewferry Rd NTHWD HA6 ....40 A2
Kew Foot Rd RCH/KEW TW9 ....137 F5
Kew Gardens Rd RCH/KEW TW9 ....137 G1
Kew Gn RCH/KEW TW9 ....117 G6
Kew Meadow Pth
RCH/KEW TW9 ....137 J2
Kew Rd RCH/KEW TW9 ....117 G6
RCH/KEW TW9 ....137 F5
Key Cl WCHPL E1 ....104 D3
Keyes Rd CRICK NW2 ....82 B3
DART DA1 ....151 K5
Keymer Rd BRXS/STRHM SW2 ....162 A4
Keynes Cl EFNCH N2 ....47 K6
Keynsham Av WFD IG8 ....38 C6
Keynsham Gdns ELTH/MOT SE9 ....146 D6
Keynsham Rd ELTH/MOT SE9 ....146 C6
MRDN SM4 ....194 A5
Keyse Rd STHWK SE1 ....19 J5
Keysham Av HEST TW5 ....133 K2
Keystone Crs IS N1 ....5 F3
Keyworth Cl CLPT E5 ....87 G2
Keyworth St STHWK SE1 ....18 B4
Kezia St DEPT SE8 ....124 B5
Khama Rd TOOT SW17 ....160 D6
Khartoum Rd IL IG1 ....90 B3
PLSTW E13 ....107 F2
TOOT SW17 ....160 C6
Khyber Rd BTSEA SW11 ....140 D3
Kibworth St VX/NE SW8 ....142 A1
Kidbrooke Gdns
BKHTH/KID SE3 ....145 K3
Kidbrooke Gv BKHTH/KID SE3 ....145 K2
Kidbrooke La ELTH/MOT SE9 ....146 D5
Kidbrooke Park Cl
BKHTH/KID SE3 ....146 A2
Kidbrooke Park Rd
BKHTH/KID SE3 ....146 A2
Kidbrooke Wy BKHTH/KID SE3 ....146 A3
Kidderminster Pl CROY/NA CR0 ....196 C5
Kidderminster Rd
CROY/NA CR0 ....196 C5
Kidderpore Av HAMP NW3 ....82 E2
Kidderpore Gdns HAMP NW3 ....82 E2
Kidd Pl CHARL SE7 ....126 D5
Kidlington Wy CDALE/KGS NW9 ....45 G5
Kielder Cl BARK/HLT IG6 ....55 F2
Kilberry Cl ISLW TW7 ....135 J2
Kilburn Br KIL/WHAMP NW6 ....82 E6
Kilburn High Rd
KIL/WHAMP NW6 ....82 E5
Kilburn La NKENS W10 ....100 B2
Kilburn Park Rd
KIL/WHAMP NW6 ....100 E1
Kilburn Pl KIL/WHAMP NW6 ....82 E6
Kilburn Priory KIL/WHAMP NW6 ....83 F6
Kilburn Sq KIL/WHAMP NW6 ....82 E6
Kilburn V KIL/WHAMP NW6 ....82 E6
Kildare Cl RSLP HA4 ....59 G5
Kildare Rd CAN/RD E16 ....106 E4
Kildare Ter BAY/PAD W2 ....100 E5
Kildoran Rd BRXS/STRHM SW2 ....141 K6
Kildowan Rd GDMY/SEVK IG3 ....73 G5
Kilgour Rd FSTH SE23 ....164 B1
Kilkie St FUL/PGN SW6 ....140 B3
Killarney Rd WAND/EARL SW18 ....160 B1
Killburns Mill Cl WLGTN SM6 ....195 G6
Killearn Rd CAT SE6 ....165 G3
Killester Gdns EW KT17 ....207 K2
Killewarren Wy
STMC/STPC BR5 ....202 D4
Killick St IS N1 ....5 G2
Killieser Av BRXS/STRHM SW2 ....161 K4
Killip Cl CAN/RD E16 ....106 D5
Killowen Av NTHLT UB5 ....78 C3
Killowen Rd HOM * E9 ....87 F4
Killyon Rd VX/NE SW8 ....141 H3
Kilmaine Rd FUL/PGN SW6 ....139 H1
Kilmarnock Gdns BCTR RM8 ....91 J1
Kilmarnock Rd OXHEY WD19 ....27 H6
Kilmarsh Rd HMSMTH W6 ....119 F4
Kilmartin Av STRHM/NOR SW16 ....180 A5
Kilmartin Rd GDMY/SEVK IG3 ....73 G6
Kilmartin Wy HCH RM12 ....93 K3
Kilmington Rd BARN SW13 ....118 D6
Kilmorey Gdns TWK TW1 ....136 C5
Kilmorey Rd TWK TW1 ....136 C5
Kilmorie Rd FSTH SE23 ....164 B3
Kiln Cl HYS/HAR UB3 ....113 G6
Kilner St POP/IOD E14 ....105 J4
Kiln Ms TOOT SW17 ....178 C1
Kiln Pl KTTN NW5 ....84 A3
Kilnside ESH/CLAY KT10 ....205 G5
Kiln Wy NTHWD HA6 ....40 C2
Kiln Wood La CRW RM5 ....57 F1
Kilpatrick Wy YEAD UB4 ....95 J4
Kilravock St NKENS W10 ....100 C2
Kilross Rd EBED/NFELT TW14 ....153 G3
Kilsha Rd WOT/HER KT12 ....188 A3
Kilvinton Dr ENC/FH EN2 ....23 K1
Kimbell Gdns FUL/PGN SW6 ....139 H2
Kimbell Pl ELTH/MOT SE9 ....146 B5
Kimberley Av EHAM E6 ....107 J1
GNTH/NBYPK IG2 ....72 D4
PECK SE15 ....143 J3
ROMW/RG RM7 ....74 D3
Kimberley Dr SCUP DA14 ....168 E4
Kimberley Gdns EN EN1 ....24 B4
FSBYPK N4 ....67 H2
Kimberley Rd BECK BR3 ....182 A5
BRXN/ST SW9 ....141 K3
CAN/RD E16 ....106 D3
CHING E4 ....38 C3
CROY/NA CR0 ....196 C3
KIL/WHAMP NW6 ....82 C6
TOTM N17 ....50 C5
UED N18 ....50 D2
WALTH E17 ....51 G4
WAN E11 ....70 B6
Kimberley Wy CHING E4 ....38 C3
Kimber Rd WAND/EARL SW18 ....159 K2
Kimble Cl WATW * WD18 ....26 C1
Kimble Crs BUSH WD23 ....28 C2
Kimble Rd WIM/MER SW19 ....178 C2
Kimbolton Cl LEE/GVPK SE12 ....165 J1
Kimmeridge Gdns
ELTH/MOT SE9 ....166 D6
Kimmeridge Rd ELTH/MOT SE9 ....166 D6
Kimpton Rd CHEAM SM3 ....208 D1
CMBW SE5 ....142 E2
Kinburn St BERM/RHTH * SE16 ....124 A2
Kincaid Rd PECK SE15 ....143 J1
Kincardine Gdns MV/WKIL * W9 ....100 E3
Kinch Gv WBLY HA9 ....62 B4
Kinder Cl THMD SE28 ....109 J6
Kinder St WCHPL E1 ....104 D5
Kinfauns Rd BRXS/STRHM SW2 ....162 B4
GDMY/SEVK IG3 ....73 H5
Kingaby Gdns RAIN RM13 ....93 J5
King Alfred Av CAT SE6 ....164 D6
King Arthur Cl PECK SE15 ....143 K1
King Charles Crs BRYLDS KT5 ....191 G4
King Charles I Island
CHCR WC2N 10 E7
King Charles' Rd BRYLDS KT5 ....191 G3
King Charles St WHALL SW1A 16 D2
King Charles Ter WAP * E1W 104 D6
King Charles Wk
WIM/MER * SW19 ....159 H3
Kingcup Cl CROY/NA CR0 ....198 A5
King David La WCHPL E1 ....104 E6
Kingdon Rd KIL/WHAMP NW6 ....82 E4
King Edward Av DART DA1 ....171 G1
King Edward Dr SURB KT6 ....206 A1
King Edward Rd BAR EN5 ....20 E5
LEY E10 ....70 A5
OXHEY WD19 ....27 J1
ROM RM1 ....75 H3
WALTH E17 ....51 G6
King Edward's Gdns ACT W3 ....117 H1
King Edward's Gv TEDD TW11 ....174 C2
King Edward's Rd BARK IG11 ....90 D6
ED N9 ....36 D3
HACK E8 ....86 D6
PEND EN3 ....25 F5
RSLP HA4 ....58 B5
King Edward St STBT EC1A 12 C3
King Edward the Third Ms
BERM/RHTH SE16 ....123 J2
King Edward Wk STHWK SE1 ....17 K5
Kingfield Rd EA W5 ....97 K3
Kingfield St POP/IOD E14 ....125 F4
Kingfisher Cl KTN/HRWW/W HA3 ....43 F3
STMC/STPC BR5 ....202 E1
THMD SE28 ....109 J6
Kingfisher Dr
RCHPK/HAM TW10 ....156 D6
Kingfisher Pl WDGN * N22 ....49 F5
Kingfisher St EHAM E6 ....107 J4
Kingfisher Wy CROY/NA CR0 ....198 A2
WLSDN * NW10 ....81 F4
King Gdns CROY/NA CR0 ....211 H3
King Garth Ms FSTH SE23 ....163 K4
King George Av BUSH WD23 ....28 B1
CAN/RD E16 ....107 H5
GNTH/NBYPK IG2 ....72 D3
WOT/HER KT12 ....188 C5
King George Cl ROMW/RG RM7 ....56 E6
King George Sq
RCHPK/HAM TW10 ....157 G1
King George St GNWCH SE10 ....145 F1
King George VI Av MTCM CR4 ....194 E1
Kingham Cl NTGHL W11 ....119 H2
WAND/EARL SW18 ....160 B2
King Harolds Wy BXLYHN DA7 ....148 E1
King Henry Ms ORP BR6 ....217 F3
King Henry's Dr CROY/NA CR0 ....214 A6
King Henry's Rd HAMP NW3 ....83 J5
KUT KT1 ....175 J6
King Henry St STNW/STAM N16 ....86 A3
King Henry's Wk IS N1 ....86 A4
King Henry Ter WAP * E1W 104 D6
Kinghorn St STBT * EC1A 12 C2
King James St STHWK SE1 ....18 B3
King John Ct SDTCH EC2A 7 H6
King John St WCHPL E1 ....105 F4
King John's Wk ELTH/MOT SE9 ....166 D2
Kinglake Est WALW * SE17 ....123 F5
Kinglake St WALW SE17 ....123 F5
Kingly Ct REGST * W1B 10 B5
Kingly St REGST W1B 10 A4
King & Queen Cl
ELTH/MOT * SE9 ....166 D6
King & Queen St WALW * SE17 ....122 D5
King & Queen Whf
BERM/RHTH * SE16 ....124 A1
Kingsand Rd LEE/GVPK SE12 ....165 K4
Kings Arbour NWDGN UB2 ....114 D5
King's Arms Yd LOTH EC2R 12 E3
Kingsash Dr YEAD UB4 ....95 J3
Kings Av BAL SW12 ....161 J3
BMLY BR1 ....183 K2
CAR SM5 ....209 J5
CHDH RM6 ....74 B3
CLAP SW4 ....161 K1
EA W5 ....97 K5
GFD/PVL UB6 ....96 B5
HEST TW5 ....135 G2
MUSWH N10 ....48 A6
NWMAL KT3 ....192 C1
WCHMH N21 ....35 H3
WFD IG8 ....53 G1
King's Bench St STHWK SE1 ....18 B2
King's Bench Wk EMB * EC4Y 11 K5
Kingsbridge Av ACT W3 ....117 G2
Kingsbridge Ct POP/IOD E14 ....124 D4
Kingsbridge Rd BARK IG11 ....108 D1
MRDN SM4 ....193 G4
NKENS W10 ....100 A5
NWDGN UB2 ....114 E4
WOT/HER KT12 ....188 A4
Kingsbury Gn CDALE/KGS * NW9 ....62 E2
Kingsbury Rd CDALE/KGS NW9 ....62 E2
IS N1 ....86 A4
Kingsbury Ter IS N1 ....86 A4
Kings Cha E/WMO/HCT KT8 ....173 H6
Kingsclere Cl PUT/ROE SW15 ....158 D2
Kingsclere Pl ENC/FH EN2 ....23 J3
Kingscliffe Gdns
WIM/MER SW19 ....159 J3
King's Cl LEY E10 ....69 K4
DART DA1 ....150 B5
HDN NW4 ....64 B1
NTHWD HA6 ....40 D2
THDIT KT7 ....190 B3
WOT/HER * KT12 ....188 A5
King's College Rd HAMP * NW3 ....83 H5
RSLP HA4 ....58 D3
Kingscote Rd CHSWK W4 ....118 A3
CROY/NA CR0 ....197 J4
NWMAL KT3 ....176 A6
Kingscote St EMB EC4Y 12 A5
Kings Ct PLSTW E13 ....89 F6
STHWK * SE1 ....18 B2
Kingscourt Rd
STRHM/NOR SW16 ....161 J5
King's Crs HBRY N5 ....85 J1
Kingscroft Rd CRICK NW2 ....82 D4
King's Cross Br FSBYW * WC1X 5 F4
King's Cross Rd FSBYW WC1X 5 H4
Kingsdale Gdns NTGHL W11 ....119 G1
Kingsdale Rd PGE/AN SE20 ....182 A4
WOOL/PLUM SE18 ....128 A6
Kingsdown Av ACT W3 ....99 G6
SAND/SEL CR2 ....211 J6
WEA W13 ....116 C2
Kingsdown Cl
BERM/RHTH * SE16 ....123 J5
NTGHL W11 ....100 B5
Kingsdowne Ct EA * W5 ....98 A6
Kingsdowne Rd SURB KT6 ....191 F4
Kingsdown Rd ARCH N19 ....84 E1
CHEAM SM3 ....208 C3
WAN E11 ....88 C1
Kingsdown Wy HAYES BR2 ....199 K3
King's Dr THDIT KT7 ....190 C3
BRYLDS KT5 ....191 H4
EDGE HA8 ....30 B6
WBLY HA9 ....62 D6
Kingsend RSLP HA4 ....58 C5
Kingsend Ct RSLP * HA4 ....58 C5
Kings Farm WALTH * E17 ....51 K4
Kings Farm Av
RCHPK/HAM TW10 ....137 H5
Kingsfield Av RYLN/HDSTN HA2 ....60 B2
Kingsfield Ct OXHEY WD19 ....27 H1
Kingsfield Rd HRW * HA1 ....60 D4
OXHEY WD19 ....27 H2
Kingsfield Ter DART * DA1 ....171 G1
Kingsford Av WLGTN SM6 ....210 E5
Kingsford St KTTN NW5 ....83 K3
Kingsford Wy EHAM E6 ....107 K4
Kings Gdns IL IG1 ....72 D5
KIL/WHAMP NW6 ....82 E5
Kingsgate WBLY HA9 ....80 E1
Kingsgate Av FNCH N3 ....46 E6
Kingsgate Cl BXLYHN DA7 ....149 F2
STMC/STPC BR5 ....186 D6
Kingsgate Est IS * N1 ....86 A4
Kingsgate Pl KIL/WHAMP NW6 ....82 E5
Kingsgate Rd KIL/WHAMP NW6 ....82 E5
KUT KT1 ....175 F4
Kingsground ELTH/MOT SE9 ....166 D2
King's Gv PECK SE15 ....143 J2
ROM RM1 ....75 J2
Kings Hall Ms LEW * SE13 ....145 F4
Kings Hall Rd BECK BR3 ....182 A3
Kings Head Hl CHING E4 ....37 K2
King's Hwy WOOL/PLUM SE18 ....127 K6
Kingshill Av CRW RM5 ....56 E2
KTN/HRWW/W HA3 ....61 H1
WPK KT4 ....192 D4
YEAD UB4 ....94 C2
Kingshill Ct BAR * EN5 ....20 C5
Kingshill Dr KTN/HRWW/W HA3 ....43 H6
Kingshold Rd HOM E9 ....86 E5
Kingsholm Gdns ELTH/MOT SE9 ....146 C5
Kingshurst Rd LEE/GVPK SE12 ....165 K2
Kings Keep HAYES * BR2 ....183 H6
SURB * KT6 ....191 F1
Kingsland Gn STNW/STAM N16 ....86 A4
Kingsland High St HACK E8 ....86 B4
Kingsland Pas HACK E8 ....86 A4
Kingsland Rd BETH E2 ....7 H3
HACK E8 ....86 B5
PLSTW E13 ....107 G2
King's La SUT SM1 ....209 H3
Kingslawn Cl PUT/ROE SW15 ....138 E6
Kingsleigh Pl MTCM CR4 ....178 E6
Kingsleigh Wk HAYES BR2 ....199 J1
Kingsley Av DART DA1 ....151 K6
HSLW TW3 ....135 H3
STHL UB1 ....96 A6
SUT SM1 ....209 H2
WEA W13 ....97 G5
Kingsley Cl DAGE RM10 ....92 D2
GLDGN NW11 ....65 G2
Kingsley Ct EDGE * HA8 ....30 D4
GPK RM2 ....75 K3
Kingsley Dr WPK KT4 ....192 C6
Kingsley Gdns CHING E4 ....51 J1
Kingsley Ms CHST BR7 ....185 G2
KENS * W8 ....120 A3
WAP * E1W 104 D6
Kingsley Pl HGT N6 ....66 A4
Kingsley Rd BARK/HLT IG6 ....54 C4
CROY/NA CR0 ....196 B5
FSTGT E7 ....88 E5
HSLW TW3 ....135 H3
KIL/WHAMP NW6 ....82 D6
ORP BR6 ....217 F4
PIN HA5 ....59 K1
PLMGR N13 ....35 G6
RYLN/HDSTN HA2 ....78 C2
WALTH E17 ....52 A5
WIM/MER SW19 ....178 A1
Kingsley St BTSEA SW11 ....140 E4
Kingsley Wy EFNCH N2 ....65 G3
Kingsley Wood Dr
ELTH/MOT SE9 ....166 E5
Kingslyn Crs NRWD SE19 ....181 F4
Kings Ml HMSMTH * W6 ....119 F4
Kingsman St WOOL/PLUM SE18 ....126 E4
Kingsmead BAR EN5 ....20 E5
RCHPK/HAM TW10 ....157 G1
Kingsmead Av CDALE/KGS NW9 ....63 F4
ED N9 ....36 D3
MTCM CR4 ....179 H6
ROM RM1 ....75 G3
SUN TW16 ....172 B6
SURB KT6 ....191 H6
WPK KT4 ....207 K1
Kingsmead Cl BFN/LL DA15 ....168 B4
HOR/WEW KT19 ....207 F5
TEDD TW11 ....174 C2
Kingsmead Dr NTHLT UB5 ....77 K5
Kingsmead Pde NTHLT * UB5 ....77 K5
Kings Mead Pk ESH/CLAY KT10 ....204 E5
Kingsmead Rd BRXS/STRHM SW2 ....162 B4
Kingsmead Wy HOM E9 ....87 G2
Kingsmere Cl PUT/ROE SW15 ....139 G4
Kingsmere Pk CDALE/KGS NW9 ....62 E5
Kingsmere Pl STNW/STAM * N16 ....67 K5
Kingsmere Rd WIM/MER SW19 ....159 G4
King's Ms BMSBY WC1N 5 H7
Kingsmill Gdns DAGW RM9 ....92 B3
Kingsmill Rd DAGW RM9 ....92 B3
Kingsmill Ter STJWD NW8 ....2 B2
Kingsnympton Pk
KUTN/CMB KT2 ....175 J3
Kings Oak ROMW/RG RM7 ....56 C6
King's Orch ELTH/MOT SE9 ....166 D1
King's Paddock HPTN TW12 ....173 H4
Kings Pde CAR * SM5 ....209 J1
SHB * W12 ....118 D3
TOTM * N17 ....50 B6
WLSDN * NW10 ....82 A6
Kingspark Ct SWFD E18 ....52 E6
Kings Pas WAN * E11 ....70 C4
Kings Pl BKHH IG9 ....39 H4
CHSWK W4 ....117 K5
LOU IG10 ....39 H2
STHWK SE1 ....18 C3
King Sq FSBYE EC1V 6 C5
King's Quay WBPTN * SW10 ....140 B2
Kings Reach EMB * EC4Y 11 K5
Kingsridge Gdns DART DA1 ....171 G1
Kings Rd BAR EN5 ....20 A4
BARK IG11 ....90 C5
BGVA SW1W 15 H6
CHEL * SW3 ....120 C6
CHEL SW3 ....120 C6
CHING E4 ....38 B3
EA W5 ....97 K4
EHAM E6 ....89 G6
FELT TW13 ....154 B3
FUL/PGN SW6 ....140 A2
KUTN/CMB KT2 ....175 G3
MORT/ESHN SW14 ....138 A4
MTCM CR4 ....179 F6
ORP BR6 ....217 F2
RCHPK/HAM TW10 ....137 G6
ROM RM1 ....75 J2
RYLN/HDSTN HA2 ....59 K6
SNWD SE25 ....181 H6
SURB KT6 ....190 D5
TEDD TW11 ....173 J1
TOTM N17 ....50 B4
TWK TW1 ....156 C1
UED * N18 ....50 C1
WAN E11 ....70 C4
WDGN N22 ....49 F4
WDR/YW UB7 ....112 C2
WIM/MER SW19 ....177 K2
WLSDN NW10 ....81 K5
WLSDN NW10 ....81 G6
WOT/HER KT12 ....188 A6
King's Scholars' Pas WEST SW1P 16 A5
King Stairs Cl BERM/RHTH SE16 ....123 J2
King's Ter CAMTN NW1 ....4 A1
Kingsthorpe Rd SYD SE26 ....164 A6
Kingston Av CHEAM SM3 ....208 C1
EBED/NFELT TW14 ....153 H1
Kingston By-Pass BRYLDS KT5 ....191 K5
CHSGTN KT9 ....206 B1
ESH/CLAY KT10 ....204 E1
Kingston Cl CHDH RM6 ....56 A6
NTHLT UB5 ....77 K5
TEDD TW11 ....174 C2
Kingston Crs BECK BR3 ....182 C4
Kingston Gdns CROY/NA CR0 ....210 E1
Kingston Hall Rd KUT KT1 ....174 E6
Kingston Hl KUTN/CMB KT2 ....175 H4
Kingston Hill Av CHDH RM6 ....56 A6
Kingston Hill Pl KUTN/CMB KT2 ....157 K6
Kingston House Est SURB * KT6 ....190 C3
Kingston La TEDD TW11 ....174 B1
WDR/YW UB7 ....112 C2
Kingston Ldg NWMAL KT3 ....192 B1
Kingston Rd BRYLDS KT5 ....191 J6
EBAR EN4 ....21 H6
ED N9 ....36 C4
EW KT17 ....207 H5
HOR/WEW KT19 ....207 F2
IL IG1 ....90 C2
NWDGN UB2 ....114 E2
NWMAL KT3 ....192 A1
PUT/ROE SW15 ....158 E3
ROM RM1 ....75 H1
RYNPK SW20 ....177 H5
TEDD TW11 ....174 C2
Kingston Sq NRWD SE19 ....180 E1
Kingston V PUT/ROE SW15 ....158 A6
Kingstown St CAMTN NW1 ....83 K6
King St CITYW EC2V 12 D4
COVGDN WC2E 10 E5
EFNCH N2 ....47 H6
HMSMTH W6 ....118 C4
NWDGN UB2 ....114 D3
PLSTW E13 ....106 E3
RCH/KEW TW9 ....136 E6
STJS SW1Y 16 B1
TOTM N17 ....50 B4
TWK TW1 ....156 B3
King St Cloisters HMSMTH * W6 ....118 E4
King Street Pde TWK * TW1 ....156 B3
Kingswater Pl BTSEA * SW11 ....140 D1
Kings Wy CROY/NA CR0 ....211 F3
HRW HA1 ....60 E1
Kingsway HOL/ALD WC2B 11 G3
HYS/HAR UB3 ....94 A4
MORT/ESHN SW14 ....137 J4
NWMAL KT3 ....193 F1
PEND EN3 ....24 D6
STMC/STPC BR5 ....201 J2
STWL/WRAY TW19 ....152 A3
WBLY HA9 ....80 A2
WWKM BR4 ....214 D1
Kingsway Av SAND/SEL CR2 ....212 E6
Kingsway Crs RYLN/HDSTN HA2 ....60 C1
Kingsway Pde
STNW/STAM * N16 ....85 K1
Kingsway Pl CLKNW EC1R 5 K6
Kingsway Rd CHEAM SM3 ....208 C5
Kingswear Rd KTTN NW5 ....84 B1
RSLP HA4 ....58 E6
Kingswood Av BELV DA17 ....129 G4
HAYES BR2 ....183 H6
HEST TW5 ....134 E3
HPTN TW12 ....173 G2
KIL/WHAMP NW6 ....82 C6
THHTH CR7 ....196 B2
Kingswood Cl DART DA1 ....171 F1
EN EN1 ....24 B5
NWMAL KT3 ....192 C3
ORP BR6 ....201 J4
SURB KT6 ....191 F4
TRDG/WHET N20 ....33 G1
VX/NE SW8 ....141 K1
Kingswood Dr BELMT SM2 ....209 F6
CAR SM5 ....194 E5
NRWD SE19 ....163 F6
Kingswood Pk FNCH N3 ....46 D5
Kingswood Pl LEW SE13 ....145 H5
Kingswood Rd
BRXS/STRHM SW2 ....161 K1
CHSWK W4 ....117 K3
GDMY/SEVK IG3 ....73 G5
HAYES BR2 ....183 H6
PGE/AN SE20 ....181 K2
WAN E11 ....70 C4

WIM/MER SW19 177 J4
Kingswood Ter CHSWK W4 117 K3
Kingswood Wy WLGTN SM6 210 E3
Kingsworth Cl BECK BR3 198 B2
Kingsworthy Cl KUT KT1 175 G5
Kings Yd PUT/ROE * SW15 139 G4
SRTFD * E15 87 J4
Kingthorpe Rd WLSDN NW10 81 F5
Kingthorpe Ter WLSDN * NW10 81 F5
Kingwell Rd EBAR EN4 21 H1
King William La GNWCH SE10 125 H5
King William St CANST EC4R 13 F6
King William Wk GNWCH SE10 125 F6
Kingwood Rd FUL/PGN SW6 139 H1
Kinlet Rd WOOL/PLUM SE18 147 H1
Kinloch Dr CDALE/KGS NW9 63 G4
Kinloch St HOLWY N7 85 F1
Kinloss Gdns FNCH N3 46 D6
Kinloss Rd CAR SM5 194 B4
Kinnaird Av BMLY BR1 183 J2
CHSWK W4 137 K1
Kinnaird Cl BMLY BR1 183 J2
Kinnaird Wy WFD IG8 53 K2
Kinnear Rd SHB W12 118 C2
Kinnerton Pl North KTBR * SW1X 15 F3
Kinnerton Pl South KTBR * SW1X 15 F3
Kinnerton St KTBR SW1X 15 G3
Kinnerton Yd KTBR * SW1X 15 G3
Kinnoul Rd HMSMTH W6 119 H6
Kinross Av WPK KT4 192 D6
Kinross Cl KTN/HRWW/W HA3 62 B2
Kinross Ter WALTH E17 51 H5
Kinsale Rd PECK SE15 143 H4
Kintyre Cl STRHM/NOR SW16 180 A5
Kinveachy Gdns CHARL SE7 126 D5
Kinver Rd SYD SE26 163 K6
Kipling Dr WIM/MER SW19 178 C2
Kipling Est STHWK SE1 19 F3
Kipling Rd BXLYHN DA7 149 F2
Kipling St STHWK SE1 19 F3
Kipling Ter ED * N9 35 K5
Kippington Dr ELTH/MOT SE9 166 C3
Kirby Cl BARK/HLT IG6 54 E2
HOR/WEW KT19 207 H3
LOU IG10 39 J2
NTHWD HA6 40 D2
Kirby Est BERM/RHTH * SE16 123 J3
Kirby Gv STHWK SE1 19 G2
Kirby St HCIRC EC1N 11 K1
Kirchen Rd WEA W13 97 H6
Kirkcaldy Gn OXHEY WD19 27 G5
Kirkdale SYD SE26 163 J4
Kirkdale Cnr SYD * SE26 163 K6
Kirkdale Rd WAN E11 70 C5
Kirkfield Cl WEA W13 116 C1
Kirkham Rd EHAM E6 107 J5
Kirkham St WOOL/PLUM SE18 127 K6
Kirkland Av CLAY IG5 54 A5
Kirkland Cl BFN/LL DA15 167 K1
Kirkland Dr ENC/FH EN2 23 J2
Kirkland Wk HACK E8 86 B4
Kirk La WOOL/PLUM SE18 127 H6
Kirkleas Rd SURB KT6 191 F5
Kirklees Rd BCTR RM8 91 J3
THHTH CR7 196 B2
Kirkley Rd WIM/MER SW19 177 K4
Kirkly Cl SAND/SEL CR2 212 A6
Kirkmichael Rd POP/IOD E14 106 A5
Kirk Rd WALTH E17 69 H3
Kirkside Rd BKHTH/KID SE3 125 K6
Kirk's Pl POP/IOD E14 105 H4
Kirkstall Av TOTM N17 67 K1
Kirkstall Gdns
BRXS/STRHM SW2 161 J3
Kirkstall Rd BRXS/STRHM SW2 161 K3
Kirksted Rd MRDN SM4 194 A5
Kirkstone Wy BMLY BR1 183 H3
Kirkton Rd SEVS/STOTM N15 68 A1
Kirkwall Pl BETH * E2 104 E2
Kirkwood Rd PECK SE15 143 J3
Kirn Rd WEA W13 97 H6
Kirrane Cl NWMAL KT3 192 C2
Kirtley Rd SYD SE26 164 B6
Kirtling St VX/NE SW8 141 H1
Kirton Cl CHSWK W4 118 A4
Kirton Gdns BETH E2 7 K5
Kirton Ldg WAND/EARL * SW18 160 A1
Kirton Rd PLSTW E13 107 G1
Kirton Wk EDGE HA8 44 E3
Kirwyn Wy CMBW SE5 142 D1
Kitcat Ter BOW E3 105 J2
Kitchener Rd EFNCH N2 47 J6
FSTGT E7 89 F4
THHTH CR7 180 E6
TOTM N17 50 A6
WALTH E17 51 K4
Kite Pl BETH * E2 104 C2
Kite Yd BTSEA * SW11 140 E2
Kitley Gdns NRWD SE19 181 G4
Kitson Rd BARN SW13 138 D2
CMBW SE5 142 D1
Kittiwake Rd NTHLT UB5 95 H2
Kittiwake Wy YEAD UB4 95 H4
Kitto Rd NWCR SE14 144 A3
Kiver Rd ARCH N19 66 E6
Klea Av CLAP SW4 161 H1
Knapdale Cl FSTH SE23 163 J4
Knapmill Rd CAT SE6 164 D4
Knapmill Wy CAT SE6 164 D4
Knapp Cl WLSDN NW10 81 G4
Knapp Rd ASHF TW15 152 C6
BOW E3 105 J3
Knapton Ms TOOT SW17 179 F2
Knaresborough Dr
WAND/EARL SW18 160 A3
Knaresborough Pl ECT SW5 120 A4
Knatchbull Rd CMBW SE5 142 C3
WLSDN NW10 81 F6
Knebworth Av WALTH E17 51 J4
Knebworth Rd
STNW/STAM * N16 86 A2
Knee Hl ABYW SE2 128 D5
Knee Hill Crs ABYW SE2 128 D4
Kneller Gdns ISLW TW7 155 J1
Kneller Rd BROCKY SE4 144 B5
NWMAL KT3 192 B4
WHTN TW2 155 H1
Knight Cl BCTR RM8 73 J6
Knighten St WAP E1W 123 J1
Knighthead Point
POP/IOD * E14 124 D2
Knightland Rd CLPT E5 68 D6
Knighton Cl ROMW/RG RM7 75 F3
SAND/SEL CR2 211 H6
WFD IG8 39 F6
Knighton Dr WFD IG8 39 F6
Knighton La BKHH IG9 39 F4
Knighton Park Rd SYD SE26 182 A1
Knighton Rd FSTGT E7 88 E1
ROMW/RG RM7 74 E3
Knightrider Ct BLKFR * EC4V 12 B5
Knightrider St BLKFR EC4V 12 C5
Knight's Av EA W5 117 F2
Knightsbridge SKENS SW7 14 D3
Knightsbridge Gdns
ROMW/RG RM7 75 F2
Knightsbridge Gn KTBR * SW1X 14 E3
Knights Chambers ED * N9 36 C5
Knight's Hl WNWD SE27 180 C1
Knight's Hill Sq WNWD SE27 162 C6
Knight's La ED N9 36 C5
Knights Manor Wy DART DA1 171 J1
Knight's Pk KUT KT1 175 F6
Knights Rdg ORP BR6 217 H3
Knights Rd CAN/RD E16 125 K1
STAN HA7 29 J6
Knights Wk LBTH SE11 18 A7
Knights Wy BARK/HLT IG6 54 C2
Knightswood Cl EDGE HA8 30 E4
Knightswood Rd RAIN RM13 111 H1
Knightwood Crs NWMAL KT3 192 B3
Knivet Rd FUL/PGN SW6 119 K6
Knobs Hill Rd SRTFD E15 87 K6
Knockholt Rd ELTH/MOT SE9 146 C6
The Knole ELTH/MOT SE9 167 F6
Knole Cl CROY/NA * CR0 197 K3
Knole Rd DART DA1 170 D2
Knoll Crs NTHWD HA6 40 C5
Knoll Dr STHGT/OAK N14 34 A2
Knollmead BRYLDS KT5 191 K5
Knoll Ri ORP BR6 202 A5
Knoll Rd BXLY DA5 169 H2
SCUP DA14 186 C1
WAND/EARL SW18 140 B6
The Knoll BECK BR3 182 E4
HAYES BR2 199 K6
PIN * HA5 41 H5
WEA W13 97 J4
Knolls Cl WPK KT4 207 K1
Knollys Cl WNWD * SE27 162 C5
STRHM/NOR SW16 162 B5
Knolly's Rd STRHM/NOR SW16 162 B5
Knottisford St BETH E2 105 F2
Knotts Green Rd LEY E10 69 K3
Knowle Av BXLYHN DA7 149 F1
Knowle Cl BRXN/ST SW9 142 B4
Knowle Rd HAYES BR2 200 D6
WHTN TW2 155 K3
Knowles Cl WDR/YW UB7 112 B1
Knowles Ct HRW HA1 61 F3
Knowles Hill Crs LEW SE13 145 G6
Knowlton Gn HAYES BR2 199 J2
Knowsley Av STHL UB1 115 G1
Knowsley Rd BTSEA SW11 140 E3
Knox Rd FSTGT E7 88 E4
Knox St MBLAR W1H 8 E1
Knoyle St NWCR SE14 124 B6
Kohat Rd WIM/MER SW19 178 A1
Koh-i-noor Av BUSH WD23 28 A1
Kossuth St GNWCH SE10 125 H5
Kramer Ms ECT * SW5 119 K5
Kreedman Wk HACK * E8 86 C3
Kuala Gdns STRHM/NOR SW16 180 A4
Kydbrook Cl STMC/STPC BR5 201 H4
Kylemore Cl EHAM E6 107 H1
Kylemore Rd KIL/WHAMP NW6 82 E5
Kymberley Rd HRW * HA1 60 E3
Kyme Rd ROM RM1 75 H3
Kynance Gdns STAN HA7 43 J4
Kynance Ms KENS W8 120 A3
Kynance Pl SKENS SW7 120 B3
Kynaston Av THHTH CR7 196 D2
Kynaston Cl KTN/HRWW/W HA3 42 D3
Kynaston Crs THHTH CR7 196 D2
Kynaston Rd BMLY BR1 183 K1
ENC/FH EN2 23 K2
STMC/STPC BR5 202 C4
STNW/STAM N16 86 A1
THHTH CR7 196 D2
Kynaston Wd
KTN/HRWW/W HA3 42 D3
Kynersley Cl CAR SM5 209 K1
Kynoch Rd UED N18 37 F6
Kyrle Rd BTSEA SW11 161 F1
Kyverdale Rd STNW/STAM N16 68 B4

L

Laburnum Av DART DA1 171 F3
ED N9 36 A4
HCH RM12 75 J6
SUT SM1 209 J1
TOTM N17 49 K3
Laburnum Cl CHING E4 51 H2
Laburnum Ct STAN HA7 29 J6
Laburnum Crs SUN TW16 172 A4
Laburnum Gdns CROY/NA CR0 198 A4
Laburnum Gv CDALE/KGS NW9 62 E4
HSLW TW3 134 E5
NWMAL KT3 176 A5
STHL UB1 95 K3
WCHMH N21 35 J4
Laburnum Pl ELTH/MOT * SE9 147 F6
Laburnum Rd HYS/HAR UB3 113 J4
MTCM CR4 179 F5
WIM/MER SW19 178 B3
Laburnum St BETH E2 7 J1
Laburnum Wy HAYES BR2 201 G4
STWL/WRAY TW19 152 C3
Lacebark Cl BFN/LL DA15 168 A2
Lacey Cl ED N9 36 C4
Lacey Dr BCTR RM8 91 J1
EDGE HA8 30 A6
HPTN TW12 172 E4
Lackington St SDTCH EC2A 13 F1
Lacock Cl WIM/MER SW19 178 B2
Lacon Rd EDUL SE22 143 H5
Lacrosse Wy STRHM/NOR SW16 179 J4
Lacy Rd PUT/ROE SW15 139 G5
Ladas Rd WNWD SE27 180 D1
Ladbroke Crs NTGHL W11 100 C5
Ladbroke Gdns NTGHL W11 100 D6
Ladbroke Gv NKENS W10 100 B3
Ladbroke Ms NTGHL W11 119 H1
Ladbroke Rd EN EN1 36 B1
NTGHL W11 119 J1
Ladbroke Sq NTGHL W11 100 D6
Ladbroke Ter NTGHL W11 100 D6
Ladbroke Wk NTGHL W11 119 J1
Ladbrook Cl PIN HA5 59 K2
Ladbrooke Crs SCUP DA14 168 E5
Ladbrook Rd SNWD SE25 180 E6
Ladderstile Ride
RCHPK/HAM TW10 175 J1
Ladderswood Wy
FBAR/BDGN N11 48 C1
Lady Alesford Av STAN HA7 43 H1
Lady Booth Rd KUT KT1 175 F5
Ladycroft Gdns ORP BR6 216 C3
Ladycroft Rd LEW SE13 144 E4
Ladycroft Wk STAN HA7 43 K4
Ladycroft Wy ORP BR6 216 C3
Lady Forsdyke Wy
HOR/WEW KT19 206 C6
Ladygate La RSLP HA4 58 A3
Ladygrove CROY/NA CR0 213 G6
Lady Harewood Wy
HOR/WEW KT19 206 C6
Lady Hay WPK KT4 192 C6
Lady Margaret Rd ARCH N19 84 C2
STHL UB1 95 K3
Ladymount WLGTN SM6 210 D2
Ladyship Ter EDUL * SE22 163 J2
Ladysmith Av EHAM E6 107 J1
GNTH/NBYPK IG2 72 D4
Ladysmith Rd CAN/RD E16 106 D2
ELTH/MOT SE9 167 F1
EN EN1 24 B3
KTN/HRWW/W HA3 42 E5
TOTM N17 50 C5
UED N18 50 D1
Lady Somerset Rd KTTN NW5 84 B2
Ladywell Rd LEW SE13 144 E6
Ladywell St SRTFD E15 88 D6
Ladywell Water Tower
BROCKY * SE4 144 C4
Ladywood Av STMC/STPC BR5 201 K2
Ladywood Rd SURB KT6 191 H6
Lafone Av FELT TW13 154 B3
Lafone St STHWK SE1 19 J2
Lagado Ms BERM/RHTH SE16 124 A1
Lagonda Av BARK/HLT IG6 55 F2
Lagonda Wy DART DA1 151 F5
Lagoon Rd STMC/STPC BR5 202 C2
Laidlaw Dr WCHMH N21 23 F6
Laing Cl CHIG IG7 54 D2
Laing Dean NTHLT UB5 77 G6
Laings Av MTCM CR4 178 E5
Lainlock Pl HSLW TW3 135 G2
Lainson St WAND/EARL SW18 159 K2
Lairdale Cl DUL SE21 162 D3
Lairs Cl HOLWY * N7 84 E4
Laitwood Rd BAL SW12 161 G3
The Lake BUSH WD23 28 D3
Lake Av BMLY BR1 183 K2
Lake Cl BCTR RM8 91 K1
Lakedale Rd WOOL/PLUM SE18 127 K5
Lake Dr BUSH WD23 28 C4
Lakefield Rd WDGN N22 49 H5
Lake Gdns DAGE RM10 92 C3
RCHPK/HAM TW10 156 C5
WLGTN SM6 210 B1
Lakehall Gdns THHTH CR7 196 C2
Lakehall Rd THHTH CR7 196 C2
Lake House Rd WAN E11 88 E1
Lakehurst Rd HOR/WEW KT19 207 G3
Lakeland Cl KTN/HRWW/W HA3 42 D2
Lakenheath STHGT/OAK N14 22 D6
Lake Ri ROM RM1 57 H6
Lake Rd CHDH RM6 73 K1
CROY/NA CR0 198 C6
DAGW RM9 110 D2
WIM/MER SW19 177 J1
Lakeside BECK BR3 182 E6
ENC/FH EN2 22 D5
HOR/WEW KT19 207 G4
WEA W13 97 J5
WLGTN SM6 210 B2
Lakeside Av REDBR IG4 71 H1
THMD SE28 128 B1
Lakeside Cl BFN/LL DA15 148 D6
RSLP HA4 58 B1
SNWD SE25 181 H5
Lakeside Crs EBAR EN4 33 K1
Lakeside Dr ESH/CLAY KT10 204 C4
HAYES BR2 215 J1
Lakeside Rd PLMGR N13 35 F6
WKENS W14 119 G3
Lakeside Wy WBLY HA9 80 C2
Lakes Rd HAYES BR2 215 G3
Lakeswood Rd STMC/STPC BR5 201 G3
Lake Vw EDGE HA8 44 B1
Lake View Est BOW * E3 105 F1
Lakeview Rd WELL DA16 148 C5
WNWD SE27 180 B1
Lake View Ter UED * N18 36 B6
Lakis Cl HAMP NW3 83 G2
Laleham Av MLHL NW7 31 F5
Laleham Ct SUT * SM1 209 G3
Laleham Rd CAT SE6 165 F2
Lalor St FUL/PGN SW6 139 H3
Lambarde Av ELTH/MOT SE9 167 F6
Lamberhurst Cl
STMC/STPC BR5 202 E5
Lamberhurst Rd BCTR RM8 74 A5
WNWD SE27 162 B6
Lambert Av RCH/KEW TW9 137 H4
Lambert Jones Ms BARB * EC2Y 12 C1
Lambert Rd BRXS/STRHM SW2 141 K6
CAN/RD E16 107 F5
NFNCH/WDSP N12 47 H1
Lambert's Pl CROY/NA CR0 196 E5
Lambert's Rd SURB KT6 191 F2
Lambert St IS N1 85 G5
Lambert Wy NFNCH/WDSP N12 47 G1
Lambeth Br WEST SW1P 17 F6
Lambeth High St STHWK SE1 17 G7
Lambeth Hl BLKFR * EC4V 12 C5
Lambeth Palace Rd STHWK SE1 17 G5
Lambeth Rd CROY/NA CR0 196 B5
STHWK SE1 17 J5
Lambeth Wk LBTH SE11 17 H7
Lamb La HACK E8 86 D5
Lamble St KTTN NW5 84 A3
Lambley Rd DAGW RM9 91 H4
Lambolle Pl HAMP NW3 83 J4
Lambolle Rd HAMP NW3 83 J4
Lambourn Cl HNWL W7 116 A2
KTTN * NW5 84 C2
Lambourne Av WIM/MER SW19 159 J6
Lambourne Gdns BARK IG11 91 F5
CHING E4 37 J4
EN EN1 24 B3
Lambourne Gv KUT KT1 175 J5
Lambourne Pl BKHTH/KID SE3 146 A2
Lambourne Rd BARK IG11 90 E5
GDMY/SEVK IG3 72 E6
WAN E11 70 A4
Lambourn Rd CLAP SW4 141 G4
Lambrook Ter FUL/PGN SW6 139 H2
Lambs Cl ED * N9 36 C4
Lamb's Conduit Pas
FSBYW WC1X 11 G1
Lamb's Conduit St BMSBY WC1N 5 G7
Lambscroft Av ELTH/MOT SE9 166 B5
Lambs Meadow WFD IG8 53 H5
Lambs Ms IS N1 6 A1
Lamb's Pas STLK EC1Y 6 E7
Lambs Ter ED * N9 35 K4
Lamb St WCHPL E1 13 J1
Lambs Wk ENC/FH EN2 23 J3
Lambton Pl NTGHL * W11 100 D6
Lambton Rd ARCH N19 66 E5
RYNPK SW20 177 F5
Lamb Wk STHWK SE1 19 G3
Lamerock Rd BMLY BR1 165 J6
Lamerton Rd BARK/HLT IG6 54 B5
Lamerton St DEPT SE8 124 D6
Lamford Cl TOTM N17 49 K3
Lamington St HMSMTH W6 118 E4
Lamlash St LBTH SE11 18 A6
Lammas Av MTCM CR4 179 F5
Lammas La ESH/CLAY KT10 204 A2
Lammas Park Gdns EA W5 116 D1
Lammas Rd HOM E9 87 F5
LEY E10 69 G6
RCHPK/HAM TW10 156 D6
Lammermoor Rd BAL * SW12 161 G2
Lamont Rd WBPTN SW10 120 C6
Lamont Road Pas
WBPTN * SW10 120 C6
Lamorbey Cl BFN/LL DA15 168 A4
Lamorbey Pk BFN/LL * DA15 168 C3
Lamorna Cl ORP BR6 202 B4
WALTH E17 52 A5
Lamorna Gv STAN HA7 43 K4
Lampard Gv STNW/STAM N16 68 B5
Lampern Sq BETH * E2 104 C2
Lampeter Sq HMSMTH W6 119 H6
Lamplighter Cl WCHPL E1 104 E3
Lamplighters Cl DART DA1 171 J1
Lampmead Rd LEW SE13 145 H6
Lamport Cl WOOL/PLUM SE18 126 E4
Lampton Av HEST TW5 135 F2
Lampton House Cl
WIM/MER SW19 159 G6
Lampton Park Rd HSLW TW3 135 G3
Lampton Rd HSLW TW3 135 G3
Lamson Rd RAIN RM13 111 H4
Lanacre Av CDALE/KGS NW9 45 G4
Lanark Cl EA W5 97 J4
Lanark Pl MV/WKIL W9 101 G3
Lanark Rd MV/WKIL W9 101 F1
Lanbury Rd PECK SE15 144 A5
Lancashire Ct MYFR/PKLN W1K 9 J5
Lancaster Av BARK IG11 90 E5
EBAR EN4 21 H1
MTCM CR4 195 K2
WAN E11 71 F1
WIM/MER SW19 177 G1
WNWD SE27 162 C4
Lancaster Cl CDALE/KGS NW9 45 H3
HAYES BR2 199 J1
IS N1 86 A5
STWL/WRAY TW19 152 B1
TOTM * N17 50 C3
Lancaster Dr HAMP NW3 83 J4
HCH RM12 93 K3
POP/IOD E14 125 F1
Lancaster Gdn KUTN/CMB KT2 174 E1
Lancaster Gdns
WIM/MER SW19 177 H1
Lancaster Ga BAY/PAD W2 101 G6
Lancaster Gv HAMP NW3 83 H4
Lancaster Ms BAY/PAD * W2 101 G6
RCHPK/HAM TW10 157 F1
WAND/EARL * SW18 140 A6
Lancaster Pk
RCHPK/HAM TW10 137 F6
Lancaster Pl TPL/STR WC2R 11 G5
TWK TW1 156 B2
WIM/MER SW19 177 G1
Lancaster Rd EBAR EN4 21 H6
ENC/FH EN2 23 K2
FBAR/BDGN N11 48 D2
FSBYPK N4 67 G4
FSTGT E7 88 E5
NTGHL W11 100 C5
NTHLT UB5 78 C4
RYLN/HDSTN HA2 60 A2
SNWD SE25 181 G5
STHL UB1 95 J6
UED N18 50 B1
WALTH E17 51 F5
WAN E11 70 C6
WIM/MER SW19 177 G1
WLSDN NW10 81 H3
Lancaster Stables HAMP * NW3 83 J4
Lancaster St STHWK SE1 18 A3
Lancaster Ter BAY/PAD W2 8 A5
Lancaster Wk HYS/HAR UB3 94 A5
Lancaster West NTGHL * W11 100 C5
Lancastrian Rd WLGTN SM6 210 E5
Lancefield St MV/WKIL W9 100 D2
Lancell St STNW/STAM N16 68 A6
Lancelot Av ALP/SUD HA0 79 K2
Lancelot Crs ALP/SUD HA0 79 K2
Lancelot Gdns EBAR EN4 34 A2
Lancelot Pde ALP/SUD * HA0 80 A3
Lancelot Pl SKENS SW7 14 E3
Lancelot Rd ALP/SUD HA0 79 K2
BARK/HLT IG6 54 E2
WELL DA16 148 B5
Lance Rd HRW HA1 60 C4
Lancer Sq KENS * W8 120 A2
Lancey Cl CHARL SE7 126 C4
Lanchester Rd HGT N6 65 K2
Lancing Gdns ED N9 36 B3
Lancing Rd CROY/NA CR0 196 A3
FELT TW13 153 J4
GNTH/NBYPK IG2 72 D3
ORP BR6 202 C6
WEA W13 97 H6
Lancing St CAMTN NW1 4 C5
Landale Gdns DART DA1 171 F3
Landau Wy ERITH DA8 131 G5
Landcroft Rd EDUL SE22 163 G1
Landells Rd EDUL SE22 163 G1
Landford Rd PUT/ROE SW15 139 F4
Landgrove Rd WIM/MER SW19 177 K1
Landleys Flds HOLWY * N7 84 D3
Landmann Wy NWCR SE14 124 A6
Landon Pl KTBR SW1X 14 E4
Landons Cl POP/IOD E14 125 F1
Landor Rd BRXN/ST SW9 141 K4
Landor Wk SHB W12 118 D2
Landra Gdns WCHMH N21 35 H1
Landridge Dr EN EN1 24 D1
Landridge Rd FUL/PGN SW6 139 H3
Landrock Rd CEND/HSY/T N8 66 E3
Landscape Rd WFD IG8 53 F3
Landseer Av MNPK E12 90 A3
Landseer Cl EDGE HA8 44 C5
EMPK RM11 75 K5
WIM/MER SW19 178 B4
Landseer Rd ARCH N19 84 E1
EN EN1 24 C6
NWMAL KT3 192 A4
SUT SM1 208 E4
Lands' End BORE WD6 29 K1
Landstead Rd
WOOL/PLUM SE18 147 J1
The Landway STMC/STPC BR5 186 D6
The Lane BKHTH/KID SE3 145 K4
Lane Ap MLHL * NW7 46 C1
Lane Cl CRICK NW2 81 K1
Lane End BXLYHN DA7 149 J4
Lane Gdns BUSH WD23 28 E3
Lanercost Gdns STHGT/OAK N14 34 E1
Lanercost Rd
BRXS/STRHM SW2 162 B4
Laneside CHST BR7 185 G1
EDGE HA8 44 E1
Laneside Av BCTR RM8 74 B4
STJWD NW8 101 G1
Laneway PUT/ROE SW15 138 E6
Lanfranc Rd BOW E3 105 G1
Lanfrey Pl WKENS W14 119 J5
Langbourne Av HGT N6 66 A6
Langbourne Wy ESH/CLAY KT10 205 F4
Langbrook Rd BKHTH/KID SE3 146 C4
Langcroft Cl CAR SM5 209 K1
Langdale Av MTCM CR4 178 E6
Langdale Cl BCTR RM8 73 J5
MORT/ESHN SW14 137 J5
ORP BR6 216 B1
Langdale Crs BXLYHN DA7 149 H2
Langdale Dr YEAD UB4 94 C1
Langdale Gdns HCH RM12 93 J3
Langdale Pde MTCM * CR4 178 E5
Langdale Rd GNWCH SE10 145 F1
THHTH CR7 196 B1
Langdale St WCHPL * E1 104 D5
Langdon Ct WLSDN NW10 81 G6
Langdon Crs EHAM E6 108 A1
Langdon Dr CDALE/KGS NW9 62 E5
Langdon Park Rd HGT N6 66 B4
Langdon Pl MORT/ESHN SW14 137 K4
Langdon Rd EHAM E6 90 A6
HAYES BR2 184 A6
MRDN SM4 194 B2
Langdon Shaw SCUP DA14 186 A1
Langdon Wk MRDN SM4 194 B2
Langdon Wy STHWK SE1 123 H4
Langford Cl HACK E8 86 C3
SEVS/STOTM N15 68 A3
Langford Crs EBAR EN4 21 K5
Langford Gn CMBW SE5 143 F4
Langford Pl SCUP DA14 168 B5
STJWD NW8 101 G1
Langford Rd EBAR EN4 21 K5
FUL/PGN SW6 140 A3
WFD IG8 53 G2
Langfords BKHH IG9 39 H4
Langham Ct RSLP * HA4 77 F3
Langham Dr GDMY/SEVK IG3 73 H3
Langham Gdns ALP/SUD HA0 61 J6
EDGE HA8 44 E3
RCHPK/HAM TW10 156 D6
WCHMH N21 23 G6
WEA W13 97 H6
Langham House Cl
RCHPK/HAM TW10 156 E6
Langham Pde
SEVS/STOTM * N15 49 H6
Langham Park Pl HAYES BR2 199 J1
Langham Pl CAVSQ/HST W1G 9 K2
CHSWK W4 118 B6
SEVS/STOTM N15 49 H6
Langham Rd EDGE HA8 44 E2
RYNPK SW20 177 F4
SEVS/STOTM N15 49 H6
TEDD TW11 174 C1
Langham St REGST W1B 9 K2
Langhedge Cl UED N18 50 B2
Langhedge La UED N18 50 B1
Langholm Cl BAL SW12 161 J2
Langholme BUSH WD23 28 C3
Langhorn Dr WHTN TW2 155 K2
Langhorne Rd DAGE RM10 92 C5
Langland Ct NTHWD HA6 40 A3
Langland Crs STAN HA7 43 K6
Langland Dr PIN HA5 41 J3
Langland Gdns CROY/NA CR0 198 C6
HAMP NW3 83 F3
Langler Rd WLSDN NW10 100 A1
Langley Av RSLP HA4 59 F6
SURB KT6 190 E5
WPK KT4 193 G6
Langley Ct BECK * BR3 198 E1
COVGDN WC2E 10 E5
Langley Crs DAGW RM9 91 J5
EDGE HA8 30 E5
HYS/HAR UB3 133 J1
WAN E11 71 F4
Langley Dr ACT W3 117 J2
WAN E11 71 F4
Langley Gdns DAGW RM9 91 K5
STMC/STPC BR5 201 G3
Langley Gv NWMAL KT3 176 A5
Langley La VX/NE SW8 121 K6
Langley Pk EDGE HA8 45 G2
Langley Park Rd BELMT SM2 209 G4
Langley Rd BECK BR3 198 A1
ISLW TW7 136 A3
SAND/SEL CR2 213 F6
SURB KT6 191 F4
WELL DA16 128 D6
WIM/MER SW19 177 J4
Langley Rw BAR EN5 20 D2
Langley St LSQ/SEVD WC2H 10 E4
Langley Wy WWKM BR4 199 G5
Langley Wd BECK * BR3 199 H2
Langmead Dr BUSH WD23 28 D3
Langmead St WNWD SE27 162 C6
Langport Ct WOT/HER KT12 188 B5
Langridge Ms HPTN TW12 172 E2
Langroyd Rd TOOT SW17 160 E4
Langside Av PUT/ROE SW15 138 D5
Langside Crs STHGT/OAK N14 34 D5
Langston Hughes Cl
HNHL * SE24 142 C5

Lang St *WCHPL* E1 104 E3
Langthorn Ct *LOTH* * EC2R 13 F4
Langthorne Rd *WAN* E11 88 B1
Langthorne St *FUL/PGN* SW6 139 G2
Langton Av *EHAM* E6 108 A2
TRDG/WHET N20 33 G2
Langton Cl *FSBYW* WC1X 5 H5
Langton Gv *NTHWD* HA6 40 A1
Langton Ri *FSTH* SE23 163 J2
Langton Rd *BRXN/ST* SW9 142 C1
CRICK NW2 82 A1
E/WMO/HCT KT8 189 H2
KTN/HRWW/W HA3 42 C3
Langton St *WBPTN* SW10 120 B6
Langton Vls *TOTM* * N17 50 C4
Langton Wy *BKHTH/KID* SE3 145 K2
CROY/NA CR0 212 A2
Langtry Pl *FUL/PGN* SW6 119 K6
NTHLT UB5 95 H1
Langtry Rd *STJWD* NW8 83 F6
Langtry Wk *KIL/WHAMP* NW6 83 G6
Langwood Cha *TEDD* TW11 174 D2
Langworth Cl *RDART* DA2 171 G5
Langworth Dr *YEAD* UB4 95 F5
Lanhill Rd *MV/WKIL* W9 100 E3
Lanier Rd *LEW* SE13 165 F1
Lanigan Dr *HSLW* TW3 135 G6
Lankaster Gdns *EFNCH* N2 47 H4
Lankers Dr *RYLN/HDSTN* HA2 59 K3
Lankton Cl *BECK* BR3 183 F4
Lannock Rd *HYS/HAR* UB3 113 J1
Lannoy Rd *ELTH/MOT* SE9 167 H3
Lanrick Rd *POP/IOD* E14 106 B5
Lanridge Rd *ABYW* SE2 128 E3
Lansbury Av *BARK* IG11 91 G5
CHDH RM6 74 A2
EBED/NFELT TW14 154 A1
UED N18 49 K1
Lansbury Cl *WLSDN* NW10 80 E3
Lansbury Crs *DART* DA1 151 K6
Lansbury Dr *YEAD* UB4 94 D2
Lansbury Gdns *POP/IOD* * E14 106 B5
Lansbury Rd *PEND* EN3 25 F2
Lansbury Wy *UED* N18 50 A1
Lanscombe Wk *VX/NE* * SW8 141 K1
Lansdell Rd *MTCM* CR4 179 F5
Lansdown Cl *WOT/HER* KT12 188 B5
Lansdowne Av *BXLYHN* DA7 148 D1
ORP BR6 201 G5
Lansdowne Cl *BRYLDS* KT5 191 J6
RYNPK SW20 177 G3
TWK TW1 156 A3
Lansdowne Copse *WPK* * KT4 192 D6
Lansdowne Ct *WPK* KT4 192 D6
Lansdowne Crs *NTGHL* W11 100 C6
Lansdowne Dr *HACK* E8 86 D6
Lansdowne Gdns *VX/NE* SW8 141 K2
Lansdowne Gn *VX/NE* SW8 141 K1
Lansdowne Gv *WLSDN* NW10 81 G2
Lansdowne Hl *WNWD* SE27 162 C5
Lansdowne La *CHARL* SE7 126 C5
Lansdowne Ms *CHARL* SE7 126 C5
NTGHL W11 119 J1
Lansdowne Pl *NRWD* SE19 181 G3
STHWK SE1 19 F4
Lansdowne Ri *NTGHL* W11 100 C6
Lansdowne Rd *BMLY* BR1 183 K5
CHING E4 37 J4
CROY/NA CR0 196 D6
FNCH N3 46 D3
GDMY/SEVK IG3 73 F5
HACK E8 86 C5
HOR/WEW KT19 206 E5
HSLW TW3 135 G4
MUSWH N10 48 C5
NTGHL W11 100 C6
RYNPK SW20 177 F3
STAN HA7 43 J2
SWFD E18 52 E6
TOTM N17 50 C4
WALTH E17 69 J3
WAN E11 70 D6
Lansdowne Ter *BMSBY* WC1N 5 F7
Lansdowne Wk *NTGHL* W11 119 H1
Lansdowne Wy *VX/NE* SW8 141 K2
Lansdowne Wood Cl
WNWD SE27 162 C5
Lansdown Rd *FSTGT* E7 89 G5
SCUP DA14 168 C5
Lansfield Av *UED* N18 36 C6
Lantern Cl *ALP/SUD* HA0 79 K3
PUT/ROE SW15 138 D5
Lanterns Ct *POP/IOD* E14 124 D3
Lantern Wy *WDR/YW* UB7 112 B2
Lant St *STHWK* SE1 18 C2
Lanvanor Rd *PECK* SE15 143 K3
Lapford Cl *MV/WKIL* * W9 100 D3
Lapse Wood Wk *FSTH* SE23 163 J3
Lapstone Gdns
KTN/HRWW/W HA3 61 J3
Lapwing Cl *ERITH* * DA8 150 E1
Lapwing Wy *YEAD* UB4 95 H5
Lapworth Cl *ORP* BR6 202 D6
Lapworth Ct *BAY/PAD* W2 101 F4
Lara Cl *CHSGTN* KT9 206 A5
LEW SE13 165 F1
Larbert Rd *STRHM/NOR* SW16 179 H4
The Larches *PLMGR* N13 35 J5
Larch Av *ACT* W3 118 B1
Larch Cl *BAL* SW12 161 G4
DEPT SE8 124 C6
FBAR/BDGN N11 48 A2
Larch Crs *HOR/WEW* KT19 206 D4
YEAD UB4 95 G4
Larch Dene *ORP* BR6 201 F6
Larch Dr *CHSWK* * W4 117 H5
Larches Av *MORT/ESHN* SW14 138 A5
Larch Gv *BFN/LL* DA15 168 A3
Larch Rd *CRICK* NW2 82 A2
DART DA1 171 G3
LEY E10 69 J6
Larch Tree Wy *CROY/NA* CR0 213 J1
Larch Wy *HAYES* BR2 201 F4
Larchwood Av *CRW* RM5 56 D2
Larchwood Cl *CRW* RM5 56 E2
Larchwood Rd *ELTH/MOT* SE9 167 G4
Larcombe Cl *CROY/NA* CR0 212 B2
Larcom St *WALW* SE17 18 D7
Larden Rd *ACT* W3 118 B2
Largewood Av *SURB* KT6 191 H6
Larissa St *WALW* * SE17 19 F7
Larkbere Rd *SYD* SE26 164 B6
Larken Cl *BUSH* WD23 28 C3
Larken Dr *BUSH* WD23 28 C3
Larkfield Av *KTN/HRWW/W* HA3 43 H6
Larkfield Rd *RCH/KEW* TW9 137 F5
SCUP DA14 168 A5
Larkhall La *CLAP* SW4 141 K3
Larkhall Ri *CLAP* SW4 141 H4
Larkham Cl *FELT* TW13 153 H5
Larkhill Ter *WOOL/PLUM* * SE18 147 F1
Lark Rw *BETH* E2 86 E6
Larkshall Crs *CHING* E4 38 A6
Larkshall Rd *CHING* E4 52 A1
Larkspur Cl *CDALE/KGS* NW9 62 D2
ORP BR6 202 D6
TOTM N17 49 K3
Larkspur Gv *EDGW* HA8 30 E6
Larkspur Wy *HOR/WEW* KT19 206 E3
Larkswood Cl *ERITH* DA8 150 D2
Larkswood Ri *PIN* HA5 59 G1
Larkswood Rd *CHING* E4 37 J6
Lark Wy *CAR* SM5 194 D4
Larkway Cl *CDALE/KGS* NW9 63 F1
Larnach Rd *HMSMTH* W6 119 G6
Larne Rd *RSLP* HA4 58 D4
Larner Rd *ERITH* DA8 150 B1
Larpent Av *PUT/ROE* SW15 139 F6
Larwood Cl *GFD/PVL* UB6 78 D3
Lascelles Av *HRW* HA1 60 D4
Lascelles Cl *WAN* E11 70 B6
Lascott's Rd *WDGN* N22 49 F2
Lassa Rd *ELTH/MOT* SE9 146 D6
Lassell St *GNWCH* SE10 125 G5
Latchett Rd *SWFD* E18 53 F4
Latchingdon Gdns *WFD* IG8 53 J2
Latchmere Cl
RCHPK/HAM TW10 175 F1
Latchmere La *KUTN/CMB* KT2 175 G2
Latchmere Rd *BTSEA* SW11 140 E3
KUTN/CMB KT2 175 F2
Latchmere St *BTSEA* SW11 140 E3
Lateward Rd *BTFD* TW8 116 E6
Latham Cl *EHAM* E6 107 J5
Latham Rd *BXLYHS* DA6 149 H6
TWK TW1 156 A2
Latham's Wy *CROY/NA* CR0 196 A5
Lathkill Cl *EN* EN1 36 C2
Lathom Rd *EHAM* E6 89 K5
Latimer Av *EHAM* E6 89 K6
Latimer Cl *PIN* HA5 41 G4
WATW WD18 26 C2
WPK KT4 207 K2
Latimer Gdns *PIN* HA5 41 G4
Latimer Pl *NKENS* W10 100 A5
Latimer Rd *BAR* EN5 21 F4
CROY/NA * CR0 211 H1
FSTGT E7 89 F2
NKENS W10 100 A4
SEVS/STOTM N15 68 A3
TEDD TW11 174 A1
WIM/MER SW19 178 A2
Latona Rd *PECK* SE15 123 H6
La Tourne Gdns *ORP* BR6 216 C1
Lattimer Pl *CHSWK* W4 138 B1
Latton Cl *ESH/CLAY* KT10 204 B2
WOT/HER KT12 188 E4
Latymer Gdns *FNCH* * N3 46 C5
Latymer Rd *ED* N9 36 B3
Latymer Wy *ED* N9 35 K4
Lauder Cl *NTHLT* UB5 95 H1
Lauderdale Dr
RCHPK/HAM TW10 156 E5
Lauderdale Pde *MV/WKIL* * W9 101 F2
Lauderdale Pl *BARB* * EC2Y 12 D2
Lauderdale Rd *MV/WKIL* W9 101 F2
Laud St *CROY/NA* CR0 211 J1
LBTH SE11 122 A5
Laughton Rd *NTHLT* UB5 95 H1
Launcelot Rd *BMLY* BR1 165 K6
Launcelot St *STHWK* SE1 17 J3
Launceston Gdns *GFD/PVL* UB6 79 J6
Launceston Pl *KENS* W8 120 B3
Launceston Rd *GFD/PVL* UB6 79 J6
Launch St *POP/IOD* E14 125 F3
Launders Ga *ACT* * W3 117 J2
Laundress La *CLPT* * E5 86 C1
Laundry Rd *HMSMTH* W6 119 H6
Laura Cl *EN* EN1 24 A6
WAN E11 71 G2
Lauradale Rd *EFNCH* N2 65 K1
Laura Pl *CLPT* E5 86 E2
Laura Ter *FSBYPK* * N4 67 H6
Laurel Av *TWK* TW1 156 A3
Laurel Bank *NFNCH/WDSP* * N12 33 G6
Laurel Bank Gdns
FUL/PGN SW6 139 J3
Laurel Bank Rd *ENC/FH* EN2 23 J2
Laurel Cl *BARK/HLT* IG6 54 C2
DART DA1 171 F3
SCUP DA14 168 B5
TOOT SW17 178 D1
Laurel Crs *CROY/NA* CR0 213 J1
ROMW/RG RM7 75 G5
Laurel Dr *WCHMH* N21 35 G2
Laurel Gdns *CHING* E4 37 K2
HNWL W7 115 K1
HSLWW TW4 134 D5
MLHL NW7 31 F5
Laurel Gv *PGE/AN* SE20 181 J3
SYD SE26 182 A1
Laurel La *WDR/YW* UB7 112 B4
Laurel Pk *KTN/HRWW/W* HA3 43 F3
Laurel Rd *BARN* SW13 138 D3
HPTN TW12 173 J1
RYNPK SW20 176 E4
The Laurels *BUSH* * WD23 28 E4
CMBW * SE5 142 C1
RDART * DA2 171 F5
Laurel St *HACK* E8 86 B4
Laurel Vw *NFNCH/WDSP* N12 33 F5
Laurel Vls *HNWL* * W7 115 K2
Laurel Wy *NFNCH/WDSP* N12 32 E5
SWFD E18 70 D1
Laurence Ms *SHB* W12 118 D2
Laurence Pountney Hl
CANST * EC4R 12 E5
Laurence Pountney La
CANST EC4R 12 E5
Laurie Gv *NWCR* SE14 144 B2
Laurie Rd *HNWL* W7 96 E4
Laurier Rd *CROY/NA* CR0 197 G4
KTTN NW5 84 B1
Laurimel Cl *STAN* HA7 43 H2
Laurino Pl *BUSH* WD23 28 C4
Lauriston Rd *HOM* E9 87 F6
WIM/MER SW19 177 G2
Lausanne Rd *CEND/HSY/T* N8 67 G1
PECK SE15 143 K2
Lavender Av *CDALE/KGS* NW9 62 E5
MTCM CR4 178 D4
WPK KT4 208 A1
Lavender Cl *CAR* SM5 210 A2
CHEL SW3 120 C6
HAYES BR2 200 D3
Lavender Ct *E/WMO/HCT* KT8 173 G6
Lavender Gdns *BTSEA* SW11 140 E5
ENC/FH EN2 23 H1
KTN/HRWW/W HA3 42 E2
Lavender Gv *HACK* E8 86 C5
MTCM CR4 178 D4
Lavender Hl *BTSEA* SW11 140 E4
ENC/FH EN2 23 J2
Lavender Pl *IL* IG1 90 B3
Lavender Ri *WDR/YW* UB7 112 D2
Lavender Rd *BERM/RHTH* SE16 124 B1
BTSEA SW11 140 C4
CAR SM5 210 A3
CROY/NA CR0 196 A3
ENC/FH EN2 23 K2
HOR/WEW KT19 206 D3
SUT SM1 209 H2
Lavender St *SRTFD* E15 88 C4
Lavender Sweep *BTSEA* SW11 140 E5
Lavender Ter *BTSEA* * SW11 140 D4
Lavender V *WLGTN* SM6 210 D4
Lavender Wy *CROY/NA* CR0 198 A3
Lavengro Rd *WNWD* SE27 162 D4
Lavenham Rd
WAND/EARL SW18 159 J4
Lavernock Rd *BXLYHN* DA7 149 H3
Lavers Rd *STNW/STAM* N16 86 A1
Laverstoke Gdns
PUT/ROE SW15 158 C2
Laverton Ms *ECT* SW5 120 A4
Laverton Pl *ECT* SW5 120 A4
Lavidge Rd *ELTH/MOT* SE9 166 D4
Lavina Gv *IS* N1 5 G2
Lavington Cl *HOM* E9 87 H4
Lavington Rd *CROY/NA* CR0 211 F1
WEA W13 116 C1
Lavington St *STHWK* SE1 18 B1
Lavinia Rd *DART* DA1 171 J1
Lawdon Gdns *CROY/NA* CR0 211 H2
Lawford Cl *WLGTN* SM6 210 E6
Lawford Gdns *DART* DA1 151 F6
Lawford Rd *CHSWK* W4 137 K1
IS N1 86 A5
KTTN NW5 84 C4
Lawless St *POP/IOD* * E14 105 K6
Lawley Rd *STHGT/OAK* N14 34 B2
Lawley St *CLPT* E5 86 E2
The Lawn *NWDGN* UB2 115 F5
Lawn Cl *BMLY* BR1 184 A3
EN EN1 36 B2
NWMAL KT3 176 B5
RSLP HA4 76 D1
SWLY BR8 187 K5
Lawn Crs *RCH/KEW* TW9 137 H3
Lawn Farm Gv *CHDH* RM6 74 A1
Lawn Gdns *HNWL* W7 115 K1
Lawn House Cl *POP/IOD* E14 125 F2
Lawn La *VX/NE* SW8 121 K6
Lawn Rd *BECK* BR3 182 D3
HAMP NW3 83 K3
The Lawns *BELMT* SM2 208 C5
BKHTH/KID * SE3 145 J4
CHING E4 51 J1
NRWD SE19 180 E4
PIN HA5 42 B3
SCUP DA14 168 C6
Lawns Ct *WBLY* * HA9 62 C6
Lawns Wy *CRW* RM5 56 E3
Lawnswood *BAR* * EN5 20 C6
Lawn Ter *BKHTH/KID* SE3 145 J4
Lawn V *PIN* HA5 41 H5
Lawrence Av *MLHL* NW7 31 G6
MNPK E12 90 A2
NWMAL KT3 192 A3
PLMGR N13 35 H6
WALTH E17 51 F4
Lawrence Buildings
STNW/STAM N16 86 B1
Lawrence Cl *SEVS/STOTM* N15 68 A1
SHB * W12 99 K6
Lawrence Ct *MLHL* NW7 45 G1
OXHEY * WD19 27 H5
Lawrence Crs *DAGE* RM10 92 D1
EDGE HA8 44 C5
Lawrence Dr *HGDN/ICK* UB10 76 A2
Lawrence Gdns *MLHL* NW7 31 H5
Lawrence Hl *CHING* E4 37 J4
Lawrence Hill Gdns *DART* DA1 171 F1
Lawrence Hill Rd *DART* DA1 171 F1
Lawrence La *CITYW* EC2V 12 D4
Lawrence Pde *ISLW* * TW7 136 C4
Lawrence Pl *IS* * N1 84 E6
Lawrence Rd *EA* W5 116 D4
EHAM E6 89 J6
ERITH DA8 149 J1
GPK RM2 75 K2
HPTN TW12 172 E3
HSLWW TW4 134 B5
PIN HA5 59 H2
PLSTW E13 89 F6
RCHPK/HAM TW10 156 D6
SEVS/STOTM N15 50 A6
SNWD SE25 197 G1
UED N18 36 D6
WWKM BR4 214 E2
YEAD UB4 94 A1
Lawrence St *CAN/RD* E16 106 D4
CHEL SW3 120 D6
MLHL NW7 31 H6
Lawrence Wy *WLSDN* NW10 80 E1
Lawrence Yd *SEVS/STOTM* N15 68 A1
Lawrie Park Av *SYD* SE26 181 J1
Lawrie Park Crs *SYD* SE26 181 J1
Lawrie Park Gdns *SYD* SE26 181 J1
Lawrie Park Rd *SYD* SE26 181 K2
Lawson Cl *CAN/RD* E16 107 G5
WIM/MER SW19 159 G5
Lawson Gdns *DART* DA1 151 G6
PIN HA5 41 F6
Lawson Rd *DART* DA1 151 G5
PEND EN3 24 E2
STHL UB1 95 K3
Law St *STHWK* SE1 19 F4
Lawton Rd *BOW* E3 105 G2
EBAR EN4 21 H4
LEY E10 70 A5
Laxcon Cl *WLSDN* NW10 81 F3
Laxey Rd *ORP* BR6 217 F4
Laxley Cl *CMBW* SE5 142 C1
Laxton Pl *CAMTN* NW1 3 K6
Layard Rd *BERM/RHTH* SE16 123 J4
EN EN1 24 B2
THHTH CR7 180 E5
Layard Sq *BERM/RHTH* SE16 123 J4
Laycock St *IS* N1 85 G4
Layer Gdns *ACT* W3 98 C6
Layfield Cl *HDN* NW4 63 K4
Layfield Crs *HDN* NW4 63 K4
Layfield Rd *HDN* NW4 63 K4
Layhams Rd *HAYES* BR2 214 E5
WWKM BR4 214 C2
Laymarsh Cl *BELV* DA17 129 G3
Laymead Cl *NTHLT* UB5 77 J4
Laystall St *FSBYW* WC1X 5 J7
Layton Crs *CROY/NA* CR0 211 G3
Layton Pl *RCH/KEW* TW9 137 H2
Layton Rd *BTFD* TW8 116 E5
HSLW TW3 135 G5
Layzell Wk *ELTH/MOT* SE9 166 C3
Lazenby Ct *COVGDN* * WC2E 10 E5
Leabank Cl *HRW* HA1 78 E1
Leabank Sq *HOM* E9 87 J4
Leabank Vw *SEVS/STOTM* N15 68 C3
Leabourne Rd *STNW/STAM* N16 68 C3
Lea Bridge Rd *CLPT* E5 69 F6
Lea Cl *WHTN* TW2 154 E2
Lea Cottages *MTCM* * CR4 179 F5
Lea Crs *RSLP* HA4 76 D2
Leacroft Av *BAL* SW12 160 E2
Leacroft Cl *WCHMH* N21 35 H4
Leadale Av *CHING* E4 37 J4
Leadale Rd *STNW/STAM* N16 68 C3
Leadbeaters Cl *FBAR/BDGN* N11 47 K1
Leadenhall Pl *FENCHST* EC3M 13 G4
Leadenhall St *BANK* EC3V 13 G4
Leader Av *MNPK* E12 90 A3
The Leadings *WBLY* HA9 80 E1
Leaf Cl *NTHWD* HA6 40 B3
THDIT KT7 189 K2
Leaf Gv *STRHM/NOR* SW16 180 B1
Leafield Cl *STRHM/NOR* SW16 180 C2
Leafield La *SCUP* DA14 169 G6
Leafield Rd *RYNPK* SW20 177 J6
SUT SM1 193 K6
Leafy Gv *HAYES* BR2 215 G3
Leafy Oak Rd *LEE/GVPK* SE12 166 B6
Leafy Wy *CROY/NA* CR0 197 G6
Lea Gdns *WBLY* HA9 80 B3
Leagrave St *CLPT* E5 86 E1
Lea Hall Gdns *LEY* * E10 69 J5
Lea Hall Rd *LEY* E10 69 J5
Leahurst Rd *LEW* SE13 145 G6
Leake St *STHWK* SE1 17 H2
Lealand Rd *SEVS/STOTM* N15 68 B3
Leamington Av *BMLY* BR1 184 B1
MRDN SM4 193 J1
ORP BR6 216 E2
WALTH E17 69 J2
Leamington Cl *BMLY* BR1 166 B6
HSLW TW3 135 H6
Leamington Crs
RYLN/HDSTN HA2 77 J1
Leamington Gdns
GDMY/SEVK IG3 73 F6
Leamington Pk *ACT* W3 99 F4
Leamington Pl *YEAD* UB4 94 D3
Leamington Rd *NWDGN* UB2 114 C4
Leamington Road Vls
NTGHL W11 100 D4
Leamore St *HMSMTH* W6 118 E4
Leamouth Rd *EHAM* E6 107 J5
POP/IOD E14 106 B5
Leander Rd *BRXS/STRHM* SW2 162 A1
NTHLT UB5 96 A1
THHTH CR7 196 A1
Learner Dr *RYLN/HDSTN* HA2 60 A6
Lea Rd *BECK* BR3 182 D5
ENC/FH EN2 23 K2
NWDGN UB2 114 D4
Learoyd Gdns *EHAM* E6 108 A6
Leas Cl *CHSGTN* KT9 206 B5
Leas Dl *ELTH/MOT* SE9 167 F5
Leas Gn *CHST* BR7 186 A2
Leaside Av *MUSWH* N10 48 A6
Leaside Rd *CLPT* E5 68 E5
Leasowes Rd *LEY* E10 69 J5
Leathart Cl *HCH* RM12 93 K5
Leatherbottle Gn *ERITHM* DA18 129 G3
Leather Cl *MTCM* CR4 179 F5
Leatherdale St *WCHPL* * E1 105 F2
Leather Gdns *SRTFD* E15 88 C6
Leatherhead Cl *STNW/STAM* N16 68 A5
Leather La *CLKNW* EC1R 5 J7
HCIRC EC1N 11 J1
Leathermarket Ct *STHWK* SE1 19 G3
Leathermarket St *STHWK* SE1 19 G3
Leathersellers Cl *BAR* * EN5 20 C4
Leathsale Rd *RYLN/HDSTN* HA2 78 B1
Leathwaite Rd *BTSEA* SW11 140 E5
Leathwell Rd *DEPT* SE8 144 E3
Lea V *DART* DA1 150 A5
Lea Valley Rd *CHING* E4 37 H1
Lea Valley Wk *CLPT* E5 68 D4
TOTM N17 50 D5
Leaveland Cl *BECK* BR3 198 D1
Leaver Gdns *GFD/PVL* UB6 96 D1
Leavesden Rd *STAN* HA7 43 G2
Leaway *CLPT* * E5 68 E5
Lebanon Av *FELT* TW13 172 C1
Lebanon Gdns
WAND/EARL SW18 159 K1
Lebanon Pk *TWK* TW1 156 C2
Lebanon Rd *CROY/NA* CR0 197 F5
WAND/EARL SW18 139 K6
Lebrun Sq *BKHTH/KID* SE3 146 A5
Lechmere Ap *WFD* IG8 53 H5
Lechmere Av *CHIG* IG7 54 C1
Lechmere Rd *CRICK* NW2 81 K4
Leckford Rd *WAND/EARL* SW18 160 B4
Leckwith Av *ABYW* SE2 129 F6
Lecky St *SKENS* SW7 120 C5
Leconfield Av *BARN* SW13 138 C4
Leconfield Rd *HBRY* N5 85 K2
Leda Av *PEND* EN3 25 F2
Leda Rd *WOOL/PLUM* SE18 126 E3
Ledbury Ms North
NTGHL * W11 100 E6
Ledbury Ms West *NTGHL* W11 100 E6
Ledbury Rd *CROY/NA* CR0 211 J2
NTGHL W11 100 D5
Ledbury St *PECK* SE15 143 H1
Ledrington Rd *NRWD* SE19 181 G2
Ledway Dr *WBLY* HA9 62 B4
The Lee *NTHWD* HA6 40 D1
Lee Av *CHDH* RM6 74 A3
Leechcroft Av *BFN/LL* DA15 148 A6
Leechcroft Rd *WLGTN* SM6 210 A1
Lee Church St *LEW* SE13 145 H5
Lee Cl *WALTH* E17 51 F4
Lee Conservancy Rd *HOM* E9 87 H3
Leecroft Rd *BAR* EN5 20 C6
Leeds Cl *ORP* BR6 202 E6
Leeds Rd *IL* IG1 72 D5
Leeds St *UED* N18 50 C1
Lee Gn *STMC/STPC* BR5 202 B2
Lee High Rd *LEW* SE13 145 G5
Leeke St *FSBYW* WC1X 5 G4
Leeland Rd *WEA* W13 116 B1
Leeland Ter *WEA* W13 116 B1
Leeland Wy *WLSDN* NW10 81 G2
Leemount Cl *HDN* * NW4 64 B1
Lee Pk *BKHTH/KID* SE3 145 J5
Lee Park Wy *UED* N18 51 F1
Lee Rd *BKHTH/KID* SE3 145 J4
EN EN1 36 C1
GFD/PVL UB6 79 J6
MLHL NW7 46 B3
WIM/MER SW19 178 A4
The Lees *CROY/NA* CR0 198 C6
Lees Av *NTHWD* HA6 40 D4
Leeside *BAR* EN5 20 C6
Leeside Crs *GLDGN* NW11 64 C3
Leeside Rd *TOTM* N17 50 E2
Leeson Rd *BRXN/ST* * SW9 142 B6
Leesons Hl *CHST* BR7 185 K6
Leesons Wy *STMC/STPC* BR5 186 A5
Lees Pl *MYFR/PKLN* W1K 9 G5
Lee St *HACK* E8 86 B6
Lee Ter *BKHTH/KID* SE3 145 H4
Lee Vw *ENC/FH* EN2 23 H2
Leeward Gdns *WIM/MER* SW19 177 H2
Leeway *DEPT* SE8 124 C5
The Leeways *CHEAM* * SM3 208 C4
Leewood Cl *LEE/GVPK* * SE12 165 J1
Lefevre Wk *BOW* E3 87 H6
Leffern Rd *SHB* W12 118 D2
Lefroy Rd *SHB* W12 118 C2
Left Side *STHGT/OAK* * N14 34 D3
Legard Rd *HBRY* N5 85 H1
Legatt Rd *ELTH/MOT* SE9 146 C6
Leggatt Rd *SRTFD* E15 106 A1
Legge St *LEW* SE13 145 F6
Leghorn Rd *WLSDN* NW10 99 J1
WOOL/PLUM SE18 127 J5
Legion Cl *IS* N1 85 G4
Legion Ter *BOW* E3 87 J6
Legion Wy *NFNCH/WDSP* N12 47 J3
Legon Av *ROMW/RG* RM7 74 E5
Legrace Av *HSLWW* TW4 134 C3
Leicester Av *MTCM* CR4 195 K1
Leicester Cl *WPK* KT4 208 A2
Leicester Gdns *GDMY/SEVK* IG3 72 E4
Leicester Pl *LSQ/SEVD* * WC2H 10 D5
Leicester Rd *BAR* EN5 21 F6
CROY/NA CR0 197 F4
EFNCH N2 47 J6
WAN E11 71 F2
WLSDN NW10 81 F5
Leicester Sq *LSQ/SEVD* WC2H 10 D6
Leicester St *SOHO/SHAV* W1D 10 D5
Leigham Av *STRHM/NOR* SW16 161 K5
Leigham Court Rd
STRHM/NOR SW16 162 A5
Leigham Dr *ISLW* TW7 135 K1
Leigham Hall Pde
STRHM/NOR * SW16 161 K5
Leigham V *STRHM/NOR* SW16 162 B5
Leigh Av *REDBR* IG4 71 H1
Leigh Cl *NWMAL* KT3 192 A1
Leigh Ct *RYLN/HDSTN* * HA2 60 E5
Leigh Crs *CROY/NA* CR0 213 K5
Leigh Gdns *WLSDN* NW10 100 A1
Leigh Hunt Dr *STHGT/OAK* N14 34 D4
Leigh Orchard Cl
STRHM/NOR SW16 162 A5
Leigh Pl *WELL* DA16 148 B3
Leigh Rd *EHAM* E6 90 A5
HBRY N5 85 H2
HSLW TW3 135 J5
LEY E10 70 A4
Leigh Rodd *OXHEY* WD19 27 J5
Leigh St *STPAN* WC1H 4 E6
Leigh Ter *STMC/STPC* * BR5 186 C6
Leighton Av *MNPK* E12 90 A3
PIN HA5 41 J6
Leighton Cl *EDGW* HA8 44 C5
Leighton Crs *KTTN* NW5 84 C3
Leighton Gdns *WLSDN* NW10 100 A1
Leighton Gv *KTTN* NW5 84 C3
Leighton Pl *KTTN* NW5 84 C3
Leighton Rd *EN* EN1 24 B6
KTN/HRWW/W HA3 42 D5
KTTN NW5 84 D3
WEA W13 116 B2
Leighton St *CROY/NA* CR0 196 C5
Leila Parnell Pl *CHARL* SE7 126 B6
Leinster Av *MORT/ESHN* SW14 137 K4
Leinster Gdns *BAY/PAD* W2 101 G5
Leinster Pl *BAY/PAD* W2 101 G5
Leinster Rd *MUSWH* N10 66 B1
Leinster Sq *BAY/PAD* W2 100 E6
Leinster Ter *BAY/PAD* W2 101 G6
Leisure Wy *NFNCH/WDSP* N12 47 H3
Leith Cl *CDALE/KGS* NW9 63 F5
Leithcote Gdns
STRHM/NOR SW16 162 A6
Leithcote Pth
STRHM/NOR SW16 162 A5
Leith Hl *STMC/STPC* BR5 186 B4
Leith Rd *WDGN* N22 49 H4
Leith Towers *BELMT* * SM2 209 F5
Leith Yd *KIL/WHAMP* * NW6 82 E6
Leila Av *HSLWW* TW4 134 B3
Lelitia Cl *HACK* E8 86 C6
Leman St *WCHPL* E1 13 K4
Lemark Cl *STAN* HA7 43 J2
Le May Av *LEE/GVPK* SE12 166 A5
Lemmon Rd *GNWCH* SE10 125 H6
Lemna Rd *WAN* E11 70 C4
Lemonwell Dr *ELTH/MOT* SE9 147 G6
Lemsford Cl *SEVS/STOTM* N15 68 C3
Lena Crs *ED* N9 36 E4
Lena Gdns *HMSMTH* W6 119 F3
Lena Kennedy Cl *CHING* E4 52 A2
Lendal Ter *CLAP* * SW4 141 K4
Lenelby Rd *SURB* KT6 191 H5
Len Freeman Pl *FUL/PGN* SW6 119 J6
Lenham Rd *BXLYHN* DA7 129 G6
LEW SE13 145 J5
SUT SM1 209 F2
THHTH CR7 180 E5
Lennard Av *WWKM* BR4 199 H6
Lennard Cl *WWKM* BR4 199 H6
Lennard Rd *CROY/NA* CR0 196 D5
HAYES BR2 200 E5
SYD SE26 181 K2
Lennard Ter *SYD* * SE26 182 A2
Lennon Rd *CRICK* NW2 82 A3
Lennox Cl *ROM* RM1 75 H3
Lennox Gdns *CROY/NA* CR0 211 H2

IL IG1 71 K5
KTBR SW1X 14 E5
WLSDN NW10 81 H2
Lennox Gardens Ms CHEL SW3 14 E6
Lennox Rd FSBYPK N4 67 F6
WALTH E17 69 H3
Lenor Cl BXLYHS DA6 149 F5
Lensbury Wy ABYW SE2 128 E3
Lens Rd FSTGT E7 89 G5
Lenthall Rd HACK E8 86 B5
Lenthorp Rd GNWCH SE10 125 J5
Lentmead Rd BMLY BR1 165 J5
Lenton Ri RCH/KEW TW9 137 F4
Lenton St WOOL/PLUM SE18 127 J4
Lenton Ter FSBYPK * N4 67 G6
Leof Crs CAT SE6 182 E1
Leominster Rd MRDN SM4 194 B3
Leominster Wk MRDN SM4 194 B3
Leonard Av MRDN SM4 194 B2
ROMW/RG RM7 75 F5
Leonard Ct KENS W8 119 K3
Leonard Pl HAYES * BR2 215 J1
STNW/STAM * N16 86 A2
Leonard Rd CHING E4 51 J2
ED * N9 36 B5
FSTGT E7 88 E2
MTCM CR4 179 H4
NWDGN UB2 114 C3
Leonard St CAN/RD E16 126 D1
SDTCH EC2A 7 G6
Leontine Cl PECK SE15 143 H1
Leopold Av WIM/MER SW19 177 J1
Leopold Ms HOM E9 86 E6
Leopold Rd EA W5 117 G1
EFNCH N2 47 H6
WALTH E17 69 J2
WIM/MER SW19 159 J6
WLSDN NW10 81 G5
Leopold St BOW E3 105 H4
Leo St PECK SE15 143 J1
Leppoc Rd CLAP SW4 141 J6
Leroy St STHWK SE1 19 G6
Lerry Cl WKENS W14 119 J6
Lescombe Cl FSTH SE23 164 B5
Lescombe Rd FSTH SE23 164 B5
Lesley Cl BXLY DA5 169 J2
Leslie Gdns BELMT SM2 208 E5
Leslie Gv CROY/NA CR0 196 E5
Leslie Grove Pl CROY/NA * CR0 197 F5
Leslie Park Rd CROY/NA CR0 197 F5
Leslie Rd CAN/RD E16 107 F5
EFNCH N2 47 H6
WAN E11 88 B2
Lesney Pk ERITH DA8 130 A6
Lesney Park Rd ERITH DA8 130 A6
Lessar Av CLAP SW4 141 H6
Lessingham Av TOOT SW17 160 E6
Lessing St FSTH SE23 164 B2
Lessington Av ROMW/RG RM7 74 E3
Lessness Av BXLYHN DA7 148 E1
Lessness Pk BELV DA17 129 G5
Lessness Rd MRDN SM4 194 B3
Lester Av SRTFD E15 106 C3
Leston Cl RAIN RM13 111 K2
Leswin Pl STNW/STAM N16 86 B1
Leswin Rd STNW/STAM N16 86 B1
Letchford Gdns WLSDN NW10 99 J2
Letchford Ms WLSDN * NW10 99 J2
Letchford Ter
KTN/HRWW/W * HA3 42 B4
Letchworth Av
EBED/NFELT TW14 153 J2
Letchworth Cl HAYES BR2 199 K2
OXHEY WD19 41 H1
Letchworth Dr HAYES BR2 199 K2
Letchworth St TOOT SW17 160 E6
Letterstone Rd FUL/PGN SW6 139 J1
Lettice St FUL/PGN SW6 139 J3
Lett Rd SRTFD E15 88 B5
Leucha Rd WALTH E17 69 G2
Levana Cl WIM/MER SW19 159 H3
Levehurst Wy CLAP SW4 141 K3
Leven Cl OXHEY * WD19 41 H1
Levendale Rd FSTH SE23 164 B4
Leven Rd POP/IOD E14 106 A4
Leven Wy HYS/HAR UB3 94 C5
Leverett St CHEL SW3 14 D6
Leverholme Gdns
ELTH/MOT SE9 167 F6
Leverson St STRHM/NOR SW16 179 H2
Lever St FSBYE EC1V 6 C5
Leverton Pl KTTN NW5 84 C3
Leverton St KTTN NW5 84 C3
Levett Gdns GDMY/SEVK IG3 91 F2
Levett Rd BARK IG11 90 E4
Levine Gdns BARK IG11 109 K1
Lewes Cl NTHLT UB5 78 A4
Lewesdon Cl WIM/MER SW19 159 G3
Lewes Rd BMLY BR1 184 C5
NFNCH/WDSP N12 47 J1
Leweston Pl STNW/STAM N16 68 B4
Lewgars Av CDALE/KGS NW9 62 E3
Lewing Cl ORP BR6 201 K5
Lewin Rd BXLYHS DA6 149 F5
MORT/ESHN SW14 138 A4
STRHM/NOR SW16 179 J2
Lewis Av WALTH E17 51 J4
Lewis Cl STHGT/OAK N14 34 C2
Lewis Crs WLSDN NW10 81 F3
Lewis Gdns EFNCH N2 47 H5
Lewis Gv LEW SE13 145 F5
Lewisham High St LEW SE13 164 E1
Lewisham Hl LEW SE13 145 F3
Lewisham Pk LEW SE13 164 E1
Lewisham Rd LEW SE13 145 F3
Lewisham Wy BROCKY SE4 144 C3
Lewis Pl HACK E8 86 C3
Lewis Rd MTCM CR4 178 D5
RCHPK/HAM * TW10 136 E6
SCUP DA14 168 D5
STHL UB1 114 D2
SUT SM1 209 F2
WELL DA16 148 D4
Lewis St CAMTN NW1 84 B5
Lewis Wy DAGE RM10 92 D4
Lexden Dr CHDH RM6 73 H3
Lexden Rd ACT W3 98 D6
MTCM CR4 195 J1
Lexham Gdns KENS W8 119 K4
Lexham Ms KENS W8 119 K4
Lexington St SOHO/CST W1F 10 B4
Lexington Wy BAR EN5 20 B5
Lexton Gdns BRXS/STRHM SW2 161 J3
Leyborne Av WEA W13 116 D2
Leyborne Pk RCH/KEW TW9 137 H2
Leybourne Cl HAYES BR2 199 K2
Leybourne Rd CAMTN * NW1 84 B5
CDALE/KGS NW9 62 C2
HGDN/ICK UB10 76 A6
WAN E11 70 D5
Leybourne St CAMTN NW1 84 B5
Leyburn Cl WALTH E17 70 A1
Leyburn Gdns CROY/NA CR0 197 F6
Leyburn Gv UED N18 50 C2
Leyburn House
WOOL/PLUM SE18 146 D1
Leyburn Rd UED N18 50 C2
Leycroft Gdns ERITH DA8 150 E2
Leyden St WCHPL E1 13 J2
Leyes Rd CAN/RD E16 107 H6
Leyfield WPK KT4 192 B6
Leyland Av PEND EN3 25 G3
Leyland Rd LEE/GVPK SE12 145 J6
Leylang Rd NWCR SE14 144 A1
The Leys KTN/HRWW/W HA3 62 B3
Leys Av DAGE RM10 92 E6
Leys Cl DAGE RM10 92 E5
HRW HA1 60 D1
Leysdown Av BXLYHN DA7 149 K5
Leysdown Rd ELTH/MOT SE9 166 D4
Leysfield Rd SHB W12 118 D2
Leys Gdns EBAR EN4 22 A6
Leyspring Rd WAN E11 70 D5
Leys Rd East PEND EN3 25 G2
Leys The EFNCH N2 65 G1
Ley St IL IG1 72 C6
Leyswood Dr GNTH/NBYPK IG2 72 E2
Leythe Rd ACT W3 117 K2
Leyton Cross Rd RDART DA2 170 C5
Leyton Gra LEY E10 69 J6
Leyton Green Rd LEY E10 70 A3
Leyton Park Rd LEY E10 70 A6
Leyton Rd SRTFD E15 88 B3
WIM/MER SW19 178 B3
Leytonstone Rd SRTFD E15 88 C4
Leywick St SRTFD E15 106 C1
Lezayre Rd ORP BR6 217 F4
Liardet St NWCR SE14 124 B6
Liberia Rd HBRY N5 85 H4
Liberty Av WIM/MER SW19 178 C4
Liberty Ms WDGN * N22 49 H4
Liberty St BRXN/ST SW9 142 A2
Libra Rd BOW E3 87 H6
PLSTW E13 106 E1
Library Pde WLSDN * NW10 81 G6
Library St STHWK SE1 18 B3
Lichfield Cl EBAR EN4 21 K4
Lichfield Gdns RCH/KEW * TW9 137 F6
Lichfield Gv FNCH N3 46 E4
Lichfield Rd BCTR RM8 91 H2
BOW E3 105 G2
CRICK NW2 82 C2
ED N9 36 C4
EHAM E6 107 H2
HSLWW TW4 134 B4
NTHWD HA6 40 E6
RCH/KEW TW9 137 G2
WFD IG8 38 C6
Lichfield Ter
RCHPK/HAM * TW10 137 F6
Lidbury Rd MLHL NW7 46 C2
Lidcote Gdns BRXN/ST * SW9 142 B3
Liddall Wy WDR/YW UB7 112 C1
Liddell Cl KTN/HRWW/W HA3 43 K6
Liddell Gdns WLSDN NW10 100 A1
Liddell Rd KIL/WHAMP NW6 82 E4
Lidding Rd KTN/HRWW/W HA3 61 K2
Liddington Rd SRTFD E15 88 D6
Liddon Rd BMLY BR1 184 B6
PLSTW E13 107 F2
Liden Cl WALTH E17 69 H4
Lidfield Rd STNW/STAM N16 85 K2
Lidgate Rd PECK * SE15 143 G1
Lidiard Rd WAND/EARL SW18 160 B4
Lido Sq TOTM N17 49 K5
Lidyard Rd ARCH N19 66 C5
Liffler Rd WOOL/PLUM SE18 127 K5
Lifford St PUT/ROE SW15 139 G5
Lightcliffe Rd PLMGR N13 35 G6
Lighterman Ms WCHPL E1 105 F5
Lighterman's Rd POP/IOD E14 124 D2
Lightfoot Rd CEND/HSY/T N8 66 E2
Ligonier St BETH E2 7 J6
Lilac Cl CHING E4 51 H2
Lilac Gdns CROY/NA CR0 213 J1
EA W5 116 E3
HYS/HAR UB3 94 C5
ROMW/RG RM7 75 G5
Lilac Pl LBTH SE11 17 G7
Lilac St SHB W12 99 J6
Lilburne Gdns ELTH/MOT SE9 146 D6
Lilburne Rd ELTH/MOT SE9 146 D6
Lile Crs HNWL W7 96 E4
Lilestone St STJWD NW8 2 C6
Lilford Rd BRXN/ST SW9 142 C3
Lilian Barker Cl LEE/GVPK SE12 145 K6
Lilian Board Wy GFD/PVL UB6 78 D3
Lilian Gdns WFD IG8 53 F4
Lilian Rd MTCM CR4 179 H4
Lillechurch Rd BCTR RM8 91 H4
Lilleshall Rd MRDN SM4 194 C3
Lilley Cl WAP E1W 123 H1
Lilley La MLHL * NW7 45 G1
Lillian Av ACT W3 117 H2
Lillian Rd BARN SW13 118 D6
Lillie Rd FUL/PGN SW6 119 G6
Lillieshall Rd CLAP SW4 141 G4
Lillie Yd FUL/PGN SW6 119 K6
Lillington Gardens Est PIM SW1V 16 B7
Lilliput Av NTHLT UB5 77 J6
Lilliput Rd ROMW/RG RM7 75 F4
Lily Cl WKENS * W14 119 H4
Lily Dr WDR/YW UB7 112 A4
Lily Gdns ALP/SUD HA0 97 J1
Lily Pl HCIRC EC1N 11 K1
Lily Rd LEY E10 69 J3
Lilyville Rd FUL/PGN SW6 139 J2
Limbourne Av BCTR RM8 74 B4
Limburg Rd BTSEA SW11 140 D5
Limeburner La STP EC4M 12 A3
Lime Cl BKHH IG9 39 H4
BMLY BR1 200 D1
KTN/HRWW/W HA3 43 G5
OXHEY WD19 27 H2
ROMW/RG RM7 74 E2
RSLP HA4 40 D6
WAP E1W 123 H1
Lime Crs SUN TW16 172 B5
Limecroft Cl HOR/WEW KT19 207 F5
Limedene Cl PIN HA5 41 H4
Lime Gv BARK/HLT IG6 55 F2
BFN/LL DA15 168 A1
HYS/HAR UB3 94 B6
NWMAL KT3 176 A6
ORP BR6 201 G6
RSLP HA4 59 F3
SHB W12 119 F2
TRDG/WHET N20 32 C3
TWK TW1 156 A1
Limeharbour POP/IOD E14 124 E3
Limehouse POP/IOD * E14 105 J6
Limehouse Cswy POP/IOD E14 105 H6
Limehouse Link POP/IOD E14 105 G6
Lime Kiln Dr CHARL SE7 126 A6
Limerick Cl BAL SW12 161 H2
Limerston St WBPTN SW10 120 B6
The Limes CMBW * SE5 143 F4
PUR RM19 131 K5
WAND/EARL * SW18 159 K1
The Limes Av FBAR/BDGN N11 48 B1
Limes Av BARN SW13 138 C3
CAR SM5 194 E5
CHIG IG7 54 C1
CROY/NA CR0 211 F1
GLDGN NW11 64 C4
MLHL NW7 45 G2
NFNCH/WDSP N12 33 G6
PGE/AN SE20 181 J3
WAN E11 71 F1
Limes Cl CAR SM5 194 E6
FBAR/BDGN * N11 48 C1
Limesdale Gdns EDGE HA8 44 E5
Limes Field Rd BARN SW13 138 B4
Limesford Rd PECK SE15 144 A5
Limes Gdns WAND/EARL SW18 159 K1
Limes Gv LEW SE13 145 F5
Limes Rd BECK BR3 182 E5
CROY/NA CR0 196 E3
Limes Rw ORP BR6 216 B3
Lime St FENCHST EC3M 13 G5
WALTH E17 69 G1
Lime Street Pas BANK * EC3V 13 G4
Limes Wk EA W5 116 E2
PECK * SE15 143 K5
Lime Tree Av THDIT KT7 189 K5
Limetree Cl BRXS/STRHM SW2 162 A3
Lime Tree Ct PIN * HA5 42 A3
Lime Tree Gv CROY/NA CR0 213 H1
Limetree Pl MTCM CR4 179 G4
Lime Tree Rd HEST TW5 135 G2
Lime Tree Ter CAT * SE6 164 C3
Lime Tree Wk BUSH WD23 28 E3
ENC/FH EN2 23 J1
WWKM BR4 214 D2
Lime Wk SRTFD * E15 88 C6
Limewood Cl BECK BR3 199 F2
WALTH E17 69 H1
WEA W13 97 H5
Limewood Rd ERITH DA8 149 K1
Limpsfield Av THHTH CR7 196 A2
WIM/MER SW19 159 G4
Linacre Rd CRICK NW2 81 K4
Linchmere Rd LEE/GVPK SE12 165 K2
Lincoln Av ROMW/RG RM7 75 G5
STHGT/OAK N14 34 C5
WHTN TW2 155 H4
WIM/MER SW19 159 G5
Lincoln Cl ERITH DA8 150 C3
GFD/PVL UB6 78 C6
RYLN/HDSTN HA2 59 K2
Lincoln Crs EN EN1 24 A5
Lincoln Dr OXHEY WD19 27 G5
Lincoln Est BOW E3 105 J3
Lincoln Gdns IL IG1 71 J4
Lincoln Green Rd
STMC/STPC BR5 202 A2
Lincoln Ms KIL/WHAMP NW6 82 D6
Lincoln Pde EFNCH * N2 47 J6
Lincoln Rd ALP/SUD HA0 79 K4
EFNCH N2 47 J6
EN EN1 24 A5
ERITH DA8 150 C3
FELT TW13 154 E5
MTCM CR4 195 K2
NTHWD HA6 40 D6
NWMAL KT3 175 K6
PLSTW E13 107 F3
RYLN/HDSTN HA2 59 K2
SCUP DA14 186 C1
SNWD SE25 181 J6
SWFD E18 52 D4
WPK KT4 192 E5
The Lincolns MLHL NW7 31 H5
Lincoln's Inn Flds LINN WC2A 11 G3
Lincoln St CHEL SW3 14 E7
WAN E11 70 C6
Lincoln Ter BELMT * SM2 208 E5
Lincoln Wy EN EN1 24 D6
Lincombe Rd BMLY BR1 165 J5
Lindal Crs STHGT/OAK N14 22 E6
The Lindales TOTM N17 50 C2
Lindal Rd BROCKY SE4 144 C6
Lindbergh Rd WLGTN SM6 210 E6
Linden Av DART DA1 171 F3
EN EN1 24 C2
HSLW TW3 135 G6
RSLP HA4 58 E5
THHTH CR7 196 C1
WBLY HA9 80 B3
WLSDN NW10 100 B1
Linden Cl ORP BR6 217 G3
RSLP HA4 58 E5
STAN HA7 43 H1
STHGT/OAK N14 34 C1
THDIT KT7 190 B4
Linden Cottages
WIM/MER * SW19 177 H2
Linden Crs GFD/PVL UB6 79 F4
KUT KT1 175 G5
WFD IG8 53 F2
Lindenfield CHST BR7 185 G5
Linden Gdns BAY/PAD W2 100 E6
CHSWK W4 118 A5
EN EN1 24 C2
Linden Gv NWMAL KT3 176 B6
PECK SE15 143 J4
SYD SE26 181 K2
Linden Lea EFNCH N2 65 G2
PIN * HA5 41 K3
Linden Leas WWKM BR4 199 G6
Linden Ms IS N1 85 K3
NTGHL W11 100 E6
Linden Pl MTCM CR4 194 D1
Linden Rd FBAR/BDGN N11 33 K4
HPTN TW12 173 F4
MUSWH N10 66 B1
SEVS/STOTM N15 67 J1
The Lindens CHSWK W4 137 K2
NFNCH/WDSP * N12 47 H1
WALTH * E17 69 K1
Linden St ROMW/RG RM7 75 F1
Linden Wy STHGT/OAK N14 34 C1
Lindfield Gdns HAMP NW3 83 G3
Lindfield Rd CROY/NA CR0 197 G3
EA W5 97 J3
Lindfield St POP/IOD E14 105 J5
Lindhill Cl PEND EN3 25 F3
Lindisfarne Md HOM E9 87 G2
Lindisfarne Rd BCTR RM8 91 J1
RYNPK SW20 176 D3
Lindley Est PECK * SE15 143 H1
Lindley Pl RCH/KEW TW9 137 H2
Lindley Rd LEY E10 70 A6
Lindley St WCHPL E1 104 E4
Lindore Rd BTSEA SW11 140 E5
Lindores Rd CAR SM5 194 B4
Lindo St PECK SE15 143 K3
Lind Rd SUT SM1 209 G3
Lindrop St FUL/PGN SW6 140 B3
Lindsay Cl CHSGTN KT9 206 A5
STWL/WRAY TW19 152 A1
Lindsay Dr KTN/HRWW/W HA3 62 A3
Lindsay Rd HPTN TW12 155 G6
WPK KT4 192 E6
Lindsay Sq PIM SW1V 121 J5
Lindsell St GNWCH SE10 145 F2
Lindsey Cl BMLY BR1 184 C6
MTCM CR4 195 K1
Lindsey Gdns
EBED/NFELT * TW14 153 G2
Lindsey Ms IS N1 85 J5
Lindsey Rd BCTR RM8 91 J1
Lindsey St STBT EC1A 12 B1
Lind St DEPT SE8 144 E3
Lindum Rd TEDD TW11 174 D3
Lindway WNWD SE27 180 C1
Linfield Cl HDN NW4 46 A6
Linford Rd WALTH E17 52 A6
Linford St VX/NE SW8 141 H2
Lingards Rd LEW SE13 145 F5
Lingey Cl BFN/LL DA15 168 A4
Lingfield Av BRYLDS KT5 191 F1
Lingfield Cl EN EN1 36 A1
NTHWD HA6 40 C3
Lingfield Ct NTHLT * UB5 96 A1
Lingfield Crs ELTH/MOT SE9 147 J5
Lingfield Gdns ED N9 36 D2
Lingfield Rd WIM/MER SW19 177 G2
WPK KT4 208 A1
Lingham St BRXN/ST SW9 141 K3
Lingholm Wy BAR EN5 20 B6
Ling Rd CAN/RD E16 106 E4
ERITH DA8 129 K6
Lingwell Rd TOOT SW17 160 D5
Lingwood Gdns ISLW TW7 135 K1
Lingwood Rd STNW/STAM N16 68 C4
Linhope St CAMTN NW1 2 E6
The Link ACT W3 98 D5
ALP/SUD HA0 61 J5
NTHLT * UB5 77 K3
PEND EN3 25 G2
PIN HA5 59 G3
TEDD TW11 174 A2
Linkfield E/WMO/HCT KT8 173 F6
Link Fld HAYES BR2 199 K3
Linkfield Rd ISLW TW7 136 A3
Link La WLGTN SM6 210 D4
Linklea Cl CDALE/KGS NW9 45 G3
Link Rd DAGW RM9 110 D1
EBED/NFELT TW14 153 J2
FBAR/BDGN N11 34 A6
WLGTN SM6 195 F5
The Links WALTH E17 69 G1
Links Av GPK RM2 57 K5
MRDN SM4 193 K1
Links Dr TRDG/WHET N20 32 E3
Links Gdns STRHM/NOR SW16 180 B3
Linkside CHIG IG7 54 C1
NFNCH/WDSP N12 46 D2
NWMAL KT3 176 B5
Linkside Cl ENC/FH EN2 23 F4
Linkside Gdns ENC/FH EN2 23 F4
Links Rd ACT W3 98 C5
CRICK NW2 63 H6
TOOT SW17 179 F2
WFD IG8 52 E1
WWKM BR4 199 F5
Links Side ENC/FH EN2 23 F4
Link St HOM E9 86 E4
Links Vw DART DA1 171 F3
FNCH N3 46 D3
Links View Cl STAN HA7 43 G2
Linksview Ct HPTN * TW12 155 J6
Links View Rd CROY/NA CR0 213 J1
HPTN TW12 173 H1
Links Wy BECK BR3 198 D3
NTHWD HA6 40 A4
Linksway HDN NW4 46 B5
NTHWD HA6 40 B4
Links Yd WCHPL E1 13 K1
The Linkway BAR EN5 32 E1
BELMT SM2 209 G6
Link Wy HAYES BR2 200 D4
RCHPK/HAM TW10 156 C4
Linkway BCTR RM8 91 J2
FSBYPK N4 67 J4
PIN HA5 41 H4
RYNPK SW20 176 E6
Linkwood Wk CAMTN NW1 84 D5
Linley Crs ROMW/RG RM7 56 D6
Linley Rd TOTM N17 50 A5
Linnell Cl GLDGN NW11 65 F3
Linnell Dr GLDGN NW11 65 F3
Linnell Rd CMBW SE5 143 F3
UED N18 50 C1
Linnet Cl BUSH WD23 28 C3
ED N9 37 F3
THMD SE28 109 J6
Linnet Ms BAL SW12 161 F2
Linnett Cl CHING E4 38 A6
Linom Rd CLAP SW4 141 K5
Linscott Rd CLPT E5 86 E2
Linsdell Rd BARK IG11 90 C6
Linsey St BERM/RHTH SE16 123 H4
Linslade Cl HSLWW TW4 134 D6
PIN HA5 41 F6
Linslade Rd ORP BR6 217 G4
Linstead St KIL/WHAMP NW6 82 E5
Linstead Wy WAND/EARL SW18 159 H2
Lintaine Cl FUL/PGN * SW6 119 H6
Linthorpe Av ALP/SUD HA0 79 J4
Linthorpe Rd EBAR EN4 21 J4
STNW/STAM N16 68 A4
Linton Cl CAR SM5 194 E4
CHARL SE7 126 B5
WELL DA16 148 B2
Linton Ct ROM RM1 57 G5
Linton Gdns EHAM E6 107 J5
Linton Gv WNWD SE27 180 C1
Linton Rd BARK IG11 90 C5
Linton St IS N1 6 D1
Lintott Ct STWL/WRAY TW19 152 A1
Linver Rd FUL/PGN SW6 139 J3
Linwood Cl CMBW SE5 143 G3
Linwood Crs EN EN1 24 C2
Linzee Rd CEND/HSY/T N8 66 E1
Lion Av TWK TW1 156 A3
Lion Cl BROCKY SE4 164 D1
Lionel Gdns ELTH/MOT SE9 146 C6
Lionel Ms NKENS * W10 100 C4
Lionel Rd ELTH/MOT SE9 146 C6
Lionel Rd North BTFD TW8 117 F3
Lionel Rd South BTFD TW8 117 G5
Lion Gate Gdns RCH/KEW TW9 137 G4
Lion Mills BETH * E2 104 C1
Lion Park Av CHSGTN KT9 206 C2
Lion Rd BXLYHS DA6 149 F5
CROY/NA CR0 196 D2
ED N9 36 C4
EHAM E6 107 K4
WHTN TW2 156 A3
Lions Cl ELTH/MOT SE9 166 B5
Lion Wy BTFD TW8 136 E1
Lion Wharf Rd ISLW TW7 136 C4
Liphook Cl HCH RM12 93 H2
Liphook Crs FSTH SE23 163 K2
Liphook Rd OXHEY WD19 27 H6
Lisbon Av WHTN TW2 155 H4
Lisbon Cl WALTH E17 51 H5
Lisburne Rd HAMP NW3 83 K2
Lisford St PECK SE15 143 G2
Lisgar Ter WKENS W14 119 J4
Liskeard Gdns BKHTH/KID SE3 145 K2
Lisle Cl TOOT SW17 161 G6
Lisle St SOHO/SHAV W1D 10 D5
Lismore WIM/MER * SW19 177 J1
Lismore Circ HAMP NW3 83 K3
Lismore Cl ISLW TW7 136 B3
Lismore Rd SAND/SEL CR2 212 A4
TOTM N17 49 K6
Lismore Wk IS N1 85 J4
Lissant Cl SURB KT6 190 D4
Lissenden Gdns KTTN NW5 84 A2
Lisson Gv STJWD NW8 2 B6
Lisson St STJWD NW8 8 C1
Lister Cl ACT W3 99 F4
WIM/MER SW19 178 D4
Lister Gdns UED N18 49 J1
Lister Ms HOLWY N7 85 F2
Lister Rd WAN E11 70 C5
Liston Rd CLAP SW4 141 H4
TOTM N17 50 C4
Liston Wy WFD IG8 53 G3
Listowel Cl BRXN/ST SW9 142 B1
Listowel Rd DAGE RM10 92 C1
Listria Pk STNW/STAM N16 68 A6
Litchfield Av MRDN SM4 193 J4
SRTFD * E15 88 C4
Litchfield Gdns WLSDN NW10 81 J4
Litchfield Rd SUT SM1 209 G2
Litchfield Wy GLDGN NW11 65 G2
Lithgow's Rd HTHAIR TW6 133 H5
Lithos Rd HAMP NW3 83 F4
Little Acre BECK BR3 182 D6
Little Albany St CAMTN NW1 3 K6
Little Argyll St CONDST * W1S 10 A4
Little Benty WDR/YW UB7 112 A5
Little Birches BFN/LL DA15 167 K4
The Little Boltons WBPTN SW10 120 A5
Little Bornes DUL SE21 163 F6
Little Britain STBT EC1A 12 C2
Littlebrook Cl CROY/NA CR0 198 A3
Littlebrook Manor Wy
DART DA1 151 K6
Littlebury Rd CLAP * SW4 141 J4
Little Bury St ED N9 36 A2
Little Cedars NFNCH/WDSP N12 33 G6
Little Chester St KTBR SW1X 15 J4
Little Cloisters WEST SW1P 16 E4
Littlecombe Cl PUT/ROE * SW15 159 G1
Littlecote Cl WIM/MER SW19 159 G2
Littlecote Pl PIN HA5 41 J4
Little Ct WWKM BR4 199 H6
Littlecroft ELTH/MOT SE9 147 F4
Littledale ABYW SE2 128 B6
Little Deans Yd WEST SW1P 16 E4
Little Dimocks BAL SW12 161 G4
Little Dorrit Ct STHWK SE1 18 D2
Little Ealing La EA W5 116 D4
Little Edward St CAMTN * NW1 3 K4
Little Elms HYS/HAR UB3 133 G1
Little Essex St TPL/STR * WC2R 11 J5
Little Ferry Rd TWK * TW1 156 C3
Littlefield Cl ARCH N19 84 C2
KUT KT1 175 F5
Littlefield Rd EDGE HA8 44 E3
Little Friday Rd CHING E4 38 C4
Little Gearies BARK/HLT IG6 72 B1
Little George St WEST SW1P 16 E3
Little Green St KTTN * NW5 84 B2
Littlegrove EBAR EN4 33 J1
Little Heath CHARL SE7 126 D6
CHDH RM6 73 H1
Little Heath Rd BXLYHN DA7 149 G2
Littleheath Rd SAND/SEL CR2 212 D6
Little Ilford La MNPK E12 89 K2
Littlejohn Rd HNWL W7 97 F5
STMC/STPC BR5 202 B3
Little Marlborough St
REGST * W1B 10 A4
Littlemead ESH/CLAY KT10 204 D2
Littlemede ELTH/MOT SE9 166 E5
Littlemoor Rd IL IG1 90 D1
Littlemore Rd ABYW SE2 128 B2
Little Moss La PIN HA5 41 J5
Little Newport St
LSQ/SEVD WC2H 10 D5
Little New St FLST/FETLN EC4A 11 K3
Little Orchard Cl PIN * HA5 41 J5
Little Oxhey La OXHEY WD19 41 J1
Little Park Dr FELT TW13 154 C4
Little Park Gdns ENC/FH EN2 23 K4
Little Pluckett's Wy BKHH IG9 39 H3
Little Portland St REGST W1B 9 K3
Little Potters BUSH WD23 28 D2
Little Queens Rd TEDD TW11 174 A2
Little Queen St DART DA1 171 J2
Little Redlands BMLY BR1 184 D5
Little Rd HYS/HAR UB3 113 J2
Little Rownings FSTH SE23 163 J4
Littlers Cl WIM/MER SW19 178 C4
Little Russell St
NOXST/BSQ WC1A 10 E2
Little St James's St WHALL SW1A 16 A1

Little St Leonards
MORT/ESHN SW14 137 K4
Little Smith St WEST SW1P 16 D4
Littlestone Cl BECK BR3 182 D2
Little Strd CDALE/KGS NW9 45 H5
Little Stream Cl NTHWD HA6 40 C1
Little Thrift STMC/STPC BR5 201 H1
Little Titchfield St GTPST W1W 10 A2
Littleton Av CHING E4 38 D3
Littleton Crs HRW HA1 61 F6
Littleton Rd HRW HA1 61 F6
Littleton St WAND/EARL SW18 160 B4
Little Trinity La BLKFR EC4V 12 D5
Little Turnstile HHOL WC1V 11 G2
Littlewood LEW SE13 145 F6
Little Wood Cl STMC/STPC BR5 186 B4
Littlewood Cl WEA W13 116 C3
Littleworth Av ESH/CLAY KT10 204 D3
Littleworth Common Rd
ESH/CLAY KT10 204 D1
Littleworth La ESH/CLAY KT10 204 D2
Littleworth Pl ESH/CLAY KT10 204 D2
Littleworth Rd ESH/CLAY KT10 204 D3
Livermere Rd HACK E8 86 B6
Liverpool Gv WALW SE17 122 E5
Liverpool Rd CAN/RD E16 106 C4
EA W5 116 E2
IS N1 85 G5
KUTN/CMB KT2 175 H3
LEY E10 70 A3
THHTH CR7 180 D6
Liverpool St LVPST EC2M 13 G2
Livesey Cl KUT KT1 175 G6
Livesey Pl PECK SE15 123 H6
Livingstone Rd BTSEA SW11 140 C4
HSLW TW3 135 H5
PLMGR N13 48 E2
SRTFD E15 88 A6
STHL UB1 95 H6
THHTH CR7 180 E5
WALTH E17 69 K3
Lizard St FSBYE EC1V 6 D5
Lizban St BKHTH/KID SE3 146 A1
Llanelly Rd CRICK NW2 64 D6
Llanover Rd WBLY HA9 79 K1
WOOL/PLUM SE18 147 F1
Llanthony Rd MRDN SM4 194 C3
Llanvanor Rd CRICK NW2 64 D6
Llewellyn St BERM/RHTH SE16 123 H2
Lloyd Av STRHM/NOR SW16 179 K4
Lloyd Baker St FSBYW WC1X 5 J5
Lloyd Ct PIN HA5 59 H2
Lloyd Ms PEND EN3 25 J1
Lloyd Park Av CROY/NA CR0 212 B2
Lloyd Rd DAGW RM9 92 B4
EHAM E6 89 K6
WALTH E17 69 F1
WPK KT4 208 A1
Lloyd's Av TWRH EC3N 13 H4
Lloyd's Pl BKHTH/KID * SE3 145 H3
Lloyd Sq FSBYW WC1X 5 J5
Lloyd's Rw CLKNW EC1R 5 K5
Lloyd St FSBYW WC1X 5 J4
Lloyds Wy BECK BR3 198 B2
Lloyd Thomas Ct WDGN * N22 49 F3
Lloyd Vls BROCKY SE4 144 D3
Loampit Hl LEW SE13 144 D3
Loampit V LEW SE13 144 E4
Loanda Cl HACK E8 86 B6
Loats Rd BRXS/STRHM SW2 161 K1
Locarno Rd ACT W3 117 K1
GFD/PVL UB6 96 C3
Lochaber Rd LEW SE13 145 H5
Lochaline St HMSMTH W6 119 F6
Lochan Cl YEAD UB4 95 J3
Lochinvar St BAL SW12 161 G2
Lochmere Cl ERITH DA8 129 J6
Lochnagar St POP/IOD E14 106 A4
Lock Cha LEW SE13 145 H4
Lock Cl NWDGN * UB2 115 H2
Locke Cl RAIN RM13 93 H4
Lockesley Dr STMC/STPC BR5 202 A3
Lockesley Sq SURB * KT6 190 E3
Locket Rd KTN/HRWW/W HA3 43 F5
Lockfield Av PEND EN3 25 G3
Lockgate Cl HOM E9 87 H3
Lockhart Cl HOLWY N7 85 F4
Lockhart St BOW E3 105 H3
Lockhurst St CLPT E5 87 F2
Lockington Rd VX/NE SW8 141 G2
Lockmead Rd LEW SE13 145 F4
SEVS/STOTM N15 68 C3
Lock Rd RCHPK/HAM TW10 156 D6
Lock's La MTCM CR4 179 F4
Locksley Est POP/IOD E14 105 H5
Locksley St POP/IOD E14 105 H4
Locksmeade Rd
RCHPK/HAM TW10 156 C6
Lockwood Cl SYD SE26 164 A6
Lockwood Sq
BERM/RHTH SE16 123 J3
Lockwood Wy CHSGTN KT9 206 C3
WALTH E17 51 F5
Lockyer St STHWK SE1 19 F3
Locomotive Dr
EBED/NFELT TW14 153 K3
Locton Gn BOW * E3 87 H6
Loddiges Rd HOM E9 86 E5
Loder St PECK SE15 143 K1
The Lodge SHB * W12 119 G2
Lodge Av CROY/NA CR0 211 F1
DAGW RM9 91 H6
DART DA1 171 F1
GPK RM2 75 J2
KTN/HRWW/W HA3 62 A1
Lodge Cl EDGE * HA8 44 B2
ISLW TW7 136 C2
ORP BR6 202 C5
UED N18 49 J1
WLGTN SM6 195 F5
Lodge Ct ALP/SUD * HA0 80 A3
Lodge Crs ORP BR6 202 C5
Lodge Dr PLMGR N13 35 G6
Lodge Gdns BECK BR3 198 C2
Lodge Hl REDBR IG4 71 J1
WELL DA16 148 C1
Lodgehill Park Cl
RYLN/HDSTN HA2 60 B6
Lodge La BXLY DA5 168 E1
CROY/NA CR0 213 K5
CRW RM5 56 C3
NFNCH/WDSP N12 47 G1
Lodge Mansions Pde
PLMGR * N13 35 G6
Lodge Ms HBRY * N5 85 J2
Lodge Pl SUT SM1 209 F3
Lodge Rd BMLY BR1 184 B3
CROY/NA CR0 196 C3
HDN NW4 64 A1
STJWD NW8 2 B5
SUT SM1 209 F3
WLGTN SM6 210 B3
Lodge Vls WFD IG8 52 D3
Lodge Wy ASHF TW15 152 B4
Lodore Gdns CDALE/KGS NW9 63 G2
Lodore St POP/IOD E14 106 A5
Lofthouse Pl CHSGTN KT9 205 J4
Loftie St BERM/RHTH SE16 123 H2
Lofting Rd IS N1 85 G5
Loftus Rd SHB W12 118 E1
Loftus Vls SHB * W12 118 E1
Logan Cl HSLWW TW4 134 E4
PEND EN3 25 F2
Logan Ms KENS W8 119 K4
ROM RM1 75 G2
Logan Pl ECT SW5 119 K4
Logan Rd ED N9 36 D4
WBLY HA9 62 A6
The Logans BAR * EN5 20 B4
Logs Hl CHST BR7 184 D4
Logs Hill Cl CHST BR7 184 D4
Lolesworth Cl WCHPL * E1 13 K2
Lollard St LBTH SE11 17 H6
Loman St STHWK SE1 18 B2
Lomas Cl CROY/NA CR0 214 A5
Lomas St WCHPL E1 104 C4
Lombard Av GDMY/SEVK IG3 72 E5
PEND EN3 24 E2
Lombard Rd BTSEA SW11 140 C3
FBAR/BDGN N11 48 B1
WIM/MER SW19 178 A5
Lombard St BANK EC3V 13 F4
Lombard Vls FBAR/BDGN * N11 48 B1
Lombard Wall CHARL SE7 126 A3
Lombardy Pl BAY/PAD W2 101 F6
Lomond Cl ALP/SUD HA0 80 B5
SEVS/STOTM N15 68 A1
Lomond Gdns SAND/SEL CR2 213 G5
Lomond Gv CMBW SE5 142 E1
Loncroft Rd CMBW SE5 123 F6
Londesborough Rd
STNW/STAM N16 86 A2
London Br CANST EC4R 13 F6
London Bridge Wk STHWK * SE1 13 F7
Londonderry Pde ERITH * DA8 150 A1
London Flds HACK * E8 86 D5
London Fields East Side
HACK E8 86 D5
London Fields West Side
HACK E8 86 C5
London La BMLY BR1 183 K3
HACK E8 86 D5
London Loop BORE WD6 30 D1
CROY/NA CR0 213 F1
ENC/FH EN2 23 J1
MLHL NW7 45 J1
SAND/SEL CR2 213 F6
WWKM BR4 214 B1
London Ms BAY/PAD W2 8 B4
London Rd BARK IG11 90 B5
BMLY BR1 183 J3
BUSH WD23 27 J1
CHDH RM6 74 C3
CHEAM SM3 193 H6
CROY/NA CR0 196 C5
DART DA1 150 A6
EN EN1 23 K5
EW KT17 207 H6
FSTH SE23 163 K3
HRW HA1 60 E6
ISLW TW7 135 K3
KUT KT1 175 F5
MRDN SM4 193 K2
MTCM CR4 178 E4
MTCM CR4 194 D1
MTCM CR4 195 F4
PLSTW E13 106 E1
ROMW/RG RM7 74 E3
SOCK/AV RM15 131 J2
STAN HA7 43 J1
STHWK SE1 18 A4
STRHM/NOR SW16 180 A5
STWL/WRAY TW19 152 A4
SWLY BR8 187 K5
THHTH CR7 196 B3
TWK TW1 156 B3
WBLY HA9 80 A3
WLGTN SM6 195 G6
London Stile CHSWK W4 117 H5
London St BAY/PAD W2 8 A4
FENCHST * EC3M 13 H5
London Ter BETH * E2 104 C1
London Wall BARB EC2Y 12 E2
London Wall Buildings
LVPST EC2M 13 F2
Lonesome Wy MTCM CR4 179 G4
Long Acre COVGDN WC2E 10 E4
STMC/STPC BR5 202 E6
Long Acre Ct WEA * W13 97 G4
Longacre Pl CAR * SM5 210 A4
Longacre Rd WALTH E17 52 B4
Longbeach Rd BTSEA SW11 140 E4
Longboat Rw STHL UB1 95 K5
Longbridge Rd BARK IG11 90 D4
BCTR RM8 91 G2
Longbridge Wy LEW SE13 145 F6
Longbury Cl STMC/STPC BR5 186 C6
Longbury Dr STMC/STPC BR5 186 C6
Longcliffe Pth OXHEY WD19 26 E5
Long Ct PUR RM19 131 K4
Longcroft ELTH/MOT SE9 167 F5
Long Cft OXHEY WD19 27 F2
Longcrofte Rd EDGE HA8 43 K3
Long Deacon Rd CHING E4 38 C4
Longdon Wd HAYES BR2 215 J2
Longdown Rd CAT SE6 164 D6
Long Dr ACT W3 99 G5
GFD/PVL UB6 78 B6
RSLP HA4 77 G2
WDR/YW * UB7 112 B2
Long Elmes KTN/HRWW/W HA3 42 C4
Longfellow Rd BOW * E3 105 G2
WALTH E17 69 H3
WPK KT4 192 D5
Longfellow Wy STHWK * SE1 19 K7
Longfield BMLY BR1 183 J4
Long Fld CDALE/KGS NW9 45 G3
Longfield Av EA W5 97 J6
EMPK RM11 75 H4
MLHL NW7 45 J3
WALTH E17 69 G1
WBLY HA9 62 A5
WLGTN SM6 195 F5
Longfield Crs SYD SE26 163 K5
Longfield Dr MORT/ESHN SW14 137 J6
WIM/MER SW19 178 D4
Longfield Est STHWK SE1 19 K6
Longfield Rd EA W5 97 J5
Longfield St WAND/EARL SW18 159 K2
Longford Av EBED/NFELT TW14 153 H1
STHL UB1 96 A6
STWL/WRAY TW19 152 B3
Longford Cl FELT TW13 154 D5
HPTN TW12 155 F6
YEAD UB4 95 H6
Longford Ct HOR/WEW KT19 206 E2
HPTN TW12 173 G2
Longford Gdns SUT SM1 209 G1
YEAD UB4 95 H6
Longford Rd WHTN TW2 155 F3
Longford St CAMTN NW1 3 K6
Longford Wy
STWL/WRAY TW19 152 B3
Longhayes Av CHDH RM6 55 K6
Longheath Gdns CROY/NA CR0 197 K2
Longhedge St BTSEA SW11 141 F3
Longhill Rd CAT SE6 165 G4
Longhook Gdns NTHLT UB5 94 E1
Longhope Cl PECK SE15 123 F6
Longhurst Rd CROY/NA CR0 197 J3
LEW SE13 145 H6
Longland Dr TRDG/WHET N20 33 F5
Longlands Park Crs
BFN/LL DA15 167 K5
Longlands Rd BFN/LL DA15 167 K5
Long La BXLYHN DA7 149 F1
CROY/NA CR0 197 K3
FNCH N3 47 F4
STBT EC1A 12 B1
STHWK SE1 19 F3
STWL/WRAY TW19 152 C3
Longleat Rd EN EN1 24 A6
Longleat Wy EBED/NFELT TW14 153 F2
Longleigh La ABYW SE2 128 D6
Longley Av ALP/SUD HA0 80 B6
Longley Rd CROY/NA CR0 196 C4
HRW HA1 60 D2
TOOT SW17 178 D2
Long Leys CHING E4 51 K2
Longley St STHWK SE1 123 H4
Longley Wy CRICK NW2 82 A1
Long Mark Rd CAN/RD E16 107 H5
Long Md CDALE/KGS NW9 45 H4
Longmead CHST BR7 185 F5
Longmead Dr SCUP DA14 168 E4
Long Meadow HOLWY * N7 84 D4
Long Meadow Cl BECK BR3 199 F4
Longmeadow Rd BFN/LL DA15 167 K3
Longmead Rd HYS/HAR UB3 94 E6
THDIT KT7 189 K4
TOOT SW17 178 E1
Longmoore St PIM SW1V 16 A7
Longmore Av BAR EN5 33 G1
Longnor Rd WCHPL E1 105 F2
Long Pond Rd BKHTH/KID SE3 145 H2
Longport Cl BARK/HLT IG6 55 G2
Long Reach Rd BARK IG11 109 F3
Longreach Rd ERITH DA8 150 E1
Longridge La STHL UB1 96 B6
Longridge Rd ECT SW5 119 K4
Long Rd CLAP SW4 141 H5
Longshaw Rd CHING E4 38 B5
Longshore DEPT SE8 124 C4
Longstaff Crs
WAND/EARL SW18 159 K1
Longstaff Rd
WAND/EARL SW18 159 K1
Longstone Av WLSDN NW10 81 H5
Longstone Rd
STRHM/NOR SW16 179 G1
Long St BETH E2 7 J4
Longthornton Rd
STRHM/NOR SW16 179 H5
Longton Av SYD SE26 163 H6
Longton Gv SYD SE26 163 J6
Longview Wy CRW RM5 57 F4
Longville Rd LBTH SE11 18 A6
Long Wk NWMAL KT3 175 K6
STHWK SE1 19 H4
Longwalk Rd STKPK UB11 112 E1
Longwood Ct WPK KT4 192 D6
Longwood Dr PUT/ROE SW15 158 D1
Longwood Gdns CLAY IG5 71 K1
Longworth Cl THMD SE28 109 K5
Long Yd BMSBY WC1N 5 G7
The Loning CDALE/KGS NW9 63 H1
PEND EN3 24 E1
Lonsdale Av EHAM E6 107 H3
ROMW/RG RM7 74 E3
WBLY HA9 80 A3
Lonsdale Cl EHAM E6 107 J3
ELTH/MOT SE9 166 C5
UX/CGN UB8 94 A5
Lonsdale Crs GNTH/NBYPK IG2 72 B3
Lonsdale Dr ENC/FH EN2 22 D5
Lonsdale Dr North ENC/FH EN2 22 E6
Lonsdale Gdns
STRHM/NOR SW16 196 A1
Lonsdale Ms RCH/KEW * TW9 137 H2
Lonsdale Pl IS N1 85 G5
Lonsdale Rd BARN SW13 138 C1
BXLYHN DA7 149 G3
CHSWK W4 118 C4
KIL/WHAMP NW6 100 D1
NTGHL W11 100 D5
NWDGN UB2 114 C3
SNWD SE25 197 J1
WAN E11 70 D4
Lonsdale Sq IS * N1 85 G5
Loobert Rd SEVS/STOTM N15 50 A6
Looe Gdns BARK/HLT IG6 54 B6
Loop Rd CHST BR7 185 G1
Lopen Rd UED N18 36 A6
Loraine Cl PEND EN3 24 E6
Loraine Cottages HOLWY * N7 85 F2
Loraine Rd CHSWK W4 117 J6
HOLWY N7 85 F2
Lord Av CLAY IG5 71 K1
Lord Chancellor Wk
KUTN/CMB KT2 175 K4
Lord Gdns CLAY IG5 71 J1
Lord Hills Rd BAY/PAD W2 101 F4
Lord Holland La BRXN/ST * SW9 142 B3
Lord Knyvett Cl
STWL/WRAY TW19 152 A1
Lord Knyvetts Ct
STWL/WRAY * TW19 152 B1
Lord Napier Pl HMSMTH W6 118 D5
Lord North St WEST SW1P 16 E5
Lord Roberts Ms
FUL/PGN * SW6 140 A1
Lords Cl DUL SE21 162 D4
FELT TW13 154 D4
Lordship Gv STNW/STAM N16 67 K6
Lordship La EDUL SE22 163 G1
WDGN N22 49 H4
Lordship Pk STNW/STAM N16 67 K6
Lordship Park Ms
STNW/STAM N16 67 J6
Lordship Pl CHEL SW3 120 D6
Lordship Rd NTHLT UB5 77 J5
STNW/STAM N16 67 K6
Lordship Ter STNW/STAM N16 67 K6
Lordsmead Rd TOTM N17 50 A4
Lord St CAN/RD E16 126 D1
Lords Vw STJWD NW8 2 C5
Lord Warwick St
WOOL/PLUM SE18 126 E3
Lorenzo St FSBYW WC1X 5 G4
Loretto Gdns KTN/HRWW/W HA3 62 A1
Lorian Cl NFNCH/WDSP N12 33 F6
Loring Rd ISLW TW7 136 A3
TRDG/WHET N20 33 J4
Loris Rd HMSMTH W6 119 F3
Lorn Ct BRXN/ST SW9 142 B3
Lorne Av CROY/NA CR0 198 A4
Lorne Cl STJWD NW8 2 D5
Lorne Gdns CROY/NA CR0 198 B4
NTGHL W11 119 G2
WAN E11 71 G1
Lorne Rd FSBYPK N4 67 F5
FSTGT E7 89 F2
KTN/HRWW/W HA3 43 F5
RCHPK/HAM TW10 137 G6
WALTH E17 69 J2
Lorne Ter FNCH * N3 46 D5
Lorn Rd BRXN/ST SW9 142 A3
Lorraine Pk KTN/HRWW/W HA3 42 E3
Lorrimore Rd WALW SE17 122 C6
Lorrimore Sq WALW SE17 122 C6
Loseberry Rd ESH/CLAY KT10 204 D3
Lothair Rd EA W5 116 E2
Lothair Rd North FSBYPK N4 67 H3
Lothair Rd South FSBYPK N4 67 G4
Lothbury LOTH EC2R 12 E3
Lothian Av YEAD UB4 95 F4
Lothian Cl ALP/SUD HA0 79 G2
Lothian Rd BRXN/ST SW9 142 C2
Lothrop St NKENS W10 100 C2
Lots Rd WBPTN SW10 140 B1
Loubet St TOOT SW17 178 E2
Loudoun Av GNTH/NBYPK IG2 72 B2
Loudoun Rd STJWD NW8 83 G6
Loughborough Pk
BRXN/ST SW9 142 C5
Loughborough Rd
BRXN/ST SW9 142 C3
Loughborough St LBTH SE11 122 A5
Lough Rd HOLWY N7 85 F4
Loughton Wy BKHH IG9 39 H3
Louisa Cl HOM E9 86 E5
Louisa St WCHPL E1 105 F4
Louis Cl CHST BR7 166 E6
Louise Bennett Cl HNHL * SE24 142 C5
Louise Gdns RAIN RM13 111 G2
Louise Rd SRTFD E15 88 C4
Louisville Rd TOOT SW17 161 F5
Louvaine Rd BTSEA SW11 140 C5
Lovage Ap EHAM E6 107 J4
Lovat Cl CRICK NW2 81 H1
Lovat La FENCHST EC3M 13 G5
Lovatt Cl EDGE HA8 44 D2
Loveday Rd WEA W13 116 C1
Lovegrove St STHWK SE1 123 H5
Lovegrove Wk POP/IOD E14 125 F1
Lovekyn Cl KUTN/CMB KT2 175 F5
Lovelace Av HAYES BR2 201 F3
Lovelace Gdns BARK IG11 91 G2
SURB KT6 190 E4
Lovelace Gn ELTH/MOT SE9 146 E4
Lovelace Rd DUL SE21 162 D4
EBAR EN4 33 J2
SURB KT6 190 D4
Lovelace Vls THDIT * KT7 190 C4
Love La BXLY DA5 169 H1
CHEAM SM3 208 C4
CITYW EC2V 12 D3
MRDN SM4 193 K4
MTCM CR4 178 D6
PIN HA5 41 J6
SNWD SE25 181 J6
SURB KT6 190 E6
TOTM N17 50 B3
WFD IG8 53 K2
WOOL/PLUM SE18 127 F4
Lovel Av WELL DA16 148 B3
Lovelinch Cl PECK SE15 123 K6
Lovell Pl BERM/RHTH SE16 124 B3
Lovell Rd RCHPK/HAM TW10 156 D5
STHL UB1 96 B5
Lovell Wk RAIN RM13 93 J4
Loveridge Ms KIL/WHAMP NW6 82 D4
Loveridge Rd KIL/WHAMP NW6 82 D4
Lovett Dr CAR SM5 194 B4
Lovett Wy WLSDN NW10 80 E3
Love Wk CMBW SE5 142 E3
Lovibonds Av ORP BR6 216 B1
Lowbrook Rd IL IG1 90 B2
Lowden Rd ED N9 36 D3
HNHL SE24 142 C5
STHL UB1 95 J6
The Lowe CHIG IG7 55 G1
Lowe Av CAN/RD E16 106 E4
Lowe Cl CHIG IG7 55 G1
Lowell St POP/IOD E14 105 G5
Lowen Rd RAIN RM13 111 F1
Lower Addiscombe Rd
CROY/NA CR0 196 E5
Lower Addison Gdns
WKENS W14 119 H2
Lower Bedfords Rd ROM RM1 57 J2
Lower Belgrave St BGVA SW1W 15 J5
Lower Boston Rd HNWL W7 115 K1
Lower Broad St DAGE RM10 92 C6
Lower Camden CHST BR7 184 E4
Lower Church St
CROY/NA * CR0 196 C6
Lower Clapton Rd CLPT E5 86 D2
Lower Clarendon Wk
NTGHL W11 100 C5
Lower Common South
PUT/ROE SW15 138 E4
Lower Coombe St
CROY/NA CR0 211 J2
Lower Downs Rd RYNPK SW20 177 G4
Lower Gravel Rd HAYES BR2 200 D5
Lower Green Gdns WPK KT4 192 D5
Lower Green Rd ESH/CLAY KT10 189 G6
Lower Gn West MTCM CR4 178 D6
Lower Grosvenor Pl KTBR SW1X 15 J4
Lower Grove Rd
RCHPK/HAM TW10 157 G1
Lower Hall La CHING E4 51 G1
Lower Hampton Rd SUN TW16 172 C5
Lower Ham Rd KUTN/CMB KT2 174 E2
Lower James St
SOHO/CST * W1F 10 B5
Lower John St SOHO/CST W1F 10 B5
Lower Kenwood Av
STHGT/OAK N14 22 E6
Lower Lea Crossing
POP/IOD E14 106 C6
Lower Maidstone Rd
FBAR/BDGN N11 48 C2
Lower Mardyke Av RAIN RM13 110 E1
Lower Marsh STHWK SE1 17 J3
Lower Marsh La KUT KT1 191 H1
Lower Merton Ri HAMP NW3 83 J5
Lower Morden La MRDN SM4 193 F3
Lower Mortlake Rd
RCH/KEW TW9 137 F5
Lower Paddock Rd OXHEY WD19 27 J1
Lower Park Rd BELV DA17 129 H3
FBAR/BDGN N11 48 C1
Lower Queen's Rd BKHH IG9 39 J4
Lower Richmond Rd
PUT/ROE SW15 139 F4
RCH/KEW TW9 137 H4
Lower Rd BELV DA17 129 K3
BERM/RHTH SE16 123 K3
RYLN/HDSTN HA2 60 D6
STMC/STPC BR5 202 C3
SUT SM1 209 H3
Lower Sand Hills SURB KT6 190 D4
Lower Sloane St BGVA SW1W 15 F7
Lower Station Rd DART DA1 170 B1
Lower Strd CDALE/KGS NW9 45 H5
Lower Sunbury Rd HPTN TW12 172 E5
Lower Tail OXHEY WD19 27 J5
Lower Teddington Rd KUT KT1 174 E4
Lower Ter HAMP NW3 83 G1
Lower Thames St MON EC3R 13 H6
Lower Tub BUSH WD23 28 D2
Lower Wood Rd ESH/CLAY KT10 205 H4
Loweswater Cl WBLY HA9 61 K6
Lowfield Rd ACT W3 98 E5
KIL/WHAMP NW6 82 E5
Lowfield St DART DA1 171 H2
Low Hall Cl CHING E4 37 J2
Low Hall La WALTH E17 69 G3
Lowick Rd HRW HA1 60 E1
Lowland Gdns ROMW/RG RM7 74 D3
Lowlands Rd HRW HA1 60 E4
PIN HA5 59 G4
STWL/WRAY TW19 132 A6
Lowman Rd HOLWY N7 85 F2
Lowndes Cl KTBR SW1X 15 H5
Lowndes Ct REGST W1B 10 A4
Lowndes Pl KTBR * SW1X 15 G5
Lowndes Sq KTBR SW1X 15 F3
Lowndes St KTBR SW1X 15 F4
Lowood St WCHPL E1 104 D6
Lowry Crs MTCM CR4 178 D5
Lowry Rd BCTR RM8 91 H3
Lowshoe La ROMW/RG RM7 56 D4
Lowson Gv OXHEY WD19 27 J2
Lowswood Cl NTHWD HA6 40 A4
Lowther Dr ENC/FH EN2 22 E5
Lowther Hl FSTH SE23 164 B2
Lowther Man BARN * SW13 138 D2
Lowther Rd BARN SW13 138 C2
HOLWY * N7 85 G3
KUTN/CMB KT2 175 G4
STAN HA7 44 B6
WALTH E17 51 G5
Lowth Rd CMBW SE5 142 D3
Loxford Av EHAM E6 107 H1
Loxford La IL IG1 90 C3
Loxford Rd BARK IG11 90 B4
Loxham Rd CHING E4 51 K3
Loxham St STPAN * WC1H 5 F5
Loxley Cl SYD SE26 182 A1
Loxley Rd HPTN TW12 154 E6
WAND/EARL SW18 160 C3
Loxton Rd FSTH SE23 164 A3
Loxwood Cl EBED/NFELT TW14 153 G3
STMC/STPC BR5 202 E6
Loxwood Rd TOTM N17 50 A6
Lubbock Rd CHST BR7 184 E3
Lubbock St NWCR SE14 143 K1
Lucan Pl CHEL SW3 14 C7
Lucan Rd BAR EN5 20 C4
Lucas Av PLSTW E13 89 F6
RYLN/HDSTN HA2 60 A6
Lucas Gdns EFNCH N2 47 G5
Lucas Rd PGE/AN SE20 181 K2
Lucas Sq GLDGN NW11 64 E3
Lucas St DEPT SE8 144 D3
Lucerne Cl PLMGR N13 34 E5
Lucerne Gv WALTH E17 70 B1
Lucerne Ms KENS W8 119 K1
Lucerne Rd HBRY N5 85 H2
ORP BR6 202 A5
THHTH CR7 196 C2
Lucey Rd BERM/RHTH SE16 123 H3
Lucey Wy BERM/RHTH SE16 123 H3
Lucien Rd TOOT SW17 161 F6
WAND/EARL SW18 160 A4
Lucknow St WOOL/PLUM SE18 147 K1
Lucorn Cl LEE/GVPK SE12 165 J1
Luctons Av BKHH IG9 39 G3
Luddesdon Rd ERITH DA8 149 H1
Ludford Cl CDALE/KGS NW9 45 G5
CROY/NA CR0 211 H2
Ludgate Broadway
BLKFR * EC4V 12 B4
Ludgate Circ STP * EC4M 12 A4
Ludgate Hl STP EC4M 12 A4
Ludgate Sq BLKFR * EC4V 12 B4
Ludham Cl THMD SE28 109 J5
WFD IG8 54 C4
Ludlow Cl HAYES BR2 183 K6
RYLN/HDSTN HA2 77 K2
Ludlow Md OXHEY WD19 27 F5
Ludlow Rd EA W5 97 J3
FELT TW13 153 K5
Ludlow St FSBYE * EC1V 6 C6
Ludlow Wy EFNCH N2 65 G1
Ludovick Wk PUT/ROE SW15 138 B5
Luffield Rd ABYW SE2 128 C3
Luffman Rd LEE/GVPK SE12 166 A5
Lugard Rd PECK SE15 143 J3
Lugg Ap MNPK E12 90 A1
Luke St SDTCH EC2A 7 G6
Lukin Crs CHING E4 38 B5

Lukin St WCHPL E1 104 E6
Lullingstone Cl STMC/STPC BR5 186 C3
Lullingstone Crs
STMC/STPC BR5 186 B3
Lullingstone La LEW SE13 165 G1
Lullingstone Rd BELV DA17 129 G6
Lullington Garth BMLY * BR1 183 H3
MLHL NW7 46 D1
Lullington Rd DAGW RM9 92 A5
PGE/AN SE20 181 H3
Lulworth Av HEST TW5 135 G2
WBLY HA9 61 J4
Lulworth Cl RYLN/HDSTN HA2 77 K1
Lulworth Crs MTCM CR4 178 D5
Lulworth Dr CRW RM5 56 D1
PIN HA5 59 H4
Lulworth Gdns RYLN/HDSTN HA2 59 J6
Lulworth Rd ELTH/MOT SE9 166 D4
PECK * SE15 143 J3
WELL DA16 148 A3
Lulworth Waye YEAD UB4 95 F5
Lumen Rd WBLY * HA9 61 K6
Lumley Cl BELV DA17 129 H6
Lumley Flats BGVA * SW1W 121 F5
Lumley Gdns CHEAM SM3 208 C3
Lumley Rd CHEAM SM3 208 C4
Lumley St MYFR/PKLN W1K 9 H4
Luna Rd THHTH CR7 180 D6
Lundin Wk OXHEY * WD19 27 H6
Lundy Dr HYS/HAR UB3 113 H4
Lundy Wk IS * N1 85 J4
Lunham Rd NRWD SE19 181 F2
Lupin Cl BRXS/STRHM SW2 162 C4
CROY/NA CR0 198 A5
ROMW/RG RM7 75 F6
WDR/YW UB7 112 A5
Lupton Cl LEE/GVPK SE12 166 A6
Lupton St KTTN NW5 84 C2
Lupus St PIM SW1V 121 G5
Lurgan Av HMSMTH W6 119 G6
Lurline Gdns BTSEA SW11 141 F2
Luscombe Wy VX/NE SW8 141 K1
Lushington Rd CAT SE6 182 E1
WLSDN NW10 99 K1
Lushington Ter HACK E8 86 C3
Luther Cl EDGE HA8 30 E4
Luther King Cl WALTH E17 69 G3
Luton Pl GNWCH SE10 145 F1
Luton Rd PLSTW E13 106 E3
SCUP DA14 168 D5
WALTH E17 51 G6
Luton St STJWD NW8 2 B7
Luttrell Av PUT/ROE SW15 138 E6
Lutwyche Rd FSTH SE23 164 C4
Luxborough La CHIG IG7 39 K6
Luxborough St MHST W1U 3 G7
Luxemburg Gdns HMSMTH W6 119 G4
Luxfield Rd ELTH/MOT SE9 166 D3
Luxford St BERM/RHTH SE16 124 A4
Luxmore St BROCKY SE4 144 C2
Luxor St CMBW SE5 142 C3
Lyall Av DUL SE21 163 F6
Lyall Ms KTBR SW1X 15 G5
Lyall Ms West KTBR * SW1X 15 G5
Lyall St KTBR SW1X 15 G5
Lyal Rd BOW E3 105 G1
Lycett Pl SHB W12 118 D2
Lych Gate Rd ORP BR6 202 B5
Lych Gate Wk HYS/HAR UB3 94 D6
Lyconby Gdns CROY/NA CR0 198 B4
Lydd Cl BFN/LL DA15 167 K5
Lydden Gv WAND/EARL SW18 160 A2
Lydden Rd WAND/EARL SW18 160 A2
Lydd Rd BXLYHN DA7 149 G1
Lydeard Rd EHAM E6 89 K5
Lydford Cl STNW/STAM N16 86 A3
Lydford Rd CRICK NW2 82 B4
MV/WKIL W9 100 D3
SEVS/STOTM N15 67 K2
Lydhurst Av BRXS/STRHM SW2 162 A4
Lydia Rd ERITH DA8 130 C6
Lydney Cl PECK SE15 143 F1
WIM/MER SW19 159 H4
Lydon Rd CLAP SW4 141 H4
Lydstep Rd CHST BR7 167 F6
Lyford Rd WAND/EARL SW18 160 C2
Lyford St WOOL/PLUM SE18 126 D4
Lygon Pl BGVA * SW1W 15 J5
Lyham Cl BRXS/STRHM SW2 161 K1
Lyham Rd BRXS/STRHM SW2 141 K6
Lyle Cl MTCM CR4 195 F4
Lyme Farm Rd LEE/GVPK SE12 145 K5
Lyme Gv HOM E9 86 E5
Lymer Av NRWD SE19 181 G1
Lyme Rd WELL DA16 148 C2
Lymescote Gdns SUT SM1 193 K6
Lyme St CAMTN NW1 84 C5
Lyme Ter CAMTN NW1 84 C5
Lyminge Cl SCUP DA14 168 A6
Lyminge Gdns
WAND/EARL SW18 160 D3
Lymington Av WDGN N22 49 G5
Lymington Cl
STRHM/NOR SW16 179 J5
Lymington Dr RSLP HA4 58 B6
Lymington Gdns
HOR/WEW KT19 207 H3
Lymington Rd BCTR RM8 73 K5
KIL/WHAMP * NW6 83 F4
Lyminster Cl YEAD UB4 95 J4
Lympstone Gdns PECK SE15 143 H1
Lynbridge Gdns PLMGR N13 35 H6
Lynbrook Cl PECK SE15 143 F1
RAIN RM13 111 F1
Lynchen Cl HEST TW5 133 K2
Lyncourt BKHTH/KID * SE3 145 G3
Lyncroft Av PIN HA5 59 H2
Lyncroft Gdns EW KT17 207 H6
HSLW TW3 135 H6
KIL/WHAMP NW6 82 E3
WEA W13 116 D2
Lyndale CRICK NW2 82 D2
ESH/CLAY * KT10 189 K4
Lyndale Av CRICK NW2 82 D1
Lyndale Cl BKHTH/KID SE3 125 J6
Lyndale Hampton Court Wy
ESH/CLAY KT10 189 K4
Lynden Wy SWLY BR8 187 K6
Lyndhurst Av BRYLDS KT5 191 J5
MLHL NW7 45 G2
NFNCH/WDSP N12 47 K2
PIN HA5 41 F4
STHL UB1 115 G1
STRHM/NOR SW16 179 J5
WHTN TW2 154 E3
Lyndhurst Cl BXLYHN DA7 149 J4
CROY/NA CR0 212 B1
ORP BR6 216 B2
WLSDN NW10 81 F1
Lyndhurst Ct BELMT * SM2 208 E5
Lyndhurst Dr LEY E10 70 A4
NWMAL KT3 192 B3
Lyndhurst Gdns BARK IG11 90 E4
EN EN1 24 A5
FNCH N3 46 C4
GNTH/NBYPK IG2 72 D3
HAMP NW3 83 H3
PIN HA5 41 F4
Lyndhurst Gv CMBW SE5 143 F3
Lyndhurst Leys HAYES * BR2 183 G5
Lyndhurst Prior SNWD * SE25 181 F6
Lyndhurst Rd BXLYHN DA7 149 J4
CHING E4 52 A3
GFD/PVL UB6 96 B3
HAMP NW3 83 H3
THHTH CR7 196 B1
UED N18 36 C6
WDGN N22 49 G2
Lyndhurst Sq PECK SE15 143 G2
Lyndhurst Ter HAMP NW3 83 H3
Lyndhurst Wy BELMT SM2 208 E6
PECK SE15 143 G2
Lyndon Av BFN/LL DA15 148 A6
PIN HA5 41 J2
WLGTN SM6 210 A1
Lyndon Rd BELV DA17 129 H4
Lyndon Yd TOOT SW17 160 A6
Lyne Crs WALTH E17 51 H4
Lyneham Wk CLPT * E5 87 G3
Lynette Av CLAP SW4 161 G1
Lynford Cl EDGE HA8 44 E4
Lynford Gdns EDGE HA8 30 D6
GDMY/SEVK IG3 73 F6
Lynford Ter ED * N9 36 B3
Lynhurst Crs HGDN/ICK UB10 76 A5
Lynhurst Rd HGDN/ICK UB10 76 A5
Lynmere Rd WELL DA16 148 C3
Lyn Ms STNW/STAM * N16 86 B2
Lynmouth Av EN EN1 36 B1
MRDN SM4 193 G4
Lynmouth Dr RSLP HA4 59 F6
Lynmouth Gdns GFD/PVL UB6 79 H6
HEST TW5 134 C2
Lynmouth Ri STMC/STPC BR5 202 C1
Lynmouth Rd EFNCH N2 47 K6
GFD/PVL UB6 79 H6
STNW/STAM N16 68 B5
WALTH E17 69 G3
Lynn Cl KTN/HRWW/W HA3 42 D5
Lynne Cl ORP * BR6 217 F4
Lynnett Rd BCTR RM8 73 K6
Lynne Wk ESH/CLAY KT10 204 C3
Lynne Wy NTHLT UB5 95 H1
WLSDN NW10 81 G4
Lynn Ms WAN E11 70 C6
Lynn Rd BAL SW12 161 G2
GNTH/NBYPK IG2 72 D4
WAN E11 70 C6
Lynn St ENC/FH EN2 23 K2
Lynscott Wy SAND/SEL CR2 211 H6
Lynstead Cl BMLY BR1 184 B5
Lynsted Cl BXLYHS DA6 149 J6
Lynsted Ct BECK BR3 182 B5
Lynsted Gdns ELTH/MOT SE9 146 C5
Lynton Av ACT W3 98 E5
CDALE/KGS NW9 63 H1
NFNCH/WDSP N12 33 H6
ROMW/RG RM7 56 D4
STMC/STPC BR5 202 C1
WEA W13 97 G5
Lynton Cl CHSGTN KT9 206 A2
ISLW TW7 136 A5
WLSDN NW10 81 G3
Lynton Crs GNTH/NBYPK IG2 72 B3
Lynton Est STHWK SE1 19 K7
Lynton Gdns EN EN1 36 A2
FBAR/BDGN N11 48 D2
Lynton Md TRDG/WHET N20 32 E5
Lynton Rd ACT W3 98 C6
CEND/HSY/T N8 66 D2
CHING E4 51 K1
CROY/NA CR0 196 B3
KIL/WHAMP NW6 82 D6
NWMAL KT3 192 A2
RYLN/HDSTN HA2 59 J6
STHWK SE1 19 K7
Lynton Ter ACT * W3 98 E5
Lynwood Cl CRW RM5 56 D2
RYLN/HDSTN HA2 77 J1
SWFD E18 53 G4
Lynwood Dr CRW RM5 56 D2
NTHWD HA6 40 C4
WPK KT4 192 D6
Lynwood Gdns CROY/NA CR0 211 F2
STHL UB1 95 K5
Lynwood Gv ORP BR6 201 K4
WCHMH N21 35 G3
Lynwood Rd EA W5 97 K2
ESH/CLAY KT10 190 A6
TOOT SW17 160 E5
Lynwood Ter WIM/MER * SW19 177 J4
Lyon Meade STAN HA7 43 J4
Lyon Park Av ALP/SUD HA0 80 A4
Lyon Rd HRW HA1 61 F3
ROM RM1 75 H4
WIM/MER SW19 178 B4
WOT/HER KT12 188 D6
Lyonsdown Av BAR EN5 33 G1
Lyonsdown Rd BAR EN5 21 G6
Lyons Pl STJWD NW8 2 A7
Lyon St IS N1 85 F5
Lyons Wk WKENS W14 119 H4
Lyon Wy GFD/PVL UB6 78 E6
Lyoth Rd STMC/STPC BR5 201 H6
Lyric Dr GFD/PVL UB6 96 B3
Lyric Ms SYD SE26 163 K6
Lyric Rd BARN SW13 138 C2
Lysander CDALE/KGS * NW9 45 H4
Lysander Gdns SURB KT6 191 G3
Lysander Gv ARCH N19 66 D5
Lysander Ms ARCH * N19 66 E5
Lysander Rd CROY/NA CR0 211 F4
RSLP HA4 58 B6
Lysander Wy ORP BR6 216 C1
Lysias Rd BAL SW12 161 F1
Lysia St FUL/PGN SW6 139 G1
Lysons Wk PUT/ROE * SW15 138 D6
Lytchet Rd BMLY BR1 183 K3
Lytchet Wy PEND EN3 24 E2
Lytchgate Cl SAND/SEL CR2 212 A5
Lytcott Dr E/WMO/HCT KT8 172 E6
Lytcott Gv EDUL SE22 143 G6
Lytham Av OXHEY WD19 41 H1
Lytham Cl THMD SE28 110 A5
Lytham Gv EA W5 98 A2
Lytham St WALW SE17 122 E5
Lyttelton Rd EFNCH N2 65 G2
LEY E10 87 K1
Lyttleton Cl HAMP NW3 83 J5
Lyttleton Rd CEND/HSY/T * N8 49 G6
Lytton Av PEND EN3 25 G1
PLMGR N13 35 G4
Lytton Cl EFNCH N2 65 H2
NTHLT UB5 77 K5
Lytton Gdns WLGTN SM6 210 D2
Lytton Gv PUT/ROE SW15 139 G6
Lytton Rd BAR EN5 21 G5
GPK RM2 75 K2
PIN HA5 41 J3
WAN E11 70 C4
Lyveden Rd BKHTH/KID SE3 146 A1
WIM/MER SW19 178 D2

M

Maberley Crs NRWD SE19 181 H3
Maberley Rd BECK BR3 182 A6
NRWD SE19 181 G4
Mabledon Pl CAMTN NW1 4 D5
Mablethorpe Rd FUL/PGN SW6 139 H1
Mabley St HOM E9 87 G3
Macaret Cl TRDG/WHET N20 33 F2
Macarthur Cl FSTGT E7 88 E4
Macarthur Ter CHARL * SE7 126 C6
Macaulay Av ESH/CLAY KT10 189 K6
Macaulay Rd CLAP SW4 141 G4
EHAM E6 107 H1
Macbean St WOOL/PLUM SE18 127 F3
Macbeth St HMSMTH W6 118 E5
Macclesfield Br STJWD NW8 2 D2
Macclesfield Rd FSBYE EC1V 6 C4
SNWD SE25 197 J2
Macclesfield St
SOHO/SHAV * W1D 10 D5
Macdonald Av DAGE RM10 92 D1
Macdonald Rd ARCH N19 66 C6
FBAR/BDGN N11 47 K1
FSTGT E7 88 E2
WALTH E17 52 A5
Macduff Rd BTSEA SW11 141 F2
Mace Cl WAP E1W 123 J1
Mace Gtwy CAN/RD E16 106 E6
Mace St BETH E2 105 F1
Macfarlane La ISLW TW7 116 A6
Macfarlane Rd SHB W12 119 F1
Mac Farren Pl CAMTN NW1 3 H7
Macgregor Rd CAN/RD E16 107 G4
Machell Rd PECK SE15 143 K4
Mackay Rd CLAP SW4 141 G4
Mackennal St STJWD NW8 2 D3
Mackenzie Cl SHB * W12 99 K6
Mackenzie Rd BECK BR3 182 A5
HOLWY N7 85 F4
Mackeson Rd HAMP * NW3 83 K2
Mackie Rd BRXS/STRHM SW2 162 B2
Mackintosh La HOM E9 87 F3
Macklin St HOL/ALD * WC2B 11 F3
Macks Rd BERM/RHTH SE16 123 H4
Mackworth St CAMTN NW1 4 A4
Maclean Rd FSTH SE23 164 B1
Macleod House
WOOL/PLUM SE18 146 D1
Macleod Rd STHGT/OAK N14 22 E6
Macleod St WALW SE17 122 D5
Maclise Rd WKENS W14 119 H3
Macoma Rd WOOL/PLUM SE18 127 J6
Macoma Ter WOOL/PLUM SE18 127 J6
Maconochies Rd POP/IOD * E14 124 E5
Macquarie Wy POP/IOD E14 124 E4
Macroom Rd MV/WKIL W9 100 D2
Mada Rd ORP BR6 216 B1
Maddams St BOW E3 105 K3
Maddison Cl TEDD TW11 174 A2
Maddocks Cl SCUP DA14 186 E2
Maddock Wy WALW SE17 122 C6
Maddox St MYFR/PKLN W1K 9 K5
Madeira Av BMLY BR1 183 H4
Madeira Gv WFD IG8 53 G2
Madeira Rd MTCM CR4 194 E1
PLMGR N13 35 H6
STRHM/NOR SW16 179 K1
WAN E11 70 B5
Madeley Rd EA W5 97 K6
Madeline Gv IL IG1 90 D3
Madeline Rd PGE/AN SE20 181 H3
Madge Gill Wy EHAM E6 89 J6
Madge Hl HNWL * W7 96 E6
Madinah Rd HACK E8 86 C4
Madison Crs WELL DA16 148 D1
Madison Gdns BXLYHN DA7 148 D1
Madras Pl HOLWY N7 85 G4
Madras Rd IL IG1 90 B2
Madrid Rd BARN SW13 138 D2
Madron St STHWK SE1 123 F5
Mafeking Av BTFD TW8 117 F6
EHAM E6 107 H1
GNTH/NBYPK IG2 72 D4
Mafeking Rd CAN/RD E16 106 D3
EN EN1 24 B4
TOTM N17 50 C5
Magazine Ga BAY/PAD * W2 8 D7
Magdala Av ARCH N19 66 C6
Magdala Rd ISLW TW7 136 B4
SAND/SEL CR2 211 K5
Magdalene Gdns EHAM E6 108 A3
Magdalen Rd
WAND/EARL SW18 160 B3
Magdalen St STHWK SE1 19 G1
Magdelan Gv ORP BR6 217 H2
Magee St LBTH SE11 122 B6
Magnaville Rd BUSH WD23 28 E2
Magnet Rd WBLY * HA9 61 K6
Magnin Cl HACK E8 86 C6
Magnolia Cl KUTN/CMB KT2 175 J2
LEY E10 69 J6
Magnolia Ct KTN/HRWW/W HA3 62 B4
Magnolia Gdns EDGE HA8 30 E6
Magnolia Pl CLAP * SW4 141 K6
EA * W5 97 K4
Magnolia Rd CHSWK W4 117 J6
Magnolia St WDR/YW UB7 112 A4
Magnolia Wy HOR/WEW KT19 206 E3
Magnolia Whf CHSWK * W4 117 J6
Magpie Cl CDALE/KGS NW9 45 G5
EN EN1 24 C2
FSTGT E7 88 D3
Magpie Hall Cl HAYES BR2 200 D3
Magpie Hall La HAYES BR2 200 D4
Magpie Hall Rd BUSH WD23 28 E4
Magpie Pl NWCR * SE14 124 B6
Magri Wk WCHPL E1 104 E4
Maguire Dr RCHPK/HAM TW10 156 D6
Maguire St STHWK SE1 19 K2
Mahlon Av RSLP HA4 77 F3
Mahogany Cl BERM/RHTH SE16 124 B1
Mahon Cl EN EN1 24 B2
Maida Av BAY/PAD W2 101 G4
CHING E4 37 K2
Maida Rd BELV DA17 129 H3
Maida V MV/WKIL W9 101 G2
STJWD NW8 2 A6
Maida Vale Rd DART DA1 170 D1
Maida Wy CHING E4 37 K2
Maiden Erlegh Av BXLY DA5 169 F3
Maiden La CAMTN NW1 84 D5
COVGDN WC2E 11 F6
DART DA1 150 D5
STHWK SE1 18 D1
Maiden Rd SRTFD E15 88 C5
Maidenstone Hl GNWCH SE10 145 F2
Maidstone Av CRW RM5 56 E5
Maidstone Buildings Ms
STHWK SE1 18 D1
Maidstone Rd FBAR/BDGN N11 48 D2
SCUP DA14 186 E2
Main Av EN EN1 24 B6
NTHWD HA6 26 A5
Main Barracks
WOOL/PLUM * SE18 126 E5
Main Dr GFD/PVL * UB6 97 G2
WBLY * HA9 79 K1
Mainridge Rd CHST BR7 167 F6
Main Rd BFN/LL DA15 167 K5
GPK RM2 75 H1
ORP * BR6 217 J6
STMC/STPC BR5 186 D4
SWLY BR8 203 K3
Main St FELT TW13 172 C1
Maise Webster Cl
STWL/WRAY * TW19 152 A2
Maismore St PECK SE15 123 H6
The Maisonettes SUT * SM1 208 D3
Maitland Cl GNWCH SE10 144 E1
HSLWW TW4 134 E4
WOT/HER KT12 188 D6
Maitland Park Rd HAMP NW3 83 K4
Maitland Park Vls HAMP NW3 83 K4
Maitland Rd SRTFD * E15 88 D4
SYD SE26 182 A2
Majendie Rd WOOL/PLUM SE18 127 J5
Major Rd BERM/RHTH * SE16 123 H3
SRTFD E15 88 B3
Makepeace Av HGT N6 66 A6
Makepeace Rd NTHLT UB5 95 J1
WAN E11 70 E1
Makins St CHEL SW3 14 D7
Malabar St POP/IOD E14 124 D2
Malam Gdns POP/IOD E14 105 K6
Malan Sq RAIN RM13 93 K4
Malbrook Rd PUT/ROE SW15 138 E5
Malcolm Cl PGE/AN * SE20 181 K3
Malcolm Ct STAN HA7 43 J1
Malcolm Crs HDN NW4 63 J2
Malcolm Dr SURB KT6 190 E5
Malcolm Gavin Cl TOOT SW17 160 D4
Malcolm Pl BETH E2 104 E3
Malcolm Rd PGE/AN SE20 181 K3
SNWD SE25 197 H3
WCHPL E1 104 E3
WIM/MER SW19 177 H2
Malcolm Wy WAN E11 70 E2
Malden Av GFD/PVL UB6 78 E4
SNWD SE25 197 J1
Malden Green Av WPK KT4 192 C5
Malden Hl NWMAL KT3 192 C1
Malden Hill Gdns NWMAL KT3 176 C6
Malden Pk NWMAL KT3 192 C3
Malden Pl KTTN NW5 84 A3
Malden Rd CHEAM SM3 208 B2
KTTN NW5 83 K3
NWMAL KT3 192 C4
Malden Wy NWMAL KT3 192 A3
Malden Wy (Kingston By-Pass)
NWMAL KT3 192 B3
Maldon Cl CMBW * SE5 143 F4
IS N1 85 J6
Maldon Rd ACT W3 98 E6
ED N9 36 B5
ROMW/RG RM7 74 E4
WLGTN SM6 210 B3
Maldon Wk WFD IG8 53 G2
Malet St GWRST WC1E 4 C7
Maley Av WNWD SE27 162 C4
Malford Gv SWFD E18 52 E6
Malfort Rd CMBW SE5 143 F4
Malham Cl FBAR/BDGN N11 48 A2
Malham Rd FSTH SE23 164 A3
Malham Ter UED * N18 50 D2
The Mall BTFD * TW8 116 E6
BXLYHS * DA6 149 H5
EA W5 98 A6
EMPK RM11 75 K5
KTN/HRWW/W HA3 62 B3
MORT/ESHN SW14 137 K6
SRTFD * E15 88 B5
STHGT/OAK N14 34 E5
SURB KT6 190 E2
WHALL SW1A 16 A2
Mallams Ms BRXN/ST SW9 142 B4
Mallard Cl BAR * EN5 33 H1
DART DA1 151 J6
KIL/WHAMP NW6 100 E1
WHTN TW2 155 F2
Mallard Ct WALTH * E17 52 B6
Mallard Pl TWK TW1 156 B5
WDGN * N22 49 F5
Mallards Ct OXHEY * WD19 27 K5
Mallards Rd BARK IG11 109 G2
WFD IG8 53 F3
Mallard Wk CROY/NA CR0 198 A2
Mallard Wy CDALE/KGS NW9 62 E4
NTHWD HA6 40 A3
WLGTN SM6 210 C6
Mall Chambers KENS * W8 119 K1
Mallet Dr NTHLT UB5 77 K3
Mallet Rd LEW SE13 165 G1
Malling Cl CROY/NA * CR0 197 K3
Malling Gdns MRDN SM4 194 B3
Malling Wy HAYES BR2 199 J4
Mallinson Rd BTSEA SW11 140 D6
CROY/NA CR0 210 D1
Mallord St CHEL SW3 120 C6
Mallory Cl BROCKY SE4 144 B5
Mallory Gdns EBAR EN4 34 A2
Mallory St STJWD NW8 2 D7
Mallow Cl CROY/NA CR0 198 A5
Mallow Md MLHL NW7 46 C3
Mallow St FSBYE EC1V 6 E6
Mall Rd HMSMTH W6 118 E5
Mall Vls HMSMTH * W6 118 E5
Malmains Cl BECK BR3 199 G2
Malmains Wy BECK BR3 199 F1
Malmesbury Cl PIN HA5 58 E1
Malmesbury Rd BOW E3 105 H2
CAN/RD E16 106 C4
MRDN SM4 194 B4
SWFD E18 52 D4
Malmesbury Ter CAN/RD E16 106 D4
Malmesbury West Est BOW E3 105 H2
Malpas Dr PIN HA5 59 H2
Malpas Rd BROCKY SE4 144 C3
DAGW RM9 91 K4
HACK E8 86 D4
Malta Rd LEY E10 69 J5
Malta St FSBYE EC1V 6 A6
Maltby Cl ORP BR6 202 B5
Maltby Dr EN EN1 24 D1
Maltby Rd CHSGTN KT9 206 C4
Maltby St STHWK SE1 19 J4
Malthouse Dr FELT TW13 172 C1
The Maltings ORP BR6 202 A5
ROM RM1 75 H4
SNWD * SE25 181 F6
Maltings Pl FUL/PGN SW6 140 A2
STHWK SE1 19 H2
Malting Wy ISLW TW7 136 A4
Malton Ms NKENS * W10 100 C5
WOOL/PLUM SE18 127 K6
Malton Rd NKENS W10 100 C5
Malton St WOOL/PLUM SE18 127 K6
Maltravers St TPL/STR WC2R 11 H5
Malt St STHWK SE1 123 H6
Malva Cl WAND/EARL SW18 140 A6
Malvern Av BXLYHN DA7 149 F1
CHING E4 52 B3
RYLN/HDSTN HA2 77 J1
Malvern Cl MTCM CR4 179 H6
NKENS W10 100 D4
SURB KT6 191 F5
Malvern Dr FELT TW13 172 C1
GDMY/SEVK IG3 91 F2
WFD IG8 53 G1
Malvern Gdns CRICK NW2 64 C6
KTN/HRWW/W HA3 62 A1
LOU IG10 39 K1
Malvern Ms KIL/WHAMP NW6 100 E2
Malvern Pl MV/WKIL * W9 100 D2
Malvern Rd CEND/HSY/T N8 49 F6
EHAM E6 89 J6
EMPK RM11 75 J3
HACK E8 86 C5
HPTN TW12 173 F4
HYS/HAR UB3 133 H1
MV/WKIL * W9 100 D2
ORP BR6 217 H2
SURB KT6 191 F6
THHTH CR7 196 B1
TOTM N17 50 C6
WAN E11 70 C6
Malvern Ter ED N9 36 B3
IS N1 85 G6
Malvern Wy WEA W13 97 H4
Malwood Rd BAL SW12 161 G1
Malyons Rd LEW SE13 144 E6
Malyons Ter LEW SE13 144 E6
Managers St POP/IOD * E14 125 F1
Manaton Cl PECK SE15 143 J4
Manaton Crs STHL UB1 96 A5
Manbey Gv SRTFD E15 88 C4
Manbey Park Rd SRTFD E15 88 C4
Manbey Rd SRTFD * E15 88 C4
Manbey St SRTFD E15 88 C4
Manbre Rd HMSMTH W6 119 F6
Manbrough Av EHAM E6 107 K2
Manchester Dr NKENS * W10 100 C3
Manchester Gv POP/IOD E14 125 F5
Manchester Ms MHST W1U 9 G2
Manchester Rd POP/IOD E14 125 F5
SEVS/STOTM N15 67 K3
THHTH CR7 180 D6
Manchester Sq MBLAR W1H 9 H3
Manchester St MHST W1U 9 G2
Manchester Wy DAGE * RM10 92 D2
Manchuria Rd BTSEA SW11 161 F1
Manciple St STHWK SE1 19 F3
Mandalay Rd CLAP SW4 141 H6
Mandarin Wy YEAD UB4 95 H5
Mandela Cl WLSDN NW10 80 E5
Mandela Rd CAN/RD E16 106 E5
Mandela St BRXN/ST SW9 142 B1
CAMTN NW1 84 C6
Mandela Wy STHWK SE1 19 H6
Mandeville Cl WIM/MER SW19 177 H3
Mandeville Dr SURB KT6 190 E5
Mandeville Pl MHST W1U 9 H3
Mandeville Rd ISLW TW7 136 B3
NTHLT UB5 78 A4
STHGT/OAK N14 34 B4
Mandeville St CLPT E5 87 G1
Mandrake Rd TOOT SW17 160 E5
Mandrake Wy SRTFD * E15 88 C5
Mandrell Rd BRXS/STRHM SW2 141 K6
Manette St SOHO/SHAV W1D 10 D4
Manford Cross CHIG IG7 55 G1
Manford Wy CHIG IG7 54 E1
Manfred Rd PUT/ROE SW15 139 J6
Manger Rd HOLWY N7 84 E4
Manilla St POP/IOD E14 124 D2
Manister Rd ABYW SE2 128 B3
Manley Ct STNW/STAM N16 86 B1
Manley St CAMTN NW1 84 A6
Mann Cl CROY/NA CR0 211 J1
Manningford Cl FSBYE * EC1V 6 A4
Manning Gdns
KTN/HRWW/W HA3 61 K4
Manning Pl RCHPK/HAM TW10 157 G1
Manning Rd DAGE RM10 92 C5
STMC/STPC BR5 202 E2
WALTH E17 69 G1
Manningtree Cl
WIM/MER SW19 159 H3
Manningtree Rd RSLP HA4 77 F2
Manningtree St WCHPL E1 104 C5
Mannin Rd CHDH RM6 73 H4
Mannock Rd DART DA1 151 J4
WDGN N22 49 H6
Mann's Cl ISLW TW7 136 A6
Manns Rd EDGE HA8 44 C2
Manoel Rd WHTN TW2 155 H4
Manor Av BROCKY SE4 144 C3
HSLWW TW4 134 C4
NTHLT UB5 77 K5

Manorbrook BKHTH/KID SE3 145 K5
Manor Cl BAR EN5 20 C5
CDALE/KGS NW9 62 D1
DAGE RM10 93 F4
DART DA1 150 A5
MLHL * NW7 45 F1
RDART DA2 170 D5
ROM RM1 75 J2
RSLP HA4 58 D5
THMD SE28 109 J5
WPK KT4 192 B5
Manor Cottages NTHWD HA6 40 D4
Manor Cottages Ap EFNCH N2 47 G5
Manor Ct ACT * W3 117 H4
E/WMO/HCT * KT8 189 F1
HRW * HA1 61 F3
KUTN/CMB * KT2 175 H4
WBLY * HA9 80 B2
Manor Court Rd HNWL W7 96 E6
Manor Crs BRYLDS KT5 191 H3
Manor Cft EDGE * HA8 44 C2
Manordene Cl THDIT KT7 190 B5
Manordene Rd THMD SE28 109 J5
The Manor Dr WPK KT4 192 B5
Manor Dr BRYLDS KT5 191 H3
ESH/CLAY KT10 205 F1
FELT TW13 172 C1
HOR/WEW KT19 207 G4
MLHL NW7 45 F1
STHGT/OAK N14 34 B2
TRDG/WHET N20 33 J5
WBLY HA9 80 B2
Manor Dr North NWMAL KT3 192 A4
Manor Est BERM/RHTH SE16 123 J4
Manor Farm Dr CHING E4 38 C5
Manor Farm Rd ALP/SUD HA0 97 K1
STRHM/NOR SW16 180 B5
Manorfields Cl CHST BR7 186 A6
Manor Gdns ACT W3 117 H4
HOLWY N7 84 E1
HPTN TW12 173 G3
RCH/KEW TW9 137 G5
RSLP HA4 77 G3
RYNPK SW20 177 J5
SAND/SEL CR2 212 B4
VX/NE * SW8 141 H3
Manor Ga NTHLT UB5 77 J5
Manorgate Rd KUTN/CMB KT2 175 H4
Manor Gv BECK BR3 182 E5
PECK SE15 123 K6
RCH/KEW TW9 137 H5
Manor Hall Av HDN NW4 46 A5
Manor Hall Dr HDN NW4 46 B5
Manor Hall Gdns LEY E10 69 J5
Manor House Dr
KIL/WHAMP NW6 82 B5
Manor House Wy ISLW TW7 136 C4
Manor La FELT TW13 153 K4
HYS/HAR UB3 133 G6
LEW SE13 145 H6
SUN TW16 172 A5
SUT SM1 209 G3
Manor Lane Ter LEW SE13 145 H5
Manor Ms KIL/WHAMP NW6 100 E1
Manor Mt FSTH SE23 163 K3
Manor Pde HRW * HA1 61 F3
STNW/STAM * N16 68 B6
Manor Pk CHST BR7 185 J5
LEW SE13 145 G6
RCH/KEW TW9 137 G5
Manor Park Cl WWKM BR4 198 E5
Manor Park Crs EDGE HA8 44 C2
Manor Park Dr RYLN/HDSTN HA2 42 B6
Manor Park Gdns EDGE HA8 44 C1
Manor Park Rd CHST BR7 185 H4
EFNCH N2 47 G6
MNPK E12 89 H2
SUT SM1 209 G3
WLSDN NW10 81 G6
WWKM BR4 198 E5
Manor Pl CHST BR7 185 J5
EBED/NFELT TW14 153 K3
MTCM CR4 179 H6
SUT SM1 209 F3
WALW SE17 122 D5
Manor Rd BAR EN5 20 C5
BECK BR3 182 D5
BELMT SM2 208 D5
BFN/LL DA15 168 A5
BXLY DA5 169 J3
CAN/RD E16 106 C4
CHDH RM6 73 K3
CHIG IG7 54 A2
DAGE RM10 92 E4
DART DA1 150 B5
E/WMO/HCT KT8 189 J1
ENC/FH EN2 23 K3
ERITH DA8 130 C6
HRW HA1 61 G3
HYS/HAR UB3 94 E5
LEY E10 69 J4
LOU IG10 39 F1
MTCM CR4 179 H6
RCH/KEW TW9 137 G4
ROM RM1 75 J2
RSLP HA4 58 B5
RYNPK SW20 177 J5
SNWD SE25 181 H6
STNW/STAM N16 68 A5
TEDD TW11 174 B1
TOTM N17 50 C4
WALTH E17 51 G5
WDGN N22 48 E2
WEA W13 97 G6
WHTN TW2 155 H4
WLGTN SM6 210 B2
WWKM BR4 198 E6
Manor Rd North
ESH/CLAY KT10 205 F1
WLGTN SM6 210 B2
Manor Rd South
ESH/CLAY KT10 204 E2
Manorside BAR EN5 20 C5
Manor Sq BCTR RM8 73 J6
Manor V BTFD TW8 116 D5
Manor Vw FNCH N3 47 F5
Manor Wy BECK BR3 182 D6
BKHTH/KID SE3 145 K5
BXLY DA5 169 H3
BXLYHN DA7 150 A4
CDALE/KGS NW9 63 G1
CHING E4 38 B6
HAYES BR2 200 D3
MTCM CR4 179 H6
NWDGN UB2 114 C4
RAIN RM13 111 G3
RSLP HA4 58 C4
RYLN/HDSTN HA2 60 B1
SAND/SEL CR2 212 A4
STMC/STPC BR5 201 H1
Manorway EN EN1 36 A2
WFD IG8 53 G1
The Manor Wy WLGTN SM6 210 B2
Manor Wy WPK KT4 192 B5
Manresa Rd CHEL * SW3 120 C5
Mansard Beeches TOOT SW17 179 F1
Mansard Cl HCH RM12 75 J6
PIN HA5 41 H6
Manse Cl HYS/HAR UB3 113 G6
Mansel Gv WALTH E17 51 J4
Mansell Rd ACT W3 118 A1
GFD/PVL UB6 96 B4
Mansell St WCHPL E1 13 K4
Mansel Rd WIM/MER SW19 177 H2
Mansergh Cl WOOL/PLUM SE18 146 D1
Manse Rd STNW/STAM N16 86 B1
Manser Rd RAIN RM13 111 G2
Mansfield Av EBAR EN4 33 K1
RSLP HA4 59 F5
SEVS/STOTM N15 67 K1
Mansfield Cl ED N9 36 C1
STMC/STPC BR5 202 E4
Mansfield Dr YEAD UB4 94 C3
Mansfield Hl CHING E4 37 K3
Mansfield Ms CAVSQ/HST W1G 9 J2
Mansfield Rd ACT W3 98 D3
CHSGTN KT9 205 J3
HAMP NW3 83 K3
IL IG1 72 A6
SAND/SEL CR2 211 K4
WALTH E17 69 H1
WAN E11 71 F3
Mansfield St CAVSQ/HST W1G 9 J2
Mansford St BETH E2 104 C1
Manship Rd MTCM CR4 179 F4
Mansion House Pl
MANHO * EC4N 12 E4
The Mansions ECT * SW5 120 A5
Manson Ms SKENS * SW7 120 B4
Manson Pl SKENS SW7 14 A7
Manstead Gdns CHDH RM6 73 J4
RAIN RM13 111 K5
Manston Av NWDGN UB2 115 F4
Manston Cl PGE/AN SE20 181 K4
Manstone Rd CRICK NW2 82 C3
Manston Gv KUTN/CMB KT2 174 E1
Manston Wy HCH RM12 93 K4
Manthorpe Rd
WOOL/PLUM SE18 127 H5
Mantilla Rd TOOT SW17 161 F6
Mantle Rd BROCKY SE4 144 B4
Mantlet Cl STRHM/NOR SW16 179 H3
Mantle Wy SRTFD E15 88 C5
Manton Av HNWL W7 116 A2
Manton Cl HYS/HAR UB3 94 C6
Manton Rd ABYW SE2 128 B4
Mantua St BTSEA SW11 140 C4
Mantus Cl WCHPL E1 104 E3
Mantus Rd WCHPL E1 104 E3
Manus Wy TRDG/WHET N20 33 G4
Manville Gdns TOOT SW17 161 G5
Manville Rd TOOT SW17 161 F4
Manwood Rd BROCKY SE4 164 C1
Manwood St CAN/RD E16 126 E1
Many Gates BAL SW12 161 G4
Mapesbury Rd CRICK NW2 82 C4
Mapeshill Pl CRICK NW2 82 A4
Mape St BETH E2 104 D3
Maple Av ACT W3 118 B1
CHING E4 51 H2
RYLN/HDSTN HA2 60 B6
Maple Cl BARK/HLT IG6 54 E2
BKHH IG9 39 H5
CLAP SW4 161 J1
FNCH N3 46 E2
HCH RM12 93 K1
HPTN TW12 172 E2
MTCM CR4 179 G4
RSLP HA4 59 F3
STMC/STPC BR5 201 J2
STNW/STAM N16 68 C3
YEAD UB4 95 H2
Maple Ct NWMAL KT3 176 A6
Maple Crs BFN/LL DA15 168 B1
Maplecroft Cl EHAM E6 107 H5
Mapledale Av CROY/NA CR0 212 D1
Mapledene Est HACK * E8 86 C5
Mapledene Rd HACK E8 86 B5
Maple Gdns ASHF TW15 152 B4
EDGE HA8 45 G3
Maple Gv BTFD TW8 136 C1
CDALE/KGS NW9 62 E4
EA W5 116 E3
STHL UB1 95 K4
Maplehurst Cl KUT KT1 191 F1
Maple Leaf Dr BFN/LL DA15 168 A3
Mapleleafe Gdns BARK/HLT IG6 54 B6
Maple Leaf Sq
BERM/RHTH * SE16 124 A2
Maple Ms KIL/WHAMP * NW6 101 F1
STRHM/NOR SW16 180 A1
Maple Pl FITZ W1T 10 B1
WDR/YW UB7 112 B1
Maple Rd DART DA1 171 F3
PGE/AN SE20 181 J4
SURB KT6 190 E2
WAN E11 70 C3
YEAD UB4 95 G2
The Maples E/WMO/HCT * KT8 174 D3
ESH/CLAY * KT10 205 G5
Maples Pl WCHPL * E1 104 D4
Maplestead Rd
BRXS/STRHM SW2 162 A2
DAGW RM9 91 H6
Maple St FITZ W1T 10 A1
ROMW/RG RM7 74 E1
Maplethorpe Rd THHTH CR7 196 B1
Mapleton Cl HAYES BR2 199 K2
Mapleton Crs PEND EN3 24 E1
WAND/EARL SW18 160 A1
Mapleton Rd CHING E4 38 A5
EN EN1 24 D3
WAND/EARL SW18 159 K1
Maple Wk NKENS * W10 100 B3
Maple Wy FELT TW13 153 K5
Maplin Cl WCHMH N21 35 F1
Maplin Rd CAN/RD E16 106 E5
Maplin St BOW E3 105 H2
Mapperley Dr WFD IG8 52 C3
Maran Wy ERITHM DA18 128 E3
Marathon Wy THMD SE28 128 A2
Marban Rd MV/WKIL W9 100 D2
Marble Cl ACT W3 117 J1
Marble Dr CRICK NW2 64 B5
Marble Hill Cl TWK TW1 156 C2
Marble Hill Gdns TWK TW1 156 C2
Marble Quay WAP E1W 13 K7
Marbrook Ct LEE/GVPK SE12 166 B5
Marcella Rd BRXN/ST SW9 142 B3
Marcellina Wy ORP BR6 216 E1
Marcet Rd DART DA1 151 F6
Marchant Rd WAN E11 70 B6
Marchant St NWCR SE14 124 B6
Marchbank Rd WKENS W14 119 J6
Marchmont Rd
RCHPK/HAM TW10 137 G6
WLGTN SM6 210 C6
Marchmont St BMSBY WC1N 4 E6
March Rd TWK TW1 156 A2
Marchside Cl HEST TW5 134 C2
Marchwood Cl CMBW SE5 143 F1
Marchwood Crs EA W5 97 J5
Marcia Rd STHWK SE1 19 H7
Marcilly Rd WAND/EARL SW18 140 C6
Marconi Pl FBAR/BDGN N11 34 B6
Marconi Rd LEY E10 69 J5
Marconi Wy STHL UB1 96 B5
Marcon Pl HACK E8 86 D4
Marco Rd HMSMTH W6 118 E3
Marcus Garvey Ms EDUL SE22 163 J1
Marcus Garvey Wy
BRXN/ST SW9 142 B5
Marcus Rd DART DA1 170 D2
Marcus St SRTFD E15 88 C6
WAND/EARL SW18 160 A1
Marcus Ter WAND/EARL SW18 160 A1
Mardale Dr CDALE/KGS NW9 63 F2
Mardell Rd CROY/NA CR0 198 A2
Marden Av HAYES BR2 199 K3
Marden Crs BXLY DA5 149 K6
CROY/NA CR0 196 A3
Marden Rd CROY/NA CR0 196 A3
ROM RM1 75 G3
TOTM N17 50 A5
Marden Sq BERM/RHTH SE16 123 J3
Marder Rd WEA W13 116 B2
Marechal Niel Av BFN/LL DA15 167 J5
Marechal Niel Pde
BFN/LL * DA15 167 J5
Maresfield CROY/NA CR0 212 A1
Maresfield Gdns HAMP NW3 83 G3
Mare St HACK E8 86 D3
Marfleet Cl CAR SM5 194 D6
Margaret Av CHING E4 37 K1
Margaret Bondfield Av
BARK IG11 91 G5
Margaret Cl GPK RM2 75 K2
Margaret Gardner Dr
ELTH/MOT SE9 166 E4
Margaret Ingram Cl
FUL/PGN * SW6 119 J6
Margaret Lockwood Cl
KUT * KT1 191 G1
Margaret Rd BXLY DA5 168 E1
EBAR EN4 21 H6
GPK RM2 75 K2
STNW/STAM * N16 68 B5
Margaret St GTPST W1W 10 A3
Margaretta Ter CHEL SW3 120 D6
Margaretting Rd MNPK E12 71 G6
Margaret Wy REDBR IG4 71 J3
Margate Rd BRXS/STRHM SW2 141 K6
Margeholes OXHEY WD19 27 J4
Margery Rd BCTR RM8 91 K1
Margery St FSBYW WC1X 5 J5
Margin Dr WIM/MER SW19 177 G1
Margravine Gdns HMSMTH W6 119 G5
Margravine Rd HMSMTH W6 119 G6
Marguerite Vls RYNPK * SW20 176 E3
Marham Gdns MRDN SM4 194 B3
WAND/EARL SW18 160 D3
Maria Cl BERM/RHTH SE16 123 H4
Marian Cl YEAD UB4 95 H3
Marian Pl BETH E2 104 D1
Marian Rd STRHM/NOR SW16 179 H4
Marian Sq BETH E2 104 C1
Marian St BETH * E2 104 D1
Marian Wy WLSDN NW10 81 H5
Maria Ter WCHPL E1 105 F4
Maria Theresa Cl NWMAL KT3 192 A2
Maricas Av KTN/HRWW/W HA3 42 D4
Marie Curie CMBW * SE5 143 F2
Marie Lloyd Wk HACK * E8 86 C4
Mariette Wy WLGTN SM6 210 E6
Marigold Aly STHWK SE1 12 A6
Marigold Cl STHL UB1 95 J6
Marigold St BERM/RHTH SE16 123 J2
Marigold Wy CROY/NA CR0 198 A5
Marina Ap YEAD UB4 95 J4
Marina Av NWMAL KT3 192 E3
Marina Dr DART DA1 171 K3
WELL DA16 147 K3
Marina Gdns ROMW/RG RM7 74 D2
Marina Wy TEDD TW11 174 E3
Marine Ct PUR RM19 131 J4
Marine Dr BARK IG11 109 G3
WOOL/PLUM SE18 126 E4
Marinefield Rd FUL/PGN SW6 140 A3
Mariner Gdns
RCHPK/HAM TW10 156 C5
Mariner Rd MNPK E12 90 A2
Mariners Ms POP/IOD E14 125 G4
Marine St BERM/RHTH SE16 123 H3
Marion Cl BARK/HLT IG6 54 D3
Marion Crs STMC/STPC BR5 202 C2
Marion Gv WFD IG8 52 C1
Marion Rd CROY/NA CR0 196 D2
MLHL NW7 45 J1
Marischal Rd LEW SE13 145 G4
Maritime Quay POP/IOD E14 124 D5
Maritime St BOW E3 105 H3
Marius Rd TOOT SW17 161 F4
Marjorie Gv BTSEA SW11 140 E5
Mark Av CHING E4 37 K1
Mark Cl BXLYHN DA7 149 F2
HAYES BR2 215 J2
STHL UB1 115 F1
The Market COVGDN * WC2E 11 F5
HNWL * W7 116 A2
PECK * SE15 143 H3
RCH/KEW * TW9 136 E6
SUT * SM1 194 B5
Markeston Gn OXHEY WD19 27 H6
Market Chambers ENC/FH * EN2 23 K4
Market Est HOLWY N7 84 E4
Market La EDGE HA8 44 E4
Market Link ROM RM1 75 G1
Market Meadow
STMC/STPC BR5 202 D1
Market Ms MYFR/PICC W1J 15 J1
Market Pde BMLY * BR1 183 K4
ED * N9 36 C4
EW * KT17 207 H6
FELT * TW13 154 D4
LEY * E10 69 K3
SCUP * DA14 168 B6
SNWD * SE25 197 H1
STNW/STAM * N16 68 C5
WALTH * E17 51 H6
Market Pl ACT W3 117 K1
BERM/RHTH * SE16 123 H4
BTFD TW8 136 D1
BXLYHN DA7 149 H5
DART DA1 171 H2
EFNCH N2 47 H6
KUT * KT1 174 E5
ROM RM1 75 G2
SOHO/SHAV W1D 10 A3
Market Rd HOLWY N7 84 E4
RCH/KEW TW9 137 H4
Market Sq BMLY BR1 183 K5
ED N9 36 D4
Market St DART DA1 171 H2
EHAM E6 107 K1
WOOL/PLUM SE18 127 F4
Market Ter BTFD * TW8 117 F6
Markfield Gdns CHING E4 37 K2
Markfield Rd SEVS/STOTM N15 68 C1
Markham Pl CHEL SW3 120 E5
Markham Sq CHEL SW3 120 E5
Markham St CHEL SW3 120 D5
Markhole Cl HPTN TW12 172 E3
Markhouse Av WALTH E17 69 G3
Markhouse Rd WALTH E17 69 H3
Mark La MON EC3R 13 H5
Markmanor Av WALTH E17 69 G4
Mark Rd WDGN N22 49 H5
Marksbury Av RCH/KEW TW9 137 H4
Marks Rd ROMW/RG RM7 74 E2
Markstone Ter ORP * BR6 202 B4
Mark St SDTCH EC2A 7 G6
SRTFD E15 88 C5
Mark Ter RYNPK * SW20 177 F3
The Markway SUN TW16 172 B5
Markwell Cl SYD SE26 163 J6
Markyate Rd BCTR RM8 91 H3
Marlands Rd CLAY IG5 53 J6
Marlborough Rd ISLW TW7 136 C1
Marlborough Av EDGE HA8 30 D5
HACK * E8 86 C6
RSLP HA4 58 A3
STHGT/OAK N14 34 C5
Marlborough Cl ORP BR6 202 A4
TRDG/WHET N20 33 K5
WALW SE17 18 B7
WIM/MER SW19 178 D2
Marlborough Ct REGST W1B 10 A4
Marlborough Crs CHSWK W4 118 A3
Marlborough Dr CLAY IG5 53 J6
Marlborough Gdns
TRDG/WHET N20 33 K5
Marlborough Ga BAY/PAD W2 8 A6
Marlborough Gv STHWK SE1 123 H5
Marlborough Hl HRW HA1 60 E1
STJWD NW8 83 G6
Marlborough La CHARL SE7 126 B6
Marlborough Ms BRXN/ST SW9 142 A5
Marlborough Pde FSBYPK * N4 67 J5
Marlborough Park Av
BFN/LL DA15 168 B3
Marlborough Pl STJWD NW8 101 G1
Marlborough Rd ARCH N19 66 E6
BCTR RM8 91 J2
BXLYHN DA7 148 E4
CHING E4 51 K2
CHSWK W4 117 K5
DART DA1 171 F1
EA W5 116 E2
ED N9 36 B3
FELT TW13 154 C4
FSTGT E7 89 G5
HAYES BR2 200 B1
HPTN TW12 173 F2
HYS/HAR UB3 133 G1
NWDGN UB2 114 B3
RCHPK/HAM TW10 157 F1
ROMW/RG RM7 74 C1
SAND/SEL CR2 211 J5
SRTFD * E15 88 C2
SUT SM1 208 E1
SWFD E18 52 E6
WDGN N22 49 F3
WHALL SW1A 16 B1
WIM/MER SW19 178 D2
WOOL/PLUM SE18 127 G3
Marlborough St CHEL SW3 14 C7
Marlborough Yd ARCH N19 66 D6
Marler Rd FSTH SE23 164 C3
Marley Av BXLYHN DA7 128 E6
Marley Cl GFD/PVL UB6 96 A2
SEVS/STOTM N15 67 H1
Marlingdene Cl HPTN TW12 173 F2
Marlings Cl CHST BR7 201 K1
Marlings Park Av CHST BR7 201 K1
The Marlins NTHWD HA6 40 D2
Marlins Cl SUT * SM1 209 G3
Marlins Meadow WATW WD18 26 B1
Marloes Cl ALP/SUD HA0 79 K2
Marloes Rd KENS W8 120 A3
Marlow Av PUR RM19 131 K4
Marlow Cl PGE/AN SE20 181 J6
Marlow Ct CDALE/KGS NW9 45 H6
Marlow Crs TWK TW1 156 A1
Marlow Dr CHEAM SM3 208 B1
Marlowe Cl BARK/HLT IG6 54 C4
CHST BR7 185 J2
Marlowe Rd WALTH E17 70 A1
The Marlowes DART DA1 150 A5
STJWD NW8 2 A1
Marlowe Wy CROY/NA CR0 195 K6
Marlow Gdns HYS/HAR UB3 113 G3
Marlow Rd EHAM E6 107 K2
NWDGN UB2 114 E3
PGE/AN SE20 181 J6
Marlow Wy BERM/RHTH SE16 124 A2
Marl Rd WAND/EARL SW18 140 A5
Marlton St GNWCH SE10 125 J5
Marlwood Cl BFN/LL DA15 167 K4
Marlyon Rd BARK/HLT IG6 55 H1
Marmadon Rd
WOOL/PLUM SE18 128 A4
Marmion Ap CHING E4 37 J6
Marmion Av CHING E4 37 H6
Marmion Cl CHING E4 37 H6
Marmion Ms BTSEA * SW11 141 F4
Marmion Rd BTSEA SW11 141 F5
Marmont Rd PECK SE15 143 H2
Marmora Rd EDUL SE22 163 K1
Marmot Rd HSLWW TW4 134 C4
Marne Av FBAR/BDGN N11 34 B6
WELL DA16 148 B4
Marnell Wy HSLWW TW4 134 C4
Marne St NKENS W10 100 C2
Marney Rd BTSEA SW11 141 F5
Marnfield Crs
BRXS/STRHM SW2 162 A3
Marnham Av CRICK NW2 82 C2
Marnham Crs GFD/PVL UB6 96 B2
Marnock Rd BROCKY SE4 144 C6
Maroon St POP/IOD E14 105 G4
Maroons Wy CAT SE6 182 D1
Marquess Rd IS N1 85 K4
Marquess Rd North IS N1 85 J4
Marquess Rd South IS * N1 85 J4
Marquis Cl ALP/SUD HA0 80 B5
Marquis Rd CAMTN NW1 84 D4
FSBYPK N4 67 F5
WDGN N22 49 F2
Marrabon Cl BFN/LL DA15 168 B3
Marrick Cl PUT/ROE SW15 138 D5
Marrilyne Av PEND EN3 25 H1
Mariner Ct HYS/HAR * UB3 94 C6
Marriot Rd MUSWH N10 47 K4
Marriott Cl EBED/NFELT TW14 153 G1
Marriott Rd BAR EN5 20 B4
DART DA1 171 K2
FSBYPK N4 67 F5
SRTFD E15 88 C6
Marriotts Cl CDALE/KGS NW9 63 H3
Marriotts Yd BAR * EN5 20 B4
Marryat Pl WIM/MER SW19 159 H6
Marryat Rd WIM/MER SW19 177 G1
Marryat Sq FUL/PGN * SW6 139 H2
Marsala Rd LEW SE13 144 E5
Marsden Rd ED N9 36 D4
PECK SE15 143 G4
Marsden St KTTN NW5 84 A4
Marsden Wy ORP BR6 217 F2
Marshall Cl FBAR/BDGN N11 34 B6
HRW HA1 60 D4
HSLWW TW4 134 E6
WAND/EARL SW18 160 B1
Marshall Dr YEAD UB4 94 D4
Marshall Est MLHL * NW7 31 J6
Marshall Rd LEY E10 87 K2
TOTM N17 49 K4
Marshalls Dr ROM RM1 57 G6
Marshalls Gv WOOL/PLUM SE18 126 D4
Marshalls Rd ROMW/RG RM7 75 F1
SUT SM1 209 F2
Marshall St SOHO/CST W1F 10 B4
Marshalsea Rd STHWK SE1 18 D2
Marsham Cl CHST * BR7 185 G1
Marsham St WEST SW1P 16 D6
Marsh Av MTCM CR4 178 E5
Marshbrook Cl BKHTH/KID SE3 146 C4
Marsh Cl MLHL NW7 31 H5
Marsh Dr CDALE/KGS NW9 63 H3
Marsh Farm Rd WHTN TW2 156 A3
Marshfield St POP/IOD E14 125 F3
Marshgate La SRTFD E15 87 K6
Marsh Green Rd DAGE RM10 92 C6
Marsh Hl HOM E9 87 G3
Marsh La LEY E10 69 H6
MLHL NW7 31 G5
STAN HA7 43 J1
TOTM N17 50 D3
Marsh Rd ALP/SUD HA0 97 K2
PIN HA5 59 K1
Marshside Cl ED N9 36 E3
Marsh St DART DA1 151 K4
POP/IOD * E14 124 E4
Marsh Ter STMC/STPC * BR5 202 E1
Marsh Wall POP/IOD E14 124 D2
Marsh Wy DAGW RM9 111 F3
Marsland Cl WALW SE17 122 C5
Marston Av CHSGTN KT9 206 A4
DAGE RM10 92 C1
Marston Cl DAGE RM10 92 C1
KIL/WHAMP NW6 83 G5
Marston Ct WOT/HER * KT12 188 B5
Marston Rd CLAY IG5 53 J5
TEDD TW11 174 C1
Marston Wy NRWD SE19 180 C3
Marsworth Av PIN HA5 41 H4
Marsworth Cl WATW * WD18 26 C1
YEAD UB4 95 J4
Martaban Rd STNW/STAM N16 68 A6
Martara Ms WALW SE17 122 D5
Martello St HACK E8 86 D5
Martell Rd DUL SE21 162 E5
Martel Pl HACK E8 86 B4
Marten Rd WALTH E17 51 J5
Martens Av BXLYHN DA7 149 K5
Martens Cl BXLYHN DA7 149 K5
Martham Cl BARK/HLT IG6 54 B4
THMD SE28 109 K6
Martha Rd SRTFD E15 88 C4
Martha's Buildings FSBYE EC1V 6 E6
Martha St WCHPL E1 104 E5
Marthorne Crs
KTN/HRWW/W HA3 42 D5
Martin Bowes Rd
ELTH/MOT SE9 146 E4
Martin Cl ED N9 37 F3
Martin Crs CROY/NA CR0 196 A5
Martindale MORT/ESHN SW14 137 K6
Martindale Av CAN/RD E16 106 E6
ORP BR6 217 G3
Martindale Rd BAL SW12 161 G2
HSLWW TW4 134 D5
Martin Dene BXLYHS DA6 149 G6
Martin Dr NTHLT UB5 77 K3
RAIN RM13 111 K3
Martineau Cl ESH/CLAY KT10 204 D2
Martineau Rd HBRY N5 85 H2
Martineau St WCHPL E1 104 E6
Martingales Cl
RCHPK/HAM TW10 156 E5
Martin Gdns BCTR RM8 91 J2
Martin Gv WIM/MER SW19 177 K6
Martin La CANST EC4R 13 F5
Martin Ri BXLYHS DA6 149 G6
Martin Rd BCTR RM8 91 J2
RDART DA2 171 F5
The Martins SYD SE26 181 J1
WBLY * HA9 80 B1
Martins Cl STMC/STPC BR5 186 E6
WWKM BR4 199 G6
Martins Mt BAR EN5 20 E5
Martin's Rd HAYES BR2 183 H5
Martin St THMD SE28 127 K1
Martins Wk MUSWH * N10 48 A4
Martin Wy RYNPK SW20 177 H6
Martlet Gv NTHLT UB5 95 H2

Martlett Ct HOL/ALD WC2B 11 F4
Martley Dr IL IG1 72 B2
Martock Cl KTN/HRWW/W HA3 61 G1
Marton Cl CAT SE6 164 D5
Marton Rd STNW/STAM * N16 68 A6
Martys Yd HAMP * NW3 83 H2
Marvell Av YEAD UB4 94 E4
Marvels Cl LEE/GVPK SE12 166 A4
Marvels La LEE/GVPK SE12 166 A4
Marville Rd FUL/PGN SW6 139 J1
Marvin St HACK * E8 86 D4
Marwell Cl ROM RM1 75 J3
WWKM BR4 199 J6
Marwood Cl WELL DA16 148 C4
Mary Adelaide Cl
PUT/ROE SW15 158 B5
Mary Ann Buildings DEPT SE8 124 D6
Maryatt Av RYLN/HDSTN HA2 60 B6
Marybank WOOL/PLUM SE18 126 E4
Mary Cl KTN/HRWW/W HA3 62 B1
Mary Datchelor Cl CMBW SE5 142 E2
Maryfield Cl BXLY DA5 170 B5
Mary Gn STJWD * NW8 83 F6
Maryland Pk SRTFD E15 88 C3
Maryland Rd MV/WKIL W9 100 E3
SRTFD E15 88 B3
THHTH CR7 180 C4
WDGN N22 49 G2
Maryland Sq SRTFD E15 88 C3
Marylands Rd MV/WKIL W9 100 E3
Maryland St SRTFD E15 88 B3
Maryland Wk IS * N1 85 J6
Mary Lawrencson Pl
BKHTH/KID SE3 145 J1
Marylebone High St MHST W1U 9 H2
Marylebone La MHST W1U 9 H3
Marylebone Ms CAVSQ/HST W1G 9 H2
Marylebone Pas GTPST W1W 10 B3
Marylebone Rd CAMTN NW1 3 G7
Marylebone St MHST W1U 9 H2
Marylee Wy LBTH SE11 17 H7
Maryon Gv WOOL/PLUM SE18 126 D4
Maryon Ms HAMP NW3 83 J2
Maryon Rd CHARL SE7 126 D4
Mary Peters Dr GFD/PVL UB6 78 D3
Mary Pl NTGHL W11 100 C6
Mary Rose Cl HPTN TW12 173 F4
Maryrose Wy TRDG/WHET N20 33 H4
Mary Seacole Cl HACK * E8 86 B6
Mary Secole Cl HACK E8 86 B6
Mary's Ter TWK TW1 156 B2
Mary St CAN/RD E16 106 D4
IS N1 6 D1
Mary Ter CAMTN NW1 3 K1
Masbro' Rd WKENS W14 119 G3
Mascalls Rd CHARL SE7 126 B6
Mascotts Cl CRICK NW2 81 K1
Masefield Av STAN HA7 43 F1
STHL UB1 96 A6
Masefield Cl ERITH DA8 150 C2
HARH RM3 57 K4
Masefield Crs STHGT/OAK N14 22 C6
Masefield Gdns EHAM E6 108 A3
Masefield La YEAD UB4 95 F3
Masefield Rd FELT TW13 154 E6
Masefield Vw ORP BR6 216 C1
Masefield Wy
STWL/WRAY TW19 152 C3
Mashie Rd ACT W3 99 G5
Mashiters Hl ROM RM1 57 F4
Mashiters Wk ROM RM1 57 G6
Maskall Cl BRXS/STRHM * SW2 162 B3
Maskell Rd TOOT SW17 160 B5
Maskelyne Cl BTSEA SW11 140 D2
Mason Cl BERM/RHTH SE16 123 H5
BXLYHN DA7 149 J4
HPTN TW12 172 E4
RYNPK SW20 177 G4
Mason Ct WBLY * HA9 62 C6
Mason Rd WFD IG8 38 C6
Mason's Arms Ms
CONDST * W1S 9 K4
Mason's Av CITYW EC2V 12 E3
CROY/NA CR0 211 J1
KTN/HRWW/W HA3 42 E6
Masons Ct EW * KT17 207 J6
Masons Hl HAYES BR2 183 K6
WOOL/PLUM SE18 127 G4
Mason's Pl FSBYE EC1V 6 B4
MTCM CR4 178 E4
Mason St WALW SE17 19 F6
Masons Yd FSBYE EC1V 6 C6
STJS SW1Y 10 B7
Massey Cl FBAR/BDGN N11 48 B1
Massie Rd HACK E8 86 C4
Massingberd Wy TOOT SW17 161 G6
Massinger St WALW SE17 19 G7
Massingham St WCHPL E1 105 F3
Masson Av RSLP HA4 77 G4
Master Gunners Pl
WOOL/PLUM SE18 146 D2
Masterman Rd EHAM E6 107 J2
Masters Cl STRHM/NOR SW16 179 H2
Masters Dr BERM/RHTH SE16 123 J5
Master's St WCHPL E1 105 F4
Mast House Ter POP/IOD * E14 124 D4
Masthouse Ter POP/IOD E14 124 D4
Mastmaker Rd POP/IOD E14 124 D2
Maswell Park Crs HSLW TW3 135 H6
Maswell Park Rd HSLW TW3 135 G6
Matcham Rd WAN E11 88 D1
Matchless Dr WOOL/PLUM SE18 147 F1
Matfield Cl HAYES BR2 199 K2
Matfield Rd BELV DA17 129 H6
Matham Gv EDUL SE22 143 G5
Matham Rd E/WMO/HCT KT8 189 J2
Matheson Rd WKENS W14 119 J4
Mathews Av EHAM E6 108 A1
Mathews Park Av SRTFD E15 88 D4
Mathews Yd LSQ/SEVD * WC2H 10 E4
Mathieson Ct STHWK SE1 18 B3
Matilda Cl NRWD SE19 180 E3
Matilda St IS N1 5 H1
Matlock Cl BAR EN5 20 B6
Matlock Crs CHEAM SM3 208 C2
OXHEY WD19 27 G5
Matlock Gdns CHEAM SM3 208 C2
Matlock Pl CHEAM SM3 208 C2
Matlock Rd LEY E10 70 A3
Matlock St WCHPL E1 105 G5
Matlock Wy NWMAL KT3 176 A4
Matthew Cl NKENS * W10 100 B3
Matthew Ct MTCM CR4 195 J2
Matthews Rd GFD/PVL UB6 78 D3
Matthews St BTSEA * SW11 140 E3
Matthias Rd STNW/STAM N16 85 K3
Mattingly Wy PECK SE15 143 G1
Mattison Rd FSBYPK N4 67 G3
Mattock La WEA W13 116 D1
Maud Cashmore Wy
WOOL/PLUM SE18 126 E3
Maude Rd CMBW SE5 143 F3
WALTH E17 69 G2
Maudesville Cottages
HNWL W7 115 K1
Maude Ter WALTH E17 69 G1
Maud Gdns BARK IG11 109 F1
PLSTW E13 106 D1
Maudlins Gn WAP * E1W 123 H1
Maud Rd LEY E10 88 A1
PLSTW E13 88 D6
Maudslay Rd ELTH/MOT SE9 146 E4
Maud St CAN/RD E16 106 D4
Maud Wilkes Cl KTTN NW5 84 C3
Mauleverer Rd
BRXS/STRHM SW2 141 K6
Maundeby Wk WLSDN * NW10 81 G5
Maunder Rd HNWL W7 115 K1
Maunsel St WEST SW1P 16 C6
Maurice Av WDGN N22 49 H5
Maurice Brown Cl MLHL * NW7 46 B1
Maurice St SHB W12 99 K5
Maurice Wk GLDGN NW11 65 G1
Maurier Cl NTHLT UB5 77 G6
Mauritius Rd GNWCH SE10 125 H4
Maury Rd STNW/STAM N16 68 C6
Mavelstone Rd BMLY BR1 184 C4
Maverton Rd BOW * E3 87 J6
Mavis Av HOR/WEW KT19 207 G3
Mavis Cl HOR/WEW KT19 207 G3
Mawbey Pl STHWK SE1 123 G5
Mawbey Rd STHWK SE1 123 G5
Mawbey St VX/NE SW8 141 K1
Mawney Cl ROMW/RG RM7 56 D5
Mawney Rd ROMW/RG RM7 56 D6
Mawson Cl RYNPK SW20 177 H5
Mawson La CHSWK W4 118 C6
Maxey Gdns DAGW RM9 92 A2
Maxey Rd DAGW RM9 92 A2
WOOL/PLUM SE18 127 H4
Maxfield Cl TRDG/WHET N20 33 G2
Maximfeldt Rd ERITH DA8 130 B5
Maxim Rd DART DA1 150 B6
ERITH DA8 130 B5
WCHMH N21 35 G1
Maxted Pk HRW HA1 60 E4
Maxted Rd PECK SE15 143 G4
Maxwell Cl CROY/NA CR0 195 K5
HYS/HAR UB3 94 E6
Maxwell Gdns ORP BR6 217 F1
Maxwell Ri OXHEY WD19 27 J2
Maxwell Rd FUL/PGN SW6 140 A1
NTHWD HA6 40 B3
WDR/YW UB7 112 B4
WELL DA16 148 B5
Maxwelton Av MLHL NW7 45 F1
Maxwelton Cl MLHL NW7 45 F1
Maya Cl PECK SE15 143 J3
Mayall Rd BRXN/ST SW9 142 C6
Maya Pl FBAR/BDGN N11 48 D3
Maya Rd EFNCH N2 65 G1
May Av STMC/STPC BR5 202 C2
Maybank Av ALP/SUD HA0 79 G3
HCH RM12 93 K3
SWFD E18 53 F5
Maybank Gdns PIN HA5 58 E2
Maybank Rd SWFD E18 53 G4
May Bate Av KUTN/CMB KT2 174 E4
Mayberry Pl BRYLDS KT5 191 G4
Maybourne Cl SYD * SE26 181 J2
Maybury Cl EN EN1 24 D1
STMC/STPC BR5 201 G2
Maybury Gdns WLSDN NW10 81 J5
Maybury Rd BARK IG11 109 G1
PLSTW E13 107 G3
Maybury St TOOT SW17 178 D1
Maychurch Cl STAN HA7 43 K4
May Cl CHSGTN KT9 206 B4
Maycock Gv NTHWD HA6 40 D2
Maycroft PIN HA5 41 F5
Maycross Av MRDN SM4 193 J1
Mayday Gdns BKHTH/KID SE3 146 D3
Mayday Rd THHTH CR7 196 C3
Mayefield Rd THHTH CR7 196 A1
Mayerne Rd ELTH/MOT SE9 146 C6
Mayesbrook Rd BARK IG11 91 F6
GDMY/SEVK IG3 91 G1
Mayesford Rd CHDH RM6 73 J4
Mayes Rd WDGN N22 49 F5
Mayeswood Rd LEE/GVPK SE12 166 B6
Mayfair Av BXLYHN DA7 148 E2
CHDH RM6 73 K3
IL IG1 71 K6
WHTN TW2 155 H2
WPK KT4 192 D5
Mayfair Cl BECK BR3 182 E4
SURB KT6 191 F5
Mayfair Gdns TOTM N17 49 J2
WFD IG8 52 E3
Mayfair Ms HAMP * NW3 83 K5
Mayfair Pl MYFR/PICC W1J 9 K7
Mayfair Rd DART DA1 151 G6
Mayfair Ter STHGT/OAK N14 34 D2
Mayfield BXLYHN DA7 149 G4
Mayfield Av CHSWK W4 118 B4
KTN/HRWW/W HA3 61 H2
NFNCH/WDSP N12 33 G6
ORP BR6 202 A5
STHGT/OAK N14 34 C4
WEA W13 116 C3
WFD IG8 52 E2
Mayfield Cl CLAP SW4 141 J6
HACK E8 86 B4
PGE/AN * SE20 181 J4
THDIT KT7 190 C5
Mayfield Crs ED N9 36 D1
THHTH CR7 196 A1
Mayfield Dr PIN HA5 59 K1
Mayfield Gdns HDN NW4 64 B3
HNWL W7 96 D5
Mayfield Rd ACT W3 98 D6
BCTR RM8 73 J5
BELMT SM2 209 H4
BELV DA17 129 K4
BMLY BR1 200 D2
CEND/HSY/T N8 67 F3
CHING E4 38 B4
HACK * E8 86 B5
PEND EN3 25 F3
PLSTW E13 106 D3
SAND/SEL CR2 211 K6
SHB W12 118 B2
WALTH E17 51 G5
WIM/MER SW19 177 J4
Mayfields WBLY HA9 62 C6
Mayfields Cl WBLY HA9 62 C6
Mayfield Vls SCUP * DA14 186 D2
Mayflower Cl BERM/RHTH SE16 124 A4
RSLP HA4 58 A3
Mayflower Rd
BRXN/ST SW9 141 K4
Mayflower St
BERM/RHTH SE16 123 K2
Mayfly Cl PIN HA5 59 G4
STMC/STPC BR5 202 E1
Mayford Cl BAL SW12 160 E2
BECK BR3 182 A6
Mayford Rd BAL SW12 160 E2
May Gdns BORE WD6 29 K1
GFD/PVL UB6 97 J1
Maygood St IS N1 5 H2
Maygreen Crs EMPK RM11 75 J4
Maygrove Rd KIL/WHAMP NW6 82 D4
Mayhew Cl CHING E4 37 J5
Mayhill Rd BAR EN5 20 C6
CHARL SE7 126 A6
Maylands Av HCH RM12 93 K2
Maylands Dr SCUP DA14 168 E5
Maylands Rd OXHEY WD19 27 G6
Maynard Cl ERITH DA8 150 C1
FUL/PGN SW6 140 A1
SEVS/STOTM N15 68 A2
Maynard Rd WALTH E17 70 A2
Maynards Quay WAP * E1W 104 E6
Maynooth Gdns MTCM CR4 194 E4
Mayola Rd CLPT E5 86 E2
Mayo Rd CROY/NA CR0 196 E2
WLSDN NW10 81 G4
Mayow Rd SYD SE26 164 A6
Mayplace Av DART DA1 150 D5
Mayplace Cl BXLYHN DA7 149 J4
Mayplace La WOOL/PLUM SE18 127 G6
Mayplace Rd BXLYHN DA7 149 K4
Mayplace Rd East BXLYHN DA7 149 K4
Mayplace Rd West BXLYHN DA7 149 H5
Maypole Crs BARK/HLT IG6 54 D3
ERITH DA8 131 G6
May Rd CHING E4 51 J2
PLSTW E13 106 E1
RDART DA2 171 J6
WHTN TW2 155 K3
Mayroyd Av SURB KT6 191 H6
May's Buildings Ms GNWCH SE10 145 G1
Mays Ct CHCR WC2N 10 E6
May's Hill Rd HAYES BR2 183 H5
Mays La BAR EN5 31 K2
Maysoule Rd BTSEA SW11 140 C5
Mays Rd HPTN TW12 173 J1
May St WKENS W14 119 J5
Mayswood Gdns DAGE RM10 92 E4
Maythorne Cottages LEW SE13 165 G1
Mayton St HOLWY N7 85 F1
Maytree Cl EDGE HA8 30 E5
RAIN RM13 111 G1
Maytree Ct MTCM CR4 179 F6
Maytree La STAN HA7 43 F2
Maytree Wk
BRXS/STRHM * SW2 162 B4
Mayville Est STNW/STAM * N16 86 A3
Mayville Rd IL IG1 90 B3
WAN E11 70 C6
Maywood Cl BECK * BR3 182 E3
Maze Hl BKHTH/KID SE3 145 J1
GNWCH SE10 125 H6
Mazenod Av KIL/WHAMP NW6 82 E5
Maze Rd RCH/KEW TW9 137 H1
McAdam Dr ENC/FH EN2 23 H3
McAuley Cl ELTH/MOT SE9 147 F6
STHWK SE1 17 J4
McCall Cl CLAP SW4 141 K3
McCall Crs CHARL SE7 126 D5
McCarthy Rd FELT TW13 172 C1
McCoid Wy STHWK SE1 18 C3
McCrone Ms HAMP NW3 83 H4
McCudden Rd DART DA1 151 J4
McCullum Rd BOW E3 87 H6
McDermott Cl BTSEA SW11 140 D3
McDermott Rd PECK SE15 143 H4
McDonough Cl CHSGTN KT9 206 A2
McDougall Ct RCH/KEW TW9 137 H3
McDowall Cl CAN/RD E16 106 E4
McEntee Av WALTH E17 51 G4
McEwan Wy SRTFD * E15 88 B6
McGrath Rd FSTGT E7 88 D4
McGregor Rd NTGHL W11 100 D5
McIntosh Cl ROM RM1 57 G6
WLGTN SM6 210 E5
McIntosh Rd ROM RM1 57 G6
McKay Rd RYNPK SW20 176 E3
McKellar Cl BUSH WD23 28 C4
McKerrell Rd PECK SE15 143 H2
McKillop Wy SCUP DA14 186 D3
McLeod Rd ABYW SE2 128 D4
McLeod's Ms SKENS SW7 120 A3
McMillan St DEPT * SE8 124 D6
McNair Rd NWDGN UB2 115 F3
McNeil Rd CMBW SE5 143 F3
McNicol Dr WLSDN NW10 98 E1
McRae La MTCM CR4 194 E4
The Mead BECK BR3 183 F5
EFNCH N2 47 G5
OXHEY WD19 27 J5
WEA W13 97 H4
WLGTN SM6 210 D4
WWKM BR4 199 G5
Mead Cl CAMTN * NW1 84 A5
GPK RM2 57 J5
KTN/HRWW/W HA3 42 D4
Mead Ct CDALE/KGS NW9 62 E2
Mead Crs CHING E4 38 A6
DART DA1 171 G3
SUT SM1 209 J2
Meadcroft Rd LBTH SE11 122 B6
Meade Cl CHSWK W4 117 H6
Meadfield EDGE HA8 30 D4
Mead Fld RYLN/HDSTN * HA2 77 K1
Meadfoot Rd
STRHM/NOR SW16 179 H4
Meadgate Av WFD IG8 53 J1
Mead Gv CHDH RM6 55 K6
Mead House La YEAD UB4 94 B3
Meadlands Dr RCHPK/HAM TW10 156 E4
The Meadow CHST BR7 185 H2
Meadow Av CROY/NA CR0 198 A3
Meadowbank BKHTH/KID SE3 145 J4
BRYLDS KT5 191 G3
HAMP NW3 83 K5
OXHEY WD19 27 G2
WCHMH N21 35 F1
Meadowbank Cl FUL/PGN SW6 139 F1
Meadowbank Gdns HEST TW5 133 K2
Meadowbank Rd
CDALE/KGS NW9 63 F4
Meadow Cl BAR EN5 32 D1
BXLYHS DA6 149 G6
CAT SE6 182 D1
CHING E4 37 K3
CHST BR7 185 G1
ESH/CLAY KT10 205 F1
HOM E9 87 H3
HSLWW TW4 155 F1
NTHLT UB5 96 A1
PEND EN3 25 G2
RCHPK/HAM TW10 157 F3
RSLP HA4 58 D3
RYNPK SW20 193 G1
Meadowcourt Rd
BKHTH/KID SE3 145 J5
Meadow Cft BMLY BR1 184 E6
Meadowcroft BUSH * WD23 28 B1
Meadowcroft Cl PLMGR * N13 35 H4
Meadowcroft Rd PLMGR N13 35 G4
Meadow Dr HDN NW4 46 A5
MUSWH N10 48 A6
Meadowford Cl THMD SE28 109 G6
Meadow Gdns EDGE HA8 44 D2
Meadow Garth WLSDN NW10 80 E4
Meadow Hl NWMAL KT3 192 B3
Meadow La LEE/GVPK SE12 166 A5
Meadowlea Cl WDR/YW UB7 112 A6
Meadow Ms VX/NE SW8 122 A6
Meadow Pl CHSWK * W4 138 B1
VX/NE SW8 141 K1
Meadow Rd BARK IG11 91 F5
DAGW RM9 92 B4
ESH/CLAY KT10 204 E3
FELT TW13 154 D4
HAYES BR2 183 H4
PIN HA5 59 H1
ROMW/RG RM7 74 E5
STHL UB1 95 K6
SUT SM1 209 J2
VX/NE SW8 122 A6
WIM/MER SW19 178 B3
Meadow Rw STHWK SE1 18 C5
The Meadows ORP BR6 217 J4
Meadows Cl LEY E10 69 J6
Meadowside DART DA1 171 H3
ELTH/MOT SE9 146 B5
TWK TW1 156 E2
WOT/HER KT12 188 B6
Meadowside Rd BELMT SM2 208 C6
Meadow Stile CROY/NA CR0 211 J1
Meadowsweet Cl CAN/RD E16 107 H4
NWMAL KT3 193 F2
Meadow Vw BFN/LL DA15 168 C1
HRW HA1 60 E5
Meadowview Rd BXLY DA5 169 F1
CAT SE6 164 D6
HOR/WEW KT19 207 G6
Meadow View Rd THHTH CR7 196 C2
YEAD UB4 94 B3
Meadow Wk DAGW RM9 92 B4
HOR/WEW KT19 207 G4
RDART DA2 171 F6
SWFD E18 70 E1
WLGTN SM6 210 B1
The Meadow Wy
KTN/HRWW/W HA3 42 E4
Meadow Wy CDALE/KGS NW9 63 F2
CHSGTN KT9 206 A3
ORP BR6 216 A1
RSLP HA4 59 F3
WBLY HA9 79 K2
Meadow Waye HEST TW5 134 D1
Mead Pth WIM/MER SW19 178 C2
Mead Pl CROY/NA CR0 196 C5
HOM E9 86 E4
Mead Plat WLSDN NW10 80 E4
Mead Rd CHST BR7 185 H2
DART DA1 171 G3
EDGE HA8 44 C2
RCHPK/HAM TW10 156 D5
Mead Rw STHWK SE1 17 J4
The Meads CHEAM SM3 208 B1
EDGE HA8 45 F2
MTCM * CR4 194 D2
Meadside Cl BECK BR3 182 B4
Meads La GDMY/SEVK IG3 73 F4
Meads Rd PEND EN3 25 G2
WDGN N22 49 H5
Meadvale Rd CROY/NA CR0 197 G4
EA W5 97 H3
The Meadway BKHH IG9 39 H3
BKHTH/KID SE3 145 G3
ORP BR6 217 H3
Mead Wy CROY/NA CR0 198 B6
HAYES BR2 199 K3
RSLP HA4 58 B3
Meadway ASHF TW15 152 D6
BAR EN5 20 E5
BECK BR3 183 F4
BRYLDS KT5 191 K5
ESH/CLAY KT10 204 B6
GDMY/SEVK IG3 90 E2
GLDGN NW11 65 F3
GPK RM2 57 J5
RYNPK SW20 193 F1
STHGT/OAK N14 34 D4
WFD IG8 53 G1
WHTN TW2 155 J3
Meadway Cl BAR EN5 20 E4
GLDGN NW11 65 F3
PIN HA5 42 B2
Meadway Ct EA * W5 98 B4
Meadway Gdns RSLP HA4 58 B3
Meaford Wy PGE/AN SE20 181 J3
Meanley Rd MNPK E12 89 J3
Meard St SOHO/CST W1F 10 C4
Meath Cl STMC/STPC BR5 202 C2
Meath Rd IL IG1 90 C1
SRTFD E15 106 D1
Meath St BTSEA SW11 141 G2
Mecklenburgh Pl BMSBY WC1N 5 G6
Mecklenburgh Sq BMSBY WC1N 5 G6
Mecklenburgh St BMSBY WC1N 5 G6
Medburn St CAMTN NW1 4 C2
Medcroft Gdns
MORT/ESHN SW14 137 K5
Medebourne Cl BKHTH/KID SE3 145 K4
Medesenge Wy PLMGR N13 49 H2
Medfield St PUT/ROE SW15 158 D2
Medhurst Cl BOW E3 105 G1
Median Rd CLPT E5 86 E3
Medina Av ESH/CLAY KT10 204 E1
Medina Rd HOLWY N7 85 G1
Medland Cl WLGTN SM6 195 F5
Medlar Cl NTHLT UB5 95 H1
Medlar St CMBW SE5 142 D2
Medley Rd KIL/WHAMP NW6 82 E4
Medora Rd BRXS/STRHM SW2 162 A1
ROMW/RG RM7 75 F1
Medusa Rd LEW SE13 164 E1
Medway Cl CROY/NA CR0 197 K3
IL IG1 90 C3
Medway Dr GFD/PVL UB6 97 F1
Medway Gdns ALP/SUD HA0 79 G2
Medway Pde GFD/PVL * UB6 97 F1
Medway Rd BOW E3 105 G1
DART DA1 150 D4
Medway St WEST SW1P 16 C5
Medwin St BRXN/ST SW9 142 A5
Meerbrook Rd BKHTH/KID SE3 146 B4
Meeson Rd SRTFD E15 88 D5
Meeson St CLPT E5 87 G2
Meesons Whf SRTFD * E15 106 A1
Meeting Field Pth HOM * E9 86 E4
Meeting House Aly WAP * E1W 123 J1
Meeting House La PECK SE15 143 J2
Mehetabel Rd HOM E9 86 E4
Meister Cl IL IG1 72 D5
Melanda Cl CHST BR7 184 E1
Melanie Cl BXLYHN DA7 149 F2
Melaris Ms KIL/WHAMP NW6 82 E3
Melbourne Av PLMGR N13 49 F2
RYLN/HDSTN HA2 42 B6
WEA W13 116 B1
Melbourne Cl ORP BR6 201 K4
WLGTN SM6 210 C3
Melbourne Gdns CHDH RM6 74 A2
Melbourne Gv EDUL SE22 143 G5
Melbourne Ms BRXN/ST SW9 142 B2
CAT SE6 165 F2
Melbourne Pl HOL/ALD WC2B 11 H4
Melbourne Rd EHAM E6 107 K1
IL IG1 72 B5
LEY E10 69 K4
TEDD TW11 174 D2
WALTH E17 69 G1
WIM/MER SW19 177 K4
WLGTN SM6 210 B3
Melbourne Sq BRXN/ST SW9 142 B2
Melbourne Ter EDUL * SE22 143 F5
FUL/PGN * SW6 140 A1
Melbourne Wy EN EN1 36 B1
Melbury Av NWDGN UB2 115 G3
Melbury Cl CHST BR7 184 E2
ESH/CLAY KT10 205 H4
Melbury Ct WKENS W14 119 J3
Melbury Dr CMBW SE5 143 F1
Melbury Gdns RYNPK SW20 176 E4
Melbury Rd KTN/HRWW/W HA3 62 B2
WKENS W14 119 J3
Melbury Ter CAMTN NW1 2 D7
Melcombe Gdns
KTN/HRWW/W HA3 62 B3
Melcombe Pl CAMTN NW1 8 E1
Melcombe St CAMTN NW1 3 F7
Meldon Cl FUL/PGN * SW6 140 A2
Meldone Cl BRYLDS KT5 191 J3
Meldrum Cl STMC/STPC BR5 202 D3
Meldrum Rd GDMY/SEVK IG3 73 G6
Melfield Gdns CAT SE6 164 E6
Melfont Av THHTH CR7 180 C6
Melford Av BARK IG11 90 E4
Melford Cl CHSGTN KT9 206 B3
Melford Rd EDUL SE22 163 H3
EHAM E6 107 K3
IL IG1 72 D6
WALTH E17 69 G1
WAN E11 70 C6
Melfort Rd THHTH CR7 180 C6
Melgund Rd HBRY N5 85 G3
Melina Cl HYS/HAR UB3 94 B4
Melina Pl STJWD NW8 2 A5
Melina Rd SHB W12 118 E2
Melior Pl STHWK * SE1 19 G2
Melior St STHWK SE1 19 F2
Meliot Rd CAT SE6 165 G4
Meller Cl CROY/NA CR0 210 E1
Melling Dr EN EN1 24 C2
Melling St WOOL/PLUM SE18 127 K6
Mellish Gdns WFD IG8 52 E1
Mellish St POP/IOD E14 124 D3
Mellison Rd TOOT SW17 178 D1
Melliss Av RCH/KEW TW9 137 J2
Mellitus St SHB W12 99 H5
Mellor Cl WOT/HER KT12 188 E4
Mellow La East YEAD UB4 94 A3
Mellows Rd CLAY IG5 53 K6
WLGTN SM6 210 D3
Mells Crs ELTH/MOT SE9 166 E6
Mell St GNWCH SE10 125 H5
Melody Rd WAND/EARL SW18 140 B6
Melon Pl KENS W8 119 K2
Melon Rd PECK SE15 143 H2
WAN E11 88 C1
Melrose Av CRICK NW2 82 A3
DART DA1 170 B2
GFD/PVL UB6 96 B1
MTCM CR4 179 G3
STRHM/NOR SW16 180 A6
WDGN N22 49 H4
WHTN TW2 155 G2
WIM/MER SW19 159 J4
Melrose Cl GFD/PVL UB6 96 B1
LEE/GVPK SE12 165 K3
YEAD UB4 94 E4
Melrose Crs ORP BR6 216 D2
Melrose Dr STHL UB1 115 F1
Melrose Gdns EDGE HA8 44 D6
HMSMTH W6 119 F3
NWMAL KT3 176 A6
Melrose Rd BARN SW13 138 C3
RYLN/HDSTN HA2 59 K1
WAND/EARL SW18 159 J1
WIM/MER SW19 177 K5
Melrose Ter HMSMTH W6 119 F2
Melrose Vls BECK * BR3 182 D5
Melsa Rd MRDN SM4 194 B3
Melthorne Dr RSLP HA4 77 G1
Melthorpe Gdns
WOOL/PLUM SE18 146 C2
Melton Cl RSLP HA4 59 G5
Melton Flds HOR/WEW KT19 207 F6
Melton Gdns ROM RM1 75 H4
Melton Pl HOR/WEW KT19 207 F6
Melton St CAMTN NW1 4 B5
Melville Av GFD/PVL UB6 79 F3
RYNPK SW20 176 D3
SAND/SEL CR2 212 B3
Melville Cl HGDN/ICK UB10 76 B1
Melville Ct DEPT SE8 124 A4
Melville Gdns PLMGR N13 49 G1
Melville Pl IS * N1 85 J5

Melville Rd BARN SW13 138 D2
RAIN RM13 111 J3
ROMW/RG RM7 56 D3
SCUP DA14 168 D4
WALTH E17 69 H1
WLSDN NW10 81 F5
Melville Villas Rd ACT * W3 118 A1
Melvin Rd PGE/AN SE20 181 K4
Memel St STLK EC1Y 6 C7
Memorial Av SRTFD E15 106 C2
Memorial Cl HEST TW5 114 E6
Mendip Cl HYS/HAR UB3 133 G1
SYD SE26 163 K6
WPK KT4 193 F6
Mendip Dr GLDGN NW11 64 C6
Mendip Houses BETH * E2 104 E2
Mendip Rd BTSEA SW11 140 B4
BUSH WD23 28 C1
BXLYHN DA7 150 B2
EMPK RM11 75 J4
GNTH/NBYPK IG2 72 E2
Mendora Rd FUL/PGN SW6 139 H1
Menelik Rd CRICK NW2 82 C2
Menlo Gdns NRWD SE19 180 E3
Menon Dr ED N9 36 D5
Menotti St BETH * E2 104 C3
Mentmore Cl KTN/HRWW/W HA3 61 J3
Mentmore Ter HACK E8 86 D5
Meon Rd ACT W3 117 K2
Meopham Rd MTCM CR4 179 H4
Mepham Crs
KTN/HRWW/W HA3 42 C3
Mepham Gdns
KTN/HRWW/W HA3 42 C3
Mepham St STHWK SE1 17 H1
Mera Dr BXLYHN DA7 149 H5
Merantun Wy WIM/MER SW19 178 A4
Merbury Cl LEW SE13 145 F6
Merbury Rd THMD SE28 127 J1
Merbury St WOOL/PLUM SE18 127 G3
Mercator Pl POP/IOD E14 124 D5
Mercator Rd LEW SE13 145 G5
Mercer Cl THDIT KT7 190 A4
Merceron Houses BETH * E2 104 E2
Merceron St WCHPL E1 104 D3
Mercer Pl PIN HA5 41 G5
Mercers Cl GNWCH SE10 125 J4
Mercers Cottages WCHPL * E1 105 G5
Mercers Pl HMSMTH W6 119 F4
Mercers Rd ARCH N19 84 D1
Mercer St LSQ/SEVD WC2H 10 E4
Merchant St BOW * E3 105 H2
Merchiston Rd CAT SE6 165 G4
Merchland Rd ELTH/MOT SE9 167 H3
Mercia Gv LEW SE13 145 F4
Mercier Rd PUT/ROE SW15 139 H6
Mercury Gdns ROM RM1 75 H2
Mercury House HYS/HAR * UB3 113 J2
Mercury Rd BTFD TW8 116 D5
Mercury Wy NWCR SE14 124 A6
Mercy Ter LEW SE13 144 E6
Merebank La WLGTN SM6 211 F3
Mere Cl ORP BR6 201 G6
WIM/MER SW19 159 G2
Meredith Av CRICK NW2 82 A3
Meredith Cl PIN HA5 41 H3
Meredith Ms BROCKY * SE4 144 C5
Meredith St CLKNW EC1R 6 A5
PLSTW E13 106 E2
Meredyth Rd BARN SW13 138 D3
Mere End CROY/NA CR0 198 A4
Mereside ORP BR6 201 F6
Mereside Pk ASHF * TW15 153 F6
Meretone Cl BROCKY SE4 144 B5
Merevale Crs MRDN SM4 194 B3
Mereway Rd WHTN TW2 155 J3
Merewood Cl BMLY BR1 185 F5
Merewood Rd BXLYHN DA7 149 K3
Mereworth Cl HAYES BR2 199 J2
Mereworth Dr
WOOL/PLUM SE18 147 G1
Meriden Cl BARK/HLT IG6 54 C4
BMLY BR1 184 C3
Meridian Rd CHARL SE7 146 C1
Meridian Sq SRTFD E15 88 B5
Meridian Wy UED N18 50 E2
Merifield Rd ELTH/MOT SE9 146 B5
Merino Cl WAN E11 71 G1
Merivale Rd HRW HA1 60 C4
PUT/ROE SW15 139 H5
Merlewood Dr CHST BR7 184 E4
Merley Ct CDALE/KGS NW9 62 E5
Merlin Cl CROY/NA CR0 211 F4
CROY/NA CR0 212 A2
CRW RM5 57 F2
MTCM CR4 178 D6
NTHLT UB5 95 G2
Merlin Crs EDGE HA8 44 B4
Merlin Gdns ROM RM1 57 F2
Merlin Gv BARK/HLT IG6 54 B3
BECK BR3 198 C1
Merlin Rd CRW RM5 57 F2
MNPK E12 71 H6
WELL DA16 148 B5
Merlin Rd North WELL DA16 148 B5
Merlins Av RYLN/HDSTN HA2 77 K1
Merlin St FSBYW WC1X 5 J5
Mermagen Dr RAIN RM13 93 K5
Mermaid Ct STHWK SE1 18 E2
Merredene St
BRXS/STRHM SW2 162 A1
Merriam Cl CHING E4 52 A1
Merrick Rd NWDGN UB2 114 E4
Merrick Sq STHWK SE1 18 E4
Merridene WCHMH N21 35 H1
Merrielands Crs DAGW RM9 110 B1
Merrilands Rd WPK KT4 193 F5
Merrilees Rd BFN/LL DA15 167 K2
Merrilyn Cl ESH/CLAY KT10 205 G4
Merriman Rd BKHTH/KID SE3 146 B2
Merrington Rd FUL/PGN SW6 119 K6
Merrion Av STAN HA7 43 K1
Merritt Gdns CHSGTN KT9 205 J4
Merritt Rd BROCKY SE4 144 C6
Merrivale STHGT/OAK N14 22 D6
Merrivale Av REDBR IG4 71 H1
Merrivale Ms WDR/YW * UB7 112 A1
Merrow Rd BELMT SM2 208 B6
Merrow St WALW SE17 122 E5
Merrow Wk WALW SE17 122 E5
Merrow Wy CROY/NA CR0 214 A4
Merrydown Wy CHST BR7 184 D4
Merryfield BKHTH/KID SE3 145 J3
Merryfield Gdns STAN HA7 43 J1
Merryhill Cl CHING E4 37 K2
Merry Hill Mt BUSH WD23 28 B3
Merry Hill Rd BUSH WD23 28 A2
Merryhills Dr ENC/FH EN2 22 E5
Merryweather Cl DART DA1 171 J1
Merryweather Ct NWMAL * KT3 192 B2
Mersey Rd WALTH E17 51 H6
Mersham Dr CDALE/KGS NW9 62 C2
Mersham Pl PGE/AN SE20 181 J4
THHTH CR7 180 E5
Mersham Rd THHTH CR7 180 E6
Merten Rd CHDH RM6 74 A4
Merthyr Ter BARN SW13 118 E6
Merton Av CHSWK W4 118 C4
NTHLT UB5 78 C3
Merton Gdns STMC/STPC BR5 201 G2
Merton Hall Gdns RYNPK SW20 177 H4
Merton Hall Rd WIM/MER SW19 177 H4
Merton High St
WIM/MER SW19 178 B3
Merton La HGT N6 65 K6
Merton Pl WIM/MER * SW19 178 B4
Merton Ri HAMP NW3 83 J5
Merton Rd BARK IG11 91 F5
ENC/FH EN2 23 K1
GDMY/SEVK IG3 73 F4
RYLN/HDSTN HA2 60 C5
SNWD SE25 197 G2
WALTH E17 70 A2
WAND/EARL SW18 159 K3
WIM/MER SW19 178 A3
Merton Wy E/WMO/HCT KT8 189 H1
Mertoun Ter MBLAR * W1H 8 E3
Merttins Rd PECK SE15 144 A5
Meru Cl KTTN NW5 84 A3
Mervan Rd BRXS/STRHM SW2 142 B5
Mervyn Av ELTH/MOT SE9 167 H5
Mervyn Rd WEA W13 116 B3
Messaline Av ACT W3 98 E5
Messent Rd ELTH/MOT SE9 146 B6
Messeter Pl ELTH/MOT SE9 167 F1
Messina Av KIL/WHAMP NW6 82 E5
Meteor St BTSEA SW11 141 F5
Meteor Wy WLGTN SM6 210 E5
Metford Crs PEND EN3 25 J1
Metheringham Wy
CDALE/KGS NW9 45 G5
Methley St LBTH SE11 122 B5
Methuen Cl EDGE HA8 44 C3
Methuen Pk MUSWH N10 48 B5
Methuen Rd BELV DA17 129 J4
BXLYHS DA6 149 G5
EDGE HA8 44 C3
Methwold Rd NKENS W10 100 B4
Metropolitan Cl POP/IOD E14 105 J4
Metropolitan Whf WAP * E1W 123 K1
The Mews BECK * BR3 182 D4
CEND/HSY/T N8 67 G1
NFNCH/WDSP * N12 47 F1
REDBR IG4 71 H2
ROM RM1 75 G1
STRHM/NOR * SW16 180 A4
TWK * TW1 156 C1
Mews North BGVA SW1W 15 J5
Mews Pl WFD IG8 38 E6
Mews South PIM SW1V 121 H5
Mews St WAP E1W 13 K7
Mexfield Rd PUT/ROE SW15 139 J6
Meyer Gn EN EN1 24 C1
Meyer Rd ERITH DA8 129 K6
Meymott St STHWK SE1 18 A1
Meynell Crs HOM E9 87 F5
Meynell Gdns HOM E9 87 F5
Meynell Rd HARH RM3 57 K2
HOM E9 87 F5
Meyrick Rd BTSEA SW11 140 C4
WLSDN NW10 81 J4
Mezen Cl NTHWD HA6 40 B1
Miah Ter WAP * E1W 123 H1
Micawber St IS N1 6 C4
Michael Gaynor Cl HNWL W7 116 A1
Michaelmas Cl RYNPK SW20 177 F6
Michael Rd FUL/PGN SW6 140 A2
SNWD SE25 181 F6
WAN E11 70 C5
Michaels Cl LEW SE13 145 H4
Micheldever Rd LEW SE13 165 H1
Michelham Gdns TWK TW1 156 A5
Michigan Av MNPK E12 89 J2
Michleham Down
NFNCH/WDSP N12 32 D6
Mickleham Cl STMC/STPC BR5 186 A5
Mickleham Gdns CHEAM SM3 208 C4
Mickleham Rd STMC/STPC BR5 186 A4
Mickleham Wy CROY/NA CR0 214 B5
Micklethwaite Rd
FUL/PGN SW6 119 K6
Midcroft RSLP HA4 58 C5
Middle Dartrey Wk
WBPTN * SW10 140 B1
Middle Dene MLHL NW7 31 F5
Middlefield STJWD NW8 83 H6
Middlefields CROY/NA CR0 213 G6
WEA W13 97 H4
Middle Green Cl BRYLDS KT5 191 G3
Middleham Gdns UED N18 50 C2
Middleham Rd UED N18 50 C2
Middle La CEND/HSY/T N8 66 E2
TEDD TW11 174 A2
Middle Lane Ms CEND/HSY/T N8 66 E2
Middle Park Av ELTH/MOT SE9 166 C2
Middle Rd EBAR EN4 33 J1
PLSTW E13 106 E1
RYLN/HDSTN HA2 60 D6
STRHM/NOR SW16 179 H5
Middle Rw NKENS W10 100 C3
Middlesborough Rd UED N18 50 C2
Middlesex Pl HOM E9 86 E4
Middlesex Rd MTCM CR4 195 K2
Middlesex St WCHPL E1 13 H2
Middle St CROY/NA CR0 196 D6
STBT EC1A 12 C1
Middle Temple La TPL/STR WC2R 11 J4
Middleton Av CHING E4 37 H6
GFD/PVL UB6 96 D1
SCUP DA14 186 D2
Middleton Buildings GTPST W1W 10 A2
Middleton Cl CHING E4 37 H5
Middleton Dr BERM/RHTH SE16 124 A2
PIN HA5 40 E6
Middleton Gdns
GNTH/NBYPK IG2 72 B3
Middleton Gv HOLWY N7 84 E3
Middleton Pl GTPST W1W 10 A2
Middleton Rd GLDGN NW11 64 E4
HACK E8 86 B5
HYS/HAR UB3 94 B4
MRDN SM4 194 B3
NWMAL KT3 175 K6
Middleton St BETH E2 104 D2
Middleton Wy LEW SE13 145 G5
Middleway GLDGN NW11 65 F2
The Middle Wy
KTN/HRWW/W HA3 43 F5
Middle Wy STRHM/NOR SW16 179 J5
Middle Yd STHWK SE1 13 F7
Midfield Av BXLYHN DA7 149 K4
Midfield Wy STMC/STPC BR5 186 C4
Midford Pl FITZ * W1T 4 B7
Midholm GLDGN NW11 65 F1
WBLY HA9 62 C5
Midholm Cl GLDGN * NW11 65 F1
Midholm Rd CROY/NA CR0 213 G1
Midhope St STPAN WC1H 5 F5
Midhurst Av CROY/NA CR0 196 B4
MUSWH N10 48 A6
Midhurst Cl HCH RM12 93 J2
Midhurst Gdns HGDN/ICK UB10 76 A5
Midhurst Hl BXLYHS DA6 149 H6
Midhurst Pde MUSWH * N10 48 A6
Midhurst Rd HNWL W7 116 B2
Midland Arches CRICK * NW2 63 K6
Midland Crs HAMP NW3 83 G4
Midland Rd CAMTN NW1 4 D3
LEY E10 70 A4
Midland Ter WLSDN NW10 99 G3
Midlothian Rd BOW E3 105 H3
Midmoor Rd BAL SW12 161 H3
WIM/MER SW19 177 G4
Midship Cl BERM/RHTH * SE16 124 A1
Midship Point POP/IOD * E14 124 D2
Midstrath Rd WLSDN NW10 81 G2
Midsummer Av HSLWW TW4 134 E5
Midway CHEAM SM3 193 J4
WOT/HER KT12 188 A6
Midwinter Cl WELL DA16 148 B4
Mighell Av REDBR IG4 71 H2
Milan Rd STHL UB1 114 E2
Milborne Gv WBPTN SW10 120 B5
Milborne St HOM E9 86 E4
Milborough Crs LEE/GVPK SE12 165 H1
Milbourne La ESH/CLAY KT10 204 C4
Milbrook ESH/CLAY KT10 204 C4
Milcote St STHWK SE1 18 A3
Mildenhall Rd CLPT E5 86 E2
Mildmay Av IS N1 85 K4
Mildmay Gv North IS N1 85 K3
Mildmay Gv South IS N1 85 K3
Mildmay Pk IS N1 85 K3
Mildmay Pl STNW/STAM * N16 86 A3
Mildmay Rd IL IG1 90 B1
IS N185 K3
ROMW/RG RM7 74 E2
Mildmay St IS N1 85 K4
Mildred Av HYS/HAR UB3 113 G4
NTHLT UB5 78 B3
Mildred Cl DART DA1 171 K1
Mildred Rd ERITH DA8 130 B5
The Mile End WALTH E17 51 F4
Mile End Pl WCHPL E1 105 F3
Mile End Rd WCHPL E1 104 E4
Mile Rd WLGTN SM6 195 F5
Miles Dr THMD SE28 127 K1
Milespit Hl MLHL NW7 45 K1
Miles Pl BRYLDS * KT5 191 G1
Miles Rd CEND/HSY/T N8 48 E6
MTCM CR4 178 D6
Miles St VX/NE SW8 121 K6
Milestone Cl BELMT SM2 209 H4
ED N9 36 C4
Milestone Rd NRWD SE19 181 G2
Miles Wy TRDG/WHET N20 33 J4
Milfoil St SHB W12 99 J6
Milford Cl ABYW SE2 129 F6
Milford Gdns ALP/SUD HA0 79 K3
EDGE HA8 44 C3
Milford Gv SUT SM1 209 G2
Milford La TPL/STR WC2R 11 J5
Milford Ms STRHM/NOR SW16 162 A5
Milford Rd STHL UB1 96 A6
WEA W13 116 C1
Milk St BMLY BR1 184 A2
CAN/RD E16 127 G1
CITYW EC2V 12 D3
Milkwell Gdns WFD IG8 53 F3
Milkwell Yd CMBW SE5 142 D2
Milkwood Rd HNHL SE24 142 C6
Milk Yd WAP E1W 104 E6
Millais Av MNPK E12 90 A3
Millais Gdns EDGE HA8 44 C5
Millais Rd EN EN1 24 B6
NWMAL KT3 192 B4
WAN E11 88 A2
Millais Wy HOR/WEW KT19 206 E2
Millard Cl STNW/STAM N16 86 A3
Millbank WEST SW1P 16 E6
Millbank Est WEST SW1P 16 D7
Millbank Wy LEE/GVPK SE12 145 K6
Millbourne Rd FELT TW13 154 D6
Mill Br BAR * EN5 20 D6
Millbrook Av WELL DA16 147 J5
Millbrook Gdns CHDH RM6 74 A3
GPK RM2 57 G5
Millbrook Rd BRXN/ST SW9 142 C4
ED N9 36 D3
Mill Brook Rd STMC/STPC BR5 202 D1
Mill Cl CAR * SM5 195 F6
WDR/YW UB7 112 A3
Mill Cnr BAR EN5 20 D2
Millennium Br STHWK SE1 12 C6
Millennium Cl CAN/RD E16 106 E5
Millennium Dr POP/IOD E14 125 G3
Millennium Pl BETH * E2 104 D1
Millennium Sq STHWK SE1 19 J2
Millennium Wy GNWCH SE10 125 H2
Millennium Whf POP/IOD E14 125 G4
Miller Av PEND * EN3 25 J1
Miller Cl MTCM CR4 194 E4
Miller Rd CROY/NA CR0 196 A5
WIM/MER SW19 178 C2
Miller's Av HACK E8 86 B3
Millers Cl MLHL NW7 31 J6
Miller's Ct CHSWK W4 118 C5
Millers Green Cl ENC/FH EN2 23 H4
Miller's Ter HACK E8 86 B3
Miller St CAMTN NW1 4 A2
Miller's Wy HMSMTH W6 119 F2
Millers Yd FNCH N3 47 F4
Miller Wk STHWK SE1 17 K1
Millet Rd GFD/PVL UB6 96 B2
Mill Farm Cl PIN HA5 41 G5
Mill Farm Crs HSLWW TW4 154 D3
Millfield Av WALTH E17 51 H4
Millfield La HGT N6 65 K6
Millfield Rd EDGE HA8 44 E5
HSLWW TW4 154 D3
Millfields Cl STMC/STPC BR5 202 C1
Millfields Rd CLPT E5 86 E2
Mill Gdns SYD SE26 163 J6
Mill Gn MTCM * CR4 195 F4
Mill Green Rd MTCM CR4 195 F4
Millgrove St BTSEA SW11 141 F2
Millharbour POP/IOD E14 124 E3
Millhaven Cl CHDH RM6 73 H3
Mill Hl BARN SW13 138 D4
Mill Hill Gv ACT * W3 117 J1
Mill Hill Rd ACT W3 117 J2
BARN SW13 138 E4
Mill Hill Ter ACT W3 117 J1
Millhouse Pl WNWD SE27 162 C6
Millicent Rd LEY * E10 69 H5
Milligan St POP/IOD E14 105 H6
Milling Rd EDGE HA8 45 F3
Millington Rd HYS/HAR UB3 113 H3
Mill La CAR SM5 210 A2
CHDH RM6 74 A3
CHING E4 25 K4
CRICK NW2 82 C3
CROY/NA CR0 211 G1
EW KT17 207 H6
WFD IG8 52 D1
WOOL/PLUM SE18 127 F5
Millman Ms BMSBY * WC1N 5 G7
Millman Pl BMSBY WC1N 5 G7
Millman St BMSBY WC1N 5 G7
Millmark Gv NWCR SE14 144 B3
Millmarsh La PEND EN3 25 G3
Mill Mead Rd TOTM N17 50 D6
Mill Pl CHST BR7 185 F4
DART DA1 150 D5
KUT KT1 175 G6
POP/IOD E14 105 G5
Mill Plat ISLW TW7 136 B4
Mill Plat Av ISLW TW7 136 B3
Millpond Est
BERM/RHTH * SE16 123 J2
Mill Pond Rd DART DA1 171 H1
Mill Rdg EDGE HA8 44 B1
Mill Rd CAN/RD E16 126 A1
ERITH DA8 149 K1
ESH/CLAY KT10 189 F6
IL IG1 90 A1
RDART DA2 171 J6
WDR/YW UB7 112 A3
WHTN TW2 155 H4
WIM/MER SW19 178 B3
Mill Rw BXLY * DA5 169 J2
IS N1 7 H1
Mills Gv HDN NW4 46 B6
POP/IOD E14 106 A4
Millshot Cl FUL/PGN SW6 139 F2
Millside CAR SM5 194 E6
Millside Pl ISLW TW7 136 C3
Millson Cl TRDG/WHET N20 33 H4
Mills Rw CHSWK W4 118 A4
Millstream Cl PLMGR N13 49 G1
Millstream Rd STHWK SE1 19 J3
Mill St CONDST W1S 9 K5
KUT KT1 175 F6
STHWK SE1 19 K3
Mill V HAYES BR2 183 K6
Mill View Cl EW KT17 207 H5
Mill View Gdns CROY/NA CR0 213 F1
Millwall Dock Rd POP/IOD E14 124 D3
Mill Wy EBED/NFELT TW14 134 A6
MLHL NW7 45 G1
Millway Gdns NTHLT UB5 77 K4
Millwell Crs CHIG IG7 54 D1
Millwood Rd HSLW TW3 135 H6
STMC/STPC BR5 186 D6
Millwood St NKENS W10 100 C4
Milman Cl PIN HA5 41 H6
Milman Rd KIL/WHAMP NW6 100 B1
Milmans St WBPTN * SW10 120 C6
WBPTN SW10 120 C6
Milne Fld PIN HA5 42 A3
Milne Gdns ELTH/MOT SE9 146 D6
Milner Ct BUSH WD23 28 B1
Milner Dr WHTN TW2 155 J2
Milner Pl IS N1 85 G6
Milner Rd BCTR RM8 73 J6
KUT KT1 174 E6
MRDN SM4 194 C2
SRTFD E15 106 C2
THHTH CR7 180 D6
WIM/MER SW19 178 A4
Milner Sq IS * N1 85 G5
Milner St CHEL SW3 14 E6
Milnthorpe Rd CHSWK W4 118 A6
Milo Rd EDUL SE22 163 G1
Milroy Wk STHWK SE1 11 K7
Milson Rd WKENS W14 119 H3
Milton Av BAR EN5 20 D6
CDALE/KGS NW9 44 D6
CROY/NA CR0 196 E4
EHAM E6 89 H5
HCH RM12 75 H6
HGT N6 66 C4
SUT SM1 209 H1
WLSDN NW10 81 F6
Milton Cl EFNCH N2 65 G3
STHWK SE1 19 J7
SUT SM1 209 H1
YEAD UB4 94 E5
Milton Ct BARB EC2Y 12 E1
Milton Court Rd NWCR SE14 124 B6
Milton Crs GNTH/NBYPK IG2 72 C4
Milton Gdns STWL/WRAY TW19 152 C3
Milton Gv FBAR/BDGN N11 48 C1
STNW/STAM N16 85 K2
Milton Pk HGT N6 66 C4
Milton Rd ACT W3 118 A1
BELV DA17 129 H4
CDALE/KGS * NW9 63 J4
CROY/NA CR0 196 E4
HGT N6 66 C4
HNHL SE24 142 C6
HNWL W7 97 F6
HPTN TW12 173 F3
HRW HA1 60 E1
MLHL NW7 45 J1
MORT/ESHN SW14 138 A4
MTCM CR4 179 F3
ROM RM1 75 J3
SEVS/STOTM N15 49 H6
SUT SM1 208 E1
WALTH E17 69 J1
WELL DA16 148 A2
WIM/MER SW19 178 B2
WLGTN SM6 210 C4
Milton St BARB EC2Y 12 E1
Milton Wy WDR/YW UB7 112 C4
Milverton Dr HGDN/ICK UB10 76 A2
Milverton Gdns GDMY/SEVK IG3 73 F6
Milverton Rd KIL/WHAMP NW6 82 A5
Milverton St LBTH SE11 122 B5
Milverton Wy ELTH/MOT SE9 167 F6
Milward St WCHPL E1 104 D4
Mimosa Cl ORP BR6 217 J1
Mimosa Rd YEAD UB4 95 G4
Mimosa St FUL/PGN SW6 139 J2
Minard Rd CAT SE6 165 H3
Mina Rd WALW SE17 123 F5
WIM/MER SW19 177 K4
Minchenden Crs STHGT/OAK N14 34 D5
Mincing La MON EC3R 13 G5
Minden Rd CHEAM SM3 193 H6
PGE/AN SE20 181 J4
Minehead Rd RYLN/HDSTN HA2 78 A1
STRHM/NOR SW16 180 A1
Mineral St WOOL/PLUM SE18 127 K4
Minera Ms BGVA SW1W 15 H6
Minerva Cl BRXN/ST SW9 142 B1
SCUP DA14 167 K6
Minerva Rd CHING E4 51 K3
KUT KT1 175 G5
WLSDN NW10 98 E3
Minerva St BETH E2 104 D1
Minet Av WLSDN NW10 99 G1
Minet Dr HYS/HAR UB3 113 K1
Minet Gdns HYS/HAR UB3 114 A1
WLSDN NW10 99 G1
Minet Rd CMBW SE5 142 C3
Minford Gdns WKENS W14 119 G2
Ming St POP/IOD E14 105 J6
Minimax Cl EBED/NFELT TW14 153 K1
Ministry Wy ELTH/MOT SE9 166 E4
Mink Ct HSLWW TW4 134 B3
Minniedale BRYLDS KT5 191 G2
Minnow Wk WALW SE17 19 H7
Minories TWRH EC3N 13 J4
Minshull Pl BECK * BR3 182 D3
Minshull St VX/NE * SW8 141 J2
Minson Rd HOM E9 87 F6
Minstead Gdns PUT/ROE SW15 158 C2
Minstead Wy NWMAL KT3 192 B3
Minster Av SUT SM1 193 K6
Minster Ct FENCHST * EC3M 13 G5
Minster Dr CROY/NA CR0 212 A2
Minster Gdns E/WMO/HCT KT8 188 E1
Minster Rd BMLY BR1 184 A3
CRICK NW2 82 C3
Minstrel Gdns BRYLDS KT5 191 G1
Mintern Cl PLMGR N13 35 H5
Minterne Av NWDGN UB2 115 F4
Minterne Rd KTN/HRWW/W HA3 62 B2
Minterne Waye YEAD UB4 95 G5
Mintern St IS N1 7 F2
Minton Ms KIL/WHAMP NW6 83 F4
Mint Rd WLGTN SM6 210 B3
Mint St STHWK SE1 18 C2
Mint Wk CROY/NA CR0 211 J1
Mirabel Rd FUL/PGN SW6 139 J1
Miranda Cl WCHPL E1 104 E4
Miranda Rd ARCH N19 66 C5
Mirfield St CHARL SE7 126 C3
Miriam Rd WOOL/PLUM SE18 127 K5
Mirren Cl RYLN/HDSTN HA2 77 K2
Miskin Rd DART DA1 171 F2
Missenden Cl
EBED/NFELT TW14 153 J3
Missenden Gdns MRDN SM4 194 B3
Mission Gv WALTH E17 69 H2
Mission Pl PECK SE15 143 H2
Mistletoe Cl CROY/NA CR0 198 A5
Misty's Fld WOT/HER KT12 188 B5
Mitali Pas WCHPL E1 104 C5
Mitcham La STRHM/NOR SW16 179 H1
Mitcham Pk MTCM CR4 194 E1
Mitcham Rd CROY/NA CR0 195 J3
EHAM E6 107 J2
GDMY/SEVK IG3 73 F4
TOOT SW17 178 E2
Mitchellbrook Wy WLSDN NW10 81 F4
Mitchell Cl ABYW SE2 128 D5
BELV DA17 129 K3
DART DA1 171 H4
Mitchell Rd ORP BR6 217 F2
PLMGR N13 49 H1
Mitchell St FSBYE EC1V 6 C6
Mitchell Wy BMLY BR1 183 K4
WLSDN NW10 80 E4
Mitchison Rd IS N1 85 K4
Mitchley Rd TOTM N17 50 C6
Mitford Rd FSBYPK N4 66 E6
The Mitre POP/IOD E14 105 H6
Mitre Cl BELMT SM2 209 G5
HAYES BR2 183 J5
Mitre Rd SRTFD E15 106 C1
STHWK SE1 17 K2
Mitre Sq HDTCH EC3A 13 H4
Mitre St HDTCH EC3A 13 H4
Mitre Wy WLSDN NW10 99 K4
The Moat NWMAL KT3 176 B4
Moat Cl ORP BR6 217 F4
Moat Ct ELTH/MOT * SE9 166 E1
Moat Crs EFNCH N2 47 F6
Moat Cft WELL DA16 148 D4
Moat Dr HRW HA1 60 C1
RSLP HA4 58 C4
Moat Farm Rd NTHLT UB5 77 K4
Moat La ERITH DA8 150 D2
Moat Pl ACT W3 98 D5
BRXN/ST SW9 142 A4
Moat Side FELT TW13 154 B6
PEND EN3 24 E5
Moberly Rd CLAP SW4 161 J2
Modbury Gdns HAMP NW3 84 A4
Model Cottages WEA * W13 116 C2
Model Farm Cl ELTH/MOT SE9 166 D5
Moelyn Ms HRW HA1 61 G2
Moffat Rd PLMGR N13 48 E2
THHTH CR7 180 D5
TOOT SW17 160 D6
Mogden La ISLW TW7 136 A6
Mohammad Khan Rd WAN * E11 70 D5
Moiety Rd POP/IOD E14 124 D2
Moira Cl TOTM N17 50 A5
Moira Rd ELTH/MOT SE9 146 E5
Moir Cl SAND/SEL CR2 212 C6
Molash Rd STMC/STPC BR5 202 E1
Mole Abbey Gdns
E/WMO/HCT KT8 173 F6
Mole Ct HOR/WEW KT19 206 E2
Molember Rd E/WMO/HCT KT8 189 K2
Molescroft ELTH/MOT SE9 167 H5
Molesey Av E/WMO/HCT KT8 188 E2
Molesey Dr CHEAM SM3 193 H6
Molesey Park Av
E/WMO/HCT KT8 189 G2

Molesey Park Cl
E/WMO/HCT KT8 189 H2
Molesey Park Rd
E/WMO/HCT KT8 189 G2
Molesey Rd E/WMO/HCT KT8 188 D2
Molesford Rd FUL/PGN * SW6 139 K2
Molesham Cl E/WMO/HCT KT8 173 G6
Molesham Wy E/WMO/HCT KT8 189 G1
Molesworth St LEW SE13 145 F4
Mollison Av PEND EN3 25 G4
Mollison Dr WLGTN SM6 210 E5
Mollison Wy EDGE HA8 44 C5
Molly Huggins Cl BAL SW12 161 H2
Molyneux Dr TOOT SW17 161 G6
Molyneux St MBLAR W1H 8 D2
Monarch Cl EBED/NFELT TW14 153 H2
RAIN RM13 111 J1
WWKM BR4 214 D2
Monarch Dr CAN/RD E16 107 H4
Monarch Ms WNWD SE27 180 B1
Monarch Pde MTCM * CR4 178 E5
Monarch Pl BKHH IG9 39 G4
Monarch Rd BELV DA17 129 H3
Monarch's Wy RSLP * HA4 58 B5
Mona Rd PECK SE15 143 K3
Monastery Gdns ENC/FH EN2 23 K3
Mona St CAN/RD E16 106 D4
Monaveen Gdns
E/WMO/HCT KT8 173 G6
Monck's Rw PUT/ROE * SW15 159 J1
Monck St WEST SW1P 16 D5
Monclar Rd CMBW SE5 142 E5
Moncorvo Cl SKENS SW7 14 C3
Moncrieff St PECK SE15 143 H3
Mondial Wy WDR/YW UB7 133 F1
Monega Rd FSTGT E7 89 G4
Money La WDR/YW UB7 112 A3
Monier Rd BOW E3 87 J5
Monivea Rd BECK BR3 182 C3
Monk Dr CAN/RD E16 106 E6
Monkfrith Av STHGT/OAK N14 34 B1
Monkfrith Wy STHGT/OAK N14 34 B2
Monkham's Av WFD IG8 53 F1
Monkham's Dr WFD IG8 53 F1
Monkham's La WFD IG8 39 F6
Monkleigh Rd MRDN SM4 177 H6
Monks Av BAR EN5 33 G1
E/WMO/HCT KT8 188 E2
Monks Cl ABYW SE2 128 E4
ENC/FH EN2 23 J3
RSLP HA4 77 H2
RYLN/HDSTN * HA2 60 A6
Monks Crs WOT/HER KT12 188 A5
Monksdene Gdns SUT SM1 209 F1
Monks Dr ACT W3 98 C4
Monks Orch DART DA1 171 F4
Monks Orchard Rd BECK BR3 198 D5
Monks Pk WBLY HA9 80 E4
Monks Park Gdns WBLY HA9 80 D4
Monks Rd ENC/FH EN2 23 H3
Monk St WOOL/PLUM SE18 127 F4
Monks Wy BECK BR3 198 D3
GLDGN NW11 64 D1
STMC/STPC BR5 201 H5
Monkswood Gdns CLAY IG5 54 A6
Monkton Rd WELL DA16 148 A3
Monkton St LBTH SE11 17 K6
Monkville Av GLDGN NW11 64 D1
Monkville Pde GLDGN * NW11 64 D1
Monkwell Sq BARB EC2Y 12 D2
Monkwood Cl ROM RM1 75 J2
Monmouth Av KUT KT1 174 D3
SWFD E18 71 F1
Monmouth Cl CHSWK W4 118 A3
MTCM CR4 195 K1
WELL DA16 148 B5
Monmouth Gv BTFD TW8 117 F4
Monmouth Pl BAY/PAD W2 100 E5
Monmouth Rd BAY/PAD W2 100 E5
DAGW RM9 92 B3
ED N9 36 D4
EHAM E6 107 K2
HYS/HAR UB3 113 H4
Monmouth St LSQ/SEVD WC2H 10 E4
Monnery Rd ARCH N19 84 C1
Monnow Rd STHWK SE1 123 H5
Monoux Gv WALTH E17 51 J4
Monroe Crs EN EN1 24 D2
Monroe Dr MORT/ESHN SW14 137 J6
Monro Gdns KTN/HRWW/W HA3 42 E3
Monro Pl HOR/WEW KT19 206 C6
Monsell Rd FSBYPK N4 85 H1
Monson Rd NWCR SE14 144 A1
WLSDN NW10 99 J1
Mons Wy HAYES BR2 200 D3
Montacute Rd BUSH WD23 28 E2
CAT SE6 164 C2
CROY/NA CR0 214 A6
MRDN SM4 194 C3
Montagu Crs UED N18 36 D6
Montague Av BROCKY SE4 144 C5
HNWL W7 116 A1
Montague Cl STHWK SE1 12 E7
Montague Gdns EA W5 98 C6
Montague Hall Pl BUSH WD23 28 A1
Montague Pl GWRST WC1E 10 D1
Montague Rd CEND/HSY/T N8 67 F2
CROY/NA CR0 196 C5
HACK E8 86 C3
HNWL W7 116 A2
HSLW TW3 135 G4
NWDGN UB2 114 D4
RCHPK/HAM TW10 157 F1
TOTM * N17 68 C1
WAN E11 70 D6
WEA W13 97 H5
WIM/MER SW19 178 A3
Montague Sq NWCR SE14 143 K1
Montague St RSQ WC1B 10 E1
STBT EC1A 12 C2
Montague Ter HAYES * BR2 199 K1
Montagu Gdns UED N18 36 D6
WLGTN SM6 210 C2
Montagu Man MHST W1U 9 F2
Montagu Ms North MBLAR W1H 9 F2
Montagu Ms South MBLAR W1H 9 F3
Montagu Ms West MBLAR W1H 9 F3
Montagu Pl MBLAR W1H 8 E2
Montagu Rd HDN NW4 63 J3
UED N18 50 D1
Montagu Rw MHST W1U 9 F2
Montagu Sq MBLAR W1H 9 F2
Montagu St MBLAR W1H 9 F3
Montalt Rd WFD IG8 52 D1
Montana Gdns CAT SE6 182 C1
SUT SM1 209 G3
Montana Rd RYNPK SW20 177 F4
TOOT SW17 161 F5
Montbelle Rd ELTH/MOT SE9 167 G5
Montbretia Cl STMC/STPC BR5 202 D1
Montcalm Cl HAYES BR2 199 K3
YEAD UB4 95 F2
Montcalm Rd CHARL SE7 146 C1
Montclare St BETH E2 7 J5
Monteagle Av BARK IG11 90 C4
Monteagle Wy PECK SE15 143 J4
Montefiore St VX/NE SW8 141 G3
Montem Rd FSTH SE23 164 C2
NWMAL KT3 192 B1
Montem St FSBYPK N4 67 F5
Montenotte Rd CEND/HSY/T N8 66 C2
Monterey Cl BXLY DA5 169 K4
Montesquieu Ter CAN/RD * E16 106 D5
Montford Pl LBTH SE11 122 B6
Montfort Gdns BARK/HLT IG6 54 C2
Montfort Pl WIM/MER SW19 159 G3
Montgomery Av
ESH/CLAY KT10 189 K6
Montgomery Cl BFN/LL DA15 147 K6
MTCM * CR4 195 K1
Montgomery Rd CHSWK W4 117 K4
EDGE HA8 44 B2
Montholme Rd BTSEA SW11 160 E1
Monthorpe Rd WCHPL E1 104 C4
Montolieu Gdns PUT/ROE SW15 138 E6
Montpelier Av BXLY DA5 168 E2
EA W5 97 J4
Montpelier Gdns CHDH RM6 73 J4
EHAM E6 107 H2
Montpelier Gv KTTN NW5 84 C3
Montpelier Ms SKENS SW7 14 D4
Montpelier Pl SKENS SW7 14 D4
WCHPL E1 104 E5
Montpelier Ri GLDGN NW11 64 C4
WBLY HA9 61 K5
Montpelier Rd EA W5 97 K4
FNCH N3 47 G4
PECK SE15 143 J2
SUT SM1 209 G2
Montpelier Rw BKHTH/KID SE3 145 J3
TWK TW1 156 C2
Montpelier Sq SKENS SW7 14 D4
Montpelier St SKENS SW7 14 D3
Montpelier Ter SKENS SW7 14 D3
Montpelier V BKHTH/KID * SE3 145 J3
Montpelier Wk SKENS SW7 14 D3
Montpelier Wy GLDGN NW11 64 C4
Montrave Rd PGE/AN SE20 181 K2
Montreal Pl HOL/ALD WC2B 11 G5
Montreal Rd IL IG1 72 C4
Montrell Rd BRXS/STRHM SW2 161 K3
Montrose Av BFN/LL DA15 168 B2
EDGE HA8 45 F5
KIL/WHAMP NW6 100 C1
WELL DA16 147 J4
WHTN TW2 155 G2
Montrose Cl WELL DA16 148 A4
WFD IG8 38 E6
Montrose Crs ALP/SUD HA0 80 A4
NFNCH/WDSP N12 47 F2
Montrose Gdns MTCM CR4 178 E6
SUT SM1 194 A6
Montrose Pl KTBR SW1X 15 H3
Montrose Rd
EBED/NFELT TW14 153 G1
KTN/HRWW/W HA3 42 E5
Montrose Vls HMSMTH * W6 118 D5
Montrose Wy FSTH SE23 164 A3
Montserrat Av WFD IG8 52 B3
Montserrat Cl NRWD SE19 180 E1
Montserrat Rd PUT/ROE SW15 139 H5
Monument St MON EC3R 13 F6
Monument Wy TOTM N17 50 B6
Monza St WAP E1W 104 E6
Moodkee St BERM/RHTH SE16 123 K3
Moody St WCHPL E1 105 F2
Moon Ct LEE/GVPK * SE12 145 K5
Moon La BAR EN5 20 D4
Moon St IS N1 85 H6
Moorcroft EDGE * HA8 44 D4
Moorcroft Gdns HAYES BR2 200 D2
Moorcroft Rd
STRHM/NOR SW16 161 K5
Moorcroft Wy PIN HA5 59 J2
Moordown WOOL/PLUM SE18 147 G2
Moore Cl MORT/ESHN SW14 137 K4
MTCM * CR4 179 G5
WLGTN SM6 210 E5
Moore Crs DAGW RM9 91 H6
Moorefield Rd TOTM N17 50 B6
Mooreland Rd BMLY BR1 183 J3
Moore Park Rd FUL/PGN SW6 140 A1
Moore Rd NRWD SE19 180 D2
Moore St CHEL SW3 14 E6
Moore Wy BELMT SM2 208 E6
Moorey Cl SRTFD E15 88 D6
Moorfield Av EA W5 97 K3
Moorfield Rd CHSGTN KT9 206 A3
ORP BR6 202 B4
PEND EN3 24 E2
Moorfields LVPST EC2M 12 E2
Moorfields Highwalk BARB EC2Y 12 E2
Moorgate LOTH EC2R 12 E3
Moorgate Pl LOTH * EC2R 12 E3
Moorhead Wy BKHTH/KID SE3 146 A5
Moorhen Cl ERITH DA8 150 E1
Moorhouse Rd BAY/PAD W2 100 E5
KTN/HRWW/W HA3 43 K6
The Moorings CHSWK * W4 117 H6
Moorland Cl HSLWW TW4 155 F2
ROMW/RG RM7 56 D4
Moorland Rd BRXN/ST SW9 142 C5
Moorlands Av MLHL NW7 45 K2
Moor La BARB EC2Y 12 E2
CHSGTN KT9 206 A2
Moor Lane Crossing
WATW WD18 26 A2
Moormead Dr HOR/WEW KT19 207 G3
Moor Mead Rd TWK TW1 156 B1
Moor Park Gdns
KUTN/CMB KT2 176 B3
NTHWD * HA6 26 A4
Moor Park Rd NTHWD HA6 40 B2
Moorside Rd BMLY BR1 165 H6
Moor St SOHO/SHAV W1D 10 D4
Moortown Rd OXHEY WD19 27 G6
Moor Vw WATW WD18 26 E2
Morant Gdns CRW RM5 56 D1
Morant St POP/IOD E14 105 J6
Mora Rd CRICK NW2 82 A2
Mora St FSBYE EC1V 6 D5
Morat St BRXN/ST SW9 142 A2
Moravian Pl WBPTN SW10 120 C6
Moravian St BETH E2 104 E1
Moray Av HYS/HAR UB3 113 J1
Moray Cl EDGE * HA8 30 D4
ROM RM1 57 G3
Moray Ms HOLWY N7 67 F6
Moray Rd HOLWY N7 67 F6
Moray Wy ROM RM1 57 F3
Morcambe St WALW SE17 18 D7
Mordaunt Gdns DAGW RM9 92 A5
Mordaunt Rd WLSDN NW10 81 F6
Mordaunt St BRXN/ST SW9 142 A4
Morden Ct MRDN SM4 194 A1
Morden Court Pde
WIM/MER * SW19 178 A6
Morden Gdns GFD/PVL UB6 79 F3
MTCM CR4 194 C1
Morden Hall Rd MRDN SM4 178 A6
Morden Hl LEW SE13 145 F3
Morden La LEW SE13 145 F3
Morden Rd BKHTH/KID SE3 145 K3
CHDH RM6 74 A4
WIM/MER SW19 178 A5
Morden Road Ms
BKHTH/KID SE3 145 K3
Morden St LEW SE13 144 E2
Morden Wy CHEAM SM3 193 K4
Morden Wharf Rd GNWCH SE10 125 H3
Mordon Rd GDMY/SEVK IG3 73 F4
Mordred Rd CAT SE6 165 H4
Morecambe Cl HCH RM12 93 K3
WCHPL * E1 105 F4
Morecambe Gdns STAN HA7 29 K6
Morecambe Ter UED * N18 35 K6
More Cl CAN/RD E16 106 D5
WKENS W14 119 G4
Morecoombe Cl KUTN/CMB KT2 175 J3
Moree Wy UED N18 36 C6
Moreland Cottages BOW * E3 105 J1
Moreland St FSBYE EC1V 6 B4
Moreland Wy CHING E4 37 K5
More La ESH/CLAY KT10 204 B1
Morella Rd BAL SW12 160 E2
Moremead Rd CAT SE6 164 C6
Morena St CAT SE6 164 E2
Moresby Av BRYLDS KT5 191 J4
Moresby Rd CLPT E5 68 D5
Mores Gdn CHEL * SW3 120 C6
Moretaine Rd ASHF TW15 152 A5
Moreton Av ISLW TW7 135 J2
Moreton Cl CLPT E5 68 E6
MLHL NW7 46 A2
SEVS/STOTM N15 67 K3
Moreton Ct DART DA1 150 B4
Moreton Gdns WFD IG8 53 J1
Moreton Pl PIM SW1V 121 H5
Moreton Rd SAND/SEL CR2 211 K3
SEVS/STOTM N15 67 K3
WPK KT4 192 D6
Moreton St PIM SW1V 121 H5
Moreton Ter PIM SW1V 121 H5
Moreton Terrace Ms North
PIM SW1V 121 H5
Moreton Terrace Ms South
PIM * SW1V 121 H5
Morford Cl RSLP HA4 59 F4
Morford Wy RSLP HA4 59 F4
Morgan Av WALTH E17 70 B1
Morgan Cl DAGE RM10 92 C5
NTHWD HA6 40 D1
Morgan Rd BMLY BR1 183 K3
HOLWY N7 85 G3
NKENS W10 100 D4
Morgan's La HYS/HAR UB3 94 B4
STHWK SE1 19 G1
Morgan St BOW E3 105 G2
CAN/RD E16 106 D4
Morgan Wy WFD IG8 53 J2
Moriatry Cl HOLWY N7 84 E2
Morie St WAND/EARL SW18 140 A5
Morieux Rd LEY E10 69 H5
Moring Rd TOOT SW17 161 F6
Morkyns Wk DUL * SE21 163 F5
Morland Av CROY/NA CR0 197 F5
DART DA1 150 E6
Morland Cl GLDGN NW11 65 F5
HPTN TW12 172 E1
MTCM CR4 178 D6
Morland Est HACK * E8 86 C5
Morland Gdns STHL UB1 115 G1
WLSDN NW10 81 F5
Morland Ms IS N1 85 G5
Morland Rd CROY/NA CR0 197 G4
DAGE RM10 92 C5
IL IG1 72 B6
KTN/HRWW/W HA3 62 A2
PGE/AN SE20 182 A3
SUT SM1 209 G3
WALTH E17 69 F2
Morley Av CHING E4 52 B3
UED N18 36 C6
WDGN N22 49 G5
Morley Cl ORP BR6 201 G6
Morley Crs EDGE HA8 30 E4
RSLP HA4 59 G6
Morley Crs East STAN HA7 43 J6
Morley Crs West STAN HA7 43 J6
Morley Hl ENC/FH EN2 23 K1
Morley Rd BARK IG11 90 D6
CHDH RM6 74 A2
CHEAM SM3 193 J5
CHST BR7 185 H4
LEW SE13 145 F5
LEY E10 70 A5
SRTFD E15 106 D1
TWK TW1 156 E1
Morley St STHWK SE1 17 K3
Morna Rd CMBW SE5 142 D3
Morning La HOM E9 86 E4
Morningside Rd WPK KT4 192 E6
Mornington Av BMLY BR1 184 B6
IL IG1 72 A4
WKENS W14 119 J4
Mornington Ct BXLY DA5 170 A3
Mornington Crs CAMTN NW1 4 A2
HEST TW5 134 A2
Mornington Gv BOW E3 105 J2
Mornington Ms CMBW SE5 142 D2
Mornington Pl CAMTN NW1 3 K2
Mornington Rd CHING E4 38 B2
DEPT SE8 144 C1
GFD/PVL UB6 96 B4
WAN E11 70 D5
WFD IG8 38 E6
Mornington St CAMTN NW1 3 K2
Mornington Ter CAMTN NW1 3 K1
Mornington Wk
RCHPK/HAM TW10 156 D6
Morocco St STHWK SE1 19 G3
Morpeth Gv HOM E9 87 F6
Morpeth Rd HOM E9 86 E6
Morpeth St BETH E2 105 F2
Morpeth Ter WEST SW1P 16 A5
Morpeth Wk TOTM * N17 50 D3
Morrab Gdns GDMY/SEVK IG3 91 F1
Morrel Cl BAR EN5 21 G4
Morris Av MNPK E12 89 K3
Morris Bishop Ter HGT * N6 66 A3
Morris Cl CROY/NA CR0 198 B3
ORP BR6 216 E1
Morris Ct CHING E4 37 K5
Morris Gdns DART DA1 151 K6
WAND/EARL SW18 159 K2
Morrish Rd BRXS/STRHM SW2 161 K2
Morrison Av TOTM N17 50 A6
Morrison Rd BARK IG11 110 A1
DAGW RM9 92 A6
YEAD UB4 95 F2
Morrison St BTSEA SW11 141 F4
Morris Pl FSBYPK N4 67 G6
Morris Rd BCTR RM8 74 B6
HARH RM3 57 K3
ISLW TW7 136 A4
POP/IOD E14 105 K4
WAN E11 88 C2
Morris St WCHPL E1 104 D5
Morriston Cl OXHEY WD19 41 G1
Morse Cl PLSTW E13 106 E2
Morshead Rd MV/WKIL W9 100 E2
Morson Rd PEND EN3 37 G1
Morteyne Rd TOTM N17 49 K4
Mortham St SRTFD E15 88 C6
Mortimer Cl BAL SW12 161 J4
BUSH WD23 28 B1
CRICK NW2 82 D1
Mortimer Crs KIL/WHAMP NW6 83 F6
WPK KT4 207 F1
Mortimer Dr EN EN1 23 K6
Mortimer Pl KIL/WHAMP NW6 83 F6
Mortimer Rd EHAM E6 107 K2
ERITH DA8 130 A6
IS N1 86 A5
MTCM CR4 178 E4
ORP BR6 202 B6
WEA W13 97 J5
WLSDN NW10 100 A2
Mortimer Sq NTGHL W11 100 B6
Mortimer St REGST W1B 9 K3
Mortimer Ter KTTN * NW5 84 B2
Mortlake Cl CROY/NA CR0 210 E1
Mortlake Dr MTCM CR4 178 D4
Mortlake High St
MORT/ESHN SW14 138 A4
Mortlake Rd CAN/RD E16 107 F5
IL IG1 90 C2
MORT/ESHN SW14 137 J4
Morton Cl CROY/NA CR0 211 F5
Morton Crs FBAR/BDGN N11 34 D6
Morton Gdns WLGTN SM6 210 C3
Morton Ms ECT * SW5 120 A4
Morton Pl STHWK SE1 17 J5
Morton Rd IS N1 85 J5
MRDN SM4 194 C2
SRTFD E15 88 D5
Morton Wy STHGT/OAK N14 34 C5
Morvale Cl BELV DA17 129 G4
Morval Rd BRXS/STRHM SW2 142 B6
Morven Rd TOOT SW17 160 E5
Morville St BOW E3 105 J1
Morwell St FITZ W1T 10 C2
Moscow Pl BAY/PAD * W2 101 F6
Moscow Rd BAY/PAD W2 100 E6
Moselle Av WDGN N22 49 G5
Moselle Cl CEND/HSY/T N8 49 F6
Moselle St TOTM N17 50 B3
Mossborough Cl
NFNCH/WDSP N12 47 F2
Mossbury Rd BTSEA SW11 140 D4
Moss Cl PIN HA5 41 K5
WCHPL E1 104 C4
Mossdown Cl BELV DA17 129 H4
Mossford Gn BARK/HLT IG6 54 B6
Mossford La BARK/HLT IG6 54 C5
Mossford St BOW E3 105 H3
Moss Gdns SAND/SEL CR2 213 F5
Moss Hall Crs NFNCH/WDSP N12 47 F2
Moss Hall Gv FNCH N3 47 F2
Moss La PIN HA5 41 J5
ROM RM1 75 H3
Mosslea Rd HAYES BR2 200 C2
ORP BR6 216 C1
PGE/AN SE20 181 K3
Mossop St CHEL SW3 14 D6
Moss Rd DAGE RM10 92 C5
Mossville Gdns MRDN SM4 177 J6
Moston Cl HYS/HAR UB3 113 J5
Mostyn Av WBLY HA9 80 B3
Mostyn Gdns WLSDN NW10 100 B2
Mostyn Gv BOW E3 105 H1
Mostyn Rd BRXN/ST SW9 142 B2
EDGE HA8 45 G3
WIM/MER SW19 177 J5
Mosul Wy HAYES BR2 200 D3
Mosyer Dr STMC/STPC BR5 202 E6
Motcomb St KTBR SW1X 15 G4
Moth Cl WLGTN SM6 210 E5
The Mothers Sq CLPT * E5 86 D2
Motley St VX/NE SW8 141 H3
Motspur Pk NWMAL KT3 192 C3
Mottingham Gdns
ELTH/MOT SE9 166 C3
Mottingham La ELTH/MOT SE9 166 B3
Mottingham Rd ED N9 37 F1
ELTH/MOT SE9 166 E5
Mottisfont Rd ABYW SE2 128 B3
Moulins Rd HOM E9 86 E5
Moulton Av HEST TW5 134 D3
Moundfield Rd STNW/STAM N16 68 C3
The Mount BMLY * BR1 184 D4
BXLYHS * DA6 149 J6
CLPT * E5 68 D6
ESH/CLAY KT10 204 A4
HAMP NW3 83 G2
NTHLT * UB5 78 B3
NWMAL KT3 176 C6
TRDG/WHET N20 33 G4
WBLY HA9 62 D6
WPK KT4 207 K2
Mountacre Cl SYD SE26 163 G6
Mount Adon Pk EDUL SE22 163 H2
Mountague Pl POP/IOD E14 106 A6
Mount Angelus Rd
PUT/ROE SW15 158 C2
Mount Ararat Rd
RCHPK/HAM TW10 137 F6
Mount Ash Rd SYD SE26 163 J5
Mount Av CHING E4 37 J5
STHL UB1 96 A5
Mountbatten Cl NRWD SE19 181 F1
WOOL/PLUM SE18 127 K6
Mountbatten Ct BKHH IG9 39 H4
Mountbel Rd
KTN/HRWW/W * HA3 43 G5
Mount Cl BMLY BR1 184 D4
CAR SM5 210 A6
EA * W5 97 J4
EBAR EN4 22 A5
Mountcombe Cl SURB KT6 191 F4
Mount Cottages BXLYHS * DA6 149 F5
Mount Ct WWKM BR4 199 H6
Mount Culver Av SCUP DA14 186 E2
Mount Dr CDALE/KGS NW9 62 E6
RYLN/HDSTN HA2 59 K2
Mountearl Gdns
STRHM/NOR SW16 162 A5
Mount Echo Av CHING E4 37 K3
Mount Echo Dr CHING E4 37 K3
Mount Ephraim La
STRHM/NOR SW16 161 J5
Mount Ephraim Rd
STRHM/NOR SW16 161 J5
Mountfield Cl LEW SE13 165 G2
Mountfield Rd EA W5 97 K5
EHAM E6 107 K1
FNCH N3 46 E6
Mountfield Wy STMC/STPC BR5 202 D1
Mountford St WCHPL E1 104 C5
Mountfort Crs IS N1 85 G5
Mountfort Ter IS N1 85 G5
Mount Gdns SYD SE26 163 J5
Mount Gv EDGE HA8 30 E5
Mountgrove Rd HBRY N5 85 J1
Mounthurst Rd HAYES BR2 199 K4
Mountington Park Cl
KTN/HRWW/W HA3 61 K3
Mountjoy Cl THMD SE28 128 C2
Mount Mills FSBYE EC1V 6 B5
Mount Nod Rd
STRHM/NOR SW16 162 A5
Mount Pde EBAR * EN4 21 J5
Mount Pk CAR SM5 210 A6
Mount Park Av HRW HA1 60 D6
SAND/SEL CR2 211 H6
Mount Park Crs EA W5 97 K5
Mount Park Rd EA W5 97 K4
HRW HA1 60 D6
PIN HA5 58 E2
Mount Pl ACT W3 117 J1
Mount Pleasant ALP/SUD HA0 80 A6
EBAR EN4 21 K5
FSBYW WC1X 5 H7
HRW * HA1 60 E6
RSLP HA4 77 G1
WNWD SE27 162 D6
Mount Pleasant Crs
FSBYPK * N4 67 F4
Mount Pleasant Hl CLPT E5 68 D6
Mount Pleasant La CLPT E5 68 D5
Mount Pleasant Pl
WOOL/PLUM SE18 127 J4
Mount Pleasant Rd CRW RM5 57 F2
DART DA1 171 J1
EA W5 97 J3
LEW SE13 165 F1
NWMAL KT3 175 K6
TOTM N17 50 A6
WALTH E17 51 G5
WLSDN NW10 82 A5
Mount Pleasant Vls FSBYPK N4 67 F4
Mount Ri FSTH SE23 163 K4
Mount Rd BCTR RM8 74 B5
BXLYHS DA6 149 F6
CHSGTN KT9 206 B3
CRICK NW2 81 K1
DART DA1 170 C1
EBAR EN4 21 J6
FELT TW13 154 D5
HDN NW4 63 J3
HYS/HAR UB3 113 K2
IL IG1 90 B3
MTCM CR4 178 C5
NRWD * SE19 180 E2
NWMAL KT3 176 A6
WAND/EARL SW18 159 K4
Mount Rw MYFR/PKLN W1K 9 J6
Mountside KTN/HRWW/W HA3 43 F4
Mounts Pond Rd LEW SE13 145 G3
The Mount Sq HAMP * NW3 83 G1
Mount Stewart Av
KTN/HRWW/W HA3 61 K3
Mount St MYFR/PKLN W1K 9 G6
Mount Ter WCHPL E1 104 D4
Mount Vw ENC/FH EN2 23 F1
Mountview MLHL NW7 31 F5
NTHWD HA6 40 E2
Mount Vw NWDGN * UB2 114 C4
Mount View Rd CDALE/KGS NW9 63 F1
CHING E4 38 A2
ESH/CLAY KT10 205 H5
FSBYPK N4 67 F4
Mountview Rd ORP BR6 202 B4
Mount Vls WNWD SE27 162 C5
Mount Wy CAR SM5 210 A6
Mountwood E/WMO/HCT KT8 173 G6
Movers La BARK IG11 90 D6
Mowatt Cl ARCH N19 66 D6
Mowbray Gdns NTHLT * UB5 78 A6
Mowbray Rd BAR EN5 21 G5
EDGE HA8 30 C6
KIL/WHAMP NW6 82 C5
NRWD SE19 181 G4
RCHPK/HAM TW10 156 D5
Mowbrays Cl CRW RM5 56 E4
Mowbrays Rd CRW RM5 56 E5
Mowlem St BETH E2 104 D1
Mowll St BRXN/ST SW9 142 B1
Moxon Cl PLSTW E13 106 D1
Moxon St BAR EN5 20 D4
MHST W1U 9 G2
Moye Cl BETH * E2 104 C1
Moyers Rd LEY E10 70 A5
Moylan Rd HMSMTH W6 119 H6
Moyne Pl WLSDN NW10 98 C2
Moynihan Dr STHGT/OAK N14 22 E6
Moys Cl CROY/NA CR0 195 K3
Moyser Rd STRHM/NOR SW16 179 G1
Mozart St NKENS W10 100 D2
Muchelney Rd MRDN SM4 194 B3
Muggeridge Cl SAND/SEL CR2 211 K3
Muggeridge Rd DAGE RM10 92 D2
Muir Cl WAND/EARL SW18 160 D1
Muirdown Av
MORT/ESHN SW14 137 K5

Muirfield ACT W3 99 G5
Muirfield Cl BERM/RHTH * SE16 123 J5
OXHEY * WD19 41 G1
Muirfield Crs POP/IOD E14 124 E3
Muirfield Gn OXHEY WD19 27 G6
Muirfield Rd OXHEY WD19 27 G6
Muirkirk Rd CAT SE6 165 F3
Muir Rd CLPT E5 86 C2
Muir St CAN/RD E16 126 E1
Mulberry Av STWL/WRAY TW19 152 B3
Mulberry Cl CHEL * SW3 120 C6
CHING E4 37 J4
EBAR EN4 21 H5
GPK RM2 75 K1
HDN NW4 46 A6
NTHLT UB5 95 J1
STRHM/NOR SW16 161 H6
Mulberry Crs BTFD TW8 136 C1
WDR/YW UB7 112 D2
Mulberry Dr PUR RM19 131 J4
Mulberry La CROY/NA CR0 197 G5
Mulberry Ms NWCR SE14 144 C2
Mulberry Pde WDR/YW UB7 112 D3
Mulberry Pl HMSMTH W6 118 D5
Mulberry Rd HACK E8 86 B5
Mulberry St WCHPL E1 104 C5
Mulberry Wk CHEL SW3 120 C6
Mulberry Wy BARK/HLT IG6 72 C1
BELV DA17 129 K2
SWFD E18 53 F5
Mulgrave Rd BELMT SM2 208 D5
CROY/NA CR0 211 K1
EA W5 97 K2
HRW HA1 61 G6
WKENS W14 119 J6
WLSDN NW10 81 H2
WOOL/PLUM SE18 126 E4
Mulholland Cl MTCM CR4 179 G5
Mulkern Rd ARCH N19 66 D5
Mullards Cl MTCM CR4 194 E5
Mullet Gdns BETH E2 104 C2
Mullins Pth MORT/ESHN SW14 138 A4
Mullion Cl KTN/HRWW/W HA3 42 B4
Mullion Wk OXHEY WD19 27 H6
Mull Wk IS N1 85 J4
Mulready St STJWD NW8 2 C7
Multi Wy ACT W3 118 B2
Multon Rd WAND/EARL SW18 160 C2
Mumford Ct CITYW EC2V 12 D3
Mumford Rd HNHL SE24 142 C6
Muncaster Cl ASHF TW15 152 D6
Muncaster Rd CLAP SW4 140 E5
Muncies Ms CAT SE6 165 F4
Mundania Rd EDUL SE22 163 J1
Munday Rd CAN/RD E16 106 E5
Munden St WKENS W14 119 H4
Mundesly Cl OXHEY WD19 27 G6
Mundford Rd CLPT E5 68 E6
Mundon Gdns IL IG1 72 D5
Mund St WKENS W14 119 J5
Mundy St IS N1 7 G4
Mungo-Park Cl BUSH * WD23 28 C4
Mungo Park Rd RAIN RM13 93 J4
Mungo Park Wy
STMC/STPC BR5 202 D4
Munnery Wy ORP BR6 216 A1
Munnings Gdns ISLW TW7 135 J6
Munro Dr FBAR/BDGN * N11 48 C2
Munro Ms NKENS W10 100 C4
Munslow Gdns SUT SM1 209 G2
Munster Av HSLWW TW4 134 D5
Munster Gdns PLMGR N13 35 J6
Munster Ms FUL/PGN * SW6 139 J1
Munster Rd FUL/PGN SW6 139 H1
TEDD TW11 174 D2
Munster Sq CAMTN NW1 3 K5
Munton Rd WALW SE17 18 D6
Murchison Av BXLY DA5 168 E3
Murchison Rd LEY E10 70 A6
Murdock Cl CAN/RD E16 106 D5
Murdock St PECK SE15 123 J6
Murfett Cl WIM/MER SW19 159 H4
Muriel St IS N1 5 H2
Murillo Rd LEW SE13 145 G5
Murphy St STHWK SE1 17 J3
Murray Av BMLY BR1 184 A6
HSLW TW3 135 G6
Murray Crs PIN HA5 41 H4
Murray Gv IS N1 6 E3
Murray Ms CAMTN NW1 84 D5
Murray Rd EA W5 116 D4
NTHWD HA6 40 C4
RCHPK/HAM TW10 156 C4
STMC/STPC BR5 186 C6
WIM/MER SW19 177 G2
Murray Sq CAN/RD E16 106 E5
Murray St CAMTN NW1 84 D5
Murray Ter HAMP NW3 83 G2
Murtwell Dr CHIG IG7 54 C2
Musard Rd WKENS W14 119 H6
Musbury St WCHPL E1 104 E5
Muscatel Pl CMBW SE5 143 F2
Muschamp Rd CAR SM5 194 D6
PECK SE15 143 G4
Muscovy St TWRH EC3N 13 H6
Museum St NOXST/BSQ WC1A 10 E3
Musgrave Cl EBAR EN4 21 G2
Musgrave Crs FUL/PGN SW6 139 K1
Musgrave Rd ISLW TW7 136 A2
Musgrove Rd NWCR SE14 144 A2
Musjid Rd BTSEA SW11 140 C3
Musquash Wy HSLWW TW4 134 B3
Muston Rd CLPT E5 68 D6
Muswell Av MUSWH N10 48 B5
Muswell Hl MUSWH N10 48 B6
Muswell Hill Broadway
MUSWH N10 48 B6
Muswell Hill Pl MUSWH N10 66 B1
Muswell Hill Rd MUSWH N10 66 A1
Muswell Ms MUSWH N10 48 B6
Muswell Rd MUSWH N10 48 B5
Mutrix Rd KIL/WHAMP NW6 82 E6
Mutton Pl CAMTN NW1 84 A4
Muybridge Rd NWMAL KT3 175 K5
Myatt Rd BRXN/ST SW9 142 C2
Mycenae Rd BKHTH/KID SE3 125 K6
Myddelton Av EN EN1 24 A1
Myddelton Gdns WCHMH N21 35 J2
Myddelton Pk TRDG/WHET N20 33 H5
Myddelton Pas CLKNW EC1R 5 K4
Myddelton Rd CEND/HSY/T N8 48 E6
Myddelton Sq CLKNW EC1R 5 K4
Myddelton St CLKNW EC1R 5 K5
Myddleton Av FSBYPK N4 67 H6
Myddleton Rd WDGN N22 48 E3
Myers La NWCR SE14 124 A6
Mylis Cl SYD SE26 163 J6
Mylne Cl HMSMTH * W6 118 D5
Mylne St CLKNW EC1R 5 J3
Myra St ABYW SE2 128 B5
Myrdle St WCHPL E1 104 C4
Myrna Cl WIM/MER SW19 178 D3
Myron Pl LEW SE13 145 F4
Myrtle Aly WOOL/PLUM SE18 127 F3
Myrtle Av EBED/NFELT TW14 133 H5
RSLP HA4 58 E4
Myrtleberry Cl HACK * E8 86 B4
Myrtle Cl EBAR EN4 33 K3
ERITH DA8 150 B1
WDR/YW UB7 112 C4
Myrtledene Rd ABYW SE2 128 B5
Myrtle Gdns HNWL W7 115 K1
Myrtle Gv ENC/FH EN2 23 K1
NWMAL KT3 175 K5
Myrtle Rd ACT W3 117 K1
CROY/NA CR0 213 J1
DART DA1 171 G4
EHAM E6 89 J6
HPTN TW12 173 H2
HSLW TW3 135 H3
IL IG1 72 B6
PLMGR N13 35 J5
SUT SM1 209 G3
WALTH E17 69 G3
Myrtleside Cl NTHWD HA6 40 B3
Myrtle St IS N1 7 G3
Myrtle Wk IS N1 7 G3
Mysore Rd BTSEA SW11 140 E5
Myton Rd DUL SE21 162 E5

N

Nadine St CHARL SE7 126 B5
Nagle Cl WALTH E17 52 B5
Nag's Head La WELL DA16 148 C4
Nags Head Rd PEND EN3 24 E5
Nairne Gv EDUL SE22 142 E6
Nairn Gn OXHEY WD19 26 E5
Nairn Rd RSLP HA4 77 G4
Nairn St POP/IOD E14 106 A4
Nallhead Rd FELT TW13 172 B1
Namba Roy Cl
STRHM/NOR SW16 162 A6
Namton Dr STRHM/NOR SW16 196 A1
Nan Clark's La MLHL NW7 31 H4
Nancy Downs OXHEY WD19 27 G2
Nankin St POP/IOD E14 105 J5
Nansen Rd BTSEA SW11 141 F5
Nansen Village
NFNCH/WDSP * N12 33 F6
Nantes Cl WAND/EARL SW18 140 B5
Nant Rd CRICK NW2 64 D6
Nant St BETH E2 104 D2
Naoroji St FSBYW WC1X 5 J5
Napier Av FUL/PGN SW6 139 J4
POP/IOD E14 124 D5
Napier Cl DEPT SE8 144 C1
EMPK RM11 75 K5
WDR/YW UB7 112 C3
Napier Ct LEE/GVPK SE12 166 A4
Napier Gv IS N1 6 D3
Napier Pl WKENS W14 119 J3
Napier Rd ALP/SUD HA0 79 K3
BELV DA17 129 G4
EHAM E6 90 A6
HAYES BR2 184 A6
ISLW TW7 136 B5
PEND EN3 25 F6
SAND/SEL CR2 211 K5
SNWD SE25 197 J1
SRTFD E15 106 C1
TOTM N17 50 A5
WAN E11 88 C1
WDR/YW UB7 132 A2
WKENS W14 119 J3
WLSDN NW10 99 K2
Napier Ter IS N1 85 H5
Napoleon Rd CLPT E5 86 D1
TWK * TW1 156 C2
Napton Cl YEAD UB4 95 J3
Narbonne Av CLAP SW4 161 H1
Narboro Ct ROM RM1 75 J3
Narborough Cl HGDN/ICK UB10 58 D6
Narborough St FUL/PGN SW6 140 A3
Narcissus Rd KIL/WHAMP NW6 82 E3
Narford Rd CLPT E5 86 C1
Narrow Boat Cl THMD SE28 127 J2
Narrow St ACT W3 117 J1
POP/IOD E14 105 G6
Narrow Wy HAYES BR2 200 D3
Nascot St SHB W12 100 A5
Naseby Cl ISLW TW7 135 K2
KIL/WHAMP * NW6 83 G5
Naseby Ct WOT/HER * KT12 188 B6
Naseby Rd CLAY IG5 53 K4
DAGE RM10 92 C1
NRWD SE19 180 E2
Nash Cl SUT SM1 209 H1
Nash Gn BMLY BR1 183 K3
Nash La HAYES BR2 214 E4
Nash Rd BROCKY SE4 144 B6
CHDH RM6 73 K1
ED N9 36 E4
Nash St CAMTN NW1 3 K4
Nash Wy KTN/HRWW/W HA3 61 H3
Nasmyth St HMSMTH W6 118 E3
Nassau Rd BARN SW13 138 C2
Nassau St GTPST W1W 10 A2
Nassington Rd HAMP NW3 83 J2
Natalie Cl EBED/NFELT TW14 153 G2
Natal Rd FBAR/BDGN N11 48 E1
IL IG1 90 B2
STRHM/NOR SW16 179 J2
THHTH CR7 180 E6
Nathaniel Cl WCHPL E1 13 K2
Nathans Rd ALP/SUD HA0 61 J6
Nathan Wy THMD SE28 128 A3
National Ter
BERM/RHTH * SE16 123 J2
Nation Wy CHING E4 38 A3
Naval Rw POP/IOD E14 106 A6
Navarino Gv HACK E8 86 C4
Navarino Rd HACK E8 86 C4
Navarre Gdns CRW RM5 56 D2
Navarre Rd EHAM E6 107 J1
Navarre St BETH E2 7 J6
Navestock Cl CHING * E4 38 A5
Navestock Crs WFD IG8 53 G4
Navestock Ter WFD IG8 53 G3
Navigator Dr NWDGN UB2 115 H2
Navy St CLAP SW4 141 J4
Nayim Pl HACK E8 86 D4
Naylor Gv PEND EN3 25 F6
Naylor Rd PECK SE15 143 J1
TRDG/WHET N20 33 G4
Nazareth Cl PECK SE15 143 K3
Nazrul St BETH E2 7 J4
Neal Av STHL UB1 95 K3
Neal Cl NTHWD HA6 40 E4
Nealden St BRXN/ST SW9 142 A4
Neale Cl EFNCH N2 47 G6
Neal St LSQ/SEVD WC2H 10 E4
Neal Ter FSTH * SE23 164 A3
Neal Yd LSQ/SEVD WC2H 10 E4
Near Acre CDALE/KGS NW9 45 H4
Neasden Cl WLSDN NW10 81 G3
Neasden La WLSDN NW10 81 G1
Neasden La North WLSDN NW10 81 G1
Neasham Rd BCTR RM8 91 H3
Neate St CMBW SE5 123 F6
Neath Gdns MRDN SM4 194 B3
Neathouse Pl PIM SW1V 16 A6
Neats Acre RSLP HA4 58 B4
Neatscourt Rd EHAM E6 107 H4
Neckinger STHWK SE1 19 K4
Neckinger Est BERM/RHTH SE16 19 K4
Neckinger St STHWK SE1 19 K3
Nectarine Wy LEW SE13 144 E3
Needham Rd BAY/PAD W2 100 E5
Needleman St
BERM/RHTH SE16 124 A2
Neeld Crs HDN NW4 63 K2
WBLY HA9 80 C3
Neils Yd LSQ/SEVD * WC2H 10 E4
Nelgarde Rd CAT SE6 164 D2
Nella Rd HMSMTH W6 119 G6
Nelldale Rd BERM/RHTH SE16 123 J4
Nello James Gdns WNWD SE27 162 E6
Nelson Cl CROY/NA CR0 196 C5
EBED/NFELT * TW14 153 J3
KIL/WHAMP NW6 100 E2
ROMW/RG RM7 56 D4
WOT/HER KT12 188 A5
Nelson Gdns BETH E2 104 C2
HSLW TW3 155 F1
Nelson Grove Rd
WIM/MER SW19 178 A4
Nelson Mandela Cl MUSWH N10 47 K5
Nelson Mandela Rd
BKHTH/KID SE3 146 B4
Nelson Pl IS N1 6 B3
SCUP DA14 168 B6
Nelson Rd BELV DA17 129 G5
CEND/HSY/T N8 67 F2
CHING E4 51 K2
DART DA1 171 F1
ED N9 36 D5
GNWCH SE10 125 F6
HAYES BR2 200 B1
HRW HA1 60 D5
HSLW TW3 155 F1
NWMAL KT3 192 A2
PEND EN3 37 F1
RAIN RM13 111 H1
SCUP DA14 168 B6
SEVS/STOTM N15 68 A1
STAN HA7 43 J2
WAN E11 70 E1
WDR/YW UB7 132 C2
WIM/MER SW19 178 A3
Nelson Sq STHWK SE1 18 A2
Nelsons Rw CLAP SW4 141 J5
Nelson St CAN/RD E16 106 D6
EHAM E6 107 K1
WCHPL E1 104 D5
Nelsons Yd CAMTN NW1 4 A2
Nelson Ter FSBYE EC1V 6 B3
Nelson Wk HOR/WEW KT19 206 C6
Nemoure Rd ACT W3 98 E6
Nene Gdns FELT TW13 154 E4
Nene Rd HTHAIR TW6 132 E2
Nepaul Rd BTSEA SW11 140 D3
Nepean St PUT/ROE SW15 158 D1
Neptune Cl RAIN RM13 111 H1
Neptune Rd HRW HA1 60 D3
HTHAIR * TW6 133 F2
Neptune St BERM/RHTH SE16 123 K3
Nesbit Cl BKHTH/KID SE3 145 H4
Nesbit Rd ELTH/MOT SE9 146 C5
Nesbitts Aly BAR * EN5 20 D4
Nesbitt Sq NRWD * SE19 181 F3
Nesham St WAP E1W 123 H1
Ness Rd ERITH DA8 131 G6
Ness St BERM/RHTH SE16 123 H3
Nesta Rd WFD IG8 52 D2
Nestle's Av HYS/HAR UB3 113 J3
Nestor Av WCHMH N21 35 H1
Netheravon Rd CHSWK W4 118 C5
HNWL W7 116 A1
Netheravon Rd South
CHSWK W4 118 C6
Netherbury Rd EA W5 116 E3
Netherby Gdns ENC/FH EN2 22 E5
Netherby Rd FSTH SE23 163 K2
Nether Cl FNCH N3 46 E3
Nether Ct MLHL * NW7 46 D2
Nethercourt Av FNCH N3 46 E2
Netherfield Gdns BARK IG11 90 D4
Netherfield Rd
NFNCH/WDSP N12 47 F1
TOOT SW17 161 F5
Netherford Rd CLAP SW4 141 H3
Netherhall Gdns HAMP NW3 83 G3
Netherhall Wy HAMP NW3 83 G3
Netherlands Rd BAR EN5 33 H1
Netherleigh Cl ARCH * N19 66 B5
Netherpark Dr GPK RM2 57 H5
Nether St FNCH N3 46 E4
Netherton Gv WBPTN SW10 120 B6
Netherton Rd SEVS/STOTM N15 67 K3
TWK TW1 136 B6
Netherwood Pl WKENS * W14 119 G3
Netherwood Rd WKENS W14 119 G3
Netherwood St
KIL/WHAMP NW6 82 D5
Netley Cl CHEAM SM3 208 B3
CROY/NA CR0 214 A5
Netley Dr WOT/HER KT12 188 E4
Netley Gdns MRDN SM4 194 B4
Netley Rd BTFD TW8 117 F6
GNTH/NBYPK IG2 72 D2
MRDN SM4 194 B4
WALTH E17 69 H2
Netley St CAMTN NW1 4 A5
Nettlecombe Cl BELMT SM2 209 F6
Nettleden Av WBLY HA9 80 C4
Nettlefold Pl WNWD SE27 162 C5
Nettlestead Cl BECK BR3 182 C3
Nettleton Rd HTHAIR TW6 132 E2
NWCR SE14 144 A1
Nettlewood Rd
STRHM/NOR SW16 179 J3
Neuchatel Rd CAT SE6 164 C4
Nevada Cl NWMAL KT3 191 K1
Nevada St GNWCH SE10 145 F1
Nevern Pl ECT SW5 119 K4
Nevern Rd ECT SW5 119 K4
Nevern Sq ECT SW5 119 K4
Nevil Cl NTHWD HA6 40 B1
Neville Av NWMAL KT3 176 A4
Neville Cl ACT W3 117 K2
BFN/LL DA15 168 A6
HSLW TW3 135 F3
KIL/WHAMP NW6 100 D1
PECK SE15 143 H1
WAN E11 88 D1
Neville Dr EFNCH N2 65 G3
Neville Gdns BCTR RM8 91 K1
Neville Gill Cl WAND/EARL SW18 159 K1
Neville Pl WDGN N22 49 F4
Neville Rd BARK/HLT IG6 54 C4
BCTR RM8 73 K6
CROY/NA CR0 196 E4
EA W5 97 K3
FSTGT E7 88 E5
KIL/WHAMP * NW6 100 D1
KUT KT1 175 H5
RCHPK/HAM TW10 156 D5
Neville St SKENS SW7 120 C5
Neville Ter SKENS * SW7 120 C5
Neville Wk CAR SM5 194 D4
Nevill Rd STNW/STAM N16 86 A2
Nevill Wy LOU IG10 39 J1
Nevil Wk CAR * SM5 194 D4
Nevin Dr CHING E4 37 K3
Nevinson Cl WAND/EARL SW18 160 C1
Nevis Cl ROM RM1 57 G2
Nevis Rd TOOT SW17 161 F4
New Acres Rd THMD SE28 127 K2
Newall Rd HTHAIR TW6 133 F2
Newark Ct WOT/HER KT12 188 B5
Newark Crs WLSDN NW10 99 F2
Newark Knok EHAM E6 108 A5
Newark Rd SAND/SEL CR2 211 K4
Newark St WCHPL E1 104 D4
Newark Wy HDN NW4 63 J1
New Ash Cl EFNCH N2 47 H6
New Barn Cl CROY/NA CR0 211 F4
New Barns Av MTCM CR4 195 J1
New Barn St PLSTW E13 106 E3
Newbery Rd ERITH DA8 150 C2
Newbiggin Pth OXHEY WD19 27 G6
Newbold Cottages WCHPL * E1 104 E5
Newbolt Av CHEAM SM3 208 A3
Newbolt Rd STAN HA7 43 F2
New Bond St MYFR/PICC W1J 9 K5
Newborough Gn NWMAL KT3 192 A1
New Brent St HDN NW4 64 A2
New Bridge St STP EC4M 12 A4
New Broad St LVPST EC2M 13 F2
New Broadway EA W5 97 K6
Newburgh Rd ACT W3 117 K1
Newburgh St SOHO/CST W1F 10 A4
New Burlington Ms CONDST W1S 10 A5
New Burlington Pl CONDST W1S 10 A5
New Burlington St CONDST W1S 10 A5
Newburn St LBTH SE11 122 A5
Newbury Cl NTHLT UB5 77 K4
Newbury Gdns HOR/WEW KT19 207 H2
Newbury Ms KTTN NW5 84 A4
Newbury Rd CHING E4 52 A2
GNTH/NBYPK IG2 72 D3
HAYES BR2 183 K6
WDR/YW UB7 132 C2
Newbury St STBT EC1A 12 C2
Newbury Wy NTHLT UB5 77 J4
New Butt La DEPT * SE8 144 D1
Newby Cl EN EN1 24 A3
Newby Pl POP/IOD E14 106 A6
Newby St VX/NE SW8 141 G4
Newcastle Av BARK/HLT IG6 55 G2
Newcastle Cl STP EC4M 12 A3
Newcastle Pl BAY/PAD W2 8 B2
Newcastle Rw CLKNW EC1R 5 K7
New Cavendish St MHST W1U 9 H2
New Change STP EC4M 12 C4
New Charles St FSBYE EC1V 6 B4
New Church Rd CMBW SE5 142 E1
New City Rd PLSTW E13 107 G2
New Cl FELT TW13 172 D1
WIM/MER SW19 178 B6
New College Ms IS * N1 85 G5
New College Pde HAMP * NW3 83 G4
Newcombe Pk ALP/SUD HA0 80 B6
MLHL NW7 45 G1
Newcombe St KENS * W8 119 K1
Newcome Gdns
STRHM/NOR SW16 161 K6
Newcomen Rd BTSEA SW11 140 C4
WAN * E11 88 D1
Newcomen St STHWK SE1 18 E2
New Compton St
LSQ/SEVD * WC2H 10 D4
New Ct NTHLT UB5 78 B3
TPL/STR * WC2R 11 J5
Newcourt St STJWD NW8 2 C3
New Crane Pl WAP * E1W 123 K1
New Crescent Yd
WLSDN * NW10 99 H1
New Cross Rd NWCR SE14 143 K1
Newdales Cl ED N9 36 C4
Newdene Av NTHLT UB5 95 H1
Newdigate STRHM/NOR * SW16 162 B6
Newell St POP/IOD E14 105 H5
New End HAMP NW3 83 G2
New End Sq HAMP NW3 83 H2
Newent Cl CAR SM5 194 E5
PECK SE15 143 F1
New Era Est IS N1 7 G1
New Farm Av HAYES BR2 199 K1
New Farm La NTHWD HA6 40 C4
New Ferry Ap
WOOL/PLUM SE18 127 F3
New Fetter La FLST/FETLN EC4A 11 K3
Newfield Cl HPTN TW12 173 F4
Newfield Ri CRICK NW2 81 J1
New Forest La CHIG IG7 54 A2
Newgale Gdns EDGE HA8 44 B4
New Garden Dr WDR/YW UB7 112 B2
Newgate CROY/NA CR0 196 D5
Newgate Cl FELT TW13 154 D4
Newgate St CHING E4 38 C5
STBT EC1A 12 B3
New Globe Wk STHWK SE1 12 C7
New Goulston St WCHPL E1 13 J3
New Green Pl NRWD SE19 181 F2
Newhall Gdns WOT/HER KT12 188 B6
Newham's Rw STHWK SE1 19 H3
Newham Wy CAN/RD E16 106 D4
Newhaven Cl HYS/HAR UB3 113 J4
Newhaven Gdns ELTH/MOT SE9 146 C5
Newhaven La CAN/RD E16 106 E4
Newhaven Rd SNWD SE25 196 E2
New Heston Rd HEST TW5 134 E1
Newhouse Av CHDH RM6 55 K6
Newhouse Cl NWMAL KT3 192 B4
Newhouse Wk MRDN SM4 194 B4
Newick Cl BXLY DA5 169 J1
Newick Rd CLPT E5 86 D1
Newing Gn BMLY BR1 184 C3
Newington Barrow Wy
HOLWY N7 85 F1
Newington Butts LBTH SE11 18 B7
Newington Cswy STHWK SE1 18 C4
Newington Gn STNW/STAM N16 85 K3
Newington Green Rd IS N1 85 K3
New Inn Broadway SDTCH * EC2A 7 H6
New Inn Sq SDTCH * EC2A 7 H6
New Inn St SDTCH * EC2A 7 H6
New Inn Yd SDTCH EC2A 7 H6
New Kelvin Av TEDD TW11 173 K2
New Kent Rd STHWK SE1 18 C6
New Kings Rd FUL/PGN SW6 139 J3
FUL/PGN SW6 139 K3
New King St DEPT SE8 124 D6
Newland Cl PIN HA5 41 J2
Newland Dr EN EN1 24 D2
Newland Gdns HNWL W7 116 B2
Newland Rd CEND/HSY/T N8 48 E6
The Newlands WLGTN SM6 210 C5
Newlands Av THDIT KT7 189 K5
Newlands Cl ALP/SUD HA0 79 J4
EDGE HA8 30 A5
NWDGN UB2 114 D5
Newlands Ct WBLY HA9 62 C6
Newlands Pk SYD SE26 181 K2
Newlands Pl BAR EN5 20 B6
Newlands Quay WAP E1W 104 E6
Newlands Rd
STRHM/NOR SW16 179 K5
WFD IG8 38 D4
Newland St CAN/RD E16 126 D1
Newlands Wy CHSGTN KT9 205 J3
Newlands Wd CROY/NA CR0 213 H6
Newlands Woods
CROY/NA * CR0 213 H6
Newling Cl EHAM E6 107 K5
Newling Est BETH E2 7 K5
New London St MON * EC3R 13 H5
New Lydenburg St CHARL SE7 126 B3
Newlyn Cl ORP BR6 217 F2
Newlyn Gdns RYLN/HDSTN HA2 59 K4
Newlyn Rd BAR EN5 20 D5
TOTM N17 50 B4
WELL DA16 148 A3
Newman Rd BMLY BR1 183 K4
CROY/NA CR0 196 A4
HYS/HAR UB3 95 F6
PLSTW E13 107 F2
WALTH E17 69 F2
Newman's Rw LINN WC2A 11 H2
Newman St FITZ W1T 10 B2
Newman's Wy EBAR EN4 21 G3
Newmarket Av NTHLT UB5 78 A3
Newmarsh Rd THMD SE28 128 A1
New Mill Rd STMC/STPC BR5 186 D4
Newminster Ct ENC/FH * EN2 23 H3
Newminster Rd MRDN SM4 194 B3
New Mount St SRTFD E15 88 B5
Newnham Av RSLP HA4 59 G5
Newnham Cl LOU IG10 39 H1
NTHLT UB5 78 C4
THHTH CR7 180 D5
Newnham Gdns NTHLT UB5 78 C4
Newnham Gn WDGN * N22 49 G4
Newnham Rd WDGN N22 49 F4
Newnhams Cl BMLY BR1 184 E6
Newnham Ter STHWK SE1 17 J4
Newnham Wy
KTN/HRWW/W HA3 62 A2
New North Pl SDTCH EC2A 7 G6
New North Rd BARK/HLT IG6 54 D3
IS N1 7 F3
New North St BMSBY WC1N 11 G1
Newnton Cl FSBYPK N4 67 K4
New Oak Rd EFNCH N2 47 G5
New Oxford St
NOXST/BSQ WC1A 10 E3
New Pde ASHF * TW15 152 C6
WDR/YW * UB7 112 B1
New Park Av PLMGR N13 35 J5
New Park Cl NTHLT UB5 77 J4
New Park Est UED N18 50 E1
New Park Rd BRXS/STRHM SW2 161 K3
New Place Sq
BERM/RHTH * SE16 123 J3
New Plaistow Rd SRTFD E15 88 C6
New Pond Pde RSLP * HA4 76 E1
Newport Av POP/IOD E14 106 B6
Newport Ct SOHO/SHAV W1D 10 D5
Newport Md OXHEY * WD19 27 H6
Newport Pl SOHO/SHAV * W1D 10 D5
Newport Rd BARN SW13 138 D2
HTHAIR TW6 132 D2
LEY E10 70 B6
WALTH * E17 69 G1
YEAD UB4 94 B4
Newport St LBTH SE11 17 G7
Newquay Crs RYLN/HDSTN HA2 59 J6
Newquay Gdns OXHEY WD19 27 F4
Newquay Rd CAT SE6 164 E4
New Quebec St MBLAR W1H 9 F4
New River Crs PLMGR N13 35 H6
New River Wy STNW/STAM N16 67 K4
New Rd ABYW SE2 128 E4
BTFD * TW8 116 E6
CEND/HSY/T N8 66 D2
CHING E4 37 K6
DAGW RM9 92 C6
E/WMO/HCT KT8 173 F6
EBED/NFELT TW14 153 G1
EBED/NFELT TW14 154 A3
ED N9 36 C5
ESH/CLAY KT10 204 C2
FELT TW13 172 D1
GDMY/SEVK IG3 72 E6
HGDN/ICK UB10 94 A3
HRW HA1 79 F2
HSLW TW3 135 G5
HYS/HAR UB3 133 F1
KUTN/CMB KT2 175 H3
MLHL NW7 46 C3

MTCM CR4 195 F5
ORP BR6 202 B4
RAIN RM13 111 J2
RAIN RM13 131 J1
RCHPK/HAM TW10 156 D6
WCHPL E1 104 D4
WDGN N22 49 J4
WELL DA16 148 C3
New Road Hl HAYES BR2 215 J6
New Rw CHCR WC2N 10 E5
Newry Rd TWK TW1 136 B5
Newsam Av SEVS/STOTM N15 67 K2
Newsholme Dr WCHMH N21 23 F6
New Spring Gardens Wk
LBTH * SE11 121 K5
New Sq LINN WC2A 11 H3
Newstead Av ORP BR6 216 D1
Newstead Cl NFNCH/WDSP N12 47 J2
Newstead Ct NTHLT * UB5 95 J2
Newstead Rd LEE/GVPK SE12 165 J2
Newstead Wk MRDN SM4 194 B4
Newstead Wy WIM/MER SW19 159 G6
New St LVPST EC2M 13 H2
New Street Hl BMLY BR1 184 A1
New Street Sq FLST/FETLN EC4A 11 K3
Newton Av ACT W3 117 K2
MUSWH N10 48 A4
Newton Cl RYLN/HDSTN HA2 60 A6
WALTH E17 69 G3
Newton Gv CHSWK W4 118 B3
Newton Rd ALP/SUD HA0 80 B5
BAY/PAD W2 101 F5
CRICK NW2 82 A2
ISLW TW7 136 A3
KTN/HRWW/W HA3 42 E4
SEVS/STOTM N15 68 B2
SRTFD * E15 88 B3
WDR/YW UB7 132 B2
WELL DA16 148 B4
WIM/MER SW19 177 H3
Newtons Cl RAIN RM13 93 G5
Newton St HOL/ALD WC2B 11 F3
Newton's Yd WAND/EARL SW18 139 K6
Newton Ter HAYES BR2 200 C3
Newton Wk EDGE HA8 44 D4
Newton Wy UED N18 49 J1
New Tower Buildings
WAP * E1W 123 J1
Newtown St BTSEA SW11 141 G2
New Trinity Rd EFNCH N2 47 H6
New Union Cl POP/IOD E14 125 F3
New Union St BARB EC2Y 12 E2
New Vls TOTM * N17 50 C4
New Wanstead WAN E11 70 E3
New Way Rd CDALE/KGS NW9 63 G1
New Wharf Rd IS N1 5 F2
New Zealand Wy RAIN RM13 111 H2
Niagara Av EA W5 116 D4
Niagara Cl IS N1 6 D2
Nibthwaite Rd HRW HA1 60 E2
Nicholas Cl GFD/PVL UB6 96 B1
Nicholas Gdns EA W5 116 E1
Nicholas La MANHO EC4N 13 F5
Nicholas Rd BCTR RM8 74 B6
BORE WD6 30 B1
CROY/NA CR0 210 E2
WCHPL E1 104 E3
Nicholas Wy NTHWD HA6 40 A4
Nicholay Rd ARCH N19 66 D5
Nicholes Rd HSLW TW3 135 F5
Nichol La BMLY BR1 183 K3
Nichollsfield Wk HOLWY N7 84 E3
Nicholl St BETH E2 86 C6
Nichols Cl FSBYPK * N4 67 G5
Nichols Gn EA W5 98 A4
Nicholson Dr BUSH WD23 28 C3
Nicholson Ms KUT KT1 191 F1
Nicholson Rd CROY/NA CR0 197 G5
Nicholson St STHWK SE1 18 A1
Nickelby Cl THMD SE28 109 J5
Nicola Cl KTN/HRWW/W HA3 42 D5
SAND/SEL CR2 211 J4
Nicola Ms BARK/HLT IG6 54 B3
Nicoll Pl HDN NW4 63 K3
Nicoll Rd WLSDN NW10 81 G6
Nicolson Rd STMC/STPC BR5 202 D4
Nicosia Rd WAND/EARL SW18 160 D2
Niederwald Rd SYD SE26 164 B6
Nield Rd HYS/HAR UB3 113 J2
Nigel Cl NTHLT UB5 77 J6
Nigel Fisher Wy CHSGTN KT9 205 J5
Nigel Ms IL IG1 90 B2
Nigel Playfair Av HMSMTH W6 118 E5
Nigel Rd FSTGT E7 89 G3
PECK SE15 143 H4
Nigeria Rd CHARL SE7 146 B1
Nightingale Av CHING E4 52 C1
Nightingale Cl CAR SM5 195 F6
CHING E4 38 C6
CHSWK W4 117 K6
PIN HA5 59 G2
Nightingale Cnr
STMC/STPC * BR5 202 E1
Nightingale Dr HOR/WEW KT19 206 D4
Nightingale Gv LEW SE13 145 G6
Nightingale La BAL SW12 160 E2
BMLY BR1 184 B5
CEND/HSY/T N8 66 E1
RCHPK/HAM TW10 157 F2
WAN E11 71 F2
Nightingale Ms KUT * KT1 174 E6
LBTH SE11 17 K6
Nightingale Pl WBPTN SW10 120 B6
WOOL/PLUM SE18 127 F6
Nightingale Rd CAR SM5 209 K1
CLPT E5 86 D1
E/WMO/HCT KT8 189 G2
ED N9 36 E2
HNWL W7 116 A1
HPTN TW12 173 F2
STMC/STPC BR5 201 H3
WDGN N22 48 E4
WLSDN NW10 99 H1
WOT/HER * KT12 188 B4
The Nightingales
STWL/WRAY TW19 152 C3
Nightingale Sq BAL SW12 161 F2
Nightingale V
WOOL/PLUM SE18 127 F6
Nightingale Wk BAL SW12 161 G1
Nightingale Wy EHAM E6 107 J4
Nigntingale Av HRW HA1 61 H4
Nile Cl STNW/STAM N16 86 B1
Nile Dr ED N9 36 E5
Nile Rd PLSTW E13 107 G1
Nile St IS N1 6 E4
Nile Ter PECK SE15 123 G5
Nimmo Dr BUSH WD23 28 D2
Nimrod Cl NTHLT UB5 95 H2
Nimrod Pas IS N1 86 A4
Nimrod Rd STRHM/NOR SW16 179 G2
Nina Mackay Cl SRTFD * E15 88 C6
Nine Acres Cl MNPK E12 89 J3
Nine Elms Cl EBED/NFELT TW14 153 J3
Nine Elms La VX/NE SW8 141 H1
Nineteenth Rd MTCM CR4 195 K1
Ninhams Wd ORP BR6 216 A2
Ninth Av HYS/HAR UB3 94 E6
Nithdale Rd WOOL/PLUM SE18 147 G1
Nithsdale Gv HGDN/ICK UB10 76 A1
Niton Cl BAR EN5 32 B1
Niton Rd RCH/KEW * TW9 137 H4
Niton St FUL/PGN SW6 139 G1
No 1 St WOOL/PLUM SE18 127 G3
No 2 St WOOL/PLUM SE18 127 G3
Noak Hill Rd HARH RM3 57 K1
Nobel Dr HYS/HAR UB3 133 H1
Nobel Rd UED N18 36 E6
Noble Cnr HEST * TW5 135 F2
Noble St CITYW EC2V 12 C3
Noel Rd ACT W3 98 C5
EHAM E6 107 J3
IS N1 6 A2
Noel St SOHO/CST * W1F 10 B4
Nolan Wy CLPT E5 86 C2
Nolton Pl EDGE HA8 44 B4
Nonsuch Cl BARK/HLT IG6 54 B2
Nonsuch Pl CHEAM * SM3 208 B5
Norbiton Av KUT KT1 175 H5
Norbiton Common Rd
NWMAL KT3 175 J6
Norbiton Rd POP/IOD E14 105 H5
Norbroke St ACT W3 99 H6
Norburn St NKENS W10 100 C4
Norbury Av HSLW TW3 135 J6
STRHM/NOR SW16 180 A4
Norbury Cl STRHM/NOR SW16 180 B4
Norbury Court Rd
STRHM/NOR SW16 179 K5
Norbury Crs STRHM/NOR SW16 180 B5
Norbury Cross
STRHM/NOR SW16 179 K6
Norbury Gdns CHDH RM6 73 K2
Norbury Gv MLHL NW7 31 G5
Norbury Hl STRHM/NOR SW16 180 B3
Norbury Ri STRHM/NOR SW16 179 K6
Norbury Rd CHING E4 51 J1
THHTH CR7 180 D5
Norbury Vls KUT * KT1 175 G5
Norcombe Gdns
KTN/HRWW/W HA3 61 J3
Norcott Cl YEAD UB4 95 G3
Norcott Rd STNW/STAM N16 68 C6
Norcroft Gdns EDUL SE22 163 H2
Norcutt Rd WHTN TW2 155 K3
Nordenfeldt Rd ERITH DA8 130 A5
Norfield Rd RDART DA2 169 K6
Norfolk Av PLMGR N13 49 H2
SEVS/STOTM N15 68 B3
Norfolk Cl DART DA1 171 K1
EBAR EN4 22 A5
EFNCH N2 47 J6
PLMGR N13 49 H2
TWK * TW1 156 C1
Norfolk Ct BAR * EN5 20 C5
Norfolk Crs BAY/PAD W2 8 C3
BFN/LL DA15 167 K2
Norfolk Gdns BXLYHN DA7 149 G2
Norfolk House Rd
STRHM/NOR SW16 161 J5
Norfolk Ms NKENS W10 100 C4
Norfolk Pl BAY/PAD W2 8 B3
WELL DA16 148 B3
Norfolk Rd BAR EN5 20 E4
BARK IG11 90 E5
DAGE RM10 92 D3
EHAM E6 89 K6
ESH/CLAY KT10 204 E3
FELT TW13 154 B3
GDMY/SEVK IG3 72 E5
HRW HA1 60 B2
PEND EN3 24 D6
ROMW/RG RM7 74 E3
STJWD NW8 2 B1
THHTH CR7 180 D6
WALTH E17 51 G4
WIM/MER SW19 178 D3
WLSDN NW10 81 G5
Norfolk Rw STHWK SE1 17 G6
Norfolk Sq BAY/PAD W2 8 B4
Norfolk Square Ms BAY/PAD W2 8 B4
Norfolk St FSTGT E7 88 E3
Norgrove St BAL SW12 161 F3
Norhyrst Av SNWD SE25 181 G6
Norland Pl NTGHL W11 119 H1
Norland Rd NTGHL W11 119 G1
Norlands Crs CHST BR7 185 G4
Norlands Ga CHST * BR7 185 G4
Norland Sq NTGHL W11 119 H1
Norley V PUT/ROE SW15 158 D3
Norlington Rd WAN E11 70 A5
Norman Av FELT TW13 154 D4
STHL UB1 95 J6
TWK TW1 156 C2
WDGN N22 49 J4
Normanby Cl PUT/ROE SW15 139 J6
Normanby Rd WLSDN NW10 81 H3
Norman Cl ORP BR6 216 C1
ROMW/RG RM7 56 D5
Norman Crs HEST TW5 134 C1
PIN HA5 41 G4
Normand Gdns WKENS * W14 119 H6
Normand Ms WKENS W14 119 H6
Normand Rd WKENS W14 119 J6
Normandy Av BAR EN5 20 D6
Normandy Cl SYD SE26 164 B5
Normandy Dr HYS/HAR UB3 94 A5
Normandy Rd BRXN/ST SW9 142 B2
Normandy Ter CAN/RD E16 107 F5
Normandy Wy ERITH DA8 150 B2
Norman Gv BOW E3 105 G1
Normanhurst Av WELL DA16 148 E2
Normanhurst Dr TWK TW1 136 C6
Normanhurst Rd
BRXS/STRHM SW2 162 A4
STMC/STPC BR5 186 C5
WOT/HER KT12 188 C6
Norman Pde SCUP * DA14 169 F5
Norman Rd BELV DA17 129 J2
DART DA1 171 H3
EHAM E6 107 K3
EMPK RM11 75 J4
GNWCH SE10 144 E1
IL IG1 90 B3
SEVS/STOTM N15 68 B2
SUT SM1 208 E3
THHTH CR7 196 C2
WAN E11 70 C6
WIM/MER SW19 178 B3
Normans Cl WDGN * N22 49 J4
WLSDN NW10 81 F4
Normansfield Av
E/WMO/HCT KT8 174 D3
Normansfield Cl BUSH WD23 28 B2
Normanshire Dr CHING E4 37 J6
Normans Md WLSDN NW10 81 F4
Norman St FSBYE EC1V 6 C5
Norman Ter KIL/WHAMP * NW6 82 D3
Normanton Av
WAND/EARL SW18 159 K4
Normanton Pk CHING E4 38 C5
Normanton Rd SAND/SEL CR2 212 A4
Normanton St FSTH SE23 164 A4
Norman Wy ACT W3 98 D4
STHGT/OAK N14 34 E4
Normington Cl
STRHM/NOR SW16 180 B1
Norrice Lea EFNCH N2 65 H2
Norris St STJS SW1Y 10 C6
Norris Wy DART DA1 150 C4
Norroy Rd PUT/ROE SW15 139 G5
Norrys Cl EBAR EN4 21 K6
Norrys Rd EBAR EN4 21 K5
Norseman Cl GDMY/SEVK IG3 73 H5
Norseman Wy GFD/PVL UB6 78 B6
Norstead Pl PUT/ROE SW15 158 D4
North Access Rd WALTH E17 69 F3
North Acre CDALE/KGS NW9 45 G4
North Acton Rd WLSDN NW10 99 F1
Northall Rd BXLYHN DA7 149 K3
Northampton Gv IS N1 85 J3
Northampton Pk IS N1 85 J4
Northampton Rd CLKNW EC1R 5 K6
CROY/NA CR0 197 H6
PEND EN3 25 G5
Northampton Rw CLKNW * EC1R 5 K6
Northampton Sq FSBYE EC1V 6 A5
Northampton St IS * N1 85 J5
Northanger Rd
STRHM/NOR SW16 179 K2
North Ap RKW/CH/CXG WD3 26 A4
North Audley St MYFR/PKLN W1K 9 G4
North Av CAR SM5 210 A5
HYS/HAR UB3 94 E6
RCH/KEW TW9 137 H2
RYLN/HDSTN HA2 60 B3
STHL UB1 95 K6
UED N18 36 C6
WEA W13 97 H5
North Bank STJWD NW8 2 C5
Northbank Rd WALTH E17 52 A5
North Birkbeck Rd WAN E11 88 B1
Northborough Rd
STRHM/NOR SW16 179 K5
Northbourne HAYES BR2 199 K4
Northbourne Rd CLAP SW4 141 J5
Northbrook Dr NTHWD HA6 40 C4
Northbrook Rd BAR EN5 32 C1
CROY/NA CR0 196 E2
IL IG1 72 A6
LEW SE13 145 G6
WDGN N22 48 E2
Northburgh St FSBYE EC1V 6 B7
North Carriage Dr BAY/PAD W2 8 D5
Northchurch Rd IS N1 85 K5
WBLY HA9 80 C4
Northchurch Ter IS N1 86 A5
North Circular PLMGR N13 49 G1
WALTH E17 51 K4
North Circular Rd CHING * E4 51 G2
CRICK NW2 81 G1
EFNCH N2 47 G5
GLDGN NW11 64 C1
SWFD E18 53 G6
WLSDN NW10 98 B1
Northcliffe Cl WPK KT4 207 G1
Northcliffe Dr TRDG/WHET N20 32 D3
North Cl BAR EN5 20 A6
BXLYHS DA6 148 E5
CHIG IG7 55 G1
DAGE RM10 92 C6
EBED/NFELT TW14 153 G1
MRDN SM4 193 H1
North Colonnade POP/IOD E14 124 D1
North Common Rd EA W5 98 A6
Northcote Av BRYLDS KT5 191 H4
EA W5 98 A6
ISLW TW7 136 B6
STHL UB1 95 J6
Northcote Rd BTSEA SW11 140 D5
CROY/NA CR0 196 E3
NWMAL KT3 175 K6
SCUP DA14 167 K6
TWK TW1 136 B6
WALTH E17 69 G1
WLSDN NW10 81 G5
Northcott Av WDGN N22 48 E4
North Countess Rd WALTH E17 51 H5
North Cray Rd BXLY DA5 169 H4
SCUP DA14 187 F2
North Crs CAN/RD E16 106 B3
FITZ W1T 10 C1
FNCH N3 46 D5
Northcroft Rd HOR/WEW KT19 207 G5
WEA W13 116 C2
North Cross Rd BARK/HLT IG6 72 C1
EDUL SE22 143 G6
Northdene CHIG IG7 54 D1
North Dene HEST TW5 135 G2
MLHL NW7 31 F5
Northdene Gdns
SEVS/STOTM N15 68 B3
Northdown Cl RSLP HA4 76 D1
Northdown Gdns
GNTH/NBYPK IG2 72 E2
Northdown Rd EMPK RM11 75 K4
WELL DA16 148 C3
Northdown St IS N1 5 G3
North Dr BECK BR3 198 E2
HSLW TW3 135 H3
ORP BR6 216 E2
RSLP HA4 58 C4
STRHM/NOR SW16 161 H6
North End BKHH IG9 39 G2
CROY/NA CR0 196 D6
HAMP NW3 65 G6
North End Av HAMP NW3 65 G6
North End Crs WKENS W14 119 J4
North End La ORP BR6 216 B6
Northend Rd ERITH DA8 150 C2
North End Rd FUL/PGN SW6 139 K1
GLDGN NW11 64 E5
WBLY HA9 80 C1
WKENS W14 119 H4
North End Wy HAMP NW3 65 G6
Northern Av ED N9 36 B4
Northernhay Wk MRDN SM4 193 H1
Northern Perimeter Rd
HTHAIR TW6 133 F2
Northern Perimeter Rd (West)
HTHAIR TW6 132 B2
Northern Relief Rd BARK IG11 90 C5
North Eyot Gdns
HMSMTH * W6 118 C5
Northey St POP/IOD E14 105 G6
North Farm LOU IG10 39 K1
Northfield Av PIN HA5 59 H1
STMC/STPC BR5 202 D3
WEA W13 116 C2
Northfield Cl BMLY BR1 184 D4
HYS/HAR UB3 113 J3
Northfield Crs CHEAM SM3 208 C2
Northfield Pde HYS/HAR * UB3 113 J3
Northfield Pk HYS/HAR UB3 113 H3
North Field Rd HEST TW5 114 C6
Northfield Rd DAGW RM9 92 B2
EBAR EN4 21 J4
EHAM E6 89 K4
PEND * EN3 24 D6
STNW/STAM N16 68 A4
WEA W13 116 C2
Northfields WAND/EARL SW18 139 K5
Northfields Rd ACT W3 98 E4
North Gdns WIM/MER SW19 178 C3
Northgate NTHWD HA6 40 A3
Northgate Dr CDALE/KGS NW9 63 G3
North Gower St CAMTN NW1 4 A5
North Gv HGT N6 66 A4
SEVS/STOTM N15 67 K2
North Hl HGT N6 65 K3
North Hill Av HGT N6 65 K3
North Hyde Gdns HYS/HAR UB3 113 K3
North Hyde La NWDGN UB2 114 D5
North Hyde Rd HYS/HAR UB3 113 H3
North Hyde Whf NWDGN * UB2 114 B4
Northiam NFNCH/WDSP N12 32 E6
Northiam St HACK E8 86 D6
Northington St BMSBY WC1N 11 G1
Northlands Av ORP BR6 216 E2
Northlands St CMBW SE5 142 D3
North La TEDD TW11 174 A2
North Lodge Cl
PUT/ROE * SW15 139 G6
North Ms BMSBY WC1N 5 H7
North Mt TRDG/WHET * N20 33 G4
Northolm EDGE HA8 31 F6
Northolme Gdns EDGE HA8 44 C4
Northolme Ri ORP BR6 201 K6
Northolme Rd HBRY N5 85 J2
Northolt Av RSLP HA4 77 F3
Northolt Gdns GFD/PVL UB6 79 F3
Northolt Rd RYLN/HDSTN HA2 78 B2
WDR/YW UB7 132 A2
Northover BMLY BR1 165 J6
North Pde CHSGTN KT9 206 B3
EDGE * HA8 44 C5
STHL * UB1 96 A5
North Pk ELTH/MOT SE9 166 E1
North Pas WAND/EARL SW18 139 K6
North Peckham Est PECK SE15 143 G1
North Pl TEDD TW11 174 A2
WIM/MER SW19 178 E3
North Pole La HAYES BR2 214 E4
North Pole Rd SHB W12 100 A5
Northport St IS N1 7 F1
North Ri BAY/PAD * W2 8 D4
North Rd BELV DA17 129 J3
BMLY BR1 184 A4
BTFD TW8 117 F6
CHDH RM6 74 A2
DART DA1 170 C1
EA W5 116 E3
EBED/NFELT TW14 153 G1
ED N9 36 D3
EDGE HA8 44 D4
EFNCH N2 47 J4
GDMY/SEVK IG3 72 E6
HEST TW5 114 B6
HGT N6 66 A4
HOLWY N7 84 E4
HYS/HAR UB3 94 B4
RCH/KEW TW9 137 H3
STHL UB1 96 A6
SURB KT6 190 E3
WDR/YW UB7 112 C3
WIM/MER SW19 178 C2
WOOL/PLUM SE18 127 K4
WWKM BR4 198 E5
Northrop Rd HTHAIR TW6 133 H2
North Rw MYFR/PKLN W1K 9 G5
North Several
BKHTH/KID * SE3 145 G3
Northside Rd BMLY BR1 183 K4
North Side
Wandsworth Common
WAND/EARL SW18 140 B6
Northspur Rd SUT SM1 208 E1
North Sq ED N9 36 D4
GLDGN NW11 64 E3
Northstead Rd
BRXS/STRHM SW2 162 B4
North St BARK IG11 90 C5
BMLY BR1 183 K5
BXLYHN DA7 149 H5
CAR SM5 209 K2
DART DA1 171 G2
HDN NW4 64 A2
ISLW TW7 136 B4
PLSTW E13 107 F1
ROM RM1 75 F1
VX/NE SW8 141 G4
North Tenter St WCHPL E1 13 K4
North Ter CHEL SW3 14 C6
Northumberland Aly
TWRH * EC3N 13 H4
Northumberland Av
CHCR WC2N 10 E7
EN EN1 24 D1
ISLW TW7 136 A2
MNPK E12 71 G5
WELL DA16 147 K5
Northumberland Cl ERITH DA8 149 K1
STWL/WRAY TW19 152 B1
Northumberland Crs
EBED/NFELT TW14 153 H1
Northumberland Gdns
BMLY BR1 201 F1
ED N9 36 B5
MTCM CR4 195 K2
Northumberland Gv TOTM N17 50 D3
Northumberland Pk ERITH DA8 149 K1
TOTM N17 50 C3
Northumberland Pl
BAY/PAD W2 100 E5
Northumberland Rd BAR EN5 33 G1
EHAM E6 107 J5
RYLN/HDSTN HA2 59 K2
WALTH E17 69 J4
Northumberland St CHCR WC2N 10 E7
Northumberland Wy
ERITH DA8 149 K2
Northumbria St POP/IOD E14 105 J5
North Verbena Gdns
HMSMTH * W6 118 D5
North Vw EA W5 97 J3
PIN HA5 59 G4
WIM/MER SW19 176 E1
Northview Crs WLSDN NW10 81 H2
Northview Dr WFD IG8 53 H5
Northview Pde HOLWY * N7 84 E1
North View Rd CEND/HSY/T N8 48 D6
North Vls CAMTN NW1 84 D4
North Wy CDALE/KGS NW9 44 D6
ED N9 36 E4
FBAR/BDGN N11 48 C2
PIN HA5 41 G6
Northway GLDGN NW11 65 F2
RYNPK SW20 177 H6
WLGTN SM6 210 C2
Northway Crs MLHL NW7 31 G6
Northway Rd CMBW SE5 142 D4
CROY/NA CR0 197 G3
Northways Pde HAMP * NW3 83 H5
North Weald La KUTN/CMB KT2 174 D1
North Western Av
(Watford By-Pass)
STAN HA7 29 G1
North Wharf Rd BAY/PAD W2 8 A2
Northwick Av HRW HA1 61 G3
Northwick Cir
KTN/HRWW/W HA3 61 J3
Northwick Cl STJWD NW8 2 A6
Northwick Park Rd HRW HA1 61 F3
Northwick Rd ALP/SUD HA0 79 K6
OXHEY WD19 27 G6
Northwick Ter STJWD NW8 2 A6
Northwold Dr PIN HA5 41 G6
Northwold Rd STNW/STAM N16 68 C6
Northwood Av HCH RM12 93 J2
Northwood Gdns CLAY IG5 72 A1
GFD/PVL UB6 79 F3
NFNCH/WDSP N12 47 H1
Northwood Pl ERITHM DA18 129 G3
Northwood Rd CAR SM5 210 A4
FSTH SE23 164 C3
HGT N6 66 B4
HTHAIR TW6 132 A2
THHTH CR7 180 D5
Northwood Wy NTHWD HA6 40 E4
North Woolwich Rd
CAN/RD E16 126 A1
North Worple Wy
MORT/ESHN SW14 138 A4
Norton Av BRYLDS KT5 191 J4
Norton Cl CHING E4 51 J1
Norton Folgate WCHPL E1 7 H7
Norton Gdns STRHM/NOR SW16 179 K5
Norton Rd ALP/SUD HA0 79 K4
DAGE RM10 93 F4
LEY E10 69 H5
Norval Gn BRXN/ST * SW9 142 B3
Norval Rd ALP/SUD HA0 61 H6
Norway Ga BERM/RHTH SE16 124 B3
Norway Pl POP/IOD E14 105 H5
Norway St GNWCH SE10 124 E6
Norwich Pl BXLYHS DA6 149 H5
Norwich Rd FSTGT E7 88 E4
GFD/PVL UB6 78 B6
PIN HA5 40 D6
THHTH CR7 180 D6
Norwich St FLST/FETLN EC4A 11 J3
Norwich Wk EDGE HA8 44 E3
Norwood Av ALP/SUD HA0 80 B6
ROMW/RG RM7 75 F4
Norwood Cl NWDGN UB2 115 F4
WHTN TW2 155 J4
Norwood Crs HTHAIR TW6 133 F2
Norwood Dr RYLN/HDSTN HA2 59 K3
Norwood Gdns NWDGN UB2 114 E4
YEAD UB4 95 G3
Norwood Green Rd
NWDGN UB2 115 F4
Norwood High St WNWD SE27 162 C5
Norwood Park Rd WNWD SE27 180 D1
Norwood Rd HNHL SE24 162 C3
NWDGN UB2 114 D3
Notley St CMBW SE5 142 E1
Notson Rd SNWD SE25 197 J1
Notting Barn Rd NKENS W10 100 B3
Nottingdale Sq NTGHL * W11 119 H1
Nottingham Av CAN/RD E16 107 G4
Nottingham Ct
LSQ/SEVD * WC2H 10 E4
Nottingham Pl MHST W1U 3 G7
Nottingham Rd ISLW TW7 136 A3
LEY E10 70 A3
SAND/SEL CR2 211 J3
TOOT SW17 160 E3
Nottingham St MHST W1U 9 G1
Nottingham Ter CAMTN NW1 3 G7
Notting Hill Ga NTGHL W11 119 K1
Nova Ms MRDN SM4 193 H4
Novar Cl ORP BR6 202 A4
Nova Rd CROY/NA CR0 196 C5
Novar Rd ELTH/MOT SE9 167 H3
Novello St FUL/PGN SW6 139 K2
Nowell Rd BARN SW13 118 D6
Nower Hl PIN HA5 59 K1
Noyna Rd TOOT SW17 160 E5
Nubia Wy BMLY BR1 165 H6
Nuding Cl LEW SE13 144 D4
Nugent Rd ARCH N19 66 E5
SNWD SE25 181 G6
Nugents Ct PIN * HA5 41 J4
Nugent's Pk PIN HA5 41 K4
Nugent Ter STJWD NW8 101 G1
Nuneaton Rd DAGW RM9 91 K5
Nunhead Gv PECK SE15 143 J4
Nunhead La PECK SE15 143 J4
Nunnington Cl ELTH/MOT SE9 166 D5
Nunn's Rd ENC/FH EN2 23 J3
Nupton Dr BAR EN5 32 A1
Nurse Cl EDGE HA8 44 E4
The Nursery ERITH DA8 150 C1
Nursery Av BXLYHN DA7 149 G4

CROY/NA CR0 198 A6
FNCH N3 47 F5
Nursery Cl BROCKY SE4 144 C3
CHDH RM6 73 K3
CROY/NA CR0 198 A6
EBED/NFELT TW14 154 A2
ORP BR6 202 A4
PEND EN3 25 F2
SWLY BR8 187 K5
WFD IG8 53 F1
Nursery Gdns CHST BR7 185 G2
HSLWW TW4 134 E6
PEND EN3 25 F2
Nursery La BETH E2 7 J1
FSTGT E7 88 E4
NKENS W10 100 A4
Nurserymans Rd
FBAR/BDGN N11 34 A4
Nursery Rd BRXN/ST SW9 142 A5
EFNCH N2 47 H4
HOM E9 86 E4
MTCM CR4 194 D1
PIN HA5 41 G6
STHGT/OAK N14 34 C2
SUT SM1 209 G2
THHTH CR7 196 E1
WIM/MER SW19 177 H3
WIM/MER SW19 178 A5
Nursery Rw BAR * EN5 20 C4
WALW SE17 18 E7
Nursery St TOTM N17 50 B3
Nursery Wk HDN NW4 45 K6
Nurstead Rd ERITH DA8 149 H1
Nutbourne St NKENS W10 100 C2
Nutbrook St PECK SE15 143 G4
Nutbrowne Rd DAGW RM9 92 B6
Nutcroft Rd PECK SE15 143 J1
Nutfield Cl CAR SM5 209 J1
UED N18 50 C2
Nutfield Gdns GDMY/SEVK IG3 73 F6
NTHLT UB5 95 G1
Nutfield Rd CRICK NW2 63 J6
EDUL SE22 143 G6
SRTFD E15 88 A2
THHTH CR7 196 C1
Nutfield Wy ORP BR6 201 F6
Nutford Pl BAY/PAD W2 8 D3
Nuthatch Gdns THMD SE28 127 J2
Nuthurst Av BRXS/STRHM SW2 162 A4
Nutley Ter HAMP NW3 83 H4
Nutmead Cl BXLY DA5 169 K3
Nutmeg Cl CAN/RD E16 106 C3
Nutmeg La POP/IOD E14 106 B5
Nuttall St IS N1 7 H2
Nutter La WAN E11 71 G2
Nutt Gv EDGE HA8 29 K4
Nut Tree Cl ORP BR6 217 K1
Nutt St PECK SE15 143 G1
Nutwell St TOOT SW17 178 D1
Nuxley Rd BELV DA17 129 G6
Nyanza St WOOL/PLUM SE18 127 J6
Nylands Av RCH/KEW TW9 137 H3
Nymans Gdns RYNPK SW20 176 E6
Nynehead St NWCR SE14 144 B1
Nyon Gv FSTH SE23 164 C4
Nyssa Cl WFD IG8 53 K2

O

Oak Av CEND/HSY/T N8 66 E1
CROY/NA CR0 198 D6
ENC/FH EN2 23 F2
HEST TW5 134 C1
HPTN TW12 172 D1
MUSWH N10 48 B3
TOTM N17 49 K3
WDR/YW UB7 112 D3
Oakbank Av WOT/HER KT12 188 E4
Oakbank Gv HNHL SE24 142 D5
Oakbrook Cl BMLY BR1 166 A6
Oakbury Rd FUL/PGN SW6 140 A3
Oak Cl DART DA1 150 B5
STHGT/OAK N14 34 B2
Oakcombe Cl NWMAL KT3 176 B4
Oak Cottage Cl CAT SE6 165 H3
Oak Cottages HNWL * W7 115 K2
Oak Crs CAN/RD E16 106 C4
Oakcroft Cl PIN HA5 41 F5
Oakcroft Rd CHSGTN KT9 206 B2
LEW SE13 145 G3
Oakcroft Vls CHSGTN KT9 206 B2
Oakdale STHGT/OAK N14 34 B2
Oakdale Av KTN/HRWW/W HA3 62 A2
NTHWD HA6 40 E5
Oakdale Cl OXHEY WD19 27 G6
Oakdale Gdns CHING E4 52 A1
Oakdale Rd FSBYPK N4 67 J3
FSTGT E7 89 F5
HOR/WEW KT19 207 F6
OXHEY WD19 27 G5
PECK SE15 143 K4
STRHM/NOR SW16 179 K1
SWFD E18 53 F5
WAN E11 70 B6
Oakdale Wy MTCM CR4 195 F4
Oakdene Av CHST BR7 185 F1
ERITH DA8 129 K6
THDIT KT7 190 B5
Oakdene Cl PIN HA5 41 K3
Oak Dene Cl ROM RM1 75 K3
Oakdene Dr BRYLDS KT5 191 K5
Oakdene Ms CHEAM SM3 193 J5
Oakdene Pk FNCH N3 46 D3
Oakdene Rd STMC/STPC BR5 202 B3
Oakden St LBTH SE11 17 K6
Oaken Dr ESH/CLAY KT10 205 F4
Oaken La ESH/CLAY KT10 204 E2
Oakenshaw Cl SURB KT6 191 F4
Oakeshott Av HGT N6 66 A6
Oakey La STHWK SE1 17 J4
Oakfield CHING E4 51 K1
Oakfield Av KTN/HRWW/W HA3 43 H6
Oakfield Cl NWMAL KT3 192 C2
Oakfield Gdns BECK BR3 198 D2
CAR SM5 194 D5
GFD/PVL UB6 96 D3
UED N18 36 A6
Oakfield La HAYES BR2 215 G2
RDART DA2 170 D4
Oakfield Park Rd DART DA1 171 G4
Oakfield Pl DART DA1 171 G4
Oakfield Rd ASHF TW15 152 E6
CROY/NA CR0 196 D5
EHAM E6 89 J6
FNCH N3 47 F4
FSBYPK N4 67 G3
IL IG1 90 B1
PGE/AN SE20 181 J4
STHGT/OAK N14 34 E4
WALTH E17 51 G5
WIM/MER SW19 159 G5
Oakfields Rd GLDGN NW11 64 C3
Oakfield St WBPTN SW10 120 B6
Oakford Rd KTTN NW5 84 C2
Oak Gdns CROY/NA CR0 198 D6
EDGE HA8 44 E5
Oak Gv CRICK NW2 82 B2
RSLP HA4 59 F5
SUN TW16 172 A3
WWKM BR4 199 F6
Oak Grove Rd PGE/AN SE20 181 K4
Oak Hall Rd WAN E11 71 F3
Oakham Cl CAT * SE6 164 C4
Oakham Dr HAYES BR2 199 K1
Oakhampton Rd MLHL NW7 46 B4
Oakhill ESH/CLAY KT10 205 G4
Oak Hl SURB KT6 191 F4
WFD IG8 52 B3
Oakhill Av HAMP NW3 83 F2
PIN HA5 41 J5
Oak Hill Crs SURB KT6 191 F4
WFD IG8 52 C3
Oak Hill Gdns WALTH E17 52 C4
Oak Hill Gv SURB KT6 191 F3
Oak Hill Pk HAMP NW3 83 F2
Oak Hill Park Ms HAMP NW3 83 G2
Oakhill Pl WAND/EARL SW18 139 K6
Oak Hill Rd SURB * KT6 191 F3
Oakhill Rd BECK BR3 183 F5
ORP BR6 202 A6
PUT/ROE SW15 139 J6
STRHM/NOR SW16 179 K4
SUT SM1 209 F1
Oak Hill Wy HAMP NW3 83 G2
Oakhouse Rd BXLYHS DA6 149 H6
Oakhurst Av BXLYHN DA7 149 F1
EBAR EN4 33 J2
Oakhurst Cl BARK/HLT IG6 54 C4
CHST BR7 184 E4
TEDD TW11 173 K1
WALTH E17 70 C1
Oakhurst Gdns BXLYHN DA7 149 F1
CHING E4 38 D3
WALTH E17 70 C1
Oakhurst Gv EDUL SE22 143 H5
Oakhurst Rd HOR/WEW KT19 206 E4
Oakington Av HYS/HAR UB3 113 G4
RYLN/HDSTN HA2 60 A4
WBLY HA9 80 B1
Oakington Dr SUN TW16 172 B5
Oakington Manor Dr WBLY HA9 80 C3
Oakington Rd MV/WKIL * W9 100 E3
Oakington Wy CEND/HSY/T N8 66 E3
Oakland Pl BKHH IG9 38 E4
Oakland Rd SRTFD E15 88 C2
Oaklands PLMGR N13 35 F4
Oaklands Av BFN/LL DA15 168 A2
ED N9 36 D1
ESH/CLAY KT10 189 J5
ISLW TW7 116 A6
OXHEY WD19 27 F3
ROM RM1 57 G6
THHTH CR7 196 B1
WWKM BR4 213 K1
Oaklands Cl ALP/SUD HA0 79 K3
BXLYHS DA6 149 G6
CHSGTN KT9 205 J2
STMC/STPC BR5 201 K3
Oaklands Ga NTHWD HA6 40 C2
Oaklands Gv SHB W12 118 D1
Oaklands Ms CRICK NW2 82 B2
Oaklands Park Av IL IG1 72 C6
Oaklands Pl CLAP SW4 141 J5
Oaklands Rd BMLY BR1 183 H3
BXLYHS DA6 149 G5
CRICK NW2 82 B2
HNWL W7 116 A2
MORT/ESHN SW14 138 A4
TRDG/WHET N20 32 D2
Oaklands Wy WLGTN SM6 210 C5
Oakland Wy HOR/WEW KT19 207 F4
Oak La EFNCH N2 47 H5
FBAR/BDGN N11 48 D2
ISLW TW7 135 K5
POP/IOD E14 105 H6
TWK TW1 156 B2
WFD IG8 38 D6
Oakleafe Gdns CLAY IG5 54 B6
Oakleigh Av EDGE HA8 44 D5
SURB KT6 191 H5
TRDG/WHET N20 33 H3
Oakleigh Cl TRDG/WHET N20 33 K5
Oakleigh Ct EDGE * HA8 44 E5
Oakleigh Crs TRDG/WHET N20 33 J5
Oakleigh Dr RKW/CH/CXG WD3 26 A1
Oakleigh Gdns EDGE HA8 44 B1
ORP BR6 216 E2
TRDG/WHET N20 33 G3
Oakleigh Ms TRDG/WHET * N20 33 G4
Oakleigh Park Av CHST BR7 185 F5
Oakleigh Pk North
TRDG/WHET N20 33 H3
Oakleigh Pk South
TRDG/WHET N20 33 J3
Oakleigh Rd HGDN/ICK UB10 76 A5
PIN HA5 41 K2
Oakleigh Rd North
TRDG/WHET N20 33 H4
Oakleigh Rd South
FBAR/BDGN N11 34 A6
Oakleigh Wy MTCM CR4 179 G4
SURB KT6 191 H5
Oakley Av BARK IG11 91 F4
CROY/NA CR0 210 E2
EA W5 98 C6
Oakley Cl CHING E4 38 B4
HNWL W7 96 E6
ISLW TW7 135 J2
Oakley Crs FSBYE * EC1V 6 B3
Oakley Dr BFN/LL DA15 167 J4
HAYES BR2 215 J1
LEW SE13 165 G1
Oakley Gdns CEND/HSY/T N8 67 F2
CHEL SW3 120 D6
Oakley Pk BFN/LL DA15 168 D2
Oakley Pl STHWK SE1 123 G5
Oakley Rd HAYES BR2 215 J1
HRW HA1 60 E3
IS N1 85 K5
SNWD SE25 197 J2
Oakley Sq CAMTN NW1 4 B2
Oakley St CHEL SW3 120 D6
Oakley Yd BETH * E2 7 K6
Oak Lodge Av CHIG IG7 54 D1
Oak Lodge Cl STAN HA7 43 J1
Oak Lodge Dr WWKM BR4 198 E4
Oakmead Av HAYES BR2 199 K3
Oakmeade PIN HA5 42 A2
Oakmead Gdns EDGE HA8 31 F6
Oakmead Pl MTCM CR4 178 D4
Oakmead Rd BAL SW12 161 G3
CROY/NA CR0 195 J3
Oakmere Rd ABYW SE2 128 B6
Oakmoor Wy CHIG IG7 55 K1
Oakmore Gdns STMC/STPC BR5 202 D1
Oak Park Gdns WIM/MER SW19 159 G3
Oakridge Dr EFNCH N2 47 H6
Oakridge Rd BMLY BR1 165 H6
Oak Ri BKHH IG9 39 H5
Oak Rd EA W5 97 K6
ERITH DA8 149 K1
ERITH DA8 150 D2
NWMAL KT3 176 A5
ORP BR6 217 G5
Oak Rw MTCM CR4 179 H5
The Oaks FELT * TW13 154 D4
HAYES * BR2 201 F3
MRDN * SM4 193 H1
NFNCH/WDSP N12 33 F6
OXHEY WD19 27 G3
RSLP HA4 58 B4
SURB KT6 205 J1
WFD IG8 52 C3
WOOL/PLUM SE18 127 H5
YEAD UB4 94 A1
Oaks Av CRW RM5 56 E5
FELT TW13 154 D4
NRWD SE19 181 F1
WPK KT4 207 K2
Oaksford Av SYD SE26 163 J5
Oaks Gv CHING E4 38 C4
Oakshade Rd BMLY BR1 165 G6
Oakshaw Rd WAND/EARL SW18 160 A2
Oaks La CROY/NA CR0 212 E1
GNTH/NBYPK IG2 72 E2
Oaks Rd CROY/NA CR0 212 D3
STWL/WRAY TW19 132 A6
Oak St ROMW/RG RM7 74 E2
Oaks Wy CAR SM5 209 K5
SURB KT6 190 E6
Oakthorpe Rd PLMGR N13 49 G1
Oaktree Av PLMGR N13 35 G5
Oak Tree Cl STAN HA7 43 J3
WEA * W13 97 J5
Oak Tree Ct BORE * WD6 29 K1
Oak Tree Dell CDALE/KGS NW9 62 E2
Oak Tree Dr TRDG/WHET N20 33 F3
Oak Tree Gdns BMLY BR1 184 A1
Oaktree Gv IL IG1 90 D3
Oak Tree Rd STJWD NW8 2 B5
Oakview Gdns EFNCH N2 65 H1
Oakview Gv CROY/NA CR0 198 B5
Oakview Rd CAT SE6 182 E1
Oak Village HAMP NW3 84 A2
Oak Vls GLDGN * NW11 64 D3
Oak Wy ACT W3 118 B1
CROY/NA CR0 198 A3
EBED/NFELT TW14 153 H3
STHGT/OAK N14 34 B2
Oakway HAYES BR2 183 G5
RYNPK SW20 193 F1
Oakway Cl BXLY DA5 169 F1
Oakways ELTH/MOT SE9 167 G1
Oakwood WLGTN SM6 210 B6
Oakwood Av BECK BR3 183 F5
HAYES BR2 184 A6
HOR/WEW KT19 206 C6
MTCM CR4 178 C5
STHGT/OAK N14 34 D2
STHL UB1 96 A6
Oakwood Cl CHST BR7 184 E2
STHGT/OAK N14 34 C1
WFD IG8 53 J2
Oakwood Ct WKENS W14 119 J3
Oakwood Crs GFD/PVL UB6 79 G4
WCHMH N21 34 E1
Oakwood Dr BXLYHN DA7 149 K5
EDGE HA8 44 E2
NRWD SE19 180 E2
Oakwood Gdns GDMY/SEVK IG3 73 F6
ORP BR6 216 B1
SUT SM1 193 K6
Oakwood La WKENS W14 119 J3
Oakwood Pde EBAR * EN4 22 C6
Oakwood Park Cottages
STHGT/OAK * N14 35 F1
Oakwood Park Rd
STHGT/OAK N14 34 E1
Oakwood Pl CROY/NA CR0 196 B3
Oakwood Rd CROY/NA CR0 196 B3
GLDGN NW11 64 E2
ORP BR6 201 H6
PIN HA5 41 F5
RYNPK SW20 176 D4
Oakworth Rd NKENS W10 100 A4
Oarsman Pl E/WMO/HCT KT8 189 K1
Oast House Wy STMC/STPC BR5 202 C1
Oates Cl HAYES BR2 183 G6
Oates Rd CRW RM5 56 D1
Oatfield Rd ORP BR6 202 A5
Oatland Ri WALTH E17 51 G5
Oatlands Rd PEND EN3 24 E2
Oat La CITYW EC2V 12 C3
Oban Cl PLSTW E13 107 G3
Oban Rd PLSTW E13 107 G2
SNWD SE25 196 E1
Oban St POP/IOD E14 106 B5
Oberstein Rd BTSEA SW11 140 C5
Oborne Cl HNHL SE24 142 C6
Observatory Gdns KENS W8 119 K2
Observatory Rd
MORT/ESHN SW14 137 K5
SKENS SW7 14 B4
Occupation La EA W5 116 E4
WOOL/PLUM SE18 147 G2
Occupation Rd WALW SE17 122 D5
WEA W13 116 C2
Ocean Est WCHPL E1 105 F3
Ocean St WCHPL E1 105 F4
Ockendon Ms IS * N1 85 K4
Ockendon Rd IS N1 85 K4
Ockham Dr STMC/STPC BR5 186 B3
Ockley Rd CROY/NA CR0 196 A4
STRHM/NOR SW16 161 K6
Octagon Ar LVPST * EC2M 13 G2
Octavia Cl MTCM CR4 194 D2
Octavia Ms CRICK * NW2 81 K4
Octavia Rd ISLW TW7 136 A4
Octavia St BTSEA SW11 140 D2
Octavius St DEPT SE8 144 D1
October Pl HDN * NW4 46 B6
Odard Rd E/WMO/HCT KT8 189 F1
Odeon Pde ELTH/MOT * SE9 146 D5
GFD/PVL * UB6 79 H4
HOLWY * N7 84 E1
ISLW * TW7 135 K3
Odessa Rd FSTGT E7 88 D2
WLSDN NW10 99 J1
Odessa St BERM/RHTH SE16 124 C3
Odger St BTSEA SW11 140 E3
Odhams Wk LSQ/SEVD * WC2H 10 E4
Odsey Vls FSBYPK * N4 67 G3
Offa's Md HOM E9 87 G2
Offenham Rd ELTH/MOT SE9 166 E6
Offerton Rd CLAP SW4 141 H4
Offham Slope NFNCH/WDSP N12 46 D1
Offley Rd BRXN/ST SW9 142 B1
Offord Cl TOTM N17 50 C3
Offord Rd IS N1 85 G5
Offord St IS N1 85 F5
Ogilby St WOOL/PLUM SE18 126 E4
Oglander Rd PECK SE15 143 G5
Ogle St GTPST W1W 10 A1
Oglethorpe Rd DAGE RM10 92 B1
Ohio Rd PLSTW E13 106 D3
Oil Mill La HMSMTH W6 118 D5
Okeburn Rd TOOT SW17 179 F1
Okehampton Crs WELL DA16 148 C2
Okehampton Rd WLSDN NW10 82 A6
Olaf St NTGHL W11 100 B6
Old Bailey STP EC4M 12 B4
Old Barn Cl BELMT SM2 208 C5
Old Barn Wy BXLYHN DA7 150 A5
Old Barrack Yd KTBR SW1X 15 G2
Oldberry Rd EDGE HA8 45 F2
Old Bethnal Green Rd BETH E2 104 D2
Old Bexley La BXLY DA5 170 A4
Old Bond St CONDST W1S 10 A6
Oldborough Rd ALP/SUD HA0 61 J6
Old Brewery Ms HAMP NW3 83 H2
Old Bridge Cl NTHLT UB5 96 A1
Old Bridge St KUT KT1 174 E5
Old Broad St LVPST EC2M 13 G3
Old Bromley Rd BMLY BR1 183 G1
Old Brompton Rd ECT SW5 119 K5
Old Buildings LINN WC2A 11 J3
Old Burlington St CONDST W1S 10 A5
Oldbury Cl STMC/STPC BR5 202 E1
Oldbury Pl MHST W1U 9 H1
Oldbury Rd EN EN1 24 C3
Old Castle St WCHPL E1 13 J3
Old Cavendish St
W1G 9 J3
Old Chapel Rd SWLY BR8 203 K4
Old Chestnut Av
ESH/CLAY KT10 204 A4
Old Church La CDALE/KGS NW9 62 E6
GFD/PVL UB6 97 G2
STAN HA7 43 H2
Old Church Pth ESH/CLAY KT10 204 B2
Oldchurch Ri ROMW/RG RM7 75 G3
Oldchurch Rd ROMW/RG RM7 75 F4
Old Church Rd WCHPL * E1 105 F5
CHING E4 37 J5
Old Church St CHEL SW3 120 C6
Old Claygate La ESH/CLAY KT10 205 G4
Old Compton St
SOHO/SHAV W1D 10 C5
Old Cote Dr HEST TW5 115 F6
Old Court Pl KENS W8 120 A2
The Old Ctyd BMLY BR1 184 A4
Old Dairy Ms BAL SW12 161 F3
KTTN * NW5 84 B4
Old Deer Pk RCH/KEW * TW9 137 G4
Old Deer Park Gdns
RCH/KEW TW9 137 F4
Old Devonshire Rd BAL SW12 161 G2
Old Dock Cl RCH/KEW TW9 117 H6
Old Dover Rd BKHTH/KID SE3 145 K1
Old Farm Av BFN/LL DA15 167 J3
STHGT/OAK N14 34 C2
Old Farm Cl HSLW TW3 134 E5
Old Farm Rd EFNCH N2 47 H4
HPTN TW12 172 E2
WDR/YW UB7 112 A2
Old Farm Rd East BFN/LL DA15 168 B4
Old Farm Rd West BFN/LL DA15 168 A4
Oldfield Cl BMLY BR1 200 E1
GFD/PVL UB6 78 E3
STAN HA7 43 G1
Oldfield Farm Gdns
GFD/PVL UB6 78 D6
Oldfield Gv DEPT SE8 124 A4
Oldfield La North GFD/PVL UB6 78 D4
Oldfield La South GFD/PVL UB6 96 C2
Oldfield Ms HGT N6 66 C4
Oldfield Rd ACT W3 118 C2
BMLY BR1 200 E1
BXLYHN DA7 149 F3
HPTN TW12 173 F4
STNW/STAM N16 86 A1
WIM/MER SW19 177 H2
WLSDN NW10 81 H5
Oldfields Circ NTHLT UB5 78 C4
Oldfields Rd CHEAM SM3 193 K6
Old Fish Street Hl BLKFR * EC4V 12 C5
Old Fleet La STP EC4M 12 A3
Old Fold Cl BAR * EN5 20 D2
Old Fold La BAR EN5 20 D2
Old Fold Vw BAR EN5 20 A4
Old Ford Lock SRTFD * E15 87 J5
Old Ford Rd BETH E2 104 E1
BOW E3 87 H6
Old Forge Cl STAN HA7 29 G6
Old Forge Rd EN EN1 24 B1
Old Forge Wy SCUP DA14 168 C6
Old Gannon Cl NTHWD HA6 26 A6
Old Gloucester St BMSBY WC1N 11 F1
Old Hall Cl PIN HA5 41 J4
Old Hall Dr PIN HA5 41 J4
Oldham Ter ACT W3 117 K1
Old Hl CHST BR7 185 F4
ORP BR6 216 E4
Oldhill St STNW/STAM N16 68 C5
Old Homesdale Rd HAYES BR2 200 B1
Old Hospital Cl TOOT * SW17 160 E3
Old House Cl WIM/MER SW19 177 H1
Old House Gdns TWK * TW1 156 D1
Old Howlett's La RSLP * HA4 58 B3
Old Jamaica Rd STHWK SE1 123 H3
Old James St PECK SE15 143 J4
Old Jewry LOTH * EC2R 12 E4
Old Kenton La CDALE/KGS NW9 62 D2
Old Kent Rd STHWK SE1 123 F5
Old Kingston Rd WPK KT4 206 E1
Old Lodge Wy STAN HA7 43 G1
Old London Rd KUTN/CMB KT2 175 H5
Old Maidstone Rd SCUP DA14 187 G3
Old Malden La WPK KT4 192 B6
Old Manor Dr ISLW TW7 155 H1
Old Manor Wy BXLYHN DA7 150 A3
ELTH/MOT SE9 184 E1
Old Manor Yd ECT * SW5 120 A4
Old Market Sq BETH E2 7 J4
Old Marylebone Rd CAMTN NW1 8 D2
Old Mill Ct SWFD E18 53 G6
Old Mill Rd KUT KT1 175 G6
WOOL/PLUM SE18 127 J6
Old Mitre Ct EMB * EC4Y 11 K4
Old Montague St WCHPL E1 104 C4
Old Nichol St BETH E2 7 J6
Old North St FSBYW * WC1X 11 G1
Old Oak Common La
WLSDN NW10 99 G3
Old Oak La WLSDN NW10 99 H2
Old Oak Rd ACT W3 99 H6
The Old Orch HAMP * NW3 83 K2
Old Orch SUN TW16 172 B5
Old Palace Rd CROY/NA CR0 211 J1
Old Palace Yd RCH/KEW TW9 136 D6
Old Paradise St LBTH SE11 17 G6
Old Park Av BAL SW12 161 F1
ENC/FH EN2 23 J5
Old Park Gv WCHMH N21 23 J5
Old Park La MYFR/PICC W1J 15 H1
Old Park Ms HEST TW5 134 E1
Old Park Ridings WCHMH N21 35 H1
Old Park Rd ABYW SE2 128 B5
ENC/FH EN2 23 H4
PLMGR N13 35 F5
Old Park Rd South ENC/FH EN2 23 H5
Old Park Vw ENC/FH EN2 23 G4
Old Perry St CHST BR7 185 K3
Old Pound Cl ISLW TW7 136 B2
Old Pye St WEST SW1P 16 C4
Old Quebec St MBLAR W1H 9 F4
Old Queen St STJSPK SW1H 16 D3
Old Rectory Gdns EDGE HA8 44 C2
Old Redding KTN/HRWW/W HA3 42 B1
Oldridge Rd BAL SW12 161 F2
Old Rd DART DA1 150 A5
LEW SE13 145 H5
PEND EN3 24 E2
Old Royal Free Sq IS N1 5 K1
Old Ruislip Rd NTHLT UB5 95 H1
Old's Ap WATW WD18 26 A3
Old School Cl BECK BR3 182 A5
Old School Crs FSTGT E7 88 E4
Old Schools La EW KT17 207 H6
Old School Sq THDIT KT7 190 A3
Old School Ter CHEAM * SM3 208 B5
Old Seacoal La STP * EC4M 12 A4
Old South Cl PIN HA5 41 H4
Old South Lambeth Rd
VX/NE * SW8 141 K1
Old Sq LINN WC2A 11 H3
Old Stable Ms HBRY * N5 85 J1
Old Station Gdns TEDD * TW11 174 B2
Old Station Rd HYS/HAR UB3 113 J3
Oldstead Rd BMLY BR1 165 G6
Old St FSBYE EC1V 6 C6
PLSTW E13 107 F1
Old Swan Yd CAR SM5 209 K2
Old Town CLAP SW4 141 H5
CROY/NA CR0 211 H1
Old Tramyard
WOOL/PLUM SE18 127 K4
Old Woolwich Rd GNWCH SE10 125 G6
Old York Rd WAND/EARL SW18 140 A6
Oleander Cl ORP BR6 216 D3
O'leary Sq WCHPL E1 104 E4
Olga St BOW E3 105 G1
Olinda Rd STNW/STAM N16 68 B3
Oliphant St NKENS W10 100 C2
Oliver Av SNWD SE25 181 G6
Oliver Cl CHSWK W4 117 J6
Oliver Gdns EHAM E6 107 J4
Oliver Gv SNWD SE25 197 G1
Oliver Ms PECK SE15 143 H3
Olive Rd CRICK NW2 82 A2
DART DA1 171 G3
EA W5 116 E3
PLSTW E13 107 G2
WIM/MER * SW19 178 B3
Oliver Rd LEY E10 69 K6
NWMAL KT3 175 K5
RAIN RM13 93 H6
SUT SM1 209 H2
WALTH E17 70 A2
Oliver's Yd STLK EC1Y 7 F6
Olive St ROMW/RG RM7 75 F2
Ollerton Gn BOW E3 87 H6
Ollerton Rd FBAR/BDGN N11 48 D1
Olley Cl WLGTN SM6 210 E5
Ollgar Cl ACT W3 118 C1
Olliffe St POP/IOD E14 125 F3
Olmar St STHWK SE1 123 H6
Olney Rd WALW SE17 122 D6
Olron Crs BXLYHS DA6 148 E6
Olven Rd WOOL/PLUM SE18 147 H1
Olveston Wk MRDN SM4 194 C3
Olwen Ms PIN HA5 41 H5
Olyffe Av WELL DA16 148 B3
Olyffe Dr BECK BR3 183 F4
Olympia Wy WKENS W14 119 H3
Olympic Wy GFD/PVL UB6 78 B6
WBLY HA9 80 C2
Oman Av CRICK NW2 82 A3
O'Meara St STHWK SE1 18 D1
Omega Pl IS N1 5 F3
Omega St NWCR SE14 144 C2
Ommaney Rd NWCR SE14 144 A2
Omnibus Wy WALTH E17 51 J5
Ondine Rd EDUL SE22 143 G5
Onega Ga BERM/RHTH SE16 124 B3
One Tree Cl FSTH SE23 163 K1
Ongar Cl CHDH RM6 73 J2
Ongar Rd FUL/PGN SW6 119 K6
Ongar Wy RAIN RM13 93 G6
Onra Rd WALTH E17 69 J4
Onslow Av RCHPK/HAM TW10 137 F6
Onslow Cl CHING E4 38 B4
Onslow Crs CHST BR7 185 G4
Onslow Dr SCUP DA14 168 E5
Onslow Gdns MUSWH N10 66 B2
SKENS SW7 14 A7
SWFD E18 53 F6
THDIT KT7 189 K5
WCHMH N21 23 G6
WLGTN SM6 210 C5
Onslow Ms East SKENS SW7 14 A7
Onslow Ms West SKENS SW7 14 A7

Onslow Pde STHGT/OAK * N14 34 B3
Onslow Rd CROY/NA CR0 196 B4
NWMAL KT3 192 D1
RCHPK/HAM TW10 157 F1
Onslow Sq SKENS SW7 14 B7
Onslow St FARR EC1M 5 K7
Onslow Wy THDIT KT7 189 K5
Ontario St STHWK SE1 18 B5
Ontario Wy POP/IOD E14 105 J6
On the Hl OXHEY WD19 27 J4
Opal Cl CAN/RD E16 107 H5
Openshaw Rd ABYW SE2 128 C5
Openview WAND/EARL SW18 160 B3
Ophir Ter PECK SE15 143 H2
Opossum Wy HSLWW TW4 134 B4
Oppenheim Rd LEW SE13 145 F3
Oppidans Rd HAMP NW3 83 K5
Optima Pk DART * DA1 150 D4
Orange Court La ORP BR6 216 A6
Orange Gv CHIG IG7 54 C2
WAN E11 88 C1
Orange Hill Rd EDGE HA8 44 E3
Orange Pl BERM/RHTH SE16 123 K3
The Orangery
RCHPK/HAM TW10 156 D4
Orangery La ELTH/MOT SE9 146 E6
Orange St LSQ/SEVD WC2H 10 D6
WAP E1W 123 H1
Orange Tree Hl ROM RM1 57 F1
Oransay Rd IS N1 85 J4
Oratory La CHEL * SW3 120 C5
Orbain Rd FUL/PGN SW6 139 H1
Orbel St BTSEA SW11 140 D2
Orb St WALW SE17 18 E7
The Orchard BKHTH/KID SE3 145 G3
CHSWK W4 118 A4
EW KT17 207 H5
GLDGN NW11 64 E2
WCHMH N21 35 K1
Orchard BUSH WD23 28 D3
Orchard Av BELV DA17 129 G6
CROY/NA CR0 198 B6
DART DA1 170 E2
EBED/NFELT TW14 133 G6
FNCH N3 46 E6
HEST TW5 134 D1
MTCM CR4 195 F5
NWMAL KT3 176 B5
STHGT/OAK N14 34 C1
STHL UB1 114 D1
THDIT KT7 190 B5
TRDG/WHET N20 33 H4
Orchard Cl ALP/SUD HA0 80 A6
BXLYHN DA7 149 F2
CHING E4 37 J6
CRICK NW2 81 J1
EDGE HA8 44 A2
FSTH SE23 163 K1
HOR/WEW * KT19 206 D4
NKENS W10 100 C4
RSLP HA4 58 A4
RYNPK SW20 193 F1
WOT/HER KT12 188 A4
Orchard Cottages
HYS/HAR * UB3 113 H2
KUTN/CMB * KT2 175 H4
Orchard Ct WLGTN * SM6 210 B3
WPK * KT4 192 D5
Orchard Crs EDGE HA8 44 E1
EN EN1 24 B2
Orchard Dr BKHTH/KID SE3 145 H3
EDGE HA8 44 B1
Orchard Gdns CHSGTN KT9 206 A2
Orchard Ga CDALE/KGS NW9 63 G1
ESH/CLAY KT10 189 J5
GFD/PVL UB6 79 H4
Orchard Gn ORP BR6 201 K6
Orchard Gv CROY/NA CR0 198 B4
EDGE HA8 44 C4
KTN/HRWW/W HA3 62 B2
ORP BR6 202 A6
PGE/AN SE20 181 H3
Orchard Hl DART DA1 150 B6
LEW SE13 144 E3
Orchard La E/WMO/HCT KT8 189 J3
RYNPK SW20 176 E4
WFD IG8 39 G6
Orchardleigh Av PEND EN3 24 E3
Orchardmede EN EN1 35 K1
Orchard Ms IS N1 85 K5
Orchard Pl POP/IOD E14 106 C6
STMC/STPC * BR5 186 D6
TOTM N17 50 B3
Orchard Ri CROY/NA CR0 198 B5
KUTN/CMB KT2 175 K4
RCHPK/HAM TW10 137 J5
RSLP HA4 40 D6
Orchard Ri East BFN/LL DA15 147 K6
Orchard Ri West BFN/LL DA15 147 K6
Orchard Rd BAR EN5 20 C5
BELV DA17 129 H4
BMLY BR1 184 B4
BTFD TW8 116 D6
CHSGTN KT9 206 A2
DAGE RM10 92 C6
HGT N6 66 B4
HPTN TW12 172 E3
HSLWW TW4 134 E6
HYS/HAR UB3 94 E6
KUT KT1 175 F5
ORP BR6 216 B3
ORP BR6 217 J6
PEND EN3 24 E6
RCH/KEW TW9 137 H4
ROMW/RG RM7 56 D5
SCUP DA14 167 K6
SUN TW16 172 A3
SUT SM1 208 E3
TWK TW1 136 B6
WELL DA16 148 C4
Orchardson St STJWD NW8 2 A7
Orchard Sq WKENS * W14 119 J5
Orchard St DART DA1 171 H1
MBLAR W1H 9 G4
THDIT KT7 190 C5
WALTH E17 69 G1
Orchard Ter EN * EN1 36 C1
WLSDN * NW10 81 H2
Orchard Vls SCUP * DA14 186 D2
Orchard Wy ASHF TW15 152 C4
CROY/NA CR0 198 B4
EN EN1 24 A4
ESH/CLAY KT10 204 C4
RDART DA2 171 G5
SUT SM1 209 H2
Orchid Cl CHSGTN KT9 205 J5
STHL UB1 95 J5
Orchid Rd STHGT/OAK N14 34 C2
Orchid St SHB W12 99 J6
Orde Hall St BMSBY * WC1N 11 G1
Ordell Rd BOW E3 105 H1
Ordnance Cl FELT TW13 153 K4
Ordnance Crs GNWCH SE10 125 H2
Ordnance Hl STJWD NW8 2 B1
Ordnance Ms STJWD NW8 2 B2
Ordnance Rd CAN/RD E16 106 D4
WOOL/PLUM SE18 127 F6
Oregon Av MNPK E12 89 K2
Oregon Cl NWMAL KT3 191 K1
Oregon Sq ORP BR6 201 J5
Orestes Ms KIL/WHAMP * NW6 82 E3
Orford Gdns TWK TW1 156 A4
Orford Rd CAT SE6 164 E5
SWFD E18 53 F6
WALTH E17 69 K2
Oriel Cl MTCM CR4 195 J1
Oriel Ct HAMP NW3 83 G2
Oriel Dr BARN SW13 119 F6
Oriel Gdns CLAY IG5 53 K6
Oriel Rd HOM E9 87 F4
Oriel Wy NTHLT UB5 78 B5
Oriental Rd CAN/RD E16 126 C1
Orient St LBTH SE11 18 A6
Orient Wy CLPT E5 87 F1
LEY E10 87 J1
Oriole Wy THMD SE28 109 H6
Orion Rd MUSWH N10 48 A2
Orion Wy NTHWD HA6 26 D6
Orissa Rd WOOL/PLUM SE18 127 K5
Orkney St BTSEA SW11 141 F3
Orlando Rd CLAP SW4 141 H4
Orleans Rd NRWD SE19 180 E2
TWK TW1 156 C2
Orleston Ms HOLWY N7 85 G4
Orleston Rd HOLWY N7 85 G4
Orley Farm Rd HRW HA1 78 E1
Ormanton Rd SYD SE26 163 H6
Orme Ct BAY/PAD W2 101 F6
Ormeley Rd BAL SW12 161 G2
Orme Rd KUT KT1 175 J5
SUT SM1 209 F4
Ormerod Gdns MTCM CR4 179 F5
Ormesby Cl THMD SE28 109 K6
Ormesby Wy KTN/HRWW/W HA3 62 B3
Orme Sq BAY/PAD W2 101 F6
Orme Square Ga KENS W8 101 F6
Ormiston Gv SHB W12 118 E1
Ormiston Rd GNWCH SE10 125 K5
Ormond Av HPTN TW12 173 G4
ORP BR6 201 H6
Ormond Cl BMSBY WC1N 11 F1
Ormond Crs HPTN TW12 173 G3
Ormond Dr HPTN TW12 173 G3
Ormonde Av HOR/WEW KT19 207 F6
Ormonde Ct STJWD * NW8 2 E1
Ormonde Ga CHEL * SW3 120 E5
Ormonde Pl BGVA SW1W 15 H7
Ormonde Ri BKHH IG9 39 G3
Ormonde Rd MORT/ESHN SW14 137 J4
NTHWD HA6 26 B6
Ormonde Ter STJWD NW8 2 E1
Ormond Rd ARCH N19 66 E5
RCHPK/HAM TW10 136 E6
Ormond Yd STJS SW1Y 10 B7
Ormsby BELMT * SM2 209 F5
Ormsby Gdns GFD/PVL UB6 96 C1
Ormsby Pl STNW/STAM N16 86 B1
Ormsby St BETH E2 7 J2
Ormside St PECK SE15 123 K6
Ormskirk Rd OXHEY WD19 27 H6
Ornan Rd HAMP NW3 83 J3
Oronsay Wk IS * N1 85 J4
Orpheus St CMBW SE5 142 E2
Orpington Gdns ED N9 36 A5
Orpington Rd CHST BR7 185 K6
WCHMH N21 35 G3
Orpwood Cl HPTN TW12 172 E2
Orsett Ms BAY/PAD * W2 101 G5
Orsett St LBTH SE11 122 A5
Orsett Ter BAY/PAD W2 101 F5
WFD IG8 53 G4
Orsman Rd IS N1 7 G1
Orton St WAP E1W 123 H1
Orville Rd BTSEA SW11 140 C3
Orwell Cl HYS/HAR UB3 94 C6
Orwell Rd PLSTW E13 107 G1
Osbaldeston Rd
STNW/STAM N16 68 C6
Osberton Rd LEE/GVPK SE12 145 K6
Osbert St WEST SW1P 16 C7
Osborn Cl HACK E8 86 C6
Osborne Av STWL/WRAY TW19 152 B3
Osborne Cl BECK BR3 198 B1
EBAR EN4 21 K4
EMPK RM11 75 K3
FELT TW13 172 C1
Osborne Ct EA * W5 98 A4
Osborne Gdns THHTH CR7 180 D5
Osborne Gv WALTH E17 69 H1
Osborne Rd ACT W3 117 J2
BELV DA17 129 G5
BKHH IG9 39 F3
CRICK NW2 81 K4
EMPK RM11 75 K3
FSBYPK N4 67 G5
FSTGT E7 89 F3
HOM E9 87 H4
HSLW TW3 134 E4
KUTN/CMB KT2 175 F3
LEY E10 87 K1
PEND EN3 25 G3
PLMGR N13 35 G5
STHL UB1 96 C5
THHTH CR7 180 D5
Osborne Sq DAGW RM9 92 B2
Osborne Ter TOOT * SW17 179 F1
Osborne Wy CHSGTN KT9 206 B3
Osborn Gdns MLHL NW7 46 B3
Osborn La FSTH SE23 164 B2
Osborn St WCHPL E1 13 K2
Osborn Ter BKHTH/KID SE3 145 J5
Osbourne Ct RYLN/HDSTN * HA2 60 B1
Oscar Faber Pl IS * N1 86 A5
Oscar St DEPT SE8 144 D3
Oseney Crs KTTN NW5 84 C4
Osgood Av ORP BR6 217 F3
Osgood Gdns ORP BR6 217 F3
O'shea Gv BOW E3 87 H6
Osidge La STHGT/OAK N14 34 A3
Osier Crs MUSWH N10 47 K4
Osiers Rd WAND/EARL SW18 139 K5
Osier St WCHPL E1 104 E3
Osier Wy LEY E10 87 K1
MTCM CR4 194 D2
Oslac Rd CAT SE6 182 E1
Osman Rd ED N9 36 C5
HMSMTH * W6 119 F3
Osmond Cl RYLN/HDSTN HA2 60 C6
Osmond Gdns WLGTN SM6 210 C3
Osmund St SHB W12 99 H5
Osnaburgh St CAMTN NW1 3 K7
Osnaburgh Ter CAMTN NW1 3 K6
Osney Wk MRDN SM4 194 C3
Osprey Cl EHAM E6 107 J4
SWFD E18 70 E1
WALTH E17 51 G3
WDR/YW UB7 112 A2
Osprey Est BERM/RHTH SE16 124 A4
Osprey Ms PEND EN3 24 D6
Ospringe Cl PGE/AN SE20 181 K3
Ospringe Rd KTTN NW5 84 C2
Osram Rd WBLY * HA9 79 K1
Ossian Rd FSBYPK N4 67 F4
Ossington Buildings
MHST * W1U 9 G1
Ossington Cl BAY/PAD * W2 100 E6
Ossington St BAY/PAD * W2 101 F6
Ossory Rd STHWK SE1 123 H6
Ossulston St CAMTN NW1 4 D3
Ossulton Pl EFNCH * N2 47 G6
Ossulton Wy EFNCH N2 65 G1
Ostade Rd BRXS/STRHM SW2 162 A2
Ostell Crs PEND EN3 25 J1
Osten Ms SKENS * SW7 120 A3
Osterberg Rd DART DA1 151 J5
Osterley Av ISLW TW7 135 J1
Osterley Crs ISLW TW7 135 K2
Osterley Gdns THHTH CR7 180 D5
Osterley La NWDGN UB2 115 G5
Osterley Park Rd NWDGN * UB2 114 E3
Osterley Park View Rd
HNWL W7 115 K2
Osterley Rd ISLW TW7 135 K1
STNW/STAM N16 86 A2
Ostliffe Rd PLMGR N13 49 H1
Oswald Rd STHL UB1 114 D1
Oswald's Md CLPT E5 87 G2
Oswald St CLPT E5 87 F1
Oswald Ter CRICK * NW2 82 A1
Osward CROY/NA * CR0 213 H6
Osward Pl ED N9 36 C4
Osward Rd BAL SW12 160 E4
Oswin St LBTH SE11 18 B6
Oswyth Rd CMBW SE5 143 F3
Otford Cl BMLY BR1 185 F6
BXLY DA5 169 J1
PGE/AN SE20 181 K4
Otford Crs BROCKY SE4 164 C1
Othello Cl LBTH SE11 122 C5
Otis St BOW E3 106 A2
Otley Dr GNTH/NBYPK IG2 72 B3
Otley Rd CAN/RD E16 107 G5
Otley Ter CLPT E5 68 E6
Otley Wy OXHEY WD19 27 G5
Otlinge Rd STMC/STPC BR5 202 E1
Ottawa Gdns DAGE RM10 93 F5
Ottaway St CLPT E5 86 C1
Otterbourne Rd CHING E4 38 B5
CROY/NA CR0 196 D6
Otterburn Gdns ISLW TW7 136 B1
Otterburn St TOOT SW17 178 E2
Otterden Cl ORP BR6 216 E2
Otterden St CAT SE6 164 D6
Otter Rd GFD/PVL UB6 96 C3
Otters Cl STMC/STPC BR5 202 E1
Otto Cl SYD * SE26 163 J4
Otto St WALW SE17 122 C6
Otway Gdns BUSH WD23 28 E2
Oulton Cl THMD SE28 109 J5
Oulton Crs BARK IG11 91 F4
Oulton Rd SEVS/STOTM N15 67 K2
Oulton Wy OXHEY WD19 27 K6
Oundle Av BUSH WD23 28 C1
Ouseley Rd BAL SW12 160 E3
Outer Cir CAMTN NW1 2 E6
Outgate Rd WLSDN NW10 81 H5
Outram Pl IS N1 84 E6
Outram Rd CROY/NA CR0 197 G6
EHAM E6 89 J6
WDGN N22 48 D4
Outwich St HDTCH * EC3A 13 H3
The Oval BETH E2 104 D1
BFN/LL DA15 168 B2
Oval Ct EDGE * HA8 44 E3
Oval Pl VX/NE SW8 142 A1
Oval Rd CAMTN NW1 84 B6
CROY/NA CR0 196 E6
Oval Rd North DAGE RM10 92 E6
Oval Rd South DAGE RM10 110 E1
Oval Wy LBTH SE11 122 A5
Overbrae BECK BR3 182 D2
Overbrook Wk EDGE HA8 44 C3
Overbury Av BECK BR3 182 E6
Overbury Rd SEVS/STOTM N15 67 K3
Overbury St CLPT E5 87 F2
Overcliff Rd LEW SE13 144 D4
Overcourt Cl BFN/LL DA15 168 C1
Overdale Av NWMAL KT3 175 K5
Overdale Rd EA W5 116 D3
Overdown Rd CAT SE6 164 D6
Overhill Cottages MTCM * CR4 179 F5
Overhill Rd EDUL SE22 163 H2
PUR/KEN CR8 211 G6
Overhill Wy BECK BR3 199 G2
Overlea Rd CLPT E5 68 C4
Overmead ELTH/MOT SE9 167 J2
Overstand Cl BECK BR3 198 D2
Overstone Gdns CROY/NA CR0 198 C4
Overstone Rd HMSMTH W6 119 F4
Overton Cl ISLW TW7 136 A2
WLSDN NW10 80 E4
Overton Dr CHDH RM6 73 J4
WAN E11 71 F4
Overton Rd ABYW SE2 128 D3
BELMT SM2 208 E5
BRXN/ST SW9 142 B3
LEY E10 69 G5
STHGT/OAK N14 22 E6
Overton's Yd CROY/NA CR0 211 J1
Overy Liberty DART DA1 171 H2
Overy St DART DA1 171 J1
Ovesdon Av RYLN/HDSTN HA2 59 K5
Ovett Cl NRWD SE19 181 F2
Ovex Cl POP/IOD E14 125 F3
Ovington Gdns CHEL SW3 14 D5
Ovington Ms CHEL SW3 14 D5
Ovington Sq CHEL SW3 14 D5
Ovington St CHEL SW3 14 D5
Owen Cl CROY/NA CR0 196 E3
CRW RM5 56 C2
NTHLT * UB5 95 F2
THMD SE28 128 D1
Owen Gdns WFD IG8 53 J2
Owenite St ABYW SE2 128 C4
Owen Rd PLMGR N13 49 J1
Owen's Rw FSBYE EC1V 6 A4
Owen St FSBYE EC1V 5 K3
Owens Wy FSTH SE23 164 B2
Owen Wy WLSDN NW10 80 E4
Owgan Cl CMBW SE5 142 E1
Oxberry Av FUL/PGN SW6 139 H3
Oxenden Wood Rd ORP BR6 217 H4
Oxendon St SOHO/SHAV * W1D 10 C6
Oxenford St PECK SE15 143 G4
Oxenpark Av WBLY HA9 62 A4
Oxestalls Rd DEPT SE8 124 B5
Oxford Av HEST TW5 115 F5
HYS/HAR UB3 133 J1
RYNPK SW20 177 H5
Oxford Cl ED N9 36 D4
MTCM CR4 179 H6
NTHWD HA6 26 A6
Oxford Ct MANHO EC4N 12 E5
Oxford Crs NWMAL KT3 192 A3
Oxford Dr RSLP HA4 59 G6
Oxford Gdns CHSWK W4 117 H5
NKENS W10 100 B5
TRDG/WHET N20 33 H3
WCHMH N21 35 J2
Oxford Ga WKENS * W14 119 G4
Oxford Ms BXLY DA5 169 H3
Oxford Rd CAR SM5 209 J4
EA W5 97 K6
ED N9 36 D4
FSBYPK N4 67 G5
HPTN TW12 173 J1
HRW HA1 60 C3
IL IG1 90 C2
KIL/WHAMP NW6 100 E1
KTN/HRWW/W HA3 43 F6
NRWD SE19 180 E2
PEND EN3 24 D6
PUT/ROE SW15 139 H5
SCUP DA14 186 C1
SRTFD E15 88 B4
WFD IG8 53 H1
WLGTN * SM6 210 C3
Oxford Rd North CHSWK W4 117 J5
Oxford Rd South CHSWK W4 117 H5
Oxford Rw SUN * TW16 172 B6
Oxford Sq BAY/PAD W2 8 D4
Oxford St MYFR/PKLN W1K 9 G4
Oxford Wk STHL UB1 114 E1
Oxford Wy FELT TW13 154 C6
Oxgate Court Pde CRICK * NW2 63 K6
Oxgate Gdns CRICK NW2 81 K1
Oxgate La CRICK NW2 63 K6
Oxhawth Crs HAYES BR2 201 F2
Oxhey Av OXHEY WD19 27 H2
Oxhey Dr OXHEY WD19 27 F6
Oxhey La OXHEY WD19 27 H2
PIN HA5 42 A1
Oxhey Ridge Cl OXHEY WD19 40 E1
Oxhey Rd OXHEY WD19 27 G2
Oxleas EHAM E6 108 B5
Oxleas Cl WELL DA16 147 J3
Oxleay Rd RYLN/HDSTN HA2 60 A5
Oxleigh Cl NWMAL KT3 192 B2
Oxley Cl STHWK SE1 123 G5
Oxleys Rd CRICK NW2 81 K1
Oxlow La DAGE RM10 92 C2
Oxonian St EDUL SE22 143 G5
Oxted Cl MTCM CR4 178 C6
Oxtoby Wy STRHM/NOR SW16 179 J4
Oyster Catchers Cl CAN/RD E16 107 F5
Oyster Rw WCHPL E1 104 E5
Ozolins Wy CAN/RD E16 106 D5

P

Paceheath Cl CRW RM5 57 F2
Pace Pl WCHPL E1 104 D5
Pacific Cl EBED/NFELT TW14 153 J3
Pacific Rd CAN/RD E16 106 E5
Packington Sq IS N1 6 C1
Packington St IS N1 6 B1
Packmores Rd ELTH/MOT SE9 147 J6
Padbury Cl EBED/NFELT TW14 153 G3
Padbury Ct BETH E2 7 K5
Padcroft Rd WDR/YW UB7 112 A1
Paddenswick Rd HMSMTH W6 118 D3
Paddington Cl NTHLT UB5 95 H3
Paddington Gn BAY/PAD W2 8 A2
Paddington St MHST W1U 9 G1
Paddock Cl BKHTH/KID SE3 145 K4
NTHLT UB5 96 A1
ORP BR6 216 B2
OXHEY WD19 27 J1
SYD SE26 164 A6
WPK KT4 192 B5
Paddock Gdns NRWD SE19 181 F2
Paddock Rd BXLYHS DA6 149 F5
CRICK NW2 81 J1
RSLP HA4 77 H1
The Paddocks EA * W5 116 E3
EBAR EN4 21 K4
MLHL * NW7 46 D2
WBLY HA9 62 D6
Paddocks Cl RYLN/HDSTN HA2 78 B2
STMC/STPC BR5 202 E6
Paddock Wy CHST BR7 185 J3
Padfield Rd CMBW SE5 142 D4
Padley Cl CHSGTN KT9 206 B3
Padnall Rd CHDH RM6 55 K6
Padstow Cl ORP BR6 217 G2
Padstow Rd ENC/FH EN2 23 H3
Padstow Wk EBED/NFELT TW14 153 J4
Padua Rd PGE/AN SE20 181 K4
Pagden St VX/NE SW8 141 G2
Pageant Crs BERM/RHTH SE16 124 C1
Pageant Wk CROY/NA CR0 212 A1
Page Cl DAGW RM9 92 A3
FELT TW13 172 D2
KTN/HRWW/W HA3 62 B3
Page Crs CROY/NA CR0 211 H3
ERITH DA8 150 C1
Page Green Rd
SEVS/STOTM * N15 68 C2
Page Heath La BMLY BR1 184 C6
Page Heath Vls BMLY BR1 184 C6
Pagehurst Rd CROY/NA CR0 197 H4
Page Meadow MLHL NW7 45 J3
Page Rd EBED/NFELT TW14 153 G1
Page's Hl MUSWH N10 48 A5
Page's La MUSWH N10 48 A5
Page St MLHL NW7 45 J4
WEST SW1P 16 D6
Page's Wk STHWK SE1 19 G6
Pages Yd CHSWK * W4 118 B6
Paget Av SUT SM1 209 H1
Paget Cl HPTN TW12 155 J6
Paget Gdns CHST BR7 185 G4
Paget La ISLW TW7 135 J4
Paget Pl KUTN/CMB * KT2 175 K2
THDIT KT7 190 A5
Paget Ri WOOL/PLUM SE18 147 F1
Paget Rd HGDN/ICK UB10 94 A3
IL IG1 90 B2
STNW/STAM N16 67 K5
Paget St FSBYE EC1V 6 A4
Paget Ter WOOL/PLUM SE18 127 G6
Pagitts Gv EBAR EN4 21 F2
Pagnell St NWCR SE14 144 C1
Pagoda Av RCH/KEW TW9 137 G4
Pagoda Gdns BKHTH/KID SE3 145 G3
Paignton Rd RSLP HA4 76 E1
SEVS/STOTM N15 68 A3
Paines Cl PIN HA5 41 J6
Paine's La PIN HA5 41 J5
Pain's Cl MTCM CR4 179 G5
Painsthorpe Rd
STNW/STAM N16 86 A1
Painters Rd GNTH/NBYPK IG2 55 G6
Paisley Rd CAR SM5 194 C5
WDGN N22 49 H4
Pakeman St HOLWY N7 85 F1
Pakenham Cl BAL SW12 161 F3
Pakenham St FSBYW WC1X 5 H5
Palace Av KENS W8 120 A2
Palace Ct BAY/PAD W2 101 F6
KTN/HRWW/W HA3 62 A3
Palace Court Gdns MUSWH N10 48 C6
Palace Garden Ms KENS W8 120 A1
Palace Gdns BKHH IG9 39 H3
Palace Gardens Ter KENS W8 120 A1
Palace Ga KENS W8 120 B2
Palace Gates Rd WDGN N22 48 E4
Palace Gn CROY/NA CR0 213 H5
KENS W8 120 A1
Palace Gv BMLY BR1 184 A4
NRWD SE19 181 G3
Palace Ms FUL/PGN * SW6 139 J1
Palace Pde WALTH * E17 69 H1
Palace Pl WESTW SW1E 16 A4
Palace Rd BMLY BR1 184 A4
BRXS/STRHM SW2 162 A3
CEND/HSY/T N8 66 D2
E/WMO/HCT KT8 173 H6
FBAR/BDGN N11 48 E3
KUT KT1 190 E1
NRWD SE19 181 G3
RSLP HA4 77 J2
Palace Sq NRWD SE19 181 G3
Palace St WESTW SW1E 16 A4
Palace Vw BMLY BR1 184 A6
CROY/NA CR0 213 H2
LEE/GVPK SE12 165 K4
Palace View Rd CHING E4 51 K1
Palamos Rd LEY E10 69 J5
Palatine Av STNW/STAM N16 86 A2
Palatine Rd STNW/STAM N16 86 A2
Palemead Cl FUL/PGN SW6 139 G2
Palermo Rd WLSDN NW10 99 J1
Palestine Gv WIM/MER SW19 178 C4
Palewell Cl STMC/STPC BR5 186 C5
Palewell Common Dr
MORT/ESHN SW14 138 A6
Palewell Pk MORT/ESHN SW14 138 A6
Palfrey Pl BRXN/ST SW9 142 A1
Palgrave Av STHL UB1 96 A6
Palgrave Gdns CAMTN NW1 2 D6
Palgrave Rd SHB W12 118 C3
Palissy St BETH E2 7 J5
Pallant Wy ORP BR6 216 A1
Pallet Wy WOOL/PLUM SE18 146 D2
Palliser Dr RAIN RM13 111 J4
Palliser Rd WKENS W14 119 H5
Pall Ml STJS SW1Y 16 C1
Pall Ml East STJS SW1Y 10 C7
Pall Mall Pl STJS SW1Y 16 B1
Palmar Crs BXLYHN DA7 149 H4
Palmar Rd BXLYHN DA7 149 H3
Palmarsh Rd STMC/STPC BR5 202 E1
Palm Av SCUP DA14 186 E2
Palm Cl LEY E10 87 K1
Palmeira Rd BXLYHN DA7 148 E4
Palmer Av BUSH WD23 28 B1
CHEAM SM3 208 A2
Palmer Cl HEST TW5 135 F2
WWKM BR4 199 G6
Palmer Crs KUT KT1 175 F6
Palmer Gdns BAR EN5 20 B6
Palmer Pl HOLWY N7 85 G3
Palmer Rd BCTR RM8 73 K5
PLSTW E13 107 F3
Palmers Gv E/WMO/HCT KT8 189 F1
Palmers La PEND EN3 24 E2
Palmers Rd BETH E2 105 F1
FBAR/BDGN N11 48 C1
MORT/ESHN SW14 137 K4
STRHM/NOR SW16 180 A5
Palmerston Crs PLMGR N13 49 F1
WOOL/PLUM SE18 127 H6
Palmerston Gv WIM/MER SW19 177 K3
Palmerston Rd ACT W3 117 K3
BKHH IG9 39 G4
CAR SM5 209 K2
CROY/NA CR0 196 E2
FSTGT E7 89 F3
HSLW TW3 135 H2
KIL/WHAMP NW6 82 D5
KTN/HRWW/W * HA3 42 E6
MORT/ESHN SW14 137 K5
ORP BR6 216 C2
SUT SM1 209 G3
WALTH E17 69 H1
WDGN N22 49 F3
WHTN TW2 155 K1
WIM/MER SW19 177 K3
Palmerston Wy VX/NE * SW8 141 G1
Palmer St STJSPK SW1H 16 C4
Palmers Whf KUT * KT1 174 E5
Palm Gv EA W5 117 F3
Palm Rd ROMW/RG RM7 74 E2
Pamela Ct FNCH * N3 47 F2
Pamela Gdns PIN HA5 59 F2
Pams Wy HOR/WEW KT19 207 F3
Pancras La MANHO EC4N 12 D4
Pancras Rd CAMTN NW1 4 D2
Pandora Rd KIL/WHAMP NW6 82 E4
Panfield Ms GNTH/NBYPK IG2 72 A3
Panfield Rd ABYW SE2 128 B3

Pangbourne Av NKENS * W10 ....100 A4
Pangbourne Dr STAN HA7 ....43 K1
Panhard Pl STHL UB1 ....96 B6
Pank Av BAR EN5 ....21 H6
Pankhurst Cl ISLW TW7 ....136 A4
Pankhurst Rd WOT/HER KT12 ....188 B4
Pankridge OXHEY * WD19 ....27 H4
Panmuir Rd RYNPK SW20 ....176 E4
Panmure Cl HBRY N5 ....85 H2
Panmure Rd SYD SE26 ....163 J5
Pansy Gdns SHB W12 ....99 J6
Panther Dr WLSDN NW10 ....81 F3
The Pantiles BMLY BR1 ....184 D6
BUSH WD23 ....28 D3
BXLYHN DA7 ....149 G1
Pantiles Cl PLMGR N13 ....49 H1
Panton Cl CROY/NA CR0 ....196 C5
Panton St LSQ/SEVD WC2H 10 D6
Paper Buildings EMB * EC4Y 11 K5
Papermill Cl CAR SM5 ....210 A2
Papillons Wk BKHTH/KID SE3 ....145 K3
Papworth Gdns HOLWY N7 ....85 F3
Papworth Wy
BRXS/STRHM SW2 ....162 B2
The Parade ALP/SUD * HA0 ....79 H4
BROCKY * SE4 ....144 C2
BTSEA * SW11 ....140 C5
CAR * SM5 ....209 K3
CROY/NA * CR0 ....195 K3
CROY/NA * CR0 ....211 F3
DART * DA1 ....150 C6
EA * W5 ....97 K5
EDUL * SE22 ....143 F4
ESH/CLAY KT10 ....204 E4
FSBYPK * N4 ....67 G6
KUT * KT1 ....175 F5
OXHEY * WD19 ....27 H5
PGE/AN * SE20 ....181 K4
RCH/KEW * TW9 ....137 H4
SUT * SM1 ....208 D1
SYD * SE26 ....163 J6
Parade Ms BRXS/STRHM SW2 ....162 C4
Parade Ter CDALE/KGS * NW9 ....63 J3
Paradise Pas HOLWY N7 ....85 G3
Paradise Rd CLAP SW4 ....141 K3
RCHPK/HAM TW10 ....137 F6
Paradise Rw BETH * E2 ....104 D2
Paradise St BERM/RHTH SE16 ....123 J2
Paradise Wk CHEL SW3 ....120 E6
The Paragon BKHTH/KID SE3 ....145 K3
Paragon Cl CAN/RD E16 ....106 E5
Paragon Gv BRYLDS KT5 ....191 G3
Paragon Ms WALW SE17 ....19 F6
Paragon Pl BKHTH/KID SE3 ....145 J3
Paragon Rd HACK E8 ....86 D4
Parbury Ri CHSGTN KT9 ....206 A4
Parbury Rd FSTH SE23 ....164 B1
Parchmore Rd THHTH CR7 ....180 C5
Parchmore Wy THHTH CR7 ....180 C5
Pardoner St STHWK SE1 ....19 F4
Pardon St FSBYE EC1V 6 B6
Parfett St WCHPL E1 ....104 C4
Parfrey St HMSMTH W6 ....119 F6
Parham Dr GNTH/NBYPK IG2 ....72 B3
Paris Gdn STHWK SE1 ....12 A7
Parish Cl EMPK RM11 ....75 K6
Parish Gate Dr BFN/LL DA15 ....167 K1
Parish La PGE/AN SE20 ....182 A3
Parish Whf WOOL/PLUM SE18 ....126 D4
The Park CAR SM5 ....209 K3
EA W5 ....116 E1
GLDGN NW11 ....65 F5
HGT N6 ....66 A4
SCUP DA14 ....186 A1
Park Ap BERM/RHTH * SE16 ....123 K3
WELL DA16 ....148 C5
Park Av BMLY BR1 ....183 K2
CAR SM5 ....210 A4
CRICK NW2 ....82 A4
EHAM E6 ....90 A6
EN EN1 ....23 K6
FNCH N3 ....47 F4
GLDGN NW11 ....65 F5
HSLW TW3 ....155 G1
IL IG1 ....72 A6
MORT/ESHN SW14 ....138 A5
MTCM CR4 ....179 G3
ORP BR6 ....200 E6
ORP BR6 ....217 G1
PLMGR N13 ....35 G5
RSLP HA4 ....58 C3
SRTFD E15 ....88 C4
STHL UB1 ....114 E2
UED N18 ....36 C6
WDGN N22 ....48 E5
WFD IG8 ....53 F1
WLSDN NW10 ....98 B2
WWKM BR4 ....199 F6
Park Av East EW KT17 ....207 J4
Park Av North CEND/HSY/T N8 ....66 D1
WLSDN NW10 ....81 K3
Park Avenue Rd TOTM N17 ....50 D3
Park Av South CEND/HSY/T N8 ....66 D1
Park Av West EW KT17 ....207 J4
Park Bvd GPK RM2 ....57 H4
Park Cha WBLY HA9 ....80 B2
Park Cl CAR SM5 ....209 K4
CRICK NW2 ....81 J1
HOM E9 ....86 E6
HPTN TW12 ....173 H4
HSLW TW3 ....135 H6
KTN/HRWW/W HA3 ....42 E4
KUTN/CMB KT2 ....175 H4
SKENS * SW7 ....14 E3
TRDG/WHET * N20 ....33 H6
WKENS W14 ....119 J3
WLSDN NW10 ....98 B2
Park Cottages FNCH * N3 ....46 D5
Park Ct DUL * SE21 ....162 E5
NWMAL KT3 ....192 A1
SYD * SE26 ....181 J2
WBLY HA9 ....80 A3
Park Crs EMPK RM11 ....75 J4
ENC/FH EN2 ....23 K5
ERITH DA8 ....129 K6
FNCH N3 ....47 F3
KTN/HRWW/W HA3 ....42 E4
REGST W1B 3 J7
WHTN TW2 ....155 J3
Park Crescent Ms East
REGST W1B 3 K7
Park Crescent Ms West
CAVSQ/HST W1G 3 J7
Park Cft EDGE HA8 ....44 E4
Parkcroft Rd LEE/GVPK SE12 ....165 J2
Parkdale Crs WPK KT4 ....207 F1
Parkdale Rd WOOL/PLUM SE18 ....127 K5
Park Dr ACT W3 ....117 H3
CHARL SE7 ....126 D6
DAGE RM10 ....92 E1
GLDGN NW11 ....65 F5
KTN/HRWW/W HA3 ....42 D2
MORT/ESHN SW14 ....138 A6
ROM RM1 ....75 F1
RYLN/HDSTN HA2 ....60 A4
WCHMH N21 ....35 J1
Park End BMLY BR1 ....183 J4
HAMP NW3 ....83 J2
Park End Rd ROM RM1 ....75 G1
Parker Cl CAN/RD E16 ....126 D1
CAR SM5 ....209 K4
Parker Ms HOL/ALD * WC2B 11 F3
Parke Rd BARN SW13 ....138 D2
Parker Rd CROY/NA CR0 ....211 J2
Parker's Rw STHWK SE1 ....19 K3
Parker St CAN/RD E16 ....126 D1
HOL/ALD WC2B 11 F3
Parkes Rd CHIG IG7 ....55 F1
Park Farm Cl EFNCH N2 ....47 G6
Park Farm Rd BMLY BR1 ....184 C4
KUTN/CMB KT2 ....175 F3
Parkfield Av FELT TW13 ....153 K5
MORT/ESHN SW14 ....138 B5
NTHLT UB5 ....95 H1
RYLN/HDSTN HA2 ....42 C5
Parkfield Cl EDGE HA8 ....44 D2
NTHLT UB5 ....95 J1
Parkfield Crs FELT TW13 ....153 K5
RSLP HA4 ....59 J6
RYLN/HDSTN HA2 ....42 C5
Parkfield Dr NTHLT UB5 ....95 H1
Parkfield Gdns RYLN/HDSTN HA2 ....42 B6
Parkfield Pde FELT * TW13 ....153 K5
Parkfield Rd FELT TW13 ....153 K5
NTHLT UB5 ....95 J1
NWCR SE14 ....144 C2
RYLN/HDSTN HA2 ....78 C1
WLSDN NW10 ....81 J5
Parkfields CROY/NA CR0 ....198 C5
PUT/ROE SW15 ....139 F5
Parkfields Av CDALE/KGS NW9 ....63 F5
RYNPK SW20 ....176 E4
Parkfields Cl CAR SM5 ....210 A2
Parkfields Rd KUTN/CMB KT2 ....175 G1
Parkfield St IS N1 ....5 K2
Parkfield Wy HAYES BR2 ....200 E3
Park Gdns CDALE/KGS NW9 ....44 D6
ERITH DA8 ....130 A4
KUTN/CMB KT2 ....175 G1
Parkgate BKHTH/KID SE3 ....145 J4
Park Ga EA W5 ....97 K4
EFNCH N2 ....47 H6
WCHMH N21 ....35 F2
Parkgate Av EBAR EN4 ....21 G2
Parkgate Cl KUTN/CMB KT2 ....175 J2
Park Gate Ct HPTN * TW12 ....173 H1
Parkgate Crs EBAR EN4 ....21 G2
Parkgate Gdns
MORT/ESHN SW14 ....138 A6
Parkgate Rd BTSEA SW11 ....140 D1
CAR SM5 ....210 A3
Park Gates RYLN/HDSTN * HA2 ....78 A2
Park Gv BMLY BR1 ....184 A4
BXLYHN DA7 ....149 K5
EDGE HA8 ....44 B1
FBAR/BDGN N11 ....48 D3
SRTFD E15 ....88 E6
Park Grove Rd WAN E11 ....70 C6
Park Hall Rd DUL SE21 ....162 E5
EFNCH N2 ....65 J1
Parkham St BTSEA SW11 ....140 C2
Park Hl BMLY BR1 ....200 D1
CAR SM5 ....209 K4
CLAP SW4 ....141 J6
EA W5 ....97 K4
FSTH SE23 ....163 J4
RCHPK/HAM TW10 ....157 G1
Park Hill Cl CAR SM5 ....209 J3
Park Hill Ri CROY/NA CR0 ....197 F6
Parkhill Rd BFN/LL DA15 ....167 K5
BXLY DA5 ....169 G2
CHING E4 ....38 A2
HAMP NW3 ....83 K3
Park Hill Rd CROY/NA CR0 ....197 F6
HAYES BR2 ....183 H5
WLGTN SM6 ....210 B5
Parkhill Wk HAMP NW3 ....83 K3
Parkholme Rd HACK E8 ....86 C4
Park House Gdns TWK TW1 ....136 D6
Parkhouse St CMBW SE5 ....142 E1
Parkhurst Gdns BXLY DA5 ....169 H2
Parkhurst Rd BXLY DA5 ....169 H2
FBAR/BDGN N11 ....34 A6
HOLWY N7 ....84 E2
MNPK E12 ....90 A2
SUT SM1 ....209 H2
TOTM N17 ....50 C5
WALTH * E17 ....69 G1
WDGN N22 ....49 F3
Parkland Av ROM RM1 ....57 G5
Parkland Gv ASHF TW15 ....152 D6
Parkland Rd ASHF TW15 ....152 D6
WDGN N22 ....49 F5
WFD IG8 ....53 F3
Parklands BRYLDS KT5 ....191 G2
BUSH * WD23 ....28 C1
HGT N6 ....66 B4
Parklands Cl EBAR EN4 ....21 H1
GNTH/NBYPK IG2 ....72 C4
MORT/ESHN SW14 ....137 K6
Parklands Dr FNCH N3 ....46 C6
Parklands Pde HEST * TW5 ....134 C3
Parklands Rd TOOT SW17 ....179 G1
Parklands Wy WPK KT4 ....192 B6
Park La CAR SM5 ....210 A3
CHDH RM6 ....73 K3
CHEAM SM3 ....208 C4
CROY/NA CR0 ....196 E6
ED N9 ....36 B5
EMPK RM11 ....75 J4
HCH RM12 ....93 K4
HYS/HAR UB3 ....133 K1
MBLAR W1H 9 F5
MYFR/PICC W1J 15 H2
RCH/KEW * TW9 ....136 E5
RYLN/HDSTN HA2 ....78 B1
SRTFD * E15 ....88 A6
STAN HA7 ....29 G5
TEDD TW11 ....174 A2
TOTM N17 ....50 C3
WBLY HA9 ....80 B2
YEAD UB4 ....94 C4
Park Lane Cl TOTM N17 ....50 C3
Parklea Cl CDALE/KGS NW9 ....45 G4
Parkleigh Rd WIM/MER SW19 ....178 A5
Parkleys KUTN/CMB KT2 ....156 E6
Parkleys Pde KUTN/CMB * KT2 ....156 E6
Park Md BFN/LL DA15 ....148 B6
RYLN/HDSTN HA2 ....78 B1
Parkmead PUT/ROE SW15 ....158 E1
Parkmead Gdns MLHL NW7 ....45 H2
Park Ms CHST BR7 ....185 G2
NKENS W10 ....100 C1
STWL/WRAY TW19 ....152 C2
Park Pde ACT * W3 ....117 H3
HYS/HAR * UB3 ....94 C5
WLSDN NW10 ....99 H1
Park Pl ACT W3 ....117 H4
BMLY * BR1 ....184 A4
EA W5 ....116 E1
HPTN TW12 ....173 H2
POP/IOD E14 ....124 D1
WBLY HA9 ....80 B2
WHALL SW1A 16 A1
Park Place Vls BAY/PAD W2 ....101 G4
Park Ridings CEND/HSY/T N8 ....49 G6
Park Ri KTN/HRWW/W HA3 ....42 E4
Park Rise Rd FSTH SE23 ....164 B3
Park Rd ALP/SUD HA0 ....80 A4
BAR EN5 ....20 D5
BECK BR3 ....182 C3
BMLY BR1 ....184 A4
BRYLDS KT5 ....191 G3
BUSH WD23 ....28 A1
CAMTN NW1 ....3 F7
CDALE/KGS NW9 ....63 F4
CEND/HSY/T N8 ....66 D2
CEND/HSY/T N8 ....67 H1
CHEAM SM3 ....208 C4
CHST BR7 ....185 G2
CHSWK W4 ....118 A6
DART DA1 ....171 K2
E/WMO/HCT KT8 ....174 D4
E/WMO/HCT KT8 ....189 H1
EBAR EN4 ....21 H5
ED N9 ....36 B6
EFNCH N2 ....47 H6
EHAM E6 ....89 G6
ESH/CLAY KT10 ....204 B2
FBAR/BDGN N11 ....48 D3
FELT TW13 ....154 C6
HNWL W7 ....97 F6
HPTN TW12 ....173 H1
HSLW TW3 ....135 H6
IL IG1 ....90 D1
ISLW TW7 ....136 C2
KUT KT1 ....174 D4
KUTN/CMB KT2 ....175 G1
LEY E10 ....69 J5
MNPK E12 ....71 F6
MNPK E12 ....89 H2
NWMAL KT3 ....192 A1
RCHPK/HAM TW10 ....157 G1
SNWD SE25 ....197 F1
SRTFD E15 ....88 E6
STHGT/OAK N14 ....34 D2
STJWD NW8 ....2 D5
STMC/STPC BR5 ....202 D3
SUN TW16 ....172 A3
TEDD TW11 ....174 A3
TWK TW1 ....156 D1
WALTH E17 ....69 H2
WAN E11 ....71 F5
WIM/MER SW19 ....178 C3
WLGTN SM6 ....195 G6
WLGTN SM6 ....210 B3
WLSDN * NW10 ....81 G6
YEAD UB4 ....94 C4
Park Rd East ACT W3 ....117 K2
Park Rd North ACT W3 ....117 J2
CHSWK W4 ....118 A6
Park Rw GNWCH SE10 ....125 G6
Park Royal Rd WLSDN NW10 ....98 E2
Parkshot RCH/KEW TW9 ....136 E5
Park Side BKHH IG9 ....39 F4
CRICK NW2 ....81 J1
HYS/HAR * UB3 ....94 C6
Parkside BECK * BR3 ....182 E5
BKHTH/KID * SE3 ....145 J1
CHEAM SM3 ....208 C4
FNCH N3 ....47 F4
HPTN TW12 ....173 J1
MLHL NW7 ....45 J2
OXHEY * WD19 ....27 G1
SCUP DA14 ....168 C4
WIM/MER SW19 ....159 G6
Parkside Av BMLY BR1 ....200 D1
BXLYHN DA7 ....150 A3
ROM RM1 ....57 F5
WIM/MER SW19 ....177 G1
Parkside Cl PGE/AN SE20 ....181 K3
Parkside Crs BRYLDS KT5 ....191 K3
HOLWY N7 ....85 G1
Parkside Cross BXLYHN DA7 ....150 B3
Parkside Dr EDGE HA8 ....30 C5
Parkside Est HOM * E9 ....87 F6
Parkside Gdns EBAR EN4 ....33 K3
WIM/MER SW19 ....159 G6
Parkside Pde ERITH * DA8 ....150 C3
Parkside Rd BELV DA17 ....129 J4
HSLW TW3 ....135 G6
NTHWD HA6 ....40 D1
Parkside St BTSEA SW11 ....141 F2
Parkside Ter ORP * BR6 ....202 B5
UED * N18 ....35 K6
Parkside Wy RYLN/HDSTN HA2 ....60 B1
Park Sq East CAMTN NW1 ....3 J6
Park Square Ms CAMTN NW1 ....3 J7
Park Sq West CAMTN NW1 ....3 J6
Parkstead Rd PUT/ROE SW15 ....138 D6
Park Steps BAY/PAD * W2 ....8 D5
Parkstone Av UED N18 ....50 B1
Parkstone Rd PECK * SE15 ....143 H3
Park St CROY/NA CR0 ....211 J1
MYFR/PKLN W1K 9 G6
STHWK SE1 ....12 C7
TEDD TW11 ....173 K2
Park Ter CAR * SM5 ....209 J1
PEND * EN3 ....25 G1
WPK KT4 ....192 D5
Parkthorne Cl
RYLN/HDSTN * HA2 ....60 B3
Parkthorne Dr RYLN/HDSTN HA2 ....60 A3
Parkthorne Rd BAL SW12 ....161 J2
Park Vw ACT W3 ....98 E4
NWMAL KT3 ....176 C6
PIN HA5 ....41 K4
WBLY HA9 ....80 D3
WCHMH N21 ....35 F2
Park View Ct
NFNCH/WDSP * N12 ....33 J6
Park View Crs FBAR/BDGN N11 ....34 B6
Park View Dr MTCM CR4 ....178 C5
Park View Est HBRY * N5 ....85 J2
Parkview Gdns CLAY IG5 ....71 K1
Park View Gdns HDN NW4 ....64 A2
WDGN * N22 ....49 G4
Park View Rd CRICK NW2 ....81 H2
EA W5 ....98 A4
ELTH/MOT SE9 ....167 G3
FNCH N3 ....47 F4
PIN HA5 ....41 F2
STHL UB1 ....115 F1
TOTM N17 ....50 C6
WELL DA16 ....148 E4
Parkview Rd CROY/NA CR0 ....197 H5
Park Village East CAMTN NW1 ....3 J2
Park Village West CAMTN NW1 ....3 J2
Park Vls TOOT * SW17 ....178 D1
Parkville Rd FUL/PGN SW6 ....139 J1
Park Vis GNWCH SE10 ....125 G6
Park Wk WBPTN SW10 ....120 B6
The Parkway HEST TW5 ....113 K6
HEST TW5 ....114 A4
NTHLT UB5 ....95 H2
Park Wy BXLY DA5 ....170 C5
E/WMO/HCT KT8 ....173 H6
EBED/NFELT TW14 ....154 A2
EDGE HA8 ....44 D4
ENC/FH EN2 ....23 G3
GLDGN NW11 ....64 C2
RSLP HA4 ....58 E5
TRDG/WHET N20 ....33 K6
Parkway CROY/NA CR0 ....214 A6
ERITHM DA18 ....129 F3
GDMY/SEVK IG3 ....91 F1
GPK RM2 ....57 H5
RAIN RM13 ....111 J3
RYNPK SW20 ....193 G1
STHGT/OAK N14 ....34 E4
WFD IG8 ....53 G1
Park West BAY/PAD W2 ....8 D3
Park West Pl BAY/PAD W2 ....8 D3
Parkwood BECK BR3 ....182 D3
Parkwood Av ESH/CLAY KT10 ....189 H5
Parkwood Ms HGT N6 ....66 B3
Parkwood Rd BXLY DA5 ....169 G2
ISLW TW7 ....136 A2
WIM/MER SW19 ....177 J1
Parliament Ct WCHPL * E1 ....13 H2
Parliament Hl HAMP NW3 ....83 J2
Parliament Hill Flds KTTN * NW5 ....84 A1
Parliament Sq WEST SW1P 16 E3
Parliament St WHALL SW1A 16 E2
Parma Crs BTSEA SW11 ....140 E5
Parmiter St BETH E2 ....104 D1
Parnell Cl EDGE HA8 ....30 D6
SHB W12 ....118 E3
Parnell Rd BOW E3 ....87 H6
Parnham St POP/IOD * E14 ....105 G5
Parolles Rd ARCH N19 ....66 C5
Paroma Rd BELV DA17 ....129 H3
Parr Av EW KT17 ....207 K6
Parr Cl ED N9 ....36 D6
Parr Rd EHAM E6 ....89 H6
STAN HA7 ....43 K4
Parrs Cl SAND/SEL CR2 ....211 K6
Parr's Pl HPTN TW12 ....173 F3
Parr St IS N1 ....6 E2
Parry Av EHAM E6 ....107 K5
Parry Cl EW KT17 ....207 J5
Parry Pl WOOL/PLUM SE18 ....127 G4
Parry Rd NKENS W10 ....100 C2
SNWD SE25 ....181 F6
Parry St VX/NE SW8 ....121 K6
Parsifal Rd KIL/WHAMP NW6 ....82 E3
Parsloes Av DAGW RM9 ....92 A3
Parsonage Cl HYS/HAR UB3 ....94 D5
Parsonage Gdns ENC/FH EN2 ....23 J3
Parsonage La ENC/FH EN2 ....23 K3
SCUP DA14 ....169 G6
Parsonage Manorway
ERITH DA8 ....129 H6
Parsonage St POP/IOD E14 ....125 F4
Parsons Crs EDGE HA8 ....30 C5
Parsons Gn FUL/PGN SW6 ....139 K2
Parsons Green La
FUL/PGN SW6 ....139 K2
Parsons Gv EDGE HA8 ....30 C5
Parsons La RDART DA2 ....170 E5
Parson's Md CROY/NA CR0 ....196 C5
E/WMO/HCT KT8 ....173 H6
Parsons Rd PLSTW E13 ....107 G1
Parson St HDN NW4 ....46 A6
Parthenia Rd FUL/PGN SW6 ....139 K2
Partingdale La MLHL NW7 ....46 B1
Partridge Cl BAR EN5 ....32 A1
BUSH * WD23 ....28 C3
CAN/RD E16 ....107 H4
STAN HA7 ....30 A6
Partridge Dr ORP BR6 ....216 C1
Partridge Gn ELTH/MOT SE9 ....167 F5
Partridge Rd HPTN TW12 ....172 E2
SCUP DA14 ....167 K5
Partridge Sq EHAM E6 ....107 J4
Partridge Wy WDGN N22 ....48 E4
Pasadena Cl HYS/HAR UB3 ....113 K2
Pascal St VX/NE SW8 ....141 J1
Pascoe Rd LEW SE13 ....145 G6
Pasley Cl WALW SE17 ....122 C5
Pasquier Rd WALTH E17 ....51 G6
Passey Pl ELTH/MOT SE9 ....166 E1
Passfield Dr POP/IOD E14 ....105 K4
Passmore Gdns FBAR/BDGN N11 ....48 D2
Passmore St BGVA SW1W 15 G7
Pasteur Cl CDALE/KGS NW9 ....45 G5
Pasteur Gdns UED N18 ....49 J1
Paston Cl WLGTN SM6 ....210 C1
Paston Crs LEE/GVPK SE12 ....166 A2
Pastor St LBTH SE11 ....18 B6
Pasture Cl ALP/SUD HA0 ....79 H1
BUSH WD23 ....28 C2
Pasture Rd ALP/SUD HA0 ....61 H6
CAT SE6 ....165 H3
DAGW RM9 ....92 B3
The Pastures OXHEY WD19 ....27 F2
TRDG/WHET N20 ....32 D3
Patcham Ter VX/NE SW8 ....141 G2
Patching Wy YEAD UB4 ....95 J4
Paternoster Rw STP EC4M 12 B4
Pater St KENS W8 ....119 K3
Pates Manor Dr
EBED/NFELT TW14 ....153 G2
The Path WIM/MER SW19 ....178 A4
Pathfield Rd STRHM/NOR SW16 ....179 J2
The Pathway OXHEY WD19 ....27 H3
Patience Rd BTSEA SW11 ....140 D3
Patio Cl CLAP SW4 ....161 J1
Patmore St VX/NE SW8 ....141 H2
Patmore Wy CRW RM5 ....56 D1
Patmos Rd BRXN/ST SW9 ....142 C1
Paton Cl BOW E3 ....105 J2
Patricia Ct WELL DA16 ....148 C1
Patricia Vls TOTM * N17 ....50 D4
Patrick Rd PLSTW E13 ....107 G2
Patriot Sq BETH E2 ....104 D1
Patrol Pl CAT SE6 ....164 E1
Patshull Pl KTTN NW5 ....84 C4
Patshull Rd KTTN NW5 ....84 C4
Pattenden Rd CAT SE6 ....164 C3
Patten Rd WAND/EARL SW18 ....160 D2
Patterdale Cl BMLY BR1 ....183 H2
Patterdale Rd PECK SE15 ....143 K1
Patterson Rd NRWD SE19 ....181 G2
Pattina Wk BERM/RHTH SE16 ....124 B1
Pattison Rd CRICK NW2 ....82 E1
Paul Cl SRTFD E15 ....88 C5
Paulet Rd CMBW SE5 ....142 C3
Paul Gdns CROY/NA CR0 ....197 G6
Paulhan Rd KTN/HRWW/W HA3 ....61 K1
Paulin Dr WCHMH N21 ....35 G2
Pauline Crs WHTN TW2 ....155 H3
Paulinus Cl STMC/STPC BR5 ....186 D5
Paul Julius Cl POP/IOD E14 ....106 B6
Paul Robeson Cl EHAM E6 ....108 A2
Paul St SDTCH EC2A 7 G6
SRTFD E15 ....88 C6
Paultons Sq CHEL SW3 ....120 C6
Paultons St CHEL SW3 ....120 C6
Pauntley St ARCH N19 ....66 C5
Paveley Dr BTSEA SW11 ....140 D1
Paveley St STJWD NW8 ....2 D6
The Pavement CLAP SW4 ....141 H5
EA * W5 ....117 F3
TEDD * TW11 ....174 C3
WAN * E11 ....70 A5
WIM/MER * SW19 ....177 J2
WNWD * SE27 ....162 D6
Pavet Cl DAGE RM10 ....92 D4
The Pavilion VX/NE * SW8 ....141 J1
Pavilion Ldg RYLN/HDSTN * HA2 ....60 D5
Pavilion Pde SHB * W12 ....100 A5
Pavilion Rd IL IG1 ....71 K4
KTBR SW1X 15 F3
Pavilion St KTBR SW1X 15 F5
Pavilion Wy EDGE HA8 ....44 E3
RSLP HA4 ....59 G6
Pavillion Ter SHB * W12 ....100 A5
Pawleyne Cl PGE/AN SE20 ....181 K3
Pawsey Cl PLSTW E13 ....88 E6
Pawson's Rd CROY/NA CR0 ....196 D3
Paxford Rd ALP/SUD HA0 ....61 H6
Paxton Cl RCH/KEW TW9 ....137 G3
WOT/HER * KT12 ....188 B4
Paxton Pl WNWD SE27 ....163 F6
Paxton Rd BMLY BR1 ....183 K3
CHSWK W4 ....118 B6
FSTH SE23 ....164 B5
TOTM N17 ....50 C3
Paxton Ter PIM SW1V 121 G6
Payne Cl BARK IG11 ....90 E5
Paynell Ct BKHTH/KID SE3 ....145 H4
Payne Rd BOW E3 ....105 K1
Paynesfield Av
MORT/ESHN SW14 ....138 A4
Paynesfield Rd BUSH WD23 ....29 F2
Payne St DEPT SE8 ....124 C6
Paynes Wk HMSMTH W6 ....119 H6
Payzes Gdns WFD * IG8 ....52 D2
Peabody Av PIM * SW1V 121 G5
Peabody Cl CROY/NA CR0 ....197 K5
GNWCH * SE10 ....144 E2
PIM SW1V 121 G5
Peabody Cottages HNHL * SE24 ....162 D2
Peabody Est BTSEA * SW11 ....140 D5
CHEL * SW3 ....120 D6
CLKNW * EC1R 5 K7
CMBW * SE5 ....142 E2
FUL/PGN * SW6 ....119 K6
HMSMTH * W6 ....119 F5
HNHL SE24 ....162 C2
NKENS * W10 ....100 A4
STHWK * SE1 ....11 K7
STHWK * SE1 ....12 C7
STLK * EC1Y 6 D7
TOTM * N17 ....50 A4
Peabody Hl DUL SE21 ....162 C3
Peabody Sq IS * N1 ....85 J6
Peabody Ter CLKNW * EC1R 5 K7
Peace Cl GFD/PVL UB6 ....78 D6
SNWD SE25 ....197 F1
STHGT/OAK N14 ....22 B6
Peace Gv WBLY HA9 ....80 D1
Peace St WOOL/PLUM SE18 ....127 F6
Peaches Cl BELMT SM2 ....208 C5
Peach Rd NKENS W10 ....100 B2
Peachum Rd BKHTH/KID SE3 ....125 J6
Peacock Av EBED/NFELT TW14 ....153 G3
Peacock St WALW SE17 ....18 B7
Peacock Yd WALW SE17 ....18 B7
The Peak SYD SE26 ....163 K5
Peaketon Av REDBR IG4 ....71 H2
Peak Hl SYD SE26 ....163 K6
Peak Hill Av SYD SE26 ....163 K6
Peak Hill Gdns SYD SE26 ....163 K6
Peal Gdns WEA W13 ....97 G2
Peall Rd CROY/NA CR0 ....196 A3
Pearce Cl MTCM CR4 ....179 F5
Pearcefield Av FSTH SE23 ....163 K3
Pear Cl CDALE/KGS NW9 ....63 F1
NWCR SE14 ....144 B1
Pearcroft Rd WAN E11 ....70 B6
Peardon St VX/NE SW8 ....141 G3
Peareswood Gdns STAN HA7 ....43 K4
Peareswood Rd ERITH DA8 ....150 C2
Pearfield Rd FSTH SE23 ....164 B5
Pear Gv WAN E11 ....88 B1
Pearl Cl CRICK NW2 ....64 B4
EHAM E6 ....108 A5
Pearl Rd WALTH E17 ....51 J6
Pearl St WAP E1W 123 J1
Pearman St STHWK SE1 ....17 K4
Pear Pl STHWK SE1 ....17 J2
Pearscroft Ct FUL/PGN SW6 ....140 A2
Pearscroft Rd FUL/PGN SW6 ....140 A3
Pearson's Av NWCR SE14 ....144 D2
Pearson St BETH E2 ....7 J2
Pearson Wy DART DA1 ....171 J4
Pears Rd HSLW TW3 ....135 H4
Pear Tree Cl BETH E2 ....7 J1
ERITH DA8 ....150 A2
MTCM CR4 ....178 D5
Pear Tree Ct CLKNW EC1R 5 K7
Peartree Gdns BCTR RM8 ....91 H3
ROMW/RG RM7 ....56 D5

Peartree La WAP * E1W 104 E6
Peartree Rd EN EN1 24 A4
Peartree St FSBYE EC1V 6 B6
Peartree Wy GNWCH SE10 125 K4
Pearwood Cottages STAN * HA7 29 J4
Peary Pl BETH E2 104 E2
Pease Cl HCH RM12 93 K5
Peasmead Ter CHING * E4 38 A6
Peatfield Cl BFN/LL DA15 167 K5
Pebworth Rd HRW HA1 61 G6
Peckarmans Wd SYD SE26 163 H5
Peckett Sq HBRY * N5 85 J2
Peckford Pl BRXN/ST SW9 142 B3
Peckham Gv PECK SE15 143 F1
Peckham High St PECK SE15 143 H2
Peckham Hill St PECK SE15 143 H1
Peckham Park Rd PECK SE15 143 H1
Peckham Rd CMBW SE5 143 F2
Peckham Rye EDUL SE22 143 H5
Pecks Yd WCHPL * E1 13 J1
Peckwater St KTTN NW5 84 C3
Pedlars Wk HOLWY * N7 84 E3
Pedley Rd BCTR RM8 73 J5
Pedley St BETH E2 104 C3
WCHPL E1 7 K7
Pedro St CLPT E5 87 F1
Peek Crs WIM/MER SW19 177 G1
Peel Cl CHING E4 37 K4
ED N9 36 C5
Peel Dr CDALE/KGS NW9 45 H6
CLAY IG5 53 J6
Peel Gv BETH E2 104 E1
Peel Pas KENS W8 119 K1
Peel Pl CLAY IG5 53 J5
Peel Prec KIL/WHAMP NW6 100 D1
Peel Rd ALP/SUD HA0 79 J1
KIL/WHAMP NW6 100 E2
KTN/HRWW/W HA3 42 E6
ORP BR6 216 C2
SWFD E18 52 D4
Peel St KENS W8 119 K1
Peerglow Est PEND * EN3 24 E6
Peerless St FSBYE EC1V 6 E5
Pegamoid Rd UED N18 36 E5
Pegasus Cl STNW/STAM * N16 85 K2
Pegasus Ct BTFD TW8 117 G5
Pegasus Pl FUL/PGN * SW6 139 K2
LBTH * SE11 122 B6
Pegasus Rd CROY/NA CR0 211 G4
Pegasus Wy FBAR/BDGN N11 48 B2
Pegg Rd HEST TW5 134 C1
Pegley Gdns LEE/GVPK SE12 165 K4
Pegwell St WOOL/PLUM SE18 147 K1
Pekin St POP/IOD E14 105 J5
Peldon Wk IS * N1 85 H6
Pelham Av BARK IG11 91 F6
Pelham Cl CMBW SE5 143 F4
Pelham Cottages BXLY * DA5 169 J3
Pelham Crs SKENS SW7 14 C7
Pelham Pl SKENS SW7 14 C6
Pelham Rd BXLYHN DA7 149 H4
IL IG1 72 D6
PGE/AN SE20 181 K5
SEVS/STOTM N15 68 B1
SWFD E18 53 F6
WDGN N22 49 G5
WIM/MER SW19 177 K3
Pelhams Cl ESH/CLAY KT10 204 A2
Pelham St SKENS SW7 14 B6
Pelhams Wk ESH/CLAY KT10 204 A2
Pelier St WALW SE17 122 D6
Pelinore Rd CAT SE6 165 H4
Pellant Rd FUL/PGN SW6 139 H1
Pellatt Gv WDGN N22 49 G4
Pellatt Rd EDUL SE22 143 G6
WBLY HA9 61 K6
Pellerin Rd STNW/STAM N16 86 A3
Pelling St POP/IOD E14 105 H5
Pellipar Cl PLMGR N13 35 G5
Pellipar Rd WOOL/PLUM SE18 126 E5
Pelly Rd PLSTW E13 88 E6
Pelter St BETH E2 7 J4
Pelton Rd GNWCH SE10 125 H5
Pembar Av WALTH * E17 51 G6
Pemberley Cha HOR/WEW KT19 206 D3
Pemberley Cl HOR/WEW KT19 206 D3
Pember Rd WLSDN NW10 100 B2
Pemberton Av GPK RM2 57 K6
Pemberton Gdns ARCH N19 84 C1
CHDH RM6 74 A2
Pemberton Pl ESH/CLAY KT10 204 C1
HACK E8 86 D5
Pemberton Rd
E/WMO/HCT KT8 189 H1
FSBYPK N4 67 G2
Pemberton Rw
FLST/FETLN EC4A 11 K3
Pemberton Ter ARCH N19 84 C1
Pembridge Av HSLWW TW4 154 E3
Pembridge Crs NTGHL W11 100 D6
Pembridge Gdns BAY/PAD * W2 100 E6
Pembridge Ms NTGHL W11 100 E6
Pembridge Pl BAY/PAD W2 100 E6
Pembridge Rd NTGHL W11 100 E6
Pembridge Sq BAY/PAD W2 100 E6
Pembridge Vls NTGHL W11 100 E6
Pembroke Av BRYLDS KT5 191 J2
EN EN1 24 D2
KTN/HRWW/W HA3 43 G6
RSLP HA4 59 H5
Pembroke Cl ERITH DA8 129 K4
KTBR SW1X 15 H3
Pembroke Gdns DAGE RM10 92 D1
KENS W8 119 J3
Pembroke Gardens Cl KENS W8 119 J3
Pembroke Ldg STAN * HA7 43 J2
Pembroke Ms KENS W8 119 K3
MUSWH N10 48 A4
Pembroke Pde ERITH * DA8 129 K5
Pembroke Pl EDGE HA8 44 C3
ISLW TW7 135 K3
KENS W8 119 K3
Pembroke Rd BMLY BR1 184 B5
CEND/HSY/T N8 66 E1
ECT SW5 119 K4
EHAM E6 107 K4
ERITH DA8 129 K5
GDMY/SEVK IG3 73 F5
GFD/PVL UB6 96 B3
MTCM CR4 179 F5
MUSWH N10 48 A4
NTHWD HA6 26 A5
PLMGR N13 35 J5
RSLP HA4 58 C5
SEVS/STOTM N15 68 B2
SNWD SE25 197 F1
WALTH E17 69 K2
WBLY HA9 79 K1
Pembroke Sq KENS W8 119 K3
Pembroke St IS N1 84 E5
Pembroke Ter STJWD * NW8 2 A1
Pembroke Vls KENS W8 119 K4
Pembroke Wk KENS W8 119 K4
Pembrook Ms BTSEA * SW11 140 C5
Pembry Cl BRXN/ST SW9 142 B2
Pembury Av WPK KT4 192 D5
Pembury Cl CLPT * E5 86 D3
HAYES BR2 199 J4
Pembury Ct HYS/HAR UB3 113 G6
Pembury Crs SCUP DA14 169 F4
Pembury Rd BXLYHN DA7 149 F1
CLPT E5 86 D3
SNWD SE25 197 H1
TOTM N17 50 B5
Pemdevon Rd CROY/NA CR0 196 B4
Pemell Cl WCHPL E1 104 E3
Pemerich Cl HYS/HAR * UB3 113 J5
Pempath Pl WBLY HA9 61 K6
Penally Pl IS N1 85 K6
Penang St WAP E1W 123 J1
Penard Rd NWDGN UB2 115 F3
Penarth St PECK SE15 123 K6
Penates ESH/CLAY KT10 204 D2
Penberth Rd CAT SE6 165 F4
Penbury Rd NWDGN UB2 114 E5
Pencombe Ms NTGHL W11 100 D6
Pencraig Wy PECK * SE15 123 J6
Pencroft Dr DART DA1 171 F2
Pendall Cl EBAR EN4 21 J5
Penda Rd ERITH DA8 149 J1
Pendarves Rd RYNPK SW20 177 F4
Penda's Md HOM E9 87 G2
Pendell Av HYS/HAR UB3 133 J1
Pendennis Rd ORP BR6 202 D6
STRHM/NOR SW16 161 K6
TOTM N17 49 K6
Penderel Rd HSLW TW3 135 F6
Penderry Ri CAT SE6 165 G4
Penderyn Wy HOLWY N7 84 D2
Pendlebury House
WOOL/PLUM SE18 146 D2
Pendle Rd STRHM/NOR SW16 179 G2
Pendlestone Rd WALTH E17 69 K2
Pendragon Rd BMLY BR1 165 K5
Pendrell Rd BROCKY SE4 144 B4
Pendrell St WOOL/PLUM SE18 127 J6
Pendula Dr YEAD UB4 95 H3
Pendulum Ms HACK * E8 86 B3
Penerley Rd CAT SE6 164 E3
RAIN RM13 111 K4
Penfold Cl CROY/NA CR0 211 G1
Penfold Pl BAY/PAD W2 8 C1
Penfold Rd ED N9 37 F3
Penfold St STJWD NW8 2 B7
Penford Gdns ELTH/MOT SE9 146 C5
Penford St CMBW SE5 142 C3
Pengarth Rd BXLY DA5 148 E6
Penge La PGE/AN SE20 181 K3
Penge Rd PLSTW E13 89 G5
SNWD SE25 181 H6
Penhale Cl ORP BR6 217 G2
Penhall Rd CHARL SE7 126 C4
Penhill Rd BXLY DA5 168 D2
Penhurst Rd BARK/HLT IG6 54 B3
Penifather La GFD/PVL UB6 96 D2
Peninsular Cl
EBED/NFELT TW14 153 G1
Peninsular Park Rd CHARL SE7 125 K5
Penistone Rd
STRHM/NOR SW16 179 K3
Penmon Rd ABYW SE2 128 B3
Pennack Rd PECK SE15 123 G6
Pennant Ms KENS W8 120 A4
Pennant Ter WALTH E17 51 H5
Pennard Rd SHB W12 119 F2
The Pennards SUN TW16 172 B6
Penn Cl GFD/PVL UB6 96 B1
KTN/HRWW/W HA3 61 J1
Penner Cl WIM/MER SW19 159 H4
Penners Gdns SURB KT6 191 F4
Pennethorne Cl HOM E9 86 E6
Pennethorne Rd PECK SE15 143 J1
Penney Cl DART DA1 171 G2
Penn Gdns CHST BR7 185 G5
CRW RM5 56 C3
Pennine Dr CRICK NW2 64 C6
Pennine La CRICK NW2 64 C6
Pennine Pde CRICK * NW2 64 C6
Pennine Wy BXLYHN DA7 150 B2
HYS/HAR UB3 133 G1
Pennington Cl CRW RM5 56 C2
Pennington Dr STHGT/OAK N14 22 E6
Pennington St WAP E1W 104 D6
Pennington Wy LEE/GVPK SE12 166 A4
Penniston Cl WDGN N22 49 J5
Penn La BXLY DA5 168 E1
Penn Rd HOLWY N7 84 E3
Penn St IS N1 7 F1
Penny Cl RAIN RM13 111 K2
Pennycroft SAND/SEL CR2 213 G6
Pennyfields POP/IOD E14 105 J6
Pennymoor Wk MV/WKIL W9 100 D3
Pennyroyal Av EHAM E6 108 A5
Penpoll Rd HACK E8 86 D4
Penpool La WELL DA16 148 C4
Penrhyn Av WALTH E17 51 J4
Penrhyn Crs MORT/ESHN SW14 137 K5
WALTH E17 51 J4
Penrhyn Gdns KUT * KT1 191 F1
Penrhyn Gv WALTH E17 51 J4
Penrhyn Rd KUT KT1 175 F6
Penrith Cl BECK BR3 182 E4
PUT/ROE SW15 139 H6
Penrith Crs HCH RM12 93 J3
Penrith Pl STRHM/NOR SW16 162 C4
Penrith Rd BARK/HLT IG6 55 F2
NWMAL KT3 192 A1
SEVS/STOTM N15 67 K2
THHTH CR7 180 D5
Penrith St STRHM/NOR SW16 179 H2
Penrose Av OXHEY WD19 27 J4
Penrose Gv WALW SE17 122 D5
Penrose St WALW SE17 122 D5
Penryn St CAMTN NW1 4 C2
Penry St STHWK SE1 19 H7
Pensbury Pl VX/NE SW8 141 H3
Pensbury St VX/NE SW8 141 H3
Pensford Av RCH/KEW TW9 137 H3
Penshurst Av BFN/LL DA15 168 B1
Penshurst Gdns EDGE HA8 44 D1
Penshurst Gn HAYES BR2 199 J2
Penshurst Rd BXLYHN DA7 149 G2
HOM E9 87 F5
THHTH CR7 196 C2
TOTM N17 50 B3
Penshurst Wy BELMT SM2 208 E5
STMC/STPC BR5 202 D1
Pensilver Cl EBAR * EN4 21 J5
Penstemon Cl FNCH N3 46 E2
Pentelow Gdns
EBED/NFELT TW14 153 K1
Pentire Rd WALTH E17 52 B4
Pentland Av EDGE HA8 30 D4
Pentland Cl CRICK NW2 64 C6
ED N9 36 E4
Pentland Pl NTHLT UB5 77 J6
Pentland Rd BUSH WD23 28 C1
Pentlands Cl MTCM CR4 179 G6
Pentland St WAND/EARL SW18 160 B1
Pentland Wy HGDN/ICK UB10 76 A1
Pentlow St PUT/ROE SW15 139 F3
Pentlow Wy BKHH IG9 39 J2
Pentney Rd BAL SW12 161 H3
CHING E4 38 B3
WIM/MER SW19 177 H4
Penton Gv IS N1 5 J3
Penton Pl WALW SE17 18 B7
Penton Ri FSBYW WC1X 5 H4
Penton St IS N1 5 J2
Pentonville Rd IS N1 5 H3
Pentrich Av EN EN1 24 C1
Pentridge St PECK SE15 143 G1
Pentyre Av UED N18 49 K1
Penwerris Av ISLW TW7 135 H1
Penwith Rd WAND/EARL SW18 160 A4
Penwortham Rd
STRHM/NOR SW16 179 G2
Penylan Pl EDGE * HA8 44 C4
Penywern Rd ECT SW5 119 K5
Penzance Pl NTGHL W11 119 H1
Penzance St NTGHL W11 119 H1
Peony Gdns SHB W12 99 J6
Peploe Rd KIL/WHAMP NW6 100 B1
Peplow Cl WDR/YW UB7 112 A1
Pepper Cl EHAM E6 107 K4
Peppercorn Cl THHTH CR7 180 E5
Peppermead Sq LEW * SE13 144 D6
Peppermint Cl CROY/NA CR0 195 K4
Peppermint Pl WAN E11 88 C1
Pepper St POP/IOD E14 124 E3
STHWK SE1 18 C2
Peppie Cl STNW/STAM N16 68 A6
Pepys Crs BAR EN5 20 A6
Pepys Est DEPT SE8 124 B4
Pepys Park Est DEPT SE8 124 C4
Pepys Ri ORP BR6 202 A5
Pepys Rd NWCR SE14 144 A3
RYNPK SW20 177 F5
Pepys St TWRH EC3N 13 H5
Perceval Av HAMP NW3 83 J3
Percheron Rd BORE WD6 31 F1
Perch St HACK E8 86 B2
Percival Ct TOTM N17 50 B3
Percival Gdns CHDH RM6 73 J3
Percival Rd EN EN1 24 B5
FELT TW13 153 J4
MORT/ESHN SW14 137 K6
ORP BR6 201 G6
Percival St FSBYE EC1V 6 A6
Percival Wy HOR/WEW KT19 206 E2
Percy Bush Rd WDR/YW UB7 112 C3
Percy Gdns PEND EN3 25 F6
WPK KT4 192 A5
YEAD UB4 94 C2
Percy Ms FITZ W1T 10 C2
Percy Rd BXLYHN DA7 149 F3
CAN/RD E16 106 C4
GDMY/SEVK IG3 73 G4
HPTN TW12 173 F3
ISLW TW7 136 B5
MTCM CR4 195 F4
NFNCH/WDSP N12 47 G1
PGE/AN SE20 182 A4
ROMW/RG RM7 56 E6
SHB W12 118 D2
SNWD SE25 197 G2
WAN E11 70 C4
WCHMH N21 35 J2
WHTN TW2 155 G3
Percy St FITZ W1T 10 C2
Percy Wy WHTN TW2 155 H3
Peregrine Cl WLSDN NW10 81 F3
Peregrine Ct WELL DA16 148 A2
Peregrine Gdns CROY/NA CR0 198 B6
Peregrine Rd BARK/HLT IG6 55 H1
Peregrine Wy WIM/MER SW19 177 F3
Perham Rd WKENS W14 119 H5
Peridot St EHAM E6 107 J4
Perifield DUL SE21 162 D3
Perimeade Rd GFD/PVL UB6 97 J1
Periton Rd ELTH/MOT SE9 146 C5
Perivale Gdns WEA W13 97 H3
Perivale La GFD/PVL UB6 97 G2
Perivale Village GFD/PVL * UB6 97 J2
Perkin Cl ALP/SUD HA0 79 H3
Perkin's Rents WEST SW1P 16 C4
Perkins Rd BARK/HLT IG6 72 D2
Perkins Sq STHWK SE1 12 D7
Perks Cl BKHTH/KID SE3 145 H3
Perpins Rd ELTH/MOT SE9 167 K1
Perran Rd BRXS/STRHM SW2 162 C4
Perrers Rd HMSMTH W6 118 E3
Perrin Rd ALP/SUD HA0 79 G2
Perrin's Ct HAMP * NW3 83 G2
Perrin's Wk HAMP NW3 83 G2
Perry Av ACT W3 99 F5
Perry Cl RAIN RM13 111 F1
Perry Ct SEVS/STOTM * N15 68 A3
Perryfield Wy CDALE/KGS NW9 63 H3
RCHPK/HAM TW10 156 C4
Perry Gdns ED N9 36 A5
Perry Garth NTHLT UB5 77 G6
Perry Gv DART DA1 151 K5
Perry Hall Cl ORP BR6 202 B4
Perry Hall Rd ORP BR6 202 A3
Perry Hl CAT SE6 164 C4
Perry How WPK KT4 192 C5
Perry Mnr CHST BR7 185 K2
Perrymans Farm Rd
GNTH/NBYPK IG2 72 D3
Perry Md BUSH WD23 28 C1
ENC/FH EN2 23 H3
Perrymead St FUL/PGN SW6 139 K2
Perryn Rd ACT W3 99 F6
BERM/RHTH SE16 123 J3
Perry Oak Dr HTHAIR TW6 132 A3
Perry Ri FSTH SE23 164 B5
Perry St CHST BR7 185 K2
DART DA1 150 B4
Perry V FSTH SE23 163 K4
Persant Rd CAT SE6 165 H5
Perseverance Pl
BRXN/ST * SW9 142 B1
Pershore Cl GNTH/NBYPK IG2 72 B2
Pershore Gv CAR SM5 194 C3
Pert Cl MUSWH N10 48 B3
Perth Av CDALE/KGS NW9 63 F4
YEAD UB4 95 G3
Perth Cl RYNPK SW20 176 D5
Perth Rd BARK IG11 108 D1
BECK BR3 183 F5
FSBYPK N4 67 G5
GNTH/NBYPK IG2 72 B3
LEY E10 69 G5
PLSTW E13 107 F1
WDGN N22 49 H4
Perth Ter GNTH/NBYPK IG2 72 C4
Perwell Av RYLN/HDSTN HA2 59 K5
Petauel Rd TEDD TW11 173 K1
Petavel Rd TEDD TW11 173 K2
Peter Av WLSDN NW10 81 K5
Peterboat Cl GNWCH SE10 125 H4
Peterborough Ms
FUL/PGN SW6 139 K3
Peterborough Rd CAR SM5 194 D3
FUL/PGN SW6 139 K3
HRW HA1 60 E5
LEY E10 70 A2
Peterborough Vls
FUL/PGN SW6 140 A2
Petergate BTSEA SW11 140 B5
Peters Cl BCTR RM8 73 K5
EDGE HA8 43 K2
WELL DA16 147 K3
Petersfield Cl UED N18 49 J1
Petersfield Ri PUT/ROE SW15 158 E3
Petersfield Rd ACT W3 117 K2
Petersham Cl
RCHPK/HAM TW10 156 E4
SUT SM1 208 D3
Petersham Dr STMC/STPC BR5 186 A5
Petersham Gdns
STMC/STPC BR5 186 B5
Petersham La SKENS * SW7 120 B3
Petersham Ms SKENS SW7 120 B3
Petersham Pl SKENS SW7 120 B3
Petersham Rd
RCHPK/HAM TW10 156 E5
RCHPK/HAM TW10 157 F1
Petersham Ter CROY/NA * CR0 210 E1
Peter's Hl BLKFR EC4V 12 C5
Peterstone Rd ABYW SE2 128 C2
Peterstow Cl WIM/MER SW19 159 H4
Peter St SOHO/CST W1F 10 C5
Peterwood Wy CROY/NA CR0 196 A6
Petherton Rd HBRY N5 85 J3
Petiver Cl HOM * E9 86 E5
Petley Rd HMSMTH W6 119 F6
Peto Pl CAMTN NW1 3 K6
Petrie Cl CRICK * NW2 82 C4
Petros Gdns HAMP * NW3 83 F3
Petro St South CAN/RD E16 106 D6
Pett Cl EMPK RM11 75 K6
Petten Cl STMC/STPC BR5 202 E5
Petten Gv STMC/STPC BR5 202 D5
Petticoat Sq WCHPL E1 13 J3
Petticoat Tower WCHPL * E1 13 J3
Pettits Bvd ROM RM1 57 G5
Pettits Cl ROM RM1 57 G5
Pettits La ROM RM1 57 G6
Pettits La North ROM RM1 57 F4
Pettit's Pl DAGE RM10 92 C3
Pettit's Rd DAGE RM10 92 C3
Pettiward Cl PUT/ROE SW15 139 F5
Pettley Gdns ROMW/RG RM7 75 F2
Pettman Crs THMD SE28 127 J4
Pettsgrove Av ALP/SUD HA0 79 J3
Pett's Hl RYLN/HDSTN HA2 78 B2
Pett St WOOL/PLUM SE18 126 D4
Petts Wood Rd STMC/STPC BR5 201 J2
Petty France STJSPK SW1H 16 B4
Petworth Cl NTHLT UB5 77 K5
Petworth Gdns HGDN/ICK UB10 76 A6
RYNPK SW20 176 E6
Petworth Rd BXLYHS DA6 149 H6
NFNCH/WDSP N12 47 J1
Petworth St BTSEA SW11 140 D2
Petworth Wy HCH RM12 93 H2
Petyt Pl CHEL * SW3 120 D6
Petyward CHEL SW3 14 D7
Pevensey Av EN EN1 23 K3
FBAR/BDGN N11 48 D1
Pevensey Cl ISLW TW7 135 H1
Pevensey Rd FELT TW13 154 D3
FSTGT E7 88 E2
TOOT SW17 160 C6
Peveret Cl FBAR/BDGN * N11 48 B1
Peveril Dr TEDD TW11 173 J1
Pewsey Cl CHING E4 51 J1
Peyton Pl GNWCH SE10 145 F1
Pharaoh Cl MTCM CR4 194 E4
Pheasant Cl CAN/RD E16 107 F5
Phelp St WALW SE17 122 E6
Phelps Wy HYS/HAR UB3 113 J4
Phene St CHEL SW3 120 D6
Philan Wy CRW RM5 57 F2
Philbeach Gdns ECT SW5 119 K5
Philchurch Pl WCHPL E1 104 C5
Philimore Cl WOOL/PLUM SE18 127 K5
Philip Av ROMW/RG RM7 75 F5
Philip Gdns CROY/NA CR0 198 C6
Philip La SEVS/STOTM N15 67 K1
Philippa Gdns ELTH/MOT SE9 146 C6
Philip Rd PECK SE15 143 H4
RAIN RM13 111 G2
Philips Cl MTCM CR4 195 F5
Philip St PLSTW E13 106 E3
Phillimore Gdns KENS W8 119 K2
WLSDN NW10 82 A6
Phillimore Gardens Cl KENS W8 119 K3
Phillimore Pl KENS * W8 119 K2
Phillimore Ter KENS * W8 119 K3
Phillimore Wk KENS W8 119 K3
Phillipp St IS N1 7 H1
Phillips Cl DART DA1 170 E1
Philpot La FENCHST EC3M 13 G5
Philpot St WCHPL * E1 104 D5
Phineas Pett Road Rd
ELTH/MOT SE9 146 D4
Phipp's Bridge Rd
WIM/MER SW19 178 B5
Phipps Hatch La ENC/FH EN2 23 J1
Phipp's Ms BGVA SW1W 15 J5
Phipp St SDTCH EC2A 7 G6
Phoebeth Rd LEW SE13 144 D6
Phoenix Cl HACK * E8 86 B6
NTHWD HA6 26 D6
WWKM BR4 199 G6
Phoenix Ct BTFD TW8 117 F5
Phoenix Dr HAYES BR2 215 H2
Phoenix Pk BTFD * TW8 116 E5
Phoenix Pl DART DA1 171 G2
FSBYW WC1X 5 H6
Phoenix Rd CAMTN NW1 4 C4
PGE/AN SE20 181 K2
Phoenix St LSQ/SEVD WC2H 10 D4
Phoenix Wy HEST TW5 114 C6
Phoenix Wharf Rd STHWK SE1 19 K3
Phyllis Av NWMAL KT3 192 E2
Physic Pl CHEL SW3 120 E6
Picardy Manorway BELV DA17 129 J3
Picardy Rd BELV DA17 129 H5
Picardy St BELV DA17 129 H3
Piccadilly MYFR/PICC W1J 15 J1
Piccadilly Ar MYFR/PICC W1J 10 A7
Piccadilly Circ MYFR/PICC W1J 10 B6
Pickard St FSBYE EC1V 6 B4
Pickering Av EHAM E6 108 A1
Pickering Gdns FBAR/BDGN N11 48 A2
SNWD SE25 197 G3
Pickering Pl STJS * SW1Y 16 B1
Pickering St IS N1 85 H6
Pickets Cl BUSH WD23 28 D3
Pickets St BAL SW12 161 F2
Pickett Cft STAN HA7 43 K4
Pickett's Lock La ED N9 37 F4
Pickford Cl BXLYHN DA7 149 F3
Pickford La BXLYHN DA7 149 F3
Pickford Rd BXLYHN DA7 149 F4
Pickfords Whf IS * N1 6 C3
Pickhurst Gn HAYES BR2 199 J4
Pickhurst La HAYES BR2 199 K5
Pickhurst Md HAYES BR2 199 J4
Pickhurst Pk HAYES BR2 199 H3
Pickhurst Ri WWKM BR4 199 G5
Pickwick Cl HSLWW TW4 134 D6
Pickwick Ms UED N18 50 A1
Pickwick Pl HRW HA1 60 E4
Pickwick Rd DUL SE21 162 E2
Pickwick St STHWK SE1 18 C3
Pickwick Wy CHST BR7 185 H2
Pickworth Cl VX/NE * SW8 141 K1
Picton Pl MBLAR W1H 9 H4
Picton St CMBW SE5 142 E1
Piedmont Rd
WOOL/PLUM SE18 127 J5
Pier Head WAP * E1W 123 J1
Piermont Pl BMLY BR1 184 C5
Piermont Rd EDUL SE22 143 J6
Pierrepoint Ar IS * N1 6 A2
Pierrepoint Rd ACT W3 98 D6
Pierrepoint Rw IS N1 6 A2
Pier Rd CAN/RD E16 126 E2
EBED/NFELT TW14 134 A6
ERITH DA8 130 B6
Pier St POP/IOD E14 125 F4
Pier Ter WAND/EARL SW18 140 A5
Pier Wy WOOL/PLUM SE18 127 J3
Pigeon La HPTN TW12 155 F6
Pigott St POP/IOD E14 105 J5
Pike Cl BMLY BR1 184 A1
Pike Rd MLHL NW7 31 F6
Pike's End PIN HA5 59 F1
Pikestone Cl YEAD * UB4 95 J3
Pilgrimage St STHWK SE1 18 E3
Pilgrim Cl MRDN SM4 194 A4
Pilgrim Hl WNWD SE27 162 D6
Pilgrims Cl NTHLT UB5 78 C3
PLMGR N13 35 F6
Pilgrims Ct DART DA1 151 K6
Pilgrim's La HAMP NW3 83 H2
Pilgrims Ms POP/IOD E14 106 B6
Pilgrims Pl ASHF * TW15 152 C6
Pilgrim's Ri EBAR EN4 21 J6
Pilgrim St BLKFR * EC4V 12 A4
Pilgrims Wy ARCH N19 66 D5
SAND/SEL * CR2 212 B3
WBLY HA9 62 D5
SAND/SEL CR2 212 B4
Pilkington Rd ORP BR6 216 C1
PECK SE15 143 J3
Pilot Cl DEPT SE8 124 C6
Pilsden Cl WIM/MER * SW19 159 G3
Piltdown Rd OXHEY WD19 27 H6
Pilton Pl WALW SE17 122 D5
Pimlico Rd BGVA SW1W 121 F5
Pinchbeck Rd ORP BR6 217 F4
Pinchin & Johnsons Yd
WCHPL * E1 104 C6
Pinchin St WCHPL E1 104 C6
Pincott Pl BROCKY SE4 144 A4
Pincott Rd BXLYHS DA6 149 H6
WIM/MER SW19 178 B4
Pindar St SDTCH EC2A 13 G1
Pindock Ms MV/WKIL W9 101 F3
Pine Apple Ct WESTW * SW1E 16 A4
Pine Av SRTFD E15 88 B3
WWKM BR4 198 E5
Pine Cl LEY E10 69 J6
NTHWD HA6 40 C2
PGE/AN SE20 181 K4
STAN HA7 29 H6
STHGT/OAK N14 34 C2
Pine Coombe CROY/NA CR0 213 F2
Pinecrest Gdns ORP BR6 216 B2
Pinecroft KTN/HRWW/W HA3 62 B2
WELL DA16 148 B1
Pinecroft Crs BAR EN5 20 C5
Pinefield Cl POP/IOD * E14 105 J6
Pine Gdns BRYLDS KT5 191 H3
RSLP HA4 59 F5
Pine Gld ORP BR6 215 K2
Pine Gv FSBYPK N4 66 E6
TRDG/WHET N20 32 D3
WIM/MER SW19 177 J1
Pinelands Cl BKHTH/KID * SE3 145 J1
Pinelees Ct MORT/ESHN * SW14 137 K5
Pinemartin Cl CRICK NW2 82 A1
Pine Rdg CAR SM5 210 A6
Pine Rd CRICK NW2 82 A2
FBAR/BDGN N11 34 A4
Pines Rd BMLY BR1 184 D5
The Pines NRWD * SE19 180 C2
WFD IG8 38 E5
Pine St CLKNW EC1R 5 J6
Pine Tree Cl HEST TW5 134 A2
Pine Wk BRYLDS KT5 191 H3
Pinewood Av BFN/LL DA15 167 K3
PIN HA5 42 B2
RAIN RM13 111 K3
Pinewood Cl CROY/NA CR0 213 G1
ORP BR6 201 J5
PIN HA5 42 B2
Pinewood Dr ORP BR6 216 E3
Pinewood Gv WEA W13 97 J5

Pinewood Ldg BUSH * WD23 28 D3
Pinewood Ms
STWL/WRAY TW19 152 A1
Pinewood Rd ABYW SE2 128 E6
FELT TW13 154 A5
HAYES BR2 199 K1
Pinfold Rd STRHM/NOR SW16 161 K6
Pinglestone Cl WDR/YW UB7 132 B1
Pinkcoat Cl FELT TW13 154 A5
Pinkham Wy North Circular Rd
MUSWH N10 47 K3
Pinkwell Av HYS/HAR UB3 113 G4
Pinkwell La HYS/HAR UB3 113 F4
Pinley Gdns DAGW RM9 91 H6
Pinnacle Hl BXLYHN DA7 149 J5
Pinnacle Hl North BXLYHN DA7 149 J4
Pinnell Rd ELTH/MOT SE9 146 C5
Pinner Ct PIN HA5 60 A1
Pinner Gn PIN HA5 41 G5
Pinner Gv PIN HA5 59 J1
Pinner Hl PIN HA5 41 F3
Pinner Hill Rd PIN HA5 41 G4
Pinner Park Av
RYLN/HDSTN HA2 42 C5
Pinner Park Gdns
RYLN/HDSTN HA2 42 C5
Pinner Rd HRW HA1 60 B2
NTHWD HA6 40 D4
OXHEY WD19 27 H1
PIN HA5 59 K1
Pinner Vw RYLN/HDSTN HA2 60 C1
Pinn Wy RSLP HA4 58 B4
Pintail Cl EHAM E6 107 J4
Pintail Rd WFD IG8 53 F3
Pintail Wy YEAD UB4 95 H4
Pinto Cl BORE * WD6 31 F1
Pinto Wy BKHTH/KID SE3 146 A5
Pioneer Cl SHB W12 99 K5
Pioneer St PECK SE15 143 H2
Pioneer Wy SHB W12 100 A5
WATW WD18 26 D1
Piper Cl HOLWY N7 85 F3
Piper Rd KUT KT1 175 H6
Pipers Gdns CROY/NA CR0 198 B4
Pipers Gn CDALE/KGS NW9 62 E2
Pipers Green La EDGE HA8 30 A5
Pipewell Rd CAR SM5 194 D3
Pippin Cl CRICK NW2 81 J1
CROY/NA CR0 198 C5
Pippins Cl WDR/YW UB7 112 A3
Piquet Rd PGE/AN SE20 181 K5
Pirbright Crs CROY/NA CR0 214 A4
Pirbright Rd WAND/EARL SW18 159 J3
Pirie St CAN/RD E16 126 A1
Pitcairn Cl ROMW/RG RM7 74 C1
Pitcairn Rd MTCM CR4 178 E3
Pitchford St SRTFD E15 88 B5
Pitfield Crs THMD SE28 128 B1
Pitfield St IS N1 7 G4
Pitfield Wy PEND * EN3 24 E2
WLSDN NW10 80 E4
Pitfold Rd LEE/GVPK SE12 165 K2
Pitlake CROY/NA CR0 196 C6
Pitman St CMBW SE5 142 D1
Pitsea Pl WCHPL E1 105 F5
Pitsea St WCHPL E1 105 F5
Pitshanger La EA W5 97 H3
Pitt Crs WIM/MER SW19 160 A6
Pittman Gdns IL IG1 90 C3
Pitt Rd ORP BR6 216 C2
RYLN/HDSTN HA2 60 C6
THHTH CR7 196 D2
Pitt's Head Ms MYFR/PKLN W1K 15 H1
Pittsmead Av HAYES BR2 199 K4
Pitt St KENS W8 119 K2
Pittville Gdns SNWD SE25 181 H6
Pixley St POP/IOD E14 105 H5
Pixton Wy CROY/NA CR0 213 G6
Place Farm Av ORP BR6 201 J5
Plaistow Gv BMLY BR1 184 A3
SRTFD E15 88 D6
Plaistow La BMLY BR1 183 K3
Plaistow Park Rd PLSTW E13 107 F1
Plaistow Rd PLSTW E13 106 E1
SRTFD E15 88 D6
Plane St SYD SE26 163 J5
Plane Tree Crs FELT TW13 154 A5
Plantagenet Cl HOR/WEW KT19 207 F2
Plantagenet Gdns CHDH RM6 73 K4
Plantagenet Pl CHDH RM6 73 K4
Plantagenet Rd BAR EN5 21 G5
Plantain Gdns WAN * E11 88 B1
Plantain Pl STHWK SE1 18 E2
The Plantation BKHTH/KID SE3 145 K3
Plantation Dr STMC/STPC BR5 202 E5
Plantation Rd ERITH DA8 150 D2
Plashet Gv EHAM E6 89 G6
Plashet Rd PLSTW E13 88 E6
Plassy Rd CAT SE6 164 E2
Platina St SDTCH EC2A 7 F6
Plato Rd CLAP SW4 141 K5
Platt's La HAMP NW3 82 E1
Platts Rd PEND EN3 24 E2
Platt St CAMTN NW1 4 C2
Plawsfield Rd BECK BR3 182 A4
Plaxtol Cl BMLY BR1 184 B4
Plaxtol Rd ERITH DA8 149 H1
Playfair St HMSMTH * W6 119 F5
Playfield Av CRW RM5 56 E4
Playfield Crs EDUL SE22 143 F6
Playfield Rd EDGE HA8 44 E5
Playford Rd FSBYPK N4 67 G6
Playgreen Wy CAT SE6 164 D6
Playground Cl BECK BR3 182 A5
Playhouse Yd BLKFR EC4V 12 A4
Plaza Pde ALP/SUD * HA0 80 A4
The Pleasance PUT/ROE SW15 138 E5
Pleasance Rd PUT/ROE SW15 138 E6
STMC/STPC BR5 186 C5
Pleasant Gv CROY/NA CR0 213 H1
Pleasant Pl IS N1 85 H5
Pleasant Vw ERITH DA8 130 B5
ORP BR6 216 C3
Pleasant Wy ALP/SUD HA0 97 J1
Plender St CAMTN NW1 4 A1
Pleshey Rd HOLWY N7 84 D2
Plesman Wy WLGTN * SM6 210 E6
Plevna Crs SEVS/STOTM N15 68 A3
Plevna Rd ED N9 36 C5
HPTN TW12 173 G4
Plevna St POP/IOD E14 125 F3
Pleydell Av HMSMTH W6 118 C3
NRWD SE19 181 G3
Pleydell Est FSBYE * EC1V 6 D5
Pleydell Gdns NRWD * SE19 181 G2
Pleydell St EMB EC4Y 11 K4
Plimsoll Cl POP/IOD E14 105 K5
Plimsoll Rd FSBYPK N4 85 H1
Plough Farm Cl RSLP HA4 58 B3
Plough La CROY/NA CR0 210 E2
EDUL SE22 163 G1
TEDD * TW11 174 B1
WIM/MER SW19 178 A1
WLGTN SM6 210 E6
Plough Lane Cl WLGTN SM6 210 E3
Ploughmans Cl CAMTN NW1 84 D6
Ploughmans End ISLW TW7 135 J6
Plough Pl FLST/FETLN EC4A 11 K3
Plough Rd BTSEA SW11 140 C4
HOR/WEW KT19 207 F5
Plough St WCHPL * E1 104 C5
Plough Ter BTSEA SW11 140 C5
Plough Wy BERM/RHTH SE16 124 A4
Plough Yd SDTCH EC2A 7 H7
Plover Wy BERM/RHTH SE16 124 B3
YEAD UB4 95 H5
Plowden Buildings EMB * EC4Y 11 J5
Plowman Cl UED N18 49 K1
Plowman Wy BCTR RM8 73 J5
Plumbers Rw WCHPL E1 104 C4
Plumbridge St GNWCH * SE10 145 F2
Plum Cl FELT TW13 153 K3
Plum Garth BTFD TW8 116 E4
Plum La WOOL/PLUM SE18 147 G1
Plummer La MTCM CR4 178 E4
Plummer Rd CLAP SW4 161 H1
Plumpton Cl NTHLT UB5 78 A4
Plumpton Wy CAR SM5 209 J1
Plumstead Common Rd
WOOL/PLUM SE18 127 H6
Plumstead High St
WOOL/PLUM SE18 127 J4
Plumstead Rd
WOOL/PLUM SE18 127 H4
Plumtree Cl DAGE RM10 92 D4
Plumtree Ct FLST/FETLN EC4A 11 K3
Plymouth Rd BMLY BR1 184 A4
CAN/RD E16 106 E4
Plymouth Whf POP/IOD E14 125 G4
Plympton Av KIL/WHAMP NW6 82 D5
Plympton Cl BELV DA17 129 F3
Plympton Pl STJWD * NW8 2 C7
Plympton Rd KIL/WHAMP NW6 82 D5
Plympton St STJWD NW8 2 C7
Plymstock Rd WELL DA16 148 D1
Pocklington Cl CDALE/KGS NW9 45 G5
Pocock Av WDR/YW UB7 112 C3
Pocock St STHWK SE1 18 A2
Podmore Rd WAND/EARL SW18 140 B5
Poet's Rd HBRY N5 85 K3
Poets Wy HRW HA1 60 E1
Pointalls Cl FNCH N3 47 G5
Point Cl GNWCH SE10 145 F2
Pointer Cl THMD SE28 109 K5
Pointers Cl POP/IOD E14 124 E5
Point Hl GNWCH SE10 145 F2
Point Pl WBLY HA9 80 D5
Point Pleasant
WAND/EARL SW18 139 K5
Poland St SOHO/CST W1F 10 B3
Polebrook Rd BKHTH/KID SE3 146 B4
Polecroft La CAT SE6 164 C4
Pole Hill Rd CHING E4 38 A2
Polesden Gdns RYNPK SW20 176 E6
Polesworth Rd DAGW RM9 110 B1
Pollard Cl CAN/RD E16 106 E6
CHIG IG7 55 G1
HOLWY N7 85 F3
Pollard Rd MRDN SM4 194 C2
TRDG/WHET N20 33 J4
Pollard Rw BETH E2 104 C2
Pollards Crs STRHM/NOR SW16 179 K6
Pollards Hl East
STRHM/NOR SW16 180 A6
Pollards Hl North
STRHM/NOR SW16 180 A6
Pollards Hl South
STRHM/NOR SW16 179 K6
Pollards Hl West
STRHM/NOR SW16 179 K6
Pollard St BETH * E2 104 C2
Pollards Wood Rd
STRHM/NOR SW16 179 K5
Pollen St CONDST W1S 9 K4
Pollitt Dr STJWD NW8 2 A6
Polperro Cl ORP BR6 202 A3
Polperro Ms LBTH SE11 17 K6
Polsted Rd CAT SE6 164 C2
Polthorne Gv
WOOL/PLUM SE18 127 H4
Polworth Rd STRHM/NOR SW16 179 K1
The Polygon CLAP * SW4 141 H5
Polygon Rd CAMTN NW1 4 C3
Polytechnic St
WOOL/PLUM SE18 127 F4
Pomell Wy WCHPL E1 13 K3
Pomeroy St NWCR SE14 143 K1
Pomfret Rd CMBW SE5 142 C4
Pomoja La ARCH N19 66 E6
Pond Cl BKHTH/KID SE3 145 K3
NFNCH/WDSP N12 47 J2
Pond Cottage La BECK BR3 198 D5
Ponder St HOLWY * N7 85 F5
Pond Farm Est CLPT * E5 86 E1
Pondfield Rd DAGE RM10 92 D3
HAYES BR2 199 H5
ORP BR6 216 B1
Pond Gn RSLP HA4 58 C6
Pond Hill Gdns CHEAM * SM3 208 C4
Pond Md EDUL SE22 162 E1
Pond Pl CHEL SW3 14 C7
Pond Rd BKHTH/KID SE3 145 J4
SRTFD E15 106 C1
Pondside Cl HYS/HAR UB3 133 G1
Pond St HAMP NW3 83 J3
Pond Wy TEDD TW11 174 D2
Pondwood Ri ORP BR6 201 K4
Ponler St WCHPL E1 104 D5
Ponsard Rd WLSDN NW10 99 K2
Ponsford St HOM E9 86 E4
Ponsonby Pl WEST SW1P 121 J5
Ponsonby Rd PUT/ROE SW15 158 E2
Ponsonby Ter WEST SW1P 121 J5
Pontefract Rd BMLY BR1 183 K1
Ponton Rd VX/NE SW8 141 J1
Pont St KTBR SW1X 14 E5
Pont Street Ms CHEL SW3 14 E5
Pool Cl BECK BR3 182 D1
E/WMO/HCT KT8 188 E2
Pool Ct CAT SE6 164 D4
Poole Cl RSLP HA4 58 C6
Poole Court Rd HEST TW5 134 D3
Poole Rd HOM E9 87 F4
HOR/WEW KT19 207 F4
Pooles Buildings FSBYW WC1X 5 J7
Pooles La WBPTN * SW10 140 B1
Pooles Pk FSBYPK N4 67 G6
Poole St IS N1 6 E1
Poole Wy YEAD * UB4 94 C2
Poolmans St BERM/RHTH SE16 124 A2
Pool Rd E/WMO/HCT KT8 188 E2
HRW HA1 60 D4
Poolsford Rd CDALE/KGS NW9 63 G1
Poonah St WCHPL E1 104 E5
Pope Cl EBED/NFELT TW14 153 J3
WIM/MER * SW19 178 C2
Pope Rd HAYES BR2 200 C2
Pope's Av WHTN TW2 155 K4
Popes Dr FNCH N3 46 E4
Popes Gv CROY/NA CR0 213 H1
WHTN TW2 155 K4
Pope's La EA W5 116 E3
Pope's Rd BRXN/ST * SW9 142 B5
Pope St STHWK SE1 19 H3
Popham Cl FELT TW13 154 D5
Popham Gdns RCH/KEW * TW9 137 J4
Popham Rd IS N1 85 J6
Popham St IS N1 85 H6
Popinjays Rw CHEAM * SM3 208 B3
Poplar Av MTCM CR4 178 E4
NWDGN UB2 115 G3
ORP BR6 201 G6
Poplar Bath St POP/IOD E14 105 K6
Poplar Cl HOM E9 87 H3
PIN HA5 41 H4
Poplar Court Pde TWK * TW1 156 D1
Poplar Crs HMSMTH W6 119 F2
HOR/WEW KT19 206 E4
Poplar Farm Cl HOR/WEW KT19 206 E4
Poplar Gdns NWMAL KT3 176 A5
Poplar Gv FBAR/BDGN N11 48 A2
NWMAL KT3 176 A6
WBLY HA9 80 E1
Poplar High St POP/IOD E14 105 K6
Poplar Ms SHB W12 119 F1
Poplar Mt BELV DA17 129 J4
Poplar Pl BAY/PAD W2 101 F6
HYS/HAR UB3 94 E6
THMD SE28 109 J6
Poplar Rd CHEAM SM3 193 J5
HNHL SE24 142 D5
WIM/MER SW19 177 K5
Poplar Rd South
WIM/MER SW19 177 K6
Poplars Cl RSLP HA4 58 C5
Poplars Rd WALTH E17 69 K3
Poplar St ROMW/RG RM7 74 E1
Poplar Vw WBLY * HA9 61 K6
Poplar Wk CROY/NA CR0 196 D6
HNHL SE24 142 D5
Poplar Wy BARK/HLT IG6 72 C1
FELT TW13 153 K5
Poppins Ct FLST/FETLN EC4A 12 A4
Poppleton Rd WAN E11 70 C3
Poppy Cl MTCM CR4 195 F5
Poppy La CROY/NA CR0 197 K4
Porchester Garden Ms
BAY/PAD * W2 101 F5
Porchester Gdns BAY/PAD W2 101 F6
Porchester Ga BAY/PAD * W2 101 G6
Porchester Md BECK BR3 182 E2
Porchester Pl BAY/PAD W2 8 D4
Porchester Rd BAY/PAD W2 101 F5
KUT KT1 175 J5
Porchester Sq BAY/PAD W2 101 F5
Porchester Square Ms
BAY/PAD * W2 101 F5
Porchester Ter BAY/PAD W2 101 G6
Porch Wy TRDG/WHET N20 33 K5
Porcupine Cl ELTH/MOT SE9 166 D4
Porden Rd BRXS/STRHM SW2 142 A5
Porlock Av RYLN/HDSTN HA2 60 C5
Porlock Rd EN EN1 36 B2
Porlock St STHWK SE1 19 F2
Porrington Cl CHST BR7 184 E4
Portal Cl RSLP HA4 76 E2
WNWD SE27 162 B5
Portbury Cl PECK SE15 143 H2
Portchester Cl CMBW SE5 142 D5
Portcullis Lodge Rd
ENC/FH EN2 23 K4
Portelet Rd WCHPL E1 105 F2
Porten Houses WKENS * W14 119 H3
Porten Rd WKENS W14 119 H3
Porter Rd EHAM E6 107 K5
Porters Av DAGW RM9 91 H4
Porter St MHST W1U 9 F1
STHWK SE1 12 D7
Porters Wk WAP * E1W 104 D6
Porters Wy WDR/YW UB7 112 C3
Porteus Rd BAY/PAD W2 101 G4
Portgate Cl MV/WKIL W9 100 D3
Porthcawe Rd SYD SE26 164 B6
Porthkerry Av WELL DA16 148 B5
Portia Wy BOW E3 105 H3
The Porticos WBPTN * SW10 120 C6
Portinscale Rd PUT/ROE SW15 139 H6
Portland Av BFN/LL DA15 168 B1
NWMAL KT3 192 C4
STNW/STAM N16 68 B5
Portland Cl CHDH RM6 74 A2
Portland Cottages
CROY/NA * CR0 195 J4
Portland Crs ELTH/MOT SE9 166 D4
FELT TW13 153 G6
GFD/PVL UB6 96 B4
STAN HA7 43 K5
Portland Crs West STAN HA7 43 K6
Portland Dr ENC/FH EN2 24 A1
Portland Gdns CHDH RM6 73 K2
FSBYPK N4 67 H3
Portland Gv VX/NE SW8 142 A2
Portland Ms SOHO/CST W1F 10 B4
Portland Pl CAVSQ/HST W1G 3 J7
SNWD SE25 197 H1
Portland Ri FSBYPK N4 67 H5
Portland Rd ASHF TW15 152 B5
BMLY BR1 166 B6
KUT KT1 175 F6
MTCM CR4 178 D5
NTGHL W11 100 C6
NWDGN UB2 114 E3
SEVS/STOTM N15 68 A1
SNWD SE25 197 J1
YEAD UB4 94 C2
Portland Sq WAP E1W 123 J1
Portland St WALW SE17 122 E5
Portland Ter RCH/KEW * TW9 136 E5
Portman Av MORT/ESHN SW14 138 A4
Portman Cl BXLY DA5 170 B3
BXLYHN DA7 148 E4
MBLAR W1H 9 G3
Portman Dr WFD IG8 53 H5
Portman Gdns CDALE/KGS NW9 45 F6
Portman Ga STJWD NW8 2 D7
Portman Ms South MBLAR W1H 9 G4
Portman Pl BETH E2 104 E2
Portman Rd KUT KT1 175 G5
Portman Sq MBLAR W1H 9 F3
Portman St MBLAR W1H 9 G4
Portman Towers MBLAR W1H 9 F3
Portmeers Cl WALTH * E17 69 H3
Portmore Gdns CRW RM5 56 C1
Portnall Rd MV/WKIL W9 100 D2
Portnoi Cl ROM RM1 57 F5
Portobello Ct NTGHL * W11 100 D6
Portobello Ms NTGHL W11 100 E6
Portobello Rd NKENS W10 100 C4
Portpool La FSBYW WC1X 11 J1
Portree St POP/IOD E14 106 B5
Portsdown Av GLDGN NW11 64 D3
Portsdown Ms GLDGN NW11 64 D3
Portsea Ms BAY/PAD W2 8 D4
Portsea Pl BAY/PAD W2 8 D4
Portslade Rd VX/NE SW8 141 H3
Portsmouth Av THDIT KT7 190 B4
Portsmouth Rd ESH/CLAY KT10 204 A4
KUT KT1 174 E6
PUT/ROE SW15 158 E3
Portsmouth St LINN WC2A 11 G3
Portsoken St TWRH EC3N 13 J5
Portugal Gdns WHTN * TW2 155 H4
Portugal St LINN WC2A 11 H4
Portway SRTFD E15 88 E6
Portway Crs EW KT17 207 J6
Portway Gdns
WOOL/PLUM SE18 146 C2
The Postern BARB * EC2Y 12 D2
Postern Gn ENC/FH EN2 23 G3
Post La WHTN TW2 155 J3
Postmill Cl CROY/NA CR0 212 E1
Post Office Ap FSTGT E7 89 F3
Post Rd NWDGN UB2 115 G3
Postway Ms IL IG1 90 B1
Potier St STHWK SE1 19 F5
Potter Cl MTCM * CR4 179 G5
The Potteries BAR * EN5 20 E6
Potterne Cl WIM/MER SW19 159 G2
Potters Cl CROY/NA CR0 198 B5
Potters Fld EN * EN1 24 A5
Potters Flds STHWK SE1 19 H1
Potters Gv NWMAL KT3 191 K1
Potters Heights Cl PIN HA5 41 F3
Potter's La BAR EN5 20 E5
STRHM/NOR * SW16 179 J2
Potter's Rd BAR EN5 21 F5
FUL/PGN SW6 140 B3
Potter St NTHWD HA6 40 E4
Potter Street Hl NTHWD HA6 41 F2
Pottery La NTGHL W11 119 H1
Pottery Rd BTFD TW8 117 F6
BXLY DA5 169 K4
Pottery St BERM/RHTH * SE16 123 J2
Pott St BETH E2 104 D2
Poulett Gdns TWK TW1 156 A4
Poulett Rd EHAM E6 107 K1
Poulter Pk MTCM * CR4 194 D3
Poulters Wd HAYES BR2 215 H3
Poulton Av SUT SM1 209 H1
Poulton Cl HACK E8 86 D4
Poultry LOTH EC2R 12 E4
Pound Cl ORP BR6 201 J6
SURB KT6 190 D5
Pound Court Dr ORP BR6 201 J6
Pound Farm La ESH/CLAY KT10 189 J5
Pound La WLSDN NW10 81 J4
Pound Park Rd CHARL SE7 126 C4
Pound Pl ELTH/MOT SE9 167 F1
Pound St CAR SM5 209 K3
Pountney Rd BTSEA SW11 141 F4
Poverest Rd STMC/STPC BR5 202 A2
Powder Mill La DART DA1 171 H4
WHTN TW2 154 E3
Powell Cl EDGE HA8 44 B2
Powell Gdns DAGE RM10 92 C2
Powell Rd BKHH IG9 39 G2
CLPT E5 86 D1
Power Rd CHSWK W4 117 H4
Powers Ct TWK TW1 156 E2
Powerscroft Rd CLPT E5 86 E2
SCUP DA14 186 D2
Powis Ct BUSH * WD23 28 D3
Powis Gdns GLDGN NW11 64 D4
NTGHL W11 100 D5
Powis Ms NTGHL W11 100 D5
Powis Pl BMSBY WC1N 5 F7
Powis Rd BOW E3 105 K2
Powis Sq NTGHL W11 100 D5
Powis St WOOL/PLUM SE18 127 F3
Powis Ter NTGHL W11 100 D5
Powlett Pl CAMTN * NW1 84 B5
Pownall Gdns HSLW TW3 135 G5
Pownall Rd HACK E8 86 C6
HSLW TW3 135 G5
Pownsett Ter IL IG1 90 C3
Powster Rd BMLY BR1 183 K1
Powys Cl BXLYHN DA7 128 E6
Powys La PLMGR N13 34 E6
Poynders Rd CLAP SW4 161 H2
Poynings Cl ORP BR6 202 D6
Poynings Rd ARCH N19 84 C1
Poynings Wy NFNCH/WDSP N12 46 E1
Poyntell Crs CHST BR7 185 J4
Poynter Rd EN EN1 24 B6
Poynton Rd TOTM N17 50 C5
Poyntz Rd BTSEA SW11 140 E3
Poyser St BETH E2 104 D2
Praed Ms BAY/PAD W2 8 B3
Praed St BAY/PAD W2 8 B3
Pragel St PLSTW E13 107 F1
Pragnell Rd LEE/GVPK SE12 166 A4
Prague Pl BRXS/STRHM SW2 141 K6
Prah Rd FSBYPK N4 67 G6
Prairie St VX/NE SW8 141 F3
Pratt Ms CAMTN NW1 4 A1
Pratt St CAMTN NW1 4 A1
Pratt Wk LBTH SE11 17 H6
Prayle Gv CRICK NW2 64 B5
Prebend Gdns CHSWK W4 118 C4
Prebend St IS N1 6 C1
The Precinct IS * N1 6 C2
Precinct Rd HYS/HAR UB3 94 E6
Premiere Pl POP/IOD E14 105 J6
Premier Park Rd WLSDN NW10 98 D1
Prentis Rd STRHM/NOR SW16 161 J6
Prentiss Ct CHARL SE7 126 C4
Presburg Rd NWMAL KT3 192 B2
Prescelly Pl EDGE HA8 44 B4
Prescot St WCHPL E1 13 K5
Prescott Av STMC/STPC BR5 201 G3
Prescott Cl EMPK RM11 75 K5
Prescott Pl CLAP SW4 141 J4
Presentation Ms
BRXS/STRHM SW2 162 A4
Presidents Dr WAP E1W 123 J1
President St FSBYE * EC1V 6 C4
Press Rd WLSDN NW10 81 F1
Prestage Wy POP/IOD E14 106 A6
Prestbury Rd FSTGT E7 89 G5
Prestbury Sq ELTH/MOT SE9 166 E6
Prested Rd BTSEA SW11 140 D5
Preston Av CHING E4 52 B2
Preston Cl STHWK * SE1 19 G6
WHTN TW2 155 K5
Preston Ct WOT/HER KT12 188 B5
Preston Dr BXLYHN DA7 148 E2
HOR/WEW KT19 207 G4
WAN E11 71 G2
Preston Gdns IL IG1 71 J3
WLSDN * NW10 81 G4
Preston Hl KTN/HRWW/W HA3 62 A4
Preston Pl RCHPK/HAM TW10 137 F6
WLSDN NW10 81 J4
Preston Rd NRWD SE19 180 C2
RYNPK SW20 176 D3
WAN E11 70 C3
WBLY HA9 62 A6
Prestons Rd HAYES BR2 214 E1
POP/IOD E14 106 A6
Preston Vls KUT * KT1 175 G5
Preston Waye
KTN/HRWW/W HA3 62 A5
Prestwich Ter CLAP * SW4 141 J6
Prestwick Cl NWDGN UB2 114 D5
Prestwick Rd OXHEY WD19 27 H5
Prestwood OXHEY * WD19 27 J4
Prestwood Av
KTN/HRWW/W HA3 61 H1
Prestwood Cl
KTN/HRWW/W HA3 61 H1
WOOL/PLUM SE18 148 B1
Prestwood Dr CRW RM5 56 E1
Prestwood Gdns CROY/NA CR0 196 D4
Prestwood St IS * N1 6 D3
Pretoria Av WALTH E17 69 G1
Pretoria Crs CHING E4 38 A3
Pretoria Pde LEW * SE13 144 D3
Pretoria Rd CAN/RD E16 106 D2
CHING E4 38 A3
IL IG1 90 B2
ROMW/RG RM7 74 E1
STRHM/NOR SW16 179 G2
TOTM N17 50 B2
WAN E11 70 B5
Pretoria Rd North UED N18 50 B2
Prevost Rd FBAR/BDGN N11 34 A4
Price Cl MLHL NW7 46 C2
TOOT SW17 160 E5
Price Rd CROY/NA CR0 211 H3
Price's St STHWK SE1 18 B1
Pricklers Hl BAR EN5 21 F6
Prickley Wd HAYES BR2 199 J5
Prideaux Pl ACT W3 99 F6
FSBYW WC1X 5 H4
Prideaux Rd BRXN/ST SW9 141 K4
Pridham Rd THHTH CR7 196 E1
Priestfield Rd FSTH SE23 164 B5
Priestlands Park Rd
BFN/LL DA15 168 A5
Priestley Cl STNW/STAM * N16 68 B4
Priestley Gdns CHDH RM6 73 H3
Priestley Rd MTCM CR4 179 F5
Priestley Wy CRICK NW2 63 J5
WALTH E17 51 F6
Priest Park Av RYLN/HDSTN HA2 60 A6
Priests Av ROM RM1 57 F5
Priests Br MORT/ESHN SW14 138 B4
Prima Rd BRXN/ST SW9 142 B1
Primrose Av ENC/FH EN2 23 K2
GDMY/SEVK IG3 73 G4
Primrose Cl CAT SE6 183 F1
RYLN/HDSTN HA2 77 K1
WLGTN SM6 195 G5
Primrose Dr WDR/YW UB7 112 A4
Primrose Gdns BUSH WD23 28 B2
HAMP NW3 83 J4
RSLP HA4 77 G3
Primrose Hl EMB EC4Y 11 K4
Primrose Hill Rd HAMP NW3 83 J4
Primrose Hill Studios
CAMTN NW1 84 A6
Primrose La CROY/NA CR0 197 K5
Primrose Ms CAMTN * NW1 83 K5
Primrose Rd LEY E10 69 K5
SWFD E18 53 F5
Primrose Sq HOM E9 86 E5
Primrose St SDTCH EC2A 13 G1
Primrose Wk EW KT17 207 H5
NWCR SE14 144 B1
Primrose Wy ALP/SUD HA0 97 K1
Primula St SHB W12 99 J6
Prince Albert STJWD NW8 2 D2
Prince Albert Rd STJWD NW8 2 C4
Prince Arthur Rd HAMP NW3 83 G3
Prince Charles Dr HDN NW4 64 A4
Prince Charles Rd
BKHTH/KID SE3 145 J2
Prince Charles Wy WLGTN SM6 210 B1
Prince Consort Dr CHST BR7 185 J4
Prince Consort Rd SKENS SW7 14 A4
Princedale Rd NTGHL W11 119 H1
Prince Edward Rd HOM E9 87 H4
Prince George Av
STHGT/OAK N14 22 C6
Prince George Rd
STNW/STAM N16 86 A2
Prince George's Av
RYNPK SW20 177 F5
Prince Georges Rd
WIM/MER SW19 178 C4
Prince Henry Rd CHARL SE7 146 C1
Prince Imperial Rd CHST BR7 185 G3
WOOL/PLUM SE18 146 E2
Prince John Rd ELTH/MOT SE9 146 D6
Princelet St WCHPL E1 13 K1
Prince of Orange La
GNWCH * SE10 145 F1
Prince of Wales Cl HDN NW4 63 K1
Prince of Wales Dr BTSEA SW11 140 E2
Prince of Wales Ga SKENS SW7 14 C2
Prince of Wales Pas
CAMTN * NW1 4 A5
Prince of Wales Rd
BKHTH/KID SE3 145 J2
CAN/RD E16 107 G5

KTTN NW5 84 A4
SUT SM1 194 C6
Prince of Wales Ter CHSWK W4 118 B5
KENS * W8 120 A2
Prince Regent La PLSTW E13 107 G3
Prince Regent Ms CAMTN NW1 4 A5
Prince Regent Rd HSLW TW3 135 H4
Prince Rd SNWD SE25 197 F2
Prince Rupert Rd
ELTH/MOT SE9 146 E5
Princes Ar MYFR/PICC W1J 10 B7
Princes Av ACT W3 117 H3
CAR SM5 209 K5
CDALE/KGS NW9 62 C1
FNCH N3 47 F4
MUSWH N10 48 B6
PLMGR N13 49 G1
STMC/STPC BR5 201 K2
SURB KT6 191 H6
WDGN N22 48 D4
WFD IG8 39 F6
Prince's Cl HPTN TW12 155 J6
CDALE/KGS NW9 62 C1
EDGE HA8 44 C1
SCUP DA14 168 E5
Princes Ct WBLY HA9 80 A3
Princes Dr HRW HA1 42 E6
Princes Gdns ACT W3 98 C5
EA W5 97 J3
SKENS SW7 14 B4
Prince's Ga SKENS SW7 14 C3
SKENS SW7 14 B4
Princes Gate Ct SKENS SW7 14 A3
Princes Gate Ms SKENS SW7 14 B4
Princes La MUSWH N10 48 A6
Prince's Ms BAY/PAD W2 100 E6
HMSMTH * W6 118 E5
Princes Pde GLDGN * NW11 64 C3
Princes Pk RAIN RM13 93 J5
Princes Park Av GLDGN NW11 64 C3
HYS/HAR UB3 94 B6
Princes Park Cir HYS/HAR UB3 94 B6
Princes Park Cl HYS/HAR UB3 94 B6
Princes Park La HYS/HAR UB3 94 B6
Princes Park Pde HYS/HAR UB3 94 B6
Princes Pl NTGHL W11 119 H1
Prince's Pln HAYES BR2 200 D4
Princes Ri LEW SE13 145 F3
Princes Riverside Rd
BERM/RHTH SE16 124 A1
Prince's Rd HPTN TW12 155 J6
MORT/ESHN SW14 138 A4
WIM/MER SW19 177 K2
BARK/HLT IG6 72 D1
BKHH IG9 39 G4
DART DA1 170 E2
DART DA1 171 J3
FELT TW13 153 J5
KUTN/CMB KT2 175 H4
PGE/AN SE20 182 A2
RCH/KEW TW9 137 G2
RCHPK/HAM TW10 137 G6
ROM RM1 75 J2
UED N18 36 E6
WEA W13 116 C1
Princess Alice Wy THMD SE28 127 J2
Princess Av WBLY HA9 62 A6
Princess Crs FSBYPK N4 67 H6
Princesses Pde DART * DA1 150 C6
Princess La RSLP HA4 58 C5
Princess Louise Cl BAY/PAD W2 8 B1
Princess May Rd
STNW/STAM N16 86 A2
Princess Ms HAMP NW3 83 H4
Princess Pde ORP * BR6 216 A1
Prince's Sq BAY/PAD W2 100 E6
Princess Rd CAMTN NW1 84 A6
CROY/NA CR0 196 D3
KIL/WHAMP NW6 100 E1
Princess St BXLYHN DA7 149 G4
STHWK SE1 18 B5
Prince's St LOTH EC2R 12 E4
RCH/KEW TW9 137 F5
CONDST W1S 9 K4
SUT SM1 209 H2
TOTM N17 50 A2
Prince's Ter PLSTW E13 89 F6
Prince St DEPT SE8 124 C6
Princes Vw DART DA1 171 K3
Princes Wy BKHH IG9 39 G4
CROY/NA CR0 211 F3
RSLP HA4 77 J2
WIM/MER SW19 159 G2
WWKM BR4 214 D2
Prince's Yd NTGHL W11 119 H1
Princethorpe Rd SYD SE26 164 A6
Princeton St GINN WC1R 11 G2
Pringle Gdns STRHM/NOR SW16 161 H6
Printers Inn Ct FLST/FETLN EC4A 11 J3
Printinghouse La HYS/HAR UB3 113 H2
Printing House Yd BETH * E2 7 H5
Priolo Rd CHARL SE7 126 B5
Prior Av BELMT SM2 209 J5
Prior Bolton St IS N1 85 H4
Prioress Rd WNWD SE27 162 C5
Prioress St STHWK SE1 19 F5
Prior Rd IL IG1 90 A1
Priors Cft WALTH E17 51 G5
Priors Fld NTHLT UB5 77 J4
Priorsford Av STMC/STPC BR5 202 B1
Priors Gdns RSLP HA4 77 G3
Priors Md EN EN1 24 A2
Prior St GNWCH SE10 145 F1
The Priory BKHTH/KID SE3 145 J4
CROY/NA * CR0 211 G1
ORP * BR6 202 C4
Priory Av ALP/SUD HA0 79 F2
CEND/HSY/T N8 66 D1
CHEAM SM3 208 B2
CHING E4 37 H5
CHSWK W4 118 B3
STMC/STPC BR5 201 J3
WALTH E17 69 J2
Priory Cl ALP/SUD HA0 79 F2
BECK BR3 182 B6
BMLY BR1 184 E4
CHING E4 37 H5
DART DA1 151 F6
HPTN TW12 172 E4
HYS/HAR UB3 95 F6
RSLP HA4 58 D5
STAN HA7 29 F5
STHGT/OAK N14 22 B6
SWFD E18 52 E4
TRDG/WHET N20 32 D2
WIM/MER * SW19 178 A4
Priory Cottages EA * W5 98 B4
Priory Ct BLKFR * EC4V 12 B4
VX/NE SW8 141 J2
WALTH E17 51 H6
Priory Crs ALP/SUD HA0 79 G1
CHEAM SM3 208 B2
NRWD SE19 180 D3
Priory Dr ABYW SE2 128 E5
STAN HA7 29 F5
Priory Field Dr EDGE HA8 30 D6
Priory Gdns ALP/SUD HA0 79 G2
BARN SW13 138 C4
CHSWK * W4 118 B4
DART DA1 151 G6
HGT N6 66 B3
HPTN TW12 172 E3
SNWD SE25 197 G1
Priory Green Est IS N1 5 G2
Priory Gv CLAP SW4 141 K2
Priory Hl ALP/SUD HA0 79 G2
DART DA1 171 G1
Priory La E/WMO/HCT KT8 189 F1
PUT/ROE SW15 138 C6
Priory Leas ELTH/MOT * SE9 166 D3
Priory Ms EMPK RM11 75 K5
Priory Pk BKHTH/KID SE3 145 J4
Priory Park Rd ALP/SUD HA0 79 G2
KIL/WHAMP NW6 82 D6
Priory Pl DART DA1 171 G1
Priory Rd BARK IG11 90 D5
CEND/HSY/T N8 66 D1
CHEAM SM3 208 B2
CHSGTN KT9 206 A1
CHSWK W4 118 A3
CROY/NA CR0 196 B4
DART DA1 151 G5
EHAM E6 89 H6
HPTN TW12 172 E3
HSLW TW3 135 H6
KIL/WHAMP NW6 83 F5
MUSWH N10 66 C1
RCH/KEW TW9 117 H6
WIM/MER SW19 178 C3
Priory St BOW E3 105 K2
Priory Ter KIL/WHAMP NW6 83 F6
Priory Vw BUSH WD23 28 E2
Priory Vls FBAR/BDGN * N11 47 K2
Priory Wk WBPTN SW10 120 B5
Priory Wy NWDGN UB2 114 C3
RYLN/HDSTN HA2 60 B1
WDR/YW UB7 112 B6
Pritchard's Rd BETH E2 104 C1
Priter Rd BERM/RHTH * SE16 123 H3
Private Rd EN EN1 23 K6
Probert Rd BRXS/STRHM SW2 142 B6
Probyn Rd BRXS/STRHM SW2 162 C4
Procter St GINN WC1R 11 G2
Proctor Cl MTCM CR4 179 F4
Proctors Cl EBED/NFELT TW14 153 K3
Progress Wy CROY/NA CR0 196 A6
EN EN1 24 C6
WDGN N22 49 G4
The Promenade CHSWK W4 138 B2
EDGE * HA8 44 C1
Promenade Approach Rd
CHSWK W4 138 B1
Prospect Cl BELV DA17 129 H4
HEST TW5 134 E2
RSLP HA4 59 H4
SYD SE26 163 J6
Prospect Cottages
WAND/EARL SW18 139 K5
Prospect Crs WHTN TW2 155 H1
Prospect Hl WALTH E17 69 K1
Prospect Pl CHSWK W4 118 A5
CRICK NW2 82 D1
DART DA1 171 H1
EFNCH N2 65 H1
HAYES BR2 184 A6
ROMW/RG RM7 56 E5
RYNPK SW20 176 E3
WAP E1W 123 K1
Prospect Rd BAR EN5 20 E5
CRICK NW2 82 D1
SURB KT6 190 D3
WFD IG8 53 G1
Prospect St BERM/RHTH SE16 123 J2
Prospect V WOOL/PLUM SE18 126 D4
Prospero Rd ARCH N19 66 D5
Prothero Gdns HDN NW4 63 K2
Prothero Rd FUL/PGN SW6 139 H1
Prout Gv WLSDN NW10 81 G2
Prout Rd CLPT E5 86 D1
Providence Cl HOM * E9 87 F6
Providence Ct MYFR/PKLN W1K 9 H5
Providence La HYS/HAR UB3 133 G1
Providence Pl IS N1 6 A1
ROMW/RG RM7 56 B4
Providence Rd WDR/YW UB7 112 B1
Providence Row Cl BETH E2 104 D2
Providence Sq STHWK SE1 19 G2
Providence Yd BETH * E2 104 C2
Provincial Ter PGE/AN * SE20 182 A3
Provost Est IS N1 6 E4
Provost Rd HAMP NW3 83 K5
Provost St IS N1 6 E3
Prowse Av BUSH WD23 28 C4
Prowse Pl CAMTN NW1 84 C5
Pruden Cl STHGT/OAK * N14 34 C4
Prusom St WAP E1W 123 J1
Pudding La MON EC3R 13 F5
Pudding Mill La SRTFD E15 87 K6
Puddle Dock BLKFR EC4V 12 B5
Puffin Cl BARK IG11 109 H2
CROY/NA CR0 198 A2
Pulborough Rd
WAND/EARL SW18 159 J2
Pulborough Wy HSLWW TW4 134 B5
Pulford Rd SEVS/STOTM N15 67 K3
Pulham Av EFNCH N2 65 G1
Puller Rd BAR EN5 20 C3
Pulleyns Av EHAM E6 107 J2
Pullman Gdns PUT/ROE SW15 159 F1
Pullman Ms LEE/GVPK SE12 166 A5
Pullman Pl ELTH/MOT SE9 146 D6
Pulross Rd BRXN/ST SW9 142 A4
Pulteney Cl BOW E3 87 H6
Pulteney Rd SWFD E18 53 F6
Pulton Pl FUL/PGN SW6 139 K1
Puma Ct WCHPL E1 13 J1
Pump Aly BTFD TW8 136 E1
Pump Cl NTHLT UB5 96 A1
Pump Ct EMB * EC4Y 11 J4
Pump House Cl HAYES BR2 183 J5
Pumping Station Rd
CHSWK W4 138 B1
Pump La HYS/HAR UB3 113 K2
NWCR SE14 143 K1
Punderson's Gdns BETH E2 104 D2
Purbeck Av NWMAL KT3 192 C3
Purbeck Dr CRICK NW2 64 B6
Purbeck Rd EMPK RM11 75 J4
Purbrook St STHWK SE1 19 H4
Purcell Crs FUL/PGN * SW6 119 G6
Purcell Ms WLSDN * NW10 81 G5
Purcell Rd GFD/PVL UB6 96 B4
Purcells Av EDGE HA8 44 C1
Purcell St IS N1 7 G2
Purchese St CAMTN NW1 4 C2
Purdy St BOW E3 105 K3
Purelake Ms LEW * SE13 145 G4
Purland Cl BCTR RM8 74 B5
Purland Rd THMD SE28 128 A2
Purleigh Av WFD IG8 53 J2
Purley Av CRICK NW2 64 C6
Purley Cl CLAY IG5 54 A5
Purley Pl IS N1 85 H5
Purley Rd ED N9 35 K5
SAND/SEL CR2 211 K5
Purley Wy CROY/NA CR0 196 A5
CROY/NA CR0 211 G2
Purneys Rd ELTH/MOT SE9 146 C5
Purrett Rd WOOL/PLUM SE18 128 A5
Pursers Cross Rd
FUL/PGN * SW6 139 J2
Pursewardens Cl WEA W13 116 D1
Pursley Rd MLHL NW7 45 K3
Purves Rd WLSDN NW10 99 K2
Putney Br PUT/ROE SW15 139 H4
Putney Bridge Ap
PUT/ROE SW15 139 H4
Putney Bridge Rd
PUT/ROE SW15 139 H5
Putney Common
PUT/ROE SW15 139 F4
Putney Ex PUT/ROE * SW15 139 G5
Putney Heath PUT/ROE SW15 158 E1
Putney Heath La
PUT/ROE SW15 159 G1
Putney High St PUT/ROE SW15 139 H5
Putney Hl PUT/ROE SW15 159 G2
Putney Park Av PUT/ROE SW15 138 D5
Putney Park La PUT/ROE SW15 138 E5
Puttenham Cl OXHEY WD19 27 G5
Pycombe Cnr NFNCH/WDSP N12 32 D6
Pycroft Wy ED N9 36 C6
Pylbrook Rd SUT SM1 208 E1
Pym Cl EBAR EN4 21 H6
Pymers Md DUL SE21 162 D3
Pymmes Brook Trail EBAR EN4 21 J6
EBAR EN4 33 K2
PLMGR N13 34 E6
Pymmes Cl PLMGR N13 49 F1
TOTM N17 50 D4
Pymmes Gdns North ED N9 36 B5
Pymmes Gdns South ED N9 36 B5
Pymmes Green Rd
FBAR/BDGN N11 34 B6
Pymmes Rd PLMGR N13 48 E2
Pymms Brook Dr EBAR EN4 21 J5
Pyne Rd SURB KT6 191 H5
Pynham Cl ABYW SE2 128 B3
Pynnacles Cl STAN HA7 43 H1
Pyrland Rd HBRY N5 85 K3
RCHPK/HAM TW10 157 G1
Pyrmont Gv WNWD SE27 162 C5
Pyrmont Rd CHSWK W4 117 H6
Pytchley Crs NRWD SE19 180 D2
Pytchley Rd EDUL SE22 143 F4

Q

The Quadrangle BAY/PAD W2 8 C3
HNHL * SE24 142 D6
WBPTN * SW10 140 B2
The Quadrant BELMT SM2 209 G4
BXLYHN DA7 148 E1
EDGE * HA8 44 C2
NKENS * W10 100 B2
RCH/KEW TW9 136 E6
RYLN/HDSTN * HA2 42 D6
RYNPK SW20 177 H4
Quadrant Ar REGST W1B 10 B6
Quadrant Cl HDN * NW4 63 K2
Quadrant Gv HAMP NW3 83 K3
Quadrant Rd RCH/KEW TW9 136 E5
THHTH CR7 196 C1
Quad Rd WBLY * HA9 79 K1
Quaggy Wk BKHTH/KID SE3 145 K5
Quainton St WLSDN NW10 81 F1
Quaker La NWDGN UB2 115 F3
Quakers Course CDALE/KGS NW9 45 H4
Quakers Pl FSTGT E7 89 H3
Quaker St WCHPL E1 7 J7
Quakers Wk WCHMH N21 35 K1
Quality Ct LINN WC2A 11 J3
Quantock Cl HYS/HAR UB3 133 G1
Quantock Gdns CRICK * NW2 64 B6
Quantock Rd BXLYHN DA7 150 B3
Quarles Cl CRW RM5 56 C3
Quarrendon St FUL/PGN SW6 139 K2
Quarr Rd CAR SM5 194 C3
Quarry Ms PUR RM19 131 K4
Quarry Park Rd SUT SM1 208 D4
Quarry Ri SUT SM1 208 D4
Quarry Rd WAND/EARL SW18 160 B1
Quartermile La LEY E10 87 K2
Quatre Ports CHING * E4 52 B1
Quay House POP/IOD * E14 124 D2
Quebec Ms MBLAR W1H 9 F4
Quebec Rd GNTH/NBYPK IG2 72 C4
YEAD UB4 95 G6
Quebec Wy BERM/RHTH SE16 124 A2
Queen Adelaide Rd
PGE/AN SE20 181 K2
Queen Anne Av HAYES BR2 183 K6
Queen Anne Dr ESH/CLAY KT10 204 E5
Queen Anne Ga BXLYHN DA7 148 E4
Queen Anne Ms CAVSQ/HST W1G 9 K2
Queen Anne Rd HOM E9 87 F4
Queen Annes Cl WHTN TW2 155 J5
Queen Anne's Gdns CHSWK W4 118 B3
EA W5 117 F2
EN EN1 36 A1
MTCM * CR4 178 E6
Queen Anne's Ga STJSPK SW1H 16 C3
Queen Anne's Gv CHSWK W4 118 B3
EA W5 117 F2
EN EN1 35 K2
Queen Anne's Pl EN EN1 36 A1
Queen Anne St CAVSQ/HST W1G 9 J2
Queen Anne Ter WAP * E1W 104 D6
Queenborough Gdns CHST BR7 185 J2
GNTH/NBYPK IG2 72 A1
Queen Caroline Est
HMSMTH W6 119 F5
Queen Caroline St HMSMTH W6 119 F5
Queen Elizabeth Buildings
EMB * EC4Y 11 J5
Queen Elizabeth College
GNWCH * SE10 145 F1
Queen Elizabeth Gdns
MRDN SM4 193 K1
Queen Elizabeth Rd
KUTN/CMB * KT2 175 G4
WALTH E17 51 G6
Queen Elizabeth's Cl
STNW/STAM N16 67 K6
Queen Elizabeth's Dr
STHGT/OAK N14 34 E3
Queen Elizabeth St STHWK SE1 19 H2
Queen Elizabeth's Wk
STNW/STAM N16 67 K6
WLGTN SM6 210 D2
Queen Elizabeth Wk
BARN SW13 138 D2
Queenhithe BLKFR EC4V 12 D6
Queen Margaret's Gv IS N1 86 A3
Queen Mary Av MRDN SM4 193 G2
Queen Mary Cl CHSGTN KT9 206 C1
ROM RM1 75 H3
Queen Mary Rd NRWD SE19 180 C2
Queen Mary's Av CAR SM5 209 K5
Queen Mother Ga BAY/PAD W2 15 H1
Queens Acre CHEAM SM3 208 B5
Queens Av FELT TW13 154 B6
FNCH N3 47 G3
GFD/PVL UB6 96 B5
KTN/HRWW/W HA3 43 H6
MUSWH N10 48 A6
TRDG/WHET N20 33 H4
WCHMH N21 35 H3
WFD IG8 53 F1
Queensberry Ms West
SKENS * SW7 14 A6
Queensberry Pl FSTGT E7 89 H3
SKENS SW7 14 A6
Queensberry Wy SKENS * SW7 14 A6
Queensborough Ms
BAY/PAD * W2 101 G6
Queensborough Studios
BAY/PAD * W2 101 F6
Queensborough Ter
BAY/PAD W2 101 F6
Queensbridge Pk ISLW TW7 155 J1
Queensbridge Rd HACK E8 86 B5
Queensbury Rd ALP/SUD HA0 98 B1
CDALE/KGS NW9 63 F4
Queensbury Station Pde
EDGE HA8 44 B6
Queensbury St IS N1 85 J5
Queens Circ VX/NE SW8 141 G1
Queens Cl ESH/CLAY * KT10 204 B2
EDGE HA8 44 C1
WLGTN SM6 210 B3
Queens Club Gdns
WKENS * W14 119 H6
WKENS W14 119 H6
Queens Club Ter WKENS * W14 119 J6
Queenscourt WBLY HA9 80 A2
Queen's Crs KTTN NW5 84 A4
RCHPK/HAM TW10 137 G6
Queenscroft Rd ELTH/MOT SE9 146 C6
Queensdale Crs NTGHL W11 119 G1
Queensdale Pl NTGHL W11 119 H1
Queensdale Rd NTGHL W11 119 G1
Queensdale Wk NTGHL W11 119 H1
Queens Down Rd CLPT E5 86 D2
Queens Dr BRYLDS KT5 191 H4
EA W5 98 B5
FSBYPK N4 67 H6
LEY E10 69 J4
THDIT KT7 190 B3
Queen's Elm Sq WBPTN SW10 120 C5
Queen's Gdns BAY/PAD W2 101 G6
EA W5 97 J4
HDN NW4 64 A2
HEST TW5 134 D2
RAIN RM13 111 F1
Queens Garth FSTH * SE23 163 K4
Queen's Ga SKENS SW7 120 B2
Queensgate Gdns
PUT/ROE SW15 138 E5
Queens Gate Gdns CHST BR7 185 J4
SKENS * SW7 120 B3
SKENS SW7 120 B3
Queen's Gate Ms SKENS SW7 120 B3
Queensgate Pl KIL/WHAMP NW6 82 E5
Queen's Gate Pl SKENS * SW7 120 B3
Queen's Gate Place Ms
SKENS * SW7 120 B3
Queen's Gate Ter SKENS * SW7 120 B3
Queen's Gv STJWD NW8 2 A1
Queen's Grove Rd CHING E4 38 B3
Queen's Head St IS N1 6 B1
Queens Keep TWK * TW1 156 D1
Queensland Av UED N18 49 J2
WIM/MER SW19 178 A4
Queensland Pl HOLWY N7 85 G2
Queensland Rd HOLWY N7 85 G2
Queens La MUSWH N10 48 B6
Queensmead STJWD NW8 83 H6
Queen's Mead Rd HAYES BR2 183 J5
Queensmere Cl
WIM/MER SW19 159 G4
Queensmere Rd
WIM/MER SW19 159 G4
Queensmill Rd FUL/PGN SW6 139 G1
Queens Pde CEND/HSY/T * N8 67 H1
CRICK * NW2 82 A4
EA * W5 98 B5
FBAR/BDGN * N11 47 K1
FBAR/BDGN * N11 48 E3
HDN * NW4 63 K2
Queens Parade Cl
FBAR/BDGN N11 47 K1
Queens Park Gdns FELT * TW13 153 J5
Queen's Pl MRDN SM4 193 K1
Queens promenade SURB KT6 190 E1
Queen Sq BMSBY WC1N 5 F7
Queen's Ride BARN SW13 138 E4
Queen's Ri RCHPK/HAM TW10 157 G1
Queens Rd BAR EN5 20 B4
BARK IG11 90 C5
BECK BR3 182 B5
BKHH IG9 39 F4
BMLY BR1 183 K5
CHST BR7 185 G2
CROY/NA CR0 196 C3
EA W5 98 A5
ED N9 36 D4
EN EN1 24 A5
ERITH DA8 130 B6
FBAR/BDGN N11 48 E3
FELT TW13 154 A3
FNCH N3 47 G4
HDN NW4 64 A2
HPTN TW12 155 G6
HSLW TW3 135 G4
HYS/HAR UB3 94 C5
KUTN/CMB KT2 175 H3
MORT/ESHN SW14 138 A4
MRDN SM4 193 K1
MTCM CR4 178 C6
NWDGN UB2 114 C2
NWMAL KT3 192 C1
PECK SE15 143 K2
PLSTW E13 89 F6
RCHPK/HAM TW10 157 G1
TEDD TW11 174 A2
THDIT KT7 190 A2
TWK TW1 156 A3
WALTH E17 69 H3
WAN E11 70 C4
WDR/YW UB7 112 C2
WELL DA16 148 C3
WIM/MER SW19 177 K2
WLGTN SM6 210 B3
Queen's Rd West PLSTW E13 106 E1
Queens Rw WALW * SE17 122 E6
WALW SE17 122 E6
Queen's Ter ISLW TW7 136 B5
PLSTW E13 89 F6
STJWD NW8 2 A1
THDIT * KT7 190 B3
WCHPL * E1 104 E3
Queens Ter Cottages
HNWL * W7 115 K2
Queensthorpe Ms SYD * SE26 164 A6
Queensthorpe Rd SYD SE26 164 A6
Queens Town Gdns RAIN RM13 111 H2
Queenstown Rd CHEL SW3 121 G6
VX/NE SW8 141 G3
Queen St BXLYHN DA7 149 G4
CROY/NA CR0 211 J2
ERITH * DA8 130 B6
MANHO EC4N 12 D4
MYFR/PICC W1J 9 J7
ROMW/RG RM7 75 F3
TOTM N17 50 A2
Queen Street Pl CANST EC4R 12 D6
Queensville Rd CLAP SW4 161 J2
Queens Wk ASHF TW15 152 A6
CDALE/KGS NW9 62 E6
CHING E4 38 B3
EA W5 97 J3
HRW HA1 60 E1
RSLP HA4 77 G1
Queens Walk Ter RSLP * HA4 77 G1
Queens Wy FELT TW13 154 B6
HDN NW4 64 A2
Queensway BAY/PAD W2 101 F6
CROY/NA CR0 211 F3
PEND EN3 24 E5
STMC/STPC BR5 201 H2
SUN TW16 172 A5
WWKM BR4 214 E2
Queens Well Av
TRDG/WHET N20 33 J6
Queenswood Av HEST TW5 134 E3
HPTN TW12 173 G2
THHTH CR7 196 B2
WALTH E17 52 A4
WLGTN SM6 210 D2
Queenswood Gdns WAN E11 70 E5
Queenswood Pk FNCH N3 46 C5
Queenswood Rd BFN/LL DA15 148 A6
FSTH SE23 164 B5
Queen's Wood Rd HGT N6 66 B3
Queen's Yd FITZ W1T 4 B7
Queen Victoria Av ALP/SUD HA0 79 K5
Queen Victoria St BLKFR EC4V 12 A5
Queen Victoria Ter WAP * E1W 104 D6
Quemerford Rd HOLWY N7 85 F3
Quentin Pl LEW SE13 145 H4
Quentin Rd BKHTH/KID SE3 145 H4
Quernmore Cl BMLY BR1 183 K2
Quernmore Rd BMLY BR1 183 K2
FSBYPK N4 67 G3
Querrin St FUL/PGN SW6 140 B3
Questor DART * DA1 171 J4
Quex Ms KIL/WHAMP NW6 82 E6
Quex Rd KIL/WHAMP NW6 82 E6
Quick Rd CHSWK W4 118 B5
Quicks Rd WIM/MER SW19 178 A3
Quick St IS N1 6 B3
Quickswood HAMP NW3 83 J5
Quiet Nook HAYES BR2 215 H1
Quill St EA W5 98 A2
FSBYPK N4 85 G1
Quilp St STHWK SE1 18 C2
Quilter Rd STMC/STPC BR5 202 D5
Quilter St BETH E2 104 C2
WOOL/PLUM SE18 128 A5
Quintin Av RYNPK SW20 177 H4
Quinton Cl BECK BR3 183 F6
HEST TW5 134 A1
WLGTN SM6 210 B2
Quinton Rd THDIT KT7 190 B5
Quinton St WAND/EARL SW18 160 B4
Quixley St POP/IOD E14 106 B6
Quorn Rd EDUL SE22 143 F5

R

Rabbit Rw KENS * W8 119 K1
Rabbits Rd MNPK E12 89 J2
Rabournmead Dr RSLP HA4 77 J3
Raby Rd NWMAL KT3 192 A1
Raby St POP/IOD * E14 105 G5
Raccoon Wy HSLWW TW4 134 B3
Rachel Cl BARK/HLT IG6 54 D6
Rackham Cl WELL DA16 148 C3
Rackham Ms STRHM/NOR SW16 179 H2
Racton Rd FUL/PGN SW6 119 K6
Radbourne Av EA W5 116 D4
Radbourne Cl CLPT E5 87 F2
Radbourne Ct
KTN/HRWW/W * HA3 61 H3
Radbourne Crs WALTH E17 52 B6
Radbourne Rd BAL SW12 161 H2
Radcliffe Av ENC/FH EN2 23 J2
WLSDN NW10 99 J1

Radcliffe Gdns CAR SM5 209 J5
Radcliffe Rd CROY/NA CR0 197 G6
KTN/HRWW/W HA3 43 G5
STHWK SE1 19 H4
WCHMH N21 35 H3
Radcliffe Wy NTHLT UB5 95 H2
Radcot St LBTH SE11 122 B5
Raddington Rd NKENS W10 100 C4
Radfield Wy ELTH/MOT SE9 167 J2
Radford Est WLSDN * NW10 99 G2
Radford Rd LEW SE13 165 F1
Radford Wy BARK IG11 109 F2
Radipole Rd FUL/PGN SW6 139 J2
Radius Pk EBED/NFELT * TW14 133 J5
Radland Rd CAN/RD E16 106 E5
Radlet Av SYD SE26 163 J5
Radlett Cl FSTGT E7 88 D4
Radlett Pl STJWD NW8 2 C1
Radley Av GDMY/SEVK IG3 91 F2
Radley Cl EBED/NFELT TW14 153 J3
Radley Ct BERM/RHTH SE16 124 A2
Radley Gdns KTN/HRWW/W HA3 62 A1
Radley Ms KENS W8 119 K3
Radley Rd TOTM N17 50 A5
Radley's La SWFD E18 52 E5
Radleys Md DAGE RM10 92 D4
Radley Sq CLPT * E5 68 E6
Radley Ter CAN/RD * E16 106 D4
Radlix Rd LEY E10 69 J5
Radnor Av HRW HA1 60 E2
WELL DA16 148 C6
Radnor Cl CHST BR7 185 K2
MTCM CR4 195 K2
Radnor Crs REDBR IG4 71 K2
WOOL/PLUM SE18 148 B1
Radnor Gdns EN EN1 24 A2
TWK TW1 156 A4
Radnor Ms BAY/PAD W2 8 B4
Radnor Pl BAY/PAD W2 8 C4
Radnor Rd HRW HA1 60 D2
KIL/WHAMP NW6 82 C6
PECK SE15 143 H1
TWK TW1 156 A4
Radnor St FSBYE EC1V 6 D5
Radnor Ter WKENS W14 119 J4
Radnor Wk CHEL SW3 120 D5
CROY/NA CR0 198 B4
Radnor Wy WLSDN NW10 98 D3
Radstock Av KTN/HRWW/W HA3 43 G6
Radstock Cl FBAR/BDGN N11 48 A1
Radstock St BTSEA * SW11 140 D1
Raeburn Av BRYLDS KT5 191 J3
DART DA1 150 E6
Raeburn Cl EFNCH N2 65 G3
KUT KT1 174 E3
Raeburn Rd BFN/LL DA15 167 K1
EDGE HA8 44 C5
YEAD UB4 94 B1
Raeburn St BRXS/STRHM SW2 141 K5
Rafford Wy BMLY BR1 184 A5
Raggleswood CHST BR7 185 F4
Raglan Cl HSLWW TW4 134 D6
Raglan Ct CROY/NA CR0 211 H3
Raglan Gdns OXHEY WD19 27 F3
Raglan Rd BELV DA17 129 G4
EN EN1 36 A2
HAYES BR2 200 B1
WALTH E17 70 A2
WOOL/PLUM SE18 127 H5
Raglan St KTTN NW5 84 B4
Raglan Ter RYLN/HDSTN * HA2 78 B2
Raglan Vls WALTH * E17 70 A2
Raglan Wy NTHLT UB5 78 D4
Ragley Cl ACT W3 117 K2
Raider Cl ROMW/RG RM7 56 D4
Railey Ms KTTN NW5 84 C3
Railshead Rd ISLW TW7 136 C5
Railton Rd HNHL SE24 142 B6
Railway Ap HRW HA1 61 F1
STHWK SE1 13 F7
TWK TW1 156 B2
WLGTN * SM6 210 B4
Railway Ar BRXN/ST * SW9 142 B5
Railway Av BERM/RHTH SE16 123 K2
Railway Cottages SHB * W12 119 F2
SRTFD * E15 106 C1
WIM/MER * SW19 160 A6
Railway Gv NWCR SE14 144 C1
Railway Pl BELV DA17 129 H3
Railway Ri EDUL SE22 143 F5
Railway Rd TEDD TW11 155 K6
Railway Side BARN SW13 138 B4
Railway Station Whf LEY * E10 69 G5
Railway St BCTR RM8 73 J5
IS N1 5 F3
Railway Ter FELT TW13 153 K3
LEW SE13 144 E6
WALTH E17 52 A4
Rainborough Cl WBLY HA9 80 E4
Rainbow Av POP/IOD E14 124 E5
Rainbow Ct OXHEY WD19 27 G1
Rainbow St CMBW SE5 143 F1
Raine St WAP E1W 123 J1
Rainham Cl BTSEA SW11 160 D1
ELTH/MOT SE9 167 K1
Rainham Rd RAIN RM13 93 H5
RAIN RM13 111 J2
WLSDN NW10 100 A2
Rainham Rd North DAGE RM10 74 D6
Rainham Rd South DAGE RM10 92 E2
Rainhill Wy BOW E3 105 J2
Rainsborough Av DEPT SE8 124 B4
Rainsford Rd WLSDN NW10 98 D2
Rainsford St BAY/PAD W2 8 C3
Rainsford Wy HCH RM12 75 J5
Rainton Rd CHARL SE7 125 H5
Rainville Rd HMSMTH W6 119 F6
Raisins Hl PIN HA5 41 G6
Raith Av STHGT/OAK N14 34 D5
Raleana Rd POP/IOD E14 125 F1
Raleigh Av WLGTN SM6 210 D2
YEAD UB4 95 F4
Raleigh Cl ERITH DA8 130 C6
HDN NW4 64 A2
PIN HA5 59 H4
RSLP HA4 58 D6
Raleigh Dr BRYLDS KT5 191 K5
ESH/CLAY KT10 204 D3
TRDG/WHET N20 33 J5
Raleigh Gdns MTCM CR4 178 E6
Raleigh Ms IS N1 6 B1
ORP BR6 217 F3
Raleigh Rd CEND/HSY/T N8 67 G1
ENC/FH EN2 23 K5
FELT TW13 153 J4
MUSWH N10 47 J4
NWDGN UB2 114 D5
PGE/AN SE20 182 A3
RCH/KEW TW9 137 G4
Raleigh St IS N1 6 B1
Raleigh Wy FELT TW13 172 B1
STHGT/OAK N14 34 D3
Ralph Perring Ct BECK BR3 198 D1
Ralston St CHEL SW3 120 E5
Ralston Wy OXHEY WD19 27 H4
Rama Cl STRHM/NOR SW16 179 K3
Ramac Wy CHARL SE7 126 A4
Rambler Cl STRHM/NOR SW16 161 H6
Rame Cl TOOT SW17 179 F1
Ramilles Cl BRXS/STRHM SW2 161 K1
Ramillies Pl SOHO/CST W1F 10 A4
Ramillies Rd BFN/LL DA15 168 C1
CHSWK W4 118 A3
MLHL NW7 31 G4
Ramillies St SOHO/CST W1F 10 A4
Ramones Ter MTCM * CR4 195 H1
Rampart St WCHPL E1 104 D5
Ram Pas KUT KT1 174 E5
Rampayne St PIM SW1V 121 J5
Rampton Cl CHING E4 37 J5
Ramsay Gdns GPK RM2 57 K4
Ramsay Rd ACT W3 117 K3
FSTGT E7 88 D2
Ramscroft Cl ED N9 36 A2
Ramsdale Rd TOOT SW17 179 F1
Ramsden Cl STMC/STPC BR5 202 D5
Ramsden Dr CRW RM5 56 C3
Ramsden Ga BAL * SW12 161 G2
Ramsden Rd BAL SW12 161 F2
ERITH DA8 150 A1
FBAR/BDGN N11 47 K1
ORP BR6 202 C4
Ramsey Cl CDALE/KGS NW9 63 H3
GFD/PVL UB6 78 D3
Ramsey Rd THHTH CR7 196 A3
Ramsey St BETH E2 104 C3
Ramsey Wk IS * N1 85 K4
Ramsey Wy STHGT/OAK N14 34 C2
Ramsgate St HACK * E8 86 B4
Ramsgill Ap GNTH/NBYPK IG2 73 F1
Ramsgill Dr GNTH/NBYPK IG2 73 F2
Rams Gv CHDH RM6 74 A1
Ram St WAND/EARL SW18 140 A6
Ramulis Dr YEAD UB4 95 J3
Ramus Wood Av ORP BR6 216 E3
Rancliffe Gdns ELTH/MOT SE9 146 D5
Rancliffe Rd EHAM E6 107 J1
Randall Av CRICK NW2 63 G6
Randall Cl BTSEA SW11 140 D2
ERITH DA8 129 K6
Randall Pl GNWCH SE10 145 F1
Randall Rd LBTH SE11 122 A5
Randall Rw LBTH SE11 17 G7
Randell's Rd IS N1 84 E6
Randisbourne Gdns CAT * SE6 164 E5
Randle Rd RCHPK/HAM TW10 156 D6
Randlesdown Rd CAT SE6 164 D6
Randolph Ap CAN/RD E16 107 G5
Randolph Av MV/WKIL W9 101 F1
Randolph Cl BXLYHN DA7 149 K4
KUTN/CMB * KT2 175 K1
Randolph Crs MV/WKIL W9 101 G3
Randolph Gdns
KIL/WHAMP NW6 101 F1
Randolph Ms MV/WKIL W9 101 G3
Randolph Rd HAYES BR2 200 E5
MV/WKIL W9 101 G3
STHL * UB1 114 E2
WALTH * E17 69 K2
Randon Cl PIN HA5 42 B5
Ranelagh Av BARN SW13 138 D3
FUL/PGN SW6 139 J4
Ranelagh Cl EDGE HA8 30 C6
Ranelagh Dr EDGE HA8 30 C6
TWK TW1 136 C5
Ranelagh Gdns CHSWK W4 137 K1
FUL/PGN SW6 139 H4
IL IG1 72 A5
WAN E11 71 G2
Ranelagh Gv BGVA SW1W 121 F5
Ranelagh Pl NWMAL KT3 192 B2
Ranelagh Rd ALP/SUD HA0 79 K3
EA W5 116 E2
EHAM E6 90 A6
PIM SW1V 121 H5
SRTFD E15 88 C6
STHL UB1 114 C1
TOTM N17 50 A6
WAN E11 88 C2
WDGN N22 49 F4
WLSDN NW10 99 H1
Ranfurly Rd SUT SM1 193 K6
Rangefield Rd BMLY BR1 183 K2
Rangemoor Rd
SEVS/STOTM N15 68 B2
Rangers Rd BKHH IG9 38 E2
Rangeworth Pl BFN/LL DA15 168 A5
Rangoon St TWRH * EC3N 13 J4
Rankin Cl CDALE/KGS NW9 45 G6
Ranleigh Gdns BXLYHN DA7 149 G1
Ranmere St BAL SW12 161 G3
Ranmoor Gdns HRW HA1 60 D1
Ranmore Av CROY/NA CR0 212 B1
Ranmore Pth STMC/STPC BR5 202 B1
Ranmore Rd BELMT SM2 208 B6
Rannoch Cl EDGE HA8 30 D4
Rannoch Rd HMSMTH W6 119 F6
Rannock Av CDALE/KGS NW9 63 F4
Ransom Cl OXHEY WD19 27 G2
Ransom Rd CHARL * SE7 126 B5
Ranston St STJWD NW8 8 C1
Ranulf Rd CRICK NW2 82 D2
Ranwell Cl BOW * E3 87 H6
Ranworth Cl ERITH DA8 150 B3
Ranworth Rd ED N9 36 E4
Ranyard Cl CHSGTN KT9 206 B1
Raphael Av ROM RM1 57 H6
Raphael Dr THDIT KT7 190 A5
Raphael St SKENS SW7 14 E3
Rapier Cl PUR RM19 131 J4
Rasper Rd TRDG/WHET N20 33 G4
Rastell Av BRXS/STRHM SW2 161 J4
Ratcliffe Cl LEE/GVPK SE12 165 K2
Ratcliffe Cross St WCHPL * E1 105 F5
Ratcliffe La POP/IOD E14 105 G5
Ratcliff Rd FSTGT E7 89 G3
Rathbone Market
CAN/RD * E16 106 D4
Rathbone Pl FITZ W1T 10 C2
Rathbone Sq CROY/NA * CR0 211 J2
Rathbone St CAN/RD E16 106 D4
FITZ W1T 10 B2
Rathcoole Av CEND/HSY/T N8 67 F2
Rathcoole Gdns CEND/HSY/T N8 67 F2
Rathfern Rd CAT SE6 164 C3
Rathgar Av WEA W13 116 C1
Rathgar Cl FNCH N3 46 D5
Rathgar Rd BRXN/ST SW9 142 C4
Rathmell Dr CLAP SW4 161 J1
Rathmore Rd CHARL SE7 126 A5
Rattray Rd BRXS/STRHM SW2 142 B5
Raul Rd PECK SE15 143 H3
Raveley St KTTN NW5 84 C2
Raven Cl CDALE/KGS NW9 45 H5
Ravencroft Crs ELTH/MOT SE9 166 E5
Ravenet St BTSEA SW11 141 G2
Ravenfield Rd TOOT SW17 160 E5
Ravenhill Rd PLSTW E13 89 G6
Ravenna Rd PUT/ROE SW15 139 G6
Ravenoak Wy CHIG IG7 54 E1
Ravenor Park Rd GFD/PVL UB6 96 B2
Raven Rd SWFD E18 53 G5
Raven Rw WCHPL E1 104 D4
Ravens Ait SURB * KT6 190 E2
Ravensbourne Av HAYES BR2 183 G4
STWL/WRAY TW19 152 B3
Ravensbourne Gdns CLAY IG5 54 A4
WEA W13 97 H4
Ravensbourne Pk BROCKY SE4 164 D2
Ravensbourne Park Crs
CAT SE6 164 C2
Ravensbourne Pl DEPT SE8 144 E3
Ravensbourne Rd BMLY BR1 183 K6
CAT SE6 164 C2
DART DA1 150 D4
TWK TW1 156 D1
Ravensbury Av MRDN SM4 194 B2
Ravensbury Gv MTCM CR4 194 C1
Ravensbury La MTCM CR4 194 C1
Ravensbury Rd
STMC/STPC BR5 202 A1
WAND/EARL SW18 160 A4
Ravensbury Ter
WAND/EARL SW18 160 A4
Ravenscar Rd BMLY BR1 165 H6
SURB KT6 191 G6
Ravens Cl CDALE/KGS NW9 45 G5
EN EN1 24 A3
HAYES BR2 183 J5
Ravenscourt Av HMSMTH W6 118 D4
Ravenscourt Cl RSLP HA4 58 A4
Ravenscourt Gdns
HMSMTH W6 118 C4
Ravenscourt Pk HMSMTH W6 118 D4
Ravenscourt Pl HMSMTH W6 118 E4
Ravenscourt Rd HMSMTH W6 118 E4
STMC/STPC BR5 186 B6
Ravenscourt Sq HMSMTH W6 118 D3
Ravenscraig Rd FBAR/BDGN N11 34 B6
Ravenscroft Av GLDGN NW11 64 D4
WBLY HA9 62 A5
Ravenscroft Cl CAN/RD E16 106 E4
Ravenscroft Cottages
BAR * EN5 20 E5
Ravenscroft Pk BAR EN5 20 B5
Ravenscroft Rd BECK BR3 181 K5
CAN/RD E16 106 E4
CHSWK W4 117 K4
Ravenscroft St BETH E2 7 K3
Ravensdale Av
NFNCH/WDSP N12 33 G6
Ravensdale Gdns NRWD SE19 180 E3
Ravensdale Rd HSLWW TW4 134 D4
STNW/STAM N16 68 B4
Ravensdon St LBTH SE11 122 B5
Ravensfield DAGW RM9 91 K2
Ravensfield Gdns
HOR/WEW KT19 207 G3
Ravenshaw St
KIL/WHAMP NW6 82 D3
Ravenshill CHST BR7 185 G4
Ravenshurst Av HDN NW4 64 A1
Ravenside Cl UED N18 51 F1
Ravenslea Rd BAL SW12 160 E2
Ravensmead Rd HAYES BR2 183 G3
Ravensmede Wy CHSWK W4 118 C4
Ravens Ms BKHTH/KID * SE3 145 K6
Ravenstone Rd
CDALE/KGS * NW9 63 H3
CEND/HSY/T N8 49 F6
Ravenstone St BAL SW12 161 F3
Ravens Wy LEE/GVPK SE12 145 K6
Ravenswood BXLY DA5 169 F3
Ravenswood Av SURB KT6 191 G6
WWKM BR4 199 F5
Ravenswood Cl CRW RM5 56 D1
Ravenswood Ct
KUTN/CMB * KT2 175 K2
Ravenswood Crs
RYLN/HDSTN HA2 59 K6
WWKM BR4 199 F5
Ravenswood Gdns ISLW TW7 135 K2
Ravenswood Pk NTHWD HA6 40 E2
Ravenswood Rd BAL SW12 161 G2
CROY/NA CR0 211 H1
WALTH E17 70 A1
Ravensworth Rd
ELTH/MOT SE9 166 E6
WLSDN * NW10 99 K2
Ravent Rd LBTH SE11 17 H7
Ravey St SDTCH EC2A 7 G6
Ravine Gv WOOL/PLUM SE18 127 K6
Rav Pinter Cl STNW/STAM N16 68 A4
Rawlings Cl ORP BR6 217 F3
Rawlings St CHEL SW3 14 E6
Rawlins Cl FNCH N3 46 C6
SAND/SEL CR2 213 H5
Rawnsley Av MTCM CR4 194 C2
Rawreth Wk IS * N1 85 J6
Rawson St BTSEA SW11 141 G2
Rawsthorne Cl CAN/RD E16 126 E1
Rawstorne Pl FSBYE * EC1V 6 A4
Rawstorne St FSBYE EC1V 6 A4
Ray Bell Ct BROCKY * SE4 144 C3
Raydean Rd BAR EN5 20 E6
Raydons Gdns DAGW RM9 92 A2
Raydons Rd DAGW RM9 92 A3
Raydon St ARCH N19 66 B6
Rayfield Cl HAYES BR2 200 D3
Rayford Av LEE/GVPK SE12 165 J2
Rayford Cl DART DA1 151 F6
Ray Gdns BARK IG11 109 G1
STAN HA7 43 H1
Ray Lamb Wy ERITH DA8 130 E6
Rayleas Cl WOOL/PLUM SE18 147 G2
Rayleigh Av TEDD TW11 173 K2
Rayleigh Cl PLMGR N13 35 K5
Rayleigh Ct KUT KT1 175 H5
Rayleigh Ri SAND/SEL CR2 212 A4
Rayleigh Rd CAN/RD E16 126 A1
PLMGR N13 35 J5
WFD IG8 53 G3
WIM/MER SW19 177 J4
Ray Lodge Rd WFD IG8 53 G2
Raymead Av THHTH CR7 196 B2
Raymere Gdns
WOOL/PLUM SE18 147 J1
Raymond Av HNWL W7 116 B3
SWFD E18 52 D6
Raymond Buildings
GINN * WC1R 11 H1
Raymond Cl SYD SE26 181 K1
Raymond Rd BECK BR3 198 B1
GNTH/NBYPK IG2 72 D4
PLSTW E13 89 G5
WIM/MER SW19 177 H2
Raymond Wy ESH/CLAY * KT10 205 G4
Raymouth Rd
BERM/RHTH SE16 123 J4
Rayne Ct SWFD E18 70 D1
Rayners Cl ALP/SUD HA0 79 K3
Rayners Gdns NTHLT UB5 95 F2
Rayners La PIN HA5 59 K3
Rayner's Rd PUT/ROE SW15 139 H6
Raynes Av WAN E11 71 G4
Raynham Av UED N18 50 C2
Raynham Rd HMSMTH W6 118 E4
UED N18 50 C1
Raynham Ter UED N18 50 C1
Raynor Cl STHL UB1 114 E1
Raynor Pl IS N1 85 J6
Raynton Cl RYLN/HDSTN HA2 59 J5
YEAD UB4 94 D3
Raynton Dr YEAD UB4 94 C1
Ray Rd CRW RM5 56 D1
E/WMO/HCT KT8 189 G2
Rays Av UED N18 36 E6
Rays Rd UED N18 36 E6
WWKM BR4 199 F4
Ray St CLKNW EC1R 5 K7
Ray Street Br CLKNW * EC1R 5 K7
Raywood Cl WDR/YW UB7 133 F1
Reachview Cl CAMTN NW1 84 C5
Reading La HACK E8 86 D4
Reading Rd NTHLT UB5 78 B3
SUT SM1 209 G3
Reading Wy MLHL NW7 46 C1
Reads Cl IL IG1 90 B1
Reapers Cl CAMTN NW1 84 D6
Reapers Wy ISLW TW7 135 J6
Reardon Pth WAP E1W 123 J1
Reardon St WAP E1W 123 J1
Reaston St NWCR SE14 143 K1
Reckitt Rd CHSWK W4 118 B5
Record St PECK SE15 123 K6
Recovery St TOOT SW17 178 D1
Recreation Av ROMW/RG RM7 74 E2
Recreation Rd HAYES BR2 183 J5
NWDGN UB2 114 D4
SYD SE26 164 A6
Recreation Wy MTCM CR4 179 K6
Rector St IS N1 6 C1
Rectory Cl CHING E4 37 J5
DART DA1 150 B5
FNCH N3 46 D4
RYNPK SW20 177 F5
SCUP DA14 168 C6
STAN HA7 43 H2
SURB KT6 190 D5
Rectory Field Crs CHARL SE7 146 B1
Rectory Gdns BECK * BR3 182 D4
CEND/HSY/T N8 66 E1
CHST * BR7 185 H4
NTHLT UB5 77 K6
Rectory Gn BECK BR3 182 C4
Rectory Gv CLAP SW4 141 H4
CROY/NA CR0 196 C6
FELT TW13 154 E6
Rectory La EDGE HA8 44 C2
SCUP DA14 168 C6
STAN HA7 43 H1
SURB KT6 190 D5
TOOT SW17 179 F1
WLGTN SM6 210 C2
Rectory Orch WIM/MER SW19 159 H6
Rectory Park Av NTHLT UB5 95 K2
Rectory Pl CHST * BR7 185 H4
WOOL/PLUM SE18 127 F4
Rectory Rd BARN SW13 138 D3
BECK BR3 182 D4
DAGE RM10 92 C4
HAYES BR2 215 H5
HEST TW5 134 A3
HYS/HAR UB3 94 E5
MNPK E12 89 K3
NWDGN UB2 114 E3
STNW/STAM N16 68 B6
SUT SM1 208 E1
WALTH E17 69 K1
Rectory Sq WCHPL E1 105 F4
Reculver Ms UED N18 36 C6
Reculver Rd BERM/RHTH SE16 123 K5
Red Anchor Cl CHEL * SW3 120 C6
Redan Pl BAY/PAD * W2 101 F5
Redan St WKENS W14 119 G3
Redan Ter CMBW SE5 142 C3
Red Barracks Rd
WOOL/PLUM SE18 126 E4
Redberry Gv SYD SE26 163 K5
Redbourne Av FNCH N3 46 E4
Redbourne Dr THMD SE28 109 K5
Redbridge Gdns CMBW SE5 143 F1
Redbridge La East REDBR IG4 71 H3
Redbridge La West WAN E11 71 F3
Redburn St CHEL SW3 120 E6
Redbury Cl RAIN RM13 111 K3
Redcar Cl NTHLT UB5 78 B4
Redcar St CMBW * SE5 142 D1
Redcastle Cl WCHPL E1 104 E6
Red Cedars Rd ORP BR6 201 K4
Redchurch St BETH E2 7 J6
Redcliffe Cl ECT SW5 120 A5
Redcliffe Gdns IL IG1 72 A5
WBPTN SW10 120 A5
Redcliffe Ms WBPTN SW10 120 A5
Redcliffe Pl WBPTN SW10 120 B6
Redcliffe Rd WBPTN SW10 120 B5
Redcliffe Sq WBPTN SW10 120 A5
Redcliffe St WBPTN * SW10 120 A6
Redclose Av MRDN SM4 193 K2
Redclyffe Rd EHAM E6 89 G6
Redcroft Rd STHL UB1 96 C6
Redcross Wy STHWK SE1 18 D2
The Reddings MLHL NW7 31 H5
Reddings Cl MLHL NW7 31 H6
Reddington Cl SAND/SEL CR2 211 K6
Reddins Rd PECK SE15 143 H1
Reddons Rd BECK BR3 182 B3
Reddy Rd ERITH DA8 130 C6
Rede Pl BAY/PAD W2 100 E5
Redesdale Gdns ISLW TW7 136 B1
Redesdale St CHEL SW3 120 E6
Redfern Av HSLWW TW4 155 F2
Redfern Rd CAT SE6 165 F2
WLSDN NW10 81 G5
Redfield La ECT SW5 119 K4
Redfield Ms ECT SW5 119 K4
Redford Av THHTH CR7 196 A1
WLGTN SM6 210 E4
Redford Cl FELT TW13 153 J4
Redford Wk IS * N1 85 H6
Redgate Dr HAYES BR2 200 A6
Redgate Ter PUT/ROE SW15 159 G1
Redgrave Cl SNWD SE25 197 G3
Redgrave Rd PUT/ROE SW15 139 G5
Redgrave Ter BETH * E2 104 C2
Redhall Ter EA * W5 98 C6
Red Hl CHST BR7 185 F1
Redhill Dr EDGE HA8 44 E5
Redhill St CAMTN NW1 3 K4
Red House La BXLYHS DA6 148 E5
Red House Rd CROY/NA CR0 195 J3
Red House Sq IS * N1 85 J5
Redington Gdns HAMP NW3 83 F2
Redington Rd HAMP NW3 83 F1
Redland Gdns
E/WMO/HCT * KT8 188 E1
Redlands Rd PEND EN3 25 G2
Redlands Wy BRXS/STRHM SW2 161 K2
Red La ESH/CLAY KT10 205 G4
Redleaf Cl BELV DA17 129 H6
Redlees Cl ISLW TW7 136 B5
Red Lion Cl STMC/STPC BR5 202 D3
WALW SE17 122 E6
Red Lion Ct FLST/FETLN EC4A 11 K4
HSLW * TW3 135 G4
Red Lion Hl EFNCH N2 47 H5
Red Lion La WOOL/PLUM SE18 147 F2
Red Lion Pde PIN * HA5 41 J6
Red Lion Pl WOOL/PLUM * SE18 147 F2
Red Lion Rd SURB KT6 191 G6
Red Lion Rw WALW SE17 122 D6
Red Lion Sq BMSBY WC1N 11 G2
WAND/EARL * SW18 139 K6
Red Lion St GINN WC1R 11 G2
RCHPK/HAM TW10 136 E6
Red Lion Yd MYFR/PKLN * W1K 9 H7
Red Lodge Crs BXLY DA5 170 A5
Red Lodge Rd BXLY DA5 170 A5
WWKM BR4 199 F5
Redman Cl NTHLT UB5 95 G1
Redman's Rd WCHPL E1 104 E4
Redmead La WAP E1W 123 H1
Redmead Rd HYS/HAR UB3 113 H4
Redmore Rd HMSMTH * W6 118 E4
Red Oak Cl ORP BR6 216 B1
Red Pl MYFR/PKLN W1K 9 G5
Red Post Hl HNHL SE24 142 E6
Redriffe Rd PLSTW E13 106 D1
Redriff Rd BERM/RHTH SE16 124 B3
ROMW/RG RM7 56 D5
Redroofs Cl BECK BR3 182 E4
Redruth Cl WDGN N22 49 F3
Redruth Rd HOM E9 86 E6
Redstart Cl EHAM E6 107 J4
NWCR * SE14 144 B1
Redston Rd CEND/HSY/T N8 66 D1
Redvers Rd WDGN N22 49 G5
Redvers St IS N1 7 H4
Redwald Rd CLPT E5 87 F2
Redway Dr WHTN TW2 155 H2
Redwing Rd WLGTN SM6 210 E4
Redwood Cl BERM/RHTH SE16 124 B1
BFN/LL DA15 168 B3
OXHEY WD19 27 G6
STHGT/OAK N14 34 D2
Redwood Gdns CHING * E4 37 K2
Redwood Wy BAR EN5 20 B6
Reece Ms SKENS SW7 14 A6
Reed Av ORP BR6 216 E1
Reed Cl CAN/RD E16 106 E4
LEE/GVPK SE12 145 K6
Reede Rd DAGE RM10 92 C4
Reede Wy DAGE RM10 92 D4
Reedham Cl TOTM N17 68 D1
Reedham St PECK * SE15 143 H3
Reedholm Vls STNW/STAM N16 85 K2
Reed Pond Wk GPK RM2 57 H5
Reed Rd TOTM N17 50 B6
Reedsfield Cl ASHF TW15 152 E5
Reedsfield Rd ASHF TW15 152 E6
Reed's Pl CAMTN NW1 84 C5
Reedworth St LBTH SE11 17 K7
Reenglass Rd STAN * HA7 29 K6
Rees Dr STAN HA7 30 A6
Rees Gdns CROY/NA CR0 197 G3
Reesland Cl MNPK E12 90 A4
Rees St IS N1 6 D1
Reets Farm Cl CDALE/KGS NW9 63 G3
Reeves Av CDALE/KGS NW9 63 F4
Reeves Cnr CROY/NA CR0 196 C6
Reeves Ms MYFR/PKLN W1K 9 G6
Reeves Rd BOW E3 105 K3
WOOL/PLUM SE18 127 G6
Reform Rw TOTM N17 50 B5
Reform St BTSEA SW11 140 E3
Regal Cl EA W5 97 K4
WCHPL E1 104 C4
Regal Ct MTCM CR4 178 E6
UED N18 50 B1
Regal Crs WLGTN SM6 210 B1
Regal Dr FBAR/BDGN N11 48 B1
Regal La CAMTN NW1 3 H1
Regal Wy KTN/HRWW/W HA3 62 A3
Regan Wy IS N1 7 G3
Regarder Rd CHIG IG7 55 H1
Regarth Av ROM RM1 75 G3
Regency Cl CHIG IG7 54 C1
EA W5 98 A5
HPTN TW12 172 E1
Regency Ct EN EN1 23 K6
Regency Dr RSLP HA4 58 C5
Regency Gdns WOT/HER KT12 188 C5
Regency Lawn KTTN * NW5 84 B1
Regency Ms BECK BR3 183 F4
WLSDN NW10 81 J4
Regency Pde HAMP * NW3 83 H5
Regency Pl WEST * SW1P 16 C6
Regency St WEST SW1P 16 D7
Regency Ter HGT * N6 65 K3
SKENS * SW7 120 C5
Regency Wk CROY/NA CR0 198 B3
Regency Wy BXLYHN DA7 148 E4
Regent Cl HEST TW5 134 A2
KTN/HRWW/W HA3 62 A3

NFNCH/WDSP N12 47 G1
Regent Gdns GDMY/SEVK IG3 73 G5
Regent Pde BELMT * SM2 209 G4
STNW/STAM * N16 68 B4
Regent Pl WIM/MER SW19 178 B1
Regent Rd BRYLDS KT5 191 G2
HNHL SE24 162 C1
Regents Av PLMGR N13 49 G1
Regents Bridge Gdns
VX/NE SW8 121 K6
Regents Cl SAND/SEL CR2 212 A4
YEAD UB4 94 C4
Regents Dr HAYES BR2 215 H3
WFD IG8 54 A2
Regents Ms STJWD NW8 101 G1
Regent's Park Rd FNCH N3 46 D6
HAMP NW3 83 K6
Regent's Park Ter CAMTN NW1 84 B6
Regents Pl LOU IG10 39 H2
Regents Plaza
KIL/WHAMP * NW6 101 F1
Regent Sq BELV DA17 129 J4
BOW E3 105 K2
STPAN WC1H 5 F5
Regent's Rw HACK E8 86 C6
Regent St CHSWK W4 117 H5
CONDST W1S 10 A4
WLSDN NW10 100 B2
Regents Whf IS * N1 5 G2
Reginald Rd DEPT SE8 144 D1
FSTGT E7 88 E5
NTHWD HA6 40 D4
Reginald Sq DEPT SE8 144 D1
Regina Rd FSBYPK N4 67 F5
NWDGN UB2 114 D4
SNWD SE25 181 H6
WEA W13 116 B1
Regina Ter WEA W13 116 B1
Regis Rd KTTN NW5 84 B3
Regnart Buildings CAMTN NW1 4 B5
Reid Cl PIN HA5 40 E6
Reidhaven Rd
WOOL/PLUM SE18 127 K4
Reigate Av SUT SM1 194 A5
Reigate Rd BMLY BR1 165 K4
GDMY/SEVK IG3 73 F6
Reigate Wy WLGTN SM6 210 E3
Reighton Rd CLPT E5 86 C1
Relay Rd SHB W12 100 A6
Relf Rd PECK SE15 143 H4
Reliance Ar BRXN/ST * SW9 142 B5
Relton Ms SKENS SW7 14 D4
Rembrandt Cl BGVA * SW1W 121 F5
POP/IOD E14 125 G3
Rembrandt Ct HOR/WEW KT19 207 H4
Rembrandt Rd EDGE * HA8 44 C5
LEW SE13 145 H5
Remington Rd EHAM E6 107 J5
SEVS/STOTM N15 67 K3
Remington St IS N1 6 B3
Remnant St HOL/ALD WC2B 11 G3
Remus Rd BOW E3 87 J5
Rendle Cl CROY/NA CR0 197 G2
Rendlesham Rd CLPT E5 86 C2
ENC/FH EN2 23 H2
Renforth St BERM/RHTH SE16 123 K2
Renfrew Cl EHAM E6 108 A6
Renfrew Rd HEST TW5 134 C3
KUTN/CMB KT2 175 K3
LBTH SE11 18 A6
Renmuir St TOOT SW17 178 E2
Rennell St LEW SE13 145 F4
Renness Rd WALTH E17 51 G6
Rennets Cl ELTH/MOT SE9 147 J6
Rennets Wood Rd
ELTH/MOT SE9 147 J6
Rennie Cl ASHF TW15 152 A5
Rennie Est BERM/RHTH SE16 123 J4
Rennie St STHWK SE1 12 A7
Renown Cl CROY/NA CR0 196 C5
ROMW/RG RM7 56 C4
Rensburg Rd WALTH E17 69 F2
Rensburg Vls WALTH * E17 69 F2
Renshaw Cl BELV DA17 129 G6
Renters Av HDN NW4 64 A3
Renton Cl BRXS/STRHM * SW2 162 A1
Renton Dr STMC/STPC BR5 202 E4
Renwick Rd BARK IG11 109 H3
Repens Wy YEAD UB4 95 H3
Rephidim St STHWK SE1 19 F5
Replingham Rd
WAND/EARL SW18 159 J3
Reporton Rd FUL/PGN SW6 139 H2
Repository Rd
WOOL/PLUM SE18 126 E6
Repton Av ALP/SUD HA0 79 J2
GPK RM2 57 J6
HYS/HAR UB3 113 G4
Repton Cl SUT SM1 209 J3
Repton Ct BECK BR3 182 E4
Repton Dr GPK RM2 75 J1
Repton Gdns GPK RM2 57 J6
Repton Gv CLAY IG5 53 K4
Repton Rd KTN/HRWW/W HA3 62 B1
ORP BR6 217 G2
Repton St POP/IOD E14 105 G5
Repulse Cl ROMW/RG RM7 56 D4
Reservoir Cl THHTH CR7 180 E6
Reservoir Rd BROCKY SE4 144 B3
RSLP HA4 58 A2
STHGT/OAK N14 22 C6
Resolution Wy DEPT SE8 144 D1
Restell Cl BKHTH/KID SE3 125 H6
Restmor Wy WLGTN SM6 195 F6
Reston Pl SKENS SW7 120 B2
Restons Crs ELTH/MOT SE9 167 J1
Retford St BETH * E2 7 H3
BETH * E2 7 J4
Retingham Wy CHING E4 37 K4
The Retreat BARN SW13 138 B4
BRYLDS KT5 191 G3
CDALE/KGS NW9 63 F2
ORP BR6 217 H4
RYLN/HDSTN HA2 60 A4
THHTH CR7 196 E1
WPK KT4 207 K1
Retreat Cl KTN/HRWW/W HA3 61 J2
Retreat Pl HOM E9 86 E4
Retreat Rd RCH/KEW TW9 136 E6
Reunion Rw WAP * E1W 104 D6
Reveley Sq BERM/RHTH SE16 124 B2
Revell Ri WOOL/PLUM SE18 128 A6
Revell Rd KUT KT1 175 J5
SUT SM1 208 D4
Revelon Rd BROCKY SE4 144 B5
Revelstoke Rd WAND/EARL SW18 159 K4
Reventlow Rd ELTH/MOT SE9 167 H3
Reverdy Rd STHWK SE1 123 H4
Reverend Cl RYLN/HDSTN HA2 78 B1
Revesby Rd CAR SM5 194 D3
Review Rd CRICK NW2 63 H6
DAGE RM10 110 D1
Rewell St FUL/PGN * SW6 140 B1
Rewley Rd CAR SM5 194 C3
Rex Pl MYFR/PKLN W1K 9 H7
Reydon Av WAN E11 71 G3
Reynard Cl BMLY BR1 184 E6
Reynard Dr NRWD SE19 181 G3
Reynard Pl NWCR * SE14 124 B6
Reynardson Rd TOTM N17 49 J3
Reynolds Av CHDH RM6 73 J4
CHSGTN KT9 206 A5
MNPK E12 90 A3
Reynolds Cl CAR SM5 194 E5
GLDGN NW11 65 F4
WIM/MER SW19 178 C4
Reynolds Dr EDGE HA8 44 B6
Reynolds Pl BKHTH/KID SE3 146 A1
RCHPK/HAM TW10 157 G1
Reynolds Rd CHSWK W4 117 K3
NWMAL KT3 192 A4
PECK SE15 143 K6
YEAD UB4 95 G3
Reynolds Wy CROY/NA CR0 212 A2
Rheidol Ms IS N1 6 C2
Rheidol Ter IS N1 6 B2
Rheingold Wy WLGTN SM6 210 E6
Rheola Cl TOTM N17 50 B4
Rhoda St BETH E2 7 K6
Rhodes Av WDGN N22 48 C4
Rhodesia Rd BRXN/ST SW9 141 K3
WAN E11 70 B6
Rhodes St HOLWY N7 85 F3
Rhodeswell Rd BOW E3 105 G4
Rhodrons Av CHSGTN KT9 206 A3
Rhondda Gv BOW E3 105 G2
Rhyl Rd GFD/PVL UB6 97 F1
Rhyl St KTTN NW5 84 A4
Rhys Av FBAR/BDGN N11 48 D3
Rialto Rd MTCM CR4 179 F5
Ribble Cl WFD IG8 53 G2
Ribblesdale Av FBAR/BDGN N11 47 K2
NTHLT UB5 78 B4
Ribblesdale Rd CEND/HSY/T N8 67 F1
STRHM/NOR SW16 179 G1
Ribbon Dance Ms CMBW SE5 142 E2
Ribchester Av GFD/PVL UB6 97 F2
Ribston Cl HAYES BR2 200 E5
Ricardo St POP/IOD E14 105 K5
Ricards Rd WIM/MER SW19 177 J1
Rice Pde STMC/STPC * BR5 201 J2
Richard Cl WOOL/PLUM SE18 126 D4
Richard House Dr CAN/RD E16 107 H5
Richards Av ROMW/RG RM7 74 E2
Richards Cl BUSH WD23 28 D2
HRW HA1 61 G2
HYS/HAR UB3 113 G6
Richards Cottages CAR * SM5 209 K3
Richards Fld HOR/WEW KT19 207 F6
Richardson Cl HACK * E8 86 B6
Richardson Rd SRTFD * E15 106 C1
Richardson's Ms FITZ W1T 4 A7
Richard's Pl CHEL SW3 14 D6
WALTH E17 51 J6
Richard St WCHPL E1 104 D5
Richbell Pl BMSBY WC1N 11 G1
Richborne Ter VX/NE SW8 142 A1
Richborough Cl
STMC/STPC BR5 202 E1
Richborough Rd CRICK NW2 82 B2
Riches Rd IL IG1 72 C6
Richfield Rd BUSH WD23 28 C2
Richford Ga HMSMTH * W6 119 F3
Richford Rd SRTFD E15 88 D6
Richford St SHB W12 119 F2
Richlands Av EW KT17 207 J2
Richmer Rd ERITH DA8 150 D1
Richmond Av CHING E4 52 B1
EBED/NFELT TW14 153 H1
IS N1 85 F6
RYNPK SW20 177 H4
WLSDN NW10 81 K4
Richmond Buildings
SOHO/CST W1F 10 C4
Richmond Cl WALTH E17 69 H3
Richmond Crs CHING E4 52 B1
ED N9 36 C3
IS N1 85 F6
Richmond Dr WFD IG8 54 A3
Richmond Gdns HDN NW4 63 J2
KTN/HRWW/W HA3 43 F3
Richmond Gn CROY/NA CR0 210 E1
Richmond Gv IS N1 85 H5
Richmond Hl
RCHPK/HAM TW10 157 F1
Richmond Ms SOHO/CST W1F 10 C4
Richmond Pde TWK * TW1 156 D1
Richmond Park Rd
KUTN/CMB KT2 175 F3
MORT/ESHN SW14 137 K6
Richmond Pl WOOL/PLUM SE18 127 H4
Richmond Rd BAR EN5 21 G6
CHING * E4 38 B3
CROY/NA CR0 210 E1
EA W5 117 F2
EFNCH * N2 47 G5
FBAR/BDGN N11 48 E2
FSTGT E7 89 F3
HACK E8 86 C5
IL IG1 90 C1
ISLW TW7 136 B5
KUTN/CMB KT2 174 E1
ROM RM1 75 H3
RYNPK SW20 176 E4
SEVS/STOTM N15 68 A3
THHTH CR7 196 C1
TWK TW1 156 C2
WAN E11 70 B6
Richmond St PLSTW E13 106 E1
Richmond Ter WHALL SW1A 16 E2
Richmond Vls WALTH * E17 51 K4
Richmond Wy SHB W12 119 G2
WAN E11 70 E6
Richmount Gdns
BKHTH/KID SE3 145 K4
Rich St POP/IOD E14 105 H6
Rickard Cl BRXS/STRHM SW2 162 B3
HDN NW4 63 J1
WDR/YW UB7 112 A3
Rickards Cl SURB KT6 191 F6
Rickett St FUL/PGN SW6 119 K6
Rickman St WCHPL E1 104 E3
Rickmansworth Rd NTHWD HA6 40 B3
Rick Roberts Wy SRTFD E15 88 B6
Rickthorne Rd ARCH N19 66 E6
Ridding La GFD/PVL UB6 79 F3
Riddons Rd LEE/GVPK SE12 166 B5
The Ride BTFD TW8 116 C5
PEND EN3 24 E4
Rideout St WOOL/PLUM SE18 126 E4
Rider Cl BFN/LL DA15 167 K1
Ridgdale St BOW E3 105 J1
The Ridge BAR * EN5 20 D6
BRYLDS KT5 191 H2
BXLY DA5 169 G2
ORP BR6 201 J6
WHTN TW2 155 J2
Ridge Av DART DA1 170 C1
WCHMH N21 35 J2
Ridgebrook Rd BKHTH/KID SE3 146 B5
Ridge Cl CDALE/KGS NW9 63 F1
HDN NW4 46 B5
THMD SE28 127 J2
Ridge Crest ENC/FH EN2 23 F2
Ridgecroft Cl BXLY DA5 169 K3
Ridge Hl GLDGN NW11 64 C5
Ridgemead Cl STHGT/OAK N14 34 E4
Ridgemont Gdns EDGE HA8 30 E6
Ridgemount Av CROY/NA CR0 198 A6
Ridgemount Gdns ENC/FH EN2 23 H4
Ridge Rd CEND/HSY/T N8 67 F3
CHEAM SM3 193 J5
CRICK NW2 82 D1
MTCM CR4 179 G3
WCHMH N21 35 K3
Ridge Ter WCHMH * N21 35 J2
Ridgeview Cl BAR EN5 32 B1
Ridgeview Rd NFNCH/WDSP N12 33 F5
The Ridgway BELMT SM2 209 H5
The Ridgeway ACT W3 117 H3
CDALE/KGS NW9 63 F1
CHING E4 38 A3
CROY/NA CR0 211 F1
ENC/FH EN2 23 G2
FBAR/BDGN N11 33 K6
FNCH N3 47 F5
GLDGN NW11 64 D5
GPK RM2 75 J1
KTN/HRWW/W HA3 61 J3
MLHL NW7 31 K6
RSLP HA4 58 E4
RYLN/HDSTN HA2 59 K2
STAN HA7 43 J2
STHGT/OAK N14 34 E4
Ridge Wy DART DA1 170 C1
FELT TW13 154 D5
Ridgeway HAYES BR2 199 K6
WFD IG8 39 G6
Ridgeway Av EBAR EN4 33 K1
Ridgeway Crs ORP BR6 216 E1
Ridgeway Crescent Gdns
ORP BR6 201 K6
Ridgeway Dr BMLY BR1 166 A6
Ridgeway East BFN/LL DA15 148 A6
Ridgeway Gdns REDBR IG4 71 K3
Ridgeway Rd ISLW TW7 135 K1
Ridgeway Rd North ISLW TW7 135 K1
Ridgeway West BFN/LL DA15 147 K6
Ridgewell Cl DAGE RM10 92 D6
IS N1 85 J6
SYD SE26 164 C6
Ridgmount Gdns GWRST WC1E 10 C1
Ridgmount Rd
WAND/EARL SW18 140 A6
Ridgmount St GWRST WC1E 10 C1
Ridgway RCHPK/HAM * TW10 157 F1
WIM/MER SW19 177 F3
Ridgway Gdns WIM/MER SW19 177 G3
Ridgway Pl WIM/MER SW19 177 H2
Ridgway Rd BRXN/ST SW9 142 C4
Ridgwell Rd CAN/RD E16 107 G4
Riding House St REGST * W1B 9 K2
The Ridings BRYLDS KT5 191 H2
EA W5 98 B3
EBAR * EN4 33 J2
EW KT17 207 H6
The Riding GLDGN NW11 64 D4
Ridings Av WCHMH N21 23 H5
Ridler Rd EN EN1 24 A1
Ridley Av WEA W13 116 C3
Ridley Cl HARH RM3 57 K4
Ridley Rd FSTGT E7 89 G2
HACK E8 86 B3
HAYES BR2 183 J6
WELL DA16 148 C2
WIM/MER SW19 178 A3
WLSDN NW10 99 J1
Ridsdale Rd PGE/AN SE20 181 J4
Riefield Rd ELTH/MOT SE9 147 H5
Riesco Dr CROY/NA CR0 212 E4
Riffel Rd CRICK NW2 82 A3
Rifle Pl NTGHL W11 119 G1
Rifle Range La HRW HA1 61 F5
Rifle St POP/IOD E14 105 K4
Rigault Rd FUL/PGN SW6 139 H3
Rigby Cl CROY/NA CR0 211 G1
Rigby La HYS/HAR UB3 113 G2
Rigby Ms IL IG1 72 A6
Rigden St POP/IOD E14 105 K5
Rigeley Rd WLSDN NW10 99 J2
Rigg Ap LEY E10 69 F5
Rigge Pl CLAP SW4 141 J5
Riggindale Rd
STRHM/NOR SW16 179 J1
Right Side STHGT/OAK * N14 34 D3
Riley Rd PEND EN3 24 E1
STHWK SE1 19 J4
Riley St WBPTN SW10 140 C1
Rinaldo Rd BAL SW12 161 G2
Ring Cl BMLY BR1 184 A3
Ringcroft St HOLWY N7 85 G3
Ringer's Rd BMLY BR1 183 K6
Ringford Rd WAND/EARL SW18 139 J6
Ringlet Cl CAN/RD E16 107 F4
Ringmer Av FUL/PGN SW6 139 H2
Ringmer Pl WCHMH N21 23 K6
Ringmer Wy BMLY BR1 200 E2
Ringmore Ri FSTH SE23 163 J2
Ringshall Rd CHST BR7 186 B6
Ringslade Rd WDGN N22 49 F5
Ringstead Rd CAT SE6 164 E2
SUT SM1 209 H2
Ring Wy FBAR/BDGN N11 48 C2
Ringway NWDGN UB2 114 D5
Ringwold Cl BECK BR3 182 B3
Ringwood Av CROY/NA CR0 195 K4
EFNCH N2 47 K6
Ringwood Cl PIN * HA5 41 G6
Ringwood Gdns PUT/ROE SW15 158 D4
Ringwood Rd WALTH E17 69 H3
Ringwood Wy HPTN TW12 155 F6
WCHMH N21 35 H2
Ripley Cl BMLY BR1 200 E2
CROY/NA CR0 214 A4
Ripley Gdns MORT/ESHN SW14 138 A4
Ripley Ms WAN * E11 70 C3
Ripley Rd BELV DA17 129 H4
CAN/RD E16 107 G5
ENC/FH EN2 23 J2
GDMY/SEVK IG3 73 F6
HPTN TW12 173 F3
Ripleys Market DART * DA1 171 H2
Ripley Vls WEA * W13 97 J5
Ripon Cl NTHLT UB5 78 A3
Ripon Gdns CHSGTN KT9 205 K3
IL IG1 71 J3
Ripon Rd ED N9 36 D2
TOTM N17 49 K6
WOOL/PLUM SE18 127 G6
Rippersley Rd WELL DA16 148 B2
Ripple Rd BARK IG11 90 C5
BARK IG11 90 E6
BARK IG11 91 H6
BARK IG11 92 A6
Ripplevale Gv IS N1 85 F5
Rippolson Rd
WOOL/PLUM SE18 128 A5
Risborough Cl MUSWH * N10 48 B6
Risborough Dr WPK KT4 192 D4
Risborough St STHWK SE1 18 B2
Risdon St BERM/RHTH SE16 123 K2
The Rise BKHH IG9 39 H3
BXLY DA5 168 D2
DART DA1 150 C5
EDGE HA8 44 D1
GFD/PVL UB6 79 G3
MLHL NW7 45 H2
PLMGR N13 35 G6
SAND/SEL CR2 212 E6
WAN E11 70 E2
WLSDN NW10 81 F1
Risebridge Cha ROM RM1 57 H3
Risebridge Rd GPK RM2 57 H5
Risedale Rd BXLYHN DA7 149 J4
Riseldine Rd FSTH SE23 164 B1
Rise Park Bvd ROM RM1 57 H4
Rise Park Pde ROM RM1 57 G5
Rising Hill Cl NTHWD * HA6 40 A2
Risinghill St IS N1 5 J2
Risingholme Cl BUSH WD23 28 B2
KTN/HRWW/W HA3 42 E4
Risingholme Rd
KTN/HRWW/W HA3 42 E5
The Risings WALTH E17 70 B1
Risley Av TOTM N17 49 J4
Rita Rd VX/NE SW8 141 K1
Ritches Rd SEVS/STOTM N15 67 J2
Ritchie Rd CROY/NA CR0 197 J3
Ritchie St IS N1 5 K2
Ritchings Av WALTH E17 69 G1
Ritherdon Rd TOOT SW17 161 F4
Ritson Rd HACK E8 86 B4
Ritter St WOOL/PLUM SE18 127 F6
Rivaz Pl HOM E9 86 E4
Rivenhall Gdns SWFD E18 70 D1
River Av PLMGR N13 35 H5
THDIT KT7 190 B4
Riverbank E/WMO/HCT KT8 173 K6
River Bank THDIT KT7 190 A2
WCHMH N21 35 J2
Riverbank Rd BMLY BR1 165 K5
Riverbank Wy BTFD TW8 116 D6
River Barge Cl POP/IOD E14 125 F2
River Cl NWDGN UB2 115 H2
RAIN RM13 111 K4
RSLP HA4 58 D3
WAN E11 71 G3
Rivercourt Rd HMSMTH W6 118 E4
Riverdale Dr WAND/EARL SW18 160 A3
Riverdale Gdns TWK TW1 136 D6
Riverdale Rd BXLY DA5 169 G2
ERITH DA8 129 J5
FELT TW13 154 D6
TWK TW1 156 D1
WOOL/PLUM SE18 128 A5
Riverdene EDGE HA8 30 E6
Riverdene Rd IL IG1 90 A1
River Front EN EN1 23 K4
River Gdns CAR SM5 195 F6
EBED/NFELT TW14 134 A6
River Grove Pk BECK BR3 182 C4
Riverhead Cl WALTH E17 51 F5
Riverholme Dr HOR/WEW KT19 207 F6
River La RCHPK/HAM TW10 156 E3
Rivermead E/WMO/HCT KT8 173 H6
SURB * KT6 190 E2
Rivermead Cl TEDD TW11 174 C1
Rivermead Rd UED * N18 51 F1
River Meads Av WHTN TW2 155 G5
Rivernook Cl WOT/HER KT12 188 B2
Riverpark Gdns HAYES BR2 183 G5
River Park Rd WDGN N22 49 F5
River Park Vw ORP BR6 202 C4
River Pl IS N1 85 J5
River Reach TEDD TW11 174 D2
River Rd BARK IG11 108 E1
BKHH IG9 39 J3
Riversdale Rd CRW RM5 56 D3
HBRY N5 85 H1
THDIT KT7 190 B2
Riversfield Rd EN EN1 24 A4
Riverside CHARL SE7 126 A3
HDN NW4 63 K4
RCH/KEW * TW9 117 H6
SUN * TW16 172 C5
TWK TW1 156 C3
Riverside Av E/WMO/HCT KT8 189 J2
Riverside Cl CLPT E5 68 E5
HNWL W7 96 E3
KUT KT1 190 E1
STMC/STPC BR5 186 D5
WLGTN SM6 210 B1
Riverside Ct CHING * E4 37 K1
Riverside Dr CHSWK W4 138 B1
ESH/CLAY KT10 204 A2
GLDGN * NW11 64 C3
MTCM CR4 194 D2
RCHPK/HAM TW10 156 C5
Riverside Gdns ALP/SUD HA0 98 A1
ENC/FH EN2 23 J3
HMSMTH W6 118 E5
Riverside Ms CROY/NA * CR0 210 E1
Riverside Pl FBAR/BDGN * N11 34 C5
STWL/WRAY TW19 152 A1
Riverside Rd IL IG1 90 B1
OXHEY WD19 27 F1
SCUP DA14 169 F5
SEVS/STOTM N15 68 C3
SRTFD E15 106 A1
STWL/WRAY TW19 132 A6
TOOT SW17 160 A6
The Riverside
E/WMO/HCT * KT8 173 J6
Riverside Vls SURB * KT6 190 D3
Riverside Wk ISLW TW7 135 K4
KUT KT1 174 E5
Riverside Wy DART DA1 151 H6
River St CLKNW EC1R 5 J4
River Ter HMSMTH W6 119 F5
Riverton Cl MV/WKIL * W9 100 D2
Riverview Gdns BARN SW13 118 E6
River View Gdns TWK TW1 156 A4
Riverview Pk CAT SE6 164 D4
Riverview Rd CHSWK W4 137 J1
HOR/WEW KT19 206 E2
River Wk SUN TW16 172 C5
River Wy FELT TW13 155 G4
GNWCH SE10 125 J3
HOR/WEW KT19 207 F3
Riverway PLMGR N13 49 G1
River Whf BELV * DA17 130 A2
Riverwood La CHST BR7 185 J5
Rivington Av WFD IG8 53 H5
Rivington Crs CDALE/KGS NW9 45 G3
Rivington Pl SDTCH EC2A 7 H5
Rivington St SDTCH EC2A 7 H5
Rivington Wk HACK * E8 86 C6
Rivulet Rd TOTM N17 49 J3
Rixon St HOLWY N7 85 G1
Rixsen Rd MNPK E12 89 J3
Roach Rd BOW E3 87 J5
Roads Pl FSBYPK N4 66 E6
Roan St GNWCH SE10 125 F6
Robarts Cl PIN HA5 59 F2
Robb Rd STAN HA7 43 G2
Robert Adam St MBLAR W1H 9 G3
Roberta St BETH E2 104 C2
Robert Cl CHIG IG7 55 F1
MV/WKIL W9 101 G3
Robert Keen Cl PECK SE15 143 H2
Robert Lowe Cl NWCR SE14 144 A1
Robertson Dr BMLY BR1 184 B5
Robertsbridge Rd CAR SM5 194 B4
Roberts Cl CHEAM SM3 208 B5
ELTH/MOT SE9 167 J3
HARH RM3 57 K4
STMC/STPC BR5 202 D2
THHTH CR7 180 E6
WDR/YW UB7 112 B1
Roberts Ct CHSGTN * KT9 205 K3
WLSDN NW10 81 G4
Roberts House
WOOL/PLUM SE18 146 D2
Roberts Ms KTBR * SW1X 15 G5
Robertson Rd SRTFD E15 88 A6
Robertson St VX/NE SW8 141 G4
Robert's Pl CLKNW * EC1R 5 K6
Roberts Rd BELV DA17 129 H5
MLHL NW7 46 C1
WALTH E17 51 K4
Robert St CAMTN NW1 3 K5
CHCR WC2N 11 F6
CROY/NA CR0 211 J1
WOOL/PLUM SE18 127 J5
Robeson St BOW E3 105 H4
Robina Cl BXLYHS DA6 148 E5
NTHWD HA6 40 D5
Robin Cl CRW RM5 57 F3
HPTN TW12 172 D1
MLHL NW7 31 G5
Robin Gv BTFD TW8 116 D6
HGT N6 66 A6
KTN/HRWW/W HA3 62 B3
Robin Hill Dr CHST BR7 184 D2
Robinhood Cl MTCM CR4 195 H1
Robin Hood Dr
KTN/HRWW/W HA3 43 F3
Robin Hood Gdns
POP/IOD * E14 106 A6
Robin Hood Gn STMC/STPC BR5 202 B2
Robinhood La MTCM CR4 179 H6
Robin Hood La BXLYHS DA6 149 F6
POP/IOD E14 106 A6
PUT/ROE SW15 158 B5
SUT SM1 208 E3
Robin Hood Rd PUT/ROE SW15 158 B6
Robin Hood Wy GFD/PVL UB6 79 F4
PUT/ROE SW15 158 B6
Robin Hood Wy
(Kingston By-Pass)
PUT/ROE SW15 158 B6
Robinia Cl BARK/HLT IG6 54 E2
PGE/AN SE20 181 H4
Robinia Crs LEY E10 69 K6
Robins Gv WWKM BR4 214 E1
Robinson Cl HCH RM12 93 K5
Robinson Crs BUSH WD23 28 C3
Robinson Rd BETH E2 104 E1
DAGE RM10 92 C2
WIM/MER SW19 178 D2
Robinson's Cl WEA W13 97 G4
Robinson St CHEL SW3 120 E6
Robin Wy STMC/STPC BR5 186 C6
Robinwood Pl
RCHPK/HAM TW10 158 A6
Robsart St BRXN/ST SW9 142 A3
Robson Av WLSDN NW10 81 J6
Robson Cl EHAM E6 107 J5
ENC/FH EN2 23 H3
Robson Rd WNWD SE27 162 C5
Roch Av EDGE HA8 44 B5
Rochdale Rd ABYW SE2 128 C5
Rochdale Wy DEPT SE8 144 D1
Rochelle Cl BTSEA SW11 140 C5
Rochelle St BETH E2 7 J5
Rochemont Wk HACK * E8 7 K1
Roche Rd STRHM/NOR SW16 179 K4
Rochester Av BMLY BR1 184 A5
FELT TW13 153 J4
PLSTW E13 89 G6
Rochester Cl BFN/LL DA15 168 C1
EN EN1 24 A2
STRHM/NOR * SW16 179 K3
Rochester Dr BXLY DA5 169 H1
PIN HA5 59 H2
Rochester Gdns CROY/NA CR0 212 A1
IL IG1 71 K4
Rochester Ms CAMTN NW1 84 C5
EA * W5 116 D4
Rochester Pde FELT * TW13 153 K5
Rochester Pl CAMTN NW1 84 C4
Rochester Rd CAMTN NW1 84 C4
CAR SM5 209 K2
DART DA1 171 K2

NTHWD HA6 40 D6
Rochester Rw WEST SW1P 16 B6
Rochester Sq CAMTN NW1 84 C5
Rochester St WEST SW1P 16 C5
Rochester Ter CAMTN NW1 84 C4
Rochester Wk STHWK * SE1 12 E7
Rochester Wy BKHTH/KID SE3 146 A2
DART DA1 170 B2
Rochester Wy Relief Rd
ELTH/MOT SE9 146 D6
Roche Wk MRDN SM4 194 C3
Rochford Av CHDH RM6 73 J2
Rochford Cl EHAM E6 107 H1
HCH RM12 93 K4
Rochford Wk HACK * E8 86 C5
Rochford Wy CROY/NA CR0 195 K3
Rock Av MORT/ESHN SW14 138 A4
Rockbourne Rd FSTH SE23 164 A3
Rock Cl MTCM CR4 178 C5
Rockell's Pl EDUL SE22 163 J1
Rockford Av GFD/PVL UB6 97 H1
Rock Grove Wy
BERM/RHTH SE16 123 H4
Rockhall Rd CRICK NW2 82 B2
Rockhampton Rd
SAND/SEL CR2 212 A4
STRHM/NOR SW16 162 B6
Rock Hl SYD SE26 163 G6
Rockingham Av EMPK RM11 75 K3
Rockingham Cl PUT/ROE SW15 138 C5
Rockingham Ga BUSH WD23 28 C1
Rockingham St STHWK SE1 18 C5
Rockland Rd PUT/ROE SW15 139 H5
Rocklands Dr
KTN/HRWW/W HA3 43 H5
Rockley Rd SHB W12 119 G2
Rockmount Rd NRWD SE19 180 E2
WOOL/PLUM SE18 128 A5
Rocks La BARN SW13 138 D4
Rock St FSBYPK N4 67 G6
Rockware Av GFD/PVL UB6 78 E6
Rockways BAR EN5 31 H1
Rockwell Gdns NRWD SE19 163 F6
Rockwell Rd DAGE RM10 92 D3
Rocliffe St IS N1 6 B3
Rocombe Crs FSTH * SE23 163 K2
Rocque La BKHTH/KID SE3 145 J4
Rodborough Rd GLDGN NW11 64 E5
Roden Gdns CROY/NA CR0 197 F3
Rodenhurst Rd CLAP SW4 161 H2
Roden St HOLWY N7 85 F1
IL IG1 90 A1
Rodeo Cl ERITH DA8 150 E2
Roderick Rd HAMP NW3 83 K2
Rodgers Cl BORE WD6 29 K1
Roding Gdns LOU IG10 39 J1
Roding La BKHH IG9 39 J3
Roding La North WFD IG8 53 J5
Roding La South REDBR IG4 71 H2
Roding Ms WAP E1W 123 H1
Roding Rd CLPT E5 87 F2
EHAM E6 108 B4
Rodings Rw BAR * EN5 20 C5
Roding Vw BKHH IG9 39 H3
Rodmarton St MHST W1U 9 F2
Rodmell Cl YEAD UB4 95 J3
Rodmell Slope
NFNCH/WDSP N12 46 D1
Rodmere St GNWCH SE10 125 H5
Rodmill La BRXS/STRHM SW2 161 K2
Rodney Cl CROY/NA CR0 196 C5
NWMAL KT3 192 B2
PIN HA5 59 J4
WOT/HER * KT12 188 B5
Rodney Gdns PIN HA5 59 G2
WWKM BR4 214 E2
Rodney Pl STHWK SE1 18 D6
WALTH E17 51 G5
WIM/MER SW19 178 B4
Rodney Rd HSLW TW3 155 F1
MTCM CR4 178 D5
NWMAL KT3 192 B2
WALW SE17 18 D7
WAN E11 71 F1
WOT/HER KT12 188 B6
Rodney St IS N1 5 H2
Rodney Wy ROMW/RG RM7 56 D4
Rodway Rd BMLY BR1 184 A4
PUT/ROE SW15 158 D2
Rodwell Cl RSLP * HA4 59 G5
Rodwell Rd EDUL SE22 163 G1
Roebuck Cl FELT TW13 154 A6
Roebuck La BKHH IG9 39 G3
Roebuck Rd BARK/HLT IG6 55 H2
CHSGTN KT9 206 C3
Roedean Av PEND EN3 24 E2
Roedean Cl ORP BR6 217 H2
PEND EN3 24 E2
Roedean Crs PUT/ROE SW15 158 B1
Roe End CDALE/KGS NW9 62 E1
Roe Gn CDALE/KGS NW9 62 E2
Roehampton Cl PUT/ROE SW15 138 D5
Roehampton Dr CHST BR7 185 H2
Roehampton Ga
PUT/ROE SW15 158 B1
Roehampton High St
PUT/ROE SW15 158 D2
Roehampton La
PUT/ROE SW15 138 D6
Roehampton V PUT/ROE SW15 158 C5
Roe La CDALE/KGS NW9 62 E1
Roe Wy WLGTN SM6 210 E5
Rofant Rd NTHWD HA6 40 C2
Roffey St POP/IOD E14 125 F2
Rogers Gdns DAGE RM10 92 C3
Rogers Rd CAN/RD E16 106 D5
DAGE RM10 92 C3
TOOT SW17 160 C6
Rogers Ruff NTHWD HA6 40 A4
Roger St BMSBY WC1N 5 H7
Rojack Rd FSTH SE23 164 A3
Rokeby Gdns WFD IG8 52 E4
Rokeby Pl RYNPK SW20 176 E3
Rokeby Rd BROCKY * SE4 144 C3
Rokeby St SRTFD E15 88 C6
Rokesby Cl WELL DA16 147 J3
Rokesby Pl ALP/SUD HA0 79 K3
Rokesly Av CEND/HSY/T N8 66 E2
Roland Gdns SKENS SW7 120 B5
Roland Ms WCHPL * E1 105 F4
Roland Rd WALTH E17 70 B1
Roland Wy WALW SE17 122 E5
WBPTN SW10 120 B5
WPK KT4 192 C6
Roles Gv CHDH RM6 73 K1
Rolfe Cl EBAR EN4 21 J5
Rolinsden Wy HAYES BR2 215 H2
Rollesby Rd CHSGTN KT9 206 C4
Rollesby Wy THMD SE28 109 J6
Rolleston Av STMC/STPC BR5 201 G3
Rolleston Cl STMC/STPC BR5 201 G4
Rolleston Rd SAND/SEL CR2 211 K5
Roll Gdns GNTH/NBYPK IG2 72 A2
Rollins St NWCR SE14 123 K6
Rollit Crs HSLW TW3 135 F6
Rollit St HOLWY N7 85 G3
Rolls Buildings FLST/FETLN EC4A 11 J3
Rollscourt Av HNHL SE24 142 D6
Rolls Park Av CHING E4 51 J2
Rolls Park Rd CHING E4 51 K1
Rolls Rd STHWK SE1 123 G5
Rolt St DEPT SE8 124 B6
Rolvenden Gdns BMLY BR1 184 C4
Rolvenden Pl TOTM N17 50 C4
Roman Cl ACT W3 117 J2
EBED/NFELT TW14 134 B6
RAIN RM13 111 F1
Romanfield Rd
BRXS/STRHM SW2 162 A2
Romanhurst Av HAYES BR2 199 H1
Romanhurst Gdns BECK BR3 199 H1
Roman Ri NRWD SE19 180 E2
Roman Rd BETH E2 105 F1
BOW E3 87 H6
CHSWK W4 118 B4
EHAM E6 107 J3
IL IG1 90 B4
MUSWH N10 48 B3
Roman Sq THMD SE28 128 B1
Roman Wy CROY/NA CR0 196 C6
DART DA1 150 B6
EN EN1 24 B6
HOLWY N7 85 F4
Romany Gdns CHEAM SM3 193 K4
Romany Ri STMC/STPC BR5 201 H5
Roma Rd WALTH E17 51 G6
Romberg Rd TOOT SW17 161 F5
Romborough Gdns LEW SE13 145 F6
Romborough Wy LEW SE13 145 F6
Rom Crs ROMW/RG RM7 75 G4
Romeland BORE WD6 29 K1
Romero Sq BKHTH/KID SE3 146 B5
Romeyn Rd STRHM/NOR SW16 162 A5
Romford Rd CHDH RM6 55 K2
FSTGT E7 88 E4
MNPK E12 90 A1
SRTFD E15 88 C5
Romford St WCHPL E1 104 C4
Romilly Dr OXHEY WD19 27 J6
Romilly Rd FSBYPK N4 67 H6
Romilly St SOHO/SHAV W1D 10 D5
Rommany Rd WNWD SE27 162 E6
Romney Cl CHSGTN KT9 206 A2
GLDGN NW11 65 F5
RYLN/HDSTN HA2 60 A4
TOTM N17 50 D4
Romney Dr BMLY BR1 184 C3
RYLN/HDSTN HA2 60 A4
Romney Gdns BXLYHN DA7 149 G2
Romney Rd GNWCH SE10 125 F6
NWMAL KT3 192 A3
WOOL/PLUM SE18 127 G3
YEAD UB4 94 B1
Romney Rw CRICK * NW2 64 B6
Romola Rd BRXS/STRHM SW2 162 C3
Romsey Cl ORP BR6 216 C2
Romsey Rd DAGW RM9 91 K6
WEA * W13 97 G6
Rom Valley Wy ROMW/RG RM7 75 G3
Ronald Av SRTFD E15 106 C2
Ronald Cl BECK BR3 198 C2
Ronalds Rd BMLY BR1 183 K4
HBRY N5 85 H3
Ronaldstone Rd BFN/LL DA15 167 K1
Ronald St WCHPL E1 104 E5
Rona Rd HAMP NW3 84 A2
Ronart St KTN/HRWW/W HA3 43 F6
Rona Wk IS N1 85 K4
Rondu Rd CRICK NW2 82 C3
Ronelean Rd SURB KT6 191 G6
Roneo Cnr ROMW/RG RM7 75 H5
Roneo Link HCH RM12 75 H5
Ronfearn Av STMC/STPC BR5 202 E2
Ron Green Ct ERITH DA8 130 A5
Ron Leighton Wy EHAM E6 89 J6
Ronver Rd LEE/GVPK SE12 165 K3
Rood La FENCHST EC3M 13 G5
Rookby Ct WCHMH N21 35 H4
Rook Cl WBLY HA9 80 D1
Rookeries Cl FELT TW13 154 A5
The Rookery
STRHM/NOR * SW16 180 A2
Rookery Dr CHST BR7 185 F4
Rookery Gdns STMC/STPC BR5 202 D2
Rookery La HAYES BR2 200 C3
Rookery Rd CLAP SW4 141 H5
Rookery Wy CDALE/KGS NW9 63 H2
Rookesley Rd STMC/STPC BR5 202 E4
Rookfield Av MUSWH N10 66 C1
Rookfield Cl MUSWH N10 66 C1
Rooks Ter WDR/YW * UB7 112 B2
Rookstone Rd TOOT SW17 178 E1
Rookwood Av NWMAL KT3 192 D1
WLGTN SM6 210 D2
Rookwood Gdns CHING * E4 38 D4
Rookwood Rd STNW/STAM N16 68 B3
Roosevelt Wy DAGE RM10 93 F4
Rootes Dr NKENS W10 100 B3
Ropemaker Rd
BERM/RHTH SE16 124 B2
Ropemaker's Flds
POP/IOD * E14 105 H6
Ropemaker St BARB EC2Y 12 E1
Roper La STHWK SE1 19 H3
Ropers Av CHING E4 52 A1
Ropers Orch CHEL * SW3 120 D6
Roper St ELTH/MOT SE9 146 E6
Roper Wy MTCM CR4 179 F5
Ropery St BOW E3 105 H3
Rope St BERM/RHTH SE16 124 B3
Ropewalk Gdns WCHPL E1 104 C5
Ropewalk Ms HACK * E8 86 B5
Rope Yard Rails
WOOL/PLUM SE18 127 G3
Ropley St BETH E2 104 C1
Rosa Alba Ms HBRY N5 85 J2
Rosa Av ASHF TW15 152 D6
Rosaline Rd FUL/PGN SW6 139 H1
Rosaline Ter FUL/PGN * SW6 139 H1
Rosamond St SYD SE26 163 J5
Rosamond Vls
MORT/ESHN * SW14 138 A5
Rosamund Cl SAND/SEL CR2 211 K2
Rosary Cl HSLW TW3 134 D3
Rosary Gdns ASHF TW15 152 E6
BUSH WD23 28 E2
SKENS SW7 120 B4
Rosary Ga BTSEA SW11 141 G1
Rosaville Rd FUL/PGN SW6 139 J1
Roscoe St STLK EC1Y 6 D7
Roscoff Cl EDGE HA8 44 D4
Roseacre Cl WEA W13 97 H4
Roseacre Rd WELL DA16 148 C4
Rose Aly STHWK SE1 12 D7
Rose & Crown Yd STJS * SW1Y 16 B1
Roseary Cl WDR/YW UB7 112 A4
Rose Av MRDN SM4 194 B2
MTCM CR4 178 E4
SWFD E18 53 F5
Rosebank PGE/AN SE20 181 J3
Rosebank Av HRW HA1 79 F2
Rose Bank Cl NFNCH/WDSP N12 47 J1
Rosebank Cl TEDD TW11 174 B2
Rosebank Est BOW E3 105 H1
Rosebank Gdns ACT * W3 99 F5
BOW * E3 105 G1
Rosebank Gv WALTH E17 51 H6
Rosebank Rd HNWL W7 115 K2
WALTH E17 69 J3
Rosebank Wk CAMTN * NW1 84 D5
Rosebank Wy ACT W3 99 F5
Rose Bates Dr CDALE/KGS NW9 62 C1
Roseberry Gdns DART DA1 171 F2
FSBYPK N4 67 H3
ORP BR6 216 E1
Roseberry Pl HACK E8 86 B4
Roseberry St BERM/RHTH SE16 123 J4
Rosebery Av BFN/LL DA15 167 K2
CLKNW EC1R 5 J7
MNPK E12 89 J4
NWMAL KT3 176 C5
RYLN/HDSTN HA2 77 J2
THHTH CR7 180 D5
TOTM N17 50 C5
Rosebery Cl MRDN SM4 193 G3
Rosebery Ct CLKNW EC1R 5 J6
Rosebery Gdns
CEND/HSY/T * N8 66 E2
SUT SM1 209 F2
WEA W13 97 G5
Rosebery Ms MUSWH N10 48 C5
Rosebery Pde EW * KT17 207 H5
Rosebery Rd BUSH WD23 28 B3
CLAP SW4 161 K1
ED N9 36 C5
HSLW TW3 135 H6
KUT KT1 175 J5
MUSWH N10 48 C5
SUT SM1 208 D4
Rosebine Av WHTN TW2 155 J2
Rosebriars ESH/CLAY KT10 204 C3
Rosebury Rd FUL/PGN SW6 140 A3
Rosebury Sq WFD IG8 54 A3
Rosebury V RSLP HA4 58 E6
Rose Ct WCHPL E1 13 J2
Rosecourt Rd CROY/NA CR0 196 A3
Rosecroft Av HAMP NW3 82 E1
Rosecroft Cl STMC/STPC BR5 202 D3
Rosecroft Ct NTHWD * HA6 40 A2
Rose Croft Gdns CRICK NW2 81 J1
Rosecroft Gdns WHTN TW2 155 J3
Rosecroft Rd STHL UB1 96 A3
Rosecroft Wk ALP/SUD HA0 79 K3
PIN HA5 59 H2
Rose Dl ORP BR6 201 G6
Rosedale Av HYS/HAR UB3 94 B4
Rosedale Cl ABYW SE2 128 C3
HNWL W7 116 A2
STAN HA7 43 H2
Rosedale Gdns DAGW RM9 91 H5
Rosedale Rd DAGW RM9 91 H5
EW KT17 207 J3
FSTGT E7 89 G3
RCH/KEW TW9 137 F5
ROM RM1 56 E6
Rosedene Av CROY/NA CR0 195 K4
GFD/PVL UB6 96 A2
MRDN SM4 193 K2
STRHM/NOR SW16 162 A5
Rosedene Cl DART DA1 171 F2
Rosedene Gdns
GNTH/NBYPK IG2 72 A1
Rosedene Ter LEY E10 69 K6
Rosedew Rd HMSMTH W6 119 G6
Rose End WPK KT4 193 G5
Rosefield POP/IOD E14 105 J6
Rosefield Cl CAR SM5 209 J3
Rosefield Gdns POP/IOD E14 105 J6
Rose Garden Cl EDGE HA8 44 A2
Rose Gdns EA W5 116 E3
FELT TW13 153 K4
STHL UB1 96 A3
STWL/WRAY TW19 152 A2
Rose Gln CDALE/KGS NW9 63 F1
ROMW/RG RM7 75 G5
Rosehart Ms NTGHL W11 100 E5
Rosehatch Av CHDH RM6 55 K6
Roseheath Rd HSLWW TW4 134 E6
Rosehill ESH/CLAY KT10 205 G4
HPTN TW12 173 F4
Rose Hl SUT SM1 194 A6
Rosehill Av SUT SM1 194 B5
Rosehill Court Pde MRDN * SM4 194 B4
Rosehill Gdns GFD/PVL UB6 79 F3
SUT SM1 194 A6
Rose Hill Pk West SUT SM1 194 B5
Rosehill Rd WAND/EARL SW18 160 B1
Roseland Cl TOTM N17 49 K3
Rose La CHDH RM6 74 A1
Rose Lawn BUSH WD23 28 C3
Roseleigh Av HBRY N5 85 H2
Roseleigh Cl TWK TW1 156 E1
Rosemary Av E/WMO/HCT KT8 173 F6
ED N9 36 D3
ENC/FH EN2 23 K2
FNCH N3 47 F5
HSLWW TW4 134 C3
ROM RM1 57 H6
Rosemary Cl CROY/NA CR0 195 K4
Rosemary Dr POP/IOD E14 106 B5
REDBR IG4 71 H2
Rosemary Gdns BCTR RM8 74 B5
CHSGTN KT9 206 A2
Rosemary La
MORT/ESHN SW14 137 K4
Rosemary Rd PECK SE15 143 G1
TOOT SW17 160 A5
WELL DA16 148 A2
Rosemary St IS N1 85 K6
Rosemead CDALE/KGS NW9 63 H4
Rosemead Av FELT TW13 153 J4
MTCM CR4 179 H6
WBLY HA9 80 A3
Rosemont Av NFNCH/WDSP N12 47 G2
Rosemont Rd ACT W3 98 D6
HAMP NW3 83 G4
NWMAL KT3 175 K6
RCHPK/HAM TW10 157 F1
Rosemoor St CHEL SW3 14 E7
Rosemount Cl WFD IG8 53 K2
Rosemount Dr BMLY BR1 200 E1
Rosemount Rd ALP/SUD HA0 80 A6
WEA W13 97 G5
Rosenau Crs BTSEA SW11 140 E2
Rosenau Rd BTSEA SW11 140 D2
Rosendale Rd HNHL SE24 162 D2
Roseneath Av WCHMH N21 35 H3
Roseneath Rd BTSEA SW11 161 F1
Roseneath Wk EN EN1 24 A5
Rosenheath Cl ORP BR6 217 H5
Rosens Wk EDGE HA8 30 D5
Rosenthal Rd CAT SE6 164 E1
Rosenthorpe Rd PECK SE15 144 A6
Rose Park Cl YEAD UB4 95 G3
Roserton St POP/IOD E14 125 F2
The Rosery CROY/NA CR0 198 A3
The Roses WFD * IG8 52 D3
Rose Sq CHEL * SW3 120 C5
Rose St COVGDN WC2E 10 E5
Rosethorn Cl BAL SW12 161 H2
Rosetta Cl VX/NE SW8 141 K1
Roseveare Rd LEE/GVPK SE12 166 B6
Roseville Av HSLW TW3 135 F6
Roseville Rd HYS/HAR UB3 113 K5
Rosevine Rd RYNPK SW20 177 F4
Rose Wk BRYLDS KT5 191 J2
WWKM BR4 199 G6
Roseway DUL SE21 162 E1
EDGE HA8 30 E6
Rose Wy LEE/GVPK SE12 145 K6
Rosewell Cl PGE/AN SE20 181 J3
Rosewood RDART DA2 170 B6
Rosewood Av GFD/PVL UB6 79 G3
HCH RM12 93 J3
Rosewood Cl SCUP DA14 168 D5
Rosewood Ct KUTN/CMB KT2 175 H3
Rosewood Gv SUT SM1 194 B6
Rosewood Ter PGE/AN * SE20 181 K3
Rosher Cl SRTFD E15 88 B5
Rosina St HOM E9 87 F3
Roskell Rd PUT/ROE SW15 139 G4
Roslin Rd ACT W3 117 J3
Roslin Wy BMLY BR1 183 K1
Roslyn Cl MTCM CR4 178 C5
Roslyn Gdns GPK RM2 57 H5
Roslyn Ms SEVS/STOTM * N15 68 A2
Roslyn Rd SEVS/STOTM N15 67 K2
Rosmead Rd NTGHL W11 100 C6
Rosoman Pl CLKNW EC1R 5 K6
Rosoman St CLKNW EC1R 5 K5
Rossall Cl EMPK RM11 75 J3
Rossall Crs WLSDN NW10 98 B2
Ross Av BCTR RM8 74 B6
MLHL NW7 46 C1
Ross Cl HYS/HAR UB3 113 G4
KTN/HRWW/W HA3 42 C3
Rossdale SUT SM1 209 J3
Rossdale Dr CDALE/KGS NW9 62 E5
ED N9 36 E1
Rossdale Rd PUT/ROE SW15 139 F5
Rosse Ms BKHTH/KID SE3 146 A2
Rossendale St CLPT E5 68 D6
Rossendale Wy CAMTN NW1 84 C6
Rossetti Rd BERM/RHTH SE16 123 J5
Ross House WOOL/PLUM SE18 146 D2
Rossignol Gdns CAR SM5 195 F6
Rossindel Rd HSLW TW3 135 F6
Rossington Cl EN EN1 24 D1
Rossington St CLPT * E5 68 D6
Rossiter Flds BAR EN5 32 C1
Rossiter Rd BAL SW12 161 G3
Rossland Cl BXLYHS DA6 149 H6
Rosslyn Av BARN SW13 138 B4
BCTR RM8 74 B4
CHING E4 38 D4
EBAR EN4 33 J1
EBED/NFELT TW14 153 K1
Rosslyn Cl HYS/HAR UB3 94 B4
WWKM BR4 214 D1
Rosslyn Crs HRW HA1 61 F1
WBLY HA9 80 A1
Rosslyn Hl HAMP NW3 83 H3
Rosslyn Park Ms HAMP NW3 83 H3
Rosslyn Rd BARK IG11 90 D5
TWK TW1 156 D1
WALTH * E17 70 A1
Rossmore Cl STJWD * NW8 2 D7
Rossmore Rd STJWD NW8 2 D6
Ross Pde WLGTN SM6 210 B4
Ross Rd DART DA1 170 D1
SNWD SE25 181 F6
WHTN TW2 155 H3
WLGTN SM6 210 C4
Ross Wy ELTH/MOT SE9 146 D4
NTHWD HA6 26 D6
Rosswood Gdns WLGTN SM6 210 B4
Rostella Rd TOOT SW17 160 C6
Rostrever Gdns HYS/HAR UB3 113 H1
Rostrevor Av SEVS/STOTM N15 68 B3
Rostrevor Gdns NWDGN UB2 114 D5
Rostrevor Rd FUL/PGN SW6 139 J2
WIM/MER SW19 177 K1
Rotary St STHWK SE1 18 A4
Rothbury Av RAIN RM13 111 K4
Rothbury Gdns ISLW TW7 136 B1
Rothbury Rd HOM E9 87 H5
Rotherfield Rd CAR SM5 210 A2
Rotherfield St IS N1 85 J5
Rotherham Wk STHWK * SE1 18 B1
Rotherhill Av
STRHM/NOR SW16 179 J2
Rotherhithe New Rd
BERM/RHTH SE16 123 J5
Rotherhithe Old Rd
BERM/RHTH SE16 124 A4
Rotherhithe St
BERM/RHTH SE16 123 K2
Rotherhithe Tnl
BERM/RHTH SE16 123 K2
Rothermere Rd CROY/NA CR0 211 F3
Rotherwick Hl EA W5 98 B3
Rotherwick Rd GLDGN NW11 64 E4
Rotherwood Cl
WIM/MER SW19 177 H4
Rotherwood Rd
PUT/ROE SW15 139 G4
Rothery St IS N1 85 H6
Rothery Ter BRXN/ST * SW9 142 C1
Rothesay Av GFD/PVL UB6 78 D4
RCHPK/HAM TW10 137 J5
RYNPK SW20 177 H5
Rothesay Rd SNWD SE25 196 E1
Rothsay Rd FSTGT E7 89 G5
Rothsay St STHWK SE1 19 G4
Rothschild Rd CHSWK W4 117 K4
Rothschild St WNWD SE27 162 C6
Rothwell Gdns DAGW RM9 91 J5
Rothwell Rd DAGW RM9 91 J6
Rothwell St CAMTN NW1 83 K6
Rotterdam Dr POP/IOD E14 125 F3
Rouel Rd BERM/RHTH SE16 123 H4
Rougemont Av MRDN SM4 193 K3
The Roughs NTHWD HA6 26 C5
Roundaway Rd CLAY IG5 53 K5
Roundel Cl BROCKY SE4 144 C5
Round Gv CROY/NA CR0 198 A4
Roundhay Cl FSTH SE23 164 A4
Roundhedge Wy ENC/FH EN2 23 F1
Round Hl SYD SE26 163 J4
Roundhill Dr ENC/FH EN2 23 F5
Roundlyn Gdns
STMC/STPC BR5 202 C1
Roundtable Rd BMLY BR1 165 K5
Roundtree Rd ALP/SUD HA0 79 H3
The Roundway ESH/CLAY KT10 205 F4
TOTM N17 49 K4
WATW WD18 26 D2
Roundways RSLP HA4 76 D1
Roundwood CHST BR7 185 G5
Roundwood Av STKPK UB11 113 F1
Roundwood Cl RSLP * HA4 58 B4
Roundwood Pk WLSDN * NW10 81 J6
Roundwood Rd WLSDN NW10 81 G4
Rounton Rd BOW E3 105 J3
Roupell Rd BRXS/STRHM SW2 162 A3
Roupell St STHWK SE1 17 K1
Rousden St CAMTN NW1 84 C5
Rouse Gdns DUL SE21 163 F6
Rous Rd BKHH IG9 39 J3
Routemaster Cl PLSTW E13 107 F2
Routh Rd WAND/EARL SW18 160 D2
Routh St EHAM E6 107 K4
Rover Av BARK/HLT IG6 55 F2
Rowallan Rd FUL/PGN SW6 139 H1
Rowan Av CHING E4 51 H2
Rowan Cl ALP/SUD HA0 79 G1
EA W5 117 F2
IL IG1 90 D3
KTN/HRWW/W HA3 43 F2
NWMAL KT3 176 B5
STRHM/NOR SW16 179 H4
Rowan Crs DART DA1 171 F3
STRHM/NOR SW16 179 H4
Rowan Dr CDALE/KGS NW9 45 J6
Rowan Gdns CROY/NA CR0 212 B1
Rowan Pl HYS/HAR UB3 94 D6
Rowan Rd BTFD TW8 136 C1
BXLYHN DA7 149 F4
HMSMTH W6 119 G4
STRHM/NOR SW16 179 H5
WDR/YW UB7 112 A4
The Rowans PLMGR N13 35 J5
Rowan Ter PGE/AN * SE20 181 H4
WIM/MER * SW19 177 H3
Rowantree Cl WCHMH N21 35 K3
Rowantree Ms ENC/FH EN2 23 H3
Rowantree Rd ENC/FH EN2 23 H3
WCHMH N21 35 K3
Rowan Wk EFNCH N2 65 G3
HAYES BR2 215 K1
NKENS * W10 100 C3
Rowan Wy CHDH RM6 55 J6
Rowanwood Av BFN/LL DA15 168 B3
Rowben Cl TRDG/WHET N20 33 F3
Rowberry Cl FUL/PGN SW6 139 G1
Rowcross St STHWK SE1 123 G5
Rowdell Rd NTHLT UB5 78 A6
Rowden Pde CHING * E4 51 J2
Rowden Rd BECK BR3 182 B4
CHING E4 51 K2
HOR/WEW KT19 206 E2
Rowditch La BTSEA SW11 141 F3
Rowdon Av WLSDN NW10 81 K5
Rowdown Crs CROY/NA CR0 214 B6
Rowdowns Rd DAGW RM9 92 B6
Rowe Gdns BARK IG11 109 F1
Rowe La HOM E9 86 E3
Rowena Crs BTSEA SW11 140 D3
Rowe Wk RYLN/HDSTN HA2 78 A1
Rowfant Rd TOOT SW17 161 F4
Rowhill Rd CLPT E5 86 D2
Rowington Cl BAY/PAD W2 101 F4
Rowland Av KTN/HRWW/W HA3 43 J6
Rowland Gv SYD SE26 163 J5
Rowland Hill Av TOTM N17 49 J3
Rowland Hill St HAMP NW3 83 J3
Rowland Pl NTHWD * HA6 40 C3
Rowlands Av PIN HA5 42 A2
Rowlands Cl HGT * N6 66 A3
MLHL NW7 45 J3
Rowlands Rd BCTR RM8 74 B6
Rowland Wy WIM/MER SW19 178 A4
Rowlatt Cl RDART DA2 171 F6
Rowley Av BFN/LL DA15 168 C2
Rowley Cl ALP/SUD HA0 80 B5
OXHEY WD19 27 J1
Rowley Cottages WKENS * W14 119 J4
Rowley Gdns FSBYPK N4 67 J4
Rowley Rd SEVS/STOTM N15 67 J2
Rowley Wy STJWD NW8 83 G6
Rowlheys Pl WDR/YW UB7 112 B3
Rowlls Rd KUT KT1 175 G6
Rowney Gdns DAGW RM9 91 J4
Rowney Rd DAGW RM9 91 H4
Rowntree Cl KIL/WHAMP * NW6 82 E4
PLSTW E13 107 F3
Rowntree Rd WHTN TW2 155 K3
Rowse Cl SRTFD E15 88 A6
Rowsley Av HDN NW4 46 A6
Rowstock Gdns HOLWY N7 84 D3
Rowton Rd WOOL/PLUM SE18 147 H1
Roxborough Av HRW HA1 60 D4
ISLW TW7 136 A1
Roxborough Pk HRW HA1 60 E4
Roxborough Rd HRW HA1 60 D2
Roxbourne Cl NTHLT UB5 77 H4
Roxburgh Rd WNWD SE27 180 C1
Roxburn Wy RSLP HA4 76 D1
Roxby Pl FUL/PGN SW6 119 K6
Roxeth Green Av
RYLN/HDSTN HA2 78 B1
Roxeth Gv RYLN/HDSTN HA2 78 B2
Roxeth Hl RYLN/HDSTN HA2 60 D6
Roxley Rd LEW SE13 164 E1
Roxton Gdns CROY/NA CR0 213 H4

Roxwell Rd BARK IG11 ....109 G1
SHB W12 ....118 D2
Roxwell Wy WFD IG8 ....53 G3
Roxy Av CHDH RM6 ....73 J4
Royal Albert Rd EHAM E6 ....108 A6
Royal Albert Wy CAN/RD E16 ....107 H6
Royal Ar CONDST W1S 10 A6
Royal Arsenal West
WOOL/PLUM * SE18 ....127 F5
Royal Av CHEL SW3 ....120 E5
WPK KT4 ....192 B6
Royal Circ WNWD SE27 ....162 B5
Royal Cl DEPT SE8 ....124 C6
GDMY/SEVK IG3 ....73 G4
ORP BR6 ....216 B2
STNW/STAM * N16 ....68 A5
WPK KT4 ....192 B6
Royal College St CAMTN NW1 ....84 C5
Royal Ct BANK EC3V 13 F4
ELTH/MOT * SE9 ....166 E3
EN * EN1 ....36 A1
Royal Crs NTGHL W11 ....119 G2
RSLP HA4 ....77 J2
Royal Crescent Ms NTGHL W11 ....119 G2
Royal Docks Rd EHAM E6 ....108 B4
Royal Herbert Pavilions
WOOL/PLUM * SE18 ....146 E2
Royal Hl GNWCH SE10 ....145 F1
Royal Hospital Rd CHEL SW3 ....120 E6
Royal Ms BAL SW12 ....161 G2
Royal Mint Pl WCHPL E1 ....13 K5
Royal Mint St TWRH EC3N 13 K5
Royal Naval Pl NWCR SE14 ....144 C1
Royal Oak Pl EDUL SE22 ....163 J1
Royal Oak Rd BXLYHS DA6 ....149 G6
HACK E8 ....86 D4
Royal Opera Ar STJS * SW1Y 10 C7
Royal Orchard Cl
WAND/EARL SW18 ....159 H2
Royal Pde BKHTH/KID SE3 ....145 J3
CHST BR7 ....185 H3
FUL/PGN * SW6 ....139 H1
Royal Pl GNWCH SE10 ....145 F1
Royal Rd CAN/RD E16 ....107 H5
SCUP DA14 ....168 E5
TEDD TW11 ....173 J1
WALW SE17 ....122 C6
Royal Route WBLY HA9 ....80 B2
Royal St STHWK SE1 ....17 H4
Royal Victor Pl BOW E3 ....105 F1
Roycraft Av BARK IG11 ....109 F1
Roycroft Cl BRXS/STRHM * SW2 ....162 B3
SWFD E18 ....53 F4
Roydene Rd WOOL/PLUM SE18 ....127 K6
Roydon Cl LOU IG10 ....39 J2
Roy Gdns GNTH/NBYPK IG2 ....72 E1
Roy Gv HPTN TW12 ....173 G2
Royle Cl GPK RM2 ....75 K2
Royle Crs WEA W13 ....97 G3
Roy Rd NTHWD HA6 ....40 D3
Royston Av CHING E4 ....51 J1
SUT SM1 ....209 H1
WLGTN SM6 ....210 D2
Royston Cl HEST TW5 ....134 A2
Royston Gdns IL IG1 ....71 H3
Royston Gv PIN HA5 ....41 K2
Royston Park Rd PIN HA5 ....41 K2
Royston Rd DART DA1 ....170 C1
PGE/AN SE20 ....182 A4
RCHPK/HAM TW10 ....137 F6
The Roystons BRYLDS KT5 ....191 J2
Royston St BETH E2 ....104 E1
Rozel Rd CLAP SW4 ....141 H3
Rubastic Rd NWDGN UB2 ....114 B3
Rubens Rd NTHLT UB5 ....95 G1
Rubens St CAT SE6 ....164 C4
Ruby Ms WALTH * E17 ....51 J6
Ruby Rd WALTH E17 ....51 J6
Ruby St PECK SE15 ....123 J6
Ruby Triangle PECK * SE15 ....123 J6
Ruckholt Cl LEY E10 ....87 K1
Ruckholt Rd LEY E10 ....87 K2
Rucklidge Av WLSDN NW10 ....99 H1
Rudall Crs HAMP NW3 ....83 H2
Ruddington Cl CLPT E5 ....87 G2
Ruddock Cl EDGE HA8 ....44 E3
Ruddstreet Cl
WOOL/PLUM SE18 ....127 G4
Rudgwick Ter STJWD * NW8 ....2 D1
Rudland Rd BXLYHN DA7 ....149 J4
Rudloe Rd BAL SW12 ....161 H2
Rudolf Pl VX/NE SW8 ....121 K6
Rudolph Rd BUSH WD23 ....28 A1
KIL/WHAMP NW6 ....100 E1
PLSTW E13 ....106 E1
Rudyard Gv EDGE HA8 ....44 E2
Ruffetts Cl SAND/SEL CR2 ....212 D5
The Ruffetts SAND/SEL CR2 ....212 D5
Ruffle Cl WDR/YW UB7 ....112 B2
Rufford Cl HRW HA1 ....61 G3
Rufford St IS N1 ....84 E6
Rufus Cl RSLP HA4 ....77 H1
Rufus St IS N1 ....7 G5
Rugby Av ALP/SUD HA0 ....79 J2
ED N9 ....36 B3
GFD/PVL UB6 ....78 D4
Rugby Cl HRW HA1 ....60 E1
Rugby Gdns DAGW RM9 ....91 J4
Rugby La BELMT SM2 ....208 B6
Rugby Rd CDALE/KGS NW9 ....62 C1
CHSWK W4 ....118 B2
DAGW RM9 ....91 H5
WHTN TW2 ....155 K1
Rugby St BMSBY WC1N 5 G7
Rugg St POP/IOD E14 ....105 J6
Ruislip Cl GFD/PVL UB6 ....96 B3
Ruislip Ct RSLP * HA4 ....58 D6
Ruislip Rd NTHLT UB5 ....77 G6
Ruislip Rd East GFD/PVL UB6 ....96 C3
Ruislip St TOOT SW17 ....160 E6
Rumbold Rd FUL/PGN SW6 ....140 A1
Rum Cl WAP E1W 104 D6
Rumsey Cl HPTN TW12 ....172 E2
Rumsey Rd BRXN/ST SW9 ....142 A4
Runbury Cir CDALE/KGS NW9 ....63 F6
Runcorn Cl TOTM N17 ....68 D1
Runcorn Pl NTGHL W11 ....100 C6
Rundell Crs HDN NW4 ....63 K2
Runes Cl MTCM CR4 ....194 C1
Runnelfield HRW HA1 ....78 E1
Runnymede WIM/MER SW19 ....178 C4
Runnymede Cl WHTN TW2 ....155 G1
Runnymede Crs
STRHM/NOR SW16 ....179 J4
Runnymede Gdns GFD/PVL UB6 ....96 D1
WHTN TW2 ....155 G1
Runnymede Rd HSLW TW3 ....155 G1
The Runway RSLP HA4 ....77 F3
Rupack St BERM/RHTH * SE16 ....123 K2
Rupert Av WBLY HA9 ....80 A3
Rupert Ct E/WMO/HCT * KT8 ....189 F1
SOHO/SHAV W1D 10 C5
Rupert Gdns BRXN/ST SW9 ....142 C3
Rupert Rd ARCH N19 ....84 D1
CHSWK W4 ....118 B3
KIL/WHAMP NW6 ....100 D1
Rupert St SOHO/SHAV * W1D 10 C5
Rural Cl EMPK RM11 ....75 K5
Rural Wy STRHM/NOR SW16 ....179 G3
Rusbridge Cl HACK E8 ....86 C3
Ruscoe Rd CAN/RD E16 ....106 D5
Ruscombe Wy
EBED/NFELT TW14 ....153 J2
Rusham Rd BAL SW12 ....160 E1
Rushbrook Crs WALTH E17 ....51 H4
Rushbrook Rd ELTH/MOT SE9 ....167 H4
Rush Common Ms
BRXS/STRHM SW2 ....161 K2
Rushcroft Rd
BRXS/STRHM SW2 ....142 B5
CHING E4 ....51 K3
Rushden Cl NRWD SE19 ....180 E3
Rushdene ABYW SE2 ....128 D3
Rushdene Av EBAR EN4 ....33 J2
Rushdene Cl NTHLT UB5 ....95 G1
Rushdene Crs NTHLT UB5 ....95 F1
Rushdene Rd PIN HA5 ....59 G3
Rushden Gdns CLAY IG5 ....54 A6
MLHL NW7 ....46 A2
Rushdon Cl ROM RM1 ....75 J2
Rushet Rd STMC/STPC BR5 ....186 B5
Rushett Cl THDIT KT7 ....190 C5
Rushett Rd THDIT KT7 ....190 C4
Rushey Cl NWMAL KT3 ....192 A1
Rushey Gn CAT SE6 ....164 E2
Rushey Hl ENC/FH EN2 ....23 F5
Rushey Md BROCKY SE4 ....144 D6
Rushford Rd BROCKY SE4 ....164 C1
Rush Green Gdns
ROMW/RG RM7 ....74 E5
Rush Green Rd ROMW/RG RM7 ....74 E5
Rushgrove Av CDALE/KGS NW9 ....63 H1
Rushgrove Pde
CDALE/KGS * NW9 ....63 H2
Rushgrove St
WOOL/PLUM SE18 ....126 E4
Rush Hill Ms BTSEA SW11 ....141 F4
Rush Hill Rd BTSEA SW11 ....141 F4
Rushley Cl HAYES BR2 ....215 H2
Rushmead BETH E2 ....104 D2
RCHPK/HAM TW10 ....156 C5
Rushmead Cl CROY/NA CR0 ....212 B2
Rushmere Ct WPK KT4 ....192 D6
Rushmere Pl WIM/MER SW19 ....177 G1
Rushmon Pl CHEAM * SM3 ....208 C4
Rushmon Vls NWMAL * KT3 ....192 C1
Rushmoor Cl PIN HA5 ....59 F1
Rushmore Cl BMLY BR1 ....184 D6
Rushmore Ct WATW * WD18 ....26 B1
Rushmore Rd CLPT E5 ....86 E2
Rusholme Av DAGE RM10 ....92 C1
Rusholme Gv NRWD SE19 ....181 F1
Rusholme Rd PUT/ROE SW15 ....159 G1
Rushout Av KTN/HRWW/W HA3 ....61 H3
Rushton St IS N1 ....7 F2
Rushworth St STHWK SE1 ....18 B2
Rushy Meadow La CAR SM5 ....194 D6
Ruskin Av EBED/NFELT TW14 ....153 J2
MNPK E12 ....89 K4
RCH/KEW TW9 ....137 H1
WELL DA16 ....148 B4
Ruskin Cl GLDGN NW11 ....65 F3
Ruskin Dr ORP BR6 ....216 E1
WELL DA16 ....148 B4
WPK KT4 ....192 E6
Ruskin Gdns EA W5 ....97 K3
HARH RM3 ....57 K4
KTN/HRWW/W HA3 ....62 B2
Ruskin Gv DART DA1 ....151 K6
WELL DA16 ....148 B3
Ruskin Rd BELV DA17 ....129 H4
CAR SM5 ....210 A3
CROY/NA CR0 ....196 C6
ISLW TW7 ....136 A4
STHL UB1 ....95 J6
TOTM N17 ....50 B4
Ruskin Wk ED N9 ....36 C4
HAYES BR2 ....200 D3
HNHL SE24 ....142 D6
Ruskin Wy WIM/MER SW19 ....178 C5
Rusland Av ORP BR6 ....216 D1
Rusland Park Rd HRW HA1 ....60 E1
Rusper Cl CRICK NW2 ....82 A1
STAN HA7 ....29 J6
Rusper Rd DAGW RM9 ....91 J4
WDGN N22 ....49 H5
Russel Cl BECK BR3 ....182 E6
Russell Av WDGN N22 ....49 H5
Russell Cl BXLYHN DA7 ....149 H5
CHARL SE7 ....146 B1
DART DA1 ....150 D4
NTHWD HA6 ....40 A1
RSLP HA4 ....59 G6
WLSDN NW10 ....80 E5
Russell Ct BAR * EN5 ....21 G5
WHALL SW1A 16 B1
Russell Dr STWL/WRAY TW19 ....152 A1
Russell Gdns GLDGN NW11 ....64 C3
RCHPK/HAM TW10 ....156 D4
TRDG/WHET N20 ....33 J4
WDR/YW UB7 ....112 D5
WKENS * W14 ....119 H3
Russell Gardens Ms
WKENS W14 ....119 H2
Russell Gv BRXN/ST SW9 ....142 B2
MLHL NW7 ....45 G1
Russell Kerr Cl CHSWK * W4 ....137 K1
Russell La TRDG/WHET N20 ....33 K4
Russell Pde GLDGN * NW11 ....64 C3
Russell Pl HAMP NW3 ....83 J3
Russell Rd BKHH IG9 ....39 G3
CAN/RD E16 ....106 E5
CDALE/KGS NW9 ....63 H3
CEND/HSY/T N8 ....66 D3
CHING E4 ....37 H6
EN EN1 ....24 B1
LEY E10 ....69 K3
MTCM CR4 ....178 D6
NTHLT UB5 ....78 C3
NTHWD HA6 ....26 A5
SEVS/STOTM N15 ....68 A2
TRDG/WHET N20 ....33 J4
WALTH E17 ....51 H6
WDGN N22 ....49 F2
WHTN TW2 ....156 A1
WIM/MER SW19 ....177 K3
WKENS W14 ....119 H3
Russell Sq GWRST WC1E 10 D1
RSQ WC1B 4 E7
Russell St HOL/ALD WC2B 11 G4
Russell Wy OXHEY WD19 ....27 F2
SUT SM1 ....209 F3
Russet Cl HGDN/ICK UB10 ....94 A3
Russet Crs HOLWY * N7 ....85 F3
Russet Dr CROY/NA CR0 ....198 B5
Russets Cl CHING E4 ....38 B6
Russett Cl ORP BR6 ....217 H3
Russia Dock Rd
BERM/RHTH * SE16 ....124 B1
Russia La BETH E2 ....104 E1
Russia Rw CITYW EC2V 12 D4
Rusthall Av CHSWK W4 ....118 A3
Rusthall Cl CROY/NA CR0 ....197 K3
Rustic Av STRHM/NOR SW16 ....179 G3
Rustic Pl ALP/SUD HA0 ....79 K2
Rustington Wk MRDN SM4 ....193 J4
Ruston Av BRYLDS KT5 ....191 J4
Ruston Ms NTGHL * W11 ....100 C5
Ruston Rd WOOL/PLUM SE18 ....126 D3
Ruston St BOW E3 ....87 H6
Rust Sq CMBW SE5 ....142 E1
Rutford Rd STRHM/NOR SW16 ....179 K1
Ruth Cl KTN/HRWW/W HA3 ....62 B1
Ruthen Cl EW KT17 ....207 H6
Rutherford Cl BELMT SM2 ....209 H4
Rutherford St WEST SW1P 16 C6
Rutherford Wy BUSH WD23 ....28 D3
WBLY HA9 ....80 C1
Rutherglen Rd ABYW SE2 ....128 B6
Rutherwyke Cl EW KT17 ....207 J4
Ruthin Cl CDALE/KGS NW9 ....63 G3
Ruthin Rd BKHTH/KID SE3 ....125 K6
Ruthven St HOM E9 ....87 F6
Rutland Av BFN/LL DA15 ....168 B2
Rutland Cl BXLY DA5 ....168 E3
DART DA1 ....171 G2
MORT/ESHN SW14 ....137 J4
Rutland Ct CHST BR7 ....185 F4
SKENS SW7 ....14 D3
Rutland Dr MRDN SM4 ....193 K4
RCHPK/HAM TW10 ....156 E3
Rutland Gdns BCTR RM8 ....91 J3
CROY/NA CR0 ....212 A2
FSBYPK N4 ....67 H3
SKENS SW7 ....14 D3
WEA * W13 ....97 G4
Rutland Ga BELV DA17 ....129 J5
HAYES BR2 ....199 J1
SKENS SW7 ....14 C4
Rutland Gate Ms SKENS * SW7 ....14 C3
Rutland Gv HMSMTH W6 ....118 E5
Rutland Ms STJWD * NW8 ....83 F6
Rutland Ms South SKENS * SW7 ....14 C4
Rutland Pk CAT SE6 ....164 C4
CRICK NW2 ....82 A4
Rutland Pl BUSH * WD23 ....28 D3
FARR * EC1M 12 B1
Rutland Rd FSTGT E7 ....89 H5
HOM E9 ....87 F6
HRW HA1 ....60 C3
HYS/HAR UB3 ....113 G4
IL IG1 ....90 B2
STHL UB1 ....96 A3
WALTH E17 ....69 J3
WAN E11 ....71 F2
WHTN TW2 ....155 J4
WIM/MER SW19 ....178 D3
Rutland St SKENS SW7 ....14 D4
Rutland Wk CAT SE6 ....164 C4
Rutland Wy STMC/STPC BR5 ....202 D3
Rutley Cl LBTH SE11 ....122 C6
Rutlish Rd WIM/MER SW19 ....177 K4
Rutter Gdns MTCM CR4 ....194 C1
Rutters Cl WDR/YW UB7 ....112 D2
The Rutts BUSH WD23 ....28 D3
Rutt's Ter NWCR SE14 ....144 A2
Ruvigny Gdns PUT/ROE SW15 ....139 G4
Ruxley Cl HOR/WEW KT19 ....206 D3
SCUP DA14 ....186 E2
Ruxley Crs ESH/CLAY KT10 ....205 H5
Ruxley La HOR/WEW KT19 ....206 D4
Ruxley Ms HOR/WEW KT19 ....206 D3
Ruxley Rdg ESH/CLAY KT10 ....205 G5
Ruxley Towers
ESH/CLAY * KT10 ....205 G5
Ryan Cl BKHTH/KID SE3 ....146 A5
RSLP HA4 ....59 F5
Ryan Ct OXHEY * WD19 ....27 J2
Ryan Dr BTFD TW8 ....116 B6
Ryarsh Crs ORP BR6 ....216 E2
Rycroft Wy TOTM * N17 ....50 B6
Rycullf Sq BKHTH/KID SE3 ....145 J3
Rydal Cl HDN NW4 ....46 C4
Rydal Crs GFD/PVL UB6 ....97 H2
Rydal Dr BXLYHN DA7 ....149 H2
WWKM BR4 ....199 H6
Rydal Gdns CDALE/KGS NW9 ....63 G2
HSLW TW3 ....155 G1
PUT/ROE SW15 ....176 B1
WBLY HA9 ....61 J5
Rydal Mt HAYES * BR2 ....199 J1
Rydal Rd STRHM/NOR SW16 ....179 J1
Rydal Wy PEND EN3 ....36 E1
RSLP HA4 ....77 G2
Rydens Av WOT/HER KT12 ....188 B6
Rydens Cl WOT/HER KT12 ....188 B6
Rydens Pk WOT/HER KT12 ....188 C6
Ryde Pl TWK TW1 ....156 D1
Ryder Cl BUSH WD23 ....28 B1
Ryder Dr BERM/RHTH SE16 ....123 J5
Ryder Gdns RAIN RM13 ....93 H4
Ryder St STJS SW1Y 10 B7
Ryde Vale Rd BAL SW12 ....161 G4
Rydon St IS N1 ....6 D1
Rydston Cl HOLWY N7 ....85 F5
The Rye STHGT/OAK N14 ....34 C2
Rye Cl BXLY DA5 ....169 J1
Ryecotes Md DUL SE21 ....163 F3
Rye Crs STMC/STPC BR5 ....202 D5
Ryecroft Av CLAY IG5 ....54 B5
WHTN TW2 ....155 G3
Ryecroft Rd LEW SE13 ....145 F6
STMC/STPC BR5 ....201 J3
STRHM/NOR SW16 ....180 B2
Ryecroft St FUL/PGN SW6 ....140 A2
Ryedale EDUL SE22 ....163 J1
Ryefield Av HGDN/ICK UB10 ....76 A6
Ryefield Crs PIN * HA5 ....40 E5
Ryefield Pde NTHWD * HA6 ....40 E5
Ryefield Rd NRWD SE19 ....180 D2
Rye Hill Pk PECK SE15 ....143 K5
Ryelands Crs LEE/GVPK SE12 ....166 B1
Rye La PECK SE15 ....143 H2
Rye Rd PECK SE15 ....144 A5
Rye Wk PUT/ROE SW15 ....139 G6
Rye Wy EDGE HA8 ....44 B2
Ryfold Rd WIM/MER SW19 ....159 K5
Ryhope Rd FBAR/BDGN N11 ....34 B6
Ryland Cl FELT TW13 ....153 J6
Rylandes Rd CRICK NW2 ....81 J1
SAND/SEL CR2 ....212 D6
Ryland Rd KTTN * NW5 ....84 B4
Rylett Crs SHB W12 ....118 C3
Rylett Rd SHB W12 ....118 C2
Rylston Rd FUL/PGN SW6 ....119 J6
PLMGR N13 ....35 K5
Rymer Rd CROY/NA CR0 ....197 F4
Rymer St HNHL SE24 ....162 C1
Rymill St CAN/RD E16 ....127 F1
Rysbrack St CHEL SW3 ....14 E4
Rythe Cl CHSGTN KT9 ....205 J5
Rythe Ct THDIT KT7 ....190 B4
Rythe Rd ESH/CLAY KT10 ....204 D3
Ryves Cottages MTCM * CR4 ....179 F5

S

Sabbarton St CAN/RD E16 ....106 D5
Sabine Rd BTSEA SW11 ....140 E4
Sable Cl HSLWW TW4 ....134 B4
Sable St IS N1 ....85 H5
Sach Rd CLPT E5 ....68 D6
Sackville Av HAYES BR2 ....199 K5
Sackville Cl RYLN/HDSTN HA2 ....78 D1
Sackville Est STRHM/NOR SW16 ....161 K5
Sackville Gdns IL IG1 ....71 K5
Sackville Rd BELMT SM2 ....208 E5
DART DA1 ....171 G4
Sackville St MYFR/PICC W1J 10 B6
Saddlers Cl PIN HA5 ....42 A1
Saddlers Ms KUT * KT1 ....174 D4
Saddlescombe Wy
NFNCH/WDSP N12 ....46 E1
Sadler Cl MTCM CR4 ....178 E5
Sadlers Ride E/WMO/HCT KT8 ....173 H5
Saffron Av POP/IOD E14 ....106 B6
Saffron Cl CROY/NA CR0 ....195 K3
Saffron Hl HCIRC EC1N 11 K2
Saffron Rd CRW RM5 ....57 F5
Saffron St FARR EC1M 11 K1
Saffron Wy SURB KT6 ....190 E5
Sage Cl EHAM E6 ....107 K4
Sage St WCHPL E1 ....104 E6
Sage Wy FSBYW WC1X 5 G5
Sage Yd SURB * KT6 ....191 G5
Saigasso Cl CAN/RD E16 ....107 H5
Sail St LBTH SE11 ....17 H6
Sainfoin Rd TOOT SW17 ....161 F4
Sainsbury Rd NRWD SE19 ....181 F1
St Agatha's Dr KUTN/CMB KT2 ....175 G2
St Agatha's Gv CAR SM5 ....194 E5
St Agnes Cl HOM * E9 ....86 E6
St Agnes Pl CMBW SE5 ....122 C6
St Agnes Well STLK EC1Y 7 F6
St Aidan's Rd EDUL SE22 ....163 J1
WEA W13 ....116 C2
St Albans Av CHSWK W4 ....118 A3
EHAM E6 ....107 K2
FELT TW13 ....172 C1
St Albans Crs WDGN N22 ....49 G4
St Albans Farm HSLWW * TW4 ....134 B6
St Alban's Gdns TEDD TW11 ....174 B1
St Alban's Gv CAR SM5 ....194 D4
KENS W8 ....120 A3
KENS * W8 ....120 A3
St Albans La GLDGN NW11 ....64 E5
St Alban's Ms BAY/PAD W2 ....8 B1
St Alban's Pl IS N1 ....6 A1
St Albans Rd GDMY/SEVK IG3 ....73 F5
KUTN/CMB KT2 ....175 F2
SUT SM1 ....208 D2
BAR EN5 ....20 C2
DART DA1 ....171 J1
KTTN NW5 ....84 A1
WFD IG8 ....52 E3
WLSDN NW10 ....81 G6
St Alban's St STJS SW1Y 10 C6
St Albans Ter HMSMTH * W6 ....119 H6
St Alfege Rd CHARL SE7 ....126 C6
St Alphage Gdn BARB EC2Y 12 D2
St Alphage Gdns BARB * EC2Y 12 D2
St Alphage Highwalk BARB EC2Y 12 D2
St Alphage Wk EDGE * HA8 ....44 E5
St Alphege Rd ED N9 ....36 E2
St Alphonsus Rd CLAP SW4 ....141 H5
St Amunds Cl CAT SE6 ....164 D6
St Andrews Av ALP/SUD HA0 ....79 G2
HCH RM12 ....93 H3
St Andrew's Cl CRICK * NW2 ....81 K1
NFNCH/WDSP * N12 ....33 G6
BERM/RHTH * SE16 ....123 J5
RSLP HA4 ....59 H6
STAN * HA7 ....43 J5
THDIT KT7 ....190 C5
THMD SE28 ....109 K5
St Andrew's Ct
WAND/EARL SW18 ....160 B4
St Andrews Dr ORP BR6 ....202 C3
STAN HA7 ....43 J4
St Andrew's Gv STNW/STAM N16 ....67 K5
St Andrew's Hl BLKFR EC4V 12 B5
St Andrews Ms BAL SW12 ....161 J3
STNW/STAM * N16 ....68 A4
St Andrew's Pl CAMTN NW1 ....3 J6
St Andrew's Rd CROY/NA CR0 ....211 J2
ACT W3 ....99 G5
EN EN1 ....23 K4
GLDGN NW11 ....64 D3
HNWL W7 ....115 K2
IL IG1 ....71 K4
PLSTW E13 ....107 F2
SURB KT6 ....190 E3
WAN E11 ....70 C3
WKENS W14 ....119 H6
WLSDN NW10 ....81 K4
CAR SM5 ....209 J1
CDALE/KGS NW9 ....63 F5
ED N9 ....36 E2
ROMW/RG RM7 ....75 F3
SCUP DA14 ....168 E5
WALTH E17 ....51 F5
WKENS * W14 ....119 H6
St Andrew's Sq NTGHL * W11 ....100 C5
SURB KT6 ....190 E3
St Andrews Ter OXHEY * WD19 ....41 G1
St Andrew St HCIRC EC1N 11 K2
St Andrews Wy BOW E3 ....105 K3
St Anna Rd BAR * EN5 ....20 B6
St Anne's Av STWL/WRAY TW19 ....152 A2
St Anne's Cl HGT N6 ....84 A1
OXHEY WD19 ....27 G6
St Annes Ct SOHO/CST W1F 10 C4
St Annes Gdns WLSDN NW10 ....98 B2
St Anne's Pas POP/IOD * E14 ....105 H5
St Anne's Rd ALP/SUD HA0 ....79 K3
LEY E10 ....70 B6
St Anne's Rw POP/IOD E14 ....105 H5
St Anne St POP/IOD E14 ....105 H5
St Ann's BARK IG11 ....90 C6
St Anns Ct HDN * NW4 ....45 K6
St Ann's Crs WAND/EARL SW18 ....160 A1
St Ann's Gdns HAMP NW3 ....84 A4
St Ann's Hl WAND/EARL SW18 ....140 A6
St Ann's Park Rd
WAND/EARL SW18 ....160 B1
St Ann's Rd BARK IG11 ....90 C6
BARN * SW13 ....138 C3
ED N9 ....36 B4
HRW HA1 ....60 E3
NTGHL W11 ....100 B6
SEVS/STOTM N15 ....67 K2
St Ann's St WEST SW1P 16 D5
St Ann's Ter STJWD NW8 ....2 B2
St Ann's Vls NTGHL W11 ....119 G1
St Ann's Wy CROY/NA CR0 ....211 H4
St Anselm's Pl MYFR/PKLN W1K 9 J5
St Anselms Rd HYS/HAR UB3 ....113 J2
St Anthony's Av WFD IG8 ....53 G2
St Anthonys Cl TOOT SW17 ....160 D4
WAP * E1W 123 H1
St Anthony's Ct HAYES BR2 ....201 G5
St Anthony's Wy
EBED/NFELT TW14 ....133 J5
St Antony's Rd FSTGT E7 ....89 F5
St Arvans Cl CROY/NA CR0 ....212 A1
St Asaph Rd BROCKY SE4 ....144 A4
St Aubyn's Av HSLW TW3 ....135 F6
WIM/MER SW19 ....177 J1
St Aubyns Cl ORP BR6 ....217 F1
St Aubyns Gdns ORP BR6 ....202 A6
St Aubyn's Rd NRWD SE19 ....181 G2
St Audrey Av BXLYHN DA7 ....149 H3
St Augustine's Av BMLY BR1 ....200 D2
EA W5 ....98 A1
SAND/SEL CR2 ....211 J5
WBLY HA9 ....80 A1
St Augustine's Rd BELV DA17 ....129 G4
CAMTN NW1 ....84 D5
St Austell Cl EDGE HA8 ....44 B5
St Austell Rd BKHTH/KID SE3 ....145 F3
St Awdry's Rd BARK IG11 ....90 D5
St Barnabas Cl BECK BR3 ....183 F5
St Barnabas' Gdns
E/WMO/HCT KT8 ....189 F2
St Barnabas Rd MTCM CR4 ....179 F3
SUT SM1 ....209 H3
SWFD E18 ....53 F4
WALTH E17 ....69 J3
St Barnabas Ter HOM E9 ....87 F3
St Barnabas Vls VX/NE SW8 ....141 K2
St Barnabus St BGVA SW1W 121 F5
St Bartholomew's Cl SYD SE26 ....163 K6
St Bartholomew's Rd EHAM E6 ....89 J6
St Benets Cl TOOT * SW17 ....160 D4
St Benet's Gv MRDN SM4 ....194 B4
St Benjamins Dr ORP BR6 ....217 J6
St Bernards CROY/NA CR0 ....212 A1
St Bernards Cl WNWD SE27 ....162 E6
St Bernard's Rd EHAM E6 ....89 H6
St Blaise Av BMLY BR1 ....184 A5
St Botolph St HDTCH EC3A 13 J3
St Bride's Av EDGE HA8 ....44 B4
St Brides Cl ERITHM DA18 ....128 E2
St Bride St FLST/FETLN EC4A 12 A3
St Catherines Cl CHSGTN KT9 ....205 K4
TOOT * SW17 ....160 D4
St Catherines Ct FELT TW13 ....153 K3
St Catherine's Dr NWCR SE14 ....144 A3
St Catherines Ms CHEL SW3 ....14 E6
St Catherines Rd CHING E4 ....37 J4
St Chads Cl SURB KT6 ....190 D4
St Chad's Gdns CHDH RM6 ....74 A4
St Chad's Pl FSBYW WC1X 5 F4
St Chad's Rd CHDH RM6 ....74 A3
St Chad's St STPAN WC1H 5 F4
St Charles Pl NKENS W10 ....100 C4
St Charles Sq NKENS W10 ....100 C4
St Christopher's Cl ISLW TW7 ....135 K2
St Christophers Dr HYS/HAR UB3 ....95 F6
St Christopher's Ms
WLGTN SM6 ....210 C3
St Christopher's Pl MHST W1U 9 H4
St Clair Cl CLAY IG5 ....53 K5
St Clair Dr WPK KT4 ....207 K1
St Clair Rd PLSTW E13 ....107 F1
St Clair's Rd CROY/NA CR0 ....197 F6
St Clare St TWRH EC3N 13 J4
St Clements Ct PUR RM19 ....131 K4
St Clement's La LINN WC2A 11 H4
St Clements St HOLWY N7 ....85 G5
St Clements Yd EDUL * SE22 ....143 G6
St Cloud Rd WNWD SE27 ....162 D6
St Crispins Cl HAMP NW3 ....83 J2
STHL UB1 ....95 K5
St Cross St HCIRC EC1N 11 K1
St Cuthberts Gdns PIN * HA5 ....41 K3
St Cuthbert's Rd CRICK NW2 ....82 D4
PLMGR N13 ....49 G2
St Cyprian's St TOOT SW17 ....160 E6
St Davids Cl BERM/RHTH * SE16 ....123 J5
WBLY HA9 ....80 E1
WWKM BR4 ....198 E4
St David's Dr EDGE HA8 ....44 B4
St Davids Ms BOW * E3 ....105 G2
St David's Pl HDN NW4 ....63 K4
St Davids Sq POP/IOD E14 ....124 E5
St Denis Rd WNWD SE27 ....162 E6
St Dionis Rd FUL/PGN SW6 ....139 J3
St Donatt's Rd NWCR SE14 ....144 C2
St Dunstan's Av ACT W3 ....99 F6
St Dunstans Cl HYS/HAR UB3 ....113 J4
St Dunstan's Gdns ACT W3 ....99 F6
St Dunstan's Hl MON * EC3R 13 G6
SUT SM1 ....208 C2
St Dunstan's La BECK BR3 ....199 F3
MON * EC3R 13 G6
St Dunstans Rd FSTGT E7 ....89 F4
FELT TW13 ....153 J5
HMSMTH W6 ....119 G5
HNWL W7 ....115 K2
HSLWW TW4 ....134 A3
SNWD SE25 ....197 G1
St Edmunds Av RSLP HA4 ....58 B3

St Edmunds Cl ABYW SE2 128 E2
STJWD NW8 2 E1
TOOT SW17 160 D4
St Edmunds Dr STAN HA7 43 G4
St Edmund's La WHTN TW2 155 G2
St Edmunds Rd DART DA1 151 J5
ED N9 36 C2
IL IG1 71 K3
St Edmunds Sq BARN SW13 119 F6
St Edmund's Ter STJWD NW8 2 D2
St Edward's Cl GLDGN NW11 64 E3
St Edwards Wy ROMW/RG RM7 75 F2
St Egberts Wy CHING E4 38 A3
St Elmo Rd ACT W3 118 C2
St Elmos Rd BERM/RHTH SE16 124 B2
St Erkenwald Ms BARK IG11 90 D6
St Erkenwald Rd BARK IG11 90 D6
St Ervans Rd NKENS W10 100 C4
St Faith's Cl ENC/FH EN2 23 J2
St Faith's Rd HNHL SE24 162 C3
St Fidelis' Rd ERITH DA8 130 A4
St Fillans Rd CAT SE6 165 F3
St Francis Cl ORP BR6 201 K3
OXHEY WD19 27 F3
St Francis Rd EDUL SE22 143 F5
St Francis Wy IL IG1 90 D2
St Gabriel's Cl WAN E11 71 F5
St Gabriel's Rd CRICK NW2 82 B3
St George's Av CDALE/KGS NW9 62 E1
EA W5 116 E2
FSTGT E7 89 F5
HOLWY N7 84 D2
STHL UB1 95 K6
St George's Circ STHWK SE1 18 A3
St Georges Cl ALP/SUD HA0 79 G1
THMD SE28 109 K5
GLDGN NW11 64 D3
St George's Dr OXHEY WD19 27 J5
PIM SW1V 121 G5
PIM * SW1V 121 G5
St Georges Flds BAY/PAD W2 8 D5
St Georges Gdns SURB KT6 191 J6
St George's Gv TOOT SW17 160 C5
St George's La MON * EC3R 13 F5
St George's Ms CAMTN NW1 83 K5
CHSWK * W4 117 K6
DEPT SE8 124 C4
St Georges Pde CAT * SE6 164 C4
St George's Rd BECK BR3 182 E4
ED N9 36 C5
EN EN1 24 B1
FELT TW13 154 C6
FSTGT E7 89 F5
GLDGN NW11 64 D3
HNWL W7 116 A1
IL IG1 71 K4
KUTN/CMB KT2 175 H3
LEY E10 88 A1
MTCM CR4 179 G6
PLMGR N13 35 F5
RCH/KEW TW9 137 G4
SCUP DA14 186 E2
STHWK SE1 18 A5
TWK TW1 136 C6
WIM/MER SW19 177 J2
WLGTN SM6 210 B3
BMLY BR1 184 E5
CHSWK W4 118 A2
DAGW RM9 92 A3
STMC/STPC BR5 201 J3
St Georges Rd West BMLY BR1 184 D5
St Georges's Ct STP * EC4M 12 A3
St George's Sq FSTGT E7 89 F5
NWMAL * KT3 176 B6
PIM SW1V 121 J5
PIM * SW1V 121 J5
St George's Square Ms
PIM SW1V 121 J5
St George's Ter CAMTN NW1 83 K5
PECK * SE15 143 H1
St George St CONDST W1S 9 K5
St George's Wk CROY/NA CR0 196 D6
St George's Wy PECK SE15 123 F6
PECK * SE15 123 F6
St Gerards Cl CLAP SW4 141 H6
St German's Pl BKHTH/KID SE3 145 K3
St German's Rd FSTH SE23 164 B3
St Giles Av DAGE RM10 92 D5
HGDN/ICK UB10 76 A2
St Giles Churchyard BARB * EC2Y 12 D2
St Giles Cl DAGE RM10 92 D5
ORP BR6 216 D3
St Giles High St LSQ/SEVD WC2H 10 D3
St Giles Rd CMBW SE5 143 F2
St Gothard Rd WNWD SE27 162 E6
St Gregory Cl RSLP HA4 77 G2
St Helena Rd BERM/RHTH SE16 124 A4
St Helena St FSBYW * WC1X 5 J5
St Helena Ter RCH/KEW * TW9 136 E6
St Helens THDIT * KT7 189 K4
St Helen's Crs STRHM/NOR SW16 180 A4
St Helen's Gdns NKENS W10 100 B5
St Helen's Pl OBST EC2N 13 G3
St Helens Rd ERITHM DA18 128 E2
IL IG1 71 K3
STRHM/NOR SW16 180 A5
WEA W13 116 C1
St Helier Av MRDN SM4 194 B4
St Heliers Av HSLWW TW4 135 F6
St Helier's Rd LEY E10 69 K3
St Hildas Cl KIL/WHAMP * NW6 82 B6
TOOT SW17 160 D4
St Hilda's Rd BARN SW13 118 E6
St Hughes Cl TOOT * SW17 160 D4
St Hugh's Rd PGE/AN * SE20 181 J4
St Ivians Dr GPK RM2 57 J6
St James Av SUT SM1 208 E3
TRDG/WHET N20 33 J5
WEA W13 116 B1
St James Cl STJWD NW8 2 E2
TRDG/WHET N20 33 J5
NWMAL KT3 192 C2
RSLP HA4 59 G6
St James' Ct WESTW * SW1E 16 B4
St James' Gdns ALP/SUD HA0 79 K5
St James Ms POP/IOD * E14 125 F3
St James Pl DART DA1 171 G1
St James Rd CAR SM5 209 J1
EBAR EN4 21 H4
ED N9 36 D4
FSTGT E7 88 D3
MTCM CR4 179 F3
SURB KT6 190 E3
SUT SM1 208 E4
St James's NWCR SE14 144 B2
St James's Av BECK BR3 182 B6
BETH E2 104 E1
HPTN TW12 173 H1
St James's Chambers
STJS * SW1Y 10 B7
St James's Cl TOOT * SW17 160 E4
TOOT * SW17 179 F1
WOOL/PLUM SE18 127 H5
St James's Cottages
RCHPK/HAM * TW10 136 E6
St James's Ct KUT * KT1 175 F6
WESTW SW1E 16 B4
St James's Crs BRXN/ST SW9 142 B4
St James's Dr BAL SW12 160 E3
St James's Gdns CAMTN * NW1 4 A5
NTGHL W11 119 H1
St James's Gv BTSEA * SW11 140 E3
St James's La MUSWH N10 66 B1
St James's Market STJS * SW1Y 10 C6
St James's Ms WALTH E17 69 G2
St James's Pk CROY/NA CR0 196 D4
St James's Pl WHALL SW1A 16 A1
St James Sq SURB KT6 190 D4
St James's Rd
BERM/RHTH SE16 123 H5
CROY/NA CR0 196 D4
HPTN TW12 173 G1
KUT KT1 174 E5
STHWK SE1 123 H5
St James's Rw CHSGTN * KT9 205 K4
St James's Sq STJS SW1Y 10 C7
St James's St WALTH E17 69 G2
WHALL SW1A 10 A7
St James's Ter STJWD NW8 2 E1
St James's Terrace Ms
STJWD NW8 2 E1
St James St HMSMTH W6 119 F5
St James Ter BAL * SW12 161 F3
ORP * BR6 217 J6
St James Wk CLKNW EC1R 6 A6
St James Wy SCUP DA14 187 F1
St Jerome's Gv HYS/HAR UB3 94 A5
St Joan's Rd ED N9 36 B4
St John Cl FUL/PGN * SW6 139 K1
St John's Av FBAR/BDGN N11 47 K1
PUT/ROE SW15 139 G6
WLSDN NW10 81 H6
St John's Church Rd HOM * E9 86 E3
St Johns Cl STHGT/OAK * N14 34 C1
FUL/PGN * SW6 139 K1
RAIN RM13 93 J5
TRDG/WHET * N20 33 G4
WBLY HA9 80 A3
St Johns Cottages
PGE/AN * SE20 181 K3
St Johns Ct BKHH * IG9 39 F3
BKHH IG9 39 F3
ISLW TW7 136 A3
St John's Crs BRXN/ST SW9 142 B4
St John's Dr WAND/EARL SW18 160 A3
WOT/HER KT12 188 B5
St John's Est IS N1 7 F3
STHWK SE1 19 J2
St John's Gdns NTGHL W11 100 D6
St John's Gv ARCH N19 66 C6
BARN * SW13 138 C3
RCH/KEW * TW9 137 F5
St John's Hl BTSEA SW11 140 D5
St John's Hill Gv BTSEA SW11 140 C5
St John's La FARR EC1M 6 A7
St Johns Pde SCUP * DA14 168 C6
WEA * W13 116 C1
St John's Pk BKHTH/KID SE3 145 K1
St John's Pl FARR EC1M 6 A7
St Johns Rd GNTH/NBYPK IG2 72 E4
NWMAL KT3 175 K6
BARK IG11 90 E6
BTSEA SW11 140 D5
CAN/RD E16 106 E5
CAR SM5 209 J1
CHING E4 37 K5
CROY/NA CR0 211 H1
CRW RM5 56 E1
E/WMO/HCT KT8 189 J1
EHAM E6 89 J6
ERITH DA8 130 A5
FELT TW13 154 E6
GLDGN NW11 64 D3
HRW HA1 61 F3
ISLW TW7 136 A3
KUT KT1 174 D5
NWDGN UB2 114 D3
PGE/AN SE20 181 K3
RCH/KEW TW9 137 F5
SCUP DA14 168 C6
SEVS/STOTM N15 68 A3
STMC/STPC BR5 201 J3
SUT SM1 193 K6
WALTH E17 51 K5
WBLY HA9 79 K2
WELL DA16 148 C4
WIM/MER SW19 177 H3
St John's Sq FARR EC1M 6 A7
St John's Ter FSTGT E7 89 F4
NKENS W10 100 B3
WOOL/PLUM SE18 127 H6
St John St FSBYE EC1V 5 K3
St John's V DEPT SE8 144 D3
St John's Vls ARCH N19 66 D6
KENS * W8 120 A3
KENS * W8 120 A3
St John's Wy ARCH N19 66 C6
St John's Wood High St
STJWD NW8 2 B3
St John's Wood Pk STJWD NW8 2 A1
St John's Wood Rd STJWD NW8 2 A6
St John's Wood Ter STJWD NW8 2 C2
St Josephs Cl NKENS W10 100 C4
ORP BR6 217 F2
St Joseph's Dr STHL UB1 114 D1
St Josephs Gv HDN NW4 63 K1
St Joseph's Rd ED N9 36 D2
St Joseph's St VX/NE * SW8 141 G2
St Joseph's V BKHTH/KID SE3 145 G3
St Jude's Rd BETH E2 104 D1
St Jude St STNW/STAM N16 86 A3
St Julian's Cl
STRHM/NOR * SW16 162 B6
St Julian's Farm Rd
WNWD SE27 162 B6
St Julian's Rd KIL/WHAMP NW6 82 D5
St Justin Cl STMC/STPC BR5 186 E6
St Katharine's Prec CAMTN * NW1 3 J2
St Katharine's Wy TWRH EC3N 13 K7
St Katherines Rd ERITHM DA18 128 E2
St Katherines Wk NTGHL * W11 100 B6
St Keverne Rd ELTH/MOT SE9 166 D6
St Kilda Rd ORP BR6 202 A5
WEA W13 116 B2
St Kilda's Rd HRW HA1 60 E3
STNW/STAM N16 67 K5
St Kitts Ter NRWD SE19 181 F1
St Laurence Cl STMC/STPC BR5 186 E6
St Laurence's Cl
KIL/WHAMP NW6 82 B6
St Lawrence Cl EDGW HA8 44 B3
St Lawrence Cottages
POP/IOD * E14 125 F1
St Lawrence Dr PIN HA5 59 F2
St Lawrence St POP/IOD E14 125 F1
St Lawrence Ter NKENS W10 100 C4
St Lawrence Wy
BRXN/ST * SW9 142 B3
St Leonard's Av CHING E4 52 B2
KTN/HRWW/W HA3 61 J2
St Leonards Cl WELL DA16 148 B4
St Leonard's Gdns HEST TW5 134 D1
IL IG1 90 C3
St Leonards Ri ORP BR6 216 E2
St Leonards Rd
MORT/ESHN SW14 137 K4
CROY/NA CR0 211 H1
ESH/CLAY KT10 205 F4
POP/IOD E14 106 A5
SURB KT6 190 E2
THDIT KT7 190 B3
WEA W13 97 J6
WLSDN NW10 99 F3
St Leonards Sq KTTN NW5 84 A4
St Leonard's St BOW E3 105 K2
St Leonard's Ter CHEL SW3 120 E5
CHEL * SW3 120 E5
St Leonard's Wk
STRHM/NOR SW16 180 A3
St Leonards Wy EMPK RM11 75 K5
St Loo Av CHEL SW3 120 D6
St Louis Rd WNWD SE27 162 D6
St Loy's Rd TOTM N17 50 A5
St Lucia Dr SRTFD E15 88 D6
St Luke's Av CLAP SW4 141 J5
ENC/FH EN2 23 K1
IL IG1 90 B3
St Luke's Cl SNWD SE25 197 J3
St Luke's Ms NTGHL W11 100 D5
St Luke's Rd NTGHL W11 100 D4
St Lukes's Cl FSBYE EC1V 6 D6
St Luke's Sq CAN/RD E16 106 D5
St Luke's St CHEL SW3 120 D5
St Lukes Yd MV/WKIL * W9 100 D1
St Malo Av ED N9 36 E5
St Margarets BARK IG11 90 D6
RCHPK/HAM * TW10 175 K1
St Margarets Av BFN/LL DA15 167 J5
TRDG/WHET N20 33 G3
CHEAM SM3 208 C1
RYLN/HDSTN HA2 78 C1
SEVS/STOTM N15 67 H1
St Margarets Cl ORP BR6 217 H2
St Margarets Ct
PUT/ROE * SW15 138 E5
St Margaret's Crs
PUT/ROE * SW15 138 E6
St Margaret's Dr TWK TW1 136 C6
St Margaret's Gv TWK TW1 156 B1
WAN E11 88 D1
WOOL/PLUM SE18 127 H6
St Margarets La KENS * W8 120 A3
St Margarets Ms
RCHPK/HAM * TW10 175 K1
St Margarets Rd EDGE HA8 44 D1
RSLP HA4 58 B3
BROCKY SE4 144 C5
HNWL W7 115 K2
MNPK E12 71 G6
TOTM N17 50 A6
TWK TW1 136 C5
WLSDN NW10 100 A2
St Margaret's Ter
WOOL/PLUM SE18 127 H5
St Margaret St WEST SW1P 16 E3
St Mark's Cl BAR EN5 21 F4
FUL/PGN SW6 139 K2
St Mark's Crs CAMTN * NW1 84 A6
St Marks Ga HOM E9 87 G5
St Mark's Gv WBPTN * SW10 140 A1
St Mark's Hl SURB KT6 191 F3
St Mark's Pl NTGHL W11 100 C5
WIM/MER * SW19 177 J2
St Mark's Ri HACK E8 86 B3
St Mark's Rd EA W5 117 F1
EN EN1 36 B1
HAYES BR2 184 A6
HNWL W7 115 K2
MTCM CR4 178 E5
NKENS W10 100 B5
SNWD SE25 197 H1
TEDD TW11 174 C3
St Mark's Sq CAMTN NW1 84 A6
St Mark St WCHPL E1 13 K4
St Marks Vls FSBYPK * N4 67 F6
St Martin's Ap RSLP HA4 58 C4
St Martin's Av EHAM E6 107 H1
St Martin's Cl CAMTN NW1 84 C6
EN EN1 24 D2
ERITHM DA18 128 E2
OXHEY WD19 27 G6
St Martins Ct LSQ/SEVD WC2H 10 E5
LSQ/SEVD * WC2H 10 E5
St Martin's La BECK BR3 198 E2
CHCR WC2N 10 E5
St Martin's Le Grand STBT EC1A 12 C3
St Martin's Pl CHCR WC2N 10 E6
St Martin's Rd BRXN/ST SW9 142 A3
DART DA1 171 J1
ED N9 36 D4
St Martin's St LSQ/SEVD * WC2H 10 D6
St Martin's Wy TOOT SW17 160 B5
St Mary Abbot's Pl KENS W8 119 J3
KENS * W8 119 J3
St Mary Abbots Ter
WKENS * W14 119 J3
St Mary At Hl MON EC3R 13 G6
St Mary Av WLGTN SM6 210 A1
St Mary Axe HDTCH EC3A 13 G4
St Marychurch St
BERM/RHTH SE16 123 K2
St Mary Graces Ct TWRH * EC3N 13 K6
St Mary Newington Cl
WALW * SE17 123 F5
St Mary Rd WALTH E17 69 J1
St Marys BARK IG11 108 D1
St Mary's Ap MNPK E12 89 K3
St Marys Av NWDGN UB2 115 G4
FNCH N3 46 C5
HAYES BR2 183 H6
NTHWD HA6 40 C1
STWL/WRAY TW19 152 A2
TEDD * TW11 174 A2
WAN E11 71 F3
St Mary's Cl CHSGTN KT9 206 B5
EW KT17 207 H5
STMC/STPC BR5 186 C5
TOTM * N17 50 B5
St Marys Ct SHB * W12 118 C3
St Mary's Crs HDN NW4 45 K6
HYS/HAR UB3 94 D6
ISLW TW7 135 J1
STWL/WRAY TW19 152 A2
St Mary's Dr EBED/NFELT TW14 153 F2
St Marys Est
BERM/RHTH * SE16 123 K2
St Mary's Gdns LBTH SE11 17 K6
LBTH * SE11 17 K6
St Mary's Ga KENS W8 120 A3
KENS * W8 120 A3
St Mary's Gn EFNCH N2 47 G6
St Mary's Gv BARN SW13 138 E4
CHSWK W4 117 J6
IS N1 85 H4
RCH/KEW TW9 137 G5
St Mary's Ms KIL/WHAMP * NW6 83 F5
St Mary's Pth IS * N1 85 H6
St Mary's Pl EA W5 116 E2
KENS * W8 120 A3
KENS * W8 120 A3
St Marys Rd IL IG1 72 C6
BXLY DA5 169 K3
CEND/HSY/T * N8 66 E1
E/WMO/HCT KT8 189 J2
EA W5 116 E2
EBAR EN4 33 K2
ED N9 36 E3
GLDGN NW11 64 C4
HYS/HAR UB3 94 D6
LEY E10 88 A1
PECK SE15 143 K3
PLSTW E13 107 F1
SNWD SE25 181 F6
SURB KT6 190 D4
WIM/MER SW19 177 H1
WLSDN NW10 81 G6
WPK KT4 192 B6
St Mary's Sq BAY/PAD W2 8 A1
EA * W5 116 E2
St Mary's Ter BAY/PAD W2 8 A1
BORE * WD6 29 K1
St Mary St WOOL/PLUM SE18 126 E4
St Marys Vw KTN/HRWW/W HA3 61 J2
St Mary's Wk HYS/HAR UB3 94 D6
LBTH SE11 17 K6
LBTH * SE11 17 K6
St Marys Wy CHIG IG7 54 A1
St Matthew's Av SURB KT6 191 F5
St Matthews Cl OXHEY WD19 27 H1
RAIN RM13 93 J5
St Matthews Dr BMLY BR1 184 E6
St Matthew's Rd
BRXS/STRHM SW2 142 A6
EA W5 117 F1
St Matthew's Rw BETH E2 104 C2
St Matthew St WEST SW1P 16 C4
St Matthias Cl CDALE/KGS NW9 63 H2
St Maur Rd FUL/PGN SW6 139 J2
St Meddens CHST * BR7 185 J3
St Mellion Cl THMD SE28 109 K5
St Merryn Cl WOOL/PLUM SE18 147 J1
St Michael's Aly BANK EC3V 13 F4
St Michaels Av ED N9 36 E2
WBLY HA9 80 C4
St Michaels Cl BMLY BR1 184 D6
CAN/RD E16 107 H4
ERITHM * DA18 128 E2
FNCH N3 46 D5
NFNCH/WDSP N12 47 J1
WOT/HER KT12 188 B6
WPK KT4 192 C6
St Michaels Ct GLDGN * NW11 64 D4
St Michael's Crs PIN HA5 59 J3
St Michael's Gdns NKENS W10 100 B4
St Michaels Ri WELL * DA16 148 C2
St Michael's Rd BRXN/ST SW9 142 A3
CRICK NW2 82 A2
CROY/NA * CR0 196 D5
WELL DA16 148 C4
WLGTN SM6 210 C4
St Michael's St BAY/PAD W2 8 B3
St Michaels Ter HGT * N6 66 A5
WDGN N22 48 E5
St Mildred's Ct LOTH * EC2R 12 E4
St Mildreds Rd CAT SE6 165 H2
St Nicholas Av HCH RM12 93 J1
St Nicholas Cl BORE WD6 29 K1
St Nicholas Glebe TOOT SW17 179 F2
St Nicholas Rd SUT SM1 209 F3
THDIT KT7 190 A3
WOOL/PLUM SE18 128 A5
St Nicholas St DEPT SE8 144 C2
St Nicholas Wy SUT SM1 209 F2
St Nicolas La CHST BR7 184 D4
St Ninian's Ct TRDG/WHET N20 33 K5
St Norbert Rd BROCKY SE4 144 B5
St Olaf's Rd FUL/PGN SW6 139 H1
St Olave's Rd EHAM E6 90 A6
St Olave's Wk
STRHM/NOR SW16 179 H5
St Onge Pde EN * EN1 23 K4
St Oswald's Pl LBTH SE11 122 A5
LBTH * SE11 122 A5
St Oswald's Rd
STRHM/NOR SW16 180 C4
St Oswulf St WEST * SW1P 16 D7
St Pancras Gdns CAMTN * NW1 4 D1
St Pancras Wy CAMTN NW1 84 C5
St Paul's Av BERM/RHTH * SE16 124 A1
CRICK NW2 81 K4
KTN/HRWW/W HA3 62 B2
St Paul's Church Yd
BLKFR * EC4V 12 B4
St Paul's Cl CAR SM5 194 D4
CHARL SE7 126 C5
CHSGTN KT9 205 K2
EA W5 117 G2
EA W5 117 G2
HSLW TW3 134 E3
HYS/HAR UB3 113 G5
St Paul's Cray Rd CHST BR7 185 J4
St Pauls Crs CAMTN NW1 84 D5
CAMTN NW1 84 D5
St Paul's Dr SRTFD E15 88 B3
St Pauls Ms CAMTN NW1 84 D5
St Paul's Pl IS N1 85 K4
St Pauls Ri PLMGR N13 49 H2
St Pauls Rd BARK IG11 90 C6
RCH/KEW TW9 137 G4
BTFD TW8 116 E6
ERITH DA8 149 K1
IS N1 85 H4
THHTH CR7 180 D6
TOTM N17 50 C3
St Pauls Ter WALW * SE17 122 C6
St Paul St IS N1 6 C1
St Paul's Wy FNCH N3 47 F3
POP/IOD E14 105 H4
St Paul's Wood Hl
STMC/STPC BR5 185 K5
St Peter's Av BETH E2 104 C1
UED N18 36 C6
St Petersburgh Ms
BAY/PAD * W2 101 F6
St Petersburgh Pl BAY/PAD W2 101 F6
St Peters Cl CHST BR7 185 J3
GNTH/NBYPK IG2 72 E1
TOOT SW17 160 D4
BETH E2 104 C1
BUSH WD23 28 D3
RSLP HA4 59 H6
St Peters Ct E/WMO/HCT KT8 189 F1
LEE/GVPK * SE12 145 J6
HDN * NW4 64 A2
St Peter's Gdns WNWD SE27 162 B5
St Peter's Gv HMSMTH W6 118 D4
St Peter's Pth WALTH E17 70 C1
St Peters Pl MV/WKIL W9 101 F3
St Peters Rd KUT KT1 175 H5
CROY/NA CR0 211 K2
E/WMO/HCT KT8 189 F1
ED N9 36 D3
HMSMTH * W6 118 D5
STHL UB1 96 A4
TWK TW1 136 C6
St Peter's Sq BETH * E2 104 C1
HMSMTH W6 118 C5
St Peter's St IS N1 6 B1
SAND/SEL CR2 211 K3
St Peter's Ter FUL/PGN SW6 139 H1
St Peter's Vls HMSMTH W6 118 D4
St Peter's Wy EA W5 97 K4
HYS/HAR UB3 113 G5
IS * N1 86 A5
St Philip's Av WPK KT4 192 E6
St Philip Sq VX/NE * SW8 141 G3
St Philip's Rd HACK E8 86 C4
SURB KT6 190 E3
St Philip St VX/NE SW8 141 G3
St Philip's Wy IS N1 6 D1
St Quentin Rd WELL DA16 148 A4
St Quintin Av NKENS W10 100 A4
St Quintin Rd PLSTW E13 107 F2
St Raphael's Wy WLSDN NW10 80 E3
St Regis Cl MUSWH N10 48 B5
St Ronans Cl EBAR EN4 21 H1
St Ronans Crs WFD IG8 52 E3
St Rule St VX/NE SW8 141 H3
St Saviour's Rd
BRXS/STRHM SW2 142 A6
CROY/NA CR0 196 D3
Saints Cl WNWD SE27 162 C6
Saints Dr FSTGT E7 89 H3
St Silas Pl KTTN NW5 84 A4
St Simon's Av PUT/ROE SW15 139 F6
St Stephen's Av SHB W12 118 E2
WALTH E17 70 A2
WEA W13 97 H5
St Stephens Cl KTTN * NW5 83 K3
STHL UB1 96 A4
STJWD NW8 2 C1
WALTH E17 69 K2
St Stephen's Crs BAY/PAD W2 100 E5
THHTH CR7 180 B6
St Stephen's Gdns BAY/PAD W2 100 E5
TWK TW1 156 D1
St Stephen's Gv LEW SE13 145 F4
St Stephen's Ms BAY/PAD W2 100 E4
St Stephens Pde WHALL SW1A 16 E2
St Stephens Rd EHAM E6 89 G5
BAR EN5 20 B6
BOW E3 87 G6
BOW E3 105 H1
HSLW TW3 155 F1
WALTH E17 69 K2
WDR/YW UB7 112 A1
WEA W13 97 H5
St Stephens Ter VX/NE * SW8 141 K1
VX/NE SW8 142 A1
St Stephen's Wk SKENS * SW7 120 B4
St Swithin's La MANHO EC4N 12 E5
St Swithun's Rd LEW * SE13 145 G6
St Theresa's Rd
EBED/NFELT TW14 133 J5
St Thomas Cl SURB KT6 191 G5
St Thomas Ct BXLY DA5 169 H2
St Thomas' Dr PIN HA5 41 J4
STMC/STPC BR5 201 H5
St Thomas Gdns IL IG1 90 C4
St Thomas' Rd CHSWK W4 137 K1
BELV DA17 129 K3
CAN/RD E16 106 E5
STHGT/OAK N14 34 D2
St Thomas's Gdns HAMP NW3 84 A4
St Thomas's Pl HOM * E9 86 E5
Saint Thomas's Rd FSBYPK N4 67 G6
St Thomas's Rd WLSDN NW10 81 G6
St Thomas's Sq HACK E8 86 D5
St Thomas St STHWK SE1 19 F1
St Thomas's Wy FUL/PGN SW6 139 J1
St Ursula Gv PIN HA5 59 H2
St Ursula Rd STHL UB1 96 A5
St Vincent Cl WNWD SE27 180 C1
St Vincent Rd WHTN TW2 155 H1
St Vincents Rd DART DA1 171 K1
St Vincent St MHST W1U 9 H2
St Wilfrid's Cl EBAR * EN4 21 J6
St Wilfrid's Rd EBAR EN4 21 H6
St Winefride's Av MNPK E12 89 K3
St Winifred's Cl CHIG IG7 54 C1
St Winifred's Rd TEDD TW11 174 C2
Saladin Dr PUR RM19 131 K4
Salamanca Pl LBTH SE11 17 G7
Salamanca St LBTH SE11 17 G7
Salamander Cl KUTN/CMB KT2 174 D1
Salamander Quay KUT * KT1 174 E4
Salamons Wy RAIN RM13 111 G5
Salcombe Dr CHDH RM6 74 B3
MRDN SM4 193 G5
Salcombe Gdns MLHL NW7 46 A2
Salcombe Rd ASHF TW15 152 B6
STNW/STAM N16 86 B3
WALTH E17 69 H4
Salcombe Wy RSLP HA4 58 E6
Salcott Rd BTSEA SW11 140 E6

CROY/NA CR0 210 E1
Salehurst Cl KTN/HRWW/W HA3 62 A2
Salehurst Rd BROCKY SE4 164 C1
Salem Pl CROY/NA CR0 211 J1
Sale Pl BAY/PAD W2 8 C2
Sale St BETH E2 104 C3
Salford Rd BRXS/STRHM SW2 161 J3
Salhouse Cl THMD SE28 109 J5
Salisbury Av BARK IG11 90 D5
FNCH N3 46 D5
SUT SM1 208 D4
Salisbury Cl WALW SE17 18 E6
WPK KT4 207 H1
Salisbury Ct EMB EC4Y 11 K4
Salisbury Gdns
WIM/MER * SW19 177 H3
Salisbury Pavement
FUL/PGN * SW6 139 K1
Salisbury Pl BRXN/ST SW9 142 C1
MBLAR W1H 8 E1
Salisbury Prom
CEND/HSY/T * N8 67 H2
Salisbury Rd BAR EN5 20 C4
BXLY DA5 169 H3
CAR SM5 209 K4
CHING E4 37 J5
CROY/NA CR0 197 H3
DAGE RM10 92 D4
ED N9 36 C5
FELT TW13 154 B3
FSBYPK N4 67 H2
FSTGT E7 88 E4
GDMY/SEVK IG3 72 E6
GPK RM2 75 K2
HAYES BR2 200 D2
HOR/WEW KT19 207 F2
HRW HA1 60 D2
HSLWW TW4 134 B4
LEY E10 70 A6
MNPK E12 89 H3
NWDGN * UB2 114 D4
NWMAL KT3 176 A6
PIN HA5 58 E1
RCH/KEW TW9 137 F5
WALTH E17 70 A2
WDGN N22 49 H5
WEA W13 116 C2
WIM/MER SW19 177 H3
Salisbury Sq EMB * EC4Y 11 K4
Salisbury St ACT W3 117 K2
STJWD NW8 2 C7
Salisbury Ter PECK SE15 143 K4
Salix Cl SUN TW16 172 A3
Sally Murray Cl MNPK E12 90 A2
Salmen Rd PLSTW E13 106 D1
Salmon La POP/IOD E14 105 G5
Salmon Ms KIL/WHAMP * NW6 82 E3
Salmon Rd BELV DA17 129 H5
DART DA1 151 J4
Salmons Rd CHSGTN KT9 206 A4
ED N9 36 C3
Salmon St CDALE/KGS NW9 62 D5
CDALE/KGS NW9 62 E4
POP/IOD * E14 105 H5
Salomons Rd PLSTW E13 107 G4
Salop Rd WALTH E17 69 F3
Saltash Cl SUT SM1 208 D2
Saltash Rd BARK/HLT IG6 54 D3
WELL DA16 148 D2
Saltcoats Rd CHSWK W4 118 B2
Saltcote Cl DART DA1 170 B1
Saltcroft Cl WBLY HA9 62 D5
Salter Cl RYLN/HDSTN HA2 77 K1
Salterford Rd TOOT SW17 179 F2
Salter Rd BERM/RHTH SE16 124 A1
Salters' Hall Ct MANHO * EC4N 12 E5
Salter's Hl NRWD SE19 180 E1
Salters Rd NKENS W10 100 B3
WALTH E17 70 B1
Salters Rw IS * N1 85 K4
Salter St POP/IOD E14 105 J6
WLSDN NW10 99 J2
Salterton Rd HOLWY N7 84 E1
Saltford Cl ERITH DA8 130 B5
Saltley Cl EHAM E6 107 J5
Saltoun Rd BRXS/STRHM SW2 142 B5
Saltram Crs MV/WKIL W9 100 D2
Saltwell St POP/IOD E14 105 J6
Saltwood Cl ORP BR6 217 J2
Saltwood Gv WALW * SE17 122 E5
Salusbury Rd KIL/WHAMP NW6 82 C6
Salvador TOOT SW17 178 D1
Salvia Gdns GFD/PVL UB6 97 G1
Salvin Rd PUT/ROE SW15 139 G4
Salway Cl WFD IG8 52 E3
Salway Pl SRTFD E15 88 B4
Salway Rd SRTFD E15 88 B4
Samantha Cl WALTH E17 69 H4
Sam Bartram Cl CHARL SE7 126 B5
Samels Ct HMSMTH W6 118 D5
Samford St STJWD NW8 2 C7
Samos Rd PGE/AN SE20 181 J5
Sampson Av BAR EN5 20 B6
Sampson Cl BELV DA17 128 E3
Sampson St WAP * E1W 123 H1
Samson St PLSTW E13 107 G1
Samuel Cl HACK E8 86 B6
NWCR SE14 124 A6
WOOL/PLUM SE18 126 D4
Samuel Gray Gdns
KUTN/CMB KT2 174 E4
Samuel St PECK SE15 143 G1
WOOL/PLUM SE18 126 E4
Sancroft Cl CRICK NW2 81 K1
Sancroft Rd KTN/HRWW/W HA3 43 F5
Sancroft St LBTH SE11 122 B5
The Sanctuary BXLY DA5 168 E1
WEST SW1P 16 D4
Sanctuary Cl DART DA1 171 F1
Sanctuary Rd
STWL/WRAY TW19 152 D1
Sanctuary St STHWK SE1 18 D3
Sandall Cl EA W5 98 A3
Sandall Rd EA W5 98 A3
KTTN NW5 84 C4
Sandal Rd NWMAL KT3 192 B1
UED N18 50 C1
Sandal St SRTFD E15 88 C6
Sandalwood Cl WCHPL E1 105 G3
Sandalwood Dr RSLP HA4 58 A4
Sandalwood Rd FELT TW13 154 A5
Sandbach Pl WOOL/PLUM SE18 127 H5
Sandbourne Av
WIM/MER SW19 178 A6
Sandbourne Rd BROCKY SE4 144 B3
Sandbrook Cl MLHL NW7 45 F2
Sandbrook Rd STNW/STAM N16 86 A1
Sandby Gn ELTH/MOT SE9 146 D4
Sandcliff Rd ERITH DA8 130 A4
Sandcroft Cl PLMGR N13 49 H2
Sandell's Av ASHF TW15 153 F6
Sandell St STHWK SE1 17 J2
Sanders Cl HPTN TW12 173 H1
Sanders La MLHL NW7 46 B3
Sanderson Cl KTTN * NW5 84 B2
Sanders Pde
STRHM/NOR * SW16 179 K2
Sanderstead Av CRICK NW2 64 C6
Sanderstead Cl CLAP SW4 161 H2
Sanderstead Rd LEY E10 69 G5
SAND/SEL CR2 211 K5
STMC/STPC BR5 202 C3
Sandfield Gdns THHTH CR7 180 C6
Sandfield Pl THHTH CR7 180 D6
Sandfield Rd THHTH CR7 180 C6
Sandford Av WDGN N22 49 H4
Sandford Rd BXLYHS DA6 149 F5
EHAM E6 107 K2
HAYES BR2 199 K1
Sandford Rw WALW SE17 122 E5
Sandford St FUL/PGN SW6 140 A1
Sandgate Cl ROMW/RG RM7 74 E4
Sandgate La WAND/EARL SW18 160 D3
Sandgate Rd WELL DA16 148 D1
Sandgate St PECK SE15 123 J6
The Sandhills WBPTN * SW10 120 B6
Sandhills WLGTN SM6 210 D2
Sandhurst Av BRYLDS KT5 191 J4
RYLN/HDSTN HA2 60 B3
Sandhurst Cl CDALE/KGS NW9 44 C6
SAND/SEL CR2 212 A6
Sandhurst Dr GDMY/SEVK IG3 91 F2
Sandhurst Market CAT * SE6 165 F3
Sandhurst Pde CAT * SE6 165 F3
Sandhurst Rd BFN/LL DA15 168 A5
BXLY DA5 148 E6
CAT SE6 165 G3
CDALE/KGS NW9 44 C6
ED N9 36 E1
ORP BR6 217 G1
Sandhurst Wy SAND/SEL CR2 212 A5
Sandifer Dr CRICK NW2 82 B1
Sandiford Rd CHEAM SM3 193 J6
Sandiland Crs HAYES BR2 199 J6
Sandilands CROY/NA CR0 212 C1
Sandilands Rd FUL/PGN SW6 140 A2
Sandison St PECK SE15 143 G4
Sandland St GINN WC1R 11 H2
Sandling Ri ELTH/MOT SE9 167 F5
Sandlings Cl PECK SE15 143 J3
Sandmere Rd CLAP SW4 141 K5
Sandon Cl ESH/CLAY KT10 189 J4
Sandow Crs HYS/HAR UB3 113 J3
Sandown Av DAGE RM10 92 E4
ESH/CLAY KT10 204 C3
Sandown Cl HEST TW5 133 K2
Sandown Ct BELMT * SM2 209 F5
DAGE RM10 92 E4
SYD * SE26 163 J5
Sandown Dr CAR SM5 210 A6
Sandown Ga ESH/CLAY KT10 189 J6
Sandown Rd ESH/CLAY KT10 204 C2
SNWD SE25 197 J2
Sandown Wy NTHLT UB5 77 J4
Sandpiper Cl BERM/RHTH SE16 124 C2
WALTH E17 51 F3
Sandpiper Dr ERITH DA8 150 E1
Sandpiper Rd SUT SM1 208 D3
Sandpiper Ter CLAY * IG5 54 B6
Sandpiper Wy STMC/STPC BR5 202 E1
Sandpit Pl CHARL SE7 126 D5
Sandpit Rd BMLY BR1 183 H1
DART DA1 151 F5
Sandpits Rd CROY/NA CR0 213 F2
RCHPK/HAM TW10 156 E4
Sandra Cl HSLW TW3 135 G6
WDGN N22 49 J4
Sandridge Cl HRW HA1 60 E1
Sandridge St ARCH N19 66 C6
Sandringham Av RYNPK SW20 177 H4
Sandringham Cl EN EN1 24 A3
WIM/MER * SW19 159 G3
Sandringham Crs
RYLN/HDSTN HA2 78 A1
Sandringham Dr ASHF TW15 152 A6
BXLY DA5 170 B4
WELL DA16 147 K3
Sandringham Gdns
BARK/HLT IG6 54 C6
CEND/HSY/T N8 66 E3
HEST TW5 133 K2
NFNCH/WDSP N12 47 H2
Sandringham Pl
E/WMO/HCT KT8 189 F1
Sandringham Rd BARK IG11 91 F4
BMLY BR1 183 K1
CRICK NW2 81 K3
CROY/NA CR0 196 D2
FSTGT E7 89 G3
GLDGN NW11 64 C4
HACK E8 86 C3
HTHAIR TW6 132 B6
LEY E10 70 B4
NTHLT UB5 78 A5
WDGN N22 49 J6
WPK KT4 207 J1
Sandrock Pl CROY/NA CR0 213 F2
Sandrock Rd LEW SE13 144 D4
Sands End La FUL/PGN SW6 140 A2
Sandstone Rd LEE/GVPK SE12 166 A4
Sands Wy WFD IG8 53 K2
Sandtoft Rd CHARL SE7 126 A6
Sandway Rd STMC/STPC BR5 202 D1
Sandwell Crs KIL/WHAMP NW6 82 E4
Sandwich St STPAN WC1H 4 E5
Sandwick Cl MLHL NW7 45 J3
Sandy Bury ORP BR6 216 D1
Sandycombe Rd
EBED/NFELT TW14 153 K3
RCH/KEW TW9 137 H3
Sandycoombe Rd TWK TW1 156 D1
Sandycroft ABYW SE2 128 B6
Sandy Dr EBED/NFELT TW14 153 H3
Sandy Hill Av WOOL/PLUM SE18 127 G5
Sandy Hill La WOOL/PLUM SE18 127 G4
Sandyhill Rd IL IG1 90 B2
Sandy Hill Rd WLGTN SM6 210 C6
WOOL/PLUM SE18 127 G5
Sandy La BELMT SM2 208 C6
KTN/HRWW/W HA3 62 B3
MTCM CR4 179 F4
NTHWD HA6 26 D4
ORP BR6 202 B4
RCHPK/HAM TW10 156 D4
STMC/STPC BR5 186 E3
TEDD TW11 174 B3
WOT/HER KT12 188 A3
Sandy La North WLGTN SM6 210 D3
Sandy La South WLGTN SM6 210 C6
Sandy Ldg PIN * HA5 42 A2
Sandy Lodge Ct NTHWD * HA6 40 C1
Sandy Lodge La NTHWD HA6 26 B4
Sandy Lodge Wy NTHWD HA6 40 C1
Sandymount Av STAN HA7 43 J1
Sandy Rdg CHST BR7 185 F2
Sandy Rd HAMP NW3 65 F6
Sandy's Rw WCHPL E1 13 H2
Sandy Wy CROY/NA CR0 213 H1
Sanford La STNW/STAM N16 68 B6
Sanford St NWCR SE14 124 B6
Sanford Ter STNW/STAM N16 86 B1
Sanger Av CHSGTN KT9 206 B3
Sangley Rd CAT SE6 164 E3
SNWD SE25 197 F1
Sangora Rd BTSEA SW11 140 C5
Sansom Rd WAN * E11 70 D6
Sansom St CMBW SE5 142 E1
Sans Wk CLKNW EC1R 6 A6
Santley St BRXS/STRHM SW2 141 K5
Santos Rd PUT/ROE SW15 139 K6
Saperton Wk LBTH SE11 17 H6
Saphora Cl ORP BR6 216 D3
Sapphire Cl BCTR RM8 73 J5
Sapphire Rd DEPT SE8 124 B4
Saracen Cl CROY/NA CR0 196 E3
Saracen St POP/IOD E14 105 J5
Sarah St BETH E2 7 H4
Saratoga Rd CLPT E5 86 E2
Sardinia St HOL/ALD WC2B 11 G4
Sarita Cl KTN/HRWW/W HA3 42 D5
Sark Cl HEST TW5 135 F1
Sarnesfield Rd ENC/FH * EN2 23 K5
Sarre Rd KIL/WHAMP NW6 82 D3
Sarsen Av HSLW TW3 134 E3
Sarsfeld Rd BAL SW12 160 E3
Sarsfield Rd GFD/PVL UB6 97 H1
Sartor Rd PECK SE15 144 A5
Sarum Ter BOW * E3 105 H3
Satanita Cl CAN/RD E16 107 H5
Satchell Md CDALE/KGS NW9 45 H4
Satchwell Rd BETH E2 104 C2
Sattar Ms STNW/STAM * N16 85 K1
Sauls Gn WAN E11 88 C1
Saunders Cl POP/IOD * E14 105 H6
Saunders Ness Rd POP/IOD E14 125 G4
Saunders Rd WOOL/PLUM SE18 128 A5
Saunders St LBTH SE11 17 J6
Saunders Wy DART DA1 171 J4
THMD SE28 109 H6
Saunderton Rd ALP/SUD HA0 79 H3
Saunton Av HYS/HAR UB3 133 J1
Saunton Rd HCH RM12 75 J6
Savage Gdns EHAM E6 107 K5
TWRH EC3N 13 H5
Savernake Ct STAN * HA7 43 H2
Savernake Rd ED N9 36 C1
HAMP NW3 83 K2
Savery Dr SURB KT6 190 D4
Savile Cl NWMAL KT3 192 B2
THDIT KT7 190 A5
Savile Gdns CROY/NA CR0 197 G6
Savile Rw CONDST W1S 10 A5
Saville Rd CAN/RD E16 126 D1
CHDH RM6 74 B3
CHSWK W4 118 A3
TWK TW1 156 A3
Saville Rw HAYES BR2 199 J5
Savill Gdns RYNPK SW20 176 D6
Savill Rw WFD IG8 52 D2
Savona Cl WIM/MER SW19 177 G3
Savona St VX/NE SW8 141 H1
Savoy Av HYS/HAR UB3 113 H5
Savoy Cl EDGE HA8 44 C1
SRTFD E15 88 C6
Savoy Ct TPL/STR * WC2R 11 F6
Savoy Hl TPL/STR WC2R 11 G6
Savoy Pde EN * EN1 24 A4
Savoy Pl CHCR WC2N 11 F6
Savoy Rd DART DA1 151 F6
Savoy Rw TPL/STR WC2R 11 G5
Savoy Steps TPL/STR * WC2R 11 G6
Savoy St TPL/STR WC2R 11 G5
Savoy Wy TPL/STR WC2R 11 G6
Sawbill Cl YEAD UB4 95 H4
Sawkins Cl WIM/MER SW19 159 G4
Sawley Rd SHB W12 118 D1
Sawtry Cl CAR SM5 194 C4
Sawyer Cl ED N9 36 C4
Sawyer's Hl RCHPK/HAM TW10 157 G2
Sawyers Lawn WEA W13 97 F5
Sawyer St STHWK SE1 18 C2
Saxby Rd BRXS/STRHM SW2 161 K2
Saxham Rd BARK IG11 90 E6
Saxlingham Rd CHING E4 38 B5
Saxon Av FELT TW13 154 E4
Saxonbury Av SUN TW16 172 A6
Saxonbury Cl MTCM CR4 178 C6
Saxonbury Gdns SURB KT6 190 D5
Saxon Cl SURB KT6 190 E3
WALTH E17 69 J4
Saxon Dr ACT W3 98 D5
Saxonfield Cl BRXS/STRHM SW2 162 A2
Saxon Rd BMLY BR1 183 J3
BOW E3 105 H1
CROY/NA CR0 196 E2
EHAM E6 107 K3
IL IG1 90 B4
RDART DA2 171 H6
STHL UB1 95 J6
WBLY HA9 80 E1
WDGN N22 49 H4
Saxon Wy STHGT/OAK N14 34 D1
Saxony Pde HYS/HAR UB3 94 A4
Saxton Cl LEW SE13 145 G4
Saxville Rd STMC/STPC BR5 186 C6
Sayesbury La UED N18 50 C1
Sayes Court Rd STMC/STPC BR5 186 B6
Sayes Court St DEPT SE8 124 C5
Scadbury Gdns STMC/STPC BR5 186 B5
Scads Hill Cl ORP BR6 202 A3
Scala St FITZ W1T 10 B1
Scales Rd TOTM N17 50 B6
Scammell Wy WATW WD18 26 D1
Scampston Ms NKENS W10 100 B5
Scampton Rd HTHAIR TW6 152 C1
Scandrett St WAP * E1W 123 J1
Scarba Wk IS N1 85 K4
Scarborough Rd ED N9 36 E2
FSBYPK N4 67 G4
HTHAIR TW6 153 F1
WAN E11 70 B5
Scarborough St WCHPL E1 13 K4
Scarbrook Rd CROY/NA CR0 211 J1
Scarle Rd ALP/SUD HA0 79 K4
Scarlet Cl STMC/STPC BR5 202 C1
Scarlet Rd CAT SE6 165 H5
Scarsbrook Rd BKHTH/KID SE3 146 C4
Scarsdale Pl KENS W8 120 A3
Scarsdale Rd RYLN/HDSTN HA2 78 C1
Scarsdale Vls KENS W8 119 K3
Scarth Rd BARN SW13 138 C4
Scawen Cl CAR SM5 210 A2
Scawen Rd DEPT SE8 124 B5
Scawfell St BETH E2 7 K3
Scaynes Link NFNCH/WDSP N12 32 E6
Sceptre Rd BETH E2 104 E2
Scholars Rd BAL SW12 161 H3
CHING E4 38 A3
Scholefield Rd ARCH N19 66 D5
Schonfeld Sq STNW/STAM N16 67 K6
School Cl DART DA1 150 C5
School House La TEDD TW11 174 C3
Schoolhouse La WAP * E1W 105 F6
School La BUSH WD23 28 B2
KUT KT1 174 D4
PIN * HA5 59 J1
SURB KT6 191 H5
WELL DA16 148 C4
School Pas KUT KT1 175 G5
STHL UB1 114 E1
School Rd CHST BR7 185 H4
DAGE RM10 92 C6
E/WMO/HCT KT8 189 J1
HPTN TW12 173 H2
HSLW TW3 135 H4
KUT * KT1 174 D4
MNPK E12 89 K2
WDR/YW UB7 112 A6
WLSDN NW10 99 F3
School Road Av HPTN TW12 173 H2
School Wy BCTR RM8 91 H1
Schoolway NFNCH/WDSP N12 47 H2
Schooner Cl BARK IG11 109 H2
POP/IOD E14 125 G3
Schubert Rd BORE WD6 29 K1
PUT/ROE SW15 139 J6
Sclater St WCHPL E1 7 J6
Scoles Crs BRXS/STRHM SW2 162 B3
Scope Wy KUT KT1 191 F1
Scoresby St STHWK SE1 18 A1
Scorton Av GFD/PVL UB6 97 G1
Scotch Common WEA W13 97 G4
Scot Gv PIN HA5 41 H3
Scotia Rd BRXS/STRHM SW2 162 B2
Scotland Gn TOTM N17 50 B5
Scotland Green Rd PEND EN3 25 F6
Scotland Green Rd North
PEND EN3 25 F5
Scotland Rd BKHH IG9 39 G3
Scotney Cl ORP BR6 216 A2
Scots Cl STWL/WRAY TW19 152 A3
Scotsdale Cl BELMT SM2 208 C5
CHST BR7 201 K1
Scotsdale Rd LEE/GVPK SE12 146 A6
Scotswood St CLKNW * EC1R 5 K6
Scotswood Wk TOTM * N17 50 D3
Scott Cl HOR/WEW KT19 206 E3
STRHM/NOR SW16 180 A4
WDR/YW UB7 112 C4
Scott Crs ERITH DA8 150 C2
RYLN/HDSTN HA2 60 B5
Scott Ellis Gdns STJWD NW8 2 A5
Scottes La BCTR RM8 73 K5
Scott Farm Cl THDIT KT7 190 C5
Scott Gdns HEST TW5 134 C1
Scott Lidgett Crs
BERM/RHTH SE16 123 H2
Scotts Av HAYES BR2 183 G5
Scotts Dr HPTN TW12 173 G3
Scotts Farm Rd
HOR/WEW KT19 206 E4
Scott's La HAYES BR2 183 G6
Scotts Pas WOOL/PLUM * SE18 127 G4
Scotts Rd NWDGN UB2 114 B3
BMLY BR1 183 K3
LEY E10 70 A5
SHB W12 118 E2
Scott St WCHPL E1 104 D3
Scott Trimmer Wy HEST TW5 134 D3
Scottwell Dr CDALE/KGS NW9 63 H2
Scoulding Rd CAN/RD E16 106 D5
Scouler St POP/IOD E14 106 B6
Scout La CLAP SW4 141 H4
Scout Wy MLHL NW7 31 F6
Scovell Crs STHWK * SE1 18 C3
Scovell Rd STHWK SE1 18 C3
Scrattons Ter BARK IG11 109 K1
Scriven St HACK E8 86 B6
Scrooby St CAT SE6 164 E1
Scrubs La WLSDN NW10 99 J2
Scrutton St SDTCH EC2A 7 G7
Scutari Rd EDUL SE22 143 J6
Scylla Crs HTHAIR TW6 152 E2
Scylla Rd HTHAIR TW6 152 E1
PECK SE15 143 J4
Seabright St BETH E2 104 D2
Seabrook Dr WWKM BR4 199 H6
Seabrook Gdns ROMW/RG RM7 74 C4
Seabrook Rd BCTR RM8 91 K1
Seaburn Cl RAIN RM13 111 G2
Seacole Cl ACT W3 99 F5
Seacourt Rd ABYW SE2 128 E2
Seacroft Gdns OXHEY WD19 27 H5
Seafield Rd FBAR/BDGN N11 34 D6
Seaford Cl RSLP HA4 58 B6
Seaford Rd EN EN1 24 A5
HTHAIR TW6 132 A6
SEVS/STOTM N15 67 K2
WALTH E17 51 K6
WEA W13 116 C1
Seaford St STPAN WC1H 5 F5
Seaforth Av NWMAL KT3 192 E2
Seaforth Cl ROM RM1 57 G3
Seaforth Crs HBRY N5 85 J3
Seaforth Gdns HOR/WEW KT19 207 H2
WCHMH N21 35 F2
WFD IG8 53 G1
Seager Buildings DEPT * SE8 144 D2
Seager Pl BOW E3 105 H4
Seagrave Cl WCHPL * E1 105 F4
Seagrave Rd FUL/PGN SW6 119 K6
Seagry Rd WAN E11 70 E3
Sealand Rd HTHAIR TW6 152 D1
Seal St HACK E8 86 B2
Searles Cl BTSEA SW11 140 D1
Searles Dr EHAM E6 108 B4
Searles Rd STHWK SE1 19 F6
Sears St CMBW SE5 142 E1
Seasprite Cl NTHLT UB5 95 H2
Seaton Av GDMY/SEVK IG3 90 E3
Seaton Cl LBTH SE11 122 C5
PLSTW E13 106 E3
PUT/ROE SW15 158 E2
WHTN TW2 155 J1
Seaton Dr ASHF TW15 152 B4
Seaton Gdns RSLP HA4 76 E1
Seaton Rd ALP/SUD * HA0 98 A1
DART DA1 170 D2
HYS/HAR UB3 113 G4
MTCM CR4 178 D5
WELL DA16 148 D1
WHTN TW2 155 H1
Seaton St UED N18 50 C1
Sebastian St FSBYE EC1V 6 B5
Sebastopol Rd ED N9 36 C6
Sebbon St IS N1 85 H5
Sebergham Gv MLHL NW7 45 J3
Sebert Rd FSTGT E7 89 F3
Sebright Rd BAR EN5 20 B3
Secker Crs KTN/HRWW/W HA3 42 C4
Secker St STHWK SE1 17 J1
Second Av ACT W3 118 C1
CHDH RM6 73 J2
DAGE RM10 110 D1
EN EN1 24 B6
HDN NW4 64 B1
HYS/HAR UB3 113 J1
MNPK E12 89 J2
MORT/ESHN SW14 138 B4
NKENS W10 100 C3
PLSTW E13 106 E2
UED N18 36 E6
WALTH E17 69 J2
WBLY HA9 61 K6
WOT/HER KT12 188 A3
Second Cl E/WMO/HCT KT8 189 G1
Second Cross Rd WHTN TW2 155 J4
Second Wy WBLY HA9 80 D2
Sedan Wy WALW SE17 123 F5
Sedcombe Cl SCUP DA14 168 C6
Sedcote Rd PEND EN3 24 E6
Sedding St KTBR SW1X 15 G6
Seddon Rd MRDN SM4 194 C2
Seddon St FSBYW WC1X 5 G5
Sedgebrook Rd BKHTH/KID SE3 146 C3
Sedgecombe Av
KTN/HRWW/W HA3 61 J2
Sedgeford Rd SHB W12 118 C1
Sedgehill Rd CAT SE6 182 D1
Sedgemere Av EFNCH N2 47 G6
Sedgemere Rd ABYW SE2 128 D3
Sedgemoor Dr DAGE RM10 92 C2
Sedge Rd TOTM N17 50 E3
Sedgeway CAT SE6 165 J3
Sedgewood Cl HAYES BR2 199 J4
Sedgmoor Pl CMBW SE5 143 F1
Sedgwick Rd LEY E10 70 A6
Sedgwick St HOM E9 87 F3
Sedleigh Rd WAND/EARL SW18 159 J1
Sedlescombe Rd FUL/PGN SW6 119 J6
Sedley Cl EN EN1 24 D1
Sedley Pl MYFR/PKLN W1K 9 J4
Sedum Cl CDALE/KGS NW9 62 D2
Seeley Dr DUL SE21 163 F6
Seelig Av CDALE/KGS NW9 63 J4
Seely Rd TOOT SW17 179 F2
Seething La TWRH EC3N 13 H5
Seething Wells La SURB KT6 190 D3
Sefton Av KTN/HRWW/W HA3 42 D5
MLHL NW7 45 F1
Sefton Cl STMC/STPC BR5 202 A1
Sefton Ct ENC/FH * EN2 23 H3
Sefton Rd CROY/NA CR0 197 H5
STMC/STPC BR5 202 A1
Sefton St PUT/ROE SW15 139 F3
Sekforde St CLKNW EC1R 6 A7
Sekhon Ter FELT TW13 155 F5
Selah Dr SWLY BR8 187 K4
Selan Gdns YEAD UB4 95 F4
Selbie Av WLSDN NW10 81 H3
Selborne Av BXLY DA5 169 F3
MNPK E12 90 A2
Selborne Gdns GFD/PVL UB6 97 G1
HDN NW4 63 J1
Selborne Rd CMBW SE5 142 E3
CROY/NA CR0 212 A1
IL IG1 72 A6
NWMAL KT3 176 B5
SCUP DA14 168 C6
STHGT/OAK N14 34 E5
WALTH E17 69 H2
WDGN N22 49 F4
Selbourne Av SURB KT6 191 G6
Selby Cha RSLP HA4 59 F6
Selby Cl CHSGTN KT9 206 A5
CHST BR7 185 F2
Selby Gdns STHL UB1 96 A3
Selby Gn CAR SM5 194 D4
Selby Rd CAR SM5 194 D4
EA W5 97 H3
PGE/AN SE20 181 H5
PLSTW E13 107 F4
TOTM N17 50 A2
WAN E11 88 C1
Selby St WCHPL E1 104 C3
Selden Rd PECK SE15 143 K3
Selhurst Cl WIM/MER SW19 159 G3
Selhurst New Rd SNWD SE25 197 F3
Selhurst Pl CROY/NA CR0 197 F3
Selhurst Rd ED N9 35 K5
SNWD SE25 197 F2
Selinas La BCTR RM8 74 A4
Selkirk Dr ERITH DA8 150 B2
Selkirk Rd TOOT SW17 160 D6
WHTN TW2 155 H4
Sellers Hall Cl FNCH N3 46 E3
Sellincourt Rd
TOOT SW17 178 D1
Sellindge Cl BECK BR3 182 C3
Sellons Av WLSDN NW10 81 H6
Sellwood Dr BAR EN5 20 B6
Selsdon Av SAND/SEL CR2 211 K4
Selsdon Cl CRW RM5 56 E4
SURB KT6 191 F2
Selsdon Rd CRICK NW2 63 H6
PLSTW E13 89 G6
SAND/SEL CR2 211 K3
WAN E11 70 E4
WNWD SE27 162 C5
Selsdon Wy POP/IOD E14 124 E3
Selsea Pl STNW/STAM N16 86 A3
Selsey Crs WELL DA16 148 E2
Selsey St POP/IOD E14 105 J4
Selvage La MLHL NW7 45 F1
Selway Cl PIN HA5 59 F1

Selwood Pl SKENS SW7 120 C5
Selwood Rd CHEAM SM3 193 J5
CHSGTN KT9 205 K2
CROY/NA CR0 197 J6
Selwood Ter SKENS SW7 120 C5
Selworthy Cl WAN E11 70 E2
Selworthy Rd CAT SE6 164 C5
Selwyn Av CHING E4 52 A2
GDMY/SEVK IG3 73 F3
RCH/KEW TW9 137 G4
Selwyn Cl HSLWW TW4 134 D5
Selwyn Ct EDGE HA8 44 D3
Selwyn Crs WELL DA16 148 C5
Selwyn Rd BOW E3 105 H1
NWMAL KT3 192 A2
PLSTW E13 89 F6
WLSDN NW10 81 G5
Semley Pl BGVA SW1W 15 H7
Semley Rd STRHM/NOR SW16 179 K5
Senate St PECK SE15 143 K3
Seneca Rd THHTH CR7 196 D1
Senga Rd WLGTN SM6 195 F5
Senhouse Rd CHEAM SM3 208 B1
Senior St BAY/PAD W2 101 F4
Senlac Rd LEE/GVPK SE12 166 A3
Sennen Rd EN EN1 36 B2
Senrab St WCHPL E1 105 F5
Sentinel Cl NTHLT UB5 95 J3
September Wy STAN HA7 43 H2
Sequoia Cl BUSH WD23 28 D3
Sequoia Gdns ORP BR6 202 A4
Sequoia Pk PIN HA5 42 B2
Serbin Cl LEY E10 70 A4
Serenaders Rd BRXN/ST SW9 142 B3
Serjeant's Inn EMB * EC4Y 11 K4
Serle St LINN WC2A 11 H3
Sermon Dr SWLY BR8 187 K6
Sermon La BLKFR EC4V 12 C4
Serpentine Rd BAY/PAD W2 14 D1
Service Route No 1 SRTFD E15 88 B5
Service Route No 2 SRTFD E15 88 B5
Service Route No 3 SRTFD E15 88 B4
Servilden Dr BMLY BR1 184 C4
Setchell Est STHWK SE1 19 J6
Setchell Rd STHWK SE1 19 J6
Setchell Wy STHWK SE1 19 J6
Seton Gdns DAGW RM9 91 J5
Settles St WCHPL E1 104 C5
Settrington Rd FUL/PGN SW6 140 A3
Seven Acres CAR SM5 194 D6
NTHWD HA6 40 E2
Sevenex Pde WBLY * HA9 80 A3
Seven Kings Rd GDMY/SEVK IG3 72 E5
Sevenoaks Rd BROCKY SE4 164 C1
ORP BR6 217 F2
Sevenoaks Wy STMC/STPC BR5 186 D6
Seven Sisters Rd FSBYPK N4 67 H6
HOLWY N7 85 F1
Seventh Av HYS/HAR UB3 113 K1
MNPK E12 89 K2
Severnake Cl POP/IOD E14 124 D4
Severn Av GPK RM2 57 K6
NKENS W10 100 C2
Severn Dr EN EN1 24 C1
ESH/CLAY KT10 190 B6
WOT/HER KT12 188 C6
Severn Wy WLSDN NW10 81 H3
Severus Rd BTSEA SW11 140 D5
Seville Ms IS N1 86 A5
Seville St KTBR SW1X 15 F3
Sevington Rd HDN NW4 63 K3
Sevington St MV/WKIL W9 101 F3
Seward Rd BECK BR3 182 A5
HNWL W7 116 B2
Sewardstone Rd BETH E2 104 E1
CHING E4 25 K5
Seward St FSBYE EC1V 6 B6
Sewdley St CLPT E5 87 F1
Sewell Rd ABYW SE2 128 B3
Sewell St PLSTW E13 106 E2
Sextant Av POP/IOD E14 125 G4
Sexton Cl RAIN RM13 93 H6
Seymer Rd ROM RM1 57 F6
Seymour Av EW KT17 207 K6
MRDN SM4 193 G4
TOTM N17 50 C5
Seymour Cl E/WMO/HCT KT8 189 H2
LOU IG10 39 J1
PIN HA5 41 K4
Seymour Dr HAYES BR2 200 E5
Seymour Gdns BROCKY SE4 144 A4
BRYLDS KT5 191 G2
FELT TW13 154 A6
IL IG1 71 K5
RSLP HA4 59 H5
TWK TW1 156 C2
Seymour Ms MBLAR W1H 9 G3
Seymour Pl MBLAR W1H 8 E2
SNWD SE25 197 J1
Seymour Rd CAR SM5 210 A3
CEND/HSY/T N8 67 H2
CHING E4 37 K3
CHSWK W4 117 K4
E/WMO/HCT KT8 189 H2
ED N9 36 D4
EHAM E6 89 H6
FNCH N3 47 F3
HPTN TW12 173 H1
KUT KT1 174 E4
LEY E10 69 H5
MTCM CR4 195 F4
WAND/EARL SW18 159 J2
WIM/MER SW19 159 G5
Seymour St BAY/PAD W2 8 E4
WOOL/PLUM SE18 127 H4
Seymour Ter PGE/AN SE20 181 J4
Seymour Vls PGE/AN SE20 181 J4
Seymour Wk WBPTN SW10 120 B6
Seyssel St POP/IOD E14 125 F4
Shaa Rd ACT W3 99 F6
Shacklegate La TEDD TW11 155 K6
Shackleton Cl FSTH SE23 163 J4
Shackleton Rd STHL UB1 95 K6
Shacklewell La HACK E8 86 B3
Shacklewell Rd STNW/STAM N16 86 B2
Shacklewell Rw HACK E8 86 B2
Shacklewell St BETH E2 7 K6
Shadbolt Av CHING E4 51 G1
Shadbolt Cl WPK KT4 192 C6
Shad Thames STHWK SE1 19 J1
Shadwell Dr NTHLT UB5 95 K2
Shadwell Gdns WCHPL * E1 104 E6
Shadwell Pierhead WAP E1W 104 E6
Shady Bush Cl BUSH WD23 28 C2
Shaef Wy TEDD TW11 174 B3
Shafter Rd DAGE RM10 92 E4
Shaftesbury Av BAR EN5 21 G5
EBED/NFELT TW14 153 K1
KTN/HRWW/W HA3 61 K3
MYFR/PICC W1J 10 C5
NWDGN UB2 115 F4
PEND EN3 25 F3
RYLN/HDSTN HA2 60 C5
Shaftesbury Cir
RYLN/HDSTN * HA2 60 C5
Shaftesbury Gdns WLSDN NW10 99 G3
Shaftesbury Ms KENS W8 119 K3
Shaftesbury Pde
RYLN/HDSTN * HA2 60 C5
Shaftesbury Pl BARB * EC2Y 12 C2
Shaftesbury Rd ARCH N19 66 E5
BECK BR3 182 C5
CAR SM5 194 C4
CHING E4 38 B3
FSTGT E7 89 G5
LEY * E10 69 J5
RCH/KEW TW9 137 F4
ROM RM1 75 H3
UED N18 50 A2
WALTH E17 69 K2
The Shaftesburys BARK IG11 108 C1
Shaftesbury St IS N1 6 D3
Shaftesbury Ter HMSMTH * W6 118 C4
Shaftesbury Wy WHTN TW2 155 J5
Shaftesbury Waye YEAD UB4 95 F4
Shafto Ms KTBR SW1X 14 E5
Shafton Ms HOM * E9 87 F6
Shafton Rd HOM E9 87 F6
Shakespeare Av
EBED/NFELT TW14 153 K1
FBAR/BDGN N11 48 C1
WLSDN NW10 80 E6
YEAD UB4 94 E5
Shakespeare Crs MNPK E12 89 K5
WLSDN NW10 81 F6
Shakespeare Dr
KTN/HRWW/W HA3 62 B3
Shakespeare Gdns EFNCH N2 65 K1
Shakespeare Rd ACT W3 117 K1
BXLYHN DA7 149 F2
DART DA1 151 K5
FNCH * N3 46 E4
HNHL SE24 142 C6
HNWL W7 97 F6
MLHL NW7 31 J6
ROM RM1 75 H3
WALTH E17 51 F5
Shakespeare Sq BARK/HLT IG6 54 B2
Shakespeare Ter
RCH/KEW * TW9 137 H4
Shakespeare Wy FELT TW13 154 B6
Shakspeare Ms STNW/STAM N16 86 A2
Shakspeare Wk
STNW/STAM N16 86 A2
Shalbourne Sq HOM E9 87 H4
Shalcomb St WBPTN SW10 120 B6
Shaldon Dr MRDN SM4 193 H2
RSLP HA4 77 G1
Shaldon Rd EDGE HA8 44 B5
Shalfleet Dr NKENS W10 100 B6
Shalford Cl ORP BR6 216 C2
Shalford Ct IS * N1 6 A2
Shalimar Gdns ACT W3 98 E6
Shalimar Rd ACT W3 98 E6
Shallons Rd ELTH/MOT SE9 167 G6
Shalstone Rd
MORT/ESHN SW14 137 J4
Shalston Vls SURB KT6 191 G3
Shamrock Rd CROY/NA CR0 196 A3
Shamrock St CLAP SW4 141 J4
Shamrock Wy STHGT/OAK N14 34 B3
Shandon Rd CLAP SW4 161 H1
Shand St STHWK SE1 19 H2
Shandy St WCHPL E1 105 F4
Shanklin Gdns OXHEY WD19 27 G6
Shanklin Rd CEND/HSY/T N8 66 D2
SEVS/STOTM N15 68 C2
Shannon Cl CRICK NW2 82 B1
HEST TW5 114 C5
Shannon Gv BRXN/ST SW9 142 A5
Shannon Pl STJWD NW8 2 D2
Shannon Wy BECK BR3 182 E2
Shap Crs CAR SM5 194 E5
Shapland Wy PLMGR N13 49 F1
Shapwick Cl FBAR/BDGN N11 47 K1
Shardcroft Av HNHL SE24 142 C6
Shardeloes Rd BROCKY * SE4 144 C6
BROCKY SE4 144 C3
Shard's Sq PECK SE15 123 H6
Sharland Cl THHTH CR7 196 B3
Sharman Ct SCUP DA14 168 B6
Sharnbrooke Cl WELL DA16 148 D4
Sharon Cl SURB KT6 190 D5
Sharon Gdns HOM E9 86 E6
Sharon Rd CHSWK W4 118 A5
PEND EN3 25 G3
Sharples Hall St CAMTN NW1 83 K5
Sharps La RSLP HA4 58 B5
Sharp Wy DART DA1 151 J4
Sharratt St PECK SE15 123 K6
Sharsted St WALW SE17 122 C5
Sharvel La NTHLT UB5 76 E6
Shavers Pl MYFR/PICC W1J 10 C6
The Shaw CHST * BR7 185 H3
Shaw Av BARK IG11 110 A1
Shawbrooke Rd ELTH/MOT SE9 146 C5
Shawbury Rd EDUL SE22 143 G6
Shaw Cl BUSH WD23 28 E4
EMPK RM11 75 K5
THMD SE28 128 C1
Shaw Dr WOT/HER KT12 188 B4
Shawfield Pk BMLY BR1 184 C5
Shawfield St CHEL SW3 120 D5
Shawford Rd HOR/WEW KT19 207 F4
Shaw Gdns BARK IG11 110 A1
Shaw Rd BMLY BR1 165 J5
EDUL SE22 143 F5
PEND EN3 25 F2
Shaw's Cottages FSTH SE23 164 B5
Shaw Sq WALTH E17 51 G4
Shaw Wy WLGTN SM6 210 E5
Shaxton Crs CROY/NA CR0 214 A6
Sheaf Cottages THDIT * KT7 189 K5
Shearing Dr MRDN SM4 194 B4
Shearling Wy HOLWY N7 84 E4
Shearman Rd BKHTH/KID SE3 145 J5
Shearwater Rd SUT SM1 208 D3
Shearwater Wy YEAD UB4 95 H5
Shearwood Cresent DART DA1 150 C4
Sheaths Cottages THDIT * KT7 190 C4
Sheaveshill Av CDALE/KGS NW9 45 G6
Sheaveshill Pde
CDALE/KGS * NW9 63 G1
Sheen Common Dr
RCHPK/HAM TW10 137 H5
Sheen Court Rd
RCHPK/HAM TW10 137 H5
Sheendale Rd RCH/KEW TW9 137 G5
Sheenewood SYD SE26 181 J1
Sheen Gate Gdns
MORT/ESHN SW14 137 K5
Sheen Gv IS N1 85 G6
Sheen La MORT/ESHN SW14 137 K5
Sheen Pk RCH/KEW TW9 137 G5
Sheen Rd RCHPK/HAM TW10 137 F5
STMC/STPC BR5 202 A1
Sheen Wy WLGTN SM6 211 F3
Sheen Wd MORT/ESHN SW14 137 K6
Sheepcote Cl HEST TW5 133 K1
Sheepcote La BTSEA SW11 140 E3
STMC/STPC BR5 203 H1
Sheepcote Rd HRW HA1 61 F3
Sheepcotes Rd CHDH RM6 73 K1
Sheephouse Wy NWMAL KT3 192 A5
Sheep La HACK E8 86 D6
Sheep Walk Ms WIM/MER SW19 177 G2
Sheerwater Rd CAN/RD E16 107 H4
Sheffield Rd HTHAIR TW6 153 F1
Sheffield St LINN * WC2A 11 G4
Sheffield Ter KENS W8 119 K2
Sheffield Wy HTHAIR TW6 133 G6
Shefton Ri NTHWD HA6 40 E3
Sheila Rd CRW RM5 56 D3
Shelbourne Cl PIN HA5 41 K6
Shelbourne Rd TOTM N17 50 D4
Shelburne Dr HSLWW TW4 155 F1
Shelburne Rd HOLWY N7 85 F2
Shelbury Cl SCUP DA14 168 B5
Shelbury Rd EDUL SE22 143 J6
Sheldon Av CLAY IG5 54 B5
HGT N6 65 K4
Sheldon Cl LEE/GVPK SE12 146 A6
PGE/AN SE20 181 J4
Sheldon Rd BXLYHN DA7 149 G2
CRICK NW2 82 B2
DAGW RM9 92 A5
UED N18 36 A6
Sheldon St CROY/NA CR0 211 J1
Sheldrake Cl CAN/RD E16 126 E1
Sheldrake Pl KENS W8 119 J2
Sheldrick Cl MTCM CR4 178 C5
Shelduck Cl FSTGT E7 88 D3
Sheldwich Ter HAYES * BR2 200 D3
Shelford Pl STNW/STAM N16 85 K1
Shelford Ri NRWD SE19 181 F3
Shelford Rd BAR EN5 32 A1
Shelgate Rd BTSEA SW11 140 E6
Shell Cl HAYES BR2 200 D3
Shellduck Cl CDALE/KGS NW9 45 G5
Shelley Av GFD/PVL UB6 96 D2
HCH RM12 75 H6
MNPK E12 89 J4
Shelley Cl EDGE HA8 30 C6
GFD/PVL UB6 96 D2
NTHWD HA6 40 D1
ORP BR6 216 E1
YEAD UB4 94 E4
Shelley Crs HEST TW5 134 C2
STHL UB1 95 K5
Shelley Dr WELL DA16 147 K2
Shelley Gdns ALP/SUD HA0 61 K6
Shelley Rd WLSDN NW10 81 F6
Shelley Wy WIM/MER SW19 178 C2
Shellgrove Rd STNW/STAM * N16 86 A3
Shellness Rd CLPT E5 86 D3
Shell Rd LEW SE13 144 E4
Shellwood Rd BTSEA SW11 140 E3
Shelmerdine Cl BOW E3 105 J4
Shelson Av FELT TW13 153 J6
Shelson Pde FELT * TW13 153 J5
Shelton Rd WIM/MER SW19 177 K4
Shelton St LSQ/SEVD * WC2H 11 E4
Shenfield Rd WFD IG8 53 F3
Shenfield St IS N1 7 H3
Shenley Av RSLP HA4 58 D6
Shenley Rd CMBW SE5 143 F2
DART DA1 171 K1
HEST TW5 134 D2
Shepherd Cl FELT TW13 154 D6
Shepherdess Pl FSBYE EC1V 6 D4
Shepherdess Wk IS N1 6 D3
Shepherd Market
MYFR/PICC * W1J 15 J1
Shepherd's Bush Gn SHB W12 119 F2
Shepherd's Bush Market
SHB W12 119 F2
Shepherd's Bush Pl SHB * W12 119 G2
Shepherd's Bush Rd
WKENS W14 119 F3
Shepherd's Cl HGT N6 66 B3
CHDH RM6 73 K2
ORP BR6 217 F1
Shepherds Gn CHST BR7 185 J3
Shepherd's Hl HGT N6 66 B3
Shepherds La DART DA1 170 D3
HOM * E9 87 F3
Shepherd's Leas
ELTH/MOT * SE9 147 J5
Shepherds Pl MYFR/PKLN W1K 9 G5
Shepherds St MYFR/PICC W1J 15 J1
Shepherds Wk BUSH WD23 28 D4
CRICK NW2 63 J6
HAMP NW3 83 H3
Shepherds Wy SAND/SEL CR2 213 F5
Shepiston La WDR/YW UB7 112 E4
Shepley Cl CAR SM5 210 A1
Shepley Ms PEND EN3 25 J1
Sheppard Cl EN EN1 24 D1
SURB KT6 191 F1
Sheppard Dr BERM/RHTH SE16 123 J5
Sheppard St CAN/RD E16 106 D3
Shepperton Rd IS N1 85 K6
STMC/STPC BR5 201 H3
Sheppey Cl ERITH DA8 150 E1
Sheppey Gdns DAGW RM9 91 J5
Sheppey Rd DAGW RM9 91 H5
Sheppey Wk IS * N1 85 J5
Shepton Houses BETH * E2 104 E2
Sherard Rd ELTH/MOT SE9 146 D6
Sherborne Av NWDGN UB2 115 F4
PEND EN3 24 E3
Sherborne Cl YEAD UB4 95 G5
Sherborne Crs CAR SM5 194 D4
Sherborne Gdns
CDALE/KGS NW9 44 C6
WEA W13 97 H5
Sherborne La MANHO EC4N 12 E5
Sherborne Pl NTHWD HA6 40 B2
Sherborne Rd CHEAM SM3 193 K6
CHSGTN KT9 206 A3
EBED/NFELT TW14 153 G3
STMC/STPC BR5 202 A2
Sherborne St IS N1 85 K6
Sherborne Vls WEA * W13 97 H4
Sherboro Rd SEVS/STOTM N15 68 B3
Sherbrooke Cl BXLYHN DA7 149 H5
Sherbrooke Rd FUL/PGN SW6 139 H1
Sherbrooke Ter FUL/PGN * SW6 139 H1
Sherbrook Gdns WCHMH N21 35 H2
Shere Cl CHSGTN KT9 205 K3
Sheredan Rd CHING E4 52 B1
Shere Rd GNTH/NBYPK IG2 72 A2
Sherfield Cl NWMAL KT3 191 J1
Sherfield Gdns PUT/ROE SW15 158 C1
Sheridan Cl HARH RM3 57 K3
Sheridan Ct DART DA1 151 K5
HSLWW TW4 134 D6
Sheridan Crs CHST BR7 185 G5
Sheridan Gdns
KTN/HRWW/W HA3 61 K3
Sheridan Pl HPTN TW12 173 G4
Sheridan Rd BELV DA17 129 H4
BXLYHN DA7 149 F4
FSTGT E7 88 D1
MNPK E12 89 J3
OXHEY WD19 27 H2
RCHPK/HAM TW10 156 D5
WIM/MER SW19 177 J4
Sheridan St WCHPL E1 104 D5
Sheridan Ter NTHLT * UB5 78 B3
Sheridan Wk CAR SM5 209 K3
GLDGN NW11 64 E3
Sheridan Wy BECK BR3 182 C4
Sheringham Av MNPK E12 89 K2
ROMW/RG RM7 74 E3
STHGT/OAK N14 22 D6
WHTN TW2 154 E3
Sheringham Dr BARK IG11 91 F3
Sheringham Rd HOLWY N7 85 G4
PGE/AN SE20 181 J5
Sherington Av PIN HA5 42 A3
Sherington Rd CHARL SE7 126 A6
Sherland Rd TWK TW1 156 A3
Sherlies Av ORP BR6 201 K6
Sherlock Ms MHST W1U 9 G1
Sherman Rd BMLY BR1 183 K4
Shernhall St WALTH E17 52 A6
Sherrard Rd FSTGT E7 89 G4
Sherrards Wy BAR EN5 20 E6
Sherrick Green Rd WLSDN NW10 81 K3
Sherriff Rd KIL/WHAMP NW6 82 E4
Sherringham Av FELT TW13 153 K5
TOTM N17 50 C5
Sherrock Gdns HDN NW4 63 J1
Sherry Ms BARK IG11 90 D5
Sherwin Rd NWCR SE14 144 A2
Sherwood SURB KT6 190 E6
Sherwood Av GFD/PVL UB6 78 E4
RSLP HA4 58 C3
STRHM/NOR SW16 179 J3
SWFD E18 53 F6
YEAD UB4 95 F3
Sherwood Cl BXLY DA5 168 D1
WALTH E17 51 H5
WEA W13 116 C1
Sherwood Ct MBLAR * W1H 8 E2
Sherwood Gdns BARK IG11 90 D5
POP/IOD E14 124 D4
STHWK SE1 123 H5
Sherwood House
RYLN/HDSTN * HA2 78 C1
Sherwood Park Av
BFN/LL DA15 168 B2
Sherwood Park Rd MTCM CR4 195 H1
SUT SM1 208 E3
Sherwood Rd BARK/HLT IG6 72 D1
CROY/NA CR0 197 J4
HDN NW4 46 A6
HPTN TW12 173 H1
RYLN/HDSTN HA2 60 C6
WELL DA16 147 K4
WIM/MER SW19 177 J3
Sherwoods Rd OXHEY WD19 27 J2
Sherwood St SOHO/SHAV W1D 10 B5
TRDG/WHET N20 33 H5
Sherwood Ter TRDG/WHET N20 33 H5
Sherwood Wy WWKM BR4 199 F6
Shetland Cl BORE WD6 31 F1
Shetland Rd BOW E3 105 H1
Shield Dr BTFD TW8 116 C6
Shieldhall St ABYW SE2 128 D4
Shield Rd ASHF TW15 153 F6
Shifford Pth FSTH * SE23 164 A5
Shillibeer Pl MBLAR W1H 8 D2
Shillingford St IS N1 85 H6
Shilling Pl HNWL * W7 116 B1
Shinfield St SHB W12 100 A5
Shinglewell Rd ERITH DA8 149 H1
Shinners Cl SNWD SE25 197 H2
Ship & Mermaid Rw
STHWK * SE1 19 F2
Shipka Rd BAL SW12 161 G3
Ship La MORT/ESHN SW14 137 K4
Shipman Rd CAN/RD E16 107 F5
FSTH SE23 164 A4
Ship St DEPT SE8 144 D2
Ship Tavern Pas BANK EC3V 13 G5
Shipton Cl BCTR RM8 91 K1
Shipton St BETH E2 7 K4
Shipwright Rd
BERM/RHTH SE16 124 B2
Shipwright Yd STHWK * SE1 19 G1
Shirburn Cl FSTH SE23 163 K2
Shirbutt St POP/IOD E14 105 J6
Shirebrook Rd BKHTH/KID SE3 146 C3
Shire Ct EW KT17 207 H5
Shirehall Cl HDN NW4 64 B3
Shirehall Gdns HDN NW4 64 B3
Shirehall La HDN NW4 64 B3
Shirehall Pk HDN NW4 64 B3
Shire Horse Wy ISLW TW7 136 A4
Shire La ORP BR6 215 K5
ORP BR6 216 E3
The Shires RCHPK/HAM TW10 157 F6
Shirland Ms MV/WKIL W9 100 D2
Shirland Rd MV/WKIL W9 100 D2
Shirley Av BXLY DA5 168 E2
CROY/NA CR0 197 K5
SUT SM1 209 J2
Shirley Church Rd
CROY/NA CR0 213 F1
Shirley Cl DART DA1 151 F5
HSLW TW3 135 H6
WALTH * E17 69 K2
Shirley Crs BECK BR3 198 B1
Shirley Dr HSLW TW3 135 H6
Shirley Gdns BARK IG11 90 E4
HNWL W7 116 A1
Shirley Gv BTSEA SW11 141 F4
ED N9 36 E2
Shirley Hills Rd CROY/NA CR0 213 F3
Shirley Oaks Rd CROY/NA CR0 198 A5
Shirley Park Rd CROY/NA CR0 197 J5
Shirley Rd BFN/LL DA15 167 K5
CHSWK W4 118 A2
CROY/NA CR0 197 J5
ENC/FH EN2 23 J4
SRTFD E15 88 C5
WLGTN SM6 210 C6
Shirley Rw SNWD * SE25 181 H5
Shirley St CAN/RD E16 106 D5
Shirley Wy CROY/NA CR0 213 H1
Shirlock Rd HAMP NW3 83 K2
Shobden Rd TOTM N17 49 K4
Shobroke Cl CRICK NW2 82 A1
Shoebury Rd EHAM E6 89 K5
Shoe La FLST/FETLN EC4A 11 K3
Sholden Gdns STMC/STPC BR5 202 D2
Shooters Av KTN/HRWW/W HA3 61 J1
Shooters Hl WOOL/PLUM SE18 146 E2
Shooters Hill Rd
BKHTH/KID SE3 145 H2
Shooters Rd ENC/FH EN2 23 G1
Shoot-up Hl CRICK NW2 82 C4
Shops SYD * SE26 182 A1
Shore Cl EBED/NFELT TW14 153 K2
HPTN TW12 172 D1
Shoreditch High St BETH E2 7 H5
WCHPL E1 13 H1
Shore Gv FELT TW13 155 F4
Shoreham Cl CROY/NA CR0 197 K3
WAND/EARL SW18 140 A6
Shoreham Rd STMC/STPC BR5 186 C4
Shoreham Rd (East)
HTHAIR TW6 132 B6
Shoreham Rd (West)
HTHAIR TW6 132 B6
Shoreham Wy HAYES BR2 199 K3
Shore Pl HOM E9 86 E5
Shore Rd HOM E9 86 E5
Shorncliffe Rd STHWK SE1 123 G5
Shorndean St CAT SE6 165 F3
Shorne Cl BFN/LL DA15 168 C1
STMC/STPC BR5 202 E1
Shornefield Cl BMLY BR1 185 F6
Shorrolds Rd FUL/PGN SW6 139 K1
Shortcroft Rd EW KT17 207 H5
Shorter St WCHPL E1 13 J5
Shortgate NFNCH/WDSP N12 32 D6
Shortlands HMSMTH W6 119 G4
HYS/HAR UB3 113 G6
Shortlands Cl BELV DA17 129 G3
UED N18 35 K5
Shortlands Gdns HAYES BR2 183 H5
Shortlands Gv HAYES BR2 183 G6
Shortlands Rd HAYES BR2 183 G6
KUTN/CMB KT2 175 G3
LEY E10 69 K4
Short La STWL/WRAY TW19 152 C2
Short Rd CHSWK W4 118 B6
STWL/WRAY TW19 152 B1
WAN E11 70 C6
Shorts Cft CDALE/KGS NW9 62 D1
Shorts Gdns LSQ/SEVD * WC2H 10 E4
Shorts Rd CAR SM5 209 J2
Short St STHWK SE1 17 K2
Shortway ELTH/MOT SE9 146 D4
Short Wy NFNCH/WDSP N12 47 J2
WHTN TW2 155 H2
Shotfield WLGTN SM6 210 B4
Shott Cl SUT SM1 209 G3
Shottendane Rd
FUL/PGN * SW6 139 K2
Shottery Cl ELTH/MOT SE9 166 D5
Shottfield Av
MORT/ESHN SW14 138 B5
Shoulder of Mutton Aly
POP/IOD E14 105 G6
Shouldham St MBLAR W1H 8 D2
Showers Wy HYS/HAR UB3 113 K1
Shrapnel Cl WOOL/PLUM SE18 146 D1
Shrapnel Rd ELTH/MOT SE9 146 E4
Shrewsbury Av
KTN/HRWW/W HA3 62 A1
MORT/ESHN SW14 137 K5
Shrewsbury Cl SURB KT6 191 F6
Shrewsbury Crs WLSDN NW10 81 F6
Shrewsbury La
WOOL/PLUM SE18 147 G2
Shrewsbury Ms BAY/PAD W2 100 E5
Shrewsbury Rd BAY/PAD W2 100 E5
BECK BR3 182 B6
CAR SM5 194 D4
EBED/NFELT TW14 153 F1
FBAR/BDGN N11 48 D2
MNPK E12 89 H4
Shrewsbury St NKENS W10 100 A3
Shrewton Rd TOOT * SW17 178 E3
Shroffold Rd BMLY BR1 165 H6
Shropshire Cl MTCM CR4 195 K1
Shropshire Rd WDGN N22 49 F3
Shroton St CAMTN NW1 8 C1
The Shrubberies CHIG IG7 54 C1
SWFD E18 52 E5
The Shrubbery SURB * KT6 191 F5
Shrubbery Gdns WCHMH N21 35 H2
Shrubbery Rd STHL UB1 114 E1
STRHM/NOR SW16 161 K6
Shrubland Cl TRDG/WHET * N20 33 H4
Shrubland Gv WPK KT4 208 A1
Shrubland Rd HACK E8 86 C6
LEY E10 69 J4
WALTH E17 69 J2
Shrublands Av CROY/NA CR0 213 J2
Shrublands Cl CHIG IG7 54 C2
SYD SE26 163 K5
Shrubsall Cl ELTH/MOT SE9 166 D3
Shuna Wk IS * N1 85 K4
Shurland Av EBAR EN4 33 K1
Shurland Gdns PECK * SE15 143 G1
Shurlock Dr ORP BR6 216 C2
Shuters Sq WKENS * W14 119 J5
Shuttle Cl BFN/LL DA15 168 A2
Shuttlemead BXLY DA5 169 G2
Shuttle Rd DART DA1 150 D4
Shuttle St WCHPL E1 104 C3
Shuttleworth Rd BTSEA SW11 140 C3
Sibella Rd CLAP SW4 141 J3
Sibley Cl BXLYHS DA6 149 F6
Sibley Ct UX/CGN UB8 94 A4
Sibley Gv MNPK E12 89 J5
Sibthorpe Rd LEE/GVPK SE12 166 A2
Sibthorp Rd MTCM * CR4 178 E5
Sibton Rd CAR SM5 194 D4

Sicilian Av NOXST/BSQ * WC1A 11 F2
Sidbury St FUL/PGN SW6 139 H2
Sidcup By-Pass Rd SCUP DA14 167 K6
Sidcup Hl SCUP DA14 186 C1
Sidcup Hill Gdns SCUP * DA14 186 D1
Sidcup Pl SCUP DA14 186 B1
Sidcup Rd LEE/GVPK SE12 146 A6
Siddeley Dr HSLWW TW4 134 D4
Siddons La CAMTN NW1 3 F7
Siddons Rd CROY/NA CR0 211 G1
FSTH SE23 164 B4
TOTM N17 50 C4
Side Rd WALTH E17 69 H2
Sidewood Rd ELTH/MOT SE9 167 J3
Sidford Pl STHWK SE1 17 H5
The Sidings LOU IG10 39 J1
WAN E11 70 A5
Sidmouth Av ISLW TW7 135 K3
Sidmouth Cl OXHEY WD19 27 F4
Sidmouth Dr RSLP HA4 76 E1
Sidmouth Pde CRICK * NW2 82 A5
Sidmouth Rd LEY E10 88 A1
PECK SE15 143 G2
STMC/STPC BR5 202 C2
WELL DA16 148 D1
WLSDN NW10 82 A5
Sidmouth St STPAN WC1H 5 F5
Sidney Av PLMGR N13 49 F2
Sidney Elson Wy EHAM E6 108 A1
Sidney Gdns BTFD TW8 116 E6
Sidney Gv FSBYE EC1V 6 A3
Sidney Rd BECK BR3 182 B5
BRXN/ST SW9 142 A3
FSTGT E7 88 E1
RYLN/HDSTN HA2 42 C6
SNWD SE25 197 H2
TWK TW1 156 B1
WDGN N22 49 F3
Sidney Sq WCHPL * E1 104 E4
Sidney St WCHPL E1 104 D4
Sidworth St HACK E8 86 D5
Siebert Rd BKHTH/KID SE3 125 K6
Siemens Rd WOOL/PLUM SE18 126 C3
Sienna Ter CRICK * NW2 63 J6
Sierra Dr DAGW RM9 110 E1
Sigdon Rd HACK E8 86 C3
The Sigers RSLP HA4 59 F3
Signmakers Yd CAMTN * NW1 3 K1
Sigrist Sq KUTN/CMB KT2 175 F4
Silbury Av MTCM CR4 178 D4
Silbury St IS * N1 6 E4
Silchester Rd NKENS W10 100 B5
Silecroft Rd BXLYHN DA7 149 H2
Silesia Buildings HACK E8 86 D5
Silex St STHWK SE1 18 B3
Silk Cl LEE/GVPK SE12 145 K6
Silkfield Rd CDALE/KGS NW9 63 G2
Silk Mill Rd OXHEY WD19 27 F2
Silk Mills Pth LEW SE13 145 F4
Silkstream Pde EDGE * HA8 44 E4
Silkstream Rd EDGE HA8 44 E4
Silk St BARB EC2Y 12 D1
Silsoe Rd WDGN N22 49 F6
Silver Birch Av CHING E4 51 H1
Silver Birch Cl CAT SE6 164 C5
FBAR/BDGN N11 48 A2
RDART DA2 170 B6
THMD SE28 128 B1
Silver Birch Ms BARK/HLT IG6 54 C2
Silverbirch Wk HAMP * NW3 83 K4
Silvercliffe Gdns EBAR EN4 21 J5
Silver Cl KTN/HRWW/W HA3 42 D3
NWCR * SE14 144 B1
Silver Crs CHSWK W4 117 J4
Silverdale CAMTN NW1 4 A3
ENC/FH EN2 22 E5
SYD SE26 163 K6
Silverdale Cl HNWL W7 115 K1
NTHLT UB5 77 K3
SUT SM1 208 D2
Silverdale Dr ELTH/MOT SE9 166 D4
HCH RM12 93 K3
SUN TW16 172 A5
Silverdale Gdns HYS/HAR UB3 113 K2
Silverdale Rd BXLYHN DA7 149 J3
CHING E4 52 B2
HYS/HAR UB3 113 K2
STMC/STPC BR5 186 B6
STMC/STPC BR5 201 H1
Silverdene NFNCH/WDSP * N12 47 F2
Silver Dene PUT/ROE * SW15 139 F6
Silverhall St ISLW TW7 136 B4
Silverholme Cl
KTN/HRWW/W HA3 62 A4
Silver La WWKM BR4 199 G6
Silverleigh Rd THHTH CR7 196 A1
Silvermere Av CRW RM5 56 D2
Silvermere Dr UED * N18 51 F1
Silvermere Rd LEW SE13 164 D1
Silvermere Rw SNWD * SE25 181 H5
Silver Rd SHB W12 100 B6
Silver Spring Cl ERITH DA8 129 J6
Silverston Wy STAN HA7 43 J2
Silver St EN EN1 23 K4
UED N18 35 K6
Silverthorne Rd VX/NE SW8 141 G3
Silverthorn Gdns CHING E4 37 J4
Silverton Rd HMSMTH W6 139 G1
Silvertown Wy CAN/RD E16 106 D6
Silvertree La GFD/PVL UB6 96 D2
Silver Wk BERM/RHTH SE16 124 C1
Silver Wy ROMW/RG RM7 56 D6
Silverwood Cl BECK BR3 182 D3
CROY/NA CR0 213 H6
NTHWD HA6 40 A4
Silvester Rd EDUL SE22 143 G6
Silvester St STHWK SE1 18 E3
Silwood St BERM/RHTH SE16 124 A5
Simmil Rd ESH/CLAY KT10 204 E3
Simmons Cl TRDG/WHET N20 33 J3
Simmons Ga ESH/CLAY KT10 204 C3
Simmons La CHING E4 38 B4
Simmons Rd WOOL/PLUM SE18 127 G5
Simmons' Wy TRDG/WHET N20 33 J4
Simms Cl CAR SM5 194 D6
Simms Gdns EFNCH N2 47 G5
Simms Rd STHWK SE1 123 H4
Simnel Rd LEE/GVPK SE12 166 A2
Simon Cl NTGHL W11 100 D6
Simonds Rd LEY E10 69 J6
Simone Cl BMLY BR1 184 C4
Simons Wk SRTFD E15 88 B3
Simpson Cl WCHMH N21 23 F6
Simpson Dr ACT W3 99 F5
Simpson Rd HSLWW TW4 154 E1
RAIN RM13 93 H4
RCHPK/HAM TW10 156 D6
Simpson's Rd HAYES BR2 183 K6
POP/IOD E14 105 K6
Simpson St BTSEA SW11 140 D3
Simpson Wy SURB KT6 190 D3
Sims Cl ROM RM1 75 H1
Sinclair Dr BELMT SM2 209 F6
Sinclair Gdns WKENS W14 119 G2
Sinclair Gv GLDGN NW11 64 B3
Sinclair Rd CHING E4 51 H1
WKENS W14 119 H3
Sinclare Cl EN EN1 24 B2
Singapore Rd HNWL W7 116 B1
Singer St FSBYE EC1V 7 F5
Singleton Cl CROY/NA CR0 196 D4
HCH RM12 93 H2
WIM/MER SW19 178 E3
Singleton Rd DAGW RM9 92 B3
Singleton Scarp
NFNCH/WDSP N12 46 E1
Sinnott Rd WALTH E17 51 F4
Sion Rd TWK TW1 156 C3
Sipson Cl WDR/YW UB7 112 D6
Sipson La WDR/YW UB7 112 E6
Sipson Rd WDR/YW UB7 112 C4
Sipson Wy WDR/YW UB7 132 D1
Sir Abraham Dawes Cottages
PUT/ROE * SW15 139 H5
Sir Alexander Cl ACT W3 118 C1
Sir Cyril Black Wy
WIM/MER SW19 177 J3
Sirdar Rd MTCM CR4 179 F2
NTGHL W11 100 B6
WDGN N22 49 H6
Sir John Kirk Cl CMBW SE5 142 D1
Sir Thomas Moore Est
CHEL SW3 120 C6
Sirus Rd NTHWD HA6 40 E1
Sise La MANHO * EC4N 12 E4
Sisley Rd BARK IG11 90 E6
Sispara Gdns WAND/EARL SW18 159 J1
Sissinghurst Cl BMLY BR1 183 H1
Sissinghurst Rd CROY/NA CR0 197 H4
Sister Mabel's Wy PECK * SE15 143 H1
Sisters Av BTSEA SW11 140 E5
Sistova Rd BAL SW12 161 G3
Sisulu Pl BRXN/ST SW9 142 B4
Sittingbourne Av EN EN1 35 K1
Sitwell Gv STAN HA7 43 F1
Siverst Cl NTHLT UB5 78 B4
Siviter Wy DAGE RM10 92 D5
Siward Rd HAYES BR2 184 A6
TOOT SW17 160 B5
TOTM N17 49 K4
Sixth Av HYS/HAR UB3 113 J1
MNPK E12 89 K2
NKENS W10 100 C3
Sixth Cross Rd WHTN TW2 155 H5
Skardu Rd CRICK NW2 82 C3
Skeena Hl WAND/EARL SW18 159 H2
Skeet Hill La STMC/STPC BR5 203 G6
Skeffington Rd EHAM E6 89 K6
Skelbrook St WAND/EARL SW18 160 A4
Skelgill Rd PUT/ROE SW15 139 J5
Skelley Rd SRTFD E15 88 D5
Skelton Cl HACK * E8 86 B4
Skelton Rd FSTGT E7 88 E4
Skelton's La LEY E10 69 K4
Skelwith Rd HMSMTH W6 119 F6
Skerne Rd KUTN/CMB KT2 174 E4
Sketchley Gdns
BERM/RHTH SE16 124 A5
Sketty Rd EN EN1 24 B4
Skiers St SRTFD E15 88 C6
Skiffington Cl
BRXS/STRHM SW2 162 B3
Skinner Pl BGVA * SW1W 15 G7
Skinners La BLKFR EC4V 12 D5
HEST TW5 135 G2
Skinner St CLKNW EC1R 5 K5
Skipsey Av EHAM E6 107 K2
Skipton Cl FBAR/BDGN N11 48 A2
Skipton Dr HYS/HAR UB3 113 F3
Skipworth Rd HOM E9 86 E6
Skylines Village POP/IOD * E14 125 F2
Sky Peals Rd WFD IG8 52 B4
Skyport Dr WDR/YW UB7 132 A1
The Slade WOOL/PLUM SE18 127 K6
Sladebrook Rd BKHTH/KID SE3 146 C4
Sladedale Rd WOOL/PLUM SE18 127 K5
Slade Gdns ERITH DA8 150 C2
Slade Green Rd ERITH DA8 150 C2
Sladen Pl CLPT E5 86 D2
Slades Cl ENC/FH EN2 23 G4
Slades Dr CHST BR7 167 H6
Slades Gdns ENC/FH EN2 23 G3
Slades Hl ENC/FH EN2 23 G4
Slades Ri ENC/FH EN2 23 G4
Slade Wk WALW SE17 122 C6
Slagrove Pl LEW SE13 144 D6
Slaidburn St WBPTN SW10 120 B6
Slaithwaite Rd LEW SE13 145 F5
Slaney Pl HOLWY N7 85 G3
Slaney Rd ROM RM1 75 G2
Slattery Rd FELT TW13 154 B3
Sleaford Gn OXHEY WD19 27 H5
Sleaford St VX/NE SW8 141 H1
Slievemore Cl CLAP SW4 141 J4
Slingsby Pl COVGDN WC2E 10 E5
Slippers Pl BERM/RHTH SE16 123 J3
Sloane Av CHEL SW3 14 D7
Sloane Ct East CHEL SW3 121 F5
Sloane Ct West CHEL SW3 121 F5
Sloane Gdns BGVA SW1W 15 G7
ORP BR6 216 C1
Sloane Sq BGVA SW1W 15 F7
Sloane St KTBR SW1X 15 F3
Sloane Ter KTBR SW1X 15 F6
Sloane Wk CROY/NA CR0 198 C3
Slocum Cl THMD SE28 109 J6
Slough La CDALE/KGS NW9 62 E3
Sly St WCHPL * E1 104 D5
Smaldon Cl WDR/YW UB7 112 D3
Smallberry Av ISLW TW7 136 A3
Smallbrook Ms BAY/PAD W2 8 A4
Smalley Cl STNW/STAM N16 86 B1
Smallwood Rd TOOT SW17 160 C6
Smarden Cl BELV DA17 129 H5
Smart Cl HARH RM3 57 K4
Smart's Pl HHOL WC1V 11 F3
UED N18 50 C1
Smart St BETH E2 105 F2
Smeaton Rd WAND/EARL SW18 159 K2
WFD IG8 53 K1
Smeaton St WAP E1W 123 J1
Smedley St VX/NE SW8 141 J3
Smeed Rd BOW E3 87 J5
Smiles Pl LEW SE13 145 F3
Smith Cl BERM/RHTH SE16 124 A1
Smithfield St STBT EC1A 12 A2
Smithies Rd ABYW SE2 128 C4
Smith's Ct SOHO/SHAV * W1D 10 C5
Smithson Rd TOTM N17 49 K4
Smith St BRYLDS KT5 191 G3
CHEL SW3 120 E5
Smith Ter CHEL SW3 120 E5
Smithwood Cl WIM/MER SW19 159 H4
Smithy St WCHPL E1 104 E4
Smugglers Wy
WAND/EARL SW18 140 A5
Smyrks Rd WALW * SE17 123 F5
WALW SE17 123 F5
Smyrna Rd KIL/WHAMP NW6 82 E5
Smythe St POP/IOD E14 105 K6
Snakes La EBAR EN4 22 B4
Snakes La East WFD IG8 53 G2
Snakes La West WFD IG8 52 E2
Snaresbrook Dr STAN HA7 29 K6
Snaresbrook Rd WAN E11 70 D1
Snarsgate St NKENS W10 100 A4
Sneath Av GLDGN NW11 64 D4
Snell's Pk UED N18 50 B2
Sneyd Rd CRICK NW2 82 A3
Snipe Cl ERITH DA8 150 E1
Snowbury Rd FUL/PGN SW6 140 A3
Snowden Dr CDALE/KGS NW9 63 G3
Snowdon Crs HYS/HAR UB3 113 F3
Snowdon Rd West HTHAIR TW6 153 F1
Snowdown Cl PGE/AN SE20 181 K4
Snowdrop Cl HPTN TW12 173 F2
Snow Hl STBT EC1A 12 A2
Snowsfields STHWK SE1 19 F2
Snowshill Rd MNPK E12 89 J3
Snowy Fielder Waye ISLW TW7 136 C3
Soames St PECK SE15 143 G4
Soames Wk NWMAL KT3 176 B4
Soho Sq SOHO/SHAV W1D 10 C4
Soho St SOHO/SHAV W1D 10 C3
Sojourner Truth Cl HACK * E8 86 D4
Solander Gdns WCHPL E1 104 D6
Solebay St WCHPL E1 105 G3
Solent Ri PLSTW E13 106 E2
Solent Rd KIL/WHAMP NW6 82 E3
Solna Av PUT/ROE SW15 139 F6
Solna Rd WCHMH N21 35 K3
Solomon Av UED N18 36 C6
Solomon's Pas PECK SE15 143 J5
Solon New Rd CLAP SW4 141 K5
Solon Rd CLAP SW4 141 K5
Solway Cl HACK E8 86 B4
HSLWW TW4 134 D4
Solway Rd EDUL SE22 143 H5
WDGN N22 49 H4
Somaford Gv EBAR EN4 33 H1
Somali Rd CRICK NW2 82 D2
Somerby Rd BARK IG11 90 D5
Somercoates Cl EBAR EN4 21 J4
Somerden Rd STMC/STPC BR5 202 E4
Somerfield Rd FSBYPK N4 67 H6
Somerford Cl PIN HA5 58 E1
Somerford Gv STNW/STAM N16 86 B2
TOTM N17 50 C3
Somerford St WCHPL * E1 104 D3
Somerford Wy
BERM/RHTH SE16 124 B2
Somerhill Av BFN/LL DA15 168 C2
Somerhill Rd WELL DA16 148 C3
Somerleyton Rd BRXN/ST SW9 142 B5
Somersby Gdns REDBR IG4 71 K2
Somers Cl CAMTN * NW1 4 C2
Somers Crs BAY/PAD W2 8 C4
Somerset Av CHSGTN KT9 205 K2
RYNPK SW20 176 E5
WELL DA16 148 A6
Somerset Cl NWMAL KT3 192 B3
TOTM N17 49 K5
WFD IG8 52 E4
Somerset Gdns HGT N6 66 A4
LEW SE13 144 E3
STRHM/NOR SW16 180 A6
TEDD TW11 173 K1
TOTM * N17 50 A3
Somerset Rd BAR EN5 21 F6
BTFD TW8 116 D6
CHSWK W4 118 A3
DART DA1 170 E1
HDN NW4 64 A1
HRW HA1 60 C3
KUT KT1 175 G5
ORP BR6 202 B4
PEND EN3 25 J1
STHL UB1 96 A4
TEDD TW11 173 K1
TOTM N17 50 B6
UED N18 50 B1
WALTH E17 69 J2
WEA W13 116 C1
WIM/MER SW19 159 H5
Somerset Sq WKENS * W14 119 H3
Somerset Street Little
TWRH EC3N 13 J4
Somerset Waye HEST TW5 114 D6
Somersham Rd BXLYHN DA7 149 F3
Somers Pl BRXS/STRHM SW2 162 A2
Somers Rd BRXS/STRHM SW2 162 A1
WALTH E17 69 H1
Somers Wy BUSH WD23 28 C2
Somerton Av RCH/KEW TW9 137 J4
Somerton Rd CRICK NW2 82 B1
PECK SE15 143 J5
Somertrees Av LEE/GVPK SE12 166 A4
Somervell Rd RYLN/HDSTN HA2 77 K3
Somerville Av BARN SW13 119 F6
Somerville Rd CHDH RM6 73 J2
DART DA1 171 J1
PGE/AN SE20 182 A3
Sonderburg Rd HOLWY N7 67 F6
Sondes St WALW SE17 122 E6
Sonia Cl OXHEY WD19 27 G2
Sonia Gdns CRICK NW2 81 H2
HEST TW5 135 F1
NFNCH/WDSP N12 33 G6
Sonning Gdns HPTN TW12 172 D2
Sonning Rd CROY/NA CR0 197 H3
Soper Cl CHING E4 51 H1
FSTH SE23 164 A3
Soper Ms PEND EN3 25 J1
Sophia Cl HOLWY N7 85 F4
Sophia Rd CAN/RD E16 107 F5
LEY E10 69 K5
Sophia Sq POP/IOD E14 105 G6
Sopwith Av CHSGTN KT9 206 A3
Sopwith Cl RCHPK/HAM TW10 175 G1
Sopwith Rd HEST TW5 134 B1
Sopwith Wy KUTN/CMB KT2 175 F4
VX/NE SW8 141 G1
Sorrel Bank CROY/NA CR0 213 G6
Sorrel Cl THMD SE28 128 B1
Sorrel Gdns EHAM E6 107 J4
Sorrel La POP/IOD E14 106 B5
Sorrell Cl BRXN/ST * SW9 142 B3
NWCR SE14 144 B1
Sorrel Wk ROM RM1 57 H6
Sorrento Rd SUT SM1 209 F1
Sotheby Rd HBRY N5 85 J2
Sotheran Cl HACK E8 86 C6
Soudan Rd BTSEA SW11 140 E2
Souldern Rd WKENS * W14 119 G3
Sounds Ldg SWLY BR8 203 K3
South Access Rd WALTH E17 69 G4
South Acre CDALE/KGS NW9 45 H5
Southacre Wy PIN HA5 41 G4
South Africa Rd SHB W12 99 K6
Southall Ct STHL * UB1 95 K6
Southall La HEST TW5 114 A5
Southall Pl STHWK SE1 18 E3
Southampton Buildings
LINN * WC2A 11 J2
Southampton Gdns MTCM CR4 195 K2
Southampton Pl
NOXST/BSQ WC1A 11 F2
Southampton Rd HAMP NW3 83 K3
HTHAIR TW6 152 C1
Southampton Rw RSQ WC1B 11 F2
Southampton St COVGDN WC2E 11 F5
Southampton Wy CMBW SE5 142 E1
Southam St NKENS W10 100 C3
South Ap NTHWD HA6 26 B5
South Audley St
MYFR/PKLN W1K 9 H6
South Av CAR SM5 210 A5
CHING E4 37 K2
RCH/KEW * TW9 137 H3
STHL UB1 95 K6
South Av Gdns STHL UB1 95 K6
South Bank STHWK SE1 11 K6
SURB KT6 191 F3
Southbank THDIT KT7 190 C4
South Bank Ter SURB * KT6 191 F3
South Birkbeck Rd WAN E11 88 B1
South Black Lion La
HMSMTH W6 118 D5
South Bolton Gdns
WBPTN SW10 120 A5
Southborough Cl SURB KT6 190 E5
Southborough La HAYES BR2 200 E2
Southborough Rd BMLY BR1 184 D6
HOM E9 86 E6
SURB KT6 191 F5
Southborough Rd (The Lane)
SURB * KT6 191 F5
Southbourne HAYES BR2 199 K4
Southbourne Av
CDALE/KGS NW9 44 E5
Southbourne Cl PIN HA5 59 J4
Southbourne Crs HDN NW4 64 C1
Southbourne Gdns IL IG1 90 C3
LEE/GVPK SE12 146 A6
RSLP HA4 59 F5
Southbridge Pl CROY/NA CR0 211 J2
Southbridge Rd CROY/NA CR0 211 J2
Southbridge Wy NWDGN UB2 114 D2
Southbrook Rd LEW SE13 165 H1
STRHM/NOR SW16 179 K4
Southbury Av EN EN1 24 C5
Southbury Rd EN EN1 24 B5
South Carriage Dr SKENS SW7 14 C3
Southchurch Ct PLMGR N13 49 F1
Southchurch Rd EHAM E6 107 K1
South Cl BAR EN5 20 D4
BXLYHS DA6 148 E5
DAGE RM10 92 C6
FELT TW13 155 F5
HGT N6 66 B3
PIN HA5 59 K4
WDR/YW UB7 112 C3
The South Colonnade
POP/IOD E14 124 E1
South Colonnade POP/IOD E14 124 D1
Southcombe St WKENS W14 119 H4
Southcote Av BRYLDS KT5 191 J4
FELT TW13 153 K4
Southcote Ri RSLP HA4 58 B4
Southcote Rd ARCH N19 84 C2
SNWD SE25 197 J2
WALTH E17 69 F2
South Countess Rd WALTH E17 51 H6
South Crs CAN/RD E16 106 B4
Southcroft Av WELL DA16 147 K4
WWKM BR4 199 F6
Southcroft Rd ORP BR6 216 E1
STRHM/NOR SW16 179 G2
South Cross Rd BARK/HLT IG6 72 C2
South Croxted Rd DUL SE21 162 E5
Southdale CHIG IG7 54 D2
Southdean Gdns
WIM/MER SW19 159 J4
South Dene MLHL NW7 31 F5
Southdown Av HNWL W7 116 B3
Southdown Crs
GNTH/NBYPK IG2 72 E2
RYLN/HDSTN HA2 60 C5
Southdown Dr RYNPK SW20 177 G3
Southdown Rd CAR SM5 210 A6
EMPK RM11 75 K4
RYNPK SW20 177 G4
Southdown Vls
SEVS/STOTM * N15 67 H2
South Dr ORP BR6 216 E3
RSLP HA4 58 C5
South Ealing Rd EA W5 116 E2
South Eastern Av ED N9 36 B5
South Eaton Pl BGVA SW1W 15 H6
South Eden Park Rd BECK BR3 198 E1
South Edwardes Sq KENS W8 119 J3
South End CROY/NA CR0 211 J3
KENS * W8 120 A3
Southend Cl ELTH/MOT SE9 167 G1
Southend Crs ELTH/MOT SE9 167 F1
Southend La CAT SE6 164 D6
Southend Rd BECK BR3 182 D4
South End Rd HAMP NW3 83 J2
RAIN RM13 93 J6
Southend Rd REDBR IG4 53 J6
Southend Rd (North Circular)
WALTH E17 52 B4
South End Rw KENS W8 120 A3
Southern Av EBED/NFELT TW14 153 K3
SNWD SE25 181 G6
Southern Down FELT * TW13 154 B3
Southern Dr LOU IG10 39 K1
Southerngate Wy NWCR SE14 144 B1
Southern Gv BOW E3 105 H2
Southern Perimeter Rd
HTHAIR TW6 133 F6
Southern Rd EFNCH N2 65 K1
PLSTW E13 107 F1
Southern Rw NKENS W10 100 B3
Southern St IS N1 5 G2
Southern Wy CHDH RM6 74 C3
Southerton Rd HMSMTH * W6 119 F4
South Esk Rd FSTGT E7 89 G4
Southey Rd BRXN/ST SW9 142 B2
SEVS/STOTM N15 68 A2
WIM/MER SW19 177 K3
Southey St PGE/AN SE20 182 A3
Southfield BAR EN5 32 B1
Southfield Gdns TWK TW1 156 A6
Southfield Pk RYLN/HDSTN HA2 60 B1
Southfield Rd CHST BR7 186 A6
CHSWK W4 118 A2
PEND EN3 36 D1
Southfields E/WMO/HCT KT8 189 K3
HDN NW4 45 K6
Southfields Ms
WAND/EARL * SW18 159 K1
Southfields Rd
WAND/EARL SW18 159 K1
Southfleet Rd ORP BR6 216 E1
South Gdns WBLY * HA9 62 C6
WIM/MER SW19 178 C3
South Gate Av FELT TW13 153 G6
Southgate Gv IS N1 85 K5
Southgate Rd IS N1 85 K6
South Gipsy Rd WELL DA16 148 E4
South Gv HGT N6 66 A5
SEVS/STOTM N15 67 K2
WALTH E17 69 H2
South Hall Dr RAIN RM13 111 K4
South Hl CHST BR7 184 E2
NTHWD * HA6 40 C4
South Hill Av RYLN/HDSTN HA2 78 C1
South Hill Gv HRW HA1 78 E2
South Hill Pk HAMP NW3 83 J2
South Hill Park Gdns HAMP NW3 83 J2
South Hill Rd HAYES BR2 183 H6
Southholme Cl NRWD SE19 181 F4
Southill La PIN HA5 58 E1
Southill Rd CHST BR7 184 D3
Southill St POP/IOD E14 105 K5
South Island Pl BRXN/ST SW9 142 A1
South Kensington Station Ar
SKENS SW7 14 B6
South Lambeth Pl VX/NE SW8 121 K6
South Lambeth Rd VX/NE SW8 121 K6
Southland Rd
WOOL/PLUM SE18 148 A1
Southlands Av ORP BR6 216 E2
Southlands Dr WIM/MER SW19 159 G4
Southlands Gv BMLY BR1 184 D6
Southlands Rd HAYES BR2 200 C1
Southland Wy HSLW TW3 135 J6
South La KUT KT1 174 E6
NWMAL KT3 192 A1
South La West NWMAL KT3 192 A1
South Lodge Av MTCM CR4 195 K1
South Lodge Crs ENC/FH EN2 22 D5
South Lodge Dr STHGT/OAK N14 22 D6
South Md CDALE/KGS NW9 45 H4
HOR/WEW KT19 207 H5
Southmead Rd WIM/MER SW19 159 H3
South Molton La
MYFR/PKLN W1K 9 J4
South Molton Rd CAN/RD E16 106 E5
South Molton St
MYFR/PKLN W1K 9 J4
Southmont Rd ESH/CLAY KT10 189 K6
Southmoor Wy HOM E9 87 H4
South Mt TRDG/WHET * N20 33 G4
South Norwood Hl SNWD SE25 181 F5
South Oak Rd
STRHM/NOR SW16 162 A6
Southold Ri ELTH/MOT SE9 166 E5
Southolm St VX/NE SW8 141 G2
Southover BMLY BR1 183 K1
NFNCH/WDSP N12 32 E6
South Pde CHEL SW3 120 C5
CHSWK W4 118 A4
EDGE * HA8 44 C5
WLGTN * SM6 210 C4
South Park Crs CAT SE6 165 H3
IL IG1 90 D1
South Park Dr IL IG1 90 E1
South Park Gv NWMAL KT3 191 K1
South Park Hill Rd
SAND/SEL CR2 211 K3
South Park Ms FUL/PGN SW6 140 A4
South Park Rd IL IG1 90 D1
WIM/MER SW19 177 K2
South Park Ter IL IG1 90 D1
South Park Wy RSLP HA4 77 G4
South Pl BRYLDS KT5 191 G4
LVPST EC2M 13 F2
PEND EN3 24 E6
South Place Ms LVPST EC2M 13 F2
Southport Rd
WOOL/PLUM SE18 127 J4
Southridge Pl RYNPK SW20 177 G3
South Ri BAY/PAD * W2 8 D5
CAR SM5 209 J6
South Rd CHDH RM6 73 J2
EA W5 116 E4
ED N9 36 C3
EDGE HA8 44 D4
ERITH DA8 130 C6
FELT TW13 172 C1
FSTH SE23 164 A4
NWDGN UB2 114 E2
WDR/YW UB7 112 D3
WHTN TW2 155 J5
WIM/MER SW19 178 C2
South Rw BKHTH/KID SE3 145 K3
Southsea Rd KUT KT1 191 F1
South Sea St BERM/RHTH SE16 124 C3
South Side HMSMTH W6 118 C3
SEVS/STOTM * N15 68 B1
Southside Common
WIM/MER SW19 177 G2
Southspring ELTH/MOT SE9 167 J2
South Sq GINN WC1R 11 J2
GLDGN NW11 64 E3
South St BMLY BR1 183 K5
ISLW TW7 136 B4
MYFR/PKLN W1K 9 H7
PEND EN3 25 F6
RAIN RM13 110 E1
ROM RM1 75 G2
South Tenter St WCHPL E1 13 K5
South Ter SKENS SW7 14 C6

SURB KT6 191 F3
WDGN N22 48 E5
South V HRW HA1 78 E2
NRWD SE19 181 F2
Southvale Rd BKHTH/KID SE3 145 H3
South Vale Rd SURB KT6 191 F6
South Vw BMLY BR1 184 B5
Southview Av WLSDN NW10 81 H3
South View Cl BXLY DA5 169 G1
Southview Cl TOOT SW17 179 F1
South View Ct NRWD * SE19 180 D3
South View Crs GNTH/NBYPK IG2 72 B3
Southview Dr SWFD E18 53 F6
Southview Gdns WLGTN SM6 210 C5
Southview Rd BMLY BR1 165 G6
South View Rd CEND/HSY/T N8 48 D6
LOU IG10 39 K1
PIN HA5 41 F2
RDART DA2 171 G5
Southviews SAND/SEL CR2 213 F6
South Vls CAMTN NW1 84 D4
Southville VX/NE SW8 141 J2
Southville Cl EBED/NFELT TW14 153 H2
HOR/WEW KT19 207 F6
Southville Crs
EBED/NFELT TW14 153 H3
Southville Rd
EBED/NFELT TW14 153 H3
THDIT KT7 190 B4
South Wk WWKM BR4 214 C1
Southwark Br CANST EC4R 12 D6
Southwark Bridge Rd
STHWK SE1 12 D7
Southwark Park Est
BERM/RHTH * SE16 123 J4
Southwark Park Rd
BERM/RHTH SE16 19 K6
Southwark Pl BMLY BR1 184 E6
Southwark St STHWK SE1 12 B7
Southwater Cl BECK BR3 182 E3
South Wy CROY/NA CR0 213 G1
FBAR/BDGN N11 48 C2
RYLN/HDSTN HA2 60 A1
WBLY HA9 80 C3
Southway GLDGN NW11 65 F3
HAYES BR2 199 K4
RYNPK SW20 193 G1
TRDG/WHET N20 32 E4
WLGTN SM6 210 C2
Southwell Av NTHLT UB5 78 A4
Southwell Gdns SKENS SW7 120 B4
Southwell Grove Rd WAN E11 70 C6
Southwell Rd CMBW SE5 142 D4
CROY/NA CR0 196 B3
KTN/HRWW/W HA3 61 K3
South Western Rd TWK TW1 156 B1
Southwest Rd WAN E11 70 B5
South Wharf Rd BAY/PAD W2 8 A3
Southwick Ms BAY/PAD W2 8 B3
Southwick Pl BAY/PAD W2 8 C4
Southwick St BAY/PAD W2 8 C3
Southwick Yd BAY/PAD * W2 8 D4
Southwold Dr BARK IG11 91 G3
Southwold Rd BXLY DA5 169 J1
CLPT E5 68 D6
Southwood Av HGT N6 66 B4
KUTN/CMB KT2 175 K4
Southwood Cl BMLY BR1 200 E1
WPK KT4 193 G5
Southwood Dr BRYLDS KT5 191 K4
Southwood Gdns BARK/HLT IG6 72 B1
ESH/CLAY KT10 205 G1
Southwood La HGT N6 66 A4
Southwood Lawn Rd HGT N6 66 B4
Southwood Pk HGT * N6 66 B4
Southwood Rd ELTH/MOT SE9 167 G4
THMD SE28 128 C1
South Worple Wy
MORT/ESHN SW14 138 A4
Sovereign Cl EA W5 97 J4
RSLP HA4 58 C5
WAP E1W 104 D6
Sovereign Ct E/WMO/HCT KT8 188 E1
Sovereign Crs POP/IOD E14 105 G6
Sovereign Gv ALP/SUD HA0 79 K1
Sovereign Ms BETH * E2 7 J2
Sovereign Pk WLSDN * NW10 98 D3
Sovereign Rd BARK IG11 109 J2
Sowerby Cl ELTH/MOT SE9 146 E6
Sowrey Av RAIN RM13 93 H4
Space Waye EBED/NFELT TW14 133 K6
Spa Cl NRWD SE19 181 F4
Spafield St CLKNW * EC1R 5 J6
Spa Green Est CLKNW * EC1R 5 K4
Spa Hl THHTH CR7 180 E4
Spalding Cl EDGE HA8 45 G3
Spalding Rd HDN NW4 64 A3
TOOT SW17 179 G1
Spanby Rd BOW E3 105 J3
Spaniards Cl GLDGN NW11 65 G5
Spaniards End GLDGN NW11 65 G5
Spaniards Rd HAMP NW3 65 G6
Spanish Pl MHST * W1U 9 H3
Spanish Rd WAND/EARL SW18 140 B6
Sparkbridge Rd HRW HA1 60 E1
Sparke Ter CAN/RD * E16 106 D5
Sparkford Gdns FBAR/BDGN N11 48 A1
Sparks Cl ACT W3 99 F5
BCTR RM8 73 K6
HPTN TW12 172 D2
Spa Rd BERM/RHTH SE16 19 J5
Sparrow Cl HPTN TW12 172 D2
Sparrow Dr STMC/STPC BR5 201 H5
Sparrow Farm Dr
EBED/NFELT TW14 154 C2
Sparrow Farm Rd EW KT17 207 J2
Sparrow Gn DAGE RM10 92 D1
Sparrows Herne BUSH WD23 28 B2
Sparrows La ELTH/MOT SE9 167 H3
Sparrows Wy BUSH * WD23 28 C2
Sparrows Wick BUSH * WD23 28 C3
Sparsholt Rd ARCH N19 67 F5
BARK IG11 90 E6
Sparta St GNWCH SE10 145 F2
Speakers Ct CROY/NA * CR0 196 E5
Spearman St
WOOL/PLUM * SE18 127 F6
Spear Ms ECT SW5 119 K4
Spears Rd ARCH N19 66 E5
Speart La HEST TW5 134 D1
Spedan Cl HAMP NW3 83 F1
Speedwell St DEPT SE8 144 D1
Speer Rd THDIT KT7 190 A3
Speirs Cl NWMAL KT3 192 C3
Spekehill ELTH/MOT SE9 166 E5
Speke Rd THHTH CR7 180 E5
Speldhurst Cl HAYES BR2 199 J2
Speldhurst Rd CHSWK W4 118 A3
HOM E9 87 F5
Spellbrook Wk IS * N1 85 J6
Spelman St WCHPL E1 104 C4
Spence Cl BERM/RHTH SE16 124 C2
Spencer Av PLMGR N13 49 F2
YEAD UB4 94 E4
Spencer Cl FNCH N3 46 D5
ORP BR6 201 K6
WFD IG8 53 G1
WLSDN NW10 98 B2
Spencer Dr EFNCH N2 65 G3
Spencer Gdns
MORT/ESHN SW14 137 K6
Spencer Hl WIM/MER SW19 177 H2
Spencer Hill Rd WIM/MER SW19 177 H3
Spencer House SURB * KT6 191 F2
Spencer Ms HMSMTH W6 119 H6
Spencer Pk WAND/EARL SW18 140 C6
Spencer Pl CROY/NA CR0 196 E4
IS N1 85 H5
WEST SW1P 16 B5
Spencer Ri KTTN NW5 84 B2
Spencer Rd ACT W3 117 K1
ALP/SUD HA0 61 J6
BMLY BR1 183 J3
BTSEA SW11 140 C5
CEND/HSY/T N8 67 F2
CHSWK W4 137 K1
E/WMO/HCT KT8 189 H1
EHAM E6 89 H6
FBAR/BDGN N11 34 B6
GDMY/SEVK IG3 73 F5
ISLW TW7 135 J2
KTN/HRWW/W HA3 42 E5
MTCM CR4 179 F6
MTCM CR4 194 E4
RAIN RM13 111 F2
RYNPK SW20 176 E4
SAND/SEL CR2 212 A3
TOTM N17 50 C4
WALTH E17 52 A5
WHTN TW2 155 K5
Spencer St FSBYE EC1V 6 A5
NWDGN UB2 114 C3
Spencer Wk PUT/ROE SW15 139 G5
Spenser Gv STNW/STAM N16 86 A2
Spenser Ms DUL SE21 162 E3
Spenser Rd HNHL SE24 142 C6
Spenser St WESTW SW1E 16 B4
Spensley Wk STNW/STAM N16 85 K1
Speranza St WOOL/PLUM SE18 128 A5
Sperling Rd TOTM N17 50 B5
Spert St POP/IOD E14 105 G6
Speyside STHGT/OAK N14 34 C1
Spey St POP/IOD E14 106 A4
Spey Wy ROM RM1 57 G3
Spezia Rd WLSDN NW10 99 J1
Spicer Cl CMBW SE5 142 C3
WOT/HER KT12 188 B3
Spices Yd CROY/NA CR0 211 J2
Spielman Rd DART DA1 151 J5
Spigurnell Rd TOTM N17 49 K4
Spikes Bridge Rd STHL UB1 95 J5
Spilsby Cl CDALE/KGS NW9 45 G5
Spindle Cl WOOL/PLUM SE18 126 D3
Spindlewood Gdns
CROY/NA CR0 211 K2
Spindrift Av POP/IOD E14 124 E4
Spinel Cl WOOL/PLUM SE18 128 A5
Spinnaker Cl BARK IG11 109 H2
Spinnells Rd RYLN/HDSTN HA2 59 K5
The Spinney ALP/SUD HA0 79 G1
BARN * SW13 118 E6
CHEAM SM3 208 A2
NFNCH/WDSP * N12 47 G3
SCUP DA14 187 F1
STAN HA7 30 A6
STRHM/NOR SW16 161 H5
WCHMH N21 35 G2
Spinney Cl BECK BR3 198 E1
NWMAL KT3 192 B2
RAIN RM13 111 G1
WPK KT4 207 H1
Spinney Dr EBED/NFELT TW14 153 F2
Spinney Gdns DAGW RM9 92 A3
NRWD SE19 181 G1
Spinney Oak BMLY BR1 184 D5
The Spinneys BMLY BR1 184 E5
The Spires DART DA1 171 G4
Spirit Quay WAP E1W 123 H1
Spital Sq WCHPL E1 13 H1
Spital St DART DA1 171 G1
WCHPL E1 104 C4
Spital Yd WCHPL * E1 13 H1
Spitfire Est HEST * TW5 114 B5
Spitfire Wy HEST TW5 114 B5
Spode Wk KIL/WHAMP * NW6 83 F3
Spondon Rd SEVS/STOTM N15 68 C1
Spoonbill Wy YEAD UB4 95 H4
Spooner Wk WLGTN SM6 210 D3
Sportsbank St CAT SE6 165 F2
Spottons Gv TOTM N17 49 J4
Spout Hl CROY/NA CR0 213 J3
Spratt Hall Rd WAN E11 70 E3
Spray St WOOL/PLUM SE18 127 G4
Spreighton Rd
E/WMO/HCT KT8 189 G1
Sprimont Pl CHEL SW3 120 E5
Springall St PECK SE15 143 J1
Springbank WCHMH N21 35 F1
Springbank Rd LEW SE13 165 H1
Springbank Wk CAMTN NW1 84 D5
Springbourne Ct BECK BR3 183 F4
Spring Bridge Rd EA W5 97 K6
Spring Cl BAR EN5 20 B6
BCTR RM8 73 K5
Springclose La CHEAM SM3 208 C4
Spring Cnr FELT * TW13 153 K5
Spring Cottages SURB * KT6 190 E2
Spring Court Rd ENC/FH EN2 23 G1
Springcroft Av EFNCH N2 47 K6
Springdale Rd STNW/STAM N16 85 K2
Spring Dr PIN HA5 58 E3
Springfield BUSH WD23 28 D3
CLPT E5 68 D5
Springfield Av HPTN TW12 173 G2
MUSWH N10 48 C6
RYNPK SW20 177 J6
Springfield Cl NFNCH/WDSP N12 47 F1
STAN HA7 29 G5
Springfield Dr GNTH/NBYPK IG2 72 C2
Springfield Gdns BMLY BR1 200 E1
CDALE/KGS NW9 63 F2
CLPT E5 68 D5
RSLP HA4 59 F5
WFD IG8 53 G3
WWKM BR4 198 E6
Springfield Gv CHARL SE7 126 B6
Springfield La KIL/WHAMP NW6 82 E6
Springfield Mt CDALE/KGS NW9 63 G2
Springfield Pl NWMAL KT3 191 K1
Springfield Ri SYD SE26 163 J6
Springfield Rd BMLY BR1 200 E1
BXLYHN DA7 149 J4
CHING E4 38 C3
EHAM E6 89 K5
FBAR/BDGN N11 48 C1
HNWL W7 115 K1
HRW HA1 60 E3
HYS/HAR UB3 114 B1
KUT KT1 191 F1
SEVS/STOTM N15 68 C1
SRTFD * E15 106 C2
STJWD NW8 83 G6
SYD SE26 181 J1
TEDD TW11 174 B1
THHTH CR7 180 D4
WALTH E17 69 H3
WELL DA16 148 C4
WHTN TW2 155 F3
WIM/MER SW19 177 J1
WLGTN SM6 210 B3
Springfield Wk
KIL/WHAMP NW6 83 F6
Springfield Wy STMC/STPC BR5 186 D6
Spring Gdns E/WMO/HCT KT8 189 H2
HBRY N5 85 J3
HCH RM12 93 K2
ORP BR6 217 H4
ROMW/RG RM7 74 E2
WFD IG8 53 G3
WHALL SW1A 10 E7
WLGTN SM6 210 C3
Spring Gv CHSWK W4 117 H5
HPTN TW12 173 G4
LOU IG10 39 H1
MTCM CR4 179 F4
Spring Grove Crs HEST TW5 135 H2
Spring Grove Rd HSLW TW3 135 H2
RCHPK/HAM TW10 137 G6
Springhead Rd ERITH DA8 130 C6
Spring Hl CLPT E5 68 C4
SYD SE26 163 K6
Springhurst Cl CROY/NA CR0 213 H2
Spring Lake STAN HA7 29 H6
Spring La CLPT E5 68 D5
MUSWH N10 48 A6
SNWD SE25 197 J3
Spring Ms MHST * W1U 9 F1
Spring Park Av CROY/NA CR0 198 A6
Springpark Dr BECK BR3 183 F6
FSBYPK N4 67 J5
Spring Park Rd CROY/NA CR0 198 A6
Spring Pl FNCH N3 46 E5
KTTN NW5 84 A3
Springpond Rd DAGW RM9 92 A3
Springrice Rd LEW SE13 165 F1
Spring Rd FELT TW13 153 J5
Spring Shaw Rd
STMC/STPC BR5 186 B4
Spring St BAY/PAD W2 8 A4
EW KT17 207 H6
Spring Tide Cl PECK * SE15 143 H2
Spring V BXLYHN DA7 149 J5
Springvale Av BTFD TW8 116 E5
Spring V North DART DA1 171 G2
Spring V South DART * DA1 171 G2
Springvale Ter WKENS W14 119 G3
Spring Villa Rd EDGE HA8 44 C3
Spring Vls WEA * W13 116 C1
Spring Wk WCHPL E1 104 C4
Springwater Cl
WOOL/PLUM * SE18 147 F2
Springwell Av WLSDN NW10 81 H6
Springwell Rd HEST TW5 134 C2
STRHM/NOR SW16 162 B6
Springwood Crs EDGE HA8 30 E4
Springwood Wy ROM RM1 75 J2
Sprowston Ms FSTGT E7 88 E4
Sprowston Rd FSTGT E7 88 E3
Sprucedale Gdns CROY/NA CR0 213 F2
PUR/KEN CR8 210 E6
Spruce Hills Rd WALTH E17 51 K5
Sprules Rd BROCKY SE4 144 B3
Spurfield E/WMO/HCT KT8 173 G6
Spurgeon Av NRWD SE19 180 E4
Spurgeon Rd NRWD SE19 180 E3
Spurgeon St STHWK SE1 18 E5
Spurling Rd DAGW RM9 92 B4
EDUL * SE22 143 G5
Spurrell Av RDART DA2 170 A6
Spur Rd BARK IG11 108 C2
EBED/NFELT TW14 134 A6
EDGE HA8 30 A6
ISLW TW7 136 B1
ORP BR6 202 B6
SEVS/STOTM * N15 67 K1
STHWK SE1 17 J2
WHALL SW1A 16 A3
Spurstowe Rd HACK E8 86 D4
Spurstowe Ter HACK E8 86 C3
The Square CAR SM5 210 A3
HMSMTH W6 119 F5
RCHPK/HAM TW10 137 F6
STKPK UB11 113 G1
WFD IG8 52 E1
Squarey St TOOT SW17 160 B5
Squire Gdns STJWD NW8 2 A5
Squires Ct WIM/MER SW19 159 K6
Squires La FNCH N3 47 F5
Squire's Mt HAMP NW3 83 H1
Squires Wy RDART DA2 170 A6
Squires Wood Dr CHST * BR7 184 E3
Squirrel Cl HSLWW TW4 134 B4
Squirrel Ms HNWL * W7 97 G6
The Squirrels BUSH WD23 28 D1
LEW SE13 145 G4
PIN HA5 41 K6
Squirrels Cl NFNCH/WDSP N12 33 G6
Squirrels Gn WPK KT4 192 C6
Squirrel's Heath Av GPK RM2 57 K6
Squirries St BETH E2 104 C2
Stable Cl NTHLT UB5 96 A1
Stable Ms WNWD SE27 180 D1
Stables End ORP BR6 216 C1
Stables Wy LBTH SE11 122 B5
Stable Wk EFNCH * N2 47 H4
Stable Wy NKENS W10 100 A5
Stable Yard Rd WHALL SW1A 16 B2
Stacey Av UED N18 36 E6
Stacey Cl LEY E10 70 B2
Stacey St HOLWY N7 85 G1
LSQ/SEVD WC2H 10 D4
Stackhouse St KTBR SW1X 14 E4
Stacy Pth CMBW * SE5 143 F1
Stadium Rd WOOL/PLUM SE18 146 E1
Stadium St WBPTN SW10 140 B1
Stadium Wy DART DA1 170 B1
WBLY HA9 80 B2
Staffa Rd LEY E10 69 G5
Stafford Cl CHEAM SM3 208 C4
KIL/WHAMP NW6 100 E2
STHGT/OAK N14 22 C6
WALTH E17 69 H3
Stafford Gdns CROY/NA CR0 211 F3
Stafford Pl RCHPK/HAM TW10 157 G2
WESTW SW1E 16 A4
Stafford Rd BOW E3 105 H1
CROY/NA CR0 211 G2
FSTGT E7 89 G5
KIL/WHAMP NW6 100 E2
KTN/HRWW/W HA3 42 C3
NWMAL KT3 175 K6
RSLP HA4 76 D2
SCUP DA14 167 K6
WLGTN SM6 210 C4
Staffordshire St PECK SE15 143 H2
Stafford Ter KENS W8 119 K3
Stag Cl EDGE HA8 44 D5
Staggart Gn BARK/HLT IG6 55 F1
Stag La BKHH IG9 39 F4
EDGE HA8 44 D5
PUT/ROE SW15 158 C5
Stag Pl WESTW SW1E 16 A4
Stags Wy ISLW TW7 116 A6
Stainbank Rd MTCM CR4 179 G6
Stainby Cl WDR/YW UB7 112 B3
Stainby Rd TOTM N17 50 B6
Stainer St STHWK SE1 19 F1
Staines Av CHEAM SM3 193 G6
Staines Rd EBED/NFELT TW14 153 F3
HSLWW TW4 134 C6
IL IG1 90 D2
WHTN TW2 155 H5
Staines Rd East SUN TW16 172 B4
Stainforth Rd GNTH/NBYPK IG2 72 D4
WALTH E17 69 J1
Staining La CITYW EC2V 12 D3
Stainmore Cl CHST BR7 185 J4
Stainsbury St BETH E2 104 E1
Stainsby Pl POP/IOD * E14 105 J5
Stainsby Rd POP/IOD E14 105 J5
Stainton Rd LEW SE13 165 G2
PEND EN3 24 E2
Stalbridge St CAMTN NW1 8 D1
Stalham St BERM/RHTH SE16 123 J3
Stalham Wy WFD IG8 54 B4
Stambourne Wy NRWD SE19 181 F3
WWKM BR4 214 A1
Stamford Brook Av
HMSMTH W6 118 C3
Stamford Brook Gdns
HMSMTH W6 118 C3
Stamford Brook Rd
HMSMTH W6 118 C3
Stamford Cl KTN/HRWW/W HA3 42 E3
SEVS/STOTM N15 68 C1
STHL UB1 96 A6
Stamford Cottages
WBPTN * SW10 140 A1
Stamford Dr HAYES BR2 199 J1
Stamford Gdns DAGW RM9 91 J5
Stamford Gv East
STNW/STAM N16 68 C5
Stamford Gv West
STNW/STAM N16 68 C5
Stamford Hl STNW/STAM N16 68 B5
Stamford Rd DAGW RM9 91 G6
EHAM E6 89 J6
IS N1 86 A5
SEVS/STOTM N15 68 C2
Stamford St STHWK SE1 11 J7
Stamp Pl BETH E2 7 J4
Stanborough HACK E8 86 B4
Stanborough Cl HPTN TW12 172 E2
Stanborough Rd HSLW TW3 135 J4
Stanbridge Pl WCHMH N21 35 H4
Stanbridge Rd PUT/ROE SW15 139 F4
Stanbrook Rd ABYW SE2 128 C2
Stanbury Ct HAMP NW3 83 K4
Stanbury Rd PECK SE15 143 J2
Stancroft CDALE/KGS NW9 63 G1
Standale Gv RSLP HA4 58 A2
Standard Pl SDTCH EC2A 7 H5
Standard Rd BELV DA17 129 H5
BXLYHS DA6 149 F5
HSLWW TW4 134 D4
PEND EN3 25 G1
WLSDN NW10 98 E3
Standen Rd WAND/EARL SW18 159 K2
Standfield Rd DAGE RM10 92 C3
Standish Rd HMSMTH W6 118 D4
Stane Cl WIM/MER SW19 178 A3
Stane Wy WOOL/PLUM SE18 146 C1
Stanfield Rd BOW E3 105 G1
Stanford Cl HPTN TW12 172 E2
ROMW/RG RM7 74 D3
RSLP HA4 58 A3
WFD IG8 53 J1
Stanford Pl STHWK SE1 19 G7
Stanford Rd FBAR/BDGN N11 47 K1
KENS W8 120 A3
STRHM/NOR SW16 179 K5
Stanford St WEST SW1P 16 C7
Stanford Wy STRHM/NOR SW16 179 J5
Stangate Gdns STAN HA7 29 H6
Stanger Rd SNWD SE25 197 H1
Stanham Pl DART DA1 150 D5
Stanham Rd DART DA1 151 F6
Stanhope Av FNCH N3 46 D6
HAYES BR2 199 K5
KTN/HRWW/W HA3 42 D4
Stanhope Cl
BERM/RHTH * SE16 124 A2
Stanhope Gdns FSBYPK N4 67 H3
HGT N6 66 B3
IL IG1 71 K5
MLHL NW7 45 H1
SKENS SW7 120 B4
Stanhope Ga BAY/PAD W2 8 E5
MYFR/PKLN W1K 15 H1
Stanhope Gv BECK BR3 198 C2
Stanhope Ms East SKENS SW7 120 B4
Stanhope Ms South SKENS SW7 120 B4
Stanhope Ms West SKENS SW7 120 B4
Stanhope Pde CAMTN NW1 3 K4
Stanhope Park Rd GFD/PVL UB6 96 C3
Stanhope Pl BAY/PAD W2 8 E4
Stanhope Rd BAR EN5 32 B1
BCTR RM8 74 B6
BFN/LL DA15 168 B6
BXLYHN DA7 149 F3
CAR SM5 210 A5
CROY/NA CR0 212 A1
GFD/PVL UB6 96 C4
HGT N6 66 C3
NFNCH/WDSP N12 47 G1
RAIN RM13 111 J1
WALTH E17 69 K2
Stanhope Rw MYFR/PICC * W1J 15 J1
Stanhope St CAMTN NW1 4 A4
Stanhope Ter BAY/PAD W2 8 B5
TWK * TW1 156 A2
Stanier Cl WKENS W14 119 J5
Stanlake Rd SHB W12 119 F1
Stanlake Vls SHB W12 119 F1
Stanley Av ALP/SUD HA0 80 A5
BARK IG11 109 F2
BCTR RM8 74 B5
BECK BR3 183 F6
GFD/PVL UB6 78 C6
GPK RM2 75 J1
NWMAL KT3 192 D2
Stanley Cl ALP/SUD HA0 80 A5
GPK RM2 75 J1
Stanley Crs NTGHL W11 100 D6
Stanleycroft Cl ISLW TW7 135 K2
Stanley Gdns ACT W3 118 B2
CRICK NW2 82 A3
MTCM * CR4 179 F2
NTGHL W11 100 D6
WLGTN SM6 210 C4
Stanley Gardens Rd TEDD TW11 173 K1
Stanley Gv THHTH CR7 196 B3
VX/NE SW8 141 F3
Stanley Park Dr ALP/SUD HA0 80 B5
Stanley Park Rd CAR SM5 209 K5
Stanley Pas CAMTN NW1 4 E3
Stanley Rd ACT W3 117 J3
BELMT SM2 209 F4
CAR SM5 210 A5
CHING E4 38 B3
CROY/NA CR0 196 B4
ED N9 36 B3
EFNCH N2 65 H1
EN EN1 24 A4
FBAR/BDGN N11 48 D2
HAYES BR2 184 B6
HSLW TW3 135 H5
IL IG1 72 D6
MNPK E12 89 J3
MORT/ESHN SW14 137 J5
MRDN SM4 193 K1
MTCM CR4 179 F3
MUSWH N10 48 B3
NTHWD HA6 40 E4
ORP BR6 202 A5
RYLN/HDSTN HA2 60 C6
SCUP DA14 168 B5
SEVS/STOTM N15 67 H1
SRTFD E15 88 B6
STHL UB1 95 J6
SWFD E18 52 D4
TEDD TW11 173 K1
WALTH E17 69 K3
WBLY HA9 80 B4
WHTN TW2 155 J5
WIM/MER SW19 177 K3
Stanley Rd North RAIN RM13 93 G6
Stanley Rd South RAIN RM13 111 H1
Stanley Sq CAR SM5 209 K6
Stanley St DEPT SE8 144 C1
Stanley Ter ARCH * N19 66 E6
BXLYHS * DA6 149 H5
Stanley Wy STMC/STPC BR5 202 C2
Stanmer St BTSEA SW11 140 D2
Stanmore Gdns RCH/KEW TW9 137 G4
SUT SM1 209 G1
Stanmore Hl STAN HA7 29 H6
Stanmore Rd BELV DA17 129 K4
RCH/KEW TW9 137 G4
SEVS/STOTM N15 67 H1
WAN E11 70 D5
Stanmore St IS N1 85 F6
Stanmore Ter BECK BR3 182 D5
Stannard Ms HACK * E8 86 C4
Stannard Rd HACK E8 86 C4
Stannary St LBTH SE11 122 B6
Stannet Wy WLGTN SM6 210 C2
Stansfeld Rd CAN/RD E16 107 H5
Stansfield Rd BRXN/ST SW9 142 A4
HSLWW TW4 134 A3
Stansgate Rd DAGE RM10 74 C6
Stanstead Cl HAYES BR2 199 J2
Stanstead Gv CAT SE6 164 C3
Stanstead Rd FSTH SE23 164 B3
WAN E11 71 F2
Stansted Cl HCH RM12 93 K4
Stansted Crs BXLY DA5 168 E3
Stansted Rd HTHAIR TW6 152 C1
Stanswood Gdns CMBW SE5 143 F1
Stanthorpe Cl
STRHM/NOR * SW16 179 K1
Stanthorpe Rd
STRHM/NOR SW16 179 K1
Stanton Av TEDD TW11 173 K2
Stanton Cl HOR/WEW KT19 206 D3
STMC/STPC BR5 202 D4
WPK KT4 193 G5
Stanton Rd BARN SW13 138 C3
CROY/NA CR0 196 D4
RYNPK SW20 177 G5
Stanton St PECK * SE15 143 H2
Stanton Wy SYD SE26 164 C6
Stanway Cl CHIG IG7 54 E1
Stanway Gdns ACT W3 117 H1
EDGE HA8 44 E2
Stanway St IS N1 7 H2
Stanwell Cl STWL/WRAY TW19 152 A1
Stanwell Gdns
STWL/WRAY TW19 152 A1
Stanwell Rd ASHF TW15 152 B6
EBED/NFELT TW14 152 E2
Stanwick Rd WKENS W14 119 J4
Stanworth St STHWK SE1 19 J3
Stanwyck Gdns HARH RM3 57 K1
Stapenhill Rd ALP/SUD HA0 79 H1
Staple Cl BXLY DA5 170 A5
Staplefield Cl
BRXS/STRHM * SW2 161 K3
PIN HA5 41 J3
Stapleford Av GNTH/NBYPK IG2 72 E2
Stapleford Cl CHING E4 38 A5
KUT KT1 175 H5
WIM/MER SW19 159 H2
Stapleford Gdns CRW RM5 56 C2
Stapleford Rd ALP/SUD HA0 79 K5

Stapleford Wy BARK IG11 109 H2
Staplehurst Rd CAR SM5 209 J5
LEW SE13 145 G6
Staple Inn HHOL WC1V 11 J2
Staples Cl BERM/RHTH SE16 124 B1
Staple St STHWK SE1 19 F3
Stapleton Crs RAIN RM13 93 J4
Stapleton Gdns CROY/NA CR0 211 G3
Stapleton Hall Rd FSBYPK N4 67 F4
Stapleton Rd BXLYHN DA7 149 G1
ORP BR6 217 F1
TOOT SW17 161 F5
Stapleton Vls STNW/STAM * N16 86 A2
Stapley Rd BELV DA17 129 H5
Staplyton Rd BAR EN5 20 C4
Star & Garter Hl
RCHPK/HAM TW10 157 F3
Starboard Wy POP/IOD E14 124 D3
Starch House La BARK/HLT IG6 54 D5
Starcross St CAMTN NW1 4 B5
Starfield Rd SHB W12 118 D2
Star Hl DART DA1 150 B6
Star La CAN/RD E16 106 C3
STMC/STPC BR5 202 E1
Starling Cl BKHH IG9 38 E3
PIN HA5 41 G6
Starmans Cl DAGW RM9 92 A6
Star Rd HGDN/ICK UB10 94 A3
ISLW TW7 135 J3
WKENS W14 119 J6
Star St BAY/PAD W2 8 B3
Starts Cl ORP BR6 216 A1
Starts Hill Av ORP BR6 216 B3
Starts Hill Rd ORP BR6 216 B1
Starveall Cl WDR/YW UB7 112 C3
Star Yd LINN WC2A 11 J3
State Farm Av ORP BR6 216 B2
Staten Gdns TWK TW1 156 A3
Statham Gv STNW/STAM N16 85 K1
UED N18 50 A1
Station Ap ALP/SUD HA0 79 H4
BAR EN5 21 G5
BECK BR3 182 B4
BELMT SM2 208 C5
BKHH * IG9 39 H6
BKHTH/KID SE3 146 A4
BXLYHN DA7 149 F3
BXLYHN DA7 149 K3
CAMTN * NW1 3 G7
CAT SE6 182 C1
CHING * E4 38 C2
CHING * E4 52 B2
CHST BR7 184 D2
CHST BR7 185 F4
CROY/NA * CR0 196 E6
DART DA1 171 H1
ESH/CLAY KT10 205 F1
FBAR/BDGN N11 48 B1
FSTGT * E7 89 F2
FUL/PGN * SW6 139 H4
GFD/PVL UB6 78 C5
GLDGN * NW11 64 B4
HAYES BR2 199 K5
HOR/WEW KT19 207 H3
HPTN TW12 173 F4
HYS/HAR UB3 113 J3
KUT KT1 175 H5
NTHWD HA6 40 C3
ORP BR6 202 A6
ORP BR6 217 H3
OXHEY WD19 27 H5
PIN HA5 41 J6
RCH/KEW TW9 137 H2
RSLP HA4 58 C5
RSLP HA4 77 F3
SAND/SEL CR2 211 K6
STMC/STPC BR5 202 C1
STRHM/NOR SW16 179 J1
SWFD * E18 53 F5
WALTH * E17 69 J2
WAN E11 70 E2
WAN * E11 88 C2
WDR/YW UB7 112 B1
WELL DA16 148 B3
WFD * IG8 53 G2
WLSDN NW10 99 H2
Station Ap Rd CHSWK W4 137 K1
Station Ar GTPST * W1W 3 K7
Station Av HOR/WEW KT19 207 G6
NWMAL KT3 176 B6
Station Buildings HAYES * BR2 199 K5
Station Chambers EA * W5 98 C3
Station Cl HPTN TW12 173 G4
Station Cottages WDGN * N22 48 E5
Station Crs ALP/SUD HA0 79 H4
ASHF TW15 152 A6
BKHTH/KID SE3 125 K5
SEVS/STOTM N15 67 K1
Stationers Hall Ct STP * EC4M 12 B4
Station Est BECK BR3 198 A1
Station Estate Rd
EBED/NFELT TW14 154 A3
Station Garage Ms
STRHM/NOR * SW16 179 J2
Station Gdns CHSWK W4 137 K1
Station Gv ALP/SUD HA0 80 A4
Station Hl HAYES BR2 199 K6
Station House Ms ED N9 36 C6
Station Pde ACT * W3 98 C5
BAL * SW12 161 F3
BARK IG11 90 C5
BECK * BR3 198 A1
BELMT * SM2 209 G4
BMLY * BR1 183 K4
BXLYHN * DA7 149 F3
CHSWK * W4 117 K4
CHSWK * W4 137 K1
CLPT * E5 86 D1
CRICK NW2 82 A4
EA * W5 117 G1
EBAR * EN4 22 A5
EBED/NFELT * TW14 154 A2
EDGE * HA8 44 A3
EHAM * E6 89 G6
EHAM * E6 89 J5
HCH RM12 93 K2
KTN/HRWW/W * HA3 43 H5
NTHLT * UB5 78 A5
NTHLT * UB5 78 B3
RCH/KEW TW9 137 H2
ROM * RM1 75 G3
RSLP * HA4 58 A6
RYLN/HDSTN * HA2 78 B2
STHGT/OAK N14 34 D3
Station Pas PECK SE15 143 K2
SWFD E18 53 F5
Station Pl FSBYPK N4 67 G6
Station Ri WNWD SE27 162 C4
Station Rd ARCH N19 84 C1
ASHF TW15 152 C6
BAR EN5 21 F6
BARK/HLT IG6 54 D6
BARN SW13 138 C3
BCTR RM8 73 K5
BELV DA17 129 H3
BFN/LL DA15 168 B4
BMLY BR1 183 K4
BXLYHN DA7 149 F4
CAR SM5 209 K2
CHING E4 38 B3
CHSGTN KT9 206 A3
CROY/NA CR0 196 D5
DART DA1 170 C1
EA W5 98 B5
EDGE HA8 44 C2
ESH/CLAY KT10 189 J5
ESH/CLAY KT10 204 D3
FBAR/BDGN N11 48 B1
FNCH N3 46 E4
GPK RM2 75 K1
HAYES BR2 183 H5
HDN NW4 63 J3
HNWL W7 115 K1
HOLWY N7 84 E2
HPTN TW12 173 G4
HRW HA1 61 F1
HSLW TW3 135 G5
HYS/HAR UB3 113 H4
IL IG1 90 B1
KUT KT1 174 E4
KUTN/CMB KT2 175 H4
LEW SE13 145 F4
MLHL NW7 45 G2
MNPK E12 89 H2
NRWD SE19 181 H2
NWMAL KT3 192 E2
ORP BR6 202 A6
PGE/AN SE20 181 K2
RYLN/HDSTN HA2 60 B2
SCUP DA14 168 B5
SNWD SE25 197 G1
STMC/STPC BR5 202 D1
TEDD TW11 174 B2
THDIT KT7 190 A4
TOTM N17 50 C6
TWK TW1 156 A3
WALTH E17 69 G3
WCHMH N21 35 H3
WDGN N22 48 E5
WDR/YW UB7 112 B2
WIM/MER SW19 178 B4
WLSDN NW10 99 H1
WWKM BR4 199 F5
Station Rd North BELV DA17 129 J3
Station Sq STMC/STPC BR5 201 H2
Station St SRTFD E15 88 B5
Station Ter CMBW SE5 142 D2
WLSDN NW10 100 B1
Station Vw GFD/PVL UB6 78 D6
Station Wy BKHH IG9 39 H6
CHEAM SM3 208 C4
Station Yd ASHF * TW15 152 C6
RSLP * HA4 58 B6
STHL * UB1 114 E2
TWK TW1 156 B2
Staunton Rd KUTN/CMB KT2 175 G3
Staunton St DEPT SE8 124 C6
Staveley Cl HOLWY * N7 84 E2
PECK SE15 143 K2
Staveley Gdns CHSWK W4 138 A2
Staveley Rd CHSWK W4 117 K6
Staverton Rd CRICK NW2 82 A6
Stave Yard Rd
BERM/RHTH SE16 124 B1
Stavordale Rd CAR SM5 194 B4
HBRY N5 85 G2
Stayner's Rd WCHPL E1 105 F3
Stayton Rd SUT SM1 208 E1
St Catherines Rd RSLP HA4 58 A2
Steadfast Rd KUT KT1 174 E4
Stead St WALW SE17 18 E7
Steam Farm La
EBED/NFELT TW14 133 J5
Stean St HACK E8 86 B6
Stebbing Wy BARK IG11 109 G1
Stebondale St POP/IOD E14 125 F5
Stedly SCUP * DA14 168 B6
Stedman Cl BXLY DA5 170 B5
Steed Cl EMPK RM11 75 K6
Steedman St WALW SE17 18 C7
Steeds Rd MUSWH N10 47 K4
Steel Ap BARK IG11 109 H1
Steele Rd CHSWK W4 117 K3
ISLW TW7 136 B5
TOTM N17 50 A6
WAN E11 88 C3
WLSDN NW10 98 E1
Steele's Ms North HAMP * NW3 83 K4
Steele's Ms South HAMP NW3 83 K4
Steele's Rd HAMP NW3 83 K4
Steeles Studios HAMP * NW3 83 K4
Steel's La WCHPL E1 104 E5
Steelyard Pas CANST EC4R 12 E6
Steep Cl ORP BR6 217 F4
Steep Hl CROY/NA CR0 212 A2
STRHM/NOR SW16 161 J5
Steeplands BUSH WD23 28 B2
Steeple Cl FUL/PGN SW6 139 H4
WIM/MER SW19 159 H6
Steeplestone Cl UED N18 49 J1
Steeple Wk IS * N1 85 J6
Steerforth St
WAND/EARL SW18 160 A4
Steers Md MTCM CR4 178 E4
Steers Wy BERM/RHTH SE16 124 B2
Stella Rd TOOT SW17 178 E2
Stelling Rd ERITH DA8 150 A1
Stellman Cl CLPT E5 86 C1
Stembridge Rd PGE/AN SE20 181 J5
Stephan Cl HACK E8 86 C6
Stephen Av RAIN RM13 93 J4
Stephen Cl ORP BR6 217 F1
Stephendale Rd FUL/PGN SW6 140 A4
Stephen Ms FITZ W1T 10 C2
Stephen Pl CLAP SW4 141 H4
Stephen Rd BXLYHN DA7 149 K4
Stephenson Rd HNWL W7 97 F5
WALTH * E17 69 G2
WHTN TW2 155 F2
Stephenson St CAN/RD E16 106 C4
WLSDN NW10 99 G2
Stephenson Wy CAMTN NW1 4 B6
Stephen's Rd SRTFD E15 88 D6
Stephen St FITZ W1T 10 C3
Stepney Cswy WCHPL E1 105 F5
Stepney Gn WCHPL E1 104 E4
Stepney High St WCHPL E1 105 F4
Stepney Wy WCHPL E1 104 E4
Sterling Av EDGE HA8 30 B6
Sterling Cl WLSDN NW10 81 J5
Sterling Gdns NWCR SE14 124 B6
Sterling Pl BTFD TW8 117 F4
Sterling Rd ENC/FH EN2 23 K2
Sterling St SKENS SW7 14 D3
Sterling Wy (North Circular)
UED N18 49 K1
Stern Cl BARK IG11 109 J1
Sterndale Rd DART DA1 171 J2
WKENS * W14 119 G3
Sterne St SHB W12 119 G2
Sternhall La PECK SE15 143 H4
Sternhold Av BRXS/STRHM SW2 161 K4
Sterry Crs DAGE RM10 92 C3
Sterry Dr HOR/WEW KT19 207 G2
THDIT KT7 189 K3
Sterry Gdns DAGE RM10 92 C4
Sterry Rd BARK IG11 91 F6
DAGE RM10 92 C2
Sterry St STHWK SE1 18 E3
Steucers La FSTH SE23 164 B3
Steve Biko La CAT SE6 164 D6
Steve Biko Rd HOLWY N7 85 G1
Steve Biko Wy HSLW TW3 135 F4
Stevedale Rd WELL DA16 148 D3
Stevedore St WAP E1W 123 J1
Stevenage Rd EHAM E6 90 A4
FUL/PGN SW6 139 G2
Stevens Av HOM E9 86 E4
Stevens Cl BECK BR3 182 D2
BXLY DA5 170 A6
HPTN TW12 172 E2
PIN HA5 59 G2
Stevens Gn BUSH WD23 28 C3
Stevens' La ESH/CLAY KT10 205 G5
Stevenson Cl BAR EN5 33 H1
ERITH DA8 150 E1
Stevenson Crs
BERM/RHTH SE16 123 H5
Stevens Rd BCTR RM8 73 H6
Stevens St STHWK SE1 19 H4
Steventon Rd SHB W12 99 H6
Steward St WCHPL E1 13 H1
Stewart Cl CDALE/KGS * NW9 62 E3
CHST BR7 185 G1
HPTN TW12 172 D2
Stewart Rd WAN E11 88 B2
Stewartsby Cl UED N18 49 J1
Stewarts Gv CHEL * SW3 120 C5
CHEL SW3 120 C5
Stewart's La VX/NE SW8 141 G1
Stewarts Rd VX/NE SW8 141 H1
VX/NE SW8 141 H2
Stewart St POP/IOD E14 125 F2
Stew La BLKFR EC4V 12 C5
Steyne Rd ACT W3 117 J1
Steyning Gv ELTH/MOT SE9 166 E6
Steynings Wy
NFNCH/WDSP N12 46 E1
Steyning Wy HSLWW TW4 134 B5
Steynton Av BXLY DA5 169 F4
Stickland Rd BELV DA17 129 H4
Stickleton Cl GFD/PVL UB6 96 B2
Stilecroft Gdns ALP/SUD HA0 79 H1
Stile Hall Gdns CHSWK W4 117 H5
Stiles Cl ERITH DA8 129 J5
HAYES BR2 200 E3
Stillingfleet Rd BARN SW13 138 D1
Stillington St WEST SW1P 16 B6
Stillness Rd FSTH SE23 164 B1
Stipularis Dr YEAD UB4 95 H3
Stirling Av PIN HA5 59 H4
Stirling Cl RAIN RM13 111 K2
STRHM/NOR SW16 179 H4
Stirling Dr ORP BR6 217 H3
Stirling Gv HSLW TW3 135 H3
Stirling Rd ACT W3 117 J3
BRXN/ST SW9 141 K3
HYS/HAR UB3 95 F6
KTN/HRWW/W HA3 43 F6
PLSTW E13 107 F1
TOTM N17 50 C4
WALTH E17 51 G6
WDGN N22 49 H4
WHTN TW2 155 F2
Stirling Wk BRYLDS KT5 191 J3
Stirling Wy BORE WD6 31 F1
Stiven Crs RYLN/HDSTN HA2 77 K1
St Luke's Est FSBYE EC1V 6 E5
Stockbury Rd CROY/NA CR0 197 K3
Stockdale Rd BCTR RM8 74 B6
Stockdove Wy GFD/PVL UB6 97 F2
Stocker Gdns DAGW RM9 91 J5
Stockfield Rd ESH/CLAY KT10 204 E3
STRHM/NOR SW16 162 A5
Stockholm Rd
BERM/RHTH SE16 123 K5
Stockholm Wy WAP * E1W 123 H1
Stockhurst Cl PUT/ROE SW15 139 F3
Stockingswater La PEND EN3 25 G4
Stockland Rd ROMW/RG RM7 75 F3
Stock La RDART DA2 171 F6
Stockley Cl WDR/YW UB7 112 E2
Stockley Farm Rd WDR/YW UB7 112 E3
Stockley Rd WDR/YW UB7 112 E3
Stock Orchard Crs HOLWY * N7 85 F2
Stock Orchard St HOLWY N7 85 F3
Stockport Rd
STRHM/NOR SW16 179 J4
Stocksfield Rd WALTH * E17 52 A6
Stocks Pl POP/IOD E14 105 H6
Stock St PLSTW E13 106 E1
Stockton Cl BAR EN5 21 G5
Stockton Gdns MLHL NW7 31 F5
TOTM N17 49 J3
Stockton Rd TOTM N17 49 J3
UED N18 50 C2
Stockwell Av BRXN/ST SW9 142 A4
Stockwell Cl BMLY BR1 184 A5
Stockwell Gdns BRXN/ST SW9 142 A2
Stockwell Gn BRXN/ST SW9 142 A3
Stockwell La BRXN/ST SW9 142 A3
Stockwell Park Crs
BRXN/ST SW9 142 A3
Stockwell Park Rd
BRXN/ST SW9 142 A2
Stockwell Park Wk
BRXN/ST SW9 142 A4
Stockwell Rd BRXN/ST SW9 142 A3
Stockwell St GNWCH SE10 125 F6
Stockwell Ter BRXN/ST SW9 142 A2
Stodart Rd PGE/AN SE20 181 K4
Stoford Cl WIM/MER SW19 159 H3
Stoke Av BARK/HLT IG6 55 G2
Stokenchurch St FUL/PGN SW6 140 A2
Stoke Newington Church St
STNW/STAM N16 68 A6
Stoke Newington Common
STNW/STAM N16 86 B1
Stoke Newington High St
STNW/STAM N16 86 B1
Stoke Newington Rd
STNW/STAM N16 86 B3
Stoke Pl WLSDN NW10 99 H2
Stoke Rd KUTN/CMB KT2 175 K3
Stokesby Rd CHSGTN KT9 206 B4
Stokesley St SHB W12 99 H5
Stokes Rd CROY/NA CR0 198 A3
EHAM E6 107 J3
Stoll Cl CRICK NW2 82 A1
Stonard Rd BCTR RM8 91 H3
PLMGR N13 35 G5
Stonards Hl LOU IG10 39 K1
Stondon Pk FSTH SE23 164 B2
Stonebridge Pk WLSDN NW10 81 F5
Stonebridge Rd
SEVS/STOTM N15 68 A2
Stonebridge Wy WBLY HA9 80 D4
Stone Buildings LINN WC2A 11 H2
Stonechat Sq EHAM E6 107 J4
Stone Cl BCTR RM8 74 B6
CLAP SW4 141 H3
WDR/YW UB7 112 C1
Stonecot Cl MRDN SM4 193 H5
Stonecot Hl MRDN SM4 193 H5
Stone Crs EBED/NFELT TW14 153 J2
Stonecroft Rd ERITH DA8 149 K1
Stonecroft Wy CROY/NA CR0 195 K4
Stonecutter St FLST/FETLN EC4A 12 A3
Stonefield Cl BXLYHN DA7 149 H4
RSLP HA4 77 J3
Stonefield St IS N1 85 G6
Stonefield Wy CHARL SE7 146 C1
RSLP HA4 77 H3
Stonegate Cl STMC/STPC BR5 186 D6
Stone Gv EDGE HA8 30 A6
Stonegrove Gdns EDGE HA8 44 B1
Stonehall Av IL IG1 71 J3
Stone Hall Gdns KENS * W8 120 A3
Stone Hall Pl KENS * W8 120 A3
Stone Hall Rd WCHMH N21 35 F2
Stoneham Rd FBAR/BDGN N11 48 C1
Stonehill Cl MORT/ESHN SW14 138 A6
Stonehill Rd CHSWK W4 117 H5
MORT/ESHN SW14 137 K6
Stonehills Ct DUL SE21 163 F5
Stonehill Woods Pk
RDART * DA2 187 J2
Stonehorse Rd PEND EN3 24 E6
Stone House Ct HDTCH EC3A 13 H3
Stonehouse La ORP BR6 217 K6
Stonehouse Rd ORP BR6 217 K6
Stoneleigh Av EN EN1 24 D1
WPK KT4 207 J1
Stoneleigh Broadway EW KT17 207 J3
Stoneleigh Crs HOR/WEW KT19 207 J3
Stoneleigh Park Av
CROY/NA CR0 198 A3
Stoneleigh Park Rd
HOR/WEW KT19 207 H4
Stoneleigh Pl NTGHL W11 100 B6
Stoneleigh Rd CAR SM5 194 D4
CLAY IG5 53 J6
TOTM N17 50 B5
Stoneleigh St NTGHL W11 100 B6
Stonemasons Cl
SEVS/STOTM * N15 67 K1
Stonenest St FSBYPK N4 67 F5
Stone Park Av BECK BR3 198 D1
Stone Pl WPK KT4 192 D6
Stone Rd HAYES BR2 199 J2
Stones Cross Rd SWLY BR8 203 K2
Stones End St STHWK SE1 18 C3
Stone St CROY/NA CR0 211 G3
Stonewall EHAM E6 108 A4
Stonewood Rd ERITH DA8 130 B5
Stoney Aly WOOL/PLUM SE18 147 F3
Stoneyard La POP/IOD E14 105 K6
Stoneycroft Cl LEE/GVPK SE12 165 J2
Stoneycroft Rd WFD IG8 53 J2
Stoneydown WALTH E17 69 G1
Stoneydown Av WALTH E17 69 G1
Stoneyfields Gdns EDGE HA8 30 E6
Stoneyfields La EDGE HA8 44 E1
Stoney La HDTCH EC3A 13 H3
NRWD SE19 181 G2
Stoney St STHWK SE1 12 E7
Stonhouse St CLAP SW4 141 H4
Stonnell's Rd BTSEA SW11 140 E6
Stonor Rd WKENS W14 119 J4
Stonycroft Cl PEND EN3 25 G3
Stopes St PECK SE15 143 G1
Stopford Rd PLSTW E13 88 E6
WALW SE17 122 C5
Store Rd CAN/RD E16 127 F2
Storers Quay POP/IOD E14 125 G4
Store St GWRST WC1E 10 C2
SRTFD E15 88 B3
Storey Rd HGT N6 65 K3
WALTH E17 69 H1
Storeys Ga STJSPK * SW1H 16 D3
WEST SW1P 16 D3
Stories Ms CMBW * SE5 143 F3
Stories Rd CMBW SE5 143 F4
Stork Rd FSTGT E7 88 D4
Storksmead Rd EDGE HA8 45 G3
Storks Rd BERM/RHTH * SE16 123 H3
Stormont Rd BTSEA SW11 141 F5
HGT N6 65 K4
Stormont Wy CHSGTN KT9 205 J3
Stormount Dr HYS/HAR UB3 113 F2
Storrington Rd CROY/NA CR0 197 G5
Story St IS N1 85 F5
Stothard St WCHPL E1 104 E3
Stott Cl WAND/EARL SW18 160 C1
Stoughton Av CHEAM SM3 208 B3
Stoughton Cl PUT/ROE SW15 158 D3
Stour Av NWDGN UB2 115 F3
Stourcliffe St BAY/PAD W2 8 E4
Stour Cl HAYES BR2 215 G2
Stourhead Cl WIM/MER SW19 159 G2
Stourhead Gdns RYNPK SW20 176 D6
Stour Rd BOW E3 87 J5
DAGE RM10 74 C6
DART DA1 150 D4
Stourton Av FELT TW13 154 E6
Stowage DEPT SE8 124 E6
Stow Crs WALTH E17 51 G4
Stowe Gdns ED N9 36 B3
Stowe Pl SEVS/STOTM N15 50 A6
Stowe Rd ORP BR6 217 H2
SHB W12 118 E2
Stowting Rd ORP BR6 216 E2
Stox Md KTN/HRWW/W HA3 42 D4
Stracey Rd WLSDN NW10 81 F6
Strachan Pl RYNPK SW20 177 F2
Stradbroke Dr CHIG IG7 54 B2
Stradbroke Gv BKHH IG9 39 H3
CLAY IG5 53 J6
Stradbroke Pk CHIG IG7 54 B2
Stradbroke Rd HBRY N5 85 J2
Stradbrook Cl RYLN/HDSTN HA2 77 K1
Stradella Rd HNHL SE24 162 D1
Strafford Av CLAY IG5 54 A5
Strafford Rd ACT W3 117 K2
BAR EN5 20 C4
HSLW TW3 134 E4
TWK TW1 156 B2
Strafford St POP/IOD E14 124 D2
Strahan Rd BOW E3 105 G2
The Straight NWDGN UB2 114 C2
Straight Rd HARH RM3 57 K1
Straightsmouth GNWCH SE10 145 F1
Strait Rd EHAM E6 107 J6
Straker's Rd EDUL SE22 143 J5
Strand TPL/STR WC2R 11 F6
Strandfield Cl
WOOL/PLUM SE18 127 K5
Strand-on-the-Green
CHSWK W4 117 H6
Strand Pl UED N18 36 A6
Strangways Ter WKENS W14 119 J3
Stranraer Wy IS N1 84 E5
Strasburg Rd BTSEA SW11 141 F2
Stratfield Park Cl WCHMH N21 35 H2
Stratford Cl BARK IG11 91 G5
DAGE RM10 92 E5
Stratford Ct NWMAL KT3 192 A1
Stratford Gv PUT/ROE SW15 139 G5
Stratford House Av BMLY BR1 184 D6
Stratford Pl MHST W1U 9 J4
Stratford Rd HTHAIR TW6 152 E1
KENS W8 119 K4
NWDGN UB2 114 D4
PLSTW E13 88 E6
THHTH CR7 196 B1
YEAD UB4 95 F3
Stratford Vls CAMTN NW1 84 C5
Strathan Cl WAND/EARL SW18 159 H1
Strathaven Rd LEE/GVPK SE12 166 A1
Strathblaine Rd BTSEA SW11 140 C6
Strathbrook Rd
STRHM/NOR SW16 180 A3
Strathcona Rd WBLY HA9 61 K6
Strathdale STRHM/NOR SW16 180 A1
Strathdon Dr TOOT SW17 160 C5
Strathearn Av HYS/HAR UB3 133 J1
WHTN TW2 155 H3
Strathearn Cottages
TRDG/WHET * N20 32 E5
Strathearn Pl BAY/PAD W2 8 C5
Strathearn Rd SUT SM1 208 E3
WIM/MER SW19 177 K1
Stratheden Rd BKHTH/KID SE3 145 K2
Strathfield Gdns BARK IG11 90 D4
Strathleven Rd
BRXS/STRHM SW2 141 K6
Strathmore Gdns EDGE HA8 44 D5
FNCH N3 47 F4
HCH RM12 75 H5
KENS W8 119 K1
Strathmore Rd CROY/NA CR0 196 D4
TEDD TW11 155 K6
WIM/MER SW19 159 K5
Strathnairn St STHWK SE1 123 H4
Strathray Gdns HAMP * NW3 83 J4
Strath Ter BTSEA SW11 140 D5
Strathville Rd
WAND/EARL SW18 159 K4
Strathyre Av
STRHM/NOR SW16 180 B6
Stratton Av WLGTN SM6 210 D6
Stratton Cl BXLYHN DA7 149 F4
EDGE HA8 44 B2
HEST TW5 134 E2
WIM/MER SW19 177 J5
WOT/HER * KT12 188 B5
Strattondale St POP/IOD E14 125 F3
Stratton Dr BARK IG11 90 E3
Stratton Gdns STHL UB1 95 K5
Stratton Rd BXLYHN DA7 149 F4
WIM/MER SW19 177 K5
Stratton St MYFR/PICC W1J 9 K7
Strauss Rd CHSWK * W4 118 A2
Strawberry Hill Rd TWK TW1 156 A5
Strawberry La CAR SM5 209 K1
Strawberry Ter MUSWH * N10 47 K4
Strawberry V EFNCH N2 47 H4
TWK TW1 156 A5
Streakes Field Rd CRICK NW2 63 J6
Streamdale ABYW SE2 128 C6
Streamline Ms EDUL SE22 163 J3
Streamside Cl ED N9 36 B3
HAYES BR2 199 K1
Stream Wy BELV DA17 129 H6
Streatfeild Av EHAM E6 89 K6
Streatfield Rd
KTN/HRWW/W HA3 43 J6
Streatham Cl
STRHM/NOR * SW16 161 K4
Streatham Common
STRHM/NOR * SW16 179 J3
Streatham Common North
STRHM/NOR SW16 180 A1
Streatham Common South
STRHM/NOR SW16 179 K2
Streatham Ct
STRHM/NOR SW16 161 K5
Streatham Gn
STRHM/NOR * SW16 161 K6
Streatham High Rd
STRHM/NOR SW16 161 K6
Streatham Hl
BRXS/STRHM SW2 161 K3
Streatham Pl
BRXS/STRHM SW2 161 K2
Streatham Rd MTCM CR4 179 F4
Streatham St NOXST/BSQ WC1A 10 E3
Streatham V STRHM/NOR SW16 179 H4
Streathbourne Rd TOOT SW17 161 F4
Streatleigh Pde
STRHM/NOR * SW16 161 K4
Streatley Pl HAMP NW3 83 H2
Streatley Rd KIL/WHAMP NW6 82 D5
Streeters La WLGTN SM6 210 D1
Streetfield Ms BKHTH/KID SE3 145 K3

Streimer Rd SRTFD E15 106 A1
Strelley Wy ACT W3 99 G6
Stretton Rd CROY/NA CR0 197 F4
RCHPK/HAM TW10 156 D4
Strickland Av DART DA1 151 J5
Strickland Rw
WAND/EARL SW18 160 C2
Strickland St DEPT SE8 144 D3
Strickland Wy ORP BR6 217 F2
Stride Rd PLSTW E13 106 D1
Strimon Cl ED N9 36 E4
Stripling Wy WATW WD18 26 E1
Strode Cl MUSWH N10 48 A3
Strode Rd FSTGT E7 88 E2
FUL/PGN SW6 139 G1
TOTM N17 50 A5
WLSDN NW10 81 J4
Strone Rd FSTGT E7 89 G4
Strone Wy YEAD UB4 95 J3
Strongbow Crs ELTH/MOT SE9 146 E6
Strongbow Rd ELTH/MOT SE9 146 E6
Strongbridge Cl
RYLN/HDSTN HA2 60 A5
Stronsa Rd SHB W12 118 C2
Strood Av ROMW/RG RM7 75 F5
Stroud Crs PUT/ROE SW15 158 C5
Stroudes Cl WPK KT4 192 C4
Stroud Fld NTHLT UB5 77 J4
Stroud Ga RYLN/HDSTN HA2 78 B2
Stroud Green Rd FSBYPK N4 67 F5
Stroud Green Wy CROY/NA CR0 197 J4
Stroud Rd SNWD SE25 197 H3
WIM/MER SW19 159 K5
Strouds Cl CHDH RM6 73 H2
Stroughton Cl LBTH SE11 17 H7
Strout's Pl BETH E2 7 J4
Strutton Gnd WEST SW1P 16 C4
Strype St WCHPL E1 13 J2
St Saviour's Est STHWK SE1 19 J4
Stuart Av CDALE/KGS NW9 63 J4
EA W5 117 G2
HAYES BR2 199 K5
RYLN/HDSTN HA2 77 K1
WOT/HER KT12 188 B5
Stuart Ct BORE WD6 29 K1
Stuart Crs CROY/NA CR0 213 H1
HYS/HAR UB3 94 A5
WDGN N22 49 F4
Stuart Evans Cl WELL DA16 148 D4
Stuart Gv TEDD TW11 173 K1
Stuart Mantle Wy ERITH DA8 150 A1
Stuart Pl MTCM CR4 178 E4
Stuart Rd ACT W3 117 K1
BARK IG11 91 F6
EBAR EN4 33 J2
KIL/WHAMP NW6 100 E2
KTN/HRWW/W HA3 43 F6
PECK SE15 143 K5
RCHPK/HAM TW10 156 C4
THHTH CR7 196 D1
WELL DA16 148 C2
WIM/MER SW19 159 K5
Stubbs Cl CDALE/KGS NW9 62 E2
Stubbs Dr BERM/RHTH SE16 123 J5
Stubbs Wy WIM/MER SW19 178 C4
Stucley Pl CAMTN NW1 84 B5
Stucley Rd ISLW TW7 135 H1
Studdridge St FUL/PGN SW6 139 K3
Studd St IS N1 85 H6
Studholme Ct HAMP * NW3 82 E2
Studholme St PECK SE15 143 J1
The Studios BUSH WD23 28 A1
Studio Pl KTBR * SW1X 15 F3
Studland Cl BFN/LL DA15 168 A5
Studland Rd HNWL W7 96 D5
KUTN/CMB KT2 175 F2
SYD SE26 182 A1
Studland St HMSMTH W6 118 E4
Studley Av CHING E4 52 B3
Studley Cl CLPT E5 87 G3
Studley Ct SCUP DA14 186 C1
Studley Dr REDBR IG4 71 H3
Studley Grange Rd HNWL W7 115 K3
Studley Rd CLAP SW4 141 K2
DAGW RM9 91 K5
FSTGT E7 89 F4
Stukeley Rd FSTGT E7 89 F5
Stukeley St HOL/ALD WC2B 11 F3
Stumps Hill La BECK BR3 182 D2
Sturdy Rd PECK SE15 143 J3
Sturge Av WALTH E17 51 K4
Sturgeon Rd WALW SE17 122 D5
Sturges Fld CHST BR7 185 J3
Sturgess Av HDN NW4 63 K4
Sturge St STHWK SE1 18 C3
Sturmer Wy HOLWY N7 85 F3
Sturminster Cl YEAD UB4 95 G5
Sturrock Cl SEVS/STOTM N15 67 K1
Sturry St POP/IOD E14 105 K5
Sturt St IS N1 6 D3
Stutfield St WCHPL E1 104 C5
Styles Gdns BRXN/ST SW9 142 C4
Styles Wy BECK BR3 199 F1
Sudbourne Rd
BRXS/STRHM SW2 141 K6
Sudbrooke Rd BAL SW12 160 E1
Sudbrook Gdns
RCHPK/HAM TW10 157 F5
Sudbrook La RCHPK/HAM TW10 157 F3
Sudbury EHAM E6 108 A5
Sudbury Av ALP/SUD HA0 79 J1
Sudbury Court Dr HRW HA1 61 G6
Sudbury Court Rd ALP/SUD HA0 79 G1
Sudbury Crs ALP/SUD HA0 79 H3
BMLY BR1 183 K1
Sudbury Cft ALP/SUD HA0 79 F2
Sudbury Gdns CROY/NA CR0 212 A2
Sudbury Heights Av
GFD/PVL UB6 79 F3
Sudbury Hl HRW HA1 78 E1
Sudbury Hill Cl ALP/SUD HA0 79 F2
Sudbury Rd BARK IG11 91 F3
Sudeley St IS N1 6 B3
Sudlow Rd WAND/EARL SW18 139 K5
Sudrey St STHWK SE1 18 C3
Suez Av GFD/PVL UB6 97 F1
Suez Rd PEND EN3 25 G5
Suffield Rd CHING E4 37 K5
PGE/AN SE20 181 K5
SEVS/STOTM * N15 68 B2
Suffolk La CANST EC4R 12 E5
Suffolk Park Rd WALTH E17 69 G1
Suffolk Rd BARK IG11 90 D5
BARN SW13 138 C1
DAGE RM10 92 D3
DART DA1 171 H1
GDMY/SEVK IG3 72 E3
PEND EN3 24 D6
PLSTW E13 106 D2
RYLN/HDSTN HA2 59 K3
SCUP DA14 186 D2
SEVS/STOTM N15 67 K3
SNWD SE25 197 G1
WLSDN NW10 81 G5
WPK KT4 192 C6
Suffolk St FSTGT E7 88 E3
STJS SW1Y 10 D7
Suffolk Vls WAND/EARL * SW18 159 K2
Sugar House La SRTFD E15 106 A1
Sugar Loaf Wk BETH * E2 104 E2
Sugden Rd BTSEA SW11 141 F4
THDIT KT7 190 B5
Sugden Wy BARK IG11 109 F1
Sulgrave Gdns SHB W12 119 F2
Sulgrave Rd SHB W12 119 F2
Sulina Rd BRXS/STRHM SW2 161 K2
Sulivan Ct FUL/PGN SW6 139 K3
Sulivan Rd FUL/PGN SW6 139 K4
Sullivan Av CAN/RD E16 107 H4
Sullivan Cl BTSEA SW11 140 D4
DART DA1 170 E1
E/WMO/HCT KT8 173 G6
YEAD UB4 95 G4
Sullivan Rd LBTH SE11 17 K6
Sullivan Wy BORE WD6 29 J1
Sultan Rd WAN E11 71 F1
Sultan St BECK BR3 182 A5
CMBW SE5 142 D1
Sumatra Rd KIL/WHAMP NW6 82 E4
Sumburgh Rd BAL SW12 161 F1
Summer Av E/WMO/HCT KT8 189 K2
Summercourt Rd WCHPL E1 104 E5
Summerene Cl
STRHM/NOR SW16 179 H3
Summerfield Av
KIL/WHAMP NW6 100 C1
NFNCH/WDSP N12 47 J2
Summerfield La SURB KT6 190 E6
Summerfield Rd LOU IG10 39 H1
WEA W13 97 H3
Summerfield St LEE/GVPK SE12 165 J2
Summer Gdns E/WMO/HCT KT8 189 K2
Summer Gv BORE WD6 29 K1
Summer Hl CHST BR7 185 F5
Summerhill Cl ORP BR6 216 E2
Summerhill Gv EN EN1 36 A1
Summerhill Rd DART DA1 171 G2
SEVS/STOTM N15 67 K1
Summerhill Wy MTCM CR4 179 F4
Summerhouse Av HEST TW5 134 D2
Summerhouse La
WDR/YW UB7 112 A6
Summerhouse Rd
STNW/STAM N16 68 A6
Summerland Gdns MUSWH N10 48 B6
Summerlands Av ACT W3 98 E6
Summerlee Av EFNCH N2 65 K1
Summerlee Gdns EFNCH N2 65 K1
Summerley St
WAND/EARL SW18 160 A4
Summer Pl WATW * WD18 26 D1
Summer Rd E/WMO/HCT KT8 189 K2
Summersby Rd HGT N6 66 B3
Summers Cl BELMT SM2 208 E5
WBLY HA9 62 D5
Summerskille Cl ED N9 36 D4
Summers La NFNCH/WDSP N12 47 H3
Summers Rw NFNCH/WDSP N12 47 J2
Summers St CLKNW EC1R 5 J7
Summerstown TOOT SW17 160 B5
Summerton Wy THMD SE28 109 K6
Summer Trees SUN TW16 172 A4
Summerville Gdns SUT SM1 208 D4
Summerwood Rd ISLW TW7 156 A1
Summit Av CDALE/KGS NW9 63 F2
Summit Centre WDR/YW * UB7 132 A1
Summit Cl CDALE/KGS NW9 63 F1
EDGE HA8 44 C3
STHGT/OAK N14 34 C4
Summit Dr WFD IG8 53 H5
Summit Est STNW/STAM * N16 68 C4
Summit Rd NTHLT UB5 78 A5
WALTH E17 69 K1
Summit Wy NRWD SE19 181 F3
STHGT/OAK N14 34 B4
Sumner Av PECK SE15 143 G2
Sumner Cl ORP BR6 216 C2
Sumner Gdns CROY/NA CR0 196 B5
Sumner Pl SKENS SW7 14 B7
Sumner Place Ms SKENS SW7 14 B7
Sumner Rd CROY/NA CR0 196 C5
HRW HA1 60 C4
PECK SE15 123 G6
Sumner Rd South
CROY/NA CR0 196 B5
Sumner St STHWK SE1 12 C7
Sumpter Cl HAMP NW3 83 G4
Sunbeam Crs NKENS W10 100 A3
Sunbeam Rd WLSDN NW10 98 E3
Sunbury Av MLHL NW7 45 F1
MORT/ESHN SW14 138 A5
Sunbury Ct BAR * EN5 20 C5
SUN TW16 172 C5
Sunbury Court Rd SUN TW16 172 B5
Sunbury Gdns MLHL NW7 45 F1
Sunbury La BTSEA SW11 140 C2
Sunbury Rd CHEAM SM3 208 B1
FELT TW13 153 J5
Sunbury St WOOL/PLUM SE18 126 E3
Sunbury Wy FELT TW13 172 B1
Sun Ct ERITH DA8 150 C3
Suncroft Pl SYD SE26 163 K5
Sunderland Mt FSTH * SE23 164 A4
Sunderland Rd EA W5 116 E3
FSTH SE23 164 A4
Sunderland Ter BAY/PAD * W2 101 F5
Sunderland Wy MNPK E12 71 H6
Sundew Av SHB W12 99 J6
Sundew Ct ALP/SUD * HA0 98 A1
Sundial Av SNWD SE25 181 G5
Sundorne Rd CHARL SE7 126 A5
Sundridge Av BMLY BR1 184 C4
WELL DA16 147 J3
Sundridge Cl DART DA1 171 K1
Sundridge Pde BMLY * BR1 184 A3
Sundridge Rd CROY/NA CR0 197 G5
Sunfields Pl BKHTH/KID SE3 146 A1
Sun in Sands Rbt
BKHTH/KID SE3 146 A1
Sunken Rd CROY/NA CR0 212 E3
Sunkist Wy WLGTN SM6 210 E6
Sunland Av BXLYHS DA6 149 F5
Sun La BKHTH/KID SE3 146 A1
Sunleigh Rd ALP/SUD HA0 80 A6
Sunley Gdns GFD/PVL UB6 97 G1
Sunlight Cl WIM/MER * SW19 178 B2
Sunlight Sq BETH E2 104 D2
Sunna Gdns SUN TW16 172 A5
Sunningdale STHGT/OAK N14 48 D1
Sunningdale Av ACT W3 99 G6
BARK IG11 90 D6
FELT TW13 154 D4
RAIN RM13 111 K3
RSLP HA4 59 G5
Sunningdale Cl
BERM/RHTH * SE16 123 J5
STAN HA7 43 G3
SURB KT6 191 F6
THMD SE28 110 A5
Sunningdale Gdns
CDALE/KGS NW9 62 E2
KENS * W8 119 K3
Sunningdale Ldg EDGE * HA8 44 B1
Sunningdale Rd HAYES BR2 200 D1
RAIN RM13 93 J5
SUT SM1 208 D1
Sunningfield Rd HDN NW4 45 K6
Sunningfields Crs HDN NW4 45 K5
Sunninghill Ct ACT * W3 117 K2
Sunninghill Rd LEW SE13 144 E3
Sunny Bank SNWD SE25 181 H6
Sunny Crs WLSDN NW10 80 E5
Sunnycroft Rd HSLW TW3 135 G3
SNWD SE25 181 H6
STHL UB1 96 A4
Sunnydale ORP BR6 201 F6
Sunnydale Gdns MLHL NW7 45 F2
Sunnydale Rd LEE/GVPK SE12 146 A6
Sunnydene Av CHING E4 52 B1
RSLP HA4 58 E5
Sunnydene Gdns ALP/SUD HA0 79 J4
Sunnydene St SYD SE26 164 B6
Sunnyfield MLHL NW7 31 H6
Sunny Gardens Rd HDN NW4 46 A6
Sunny Hl HDN NW4 45 K6
Sunnyhill Cl CLPT E5 87 G2
Sunnyhill Rd STRHM/NOR SW16 161 K6
Sunnyhurst Cl SUT SM1 208 E1
Sunnymead Av MTCM CR4 179 J6
Sunnymead Rd
CDALE/KGS NW9 63 F4
PUT/ROE SW15 138 E6
Sunnymede Av HOR/WEW KT19 207 G6
Sunnymede Dr BARK/HLT IG6 72 B1
Sunny Ms CRW RM5 56 E3
Sunny Nook Gdns
SAND/SEL CR2 211 K4
Sunny Pl HDN NW4 64 A1
The Sunny Rd PEND EN3 25 F2
Sunnyside CAT * SE6 164 C2
CRICK NW2 82 D1
WIM/MER SW19 177 H2
WOT/HER KT12 188 B2
Sunnyside Dr CHING E4 38 A2
Sunnyside Rd ARCH N19 66 D4
EA W5 116 E1
IL IG1 90 C1
LEY E10 69 J5
TEDD TW11 155 J6
Sunnyside Rd East ED N9 36 C5
Sunnyside Rd North ED * N9 36 B5
Sunnyside Rd South ED * N9 36 B5
Sunny Vw CDALE/KGS NW9 63 F2
Sunny Wy NFNCH/WDSP N12 47 J3
Sun Pas BERM/RHTH SE16 123 H3
Sunray Av BRYLDS KT5 191 J6
CMBW SE5 142 E5
HAYES BR2 200 D3
WDR/YW UB7 112 A2
Sunrise Cl FELT TW13 154 E5
Sun Rd WKENS W14 119 J5
Sunset Av CHING E4 37 K3
WFD IG8 52 E1
Sunset Cl ERITH DA8 150 E1
Sunset Gdns NRWD SE19 181 F5
Sunset Rd CMBW SE5 142 D5
THMD SE28 128 B2
WIM/MER SW19 176 E1
Sunset Vw BAR EN5 20 C3
Sunshine Wy MTCM CR4 178 E5
Sun St SDTCH EC2A 13 F1
Superior Dr ORP BR6 217 F4
Surbiton Ct SURB KT6 190 D3
Surbiton Crs SURB KT6 191 F1
Surbiton Hall Cl KUT KT1 191 F1
Surbiton Hill Pk BRYLDS KT5 191 G2
Surbiton Hill Rd SURB KT6 191 F1
Surbiton Rd KUT KT1 190 E1
Surlingham Cl THMD SE28 109 K6
Surma Cl WCHPL E1 104 C3
Surmans Cl DAGW RM9 91 J6
Surrendale Pl MV/WKIL W9 100 E3
Surrey Canal Rd
BERM/RHTH SE16 123 K6
Surrey Crs CHSWK W4 117 H5
Surrey Gdns FSBYPK N4 67 J3
Surrey Gv SUT SM1 209 H1
WALW SE17 123 F5
Surrey La BTSEA SW11 140 D2
Surrey Ms WNWD SE27 163 F6
Surrey Quays Rd
BERM/RHTH SE16 123 K3
Surrey Rd BARK IG11 90 E5
DAGE RM10 92 E3
HRW HA1 60 C3
PECK SE15 144 A6
WWKM BR4 198 E5
Surrey Rw STHWK SE1 18 A2
Surrey Sq WALW SE17 123 F5
Surrey St CROY/NA CR0 211 J1
PLSTW E13 107 F2
TPL/STR WC2R 11 H5
Surrey Ter WALW SE17 19 H7
Surrey Water Rd
BERM/RHTH SE16 124 A1
Surridge Gdns NRWD SE19 180 E2
Surr St HOLWY N7 84 E3
Susan Cl ROMW/RG RM7 56 E6
Susannah St POP/IOD E14 105 K5
Susan Rd BKHTH/KID SE3 146 A3
Susan Wd CHST BR7 185 F4
Sussex Av ISLW TW7 135 K4
Sussex Cl ARCH * N19 66 E6
NWMAL KT3 192 B1
REDBR IG4 71 K3
TWK TW1 156 C1
Sussex Crs NTHLT UB5 78 A4
Sussex Gdns BAY/PAD W2 8 B5
CHSGTN KT9 205 K4
EFNCH N2 65 K2
FSBYPK N4 67 J2
Sussex Ga EFNCH * N2 65 K2
Sussex Ms East BAY/PAD * W2 8 B5
Sussex Ms West BAY/PAD W2 8 B5
Sussex Pl BAY/PAD W2 8 B4
CAMTN NW1 2 E6
HMSMTH W6 119 F5
NWMAL KT3 192 B1
Sussex Rd CAR SM5 209 K4
DART DA1 171 K2
EHAM E6 108 A1
ERITH DA8 149 J1
HGDN/ICK UB10 76 A2
HRW HA1 60 C2
MTCM * CR4 195 K2
NWDGN UB2 114 C3
NWMAL KT3 192 B1
SAND/SEL CR2 211 K4
SCUP DA14 186 C1
STMC/STPC BR5 202 D3
WWKM BR4 198 E5
Sussex Sq BAY/PAD W2 8 B5
Sussex St PIM SW1V 121 G5
PLSTW E13 107 F2
Sussex Ter PGE/AN * SE20 181 K3
Sussex Wy ARCH N19 66 D5
EBAR EN4 22 B6
Sutcliffe Cl GLDGN NW11 65 F2
Sutcliffe Rd WELL DA16 148 D3
WOOL/PLUM SE18 127 K6
Sutherland Av HYS/HAR UB3 113 K4
MV/WKIL W9 100 E3
STMC/STPC BR5 202 A3
WEA W13 97 H5
WELL DA16 147 J5
Sutherland Cl BAR EN5 20 C5
Sutherland Ct CDALE/KGS NW9 62 D1
Sutherland Dr WIM/MER SW19 178 C4
Sutherland Gdns
MORT/ESHN SW14 138 B4
WPK KT4 192 E5
Sutherland Gv TEDD TW11 173 K1
WAND/EARL SW18 159 J2
Sutherland House WALTH * E17 51 G6
Sutherland Pl BAY/PAD W2 100 E5
Sutherland Rd BELV DA17 129 H3
BOW E3 105 H1
CHSWK W4 118 A6
CROY/NA CR0 196 B4
ED N9 36 C3
PEND EN3 37 F1
STHL UB1 95 K5
TOTM N17 50 C3
WALTH E17 51 F5
WEA W13 97 G5
Sutherland Rw PIM * SW1V 121 G5
Sutherland Sq WALW SE17 122 D5
Sutherland St PIM SW1V 121 G5
Sutherland Vls WEA * W13 97 G6
Sutherland Wk WALW SE17 122 D5
Sutlej Rd CHARL SE7 146 B1
Sutterton St HOLWY N7 85 F4
The Sutton Est IS * N1 85 H5
Sutton Cl BECK BR3 182 E4
CHSWK * W4 117 K6
LOU IG10 39 J2
PIN HA5 58 E2
Sutton Common Rd
CHEAM SM3 193 J4
Sutton Ct BELMT SM2 209 G5
CHSWK * W4 117 K6
EA * W5 117 F1
Sutton Court Rd BELMT SM2 209 G4
CHSWK W4 117 K6
PLSTW E13 107 G2
Sutton Crs BAR EN5 20 B6
Sutton Dene HSLW TW3 135 G2
Sutton Dwelling Est CHEL SW3 120 D5
Sutton Est IS * N1 85 H5
Sutton Gdns CROY/NA CR0 197 G2
Sutton Gv SUT SM1 209 H3
Sutton Hall HEST TW5 135 F1
Sutton La CHSWK W4 117 K5
HSLW TW3 134 E3
Sutton La South CHSWK W4 117 K6
Sutton Park Rd SUT SM1 209 F4
Sutton Pl HOM E9 86 E3
Sutton Rd BARK IG11 108 E1
HEST TW5 135 F2
MUSWH N10 48 A4
PLSTW E13 106 D3
WALTH E17 51 F4
Sutton Rw SOHO/SHAV W1D 10 C3
Sutton Sq HEST TW5 134 E2
HOM * E9 86 E3
Sutton St WCHPL E1 104 E5
Sutton Wy HEST TW5 134 E2
NKENS W10 100 A4
Swaby Rd WAND/EARL SW18 160 B4
Swaffield Rd WAND/EARL SW18 160 B2
Swain Cl STRHM/NOR SW16 179 G2
Swain Rd THHTH CR7 196 D2
Swains Cl WDR/YW UB7 112 B2
Swain's La HGT N6 66 A5
KTTN NW5 84 A1
Swainson Rd ACT W3 118 C2
Swains Rd MTCM CR4 178 E3
Swain St STJWD NW8 2 B7
Swaisland Rd DART DA1 150 E6
Swaislands Dr DART DA1 150 C6
Swaledale Cl FBAR/BDGN N11 48 A2
Swale Rd DART DA1 150 D4
Swallands Rd CAT SE6 164 D5
Swallow Cl BUSH WD23 28 B3
BXLYHN DA7 150 B2
NWCR SE14 143 K2
Swallow Ct RSLP * HA4 59 G5
Swallowdale SAND/SEL CR2 213 F6
Swallow Dr NTHLT UB5 96 A1
WLSDN NW10 81 F4
Swallowfield Rd CHARL SE7 126 A5
Swallowfield Wy HYS/HAR UB3 113 G2
Swallow Gdns
STRHM/NOR SW16 179 J1
Swallow Pl REGST W1B 9 K4
Swallow St CONDST W1S 10 B6
EHAM E6 107 J4
Swallowtail Cl STMC/STPC BR5 202 E1
Swanage Rd CHING E4 52 A3
WAND/EARL SW18 160 B1
Swanage Waye YEAD UB4 95 G5
Swan And Pike Rd PEND EN3 25 J1
Swan Ap EHAM E6 107 J4
Swanbridge Rd BXLYHN DA7 149 H2
Swan Cl CROY/NA * CR0 197 F4
FELT TW13 154 D6
STMC/STPC BR5 186 B6
WALTH E17 51 G4
Swandon Wy
WAND/EARL SW18 140 A5
Swan Dr CDALE/KGS NW9 45 G5
Swanfield St BETH E2 7 J5
Swan Island TWK * TW1 156 B5
Swan La CANST EC4R 13 F6
DART DA1 170 C2
LOU IG10 39 G2
TRDG/WHET N20 33 G5
Swanley Rd WELL DA16 148 D2
Swan Md STHWK SE1 19 G5
Swan Ms BRXN/ST SW9 142 A3
Swan Pas WCHPL E1 13 K6
Swan Pl BARN SW13 138 C3
Swan Rd BERM/RHTH SE16 123 K2
FELT TW13 154 D6
GFD/PVL UB6 96 B5
WDR/YW UB7 112 A2
Swanscombe Rd CHSWK W4 118 B5
NTGHL W11 119 G1
Swansea Rd HTHAIR TW6 153 F1
PEND EN3 24 E5
Swanston Pth OXHEY WD19 27 G5
Swan St ISLW TW7 136 C4
STHWK SE1 18 D3
Swanton Gdns WIM/MER SW19 159 G3
Swanton Rd ERITH DA8 149 H1
Swan Wk CHEL SW3 120 E6
Swan Wy PEND EN3 25 F3
Swanwick Cl PUT/ROE SW15 158 C2
Swan Yd IS N1 85 H4
Sward Rd STMC/STPC BR5 202 B3
Swaton Rd BOW E3 105 J3
Swaylands Rd BELV DA17 129 H6
Swaythling Cl UED N18 36 D6
Sweden Ga BERM/RHTH SE16 124 B4
Sweeney Crs STHWK SE1 19 K3
Sweeps La STMC/STPC BR5 202 E2
Sweet Briar Gn ED N9 36 B5
Sweet Briar Gv ED N9 36 B5
Sweet Briar Wk UED N18 36 B6
Sweetmans Av PIN HA5 41 H6
Sweets Wy TRDG/WHET N20 33 H4
Swete St PLSTW E13 106 E1
Sweyn Pl BKHTH/KID SE3 145 K3
Swift Cl RYLN/HDSTN HA2 60 B6
WALTH E17 51 G3
YEAD UB4 94 D5
Swift Rd FELT TW13 154 C6
NWDGN UB2 114 E3
Swiftsden Wy BMLY BR1 183 H2
Swift St FUL/PGN SW6 139 H2
Swinbrook Rd NKENS W10 100 C4
Swinburne Crs CROY/NA CR0 197 K3
Swinburne Rd PUT/ROE SW15 138 D5
Swinderby Rd ALP/SUD HA0 80 A4
Swindon Cl GDMY/SEVK IG3 72 E6
Swindon Rd HTHAIR TW6 133 F6
Swindon St SHB * W12 118 E1
Swinfield Cl FELT TW13 154 D6
Swinford Gdns BRXN/ST SW9 142 C4
Swingate La WOOL/PLUM SE18 147 K1
Swinnerton St HOM E9 87 G3
Swinton Cl WBLY HA9 62 D5
Swinton Pl FSBYW WC1X 5 G4
Swinton St FSBYW WC1X 5 G4
Swires Shaw HAYES BR2 215 H2
Swithland Gdns ELTH/MOT SE9 166 E6
Swyncombe Av BTFD TW8 116 C4
Swynford Gdns HDN NW4 63 J1
Sybil Phoenix Cl DEPT SE8 124 A5
Sybourn St WALTH E17 69 H4
Sycamore Av BFN/LL DA15 168 A1
BOW E3 87 H6
EA W5 116 E3
HYS/HAR UB3 94 C6
Sycamore Cl ACT W3 118 B1
CAN/RD E16 106 C3
CAR SM5 209 K2
EBAR EN4 33 H1
ED N9 36 C6
EDGE HA8 30 E6
FELT TW13 153 K5
NTHLT UB5 77 J6
SAND/SEL CR2 212 A3
Sycamore Gdns MTCM CR4 178 C5
SHB W12 118 E2
Sycamore Gv CAT SE6 165 F1
CDALE/KGS NW9 62 E4
NWMAL KT3 176 B6
PGE/AN SE20 181 H4
Sycamore Hl FBAR/BDGN N11 48 A2
Sycamore Ms CLAP SW4 141 H4
ERITH * DA8 130 A5
Sycamore Rd DART DA1 171 G2
WIM/MER SW19 177 F2
Sycamore St FSBYE EC1V 6 C7
Sycamore Wk NKENS W10 100 C3
Sycamore Wy TEDD TW11 174 D2
Sydcote DUL * SE21 162 D4
Sydenham Av SYD SE26 181 J1
WCHMH N21 23 F6
Sydenham Cl ROM RM1 75 H1
Sydenham Cottages
LEE/GVPK * SE12 166 B4
Sydenham Hl SYD SE26 163 H5
Sydenham Pk SYD SE26 163 K5
Sydenham Park Rd FSTH SE23 163 K5
Sydenham Ri FSTH SE23 163 J4
Sydenham Rd CROY/NA CR0 196 D6
SYD SE26 182 A1
Sydenham Station Ap
SYD SE26 163 K6
Sydmons Ct FSTH * SE23 163 K2
Sydner Rd STNW/STAM N16 86 B2
Sydney Cl SKENS SW7 14 B7
Sydney Gv HDN NW4 64 A2
Sydney Ms SKENS SW7 14 B7
Sydney Pl SKENS SW7 14 B7
Sydney Rd ABYW SE2 128 E3
BARK/HLT IG6 54 C5
BXLYHS DA6 148 E5
CEND/HSY/T N8 67 G1
EBED/NFELT TW14 153 K3
ENC/FH EN2 23 K5
MUSWH N10 48 B4
RCH/KEW TW9 137 F5
RYNPK SW20 177 G5
SCUP DA14 167 K6
SUT SM1 208 E2
TEDD TW11 174 A1
WAN E11 71 F3
WEA W13 116 B1
Sydney St CHEL SW3 120 D5
Sydney Ter ESH/CLAY * KT10 205 F4
Sylvan Av CHDH RM6 74 B3
MLHL NW7 45 G2

WDGN N22 49 G3
Sylvan Gdns SURB KT6 190 E4
Sylvan Gv CRICK NW2 82 B2
PECK SE15 123 J6
Sylvan Hl NRWD SE19 181 F4
Sylvan Rd FSTGT E7 88 E4
IL IG1 72 C6
NRWD SE19 181 G4
WALTH * E17 69 J2
WAN E11 70 E2
Sylvan Ter PECK * SE15 143 J1
Sylvan Wy BCTR RM8 91 H1
WWKM BR4 214 C2
Sylverdale Rd CROY/NA CR0 211 H1
Sylvester Av CHST BR7 184 E2
Sylvester Pth HACK * E8 86 D4
Sylvester Rd ALP/SUD HA0 79 J3
EFNCH N2 47 G5
HACK * E8 86 D4
WALTH * E17 69 H4
Sylvia Av PIN HA5 41 K2
Sylvia Gdns WBLY HA9 80 D5
Symes Ms CAMTN NW1 4 A2
Symington Ms HOM * E9 87 F3
Symister Ms IS * N1 7 G5
Symons St BCVA SW1W 15 G7
Symphony Ms NKENS * W10 100 C2
Syon Gate Wy BTFD TW8 136 C1
Syon La BTFD TW8 136 C1
ISLW TW7 116 A6
Syon Pk ISLW * TW7 136 C4
Syon Park Gdns ISLW TW7 136 A1

T

Tabard Garden Est STHWK SE1 18 E2
Tabard St STHWK SE1 18 E4
Tabernacle Av PLSTW E13 106 E3
Tabernacle St SDTCH EC2A 7 F7
Tableer Av CLAP SW4 141 H6
Tabley Rd HOLWY N7 84 E2
Tabor Gdns CHEAM SM3 208 D4
Tabor Gv WIM/MER SW19 177 H3
Tabor Rd HMSMTH W6 118 E3
Tachbrook Rd
EBED/NFELT TW14 153 J2
NWDGN UB2 114 C4
Tachbrook St PIM SW1V 16 B7
Tack Ms BROCKY SE4 144 D4
Tadema Rd WBPTN SW10 140 B1
Tadmor St SHB W12 119 G1
Tadworth Av NWMAL KT3 192 C1
Tadworth Pde HCH RM12 93 K2
Tadworth Rd CRICK NW2 63 J6
Taeping St POP/IOD E14 124 E4
Taffy's How MTCM CR4 178 D6
Tait Rd CROY/NA CR0 197 F4
Takeley Cl CRW RM5 57 F5
Talacre Rd KTTN NW5 84 A4
Talbot Av EFNCH N2 47 H6
OXHEY WD19 27 J2
Talbot Cl SEVS/STOTM N15 68 B1
Talbot Ct BANK EC3V 13 F5
Talbot Crs HDN NW4 63 J2
Talbot Gdns GDMY/SEVK IG3 73 G6
Talbot Pl BKHTH/KID SE3 145 H3
Talbot Rd ALP/SUD HA0 79 K3
CAR SM5 210 A3
DAGW RM9 92 B5
EDUL SE22 143 F5
EHAM E6 107 K1
FSTGT E7 88 E2
HGT N6 66 A3
ISLW TW7 136 B5
KTN/HRWW/W HA3 43 F5
NTGHL W11 100 D5
NWDGN UB2 114 D4
SEVS/STOTM N15 68 B1
THHTH CR7 196 E1
WDGN N22 48 C5
WEA * W13 97 G6
WHTN TW2 155 K3
Talbot Sq BAY/PAD W2 8 A4
Talbot Wk NTGHL W11 100 C5
WLSDN * NW10 81 G4
Talbot Yd STHWK SE1 18 E1
Talcott Pth
BRXS/STRHM * SW2 162 B3
Talfourd Pl PECK SE15 143 G2
Talfourd Rd PECK SE15 143 G2
Talgarth Rd HMSMTH W6 119 G5
Talisman Cl GDMY/SEVK IG3 73 H5
Talisman Sq SYD SE26 163 H6
Talisman Wy WBLY HA9 80 B1
Tallack Rd LEY E10 69 H5
Tall Elms Cl HAYES BR2 199 J2
Tallis Cl CAN/RD E16 107 F5
Tallis Gv CHARL SE7 126 A6
Tallis St EMB EC4Y 11 K5
Tallis Vw WLSDN NW10 81 F4
Tall Trees STRHM/NOR SW16 180 A6
Talma Gdns WHTN TW2 155 K2
Talmage Cl FSTH SE23 163 K2
Talman Gv STAN HA7 43 K2
Talma Rd BRXS/STRHM SW2 142 B5
Talwin St BOW E3 105 K2
Tamar Cl BOW * E3 87 H6
Tamarind Yd WAP E1W 123 H1
Tamarisk Sq SHB W12 99 H6
Tamar St WOOL/PLUM SE18 126 D4
Tamesis Gdns WPK KT4 192 B6
Tamian Wy HSLWW TW4 134 B5
Tamworth Av WFD IG8 52 C2
Tamworth La MTCM CR4 179 G6
Tamworth Pk MTCM CR4 195 G1
Tamworth Pl CROY/NA * CR0 196 D6
Tamworth Rd CROY/NA CR0 196 D6
Tamworth St FUL/PGN SW6 119 K6
Tancred Rd FSBYPK N4 67 H3
Tandridge Dr ORP BR6 201 J5
Tanfield Av CRICK NW2 81 H2
Tanfield Rd CROY/NA CR0 211 J2
Tangier Rd RCHPK/HAM TW10 137 H5
Tangleberry Cl BMLY BR1 200 E1
Tangle Tree Cl EFNCH N2 47 F5
Tanglewood Cl CROY/NA CR0 212 E1
STAN HA7 28 E4
Tanglewood Wy FELT TW13 154 A5
Tangley Gv PUT/ROE SW15 158 C2
Tangley Park Rd HPTN * TW12 172 E1
Tangmere Crs HCH RM12 93 K4
Tangmere Gdns NTHLT UB5 95 G1
Tangmere Gv KUTN/CMB KT2 174 E1
Tangmere Wy CDALE/KGS NW9 45 G5
Tanhouse Fld KTTN * NW5 84 D3
Tankerton Houses STPAN * WC1H 5 F5
Tankerton Rd SURB KT6 191 G6
Tankerton St STPAN WC1H 5 F5
Tankerton Ter CROY/NA * CR0 196 A4
Tankerville Rd
STRHM/NOR SW16 179 J3
Tank Hill Rd PUR RM19 131 K4
Tank La PUR RM19 131 K4
Tankridge Rd CRICK NW2 63 K6
The Tanneries WCHPL * E1 104 E3
Tanners Cl WOT/HER KT12 188 A3
Tanners End La UED N18 36 A6
Tanner's Hl DEPT SE8 144 D2
Tanners La BARK/HLT IG6 54 C6
Tanner St BARK IG11 90 C4
STHWK SE1 19 H3
Tannery Cl CROY/NA CR0 198 A2
DAGE RM10 92 D1
Tannington Ter FSBYPK * N4 85 G1
Tannsfeld Rd SYD SE26 182 A1
Tansley Cl HOLWY * N7 84 D3
Tanswell St STHWK * SE1 17 J3
Tansy Cl EHAM E6 108 A5
Tantallon Rd BAL SW12 161 F3
Tant Av CAN/RD E16 106 D5
Tantony Gv CHDH RM6 55 K6
Tanworth Cl NTHWD HA6 40 A2
Tanworth Gdns PIN HA5 41 F5
Tan Yard La BXLY * DA5 169 H2
Tanza Rd HAMP NW3 83 K2
Tapestry Cl BELMT SM2 209 F5
Taplow Ct MTCM CR4 194 D1
Taplow St IS N1 6 D3
Tappesfield Rd PECK SE15 143 K4
Tapping Cl KUTN/CMB * KT2 175 H3
Tapp St BETH * E2 104 D3
Tapster St BAR EN5 20 D4
Taransay Wk IS N1 85 K4
Tara Ter BROCKY * SE4 144 B4
Tarbert Rd EDUL SE22 143 F6
Tarbert Wk WCHPL E1 104 E6
Target Cl EBED/NFELT TW14 153 H1
Tariff Rd UED N18 50 D1
Tarleton Gdns FSTH SE23 163 J3
Tarling Cl SCUP DA14 168 C5
Tarling Rd CAN/RD E16 106 D5
EFNCH N2 47 G5
Tarling St WCHPL E1 104 D5
Tarnbank ENC/FH EN2 22 E6
Tarn St STHWK SE1 18 C5
Tarnwood Pk ELTH/MOT SE9 166 E3
Tarragon Cl NWCR * SE14 144 B1
Tarragon Gv SYD SE26 182 A2
Tarrant Pl MBLAR W1H 8 E2
Tarriff Crs DEPT SE8 124 C4
Tarrington Cl
STRHM/NOR * SW16 161 J6
Tarver Rd WALW SE17 122 C5
Tarves Wy GNWCH SE10 144 E1
Tash Pl FBAR/BDGN * N11 48 B1
Tasker Cl HYS/HAR UB3 133 F1
Tasker Rd HAMP NW3 83 K3
Tasmania Ter UED N18 49 J2
Tasman Rd BRXN/ST SW9 141 K4
Tasso Rd HMSMTH W6 119 H6
Tate Gdns BUSH WD23 28 E2
Tate Rd CAN/RD E16 126 E1
SUT SM1 208 E3
Tatnell Rd FSTH SE23 164 B1
Tattersall Cl ELTH/MOT SE9 146 D6
Tatton Crs STNW/STAM N16 68 B4
Tatum Rd WLSDN NW10 80 E5
Tatum St WALW SE17 19 F7
Tauheed Cl FSBYPK N4 67 J6
Taunton Av HSLW TW3 135 H3
RYNPK SW20 176 E5
Taunton Cl BARK/HLT IG6 55 F2
BXLYHN DA7 150 A4
CHEAM SM3 193 K5
Taunton Dr EFNCH N2 47 G5
ENC/FH EN2 23 G4
Taunton Ms CAMTN NW1 2 E7
Taunton Pl CAMTN NW1 2 E6
Taunton Rd GFD/PVL UB6 78 B5
LEW SE13 145 H6
Taunton Wy STAN HA7 44 A5
Tavern Cl CAR SM5 194 D4
Taverners Cl NTGHL * W11 119 H1
Taverner Sq HBRY * N5 85 J2
Taverners Wy CHING E4 38 C3
Tavistock Av GFD/PVL UB6 97 G1
WALTH E17 51 F6
Tavistock Cl STNW/STAM * N16 86 A3
Tavistock Ct COVGDN * WC2E 11 F5
Tavistock Crs MTCM CR4 195 K1
NTGHL W11 100 D5
Tavistock Gdns GDMY/SEVK IG3 90 E2
Tavistock Gv CROY/NA CR0 196 E4
Tavistock Ms NTGHL * W11 100 D5
Tavistock Pl STHGT/OAK * N14 34 B1
STPAN WC1H 4 D6
Tavistock Rd CAR SM5 194 C5
CROY/NA CR0 196 E5
EDGE HA8 44 B4
FSBYPK N4 67 K3
HAYES BR2 199 K1
HGDN/ICK UB10 76 B3
NTGHL W11 100 D4
SWFD E18 52 E6
WAN E11 88 D2
WDR/YW UB7 112 A1
WELL DA16 148 D2
WLSDN NW10 99 H1
Tavistock Sq STPAN WC1H 4 D6
Tavistock St COVGDN WC2E 11 F5
Tavistock Ter ARCH N19 84 D1
Taviton St STPAN WC1H 4 C6
Tavy Cl LBTH SE11 122 B5
Tawney Rd THMD SE28 109 H6
Tawny Cl FELT TW13 153 K5
WEA W13 116 C1
Tawny Wy BERM/RHTH SE16 124 A4
Tayben Av WHTN TW2 155 K1
Taybridge Rd BTSEA SW11 141 F4
Tayburn Cl POP/IOD E14 106 A5
Tayfield Cl HGDN/ICK UB10 76 A1
Taylor Av RCH/KEW TW9 137 J3
Taylor Cl CRW RM5 56 C3
DEPT SE8 124 C6
HPTN TW12 173 H1
HSLW TW3 135 H2
ORP BR6 217 F2
TOTM N17 50 C3
Taylor Rd WIM/MER SW19 178 D3
WLGTN SM6 210 B3
Taylor Rw RDART DA2 171 F5
Taylor's Buildings
WOOL/PLUM SE18 127 G4
Taylors Cl SCUP DA14 168 A6
Taylors Ct FELT TW13 153 K4
Taylor's Gn ACT * W3 99 G5
Taylor's La BAR EN5 20 D2
SYD SE26 163 J6
WLSDN NW10 81 G5
Taylors Md MLHL * NW7 45 J1
Taymount Ri FSTH SE23 163 K4
Tayport Cl IS N1 85 F5
Tayside Dr EDGE HA8 30 D5
Tay Wy ROM RM1 57 H4
Taywood Rd STHL UB1 95 K2
Teak Cl BERM/RHTH SE16 124 B1
Teal Av STMC/STPC BR5 202 E1
Teal Cl CAN/RD E16 107 H4
Teal Dr NTHWD HA6 40 A3
Teale St BETH E2 104 C1
Tealing Dr HOR/WEW KT19 207 F2
Teasel Cl CROY/NA CR0 198 A5
Teasel Wy SRTFD E15 106 C2
Tebworth Rd TOTM N17 50 B3
Technology Pk
CDALE/KGS * NW9 45 F6
Teck Cl ISLW TW7 136 B3
Tedder Cl CHSGTN KT9 205 J3
Tedder Rd SAND/SEL CR2 213 F5
Teddington Pk TEDD TW11 174 A1
Teddington Park Rd
TEDD TW11 156 A6
Tedworth Gdns CHEL SW3 120 E5
Tedworth Sq CHEL * SW3 120 E5
The Tee ACT W3 99 G5
Tees Av GFD/PVL UB6 96 E1
Teesdale Av ISLW TW7 136 B2
Teesdale Cl BETH E2 104 C1
Teesdale Gdns ISLW TW7 136 B2
SNWD SE25 181 F5
Teesdale Rd WAN E11 70 D3
Teesdale St BETH E2 104 D1
Teesdale Yd BETH * E2 104 D1
Teevan Cl CROY/NA CR0 197 H4
Teevan Rd CROY/NA CR0 197 H4
Teignmouth Cl CLAP SW4 141 J5
EDGE HA8 44 B5
Teignmouth Rd CRICK NW2 82 B3
WELL DA16 148 D3
Telcote Wy RSLP * HA4 59 G4
Telegraph Hl HAMP NW3 83 F1
Telegraph La ESH/CLAY KT10 205 F2
Telegraph Pas
BRXS/STRHM SW2 161 K2
Telegraph Pl POP/IOD E14 124 E4
Telegraph Rd PUT/ROE SW15 158 E2
Telegraph St LOTH EC2R 12 E3
Telephone Pl WKENS * W14 119 J6
Telferscot Rd BAL SW12 161 J3
Telford Av BAL SW12 161 J3
Telford Cl NRWD SE19 181 G2
WALTH E17 69 G4
Telford Dr WOT/HER KT12 188 B4
Telford Rd CDALE/KGS NW9 63 H3
CHST BR7 167 J4
NKENS W10 100 C4
STHL UB1 96 B6
WHTN TW2 155 F2
Telford Road North Circular Rd
FBAR/BDGN N11 48 C2
Telfords Yd WAP * E1W 104 C6
Telford Ter PIM * SW1V 121 H6
Telford Wy ACT W3 99 G4
YEAD UB4 95 J4
Telham Rd EHAM E6 108 A1
Tell Gv EDUL SE22 143 G5
Tellisford ESH/CLAY KT10 204 B2
Tellson Av WOOL/PLUM SE18 146 C2
Telscombe Cl ORP BR6 201 K6
Temeraire St BERM/RHTH SE16 123 K2
Tempelhof Av HDN NW4 64 A4
Temperley Rd BAL SW12 161 F2
Tempest Wy RAIN RM13 93 J4
Templar Dr THMD SE28 109 K5
Templar Pl HPTN TW12 173 F3
Templars Av GLDGN NW11 64 D3
Templars Ct DART * DA1 151 K6
Templars Crs FNCH N3 46 E5
Templars Dr
KTN/HRWW/W * HA3 42 D2
Templar St CMBW SE5 142 C3
Temple Av BCTR RM8 74 C5
CROY/NA CR0 213 H1
EMB EC4Y 11 K5
TRDG/WHET N20 33 H2
Temple Cl FNCH N3 46 D5
WAN E11 70 C4
WOOL/PLUM SE18 127 H3
Templecombe Rd HOM E9 86 E6
Templecombe Wy MRDN SM4 193 H2
Temple Dwellings BETH * E2 104 D1
Temple Fortune Hl GLDGN NW11 64 E2
Temple Fortune La GLDGN NW11 64 D3
Temple Gdns BCTR RM8 91 K1
EMB * EC4Y 11 J5
GLDGN NW11 64 D3
WCHMH * N21 35 H4
Temple Gv ENC/FH EN2 23 H4
GLDGN NW11 64 E3
Temple Hl DART DA1 151 J6
Temple Hill Sq DART DA1 151 J6
Temple La EMB EC4Y 11 K4
Templeman Rd HNWL W7 97 F4
Templemead Cl ACT W3 99 G5
Temple Mead Cl STAN HA7 43 H2
Temple Mills La LEY E10 87 K2
Temple Pde BAR * EN5 33 H2
Temple Pl TPL/STR WC2R 11 H5
Temple Rd CEND/HSY/T N8 67 F1
CHSWK W4 117 K3
CRICK NW2 82 A2
CROY/NA CR0 211 K2
EA W5 116 E3
EHAM E6 89 J6
HSLW TW3 135 G5
RCH/KEW TW9 137 G3
Temple Sheen Rd
MORT/ESHN SW14 137 K5
Temple St BETH E2 104 D1
Temple Ter WDGN * N22 49 G5
Templeton Av CHING E4 37 J6
Templeton Cl
STNW/STAM * N16 86 A3
THHTH CR7 180 E4
Templeton Pl ECT SW5 119 K4
Templeton Rd FSBYPK N4 67 K3
Temple Wy SUT SM1 209 H1
Templewood WEA W13 97 H4
Templewood Av HAMP NW3 83 F1
Templewood Gdns HAMP NW3 83 F1
Temple Yd BETH E2 104 C2
Tempsford Cl ENC/FH EN2 23 J4
Temsford Cl RYLN/HDSTN HA2 42 C5
Tenbury Cl FSTGT E7 89 H3
Tenbury Ct BRXS/STRHM SW2 161 J3
Tenby Av KTN/HRWW/W HA3 43 H5
Tenby Cl CHDH RM6 74 A3
Tenby Gdns NTHLT UB5 78 A4
Tenby Rd CHDH RM6 74 A3
EDGE HA8 44 B4
PEND EN3 24 E4
WALTH E17 69 G2
WELL DA16 148 E2
Tench St WAP * E1W 123 J1
Tenda Rd BERM/RHTH SE16 123 J4
Tendring Wy CHDH RM6 73 J2
Tenham Av BRXS/STRHM SW2 161 J4
Tenniel Cl BAY/PAD W2 101 G5
Tennison Rd SNWD SE25 197 G1
Tennis St STHWK SE1 18 E2
Tenniswood Rd EN EN1 24 B2
Tennyson Av CDALE/KGS NW9 44 E6
MNPK E12 89 J5
NWMAL KT3 192 E2
TWK TW1 156 A3
WAN E11 70 E4
Tennyson Cl EBED/NFELT TW14 153 K1
PEND EN3 25 F6
WELL DA16 147 K2
Tennyson Rd DART DA1 151 K6
HNWL W7 97 F6
HSLW TW3 135 H3
KIL/WHAMP NW6 82 D6
LEY E10 69 K5
MLHL NW7 45 H1
PGE/AN SE20 182 A3
SRTFD E15 88 C5
WALTH E17 69 H3
WIM/MER SW19 178 B2
Tennyson St VX/NE SW8 141 G3
Tennyson Wy HCH RM12 75 H5
Tensing Rd NWDGN UB2 115 F3
Tentelow La NWDGN UB2 115 G3
Tenterden Cl ELTH/MOT SE9 166 E6
HDN NW4 46 B6
Tenterden Dr HDN NW4 46 B6
Tenterden Gdns CROY/NA CR0 197 H4
HDN NW4 46 B6
Tenterden Gv HDN NW4 64 A1
Tenterden Rd BCTR RM8 74 B6
CROY/NA CR0 197 H4
TOTM N17 50 B3
Tenterden St CONDST W1S 9 K4
Tenter Gnd WCHPL * E1 13 J2
Tent Peg La STMC/STPC BR5 201 H2
Tent St WCHPL E1 104 D3
Terling Cl WAN E11 88 D1
Terling Rd BCTR RM8 74 C6
Terling Wk IS * N1 85 J6
Terminus Pl PIM SW1V 15 K5
The Terrace BARN SW13 138 B3
BETH * E2 104 E2
CHING * E4 38 C5
DEPT * SE8 124 C4
EFNCH * N2 66 A1
FNCH * N3 46 D5
FSTH * SE23 164 B2
KIL/WHAMP NW6 82 E6
Terrace Gdns BARN SW13 138 C3
Terrace La RCHPK/HAM TW10 157 F1
Terrace Rd HOM E9 87 F5
PLSTW E13 88 E6
WOT/HER KT12 188 A4
Terrace Vls HMSMTH * W6 118 D5
Terrace Wk DAGW RM9 92 A3
Terrac St RCH/KEW TW9 137 G5
Terrapin Rd TOOT SW17 161 G5
Terretts Pl IS N1 85 H5
Terrick Rd WDGN N22 48 E4
Terrick St SHB W12 99 K5
Terrilands PIN HA5 41 K6
Terront Rd SEVS/STOTM N15 67 J2
Tessa Sanderson Wy
GFD/PVL UB6 78 D3
Testerton Wk NTGHL * W11 100 B6
Tetcott Rd WBPTN SW10 140 B1
Tetherdown MUSWH N10 48 A6
Tetty Wy HAYES BR2 183 K5
Teversham La VX/NE SW8 141 K2
Teviot Cl WELL DA16 148 C2
Teviot St POP/IOD E14 106 A4
Tewkesbury Av FSTH SE23 163 J3
PIN HA5 59 J2
Tewkesbury Cl LOU IG10 39 J1
Tewkesbury Gdns
CDALE/KGS NW9 44 D6
Tewkesbury Rd CAR SM5 194 C5
SEVS/STOTM N15 67 K4
WEA W13 116 B1
Tewkesbury Ter
FBAR/BDGN N11 48 C2
Tewson Rd WOOL/PLUM SE18 127 K5
Teynham Av EN EN1 35 K1
Teynham Gn HAYES BR2 199 K2
Teynton Ter TOTM N17 49 J4
Thackeray Av TOTM N17 50 C5
Thackeray Cl ISLW TW7 136 B3
RYLN/HDSTN HA2 60 A5
WIM/MER SW19 177 G3
Thackeray Dr CHDH RM6 73 G4
Thackeray Ms HACK * E8 86 C4
Thackeray Rd EHAM E6 107 H1
VX/NE SW8 141 G3
Thackeray St KENS W8 120 A3
Thakeham Cl SYD SE26 181 J1
Thalia Cl GNWCH SE10 125 G6
Thame Rd BERM/RHTH SE16 124 A2
Thames Av DAGW RM9 110 D3
GFD/PVL UB6 97 F1
WBPTN SW10 140 B2
Thames Bank
MORT/ESHN SW14 137 K3
Thamesbank Pl THMD SE28 109 J5
Thames Cir POP/IOD E14 124 D4
Thames Cl HPTN TW12 173 G5
RAIN RM13 111 K5
Thames Down Link
CHSGTN KT9 206 E2
Thames Dr RSLP HA4 58 A3
Thames Eyot TWK * TW1 156 B4
Thames Ga DART DA1 151 K6
Thamesgate Cl
RCHPK/HAM TW10 156 C6
Thameside TEDD TW11 174 E3
Thames Meadow
E/WMO/HCT KT8 173 F6
Thamesmere Dr THMD SE28 109 G6
Thames Pth BERM/RHTH SE16 124 C3
BOW E3 106 A1
CHSWK W4 138 C2
CLPT E5 87 F1
GNWCH SE10 125 F6
LBTH SE11 121 K5
RCH/KEW TW9 136 D3
TWRH EC3N 13 H7
WEST SW1P 17 F5
WOT/HER KT12 172 B6
Thames Pl PUT/ROE SW15 139 G4
Thamespoint TEDD * TW11 174 E3
Thames Quay WBPTN * SW10 140 B2
Thames Reach KUT * KT1 174 E4
Thames Rd BARK IG11 109 G2
CAN/RD E16 126 C1
CHSWK W4 117 J6
DART DA1 150 D4
Thames Side KUTN/CMB KT2 174 E4
THDIT KT7 190 C3
Thames St GNWCH SE10 124 E6
HPTN TW12 173 G5
KUT KT1 174 E5
SUN TW16 172 A6
Thamesvale Cl HSLW TW3 135 F3
Thames Village CHSWK W4 137 K2
Thamley PUR RM19 131 K4
Thanescroft Gdns
CROY/NA CR0 212 A1
Thanet Dr HAYES BR2 215 H1
Thanet Pl CROY/NA CR0 211 J2
Thanet Rd BXLY DA5 169 H2
ERITH DA8 150 B1
Thanet St STPAN WC1H 4 E5
Thane Vls HOLWY N7 85 F1
Thant Cl LEY E10 87 K2
Tharp Rd WLGTN SM6 210 D3
Thatcham Gdns
TRDG/WHET N20 33 G2
Thatchers Wy ISLW TW7 135 J6
Thatches Gv CHDH RM6 74 A1
Thaxted Pl RYNPK SW20 177 G3
Thaxted Rd BKHH IG9 39 J2
ELTH/MOT SE9 167 H4
Thaxton Rd WKENS W14 119 J6
Thayers Farm Rd BECK BR3 182 B4
Thayer St MHST W1U 9 H2
Theatre St BTSEA SW11 140 E4
Theberton St IS N1 85 G6
Theed St STHWK SE1 17 J1
Thelma Gv TEDD TW11 174 B2
Theobald Crs
KTN/HRWW/W HA3 42 B4
Theobald Rd CROY/NA CR0 196 C6
WALTH E17 69 H4
Theobald's Rd FSBYW WC1X 11 G1
Theobald St STHWK SE1 18 E5
Theodora Wy PIN HA5 40 D6
Theodore Rd LEW SE13 165 G1
Therapia La CROY/NA CR0 195 K4
Therapia Rd EDUL SE22 163 K1
Theresa Rd HMSMTH W6 118 D4
Theresa's Wk SAND/SEL CR2 211 K6
Thermopylae Ga POP/IOD E14 124 E4
Theseus Wk IS N1 6 B3
Thesiger Rd PGE/AN SE20 182 A3
Thessaly Rd VX/NE SW8 141 J2
Thetford Cl PLMGR N13 49 H2
Thetford Rd ASHF TW15 152 B6
DAGW RM9 91 K5
NWMAL KT3 192 A3
Theydon Gdns RAIN RM13 93 G5
Theydon Gv WFD IG8 53 G2
Theydon Rd CLPT E5 68 E6
Theydon St WALTH E17 69 H4
Thicket Crs SUT SM1 209 G2
Thicket Gv DAGW RM9 91 J4
PGE/AN SE20 181 H3
Thicket Rd PGE/AN SE20 181 J3
SUT SM1 209 G2
Thicket Ter PGE/AN * SE20 181 H3
Third Av ACT W3 118 C1
CHDH RM6 73 J3
DAGE RM10 92 D6
EN EN1 24 B6
HYS/HAR UB3 113 J1
MNPK E12 89 J2
NKENS W10 100 C2
PLSTW E13 106 E2
WALTH E17 69 J2
WBLY HA9 61 K6
Third Cl E/WMO/HCT KT8 189 G1
Third Cross Rd WHTN TW2 155 J4
Third Wy WBLY HA9 80 D2
Thirleby Rd EDGE HA8 45 F4
WEST SW1P 16 B5
Thirlmere Av GFD/PVL UB6 97 J2
Thirlmere Gdns WBLY HA9 61 J5
Thirlmere Ri BMLY BR1 183 J2
Thirlmere Rd BXLYHN DA7 149 K3
MUSWH N10 48 B4
STRHM/NOR SW16 161 J6
Thirsk Cl NTHLT UB5 78 A4
Thirsk Rd BTSEA SW11 141 F4
MTCM CR4 179 F3
SNWD SE25 196 E1
Thirza Rd DART DA1 171 J1
Thislefield Cl BXLY DA5 168 E3
Thistlebrook ABYW SE2 128 D3
Thistlecroft Gdns STAN HA7 43 K4
Thistledene THDIT KT7 189 K3
Thistledene Av CRW RM5 56 D1
RYLN/HDSTN HA2 77 J1
Thistle Gv WBPTN * SW10 120 B5
Thistlemead CHST BR7 185 G5
Thistlewaite Rd CLPT E5 86 D1
Thistlewood Cl HOLWY N7 67 F6
Thistleworth Cl ISLW TW7 135 J1
Thistley Cl NFNCH/WDSP N12 47 J2
Thomas A'beckett Cl
ALP/SUD HA0 79 F2
Thomas Baines Rd BTSEA SW11 140 C4
Thomas Cribb Ms EHAM E6 107 K5
Thomas Dean Rd SYD * SE26 164 C6
Thomas Dinwiddy Rd
LEE/GVPK SE12 166 A4
Thomas Doyle St STHWK SE1 18 A4
Thomas' La CAT SE6 164 E2
Thomas Moore Wy EFNCH N2 47 G6
Thomas More St WAP * E1W 104 C6
Thomas North Ter
CAN/RD * E16 106 D4
Thomas Pl KENS * W8 120 A3
Thomas Rd POP/IOD E14 105 H5

Thomas St WOOL/PLUM SE18 127 F4
Thomas Wall Cl SUT SM1 209 F3
Thompson Av RCH/KEW TW9 137 J4
Thompson Cl CHEAM SM3 193 K5
IL IG1 72 C6
Thompson Rd DAGW RM9 92 B1
EDUL SE22 163 G1
HSLW TW3 135 G5
Thompson's Av CMBW * SE5 142 D1
Thomson Crs CROY/NA CR0 196 B5
Thomson Rd KTN/HRWW/W HA3 42 E6
Thorburn Sq STHWK SE1 123 H4
Thorburn Wy WIM/MER * SW19 178 C4
Thoresby St IS N1 6 D4
Thorkhill Gdns THDIT KT7 190 B5
Thorkhill Rd THDIT KT7 190 C5
Thornaby Gdns UED N18 50 C2
Thorn Av BUSH WD23 28 C3
Thornbury Av ISLW TW7 135 J1
Thornbury Cl STNW/STAM N16 86 A3
Thornbury Rd CLAP SW4 161 K1
ISLW TW7 135 J1
Thornby Rd CLPT E5 86 E1
Thorncliffe Rd CLAP SW4 161 J1
NWDGN UB2 114 E5
Thorn Cl HAYES BR2 201 F3
NTHLT UB5 95 K2
Thorncombe Rd EDUL SE22 143 F6
Thorn Ct BELMT * SM2 209 F5
Thorncroft EMPK RM11 75 K3
Thorncroft Rd SUT SM1 209 F2
Thorncroft St VX/NE SW8 141 K1
Thorndean St
WAND/EARL SW18 160 B4
Thorndene Av TRDG/WHET N20 34 A3
Thorndike Av NTHLT UB5 77 H6
Thorndike Cl WBPTN SW10 140 B1
Thorndike St PIM * SW1V 16 C7
Thorndon Cl STMC/STPC BR5 186 A5
Thorndon Gdns
HOR/WEW KT19 207 G2
Thorndon Rd STMC/STPC BR5 186 A5
Thorndyke Ct PIN * HA5 41 K3
Thorne Cl CAN/RD E16 106 E5
ERITH DA8 129 J6
WAN * E11 88 C2
Thorneloe Gdns CROY/NA CR0 211 H3
Thorne Rd VX/NE SW8 141 K1
Thorne's Cl BECK BR3 183 F6
Thorne St BARN SW13 138 B4
Thornet Wood Rd BMLY BR1 185 F6
Thorney Crs BTSEA * SW11 140 C1
Thorneycroft Cl WOT/HER KT12 188 B3
Thorneycroft Dr PEND EN3 25 J1
Thorney Hedge Rd CHSWK W4 117 J4
Thorney St WEST SW1P 16 E6
Thornfield Av MLHL NW7 46 C4
Thornfield Pde MLHL * NW7 46 C3
Thornfield Rd SHB W12 118 E2
Thornford Rd LEW SE13 145 F6
Thorngate Rd MV/WKIL W9 100 E3
Thorngrove Rd PLSTW E13 89 F6
Thornham Gv SRTFD E15 88 B3
Thornham St GNWCH SE10 124 E6
Thornhaugh St STPAN WC1H 4 D7
Thornhill Av SURB KT6 191 F6
WOOL/PLUM SE18 147 K1
Thornhill Bridge Whf IS N1 5 G1
Thornhill Crs IS N1 85 F5
Thornhill Gdns BARK IG11 90 E5
LEY E10 69 K6
Thornhill Gv IS N1 85 F5
Thornhill Rd CROY/NA CR0 196 D4
IS N1 85 G5
LEY E10 69 K6
NTHWD HA6 26 A6
SURB KT6 191 F6
Thornhill Sq IS N1 85 F6
Thornlaw Rd WNWD SE27 162 B6
Thornley Cl TOTM N17 50 C3
Thornley Dr RYLN/HDSTN HA2 60 B6
Thornsbeach Rd CAT SE6 165 F3
Thornsett Pl PGE/AN SE20 181 J5
Thornsett Rd PGE/AN SE20 181 J5
WAND/EARL SW18 160 A4
Thornsett Ter PGE/AN * SE20 181 J5
Thornton Av BAL SW12 161 J3
CHSWK W4 118 B4
CROY/NA CR0 196 A3
WDR/YW UB7 112 C3
Thornton Cl WDR/YW UB7 112 C3
Thornton Dene BECK BR3 182 D5
Thornton Gdns BAL SW12 161 J3
Thornton Gv PIN HA5 42 A2
Thornton Hl WIM/MER SW19 177 H3
Thornton Pl MBLAR W1H 8 E1
Thornton Rd BAL SW12 161 J2
BAR EN5 20 C4
BELV * DA17 129 J4
BMLY BR1 183 K1
CAR SM5 194 C5
IL IG1 90 B2
MORT/ESHN SW14 138 A4
THHTH CR7 196 B2
UED N18 36 E5
WAN E11 70 B6
WIM/MER SW19 177 G2
Thornton Rw THHTH CR7 196 B2
Thorntons Farm Av
ROMW/RG RM7 74 E6
Thornton St BRXN/ST SW9 142 B3
Thornton Wy GLDGN NW11 65 F2
Thorntree Rd CHARL SE7 126 C5
Thornville Gv MTCM CR4 178 B5
Thornville St DEPT SE8 144 D2
Thornwood Cl SWFD E18 53 F5
Thornwood Rd LEW SE13 145 H6
Thorogood Gdns SRTFD E15 88 C3
Thorogood Wy RAIN RM13 93 G6
Thorold Rd IL IG1 72 B6
WDGN N22 48 E3
Thorparch Rd VX/NE SW8 141 J2
Thorpebank Rd SHB W12 118 D1
Thorpe Cl NKENS W10 100 C5
ORP BR6 201 K6
SYD * SE26 164 A6
Thorpe Crs OXHEY WD19 27 F2
WALTH E17 51 H5
Thorpedale Gdns
GNTH/NBYPK IG2 72 A1
Thorpedale Rd FSBYPK N4 66 E5
Thorpe Hall Rd WALTH E17 52 A4
Thorpe Rd BARK IG11 90 D5
EHAM E6 89 K6
FSTGT E7 88 E1
KUTN/CMB KT2 175 F3
SEVS/STOTM N15 68 A3
WALTH E17 52 A5
Thorpewood Av SYD SE26 163 J4
Thorpland Av HGDN/ICK UB10 76 A1
Thorsden Wy NRWD * SE19 181 F1
Thorverton Rd CRICK NW2 82 C1
Thoydon Rd BOW E3 105 G1
Thrale Rd STRHM/NOR SW16 179 H1
Thrale St STHWK SE1 18 D1
Thrasher Cl HACK * E8 86 B6
Thrawl St WCHPL E1 13 K2
Threadneedle St LOTH EC2R 13 F4
Three Colts La BETH E2 104 D3
Three Colt St POP/IOD * E14 105 H6
Three Corners BXLYHN DA7 149 J3
Three Kings Yd MYFR/PKLN W1K 9 J5
Three Meadows Ms
KTN/HRWW/W HA3 43 F4
Three Mill La SRTFD E15 106 A2
Three Oak La STHWK SE1 19 J2
Threshers Pl NTGHL W11 100 C6
Thriffwood FSTH SE23 163 K5
Thrigby Rd CHSGTN KT9 206 B4
Throckmorten Rd CAN/RD E16 107 F5
Throgmorton Av OBST EC2N 13 F3
Throgmorton St LOTH EC2R 13 F3
Throwley Cl ABYW SE2 128 D3
Throwley Rd SUT SM1 209 F3
Throwley Wy SUT SM1 209 F2
Thrupp Cl MTCM CR4 179 G5
Thrush Gn RYLN/HDSTN HA2 60 A1
Thrush St WALW SE17 122 D5
Thunderer Rd DAGW RM9 110 A3
Thurbarn Rd CAT SE6 182 E1
Thurland Rd BERM/RHTH SE16 123 H3
Thurlby Cl WFD IG8 53 K2
Thurlby Rd ALP/SUD HA0 79 K4
WNWD SE27 162 B6
Thurleigh Av BAL SW12 161 F1
Thurleigh Rd BAL SW12 160 E1
Thurleston Av MRDN SM4 193 H2
Thurlestone Av GDMY/SEVK IG3 91 F2
NFNCH/WDSP N12 47 K2
Thurlestone Rd WNWD SE27 162 B5
Thurloe Cl SKENS SW7 14 C6
Thurloe Gdns ROM RM1 75 G3
Thurloe Pl SKENS SW7 14 B6
Thurloe Place Ms SKENS * SW7 14 B6
Thurloe Sq SKENS SW7 14 C6
Thurloe St SKENS SW7 14 B6
Thurlow Cl CHING E4 51 K2
Thurlow Gdns ALP/SUD * HA0 79 K3
CHIG IG7 54 D2
Thurlow Hl DUL SE21 162 D3
Thurlow Park Rd DUL SE21 162 C4
Thurlow Rd HAMP NW3 83 H3
HNWL W7 116 B2
Thurlow St WALW SE17 123 F5
Thurlow Ter KTTN NW5 83 K3
Thurlow Wk WALW SE17 123 F5
Thurlston Rd RSLP HA4 76 E1
Thursland Rd SCUP DA14 187 F1
Thursley Crs CROY/NA CR0 214 B5
Thursley Gdns
WIM/MER SW19 159 G4
Thursley Rd ELTH/MOT SE9 166 E5
Thurso St TOOT SW17 160 C6
Thurstan Rd RYNPK SW20 176 E3
Thurston Rd DEPT SE8 144 E3
STHL UB1 95 K5
Thurtle Rd BETH E2 7 K2
Thwaite Cl ERITH DA8 129 K6
Thyer Cl ORP BR6 216 C2
Thyra Gv NFNCH/WDSP N12 47 F2
Tibbatt's Rd BOW E3 105 K3
Tibbenham Pl CAT SE6 164 D4
Tibberton Sq IS * N1 85 J5
Tibbets Cl WIM/MER SW19 159 G3
Tibbet's Ride PUT/ROE SW15 159 G2
Tiber Gdns IS N1 5 F1
Ticehurst Cl STMC/STPC BR5 186 B3
Ticehurst Rd FSTH SE23 164 B4
Tickford Cl ABYW SE2 128 D2
Tidal Basin Rd CAN/RD E16 106 D6
Tidenham Gdns CROY/NA CR0 212 A1
Tideswell Rd CROY/NA CR0 213 J1
PUT/ROE SW15 139 F5
Tideway Cl RCHPK/HAM TW10 156 C6
Tideway Wk VX/NE * SW8 121 H6
Tidey St BOW E3 105 J4
Tidford Rd WELL DA16 148 A3
Tidworth Rd BOW E3 105 J3
Tiepigs La WWKM BR4 199 H6
Tierney Rd BRXS/STRHM SW2 161 K3
Tierney Ter BRXS/STRHM * SW2 161 K3
Tiger La HAYES BR2 200 A1
Tiger Wy CLPT E5 86 D2
Tigres Cl ED N9 36 E4
Tilbrook Rd BKHTH/KID SE3 146 B4
Tilbury Cl PECK SE15 143 G1
STMC/STPC BR5 186 C5
Tilbury Rd EHAM E6 107 K1
LEY E10 70 A4
Tildesley Rd PUT/ROE SW15 159 F1
Tile Farm Rd ORP BR6 216 D1
Tilehurst Rd CHEAM SM3 208 C3
WAND/EARL SW18 160 C3
Tile Kiln La BXLY DA5 170 A4
HGT N6 66 B5
PLMGR N13 49 J1
Tileyard Rd HOLWY N7 84 E5
Tilford Av CROY/NA CR0 214 A5
Tilford Gdns WIM/MER SW19 159 G3
Tilia Rd CLPT E5 86 D2
Tiller Rd POP/IOD E14 124 D3
Tillett Cl WLSDN NW10 80 E4
Tillet Wy BETH E2 104 C2
Tillingbourne Gdns FNCH N3 46 D6
Tillingbourne Gn
STMC/STPC BR5 202 B2
Tillingbourne Wy GLDGN NW11 64 D1
Tillingham Wy
NFNCH/WDSP N12 32 E6
Tilling Rd CRICK NW2 63 K5
Tilling Wy WBLY * HA9 79 K1
Tillman St WCHPL E1 104 D5
Tilloch St IS * N1 85 F5
Tillotson Rd ED N9 36 B4
IL IG1 72 A4
KTN/HRWW/W HA3 42 B3
Tilney Gdns IS N1 85 K4
Tilney Rd DAGW RM9 92 B4
NWDGN UB2 114 B4
Tilney St MYFR/PKLN W1K 9 H7
Tilson Cl CMBW SE5 143 F1
Tilson Gdns BRXS/STRHM SW2 161 K2
Tilson Rd TOTM N17 50 C4
Tilston Cl WAN E11 88 D1
Tilton St FUL/PGN SW6 119 H6
The Tiltwood ACT W3 98 E6
Tilt Yard Ap ELTH/MOT SE9 166 E1
Timber Cl CHST BR7 185 F5
Timbercroft HOR/WEW KT19 207 G2
Timbercroft La
WOOL/PLUM SE18 127 K6
Timberdene Av BARK/HLT IG6 54 C4
Timberland Cl PECK * SE15 143 H1
Timberland Rd WCHPL * E1 104 D5
Timber Mill Wy CLAP SW4 141 J4
Timber Pond Rd
BERM/RHTH SE16 124 A2
Timberslip Dr WLGTN SM6 210 D6
The Timbers CHEAM * SM3 208 C4
Timber St FSBYE * EC1V 6 C6
Timberwharf Rd
SEVS/STOTM N15 68 C3
Time Sq HACK * E8 86 B3
Times Sq SUT * SM1 209 F3
Timothy Cl BXLYHS DA6 149 F6
Timothy Rd POP/IOD E14 105 H4
Tindal St BRXN/ST SW9 142 C2
Tine Rd CHIG IG7 54 E1
Tinniswood Cl HOLWY * N7 85 G3
Tinsley Rd WCHPL E1 104 E4
Tintagel Crs EDUL SE22 143 G5
Tintagel Dr STAN HA7 43 K1
Tintagel Rd STMC/STPC BR5 202 D6
Tintern Av CDALE/KGS NW9 44 D6
Tintern Cl PUT/ROE SW15 139 H6
WIM/MER SW19 178 B3
Tintern Gdns WCHMH N21 34 E2
Tintern Rd CAR SM5 194 C5
WDGN N22 49 J4
Tintern St CLAP SW4 141 K5
Tintern Wy RYLN/HDSTN HA2 60 B5
Tinto Rd CAN/RD E16 106 E4
Tinworth St LBTH SE11 121 K5
Tippetts Cl ENC/FH EN2 23 J2
Tipthorpe Rd BTSEA SW11 141 F4
Tipton Dr CROY/NA CR0 212 A2
Tiptree Cl CHING E4 38 A5
Tiptree Crs CLAY IG5 54 A6
Tiptree Dr ENC/FH EN2 23 K5
Tiptree Rd RSLP HA4 77 F2
Tirlemont Rd SAND/SEL CR2 211 J5
Tirrell Rd CROY/NA CR0 196 D3
Tisbury Rd STRHM/NOR SW16 179 K5
Tisdall Pl WALW SE17 19 F7
Titan Ct BTFD TW8 117 G5
Titchborne Rw BAY/PAD W2 8 D4
Titchfield Rd CAR SM5 194 C5
STJWD NW8 2 D1
Titchfield Wk CAR SM5 194 C4
Titchwell Rd WAND/EARL SW18 160 C2
Tite St CHEL SW3 120 E6
Tithe Barn Cl KUTN/CMB KT2 175 G4
Tithe Barn Wy NTHLT UB5 95 F1
Tithe Cl MLHL NW7 45 J4
WOT/HER KT12 188 A3
YEAD UB4 94 D4
Tithe Ct HDN * NW4 45 J4
Tithe Farm Av RYLN/HDSTN HA2 78 A1
Tithe Farm Cl RYLN/HDSTN HA2 78 A1
Tithe Wk MLHL NW7 45 J4
Titian Av BUSH WD23 28 E2
Titley Cl CHING E4 51 J1
Titmus Cl UX/CGN UB8 94 A5
Titmuss Av THMD SE28 109 H6
Titmuss St SHB * W12 118 E2
Tiverton Av CLAY IG5 54 A6
Tiverton Dr ELTH/MOT SE9 167 H3
Tiverton Rd ALP/SUD HA0 98 A1
EDGE HA8 44 B5
HSLW TW3 135 G3
RSLP HA4 76 E1
SEVS/STOTM N15 67 K3
UED N18 50 A1
WLSDN NW10 82 B6
Tiverton St STHWK SE1 18 C4
Tiverton Wy CHSGTN KT9 205 J3
Tivoli Gdns WOOL/PLUM SE18 126 D4
Tivoli Rd CEND/HSY/T N8 66 D2
HSLWW TW4 134 D5
WNWD SE27 180 D1
Toad La HSLWW TW4 134 E5
Tobago St POP/IOD * E14 124 D2
Tobin Cl HAMP NW3 83 J5
Toby Wy SURB KT6 191 J6
Tokenhouse Yd LOTH EC2R 12 E3
Tokyngton Av WBLY HA9 80 C4
Toland Sq PUT/ROE SW15 138 D6
Tolcarne Dr PIN HA5 40 E5
Toley Av KTN/HRWW/W HA3 62 A4
Tollbridge Cl NKENS W10 100 C3
Tollesbury Gdns BARK/HLT IG6 54 D6
Tollet St WCHPL E1 105 F3
Tollgate Dr DUL SE21 163 F4
YEAD UB4 95 H6
Tollgate Gdns
KIL/WHAMP * NW6 100 E1
Tollgate Rd EHAM E6 107 J4
Tollhouse La WLGTN SM6 210 C6
Tollhouse Wy ARCH N19 66 C6
Tollington Pk FSBYPK N4 67 F6
Tollington Pl FSBYPK N4 67 F6
Tollington Rd HOLWY N7 85 F2
Tollington Wy HOLWY N7 84 E1
Tolmer's Sq CAMTN NW1 4 B6
Tolpits La WATW WD18 26 B2
Tolpuddle Av PLSTW E13 89 G6
Tolpuddle St IS N1 5 J2
Tolsford Rd CLPT E5 86 D3
Tolson Rd ISLW TW7 136 B4
Tolverne Rd RYNPK SW20 177 F4
Tolworth Cl SURB KT6 191 J5
Tolworth Gdns CHDH RM6 73 K2
Tolworth Park Rd SURB KT6 191 G6
Tolworth Ri North BRYLDS KT5 191 K4
Tolworth Ri South BRYLDS KT5 191 K5
Tolworth Rd SURB KT6 191 F6
Tom Cribb Rd
WOOL/PLUM SE18 127 H3
Tom Jenkinson Rd CAN/RD E16 125 K1
Tomlin's Gv BOW E3 105 J2
Tomlinson Cl BETH E2 7 K5
CHSWK W4 117 J5
Tomlins Orch BARK IG11 90 C6
Tomlin's Ter POP/IOD E14 105 G5
Tom Mann Cl BARK IG11 90 E6
Tom Nolan Cl SRTFD E15 106 C1
Tompion St FSBYE EC1V 6 A5
Tom Smith Cl GNWCH SE10 125 H6
Tomswood Hl BARK/HLT IG6 54 B3
Tomswood Rd CHIG IG7 54 A2
Tonbridge Crs
KTN/HRWW/W HA3 62 A1
Tonbridge Rd E/WMO/HCT KT8 188 D1
Tonbridge St STPAN WC1H 4 E5
Tonfield Rd CHEAM SM3 193 J5
Tonsley Hl WAND/EARL SW18 140 A6
Tonsley Pl WAND/EARL SW18 140 A6
Tonsley Rd WAND/EARL SW18 140 A6
Tonsley St WAND/EARL SW18 140 A6
Tonstall Rd MTCM CR4 179 F5
Tooke Cl PIN HA5 41 J4
Tookey Cl WBLY HA9 62 B4
Took's Ct FLST/FETLN EC4A 11 J3
Tooley St STHWK SE1 13 F7
Toorack Rd KTN/HRWW/W HA3 42 D5
Tooting Bec Gdns
STRHM/NOR SW16 161 J6
Tooting Bec Rd TOOT SW17 161 F5
Tooting Gv TOOT SW17 178 D1
Tooting High St TOOT SW17 160 D6
Tooting Market TOOT * SW17 160 E6
Tootswood Rd HAYES BR2 199 H2
Topcliffe Dr ORP BR6 216 D2
Topham Sq TOTM N17 49 J4
Topham St CLKNW * EC1R 5 J6
Top House Ri CHING E4 38 A2
Topiary Sq RCH/KEW TW9 137 G4
Topley St ELTH/MOT SE9 146 B5
Topmast Point POP/IOD * E14 124 D2
Top Pk BECK BR3 199 H2
Topsfield Pde CEND/HSY/T * N8 66 E2
Topsfield Rd CEND/HSY/T N8 66 E2
Topsham Rd TOOT SW17 160 E5
Torbay Rd KIL/WHAMP NW6 82 D5
RYLN/HDSTN HA2 59 J6
Torbay St CAMTN * NW1 84 B5
Torbridge Cl EDGE HA8 44 A3
Torcross Dr FSTH SE23 163 K4
Torcross Rd RSLP HA4 77 F1
Tor Gdns KENS W8 119 K2
Tormead Cl SUT SM1 208 E4
Tormount Rd
WOOL/PLUM SE18 127 K6
Toronto Av MNPK E12 89 K2
Toronto Rd IL IG1 72 B5
Torquay Gdns REDBR IG4 71 H1
Torquay St BAY/PAD W2 101 F4
Torrens Rd BRXS/STRHM SW2 142 A6
Torrens Sq SRTFD E15 88 D4
Torrens St FSBYE EC1V 6 A3
Torriano Av KTTN NW5 84 D3
Torriano Ms HOLWY N7 84 C3
Torridge Gdns PECK SE15 143 K5
Torridge Rd THHTH CR7 196 C2
Torridon Rd CAT SE6 165 G3
Torrington Av
NFNCH/WDSP N12 47 H1
Torrington Cl ESH/CLAY KT10 204 E4
Torrington Dr RYLN/HDSTN HA2 78 B2
Torrington Gdns
FBAR/BDGN N11 48 C2
GFD/PVL UB6 79 J6
Torrington Gv
NFNCH/WDSP N12 47 J1
Torrington Pk
NFNCH/WDSP N12 33 H6
Torrington Pl FITZ W1T 10 B1
WAP E1W 123 H1
Torrington Rd BCTR RM8 74 B5
ESH/CLAY KT10 204 E4
GFD/PVL UB6 79 J6
RSLP HA4 76 E1
Torrington Sq CROY/NA * CR0 196 E4
GWRST WC1E 4 D7
Torrington Wy MRDN SM4 193 K4
Tor Rd WELL DA16 148 D2
Torr Rd PGE/AN SE20 182 A3
Torver Rd HRW HA1 60 E1
Torver Wy ORP BR6 216 D1
Torwood Rd PUT/ROE SW15 138 D6
Tothill St STJSPK SW1H 16 C3
Totnes Rd WELL DA16 148 C1
Totnes Vls FBAR/BDGN * N11 48 C1
Totnes Wk EFNCH N2 65 H1
Tottan Ter WCHPL * E1 105 F5
Tottenhall Rd PLMGR N13 49 G2
Tottenham Court Rd FITZ W1T 4 B7
Tottenham Gn East
SEVS/STOTM N15 68 B1
Tottenham La CEND/HSY/T N8 66 E3
Tottenham Ms FITZ * W1T 10 B1
Tottenham Rd IS N1 86 A4
Tottenham South Side
SEVS/STOTM N15 68 B1
Tottenham St GTPST W1W 10 B2
Totterdown St TOOT SW17 160 E6
Totteridge Common
TRDG/WHET N20 31 J4
Totteridge La TRDG/WHET N20 32 E4
Totteridge Village
TRDG/WHET N20 32 D3
Totternhoe Cl
KTN/HRWW/W HA3 61 J2
Totton Rd THHTH CR7 180 B6
Toulmin St STHWK SE1 18 C3
Toulon St CMBW SE5 142 D1
Tournay Rd FUL/PGN SW6 139 J1
Toussaint Wk
BERM/RHTH SE16 123 H3
Tovil Cl PGE/AN SE20 181 H5
Towcester Rd BOW E3 105 K3
Tower Br TWRH EC3N 13 J7
Tower Bridge Ap TWRH EC3N 13 J7
Tower Bridge Rd STHWK SE1 19 G6
Tower Buildings WAP * E1W 123 J1
Tower Cl CHIG IG7 54 B2
HAMP NW3 83 H3
ORP BR6 202 A6
PGE/AN SE20 181 J3
Tower Ct LSQ/SEVD * WC2H 10 E4
Tower Gdns ESH/CLAY KT10 205 H5
Tower Gardens Rd TOTM N17 49 J4
Tower Hamlets Rd FSTGT E7 88 D3
WALTH E17 51 J6
Tower Hl TWRH EC3N 13 H6
Tower Hill Ter MON EC3R 13 H6
Tower La WBLY * HA9 79 K1
Tower Ms CLPT * E5 87 G3
Tower Mill Rd PECK * SE15 143 F1
Tower Park Rd DART DA1 150 C6
Tower Pl MON EC3R 13 H6
Tower Ri RCH/KEW TW9 137 F4
Tower Rd BELV DA17 129 K4
BXLYHN DA7 149 J5
DART DA1 171 F2
ORP BR6 202 A6
WHTN TW2 155 K5
WLSDN NW10 81 J5
Tower Royal MANHO * EC4N 12 D5
Towers Av HGDN/ICK UB10 94 A2
Towers Ct HGDN/ICK * UB10 94 A2
Towers Pl RCHPK/HAM TW10 137 F6
Towers Rd PIN HA5 41 J4
STHL UB1 96 A3
Tower St LSQ/SEVD * WC2H 10 D4
Tower Ter WDGN N22 49 F5
Tower Vw CROY/NA CR0 198 B5
Towfield Rd FELT TW13 154 E4
Towncourt Crs STMC/STPC BR5 201 H2
Towncourt La STMC/STPC BR5 201 J3
Towncourt Pth FSBYPK N4 67 J5
Town End Pde KUT * KT1 174 E6
Towney Md NTHLT UB5 95 K1
Town Farm Wy
STWL/WRAY * TW19 152 A2
Townfield Rd HYS/HAR UB3 113 K1
Townfield Sq HYS/HAR UB3 113 J1
Town Field Wy ISLW TW7 136 B3
Town Hall Approach Rd
SEVS/STOTM N15 68 B1
Townhall Av CHSWK W4 118 A5
Town Hall Pde
BRXS/STRHM * SW2 142 A5
Town Hall Rd BTSEA SW11 140 E4
Townholm Crs HNWL W7 116 A3
Town La STWL/WRAY TW19 152 A2
Townley Ct SRTFD E15 88 D4
Townley Rd BXLYHS DA6 149 G6
EDUL SE22 143 F6
Townley St WALW * SE17 122 E5
Town Meadow BTFD TW8 136 E1
Townmead Rd FUL/PGN SW6 140 A4
RCH/KEW TW9 137 J3
Town Quay BARK IG11 90 B6
Town Rd ED N9 36 D4
Townsend Av STHGT/OAK N14 34 D6
Townsend La CDALE/KGS NW9 63 F4
Townsend Rd SEVS/STOTM N15 68 B2
STHL UB1 114 D1
WOOL/PLUM SE18 127 G3
Townsend St WALW SE17 19 F7
Townsend Wy NTHWD HA6 40 D3
Townsend Yd HGT N6 66 B5
Townshend Cl SCUP DA14 186 C2
Townshend Est STJWD NW8 2 C2
Townshend Rd CHST BR7 185 G1
RCH/KEW TW9 137 G5
STJWD NW8 2 C1
Townshend Ter RCH/KEW TW9 137 G5
Townson Av NTHLT UB5 95 F1
Townson Wy NTHLT UB5 94 E1
Town Whf ISLW * TW7 136 C4
Towpath WOT/HER * KT12 188 A1
Towpath Rd UED * N18 51 F1
Towpath Wy CROY/NA CR0 197 G3
Towton Rd WNWD SE27 162 D4
Toynbec Cl CHST BR7 167 G6
Toynbee Rd RYNPK SW20 177 H4
Toynbee St WCHPL E1 13 J2
Toyne Wy HGT N6 65 K3
Tracey Av CRICK * NW2 82 A3
Trade Cl PLMGR N13 35 G6
Trader Rd EHAM E6 108 B5
Tradescant Rd VX/NE SW8 141 K1
Trading Estate Rd
WLSDN * NW10 98 E3
Trafalgar Av PECK SE15 123 G6
TOTM N17 50 A2
WPK KT4 193 G5
Trafalgar Chambers
CHEL * SW3 120 C5
Trafalgar Gdns KENS * W8 120 A3
WCHPL E1 105 F4
Trafalgar Gv GNWCH SE10 125 G6
Trafalgar Pl UED N18 50 C1
WAN E11 70 E1
Trafalgar Rd DART DA1 171 H4
GNWCH SE10 125 H5
RAIN RM13 111 H1
WHTN TW2 155 J4
WIM/MER SW19 178 A3
Trafalgar Sq CHCR * WC2N 10 D7
Trafalgar St WALW SE17 122 E5
Trafalgar Wy CROY/NA CR0 196 A6
POP/IOD E14 125 F1
Trafford Cl SRTFD E15 87 K3
Trafford Rd THHTH CR7 196 A2
Tramway Av ED N9 36 D2
SRTFD E15 88 B5
Tramway Pth MTCM CR4 194 D1
Tranley Ms HAMP * NW3 83 J2
Tranmere Rd ED N9 36 B2
WAND/EARL SW18 160 B4
WHTN TW2 155 G2
Tranquil Ri ERITH DA8 130 B5
Tranquil V BKHTH/KID SE3 145 H3
Transept St CAMTN NW1 8 D2
Transmere Rd STMC/STPC BR5 201 H3
Transom Sq POP/IOD E14 124 E5
Transport Av BTFD TW8 116 B5
Tranton Rd BERM/RHTH SE16 123 J3
Traps La NWMAL KT3 176 B5
Travellers Site WALTH * E17 51 H3
Travellers Wy HEST TW5 134 B3
Travers Cl WALTH E17 51 F4
Travers Rd HOLWY N7 85 G1
Treacy Cl BUSH WD23 28 C4
Treadgold St NTGHL W11 100 B6
Treadway St BETH E2 104 D1
Treaty St IS N1 5 G1
Trebeck St MYFR/PICC W1J 9 J7
Trebovir Rd ECT SW5 119 K5
Treby St BOW E3 105 H3
Trecastle Wy HOLWY * N7 84 D2
Tredegar Rd BOW E3 105 H1
FBAR/BDGN N11 48 D3
RDART DA2 170 D5
Tredegar Sq BOW E3 105 H2
Trederwen Rd HACK E8 86 C6
Tredown Rd SYD SE26 181 K1
Tredwell Cl HAYES BR2 200 C1
Tredwell Rd WNWD SE27 162 C6
Tree Cl RCHPK/HAM TW10 156 E3
Treen Av BARN SW13 138 B4
Tree Rd CAN/RD E16 107 G5
Treeside Cl WDR/YW UB7 112 A4
Treetops Cl ABYW SE2 129 F5
NTHWD HA6 40 B1
Treetops Vw LOU IG10 39 H1
Tree View Cl NRWD SE19 181 F4
Treewall Gdns BMLY BR1 166 A6
Trefgarne Rd DAGE RM10 74 C6
Trefoil Rd WAND/EARL SW18 140 B6
Tregaron Av CEND/HSY/T N8 66 E4

Tregaron Gdns NWMAL KT3 192 B1
Tregarvon Rd BTSEA SW11 141 F5
Tregenna Av RYLN/HDSTN HA2 78 A2
Tregenna Cl STHGT/OAK N14 22 C6
Tregony Rd ORP BR6 217 F2
Trego Rd HOM E9 87 J5
Tregothnan Rd BRXN/ST SW9 141 K4
Tregunter Rd WBPTN SW10 120 B6
Trehearn Rd BARK/HLT IG6 54 D3
Treherne Ct BRXN/ST * SW9 142 C2
Trehern Rd MORT/ESHN SW14 138 A4
Trehurst St CLPT E5 87 G3
Trelawney Est HOM * E9 86 E4
Trelawney Rd BARK/HLT IG6 54 D3
Trelawn Rd BRXS/STRHM SW2 142 B6
WAN E11 88 A1
Trelawny Cl WALTH E17 69 K1
Treloar Gdns NRWD SE19 180 E2
Trelwney Est HOM * E9 86 E4
Tremadoc Rd CLAP SW4 141 J5
Tremaine Rd PGE/AN SE20 181 J5
Tremlett Gv ARCH N19 84 C1
Tremlett Ms ARCH * N19 84 C1
Trenance Gdns GDMY/SEVK IG3 91 G1
Trenchard Av RSLP HA4 77 F3
Trenchard Cl CDALE/KGS NW9 45 G4
STAN HA7 43 H2
Trenchard St GNWCH SE10 125 G5
Trenchold St VX/NE * SW8 121 K6
Trenear Cl ORP BR6 217 G2
Trenholme Rd PGE/AN SE20 181 J3
Trenholme Ter PGE/AN SE20 181 J3
Trenmar Gdns WLSDN NW10 99 K2
Trent Av EA W5 116 D3
Trentbridge Cl BARK/HLT IG6 55 F2
Trent Ct WAN E11 70 E2
Trent Gdns STHGT/OAK N14 34 B1
Trentham Dr STMC/STPC BR5 202 B1
Trentham St WAND/EARL SW18 159 K3
Trent Pk EBAR * EN4 22 C3
Trent Rd BKHH IG9 39 F3
BRXS/STRHM SW2 142 A6
Trent Wy WPK KT4 208 A1
YEAD UB4 94 C2
Trentwood Side ENC/FH EN2 23 F4
Treport St WAND/EARL SW18 160 A2
Tresco Cl BMLY BR1 183 H2
Trescoe Gdns CRW RM5 56 E1
PIN HA5 59 J4
Tresco Gdns GDMY/SEVK IG3 73 F6
Tresco Rd PECK SE15 143 J5
Tresham Crs STJWD NW8 2 C6
Tresham Rd BARK IG11 91 F5
Tresilian Av WCHMH N21 23 F6
Tressell Cl IS N1 85 H5
Tressillian Crs BROCKY SE4 144 D4
Tressillian Rd BROCKY SE4 144 D4
Trestis Cl YEAD UB4 95 H3
Treswell Rd DAGW RM9 92 A6
Tretawn Gdns MLHL NW7 31 G6
Tretawn Pk MLHL NW7 31 G6
Trevanion Rd WKENS * W14 119 H5
Treve Av HRW HA1 60 C4
Trevelyan Av MNPK E12 89 K2
Trevelyan Cl DART DA1 151 J5
Trevelyan Crs
KTN/HRWW/W HA3 61 K4
Trevelyan Gdns WLSDN * NW10 82 A6
Trevelyan Rd SRTFD E15 88 C2
TOOT SW17 178 E2
Treveris St STHWK SE1 18 B1
Treverton St NKENS W10 100 B3
Treves Cl WCHMH N21 23 F6
Treville St PUT/ROE SW15 158 E2
Treviso Rd FSTH SE23 164 A4
Trevithick Cl EBED/NFELT TW14 153 J3
Trevithick Dr DART DA1 151 J5
Trevithick St DEPT SE8 124 D6
Trevone Gdns PIN HA5 59 J3
Trevor Cl EBAR EN4 33 H1
HAYES BR2 199 J4
ISLW TW7 136 A6
KTN/HRWW/W HA3 43 F5
NTHLT UB5 95 G1
Trevor Crs RSLP HA4 76 D2
Trevor Gdns EDGE HA8 45 F4
Trevor Pl SKENS SW7 14 D3
Trevor Rd EDGE HA8 45 F4
HYS/HAR UB3 113 H2
WFD IG8 52 E3
WIM/MER SW19 177 H3
Trevor Sq SKENS SW7 14 D3
Trevor St SKENS SW7 14 D3
Trevose Rd WALTH E17 52 B4
Trevose Wy OXHEY WD19 27 G5
Trewenna Dr CHSGTN KT9 205 K3
Trewince Rd RYNPK SW20 177 F4
Trewint St WAND/EARL SW18 160 B4
Trewsbury Rd SYD SE26 182 A1
Triandra Wy YEAD UB4 95 H4
The Triangle BFN/LL * DA15 168 B2
NWMAL KT3 175 K5
Triangle Est LBTH * SE11 122 A5
Triangle Pas BAR * EN5 21 G5
Triangle Pl CLAP SW4 141 J5
Triangle Rd HACK E8 86 D6
Trident Pl CHEL * SW3 120 C6
Trident St BERM/RHTH SE16 124 A4
Trident Wy NWDGN UB2 114 A3
Trig La BLKFR EC4V 12 C5
Trigon Rd VX/NE SW8 142 A1
Trilby Rd FSTH SE23 164 A4
Trim St NWCR SE14 124 C6
Trinder Rd ARCH N19 66 E5
BAR EN5 20 A6
Tring Av EA W5 117 G1
STHL UB1 95 K5
WBLY HA9 80 C4
Tring Cl BARK/HLT IG6 72 C2
Trinidad Gdns DAGE RM10 93 F5
Trinidad St POP/IOD E14 105 H6
Trinity Av EFNCH N2 47 H6
EN EN1 36 B1
Trinity Buoy Whf
POP/IOD * E14 106 B4
Trinity Church Rd BARN SW13 118 E6
Trinity Church Sq STHWK SE1 18 E4
Trinity Cl CLAP * SW4 141 H5
HACK * E8 86 B4
HAYES BR2 200 D5
HSLWW TW4 134 D4
LEW SE13 145 G5
NTHWD HA6 40 C2
SAND/SEL CR2 212 A6
WAN E11 70 C6
Trinity Ct ELTH/MOT SE9 167 G1
Trinity Crs TOOT SW17 160 E4
Trinity Gdns BRXN/ST SW9 142 A5
CAN/RD E16 106 D4
DART DA1 171 G1
Trinity Gn WCHPL * E1 104 E4
Trinity Gv GNWCH SE10 145 F2
Trinity Ms PGE/AN * SE20 181 K4
Trinity Pde HSLW * TW3 135 G4
Trinity Pk CHING * E4 51 H2
Trinity Pl BXLYHS DA6 149 G5
Trinity Ri BRXS/STRHM SW2 162 C2
Trinity Rd BARK/HLT IG6 54 C6
EFNCH N2 47 H6
RCH/KEW * TW9 137 G4
STHL UB1 114 D1
TOOT SW17 160 E4
WAND/EARL SW18 160 C1
WDGN N22 48 E3
WIM/MER SW19 177 K2
Trinity Sq TWRH EC3N 13 H6
Trinity St CAN/RD E16 106 D4
ENC/FH EN2 23 J3
STHWK SE1 18 D3
Trinity Wy ACT W3 99 G6
CHING E4 51 H2
Trio Pl STHWK SE1 18 D3
Tristan Sq BKHTH/KID SE3 145 H4
Tristram Cl WALTH E17 52 B6
Tristram Rd BMLY BR1 165 J6
Triton Sq CAMTN NW1 4 A6
Tritton Av CROY/NA CR0 210 E2
Tritton Rd WNWD SE27 162 E5
Triumph Cl HYS/HAR UB3 133 F2
Triumph Rd EHAM E6 107 K5
Trojan Wy CROY/NA CR0 211 F1
Troon Cl BERM/RHTH * SE16 123 J5
Troon St WCHPL E1 105 G5
Trosley Rd BELV DA17 129 H6
Trossachs Rd EDUL SE22 143 F6
Trothy Rd STHWK SE1 123 H4
Trott Rd MUSWH N10 48 A3
Trott St BTSEA SW11 140 C2
Trotwood CHIG IG7 54 D2
Troughton Rd CHARL SE7 126 A5
Troutbeck Rd NWCR SE14 144 B2
Trout Rd WDR/YW UB7 112 A1
Trouville Rd CLAP SW4 161 H1
Trowbridge Rd HOM E9 87 H4
Trowlock Av TEDD TW11 174 D2
Trowlock Island TEDD TW11 174 E2
Trowlock Wy TEDD TW11 174 D2
Troy Ct KENS W8 119 K3
Troy Rd NRWD SE19 180 E2
Troy Town PECK SE15 143 H4
Trubshaw Rd NWDGN UB2 115 F3
Trueman Cl EDGE * HA8 44 D3
Trulock Rd TOTM N17 50 C3
Truman's Rd STNW/STAM N16 86 A3
Trumpers Wy HNWL W7 116 A3
Trumpington Rd FSTGT E7 88 D2
Trump St CITYW EC2V 12 D4
Trundlers Wy BUSH WD23 28 E3
Trundle St STHWK SE1 18 C2
Trundley's Rd DEPT SE8 124 A5
DEPT SE8 124 B6
Trundley's Ter DEPT SE8 124 A4
Truro Gdns IL IG1 71 J4
Truro Rd WALTH E17 69 H1
WDGN N22 48 E3
Truro St KTTN NW5 84 A4
Truro Wy YEAD UB4 94 C2
Trusedale Rd EHAM E6 107 K5
Truslove Rd WNWD SE27 180 B1
Trussley Rd HMSMTH W6 119 F3
Trustons Gdns EMPK RM11 75 J4
Tryfan Cl REDBR IG4 71 H2
Tryon Crs HOM E9 86 E6
Tryon St CHEL SW3 120 E5
Trystings Cl ESH/CLAY KT10 205 G4
Tuam Rd WOOL/PLUM SE18 127 J6
Tubbenden Cl ORP BR6 201 K6
Tubbenden Dr ORP BR6 216 D2
Tubbenden La ORP BR6 216 D2
Tubbenden La South ORP BR6 216 D3
Tubbs Rd WLSDN NW10 99 H1
Tuck Rd RAIN RM13 93 J4
Tudor Av GPK RM2 57 J6
HPTN TW12 173 F2
WPK KT4 207 K1
Tudor Cl ASHF TW15 152 B6
BRXS/STRHM * SW2 162 A1
CDALE/KGS NW9 62 E6
CHEAM SM3 208 B3
CHSGTN KT9 206 A3
CHST BR7 184 E4
DART DA1 170 E1
HAMP NW3 83 J3
HGT N6 66 C4
HPTN TW12 173 H1
MLHL NW7 45 J2
PIN HA5 58 E2
WFD IG8 53 F1
WLGTN SM6 210 C5
Tudor Ct ELTH/MOT * SE9 146 D5
SWLY BR8 203 K4
WALTH E17 69 H4
Tudor Ct North WBLY HA9 80 C3
Tudor Ct South WBLY HA9 80 C3
Tudor Crs BARK/HLT IG6 54 C2
ENC/FH EN2 23 J2
Tudor Dr GPK RM2 75 J1
KUTN/CMB KT2 175 F1
MRDN SM4 193 G3
WOT/HER KT12 188 C5
Tudor Est WLSDN * NW10 98 D1
Tudor Gdns ACT W3 98 C5
BARN SW13 138 B4
CDALE/KGS NW9 62 E6
GPK RM2 75 J1
TWK TW1 156 A3
WWKM BR4 214 A1
Tudor Gv HOM E9 86 E5
Tudor Pde ELTH/MOT * SE9 146 D5
Tudor Pl NRWD * SE19 181 G3
WIM/MER SW19 178 D3
Tudor Rd BAR EN5 20 E4
BARK IG11 91 F5
BECK BR3 183 F6
CHING E4 51 K2
ED N9 36 D2
EHAM E6 89 G6
HACK E8 86 D6
HPTN TW12 173 F3
HSLW TW3 135 J5
HYS/HAR UB3 94 B5
KTN/HRWW/W HA3 42 D5
KUTN/CMB KT2 175 H3
NRWD SE19 181 G3
PIN HA5 41 G5
SNWD SE25 197 J2
STHL UB1 95 J6
Tudor Sq HYS/HAR UB3 94 B4
Tudor St EMB EC4Y 11 K5
Tudor Wy ACT W3 117 H2
STHGT/OAK N14 34 D3
STMC/STPC BR5 201 J3
Tudor Well Cl STAN HA7 43 H1
Tudway Rd BKHTH/KID SE3 146 B5
Tufnail Rd DART DA1 171 J1
Tufnell Park Rd HOLWY N7 84 D2
Tufter Rd CHIG IG7 55 F1
Tufton Gdns E/WMO/HCT KT8 173 G5
Tufton Rd CHING E4 37 J6
Tufton St WEST SW1P 16 E5
Tugboat St THMD SE28 127 K2
Tugela Rd CROY/NA CR0 196 E3
Tugela St CAT SE6 164 C4
Tugmutton Cl ORP BR6 216 B2
Tulip Cl CROY/NA CR0 198 A5
EHAM E6 107 K4
HPTN TW12 172 E2
NWDGN UB2 115 H2
Tulip Gdns CHING * E4 38 B5
IL IG1 90 B4
Tulip Wy WDR/YW UB7 112 A4
Tull St MTCM CR4 194 E4
Tulse Cl BECK BR3 183 F6
Tulse Hl BRXS/STRHM SW2 162 B2
Tulsemere Rd WNWD SE27 162 D4
Tummons Gdns SNWD SE25 181 F5
Tuncombe Rd UED N18 36 A6
Tunis Rd SHB W12 119 F1
Tunley Rd BAL SW12 161 F4
WLSDN NW10 81 G6
Tunmarsh La PLSTW E13 107 G2
Tunnan Leys EHAM E6 108 A5
Tunnel Av GNWCH SE10 125 G2
Tunnel Gdns FBAR/BDGN N11 48 C3
Tunnel Link Rd HTHAIR TW6 132 D6
Tunnel Rd BERM/RHTH SE16 123 K2
Tunnel Rd East WDR/YW UB7 132 E1
Tunnel Rd West WDR/YW UB7 132 D2
Tunstall Av BARK/HLT IG6 55 G2
Tunstall Cl ORP BR6 216 E2
Tunstall Rd BRXN/ST SW9 142 A5
CROY/NA CR0 197 F5
Tunstock Wy BELV DA17 129 F3
Tunworth Cl CDALE/KGS NW9 62 E3
Tunworth Crs PUT/ROE SW15 158 C1
Tupelo Rd LEY E10 69 K6
Turene Cl BTSEA SW11 140 B5
Turin Rd ED N9 36 E2
Turin St BETH E2 104 C2
Turkey Oak Cl NRWD SE19 181 F4
Turks Rw CHEL SW3 120 E5
Turle Rd FSBYPK * N4 67 F6
STRHM/NOR SW16 179 K5
Turlewray Cl FSBYPK N4 67 F5
Turley Cl SRTFD E15 88 C6
Turnagain La STP * EC4M 12 A3
Turnage Rd BCTR RM8 74 A5
Turnant Rd TOTM N17 49 J4
Turnberry Cl
BERM/RHTH * SE16 123 J5
Turnberry Ct OXHEY * WD19 27 G5
Turnberry Wy ORP BR6 201 J5
Turnbury Cl THMD SE28 109 K5
Turner Av MTCM CR4 178 E4
SEVS/STOTM N15 68 A1
WHTN TW2 155 H5
Turner Cl ALP/SUD HA0 79 K3
CMBW SE5 142 C2
GLDGN NW11 65 F3
Turner Ct CMBW * SE5 142 E5
DART DA1 151 F6
Turner Dr GLDGN NW11 65 F3
Turner Rd EDGE HA8 44 A5
NWMAL KT3 192 A4
WALTH E17 70 A1
Turners Meadow Wy BECK BR3 182 C4
Turner's Rd POP/IOD E14 105 H4
Turner St CAN/RD E16 106 D5
WCHPL E1 104 D4
Turners Wy CROY/NA CR0 196 B6
Turner's Wd GLDGN NW11 65 G5
Turneville Rd WKENS W14 119 J6
Turney Rd DUL SE21 162 D2
Turnham Green Ter CHSWK W4 118 B4
Turnham Rd BROCKY SE4 144 B6
Turnmill St FARR EC1M 5 K7
Turnpike Cl DEPT SE8 144 C1
Turnpike Dr ORP BR6 217 J6
Turnpike La CEND/HSY/T N8 67 G1
SUT SM1 209 G3
Turnpike Link CROY/NA CR0 197 F6
Turnpike Ms CEND/HSY/T * N8 49 G6
Turnpike Pde CEND/HSY/T * N8 49 H6
Turnpike Wy ISLW TW7 136 B2
Turnstone Cl CDALE/KGS * NW9 45 G5
PLSTW E13 106 E2
Turnstone Ter WEA * W13 97 F3
Turpentine La PIM SW1V 121 G5
Turpin Av CRW RM5 56 C3
Turpington Cl HAYES BR2 200 D3
Turpington La HAYES BR2 200 D2
Turpin La ERITH DA8 130 D6
Turpin Rd EBED/NFELT TW14 153 J1
Turpin's La WFD IG8 53 K1
Turpins Yd CRICK * NW2 63 K6
Turpin Wy WLGTN SM6 210 B5
Turquand St WALW SE17 18 D7
Turret Gv CLAP SW4 141 H4
Turton Rd ALP/SUD HA0 80 A3
Turville St BETH * E2 7 J6
Tuscan Rd WOOL/PLUM SE18 127 J5
Tuskar St GNWCH SE10 125 H5
Tweeddale Gv HGDN/ICK UB10 76 A1
Tweeddale Rd CAR SM5 194 C5
Tweedmouth Rd PLSTW E13 107 F1
Tweed Wy ROM RM1 57 F3
Tweedy Rd BMLY BR1 183 K4
Twelvetrees Crs BOW E3 106 A3
Twentyman Cl WFD IG8 52 E1
Twickenham Br TWK TW1 136 E6
Twickenham Cl CROY/NA CR0 211 F1
Twickenham Gdns GFD/PVL UB6 79 G3
KTN/HRWW/W HA3 42 E3
Twickenham Rd FELT TW13 154 D6
ISLW TW7 136 A6
TEDD TW11 156 B6
WAN E11 70 B6
Twig Folly Cl BOW E3 105 F1
Twig Folly Whf BETH * E2 105 F1
Twigg Cl ERITH DA8 150 B1
Twilley St WAND/EARL SW18 160 A2
Twine Cl BARK IG11 109 H2
Twine Ct WCHPL E1 104 E6
Twineham Gn NFNCH/WDSP N12 32 E6
Twine Ter BOW * E3 105 H3
Twining Av WHTN TW2 155 H5
Twinn Rd MLHL NW7 46 C2
Twisden Rd KTTN NW5 84 B2
Twisleton Ct DART DA1 171 G1
Twybridge Wy WLSDN NW10 80 E5
Twyford Abbey Rd
WLSDN NW10 98 B2
Twyford Av ACT W3 98 C6
EFNCH N2 47 K6
Twyford Crs ACT W3 117 H1
Twyford Rd CAR SM5 194 C5
IL IG1 90 C3
RYLN/HDSTN HA2 60 B4
Twyford St IS N1 85 F6
Tyas Rd CAN/RD E16 106 D3
Tybenham Rd WIM/MER SW19 177 K6
Tyberry Rd PEND EN3 24 D4
Tyburn La HRW HA1 60 E4
Tyburn Wy MBLAR W1H 9 F5
Tye La ORP BR6 216 C3
Tyers Ga STHWK SE1 19 G3
Tyers St LBTH SE11 122 A5
Tyers Ter LBTH SE11 122 A5
Tyeshurst Cl ABYW SE2 129 F5
Tylecroft Rd STRHM/NOR SW16 179 K5
Tylehurst Gdns IL IG1 90 C3
Tyler Cl BETH E2 7 J2
Tylers Ga KTN/HRWW/W HA3 62 A3
Tylers Green Rd SWLY BR8 203 K3
Tyler St GNWCH SE10 125 H5
Tylney Av NRWD SE19 181 G1
Tylney Rd BMLY BR1 184 C5
FSTGT E7 89 G2
Tynan Cl EBED/NFELT TW14 153 K3
Tyndale La IS N1 85 H5
Tyndale Ter IS N1 85 H5
Tyndall Rd LEY E10 70 A6
WELL DA16 148 A4
Tyneham Cl BTSEA * SW11 141 F4
Tyneham Rd BTSEA SW11 141 F3
Tynemouth Cl EHAM E6 108 B5
Tynemouth Dr EN EN1 24 C1
Tynemouth Rd MTCM CR4 179 F3
SEVS/STOTM N15 68 B1
WOOL/PLUM SE18 127 K5
Tynemouth St FUL/PGN SW6 140 B3
Tynemouth Ter
SEVS/STOTM * N15 68 B1
Type St WCHPL E1 13 K3
Tynsdale Rd WLSDN NW10 81 G4
Type St BETH E2 105 F1
Tyrawley Rd FUL/PGN SW6 140 A2
Tyre La CDALE/KGS * NW9 63 G1
Tyrell Cl HRW HA1 78 E2
Tyrone Rd EHAM E6 107 K1
Tyron Wy SCUP DA14 167 K6
Tyrrell Av WELL DA16 148 B6
Tyrrell Rd EDUL SE22 143 H5
Tyrrel Wy CDALE/KGS NW9 63 H4
Tyrwhitt Rd LEW SE13 144 D4
Tysoe St CLKNW EC1R 5 J5
CLKNW EC1R 6 A6
Tyson Gdns FSTH * SE23 163 K2
Tyson Rd FSTH SE23 163 K2
Tyssen Rd STNW/STAM * N16 86 B1
Tyssen St HACK E8 86 B4
Tytherton Rd ARCH N19 84 D1

U

Uamvar St POP/IOD E14 105 K4
Uckfield Gv MTCM CR4 179 F4
Udall Gdns CRW RM5 56 C2
Udall St WEST SW1P 16 B7
Udney Park Rd TEDD TW11 174 B1
Uffington Rd WLSDN NW10 81 J6
WNWD SE27 162 B6
Ufford Cl KTN/HRWW/W HA3 42 B3
Ufford Rd KTN/HRWW/W HA3 42 B3
Ufford St STHWK SE1 17 K2
Ufton Rd IS N1 86 A5
Uhura Sq STNW/STAM * N16 86 A1
Ullathorne Rd STRHM/NOR SW16 161 H6
Ulleswater Rd PLMGR N13 34 E6
Ulleswater Vls PLMGR * N13 34 E6
Ullin St POP/IOD E14 106 A4
Ullswater Cl BMLY BR1 183 H2
KUTN/CMB * KT2 158 A6
YEAD UB4 94 C1
Ullswater Ct RYLN/HDSTN * HA2 60 A4
Ullswater Crs PUT/ROE SW15 158 A6
Ullswater Rd BARN SW13 138 D1
WNWD SE27 162 C5
Ullswater Wy HCH RM12 93 J3
Ulster Gdns PLMGR N13 35 J6
Ulster Pl CAMTN NW1 3 J7
Ulundi Rd BKHTH/KID SE3 125 H6
Ulva Rd PUT/ROE SW15 139 G5
Ulverscroft Rd EDUL SE22 143 H6
Ulverston Rd WALTH E17 52 B5
Ulysses Rd KIL/WHAMP NW6 82 D3
Umberston St WCHPL * E1 104 C5
Umbria St PUT/ROE SW15 158 D1
Umfreville Rd FSBYPK N4 67 H3
Undercliff Rd LEW SE13 144 D4
Underhill BAR EN5 20 E6
Underhill Ct BAR * EN5 20 E6
Underhill Rd EDUL SE22 143 H6
Underhill St CAMTN NW1 3 K1
Underne Av STHGT/OAK N14 34 B4
Undershaft HDTCH EC3A 13 G4
Undershaw Rd BMLY BR1 165 H5
The Underwood ELTH/MOT SE9 166 E4
Underwood Rd CHING E4 51 K1
WCHPL E1 104 C3
WFD IG8 53 H3
Underwood Rw IS N1 6 D4
Underwood St IS N1 6 D4
Undine Rd POP/IOD E14 124 E4
Undine St TOOT SW17 178 E1
Uneeda Dr GFD/PVL UB6 78 D6
Union Cl WAN E11 88 B2
Union Ct CLAP SW4 141 K3
Union Dr WCHPL * E1 105 G3
Union Gv VX/NE SW8 141 J3
Union Rd ALP/SUD HA0 80 A4
CLAP SW4 141 J3
CROY/NA CR0 196 D4
FBAR/BDGN N11 48 D2
HAYES BR2 200 C2
NTHLT UB5 96 A1
Union Sq IS N1 6 C1
Union St BAR EN5 20 C5
KUT KT1 174 E5
SRTFD E15 88 B6
STHWK SE1 18 B1
Union Wk BETH E2 7 J4
Unity Cl CROY/NA CR0 213 K6
WLSDN NW10 81 J4
WNWD SE27 180 D1
Unity Ms CAMTN NW1 4 C2
Unity Wy WOOL/PLUM SE18 126 C3
University Cl CDALE/KGS NW9 45 H3
University Gdns BXLY DA5 169 G2
University Rd WIM/MER SW19 178 C2
University St FITZ W1T 4 B7
University Wy DART DA1 151 K5
EHAM E6 108 A6
Unwin Av EBED/NFELT TW14 133 G6
Unwin Cl PECK SE15 123 H6
Unwin Rd ISLW TW7 135 K4
SKENS SW7 14 B4
Upbrook Ms BAY/PAD W2 101 G5
Upcerne Rd WBPTN SW10 140 B1
Upcroft Av EDGE HA8 44 E1
Updale Rd SCUP DA14 168 A6
Upfield CROY/NA CR0 197 J6
Upfield Rd HNWL W7 97 F3
Uphall Rd IL IG1 90 B3
Upham Park Rd CHSWK W4 118 B4
Uphill Dr CDALE/KGS NW9 62 E2
MLHL NW7 45 G1
Uphill Gv MLHL NW7 31 G6
Uphill Rd MLHL NW7 31 G6
Upland Rd BELMT SM2 209 H5
BXLYHN DA7 149 G4
EDUL SE22 143 H6
PLSTW E13 106 E3
SAND/SEL CR2 211 K3
The Uplands RSLP HA4 58 E5
Uplands BECK BR3 182 D5
Uplands Av WALTH E17 51 F6
Uplands Cl MORT/ESHN SW14 137 J6
Uplands Park Rd ENC/FH EN2 23 G3
Uplands Rd CEND/HSY/T N8 67 F2
CHDH RM6 55 K6
EBAR EN4 34 A3
ORP BR6 202 C5
WFD IG8 53 J3
Uplands Wy WCHMH N21 23 G6
Upminster Rd South
RAIN RM13 111 J3
Upney La BARK IG11 91 F5
Upnor Wy WALW SE17 123 F5
Uppark Dr GNTH/NBYPK IG2 72 C3
Upper Abbey Rd BELV DA17 129 G4
Upper Addison Gdns
WKENS W14 119 H2
Upper Bardsey Wk IS * N1 85 J4
Upper Belgrave St KTBR SW1X 15 H4
Upper Berenger Wk
WBPTN * SW10 140 C1
Upper Berkeley St BAY/PAD W2 8 E4
Upper Beulah Hl NRWD SE19 181 F4
Upper Blantyre Wk
WBPTN * SW10 140 C1
Upper Brighton Rd SURB KT6 190 E3
Upper Brockley Rd BROCKY SE4 144 C4
Upper Brook St
MYFR/PKLN W1K 9 G5
Upper Butts BTFD TW8 116 D6
Upper Caldy Wk IS * N1 85 J4
Upper Camelford Wk
NTGHL * W11 100 C5
Upper Cheyne Rw CHEL SW3 120 D6
Upper Clapton Rd CLPT E5 68 D6
Upper Clarendon Wk
NTGHL * W11 100 C5
Upper Dartrey Wk
WBPTN * SW10 140 B1
Upper Dengie Wk IS * N1 85 J6
Upper Elmers End Rd
BECK BR3 198 B1
Upper Farm Rd
E/WMO/HCT KT8 188 E1
Upper Gn East MTCM CR4 178 E6
Upper Gn West MTCM CR4 178 E5
Upper Grosvenor St
MYFR/PKLN W1K 9 G6
Upper Grotto Rd TWK TW1 156 A4
Upper Gnd STHWK SE1 11 J7
Upper Gv SNWD SE25 197 F1
Upper Grove Rd BELV DA17 129 G6
Upper Gulland Wk IS * N1 85 J4
Upper Ham Rd
RCHPK/HAM TW10 156 E6
Upper Handa Wk IS * N1 85 K4
Upper Harley St CAMTN NW1 3 H7
Upper Hawkwell Wk IS * N1 85 J6
Upper Hitch OXHEY WD19 27 J3
Upper Holly Hill Rd BELV DA17 129 J5
Upper John St REGST W1B 10 B5
Upper Lismore Wk IS * N1 85 J4
Upper Ldg KENS * W8 120 A1
Upper Ml HMSMTH W6 118 D5
Upper Marsh STHWK SE1 17 H4
Upper Montagu St MBLAR W1H 8 E1
Upper Mulgrave Rd BELMT SM2 208 C5
Upper North St POP/IOD E14 105 J4
Upper Paddock Rd OXHEY WD19 27 J1
Upper Park Rd BELV DA17 129 J4
BMLY BR1 184 A4
FBAR/BDGN N11 48 B1
HAMP NW3 83 K4
KUTN/CMB KT2 175 H2
Upper Phillimore Gdns
KENS * W8 119 K2
Upper Rainham Rd HCH RM12 75 H5
Upper Ramsey Wk IS N1 85 K4
Upper Rawreth Wk IS * N1 85 J6
Upper Richmond Rd
PUT/ROE SW15 138 E5
Upper Richmond Rd West
RCHPK/HAM TW10 137 H5
Upper Rd PLSTW E13 106 E2
WLGTN SM6 210 D3
Upper St Martin's La
LSQ/SEVD WC2H 10 E4
Upper Selsdon Rd
SAND/SEL CR2 212 B6
Upper Sheppey Wk IS N1 85 J4
Upper Sheridan Rd BELV DA17 129 H4
Upper Shirley Rd CROY/NA CR0 212 E1
Upper Sq ISLW TW7 136 B4
Upper St IS N1 5 K3
Upper Sunbury Rd HPTN TW12 172 E4
Upper Sutton La HEST TW5 135 F2

Upper Tachbrook St PIM SW1V 16 B6
Upper Tail OXHEY WD19 27 J5
Upper Talbot Wk NTGHL * W11 100 C5
Upper Teddington Rd KUT KT1 174 D4
Upper Ter HAMP NW3 83 G1
Upper Thames St BLKFR EC4V 12 C5
Upper Tollington Pk FSBYPK N4 67 G5
Upperton Rd SCUP DA14 186 A1
Upperton Rd East PLSTW E13 107 G2
Upperton Rd West PLSTW E13 107 G2
Upper Tooting Pk TOOT SW17 160 E4
Upper Tooting Rd TOOT SW17 160 E6
Upper Town Rd GFD/PVL UB6 96 B3
Upper Tulse Hl
BRXS/STRHM SW2 162 A2
Upper Vernon Rd SUT SM1 209 H3
Upper Walthamstow Rd
WALTH E17 70 B1
Upper Whistler Wk
WBPTN * SW10 140 B1
Upper Wickham La WELL DA16 148 C3
Upper Wimpole St
CAVSQ/HST W1G 9 H1
Upper Woburn Pl CAMTN NW1 4 D5
Uppingham Av STAN HA7 43 J6
Upsdell Av PLMGR N13 49 G2
Upstall St CMBW SE5 142 C2
Upton Av FSTGT E7 88 E5
Upton Cl BXLY DA5 169 G1
Upton Dene BELMT SM2 209 F5
Upton Gdns KTN/HRWW/W HA3 61 J3
Upton La FSTGT E7 89 F4
Upton Lodge Cl BUSH WD23 28 C2
Upton Park Rd FSTGT E7 89 F5
Upton Rd BXLYHS DA6 149 F5
HSLW TW3 135 F4
THHTH CR7 180 E5
UED N18 50 C1
WOOL/PLUM SE18 127 H6
Upton Rd South BXLY DA5 169 G1
Upway NFNCH/WDSP N12 47 J3
Upwood Rd LEE/GVPK SE12 165 K1
STRHM/NOR SW16 179 K4
Urlwin St CMBW SE5 122 D6
Urlwin Wk BRXN/ST SW9 142 B2
Urmston Dr WIM/MER SW19 159 H3
Ursula Ms FSBYPK N4 67 H5
Ursula St BTSEA SW11 140 D2
Urswick Rd CLPT E5 86 E3
DAGW RM9 92 A5
Usborne Ms VX/NE SW8 142 A1
Usher Rd BOW E3 87 H6
Usk Rd BTSEA SW11 140 B5
Usk St BETH E2 105 F2
Uvedale Rd DAGE RM10 92 C1
ENC/FH EN2 23 K6
Uverdale Rd WBPTN SW10 140 B1
Uxbridge Rd EA W5 98 A6
FELT TW13 154 C4
HGDN/ICK UB10 94 A3
HPTN TW12 155 F6
SHB W12 118 D1
STHL UB1 115 F1
SURB KT6 190 E1
WEA W13 116 C1
Uxbridge Rd (Harrow Weald)
KTN/HRWW/W HA3 42 B3
Uxbridge Rd (Hatch End)
PIN HA5 41 J4
Uxbridge Rd (High St)
STHL UB1 114 E1
Uxbridge Rd (Pinner) PIN HA5 41 H5
Uxbridge Rd (Stanmore)
STAN HA7 43 F2
Uxbridge Rd (The Broadway)
YEAD UB4 95 H6
Uxbridge St KENS W8 119 K1
Uxendon Crs WBLY HA9 62 A5
Uxendon Hl WBLY HA9 62 B5

V

Valance Av CHING E4 38 D3
Valan Leas HAYES BR2 183 H6
Vale Cl EFNCH N2 47 K6
MV/WKIL W9 101 G2
ORP BR6 216 A2
TWK * TW1 156 B5
Vale Cottages PUT/ROE * SW15 158 B5
Vale Ct ACT * W3 118 C1
Vale Crs PUT/ROE SW15 158 B6
Vale Cft ESH/CLAY KT10 205 F5
PIN HA5 59 J2
Vale Dr BAR EN5 20 D5
Vale End EDUL SE22 143 G5
Vale Gv ACT W3 118 A1
FSBYPK N4 67 J4
Vale La ACT W3 98 C4
Valence Av BCTR RM8 73 K5
Valence Circ BCTR RM8 91 K1
Valence Rd ERITH DA8 150 A1
Valence Wood Rd BCTR RM8 91 K1
Valencia Rd STAN HA7 29 J6
Valency Cl NTHWD HA6 26 D6
Valentia Pl BRXN/ST SW9 142 B5
Valentine Av BXLY DA5 169 F4
Valentine Pl STHWK SE1 18 A2
Valentine Rd HOM * E9 87 F4
RYLN/HDSTN HA2 78 B1
Valentines Rd IL IG1 72 B5
Valentines Wy DAGE RM10 75 G6
Vale of Health HAMP NW3 83 G1
Valerian Wy SRTFD E15 106 C2
The Vale ACT W3 118 A1
CHEL SW3 120 C6
CRICK NW2 82 B1
CROY/NA CR0 198 A6
EBED/NFELT TW14 154 A1
GLDGN NW11 64 D5
HEST TW5 114 D6
MUSWH N10 48 A4
RSLP HA4 77 G2
STHGT/OAK N14 34 E2
WFD IG8 52 E3
Vale Ri GLDGN NW11 64 D5
Vale Rd BMLY BR1 185 F5
DART DA1 170 E3
ESH/CLAY KT10 204 E6
FSBYPK N4 67 J4
FSTGT E7 89 F4
MTCM CR4 179 J6
SUT SM1 209 F2
WPK KT4 207 H1
Vale Rd North SURB KT6 191 F6
Vale Royal HOLWY N7 84 E5
Valeswood Rd BMLY BR1 183 J1
Vale Ter FSBYPK N4 67 J3
Valetta Gv PLSTW E13 106 E1
Valetta Rd ACT W3 118 B2
Valette St HACK * E8 86 D4
Valiant Cl NTHLT UB5 95 H2
ROMW/RG RM7 56 C5
Valiant Wy EHAM E6 107 K4
Vallance Rd WCHPL E1 104 C3
WDGN N22 48 C5
Vallentin Rd WALTH E17 70 A1
Valley Av NFNCH/WDSP N12 33 H6
Valley Cl DART DA1 170 C1
LOU IG10 39 K1
PIN HA5 41 F5
Valley Dr CDALE/KGS NW9 62 D2
Valleyfield Rd
STRHM/NOR SW16 180 A1
Valley Fields Crs ENC/FH EN2 23 G3
Valley Gdns ALP/SUD HA0 80 B5
WIM/MER SW19 178 C3
Valley Gv CHARL SE7 126 B5
Valley Hl LOU IG10 39 J2
Valley Pk WATW * WD18 26 A2
Valley Rd DART DA1 170 C1
ERITH DA8 129 K4
HAYES BR2 183 H5
STMC/STPC BR5 186 C4
STRHM/NOR SW16 162 A6
Valley Side CHING E4 37 J3
Valley Vw BAR EN5 32 C1
Valley Wk CROY/NA CR0 197 K6
Valliere Rd WLSDN NW10 99 J2
Valliers Wood Rd BFN/LL DA15 167 K3
Vallis Wy CHSGTN KT9 205 K2
WEA W13 97 G4
Valmar Rd CMBW SE5 142 D2
Valnay St TOOT SW17 178 E1
Valognes Av WALTH E17 51 G4
Valonia Gdns WAND/EARL SW18 159 J1
Vambery Rd WOOL/PLUM SE18 127 H6
Vanbrough Crs NTHLT UB5 95 G1
Vanbrugh Dr WOT/HER KT12 188 B4
Vanbrugh Flds BKHTH/KID SE3 125 J6
Vanbrugh Hl GNWCH SE10 125 H5
Vanbrugh Pk BKHTH/KID SE3 145 K1
Vanbrugh Park Rd
BKHTH/KID SE3 145 J1
Vanbrugh Park Rd West
BKHTH/KID SE3 145 J1
Vanbrugh Rd CHSWK W4 118 A3
Vanbrugh Ter BKHTH/KID SE3 145 J2
Vanburgh Cl CAN/RD E16 107 H4
ORP BR6 201 K5
Vancouver Cl ORP BR6 217 G2
Vancouver Man EDGE * HA8 44 D4
Vancouver Rd EDGE HA8 44 D4
FSTH SE23 164 B4
RCHPK/HAM TW10 156 D6
YEAD UB4 95 F3
Vanderbilt Rd
WAND/EARL SW18 160 A3
Vanderbilt Vls SHB * W12 119 G2
Vandome Cl CAN/RD E16 107 F5
Vandon St STJSPK SW1H 16 B4
Van Dyck Av NWMAL KT3 192 A4
Vandyke Cl PUT/ROE SW15 159 G1
Vandyke Cross ELTH/MOT SE9 146 D6
Vandy St SDTCH EC2A 7 G7
Vane Cl HAMP NW3 83 H3
KTN/HRWW/W HA3 62 B3
Vanessa Cl BELV DA17 129 H5
Vanessa Wy BXLY DA5 170 A5
Vanguard CDALE/KGS * NW9 45 G3
Vanguard Cl CAN/RD E16 106 E4
CROY/NA CR0 196 C5
ROMW/RG RM7 56 E4
Vanguard St DEPT SE8 144 D2
Vanguard Wy CROY/NA CR0 212 B2
HTHAIR TW6 133 H3
WLGTN SM6 210 E5
Vanneck Sq PUT/ROE * SW15 138 D6
Vanoc Gdns BMLY BR1 165 K6
Vansittart Rd FSTGT E7 88 E2
Vansittart St NWCR SE14 144 B1
Vanston Pl FUL/PGN SW6 139 K1
Vantage Pl KENS W8 119 K3
Vant Rd TOOT SW17 178 E1
Varcoe Rd BERM/RHTH SE16 123 J5
Vardens Rd BTSEA SW11 140 C5
Varden St WCHPL E1 104 D5
Varley Rd CAN/RD E16 107 F5
Varley Wy MTCM CR4 178 C5
Varna Rd FUL/PGN SW6 139 H1
HPTN * TW12 173 G4
Varndell St CAMTN NW1 4 A4
Varsity Dr WHTN TW2 135 K6
Varsity Rw MORT/ESHN SW14 137 K3
Vartry Rd SEVS/STOTM N15 68 A3
Vassall Rd BRXN/ST SW9 142 B1
Vauban Est BERM/RHTH SE16 19 K5
Vauban St BERM/RHTH SE16 19 K5
Vaughan Av HDN NW4 63 J2
HMSMTH W6 118 C4
Vaughan Est BETH * E2 7 J4
Vaughan Gdns IL IG1 71 K4
Vaughan Rd CMBW SE5 142 D3
HRW HA1 60 C4
SRTFD E15 88 D4
THDIT KT7 190 C4
WELL DA16 148 A3
Vaughan St BERM/RHTH SE16 124 C2
Vaughan Wy WAP E1W 104 C6
Vaughan Williams Cl DEPT SE8 144 D1
Vauxhall Br VX/NE SW8 121 K5
Vauxhall Bridge Rd PIM SW1V 16 A5
Vauxhall Gdns SAND/SEL CR2 211 J4
Vauxhall Gv VX/NE SW8 122 A6
Vauxhall Pl DART DA1 171 H2
Vauxhall St LBTH SE11 122 A5
Vauxhall Wk LBTH SE11 122 A5
Vawdrey Cl WCHPL E1 104 E3
Veals Md MTCM CR4 178 D4
Vectis Gdns TOOT SW17 179 G2
Vectis Rd TOOT SW17 179 G2
Veda Rd LEW SE13 144 D5
Vega Crs NTHWD HA6 40 D1
Vega Rd BUSH WD23 28 C2
Veldene Wy RYLN/HDSTN HA2 77 K1
Vellum Dr CAR SM5 210 A1
Venables Cl DAGE RM10 92 D2
Venables St STJWD NW8 2 B7
Vencourt Pl HMSMTH W6 118 D5
Venetian Rd CMBW SE5 142 D3
Venetia Rd EA W5 116 E2
FSBYPK N4 67 H3
Venette Cl RAIN RM13 111 K4
Venner Rd SYD SE26 181 K2
Venners Cl BXLYHN DA7 150 B3
Venn St CLAP SW4 141 H5
Ventnor Av STAN HA7 43 H4
Ventnor Dr NFNCH/WDSP N12 33 F5
Ventnor Gdns BARK IG11 90 E4
Ventnor Rd BELMT SM2 209 F5
NWCR SE14 144 A1
Ventnor Ter SEVS/STOTM * N15 68 C1
Venture Cl BXLY DA5 169 F2
Venue St POP/IOD E14 105 K4
Venus Rd WOOL/PLUM SE18 126 E3
Vera Av WCHMH N21 23 G6
Vera Ct OXHEY WD19 27 H2
Vera Lynn Cl FSTGT E7 88 E2
Vera Rd FUL/PGN SW6 139 H2
Verbena Cl CAN/RD E16 106 D3
WDR/YW UB7 112 A5
Verbena Gdns HMSMTH W6 118 D5
Verdant La CAT SE6 165 H3
Verdayne Av CROY/NA CR0 198 A5
Verderers Rd CHIG IG7 55 G1
Verdun Rd BARN SW13 138 D1
WOOL/PLUM SE18 128 B6
Vereker Rd WKENS * W14 119 H5
Vere St MHST W1U 9 J4
Vermont Cl ENC/FH EN2 23 H5
Vermont Rd NRWD SE19 180 E2
SUT SM1 209 F1
WAND/EARL SW18 160 A1
Verney Gdns DAGW RM9 92 A2
Verney Rd BERM/RHTH SE16 123 J5
DAGW RM9 92 A3
Verney St WLSDN NW10 81 F1
Verney Wy BERM/RHTH SE16 123 J5
Vernham Rd WOOL/PLUM SE18 127 H6
Vernon Av MNPK E12 89 K2
RYNPK SW20 177 G5
WFD IG8 53 F2
Vernon Cl HOR/WEW KT19 206 E4
STMC/STPC BR5 186 C6
Vernon Crs EBAR EN4 22 A6
Vernon Dr STAN HA7 43 G4
Vernon Pl BMSBY WC1N 11 F2
Vernon Ri FSBYW WC1X 5 H4
GFD/PVL UB6 78 D3
Vernon Rd BOW E3 105 H1
CEND/HSY/T * N8 49 G6
CRW RM5 56 E1
FELT TW13 153 J4
GDMY/SEVK IG3 73 F5
MORT/ESHN SW14 138 A4
SRTFD E15 88 C5
SUT SM1 209 G3
WALTH E17 69 H1
WAN E11 70 C5
Vernon Sq FSBYW * WC1X 5 H4
Vernon St WKENS W14 119 H4
Vernon Yd NTGHL W11 100 D6
Veroan Rd BXLYHN DA7 149 F3
Verona Dr SURB KT6 191 F6
Veronica Gdns MTCM CR4 179 H4
Veronica Rd TOOT SW17 161 G5
Veronique Gdns
GNTH/NBYPK IG2 72 C2
Verran Rd BAL * SW12 161 G2
Versailles Rd PGE/AN SE20 181 H3
Verulam Av WALTH E17 69 H4
Verulam Ct CDALE/KGS * NW9 63 J4
Verulam Rd GFD/PVL UB6 96 A3
Verulam St FSBYW WC1X 11 J1
Verwood Dr EBAR EN4 21 K4
Verwood Rd RYLN/HDSTN HA2 42 C5
Veryan Cl STMC/STPC BR5 202 D1
Vesey Pth POP/IOD E14 105 K5
Vespan Rd SHB W12 118 D2
Vesta Rd BROCKY SE4 144 B3
Vestris Rd FSTH SE23 164 A4
Vestry Rd CMBW SE5 143 F2
WALTH E17 69 K2
Vestry St IS N1 6 E4
Vevey St FSTH SE23 164 C4
The Viaduct MUSWH * N10 66 B1
SWFD E18 52 E5
Viaduct Pl BETH E2 104 D2
Viaduct Rd EFNCH N2 47 H5
Viaduct St BETH E2 104 D2
Vian St LEW SE13 144 E4
Vibart Gdns BRXS/STRHM SW2 162 A2
Vibart Wk IS * N1 84 E6
Vibia Cl STWL/WRAY TW19 152 A2
Vicarage Cl ERITH DA8 129 K6
NTHLT UB5 77 K6
RSLP HA4 58 B4
WPK KT4 192 B5
Vicarage Ct BECK * BR3 182 B6
Vicarage Crs BTSEA SW11 140 C2
Vicarage Dr BARK IG11 90 C5
BECK BR3 182 D4
MORT/ESHN SW14 138 A6
Vicarage Farm Rd HEST TW5 134 D2
Vicarage Flds WOT/HER KT12 188 B3
Vicarage Gdns MTCM CR4 178 D6
Vicarage Ga KENS W8 120 A2
Vicarage Gv CMBW SE5 142 E2
Vicarage La EHAM E6 107 K2
IL IG1 72 D5
SRTFD E15 88 C4
Vicarage Ms CHSWK * W4 118 B6
Vicarage Pde SEVS/STOTM * N15 67 J1
Vicarage Pk WOOL/PLUM SE18 127 H5
Vicarage Rd BXLY DA5 169 J3
CROY/NA CR0 211 G1
DAGE RM10 92 D5
E/WMO/HCT KT8 174 D4
EMPK RM11 75 J5
HDN NW4 63 J4
LEY E10 69 K4
MORT/ESHN SW14 137 K6
SRTFD E15 88 D5
SUT SM1 208 E2
TEDD TW11 174 B1
TOTM N17 50 C3
WATW WD18 26 E2
WFD IG8 53 J3
WHTN TW2 155 H1
WHTN TW2 155 K4
WOOL/PLUM SE18 127 H5
Vicarage Wk BTSEA * SW11 140 C2
Vicarage Wy RYLN/HDSTN HA2 60 A4
WLSDN NW10 81 F1
Vicars Bridge Cl ALP/SUD HA0 98 A1
Vicar's Cl EN EN1 24 A3
HACK E8 86 E6
SRTFD E15 88 E6
Vicars Hl LEW SE13 144 E5
Vicar's Moor La WCHMH N21 35 G2
Vicars Oak Rd NRWD SE19 181 F2
Vicar's Rd KTTN NW5 84 A3
Viceroy Cl EFNCH * N2 65 J1
Viceroy Pde EFNCH * N2 65 J1
Viceroy Rd VX/NE SW8 141 K2
Vickers Cl CROY/NA CR0 211 F5
Vickers Rd ERITH DA8 130 A5
Victor Gv ALP/SUD HA0 80 A5
Victoria Ar PIM SW1V 15 K5
Victoria Av CRW RM5 56 D2
E/WMO/HCT KT8 173 G6
EHAM E6 89 H6
FNCH N3 46 D4
HSLW TW3 135 F6
SURB KT6 190 E3
WBLY HA9 80 D4
WLGTN SM6 210 A1
Victoria Cl E/WMO/HCT KT8 173 F6
EBAR EN4 21 H5
HRW * HA1 61 F3
HYS/HAR UB3 94 B5
Victoria Cottages
RCH/KEW TW9 137 G2
WCHPL * E1 104 C4
Victoria Ct WBLY HA9 80 C4
Victoria Crs NRWD SE19 181 F2
SEVS/STOTM N15 68 A2
WIM/MER * SW19 177 J3
Victoria Dock Rd CAN/RD E16 106 D5
Victoria Dr WIM/MER SW19 159 G3
Victoria Emb TPL/STR WC2R 11 G6
WHALL SW1A 17 F3
Victoria Embankment Gdns
CHCR * WC2N 11 F6
Victoria Gdns HEST TW5 134 D2
NTGHL W11 119 K1
Victoria Ga BAY/PAD W2 8 B5
Victoria Gv KENS W8 120 B3
NFNCH/WDSP N12 47 H1
Victoria Grove Ms BAY/PAD W2 101 F6
Victoria La HYS/HAR UB3 113 G5
Victoria Ms KIL/WHAMP NW6 82 E6
WAND/EARL SW18 160 B3
Victorian Gv STNW/STAM N16 86 A1
Victorian Rd STNW/STAM N16 86 A1
Victoria Pde RCH/KEW * TW9 137 H2
Victoria Park Rd HOM E9 87 F6
Victoria Park Sq BETH E2 104 E2
Victoria Park Studios HOM * E9 86 E6
Victoria Pl RCHPK/HAM TW10 136 E6
Victoria Ri CLAP SW4 141 G4
Victoria Rd ACT W3 99 F4
BARK IG11 90 B4
BFN/LL DA15 168 A5
BKHH IG9 39 H4
BUSH WD23 28 B3
BXLYHS DA6 149 H5
CHING E4 38 C3
CHST BR7 185 F1
DAGE RM10 92 E3
DART DA1 151 G6
EBAR EN4 21 H5
ED N9 36 B5
ERITH DA8 130 B5
FELT TW13 154 A3
FSBYPK N4 67 F4
HAYES BR2 200 C2
HDN NW4 64 A1
KENS W8 120 B3
KIL/WHAMP NW6 100 D1
KUT KT1 175 G5
MLHL NW7 45 H1
MORT/ESHN SW14 138 A4
MTCM CR4 178 D3
NWDGN UB2 114 E3
PLSTW E13 106 E1
ROM RM1 75 H2
RSLP HA4 58 E6
SEVS/STOTM * N15 68 C1
SURB KT6 190 E3
SUT SM1 209 H3
SWFD E18 53 F6
TEDD TW11 174 B2
TWK TW1 156 C2
WALTH E17 52 A5
WAN E11 88 C2
WDGN N22 48 D4
WEA W13 97 H4
WLSDN NW10 99 G3
Victoria Sq BGVA SW1W 15 K4
Victoria St BELV DA17 129 G5
PIM SW1V 15 K5
SRTFD E15 88 C5
Victoria Ter EA * W5 116 E1
FSBYPK N4 67 G5
HRW HA1 60 E5
Victoria Vls RCH/KEW TW9 137 G4
Victoria Wy CHARL SE7 126 A5
Victoria Yd WCHPL * E1 104 C5
Victor Rd PGE/AN SE20 182 A3
RYLN/HDSTN HA2 42 C6
TEDD TW11 173 K1
WLSDN NW10 99 K2
Victors Dr HPTN * TW12 172 D2
Victors Wy BAR EN5 20 D4
Victor Vls UED * N18 35 K5
Victory Av MRDN SM4 194 B2
Victory Pk WBLY * HA9 79 K1
Victory Pl NRWD * SE19 181 F2
WALW SE17 18 D6
Victory Rd RAIN RM13 111 J1
WAN E11 71 F1
WIM/MER SW19 178 B3
Victory Wy BERM/RHTH SE16 124 B2
HEST TW5 114 B5
ROMW/RG RM7 56 D5
Vienna Cl CLAY IG5 53 H5
The View ABYW SE2 129 F5
View Cl CHIG IG7 54 D1
HGT N6 65 K4
HRW HA1 60 D1
View Crs CEND/HSY/T N8 66 D2
Viewfield Cl KTN/HRWW/W HA3 62 A4
Viewfield Rd BFN/LL DA15 168 D3
WAND/EARL SW18 159 J1
Viewland Rd WOOL/PLUM SE18 128 A5
View Rd HGT N6 65 K4
Viga Rd WCHMH N21 35 G1
Vigilant Cl SYD SE26 163 H6
Vignoles Rd ROMW/RG RM7 74 C4
Vigo St MYFR/PICC W1J 10 A6
Viking Gdns EHAM E6 107 J4
Viking Pl LEY E10 69 H5
Viking Rd STHL UB1 95 J6
Viking Wy BELV DA17 129 K3
Villacourt Rd WOOL/PLUM SE18 148 B1
The Village CHARL SE7 126 B6
HAMP * NW3 65 G6
Village Ar CHING * E4 38 B3
Village Cl CHING E4 52 A1
HAMP * NW3 83 H3
Village Green Rd DART DA1 150 D5
Village Ms CDALE/KGS * NW9 63 F6
Village Mt HAMP * NW3 83 G2
Village Park Cl EN EN1 36 A1
Village Rd EN EN1 35 K1
FNCH N3 46 C5
Village Rw BELMT SM2 208 E5
Village Wy ASHF TW15 152 C6
BECK BR3 182 D6
HNHL SE24 162 E1
PIN HA5 59 J4
WLSDN NW10 81 F2
Village Wy East
RYLN/HDSTN HA2 59 K4
Villa Rd BRXN/ST SW9 142 B4
Villas Rd WOOL/PLUM SE18 127 H4
Villa St WALW SE17 122 E5
Villiers Av BRYLDS KT5 191 G2
WHTN TW2 154 E3
Villiers Cl BRYLDS KT5 191 G1
Villiers Gv BELMT SM2 208 B6
Villiers Rd BECK BR3 182 A5
CRICK NW2 81 J4
ISLW TW7 135 K3
KUT KT1 175 G6
OXHEY WD19 27 J1
STHL UB1 114 E1
Villiers St CHCR WC2N 11 F7
Vincam Cl WHTN TW2 155 F2
Vincennes Est WNWD * SE27 162 E6
Vincent Av BRYLDS KT5 191 J5
Vincent Cl BAR EN5 20 E4
BARK/HLT IG6 54 D2
BFN/LL DA15 167 K3
ESH/CLAY KT10 204 B1
HAYES BR2 200 A1
WDR/YW UB7 112 D6
Vincent Gdns CRICK NW2 81 H1
Vincent Pde FSBYPK * N4 66 E5
Vincent Rd ACT W3 117 K3
ALP/SUD HA0 80 B5
CHING E4 52 B2
CROY/NA CR0 197 F4
DAGW RM9 92 A5
HSLWW TW4 134 C4
ISLW TW7 135 J2
KUT KT1 175 H6
SEVS/STOTM N15 67 J1
WDGN N22 49 G5
WOOL/PLUM * SE18 127 G4
Vincent Rw HPTN TW12 173 H2
Vincents Cl BERM/RHTH SE16 124 B2
Vincent Sq WDGN * N22 49 G5
WEST SW1P 16 B6
Vincent St CAN/RD E16 106 E4
WEST SW1P 16 C6
Vincent Ter IS N1 6 A2
Vincent Vls SEVS/STOTM * N15 67 J1
Vince St FSBYE EC1V 7 F5
Vine Cl BRYLDS KT5 191 G3
SUT SM1 209 G1
WDR/YW UB7 112 D4
Vine Cottages HNWL * W7 115 K1
WCHPL * E1 104 E5
Vine Ct KTN/HRWW/W HA3 62 A3
WCHPL E1 104 C4
Vine Gdns IL IG1 90 C3
Vinegar St WAP E1W 123 J1
Vinegar Yd STHWK SE1 19 G2
Vine Hl CLKNW EC1R 5 J7
Vine La STHWK SE1 19 H1
Vine Pl HSLW TW3 135 G5
The Vineries CAT * SE6 164 D3
EN EN1 24 A4
STHGT/OAK N14 34 C1
Vineries Bank MLHL NW7 45 K1
Vineries Cl WDR/YW UB7 112 D6
Vine Rd BARN SW13 138 C4
E/WMO/HCT KT8 189 H1
ORP BR6 217 F4
SRTFD E15 88 D5
Vine Rw RCHPK/HAM * TW10 137 F6
Viners Cl WOT/HER KT12 188 B3
Vines Av FNCH N3 47 F4
Vine Sq WKENS * W14 119 J5
Vine St CONDST W1S 10 B6
ROMW/RG RM7 74 E2
TWRH EC3N 13 J4
Vine Street Br FARR EC1M 5 K7
Vine Street Crs TWRH * EC3N 13 J5
The Vineyard
RCHPK/HAM TW10 136 E6
Vine Yd STHWK SE1 18 D2
Vineyard Av MLHL NW7 46 C3
Vineyard Cl CAT SE6 164 D3
KUT KT1 175 G6
Vineyard Gv FNCH N3 47 F4
Vineyard Hill Rd
WIM/MER SW19 159 K6
Vineyard Ms CLKNW * EC1R 5 J6
Vineyard Pth
MORT/ESHN SW14 138 A4
Vineyard Rd FELT TW13 153 K5
Vineyard Rw E/WMO/HCT KT8 174 D4
Vineyard Wk CLKNW EC1R 5 J6
Viney Bank CROY/NA CR0 213 H6
Viney Rd LEW SE13 144 E4
Vining St BRXN/ST SW9 142 B5
Vinson Cl ORP BR6 202 B5
Vintry Ms WALTH E17 69 J1
Viola Av ABYW SE2 128 C4
EBED/NFELT TW14 154 B1
STWL/WRAY TW19 152 B4
Viola Sq SHB W12 99 H6
Violet Av ENC/FH EN2 23 K1
Violet Cl CAN/RD E16 106 C3
DEPT SE8 124 C6
WLGTN SM6 195 F5
Violet Gdns CROY/NA CR0 211 H3
Violet Hl STJWD NW8 101 G1
Violet La CROY/NA CR0 211 H3
Violet Rd BOW E3 105 K3
SWFD E18 53 F5
WALTH E17 69 J3
Violet St BETH E2 104 D3
Virgil St STHWK SE1 17 H4
Virginia Cl CRW RM5 56 E3
NWMAL KT3 191 K1
Virginia Gdns BARK/HLT IG6 54 D5
Virginia Rd BETH E2 7 J5
THHTH CR7 180 D4
Virginia St WAP * E1W 104 C6
Viscount Cl FBAR/BDGN N11 48 A1

Viscount Dr EHAM E6 107 K4
Viscount Gv NTHLT UB5 95 H2
Viscount Rd STWL/WRAY TW19 152 A2
Viscount St STLK EC1Y 6 C7
Viscount Wy HTHAIR TW6 133 H5
The Vista ELTH/MOT SE9 166 C1
Vista Av PEND EN3 25 F3
Vista Dr REDBR IG4 71 H2
Vista Wy KTN/HRWW/W HA3 62 A3
Viveash Cl HYS/HAR UB3 113 J3
Vivian Av HDN NW4 63 K2
WBLY HA9 80 C4
Vivian Cl OXHEY WD19 26 E4
Vivian Gdns OXHEY WD19 26 E3
WBLY HA9 80 C3
Vivian Rd BOW E3 105 G1
Vivian Sq PECK SE15 143 J4
Vivian Wy EFNCH N2 65 H2
Vivien Cl CHSGTN KT9 206 A5
Vivienne Cl TWK TW1 156 E1
Vixen Ms HACK * E8 86 B6
Voce Rd WOOL/PLUM SE18 147 J1
Voewood Cl NWMAL KT3 192 C3
Voltaire Rd CLAP SW4 141 J4
Volt Av WLSDN NW10 99 F2
Volta Wy CROY/NA CR0 196 A5
Voluntary Pl WAN E11 70 E3
Vorley Rd ARCH N19 66 C6
Voss Ct STRHM/NOR SW16 179 K2
Voss St BETH E2 104 C2
Voyagers Cl THMD SE28 109 J5
Vulcan Cl EHAM E6 108 A5
Vulcan Ga ENC/FH EN2 23 G3
Vulcan Rd BROCKY SE4 144 C3
Vulcan Ter BROCKY SE4 144 C3
Vulcan Wy HOLWY N7 85 F4
The Vyne BXLYHN DA7 149 J4
Vyner Rd ACT W3 99 F6
Vyner St BETH E2 104 D1
Vyse Cl BAR EN5 20 A5

W

Wadding St WALW SE17 18 E7
Waddington Cl EN EN1 24 A5
Waddington Rd SRTFD E15 88 B3
Waddington St SRTFD E15 88 B4
Waddington Wy NRWD SE19 180 D4
Waddon Cl CROY/NA CR0 211 G1
Waddon Court Rd
CROY/NA CR0 211 G2
Waddon Marsh Wy
CROY/NA CR0 196 A6
Waddon New Rd CROY/NA CR0 211 H1
Waddon Park Av CROY/NA CR0 211 G2
Waddon Rd CROY/NA CR0 211 H1
Waddon Wy CROY/NA CR0 211 G4
Wade Av STMC/STPC BR5 202 E4
Wade House STHWK * SE1 123 H2
Wade Rd CAN/RD E16 107 G5
Wade's Gv WCHMH N21 35 G2
Wade's Hl WCHMH N21 35 G1
Wade's La TEDD TW11 174 B1
Wadeson St BETH E2 104 D1
Wade's Pl POP/IOD E14 105 K6
Wadeville Av CHDH RM6 74 A3
Wadeville Cl BELV DA17 129 H5
Wadham Av CHING E4 51 K3
Wadham Gdns GFD/PVL UB6 78 D4
HAMP NW3 83 J5
Wadham Rd CHING E4 51 K3
PUT/ROE SW15 139 H5
Wadhurst Cl PGE/AN SE20 181 J5
Wadhurst Rd CHSWK W4 118 A3
Wadley Rd WAN E11 70 C4
Wadsworth Cl GFD/PVL UB6 97 J1
PEND EN3 25 F6
Wadsworth Rd GFD/PVL UB6 97 H1
Wager St BOW E3 105 H3
Waghorn Rd KTN/HRWW/W HA3 43 K6
PLSTW E13 89 G6
Waghorn St PECK SE15 143 H4
Wagner St PECK SE15 143 K1
Wagstaff Gdns DAGW RM9 91 J5
Wagtail Cl CDALE/KGS NW9 45 G5
Wagtail Wk BECK BR3 199 F2
Wagtail Wy STMC/STPC BR5 202 E1
Waid Cl DART DA1 171 J1
Waights Ct KUTN/CMB KT2 175 F4
Wainfleet Av CRW RM5 56 E5
Wainford Cl WIM/MER SW19 159 G3
Wainwright Gv ISLW TW7 135 J5
Waite Davies Rd
LEE/GVPK SE12 165 J2
Waite St PECK SE15 123 G6
Wakefield Gdns IL IG1 71 J3
NRWD SE19 181 F3
Wakefield Ms STPAN WC1H 5 F5
Wakefield Rd FBAR/BDGN N11 48 D1
RCHPK/HAM TW10 136 E6
SEVS/STOTM N15 68 B2
Wakefield St BMSBY WC1N 5 F6
EHAM E6 89 J6
UED N18 50 C1
Wakehams Hl PIN HA5 41 K6
Wakeham St IS N1 85 K4
Wakehurst Rd BTSEA SW11 140 E6
Wakeling Rd HNWL W7 97 F4
Wakeling St WCHPL * E1 105 G5
Wakelin Rd SRTFD E15 106 C1
Wakeman Rd WLSDN NW10 100 A2
Wakemans Hill Av
CDALE/KGS NW9 63 F2
Wakering Rd BARK IG11 90 C5
Wakerly Cl EHAM E6 107 K5
Wakley St FSBYE EC1V 6 A4
Walberswick St VX/NE SW8 141 K1
Walbrook MANHO EC4N 12 E5
Walburgh St WCHPL E1 104 D5
Walcorde Av WALW SE17 18 D7
Walcot Rd PEND EN3 25 H3
Walcot Sq LBTH SE11 17 K6
Walcott St WEST * SW1P 16 B6
Waldeck Gv WNWD SE27 162 C5
Waldeck Rd CHSWK W4 117 H6
DART DA1 171 J2
MORT/ESHN SW14 137 K4
SEVS/STOTM N15 49 H6
WEA W13 97 H5
Waldegrave Gdns TWK TW1 156 A4
Waldegrave Pk TWK TW1 156 A6
Waldegrave Rd BCTR RM8 73 J6
BMLY BR1 200 D2
CEND/HSY/T * N8 49 G6
EA W5 98 B6
NRWD SE19 181 G3
TWK TW1 156 A6
Waldegrove CROY/NA CR0 212 B1
Waldemar Av FUL/PGN SW6 139 H2
WEA W13 116 D1
Waldemar Rd WIM/MER SW19 177 K1
Walden Av CHST BR7 166 E6
PLMGR N13 35 J6
RAIN RM13 111 F1
Walden Cl BELV DA17 129 G5
Walden Gdns THHTH CR7 196 A1
Waldenhurst Rd
STMC/STPC BR5 202 E4
Walden Pde CHST * BR7 184 E2
Walden Rd CHST BR7 184 E2
TOTM N17 49 K4
Waldens Cl STMC/STPC BR5 202 E4
Waldenshaw Rd FSTH SE23 163 K3
Waldens Rd STMC/STPC BR5 203 F3
Walden St WCHPL * E1 104 D5
Walden Wy BARK/HLT IG6 54 E3
MLHL NW7 46 B2
Waldo Cl CLAP SW4 141 H6
Waldo Pl WIM/MER SW19 178 D3
Waldorf Cl SAND/SEL CR2 211 H6
Waldo Rd BMLY BR1 184 B6
WLSDN NW10 99 K2
Waldram Crs FSTH SE23 163 K3
Waldram Park Rd FSTH SE23 164 A3
Waldrist Wy ERITHM DA18 129 G2
Waldron Gdns HAYES BR2 183 G6
Waldronhyrst CROY/NA CR0 211 H2
Waldron Ms CHEL SW3 120 C6
Waldron Rd HRW HA1 60 E5
WAND/EARL SW18 160 B5
The Waldrons CROY/NA CR0 211 J2
Waldron's Yd RYLN/HDSTN HA2 60 D6
Waldstock Rd THMD SE28 109 G6
Waleran Cl STAN HA7 43 F2
Walerand Rd LEW SE13 145 F3
Wales Av CAR SM5 209 K3
Wales Cl PECK SE15 143 J1
Wales Farm Rd ACT W3 99 F4
Waleton Acres WLGTN * SM6 210 C4
Waley St WCHPL * E1 105 F4
Walfield Av TRDG/WHET N20 33 F2
Walford Rd STNW/STAM N16 86 A2
Walfrey Gdns DAGW RM9 92 A5
Walham Green Ct
FUL/PGN * SW6 140 A1
Walham Gv FUL/PGN SW6 139 K1
Walham Ri WIM/MER SW19 177 H2
Walham Yd FUL/PGN SW6 139 K1
The Walk PLMGR * N13 35 G5
Walkden Rd CHST BR7 167 F6
Walker Cl DART DA1 150 C4
EBED/NFELT TW14 153 J2
FBAR/BDGN N11 34 C6
HNWL W7 115 K1
HPTN TW12 172 E2
WOOL/PLUM SE18 127 H4
Walker's Ct SOHO/CST W1F 10 C5
Walkerscroft Md DUL SE21 162 D3
Walker's Pl PUT/ROE * SW15 139 H5
Walkley Rd DART DA1 150 E6
The Walks EFNCH N2 47 H6
Wallace Cl THMD SE28 109 K6
Wallace Crs CAR SM5 209 K3
Wallace Rd IS N1 85 J4
Wallbutton Rd BROCKY SE4 144 B3
Wallcote Av CRICK NW2 64 B5
Wall End Rd EHAM E6 90 A5
Wallenger Av GPK RM2 57 K6
Waller Dr NTHWD HA6 40 E5
Waller Rd NWCR SE14 144 A3
Wallers Cl DAGW RM9 92 A6
WFD IG8 53 K2
Wallflower St SHB W12 99 H6
Wallgrave Rd ECT SW5 120 A4
Wallhouse Rd ERITH DA8 151 F1
Wallingford Av NKENS W10 100 B4
Wallington Cl RSLP HA4 58 A3
Wallington Rd GDMY/SEVK IG3 73 F4
Wallis Cl BTSEA SW11 140 C4
EMPK RM11 75 K5
RDART DA2 170 D5
Wallis Rd HOM E9 87 H4
STHL UB1 96 B5
Wallorton Gdns
MORT/ESHN SW14 138 A5
Wallside BARB * EC2Y 12 D2
Wall St IS N1 85 K4
Wallwood Rd WAN E11 70 B4
Wallwood St POP/IOD E14 105 H4
Walmar Cl EBAR EN4 21 H2
Walmer Cl CHING E4 37 K4
ORP BR6 216 D2
ROMW/RG RM7 56 D5
Walmer Gdns HNWL W7 116 B2
Walmer Rd NTGHL W11 100 C6
Walmer Ter WOOL/PLUM SE18 127 H4
Walmgate Rd GFD/PVL UB6 79 H6
Walmington Fold
NFNCH/WDSP N12 46 E2
Walm La CRICK NW2 82 B4
Walney Wk IS * N1 85 J3
Walnut Av WDR/YW UB7 112 D3
Walnut Cl BARK/HLT IG6 72 C1
CAR SM5 209 K3
DEPT SE8 124 C6
HYS/HAR UB3 94 C6
Walnut Ct EA * W5 117 F2
Walnut Gdns SRTFD E15 88 C3
Walnut Gv EN EN1 23 K6
Walnut Ms BELMT SM2 209 G5
Walnut Rd LEY E10 69 J6
Walnuts Rd ORP BR6 202 B5
Walnut Tree Av DART DA1 171 H4
MTCM * CR4 178 D6
Walnut Tree Cl BARN SW13 138 C2
CHST BR7 185 H4
Walnut Tree Rd BCTR RM8 73 K6
BTFD TW8 117 F6
ERITH DA8 130 B5
GNWCH * SE10 125 H5
HEST * TW5 114 E6
Walnut Tree Wk LBTH SE11 17 J6
Walnut Wy BKHH IG9 39 H5
RSLP HA4 77 G4
Walpole Av RCH/KEW TW9 137 G3
Walpole Cl PIN HA5 42 A3
WEA W13 116 D2
Walpole Crs TEDD TW11 174 A1
Walpole Gdns CHSWK W4 117 K5
WHTN TW2 155 K4
Walpole Ms STJWD NW8 2 A1
Walpole Pl TEDD TW11 174 A1
Walpole Rd CROY/NA CR0 196 E6
EHAM E6 89 G5
HAYES BR2 200 C2
SURB KT6 191 F4
SWFD E18 52 D4
TEDD TW11 174 A1
TOTM N17 49 J5
WALTH E17 69 G1
WHTN TW2 155 K4
WIM/MER SW19 178 C2
Walpole St CHEL SW3 120 E5
Walrond Av WBLY HA9 80 A3
Walsham Cl STNW/STAM N16 68 C5
THMD SE28 109 K6
Walsham Rd EBED/NFELT TW14 154 A2
NWCR SE14 144 A3
Walsingham Gdns
HOR/WEW KT19 207 G2
Walsingham Pk CHST BR7 185 J5
Walsingham Rd CLAP SW4 161 F1
CLPT E5 86 C1
ENC/FH EN2 23 K5
MTCM CR4 194 E2
STMC/STPC BR5 186 C4
WEA * W13 116 B1
Walsingham Wk BELV DA17 129 H6
Walters Rd PEND EN3 24 E6
SNWD SE25 197 F1
Walter St BETH E2 105 F2
KUTN/CMB * KT2 175 F4
Walters Wy FSTH SE23 164 A1
Walters Yd BMLY BR1 183 K5
Walter Ter WCHPL E1 105 F5
Walterton Rd MV/WKIL W9 100 D3
Walter Wk EDGE HA8 44 E2
Waltham Av CDALE/KGS NW9 62 C3
HYS/HAR UB3 113 F3
Waltham Cl DART DA1 170 D1
STMC/STPC BR5 202 E5
Waltham Dr EDGE HA8 44 C5
Waltham Pk WALTH E17 51 J3
Waltham Rd CAR SM5 194 C5
NWDGN UB2 114 D3
WFD IG8 53 J2
Walthamstow Av CHING E4 51 J3
Walthamstow Av (North Circular)
CHING E4 51 G1
Waltham Wy CHING E4 37 H5
Waltheof Av TOTM N17 49 K4
Waltheof Gdns TOTM N17 49 K4
Walton Av CHEAM SM3 208 D1
NWMAL KT3 192 C1
RYLN/HDSTN HA2 77 K3
Walton Cl CRICK NW2 63 K6
HRW HA1 60 D1
VX/NE SW8 141 K1
Walton Dr HRW HA1 60 D1
WLSDN NW10 81 F4
Walton Gdns ACT W3 98 D4
FELT TW13 153 J6
WBLY HA9 62 A6
Walton Gn CROY/NA CR0 213 K6
Walton Pk WOT/HER KT12 188 C6
Walton Park La WOT/HER KT12 188 D6
Walton Pl CHEL SW3 14 E4
Walton Rd CRW RM5 56 B3
HRW HA1 60 D1
MNPK E12 90 A2
PLSTW E13 107 G1
SCUP DA14 168 C5
SEVS/STOTM * N15 68 B1
WOT/HER KT12 188 C2
Walton St CHEL SW3 14 D6
ENC/FH EN2 23 K2
Walton Vls IS * N1 86 A5
Walton Wy ACT W3 98 D4
MTCM CR4 195 H1
Walt Whitman Cl HNHL * SE24 142 C5
Walverns Cl OXHEY WD19 27 G1
Walworth Pl WALW SE17 122 D5
Walworth Rd WALW SE17 18 C6
Walwyn Av BMLY BR1 184 C6
Wanborough Dr
PUT/ROE SW15 158 E3
Wanderer Dr BARK IG11 109 H2
Wandle Bank CROY/NA CR0 210 E1
WIM/MER SW19 178 C2
Wandle Ct HOR/WEW KT19 206 E2
Wandle Court Gdns
CROY/NA CR0 210 E1
Wandle Rd CROY/NA CR0 210 E1
CROY/NA CR0 211 J1
MRDN SM4 194 C2
TOOT SW17 160 D4
WLGTN SM6 195 G6
Wandle Side CROY/NA CR0 211 F1
WLGTN SM6 210 B1
Wandle Wy MTCM CR4 194 E2
WAND/EARL SW18 160 A3
Wandon Rd FUL/PGN SW6 140 A1
Wandsworth Br
WAND/EARL SW18 140 B4
Wandsworth Bridge Rd
FUL/PGN SW6 140 A2
Wandsworth Common West Side
WAND/EARL SW18 140 B6
Wandsworth High St
WAND/EARL SW18 139 K6
Wandsworth Rd CLAP SW4 141 G4
Wangey Rd CHDH RM6 73 K4
Wanless Rd HNHL SE24 142 D4
Wanley Rd CMBW SE5 142 E5
Wanlip Rd PLSTW E13 107 F3
Wannock Gdns BARK/HLT IG6 54 B4
Wansbeck Rd HOM E9 87 H5
Wansdown Pl FUL/PGN SW6 140 A1
Wansey St WALW SE17 18 D7
Wansford Rd WFD IG8 53 G4
Wanstead Cl BMLY BR1 184 B5
Wanstead La IL IG1 71 J3
Wanstead Park Av MNPK E12 71 H6
Wanstead Park Rd IL IG1 71 J5
Wanstead Pl WAN E11 70 E3
Wanstead Rd BMLY BR1 184 B5
Wansunt Rd BXLY DA5 169 K3
Wantage Rd LEE/GVPK SE12 145 J6
Wantz La RAIN RM13 111 K3
Wantz Rd DAGE RM10 92 D2
Wapping Dock St WAP * E1W 123 J1
Wapping High St WAP E1W 123 H1
Wapping La WAP E1W 104 D6
Wapping Wall WAP E1W 123 K1
Warbank La KUTN/CMB KT2 176 C3
Warbeck Rd SHB W12 118 E1
Warberry Rd WDGN N22 49 F5
Warboys Ap KUTN/CMB KT2 175 J2
Warboys Crs CHING E4 52 A1
Warboys Rd KUTN/CMB KT2 175 J2
Warburton Cl IS N1 86 A4
KTN/HRWW/W HA3 42 D2
Warburton Rd HACK E8 86 D6
WHTN TW2 155 G3
Warburton St HACK E8 86 D6
Warburton Ter WALTH E17 51 K5
Wardalls Gv NWCR * SE14 143 K1
Ward Cl ERITH DA8 130 A6
SAND/SEL CR2 212 A3
Wardell Cl CDALE/KGS NW9 45 G5
Warden Av CRW RM5 56 E1
RYLN/HDSTN HA2 59 J5
Warden Rd KTTN NW5 84 A4
Wardens Gv STHWK SE1 18 C1
Wardle St HOM E9 87 F3
Wardley St WAND/EARL SW18 160 A2
Wardo Av FUL/PGN SW6 139 H2
Wardour Ms SOHO/CST W1F 10 B4
Wardour St SOHO/CST W1F 10 B3
Ward Rd ARCH N19 84 C2
SRTFD * E15 88 B6
The Wardrobe RCH/KEW * TW9 136 E6
Wardrobe Pl BLKFR * EC4V 12 B4
Wards Rd GNTH/NBYPK IG2 72 D4
Wareham Cl HSLW TW3 135 G5
Waremead Rd GNTH/NBYPK IG2 72 B2
Warepoint Dr THMD SE28 127 J2
Warfield Rd EBED/NFELT TW14 153 H2
HPTN TW12 173 G4
WLSDN NW10 100 B2
Warfield Yd WLSDN * NW10 100 B2
Wargrave Av SEVS/STOTM N15 68 C3
Wargrave Rd RYLN/HDSTN HA2 78 C1
Warham Rd FSBYPK N4 67 G2
KTN/HRWW/W HA3 43 F6
SAND/SEL CR2 211 J3
Warham St CMBW SE5 142 C1
Waring Cl ORP BR6 217 F4
Waring Dr ORP BR6 217 F4
Waring Rd SCUP DA14 186 D2
Waring St WNWD SE27 162 D6
Warkworth Gdns ISLW TW7 136 B1
Warkworth Rd TOTM N17 49 K3
Warland Rd WOOL/PLUM SE18 147 J1
Warley Av ROMW/RG RM7 74 B4
YEAD UB4 94 E5
Warley Rd CLAY IG5 54 A4
ED N9 36 E4
WFD IG8 53 F3
YEAD UB4 94 E5
Warley St BETH E2 105 F2
Warlingham Rd THHTH CR7 196 C1
Warlock Rd MV/WKIL W9 100 D3
Warlters Cl HOLWY * N7 84 E2
Warlters Rd HOLWY N7 84 E2
Warltersville Rd ARCH N19 66 E4
Warming Cl CLPT * E5 87 F1
Warmington Rd HNHL SE24 162 D1
Warmington St PLSTW E13 106 E3
Warminster Rd SNWD SE25 181 H5
Warminster Sq SNWD SE25 181 H5
Warminster Wy MTCM CR4 179 G4
Warndon St BERM/RHTH SE16 123 K4
Warneford Pl OXHEY WD19 27 J1
Warneford Rd
KTN/HRWW/W HA3 43 K6
Warneford St HOM E9 86 D6
Warne Pl BFN/LL DA15 168 C1
Warner Av CHEAM SM3 193 H6
Warner Cl CDALE/KGS NW9 63 H4
HPTN TW12 172 E1
HYS/HAR UB3 133 G1
SRTFD E15 88 C3
Warner Pl BETH E2 104 C1
Warner Rd BMLY BR1 183 J3
CEND/HSY/T N8 66 D1
CMBW SE5 142 D2
WALTH E17 69 G1
Warner St CLKNW EC1R 5 J7
Warner Ter POP/IOD * E14 105 J4
Warner Yd CLKNW EC1R 5 J7
Warnford Rd ORP BR6 217 F3
Warnham Court Rd CAR SM5 209 K5
Warnham Rd NFNCH/WDSP N12 47 H1
Warple Ms ACT * W3 118 B2
Warple Wy ACT W3 118 B2
The Warren CAR SM5 209 H6
HEST TW5 134 E1
HOR/WEW KT19 207 F2
MNPK E12 89 J2
YEAD UB4 94 E5
Warren Av BMLY BR1 183 H3
ORP BR6 217 F3
RCHPK/HAM TW10 137 J5
SAND/SEL CR2 213 F5
WAN * E11 88 B1
Warren Cl BXLYHS DA6 149 H6
ED N9 37 F2
ESH/CLAY KT10 204 B2
WBLY HA9 61 K6
YEAD UB4 95 G4
Warren Crs ED N9 36 B2
Warren Cutting KUTN/CMB KT2 176 A3
Warrender Rd ARCH N19 84 C1
Warrender Wy RSLP HA4 58 E4
The Warren Dr WAN E11 71 G4
Warren Dr GFD/PVL UB6 96 B3
HCH RM12 93 J1
ORP BR6 217 H3
RSLP HA4 59 H4
Warren Dr North BRYLDS KT5 191 J5
Warren Dr South BRYLDS KT5 191 K5
Warren Flds STAN * HA7 29 J6
Warren Gdns ORP BR6 217 G3
Warren La STAN HA7 29 G4
WOOL/PLUM SE18 127 G3
Warren Ms GTPST W1W 4 A7
Warren Pk KUTN/CMB KT2 175 K2
Warren Park Rd SUT SM1 209 H4
Warren Pond Rd CHING E4 38 D2
Warren Ri NWMAL KT3 176 A4
Warren Rd BARK/HLT IG6 72 D2
BUSH WD23 28 C3
BXLYHS DA6 149 H6
CHING E4 38 A4
CRICK NW2 63 H6
CROY/NA CR0 197 F5
DART DA1 171 H5
HAYES BR2 199 K6
KUTN/CMB KT2 175 K2
LEY E10 88 A1
ORP BR6 217 F3
SCUP DA14 168 D5
WAN E11 71 G3
WHTN TW2 155 J1
WIM/MER SW19 178 D2
Warrens Shawe La EDGE HA8 30 D4
Warren St FITZ W1T 4 A7
Warren Wy MLHL NW7 46 C2
Warren Wood Cl HAYES BR2 199 K6
Warriner Dr ED N9 36 C5
Warriner Gdns BTSEA SW11 140 E2
Warrington Crs MV/WKIL W9 101 G3
Warrington Gdns MV/WKIL W9 101 G3
Warrington Pl POP/IOD * E14 125 F1
Warrington Rd BCTR RM8 73 K6
CROY/NA CR0 211 H1
HRW HA1 60 E2
RCHPK/HAM TW10 136 E6
Warrington Sq BCTR RM8 73 K6
Warrior Sq MNPK E12 90 A2
Warsaw Cl RSLP HA4 77 F4
Warspite Rd WOOL/PLUM SE18 126 D3
Warton Rd SRTFD E15 88 A6
Warwall EHAM E6 108 B5
Warwick Av EDGE HA8 30 D5
MV/WKIL W9 101 F3
RYLN/HDSTN HA2 77 K2
Warwick Chambers KENS * W8 119 K3
Warwick Cl BUSH WD23 28 E2
BXLY DA5 169 G2
EBAR EN4 21 H6
HPTN TW12 173 H3
ORP BR6 217 G1
Warwick Ct HHOL WC1V 11 H2
Warwick Crs BAY/PAD W2 101 G4
YEAD UB4 94 D3
Warwick Dene EA W5 117 F1
Warwick Dr BARN SW13 138 E4
Warwick Gdns FSBYPK N4 67 J2
IL IG1 72 B5
THDIT KT7 190 A2
THHTH * CR7 196 B1
WKENS W14 119 J3
Warwick Gv BRYLDS KT5 191 G4
CLPT E5 68 D5
Warwick House St STJS SW1Y 10 C7
Warwick La STP EC4M 12 B3
Warwick Pde
KTN/HRWW/W * HA3 43 H5
Warwick Pl EA W5 116 E2
MV/WKIL W9 101 G4
THDIT * KT7 190 B3
Warwick Pl North PIM * SW1V 16 A7
Warwick Rd BAR EN5 21 F5
CHING E4 51 J1
EA W5 117 F1
FBAR/BDGN N11 48 D2
FSTGT E7 88 D4
HSLWW TW4 134 A4
KUT KT1 174 D4
MNPK E12 89 J3
NWDGN UB2 114 E3
NWMAL KT3 175 K6
PGE/AN SE20 181 J6
SCUP DA14 186 C1
SUT SM1 209 G3
THDIT KT7 190 A2
THHTH CR7 180 B6
UED N18 36 A6
WALTH E17 51 H4
WAN E11 71 F2
WDR/YW UB7 112 B1
WELL DA16 148 D4
WHTN TW2 155 K3
WKENS W14 119 J4
Warwick Rw WESTW SW1E 16 A4
Warwickshire Pth DEPT SE8 144 C1
Warwick Sq PIM SW1V 121 H5
STP * EC4M 12 B3
Warwick Square Ms PIM SW1V 16 A7
Warwick St REGST W1B 10 B5
Warwick Ter WALTH * E17 70 B2
WOOL/PLUM SE18 127 J6
Warwick Wy PIM SW1V 15 K7
Warwick Yd STLK * EC1Y 6 D7
Washington Av MNPK E12 89 J2
Washington Cl BOW E3 105 K2
Washington Rd BARN SW13 138 D1
EHAM E6 89 G5
KUT KT1 175 H5
SWFD E18 52 D5
WPK KT4 192 E6
Wastdale Rd FSTH SE23 164 A3
The Watch NFNCH/WDSP * N12 33 G6
Watchfield Ct CHSWK * W4 117 K5
Watcombe Rd SNWD SE25 197 J2
Waterbank Rd CAT SE6 164 E5
Waterbeach Rd DAGW RM9 91 J4
Water Brook La HDN * NW4 64 A2
Watercress Pl IS N1 86 A5
Waterdale Rd ABYW SE2 128 B6
Waterden Rd SRTFD E15 87 J3
Waterer Ri WLGTN SM6 210 D4
Waterfall Cottages
WIM/MER SW19 178 C2
Waterfall Rd FBAR/BDGN N11 34 B6
WIM/MER SW19 178 C2
Waterfall Ter TOOT SW17 178 D2
Waterfield Cl BELV DA17 129 H3
THMD SE28 128 C1
Waterfield Cottages
MORT/ESHN * SW14 137 J5
Waterfield Gdns SNWD SE25 197 F1
Waterford Rd FUL/PGN SW6 140 A2
The Waterfront BORE * WD6 29 H1
The Water Gdns BAY/PAD W2 8 C3
Water Gdns STAN HA7 43 H2
The Watergate OXHEY WD19 27 H4
Watergate St DEPT SE8 124 D6
Waterhall Av CHING E4 38 C6
Waterhall Cl WALTH E17 51 F4
Waterhead Cl ERITH DA8 150 B1
Waterhouse Cl HAMP NW3 83 H3
Wateringbury Cl
STMC/STPC BR5 186 C6
Water La CAMTN NW1 84 B5
ED N9 36 D3
GDMY/SEVK IG3 91 F1
KUT KT1 174 E4
NWCR SE14 143 K1
PUR RM19 131 K4
RCH/KEW TW9 136 E6
SCUP DA14 169 G5
SRTFD E15 88 C4
TWK TW1 156 B3
Water Lily Cl NWDGN UB2 115 H2
Waterloo Br STHWK SE1 11 H6
Waterloo Cl EBED/NFELT TW14 153 J3
Waterloo Gdns BETH E2 104 E1
ROMW/RG RM7 75 F3
Waterloo Pl CAR * SM5 209 K1

RCH/KEW TW9 117 H6
STJS SW1Y 10 C7
Waterloo Rd BARK/HLT IG6 54 C5
CRICK NW2 63 J6
EHAM E6 89 G5
FSTGT E7 88 D3
LEY E10 69 J4
ROMW/RG RM7 75 F2
STHWK SE1 11 H7
SUT SM1 209 H3
Waterloo Ter IS N1 85 H5
Waterlow Rd ARCH N19 66 C5
Waterman Cl OXHEY WD19 27 F1
Watermans Cl KUTN/CMB * KT2 175 F3
Watermans Ms EA * W5 98 A6
Waterman St PUT/ROE SW15 139 G4
Waterman Wy WAP E1W 123 J1
Watermead EBED/NFELT TW14 153 H3
Watermead La MTCM CR4 194 E3
Watermeadow Cl ERITH DA8 150 E1
Watermeadow La
FUL/PGN SW6 140 B3
Watermead Rd CAT SE6 165 F6
Watermead Wy TOTM N17 50 D5
Watermens Sq PGE/AN * SE20 181 K3
Water Ms PECK SE15 143 K5
Watermill Cl RCHPK/HAM TW10 156 D5
Watermill La UED N18 50 A1
Water Mill Wy FELT TW13 154 E4
Watermill Wy WIM/MER SW19 178 B4
Watermint Cl STMC/STPC BR5 202 E1
Watermint Quay
STNW/STAM N16 68 C4
Water Rd ALP/SUD HA0 80 B6
Water's Edge FUL/PGN * SW6 139 G2
Watersedge HOR/WEW KT19 206 E2
Watersfield Wy EDGE HA8 43 K3
Waterside DART DA1 150 B6
WALTH E17 68 E3
Waterside Cl BARK IG11 91 G2
BERM/RHTH SE16 123 H2
HOM E9 87 H6
NTHLT UB5 95 K2
SURB KT6 191 F6
Waterside Ct LEW * SE13 145 G5
Waterside Dr WOT/HER KT12 188 A2
Waterside Rd NWDGN UB2 115 F3
Waterside Wy TOOT SW17 160 B6
Watersmeet Wy THMD SE28 109 K5
Waterson St BETH E2 7 H4
Watersplash Cl KUT KT1 175 F6
Watersplash La HYS/HAR UB3 113 K4
Waters Rd CAT SE6 165 H5
KUT KT1 175 J5
Waters Sq KUT KT1 175 J6
Water St TPL/STR WC2R 11 J5
Water Tower Hl CROY/NA CR0 211 K2
Water Tower Pl IS N1 5 K1
Waterworks La CLPT E5 69 F6
Waterworks Rd
BRXS/STRHM SW2 161 K1
Watery La HYS/HAR UB3 113 G5
NTHLT UB5 95 G1
RYNPK SW20 177 J5
SCUP DA14 186 C2
Wates Wy MTCM CR4 194 E3
Wateville Rd TOTM N17 49 J4
Watford Cl BTSEA SW11 140 D2
Watford Heath OXHEY WD19 27 H2
Watford Rd BORE WD6 29 J1
CAN/RD E16 106 E4
HRW HA1 61 G6
NTHWD HA6 40 D3
Watford Wy HDN NW4 45 J5
Watford Wy (Barnet By-Pass)
MLHL NW7 31 G6
Watkin Rd WBLY HA9 80 D1
Watkinson Rd HOLWY N7 85 F4
Watling Av EDGE HA8 44 E4
Watling Ct STP EC4M 12 D4
Watlings Cl CROY/NA CR0 198 B3
Watling St BXLYHS DA6 149 J5
STP EC4M 12 C4
Watlington Gv SYD SE26 182 B1
Watney Market WCHPL E1 104 D5
Watney Rd MORT/ESHN SW14 137 K4
Watneys Rd MTCM CR4 195 J2
Watney St WCHPL E1 104 E5
Watson Av CHEAM SM3 193 H6
EHAM E6 90 A5
Watson Cl STNW/STAM N16 85 K3
WIM/MER SW19 178 D2
Watson's Ms MBLAR W1H 8 D2
Watsons Rd WDGN N22 49 F4
Watson's St DEPT SE8 144 D1
Wattisfield Rd CLPT E5 86 E1
Watts Cl SEVS/STOTM N15 68 A2
Watts Gv BOW E3 105 J4
Watt's La CHST BR7 185 G4
TEDD TW11 174 B1
Watts Rd THDIT KT7 190 B4
Watts St WAP E1W 123 J1
Wat Tyler Rd BKHTH/KID SE3 145 F3
Wauthier Cl PLMGR N13 49 H1
Wavell Dr BFN/LL DA15 167 K1
Wavel Ms KIL/WHAMP NW6 83 F5
Wavel Pl SYD SE26 163 G6
Wavendon Av CHSWK W4 118 A5
Waveney Av PECK SE15 143 J5
Waveney Cl WAP E1W 123 H1
Waverley Av BRYLDS KT5 191 J3
CHING E4 37 H6
SUT SM1 194 A6
WALTH E17 52 B6
WBLY HA9 80 B3
WHTN TW2 154 E3
Waverley Cl E/WMO/HCT KT8 189 F2
HAYES BR2 200 C2
HYS/HAR UB3 113 G4
Waverley Crs
WOOL/PLUM SE18 127 J6
Waverley Gdns BARK IG11 108 E1
BARK/HLT IG6 54 C5
EHAM E6 107 J4
NTHWD HA6 40 E4
Waverley Gv HDN NW4 46 B6
Waverley Pl FSBYPK * N4 67 H5
STJWD NW8 2 A2
Waverley Rd CEND/HSY/T N8 66 D3
ENC/FH EN2 23 H5
EW KT17 207 K3
RAIN RM13 111 K2
RYLN/HDSTN HA2 59 J4
SNWD SE25 197 J1
STHL UB1 96 A6
SWFD E18 53 G4
TOTM N17 50 D3
WALTH E17 52 A6
WOOL/PLUM SE18 127 H5
Waverley Wy CAR SM5 209 J4
Waverton Rd
WAND/EARL SW18 160 B2
Waverton St MYFR/PICC W1J 9 H7
Wavertree Rd
BRXS/STRHM SW2 162 A3
SWFD E18 52 E5
Waxlow Crs STHL UB1 96 A5
Waxlow Rd WLSDN NW10 98 E1
Waxwell La PIN HA5 41 H6
Wayborne Gv RSLP HA4 58 A3
Waye Av HEST TW5 133 K2
Wayfarer Rd NTHLT UB5 95 J2
Wayford St BTSEA SW11 140 D3
Wayland Av HACK E8 86 C3
Waylands HYS/HAR UB3 94 B4
Waylett Pl ALP/SUD * HA0 79 K2
WNWD SE27 162 C5
Wayne Cl ORP BR6 217 F1
Wayneflete Tower Av
ESH/CLAY KT10 204 A1
Waynflete Av CROY/NA CR0 211 H1
Waynflete Sq NKENS W10 100 B6
Waynflete St WAND/EARL SW18 160 B4
Wayside CRICK NW2 64 C5
CROY/NA * CR0 213 K4
MORT/ESHN SW14 137 K5
Wayside Av BUSH WD23 28 D1
Wayside Cl ROM RM1 57 H6
STHGT/OAK N14 34 C1
Wayside Ct TWK TW1 156 D1
Wayside Gdns DAGE RM10 92 D3
Wayside Gv CHST BR7 166 E6
Wayside Ms GNTH/NBYPK IG2 72 A3
The Weald CHST BR7 184 E2
Weald Cl BERM/RHTH SE16 123 J5
HAYES BR2 200 D6
Weald La KTN/HRWW/W HA3 42 D5
Weald Ri KTN/HRWW/W HA3 43 F3
Weald Sq CLPT * E5 68 D6
Wealdstone Rd CHEAM SM3 193 J6
Weald Wy ROMW/RG RM7 74 D3
YEAD UB4 94 C2
Wealdwood Gdns PIN HA5 42 B2
Weale Rd CHING E4 38 B5
Weardale Gdns ENC/FH EN2 23 K2
Weardale Rd LEW SE13 145 G6
Wear Pl BETH E2 104 D2
Wearside Rd LEW SE13 144 E5
Weaver Cl EHAM E6 108 B6
Weavers Cl ISLW TW7 135 K5
Weaver's La STHWK SE1 19 H1
Weavers Ter FUL/PGN * SW6 119 K6
Weaver St WCHPL E1 104 C3
Weavers Wy CAMTN NW1 84 D6
Weaver Wk WNWD SE27 162 C6
Webb Cl NKENS W10 100 A3
Webber Cl BORE WD6 29 K1
ERITH DA8 150 E1
Webber Rw STHWK SE1 17 K3
Webber St STHWK SE1 17 K2
Webb Est CLPT * E5 68 C4
Webb Pl WLSDN NW10 99 H2
Webb Rd BKHTH/KID SE3 125 J6
Webbscroft Rd DAGE RM10 92 D2
Webb's Rd BTSEA SW11 140 E6
YEAD UB4 94 E2
Webb St STHWK SE1 19 G5
Webster Gdns EA W5 116 E1
Webster Rd BERM/RHTH SE16 123 H3
WAN E11 88 A1
Wedderburn Rd BARK IG11 90 D6
HAMP NW3 83 H3
Wedgewood Cl NTHWD * HA6 40 A3
Wedgwood Wk
KIL/WHAMP * NW6 83 F3
Wedgwood Wy NRWD SE19 180 D3
Wedlake St NKENS W10 100 C3
Wedmore Av CLAY IG5 54 A4
Wedmore Gdns ARCH N19 66 E6
Wedmore Rd GFD/PVL UB6 96 D2
Wedmore St ARCH N19 84 D1
Weech Rd KIL/WHAMP NW6 82 E2
Weedington Rd KTTN NW5 84 A3
Weekley Sq BTSEA * SW11 140 C4
Weigall Rd LEE/GVPK SE12 145 K5
Weighhouse St MYFR/PKLN W1K 9 H5
Weighton Rd
KTN/HRWW/W HA3 42 D4
PGE/AN SE20 181 J5
Weihurst Gdns SUT SM1 209 H3
Weimar St PUT/ROE SW15 139 H4
Weirdale Av TRDG/WHET N20 33 K4
Weir Hall Av UED N18 49 K2
Weir Hall Gdns UED N18 49 K1
Weir Hall Rd UED N18 49 K2
Weir Rd BAL SW12 161 H3
BXLY DA5 169 J2
WIM/MER SW19 160 A5
Weirside Gdns WDR/YW UB7 112 A1
Weirs Pas CAMTN NW1 4 D4
Weiss Rd PUT/ROE SW15 139 G4
Welbeck Av BFN/LL DA15 168 B3
BMLY BR1 165 K6
YEAD UB4 95 F3
Welbeck Cl EW KT17 207 J5
NWMAL KT3 192 C2
Welbeck Rd EBAR EN4 33 H1
EHAM E6 107 H2
RYLN/HDSTN HA2 60 B5
SUT SM1 194 C6
Welbeck St MHST W1U 9 H2
Welbeck Vls WCHMH * N21 35 J3
Welbeck Wy MHST W1U 9 J3
Welby St CMBW SE5 142 C2
Welch Pl PIN * HA5 41 G4
Weldon Cl RSLP HA4 77 F4
Weldon Dr E/WMO/HCT KT8 188 E1
Weld Pl FBAR/BDGN N11 48 B1
Welfare Rd SRTFD E15 88 C5
Welford Cl CLPT E5 87 F1
Welford Pl WIM/MER SW19 159 H6
Welham Rd TOOT SW17 179 F2
Welhouse Rd CAR SM5 194 D5
Wellacre Rd KTN/HRWW/W HA3 61 H3
Wellan Cl BFN/LL DA15 148 C6
Welland Gdns GFD/PVL UB6 97 F1
Welland Ms WAP E1W 123 H1
Wellands Cl BMLY BR1 184 E5
Welland St GNWCH SE10 125 F6
Well Ap BAR EN5 20 A6
Wellbrook Rd ORP BR6 216 A2
Well Cl RSLP HA4 77 J1
STRHM/NOR SW16 162 A6
Wellclose Sq WAP E1W 104 C6
Wellclose St WAP E1W 104 C6
Wellcome Av DART DA1 151 H5
Well Cottage Cl WAN E11 71 G4
Well Ct MANHO EC4N 12 D4
Welldon Crs HRW HA1 60 E3
Wellers Ct CAMTN NW1 4 E3
Weller St STHWK SE1 18 C2
Wellesley Av HMSMTH W6 118 E3
NTHWD HA6 40 D1
Wellesley Cl CHARL * SE7 126 B5
Wellesley Ct STJWD NW8 101 G2
Wellesley Court Rd
CROY/NA * CR0 196 E6
Wellesley Crs WHTN TW2 155 K4
Wellesley Gv CROY/NA CR0 196 E6
Wellesley Pde WHTN * TW2 155 K5
Wellesley Park Ms ENC/FH EN2 23 H3
Wellesley Pl CAMTN * NW1 4 C5
KTTN NW5 84 A3
Wellesley Rd BELMT SM2 209 G4
CHSWK W4 117 H5
CROY/NA CR0 196 D5
HRW HA1 60 E2
IL IG1 72 B6
KTTN NW5 84 A3
WALTH E17 69 J3
WAN E11 70 E2
WHTN TW2 155 J5
Wellesley St WCHPL E1 105 F4
Wellesley Ter IS N1 6 D4
Wellfield Av MUSWH N10 48 B6
Wellfield Gdns CAR SM5 209 J6
Wellfield Rd STRHM/NOR SW16 161 K6
Wellfit St HNHL SE24 142 C4
Wellgarth GFD/PVL UB6 79 H4
Wellgarth Rd GLDGN NW11 65 F5
Well Gv TRDG/WHET N20 33 G3
Well Hall Pde ELTH/MOT SE9 146 E5
Well Hall Rd ELTH/MOT SE9 146 E5
Wellhouse La BAR EN5 20 A5
Wellhouse Rd BECK BR3 198 C1
Welling High St WELL DA16 148 C4
Wellington Av BFN/LL DA15 168 B1
CHING E4 37 J4
ED N9 36 D5
HSLW TW3 135 F6
PIN HA5 41 K4
SEVS/STOTM N15 68 C3
WOOL/PLUM SE18 127 H3
WPK KT4 208 A1
Wellington Cl DAGE RM10 92 E5
NTGHL W11 100 E5
NWCR SE14 144 A2
OXHEY WD19 27 J5
Wellington Crs NWMAL KT3 175 K6
Wellington Dr DAGE RM10 92 E5
Wellington Gdns CHARL SE7 126 B5
HPTN TW12 155 J6
Wellington Gv GNWCH SE10 145 G1
Wellington Ms HOLWY N7 85 F4
Wellington Pde BFN/LL * DA15 148 B6
Wellington Park Est
CRICK * NW2 63 J6
Wellington Pl EFNCH * N2 65 J2
STJWD NW8 2 B4
Wellington Rd BELV DA17 129 G5
BXLY DA5 168 E1
CROY/NA CR0 196 C4
DART DA1 171 F1
EA W5 116 D4
EBED/NFELT TW14 133 H6
EHAM E6 89 K6
EN EN1 24 A6
FSTGT E7 88 E3
HAYES BR2 200 B1
HPTN TW12 155 J6
KTN/HRWW/W HA3 42 E6
LEY E10 69 G5
PIN HA5 41 K4
STJWD NW8 2 B3
STMC/STPC BR5 202 C3
WALTH E17 51 G6
WAN E11 70 E2
WIM/MER SW19 159 K4
WLSDN * NW10 100 B2
Wellington Rd North
HSLWW TW4 134 E4
Wellington Rd South
HSLWW TW4 134 E5
Wellington Rw BETH E2 7 K4
Wellington Sq CHEL SW3 120 E5
Wellington St COVGDN WC2E 11 F5
WOOL/PLUM SE18 127 F4
Wellington Ter
CEND/HSY/T * N8 49 G6
HRW HA1 60 D5
NTGHL * W11 100 E6
WAP * E1W 123 J1
Wellington Wy BOW E3 105 J2
Welling Wy ELTH/MOT SE9 147 J4
Well La MORT/ESHN SW14 137 K6
Wellmeadow Rd HNWL W7 116 B4
LEW SE13 165 H1
Well Rd BAR EN5 20 A6
HAMP NW3 83 H1
The Wells STHGT/OAK N14 34 D3
Wells Cl NTHLT UB5 95 G2
SAND/SEL CR2 212 A3
Wells Dr CDALE/KGS NW9 63 F5
Wells Gdns IL IG1 71 J4
RAIN RM13 93 H4
Wells House Rd WLSDN NW10 99 G4
Wellside Cl BAR EN5 20 A5
Wellside Gdns
MORT/ESHN SW14 137 K5
Wells Ms FITZ * W1T 10 B2
Wellsmoor Gdns BMLY BR1 185 F6
Wells Park Rd SYD SE26 163 H5
Wells Pl CMBW SE5 143 F1
WAND/EARL SW18 160 B2
Wells Ri STJWD NW8 2 E1
Wells Rd BMLY BR1 184 E5
SHB W12 119 G1
Wells Sq FSBYW WC1X 5 G5
Wells St GTPST W1W 10 A2
Wellstead Av ED N9 36 E2
Wellstead Rd EHAM E6 108 A1
Wells Ter FSBYPK N4 67 G6
Well St HOM E9 86 E5
SRTFD E15 88 C4
Wells Wy CMBW SE5 122 E6
SKENS SW7 14 A4
Well Wk HAMP NW3 83 H1
Wellwood Rd GDMY/SEVK IG3 73 G5
Welsford St STHWK SE1 123 H5
Welsh Cl PLSTW E13 106 E2
Welshpool St HACK * E8 86 C6
Welshside CDALE/KGS * NW9 63 G2
Welstead Wy CHSWK W4 118 C3
Weltje Rd HMSMTH W6 118 D5
Welton Rd WOOL/PLUM SE18 147 K1
Welwyn Av EBED/NFELT TW14 153 J1
Welwyn St BETH E2 104 E2
Welwyn Wy YEAD UB4 94 C3
Wembley Hill Rd WBLY HA9 80 B3
Wembley Park Dr WBLY HA9 80 B2
Wembley Rd HPTN TW12 173 F4
Wembley Wy WBLY HA9 80 D4
Wemborough Rd STAN HA7 43 H4
Wembury Rd HGT N6 66 B4
Wemyss Rd BKHTH/KID SE3 145 J3
Wendela Ct HRW HA1 78 E1
Wendell Rd SHB W12 118 C2
Wendling Rd CAR SM5 194 C5
Wendon St BOW E3 87 H6
Wendover Cl YEAD UB4 95 H3
Wendover Dr NWMAL KT3 192 C3
Wendover Rd ELTH/MOT SE9 146 C4
HAYES BR2 200 A1
WLSDN NW10 99 H1
Wendover Wy BUSH WD23 28 C1
ORP BR6 202 B3
WELL DA16 148 B6
Wendy Cl EN EN1 36 B1
Wendy Wy ALP/SUD HA0 80 A6
Wenlock Gdns HDN * NW4 63 J1
Wenlock Rd EDGE HA8 44 D2
IS N1 6 C3
Wenlock St IS N1 6 D3
Wennington Rd BOW E3 105 F1
RAIN RM13 111 K4
Wensley Av WFD IG8 52 E3
Wensley Cl CRW RM5 56 C1
ELTH/MOT SE9 166 E1
FBAR/BDGN N11 48 A2
Wensleydale Av CLAY IG5 53 J5
Wensleydale Gdns HPTN TW12 173 G3
Wensleydale Rd HPTN TW12 173 F4
Wensley Rd UED N18 50 D2
Wentland Cl CAT SE6 165 G4
Wentland Rd CAT SE6 165 G4
Wentworth Av FNCH N3 46 E3
Wentworth Cl ASHF TW15 152 E6
FNCH N3 47 F3
HAYES * BR2 199 K6
MRDN SM4 193 K4
ORP BR6 216 E3
SURB KT6 190 E6
THMD SE28 109 K5
Wentworth Crs HYS/HAR UB3 113 G3
PECK SE15 143 H1
Wentworth Dr DART DA1 170 D2
PIN HA5 58 E2
Wentworth Gdns PLMGR N13 35 H5
Wentworth Hl WBLY HA9 62 B5
Wentworth Ms BOW E3 105 G3
Wentworth Pk FNCH N3 47 F3
Wentworth Pl STAN * HA7 43 H2
Wentworth Rd BAR EN5 20 B3
CROY/NA CR0 196 B4
GLDGN NW11 64 D3
MNPK E12 89 H2
NWDGN UB2 114 B4
Wentworth St WCHPL E1 13 J3
Wentworth Wy PIN HA5 59 H1
RAIN RM13 111 K2
Wenvoe Av BXLYHN DA7 149 J3
Wepham Cl YEAD UB4 95 H4
Wernbrook St
WOOL/PLUM SE18 127 H6
Werndee Rd SNWD SE25 197 H1
Werneth Hall Rd CLAY IG5 53 K6
Werrington St CAMTN NW1 4 B3
Werter Rd PUT/ROE SW15 139 H5
Wesleyan Pl KTTN NW5 84 B2
Wesley Av CAN/RD E16 125 K1
HSLW TW3 134 D3
WLSDN NW10 99 F2
Wesley Cl HOLWY N7 67 F6
RYLN/HDSTN HA2 60 C6
STMC/STPC BR5 186 D6
WALW SE17 18 B7
Wesley Rd EFNCH N2 47 J5
HYS/HAR UB3 94 E6
LEY E10 70 A4
WLSDN NW10 80 E6
Wesley Sq NTGHL W11 100 B5
Wesley St CAVSQ/HST W1G 9 H2
Wessex Av WIM/MER SW19 177 K5
Wessex Cl ESH/CLAY KT10 190 A6
GDMY/SEVK IG3 72 E3
KUTN/CMB KT2 175 J4
Wessex Ct BECK * BR3 182 B4
Wessex Dr ERITH DA8 150 B3
PIN HA5 41 J3
Wessex Gdns CRICK NW2 64 C5
Wessex La GFD/PVL UB6 96 D1
Wessex St BETH E2 104 E2
Wessex Ter MTCM * CR4 194 D2
Wessex Wy GLDGN NW11 64 C4
Wesson Md CMBW * SE5 142 D1
Westacott YEAD UB4 94 C4
West Ap STMC/STPC BR5 201 H2
West Arbour St WCHPL E1 105 F5
West Av FNCH N3 46 E2
HDN NW4 64 B2
HYS/HAR UB3 94 D6
PIN HA5 59 K4
STHL UB1 95 K6
WALTH E17 69 K2
WLGTN SM6 210 E3
West Avenue Rd WALTH E17 69 J1
West Bank BARK IG11 90 B6
ENC/FH EN2 23 J4
STNW/STAM N16 68 A4
Westbank Rd HPTN TW12 173 H2
West Barnes La NWMAL KT3 192 E2
RYNPK SW20 176 E6
Westbeech Rd WDGN N22 49 G6
Westbere Dr STAN HA7 43 K1
Westbere Rd CRICK NW2 82 C2
Westbourne Av ACT W3 99 F5
CHEAM SM3 193 H6
Westbourne Cl YEAD UB4 95 G3
Westbourne Crs BAY/PAD W2 8 A5
Westbourne Crescent Ms
BAY/PAD W2 8 A5
Westbourne Dr FSTH SE23 164 A3
Westbourne Gdns BAY/PAD W2 101 F5
Westbourne Ga BAY/PAD W2 8 B6
Westbourne Gv BAY/PAD W2 100 E5
Westbourne Grove Ms
NTGHL * W11 100 E5
Westbourne Grove Ter
BAY/PAD W2 101 F5
Westbourne Park Rd
BAY/PAD W2 100 E5
Westbourne Pl ED N9 36 D5
Westbourne Rd BXLYHN DA7 148 E1
CROY/NA CR0 197 G3
FELT TW13 153 J5
HOLWY N7 85 G4
SYD SE26 182 A2
Westbourne St BAY/PAD W2 8 A5
Westbourne Ter BAY/PAD W2 8 A4
Westbourne Terrace Ms
BAY/PAD W2 101 G5
Westbourne Terrace Rd
BAY/PAD W2 101 G4
Westbridge Cl SHB W12 118 D1
Westbridge Rd BTSEA SW11 140 C2
Westbrook Av HPTN TW12 172 E3
Westbrook Cl EBAR EN4 21 H4
Westbrook Crs EBAR EN4 21 H4
Westbrook Dr STMC/STPC BR5 202 E5
Westbrooke Crs WELL DA16 148 D4
Westbrooke Rd BFN/LL DA15 167 J4
WELL DA16 148 D4
Westbrook Rd BKHTH/KID SE3 145 K2
HEST TW5 134 E1
THHTH CR7 180 E4
Westbury Ar WDGN * N22 49 H6
Westbury Av ALP/SUD HA0 80 A5
ESH/CLAY KT10 205 F4
STHL UB1 96 A3
WDGN N22 49 H6
Westbury Cl RSLP HA4 58 E4
Westbury Gv FNCH N3 46 E2
Westbury La BKHH IG9 39 G4
Westbury Lodge Cl PIN HA5 41 H6
Westbury Pl BTFD TW8 116 E6
Westbury Rd ALP/SUD HA0 80 A5
BARK IG11 90 D6
BECK BR3 182 B6
BKHH IG9 39 G3
BMLY BR1 184 C4
CROY/NA CR0 196 E3
EA W5 98 A5
FBAR/BDGN N11 48 E2
FELT TW13 154 C3
FSTGT E7 89 F3
IL IG1 71 K5
NFNCH/WDSP N12 46 E2
NTHWD HA6 26 C6
NWMAL KT3 192 A1
PGE/AN SE20 182 A4
WALTH E17 69 J1
Westbury Ter FSTGT E7 89 F4
West Carriage Dr BAY/PAD W2 8 B6
West Central St
NOXST/BSQ WC1A 10 E3
West Chantry RYLN/HDSTN HA2 42 B4
Westchester Dr HDN NW4 46 B6
Westcliffe Vls KUT * KT1 175 G5
West Cl ASHF TW15 152 B6
EBAR EN4 22 A5
ED N9 36 B5
GFD/PVL UB6 96 C1
RAIN RM13 111 K3
WBLY HA9 62 B5
Westcombe Av CROY/NA CR0 195 K3
Westcombe Dr BAR EN5 20 E6
Westcombe Hl BKHTH/KID SE3 125 K6
Westcombe Park Rd
BKHTH/KID SE3 145 K1
West Common Rd HAYES BR2 199 K6
Westcoombe Av RYNPK SW20 176 C4
Westcote Ri RSLP HA4 58 A4
Westcote Rd
STRHM/NOR SW16 179 H1
Westcott Cl BMLY BR1 200 D2
CROY/NA CR0 213 K6
SEVS/STOTM N15 68 B3
Westcott Crs HNWL W7 96 E4
Westcott House POP/IOD * E14 105 J6
Westcott Rd WALW SE17 122 C6
West Ct ALP/SUD HA0 61 J6
Westcroft Cl CRICK NW2 82 C2
PEND EN3 24 E1
Westcroft Gdns MRDN SM4 177 J6
Westcroft Ms HMSMTH * W6 118 D4
Westcroft Rd CAR SM5 210 A2
Westcroft Sq HMSMTH W6 118 D4
Westcroft Wy CRICK NW2 82 C2
West Cromwell Rd ECT SW5 119 K4
West Cross Route NTGHL W11 100 B6
West Cross Wy BTFD TW8 116 C6
Westdale Rd WOOL/PLUM SE18 127 G6
Westdean Av LEE/GVPK SE12 166 A3
Westdean Cl WAND/EARL SW18 160 A1
Westdown Rd CAT SE6 164 D2
SRTFD E15 88 A2
West Drayton Park Av
WDR/YW UB7 112 B3
West Drayton Rd UX/CGN UB8 94 A4
West Dr BELMT SM2 208 B6
KTN/HRWW/W HA3 42 D2
TOOT SW17 161 G6
West Drive Gdns
KTN/HRWW/W HA3 42 D2
West Eaton Pl KTBR SW1X 15 G6
West Eaton Place Ms
KTBR SW1X 15 G6
West Ella Rd WLSDN NW10 81 G5
West End Av PIN HA5 59 H1
WALTH E17 70 A2
West End Cl WLSDN NW10 80 E5
West End Ct PIN * HA5 59 H1
West End Gdns NTHLT UB5 95 G1
West End La BAR EN5 20 B5
HYS/HAR UB3 133 F1
KIL/WHAMP NW6 82 E3
PIN HA5 41 H6
West End Rd RSLP HA4 76 D1
STHL UB1 114 D1
Westerdale Rd GNWCH SE10 125 K5
Westerfield Rd
SEVS/STOTM * N15 68 B2
Westergate Rd ABYW SE2 129 F6
Westerham Av UED N18 35 K5
Westerham Dr BFN/LL DA15 168 D1
Westerham Rd HAYES BR2 215 H4
LEY E10 69 K3
Westerley Crs SYD * SE26 182 C1
Western Av ACT W3 98 E3
DAGE RM10 92 E4
GFD/PVL UB6 97 F2
GLDGN NW11 64 B3
NTHLT UB5 77 F5
NTHLT UB5 77 J5

Western Ct FNCH * N3 46 E2
Western Gdns EA W5 98 C6
Western Gtwy CAN/RD E16 107 F6
Western La BAL SW12 161 F2
Western Man BAR * EN5 21 F6
Western Ms MV/WKIL W9 100 D3
Western Pde BAR EN5 20 E6
Western Rd BRXN/ST SW9 142 B4
EA W5 97 K6
EFNCH N2 47 K6
MTCM CR4 178 D4
NWDGN UB2 114 B4
PLSTW E13 89 F6
ROM RM1 75 H2
SUT SM1 208 E3
WALTH E17 70 A2
WDGN N22 49 F6
WLSDN NW10 98 E3
Western Ter HMSMTH * W6 118 D5
Western Vw HYS/HAR UB3 113 J2
Westernville Gdns
GNTH/NBYPK IG2 72 C4
Western Wy BAR EN5 32 E1
THMD SE28 127 K2
Westferry Circ POP/IOD E14 124 D1
Westferry Rd POP/IOD E14 105 H6
Westfield Cl CDALE/KGS NW9 44 E6
FUL/PGN * SW6 140 B1
PEND EN3 25 G4
SUT SM1 208 D2
Westfield Dr
KTN/HRWW/W HA3 61 K2
Westfield Gdns
KTN/HRWW/W HA3 61 K1
Westfield La KTN/HRWW/W HA3 61 K1
Westfield Pk PIN HA5 41 K3
Westfield Park Dr WFD IG8 53 J2
Westfield Rd BECK BR3 182 C5
BXLYHN DA7 149 K4
CROY/NA CR0 196 C6
DAGW RM9 92 A2
MLHL NW7 31 F5
MTCM CR4 178 D5
SURB KT6 190 E2
SUT SM1 208 D2
WEA W13 116 B1
WOT/HER KT12 188 D4
Westfields BARN SW13 138 C4
Westfields Av BARN SW13 138 B4
Westfields Rd ACT W3 98 D4
Westfield St WOOL/PLUM SE18 126 C3
Westfield Wy RSLP HA4 76 C1
WCHPL E1 105 G2
West Gdns WAP E1W 104 D6
WIM/MER SW19 178 D2
West Ga EA W5 98 A2
Westgate Est
EBED/NFELT * TW14 152 E3
Westgate Rd BECK BR3 183 F4
DART DA1 171 G1
SNWD SE25 197 J1
Westgate St HACK E8 86 D6
Westgate Ter WBPTN SW10 120 A5
Westglade Ct
KTN/HRWW/W HA3 61 K2
West Green Pl GFD/PVL UB6 78 D6
West Green Rd SEVS/STOTM N15 67 K1
West Gv GNWCH SE10 145 F2
WFD IG8 53 G2
Westgrove La GNWCH SE10 145 F2
West Halkin St KTBR SW1X 15 G4
West Hallowes ELTH/MOT SE9 166 C3
West Hall Rd RCH/KEW TW9 137 J2
West Ham La SRTFD E15 88 C5
West Hampstead Ms
KIL/WHAMP NW6 83 F4
West Harding St
FLST/FETLN * EC4A 11 K3
West Hatch Mnr RSLP HA4 58 D5
Westhay Gdns
MORT/ESHN SW14 137 J6
West Heath Av GLDGN NW11 64 E5
West Heath Cl DART * DA1 170 C1
HAMP NW3 82 E1
West Heath Dr GLDGN NW11 64 E5
West Heath Gdns HAMP NW3 64 E6
West Heath Rd BXLYHN DA7 128 E6
DART DA1 170 C1
HAMP NW3 64 E6
West Hl DART DA1 171 G1
HGT N6 66 A5
PUT/ROE SW15 159 G2
RYLN/HDSTN HA2 60 E6
SAND/SEL CR2 212 A6
WAND/EARL SW18 139 K6
WBLY HA9 62 B5
West Hill Dr DART DA1 171 F1
Westhill Pk HGT N6 65 K6
West Hill Ri DART DA1 171 G1
West Hill Rd PUT/ROE SW15 159 J1
West Hill Wy TRDG/WHET N20 33 F3
Westholm GLDGN NW11 65 F1
West Holme ERITH DA8 149 K2
Westholme ORP BR6 201 K4
Westholme Gdns RSLP HA4 58 E5
Westhorne Av ELTH/MOT SE9 166 B1
Westhorpe Gdns HDN NW4 46 A6
Westhorpe Rd PUT/ROE SW15 139 F4
West House Cl WIM/MER SW19 159 H3
Westhurst Dr CHST BR7 185 G1
West India Av POP/IOD E14 124 D1
West India Dock Rd
POP/IOD E14 105 H5
Westlake Cl PLMGR N13 35 G5
YEAD UB4 95 J3
Westland Cl
STWL/WRAY * TW19 152 B1
Westland Dr HAYES BR2 199 J6
Westland Pl FSBYE EC1V 6 E5
Westlands Cl HYS/HAR UB3 113 K4
Westlands Ter BAL SW12 161 H1
West La BERM/RHTH SE16 123 J2
Westlea Rd HNWL W7 116 B3
Westleigh Av PUT/ROE SW15 139 F6
Westleigh Dr BMLY BR1 184 D5
Westleigh Gdns EDGE HA8 44 C4
West Links ALP/SUD HA0 97 K2
Westlinton Cl MLHL NW7 46 C2
West Lodge Av ACT W3 117 H1
West Lodge Ct ACT * W3 117 H1
Westmacott Dr
EBED/NFELT TW14 153 J2
West Ml KENS * W8 119 K1
West Malling Wy HCH RM12 93 K3
West Md HOR/WEW KT19 207 G4
RSLP HA4 77 G2
Westmead PUT/ROE SW15 158 E2
Westmead Rd SUT SM1 209 H2
Westmede BARK/HLT IG6 54 C2
Westmere Dr MLHL NW7 31 F5
West Ms PIM SW1V 15 K7
TOTM * N17 50 D3
Westminster Av THHTH CR7 180 C5
Westminster Br WEST SW1P 17 F3
Westminster Bridge Rd
STHWK SE1 17 G3
Westminster Cl
EBED/NFELT TW14 153 K3
TEDD TW11 174 B1
Westminster Dr PLMGR N13 48 E1
Westminster Gdns BARK IG11 108 E1
BARK/HLT IG6 54 D5
CHING E4 38 C3
Westminster Rd ED N9 36 D3
HNWL W7 115 K1
SUT SM1 194 C6
Westmoat Cl BECK BR3 183 F3
Westmont Rd ESH/CLAY KT10 189 K6
Westmoor Gdns PEND EN3 25 F3
Westmoor Rd PEND EN3 25 F3
Westmoor St CHARL SE7 126 C4
Westmoreland Av WELL DA16 147 K4
Westmoreland Dr BELMT SM2 209 F6
Westmoreland Pl EA * W5 97 K4
HAYES * BR2 183 K6
PIM * SW1V 121 G5
Westmoreland Rd BARN SW13 138 C2
CDALE/KGS NW9 62 B1
HAYES BR2 199 H2
WALW SE17 122 E6
Westmoreland St
CAVSQ/HST W1G 9 H2
Westmoreland Ter
PGE/AN * SE20 181 J3
PIM SW1V 121 G5
Westmorland Cl MNPK E12 71 H6
TWK TW1 156 C1
Westmorland Rd HRW HA1 60 B2
WALTH E17 69 J3
Westmorland Wy MTCM CR4 195 J1
Westmount Ct EA * W5 98 B4
Westmount Rd ELTH/MOT SE9 146 E4
West Oak BECK BR3 183 G4
Westoe Rd ED N9 36 D4
Weston Av E/WMO/HCT KT8 188 D1
ESH/CLAY KT10 189 K4
Weston Dr KTN/HRWW/W HA3 43 H4
Weston Gdns ISLW TW7 135 J2
Weston Gn DAGW RM9 92 A2
THDIT KT7 189 K6
Weston Green Rd
ESH/CLAY KT10 189 J5
Weston Gv BMLY BR1 183 J3
Weston Pk CEND/HSY/T N8 66 E3
KUT KT1 175 F5
THDIT KT7 189 K5
Weston Park Cl THDIT * KT7 189 K5
Weston Ri FSBYW WC1X 5 H4
Weston Rd BMLY BR1 183 J4
CHSWK W4 117 K3
DAGW RM9 92 A2
EN EN1 23 K3
THDIT KT7 189 K5
Weston St STHWK SE1 19 F2
Weston Wk HACK E8 86 D5
Westover Cl BELMT SM2 209 F6
Westover Hl HAMP NW3 64 E6
Westover Rd WAND/EARL SW18 160 B1
Westow Hl NRWD SE19 181 F2
Westow St NRWD SE19 181 F2
West Pk ELTH/MOT SE9 166 D4
West Park Av RCH/KEW TW9 137 H2
West Park Cl CHDH RM6 73 K2
HEST TW5 114 E6
West Park Rd NWDGN UB2 115 H1
RCH/KEW TW9 137 H2
West Parkside GNWCH SE10 125 H2
West Pl NWDGN * UB2 115 G4
WIM/MER SW19 177 F1
Westpole Av EBAR EN4 22 B5
Westport Rd PLSTW E13 107 F3
Westport St WCHPL E1 105 F5
West Poultry Av FARR EC1M 12 A2
West Quarters SHB W12 99 J5
West Quay Dr YEAD UB4 95 J4
West Rp HTHAIR TW6 132 D2
West Ri BAY/PAD * W2 8 D5
West Rd CHDH RM6 74 A3
CHEL SW3 120 E5
CLAP SW4 141 J6
EA W5 98 A4
EBAR EN4 34 A3
EBED/NFELT TW14 153 G2
EFNCH N2 47 H5
KUTN/CMB KT2 175 K4
ROMW/RG RM7 75 F4
SRTFD E15 88 D6
TOTM N17 50 D2
WDR/YW UB7 112 C3
West Rw NKENS W10 100 C3
Westrow Dr BARK IG11 91 F4
Westrow Gdns GDMY/SEVK IG3 73 F6
West Sheen V RCH/KEW TW9 137 G5
Westside HDN NW4 45 K5
West Side Common
WIM/MER SW19 177 F2
West Smithfield STBT EC1A 12 B2
West Sq LBTH SE11 18 A5
West St BETH E2 104 D1
BMLY BR1 183 K4
BXLYHN DA7 149 G5
CAR SM5 209 K2
CROY/NA CR0 211 J2
ERITH DA8 130 A4
HRW HA1 60 D5
SUT SM1 209 F3
WALTH E17 69 K2
WAN E11 88 C1
West Street La CAR SM5 209 K2
West Street Pl CROY/NA * CR0 211 J2
West Temple Sheen
MORT/ESHN SW14 137 J6
West Tenter St WCHPL E1 13 K4
West Ter BFN/LL * DA15 167 K3
West Towers PIN HA5 59 H3
West Vw EBED/NFELT TW14 153 F3
Westview HNWL W7 96 E5
Westview Cl NKENS W10 100 A5
WLSDN NW10 81 H3
Westview Ct BORE WD6 29 K1
Westview Crs EN EN1 36 A2
Westview Dr WFD IG8 53 H5
West View Gdns BORE WD6 29 K1
West View Rd DART DA1 171 J1
Westville Rd SHB W12 118 D2
THDIT KT7 190 B4
West Wk EBAR EN4 34 A3
HYS/HAR UB3 113 K1
Westward Rd CHING E4 51 H1
Westward Wy
KTN/HRWW/W HA3 62 A3
West Warwick Pl PIM * SW1V 16 A7
Westway NTGHL W11 100 D4
RYNPK SW20 192 E1
SHB W12 99 H6
West Wy STMC/STPC BR5 201 J2
UED N18 35 K6
WLSDN NW10 81 F2
WWKM BR4 199 G3
CROY/NA CR0 198 B6
EDGE HA8 44 D2
HEST TW5 134 E2
PIN HA5 59 H1
RSLP HA4 58 D5
Westway Cl RYNPK SW20 176 E6
West Way Gdns CROY/NA CR0 198 A6
Westways HOR/WEW KT19 207 H2
Westwell Cl STMC/STPC BR5 202 E5
Westwell Rd STRHM/NOR SW16 179 K2
Westwell Road Ap
STRHM/NOR SW16 179 K2
Westwick Gdns HEST TW5 134 A3
WKENS W14 119 G2
Westwood Av NRWD SE19 180 D4
RYLN/HDSTN HA2 78 B2
Westwood Cl BMLY BR1 184 C6
ESH/CLAY KT10 204 C1
Westwood Gdns BARN SW13 138 C4
Westwood Hl SYD SE26 181 H1
Westwood La WELL DA16 148 B5
Westwood Pk FSTH SE23 163 J2
Westwood Pl SYD * SE26 181 H1
Westwood Rd BARN SW13 138 C4
CAN/RD E16 126 A1
GDMY/SEVK IG3 73 F5
West Woodside BXLY DA5 169 F3
Wetheral Dr STAN HA7 43 H4
Wetherby Cl NTHLT UB5 78 B4
Wetherby Gdns ECT SW5 120 B5
Wetherby Ms ECT SW5 120 A5
Wetherby Pl ECT SW5 120 B4
Wetherby Rd ENC/FH EN2 23 J2
Wetherby Wy CHSGTN KT9 206 A5
Wetherden St WALTH E17 69 H4
Wetherell Rd HOM E9 87 F6
Wetherill Rd MUSWH N10 48 A4
Wexford Rd BAL SW12 160 E2
Weybourne St
WAND/EARL SW18 160 B4
Weybridge Ct STHWK * SE1 123 J5
Weybridge Rd THHTH CR7 196 B1
Wey Ct HOR/WEW KT19 206 E2
Weydown Cl WIM/MER SW19 159 H3
Weyhill Rd WCHPL * E1 104 C5
Weylond Rd BCTR RM8 92 B1
Weyman Rd BKHTH/KID SE3 146 B2
Weymouth Av EA W5 116 D3
MLHL NW7 45 G1
Weymouth Cl EHAM E6 108 B5
Weymouth Ct BELMT * SM2 209 F5
Weymouth Ms CAVSQ/HST W1G 9 J1
Weymouth Rd YEAD UB4 94 C2
Weymouth St CAVSQ/HST W1G 9 H1
Weymouth Ter BETH E2 7 K2
Weymouth Vls FSBYPK * N4 67 F6
Weymouth Wk STAN HA7 43 G2
Whadcoat St FSBYPK N4 67 G6
Whalebone Av CHDH RM6 74 B3
Whalebone Gv CHDH RM6 74 B3
Whalebone La North CHDH RM6 56 A3
Whalebone La South BCTR RM8 74 B5
Whales Yd SRTFD * E15 88 C5
Wharf Bridge Rd ISLW TW7 136 C4
Wharfdale Cl FBAR/BDGN N11 48 A2
Wharfdale Rd IS N1 5 F2
Wharfedale Gdns
STRHM/NOR SW16 196 A1
Wharfedale St WBPTN SW10 120 A5
Wharf La TWK TW1 156 B3
Wharf Pl BETH E2 86 C6
Wharf Rd IS N1 6 C3
PEND EN3 37 G1
SRTFD E15 88 B6
Wharfside Rd CAN/RD E16 106 C5
Wharf St CAN/RD E16 106 C4
Wharncliffe Dr STHL UB1 115 J1
Wharncliffe Gdns SNWD SE25 181 F5
Wharncliffe Rd SNWD SE25 180 E5
Wharton Cl WLSDN NW10 81 G4
Wharton Cottages
FSBYW * WC1X 5 H5
Wharton Rd BMLY BR1 184 A4
Wharton St FSBYW WC1X 5 H5
Whateley Rd EDUL SE22 143 G6
PGE/AN SE20 182 A3
Whatley Av RYNPK SW20 177 G6
Whatman Rd FSTH SE23 164 A2
Wheastone Rd NKENS * W10 100 C4
Wheatfields PEND EN3 25 G2
Wheatfield Wy KUT KT1 175 F6
Wheathill Rd PGE/AN SE20 181 J5
Wheatlands HEST TW5 115 F6
Wheatlands Rd TOOT SW17 161 F5
Wheatley Cl HDN NW4 45 J5
Wheatley Crs HYS/HAR UB3 94 E6
Wheatley Gdns ED N9 36 A4
Wheatley Rd ISLW TW7 136 A4
Wheatley St CAVSQ/HST W1G 9 H2
Wheatley Terrace Rd
ERITH DA8 130 C6
Wheat Sheaf Cl POP/IOD E14 124 D4
Wheatsheaf Cl RSLP HA4 77 J3
Wheatsheaf La FUL/PGN SW6 139 F1
VX/NE SW8 141 K1
Wheatsheaf Rd ROM RM1 75 H3
Wheatsheaf Ter
FUL/PGN * SW6 139 J1
Wheatstone Cl WIM/MER SW19 178 C4
Wheatstone Rd NKENS W10 100 C4
Wheeler Gdns IS N1 84 E6
Wheeler La WCHPL E1 13 J1
Wheelers Cross BARK IG11 108 D1
Wheelers Dr RSLP HA4 58 A3
Wheel Farm Dr DAGE RM10 92 E1
Wheelock Cl ERITH DA8 149 J1
Wheelright Cl BUSH WD23 28 B1
Wheelwright St HOLWY N7 85 F5
Whelan Wy WLGTN SM6 210 D1
Wheler St WCHPL E1 7 J7
Whellock Rd CHSWK W4 118 B3
Whenman Av BXLY DA5 169 K4
Whetstone Cl TRDG/WHET N20 33 H4
Whetstone Pk LINN WC2A 11 G3
Whetstone Rd BKHTH/KID SE3 146 B3
Whewell Rd ARCH N19 66 E6
Whichcote St STHWK * SE1 17 J1
Whidborne Cl DEPT SE8 144 D3
Whidborne St STPAN WC1H 5 F5
Whimbrel Wy YEAD UB4 95 H5
Whinchat Rd THMD SE28 127 J3
Whinfell Cl STRHM/NOR SW16 179 J1
Whinyates Rd ELTH/MOT SE9 146 D4
Whippendell Cl STMC/STPC BR5 186 C4
Whippendell Wy
STMC/STPC BR5 186 C4
Whipps Cross Rd WAN E11 70 C2
Whiskin St CLKNW EC1R 6 A5
Whistler Gdns EDGE HA8 44 B5
Whistlers Av BTSEA * SW11 140 C1
Whistler St HBRY N5 85 H2
Whistler Wk WBPTN * SW10 140 B1
Whiston Rd BETH E2 7 J2
Whitbread Cl TOTM N17 50 C4
Whitbread Rd BROCKY SE4 144 B5
Whitburn Rd LEW SE13 144 E6
Whitby Av WLSDN NW10 98 D2
Whitby Gdns CDALE/KGS NW9 44 C6
SUT SM1 194 C6
Whitby Pde RSLP * HA4 59 G6
Whitby Rd RSLP HA4 77 F1
RYLN/HDSTN HA2 78 C1
SUT SM1 194 C6
WOOL/PLUM SE18 126 E4
Whitby St WCHPL E1 7 J6
Whitcher Cl NWCR SE14 124 B6
Whitcher Pl KTTN NW5 84 C4
Whitchurch Av EDGE HA8 44 B3
Whitchurch Cl EDGE HA8 44 B2
Whitchurch Gdns EDGE HA8 44 B3
Whitchurch La EDGE HA8 44 A3
Whitchurch Pde EDGE * HA8 44 C3
Whitchurch Rd NTGHL W11 100 B6
Whitcomb St SOHO/SHAV W1D 10 C5
Whitcome Ms RCH/KEW TW9 137 J2
Whitear Wk SRTFD E15 88 B4
Whitebarn La DAGE RM10 110 C1
Whitebeam Av HAYES BR2 201 F4
Whitebeam Cl BRXN/ST * SW9 142 A1
White Bear Pl HAMP * NW3 83 H2
White Bear Yd CLKNW * EC1R 5 J7
White Bridge Av MTCM CR4 194 C1
White Bridge Cl
EBED/NFELT TW14 153 J1
White Butts Rd RSLP HA4 77 H1
Whitechapel High St WCHPL E1 13 K3
Whitechapel Rd WCHPL E1 104 C5
White Church La WCHPL E1 104 C5
White City Cl SHB W12 100 A6
White City Rd SHB W12 99 K6
White Conduit St IS N1 5 K2
Whitecote Rd STHL UB1 96 B5
White Craig Cl PIN HA5 42 A1
Whitecroft Cl BECK BR3 199 G1
Whitecroft Wy BECK BR3 199 F1
Whitecross St STLK EC1Y 6 D6
Whitefield Av CRICK NW2 64 A4
Whitefield Cl STMC/STPC BR5 186 D6
WAND/EARL SW18 159 H1
Whitefoot La CAT SE6 165 G6
Whitefoot Ter BMLY BR1 165 J5
Whitefriars Dr
KTN/HRWW/W HA3 42 E5
Whitefriars St EMB EC4Y 11 K4
White Gate Gdns
KTN/HRWW/W HA3 42 E3
Whitehall WHALL SW1A 16 E1
Whitehall Ct WHALL SW1A 16 E1
Whitehall Crs CHSGTN KT9 205 K3
Whitehall Gdns ACT W3 117 H1
CHING E4 38 B3
CHSWK W4 117 J6
WHALL SW1A 16 E1
Whitehall La BKHH IG9 38 E4
ERITH DA8 150 C3
Whitehall Pk ARCH N19 66 C5
Whitehall Park Rd CHSWK W4 117 J6
Whitehall Pl CAR SM5 210 B2
WHALL SW1A 16 E1
Whitehall Rd CHING E4 38 C4
HAYES BR2 200 C2
HNWL W7 116 B2
HRW HA1 60 E4
THHTH CR7 196 B2
Whitehall St TOTM N17 50 B3
White Hart La BARN SW13 138 B3
ROMW/RG RM7 56 C4
WDGN N22 49 G4
White Hart Rd ORP BR6 202 B4
WOOL/PLUM SE18 127 K4
White Hart St LBTH SE11 122 B5
White Hart Ter TOTM * N17 50 B3
White Hart Yd STHWK SE1 18 E1
Whitehaven Cl HAYES BR2 199 K1
Whitehaven St STJWD NW8 2 C7
Whitehead Cl RDART DA2 171 F5
UED N18 49 K1
WAND/EARL SW18 160 B2
Whiteheads Gv CHEL SW3 14 D7
CHEL SW3 120 D5
White Heart Av UX/CGN UB8 94 A4
Whiteheath Av RSLP HA4 58 A4
White Heron Ms TEDD * TW11 174 A2
Whitehill Rd DART DA1 150 D6
Whitehorn Pl WDR/YW UB7 112 C1
White Horse Hl CHST BR7 167 F6
Whitehorse La SNWD SE25 197 F1
White Horse La WCHPL E1 105 F3
White Horse Rd EHAM E6 107 K2
Whitehorse Rd CROY/NA CR0 196 D4
WCHPL E1 105 G4
White Horse St MYFR/PICC W1J 15 K1
White House Dr STAN HA7 29 J6
White House La ENC/FH EN2 23 J2
Whitehouse Wy STHGT/OAK N14 34 B4
Whitehurst Dr UED * N18 51 F1
White Kennett St WCHPL E1 13 H3
White Ledges WEA W13 97 J5
Whitelegg Rd PLSTW E13 106 D1
Whiteley Rd NRWD SE19 180 E1
Whiteleys Wy FELT TW13 155 F5
White Lion Ct BANK EC3V 13 G4
PECK * SE15 123 K6
White Lion Hl BLKFR EC4V 12 B5
White Lion St IS N1 5 J3
The White Ldg BAR * EN5 20 C4
White Ldg NRWD SE19 180 C3
White Lodge Cl BELMT SM2 209 G5
EFNCH N2 65 H3
White Lyon Ct BARB EC2Y 12 C1
White Oak Dr BECK BR3 183 F5
White Oak Gdns BFN/LL DA15 168 A2
Whiteoaks La GFD/PVL UB6 96 D1
White Orchards STAN HA7 43 G1
TRDG/WHET N20 32 D2
White Post La HOM E9 87 H5
White Post St PECK SE15 143 K1
White Rd SRTFD E15 88 C5
Whites Av GNTH/NBYPK IG2 72 E3
White's Grounds STHWK SE1 19 H2
Whites Grounds Est STHWK SE1 19 H2
Whites Meadow BMLY * BR1 201 F1
White's Rw WCHPL E1 13 J2
White's Sq CLAP SW4 141 J5
Whitestile Rd BTFD TW8 116 D5
Whitestone La HAMP NW3 83 G1
Whitestone Wk HAMP NW3 83 G1
White St NWDGN UB2 114 C2
Whitethorn Gdns CROY/NA CR0 197 J6
ENC/FH EN2 23 K6
Whitethorn St BOW E3 105 J3
Whitewebbs Wy
STMC/STPC BR5 186 A4
Whitfield Pl FITZ W1T 4 A7
Whitfield Rd BXLYHN DA7 149 G1
EHAM E6 89 G5
GNWCH SE10 145 G2
Whitfield St FITZ W1T 10 B1
Whitford Gdns MTCM CR4 178 E6
Whitgift Av SAND/SEL CR2 211 J3
Whitgift St CROY/NA CR0 211 J1
LBTH SE11 17 G6
Whitings Rd BAR EN5 20 A6
Whitings Wy EHAM E6 108 A4
Whitland Rd CAR SM5 194 C5
Whitley Cl STWL/WRAY TW19 152 B1
Whitley Rd TOTM N17 50 A5
Whitlock Dr WAND/EARL SW18 159 H2
Whitman Rd BOW E3 105 G3
Whitmead Cl SAND/SEL CR2 211 K4
Whitmore Cl FBAR/BDGN N11 48 B1
Whitmore Est IS N1 7 H1
Whitmore Gdns WLSDN NW10 100 A1
Whitmore Rd BECK BR3 182 C6
HRW HA1 60 D4
IS N1 7 G1
Whitnell Wy PUT/ROE * SW15 139 F6
Whitney Av REDBR IG4 71 H1
Whitney Rd LEY E10 69 J4
Whitney Wk SCUP DA14 187 F2
Whitstable Cl BECK BR3 182 C4
Whitstable Pl CROY/NA CR0 211 J2
Whittaker Av RCH/KEW * TW9 136 E6
Whittaker Rd CHEAM SM3 208 D1
EHAM E6 89 G5
Whittaker St BGVA SW1W 15 G7
Whitta Rd MNPK E12 89 H2
Whittell Gdns SYD SE26 163 K5
Whittingstall Rd FUL/PGN SW6 139 J2
Whittington Av BANK EC3V 13 G4
YEAD UB4 94 D4
Whittington Ms
NFNCH/WDSP N12 33 G6
Whittington Rd WDGN N22 48 E3
Whittington Wy PIN HA5 59 J2
Whittlebury Cl CAR SM5 209 K5
Whittle Cl GFD/PVL UB6 96 B5
WALTH E17 69 G3
Whittle Rd HEST TW5 134 B1
NWDGN UB2 115 G2
Whittlesea Rd KTN/HRWW/W HA3 42 C3
Whittlesey St STHWK SE1 17 K1
Whitton Av East GFD/PVL UB6 79 F3
Whitton Av West NTHLT UB5 78 B3
Whitton Cl GFD/PVL UB6 79 H4
Whitton Dene HSLW TW3 135 G6
Whitton Dr GFD/PVL UB6 79 G4
Whitton Manor Rd ISLW TW7 155 H1
Whitton Rd HSLW TW3 135 G6
WHTN TW2 155 K1
Whitton Waye HSLW TW3 155 F1
Whitwell Rd PLSTW E13 106 E2
Whitworth Rd SNWD SE25 181 F6
WOOL/PLUM SE18 147 F1
Whitworth St GNWCH SE10 125 H5
Whorlton Rd PECK SE15 143 H4
Whybridge Cl RAIN RM13 93 G6
Whymark Av WDGN N22 49 G6
Whytecroft HEST TW5 134 C1
Whyteville Rd FSTGT E7 89 F4
Wichling Cl STMC/STPC BR5 202 E5
Wickersley Rd BTSEA SW11 141 F4
Wickers Oake NRWD * SE19 163 G6
Wicker St WCHPL * E1 104 C5
The Wicket CROY/NA CR0 213 J3
Wicket Rd GFD/PVL UB6 97 G2
The Wickets ASHF TW15 152 B6
Wickets Wy BARK/HLT IG6 55 F2
Wickford St WCHPL E1 104 E3
Wickford Wy WALTH E17 69 F1
Wickham Av CHEAM SM3 208 A3
CROY/NA CR0 198 B6
Wickham Cha WWKM BR4 199 G4
Wickham Cl NWMAL KT3 192 C2
PEND EN3 24 D4
WCHPL E1 104 E4
Wickham Ct WWKM * BR4 214 B2
Wickham Court Rd WWKM BR4 199 F6
Wickham Crs WWKM BR4 199 F6
Wickham Gdns BROCKY SE4 144 C4
Wickham La ABYW SE2 128 B6
Wickham Rd BECK BR3 182 E6
BROCKY SE4 144 C4
CHING E4 52 A3
CROY/NA CR0 197 K6
CROY/NA CR0 198 C5
KTN/HRWW/W HA3 42 D5
Wickham St LBTH SE11 122 A5
WELL DA16 147 K3
Wickham Wy BECK BR3 199 F1
Wick La BOW E3 87 J6
Wickliffe Av FNCH N3 46 C5
Wickliffe Gdns WBLY HA9 62 C6
Wicklow St FSBYW WC1X 5 G4
Wick Rd HOM E9 87 G4
TEDD TW11 174 C3
Wicks Cl ELTH/MOT SE9 166 C6
Wicksteed Cl BXLY DA5 170 A5
Wickwood St CMBW SE5 142 C3
Widdenham Rd HOLWY N7 85 F2
Widdicombe Av
RYLN/HDSTN HA2 59 J6
Widdin St SRTFD E15 88 C5
Widecombe Gdns REDBR IG4 71 J1
Widecombe Rd ELTH/MOT SE9 166 D5
Widecombe Wy EFNCH N2 65 H2

Widegate St WCHPL E1 13 H2
Widenham Cl PIN HA5 59 G2
Wide Wy STRHM/NOR SW16 179 J6
Widgeon Cl CAN/RD E16 107 F5
Widgeon Rd ERITH DA8 150 E1
Widley Rd MV/WKIL W9 100 E2
Widmore Lodge Rd BMLY BR1 184 C5
Widmore Rd BMLY BR1 184 B5
Wieland Rd NTHWD HA6 40 E3
Wigeon Wy YEAD UB4 95 H5
Wiggins Md CDALE/KGS NW9 45 H3
Wigginton Av WBLY HA9 80 C4
Wightman Rd CEND/HSY/T N8 67 G1
Wigley Rd FELT TW13 154 C4
Wigmore Pl CAVSQ/HST * W1G 9 J3
Wigmore Rd CAR SM5 194 C6
Wigmore St MBLAR W1H 9 H3
Wigram Rd WAN E11 71 G3
Wigram Sq WALTH E17 52 A6
Wigston Cl UED N18 50 A1
Wigston Rd PLSTW E13 107 F3
Wigton Gdns STAN HA7 44 A4
Wigton Pl LBTH SE11 122 B5
Wigton Rd WALTH E17 51 H4
Wilberforce Rd CDALE/KGS NW9 63 H2
FSBYPK N4 67 H6
Wilberforce Wy
WIM/MER SW19 177 G2
Wilbraham Pl KTBR SW1X 15 G6
Wilbury Wy UED N18 49 K1
Wilby Ms NTGHL W11 100 D6
Wilcot Av OXHEY WD19 27 J2
Wilcot Cl OXHEY WD19 27 J2
Wilcox Cl VX/NE SW8 141 K1
Wilcox Rd SUT * SM1 209 F2
TEDD TW11 155 J6
VX/NE SW8 141 K1
Wildacres NTHWD HA6 26 D6
Wild Ct HOL/ALD WC2B 11 G3
Wildcroft Gdns STAN HA7 43 K2
Wildcroft Rd PUT/ROE SW15 159 F2
Wilde Cl HACK E8 86 C6
Wilde Pl PLMGR N13 49 H2
Wilder Cl RSLP HA4 59 F5
The Wilderness
E/WMO/HCT KT8 189 H2
HPTN * TW12 155 G6
Wilderness Rd CHST BR7 185 G3
Wilde Rd ERITH DA8 149 J1
Wilderton Rd STNW/STAM N16 68 A4
Wildfell Rd CAT SE6 164 E2
Wild Goose Dr PECK SE15 143 K2
Wild Hatch GLDGN NW11 64 E3
Wild Oaks Cl NTHWD HA6 40 D2
Wild's Rents STHWK SE1 19 G4
Wild St HOL/ALD WC2B 11 F4
Wildwood NTHWD HA6 40 B2
Wildwood Cl LEE/GVPK SE12 165 J2
Wildwood Gv HAMP NW3 65 G5
Wildwood Ri GLDGN NW11 65 G5
Wildwood Rd GLDGN NW11 65 G4
Wilford Cl ENC/FH * EN2 23 K4
NTHWD HA6 40 B3
Wilford Rd CROY/NA CR0 196 D3
Wilfred Av RAIN RM13 111 J4
Wilfred St WESTW SW1E 16 A4
Wilfrid Gdns ACT W3 98 E4
Wilkes Rd BTFD TW8 117 F6
Wilkes St WCHPL E1 13 K1
Wilkins Cl HYS/HAR UB3 113 J5
MTCM CR4 178 D4
Wilkinson Rd CAN/RD E16 107 G5
Wilkinson St VX/NE SW8 142 A1
Wilkinson Wy CHSWK W4 118 A2
Wilkin St KTTN NW5 84 A4
Wilkin Street Ms KTTN * NW5 84 B4
Wilks Av DART DA1 171 J4
Wilks Gdns CROY/NA CR0 198 B5
Wilks Pl IS N1 7 H3
Willan Rd TOTM N17 49 K5
Willan Wall CAN/RD E16 106 D6
Willard St VX/NE SW8 141 G4
Willcocks Cl CHSGTN KT9 206 A1
Willcott Rd ACT W3 117 J1
Will Crooks Gdns
ELTH/MOT SE9 146 C5
Willenhall Av BAR EN5 33 G1
Willenhall Dr HYS/HAR UB3 94 C6
Willenhall Rd WOOL/PLUM SE18 127 G5
Willerfield Rd WLSDN NW10 98 E2
Willersley Av BFN/LL DA15 168 A3
ORP BR6 216 D1
Willersley Cl BFN/LL DA15 168 A3
Willesden La KIL/WHAMP NW6 82 B5
Willes Rd KTTN NW5 84 B4
Willett Cl NTHLT UB5 95 G2
STMC/STPC BR5 201 K3
Willett Rd THHTH CR7 196 B2
Willett Wy STMC/STPC BR5 201 J2
William Barefoot Dr
ELTH/MOT SE9 167 F4
William Booth Rd PGE/AN SE20 181 H4
William Carey Wy HRW HA1 60 E3
William Cl CRW RM5 56 E4
EFNCH N2 47 H5
LEW SE13 145 F4
NWDGN UB2 115 H2
William Covell Cl ENC/FH * EN2 23 F1
William Ellis Wy
BERM/RHTH * SE16 123 H3
William Gdns PUT/ROE SW15 138 E6
William Guy Gdns BOW E3 105 K2
William IV St CHCR WC2N 10 E6
William Margrie Cl PECK * SE15 143 H3
William Ms KTBR SW1X 15 F3
William Morley Cl EHAM E6 89 H6
William Morris Cl WALTH E17 51 H6
William Morris Wy
FUL/PGN SW6 140 B4
William Rd CAMTN NW1 4 A5
SUT SM1 209 G3
WIM/MER SW19 177 H3
Williams Av WALTH E17 51 H4
William's Buildings BETH * E2 104 E3
Williams Cl CEND/HSY/T * N8 66 D3
FUL/PGN SW6 139 H1
Williams Dr HSLW TW3 135 F5
Williams Gv SURB KT6 190 D3
WDGN N22 49 G4
Williams La MORT/ESHN SW14 137 K4
MRDN SM4 194 B3
Williamson Cl GNWCH SE10 125 J5
Williamson Rd FSBYPK N4 67 H3
Williamson St HOLWY * N7 84 E2
Williamson Wy MLHL NW7 46 C2
William Sq BERM/RHTH SE16 124 B1
Williams Rd NWDGN UB2 114 D4
WEA * W13 116 B1
Williams Ter CROY/NA CR0 211 G4
William St BARK IG11 90 C5
CAR SM5 209 J1
KTBR SW1X 15 F3
LEY E10 69 K3
TOTM N17 50 B3
Willifield Wy GLDGN NW11 64 E2
Willingdon Rd WDGN N22 49 H5
Willingham Cl KTTN NW5 84 C3
Willingham Ter KTTN * NW5 84 C3
Willingham Wy KUT KT1 175 H5
Willington Rd BRXN/ST SW9 141 K4
Willis Av BELMT SM2 209 J4
Willis Rd CROY/NA CR0 196 D4
ERITH DA8 129 K4
SRTFD E15 106 D1
Willis St POP/IOD E14 105 K5
Willmore End WIM/MER SW19 178 A4
Willoughby Av CROY/NA CR0 211 F2
Willoughby Dr RAIN RM13 93 G5
Willoughby Gv TOTM N17 50 D3
Willoughby La TOTM N17 50 D3
Willoughby Ms TOTM N17 50 D3
Willoughby Park Rd TOTM N17 50 D3
Willoughby Rd CEND/HSY/T N8 49 G6
HAMP NW3 83 H2
KUTN/CMB KT2 175 G4
TWK TW1 136 D6
Willoughby Wy CHARL SE7 126 A4
Willow Av BARN SW13 138 C3
BFN/LL DA15 168 B1
Willow Bridge Rd IS * N1 85 J4
Willowbrook HPTN * TW12 173 G1
Willowbrook Est PECK * SE15 143 G1
Willowbrook Rd NWDGN UB2 114 E3
PECK SE15 123 G6
STWL/WRAY TW19 152 B3
Willow Cl BKHH IG9 39 H5
BTFD TW8 116 D6
BXLY DA5 169 G1
HAYES BR2 200 E2
HCH RM12 93 K1
STMC/STPC BR5 202 C3
Willow Ct STAN * HA7 43 K3
Willowcourt Av
KTN/HRWW/W HA3 61 H2
Willow Dean PIN * HA5 41 H5
Willow Dene BUSH WD23 28 E2
Willowdene HGT * N6 65 K4
Willow Dene PIN HA5 41 H5
Willowdene Cl WHTN TW2 155 H2
Willow Dr BAR EN5 20 C5
Willow End NTHWD HA6 40 C3
TRDG/WHET N20 32 E4
Willowfields Cl
WOOL/PLUM SE18 127 K5
Willow Gdns HEST * TW5 135 F2
RSLP HA4 58 D6
Willow Gv CHST BR7 185 G2
RSLP HA4 58 D6
Willowhayne Dr WOT/HER KT12 188 A4
Willowhayne Gdns WPK KT4 208 A2
Willow La MTCM CR4 194 E2
WOOL/PLUM SE18 126 E4
Willowmead Cl EA W5 97 K4
Willowmere ESH/CLAY KT10 204 C2
Willow Mt CROY/NA CR0 212 A2
Willow Pl WEST SW1P 16 B6
Willow Rd CHDH RM6 74 A3
DART DA1 171 F3
EA W5 117 F2
EN EN1 24 A3
ERITH DA8 150 D2
HAMP NW3 83 H2
NWMAL KT3 191 K1
WLGTN SM6 210 B5
The Willows BECK * BR3 182 D4
EBAR * EN4 33 J1
ESH/CLAY KT10 204 E4
OXHEY WD19 27 F2
Willows Av MRDN SM4 194 A2
Willows Cl PIN HA5 41 G5
Willows Ter WLSDN * NW10 99 H1
Willow St CHING E4 38 B2
ROMW/RG RM7 74 E1
SDTCH EC2A 7 G6
Willow Ter PGE/AN * SE20 181 J4
Willowtree Cl HGDN/ICK UB10 76 A1
Willow Tree Cl HOM E9 87 G6
WAND/EARL SW18 160 A3
YEAD UB4 95 G3
Willow Tree La YEAD UB4 95 G3
Willow Tree Wk BMLY BR1 184 A4
Willowtree Wy
STRHM/NOR SW16 180 B4
Willow V CHST BR7 185 F2
SHB W12 118 D1
Willow Vw WIM/MER SW19 178 C4
Willow Wk CHEAM SM3 208 D1
DART * DA1 151 H6
ORP BR6 216 B1
SEVS/STOTM N15 67 H1
STHWK SE1 19 H6
WALTH E17 69 H2
WCHMH N21 35 F1
Willow Wy ALP/SUD * HA0 79 G1
FNCH N3 47 F3
HOR/WEW KT19 207 F4
NTGHL W11 100 B6
SYD SE26 163 J5
WHTN TW2 155 G4
Willow Wood Crs SNWD SE25 197 F3
Willow Wren Whf
NWDGN * UB2 114 A4
Willrose Crs ABYW SE2 128 C5
Wills Crs HSLW TW3 155 G1
Wills Gv MLHL NW7 45 J1
Willshaw St NWCR SE14 144 D2
Wilman Gv HACK E8 86 C5
Wilmar Cl YEAD UB4 94 B3
Wilmar Gdns WWKM BR4 198 E5
Wilmer Cl RCHPK/HAM TW10 175 G1
Wilmer Crs RCHPK/HAM TW10 175 G1
Wilmer Gdns IS N1 7 H1
Wilmer Lea Cl SRTFD E15 88 A5
Wilmer Pl STNW/STAM N16 68 B6
Wilmer Wy STHGT/OAK N14 48 D1
Wilmington Av CHSWK W4 138 A1
ORP BR6 202 D6
Wilmington Court Rd
RDART DA2 170 D5
Wilmington Gdns BARK IG11 90 D5
Wilmington Sq FSBYW WC1X 5 J5
Wilmington St FSBYW WC1X 5 J5
Wilmot Cl PECK * SE15 143 H1
Wilmot Pl CAMTN NW1 84 C5
HNWL W7 115 K1
Wilmot Rd CAR * SM5 209 K3
DART DA1 150 E6
LEY E10 69 K6
TOTM N17 49 K6
Wilmot St BETH E2 104 D3
Wilmount St WOOL/PLUM SE18 127 G4
Wilna Rd WAND/EARL SW18 160 B2
Wilsham St NTGHL W11 119 G1
Wilsmere Dr KTN/HRWW/W HA3 42 E3
NTHLT UB5 77 J4
Wilson Av MTCM CR4 178 D3
Wilson Cl SAND/SEL CR2 211 K3
WBLY HA9 62 B4
Wilson Dr WBLY HA9 62 B4
Wilson Gdns HRW HA1 60 C4
Wilson Gv BERM/RHTH SE16 123 J2
Wilson Rd CHSGTN KT9 206 B4
CMBW SE5 142 E2
IL IG1 71 K4
PLSTW E13 107 H2
Wilson's Av TOTM N17 50 B5
Wilson's Pl POP/IOD E14 105 H5
Wilson's Rd HMSMTH W6 119 G5
Wilson St SDTCH EC2A 13 F1
WALTH E17 70 A2
WCHMH N21 35 G2
Wilson Wk HMSMTH * W6 118 C4
Wilstone Cl NTHLT UB5 95 J3
Wilthorne Gdns DAGE RM10 92 D5
Wilton Av CHSWK W4 118 C5
Wilton Cl WDR/YW UB7 112 A6
Wilton Crs KTBR SW1X 15 G3
WIM/MER SW19 177 J4
Wilton Dr CRW RM5 56 E3
Wilton Est HACK * E8 86 C4
Wilton Gdns E/WMO/HCT KT8 173 F6
WOT/HER KT12 188 C5
Wilton Gv NWMAL KT3 192 C3
WIM/MER SW19 177 J3
Wilton Ms HACK * E8 86 D4
KTBR SW1X 15 H4
Wilton Pl KTBR SW1X 15 G3
Wilton Rd ABYW SE2 128 D3
EBAR EN4 21 K5
HSLWW TW4 134 C4
MUSWH N10 48 A5
PIM SW1V 16 A6
WIM/MER SW19 178 D3
Wilton Rw KTBR SW1X 15 G3
Wilton Sq IS N1 85 K6
Wilton St KTBR SW1X 15 J4
Wilton Ter KTBR SW1X 15 G4
Wilton Vls IS N1 6 E1
Wilton Wk FELT * TW13 154 A4
Wilton Wy HACK E8 86 C4
Wiltshire Cl CHEL SW3 14 D7
MLHL * NW7 45 H1
Wiltshire Gdns FSBYPK N4 67 J3
WHTN TW2 155 H3
Wiltshire La PIN HA5 58 E1
RSLP HA4 40 D6
Wiltshire Rd BRXN/ST SW9 142 B4
ORP BR6 202 B4
THHTH CR7 180 B6
Wiltshire Rw IS N1 6 E1
Wilverley Crs NWMAL KT3 192 B3
Wimbart Rd
BRXS/STRHM * SW2 162 A2
Wimbledon Br WIM/MER SW19 177 J2
Wimbledon Hill Rd
WIM/MER SW19 177 H2
Wimbledon Park Rd
WIM/MER SW19 159 H5
Wimbledon Park Side
WIM/MER SW19 159 G4
Wimbledon Rd TOOT SW17 160 B6
Wimbolt St BETH E2 104 C2
Wimborne Av NWDGN UB2 115 F4
STMC/STPC BR5 186 A6
YEAD UB4 95 F5
Wimborne Cl BKHH IG9 39 G4
LEE/GVPK SE12 145 J6
WPK KT4 193 F5
Wimborne Dr CDALE/KGS NW9 44 C6
PIN HA5 59 H4
Wimborne Gdns WEA W13 97 H5
Wimborne Rd ED N9 36 C4
TOTM N17 50 A5
Wimborne Wy BECK BR3 182 A6
Wimbourne St IS N1 6 E2
Wimpole Cl HAYES BR2 200 B1
KUT KT1 175 G5
Wimpole Ms CAVSQ/HST W1G 9 J1
Wimpole Rd WDR/YW UB7 112 A1
Wimpole St CAVSQ/HST W1G 9 J3
Wimshurst Cl CROY/NA CR0 195 K5
Winans Wk BRXN/ST SW9 142 B3
Wincanton Crs NTHLT UB5 78 A3
Wincanton Gdns BARK/HLT IG6 54 B6
Wincanton Rd
WAND/EARL SW18 159 J2
Winchcombe Rd CAR SM5 194 C4
Winchcomb Gdns
ELTH/MOT SE9 146 D4
Winchelsea Av BXLYHN DA7 149 G1
Winchelsea Cl PUT/ROE SW15 139 G6
Winchelsea Rd FSTGT E7 88 E2
TOTM N17 50 A6
WLSDN NW10 81 F6
Winchelsey Ri SAND/SEL CR2 212 B4
Winchendon Rd FUL/PGN SW6 139 J1
TEDD TW11 155 J6
Winchester Av CDALE/KGS NW9 44 B6
HEST TW5 114 E6
KIL/WHAMP NW6 82 C6
Winchester Cl EN * EN1 24 A6
ESH/CLAY KT10 204 A3
HAYES BR2 183 J6
KUTN/CMB KT2 175 J3
LBTH * SE11 18 B7
Winchester Dr PIN HA5 59 H2
Winchester Pk HAYES BR2 183 J6
Winchester Pl HACK E8 86 B3
HGT N6 66 B5
Winchester Rd BXLYHN DA7 148 E3
CHING E4 52 A3
ED N9 36 B3
FELT TW13 154 E5
HAMP NW3 83 H5
HAYES BR2 183 J6
HGT N6 66 B5
HYS/HAR UB3 133 H1
IL IG1 90 D1
KTN/HRWW/W HA3 62 A1
ORP BR6 217 J2
TWK TW1 156 C1
Winchester Sq STHWK SE1 12 E7
Winchester St ACT W3 117 K1
PIM SW1V 121 G5
Winchester Wk STHWK SE1 12 E7
Winchfield Cl
KTN/HRWW/W HA3 61 J3
Winchfield Rd SYD SE26 182 B1
Winchilsea Crs
E/WMO/HCT KT8 173 H5
Winchmore Hill Rd
STHGT/OAK N14 34 E2
Winchmore Vls WCHMH * N21 35 F2
Winckley Cl KTN/HRWW/W HA3 62 B2
Wincott St LBTH SE11 17 K6
Wincrofts Dr ELTH/MOT SE9 147 J5
Windall Cl NRWD SE19 181 H4
Windborough Rd CAR SM5 210 A5
Windermere Av FNCH N3 46 E6
HCH RM12 93 J3
KIL/WHAMP NW6 82 C6
RSLP HA4 59 G4
WBLY HA9 61 J5
WIM/MER SW19 178 A6
Windermere Cl DART DA1 170 E3
EBED/NFELT TW14 153 H3
ORP BR6 216 B1
STWL/WRAY TW19 152 A4
Windermere Gdns REDBR IG4 71 J2
Windermere Gv WBLY HA9 61 J5
Windermere Hall EDGE * HA8 44 B1
Windermere Rd ARCH * N19 66 C6
BXLYHN DA7 149 K3
CROY/NA CR0 197 G5
EA W5 116 D3
MUSWH N10 48 B4
PUT/ROE SW15 158 B6
STHL UB1 95 K4
STRHM/NOR SW16 179 H4
WWKM BR4 199 H6
Windermere Wy WDR/YW UB7 112 B1
Winders Rd BTSEA * SW11 140 D3
Windfield Cl SYD SE26 164 A6
Windham Rd RCH/KEW TW9 137 G4
Winding Wy BCTR RM8 91 J1
Windlass Pl DEPT SE8 124 B4
Windlesham Gv
WIM/MER SW19 159 G3
Windley Cl FSTH SE23 163 K4
Windmill Cl BERM/RHTH * SE16 123 H4
LEW * SE13 145 F3
SURB KT6 190 D5
Windmill Dr CLAP SW4 141 G6
HAYES BR2 215 G2
Windmill Gdns ENC/FH EN2 23 G3
Windmill Gv CROY/NA CR0 196 D4
Windmill Hl ENC/FH EN2 23 H4
HAMP * NW3 83 G1
RSLP HA4 58 D5
Windmill La BAR EN5 31 H1
BUSH WD23 28 E3
GFD/PVL UB6 96 C4
NWDGN UB2 115 H2
SRTFD E15 88 B4
THDIT KT7 190 C4
Windmill Pas CHSWK * W4 118 B4
Windmill Ri KUTN/CMB KT2 175 J3
Windmill Rd CHSWK W4 118 B4
CROY/NA CR0 196 D4
EA W5 116 D4
HPTN TW12 173 G1
MTCM CR4 195 H2
UED N18 35 K6
WAND/EARL SW18 160 C1
WIM/MER SW19 176 E1
Windmill Rw LBTH * SE11 122 B5
Windmill St BUSH WD23 28 E3
FITZ W1T 10 C2
Windmill Wk STHWK * SE1 17 K1
Windmill Wy RSLP HA4 58 D5
Windrose Cl BERM/RHTH SE16 124 A2
Windrush NWMAL KT3 191 J1
Windrush Cl BTSEA * SW11 140 C5
CHSWK * W4 137 K1
Windrush La FSTH SE23 164 A5
Windrush Rd WLSDN NW10 81 F6
Windsor Av CHEAM SM3 208 C1
E/WMO/HCT KT8 173 F6
EDGE HA8 30 D6
NWMAL KT3 191 K2
WALTH E17 51 G5
WIM/MER SW19 178 B4
Windsor Cl CHST BR7 185 G1
FNCH N3 46 C5
NTHWD HA6 40 E5
RYLN/HDSTN HA2 78 A1
WNWD SE27 162 D6
Windsor Ct PIN * HA5 41 H6
STHGT/OAK N14 34 C2
Windsor Crs RYLN/HDSTN HA2 78 A1
WBLY HA9 80 C1
Windsor Dr ASHF TW15 152 A6
DART DA1 170 D1
EBAR EN4 33 K1
ORP BR6 217 G4
Windsor Gdns CROY/NA CR0 210 E1
HYS/HAR UB3 113 G3
MV/WKIL * W9 100 E4
Windsor Gv WNWD SE27 162 D6
Windsor Ms CAT SE6 165 F3
Windsor Park Rd HYS/HAR UB3 133 J1
Windsor Rd BAR EN5 32 B1
BCTR RM8 92 A1
BXLYHS DA6 149 F5
CHING E4 37 K6
CRICK NW2 81 K4
EA W5 98 A6
FNCH N3 46 C5
FSTGT E7 89 F3
HOLWY N7 84 E1
HSLWW TW4 134 A3
IL IG1 90 C2
KTN/HRWW/W HA3 42 C4
KUTN/CMB KT2 175 F3
LEY E10 69 K6
NWDGN UB2 114 E3
PLMGR N13 35 G5
RCH/KEW TW9 137 G3
TEDD TW11 173 J1
THHTH CR7 180 C5
TOTM N17 50 C5
WAN E11 70 E5
WPK KT4 192 D6
The Windsors BKHH IG9 39 J4
Windsor St IS N1 6 B1
Windsor Ter IS N1 6 D4
Windsor Wk CMBW SE5 142 E3
Windsor Wy WKENS W14 119 G4
Windspoint Dr PECK * SE15 123 H6
Windus Rd STNW/STAM N16 68 B5
Windy Rdg BMLY BR1 184 D4
Windy Ridge Cl WIM/MER SW19 177 G1
Wine Cl WAP E1W 104 E6
Winery La KUT KT1 175 G6
Winey Cl CHSGTN KT9 205 J5
Winforton St GNWCH SE10 145 F2
Winfrith Rd WAND/EARL SW18 160 B2
Wingate Crs CROY/NA CR0 195 K3
Wingate Rd HMSMTH W6 118 E3
IL IG1 90 B3
SCUP DA14 186 D1
Wingfield Ct WATW * WD18 26 B1
Wingfield Ms PECK * SE15 143 H4
Wingfield Rd KUTN/CMB KT2 175 G2
SRTFD E15 88 C3
WALTH E17 69 K2
Wingfield St PECK SE15 143 H4
Wingfield Wy RSLP HA4 77 F4
Wingford Rd BRXS/STRHM SW2 161 K1
Wingmore Rd HNHL SE24 142 D4
Wingrave Rd HMSMTH W6 119 F6
Wingrove Rd CAT SE6 165 H4
Wings Cl SUT SM1 208 E2
Winifred Cl MLHL NW7 31 H1
Winifred Pl NFNCH/WDSP N12 47 G1
Winifred Rd BCTR RM8 74 A6
DART DA1 150 E6
ERITH DA8 130 B5
HPTN TW12 155 F6
WIM/MER SW19 177 K4
Winifred St CAN/RD E16 126 E1
Winifred Ter EN EN1 36 B2
Winkfield Rd WDGN N22 49 G4
Winkley St BETH E2 104 D1
Winkworth Cottages
WCHPL * E1 104 E3
Winlaton Rd BMLY BR1 165 G6
Winmill Rd BCTR RM8 92 B1
Winn Bridge Cl WFD IG8 53 H4
Winn Common Rd
WOOL/PLUM SE18 127 K6
Winnett St SOHO/SHAV W1D 10 C5
Winnington Cl EFNCH N2 65 H3
Winnington Rd EFNCH N2 65 H4
PEND EN3 24 E1
Winnipeg Dr ORP BR6 217 F4
Winnock Rd WDR/YW UB7 112 A1
Winn Rd LEE/GVPK SE12 165 K3
Winns Av WALTH E17 51 H6
Winns Ms SEVS/STOTM N15 68 A1
Winns Ter WALTH E17 51 J5
Winsbeach WALTH E17 52 B6
Winscombe Crs EA W5 97 K3
Winscombe St KTTN NW5 84 B1
Winscombe Wy STAN HA7 43 G1
Winsford Rd CAT SE6 164 C5
Winsford Ter UED * N18 49 K1
Winsham Gv BTSEA SW11 141 F6
Winslade Rd BRXS/STRHM SW2 141 K6
Winsland Ms BAY/PAD W2 8 A3
Winsland St BAY/PAD W2 8 A3
Winsley St GTPST W1W 10 A3
Winslow Cl PIN HA5 59 F3
WLSDN NW10 81 G1
Winslow Gv CHING E4 38 C4
Winslow Rd HMSMTH W6 119 F6
Winslow Wy FELT TW13 154 C5
Winsor Ter EHAM E6 108 B4
Winstanley Rd BTSEA SW11 140 C4
Winstead Gdns DAGE RM10 92 E3
Winston Av CDALE/KGS NW9 63 G4
Winston Cl KTN/HRWW/W HA3 43 F2
ROMW/RG RM7 74 D1
Winston Ct PIN HA5 42 B3
Winston House SURB * KT6 191 F2
Winston Rd STNW/STAM N16 85 K2
Winston Wy IL IG1 90 B1
Winter Av EHAM E6 89 J6
Winterborne Av ORP BR6 216 D1
Winterbourne Rd BCTR RM8 73 J6
CAT SE6 164 C3
THHTH CR7 196 B1
Winter Box Wk
RCHPK/HAM TW10 137 G6
Winterbrook Rd HNHL SE24 162 D1
Winterburn Cl FBAR/BDGN N11 48 A2
Winterfold Cl WIM/MER SW19 159 H4
Winters Rd THDIT KT7 190 C4
Winterstoke Rd CAT SE6 164 C3
Winterton Pl WBPTN SW10 120 B6
Winterwell Rd
BRXS/STRHM SW2 141 K6
Winthorpe Rd PUT/ROE SW15 139 H5
Winthorpe St WCHPL E1 104 D4
Winthrop St WCHPL * E1 104 D4
Winton Av FBAR/BDGN N11 48 C3
Winton Cl ED N9 37 F2
Winton Gdns EDGE HA8 44 B3
Winton Rd ORP BR6 216 B2
The Wintons BUSH * WD23 28 D3
Winton Wy STRHM/NOR SW16 180 B1
Wirral Wood Cl CHST BR7 185 F2
Wisbeach Rd CROY/NA CR0 196 E2
Wisborough Rd SAND/SEL CR2 212 B6
Wisdons Cl DAGE RM10 74 D5
Wise La MLHL NW7 45 J2
WDR/YW UB7 112 A4
Wiseman Rd LEY * E10 69 J6
Wise Rd SRTFD E15 88 A6
Wiseton Rd TOOT SW17 160 D3
Wishart Rd BKHTH/KID SE3 146 C2
Wisley Rd BTSEA SW11 140 E6
STMC/STPC BR5 186 B3
Wistaria Cl ORP BR6 201 G6
Wisteria Cl IL IG1 90 B3
Wisteria Rd LEW SE13 145 G5
Witan St BETH E2 104 D2
Witham Cl LOU IG10 39 J1
Witham Rd DAGE RM10 92 C3
GPK RM2 75 K2
ISLW TW7 135 J2
PGE/AN SE20 181 K6
WEA W13 116 B1
Withens Cl STMC/STPC * BR5 202 D1
Witherby Cl SAND/SEL CR2 212 A3
Witherington Rd HBRY * N5 85 G3
Withers Md CDALE/KGS NW9 45 H4
Witherston Wy ELTH/MOT SE9 167 F4
Withy La RSLP HA4 58 A4
Withy Md CHING E4 38 B5
Witley Crs CROY/NA CR0 214 A4
Witley Gdns NWDGN UB2 114 E4
Witley Rd ARCH N19 66 C6
Witney Cl PIN HA5 41 K2
Witney Pth FSTH * SE23 164 A5

Wittenham Wy CHING E4 38 B5
Wittering Cl KUTN/CMB KT2 174 E1
Wittersham Rd BMLY BR1 183 J1
Wivenhoe Cl PECK SE15 143 H4
Wivenhoe Ct HSLW TW3 134 E5
Wivenhoe Rd BARK IG11 109 G1
Wiverton Rd SYD SE26 181 K2
Wix Rd DAGW RM9 91 K6
Wix's La CLAP SW4 141 G5
Woburn WEA * W13 97 H4
Woburn Av HCH RM12 93 J2
Woburn Cl BUSH WD23 28 C1
WIM/MER SW19 178 B2
Woburn Pl STPAN WC1H 4 E6
Woburn Rd CAR SM5 194 D5
CROY/NA CR0 196 D5
Woburn Sq STPAN WC1H 4 D7
Woburn Wk STPAN WC1H 4 D5
Wodehouse Av PECK SE15 143 G2
Wodehouse Rd DART DA1 151 K5
Woffington Cl E/WMO/HCT KT8 174 D4
Woking Cl PUT/ROE SW15 138 C5
Woldham Pl HAYES BR2 200 B1
Woldham Rd HAYES BR2 200 B1
Wolds Dr ORP BR6 216 A2
Wolfe Cl HAYES BR2 199 K3
YEAD UB4 95 F2
Wolfe Crs CHARL SE7 126 C5
Wolferton Rd MNPK E12 89 K2
Wolfington Rd WNWD SE27 162 C6
Wolfram Cl LEW SE13 145 H6
Wolftencroft Cl BTSEA SW11 140 D4
Wollaston Cl WALW SE17 18 B7
Wolmer Cl EDGE HA8 30 C6
Wolmer Gdns EDGE HA8 30 C5
Wolseley Av WAND/EARL SW18 159 K4
Wolseley Gdns CHSWK W4 117 J6
Wolseley Rd CEND/HSY/T N8 66 D3
CHSWK W4 117 K4
FSTGT E7 89 F5
KTN/HRWW/W HA3 42 E6
MTCM CR4 195 F4
ROMW/RG RM7 75 F4
WDGN N22 49 F4
Wolseley St STHWK SE1 19 K3
Wolsey Av EHAM E6 108 A2
WALTH E17 51 H6
Wolsey Cl HSLW TW3 135 H5
KUTN/CMB KT2 175 J4
NWDGN UB2 115 H3
RYNPK SW20 176 E3
WPK KT4 207 J2
Wolsey Ct ELTH/MOT * SE9 166 E1
Wolsey Crs CROY/NA CR0 214 A6
MRDN SM4 193 J4
Wolsey Dr KUTN/CMB KT2 175 F1
WOT/HER KT12 188 C5
Wolsey Gdns BARK/HLT IG6 54 C2
Wolsey Gv EDGE HA8 45 F3
ESH/CLAY KT10 204 B2
Wolsey Ms KTTN NW5 84 C4
ORP BR6 217 F3
Wolsey Rd ASHF TW15 152 B6
E/WMO/HCT KT8 189 J1
EN EN1 24 D3
ESH/CLAY KT10 204 B2
HPTN TW12 173 G2
IS N1 85 K3
RKW/CH/CXG WD3 26 A4
Wolsey St WCHPL E1 104 E4
Wolsey Wy CHSGTN KT9 206 C3
Wolsley Cl DART DA1 150 B6
Wolstonbury NFNCH/WDSP N12 46 E1
Wolvercote Rd ABYW SE2 128 E2
Wolverley St BETH * E2 104 D2
Wolverton Av KUTN/CMB KT2 175 H4
Wolverton Gdns EA W5 98 B6
HMSMTH W6 119 G4
Wolverton Rd STAN HA7 43 H2
Wolverton Wy STHGT/OAK N14 22 C6
Wolves La WDGN N22 49 G3
Womersley Rd CEND/HSY/T N8 67 F3
Wonersh Wy BELMT SM2 208 B6
Wonford Cl NWMAL KT3 176 B4
Wontner Cl IS * N1 85 J5
Wontner Rd BAL SW12 160 E4
Woodall Cl CHSGTN KT9 205 J5
Woodall Rd PEND EN3 25 F6
Woodbank Rd BMLY BR1 165 J5
Woodbastwick Rd SYD SE26 182 A2
Woodberry Av RYLN/HDSTN HA2 60 C1
WCHMH N21 35 G4
Woodberry Crs MUSWH N10 48 B6
Woodberry Down FSBYPK N4 67 J5
Woodberry Gdns
NFNCH/WDSP N12 47 G2
Woodberry Gv BXLY DA5 170 A5
FSBYPK N4 67 J4
NFNCH/WDSP N12 47 G2
Woodberry Wy CHING E4 38 A2
NFNCH/WDSP N12 47 G2
Woodbine Cl WHTN TW2 155 J4
Woodbine Gv ENC/FH EN2 23 K1
PGE/AN SE20 181 J3
Woodbine La WPK KT4 207 K1
Woodbine Pl WAN E11 70 E3
Woodbine Rd BFN/LL DA15 167 K3
Woodbines Av KUT KT1 174 E6
Woodbine Ter HOM E9 86 E4
Woodborough Rd
PUT/ROE SW15 138 E5
Woodbourne Av
STRHM/NOR SW16 161 J5
Woodbourne Dr
ESH/CLAY KT10 205 F4
Woodbourne Gdns WLGTN SM6 210 B5
Woodbridge Cl HOLWY N7 67 F6
Woodbridge Rd BARK IG11 91 F3
Woodbridge St CLKNW EC1R 6 A6
Woodbrook Rd ABYW SE2 128 B6
Woodburn Cl HDN NW4 64 B2
Woodbury Cl CROY/NA CR0 197 G6
WAN E11 71 F1
Woodbury Park Rd WEA W13 97 H3
Woodbury Rd WALTH E17 69 K1
Woodbury St TOOT SW17 178 D1
Woodchester Sq BAY/PAD W2 101 F4
Woodchurch Cl BFN/LL DA15 167 J5
Woodchurch Dr BMLY BR1 184 C3
Woodchurch Rd
KIL/WHAMP NW6 82 E5
Wood Cl BETH E2 104 C3
BXLY DA5 170 B5
CDALE/KGS NW9 63 F4
HRW HA1 60 D4
Woodclyffe Dr CHST BR7 185 F5
Woodcock Ct
KTN/HRWW/W HA3 62 A4
Woodcock Dell Av
KTN/HRWW/W HA3 61 J4
Woodcock Hl
KTN/HRWW/W HA3 61 J2
Woodcocks CAN/RD E16 107 G4
Woodcombe Crs FSTH SE23 163 K3
Woodcot Cl ED N9 36 E1
Woodcote Av HCH RM12 93 J2
MLHL NW7 46 A2
THHTH CR7 196 C1
WLGTN SM6 210 B6
Woodcote Cl KUTN/CMB KT2 175 G1
Woodcote Dr ORP BR6 201 J4
Woodcote Gn WLGTN SM6 210 C6
Woodcote Ms LOU IG10 39 H2
WLGTN SM6 210 B4
Woodcote Pl WNWD * SE27 180 C1
Woodcote Rd WAN E11 70 E4
WLGTN SM6 210 B4
Wood Crest BELMT * SM2 209 G5
Woodcroft ELTH/MOT SE9 166 E5
GFD/PVL UB6 79 G4
WCHMH N21 35 F3
Woodcroft Av MLHL NW7 45 G3
STAN HA7 43 G4
Woodcroft Ms DEPT SE8 124 B4
Woodcroft Rd THHTH CR7 196 C2
Wood Dene PECK * SE15 143 J2
Wood Dr CHST BR7 184 D2
Woodedge Cl CHING E4 38 D3
Wooden Bridge Ter
WNWD * SE27 162 C5
The Wood End WLGTN SM6 210 B6
Woodend ESH/CLAY KT10 189 H6
Wood End HYS/HAR UB3 94 C5
Woodend NRWD SE19 180 D2
SUT SM1 194 B6
Wood End SWLY BR8 203 K1
Wood End Av RYLN/HDSTN HA2 78 B2
Wood End Cl NTHLT UB5 78 D3
Woodend Gdns ENC/FH EN2 22 E5
Wood End Gdns NTHLT UB5 78 C3
Wood End Gn YEAD UB4 94 D4
Wood End Green Rd
HYS/HAR UB3 94 B4
Wood End La NTHLT UB5 78 B4
Wood End Rd HRW HA1 78 D2
Woodend Rd WALTH E17 52 A5
Wood End Wy NTHLT UB5 78 C3
Wooder Gdns FSTGT E7 88 D2
Wooderson Cl SNWD SE25 197 F1
Woodfall Av BAR EN5 20 D6
Woodfall Dr DART DA1 150 C5
Woodfall Rd FSBYPK N4 67 G5
Woodfall St CHEL SW3 120 E5
Woodfarrs CMBW SE5 142 E5
Wood Fld HAMP * NW3 83 K3
Woodfield Av ALP/SUD HA0 79 J1
CAR SM5 210 A4
CDALE/KGS NW9 63 G1
EA W5 97 J3
NTHWD HA6 26 C6
STRHM/NOR SW16 161 J5
Woodfield Cl EN EN1 24 A5
NRWD SE19 180 D3
Woodfield Crs EA W5 97 K3
Woodfield Dr EBAR EN4 34 A3
GPK RM2 75 J1
Woodfield Gdns NWMAL KT3 192 C2
Woodfield Gv
STRHM/NOR SW16 161 J5
Woodfield Pl MV/WKIL W9 100 D4
Woodfield Ri BUSH WD23 28 D2
Woodfield Rd EA W5 97 J3
ESH/CLAY KT10 190 A6
HSLWW TW4 134 A3
MV/WKIL W9 100 D4
Woodfield Wy FBAR/BDGN N11 48 D3
Woodford Av GNTH/NBYPK IG2 71 K2
Woodford Bridge Rd REDBR IG4 53 H6
Woodford Crs PIN HA5 41 F5
Woodford New Rd WALTH E17 70 C1
WFD IG8 52 D3
Woodford Pl WBLY HA9 62 A5
Woodford Rd FSTGT E7 89 F2
SWFD E18 70 E1
Woodgate Av CHSGTN KT9 205 K3
Woodgate Crs NTHWD HA6 40 E2
Woodgate Dr
STRHM/NOR SW16 179 J3
Woodger Rd SHB W12 119 F2
Woodget Cl EHAM E6 107 J5
Woodgrange Av EA W5 117 G1
EN EN1 36 C1
KTN/HRWW/W HA3 61 J2
NFNCH/WDSP N12 47 H2
Woodgrange Cl
KTN/HRWW/W HA3 61 K2
Woodgrange Gdns EN EN1 36 C1
Woodgrange Ter EN * EN1 36 C1
Woodgrave Rd FSTGT E7 88 E3
Woodhall Av DUL SE21 163 G5
PIN HA5 41 J4
Woodhall Dr DUL SE21 163 G5
PIN HA5 41 H4
Woodhall Ga PIN HA5 41 H3
Woodhall La OXHEY WD19 27 H5
Woodham Ct SWFD E18 70 D1
Woodham Rd CAT SE6 165 F5
Woodhatch Cl EHAM E6 107 J4
Woodhaven Gdns BARK/HLT IG6 72 C1
Woodhayes Rd RYNPK SW20 177 F3
Woodhead Dr ORP BR6 216 E1
Woodheyes Rd WLSDN NW10 81 G3
Woodhill WOOL/PLUM SE18 126 D4
Woodhill Crs KTN/HRWW/W HA3 61 K3
Woodhouse Av GFD/PVL UB6 97 F1
Woodhouse Cl GFD/PVL UB6 97 F1
HYS/HAR UB3 113 H3
Woodhouse Eaves NTHWD HA6 40 E1
Woodhouse Gv MNPK E12 89 J4
Woodhouse Rd
NFNCH/WDSP N12 47 G2
WAN E11 88 D1
Woodhurst Av STMC/STPC BR5 201 H3
Woodhurst Rd ABYW SE2 128 B5
ACT W3 117 K1
Woodington Cl ELTH/MOT SE9 167 F1
Woodison St BOW E3 105 G3
Woodknoll Dr CHST BR7 184 E4
The Woodlands CMBW * SE5 142 C1
ESH/CLAY KT10 189 H6
HRW * HA1 60 E6
ISLW TW7 136 A3
LEW SE13 165 G2
NRWD SE19 180 D3
ORP BR6 217 H4
STAN * HA7 43 H1
STHGT/OAK N14 34 B3
WLGTN SM6 210 B6
Woodland Ap GFD/PVL UB6 79 G4
Woodland Cl CDALE/KGS NW9 62 E3
HOR/WEW * KT19 207 G4
NRWD SE19 181 F2
WFD IG8 39 F5
Woodland Ct GLDGN * NW11 64 C2
Woodland Crs GNWCH SE10 125 H6
Woodland Gdns ISLW TW7 135 K4
MUSWH N10 66 B2
Woodland Hl NRWD SE19 181 F2
Woodland Ri GFD/PVL UB6 79 G4
MUSWH N10 66 B1
Woodland Rd CHING E4 38 A3
FBAR/BDGN N11 48 B1
NRWD SE19 181 F1
THHTH CR7 196 B1
Woodlands GLDGN NW11 64 C2
RYLN/HDSTN HA2 60 A1
RYNPK SW20 193 F1
Woodlands Av ACT W3 117 J1
BFN/LL DA15 167 K3
CHDH RM6 74 A3
FNCH N3 47 G3
NWMAL KT3 176 A4
RSLP HA4 59 G5
WAN E11 71 F5
WPK KT4 192 C6
Woodlands Cl BMLY BR1 184 E5
ESH/CLAY KT10 205 F5
GLDGN NW11 64 C2
Woodlands Dr STAN HA7 43 F2
SUN TW16 172 B5
Woodlands Gdns WALTH * E17 70 C1
Woodlands Gv GNWCH SE10 125 H5
ISLW TW7 135 K3
Woodlands Pk BXLY DA5 169 K6
Woodlands Park Rd
BKHTH/KID SE3 125 H6
SEVS/STOTM N15 67 J2
Woodlands Rd BARN SW13 138 C4
BMLY BR1 184 E5
BXLYHN DA7 149 F4
ED N9 36 E3
ENC/FH EN2 23 K1
HRW HA1 61 F2
IL IG1 90 C1
ISLW TW7 135 K4
ORP BR6 217 G4
ROM RM1 57 H6
STHL UB1 114 C1
SURB KT6 190 E4
WALTH E17 52 A6
WAN * E11 70 C6
Woodlands St LEW SE13 165 G2
Woodlands Ter SWLY * BR8 203 K3
Woodland St HACK * E8 86 B4
Woodlands Wy PUT/ROE SW15 139 J6
Woodland Ter CHARL SE7 126 D4
Woodland Wk HAMP NW3 83 J3
HOR/WEW KT19 206 C4
Woodland Wy ABYW SE2 128 E4
BRYLDS KT5 191 J6
CROY/NA CR0 198 B5
MLHL NW7 45 G2
MRDN SM4 193 J1
MTCM CR4 179 F3
STMC/STPC BR5 201 H1
WCHMH N21 35 G4
WFD IG8 39 F5
WWKM BR4 214 A1
Wood La CDALE/KGS NW9 63 F4
DAGE RM10 74 C6
HCH RM12 93 J3
HGT N6 66 B3
ISLW TW7 115 K6
RSLP HA4 58 C6
SHB W12 100 A5
STAN HA7 29 H5
WFD IG8 52 D1
Woodlawn Cl PUT/ROE SW15 139 J6
Woodlawn Crs WHTN TW2 155 G4
Woodlawn Dr FELT TW13 154 C4
Woodlawn Rd FUL/PGN SW6 139 G1
Woodlea Dr HAYES BR2 199 H2
Woodlea Gv NTHWD HA6 40 A2
Woodlea Rd STNW/STAM N16 86 A1
Woodleigh Av
NFNCH/WDSP N12 47 J2
Woodleigh Gdns
STRHM/NOR SW16 161 K5
Woodley Cl TOOT SW17 178 E3
Woodley La SUT SM1 209 J1
Woodley Rd ORP BR6 202 D6
Wood Lodge Gdns BMLY BR1 184 D3
Wood Lodge La WWKM BR4 214 A1
Woodman Pth BARK/HLT IG6 54 E1
Woodmans Gv WLSDN NW10 81 H3
Woodmansterne Rd
STRHM/NOR SW16 179 H3
Woodman St CAN/RD E16 127 F1
Wood Md TOTM * N17 50 C2
Woodmere ELTH/MOT SE9 166 E2
Woodmere Av CROY/NA CR0 198 A4
Woodmere Cl BTSEA SW11 141 F4
CROY/NA CR0 198 A4
Woodmere Gdns CROY/NA CR0 198 A4
Woodmere Wy BECK BR3 199 G2
Woodnook Rd
STRHM/NOR SW16 179 G1
Woodpecker Cl BUSH WD23 28 C3
ED N9 36 D1
KTN/HRWW/W HA3 43 F4
Woodpecker Ms LEW SE13 145 G5
Woodpecker Mt CROY/NA CR0 213 G6
Woodpecker Rd THMD SE28 109 J6
Woodquest Av HNHL SE24 142 C6
Wood Ride EBAR EN4 21 H2
STMC/STPC BR5 201 J1
Woodridge Cl ENC/FH * EN2 23 G2
Woodridge Wy NTHWD HA6 40 C2
Woodridings Av PIN HA5 41 K4
Woodridings Cl PIN HA5 41 K3
Woodriffe Rd WAN E11 70 B4
Wood Ri PIN HA5 58 E2
Woodrow WOOL/PLUM SE18 126 D4
Woodrow Av YEAD UB4 94 D4
Woodrow Cl GFD/PVL UB6 79 H5
Woodrow Ct TOTM N17 50 D3
Woodrush Cl NWCR SE14 144 B1
Woodrush Wy CHDH RM6 73 K1
The Woods NTHWD HA6 40 E1
Woodseer St WCHPL E1 13 K1
Woodsford Sq WKENS W14 119 H2
Woodshire Rd DAGE RM10 92 E1
Woodside BKHH IG9 39 G4
GLDGN NW11 64 E2
ORP BR6 217 G3
WIM/MER SW19 177 J1
Woodside Av ALP/SUD HA0 80 A6
CHST BR7 185 H1
ESH/CLAY KT10 189 K4
HGT N6 65 K2
NFNCH/WDSP N12 33 G6
SNWD SE25 197 J3
Woodside Cl ALP/SUD HA0 80 A6
BRYLDS KT5 191 K4
BXLYHN DA7 150 A5
RSLP HA4 58 B3
STAN HA7 43 G1
Woodside Ct EA * W5 117 F1
Woodside Court Rd
CROY/NA CR0 197 H4
Woodside Crs BFN/LL DA15 167 K5
Woodside Dr RDART DA2 170 B6
Woodside End ALP/SUD HA0 80 A6
Woodside Gdns CHING E4 51 K1
TOTM N17 50 B5
Woodside Grange Rd
NFNCH/WDSP N12 33 F6
Woodside Gn CROY/NA CR0 197 H4
Woodside Gv NFNCH/WDSP N12 33 G5
Woodside La BXLY DA5 168 E1
NFNCH/WDSP N12 33 F5
Woodside Pde BFN/LL * DA15 167 K5
Woodside Pk SNWD SE25 197 H3
Woodside Park Av WALTH E17 70 B1
Woodside Park Rd
NFNCH/WDSP N12 33 F6
Woodside Pl ALP/SUD HA0 80 A6
Woodside Rd BFN/LL DA15 167 K5
BMLY BR1 200 D2
BXLYHN DA7 150 A5
KUTN/CMB KT2 175 F3
NTHWD HA6 40 D3
NWMAL KT3 176 A5
PLSTW E13 107 G3
SNWD SE25 197 J3
SUT SM1 209 G1
WDGN N22 49 G3
WFD IG8 38 E6
Woodside Wy CROY/NA CR0 197 K3
MTCM CR4 179 G4
Wood's Ms MYFR/PKLN W1K 9 F5
Woodsome Rd KTTN NW5 84 A1
Wood's Pl STHWK SE1 19 H5
Woodspring Rd
WIM/MER SW19 159 H4
Wood's Rd PECK SE15 143 J2
Woodstead Gv EDGE HA8 44 A2
Woodstock Av CHEAM SM3 193 J4
GLDGN NW11 64 C4
HNWL W7 116 B3
ISLW TW7 136 B6
STHL UB1 95 K2
Woodstock Cl BXLY DA5 169 G3
STAN HA7 44 A5
Woodstock Crs ED N9 36 D1
Woodstock Gdns BECK BR3 182 E4
GDMY/SEVK IG3 73 G6
YEAD UB4 94 D4
Woodstock Gra EA * W5 117 F1
Woodstock Gv SHB W12 119 G2
Woodstock La North SURB KT6 190 D6
Woodstock La South
ESH/CLAY KT10 205 H3
Woodstock Ms CAVSQ/HST W1G 9 H2
Woodstock Ri CHEAM SM3 193 J5
Woodstock Rd ALP/SUD HA0 80 B5
BUSH WD23 28 E2
CAR SM5 210 A3
CHSWK W4 118 B4
CROY/NA CR0 211 K1
FSBYPK N4 67 G5
FSTGT E7 89 G5
GLDGN NW11 64 D4
WALTH E17 52 B5
Woodstock St CAN/RD E16 106 D5
MYFR/PKLN W1K 9 J4
Woodstock Ter POP/IOD E14 105 K6
Woodstock Wy MTCM CR4 179 H5
Woodstone Av EW KT17 207 J3
Wood St BAR EN5 20 A5
BARB EC2Y 12 D2
CAN/RD E16 107 F6
CHSWK W4 118 B5
KUT KT1 174 E5
MTCM CR4 195 F4
WALTH E17 52 A6
Woodsyre SYD SE26 163 G6
Wood Ter CRICK * NW2 63 H6
Woodthorpe Rd
PUT/ROE SW15 138 E5
Woodtree Cl HDN NW4 46 A5
Wood V FSTH SE23 163 J3
MUSWH N10 66 C2
Woodvale Av SNWD SE25 181 G6
Woodvale Wy CRICK NW2 82 B1
Woodview Av CHING E4 38 A6
Woodview Cl KUTN/CMB KT2 158 A6
ORP BR6 201 H6
Woodview Rd SWLY BR8 187 K5
Woodville Cl LEE/GVPK SE12 145 K6
TEDD TW11 156 B6
Woodville Gdns BARK/HLT IG6 54 B6
EA W5 98 A5
RSLP HA4 58 A4
SURB * KT6 190 E4
Woodville Gv WELL * DA16 148 B4
Woodville Rd BAR EN5 21 F4
EA W5 98 A5
GLDGN NW11 64 C4
KIL/WHAMP * NW6 100 D1
MRDN SM4 193 K1
RCHPK/HAM TW10 156 C5
STNW/STAM N16 86 A3
SWFD E18 53 F5
THHTH CR7 180 E6
WALTH E17 69 G1
WAN E11 70 D5
Woodville St WOOL/PLUM SE18 126 D4
Woodward Av HDN NW4 63 J2
Woodward Cl ESH/CLAY KT10 205 F4
Woodwarde Rd EDUL SE22 163 F1
Woodward Gdns DAGW RM9 91 J5
STAN HA7 43 F3
Woodward Rd DAGW RM9 91 H5
Wood Wy ORP BR6 201 F6
Woodway Crs HRW HA1 61 G3
Woodwaye OXHEY WD19 27 G2
Woodwell St WAND/EARL SW18 140 B6
Wood Whf GNWCH SE10 124 E6
Woodyard Cl KTTN NW5 84 A3
Woodyard La DUL SE21 163 F2
Woodyates Rd LEE/GVPK SE12 165 K1
Woolacombe Rd
BKHTH/KID SE3 146 B3
Woolacombe Wy HYS/HAR UB3 113 H4
Woolands Rd WAN E11 70 C6
Woolbrook Rd DART DA1 170 B1
Wooler St WALW SE17 122 E5
Woolf Cl THMD SE28 128 C1
Woolf Ms STPAN WC1H 4 E6
Woollaston Rd FSBYPK N4 67 H3
Woollett Cl DART DA1 150 D5
Woolmead Av CDALE/KGS NW9 63 J4
Woolmer Gdns UED N18 50 C2
Woolmer Rd UED N18 50 C1
Woolmore St POP/IOD E14 106 A6
Woolneigh St FUL/PGN SW6 140 A4
Woolridge Wy HOM * E9 86 E5
Wool Rd RYNPK SW20 176 E2
Woolstaplers Wy
BERM/RHTH SE16 123 H3
Woolston Cl WALTH E17 51 F5
Woolstone Rd FSTH SE23 164 B4
Woolwich Church St CHARL SE7 126 C4
Woolwich Common
WOOL/PLUM SE18 127 F6
Woolwich High St
WOOL/PLUM SE18 127 F3
Woolwich Manorway
CAN/RD E16 127 G2
Woolwich Manor Wy
CAN/RD E16 127 G1
EHAM E6 107 K3
Woolwich New Rd
WOOL/PLUM SE18 127 F6
Woolwich Rd ABYW SE2 128 E6
BXLYHN DA7 149 H4
GNWCH SE10 125 K5
Wooster Gdns POP/IOD E14 106 B5
Wootton Gv FNCH N3 46 E4
Wootton St STHWK SE1 17 K2
Worbeck Rd PGE/AN SE20 181 J5
Worcester Av TOTM N17 50 C3
Worcester Cl CRICK NW2 81 J1
CROY/NA CR0 198 C6
MTCM CR4 179 F5
Worcester Ct WOT/HER KT12 188 B6
Worcester Crs MLHL NW7 31 G5
WFD IG8 53 F1
Worcester Dr CHSWK W4 118 B3
Worcester Gdns GFD/PVL UB6 78 C4
IL IG1 71 J4
WPK KT4 207 G1
Worcester Ms KIL/WHAMP NW6 83 F4
Worcester Park Rd WPK KT4 206 E1
Worcester Rd BELMT SM2 208 E5
MNPK E12 89 K1
WALTH E17 51 F5
WIM/MER SW19 177 J1
Worcesters Av EN EN1 24 C1
Wordsworth Av GFD/PVL UB6 96 D1
MNPK E12 89 J5
SWFD E18 52 D6
Wordsworth Dr CHEAM SM3 208 A2
Wordsworth Pde
CEND/HSY/T * N8 67 H1
Wordsworth Pl HAMP NW3 83 K3
Wordsworth Rd FELT TW13 154 E6
PGE/AN SE20 182 A3
STHWK SE1 19 J7
STNW/STAM N16 86 A2
WELL DA16 147 K2
WLGTN SM6 210 C4
Wordsworth Wk GLDGN NW11 64 D1
Wordsworth Wy DART DA1 151 K5
WDR/YW UB7 112 B4
Worfield St BTSEA SW11 140 D1
Worgan St BERM/RHTH SE16 124 A3
LBTH SE11 122 A5
Worland Rd SRTFD E15 88 C5
Worlds End Est WBPTN * SW10 140 C1
Worlds End La ORP BR6 217 G5
WCHMH N21 23 F6
Worlds End Pas WBPTN * SW10 140 C1
Worlidge St HMSMTH W6 119 F5
Worlingham Rd EDUL SE22 143 G5
Wormholt Rd SHB W12 118 D1
Wormholt Ter SHB * W12 118 D1
Wormwood St LVPST EC2M 13 G3
Wornington Rd NKENS W10 100 C4
Woronzow Rd STJWD NW8 2 B1
Worple Av ISLW TW7 136 B6
WIM/MER SW19 177 G3
Worple Cl RYLN/HDSTN HA2 59 K5
Worple Rd ISLW TW7 136 B5
RYNPK SW20 177 F5
Worple Road Ms
WIM/MER SW19 177 J2
Worple St MORT/ESHN SW14 138 A4
Worple Wy RCHPK/HAM TW10 137 F6
RYLN/HDSTN HA2 59 K5
Worship St SDTCH EC2A 7 G7
Worslade Rd TOOT SW17 160 C6
Worsley Bridge Rd CAT SE6 182 C1
Worsley Gv CLPT E5 86 C2
Worsley Rd WAN E11 88 C2
Worsopp Dr CLAP SW4 141 H6
Worth Cl ORP BR6 216 E2
Worthfield Cl HOR/WEW KT19 207 F5
Worth Gv WALW * SE17 122 E5
Worthing Cl SRTFD E15 88 C6
Worthing Rd HEST TW5 114 E6
Worthington Cl MTCM CR4 195 G1
Worthington Rd SURB KT6 191 G5
Wortley Rd CROY/NA CR0 196 B4
EHAM E6 89 H5
Worton Gdns ISLW TW7 135 J3
Worton Rd ISLW TW7 136 A4
Worton Wy ISLW TW7 135 J3
Wotton Gn STMC/STPC BR5 202 E1
Wotton Rd CRICK NW2 82 A2
Wouldham Rd CAN/RD E16 106 D5
Wouldham Ter
STMC/STPC * BR5 186 C6
Wragby Rd WAN * E11 88 C1
Wrampling Pl ED N9 36 C4
Wray Av CLAY IG5 54 A6
Wray Crs FSBYPK N4 66 E6
Wrayfield Rd CHEAM SM3 208 B1
Wray Rd BELMT SM2 208 D6
Wraysbury Cl HSLWW TW4 134 D6
Wrays Wy YEAD UB4 94 C4
Wrekin Rd WOOL/PLUM SE18 147 H1
Wren Av CRICK NW2 82 A2

NWDGN UB2 114 E4
Wren Cl CAN/RD E16 106 D5
ED N9 37 F3
STMC/STPC BR5 186 E6
Wren Crs BUSH WD23 28 C3
Wren Dr WDR/YW UB7 112 A3
Wren Gdns DAGW RM9 91 K3
HCH RM12 75 H5
Wren Ms LEW * SE13 145 H5
Wren Rd CMBW SE5 142 E2
DAGW RM9 91 K3
SCUP DA14 168 D5
Wren St FSBYW WC1X 5 H6
Wrentham Av WLSDN NW10 100 B1
Wrenthorpe Rd BMLY BR1 165 H6
Wrenwood Wy PIN HA5 59 F1
Wrexham Rd BOW E3 105 J1
Wricklemarsh Rd
BKHTH/KID SE3 146 A3
Wrigglesworth St NWCR SE14 144 A1
Wright Cl LEW SE13 145 G5
Wright Rd HEST TW5 134 B1
Wrights Cl DAGE RM10 92 D2
Wright's La KENS W8 119 K2
KENS * W8 119 K3
Wrights Pl WLSDN * NW10 80 E4
Wright's Rd BOW E3 105 H1
SNWD SE25 181 F6
Wright's Rw CAR SM5 210 B2
Wrigley Cl CHING * E4 52 B1
Wrotham Rd BAR EN5 20 C3
CAMTN * NW1 84 C5
WEA W13 116 D1
WELL DA16 148 D2
Wrottesley Rd WLSDN NW10 99 K1
WOOL/PLUM SE18 127 H6
Wroughton Rd BTSEA SW11 160 E1
Wroughton Ter HDN * NW4 63 K1
Wroxall Rd DAGW RM9 91 J4
Wroxham Gdns FBAR/BDGN N11 48 C3
Wroxham Rd THMD SE28 109 K6
Wroxton Rd PECK SE15 143 J3
Wrythe Gn CAR SM5 209 K1
Wrythe Green Rd CAR SM5 209 K1
Wrythe La CAR SM5 194 C5
Wulfstan St SHB W12 99 H5
Wyatt Cl BUSH WD23 28 E2
FELT TW13 154 C3
YEAD UB4 94 E4
Wyatt Dr BARN SW13 118 E6
Wyatt Park Rd
BRXS/STRHM SW2 162 A4
Wyatt Rd DART DA1 150 C4
FSTGT E7 88 E4
HBRY N5 85 J1
Wyatt's La WALTH E17 52 A6
Wybert St CAMTN NW1 3 K6
Wyborne Wy WLSDN NW10 80 E5
Wyburn Av BAR EN5 20 D4
Wychcombe Studios
HAMP * NW3 83 K4
Wyche Gv SAND/SEL CR2 211 J5
Wycherley Cl BKHTH/KID SE3 145 J1
Wycherley Crs BAR EN5 33 F1
Wychwood Av EDGE HA8 43 K2
THHTH CR7 180 C6
Wychwood Cl EDGE HA8 43 K2
Wychwood End HGT N6 66 C4
Wychwood Gdns CLAY IG5 71 K1
Wychwood Wy NTHWD HA6 40 D3
Wycliffe Cl WELL DA16 148 A2
Wycliffe Rd BTSEA SW11 141 F3
WIM/MER SW19 178 A2
Wyclif St FSBYE EC1V 6 A5
Wycombe Gdns CRICK NW2 64 D6
Wycombe Pl WAND/EARL SW18 160 B1
Wycombe Rd ALP/SUD HA0 80 C6
GNTH/NBYPK IG2 71 K2
TOTM N17 50 C4
Wydell Cl MRDN SM4 193 F3
Wydenhurst Rd CROY/NA CR0 197 H4
Wydeville Manor Rd
LEE/GVPK SE12 166 A6
Wye Cl ASHF TW15 152 E6
ORP BR6 202 A4
RSLP HA4 58 A3
Wyemead Crs CHING E4 38 C4
Wye St BTSEA SW11 140 C4
Wyevale Cl PIN HA5 40 E6
Wyfields CLAY IG5 54 B4
Wyfold Rd FUL/PGN SW6 139 H2
Wyke Cl ISLW TW7 116 A6
Wyke Gdns HNWL W7 116 A3
Wykeham Av DAGW RM9 91 J4
Wykeham Cl WDR/YW UB7 112 D6
Wykeham Gn DAGW RM9 91 J4
Wykeham Hl WBLY HA9 62 B5
Wykeham Ri TRDG/WHET N20 32 C3
Wykeham Rd HDN NW4 64 A2
KTN/HRWW/W HA3 61 H1
Wyke Rd BOW E3 87 J5
RYNPK SW20 177 F5
Wylchin Cl PIN HA5 58 D1
Wyldes Cl GLDGN NW11 65 G5
Wyldfield Gdns ED N9 36 B4
Wyld Wy WBLY HA9 80 D4
Wyleu St FSTH SE23 164 B2
Wylie Rd NWDGN UB2 115 F3
Wyllen Cl WCHPL E1 104 E3
Wylo Dr BAR EN5 31 J1
Wymark Cl RAIN RM13 111 H1
Wymering Rd MV/WKIL W9 100 E2
Wymond St PUT/ROE SW15 139 F4
Wynan Rd POP/IOD E14 124 E5
Wynaud Ct WDGN N22 49 F2
Wyncham Av BFN/LL DA15 167 K3
Wynchgate KTN/HRWW/W HA3 42 E3
STHGT/OAK N14 34 E2
Wyncote Wy SAND/SEL CR2 213 F6
Wyncroft Cl BMLY BR1 184 E6
Wyndale Av CDALE/KGS NW9 62 C3
Wyndcliff Rd CHARL SE7 126 A6
Wyndcroft Cl ENC/FH EN2 23 H4
Wyndham Cl BELMT SM2 208 E5
ORP BR6 201 H5
Wyndham Crs HSLWW TW4 154 E1
KTTN NW5 84 C1
Wyndham Est CMBW SE5 142 D1
Wyndham Ms MBLAR W1H 8 E2
Wyndham Pl MBLAR W1H 8 E2
Wyndham Rd CMBW SE5 142 D1
EBAR EN4 33 K3
EHAM E6 89 H5
KUTN/CMB KT2 175 G3
WEA W13 116 C3
Wyndham St MBLAR W1H 8 E1
Wyneham Rd HNHL SE24 142 E6
Wynell Rd FSTH SE23 164 A5
Wynford Gv STMC/STPC BR5 186 C6
Wynford Pl BELV DA17 129 H6
Wynford Rd IS N1 5 G2
Wynford Wy ELTH/MOT SE9 166 E5
Wynlie Gdns PIN HA5 41 F5
Wynndale Rd SWFD E18 53 F4
Wynne Rd BRXN/ST SW9 142 B3
Wynn's Av BFN/LL DA15 148 B6
Wynnstay Gdns KENS * W8 119 K3
Wynter St BTSEA SW11 140 B5
Wynton Gdns SNWD SE25 197 F2
Wynton Pl ACT W3 98 D5
Wynyard Ter LBTH * SE11 122 A5
Wynyatt St FSBYE EC1V 6 A4
Wyre Gv EDGE HA8 30 E5
HYS/HAR UB3 113 K4
Wyresdale Crs GFD/PVL UB6 97 F2
Wyteleaf Cl RSLP HA4 58 A3
Wythburn Pl MBLAR W1H 8 E4
Wythenshawe Rd DAGE RM10 92 C1
Wythes Cl BMLY BR1 184 E5
Wythes Rd CAN/RD E16 126 D1
Wythfield Rd ELTH/MOT SE9 166 E1
Wyvenhoe Rd RYLN/HDSTN HA2 78 C1
Wyvern Cl DART DA1 171 F2
ORP BR6 217 H1
Wyvern Est NWMAL * KT3 176 D6
Wyvil Rd VX/NE SW8 141 K1
Wyvis St POP/IOD E14 105 K4

Y

Yabsley St POP/IOD E14 125 F1
Yalding Gv STMC/STPC BR5 202 E1
Yalding Rd BERM/RHTH SE16 123 H3
Yale Cl HSLWW TW4 134 E6
Yale Wy HCH RM12 93 J2
Yarborough Rd
WIM/MER SW19 178 C4
Yardley Cl CHING E4 25 K6
Yardley La CHING E4 25 K6
Yardley St FSBYW WC1X 5 J6
Yarmouth Crs TOTM N17 68 D2
Yarmouth Pl MYFR/PICC W1J 15 J1
Yarnton Wy ABYW SE2 128 D2
Yarrow Crs EHAM E6 107 J4
Yateley St WOOL/PLUM SE18 126 C3
Yeading Av RSLP HA4 59 J6
Yeading Fk YEAD UB4 95 G4
Yeading Gdns YEAD UB4 95 F4
Yeading La YEAD UB4 95 F5
Yeames Cl WEA W13 97 G5
Yeate St IS N1 85 K5
Yeatman Rd HGT N6 65 K3
Yeats Cl LEW * SE13 145 G3
WLSDN NW10 81 G4
Ye Cnr BUSH WD23 27 H1
Yeend Cl E/WMO/HCT KT8 189 F1
Yeldham Rd HMSMTH W6 119 G5
Yeldham Vls HMSMTH * W6 119 G5
Yelverton Rd BTSEA SW11 140 C3
Yenston Cl MRDN SM4 193 K3
Yeoman Cl EHAM E6 108 B6
Yeoman Rd NTHLT UB5 77 J5
Yeomans Acre RSLP HA4 58 E3
Yeoman's Rw CHEL SW3 14 D5
Yeoman St BERM/RHTH SE16 124 B4
Yeomans Wy PEND * EN3 24 D3
Yeomen Wy BARK/HLT IG6 54 C2
Yeo St BOW E3 105 K4
Yeovil Cl ORP BR6 201 K6
Yeovilton Pl KUTN/CMB KT2 174 E1
Yerbury Rd ARCH N19 84 D1
Yester Dr CHST BR7 184 D3
Yester Pk CHST BR7 184 E3
Yester Rd CHST BR7 184 E3
Yew Cl BKHH IG9 39 H4
Yewdale Cl BMLY BR1 183 H2
Yewfield Rd WLSDN NW10 81 H5
Yew Gv CRICK NW2 82 B2
The Yews ASHF * TW15 152 E6
Yewtree Cl RYLN/HDSTN HA2 60 B1
Yew Tree Cl WCHMH N21 35 G2
WELL DA16 148 B2
WPK KT4 192 B5
Yew Tree Ct BORE WD6 29 K1
Yew Tree Gdns CHDH RM6 74 A2
ROMW/RG RM7 75 F2
Yewtree Rd BECK BR3 182 C6
Yew Tree Rd SHB W12 99 H6
Yew Tree Wk HSLWW TW4 134 E6
Yew Wk HRW HA1 60 E5
Yoakley Rd STNW/STAM N16 68 A6
Yoke Cl HOLWY N7 84 E4
Yolande Gdns ELTH/MOT SE9 146 D6
Yonge Pk HOLWY N7 85 G1
York Av BFN/LL DA15 167 K4
HNWL W7 115 K1
HYS/HAR UB3 94 A5
KTN/HRWW/W HA3 43 H4
MORT/ESHN SW14 137 K6
York Br CAMTN NW1 3 G6
York Buildings CHCR WC2N 11 F6
York Cl CMBW * SE5 142 D3
EHAM E6 107 K5
HNWL W7 115 K1
MRDN SM4 194 A1
York Gdns WOT/HER KT12 188 C6
York Ga CAMTN NW1 3 H7
STHGT/OAK N14 34 E2
York Gv PECK SE15 143 K2
York Hl STRHM/NOR SW16 162 C5
York House Pl KENS * W8 120 A2
Yorkland Av WELL DA16 148 A5
York Ms IL IG1 72 A6
KTTN NW5 84 B3
York Pde BTFD * TW8 116 E5
CDALE/KGS * NW9 63 J3
York Pl BTSEA SW11 140 B4
IL IG1 72 A6
York Ri KTTN NW5 84 B1
ORP BR6 201 K5
York Rd ACT W3 98 E5
BAR EN5 21 G6
BELMT SM2 208 E4
BTFD TW8 116 E5
BTSEA SW11 140 B5
CHING E4 51 J1
CROY/NA CR0 196 B4
DART DA1 171 J2
EA W5 116 D3
FBAR/BDGN N11 48 D2
FSTGT E7 88 E4
HSLW TW3 135 G4
IL IG1 90 A1
KUTN/CMB KT2 175 G3
LEY E10 88 A1
NTHWD HA6 40 E5
RAIN RM13 93 F5
RCHPK/HAM TW10 137 G6
STHWK SE1 17 H2
TEDD TW11 155 K6
UED N18 50 D1
WALTH E17 69 F2
WCHMH N21 35 K2
WIM/MER SW19 178 A2
Yorkshire Cl STNW/STAM N16 86 A1
Yorkshire Gdns UED N18 50 D1
Yorkshire Grey Yd HHOL * WC1V 11 G2
Yorkshire Rd MTCM CR4 195 K2
POP/IOD E14 105 G5
York Sq POP/IOD * E14 105 G5
York St BARK IG11 90 B6
MBLAR W1H 8 E2
MTCM CR4 195 F4
TWK TW1 156 B3
York St Chambers MHST * W1U 9 F1
York Ter ENC/FH EN2 23 J1
ERITH DA8 149 K2
York Ter East CAMTN NW1 3 H7
York Ter West CAMTN NW1 3 G7
Yorkton St BETH E2 104 C1
York Wy CHSGTN KT9 205 K5
FELT TW13 154 E5
IS N1 5 F2
TRDG/WHET N20 33 K5
York Way Ct IS N1 5 F1
York Way Est HOLWY N7 84 E4
Youngmans Cl ENC/FH EN2 23 J2
Young Rd CAN/RD E16 107 G5
Youngs Rd GNTH/NBYPK IG2 72 D2
Young St KENS W8 120 A2
Yoxley Ap GNTH/NBYPK IG2 72 C3
Yoxley Dr GNTH/NBYPK IG2 72 C3
Yukon Rd BAL SW12 161 G2
Yuletide Cl WLSDN NW10 81 G4
Yunus Khan Cl WALTH E17 69 J2

Z

Zampa Rd BERM/RHTH SE16 123 K5
Zander Ct BETH E2 104 C2
Zangwill Rd BKHTH/KID SE3 146 C2
Zealand Av WDR/YW UB7 132 A1
Zealand Rd BOW E3 105 G1
Zelah Rd STMC/STPC BR5 202 C4
Zennor Rd BAL SW12 161 H3
Zenoria St EDUL SE22 143 G5
Zermatt Rd THHTH CR7 196 D1
Zetland St POP/IOD E14 106 A4
Zion Pl THHTH CR7 196 E1
Zion Rd THHTH CR7 196 E1
Zoar St STHWK SE1 12 C7
Zoffany St ARCH N19 66 D6

Index - featured places

AAIS
DART DA1 171 H2
Aarotya Medical Centre
TOTM N17 67 J1
Abbey Business Centre
VX/NE SW8 141 H2
The Abbey Clinic
BELV DA17 129 G5
Abbey Industrial Estate
ALP/SUD HA0 80 B6
MTCM CR4 194 E2
Abbey Medical Centre
STJWD NW8 83 F6
Abbey Mills
WIM/MER SW19 178 B4
Abbey Park Industrial Estate
BARK IG11 108 B1
Abbey Primary School
ABYW SE2 128 D3
Abbey (rems of)
ABYW SE2 128 C6
Abbey Road Health Centre
SRTFD E15 88 C6
Abbey School for the English Language
STJWD NW8 101 G1
Abbey Sports Centre
BARK IG11 90 C6
Abbey Trading Estate
SYD SE26 182 B1
Abbey Tutorial College
BAY/PAD W2 100 E5
Abbey Wharf Industrial Estate
BARK IG11 108 D2
Abbey Wood School
ABYW SE2 128 B3
Abbotsbury First School
MRDN SM4 194 A2
ABC Cinema
CAT SE6 164 E3
ESH/CLAY KT10 204 B2
HAMP NW3 83 J3
KUTN/CMB KT2 175 F5
PUT/ROE SW15 139 H4
STRHM/NOR SW16 161 K4
Abercorn Place School
STJWD NW8 101 G1
Abercorn Trading Estate
ALP/SUD HA0 79 K6
Aberdeen Wharf
WAP E1W 123 J1
Aberglen Industrial Estate
HYS/HAR UB3 113 G2
Abney Park Cemetery
STNW/STAM N16 68 A6
Acacia Business Centre
WAN E11 88 C1
Acland Burghley School
KTTN NW5 84 B2
Acorn Industrial Park
DART DA1 150 D6
Acre Road Health Clinic
KUTN/CMB KT2 175 G3
Acton Business Centre
WLSDN NW10 99 F3
Acton Central Industrial Estate
ACT W3 98 D6
Acton Health Centre
ACT W3 117 K1
Acton High School
ACT W3 117 H2
Acton Hospital
ACT W3 117 H2
Acton Lane Medical Centre
CHSWK W4 118 A2
Acton Park Industrial Estate
ACT W3 118 C1
CHSWK W4 118 A2
Acton Superbowl
ACT W3 98 C3
Acton Swimming Baths
ACT W3 117 K1
Acumen (Anglo School)
NRWD SE19 181 F3
Adams Bridge Business Centre
WBLY HA9 80 D3
Adamsrill Primary School
FSTH SE23 164 B5
Adath Yisroel Cemetery
EN EN1 24 B2
Addey & Stanhope School
NWCR SE14 144 C2
The Addington Golf Club
CROY/NA CR0 213 H6
Addington Palace Golf Club
CROY/NA CR0 213 G4
Addiscombe Cricket Club
CROY/NA CR0 212 B1
Addison Primary School
WKENS W14 119 G3
Adelphi Theatre
COVGDN WC2E 11 F6
Adler Industrial Estate
HYS/HAR UB3 113 G2
Admiral Hyson Industrial Estate
BERM/RHTH SE16 123 J4
Admiralty Arch
STJS SW1Y 10 D7
ADT Technology College
PUT/ROE SW15 139 J6
The Adult College of Barking & Dagenham
BARK IG11 90 E4
Adult Education Centre
DART DA1 171 J2
POP/IOD E14 125 F3
Africa Centre
COVGDN WC2E 11 F5
Agora Shopping Centre
PECK SE15 143 H3
Ainslie Wood Primary School
CHING E4 51 K1
Airbase Unity Elementary School
HGDN/ICK UB10 58 A6
Airbus Coach Station
HTHAIR TW6 132 C4
Air Call Business Centre
CDALE/KGS NW9 45 F6
Airedale Physiotherapy Clinic
CHSWK W4 118 C5
Airlinks Golf Club
NWDGN UB2 114 B4
Air Links Industrial Estate
HEST TW5 114 B5
Airport Gate Business Centre
WDR/YW UB7 132 C1
Aksaray Sports Club
STNW/STAM N16 85 K2
Albany Centre & Theatre
DEPT SE8 144 C1
Albany Clinic
BFN/LL DA15 168 B6
WIM/MER SW19 178 A3
The Albany College
HDN NW4 63 K2
Albany Park Canoe & Sailing Centre
KUTN/CMB KT2 174 E2
Albany School Grant Maintained
PEND EN3 25 F1
The Albany School
HCH RM12 75 K6
Albemarle Independant College
BAY/PAD W2 101 F6
Albemarle Primary School
WIM/MER SW19 159 H4
Albert Memorial
SKENS SW7 14 A2
Albery Theatre
CHCR WC2N 10 E5
Albion Health Centre
WCHPL E1 104 D4
Albion J & I School
BERM/RHTH SE16 123 K2
Albion Street Health Centre
BERM/RHTH SE16 123 K2
Albright Industrial Estate
RAIN RM13 111 H4
The Alchemy Gallery
CLKNW EC1R 5 J6
Alderbrook Primary School
BAL SW12 161 G2
Aldersbrook County Secondary School
MNPK E12 71 G5
Aldersbrook Primary School
WAN E11 71 G5
Alderwood Primary School
ELTH/MOT SE9 167 J1
Aldwych Theatre
HOL/ALD WC2B 11 G4
Alexander Mcleod Primary School
ABYW SE2 128 C5
Alexandra Avenue Clinic
RYLN/HDSTN HA2 59 K6
Alexandra Business Centre
PEND EN3 25 F5
Alexandra Infant School
KUTN/CMB KT2 175 H3
PGE/AN SE20 182 A3
Alexandra Junior School
HSLW TW3 135 G3
SYD SE26 182 A2
Alexandra Palace
WDGN N22 48 D6
Alexandra Palace Ice Rink
WDGN N22 48 D5
Alexandra Primary School
WDGN N22 49 F5
Alexandra School
RYLN/HDSTN HA2 59 K6
Alfred Mizen First School
MTCM CR4 179 J6
Alfred Salter Primary School
BERM/RHTH SE16 124 A2
Alfreds Way Industrial Estate
BARK IG11 91 G6
Allegery Clinic
CAVSQ/HST W1G 9 J2
Allenby Infant School
STHL UB1 96 A5
Allen Edwards Primary School
CLAP SW4 141 K2
The All England Lawn Tennis & Croquet Club
WIM/MER SW19 159 G5
Alleyns School
EDUL SE22 143 F6
Allfarthing JMI School
WAND/EARL SW18 160 B1
All Saints Benhilton School
SUT SM1 209 F1
All Saints Catholic School
BCTR RM8 74 C5
All Saints CE First School
WIM/MER SW19 178 B3
All Saints CE Junior School
NRWD SE19 181 F4
All Saints CE Primary School
BKHTH/KID SE3 145 H3
CRICK NW2 82 D1
FUL/PGN SW6 139 H3
PUT/ROE SW15 139 F4
TRDG/WHET N20 33 H4
All Souls CE Primary School
GTPST W1W 10 A2
Allum Medical Centre
WAN E11 70 B4
Alma Primary School
BERM/RHTH SE16 123 H4
PEND EN3 25 G6
Almeida Theatre
IS N1 85 H5
Al Muntada Islamic School
FUL/PGN SW6 139 J2
Alperton Cemetery
ALP/SUD HA0 79 K6
Alperton Community School
ALP/SUD HA0 80 A5
Alperton High School
ALP/SUD HA0 79 K6
Alperton Sports Ground
ALP/SUD HA0 97 K1
Alpha Business Centre
WALTH E17 69 H2
Alpha Preparatory School
HRW HA1 60 E2
Alpine Business Centre
EHAM E6 108 A4
Alscot Road Industrial Estate
STHWK SE1 19 K6
Altmore Infant School
EHAM E6 89 K5
The Alton School
PUT/ROE SW15 158 C2
Ambler Primary School
FSBYPK N4 85 H1
Ambleside Junior School
WOT/HER KT12 188 B5
AMC Business Centre
WLSDN NW10 98 D2
American Intercontinental University
MHST W1U 9 H2
AMF Bowling
LEW SE13 145 F4
Amherst Primary School
HACK E8 86 C3
Ampthill Square Medical Centre
CAMTN NW1 4 A3
Amy Johnson Primary School
WLGTN SM6 210 E5
Anchorage Point Industrial Estate
CHARL SE7 126 B3
Anchor Bay Industrial Estate
ERITH DA8 150 C1
Anchor Retail Park
WCHPL E1 104 E3
Andover Medical Centre
HOLWY N7 85 F1
The Andrew Ewing Primary School
HEST TW5 134 E1

Andrew Sketchley Theatre
WCHPL E1 104 C4
Anerley Primary School
PGE/AN SE20 181 H4
Anerley School
PGE/AN SE20 181 H4
Angel Centre
DART DA1 171 H1
Angerstein Business Park
GNWCH SE10 125 K4
Angerstein Works
BKHTH/KID SE3 125 K6
Anglian Industrial Estate
BARK IG11 109 F3
Animal Cemetery
REDBR IG4 53 H6
Annandale Primary School
GNWCH SE10 125 J2
GNWCH SE10 125 J5
Annemount School
EFNCH N2 65 G3
Annunciation RC Infant School
EDGE HA8 45 F4
The Annunciation RC Junior School
MLHL NW7 45 F2
Anson Primary School
CRICK NW2 82 B3
Ante Natal Clinic
MUSWH N10 48 A6
Apex Industrial Estate
WLSDN NW10 99 H3
Apex Retail Park
FELT TW13 154 E5
Apollo Theatre
SOHO/SHAV W1D 10 C5
Apollo Victoria Theatre
PIM SW1V 16 A5
Apostolic Nuncio
WIM/MER SW19 159 F5
Applegarth Primary School
CROY/NA CR0 213 K4
Apsley House, The Wellington Museum
BAY/PAD W2 15 G2
Aquarius Business Park
CRICK NW2 63 J5
Aquarius Golf Club
PECK SE15 143 K6
Arcadia Shopping Centre
EA W5 97 K6
The Archbishop Lanfranc School
CROY/NA CR0 195 K3
Archbishop Michael Ramsey Technology College
CMBW SE5 142 C1
Archbishop Sumners CE Primary School
LBTH SE11 17 K7
Archbishop Tenisons CE School
CROY/NA CR0 212 B1
Archbishop Tenison's School
VX/NE SW8 122 A6
Archdale Business Centre
RYLN/HDSTN HA2 60 C6
Archdeacon Cambridge's CE Primary School
WHTN TW2 155 K4
Arches Business Centre
NWDGN UB2 114 E2
Arches Leisure Centre
GNWCH SE10 125 G6
Archgate Business Centre
NFNCH/WDSP N12 33 G6
Archway Business Centre
ARCH N19 84 D1
Archway Leisure Centre
ARCH N19 66 C6
Arena Estate
FSBYPK N4 67 H3
Argyle Primary School
STPAN WC1H 4 E4
Arklow Trading Estate
NWCR SE14 124 B6
Armourers & Braziers' Hall
LOTH EC2R 12 E2
Arndale Health Centre
WAND/EARL SW18 159 K1
Arnhem Wharf Primary School
BERM/RHTH SE16 124 C3
Arnold House School
STJWD NW8 2 A2
Arnos Pool
FBAR/BDGN N11 48 D1
Arnot Abbey
FARR EC1M 12 A1
Arsenal FC (Highbury)
HBRY N5 85 G1
Arts Centre
BMLY BR1 184 C4
HAMP NW3 83 F3
Art School
BECK BR3 198 B2
Arts Theatre
LSQ/SEVD WC2H 10 E5
PUT/ROE SW15 139 G5
Ashbourne Independent Sixth Form College
KENS W8 120 A2
Ashburnham Primary School
WBPTN SW10 140 C1
Ashburton High School
CROY/NA CR0 197 J4
Ashburton Primary School
CROY/NA CR0 197 J3
Ashby Mill School
CLAP SW4 141 K6
Ashfield Junior School
BUSH WD23 28 B2
Ashford Clinic
ASHF TW15 152 B5
Ashford High School
ASHF TW15 152 B5
Ashford Hospital A & E
STWL/WRAY TW19 152 B4
Ashford Industrial Estate
ASHF TW15 153 F6
Ashford Sports Club
ASHF TW15 152 A6
STWL/WRAY TW19 152 C3
Ashgrove College
WALTH E17 51 J6
Ashgrove Estate
BMLY BR1 183 G2
Ashgrove School
BMLY BR1 184 A5
Ashleigh Commercial Estate
CHARL SE7 126 B4
Ashmead Primary School
DEPT SE8 144 D3
Ashmole Centre
STHGT/OAK N14 34 C3
Ashmole Primary School
VX/NE SW8 122 A6
Ashmole School
STHGT/OAK N14 34 C3
Ashmount Primary School
ARCH N19 66 C4
Ashton House School
ISLW TW7 135 J2
Ashton Playing Fields Track
WFD IG8 53 J2
Aspen House School
LBTH SE11 122 C6
Aspen House Secondary & Primary School
BRXS/STRHM SW2 161 K3
Asquith Court School
KTN/HRWW/W HA3 61 H3
Asquith School
PEND EN3 24 E5
Assembly Rooms
KUT KT1 191 F1
Associated Newspapers
BERM/RHTH SE16 124 A3
Aston Clinic
NWMAL KT3 192 B1
Aston House School
EA W5 97 K5
Asylum Medical Centre
CEND/HSY/T N8 49 G6
Athelney Primary School
CAT SE6 164 D5
Athelstan House School
HPTN TW12 173 F4
Athena Medical Centre
CLPT E5 86 E2
Atherton Leisure Centre
FSTGT E7 88 D4
Athlone House Hospital
HGT N6 65 K5
Athlon Industrial Estate
ALP/SUD HA0 97 K1
Atkinson Morley Hospital
RYNPK SW20 176 E3
Atlas Business Centre
CRICK NW2 63 K6
Atlas Transport Estate
BTSEA SW11 140 B3
Auriol Junior School
HOR/WEW KT19 207 H2
Australia House
HOL/ALD WC2B 11 H4
Aveling Park School
WALTH E17 51 J5
Avenue House School
WEA W13 97 H5
Avenue Industrial Estate
CHING E4 51 H2
Avenue Primary School
KIL/WHAMP NW6 82 C5
MNPK E12 89 J2
Avigdor Primary School
STNW/STAM N16 67 K6
Avondale Park Primary School
NTGHL W11 100 B6
Avon House School
WFD IG8 38 E6
Avon Trading Estate
WKENS W14 119 J4
Axis Business Centre
SRTFD E15 87 K6
The Aylesham Centre
PECK SE15 143 H2
Ayloff Primary School
HCH RM12 93 K2
Aylward First & Middle Schools
STAN HA7 43 K1
Aylward School
UED N18 35 K6
Aylwin Girls School
BERM/RHTH SE16 19 K6
BAA Heathrow Visitor Centre
HTHAIR TW6 132 E2
Babington House School
CHST BR7 184 E2
Back Care Clinic
WPK KT4 192 D5
Bacons City Technology College
BERM/RHTH SE16 124 A2
Bacon's College
BERM/RHTH SE16 124 B1
Baden Powell House
SKENS SW7 120 B4
Baden Powell Primary School
CLPT E5 86 D1
Bakers Hall
MON EC3R 13 H6
Balaam Leisure Centre
PLSTW E13 106 E3
Bales College
NKENS W10 100 B2
Balfour Business Centre
NWDGN UB2 114 C3
Balgowan Primary School
BECK BR3 182 B5
Balham Health Centre
BAL SW12 161 G4
Balham Leisure Centre
TOOT SW17 161 F4
Balham Preparatory School
TOOT SW17 160 E6
Balmoral Trading
BARK IG11 109 F4
Baltic Exchange
HDTCH EC3A 13 H3
Bancrofts School
WFD IG8 38 E5
Bandon Hill Cemetery
WLGTN SM6 210 D3
Bandon Hill Primary School
WLGTN SM6 210 D4
Bangabandhu Primary School
BETH E2 104 E2
Bank of England Extension
STP EC4M 12 C4
Bank of England (& Museum)
LOTH EC2R 12 E4
Bankside Gallery
STHWK SE1 12 B6
Bankside Jetty
STHWK SE1 12 C6
Bankside Park Industrial Estate
BARK IG11 109 G2
Bannister Stadium
KTN/HRWW/W HA3 42 C2
Bannockburn Primary School
WOOL/PLUM SE18 128 A4
Banqueting House
WHALL SW1A 16 E1
Barber Surgeons' Hall
BARB EC2Y 12 D2
Barbican Cinema
BARB EC2Y 12 C1
Barbican Station
STBT EC1A 12 B1
The Barbican
BARB EC2Y 12 C1
Barbican Theatre
BARB EC2Y 12 D1
Barclay J & I School
LEY E10 70 B3
Barham Primary School
ALP/SUD HA0 79 J4
Baring Primary School
LEE/GVPK SE12 165 K2
Baring Road Medical Centre
LEE/GVPK SE12 165 K4
Barkantine Clinic
POP/IOD E14 124 D2
Barking Abbey Comprehensive School
BARK IG11 90 D3
BARK IG11 91 F4
Barking Abbey Industrial Estate
BARK IG11 90 B6
Barking Abbey Leisure Centre
BARK IG11 91 G4
Barking College
ROMW/RG RM7 75 F6
Barking FC
BCTR RM8 91 H3
Barking Hospital
BARK IG11 91 F5
Barking Industrial Park
BARK IG11 91 F6
Barking RUFC
DAGW RM9 91 K6
Barkingside Cemetery
BARK/HLT IG6 54 B6
Barkingside FC
BARK/HLT IG6 72 D1
Barlby Primary School
NKENS W10 100 B3
Barley Lane Primary School
GDMY/SEVK IG3 73 G4
Barnabas Medical Centre
NTHLT UB5 78 C4
Barn Croft Primary School
WALTH E17 69 G3
Barnehurst Primary School
BXLYHN DA7 149 K2
Barnehurst Public Pay & Play Golf Club
BXLYHN DA7 150 A4
Barn Elms Athletics Track
BARN SW13 138 E3
Barn Elms Water Sports Centre
BARN SW13 139 F3
Barnes Cray Primary School
DART DA1 150 D5
Barnes Hospital
MORT/ESHN SW14 138 B4
Barnes Sports Club
BARN SW13 138 C2
Barnet College
BAR EN5 20 D5
NFNCH/WDSP N12 47 G1
Barnet Copthall Pool & Stadium
HDN NW4 45 K3
Barnet Copthall Stadium
HDN NW4 46 A4
Barnet County Court
BAR EN5 21 G5
FNCH N3 46 E4
Barnet FC (Underhill)
BAR EN5 20 E6
Barnet General Hospital
BAR EN5 20 B5
Barnet Health Centre
BAR EN5 20 E6
Barnet Hill JMI School
BAR EN5 20 D6
Barnet Hospital Chest Clinic
BAR EN5 20 B5
Barnet Magistrates Court
BAR EN5 20 D5
Barnet Museum
BAR EN5 20 C5
Barnet Trading Estate
BAR EN5 20 D4
Barnfield Primary School
EDGE HA8 44 E4
Barnhill Community High School
YEAD UB4 95 F2
Barnsbury School for Girls
IS N1 85 G4
Barons Court Theatre
WKENS W14 119 H5
Barratt Industrial Park
BOW E3 106 A3
Barrett Industrial Park
STHL UB1 115 F1
Barrett Way Industrial Estate
HRW HA1 42 D6
Barrington Primary School
BXLYHN DA7 148 E3
Barrow Hedges Primary School
CAR SM5 209 J5
Barrow Hill Junior School
STJWD NW8 2 C3
Barton House Health Centre
STNW/STAM N16 85 K1
Barwell Business Park
CHSGTN KT9 205 K5
Bassett House School
NKENS W10 100 B5
Baston School
HAYES BR2 200 A6
Bath Factory Estate
HNHL SE24 162 D1
Battersea Business Centre
BTSEA SW11 141 F4
Battersea Dogs' Home
VX/NE SW8 141 G1
Battersea Power Station (disused)
VX/NE SW8 121 G6
Battersea Sports Centre
BTSEA SW11 140 C4
Battersea Technology College
BTSEA SW11 140 E2
Battersea Tutorial College
TOOT SW17 161 F4
BBC Studios
MV/WKIL W9 101 F3
BBC Television Centre
SHB W12 100 A6
Beacon House School
EA W5 117 G1
Beaconsfield Primary School
HYS/HAR UB3 114 B1
Beal High School
REDBR IG4 53 J6
Beam Primary School
DAGE RM10 110 E1
Beatrix Potter Primary School
WAND/EARL SW18 160 B3
Beauclerc Infant School
SUN TW16 172 B6
Beaumont Primary School
LEY E10 69 K4
Beaver College
BAY/PAD W2 100 E6
The Beavers Community Primary School
HSLWW TW4 134 B4
Beaverwood School for Girls
CHST BR7 185 K2
Beckenham Business Centre
BECK BR3 182 B2
Beckenham Crematorium
SNWD SE25 181 K6
Beckenham Cricket Club
BECK BR3 182 E3
Beckenham Hospital
BECK BR3 182 C5
Beckenham Leisure Centre
BECK BR3 182 B4
Beckenham Place Park Golf Course
BECK BR3 182 E2
Beckenham RFC
BECK BR3 198 B1
Beckenham Town FC
BECK BR3 198 D2
Becket Sports Centre
DART DA1 171 F1
Beckford Primary School
KIL/WHAMP NW6 82 D3
Beckmead School
BECK BR3 198 D5
The Beck Theatre
HYS/HAR UB3 94 D5
Beckton Ski Centre
EHAM E6 108 A3
Beckton Special School
CAN/RD E16 107 H4
Beckton Triangle Retail Park
EHAM E6 108 B2
Becontree Day Hospital
BCTR RM8 74 A6
Becontree Primary School
BCTR RM8 91 H1
Bective House Clinic
PUT/ROE SW15 139 J5
Beddington Infants School
WLGTN SM6 210 C1
Beddington Medical Centre
CROY/NA CR0 210 E2
Beddington Park Primary School
CROY/NA CR0 210 D1
Beddington Trading Estate
CROY/NA CR0 195 K5
Bedelsford School
KUT KT1 175 F6
Bedensfield Clinic
SCUP DA14 187 F1
Bedfont Health Clinic
EBED/NFELT TW14 153 H2
Bedfont Industrial Park
FELT TW13 153 G5
Bedfont J & I School
EBED/NFELT TW14 153 H1
Bedfont Lakes Country Park
EBED/NFELT TW14 153 F4
Bedington Infant School
WLGTN SM6 210 C2
Bedonwell Clinic
ABYW SE2 129 F6
Bedonwell Medical Centre
BELV DA17 129 G5
Bedonwell Primary School
BELV DA17 129 F6
Beecholme First School
MTCM CR4 179 G4
Beechwood School
STRHM/NOR SW16 161 K4
Beehive Preparatory School
REDBR IG4 71 K1
The Beehive School
ARCH N19 66 D4
Beis Rochel D'satmar Girls School
STNW/STAM N16 68 A4
Beis Yaakov Primary School
CDALE/KGS NW9 45 F6
Bellamy's Wharf
BERM/RHTH SE16 124 A1
Bellenden Primary School
PECK SE15 143 H4
Bellenden Road Business Centre
PECK SE15 143 G3
Bellenden Road Retail Park
PECK SE15 143 G2
Belleville Primary School
BTSEA SW11 140 E6
Belle Vue Cinema
EDGE HA8 44 C2
WLSDN NW10 81 K5
Bell Industrial Estate
CHSWK W4 117 K4
Bellingham Trading Estate
CAT SE6 164 E5
Bell Lane JMI School
HDN NW4 64 B1
Belmont First & Middle School
KTN/HRWW/W HA3 43 F5
Belmont J & I School
WDGN N22 49 J6
Belmont (Mill Hill Junior School)
MLHL NW7 31 J5
Belmont Park School
LEY E10 70 A3
Belmont Primary School
BXLYHN DA7 149 H1
CHSWK W4 118 A4
Belmore Primary School
YEAD UB4 95 F2
Belvedere Day Hospital
WLSDN NW10 81 J6
Belvedere Industrial Estate
BELV DA17 130 A1
Belvedere Link Business Park
BELV DA17 129 K3
Belvedere Primary School
BELV DA17 129 J4
Belvue Business Centre
NTHLT UB5 78 B5
Belvue School
NTHLT UB5 78 A6
Benedict House Preparatory School
BFN/LL DA15 168 A6
Benhurst JMI School
HCH RM12 93 K1
Ben Jonson Primary School
WCHPL E1 105 G3
Bensham Manor School
THHTH CR7 196 D2
Benson Primary School
CROY/NA CR0 213 G1
Bentalls Shopping Centre
KUT KT1 174 E5
Benthal Primary School
STNW/STAM N16 86 C1
Bentley Wood Girls School
STAN HA7 43 F1
Bentworth Primary School
SHB W12 99 K5
Beormund School
STHWK SE1 18 E3
Berger Primary School
HOM E9 87 F4
Berkeley Primary School
HEST TW5 114 C6
Berlitz Schools of Languages
LINN WC2A 11 H2
Bermondsey Town Hall
STHWK SE1 19 K5
Bermondsey Trading Estate
BERM/RHTH SE16 123 K4
Berrymede Infant School
ACT W3 117 J2
Berrymede Junior School
ACT W3 117 J2
Bertram House School
TOOT SW17 161 F4
Bessemer Grange J & I School
EDUL SE22 143 F5
Bessemer Park Industrial Estate
BRXN/ST SW9 142 C5
Bethlem Royal Hospital
BECK BR3 198 D4
Bethnal Green Museum of Childhood
BETH E2 104 D2
Bethnal Green Technology College
BETH E2 7 K5
Beulah J & I School
THHTH CR7 180 D5
Beverley School
NWMAL KT3 192 D2
Beverley Trading Estate
MRDN SM4 193 G4
Bevington Primary School
NKENS W10 100 C4
Bexley College
ABYW SE2 128 E6
ERITH DA8 129 K4
Bexley Cricket Club
BXLY DA5 169 H3
Bexley Erith Technical High School
BXLY DA5 169 H1
Bexley Grammar School
WELL DA16 148 C5
Bexleyheath Centre
BXLYHS DA6 149 F5
Bexleyheath Golf Club
BXLYHS DA6 149 F6
Bexleyheath School
BXLYHN DA7 149 H4
Bexley Hospital
BXLY DA5 170 B4
Bexley RFC
BXLY DA5 169 H2
BFI London IMAX Cinema
STHWK SE1 17 H1
Bickley Park Cricket Club
BMLY BR1 184 D5
Bickley Park Prep School
BMLY BR1 184 C6
Bickley Park School
BMLY BR1 184 D6
Big Ben
WEST SW1P 17 F3
Bigland Green Primary School
WCHPL E1 104 D5
Billingsgate Fish Market
POP/IOD E14 124 E1
Birch Court Colindale Hospital
CDALE/KGS NW9 45 G5
Birchwood Park Golf Club
RDART DA2 187 K3
Birkbeck College
STPAN WC1H 4 C6
Birkbeck Primary School
SCUP DA14 168 C5
Bishop Challenor RC School
WCHPL E1 104 E6
Bishop Challoner RC Secondary School
WCHPL E1 104 E5
Bishop Challoner School
HAYES BR2 183 G5
Bishop Douglas RC School
EFNCH N2 47 G5
Bishop Gilpin Primary School
WIM/MER SW19 177 J1
Bishop John Robinson CE Primary
THMD SE28 109 J6
Bishop Perrin CE Primary School
WHTN TW2 155 G2
Bishop Ramsey CE School
RSLP HA4 58 E4
RSLP HA4 58 D4
Bishopsgate Institute
WCHPL E1 13 H2

Bishop Stopford School *EN* EN1 24 D3
Bishop Thomas Grant School *STRHM/NOR* SW16 180 A1
Bishop Winnington-Ingram CE Primary School *RSLP* HA4 58 B4
Bittacy Business Centre *MLHL* NW7 46 C2
Blackburn Trading Estate *STWL/WRAY* TW19 152 C1
Blackfen School for Girls *BFN/LL* DA15 168 C1
Blackfriars Millennium Pier *EMB* EC4Y 11 K5
Blackfriars Pier *BLKFR* EC4V 12 B5
Blackfriars Station *BLKFR* EC4V 12 A5
Blackheath Bluecoat CE School *BKHTH/KID* SE3 146 A1
Blackheath Business Estate *GNWCH* SE10 145 F2
The Blackheath Clinic *BKHTH/KID* SE3 145 K5
Blackheath High School *BKHTH/KID* SE3 145 J3
Blackheath High Senior School *BKHTH/KID* SE3 145 K1
Blackheath Hospital *BKHTH/KID* SE3 145 J4
Blackwall Trading Estate *POP/IOD* E14 106 B4
Blaire Peach School *STHL* UB1 114 C1
Blake College *GTPST* W1W 10 A1
Blanche Neville School *WDGN* N22 49 G4
Blenheim Business Centre *MTCM* CR4 178 E4
Blenheim J & I School *ORP* BR6 202 D6
Blenheim Shopping Centre *PGE/AN* SE20 181 K3
Blessed Dominic RC Primary School *CDALE/KGS* NW9 45 G5
Blessed John Roche Catholic School *POP/IOD* E14 105 J5
Blessed Sacrament RC Primary School *IS* N1 5 F1
Blood Transfusion Centre *EDGE* HA8 44 D3
Bloomfield Clinic (Guys Hospital) *STHWK* SE1 19 F2
Bloomsbury College *FUL/PGN* SW6 139 K1
Bloomsbury Theatre *STPAN* WC1H 4 C6
Blossom House School *RYNPK* SW20 177 F3
Blossoms Inn Medical Centre *BLKFR* EC4V 12 D5
Blue Gate Fields Primary School *WCHPL* E1 104 E6
BML Medical Centre *CAVSQ/HST* W1G 9 H2
Bnois Jerusalem School *STNW/STAM* N16 67 K4
The Bob Hope Theatre *ELTH/MOT* SE9 166 E1
Bodywise Natural Health Centre *BETH* E2 104 E2
Boleyn Cinema *EHAM* E6 107 H1
Bolingbroke Hospital *BTSEA* SW11 140 D6
Bolingbroke Primary School *BTSEA* SW11 140 C2
Bond First School *MTCM* CR4 178 E5
Bond Road School *MTCM* CR4 178 E5
Bonner Primary School *BETH* E2 105 F1
Bonneville Primary School *CLAP* SW4 161 H1
Bonus Pastor School *BMLY* BR1 165 H6
Boomes Industrial Estate *RAIN* RM13 111 H3
Booster Cushion Theatre *WDGN* N22 49 F5
Borough Market *STHWK* SE1 12 E7
Boston Business Park *HNWL* W7 115 K3
Boston University *ECT* SW5 120 B4
Botwell RC Primary School *HYS/HAR* UB3 113 J2
Boundary Business Park *MTCM* CR4 178 C5
Bounds Green Health Centre *FBAR/BDGN* N11 48 D3
Bounds Green Industrial Estate *FBAR/BDGN* N11 48 C2
Bounds Green Primary School *FBAR/BDGN* N11 48 E3
Bourne CP School *RSLP* HA4 77 G3
Bourne Hall Health Centre *EW* KT17 207 H6
Bourne Hall Museum *EW* KT17 207 H6
Bourne Road Industrial Park *DART* DA1 150 A6
Bourneside Sports Club *STHGT/OAK* N14 34 E3
Bousfield Primary School *ECT* SW5 120 A5
Boutcher CE Primary School *STHWK* SE1 19 J5
Bowater House *SKENS* SW7 14 E3
Bow County Court *SRTFD* E15 88 D4
Bow County Secondary School *BOW* E3 105 J2
Bowden House Clinic *HRW* HA1 60 E6
Bower Park School *ROM* RM1 57 G2
Bowes Primary School *FBAR/BDGN* N11 48 D1
Bowes Road Clinic *FBAR/BDGN* N11 48 C1
Bow Industrial Park *SRTFD* E15 87 J5
Bowman Trading Estate *CDALE/KGS* NW9 44 C6
Bow Street Magistrates Court *HOL/ALD* WC2B 11 F4
Bow Triangle Business Centre *BOW* E3 105 J3
Boxgrove Primary School *ABYW* SE2 128 D3
Boys' Club *EDGE* HA8 44 C3
Brackenbury Health Centre *HMSMTH* W6 118 E3
Brackenbury Primary School *HMSMTH* W6 118 E3
Bracken Industrial Estate *BARK/HLT* IG6 55 F3
Brady Recreation Centre *WCHPL* E1 104 C4
Braeside Junior School *BKHH* IG9 39 G3
Braeside Senior School *BKHH* IG9 39 F3
Braincroft Primary School *CRICK* NW2 81 H1
Braintree Road Industrial Estate *RSLP* HA4 77 F2
Bramah's Tea & Coffee Museum *STHWK* SE1 18 D1
Brampton Manor School *PLSTW* E13 107 H3
Brampton Primary School *BXLYHN* DA7 148 E3
EHAM E6 107 J2
Brandlehow Primary School *PUT/ROE* SW15 139 J5
Branollys Health Centre *PLSTW* E13 106 E3
Breakspear Crematorium *RSLP* HA4 58 A2
Breaside Pre Prep School *BMLY* BR1 183 K3
Brecknock Primary School *HOLWY* N7 84 D4
Bredinghurst School *PECK* SE15 143 K5
Brent Adult College *WLSDN* NW10 81 F6
Brent Arts Council *CRICK* NW2 81 J1
Brent Child & Family Clinic *WLSDN* NW10 81 H3
Brent Cross Shopping Centre *HDN* NW4 64 A4
Brentfield Medical Centre *WLSDN* NW10 81 F4
Brentfield Primary School *WLSDN* NW10 81 F4
Brentford Business Centre *BTFD* TW8 136 D1
The Brentford Clinic *BTFD* TW8 117 F6
Brentford County Court *BTFD* TW8 136 E1
Brentford FC (Griffin Park) *BTFD* TW8 116 E6
Brentford Fountain Leisure Centre *CHSWK* W4 117 G5
Brentford Health Centre *BTFD* TW8 116 D6
Brentford Medical Centre *BTFD* TW8 136 E1
Brentford School for Girls *BTFD* TW8 116 E6
Brent Knoll School *FSTH* SE23 164 A5
Brent Magistrates Court House *WLSDN* NW10 81 G4
Brent Park Industrial Estate *NWDGN* UB2 114 A3
Brentside First School *HNWL* W7 96 E4
Brentside High School *HNWL* W7 96 E3
Brentside Primary School *HNWL* W7 96 E3
Brent Trading Estate *WLSDN* NW10 81 G3
Brent Valley Golf Club *HNWL* W7 96 E6
Brentwaters Business Park *BTFD* TW8 136 D1
Brewers' Hall *CITYW* EC2V 12 D2
Brewery Industrial Estate *IS* N1 6 C3
Brewery Mews Business Centre *ISLW* TW7 136 A4
Brick Lane Music Hall *SDTCH* EC2A 7 H5
Brick Lane Music House *WCHPL* E1 7 K7
Bricklayer Arms Industrial Estate *STHWK* SE1 19 J7
The Bridewell Theatre *EMB* EC4Y 12 A4
The Bridge Business Centre *NWDGN* UB2 115 F2
Bridge Lane Theatre *BTSEA* SW11 140 D2
The Bridge Leisure Centre *SYD* SE26 182 C1
Bridge Park Business & Leisure Centre *WLSDN* NW10 80 D5
Brigham Young University *BAY/PAD* W2 100 E6
Bright Sparks Montessori School *WKENS* W14 119 G2
Bright Sparks School *STRHM/NOR* SW16 161 K6
Brigstock Medical Centre *THHTH* CR7 196 C2
Brimsdown Industrial Estate *PEND* EN3 24 E3
Brimsdown Primary School *PEND* EN3 25 F4
Brindishe Primary School *LEE/GVPK* SE12 145 J6
Britannia Business Centre *CRICK* NW2 82 B2
Britannia Leisure Centre *IS* N1 7 F1
Britannia Sports Ground *WALTH* E17 51 J3
Britannia Village Primary School *CAN/RD* E16 126 A1
British Airways London Eye *WHALL* SW1A 17 F2
British Cartoon Centre *BMSBY* WC1N 5 F7
British Dental Association *CAVSQ/HST* W1G 9 J2
British Library *CAMTN* NW1 4 D4
British Library Newspaper Library *CDALE/KGS* NW9 45 G6
British Medical Association *STPAN* WC1H 4 D6
British Museum *RSQ* WC1B 10 E2
The British Museum Shop *HTHAIR* TW6 132 E6
British Telecom Tower *GTPST* W1W 10 A1
The Brit School *SNWD* SE25 196 E3
Brittons School *RAIN* RM13 93 H5
Brixton Academy *BRXN/ST* SW9 142 B4
Brixton College for Further Education *BRXS/STRHM* SW2 142 A6
Brixton Recreation Centre *BRXN/ST* SW9 142 B4
Broadfields Infant School *EDGE* HA8 30 C4
Broadfields Junior School *EDGE* HA8 30 D4
Broadgate *LVPST* EC2M 13 F1
Broadgate Ice Arena *LVPST* EC2M 13 G2
Broadhurst School *KIL/WHAMP* NW6 83 G5
Broadmead Primary School *CROY/NA* CR0 196 E3
Broadwalk Shopping Centre *EDGE* HA8 44 C2
Broadwater Farm Primary School *TOTM* N17 49 K5
Broadwater Primary School *TOOT* SW17 160 C6
Broadway Clinic *EDGE* HA8 44 D4
Broadway Retail Park *CRICK* NW2 82 B2
Broadway Shopping Centre *BXLYHS* DA6 149 H5
HMSMTH W6 119 F5
Broadway Square Shopping Centre *BXLYHN* DA7 149 H5
Broadway Squash & Fitness Centre *HMSMTH* W6 119 G4
Brocklebank Health Centre *WAND/EARL* SW18 160 A2
Brocklebank Industrial Estate *GNWCH* SE10 125 K4
Brockley Cross Business Centre *BROCKY* SE4 144 B4
Brockley Primary School *BROCKY* SE4 144 C6
Brockwell Lido *HNHL* SE24 162 C1
Brockwell Primary School *BRXS/STRHM* SW2 162 B1
Bromet Primary School *OXHEY* WD19 27 H2
Bromley Cemetery *BMLY* BR1 183 J3
Bromley College of Further & Higher Education *BMLY* BR1 183 K4
HAYES BR2 200 C3
Bromley County Court *BMLY* BR1 183 K4
Bromley FC *HAYES* BR2 200 A2
Bromley Golf Club *HAYES* BR2 200 D4
Bromley High School *BMLY* BR1 201 F1
Bromley Hospital *HAYES* BR2 200 A1
Bromley Hospitals NHS Trust *ORP* BR6 216 A2
ORP BR6 217 F2
Bromley Industrial Centre *BMLY* BR1 184 C6
Bromley Mall Indoor Market *BMLY* BR1 183 K5
Bromley Museum *ORP* BR6 202 C4
Bromley Road Infant School *BECK* BR3 182 E4
Bromley Road Retail Park *CAT* SE6 164 E4
Brompton Cemetery *WBPTN* SW10 120 A6
Brompton Medical Centre *WBPTN* SW10 120 A5
Brompton Oratory *SKENS* SW7 14 C5
Bromyard Leisure Centre *ACT* W3 118 B1
Brondesbury College for Boys *KIL/WHAMP* NW6 82 B5
Brooke Trading Estate *ROM* RM1 75 H4
Brookfield Primary School *CHEAM* SM3 193 H5
HGT N6 66 B6
Brook House FC *YEAD* UB4 94 D2
Brook Industrial Estate *YEAD* UB4 114 C1
Brookland Primary School *GLDGN* NW11 65 F1
Brooklands Primary School *BKHTH/KID* SE3 145 K4
Brook Lane Business Centre *BTFD* TW8 116 E5
Brookmarsh Trading Estate *DEPT* SE8 144 E1
Brookmead Industrial Estate *MTCM* CR4 195 H3
Brookside J & I School *YEAD* UB4 95 G2
Broomfield House School *RCH/KEW* TW9 137 G2
Broomfield School *STHGT/OAK* N14 48 D1
Broomsleigh Business Park *CAT* SE6 182 C1
Broomwood Hall School *BAL* SW12 161 F2
Brothwick Wharf *DEPT* SE8 124 D5
Brownlow Medical Centre *FBAR/BDGN* N11 48 E1
Bruce Castle Museum *TOTM* N17 50 A4
Bruce Grove Primary School *TOTM* N17 50 B5
Brunel Engine House *BERM/RHTH* SE16 123 K2
Brunel University *ISLW* TW7 135 K1
TWK TW1 136 C5
Brunel University (Osterley Campus) Track *ISLW* TW7 135 K1
Brunswick Health Centre *FBAR/BDGN* N11 34 A4
Brunswick Housing & Shopping Centre *BMSBY* WC1N 5 F6
Brunswick Industrial Park *FBAR/BDGN* N11 34 B6
Brunswick Medical Centre *BMSBY* WC1N 4 E6
Brunswick Park JMI School *FBAR/BDGN* N11 34 A3
Brunswick Park Primary School *CMBW* SE5 142 E1
BT Centre *STBT* EC1A 12 C3
Buckhurst Hill FC *BKHH* IG9 39 J3
Buckhurst Hill Primary School *BKHH* IG9 39 J4
Buckingham College Preparatory School *PIN* HA5 59 K3
Buckingham College School *HRW* HA1 60 E2
Buckingham Palace *WHALL* SW1A 15 K3
Buckingham Primary School *HPTN* TW12 172 E1
Buckingham Road Cemetery *IL* IG1 72 D6
Buckland Infant School *CHSGTN* KT9 206 B3
Building Centre *GWRST* WC1E 10 C2
Bullers Wood School *CHST* BR7 184 E4
Bullsbridge Industrial Estate *NWDGN* UB2 114 A4
The Bull Theatre *BAR* EN5 20 D5
Bupa Roding Hospital *REDBR* IG4 53 H6
Burbage School *IS* N1 7 G2
Burdett Coutts CE Primary School *WEST* SW1P 16 C6
Burgess Industrial Park *CMBW* SE5 142 E1
Burlington Danes School *SHB* W12 99 K5
Burlington Primary School *NWMAL* KT3 192 C1
Burnham Trading Estate *DART* DA1 151 G5
Burnhill Business Centre *BECK* BR3 182 D4
Burnley Road Clinic *WLSDN* NW10 81 J3
Burnside Industrial Estate *BARK/HLT* IG6 55 H1
Burnt Ash Infant School *BMLY* BR1 183 K1
Burnt Ash School *BMLY* BR1 183 J1
Burnt Oak Junior School *BFN/LL* DA15 168 B3
Burntwood School *TOOT* SW17 160 C4
Burrels Wharf *POP/IOD* E14 124 E5
Bursted Woodprimary School *BXLYHN* DA7 149 J3
Burwell Industrial Estate *LEY* E10 69 G5
Burwood School *ORP* BR6 202 E6
Bushey Golf & Country Club *BUSH* WD23 28 A1
Bushey Hall School *BUSH* WD23 27 K1
Bushey Health Centre *BUSH* WD23 27 K1
Bushey Heath Primary School *BUSH* WD23 28 D3
Bushey Middle School *RYNPK* SW20 176 E6
Bushey Museum & Art Gallery *BUSH* WD23 28 A1
Bush Hill Park Golf Club *WCHMH* N21 23 J6
Bush Hill Park Medical Centre *EN* EN1 36 B1
Bush Hill Park Primary School *EN* EN1 24 C6
Bush House (BBC) *HOL/ALD* WC2B 11 G4
Bush Industrial Estate *ARCH* N19 84 C1
WLSDN NW10 99 F2
The Business Design Centre *IS* N1 5 K1
Bute House Preparatory School for Girls *HMSMTH* W6 119 F4
Butlers Wharf *STHWK* SE1 19 K1
Butler's Wharf Business Centre *STHWK* SE1 19 K2
Butler's Wharf Pier *STHWK* SE1 19 K1
Butterfly House *BTFD* TW8 136 C2
Butterfly Sports Club *ELTH/MOT* SE9 167 G1
Buxlow Preparatory School *WBLY* HA9 80 A1
Buzzard Creek Industrial Estate *BARK* IG11 109 F2
Byam Shaw School of Art *ARCH* N19 66 C6
Byfleet Industrial Estate *WATW* WD18 26 A3
Bygrove JMI School *POP/IOD* E14 105 K5
Byron Court Primary School *ALP/SUD* HA0 61 J6
Cabinet War Rooms *WHALL* SW1A 16 D2
Calder House School *BTSEA* SW11 140 E2
Caledonian Market *STHWK* SE1 19 H4
Cally Pool *IS* N1 85 F6
Calverton Primary School *CAN/RD* E16 107 H5
Cambell Primary School *DAGW* RM9 91 K5
Camberwell Business Centre *CMBW* SE5 142 E1
Camberwell College of Arts *CMBW* SE5 143 F2
Camberwell Leisure Centre *CMBW* SE5 142 E2
Camberwell New Cemetery *FSTH* SE23 164 A1
Camberwell Trading Estate *CMBW* SE5 142 C3
Cambridge Park Bowling & Sports Club *TWK* TW1 156 D1
Cambridge School *HMSMTH* W6 118 E4
Cambridge Theatre *LSQ/SEVD* WC2H 10 E4
Camden Community Trust Day Hospital *KTTN* NW5 84 C4
Camden House Clinic *BKHTH/KID* SE3 145 H3
Camden Junior School *CAR* SM5 209 K2
Camden Market *CAMTN* NW1 84 A5
Camden Peoples Theatre *CAMTN* NW1 4 A5
Camden School for Girls *KTTN* NW5 84 C4
Camden Theatre *CAMTN* NW1 4 A2
Camden Town Hall & St Pancras Library *CAMTN* NW1 4 E4
Camelot Primary School *PECK* SE15 143 J1
Cameron House School *CHEL* SW3 120 C6
Camperdown House *WCHPL* E1 13 K4
Campion House College *ISLW* TW7 135 J1
Campsbourne Infant School *CEND/HSY/T* N8 48 E6
Campsbourne Junior School *CEND/HSY/T* N8 48 E6
Canada House *STJS* SW1Y 10 D7
Canada House Business Centre *RSLP* HA4 59 G5
Canada Square *POP/IOD* E14 124 D1
Canada Water Retail Park *BERM/RHTH* SE16 124 A3
Canada Wharf Museum *BERM/RHTH* SE16 124 C1
Canal Cafe Theatre *BAY/PAD* W2 101 G4
Canary Riverside *BERM/RHTH* SE16 124 C1
Canary Wharf Pier *BERM/RHTH* SE16 124 C1
Canary Wharf Tower *POP/IOD* E14 124 E1
Canberra Primary School *SHB* W12 99 K6
Canbury Business Centre *KUTN/CMB* KT2 175 F4
Canbury 2000 Business Park *KUTN/CMB* KT2 175 F4
Canbury Medical Centre *KUTN/CMB* KT2 175 G4
Canbury School *RCHPK/HAM* TW10 175 J2
Cann Hall Primary School *WAN* E11 88 D1
The Canning School *KENS* W8 119 K3
Cannon Hill Clinic *STHGT/OAK* N14 34 E5
Cannon Lane Primary School *PIN* HA5 59 H3
Cannon Sports Club *CANST* EC4R 12 D5
Cannon Street Station *CANST* EC4R 12 E5
Cannon Trading Estate *WBLY* HA9 80 D2
Cannon Wharf Business Centre *DEPT* SE8 124 B4
Cannon Workshops *POP/IOD* E14 105 J6
Canon Barnett Primary School *WCHPL* E1 13 K3
Canonbury Business Centre *IS* N1 85 J6

Canonbury Primary School IS N1 85 H4
Canon Palmer RC High School IL IG1 72 E5
Canons High School EDGE HA8 44 B5
The Canons Leisure Centre MTCM CR4 194 E1
Canterbury Industrial Estate NWCR SE14 124 A6
Cantium Retail Park STHWK SE1 123 H6
Capital Business Centre ALP/SUD HA0 97 K1; MTCM CR4 194 E2
Capital Industrial Estate BELV DA17 129 J4; BELV DA17 129 K1
Capital Radio LSQ/SEVD WC2H 10 D6
Capital Wharf WAP E1W 123 H1
Capitol Industrial Park CDALE/KGS NW9 44 E6
Caplan Estate MTCM CR4 179 H4
Cardiff Road Industrial Estate WATW WD18 27 F1
Cardinal Hinsley High School WLSDN NW10 81 J6
Cardinal Pole RC School HOM E9 87 G4
Cardinal Pole RC Secondary Lower School HOM E9 87 F5
Cardinal Road Infant School FELT TW13 154 A3
Cardinal Vaughan Memorial School WKENS W14 119 H2
The Cardinal Wiseman ARC School Technology & Art College GFD/PVL UB6 96 C4
Cardwell Primary School WOOL/PLUM SE18 126 E4
Carew Manor School WLGTN SM6 210 D1
Carlisle Infant School HPTN TW12 173 G2
Carlton Gate Development MV/WKIL W9 100 E4
Carlton House STJS SW1Y 16 C1
Carlton Primary School KTTN NW5 84 A3
Carlton Vale Infant School KIL/WHAMP NW6 100 D2
Carlyle's House (NT) CHEL SW3 120 D6
Carnwath Road Industrial Estate FUL/PGN SW6 140 A4
Carolyn School Shop PIN HA5 59 J1
Carpenders Park Cemetery OXHEY WD19 27 K6
Carpenters Business Park HOM E9 87 J4
Carpenters' Hall LVPST EC2M 13 F2
Carpenters Primary School SRTFD E15 88 A6
Carshalton AFC SUT SM1 209 J1
Carshalton College of Further Education CAR SM5 209 K1
Carshalton High School for Boys CAR SM5 194 C6
Carshalton High School for Girls CAR SM5 209 J1
Carshalton War Memorial Hospital CAR SM5 209 K3
Carterhatch Primary School EN EN1 24 D2
Caryl Thomas Clinic HRW HA1 60 E1
The Cassel Hospital RCHPK/HAM TW10 156 E6
Cassidy Medical Centre FUL/PGN SW6 139 K1
Castilion Primary School THMD SE28 109 J5
Castlebar Special School WEA W13 97 G4
Castlecombe Primary School ELTH/MOT SE9 184 D1
Castle Industrial Estate WALW SE17 18 C6
Caterham High School CLAY IG5 53 K5
Catford Cricket & Sports Club CAT SE6 164 E3
Catford Cyphers Cricket Club CAT SE6 164 C4
Catford Girls School CAT SE6 165 G5
Catford Trading Estate CAT SE6 164 E4
Catford Wanderers Sports Club CAT SE6 165 F6
Cathall Leisure Centre WAN E11 88 B1
Cathedral School of St Saviour & St Mary Overie STHWK SE1 18 D2
Cator Park School for Girls BECK BR3 182 B3
Cavendish College FITZ W1T 10 C2
Cavendish Primary School CHSWK W4 138 B1
The Cavendish School CAMTN NW1 84 B6
Cavendish Special School HNWL W7 97 F5
Caxton Hall STJSPK SW1H 16 C4
Caxton Trading Estate HYS/HAR UB3 113 H2
Cayley Primary School POP/IOD E14 105 G4
Cecil Park Clinic PIN HA5 59 J1
The Cedar School FSTGT E7 89 G4
Cedars First School KTN/HRWW/W HA3 42 C4
Cedars Middle School KTN/HRWW/W HA3 42 C4
The Cedars Primary School HEST TW5 133 K1
Cedar Way Industrial Estate CAMTN NW1 84 D5
Cenotaph WHALL SW1A 16 E2
Centaurs Business Centre ISLW TW7 116 B6
Centaurs RFC ISLW TW7 116 A6
Central Business Centre WLSDN NW10 81 G3
Central Criminal Court STP EC4M 12 A3
Central Foundation Boys School SDTCH EC2A 7 F6
Central Foundation Girls School BOW E3 105 G2
Central Hall STJSPK SW1H 16 D3
Central Hendon Clinic HDN NW4 63 K1
Central London County Court CAVSQ/HST W1G 3 J7
Central London Golf Club TOOT SW17 160 C4
Central London Markets FARR EC1M 12 A2
Central Medical Centre MRDN SM4 194 B1
Central Middlesex Hospital WLSDN NW10 98 E2
Central Park Arena DART DA1 171 H3
Central Park Primary School EHAM E6 107 H1
Central St Martins College of Art and Design RSQ WC1B 11 F2
Central School of Ballet CLKNW EC1R 5 K7
Central School of Fashion GTPST W1W 10 A2
Central School of Speech & Drama HAMP NW3 83 H5
Central School Speech & Drama CAMTN NW1 4 C1
Central Square Shopping Centre ALP/SUD HA0 80 A4
Centre Court Shopping Centre WIM/MER SW19 177 J2
Centre Point LSQ/SEVD WC2H 10 D3
Chace Community School EN EN1 24 A2
Chadwell Heath Hospital CHDH RM6 73 H2
Chadwell Heath Industrial Park BCTR RM8 74 A5
Chadwell Heath Luncheon & Leisure Centre CHDH RM6 73 K3
Chadwell Heath School CHDH RM6 73 H3
Chadwell Primary School CHDH RM6 73 J4
Chaffinch Business Park BECK BR3 182 A6
Chailey Industrial Estate HYS/HAR UB3 113 K2
Chalcot School CAMTN NW1 84 B4
Chalgrove Primary School FNCH N3 46 C6
Chalkhill Primary School WBLY HA9 80 D1
Chambers Business Park WDR/YW UB7 112 D6
Chambers Wharf STHWK SE1 123 H2
Chandlers Field Primary School E/WMO/HCT KT8 189 F2
Chandos Business Centre WLGTN SM6 210 C4
Channelsea Business Centre SRTFD E15 106 B1
Channing School HGT N6 66 B5
Chapel End Infant School WALTH E17 51 K4
Chapel End Junior School WALTH E17 51 K4
Chapman Park Industrial Estate WLSDN NW10 81 H4
Charing Cross Hospital HMSMTH W6 119 G6
Charing Cross Station CHCR WC2N 11 F7
Charing Cross & Westminster Medical School HMSMTH W6 119 G5
The Charles Dickens Museum BMSBY WC1N 5 G7
Charles Dickens Primary School STHWK SE1 18 C3
Charles Edward Brook Lower School CMBW SE5 142 C2
Charles Edward Brook Upper School CMBW SE5 142 C2
Charles Lamb Primary School IS N1 85 J6
Charlotte Sharman Primary School LBTH SE11 18 A5
Charlton Athletic FC (The Valley) CHARL SE7 126 B5
Charlton Health & Fitness Centre CHARL SE7 126 B5
Charlton House CHARL SE7 126 C6
Charlton Manor Primary School CHARL SE7 146 C1
Charlton RFC ELTH/MOT SE9 167 G2
Charlton School CHARL SE7 126 D6
Charrington Bowl SURB KT6 191 J6
Charville Primary School YEAD UB4 94 C1
Charter Clinic CHEL SW3 120 E5
Charterhouse FARR EC1M 12 B1
Charteris Road Sports Centre HAMP NW3 83 J3; KIL/WHAMP NW6 82 D6
Charter Nightingale Hospital & Counselling Centre CAMTN NW1 8 D1
The Charter School EDUL SE22 142 E6
Chartfield School PUT/ROE SW15 138 E6
Chartwell Business Centre BMLY BR1 184 C6
Chase Bridge Primary School WHTN TW2 155 K1
Chase Farm Hospital ENC/FH EN2 23 G1
Chase Lane Primary School CHING E4 37 H6
Chase Road Trading Estate WLSDN NW10 99 F3
Chase Side J & I School ENC/FH EN2 23 J3
Chaseville Clinic WCHMH N21 35 F1
Chatsworth Infant School BFN/LL DA15 168 B3
Chatsworth J & I School HSLW TW3 135 H5
Chaucer Clinic NWDGN UB2 115 J2
Cheam Common Infant School WPK KT4 192 E6
Cheam Common Junior School WPK KT4 207 K1
Cheam Fields Primary School CHEAM SM3 208 C3
Cheam High School CHEAM SM3 208 C2
Cheam Leisure Centre CHEAM SM3 208 B2
Cheam Park Farm Junior School CHEAM SM3 208 C1
Cheam Sports Club BELMT SM2 208 B5
Chelsea Barracks BGVA SW1W 121 F5
Chelsea Bridge Business Centre VX/NE SW8 141 G1
Chelsea Centre & Theatre WBPTN SW10 140 C1
Chelsea Cinema CHEL SW3 120 D5
The Chelsea Club Leisure Centre FUL/PGN SW6 120 A6
Chelsea College of Art & Design CHEL SW3 120 C5; FUL/PGN SW6 140 B3
Chelsea FC (Stamford Bridge) FUL/PGN SW6 140 A1
Chelsea Fields Industrial Estate WIM/MER SW19 178 C4
Chelsea Leisure Centre CHEL SW3 120 D5
Chelsea Old Town Hall CHEL SW3 120 D5
Chelsea Physic Garden CHEL SW3 120 E6
Chelsea & Westminster Hospital WBPTN SW10 120 B6
Chelsea Wharf WBPTN SW10 140 C1
Chennestone Community School SUN TW16 172 A5
Cherington House Health Centre HNWL W7 116 A1
Cherry Garden School BERM/RHTH SE16 123 H4
Cherry Lane Primary School WDR/YW UB7 112 C4
Cherry Orchard Primary School CHARL SE7 146 B1
Chessington Community College & Sports Centre CHSGTN KT9 205 K5
Chessington Cricket Club CHSGTN KT9 205 J5
Chessington Golf Club CHSGTN KT9 205 K5
Chesterton Primary School BTSEA SW11 141 F2
Chestnut Grove School BAL SW12 161 F3
Cheyne Centre CHEL SW3 120 D6
Chigwell Golf Club CHIG IG7 54 A1
Childeric Primary School NWCR SE14 144 B1
Childs Hill Clinic CRICK NW2 64 D6
Childs Hill Primary School CRICK NW2 82 C1
Childs Welfare Clinic DAGW RM9 91 J3
Chiltonian Industrial Estate LEE/GVPK SE12 165 J1
Chimnocks Wharf POP/IOD E14 105 G6
Chingford CE Infant School CHING E4 38 B3
Chingford CE Junior School CHING E4 38 B3
Chingford Hall Primary School CHING E4 51 H2
Chingford Health Centre CHING E4 37 H6
Chingford Industrial Centre CHING E4 51 G1
Chingford RFC CHING E4 37 J3
Chingford School CHING E4 37 K3
Chisenhale Primary School BOW E3 105 G1
Chislehurst Caves CHST BR7 185 F4
Chislehurst Cemetery CHST BR7 185 K1
Chislehurst Golf Club CHST BR7 185 G3
Chislehurst Natural Health Centre CHST BR7 185 G2
Chislehurst & Sidcup Grammar School BFN/LL DA15 168 C4
Chiswick & Bedford Park Preparatory School CHSWK W4 118 B4
Chiswick Business Park CHSWK W4 117 J4
Chiswick Community School CHSWK W4 138 A1
Chiswick House CHSWK W4 118 A6
Chrisp Street Health Centre POP/IOD E14 105 K5
Christ Church Bentinck CE Primary School CAMTN NW1 8 C1
Christ Church Brondesbury CE J & I School KIL/WHAMP NW6 82 D6
Christ Church CE Infant School NWMAL KT3 176 B6
Christ Church CE Junior School NWMAL KT3 176 A6
Christ Church CE Primary School BAR EN5 20 B3; BRXN/ST SW9 142 B2; BRXS/STRHM SW2 162 A3; BRYLDS KT5 191 H3; CHEL SW3 120 E6; FSTH SE23 164 A4
Christchurch CE Primary School HAMP NW3 83 H1; WCHPL E1 13 K2
Christ Church CE Primary School WOOL/PLUM SE18 147 F2
Christchurch CE School NFNCH/WDSP N12 47 H1
Christ Church CE Middle School EA W5 97 K6
Christ Church CE Primary School CHEL SW3 120 E6
Christchurch Industrial Centre STHWK SE1 12 A7
Christ Church Primary School BTSEA SW11 140 D4
Christchurch Primary School IL IG1 72 C5
Christ Church School CAMTN NW1 3 K3
Christian Meeting Hall BECK BR3 182 D4
Christine King 6th Form College LEW SE13 145 G4
Christopher Hatton Primary School FSBYW WC1X 5 J7
Christs College BKHTH/KID SE3 145 K2; EFNCH N2 47 F6
Christs College School EFNCH N2 47 F6
Christs School RCHPK/HAM TW10 137 G6
Christ the King RC First School STWL/WRAY TW19 152 A1
Christ the King RC Primary School FSBYPK N4 67 F6
Chrysalis Theatre BAL SW12 161 F3
Chrysanthemum Clinic CHSWK W4 137 K1
Chrysolyta Primary School STHWK SE1 19 F4
Church Down Adult School LEE/GVPK SE12 165 K4
Church End Medical Centre WLSDN NW10 81 G4
Church Farm House Museum HDN NW4 45 K6
Church Farm Swimming Pool EBAR EN4 33 K3
Churchfield Primary School ED N9 36 B3
Churchfield School WOOL/PLUM SE18 128 A4
Churchfields J & I School SWFD E18 52 E4
Churchfields Primary School BECK BR3 182 A6
Church Hill Primary School EBAR EN4 33 K2
Church House WEST SW1P 16 D4
Churchill Clinic STHWK SE1 17 K4
Churchill College RYNPK SW20 177 F5; TOOT SW17 160 E4
Churchill Gardens Primary School PIM SW1V 121 H5
Churchill Theatre HAYES BR2 183 K5
Church Mead Infant School LEY E10 69 J5
Church Mead Junior School LEY E10 69 J5
The Church School BTFD TW8 117 F6
Church Stairs BERM/RHTH SE16 123 J2
Church Trading Estate ERITH DA8 150 D1
Cineworld Cinema BXLYHS DA6 149 J5; FELT TW13 154 A4; WDGN N22 49 G5
City Banking College STHWK SE1 19 F2
City Business Centre BERM/RHTH SE16 123 K2
City Business College FSBYE EC1V 6 B5
City Central Estate FSBYE EC1V 6 C5
City College of Higher Education IS N1 7 F4
City & Guilds of London Art School LBTH SE11 122 C5
City Health Centre FSBYE EC1V 6 E6
City & Islington College FSBYE EC1V 6 D5; FSBYPK N4 67 H6; HOLWY N7 84 E2; IS N1 85 J6; STLK EC1Y 6 E7
City & Islington College Sixth Form Centre HOLWY N7 85 F2
City of London Cemetery MNPK E12 71 J6
City of London Club OBST EC2N 13 G3
City of London College WCHPL E1 104 C5
City of London Crematorium MNPK E12 89 H1
City of London Magistrates Court MANHO EC4N 12 E4
City of London Polytechnic Sports Ground ELTH/MOT SE9 166 B4
City of London School BLKFR EC4V 12 B5
City of London School for Girls BARB EC2Y 12 C1
City of Westminster Cemetery HNWL W7 116 A1
City of Westminster College BAY/PAD W2 8 A1; MV/WKIL W9 100 D2
City of Westminster Vehicle Pound BAY/PAD W2 9 F6
City Thameslink Station FLST/FETLN EC4A 12 A4
City University FSBYE EC1V 6 A3; FSBYE EC1V 6 B5
City University Business School BARB EC2Y 12 D1
Civic Centre & Bromley Palace BMLY BR1 184 A5
Civic Medical Centre HRW HA1 60 E2
Civil Service Recreation Centre WEST SW1P 16 D5
Civil Service Sports Ground ELTH/MOT SE9 166 B1
Clapham Common Clinic CLAP SW4 141 J5
Clapham Manor Primary School CLAP SW4 141 H4
Clapham Manor Street Public Baths CLAP SW4 141 J4
Clapham North Business Centre CLAP SW4 141 J4
Clapham Park School CLAP SW4 141 J6
Clapham Picture House CLAP SW4 141 H5
Clapton Girls' Technology College CLPT E5 86 E2
Clapton Jewish Boys School STNW/STAM N16 68 B4
Clara Grant Primary School BOW E3 105 J3
Clare House Primary School BECK BR3 183 F5
Claremont Clinic FSTGT E7 89 F3
Claremont Fan Court School ESH/CLAY KT10 204 B4
Claremont High School KTN/HRWW/W HA3 62 A2
Claremont Way Industrial Estate CRICK NW2 64 A5
Clarence House WHALL SW1A 16 B2
Clarendon Primary School ASHF TW15 152 C5
Clarendon Special School HPTN TW12 173 G2
Claridges Hotel MYFR/PKLN W1K 9 J5
Claverings Industrial Estate ED N9 36 E4
Claygate Primary School ESH/CLAY KT10 204 E5
Clayhall Clinic CLAY IG5 53 J6
Clayponds Hospital BTFD TW8 117 F4
Cleeve Park School SCUP DA14 168 D5
Clementine Churchill Hospital HRW HA1 79 F1
Cleopatra's Needle CHCR WC2N 11 G7
Clerkenwell County Court IS N1 6 A2
Clerkenwell Heritage Centre FARR EC1M 6 A7
Clerkenwell Parochial CE Primary School CLKNW EC1R 5 J5
Cleveland Primary School IL IG1 90 B2
Cleves Primary School EHAM E6 89 H6
C & L Golf & Country Club NTHLT UB5 77 F5
Clifton Lodge School EA W5 97 K6
Clifton Primary School NWDGN UB2 114 D4
Clink Exhibition STHWK SE1 12 E7

Clissold Leisure Centre STNW/STAM N16 85 K1
Clissold Park Natural Health Centre STNW/STAM N16 68 A6
Clitterhouse Primary School CRICK NW2 64 B6
C & L Leisure Centre NTHLT UB5 77 F5
Clockhouse Industrial Estate EBED/NFELT TW14 152 E3
Clockhouse Primary School CRW RM5 56 D2
Clock Museum CITYW EC2V 12 D3
Cloisters Business Centre VX/NE SW8 141 G1
Clore Gallery WEST SW1P 16 E7
The Clore Tikva School BARK/HLT IG6 54 C5
Clothworkers' Hall FENCHST EC3M 13 H5
Clouster's Green WAP E1W 123 H1
Cobbold Estate WLSDN NW10 81 H4
Cobourg Primary School CMBW SE5 123 G5
Cochrane Theatre GINN WC1R 11 G2
Cockfosters Sports Ground EBAR EN4 21 K4
The Cockpit Theatre STJWD NW8 2 C7
Coldharbour Industrial Estate CMBW SE5 142 D3
Coldharbour Leisure Centre ELTH/MOT SE9 166 E4
Coldharbour Sports Ground ELTH/MOT SE9 167 F4
Colebrooke Primary School IS N1 6 A2
Colegrave Primary School SRTFD E15 88 B3
Coleraine Park Primary School TOTM N17 50 D4
Coleridge Primary School HGT N6 66 D4
Colfes Preparatory School LEE/GVPK SE12 166 A1
Colindale Business Park CDALE/KGS NW9 44 E6
Colindale Hospital CDALE/KGS NW9 45 G6
Colindale Primary School CDALE/KGS NW9 63 H1
Coliseum Theatre CHCR WC2N 10 E6
College Fields Business Centre WIM/MER SW19 178 D4
College Library & Civic Centre SUT SM1 209 F3
College of Arms BLKFR EC4V 12 C4
College of Central London SDTCH EC2A 7 G6
College of Fuel Technology HGT N6 66 A3
College of Law GWRST WC1E 10 C1
The College of Law FLST/FETLN EC4A 11 J3
GWRST WC1E 10 C1
College of North East London CEND/HSY/T N8 67 G1
FBAR/BDGN N11 48 C4
SEVS/STOTM N15 68 B1
College of North West London KIL/WHAMP NW6 82 E6
WBLY HA9 80 C1
WLSDN NW10 81 H3
College of Organists FLST/FETLN EC4A 11 K3
College Park School BAY/PAD W2 101 F5
Collier Row Clinic ROMW/RG RM7 56 D4
Collier Row FC ROMW/RG RM7 56 B4
Collingwood Business Centre ARCH N19 84 E1
Collingwood Preparatory School WLGTN SM6 210 B3
Collins Method School CRICK NW2 82 A4
Collis Primary School TEDD TW11 174 C2
Colnbrook School OXHEY WD19 27 G4
Coloma Convent Girls School CROY/NA CR0 213 F1
The Colonnades Shopping Centre BGVA SW1W 15 J6
Colours Sports Club SUT SM1 209 G3
Columbia Primary School BETH E2 7 K4
Colvestone Primary School HACK E8 86 B3
Colville Primary School NTGHL W11 100 D5
Colyers Lane Medical Centre ERITH DA8 150 A2
Colyers Primary School ERITH DA8 150 A2
Comber Grove Primary School CMBW SE5 142 D1
Comedy Theatre STJS SW1Y 10 C6
Comelle House Trading Estate DEPT SE8 124 B5
Commonwealth Institute KENS W8 119 J3
Community Arts Centre GNWCH SE10 144 E1
Community Care Centre ENC/FH EN2 23 K2
Community Centre (Island History Trust) POP/IOD E14 125 F4
Community College and School GNWCH SE10 145 F1
Community Health Centre HOM E9 86 E6
Compass Theatre HGDN/ICK UB10 76 A1
Complementary Health Centre LEW SE13 165 H1
Compton Leisure Centre NTHLT UB5 77 J6
The Compton School NFNCH/WDSP N12 47 J2
Compton Sports Centre NFNCH/WDSP N12 47 J2
Concord Business Centre ACT W3 98 D4
Coney Hill School HAYES BR2 199 J6
Connaught Business Centre CDALE/KGS NW9 63 H2
CROY/NA CR0 211 F4
MTCM CR4 194 E2
Connaught Girls School WAN E11 70 C5
Connaught House School BAY/PAD W2 8 E4
Consort Clinic PECK SE15 143 J4
Consulate General of Monaco SKENS SW7 14 A6
Consulate of Burkina Faso BTSEA SW11 140 B4
Consulate of Chile CAVSQ/HST W1G 3 J7
Consulate of Colombia GTPST W1W 10 A3
Consulate of Eritrea IS N1 5 K2
Consulate of Guinea MYFR/PKLN W1K 9 G6
Consulate of Panama MYFR/PICC W1J 15 J1
Control Tower HTHAIR TW6 132 E4
Convent of Jesus & Mary Infant School CRICK NW2 82 A4
Convent of Jesus & Mary Language College WLSDN NW10 81 H6
Conway Hall FSBYW WC1X 11 G1
Conway Medical Centre WOOL/PLUM SE18 127 J5
Conway Primary School WOOL/PLUM SE18 127 K4
Coombe Girls School NWMAL KT3 176 A5
Coombe Hill Golf Club KUTN/CMB KT2 176 A3
Coombe Hill J & I School NWMAL KT3 176 A4
Coombe Wood Golf Club KUTN/CMB KT2 175 J3
Coopers' Hall LVPST EC2M 13 H2
Coopers Lane Primary School LEE/GVPK SE12 165 K4
Coopers School CHST BR7 185 H4
Copenhagen Primary School IS N1 5 F1
Copland Community School & Technology Centre WBLY HA9 80 B3
Coppermill Primary School WALTH E17 69 F2
Coppetts Wood Hospital MUSWH N10 47 K4
Coppetts Wood Primary School MUSWH N10 48 A4
Coppice Primary School CHIG IG7 55 G1
Copthall School MLHL NW7 45 K2
Cordwainers College HOM E9 86 E5
Corinthian Casuals FC CHSGTN KT9 206 C1
Cornhill Sports Club BECK BR3 182 D1
Coronet Cinema NTGHL W11 119 K1
SEVS/STOTM N15 49 H6
Corpus Christi RC Primary School BRXS/STRHM SW2 142 A6
Cosmopolitan College IS N1 5 G3
Coston Secondary Modern Girls School GFD/PVL UB6 96 C2
Coteford Infant School RSLP HA4 58 E3
Courtauld Institute HOL/ALD WC2B 11 G5
Court Farm Industrial Estate STWL/WRAY TW19 152 C1
Courtfield Medical Centre ECT SW5 120 A4
Courtland JMI School MLHL NW7 31 G4
Covent Garden Flower Market VX/NE SW8 121 K6
Covent Garden Medical Centre LSQ/SEVD WC2H 10 E4
CPFC Soccer & Sports Centre BRXN/ST SW9 142 A4
Crafts Council IS N1 5 K3
Crampton Primary School WALW SE17 18 B7
Cranbrook College IL IG1 72 A6
Crane Infant School FELT TW13 154 E4
Crane Junior School FELT TW13 154 D4
Cranford Community College HEST TW5 114 A6
Cranford Infant School HSLWW TW4 133 K3
Cranford Junior School HSLWW TW4 134 A3
Cranford Park Junior School HYS/HAR UB3 113 J4
Cranford Park Primary School HYS/HAR UB3 113 J2
Cranleigh Gardens Industrial Estate STHL UB1 95 K4
Cranmer School MTCM CR4 194 E2
The Craven Clinic HMSMTH W6 118 E4
Craven Park Health Centre WLSDN NW10 81 F6
Craven Park Medical Centre WLSDN NW10 81 F6
Craven Park Primary School SEVS/STOTM N15 68 C3
Crawford Primary School CMBW SE5 142 D2
Crawford Upper School MBLAR W1H 8 E2
Crayfield Industrial Park STMC/STPC BR5 186 D5
Crayfields Business Park STMC/STPC BR5 186 D4
STMC/STPC BR5 202 D2
Crayford Commercial Centre DART DA1 150 B6
Crayford Industrial Estate DART DA1 150 C6
Crayford Leisure Centre & Greyhound Stadium DART DA1 170 B1
Crayford Medical Centre DART DA1 150 C6
Crayside Industrial Estate DART DA1 150 D4
Cray Valley Golf Club STMC/STPC BR5 187 F4
Creekmouth Industrial Estate BARK IG11 109 F3
Creek Road Health Centre DEPT SE8 124 D6
Creek Road Industrial Estate DEPT SE8 124 E6
Cremer Business Centre BETH E2 7 J3
Crewe House MYFR/PICC W1J 9 J7
Cricket Pavilion WEST SW1P 16 C6
Cricklefield Stadium IL IG1 72 E6
Cricklewood Trading Estate CRICK NW2 82 C1
Crispin Industrial Centre UED N18 50 E1
Criterion Theatre MYFR/PICC W1J 10 B6
Crockenhill Primary School SWLY BR8 203 K3
Crofton Leisure Centre BROCKY SE4 164 D1
Crofton School BROCKY SE4 164 D1
Croham Hurst Golf Club SAND/SEL CR2 212 B4
Croham Hurst School SAND/SEL CR2 212 B3
Cromer Road JMI School BAR EN5 21 F4
Cromwell Business Centre BARK IG11 108 E2
Cromwell Hospital KENS W8 119 K4
Cromwell Industrial Estate LEY E10 69 G5
Crook Log Primary School BXLYHS DA6 148 E5
Crook Log Sports Centre WELL DA16 148 E4
Crouch End Art School CEND/HSY/T N8 66 E2
Crouch End Health Centre CEND/HSY/T N8 66 E2
Crouch Hill Recreation Centre ARCH N19 66 E4
Crowland Primary School SEVS/STOTM N15 68 B2
Crowlands Primary School ROMW/RG RM7 74 E3
Crown Business Centre WDR/YW UB7 112 C1
Crown Close Business Centre BOW E3 87 J6
Crown Court at the Borough STHWK SE1 18 B2
Crowndale Health Centre CAMTN NW1 4 B2
Crownfield Primary School ROMW/RG RM7 56 C5
Crown Lane Clinic STHGT/OAK N14 34 C3
Crown Lane Primary School WNWD SE27 180 C1
Crown Trading Centre HYS/HAR UB3 113 H2
Crown Woods School ELTH/MOT SE9 147 H6
Croydon Airport Industrial Estate CROY/NA CR0 211 G5
Croydon Cemetery THHTH CR7 196 A2
Croydon Clocktower Cinema CROY/NA CR0 211 J1
Croydon College CROY/NA CR0 196 E6
Croydon Fairfield Halls Cinema CROY/NA CR0 211 K1
Croydon FC SNWD SE25 197 K2
Croydon Indoor Bowling Club SAND/SEL CR2 211 J3
Croydon Road Industrial Estate SNWD SE25 197 K1
Croydon Sports Arena SNWD SE25 197 K2
Crusader Industrial Estate FSBYPK N4 67 J3
Crusoe House School IS N1 6 E4
Crystal Palace NRWD SE19 181 H2
Crystal Palace Athletics Stadium NRWD SE19 181 H2
Crystal Palace FC 1986 (Selhurst Park) SNWD SE25 197 F1
Crystal Palace Museum NRWD SE19 181 G2
Cuaco Sports Ground BECK BR3 182 D2
Cubitt Town Primary School POP/IOD E14 125 F3
Cuddington Cemetery WPK KT4 192 E6
Cuddington CP School HOR/WEW KT19 207 H1
Culloden Primary School POP/IOD E14 106 B5
Culvers House Primary School MTCM CR4 195 F5
Cumberland Business Park WLSDN NW10 98 D2
Cumberland Comprehensive School CAN/RD E16 106 D4
Cumberland Park Industrial Estate WLSDN NW10 99 J2
The Cuming Museum WALW SE17 18 C7
Cumnor House School SAND/SEL CR2 211 H6
Curwen Primary School PLSTW E13 106 E1
Curzon Mayfair Cinema MYFR/PICC W1J 15 J1
Curzon Soho Cinema SOHO/SHAV W1D 10 D5
Custom House MON EC3R 13 G6
Cutlers' Hall STP EC4M 12 B3
Cutty Sark GNWCH SE10 125 F6
Cygnet Clinic Beckton EHAM E6 108 B4
Cygnus Business Centre WLSDN NW10 81 H3
Cypress Infant School SNWD SE25 181 F5
Cypress Junior School SNWD SE25 181 F5
Cyprus College of Art WNWD SE27 162 C6
Cyril Jackson Primary School POP/IOD E14 105 H6
Dagenham Chest Clinic BCTR RM8 92 B1
Dagenham Civic Centre DAGE RM10 74 D6
Dagenham Priory Comprehensive School DAGE RM10 92 D5
Dagenham & Redbridge FC DAGE RM10 92 D3
Dagenham Superbowl DAGE RM10 110 D1
Dagenham Swimming Pool BCTR RM8 74 B6
Daiglen School BKHH IG9 39 G3
Daily Mirror Office FLST/FETLN EC4A 11 K2
Daily Telegraph POP/IOD E14 124 D3
Dairy Meadow Primary School NWDGN UB2 114 E3
D'Albiac House HTHAIR TW6 132 D3
Dali Universal Exhibition STHWK SE1 17 G2
Dallington School FSBYE EC1V 6 B6
Dalmain Primary School FSTH SE23 164 B3
Damilola Taylor Centre PECK SE15 143 G1
Danegrove Primary School EBAR EN4 33 J1
Danesfield Manor School WOT/HER KT12 188 A6
Danetree School HOR/WEW KT19 206 E5
Danson Primary School WELL DA16 148 C5
Danson Watersports Centre BXLYHS DA6 148 D6
Darell Primary School RCH/KEW TW9 137 H4
Darent Industrial Park ERITH DA8 131 G5
Darrick Wood Primary School ORP BR6 216 B2
Darrick Wood School ORP BR6 216 B1
Darrick Wood Sports Centre ORP BR6 216 C1
Darrick Wood Swimming Pool ORP BR6 216 B1
Dartford County Court DART DA1 171 H1
Dartford Golf Club DART DA1 170 E4
Dartford Grammar School for Boys DART DA1 171 F1
Dartford Grammar School for Girls DART DA1 171 F2
Dartford Magistrates Court DART DA1 171 G1
Dartford Museum & Library DART DA1 171 H2
Dartford Natural Health Centre DART DA1 171 H2
Dartford West Health Centre DART DA1 171 F1
Dartford West Technology College DART DA1 171 F2
Darwin Centre SKENS SW7 14 A5
Datapoint Business Centre CAN/RD E16 106 B3
Daubeney Primary School CLPT E5 87 G2
David Game College NTGHL W11 119 K1
David Game Tutorial College SKENS SW7 14 A7
David Livingstone Primary School THHTH CR7 180 D4
David Lloyd Leisure Centre KENS W8 120 A4
David Lloyd Sports Centre EN EN1 24 C3
David Lloyd Tennis Centre SCUP DA14 186 D1
Davidson J & I School CROY/NA CR0 197 G4
Davies Lane Infant School WAN E11 70 D6
Davies's College STHWK SE1 18 D2
Dawlish Primary School LEY E10 70 A6
Days Lane Primary School BFN/LL DA15 168 A1
Deanesfield Primary School RSLP HA4 77 H2
Deansbrook Primary School MLHL NW7 44 E2
Deansfield Primary School ELTH/MOT SE9 147 F4
De Beauvoir Primary School IS N1 86 A4
De Bohun Primary School STHGT/OAK N14 22 A6
Delta Wharf GNWCH SE10 125 G2
De Lucy Primary School ABYW SE2 128 C2
Denmead School HPTN TW12 173 F3
Denver Industrial Estate RAIN RM13 111 H4
Department for Environment, Food & Rural Affairs WHALL SW1A 10 E7
Department of Health WHALL SW1A 16 E2
Department of Trade & Industry STJSPK SW1H 16 D4
Deptford Business Centre DEPT SE8 124 A5
Deptford Green School NWCR SE14 144 C1
Deptford Park Business Centre DEPT SE8 124 B5
Deptford Park Primary School DEPT SE8 124 B5
Deptford Trading Estate DEPT SE8 124 B5
Dersingham Infant School MNPK E12 89 K3
Derwentwater Primary School ACT W3 117 K1
Descovery Business Park BERM/RHTH SE16 123 H3
Design Museum STHWK SE1 19 K1
Deutsche Schule RCHPK/HAM TW10 156 E3
Devonshire Hill Primary School TOTM N17 49 K2
Devonshire Hospital MHST W1U 9 H1
Devonshire House Preparatory School HAMP NW3 83 H3
Devonshire House School HAMP NW3 83 G3
Devonshire Primary School BELMT SM2 209 G5
Diamond College SOHO/SHAV W1D 10 D3
Diana Fountain E/WMO/HCT KT8 174 A5
Diane Matthews Clinic ROMW/RG RM7 75 F1
Dilloway Industrial Estate NWDGN UB2 114 D2
Docklands Medical Centre POP/IOD E14 124 D4
Docklands Sailing Centre POP/IOD E14 124 D3
Docklands Sailing & Watersports Centre BERM/RHTH SE16 124 C3
Dockmaster's House POP/IOD E14 105 J6
Dockwell's Industrial Estate EBED/NFELT TW14 134 A6
Dockyard Industrial Estate WOOL/PLUM SE18 126 D3
Dog Kennel Hill Primary School CMBW SE5 143 F4
Dokal Industrial Estate NWDGN UB2 114 D2
Dollis Hill Synagogue & Torah Temimah Primary School CRICK NW2 81 K2
Dollis Infant School MLHL NW7 46 A3
Dollis Junior School MLHL NW7 46 A3
The Dolphin Leisure Centre ROM RM1 75 H1
Dolphin School BTSEA SW11 140 E6
Dome GNWCH SE10 125 H1
The Dominican Republic Embassy BAY/PAD W2 101 F5
Dominion Business Park ED N9 37 F4
Dominion Theatre NOXST/BSQ WC1A 10 D3
Donmar Warehouse Theatre LSQ/SEVD WC2H 10 E4
Donnington Primary School WLSDN NW10 81 K5
Dorchester Primary School WPK KT4 193 F5
Dorma Trading Park LEY E10 69 F5
Dormers Wells Leisure Centre STHL UB1 96 B5
Dormers Wells Medical Centre STHL UB1 96 A5
Dormers Wells Primary School STHL UB1 96 B6
Dormers Wells School STHL UB1 96 A5
Dorothy Barley Primary School BCTR RM8 91 H3
Dorset Road Infant School ELTH/MOT SE9 166 D4
Douglas Bader Foundation PUT/ROE SW15 158 D1

Dovers Corner Industrial Estate RAIN RM13 111 H2
Downderry Primary School BMLY BR1 165 H6
Downe Manor Primary School NTHLT UB5 95 F2
Downham Health Centre BMLY BR1 165 H6
Downhills Primary School TOTM N17 67 K1
Down Lane Junior School TOTM N17 50 B5
Downsell Junior School WAN E11 88 B2
Downshall Primary School GNTH/NBYPK IG2 72 E4
Downsview Primary School NRWD SE19 180 D3
Downsview School CLPT E5 86 D2
Drapers Hall LOTH EC2R 13 F3
Drapers Sports Ground SRTFD E15 88 A2
Drayton Green Primary School WEA W13 97 G6
Drayton Manor High School HNWL W7 97 F6
Drayton Park Primary School HBRY N5 85 G3
DRCA Business Centre BTSEA SW11 141 F2
Drew Primary School CAN/RD E16 126 D1
Driving School & Road Safety Centre KTN/HRWW/W HA3 43 G6
Dr Johnson's House FLST/FETLN EC4A 11 K4
Dr Rolfes Montessori School BAY/PAD W2 100 E6
Dr Tripletts CE J & I School HYS/HAR UB3 94 D5
Drummond Shopping Centre CROY/NA CR0 196 D6
Drury Way Industrial Estate WLSDN NW10 81 F2
Duchess Theatre COVGDN WC2E 11 G5
Duff Miller College SKENS SW7 120 B3
Duke of York Column STJS SW1Y 16 C1
Duke of York's HQ CHEL SW3 15 F7
Duke of York Theatre CHCR WC2N 10 E6
Dulverton Primary School BFN/LL DA15 167 J4
Dulwich College DUL SE21 163 F3
Dulwich College Preparatory School DUL SE21 163 F5
Dulwich College Track DUL SE21 163 F4
Dulwich Hamlet FC EDUL SE22 143 F5
Dulwich Hamlet Junior School DUL SE21 162 E1
Dulwich Hospital EDUL SE22 143 F5
Dulwich Leisure Centre EDUL SE22 143 H5
Dulwich Medical Centre EDUL SE22 143 H6
Dulwich Picture Gallery DUL SE21 162 E2
Dulwich & Sydenham Hill Golf Club DUL SE21 163 H4
Dulwich Village CE Infant School DUL SE21 163 F1
Dunbar Wharf POP/IOD E14 105 H6
Duncombe Primary School ARCH N19 66 E5
Dundee Wharf POP/IOD E14 105 H6
Dundonald First School WIM/MER SW19 177 J3
Dunningford Primary School HCH RM12 93 H3
Dunraven School (Lower School) STRHM/NOR SW16 162 A5
Dunraven School (Upper School) STRHM/NOR SW16 162 A5
Duppas Junior School CROY/NA CR0 211 H3
Durand Primary School BRXN/ST SW9 142 A2
Durands Wharf BERM/RHTH SE16 124 C2
Durants School PEND EN3 24 E2
Durdans Park Primary School STHL UB1 95 K4
Durston House School EA W5 97 K5
Dysart School KUTN/CMB KT2 156 E6
Dysart Special School SURB KT6 191 F4
Eaglesfield School WOOL/PLUM SE18 147 F2
Eagle Trading Estate MTCM CR4 194 E3
Ealdham Primary School ELTH/MOT SE9 146 B5
Ealing Abbey EA W5 97 J5
Ealing Abbey Scriptorium WEA W13 97 J5
The Ealing Broadway Centre EA W5 97 K6
Ealing Central Sports Ground GFD/PVL UB6 97 G1
Ealing Civic Centre EA W5 97 J6
Ealing College Upper School WEA W13 97 H5
Ealing Cricket Club EA W5 98 A5
Ealing Film Studios EA W5 116 D1
Ealing Golf Club GFD/PVL UB6 97 H2
Ealing Hospital NWDGN UB2 115 J2
Ealing Northern Sports Centre GFD/PVL UB6 78 D2
Ealing Park Health Centre EA W5 116 E4
Ealing Road Trading Estate BTFD TW8 116 E5
Ealing Sports Centre EA W5 98 A6
Ealing Tertiary College EA W5 116 D1
Ealing Tutorial College EA W5 97 J6
Eardley Primary School STRHM/NOR SW16 179 H2
Earlham J & I School WDGN N22 49 G3
Earlham Primary School FSTGT E7 88 D3
Earl's Court Exhibition Centre ECT SW5 119 K5
Earlsfield Primary School WAND/EARL SW18 160 B4
Earlsmead First & Middle School RYLN/HDSTN HA2 77 K2
Earlsmead Primary School SEVS/STOTM N15 68 B1
Earth Gallery SKENS SW7 14 B5
East Acton Primary School ACT W3 99 G6
East Barking Luncheon & Leisure Centre BCTR RM8 91 J3
East Barnet Health Centre EBAR EN4 21 H6
East Barnet School EBAR EN4 21 H4
EBAR EN4 33 K1
East Beckton District Centre EHAM E6 107 K5
Eastbrook Comprehensive School DAGE RM10 92 E2
Eastbrook End Cemetery DAGE RM10 93 G1
Eastbrookend Country Park DAGE RM10 93 F2
Eastbury Comprehensive School BARK IG11 90 E5
Eastbury Farm JMI School NTHWD HA6 26 D6
Eastbury Infant School BARK IG11 91 F5
Eastcote Cricket Club PIN HA5 59 F2
Eastcote Health Centre PIN HA5 59 G4
Eastcote Industrial Estate RSLP HA4 59 G4
Eastcote Lane Cemetery RYLN/HDSTN HA2 78 B1
Eastcote Primary School ELTH/MOT SE9 147 J4
Eastcourt Independent School GDMY/SEVK IG3 73 G5
Eastern Business Park HTHAIR TW6 133 J3
Eastfield Primary School PEND EN3 25 F1
Eastfields High School MTCM CR4 179 G5
East Finchley Cemetery EFNCH N2 47 F6
East Finchley Medical Centre EFNCH N2 65 J1
East Finchley School of English EFNCH N2 47 J6
East Greenwich Christ Church CE Primary School GNWCH SE10 125 H4
East Ham Industrial Estate CAN/RD E16 107 H3
East Ham Jewish Cemetery EHAM E6 107 J2
East Ham Leisure Centre EHAM E6 89 K6
East Ham Memorial Hospital FSTGT E7 89 H5
East Ham Nature Reserve EHAM E6 107 K3
East Lane Business Park WBLY HA9 61 K6
Eastlea Community School CAN/RD E16 106 C3
East London Business College WAN E11 70 C5
East London Cemetery PLSTW E13 106 D2
East London Crematorium PLSTW E13 106 D2
East London RFC EHAM E6 107 K4
East London RUFC PLSTW E13 106 D1
Eastman Dental Hospital FSBYW WC1X 5 G6
East Molesey Cricket Club E/WMO/HCT KT8 173 H6
East Sheen Cemetery RCHPK/HAM TW10 137 H6
East Sheen Primary School MORT/ESHN SW14 138 B5
East Thamesmead Business Park ERITHM DA18 129 G2
East Wickham Primary School WELL DA16 148 A2
Eaton House School KTBR SW1X 15 G6
Eaton Manor RFC WAN E11 71 G2
Eaton Square Preparatory School BGVA SW1W 15 J6
Eaton Square School PIM SW1V 16 A7
Ecclesbourne Primary School IS N1 85 K5
THHTH CR7 196 D2
Eckerd College GWRST WC1E 10 C1
Ecole De Mime Corporel Theatre De Lange Fou FSBYPK N4 66 E6
Eden College STHWK SE1 18 B4
Edenham High School CROY/NA CR0 198 B4
Eden Medical Centre WKENS W14 119 J4
Edenvale Child Health Clinic TOOT SW17 179 F3
Eden Walk Shopping Centre KUT KT1 175 F5
Edes Business Park WLGTN SM6 195 F6
Edgebury Primary School CHST BR7 167 H6
Edge Business Centre CRICK NW2 63 K6
Edgwarebury Cemetery EDGE HA8 30 C4
Edgware Clinic EDGE HA8 44 C2
Edgware College HAMP NW3 83 G4
Edgware Community Hospital EDGE HA8 44 D3
Edgware FC & Wealdstone FC EDGE HA8 44 C3
Edgware Infant School EDGE HA8 44 C2
Edgware Junior School EDGE HA8 44 C2
The Edgware School EDGE HA8 30 B6
Edinburgh Primary School WALTH E17 69 H2
Edith Neville Primary School CAMTN NW1 4 C3
Edmonton Cemetery ED N9 35 K4
Edmonton County Court UED N18 50 C1
Edmonton Green Shopping Centre ED N9 36 D4
Edmonton Leisure Centre ED N9 36 C5
Edmonton Upper School EN EN1 36 B2
Edmund Waller Primary School NWCR SE14 144 A3
Education Centre WOOL/PLUM SE18 127 G5
Edward Betham CE Primary School GFD/PVL UB6 96 D2
Edward Pauling School FELT TW13 153 H4
Edward Redhead Primary School WALTH E17 51 G6
Edward Wilson Primary School BAY/PAD W2 101 F4
Edwin Lambert Schooll EMPK RM11 75 J3
Effra Primary School BRXS/STRHM SW2 142 B6
Effra Road Retail Park BRXS/STRHM SW2 142 B6
Eglinton Infant School WOOL/PLUM SE18 147 F1
Eglinton Junior School WOOL/PLUM SE18 127 F6
Elbourne Trading Estate BELV DA17 129 J3
Eldenwall Industrial Estate BCTR RM8 74 A5
Eldon JMI School ED N9 36 E3
Eleanor Palmer Primary School KTTN NW5 84 C2
Eleanor Smith Special School & Primary Support Service PLSTW E13 106 E1
Electrical Trades Union College ESH/CLAY KT10 204 A2
Electric Cinema NTGHL W11 100 D5
Elephant and Castle Station STHWK SE1 18 C6
Elephant & Castle Leisure Centre LBTH SE11 18 B6
Elephant & Castle Shopping Centre STHWK SE1 18 B5
Elers Clinic HYS/HAR UB3 113 G4
Elfrida Primary School CAT SE6 164 E6
Eliot Bank Primary School FSTH SE23 163 J4
Elizabeth Garrett Anderson Hospital CAMTN NW1 4 D5
Elizabeth Garrett Anderson School IS N1 5 H2
Elizabeth Selby Infant School BETH E2 104 C2
Elizabeth Trading Estate NWCR SE14 124 A6
Ellen Wilkinson Primary School EHAM E6 107 H4
Ellen Wilkinson School for Girls ACT W3 98 B5
Ellerslie Square Industrial Estate BRXS/STRHM SW2 141 K5
Ellingham Primary School CHSGTN KT9 205 K5
Elliott Foundation School PUT/ROE SW15 159 F1
Elmbridge Leisure Centre WOT/HER KT12 188 A2
Elm Court School WNWD SE27 162 C4
Elmgrove First & Middle School KTN/HRWW/W HA3 61 G1
Elmhurst Preparatory School BECK BR3 198 A1
Elmhurst Primary School FSTGT E7 89 F5
Elmhurst School CROY/NA CR0 211 K2
Elm Lea Trading Estate TOTM N17 50 C3
Elmwood Primary School CROY/NA CR0 196 C4
Elm Wood Primary School WNWD SE27 162 E5
Elsdale Street Health Centre HOM E9 86 E5
Elsley Primary School WBLY HA9 80 B4
Elsley School BTSEA SW11 141 F4
Eltham Bus Station ELTH/MOT SE9 146 E6
Eltham Cemetery ELTH/MOT SE9 147 H5
Eltham CE Primary School ELTH/MOT SE9 146 E6
Eltham College ELTH/MOT SE9 166 C4
Eltham College Junior School ELTH/MOT SE9 166 C3
Eltham Crematorium ELTH/MOT SE9 147 J5
Eltham Green School ELTH/MOT SE9 166 C1
Eltham Health Clinic ELTH/MOT SE9 146 D6
Eltham Health & Fitness Centre ELTH/MOT SE9 167 F1
Eltham Hill Technology College ELTH/MOT SE9 166 D1
Eltham Palace (remains) ELTH/MOT SE9 166 D2
Eltham Pools ELTH/MOT SE9 146 D6
Eltham Warren Golf Club ELTH/MOT SE9 147 G6
Elthorne Park High School HNWL W7 116 A3
Elthorne Sports Centre HNWL W7 116 A3
Elystan Business Centre HYS/HAR UB3 95 G6
Emanuel School WAND/EARL SW18 140 C6
Embankment Pier CHCR WC2N 11 G7
Embassy of Afghanistan SKENS SW7 14 A3
Embassy of Albania BGVA SW1W 15 K5
Embassy of Algeria NTGHL W11 119 H1
Embassy of Angola MYFR/PKLN W1K 9 G6
Embassy of Argentina MYFR/PKLN W1K 9 J5
Embassy of Armenia KENS W8 120 A3
Embassy of Austria KTBR SW1X 15 G4
Embassy of Bahrain SKENS SW7 120 B3
Embassy of Belarus KENS W8 120 A2
Embassy of Belgium KTBR SW1X 15 H5
Embassy of Bolivia KTBR SW1X 15 H5
Embassy of Bosnia-Herzegovina CAVSQ/HST W1G 9 K3
Embassy of Brazil MYFR/PKLN W1K 9 G5
Embassy of Bulgaria SKENS SW7 120 B3
Embassy of Cameroon NTGHL W11 119 H1
Embassy of China CAVSQ/HST W1G 9 J1
Embassy of Costa Rica BAY/PAD W2 101 G6
Embassy of Cote d'Ivoire KTBR SW1X 15 H4
Embassy of Croatia GTPST W1W 3 K7
Embassy of Cuba LSQ/SEVD WC2H 10 E3
Embassy of Democratic Republic of the Congo KTBR SW1X 15 F5
Embassy of Denmark KTBR SW1X 14 E4
Embassy of Ecuador KTBR SW1X 14 E4
Embassy of Egypt MYFR/PICC W1J 9 J7
Embassy of Estonia SKENS SW7 120 B2
Embassy of Ethiopia SKENS SW7 14 B3
Embassy of Finland KTBR SW1X 15 G4
Embassy of France KTBR SW1X 15 F2
Embassy of Georgia KENS W8 120 A2
Embassy of Germany KTBR SW1X 15 G4
Embassy of Ghana HGT N6 66 B5
Embassy of Greece KENS W8 119 J1
Embassy of Guatemala WBPTN SW10 120 A6
Embassy of Honduras MBLAR W1H 9 F1
Embassy of Hungary KTBR SW1X 15 H5
Embassy of Iceland KTBR SW1X 15 G6
Embassy of Indonesia MYFR/PKLN W1K 9 H6
Embassy of Iran SKENS SW7 14 B3
Embassy of Iraq SKENS SW7 120 B3
Embassy of Ireland KTBR SW1X 15 J3
Embassy of Israel KENS W8 120 A2
Embassy of Italy MYFR/PKLN W1K 9 H5
Embassy of Japan MYFR/PICC W1J 15 K1
Embassy of Jordan KENS W8 119 J2
Embassy of Korea WESTW SW1E 16 B4
Embassy of Krygyzstan MBLAR W1H 8 E2
Embassy of Kuwait KTBR SW1X 15 F2
Embassy of Latvia CAMTN NW1 3 G7
Embassy of Lebanon KENS W8 120 A1
Embassy of Liberia BAY/PAD W2 100 E6
Embassy of Lithuania MBLAR W1H 8 E2
Embassy of Luxembourg KTBR SW1X 15 G3
Embassy of Mexico MYFR/PICC W1J 15 J1
Embassy of Mongolia KENS W8 120 A2
Embassy of Morocco SKENS SW7 120 B4
Embassy of Mozambique FITZ W1T 4 A7
Embassy of Myanmar MYFR/PICC W1J 9 J7
Embassy of Nepal KENS W8 120 A1
Embassy of Netherlands SKENS SW7 120 B2
Embassy of Norway KTBR SW1X 15 H4
Embassy of Oman SKENS SW7 120 B3
Embassy of Paraguay KENS W8 120 A3
Embassy of Peru KTBR SW1X 15 F4
Embassy of Philippines KENS W8 120 A1
Embassy of Poland CAVSQ/HST W1G 9 J1
Embassy of Portugal KTBR SW1X 15 G3
Embassy of Qatar MYFR/PKLN W1K 9 H7
Embassy of Republic of Gabon SKENS SW7 120 B3
Embassy of Republic of Senegal CRICK NW2 82 A5
Embassy of Romania KENS W8 120 A2
Embassy of Russian Federation KENS W8 120 A1
Embassy of Saudi Arabia MYFR/PICC W1J 9 J7
Embassy of Slovak Republic KENS W8 120 A1
Embassy of Slovenia CAVSQ/HST W1G 9 J3
Embassy of Spain KTBR SW1X 15 H4
Embassy of Sudan WHALL SW1A 16 A1
Embassy of Sweden MBLAR W1H 8 E2
Embassy of Switzerland MBLAR W1H 8 E2
Embassy of Syria KTBR SW1X 15 G3
Embassy of Thailand SKENS SW7 120 B3
Embassy of Tunisia SKENS SW7 14 B3
Embassy of Turkey KTBR SW1X 15 H3
Embassy of Turkmenistan GTPST W1W 10 B2
Embassy of Ukraine NTGHL W11 119 H1
Embassy of United Arab Emirates SKENS SW7 14 B2
Embassy of Uruguay SKENS SW7 14 D4
Embassy of USA MYFR/PKLN W1K 9 G5
Embassy of Uzbekistan NTGHL W11 119 J1
Embassy of Venezuela SKENS SW7 14 B5
Embassy of Yemen SKENS SW7 14 A6
Ember Sports Club ESH/CLAY KT10 189 H5
Embroidery World Business Centre WFD IG8 53 H5
EMD Walthamstow Cinema WALTH E17 69 J1
Emery Theatre POP/IOD E14 105 K5
Emmanuel CE Primary School KIL/WHAMP NW6 82 E3
Emmanuel CE School NTHWD HA6 40 D3
Empire Cinema LSQ/SEVD WC2H 10 D5
Endsleigh Industrial Estate NWDGN UB2 114 D4
Enfield Business Centre PEND EN3 24 E3
Enfield Chace Lower School ENC/FH EN2 24 A1
Enfield College PEND EN3 24 E4
Enfield County Upper School ENC/FH EN2 23 K4
Enfield Cricket Club EN EN1 24 A5
Enfield FC ED N9 36 E4
Enfield Golf Club ENC/FH EN2 23 H5
Enfield Grammar School (Upper) ENC/FH EN2 23 K4
Enfield Lower Grammar School ENC/FH EN2 23 K3
English Martyrs RC Primary School WALW SE17 18 E7
WCHPL E1 13 K4
Ennersdale Primary School LEW SE13 145 G6
Ensham Secondary School TOOT SW17 178 E1
Enterprise Business Park POP/IOD E14 124 E2

Enterprise Industrial Estate *BERM/RHTH* SE16 123 K5
Epsom & Ewell High School *HOR/WEW* KT19 206 E4
Eric Liddell Sports Centre *ELTH/MOT* SE9 166 C4
Erith Cemetery *ERITH* DA8 129 J6
Erith & District Hospital *ERITH* DA8 130 A6
Erith Health Centre *ERITH* DA8 130 B6
Erith Library & Museum *ERITH* DA8 130 B5
Erith School *ERITH* DA8 149 K1
Erith School Community Sports Centre *ERITH* DA8 149 K1
Erith Small Business Centre *ERITH* DA8 130 C6
Erith Sports Centre *ERITH* DA8 130 B6
Erith Stadium *ERITH* DA8 130 B6
Erith Theatre Guild *ERITH* DA8 130 C5
Ernest Bevin School *TOOT* SW17 160 D5
Eros *MYFR/PICC* W1J 10 C6
Esher Church School (Primary) *ESH/CLAY* KT10 204 C4
Esher College *THDIT* KT7 189 K4
Esher RFC *WOT/HER* KT12 188 D6
Essendine Primary School *KIL/WHAMP* NW6 100 E2
Essex Primary School *MNPK* E12 89 J4
Ethelburga GM School *BTSEA* SW11 140 D2
Ethel Davis School *CHDH* RM6 73 H2
Euro Business Centre *SRTFD* E15 88 D6
Eurolink Business Centre *BRXS/STRHM* SW2 142 B5
Europa Trading Estate *ERITH* DA8 130 A5
European Business Centre *CDALE/KGS* NW9 45 F6
European School of Economics *KTBR* SW1X 15 H3
European Vocational College *HDTCH* EC3A 13 H4
Euro Way School *CEND/HSY/T* N8 49 G6
Euro Way School London *FSBYPK* N4 67 H4
Euston Centre *CAMTN* NW1 4 A6
Euston Station *CAMTN* NW1 4 C5
Euston Tower *CAMTN* NW1 4 A6
Eveline Lowe Primary School *STHWK* SE1 123 H5
Evendine College *SOHO/SHAV* W1D 10 C3
Eversley Medical Centre *THHTH* CR7 196 B3
Eversley Primary School *WCHMH* N21 22 E6
Everyman Cinema *HAMP* NW3 83 G2
Evolution House *RCH/KEW* TW9 137 F3
Ewell Athletics Track *HOR/WEW* KT19 207 F4
Ewell Castle School *EW* KT17 207 J6
Ewell Grove Infant School *EW* KT17 207 H6
EW Fact/Emile Woolf Colleges *HOLWY* N7 84 E4
ExCeL Exhibition Centre *CAN/RD* E16 126 A1
Exchange Square *SDTCH* EC2A 13 G1
The Exchange *IL* IG1 72 B6
Exhibition Halls *STLK* EC1Y 12 D1
WBLY HA9 80 C2
Eye Clinic *LSQ/SEVD* WC2H 10 D3
Faircharm Trading Estate *DEPT* SE8 144 E1
IS N1 6 C2
The Faircross Complementary Medical Centre *BARK* IG11 90 E4
Fairfield Clinic *BKHH* IG9 39 F3
Fairfield Industrial Estate *KUT* KT1 175 G6
Fairfield Pool & Leisure Centre *DART* DA1 171 H2
Fairholme J & I School *EBED/NFELT* TW14 153 G3
Fairlawn Primary School *FSTH* SE23 163 K2
Fairley House School *WEST* SW1P 16 C7
Fairlop Primary School *BARK/HLT* IG6 54 C4
Fairview Industrial Centre *DAGW* RM9 111 F5
Fairview Industrial Estate *HYS/HAR* UB3 113 J2
Fairview Medical Centre *STRHM/NOR* SW16 179 K4
Fairway JMI School *MLHL* NW7 31 F4
Fairway Primary School *MLHL* NW7 31 F4
Fairways Business Park *LEY* E10 69 G6
Falconbrook JMI School *BTSEA* SW11 140 C3
Falcon Business Centre *BTSEA* SW11 140 D5
Falcon Park Industrial Estate *WLSDN* NW10 81 G3
Falkner House School *SKENS* SW7 120 B5
Fanmakers' Hall *LVPST* EC2M 13 G3
Fan Museum *GNWCH* SE10 145 F1
Faraday Building *BLKFR* EC4V 12 B4
Farm Lane Trading Estate *FUL/PGN* SW6 119 K6
Farnborough Primary School *ORP* BR6 216 D3
Farnell House Medical Centre *HSLW* TW3 135 G2
Farnham Green Primary School *GDMY/SEVK* IG3 73 G3
Farringdon Station *FARR* EC1M 11 K1
Farrington & Stratford House School *CHST* BR7 185 J3
Fashion & Textile Design Museum *STHWK* SE1 19 H3
Featherstone Industrial Estate *NWDGN* UB2 114 D2
Featherstone Primary School *NWDGN* UB2 114 D3
Featherstone Road Health Clinic *NWDGN* UB2 114 D3
Featherstone School *NWDGN* UB2 114 C4
Felnex Trading Estate *WLGTN* SM6 195 F6
Feltham Airparcs Leisure Centre *FELT* TW13 154 C4
Feltham Athletics Arena *EBED/NFELT* TW14 153 K2
Felthambrook Industrial Estate *FELT* TW13 154 A5
Feltham Community College *FELT* TW13 154 B4
Feltham Hill Infant School *FELT* TW13 153 H5
Feltham Hill Junior School *FELT* TW13 153 J5
Feltham & Hounslow Boro FC *EBED/NFELT* TW14 153 K2
Feltham Superbowl *FELT* TW13 154 A4
Fenchurch Street Station *FENCHST* EC3M 13 H5
Fenstanton J & I School *BRXS/STRHM* SW2 162 B3
Fenton House *HAMP* NW3 83 G1
Fern Hill Primary School *KUTN/CMB* KT2 175 F2
Ferrier Industrial Estate *WAND/EARL* SW18 140 A5
Ferry Island Retail Park *TOTM* N17 50 B6
Ferry Lane Industrial Estate *RAIN* RM13 111 J4
WALTH E17 50 E6
Ferry Lane Primary School *TOTM* N17 68 D1
Festival Pier *STHWK* SE1 11 H7
Field End Primary School *RSLP* HA4 59 H6
Fielding Primary School *WEA* W13 116 C3
Film House Cinema *RCH/KEW* TW9 136 E6
Financial Times *POP/IOD* E14 106 A5
STHWK SE1 12 D7
Finchley Lido *NFNCH/WDSP* N12 47 H3
Finchley Catholic High School *NFNCH/WDSP* N12 33 G5
Finchley Cricket Club *FNCH* N3 47 F5
Finchley Golf Club *MLHL* NW7 46 D2
The Finchley Industrial Centre *NFNCH/WDSP* N12 33 G6
Finchley Memorial Hospital *FNCH* N3 47 G3
Finchley Youth Theatre *EFNCH* N2 47 J6
Fine Arts College *HAMP* NW3 83 J4
Finsbury Circus Medical Centre *LVPST* EC2M 13 F2
Finsbury Health Centre *CLKNW* EC1R 5 J6
Finsbury Leisure Centre *FSBYE* EC1V 6 D5
Finsbury Park Track *FSBYPK* N4 67 H4
Finton House School *TOOT* SW17 160 E4
Fircroft Primary School *TOOT* SW17 160 E4
Fire Brigade HQ *STHWK* SE1 17 G6
Fire Brigade Museum *STHWK* SE1 18 C2
Firepower (Museum of Artillery) *WOOL/PLUM* SE18 127 G3
Firs Farm Primary School *PLMGR* N13 35 K5
Fisher Athletic FC *BERM/RHTH* SE16 124 A1
Fishmonger's Hall *CANST* EC4R 12 E6
Fitness Unlimited Leisure Centre *BOW* E3 105 J1
Fitzjohns Primary School *HAMP* NW3 83 H3
Fitzrovia Medical Centre *GTPST* W1W 4 A7
Fitzroy Nuffield Hospital *MBLAR* W1H 8 E3
Five Bridges School *LBTH* SE11 122 A5
Five Elms Primary School *DAGW* RM9 92 B1
Five Ways Business Centre *FELT* TW13 154 A5
Flamsteed House Museum *GNWCH* SE10 145 G1
Flaxman Sports Centre *CMBW* SE5 142 D3
Fleecefield Primary School *ED* N9 36 C6
Fleet Primary School *HAMP* NW3 83 K3
Fleetway Business Park *GFD/PVL* UB6 97 H1
Fleming Lab Museum *BAY/PAD* W2 8 B3
Flora Gardens Primary School *HMSMTH* W6 118 E4
Florence Nightingale Museum *STHWK* SE1 17 G3
Florida State University *RSQ* WC1B 10 D2
Flutters Leisure Centre *FUL/PGN* SW6 139 K1
FOB School *STNW/STAM* N16 68 C4
Follys End Christian High School *SNWD* SE25 197 F3
The Foot Clinic *WIM/MER* SW19 177 H1
Fordbridge Medical Centre *ASHF* TW15 152 C6
The Ford College *CONDST* W1S 9 K5
Ford Industrial Park *DAGW* RM9 110 D2
Fordview Industrial Estate *RAIN* RM13 111 F2
Foreign & Commonwealth Office *WHALL* SW1A 16 D2
Foreland Medical Centre *NTGHL* W11 100 C6
Forest Business Park *WALTH* E17 69 F4
Forestdale Primary School *CROY/NA* CR0 213 G6
Foresters Primary School *WLGTN* SM6 210 D4
Forest Gate Community School *FSTGT* E7 88 E3
Forest Hill Business Centre *FSTH* SE23 163 K4
Forest Hill Industrial Estate *FSTH* SE23 163 K4
Forest Hill School *FSTH* SE23 164 A5
Forest Hills Pools *FSTH* SE23 163 K4
Forest House Business Centre *WAN* E11 70 D4
Forest Industrial Park *BARK/HLT* IG6 54 E3
Forest Road Medical Centre *WALTH* E17 51 H6
Forest School *WALTH* E17 70 C1
Forest Trading Estate *WALTH* E17 51 F6
Forge Close Clinic *HAYES* BR2 199 K5
Forge Lane Primary School *FELT* TW13 172 D1
The Former Health Centre *CHARL* SE7 126 C4
Forster Park Primary School *CAT* SE6 165 H5
Fortismere School *EFNCH* N2 47 K5
Fortismere Secondary School *MUSWH* N10 48 A6
Fortune Theatre *HOL/ALD* WC2B 11 F4
The Forum *EDGE* HA8 44 C2
Fossdene Primary School *CHARL* SE7 126 A5
Fosters Primary School *WELL* DA16 148 D3
Foster's Primary School *WELL* DA16 148 D3
Foulds School *BAR* EN5 20 B4
The Foundling Museum *BMSBY* WC1N 5 F6
Fountayne Business Centre *SEVS/STOTM* N15 68 C1
Fountayne Road Health Centre *CLPT* E5 68 C6
Foxfield Primary School *WOOL/PLUM* SE18 127 H5
Fox Primary School *KENS* W8 119 K1
Frances Bardsley School for Girls *ROM* RM1 75 J2
Franciscan Primary School *TOOT* SW17 161 F6
Francis Holland School *BGVA* SW1W 15 H7
CAMTN NW1 2 E7
Frank Barnes Primary School *STJWD* NW8 83 H5
Franklin Industrial Estate *PGE/AN* SE20 181 K4
Freehold Industrial Centre *HSLWW* TW4 134 B6
Free Trade Wharf *WAP* E1W 105 F6
Fresh Wharf Estate *BARK* IG11 90 B6
Freuchen Medical Centre *WLSDN* NW10 99 H1
Freud Museum *HAMP* NW3 83 H4
Friars Primary Foundation School *STHWK* SE1 18 A2
Friends House *CAMTN* NW1 4 C5
Friends of Bar Ilan University *GLDGN* NW11 64 E5
Friends of the Hebrew University *CAMTN* NW1 3 J1
Friern Barnet School *FBAR/BDGN* N11 47 K1
Friern Bridge Retail Park *FBAR/BDGN* N11 48 B2
Frithwood Primary School *NTHWD* HA6 40 D2
Froebel College *PUT/ROE* SW15 158 D1
Frogmore Industrial Estate *HBRY* N5 85 J2
HYS/HAR UB3 113 H2
WLSDN NW10 98 E2
Fryent Country Park *WBLY* HA9 62 C4
Fryent Medical Centre *CDALE/KGS* NW9 62 E4
Fryent Primary School *CDALE/KGS* NW9 62 E4
Fulham Clinic *FUL/PGN* SW6 119 J6
Fulham Cross School *FUL/PGN* SW6 139 G1
Fulham FC (Craven Cottage) *BARN* SW13 139 F2
Fulham Medical Centre *FUL/PGN* SW6 140 A1
Fulham Palace *FUL/PGN* SW6 139 H3
Fulham Preparatory School *FUL/PGN* SW6 139 H3
Fulham Primary School *FUL/PGN* SW6 119 K6
Fulham & South Kensington Institute *WBPTN* SW10 120 B5
Fulham Warner Village Cinema *FUL/PGN* SW6 139 K1
Fuller Smith & Turner Sports Club *CHSWK* W4 138 B2
Fullwell Cross Health Centre *BARK/HLT* IG6 54 C5
Fullwell Cross Swimming Pool & Recreation Centre *BARK/HLT* IG6 54 C5
Fullwood Primary School *BARK/HLT* IG6 72 C1
Fulwell Golf Club *HPTN* TW12 155 J6
Furzedown Primary School *TOOT* SW17 179 G2
Furze Infant School *CHDH* RM6 74 A3
Future Business College *CONDST* W1S 9 K4
Gainsborough Clinic *PLMGR* N13 35 F6
Gainsborough Primary School *HOM* E9 87 H4
SRTFD E15 106 C2
Galleywall Primary School *BERM/RHTH* SE16 123 J4
Galliard Primary School *ED* N9 36 C1
Gallions Mount Primary School *WOOL/PLUM* SE18 128 A5
Gallions Primary School *EHAM* E6 108 B5
Gants Hill Medical Centre *GNTH/NBYPK* IG2 72 A3
Gardener Industrial Estate *BECK* BR3 182 B1
Garden House Boys School *KTBR* SW1X 14 E5
Garden House Girls School *BGVA* SW1W 121 F5
Garden Suburb Primary School *GLDGN* NW11 64 D2
Garfield Primary School *FBAR/BDGN* N11 48 B1
WIM/MER SW19 178 B2
Garratt Park Secondary Special School *WAND/EARL* SW18 160 A5
Garrick Industrial Centre *CDALE/KGS* NW9 63 H2
Garrick Theatre *LSQ/SEVD* WC2H 10 E6
Garth Primary School *MRDN* SM4 194 C2
The Garth Road Industrial Centre *MRDN* SM4 193 F4
Gascoigne Primary School *BARK* IG11 90 C6
Gate Cinema *NTGHL* W11 119 K1
Gatehouse School *BETH* E2 105 F1
The Gatehouse Theatre *HGT* N6 66 A4
Gate Theatre *NTGHL* W11 100 E6
Gateway Industrial Estate *WLSDN* NW10 99 H2
Gateway Primary School *STJWD* NW8 2 B6
Gayhurst Primary School *HACK* E8 86 C5
Gearies Infant School *GNTH/NBYPK* IG2 72 A2
Gearies Junior School *GNTH/NBYPK* IG2 72 B2
Geffrye Museum *BETH* E2 7 H3
Gemini Business Estate *NWCR* SE14 124 A5
General Medical Clinics *WCHPL* E1 13 J1
Genesis Cinema *WCHPL* E1 104 E3
Geoffrey Chaucer School *STHWK* SE1 18 E5
The Geoffrey Lloyd Foulkes Clinic *IL* IG1 72 A6
Geoffrey Whitworth Theatre *DART* DA1 150 D5
George Eliot J & I School *STJWD* NW8 83 G6
George Green Mixed School *POP/IOD* E14 125 F5
George Lowe Court *BAY/PAD* W2 101 F4
George Mitchell School *LEY* E10 69 K5
George Mitchell School Annexe *LEY* E10 69 K5
George Spicer Primary School *EN* EN1 24 B4
George Tomlinson Primary School *WAN* E11 70 C5
Germal College *FSBYPK* N4 67 G5
Gibbs Green Special School *WKENS* W14 119 J5
Gibson Business Centre *TOTM* N17 50 B2
The Gibson Business Centre *TOTM* N17 50 B3
Gidea Park College *GPK* RM2 57 J6
Gidea Park Primary School *GPK* RM2 75 H1
The Gielgud Theatre *SOHO/SHAV* W1D 10 C5
Giffin Business Centre *DEPT* SE8 144 D1
Gifford Primary School *NTHLT* UB5 95 K1
Gilbert Collection *TPL/STR* WC2R 11 G5
Gilbert Colvin Primary School *CLAY* IG5 54 A4
Gilbert Scott Primary School *SAND/SEL* CR2 213 G5
Gillespie Primary School *FSBYPK* N4 85 H1
Girdlers' Hall *CITYW* EC2V 12 D2
Glade Primary School *CLAY* IG5 53 K4
Gladesmore Community School *SEVS/STOTM* N15 68 C2
The Glades Shopping Centre *BMLY* BR1 183 K5
Gladstone Court Business Centre *VX/NE* SW8 141 H2
Gladstone Medical Centre *CRICK* NW2 81 H2
Gladstone Park Primary School *WLSDN* NW10 81 K3
Glaziers/scientific Instrument Makers Hall *STHWK* SE1 12 E7
Glebe First & Middle School *KTN/HRWW/W* HA3 61 K1
Glebe Primary School *HGDN/ICK* UB10 76 B2
Glebe School *WWKM* BR4 199 G5
Gleen Lecky Health Centre *PUT/ROE* SW15 139 G5
Glenbrook Primary School *CLAP* SW4 161 J1
Glencairn Sports Club *FBAR/BDGN* N11 48 C3
Glendower Preparatory School *SKENS* SW7 120 B4
Glenham College *IL* IG1 72 B6
Glenlyn Medical Centre *E/WMO/HCT* KT8 189 H2
Glenthorne High School *CHEAM* SM3 193 K5
Globe Primary School *BETH* E2 104 E2
Globe Wharf *WAP* E1W 105 F6
Gloucester Primary School *PECK* SE15 143 F1
Gobions JMI School *ROM* RM1 57 F2
Godolphin & Latymer School *HMSMTH* W6 118 E4
Godwin Junior School *FSTGT* E7 89 F2
Godwin Primary School *DAGW* RM9 92 A5
Golborne Medical Centre *NKENS* W10 100 D3
Goldbeaters Primary School *EDGE* HA8 45 F4
Golden Hinde Educational Museum *STHWK* SE1 12 E6
Golders Green Crematorium *GLDGN* NW11 64 E4
Golders Green Health Centre *GLDGN* NW11 65 F5
Golders Hill Health Centre *EFNCH* N2 65 G3
Golders Hill School *GLDGN* NW11 64 E4
Goldhawk Industrial Estate *SHB* W12 118 E3
Goldsmiths College *BROCKY* SE4 144 C4
DEPT SE8 124 D6
LEW SE13 145 H5
NWCR SE14 144 B2
Goldsmiths College Sports Ground *SCUP* DA14 169 G5
Goldsmiths Hall *STBT* EC1A 12 C3
Gonville Primary School *THHTH* CR7 196 A2
Goodinge Health Centre *HOLWY* N7 84 E4
Goodmayes Primary School *GDMY/SEVK* IG3 73 H5
Goodmayes Retail Park *CHDH* RM6 73 H4
Goodrich J & I School *EDUL* SE22 163 H1
Good Shepherd RC Primary School *BMLY* BR1 165 J6
CROY/NA CR0 213 K5
The Good Shepherd RC Primary School *SHB* W12 118 C2
Goodwyn School *MLHL* NW7 45 J1
Goose Green Primary School *EDUL* SE22 143 G5
Goose Green Trading Estate *EDUL* SE22 143 H5
Gordonbrock Primary School *BROCKY* SE4 144 D6
Gordon Hospital *WEST* SW1P 16 C7
Gordon House Health Centre *WEA* W13 116 D1
Gordon Infant School *IL* IG1 90 D1
Gordon Primary School *ELTH/MOT* SE9 146 E5
Goresbrook Leisure Centre *DAGW* RM9 91 K6
Goresbrook Sports Centre *DAGW* RM9 92 A6

Gorringe Park Middle School
MTCM CR4 179 F4
Gosai Cinema
WEA W13 116 C1
Gosbury Hill Health Centre
CHSGTN KT9 206 A2
Gosford Primary School
REDBR IG4 71 K2
Gospel Oak Primary School
HAMP NW3 84 A2
Gower House School
CDALE/KGS NW9 62 E6
Grace Business Centre
MTCM CR4 194 E3
Grace Theatre at the Latchmere
BTSEA SW11 140 E3
Graduate School of Management
TOTM N17 50 B4
Grafton Primary School
BCTR RM8 74 A6
HOLWY N7 84 E1
Grahame Park Health Centre
CDALE/KGS NW9 45 G4
Grahame Park J & I School
CDALE/KGS NW9 45 G4
Granard Business Centre
EDGE HA8 45 G2
Granard Primary School
PUT/ROE SW15 158 E1
Granby Sports Club
ELTH/MOT SE9 184 D1
Grand Avenue Primary School
BRYLDS KT5 191 K4
Grande Vitesse Industrial Centre
STHWK SE1 18 B1
Grand Union Industrial Estate
WLSDN NW10 98 D1
Grange First & Middle School
RYLN/HDSTN HA2 60 B5
Grange Infant School
CAN/RD E16 106 D2
The Grange Museum
CRICK NW2 81 H2
Grange Park Clinic
YEAD UB4 94 D3
Grange Park Preparatory School
WCHMH N21 35 H1
Grange Park Primary School
ENC/FH EN2 23 G5
YEAD UB4 94 D3
Grange Primary School
EA W5 116 E2
STHWK SE1 19 G5
Grangewood Independent School
FSTGT E7 89 H5
Grangewood School
RSLP HA4 58 E2
Granton Primary School
STRHM/NOR SW16 179 H3
Granville Road Industrial Estate
CRICK NW2 64 D6
Grasmere Primary School
STNW/STAM N16 85 K2
Grasshoppers RFC
ISLW TW7 116 A6
Grassroots School
HPTN TW12 173 F4
Grasvenor Avenue Infant School
BAR EN5 32 E1
Gravel Hill Primary School
BXLYHS DA6 149 J6
Graveney School
TOOT SW17 179 G2
Graves Yard Industrial Estate
WELL DA16 148 B3
Grays Farm Primary School
STMC/STPC BR5 186 C4
Grazebrook Primary School
STNW/STAM N16 68 A6
Great Cambridge Industrial Estate
EN EN1 24 D6
Great Chapel Street Medical Centre
SOHO/SHAV W1D 10 C3
Greater London Authority Headquarters (City Hall)
STHWK SE1 19 H1
Great Jubilee Wharf
WAP E1W 123 K1
Great Western Industrial Park
NWDGN UB2 115 G2
Great West Trading Estate
BTFD TW8 116 C6
Greenacres Primary School
ELTH/MOT SE9 167 F4
The Green CE Primary School
TOTM N17 50 B6
Green Dragon School
BTFD TW8 117 F5
Greenfield Medical Centre
CRICK NW2 82 C1
Greenfields Junior School
SHB W12 99 H6
Greenfields Primary School
OXHEY WD19 41 G1
Greenfields Special School
MUSWH N10 47 K4
Greenford Avenue Medical Centre
HNWL W7 96 E4
Greenford Green Clinic
GFD/PVL UB6 78 E3
Greenford High School
STHL UB1 96 A2
Greenford Industrial Estate
GFD/PVL UB6 78 B6
Greenford Park Cemetery
GFD/PVL UB6 96 B4
Greenford Road Medical Centre
GFD/PVL UB6 96 D1
Greenford Sports Centre
STHL UB1 96 A2
Greengate Medical Centre
PLSTW E13 107 F2
Greengrove College
STHGT/OAK N14 34 E4
Greenheath Business Centre
BETH E2 104 D2
Greenhill College
HRW HA1 61 F2
Greenhill Park Medical Centre
WLSDN NW10 81 G6
Greenland Pier
BERM/RHTH SE16 124 C3
Green Lane Business Park
ELTH/MOT SE9 167 F4
Green Lane Primary School
WPK KT4 192 E4
Greenleaf Primary School
WALTH E17 51 H6
Greenmead Primary School
PUT/ROE SW15 138 E6
The Green School for Girls
ISLW TW7 136 B1
Greenshaw High School
SUT SM1 194 B6
Greenshields Industrial Estate
CAN/RD E16 125 K1
Greenside Primary School
SHB W12 118 D2
Greenslade Primary School
WOOL/PLUM SE18 127 J6
Green Street Green Primary School
ORP BR6 217 F4
Greenvale School
FSTH SE23 164 B5
Greenwich Centre Business Park
DEPT SE8 144 E1
Greenwich Cinema
GNWCH SE10 145 F1
Greenwich College
GNWCH SE10 145 F1
Greenwich Community College
WOOL/PLUM SE18 127 G4
WOOL/PLUM SE18 127 J6
Greenwich Hospital
GNWCH SE10 125 J5
Greenwich Industrial Estate
CHARL SE7 126 A4
GNWCH SE10 144 E1
Greenwich Natural Health Centre
GNWCH SE10 145 F1
Greenwich Pier
POP/IOD E14 125 F5
Greenwich Theatre & Art Gallery
GNWCH SE10 145 G1
Greenwich University Library
GNWCH SE10 125 F6
Greenwood First School
MTCM CR4 179 J6
Greenwood Primary School
NTHLT UB5 78 C3
Greenwood School
WOOL/PLUM SE18 147 K2
Greenwood Theatre
STHWK SE1 19 F2
Green Wrythe Primary School
CAR SM5 194 C3
Gresham College
FLST/FETLN EC4A 11 J2
Gresham Way Industrial Estate
WIM/MER SW19 160 A5
The Greycoat Hospital
WEST SW1P 16 C7
Grey Coat Hospital Upper School
WEST SW1P 16 C5
Grey Court School
RCHPK/HAM TW10 156 E5
Griffen Manor School
WOOL/PLUM SE18 147 K2
Grimsdyke First & Middle School
PIN HA5 41 K2
Grims Dyke Golf Club
PIN HA5 28 A6
Grinling Gibbons Primary School
DEPT SE8 124 C6
Grist Memorial Sports Club
E/WMO/HCT KT8 189 K2
Grocers' Hall
CITYW EC2V 12 E4
Grosvenor Hospitals
HDN NW4 63 K2
The Grove Health Centre
SHB W12 118 E2
Grove House School
WNWD SE27 162 C4
Grovelands Priory Hospital
STHGT/OAK N14 34 E3
Grovelands School
WOT/HER KT12 188 A3
Grove Medical Centre
DEPT SE8 124 B4
The Grove Medical Centre
ARCH N19 66 C6
Grove Park Industrial Estate
CDALE/KGS NW9 63 F1
Grove Park Primary School
CHSWK W4 117 K6
Grove Park School
CDALE/KGS NW9 62 E1
Grove Primary School
CHDH RM6 73 H2
Grove Road Primary School
HSLW TW3 135 F5
The Groves Medical Centre
NWMAL KT3 176 B6
Grove Village Medical Centre
EBED/NFELT TW14 153 H3
Guardian Angels RC Primary School
BOW E3 105 G3
Guardian Newspapers
POP/IOD E14 124 E2
Guards' Chapel & Museum
WHALL SW1A 16 C3
Guildhall Annex KUT KT1 174 E6
Guildhall Art Gallery
LOTH EC2R 12 E3
Guildhall School BARB EC2Y 12 D1
Guildhall School of Music & Drama
STLK EC1Y 6 D7
Guildhall University
WCHPL E1 104 C5
Gumley House Convent School
ISLW TW7 136 B4
Gunnersbury Catholic School
BTFD TW8 116 D5
Gunnersbury Park Museum
ACT W3 117 H3
Gurnell Leisure Centre
WEA W13 97 F2
Guru Gobind Singh Khalsa College
CHIG IG7 39 K3
Guru Nanak Medical Centre
STHL UB1 114 C1
Guys Hospital
STHWK SE1 19 F1
Guys Kings & St Thomas School of Medicine
CMBW SE5 142 D3
Gwyn Jones Primary School
WAN E11 70 B4
GX Superbowl
EHAM E6 108 A4
Gypsy Moth IV
GNWCH SE10 125 F6
Haberdashers Askes Hatcham College
NWCR SE14 144 A3
NWCR SE14 144 B2
Haberdashers' Hall
CITYW EC2V 12 D3
Hackbridge Primary School
WLGTN SM6 195 F5
Hackney Business Centre
HACK E8 86 D4
Hackney Community College
CLPT E5 86 D1
IS N1 7 G3
Hackney Empire Variety Theatre
HACK E8 86 D4
Hackney Free & Parochial CE School
HOM E9 86 E4
Hackney Hospital
HOM E9 87 G3
The Hackney Museum
HOM E9 86 E6
Hackney Sports Centre
HOM E9 87 J2
Hadley Wood Golf Club
EBAR EN4 21 J2
Hadley Wood Primary School
EBAR EN4 21 G1
Hadlow College
LEE/GVPK SE12 166 B3
The Haelan Clinic
CEND/HSY/T N8 66 D3
Haggerston School
BETH E2 7 K2
Haggerston Swimming Pool
BETH E2 7 K1
Hague Primary School
BETH E2 104 D3
Hailey Road Business Park
ERITHM DA18 129 H2
Haimo Primary School
ELTH/MOT SE9 146 C6
Hainault Forest Golf Club
CHIG IG7 55 K2
Hainault Forest High School
CHIG IG7 55 G1
Hainault Industrial Estate
BARK/HLT IG6 55 J1
Hakim Qureshi Clinic
NWDGN UB2 114 D3
The Hale Clinic
REGST W1B 3 K7
Half Moon Theatre
WCHPL E1 105 F3
Haling Manor High School
CROY/NA CR0 211 H5
Halley Primary School
POP/IOD E14 105 G4
Hallfield Clinic
BAY/PAD W2 101 G5
Hallfield Primary School
BAY/PAD W2 101 G5
The Hall Junior School
HAMP NW3 83 H4
Hallmark Trading Estate
WBLY HA9 80 E2
Hall Place
BXLY DA5 169 K1
Halls Business Centre
HYS/HAR UB3 113 K3
Hall School Wimbledon
PUT/ROE SW15 158 D5
The Hall Senior School
HAMP NW3 83 H4
Hallsville Primary School
CAN/RD E16 106 E5
Halstow Primary School
GNWCH SE10 125 J5
Hambrough Primary School
STHL UB1 114 D1
Hamer Indoor Market
BOW E3 105 H1
Ham Health Clinic
RCHPK/HAM TW10 156 D5
Ham House (NT)
RCHPK/HAM TW10 156 D3
Hamilton Road Industrial Estate
WNWD SE27 162 E6
Hamlet International Industrial Estate
ERITH DA8 130 A5
Hammersmith Apollo
HMSMTH W6 119 F5
Hammersmith Cemetery
HMSMTH W6 119 G5
The Hammersmith Hospitals
SHB W12 99 J5
Hammersmith Industrial Estate
HMSMTH W6 119 F6
Hammersmith New Cemetery
RCH/KEW TW9 137 J3
Hammersmith Palais
HMSMTH W6 119 F4
Hammersmith Physio & Sports Injury Clinic
HMSMTH W6 119 F4
Hammersmith & West London College
WKENS W14 119 G4
Hampden Gurney School
MBLAR W1H 8 D3
Ham & Petersham Cricket Club
RCHPK/HAM TW10 156 E6
The Hampshire School (Knightsbridge)
SKENS SW7 14 C3
The Hampshire School
BAY/PAD W2 101 F6
Hampstead Cricket Club
KIL/WHAMP NW6 83 F3
Hampstead Golf Club
EFNCH N2 65 G4
Hampstead Hill School
HAMP NW3 83 K2
Hampstead Medical Centre
HAMP NW3 83 G2
Hampstead Parochial CE School
HAMP NW3 83 G2
Hampstead School
CRICK NW2 82 C2
Hampstead School of English
KIL/WHAMP NW6 82 E2
Hampstead Theatre
HAMP NW3 83 H5
Hampton Cemetery
HPTN TW12 173 F3
Hampton Community College
HPTN TW12 173 F1
Hampton Court Palace
E/WMO/HCT KT8 174 A6
Hampton Farm Industrial Estate
FELT TW13 154 D5
Hampton FC
HPTN TW12 173 G4
Hampton Hill Junior School
HPTN TW12 173 H1
Hampton Infant School
HPTN TW12 172 E3
Hampton Junior School
HPTN TW12 173 F4
The Hampton Medical Centre
HPTN TW12 173 F3
Hampton Open Air Pool
HPTN TW12 173 H3
Hampton Road Industrial Park
CROY/NA CR0 196 D3
Hampton School
HPTN TW12 173 F1
Hampton Wick Infants School
KUT KT1 174 D3
Handel's House
MYFR/PKLN W1K 9 J5
Handsworth Health Clinic
CHING E4 52 B2
Handsworth Primary School
CHING E4 52 B2
Hanover Primary School
IS N1 6 B2
Hanover Trading Estate
HOLWY N7 84 E3
Hanover West Industrial Estate
WLSDN NW10 98 E2
Hanworth Trading Estate
FELT TW13 154 D5
Harbinger Primary School
POP/IOD E14 124 D4
Harborough School
ARCH N19 66 D6
Harenc School
SCUP DA14 186 D1
Hargrave Park Primary School
ARCH N19 66 C6
Haringey Arts Council
ED N9 36 C4
Haringey Community Health Clinic
SEVS/STOTM N15 68 B1
Haringey Health Care
SEVS/STOTM N15 68 B1
Haringey Magistrates Court
HGT N6 66 A3
Harland Primary School
WIM/MER SW19 178 B5
Harlesden Primary School
WLSDN NW10 99 G1
Harley Medical Centre
CAVSQ/HST W1G 9 J3
The Harley Medical Centre
CANST EC4R 12 D5
Harley Street Clinic
CAVSQ/HST W1G 9 J2
Harlington Community School
HYS/HAR UB3 113 G4
Harlyn Primary School
PIN HA5 41 F6
The Harold Macmillan Medical Centre
HRW HA1 60 D4
Harp Business Centre
CRICK NW2 63 J6
Harpley School
WCHPL E1 104 E3
Harrington Hill Primary School
CLPT E5 68 D5
Harris City Technology College
NRWD SE19 181 G4
Harrodian School
BARN SW13 138 C1
Harrods Store
CHEL SW3 14 E4
Harrovian Business Village
HRW HA1 60 D4
Harrow Arts Centre
PIN HA5 42 A3
Harrow Borough FC
RYLN/HDSTN HA2 78 A2
Harrow College
HRW HA1 60 E4
Harrow Cricket Club
HRW HA1 78 E2
Harrow Crown Courts
HRW HA1 42 D6
Harrow Heritage Museum
RYLN/HDSTN HA2 42 C6
Harrow High School
HRW HA1 61 G3
Harrow Magistrates Court
HRW HA1 61 F1
Harrow RFC
STAN HA7 29 H5
Harrow Road Health Centre
BAY/PAD W2 100 E4
Harrow School
HRW HA1 60 E4
RYLN/HDSTN HA2 60 E6
Harrow Superbowl
RYLN/HDSTN HA2 60 B2
Harrow Town Cricket Club
RYLN/HDSTN HA2 60 A5
Harrow Weald Cemetery
KTN/HRWW/W HA3 42 E2
Harry Gosling Primary School
WCHPL E1 104 C5
Hartley Primary School
EHAM E6 89 J6
Hartsbourne Golf & Country Club
BUSH WD23 28 C4
Hartsbourne JMI School
BUSH WD23 28 D4
Harvington School
EA W5 97 J5
Haselrigge School
CLAP SW4 141 J5
Haseltine Primary School
CAT SE6 164 C6
Haslemere Business Centre
EN EN1 24 D5
Haslemere Industrial Estate
EBED/NFELT TW14 133 K6
WAND/EARL SW18 160 A4
Haslemere Primary School
MTCM CR4 178 C5
Hasmonean High School
HDN NW4 46 B5
MLHL NW7 45 J4
Hasmonean Primary School
HDN NW4 64 B2
Haste Hill Golf Club
NTHWD HA6 40 C5
Hastings Clinic
BRXS/STRHM SW2 142 A6
Hastingwood Trading Estate
UED N18 51 G2
Hatcham Mews Business Centre
NWCR SE14 144 A1
Hatch End High School
KTN/HRWW/W HA3 42 B3
Hatch End Swimming Pool
PIN HA5 42 A3
Hathaway Primary School
WEA W13 97 F4
Hatton School
REDBR IG4 53 H6
Havelock Primary School
NWDGN UB2 114 E3
Haven Green Clinic
EA W5 97 K5
Havering College of Further & Higher Education
EMPK RM11 75 K4
Havering Magistrates Court
ROM RM1 75 G1
Haverstock School
CAMTN NW1 84 A4
Hawes Down Clinic
WWKM BR4 199 G6
Hawes Down primary School
WWKM BR4 199 G5
The Hawker Centre
KUTN/CMB KT2 174 E1
Hawkins Clinic
PUT/ROE SW15 139 G5
RYNPK SW20 176 C4
Hawksmoor Primary School
THMD SE28 109 H6
Hawley Infant School
CAMTN NW1 84 B5
Haydon School
PIN HA5 40 D6
Hayes Bridge Middle School
NWDGN UB2 114 D2
Hayes Bridge Retail Park
HYS/HAR UB3 95 G6
Hayes Cricket Club
HYS/HAR UB3 94 D5
Hayes FC
HYS/HAR UB3 94 D6
Hayes Grove Priory Hospital
HAYES BR2 199 K6
The Hayes Manor School
HYS/HAR UB3 94 B5
Hayes Park J & I School
YEAD UB4 94 D3
Hayes Pool
HYS/HAR UB3 113 J1
Hayes Primary School
HAYES BR2 200 A5
Hayes School
HAYES BR2 200 A6
Hayes Social and Sports Club
HYS/HAR UB3 94 D6
Hayes Stadium Sports Centre
HYS/HAR UB3 94 B5
Hay Lane School
CDALE/KGS NW9 62 E1
Haymerle School
PECK SE15 123 H6
Hays Galleria
MON EC3R 13 G7
Hayward Gallery
STHWK SE1 17 H1
Hazelbury Primary School
ED N9 36 A5
Hazeldene Medical Centre
WBLY HA9 80 D4
Hazelhurst School
RYNPK SW20 177 G4
Hazelwood Infant School
PLMGR N13 35 H6
Hazelwood Junior School
PLMGR N13 35 G6
Healy Medical Centre
CLPT E5 68 D5
The Heart Hospital
CAVSQ/HST W1G 9 H2
Heathbrook Primary School
VX/NE SW8 141 H3
Heath Business Centre
HSLW TW3 135 H5
Heathcote School
CHING E4 38 C4
Heathfield College
HAYES BR2 215 G4
Heathfield Primary School
WHTN TW2 155 F3
Heathfield School (Senior)
PIN HA5 59 H3
Heath House Preparatory School
BKHTH/KID SE3 145 J3
Heathland School
HSLWW TW4 154 E1
Heathmere Primary School
PUT/ROE SW15 158 D3
Heathpark Golf Club
WDR/YW UB7 112 D3
Heathrow Airport
HTHAIR TW6 132 E3
Heathrow Airport Central Bus & Coach Station
HTHAIR TW6 132 D4

Heathrow International Trading Estate HSLWW TW4 134 A4
Heathrow Medical Centre HYS/HAR UB3 113 G5
Heathrow Primary School WDR/YW UB7 112 C6
Heathrow World Cargo Centre HTHAIR TW6 132 C6
Heathside Preparatory School HAMP NW3 83 G2
Heathway Industrial Estate DAGE RM10 92 D2
Heathway Medical Centre DAGW RM9 92 B2
Heavers Farm Primary School SNWD SE25 197 G2
Heber Primary School EDUL SE22 163 G1
Heckford Street Business Centre WAP E1W 105 F6
Hedges & Butler Estate SRTFD E15 106 A1
Hedgewood School YEAD UB4 94 C2
Helena Road Clinic WLSDN NW10 81 K2
Heliport Industrial Estate BTSEA SW11 140 C3
Hellenic College of London KTBR SW1X 14 E5
Helston Court Business Centre WIM/MER SW19 176 E1
Henderson Hospital BELMT SM2 208 E6
Hendon Cemetery HDN NW4 46 B4
Hendon College CDALE/KGS NW9 45 H4
Hendon Crematorium HDN NW4 46 B3
Hendon FC CRICK NW2 64 B6
Hendon Golf Club HDN NW4 46 A3
Hendon Preparatory School HDN NW4 46 B6
Hendon School HDN NW4 64 B2
Hendon Secretarial College HDN NW4 63 K2
Hendon Youth Sports Centre CRICK NW2 64 B4
Henry Cavendish Primary School BAL SW12 161 H3
Henry Compton School FUL/PGN SW6 139 G2
Henry Fawcett Primary School LBTH SE11 122 B6
Henry Green Primary School BCTR RM8 73 K5
Henry Maynard Infant School WALTH E17 70 A2
Henry Maynard Junior School WALTH E17 70 A2
Henwick Primary School ELTH/MOT SE9 146 C4
Herbert Morrison Primary School VX/NE SW8 141 K1
Hereward House School HAMP NW3 83 J4
Her Majestys' Theatre STJS SW1Y 10 D7
Hermitage Primary School WAP E1W 123 H1
Herne Hill School HNHL SE24 142 D6
Herne Hill Stadium (Cycle Centre) DUL SE21 162 E1
Heron Industrial Estate SRTFD E15 105 K1
Heronsgate Primary School THMD SE28 127 J3
Heron Trading Estate ACT W3 98 D4
Hersham Trading Estate WOT/HER KT12 188 D6
Heston Community School HEST TW5 135 F1
Heston Community Sports Hall HEST TW5 135 F1
Heston Industrial Mall HEST TW5 134 E1
Heston Infant School HEST TW5 135 F1
Heston Junior School HEST TW5 115 F6
Heston Park Cricket Club HEST TW5 114 E6
Heston Swimming Baths HEST TW5 114 E6
Hgs Institute Centre GLDGN NW11 65 F2
Higgs Industrial Estate BRXN/ST SW9 142 C4
Highams Lodge Business Centre WALTH E17 51 F6
Highams Park School CHING E4 52 B2
Highbury Corner Magistrates Court HOLWY N7 85 G4
Highbury Fields School HBRY N5 85 H3
Highbury Grove School HBRY N5 85 J3
Highbury Park Clinic HBRY N5 85 H1
Highbury Pool HBRY N5 85 H4
Highbury Quadrant Primary School HBRY N5 85 J2
High Commission of Angola MYFR/PKLN W1K 9 H5
High Commission of Antigua & Barbuda MHST W1U 9 G3
High Commission of Bahamas MYFR/PICC W1J 9 H7
High Commission of Bangladesh SKENS SW7 120 B3
High Commission of Barbados FITZ W1T 10 C3
High Commission of Belize CAVSQ/HST W1G 9 J3
High Commission of Botswana OXSTW W1C 9 J4
High Commission of Brunei BAY/PAD W2 8 B3
KTBR SW1X 15 G4
High Commission of Cyprus CONDST W1S 9 K4
MYFR/PKLN W1K 9 G5
High Commission of Dominica ECT SW5 120 A4
High Commission of Fiji SKENS SW7 120 B2
High Commission of Gambia KENS W8 120 A2
High Commission of Grenada ECT SW5 120 A5
High Commission of Guyana NTGHL W11 101 F6
High Commission of Jamaica SKENS SW7 14 A3
High Commission of Kenya CAVSQ/HST W1G 9 J1
High Commission of Lesotho KTBR SW1X 15 G4
High Commission of Malawi MYFR/PKLN W1K 9 J5
High Commission of Malaysia KTBR SW1X 15 H3
MBLAR W1H 8 E3
High Commission of Maldives MHST W1U 9 G1
High Commission of Malta MYFR/PICC W1J 10 B6
High Commission of Namibia CAVSQ/HST W1G 9 K2
High Commission of New Zealand STJS SW1Y 10 C7
High Commission of Nigeria CHCR WC2N 10 E7
EMB EC4Y 11 K4
High Commission of Pakistan KTBR SW1X 15 F4
High Commission of Papua New Guinea STJS SW1Y 10 C7
High Commission of St Lucia KENS W8 120 A2
High Commission of Seychelles MBLAR W1H 9 F1
High Commission of Sierra Leone OXSTW W1C 10 A3
High Commission of Singapore KTBR SW1X 15 F3
KTBR SW1X 15 G5
STJS SW1Y 10 C7
WEST SW1P 16 B6
High Commission of South Africa CHCR WC2N 10 E7
High Commission of Sri Lanka BAY/PAD W2 8 B5
High Commission of Swaziland WESTW SW1E 16 A4
High Commission of Tonga MBLAR W1H 8 D2
High Commission of Trinidad & Tobago KTBR SW1X 15 G4
High Commission of Uganda STJS SW1Y 10 D7
High Commission of Zambia BAY/PAD W2 120 B2
High Commission of Zimbabwe CHCR WC2N 10 E6
High Cross Centre SEVS/STOTM N15 68 C1
High Elms Country Park ORP BR6 216 C5
High Elms Golf Club ORP BR6 216 C5
Highfield Infant School HAYES BR2 199 H1
Highfield Junior School HAYES BR2 199 H1
Highfield Primary School WCHMH N21 35 H3
Highfield School WAND/EARL SW18 160 D2
Highgate Cemetery HGT N6 66 A5
Highgate Golf Club HGT N6 65 J3
Highgate Junior School HGT N6 65 K4
Highgate Pre-Preparatory School HGT N6 65 K4
Highgate Primary School HGT N6 65 K3
Highgate Private Hospital HGT N6 65 K3
Highgate School HGT N6 65 K4
Highgate Wood School CEND/HSY/T N8 66 C2
Highgrove Pool RSLP HA4 58 E4
Highlands J & I School IL IG1 71 K5
Highlands Primary School IL IG1 71 K5
Highshore School PECK SE15 143 G2
High View Primary School BTSEA SW11 140 C5
Highview Primary School WLGTN SM6 210 E3
The Highway Primary School ORP BR6 217 J3
The Highway Trading Centre WAP E1W 105 F6
Hillbrook Primary School TOOT SW17 160 E6
Hillcroft College SURB KT6 191 F3
Hillcross Primary School MRDN SM4 193 J1
Hill House School CHEL SW3 120 D6
Hill Mead Infant School BRXN/ST SW9 142 C5
Hillmead Primary School BRXN/ST SW9 142 C5
Hills Grove Primary School WELL DA16 148 D1
Hillside Primary School NTHWD HA6 40 E3
Hilly Fields Medical Centre BROCKY SE4 144 D6
The Hiltongrove Business Centre WALTH E17 69 J1
Hinchley Wood School ESH/CLAY KT10 190 B6
Hinley Clinic LBTH SE11 18 A7
Hispaniola WHALL SW1A 17 F1
Hitherfield Primary School STRHM/NOR SW16 162 B4
Hither Green Cemetery CAT SE6 165 J4
Hither Green Primary School LEW SE13 165 G1
HM Prison BRXS/STRHM SW2 161 K1
HOLWY N7 84 E2
HOLWY N7 85 F4
WAND/EARL SW18 160 C1
THMD SE28 127 K3
SHB W12 99 J5
HMS Belfast MON EC3R 13 H7
HMS President EMB EC4Y 11 K5
HM Young Offender Institution FELT TW13 153 G5
Hobbayne First & Middle School HNWL W7 97 F5
Hobbayne Primary School HNWL W7 96 E5
Hogarth Business Park CHSWK W4 118 B6
Hogarth Industrial Estate WLSDN NW10 99 J3
Hogarth Primary School CHSWK W4 118 B5
Hogarth's House CHSWK W4 118 A6
Holbeach Primary School CAT SE6 164 D2
Holborn College WKENS W14 119 H6
Holborn Medical Centre BMSBY WC1N 5 G7
Holborn Town Hall HHOL WC1V 11 F3
Holland House School EDGE HA8 30 C6
Holland Park School KENS W8 119 J2
Holland Park Theatre KENS W8 119 J2
Holland Street Clinic KENS W8 119 K2
Hollickwood JMI School MUSWH N10 48 B3
Holloway School HOLWY N7 84 D3
Hollydale Primary School PECK SE15 143 K3
The Hollyfield School SURB KT6 191 F2
Holly House Private Hospital BKHH IG9 39 F4
Hollymount Primary School RYNPK SW20 177 F4
Holly Park JMI School FBAR/BDGN N11 34 A6
Holmefield Preparatory School SUT SM1 208 E3
The Holme CAMTN NW1 3 F5
Holmleigh Primary School STNW/STAM N16 68 B5
Holy Cross Convent School NWMAL KT3 192 A1
Holy Cross Preparatory School KUTN/CMB KT2 175 K3
Holy Cross Primary School FUL/PGN SW6 139 K2
Holy Cross RC Primary School CAT SE6 165 F3
Holy Family College WALTH E17 52 A6
Holy Family RC Primary School BKHTH/KID SE3 146 A5
POP/IOD E14 105 J6
Holy Family Technology College WALTH E17 69 K1
Holy Ghost RC Primary School BAL SW12 160 E2
Holy Innocents Catholic Primary School ORP BR6 217 F1
Holy Trinity CE First School WIM/MER SW19 177 K2
Holy Trinity CE Junior School WLGTN SM6 210 C2
Holy Trinity CE Primary School BGVA SW1W 15 G6
BRXS/STRHM SW2 162 A2
DART DA1 151 F6
EFNCH N2 47 H6
FSTH SE23 163 K4
KIL/WHAMP NW6 83 G4
NTHWD HA6 40 A2
RCHPK/HAM TW10 137 H5
Holy Trinity College BMLY BR1 184 B4
Holy Trinity Haverstock Hill CE Primary School CAMTN NW1 84 B5
Holy Trinity Lamorbey CE Primary School BFN/LL DA15 168 B3
Holy Trinity Primary School HACK E8 86 B4
Holy Trinity School CHEL SW3 15 F6
Holywell School WATW WD18 26 D1
Home Park Golf Club E/WMO/HCT KT8 190 D2
Homerton Hospital CLPT E5 87 F3
Homerton House School HOM E9 86 E3
Homoeopathic Health Centre PLSTW E13 106 E3
The Homoeopathic Health Centre MLHL NW7 45 H1
Honeypot Business Centre STAN HA7 44 A4
Honeypot Lane Centre STAN HA7 43 K4
Honeypot Medical Centre STAN HA7 44 A5
Honeywell Primary School BTSEA SW11 160 E1
Hong Kong & Shanghai Sports Club BECK BR3 182 B2
Honor Oak Crematorium FSTH SE23 144 A6
Honor Oak Gallery FSTH SE23 164 A1
Honor Oak Health Centre BROCKY SE4 144 B5
Honourable Artillery Company Hq STLK EC1Y 6 E7
Hook Lane Primary School WELL DA16 148 B4
Hook Rise South Industrial Park CHSGTN KT9 206 C1
Horizon Business Centre ED N9 37 F4
Horizon Industrial Estate PECK SE15 123 H6
Horizon School STNW/STAM N16 86 A2
The Horniman Museum & Gardens FSTH SE23 163 J3
Horniman Primary School FSTH SE23 163 J3
Horn Park Primary School LEE/GVPK SE12 166 A2
Hornsby House School BAL SW12 161 F3
Hornsey Central Hospital CEND/HSY/T N8 66 C2
Hornsey County School FSBYPK N4 67 H2
Hornsey Rise Health Centre ARCH N19 66 D4
Hornsey School for Girls CEND/HSY/T N8 67 F2
Horseferry Road Magistrates Court WEST SW1P 16 D5
Horse Guards Parade WHALL SW1A 16 D1
Horsenden Hill Golf Club GFD/PVL UB6 79 H4
Horsenden Primary School GFD/PVL UB6 78 E4
Horton Country Park HOR/WEW KT19 206 C6
Horton Industrial Park WDR/YW UB7 112 C1
Horton Park Golf & Country Club HOR/WEW KT19 206 E5
Hortus Cemetery NWDGN UB2 114 E2
Hospital of St John & St. Elizabeth STJWD NW8 2 A3
Hotham Primary School PUT/ROE SW15 139 G5
Hotspur Industrial Estate TOTM N17 50 D2
Houndsfield Primary School ED N9 36 C2
Hounslow Business Park HSLW TW3 135 F5
Hounslow Cemetery HSLWW TW4 154 E2
Hounslow College Independent School FELT TW13 154 C6
Hounslow Cricket Club HSLW TW3 134 E3
Hounslow Heath Golf Club HSLWW TW4 134 C6
Hounslow Heath Infant School HSLWW TW4 134 D4
Hounslow Heath Junior School HSLWW TW4 134 D4
Hounslow Manor School HSLW TW3 135 G4
Hounslow Manor Sports Hall HSLW TW3 135 G4
Hounslow Town Primary School HSLW TW3 135 H4
House of Detention CLKNW EC1R 5 K6
House of St Barnabus SOHO/SHAV W1D 10 C4
Houses of Parliament WEST SW1P 17 F3
Houston Business Park YEAD UB4 114 B1
Howard Primary School CROY/NA CR0 211 J2
Howland Quay BERM/RHTH SE16 124 A3
Hoxton Hall Community Theatre IS N1 7 G2
HQS Wellington (Master Mariners) TPL/STR WC2R 11 J6
Hubbinet Industrial Estate ROMW/RG RM7 56 E6
Hughesfields Primary School DEPT SE8 124 D6
Hugh Myddelton Primary School CLKNW EC1R 5 K5
The Humana Wellington Hospital STJWD NW8 2 B4
Humber Trading Estate CRICK NW2 63 K6
Hungerford Primary School HOLWY N7 84 D4
Hunters Hall Primary School DAGE RM10 92 D3
Hunter Street Health Centre STPAN WC1H 4 E6
Huntsman Sports Club BKHTH/KID SE3 145 K5
Hurlingham Business Park FUL/PGN SW6 139 K4
Hurlingham & Chelsea School FUL/PGN SW6 139 K4
Hurlingham House FUL/PGN SW6 139 J4
Hurlingham Private School PUT/ROE SW15 139 J5
Huron University SKENS SW7 14 B4
Hurricane Trading Centre CDALE/KGS NW9 45 H4
Hurstmere School BFN/LL DA15 168 C3
Hurst Park School E/WMO/HCT KT8 173 F6
Hurst Primary School BXLY DA5 168 E3
The Hyde Industrial Estate CDALE/KGS NW9 63 H2
The Hyde School CDALE/KGS NW9 63 H2
Hyland House School WALTH E17 52 B5
Hyleford Leavers Unit School BARK/HLT IG6 54 D5
Hyleford School IL IG1 90 E3
Hythe Road Industrial Estate WLSDN NW10 99 J3
Ian Mikardo High School BOW E3 105 K2
Ibstock Place School PUT/ROE SW15 158 B1
ICA Cinema STJS SW1Y 16 D1
Ichthus Primary School CMBW SE5 142 E1
Ickburgh School CLPT E5 86 D1
Ickenham Clinic HGDN/ICK UB10 76 A1
Ihlara Sport FC HBRY N5 85 J2
Ikra Primary School STNW/STAM N16 86 A2
Ilderton Primary School BERM/RHTH SE16 123 K6
Ilford County Court IL IG1 72 D6
Ilford County High School BARK/HLT IG6 54 C5
Ilford Golf Club IL IG1 71 K5
Ilford Jewish Primary School BARK/HLT IG6 54 D6
Ilford Medical Centre IL IG1 90 B1
Ilford Preparatory School GDMY/SEVK IG3 73 F5
Ilford Retail Park IL IG1 72 C6
Ilford Swimming Pool IL IG1 72 D6
Imber Court Trading Estate E/WMO/HCT KT8 189 J3
Immanuel CE Primary School STRHM/NOR SW16 179 K2
Immanuel College BUSH WD23 28 E2
Immanuel School ROM RM1 57 G2
Imperial College PUT/ROE SW15 139 G3
SKENS SW7 14 A4
Imperial College Athletic Ground WDR/YW UB7 113 F6
Imperial College of Science FUL/PGN SW6 119 K6
Imperial College of Science & Technology SKENS SW7 14 B3
Imperial College School of Medicine PIM SW1V 16 C7
Imperial War Museum STHWK SE1 17 K5
Imperial War Museum Annexe STHWK SE1 17 K5
Independent Industrial Estate WDR/YW UB7 112 C1
Independent Jewish School HDN NW4 64 B2
India House HOL/ALD WC2B 11 G5
Infant College IL IG1 72 A6
Innellan House School PIN HA5 41 H6
Inner London Sessions House (Crown Court) STHWK SE1 18 C4
Inner Temple EMB EC4Y 11 K5
Innholders Hall CANST EC4R 12 D5
Inns of Court and Chancery TPL/STR WC2R 11 J4
Inns of Court School of Law GINN WC1R 11 H1
Institut Francais SKENS SW7 14 A6
International Community School CAMTN NW1 3 G7
International Financial Centre OBST EC2N 13 G3
International Rail Terminal STHWK SE1 17 H2
International School of London ACT W3 117 H4
International Trading Estate NWDGN UB2 114 A3
Invicta Industrial Estate SRTFD E15 106 A2
Invicta Primary School BKHTH/KID SE3 125 K6
Invicta Sports Club DART DA1 151 G6
Inwood Business Centre HSLW TW3 135 G5
IQRA Independent School BRXN/ST SW9 142 B4

Ironmonger Row Baths *FSBYE* EC1V 6 C5
Ironmongers Hall *STBT* EC1A 12 C2
Islamia Girls School *KIL/WHAMP* NW6 82 C6
Islamic College for Advanced Studies *WLSDN* NW10 81 K5
The Islamic Grammar School *WAND/EARL* SW18 159 J2
Island Clinic *POP/IOD* E14 125 F2
Isleworth Blue CE Primary School *ISLW* TW7 136 B4
Isleworth Cemetery *ISLW* TW7 136 B3
Isleworth Recreation Centre *ISLW* TW7 136 A5
Isleworth & Syon School for Boys *ISLW* TW7 135 K1
Isleworth Town Primary School *ISLW* TW7 136 A3
Islington Arts & Media School *FSBYPK* N4 67 F5
Islington Business Centre *IS* N1 85 J6
Islington Crematorium *EFNCH* N2 47 J4
Islington Green Medical Centre *IS* N1 85 H6
Islington Green School *IS* N1 6 B1
Islington Tennis Centre *HOLWY* N7 84 E4
Islington Town Hall *IS* N1 85 H5
Ismaili Centre *SKENS* SW7 14 B6
Italia Conti Academy of Theatre Arts *BRXN/ST* SW9 141 K4
Italian Hospital *WEST* SW1P 16 A6
Ithaca College *SKENS* SW7 120 B4
Ivybridge Primary School *TWK* TW1 156 A1
Ivybridge Retail Park *ISLW* TW7 136 A6
Ivydale Primary School *BROCKY* SE4 144 A5
Jack & Jill School *HPTN* TW12 173 F2
WHTN TW2 155 K4
Jack Taylor School *KIL/WHAMP* NW6 83 G6
Jack Tizzard School *FUL/PGN* SW6 139 G2
Jacques Prevert School *WKENS* W14 119 G4
Jamahiriya School *CHEL* SW3 120 D6
James Allens Preparatory Girls School *EDUL* SE22 142 E6
James Dixon Primary School *PGE/AN* SE20 181 H3
Jamestown Mental Health Centre *HAMP* NW3 83 K5
James Wolfe Primary School *GNWCH* SE10 144 E1
Janet Adegoke Leisure Centre *SHB* W12 99 J6
The Japanese School *ACT* W3 98 C6
Japan Green Medical Centre *ACT* W3 117 J1
Jenner Health Centre *FSTH* SE23 164 B3
Jenny Hammond Primary School *WAN* E11 88 C2
Jermyn Street Theatre *STJS* SW1Y 10 B6
Jessop Primary School *HNHL* SE24 142 C5
Jewel Tower *WEST* SW1P 16 E4
Jewish Cemetery *GLDGN* NW11 64 E3
Jewish Community Theatre *CMBW* SE5 142 E4
Jewish Free School *KTTN* NW5 84 D4
The Jewish Museum *CAMTN* NW1 3 J1
FNCH N3 46 E5
Jews College London *HDN* NW4 64 B1
Johanna Primary School *STHWK* SE1 17 J3
John Ball Primary School *BKHTH/KID* SE3 145 H3
John Betts Primary School *HMSMTH* W6 118 D3
John Bramston Primary School *BARK/HLT* IG6 55 G2
John Burns Primary School *BTSEA* SW11 141 F3
John Chilton School *NTHLT* UB5 77 J5
John Dixon Clinic *BERM/RHTH* SE16 123 J3
John Donne Primary School *PECK* SE15 143 J2
John F Kennedy Special School *SRTFD* E15 88 B6
John Keble CE Primary School *WLSDN* NW10 81 H6
John Kelly Boys & Girls Technology College *CRICK* NW2 81 H1
The John Loughborough School *TOTM* N17 50 B5
John Lyon School *RYLN/HDSTN* HA2 60 D5
John Milton Primary School *VX/NE* SW8 141 H1
John Nightingale School *E/WMO/HCT* KT8 172 E6
John Orwell Sports Centre *WAP* E1W 123 H1
John Paul II RC School *WIM/MER* SW19 159 G2
John Perryn Primary School *ACT* W3 99 G4
John Perry Primary School *DAGE* RM10 93 F4
John Roan Lower School *BKHTH/KID* SE3 125 J6
John Roan School *BKHTH/KID* SE3 145 H1
John Ruskin College *SAND/SEL* CR2 213 G5
John Ruskin Primary School *WALW* SE17 122 D6
John Scott Health Centre *FSBYPK* N4 67 J5
John Scurr JMI School *WCHPL* E1 104 E3
John Smith House *WALW* SE17 18 C7
Johnsons Industrial Estate *HYS/HAR* UB3 113 K3
John Stainer Primary School *BROCKY* SE4 144 B4
Joseph Clarke Special School *CHING* E4 52 B2
Joseph Hood Primary School *RYNPK* SW20 177 H5
Joseph Lancaster School *STHWK* SE1 18 D5
Joseph Tritton Primary School *BTSEA* SW11 140 B5
Joydens Wood Infant School *RDART* DA2 170 B6
Joydens Wood Junior School *BXLY* DA5 170 B6
Jubilee Country Park *HAYES* BR2 201 G1
Jubilee JMI School *STNW/STAM* N16 68 C5
Jubilee Market *COVGDN* WC2E 11 F5
Jubilee Primary School *THMD* SE28 109 J6
Jubilee Sports Ground *CHING* E4 38 B6
Julians Primary School *STRHM/NOR* SW16 162 B6
Junior & Youth Centre *POP/IOD* E14 105 H4
Juno Way Industrial Estate *NWCR* SE14 124 A6
JVC Business Park *CRICK* NW2 63 J5
Kangley Business Centre *SYD* SE26 182 C1
Katella Trading Estate *BARK* IG11 108 E2
Katherine Road Medical Centre *FSTGT* E7 89 G4
Keats House Museum *HAMP* NW3 83 H2
Keble Preparatory School *WCHMH* N21 35 G2
Keen Students Supplementary School *WCHPL* E1 104 C4
Keir Hardie Primary School *CAN/RD* E16 106 E4
Keith Davis Cue Sports Club *DAGW* RM9 91 K5
Kelmscott Leisure Centre *WALTH* E17 69 H3
Kelmscott School *WALTH* E17 69 H3
Kelsey Park School *BECK* BR3 182 D6
Kelvin Grove Primary School *SYD* SE26 163 J5
Kelvin Industrial Estate *GFD/PVL* UB6 78 B6
GFD/PVL UB6 96 D2
Kemnal Technology College *STMC/STPC* BR5 186 C3
Kempton Park Racecourse *SUN* TW16 172 A3
Ken Barrington Centre *LBTH* SE11 122 A6
Kender Primary School *NWCR* SE14 143 K2
Kenmont Primary School *WLSDN* NW10 99 J2
Kenmore Park Middle School *KTN/HRWW/W* HA3 43 K6
Kenneth More Theatre *IL* IG1 90 C1
Kensal Rise Primary School *WLSDN* NW10 100 B1
Kensington Ave Primary School *THHTH* CR7 180 B4
Kensington Business Centre *SKENS* SW7 14 D4
Kensington & Chelsea College *NKENS* W10 100 C4
WBPTN SW10 140 B1
Kensington & Chelsea Town Hall *KENS* W8 119 K2
Kensington Leisure Centre *NTGHL* W11 100 B6
Kensington Market *KENS* W8 120 A2
Kensington Palace *KENS* W8 120 A1
Kensington Park School *REGST* W1B 9 K1
Kensington Preparatory School *FUL/PGN* SW6 139 J2
Kensington Primary School *MNPK* E12 89 K4
Kensington School of Business *HCIRC* EC1N 11 K1
Kensington Wharf *WBPTN* SW10 140 C1
Kensit Memorial College *FNCH* N3 46 C5
Kentish Town Church CE Primary School *KTTN* NW5 84 C3
Kentish Town Health Centre *KTTN* NW5 84 C4
Kentish Town Industrial Estate *KTTN* NW5 84 B3
Kentish Town Sports Centre *KTTN* NW5 84 A4
Kenton Clinic *KTN/HRWW/W* HA3 62 A2
Kenton Cricket Club *KTN/HRWW/W* HA3 61 J1
Kent Park Industrial Estate *PECK* SE15 123 J6
Kenwood House *HGT* N6 65 J5
Kerem House School *EFNCH* N2 65 G2
The Kerem School *EFNCH* N2 65 H2
Keston CE Primary School *HAYES* BR2 215 H3
Kew Bridge Steam Museum *BTFD* TW8 117 G5
Kew College *RCH/KEW* TW9 137 H1
Kew Gardens (Royal Botanic Gardens) *RCH/KEW* TW9 137 F2
Kew Palace *RCH/KEW* TW9 137 F1
Kew Retail Park *RCH/KEW* TW9 137 J2
Keyplan & Roxburghe College *FITZ* W1T 4 B7
Keyworth Primary School *WALW* SE17 122 C5
Khalsa College London *HRW* HA1 61 F3
Kidbrooke Park Primary School *BKHTH/KID* SE3 146 B3
Kidbrooke School *BKHTH/KID* SE3 146 C3
Kilburn Park Junior School *KIL/WHAMP* NW6 100 D2
Killick Street Medical Centre *IS* N1 5 G2
Kilmorie Primary School *FSTH* SE23 164 B4
Kimberley Industrial Estate *WALTH* E17 51 H3
Kimpton Industrial Estate *CHEAM* SM3 193 J6
King Alfred School *GLDGN* NW11 65 F5
King Athelstan Primary School *KUT* KT1 175 G6
King Edwards Road Clinic *RSLP* HA4 58 B5
King Edward VII Hospital for Officers *MHST* W1U 9 H1
King Fahad Academy (Boys School & Girls Lower School) *ACT* W3 99 G6
King Fahad Academy (Girls Upper School) *EA* W5 116 D4
The Kingfisher Medical Centre *DEPT* SE8 124 C6
The Kingfisher Sports Centre *KUT* KT1 175 F5
Kingford Community School *PLSTW* E13 107 G3
King George Hospital *GDMY/SEVK* IG3 73 G2
Kingham Industrial Estate *WLSDN* NW10 99 F2
King Henry's Reach Development *BARN* SW13 119 F6
King & Queen Wharf *WAP* E1W 105 F6
Kings Acre Primary School *CLAP* SW4 141 K6
Kings Avenue Medical Centre *GFD/PVL* UB6 96 C5
Kingsbury Green Primary School *CDALE/KGS* NW9 62 D2
Kingsbury High School *CDALE/KGS* NW9 62 D1
Kingsbury Hospital *CDALE/KGS* NW9 62 C1
Kingsbury Tamil School *CDALE/KGS* NW9 44 D6
Kingsbury Trading Estate *CDALE/KGS* NW9 62 E3
Kings College Hospital *CMBW* SE5 142 D4
Kings College London *CMBW* SE5 142 E3
HAMP NW3 82 E2
KENS W8 119 K2
LSQ/SEVD WC2H 11 F4
STHWK SE1 12 B7
STHWK SE1 18 D1
TPL/STR WC2R 11 H5
WBPTN SW10 140 B1
WEST SW1P 16 B6
King's College School *WIM/MER* SW19 177 F2
Kings College School of Medicine & Dentistry *DUL* SE21 162 E1
Kings College Sports Ground *RSLP* HA4 58 C3
King's Cross Station *CAMTN* NW1 4 E3
King's Cross Thameslink Station *FSBYW* WC1X 5 G4
Kingsdale School *DUL* SE21 163 F5
Kings Estate *HCH* RM12 93 J2
Kingsgate Business Centre *KUTN/CMB* KT2 175 F4
Kingsgate Primary School *KIL/WHAMP* NW6 82 E5
Kings Hall Leisure Centre *CLPT* E5 86 E3
Kings Head Theatre *IS* N1 85 G6
Kings House School *RCHPK/HAM* TW10 137 G6
Kingsland Health Centre *HACK* E8 86 B5
Kingsland School *HACK* E8 86 B3
Kingsland Shopping Centre *HACK* E8 86 B4
Kingsley Primary School *CROY/NA* CR0 196 A5
Kings Mall Shopping Centre *HMSMTH* W6 119 F4
Kingsmeadow Athletics Centre *KUT* KT1 175 G6
Kingsmead Primary School *CLPT* E5 87 G2
Kingsmead School *EN* EN1 24 C5
The Kings Oak Private Hospital *ENC/FH* EN2 23 G1
King Solomon High School *BARK/HLT* IG6 54 D5
Kings Private Clinic *GDMY/SEVK* IG3 73 F5
MHST W1U 9 G1
Kings School of English *BECK* BR3 182 C5
Kings Stairs *BERM/RHTH* SE16 123 J2
Kingston Business Centre *CHSGTN* KT9 206 A1
Kingston College of Further Education *KUT* KT1 174 E6
Kingston Crematorium *KUT* KT1 175 H6
Kingston Crown Court *KUT* KT1 174 E6
Kingston Grammar School *KUT* KT1 175 G5
Kingston Hospital NHS Trust *KUTN/CMB* KT2 175 H4
Kingstonian FC *KUT* KT1 175 H6
Kingston University *KUT* KT1 175 F6
KUTN/CMB KT2 176 A1
KUTN/CMB KT2 176 A3
King Street College *HMSMTH* W6 119 F4
Kingsway Business Park *HPTN* TW12 172 E4
Kingsway College *CLKNW* EC1R 5 K6
KTTN NW5 84 B4
STPAN WC1H 5 G5
Kingswood Primary School *WNWD* SE27 162 E6
Kisharon School *GLDGN* NW11 64 D3
KLC School of Design *WBPTN* SW10 140 B2
Knightsbridge Barracks *SKENS* SW7 14 D3
Knightsbridge Medical Centre *KTBR* SW1X 15 F4
Knollmead Primary School *WPK* KT4 191 K6
Knowledge Point School *HOLWY* N7 85 F4
Kobi Nazrul Primary School *WCHPL* E1 104 C5
KP Estate *RAIN* RM13 111 G6
KS Medical Centre *STHL* UB1 96 B6
Kubrick Business Estate *FSTGT* E7 89 F2
Laban Centre *DEPT* SE8 144 E1
Laburnum Health Centre *DAGE* RM10 74 C6
Laburnum Primary School *HACK* E8 7 J1
Lady Bankes Primary School *RSLP* HA4 58 E6
Lady Edens School *KENS* W8 120 A3
The Lady Eleanor Holles School *HPTN* TW12 173 G1
Lady Margaret Primary School *STHL* UB1 95 K4
Lady Margaret School *FUL/PGN* SW6 139 K2
Ladywell Arena *LEW* SE13 164 E1
Ladywell Cemetery *BROCKY* SE4 144 C6
Ladywell Leisure Centre *LEW* SE13 145 F6
Lake Business Centre *TOTM* N17 50 C2
Laker Industrial Estate *BECK* BR3 182 B1
Lambeth Cemetery *TOOT* SW17 178 B1
Lambeth College *CLAP* SW4 141 H6
STHWK SE1 19 H1
Lambeth Crematorium *TOOT* SW17 160 B6
Lambeth Palace *STHWK* SE1 17 G5
Lambs Court *POP/IOD* E14 105 G6
Lamont Business Centre *CROY/NA* CR0 195 K4
Lamorbey Swimming Centre *BFN/LL* DA15 168 B4
Lampton School *HEST* TW5 135 F2
The Lanark Medical Centre *MV/WKIL* W9 101 F2
Lancaster House *WHALL* SW1A 16 A2
Lancasterian Primary School *TOTM* N17 50 A4
Lancaster Road Industrial Estate *EBAR* EN4 21 H6
Lancelot Medical Centre *ALP/SUD* HA0 79 K3
Lanford Obesity Clinic *ED* N9 36 D2
Langbourne Primary School *DUL* SE21 163 F5
Langdon Park Secondary School *POP/IOD* E14 105 K5
Langdon School *EHAM* E6 108 B1
Langford Primary School *FUL/PGN* SW6 140 A3
The Langham School *SEVS/STOTM* N15 67 J1
Langhedge Lane Industrial Estate *UED* N18 50 B2
Langley Park Girls School & Sports Centre *BECK* BR3 198 E2
Langley Park Golf Club *BECK* BR3 199 G3
Langley Park School for Boys *BECK* BR3 198 E3
Langthorne Health Centre *WAN* E11 88 B1
Langthorne Hospital *WAN* E11 88 B2
Lansbury Lawrence Primary School *POP/IOD* E14 105 K5
Lansdowne College *BAY/PAD* W2 101 F6
Lansdowne School *BRXN/ST* SW9 142 A4
La Retraite RC Girls School *BAL* SW12 161 H2
Lark Hall Junior School *CLAP* SW4 141 J3
Lark Hall Primary School *CLAP* SW4 141 J3
Larkshall Business Centre *CHING* E4 38 B4
Larkswood Primary School *CHING* E4 37 K6
Larmenier Infant School *HMSMTH* W6 119 G4
La Sainte Union Convent School *KTTN* NW5 84 A1
La Salette RC Primary School *RAIN* RM13 111 J2
Lasnding Stage *DEPT* SE8 124 D5
Latchmere J & I School *KUTN/CMB* KT2 175 G2
Latchmere Leisure Centre *BTSEA* SW11 140 E3
Lathom Junior School *EHAM* E6 89 J5
Latimer Industrial Estate *SHB* W12 100 A5
Latymer All Saints CE Primary School *ED* N9 36 B4
The Latymer School *ED* N9 36 A4
Latymer Upper School *HMSMTH* W6 118 D4
Launcelot Primary School *BMLY* BR1 165 K6
Laurel Clinic *EA* W5 116 D4
Laurence Haines School *WATW* WD18 26 E1
Lauriston Primary School *HOM* E9 87 F6
Lavender Primary School *ENC/FH* EN2 24 A1
Lawdale Junior School *BETH* E2 104 C2
Lawrence Trading Estate *GNWCH* SE10 125 H4
Lawrence Wharf *BERM/RHTH* SE16 124 C1
Laycock Primary School *IS* N1 85 G4
Lazards Sports Club *SUN* TW16 172 A4
Lea Bridge Industrial Estate *LEY* E10 69 G5
Leadenhall Market *BANK* EC3V 13 G4
Lea Park Trading Estate *LEY* E10 69 H4
Leaside Business Centre *PEND* EN3 25 H3
Leathermarket Gardens *STHWK* SE1 19 G3
Leathersellers Sports Ground *ELTH/MOT* SE9 166 B2
Leathers Hall *HDTCH* EC3A 13 G3
Lea Valley Primary School *TOTM* N17 50 C3
Lea Valley Trading Estate *UED* N18 36 E6
UED N18 51 F2
L'écoles Des Petits *FUL/PGN* SW6 140 A3
Lee Manor Primary School *LEW* SE13 165 H1
Leeside Court *BERM/RHTH* SE16 124 A1
Leeside Trading Estate *TOTM* N17 50 E3
Leesons Primary School *STMC/STPC* BR5 186 B6
Lee Valley Campsite *CHING* E4 25 K3
Lee Valley Ice Centre *LEY* E10 69 F6
Lee Valley Leisure Centre Camping & Caravan *ED* N9 37 F3
Lee Valley Leisure Golf Club *ED* N9 37 G2
Lee Valley Watersports Centre *CHING* E4 51 G2
The Leigh City Technology College (East Campus) *DART* DA1 171 K3
The Leigh City Technology College (West Campus) *DART* DA1 171 K3
Leigh Close Industrial Estate *NWMAL* KT3 192 A1
Leighton House Museum & Art Gallery *WKENS* W14 119 J3
Lena Gardens Primary School *HMSMTH* W6 119 F3
Leopold Primary School *WLSDN* NW10 81 H5
Leopold Street Clinic *BOW* E3 105 H4
Lesnes Abbey *ABYW* SE2 128 E4
Lesney Park Primary School *ERITH* DA8 130 A6
Lessness Heath Primary School *BELV* DA17 129 H5
Lewin Mead Community Mental Health Centre *STRHM/NOR* SW16 179 J2

Lewis Clinic
CAR SM5 210 A2
Lewisham Bridge Primary School
LEW SE13 144 E4
Lewisham Business Centre
NWCR SE14 124 A6
Lewisham Centre
LEW SE13 145 F4
Lewisham College
DEPT SE8 144 D2
Lewisham Crematorium
CAT SE6 165 J4
The Leys Primary School
DAGE RM10 92 E5
Leyton Business Centre
LEY E10 69 H6
Leyton Cross
DART DA1 170 D4
Leyton FC
LEY E10 69 H5
Leyton Industrial Village
LEY E10 69 F4
Leyton Leisure Centre
LEY E10 69 K4
Leyton Orient FC (Matchroom Stadium)
LEY E10 87 K1
Leytonstone School
WAN E11 70 C3
Leyton VI Form College
LEY E10 70 B3
Leyton Youth Sports Ground
LEY E10 69 K5
The Liberty City Clinic
SDTCH EC2A 7 G6
Liberty II Centre
ROM RM1 75 G1
Liberty Middle School
MTCM CR4 178 D5
Library & Community Centre
BTSEA SW11 140 C4
Lilian Baylis School
LBTH SE11 17 H7
VX/NE SW8 121 K6
Lillian Baylis Theatre
FSBYE EC1V 6 A4
Lillian Bishop School of English
SKENS SW7 14 A6
Lillie Road Fitness Centre
FUL/PGN SW6 119 G6
Limehouse Town Hall
POP/IOD E14 105 H5
Limes Farm Primary School
CHIG IG7 54 D2
Lime Trees Park Golf Club
NTHLT UB5 77 G6
Lincoln Road Clinic
EN EN1 24 C6
Lincoln's Inn
LINN WC2A 11 H3
Linden Bridge School
WPK KT4 207 G1
Linden Lodge School
WIM/MER SW19 159 H3
Lindon Bennett School
FELT TW13 172 C1
Linford Christie Stadium
SHB W12 99 J4
The Link Day Primary School
CROY/NA CR0 210 E2
The Link Secondary School
CROY/NA CR0 211 F2
Links Primary School
TOOT SW17 179 F2
Linley Sambourne House
KENS W8 119 J2
Linnet House Clinic
STJWD NW8 2 C3
Linton Mead Primary School
THMD SE28 109 H6
Lionel Road Primary School
BTFD TW8 117 F4
Lion House School
PUT/ROE SW15 139 G5
Lismarrine Industrial Park
BORE WD6 29 H1
Lisson Grove Health Centre
STJWD NW8 2 C6
Lister Community School
PLSTW E13 107 F1
The Lister Hospital
BGVA SW1W 121 G5
Lister House Clinic
CAVSQ/HST W1G 9 J3
Little Angel Theatre
IS N1 85 H6
Little Danson Welfare Clinic
WELL DA16 148 B5
Little Eden & Eden High School
FELT TW13 154 C6
Little Furze School
OXHEY WD19 27 F5
Little Hands Theatre
HDN NW4 64 A1
Little Heath School
CHDH RM6 73 H1
Little Ilford School
MNPK E12 89 K3
Little St Helens School
NTHWD HA6 40 D2
Little Stanmore First & Middle School
EDGE HA8 44 A4
Little Venice Medical Centre
MV/WKIL W9 101 G3
Little Wandsworth School
TOOT SW17 161 F4
Liverpool Street Station
LVPST EC2M 13 G1
Livesey Museum for Children
PECK SE15 123 J6
Livingstone Hospital
DART DA1 171 J2
Livingstone Primary School
EBAR EN4 21 H4
Lloyd's
BANK EC3V 13 G4
Lloyds Register Cricket Club
DUL SE21 162 E3
Locks View Court
POP/IOD E14 105 G6
Lockwood Industrial Park
TOTM N17 50 D6
Lombard Business Centre
BTSEA SW11 140 C3
Lombard Business Park
CROY/NA CR0 196 A4
WAND/EARL SW18 160 C1
WIM/MER SW19 178 B5
Lombard Trading Estate
CHARL SE7 126 A4
Lombardy Retail Park
HYS/HAR UB3 95 F6
London Academy of Music & Dramatic Art
HMSMTH W6 119 G5
London Aquarium
STHWK SE1 17 G3
London Area Terminal Control Centre
WDR/YW UB7 112 C2
London Arena
POP/IOD E14 124 E3
London Balloon
LBTH SE11 122 A5
London Bible College
NTHWD HA6 40 B2
London Bridge City Pier
MON EC3R 13 G7
London Bridge Hospital
STHWK SE1 13 F7
London Bridge Sports Centre
CANST EC4R 12 E6
London Bridge Station
STHWK SE1 19 G1
London Broncos RLFC (Griffin Park)
BTFD TW8 116 E6
London Business School
CAMTN NW1 2 E6
The London Canal Museum
IS N1 5 F2
London Capital College
CAMTN NW1 84 B6
London Chest Hospital
BETH E2 104 E1
London City Airport
CAN/RD E16 126 D1
London City College
STHWK SE1 17 J1
London City Mission
STHWK SE1 19 H2
The London Clinic
MHST W1U 3 H7
London College of Business & Computing
BETH E2 104 D1
London College of Fashion
CAVSQ/HST W1G 9 K3
MHST W1U 9 H4
SDTCH EC2A 7 H6
London College of Further Education
LBTH SE11 18 A7
London College of Higher Education
CLAP SW4 141 G4
London College of International Business Studies
HHOL WC1V 11 F2
London College of Printing
LBTH SE11 18 B5
The London College
KENS W8 119 K1
London Commodity Exchange
WAP E1W 13 K6
London Dungeon
STHWK SE1 13 F7
London Electronics College
ECT SW5 119 K5
London Executive College
TOOT SW17 161 F5
London Eye Clinic
CAVSQ/HST W1G 9 J2
London Fields Primary School
HACK E8 86 D6
London Foot Hospital
FITZ W1T 4 A7
London Gender Clinic
HDN NW4 63 K3
London Group Business Park
CRICK NW2 63 H5
London Guildhall University
LVPST EC2M 13 F2
TWRH EC3N 13 J4
London Guildhall University Sports Ground
LEE/GVPK SE12 166 B4
London Heart Clinic
CAVSQ/HST W1G 9 J2
London Hospital Medical College
WCHPL E1 104 D4
The London Industrial Estate
EHAM E6 108 A4
London Industrial Park
EHAM E6 108 B4
The London Institute
WEST SW1P 121 K5
London International Film School
LSQ/SEVD WC2H 10 E4
The London Irish Youth Theatre
HGT N6 66 B5
London Islamic School/Madrasah
WCHPL E1 104 D5
London Ladies & Girls FC
CAT SE6 182 E1
London Lane Clinic
BMLY BR1 183 J3
London Lighthouse
NTGHL W11 100 C5
London Living Theatre
SYD SE26 164 A6
London Nautical School
STHWK SE1 11 K7
London Open College
FSBYE EC1V 6 B4
London Oratory School
FUL/PGN SW6 139 K1
London Pavilion
REGST W1B 10 C6
London Road Medical Centre
THHTH CR7 196 B3
London School of Economics
HHOL WC1V 10 E3
LINN WC2A 11 H4
STHWK SE1 12 C7
London School of Hygiene & Tropical Medicine
GWRST WC1E 10 D1
London Scottish Golf Club
WIM/MER SW19 158 E5
London Silver Vaults
LINN WC2A 11 J2
The London Television Centre (LWT)
STHWK SE1 11 J7
London Tourist Board & Convention Centre
BGVA SW1W 15 J4
London Toy & Model Museum
BAY/PAD W2 101 G6
London Transport Bus Depot
BXLYHN DA7 149 J4
London Transport Museum
COVGDN WC2E 11 F5
London Underwriting Centre
MON EC3R 13 H5
London Weather Centre
CLKNW EC1R 11 J1
London Welsh FC
RCH/KEW TW9 137 F4
London Welsh School
CRICK NW2 82 A4
London Wetland Centre
BARN SW13 138 E2
London Zoo
CAMTN NW1 3 G2
Lonesome First School
MTCM CR4 179 G5
Long Ditton County Infant School
SURB KT6 190 D5
Long Ditton Ferry
THDIT KT7 190 C3
Longfield Primary School
RYLN/HDSTN HA2 60 A3
Longford Community School
EBED/NFELT TW14 153 J2
Longford Industrial Estate
HPTN TW12 173 G2
Longlands Primary School
BFN/LL DA15 167 K5
Long Lane AFC
BKHTH/KID SE3 146 B3
Longmead Primary School
WDR/YW UB7 112 A3
Longshaw Primary School
CHING E4 38 B5
Lord Lister Health Centre
FSTGT E7 88 E2
Lordship Lane Clinic
TOTM N17 50 A5
Lordship Lane Primary School
WDGN N22 49 J4
Lord's Tour & MCC Museum
STJWD NW8 2 A5
Lorimar Business Centre
RAIN RM13 111 G5
Loughborough Primary School
BRXN/ST SW9 142 C3
Lovelace Primary School
CHSGTN KT9 205 J3
Lovell's Wharf
GNWCH SE10 125 G5
Lower Clapton Health Centre
CLPT E5 86 E3
Lower Place Business Centre
WLSDN NW10 98 E1
Lower Sydenham Industrial Estate
CAT SE6 182 C1
Lowfield Medical Centre
DART DA1 171 H2
Low Hall Sports Ground
WALTH E17 69 F3
Lowther Primary School
BARN SW13 118 D6
Loxford School of Science and Technology
IL IG1 90 D3
Loyola Preparatory School
BKHH IG9 39 G3
LPR Sports Club
BARK/HLT IG6 55 F4
LSE Sports Club
NWMAL KT3 192 A3
LT Lost Property Office
CAMTN NW1 3 F7
LTR Depot
SHB W12 119 G1
Lubavitch House School
STNW/STAM N16 68 B4
Lucas Vale Primary School
DEPT SE8 144 D2
Lucie Clayton Secretarial/ Fashion Design College
KENS W8 120 B3
Lutomer House Business Centre
POP/IOD E14 124 E1
Lux Cinema
IS N1 7 G5
Lycee Francais
SKENS SW7 14 A6
The Lyceum Theatre
TPL/STR WC2R 11 G5
Lyndean Industrial Estate
ABYW SE2 128 D3
Lyndhurst House Preparatory School
HAMP NW3 83 H3
Lyndhurst Primary School
CMBW SE5 142 E3
Lyon Business Park
BARK IG11 108 E1
Lyon Park J & I School
ALP/SUD HA0 80 B5
Lyonsdown School
BAR EN5 21 G6
Lyric Theatre
HMSMTH W6 119 F4
SOHO/SHAV W1D 10 C5
Mabwin Supplementary School
ED N9 36 D4
Macaulay CE Primary School
CLAP SW4 141 G5
Madame Tussaud's
CAMTN NW1 3 G7
Madeira Grove Clinic
WFD IG8 53 F1
Madison Bowl
NTHWD HA6 40 C3
Madni Girls School
WCHPL E1 104 D5
Mahatma Gandhi Industrial Estate
BRXN/ST SW9 142 C4
Maida Vale Hospital
STJWD NW8 101 G2
Maida Vale Medical Centre
MV/WKIL W9 101 F2
Malcolm Primary School
PGE/AN SE20 181 K3
The Malden Centre
NWMAL KT3 192 C1
Malden Golf Club
NWMAL KT3 176 B5
Malden Manor Junior School
NWMAL KT3 192 B4
Malden Parochial Primary School
WPK KT4 192 B5
Malden Road Baths
CHEAM SM3 208 B2
Malham Road Industrial Estate
FSTH SE23 164 A3
Mall Galleries
STJS SW1Y 10 D7
The Mall School
WHTN TW2 155 J5
Malmesbury Middle School
MRDN SM4 194 B3
Malmesbury Primary School
BOW E3 105 H2
MRDN SM4 194 B4
Malorees J & I School
KIL/WHAMP NW6 82 B5
Malory School
BMLY BR1 165 K6
Mandeville Primary School
CLPT E5 87 G1
Mandeville Special School
NTHLT UB5 77 K4
Manford Industrial Estate
ERITH DA8 130 E6
Manford Way Health Centre
BARK/HLT IG6 55 F2
Manor Brook Medical Centre
BKHTH/KID SE3 146 A3
Manor Drive Health Centre
WPK KT4 192 C5
Manorfield Primary School
POP/IOD E14 105 K4
Manor House Hospital
GLDGN NW11 65 F5
Manor House School
HNWL W7 96 E6
Manor Infant School
BARK IG11 91 F4
Manor Oak Primary School
STMC/STPC BR5 202 E2
Manor Park Cemetery
FSTGT E7 89 H2
Manor Park Crematorium
FSTGT E7 89 G2
Manor Park Methodist School
MNPK E12 89 J2
Manor Park Primary School
SUT SM1 209 G3
Manor Primary School
SRTFD E15 106 C1
The Manor Primary School
ROM RM1 75 H2
Manorside Primary School
FNCH N3 47 F4
Manor Special School
WLSDN NW10 100 B1
Manor Way Business Centre
DAGW RM9 111 F4
Mansion House
MANHO EC4N 12 E4
Mapledown School
CRICK NW2 64 B4
Maple Grove Business Centre
HSLWW TW4 134 B5
Maple Industrial Estate
FELT TW13 153 K4
Maple Infant School
SURB KT6 190 E2
Maples Business Centre
IS N1 85 G5
Marble Arch
BAY/PAD W2 9 F5
Marble Hill House
TWK TW1 156 D2
Maria Fidelis Convent Lower School
CAMTN NW1 4 B5
Maria Fidelis Convent Upper School
CAMTN NW1 4 C4
Marion Richardson Primary School
WCHPL E1 105 F5
Marion Vian Primary School
BECK BR3 198 A2
Maritime Industrial Estate
CHARL SE7 126 A4
Maritime Museum
GNWCH SE10 125 H4
The Marjory Kinnon School
EBED/NFELT TW14 133 H6
The Market
COVGDN WC2E 11 F5
Market Trading Estate
NWDGN UB2 114 A4
Marks Gate Junior School
CHDH RM6 56 A6
Marlborough Cricket Club
DUL SE21 163 H3
Marlborough Day Hospital
STJWD NW8 101 G1
Marlborough First & Middle School
HRW HA1 60 E1
Marlborough House
STJS SW1Y 16 B1
Marlborough Park School
BFN/LL DA15 168 B3
Marlborough Primary School
CHEL SW3 14 D7
ISLW TW7 136 B2
Marlborough Trading Estate
RCH/KEW TW9 137 J2
Marlowe Business Centre
NWCR SE14 144 B1
Marner Primary School
BOW E3 105 K3
Marshalls Park School
ROM RM1 57 G5
Marshall Street Leisure Centre
SOHO/CST W1F 10 B4
Marsh Gate Business Centre
SRTFD E15 106 A1
Marshgate Trading Estate
SRTFD E15 87 K5
Marsh Green School
DAGW RM9 110 C1
Martan College
HOL/ALD WC2B 11 F3
Martinbridge Industrial Estate
EN EN1 24 C6
Martindale Industrial Estate
EN EN1 24 A6
Martin Infant School
EFNCH N2 47 J5
Marvels Lane Primary School
LEE/GVPK SE12 166 B6
Mary Boone School
WKENS W14 119 H4
Maryland Industrial Estate
SRTFD E15 88 C3
Maryland Primary School
SRTFD E15 88 C3
Marylebone Health Centre
MHST W1U 3 H7
Marylebone Magistrates Court
CAMTN NW1 8 D1
Marylebone Station
CAMTN NW1 2 D7
Marymount International School
KUTN/CMB KT2 175 K3
Mary Wallace Theatre
TWK TW1 156 B3
Maswell Park Health Centre
HSLW TW3 135 H6
Matilda Marks School
MLHL NW7 45 F1
Matrix Business Centre
DART DA1 151 H6
The Maudsley Hospital
CMBW SE5 142 E3
Mawbrey Brough Health Centre
VX/NE SW8 141 K1
The Mawney School
ROMW/RG RM7 75 F2
Mayday University Hospital
THHTH CR7 196 C3
Mayesbrook Park Arena
BCTR RM8 91 G3
Mayespark Primary School
GDMY/SEVK IG3 91 G1
Mayfair Medical Centre
MYFR/PKLN W1K 9 H4
Mayfield Primary School
GFD/PVL UB6 96 D5
Mayfield School
PIN HA5 41 J6
Mayfield School & College
BCTR RM8 73 J5
Mayflower Primary School
POP/IOD E14 105 J5
Mayplace Primary School
BXLYHN DA7 150 A5
Maypole Primary School
BXLY DA5 170 B4
Maytime School
IL IG1 90 A1
Mayville Infant School
WAN E11 88 C1
Mayville Junior School
WAN E11 70 C6
Maze Hill School
GNWCH SE10 125 H6
Mazenod RC Primary School
KIL/WHAMP NW6 82 E5
McEntee School
WALTH E17 51 H4
McKay Trading Estate
NKENS W10 100 C3
McMillan Clinic
HYS/HAR UB3 94 A6
MDQ Majidiah (UK)
WCHPL E1 104 D6
The Mead Infant School
HOR/WEW KT19 207 H1
Meadlands Primary School
RCHPK/HAM TW10 156 D6
Meadowgate School
BROCKY SE4 144 A4
Meadowside Leisure Centre
BKHTH/KID SE3 146 B5
Mead Road Infant School
CHST BR7 185 H2
The Medical Centre
BXLYHN DA7 149 K4
Mednurs Clinic
SEVS/STOTM N15 67 K3
Megabowl
BRXS/STRHM SW2 161 K4
Melcombe Primary School
HMSMTH W6 119 G6
Mellish Industrial Estate
WOOL/PLUM SE18 126 C3
Mellow Lane School
YEAD UB4 94 A3
Melrose Special School
MTCM CR4 178 D6
Memorial Hospital
WOOL/PLUM SE18 147 F3
The Menorah Foundation School
EDGE HA8 44 E3
Menorah Grammar School
GLDGN NW11 64 C4
Menorah Primary School
GLDGN NW11 64 C4
Mercers' Hall
CITYW EC2V 12 D4
The Merchant Taylors Hall
BANK EC3V 13 F4
Merchant Taylors School
NTHWD HA6 26 C3
Meridian Clinic
BRXN/ST SW9 142 A4
Meridian Locality Mental Health Centre
CHARL SE7 126 B6
Meridian Primary School
GNWCH SE10 125 G5
Meridian Sports Club
CHARL SE7 126 D6
Meridian Trading Estate
CHARL SE7 126 A4
Merlin Primary School
BMLY BR1 165 K5
Merlin School
PUT/ROE SW15 139 G6
Mermaid Theatre
BLKFR EC4V 12 B5
Merrielands Retail Park
DAGW RM9 92 B6

Merryhills Clinic
ENC/FH EN2 23 F4
Merryhills Primary School
ENC/FH EN2 23 F5
Merton Abbey First School
WIM/MER SW19 178 A4
Merton Adult College
RYNPK SW20 177 H6
Merton College
MRDN SM4 193 J2
Merton Court
Preparatory School
SCUP DA14 168 D6
Merton Industrial Park
WIM/MER SW19 178 B4
Merton Park Primary School
WIM/MER SW19 177 J5
Merton Road Industrial Estate
WAND/EARL SW18 159 K2
Metro Business Centre
SYD SE26 182 C2
The Metro Golf Centre
HDN NW4 46 A4
Metro Industrial Centre
ISLW TW7 135 K3
Metropolitan Business Centre
HACK E8 86 A5
Metropolitan Hospital
STHWK SE1 17 K4
Metropolitan Police FC
E/WMO/HCT KT8 189 J3
Metropolitan Police
Hayes Sports Club
HAYES BR2 199 J6
Metropolitan Police
(Hendon) Track
CDALE/KGS NW9 45 H6
Metropolitan Police
Training School, Hendon
CDALE/KGS NW9 45 H6
Metropolitan Tabernacle
LBTH SE11 18 B6
Metro Trading Centre
WBLY HA9 80 D2
Michael Faraday
Primary School
WALW SE17 122 E5
Michael Manley
Industrial Estate
VX/NE SW8 141 H3
Michael Sobell Sinai School
KTN/HRWW/W HA3 62 C3
The Michael Tippett School
LBTH SE11 17 K7
Midas Business Centre
DAGE RM10 92 C2
Midas Industrial Estate
DAGE RM10 92 C2
Middle Park Primary School
ELTH/MOT SE9 166 C2
Middle Row Primary School
NKENS W10 100 C3
Middlesex Business Centre
NWDGN UB2 115 F2
Middlesex CCC
(Lord's Cricket Ground)
STJWD NW8 2 B4
Middlesex Guildhall
WEST SW1P 16 D3
Middlesex Hospital
GTPST W1W 10 B2
Middlesex Hospital
Medical School
FITZ W1T 10 B1
Middlesex Hospital
Nurses Home
GTPST W1W 10 A1
Middlesex Hospital School
of Physiotherapy
FITZ W1T 10 B1
Middlesex Hospital
Sports Ground
CHST BR7 186 A1
Middlesex University
EBAR EN4 34 A1
GLDGN NW11 65 F5
TOTM N17 50 A2
WDGN N22 48 E5
Middlesex University
Business School
HDN NW4 63 K1
Middle Temple Hall
TPL/STR WC2R 11 J5
Midfield Primary School
CHST BR7 186 B3
Midway Mission Hospital
BETH E2 7 J5
Milbourne Lodge School
ESH/CLAY KT10 204 D4
Mile End &
Bow Business Centre
WCHPL E1 104 D4
Mile End Hospital
WCHPL E1 105 F2
Mile End Stadium
BOW E3 105 H4
Milehams Industrial Estate
PUR RM19 131 K3
Miles Coverdale Primary School
SHB W12 119 F2
Millbank Millennium Pier
WEST SW1P 16 E7
Millbank Primary School
WEST SW1P 16 D7
Millbank Tower
WEST SW1P 16 E7
Millbourne Lodge
Junior School
ESH/CLAY KT10 204 C3
Millennium Arena
BTSEA SW11 141 F1
Millennium Balloon
STHWK SE1 19 H1
Millennium Harbour
Development
BERM/RHTH SE16 124 C2
Millennium Quay
DEPT SE8 124 E6
Millennium Wharf Development
POP/IOD E14 125 G3
Mill Farm Business Park
HSLWW TW4 154 D2
Millfields J & I School
CLPT E5 86 E2
Millfield Theatre
UED N18 35 K6
Mill Green Business Park
MTCM CR4 194 E4
Mill Hill Cemetery
MLHL NW7 46 A2
Mill Hill County High School
MLHL NW7 31 G4
The Mill Hill Cricket Club
MLHL NW7 32 A5
Mill Hill Golf Club
MLHL NW7 31 G4
Mill Hill Industrial Estate
MLHL NW7 45 H2
Mill Hill School
MLHL NW7 31 K6
Mill Lane Medical Centre
KIL/WHAMP NW6 82 E3
Mill Lane Trading Estate
CROY/NA CR0 211 F1
Mill River Trading Estate
PEND EN3 25 G5
Millside Industrial Estate
DART DA1 151 G5
Mill Street Clinic
STHWK SE1 19 K2
Mill Trading Estate
WLSDN NW10 98 D1
Millwall FC (The New Den)
BERM/RHTH SE16 123 K5
Milmead Industrial Centre
TOTM N17 50 D5
Milton Natural Health Centre
HGT N6 66 C4
Minet Clinic
HYS/HAR UB3 113 K1
Minet J & I School
HYS/HAR UB3 114 A1
Ministry of Defence
WHALL SW1A 16 E1
Mini Town Hall
WOOL/PLUM SE18 128 A5
Mint Business Park
CAN/RD E16 106 E4
Mirravale Trading Estate
BCTR RM8 74 A4
Mission Grove Primary School
WALTH E17 69 H1
Mitcham Cricket Club
MTCM CR4 194 D1
Mitcham Golf Club
MTCM CR4 195 F2
Mitcham Industrial Estate
MTCM CR4 179 F4
Mitcham Road Crematorium
THHTH CR7 195 K2
Mitchell Brook Primary School
WLSDN NW10 81 F4
Mitre Bridge Industrial Park
WLSDN NW10 99 K3
Moatbridge School
ELTH/MOT SE9 166 C1
Moberly Sports &
Education Centre
NKENS W10 100 B2
Molesey Hospital
E/WMO/HCT KT8 189 F2
Molesey Lock
E/WMO/HCT KT8 173 K6
Mollison Drive Health Centre
WLGTN SM6 210 E5
Monega Primary School
MNPK E12 89 H3
Monken Hadley CE
Primary School
EBAR EN4 20 E2
Monkfrith Primary School
EBAR EN4 34 A2
Monks Hill Sports Centre
SAND/SEL CR2 213 F5
Monks Orchard Primary School
CROY/NA CR0 198 A2
Monson Primary School
NWCR SE14 144 A1
Montbelle Primary School
ELTH/MOT SE9 167 G5
Monteagle Primary School
DAGW RM9 91 H6
Montem Primary School
HOLWY N7 85 F1
Montpelier Primary School
EA W5 97 K4
The Monument
CANST EC4R 13 F5
Moore Place Golf Club
ESH/CLAY KT10 204 A3
Moorfields Eye Hospital
FSBYE EC1V 6 E5
Moorfields Primary School
STLK EC1Y 6 E6
Moorgate Station
BARB EC2Y 12 E2
Moor Lane Junior School
CHSGTN KT9 206 B3
Moor Park Industrial Estate
WATW WD18 26 A2
Mora Primary School
CRICK NW2 82 A2
Morden Cemetery
MRDN SM4 193 F3
Morden College Homes
BKHTH/KID SE3 145 K3
Morden First School
MRDN SM4 193 K2
Morden Hall Medical Centre
WIM/MER SW19 178 A6
Morden Mount Primary School
LEW SE13 144 E3
Morden Park Pool
MRDN SM4 193 J3
Morden Road Clinic
WIM/MER SW19 178 A6
More House School
ISLW TW7 135 K2
KTBR SW1X 15 F5
Moreland Primary School
FSBYE EC1V 6 B5
Moriah Jewish Day School
PIN HA5 59 J5
Morningside Primary School
HOM E9 86 E4
Mornington Sports &
Fitness Centre
CAMTN NW1 84 B6
Morpeth School
BETH E2 104 E2
Mortimer Road Clinic
WLSDN NW10 100 A2
Mortimer School
STRHM/NOR SW16 161 J4
Mortlake Cemetery
MORT/ESHN SW14 138 B4
Mortlake Crematorium
RCH/KEW TW9 137 J3
Moselle School
TOTM N17 50 A5
Mosiah Foundation
Supplementary School
STNW/STAM N16 68 A5
Mossford Green Primary School
BARK/HLT IG6 54 C5
Moss Hall Primary School
FNCH N3 47 F2
The Mother & Baby Clinic
HOM E9 86 E4
Mottingham Community
Health Clinic
ELTH/MOT SE9 166 D6
Mottingham Primary School
ELTH/MOT SE9 166 E5
Mount Carmel RC
Primary School
EA W5 116 D3
Mount Carmel School
ARCH N19 66 D5
The Mount Infant School
NWMAL KT3 175 J6
Mount Medical Centre
FELT TW13 154 D4
Mount School
MLHL NW7 45 K1
Mount Stewart Primary School
KTN/HRWW/W HA3 61 K3
Mowlem Primary School
BETH E2 104 E1
Mowlem Trading Estate
TOTM N17 50 E3
MS Business Centre
PIN HA5 41 H6
MSP Business Centre
WBLY HA9 80 D2
Mudchute City Farm
POP/IOD E14 125 F4
Mudlands Estate
RAIN RM13 111 G2
Mulberry Business Centre
BERM/RHTH SE16 124 A2
Mulberry House School
CRICK NW2 82 C3
Mulberry School for Girls
WCHPL E1 104 D5
Mulgrave Primary School
WOOL/PLUM SE18 127 F4
WOOL/PLUM SE18 127 G3
Murky Puddle Theatre
NWMAL KT3 176 C6
Murray Business Centre
STMC/STPC BR5 186 C6
Muschamp Primary School
CAR SM5 194 D6
Museum in Docklands
POP/IOD E14 105 J6
Museum of Archaeological
Research Centre
IS N1 6 D1
Museum of Artillery
in the Rotunda
CHARL SE7 126 E5
Museum of Domestic Design &
Architecture
EBAR EN4 21 K6
Museum of Fulham Palace
FUL/PGN SW6 139 G3
Museum of Garden History
STHWK SE1 17 F5
Museum of London
STBT EC1A 12 C2
Museum of London
(Archaeological Research
Centre)
IS N1 6 D2
Museum of Richmond
RCH/KEW TW9 136 E6
Museum of Rugby &
Twickenham Stadium Tours
WHTN TW2 155 K1
Museum of the Order of St John
FARR EC1M 6 B7
Museums of the
Royal College of Surgeons
LINN WC2A 11 H3
The Musical Museum
BTFD TW8 117 F6
Muswell Hill Bowling Club
MUSWH N10 48 A6
Muswell Hill Golf Club
FBAR/BDGN N11 48 B4
Muswell Hill Primary School
MUSWH N10 48 B6
Myatt Garden Primary School
BROCKY SE4 144 C3
Myatts Field Clinic
BRXN/ST SW9 142 C2
Nagi Business Centre
ALP/SUD HA0 97 K1
Nags Head Shopping Centre
HOLWY N7 85 F2
Naima Jewish
Preparatory School
KIL/WHAMP NW6 101 F1
National Army Museum
CHEL SW3 120 E6
National Film Theatre
STHWK SE1 11 H7
National Gallery
LSQ/SEVD WC2H 10 D6
National Hospital for Neurology
& Neurosurgery
BMSBY WC1N 4 E7
National Hospital for Sick Children
(Great Ormond St)
BMSBY WC1N 5 F7
National Maritime Museum
GNWCH SE10 125 G6
National Physical Laboratory
TEDD TW11 173 K2
National Portrait Gallery
LSQ/SEVD WC2H 10 D6
National Temperance Hospital
CAMTN NW1 4 B5
National Youth Theatre of GB
HOLWY N7 84 E1
Natural History Museum
SKENS SW7 14 A5
Natural Therapy Clinic
TOOT SW17 179 G1
Natwest Sports Club
BECK BR3 182 C2
Navigation College
MANHO EC4N 12 D5
NEC Harlequins RFC (The Stoop
Memorial Ground)
WHTN TW2 155 K2
Negus 6th Form Centre
WOOL/PLUM SE18 127 J6
Nelson Dock Museum
BERM/RHTH SE16 124 C1
Nelson Hospital
WIM/MER SW19 177 J5
Nelson Primary School
EHAM E6 108 A1
WHTN TW2 155 G1
Nelson's Column
CHCR WC2N 10 E7
Nelson Trading Estate
WIM/MER SW19 178 A4
Neo Clinic
PIM SW1V 16 A7
Netley Primary School
CAMTN NW1 4 A5
The New Ambassadors Theatre
LSQ/SEVD WC2H 10 E4
New Atlas Wharf Development
BERM/RHTH SE16 124 C3
New Brentford Cemetery
HSLW TW3 134 E3
Newbury Park Health Centre
GNTH/NBYPK IG2 72 D3
Newbury Park Primary School
GNTH/NBYPK IG2 72 D3
The New Business Centre
WLSDN NW10 99 H2
New Caledonian Wharf
BERM/RHTH SE16 124 C3
New Chiswick Pool
CHSWK W4 138 B1
New City Primary School
PLSTW E13 107 G2
New Connaught Rooms
HOL/ALD WC2B 11 F3
New Covent Garden Market
VX/NE SW8 121 J6
New Crane Wharf
WAP E1W 123 K1
New Cross Sports Arena
NWCR SE14 144 B1
New End Primary School
HAMP NW3 83 G2
New End Theatre
HAMP NW3 83 G1
New England Industrial Estate
BARK IG11 108 C1
Newfield Primary School
WLSDN NW10 81 H5
The New Furness
Primary School
WLSDN NW10 99 J1
Newham College of
Further Education
EHAM E6 107 K1
SRTFD E15 88 C5
Newham Community College
CAN/RD E16 106 C3
Newham General Hospital
PLSTW E13 107 G3
Newham Leisure Centre
PLSTW E13 107 G4
Newham Medical Centre
PLSTW E13 107 G1
Newham Sixth Form College
PLSTW E13 107 F3
New Health Centre
TOTM N17 50 A4
Newington Court
Business Centre
STHWK SE1 18 C5
Newington Green
Primary School
STNW/STAM N16 86 A3
Newington Industrial Estate
WALW SE17 18 B7
New Kings Primary School
FUL/PGN SW6 139 J3
Newland House School
TWK TW1 156 A6
New London Theatre
LSQ/SEVD WC2H 11 F3
Newnham J & I School
RSLP HA4 59 G5
Newport J & I School
LEY E10 70 A6
New River Stadium
WDGN N22 49 H3
New Rush Hall School
IL IG1 72 C6
New School
FUL/PGN SW6 139 J2
New Scotland Yard
STJSPK SW1H 16 C4
News International
WAP E1W 104 D6
New Southgate Cemetery
FBAR/BDGN N11 34 B5
New Southgate Crematorium
FBAR/BDGN N11 34 B5
New Southgate Industrial Estate
FBAR/BDGN N11 48 C1
New Southgate Pain Clinic &
Medical Centre
FBAR/BDGN N11 48 C1
New Spitalfields Market
LEY E10 87 J1
Newstead Wood
School for Girls
ORP BR6 216 D1
Newton Farm First &
Middle School
RYLN/HDSTN HA2 59 K6
Newton Industrial Estate
CHDH RM6 73 K1
Newton Medical Centre
BAY/PAD W2 101 F5
Newton Preparatory School
VX/NE SW8 141 G1
Newtons Primary School
RAIN RM13 111 F1
New Victoria Hospital
KUTN/CMB KT2 176 B3
New Woodlands School
BMLY BR1 165 H6
New York University in London
RSQ WC1B 10 D2
Nightingale Clinic
PLSTW E13 107 G1
Nightingale Primary School
CLPT E5 86 C2
SWFD E18 71 G1
WDGN N22 48 E4
WOOL/PLUM SE18 127 G5
Nightingale School
STHWK SE1 17 G3
TOOT SW17 160 D4
Nineacres School
WOOL/PLUM SE18 127 J5
Noel Park Primary School
WDGN N22 49 H5
Nonsuch High School for Girls
EW KT17 208 B5
Nonsuch Primary School
EW KT17 207 K3
Norbury Complementary
Therapy Clinic
STRHM/NOR SW16 180 A4
Norbury First & Middle School
HRW HA1 60 E2
Norbury Health Centre
STRHM/NOR SW16 180 A5
Norbury Manor Primary School
STRHM/NOR SW16 179 K4
Norbury Manor Secondary
Girls School
STRHM/NOR SW16 180 A4
Norbury Trading Estate
STRHM/NOR SW16 180 A5
Norfolk House School
MUSWH N10 48 B5
Norland Place School
NTGHL W11 119 H1
Norlington School
WAN E11 70 B5
Normand Park Primary School
WKENS W14 119 J6
Normandy Primary School
ERITH DA8 150 A2
Normanhurst School
CHING E4 38 B2
Norman Park Athletics Track
HAYES BR2 200 A3
Norman Shaw Building
(MP's Offices)
WHALL SW1A 16 E2
North Acton Business Park
ACT W3 99 F5
North Beckton Primary School
EHAM E6 107 K4
North Bridge House
HAMP NW3 83 G4
North Bridge House School
HAMP NW3 83 H4
North Bridge House
Senior School
CAMTN NW1 3 J1
Northbrook CE School
LEW SE13 145 H6
Northbury Primary School
BARK IG11 90 B4
North Clinic
BMLY BR1 183 K4
Northcote Lodge School
BTSEA SW11 160 D1
North Cray Primary School
SCUP DA14 187 F2
North Croydon Medical Centre
THHTH CR7 196 C3
North Ealing Primary School
WEA W13 97 H3
North East Surrey Crematorium
NWMAL KT3 193 F3
Northend Primary School
ERITH DA8 150 C2
North End Trading Estate
ERITH DA8 150 B1
North Feltham Trading Estate
EBED/NFELT TW14 134 A5
Northfields Industrial Estate
ALP/SUD HA0 80 C6
Northfields Prospect
Business Centre
WAND/EARL SW18 139 J5
Northgate Business Centre
EN EN1 24 D4
Northgate Clinic
CDALE/KGS NW9 63 G3
Northgate Industrial Park
ROMW/RG RM7 56 B5
North Harringey
Primary School
CEND/HSY/T N8 67 G1
North Havering College of
Adult Education
ROM RM1 75 G1
North London Collegiate School
EDGE HA8 44 A2
The North London Hospice
NFNCH/WDSP N12 33 F5
North London School of
Physiotherapy
ARCH N19 66 C5
North London Tutorial College
HDN NW4 64 A3
North Middlesex Golf Club
TRDG/WHET N20 33 H5
North Middlesex Hospital
UED N18 50 A1
Northolt Aerodrome
RSLP HA4 76 E4
Northolt High School
NTHLT UB5 77 K4
Northolt Park Infant School
NTHLT UB5 78 B3
Northolt Primary School
NTHLT UB5 77 H5
Northolt Road Clinic
RYLN/HDSTN HA2 78 C1
Northolt Swimarama
NTHLT UB5 78 A4
North Primary School
STHL UB1 95 K6
Northside Primary
NFNCH/WDSP N12 47 F1
The North Street Health Centre
CLAP SW4 141 H4
Northumberland Heath
Medical Centre
ERITH DA8 150 A1
Northumberland Heath
Primary School
ERITH DA8 149 J1
Northumberland
Park Industrial Estate
TOTM N17 50 D2
Northumberland Park School
TOTM N17 50 C3
Northview Primary School
WLSDN NW10 81 G2

Northway School
MLHL NW7 30 E5
North West Kent College of Technology
DART DA1 171 F2
North West London Jewish J & I School
CRICK NW2 82 C5
North West London Medical Centre
MV/WKIL W9 101 G2
North Westminster Community School
BAY/PAD W2 8 A2
STJWD NW8 8 C1
North Westminster Community Secondary School
MV/WKIL W9 100 E3
North Weylands Industrial Estate
WOT/HER KT12 188 D6
Northwick Park Hospital & Clinical Research Centre
HRW HA1 61 H4
Northwold Primary School
CLPT E5 68 C6
Northwood Cemetery
NTHWD HA6 40 D5
Northwood College
NTHWD HA6 40 B3
Northwood FC
NTHWD HA6 40 D5
Northwood Golf Club
NTHWD HA6 40 B3
Northwood & Pinner Community Hospital
NTHWD HA6 40 E4
Northwood Preparatory School
RKW/CH/CXG WD3 26 A4
Northwood Primary School
ERITHM DA18 129 F3
Northwood School
NTHWD HA6 41 F4
Northwood Sports Centre
PIN HA5 41 F4
Norwegian/British Monument
BAY/PAD W2 8 C7
The Norwegian School
WIM/MER SW19 177 F3
Norwood Green Infant School
NWDGN UB2 114 D5
Norwood Green Junior School
NWDGN UB2 114 D5
Norwood Heights Shopping Centre
NRWD SE19 181 F2
Norwood Park Primary School
WNWD SE27 162 D6
Norwood School
WNWD SE27 180 D1
Notre Dame RC Girls School
STHWK SE1 18 A4
Notre Dame RC Primary School
WOOL/PLUM SE18 127 G6
Notting Hill & Ealing High School
WEA W13 97 H4
Nower Hill High School
PIN HA5 60 A1
N1 Shopping Centre
IS N1 5 K2
NTGB Sports Ground
EHAM E6 90 A4
Nuffield Hospital
ENC/FH EN2 23 G3
Nugent Industrial Park
STMC/STPC BR5 202 D1
Nutrition Clinic
MHST W1U 9 G1
Oakdale Infant School
SWFD E18 53 F5
Oakdale Junior School
SWFD E18 53 G5
Oakfield Preparatory School
DUL SE21 162 E4
Oakfield Primary School
DART DA1 171 G4
Oakfield Road Industrial Estate
PGE/AN SE20 181 J3
Oak Hill College
EBAR EN4 34 A1
Oak Hill Health Centre
SURB KT6 191 F3
Oakhill Primary School
WFD IG8 52 C2
Oakington Manor School
WBLY HA9 80 D3
Oakland CP School
EBAR EN4 33 K1
Oaklands Primary School
HNWL W7 116 A2
Oaklands School
ISLW TW7 135 J4
Oaklands Secondary School
BETH E2 104 C2
Oak Lane Cemetery
TWK TW1 156 B2
Oak Lane Medical Centre
TWK TW1 156 C2
Oakleigh School
TRDG/WHET N20 33 J5
Oak Lodge JMI School
WWKM BR4 198 E4
Oak Lodge Medical Centre
EDGE HA8 44 D3
Oak Lodge School
BAL SW12 160 E2
EFNCH N2 47 G6
Oakthorpe Primary School
PLMGR N13 49 J1
Oak Tree Medical Centre
GDMY/SEVK IG3 72 E6
Oakwood Business Park
WLSDN NW10 99 F2
Oakwood Medical Centre
STHGT/OAK N14 22 C6
Oasis Sports Centre
LSQ/SEVD WC2H 10 E3
Obstetrics Hospital
GWRST WC1E 4 B7
Occupational Health Centre
CROY/NA CR0 211 K1
Odeon Cinema
ARCH N19 84 E1
BAR EN5 20 E6
BECK BR3 182 D5
CAMTN NW1 84 B6
ELTH/MOT SE9 146 D5
ESH/CLAY KT10 204 B2
FITZ W1T 10 C2
GNTH/NBYPK IG2 72 A3
HAYES BR2 183 K5
KENS W8 119 K3
KIL/WHAMP NW6 83 H5
KUTN/CMB KT2 175 F5
LSQ/SEVD WC2H 10 D6
MBLAR W1H 9 F4
MUSWH N10 66 A1
RCHPK/HAM TW10 136 E6
ROM RM1 75 H2
STJS SW1Y 10 C6
STRHM/NOR SW16 161 K5
SWFD E18 52 E5
WIM/MER SW19 177 K3
Odeon Covent Gardens Cinema
LSQ/SEVD WC2H 10 D4
Odeon Wardour Street Cinema
SOHO/SHAV W1D 10 C5
Odessa Infant School
FSTGT E7 88 E3
Odyssey Business Park
RSLP HA4 77 F3
Old Actonians Sports Club
EA W5 117 G2
Old Admiralty
WHALL SW1A 16 D1
Old Bancroftians FC
BKHH IG9 39 H6
Old Barnes Cemetery
BARN SW13 138 E3
Old Beckenhamian RFC
WWKM BR4 214 B1
Old Bellgate Wharf Development
BERM/RHTH SE16 124 C3
Old Bexley Business Park
BXLY DA5 169 J2
Old Bexley CE Primary School
BXLY DA5 169 G3
Old Brockleians Sports Ground
ELTH/MOT SE9 166 B1
Old Bromlians Cricket Club
HAYES BR2 200 A2
Old Cemetery
EDUL SE22 163 J1
Oldchurch Hospital
ROMW/RG RM7 75 F3
Old Colfeian Sports Club
LEE/GVPK SE12 145 K6
Old Curiosity Shop
LINN WC2A 11 G3
Old Elthamians Sports Club
CHST BR7 185 K2
Oldfield House Special School
HPTN TW12 172 E4
Oldfields Primary School
GFD/PVL UB6 96 D1
Oldfields Trading Estate
SUT SM1 208 E1
Old Fold Manor Golf Club
BAR EN5 20 C2
Old Ford Primary School
BOW E3 105 H1
Oldhill Medical Centre
STNW/STAM N16 68 B5
Old Jamaica Business Estate
BERM/RHTH SE16 19 K4
Old Lyonian Sports Ground
RYLN/HDSTN HA2 60 C2
Old Millhillians Sports Ground
PIN HA5 42 A4
Old Oak Primary School
SHB W12 99 H5
Old Operating Theatre Museum
STHWK SE1 18 E1
Old Owens Sports Ground
TRDG/WHET N20 33 H3
Old Palace Primary School
BOW E3 105 K2
Old Palace School
CROY/NA CR0 211 H1
Old Royal Naval College
GNWCH SE10 125 G5
Old Royal Observatory Greenwich
GNWCH SE10 145 G1
Old Station Museum
CAN/RD E16 127 F2
Old Street Station
FSBYE EC1V 6 E5
Old Sun Wharf
POP/IOD E14 105 G6
Old Tiffinians Sports Ground
E/WMO/HCT KT8 189 K2
Old Treasury
WHALL SW1A 16 E2
Old Vicarage School
RCHPK/HAM TW10 157 F1
Old Vic Theatre
STHWK SE1 17 K2
Old War Office
WHALL SW1A 16 E1
Old Wilsonians Sports Club
WWKM BR4 199 H5
Olga Primary School
BOW E3 105 G1
Oliver Business Park
WLSDN NW10 98 E1
Oliver Goldsmith Primary School
CDALE/KGS NW9 63 F2
CMBW SE5 143 G2
Olympia
WKENS W14 119 H3
Olympia Industrial Estate
WDGN N22 49 F5
Olympic Industrial Estate
WBLY HA9 80 D2
Olympic Retail Park
WBLY HA9 80 C2
Olympic Trading Estate
WBLY HA9 80 D2
The One Stanley Medical Centre
ALP/SUD HA0 80 A5
On Sai Clinic
ECT SW5 120 A4
On the Road Tours CC
WAND/EARL SW18 160 B1
Open Air Theatre
CAMTN NW1 3 G5
The Open University
FSBYW WC1X 5 G4
HAMP NW3 82 E2
Ophaboom Theatre
WLSDN NW10 99 K2
Optimax Laser Eye Clinic
HAMP NW3 83 G4
Orange Tree Theatre
RCH/KEW TW9 137 F5
Orchard Business Centre
SYD SE26 182 C1
The Orchard Health Centre
BARK IG11 108 C1
Orchard House School
CHSWK W4 118 A4
The Orchard Junior School
HSLW TW3 135 F5
Orchard Primary School
HOM E9 86 E5
The Orchard School
E/WMO/HCT KT8 189 J2
Orchard Shopping Centre
DART DA1 171 H1
The Orchard Theatre
DART DA1 171 H1
Orchard Way Primary School
CROY/NA CR0 198 B4
Oriel Primary School
FELT TW13 154 D5
Orient Industrial Park
LEY E10 69 J6
Orion Business Centre
BERM/RHTH SE16 124 A5
Orleans House Gallery
TWK TW1 156 C3
Orleans Infant School
TWK TW1 156 C2
Orleans Park School
TWK TW1 156 C2
Orley Farm School
HRW HA1 78 D1
Orpington College of Further Education
ORP BR6 202 B5
The Orpington Halls
ORP BR6 202 B6
Orpington Mental Health Centre
ORP BR6 217 F1
Orpington Retail Park
STMC/STPC BR5 202 D1
Orpington Superbowl
ORP BR6 202 B5
Osidge JMI School
STHGT/OAK N14 34 C3
Osmani Primary School
WCHPL E1 104 C4
Osteopathic Clinic
HOR/WEW KT19 207 F3
Osterley RFC
NWDGN UB2 115 G3
Our Lady Immaculate RC Primary School
BRYLDS KT5 191 J5
Our Lady of Dolours RC Primary School
BAY/PAD W2 101 F4
Our Lady of Grace RC Junior School
CRICK NW2 81 K1
Our Lady of Lourdes RC Primary School
FBAR/BDGN N11 48 C1
FNCH N3 47 G3
LEW SE13 145 G4
WAN E11 70 D3
WLSDN NW10 80 E6
Our Lady of Muswell RC Primary School
MUSWH N10 48 A5
Our Lady of St Johns
BTFD TW8 116 D5
Our Lady of the Assumption RC Infant School
BETH E2 104 E1
Our Lady of the Rosary RC Primary School
BFN/LL DA15 167 K1
Our Lady of the Sacred Heart School
HOLWY N7 85 F3
Our Lady of the Visitation RC Combined Primary School
GFD/PVL UB6 96 C3
Our Lady of Victories RC Primary School
PUT/ROE SW15 139 G5
SKENS SW7 14 A7
Our Lady Queen of Heaven RC Primary School
WIM/MER SW19 159 G2
Our Lady RC Primary School
POP/IOD E14 105 H5
Our Lady & St Joseph Primary School
IS N1 86 A4
Our Lady & St Philip Neri RC Primary School
FSTH SE23 164 A5
Our Ladys Catholic Primary School
DART DA1 171 F1
Our Ladys Convent High School
STNW/STAM N16 68 A4
Our Ladys RC Primary School
CAMTN NW1 84 C6
Oval Business Centre
LBTH SE11 122 A5
Oval House Theatre
LBTH SE11 122 B6
Oval Primary School
CROY/NA CR0 197 F5
Overton Grange School
BELMT SM2 209 F5
Oxford Gardens Primary School
NKENS W10 100 B5
Oxford House College
SOHO/SHAV W1D 10 C3
Oxhey Infant School
BUSH WD23 27 J1
Oxhey Wood Primary School
OXHEY WD19 27 G6
Oxo Tower Wharf
STHWK SE1 11 K6
Paddington Bowling & Sports Club
MV/WKIL W9 101 F3
Paddington Green Primary School
BAY/PAD W2 2 A7
Paddington Recreation Ground Athletics Track
MV/WKIL W9 100 E2
Paddington Station
BAY/PAD W2 8 A3
Paddock School
PUT/ROE SW15 138 C5
Pain Relief Clinic
HDN NW4 63 K3
Pakeman Primary School
HOLWY N7 85 F1
Palace Gardens Shopping Centre
ENC/FH EN2 23 K4
Palladium Theatre
REGST W1B 10 A4
Palmers Green High School
WCHMH N21 35 G4
Palmerston Business Centre
SUT SM1 209 G3
Palm House
RCH/KEW TW9 137 G2
Panorama Pier
STHWK SE1 12 B6
Paradise Swimming Pools
MLHL NW7 45 G1
Parayhouse School
WBPTN SW10 140 B1
Parchmore Medical Centre
THHTH CR7 180 D6
Pardes House & Beis Yaakov Boys School
FNCH N3 46 D5
Parent Infant Clinic
HAMP NW3 83 G3
Parish CE Primary School
BMLY BR1 183 K3
Parish Church CE Primary School
CROY/NA CR0 211 H1
Park Business Centre
KIL/WHAMP NW6 100 E2
Parkfield Industrial Estate
BTSEA SW11 141 F3
Parkfield JMI School
HDN NW4 63 K4
Parkgate House School
BTSEA SW11 141 F5
Park Hall Trading Estate
WNWD SE27 162 D5
Park High School
STAN HA7 43 K5
Park Hill Junior School
CROY/NA CR0 211 K1
Parkhill Primary School
CLAY IG5 53 K6
Park Hill School
KUTN/CMB KT2 175 H3
Park House Medical Centre
KIL/WHAMP NW6 100 C1
Parkhouse Middle School
WIM/MER SW19 159 J6
Park House RFC
HAYES BR2 200 B6
Parkhurst Infant School
TOTM N17 50 B5
Parklands Primary School
ROM RM1 57 F6
Park Lane Primary School
WBLY HA9 80 A2
Park Medical Centre
BERM/RHTH SE16 124 A4
Park Mews Small Business Centre
HNHL SE24 162 D1
Park Primary School
SRTFD E15 88 D5
Park Road Clinic
CEND/HSY/T N8 66 D2
Park Road Swimming Centre
CEND/HSY/T N8 66 D2
Park Royal Business Centre
WLSDN NW10 98 E3
Park School for Girls
IL IG1 72 B5
Parkside Business Estate
DEPT SE8 124 C6
Parkside Clinic
NTGHL W11 100 C5
Parkside Health
NTGHL W11 100 C5
Parkside Hospital
WIM/MER SW19 159 G5
Park Walk Primary School
WBPTN SW10 120 C6
Parkway Primary School
ERITHM DA18 129 F3
Parkway Trading Estate
HEST TW5 114 B6
Parkwood Primary School
FSBYPK N4 67 H6
Parliament Hill Fields Athletics Track
KTTN NW5 83 K2
Parliament Hill School
KTTN NW5 84 A2
Parmiter Industrial Centre
BETH E2 104 D1
Parnells Sports Ground
KTN/HRWW/W HA3 62 B3
Parsloes Primary School
DAGW RM9 92 B4
Parsons Green Health Clinic
FUL/PGN SW6 139 K2
Passport Language Schools
BMLY BR1 184 A4
Patent Office
HHOL WC1V 11 J2
The Patrick Doody Clinic & Health Centre
WIM/MER SW19 177 K3
Pattinson Clinic
RCHPK/HAM TW10 136 E6
The Paul Robeson Theatre
HSLW TW3 135 G4
Pavilion Barclays Sports Ground
EA W5 98 A4
The Pavilion Leisure Centre
BMLY BR1 183 K5
Pavilion Restaurant
RCH/KEW TW9 137 F3
Paxton Primary School
NRWD SE19 181 G2
Pdsa Hospital
REDBR IG4 53 H6
Peace Pagoda
BTSEA SW11 140 E1
Peacock Estate
TOTM N17 50 B2
Peacock Industrial Estate
TOTM N17 50 B3
The Peacock Theatre
HOL/ALD WC2B 11 G4
Peall Road Industrial Estate
CROY/NA CR0 196 A3
Peckham Leisure Centre
PECK SE15 143 H2
Peckham Park Primary School
PECK SE15 143 H1
Peckham Pulse Healthy Living Centre
PECK SE15 143 H2
Peckham Rye Primary School
PECK SE15 143 J4
Pelham Primary School
BXLYHN DA7 149 G4
WIM/MER SW19 177 K3
Pembridge Hall
BAY/PAD W2 100 E6
Pendragon Secondary School
BMLY BR1 165 K5
Pentavia Retail Park
MLHL NW7 45 H3
Penton Primary School
IS N1 5 K2
Penwortham Primary School
STRHM/NOR SW16 179 G2
Percival David Foundation of Chinese Art
STPAN WC1H 4 D6
Perivale Industrial Park
GFD/PVL UB6 79 G6
Perivale New Business Centre
GFD/PVL UB6 97 J1
Perivale Park Athletics Track
GFD/PVL UB6 96 E2
Perivale Park Golf Course
GFD/PVL UB6 96 E2
Perivale Primary School
GFD/PVL UB6 97 J1
Perrin Road Clinic
ALP/SUD HA0 79 H2
Perry Hall Primary School
ORP BR6 202 A3
Perrymount Primary School
FSTH SE23 164 A4
Peterborough Primary School
FUL/PGN SW6 139 K3
Peterborough & St Margarets High School
STAN HA7 28 E5
Peter Hills School
BERM/RHTH SE16 124 A1
Peter James Business Centre
HYS/HAR UB3 113 K2
Peterley Business Centre
BETH E2 104 D1
Peter Pan Statue
BAY/PAD W2 8 A7
Petric Museum of Egyptia Archaeology
GWRST WC1E 4 C7
Pewterers' Hall
CITYW EC2V 12 D2
Phoenix Business Centre
POP/IOD E14 105 J4
Phoenix Cinema
EFNCH N2 65 J1
Phoenix College
MRDN SM4 194 A2
TOOT SW17 160 D4
Phoenix Court
POP/IOD E14 124 D4
Phoenix High School
SHB W12 99 J6
Phoenix Industrial Estate
HRW HA1 61 F1
Phoenix Leisure Centre
CAT SE6 164 E2
Phoenix School
BOW E3 105 H2
HAMP NW3 83 H5
Phoenix Theatre
LSQ/SEVD WC2H 10 D4
Phoenix Trading Estate
GFD/PVL UB6 79 J6
Photographer's Gallery
LSQ/SEVD WC2H 10 D5
Physical Energy Statue
BAY/PAD W2 14 A1
Piccadilly Theatre
SOHO/SHAV W1D 10 C5
Pickford Lane Medical Centre
BXLYHN DA7 149 F2
Pickhurst Infant School
HAYES BR2 199 H3
Pickhurst Junior School
HAYES BR2 199 J3
Picture House Cinema
SRTFD E15 88 B4
Pilgrims Way J & I School
PECK SE15 123 K6
Pilot Industrial Centre
WLSDN NW10 99 G3
Pilton Estate
CROY/NA CR0 196 C6
Pimlico School
PIM SW1V 121 H5
Pinewood Primary School
CRW RM5 56 D1
Pinkwell Primary School
WDR/YW UB7 113 F4
Pinner Hill Golf Club
PIN HA5 41 F2
Pinner Park Primary School
RYLN/HDSTN HA2 42 B6
Pinner View Medical Centre
HRW HA1 60 C2
Pinner Wood Primary School
PIN HA5 41 G4
Pinn Medical Centre
PIN HA5 59 J1
Pioneers Industrial Park
CROY/NA CR0 195 K5
Pitshanger Manor Museum
EA W5 116 D1
Plaisterers Hall
CITYW EC2V 12 C2
Plaistow Hospital
PLSTW E13 107 F1
Planetarium
CAMTN NW1 3 G7
Plantation House Medical Centre
LOTH EC2R 13 F3

Plashet Jewish Cemetery
MNPK E12 ... 89 H4
Plashet Road Medical Centre
FSTGT E7 ... 89 F5
Plashet School
EHAM E6 ... 89 J5
Players Theatre
CHCR WC2N ... 10 E7
The Playhouse
CHCR WC2N ... 11 F7
Plaza Business Centre
PEND EN3 ... 25 H3
Pleasance Theatre
HOLWY N7 ... 84 E4
Plumcroft Primary School
WOOL/PLUM SE18 ... 127 H6
Plumstead Leisure Centre
WOOL/PLUM SE18 ... 128 A5
Plumstead Manor School
WOOL/PLUM SE18 ... 127 J5
The Pointer School
BKHTH/KID SE3 ... 145 K2
Police Cadet School
WAN E11 ... 70 E5
The Polish Institute & Sikorski Museum
SKENS SW7 ... 14 B3
Polka Theatre for Children
WIM/MER SW19 ... 178 A2
Pollock's Toy Museum
FITZ W1T ... 10 B1
Ponders End Industrial Estate
PEND EN3 ... 25 F3
PEND EN3 ... 25 H5
Poole's Park Primary School
HOLWY N7 ... 67 F6
Pools in the Park
RCH/KEW TW9 ... 136 E5
Pope John Primary School
SHB W12 ... 99 K6
Pop In Business Centre
WBLY HA9 ... 80 D3
Poplar Business Park
POP/IOD E14 ... 106 A6
Poplar First School
WIM/MER SW19 ... 177 K6
Pop Up Theatre
IS N1 ... 5 K3
Porchester Leisure Centre
BAY/PAD W2 ... 101 F5
Portcullis House
WHALL SW1A ... 17 F3
The Portland Hospital
REGST W1B ... 3 K7
Portland House Medical Centre
GFD/PVL UB6 ... 96 B3
Portland Medical Centre
SNWD SE25 ... 197 J2
Portland Place School
REGST W1B ... 9 K1
The Portman Clinic
HAMP NW3 ... 83 H4
Portobello Market
NKENS W10 ... 100 C4
Portobello Medical Centre
NTGHL W11 ... 100 C5
Portway Primary School
SRTFD E15 ... 88 E6
Pound Park Nursery School
CHARL SE7 ... 126 C5
The Pountney Clinic
HSLW TW3 ... 135 F4
Poverest Primary School
STMC/STPC BR5 ... 202 B2
Powergate Business Park
WLSDN NW10 ... 99 F2
Power Industrial Estate
ERITH DA8 ... 150 C2
Premier Cinema
PECK SE15 ... 143 H3
Prendergast School
BROCKY SE4 ... 144 D5
Preston Manor School
WBLY HA9 ... 62 B6
Preston Medical Centre
WBLY HA9 ... 80 A1
Preston Park Primary School
WBLY HA9 ... 61 K5
PR for Schools
SYD SE26 ... 163 K5
Priestmead First & Middle Schools
KTN/HRWW/W HA3 ... 43 H6
Primary School
CHEL SW3 ... 120 D5
Primrose Hill School
CAMTN NW1 ... 84 A6
Primrose Montessori School
HBRY N5 ... 85 J1
Prince Charles Cinema
SOHO/SHAV W1D ... 10 D5
Prince Edward Theatre
SOHO/SHAV W1D ... 10 C4
Prince of Wales Theatre
STJS SW1Y ... 10 C6
Princes College
NOXST/BSQ WC1A ... 10 E3
Princes Court Business Centre
WAP E1W ... 104 D6
Princess Avenue School
MUSWH N10 ... 48 B6
Princess Frederica CE J & I School
WLSDN NW10 ... 99 K1
Princess Grace Hospital
MHST W1U ... 3 G7
Princess Louise Hospital
NKENS W10 ... 100 A4
Princess May Primary School
STNW/STAM N16 ... 86 A3
Princess of Wales Conservatory
RCH/KEW TW9 ... 137 G1
Prior Western Primary School
STLK EC1Y ... 6 D7
Priory CE Middle School
WIM/MER SW19 ... 178 A1
Priory House School
CAT SE6 ... 164 E3
Priory Leisure Centre
STMC/STPC BR5 ... 202 D5
Priory Retail Park
WIM/MER SW19 ... 178 C3
Priory School
STMC/STPC BR5 ... 202 D5
Priory Shopping Centre
DART DA1 ... 171 G1
Priory Special School
SNWD SE25 ... 197 G1
The Priory
ORP BR6 ... 202 C4
Privy Council
STJS SW1Y ... 16 C1
Privy Council Office
WHALL SW1A ... 16 E1
Progress Business Park
CROY/NA CR0 ... 196 A6
Pronto Trading Estate
YEAD UB4 ... 94 C4
Prospect House School
PUT/ROE SW15 ... 159 G2
Prospect of Whitby
WAP E1W ... 123 K1
Proud Gallery
CHCR WC2N ... 10 E6
Providence Road School
WDR/YW UB7 ... 112 B1
Provident Industrial Estate
HYS/HAR UB3 ... 113 K2
Psychiatric Home
BRXN/ST SW9 ... 141 K4
Public Record Office
LINN WC2A ... 11 J3
Public Record Office Museum
RCH/KEW TW9 ... 137 J1
Pump House
BERM/RHTH SE16 ... 124 B1
Pump Lane Industrial Estate
HYS/HAR UB3 ... 114 A2
Puppet Theatre Barge
MV/WKIL W9 ... 101 G4
The Purcell School
HRW HA1 ... 78 D1
Purdy Hicks Gallery
STHWK SE1 ... 12 A7
Purfleet Industrial Park
PUR RM19 ... 131 J1
Purfleet Primary School
PUR RM19 ... 131 K4
Purley Oaks Primary School
SAND/SEL CR2 ... 211 K5
Pursuit Centre
WAP E1W ... 104 E6
Putney Animal Hospital
PUT/ROE SW15 ... 139 G5
Putney Exchange Shopping Centre
PUT/ROE SW15 ... 139 G5
Putney High School
PUT/ROE SW15 ... 139 G6
Putney Hospital
PUT/ROE SW15 ... 139 F4
Putney Leisure Centre
PUT/ROE SW15 ... 139 F5
Putney Lower Common Cemetery
PUT/ROE SW15 ... 138 E3
Putneymead Medical Centre
PUT/ROE SW15 ... 139 F5
Putney Park School
PUT/ROE SW15 ... 138 E5
Putney School of Art
PUT/ROE SW15 ... 139 H5
Putney Vale Cemetery
PUT/ROE SW15 ... 158 D4
Putney Vale Crematorium
PUT/ROE SW15 ... 158 D4
Pylon Trading Estate
CAN/RD E16 ... 106 B3
Quadrant Business Park
KIL/WHAMP NW6 ... 82 C6
Quebec Industrial Estate
BERM/RHTH SE16 ... 124 B2
Queen Charlottes & Chelsea Hospital
HMSMTH W6 ... 118 D3
Queen Charlotte's Cottage
RCH/KEW TW9 ... 137 G1
Queen Elizabeth Centre
BAR EN5 ... 20 D5
Queen Elizabeth Conference Centre
WEST SW1P ... 16 D3
Queen Elizabeth Hall
STHWK SE1 ... 11 G7
Queen Elizabeth Hospital
CHARL SE7 ... 126 E6
Queen Elizabeth II School
MV/WKIL W9 ... 100 D3
Queen Elizabeth Museum
CHING E4 ... 38 D2
Queen Elizabeths Boys School
BAR EN5 ... 20 B4
Queen Elizabeths Girls School
BAR EN5 ... 20 D5
Queen Elizabeth Stadium
EN EN1 ... 24 B3
Queenhithe Stairs
BLKFR EC4V ... 12 C6
Queen Mary's Hospital
HAMP NW3 ... 83 G1
Queen Marys Hospital
SCUP DA14 ... 186 B1
Queen Marys Hospital for Children
CAR SM5 ... 209 K6
Queen Mary's University Hospital
PUT/ROE SW15 ... 158 D1
Queen Mary & Westfield College
SWFD E18 ... 52 E4
WCHPL E1 ... 105 F3
Queen Mother Sports Centre
PIM SW1V ... 16 A6
Queensbridge Infant School
HACK E8 ... 86 B5
Queensbridge Sports Centre
HACK E8 ... 86 B5
Queen's Building
HTHAIR TW6 ... 132 E4
Queens CE Primary School
RCH/KEW TW9 ... 137 G1
Queen's Club
WKENS W14 ... 119 H5
Queens College
CAVSQ/HST W1G ... 9 J2
Queen's Gallery
WHALL SW1A ... 15 K3
Queens Gate School
SKENS SW7 ... 14 A6
The Queens House
GNWCH SE10 ... 125 G6
Queens Ice Skating Club
BAY/PAD W2 ... 101 F6
Queens Manor Primary School
FUL/PGN SW6 ... 139 F1
Queensmead School
RSLP HA4 ... 77 H2
Queensmead Sports Centre
RSLP HA4 ... 58 E6
RSLP HA4 ... 77 H3
Queens Medical Centre
RCHPK/HAM TW10 ... 137 G6
Queensmill School
FUL/PGN SW6 ... 139 K3
Queens Park Community School GM
KIL/WHAMP NW6 ... 82 A6
Queens Park Health Centre
NKENS W10 ... 100 C2
Queens Park Primary School
NKENS W10 ... 100 C2
Queens Park Rangers FC (Loftus Road Stadium)
SHB W12 ... 99 K6
Queen's Road Cemetery
CROY/NA CR0 ... 196 D3
Queens Road Practice
NWCR SE14 ... 144 A2
Queens Theatre
SOHO/SHAV W1D ... 10 C5
Queensway Business Centre
PEND EN3 ... 24 E5
Queenswell Infant School
TRDG/WHET N20 ... 33 H4
Queen Victoria Memorial
WHALL SW1A ... 16 A3
The Questors Theatre
EA W5 ... 97 J6
Quicksilver Theatre
IS N1 ... 86 A5
Radcliffe College
SOHO/CST W1F ... 10 A4
Raglan Infant School
EN EN1 ... 36 A1
Raglan Junior School
EN EN1 ... 36 A2
Raglan Primary School
HAYES BR2 ... 200 B1
Railton Road Clinic
BRXN/ST SW9 ... 142 C6
Rainbow Industrial Estate
RYNPK SW20 ... 176 E5
Rainbow Quay
BERM/RHTH SE16 ... 124 B3
Raines Foundation School
BETH E2 ... 104 D2
Rainham Hall Nt
RAIN RM13 ... 111 J3
Rainham Trading Estate
RAIN RM13 ... 111 G2
Rainham Village Primary School
RAIN RM13 ... 111 J3
Ramac Industrial Estate
CHARL SE7 ... 125 K5
Ram Brewery & Visitor Centre
WAND/EARL SW18 ... 140 A6
Randal Cremer Primary School
BETH E2 ... 7 J2
Ranelagh Gardens (Site of Chelsea Flower Show)
CHEL SW3 ... 121 F6
Ranelagh Primary School
SRTFD E15 ... 106 C1
Rangefield Primary School
BMLY BR1 ... 183 H1
Rangers House (The Wernher Collection)
GNWCH SE10 ... 145 G2
Ransomes Dock Business Centre
BTSEA SW11 ... 140 D1
Raphael School
EMPK RM11 ... 75 J3
Rathfern Primary School
CAT SE6 ... 164 C3
Ravenor Primary School
GFD/PVL UB6 ... 96 A2
Ravensbourne College of Design & Communication
CHST BR7 ... 184 E1
The Ravensbourne School
HAYES BR2 ... 200 A1
Ravenscourt Park Preparatory School
HMSMTH W6 ... 118 D4
Ravenscroft Medical Centre
GLDGN NW11 ... 64 D4
Ravenscroft Primary School
PLSTW E13 ... 106 E3
Ravenscroft School
TRDG/WHET N20 ... 32 D2
Ravenside Retail Park
UED N18 ... 51 F1
Ravensquay Business Centre
STMC/STPC BR5 ... 202 C2
Ravenstone Primary School
BAL SW12 ... 161 F3
Ravenswood Industrial Estate
WALTH E17 ... 70 A1
Ravens Wood School
HAYES BR2 ... 215 H1
Ray Lodge Primary School
WFD IG8 ... 53 H2
Raynes Park High School
NWMAL KT3 ... 176 E6
Raynes Park Sports Ground
RYNPK SW20 ... 176 D5
Raynes Park Vale FC
RYNPK SW20 ... 193 G2
Raynham Primary School
UED N18 ... 50 C1
RCA Sculpture School
BTSEA SW11 ... 140 D1
Reay Primary School
BRXN/ST SW9 ... 142 A1
Records Office
CLKNW EC1R ... 5 K6
Rectory Business Centre
SCUP DA14 ... 168 C6
Rectory Paddock School
STMC/STPC BR5 ... 186 D5
Redbridge College
CHDH RM6 ... 73 H2
Redbridge Museum
IL IG1 ... 90 B1
Redbridge Primary School
REDBR IG4 ... 71 J2
Redbridge Sports Centre
BARK/HLT IG6 ... 54 D4
Redburn Industrial Estate
PEND EN3 ... 37 F1
Redcliffe School
WBPTN SW10 ... 120 B6
Reddiford School
PIN HA5 ... 59 J1
Redford Lodge Psychiatric Hospital
ED N9 ... 36 C4
Redhill Junior School
CHST BR7 ... 185 G1
Redlands Primary School
WCHPL E1 ... 104 E4
Red Lion Business Park
SURB KT6 ... 191 G6
Redriff Community Primary School
BERM/RHTH SE16 ... 124 B1
Red Rose Trading Estate
EBAR EN4 ... 21 H6
Regent Business Centre
HYS/HAR UB3 ... 114 A2
Regent Clinic
CAVSQ/HST W1G ... 9 J2
Regent's College
CAMTN NW1 ... 3 G4
Regent's Park Barracks
CAMTN NW1 ... 3 J2
Regents Park Clinic
CAMTN NW1 ... 2 E6
Regents Park Medical Centre
CAMTN NW1 ... 3 K4
Regent's Park Track
CAMTN NW1 ... 2 E2
Regina Coeli RC Primary School
CROY/NA CR0 ... 211 H5
Renoir Cinema
BMSBY WC1N ... 5 F6
Renwick Industrial Estate
BARK IG11 ... 109 H1
Reynard Mills Trading Estate
BTFD TW8 ... 116 D5
Reynolds Sports Centre
EA W5 ... 117 H2
Rhodes Avenue Primary School
FBAR/BDGN N11 ... 48 C4
Rhodes Farm Clinic
MLHL NW7 ... 32 A6
Rhyl Primary School
KTTN NW5 ... 84 A4
RIBA Library Drawings & Manuscript Collection
MBLAR W1H ... 9 F3
Ricards Lodge High School
WIM/MER SW19 ... 177 J1
Richard Alibon Primary School
DAGE RM10 ... 92 C3
Richard Atkins Primary School
BRXS/STRHM SW2 ... 161 K2
Richard Cloudesley School
STLK EC1Y ... 6 C7
Richard Cobden Primary School
CAMTN NW1 ... 4 B1
Rich Industrial Estate
PECK SE15 ... 123 J6
STHWK SE1 ... 19 H5
Richmond Adult & Community College
RCH/KEW TW9 ... 136 E5
TWK TW1 ... 156 A3
The Richmond Clinic
RCHPK/HAM TW10 ... 137 G5
Richmond College
KENS W8 ... 120 A3
RCHPK/HAM TW10 ... 157 F2
Richmond FC
RCH/KEW TW9 ... 136 E5
The Richmond Golf Club
RCHPK/HAM TW10 ... 157 F4
The Richmond Green Medical Centre
RCH/KEW TW9 ... 136 E6
Richmond House School
HPTN TW12 ... 172 E1
Richmond Magistrates Court
RCH/KEW TW9 ... 136 E5
Richmond Park Golf Club
PUT/ROE SW15 ... 158 B2
Richmond Road Medical Centre
KUTN/CMB KT2 ... 175 F3
Richmond Theatre
RCH/KEW TW9 ... 136 E5
Richmond upon Thames College
WHTN TW2 ... 155 K2
Ridge House Clinic
WCHMH N21 ... 35 K2
Ridgeway Primary School
SAND/SEL CR2 ... 212 A6
Rio Cinema
HACK E8 ... 86 B3
Ripple J & I School
BARK IG11 ... 90 D6
Risebridge Golf Club
ROM RM1 ... 57 H3
Rise Park Primary School
ROM RM1 ... 57 F4
Risley Avenue Primary School
TOTM N17 ... 50 A4
Ritzy Cinema
BRXN/ST SW9 ... 142 B5
River Brent Business Park
NWDGN UB2 ... 115 K3
River Gardens Business Centre
EBED/NFELT TW14 ... 134 A5
River Mole Business Park
ESH/CLAY KT10 ... 189 F5
River Place Health Centre
IS N1 ... 85 J5
River Road Business Park
BARK IG11 ... 108 E2
Riversdale Primary School
WAND/EARL SW18 ... 159 K3
Riverside Business Centre
WAND/EARL SW18 ... 160 A3
Riverside Business Park
WIM/MER SW19 ... 178 B4
Riverside Community Health Care
WKENS W14 ... 119 G3
Riverside Golf Club
THMD SE28 ... 110 A5
Riverside Industrial Estate
BARK IG11 ... 109 G2
DART DA1 ... 151 H6
ED N9 ... 37 G1
Riverside Primary School
BERM/RHTH SE16 ... 123 H2
Riverside Studios Cinema
BARN SW13 ... 119 F5
Riverside Swimming Centre
ERITH DA8 ... 130 B5
Riverside Wandle Trading Estate
MTCM CR4 ... 194 E4
Riverston School
LEE/GVPK SE12 ... 145 K6
Riverview C E Primary School
HOR/WEW KT19 ... 206 E2
RJ Mitchell Primary School
HCH RM12 ... 93 K4
RNIB Sunshine House School
NTHWD HA6 ... 40 B2
RNLI Lifeboat Station
MON EC3R ... 13 H7
Roan Industrial Estate
MTCM CR4 ... 178 D4
Robert Blair Primary School
HOLWY N7 ... 84 E4
Robert Browning Primary School
WALW SE17 ... 122 E5
Robert Clack School
BCTR RM8 ... 74 B5
Robin Hood Infant School
SUT SM1 ... 208 E3
Robin Hood Junior School
SUT SM1 ... 209 F3
Robin Hood Lane Health Centre
SUT SM1 ... 208 E3
Robin Hood Primary School
KUTN/CMB KT2 ... 176 A1
Robinsfield Infant School
STJWD NW8 ... 2 B2
The Roche School
WAND/EARL SW18 ... 139 K6
Rockcliffe Manor Primary School
WOOL/PLUM SE18 ... 147 K1
Rockmount School
NRWD SE19 ... 180 D2
Rockware Business Centre
GFD/PVL UB6 ... 78 D6
Roding Primary School
BCTR RM8 ... 91 J2
WFD IG8 ... 53 J3
Roebuck Road Trading Estate
BARK/HLT IG6 ... 55 H2
Roe Green J & I School
CDALE/KGS NW9 ... 62 D1
Roehampton Church School
PUT/ROE SW15 ... 158 E2
Roehampton Golf Club
PUT/ROE SW15 ... 138 C5
Roehampton Institute
PUT/ROE SW15 ... 138 C6
WAND/EARL SW18 ... 159 H1
The Roehampton Priory Hospital
PUT/ROE SW15 ... 138 C5
Roehampton Recreation Centre
PUT/ROE SW15 ... 158 D2
Roger Ascham Primary School
WALTH E17 ... 51 H4
Roger Bannister Sports Ground
KTN/HRWW/W HA3 ... 42 C2
Rokeby School
KUTN/CMB KT2 ... 175 K3
SRTFD E15 ... 88 B5
Rokesly Primary School
CEND/HSY/T N8 ... 66 E2
Roman Bath
TPL/STR WC2R ... 11 H5
Roman Industrial Estate
CROY/NA CR0 ... 197 F4
Roman Road Primary School
EHAM E6 ... 107 H3
Roman Wall Remains
BARB EC2Y ... 12 C2
Romford Cemetery
ROMW/RG RM7 ... 74 E4
Romford Clinic
ROM RM1 ... 75 H1
Romford County Court
ROM RM1 ... 75 H1
Romford Golf Club
GPK RM2 ... 57 J6
Romford Ice Rink
ROMW/RG RM7 ... 75 G4
Ronald Rose Primary School
WIM/MER SW19 ... 159 G2
Rood Lane Medical Centre
FENCHST EC3M ... 13 G5
Rooks Heath School
RYLN/HDSTN HA2 ... 78 A1
Roosevelt Memorial
MYFR/PKLN W1K ... 9 H5
Ropery Business Park
CHARL SE7 ... 126 B4
Rosary Priory High School
BUSH WD23 ... 28 E1
Rosary RC Infant School
HEST TW5 ... 114 E6
The Rosary RC Primary School
HAMP NW3 ... 83 J3
Rosebery Industrial Park
TOTM N17 ... 50 D5
Rose Bruford College of Speech & Drama
BFN/LL DA15 ... 168 C3
Roselands Clinic
NWMAL KT3 ... 191 K1
Rosemary School (Primary)
IS N1 ... 85 J6
Rosemary Secondary School
CLKNW EC1R ... 6 A6
Rose McAndrew Clinic
BRXN/ST SW9 ... 142 A3
Rosemead Preparatory School
DUL SE21 ... 162 D4
Rosendale Primary School
DUL SE21 ... 162 D2
Rose Theatre Exhibition
STHWK SE1 ... 12 C7
Rosetta Primary School
CAN/RD E16 ... 107 F4
Rosewood Medical Centre
HCH RM12 ... 93 K3
Rosh Pinah Primary School
EDGE HA8 ... 30 D4
Rosslyn Park RFC
PUT/ROE SW15 ... 138 C5
Rotherfield Primary School
IS N1 ... 85 J6
Rotherhithe Civic Centre
BERM/RHTH SE16 ... 123 K2

Rotherhithe Primary School
BERM/RHTH SE16 ... 123 K4
The Rotunda
KUT KT1 ... 175 F5
The Roundhouse Theatre
CAMTN NW1 ... 84 A5
Roundwood Park Medical Centre
WLSDN NW10 ... 81 J5
Rowan High School
CLAP SW4 ... 161 J1
MTCM CR4 ... 179 H5
Rowans School
RYNPK SW20 ... 176 D3
Rowhill School
RDART DA2 ... 171 F6
Rowley Industrial Park
ACT W3 ... 117 J3
Roxbourne Medical Centre
RYLN/HDSTN HA2 ... 60 B6
Roxbourne Middle School
RSLP HA4 ... 59 H6
Roxeth First & Middle School
RYLN/HDSTN HA2 ... 60 D6
Roxeth Manor First School
RYLN/HDSTN HA2 ... 78 A1
Roxeth Mead School
RYLN/HDSTN HA2 ... 60 D6
Roxwell Trading Park
WALTH E17 ... 69 G4
Royal Academy of Arts
MYFR/PICC W1J ... 10 A6
Royal Academy of Dramatic Art
GWRST WC1E ... 4 D7
Royal Academy of Music
CAMTN NW1 ... 3 H7
Royal Air Force Museum
CDALE/KGS NW9 ... 45 J5
Royal Albert Hall
SKENS SW7 ... 14 A3
Royal Arsenal
WOOL/PLUM SE18 ... 127 G3
Royal Ballet School
LSQ/SEVD WC2H ... 11 F4
The Royal Ballet School
RCHPK/HAM TW10 ... 158 A3
Royal Blackheath Golf Club
ELTH/MOT SE9 ... 166 E2
Royal Botanic Gardens Kew School
RCH/KEW TW9 ... 137 G1
Royal Brompton & National Heart Hospitals
CHEL SW3 ... 120 C5
Royal College of Anaesthetists
RSQ WC1B ... 10 E1
Royal College of Art
SKENS SW7 ... 120 B2
Royal College of Music
SHB W12 ... 118 D3
SKENS SW7 ... 14 A4
Royal College of Nursing
CAMTN NW1 ... 4 B6
IS N1 ... 6 A1
Royal College of Obstetricians & Gynaecologists
CAMTN NW1 ... 2 E6
Royal College of Ophthalmologists
CAMTN NW1 ... 3 G7
Royal College of Paediatrics & Child Health
GTPST W1W ... 9 K1
The Royal College of Pathology
STJS SW1Y ... 16 C1
Royal College of Physicians
CAMTN NW1 ... 3 J6
Royal College of Surgeons
LINN WC2A ... 11 H3
Royal Courts of Justice
LINN WC2A ... 11 H4
Royal Court Theatre
BGVA SW1W ... 15 G7
Royal Court Young Peoples Theatre
NKENS W10 ... 100 C4
The Royal Dock Community School
CAN/RD E16 ... 107 G5
Royal Docks Medical Centre
EHAM E6 ... 108 A5
Royal Epping Forest Golf Club
CHING E4 ... 38 C2
Royal Exchange
LOTH EC2R ... 13 F4
Royal Festival Hall
STHWK SE1 ... 17 G1
Royal Foundation of Grey Coat Hospital
WESTW SW1E ... 16 A4
Royal Free Hospital
HAMP NW3 ... 83 J3
Royal Free Hospital School of Medicine
HAMP NW3 ... 83 J3
Royal Geographical Soc
SKENS SW7 ... 14 A3
Royal Horticultural Society New Hall
WEST SW1P ... 16 C5
Royal Horticultural Society Old Hall
WEST SW1P ... 16 C6
Royal Hospital
RCH/KEW TW9 ... 137 F4
Royal Hospital Chelsea
CHEL SW3 ... 120 E5
Royal Hospital for Neuro-Disability
WAND/EARL SW18 ... 159 H1
Royal Hospital & Home
PUT/ROE SW15 ... 158 E2
Royal Hospital Museum
CHEL SW3 ... 121 F5
Royal Institute of British Architects
REGST W1B ... 9 K1
Royal Institution's Faraday Museum
MYFR/PICC W1J ... 9 K6
The Royal London Estate
TOTM N17 ... 50 D3
Royal London Homeopathic Hospital
BMSBY WC1N ... 11 F1
The Royal London Hospital (Whitechapel) A & E
WCHPL E1 ... 104 D4
Royal Marsden Hospital
CHEL SW3 ... 120 C5
The Royal Mews
WHALL SW1A ... 15 K4
Royal Mid-Surrey Golf Club
RCH/KEW TW9 ... 136 E4
Royal Mint Court
TWRH EC3N ... 13 K6
Royal National Orthopaedic Hospital
GTPST W1W ... 3 K7
STAN HA7 ... 29 H3
Royal National Theatre
CMBW SE5 ... 142 B1
STHWK SE1 ... 11 J7
Royal National Throat Nose & Ear Hospital
FSBYW WC1X ... 5 G4
Royal Observatory Greenwich
GNWCH SE10 ... 125 G6
Royal Opera House
COVGDN WC2E ... 11 F4
Royal Park Primary School
SCUP DA14 ... 169 F5
Royal Russell School
CROY/NA CR0 ... 212 D4
The Royal School
HAMP NW3 ... 83 H2
Royal Society of Arts
TPL/STR WC2R ... 11 F6
Royal Society of Medicine
CAVSQ/HST W1G ... 9 J3
Royal Veterinary College
CAMTN NW1 ... 4 B1
Royal Victoria Docks Watersports Centre
CAN/RD E16 ... 106 E6
Royal Wimbledon Golf Club
WIM/MER SW19 ... 176 E1
Royston Primary School
BECK BR3 ... 182 A4
RSPCA Animal Hospital
HOLWY N7 ... 67 F6
Rudolph Steiner Hall
CAMTN NW1 ... 2 E6
Rufus Business Centre
WAND/EARL SW18 ... 160 A4
Ruislip Gardens Primary School
HGDN/ICK UB10 ... 76 C2
Ruislip Golf Club
RSLP HA4 ... 58 A6
Ruislip Manor FC
RSLP HA4 ... 58 D6
Ruislip RFC
RSLP HA4 ... 58 C6
Rumford Shopping Hall
ROM RM1 ... 75 G1
Rush Croft School
CHING E4 ... 51 K3
Rushey Green Primary School
CAT SE6 ... 164 E3
Rush Green Primary School
ROMW/RG RM7 ... 75 F5
Rushmore Junior School
CLPT E5 ... 86 E2
Ruskin House School
HNHL SE24 ... 142 D6
The Russell JMI School
RCHPK/HAM TW10 ... 156 E4
The Russell School
RCHPK/HAM TW10 ... 156 E3
Russet House School
EN EN1 ... 24 D2
Rutlish School
RYNPK SW20 ... 177 J5
Ruxley Corner Industrial Estate
SCUP DA14 ... 186 E2
Ruxley Manor School
ELTH/MOT SE9 ... 167 F6
Ruxley Park Golf Centre
STMC/STPC BR5 ... 186 E4
Ryde College
WATW WD18 ... 26 C1
Ryefield Primary School
HGDN/ICK UB10 ... 76 B6
Ryelands Primary School
SNWD SE25 ... 197 J2
Saatchi Gallery
STHWK SE1 ... 17 G2
Sacred Heart High School
HMSMTH W6 ... 119 F4
Sacred Heart High School for Girls
KTN/HRWW/W HA3 ... 42 E5
Sacred Heart Junior Middle & Infant School
OXHEY WD19 ... 27 K1
Sacred Heart Junior School
HMSMTH W6 ... 119 G4
Sacred Heart RC Infant School
BTSEA SW11 ... 140 D3
Sacred Heart RC J & I School
RSLP HA4 ... 58 C6
Sacred Heart RC Junior & Middle School
BTSEA SW11 ... 140 D4
Sacred Heart RC Primary School
NWMAL KT3 ... 192 D1
PUT/ROE SW15 ... 138 D6
TEDD TW11 ... 174 C3
Sacred Heart RC School
CMBW SE5 ... 142 D2
Sacred Heart School
HOLWY N7 ... 85 F3
Saddlers Hall
CITYW EC2V ... 12 C4
Sadler's Wells Theatre
CLKNW EC1R ... 5 K4
SAE Technology College
HOLWY N7 ... 84 E3
Safari Cinema
CROY/NA CR0 ... 196 C4
Safari Cinema & Bingo
HRW HA1 ... 61 F2
Sai Medical Centre
POP/IOD E14 ... 125 F1
St Agathas RC Primary School
KUTN/CMB KT2 ... 175 G2
St Agnes RC Primary School
BOW E3 ... 105 J2
CRICK NW2 ... 82 C1
St Aidans Primary School
FSBYPK N4 ... 67 G4
St Aidans RC Primary School
IL IG1 ... 72 D5
St Albans CE Primary School
FSBYW WC1X ... 11 J1
St Albans Health Clinic
KTTN NW5 ... 84 A1
St Albans RC Aided Primary School
E/WMO/HCT KT8 ... 189 G2
St Albans RC Church & School Presbytery
HCH RM12 ... 93 J3
St Albans RC JMI School
HCH RM12 ... 93 K5
St Albans Road Infant School
DART DA1 ... 171 J1
St Alfege with St Peter CE Primary School
GNWCH SE10 ... 125 F6
St Aloysius College
ARCH N19 ... 66 C5
St Aloysius RC Infant School
CAMTN NW1 ... 4 C4
St Aloysius RC Junior School
CAMTN NW1 ... 4 B3
St Andrew & St Francis CE JMI School
CRICK NW2 ... 81 J4
St Andrews CE JMI School
TRDG/WHET N20 ... 32 D4
St Andrews CE Primary School
EN EN1 ... 23 K3
STHGT/OAK N14 ... 34 D3
St Andrews Greek School
CAMTN NW1 ... 84 B4
St Andrews Hospital
BOW E3 ... 105 K3
St Andrews Primary School
BRXN/ST SW9 ... 142 A3
IS N1 ... 85 F6
St Andrews School
RYLN/HDSTN HA2 ... 60 B2
WLSDN NW10 ... 81 K5
St Angelas RC School
FSTGT E7 ... 89 F4
St Annes Catholic High School
PLMGR N13 ... 35 G6
St Annes CE Primary School
WAND/EARL SW18 ... 140 A6
St Annes Convent School
EN EN1 ... 23 K5
St Annes Primary School
STWL/WRAY TW19 ... 152 B2
St Annes RC Primary School
LBTH SE11 ... 122 A6
St Annes Special School
MRDN SM4 ... 194 A2
St Anne's Trading Estate
POP/IOD E14 ... 105 H5
St Anns CE Primary School
SEVS/STOTM N15 ... 67 K2
St Ann's General Hospital
SEVS/STOTM N15 ... 67 J2
St Anns School
HNWL W7 ... 115 K1
St Ann's Shopping Centre
HRW HA1 ... 60 E3
St Anselms RC First & Middle School
HRW HA1 ... 60 E4
St Anselms RC Primary School
DART DA1 ... 151 K6
NWDGN UB2 ... 114 E3
St Anslems RC Primary School
TOOT SW17 ... 161 F5
St Anthonys Hospital
WPK KT4 ... 193 G5
St Anthony's Preparatory School
HAMP NW3 ... 83 H2
St Anthonys RC Primary School
EDUL SE22 ... 163 G1
FSTGT E7 ... 88 E5
PGE/AN SE20 ... 181 J4
St Anthony's School
HAMP NW3 ... 83 G3
St Antonys RC Primary School
WFD IG8 ... 38 E6
St Aubyns School
WFD IG8 ... 52 D3
St Augustines CE School
KIL/WHAMP NW6 ... 100 E1
St Augustines Primary School
BELV DA17 ... 129 G3
KIL/WHAMP NW6 ... 101 F1
St Augustines Priory School
EA W5 ... 98 A4
St Augustines RC Infant School
GNTH/NBYPK IG2 ... 72 B2
St Augustines RC Primary School
CAT SE6 ... 182 E1
GNTH/NBYPK IG2 ... 72 B2
WKENS W14 ... 119 H6
St Barnabas & Philip CE Primary
KENS W8 ... 119 K3
St Bartholomews CE Primary School
SYD SE26 ... 163 K6
St Bartholomews Hospital
STBT EC1A ... 12 B2
St Bartholomews Medical School
FARR EC1M ... 6 B7
St Bartholomews & Royal London School of Medicine
FARR EC1M ... 12 C1
St Bartholomew's the Great
STBT EC1A ... 12 B2
St Barts Hospital Sports Ground
CHST BR7 ... 185 J2
St Bedes RC Infant School
BAL SW12 ... 161 J3
St Bedes RC Primary School
CHDH RM6 ... 73 J2
St Benedicts Junior School
EA W5 ... 97 J4
St Benedicts School
EA W5 ... 97 K4
St Bernadettes RC First & Middle School
KTN/HRWW/W HA3 ... 62 B1
St Bonaventure's School
FSTGT E7 ... 88 E5
St Boniface RC Primary School
TOOT SW17 ... 178 E1
St Catherines RC Girls School
BXLYHS DA6 ... 149 J6
St Catherines RC Middle School
NWMAL KT3 ... 193 F2
St Catherines RC Primary School
WDR/YW UB7 ... 112 A2
St Catherines School
TWK TW1 ... 156 A4
St Cecilias RC Primary School
WPK KT4 ... 193 G6
St Chads RC Primary School
SNWD SE25 ... 197 F2
St Charles Hospital
NKENS W10 ... 100 B4
St Charles RC Primary School
NKENS W10 ... 100 B4
St Christinas Prep School
STJWD NW8 ... 2 D2
St Christopher House
STHWK SE1 ... 12 C7
St Christophers School
BECK BR3 ... 183 F5
HAMP NW3 ... 83 H3
WBLY HA9 ... 80 B1
St Clare Business Park
HPTN TW12 ... 173 H2
St Clement Danes CE Primary School
HOL/ALD WC2B ... 11 G4
St Clement & James CE Primary School
NTGHL W11 ... 119 H1
St Clements Hospital
BOW E3 ... 105 H2
St Clements RC Primary School
EW KT17 ... 207 H6
St Columbas RC Boys School
BXLYHS DA6 ... 149 J6
St Cuthbert With St Matthias CE Primary School
ECT SW5 ... 120 A5
St Davids College
WWKM BR4 ... 198 E4
St Davids Health Centre
STWL/WRAY TW19 ... 152 A2
St Davids School
ASHF TW15 ... 152 C5
St Dominics RC J & I School
HOM E9 ... 87 F4
St Dominics RC Primary School
HAMP NW3 ... 83 K3
St Dominics 6th Form College
HRW HA1 ... 60 E6
St Dunstans CE Primary School
CHEAM SM3 ... 208 C5
St Dunstans College
CAT SE6 ... 164 C3
St Ebba's Hospital
HOR/WEW KT19 ... 206 E6
St Edmunds RC Primary School
ED N9 ... 36 D3
POP/IOD E14 ... 124 D4
WHTN TW2 ... 155 G2
St Edwards CE Comprehensive School
CHDH RM6 ... 74 C3
St Edwards CE Primary School
ROM RM1 ... 75 F1
St Edwards RC JMI School
STJWD NW8 ... 2 C7
St Elizabeths RC Primary School
RCHPK/HAM TW10 ... 157 G1
St Elpheges RC Primary School
WLGTN SM6 ... 210 E4
St Faiths CE School
WAND/EARL SW18 ... 140 A6
St Fidelis Catholic Primary School
ERITH DA8 ... 129 K6
St Francesca Cabrini Primary School
FSTH SE23 ... 163 K1
St Francis of Assisi Primary School
NTGHL W11 ... 100 B6
St Francis RC Primary School
PECK SE15 ... 123 H6
SRTFD E15 ... 88 C3
St Francis Xavier College
BAL SW12 ... 161 G1
St Gabriels CE Primary School
PIM SW1V ... 121 H5
St George's Cathedral
STHWK SE1 ... 17 K4
St George's Cathedral RC Primary
STHWK SE1 ... 18 A4
St Georges CE Primary School
BMLY BR1 ... 184 B5
PECK SE15 ... 143 F1
VX/NE SW8 ... 141 H1
St Georges College
HOLWY N7 ... 85 G1
St Georges Elizabethan Theatre
HOLWY N7 ... 84 D2
St Georges Hanover Square CE Primary School
MYFR/PKLN W1K ... 9 H6
St Georges Hospital
TOOT SW17 ... 178 D1
St Georges Industrial Estate
KUTN/CMB KT2 ... 174 E1
WDGN N22 ... 49 H3
St Georges Medical Centre
HDN NW4 ... 45 K6
St Georges Pool
WCHPL E1 ... 104 C6
St Georges RC First & Middle School
HRW HA1 ... 79 F1
St Georges RC Primary School
ENC/FH EN2 ... 23 K3
St Georges RC School
MV/WKIL W9 ... 101 F1
St Georges Shopping Centre & Cinema
HRW HA1 ... 60 D3
St George the Martyr CE Primary School
BMSBY WC1N ... 5 G7
St George Wharf
VX/NE SW8 ... 121 K5
St Gildas RC Junior School
CEND/HSY/T N8 ... 66 E4
St Giles College London Central
RSQ WC1B ... 10 E1
St Giles School
CROY/NA CR0 ... 211 H4
St Gregorys High School
KTN/HRWW/W HA3 ... 61 K2
St Gregorys RC Primary School
EA W5 ... 97 J3
St Helens Catholic Infant School
WALTH E17 ... 70 A2
St Helens RC Primary School
BRXN/ST SW9 ... 142 B4
PLSTW E13 ... 106 D3
St Helens School for Girls
NTHWD HA6 ... 40 C2
St Helier Hospital
SUT SM1 ... 194 B5
St Hildas School
BUSH WD23 ... 28 B2
St Ignatius RC Primary School
SEVS/STOTM N15 ... 68 A3
St James CE J & I School
BERM/RHTH SE16 ... 123 H3
St James CE Primary School
MUSWH N10 ... 66 A1
PEND EN3 ... 24 E3
St James CE Junior School
FSTGT E7 ... 88 D3
St James Hatcham CE Primary School
NWCR SE14 ... 144 B2
St James Independent School
TWK TW1 ... 156 B4
St James Medical Centre
CROY/NA CR0 ... 196 E4
St James RC Primary School
HAYES BR2 ... 201 G2
WHTN TW2 ... 155 K5
St James & St Michaels CE Primary School
BAY/PAD W2 ... 101 G6
St James's Health Centre
WALTH E17 ... 69 G2
St James's Palace
WHALL SW1A ... 16 B1
St James the Great Catholic School
PECK SE15 ... 143 G2
St James the Great RC Primary School
THHTH CR7 ... 180 C5
St Joachims RC Primary School
CAN/RD E16 ... 107 G5
St Joan of Arc RC Primary School
HBRY N5 ... 85 H2
St John Fisher RC First and Middle School
RYLN/HDSTN HA2 ... 60 A1
St John Fisher RC Primary School
ERITHM DA18 ... 129 F3
GFD/PVL UB6 ... 97 J2
NWMAL KT3 ... 193 F2
St John of Jerusalem CE Primary School
HOM E9 ... 86 E5
St John Rigby Catholic College
WWKM BR4 ... 214 B2
St John & St James CE Primary School
HACK E8 ... 86 E3
St Johns & St James CE School
UED N18 ... 50 B1
St Johns Angell Town CE Primary School
BRXN/ST SW9 ... 142 B3
St Johns CE First School
STAN HA7 ... 29 G6
St Johns CE Middle School
STAN HA7 ... 29 G6
St Johns CE Primary School
BETH E2 ... 104 E1
BKHH IG9 ... 39 F3
FBAR/BDGN N11 ... 33 K6
KUT KT1 ... 175 F6
PGE/AN SE20 ... 181 K3
TRDG/WHET N20 ... 33 G4
WALW SE17 ... 18 D7
St Johns C E School
CDALE/KGS NW9 ... 63 G2
St John's CE Walham Green
FUL/PGN SW6 ... 139 H2
St Johns CE Infant School
HDN NW4 ... 63 K2
St John's Concert Hall
WEST SW1P ... 16 E5
St Johns Highbury Vale CE Primary School
HBRY N5 ... 85 H1
St John's Hospital
SOHO/SHAV W1D ... 10 D5
St John's Hospital Day Centre
BTSEA SW11 ... 140 C5
St Johns Primary School
WEA W13 ... 97 G6
St Johns RC Primary School
BERM/RHTH SE16 ... 124 B2
St Johns RC Special School
WFD IG8 ... 54 A1
St Johns School
ENC/FH EN2 ... 23 G3
NTHWD HA6 ... 41 F2
St Johns Upper Holloway CE Primary School
ARCH N19 ... 84 D1
St Johns Way Medical Centre
ARCH N19 ... 66 D5
St Johns Wood School
STJWD NW8 ... 2 C4
St John the Baptist CE Junior School
KUT KT1 ... 174 E3
St John the Baptist CE Primary School
CAT SE6 ... 165 F6
IS N1 ... 7 G3
St John the Baptist RC Junior School
BETH E2 ... 104 E1
St John the Divine CE Primary School
CMBW SE5 ... 142 C1
St John the Evangelist RC Primary School
IS N1 ... 6 A2
St John Vianney RC Primary School
SEVS/STOTM N15 ... 67 H1
St Josephs Academic RC School
BKHTH/KID SE3 ... 145 H4
St Josephs Catholic Infant School
LEY E10 ... 69 H5

St Josephs Catholic Primary School
BMLY BR1 .... 184 B3
St Josephs College
STRHM/NOR SW16 .... 180 C2
St Josephs Convent School
WAN E11 .... 70 E3
St Josephs Primary School
HDN NW4 .... 63 K1
PUT/ROE SW15 .... 139 K6
St Joseph's RC College
MLHL NW7 .... 31 H6
St Josephs RC First & Middle School
KTN/HRWW/W HA3 .... 43 G5
St Josephs RC Infant School
NRWD SE19 .... 180 D2
WBLY HA9 .... 80 B4
St Josephs RC Junior School
CMBW SE5 .... 142 D1
LEY E10 .... 69 K5
NRWD SE19 .... 180 D2
WBLY HA9 .... 80 B3
St Josephs RC Primary School
ARCH N19 .... 66 B5
BARK IG11 .... 90 C6
BERM/RHTH SE16 .... 123 K3
CHEL SW3 .... 14 E7
DAGW RM9 .... 92 B2
DART DA1 .... 150 A5
DEPT SE8 .... 144 D1
GNWCH SE10 .... 125 H5
HNWL W7 .... 115 K1
HOL/ALD WC2B 11 F3
KUT KT1 .... 175 F5
MV/WKIL W9 .... 101 G3
STHWK SE1 .... 18 D2
STHWK SE1 .... 123 H2
WLSDN NW10 .... 81 G5
St Josephs RC School
OXHEY WD19 .... 27 F5
St Judes CE Primary School
STHWK SE1 .... 18 A5
St Jude's CE Prim School
HNHL SE24 .... 162 C1
St Judes & St Pauls CE Primary School
IS N1 .... 86 A4
St Katharine Pier
TWRH EC3N 13 K7
St Lawrence Business Centre
FELT TW13 .... 154 A4
St Lawrence Catholic School
FELT TW13 .... 154 A4
St Lawrence Junior School
E/WMO/HCT KT8 .... 173 J6
St Lawrence University
FSBYW WC1X 5 H7
St Leonards CE Primary School
STRHM/NOR SW16 .... 179 J1
St Leonards Hospital
IS N1 .... 7 H2
St Lukes CE Primary School
CAN/RD E16 .... 106 D5
FSBYE EC1V 6 D5
KUTN/CMB KT2 .... 175 G4
MV/WKIL W9 .... 100 D1
POP/IOD E14 .... 125 G4
WNWD SE27 .... 180 D1
St Luke's Health Centre
CAN/RD E16 .... 106 D5
St Lukes Hospital for the Clergy
FITZ W1T 4 A7
St Lukes School
THHTH CR7 .... 196 B1
St Lukes Woodside Hospital
MUSWH N10 .... 66 A1
St Margaret Clitherow RC Primary
THMD SE28 .... 128 C1
St Margaret Lee CE Primary School
LEW SE13 .... 145 H5
St Margarets Business Centre
TWK TW1 .... 156 B2
St Margarets CE Primary School
WOOL/PLUM SE18 .... 127 H6
St Margarets Clitherow RC Primary School
WLSDN NW10 .... 81 F1
St Margarets Primary School
BARK IG11 .... 90 B6
St Margarets School
BUSH WD23 .... 28 A2
HAMP NW3 .... 83 F2
St Marks CE Primary School
ARCH N19 .... 66 E6
HAYES BR2 .... 183 K6
LBTH SE11 .... 122 A6
SNWD SE25 .... 197 H1
St Marks Industrial Estate
CAN/RD E16 .... 126 C1
St Marks Primary School
MTCM CR4 .... 178 E5
NWDGN UB2 .... 115 K2
St Marks RC School
HSLW TW3 .... 134 E4
St Marthas Convent Senior School
EBAR EN4 .... 20 E2
St Martin-in-the-Fields High School
BRXS/STRHM SW2 .... 162 C3
St Martin of Pores RC Primary School
FBAR/BDGN N11 .... 48 C2
St Martins Hospital
MYFR/PKLN W1K 9 G5
St Martins Medical Centre
RSLP HA4 .... 58 C4
St Martins School
MLHL NW7 .... 45 G1
NTHWD HA6 .... 40 B1
St Martins School of Art
SOHO/SHAV W1D 10 D4
St Martins Theatre
LSQ/SEVD WC2H 10 D5
St Mary Abbots CE Primary School
KENS W8 .... 120 A2
St Mary & St Josephs GM School
SCUP DA14 .... 186 A1
St Mary CE Primary School
PUT/ROE SW15 .... 139 G4
St Marylebone CE Secondary School
MHST W1U 9 H1
St Marylebone Crematorium
EFNCH N2 .... 47 F6
St Mary Magdalene CE Primary School
MV/WKIL W9 .... 101 F4
WOOL/PLUM SE18 .... 126 E4
PECK SE15 .... 143 J3
St Mary Magdalene Primary School
HOLWY N7 .... 85 G4
St Mary Magdalen RC Junior School
CRICK NW2 .... 81 K4
St Mary Magdalens RC Primary School
MORT/ESHN SW14 .... 138 A4
St Mary of the Angels RC Primary School
BAY/PAD W2 .... 100 E5
St Marys Abbey
MLHL NW7 .... 31 J5
St Mary & St Pancras CE Primary School
CAMTN NW1 .... 4 C3
St Marys Bryanston Square CE Primary School
MBLAR W1H 8 E2
St Marys Catholic Primary School
CHING E4 .... 38 B3
St Marys CE High School
HDN NW4 .... 46 A6
St Marys CE Infant School
CEND/HSY/T N8 .... 67 F1
St Marys CE Junior School
CEND/HSY/T N8 .... 66 E1
STWL/WRAY TW19 .... 152 B1
THDIT KT7 .... 190 C5
St Mary's Cemetery
BTSEA SW11 .... 140 D6
St Marys CE Primary School
CHSGTN KT9 .... 206 A4
EBAR EN4 .... 33 J1
FNCH N3 .... 46 D4
IS N1 .... 85 H5
LEW SE13 .... 144 E6
TWK TW1 .... 156 B2
WALTH E17 .... 69 K1
WLSDN NW10 .... 81 G4
St Marys Church of England High School
HDN NW4 .... 46 A6
St Marys Greek Cathedral
WDGN N22 .... 49 F4
St Marys High School
CROY/NA CR0 .... 196 D5
St Marys Hospital
BAY/PAD W2 .... 8 B3
St Marys Hospital Medical School
BAY/PAD W2 .... 8 B3
St Marys Infant School
CAR SM5 .... 209 J2
St Mary's Kilburn Primary School
KIL/WHAMP NW6 .... 82 E6
St Marys Magdalens RC Primary School
BROCKY SE4 .... 144 B5
St Mary's Primary School
WKENS W14 .... 119 G3
St Marys RC Infant School
CAR SM5 .... 209 K2
CROY/NA CR0 .... 196 E5
St Marys RC JMI School
HCH RM12 .... 75 J5
St Marys RC Junior School
CROY/NA CR0 .... 196 E5
WALTH E17 .... 52 A6
St Marys RC Primary School
BECK BR3 .... 183 F3
CHSWK W4 .... 118 A5
CLAP SW4 .... 141 H6
ELTH/MOT SE9 .... 147 F6
ISLW TW7 .... 136 B4
KIL/WHAMP NW6 .... 100 E1
NKENS W10 .... 100 C3
PEND EN3 .... 25 F5
SEVS/STOTM N15 .... 67 K2
VX/NE SW8 .... 141 G2
WIM/MER SW19 .... 177 K3
St Marys & St Peters CE Primary School
TEDD TW11 .... 173 K1
St Marys School
CEND/HSY/T N8 .... 67 F2
HAMP NW3 .... 83 G3
St Marys Stoke Newington CE Primary School
STNW/STAM N16 .... 68 A6
St Marys University College
TWK TW1 .... 156 A5
St Matthews CE Primary School
PEND EN3 .... 24 E6
RYNPK SW20 .... 176 D4
SURB KT6 .... 191 F4
WDR/YW UB7 .... 112 A1
WEST SW1P 16 D5
St Matthias CE Primary School
BETH E2 .... 7 K6
STNW/STAM N16 .... 86 A3
St Meryl Junior Middle & Infant School
OXHEY WD19 .... 27 J5
St Michael At Bowes CE Junior School
PLMGR N13 .... 49 G2
St Michaels and St Martins RC Primary School
HSLWW TW4 .... 134 E4
St Michaels Catholic Grammar School
NFNCH/WDSP N12 .... 47 F1
St Michaels CE Primary School
ENC/FH EN2 .... 23 J2
HGT N6 .... 66 A4
WAND/EARL SW18 .... 159 J2
WDGN N22 .... 49 F4
St Michaels CE Aided Primary School Hall
WELL DA16 .... 148 D2
St Michaels RC Primary School
EHAM E6 .... 107 K1
St Michaels RC Secondary School
BERM/RHTH SE16 .... 123 H2
St Michaels Sydenham CE Primary
SYD SE26 .... 164 B6
St Monicas RC Primary School
IS N1 .... 7 G4
St Monica's RC Primary School
IS N1 .... 7 G4
St Monicas RC Primary School
STHGT/OAK N14 .... 34 E5
St Nicholas Centre
SUT SM1 .... 209 F3
St Nicholas Preparatory School
CDALE/KGS NW9 .... 62 E6
St Nicholas School
BORE WD6 .... 30 A1
CHST BR7 .... 185 H3
St Olaves Preparatory School
ELTH/MOT SE9 .... 167 G4
St Olave's & St Saviour's Grammar School
ORP BR6 .... 217 H1
St Osmunds RC Primary School
BARN SW13 .... 138 C2
St Pancras & Islington Cemetery
EFNCH N2 .... 47 J4
St Pancras Hospital
CAMTN NW1 .... 4 C1
St Pancras Station
CAMTN NW1 .... 4 E4
St Patricks Church School
STHWK SE1 .... 17 J1
St Patricks Infants School
WAP E1W 123 J1
St Patricks International School
SOHO/CST W1F 10 B3
St Patricks Primary School
KTTN NW5 .... 84 B4
St Patricks RC JMI School
ROMW/RG RM7 .... 56 D4
St Patricks RC Primary School
WALTH E17 .... 69 G1
WAP E1W 123 J1
WOOL/PLUM SE18 .... 127 J4
St Paulinus CE Primary School
DART DA1 .... 150 B5
St Pauls & All Hallows CE Infant School
TOTM N17 .... 50 C3
St Paul's Cathedral
STP EC4M 12 B4
St Paul's Cathedral School
STP EC4M 12 C4
St Pauls CE JMI School
MLHL NW7 .... 31 K6
St Pauls CE Primary School
BTFD TW8 .... 116 E6
CHSGTN KT9 .... 206 A2
FBAR/BDGN N11 .... 48 A1
HAMP NW3 .... 83 J5
WALW SE17 .... 122 C5
WCHMH N21 .... 35 H2
St Pauls CE Junior School
KUTN/CMB KT2 .... 175 H3
St Pauls CE Primary School
WCHPL E1 .... 104 C6
St Pauls Cray CE Primary School
STMC/STPC BR5 .... 186 D6
St Pauls Cray Health Clinic
STMC/STPC BR5 .... 186 B5
St Pauls Girls School
HMSMTH W6 .... 119 G4
St Pauls Preparatory School
BARN SW13 .... 118 D5
St Paul's Primary School
HMSMTH W6 .... 119 F5
St Pauls RC Primary School
THDIT KT7 .... 189 K4
WDGN N22 .... 49 F5
St Pauls RC School
WOOL/PLUM SE18 .... 128 B6
St Pauls Road Medical Centre
IS N1 .... 85 H4
St Pauls Way School
BOW E3 .... 105 J3
St Pauls With St Lukes CE Primary School
BOW E3 .... 105 H4
St Paul's with St Michael's CE Primary School
HACK E8 .... 86 C6
St Paul with St Luke CE Primary School
POP/IOD E14 .... 105 H4
St Peter and St Paul RC Primary School
MTCM CR4 .... 194 E1
St Peter Chanel RC Primary School
SCUP DA14 .... 186 D1
St Peter & Pauls RC Primary School
IL IG1 .... 90 D1
St Peter & St Pauls Primary School
FSBYE EC1V 6 B6
St Peters Catholic Primary School
ROM RM1 .... 57 F6
St Peters CE Primary School
HMSMTH W6 .... 118 D5
MV/WKIL W9 .... 100 E3
WALW SE17 .... 122 E5
St Peters Eaton Square CE Primary School
BGVA SW1W 15 J5
St Peter's Hospital
COVGDN WC2E 11 F5
St Peters Primary School
SAND/SEL CR2 .... 211 K4
WAP E1W 123 K1
St Peters RC Primary School
DAGW RM9 .... 92 B6
WOOL/PLUM SE18 .... 127 G5
St Philips School
CHSGTN KT9 .... 205 K4
SKENS SW7 .... 120 B4
St Phillips Infant School
SYD SE26 .... 163 J6
St Philomenas RC High School
CAR SM5 .... 209 K3
St Philomenas RC Primary School
STMC/STPC BR5 .... 202 D4
St Quintins Health Centre
NKENS W10 .... 100 A4
St Raphaels Hospice
WPK KT4 .... 193 G6
St Raphael's RC Primary School
NTHLT UB5 .... 95 F1
St Raphaels Way Medical Centre
WBLY HA9 .... 80 E3
St Richards with St Andrews CE Primary School
RCHPK/HAM TW10 .... 156 C5
St Robert Southwell RC Primary School
CDALE/KGS NW9 .... 62 E3
St Saviour & St Olaves School
STHWK SE1 .... 19 F5
St Saviours CE Infant School
EA W5 .... 116 E1
St Saviours CE Primary School
HNHL SE24 .... 142 D4
MV/WKIL W9 .... 101 F3
POP/IOD E14 .... 105 K4
WALTH E17 .... 69 H4
St Saviours RC Primary School
LEW SE13 .... 145 F5
St Scholastica's RC Primary School
STNW/STAM N16 .... 86 C1
St Stephens CE Junior School
TWK TW1 .... 156 B1
St Stephens CE Primary School
BAY/PAD W2 .... 100 E4
DEPT SE8 .... 144 D3
SHB W12 .... 119 F1
St Stephens CE School
VX/NE SW8 .... 141 K1
St Stephens Primary School
EHAM E6 .... 89 G5
St Stephens RC Primary School
WELL DA16 .... 148 B4
St Swithun Wells RC Primary School
RSLP HA4 .... 77 H1
St Teresa RC Primary School
BCTR RM8 .... 91 J2
St Teresas RC School
KTN/HRWW/W HA3 .... 42 C4
St Theresas RC Primary School
FNCH N3 .... 46 E6
St Thomas a' Becket RC Primary School
ABYW SE2 .... 128 B3
St Thomas CE Primary School
NKENS W10 .... 100 C3
STNW/STAM N16 .... 68 B5
St Thomas' Hospital
STHWK SE1 .... 17 G4
St Thomas' Hospital Operation Theatre
STHWK SE1 .... 18 E1
St Thomas More RC Primary School
BXLYHN DA7 .... 149 G3
ELTH/MOT SE9 .... 146 D4
St Thomas More RC School
CHEL SW3 .... 14 E7
ELTH/MOT SE9 .... 167 F1
St Thomas More School
WDGN N22 .... 49 F3
St Thomas of Canterbury RC Middle School
MTCM CR4 .... 179 F6
St Thomas of Canterbury RC Primary School
FUL/PGN SW6 .... 139 J1
St Thomas the Apostle College
PECK SE15 .... 143 K2
St Ursulas Convent School
GNWCH SE10 .... 145 G1
St Ursulas RC Infant School
HARH RM3 .... 57 K2
St Ursulas RC Junior School
HARH RM3 .... 57 K2
St Vincent de Paul RC Primary School
WEST SW1P 16 A5
St Vincents Catholic Primary School
ELTH/MOT SE9 .... 166 D6
St Vincents Hospital
RSLP HA4 .... 40 C6
St Vincents RC Primary School
ACT W3 .... 98 D6
BCTR RM8 .... 73 J6
MHST W1U 9 G2
MLHL NW7 .... 32 A6
St Walter & St John Sports Ground
TOOT SW17 .... 160 D3
St William of York Primary School
FSTH SE23 .... 164 B3
St Winefreds Junior School
LEE/GVPK SE12 .... 165 J1
St Winefreds RC Infant School
LEW SE13 .... 145 H6
St Winefrides Catholic Primary School
MNPK E12 .... 89 K3
Salcombe School
STHGT/OAK N14 .... 34 D2
Salesian College
BTSEA SW11 .... 140 D2
Salisbury Primary School
MNPK E12 .... 89 H3
Salisbury School
ED N9 .... 36 E3
Salisbury Upper School
ED N9 .... 36 E2
Salters' Hall
BARB EC2Y 12 D2
Salusbury Primary School
KIL/WHAMP NW6 .... 82 C6
Salvation Army Heritage Centre
BLKFR EC4V 12 C5
Salvatorian College
KTN/HRWW/W HA3 .... 42 E5
Samaritan & Western Ophthalmic Hospital
MBLAR W1H 8 E1
Samuel Jones Industrial Estate
PECK SE15 .... 143 F1
Samuel Rhodes School
IS N1 .... 85 G6
Sanderstead Junior School
SAND/SEL CR2 .... 211 K6
Sandgate Trading Estate
BERM/RHTH SE16 .... 123 J5
Sandhurst Primary School
CAT SE6 .... 165 H2
Sandown Golf Centre
ESH/CLAY KT10 .... 204 B1
Sandown Industrial Park
ESH/CLAY KT10 .... 189 F6
Sandown Park Racecourse
ESH/CLAY KT10 .... 204 B1
Sandringham Primary School
FSTGT E7 .... 89 G4
Sandy Lodge Golf Club
NTHWD HA6 .... 26 B4
Sapcote Trading Centre
WLSDN NW10 .... 81 H3
Sarah Bonnell School
SRTFD E15 .... 88 C4
Sarum Hall School
HAMP NW3 .... 83 J5
Satmer Trust School
STNW/STAM N16 .... 68 C6
Savoy Pier
TPL/STR WC2R 11 G6
Savoy Theatre
TPL/STR WC2R 11 G6
Saxon Business Centre
WIM/MER SW19 .... 178 B5
Sayer Clinic
CROY/NA CR0 .... 211 F2
Sayer Clinics
MBLAR W1H 9 F4
Schiller International School
STHWK SE1 .... 17 J1
Schomberg House
STJS SW1Y 16 B1
School of Art
RCH/KEW TW9 .... 137 F5
School of English
GLDGN NW11 .... 64 E5
School of Oriental & African Studies
STPAN WC1H 4 D7
The School of Pharmacy
BMSBY WC1N 5 F6
The School of St David & St Katharine
CEND/HSY/T N8 .... 66 E1
Science Museum
SKENS SW7 .... 14 A6
Science Museum IMAX Cinema
SKENS SW7 .... 14 A5
The Science Museum Library
SKENS SW7 .... 14 A4
Scotts Park Primary School
BMLY BR1 .... 184 B4
Scott Wilkie Primary School
CAN/RD E16 .... 107 G5
Screen on Baker Street Cinema
MHST W1U 9 F1
Screen on the Green Cinema
IS N1 .... 6 A1
Screen on the Hill Cinema
HAMP NW3 .... 83 J3
Sebright Primary School
BETH E2 .... 104 C1
Secombe Centre
SUT SM1 .... 208 E3
Sedgehill School
CAT SE6 .... 182 E1
Sedgewick Centre
WCHPL E1 .... 13 K3
Selborne Primary School
GFD/PVL UB6 .... 97 F1
The Selhurst Medical Centre
SNWD SE25 .... 196 E3
Sellincourt School
TOOT SW17 .... 178 D2
Selsdon High School
SAND/SEL CR2 .... 213 F5
Selsdon Primary School
SAND/SEL CR2 .... 212 E6
Selsdon Road Industrial Estate
SAND/SEL CR2 .... 211 K5
Selwyn Primary School
CHING E4 .... 52 A2
PLSTW E13 .... 88 E6
Sergeant Industrial Estate
WAND/EARL SW18 .... 160 A1
Serpentine Gallery
BAY/PAD W2 .... 14 B1
Servite RC Primary School
WBPTN SW10 .... 120 B6
Seven Islands Leisure Centre
BERM/RHTH SE16 .... 123 K3
Seven Kings Health Centre
GDMY/SEVK IG3 .... 72 E5
Seven Kings High School
GNTH/NBYPK IG2 .... 72 D4
Seven Mills Primary School
POP/IOD E14 .... 124 D2
Sevenoaks Way Industrial Estate
STMC/STPC BR5 .... 186 D6
Seven Sisters Primary School
SEVS/STOTM N15 .... 68 A2
Seymour Gardens Medical Centre
IL IG1 .... 71 K5
Seymour Leasure Centre
MBLAR W1H 8 E2
Shaare Zedek Medical Centre
GLDGN NW11 .... 64 D3
Shacklewell Primary School
STNW/STAM N16 .... 86 B2
Shaftesbury High School
KTN/HRWW/W HA3 .... 42 B4
Shaftesbury Hospital
LSQ/SEVD WC2H 10 D4
Shaftesbury Medical Centre
RYLN/HDSTN HA2 .... 60 C5
Shaftesbury Park Primary School
BTSEA SW11 .... 141 F4
Shaftesbury Primary School
FSTGT E7 .... 89 G5
Shaftesbury Theatre
LSQ/SEVD WC2H 10 E3
Shahjalal Medical Centre
WCHPL E1 .... 104 C5
Shakespeare Business Centre
BRXN/ST SW9 .... 142 C4
Shakespeare's Globe Theatre
STHWK SE1 .... 12 B6
The Shamrock Sports Club
ACT W3 .... 98 E5
Shannon Corner Retail Park
NWMAL KT3 .... 192 D1
Shapla J & I School
WCHPL E1 .... 104 C6
Sharp Sports Centre
EDGE HA8 .... 44 C2
Shawcroft School
STMC/STPC BR5 .... 203 F2
Sheen Lane Health Centre
MORT/ESHN SW14 .... 137 K4

Sheen Mount Primary School *RCHPK/HAM* TW10 .... 137 J6
Sheen School *MORT/ESHN* SW14 .... 138 B5
Sheen Sports Centre *MORT/ESHN* SW14 .... 138 B5
Shell Centre *STHWK* SE1 .... 17 H1
Shelley School *CLAP* SW4 .... 141 H4
Shenstone School *DART* DA1 .... 150 A6
Shepherd's Bush Cricket Club *ACT* W3 .... 99 G6
Shepherd's Bush Empire *SHB* W12 .... 119 F2
Shepherds Community School YWAM *BROCKY* SE4 .... 144 D4
Sheraton Business Centre *GFD/PVL* UB6 .... 97 J1
Sheringdale Primary School *WAND/EARL* SW18 .... 159 J3
Sheringham Junior School *MNPK* E12 .... 89 K2
Sherington Primary School *CHARL* SE7 .... 126 A6
Sherlock Holmes Museum *CAMTN* NW1 .... 3 F7
Sherwood First School *MTCM* CR4 .... 195 H1
Sherwood Park Primary School *BFN/LL* DA15 .... 168 C1
Sherwood Park School *WLGTN* SM6 .... 210 D1
Shirley Clinic *CROY/NA* CR0 .... 197 K5
Shirley High School *CROY/NA* CR0 .... 213 F1
Shirley Park Golf Club *CROY/NA* CR0 .... 197 J6
Shirley Wanderers RFC *WWKM* BR4 .... 214 A2
Shooters Hill Golf Club *WOOL/PLUM* SE18 .... 147 H2
Shopping City *WDGN* N22 .... 49 F5
The Shopping Hall *EHAM* E6 .... 89 J6
Shore Business Centre *HOM* E9 .... 86 E5
Shoreditch Comprehensive School *IS* N1 .... 7 H3
Shoreditch County Court *STLK* EC1Y 7 F6
Shortlands Golf Club *HAYES* BR2 .... 183 H4
Shotfield Health Clinic *WLGTN* SM6 .... 210 B4
Showcase Cinema *WDGN* N22 .... 49 G5
Showcase Newham Cinema *BARK* IG11 .... 108 C2
Shrewsbury House School *SURB* KT6 .... 190 E6
Shrewsbury Road Health Centre *FSTGT* E7 .... 89 H5
Sidcup Cemetery *BXLY* DA5 .... 168 E4
Sidcup Golf Club *BFN/LL* DA15 .... 168 B4
Sidcup Health Centre *SCUP* DA14 .... 168 B5
Sidcup Hill Primary School *SCUP* DA14 .... 186 C1
Sidcup Sports Club *SCUP* DA14 .... 168 A6
Sidney Russell School *DAGW* RM9 .... 92 A2
Silicon Business Centre *GFD/PVL* UB6 .... 97 J1
Silverdale Industrial Estate *HYS/HAR* UB3 .... 113 K1
Silver Industrial Estate *TOTM* N17 .... 50 B5
Silver Street Medical Centre *UED* N18 .... 36 A6
Silver Wing Industrial Estate *CROY/NA* CR0 .... 211 F4
Simon Marks Jewish Primary School *STNW/STAM* N16 .... 68 B5
Sinclair House School *FUL/PGN* SW6 .... 139 H2
Singlegate First School *WIM/MER* SW19 .... 178 C3
Sion College *EMB* EC4Y 11 K5
Sion Manning RC Girls School *NKENS* W10 .... 100 B4
Sir Francis Drake Primary School *DEPT* SE8 .... 124 B5
Sir George Monoux College *WALTH* E17 .... 51 K5
Sir James Barrie School *VX/NE* SW8 .... 141 H2
Sir John Cass Foundation/ Redcoat School *WCHPL* E1 .... 105 F4
Sir John Cass Foundation School *TWRH* EC3N 13 J4
Sir John Lillie Primary School *HMSMTH* W6 .... 119 H6
Sir John Soane's Museum *LINN* WC2A 11 H3
Sir Thomas Abney Primary School *STNW/STAM* N16 .... 67 K4
Sir Thomas Lipton Memorial Hospital *STHGT/OAK* N14 .... 34 B2
Sir William Burrough Primary School *POP/IOD* E14 .... 105 G5
Six Bridges Trading Estate *STHWK* SE1 .... 123 H5
Sixth Form Centre *FSTGT* E7 .... 89 F4
Skillion Business Park *BARK* IG11 .... 109 F2
Skinners Companys Lower Girls School *CLPT* E5 .... 68 D5
Skinners Companys School For Girls *STNW/STAM* N16 .... 68 B4
Ski Slope *STMC/STPC* BR5 .... 186 E4
Slade Green FC *ERITH* DA8 .... 150 E2
Slade Green Primary School *ERITH* DA8 .... 150 D1
Slade School of Fine Art *STPAN* WC1H 4 D5
Sleaford Industrial Estate *VX/NE* SW8 .... 141 H1
Sloane Hospital *BECK* BR3 .... 183 G4
Smallberry Green Primary School *ISLW* TW7 .... 136 B3
Smallwood Primary School *TOOT* SW17 .... 160 C6
SMA Medical Centre *LEY* E10 .... 69 K4
Smithy Street School *WCHPL* E1 .... 104 E4
Snaresbrook College *SWFD* E18 .... 52 E5
Snaresbrook Crown Court *WAN* E11 .... 70 D2
Snaresbrook Primary School *SWFD* E18 .... 70 E1
Snooker Club *WEA* W13 .... 116 C1
Snowsfields Primary School *STHWK* SE1 .... 19 G2
Sobell Leisure Centre *HOLWY* N7 .... 85 F1
Sobell Medical Centre *HOLWY* N7 .... 85 G2
Soho Parish CE Primary School *SOHO/CST* W1F 10 C5
Solent Road Health Centre *KIL/WHAMP* NW6 .... 82 E4
Somerset House *COVGDN* WC2E 11 G5
Somers Town Community Sports Centre *CAMTN* NW1 .... 4 B3
Sorsby Health Centre *CLPT* E5 .... 87 F2
South Bank Business Centre *BTSEA* SW11 .... 141 F2
VX/NE SW8 .... 121 J6
Southbank International School *HAMP* NW3 .... 83 G4
NTGHL W11 .... 100 E6
Southbank University *STHWK* SE1 .... 18 A3
STHWK SE1 .... 18 C4
VX/NE SW8 .... 141 J2
Southborough Primary School *HAYES* BR2 .... 201 F2
Southborough School *SURB* KT6 .... 206 A1
Southbury Primary School *PEND* EN3 .... 24 D5
South Camden Community School *CAMTN* NW1 .... 4 B2
South Chelsea College *BRXN/ST* SW9 .... 142 A5
South Croydon Medical Centre *SAND/SEL* CR2 .... 211 J5
South Croydon Sports Club *SAND/SEL* CR2 .... 212 A3
South Eastern University *HOLWY* N7 .... 85 F1
Southern Road Primary School *PLSTW* E13 .... 107 F1
Southfield First & Middle School *CHSWK* W4 .... 118 B2
Southfield Medical Centre *CHSWK* W4 .... 118 A2
The Southfields Clinic *WAND/EARL* SW18 .... 159 K1
Southfields Community School *WAND/EARL* SW18 .... 159 K3
Southgate Cemetery *STHGT/OAK* N14 .... 34 C4
Southgate College *STHGT/OAK* N14 .... 34 C4
Southgate Compton Cricket Club *EBAR* EN4 .... 21 K5
Southgate Leisure Centre *STHGT/OAK* N14 .... 34 D2
Southgate Road Medical Centre *IS* N1 .... 85 K5
Southgate School *EBAR* EN4 .... 22 B6
South Grove Primary School *WALTH* E17 .... 69 G3
South Hampstead Cricket Club *CRICK* NW2 .... 82 A5
South Hampstead High School (Senior) *HAMP* NW3 .... 83 H4
South Harringay Junior School *FSBYPK* N4 .... 67 G2
South Herts Golf Club *TRDG/WHET* N20 .... 32 E3
Southlake Primary School *ABYW* SE2 .... 128 E2
Southlands College *PUT/ROE* SW15 .... 138 C5
South Lewisham Health Centre *CAT* SE6 .... 165 F6
South London Crematorium *MTCM* CR4 .... 179 H5
South London Gallery *CMBW* SE5 .... 143 F2
South London Montessori School *BTSEA* SW11 .... 140 D2
The South London Natural Health Centre *CLAP* SW4 .... 141 H5
South London Tamil School *CROY/NA* CR0 .... 196 D4
South London Theatre *WNWD* SE27 .... 162 D5
Southmead Primary School *WIM/MER* SW19 .... 159 H3
South Norwood Country Park *SNWD* SE25 .... 197 K1
South Norwood Hill Medical Centre *SNWD* SE25 .... 181 F5
South Norwood Medical Centre *SNWD* SE25 .... 197 F1
South Norwood Primary School *SNWD* SE25 .... 197 H1
South Park Business Centre *IL* IG1 .... 72 E6
South Park Clinic *IL* IG1 .... 90 E2
South Park Primary School *GDMY/SEVK* IG3 .... 90 E1
South Quay Plaza *POP/IOD* E14 .... 124 E2
South Rise Primary School *WOOL/PLUM* SE18 .... 127 J5
Southside Industrial Estate *VX/NE* SW8 .... 141 H1
South Thames College *PUT/ROE* SW15 .... 139 G6
South Thames College/ Wandsworth Adult College *PUT/ROE* SW15 .... 158 C1
Southville Junior School *EBED/NFELT* TW14 .... 153 J3
Southwark Bridge Business Centre *STHWK* SE1 .... 18 D1
Southwark Bridge Stairs *BLKFR* EC4V 12 C6
Southwark Cathedral *STHWK* SE1 .... 12 E7
Southwark College *BERM/RHTH* SE16 .... 123 J3
CMBW SE5 .... 143 F1
STHWK SE1 .... 18 A2
STHWK SE1 .... 19 H4
Southwark Crown Court *MON* EC3R 13 G7
Southwark Park Primary School *BERM/RHTH* SE16 .... 123 J3
Southwark Park Sports Centre *BERM/RHTH* SE16 .... 123 K4
Southwark Sports Ground *DUL* SE21 .... 163 G3
South West Middlesex Crematorium *FELT* TW13 .... 154 D3
Southwold Primary School *CLPT* E5 .... 68 E6
South Woodford Health Centre *SWFD* E18 .... 52 E4
Southwood Hospital *HGT* N6 .... 66 A4
Southwood Primary School *DAGW* RM9 .... 92 A2
Sovereign Business Centre *PEND* EN3 .... 25 H4
The Space Arts Centre Cinema *DEPT* SE8 .... 124 C4
Sparrow Farm County Junior School *EW* KT17 .... 207 K3
Sparrow Farm Junior School *EBED/NFELT* TW14 .... 154 B2
Sparrow Farm Nursery School *EBED/NFELT* TW14 .... 154 B2
Speakers Corner *BAY/PAD* W2 .... 9 F5
Spectators Viewing Area *HTHAIR* TW6 .... 132 E4
Speedway Industrial Estate *HYS/HAR* UB3 .... 113 G2
Speke's Monument *BAY/PAD* W2 .... 120 B1
Spelthorne Sixth Form College *ASHF* TW15 .... 152 C6
Spencer House *WHALL* SW1A 16 A1
The Spires Shopping Centre *BAR* EN5 .... 20 C4
Spiritualist University *WLSDN* NW10 .... 81 J5
Spitalfields Health Centre *WCHPL* E1 .... 13 K2
Spitalfields Market Hall *WCHPL* E1 .... 13 J1
Splashworld Swimming Centre *WELL* DA16 .... 148 E5
Springfield Christian School *PECK* SE15 .... 143 G1
Springfield Hospital *TOOT* SW17 .... 160 D5
Springfield Primary School *VX/NE* SW8 .... 141 J1
Spring Grove Primary School *ISLW* TW7 .... 135 J3
Springhallow School *HNWL* W7 .... 97 F5
Spring Park Primary School *CROY/NA* CR0 .... 213 J1
Springvale Retail Park *STMC/STPC* BR5 .... 186 D6
STMC/STPC BR5 .... 202 E2
Springwell Infant School *HEST* TW5 .... 134 D1
Springwell Junior School *HEST* TW5 .... 134 D1
Spurgeons College *SNWD* SE25 .... 181 F5
Squash and Badminton Club *WIM/MER* SW19 .... 177 H3
Squirrels Heath Junior School *GPK* RM2 .... 75 K2
Squirrels Trading Estate *HYS/HAR* UB3 .... 113 J3
The Stables Gallery & Art Centre *CRICK* NW2 .... 81 J2
Stadium Business Centre *WBLY* HA9 .... 80 D1
Stadium Industrial Estate *WBLY* HA9 .... 80 D3
Stadium Retail Park *WBLY* HA9 .... 80 C1
Stafford Cross Business Park *CROY/NA* CR0 .... 211 F3
Stag Lane Medical Centre *CDALE/KGS* NW9 .... 44 E6
Stag Lane Primary School *EDGE* HA8 .... 44 C5
Stamford Clinic *HMSMTH* W6 .... 118 D4
Stamford Hill Primary School *SEVS/STOTM* N15 .... 67 K3
Stanburn Middle School *STAN* HA7 .... 43 J3
Standard Industrial Estate *CAN/RD* E16 .... 126 C2
CAN/RD E16 .... 126 E2
Stanford Middle School *STRHM/NOR* SW16 .... 179 J4
Stanhope Primary School *GFD/PVL* UB6 .... 96 C3
Stanley Infant School *TEDD* TW11 .... 155 K6
Stanley Junior School *TEDD* TW11 .... 155 K6
Stanley Park High School *CAR* SM5 .... 210 A4
Stanley Park Junior School *CAR* SM5 .... 209 K5
Stanley Technical Boys High School *SNWD* SE25 .... 181 G6
Stanmore College *STAN* HA7 .... 43 H2
Stanmore Golf Club *STAN* HA7 .... 43 H3
Stanton School of English *BAY/PAD* W2 .... 101 F5
Stanton Square Industrial Estate *CAT* SE6 .... 164 C6
Staple Inn Buildings *HHOL* WC1V 11 J2
Staples Corner Business Park *CRICK* NW2 .... 63 J5
Star Business Centre *DAGW* RM9 .... 111 F4
Star Primary School *CAN/RD* E16 .... 106 C3
Stationers Hall *STP* EC4M 12 B4
Stationery Office *HOL/ALD* WC2B 11 G3
Stephen Hawking Primary School *POP/IOD* E14 .... 105 G5
Stepney Day Hospital *WCHPL* E1 .... 104 E5
Stepney Greencoat CE Primary School *POP/IOD* E14 .... 105 H5
Stepney Green School *WCHPL* E1 .... 105 F4
Ster Century Cinema *ROM* RM1 .... 75 G2
Sterling Industrial Estate *DAGE* RM10 .... 92 D2
Sterling Way Clinic *UED* N18 .... 50 B1
Stewart Fleming Primary School *PGE/AN* SE20 .... 181 K6
Stewart Headlam Primary School *WCHPL* E1 .... 104 D3
Stillness Primary School *BROCKY* SE4 .... 164 B1
Stirling Retail Park *BORE* WD6 .... 31 F1
Stirling Way Industrial Estates *CROY/NA* CR0 .... 195 K4
Stock Exchange *OBST* EC2N 13 F3
Stockley Park Business Centre *STKPK* UB11 .... 113 F1
Stockley Park Golf Club *STKPK* UB11 .... 94 A6
Stockwell Park School *BRXN/ST* SW9 .... 142 A2
Stockwell Primary School *BRXN/ST* SW9 .... 142 A4
Stoke Newington School *STNW/STAM* N16 .... 85 K1
The Stonebridge Primary School *WLSDN* NW10 .... 80 E6
Stonebridge Shopping Centre *WLSDN* NW10 .... 81 F6
Stonehill Business Centre *UED* N18 .... 51 F2
Stonehill Business Park *UED* N18 .... 51 F1
Stone Lake Retail Park *CHARL* SE7 .... 126 B4
Stoneydown Park Primary School *WALTH* E17 .... 69 G1
Storey Primary School *CAN/RD* E16 .... 127 F1
Stormont House School *CLPT* E5 .... 86 D2
Stowford College *BELMT* SM2 .... 209 G5
Strand on the Green J & I School *CHSWK* W4 .... 117 H6
Strand Theatre *HOL/ALD* WC2B 11 G5
Stratford Magistrates Court *SRTFD* E15 .... 88 B5
Stratford School *FSTGT* E7 .... 88 E5
Stratford Shopping Centre *SRTFD* E15 .... 88 B5
Strathmore School *RCHPK/HAM* TW10 .... 156 E3
Strawberry Fields School *BAY/PAD* W2 .... 100 E5
Strawberry Hill Golf Club *WHTN* TW2 .... 155 K5
Streatham Cemetery *TOOT* SW17 .... 160 D5
Streatham & Clapham High School *STRHM/NOR* SW16 .... 161 H5
Streatham & Clapham High School Preparatory Site *BRXS/STRHM* SW2 .... 162 A3
Streatham & Croydon RFC *THHTH* CR7 .... 196 B2
Streatham Ice Rink *STRHM/NOR* SW16 .... 179 K1
Streatham Modern School *STRHM/NOR* SW16 .... 179 K2
Streatham Park Cemetery *MTCM* CR4 .... 179 H5
Streatham Swimming Pool *STRHM/NOR* SW16 .... 179 K1
Streatham Vale Sports Club *STRHM/NOR* SW16 .... 179 H3
Streatham Wells Primary School *BRXS/STRHM* SW2 .... 162 A4
Stroud Green Primary School *FSBYPK* N4 .... 67 G5
Studholme Medical Centre *ASHF* TW15 .... 152 C6
The Study Preparatory School *WIM/MER* SW19 .... 177 G1
The Study School *NWMAL* KT3 .... 192 B2
Sudbourne Primary School *BRXS/STRHM* SW2 .... 142 A6
Sudbury Court Sports Club *ALP/SUD* HA0 .... 79 J1
Sudbury Golf Club *GFD/PVL* UB6 .... 79 J4
Sudbury Primary School *ALP/SUD* HA0 .... 79 H2
Suffolks Primary School *EN* EN1 .... 24 D3
Sulivan Primary School *FUL/PGN* SW6 .... 139 K3
Summerside JMI School *NFNCH/WDSP* N12 .... 47 H2
Sunbury Court *SUN* TW16 .... 172 C5
Sunbury Lock *WOT/HER* KT12 .... 172 A6
Sundridge Park Golf Club *BMLY* BR1 .... 184 B2
Sun Life Trading Estate *EBED/NFELT* TW14 .... 133 K4
Sunnyfields Primary School *HDN* NW4 .... 45 K6
Sunnyhill Primary School *STRHM/NOR* SW16 .... 162 A6
Super Bowl *BXLYHS* DA6 .... 149 G5
Surbiton Business Centre *SURB* KT6 .... 190 E3
Surbiton Cemetery *BRYLDS* KT5 .... 191 H1
Surbiton Golf Club *ESH/CLAY* KT10 .... 205 H2
Surbiton High School *KUT* KT1 .... 191 F1
Surbiton Hospital *SURB* KT6 .... 191 F3
Surbiton Natural Health Centre *SURB* KT6 .... 191 F3
Surrey Docks Farm *BERM/RHTH* SE16 .... 124 C2
Surrey Docks Health Centre *BERM/RHTH* SE16 .... 124 B2
Surrey Docks Watersports Centre *BERM/RHTH* SE16 .... 124 B3
Surrey Quays Leisure Park *BERM/RHTH* SE16 .... 124 A3
Surrey Quays Shopping Centre *BERM/RHTH* SE16 .... 124 A3
Surrey Square J & I School *WALW* SE17 .... 122 E5
Surry CCC (The Oval) *LBTH* SE11 .... 122 A6
Sussex House Preparatory School *KTBR* SW1X 14 E6
Sutcliffe Park Athletics Track *ELTH/MOT* SE9 .... 146 A6
Sutton Alternative Health Centre *SUT* SM1 .... 209 F3
Sutton Arena *CAR* SM5 .... 194 C4
Sutton Bowling Club *BELMT* SM2 .... 208 E6
Sutton Cemetery *CHEAM* SM3 .... 193 J6
Sutton Grammar School for Boys *SUT* SM1 .... 209 G3
Sutton High Junior School *SUT* SM1 .... 209 F4
Sutton High School for Girls Gdst *SUT* SM1 .... 208 E4
Sutton House *HOM* E9 .... 86 E3
Suttons Business Park *RAIN* RM13 .... 111 F2
Sutton Superbowl *SUT* SM1 .... 209 F3
Sutton United FC *SUT* SM1 .... 208 E2
Sutton West Centre *SUT* SM1 .... 208 E3
Swaffield Primary School *WAND/EARL* SW18 .... 160 B1
Swakeleys School *HGDN/ICK* UB10 .... 94 A1
Swaminarayan School *WLSDN* NW10 .... 81 F4
Swan Business Centre *CHSWK* W4 .... 118 A4
Swan Business Park *DART* DA1 .... 151 G5
Swan Lane Pier *CANST* EC4R 12 E6
Swanlea School *WCHPL* E1 .... 104 D3
Swansmere School *WOT/HER* KT12 .... 188 B5
Swedish School *BARN* SW13 .... 118 D6
Swiss Cottage School *HAMP* NW3 .... 83 H6
Swiss Re-Insurance Tower *LVPST* EC2M 13 H4
Sybil Elgar School *EA* W5 .... 98 A6
NWDGN UB2 .... 114 E3
Sybourn Infant School *LEY* E10 .... 69 G5
Sybourn Junior School *WALTH* E17 .... 69 H4
Sydenham Girls School *SYD* SE26 .... 163 J5
Sydenham High School *SYD* SE26 .... 181 J1
Sydenham (Junior) High School *SYD* SE26 .... 163 J6
Sydney Russell Comprehensive School *DAGW* RM9 .... 91 K3
Syon House *BTFD* TW8 .... 136 D2
Syon Park *BTFD* TW8 .... 136 D3
Syon Park School *ISLW* TW7 .... 136 C2

Syracuse University London Centre
NTGHL W11 ... 100 D6
Tabard Theatre
CHSWK W4 ... 118 B4
Taberner House
CROY/NA CR0 ... 211 J1
TA Centre
EDGE HA8 ... 44 D3
HRW HA1 ... 61 F2
NFNCH/WDSP N12 ... 47 H4
Tait Road Industrial Estate
CROY/NA CR0 ... 196 E4
Talmud Torah School
STNW/STAM N16 ... 67 K4
Tamian Industrial Estate
HSLWW TW4 ... 134 B5
Tamworth Manor High School
STRHM/NOR SW16 ... 179 J6
Tandem Centre
WIM/MER SW19 ... 178 C4
Tate Britain
WEST SW1P ... 16 E7
Tate Modern
STHWK SE1 ... 12 B7
Tavistock Clinic
HAMP NW3 ... 83 H4
Tavr Centre
KUT KT1 ... 190 E1
Tavy Clinic
ABYW SE2 ... 128 D2
Teddington Business Park
TEDD TW11 ... 174 A1
Teddington Cemetery
TEDD TW11 ... 155 K6
Teddington Clinic
TEDD TW11 ... 173 K2
Teddington Lock
TEDD TW11 ... 156 C6
Teddington Memorial Hospital
TEDD TW11 ... 173 K2
Teddington Pool & Fitness Centre
TEDD TW11 ... 174 B1
Teddington School
TEDD TW11 ... 174 E2
The Teddington Theatre Club
E/WMO/HCT KT8 ... 189 J2
Telegraph Hill School
BROCKY SE4 ... 144 B3
Telferscot Primary School
BAL SW12 ... 161 H3
Temperate House
RCH/KEW TW9 ... 137 G3
Temple Hill Primary School
DART DA1 ... 151 K6
Temple of Bacchus
CMBW SE5 ... 142 D3
Temple of Mithras
MANHO EC4N ... 12 E4
Tenby Road Clinic
EDGE HA8 ... 44 B5
Tennis and Squash Club
FNCH N3 ... 46 C4
Tennis Centre
CHIG IG7 ... 39 K3
Tennis Club
HAYES BR2 ... 200 A1
STAN HA7 ... 43 H1
Tenterden Sports Ground
KTN/HRWW/W HA3 ... 62 A4
Terence McMillan Stadium
PLSTW E13 ... 107 G3
Tetherdown Primary School
MUSWH N10 ... 66 A1
Thames Barrier
CAN/RD E16 ... 126 C2
Thames Barriervisitor Centre
WOOL/PLUM SE18 ... 126 C3
Thames Christian College
BTSEA SW11 ... 140 C4
Thames Ditton Infant School
THDIT KT7 ... 190 A3
Thames Ditton Junior School
THDIT KT7 ... 190 A4
Thames House
WEST SW1P ... 16 E6
Thameside Industrial Estate
CAN/RD E16 ... 126 C1
Thames Magistrates Court
BOW E3 ... 105 J2
Thamesmead Community College
ERITHM DA18 ... 129 F2
Thamesmead Leisure Centre
THMD SE28 ... 109 G6
Thamesmead Shopping Centre
THMD SE28 ... 109 G6
Thames Valley University
EA W5 ... 116 E1
Thamesview Business Centre
RAIN RM13 ... 111 G4
Thames View Clinic
BARK IG11 ... 109 F1
Thames View J & I School
BARK IG11 ... 109 G1
Thames Water Tower
NTGHL W11 ... 119 G2
Theatre Centre
BECK BR3 ... 182 E5
Théâtre De Complicité
HOLWY N7 ... 85 F3
Theatre for Mankind
FSBYPK N4 ... 67 F5
Theatre Museum Library & Archive
COVGDN WC2E ... 11 F5
Theatre of the Dispossessed
WIM/MER SW19 ... 159 G3
Theatre Royal
HOL/ALD WC2B ... 11 F4
SRTFD E15 ... 88 B4
Theatre Royal Haymarket
STJS SW1Y ... 10 D6
Theodore Mcleary Primary School
BRXS/STRHM SW2 ... 142 A5
Therapia Trading Estate
CROY/NA CR0 ... 195 J4
Thistlebrook Industrial Estate
ABYW SE2 ... 128 D3
Thomas Arnold Primary School
DAGW RM9 ... 92 B5
Thomas Becket RC Primary School
SNWD SE25 ... 197 H3
Thomas Buxton Primary School
WCHPL E1 ... 104 C3
Thomas Fairchild Primary School
IS N1 ... 6 E2
Thomas Gamuel Primary School
WALTH E17 ... 69 J3
Thomas Jones Primary School
NTGHL W11 ... 100 C5
Thomas London Independent Day School
KENS W8 ... 120 A3
Thomas Road Industrial Estate
POP/IOD E14 ... 105 J4
Thomas's Preparatory School
BTSEA SW11 ... 140 C2
Thomas Tallis School
BKHTH/KID SE3 ... 146 A4
Thornhill Primary School
IS N1 ... 85 G5
Thornton Heath Health Centre
THHTH CR7 ... 196 D1
Thornton Heath Pools & Fitness Centre
SNWD SE25 ... 197 H2
THHTH CR7 ... 196 D1
Thornton Road Industrial Estate
CROY/NA CR0 ... 195 K3
Thorntree Primary School
CHARL SE7 ... 126 C5
Thorpe Hall Primary School
WALTH E17 ... 52 A4
Three Bridges Business Centre
NWDGN UB2 ... 115 H2
Three Bridges Primary School
NWDGN UB2 ... 114 B4
NWDGN UB2 ... 115 G3
Three Mills Heritage Centre
SRTFD E15 ... 106 A2
Thurlow Park School
WNWD SE27 ... 162 C4
Thurston Industrial Estate
LEW SE13 ... 144 E4
Tidemill Primary School
DEPT SE8 ... 144 D1
Tideway Industrial Estate
VX/NE SW8 ... 121 H6
Tiffin Girls School
KUTN/CMB KT2 ... 175 F2
Tiffin School
KUTN/CMB KT2 ... 175 G5
Tiller Centre (Swimming Baths)
POP/IOD E14 ... 124 D3
Tiller Leisure Centre
POP/IOD E14 ... 124 D3
Timbercroft Primary School
WOOL/PLUM SE18 ... 147 K1
Timbers Clinic
KTN/HRWW/W HA3 ... 42 D2
Times Square Shopping Centre
SUT SM1 ... 209 F3
Tiverton Primary School
SEVS/STOTM N15 ... 67 K3
Tobacco Dock
WAP E1W ... 104 D6
Tokyngton Community Centre
WBLY HA9 ... 80 D3
Toldos School
STNW/STAM N16 ... 67 K5
Tollgate Primary School
CROY/NA CR0 ... 197 K3
PLSTW E13 ... 107 G3
Tolworth CP School
SURB KT6 ... 191 G5
Tolworth Girls School & Centre for Continuing Education
SURB KT6 ... 206 B1
Tolworth Recreation Centre
CHSGTN KT9 ... 206 B1
Tolworth Tower
SURB KT6 ... 191 J5
Tom Hood School
WAN E11 ... 88 D1
Tooting Bec Athletics Track
TOOT SW17 ... 161 G6
Tooting Leisure Centre
TOOT SW17 ... 160 C6
Tooting & Mitcham United FC
MTCM CR4 ... 179 F4
Torriano J & I School
KTTN NW5 ... 84 C3
Torridon Primary School
CAT SE6 ... 165 G4
Torrington Clinic
NFNCH/WDSP N12 ... 47 G1
Torrington Park Health Centre
NFNCH/WDSP N12 ... 33 G6
Total Health Clinic
SHB W12 ... 118 E2
Tottenhall Infants School
PLMGR N13 ... 49 G1
Tottenham Green Leisure Centre
SEVS/STOTM N15 ... 68 A1
Tottenham Hale Retail Park
SEVS/STOTM N15 ... 68 C1
Tottenham Hotspur FC (White Hart Lane)
TOTM N17 ... 50 B3
Tottenham Park Cemetery
ED N9 ... 36 D5
Tottenham Sports Centre
TOTM N17 ... 50 B4
Totteridge Cricket Club
TRDG/WHET N20 ... 32 E4
The Tower Bridge Experience
STHWK SE1 ... 19 J1
Tower Bridge Primary School
STHWK SE1 ... 19 J2
Tower Bridge Wharf
WAP E1W ... 123 H1
Tower Hamlets College
POP/IOD E14 ... 105 K6
WCHPL E1 ... 104 E4
Tower House School
MORT/ESHN SW14 ... 137 K5
Tower Industrial Estate
SNWD SE25 ... 197 H1
Tower Medical Centre
WCHPL E1 ... 104 C5
Tower Millennium Pier
MON EC3R ... 13 H7
Tower of London
TWRH EC3N ... 13 J6
Tower Retail Park
DART DA1 ... 150 C6
Towers Business Park
WBLY HA9 ... 80 D2
Tower Stairs
MON EC3R ... 13 G6
Tower Theatre
IS N1 ... 85 H5
Town Farm Primary School
STWL/WRAY TW19 ... 152 A2
Townley Grammar School for Girls
BXLYHS DA6 ... 169 G1
Townmead Business Centre
FUL/PGN SW6 ... 140 B4
Townsend Industrial Estate
WLSDN NW10 ... 80 E6
Townsend Primary School
STHWK SE1 ... 19 G6
Toynbee Hall & Curtain Theatre
WCHPL E1 ... 13 J3
Trabzon Spor FC
STNW/STAM N16 ... 85 K2
Trade Union Congress
NOXST/BSQ WC1A ... 10 D3
Trafalgar Business Centre
BARK IG11 ... 109 F3
Trafalgar Primary School
WHTN TW2 ... 155 J4
Trafalgar Square
CHCR WC2N ... 10 D7
Trafalgar Trading Estate
PEND EN3 ... 25 H5
Tramshed Theatre
WOOL/PLUM SE18 ... 127 G4
Trans Atlantic College
BETH E2 ... 7 J2
Transport House
WEST SW1P ... 16 E5
Treasury
WHALL SW1A ... 16 E3
The Treaty Centre
HSLW TW3 ... 135 G4
The Treehouse School
BMSBY WC1N ... 5 G6
Trent CE Primary School
EBAR EN4 ... 21 K5
Trent Country Park
EBAR EN4 ... 22 A3
Trent Park Cemetery
EBAR EN4 ... 22 A4
Trent Park Golf Club
EBAR EN4 ... 22 C5
Trevor Roberts School
HAMP NW3 ... 83 H5
Tricycle Cinema
KIL/WHAMP NW6 ... 82 D5
Trident Business Centre
TOOT SW17 ... 178 E1
Trinity Business Centre
BERM/RHTH SE16 ... 124 C2
Trinity Catholic Lower High School
WFD IG8 ... 38 E6
Trinity College Centre
PECK SE15 ... 143 F1
Trinity College of Music
GNWCH SE10 ... 125 F6
MHST W1U ... 9 H2
Trinity Hospital
GNWCH SE10 ... 125 G5
Trinity House
TWRH EC3N ... 13 H5
Trinity RC High School (Upper)
WFD IG8 ... 38 E6
Trinity St Marys Primary School
BAL SW12 ... 161 F3
Trinity School
CROY/NA CR0 ... 197 K6
DAGE RM10 ... 92 C1
Trinity School Belvedere
BELV DA17 ... 129 K4
Trinity Trading Estate
HYS/HAR UB3 ... 113 K3
Triumph Trading Estate
TOTM N17 ... 50 C2
Trocadero Centre
MYFR/PICC W1J ... 10 C6
Trojan Business Centre
WLSDN NW10 ... 81 H4
Troy Industrial Estate
HRW HA1 ... 61 F2
True Buddha School
IS N1 ... 5 G1
Tudor Lodge Health Centre
WIM/MER SW19 ... 159 G2
Tudor Primary School
FNCH N3 ... 47 G4
STHL UB1 ... 95 J6
Tufnell Park Primary School
HOLWY N7 ... 84 D2
Tuke School
PECK SE15 ... 143 J2
Tulloch Clinic
SHB W12 ... 119 G1
Tunnel Avenue Trading Estate
GNWCH SE10 ... 125 G2
Turney School
DUL SE21 ... 162 D2
Turnham Primary School
BROCKY SE4 ... 144 B5
Tweeddale Infant School
CAR SM5 ... 194 C4
Tweeddale Junior School
CAR SM5 ... 194 C4
Twickenham Cemetery
WHTN TW2 ... 155 G3
Twickenham Golf Club
FELT TW13 ... 155 F5
Twickenham Park Health Centre
TWK TW1 ... 156 D1
Twickenham Stadium
WHTN TW2 ... 155 K1
Twickenham Trading Estate
TWK TW1 ... 156 A1
Two Bridges Business Park
SAND/SEL CR2 ... 211 K4
Twyford CE High School
ACT W3 ... 117 J1
Twyford Sports Centre
ACT W3 ... 117 J1
Tyburn Infant School
STJWD NW8 ... 2 B6
The Type Museum
BRXN/ST SW9 ... 142 A2
Tyssen Primary School
STNW/STAM N16 ... 68 C5
UCI Cinema
BAY/PAD W2 ... 101 F6
ED N9 ... 37 F2
SUT SM1 ... 209 F3
BERM/RHTH SE16 ... 124 A3
UCI Empire Cinema
LSQ/SEVD WC2H ... 10 D6
UCI Filmworks Cinema
GNWCH SE10 ... 125 J4
UCL Hospitals
FITZ W1T ... 4 B7
UGC CinemaCHEL SW3 ... 120 C6
CRICK NW2 ... 63 K5
EA W5 ... 97 K6
EN EN1 ... 24 C5
HMSMTH W6 ... 118 E4
SOHO/SHAV W1D ... 10 C5
Underhill J & I School
BAR EN5 ... 20 C6
Unicorn School
RCH/KEW TW9 ... 137 G2
United Medical & Dental Schools
STHWK SE1 ... 17 G4
United Services Sports Ground
CHSWK W4 ... 138 B2
Unity College
KTTN NW5 ... 84 B2
Unity Trading Estate
WFD IG8 ... 53 H6
University Church of Christ the King
STPAN WC1H ... 4 C7
University College Hospital
GWRST WC1E ... 4 B7
HAMP NW3 ... 83 H4
University College Junior School
HAMP NW3 ... 83 G2
University College London
FITZ W1T ... 10 B1
GWRST WC1E ... 4 C7
STPAN WC1H ... 4 C6
University College London, Astor College
FITZ W1T ... 10 B1
University College London, Department of Clinical Haematology
GWRST WC1E ... 4 C7
University College London Medical School
FITZ W1T ... 10 A1
University College School
HAMP NW3 ... 83 G3
University Hospital Lewisham
LEW SE13 ... 144 E6
University of California
WHALL SW1A ... 16 A1
University of East London
BCTR RM8 ... 91 G2
PLSTW E13 ... 107 F2
University of East London Campus
EHAM E6 ... 108 A6
University of Greenwich
DART DA1 ... 171 F4
DART DA1 ... 171 J4
GNWCH SE10 ... 125 G5
WOOL/PLUM SE18 ... 127 F3
University of Greenwich (Mansion Site)
ELTH/MOT SE9 ... 167 H1
University of Greenwich (Southwood Site)
ELTH/MOT SE9 ... 167 H1
University of Greenwich Sports Ground
ELTH/MOT SE9 ... 146 D5
ELTH/MOT SE9 ... 167 H2
University of London
BAY/PAD W2 ... 8 A4
BMSBY WC1N ... 5 F7
FITZ W1T ... 10 C3
GWRST WC1E ... 10 D1
NWCR SE14 ... 144 B2
STPAN WC1H ... 4 D6
University of London Athletics Ground
NWMAL KT3 ... 192 D2
University of Middlesex
EBAR EN4 ... 22 C3
PEND EN3 ... 24 D6
University of North London
HOLWY N7 ... 85 F2
University of Notre Dame
LSQ/SEVD WC2H ... 10 D6
University of Westminster
CAMTN NW1 ... 4 A6
CHSWK W4 ... 137 K2
GTPST W1W ... 9 K1
GTPST W1W ... 10 A2
HGT N6 ... 66 B5
MHST W1U ... 9 G1
University of Westminster (Harrow Campus)
HRW HA1 ... 61 G4
Uphall Primary School
IL IG1 ... 90 B3
Upland Primary School
BXLYHN DA7 ... 149 G4
Uplands Business Park
WALTH E17 ... 51 F5
Upper Montagu Street Clinic
MBLAR W1H ... 8 E1
Upper Tooting Independent High School
TOOT SW17 ... 160 D4
Upton Cross Primary School
PLSTW E13 ... 89 F6
Upton Day Hospital
BXLYHS DA6 ... 149 F5
Upton Lane Medical Centre
FSTGT E7 ... 89 F4
Upton Primary School
BXLY DA5 ... 149 F6
Upton Road School
BXLYHS DA6 ... 149 F6
Ursuline High School
IL IG1 ... 72 B6
RYNPK SW20 ... 177 G3
Uxbridge College
HYS/HAR UB3 ... 94 E6
Uxbridge County Court
YEAD UB4 ... 94 C4
Uxendon Manor JMI School
KTN/HRWW/W HA3 ... 62 A2
Vale Farm Sports Centre
ALP/SUD HA0 ... 79 H2
Vale Industrial Estate
WATW WD18 ... 26 A3
The Vale Medical Centre
FSTH SE23 ... 164 B4
Valence House Museum & Library
BCTR RM8 ... 73 K6
Valence Junior School
BCTR RM8 ... 73 K6
Valentine High School
IL IG1 ... 72 A3
Valentines High Lower School
GNTH/NBYPK IG2 ... 72 B2
Vale Park Industrial
ACT W3 ... 118 B2
The Vale School
SKENS SW7 ... 120 B3
Valley Primary School
HAYES BR2 ... 183 H5
Valmar Trading Estate
CMBW SE5 ... 142 D2
Vanbrugh Theatre
GWRST WC1E ... 4 C7
Vanguard Trading Estate
SRTFD E15 ... 88 A6
Vaudeville Theatre
COVGDN WC2E ... 11 F5
Vaughan First & Middle School
RYLN/HDSTN HA2 ... 60 C3
Vauxhall Primary School
LBTH SE11 ... 122 A5
Vauxhall Station
LBTH SE11 ... 121 K5
Vernon House Special School
WLSDN NW10 ... 80 E3
Vestry Hall
MTCM CR4 ... 178 E6
Vestry House Museum
WALTH E17 ... 69 K1
Vicarage Fields Health Clinic
BARK IG11 ... 90 C5
The Vicarage Field Shopping Centre
BARK IG11 ... 90 C5
Vicarage Primary School
EHAM E6 ... 107 K2
Vicars Green Primary School
GFD/PVL UB6 ... 97 J1
VI Components Industrial Park
ERITH DA8 ... 130 B5
Victoria & Albert Museum
SKENS SW7 ... 14 B5
Victoria Business Centre
WELL DA16 ... 148 B3
Victoria Chiropractic Clinic
CHEL SW3 ... 14 E3
Victoria Coach Station
BGVA SW1W ... 15 J7
Victoria Hall
FNCH N3 ... 46 D4
Victoria Industrial Estate
ACT W3 ... 99 F4
Victoria Industrial Park
DART DA1 ... 151 G6
Victoria Junior School
FELT TW13 ... 154 A3
Victoria Medical Centre
PIM SW1V ... 16 A7
Victoria Palace Theatre
WESTW SW1E ... 15 K5
Victoria Park Industrial Centre
HOM E9 ... 87 H5
Victoria Place Shopping Centre
PIM SW1V ... 15 K6
Victoria Rail/Air Terminal
PIM SW1V ... 15 K6
Victoria Retail Park
RSLP HA4 ... 77 H3
Victoria Station
PIM SW1V ... 15 K6
Victoria Wharf
POP/IOD E14 ... 105 G6
Victoria Wharf Industrial Estate
DEPT SE8 ... 124 C5
Victor Seymour Infant School
CAR SM5 ... 209 K1
Victory Business Centre
ISLW TW7 ... 136 A5
Victory Primary School
WALW SE17 ... 18 D6
Viking Business Centre
ROMW/RG RM7 ... 74 E4
Viking Primary School
NTHLT UB5 ... 95 H2
Village Infant School
DAGE RM10 ... 92 C5
The Village School
HAMP NW3 ... 83 K4
Villiers High School
STHL UB1 ... 115 F1
The Vine Clinic
KUTN/CMB KT2 ... 175 F2
Vine Medical Centre
E/WMO/HCT KT8 ... 173 H6
The Vines School
BTSEA SW11 ... 141 F5
The Vineyard Primary School
RCHPK/HAM TW10 ... 157 F1
Vinopolis, City of Wine
STHWK SE1 ... 12 D7
Vinters' Hall
BLKFR EC4V ... 12 D5
VIP Trading Estate
CHARL SE7 ... 126 B4
Virginia Primary School
BETH E2 ... 7 J5
Virgo Fidelis Convent Schools
NRWD SE19 ... 180 D2
Vitoria Primary School
IS N1 ... 5 H1
Voyager Business Estate
BERM/RHTH SE16 ... 123 H3
Vulcan Business Centre
CROY/NA CR0 ... 214 C6
Waddon Clinic
CROY/NA CR0 ... 211 G3
Waddon Infant School
CROY/NA CR0 ... 211 G3
Wadham Lodge Sports Centre
WALTH E17 ... 51 K4
Wadsworth Business Centre
GFD/PVL UB6 ... 97 J1
The Waldegrave Clinic
TEDD TW11 ... 174 A1
Waldegrave Girls School
WHTN TW2 ... 155 J5
Waldo Industrial Estate
BMLY BR1 ... 184 B6
Waldorf School of SW London
STRHM/NOR SW16 ... 161 H4

Waldorf Steiner School of SW London STRHM/NOR SW16 161 J6
Walford Secondary School NTHLT UB5 77 J6
Walker Primary School STHGT/OAK N14 34 D4
Wallace Collection MHST W1U 9 G3
Wallbrook Business Centre HSLWW TW4 134 A4
Wallington County Grammar School WLGTN SM6 210 B1
Wallington High School for Girls WLGTN SM6 210 B6
Walmer Road Clinic NTGHL W11 100 C6
Walm Lane Clinic CRICK NW2 82 B3
Walnut Leisure Centre ORP BR6 202 B5
Walnuts Shopping Centre ORP BR6 202 B5
Walnut Tree Walk Primary School LBTH SE11 17 J6
Waltham Forest College WALTH E17 51 F5
WALTH E17 51 K6
Waltham Forest Magistrates Court WALTH E17 51 K6
Waltham Forest Theatre WALTH E17 51 H6
Waltham Forest Track WALTH E17 51 K5
Walthamstow Business Centre WALTH E17 52 A5
Walthamstow Greyhound Stadium CHING E4 51 K3
Walthamstow School for Girls WALTH E17 69 K1
Walton Business Centre WOT/HER KT12 188 A4
Walton Casuals FC WOT/HER KT12 188 A2
Walton Community Hospital WOT/HER KT12 188 A6
Walton Swimming Pool WOT/HER KT12 188 A5
Walworth Lower School WALW SE17 122 E5
Walworth Town Hall WALW SE17 18 C7
Walworth Upper School WALW SE17 123 F5
Wandle Primary School WAND/EARL SW18 160 A3
Wandle Recreation Centre WAND/EARL SW18 160 A1
Wandle Trading Estate MTCM CR4 194 E4
Wandsworth Adult College TOOT SW17 160 D6
The Wandsworth Arndale Centre WAND/EARL SW18 160 A1
Wandsworth Cemetery WAND/EARL SW18 160 B3
Wandsworth Community Health Trust TOOT SW17 179 F1
Wandsworth County Court PUT/ROE SW15 139 H6
Wandsworth Trading Estate WAND/EARL SW18 160 A2
Wanstead CE Primary School WAN E11 70 E2
Wanstead Cricket Club WAN E11 71 F4
Wanstead Golf Club WAN E11 71 G4
Wanstead High School WAN E11 71 G3
Wanstead Hospital WAN E11 71 F1
Wanstead Leisure Centre WAN E11 71 G3
Wapping Sports Centre WAP E1W 123 J1
Wapping Wharf WAP E1W 123 K1
Warehouse Theatre CROY/NA CR0 196 E6
War Memorial Sports Ground SUT SM1 209 J2
Warner Village Cinema ACT W3 98 C3
CROY/NA CR0 196 A6
DAGW RM9 92 A6
HAMP NW3 83 F4
HRW HA1 60 E3
NFNCH/WDSP N12 47 H4
SHB W12 119 G2
SOHO/SHAV W1D 10 D5
Warnford Industrial Estate HYS/HAR UB3 113 H2
Warren Comprehensive School CHDH RM6 74 B2
Warren Dell Primary School OXHEY WD19 27 G5
Warrender School RSLP HA4 58 D4
Warren Junior School CHDH RM6 74 B2
The Warren Medical Centre YEAD UB4 95 F5
Warren Road Primary School ORP BR6 217 F2
Warren Sports Centre CHDH RM6 74 B2
Warwick Estate BAY/PAD W2 101 F4
Warwick Leadlay Gallery GNWCH SE10 125 F6
Warwick Park School PECK SE15 143 G2
Warwick School for Boys WALTH E17 70 A1
Waterfront Leisure Centre WOOL/PLUM SE18 127 F3
Watergate School LEW SE13 144 E5
Waterloo East Station STHWK SE1 17 K1
Waterloo Health Centre STHWK SE1 17 J3
Waterloo Station STHWK SE1 17 J2
Watermans Arts, Cinema & Theatre Centre BTFD TW8 117 F6
The Watermans Hall MON EC3R 13 G6
Watermeads High School MRDN SM4 194 C3
Watermill Business Centre PEND EN3 25 H3
Water Rats Theatre STPAN WC1H 5 F4
Waterside Business Centre ISLW TW7 136 C5
The Waterside Trading Centre HNWL W7 115 K3
Watersports Centre FSBYPK N4 67 J5
Waterways Business Centre PEND EN3 25 H1
Watling Clinic EDGE HA8 45 F3
Watling Medical Centre EDGE HA8 44 E4
Wavelengths Leisure Pool & Library DEPT SE8 144 D1
Waverley Industrial Estate HRW HA1 42 D6
Waverley Lower Secondary School EDUL SE22 143 J6
Waverley School PECK SE15 143 K6
PEND EN3 24 E5
Waxchandlers' Hall CITYW EC2V 12 D3
Weald College KTN/HRWW/W HA3 42 E2
Weald First & Middle School KTN/HRWW/W HA3 43 F3
Welbeck Clinic CRICK NW2 82 E1
Welbourne Primary School TOTM N17 68 C1
Welfare Clinic CMBW SE5 142 E4
GNWCH SE10 145 F1
HGT N6 66 A3
Wellcome Institute CAMTN NW1 4 C6
Welldon Park Middle School RYLN/HDSTN HA2 78 C2
The Welling Clinic WELL DA16 148 B3
Welling Medical Centre WELL DA16 148 A5
Welling School WELL DA16 148 C2
Wellington Arch MYFR/PICC W1J 15 H2
Wellington Barracks STJSPK SW1H 16 B3
Wellington Primary School BOW E3 105 J2
HSLW TW3 134 E3
Welling United FC WELL DA16 148 D4
Wells Primary School WFD IG8 39 F6
Wembley Arena WBLY HA9 80 C2
Wembley Conference Centre WBLY HA9 80 B2
Wembley FC ALP/SUD HA0 79 H2
Wembley High School ALP/SUD HA0 79 J1
Wembley Hospital ALP/SUD HA0 79 K4
Wembley Manor Primary School WBLY HA9 80 A1
Wembley Park Business Centre WBLY HA9 80 D1
Wembley Stadium Industrial Estate WBLY HA9 80 C2
WBLY HA9 80 E1
Wembley Stadium (under development) WBLY HA9 80 C2
Wendell Park Primary School SHB W12 118 C2
Wentworth Primary School DART DA1 170 C2
Wentworth Tutorial College GLDGN NW11 64 B3
Wesley's Chapel, House & Museum STLK EC1Y 6 E6
Wessex Gardens Primary School CRICK NW2 64 C5
West Acton Primary School ACT W3 98 D5
West Becton Health Centre CAN/RD E16 107 H5
Westbourne Green Sports Complex BAY/PAD W2 100 E4
Westbourne Primary School SUT SM1 208 E1
Westbridge College BTSEA SW11 140 D2
Westbrooke School WELL DA16 148 E4
Westbury Medical Centre WDGN N22 49 J5
Westcroft Leisure Centre CAR SM5 210 A2
West Drayton Primary School WDR/YW UB7 112 B2
West Ealing Business Centre WEA W13 97 G6
Western Avenue Business Park ACT W3 98 D3
Western Trading Estate WLSDN NW10 98 E3
West Ewell County Infant School HOR/WEW KT19 207 F3
Westfield School WATW WD18 26 D1
Westfields Primary School BARN SW13 138 C3
Westgate Business Centre NKENS W10 100 C3
Westgate Primary School DART DA1 171 G2
West Green Primary School SEVS/STOTM N15 67 J1
West Grove Primary School STHGT/OAK N14 34 D2
West Ham Church Primary School SRTFD E15 88 D6
West Ham Lane Clinic SRTFD E15 88 C6
West Hampstead Clinic KIL/WHAMP NW6 82 E5
West Ham United FC (Upton Park) EHAM E6 107 H1
West Hatch High School CHIG IG7 53 K1
West Hendon Clinic CDALE/KGS NW9 63 H3
West Hill Primary School DART DA1 171 F1
WAND/EARL SW18 139 K6
West India Pier BERM/RHTH SE16 124 C2
West India Shopping Centre POP/IOD E14 124 D1
Westland Heliport BTSEA SW11 140 C4
West Lea School ED N9 36 A5
West Lodge Preparatory School BFN/LL DA15 168 A5
West Lodge Primary School PIN HA5 59 H1
West London County Court WKENS W14 119 H4
West London Magistrates Court HMSMTH W6 119 G5
West London Tamil School WLSDN NW10 99 H1
West Mead Clinic RSLP HA4 77 G1
West Middlesex Golf Club STHL UB1 96 C6
West Middlesex University Hospital ISLW TW7 136 B3
Westminster Abbey WEST SW1P 16 E4
Westminster Abbey Choir School WEST SW1P 16 D4
Westminster Business Square LBTH SE11 122 A5
Westminster Cathedral WEST SW1P 16 A5
Westminster Cathedral Choir School WEST SW1P 16 B6
Westminster Cathedral RC Primary School PIM SW1V 121 J5
Westminster City Hall WESTW SW1E 16 B4
Westminster City School WESTW SW1E 16 B4
Westminster College BTSEA SW11 141 F2
SOHO/SHAV W1D 10 B5
Westminster Industrial Estate WOOL/PLUM SE18 126 C3
Westminster Natural Health Centre PIM SW1V 16 A7
Westminster Pier WHALL SW1A 17 F3
Westminster School WEST SW1P 16 E4
Westminster Technical College WEST SW1P 16 B6
Westminster Theatre WESTW SW1E 16 A4
Westminster Under School WEST SW1P 16 C7
Westmoor Community Clinic PUT/ROE SW15 158 D2
West Norwood Clinic WNWD SE27 162 D4
West Norwood Crematorium WNWD SE27 162 D5
West One Shopping Centre MYFR/PKLN W1K 9 H4
Weston Green School THDIT KT7 189 K5
Weston Park Clinic CEND/HSY/T N8 66 E2
Weston Park Primary School CEND/HSY/T N8 67 F2
Westpoint Trading Estate ACT W3 98 D4
West Ramp Coach Park WDR/YW UB7 132 D2
West Ruislip Elementary School HGDN/ICK UB10 76 A1
West 12 Shopping & Leisure Centre WKENS W14 119 G2
West Thames College ISLW TW7 135 K2
West Thornton Primary School CROY/NA CR0 196 A4
West Twyford Primary School WLSDN NW10 98 C1
Westway Business Centre BAY/PAD W2 101 F4
Westway Sports Centre NKENS W10 100 B5
West Wickham Swimming Baths WWKM BR4 199 F5
Westwood High School for Girls NRWD SE19 180 D3
Westwood Primary School WELL DA16 147 K5
Westwood School BUSH WD23 28 D4
Westwood Technology College WELL DA16 147 J5
Whaddon House Clinic CMBW SE5 143 F4
Whipps Cross Hospital LEY E10 70 B3
White Bridge Primary School LOU IG10 39 J2
Whitechapel Art Gallery WCHPL E1 13 K3
Whitechapel Sports Centre WCHPL E1 104 C3
Whitefield School CRICK NW2 64 B4
Whitefield School & Leisure Centre WALTH E17 52 B4
Whitefriars First & Middle School KTN/HRWW/W HA3 42 E5
Whitefriars Trading Estate KTN/HRWW/W HA3 42 D5
Whitehall Primary School CHING E4 38 C4
Whitehall Theatre WHALL SW1A 10 D7
White Hart Lane School WDGN N22 49 H3
Whiteheath Junior School RSLP HA4 58 A3
Whitehorse Manor Primary School THHTH CR7 196 E1
Whiteleys Shopping Centre BAY/PAD W2 101 F5
Whiterose Trading Estate EBAR EN4 33 J2
Whitgift School SAND/SEL CR2 211 J3
Whitgift Shopping Centre CROY/NA CR0 196 D6
Whitings Hill Primary School BAR EN5 20 A6
Whitmore High School RYLN/HDSTN HA2 60 C5
Whitmore Primary School IS N1 7 F1
Whittingham Community Primary School WALTH E17 51 G4
Whittington Hospital ARCH N19 66 B6
Whittlesea School KTN/HRWW/W HA3 42 C3
Whitton Health Centre WHTN TW2 155 H3
Whitton Health Clinic WHTN TW2 155 G3
Whitton School WHTN TW2 155 G4
Whitton Sports & Fitness Centre WHTN TW2 155 G4
Whybridge Infant School RAIN RM13 93 J6
Whybridge Junior School RAIN RM13 93 H6
Wickham Theatre WWKM BR4 214 B1
Wide Way Health Clinic MTCM CR4 179 J6
Widmore Centre BMLY BR1 184 B5
Wigmore Hall MHST W1U 9 J3
Wilberforce Primary School NKENS W10 100 C2
Wilbury Primary School UED N18 49 K1
Willesden Community Hospital WLSDN NW10 81 J5
Willesden County Court WLSDN NW10 99 G1
Willesden High School WLSDN NW10 81 K6
Willesden Medical Centre CRICK NW2 81 K4
Willesden Sports Centre WLSDN NW10 81 K6
Willesden Sports Stadium WLSDN NW10 81 K6
William Bellamy J & I School DAGE RM10 74 C6
William Byrd School HYS/HAR UB3 113 F6
William C Harvey Special School TOTM N17 49 K5
William Davies Primary School FSTGT E7 89 H4
William Ellis School KTTN NW5 84 A1
William Ellis Sports Ground EDGE HA8 44 C4
William Ford CE Junior School DAGE RM10 92 C5
William Morris Academy HMSMTH W6 119 G5
William Morris Gallery WALTH E17 51 J6
William Morris Middle School MTCM CR4 179 J6
William Morris School WALTH E17 51 G4
William Patten Primary School STNW/STAM N16 68 B6
William Torbitt J & I School GNTH/NBYPK IG2 72 E2
William Tyndale Primary School IS N1 85 H5
Willington School WIM/MER SW19 177 J2
Willoughby Hall School HAMP NW3 83 H2
Willow Business Centre MTCM CR4 194 E2
Willow Business Park SYD SE26 163 K5
Willow Court Colindale Hospital CDALE/KGS NW9 45 F5
Willowfield Adult Education Centre WALTH E17 51 F6
Willowfield School HNHL SE24 142 D5
WALTH E17 51 G6
The Willows Clinic CHST BR7 185 F2
The Willows YEAD UB4 95 H3
Willow Tree Primary School NTHLT UB5 77 J4
Wilmington Boys Grammar School RDART DA2 170 E5
Wilmington Grammar School for Girls RDART DA2 170 E4
Wilmington Hall School RDART DA2 170 D5
Wilmington Primary School RDART DA2 170 E5
Wilsons School WLGTN SM6 210 E4
Wimbledon Chase Middle School RYNPK SW20 177 H4
Wimbledon College High School WIM/MER SW19 177 G3
Wimbledon Common Golf Club WIM/MER SW19 176 E1
Wimbledon Common Pre-Preparatory School WIM/MER SW19 177 F2
Wimbledon FC (Selhurst Park) SNWD SE25 197 F1
Wimbledon (Gap Road) Cemetery WIM/MER SW19 160 A6
Wimbledon High School WIM/MER SW19 177 H2
Wimbledon House School WIM/MER SW19 177 K4
Wimbledon Magistrates Court WIM/MER SW19 177 K2
Wimbledon Park Athletics Track WIM/MER SW19 159 J4
Wimbledon Park Golf Club WIM/MER SW19 159 J5
Wimbledon Park Primary School WIM/MER SW19 159 K4
Wimbledon Recreation Centre WIM/MER SW19 178 A2
Wimbledon RFC RYNPK SW20 176 C3
Wimbledon School of Art WIM/MER SW19 177 H4
WIM/MER SW19 177 K3
Wimbledon School of English WIM/MER SW19 177 H2
Wimbledon Stadium TOOT SW17 160 A6
Wimbledon Stadium Business Centre WIM/MER SW19 160 A5
Wimbledon Theatre WIM/MER SW19 177 K3
Winchcombe Business Centre PECK SE15 123 F6
Winchmore Hill Clinic WCHMH N21 35 H3
Winchmore Hill Cricket Club WCHMH N21 35 J3
Winchmore School WCHMH N21 35 J4
Windmill Business Centre NWDGN UB2 115 H1
Windmill School BRXS/STRHM SW2 141 K6
Windmill Trading Estate MTCM CR4 195 H2
Windrush Primary School THMD SE28 128 C1
Winfield House CAMTN NW1 2 D4
Wingate & Finchley FC NFNCH/WDSP N12 47 H3
Wingate Trading Estate TOTM N17 50 B3
Wingfield Primary School BKHTH/KID SE3 145 K4
Winns Primary School WALTH E17 51 H5
Winsor Primary School EHAM E6 108 A5
Winston Churchill's Britain at War Experience STHWK SE1 19 F1
Winterbourne Junior Girls School THHTH CR7 196 B1
Winton Primary School IS N1 5 G3
Witley Industrial Estate NWDGN UB2 114 E4
Witnitz School STNW/STAM N16 68 B5
Wix Primary School CLAP SW4 141 G4
Wolf Fields Primary School NWDGN UB2 114 E4
Wolfson-hillel Primary School STHGT/OAK N14 34 D1
Wolfson Medical Centre RYNPK SW20 176 D3
Wolsey Business Park WATW WD18 26 B2
The Woodberry Clinic MUSWH N10 48 B6
Woodbridge High School & Language College WFD IG8 53 F3
Woodbrook School BECK BR3 182 C4
Woodbury Down Primary School FSBYPK N4 67 J4
Woodcroft Primary School EDGE HA8 45 F3
Wood End J & I Schools GFD/PVL UB6 78 D3
Wood End Park Junior School HYS/HAR UB3 94 A6
Woodentops School BAL SW12 161 J3
Woodfield School CDALE/KGS NW9 63 G5
Woodford County High School WFD IG8 52 D2
Woodford Golf Club WFD IG8 52 D1
Woodford Green Preparatory School WFD IG8 52 E2
Woodford Green Primary School WFD IG8 52 D1
Woodford Trading Estate WFD IG8 53 G5

Woodgrange Infant School
FSTGT E7 .... **89** F2
Woodgrange Park Cemetery
FSTGT E7 .... **89** H3
Wood Green Crown Court
WDGN N22 .... **49** G4
Wood Green Health Centre
WDGN N22 .... **49** F4
Wood Green Old Boys FC
WDGN N22 .... **49** G3
Woodhall School
OXHEY WD19 .... **27** J6
Woodhill Primary School
CHARL SE7 .... **126** D4
Woodhouse Sixth Form College
NFNCH/WDSP N12 .... **47** H1
Woodlands Infant & Junior School
IL IG1 .... **90** D3
Woodlands Park Primary School
SEVS/STOTM N15 .... **67** J2
Wood Lane Medical Centre
RSLP HA4 .... **58** C5
Wood Lane School
FUL/PGN SW6 .... **140** B2
Wood Lane Sports Centre
BCTR RM8 .... **74** D5
Woodmansterne Primary School
STRHM/NOR SW16 .... **179** J4
Woodridge Primary School
NFNCH/WDSP N12 .... **32** D5
Woodside Health Centre
SNWD SE25 .... **197** J2
Woodside Junior School
CROY/NA CR0 .... **197** H4
WALTH E17 .... **52** A6
Woodside Park Golf Club
NFNCH/WDSP N12 .... **32** E6
Woodside Park School
FBAR/BDGN N11 .... **47** K1
NFNCH/WDSP N12 .... **33** F6
Woodside School
BELV DA17 .... **129** J4
Wood Street Medical Centre
WALTH E17 .... **52** A6
Wood Wharf
POP/IOD E14 .... **124** E1
Wood Wharf Business Park
POP/IOD E14 .... **125** F2
Woolmore Primary School
POP/IOD E14 .... **106** A6
Woolwich Cemetery
WOOL/PLUM SE18 .... **148** A1
Woolwich College
WOOL/PLUM SE18 .... **126** C4
WOOL/PLUM SE18 .... **127** H4
Woolwich County Court
WOOL/PLUM SE18 .... **127** F3
Woolwich Crown Court
THMD SE28 .... **127** K2
Woolwich Polytechnic School
THMD SE28 .... **128** B1
Worcesters Primary School
EN EN1 .... **24** B1
Working Mens College
CAMTN NW1 .... **4** B2
World Business Centre Heathrow
HTHAIR TW6 .... **133** F2
Worlds End Place
WBPTN SW10 .... **140** B1
World Trade Centre
TWRH EC3N **13** K6
World University Service
STLK EC1Y **6** E7
Wormholt Park Primary School
SHB W12 .... **99** J6
Worple Primary School
ISLW TW7 .... **136** B5
Worsley Bridge Junior School
BECK BR3 .... **182** D3
Worton Hall Industrial Estate
ISLW TW7 .... **135** K5
Wrencote
CROY/NA CR0 .... **211** J1
Wyborne Primary School
ELTH/MOT SE9 .... **167** G3
Wyke Green Golf Club
ISLW TW7 .... **116** A6
Wykeham Primary School
HCH RM12 .... **75** J5
WLSDN NW10 .... **81** F1
Wyndhams Theatre
LSQ/SEVD WC2H **10** D5
Wyvil Primary School
VX/NE SW8 .... **141** K1
Yale University Press
HAMP NW3 .... **83** J2
Yardley Primary School
CHING E4 .... **25** K6
Yeading FC
HYS/HAR UB3 .... **114** B1
Yeading Medical Centre
NTHLT UB5 .... **95** G2
Yeading Primary School
YEAD UB4 .... **95** G4
Yerbury Primary School
ARCH N19 .... **84** D1
Yeshivo Horomo Talmudical College
STNW/STAM N16 .... **67** K5
Yesodey Hatorah Jewish School
STNW/STAM N16 .... **68** B4
Yetev Lev Day School for Boys
STNW/STAM N16 .... **68** C5
Yiewsley Health Centre
WDR/YW UB7 .... **112** B1
York Clinic
STHWK SE1 .... **18** E1
York Hall
BETH E2 .... **104** D1
York Road Junior School
DART DA1 .... **171** J2
York Water Gate
CHCR WC2N **11** F7
Young England RFC
VX/NE SW8 .... **121** K6
Young Vic Theatre
STHWK SE1 .... **17** K2
Zennor Road Industrial Estate
BAL SW12 .... **161** H3
Zephyr Business Centre
SEVS/STOTM N15 .... **68** A1
Ziam Trading Estate
WALTH E17 .... **68** E5

Acknowledgements

The Post Office is a registered trademark of Post Office Ltd. in the UK and other countries.

Schools address data provided by Education Direct.

Petrol station information supplied by Johnsons

One-way street data provided by © Tele Atlas N.V. Tele Atlas

The boundary of the London congestion charging zone supplied by Transport for London